A BIOGRAPHICAL HISTORY
OF MEDICINE

A BIOGRAPHICAL HISTORY OF MEDICINE

Excerpts and Essays
on the Men and Their Work

JOHN H. TALBOTT, M.D.

Formerly
Professor of Medicine
University of Buffalo School of Medicine,
Physician-in-Chief, Buffalo General Hospital

and

Editor, Journal of the American
Medical Association and Director
of the Division of Scientific Publications

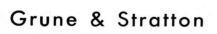 

Grune & Stratton   New York · London

Grune & Stratton, Inc., 757 Third Avenue, New York, New York 10017

Library of Congress Catalog Card Number 78-109574
International Standard Book Number 0-8089-0657-7

Printed in the United States of America (PC-B)

To Mildred Cherry Talbott

who is deserving of almost everything said by authors in dedications to their wives who allowed their husbands to devote themselves to literary endeavors which they cannot entirely share. This work was done largely at home at night and on weekends but my wife, a dedicated reader, kept busy with her review of contemporary books and literature while I, in a neighboring chair and as eager as a schoolboy, was reviewing the growth of medicine over the centuries

CONTENTS

PREFACE

THE PREFACE for a book of this size can be little more than a suggestion of the accolades worthy of a large number of associates and friends who contributed to the contents. Several are mentioned especially in the Preface; an extended list appears after the text under Acknowledgments. I have no evidence to measure the popularity of prefaces in medical books. In my instance, however, I would be grossly negligent in my social and professional responsibilities if I failed to make clear my great debt to so many who contributed their various talents and participated at various stages in the preparation of this book. These biographical studies were started more than a decade ago as isolated essays without any serious thought either that the project would continue regularly or that the number and extent would be so comprehensive and cohesive as to justify a publication of this size.

These essays, which were published in the *Journal of the American Medical Association* as historical editorial material, were part of a grand design to provide a diversity of subjects for the regular readers. I am grateful to *JAMA* for permission to present these essays as revised and expanded here. Each biographical essay was a unit and in most instances contained brief excerpts of published critical contributions, reproduced in small type.

The composition in standard type is mine. However, I owe a great debt to Lulu Fisher, manuscript editor during several of my earliest years on the *JAMA* staff and more recently to Raymond Verrill, who came into my life many years ago as my son's English teacher when he was a preparatory student at Nichols School, Buffalo, New York.

I was intensely interested both in the choice of words within my composition and in the preciseness of reproduction of the excerpts of material previously published. I was and am less concerned about the uniformity of punctuation of the references. The reader will appreciate many lapses. My primary purpose was and is the clear presentation of biographical material so that the original work could be retrieved as simply as possible. Some of the punctuation in the text may appear too simplified. I believe, however, that it follows a worthwhile trend and I support it.

Many times English translations were available for excerpting. When English translations were not available, I selected excerpted material from the work of qualified professionals. In the former category I relied heavily on the translations by the New Sydenham Society; *Medical Classics* by Crosby, published by Williams & Wilkins; *Classics in Clinical Dermatology* by Shelley and Crissey, published by Charles C Thomas;

Cardiac Classics by Williams and Keys, published by C. V. Mosby; *Classic Descriptions of Diseases* by Major, published by Charles C Thomas; and *Selected Readings in the History of Physiology* by Fulton, published by Charles C Thomas. When English translations were not available, and this happened many times, excerpted material selected by me was translated by Z. Danilevicius, a Senior Editor of *JAMA*. Others who prepared one or more translations are listed in the Acknowledgments.

The typing of the drafts, was considered by some of the secretaries to be less interesting than the typing of my letters; others looked forward to the challenge of a new draft, even though many revisions tended toward tedium. It is not an exaggeration to confess, neither in boast nor in shame, that each of the essays was revised a minimum of five, six, or seven times during as many weeks. The record was ten revisions. (Sigmund Freud was the subject, and probably fittingly so). A listing of the secretaries is hardly any reward for their efforts, but is given chronologically under Acknowledgments.

In the earlier years of preparation most of the editorials were reviewed out of the office by someone especially familiar with the man or the subject. The long list of reviewers begins with Chauncey D. Leake and the late Henry L. Viets and is continued in Acknowledgments. The overwhelming generosity of the many who gladly accepted this task allows the few exceptions to fade from the memory as an unaccountable unscholarly experience. I willingly sought and gladly accepted any opinions contrary to my own. However, the final presentation of each man carries my own conviction as to its accuracy. I confidently leave the final verdict to my readers.

Particular credit is due to the librarians who provided counsel, books, or illustrations or all three. Especially helpful were Gertrude Annan, Library of the New York Academy of Medicine; Elliott Morse and W. B. McDaniel, II, the Library of the College of Physicians, Philadelphia; William Beatty, Northwestern University Medical School; and John B. Blake and Martin M. Cummings, National Library of Medicine, Bethesda; John M. Connor, Los Angeles County Medical Library; and the staff of the Countway (Boston Medical-Harvard) Library.

Especially creditable are the line drawings prepared by Gabriel Bako. They are labeled as composites; if two portraits were available, both served as models. I think they are an outstanding group of illustrations.

A word should be said about the organization of this book. The essays are grouped by specialties within an era. For example, in the medieval period, surgeons are in one group, anatomists in another and physiologists in yet a third.

Although some of the men included in this book lived in the 20th century, this work makes no attempt to penetrate deeply into contemporary medicine. Several of the subjects were my teachers in medical school and I hope that I may be forgiven for any bias. At the time this Preface is being written there is one man still alive, Eugene V. Opie.

It would be impossible for me to justify the inclusions and the exclusions in a comprehensive survey of medical history. I must fall back upon the whims of an editor. The selection is exclusively my judgment. Others may argue that I have included several who were probably more glamorous than scientific; I accept this charge without apology. I have attempted to trace the history of medicine as viewed by a contemporary clinical scholar who is not in any way striving to be a professional medical historian.

JOHN H. TALBOTT, MD

A BIOGRAPHICAL HISTORY
OF MEDICINE

Hammurabi (2250 BC)

THE CODE OF HAMMURABI is probably the earliest document which recognized physicians and surgeons as a separate class and regulated their activities. It was engraved in cuneiform characters on a diorite monument found early in this century on the acropolis of Susa by an expedition sent out by the French government.[1]

The King of Babylon who codified the laws was a great and God-fearing soldier who provided justice for the three classes of people in his realm: gentlemen, the freemen, and slaves. The code, a clear break from the Babylonian-Assyrian incantations and divinations, was transliterated and translated in 1904 by Harper, professor of semantic languages at the University of Chicago. A great variety of subjects is included in the 282 sections. Several which concern bodily injury[1] and physicians' fees follow.[2]

196. If a man destroy the eye of another man, they shall destroy his eye.

199. If one destroy the eye of a man's slave or break a bone of a man's slave he shall pay one-half his price.

206. If a man strike another man in a quarrel and wound him, he shall swear: "I struck him without intent," and he shall be responsible for the physician.

209. If a man strike a man's daughter and bring about a miscarriage, he shall pay ten shekels of silver for her miscarriage.

210. If that woman die, they shall put his daughter to death.

215. If a physician operate on a man for a severe wound (or make a severe wound upon a man) with a bronze lancet and save the man's life; or if he open an abscess (in the eye) of a man with a bronze lancet and save that man's eye, he shall receive ten shekels of silver (as his fee).

216. If he be a freeman, he shall receive five shekels.

217. If it be a man's slave, the owner of the slave shall give two shekels of silver to the physician.

221. If a physician set a broken bone for a man or cure his diseased bowels, the patient shall give five shekels of silver to the physician.

222. If he be a freeman, he shall give three shekels of silver.

223. If it be a man's slave, the owner of the slave shall give two shekels of silver to the physician.

1. Letienne, A.: Medicine 2000 Years Before Our Era: The Code of Hammurabi (Fr), *Presse Med* 14:273-275, 1906.

2. Harper, R. F.: *The Code of Hammurabi, King of Babylon About 2250 B.C.*, Chicago: University of Chicago Press, 1904.

1

Glyptotek, Copenhagen

Aesculapius

AESCULAPIUS, Asclepios, Asklepios, Asclepius (Latin), or Ασκλπος (Greek), if one has a yearning for the good old days of resinated wine and chariot races, is probably the most venerated physician of all times. Scholia in Homer's Iliad suggests that the name Aesculapius was derived from words meaning applying (askein) and making the limbs gentle (epia).[1] Another interpretation ascribes his name to "healing soothingly and for deferring the withering that comes with death." Yet a third writer affirms that Aesculapius was originally known as Epios because of his gentleness and calmness. After he had cured Askles, the tyrant of Epidaurus who suffered from ophthalmia, he was called Aesculapius, with the accent on the penult. Demosthenes changed the pronunciation by accenting the antepenult. Aesculapius is to be distinguished from Asclepiad, a generic appellation for a priest of the temple of Asclepius, from Asclepias, a genus of Asclepiadaceous plants, and from Asclepiades, a Bithynian physician of the second century before Christ, who practiced in Rome and openly admitted opposition to the teachings of Hippocrates.

The fact or fancy, man or myth, physical being or deity of Aesculapius probably never will be resolved. The evidence in support of a practicing physician skilled in the art and widely recognized throughout ancient Greece, and even as distant as Egypt, is impressive to the present-day traveler. Because of his clinical acumen and his skill in combating morbidity as well as mortality, the ancient writers described him as being with a serpent. The sculpturer who carved for eternity and the painter who used oils and pigments for a shorter period of time gave him a serpent, with the implication that those who avail themselves of medical science undergo a biological change making them similar to the serpent. Patients are young again after illnesses and are able to slough off old age. Also the serpent is a sign of attention, much of which is required in medical treatment. The staff around which the serpent twines is a symbol of support. "It prevents our falling into sickness and although stumbling without the staff we would fall even sooner than need be."

Whence came Aesculapius? This question is answered in the legend of the son of Apollo and Coronis. "In all Thessaly there was no fairer maid than Coronis of Larissa. She surely found favor in thy eyes, O Delphic god, so long as she was chaste—or undetected. But the bird of Thoebus discovered her unchastity and told his master that he had seen Coronis lying beside the youth of Thessaly." Aesculapius was the offspring of this union. In maturity he excelled in nature and keenness of mind; he strove after medical knowledge and discovered many of the things that tend to promote health. He advanced so far in reputation as to cure many of the sick who had been despaired of, contrary to all expectations. "He revived some who had died." The story was current that even Pluto, bringing a charge against Aesculapius, accused him before Jove on the ground that the scope of his power was diminishing, for the dead were continually growing fewer because they were healed by Aesculapius.

The Homeric Aesculapius is said to have restored life to Glaucus, the son of Minos, on the island of Crete. It is on this island that the best preserved ruins of Minoan civilization are extant today. This golden era of pre-Hellenic Greece was in flower from 3400 to 1200 BC. The most famous antiquities on the island are the partially restored palace of King Minos at Knossos and the excavation at Phaistos. Nearby is the court from which Daedalus took off in his flying machine. Aesculapius practiced medicine also at Delphi, the site of the most famous oracle of Greece. An impressive portion of this oracle remains on the side of the hill near Mount Parnassus. The two greatest Aesculapian temples that the traveler may see on the tourist trails are fabulous in extent and remarkable in their state of preservation. On the island of Cos, the Sacred Spring is still flowing in the Aesculapian Temple. At Epidaurus on the Peloponnesus, south of Athens, a remarkably well preserved amphitheater is only a few steps from the Aesculapian Temple. c 360 BC.

Like many modern physicians, the first Aesculapius sired at least four children. His daughters were Hygieia and Panacea. Two sons, Podelirius and Machaon, became physicians. Because of their professional skill they were called into the military service in the Trojan War under Agamemnon. It was an ideal combination of internal medicine and surgery. "Podelirius treated diseases by diet while his brother Machaon having been blessed with more agile hands, practiced surgery only." It is stated that King Agamemnon summoned Machaon to cure the wounded Menelaus. Although Schliemann, the unorthodox German archeologist, was proved wrong in his assumption that he had discovered the tomb of Agamemnon, the bathroom in the palace where Orestes slew his mother is pointed out to the modern traveler. Also, the beehive tombs, huge vaulted underground chambers, may be seen on a neighboring hill. Undoubtedly Agamemnon was buried in a similar tomb nearby.

A number of anaglyphs and artifacts pertinent to Aesculapius are described in a work by Kerényi, translated from the German.[2] Four votive reliefs may be seen in the National Archeological Museum in Athens. One represents Aesculapius accompanied by two goddesses, dated about 390 BC. One from Thyrea in Argolis depicts the family of Aesculapius, c 370-360 BC. The third is from the Aesculapion of the Acropolis in Athens. The patient is depicted in the act of receiving medicine from Aesculapius; the snake staff is between the patient and physician. The fourth is from Epidaurus and represents Aesculapius and his sons. A silver coin from Epidaurus bears an effigy of the great physician. A dog lies under the throne. In Asia Minor a coin, c AD 220, was discovered portraying Aesculapius riding on a snake. This is the reverse of a medallion of Alexander Severus from Nikaia, near Pergamon. Also, a medal of Commodus, AD 180-192, portrays a ritual statue at Pergamon on the reverse. A marble head of Aesculapius, c 340 BC, was discovered in a cave on the island of Melos. The head is now reposing in London in the British Museum. The features peculiar to the "ideal type" of Aesculapius have been described by Kerényi as "The eyes seem to look upwards and into the distance without definite aim. This combined with the vivid movement gives us an impression of a greater inner emotion, one might almost say of suffering. This god does not stand before us in Olympian calm: he is assailed as it were by the sufferings of men, which it is his vocation to assuage."

The Aesculapion at Cos was not rediscovered until 1902. Excavations of the temple are incomplete. Something has been known of this sanctuary and the works of art it contained ever since 1891, at which time the Mimiamboi (mimes in choliambic verse) by the poet Herondas, 250 BC, were published. Herondas described "women offering sacrifices in the temple of Asklepios" (at Cos).

And on to Rome—a bust of Aesculapius remains on the wall that surrounds an island in the Tiber, near the Church of San Bartolomeo, amid several hospital buildings. A snake and staff are also visible, carved on travertine, near the bust. On the Pincian Hill in Rome, an enthroned Aesculapius dates from the second century after Christ. In the Capitoline Musem a bronze of Aesculapius, c 150 AD, was recovered from the port of Anzio, the port of entry where Aesculapius presumably first set foot on the Roman heartland. The Baths of Caracalla gave up a head of Aesculapius, late second century after Christ, which is now in Rome.

Hippocrates was the 18th descendant of Aesculapius through Podalirius. If Hippocrates was a man of flesh and blood, could not Aesculapius seven centuries earlier likewise have been a man and not a myth?

1. Edelstein, E. J., and Edelstein, L.: *Asclepius: Collections and Interpretations of Testimonies,* Baltimore: Johns Hopkins Press, 1945.

2. Kerényi, C.: *Asklepios: Archetypal Image of the Physician's Existence,* translated by R. Manheim, vol 3, New York: Pantheon Books Inc., 1959.

Hippocrates (460-375 BC)

HIPPOCRATES, born on the island of Cos, was the son and grandson of a physician. He separated medicine from philosophy in a rational environment, characterized as one of the most memorable epochs in the intellectual development of the human race. His contemporaries included the philosopher Democritus, the statesman Pericles, the sculptors Polycletus and Phidias, the historians Herodotus and Thucydides, the poet Pindar, and the dramatists Aeschylus, Sophocles, Euripides, and Aristophanes.

The volume of medical and general literature attributed to or associated with Hippocrates and Greek medicine of his time exceeds that of any other physician. More scholars have devoted more years to the study, translation, and interpretation of Hippocratic works than to the works of any other physician in the history of man. Those professing superior knowledge of these epo-

chal treatises generally agree that the collection of writings under his name probably represents the labors of many—some prepared even before his day, others decades

Courtesy of D. W. Richards

or centuries after his death. Even the treatises believed to be most likely his own composition were prepared at different times in his life. The current compilation in *The Genuine Works of Hippocrates*[1] proceeds from the "Prognostics" and the "Aphorisms" to the "First and Third Books of the Epidemics," to the "Regimen in Acute Diseases," "On Airs, Waters, and Places," "On the Articulations," "On Fractures," "On Wounds of the Head," and concludes with "The Oath" and "The Law," each prepared in a precise but simple style of composition.[1]

Hippocrates rejected the mysticism of his predecessors and founded the bedside method for the study of a patient with a disease, albeit acknowledging the humoral pathology which attributed all diseases to one or more baneful reactions of body fluids. Diseases were divided into acute and chronic, endemic and epidemic. He used his clinical experience and peripheral senses as diagnostic instruments; and having formulated his conclusions with transparent honesty, placed the dignity of the physician on the highest plane of social intercourse and gave Greek medicine its ethical ideas. Hippocrates recorded his failures as well as his successes in diagnosis and treatment. Without benefit of experiments in natural science, he capitalized maximally upon the clinical findings and clinical course of individual patients. He recognized, defined, and classified as many symptoms as possible in his examination before he rendered a prognosis.

With modern concepts of the approach to disease, it is natural then to expect that several of the findings derived from clinical observation remain valid. Thus, his descriptions of pulmonary phthisis, gibbous spine in patients with tuberculosis, puerperal septicemia, epilepsy, the diurnal fevers of malaria, respiratory infection, dysentery, and mania are readily recognized as current maladies. Hippocrates recommended trephining for decompression in cranial contusion and simple expectant treatment for open depressed fractures of the skull. His methods of reduction of fractures of the hip and the shoulder are first-class. He recommended irrigation of wounds with clean water or wine; dressings were to be applied about the suppurating wound rather than over it, thereby gaining exposure to the atmosphere. He gave a good description of wound healing by first and second intention. Hippocrates believed in assisting nature in convalescence and favored simple expedients such as fresh air, good diet, massage, hydrotherapy, and barley water as well as the then current practices of purgation and blood letting to allow escape of disordered humors.

The excerpts below are taken from *The Genuine Works of Hippocrates*[1] translated from the Greek by Francis Adams, one of a number of recognized English translations. Although Hippocrates was more interested in recording his clinical observations than philosophizing, the "Aphorisms" are exemplary of a blending of the thoughts of a reflective philosopher and the wisdom of an experienced practitioner. The First Aphorism has been widely used.

Life is short, and the Art long; the occasion fleeting; experience fallacious, and judgment difficult. The physician must not only be prepared to do what is right himself, but also to make the patient, the attendants, and externals cooperate.

In "Epidemics" Hippocrates presents a contemporary definition of an outstanding physician, followed by a clear description of mumps and diphtheria, and a sentence reference to Cheyne-Stokes respiration.[1]

The physician must be able to tell the antecedents, know the present and foretell the future— must meditate these things and have two special objects in view with regard to diseases, namely to do good or to do no harm. The art consists in three things—the disease the patient, and the physician. The physician is the servant of the art, and the patient must combat the disease along with the physician.

Swellings appeared about the ears, in many on either side, and in the greatest number on both sides, being unaccompanied by fever so as not to confine the patient to bed; in all cases they disappeared without giving trouble, neither did any of them come to suppuration, as is common in swellings from other causes. They were of a lax, large, diffused character, without inflammation or pain and they went away without any critical sign. . . . In some instances earlier, and in others later, inflammations with pain seized sometimes one of the testicles, and sometimes both; some of these cases were accompanied with fever and some not; the greater part of these were attended with much suffering. In other respects they were free of disease, so as not to require medical assistance.

The woman affected with quinsy, who lodged in the house of Aristion: her complaint began in the tongue; speech inarticulate; tongue red and parched. On the first day, felt chilly, and afterwards became heated. On the third day, a rigor, acute fever; a reddish and hard swelling on both sides of the neck and chest, extremities cold and livid; respiration elevated; the drink returned by the nose; she could not swallow; alvine and urinary discharges suppressed. On the fourth, all the symptoms were exacerbated. On the sixth she died of the quinsy.

Philliscus, who lived by the Wall, took to bed on the first day of acute fever; he sweated; towards night was uneasy; . . . about the middle of the sixth day he died. The respiration throughout, like that of a person recollecting himself, was rare and large. . . .

In his *"Book of Prognostics"* Hippocrates offers common sense advice and describes the appearance of approaching death, currently identified as the "Hippocrates facies."

It appears to me a most excellent thing for the physician to cultivate Prognosis; for by foreseeing and foretelling, in the presence of the sick, the present, the past, and the future, and explaining the omissions which patients have been guilty of, he will be the more readily believed to be acquainted with the circumstances of the sick; so that men will have confidence to intrust themselves to such a physician. And he will manage the cure best who has foreseen what is to happen from the present state of matters. For it is impossible to make all the sick well; this, indeed, would have been better than to be able to foretell what is going to happen.

He should observe thus in acute diseases: first, the countenance of the patient, if it be like those of persons in health, and more so, if like itself, for this is the best of all; whereas the most opposite to it is the worst, such as the following; *a sharp nose; hollow eyes, collapsed temples; the ears cold contracted, and their lobes turned out; the skin about the forehead being rough, distended and parched; the color of the whole face being green, black, livid, or lead-colored.*

The notation of contralateral convulsions in injuries of the head is followed by descriptions of the "Hippocrates nails" in empyema and by currently valid observations on the natural clinical history of gouty arthritis.

And, for the most part, convulsions seize the other side of the body; for, if the wound be situated on the left side, the convulsions will seize the right side of the body; or if the wound be on the right side of the head, the convulsion attacks the left side of the body. And some become apoplectic.

Empyema may be recognized in all cases by the following symptoms: . . . there is a desire to cough, and the patients expectorate nothing worth mentioning, the eyes become hollow, the cheeks have red spots on them, the nails of the hands are bent, the fingers are hot, especially their extremities, there are swellings in the feet, they have no desire of food, and small blisters (phlyctaenae) occur over the body. These symptoms attend chronic empyemata, . . . at the same time the patient has some difficulty of breathing. Whether they will break earlier or later may be determined by these

symptoms; if there be pain at the commencement, and if the dyspnoea, cough, and ptyalism be severe, the rupture may be expected in the course of twenty days or still earlier

Eunuchs do not take the gout, nor become bald.
A woman does not take the gout, unless her menses be stopped.
A young man does not take the gout until he indulges in coition.
For the most part, gouty affections rankle in spring and in autumn.

The "Oath of Hippocrates" needs reference only in passing. Recent evidence suggests that it was not prepared by Hippocrates but was a product of the Pythagorean school. Whether this revised identification will be confirmed at some future time, there is no doubt that the "Hippocratic Oath" will retain its eponymic authorship.

The village on the island of Cos displays the plane tree, famous as the mythical site for the Hippocratic lectures. It is only a short distance from the temple of Aesculapius built in the beginning of the 3rd century before Christ, considerable portions of which remain. Possibly the tree also served to shelter St. Luke and St. Paul, the itinerant apostles. Hippocrates himself was an ardent traveler throughout the Mediterranean countries; he practiced in Athens and received the honor of Athenian citizenship. He is believed to have died in Thessaly, and some evidence suggests that he was a centenarian. The finding of a marble bust of Hippocrates in 1940 near the ruins of Ostia Antica, the seaport of imperial Rome, is a most recent memorabilia of Hippocrates.[2] The influence of Hippocrates as a disciple in the cult of Asculapius was dominant until the second century and persists as indicated by the accolade to him—the "Father of Physic."

1. Adams, F.: *The Genuine Works of Hippocrates,* New York: William Wood & Co., 1929.
2. Richards, D. W.: Hippocrates of Ostia, JAMA 204: 1049-1056 (June 17) 1968.

The commentaries on medicine are the only extant portion of his encyclopedia, called *De artibus,* which contained sections on agriculture, military arts, rhetoric, philosophy, and jurisprudence. The contents of *De medicina,* the sixth and last section in the series, were derived from the teachings of Hippocrates and others in the Hellenistic period, from the school of Asclepiades of Bithynia, and from the Alexandrian school, where particular emphasis was placed upon anatomy and surgery. He translated medical and anatomical terms from Greek into Latin and thereby created the corpus of Latin nomenclature which has dominated Western medicine for almost two millennia. Celsus did not subscribe to any of the sects or schools then in vogue and took only what he wanted from the Methodists, the Rationalists, and the Empirics. He employed reasoning, observation, and common sense in the practice of medicine and opened the bodies of the dead to advance his knowledge.

De medicina was rediscovered in 1443 when Thomas of Sarzanne, later Pope Nicholas V, found a copy of the manuscript in the papal library at St. Ambrose, Milan. The first printed edition was prepared in Florence in 1478. The compendium consists of eight books; the first four discuss treatment by diet and medicines, the last four discuss treatment by diet and surgical management. Many translations have been prepared. The three-volume English translation from the Loeb Classical Library series is the source of the excerpts used in this essay. These will be presented without regard to their order in the original. The first excerpt discusses the approach to the patient by the physician. This is followed by the qualifications of the surgeon including ambidexterity, some general advice on prognosis, a selected list of familiar anatomical or medical terms, and the critical signs of inflammation.[3]

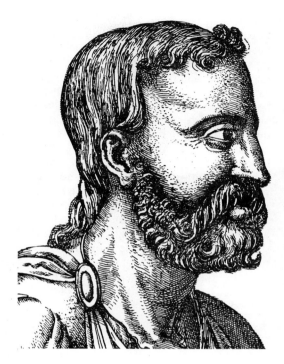

Aulus Cornelius Celsus
(30 BC-50 AD)

BETWEEN HIPPOCRATES of the third century before Christ, and Galen of the second century after Christ came Celsus, medical historian, nobleman, and landowner. He lived in the reign of Tiberius Caesar at the height of Roman civilization immediately after the founding of the Empire upon the dissolution of the Republic. Most historians have judged Celsus to be a scholar of medicine with limited clinical experience, but, since he was not a bedside practitioner, his writings were largely ignored by his colleagues.[1] In his time and for many centuries after, medicine was regarded as a branch of general knowledge and culture in which scholars were accustomed to hold varying degrees of interest. Celsus was one who held most of the contemporary knowledge of medicine within his grasp. Among several manuscripts which he composed in fine Latin style, his most famous, *De medicina,*[2] was also one of the first medical treatises to reappear with the revival of learning 15 centuries later.

. . . Fear and anger and any other feeling of the mind is often apt to excite the pulse; so that when the practitioner makes his first visit, the solicitude of the patient who is in doubt as to what the practitioner may think of his state, may disturb his pulse. On this account a practitioner of experience does not seize the patient's forearm with his hand, as soon as he comes, but first sits down and with a cheerful countenance asks how the patient finds himself; and if the patient has any fear, he calms him with entertaining talk, and only after that moves his hand to touch the patient.

Now a surgeon should be youthful or at any rate nearer youth than age; with a strong and steady hand which never trembles, and ready to use the left hand as well as the right; with vision sharp and clear, and spirit undaunted; filled with pity, so that he wishes to cure his patient, yet is not moved by his cries, to go too fast, or cut less than is necessary; but he does everything just as if the cries of pain cause him no emotion.

In this connexion, however, a practitioner should know above all which wounds are incurable, which may be cured with difficulty, and which more readily. For it is the part of a prudent man first not to touch a case he cannot save, and not to risk the appearance of having killed one whose lot is but to die; next, when there is grave fear without, however, absolute despair, to point out to the patient's relatives that hope is surrounded by difficulty, for then if the art is overcome by the malady, he will not appear to have been ignorant or mistaken. But while such steps become a prudent practitioner, it is like a mountebank to exaggerate a small matter in order to enhance his own achievement. It is right to commit himself to a statement that a case is simple in order that he may examine it with even more care for fear a case slight in itself may become worse by negligence on the doctor's part.

No attempt will be made to list each subject mentioned by Celsus, but familiar names and diseases are noteworthy. Thus, specialties are listed under medicine, surgery, dermatology, neurology, psychiatry, otolaryngology, obstetrics, gynecology, urology, and plastic surgery. He recognized the position and arrangement of single organs in dissection, understood the difference between arteries and veins, observed that the arteries spurt blood when cut, and probably referred to tuberculosis. Insanity was regarded as a general disease; tabes, a wasting disease. Fasting was prescribed for acute diarrhea, trephining was practiced for head wounds, and excision of the breast was recommended for early carcinoma.

Peripneumonia, involving the whole lung, is obviously our pneumonia. Distemper in the large intestine near the caecum, accompanying violent inflammation and pain on the right side of the abdomen, probably is appendicitis. The technique for circumcision is carefully described. Many of the derma-

tologic names which come to us from the Greek are mentioned and include elephantiasis, scabies, alopecia areata (area Celsi), erysipelas, carbuncle, pustules, phlyctenae, impetigo, vitiligo, sycosis, ulcers, tumors, exanthema, and struma. In otolaryngology, he mentions angina, the semicircular canals, and tonsillectomy. Among surgical procedures, Celsus describes lateral lithotomy, herniorrhaphy, amputation, and ligation of blood vessels. In ophthalmology, he describes couching for cataract, although the word "cataract" was not used until a thousand years later. He describes paracentesis, fasting and abstinence from fluid for abdominal ascites. Diuretics, massage, sweating, and draining of fluid from the limbs are recommended for generalized anasarca. Probably his most quoted remark is made in book 3, chapter 10, on the cardinal signs of inflammation.[3]

But if there is inflammation and pain in the chest, the first thing is to apply to it repressing plasters, lest more diseased matter should gather there, if hotter ones were applied; next, when the primary inflammation has subsided, and not before, we must go on to hot and moist plasters, in order to disperse what remains of the matter. Now the signs of an inflammation are four: redness and swelling with heat and pain. Over this Erasistratus greatly erred, when he said that no fever occurred apart from inflammation. Therefore if there is pain without inflammation, nothing is to be put on: for the actual fever at once will dissolve the pain. But if there is neither inflammation nor fever, but just pain in the chest, it is allowable to use hot and dry foments from the first.

1. Castiglioni, A.: *A History of Medicine*, ed 2, E. B. Krumbhaar (trans.-ed.), New York: Alfred A. Knopf, 1947.

2. Celsus, A. C.: *De Medicina*, Florence: Nicolaus (Laurentius), 1478.

3. Celsus, A. C.: *De Medicina*, W. G. Spencer (trans.), Cambridge, Mass: Harvard University Press, 1935-1938.

Dioscorides (c AD 54-68)

PEDACIUS DIOSCORIDES, Greek physician and surgeon, while serving in the Roman Legions, collected plants from wide areas of the ancient world for the preparation of his *Materia medica,* acknowledged as the authoritative source document on the subject for 15 centuries. He is believed to have been born in Anazarba, Cilicia, in Asia Minor, early in the first century. His early education was pursued in Nero's army in Alexandria. This was followed by campaigns in the Mediterranean countries and caring for the sick, interspersed with botanizing and planning his *Materia medica.* The first copy of the Greek *Herbal* was assembled about AD 70. In contrast to a nosologic description of disease with notes on treatment, or a book of aphorisms—traditional texts of that time—the manuscript was true to the designation, "materia medica," a term introduced into medical writing by Dioscorides. The plant or herb was identified by the enumeration of its names according to its indigenous site; special features were noted, concluding with a discussion of disorders or conditions in which it was judged useful.[1] Illustrations,

which aided in identification, probably were added in the revisions prepared in the third or fourth century. The chapters were arranged in alphabetical order at about the same time.

Sigerist has listed a number of editions and abbreviated texts that appeared during the Middle Ages, which reflect the significance and popularity of the treatise.[2] It was translated into most of the cultural languages of the ancient and modern world. There are at least 12 extant complete codices, profusely illustrated. The most important codex is a 9th century manuscript in the National Library in Paris. The Latin edition, with Greek transliteration, which was available for perusal, was published at Caesarea, Asia Minor, in 1598.[3] More than 600 plants and a smaller number of agents from the animal and mineral kingdom were included in five books in the original manuscript. At least one hundred of the items remained in the pharmacopeias prepared as recently as the early 20th century. A few herbals or their active pharmacologic ingredients continue to enjoy current use in the practice of medicine.

Items listed in this 1598 edition include acacia, aconite, aloes, cannabis, cantharides, colchicum, gentian, glycyrrhiza, black and white hellebore, thyme, tragacanth, veratrum, and more than 60 different wines. Dioscorides presented a number of examples of adulteration and the devices for recognizing such fraud. The tools for detection included the sensory organs of touch, taste, smell, and sight, and physical-chemical tests of solubility, specific gravity, diffusibility, flexibility, and reaction to ignition.[4]

During the years 1652-1655, John Goodyer, botanist of Petersfield, prepared an English translation, which was edited and published by R. T. Gunther in 1934. For almost three centuries, the early translation was held in Oxford in the Magdalen College Library.[1] The excerpts quoted from this edition were chosen as examples of herbs that possess pharmacologic activity and remain in current use because of their specific therapeutic value. These are santonin for the treatment of roundworms, colchicum (colchicine) for the treatment of arthritis (gout), castor oil for purging, and Mandragora wine for sedation and partial anesthesia in surgical operations.

27. *Apsinthion Thalassion. Artemisia maritima.* Absinthium marinum [but some call it Sandonion, some Seriphum, ye Romans Santonicum] which some call Seriphion, very much grows in the Mount Taurus about Cappadocia, & in Taphosiris of Egypt which ye Isiaci doe use instead of an olive branch. But ye herb is with thin branches like ye small Abrotonum abounding with little seels, somewhat bitter, bad for ye stomach, of a strong smell, binding with some heating, which being sodden by itself, or with Rice, & taken with honey doth kill ye Ascaridae and round worms, loosening ye belly gently. But is of force to doe ye same things with Sapa or being sod together with Lenticula. Cattle feeding on it, grow very fat.

The *Ephemeron* as described by Dioscorides is now identified as *Colchicum lingulatum,* with a lower content of colchicine than *C. autumnale.* No reference could be found which suggested that Dioscorides was familiar with its use in the treatment of gout or arthritis.[1]

85. *Ephemeron. Colchicum parnassicum* (Meadow Saffron). Ephemerum, which some call agrestis Iris, hath leaves & a stalk like to ye Lilly, but whiter, ye flowers white, bitter, & ye seed soft. The root lies under being single, ye thickness of a finger, long binding, sweet smelling. It grows in woods, & shady places. The root of this is a remedy for ye toothache, by way of collution. But ye leaves being sodden in wine & smeared on do dissolve Oedemata, & tumors, having not yet an humour.

164. *Kroton e kiki. Ricinus communis.* Ricinus, or Crotona, which some call Sesamum sylvestre, some Seseli cyprium, some Croton [ye Egyptians Systhamna, some Trixis, the Magi Sanguis febris, ye Romans Ricinus, some Lupa]. It is called Ricinus, for the likeness of ye seed to that creature. But it is a tree having ye heighth of a small fig tree, but leaves like ye plane tree, but greater, and smoother, and blacker, but it hath the trunks & the boughs hollow after ye manner of a reed, but ye seed in rough berries, which being peeled is like to ye creature Ricinus. Out of which also is pressed the oil which is called Cicinum. It is not to be eaten, but is useful for candles and plasters. But as many as 30 grains in number being made clean, & drank being beaten small, drive out through ye belly Phlegm, & choler, & water. They do also move vomiting, but ye purginging after this way is harsh & extremely laboursome, mightily overturning the stomach, but being beaten & laid on cleanse ye Vari, & sun-burnings.

76. *Mandragoras. Atropa Mandragora* (Mandrake). Mandragoras, which some call Antimelon, some call it Dircaea, some Circaea [some Circaeum, some Xeranthe, some Antimnion, some Bombochylon, some Minon, ye Egyptians Apemum, Pythagoras Anthropomorphon, some Aloitin, some Thridacian, some Cammaron, Zoroastres Diamonon, or Archinen, ye Magi Hemionous, some Gonogeonas, ye Romans Mala Canina, some Mala terrestria.].

And some do seeth the roots in wine to thirds, & straining it set it up. Using a Cyathus of it for such as cannot sleep, or are grievously pained, & upon whom being cut, or cauterized they wish to make a not-feeling pain. . . . & being put up into ye seat for a suppository, it causeth sleep. . . . Ye wine of ye bark of ye root is prepared without seething but you must cast in 3 pounds into a Metreta of sweet wine, & that there be given of it 3 Cyathi to such as shall be cut, or cauterized, as is aforesaid. For they do not apprehend the pain, because they are overborn with dead sleep, but the apples being smelled to, or eaten, are soporiferous, & ye juice that is of them. But used too much they make men speechless. . . . Physitians also, use this, when they are about to cut, or cauterize.

Dioscorides, botanist and herbalist, was considered the ultimate authority in this field for a millennium and a half. Manuscripts on the use of botanicals in medicine were largely plagiarized from revisions or editions of his great Greek manuscript as recently as the 17th century.

1. Gunther, R. T.: *The Greek Herbal of Dioscorides,* Oxford: University Press, 1934.
2. Sigerist, H. F.: Materia Medica in the Middle Ages, *Bull Hist Med* 7:417-423, 1939.
3. Dioscorides, P.: *Pedacii Dioscoridis Aanazarbaei Opera,* Caesarea: A. Wecheli, 1598.
4. Stieb, E. W.: Drug Adulteration and Its Detection, in the Writings of Theophrastus, Dioscorides and Pliny, *J Mond Pharm* 2:117-134, 1958.

Rufus of Ephesus

RUFUS (Fr. *roux,* redhead, red-beard), a common given name in Rome, of Ephesus (Asia Minor) is certainly the greatest medical link between Hippocrates and Galen. Second in stature as a Greek physician, and in clinical acclaim surpassed only by his predecessor and his successor, he lived in the reign of Trajan (AD 98-117). Remnants of his teachings were preserved by Oribasius, court physician to Emperor Julianus, a countryman and eclectic physician who lived in the fourth century after Christ. Paul of Aegina (AD 625-690) was also a chronicler of the writing of Rufus. Paul was

National Library of Medicine

the last of the Greek physicians who preserved the writings that had been compiled over the millennium. The description of the plague by Rufus, retold by Paul, recounts the environment in which it flourished, the symptoms and physical signs of the afflicted and the symptomatic treatment. The works of Rufus were also translated into Arabic, especially by Rhazes (AD 865-929). Gilbertus Anglicus (AD 1180-1250), believed to be the first Englishman to write about gout, quoted freely from Rufus. It is possible that Chaucer was referring to Rufus in his *Doctour of Physic:* "Well knew he the old Esculapius and Diuscorides, and Eekrisus (Rufus)."

Rufus studied medicine in Alexandria and practiced throughout the central and eastern Mediterranean lands. His treatise entitled *On the Interrogation of the Patient* is of particular interest. He considered the interrogation of the patient to be a fundamental stage in the examination. Brock's translation of Rufus from the Greek[1] is as follows:

One must put questions to the patient, for thereby certain aspects of the disease can be better understood, and the treatment rendered more effective. And I place the interrogation of the patient himself first, since in this way you can learn how far his mind is healthy or otherwise; also his physical strength and weakness; and you can get some idea of the disease and the part affected.—First we have to ask at what time the illness began; this is most valuable both for treatment and for reckoning the critical days; it suffices for setting us on the look-out for the periodical occurrence of the latter.—The next thing to ask is whether what has now happened is one of the diseases to which the individual is accustomed, or is something which has never happened to him before. For, speaking generally, many people fall ill more than once with the same disease, have the same symptoms and are similarly treated.—In regard to congenital diseases: it is surely not possible, is it, to find out about these in any way except by asking? Moreover, this could not be called a trivial inquiry, unless it is also trivial to determine what disease is easy to treat and what difficult. For it is justly believed that everything congenital is harder to cure than what is not.

The opposing view presumably was taken by Callimachus (identity as a physician not established). Rufus continues:

This is why I am surprised at Callimachus; he alone of all physicians of the past—or at least of those to whom one would pay any attention—maintains that it is unnecessary to make any inquiries either about any other diseases or injuries, and particularly those of the head. He holds that the physical signs in each case are enough to indicate both the disease and its cause, and that on these we can base the whole prognosis and a more efficient treatment. He considers it superfluous to ask about even the determining causes of a disease, such as the manner of life and the various occupations.—He maintains that the physician has nothing to learn from any of these, if he will but carefully consider the signs occurring in each disease.—My own view, however, is that, while one may discover a great deal by one's self about disease, yet one does this best and more definitely by means of questions; for, if the result of these corresponds with the signs found, the condition is then more easily known.

The treatise on gout attributes the malady to the accumulation of poisons in the body. Rufus uses terms which may be translated as "visceral gout" and "recurrent gout." There is little indication, however, that he distinguished this malady as another type of arthritis. Delpeuch[2] attributes to Rufus the description of tophi (calculi) in the kidney and the use of colocynth in treatment. It is well established that Alexander of Tralles five centuries later used Colchicum in treatment. Is it possible that Rufus was aware of the specific property of Colchicum and confused it with colocynth?

Rufus described filariasis: "In the country of the Arabs there occurs an ailment, the 'snake' disease, which in Greek is called a 'sinew.' This 'snake,' as thick as the chord of a lyre, moves and turns about in the flesh like a reptile, and especially in the thighs and legs, but also in other parts of the body."

The anatomical nomenclature introduced by Rufus is noteworthy. Regional anatomy was based on examination of slaves. On the other hand, dissection was carried out on monkeys because their anatomy was similar to that of man. The membrane of the ventricles of the brain was called the choroid; it resembled the chorion of the placenta. The crystalline lens, the membranes of the eye and optic chiasm were described. He noted that the pulse and the apical impulse of the heart were synchronous. He described the liver as a five-lobed organ. This error was perpetuated in the literature until Vesalius corrected it. The contributions of Rufus of Ephesus to internal medicine, surgery, anatomy, physiology, and nomenclature, justify his stature in Greek medicine not far removed from that of Hippocrates and Galen.

1. Brock, A. J.: Greek Medicine, London, J. M. Dent & Sons, Ltd., 1929.

2. Delpeuch, A.: Gout and Rheumatism, Paris, G. Carré and C. Naud, 1900.

Galen (AD 130-200)

GALEN brought to a close the medicine of ancient Greece and in its place introduced experimental physiology. More than 14 centuries were yet to elapse, however, before the modern medical era began. Galen, in the interim, was quoted endlessly, but his reputation was not threatened by any competitor, nor were his scientific contributions put to test, expanded, revised, or rejected. Thus, his word carried an authority rivaled only by Hippocrates from ancient to early modern times. No medical scientist approached the stature of Galen until Vesalius, with De fabrica, provided the first modern

Royal College of Physicians

treatise on anatomy in 1543, and Harvey established the basis for modern physiology in the discovery of the circulation of blood in 1628. But even in these notable events, the observations were built upon the contributions of Galen. In contrast, when Galen pursued studies on anatomy and physiology in the second century AD, there was little upon which to build, except for the clinical observations of Hippocrates.

Galen was born at Pergamum (parchment center), approximately 50 miles north of Smyrna (Izmir, Turkey), the son of Nicon, and died about AD 200. His name was assumed to be Claudius Galen, although Clarissimus has been suggested because of his brilliance. On the other hand, the Greek Galenos means "calm" or "serene," "a quiet sea," hardly a valid characterization of an impetuous person. His father, architect, mathematician, and land owner, has been held responsible, through a dream, for Galen's early schooling in philosophy, mathematics, and logic and the preparation for medicine. Galen studied first in the local temple of Aesculapius, an institution for medical teaching and medical healing, common to a number of cities of ancient Greece. After the death of his father, he studied under Pelops at Smyrna and for a short time at Corinth, the new capital of Greece. Formal education was concluded at the then famous university of Alexandria, the best school for the study of anatomy in the ancient world, where he remained for several years. Before the age of 30, he returned to Pergamum to begin the practice of medicine, and in due time was appointed surgeon for the gladiators at the summer games. The appointment provided surgical experience in the care of the contestants and medical experience in directing their training and planning of diets. In subsequent years, anatomy, physiology, and general medicine, rather than surgery, were Galen's chief medical interests.

As the outstanding physician of Asia Minor, it is not surprising that he was attracted to Rome, the capital of the civilized world. However, Rome was hostile to foreigners and particularly to foreigners of the professional skill and clinical capacity of a Galen. Although spurned by the citizens, his remarkable skills in diagnosis and treatment soon reached the ears of the emperor, Marcus Aurelius, who commanded him to serve as his personal physician. With fame and high prestige, Galen returned to Pergamum five years later. His departure was keenly felt, and before long he was persuaded by Marcus Aurelius to return to Rome, where he wrote and practiced for the three final decades of life.

Galen was a prolific writer and dealt with philosophy, mathematics, and grammar, in addition to medicine. Many of his treatises, prepared in Greek, were translated into Arabic, then into Latin, and in recent centuries into modern languages. A contemporary translation of books I-VIII and the first five chapters of book IX of his *Anatomy,* undertaken by Singer, was published in 1956.[2] The later books, up to and including XV, were translated by Duckworth and published in 1962.[3] The lectures which form the substance of the volumes were delivered in the Greek language in Rome in AD 177, taken down in shorthand, translated into Latin in 1531, and used by Vesalius in the preparation of *De fabrica.* Near the end of his life, many of his manuscripts and books were lost in a fire which destroyed the Temple of Peace in Rome. The selected items and excerpts offered in his *Anatomy* necessarily reflect only inadequately the magnitude of the influence of Galen's medical practice and medical thought, the products of a brilliant mind.

An elaborate system of polypharmacy was introduced by Galen, which remains in the use of the term "galenicals," applying particularly to plants and herbs. In his travels and practice throughout his known world, medicinals were collected and their therapeutic value described. A system of pathologic physiology was developed, based upon the four humors of Hippocrates: blood, phlegm, yellow bile, and black bile, and the three spirits: natural, vital, and animal. The natural spirit was assigned to the liver for generation, growth, and nutrition of the body; the vital spirit, to the heart for elaboration and dissipation of heat; and the animal spirit, to the brain for sensation and motion. The parts of the body were viewed as simple or compound, comprising the elements of fire, water, air, and earth, with the qualities of heat, cold, moisture, and dryness. Health consisted of a balanced proportion of the four elements; sickness followed an imbalance of the elements.

The physiology advanced by Galen is highly commendable as judged by current concepts, if by vital spirit, oxygen is intended, and if animal spirit is replaced by electrical potential of the nerve. He demonstrated experimentally that the arteries and veins were connected and that the arteries contained blood and air and not air alone. The left ventricle received the vital spirit from the lungs and blood from the right ventricle. The pulse rate was studied and arrhythmias recognized; the terms "systole" and "diastole" were introduced. He wrote that:[4]

The heart and all the arteries pulsate with the same rhythm, so that from one you can judge of all; not that it is possible to feel the pulsations of all to the same extent, but only in those areas where the artery is close to the surface.

But you could not find any arteries more convenient or more suitable for taking the pulse than those in the wrists, for they are easily visible, as there is little flesh over them, and it is not necessary to strip any part of the body of clothing for them.

The artery will seem to the touch to be distended in every dimension.

In an animal in a normal state of health you will find the artery quite moderately distended; but in abnormal conditions sometimes the tension is too low, sometimes too great in every dimension.

As regards special characteristics, there is swiftness and slowness. The strength of the pulse or the reverse is determined by the force with which it repels the touch; if it repels violently it is strong, if weakly the reverse.

Regularity and irregularity occur in the above-mentioned variations. By regularity is meant an even and unbroken series. . . . Irregularity means the destruction of even rhythm in whatever varieties of pulse it occurs.

For one may be irregular in size, another in rate, another in violence, feebleness, and frequency, and so on.

Sometimes too, when a number of beats are definite and regular, an uneven pulsation occurs in the midst of the even ones; and this may happen in various ways. For there may be three regular beats, then the fourth irregular, and so on continuously; or there may be four regular and the fifth irregular.

In the treatise *On the Natural Facilties,*[5] Galen assumed that the organs "attracted" what was needed for nutrition. The kidneys, specifically, attracted the serous portion of the blood in the formation of urine, and urinary difficulties were related to the kidneys.[4]

That they are the organs for separating out the urine was the belief of such physicians as Hippocrates, Diocles, Erisistratus and Praxagoras, but in truth any butcher knows this from the fact that he sees every day the position of the kidneys and the duct (called the ureter) which runs from each kidney into the bladder and by studying this anatomy he reasons what their use is and the nature of their functions. But aside from the butchers, all patients who suffer from painful urination or retention of urine call themselves nephritics or kidney patients when they have a colic in the loins or pass sandy matter in the urine.

Since dissection of the human body was forbidden in Galen's time, his studies in anatomy were conducted primarily upon animals, particularly Barbary apes. Occasionally it was possible to dissect the body of a slain enemy or a slave, and skeletons were sometimes assembled from the remains of hasty burials in shallow graves.[2]

Make it rather your serious endeavour not only to acquire accurate book-knowledge of each bone but also to examine assiduously with your own eyes the human bones themselves. This is quite easy at Alexandria because the physicians there employ ocular demonstrations in teaching osteology to students. For this reason, if for no other, try to visit Alexandria. But if you cannot, it is still possible to see something of human bones. I, at least, have done so often on the breaking open of a grave or tomb. Thus once a river, inundating a recent hastily made grave, broke it up, washing away the body. The flesh had putrefied, though the bones still held together in their proper relations. It was carried down a stadium and, reaching marshy ground, drifted ashore. This skeleton was as though deliberately prepared for such elementary teaching.

If you have not the luck to see anything of this sort, dissect an ape and, having removed the flesh, observe each bone with care. Choose those apes likest man, with short jaws and small canines.

I therefore maintain that the bones must be learnt either from man, or ape, or better from both, before dissecting the muscles, for these two (namely bones and muscles) form the groundwork of the other parts, the foundations, as it were, of a building. And next, study arteries, veins, and nerves. Familiarity with dissection of these will bring you to the inward parts and so to a knowledge of the viscera, the fat, and the glands, which also you should examine separately, in detail. Such should be the order of your training.

In his *De temperamentis,* Galen observed that animal poisons were not harmful unless they entered the blood stream; likewise, the saliva of the rabid dog or the venom of the viper produced no harmful effects on the stomach when taken internally or on the surface of the body, unless they entered through broken skin. Pneumonia was differentiated from pleurisy; aneurysm and dilatation of vessels were observed. Jaundice was declared to be a symptom not a disease. A full, not exclusively a milk, diet and climatic treatment was recommended for different forms of phthisis. The relationship between renal calculus and gout was suspected. Opium was to be used cautiously. The sympathetic ganglia were described. The pulsations of blood between the heart and a ligated artery, but not beyond, were demonstrated, as well as the beating of an excised heart outside the body. The concept of tonus as active posture was introduced. Incision and draining were recommended for treatment of suppuration, which was associated with the healing of wounds by second intention.

Galen was the first to demonstrate that contraction is the sole action of muscle and that the movement of a relaxed muscle is produced by the contraction of an opposing muscle group. Only one direction of contraction was attributed to each muscle. In discovering the force of a contracting muscle, he deduced that the stimulus originated in the brain and was communicated peripherally by the nerves. This was confirmed by serial dissection of the cord, with subsequent paralysis of the enervated skeletal muscles. When the cord was bisected, only one side of the body was paralyzed. The interruption of a nerve caused loss of motion and sensation peripherally but not centrally. Sensory and motor nerves were shown to have separate attachments to the cord. One of his best studies on the nervous system described the control of movements of the vocal cords. The recurrent laryngeal nerve was discovered accidentally while he was severing the nerves in the chest.

The conduct of a comprehensive physical examination followed logical principles. The medical history included inquiry of past social events, occupation, habits, exposure to contagious diseases, and respiratory, gastrointestinal, and urinary complaints. On physical examination, the clothing was removed; palpation and percussion were practiced; fever was detected by the warmth of the skin; the pulse rate was measured, and sputum, vomit, urine, and feces were examined. The individual was treated as well as the morbid process. Analogies and relations were seen, and the common embryologic

origin of male and female reproductive organs appreciated.

Galen, interested in natural philosophy and natural science, explored medical principles based upon critical observations in anatomy and physiology. Possibly he was the last physician cognizant of scientific medicine of the past and contemporary to him.

1. Brock, A. J.: *Greek Medicine*, E. Barker, ed., London: J. M. Dent & Sons, Ltd., 1929.
2. Singer, C.: *Galen on Anatomical Procedures*, London: Oxford University Press, 1956.
3. Duckworth, W. L. H.: *Galen on Anatomical Procedures*, Cambridge University Press, 1962.
4. "Galen," in *Source Book of Medical History*, compiled by L. Clendening, New York: Dover Publications, Inc., 1960.
5. Galen: *On the Natural Faculties*, A. J. Brock, trans., Loeb Classical Library, London: W. Heinemann, 1916.

National Library of Medicine

Aretaeus, the Cappadocian

THE A'S IN GRECO-ROMAN MEDICINE HAVE IT! Aesculapius, Aëtius (physician to Justinian I), Antyllus (Antyllian operation for aneurysm), and Aristotle span a period of almost 2,000 years, beginning with the dawn of Greek medicine and concluding with the fall of the Roman Empire. It is customary to identify historic greats before the Renaissance by a community or country of birth or residence. Aretaeus, a Greek, was born in Cappadocia, a Roman province in Asia Minor, several centuries after Hippocrates. Although the records are unclear as to his precise dates in the chronology of medicine, it is believed that he was a contemporary of Galen, the 2nd or 3rd century after Christ.[1] He studied in Alexandria, whose fame as a medical center was already on the descendancy but still recognized as a great school of medicine.

Aretaeus was a prolific writer, but few translations of his original communications remain. *De causis et signis morborum* is the only extant treatise. Aretaeus was one of the first to describe cardiac murmurs; possibly he was the first to practice direct auscultation of the chest. His style of writing is described as "Ionic, original, refined and elegant."[2] Aretaeus, a sound clinician, rejected idle speculation and superstition and added his personal experiences and observations to the aphorisms of Hippocrates. A description and understanding of form and structure of the body preceded a discussion of diagnosis and treatment. His school of medicine was Eclectic, which combined the best of Empiricism and Methodism. The heart was regarded as the central organ of man, the site of the soul. In this he accepted the philosophy of the Pneumatics. The heart, surrounded by the lungs, influenced respiration and the need of the body for air (oxygen). Arteries were recognized as the carriers of red blood, the veins the carriers of dark blood. Nerves were the organ of sensation and the source of muscular action.

A number of diseases are readily identified. His account of the insensibility of pulmonary tissue to pain, the ominous nature of hemoptysis, and the chronic cough leaves little doubt that pulmonary tuberculosis (phthisis) was the morbid state described in one section. Other features of the malady included the curved nails, weight loss, prominent ribs and shoulder blades, narrow chest, night sweats, and pallor. Diabetes, a Greek term signifying a syphon, was more common among women; it was described as the "melting down of the flesh and limbs into urine." Once the disease is fully established, death rapidly supervenes. Thirst is unquenchable. Restlessness and nausea are terminal symptoms. The development of dropsy and anasarca in the diabetic is identified in contemporary medicine as the nephrotic syndrome.

The epileptic seizure was vividly described:[1]

In the attack, the person lies insensible; the hands are clasped together by the spasm. . . . The calamity bears a resemblance to slaughtered bulls; the neck bent, the head variously distorted, for sometimes it is arched, as it were, forwards, so that the chin rests upon the breast; and sometimes it is retracted to the back . . . The tongue protrudes, so as to incur the risk of a great wound, or of a piece of it being cut off, should the teeth come forcibly together with the spasm; the eyes roll inwards . . . the lips sometimes compressed together to a sharp point. . . . As the illness increases lividity of countenance also supervenes . . . inability of speech as in suffocation; insensibility even if you call loudly. The utterance a moaning and lamentation; and the respiration a sense of suffocation, as in a person who is throttled. . . . But when they come to the termination of the illness, there are unconscious discharges of the urine, and watery discharges from the bowels.

The trephine was used in the treatment of intractable epilepsy if bleeding from the vein at the forehead and application of heat were ineffective. Mental aberrations were divided into mania, melancholia, and stable insanity.[3] Lead colic, pharyngeal diphtheria, asthma, and hysteria were described. Opium was prescribed for pain. Aretaeus had knowledge of tracheotomy. He was the first clinician to accept contagion as a fact. Decussation of nerve pathways in the spinal cord was appreciated.[1]

If, therefore, the commencement of the affection be below the head, such as the membrane of the spinal marrow, the parts which are homonymous and connected with it are paralysed: the right on the right side, and the left on the left side. But if the head be primarily affected on the right side, the left side of the body will be paralysed; and the right, if on the left side. The cause of this is the interchange in the origins of the nerves, for they do not pass along on the same side, the right on the right side, until their terminations; but each of them passes over to the other side from that of its origin, decussating each other in the form of the letter X.

The diagnosis and treatment of gout (podagra) was described.[1]

. . . for in gouty cases hellebore is the great remedy, yet only in the first attacks of the affection.

But if it has subsided for a long time already, and also if it appear to have been transmitted from the patient's forefathers, the disease sticks to him until death.

The prescription of white hellebore, a powerful purge, was empiric. Possibly it is not so strange as would appear on casual inspection. Herbs comprised a significant category of therapeutic agents in Greco-Roman medicine. Colchicine, from the yellow saffron, the only specific drug available today in the management of articular gout, also is a powerful purge. It seems reasonable to believe that some confusion might have arisen between the white hellebore and the yellow saffron in the empiric treatment of this articular malady. The tale of the Olympic runner with gout, who was a victor in the games between acute attacks, is given in this section.

Endocrinology was not overlooked. A possible case of hypopituitarism was described:[1]

For it is the semen, when possessed of vitality, which makes us to be men, hot, well braced in limbs, hairy, well voiced, spirited, strong to think and to act, as the characteristics of men prove. For when the semen is not possessed of its vitality, persons become shrivelled, have a sharp tone of voice, lose their hair and their beard, and become effeminate, as the characteristics of eunuchs prove.

Although Aretaeus lived nearly 2,000 years ago, his writings have meaning in relation to the practice of medicine today. He was a critical observer at the bedside; he reported the natural history of morbid processes and refused to dissipate his talents in useless speculation—a sound procedure for ancient Cappadocia or contemporary clinical medicine.

1. *Extant Works of Aretaeus, the Cappadocian,* F. Adams, ed. and trans., London: Printed for Sydenham Society, 1856.
2. Robinson, V.: *Pathfinders in Medicine,* 2nd ed., New York: Medical Life Press, 1929.
3. Gordon, B. L.: *Medicine Throughout Antiquity,* Philadelphia: F. A. Davis Company, 1949.

Isidore of Seville (c 560-636)

ST. ISIDORE OF SEVILLE, also known as Isidorus Hispalensis, produced an encyclopedic work, which served for generations as a text for those who cultivated medicine as a scholastic discipline within the church.[1] Neither the site nor the date of his birth is known. Born of Catholic parents he was never a monk and upon the death of his parents in boyhood remained unmarried and sympathetic toward monastic life his education was entrusted to his brother, Leander, Bishop of Seville, who had established a cathedral school. Here Isidor acquired a knowledge of Latin and Hebrew and probably some Greek. After Leander died in 599, Isidore succeeded him as Bishop and remained in the hierarchy through the supervision of the fourth Council of Toledo convened in 633.

Following the decline of Roman civilization, the eradication of the Empire by the Goths, and the widespread disappearance of learning in Europe in the waning years of the 5th century, Isidore joined a small number of scholars in an attempt to preserve the spiritual and educational amenities of the dying Western civilization. Although not an original thinker he produced a tremendous literary output. He prepared several works on history and treatises on the scriptures, theology, and liturgy. Especially was his noteworthy encyclopedia of ancient and contemporary facts, called *Etymologiae* or *Origins*, which was divided into 20 books and which carried exerted great influence throughout the Middle Ages. Book IV on medicine is of particular interest to physicians. Other portions of the encyclopedia that concern man and his parts discuss astronomy, meteorology and the elements, healing springs, and diet. Although Isidore provided no list of references as source material, his biographers believe that he relied heavily upon the writings of Hippocrates, Galen, Dioscorides, Caelius Aurelianus, Oribasius, and possibly Celsus and Soranus.

The 13 chapters of Isidore's book on medicine include a discussion of the three medical sects in vogue at the time, the four elements and the four humors, acute and chronic diseases, disorders of the skin, therapeutic agents, surgical instruments, etc. Masturbation was regarded as an effeminate habit and alcoholism was condemned. He probably refers to angina pectoris when he described sharp pains in the anterior chest accompanied by extreme apprehension. Pleurisy is identified symptomatically as a sharp pain accompanied by fever and bloody sputum. Phthisis is classified as a chronic disease, especially among young people, associated with gradual wasting of the body. From the concluding chapter, "The Study of Medicine," a rhetorical question is raised as to why medicine is not contained within the liberal arts. An enlightening answer is provided as follows.[2]

1. Some ask why the art of medicine is not included among the other liberal disciplines. It is because whereas they embrace individual subjects, medicine embraces them all. The physician ought to know literature, *grammatica,* to be able to understand or to explain what he reads.

2. Likewise also rhetoric, that he may delineate in true arguments the things which he discusses; dialetic also so that he may study the causes and cures of infirmities in the light of reason. Similarly also arithmetic, in view of the temporal relationships involved in the paroxysms of diseases and in diurnal cycles.

3. It is no different with respect to geometry because of the properties of regions and the locations of places. He should teach what must be observed in them by everyone. Moreover, music ought not be unknown by him, for many things are said to have been accomplished for ill men through the use of this art, as is said of David who cleansed Saul of an unclean spirit through the art of melody. The physician Asclepiades also restored a certain insane man to his pristine health through music.

4. Finally also, he ought to know astronomy, by which he should study the motions of the stars and the changes of the seasons, for as a certain physician said, our bodies are also changed with their courses.

5. Hence it is that medicine is called a second philosophy, for each discipline claims the whole of man for itself. Just as by philosophy the soul, so also by medicine the body is cured.

Isidore is remembered today because he kept ancient traditions of learning alive in the monasteries through his many writings and particularly his *Etymologiae.*

1. Fletcher, G. R. J.: *St. Isidore of Seville and His Book on Medicine,* London: J. Bale, Sons, & Danielsson, 1920.
2. Sharpe, W. D.: Isidore of Seville: The Medical Writings, An English Translation With an Introduction and Commentary, *Trans Amer Philos Soc* 54:1-75 (April, pt 2) 1964.

Rhazes (c 850-932)

OF THE FOUR OUTSTANDING PHYSICIANS of the Muslim world, Rhazes, Haly Ben Abbas, and Avicenna practiced in the Eastern Caliphate. Albucasis of Spain was a Westerner.[1] The surgical writings of Rhazes were followed by many physicians until the contributions of Ambroise Paré replaced them in the 16th century. Abú Bakr Muhammad ibn Zakariyyá of Ray, (Arabic, ar-Rází or Al-Kazi, Latinized in the Middle Ages to Rhazes), was born about the year 850 only a few miles north of Tehran, the modern capital of Iran (Persia). Rhazes was interested in music, particularly the lute in early life, and compiled an encyclopedia of music. Philosophy was another commanding interest. Rhazes' dedication to medicine, not manifest until the age of 30, has been attributed to hospital visits and conversations with the local pharmacist. Thereafter, his rise to fame was rapid. He walked the wards of the Azudi Hospital with students and interns in an informal, but planned, program of teaching and management of the sick similar to current practices. The pupil (clinical clerks) examined the patient initially, followed by the teacher (the preceptor or the instructor), and lastly by the chief, Rhazes, in billowing robes. Common sense psychiatry, great professional skill, and acute diagnostic ability brought him general acclaim. Between consultations and ward visits, precious hours were found for the composition of more than 200 treatises in medicine. Many as yet have never been translated from the Arabic.

It is reasonable to assume that the aggregate of significant medical knowledge from the beginning of recorded history was assembled and annotated in his 20-volume masterpiece, *Al-Hawi* or *El Hawi.* The medical lore from Greece, the Roman Empire, Syria, India, and Persia, supplemented by personal experiences and professional judgments, was tabulated. The categories included medicine, surgery, anatomy, physiology, materia medica, dietetics, hygiene, and chemistry. Specific items included renal and vesical calculi, the use of animal gut for surgical sutures, the value of white lead and mercury in ointments, a description of the recurrent laryngeal nerve, genitourinary infection, the differentiation of gout and rheumatism, and a description of spina bifida.

Rhazes conceived of fever as a defense against disease, not as the disease itself. His most celebrated treatise concerns smallpox and measles. The English copy, reprinted in *Medical Classics,*[2] was based upon the translation from the Arabic by Greenhill and was published in 1847 for the Sydenham Society in London. Smallpox, or variola, was endemic and epidemic in Asia from the dawn of history. The term "variola" appears first in the 6th century in church writings. The derivation is from the Latin, *varus,* a pimple or pustule. Rhazes in 910 at the age of 60, described the clinical symptoms and findings which differentiated smallpox from measles. Later on the word "greatpox" was selected for syphilis, to distinguish this new disease from smallpox.

One reference in this document suggests that Rhazes had some preconception of Harvey's discovery of the circulation of blood seven centuries later.[3]

For the putrid air, which has an undue proportion of heat and moisture, and also an inflamed air, promotes the eruption of this disease (smallpox), by converting the spirit in the two ventricles of the heart to its own temperament, and then by means of the heart converting the whole of the blood in the arteries into a state of corruption like itself.

Sadi accepts the premise that Rhazes was aware of the presence of blood in the heart and blood vessels, and that "corruption" could be spread from the ventricles to the peripheral arteries. However, no mention was made of the propelling action of the heart or circulation of blood as a physiologic concept.

Rhazes begins his masterpiece on smallpox with the gracious acknowledgement that Galen had recognized the malady and had described specific treatment:

The eruption of the Small-Pox is preceded by a continued fever, pain in the back, itching in the nose, and terrors in sleep. . . . A pricking which the patient feels all over his body . . . an inflamed color . . . in both the cheeks; a redness of both the eyes . . . pain in the throat and chest, with a slight difficulty in breathing, and cough . . . (the inquietude, nausea, and anxiety are more frequent in the Measles than in the Small-Pox; while the pain in the back is more peculiar to the Small-Pox than to the Measles). . . . When, therefore, you see these symptoms . . . you may be assured that the eruption of one or other of these diseases in the patient is nigh at hand.

The eruption of the Small-Pox and Measles is accelerated by well wrapping the patient up in clothes, and rubbing his body, and exposing it to the steam of hot water.

As soon as the symptoms of the Small-Pox appear, drop rose-water into the eyes from time to time; and wash the face with cold water several times in the day, and sprinkle the eyes with the same. For if the disease be favorable, and the pustules few in number, you will by this mode of treatment prevent their breaking out in the eyes.

Now the chief prognostic signs in those who recover are, a freedom of respiration, soundness of mind, appetite for food, lightness of motion, a good state of the pulse, the patient's confident opinion respecting the event of his own illness, a convenient posture in bed, and but little tossing about and inquietude of body.

The safest kind of Measles is that where the redness is not very deep. . . . When either the Small-Pox or Measles sink in suddenly after they have begun to come out, and then the patient is seized with anxiety, and a swooning comes on, it is a sign of speedy death, unless they break out afresh.

All those pustules that are very large should be pricked; and the fluid that drops from them be soaked up with a soft clean rag in which there is nothing that may hurt or excoriate the patient.

The symptoms, findings, and treatment of smallpox recounted in the first edition of Osler's *Principles and Practice of Medicine*[4] are remarkably similar to those described by Rhazes. It is curious that the old-fashioned notion prevailed, a notion which Sydenham tried so hard to combat, that smallpox patients should be kept hot and warm. Rhazes had no premonition of vaccination against smallpox. Vaccination with cowpox had been practiced for more than 100 years in Osler's day. This represents the most significant difference between the smallpox described by Rhazes and smallpox described by Osler, great physicians whose careers were separated by a thousand years.

1. Browne, E. G.: *Arabian Medicine*, Cambridge, England: Cambridge University Press, 1921.
2. Rhazes, *Med Classics* 4:1-56 (Sept.) 1939.
3. Sadi, L. M.: The Millennium of Ar-Razi (Rhazes), *Ann Med Hist* 7:62-72 (Jan.) 1935.
4. Osler, W.: *Principles and Practice of Medicine*, New York: D. Appleton and Company, 1892.

Composite by G. Bako

Avicenna (980-1037)

AVICENNA (L.), Abū 'Ali at-Husain ibn Abdullāh ibn Sinā, the most famous physician of the Persian world, was born near Bukhārā, Iran, in 980. His place in the hierarchy of the great philosophers was just below Aristotle's. His writings reflect the Neoplatonic influence of Aristotle as modified by Muslim theology. Avicenna's father, a tax collector, sought the advantages of the capital city with its schools, mosques, and institutions of higher learning for his family, but in so doing came under the spell of the missionaries of the Ismaili sect. This secret religio-political order, which used hashish in the propagation of its doctrine, conflicted with the then current orthodoxy in speculations over man's soul and spirit. The precocious Avicenna was exposed at an early age to such heretical religious doctrine and philosophical polemics. The *Koran* had been read and memorized by the age of 10. It is no surprise that he readily documented his remarkable talents in Arabic and Persian literature in his autobiography. The record of the first 21 years was dictated to his friend and pupil, Juzjāni. This described in detail professed accomplishments in mathematics, literature, and logic. It was noted that tutoring in the first five propositions of Euclid were sufficient; the remaining forms were mastered independently. In maturity, he translated Euclid. The autobiography revealed no formal modesty:[1]

Medicine is not a difficult subject, and in a short space of time, of course, I excelled in it, so that the masters of physic came to read with me, and I began to visit the sick. Consequently there were opened to me the doors to various kinds of treatment which I learnt by experience (or experiment). I was then about sixteen years of age. During the period of hard practice and study which then ensued, I never once slept the whole night through. If a problem was too difficult for me, I repaired to the mosque and prayed, invoking the Creator of all things, until the gate that had been closed to me was opened and what had been complex became simple. Always, as night fell, I returned to my house, set the lamp before me and busied myself with reading and writing. If sleep overcame me or I felt the flesh growing weak, I had recourse to a beaker of wine, so that my energies were restored.

The Arabic epoch, 640 to 1400, revered the mantle of medicine passed down from Greek culture. The Muslim movement, which encompassed the lands from India to Spain, was responsible for the great centers of learning at Bagdad, Bukhārā, Damascus, and Alexandria in the East, balanced by the learned institutions of Cordova, Toledo, Seville, and Murcia in Spain. The principles of Arabic medicine, based upon the teachings of Hippocrates and Galen, had a lesser impact upon the life and scholarship of the times than upon the erudition displayed in theology, philosophy, mathematics, physics, and astronomy. Avicenna was not averse to pursuing any branch of learning. Although the autobiography does not extend beyond his 21st birthday, writing continued at an accelerated pace. The manuscripts, according to Brockelmann,[2] included 68 books on theology and metaphysics, 11 on astronomy and natural philosophy, 16 on medicine, and 4 in verse. Several are available only in the original Arabic; others have been translated into Latin; a few into English. A discussion of cardiac drugs has not been translated.

Avicenna's greatest medical compilation was the *Canon of Medicine,* a system presented in five parts.[3] This monumental treatise required many years to assemble; it required tremendous initiative and industry, a profound knowledge of science and medicine, and a capacity for composition. Simultaneously with the preparation of the *Canon,* a comprehensive discourse on the general principles of philosophy, metaphysics, and logic (Kitāb al-shifā, sanatio) was begun. The new concepts were transmitted each evening to his pupils who gathered to hear what had been composed during the day or to review passages from other days. The evening studies concluded with minstreling, Bacchanalia, and the pleasures associated therewith.

Avicenna studied medicine at Bagdad and was qualified to teach and to practice medicine at the age of 16. His first professional appointment was physician to The Emir (Amir).[2] Free access to the royal library was the reward for his clinical skill. One tale recounts the burning of many of the manuscripts in the great library after Avicenna had read them. His detractors hint darkly of a fire deliberately set to destroy books, already mastered, in an attempt to withhold knowledge from his rivals.

The *Canon* (al Qānūn fi-l-tibb) is a huge encyclopedia of medicine of almost 1,000,000 words. Although it is based upon the works of Galen and Hippocrates, it contains many original observations. The contagious nature of tuberculosis is recognized; mediastinitis is distinguished from pleurisy; the dissemination of diseases by water and soil and selected aspects of psychiatry are

discussed. The materia medica describes more than 760 drugs of which 60 could be identified in the *British Pharmacopoeia* of 1920. Several of the excerpts from the *Canon*[3] are as follows:

Medicine is the science of which we learn the various states of the human body, in health, when not in health, the means by which health is likely to be lost, and when lost, is likely to be restored to health.

Disease is transmitted from person to person. Heredity transmission includes premature baldness and gout.

The traveler is more exposed to illness from the diversity of the drinking water than he is from the diversity of foods. Hence it is necessary to be particular about correcting the bad qualities of the drinking water, and expend every effort in purifying it. Boil the water, for as we have already pointed out, boiling sometimes clarifies the water and separates off the impurities which are admixed with the intrinsic substance of the water.

Dark urine may be evidence of renal calculus.

In puerperal women, the appearance of dark urine is premonitory in convulsions.

If the sun-stroke has already occurred, let cold water be thrown over the limbs, and lave the face with it. Sexual intercourse must be avoided.

A person who has become frostbitten must be attended to without delay; he must be warmed and the vitality restored by calefacient oils.

The basic principles that underlie the *Canon* are the four elements: earth, water, air, and fire;[4] the qualities recognized by the basic sense of touch: cold, heat, dryness, and moisture; the temperaments: sanguineous, phlegmatic, choleric, and saturnine; and the faculties: the natural, the animal, and the vital. Nutrition and reproduction belong to the natural faculty. The vital faculty includes metabolic activity and the "breath" or "spirit," the Greek equivalent of *pneuma.* The *Canon* of Avicenna, a standard reference text from the 12th to the 17th century, was used in the universities at Montpellier, Bologna, and Paris.[5] Editions for study were published as recently as 1658.

The *Cantica (Arjuzat fi't-tibb),* Avicenna's poem on medicine, was translated into Latin in the 12th century and rendered into French and German in modern times. The first translation into English appeared in 1963.[7] This is an infinitely smaller work than the *Canon* but contains what the "Prince of Physicians" adjudged important in the theory and practice of medicine.

Avicenna devoted the last ten years of his life to intense writing and intense living. As the end approached, he freed his slaves, gave his wealth to the poor, and listened to the reading of the *Koran*. He died at the age of 58 and was buried at Hamadhān.[6] When Osler was professor of medicine at Oxford, he suggested that Levy[1] determine the condition of the tomb at Hamadhān. This suggestion was acted upon in 1919. The sepulcher was a shrine and a study center. It was rebuilt in 1954 to embrace a library and a tall open-work tower in honor of the greatest Iranian physician whose influence in medicine over the centuries compares favorably with that of Hippocrates and Galen.

1. Levy, R.: Avicenna—His Life and Times, *Med Hist* 1:249 (July) 1957.
2. Browne, E. G.: *Arabian Medicine*, Cambridge, England: University Press, 1921.
3. Gruner, O. C.: *A Treatise on the Canon of Medicine of Avicenna, Incorporating a Translation of the First Book*, London: Luzac & Co., 1930.
4. Gruner, O. C.: The Interpretation of Avicenna, *Ann Med Hist* 3:354, 1921.
5. Chatard, J. A.: Avicenna and Arabian Medicine, *Bull Johns Hopkins Hosp* 19:157 (June) 1908.
6. de Vaux, C.: *Avicenne*, Paris: Felix Alcan, 1900.
7. Krueger, H. C.: *Avicenna's Poem on Medicine*, Springfield, Ill.: Charles C Thomas, 1963.

Maimonides (1135-1204)

RABBI MOSES BEN MAIMON, the great Jewish-Arabian physician, known also as Abu Imran Musa ibn Maimun ibn Abd Allah, was born in Cordova, Spain, in the Western Caliphate in 1135.[1] In his youth in spite of the apparent decadence of Arabian medicine, a century was to pass before the acceptance of leadership by the Italian and French schools. Maimonides was born in a family of scholars. Although he obtained much of his early education from his father, there is no evidence that his father practiced medicine. In Cordova, the center of Jewish learning for several centuries, Jews and Arabs were given equal opportunity to study philosophy, theology, law, and medicine. Medicine

was but one of the several intellectual disciplines and was not segregated as a specific calling or profession. Although Maimonides took full advantage of the intellectual free-

Composite by G. Bako

dom offered by the Arabs, he was subject to the restrictions of authority and the prohibition that related to anatomical dissection and study.

With the subjugation of Cordova by the Almohades (Unitarians) in 1148,[2] the Jews were given the choice of embracing Islam or leaving the country. Maimonides' father was true to the faith, and the wanderings began. They resided temporarily in the provinces in Spain, then in Morocco and Palestine. It is not unlikely that he acquired his medical training in Fez, Morocco, where he resided for several years.[3] Eventually he settled in Cairo in 1165. By then Maimonides was 30. Although he began the preparation of his first medical treatise at the age of 28, the practice of medicine was not pursued as a vocation until Egypt was accepted as his adopted land. The father died shortly after the family fortune (precious stones) was lost in a shipwreck. This and other considerations induced Maimonides to practice medicine to support the family. While previously he had lectured on astronomy and the Talmud philosophy, medicine proved more profitable. He continued, meanwhile, as a Rabbi and judge, but medicine occupied the greater portion of his time—6 days each week. His practice was built upon the manuscripts of the ancients, supplemented by clinical experience and scientific deductions. Maimonides remained in Cairo or suburban Fustat until his death in 1204, having reached the high position of court physician to the Grand Vizier Al Fadil and Sultan Saladin.

As a forerunner of the scientific renaissance, the treatises of Maimonides, written in the later decades of his life, embrace philosophy, astronomy, mathematics, and medicine. His homilies in theology preserved the Hebrew religion and culture for several centuries. He wrote in Arabic, his native language. Many of the monographs were translated subsequently into Latin, and more recently into Hebrew, German, French, and English. The 3 best known works are *Poisons and Antidotes, Regimen Sanitatis,* and *Medical Aphorisms.* The last contains 1,500 aphorisms which are based upon the pronouncements of Hippocrates, Galen, and Avicenna.[4]

Maimonides exerted great influence upon European medicine.[1] Quackery, superstition, and mysticism in the practice of medicine were severely condemned.

Man should believe nothing which is not attested (1) by rational proof as in mathematical science, (2) by evidence of the senses or (3) by authority of prophets and saints.

The four humors of the Greeks—hot, cold, moist, and dry were recognized. Health was the blending of the four. In the introduction to the *Aphorisms,* he states:

And since I know that more men are ignorant than wise, and more men have ill-will than good will, I have had the foresight to specify at the end of every aphorism, which "particula" of Galen I am citing.

Included were chapters on the fundamentals and methods of the art of medicine, signs of special diseases, causes of special diseases, treatment of diseases, the value of diet and climate in asthma, bathing, food, drink, and rules of health.

We learn . . . that the soul is subject to health and disease just as is the body. The health and disease of both . . . undoubtedly depend upon beliefs and customs which are peculiar to mankind. . . . Within the sum total of these diseases these is one which is widespread and from which men rarely escape. This disease varies in degree in different men, just as all bodily . . . diseases vary. . . . I refer to this: that every person thinks his mind . . . more clever and more learned than it is.

Poisons and Antidotes, which was translated into several languages, was a standard reference volume for several centuries. Some passages reflect sound clinical judgment even by current standards. The bites of snakes and other animals and their treatment were considered in the first portion; the second part dealt with prophylaxis. The wound of a viper bite was to be kept open and the ligature was to be applied central to the wound, to prevent the poison from reaching the more vital parts of the body. The poison was to be sucked out of the wound by a person who was free of oral abrasions or sores. The lips and buccal mucosa of the person charged with this responsibility were coated with olive oil to prevent the absorption of poison. It was recorded that symptoms of rabies do not appear for 8 or more days after the bite; meanwhile, the wound was to be kept open for at least 40 days.

In *Regimen Sanitatis,* reliance was placed upon diet and good rules of health rather than upon drugs. Maimonides appreciated that the physical condition may be influenced by the mental state. Hemorrhoids were treated by regulation of the bowels, diet, sitz baths, and an opium ointment. Drastic purges were condemned. Wine was recommended for the aged but not for the young. General rules included early rising, regular gymnastics, an afternoon rest period, and music at bedtime. The daily prayer of a physician before beginning the visiting of the sick has been attributed to Maimonides.[5]

May there never rise in me the notion that I know enough, but give me strength and leisure and zeal to enlarge my knowledge. . . . Thou hast chosen me in Thy grace to watch over the life and death of Thy creature. I am about to fulfill my duties. Guide me in this immense work so that it may be of avail.

Maimonides, a philosopher as well as physician, combined these disciplines to achieve the 12th century version of the Greek view of an integrated life. He relied upon philosophy in the practice of medicine and called upon his clinical skill and experience in the elucidation of theology and philosophy. He extended and integrated the concept of body and soul:[1]

All things and all aspects of nature and of life, of thought and of action, were part of this harmonic whole. I shall not venture to answer the question whether this harmony made him the great man or whether he found that harmony because he was a great man.

1. Friedenwald, H.: *The Jews and Medicine*, Vol. 1, Baltimore: Johns Hopkins Press, 1944.
2. Yellin, D., and Abrahams, I.: *Maimonides*, Philadelphia: Jewish Publication Society of America, 1903.
3. Minkin, J. S.: *The World of Moses Maimonides: with Selections from His Writings*, New York: Thomas Yeseloff, Inc., 1957.
4. Bragman, L. J.: Historical Medicine: Maimonides' Treatise on Poisons, *Med Rec* 124:103 (July-Dec.) 1926.
5. Kagan, S. R.: Maimonides' Prayer, *Ann Med Hist* 10:429, 1938.

Gilbertus (c 1180-1250)

GILBERTUS ANGLICUS was one of a handful of physicians in England in the 13th century, who prepared one or more major manuscripts in medicine, of sufficient significance to hold the attention of the profession into the following centuries. The surname, "Anglicus," testifies to his European reputation, since the English would probably not speak of a fellow physician as the "Englishman." The *Compendium medicinae,* his most famous tract, is a substantial treatise devoted largely to internal medicine but with chapters on wounds, fractures, lithotomy, herniotomy, and other selected surgical subjects. The manuscript is believed to have been composed about 1240. The first printed edition, published in Lyon in 1510, embraced 724 pages.[1] Beyond the inferences that may be drawn from the contents of the *Compendium* and his other manuscripts, only bare details are known of his training and the extent of his practice.

The best interpretation of his biographical data and medical writings in recent times was prepared by Henry E. Handerson of Cleveland and privately printed by the Cleveland Medical Library Association in 1918.[2] Handerson reviewed the diverse opinions of 18th and 19th century historians and concluded that Gilbert probably was born about 1180 and died about 1250. Upon completion of his early education in England he proceeded to the Continent, spending some time in the school at Salerno, where he enjoyed the instruction of Roger of Parma and Ricardus Salernitanus. He then served for a brief period on the staff of Hubert Walter, Archbishop of Canterbury, and in 1205 returned to the Continent, where he probably was affiliated with the school at Montpellier.

Gilbert was a scholastic-humoralistic physician and attributed many diseases to a variation in quantity, quality, or location of the four humors—blood, phlegm, bile, and black bile. The authorities quoted, and from whom he borrowed extensively, included Hippocrates, Aristotle, Galen, Rufus, Alexander of Tralles, Theodorus Priscianus, Rhazes, Avicenna, Averroes, and Constantine Africanus.

The *Compendium medicinae* was divided into seven books: (1) Fevers, (2) Diseases of the Head and Nerves, (3) Diseases of the Eyes and Face, (4) Diseases of the External Members, (5 and 6) Internal Diseases, and (7) Diseases of the Generative System, Gout, Cancer, Diseases of the Skin, Poisons and Toxicology. Discussions on physiology, ophthalmology, laryngology, otology, gynecology, neurology, dermatology, embryology, obstetrics, dietetics, the hygiene of travel, and the prevention of seasickness are interspersed. The terms are modern; whereas the repeated reference to charms, superstitions, polypharmacy, and disgusting remedies is medieval. Tertian and quartan fever are differentiated in the first book. In the second book (Head and Nerves), dying the hair, the removal of excess or misplaced hair, and the medicinal use of soap are discussed. Ladies who wish to retain or to renew their youthful charm should soften the skin and open the pores with steam baths and should use warm water for washing. Epilepsy, catalepsy, analepsy, apoplexy, paralysis, tetanus, and vertigo are mentioned. Binocular vision and cataracts were noted in the commentary on the eye.

It may be inferred that gout was a common affliction in the 13th century, since a discussion of this malady occupies a disproportionate part of the last book. *Podagra,* pain in the foot, was attributed to the descent of humors to the lower extremities. Palpation was found to be helpful in understanding the morbid process. Venesection from the contralateral extremity was recommended in treatment. After the general rules, there were several pages devoted to special formulae for different forms of gout. Selected prescriptions contained the herb hermodactyl, believed to be a synonym in his time for the botanical *Colchicum autumnale*.[2]

Since, therefore, the material of this variety of arthetica, in which no swelling is present, is formed of grosser and harder substance and is found in the vicinity of hard and cold localities, it is dissolved slowly and the disease is not cured until this solution takes place. That form of the disease, however, in which there is swelling from a subtile and liquid material deposited in the soft parts is the more quickly cured. Hence swelling is the best sign of curability. This is most evidently true in podagra, unless the *materies morbi,* by reason of its scarcity, produces no enlargement of the affected part.

Gilbert's consideration of leprosy attributes the disease to heredity, a corrupt diet, foul air, the breath of a leper, or cohabitation with a woman who has been promiscuous with lepers. Anesthesia of the fingers and toes, atrophy of the skin, and distortion of the joints of the hands and feet were recorded as symptoms of the disease. The four varieties were: elephantia, leonina, tyria, and alopecia. Bimanual examination for stone in the bladder is a procedure believed to have been adopted by Gilbertus from his teacher, Roger of Parma.[1]

Mark here a chapter on the cure of stone in the bladder by means of surgery, which we have omitted above. Accordingly, to determine whether

a stone exists in the bladder, let the patient take a warm bath. Then let him be placed with his buttocks elevated, and, having inserted into the anus two fingers of the right hand, press the fist of the left hand deeply above the pubes and lift and draw the entire bladder upward. If you find anything hard and heavy, it is manifest that there is a stone in the bladder. If the body feels soft and fleshy, it is fleshy excrescence (*carnositas*), which impedes the flow of urine. Now, if the stone is located in the neck of the bladder and you wish to force it to the fundus: after the use of fomentations and inunctions, inject through a syringe (*siringa*) some petroleum, and after a short interval pass the syringe again up to the neck of the bladder and cautiously and gently push the stone away from the neck to the fundus.

Although the *Compendium* has been condemned by medical historians, Handerson believes that:[2]

The book is, undoubtedly, the work of a famous and strictly orthodox physician, possessed of exceptional education in the science of his day, a man of wide reading, broadened by extensive travel and endowed with the knowledge acquired by a long experience, honest, truthful and simple minded, yet not uncritical in regard to novelties, firm in his own opinions but not arrogant, sympathetic, possessed of a high sense of professional honor, a firm believer in authority and therefore credulous, superstitious after the manner of his age, yet harboring, too, a germ of that healthy skepticism which Roger Bacon, his great contemporary, developed and illustrated.

I believe, therefore, that we may justly award to the medical pages of the Compendium not only the rather negative praise of being written as well as the work of any of Gilbert's contemporaries, but the more positive credit of being thoroughly abreast of the medical science of its age and country, an "Abstract and brief chronicle of the time."

1. Gilbertus Anglicus: *Compendium Medicinae*, Lyon: 1510.
2. Handerson, H. E.: *Gilbertus Anglicus, Medicine of the Thirteenth Century*, Cleveland: Cleveland Medical Library Association, 1918.

Theodoric (1205-1296?)

"HERE BEGINS THE SURGERY edited and compiled by the Dominican, Brother Theodoric, Lord Bishop of Cervia." The seven books of surgery by Theodoric published about 1267 have been retranslated by Campbell and Colton.[1] Theodoric was one of the small band of clinical surgeons who were skilled in physic as well as the use of the scalpel and application of splints and bandages. A Dominican Friar, he studied in Bologna, traveled widely and counseled with other men of medicine. He became Bishop of Bitonto in 1262, Bishop of Cervia in 1266, and was confessor to Pope Innocent VI.

It is noteworthy that several of the precepts of surgical practice were subject to test and found valid seven centuries ago. The translators note that the teachings of Theodoric were astonishingly similar to those of Halsted.

There is no need . . . to be rash or daring, but let them be foresighted, gentle and circumspect, in order that, with the greatest deliberateness and gentleness they may operate under all circumstances with what gentleness they can, especially around cerebral membranes, sensitive parts and other ticklish places. . . . All the things that are necessary to the art cannot be included in books, many of these frequently happen to the operator, and cannot easily be foreseen. Surgeons must need be well-read, for even though they be experienced, they will frequently fall into error and confusion, and I can scarcely think that anyone can understand surgery without letters.

The father, or at least the spiritual leader and professional teacher, of Theodoric was Hugh of Lucia (c 1160-1257), a surgeon as skilled and learned as his pupil. Hugo did not prepare a treatise on surgery, but Theodoric attributes to him the following teachings.

In the first place the lips of the wound and all about the wound should be abraded or debrided; then the wound should be completely cleaned of fuzz, hair and anything else, and let it be wiped dry with fine lint soaked in warm wine and wrung; and thus the lips of the wound may be reunited as well as possible in accordance with their original healthy state; and having made compresses of fine and clean lint soaked in warm wine and placed upon the wound so as to fit, let it be bound up with a light bandage in such a way as the reapproximation of the wound edges cannot be disturbed at all—and, just as we have said before, do not undo the dressing until the third, fourth, or fifth day if no pain occurs.

If a nose has been sliced by a sword or other weapon so that it is hanging on . . . you should be both circumspect and cautious. Replace the nose very cautiously in its proper position, so that each part is matched to the part from which it was separated . . . and having taken stitches in suitable places, let each part of the nose be sewed to its corresponding part.

When vertebrae of the back are completely dislocated, the result is inevitably fatal. If the dislocation . . . should be directed toward the interior of the chest, there is no ingenious method for treatment . . . but the type which is displaced posteriorly is called gibbous . . . sometimes the vertebrae of the spine had been separated posteriorly . . . in such a case then the physician ought to make ready two long splints which extend from the scapula, to the buttocks . . . and bind the patient down with white bands from below the arm pits to the shoulder, and lower down, over the hips and around the thigh.

Volume 2 contains discussions of fistula, goiter (bocium), abscesses, hemorrhoids, wens, nodules, and gout, or the arthritic affection. Noli-me-tangere (rodent ulcer) was cured by "the blood of some person who has suffered the same disease, for this is a special treatment for the affection, and infallible." Herpes estiomenus, also known as lupus or the self-devourer (L., estiom), was treated by cautery. The several types of imposthumes (sing., imposthume), internal and external, were described in detail. The objective in the treatment of a solid testudo was to exercise care in removal of the tunic. If the testudo was liquid the sanies was to be evacuated. "Often times there occurs certain superfluity in some people which is commonly called lipoma (nata). . . . It is not accompanied by pain, heat, nor pulsation. And perhaps it is for this that it grows so large that it surpasses all other superfluities of the body. . . . And be careful not to incise a lipoma which is dark in color and of little sensitivity, since this is a cancerous imposthume." Figs· in the anus were treated by poulticing.

1. The Surgery of Theodoric, translated by E. Campbell, M.D., and J. Colton, M.A., New York, Appleton-Century-Crofts, Inc., vol. 1, 1955, vol. 2, 1960.

Bodleian Library, Oxford

Roger Bacon (1214-1294)

ROGER BACON, who has been credited with holding all knowledge of his time within his grasp, was born near the old Roman settlement of Ilchester, Somerset. However, he spent the majority of his intellectual life in Paris within the jurisdiction of the Franciscan Order.[1] His family enjoyed good circumstances and were able to provide him with funds for learning and the pursuit of scientific experiments. Bacon attended Oxford University in his early teens; there he developed an abiding interest in mathematics, physics, philosophy, Greek, and Aristotle's *Organon*. These pursuits of learning brought him under the influence of Edmund Rich, later Archbishop of Canterbury, and Robert Grossetête, lecturer to the Franciscans shortly after their establishment.

About 1234, Bacon continued his education in Paris, the jewel of all medieval universities, where he obtained the degree of DD and the appellation "Doctor Mirabilis." During this time he concentrated on mathematical and physiological subjects, exposed the false conceit of wisdom of his contemporary scholastic pedants, joined the Franciscans, the most learned body in contemporary Europe, accepted their mendicant philosophy, but was critical of arbitrary clerical authority. Bacon was learned in Hebrew, Greek, and Latin. He prepared a common grammar for all nations, and showed that the Bible had been poorly translated and therefore wrongly interpreted through the study of the writings of the ancients in the original and the search for answers to natural phenomena by experiment. Although he had been accused of dabbling in the black arts, his main interest in life centered on reform in philosophical and scientific thinking.

Upon his return to England Bacon probably settled in Oxford, where he devoted his time to scientific rather than scholastic matters. Becoming interested in lenses and mirrors he outlined the principles of a microscope and a reflecting telescope. Understandably, his growing reputation as a learned teacher and his intellectual reputation aroused the envy, even suspicion, of the Church. Hence he was placed under the surveillance of the order in Paris in 1257, his books and instruments were removed, and his writing and communication with the outside world restricted. Near the end of a decade of intellectual privation, he was requested by Guy de Foulques, later raised to the papal throne as Clement IV, to assemble his writings on the contemporary evils so dangerous to his way of thinking. In the face of great odds and great obstacles, he completed three large treatises in less than two years: the *Opus maius,* a review of contemporary knowledge and a guide for the use of this knowledge to enhance the dignity of man and the glory of God, the *Opus minus,* a glossary, and the *Opus tertium,* which contained a summary of the trilogy.

In 1268, Bacon was permitted to return to Oxford and to resume his teaching, experimental work, and writing. During the following years he prepared the first portion of his enclopedic treatise on philosophy. This work brought him once more under the yoke of his clerical superiors and resulted in his recall to Paris in 1278, where he was confined again for no less than 14 years.

When Bacon was allowed to resume his studies in Oxford, he wrote his final text on theology, finished only two years before his death.

By the end of the 16th century only a few of his works had been printed and further spans of time elapsed before his greatest contributions were generally available. It was clear to Bacon that all sciences are interconnected and that mathematics is the key to the others. Experimental science was judged to be the ultimate in examining natural phenomena by mathematical processes as well as suggesting further researches. He was interested in the reform of the calender, exploited the laws of reflection and refraction for practical purposes, and, although he prepared no experimental models, clearly understood the concept of reading glasses and the microscope, placement of mirrors, and the telescope, excerpted as follows.[2]

If a man looks at letters or other small objects through the medium of a crystal or of glass or of some other transparent body placed above the letters, and it is the smaller part of a sphere whose convexity is toward the eye, and the eye is in the air, he will see the letters much better and they will appear larger to him. . . . Therefore this instrument is useful to the aged and to those with weak eyes.

As the wisdom of God is ordained for the direction of the universe, so is this science of vision evidently and beneficially ordained for its beauty. I shall give some examples both of refraction and reflection . . . mirrors might be erected on an elevation opposite hostile cities and armies, so that all that was being done by the enemy might be visible. . . . For in this way Julius Caesar, when he wished to subdue England, is said to have erected very large mirrors, in order that he might see in advance from the shore of Gaul the arrangement of the cities and camps of England.

The wonders of refracted vision are still greater; for it is easily shown by the rules stated above that very large objects can be made to appear very small, and the reverse, and very distant objects will seem very close at hand, and conversely. For we can so shape transparent bodies, and arrange them in such a way with respect to our sight and objects of vision, that the rays will be refracted and bent in any direction we desire, and under any angle we wish we shall see the object near or at a distance.

Bacon has been credited with the discovery of gunpowder in the description of an explosive mixture composed of nitrates and other ingredients, which produced a noise like thunder and flashes like lightning. He may have sensed the value of this experimental observation for propulsive power for travel by boat, chariot, or by air.[2] He prophesied the use of alchemy to turn base metal into gold, and offered simple rules for delay of senescence.[2]

Not only are remedies possible against the conditions of old age coming at the time of one's prime and before the time of old age, but also if the regimen of old age should be completed, the conditions of old age and senility can still be retarded, so that they do not arrive at their ordinary time, and when they do come they can be mitigated and moderated, so that both by retarding and mitigating them life may be prolonged beyond the limit.

Bacon died a disillusioned old man, convinced of his failure in his exposure of the system of education with its formulated metaphysical creeds of heaven and earth without the employment of scientific experiments to test their validity. The loyal had incorporated their physics and mathematics into a tightly organized system of logic, limited by deductive reasoning. The Church was only conceived for that which seemed best for the Church rather than what was best for the parishioners. He was accused of heresy and blasphemy since he experimented with Nature instead of accepting the manifestations of God with implicit faith; meanwhile, he searched for the secrets of God beneficial to man.[2]

Since this Experimental Science is wholly unknown to the rank and file of students, I am therefore unable to convince people of its utility unless at the same time I disclose its excellence and its proper signification.

Concluding thus the subject of this science experimental without restriction, I shall now show its advantage to theology, as I have done similarly in the case of the other sciences. For this science teaches how wonderful instruments may be made, and uses them when made, and also considers all secret things owing to the advantages they may possess for the state and for individuals; and it directs other sciences as its handmaids, and therefore the whole power of speculative science is attributed especially to this science. And now the wonderful advantage derived . . . on behalf of the Church of God against the enemies of the faith is manifest, who should be destroyed rather by the discoveries of science than by the warlike arms of combatants.

1. Bridges, J. H.: *The Life and Work of Roger Bacon, an Introduction to the Opus Majus,* London: Williams & Norgate, 1914.

2. Bacon, R.: *Opus Majus,* 1266, in Burke, R. B. (trans.): *The Opus Majus of Roger Bacon,* 2 vol, Philadelphia: University of Pennsylvania Press, 1928.

Pietro d'Abano (1250-1315)

PETER OF ABANO (Petrus Abbonus), heretic and medical scholastic, was born in Abano near Padua. In preparation for his professional calling, he studied in Greece, becoming a master of the language, then in Constantinople, and finally in Paris, where he undertook the study of philosophy, mathematics, and medicine. The University of Padua was the site of his professional activities in his mature years and to which he gave stature and support in the rise of this school to its enviable greatness in later centuries. In medicine, it was Abano's translations into Latin of many of the great tomes prior to his time that mark him as outstanding. The writings of Hippocrates, Galen, Dioscorides, Aristotle, Alexander of Aphrodisias, Cassios,

and Abraham ben Ezra were among those translations credited to him.[1]

Recognized as one of the great intellects of his time and endowed with an encylopedic mind, it is not surprising that Peter's interests covered many of the important subjects of his day. He was especially famous for his knowledge of astrology, astronomy, and poisons. Out of his translations came a treatise on poisons and *Conciliator differentiarum,*[2] his great work in the medical field, in which he attempted to reconcile conflicting opinions of Greek, Arabic, Jewish, and Latin writers on important questions. In the *Conciliator,* first printed in 1471, he reviewed pronouncements of the past, proposed a solution, and discussed probable objections. Some postulates are sensible by current appraisal, others metaphysical. Examples of each are:[1]

14. Has air weight in its own sphere?
72. Is there a mean between health and sickness?
204. Is a narcotic good for colic?
42. Is the flesh or the heart the organ of touch?
154. Should treatment begin with strong or weak medicine?
206. Is blood-letting from the left hand a proper treatment for gout in the right foot?

De venenis, an original treatise on poisons, prepared for one of the popes, possibly John XXII, is a mixture of astrology and superstition.[3] It is divided into six chapters: the classification of poisons, how they act upon the body, how to guard against them, the effects, and the cures of particular poisons, and the problem of a panacea or bezoar against all poisons.[4]

Now every poison in its degree as a poison has an opposite quality in our bodies, and this opposition makes a great doubt as to how, and by what way the poison is able to pass to the heart of man. For either the poison is drawn to the heart, just as iron is drawn to a magnet, or it goes of itself to the heart, in other or both ways, namely, the heart attracting it, or the poison running to the heart; but if neither or none of the foresaid methods may be defended, we must admit that in no way can the poison pass to the heart, and so the question of the opposition of the poison to the heart itself will cease; in which case we may say that the poison is not destructive to the heart. Opposed to which we see that if a pernicious poison like napellus is taken, at once syncope appears, which is a passion of the heart, and there is tremor of the heart and defective pulse and all of the symptoms of cardiac passion, on account of which it must be known that the heart when it is sound, like the other members, attracts to itself nothing except blood, and at the same time the spirits, of which one remains in the right ventricle of the heart, and the other in the left.

Many held Peter in contempt, believed him to be avaricious, a black magician, and irreligious. The Church was suspicious of him for his disbelief in miracles and his hesitancy in accepting orthodoxy. He was denounced by the Inquisition for alleged sorcery and necromancy, but withstood the charges and accepted the offer from the University of Padua to be a scholar among scholars and to practice medicine. However, the respite from the Inquisition was only temporary; Abano's death prevented successful consummation of a second series of accusations, which were continued even after his burial, and instead he was burned in effigy.[1]

1. Thorndike, L.: A History of Magic and Experimental Science, vol 2, New York: Columbia University Press, 1947, pp 874-947.
2. Peter of Abano: Conciliator Differentarum, Venice, 1476.
3. Brown, H. M.: De Venenis of Petrus Abbonus, Ann Med Hist 6:25-53, 1924.
4. Peter of Abano: Tractatus de Venenis, Mantua, 1473.

Henri de Mondeville
(c 1260-1320)

HENRI DE MONDEVILLE, pupil of Theodoric and preceptor of Guy de Chauliac, was born in Normandy near Caën.[1] According to ancient custom, his surname indicates his place of birth, variously spelled as Hermondaville, Amondavilla, and Armandavilla in the early manuscripts. Henri studied medicine at Montpellier and surgery under Pitart in Paris.[2] Later as cleric-physician he was with Theodoric in Bologna, where he appreciated the method of dressing wounds that ran counter to practice of the time. Returning to France, he gained stature as an original thinker, a skilled practitioner, a teacher of anatomy, and a writer whose scientific

communications were frequently enhanced with wit and sarcasm. Remaining a bachelor, he devoted his life to the practice and art of his profession. His written work was not completed according to plan; asthma troubled him and he ultimately died of tuberculosis.

Bibliothèque Nationale, Paris

In Paris, Mondeville was surgeon to King Philip the Fair and his successor Louis X, and in the field served in expeditions against the English. He qualified as a member of the elite class of surgeons, the *medicins-chirurgiens,* graduates of a medical school, and holders of the degree of master, equivalent to doctor in medicine.[2] The lay surgeons or artisans, generally untrained, unskilled, and not associated with a medical faculty, were in the second class; nevertheless, they stood above the barber-surgeons who were to assume an important place in the practice of surgery, especially in the 15th and 16th centuries.

Mondeville is first reported as having lectured on anatomy at Montpellier, using sketches of organs and later full-length anatomic drawings. The latter are reproduced in miniature in the 1314 French manuscript translated from the Latin *Chirurgie*. The 13 drawings in color show the cadaver usually in a swaying or relaxed standing position. In the illustration of the skeletal system, the body is covered with dried soft parts. In the miniature of the muscular system, the skin is carried on a stick over the shoulder. In other miniatures, the blood vessels and the heart are drawn on the surface of the body, or the body is dissected from the back, with projection of the viscera. The arrangements are recognized as original, important contributions to anatomical descriptions and, though antedating the minute dissection of Vesalius by more than two centuries, they hardly can be considered as anticipating his work.

The *Chirurgie*, a vast work, the first comprehensive surgical treatise by a native Frenchman and one of the great manuscripts of pre-Renaissance surgery, lay dormant for centuries. It remained in manuscript form in Latin and French and did not appear in print until late in the 19th century when Pagel republished the original in the *Archiv für Klinische Chirurgie*,[3] and Nicaise, the French translation, in one volume.[1] The work is divided into five treatises, and is heavily documented with references from ancient and his contemporary time. The first book discusses anatomy, particularly surgical anatomy. The second book is concerned with wounds and ulcers. The incomplete third book is a continuation of surgical conditions. Book four, which was to deal with fractures and dislocations, was not prepared. The fifth book treats of materia medica and antidotes.

Following his teachings and writings on regional anatomy, Mondeville's second great contribution to the art of medicine and practice of surgery was the empirical objection to the traditional encouragement of suppuration in the treatment of wounds. In contrast to the prodding with instruments, application of ointments and poultices, and the introduction of other foreign bodies in fresh wounds, advocated by contemporaries, de Mondeville advised cleanliness, removal of foreign matter or injured natural tissue, prompt suturing, a good diet, adequate rest, and abandonment of potions assumed to be helpful in cicatrization. These words by Mondeville on healing by first intention were written 200 years before Paré revolted against the use of scalding oils and cautery and piously noted that the surgeon dresses but God heals the wounds.[1]

VI. We say that the wound heals by first intention when the fashion in which the edges of the wound are set together remain of the same substance and of the same nature as the edges of the wound after union, and when they are homogenous; and also when the same matter as the wound unites the edges of a wound of the flesh, and if this matter is homogenous.

Thus we call it first intention because *nature* will always do better if it is left unhindered, and the *surgeon,* who *is nature's imitator,* should try to heal all wounds in all parts of the body in the same manner.

. . . (1) *It is not necessary to probe the wounds;* (2) if needed, one should forcibly remove the bone-fragments compressing or piercing the dura mater, and also the fragments which might prove harmful if left, but only if they can be easily extracted, and if not, they should remain; similarly, it is necessary to extract or to remove all other foreign bodies found between the edges of the wound; (3) it is necessary to unite the edges of the wound; (4) it is necessary to suture if it is believed to be useful and advantageous; (5) it is necessary to rinse the wound with warm wine and to sponge it with packs rinsed in wine; (6) it is necessary to apply the plaster spread on a piece of linen, then to cover the wound with pieces of linen soaked in wine and wrung dry, finally to bandage the wound according to the rules of art.

Mondeville defined the qualities of a surgeon, and argued that surgeons should first be trained as physicians, and should never undertake hopeless cases. He was firm in his insistence upon adequate remuneration for those persons able to pay and equally insistent upon gratuitous care for the poor.[2]

He is not a good surgeon who does not know the art and science of medicine and especially anatomy. . . . The surgeon should be fairly audacious; should not discuss questions before the laity; he should operate with prudence and sagacity; he should never commence perilous operations unless he has provided everything in order to avoid danger; he should have a well made hand, the fingers long and slender, supple and sure. He should promise health to all his patients; he should not conceal from the parents or the friends the dangers that may arise; he should avoid as much as possible difficult cures; he should never undertake hopeless cases; he should give the poor gratuitous care; if possible the rich should pay well; he should not sing his own praises; he should not cover his colleagues with blame; he should not cause envy among them; he should work always with the idea of acquiring a reputation of probity; he should be reassuring to his patients by kind words and acquiesce to their requests when nothing harmful will result from them as to their cure.

In the third treatise Mondeville divides disease into two categories—those from injury or accident or any visible extrinsic agent, and those that occur without visible reason, from an intrinsic or unknown cause. The soul is closely identified with maladies in the second group.[4]

The body and the soul are so closely united, one to the other, that when one is sick, whichever it may be, the other is unable to act outwardly. It is thus evident that whoever is overtaken by an illness, whether it be of a limb or of the body, or whether of the spirit, he is, like a raving maniac, unable to recognize the truth in any faculty, nor accomplish any legitimate action, work, study or teaching.

    1. Nicaise, E.: *Chirurgie de Maitre Henri de Monde-ville, Paris:* G. Baillière, 1893. Excerpt translated by Z. Danilevicius.
    2. Cumston, C. G.: Henry de Mondeville, the Man and His Writings. With Translation of Several Chapters of his Works, *Buffalo Med J,* ns 42:486-504, 549-565, 642-656, 1903.
    3. Pagel, J. L.: The Surgery of Henri de Mondeville (Hermondaville), *Arch Klin Chir* 14:253-311, 653-751, 869-904, 1890.
    4. Zimmerman, L. M., and Veith, I.: *Great Ideas in the History of Surgery,* Baltimore: Williams & Wilkins Co., 1961.

John of Gaddesden
(c 1280-1361)

JOHN OF GADDESDEN, author of *Rosa medi-cinae,* was born about the year 1280 and died in 1361—the most famous practitioner of England in the early part of the 14th century. Before completing his scholastic training, he had acquired the baccalaureate in medicine, the doctorate in medicine, and the baccalaureate in theology.[1] There is no evidence from his *curriculum vitae,* however, that he practiced theology, except as a prebendary of St. Paul's Cathedral. Rather he was a practitioner in medicine, a calling begun with a medical background derived exclusively from reading medical books. The breadth of his self-instruction may be judged by the frequent reference in his lively writings to the medical greats, including Galen, Dioscorides, Rufus, Avicenna, Albertus, and Anglicus. As a contemporary of Chaucer, he fits admirably as the "Doctour of Phisik" in the *Canterbury Tales.*[2]

> With us ther was a Doctour of Phisik; . . .
> Wel knew he the olde Esculapius,
> And Deyscorides, and eek Rufus,
> Olde Ypocras, Haly, and Galyen,
> Serapion, Razis, and Avycen,
> Averrois, Damascien, and Constantyn,
> Bernard, and Gatesden, and Gilbertyn.

John's famous treatise, *Rosa medicinae,* the first printed medical book of an Englishman, was prepared on parchment in 1314 and printed in Pavia in 1492.[3] It is not remarkable scientifically and is little more than a medical advisor for lay application. The rose in the title, a five-petaled flower, was selected because of the five divisions of the contents. Furthermore, just as the rose is the most beautiful flower, so *Rosa medicinae* was judged by the author to be a superior manuscript. A discussion of fevers, according to the Galenic system, introduces the reader to the treatise; it continues with a discussion of the natural history of a variety of disorders, and concludes with a section on surgery and antidotes. The practice of medicine was covered from top to toe, beginning with diseases of the scalp and concluding with those of the feet. Between these anatomic extremes, John discussed the sweetness of urine voided by diabetics, hydrops, the treatment of tuberculosis, and the use of charms in medicine. The prescriptions recommended are based upon superstition or tradition; there is little evidence that he possessed any particular knowledge of the anatomy or physiology of the time. In fact, he was considered by some a charlatan who had developed a lucrative practice, prescribing expensive medicines for the rich and inexpensive drugs for the poor. Some remedies were ridiculous, others nauseating or filthy. These included animal dung, human urine, the fat of green frogs, the skin of a sea cow, the bladder of a boar, the contents of a crow's egg, the brain of a crow, the testicles of a boar, milk curdled in the stomach of a hare or bear, and a wolf's heart in milk. One of his best remembered practices was the "red light" treatment for smallpox, rediscovered by Finsen late in the 19th century. The son of Edward I, during his illness, was protected from sunlight, wrapped in red bandages, and placed in a red room.[4]

Then take a cloth of scarlet or some other red color and wrap up the patient completely, as I did in the case of the son of his majesty, the king of England, when he was suffering from this disease. In this case I also had all the hangings of the couch made of red material. The case turned out very satisfactorily and the patient recovered without a mark of smallpox.

In a long discussion of epilepsy or the falling sickness, flickering retinal images and terrifying noises were accepted as inciting agents to seizures. Prognosis was discussed; regression of the affliction before adolescence or following pregnancy was recognized, and fasting was recommended in treatment, a procedure revived in the 20th century before the introduction of anticonvulsive agents.[5]

Stimulating causes [of the seizure] are: to be in lofty places and look down from them; to be whirled about in a circle, as children play; to look at a mill-wheel turning; to look at terrifying objects, such as lightning; loud noises, such as the sound of a bell when a person is in a bell-tower right next to the bell; the sound of a bass-drum; also, sudden and great fear.

The prognostication is that of Hippocrates, "Aphorisms," Particula 2, near the beginning. Those who are born epileptics experience improvement before adolescence, but those who are 25 or more years of age frequently die. If epilepsy befalls a pregnant woman, she is freed from it when her child is born.

I have found it true whether the patient be a demoniac, or a lunatic, or an epileptic. If his parents are living, let them take him to the church, after a three days' fast by both parents and son.

One of his best clinical descriptions was that of a salivary calculus.[6]

Stones may be found in almost every cavity of the body, I saw a stone in my father's mouth under his tongue, the length of half a little finger, which I have exhibited in the schools and still carry about with me. I cured him by gargles, lotions and extracting it with a fine knife; though at first I knew not what would be the result, and because I found a hardness I thought it was an inflammation.

John of Gaddesden entered the practice of medicine with a background of medical and classical literature. His *Rosa medicinae,* filled with superstition and charms, a remarkable home medical advisor, makes no scientific contributions but presents a fair description of the medicinals of his day.

1. Cholmeley, H. P.: *John of Gaddesden and the Rosa Medicinae,* Oxford: Clarendon Press, 1912.
2. Chaucer, G.: *Canterbury Tales,* New York: E. P. Dutton & Co., Inc., 1958.
3. Gaddesden, J.: *Rosa anglica practica medicine a capite ad pedes,* Pavia: J. A. Birretta, 1492.
4. Handerson, H. E.: John of Gaddesden, Variola and the Finsen Light-Cure, *Cleveland Med J* 3:433-441 (Oct) 1904.
5. Lennox, W. G.: John of Gaddesden on Epilepsy, *Ann Med Hist* 1:283-307, 1939.
6. Withington, E. T.: *Medical History from the Earliest Times,* London: Scientific Press, Ltd., 1894.

National Library of Medicine

Guy de Chauliac
(c 1300-1368)

GUY DE CHAULIAC, who followed de Monde-ville, was of even greater stature and in-fluence than his predecessor. De Chauliac was a medical scholar who practiced surgery and treated fractures, inflammations, and tumors. His doctrine, revealed in *La Grande Chirurgie,* composed in the fading years of his life as a solace to his solitude, was domi-nant in Europe for generations.[1]

Guy was born in the village of Chauliac, on the frontier of Auvergne, and died in Lyons. The years immediately preceding were spent in the papal city of Avignon, where he served Popes Clement VI, Innocent VI, and Urban V. Guy's family was poor, but, under the protection and with the sup-port of the Church (the only course that was open in his day for training in anatomy and medicine), he received the best in early and advanced education. Having taken holy or-ders and benefited professionally therefrom, he repaid at the appropriate time in service and devotion for such opportunities and privileges. He prepared for medicine first at Toulouse, more famous for law than medi-cine, then at Montpellier, where he received a medical degree of master. Later he studied anatomy under Bertrucius at Bologna and finally surgery in Paris, meanwhile learning by dissection and testing his postulates by experiment.

His great manuscript appeared in 1363 in Latin.[1] The scope of influence on Euro-pean medicine, and to a much greater extent on surgery, may be suspected from the num-ber of transcriptions of the manuscript, translations, and editions of the printed copy. The first printed edition was published in French at Lyons in 1478. This was followed by more than 100 translations and editions in Latin, French, Italian, Dutch, German, Spanish, and English. The best modern translation is that of Nicaise in French.[2] The didactic treatise referred repeatedly to Avicenna, Albucasis, and other Arabic phy-sicians, and to Galen, the Greek, with only scant acknowledgement to Hippocrates. Since Arabic medicine had been dominant during the Middle Ages, it is not surprising that most of the medical manuscripts avail-able for study and reference were Arabic translations of the early Latin and Greek compositions. The source documents were read by Guy while living and practicing at Avignon, where many literary treasures of the Western world were clustered. *La Grande Chirurgie* was presented in seven sections: Anatomy, Aposthemata, Wounds, Ulcers, Fractures and Dislocations, Special Diseases, and Therapeutics. In the introduc-tion to the general chapter of the art of surgery, Chauliac defines the character and attributes of a surgeon.[3]

The conditions necessary for the surgeon are four: first, he should be learned; second, he should be expert; third, he must be ingenious, and fourth, he should be able to adapt himself. It is required for the first that the surgeon should know not only the principles of surgery, but also those of medicine in theory and practice; for the second, that he should have seen others operate; for the third, that he should be ingenious, of good judg-ment and memory to recognize conditions; and for the fourth, that he be adaptable and able to accommodate himself to circumstances. Let the surgeon be bold in all sure things, and fearful in dangerous things; let him avoid all faulty treat-ments and practices. He ought to be gracious to the sick, considerate to his associates, cautious in his prognostications. Let him be modest, dignified, gentle, pitiful, and merciful; not covetous nor an extortionist of money; but rather let his reward be according to his work, to the means of the patient, to the quality of the issue, and to his own dignity.

In the treatment of wounds, Chauliac believed in healing by first intention, with Nature exerting the dominant effect, supported by suitable nourishment. Except for the management of complications, his principles seem sound as they stand in the light of current surgical practice.[3]

The first object requires the removal of foreign substances, if there are any such among the divided parts.
The second is to approximate the separated parts to each other.
The third is to preserve the parts thus brought together in their proper form.
The fourth to conserve and preserve the substance of the organ.
The fifth teaches how to correct complications.

Guy de Chauliac employed bandages stiffened by egg white, advocated surgery for cataract and superficial cancer, and applied cautery for fungating tumors and osteomyelitis. Hemorrhage was staunched by silk ligatures; astringents or pressure dressings were applied to cutaneous ulcers. The overhead swing was developed for bed patients. Pulleys and weight for traction were described for fractures of the lower leg. In the management of empyema, he recommended that the incision be made between the third and fourth rib rather than lower in the thorax. He revived the trephine for injuries of the calvarium, and noted that loss of brain tissue was not necessarily fatal. Conservative manipulation of a hernia was to be tried first in incarceration. Trusses were contoured to fit the patient. In surgical treatment of hernia, the sac was excised with cautery or an imbedded wire suture and the testicle sacrificed. A number of instruments were designed for the removal of foreign bodies, including a crossbow (arbalest) for retraction of arrows. Inhalation anesthesia, which was practiced at the time according to Theodoric, was accomplished by the combination of opium, hyoscyamus, and other less potent anesthetic or analgesic agents.[2]

Some prescribe medicaments which send the patient to sleep, so that the incision may not be felt, such as opium, the juice of the morel, hyoscyamus, mandrake, ivy, hemlock, lettuce. A new sponge is soaked by them in these juices and left to dry in the sun; and when they have need of it, they put this sponge into warm water and then hold it under the nostrils of the patient until he goes to sleep. Then they perform the operation.

Although the sections of his *Chirurgie* are concerned naturally with surgical matters, one of the frequently quoted passages refers to the great plague, the Black Death or bubonic type, which struck Avignon in 1348 and again in 1360. He differentiated the bubonic type from the pneumonic and described his personal affliction, remaining with the sick and not fleeing from fear.[4]

It [the plague] was of two kinds: the first lasted two months, with continued fever & expectoration of blood. And they died of it in three days.
The second was, all the rest of the time, also with continued fever & apostems & carbuncles on the external parts, principally in the armpits & groin: & they died of it in five days. And was of such great contagiousness, (especially that which had expectoration of blood) that not only in visiting but also in looking at it, one person took it from another: so that the people died without servants & were interred without Priests.
Nevertheless, towards the end of the mortality, I fell into a continued fever, with an apostem on the groin, and sick nearly six weeks, & was in such great danger that all my companions believed that I would die, but the apostem becoming mature, & treated as I have said, I escaped by the Will of God.

Guy de Chauliac wrote extensively on dentistry, quoting a great deal from the ancients on the subject. He outlined the causes of caries including the ingestion of sweets, gave an account of different abscesses of the teeth producing infection of adjacent soft tissue, and described a mildly abrasive dentifrice, appropriate instruments for prophylaxis, extraction, and replacement of missing teeth.[5]

1. Chauliac, G.: *La Grande Chirurgie*, Lyon, 1478.
2. Nicaise, E.: *The Grand Surgery of Guy de Chauliac*, Paris: F. Alcan, 1890.
3. Brennan, W. A.: *Guy de Chauliac (A.D. 1363), On Wounds and Fractures*, Chicago: W. A. Brennan, 1923
4. Major, R. H.: *Classic Descriptions of Disease*, Springfield, Ill: Charles C Thomas, 1932, pp 73-76.
5. Guerini, V.: *A History of Dentistry*, Philadelphia and New York: Lea & Febiger, 1909.

John Arderne
(1306[07]-1380[90])

JOHN ARDERNE, scholar, writer, master surgeon of England, and the first great surgeon of Britain, was contemporary with the chivalrous days of knights in armor, when constipation, ischiorectal abscess, and fistula in ano were occupational hazards. The Cavaliers should have thanked John of Arderne for his revival of corrective measures for their fundaments, patterned after the ancients.[1] Although there are no primary source documents of his education or early professional years, it has been assumed that he studied at the University of Montpellier and was a student of the ancients. This is confirmed by frequent references to Greek and Arabic physicians among the large number of manuscripts that are believed to have been prepared by his own hand. He was with King Edward III's army in France during the Hundred Years' War, probably practiced in Antwerp, then settled at Newark, and developed a large and lucrative practice. A final move to London completed his peripatetic ventures. As a modest surgeon, he respected the Masters of Physic who were superior to him in the professional hierachy of his day, and he, in turn, was charitable to the Barber-Surgeons in the lower echelon.

His treatises were prepared in Latin. Many were translated into English. In recent times these have been reviewed and edited by D'Arcy Power.[2,3] Arderne discussed diseases of the eye, used clysters, and composed a commonplace book on the art of physic, surgery, and a materia medica, without any evidence of a systematic tabulation of disease. His first important compendium, *The Works of Maister John Arderne, Surgeon, of Newark, in Nottinghamshire, Written by his own Hand in the Year of our Lord, 1349,* was prepared while practicing in Newark.[3] The secrets of surgery discussed in this volume were learned from experience; several remain as sound precepts today. He did not fear hemorrhage as did his contemporaries. Cleanliness, particularly clean hands, was respected. Wounds were to be dressed infrequently; irritants were to be avoided.

The limitations of his skill were appreciated and accepted; incurable cases were not promised hope. The ethics of a surgeon, as expressed by Arderne, are noteworthy. He should be pious, charitable, modest, wary, careful in selection of friends, studious, sober, temperate in eating, sympathetic in judgment, not jealous of others, continent, friendly to servants, chaste, easy of address, neither too rough nor too familiar, respectful of truth, clean of speech, adroit in comfortable sayings, abhorrent of harlotry, willing to listen, and not always speaking. The following is an early 15th century translation.[1]

. . . Considere he noght ouer openly the lady or the doughters or other fair wymmen in gret me*nn*es [houses] ne *pro*fre tham noght to kisse, ne touche not *pri*uely ne ap*er*tely thair pappes, ne thair handes, ne thair share, that he renne noght into the indignacion of the lord ne of noon of his. In as moche as he may, greue he no seruant, but gete he thair loue and thair gode wille. Abstene he hym fro harlotrie als wele in wordes as in dedes in euery place, for if he vse hym to harlotery in priue places som tyme in opene place ther may falle to hym vnworship of yuel vsage; . . .

The description of carcinoma of the rectum records the character of the stool, the differential diagnosis from the bloody flux, and a poor prognosis. He states in a contemporary English version.[3,4]

Of Bubo [Cancer] Within the Rectum and the Impossibility or Great Difficulty of the Cure of It.
Bubo is an apostem breeding within the anus in the rectum with great hardness but little aching. This I say, before it ulcerates, is nothing else than a hidden cancer, that may not in the beginning of it be known by the sight of the eye, for it is all hidden within the rectum.
To that also will ignorant leeches [physician-surgeon] assure the patient, that he has dysentery, that is, the bloody flux, when truly it is not. Dysentery is always with flux of the intestines, but out of bubo [cancer] goes hard excretions and sometime they may not pass, because of the constriction caused by the bubo, and they are retained firmly within the rectum, so that they may be felt with the finger and drawn out.
I never saw nor heard of any man that was cured of the bubo of the rectum but I have known many that died of the foresaid sickness.

The delayed development of tetany following a laceration was described in a fatal case of tetanus.[2,5]

There was a gardner who, while he worked amongst the vines, cut his hand with a hook upon a Friday after the feast of Saint Thomas of Canterbury in summer so that the thumb was wholly separated from the hand except at the joint. . . . The thumb was first reduced to its proper position and sewn on and the bleeding was stopped.
Also on the eleventh night about the same time the bleeding broke out again in greater quantity than it did the first time. Nevertheless, the blood was staunched, and by the morning the patient was so taken with the cramp in the cheeks and in the arm that he was not able to take any meat into his mouth, nor could he open his mouth, and on the fifteenth day the bleeding broke out again, and on the eighteenth day the blood broke out again, beyond all measure, and always the cramp continued and he died on the twentieth day.

The successful surgical treatment of fistula in ano, a frequent complication of ischiorectal abscess, is his most famous surgical contribution. The prognosis and therapeutic results of a fistula were so unsatisfactory that it was considered incurable by contemporary surgeons and barbers. Arderne exposed the fistulous tract and applied warm compresses and gentle measures during convalescence. In preparing the patient for surgery, it was directed that he be positioned in good light so that the rectum could be explored with the examining finger.[1]

A probe—called appropriately enough, sequere me—is passed through the fistula until it is felt in the rectum. The eye of the probe is then threaded with a ligature of four strands—the fraenum Caesaris—which is drawn through the fistula as the probe is pulled out of the rectum until one end hangs out of the anus and the other from the opening of the fistula. These two ends are knotted together and the whole ligature is tightened by means of a peg—the wrayste—fixed into the widest part of the gorget—the tendiculum—in the same way that a violin peg tightens the strings passing round it. The use of the ligature is partly to control the bleeding and partly to maintain a correct line while the fistula is being divided. The gorget or tendiculum is pushed well up into the fistula and a grooved director with a curved end—the acus rostrata, or snowted needle—is passed along it until the end projects into the rectum where the probe had been previously inserted. A shield—the cochlearia, or spoon—with a depression in its centre, is then passed through the anus until the grooved director engages in the depressed notch. The object of this shield is partly to prevent the surgeon cutting down upon his own finger and partly to protect the opposite wall of the rectum should the patient struggle or make a sudden movement at the moment the fistula is divided. A scalpel—the razor or lance—is passed along the groove in the acus rostrata, and the fistula is cleanly divided along its whole length by drawing the knife, the acus rostrata, and the spoon out of the rectum with a single movement, the ligature or fraenum Caesaris coming away at the same time. Each branch of the fistula may be laid open in turn if the patient can bear it, or any further operation can be postponed, as Arderne had found by experience that when the main tract was laid open the other channels often healed of themselves.

1. Arderne, J.: *Treatises of Fistula in Ano, Hemorrhoids and Clysters*, D. Power, ed., London: Paul, Trench, and Trübner, and H. Frowde, Oxford University Press, 1910.

2. Power, D.: The Lesser Writings of John Arderne, *Hist Med Section XXIII:* 107-133, 1914.

3. *De Arte Phisicali et de Cirurgia of Master John Arderne,* D. Power, trans., London: J. Bale, Sons & Danielsson Ltd., 1922.

4. Zimmerman, L. M., and Veith, I.: *Great Ideas in the History of Surgery,* Baltimore: Williams & Wilkins, 1961.

5. Power, D.: *A Mirror for Surgeons, Selected Readings in Surgery,* Boston: Little, Brown & Co., 1939.

Leonardo da Vinci
(1452-1519)

LEONARDO, born in the Tuscan village of Vinci, is probably most famous as the painter of "The Last Supper" on the refectory wall of the monastery of Santa Maria delle Grazie in Milan and the "Mona Lisa," which hangs in the Louvre. Less well known are his anatomical drawings,[1] notes on physiology, and comments on disease.[2] Leonardo was self-educated in physiology and anatomy. His anatomical dissections and illustrations compare favorably, however, with those of Vesalius on the structure of

the human body, whose contributions were made several decades later. Leonardo also preceded Harvey by more than a century, making reference meanwhile to a physiologic concept of pulsing of the blood, possibly a premonition of the concept of circulation. Leonardo possessed insatiable curiosity, limitless intellectual energy, and a great capacity for designing mechanical devices. Although it has been claimed that none of his concepts, inventive studies, or contributions was carried to fruition, fundamental observations were made in more areas than were made by any other scientist, artist, or philosopher in the history of man. His multiple interests in addition to medicine and drawing included architecture, prose, city planning, construction of canals, military engineering, underwater craft, hydraulics, aerodynamics, cryptography, botany, sculpturing, and philosophy.

Leonardo discovered the world as he discovered man. His contemporary Botticelli brought the Middle Ages to a close; Leonardo ushered in the Renaissance. He was the natural son of Ser .Piero D'Antonio, a Florentine lawyer, and Catarina, a peasant girl. His father subsequently took himself a wife of his own station and grudgingly reared the boy in an environment of financial substance. Leonardo was apprenticed to Verrocchio of Florence about the age of 15. He studied geometry with Verrocchio and the elements of mathematics with Fra Luca Paccioli. He moved to Milan in his early 30's, where his talents were exploited as a civil and military engineer, but most of all as the painter of "The Last Supper." This was executed in his early 40's. The first extant anatomical drawings, prepared in the 1470's, show evidence of the influence of Avicenna and give meager details of structure. Also, there is evidence to believe that he was familiar with Galenic anatomy. He persisted in depicting the liver of man with five lobes.

Anatomy, physiology, and medicine were approached scientifically. The volume of human cavities was measured by injection of liquid wax. He countered the low ebb of dissection late in the Middle Ages with extensive prosection of animals and cadavers. Because of the lack of suitable means of preservation, an extremity or a portion of the body only was dissected at a single sitting, and this in a hurry. Anatomy was presented by Leonardo as three-dimensional.[3]

The true knowledge of the shape of any body will be arrived at by seeing it from different aspects. Consequently in order to convey a notion of the true shape of any limb of man who ranks among the animals as first of the beasts I will observe the aforesaid rule, making four demonstrations for the four sides of each limb, and for the bones I will make five, cutting them in half and showing the hollow of each of them, one being full of marrow the other spongy or empty or solid.

After a second stay in Milan, Leonardo was forced to leave the city because of political events. He moved to Rome to enjoy the patronage of Guiliano de' Medici, brother of Giovonni de' Medici, who became Pope Leo X, sons of Lorenzo the Magnificent. The Pope put an end to Leonardo's investigations after Guiliano's death in 1516. Francis I invited him to France and gave him a castle near Amboise, where he lived the remaining years of his life. The castle has now been restored and turned into a shrine.

Many of his notebooks were left to a young disciple, Melzi, cached and forgotten for more than 120 years. Elmer Belt, a fabulous collector of Vinciana, has described the complicated trail of the 7,000-odd pages of Leonardo's notebooks.[4] At various times, segments of his unique contribution have been in possession, or under jurisdiction, of the British Museum, the South Kensington Museum, the Royal Library in Turin, the Vatican Library, the Institut de France, the Ambrosian Library, Windsor Castle, the Prado in Madrid, Cardinal Borromeo, Napoleon Bonaparte, the Earl of Arundel, Lord Leicester, the Austrian Baron of Ottenfels, Pompeo Leoni, and Count Galeazzo Arconati. The notes were composed in the obscure dialect of Leonardo's birthplace, and in a right to left script, mirror writing, natural for the great man because of his left handedness.

The appraisal of Leonardo by Francis I is recorded by Benvenuto Cellini.[3]

He did not believe that any other man had come into the world who had attained so great knowledge as Leonardo, and that not only as sculptor, painter, and architect, for beyond that he was a profound philosopher.

Leonardo has been credited with the appreciation of arteriosclerosis as well as with thickening of veins with age, from the following notes.[3]

In proportion as the veins become old they lose their straightness of direction in their ramifications, and become so much the more flexible or winding and of thicker covering as old age becomes more full with years.

The relation of nerves with muscles was described.[3]

There are as many ramifications of the nerves as there are muscles, and there cannot be either more or less, because these muscles can only be contracted or distended by reason of these nerves from which the muscles receive their sensation.
Veins which by the thickening of their tunicles in the old restrict the passage of the blood and by this lack of nourishment destroy their life without any fever, the old coming to fail little by little in slow death.

Leonardo's discussion of the action of the heart and blood vessels, in 1510, might lead one to believe that he took one step forward in revealing the physiology of circulation, a precursor of Harvey's thesis published in 1628.[3]

Heart open in the receptacle of the spirits, that is in the artery; and in it takes or rather gives the blood to the artery, and by the mouth, it refreshes itself with air from the lung, and by it fills the auricles of the heart.
Firm muscle is drawn back, and it is the first cause of the movement of the heart, and as it draws back, it thickens, and as it thickens it becomes shortened and draws back with it all the lower and upper muscles, and closes the door, and shortens the space that intervenes between the base and the apex of the heart, and consequently comes to empty it and to draw to itself the fresh air.
Of the heart. This moves of itself and does not stop unless for ever.

The relation of male hormones to emotions and libido was described.[3]

Testicles, witnesses of coition. These contain in themselves ardour, that is they are augumenters of the animosity and ferocity of the animals; and experience shows us this clearly in the castrated animals, of which one sees the bull, the boar, the ram and the cock, very fierce animals, which after having been deprived of these testicles remain very cowardly; so one sees a ram drive before it a herd of wethers, and a cock put to flight a number of capons; and I have seen the same thing happen with a hen, and also with oxen.

Leonardo studied optics and the anatomy of the human eye and appreciated the structure of the malleus and the incus of the internal ear.[5] He discussed the muscles of the tongue, the valves of the heart, and the position of the fetus in the uterus. The bladder was assumed by many of his era to be the organ for the formation of urine. Leonardo, however, attributed this function to the kidney.[3]

> The authorities say that the uretary ducts do not enter directly to carry the urine to the bladder. . . . This proof however does not hold. . . . We may say therefore . . . that the urine enters the bladder by a long and winding way.

Leonardo da Vinci, painter and scientist of the Renaissance, the greatest Italian of all time, undertook the task of preparing an inventory of the universe. This was not achieved, but he was responsible for progress toward this goal. Included were many drawings of human anatomy and physiology. He came into this world with a social handicap and left it with a rich heritage.

1. O'Malley, C. D., and Saunders, J. B. de C. M.: *Leonardo da Vinci on the Human Body*, New York: Henry Schuman, 1952.
2. Belt, E.: *Leonardo the Anatomist*, Lawrence, Kan.: University of Kansas Press, 1955.
3. McCurdy, E.: *The Notebooks of Leonardo da Vinci*, New York: George Braziller, 1955.
4. Belt, E.: *Manuscripts of Leonardo da Vinci*, Los Angeles: The Elmer Belt Library of Vinciana, 1948.
5. Braunfels-Esche, S.: *Leonardo da Vinci, Das Anatomische Werk*, Stuttgart, Germany: Friedrich-Karl Schattauer-Verlag, 1961.

Disiderius Erasmus
(1466-1536)

ERASMUS, the greatest Renaissance figure in the North, was born at Rotterdam or Gouda in the Low Countries and died scarcely two decades after the beginning of the Reformation.[1] Critical of papal power, monastic amorality, and the pedantic theologians of the Roman Catholic Church, he encouraged man to be interested in mankind, in the consciousness of self, in reality, and in simple devotion. As a humanist, Erasmus was consumed with ardor over the rediscovery of the classics and preferred the study of Greek and Latin literature to concern over the soul and spirit. Although doubt exists regarding the birthdate of Erasmus, history leaves no question that his mother was the daughter of a commonplace middle-class family; whereas his father, who never married, was studying in Rome to become a priest at the time of the birth of Erasmus, his second son. Half a century later the stigma of illegitimacy was removed by Leo X, with the granting & dispensation for the parental indiscretion.

Erasmus received a liberal education in Gouda, and spent the years from 1475-1483 at the school of St. Lebwin's, Deventer;

there members of the Brethren of the Common Life, sympathetic to the new humanism, taught him. After taking vows at the Augustinian monastery at Steyn, he was ordained in 1492. Although provided with ample opportunity to study the classics in the secular libraries, he rebelled at the constraint of the dogma and austerity of life in the order and left it in 1494. In 1495, he began his theology studies at Montaigne College in Paris and received the bachelor of theology degree in 1497. Despite periodic poor health for the remainder of his life, he wandered about Europe studying, writing, teaching, and crusading. One or more of his mature years he spent in Paris, London, Basel, Louvain, Turin, Bologna, Venice, Padua, Rome, and Freiburg. Meanwhile, he was allowed by the Pope to live beyond the spiritual and physical confines of the order and was absolved from wearing the habit when not required. As with other notable reformers, he lived a holy life but died without the sacraments of the church.

The discovery of the printing press enabled Erasmus to circulate a tremendous number of letters and to disseminate the products of his literary output. The majority of his writings appeared initially in Latin; some were great as judged by time, others were mediocre. His best writings include *Encomium moriae* (praise of folly), *Adagia* (adages), *Colloquia,* and the *New Testament,* which marked him as the first modern *New Testament* scholar. The *Adages,* a collection of proverbs culled from Greek and Roman writers and published in 1500, was well received, supplemented, and reprinted in his lifetime and posthumously.[2] They were introduced into almost every country in Europe and are as familiar today as formerly. They include Nulla Dies sine Linea (no day without a deed); Bis Pueri Senes (once a man and twice a child); Nosce te ipsum (know thyself); In Vino Veritas (wine opens the soul); In Nocte Consilium (night is the time for reflection); and Medice, cura te ipsum (physician, heal thyself).

Erasmus is of interest to physicians in addition to his scholarship and humanism. He had consulted Linacre of London, Cop

of Paris, and other prominent physicians for his recurring illnesses. His letters leave unanswered the probability that his expressed intense affection for many of his male companions might have been strengthened by sexual intimacy. The following communication to William Herman is but one of several illustration in the *Epistles.*[3]

> I am angry with you for writing so briefly and so seldom. Poor me! has it come to this, that you grudge giving up one night's sleep for my sake? Or are we fallen among pleasures? I wish I may live to share them with you. But see where ambition has cast us. We are still rolling Sisyphus's stone. I have a scheme in hand; but if it fails, I shall fly to you. As to an honorable livelihood I have no anxiety; I am eagerly courted and sought for all round. But oh, that I could live with you, or you with me! You do not know how I am tormented with the wish for you and for you alone.

Erasmus sensed the hazards of infection from the foul air of closed spaces, in the breath of confessors, or harbored in baptismal fonts. He was hypochondriacal and rationalized this to his selfish benefit. He suffered at various times from kidney stones, gouty arthritis, lumbago, malaria, yaws or syphilis, and the plague. For his gout he preferred Burgundy wine. He wrote to Thomas More, "You have kidney stones and I have the gout; we have married two sisters."[4] William Warham, Archbishop of Canterbury, wrote to him as follows.[3]

> If in beginning a letter we wish "Health" to those that are well, how much more suitable is it to wish health to you that are sick; although by a happy omen I divine that you are already purged of your stones, now that we have kept the feast of the Purification [Candlemas]. What business have you with stones? You have not, I suppose, any great buildings on hand. Therefore as stones are no affair of yours, pray free yourself as soon as you can from such a superfluous load; and spend what money is needed to have those stones carried away. . . . Take care and get well; and do not defraud us by your sickness of the fair promise and sweet fruit of your learning.

The famous portrait by Holbein has been interpreted as showing his gouty hand(s) holding the quill. In the fall of 1520, he was delayed in Cologne because of a recurrence of an acute attack of gout. His increasing physical infirmity during his last decade has been attributed to chronic gouty arthritis. When the skeleton of Erasmus was inspected in 1928 during the reconstruction of the cathedral in Basel, other osseous lesions were studied by Werthemann of the Pathological Institute of Basel University. Lesions found in the left ulna and the left tibia were examined microscopically and diagnosed as unquestionably syphilitic in origin. Since no evidence of congenital syphilis was discovered, it was assumed that the disease was acquired.[5] Pfister, however, denied the interpretation and concluded that the lesions were typical of yaws.[6] While on his extensive travels Erasmus was exposed to endemic and epidemic plague, a disease from which his mother died. During one illness, probably plague, he attributed the development of buboes on the abdominal wall to infection entering the body through the skin. The malady is mentioned a number of times in his letters and specifically in a letter to Budé as follows.[3]

At Basel I was almost always ill, and had got better in the journey; but after passing Cologne I fell back again to the lowest level, and up to the present time I keep to the house. The surgeon, after inspecting three ulcers, has pronounced it plague, but I think he is wrong.

His *Praise of the Healing Arts,* composed in Latin, has been recently reprinted and translated into contemporary German. It discloses, as do his other writings, an intimate knowledge of the works of Galen, Hippocrates, and other ancients and offers an appraisal of contemporary physicians, less equivocal than those in other works. The introduction contains the following.[7]

The special glory of the healing arts is self-sufficient and recommends itself to mankind by its value and utility. It is not necessary to praise medicine by odious comparisons or by hurling indignities at other disciplines. It has often been praised by outstanding minds and provided fresh discussion for small minds also, because of its own peculiarities. One must on the contrary fear that these peculiar gifts, that its true and inborn greatness, that its elevation which exceeds human comprehension can not fully be expressed in mortal words. . . . For those of average beauty it is customary to view themselves by comparison with the ugly or by sensuous emphasis on appearance; but for items of great inherent value, it is sufficient to show them unadorned to the world.

. . . Many sicknesses have such a power that death is the sure fate of a patient if the doctor does not interfere immediately. . . . How many thousands of humans are live today and are healthy who would not even have been born if the same skill had not discovered the many measures against the dangers of childbirth and improved the procedures of midwifery.

While I cannot condone what the ancients have done, I must praise their sentiments and their judgement, because they believed sincerely and have expressed honestly *that there is no fitting reward for a skilled and reliable physician* and any accolade would be inadequate.

1. Mangan, J. J.: *Life, Character & Influence of Desiderius Erasmus of Rotterdam,* New York: Macmillan Co., 1927.
2. Bland, R.: *Proverbs Chiefly Taken From the Adagia of Erasmus,* 2 vol, London: T. Egerton, 1814.
3. Nichols, F. M.: *The Epistles of Erasmus,* 3 vol, New York: Russell & Russell, 1962.
4. Charcot, J. M.: *Complete Works* (Fr), Paris: Lecrosnier & Babe, 1890, vol 7, p 121.
5. Werthemann, A.: Skull and Bones of Erasmus of Rotterdam (Ger), *Verh Natur Ges* 39:313-394, 1929.
6. Pfister, C. R.: The Diseases of Erasmus (Ger), *Schweiz Med Wschr* 66:846, 1936.
7. Erasmus: *In Praise of the Healing Arts* (L), 1518, facsimile (Ger), Darmstadt, Germany: E. Merck, 1960.

Bodleian Library, Oxford

Thomas Linacre
(1460-1524)

THE RENAISSANCE, the interlude between the Middle Ages and the beginning of the modern era, meant different things to different people in Europe. In Italy, the arts, music, and science were reborn. In England, a relatively small group of scholars were responsible for the restoration of learning in language and literature. Thomas Linacre, physician, grammarian, classicist, priest, and medical scholar, ignored the barriers separating the intellectual disciplines, and embraced literature as well as clinical medicine. He translated from Greek into Latin, the language of the Renaissance intellects, fresh new versions of Hippocrates, Galen, and Aristotle.

Linacre was born in Canterbury; his training began at the Monastery School of Christ Church under William de Selling, the presiding Augustinian monk, a Fellow of All Souls College, Oxford.[1] The monk, a brilliant advocate of the classical humanistic learning, inspired his star pupil with scholarly ambitions. As Linacre grew in physical and intellectual stature, he grew likewise in creative capacity in letters and medicine. After Linacre left the monastery, he studied for a short time at Oxford, the English center of Greek learning, and, in 1484, in the footsteps of his teacher, was elected a Fellow of All Souls College.

Linacre traveled to the Continent as a classical scholar and studied in Florence, Rome, Venice, Ferrara, and Padua, where he received the degree of Doctor of Medicine in 1496. In Florence, Linacre was a pupil of Poligrano and Demetrius Chalcondyles, poet and Greek scholar, respectively. One of his fellow students in the Platonic Academy was Giovanni de' Medici, later Pope Leo X.[2] Linacre studied in the libraries, enjoyed the social amenities of the Medician court, and became acquainted with Lorenzo de Medici, "The Magnificent." The Vatican library was next on the grand tour. Selling, who had preceded his pupil to Rome as an emissary of Henry VII, probably encouraged Linacre to take advantage of the books of the Vatican, the best stocked library in Christendom. While in Rome, Linacre translated one of Plato's manuscripts and became friendly with Hermolaus Barbarus, scholar and grandson of a doge, who had translated Aristotle into Latin and, with annotations, the Greek herbal of Dioscorides.[3] In Venice, Linacre studied with the master printer-

scholar Aldus Manutius. Aldus published at least two translations for Linacre, one a mathematical treatise, the other an edition of Aristotle. At Ferrara, Linacre visited the earliest of the medical humanists Nicolaus Leonicenus, the composer of a clinical treatise on syphilis.

Linacre returned to Oxford, one of a small group who brought the Greek language back to England, and received a doctorate in medicine on the basis of the degree from Padua—with honors. Erasmus of Rotterdam, who came to Oxford for intellectual stimulation and to consult Linacre on an episode interpreted as renal colic, attributed to a combination of foul English weather and good English ale. At the beginning of the 16th century, Linacre was invited to London by Henry VII to be court physician and tutor for Prince Arthur. The court appointment was continued by Henry VIII. Other famous patients and friends of Linacre included Colet, Sir Thomas More, William Norham, Archbishop of Canterbury, Richard Foxe, Bishop of Winchester, and Cardinal Wolsey, the latter afflicted with the "English sweating disease."

The increasing number of scientific works published during the Renaissance, seeking equivalents to the Latin and Greek terms, placed an intolerable strain on the inadequate English language. The deficiency forced the development of a modern Greco-Latin medical vocabulary. The terms were gathered first in glossaries, and in subsequent years, published in systematic scientific dictionaries. The advantage of Greco-Latin etymology was clearly justified. Latin continued as the language of medical writing into the 19th century; whereas Greco-Latin terms persist as the basis of current medical etymology.

A practical result of Linacre's medical interest was the founding, with five other physicians, of the Royal College of Physicians, critically needed at that time because of the unbridled empiricism and lack of regulations. As court physician to Henry VIII, he was instrumental in inducing the Crown, in 1518, to entrust the College with the sole power of licensing the practice of physic for "all those in London and seven miles around." He offered his home for its initial session, became the College's first president, and remained in office until his death. The establishment of the Royal College for licensure was preceded by a policy whereby the permission to practice was granted by the Bishop of London or the Dean of St. Paul's Cathedral, who, with the help of qualified physicians and surgeons, judged the applicants' credentials. Outside of London, the authority to license medical practitioners rested with the Archbishops of Canterbury and Oxford. The authority of the Church continued to have limited jurisdiction over licensure until the 19th century.

Linacre's writings were confined to translation and revision, except for two treatises on Latin grammar, one ranking him as the leading European grammarian of his day, and the other to make the writings of the classical physicians available to the English medical profession. The Greek manuscripts, so long buried or lost in the Western libraries stocked from the Eastern empire, provided the material for Linacre and the other great humanists of the Renaissance. They were translated into Latin and formed the basis for the new learning and the revival of studies in the classics. The Latin translations remained as the standard texts in clinical medicine until Sydenham and Boerhaave, who came two centuries later.

The preface to Galen's *Study on the Motions of Muscles* reflects Linacre's interest and his primary contribution in medicine.[4]

There is nothing I desire more than to make the works of Galen—after Hippocrates the greatest benefactor of human health—available to all who use the Roman tongue. With this in view, as far as my own health permitted, I have translated into Latin, to the best of my moderate ability, those that have come into my hands, and I am still doing so. As for this excellent little work of his (Galen's) on muscular motion which the learned Nicolaus Leonicenus has turned into Latin, and which my Florianus has sent to me from the city, I could not let students be deprived of it for long, or refrain from having it printed in many copies and as soon as possible.

The association of Linacre with the church, which had begun during his elementary schooling, was reestablished during his last 15 years. The wealthy church at that time made its assignments lucrative; but income was a secondary motive. He was un-

married and sought leisure time for scholarly pursuits as a curate in parishes in London, York, Devonshire, and Lancashire. The ecclesiastical commissions did not demand a great deal of time and interfered little with his practice of medicine. The income from his preferments and landholdings enabled him to establish two lectureships in medicine at Oxford and one at Cambridge, the "Lynacre's Lectures."[5] Only after his death were the lectureships legalized when only one of the five originally appointed trustees survived. The Bishop of London, endowed with a resolute mind, assigned the lectureships to the university colleges rather than to the administrative units of the universities convinced as he was of their corruption. Merton's College at Oxford and St. John's College at Cambridge were the recipients. The Merton Lectureship at Oxford continues today as the Linacre Professorship of Physiology. The legacy to St. John's of Cambridge was mismanaged, but the lectureship persists.

1. Johnson, J. N.: *The Life of Thomas Linacre* (ed.) Robert Graves, London: E. Lumley, 1835.

2. O'Malley, C. D.: *English Medical Humanists: Thomas Linacre and John Caius,* University of Kansas Press, Lawrence, 1965.

3. Sharpe, W. D.: Thomas Linacre, 1460-1524: An English Physician Scholar of the Renaissance, *Bull Hist Med* 34:233-256 (May-June) 1960.

4. Fulton, J. F.: Early Medical Humanists: Leonicenus, Linacre and Thomas Elyot, *New Eng J Med* 205:141-146 (July 16) 1931.

5. Osler, W.: *Thomas Linacre,* Cambridge, England: Cambridge University Press, 1908.

Fracastorius (c 1478-1553)

HIERONYMUS FRACASTORIUS, an important figure of the Italian Renaissance, was born of well-to-do parents in Verona, at that time a vassal of Venice and without a university. Although historians and biographers do not agree on the precise year of his birth, the census records at Verona suggest 1478 as the closest approximation. His death in 1553, from a stroke, is firmly documented. He studied at nearby Padua, where his brilliant scholarship was soon recognized, and he was invited to sit with the learned men on the faculty, holding the position of lecturer in logic for several years.

Caught up in the strife of a long local war and with the responsibilities of a family, he began the practice of medicine in Verona, sharing his intellectual interests with poetry,

natural philosophy, astronomy, cosmography, geology, mathematics, and physics. He divided his time between a residence in Verona and a villa at Caffi in the hills overlooking Lake Garda;[1] however, he was not removed from the effects of the wars, foreign invasions, and epidemics of syphilis and tuberculosis that swept much of the peninsula. Under these exposures, he applied his inquiring mind to the task of discovering the causes of diseases in such a way as to place his name among the great physicians of the 16th century.

There are two remarkable compositions by Fracastorius: his blank verse describing the shepherd, *Syphilis sive morbus gallicus,*[2] one of the great medical poems of all times,[3] and a treatise on contagion, *De contagione,* a startlingly modern discussion of the spread of infectious disease. It contains a clinical discourse on typhus and tuberculosis and a chapter on the treatment of syphilis.

The poem was completed in 1525 and, with revisions, was printed in Verona in 1530, and dedicated to his friend and advisor, Cardinal Bembo, a papal secretary and one of the lovers of Lucrezia Borgia. The name chosen for the "French disease" is believed to have been taken from the name of the shepherd, although other explanations have been suggested.[4] It was prepared in Latin and referred to Greek and Roman mythology. The etiology of the affliction was considered to be due to the planets Saturn, Jupiter, and Mars, but its spread was related to contagion (coitus). This was an important advance. Little progress had been made in the understanding of fevers from the time of Hippocrates and Galen, who attributed their origin to a curruption of the body humours, and along with many later writers failed to account adequately for the pathogenesis of spread. Fracastorius, endowed with a receptive mind and a brilliant intellect and with great experience with fevers and contagion, proposed a logical explanation. He also suggested that the disease may have been quiescent and only recently had increased in virulence.[5]

Through what adventures this unknown Disease
So lately did astonisht *Europe* seize,
Through *Asian* Coasts and *Libyan* Cities ran,
And from what Seeds the Malady began,
Our Song shall tell: to *Naples* first it came
From France, and justly took from *France* his
   Name,
Companion of the War—

If from the Western Climes 'twas wafted o'er,
When daring *Spaniards* left their Native shore;
Resolv'd beyond th' *Atlantick* to descry,
Conjectur'd Worlds, or in the search to dye.
For Fame Reports this Grief perpetual there,
From Skies infected and polluted Air:
From whence 'tis grown so Epidemical
Whole Cities Victims to its Fury fall;

This new Distemper from some newer Cause;
Nor Reason can allow that this Disease,
Came first by Comerce from beyond the Seas;
Since instances in divers Lands are shown,
To whom all *Indian* Traffick is unknown:
Nor could th' Infection from the Western Clime
Seize distant Nations at the self same time;
And in Remoter parts begin its Reign,
As fierce and early as it did in *Spain.*

The proud Destroyer seeks no common Game,
He scorns the well finn'd Sporters of the Flood,
He scorns the well plum'd Singers of the wood;
The Lord of Nature onely he annoys,
And humane frame, Heav'ns Images, destroys.

Yet oft the Moon four monthly rounds shall steer
Before convincing Symptoms shall appear;

So long the Malady shall lurk within,
And grow confirm'd before the danger's seen;

The thinner Parts will yet not stick so fast,
But to the Surface of the Skin are cast,
Which in foul Botches o'er the Body spread,
Prophane the Bosome, and deform the Head:
Here Puscles in the form of Achorns swell'd.
In form alone, for these with Stench are fill'd,

A Shepherd once (distrust not ancient Fame)
Possest these Downs, and *Syphilus* his Name.
A thousand Heifers in these Vales he fed,
A thousand Ews to those fair Rivers led:
For King *Alcithous* he rais'd this Stock,
And shaded in the Covert of a Rock, . . .

From whence this Malady its birth receiv'd,
And first th' offending *Syphilus* was griev'd,
Who rais'd forbidden Altars on the Hill,
And Victims bloud with impious Hands did spill;
He first wore Buboes dreadfull to the sight,
First felt strange Pains and sleepless past the Night;
From him the Malady receiv'd its name, . . .

More than 15 years after the poem appeared, Fracastorius published his narrative on contagion. The discussion of syphilis in this treatise was more scientific and less lyrical than in the poem.[3]

Some have invented a new word for it and call it Pudendagra, because it begins with the pudenda, on the analogy of Mentagra, which begins at the chin and was so called as a new disease among the ancients, according to Pliny. In my poem I have called this disease Syphilis.

In certain individuals it would arise without any contagion having been contracted from another person; in other cases, and these were the majority, it was contracted by contagion; but not from every kind of contact, nor readily, but only when two bodies in close contact with one another became extremely heated. Now this happened in sexual intercourse especially, and it was by this means that the great majority of persons were infected. However, some cases were observed by infants who, by sucking milk from a mother or nurse who was infected, were themselves infected in a precisely similar way. . . . At last, in the majority of cases, small ulcers began to appear on the sexual organs, not unlike those which arise from over-fatigue and are called "caries," but in their nature they are very different; for the kind that appears in syphilis was intractable and would not depart, but when subdued in one part of the body, it would germinate in another place and propagate itself so that it never died out. . . . When they first appeared, the pustules were small, but they soon grew little by little till they were the size of the cup of an acorn, which in fact they resembled; they were not unlike those eruptions which in children are called "achores." . . . The patients suffered from pernicious catarrh which eroded the palate or the uvula, or the pharynx

and tonsils. In some cases the lips or nose or eyes were eaten away, or in others the whole of the sexual organs. Moreover, many patients suffered from the great deformity of gummata which developed on the members; these were often as large as an egg or a roll of bread, and when opened contained a white, sticky mucus.

In the second book on contagion, Fracastorius clearly distinguishes typhus from other fevers:[2]

They are vulgarly called "lenticulae" (small lentils), or "puncticulae" (small pricks), because they produce spots which look like lentils or flea-bites. Others spell the name differently, and call them "peticulae." We must study them carefully.

This fever, then, is contagious, but it does not infect quickly or by means of fomes, or at a distance, but only from the actual handling of the sick. Though in the early stages all pestilent fevers are gentle and mild, this sort invades so very gently that the sick are hardly willing to call in a doctor. . . . For though, according to the nature of fevers of this sort, a moderate temperature was felt, nevertheless a sort of internal disturbance became obvious, then prostration of the whole body, and a lassitude such as follows over-exertion; the patient could only lie flat on his back, the head became heavy, the senses dulled, and in the majority of cases, after the fourth or seventh day, the mind would wander; the eyes became red, and the patient was garrulous; . . . About the fourth or seventh day, red, or often purplish-red spots broke out on the arms, back and chest, looking like flea-bites (punctiform), though they were often larger and in the shape of lentils, whence arose the name of the fever.

In the discussion of the treatment of phthisis, Francastorius noted that:[3]

For the phthisis that is due to contagion per se can be contracted by a person who was not previously suffering from any disease, and is in perfect health. Hence, when catarrh or other symptoms supervene in such a patient, they are, as it were, accidents of the disease, and per se do not demand treatment as primary causes. You may administer the usual remedies, heat the head, dry out by means of sinapisms, and make the sputum come easily, but you will make all these efforts in vain, if you do not endeavor to destroy the contagion as contagian. Therefore, in dealing with that form of phthisis which has been contracted from association with a phthisical person, or by some kind of fomes, you must first of all consider carefully the points which I said must be observed in general in all contagious diseases, namely the germs, the substance which tends to be corrupted, and the substance that has already been corrupted.

Fracastorius retired from active practice to his villa not long after the publication of his poem. He continued to pursue a scientific but quiet life, devoted considerable time to materia medica and botany, and in so doing rediscovered a number of herbs that had been used by the ancients. He wrote on the movements of the planets, became interested in geology, displayed some concept of the nature of the refraction of light, and was the first to refer to the magnetic poles of the earth. Verona honored its native son with a statue in the square near those of Pliny and Catullus. The marble globe in his hand identifies him with astronomy rather than with medicine or literature. As judged by Bembo, the dedicatee in *Syphilis sive morbus gallicus,* he surpassed Lucretius and equaled Virgil.[2]

You write with much more charm than Lucretius often does . . . I could ask no more from Virgil himself . . . your lament for Marco Antonio (della Torre) and what follows, makes me think that the soul of Virgil has passed into you.

1. Riddell, W. R.: *Hieronymus Fracastorius and His Poetical and Prose Works on Syphilis,* Toronto: Canadian Social Hygiene Council, 1928.

2. Singer, C., and Singer, D.: The Scientific Position of Girolamo Fracastoro, *Ann Med Hist* 1:1-34, 1917.

3. Wright, W. C.: *Hieronymi Fracastorii, De Contagione et Contagiosis Morbis et Eorum Curatione, Libi III,* New York: G. P. Putnam's Sons, 1930.

4. Hendrickson, G. L.: The "Syphilis" of Girolamo Fracastoro, *Bull Inst Hist Med* 2:515-546, 1934.

5. Tate, N.: *Syphilis: or, a Poetical History of the French Disease, Written in Latin by Fracastorius,* London: J. Tonson, 1686.

Ulrich von Hutten
(1488-1523)

ULRICH VON HUTTEN, patriot, humanist, and protagonist of Martin Luther, without formal medical training attracted great interest to his work on epidemiology and treatment of syphilis. He was born near Fulda, Germany, in the Castle of Steckelberg. His knightly family were poor but distinguished at a time when knighthood's survival was conditioned by the returns from the poverty-stricken peasants to whom the land was leased.[1] Ulrich, a sickly child, contracted syphilis early in life and died

before his prime. After six years in a monastery at Fulda, he fled from clerical discipline, believing he could better serve God outside the order. He wandered through Germany and Italy as a mendicant scholar, visiting several universities.

Hutten served for a time as a common soldier in the army of Emperor Maximilian. In 1506. he took the bachelor's degree at Frankfort. Subsequently, his widely appreciated literary talents led to his being crowned poet laureate in poetry and prose in 1517. His support of Lutheranism, attempts to inspire a new national German spirit, and his attacks on the Papacy led to his arrest by Pope Leo X, while his venereal stigma alienated Erasmus. Rejected by the Church and shunned by many, he died penniless on an island in Lake Zürich but left a legacy of letters, poems, and a treatise on syphilis based upon his own affliction.

The French Disease,[2] first published in 1519, described the epidemiology of the malady, recounted his bitter experiences with mercury inunctions for several years and his successful therapeutic trials with guaiac. However, subsidence of symptoms was probably related to the natural course of tertiary lues rather than to the consumption of great quantities of the extract of India wood. An English translation appeared first in 1539.[3] Hutten recognized the mode of spread of the disease. Although he confused leprous lesions with lues, his ability as an experimenter was demonstrated in his insistence on physicians basing their practice on observation and experience. The following excerpts are taken from the 1730 edition by Turner.[4]

. . . and it is thought this Disease in our Days ariseth not, unless by Infection from carnal Contact as in copulating with a diseased Person; since it appears now that young Children, old Men and others, not given to Fornication or bodily Lust, are very rarely diseased: Also the more a Man is addicted to these Pleasures, the sooner he catcheth it, and as they manage themselves after, either temperately or otherwise, so it the sooner leaves them, holds them a long time, or utterly consumes them.

Though this Distemper singly may be lightly accounted, yet doth it soon convert it self into many others; and indeed whatever Pains affect a Man's Joints, may seem to arise hence; for first there is a sharp Ach in these Parts, and yet nothing to be seen; but afterwards a Flux of Humours falls down, occasioning a Swelling, which beginning to harden about the Part, a most vehement Pain ariseth, which is the first Appearance of the Distemper when it begins to fortify itself as in a Castle, there resting for a long time, and thence to disperse its Emissaries into every part of the Body, kindling therein all sorts of Aches and Dolors; when the longer the Swellings are before they ripen, the more Pain is the Patient to suffer, and truly of all others, this is the most intolerable. I my self had such a Knob or hard Swelling above my left Heel on the inside, the which after it was indurated for the Space of seven Years, could by no Applications, be softened or brought to Matter, but still continued like a Bone, till by the help of *Guajacum* it gradually vanished.

In Women the Disease resteth in their secret Places, wherein are little pretty Sores, full of venomous Poison, being very dangerous for such as unknowingly meddle with them; the which Sickness, when contracted from these infected Women, is so much the more grievous, by how much they are more inwardly corrupted and polluted therewith. By this a Man's Sinews are sometimes relaxed, and again grow hard, and contact themselves. Sometimes the Disease transforms it self into the Gout; at others, into a *Palsy* and *Apoplexy*, and infecteth many also with a *Leprosy;* for it is thought these Diseases are Neighbours each to the other, by reason of some Affinity there appears between them; those who

are seized with the Pox, frequently becoming *Lepers,* and through the Acuteness of the Pain, Men will shake and quiver as in a Fever.

Whilst the Physicians were thus confounded like Men amazed, the Surgeons as wretchedly lent a helping Hand to the same Error, and first began to burn the Sores with hot Irons. But for as much, as there seemed no end of this Cruelty, they endeavoured now to avoid the same with their *Ointments,* but all in vain, unless they added *Quick-Silver* thereunto.

With these, fewer or more, they anointed the sick Man's Joints, his Arms, Thighs, his Neck and Back, with other parts of his Body. Some using these Anointings once a Day, some twice, others three times, and four times, others; the Patient being shut up in a Stove, with continual and fervent Heat, some twenty, some thirty whole days. Some lying in Bed within the Stove were thus anointed, and covered with many Clothes, being compelled to Sweat; Part at the second anointing began to faint; yet was the Ointment of such Strength, that whatsover Distemper was in the upper Parts it drew it into the Stomach, and thence to the Brain; and so the Disease was voided both by the Nose and Mouth, and put the Patient to so great Pain, that except they took good heed, their Teeth fell out, and their Throats, their Lungs, with the Roofs of their Mouths, were full of Sores; their Jaws did swell, their Teeth loosen'd, and a stinking Matter continually was voided from these places. What Part soever it touched, the same was strait corrupted thereby, so that not only their Lips, but the inside of their Cheeks, were grievously pained, and made the Place where they were, stink most abominably; which sort of Cure was indeed so terrible, that many chose rather to die than to be eased thus of their Sickness. Howbeit, scarce one sick Person in a hundred could be cured in this Way, but quickly after relapsed, so that the Cure held but for a few Days. Whereby may be infer'd what I suffered in the same Disease, who underwent the same in this Fashion for eleven times, with great Peril and Jeopardy of Life, struggling with the Disease nine Years together.

If we ought to give God thanks both for Good and Evil, how much are we bound for his Gift of *Guajacum;* yea, how much doth the Joy and Gladness for this his Bounty to us, surpass the Pains and Sorrow of our past Sickness.

1. Holborn, H.: *Ulrich von Hutten and the German Reformation,* R. H. Bainton (trans.), New Haven: Yale University Press, 1937.

2. von Hutten, U.: *Concerning the Medicine Guaiac and the French Disease* (L), Mogintiae: J. Scheffer, 1519.

3. von Hutten, U.: *Of the Wood Called Guaiacum, That Healeth the Frenche Pockes, and also helpeth the goute in the feete, the stoone, the palsey, lepree, dropsy, fallynge evyll and other dyseases,* T. Paynell (trans.), London: T. Berthelet, 1539.

4. Hutten, U.: *A Treatise of the French Disease, Published Above 200 Years Past,* D. Turner (trans.), London: J. Clarke, 1730.

National Library of Medicine

Jacobus Sylvius (1478-1555)

JACQUES DUBOIS, humanist and anatomist, the son of an impoverished weaver, was born at Louville near Amiens, France, from which he derived his Latin cognomen Jacob Sylvius Ambianus.[1] From Sylvius are derived the following eponyms: fissure, artery (middle cerebral), aqueduct, ventricle (fifth ventricle), the *caro quadrata* muscle (flexor accessorius muscle of the foot), and valve (Eustachian valve of the heart). In all except the last instance, however, the structures have been incorrectly attributed to him, for they were neither originally described nor specifically identified by him.[2] The fissure and fifth ventricle were described by Franciscus Sylvius (de le Boë), and Barengarius described the aqueduct many years before the publication of the anatomical works of Jacobus Sylvius.

Sylvius prepared at the College of Tournay near Paris, excelling in Latin, Greek, Hebrew, and mathematics; however, he was too poor to continue preparation for a degree. Turning to the instruction of anatomy in Paris, his success alarmed the medical faculty when they could not compete with him. Sylvius subsequently went to Montpellier, where he dissected human bodies and obtained a bachelor's degree in medicine in 1531. The round trip was completed by his return to Paris and resumption of his demonstrations and lectures in anatomy at the College of Tréguier. The remark-

able number of pupils was surpassed only by their performance in later years. Vesalius, Servetus, Conrad Gesner, and Charles Estienne were among the most illustrious. Other pupils, members of undisciplined bands, roamed from university to university, but their small fees sustained Sylvius for many years. His teachings, based largely upon touch and sight, followed those of Galen, but sometimes lacked direction and were not too critical; however, he named muscles identified by Galen by number only and clarified many of Galen's obscure passages. His teaching was his life, a fine art, so excellent his pupils never wearied of learning. In the Introduction to Anatomy Sylvius counselled students of anatomy as well as proposed a system of identifying skeletal muscles.[3]

I would have you look carefully and recognize by eye when you are attending dissections or when you see anyone else who may be better supplied with instruments than yourself. For my judgment is that it is much better that you should learn the manner of cutting by eye and touch than by reading and listening. For reading alone never taught anyone how to sail a ship, to lead an army, nor to compound a medicine, which is done rather by the use of one's own sight and the training of one's   hands.

Since it   ılt to remember the muscles if they are di   ıed merely by number, as first, second, third   , we have thought best to apply to them special names in order to be more clear, and that they may be better retained in the memory, sometimes taking such names from the parts to which they are attached, such as the brachialis, the tibialis, the peroneus; at others from their shape, as the scaleni, the rhomboidei, the serrati, the lumbricoides, the soleus; again from their size, as magnus, parvus, longus, brevis; or from their substance. as carnosus, membranosus; or from the number of their heads, as biceps, triceps.

A similar system of nomenclature was applied to the vessels. To Sylvius we owe the terms "jugular," "subclavian," "phrenic," "axillary," "renal," "spermatic," "pudic," "femoral," "popliteal," "gastroepiploic" and "inferior" and "superior mesentery vessels." On the other hand, nerves were never named, which probably accounts for the retention of numbered cranial and cervical nerves.

Paradoxically, the anatomical structure probably first described clearly by Sylvius— the valve of the inferior vena cava, a semilunar fold of endocardium attached to the anterior border of the vena caval opening in fetal life—is known as the Eustachian valve. The description of the valve accepted the interpretation of the Renaissance anatomists that the auricles were part of the large vessels entering the chambers, and also made mention of valves in large veins.[4]

In the foetal heart there is a certain membrane, in the nature of a covercle or lid, at the orifice of the vessel which connects the vena cava with the arteria venosa. It is readily turned towards the orifice of the vas arteriosum and thereby prevents the blood from entering the lungs.

There is a membranous process (epiphysis) of a similar kind at the commencement of the vena azygos, and others also in more than one of the great vessels, such as the jugulars, brachials, crural veins, and trunk of the cava as it leaves the liver. The use of all of these processes, says Sylvius, is the same as that of the membranes which close the orifices of the heart.

In addition to Sylvius' contributions to anatomy, he prepared a French grammar especially designed for young ladies; he cultivated a herbarium to advance his knowledge of materia medica, described the injection of blood vessels for anatomical demonstrations, and offered sound advice for poor medical students. Suggestions for conservation of body heat in cold quarters, for effective study habits, and for the benefits of simple food were in contrast to his reputation for coarse language, harsh personality, and greediness.[3] In the ebbing years of life, Sylvius was appointed professor of medicine in the Royal College of Paris, a position held until his death. He was buried in the Cemetery of the Poor Scholars.

1. Kellet, C. E.: Sylvius and the Reform of Aanatomy, *Med Hist* 5:101-116, 1961.

2. Baker, F.: The Two Sylviuses, An Historical Study, *Bull Johns Hopkins Hosp* 20:329-339, 1909.

3. Sylvius, J.: *Opera Medica* (L), by R. Moreau, Geneva, J. Chouët, 1635, except translated by F. Baker (Ref. No. 2).

4. Sylvius, J.: *Introduction to the Physiology and Anatomy of Hippocrates and Galen* (L), J. Halpeau, Paris: 1555, excerpt translated by R. Willis, in *William Harvey*, London: C. K. Paul & Co., 1878.

Jean Fernel (1497-1558)

JEAN FRANCOIS FERNEL (Joannis Fernelii), born in the purlieus of Paris in 1485, was one of the remarkable scientists of the 16th century. If Galen is credited with the earliest treatise on human physiology, Fernel rediscovered this discipline 13 centuries later. Fernel also prepared a treatise on pathology. A presentation of the clinical findings in the case of a patient with acute appendicitis and a description of the postmortem examination preceded the modern description by Reginald Fitz by more than three hundred years. As a clinician, Fernel used the Roman term "lues venerea" for the first time to describe clinical syphilis. A very readable biography of Fernel was written by Guillaume Plancey, for 10 years his associate, who lived in his home and thereby experienced an unusual opportunity to write of his master from intimate contact. The biography by Plancey and other Ferneliana was compiled by Sir Charles S. Sherrington of Cambridge and published in 1946.[1]

Fernel, having developed a passion for the humanities early in life, begged his father for permission to study rhetoric and philosophy in Paris. His father realized that[1] . . .

Just as the careful, good and productive soil promises a fine crop, so likewise with man and learning, passion for study and the budding of innate inclinations from youth up presage a maturity rich in bright accomplishment.

After receiving a master's degree for his brilliance, he was widely recognized by the faculty in the Collége de Ste Barbe and urged to accept a position and to teach dialectic. He declined because he wished to be free to concentrate on the writings of Cicero, Aristotle, and Plato.[1]

He resolved to forego entertainment, and convivialities, feasts and drinking bouts, and even talks with fellow students and acquaintances. He took account neither of food nor sleep nor exercise, of ailments and affairs; he put up with everything in order to attain knowledge of the liberal arts—he had no other delight than learning. He thought every hour lost which was not spent in reading and studying with good authors. Desire for learning filled his mind; he was in love with scholarship and knowledge.

In the cultivation of his mind, Fernel spent the mornings in the study of mathematics, the afternoons in contemplation of philosophy, and the evenings in close attention to the Latin classics. Thus, his training was at least the equivalent of a doctorate in philosophy before he turned to medicine as a career—but not completely so. Even between the hours given to the study of medicine, he found time to teach mathematics. Fernel had passed his 50th birthday before devoting himself exclusively to the teaching and practice of medicine. When he finally established himself in medical practice, he attained renown in a few short years as the foremost physician in France, if not in Central Europe. Catherine de' Medici employed his services to cure her of sterility, and with this accomplished he delivered her ten children, reportedly at a fee of 10,000 ecus each. Appointment as physician to the king, Henry II, was accepted with considerable reluctance because he was fearful that it would usurp precious time from scholarly and professional pursuits.

Fernel's precepts of practice are worthy of emulation. Arising before daylight, he pored over his books until breakfast. Throughout the day he visited his patients, gave public lectures, and examined samples of urine that were brought to his office. Until midnight, the evenings were spent in meditation and study. Always an optimist in prognosis, Fernel held out hope of recovery in spite of overwhelming odds. In substance, he was a most successful physician and widely recognized as a skillful practitioner.

Fernel is equally famous through the centuries, however, for his contributions to physiology and pathology. His De naturali parte medicinae (1542), one of the earliest treatises devoted exclusively to physiology, was the first to identify the subject by that name. There are no divisions into functions as we appreciate them today. The volume was prepared 75 years before Harvey's discovery of the circulation of blood when neither chemistry nor the miscroscope was a tool of the trade. The four humours of Hippocrates were accepted. Fernel's conclusions on the digestive tract led Sherrington to suggest that some of the observations must have been performed on a patient whose esophagus or stomach had been injured accidentally and permitted direct inspection. He was the first to suggest that a decrease occurred in the size of the ventricles in systole, with a concomitant increase in the size of the great vessels. But for him and his time there was no escape of blood from artery to vein to complete a circular motion.

Fernel's Pathology in the second division of his Medicina[2] was his best-known achievement in medical writing. It was a systematic essay on morbidity, organ by organ throughout the body. The classification of disease was based on the premise that each disorder was specialized and was confined to a localized site in an organ. Postmortem examinations were routine and at his death his own body was prosected. A localized disease was a simple one when confined to a portion of one organ. The disease was compound when it affected an entire organ and complex when it affected two or more organs. Excerpts on abscess of the kidney from the section entitled, Cause and Symptoms of Diseases of the Kidneys, which has been translated in Long, are as follows.[3]

An abscess of the kidneys in which purulent matter is gathered, rarely occurs from phlegmon, but frequently from a foul ulcer that is not cleaned out, in the manner that I shall forthwith describe. Nevertheless in the coction of the phlegmon, pus arises and shortly an abscess of such size if formed that, the kidney being swollen, a tumor projects in the region of the loins and the ilia. Horrible fevers occur; there is a greater sense of dulness than before. But once the abscess is ruptured the pus is borne off with the urine, followed subsequently by the waste matter or decayed flesh from the putrid substance of the kidneys.

Once the abscess is emptied and cleaned there remains a very persistent and almost incurable ulcer, for the portion of the substance that is consumed by putrefaction or attrition can never be restored nor grow together, since this flesh, like all other, is inherited, and the urine, constantly flowing past, does not allow the ulcer to close. For this reason it is kept perpetually raw like a fistula.

The *Physiology* and *Pathology* of Fernel were, in each respective subject, the earliest systematic treatises. Each established its respective subject under this name, each was the product of the same mind and hand. They were the companions as well as the building stones of a most successful practice of medicine by one of the great minds of France in the 16th century.

1. Sherrington, C. S.: *Endeavour of Jean Fernel*, Cambridge University Press, 1946.
2. Fernel, J.: *Medicina*, Paris: Wechel, 1554.
3. Long, E. R.: *Selected Readings in Pathology*, 2nd ed, Springfield, Ill: Thomas, 1961.

Paracelsus (1493-1541)

PHILIPPUS THEOPHRASTUS AUREOLUS BOMBASTUS VON HOHENHEIM (Paracelsus) was born near Zürich, Switzerland, the year after Columbus discovered the new world.[1] He inherited his interest in medicine from his father, a practicing physician, a humanist, and a botanist. History has never produced a satisfactory explanation for the deep interest in philosophy manifested by Paracelsus and his approach to medicine

that was at times Quixotic. Paracelsus was not a Christian name chosen by his parents. It was, in part, a nom de plume. He was fond of neologopoiesis and especially partial

to the prefix *para*. It has been supposed that Paracelsus represents a combination of para and Celsus (parallel to Celsus), the first important medical historian, who lived in the reign of Tiberius Ceasar. The medical practice of Paracelcus' father in Einsiedeln was not especially profitable, and the family relocated in Austria, in the province of Carinthia near Villach, before the son was 10 years old. Paracelsus very likely studied the arts at the University of Vienna and medicine at the University of Ferrara in Italy. Clinical instruction had not begun at that time in Padua. While he was acquiring a medical education and later while practicing the art, Paracelsus traveled widely through Europe and into Africa. The travels included the British Isles, the Scandinavian countries, Lithuania, Poland, Turkey, the Dodecanese Isles, Egypt, and Italy. These were the years of the acquisition of knowledge of a great variety of diseases under varied political, social, and environmental conditions. He formalized his own materia medica and developed his own therapy during those travels.

In this period of acquisition of knowledge and formulation of therapy, Paracelsus recognized the relative sterility of the Middle Ages. The pharmacology and empiric teachings of Galen and Avicenna had been implemented to a limited extent by Arabic physicians, but the Renaissance in the arts and sciences was just beginning. Paracelsus opposed the polypharmacy that had been in vogue for centuries and cautioned that one drug neutralized the beneficial effects of another. He advocated, therefore, simplicity in his recipes, not multiplicity. Experiences in chemistry prompted him to use heavy metals in practice. Included were sulfur, lead, antimony, mercury, iron, and copper. Opium was a valuable drug in his practice. Observation and deductive reasoning were his handmaidens.

His writings were prepared in difficult-to-translate low German rather than in Latin, preferred by scientists and scholars of his day. One of his more important books, *Volumen paramirum,* the cause and nature of disease, was completed in 1530 but was not printed until after his death. Another, *Paragranum,* was an exposition of his principles of medicine. Neither treatise has been translated into English. However, his Collected Works have been re-published in German in 14 volumes[2] while English translations of four of his treatises were prepared a generation ago in commemoration of the four hundredth anniversary of his death.[3] They present four different aspects of his work: the first, a vindication of his character and views; the second, a study of diseases of miners; the third, a discussion of psychology and psychiatry; and the fourth, a sample of his philosophy and theology.

Sigerist[1] has recounted the five spheres of Paracelsus that determine man's destiny in health and disease. The first sphere is *ens astrale;* the stars (passage of time) affect man's medical destiny. Diseases that were fatal yesterday may be prevented or cured tomorrow. The second sphere is *ens veneni.* Good as well as evil comes from the environment; poisons that kill as well as food that

nourishes are about us. Each man has his own nature (personality), *ens naturale.* The spiritual sphere of man is *ens spirituale.* His psyche may lead him into mental maladies, it may help dispel afflictions of a similar kind. The fifth sphere, the normal, the sphere of God, is *ens Dei.*

The era in which Paracelsus lived spawned spiritualism and mysticism. Paracelsus could not escape reflecting the prevailing philosophy, but he rebelled against it, nevertheless. He was a great reformer and iconoclast. His medicine was new and different from the traditional, but he was thwarted and suppressed because he lacked a school with pupils to teach and a printer to publish his manuscripts. A call to Basel appeared to him to be the turning point. Frobenius, the great printer, and Erasmus, the humanist, both in need of medical care, were responsible for Paracelsus' moving to Basel. An additional attraction was the appointment to the position of Municipal Physician. This was a dual responsibility and embodied a professorship in the medical faculty of the University. Through a series of circumstances, the appointment was terminated a little more than a year later. His teachings were adjudged to be too unorthodox, his pupils did not understand him, and the faculty was hostile. As a wandering physician he sampled life in several social strata. He died following a tavern brawl in Salzburg at the age of 48.

The last 12 years of his life were spent in practicing and in writing, but not much publishing. Printers were reluctant to accept his manuscripts. Although only one of his major works was published in his lifetime, Paracelsus will be remembered for several contributions to medicine. The introduction of chemistry into therapy ranks with his attack upon then contemporary treatment. Sigerist concludes that: "Whether we agree with Paracelsus or not, we cannot read his books without being strongly stimulated or challenged. The problems he discussed are not solved yet, and this is why his books are still alive today. They make us realize how primitive and sketchy our present theory of medicine is. We have accumulated a large number of scientifically established facts.

They are very useful and are largely responsible for the progress of medicine. But we need a philosophy to connect the facts. This is where Paracelsus—and Descartes—can still teach us a great deal."

1. Sigerist, H. E.: *On the History of Medicine,* New York, MD Publications, Inc., 1960.

2. *Theophrastus von Hohenheim (Paracelsus) Collected Works* (Ger), Assembled by K. Sudhoff and W. Mathessin, 14 vol, Munich, Berlin, O. N. Barth, R. Oldebring, 1923-1933.

3. Sigerist, H. E.: *Four Treatises of Theophrastus von Hohenheim Called Paracelsus,* Baltimore, The Johns Hopkins Press, 1941.

Los Angeles County Medical Library

Servetus (1509-1553)

MICHAEL SERVETUS, scholastic theologian, translator of Ptolemy, discoverer of the lesser circulation of blood, practicing physician and unrestrained thinker in law, philosophy, mathematics, theology, astrology, and materia medica, paid with his life for advocating his interpretation of the scriptural precepts of Christianity. He was born at Tudela, in the province of Navarre, Spain, where his father was a royal notary living in comfortable circumstances.[1] In his infancy the family moved to Villanueva de Sijena, northeast of Saragossa; at the age of 14 or 15, Michael studied Latin and Greek while secretary to a Franciscan friar, Juan Quintana, who later became confessor to the emperor Charles V. Although a devout Catholic, Michael abandoned his study for the priesthood in favor of law at the University of Toulouse. Here his discovery of the simple truths of Jesus' teaching, untrammeled by the later Church doctrines, opened his eyes and proved his undoing in these early days of the Reformation. No doubt the sight of the Pope at the coronation ceremonies in Bologna in 1530, worshipped as a god and surrounded by worldly and immoral men of high station, contributed greatly to this enlightenment.

Servetus, independent and self-reliant, reached his own conclusions regarding the wide discrepancy in the religion then taught and the simple faith of the New Testament. Since the urge was great to spread the newfound gospel, he journeyed to Basel and Strassburg to present his views of Christ and the Trinity to the leaders of the Reformation. Instead of a warm reception, the reformers feared that great harm would come to their cause. *The Errors of the Trinity* (1531) was the first published exposé by Servetus of the fallacies of the current traditional teaching. His *Dialogues,* published shortly thereafter, was designed to retract what was unpleasant to the reformers, but his views basically remained unchanged. He discovered what he thought were fallacies in the Trinity, then taught as God the Father, God the Son, and God the Holy Spirit, the foundation of contemporary Christianity, and instead advocated a return to the primary and authentic religion of Christ.[2]

Any discussion of the Trinity should start with the man. That Jesus, surnamed Christ, was not a *hypostasis* but a human being is taught both by the early Fathers and in the Scriptures, taken in their literal sense. . . . He is God, sharing God's divinity in full; and the theory of a *communicatio idiomatum* is a confusing sophistical quibble. This does not imply two Gods, but only a double use of the term God, as is clear from the Hebrew use of the term. Christ, being one with

God the Father, equal in power, came down from heaven and assumed flesh as a man. In short, all the Scriptures speak of Christ as a man.

The doctrine of the Holy Spirit as a third separate being lands us in practical tritheism no better than atheism, even though the unit of God be insisted on. Careful interpretation of the usual prooftexts shows that they teach not a union of three beings in one, but a harmony between them. The Holy Spirit as a third person of the Godhead is unknown in Scripture. It is not a separate being, but an activity of God himself. The doctrine of the Trinity can be neither established by logic nor proved from Scripture, and is in fact inconceivable.

Each of his declarations of faith, directed primarily at the dogmas of the Church of Rome, was considered heretical by the reformers as well, and Servetus found it prudent to go into voluntary exile in France. The vaguely disguised nom de plume, Michael de Villeneuve, derived from the village of his youth, was chosen and retained for two decades until his real identity was discovered by the Inquisitors. While in exile he worked as a proofreader and copy editor in the print shop of the Trechsel Brothers in Lyons and was friendly with Champier, a physician of repute and a patron of learning, who led Servetus from astronomy, mathematics, and theology to the study of medicine. He returned to Paris, still incognito, attended the prelections of Jacobus Sylvius, and succeeded Vesalius as protector to Wynder of Anderach.

Michael de Villeneuve probably graduated and received a degree from Paris; it is certain that he remained in the city to practice medicine, meanwhile writing and teaching geography and astrology. The preparation of a small volume on materia medica, entitled *Syrups,* recently translated by O'Malley,[3] provided meager royalties. His highly popular instruction in astral influence aroused such professional jealousy that he was charged by the faculty of Paris with practicing judicial astrology, a forbidden vocation, since knowledge of the future was reserved for God. He escaped death by flight, pursued medicine near Lyon for a short time, and for more than a decade was personal physician and scholastic companion of the Archbishop of Vienne in Dauphiné. His writing during this period included a transla-

tion of the *Geography* of Ptolemy, an *Apologia* against Fuchs over the antiquity of syphilis, the editorial processing of two Latin *Bibles,* and the composition of his most famous treatise on the Reformation, the *Restoration of Christianity.* An open rebellion against Catholic dogma and the exposé of the *Errors of the Trinity* were related to his divorce from the prevalent faith found in the pathological and therapeutic canons of Galen's medicine.

Servetus' inability to dissociate science from religion is best illustrated by the introduction of the concept of the movement of the blood from the right to the left heart in his *Christianismi restitutio.* A discussion of the soul and the vital and natural spirits of the blood was the transitional device and introduction to what was subsequently and accurately described as "the lesser circulation." Whereas Galen had maintained that venous blood from the right ventricle entered the left heart through pores in the intraventricular septum (although pores of the septum had been found inadequate to handle such a volume of blood), Servetus concluded that a portion of the blood filtered through the lungs, mixed with air, changed its color, and entered the left heart. However, he did not conceive of a greater and lesser circulation and said nothing that would lead to a conceptual scheme of the transit of blood throughout the body as a circulatory phenomenon.[1]

The vital spirit, then, has its origin in the left ventricle of the heart, the lungs aiding essentially in its generation. It is a fine subtle spirit, elaborated by the power of heat, of a crimson colour and fiery potency, the lucid vapour, as it were, of the purer part of the blood, comprising in itself the substance of water, air and fire, being engendered in the lungs by the mixture of the respired air with the elaborated blood which the right ventricle of the heart communicates with the left.

But this communication does not take place through the partition of the heart, as is generally believed; but by another admirable contrivance, whereby from the right ventricle the subtle blood is agitated in a lengthened course through the lungs; wherein prepared it becomes of a crimson colour, and, from the vena arterialis (pulmonary artery) is transferred into the arteria venalis (pulmonary vein). Mingled with the inspired air in the arteria venalis, freed by expiration from fuliginous matter, and become suitable home of the vital spirit, it attracted at length into the left ventricle of the heart by the diastole of the organ.

Now, that the communication is effected in the lungs in the manner described, is proclaimed by the various conjunctions of the vena arteriosa, with the arteria venosa which take place within their substance, and by the remarkable size of the vena arteriosa, which would not be of such dimensions as it is, nor pour such a stream of the purest blood into the lungs for their nourishment only. Neither would the heart have supplied the lungs in such a manner—a truth of which we seem to be assured when we see the lungs of the embryo otherwise nourished; these membranes or valves of the heart not becoming unfolded and coming into play until the hour of birth, as Galen teaches.

The blood is therefore poured in such quantities from the heart into the lungs at the moment of birth, for the purpose indicated. And then, as it is not air only, but blood mixed with air that is carried from the lungs to the heart by the arteria venosa, it is in the lungs not in the heart that the mixture is effected; as it is also in the lungs, not in the heart, that the florid colour of the spiritous blood is acquired.

Not long after the appearance of his last great book, and at the instigation of John Calvin, Servetus was arrested and prosecuted for heresy. He had previously attempted to enter into intellectual liaison or possibly polemics with Calvin. Failing this, his book was published without review by any Reformation leader. Further insult was added by the inclusion of his correspondence with Calvin. One thousand copies were secretly printed at Vienne in 1553, but they were kept from sale, except for possibly a chance copy that came into Calvin's hands. The initials, M.S.V. (Michael Servetus Villeneuve) disclosed the identity of the author. Servetus was tried, found guilty of heresy, and condemned to death. His statements were judged equally insulting to Catholics and Protestants. The first trial in the civil court was followed by one in the ecclesiastical court. In each instance he was found guilty of the charges of spreading dangerous heresies, leading an immoral life, and disturbing the public peace. He was burned at the stake at Champel, in the outskirts of Geneva, on October 27, 1553, with copies of his books of reputed heresy, *Christianismi restitutio*, contributing to the fire. Thus, Calvin put an end to the heretic but not to his heresies which were the beginning of the

Unitarian sect. Through Calvin's intrigue, all but two of the copies were destroyed; the extant ones are some of the rarest books of the Renaissance.

1. Willis, R.: *William Harvey*, London: C. K. Paul & Co., 1878.
2. The Two Treatises of Servetus on the Trinity, E. M. Wilbur, trans., *Harvard Theol Rev* (extra no. *Harvard Theol Stud* XVI) Cambridge: Harvard University Press, 1932.
3. O'Malley, C. D.: *Michael Servetus, a Translation of His Georgraphical, Medical and Astrological Writings with Introductions and Notes,* American Philosophical Society, London: Lloyd-Luke (Medical Books) Ltd., 1953.

Royal Society of Medicine

Eucharius Rosslin (?-1526)

THE POSITION OF EUCHARIUS RÖSSLIN (or Rhodion) in obstetrical history was enhanced in the English-speaking world through the translation by Thomas Raynalde of the *Rosengarten,* Rösslin's only printed work on obstetrics. No reliable records of his birth or early life and only scant details of his professional career are retained. In addition to practicing in Worms and in Frankfurt-on-

Main, he was elected physician to the city of Frankfurt in 1506 and, in 1508, entered the service of the Duchess of Brunswick and Lüneburg.[1] His famous work, *A Garden of Roses for Pregnant Women and Midwives*,[2] in which he reintroduced podalic version, appeared in 1513; it was dedicated to the Duchess and was published at Strassburg with the illustrations reproduced from woodblock prints, the first obstetrical treatise prepared in German after the invention of printing. The volume was translated by his son, also Eucharius Rösslin, into Latin under the title *De partu hominis* in 1532 and into English in 1540 under the title *The Byrthe of Mankynde*.[3] The illustrations of this edition were prepared by copper plates. A second revised and expanded translation was prepared by Raynalde in 1545; whereas the final printing of the English translation appeared in 1654, twelve editions later. Other translations include those into French, German, Italian, Spanish, Dutch, and Czech—a total of more than 100 editions.

The Garden of Roses contained little original work; it was essentially a compilation of obstetrical comments with insufficient credit to Hippocrates, Galen, Albertus, Magnus, and others. The illustrations were taken at will without acknowledgement either from Soranus of the 2nd century or from Vesalius, a contemporary of Rösslin. The treatise was more than a text for midwives; it was designed to improve the deplorable state of midwifery of the day and proved to be the authoritative tract on obstetrics for physicians throughout England and Europe for two centuries.

The unraveling of the authorship and the translator of the several English editions was thoroughly explored and satisfactorily explained by Ballantyne in the *Journal of Obstetrics and Gynecology of the British Empire*.[1] He concluded that the 1540 edition of the *Byrthe of Mankynde* was a translation by Richard Jonas; whereas the edition of 1545 was a translation with additions by Thomas Raynalde.

As physician of London and Paris, Raynalde added the Prologue and most of Book I, with its anatomical comments. The Third Book discusses the care of the child, the choice of the wet nurse, and postoperative care; the Fourth Book considers conception and the treatment of sterility. The Second Book concerns labor, the delivery of the placenta, as well as the reintroduction of the value of podalic version and the use of the delivery stool, two obstetrical aids described by Soranus. The following excerpts are taken from the 1545 translation and describe the birth stool, version, the third stage of labor, and other aspects of delivery including reassurance to the parturient.[3]

In the fyrst boke we have sufficiently set furth and descrybyd the maner, sytuation, and forme of the Matryx, Wherin man is conceauyd: with dyvers other matters appendyng, and concernynge the better understandyng of the same.

Nowe when the woman perceaueth the matrice or mother to make laxe or loose: and to be dissolued, and that the humours yssue furthe in great plente, then shall it be mete for her to syt down lening backewarde in maner upryght. For the which purpose in some regions (as in Fraunce and Germany) the mydwyfes have stooles for the nonce, which beynge but lowe and not hye frome the grounde, be made too compase wyse and caue or holowe in the middes, that that may be receaued from underneth which is loked for: and the backe of the stole lenynge backeward, receaueth the backe of the woman, the fashion of which stoole is sette in the begynnynge of the byrth fygures hereafter.

And when the tyme of labor is come, in the same stole ought to be put manye clothes or clowtes in the backe of it, the whiche the mydwyfe may remoue from one syde to another accordinge as necessitie shall requyre. The mydwyfe herselfe shall syt before the laborynge woman, and shall diligently obserue and wayte how muche and after what means the chylde steareth it selfe: also shall with her handes fyrste annointed with the oyle of almondes, or the oyle of whyte lylies rule and directe euery thing, as shall seme beste. Also the mydwyfe must enstructe and comforte the partie not only refresshyng her with good meat and drynck, but also with swete wurdes, geuynge her good hope of a spedeful delyuerance encouragyng and enstomakyng her to pacience and tolleraunce, byddynge her to hold in her brethe in so much as she may: also strekyng gentylly with her handes her belly aboue the nauell, for that helpeth to depresse the byrthe dounwarde.

But when the byrth commeth not naturally, then must the mydwyfe do all her diligence and payne, yf it may be possible, to turn the byrth tenderlye with her annoynted handes, so that it maye be reduced agayne to a naturall byrthe, as for example: Sometime it chaunseth the chylde to come the legges and both armes and handes downewarde cloose to the sydes fyrste forthe, as appearethe in the seconde of the byrth figures: in this case the mydwyfe must do all her payne with tender handelynge and annoyntynge to receaue forthe the chylde, the legges beynge stylle close to gether, and the handes lykewyse remaynyng, as appereth in the said: ii figure.

Also somtyme the byrth cometh forward with one fote only, the other beinge lefte upward, as appearth in the iiii fygure. And in this case it behoueth the laborynge woman to lay her upryght uppon her backe, holdyng up her thyghes and belly, so that her head be the lower part of her body: then let the mydwyfe with her hand returne in agayne the fote that commeth out fyrst in as tender maner as may be, and warne the woman that laboreth to stere and moue her selfe, so that by the mouynge and sterynge the byrth may be turned the head douneward, and so to make a naturall byrth of it, and then to set the woman in the stole agayne, and to do as ye dyd in the fyrste fygure but yf it to be that notwithstandyng the mothers stearynge and mouynge the byrth do not turne: then muste the mydwyfe with her hand softely fetche out the other legge which remayned behynde, euermore taking hede of this, that by handelynge of the chylde she do not remoue ne sette out of theyr place the twoo handes hangyng douneward toward the fete.

Here also somtyme it cometh to passe, that the secondine, which is wunt to come together with the byrth, remayne and tary behynde and folowe not. And that for dyuers causes: one is, for by-cause peraduenture the woman hath ben so sore weakened and feblisshed with trauell, dolour and payne, of that fyrst byrth, that she hath no strenth remaynynge to helpe her selfe to the expellyng of this seconde byrthe: another may be, that it be entangled, tyed, or let within the matrice (which chaunseth many tymes) or that it be destitute of humours, so that the water be flowen from it soner then tyme is, which shold make the places more slyppery and more easye to passe thorowe: or els that the places ouer weryed with longe and sore labour, for payne contracte or gather together, and enclose themself agayne: or that the places be swollen for anguyshe and payne, and to let the commyng furth of the seconde byrth.

1. Ballantyne, J. W.: The "Byrth of Mankynde." (Its Author and Editions.), *J Obstet Gynaec Brit Emp* 10:297-325 (Oct) 1906; 12:175-194 (Sept) 1907; 12:255-274 (Oct) 1907.

2. Rösslin, E.: *Rosengarten*, Strassburg: Germany, 1513, facsimile, Munich: Germany, C. Kuhn, 1910.

3. Raynalde, T. (physician): *The Byrth of Mankynde*, London: T. Ray (T. Raynalde, printer?), 1545.

Composite by G. Bako

Garcia da Orta
(1501-02?-1568)

GARCIA DA ORTA, clinician and student of materia medica, who spent most of his active years in India, was born in Portugal, near the Spanish border. His parents, Castilian Jews, were baptized Christians.[1] His classical and medical education, gained through the benevolence of Martin Affonso de Sousa, later viceroy in western India, was obtained at the universities of Salamanca and at Alcalá de Henares. He received his medical degree about 1525, practiced medicine for several years at Castello de Vide, the village of his birth, before he was called to Lisbon as professor of logic at the University. Not feeling secure in Lisbon where Jewish perse-cution was beginning, and attracted by the transmarine explorations and the tremendous expansion of the colonial empire, da Orta, in 1534, sailed for the Far East as personal physician to de Sousa and surgeon to the Portuguese Navy.

Da Orta was a medical man of the Renais-sance, a natural philosopher, an accurate observer of man in relation to his natural environment, a skillful clinician, and an indepent thinker. Seasoned by the experience of several military campaigns in western India, he established a residence and medical garden at Goa. Da Orta became rich in practice, and about 1554 he gained a long lease on the island of Bombay, which he sublet. A collector of medicinal plants and herbs, he corrected and amplified many accepted notions of Asian materia medica; as a horticulturist he bred plants to increase their pharmacologic potency and sent back many specimens to Portugal including the China orange.

Late in life, Da Orta prepared his illustrated monograph, *Colloquies on the Simples and Drugs of India,* the greatest work on materia medica since Dioscorides, 1,500 years earlier. The treatise was based upon his extensive herbarium and upon a critical inquiry into the description, history, clinical effects, and economic evaluation of herbs and spices. In developing the compendium he described the symptoms of cholera (cholera morbus) which included extreme dehydration, debilitating diarrhea, weak pulse, and cold and sweaty skin. Da Orta recommended small quantities of opium to control intestinal discharges, and noted the frequently fatal outcome. He is credited with bringing the disease to the attention of the Western World and in so doing probably included examples of acute (bacillary) and chronic (amebic) dysentery.

The monograph, one of the first medical treatises printed in India, was published in Goa in 1563 and contained a laudatory ode by the immortal poet Camoens, then living in India. The initial printing, prepared in Portuguese and sprinkled with Spanish, was followed by several editions and translations into French, English, German, Italian, and Latin. The book contains 57 chapters or monographs written as colloquies, a dialogue with an imaginary Spanish inquisitor. The interlocutors are two characters combined in da Orta. Excerpts of the First Colloquy, and the description of cholera in the Seventeenth Colloquy, are taken from the translation by Markham of the Lisbon edition of 1895.

FIRST COLLOQUY

In the which is introduced to the reader, Dr. Ruano, one well known to the author in Salamanca and Alcalá, and who came to India in a ship whereof his brother-in-law was purser; and came only to learn about the drugs of India and about all other simples in that country; and how he arrived at Goa and heard of the author there, they being formerly known to each other; and how he went to the author to declare the object of his voyage, and how the author answered him.

Orta

Well! we have now adopted the same life that you proposed to enter upon after we had completed our studies; but why have you come to India?

Ruano

You should know that I came because I had a share in the ship, of which my brother-in-law was the purser; but my presence, as well as your own, in this land, may well be excused, for I come with a great desire to know about the medicinal drugs (such as are called the drugs of pharmacy in Portugal) and other medicines of this country, as well as the fruits and spices. I further wish to learn their names in different languages, and the trees or herbs from which they are taken. I also desire to know how the native physicians use them; and to learn what other plants and fruits there are belonging to this land, which are not medicinal.

Orta

In all these things I will serve you, and will tell you what is true, but I fear that what I may say will be found to be unworthy of record, for so eminent a scholar, who has risen so high in speculation, will only be satisfied by very rare things.

Ruano

Is this the disease that kills many people quickly, and from which few escape? Tell me what it is called with us, and by them, and the symptoms, and the remedy that is used.

Orta

Among us it is called *Colerica Passio.* The Indians call it MORNI, and we corrupt the word into MORDEXI. The Arabs call it HACHAIZA, a word which Rasis corrupted into SAIDA. It is more acute here than in our country, for it generally kills in twenty-four hours. I have known persons who have not lasted more than ten hours, and the longest endurance of it is four days. . . .

The pulse is very low, and can scarcely be felt. Very cold, with some sweat, also cold. Complains of great heat, and a burning thirst. The eyes much sunken. Vomits much, but so weak that he is unable to discharge anything. No sleep. Cramp in the legs. Follow after me, I will show you the way.

Orta

The cholera, as you have seen, is a very strong and dangerous malady, and dysentery, when it has become old (what we call chronic), is very difficult to cure, and when there is a hot humour it is very dangerous. The treatment must be more cautious and more careful than in Portugal, for any mistake made in the course of it is difficult to remedy.

Orta

When we find that our patients do not appreciate our gentle medicines, we deliver them over to Malabars to be given the stronger medicines. Now the Malayalims give us their water, which is compounded in the royal hospital. If the Malayalims see greater urgency they mix opium with this medicine. Some Arabs cure all dysenteric illnesses with opium rectified with nutmeg.

Orta

The Malayalims never care to confess that they give opium. I cured a very honourable gentleman, whose name is well known in Spain, and who was near to death. He had a regard for a Malayalim who had saved his life in a difficult case of dysentery. Finding himself in Goa with a slight attack, he called in this doctor who, to take the shortest way, cured him with a medicine containing opium. I was afterwards sent for and found him at death's door, with all the symptoms of having taken a dose of opium. I cured him and restored him to health.

1. Boxer, C. R.: *Two Pioneers of Tropical Medicine: Garcia d'Orta and Nicholás Monardes*, London: Wellcome Historical Medical Library, 1963.

2. Da Orta, G.: *Colloquies on the Simples & Drugs of India* (Port). C. Markham (trans.), London: H. Sotheran & Co., 1913.

Ambroise Paré (1510-1590)

AMBROISE PARÉ, the father of French surgery, is best known for his gentle treatment of battle wounds occasioned by the scarcity of boiling oil, his introduction of the ligature for hemostasis in amputations, and crediting surgical success to God's active participation in the healing process. Paré was born in the suburb of Laval, province of Maine, in the north of France at the beginning of one of the most crucial centuries for the French people.[1] The greatest fault attributed to the natural scientists lay in the use of deductive reasoning about to be severely jolted by

Francis Bacon's introduction of inductive reasoning into the coming age of science. Latin was the language of communication for the doctors while a policy of rigid selec-

National Library of Medicine

tion determined membership in the profession. Physicians were the ruling hierarchy, followed in caste by the surgeons and lastly, the barber-surgeons, the artisans of the trade.

Paré's parents were humble people, too poor to pay the necessary fees for the examination for his license to practice which should have followed his apprenticeship to a barber-surgeon. Paré went to Paris to complete his training and was appointed house surgeon in the Hôtel Dieu. He served for three years in this the only charity hospital in Paris, learning anatomy, surgery, and the manifestations of divers diseases.

Paré was endowed with the attributes of an outstanding leader of surgery, especially industry, manual dexterity, a fine intellect, a charming personality and a great desire to write although his composition confined to his native tongue was sometimes heavy and obscure. Shortly after completing his hospital service, he entered the Army as a surgeon and throughout his career alternated between military campaigns and civilian practice. Depite his lack of formal education and his barber-surgeon status he was admitted into the pompous surgical guild in 1554. Beginning with Henry II in 1552, Paré served four successive kings of France, eventually achieving a position as *premier surgeon* and *counselor*.

His first monograph on military surgery, a description of a method of treatment of wounds inflicted by the arquebus and other firearms, published in 1545,[2] was based upon the observations made during his initial military campaign almost a decade earlier. In this work he described an obligatory substitute for cauldron hot oil in the dressing of gunshot wounds.[3]

In order not to fail, before using the said oil, knowing such a thing could bring the patient severe pain, I wanted to know first how to apply it, what the other Surgeons did for the first dressing. They applied the said oil as hot as possible in the wounds with tents and setons. From this I took courage to do as they did.

Finally my oil ran out and I was constrained to apply as substitute a digestive made of egg yolk, rose oil and turpentine. That night I could not sleep at my ease, fearing that from failure to cauterize, I would find the wounded in whom I had failed to put the oil, dead of poisoning. This made me get up early to visit them, where beyond my hope, I found those on whom I had used the digestive mixture feeling little pain and their wounds neither inflamed nor swollen, having rested well enough through the night. The others to whom I had applied the said scalding oil, I found febrile, with great pain and swelling around their wounds. Then I resolved never again so cruelly to burn the poor victims of gun fire.

This small practical handbook on military surgery, prepared primarily for his fellow barber-surgeons, was followed by a tremendous volume of medical and surgical writing, which comprised an astonishing list of subjects for a surgeon of the 16th century or any century.[4] These included discussions on temporal arteriotomy for headaches, hematuria from horseback riding, transmission of syphilis from a wet nurse, the suspicion of syphilis as a cause of aneurysm, plastic reconstruction of the nose, speech appliance for use following glossectomy, separation of the pubis during labor, hydatid mole, carbon monoxide poisoning, vaginal hysterectomy, treatment of snakebite, design of surgical instruments, artificial limbs, artificial eyes, and a truss of inguinal hernia. He also prepared a treatise on the plague, smallpox, and measles with a description of leprosy, and popularized podalic version which had been described centuries earlier by Soranus of Ephesus. A severe sufferer himself from gout he wrote extensively on the disease and cautioned against the use of narcotics to control pain.

The need for preventing the spread of tumor cells in the surgical treatment of cancer of the lip was appreciated.[3] "Pass a threaded needle through the cancer so the thread held in the left hand can lift and control the cancer without any of it escaping." The incision was to include normal tissue to serve as a base and foundation for regeneration of tissue. The opening of an aneurysm was decried. In its stead, a ligature was to be passed on each side of the lesion and the dilated portion excised. He described Hippocratic succussion in a patient with empyema. A native of Turin, where he first began practice, had developed empyema as a complication of pleurisy:[3]

He coughed severely, expectorating fetid pus for six weeks; then, it ceased for twenty days, at the end of which when he bent over or shook himself, one heard a sound in his body like a half-filled bottle. . . . Some days later nature drained the pus by great vomiting, following which he recovered completely by the grace of God and of Nature.

Conservative treatment of an undescended testicle in a child as suggested by Paré remains sound practice as well as the management of a fracture of the skull.[3]

I told the father to let the child run and jump to help the testis descend into its natural place, which it did little-by-litle; without any complication.

I recalled then that Hippocrates and other good practitioners had always advised against leaving the brain uncovered if possible.

After the incision was made he saw that the bone was intact. Nevertheless he had a great suspicion that the bone was fractured, since when hit the patient fell unconscious on the ground and vomited, and had other signs indicating fracture. The patient died on the twenty-first day and persuaded by M. Mats, Thierry asked me to seek the cause of death.

His most famous apothegm from the 1585 edition of his works[1] Je le pensay, & Dieu le guarit, "I dressed him, and God healed him," has had various English renditions. Each reflects Paré's credit to divine assistance.[4]

I have wanted to give these histories to guide the young Surgeon in practice, not to praise and glorify myself, but to render it to God, knowing that all good things come from Him as from a never-failing fountain and not from ourselves. By thus giving Him thanks for all good works, I pray Him to increase in us His infinite favor.

1. Malpaigne, J. F.: *Surgery and Ambroise Paré,* translated from the French and edited by W. B. Hamby, University of Oklahoma Press, Norman, 1965.
2. Paré, A.: *The Method of Curing Wounds Made by Gun-Shot* (Fr) 1545, Faithfully done into English by Walter Hammond, 1617.
3. Hamby, W. B.: *The Case Reports and Autopsy Records of Ambroise Paré,* Springfield, Ill: Charles C Thomas, Publisher, 1960.
4. Paré, A.: *The Workes of that Famous Chururgian Ambrose Parey,* 1575, translated from the Latin by Th. Johnson, Cotes & Young, 1634.

Johannes Caius (1510-1573)

JOHN KEYS, Kayse, or Keysee (there were at least ten variations), who changed his name to the Latinized form, Johannes Caius, was born in Norwich. He was a medical man of letters, endowed the first medical college in Cambridge, and published several books, including the first English description of any disease, a guide for the laity on the English "Sweatyng Sickness." At the age of 19, John entered Gonville Hall, Cambridge, the beginning of brilliant achievements that brought him not only renown in medicine but also mastery of the Greek and Latin languages and considerable competence in logic, botany, zoology, and antiquarian studies. He translated a manuscript by Chrysostom from Greek into Latin and a treatise by Erasmus from Latin into English.[1] After taking the BA degree, he was appointed Principal of Physwick Hostel, an annex of the College in Cambridge, followed by election to fellowship of Gonville Hall. His teaching duties did not prevent completion of the AM program and may have inspired his desire to take additional medical

training in Bologna and Padua, from which he soon took two medical degrees.

Although Padua was best known for medicine at that time, Aristotelian logic and

Royal College of Physicians of London

philosophy aroused more interest in Caius than the practice of medicine, and led him to tarry there to deliver public lectures. While in Padua, he lodged for several months with Vesalius of *De fabrica* fame. In 1543, Caius studied in some of the celebrated libraries of Italy, prepared translations of Hippocrates and Galen in a "pure and copious Latin style,"[1] and corrected and classified manuscripts of Celsus. In Zürich he visited Conrad Gesner, the father of bibliography, who encouraged him in zoology, botany, and the definitive study of British dogs, and judged him the most learned physician of his age."

Although Caius had acquired a considerable reputation in the humanities on the Continent, he returned to England and began a course of instruction in anatomy in the hall of the Barber-Surgeons at the request of Henry VIII. Public dissection was permitted, with two bodies a year provided by royal charter. At the age of 46, Caius was admitted a fellow of the Royal College of

Physicians of London, was elected president in 1555, and remained a great ornament to this body. Although he established part-time residency in Cambridge, he did not abandon London, and from 1551 until his death 22 years later, rented a house in the parish of St. Bartholomew-the-Less.[2] Caius was physician to three Tudor sovereigns: Edward VI, Mary, and Elizabeth. Prestige in court diminished only with his persistence in clinging to Roman Catholic convictions during a troubled era in Elizabeth's reign. Earlier he had been charged with not only the "shew of a perverse stomach to the professors of the gospel, but [also] atheism."[1]

The treatise on the "Sweatyng Sicknesse" is a curio among English medical books.[3] It was prepared originally for the laity but later revised and published in Latin for the profession under the title *De ephemera britannica.*[4]

A Boke, or Counseill against the disease, commonly caled the Sweate, or Sweatyng Sicknesse. Made by Ihon Caius, doctour in phisicke. Very necessary for everye personne, and much requisite to be had in the handes of al sortes, for their better instruction, preparacion, and defence, against the souddein comying and fearful assaulting of the same disease—12 mo. 1552.

In the fereful tyme of the sweate (ryghte honourable) many resorted unto me for counseil, among whoe some beinge my frendes and acquaintance, desired me to write unto them some little counseil howe to governe themselves therein. ... At whose requeste, at that tyme I wrote diverse counseiles so shortly as I could for the present necessite, whiche they bothe used and dyd geve abrode to many others, and further appoynted in my self to fulfill (for so much as laye in me) the other parte of their honest request for the time to come The whiche the better to execute and brynge to passe, I spared not to go to all those that sente for me, bothe poore and riche, day and night. And that not only to do them that ease that I could, and to instructe it and for their recovery: but to note also thoroughly the cases and circumstances of the disease in diverse persons, and to understande the nature and causes of the same fully, for so much as might be.

There is no general agreement concerning the modern equivalent of the English sweating sickness. Some have assumed the malady to be acute rheumatic fever; others believed it to be plague. In my judgment, the clinical findings bear considerable resemblance to the devastating influenza epidemic of 1917-18. The affiction was highly contagious. Death frequently occurred within a few days, or even hours after onset of symptoms. Fever, prostration, delirium, tachycardia, and labored breathing were observed. Although the sweating sickness was epidemic intermittently in England for three-quarters of a century, it appeared in Germany as well as in the Low Countries. According to Caius, the susceptibility of the English was related to their diet. Treatment was directed towards promoting the sweat and avoiding all agents and devices that inhibited diaphoresis.

Although the *Boke against the Sweate* was an interesting composition, Caius made a far greater contribution to medicine when he assisted in the founding of the first medical college in England. In 1557-58, while in his 48th year, he obtained a new charter from the Crown for the founding of Gonville and Caius College and from his personal funds set up a munificent endowment. A major portion of his personal property and liquid assets was eventually made part of the endowment. Although the new charter did not specify the incorporation of a medical college as the goal, the professional interests of the donor and his acceptance of the Mastership of the College could not have been ignored. He was elected MD by the University, "in accordance with his Padua degree, and with the same Academic seniority."[5] The funds given by Caius were used to enlarge the college, to erect a new square, and to build three famous gates. The first gate, low and little, was inscribed "Humilitatis"; the second, "Virtutis," a handsome portico. The third gate, "Honoris," through which each student passed for his degree, was built after his death.

Caius was treated disrespectfully by the students and fellows of Cambridge because of his religious beliefs, but this did not dampen his loyalty. In 1572, on the execution of a decree from the Vice-Chancellor of the University and afterwards Archbishop of Canterbury, his Cambridge quarters were systematically pillaged because of certain books and vestments in his possession. It was noted that[1]

. . . he might possibly affect an indifference for all religion, in order to cover his secret attachment to popery; the reality of which he infers from a quantity of vestments, and other implements of public worship after the popish ceremonial, being found in his lodgings upon a search, which were without mercy committed to the flames.

In *The Merry Wives of Windsor,* published about 1600, Shakespeare portrays a Dr. Caius, a stupid doctor, one of the losing suitors of Anne Payne. He resembles John Caius only in name. The Shakesperean scholar, C. J. Sisson, has recently suggested that Shakespeare's model was Peter Chamberlain, the Hugenot immigrant, whose family fortunes were founded on the invention of the celebrated obstetrical forceps.[6]

John Caius, successor to Linacre in medicine and literature, is worthy of commendation for his outstanding leadership in the practice of medicine in the 16th century, for the clinical description of the English "Sweatyng Sickness," for the professional care of three ruling sovereigns, for his lectures in anatomy, for administrative responsibilities in the Royal College of Physicians, but especially for the procurement of a charter and the gift of an endowment for Gonville and Caius College, Cambridge, the first school for formal medical education in England.

1. Aikin, J.: "John Kaye or Key," in *Biographical Memoirs of Medicine in Great Britain from the Revival of Literature to the Time of Harvey,* London: J. Johnson, 1780, pp 103-136.

2. Poynter, F. N. L.: A Cambridge Quartercentenary, Gonville and Caius College, *Brit Med J* 1:703-704 (March 22) 1958.

3. Macmichael, W.: "Caius," in *Lives of British Physicians,* London: J. Murray, 1830, pp 15-30.

4. Caius, J.: *A Boke or Counseill Against the Disease Called the Sweate,* (1552), A. Malloch, ed., New York: Scholars' Facsimiles & Reprints, 1937.

5. Venn, J.: *The Works of John Caius, M.D.,* Cambridge, England: University Press, 1912.

6. Sisson, C. J.: Shakespeare's Helena and Dr. William Harvey, *Essays and Studies* 13:1-20, 1960.

Andreas Vesalius (1514-1564)

ANDREAS VESALIUS, prosector par excellence, made dissection a living and a respectable science. He was born in Brussels, a member of the fourth generation of physicians. He showed an interest early in his boyhood in anatomy, studied in Paris, and finished at the University of Louvain, where he became a pupil of Jacobus Sylvius, an avid Galenist. Vesalius had the courage to emphasize the shortcomings of Galen's dissections pursued on animals and not on human cadavers. At the age of 25, Vesalius occupied the chair of anatomy at Padua, the center of anatomy for central Europe, and within a year he published his *Tabulae anatomicae sex;* within five years as teacher and public prosector, he prepared his magnificent *De fabrica humani corporis,* a monumental break from a millennium and a half of tradition. Each treatise was illustrated by Joannes Stephanus of Calcar. The woodcuts, designed with a background landscape, became traditional for over a century and were frequently imitated. The Latin treatise set the fashion for the study of anatomy for four centuries, which embraced personal dissection, excellent graphic illustrations, and a manual for dissection.

One of the first attacks on Vesalius came from his teacher, Sylvius, who called upon him to admit his Galenic heresy, but he maintained throughout support of his pupils. Vesalius was so persecuted by the authorities that he was forced to put an end to his scientific activities. He burned his manuscripts, left Padua, and became a court physician to Emperor Charles V in Madrid; there he lived a relatively quiet life in practice. In 1563, he set out on a pilgrimage to Jerusalem, possibly as penance. During the return, he proposed to stop in Padua, where he was invited to reoccupy his old chair of anatomy. It had been occupied by Fallopius, becoming vacant upon his death. But Vesalius fell a victim to an epidemic disease and died on the Island of Zante in the Mediterranean Sea.

O'Malley[1] has translated the preface of *De Fabrica* which contains the thoughts on the learning of anatomy prepared by the founder of modern human anatomy.

Now I must recall the judgment of certain men who strongly condemn the presentation of anatomy to students, not merely by words but also, no matter how exquisitely executed, by pictorial delineation of the parts of the human body, maintaining that it is necessary for these things to be learned by careful dissection and observation of the parts themselves, as if I had inserted illustrations—very correct ones, and would that the illustrations of the parts were never spoiled by the printers—in the text so that the student relying on them might refrain from dissection of cadavers; whereas, on the contrary, I, with Galen, have encouraged the candidates of medicine in every way to undertake dissection with their own hands. If the practice of the ancients had lasted down to our times, the practice by which they trained the boys at home in the conduct of dissection just as in writing and reading, I, like the ancients, would readily agree to discard not only illustrations but also all commentaries. However, when for the sake of renown they decided to write about the practice of dissection, they communicated the art not only to the boys but also to foreigners out of respect for their virtues; but as soon as the boys were no longer given the usual training in dissection, as it was no longer accustomed to begin in boyhood, naturally they learned anatomy less well, so much so that the art deserted the

family of the Asclepiads, and, by reason of its decline through many centuries, books became necessary to preserve a complete account of it.

Nevertheless, how greatly pictures assist the understanding of these matters and place them more exactly before the eyes than even the most precise language, no student of geometry and other mathematical disciplines can fail to understand. Furthermore, the illustrations of the human parts will greatly delight those for whom there is not always a supply of human bodies for dissection; or, if there is, those who have such a fastidious nature, little worthy of a physician, that, even if they are enthusiastic about that most pleasant knowledge of man attesting the wisdom of the Great Creator—if anything does—yet they cannot bring themselves even occasionally to be present at dissection. Whatever the case may be, I have done my best to this single end, to aid as many as possible in a very recondite as well as laborious matter, and truly and completely to describe the structure of the human body which is formed not of ten or twelve parts—as it may seem to the spectator—but of some thousands of different parts, and, among other monuments to that divine man Galen, to bring to posterity an understanding of those books of his requiring the help of a teacher. I bear to the candidates of medicine fruit not to be scorned.

1. O'Malley, C. D.: *Andreas Vesalius of Brussels 1514-1564.* Berkeley and Los Angeles, University of California Press, 1964.
2. Cushing, H.: A *Bio-Bibliography of Andreas Vesalius.* New York, Schuman's, 1943.

Eustachio (1520?-1574)

BARTOLOMEO DI SANSEVERINO EUSTACHIUS, the equal of Fallopius in his contributions to human morphology and censor of Vesalius, was born in San Severino near Salerno.[1] He studied and practiced and for a time was physician-in-ordinary to the Pope. In the development of anatomy, he dissected animals and cadavers and did not hesitate to take issue with Vesalius and Fallopius when he discovered incorrect observations made by either of his predecessors. Eustachius was born and died in poverty. Although he served as professor of anatomy (medicine) at the Collegio della Sapienza in Rome, he neither possessed private funds nor obtained financial support of a patron to publish his greatest work—his anatomical tables prepared on copper plates by Pini, the beginning of this type of artisanship. Several of his anatomical writings, narrative and descriptive accompaniments to the tables, however, were published before his death. The anatomical plates, designed prior to Eustachius, had been little more than crude woodcuts. Although the illustrations presented lifeless structures, in contrast to the living anatomy of Vesalius, many of the morphological inaccuracies of Vesalius were corrected.

The failure of Eustachius' tables to be published prevented the dissemination of his influence, which might well have placed him equal to Vesalius, an anatomist more successful in teaching and publishing. The unpublished plates were deposited in the papal library in Rome and lay fallow for more than 150 years after his death. Had the plates been published at the time of their preparation, anatomy possibly would have reached, 200 years earlier, the state that it enjoyed early in the 18th century. When they were discovered, Pope Clement XI presented them to his physician, Lancisi, who arranged for their publication.[2] The first of many editions appeared in 1714. Albinus issued an edition in 1744, which has been judged the best. Eustachius' *Opuscula anatomica,* published first in 1564, described many of his original observations.[3]

Although Eustachius did not discover the Eustachian tube (the structure was known to the ancients), he gave the first clear description of the passage in his essay on the organ of hearing. He described the course of the thoracic duct in the horse, but did not associate it with man and did not realize its likely physiological significance. The relationship of the pulmonary arteries and veins to the bronchus was recognized and illustrated. He described the cochlea, the abducens nerve, the tensor tympani in man and dog, the stapedius muscle, the muscles of the throat and the neck, the origin of the optic nerves, the suprarenal glands, the arteries and veins of the arm, the gross anatomy of the uterus, the valve (Eustachian) in the right auricle, the fold of the lining membrane of the right auricle of the heart between the entrance of the vena cava and the auriculo-ventricular inlet, which in the fetus directs the blood of the inferior cava from the placenta into the left auricle through the foramen ovale.

In the treatise on the kidney, Eustachius rebuked Vesalius for describing the canine rather than the human kidney. The renal calyces were noted; whereas the existence of sulci and canaliculi in the renal substance suggested to Eustachius that urine flowed through the canaliculi towards the calyces. He introduced the subject of anatomical variations, referring to the kidney and the veins and arteries of the arm. His illustrations of the sympathetic nervous system are remarkably complete and precise. First and second dentition were observed and studied in the fetal skull as well as the nerve and blood supply of the teeth.

1. Singer, C.: *The Evolution of Anatomy.* New York, Alfred A. Knopf, 1926.
2. Lancisius, J. M.: *Anatomical Tables of Bartolomeo Eustachius* (L). Rome, Francisci Gonzagae, 1714.
3. Eustachio, B.: *Anatomical Works* (L). Delphis, Adrianum Beman, 1726.

National Library of Medicine

Gabriele Falloppio (1523-1562)

GABRIELE FALLOPPIO (Fallopius), one of the great Italian anatomists of the 16th century, may have exceeded Eustachius or even Vesalius, his teacher, in the number of original descriptions of structure and function. Falloppio was born in Modena, capital of the ancient Duchy, and received his early training under the aegis of the Church; however, with an interest in dissection, his mind turned to medicine and surgery.[1] Although he did not have a degree, he may have audited some of the demonstrations at the College of Medicine and later practiced surgery. This was followed by study in Ferrara which claimed one of the finest libraries in Europe, especially in the humanities. Fallopius received his doctor's degree in

1547; by then he was offering lectures in pharmacy and performed dissections for students.

Fallopius was called in 1548 by Cosimo I de' Medici to the chair of anatomy in Pisa and, in 1551, by the Senate of Venice to succeed Vesalius in the chair of anatomy, surgery, and superintendent of the botanical gardens at Padua (the genus of plants, Fallopio, has been named for him). This appointment was one step in the planned attempt of the Venetian government to restore to preeminence the great school of anatomy, which had suffered severely in stature in the immediate preceding years. His most famous student who came to Padua to study was Fabricius Aquapendente who later occupied the chair of anatomy. The tenure of Fallopius in Padua was short, his health began to fail, probably from tuberculosis, and death prevented the completion of his course of scheduled lectures. Before he died, however, he published in 1561 the only one of his planned treatises, *Observationes anatomicae.*[2]

The significance of this work is reflected in many editions that appeared. The Latin composition, adequate but not outstanding, reveals a familiarity with the ancient texts of Hippocrates, Galen, and others. *Observationes anatomicae* is a systematic description of the anatomy of man with scattered references to function and comparative anatomy. There are several references to the "divine" Vesalius.

The contents followed the pattern of *De fabrica* by Vesalius. It introduced new terms from Greek stems, corrected a number of misconceptions of Vesalius, but adhered to his unwieldy identification of muscles by numbers. In contrast to his respect for Vesalius, Fallopius did not mention in the first edition the contributions by Eustachius, his contemporary. Although the published works by Eustachius did not appear until 1561, there must have been some exchange between the anatomical schools.

The concept of two elements of muscle, the connective tissue and muscle fibers, according to modern terminology, was alluded to by Fallopius. He assumed that muscle was the contractural element; whereas the connective tissue contained the nervous elements. He included descriptions of the external muscle of the auricle, the orbicularis muscle, the dual action of the oblique muscles, the external pterygoid, the physiological action of the muscles of mastication, the tensor and levator veli palatini, division of the scaleni muscles of the thorax into the three component parts, the quadratus femoris of the thigh, and division of its adductor mass into three elements.

In the vascular system, Fallopius described the portal anastomosis of the liver, established the relationship of the lumbar veins to the origin of the azygos system, traced the origin of the jugular and vertebral vein, and recognized the venous sinuses of the spinal canal and the cranial cavity. In neuroanatomy, he recognized 11 of the 12 cranial nerves, although he classified only eight pairs. The olfactory tract was recognized as a nerve but not in the cranial series. He described much of the anatomy of the middle and inner ear, the facial canal (the Fallopian canal), and is credited with the first published account of the stapes although giving credit to Ingrassia for its discovery. He described the round and the oval window, the semicircular canals, the scala vestibuli, the tympanum, distribution of the chorda tympani, and the stapedius.

In the autonomic nervous system Fallopius identified the cardiac nerves, the cardiac and pulmonary plexuses, and the cervical and lumbar enlargements. The trochlear nerve was traced from the brain stem to its origin and the communication described between the lingual and hypoglossal nerves. In the abdomen he distinguished the mucosa, the submucosa, and the muscular coats in the viscera, described the valvulae conniventes of the small intestine, discovered the sphincter at the end of the biliary apparatus, and showed that the common bile duct did not open into the stomach, as previously described. The three muscular coats of the urinary bladder and the internal sphincter were recognized in the physiological functions of the kidney. He suggested that renal papillae were responsible for distilling the urine from the blood.

Fallopius made his greatest contribution in identifying various structures of the reproductive tract of the female. The difficulty of obtaining female cadavers and faulty understanding of generation contributed to the unsatisfactory descriptions of function and structure of the female pelvis. He described the hymen and the clitoris, gave the scientific names to the vagina and the placenta, and reiterated that the term, cervix, or neck of the uterus, should not apply to the vagina. He probably observed the graafian follicle and possibly the corpus luteum. He demonstrated the position of the round ligament, tracing it through the inguinal canal to its attachment in the pubis and described the cremasteric muscle of the female. The description of the fallopian tube has been translated as follows.[3]

That slender and narrow seminal passage arises from the horn of the uterus very white and sinewy but after it has passed outward a little way it becomes gradually broader and curls like the tendrils of a vine until it comes near the end when the tendril-like curls spread out and it terminates in a very broad ending which appears membranous and fleshy on account of its reddish colour. This ending is much shredded and worn as if it were the fringe of a worn piece of cloth and it has a broad opening which always lies closed by the coming together of those fringed ends. However if they be opened carefully and spread apart they form, as it were, the bell-like mouth of a bronze trumpet. Consequently since, whether the tendril-like curls be removed from this classical instrument or even added to, the seminal passage will extend from its head even to its uttermost ending and so it has been designated by me the trumpet of the uterus. They are aranged in this way in all animals not only in man, but also in fowls and cattle and in the corpses of all the other animals which I have studied.

1. Cushing, H.: A Bio-Bibliography of Andreas Vesalius. New York, Schuman's, 1943.
2. Falloppio, G.: Observationes Anatomicae. Venice, M. A. Ulmum, 1561.
3. Fulton, J. F.: Selected Readings in the History of Physiology, ed 2. Springfield, Ill, Charles C Thomas, 1966.

National Library of Medicine

Aquapendente (1537-1619)

HIERONYMUS FABRICIUS (Geronimo Fabrizio) ab Aquapendente, pupil of Fallopius and teacher of William Harvey, was born in the village of Aquapendente in central Italy within the territory ruled at that time by the Republic of Venice. The family of Fabricius, well-to-do but not wealthy, belonged to the nobility; their coat of arms is reproduced on the title page of one of his most famous books. Fabricius received an upper-class education and, in his late teens, began his advanced studies at the University of Padua, where he studied Greek, Latin, logic, and philosophy. By the time he was prepared for the study of medicine he had displayed an extraordinary memory, brilliant intellectual capacity, great industry, and complete sincerity. In medical school his most influential teacher was Fallopius, professor of anatomy, whom he assisted in dissection and accompanied during his attendance upon the sick. Fabricius obtained his doctorate in medicine and philosophy circum 1559. He followed the pattern of his famous teacher and began the practice of medicine and surgery, meanwhile continuing to perfect his

knowledge of anatomy. After the death of Fallopius in 1562, Fabricius inherited his teacher's reputation in dissection and probably gave private demonstrations in anatomy. Three years later the Venetian Senate appointed him to the chair of surgery at Padua. His first public course in anatomy began in 1566, a subject now added to his academic responsibilities. His scientific and scholarly accomplishments increased in brilliance with each decade, and, following periodic reevaluation by the Venetian Senate, he was assigned increased responsibilities with commensurate compensation. His final recognition before retirement in his late 70's included the title of *Professor Supraordinarius* of anatomy and surgery, with a salary for life.

In the 16th and 17th centuries, the University at Padua enjoyed a reputation unique among the great schools of anatomy. Dissections upon the cadaver, with but few exceptions, were conducted by Fabricius each year during his academic tenure and initially were held in a temporarily constructed anatomical theater. In the winter term of 1583-1584, indoor quarters were provided, probably financed in part by Fabricius. In 1594, a permanent theater in one of the upper rooms of a university building was constructed. This famous theater of Padua, which served for anatomical demonnstrations until late in the 19th century, is now preserved as a museum—essentially unchanged for more than 350 years. The relatively small, deep-welled amphitheatre, approximately 25 by 30 feet in size, rises six tiers around an oval pit scarcely large enough to contain the dissection table for the cadaver, the demonstrator, and the assistants. The vertical design of the tiers renders it imperative that the students stand, thereby making note-taking difficult. It was in 1598, while Fabricius was lecturing in the permanent structure, that Harvey arrived from Caius College to study anatomy. He remained in Padua until 1602 when he graduated MD. With no intent to derogate the fame of Harvey, one may assuredly assume that Fabricius' discussion of the valves of veins, his embryologic observations on the development of the heart and great vessels, as well as many of the detailed illustrations which were available during Harvey's years in Padua profoundly affected him, leading directly to his development of the concept of the circulation of blood.

At least four of the notable documents prepared by Fabricius from his dissections and formal lectures are illustrated by reproductions from copper plates. Great reverence for the authority of Aristotle, Galen, and others, with no attempt to document the contributions of his contemporary scientists, is apparent in the several works. Three have been translated into English in recent years. *The Formed Fetus,* published in 1600, is the last of the trilogy on generation and describes the developmental stages of the rabbit, guinea pig, mouse, dog, sheep, cat, pig, horse, ox, goat, deer, the dogfish, the viper, and man, giving particular attention to the structural changes in the vascular system at birth. The membranes, the placenta, the human gravid uterus, and the umbilical vessels are illustrated. Fabricius' efforts were directed to explaining what he saw rather than how it came about.

The texts of *The Formed Fetus* and *The Formation of the Egg and of the Chick* were translated by Adelmann and were published in 1942. An excerpt from the translation of the fate of the umbilical vessels, the foramen ovale, and the ductus arteriosus follows.[1]

I wish it were possible to reach the same conclusion about another marvelous thing which follows immediately upon birth, that is, the incredible transformation of the umbilical vessels remaining within the body, as well as of the arteries of the heart, or rather of the lungs; but we perceive even with our own eyes that there is a transformation of this sort. For it is an observed fact that when the fetus is shut up in the uterus, these umbilical vessels grow and are nourished and, in short, enjoy life with the other parts of the body. But when the fetus leaves the uterus, we see that they immediately waste away and are deprived of life—and not only this, but in addition, the more the infant is nourished and grows, the more rapidly also do these umbilical vessels decrease in size, wither, and dry up.

Why do they meet this most unfortunate and lamentable fate? Have these vessels committed some great crime, that you, O Nature, a just and provident mother to all other parts of the body, have become a stepmother to these alone, so that they deserve to be visited with an affliction so dire,

a punishment so severe as wasting and death? Did not the vein continuously supply blood to the fetus? Did not the arteries give life to it? Were they not the means of bestowing increase and nutrition upon the fetus? But now, O Nature, for so many benefits conferred, for so many labors undertaken do you make this recompense, returning to them for sustenance continually supplied to the fetus, wasting and decline; for growth, exsiccation; and finally for life, death?

In his surgical works, *Opera chirurgica in duas partes divisa,* published in 1617, Fabricius provided a chapter on tracheotomy in quinsy, in which he notes that the operation had been mentioned by Greek and Arabian writers. He presented an excellent description of the procedure and clearly defined its use, cautioning that empyema, pleurisy, pneumonia, and regressive quinsy were contraindications.[2]

On the other hand, it is necessary to do a laryngotomy when there is inflammation, whether in the mouth, or beneath the chin, or in the tonsils, or the uvula, or throat, or larynx, which are so great as to close entirely the tracheal tube, provided nonetheless that all of its branches are not filled with matter. . . . In summary, when the disease or the matter is only above the level of the larynx, it is necessary to make the incision; but if it extends below the larynx, it is necessary to abstain.

If one asks why it is advised to make the incision below the third or fourth cartilagenous circle, and not immediately below the larynx; the answer is, that it is intended that the incision should be as far as possible from the diseased part, or rather the site of derivation: for if one should make the incision close to the larynx, the inflammation resulting from the incision, would easily impart itself to the larynx.

Having done this, it is necessary to introduce a small cannula, the size of the opening, and having two wings to prevent its being pulled out, or drawn into the interior by breathing; and it must be short so as not to touch the inner wall of the trachea; otherwise it will excite coughing, and cause pain. . . . It must be kept in place until the danger of suffocation is passed, which ordinarily occurs after three or four days.

Fabricius discovered valves in the veins in 1574 and published his description in 1603. Although others had observed the structures earlier, Fabricius investigated them more thoroughly than anyone before him. However, he failed to recognize their physiological significance and persisted in the Galenical belief that the veins brought nutrients for the tissues and that their chief function was to retard the flow of blood. Although he accurately described and correctly placed the valves in the direction of blood flow in relation to the heart, he failed to appreciate what Harvey described later, namely, the motion of the blood in the veins toward the center of the body. The descriptions, published under the title, *De venarum ostiolis,* literally translated "doorlet," but better identified as "valves," follow.[3]

Valves of veins is the name I give to some extremely delicate little membranes in the lumen of veins. They occur at intervals, singly or in pairs, especially in the limb veins. They open upwards in the direction of the main venous trunk, and are closed below, while, viewed from the outside, they resemble the swellings in the stem and small branches of plants.

My theory is that Nature has formed them to delay the blood to some extent, and to prevent the whole mass of it flooding into the feet, or hands and fingers, and collecting there. Two evils are thus avoided, namely, under-nutrition of the upper parts of the limbs, and a permanently swollen condition of the hands and feet. Valves were made, therefore, to ensure a really fair general distribution of the blood for the nutrition of the various parts.

But a further justification can be advanced for the anatomists. All veins are not provided with valves. The vena cava, when it traverses the trunk of the body, the internal jugulars, and countless small superficial veins in like manner, are destitute of them.

The shape of valves is such that they resemble the nail of the index or other three fingers. They open upwards in the direction of the main stem of the veins, while below and at the sides they are united to the vein-wall.

The Formation of the Egg and of the Chick, another text recently translated into English by Adelmann, gave the best description of the reproductive tract of the hen at that time, speculated correctly on the ovary and the oviduct in the formation of the hen's egg, and gave the first illustrations of the progress of the development of the chick.[1] Other monographs include a 500-page treatise on the senses, *De visione, voce, auditu* (1600); the comparative anatomy of the caecal appendix, the structure of the esophagus, stomach, and bowels, *De gula, ventriculo, intestinis* (1618); mechanics of body movement, *De*

motu locali animalium secundum totum (1618); *De aure* (1603) in which he describes the external ligament of the malleus; *De respiratione et eius instrumentis* (1615) presenting the muscles and mechanisms of respiration; and a strange treatise on the language of animals, *De brutorum loquela* (1603). Fabricius carried on an active practice in medicine and surgery and became so famous that he was eventually known simply as "Aquapendente." He attended Galileo as well as Carlo de' Medici in Florence, whose parents presented him with two golden chains. He was honored with the Knighthood of Saint Mark by the Venetian Senate for his attention to the wounds of Paoli Sarpi. He bequeathed to the Venetian State all of his colored anatomical plates and certain published books, which have rested in the Biblioteca Marciana in Venice for more than 300 years, bound in 11 folio volumes.[1]

1. Fabricius, H.: *The Formation of the Egg and of the Chick* (L), Padua, Italy: A. Bencius, 1621, and *The Formed Fetus* (L), Venice: F. Bolzetta, 1600, in *The Embryological Treatises of Hieronymus Fabricius of Aquapendente,* facsimile edition, with an introduction, translation, and commentary by H. B. Adelmann, Ithaca, N. Y.: Cornell University Press, 1942.

2. Fabricius, H.; *Surgical Works* (L), Lyons, France; P. Ravaud, 1649, in Zimmerman, L. M., and Veith, I. (trans.): *Great Ideas in the History of Surgery,* Baltimore: Williams & Wilkins Co., 1961.

3. Fabricius, H.: *Valves in the Veins* (L), Padua, Italy: L. Pasquatus, 1603, facsimile edition, K. J. Franklin (trans.), Springfield, Ill. Charles C Thomas, 1933.

Composite by G. Bako

Felix Platter (1536-1614)

FELIX PLATTER (Platerus), anatomist, practitioner, and teacher, was born in Basel, the son of a distinguished father who provided his son with a classical education.[1] Young Platter began the study of medicine in 1552 at Montpellier; there he witnessed the dissection of human cadavers, and in 1556 became bachelor of medicine. His round trip, Basel to Montpellier, and his reaction to 16th century medical education were described in his dairy, which has attracted considerable interest. The document provides an excellent and authentic portrayal of aspects of life at Montpellier and in central Europe at the time of Rabelais. The introductory paragraph begins:[2]

From my childhood I had always dreamed of studying medicine and of becoming a doctor. My father desired it as much as I did, for he had himself once approached the same study. He often spoke to me of the esteem that doctors enjoy, and when I was still a child he made me admire them as they passed on horseback in the street. Considering, then, that I had arrived at the age of fifteen, and that I was an only son, he resolved, that I might the sooner become a doctor, and in good time be a support for the family, to send me to Montpellier, where in those days the study of medicine flourished.

The following year Platter toured France and Germany before returning to Basel, where he conducted a public dissection and received the degree of doctor of medicine. Although he was only 21 at the time, his reputation preceded him and contributed to his election to the "consilium medicum" at an unprecedentedly early age. With a classical education, a pronounced taste for poetry, an appreciation of music, and a Montpellier training in medicine, Platter straightaway developed a substantial following in medicine. In 1571, his appointment to the chair of the practice of medicine and his election to the position of city physician ("archiater"), made him overseer of the public health and director of the city hospitals. In this capacity, he displayed exceptional courage during the plague of 1563-1564, in attending the stricken while other physicians fled. He repeated this risk during the epidemics of 1575, 1582, 1593, and 1609.

A disciple of Vesalius and a generation younger, Platter emulated his predecessor in performing many dissections (more than 300) as well as founding an anatomical amphitheater. Also, he sponsored a botanical garden and established chairs in anatomy and botany at the University. Platter's great personal warmth on hospital rounds kept his students at his side and capitalized on a rich experience in anatomy and clinical medicine. The number of medical students attending Basel University increased several-fold during his tenure, a reflection of the enhanced status of the medical school. The latter was attributable to his reputation and energy in reorganizing the curriculum and building an outstanding faculty, while serving as rector of the University.

Having established a strong medical school and attracted an extensive practice, Platter began his medical writing, designed primarily for the student. *De corporis humani structura et usu*[3] appeared in 1583 when he was nearly 50 years of age. The majority of the illustrations were prepared from copper engravings and, other than correcting a few errors, were copied from Vesalius. Two more decades passed before the first volume of *Praxeos seu cognoscendis, praedicendis, praecauendis* (*Golden Practice*) appeared; the third major treatise, *Observationum in hominis affectibus* (1614), was a collection of case reports based upon five decades of clinical experience. The latter two works were translated into English in the 1660's. *A Golden Practice of Physick*,[4] which went through many editions for over a century, eventually was presented as five books in three volumes. The discussion comprised a rational classification of diseases according to their natural history and postmortem findings.

Platter's classification of psychiatric disorders is presented in volume 1, *On Injuries to the Functions,* in four chapters entitled: "On Mental Weakness, Congenital or Acquired"; "On Mental Consternation"; "On Mental Alienation"; and "On Mental Fatigue." He anticipated Pinel in protesting against the heartless treatment of the insane in seeking a cure for mental aberrations by reflecting upon their cause. The first two excerpts, pathogenesis and schizophrenia, are from the chapter on mental weakness; the third excerpt, cretinism, is from the chapter on mental alienation.

A Weakness of the Minde may be said to be, whenas any one is less able in Apprehension or Wit, in Judgment or Reason and Memory, then an ingenious and industrious Man. Which sometimes happens in Diseases, at other times befals those that are not Sick, but otherwise Well, of which we will here Treat. But somtimes these internal senses are all of them together dulled, and both Wit, Judgment and Memory fail, and then it may be called *a dulness of the Minde.* Otherwise some want Wit, when they scarcely learn to speak, and they apprehend Learning, and other Arts with difficulty; and it may be called *a slowness of Wit.*

Some have contracted and derived this weakness Haereditary *from their Parents* by inbred Causes; whence it often comes to pass that as the ingenious and industrious do beget their like, so drones beget drones which is easily collected by their Signs, that they were such from their Infancy, and had such Parents. This happens to some by reason of *Age,* whence old folks become for the most part forgetful and sometimes dul, by reason of the defect of native heat, unless it happens from some distemper of the Brain as shall be said by and by.

A Concussion or blow of the Head, leaving behind it some weakness in the Brain, may also be the cause of it.

Also *too great a shedding of Blood* from what part forgetful somtimes dul, by reason evacuation exhausting the Spirits on which score also *too much Venery* doth very much impare the senses, especially the Memory.

An Alienation or error of the Minde is called a *Paraphrosyne* when they feigne judg and remember those things which are not, as if they were, or those things which are unlikely and besides reason, and that either together or a part, whether this be done only by Cogitation, or they express the same by words and deeds.

This for the most part coming from inbred Causes is a certain innate foolishness otherwise proceeding from external causes if from things taken tis called *Temulency,* if it arise from some vehement affect it shall be called *a commotion of the Mind;* but sometimes depending upon internal causes it is deficiency, which happening either without a Feaver accompanying it, is Mellancholly, or with fury is *Mania* or Madness, or coupled with a Feaver, tis called a *Phrensie,* all whose accidents we shall explain singly.

Platter presented a relatively accurate clinical description of cretinism, "those who are born foolish," a condition endemic in certain geographic regions in Switzerland. His recognition of the relationship to goiter was noteworthy.[4]

Foolishness although it be not ascribed to children only when they are yet destitute of Judgment, and old Folks who are said to be twice Children (the which notwithstanding is rather a weakness of Minde in them, then a depravation) but also to every Age and all men upon that account, that all their humane actions seem to be foolish as *Erasmus* in his *Moria Brandus in navi Stultorum* have [sic] elegantly shewed it in all states of men; yet tis properly said of them who being borne truly Fools and Silly do presently even in their very infancy give signs of folly by gesticulations besides the custome of other Infants, and do not easily obey, are blockish, so that oftentimes they learne not to speak, much less to performe other Duties, in which any industry is required; which in some Countries is a common evil as they write of *Egypt,* and at *Bremis* a Village off Valesta as I my self have seen, and in the Valley of Carinthia, it is wont to befal many Infants, which besides an inbred foolishness, somtimes with an unshapen head, a great and swel'd Tongue, being dumb oftentimes with a strumous Throat, do shew a deformed sight, and setting in the waies and looking upon the Sun, and putting little sticks between the spaces of their Fingers, and variously wreathing their

Bodies, with an open Mouth, they move Laughter and admiration to those that pass by.

One excerpt from his *Histories and Observations* describes sudden death caused by enlargement of the thymus, and another, the clinicopathological findings of a meningioma.[5]

SUFFOCATION FROM A STRUMA HIDDEN IN THE NECK

The Son of *Mark Peres* aged five months, a goodly child, without any disease aforegoing, died suddenly with shivering and short wind: he had lost two Sons before the same way, and desired to know the cause. I opened his breast, and in his throat I found the Glandle of that part to be turned to a Struma of an ounce and half, spungy, and full of Veins, which hung by the Membranes to the great Vessels about the throat; it was like flesh full of blood, which came thither suddenly, and enlarged the Struma, and so killed the Child, by pressing the Vessels, and choaking.

OF ASTONISHMENT FROM A TUMOR IN THE BRAIN LIKE A GLANDLE

Gaspar Bonecutt a noble Knight was for two years changed in mind by degrees, and at length was wholly astonished, did nothing according to reason, he desired no meat, and took none but by force, and went not to bed but by violence: at meat he lean'd upon his Arm sleeping, and spake not but when provoked, and then to little purpose: water dropt in great quantity from his Nose; thus he was a half a year and then died. I searched into the causes, and I found nothing more probable then a stroake in his head three or four years before; he was ever after weak headed though before a strong Souldier. His skull being opened and his Brain divided, upon the hard part of the Brain, there was a round Tumor, fleshy hard and fungous, as big as a smal Apple, like a Kernel, it had a coat of its own and veins; yet free from all Connexion to the substance of the Brain; so that without cutting, I took it out, and it left a great hole behind it, which presently filled with water, with which the ventricles of the Brain were full. This Tumor pressed the brain and its passages, and caused this Disease and Death. Some before thought that it had been Witch craft, others humors only, to which Head diseases are ascribed; but by this opening, we found the hidden cause.

1. Cumston, C. G.: A Brief Notice of Felix Platter, With Extracts From His MS. Memoirs Preserved at the Library of Bâle, *Johns Hopkins Hosp Bull* 23:105-113 (April) 1912.

2. Platter, F.: *Beloved son Felix* (Ger), S. Jennett (trans.), London: F. Muller, 1962.

3. Platter, F.: *Structure and Function of the Human Body* (L), Basel: A. Froben, 1583.

4. Platter, F. A.: *A Golden Practice of Physick* (L), Basel: C. Waldkirchii, 1602, A. Cole, and N. Culpepper (trans.), London: P. Cole, 1662.

5. Platter, F.: *Histories and Observations* (L), Basel: C. Waldkirchii, 1614, A. Cole, and N. Culpepper (trans.), London: P. Cole, 1664.

Guillaume de Baillou (1538-1616)

GUILLAUME DE BAILLOU, whose writings appeared posthumously under the Latin name, Ballonius, was born in Paris, the son of a famous mathematician and architect. After studying at the University of Paris where he concentrated especially in Latin, Greek, and philosophy, Baillou qualified in succession for the baccalaureate and the doctor's degrees.[1] While preparing for the higher honors, he taught humanities and, upon completion of formal courses, was associated with the Faculty, serving eventually as Dean for a biennium beginning in 1580. He was a pupil of Jean Fernel and a follower of Hippocrates in his respect for the bedside observation of diseases. Exploiting his outstanding talents, he became a skillful physician, a brilliant teacher, and a student of epidemics. Baillou lived in Paris during the horrible period of the 16th century, with persecution and violence a way of death, and with squalor, filth, and pestilence spawning recurring epidemics as well as providing opportunities for investigating contagion. His rich clinical experiences are documented in descriptions of plague, measles, typhus, and smallpox, but especially notable are the accounts of the infectious afflictions currently identified as whooping cough, diphtheria, and acute rheumatic fever. His reference in *Consilia* to adhesive pericarditis associated with dropsy in two instances was noted by Morgagni as an early description of this complication. The case histories recorded clinical events but in some instances deviated from empirical observations to include the influence of environment as well as heredity on disease. Although Baillou prepared many manuscripts in Latin, none was published until nineteen years after his death, whereas two centuries elapsed before his *Epidemics* was translated into French. Excerpts from each of the three clinical descriptions, judged to be his best, come from his *Epidemics*. No speculations were included regarding pathogenesis of the epidemic diseases, and no hint of an infectious nature was given.

An epidemic of whooping cough appeared in Paris in 1578 following a hot summer.[2] Infants and children were attacked and a number died. The common cough, called "Quinta" or "Quintana," was associated with intractable irritation of the lungs. Attempts to expel the offending matter failed, and the afflicted were unable to establish an airway, either for inspiration or expiration.[2]

Why it is commonly called *Quinta*, is not without uncertainty. They think the word is formed from onomatopaea, from the sound & rattling which those coughing make. Others do not derive it from this, but think the cough is called *Quintana* in Latin because it is repeated at certain hours. This indeed experience proves to be true. For they are without this troublesome coughing for the space of four or five hours at a time, then this paroxysm of coughing returns, now so severe that blood is expelled with force through the nose & through the mouth. Most frequently an upset of the stomack follows, nor have I read any author, who has made mention of this cough. When it draws it, an acute fever comes from it, a dry cough, fullness in the chest, acute pain in the anterior & posterior parts, greatest around the spine with the large veins becoming too heated. They vomit sometimes a somewhat bloody at other

times a rather bluish material. They vomit phlegm & bile & become breathless. In this place moreover he explains the nature of this most distressing cough, which is called *Quinta*. And the cause of the cough is not from the head, as is thought by many, but sometimes from the lung itself, sometimes from adjacent parts.

The description of diphtheria, with labored breathing, a membrane deep in the throat, and sometimes death from suffocation, makes reference in one passage to four patients suffering from the fatal illness; whereas in another part of the treatise, mention is made of the son of a physician who died from suffocation, as indeed Baillou's father-in-law almost did.[2]

The greatest difficulty was in breathing, respiration was continuously rapid & shallow until death. They seemed to breathe as if dried up. Neither cough nor sputum. They were not able to hold their breath for a moment. They breathed thus with their bodies erect frequently & in small breaths. The fever was not great, nor should it have made such breathing necessary.

The surgeon said he sectioned the body of the boy with this difficult breathing, & with the disease (as I said) of unknown cause; sluggish resisting phlegm, was found which covered the trachea like a membrane and the entry & exit of air to the exterior was not free: thus sudden suffocation.

Baillou prepared one of the first books on arthritis, without giving a clear symptomatic differentiation of the several common arthritides. There also has been some difference of opinion among the translators of his works in the selection of the term "arthritis" as synonymous with "gout." The use of "gout" and "arthritis" in the translation by Barnard seems logical. In this work, under the varieties of fever and rheumatism, it is possible to identify the polyarthritis of acute rheumatic fever, acute gouty arthritis, and generalized rheumatoid arthritis, respectively.[3]

The whole body hurts, in some the face is flushed; the pain is most severe around the joints, so that the slightest movement of foot, hand or finger causes a cry of pain. Now this greater degree of pain in the joints corresponds exactly with the nature of the affected part, for this is endowed with heightened and special sensitivity. . . . If you feel the pulse there seems to be little or no fever, and yet it is actually fever, but not very severe.

At night, it is true, the pains become more severe and the patients cannot sleep, partly because they are unable to move from the spot; almost in the same position as when they first lie down, so they remain lying and can scarcely be moved or touched without agony and violent pain.

Now what articular gout (arthritis) is in any limb, exactly so is rheumatism in the whole body, as regards pain, tension and the "feeling" of burning heat—as I call it—others say "sensation." Both complaints are somewhat painful, but the gouty pain in the joint is repeated at definite times and periods. Not so this rheumatism, unless it be in those who have sinned in their manner of living. In that case the rheumatic disease may finally, through weakening of the nervous system and increasing corruption of the humours, bring about a state of generalised gout or "arthritic diathesis" and in fact those people who have had this *rheumatismós* two or three times, if they do not take great care of themselves, can hardly escape the torment of gout, so that such a rheumatism is, as it were, a forerunner and pioneer of articular gout.

1. Goodall, E. W.: A French Epidemiologist of the Sixteenth Century, Ann Med Hist 7:409-427, 1935.
2. Ballonii, G.: *Epidemics (Epidemiorum et Ephemeridum Libri Duo)* Paris: I. Quesnel, 1640, in Major, R.: *Classic Descriptions of Disease*, Springfield, Ill: Charles C Thomas, 1932, pp 94-96, 159-160.
3. Ballonii, G.: *Book on Rheumatism*, Paris: I. Quesnel, 1642, C. C. Barnard, (trans.), Brit J Rheum 2:141-162, 1940.

William Gilbert (1544-1603)

ALTHOUGH WILLIAM GILBERT has not been immortalized by any eponym in the physical sciences as have Volta, Faraday, Ampere, or Galvani, his epitaph describes him as "physician and the founder of the science of electricity." Gilbert's father, a prosperous burgess and recorder of Colchester, made it possible for his son to study at St. John's College, Cambridge, where he graduated AB in 1561, received the AM in 1564, and the MD in 1569. Trained as a physician and engaged in the practice of medicine in London for approximately 30 years, Gilbert examined systematically, and without outside financial support, the corporeal attraction of specific objects to amber, the performance of the lodestone and the move-

ments of the magnetic needle, natural phenomena which proved to be integral parts of the firmament of the science of terrestrial magnetism and electricity. In addition to

the ultimate worth of contributions to theoretical physics, there was great practical need for an understanding of the magnetic needle, since it was the best means at that time for explorers seeking distant shores to identify the northerly direction.

In research, carried out over a period of 30 years, Gilbert rejected the traditional reliance upon theoretical and unsound speculation and exploited scientific methods of experimental investigation. He collected all the sound knowledge that others had acquired on magnetism, extended it within the limitations imposed by the physical science of his time, and described his findings in *De magnete*. An adequate theory of magnetism of his day should have accounted for the allurement of iron by the lodestone, the static response of amber, and the five magnetic movements of the compass: attraction, orientation, variation from the meridian, variation from the horizontal, and diurnal variation. He noted the following in the preface and discussed each critical phase in the body of the monograph.[1,2]

Clearer proofs, in the discovery of secrets, and in the investigation of the hidden causes of things, being afforded by trustworthy experiments and by demonstrated arguments, than by the probable guesses and opinions of the ordinary professors of philosophy: so, therefore, that the noble substance of that great magnet, our common mother (the earth), hitherto quite unknown, and the conspicuous and exalted powers of this our globe, may be the better understood, we have proposed to begin with the common magnetick, stony, and iron material, and with magnetical bodies, and with the nearer parts of the earth which we can reach with our hands and perceive with our senses; then to proceed with demonstrable magnetick experiments; and so penetrate, for the first time, into the innermost parts of the earth. For after we had, in order finally to learn the true substance of the globe, seen and thoroughly examined many of those things which have been obtained from mountain heights or ocean depths, or from the profoundest caverns and from hidden mines: we applied much prolonged labour on investigating the magnetical forces; so wonderful indeed are they, compared with the forces of all other minerals, surpassing even the virtues of all other bodies about us.

Among the particularly helpful instruments devised by Gilbert in his experimental work were the spheroidal lodestone which, when capped with iron to increase its efficiency, he called an "armature;" a terrella (little earth); and a versorium, a magnetic needle balanced on a pivot, the forerunner of the electroscope. As he developed the theory that the north-south attraction of the compass was under the influence of the earth acting as a vast magnet, he drew several false inferences. The declination of the compass needle was attributed to the presence of unidentified large land masses. He assumed that, on a given point on the earth's surface, the declination of the compass needle remained forever the same. From this he deduced another erroneous theorem that the magnetic and geographic poles of the earth coincided. Gilbert pursued his belief that the earth was a magnet far enough to remove any personal skepticism, although his theories were rejected by many and were even considered heresy by some. The excerpts from Book I, Chapter XVII, summarize his findings on the magnetism of the earth.[3]

That the globe of the earth is magnetick. & a magnet; & *how in our hands the magnet stone has all the primary* forces of the earth, while the earth, by the *same powers remains constant in a fixed direction in the universe.*

Prior to bringing forward the causes of magnetical motions, & laying open the proofs of things hidden for so many ages, & our experiments (the true foundations of terrestrial philosophy), we have to establish & present to the view of the learned our New & unheard of doctrine about the earth, and this, when argued by us on the grounds of its probability, with subsequent experiments & proofs, will be as certainly assured as anything in philosophy ever has been considered & confirmed by clever arguments or mathematical proofs. The terrene mass, which together with the vasty ocean produces the sphaerick figure & constitutes our globe, being of a firm & constant substance, is not easily changed, does not wander about, & fluctuate with uncertain motions, like the seas, & flowing waves; but holds all its volume of moisture in certain beds & bounds, & as it were in oft-met veins, that it may be less diffused & dissipated at random. . . . Thus every part of the earth which is removed from its exhibits by sure experiments every impulse of the magnetick nature; by its various motions it observes the globe of the earth and the principle common to both.

Gilbert described his electrical discoveries in the second chapter of the second book. The word "electric" was coined from "elektron," the Greek for amber; whereas the term "electricity" was coined sometime later by Robert Boyle. Gilbert identified amber, jet, wax, alum, and other substances which attracted the needle of his versorium. Other masses such as bone, ivory, marble, silver, gold, iron, and even the lodestone were unattracted and were termed "anelectric" or "non-electric." Moist weather was found to hinder electrification; warming amber did not electrify it. Neither a mass of hot iron nor a burning torch was attracted by electrics. None of his electrics exposed to the action of the sun's rays acquired a charge. He examined the behavior of liquids and gases and found them susceptible to electrical influence. When a piece of excited amber was brought near a drop of water, it was drawn into a conical shape; whereas carbon particles in smoke were attracted by an electrified body. Gilbert failed, however, to discover the dissimilarity between conductors and insulators and overlooked the phenomenon that similarly electrified bodies repel each other.

Little is known of Gilbert's medical affairs. Shortly after settling in London

(1573), he became a Fellow of the College of Physicians, served as censor of the College for seven years, treasurer for nine years, and, in 1600, president. He lived near St. Paul's Cathedral, became personal physician to Queen Elizabeth, attended her during her final illness, and served for a few months as physician to James I. He took an active part in the preparation of the first London *Pharmacopoea,* published after his death by the College of Physicians, and investigated the medical properties of lodestone and iron. The only item of medical interest in his writings was the observation that iron filings were useful in the treatment of anemia, chlorosis, and in enlargement of the spleen in young girls. Two years after his death, two of his instruments for navigation were described by Blundeville in *The Theoriques of the Seven Planets.* Original copies of the first great book of modern science to be published in England are now rare and valuable. An English translation of the first Latin edition appeared in 1616, and a facsimile of the original in 1892.[4] Gilbert died of the plague—a wealthy bachelor. He gave the College of Physicians his library, globes, instruments, and cabinets of minerals, which were destroyed in the great fire of London in 1666.

1. Gilbert, W.: *On the Lodestone and Magnetic Bodies, and on the Great Magnet the Earth,* P. F. Mottelay (trans.), London: B. Quaritch, 1893.
2. Gilbert, W.: *De Magnete, Magneticisque Corporibus, et de Magno Magnete Tellure,* Londini: P. Short, 1600.
3. Roller, D. H. D.: *The De Magnete of William Gilbert,* Amsterdam: M. Hertzberger, 1959.
4. Gilbert, W.: *On the Magnet (De Magnete),* facsimile of Gilbert Club translation, New York, 1958.

Tagliacozzi (1545-1599)

GASPARE TAGLIACOZZI (Gaspar Taliacotius), born in Bologna and professor of anatomy and surgery in the university in its great days, described sound procedures for the plastic repair of facial disfiguration which have persisted into contemporary practice. Although reconstruction of the face and especially the nose had been performed by surgeons since ancient times, Tagliacozzi

is credited with perfecting the reparative techniques and with performing them with greater skill than his predecessors. Equally significant was the preparation of his *De*

curtorum chirurgia per insitionem (The Surgery of Deformities by Transplantation), the first treatise devoted exclusively to the theory and practice of the art.[1] The monograph contained descriptions of his surgical management including the trivia, and was illustrated with woodcuts made under the direction of the author.

Although Tagliacozzi's reputation has persisted through the centuries, valid biographic data remained unassembled until the appearance in 1950 of an excellent and exhaustive study of his social and professional life.[2] The co-authors spent more than 20 years in scholarly research, each contributing in his respective areas of competence, so that contemporary readers would have available a definitive biography of a surgeon and anatomist who was outranked in the 16th century only by a limited few such as Vesalius and Paré. Much of the substance of this essay has been prepared from this work. Gnudi and Webster began by correcting and confirming Tagliacozzi's birth date of 1545, with a previously undiscovered baptismal record. Evidence was found to support the assumption that

Gaspare's parents were friends of the nobility, and, being in well-to-do circumstances, were able to provide adequate education for their son, including advanced studies at the University of Bologna.

Gaspare's pursuit of learning followed the customary curriculum in the humanities; he wrote and spoke Latin in the style of Cicero, took up the study of dialectics in his 15th year, philosophy in his 17th year, and medicine in his 19th year. He read from Avicenna, Maimonides, Hippocrates, Galen, and others; was taught anatomy and the technique of rhinoplasty by Aranzio, professor of anatomy and surgery; and received clinical experience in the Ospedale Della Morte, the hospital of death. The degree in medicine was taken in 1570, and the doctor of philosophy six years later; in the interim he served as prosecutor in the anatomy department. Upon the death of Aranzio in 1589, Tagliacozzi was appointed one of four professors to the chair of anatomy and in this position conducted formal dissections for the university. On three occasions, the first in 1591, he served as Prior to the college of medicine.

Tagliacozzi began to receive patients in 1576 and soon his fame spread throughout Italy and beyond; commoners and noblemen alike sought his clinical counsel. His crowning professional achievement, the treatise on surgery of deformities, appeared in 1597.[1] The great need for plastic repair of the nose, lips, or ears resulted from disfiguration or loss of tissue in dueling, street brawls, clashes of armed men, amputation by decree of superior or petty tribunals, and the prevalence of cutaneous syphilis. In the dedication to the Grand Duke of Tuscany, Tagliacozzi, as his chief surgeon, notes:[2]

In our art [of plastic surgery], on the one hand, I have observed that some things have been described inadequately and other things obscurely by the earlier writers, and some things have been entirely omitted which regard the consummation of the art, and, on the other hand, I noticed that not all physicians have been aware of or able to perform this not ignoble part of surgery, which is concerned with the reconstruction of mutilated noses, ears and lips. Hence, considering it worth while that one should expand effort on this part

[of surgery] too, and particularly since I had heard that there were certain men in Calabria who practiced this art rather by irregular and haphazard methods than methods based upon reason—if art it should be called under those circumstances—therefore I applied myself to it with as much assiduity and diligence as possible, since it was part of my profession, in order that in this field too something might be achieved and published for the common good. And in doing this, I believe I have accomplished this much, not only to have been useful in treating people but to have brought this part [of surgery] at last to the true level of an art, so that it can be transmitted in writings and any man, even one of only moderate skill, can sagely and successfully operate with its rules before him. For these reasons, I have decided to send forth this my offspring, from my hearth into the world at last—now that it has, moreover, reached a mature age—and to share it with all public-spirited men.

Prior to the publication of the treatise, Tagliacozzi, in 1586, wrote to Girolamo Mercuriale, physician and anatomist in Padua and Bologna, defending his rhinoplastic procedures against unwarranted criticism.[3] In describing the preoperative preparation of the patient, he recommended a digestible diet and mental tranquility. The critical features of the operation included the use of skin and subcutaneous fat flaps rather than muscle for the transplant, fixation above the biceps of the donor flap to the nose with proper bandages between head and arm during the transfer, and severing the pedicle from the upper arm only after increasing the blood supply to the tissue to be transferred.[2]

The method of restoring noses by the art [of surgery], which you recently requested of me in a letter, illustrious Sir, I take pleasure in indicating to you now. . . . First consider the body of the patient and examine carefully the temperament of the body and the brain. For toward it, as at a target, all therapeutic measures must be directed. Thus, venery must be ruled out absolutely, and all anger, grief, and worry barred. The food given should be easily digestible, with little residue, and euchymous.

After these preliminary measures for the preparation and care of the body, an incision is made in the skin of either arm, left or right, down to the flesh, that is only as far as the surface of the muscles; in other words, simple and solid skin is taken from the anterior brachial region, where the triceps muscle ends and the biceps begins. . . . However, in order that in the various motions of the body those parts joined in this way may not be torn apart and injured, the arm should be kept bound to the head with proper bandages, while the wound and the suture are being healed with cicatrizing agents. [The time for] release of the bandaging will be indicated by the union and satisfactory nourishment of the skin; this varies considerably according to the various temperaments of patients. But when excellent union of the wound and nourishment of the skin is observed, sever the arm from the face, and care for the wound as you do for other wounds for a period of several days.

The great work remained as an unpublished manuscript for more than a decade. This time was devoted to correction of the copy, preparation of woodcuts for reproduction of selected instruments, illustrations of the several stages of the operations, and acquisition of additional surgical experience. Two assistants to the surgeon were recommended. Although Tagliacozzi mentions the possibility of heterologous skin transplants, he found it more practical to select the skin from the patient's own body. The exposed skin was protected against pressure and trauma, but suppuration was encouraged. Fourteen days was the usual period before beginning the transfer. At the time of transplant, the recipient surfaces were freshened. In anticipation of severing the flap, a paper template was prepared, sized for the missing tissue, placed on the skin flap, and the proper shape and size of the graft sculptured with the scalpel. The usual time for severing the flap after full union was about 20 days; shaping the flap to the desired contour for a nose required from three to six weeks. The concluding procedure included suturing at the base of the nose with patching in the nostrils and bandaging. For a defect in the lip, a skin flap from the arm was transferred; for a defect in the ear, cutis from the scalp was used. The following remarks in the first chapter of Tagliacozzi's treatise have been selected for their appropriateness to conclude this essay.[2]

We bring back, refashion and restore to wholeness the features which nature gave but chance destroyed, not that they may charm the eye but that they may be an advantage to the living soul, not as a mean artifice but as an alleviation of illness, not as becomes charlatans but as becomes good physicians and followers of the great Hippocrates. For although the original beauty of the face is indeed restored, yet this is only accidental, and the end for which the physician is working is that the features should fulfill their offices according to nature's decree.

1. Tagliacozzi, G.: *The Surgery of Deformities by Transplantation* (L), Venetiis: G. Bindonum, 1597.
2. Gnudi, M. T., and Webster, J. P.: *The Life and Times of Gaspare Tagliacozzi*, New York: H. Reichner, 1950.
3. Mercuriale, G.: *The Book of Adornment* (L), ed 2, Frankfort: J. Wechelum, 1587.

Peter Lowe (c 1550-1610)

PETER LOWE, Scotsman of Glasgow, had several missions in life. The two best remembered are a major responsibility in the founding of the Faculty of Physicians and Surgeons of Glasgow and the preparation of the first comprehensive text on surgery in English. Since little is known of Lowe's early life, most of the details of his professional career must be deduced from the text of the founding charter by James VI to the Faculty and the biographical items in his medical writings.[1] The year and place of Lowe's birth are not available from personal or state records; however, it has been assumed from the data in the preface to the

second edition of his *Discourse* that he was
born in the mid-16th century, went to Paris
to study when he was about 15, and subsequently qualified as master in the Faculty
of Surgery. Since he styled himself "Arel-
lian" in the title page of his monograph on
syphilis, the possibility that he studied medicine at Orleans has been suggested. Lowe
remained abroad to practice in France,
Flanders, and elsewhere for 22 years, became "chyrurgion-maior" to the Spanish
regiments at Paris, and for 6 years held an
honorary appointment to Henry IV. Good
evidence supports the supposition that he
came to London in 1596 and settled in
Glasgow two years later.

The principal event associated with his
appearance in London was the publication
of his first book, *An Easie, Certaine, and
Perfect Method, to Cure and Prevent the
Spanish Sicknes.* On the title page he is
listed as *"Peter Lowe Arrelian:* Doctor in
the facultie of Chirurgy in Paris; & Chirur-
gian ordinary to Henry the Fourth, the
most Christian King of Fraunce and Navarre." In the work he expresses the opinion
advanced by Fracastorius a century earlier
that the Spanish Sickness was[32]

. . . brought among the Christians, after y nativi-
tie of our Lord, 1492, by a Spaniard call
Christophorus Columbus, with many other
Spanyards, accompanied with some women, who
came from the new found Iles occidentalls. For
this sicknes is as common, or rather rises
amongst them, then any other disease with us,
and doth infect, as contagious sicknesses doe
among us. So divers Souldiers were infected, who
after their returne, not onely infected their owne
Country, but also divers others.

In 1599, Lowe was under contract (with
a small stipend) to the corporation of Glasgow to care for the poor of the community.
In the fall of the same year, he received
the charter for the Faculty of Physicians
and Surgeons, with eight provisions. The
charter was a notable and comprehensive
document. It provided for the licensing of
all persons professing to practice the art of
surgery, responsibility for medical inquests,
examination of those practicing medicine,
control of the dispensing of drugs by apothecaries, and medical counsel gratis to the

poor. In return, Lowe was exempt from the
bearing of armor, paying of taxes, and serving on the jury. The opening lines of the
charter disclose the sordid conditions of
the time, the absence of formal instruction
in training physicians and surgeons for practice, and the relation of physicians to surgeons and surgeons to barbers and apothecaries.[3]

James, be the Grace of God, King of Scottis,
to all Provostis, baillies of burrowis, Scheriffs,
Stewartis, baillies of regalities, and otheris minis-
teris of justice within the boundis following, and
their deputis, and all and sundrie otheris ouir
leigis and subditis, quhom . it efferis, quhase
knawledge thir our letteris sal cume, greiting, *Wit
ze we,* with auise o oure counsall, understanding
the grit abusis quhilk hes bene comitted in time
bigane, and zit daylie continuis be ignorant, un-
skillit and unlernit personis, quha, under the col-
lour of Chirurgeanis, abuisis the people to their
plesure, passing away but tryel or punishment,
and thairby destroyis infinite number of oure
subjectis, quhairwith na ordour hes bene tane in
tyme bigane, specially. . . . For avoiding of sik
inconvenientis, . . . makis, constitutis, and ordinis
Maister Peter Low, our Chirurgiane . . . with the
assistance of Mr. Robert Hamiltone, professour
of medecine, and their successouris, indwelleris
of our Citie of Glasgow . . . full power to call,
sumonnd, and convene before thame, within the
said burgh of Glascow, or onie otheris of ouir
said burrowis, or publict places of the foirsaids
boundis, all personis professing or using the said
airt of Chirurgie, to examine thame upon thair
literature, knawledge and practize; gif they be
fund wordie, to admit, allow, and approve thame,
give tham testimonial according to the airt and
knawledge that they sal be fund wordie to exercise thareftir.

Nixt, that the saidis visitouris sall visit everie hurt,
murtherit, poisonit, or onie other persoun tane
awa extraordinarly, and to report to the Magistrate of the fact as it is: . . . *Fordlie,* It sall not
be leisum . . . to exercise medicine without ane
testimonial of ane famous universitie quhair
medecine be taught, or the leave of oure and
oure dearest spouse chief medicinarie; and in case
they failzie, it sal be lesum to the saidis visitouris
to challenge, perseu and inhibite thame throu
using and exercing of the said airt of medecine,
under the pain of fourtie poundis, to be distributed, half to the Judges, half to the pure, toties
quoties they be found in useing and exercing
the same ay and quhill they bring sufficient testimonial as said is: *Fythlie,* That na manir of personis sell onie droggis within the Citie of Glasgow, except the sam be sichtit be the saidis
visitouris, and be William Spang, apothecar, under

the pane of confiscatioune of the droggis: *Sextlie,* That nane sell rotoun poison, asenick, or sublemate, under the pane of ane hundred merkis, excep onlie the apothecaries quha sall be bund to tak cautioun of the byaris, for coist, skaith, and damage: *Seventlie,* Yat the saidis visitouris, with thair bretherene and successouris, sall convene every first Mononday of ilk moneth at sum convenient place, to visite and give counsell to pure discusit folkis gratis: and, *last of all,* Gevand and grantand to the saidis visitouris indwellers of Glasgow, professouris of the saidis airtis, and thair bretherene, p"nt and to cum, immunite and exemptioune from all wappin shawengis, raidis, oistis, beiring of armour, watching, weirding, stenting taxationis, passing on assises, inquestis, justice, courtis, Scheriff or burrow Courtis, in actiounes criminal or cival.

Lowe's great work *Chyrurgerie* appeared in 1597. Although the introduction was in Latin, the body of the text was in the vernacular, one of the first to be written in English. A translation of the "Prognostics" of Hippocrates, probably taken from the French, was appended. Also, three other books are mentioned one or more times in *Chyrurgerie,* which must have failed to reach the published state and remained in manuscript form.[1] These are *The Poore Man's Guide, Treatise on Parturition, and on the Diseases of Married Women and Maidens,* and *The Booke of the Plague.*

In selecting excerpts from Lowe's *Chyrurgerie,* his various biographers have chosen portions of the preface, the interpretation of the allegory of Ecclesiastes 12 on aging and senescence, amputation, prosthetic devices, ligation of vessels, pleurisy, cancer, cataract, subcutaneous emphysema, scrofula, aneurysm, inguinal hernia, hydrops, gunshot wound, corns, the superstition of specific days of the week, pyemia, toothache and the use of artificial teeth, qualifications of a surgeon, fistula in ano, the application of a ligature, the association of liver disease and ascites, and contrecoup injuries of the skull. A footnote on nomenclature in gout has been added to the three that have been chosen for this essay.[4]

OF SPHASELL

. . . But where there is putrefaction, we stay the fluxe of bloud by Cauters actuals, and where there is no putrefaction, malignisie, nor humor venomous, we use the ligator.

In amputation without putrefaction, I find the litgator reasonable sure, providing it be quickly done. To doe it, first thous shalt cause the assister as I have said, to hold his fingers on the vaines, letting one loose, on the which thou shalt take hold with the backe Decurbin, taking a little of the flesh or muscles with it: then put through a needle with a strong thread, knit with a double knot, tying a little of the flesh with the vaine, which will make it hold the better.

OF THE TUMOR IN THE BELLIE CALLED HYDROPSIE

Hydropsie, is a Tumor against nature, ingendered of great quantite of Water, Winde, or Flegme, which sometimes is dispersed through the whole bodie, and is called Universall, otherwhiles in some part thereof, & is called particular. It is most commonly in the capacitie of the Periton, of the which there are three sorts, to wit, Ascites, Timpanites, and Anasarca.

The cause, is either externe, or interne: . . . The cause interne, commeth chiefly by the vertue alteratrix and concoctrix of the liver, and by a posthumes of the liver, passions of the stomacke, through the vice of the vaines meteraicks (mesentery), matrire (uterus), bladder, lights (lungs), melt (spleen), and kidneyes. . . .

OF WOUNDS IN THE HEAD

The fift kind of fracture, is called counterclift, that is, when the cleft of the bone is in the part opposite to the sore, and of all fractures this is the worst, and deceiveth most the Chyrurgion, for in it there is no signe but conjecture, and by feeling of the hurt man, in oft putting his hand on the place, and if he got the stroake with violence, falling after he got it, and did vomit, notwithstanding there be no cleft where he got the stroke. I have knowne sundry dye in this case, chiefly at the battle of Sandlis in Fraunce a valiant Captaine of Paris, who had a stroake on the right parietary, who notwithstanding of all handling by skillful Chyrurgions, dyed withint twentie dayes, at which time his *Cranium* was opened, and there was found great quantitie of bloud under the left parietarie, with a cleft in the same.

OF THE TUMOR OR PAINE IN THE HANCH OR HURCLE BONE, CALLED CIATICA

This disease (which commonly doth possesse the joynts, by the falling of some humor above nature betwixt the joynt-bones) is called by the Latines *Morbus articularis,* and in vulgar the Gout, of which there be divers kinds and names according to the joynt which is diseased, as for example: that which occupieth the jawes, is called *Schugonagra:* if in the Necke, it is called *Trahelagra:* in the Backe, it is called *Rachiragra:* that in the shoulders is called *Omogra:* that in the Clavicules is called *Clersagra:* that in the elbow is called *Pethyagra,* that in the hands is called *Cheiragra,* that in the foot is called *Podagra,* and that in the Hanch is called *Ischias,* that in the knees is called *Gonagra:* here I shall content me onely to speake of the last two, because they be the most common, the others I leave to the learned Physition, as matters more Physicall than Chyrurgicall.

A bronze memorial tablet to Peter Lowe within the nave of the cathedral in Glasgow reproduces the epitaph which was hewn on the tombstone in the cathedral yard.[5]

Stay · Passenger · And · Viow · This · Stone
For · Under · It · Lyis · Such · A · One
Who · Cuired · Many · Whill · He · Lieved
Soe · Gracious · He · Noe · Man · Grieved
Yea · When · His · Phisicks · Force · Oft · Failed
His · Plesant · Purpose · Then · Prevailed
For · Of · His · God · He · Got · The · Grace
To · Live · In · Mirth · And · Die · In · Peace
Heavin · Hes · His · Soul · His · Corps · This · Stone
Sigh · Passinger · And · Soe · Be · Gone

1. Finlayson, J.: *Acount of the Life and Works of Maister Peter Lowe,* Glasgow: J. Maclehose & Sons, 1889.
2. Lowe, P.: *An Easie, Certaine, and Perfect Method, to Cure and Prevent the Spanish Sicknes,* London: J. Roberts, 1596.
3. *Charter by King James VI. To the Faculty of Physicians and Surgeons of Glasgow,* November, 1599, Notarial Copy in the Possession of the Faculty, 1817.
4. Lowe, P.: *A Discourse of the Whole Art of Chyrurgie,* London: T. Purfoot, 1597, ed 3, 1634.
5. Duncan, A.: *Memorials of the Faculty of Physicians and Surgeons of Glasgow 1599-1850,* Glasgow: J. Maclehose & Sons, 1896.

Thomas Moffet (1553-1604)

THOMAS MOFFET, sometimes spelled Moffett, Muffett, or Moufet, was born in London, the son of a haberdasher. After attending grammar school he matriculated at Trinity College, Cambridge, in 1569 and later transferred to Caius College, where he graduated AB.[1] He studied medicine with Thomas Lorkin and John Caius and in 1576 received the AM from Trinity College. Moffet traveled through several European countries, gained the acquaintance of several distinguished physicians and chemists, attended the medical lectures of Felix Platter in Basel, and there received the MD degree in 1578. In the same year, he published two medical treatises. Proceeding to

Italy and Spain, Moffet spent considerable time studying all forms of insect life, especially the culture of the silkworm described in a poem.[2] While on the Continent he ac-

Royal College of Physicians

cepted the doctrines of Paracelsus documented in a well-written apology, published in 1584, in which he defended the use of chemical compounds against the attacks of the Galenists. Moffet returned to Cambridge to receive the MD degree. In 1585, he was admitted a candidate and three years later a Fellow of the Royal College of Physicians. By then he had secured a good practice, first in Ipswich and later in London. He attended many persons of the upper class and several of the nobility, spending considerable time at court. Moffet's later years were passed in Wilton near Wiltshire, where, in 1597, he was elected a member of parliament for Wilton.

Only two of Moffet's works were prepared in English. His poem, 75 pages long, is entitled *The Silkewormes, and their Flies: Lively described in verse, by T.M. a Countrie Farmar, and an apprentice in Physicke.* The last stanza of the Presentation, an ottava rima, is as follows:[2]

I sing of little Wormes and tender Flies,
Creeping along, or basking on the ground,
Grac't once with those they heav'nly-humane eies,
Which never yet on meanest scholler fround:
And able are this worke to aeternise,
From East to West about this lower Round,
    Deigne thou but breathe a sparke or little flame
    Of likeing, to enlife, for aye the same.

A popular treatise on food, filled with quaint and unsubstantiated concepts, is entitled *Health's Improvement: or, Rules Comprizing and Discovering the Nature, Method and Manner of Preparing all sorts of Food Used in this Nation*. The following excerpts are taken from a 1746 revision by Bennet of his treatise.[3]

Breakfasts are fit for all Men in stinking Houses or close Cities, as also in the time of Pestilence, and before you visit the Sick; for empty Veins draw deepest, and what they first receive, be it good or bad, with that they cleanse or infect the Blood. Contrariwise, where the Air is pure, clear and wholesome, it is best to fast till Dinner, unless you be either of growing Years, or of a choleric Stomach, for then you must not in any Case be long fasting.

Dinners and Suppers are generally necessary and convenient for all Ages, Times of the Year, and all Complexions, especially in these northern Parts of the World, where inward Heat being multiplied by outward Coldness, our radical Moisture would be soon consumed, if it were not restored by a double Meal at the least.

Whether Dinner *or* Supper *should be largest.*

Now whether at Dinner or Supper we may feed more plentifully, is a great Question amongst Physicians; either because they affirm too generally on either Side, or because they were ignorant of Distinctions.

Concerning the Manner of eating, it is not alike in all Countries. The *Jews, Grecians,* and old *Romans,* did eat lying and declining, to their right Side. Only the *Illyrians* sat boult upright as we do now, with a Woman placed, after the new Hans Fashion, betwixt every Man.

Finally, let me add one Thing more, and then an End of this Treatise; namely, that if our Breakfast be of liquid and supping Meats, our Dinner moist and of boil'd Meats, and our Supper chiefly of roasted Meats, a very good Order is observed therein, agreeable both to Art and the Natures of most Men.

1. Lee, S.: "Thomas Moffett," in *Dictionary of National Biography*, Oxford: University Press, 1894, vol 13, pp 548-550.

2. Moffet, T.: *The Silkewormes, and their Flies: Lively Described in Verse*, London: N. Linz, 1599.

3. Moffet, T.: *Health's Improvement: or, Rules Comprizing and Discovering the Nature, Method and Manner of Preparing all sorts of Food Used in this Nation*, London: T. Osborne, 1746.

Wilhelm Fabry (1560-1624)

GUILHELMUS FABRICIUS HILDANUS of Germany, who Latinized his name in keeping with the custom of the day, was a contemporary of Fabricius ab Aquapendente, brilliant surgeon and anatomist of Padua. Wilhelm Fabry was born at Hilden, near Dusseldorf, in humble circumstances. His father was a clerk in the Court and a person of some education. Wilhelm's early education included the study of classical and romance languages, in addition to medicine. He remained in school only through the financial assistance of Uttenhoven, a Dutch poet and friend of the family.[1] Although unable to take advantage of university training as did the other Fabricius, Wilhelm rose to eminence as a bold surgical craftsman, an anatomist privy to the secrets of structure, and an acquaintance of the wound-surgeons of his day. His capacity for work and intellectual powers were complemented by an opportune marriage to Marie Colinet, a capable surgeon and obstetrician on her own.

Although the ancients of medicine were respected and studied by Fabry, he relegated the theory of humors, currently in fashion in the explanation of disease, to a minor position. The practice of surgery was pursued as a science, not a metaphysical cult. He suffered intermittently from acute attacks of gouty arthritis and might have endured serious renal insufficiency associated with gout. Fabry was always on the move throughout an illustrious career, scarcely establishing residence in any community.

Professional activities embraced public dissection, collection of case records, writing, and exploration of new surgical procedures or improvement of accepted techniques. The number of subjects discussed in his writings, prepared originally in Latin and translated into German or other languages, leaves no doubt of his position in his profession and the capacity for progress in the search for sound surgical operations. The subjects appeared either in monographic discussion or in one of the collections of case reports, which reached the astonishing number of 600.[2] Dysentery, thermal burns, lithotomy, and anatomy were afforded monographic treatment. Gangrene, congenital malformations, trepanation, skull fracture, surgical removal of the globus, cholecystectomy, carcinoma of the eye, hydrocele, imperforate anus, mineral water baths, the wisdom of cutting through healthy tissue above the necrotic tissue in amputation, healing of the wall of the artery from the external coat of the vessel, carcinoma of the penis, and a special operation for hernia were discussed in his writings. Fabry designed several instruments and appliances, including a bullet extractor, a tourniquet for controlling hemorrhage, suspensory bandages, a urinal for ambulatory use, a field-chest of drugs and instruments for army use, and a tube for extraction of foreign bodies from the esophagus. Cautery and caustics were recommended for the bite of mad animals. In the monograph on lithotomy, he discloses his philosophy of the practice of surgery.[3]

Because every faithful Chyrurgion and Physitian is, bound before God the Chief of Physitian, not only to cure the sick, but by his good councel to keep those that are cured in their health; not only to take away the stone, but to provide against the breeding of any new ones;

therefore it is required principally that the Chururg know and be taught how and from what causes the stone in the Body of Man and especially in the Bladder, is generated and coagulated together.

The extraction of a foreign body of steel from the eye, with a magnet and the assistance of his wife-physician, is one of his most famous and frequently mentioned case reports.[2]

A peasant named Benoist Barquin from the St. Ymier Valley near the Lake of Biel was buying steel at a retail dealer's. On choosing the best steel Barquin struck two pieces together. A flying speck of steel lodged in the portion of the cornea over the iris and remained embedded in the tissue, causing great pain. After bystanders had tried in vain and the pain had increased with an inflammation, he came to see me at Bern on May 5, 1623. A good regimen was prescribed for him, and the body was evacuated by bloodletting and purging. A few days later, I tried several times to remove the foreign body, first with instruments. However, it was so small that I did not succeed, and this forced me to look for another expedient and to use a small cap, as I had on previous occasions. But this was also in vain. My wife conceived of the proper remedy. When I raised his eyelids with both hands she approached with a magnet as close to the eye as she was able. After I had tried this [method] several times—for he could not stand the light which was indispensable for this purpose—, at long last that tiny splinter was attracted to the magnet, as everyone of us saw it happen clearly, and after I had applied a collyrium he soon recuperated. Yet I have to point out that the magnet attracts as well as repels iron. I took advantage of what I had noticed (in the magnet which I used), in order not to make a mistake. Before application it is necessary to test the attraction of the magnet by turning it in the direction of the iron filings.

1. Jones, E.: The Life and Works of Guilhelmus Fabricius Hildanus, Med Hist 4:112-134; 196-209, 1960.

2. Fabri, G.: Observations Chirurgiques, book 5, L. Wood, trans. (excerpt), Geneva: J. A. Chover, 1679, pp 393-394.

3. Fabricius Hildanus, G.: Lithotomia Vesicae, Basle: L. König, 1628, trans. by Platt, W. B.: Fabricius Guilhelmus Hildanus: The Father of German Surgery, Johns Hopkins Hosp Bull 16:7-10, 1905.

Composite by G. Bako

Francois Ranchin (1560-1641)

FRANCOIS RANCHIN, gerontologist, born in Montpelier, France, into a patrician family, dedicated his life to his practice, his university, and his community.[1] He lived without financial worry in a family of culture. His loyalty to the crown was rewarded by church benefits, which provided prestige and security, albeit utilized unselfishly. Ranchin received the medical degree from the University of Montpellier in 1592. He then began a series of lectures in medicine and surgery, under the aegis of de Laurens, given in the French language when Latin was the prevailing academic tongue. He was elevated to professorial rank in 1605 by Henry IV and in 1612 was elected by the faculty and students as chancellor of the university.

Among his professional and administrative duties, Ranchin restored the famous anatomical amphitheater so badly damaged during the religious wars, regained for the College de Mende its intellectual prestige, and assumed many of the financial expenses of the revitalization of the university. In 1629, Ranchin was made mayor of Montpellier. At a time when he might have enjoyed the fruits of his labors, religious wars were bloodier than ever, and plague returned to the city as it had many times before.

During the respite from pestilence and strife subsequently, Ranchin completed his major literary work, *Opuscula medica.*[2] Earlier he had prepared a treatise on surgery, another on pharmacology, and shortly before death he published a treatise on medicine. His discussion on the plague which claimed his life appeared posthumously. His section on geriatrics (gerocomica) in *Opuscula medica,* an extensive scientific discussion, recognized the inadequacies of past contributors to which he added his empiric observations. He discusses conservation of health, maintenance of welfare, and management of diseases of the old. Diet and exercise are described in detail. He distinguishes between inevitable regression of the aged versus old age complicated by pathological changes. He reflects on rural versus urban environment, the advantages of the rich versus the hardships of the peasants. Alcohol, rest, sleep, and therapy are considered. Special diseases of postmaturity are recognized as well as the head and special senses, pulmonary and cardiac disorders, abdominal conditions, and joint and neurological diseases.

Translated excerpts from the foreword and the introduction are as follows:[3]

Not only physicians, but everybody else attending old people, being accustomed to their constant complaints, and knowing their ill-tempered and difficult manners, realize how noble and important, how serious and *difficult,* how *useful,* and even *indispensable* is that part of practical Medicine, called Gerocomica, which deals with the conservation of old people and the healing of their diseases.

Its *indispensability* results from the deficiencies of nature because of the hardships, the pains, the weaknesses, with which old people are afflicted almost without interruption. They are exposed to so many troubles of so many types that they seem to be in constant need of medical aid.

Its *usefulness* is demonstrated by consideration of the political fact that the administration of economical and political matters depends on the conservation of old people.

Its *difficulty* is shown not only by the peevishness of old people, but especially by the fact that this science has been neglected by our forefathers and even by modern authors, too. What has been written about the conservation of old people and the healing of the diseases of old age, is so bad and so unproductive that we get the impression not only that his noblest part of Medicine was not cultivated but even that, yes, it has been flatly suppressed and buried.

Now then, with God's help, let us start spiritedly with this important, serious, difficult, useful, and indispensable work. We like to teach how this science will aid in the conservation of old people, how it will throw light upon the genesis of the diseases of old age, and how—with what methods—it could be expanded by considering the diseases of the parents.

1. Bayle and Thillaye: "Ranchin, Francois," in *Biographie Medicale*, Paris: A. Delahays, 1855, pp 333-334.

2. Ranchini, F.: *Opuscula Medica*, Lyon, France: P. Ravaud, 1627.

3. Freeman, J. T.: Francois Ranchin, Contributor of an Early Chapter in Geriatrics, *J Hist Med* 5:422-431, 1950.

Composite by G. Bako

Santorio Santorio (1561-1636)

SANCTORIUS, physician, philosopher, meteorologist, and quantitative physiologist, was born in 1561 in the village of Capodistria, capital of Istria, an island in the Adriatic Sea a few miles below Trieste. His birthplace was a modest house on the street now named Via Santorio. His father was a Bombardier and Chief Steward of Munitions; his mother came of a noble Capodistrian family. Sanctorius was solidly schooled in languages and philosophy and, at the age of 14, enrolled in the University of Padua, recognized for its high scholastic achievements in science and the humanities. The Venetian Republic, under which Padua operated and in keeping with its reputation and fame, had granted it unusual liberties and privileges. Of the several faculties of the city's distinguished university, medicine enjoyed the highest rank and renown. After seven years at Padua studying medicine and natural philosophy, Sanctorius, upon the request of its king Maximilian, took up residence in Poland, where he practiced for more than a decade, meanwhile continuing consultations in Venice and other communities.[1]

Sanctorius returned to Padua in 1611 as professor of medicine and continued in this position until 1624, when he returned to a consulting practice in Venice, motivated partially by an unwillingness to devote full time to academic medicine. The Venetian Republic, aware of his great talents as consultant and the outstanding physician of his day, decreed that this move should not deprive him of his professional title in Padua, nor of the modest stipend associated with the rank. His clinical contributions include descriptions of the symptoms of phthisis, gastric ulcer, and carcinoma of the bladder, each with a modern inflection. They were subtly interwoven in his interpretation of the *Aphorisms* of Hippocrates, the writings of Galen, and the *Canon* of Avicenna.

The early 17th century, marked by the release of medicine from the bonds of natural philosophy, by the inception of quantitative biology, physiology, and biochemistry, and by the beginning of modern experimental medicine, provided an appropriate environment for his studies on metabolism.[2] The conclusions derived from precise measurements of physiological and pathological phenomena, which rightfully established him as the founder of modern metabolism, were published in a book of aphorisms, not in a documented pamphlet or monograph as might have been expected. The programed techniques and collected data in support of the aphorisms never appeared in print. The first edition of the aphorisms was published in 1614[3]; revisions and translations into other languages followed. The experimental procedure for the determination of insensible loss of body weight—the breathing of the skin—has been assumed from the famous etching that appeared on the flyleaf in later Latin editions. The etching portrays the experimental subject suspended on a steelyard, facing a meal on a small table. The physiological balance measured one function of biological life. Insensible loss was determined at varying intervals and under varying physiological and pathological states. The conclusions were presented in seven sections. The first section, "Concerning the Weight of Insensible Perspiration," described three variables: sensible intake—foods and fluids; sensible loss—urine and feces; and insensible loss or insensible perspiration. The latter embraced the vapor and gases expired from the lungs and transpired through the integument. The "equation of Sanctorious," which might be so appropriately identified, remains the basis of metabolic balance studies[4]:

Change in body weight equals (gas intake − gas output) + (fluid intake − fluid output) + (solid intake − solid output).

Section 1, Aphorism IV: Insensible Perspiration alone, discharges much more than all the servile Evacuations together.
Aphorism V: Insensible Perspiration is either made by the Pores of the Body, which is all over perspirable, and cover'd with a Skin like a Net; or it is performed by Respiration through the Mouth, which usually, in the Space of one Day, amounts to about the Quantity of half a Pound, as may plainly be made appear by breathing upon a Glass.
Aphorism VIII: If the Body be weighed in the Morning before and after sensible Evacuation, then it will be easy to determine the Quantity that is wasted that Night by Perspiration.
Aphorism XV: If a Body returns to the same Standard every Day, without any Change in the Quantity of Perspiration, there will be constantly preserved a perfect Health, and no need of critical Evacuations.
Aphorism LIX: Sixteen Ounces of Urine is generally evacuated in the Space of one Night; four Ounces by Stool, and forty Ounces and upwards by Perspiration.

Sanctorius was responsible either for the invention or the introduction into clinical medicine of two useful instruments: the clinical thermometer and the chronometer. The application of the clinical thermometer to the study of disease and a device for counting the pulse were described in his commentary on the *Canon* of Avicenna.[5] It has been assumed that Galileo was the actual inventor of the thermometer and the chronometer and that Sanctorius learned of them through his friendship with him. There were several different designs with various methods of application. The basis of the thermometer was a capillary tube filled with colored water, closed at the bulb, with the opposite end immersed in a container of fluid. As the bulb was exposed to body heat by the clasped hand, the pursed lips, or expired air, the liquid expanded and was forced into the receiving vessel. Sanctorius also perfected, in several forms, the pulsilogium, a chronometer for recording the pulse. The simplest type of chronometer was a ball suspended on a thread, oscillating as a pendulum, synchronous with the pulse rate, and backed by a calibrated chart. The thread could be shortened or lengthened, depending upon the pulse rate. A direct reading was derived from the chart. Just as the foundations of modern physics rest on the accurate measurement of time, the chronometer of humans is the biological clock, the pulse. Sanctorius also designed a trocar for extracting a bladder stone, a tracheal cannula for diphtheritic croup, and a balneatorium, a waterproof leather sack for bathing the bedridden patient. The device contained an opening for the head and an outlet at the foot. Water was poured in at the intake, flowed around the patient, and drained through the outlet. Although other instruments were described, including a meteorologic anemometer and an instrument for measuring relative humidity of the air, no experimental data from their use were published.

Sanctorius, friend and scientific colleague of Galileo, consultant in great demand throughout southern Europe, was sympathetic to Galileo's perception of the possibilities of the quantitative and experimental approach to physiology and medicine. Medicine's blind adherence to natural philosophy during the Middle Ages was beginning to weaken and, in turn, was replaced by observation, quantitative investigation, and experiments of many scientists, but especially through the genius and talents of Sanctorius.

1. Castiglioni, A.: Life and Work of Sanctorius, *Med Life* 38:729-786, 1931.

2. Major, R. H.: Santorio Santorio, *Ann Med Hist* 10:369-381 (Sept) 1938.

3. Santorio, S.: *De Statica Medicina*, Venice: N. Polum, 1614.

4. Quincy, J.: *Medicina Statica: Being the Aphorisms of Sanctorius*, 4th ed, London: J. Osborn and T. Longman, 1728.

5. Santorio, S.: *Commentaria in Primam Fen Primi Libri Canonis Avicennae*, Venice: M. A. Brogiollum, 1646.

Royal College of Physicians

Theodore Turquet de Mayerne (1573-1655)

SIR THEODORE TURQUET DE MAYERNE, physician to the royal families of France and England, was born into a Protestant upper-class family in Mayerne near Geneva.[1] His family had fled France because of religious persecution. He received his early education in Geneva and after four years of schooling at Heidelberg studied medicine at Montpellier. Mayerne graduated MB in 1596, MD in 1597, and began practice in Paris; there he soon attracted the attention of those in authority and received an appointment as teacher of anatomy to the surgeons and pharmacy to the apothecaries. His introduction of chemical agents in the management of disease, contrary to the teaching of the Galenists as detailed in his Apologia, subjected him to outspoken criticism by his contemporaries. This fresh approach led to the publication of a broadside in 1603 by the Galen-oriented doctors against his heretical teachings.

Such incidents strengthened rather than weakened Mayerne's reputation at court, and Henry IV appointed him physician-in-ordinary. Additional amenities were promised if he would embrace Roman Catholicism. Mayerne refused the offer but continued in high favor until 1606, when he moved to London and the court of King James I. The profession as well as the royal family in London welcomed his arrival; the University of Oxford honored him with the MD degree on the strength of his record at Montpellier. As first physician of England, he cared for Henry, Prince of Wales, during his fatal illness in 1612, which was assumed in retrospect to have been typhoid fever. Mayerne was accused of malicious practice in the management of the Prince but subsequently was exonerated by the King and his council.

In 1616, Mayerne was accepted as a Fellow by the Royal College of Physicians. He gave great assistance to the composition of the preface and preparation of the contents of the first edition of the London *Pharmacopoeia*. The monograph, dedicated to King James, was published in 1618. In 1624, Mayerne received the honor of knighthood and in 1625 attended the King in his last illness, kidney failure associated with tophaceous gout. Mayerne maintained the royal appointment on the ascension of Charles I, as well as enjoyed great favor with Queen Henrietta since he compounded formulae for her cosmetics, pastes, lotions, dentifrices, hair powders, and other feminine accessories. He employed his knowledge of chemistry to the advancement of the fine arts, devised a carnation-colored pigment for enamel miniatures, was one of the first to use calomel, and compounded a black mercurial lotion for skin disorders. Mayerne's final royal appointment was nominal first physician to Charles II; this climaxed the unusual honor of having served four kings. The remainder of his life was spent in England except for a brief revisit to France.

The only work Mayerne published was the *Apologia*.[2] Other volumes published over his name were prepared by others and appeared posthumously. He transcribed in Latin or French with equal ease but was less adept in English composition. As a meticulous auditor of clinical experiences, he prepared a tremendous number of case histories; many have been preserved. Each case report was presented under theoretical considerations, treatment, and recapitulation. The British Museum lists 23 volumes of reports in his handwriting. A relatively complete system of medicine, entitled *Praxeos mayernianae in morbis internis*,[3] and published in London in 1690, contained tremendous lists of compounded ingredients for specific maladies. It represented polypharmacy at its worst and was typical of medicinal therapy in the 17th century.

In the section on delivery, in the appendix which appeared first with the 1691 edition of *Praxeos*, placenta praevia is not mentioned by name but is described as a slipping of the placenta from its proper attachment on the uterus.[3] Complete separation of the placenta was advised to prevent fatal hemorrhage. Podalic version was recommended for occipital-posterior presentation, with the face of the child facing the mother's sacrum, so as to prevent the chin being caught under the symphysis pubis. Early delivery was advised for the control of convulsions when they appeared before or during labor. An emergency episiotomy by the fingernail was suggested in instances of excessive stretching of the vulva.

In 1674, Theophilus Bonetus edited a treatise on arthritis and podagra from Mayerne's notes; later, in 1676, Sherley translated into English a monograph on gout from his French notes. Although colchicine at that time was known to possess anti-gout properties, among the many recommended for acute or chronic gouty symp-

toms, he failed to mention this agent. The Epistle Dedicatory by the editor of the treatise on arthritis contained the following.[4]

Your Lordship hath had the unhappiness to be much and long afflicted with this torturing Disease, the Gout: And therefore I cannot but think I do you an acceptable service, (I am sure I intend it such) in presenting You this Book; in which You will find a most rational account of the Cause and Origin of this distemper; and an excellent Method, and efficacious Remedies against it.

I question not, but that it will prove a very acceptable thing to your Lordship, to find this worthy Author asserting the Gout to be Curable: For though you may have been otherways inform'd by some Physicians, yet when your Lordship shall have weigh'd the eminent Learning, (with the happy, and long experience, and success) of Sir THEODOR MAYERNE, 'tis not to be doubted, but that you will give your suffrage on his side.

Mayerne gave his library to the Royal College of Physicians of London, but it was destroyed in 1666 by the great fire. He died in Chelsea (London) and was interred in the Church of St. Martin's-in-the-Fields.

1. Aikin, J.: *Biographical Memoirs of Medicine in Great Britain*, London: J. Johnson, 1780, pp 249-271.
2. de Mayerne, T. T.: *Apologia in qua Videre est Inviolatis Hippocratis et Galeni Legibus Remedia Chymice Preparata, Tuto Usurpari Posse*, Rupel, 1603.
3. de Mayerne, T. T.: *Praxeos Mayerianae in Morbis Internis Praecipue Gravioribus et Chronicis Syntagma*, London: S. Smith, 1690.
4. de Mayerne, T. T.: *A Treatise of the Gout* (Fr), translated by T. Sherley, London: D. Newman, 1676.

Jean Baptiste van Helmont (1577-1644)

THE AGE OF SCIENTIFIC REALISM associated with Harvey's discovery of the circulation of blood and Vesalius' description of the structure of the body sired a small school of chemists and physiologists. Among these, Jean Baptiste van Helmont made contributions in both scientific areas. He described carbon dioxide, studied the growth of plants, recognized the acidity of gastric juice and its importance in the first stage of digestion, and examined quantitatively the urine of patients with nephritis. His writings, several published after his death, reveal an underlying mysticism, but, struggling with the unknown in chemistry and biology,

he found them susceptible to scientific study and measurement. Thus, he typifies the transition from alchemy to chemistry.

Jean Baptiste was born in Brussels of a good family; he studied at the University of Louvain trying first one faculty, then another, and eventually deciding that his love was medicine. Having initially spurned an academic degree, he then studied with the Jesuits. However, he accepted medicine for a second time, reading the works of Hippocrates, Galen, Avicenna, and others. He subsequently pursued the practice of medicine, took the MD degree at Louvain, married a pious, noble, and rich wife, and retired to Vilvorde, an estate near Brussels, to conduct his chemical experiments.[1] Failing to find any rationale for therapy or any potent therapeutic agents, except the chemical components of Paracelsus, his scientific godfather, he reluctantly continued a modest practice in medicine. At least one of his clinical observations in the care of the sick is noteworthy. Finding the liver normal and the kidneys diseased in patients dead from dropsy, he rejected the theory of the ancients that the liver was the cause of peripheral edema.

Van Helmont published a number of books during his productive years. His doctrine and concepts were assembled in the

Ortus medicinae (Origins of Medicine), edited by his son several years after his father's death.[2] As a devout Catholic and a natural philosopher, he interwove a fantastic supernatural concept into the interpretation of chemical investigations. However, he was first to use the term, "gas," to describe carbon dioxide (gas sylvestre—wood gas), a substance which lost its visible shape but not its specificity. Quantitative proof of the evolution of gaseous carbon dioxide was noted during an experiment on the preparation of charcoal.[3] The title "Philosopher Through Fire" is related to his use of combustion in exploring chemical phenomenon.[3]

Therefore the live coal, and generally whatsoever bodies do not immediately depart into water, nor yet are fixed, do necessarily belch forth a wild spirit [spiritum sylvestre] or breath. Suppose thou, that of 62 pounds of Oaken coal, one pound of ashes is composed: Therefore the 61 remaining pounds, are the wild spirit, which also being fired, cannot depart, the Vessel being shut.

I call this Spirit, unknown hitherto, by the new name of Gas, which can neither be constrained by Vessels, nor reduced into a visible body, unless the seed being first extinguished. But bodies do contain this Spirit, and do sometimes wholly depart into such a Spirit, not indeed, because it is actually in those very bodies (for truly it could not be detained, yea the whole composed body should flie away at once) but it is a Spirit grown together, coagulated after the manner of a body, and is stirred up by an attained ferment, as in Wine, the juyce of unripe Grapes, bread, hydromel or water and Honey, &c.

His measurements on a growing tree are frequently quoted to illustrate his quantitative approach to the study of living matter.[3]

For I took an Earthen Vessel, in which I put 200 pounds of Earth that had been dried in a Furnace, which I moystened with Rain-water, and I implanted therein the Trunk or Stem of a Willow Tree, weighing five pounds; and at length, five years being finished, the Tree sprung from thence, did weigh 169 pounds, and about three ounces: . . . I computed not the weight of the leaves that fell off in the four Autumnes. At length, I again dried the Earth of the Vessel, and there were found the same 200 pounds, wanting about two ounces. Therefore 164 pounds of Wood, Barks, and Roots, arose out of water onely.

Other quantitative studies were made on water and urine, and the weight of equal quantities was compared. He rejected the Paracelsian theory that sulfur, mercury, and salt were the only elements and substituted air, the natural atmosphere, and water. Water was everything not included as air. All matter, plants, and animals could be reduced to water. This is factual in that most salts essential to life are soluble.

The theory of fermentation which followed his observations on the fermentation of wine was pertinent to the physiology of digestion.[4] The action of saliva was ignored in the presentation of the several stages in digestion. The acidity alone was not believed to be capable of digestion; a ferment was required.[3]

> . . . if a *ferment* should consist in soureness; Vinegar, Oyl of *Vitriol*, and the like, should *ferment* the lump of bread, and should digest our meats by a perfect transmutation: but they do neither of these; Therefore the *ferment* is a free Secret, and vital, and therefore it everywhere co-fitteth to it self a retaining quality in its own Borders: Because, seeing *ferments* are of the rank of formal and seminal things, therefore they have also severed themselves plainly from the society of material qualities: But if they have associated unto them a corporeal ministring quality, whereby they may the more easily disperse their own vital strength; account that to be done for a help; and so it cannot but contain a duality with the Ferment: And therefore also, that quality may offend, as well in its excessive, as in its diminished degree.

The second stage of digestion was the neutralization of the acidity of the stomach with the alkalinity of the duodenum. It was assumed that bile was transported from the glallbladder in the third stage. The fourth and fifth stages were merely speculations about phenomena in the heart and blood vessels. The sixth stage of digestion, according to van Helmont, was consummated in the tissues.

1. Foster, M.: *Lectures on the History of Physiology*, Cambridge: University Press, 1924.
2. Van Helmont, F. M.: *Ortus Medicinae*, Amsterdam: L. Elzevirium, 1648.
3. Van Helmont, J. B.: *Oriatrike or, Physick Refined*, J. C. Sometime, trans., London: L. Loyd, 1662.
4. Pagel, W.: Van Helmont's Ideas on Gastric Digestion and the Gastric Acid, *Bull Hist Med* 30:524-536, 1956.

Stemma of Harvey in Padua

William Harvey (1578-1657)

THE GALENIC CONCEPT of the ebb and flow of blood within closed arterial and venous systems had been generally accepted by philosophers and scientists without serious challenge for 14 centuries when William Harvey was born at Folkestone, Kent, into a world in ferment.[1] The son of a yeoman, he received his preliminary education in Greek and Latin in King's School, Canterbury. In 1593, he entered Caius College, Cambridge, where dissection was allowed on cadavers of criminals. Harvey graduated AB in 1597 and, in seeking further training, travelled through France and Germany to Padua. In 1602, Harvey received the doctorate in arts and medicine with special commendation, a common honor at Padu not necessarily denoting outstanding intellectual performance.

Harvey then returned to London, receiving the MD from the University of Cambridge. In 1604, he was admitted a candidate of the College of Physicians and in 1609 was appointed to the staff at St. Bartholomew's Hospital. Harvey served his College in various capacities; especially notable was the office of Lumleian lecturer on anatomy and surgery. The handwritten notes of the first course of lectures presented in 1616 contain his first public thoughts on the circulation of the blood from the heart through the lungs to the arteries and return through the veins. However, 12 years passed before the greatest treatise in the history of physiology was published, in Latin. This work disclosed the relatively complete argument on the lesser and greater circulation of blood.

In this treatise, Harvey described the development of the physiological concepts based upon detailed observations of the anatomy and physiology of 80 species of animals, dissection of cadavers, the use of tight ligatures for compression of arteries, loose ligatures for compression of veins, and the first approximation of the volume of blood pumped by the heart in unit time. Harvey did not complete the circle, however, and neither observed nor described a capillary network. The following excerpts present the argument, the experimental observations, and the conclusions. The disclosure was contained in the Lumleian lecture of April 17, 1616, *Exercitatio anatomica de motu cordis et sanguinis in animalibus,*[2] and subsequently was published by a Frankfurt printer.[3]

The translation by Willis for the Sydenham Society in 1847 is the source of these excerpts.[3]

It is plain from the structure of the heart that the blood is passed continuously through the lungs to the aorta as by two clacks of a water bellows to raise water. It is shown by application of a ligature that the passage of blood is from the arteries into the veins. Whence it follows that the movement of the blood is constantly in a circle, and is brought about by the beat of the heart. It is a question, therefore, whether this is for the sake of nourishment or of heat, the blood cooled by warming the limbs, being in turn warmed by the heart.

When I first gave my mind to vivisections, as a means of discovering the motions and uses of the heart, and sought to discover these from actual inspection, and not from the writings of others, I found the task so truly arduous, so full of difficulties, that I was almost tempted to think, with Fracastorius, that the motion of the heart was only to be comprehended by God.

At length, and by using greater and daily diligence, having frequent recourse to vivisections, employing a variety of animals for the purpose, and collating numerous observations, I thought that I had attained to the truth, that I should extricate myself and escape from this labyrinth, and that I had discovered what I so much desired, both the motion and the use of the heart and arteries; . . .

At the moment the heart contracts, and when the breast is struck, when in short the organ is in its state of systole, the arteries are dilated, yield a pulse, and are in the state of diastole. In like manner, when the right ventricle contracts and propels its charge of blood, the arterial vein (the pulmonary artery) is distended at the same time with the other arteries of the body.

From these facts, it is manifest, in opposition to commonly received opinions, that the diastole of the arteries corresponds with the time of the heart's systole; and that the arteries are filled and distended by the blood forced into them by the contraction of the ventricles; the arteries, therefore, are distended, because they are filled like sacs or bladders, and are not filled because they expand like bellows.

There are, as it were, two motions going on together; one of the auricles, another of the ventricles; these by no means taking place simultaneously, but the motion of the auricles preceding, that of the heart itself following; the motion appearing to begin from the auricles and to extend to the ventricles.

First of all, the auricle contracts, and in the course of its contraction throws the blood, (which it contains in ample quantity as to the head of the veins, the store-house and cistern of the blood,) into the ventricle, which being filled, the heart raises itself straightway, makes all its fibres tense, contracts the ventricles, and performs a beat, by which beat it immediately sends the blood supplied to it by the auricle into the arteries; the right ventricle sending its charge into the lungs by the vessel which is called vena arteriosa, but which, in structure and function, and all things else, is an artery; the left ventricle sending its charge into the aorta, and through this by the arteries to the body at large.

The motion of the heart, then, is entirely of this description, and the one action of the heart is the transmission of the blood and its distribution, by means of the arteries, to the very extremities of the body; so that the pulse which we feel in the arteries is nothing more than the impulse of the blood derived from the heart. . . .

In this way, therefore, it may be said that the right ventricle is made for the sake of the lungs, and for the transmission of the blood through them, not for their nutrition. . . .

I began to think whether there might not be A MOTION, AS IT WERE, IN A CIRCLE. Now this I afterwards found to be true; and I finally saw that the blood, forced by the action of the left ventricle into the arteries, was distributed to the body at large, and its several parts, in the same manner as it is sent through the lungs.

These points proved, I conceive it will be manifest that the blood circulates, revolves, propelled and then returning, from the heart to the exremities to the heart, and thus that it performs a kind of circular motion.

. . . . and is in a state of ceaseless motion; that this is the act or function which the heart performs by means of its pulse; and that it is the sole and only end of the motion and contraction of the heart.

In the overshadowing greatness of *De motu cordis,* Harvey's treatise on embryology, *Exercitationes de generatione animalium* (1651),[4] deserves mention but not prime consideration. He formulated and possibly demonstrated the rudiments of epigenesis, clearly revealed later by Wolff and von Baer. Also it is frequently overlooked that Harvey was a successful practitioner of medicine and a private lecturer. In 1618, he was appointed physician extraordinary to James I and on the death of the monarch, his son, Charles I, appointed him physician-in-ordinary. In 1645, Harvey was elected to the honorary position of warden of Merton College at Oxford but held this position for only a year because of his loyalty to the king. Following the surrender of Oxford, Harvey retired from public life and gave his library and medical museum to the Royal College of Physicians. However, because of age and the infirmities from gouty arthritis, he did not accept the honor of the presidency when it was offered in 1654. His death was attributed to a cerebral hemorrhage. His name was perpetuated in many ways. Especially noteworthy are the Harveian lectures of the Royal College and the Harvey Society of New York, while his stemma can be seen high in the antrum in the old university building in Padua.

In a short presentation, a pragmatic offering is inevitable, without space to discuss or even to mention many of the important speculations or observations preceding his

discovery or the tremendous volume of literature about Harvey, which analyzes innumerable features of the science and philosophy of the times and which attribute to him varying degrees of credit. The conclusion of most historians, however, is that Harvey was one of the greatest physiologists of all time and probably the greatest physician in England in the 17th century.

1. Keynes, G.: *The Life of William Harvey,* Oxford: Clarendon Press, 1966.

2. Franklin, K. J.: *A Short History of Physiology,* London: J. Bale Sons & Danielsson, Ltd., 1933.

3. Harvey, W.: *Exercitatio de Motu Cordis et Sanguinis in Animalibus,* Frankfurt: W. Fitzer, 1628, in Willis, R. (trans.): *The Works of William Harvey,* M.D., London: Sydenham Society, 1847.

4. Harvey, W.: *Exercitationes de Generatione Animalium,* London: O. Pulleyn, 1651.

Composite by G. Bako

Gaspare Aselli (1581-1626)

GASPARE ASELLI, surgeon of Milan and descendant of an ancient noble family, was born in Cremona, Italy. After secondary schooling, he attended the University of Pavia, completed his medical training, and began the experimental study of anatomy and physiology in Milan, his principal home during his short professional life. The exceptions were service in the Spanish Army in Italy as head surgeon and the chair of anatomy and surgery in the Athenaeum of Pavia, to which he was appointed only a few months before his death.

Aselli's contributions, some in classical Latin, others in vulgar Latin, or in Italian, exemplified his curiosity and keenness of observations of natural phenomena. They included the study of poisonous drugs, fistula in ano, recurring calculi, and observations in surgery and therapeutics. He classified pharmacological agents of the period on the basis of clinical effects and collateral toxic actions. His observations on the lacteals in the mesentery of the dog, *De lactibus sive lacteis venis,* his only printed study, was published posthumously by his friends, Tadini and Settala.[2]

The original observations on the lacteals were made in Milan during an experimental study of visceral nerves. Upon examination of the network of white filaments in the mesentery of a dog in the postprandial state, Aselli assumed the cords were nervous tissue. Upon further investigation he found that they were conduits; and, when a white humour spurted from one of the larger filaments following laceration, he sensed the significance of his findings. However, when the experiment was repeated on a fasting animal, the results were negative. Aware of the alimentary state of the stomach in the first experiment, he concluded that the engorgement of the filaments was related to a recent meal. Aselli erred, however, in believing that the lymphatics led to the liver, the supposed central organ of circulation of his day. The misconception was not corrected until Jean Pecquet discovered the thoracic duct and showed that the receptaculum chyli received the products of digestion during nutrition. The discovery by Aselli culminated a dedicated scientific career and was more than a happenstance observation. The original report was illustrated with four colored woodcuts delightfully. The following translation was prepared by Michael Foster.[3]

On the 23rd of July of that year (1622) I had taken a dog in good condition and well fed, for a vivisection at the request of some of my friends, who very much wished to see the recurrent nerves. When I had finished this demonstration of the nerves, it seemed good to watch the movements of the diaphragm in the same operation. While I was attempting this, and and for that purpose had opened the abdomen and was pulling down with my hand the intestines and stomach gathered together into a mass, I suddenly beheld a great number of cords as it were, exceedingly thin and beautifully white, scattered over the whole of the mesentery and the intestine, and starting from almost innumerable beginnings. At first I did not delay, thinking them to be nerves. But presently I saw that I was mistaken in this since I noticed that the nerves belonging to the intestine were distinct from these cords, and wholly unlike them, and besides, were distributed quite separately from them. Wherefore struck by the novelty of the thing, I stood for some time silent while there came into my mind the various disputes, rich in personal quarrels no less than in words, taking place among anatomists concerning the mesaraic veins and their function. And by chance it happened that a few days before I had looked into a little book by Johannes Costaeus written about this very matter. When I gathered my wits together for the sake of experiment, having laid hold of a very sharp scalpel, I pricked one of these cords and indeed one of the largest of them. I had hardly touched it, when I saw a white liquid like milk or cream forthwith gush out. Seeing this, I could hardly restrain my delight, and turning to those who were standing by, to Alexander Tadinus, and more particularly to Senator Septalius, who was both a member of the great College of the Order of Physicians and, while I am writing this, the Medical Officer of Health, "Eureka" I exclaimed with Archimedes, and at the same time invited them to the interesting spectacle of such an unusual phenomenon. And they indeed were much struck with the novelty of the thing.

1. Donini, I.: In Memory of Gaspare Aselli, XVIIth Century Anatomist, *J Cardiov Surg* 6:562-566 (Nov-Dec) 1965.

2. Aselli, G.: *De Lactibus sive Lacteis Venis,* Milan: G. B. Bidelli, 1627.

3. Foster, M.: *Lectures on the History of Physiology,* Cambridge: University Press, 1901.

Composite by G. Bako

Jacobus Bontius (1592-1631)

JACOBUS BONTIUS, physician to the Netherlands East Indies, was born at Leyden, where his father, Gerardus Bontius, was professor of medicine in the liberal arts school associated with the university; his brothers also came to be distinguished members of the university faculty.[1] Jacobus graduated doctor of medicine in 1614 and practiced in Leyden until 1627, when he succumbed to the attractions of the East Indies. Prior to departing he became interested in botany and materia medica, interests maintained by the opportunities offered by the flora of the islands. After following a long and circuitous route, he eventually settled in Batavia, Java, his residence for the remaining years of a short life. During this time he studied the diseases indigenous to the tropics and described the native botanicals.

As a physician of great industry, he carried out several medical and official civic assignments under trying emotional and physical handicaps. His first wife died on the ocean voyage, his second wife died of cholera in Batavia, and his older son died from smallpox. He himself was attacked by beriberi, a disease for which he gave the first European description in his monograph, entitled *De medicina Indorum, Libri IV*. Also included were descriptions of cholera, dysentery, and yaws. The manuscript, finished in 1629, was published in 1642 by his brother, Willem, burgomaster of Leyden.[2] Several editions, with various arrangements of sections, were published in Latin, and an English translation appeared in 1769.[3]

The discussion by Bontius which followed the Galenical system—attributing disease to the pollution of air or water—also gave attention to nutritional factors, especially in the correction of some of the tropical disorders. In the first chapter on Diseases, several neurological symptoms associated with the dry form of beriberi are described. The wet form, which was to be treated by dietary measures, was mentioned in the discussion of dropsy. In the book of dialogues with Andreas Duraeus, a hospital surgeon acting as a naive foil, Bontius notes that wheat bread is preferred to rice; but if wheat is short in supply, white, cold rice is to be eaten, not hot rice. This is the only specific clue in the treatise that suggests a nutritional cause of beriberi (consummated by the identification and synthesis of thiamine in 1930 by R. R. Williams). The several excepts follow.[3]

The inhabitants of the East Indies are much afflicted with a troublesome disorder which they call the Beriberii (a word signifying a sheep). The disease has, probably, received this denomination on account that those who are seized with it, from a tottering of the knees, and a peculiar manner of walking, exhibit to the fancy a representation of the gait of that animal. It is a species of palsy, or rather a tremor: for, at the same time that it impairs the sensation of the feet and hands, and sometimes even of the whole body, it induces a trembling. The principal cause of this disease is a thick, viscid, pituitous humour, which seizes the nerves in the night, when people, after being fatigued by the heat of the day, unwarily throw off their bed-cloaths. It is more especially the product of a rainy season; and such is constantly the state of the weather in this climate from the beginning of November till May.

Among the chief symptoms of this disease, is a lassitude of the whole body. The motion and sensation, especially of the feet and hands, are languid and depraved; and, for the most part, a titillation is felt in these parts, similar to what seizes them in cold countries in the winter; but with this difference, that the sensation in the Barbiers is more painful. The speech is, sometimes, so much obstructed, that the patient can scarce pronounce a syllable articulately: which happened to myself in this disorder, when for a whole month my voice was so weak, that people, who sat close to me, could with difficulty understand what I spoke.

The cure of this disorder is generally very tedious; the humour being difficult to resolve. For the most part, however, it is not mortal, unless it seizes the muscles of the breast and thorax, and thereby stop respiration.

If the disorder is chronical and of long standing, nothing is more effectual than decoctions of china, sarsaparilla, and guaiac, which, by their mild and friendly warmth, attenuate the cold viscid humours, and discharge them by sweat and urine.

But if there should be a scarcity of wheat, then that rice is to be chosen which is the whitest, of a clear colour, and weighs heavy: and when baked, it ought always to be let cool before it is used. For experience evinces, that hot rice is not only hurtful to the stomach, but also to the brain and whole nervous system: and from the gross and dry vapours rising to the head from this aliment, the optic nerves are frequently so much obstructed as to induce a total blindness; of which disorder I have treated in my method of curing the diseases in India.

1. Scott, H. H.: *A History of Tropical Medicine*, 2 vol, Baltimore: Williams & Wilkins Co., 1939, pp 1012-1017.

2. Bontius, J.: *Of the Natural History and Medicaments of the East Indies* (L), Amsterdam, 1658, bound with Piso, G.: *Concerning Both the Natural History and Medicine of the Indies* (L), Amsterdam: L. & D. Elzevier, 1658.

3. Bontius, J.: *An Account of the Diseases, Natural History, and Medicines of the East Indies*, translated from Latin by a physician, London: T. Noteman, 1769.

Nicolaas Tulp (1593-1674)

MANY WHO ARE FAMILIAR with Rembrandt's masterpiece, the "Anatomy Lesson of Dr. Nicholas Tulp," may have overlooked the medical background and contributions of Dr. Tulp, the anatomy teacher and practicing physician of repute in Amsterdam, not an allegorical figure. As praelector in anatomy at the Surgeons' Guild, he conducted demonstrations in public anatomy in the

Theatrum Anatomicum. They were open to the profession and, by invitation, to lay persons. Thus, they were designed to entertain as well as instruct. Dissections were held

Composite by G. Bako

once a week, but only in mid-winter for obvious reasons. Although the Theatrum Anatomicum, where Tulp performed, can no longer be seen, one may naturally conclude it resembled the 17th century anatomical amphitheaters still extant in Uppsala and Padua.

It is believed that Rembrandt's famous painting was commissioned by the Surgeons' Guild as they had commissioned others on "Schools of Anatomy."[1] The selection of Tulp as the central figure may have been related to the physician-patient relationship enjoyed by Tulp and Rembrandt, but the evidence is not conclusive.[2] The spectators in the "Anatomy Lesson" have been identified as well as the cadaver, a criminal who had been hanged in 1631 for insolence. An anatomical error in the painting was detected by Spielmann.[3] The flexor sublimis digitorum arises medially from the elbow, not laterally as depicted. Since dissection in the 17th century probably did not begin with the arm and the hand, it is assumed that Rembrandt superimposed a dissected arm on the cadaver. Thus, while the "Anatomy Lesson" is one of the great paintings by Rembrandt, it is scarcely a true lesson in anatomy. Recently when the painting was cleaned, the signature of "Rembrandt, H.L., 1632" reappeared underneath numerous overlays.[4]

Nicholaas attended the University of Leyden Medical School and began his medical career at the age of 18. His inaugural dissertation discussed the relationship of body and soul.[2] As a practitioner of medicine as well as surgery, he soon attracted an extensive clientele. However, he was a civic-minded physician and served as a judge, treasurer, counsellor, mayor, and supervisor of orphans for his city.[5] At the age of 48, Tulp compiled a treatise in Latin on medical experiences and professional conclusions, entitled *Observationum medicarum libri tres, cum aeneis figuris.*[6] The first and second editions were dedicated to his son, a graduate of Leyden Medical School. A number of revisions were published in the subsequent half century. An English translation by Scolten in 1929, based on studies by Thyssen, contains a number of apt clinical observations. A case of cough, which persisted for at least 7 years, was attributed to the accidental swallowing of a hazelnut. During a heavy fit of coughing, the foreign body was expelled and the patient was relieved. Another patient had suffered a stab wound in a drunken brawl, followed by protrusion of a segment of lung. The extruded portion was excised and recovery was uneventful. A case of hydronephrosis of the kidney, with oliguria and anuria, was reported. Hyperhidrosis of long duration was identified as a hereditary malady. Under angina interna, he gave a vivid description of laryngeal diphtheria.

One of the oft-quoted clinical observations by Tulp was that of a young boy who sustained an injury to the left side of the skull followed by paralysis of the right side. Decussation of the nerve trunks described by Galen presumably had been overlooked, since Tulp queried the pathogenesis of the contralateral effect. Early drainage was recommended for empyema. Description of the vasa lactea in man and the ileocecal valve (valva Tulpii) were also his contributions.

The clinical findings in beriberi were original.[5]

Joost de Vogelaar, a young blood, very keen about travel, having satisfied himself to some extent with seeing the most important countries of the East, rested for a while on the coast of Chormandel. There the sun shines so powerfully, and the heat is so terrific that the foreigners, in order to avoid it and its awful consequences, are compelled for the greater part of the day to keep themselves in cold baths. These cold baths Joost de Vogelaar took by lying on deck and having pails of cold water poured over him. Because of this, he contracted a kind of lameness, which the Indians call "beri-beri" or "the lameness." The patient was transferred to Holland and was treated by Dr. Tulp, who diagnosed the disease as hemiplegia. . . . "He could manage to sit on a chair and could move to some extent; yea, he became aware in his paralyzed members of a wandering sensation, of that creeping feeling which is wont to be manifested when the vital forces begin to return to the nerves, and bring back health and strength."

Carcinoma of the bladder was observed postmortem by Tulp in a male who had been operated on for stones. Convalescence was complicated by a vesicorectal fistula. The patient died more than a decade after the operation. Upon opening the body:[7]

. . . we found the kidney on the right side not involved, but that on the left infected with pus and steatoma. And the most satisfactory cause for this overwhelming ill was a foul and irregular carcinoma surrounding the meatus on all sides and which descended a finger's breadth from the urinary bladder to the rectum, through which for ten years more or less urine had flowed with unbearable pain to his unhappy patient. In order that other sick people may not be forced to undergo such misfortunes, I advise the strongly desired lithotomy, and that in the future, whatever may be on hand, physicians take every care that the wounds made by them heal firmly.

1. De Lint, J. G.: *Great Painters and Their Works as Seen by a Doctor: I. Rembrandt,* The Hague: J. Philip Kruseman, 1930.

2. Goldwyn, R. M.: Nicholaas Tulp (1593-1647) *Med Hist* 5:270-276 (July) 1961.

3. Spielmann, M. H.: *The Iconography of Andreas Vesalius,* London: John Bale, Sons & Danielsson, Ltd., 1925, p. 116.

4. Heckscher, W. S.: *Rembrandt's Anatomy of Dr. Nicolaas Tulp,* New York: New York University Press, 1958.

5. Thyssen, E. H. M.: Nicolaas Tulp, A. Scolten, trans., *Med Life* 36:394-442 (Aug.) 1929.

6. Thyssen, E. H. M.: Nicolaas Tulp, *Med Life* 39: 317-328, 1932.

7. *Selected Readings in Pathology from Hippocrates to Virchow,* E. R. Long, ed., Springfield, Ill.: Charles C Thomas, 1929, pp. 69-70.

TAB·XVII·*Append.*

Johann Schultes (1595-1645)

JOHANN SCHULTES, one of the great German surgeons of the 17th century, illustrator and designer of instruments and bandages, is a familiar name in current hospital care for his description of the multiple-tailed, or the Scultetus binder. In keeping with the practice of his day, he titled his most famous treatise *Armamentarium Chirurgicum,* or the hardware of the surgeon, and signed it with the Latin derivation of his name, Joannis Sculteti. Johann was born at Ulm on the Danube and studied at Padua

under Fabricius ab Aquapendente and Adriaan van den Spieghel. He saw military service in the Thirty Years' War (1618-1648), and received a doctorate in medicine, surgery, and philosophy at Padua. He eventually settled in Ulm as the city physician, having practiced for a time in Padua and Vienna.

His *Armamentarium Chirurgicum,* edited by his nephew and namesake, Scultetus the Younger, was not published until several years after his death. The title was translated literally in the French edition, which appeared in 1672, as "L'Arcenal de Chirurgie de Iean Scultet."[1] It was "faithfully Englished" by E.B. in London in 1674. The treatise contains an account of surgical instruments, procedures for bandaging and splinting, a large number of operative procedures (including amputation of the breast), obstetrical delivery by forceps and passage of urethral sounds, case reports, and detailed illustrations. The title page is thoroughly descriptive.[2]

The Chyrurgeons Store-House: Furnished with Forty three TABLES Cut in BRASS, in which Are all sorts of INSTRUMENTS, both Antient and Modern; useful to the performance of all Manual Opperations, with an exact Description of every INSTRUMENT. Together with a hundred Choise OBSERVATIONS of famous CURES PERFORMED. With three Indexes. 1 of the INSTRUMENTS, 2 of CURES performed, and 3 of Things Remarkable.

The author's preface, which followed the dedication by Scultetus the Younger, discloses his faith in his Creator.[2]

That our first Parents were framed and Created by the Divine Power, in Perfection, strong in Body, blessed with an equal Temperament, Impregnated with a most pure flame of Life in the Oleaginous natural Moisture, and Absolute all manner of ways. . . . That in the State of Innocency they had power to Regulate their Bodyes without any fear of Death, and fully to restore, in the same goodness, their Radical Moisture, at any time wasted with heat; and to continue it even to immortality, if they had not been deceived by the Craftiness of the Serpent, and tasted of the forbidden Fruit, whereby they were afterwards obnoxious to death, and their Posterity like unto them.

Those also who lived before the Flood, and were not at so great a distance from their

Original, by the Holiness of their Life, and their Innocent and Simple Diet, taken only from Vegetables; some of them lived neer a thousand years, and other protracted, and extended their term of Life to many Ages; but after that, when Gluttony, and Intemperance provoked mens appetites, with divers sorts of Dishes, and the unlawful use of Venery did by degrees debilitate their Bodies, and exhaust their Spirits; the length of their days was very much shortened and their Lives were terminated in an hundred and twenty years:

But though many Diseases may [be] extirpated by the strength of Nature, alone, by the due observance of the six *Res non Naturales,* and the Alternate use of those two great helps, of Altering and Purging Medicines; yet there are some so obstinate as not to yield to any of these, or to be remedied any other way than by Chyrurgical Operations, by dividing what is united, by uniting what is disjoyned, and by extirpating what is superfluous, according to the true saying of *Hippocrates. Diseases which Medicines cure not, the Knife cureth; what the Knife cures not, Fire cureth; what the Fire cures not, they are to be esteemed uncurable.*

The Scultetus binder, usually applied today on the thorax or the abdomen, was shown in Table XXXVIII, Fig VI; its application on the lower leg was illustrated in Fig 1 and X, Table XXVII. The description that accompanies Table XVIII is the best reference.[2]

The length of the bands is divers, in respect of the variety of parts to be bound; upon the arm the length of the bands must be three cubits (by a cubit I understand the space from the top of the middle finger of the sick party, so far as the joint of the elbow); for the legs, they must be four cubits; for the shoulder, nine; for the thigh, twelve; and for the fingers, less by two fingers length. The bands, that beside their binding they may hinder inflammation, must be wet with sharp Wine and oil of Roses mingled together; because, being dry, they will not stick long fast together.

1. Scultet, I.: *L'Arcenal de Chirurgie de Iean Scultet,* F. Deboze, trans., Lyon: Antoine Galien, 1672.

2. Schultetus, J.: *The Chyrurgeons Store-House,* E. B., trans., London: J. Starker, 1674.

The House of Bartholinus

SEVENTEENTH CENTURY DANISH MEDICINE owes much to the Bartholin family.[1] Their contributions to anatomy and medicine were made at the beginning of the era when ducts, glands, and blood vessels were recognized as propelling conduits for body fluids, rather than as static tubes or reservoirs. The grandson, Casper II, is best remembered for the description of the duct of Bartholin, the larger and longer of the sublingual ducts, and of Bartholin's glands, two small reddish yellow bodies in the vestibular bulbs, one on either side of the vaginal orifice, known also as Duverney's glands or Tiedemann's glands.[2] The father, Thomas, is identified by Bartholin's anus, aditus ad aquaeductum cerebri. In-laws of Casper I included Olaus Wormius (Ole Worm), who described the bones within the sutures of the skull (Wormian bones), and Thomas Fincke, professor of medicine at Copenhagen. Olaus and Casper I married daughters of Fincke.

Caspar Bartholin, Primus
(1585-1629)

Casper I (1585-1629) was born at Malmo, now Swedish, but Danish at that time. He had his first teachers at the age of 3. At 11 he could deliver speeches in Latin and Greek. In his middle 20's he declined various professorships, which included philosophy at Basel, anatomy at Naples, and Greek at Montpellier. The amount of traveling that was possible in the 17th century seems fantastic. Each of the Bartholins knew Europe well from firsthand visiting. While Casper was on his tour of the Continent, he studied with Fabricius ab Aquapendente, of Padua, a teacher of Worm and Harvey.[3]

At the age of 28, Casper accepted the

chair of medicine at Copenhagen where he remained for 11 years. During a serious illness in 1624 caused by rheumatism and renal calculi, he pledged his life to theology if spared. He recovered and, in fulfillment of the vows, accepted the professorship of theology at Copenhagen, a chair which he held until his death at the age of 44. In addition to a great interest in medicine and theology, he reflected deeply upon astrology, philosophy, and metaphysics. Although his treatise *Anatomicae Institutiones* was a notable piece of writing, there is no anatomical structure associated with a Casper I eponym.

Thomas Bartholin (1616-1680), the second son of the first Casper, was born in Copenhagen, only a short time after Harvey's discovery of the circulation of blood. Like his father, he traveled over the Continent and studied at Leyden, Paris, Orleans, Montpellier, Padua, Rome, and Naples. The degree in medicine was granted at Basel in 1645. Having resisted offers to return to Copenhagen for several years, he acquiesced at last and accepted the chair of mathematics at the age of 31 and the professorship in anatomy the following year. Meanwhile, the treatise on anatomy, prepared by his father, was revised. The volume was so popular it enjoyed 4 editions. There were also many translations. During the years 1611-86, Bartholin's *Anatomy* appeared in 30 editions in Latin, French, English, German, Dutch, and Italian. Also, in 1658, he published the first Danish pharmacopeia entitled *Dispensatorium Hafniense*. In 1652, the thoracic duct in man was described, a structure which had been recognized in animals previously by Pecquet. Its association with lacteals had been described by Aselli in 1622. The observations on the thoracic duct were carried out on a Norwegian tailor who had died of pulmonary tuberculosis.[4] In 1654, Thomas extended his observations to include the lymphatic vessels. The Copenhagen faculty of medicine at that time had only two members. The senior professor was called *medicus primus,* the younger professor *medicus alter.* In 1656, Thomas Bartholin became *medicus primus* and in

this capacity was not obliged to teach anatomy, but he continued to do so until his health failed.[5]

Thomas Bartholin
(1616-1680)

Human dissection in Copenhagen prior to 1644 was drastically restricted. In that year it became a legal professional pursuit, with bodies of criminals provided by the Crown. For this the University built the Domus Anatomica, a rectangular amphitheatre with 4 tiers of seats. The walls were decorated with skeletons of animals. The King, with his royal box adjacent to the amphitheater, peeped at the dissections through specially concealed windows.

In addition to the studies in anatomy, Thomas described some of his cures in the practice of medicine.

When another displayed to me as a paralysis of the left side, I ordered that acquivit, which our people employ in place of brandy, with extract of the herb of paralysis abounding in our woods, be applied to his spine. I cured the commonly occurring pleurisies solely with a decoction of barley when the patients were adverse to venesection. I happily restored not a few bed-ridden scorbutics by means of our aquatic trefoil decocted in that old beer which we preserve in our cellars for its singular fragrance.

It is obvious that acquivit and Danish beer were endowed with recognized medical uses in the 17th century.

In recounting his medical travels, he described a hospital in southern Italy.

The Hospital of the Blessed Mary of the Annunciation was magnificent and splendid. All cases of fever were cared for on the lower floor and wounds on the upper, and there was a pleasant open space on the roof where those were admitted who were convalescent so that they might refresh themselves and become accustomed to the air. In the lowest part of the building to the right was a special room to receive the moribund and the noisy. . . . On the bed of each fever patient was affixed a stone tablet on which was noted daily when and how frequently he had received his medicine.

Just as his father had retired from medicine prematurely, Thomas abandoned academic life at the age of 47. This was related possibly to a recurring renal calculus, the familial affliction of the Bartholins. The remaining years of his life were devoted to literature and writing. He founded one of the oldest scientific periodicals, *Acta Medica et Philosophica Hafniensia, 1672-80*. Almost everything associated with Thomas—possessions, manuscripts, and memorabilia—was destroyed eventually by fire. This included the house where he lived as professor, the anatomical amphitheater where he worked, his place in the country to which he retired, his library, and the church in which he was buried. The description of the burning of his library was prepared as a dissertation for his sons in 1670 and has been translated only recently by O'Malley and published by the University of Kansas Libraries.[6] Thomas' library was destroyed accidentally in a century when the burning of books under religious or political persecution was a frequent occurrence.

My library paid the penalty to Vulcan for these things, but in one respect I am more fortunate because I, with no offensive impiety to God or to prince, saw the funeral pyre of my library; it contained nothing which was worthy of burning, no line had flowed from my pen which might wound God or offend the king or fail to instruct or to entertain the world.

The third Bartholin (Bartholin's duct and Bartholin's glands) in direct line was Casper Secundus (1655-1738). Under the influence of Swammerdam, this Casper described the vestibulovaginal glands. Up to this time it was believed that the ovaries secreted a seminal fluid, under sexual stimulus. Swammerdam denied that the discharge

Caspar Bartholin, Secundus
(1655-1738)

came from the ovaries. Casper showed that the secretion came from the vagina and uterus. Following the pattern of his father and grandfather, his life was not devoted exclusively to medicine. But unlike his forebears, his postmedicine years were dedicated to politics and public administration, the last member of the most famous medical family of Copenhagen.

1. Rhodes, P.: The Bartholin Family, *J. Obstet Gynaec Brit Emp* 64:741 (Oct.) 1957.
2. Hansen, E.: Thomas Bartholin, *Bull Sch Med Univ Maryland* 1:129 (Jan.) 1917.
3. Singer, C.: *Evolution of Anatomy*, New York: Alfred A. Knopf, 1925.
4. Garboe, A.: *Thomas Bartholin*, Copenhagen: Ejnar Munksgaard, 1950.
5. Skavlem, J. H.: Scientific Life of Thomas Bartholin, *Ann Med Hist* 3:67, 1921.
6. Bartholin, T.: *On the Burning of His Library and on Medical Travel*. C. D. O'Malley, trans., Lawrence, Kan.: University of Kansas Libraries, 1961.

René Descartes (1596-1650)

THE PROPONENTS of the Iatromathematical School, exemplified by Descartes, Borelli, Sanctorius, and others, regarded man as an earthly machine whose actions, directed by a rational soul, could be interpreted mathematically. The mathematical-physical laws which govern the universe also govern the human body. The time was the 17th century. Free thought was heresy to the theologians. The Inquisition continued to imprison and mutilate disbelievers and to ban or burn supposedly heretical books.

In this period of the Renaissance when the Church, Protestant and Papist alike, had sunk to a very low ebb, Descartes was born at La Haye, Touraine, France.

National Library of Medicine

From his mother, who died shortly after his birth, he inherited a dry cough and a pale complexion but sufficient property to make him financially independent. His delicate physique and inherited resources gave him the excuse and the opportunity to become a bedroom philosopher. It was his practice for many years to remain in bed late in the mornings where his mind was free from outside disturbances. By such uninterrupted deliberations he explored and revealed the fundamental concepts of mathematics and other disciplines that marked him as a genius. Philosophy, theology, physical astronomy, medicine, and psychology, as well as mathematics, were embraced by this agile mind and expressed in writing and discourse. But this was not unique, for in his day mathematicians sometimes were physicians, and physicians sometimes mathematicians. His interest in physical mathematics comes to us with such readily recognized expressions as Cartesian diver, Cartesian curve, Cartesian lens, Cartesian coordinates, Cartesian geometry, and Cartesian oval.

Although Descartes' contributions in mathematics surpassed those in medicine, he wrote the first textbook in physiology and advanced the concept of physiology of motion and sensation as Harvey, his contemporary, had revealed the concept of the circulation of blood. Furthermore, he popularized Harvey's epochal demonstration. Descartes reduced all physiology to physics. Locomotion, respiration, and digestion were treated as mechanical processes. Every organ of the body was compared to a machine; skeletal and muscular action was explained on the theory of levers; teeth were likened to a pair of shears, the chest to a bellows, and the stomach to a flask.[1]

At the age of 10, Descartes enrolled in the newly established Jesuit college of La Flèche, where his brilliance was prophetic of the profound expositions of his maturity. At 20, having graduated in law from the University of Poitiers, he was attracted to Paris—not for the purpose of dissipation of mind or body in the royal court life, where he was welcome—but to seek intellectual companionship among the natural scientists and philosophers. The cell of the Minim friar, Mersenne, his teacher at La Flèche, was a meeting place of the scholastics. The intellectual friendship with the friar continued throughout Descartes' life, irrespective of geographic separation or proximity.

In 1618, Descartes joined the army of Prince Maurice of Nassau (later Prince of Orange) as a volunteer. The first assignment was Holland, an asylum for those who fied before the Inquisitors. Shortly after Descartes' arrival, he had a chance meeting with Isaac Beeckman, an outstanding mathematician, and reported his discovery of analytic geometry, his great contribution to natural science:[2]

. . . an entirely new science which will allow of a general solution of all problems that can be proposed in any and every kind of quantity, continuous or discontinuous, each in accordance with its nature . . . so that almost nothing will remain to be discovered in geometry.

Some time after this initial meeting with Beeckman, Descartes joined the army of the Duke of Bavaria and was quartered during the winter at a remote camp on the Danube. Solitude provided the opportunity to define his views on physics. In a relatively short time, he rejected not only the most that he had learned about physics, but also other organized knowledge. His thinking and reasoning has been described as centrifugal.[2]

. . . he moved primarily outward from a firm central theoretical point, in diametrical contrast to thinkers like Francis Bacon or Isaac Newton. . . . The one set out from what he knew clearly, in order to find the cause of what he saw. The other set out from what he saw, in order to find the cause.

There are 3 contributions to medical science by Descartes worthy of note. These concern ophthalmology and the physiology of the eye, the energy of the heart, and the function of sensory and motor nerves. He constructed an experimental model for the study of the eye. The retina of an ox eye was removed and replaced with a transparent sheet. This permitted examination of the image cast upon it by an obect placed in front of the lens. The functioning of the iris, the ciliary muscle, binocular vision, optical illusions, and various forms of coordination and accommodation were described or illustrated in remarkable detail.

Although impressed with Harvey's work on the circulation of the blood, he was reluctant to accept all of the arguments. His doctrine of the action of cardiac muscle reflects more of the old and less of the new than many of his other treatises.[3]

You must know that the tissue of the heart contains in its pores one of those fires without light of which I spoke above, which makes it so hot, so ardent that no sooner does the blood enter into one or other of the two chambers or cavities which are in the heart, than it immediately expands and dilates, just as you would find the blood or the milk of an animal would do if you were to pour it drop by drop into a vessel which was very hot. And the fire which exists in the heart of the machine which I am describing serves no other purpose than that of expanding, heating and as it were subtilizing the blood which falls continually drop by drop, through the channel of the vena cava into the cavity of its right side, whence it is exhaled into the lung, and from the vein of the lung, which the anatomists call the vein-like artery, into the cavity of the other side, whence it is distributed over the whole body.

The tissue of the lung is so delicate and soft and always kept so fresh by the air breathed that so soon as the vapours of the blood which pass out from the right cavity of the heart enter into the artery which the anatomists call the artery-like vein, they are condensed and converted once more into blood, and then fall drop by drop into the left cavity of the heart, where if they entered without being condensed anew they would not be adequate to nourish the fire which exists there.

The differentiation of sensory and motor function of nerves is described.[3]

You see also that in each of these little tubes (nerves) there is a sort of marrow composed of a large number of exceedingly delicate threads starting from the proper substance of the brain. The ends of these threads terminate on the one hand at the internal surface of the brain looking towards the ventricles, and on the other hand in the skin or other tissues in which the tubes which hold them end. . . . Know then that a very large number of little threads like the above begin to separate all of them, the one from the other, at the internal surface of the brain where they take their origin, and spreading thence over all the rest of the body serve as organs of sense. . . . Through these pores the animal spirits which are in the ventricles immediately begin to make their way and thus pass into the nerves and so into the muscles which carry out in the machine of which we are speaking movements exactly like those to which we ourselves are incited when our senses are affected in the same way.

During his long residence in the Netherlands, he spent considerable time in dissection and theoretical speculation. The mechanical explanation of body action sought by Descartes and illustrated by a hypothetical model continues as a valuable concept in physiological research. The reflex blinking of the eyelids or the coordination of skeletal muscles in walking are examples. Although Descartes was inclined to sacrifice realistic anatomy to hypothetical anatomy, he was careful to point out that he was describing a hypothetical structure to imitate body functions.

The Cartesian philosophy included independent inquiry, the value of experimental evidence, and rejection of authority. Since the Church believed in an immobile earth, Descartes perjured his conscience to the extent that he rejected motion of the earth, but postulated the simile of a passenger in a stationary vehicle, carried along by the surrounding motion. It is not surprising that the theologians were deeply concerned over his intellectual expositions. If Descartes chose to reject the then current science and scholasticism, the next logical and easy step was to doubt the current faith. Although Holland was less subject to the unrelenting proscriptions of the Church, the Dutch Calvinists found him guilty of free thought. In 1643, a decree was passed which forbade propagation of the Cartesian philosophies in the schools and the publishing and sale of his books. But the authorities could not reach him, since he took refuge in his French nativity and enjoyed the protection of the Prince of Orange. Thirteen years after Descartes' death, everything that he had written was placed on the Index Librorum Prohibitorum.

One of his favorite pupils in Holland was Princess Elizabeth, daughter of the beautiful but notorious "Queen of Hearts." He was guilty of one misconception in regard to his princely pupil, and believed that persons "of exalted birth have naturally more exalted capacities than are given to their inferiors." Elizabeth became Abbess of the Herforden Convent, a haven for refugees of all religions. She sheltered the English Quakers, George Fox and William Penn. The second courtly association for Descartes was in Stockholm. Queen Christina, first upon the pretense of soliciting his opinions on love and hate and later because of her desire to have him close by at the court, invited him to come and live in Sweden. Christina, devoted to philosophers and scientists, expended lavishly on books and manuscripts, as had Catherine de Medici. She accomplished what no other person had been able to do. Instead of permittting Descartes to remain in bed until noon, she insisted that her instruction in philosophy begin at five o'clock in the morning. His weak lungs rebelled during that fateful winter in Stockholm, and he became a pulmonary invalid. He died before he reached his 54th birthday, a physician of the Renaissance, one of the great philosophers and mathematicians of all time.

1. Robinson, V.: *Pathfinders in Medicine,* 2nd ed., New York: Medical Life Press, 1929.
2. Crombie, A. C.: Descartes, *Sci Amer* 201:160 (Oct) 1959.
3. Foster, M.: *Lectures on the History of Physiology During the Sixteenth, Seventeenth and Eighteenth Centuries,* Cambridge, England: Cambridge University Press, 1901, p 260.

Royal College of Physicians

Francis Glisson (1597-1677)

FRANCIS GLISSON, regius professor of physic at Cambridge University, a founding member of the Royal Society, and president of the Royal College of Physicians of London, was born in Rampisham, Dorsetshire, the second of nine sons of William Glisson. Francis was in no haste to begin higher education and did not enter Gonville and Caius College, Cambridge, until the age of 20, several years later than many others of his day. He graduated MD at the age of 37. Although tardy in acquiring his professional training, he was not indolent, and within two years after graduation was appointed regius professor of medicine. The post was held *in absentia,* with limited teaching responsibilities, for more than 40 years, concomitant with a practice and a lectureship in London. The reading of anatomy at the College of Physicians in London and the attractions of the city were preferred to the modest academic responsibilities in Cambridge.

Glisson's scientific contributions include one of the first accounts of infantile rickets, a description of the capsule of the liver, plethysmographic experiments on the volume of the arm during contraction of the muscles, and the introduction of the concept of "irritability" of tissue as illustrated by the response of the intestines. The treatise on rickets is his best-known scientific effort, one of the earliest descriptions of a disease entity.[1] The term "rickets" was first used about 1625 and appears as a cause of death in a 1634 Bill of Mortality.[2] Although the morbid process did not appear *de novo* in England (it was prevalent in Roman days and was described but not named by Soranus of Ephesus), rickets is closely identified with the first years of the 17th century. In 1645, Daniel Whistler presented his inaugural dissertation on the malady and introduced the terrible term "paedosplanchnosteocaces" as the scientific appellation.[3] With Whistler's dissertation appearing in 1645 and Glisson's report in 1650, disputes over priority were to be expected. Admirers of each advanced arguments for their favorite physician.[2] Whistler was at some disadvantage in later years since his reputation was under a shadow because of unexplained difficulties with accounts while serving as treasurer of the Royal College of Physicians. There is every evidence, however, that Whistler was a respected member of the medical community, in spite of alleged lapses of financial integrity.

In the year that Whistler's inaugural dissertation was published, Glisson and seven associates agreed to present a monograph of the clinicopathological aspects of the disease. It is clear that Glisson was the leader of the group assembled to investigate the alarming increase in the incidence of the disease. As the clinical observations were being assembled, five of the original eight let full responsibility pass to Glisson, and two associates bowed out by default except for final review of the manuscript. The first edition of *De Rachitide* was prepared in Latin in 1650. An English translation by Armin appeared the following year,[1] and other editions and translations followed.

The clinical description is comprehensive; the pathogenesis which seemed satisfactory at the time was thought to be associated with unequal nourishment of segments of bone to account for the deformities so characteristic of the disease.[1]

. . . the Diagnostical Signs . . . are these.

First, A certain laxity and softness, if not a flaccidity of all the first affected parts . . . the musculous flesh is less rigid and firm; the joynts are easily flexible, and many times unable to sustain the body. Whereupon the Body being erected it is bent forwards or backwards, or to the right side or to the left.

. . . this debility beginneth from the very first rudiments of the Disease. For if Children be infested within the first year of their age or thereabouts, they go upon their feet later by reason of that weakness, and for the most part they speak before they walk, which amongst us English men, is vulgarly held to be a bad *Omen*. But if they be afflicted with this Disease, after they have begun to walk, by degrees they stand more and more feebly upon their legs, and they often stagger as they are going, and stumble upon every slight occasion; neither are they able to sustain themselves long upon their legs without sitting, or to move and play up and down with an unusual alacrity, till they have rested. Lastly, upon a vehement increase of the Disease they totally lose the use of their feet; yea, they can scarce sit with an erected posture, and the weak and feeble Neck doth scarcely, or not at all sustain the burthen of the Head.

Of how great moment the *Alogotrophy*, or unequal Nourishment of the Parts is in this affect, we have already shewed; . . . there appeareth the unusual bigness of the Head, and the fulness and lively complexion of the Face, compared with the other parts of the body.

. . . Certain swellings and knotty excrescences, about some of the joynts are observed in this affect; these are chiefly conspicuous in the Wrists, and somewhat less in the Ankles. The like Tumors also are in the tops of the Ribs where they are conjoyned with gristles in the Breast.

. . . Some bones wax crooked, especially the Bones called the Shank-bone, and the Fibula or the small Bone in the Leg, then afterwards the greater Shank-bone, and the undermost and lesser of the two long Bones of the Elbow, . . . From hence it comes to pass that some Children long afflicted with this Disease become Dwarfs.

. . . the Teeth come forth both slowly and with trouble, they grow loose upon every slight occasion, sometimes they wax black, and even fall out by pieces.

. . . The Breast in the higher progression of the Disease, becomes narrow on the sides, and sticking up fore-right, so that it may not be unaptly compared to the Keel of a Ship inverted, or the Breast of a Hen or Capon.

The monograph contains chapters on treatment and descriptions of orthopedic devices for correction of rachitic deformities. One especially, "Glisson's sling," contributed to his reputation as an orthopedic surgeon.[4]

Secondly, the artificial suspension of the body is performed by the help of an instrument cunningly made with swathing bands, first crossing the breast and coming under the arm-pits, then above the head and under the chin, and then receiving the hands by two handles, so that it is a pleasure to see the child hanging pendulous in the air, and moved to and fro by the spectators. This kind of exercise is thought to be many ways conducible in this affect, for it helpeth to restore the crooked bones, to erect the bended joynts, and to lengthen the short stature of the body. Moreover, it exciteth the vital heat and withal allureth a plentiful distribution of the Nourishment to the external and first affected parts: and in the meantime it is rather a pleasure than a trouble to the child.

Glisson's capsule, the capsule of the liver, was described from anatomical studies on the ox, which included, in addition, the portal vessels, the biliary tract, and the detection of biliary calculi in the radicles. Since the observations were based upon close inspection with the unaided eye, he failed to appreciate that the liver was a secretory organ. Although others had observed the capsule of the liver, Glisson is credited with its discovery as described in *Anatomia hepatis*.[5]

Moreover peculiar swellings are found in the biliary tract; in which it may happen that its tunic appears six times thicker than normal, its substance withers, and becomes less firm, & dissected becomes quite like a kind of soft cheese. These kinds of swellings are often found in the excised liver (especially in the ox). Frequently in various parts of the branches a stone is present. . . . This stony substance, inside the vessels (in which it remains) looks like a pipe. . . . I have often seen in the livers of oxen, these sort of tubules, of such length, that (if they can be removed whole) they form many branches of the biliary tract with a continued series of stones (like corals): . . . These stones, which are found in the gall bladder, are clearly of the same kind as these & the shapes alone differ.

The concept of "irritability" as a specific property of all tissues was advanced in his *Tractatus de ventriculo et intestinis* (1677). The phenomenon was not accepted generally until Haller offered experimental proof a century later. An important experiment in muscle physiology by means of a plethysmograph refuted the prevalent theory that muscles were inflated not deflated during contraction.[6]

Let there be provided a Glass Tube, in Length and Bore capacious enough to hold a Man's Arm, and to the upper Orifice of it on the Outside affix another Tube of Glass about an Inch Diameter in Bore, shaped like a common Weather-glass, only with a wide Mouth like a Funnel; so as the Lower-end may open into the greater Tube whose Bottom is firmly stopt: Then having erected both Tubes, let a Man of strong and brawny muscles thrust his whole naked Arm into the greater Tube up to the very Shoulder, about which the Orifice of the Glass must be closely luted, that no Water may flow out that way. This done, let as much Water be poured in by the Tunnel as both Glasses will receive, leaving only a little Space at the Top of the lesser, empty. In fine, let the Man strongly contract all the Muscles of his Arm by clinching his Fist, and relax them again by Turns; and you shall observe, that when he contracts his Muscles, the Water in the less Tube will sink somewhat lower, but rise again when he relaxes them: Whence it is evident, that the Muscles do not swell up, nor are inflated at the time of their Contraction, but rather are lessened and contracted in all their three Dimensions; otherwise the Water would at that time, not descend, but ascend in the Neck of the Funnel.

The impetus for the founding of the Royal Society was evident in 1645 when a small group of physicians conducted weekly meetings in London "for the purpose of promoting enquiries into natural and experimental philosophy."[7] After the Restoration, the medical group which claimed Glisson as a charter member was incorporated. In addition to his works on anatomy, physiology, orthopedics, and clinical medicine, he also prepared a treatise on natural philosophy. The depths of Aristotelian philosophy were explored in a system and manner which went out of fashion in the following century, according to Aikin:[7]

He was one of the first of that group of English anatomists, who, incited by the great example of Harvey, pursued their enquiries into the human structure, as it were in concert, and with more ardour and success than their countrymen ever since that period have done.

1. Glisson, F.: *De Rachitide, sive Morbo Puerili*, 2nd ed, P. Armin, trans., London: J. Streater, 1668.
2. Clarke, E.: Whistler and Glisson on Rickets, *Bull Hist Med* 36:45-61 (Jan-Feb) 1962.
3. Whistler, D.: *De Morbo Puerili Anglorum*, Leyden: W. C. Boxius, 1645.
4. Little, E. M.: Glisson as an Orthopaedic Surgeon, *Proc Roy Soc Med* 19:111-122 (Feb 17) 1926.
5. Glisson, F.: "Anatomia Hepatis," London: O. Pullein, 1654, in Major, R. H.: *Classic Descriptions of Disease*, Springfield, Ill.: Charles C Thomas, 1932, p 609.
6. Glisson, F.: "Tractatus de Ventriculo et Intestinis," London: Henry Brome, 1677, in Fulton, J. F.: *Selected Readings in the History of Physiology*, Springfield, Ill.: Charles C Thomas, 1930, p 202.
7. Aikin, J.: *Biographical Memoirs of Medicine in Great Britain from the Revival of Literature to the Time of Harvey*, London: J. Johnson, 1780.

Composite by G. Bako

Daniel Whistler (1619-1684)

WHETHER OR NOT DANIEL WHISTLER is worthy of premier accolade for his treatise on clinical rickets, one must not deny him credit for his comprehensive description of the disease. His monograph on the subject appeared five years prior to the publication of the dissertation edited by Francis Glisson, a more distinguished contemporary.

Whistler was born at Walthamstow in Essex, was educated at the school of Thame, Oxfordshire, and entered Merton College, Oxford, in 1639.[1] He graduated AB in 1642 and later in the year studied medicine at the University of Leyden. Returning to Oxford for an AM degree in 1644, Whistler completed formal training at Leyden the following year, with the doctor of medicine degree. His inaugural dissertation, prepared in Latin, was entitled *De morbo puerili Anglorum, quem patrio idiomate indigenae vocant rickets*.[2] This is his only published work and was the earliest written account of a group of symptoms and findings assumed to constitute a disease entity.

Whistler returned to England and in 1647 received a second doctor's degree from Oxford. Shortly after, he proceeded to London and accepted the professorship of geometry at Gresham College, holding meanwhile the Linacre readership at Oxford. In the pursuit of practice he became a candidate in the College of Physicians, was accepted as a Fellow in 1649, and over the years served in an impressive number of elected posts. Whistler delivered the Harveian oration in 1659, was Censor-Registrar for several years, treasurer for one year, and president the year before he died. The Royal Society elected him to fellowship in 1663.

The inauguration thesis on rickets contained descriptions of pertinent aspects of previous work but no original observations. The then available knowledge led Whistler to assign the Latin name, "Paedosplanchnosteocaces," to the disease entity. The treatise began with the diagnostic signs and physical findings, continued with the postmortem observations and proposed pathogenesis, and concluded with treatment. Excerpts are as follows.[3]

I admit that many symptoms, severely known to the ancients, make up the disease; but as a syndrome of those signs which together make up one pathognomonic whole, it was, to the best of my knowledge, unrecognized by them. It is said that is is some twenty-six years or thereabouts since it was first recognized in England, and its name, the rickets, is said to have been adopted from the surname of an empiric who first cured it. Others insist that the name arose as a country colloquialism from the neighbourhood around Dorchester, where those who have difficulty in inspiring (as frequently happens to sufferers from this disease) are in the idiom of the place said 'to rucket." However, on the subject of the name I won't litigate further and let it be correct only in Britain to give a native word the right of Latin citizenship—on this occasion let the infant disease of infants (with me as its godfather) bear the name of Paedosplanchnosteocaces.

III.
DIAGNOSTIC SIGNS

In listing the diagnostic signs I had rather say too much than too little.

1. In the first place, we may note an unnatural tenseness of the hypochondriac regions, or an abnormal swelling of the abdomen, with some hardness, especially on the right, below the region of the liver.

2. The epiphyses of the joints then swell up to a huge size for their age, sometimes out of all proportion to the growth of the rest of the body. This is particularly the case with those of the arms and feet—from which more notable symptom some dignify the complaint with the name Paedarthrocaces and Paedarthroncias.

3. Nodular swellings also grow from the sides of the chest at the costo-chondral junctions.

4. Furthermore, the whole bony structure is as flexible as softened wax, so that the flaccid and enervated legs can hardly support the superposed weight of the body; hence the tibiae, giving way beneath the overpowering weight of the frame, bend inwards; and for the same reason the legs are drawn together at their tops; and the back, by reason of the bending of the spine, sticks out in a hump in the lumbar region, so that, since the patients in their weakness cannot (in the more severe stages of the disease) bear to sit upright, much less stand, some people call the complaint Paedosteocaces. . . .

7. The teeth are cut later and with more trouble than they should be; and more often than not, decay when they have appeared.

8. These signs are generally accompanied by a narrow chest and a sharp and sometimes displaced sternum; sometimes the whole sternum, particularly the cartilaginous part, is depressed and inverted towards the bony margins of the ribs—which it early almost touches.

Whistler was an immensely popular individual in London, a friend of Samuel Pepys, John Evelyn, Oliver Cromwell, Robert Hooke, and other notables. In spite of his marriage to a widow of financial means, in his later days, he seems to have fallen into evil ways with money. He sank deeper into personal debt and was lax in the management of funds of the College of Physicians. His will, drawn the day before his death, bequeathed his books, collection of manuscripts, and a portion of his estate to the College. Whistler was buried at night in secret for fear that his creditors would seize his body for his debts. Such unfortunate events may have contributed to attempts by responsible biographers to lessen the importance of his inaugural dissertation in favor of the thesis *De rachitide* by Glisson, prepared by a group of accomplished practitioners and frequently recognized as the preferred, early description of infantile rickets.[4]

1. Moore, N.: "Daniel Whistler," in *Dictionary of National Biography*, London: Oxford University Press, 1959-1960, vol 21, p 9.
2. Whistler, D.: *On the Children's Disease of the English, Which the Inhabitants Idiomatically Call the Rickets* (L), Leyden, Holland: W. C. Boxii, 1645.
3. Smerdon, G. T.: Daniel Whistler and the English Disease, a Translation and Biographical Note, *J Hist Med* 5:397-415, 1950.
4. Still, G. F.: *The History of Pediatrics*, London: Oxford University Press, 1931.

Composite by G. Bako

Athanasius Kircher (1602-1680)

ATHANASIUS KIRCHER has been praised by some as one of the earliest microscopists to cast a suspicious eye upon microorganisms as the cause of infectious diseases,[1] and damned by others as a dilettante in science.[2] Some of his writings in mid-17th century Latin have been repeatedly and carefully translated for anyone interested in forming a judgment; other writings remain untranslated. It is believed that inspection of his words will defend rather than deny the originality and significance of his observations and constructive imagination.

Kircher was born near Fulda in the Grand Duchy of Saxe-Weimar, a predominantly Catholic community.[3] He studied Latin and music in the local school and later added Greek, Hebrew, and some science at the Jesuit college at Fulda. His novitiate in the Society of Jesus began at the age of 16. In the next decade his scholarly pursuits embraced philosophy, theology, logic, Oriental languages, and the natural sciences. During three years of probation as a priest at Speier, he first became acquainted with Egyptian hieroglyphics which,

in subsequent years, he repeatedly tried to decipher. His first teaching assignment was in the Jesuit University at Würzburg and included mathematics, moral philosophy, Hebrew, and Syrian. Then he began a series of scientific and cultural treatises so numerous that some doubt must be cast upon his depth of treatment inasmuch as he continued as professor until his death. Acting upon a prophetic insight, he abandoned Würzburg for Avignon just ahead of the Swedish invasion. In 1634, he became mathematics professor at the College of Rome and subsequently a friend of three successive Popes.

More than 40 works, many of them weighty tomes, are listed in his bibliography. Major tracts included discussions on magnetism, light, music, the geography of the environs of Rome, volcanology, sun dials, astronomy, harmony and discord, optics, acoustics, history, and Egyptian hieroglyphics—all in addition to his theological and philosophical works and miscellaneous communications. Since Kircher was not a physician, it is not surprising to find the priest in his autobiography attributing less importance than his successors to his revelations with the microscope and the pronouncements on the contagion of the plague. With a simple magnifying glass, he observed micro-life in putrefied meat and described minutiae in the blood of those dead from the plague. The findings are thought by some to refer only to blood corpuscles; others consider it remotely possible that he saw the bacillus *Pasteurella pestis*. However, the power of his magnifying glass remains a matter of conjecture, and no illustrations were made of these observations. In contrast, it has been noted that van Leeuwenhoek 20 years later provided suitable documentary evidence of his microscopic findings.

Kircher's *Scrutinium physico-medicum* appeared in 1658, was reprinted in Latin in 1659, and was translated into German by Lange. The lengthy communication contains the report of a series of experiments in which he used a microscope that magnified "a thousandfold or thirty-six diameters." The description of microscopic life on putrefied meat has been translated into English as follows.[4]

EXPERIMENT I. Take a piece of meat, and at night leave it exposed to the lunar moisture until dawn of the following day. Then examine it carefully with the microscope and you will find that all the putridity drawn from the moon (caused by the moon) has been transformed into numberless little worms of different sizes, which in the absence of the microscope you will be unable to detect, no matter how sharp sighted, with the exception of those which have grown to such a size as to become visible. You will have the same experience with cheese, milk, vinegar, and similar substances undergoing putrefaction. However, you must not suppose the miscroscope to be an ordinary one; but highly wrought by a careful and practised hand; such as mine is which represents objects a thousand times larger than they really are.

Continuing the development of his argument, Kircher was more concerned about the origin of living creatures from putrefying substances than their uniformity of shape and size. Although he may have advanced science little or not at all by these observations—and the infectious nature of disease had been alluded to for centuries—his thoughts on contagion as the cause of infectious disease are worthy of recounting. The title summarizes the substance of his thesis.[3]

A Physico-Medical Examination of the Contagious Pestilence Called the Plague, in Which are Brought to Light, Through a New Teaching, the Origin, Causes, Symptoms and Signs of the Plague, Together with Suitable Remedies, as Well as Unusual Events of a Malign Nature, Which, Through the Strength and Power of Celestial Influences Are Manifested at Regular Intervals, Now in the Elements, Now in the Epidemic Diseases of Men and Animals.

The title of chapter VIII notes:[4]

That the effluvia ANIMATA are composed of invisible living corpuscles is evident from the multitude of worms that are wont to swarm out of the same bodies. Some grow large enough to be seen; others remain invisible. In number they equal the corpuscles, or particles, composing the effluvium—which indeed are beyond number. Since they are exceedingly subtle, tenous and light, they are agitated, like atoms (atomi) by the least breath of air; but since they have a certain viscosity and glutinous tenacity, they insinuate themselves very easily into the inmost fibers of clothing, cords and linen stuffs; in fact, by virtue of their subtlety, they penetrate any porous

material, such as wood, bone, cork, nay, even metals; and there they bring forth new seminaria of contagion; and inasmuch as their substance is extremely tenuous, they live for a very long time merely on the moisture which comes to them from without.

The above excerpts, taken out of context, present the observations and thoughts of the Jesuit priest in their most favorable setting. Kircher did not pose as a physician or a biologist, although he made some excursions into the medical science of his day. Perhaps the inclusion of his writings in the history of the development of the doctrine of contagion is justified, if for no other reason than he was one who skirted the periphery and became a proponent of a useful generalization without affecting future scientific growth.

1. Major, R. H.: Athanasius Kircher, Ann Med Hist 1:105-120 (March) 1939.
2. Dobell, C.: Antony van Leeuwenhoek and His "Little Animals," New York: Dover Publications, Inc., 1932.
3. Torrey, H. B.: Athanasius Kircher and the Progress of Medicine, Osiris 4:246-275, 1938.
4. Kircher, A.: Scrutinium Physico-Medicum Contagiosae Luis, Quae Dictur Pestis, Lipsig: Haered, 1659, excerpts translated in Torrey.[3]

National Portrait Gallery, London

Sir Thomas Browne (1605-1682)

SIR THOMAS BROWNE, one of the great writers of English literature who belonged to the medical profession, was born in the first decade of the 17th century. This was a period of English history when mysticism, astrology, witchcraft, and the appeal of ancient writings were under critical scrutiny. Scientific inquiry was beginning to replace superstition and fantasy. The Church and State were deeply involved and were waiting for leaders to direct the course of civilization. Anglicans, Puritans, and Catholics rallied their supporters in religion as did the Cromwellians and the Royalists in political affairs. *Religio Medici, A Letter to a Friend, Vulgar Errors, and Christian Morals*[1] is the best-known work of the physician who was born in 1605, three years before the birth of Milton and 11 years before William Harvey discussed the circulation of blood. The first unauthorized edition of *Religio Medici* was published in 1642, the year Galileo died. The faith of a physician expounded by Browne in his masterpiece, *Religio medici,* written when he was only 30 years of age, has survived for more than 3 centuries. The simple essays have great appeal for those interested in good literature and the philosophy of a practicing physician.

Browne was born in Cheapside, London.[2] His parents were judged to be financially comfortable. The family ancestry could be traced to the Norman kings. At the age of 18, Browne entered Oxford where he studied for 6 years. Following this he practiced medicine for a time and then visited and studied in the great medical centers on the Continent. Montpellier, France, was his first choice, although its glory was on the decline, then Padua. His first Doctorate of Medicine was awarded in Leyden in Holland. A painting by Rembrandt entitled "The Lesson in Anatomy of Dr. John Deyman" portrays a student that bears a striking likeness to the portrait of Thomas Browne.

The record does not reveal whether Browne listened to Rabelais at Montpellier. It was disclosed in his tract *Of Languages,* however, that "Without some knowledge therein you cannot exactly understand the Works of Rabelais." Browne returned to England and resumed the practice of medicine first at Yorkshire and later at Norwich. Such a tour of duty was required before presentation for the Doctorate of Medicine at Oxford. *Religio Medici* was prepared in 1635. Apparently no attempt was made to publish the essays initially. The first unau-

thorized edition appeared 7 years later. Following the publication of *Religio Medici,* Coleridge honored him, Charles Lamb revered him, and Dr. Samuel Johnson wrote his biography (1756).[3] The simple, concise, religious tract was widely read, criticized, sometimes castigated. There were those who claimed that Browne was an atheist; others, a papist. In a world of religious and political turmoil, originality and candor were deeply appreciated. Browne pleaded for religious tolerance and the right of man to follow his own spiritual leanings. His interests, in addition to medicine and religion, included magnetism, embryology, numismatics, archaeology, music, astronomy, and agriculture.

One Samuel Duncon, a Norwich Quaker, wrote to Browne:

Haveing perused a booke of thyne called Religio Medici and . . . Judgeing thee juditious, I therewith send thee a booke to peruse; and if thou desire any personall conferrance with me, or any of my friends concernynge the principalls of our religion, (which we believe is the immortal religion, though generally accounted herisie) I shall indeaver it, in the same love I present this booke to thy vieue, who am a lover of mankinde in generall, and thyselfe in particuler.

Religio medici went through many English editions; it was translated into Latin, German, French, and Dutch. The publication of the tract led to the preparation of a number of books patterned after the original. Included were *De religione laici, Religio jurisconsulti, Religio stoici, Religio philosophi,* even *Religio clerici.*[4]

It was into such a milieu that *Religio Medici* had come, a forthright, chatty personal testimonial to a doctor's belief. The book displays a wide reading, ranging from the finest expression of the ancient Greek mind to the works of Browne's own contemporaries, and its style is enlivened by echoes of Rabelais, of Dante, of the early Church Fathers, and of the Elizabethans. It was written at a period when English prose was rich, flexible, and highly individualistic. It lent itself to the portrayal of the workings of an original and versatile mind. The suggestiveness and imaginative value of the metaphors, the copiousness of the longer passages, the zest, the élan, the search for the unusual, the bizarre phrases, the shock and violence of strong expressions, the rhetorical pomp, the quiet humor—all these contribute to the total effect. But the book's artistic greatness can be set forth more simply. Like all great human utterances, it is at once universal in its appeal, broad in its significance, expressive in its form, and unique in its individuality.

Stephen Paget exploited the title with his *Confessio medici.* Harvey Cushing entitled one of his monographs *Consecratio medici.* Sir William Osler, one of the staunchest admirers of Browne, carried an inexpensive edition of *Religio Medici* on his travels. This volume was placed in Osler's coffin as it lay in the chapel of Christ Church College, Oxford, as a symbol of his abiding love of literature and his lifetime devotion to the essays of the 17th century physician.

1. Browne, T.: *Religio Medici, Letter to a Friend &c. and Christian Morals,* edited by W. A. Greenhill, London: Macmillan & Co., Ltd., 1936.
2. Rolleston, H.: Sir Thomas Browne, M.D., *Ann Med Hist* 2:1 (Jan) 1930.
3. Wagley, M. F., and Wagley, P. F.: Comments on Samuel Johnson's Biography of Sir Thomas Browne, *Bull Hist Med* 31:318 (July-Aug) 1957.
4. Finch, J. S.: *Sir Thomas Browne: A Doctor's Life of Science and Faith,* New York: Henry Schuman, Inc., 1950.

Giovanni Alphonso Borelli (1608-1679)

BORELLI, STUDENT OF GALILEO and teacher of Malpighi, applied his knowledge of mathematics, chemistry, and physics to the explanation of physiological phenomena, such as respiration, digestion, and the secretion of urine, but especially, as described in *De motu animalium,* to the motion of animals and the coordinated action of flexor and extensor muscle groups.[1] A Neapolitan by birth, he studied mathematics at Rome under Castello. In his early 30's he was called to the University of Messina as professor of mathematics, where he prepared an account of the plague in Sicily. Later he filled a similar post at the University of Pisa at the prime period of the Medicis' promotions of the sciences and the arts. Although Borelli probably gave some attention to medical practice in each community, there is no record of apprenticeship and he de-

voted most of his talents to teaching mathematics and medical science. On the other hand, during retirement years, he was physician to ex-queen Christina of Sweden, who had chosen voluntary exile in Rome.

National Library of Medicine

The nonmedical subjects on which Borelli wrote included astronomy, the flight of birds, the parabolic path of planets, an apparatus for diving, and the eruption of Mt. Etna. His *De motu animalium* was published posthumously from observations which were assembled over a relatively long period of time and which were included in his lectures at Pisa. The scope of the discussion gives evidence of precise thinking and the correlation of the enlightened physics and mathematics of his day with the emerging physiology of Harvey and his successors. By applying an understanding of mechanics and physical principles to the interpretation of muscular action, animal movements were divided into the skeletal muscles of external movements and the visceral muscles of internal movements. The action of either group could be analyzed in relation to the mechanical principles of force and function and the changes within the muscle substance by which muscle movement is produced. The complex kinetics of standing, running, and walking were investigated by the application of the principles of mathematics and computation. Regarding the basis of muscular mechanics, the weak tonic contraction which a muscle exerts against its antagonist was distinguished from the strong voluntary contraction equivalent to heavy work.[2]

Although Nature is admirable in all her operations yet there is no one who is not in the highest degree astounded when he considers the immense force and energy of muscles, and sets about to understand more exactly the causes, organs and apparatus by which Nature carries out such a work.

Borelli, as had Stensen earlier, advanced the important fact that contraction was carried out by the muscle substance, while the fibers and tendons acted as passive and supportive structures. In developing a theory of muscular contraction, he erred in believing that contraction and hardening were caused not by a rearrangement of existing structure but by a substance found in the muscles or by a response to a substance transmitted along the nerve fibers. He accepted, however, the concept of irritability of muscle through nervous impulses.[2]

Since all muscles, with some few exceptions, do not manifest vital movement otherwise than in obedience to the will, since the commands of the will are not transmitted from the brain which is the instrument of the sensitive, and the seat of the motive soul, by any other channels than the nerves as all confess and as the most decided experiments shew, and since the action of any incorporeal agency or of spirituous gases must be rejected, it is clear that some corporeal substance must be transmitted along the nerves to the muscles or else some commotion must be communicated along some substance in the nerves, in such a way that a very powerful inflation can be brought about in the twinkling of an eye.
. . . it is evident that the substance or the influence which the nerves transmit is not taken by itself alone sufficient to bring about that inflation. It is necessary, therefore, that something else must be added, something which is to be found in the muscles themselves; or that in the muscles there is some adequate disposition of material so that on the arrival of the influence transmitted by the nerves there takes place something like a fermentation or ebullition by which the sudden inflation of the muscles is brought about.

Borelli was clear in his exposition of the mechanical force of ventricular systole effected by the spiral arrangement of the fibers of the ventricle, a logical extrapolation from Harvey's demonstration of the circulation of blood. He believed that the heart acted like a piston and calculated that the propulsive force of the heart was equal to the support of a weight of more than several thousand pounds.[2]

The true action of the muscle of the heart is the contraction of its ventricles, and the compression and expression of the blood contained in them is carried out after the manner of a winepress, and that not by the contortion of the spiral fibres of the heart but by their inflation and tension.

Considered by some as Borelli's most interesting work in mechanical forces of the heart is his treatment of resistance offered by the walls of the artery and the tissues surrounding them. He computed the proportionate blood flow through the splanchnic bed as 1/25 of the aortic flow on the basis of cross-section measurements of mesenteric arteries and celiac axis. The participation of the arteries in the cardiovascular phenomena was described as follows.[2]

The arteries are soft, distensible tubes full of blood, but as we have shewn not filled to extreme distension; and during each beat of the heart there is driven into them by the constriction of the heart, acting like a piston, a mass of blood sufficient to complete their distension or even more than sufficient, in which case the surplus is discharged beyond the arteries by the beat of the heart itself.

Two effects follow the beat of the heart, the filling of the arteries with the blood driven into them, and the exit of the same blood from the same arteries. Certainly these two events cannot take place at the same time; for the one consists in an expansion, the other in a constriction of the same arteries, and these two being opposed in nature cannot take place at the same time. Whence it must be that the filling of the arteries takes place first, and that their constriction and emptying follows afterwards.

1. Borelli, G. A.: De´motu animalium, Naples: Mosca, 1734.
2. Foster, M.: Lectures on the History of Physiology, Cambridge: University Press, 1901.

Composite by G. Bako

Nicholas Culpeper (1616-1654)

NICHOLAS CULPEPER, son of a clergyman, accomplished in a short life the preparation and translation of a prodigious number of texts on the treatment of disease, several of which were more popular in the home than as reference works in the physician's library.[1] In fact this stupendous outpouring of tracts outran the capacity of the presses and so found a number still unpublished at his death. Nicholas was born in London and studied at Cambridge, acquiring a good knowledge of Latin and Greek. After serving an apprenticeship to two apothecaries in succession, he established a practice in 1640 as a physician-astrologer in Red Lion Street, Spitalfields. During the civil war, he participated in at least one skirmish on the side of the Parliamentarians and received a battle wound.

The wrath of the professional hierarchy of London initially descended on Culpeper with his publication of an English translation in 1649 of the *Pharmacopoeia* of the College of Physicians. The Royal College had prevented general disclosure of their secret formulae by publishing in Latin. Cul-

peper, who was not a fellow of the College, probably considered his translation a righteous deed. In the third edition of *A Physical Directory; Or a Translation of the Dispensatory Made by the Colledg of Physitians of London, And by them imposed upon all the Apothecaries of England to make up their Medicines By,* he replied as follows to the castigation of the College.[2]

And now at last, (to let your Blasphemies and my own Medicines alone) I seriously advise you to consider what will become of your souls another day: How will you answer for the Lives of those poor people that have been lost, by your absconding Physick from them in their Mother Tongue? Are you a Colledg of Physitians or no? Do you know what belongs to your Duty or not? Wherefore did *K. Harry* the Eighth give you your Charter? to hide the knowledge of Physick from his Subjects yea, or no? Do you think you shal be called to an account for all you have done? I would have said for what you have left undone; Is not omission of good as great a sin as commission of evil? Look to it, look to it, For (as the Lord lives) I pity you, nay weep for you too: I tell you truly (and I am not ashamed of what I tell you) God hath given you what you desire, you are a Colledg of Physitians; You have Honor and Command, Learn to know yourselves; ... Do not think that I delight to oppose you; if you do, you are mistaken. Conscience dictated a few visions to my eyes, which were not supernatural: All the sick People in *England* presented themselves before me, and told me, They had Herbs in their Gardens that might cure them, but, knew not the Vertues of them: They praid me (for Gods sake, and as I would answer it another day) that I would help them; For the *Colledg of Physitians* were so *Proud,* so *Surly,* and so *Covetous,* that *Honesty went a begging in Amen-Corner, and could find no entertainment.*

As a physician-astrologer, Culpeper interpreted the influence of planets, stars, and comets on medicinals. Since astrology had been in vogue for centuries, even the revival of critical scientific inquiry during the Reformation could not immediately shake off its influences. It was not unusual for the alchemist and the physician to pay homage to astrology, as noted in another of his popular herbal treatises entitled, *The English Physician Enlarged With Three Hundred and Sixty-Nine Medicines, Made of English Herbs, That were not in any Impression until This. Being an Astrologo-Physical Dis-*

course of the Vulgar Herbs of this Nation, containing a complete Method of Physic, whereby a Man may preserve His Body in Health, or cure himself, being Sick, for Three-pence Charge, with such Things only as grow in England, The being Most fit for English Bodies.[3] In each category, the botanical, the place of growth, the time of year that it reaches maturity, and its preparation for use are described, concluding with the diseases for which it is of value. Almost any excerpt may be reproduced as an example. There were 39 herbs listed as useful in gout; in most instances, they were to be used as topical ointments. Pellitory of the Wall is described as useful for tussis, dyspnea, oliguria, ulcer, calculus, alopecia, hemorrhoids, and gout.[3]

It is under the dominion of Mercury. The dried herb Pellitory made up into an electuary with honey, or the juice of the herb, or the decoction thereof made up with sugar or honey, is a singular remedy for an old or dry cough, the shortness of breath, and wheezing in the throat. Three ounces of the juice thereof taken at a time, doth wonderfully help stopping of the urine, and to expel the stone or gravel in the kidneys or bladder, and is therefore usually put among other herbs used in clysters to mitigate pains in the back, sides, or bowels, proceeding of wind, stopping of urine, the gravel or stone, as aforesaid. . . . The said juice made into a liniment with ceruse, and oil of roses, and anointed therewith, cleanseth foul rotten ulcers, and stayeth spreading or creeping ulcers, and running scabs or sores in childrens heads; and helpeth to stay the hair from falling off the head: The said ointment, or the herb applied to the fundament, openeth the piles, and easeth their pains; and being mixed with goats tallow, helpeth the gout.

In explaining the influence of heavenly bodies on herbs and disease, Culpeper presented·his thesis of domination.[3]

What Planet causeth the disease; what part of the body is afflicted by Disease, and by what Planet the afflicted part of the Body is governed; as the Brain, by Herbs of Mercury; the Breast and Liver, by Herbs of Jupiter; the Heart and Vitals, by Herbs of the Sun, etc. Oppose diseases by Herbs of the Planet opposite to the planet that caused them—as, for instance, diseases of Jupiter, by herbs of Mercury, and the contrary; diseases of Mars, by Herbs of Venus, and the contrary. A way to cure Diseases by sympathy, and so, every Planet cures his own disease; as the Sun and Moon, by their herbs cure the eyes; Saturn the spleen; Jupiter the Liver; Mars the gall and diseases of Choller; and Venus, diseases in the instruments of Generation.

Although the combination of astrology and medicine was pure fantasy, Culpeper served medicine by translating several treatises from Latin into the vernacular, thereby making the texts available for those not schooled in the ancient language. (Two centuries were to elapse before English replaced Latin as the language of medical communication in England.) The titles of his pamphlets or texts included:[4] *A Treatise of Feavers in Generall, Anatomy, The Practice of Physick, A Sure Guide, or the Best and Nearest Way to Physick and Chyrurgery, A Treatise of the Pestilence, A Tractate of the Cure of Infants, Semeiotica Uranica, or an Astronomicall Judgment of Diseases,* based on Arabic and Greek writings, Galen's *Art of Physic,* and *A Directory for Midwives.* The first full-length book printed in the American colonies by John Allen for Nicholas Boone was the *Pharmacopoeia Londinensis; or, The London Dispensatory* of Culpeper, prepared for presentation in 1720.[5]

Rudyard Kipling composed a short story and a poem on Culpeper,[6] while *Punch* published an anonymous poem in 1929.[7]

NICHOLAS CULPEPER

There was a London doctor
    Who searched the starry skies
And gathered from the planets
    That poplar helped the eyes,
That clary took out splinters
    And borage cleansed the skin;
And borage grew at Deptford
    And clary by Gray's Inn.

He served his generation
    Till 1654,
Culling his easy simples
    Where we shall see no more;
But many a London doctor
    Would find a life pretty thin
If borage grew at Deptford
    And clary by Gray's Inn.

1. Chance, B.: Nicholas Culpeper, Gent: Student in Physick and Astrologie, *Ann Med Hist* n.s. 3:394-403, 1931.

2. Culpeper, N.: *A Physical Directory*, London: P. Cole, 1651.

3. Culpeper, N.: *The English Physician Enlarged,* London: J. Barker, 1653.

4. "Nicholas Culpeper," in *The Dictionary of National Biography,* vol 5, Oxford: University Press, 1959-1960.

5. Culpeper, N.: *Pharmacopoeia Londinensis; or, The London Dispensatory further Adorned by the Studies and Collections of the Fellows now living, of the said College,* Boston: printed by J. Allen for N. Boone, 1720.

6. Kipling, R.: *Rewards and Fairies,* New York: Charles Scribner's Sons, 1910.

7. Nicholas Culpeper, *Punch* 177:159, 1929.

Composite by G. Bako

Theophile Bonet (1620-1689)

THEOPHILE BONET, son and grandson of physicians, was born in Geneva, at that time a refuge for Protestants fleeing from religious persecution. Bonet visited several centers of learning before receiving the MD degree from Bologna in 1643 and returning to cosmopolitan Geneva.[1] He achieved immediate success in practice and, as physician to the Duc de Longueville at Neu-Chatel, gained financial and political security, enabling him to review in depth published postmortem protocols and to develop other scholarly pursuits. Meanwhile, he gained clinical experience at the bedside and recorded in minutia his observations of the sick. The inveterate practice of notetaking complemented his critical appraisal of ancient and contemporary works and led to an encyclopedic body of clinical and pathological material.

Bonet's interest in anatomy and his approach to the understanding of disease was a major break from tradition. Although Vesalius had challenged authority in anatomical dissection, Harvey had demonstrated the circulation of blood, and independence in theological thinking was infiltrating slowly from the North, the majority of those in a position to lead the medical thinking of the times were slow to accept new ideas. Bonet, however, gathered together the diverse pathological observations, classified diseases in relation to symptoms as far as possible, and developed a rational system of diagnosis and treatment.

Bonet's first book, *Pharos medicorum,* was published in 1668, shortly before he became deaf, which forced him to abandon clinical practice. He used the works of Ballonius as a model and rendered judgment on the writings of others. It is an early example of a compendium on the practice of medicine, a forerunner of his more extensive *Mercurius, A Guide to the Practical Physician* (1682), rendered into English in 1684. Shortly after, *Northern Medicine (Medicina septentrionalis collatitia)* appeared, which was planned to furnish physicians with reports from Danish, English, and German physicians during the two preceding decades. This was essentially a yearbook of medical practice compiled from reports sent to Bonet and included observations and recent discoveries in the basic sciences.

The following comments are taken from his *Guide to the Practical Physician.*[2]

Let a Physician be doubtful in his Prognostick, unless there be most certain and infallible signs of death: Let him be moderate in his promises: Yet let him always give hopes rather of Health, than foretel certain Death: For when the Patient is given over by the Physician, if he do recover afterwards (as he often does) either by chance or Nature, the Physican incurs Infamy. But if he gives hopes of Health, and Death does follow, the Disgrace is not so great; because many things might happen, Errors, Excesses, and some new Diseases, and the change from Health to Death is easier than from Death to Health, which by the course of Nature is impossible.

Frequent changing of Medicins argues either ignorance or diffidence in the Physician. This may be understood in a twofold sense, either as to Method, or as to Medicins. The first argues precipitance, and what the Physician is out of the way, because he knows not which the way is. . . . Nor are we always tied up to the self same things: for so the Physician may prescribe much, and the Patient take little.

Let him never prescribe two Medicins at once, and leave the Patient to his choice: Because then he is at a loss and can trust neither of them; but blames his Physician for Inconstancy.

Visits to Patients must not be too frequent nor too few. For too frequent visiting, where the Disease is but gentle, does argue either want of skill in a Physician, or Covetousness in extorting of Money. And too spare visiting in great Diseases does argue the same things and more than the frequency; namely either Covetousness, or ignorance of the greatness of the Disease, or Idleness.

Of the many treatises prepared by Bonet, the *Sepulchretum* (a monument not a burial vault), preceded by *Prodromus Anatomiae Practicae,* is his greatest work, the foundation upon which Morgagni built his *De Sedibus.* The first edition of *Sepulchretum,* prepared in 1679 after 30 years of practice, is 1700 pages long, contains references to more than 400 writers, and is based upon more than 3,000 postmortem protocols.[3] Each recorded disease from ancient to contemporary times was studied. The arrangement is in part alphabetic and in part anatomic. Book I relates to the head, Book II concerns the chest, Book III with disease of the abdominal cavity, diabetes, gonorrhea, hernia etc., and Book IV with fevers, tumors, fractures, gout, etc. The task of translation into English has never been accomplished.

1. Bayle and Thillaye: *Biographie Medicale* (Fr), Paris: A. Delahays, 1855, vol 1, pp 454-455.
2. Bonet, T.: *A Guide to the Practical Physician* (L), London: T. Flesher, 1684.
3. Bonet, T.: *Sepulchretum* (L), Geneva: L. Chouët, 1679.

National Library of Medicine

Johann Jacob Wepfer (1620-1695)

JOHANN JACOB WEPFER, son of the Canton councillor, was born at Schaffhausen, Switzerland, overlooking the Rhine.[1] He was noted for his identification of hemorrhagic extravasations in the cerebrum in patients stricken with apoplexy. Wepfer studied humanities and medicine at Basel and Strassburg and spent two years in Italy before he received the MD degree in 1647. Upon his return to Schaffhausen the authorities appointed him city physician and allowed him to perform postmortem examinations in recognition of his talents. He justified their confidence locally, developed an international practice, and served the Duke of Wirtemberg as personal and army physician. The Marquis de Dourlach, Charles, the Palatine, Elector and the army of Emperor Leopold also benefited from his clinical wisdom. Wepfer was temperate in food and drink; an intense desire for knowledge restricted his hours for sleep. He began the day with prayer and the reading of scripture in Greek or Latin.

Wepfer described from his postmortem experience the circular anastomosis of arteries at the base of the brain, later known as the circle of Willis. Also he postulated two causes of insufficiency of the cerebral vessels: intraluminal fibrous bodies and narrowing of the lumen. Other scientific works include the study of the effects of poisons, descriptions of findings from dissections of the wolf and eagles, and contributions in botany, zoology, and chemistry. His death was related to calcification of the aortic valves as disclosed by an autopsy performed at his request.

In formulating his deductions from the pathological findings and clinical symptoms of apoplexy, Wepfer rejected the unproved speculations of the ancients and instead developed a scientific approach admirable for his time. With the knowledge that the cerebrum was supplied by carotid and vertebral arteries, he correlated the clinical and postmortem findings in patients who had been deprived of speech alone when unilateral vessels only were involved. Also, in selected cases he found that massive hemorrhage within the substance of the brain scarcely interfered with normal function.

The first series of excerpts given below describe a case of apoplexy[2]; the second series present his findings on subdural hematoma.[3]

Johann Jakob Reiter of Kenzingen, Breisgau, a man about 45 years of age . . . assisted the most reverend abbott in performing the service in the morning, as was everyone's duty. When he had done this he withdrew to his chamber according to his habit; here by chance one of the servants went to call him and found him lying on the ground, deaf to all calls, a mere figure of a body, insensible to striking or pinching. . . . I saw him with a livid pallor, deprived of all senses and power of motion, excepting respiration. . . . At first the pulse was strong, full and rapid, then weaker, less full, and more frequent. The respiration also became more laborious, soon took place irregularly, and often seemed to stop. I omitted no kind of suitable remedy, but did not dare to open a vein because of the feebleness and shortness of respiration. In the tenth hour before the meridian the body was shaken by a peculiar motion, and a quantity of white, viscid, thick sputum issued from the mouth, but no blood came forth. From then on his vitality began to decrease more and more, and the extremities to grow colder. The first hour before the meridian of that day he died. . . . With the indulgence of the most reverend abbott, afore mentioned, a great patron of letters and all the fine arts, I opened the head. After I had removed the skullcap and cut away the dura mater, a great quantity of blood, which was copiously distributed in this space, flowed from the fairly large cavity between the dura mater and the leptomeninges. Nor was blood stagnating only around the base of the brain; it had reached to the vertex both anteriorly and posteriorly, and had insinuated itself into almost all the sulci of the brain. On exposing

the ventricles I found them also all filled with blood, not even excepting the fourth. The lateral ventricles, as if lacerated near the base, resembled fissures overdistended with blood. . . . It is, however, certain that no violent external means, whether a blow or a fall, could have been the cause of such a rupture of the blood-carrying veins, since not the slighest trace of any contusion appeared when the hair was shaved off and the skin taken away.

Jacob Reutinger, about fifty years of age . . . was at times out of his mind so that he often did not remember what he said or did. Three weeks before death he became totally blind, whereas there was no external damage to either eye. . . . A few days later this calamity was followed by another one; a paralysis, namely of the right leg, soon followed by one of the left.

On the eleventh day of February, eleven days before the full moon in the year 1656, he exchanged life with death. . . . After opening the dura meninx there exuded a pale serum the color of a grain of corn, and with a certain impetus, not unlike the blood erupts from the sectioned vena mediana of the arm, and indeed in such an amount that a ladle holding several ounces could be filled with it. This serum appeared to be acumulated mostly in the space which lies between the dura and pia mater which appeared to me wider and more voluminous than it exists usually in its natural state, whereby the serum, in its excessive amount, distended the dura mater everywhere where it did not meet an obstacle and depressed the cerebrum and cerebellum.

1. Donley, J. E.: John James Wepfer, A Renaissance Student of Apoplexy, Bull Hopkins Hosp 20:1-9 (Jan) 1909.

2. Wepfer, J. J.: Anatomical Observations From Cadavers Who Died With Apoplexy (L), Schaffhusii: J. C. Suteri, 1658, in Long, E. R. (ed.): Selected Readings in Pathology, From Hippocrates to Virchow, W. H. Wilder, Jr. (trans.), Sprinfield, Ill: Charles C Thomas, 1929.

3. Hoessly, G.-F.: Intracranial Hemorrhage in the Seventeenth Century: A Reappraisal of Johann Jacob Wepfer's Contribution Regarding Subdural Hematoma, J Neurosurg 24:493-496 (Feb) 1966.

Composite by G. Bako

Richard Wiseman (1621?-1676)

RICHARD WISEMAN was the most important surgeon of the turbulent era of the English Civil War of the 17th century. A Royalist by inclination he identified himself with the cause of the Stuarts, sharing their misfortunes and reaping his reward in the Restoration when he became sergeant-surgeon to Charles II.[1] His lasting contribution to surgery was his *Severall Chirurgicall Treatises* (1676), in which he summarized the extant surgical knowledge, adding to it the fruits of many years of military, naval, and civilian experience.[2]

Richard Wiseman was born in London and apprenticed to Richard Smith at the Barber-Surgeons' Hall. When the apprenticeship was completed, he served as surgeon in the Dutch navy for a number of years. Upon returning to England, he continued military service with the Royalist Army of the West under the command of Charles, Prince of Wales. After the defeat of the Crown Prince, Wiseman accompanied him into exile to France, returning to London but briefly. As a dedicated Royalist he faced hardships and dangers under the Cromwell government and, following arrest

and imprisonment, he joined the Spanish navy. With the restoration of the monarchy under Charles II, the climate had changed in his favor, and he then became the principal surgeon to the King.

Wiseman's civilian practice was necessarily interrupted by these changing political fortunes. During his brief sojourn in London under Cromwell, in 1652, he qualified as a member of the Barber-Surgeons' Company, serving for a time as assistant to Edward Molines of St. Thomas' Hospital. Here he performed, together with his chief, an external urethrotomy for gonorrheal stricture. As a "Practiser, not an Academick," Wiseman began his own practice of civilian surgery in the Old Bailey in 1660. In the practice of surgery, Wiseman considered himself only as a consultant and chose to rely upon referred cases and to be clearly identified with the referring physician whose counsel he valued. He rose in grade under royal decree and was appointed "sergeant-chirurgeon" to the King early in the 1670's.

In the "Epistle to the Reader," the introduction to Wiseman's *Severall Chirurgicall Treatises,* the author paid tribute to his distinguished predecessors, William Clowes and John Woodall. It was his original intention to put his papers in print for his own private satisfaction, but under advisement considered that they could be useful to others as well.[2]

In doing this, Reader, I have made a vertue of necessity, and imployed those hours for the publick service, which a frequently-repeated Sickness hath for twenty years last past deny'd me the use of in my private occasions. It hath pleased God by casting me into such a condition to give me opportunity of reading and thinking, as well as practising. Both which are necessary to the accomplishment not only of an Author, but indeed of a Chirurgeon.

"Tumors," "Ulcers," "Diseases of the Anus," "The King's Evil," "Wounds," "Gunshot Wounds," "Fractures and Luxations," and "Lues Venerea" are the titles of the eight chirurgical treatises. The sections, in turn, are divided into chapters; each includes a general discussion, definition, history, pathogenesis, signs, prognosis, treatment, and one or more illustrative case reports. The latter are detailed descriptions of contemporary practice, containing the minutiae of surgical treatment with the scalpel, cautery, escharotics, bandages, and emplastics. The style of presentation permits rapid and interesting reading, and much of the discussion is strikingly modern and scientifically correct. The white tumor of tuberculosis, the natural history of a case of carcinoma of the breast, and the management of inguinal hernia are excerpted in this essay. The most bizarre presentation, as judged by current scientific medicine, is the recounting of the superstition surrounding the "Royal touch" in the cure of tuberculosis, especially scrofula, known as the "King's Evil."[2]

The Latines call this Disease *Struma* and *Scrophula*, we the *Kings-Evil.* . . . *Strumae* are a hard Glandulous flesh, somewhat white, contained in a *cystis.*

A person of about 9 years of age, of a tender Constitution, subject to a Cough and other effects from an acidity in her Bloud, was afterwards discover'd to be lame of her right Knee, supposed to happen by some accident of a Fall. I being sent for saw the Bone on the inside protuberant, and covered with a white Swelling.

What great difficulty we meet with in the Cure of the Kings-Evil, the daily experience both of Physicians and Chirurgeons doth shew. I thought it therefore worth my while to spend a whole Treatise upon the Subject, and very particularly to go through the description of it, informing thereby the young Chirurgeon whatever is requisite to the Cure, at least as far as it cometh within the compass of our Art. But when upon trial he shall find the contumaciousness of the Disease, which frequently deludeth his best care and industry, he will find reason of acknowledging the goodness of God; who hath dealt so bountifully with this Nation, in giving the Kings of it, at least from *Edward* the Confessor downwards, (if not for a longer time) an extraordinary power in the miraculous Cure thereof. This our Chronicles have all along testified, and the personal experience of many thousands now living can witness for his Majesty that now reigneth, and his Royal Father and Grandfather. His Majesty that now is having exercised that faculty with wonderful success, not only here, but beyond the Seas in *Flanders, Holland* and *France* itself.

In the discussion of cancer:[2]

The remote Cause of this Tumor is, either a fault in the original Constitution of the Body;

or an acquired one, as by Bruise, Tumors, ill handling &c.

The *Differences* of *Cancers* are many; some whereof are with Ulceration, . . . and some of those affecting the Breast I have palliated a long time with easie Remedies. If any man will, in stead of *mild* or *occult* Cancers, call them *scirrhous* Cancers, I shall not gainsay him.

Such was the case of a Lady that laboured many years of an ulcerated Cancer. It had eat deep into her left Breast, and was fixed to the Ribs, but not with much pain. . . . She lived long, and in her latter age tolerably healthful.

Of all the Diseases which afflict mankind the *Cancer* is the most grievous and rebellious, and, is generally incurable, by reason of its corrosive and malign venom fermenting in the Humours, which, so far as we can yet find, yields neither to Purging, Bleeding, Repellents, Discutients, Suppuratives, nor any other Medicine inward or outward.

In the discussion of ruptures, Wiseman stressed the difference between intestinal and omental *hernia,* and the significance of the duration of the rupture and the degree of relaxation of the inguinal canal. He described the structural morphology, with reflections of the peritoneum, and also an "engine" for reducing intractable hernia, and discussed the need for surgery if other measures failed.[2]

If after the forementioned endeavours to reduce the Hernia, . . . you do not succeed, you ought to consider what the impediment is, and proceed accordingly to let bloud, purge or vomit, or put him into a Semicupium, keeping on his Bag-truss the while: after which he may if occasion require, be carried to and fro upon the back of a strong man with his Head downward, by which the prolapsed Bowels are often reduced. Mr. *Smith* the Truss-maker told me he had made such an Engine by which he set them on their Heads, and thereby had reduced many, which could not otherwise be relieved.

But the aforesaid ways, I bless God, have served the most deplorable Patient labouring of these Diseases under my hands. Yet if it should so happen, that all endeavours of this kind prove ineffectual, and the Patient's life be threatened by frequent vomiting and inflation of the *Abdomen,* and nothing pass through him by Stool, I would ask whether in such a case it be not more reasonable to offer in Consultation the laying open the Production while there is strength, than to suffer the patient miserably to perish under the Disease.

To perform this Operation, the Patient ought to be laid flat on his Back upon a Table or Form, and bound thereon; then an Incision must be made upon the upper part of the *Scrotum* to the Production, which requireth also to be divided, without touching the Intestines or *Omentum:* then you are to pass in a *Cannula* (like our common Director, but as big as a large Goose-quill into the Cavity under the Process of the *Peritoneum* upwards, avoiding the Intestines; then make your Incision of such a length as may serve to put your fingers into the *Scrotum,* and raise the Intestines and *Omentum,* which you are to reduce into their natural place within the Belly.

Few English physicians ever rose to greater prominence than Wiseman, who carried his experience in military and private practice to the Royal Court. His writings, which embraced a wide range of subjects, reflect great skill in practice and critical perception in the art of medicine. In addition to the items excerpted above, he described the treatment of varices, early amputation for serious battle wounds of the extremities, aneurysms, dropsies, use of mercury in syphilis, and reduction of a shoulder dislocation. A measure of respect that he held may be judged by the reflection that his treatises were considered the final authority for generations in evaluating the examinations at Surgeon's Hall in London.

1. Zimmerman, L. M., and Veith, I.: *Great Ideas in the History of Surgery,* Baltimore: Williams and Wilkins, 1961.
2. Wiseman, R.: *Severall Chirurgicall Treatises,* 2nd ed, London: R. Norton and J. Macock, 1686.

Thomas Willis (1621-1675)

THE "CIRCLE OF WILLIS," attributed to the 17th century Sedleian professor of natural philosophy at Oxford and one of the founders of the Royal Society, is not a true circle, but a seven-sided structure, a heptagon. Nor was Willis, the illustrious scholar and physician, the first to describe the arterial channels at the base of the brain. The published works of Casserio appearing in 1627, Vesling (1653), Fallopius (1561), and Wepfer (1658) either described or illustrated incompletely the vascular network.[1] Willis never claimed priority, although he was the first to combine a complete description with an equally complete illustration. He attributed its significance in health and disease to the assurance of an adequate blood supply to what was recognized at that time as the organ of thought.

Royal College of Physicians

Thomas was born at Great Bedwin in Wiltshire, the son of a farmer and retainer of St. John's College, who lost his life in the siege of Oxford during the civil war. Following private schooling at Oxford, Willis matriculated at Christ Church College in his 16th year, graduating AB in 1639 and AM in 1642. The city of Oxford was the seat of government for three years at the time when the king, Charles I, was in residence. Willis served his king in the university legion against the Parliamentarians, but devoted his spare time to the study of medicine. Receiving the MB degree in 1646, he began the practice of medicine at Oxford and continued his professional activities there until shortly after the Restoration.[2]

While in the practice of "physick," which has been described as large and productive, he composed the first of a notable number of weighty volumes in clinical medicine, natural philosophy, anatomy, and physiology. When Crofts, professor of natural philosophy at Oxford, was removed in 1660 as a victim of the Restoration Willis was appointed his successor. Several years later and on the invitation of the Archbishop of

Canterbury, Willis moved to London and continued his practice and writing. This liaison with the Archbishop was but one example of his close association with the church and clergy throughout his life. Another was the provision of an "Oratory" for devotions in his home. In Oxford, as well as London, Willis endowed a priest to read prayers in a neighboring church in the morning and evening for laboring persons unable to attend regular daytime services.

The "Circle of Willis" was illustrated in his *Cerebri anatome* published in London in 1664, with an imprimatur date of 1663 opposite the title page.[3] The volume contains a series of detailed drawings with descriptive legends of the anatomy of the central nervous system. Richard Lower aided in the preparation of the text, although his name does not appear as an author. Many of the illustrations were prepared by Christopher Wren, architect of St. Paul's Cathedral. The cranial nerves were classified into the first 10 plus the original description of the 11th cranial nerve, the spinal accessory.

Excerpts on typhoid fever, whooping cough, sweet and insipid diabetes, paracusis, gout, and muscle contraction have been selected. Not excerpted are discussions on epidemic cerebrospinal fever, myasthenia gravis, hysteria, headache, general paresis, puerperal fever, and the treatment of asthma. In his *Discourse of Fermentation,* published in 1684, typhoid fever was described under "Putrid Feaver." The typical febrile response, abdominal symptoms, and intestinal ulceration identitify the morbid process.[4]

In this Feaver, four times or seasons are to be observed, in which, as it were so many posts, or spaces, its course is performed: These are then the Beginning, the Augmentation, the Height, and Declination. These are wont to be finished in some sooner, in others more slowly, or in a longer time.

1. When therefore any one is taken with a putrid Feaver, the first assault is for the most part accompanied with a shivering or horror: . . . afterwards, a certain remission of the heat follows, but yet from the fire still glowing in the Bloud, a lassitude, and perturbation with thirst, and waking, continually infest: A pain arises in the Head, or Loins, partly from the ebullition of the Bloud, and partly from the motion of the nervous Juice being hindred; also a nauseousness, or a vomiting offends the Stomach.

A Dysentery is a Distemper, so frequent in continual Feavers, that some years it becomes Epidemical, and not more mild than the Plague, kills many: The cause of it is wont to be, not any humor produced within the Viscera, that corrodes the intestines with its Acrimony, (as some affirm) but a certain Infection impressed on the Bloud . . . unlocks the little mouths of the Arteries, and makes there little Ulcers, and exudations or flowings forth of the Bloud, like as when from the Feaverish Bloud, Pustles and Inflammations break forth outwardly, with a flowring towards the skin.

Whooping cough, the "chin-cough," is described by the term "whoop" and identified as convulsive cough of children.[5]

To this form, treating of a Cough not yet arrived to a Phthisis, ought to be referred the convulsive or suffocating Cough of children, and in our Idiome called the *Chin-cough*. This assaults chiefly Children and Infants; and at certain seasons, *viz.* Spring and Autumn especially, is wont to be epidemical. The diseased are taken with frequent and very fierce fits of Coughing, wherein namely the Organs of breathing do not only labour in pain, but also being affected convulsively, they do variously suspend or interrupt their actions; but for the most part the Diaphragma convulsed by it self, or by the impulse of other parts, doth so very long obstinately continue the Systole, or Diastole, that Inspiration, or Expiration being suppress'd for a space, the vital breath can scarcely be drawn; insomuch that coughing as being almost strangled they hoop, and by reason of the blood stagnating, they contract a blackness in their countenance; if perhaps, those organs not in such a measure convulsed, they are able to breathe any thing freer, notwithstanding they are forced always to cough more vehemently and longer, untill they wax faint.

The value of colchicum ("Hermodactyl") in the treatment of acute gout and in the prophylaxis of recurring attacks was described, as well as renal stones and renal involvement in gout. Currently, it is recognized that the joints of those afflicted with gout, or other rheumatic disorders, may be sensitive to changes in weather.[6]

. . . those that are obnoxious to this [gout] are also in danger of being sometimes troubled with the *Stone* or *Gravel* in the *Kidneys,* and on the contrary: moreover, the Gout increasingly gathers together every where about its chief Seats, to wit, the Joynts, a calculous matter, and there raises a *tophous mass.*

4. For the same reason changes of the places of aboad, also the revolutions of the year are wont to bring pains of the Gout, that it is become a Proverb, that *Gouty presons carry their Almanack in their Bones,* and from their pains draw most certain prognosticks, of the seasons, . . . moreover, at each quarter of the year, especially Spring and Fall, they are more sorely tormented; wherefore the AEquinoxes are always religiously observ'd by them.

Prior to Willis, diabetes was undifferentiated and was not specifically identified among the diseases associated with an excessive urine output. It was recognized only as the polyuria malady (pissing evil). Willis drew the correct deduction and distinguished sweet (Willis' disease) from insipid urine.[7]

Diabetes commonly is called chamber-pot dropsy, and some contend that both diseases actually are one and the same, that they have the causes and specific nature, and that their symptoms vary only as to the mode of serous excretion. . . . Really, if the subject be considered more accurately, there will appear a notable difference between these diseases. The anasarca (i.e., the dropsical edema) takes its origin first from the fact that weak and too cold blood is neither heated nor effervescent enough to digest and assimilate the chyle.

Why the urine of diabetic sufferers is sweet like honey:

It seems harder to explain why the urine of diabetic sufferers should be so strongly sweet or give off a honey taste. Nay, because according to my hypothesis, the flow of blood and the discharge of urine which follows and is due it, happen on account of combinations of salts, the liquid impregnated with these ought to be salty rather than sweet. And yet, in the very act of observing that the urine is lacking in salty flavor, it is appropriate to observe that many salts of diverse kinds are combined therein.

An interesting recovery or remission from diabetes was reported with the administration of a combination of several pharmacologic agents plus[7]

A diet almost solely of milk, sometimes raw or else diluted with distilled or barley water. . . . Through the use of these things he felt better day by day, so that within a month he began to seem practically cured. When he started to gain strength, his urine, now insipid, very little ex-

ceeded in quantity the liquid which he had ingested. Next it grew somewhat salty and less in amount than he had taken in the form of drink. Finally, his wonted spiritual tone returned. He flourished in strength, and returned to his original mode of life.

The paracusis of Willis—increased auditory acuity with increasing noise—was discussed in the treatise *The Soul of Animals.*[6]

Although hearing is in no sense effected by the tympanum as a proper organ of sensation, nevertheless, hearing does depend upon it to the extent that a privation of that sense or its diminution proceeds not rarely from impaired or impeded tympanic action. Indeed, a certain kind of deafness exists in which, despite the fact that its victims seem to lack the sense of hearing entirely, they perceive clearly the conversations of bystanders and reply suitable to questions so long as a tremendous din as of bombardment or of bells or of war drums is in progress close to their ears. Once the loud fracas subsides, they immediately grow deaf once more.

I have learned from a trustworthy man that he had known a woman who had been deaf yet heard clearly any and every word so long as a drum was being beaten inside the room [she was occupying]. For this reason her husband hired a drummer as a domestic servant, to be able by the latter's help to converse sometimes with his wife. Word has come to me too concerning another notably deaf person who lived close to a belltower and was able easily to hear any [person's] voice as often as several bells were sounding together, although unable to do so otherwise.

Doubtless the explanation in each of these instances was that the tympanum, of itself constantly laxed, was forced by the impact of strong sound to its due tautness and was thus able to some degree to serve its purpose.

Two noteworthy physiological discussions relate to the oxygenation of blood and muscular activity. Willis observed that the blood, which flowed into the pulmonary vessels from the right side, became crimson upon return to the heart. The discussion of muscular contraction appeared in 1670 as an appendix to his monograph on hysterical and hypochondriacal affections, a volume translated into English and published in London in 1684.[4]

As often as the motion of a living Muscle was beheld by me, I considered and weighed in my mind by what means all the fleshy fibres were contracted and released by turns, . . . [so] that in every contraction, the Spirits or certain elastick Particles did rush into the fleshy fibres from either Tendon, and did intumifie and force them nearer towards themselves or together; then the same Particles presently coming back from the flesh into the Tendons, the relaxation of the Muscles happened.

However, this being proved and granted, there yet remain very many difficulties concerning Musculary Motion.

Therefore as to the Musculary Motion in general, we shall conclude . . . that the animal Spirits being brought from the Head by the passage of the Nerves to every muscle (and as it is very likely) received from the membranaceous fibrils, are carried by their pasage into the tendinous fibres, and there they are plentifully laid up as in fit Store-houses; which Spirits, as they are naturally nimble and elastick, where ever they may, and are permitted, expanding themselves, leap into the fleshy fibres; then the force being finished, presently sinking down, they slide back into the Tendons, and so vicissively.

1. Meyer, A., and Hierons, R.: Observations on the History of the "Circle of Wills," *Med Hist* 6:119-130 (April) 1962.

2. "Thomas Willis," in *Dictionary of National Biography*, vol. 21, London: Oxford University Press, 1959-60.

3. Willis, T.: *Cerebri Anatome: Cui Accessit Nervorum Descriptio et Usus*, London: J. Flesher, 1664.

4. Willis, T.: *A Medical-Philosophical Discourse of Fermentation, or, of the Intestine Motion of Particles in Every Body*, S. Pordage, trans., London: H. Clark, 1684.

5. Willis, T.: *Pharmaceutice Rationalis: or, an Exercitation of the Operations of Medicines in Humane Bodies*, London: T Ding, C. Harper, and J. Leigh, 1679.

6. Willis, T.: *De Anima Brutorum, Que Hominis Vitalis ac Sensitiva Est, Exercitationes Duca*, L. Henderson, trans. London: R. Davis, 1672.

7. Willis, T.: *Pharmaceutice Rationalis sive Diatriba de Medicamentorum Operationibus in Humano Corpore*, L. Henderson, trans., 1674.

Thomas Sydenham (1624-1689)

THOMAS SYDENHAM, recognized by the translator of his famous medical text[1] as that "Excellent Practical Physician," and judged retrospectively as the designer of modern clinical medicine, was born into a family of Puritans during critical political times for England. He entered Magdalen Hall, Oxford University, at the age of 18, but his studies were interrupted by four years by the bearing of arms as a

cavalry officer on the side of the Parliamentarians during the civil war. The Royalist-Parliamentarian struggle, which lasted for more than a generation in the mid-17th cen-

Los Angeles County Medical Library

tury, was buttressed by social, economic, political, and religious issues. The Royalists included the landed aristocracy, the ecclesiastical hierarchy, the members of the court, and private individuals who preferred the established order to acceptance of changing events. The Parliamentarians, on the other hand, who were on the ascendancy from lower strata, included the growing commercial and industrial segments of the citizenry, the country gentry, the lesser clergy, and those who believed that a drastic change in government would benefit the greatest number. The civil war was interminable but not unduly costly in lives or money. King Charles I lost his head and life, while Cromwell, the Lord High Protector, lost his head after his life. Both sides had satisfaction in decapitation, but the country gradually resolved its constitutional problems and proceeded on its climb to greatness. The more ardent protagonists, like Sydenham, were affected for life and never abandoned their strong convictions. As an ardent iconoclast in the social and political order, it was natural for him to be an iconoclast in medicine and its milieu.

In 1646, when the Royalists were defeated and Oxford surrendered to Parliament, Sydenham returned to medicine, was appointed subsequently a Fellow of All Souls' College, and received the bachelor of medicine degree. After several years of practice in Oxford, he went to London and remained to the end of his professional career. He was awarded the MD degree by Cambridge at the age of 52; meanwhile, his clinical studies had carried him to the peak of medical fame at home but especially so on the Continent.

Although Sydenham was a close friend of John Locke and Robert Boyle, he was not an outstanding scholar, and is identified with no scientific discovery. He was not a Harvey or a Vesalius; he was the English Hippocrates. The Hippocratic method of observation and clinical experience, revealed first in the island of Cos in the fourth century before Christ prevailed in the Mediterranean countries until the third century after Christ. The revival of scientific medicine in England and on the Continent in the 16th century, notably by Vesalius and Harvey, established a foundation on which physicians in following generations might well have constructed what is now known as modern clinical medicine. But the anatomy of Vesalius and the physiology of Harvey were not blended until after Sydenham. He chose to study neither anatomy nor physiology, but rather the natural history of disease— a sick and suffering patient. He made current the Hippocratic method of observation and evaluation of prognosis upon personal clinical experience and clinical experience of others. Sydenham regarded disease as a continuing struggle of the body to correct the morbid disturbance and restore normal function and structure. Sydenham's most famous treatise, *The Whole Works,* begins as follows:

As the Human Body is so framed by Nature, that by reason of a continual Flux of Particles, and the Force of external things, it cannot always continue the same; upon which account there have been great numbers of diseases in all Ages; so without doubt the Necessity of finding out the Art of Healing has exercis'd the Wits of Men for many Ages, not only before the Grecian AEsculapius, but the AEgyptian too, who was a thousand Years his Senior. And indeed, as there is no man can tell who first contriv'd the Use of Houses and Clothes to defend us from the In-

juries of the Weather, so the Beginning of the Art of Physick can be no more discover'd than the Fountain of the River Nile: for this, as well as other Arts, has been always in use, tho it has been more or less cultivated, according to the various Dispositions of Times and Countries. How much the Antients, and amongst the chief, Hippocrates, have perform'd, is well known; from whom, and whose Writings, we have receiv'd the best part of the Therapeuticks.

In searching out the reason for the appellation, "The English Hippocrates," obviously one must conclude that the original and his namesake possessed outstanding characteristics in the practice of medicine. "The art of medicine was to be properly learnt only from its practice and its exercise." The natural history of disease was studied at the bedside. The influence of each teacher on subsequent generations of physicians was as profound as upon contemporaries. The names of the pupils of Hippocrates remain unknown, but there is good evidence that the master was accustomed to hold classes under the plane tree on the island of Cos. As for Sydenham— Thomas Dover, retriever of Alexander Selkirk (Robinson Crusoe), and Sir Hans Sloane, founder of the British Museum, were his pupils. Probably his most famous student, however, was Locke, who was diverted temporarily from philosophy to clinical medicine. For several years, Locke followed Sydenham from bed to bed and observed his professional technique, acting as his assistant and secretary. The treatise on smallpox was prepared from original notes taken in longhand by Locke.

Sydenham held no public position in any of the hospitals of London and advanced no further in the Royal College of Physicians than that of licentiate. Since he was not an MD during the major portion of his active years, he could not qualify as a Fellow of the College.[2]

It is noteworthy that, since Latin was the scientific language of the 17th century, the first drafts of Sydenham's texts were prepared in English, then translated into Latin, following the tradition of scientific communications of that era. In later generations they were translated back from Latin to English. Several of his less-well known writings have been collected and published in their original English by Dewhurst.[3] Sydenham taught that the epidemic diseases were influenced by meteorologic changes; rhythmic periodicity was believed to be related to seasonal variations. He held a rather low opinion of idle speculation and urged the development of a scientific nosology. He argued for the specificity of acute diseases and searched for specific remedies. Peruvian bark or Cinchona, favorite of Sydenham, was one of the few specifics known in the 17th century.[1]

The *Peruvian* Bark, which is commonly called the Jesuit's Powder, about 25 Years ago, if I remember well, first became famous at *London* for curing Agues, and especially Quartans; and indeed for very good reason, seeing these Diseases were rarely cured before by any other Method or Medicine, wherefore they were call'd *Opprobria Medicorum,* and were truly a Reproach to Physicians, but not very long after it was damn'd for two Reasons, and those no small ones, and so was wholly· disus'd.

So prominent was hysteria in Sydenham's practice that he judged it responsible for one-sixth of the morbidity among his patients. His discussion of this malady contains currently accepted aphorisms and one generally accepted observation concerning precipitating factors in acute gouty arthritis.[1]

I begin now, because you require it, Worthy Sir, to deliver those things which I have hitherto found by Observation concerning Hysterick Diseases, the Diagnostick whereof I readily confess is very obscure, and more difficult than other Diseases that afflict Mankind, and they are more difficultly cured: but I will endeavour to do as well as I can, and as briefly as is necessary for a Letter; which indeed my Sickness requires, especially at this Season of the Year, wherein there is a danger of occasioning precently a Fit of Gout, if I should study too hard.

A discussion of Sydenham's chorea begins:[1]

Chorea Sancti Viti is a sort of Convulsion, which chiefly invades Boys and Girls, from ten Years of Age to Puberty: First, is shews its self by a certain Lameness, or rather Instability of one of the Legs, which the Patient drags after him like a Fool; afterward it appears in the Hand of

the same side; which he that is affected with this Disease, can by no means keep in the same Posture for one moment, if it be brought to the Breast, or any other Part, but it will be distorted to another Position or Place by a certain Convulsion, let the Patient do what he can. If a Cup of Drink be put into his Hand, he represents a thousand Gestures, like Juglers, before he brings it to his mouth.

Sydenham differentiated scarlatina from measles.[4] Bastard peripneumonitis, pleurisy, dysentery, and other acute and chronic maladies were described. But none of these brought him such lasting fame as did the clinical description of the acute attack of gouty arthritis based upon personal experience. Before the age of 30, he began to suffer from attacks of acute gouty arthritis and a related phenomenon, hematuria from kidney stones. In the treatment of his personal affliction, bleeding and herbs were recommended. No mention was made of the tincture of colchicum or the extract of the meadow saffron, agents recognized at that time to be therapeutically potent in the treatment of acute gouty arthritis.[1]

Without doubt, Men will suppose, that either the Nature of the Disease I now treat of, is, in a manner, incomprehensible or, that I, who have been troubl'd with it Thirty-four Years, an a very dull Fellow, seeing my Observations about it, and the Cure of it, little answer their Expectations.

His most quoted description of an acute attack of gouty arthritis follows:

He goes to Bed and sleeps well, but about Two a Clock in the Morning, is waked by the Pain, seizing either his great Toe, the Heel, the Calf of the Leg, or the Ankle; this Pain is like that of dislocated Bones, with the Sense as it were of Water almost cold, poured upon the Membranes of the Parts affected, presently shivering and shaking follow with a feverish Disposition; the Pain is first gentle, but increases by degrees, (and in like manner the shivering and shaking go off) and that hourly, till towards Night it comes to its height, accompanying it self neatly according to the Variety of the Bones of the *Tarsus* and *Metatarsus,* whose Ligaments it seizes, sometimes resembling a violent stretching or tearing those Ligaments, sometimes the gnawing of a Dog, and sometimes a weight; moreover, the Part affected has such a quick and exquisite Pain, that it is not able to bear the weight of the Cloaths upon it, nor hard walking in the Chamber; and the Night is not passed over in Pain upon this Account only, but also by reason of the restless turning of the part hither and thither, and the continual Change of its Place. Nor is the tossing of the whole Body, which always accompanies the Fit, but especially at its coming, less than the continual Agitation and Pain of the tormented Member: There are a Thousand fruitless Endeavours used to ease the Pain, by changing the Place continually, whereon the Body, and the affected Members lie, yet there is no ease to be had.

So great was Sydenham's fame that Boerhaave was reported to have tipped his academic beret each time that he mentioned in his lectures the name of that excellent practical physician, the rediscoverer of the Hippocratic method of personal observation of the patient and of the value of clinical experience in integrating specific symptoms and findings.

1. *The Whole Works of that Excellent Practical Physician, Dr. Sydenham,* 7th ed., J. Pechey, trans., London: M. Wellington, 1717.
2. Payne J. F.: *Thomas Sydenham,* New York: Longmans, Green & Co., 1900.
3. Dewhurst, K.: *Dr. Thomas Sydenham (1624-1689) His Life and Original Writings,* Berkeley: University of California Press, 1966.
4. Comrie, J. D.: *Selected Works of Thomas Sydenham, M.D.,* London: John Bale, Sons & Danielsson, Ltd., 1922.

Marcello Malpighi (1628-1694)

PROBABLY THE BEST-KNOWN MEMBER OF THE FACULTY at the Medical School at Bologna was Malpighi, founder of embryology, physiologist, and anatomist.[1] Thaddeus of Florence, a respected practitioner and the first teacher at Bologna (1260), established a pattern of excellence in the care of the sick but was seriously handicapped by the sterility of science in this dark intellectual era. Original medical texts were unknown; the treatises current at that time were translations from the classical or medieval tomes. The result was a practice of medicine based upon the expositions from the Greek, Latin, and Arabic texts, complemented by clinical experience.

There is little recorded of Malpighi's earlier years. Born at Crevalcore, a few miles from Bologna, he entered the University at the age of 17, after the great scholastic center had passed its zenith. His parents, small landowners, presumably encour-

National Library of Medicine

aged him to seek a professional career. Ties with his native community were maintained throughout his life, in spite of intermittent harassment by the Sbaraglia family, neighbors and grabbers of the land. Malpighi began the study of medicine in 1651. Massari, the anatomist and his brother-in-law-to-be, exerted a profound influence upon his professional career. Massari formed a small anatomical society which gathered in an improvised home laboratory, to dissect man and beast. Nine students were charter members. Although the teaching of Galen and a select number of Arabic physicians were usually followed, Malpighi preferred Hippocrates because of his superior scientific judgments and extensive clinical experience.

Following graduation in medicine and philosophy at the age of 25, Malpighi remained in Bologna; 3 years later he was nominated public lecturer in medicine by the University Senate. His reputation as a teacher was not long in reaching northern Italy, where Ferdinand II, the grand duke of Tuscany, continuing the tradition of the scholastically ambitious Medici, who were always on the search for brilliance in the sciences and the humanities, offered Malpighi a special chair of theoretical medicine at the University of Pisa. Such an assignment today would be comparable to a professorship in physiology. Malpighi remained for 3 years at Pisa under most favorable auspices, a member of a brilliant faculty.[2]

Outstanding in the group was Borelli, 20 years older than Malpighi, overbearing and not always respectful of the accomplishments of others, but a remarkable physicist nevertheless. At the conclusion of their respective lectures each day, they met, dissected, discussed, and philosophized. In later years their friendship waned; bitterness appeared intermittently. After Pisa, Malpighi returned to Bologna and subsequently completed a 4-year stint at the University of Messina in Sicily. But the attraction for his alma mater was great, and he returned in 1666 for the remainder of his professional career.

An eponymic term sometimes exerts a remarkable influence upon the popularity of a scientist's accomplishments. Thus, the Malpighian corpuscle or Malpighian body is probably Malpighi's best remembered contribution to medicine. On the other hand, the concept of the capillary circulation of blood through the lungs and the integration of structure with function, as advanced by Malpighi, are considered by some as fundamental as Harvey's physiological observations. Furthermore, the experimental studies of Malpighi offered convincing proof of the Harveian concept. It seemed incongruous to Malpighi that the lung was an amorphous structure through which blood was channeled in and out.[2]

For while the heart is still beating two movements contrary in direction are observed in the vessels so that the circulation of the blood is clearly laid bare; and indeed the same may be even more happily recognized in the mesentery and in other larger veins contained in the abdomen. And thus by this impulse the blood is showered down in minute streams through the arteries after the fashion of a flood into the several cells, one or other conspicuous branch passing right through or leaving off there, and the blood thus repeatedly divided loses its red color and carried round in a sinuous manner is poured out on all sides until it approaches the walls and the angles and the absorbing branches of the veins.

The power of the eye could not be carried further in the opened living animal; hence I might have believed that the blood itself escaped into an empty space and was gathered up again by a gaping vessel, and by the structure of the walls. But an objection to this view was afforded by the movement of the blood being tortuous and scattered in different directions and by its being united again in a determinate part. . . . Hence it was clear to the senses that the blood flowed always along tortuous vessels and was not poured into spaces, but was always contained within tubules and that its dispersion is due to the multiple winding of the vessels. Nor is it a new thing in nature to join to each other the terminal mouths of vessels since the same obtains in the intestines and other parts.

Interspersed between his remarkable revelations of the capillary circulation in the lungs and the arrival of a clear conception of the structure of the kidney, meanwhile engaged in healing the sick and busy in the postmortem room, he reported a number of observations in the natural sciences. At Pisa, the anatomy of fishes was investigated. At Messina, the spiral intestinal valve of sharks, the optic nerve of the swordfish, and the connection of nerve fibers with cortical cells of the brain were described. Malpighi showed that the papillae of the tongue are not secretory in nature by the simple experiment of allowing the protruded tongue to dry. No secretion appeared. The papillae of the tongue and the papillae of the skin were believed to be similar in function, i.e., sensory. The nerve filaments of the tongue were implicated as the end-organs of taste. Racial characteristics were judged to be determined by the accumulation of pigment in the rete mucosum of the skin, the Malpighian layer. The lobules in the liver were described. Bile was believed to be secreted by the liver and not by the gallbladder. The glands or vesicles of the spleen were compared to a bunch of grapes. Glandular adenopathy was recognized, a syndrome redescribed 2 centuries later by Hodgkin and now identified by the eponymic designation.

Malpighi was interested in silkworms and their cultivation. He investigated their external form, musculature, tracheae, nerves, heart, intestines, genitourinary tract, and silk-spinning apparatus and noted that eggs did not develop unless they had been exposed to sperm. Studies in botany were almost as extensive as those in anatomy. The cells of plants were investigated and the need for oxygen recognized.

The remarkable contributions to the form and function of the kidney represented an extension of the observations of his predecessors. Aristotle had considered the bladder the organ responsible for the formation of urine. Vesalius reassigned this function to the kidney, without appreciation of the detailed mechanism involved. Highmore and Bellini were among the first to approach the modern concept of urine formation. In 1666, Malpighi postulated the function of the adult kidney on the basis of his observations on embryologic development. The glomeruli and the convoluted tubules were concentrated in the cortex of the kidney; whereas the medulla consisted largely of straight tubules. Although the intermingling of the capillaries with the glomeruli was recognized, the precise relationship between these structures was not defined. This phenomenon was not resolved until Bowman's report to the Royal Society in 1842. An excerpt of Hayman's complete translation of Malpighi's essay on the structure of the kidneys is noteworthy.[3]

Since in the previous section we have mentioned the glands that have been discovered in the kidney, which, as will be shown below, contribute a special service in the excretion of the urine, it is now proper to pause briefly to consider their structure. These glands, situated in the outer part of the kidney, are almost innumerable, and probably, as I think, correspond in number to the urinary vessels by which the mass of the kidney is formed. The number of the urinary vessels in each fasciculus, by which the small lobules which have been described are formed, exceeds forty.

As to the structure of the glands, a distinct outline cannot be obtained on account of their minute size and translucency. They appear, however, spherical, precisely like fish eggs: and when a dark fluid is perfused through the arteries they grow dark, and one would say that all around them are the extreme ends of the blood vessels, which run along like creeping tendrils, so that they appear as it were crowned, with this reservation, however, that the part which is fastened to the branch of the artery grows black; the rest retains its former color.

At the age of 63, Malpighi was invited to Rome by his friend, Pope Innocent XII, to serve as his personal physician. Presumably, this terminated his scientific accomplishments. He died in 1694 in the Quirinale Palace. An autopsy was performed 30 hours after his death, in keeping with an ante-mortem request. The right kidney was severely damaged, the bladder contained a small stone; the left ventricle was hypertrophied; the brain showed the residua of a vascular accident.

1. Adelmann, H. B.: *Marcello Malpighi and the Evolution of Embryology,* 5 vols, Cornell University Press and Oxford University Press, 1966.
2. Foster, M.: *Lectures on the History of Physiology,* Cambridge, England: University Press, 1901.
3. Hayman, J. M., Jr.: Malpighi's Concerning the Structure of the Kidneys, Ann Med Hist 7:242, 1925.

Antony van Leeuwenhoek (1632-1723)

ANTONY VAN LEEUWENHOEK, the father of protozoology and bacteriology, was not a teacher associated with a medical school or university. His scientific contributions were made at his leisure while he was serving as a janitor or beadle, "Bedellus," the Chamberlain to the sheriffs of Delft. He held this post for almost four decades and continued to draw a small salary until his death at the age of 91. He was also a wine-gauger and passed an examination for surveyor. Exposure to formal education was minimal; at the age of 16 he was apprenticed as a cashier and bookkeeper in a linen-draper shop in Amsterdam.[1] He returned to Delft at the age of 22 where he lived for the remainder of his life, except for one brief visit across the Channel to inspect the chalk cliffs of southern England.

The name of Leeuwenhoek has been associated with animalcules and protozoa, isolated from a number of sources and viewed through a simple microscope. Leeuwenhoek may not have been the first to discover microscopic organisms, nor was he the discoverer of the microscope. A hand lens had been used before his day; a compound microscope had been devised before he was born. His inquisitive nature concerning the minute world of protozoa and bacteria, combined with his mechanical skill, quite naturally led him to construct his own microscope and to describe protozoa, bacteria, the red blood corpuscle, spermatozoa and a

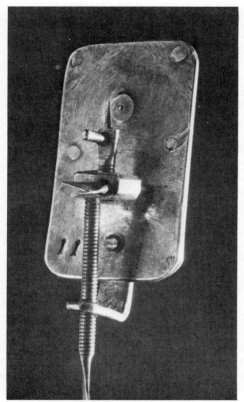

National Museum of History of Science, Leyden

great number of animate and inanimate objects.[2]

In the year 1675, I discover'd living creatures in Rain water, which had stood but few days in a new earthen pot, glased blew within. This invited me to view this water with great attention, especially those little animals appearing to me ten thousand times less than those represented by Mons. *Swamerdam,* and by him called *Water-fleas* or *Water-lice,* which may be perceived in the water with the naked eye.

Leeuwenhoek was born the same year as John Locke, Spinoza, and Vermeer (1632). When the latter died at the age of 42, the government appointed Leeuwenhoek an ex-

ecutor of the estate for the widow. Although he did not speak or write fluently in Latin, French, or English, the scientific languages of his day, and his literary style in his native Nether-Dutch was faulty and sometimes heavy, he dispatched many communications to the Royal Society of London. A part of the difficulty in composition was related to the need for new words and new concepts in the description of his investigations in the fertile fields of natural science. He was 36 before the first scientific communication was prepared. The first letter to the Royal Society of London was written at the age of 41. This followed an exchange of correspondence between his friend and fellow-townsman, the famous Dutch physician, de Graaf (Graafian follicle) and Oldenburg, the first secretary of the Royal Society. A favorable reply was prompted by the secretary's interest in getting "into communication with all men—no matter what their rank or nationality—who were working for 'the promotion of natural knowledge.' " The communication by Leeuwenhoek to the Royal Society read:[1]

I have oft-times been besought, by divers gentlemen, to set down on paper what I have beheld through my newly invented *Microscopia*: but I have generally declined; first, because I have no style, or pen, wherewith to express my thoughts properly; secondly, because I have not been brought up to languages or arts, but only to business; and in the third place, because I do not gladly suffer contradiction or censure from others. This resolve of mine, however, I have now set aside, at the intreaty of Dr. Reg. de Graaf; and I gave him a memoir on what I have noticed about mould, the sting and sundry little limbs of the bee, and also about the sting of the louse. . . . As I can't draw, I have got them drawn for me, but the proportions have not come out as well as I had hoped to see 'em; and each figure that I send you herewith was seen and drawn through a different magnifying-glass. I beg you, therefore, and those Gentlemen to whose notice these may come, please to bear in mind that my observations and thoughts are the outcome of my own unaided impulse and curiosity alone; for, besides myself, in our town there be no philosophers who practise this art; so pray take not amiss my poor pen, and the liberty I here take in setting down my random notions.

Leeuwenhoek's communications were prepared in Dutch and translated into English or Latin by friends in Delft or in London. At least 190 letters were dispatched to the Royal Society; 26 were sent to the Academy of Science of Paris. Leeuwenhoek published no detailed treatises, monographs, or books; the letters were the only outlet for his scientific endeavors. He did not attract a following of students but received many visitors. Especially notable was Peter the Great, who as he passed through Delft, requested the Bedellus to visit him on his houseboat and demonstrate the findings of the miscroscope. Circulation of blood through the tail of an eel was demonstrated to the dignitary in 1698 and described in 1708, having been inferred by inductive reasoning by Harvey decades earlier.[3]

I have formerly communicated to the Honourable Society some Discoveries of mine, relating to the Circulation of the Blood in Eels, consisting in this; to wit, that the Blood coming out of a great many small Vessels in the Tail of an Eel, falls in, and is united in one greater Blood-Vessel, where is the first beginning of the Fish Bones, and where the Blood runs thro' a Valve, which I have not only observed myself, but have likewise shoewn to several Curious Gentlemen, who view'd it with abundance of Pleasure and Surprize; for the Blood-Vein was not only moved in that part where the Valve is, but the Parts about the Blood-Vessel, of the breadth of four or five Hairs, were likewise moved or stirr'd; from whence it appear'd, that at every Protrusion of Blood into the Heart thro' the Valve, the Blood still about an instant of time, and that the same Blood falling thro' the Valve, ran with great swiftness, and was thickest just at its Protrusion out of the Valve, but ran thinner or slenderer like the Figure of a Pear; and the Vein that received this Protruded Blood, was not intirely fill'd with it, but seem'd for a small space to be as it were empty, and the Parts of it contracted, which we cou'd perceive for a small time, and further observing it, saw the Blood run slowly and leisurely along the same Vessel.

From this Observation I imagin'd, that the same thing happen'd in the Heart of a Humane Creature, *viz.* that there is a gentle and slow Protrusion of the Blood out of the Heart into that Vessel, which we call the Artery, . . .

The lenses for each of the microscopes, estimated variously between 300 and 500 in number, were ground by hand, placed between two thin sheets of metal, and, at a fixed focal distance, the object under scru-

tiny was brought into view. At a distance of 8 inches, a maximum magnification of 200 diameters was possible. Several of the microscopes were mounted in silver or gold, the others in brass. A number of drawings of the simple microscopes remain. Near the end of his life, a cabinet containing 26 models was presented to the Royal Society, but these are lost. Not more than 10 of the original microscopes are extant.

In later years *Spirilla, Bacteria, Micrococci, Leptothrix,* and *Borrelia buccale* were described in scrapings from the teeth. Five kinds of ciliates and several flagellates were identified. The striations of the muscle fibers were recognized as well as the crystalline lens of the eye. Grains of sand were used as a standard of comparison. The size of the erythrocyte as determined by Leeuwenhoek is remarkably close to current values. Insensible perspiration was measured by placing his hand in a glass vessel and occluding the circulation of air. Insensible loss from the entire body was estimated at approximately 20 fl. oz./24 hr. He refused to admit, however, that there were pores in the skin.

Although the observations of Leeuwenhoek had a profound influence upon medicine, there is no evidence that he was particularly concerned with this branch of learning. No attempt was made to correlate bacteria with contagion or disease. One hundred years and more were to elapse before irrefutable proof of this concept was revealed by Koch and Pasteur.

Leeuwenhoek was buried in the Old Church in Delft beneath a tall obelisk set in an arched niche. A circular plaque on the obelisk bears a profile with the following epitaph:[1]

To the fond and everlasting memory of Antony van Leeuwenhoek, Fellow of the English Royal Society, who, by detecting through diligent application and scrutiny the mysteries of Nature and the secrets of natural philosophy by means of microscopes invented and marvellously constructed by himself, and by describing them in the Dutch dialect, has earned the highest approbation of the whole world.

1. Dobell, C.: *Antony van Leeuwenhoek and his "Little Animals,"* New York: Dover Publications, Inc., 1960.

2. Leeuwenhoek, A. v.: *Observations, communicated to the Publisher in a Dutch Letter of the 9th of Octob. 1676. here English'd: Concerning little Animals by him observed in Rain, Well, Sea, and Snow-water; as also in water wherein Pepper hath lain infused,* London: Phil Trans 12:821-831, 1677.

3. Leeuwenhoek, A. v.: *A Letter concerning the Circulation of the Blood in Fishes, &c,* London: *Phil Trans* 26:250-257, 1710.

Nathaniel Hodges (1629-1688)

DURING THE GREAT PLAGUE OF LONDON in 1665, Nathaniel Hodges remained to tend the stricken, while others—physicians and laymen—fied the city in mortal fear. Hodges' description of the clinical symptoms, means of prevention, and modes of treatment from firsthand observations and personal affliction is the best account of the epidemic. He was born at Kensington, the son of a vicar and Dean of Hereford, prepared at Westminster School, and studied at Cambridge and at Oxford, where he received the AB and AM degrees and the MD degree in 1659.[1] London was the obvious place for the practice of medicine. He became a member of the College of Physicians just after his 30th birthday and served his College with distinction as Censor and Harveian Orator.

Hodges' great days occurred during the 1665 plague which, according to the Bills of Mortality, killed more than 68,000 persons. For professional services during the epidemic, he received an annuity from the city, but sometimes good deeds are soon forgotten, and he later fell into debt and was confined in Ludgate prison. Hodges' literary memorabilia are limited to his commonplace medical book and the account of the plague—*Loimologia* (Gr loimos, plague). The treatise, prepared in Latin, was published in 1672 and was translated into English by John Quincy nearly 50 years later. The spread of contagion and methods of prevention were important entities in the epidemiology of his time. The clinical observations were confined to the recording of buboes and carbuncles, noting the passage of clear urine, and mention of the pulse,

fever, sweating, gastrointestinal disturbances, delirium, and coma. These are of historical interest and not specifically diagnostic, except for the buboes. The use of alexipharmacs (antipoisons) was typically nonspecific. Several of the passages, especially the more dramatic descriptions, are excerpted.[2]

As soon as the Magistracy, to whom the publick Care belonged, saw how the Contagion daily increased, and had now extended it self to several Parishes, an Order was immediately issued out to shut up all the infected Houses, that neither Relations nor Acquaintance might unwarily receive it from them, and to keep the infected from carrying it about with them.

In Order whereunto, it is to be observ'd, that a Law was made for marking the Houses of infected Persons with a Red Cross, having with it this Subscription, LORD HAVE MERCY UPON US: And that a Guard should attend there continually, both to hand to the Sick the Necessaries of Food and Medicine and to restrain them from coming Abroad until Forty Days after their Recovery.

But what greatly contributed to the Loss of People thus shut up, was the wicked Practices of Nurses (for they are not to be mention'd but in the most bitter Terms): These Wretches, out of Greediness to plunder the Dead, would strangle their Patients, and charge it to the Distemper in their Throats; others would secretly convey the pestilential Taint from Sores of the infected to those who were well; and nothing indeed deterred these abandoned Miscreants from prosecuting their avaritious Purposes by all the Methods their Wickedness could invent; who, although they were without Witnesses to acuse them, yet it is not doubted but divine Vengeance will overtake such wicked Barbarities with due Punishment.

In the months of *August* and *September,* the Contagion chang'd its former flow and languid Pace, and having as it were got Master of all, made a most terrible Slaughter, so that three, four, or five Thousand died in a Week, and once eight Thousand: who can express the Calamities of such Times? The whole *British* Nation wept for the Miseries of her Metropolis. In some Houses Carcases lay waiting for Burial, and in others, Persons in their last Agonies; in one Room might be heard dying Groans, in another the Ravings of a Delirium, and not far off Relations and Friends bewailing both their Loss, and the dismal Prospect of their own sudden Departure; Death was the sure Midwife to all Children, and Infants passed immediately from the Womb to the Grave; who would not melt with Grief, to see the Stock for a future Generation hang upon the Breasts of a dead Mother? Or the Marriage-Bed changed the first Night into a Sepulchre, and the unhappy Pair meet with Death in their first Embraces? Some of the infected run about staggering like drunken Men, and fall and expire in the Streets; while others lie half-dead and comatous, but never to be waked but by the last Trumpet; some lie vomiting as if they had drank Poison; and others fall dead in the Market, while they are buying Necessaries for the Support of Life.

About the Close of the Year, that is, on the Beginning of *November,* People grew more healthful, and such a different Face was put upon the Publick, that although the Funerals were yet frequent, yet many who had made most Hast in retiring, made the most to return, and came into the City without Fear; insomuch that in *December* they crowded back as thick as they fled: The Houses which before were full of the Dead, were now again inhabited by the Living; and the Shops which had been most Part of the Year shut up, were again opened.

. . . they had the Courage now to marry again, and betake to the Means of repairing the past Mortality; and even women before deemed barren, were said to prove proliffick; so that although the Contagion had carried off, as some computed, about one hundred thousand, after a few Months their loss was hardly discernable; and thus ended this fatal Year.

1. Munk, W.: *The Roll of the Royal College of Physicians of London,* vol 1, 2nd ed, London: Royal College of Physicians, 1878.

2. Hodges, N.: *Loimologia: or, an Historical Account of the Plague in London in 1665,* 3rd ed, J. Quincy, trans., London: E. Bell, 1721.

Bernardini Ramazzini
(1633-1714)

ALTHOUGH THE TITLE of Ramazzini's famous treatise, *Diseases of Tradesmen,* marks him as the first systematic compiler of occupational diseases, one must liberally interpret the title. Tradesmen included physicians, soldiers, athletes, scholars, writers, farmers, fishermen, hunters, midwives, and grave diggers, as well as the artisans and workers susceptible to occupational hazards, such as miners, potters, painters, stone cutters, and grain sifters. As an epidemiologist, Ramazzini contributed to an understanding of the cattle plague, rinderpest, and described epidemics of malaria and lathyrism; as a meteorologist, he noted that the height of a Torcellian column of mercury varied with the weather.

Ramazzini was born in Capri in northern Italy, was well educated in elementary

National Library of Medicine

schools, studied both philosophy and medicine at the University of Parma, and received the doctorate in medicine at the age of 26. He practiced for a time in the periphery of Rome, but recurrent malaria forced him to higher ground and subsequently he chose Modena, which had recently established a medical school. After a hostile reception by the profession, counterbalanced by a successful practice and favor from the Ducal Court, Ramazzini was appointed professor of the theory of medicine at the University of Modena and discharged the duties for almost 20 years. The tenure was terminated when, in 1700, the Senate of the University of Padua persuaded him to accept a senior position. Shortly thereafter he was appointed to the first chair of the practice of medicine held in conjunction with the rectorship of the medical college.

The first edition of *Diseases of Tradesmen* appeared in Latin during the year of his transfer and was dedicated to the Moderators of Padua. An English edition appeared in 1705.[1] Several of the excerpts from the 1713 Padua edition were recently translated by Wright.[2] In the "Preface,"

Ramazzini introduced the subject of occupational disease and explained the need for an inquiry regarding occupational exposure and a procedure for establishing rapport in the examination of the patient.[1]

When a Physician therefore is call'd to visit one of the poorer and meaner sort of People, I would advise him not to clap his Hand to the Pulse as soon as he comes into a Room, without inquiring into the Circumstances of the Patient, nor to stand, as 'twere in a transient Posture, to prescribe where the Life of Man is concern'd; but to sit down by the Patient, let the Place be never so sorry, and carefully interrogate him upon such things, as both the Precepts of our Art, and the Offices of Piety require us to know. . . . To which I'd presume to add one Interrogation more; namely, what Trade he is of. . . . So, I choose to publish this Treatise of mine for the good of the Republick, or at least for the benefit of Tradesmen: And tho 'tis not very Artfully writ, I hope the Reader will vouchsafe it a civil Reception.

Hazards of the environment were distinguished from hazards of physical participation. Mercury and lead are examples of the first group. Writers' cramps, simian round shoulders of cobblers, and sciatica of tailors are examples of the second group.[1]

The various and numerous Train of Diseases that accrues to Artificers from the Exercise of their respective Trades, is in my opinion owing chiefly to two Causes: namely, first the noxious Quality of the Matter that goes thro' their hands, which by breathing out nocive Streams and thin Particles offensive to human Nature, gives rise to particular Diseases; and in the next place certain violent and disorderly Motions and improper Postures of the Body, by which the Natural Structure of the vital Machine is so undermin'd as gradually to make way for grievous Distempers.

In implicating noxious agents, Ramazzini provided an abundance of historical references and cited one or more case reports from his experience or general observations. Exposure to mercury by goldsmiths and surgeons (physicians) and exposure to lead by potters and painters are described as follows.[1]

'Tis well know what dismal Plagues are inflicted by Quicksilver upon Goldsmiths, and chiefly those who are imploy'd in Gilding Silver or Brass Work; For as this Gilding can't be perform'd without Amalgamation, (i.e. the Corrosion of the Mettal by Mercury) so when they afterwards come to dislodge this Mercury by Fire, tho they turn away their Faces, they can't possibly avoid the receiving some poysonous Steams at the Mouth, and accordingly we find that this sort of Workmen do quickly become Asthmatick, Paralytick and liable to Vertigo's; and their Complexion assumes a dangerous Ghostly Aspect.

Now-a-Days, those who rub the Mercuriad Ointments on Pocky Persons, are the meaner sort of Surgeons who undertake that Office to make a Penny by it; for the better sort of Surgeons decline such a sordid Piece of Service, which is likewise accompany'd with Danger. 'Tis true, in such Cases they make use of a Glove, but all that sence is not sufficient to keep the Mercurial Atoms from penetrating the Leather, and so reaching the Surgeons Hands.

For my part I can think of no cautionary Method so proper and so effectual for those imploy'd in such Inunctions as that of a Surgeon of our Country; who finding to his Cost that the Danger and Trouble he underwent, surpass'd the Profit, and having experienced by frequent Loosenesses, Gripes, and Salivations, upon his own Person, that such Inunctions were more afflicting to him than to the Persons anointed; did thereupon alter his Course, and continuing to prepare the Mercurial Ointment as before, and to stand by the Patients while the Friction is perform'd, order'd the Patients to rub themselves with their own Hands; by which means a double Advantage is gain'd: for not only the Surgeon avoids Danger, but the Patients thus Heating themselves by the Motion and Exercise of their Arms, make the Ointment penetrate the better; and withal have no reason to apprehend any Danger to themselves from the Remedy in which they place all their Hopes of relief.

There's scarce any City in which there are not other Workmen, . . . who receive great Prejudice from the Metallick Plagues. Among such we reckon the Potters; for what City, what Town is without such as practice that Ancientest of all Arts? Now, the Potters make use of burnt and calcin'd Lead for glazing their Ware; and for that end grind their Lead in Marble Vessels, by turning about a long Piece of Wood hung from the Roof, with a square Stone fasten'd to it at the other end. While they do this, as well as when with a pair of Tongs they daub their Vessels over with melted Lead before they put 'em into the Furnace; they receive by the Mouth and Nostrils and all the Pores of the Body all the virulent Parts of the Lead thus melted in Water and dissolv'd, and thereupon are siez'd with heavy Disorders. For first of all their Hands begin to shake and tremble, soon after they become Paralytick, Lethargick, Splenetick, Cachectick and

Toothless; and in fine, you'll scarce see a Potter that has not a Leaden Death-like Complexion.

The carrier state in a contagious affliction, cattle plague or rinderpest, was described in one of his lectures at Padua based upon the 1700 epidemic in the environs of Padua. Ramazzini made it clear that it was not beneath the dignity of medical men to discuss diseases of domestic animals. He predicted that the violence of the epidemic would subside with the coming of cold weather and noted that it was confined to cattle, affecting neither other animals nor man. Careful instructions were given for the disposal of infected carcasses. Clean stables were recommended, and the dung was to be removed regularly and not be allowed to accumulate. The carrier state was described as follows.[3]

However, it is pertinent to inquire whether, in this raging epidemic, it be safe to make use of oxen which are believed to be healthy and whether such use may not transfer infection to human bodies. For my part I am not free from some doubt as to the truth in this matter. Even though the ox appears to be vigorous and lively before it is led to the butcher's stall and though afterwards when it is killed, skinned and opened, no pathological signs are to be noted in the viscera such as have been observed in the viscera of other oxen which have perished of the epidemic disease, nevertheless, we cannot be completely certain that the ox did not harbor contagious morbific matter which is capable of transmission. For it is conceivable that there are those among our oxen which will not have experienced an overwhelming dose of infection and they will pass as being sound and healthy. Such is the deceitful cunning of the seed of this disease that it not rarely hides itself from men's eyes under another shape. Very often it happens that the one who contains the disease within himself and carries it around, feels no injury to himself and perhaps never will feel that injury although, at the same time, he may be able easily to transmit the infection to another of the same species.

The "Preface" by Dr. James to the English translation of 1746 contains a character sketch, which has been accepted by Ramazzini's biographers as a beautiful tribute to a physician who dealt at length with problems in social medicine and especially occupational diseases.[4]

Ramazini, when enter'd on the Discharge of his Office at Padua, was no less an Ornament to it than the celebrated Sanctorius,, who had formerly executed it, for never did Students of all Nations so attentively listen to the Dictates of a Master; and never did a Master take so much Pleasure, or use so much Pains, in forming the Minds of Students, and replenishing them with the most reasonable and salutary Maxims of Practice. In a Word, his singular Learning, the Sweetness of his Temper, the Candour of his Judgment, the Uprightness of his Intentions, the Honesty of his Morals, the Industry with which he discharg'd his various Offices, and the Success of his Practice render'd him so conspicuous, that he was created honorary Fellow of almost all the Academies and Universities of Europe and courted by all his learned Contemporaries, insomuch that it was thought a singular Honour to be one of Ramazzini's Correspondents. But as human Blessings are not intended to be perpetual, this Benefactor of Mankind began at last to feel the natural Effects of Age, and strong Application of Mind; for he was frequently seiz'd with a violent Palpitation of the Heart, and Disorder of the Eyes, which terminated in perfect Blindness.

1. Ramazzini, B.: *A Treatise of the Diseases of Tradesmen*, English translation, London: A Bell, R. Smith, D. Midwinter, W. Hawes, W. Davis, G. Straughan, B. Lintot, J. Round, and J. Wale, 1705.
2. Ramazzini, B.: *Diseases of Workers, Latin text of 1713*, W. C. Wright, trans., Chicago: University of Chicago Press, 1940.
3. Ramazzini, B.: "The Contagious Epidemics," *Opera Omnia, Medica, & Physica*, Geneva: Cramer & Perachon, 1716, J. M. McDonald, trans., *Bull Hist Med* 12:529-539, 1942.
4. Ramazzini, B. A.: *A Dissertation on Endemial Diseases*, Dr. James, trans., London: Thomas Osborn, 1746.

Richard Morton (1637-1698)

RICHARD MORTON, pastor turned physician, was born in Worcestershire and like his father trained for the ministry.[1] He received the AB degree at Oxford in 1656, took orders in the church, and, in 1659 after receiving the AM, was chaplain in the Foley family. Later he became Vicar of Kinver, but, when Parliament passed the Act of Uniformity with its requirement of comprehensive approval of the Book of Common Prayer, Morton began the study of medicine, being unable to accept the requirements. On the nomination of the Prince of Orange, he received the MD from Oxford in

1670, settled in London, became a Fellow of the College of Physicians, and later physician to the King.

Morton, as successful in medicine as in the ministry, left a great treatise on tuber-

Composite by G. Bako

culosis containing an excellent clinical description of wasting.[2] He described not only the physical deterioration from pulmonary tuberculosis but included other cachectic illnesses such as prolonged jaundice, gouty arthritis, and intermittent fevers. The spread of phthisis by contagion, which pursued a rapid fulminating course or developed into chronic consumption, was clearly presented. He believed that fresh air was helpful in prevention, recognized the hereditary disposition, differentiated two types of fever— the customarily persistent from intermittent pyrexia—and identified cough and loss of weight as pathognomonic signs of pulmonary consumption. His description of the tubercle, his belief that this represented the focus for independent dissemination, and speculation regarding the prevalence of the malady were based upon his own clinical experiences.[3]

. . . . a crude Tubercle or Swelling is bred from the Obstruction of some Glandulous part of the Lungs; to wit, when a greater quantity of *Serum,* or Water is separated from the Blood, than is thrown out by the Duct of the Glandule: From whence it comes to pass, that as the Part affected being too much distended by the Humour that is imprisoned in it, is deprived of its Natural Tone, and thereupon is no longer able to spew or throw out the *Serum,* or Water that flows into it, or is separated; so likewise the Humour, that is so shut up, not being any more renewed by an influx of fresh Humour, does by degrees grow dry and hard from the Natural heat of the Part: From whence arises a hardness, that resists a pressure, or a Tubercle (of which we are now speaking) which in progress of time, after the Natural Tone of the Part is in this manner destroyed, is wont to be inflam'd, and to turn to an Apostem sooner or later, according to the Nature of the *Lympha,* or included Humour, and of the Blood, from which it is separated, which indeed is the whole immediate cause of a Consumption of the Lungs, and of the dry cough which attends it.

Yea, when I consider with my self, how often in one Year there is cause enough ministred for producing these Swellings, even to those that are wont to observe the strictest Rules of Living, I cannot sufficiently admire that any one, at least after he comes to the Flower of his Youth, can dye without a touch of Consumption.

1. Osler, W.: The "Phthisiologia" of Richard Morton, M.D., *Med Libr Hist J* 2:1-7 (Jan) 1904.

2. Morton, R.: *Phthisiologia: or a Treatise of Consumptions* (L), London: S. Smith, 1689.

3. Morton, R.: *Phthisiologia,* 2nd ed, London: W. & J. Innys, 1720.

Composite by G. Bako

Niels Stensen (1638-1686)

NIELS STENSEN or Steensen or Nicholas
Steno (there are other variations also) identified with Stensen's duct, was a versatile
scientist, a pious theologian, and an astute
natural philosopher. He was born in Copenhagen and studied at the University, where
he was attracted to Thomas Bartholin, one
of the distinguished anatomists of his time.
He was equally attracted to languages, becoming proficient in German, French,
Italian, English, Greek, Latin, and, to a
lesser degree, in Hebrew and Chaldean.[1]
During the assault on Copenhagen in 1658-
1659, Stensen led a band of students in defense of the city. After the siege was lifted,
he traveled first to Amsterdam and later to
Leyden to continue the study of anatomy.
While in Amsterdam as a pupil of anatomist
Blasius (Blaes), he discovered the duct of
the parotid gland during the dissection of
the head of a sheep.[2] Sylvius of Leyden
corroborated the finding in the human,
whereas van Horne gave it the eponymic
name. The discovery provoked a public
quarrel with Blasius, who claimed priority,
and Stensen found it best to leave Amsterdam. The observation of Stensen was reported in 1661 in a letter written in Latin
to Bartholin and translated by Winter.[3]

Since you urge me in your letter to publish an
account of the exterior salivary duct, I am constrained to explain to you briefly the envy which
this bit of a discovery *(inventiuncula)* has won
for me, and also the result of this envy; not with
the purpose of seeking fame in trifles, but in
order to free myself from the hateful charge of
stealing what does not belong to me.

It is a year now since I was hospitably received by Blaes. After waiting three weeks for a
chance to secure anatomical material, I asked the
distinguished man whether I might be permitted
to dissect with my own hands such material as
I could buy for myself. He gave his consent, and
fortune so favored me that in the first sheep's
head, which I had bought on April 7 and was
dissecting alone in my room, I found a duct
which, so far as I knew, had been described by
no one before. I had removed the skin and was
preparing to dissect the brain when I decided to
examine first the ducts. With this end in view I
was exploring the courses of the veins and arteries when I noticed that the point of my knife
was no longer closely confined between tissues
but moved freely in a large cavity, and presently
I heard the teeth themselves resound, as I thrust
my knife forward.

In amazement at the discovery I called in my
host (Blaes) that I might hear his opinion. First
he ascribed the sound to the violence of my
thrust, then resorted to calling it a freak of
Nature, and finally referred to Wharton. But
inasmuch as that did not help, and the ducts,
which had been handled carelessly, allowed no
further investigation, I decided to examine them
another time more carefully. I succeeded, although not so well, a few days later with a dog's
head.

Stensen's curiosity extended from ducts
and glands to the examination of the eye,
the vessels of the nose, and the structure
and function of muscular tissue. In his dissertation on the musculature of the heart,
published at the age of 26, he clearly
stated that the muscle fiber is the contractile
element.[4]

If one desires to apply the word muscle to the
heart, one must first demonstrate the proposition
that *the heart is truly a muscle.*

Among none of the fibers of the heart does one
meet, in examination, fibers of which the center
is not fleshy, and both extremes tendinous; this
moreover is common to all the fibers of the
muscle.

And thus everything is in agreement, and truly
muscle may be attributed to the heart, nor can it
be otherwise; *truly the heart merits the name of
muscle, because it has tendons and flesh and
nerves.*

. . . thus, from the fibers proceeds all movement of the heart, occurring as a phenomenon of its own.

After four years in Holland, Stensen had acquired a firm reputation in anatomy and, upon his return to Copenhagen, conducted public dissections and demonstrations in the anatomical theater. But with multiple scientific interests and an unsatiated wanderlust, he was not quite prepared to establish final roots. Restless of mind and body, he traveled to Paris, Rome, and Florence. In 1665, while in Paris, he presented a practical and theoretical discussion of the central nervous system based upon the anatomy of the brain. In Florence he served as physician to Grand Duke Ferdinand II and was an intimate of the court of the Medicis, a center for scholars and artists. A description by Stensen of one group of congenital heart lesions, identified with Fallot, preceded Fallot by two centuries. Paralysis of the lower limbs, which followed ligation of the descending aorta, was observed. From his studies on the dogfish, he concluded that the ovarian follicles were probably eggs.

In the natural sciences, Stensen preferred the study of geology. The fundamental principles of strata formation of the earth's crust were explored in his great work *Prodromus,* published in 1669.[3] The unevenness of the strata was attributed to pressure from gases in the earth, followed by erosion by the elements and fracture of some of the layers. The foreign bodies which appeared as fossils were assumed to have been laid down in successive layers as the earth's crust was formed. A similarity between the teeth of sharks of the sea and fossil remains in the caves of Tuscany was reported.

Stensen served for a time as professor and royal anatomist in Copenhagen, but the calling to the cloth was irrepressible. In 1667, he accepted Roman Catholicism for Lutheranism and was admitted to the priesthood in 1675; then followed assignments as Vicar Apostolic of Hanover and Bishop of the diocese of Titiopolis. His devotion to the church was as sincere as his devotion had been earlier to the laboratory, and the dire poverty associated with the priesthood was of little moment to him. More than a dozen

writings on theology appeared during this period, but he was silent on scientific matters.[3]

The first portion of Stensen's professional life left a deep mark in scientific history, as he accepted only those things which were revealed by his natural senses. In a period of less than 15 years, he had made notable contributions to anatomical science. In stratography, his discoveries and logical deductions justified the appellation by von Humboldt, "the father of geology of the 19th century." A medallion portrait on the walls of the cloister at San Lorenzo, Florence, where he was buried, has been translated by Winter.[3]

Friend, you behold the likeness of Nicolaus Steno. To it more than a thousand men of learning, from all parts of the world, contributed. They made provision for the carving of it in memory of this day, the twenty-eighth of September, in the year 1881, when the Geologists, after the Congress at Bologna, under the Presidency of Cavaliere Giovanni Capellini, journeyed hither, and in the presence of delegates representing the City of Florence and the Royal Institute of Higher Studies, in the cloister of this church, as a testimonial of respect and gratitude honored with a laurel crown a man of surpassing distinction among Geologists and Anatomists.

1. Scherz, G.: *Nicolaus Steno and His Indice,* Copenhagen: Munksgaard, 1958.
2. *Nicolai Stenonis Opera Philosophica,* vol 1, V. Maar, ed., Copenhagen: V. Tryde, 1910.
3. Winter, J. G.: *The Prodromus of Nicolaus Steno's Dissertation,* New York: Macmillan Company, 1916.
4. Stenonis, N.: *De Musculis & Glandulis Observationum Specimen,* Hafniae: M. Godicchenii, 1664; excerpt in Willius F. A., and Keys T. E.: *Cardiac Classics,* St. Louis: C. V. Mosby Company, 1941.

Robert Hooke (1635-1703)

ROBERT HOOKE, curator of the Royal Society of London for 40 years and one of the brilliant minds among British scientists, was an important physiologist and anatomist. As staff scientist for the Royal Society, he produced for the enlightenment of the members an unending display of scientific experiments on an infinite variety of subjects as varied as the interests of the members. An inferior social status, together with a somewhat irascible temper, contributed to the failure of a general appreciation of Hooke's scientific contributions for many years. Currently, his biographers judge him to be similar in intellectual stature to two of his better-known contemporaries, Sir Christopher Wren and Sir Isaac Newton.

Robert Hooke was born at Freshwater on the Isle of Wight.[1] His father, a curate, died when Robert was 13, Sickly as an infant, throughout his life he suffered from headaches, vertigo, and an irritable gastrointestinal tract. His father had hoped to prepare him for the ministry, but Robert preferred instead to tinker and experiment with mechanical toys. Such an interest in machines and instruments, as well as a native talent in sketching and painting, were capitalized in the design of scientific instruments and the illustration of his scientific books in later years. After the death of his father, he entered Westminster School and became proficient in Latin and Greek, but especially in mechanics and mathematics. At the age of 18, Hooke went to Christ Church, Oxford, as a chorister and, like other choral students, acted as a servant to one of the Fellows. While at Oxford he assisted Thomas Willis in the chemistry laboratory and, in turn, was recommended to Richard Boyle, under whose direction the air pump was developed for the studies which led to the enunciation of "Boyle's law." Hooke left Oxford without a degree, but the University awarded him a master of arts in 1663; in 1691, he took the oath for doctor of physic in the Doctors' Commons.

The events that led to Hooke's appointment in the Royal Society in 1662, two years after its founding, proceeded from the deliberations of a small group of members, who met in Gresham College and found that a need for a demonstrator existed, and[2]

... propos'd a Person that was willing to be entertain'd as a Curator by the Society, offering to furnish them every day when they met, with three or four considerable Experiments; which Proposition was unanimously receiv'd, Mr. Hooke being nam'd to be the Person; and accordingly the next Day of their meeting on the twelfth of November he was unanimously accepted and taken as Curator, with the Thanks of the Society order'd to Mr. Boyle for dispensing with him for their use, and order'd that Mr. Hooke should come and sit among them, and both bring in every Day three or four of his own Experiments, and take care of such others as should be recommended to him by the Society.

This appointment permitted Hooke to design innumerable pieces of equipment and to conduct experiments in many of the natural sciences. In astronomy, he appreciated the importance of the exact measurements of time; he designed the spring escapement for watch movements and made improvements on clocks that would enable longitude to be determined at sea. In meteorology, he perfected the telescope, invented the wheel barometer which registered air pressure on a dial, and improved the thermometer, hygrometer, wind gauge, and rain gauge. He invented telescopic sights for astronomical instruments and a clock-driven telescope which could be kept constantly in motion, focusing on a designated point in the sky. In oceanography, he devised sounding machines to bring up specimens from the deep. In mechanics, he invented the universal joint now used in automobiles (Hooke's joint) and improved the spirit level; in photography, he fashioned the iris diaphragm for sharpening the image. He mentioned the phenomenon of the diffraction of light, which was later called "Newton's rings."

Hooke extended the Baconian concept of natural phenomena by mechanical inventiveness. He had some thoughts on the construction of an airplane and, in considering aerodynamics, appreciated the fact that unaided musclar power of man was insufficient to keep him aloft. A procedure for supplying air to a diver's bell by a chain of buckets was designed, As a daily companion of Sir Christopher Wren, Hooke complemented Wren in architectural accomplishments, and especially in the rebuilding of London following the great fire of 1666. While Wren was concentrating on architecture, Hooke was busy with mechanical contributions. In addition to being curator for the Royal Society, he occupied the chair of geometry and accepted the Cutlerian lectureship. The chair of anatomy at Gresham, offered to him in 1665, was retained for life.

Some of Hooke's experiments were described in his diary, others were reported in the *Philosophical Transactions,* and still others were mentioned casually by his friends. He created modern scientific instruments, sometimes from his own ideas, sometimes from ideas of others. The instrument was planned, the experiment completed, and the matter usually dropped. Only a few of his instruments were patented, and a smaller number were exploited by the inventor. In improving the design of the microscope and the illumination of the subject under examination, he noted the advantages of viewing the object in a liquid interposed between the object and the lens.[3]

By means of this instrument I can with *little trouble,* and a very small quantity of any *Liquor,* examine, most accurately, the *refraction* of it, not only for one inclination, but for all; and thereby am inabled to make very accurate Tables; several of which I have also experimentally made, and find, that *Oyl of Turpentine* has a much greater Refraction then *Spirit of Wine,* though it be *lighter; and that Spirit of wine* has a greater Refraction then *Water,* though it be lighter also; but that *salt Water* also has a greater Refraction then *fresh,* though it be *heavier.*

The transfusion of blood from a mongrel donor to the recipient, probably with the assistance of Wren, was described in Samuel Pepys' diary for November 16, 1666.[4]

This noon I met with Mr. Hooke, and he tells me the dog which was filled with another dog's blood at the College the other day is very well, and like to be so as ever, and doubts not its being found of great use to men; and so do Dr. Whistler, who dined with us at the tavern.

Middleton has suggested that Hooke's discussion of mediate auscultation appeared 150 years before Laennec's observations.[2]

There may also be a possibility of discovering the Internal Motions and Actions of Bodies by the sound they make, who knows but that as in a Watch we may hear the beating of the Balance, and the running of the Wheels, and the striking of the Hammers, and the grating of the Teeth, and multitude of other noises; who knows, I say, but that it may be possible to discover the Motions of the Internal Parts of Bodies, whether

Animal, Vegetable, or Mineral, by the sound they make, that one may discover the Works perform'd in the several offices and Shops of a Man's Body, and thereby discover what Instrument or Engine is out of order, what Works are going on at several times, . . . And somewhat more of Incouragement I have also from Experience, that I have been able to hear very plainly the beating of a Man's heart.

Probably Hooke's most important physiological experiment was the preservation of life by blowing air through the windpipe of a dog with a bellows, an experiment demonstrated before the Royal Society in 1667.[5]

I did heretofore give this *Illustrious Society* an account of an Experiment I formerly tryed of keeping a Dog alive after his *Thorax* was all display'd by the cutting away of the *Ribbs* and *Diaphragme;* and after the *Pericardium* of the Heart also was taken off. But divers persons seeming to doubt of the certainty of the Experiment (by reason that some Tryals of this matter, made by some other hands, failed of success) I caus'd at the last Meeting the same Experiment to be shewn in the presence of this *Noble Company,* and that with the same success, as it had been made by me at first; the Dog being kept alive by the Reciprocal blowing up of his Lungs with *Bellowes,* and they suffered to subside, for the space of an hour or more, after his *Thorax* had been so display'd, and his *Aspera arteria* cut off just below the *Epiglottis,* and bound on upon the nose of the Bellows.

The dog having been kept alive, (as I have now mentioned) for above an houre, in which time the Tryal had been often repeated, in suffering the Dog to fall into *Convulsive* motions by ceasing to blow the Bellows, and permitting the Lungs to subside and lye still, and of suddenly reviving him again by renewing the blast, and consequently the motion of the Lungs.

Which seem to be arguments that as the *bare* Motion of the Lungs *without fresh Air* contributes nothing to the life of the Animal, he being found to survive as well, when they were not mov'd, as when they were; so it was not the subsiding or movelesness of the Lungs, that was the immediate cause of Death, or the stopping the Circulation of the Blood through the Lungs, but the *want* of a sufficient *supply of fresh Air.*

Hooke probably was treated unfairly for many years by his biographers. The publishing of a diary, which covered eight important years in his life, has shown him to be not so dyspeptic or cantankerous as assumed earlier.[1] He was a humane and genuinely sincere scientist, whose brilliant mind was able to portray to best advantage his capabilities as designer and demonstrator of scientific instruments in the early years of the modern era. His great capacity for accurate observation and invention of instruments was equalled by his genius for theoretical insight.[6]

1. *The Diary of Robert Hooke, A.M., M.D., F.R.S., 1672-1680,* H. W. Robinson, and W. Adams, ed., London: Taylor & Francis, 1935.

2. Middleton, W. S.: The Medical Aspect of Robert Hooke, *Ann Med Hist* 9:227-243 (Sept) 1927.

3. Hooke, R.: *Micrographia: Or Some Physiological Descriptions of Minute Bodies Made by Magnifying Glasses with Observations and Inquiries Thereupon.* London: J. Martyn and J. Allestry, 1665.

4. Smith, G. G.: *The Diary of Samuel Pepys,* London: Macmillan & Co., 1929.

5. An Account of an Experiment made by M. Hook, of Preserving Animals alive by Blowing through their Lungs with Bellows, *Philos Trans* 1:539-540, 1665-1666.

6. Crowther, J. G.: *Founders of British Science,* London: Cresset Press, 1960.

National Library of Medicine

Robert Boyle (1627-1691)

ROBERT BOYLE, a self-taught natural philosopher deeply interested in the medical sciences, possessed a degree in medicine, which was not earned but was created for this 17th century genius. His name is familiar to many because of the recognition

of the reciprocal relationship between pressure and volume of a gas at a given temperature—the principle of Boyle and Mariotte. When Boyle was created doctor of physic in 1665, his contemporary, Antony à Wood, prepared the following citation:[1]

This honourable person, who was the son of Richard the first earl of Cork, was born at Lismore in Ireland, whence, after he had been well grounded in juvenile learning, he went to the univ. of Leyden, and spent some time there in good letters. Afterwards, · he travelled into France, Switzerland, Italy, &c. and . . . in Rome. . . . After his return into England, being then accounted a well-bred gentleman, he setled in Oxon, in the time of Oliver, about 1657, where he carried on his great delight in several studies, especially in experimental philosophy and chymistry, spent much money, entertained operators to work in his elaboratory which he had built for his own use, and often did repair to the club of virtuosi in the lodgings of Dr. Wilkins warden of Wadh. coll. and they to him. . . . After his majesty's restoration, when the royal society was erected, he was made one of the first members thereof, was one of the council belonging thereunto, and the greatest promoter of new philosophy of any among them. . . . The books that he hath written are many, some of which are printed beyond the seas, and are there highly valued: In all which he hath done such things for the benefit of the world and increase of knowledge, that none hath yet equall'd, much less gone beyond him. In them you'll find the greatest strength and the gentleelest smoothness, the most generous knowledge and the sweetest modesty, the noblest discoveries and the sincerest relations, the greatest self-denial and the greatest love of men, the profoundest insight into philosophy and nature, and the most devoute, affectionate sense of God and of religion, as in any works whatsoever written by other men, &c.

This rather long excerpt describes very well the geographic and hereditary environment of Boyle, his interest in science and the humanities, and his prolific literary accomplishments. He was a bachelor of means, a chemist, theologian, and medical scientist, who was well qualified to practice physic, as judged by his writings in physiology, pharmacology, pathology, and therapeutics, had he chosen to do so. Although gentle by nature and frail in constitution, he permitted neither his inherited nor acquired characteristics to deter him from a highly productive intellectual life. He pursued no single profession unless one considers polymathy a calling. He was one of the original members of the council of the Royal Society—the body that has claimed the most distinguished men of English science for three centuries.

Boyle's bibliography by John Fulton, lists more than 300 items. Contributions to chemistry, physics, medicine, philosophy, and theology are included.[1]

The Spring and Weight of the Air was Boyle's first published scientific work (1660) and one of the most noteworthy. Although the concept that air has weight should be attributed to no one person, Galileo, Torricelli, Pascal, and von Guericke are particularly deserving of sharing the honors. In the extension of the study of gases, Robert Hooke, Boyle's laboratory assistant, was charged with the design of a more efficient "wind" pump than currently available.[2] Before a regular session of the Royal Society held shortly after, Boyle demonstrated the reciprocal relationship between pressure and volume of a gas. The relationship was confirmed by Mariotte in 1676. The description by Boyle appeared in a separate tract appended to the second edition (1662) of *New Experiments , Physico-Mechanical Touching the Spring of the Air, and It's Effects, (Made for the Most Part, in a New Pneumatical Engine.).*[3]

Now that this Observation does both very well agree with and confirm our *Hypothesis,* will be easily discerned by him that takes notice that we teach, and Monsieur *Paschall* and our *English* friends Experiments prove, that the greater the weight is that leans upon the Air, the more forcible is its endeavour of Dilatation, and consequently its power of resistance (as other Springs are stronger when bent by greater weights). For this being considered it wil appear to agree rarely—well with the *Hypothesis,* that as according to it the Air in that degree of density and correspondent measure of resistance to which the weigth of the incumbent Atmosphere had brought it, was able to counter-balance and resist the pressure of a Mercurial Cylinder of about 29. Inches, as we are taught by the *Torricellian* Experiment; so here the same Air being brought to a degree of density about twice as great as that it had before, obtains a Spring twice as strong as formerly.

Another classic experiment, performed a century before Lavoisier discovered oxygen,

led to the deduction that combusion and respiration rely upon some substance in the air. Neither a flame nor an animal was found to be able to survive long in a closed chamber from which air had been removed.[4]

The flame of a lamp will last almost as little after the Exsuction of the Air, as the life of an animal. . . . That the Common flame and the Vital flame are maintained by distinct substances or parts of the Air; *or* that common Flame making a great waste of the Aereal substance, they both need to keep them alive.

In commenting on this hypothesis, Cohen discovered no experimental observations substantiating this hypothesis and speculated that the deductions were made without supporting data.

In Boyle's treatise, *The Usefulness of Experimental Philosophy*[5] (1663), "physick" was logically divisible into five parts: the physiological, pathological, semiotical, hydieinal, and the therapeutical. The division is more modern than the discussion in any area except the first. Boyle noted that the spleen is not essential to life and may be removed without obvious harm. The frog may survive after removal of the heart; the silkworm butterfly is capable of procreation after the loss of its head. A monograph on hypothermia also reveals modern concepts of the effects of cold.[6] Death from exposure to cold may be produced rapidly or slowly. The preservation of meat by freezing and revival of fish or frogs after freezing are recorded. Other physiological experiments included the transfusion of blood in animals, and comparison of the specific gravity of blood, urine, and water. Blood and urine were found to be more resistant to freezing than was water; hence, their specific gravity was higher. Experiments were made in an attempt to render sea water fit for human consumption. Studies on osmotic pressure preceded any generally accepted concept of physical chemistry. The absorption of therapeutic agents through the skin and the porosity of bodies were investigated.

In his studies on vitiated sight,[7] a case of exophthalmic ophthalmoplegia was described, without clinical evidence that the patient was suffering from hyperthyroidism.

This was a Gentlewoman about one or two and twenty years of Age, Whose Complexion and Features would have made her Handsom, if she had not had that sort of Eyes, which tho' rarely met with, some call Ox-Eyes; for Hers were swell'd much beyond the size of Human Eyes, in so much that she complain'd, they often frighted those that saw Her, and were indeed so Big, that she could not move them to the Right Hand or the Left, but was constrain'd to look strait forward; or if she would see an Object that lay Aside, she was oblig'd to turn her Whole Head that way. And so she answer'd me she was, when she set herself to Read in a Book, unless she did with her Hand move the Book from one side to another, to bring the ends of the Lines directly before her Eyes.

In his will, Boyle directed that a portion of his estate be used for the advancement of the Christian religion.[8] This was implemented by a request to "the corporation for propagating the Gospel amongst the heathen natives in New-England and other parts of America."

William and Mary College, Williamsburg, Va., was eventually

. . . a major beneficiary of the trust fund set up from the proceeds of the residue of his personalty by the direction of the Earl of Burlington and the Bishop of London, who had been designated trustees by the executors of the estate to lay out the surplus rents and profits, after incidental expenses of administration and the annuities to the Corporation for the Propagation of the Gospel in New England and Harvard College, for the advancement of the Christian religion in Virginia.

The executors of the estate invested £5,400 to purchase the manor of Brafferton in Yorkshire. The rents from the manor were conveyed to William and Mary College, to be used in the construction and operation of the Brafferton School for Indians, a unit of the college. The Court of the Chancery approved this action in 1698, which remained in effect until 1775, when "the provinces of New England and Virginia fell into a state of rebellion against the King of Great Britain." If one visits William and Mary College today, two relics of Boyle remain. A fine portrait by Frederick Causabon (alias Kerseboom), painted about 1689, hangs in the Blue Room of the Christopher Wren building. The Brafferton building, constructed in 1723, stands on the old campus and is used by the administrative branch of the college.

1. Fulton, J. F.: A Bibliography of the Honourable Robert Boyle, ed. 2, London: Oxford, 1961.

2. Turner, H. D.: Robert Hooke and Boyle's Air Pump, Nature 184:395 (Aug. 8) 1959.

3. Boyle, R.: A Defence of the Doctrine touching the Spring and Weight of the Air, Oxford, England: Henry Hall, 1662.

4. Cohen, L. A.: An Evaluation of the Classical Candle-Mouse Experiment, J Hist Med 11:127 (April) 1956.

5. Boyle, R.: Some Considerations Touching the Usefurness of Experimental Natural Philosophy, Oxford, England: Henry Hall, 1663.

6. Boyle, R.: New Experiments and Observations Touching Cold or an Experimental History of Cold, London: John Crook, 1665.

7. Boyle, R.: Final Causes and Vitiated sight, London: John Taylor, 1668.

8. Ganter, H. L.: Some Notes on "The Charity of the Honourable Robert Boyle, Esq., of the City of London, Deceased," William and Mary Quart 15:1 (Jan.); 213 (July) 1935.

John Mayow (1641?-1679)

IF JOHN MAYOW had described by name the vital substance he identified in the respiratory cycle, he would have been credited with the discovery of oxygen a century before the communications by Priestley and Lavoisier. Instead, his term for molecules "nitro-aërial" or "igneo-aërial" particles, failed to attract the scientists of his day to the significance of his experimental observations and physiological deductions. His biographers differ as to the date and place of birth, as well as to credit due for his belatedly recognized concepts.[1]

Mayow was born some time between 1640 and 1645, either in Cornwall or in London. He was accepted as a commoner of Wadham College, Oxford, and, on the recommendation of Henry Coventry, was elected to fellowship at All Souls College. There he studied law, receiving the bachelor of civil law in 1665 and the doctorate in 1670. Meanwhile, he had been elected to the Royal Society for his work on the nitro-aerial substance. There is no record of his having taken a medical degree; however, he studied physic and became sufficiently competent in medicine to practice in London and, for the summer, in the city of Bath, where he possibly included a little law. He died in his late 30's, without receiving the recognition due his important physiological observations.

Mayow, who showed that only a portion of the air is necessary for animal life, is associated with Lower, Hooke, and Boyle, eminent physiologists of Oxford. In describing the mechanics of respiration, he detected the double articulation of the ribs with the spine and the function of the intercostal muscles, recognized the composition of the supply of nutrients to the fetus, attributed contraction of skeletal muscle to a chemical reaction, and enumerated the physical findings in rickets. While at Oxford, in his 20's, he published his first treatise, *De Respiratione,* his greatest work. The monograph was expanded and complemented in the immediate subsequent years, and, in 1674, a compilation of his works entitled *Tractatus quinque medico-physici* appeared.[2] In the *Tractatus quinque,* the studies were arranged by the author in his selected order of importance. The first study explained the phenomenon of flame as arising from a part of nitre comprising the nitro-aerial spirit or igneo-aerial particles of the air. While he supported his views with ingenious and convincing arguments, he failed to identify this component as oxygen.

Mayow's views on combustion, calcination (oxidation), and respiratory exchange of gases were also supported by ingenious and convincing experiments. His separation by distillation of nitre (potassium nitrate) into two parts, one acid, the other earth, led him next to produce combustible gunpowder by the addition of sulfur to the aerial part of nitre. In experimenting with the chemical and physical properties of air, independent of Boyle but cognizant of his work, Mayow used jars inverted over water for placement of small animals, lighted candles, and susceptible combustibles, to observe that the extinction of life and flame is associated with the diminution of the volume of contained air and loss of weight by giving up its essential constituent. He reasoned from the premise that the nitro-aerial constituent, which participated in a chemical process resembling combustion in the body tissues, was extracted from the air in respiration. The substance was carried by the blood to the tissues and made arterial blood brighter and redder than venous blood. Since inspired air lost its "elastic force" (oxygen), a continual renewal from the air was imperative for life. Animals were shown to be dependent upon an environment which comprised the saline-sulfurous compounds ingested as food and replaced periodically with meals, and the second component, a supply of nitro-aerial particles, which cannot be stored and must be replaced continually. Thus, starvation does not immediately lead to death; on the other hand, the nitro-aerial particles in the air must be replaced without interruption to sustain life.[3]

. . . one can scarcely suppose that the nitre itself is all derived from the air, but merely its more volatile and subtle part, the rest of the nitre being due to the earth.

. . . something aerial . . . is necessary to the production of any flame—a fact which the experiments of Boyle have placed beyond doubt. . . . But it is not to be supposed that the air itself, but only that its more active and subtle part is the igneo-aërial food.

. . . I take it for granted that the air contains certain particles termed by us elsewhere nitro-aërial, which are absolutely indispensable for the production of fire, and that these in the burning of flame are drawn from the air and removed, so that the latter when deprived of these particles ceases to be fit for supporting fire.

. . . it is quite certain that animals in breathing draw from the air certain vital particles which are also elastic. So that there should be no doubt at all now that an aërial something absolutely necessary to life enters the blood of animals by means of respiration.

And indeed we must believe that animals and fire draw particles of the same kind from the air.

For let any animal be enclosed in a glass vessel along with a lamp so that the entrance of air from without is prevented, which is easily done if the orifice of the inverted glass be immersed in water in the manner already described. When this is done we shall soon see the lamp go out and the animal will not long survive the fatal torch. For I have ascertained by experiment that an animal enclosed in a glass vessel along with a lamp will not breathe much longer than half the time it would otherwise have lived.

Fermentation was likened to combustion, and all secretions were related to fermentative phenomena, including the ferments of the stomach, pancreas, and kidneys. The transverse fibrils inserted into the fibers of the muscle and, in turn, inserted into the tendons were associated with muscle contraction. The physiological-chemical process in muscle contraction, which required nutrients and the nitro-aërial spirit, was described as follows.[3]

. . . it has been established from what has been elsewhere said, that nitro-aërial and sulphureous particles effervesce when mixed with one another.

For, no doubt, just as the nitro-aërial spirit meeting with terrestrial sulphur excites that fermentation in which the motion and the life of vegetables consist, so also according as the same spirit, brought by means of respiration into the mass of the blood and there effervescing with the saline-sulphureous particles of the blood, produces the vital heat and motion, as I have elsewhere striven to show, it is probable that animal life and the motive function are brought about by the same particles more exalted and put in a condition of the highest vapor. For indeed I think that nitro-aërial particles springing forth from the brain into the motor parts effervesce there with the saline-sulphureous particles meeting them, and muscular contraction is caused by their mutual agitation in the way to be stated below. And hence it is that for keeping up animal motion it is essentially necessary that there should never be a deficiency in the mass of the blood of saline-sulphureous pabulum or of nitro-aërial particles; and by how much more intensely the muscular contraction takes place, as in the

harder kinds of work, so much greater is the outlay of nitro-aërial and of sulphureous particles, for the repair of which not only is the respiration increased, but besides there must be taken in greater quantity food filled with saline-sulphureous particles. Hence those articles of food which contain abundance of volatile salt and sulphur are specially fitted for restoring the powers worn by long-continued labour.

In comparative physiology and embryology, Mayow contended that the gills of fish function as lungs and the water in which the fish live contains nitro-aerial spirits to support life. When water is boiled and the vital substance extracted, it can no longer support the life of a fish. The placenta in humans was identified as the lungs of the fetus.[3]

. . . we maintain that the blood of the embryo, conveyed by the umbilical arteries to the placenta or uterine carunculae, brings not only nutritious juice, but along with this a portion of nitro-aërial particles to the foetus for its support; so that it seems that the blood of the infant is impregnated with nitro-aërial particles by its circulation in the umbilical vessels. . . . And therefore I think that the placenta should no longer be called a uterine liver but rather a uterine lung.

This liberal interpretation of Mayow's imaginative thoughts and enterprising scientific experiments has not been accepted by all who have written about him. His work was largely overlooked for a century, which has been judged consonant with his impact on physiological thinking. Some have accused him of taking his ideas on respiration and combustion from Lower, Boyle, and Hooke. Others have considered his writings largely nonsense and have assumed the abstracts in the *Philosophical Transactions* were sober, valid appraisals.[4] To come to Mayow's support, Partington of London University[1] acknowledges the achievements of Mayow as well as his shortcomings. He considers him an outstanding experimenter and speculative physiologist of his day, who, had he not died at an early age, might have continued his scientific work, adding new observations and possibly shortening the time until the identification and isolation of oxygen by Priestley and Lavoisier.

1. Partington, J. R.: The Life and Work of John Mayow (1641-1679), *Isis* 47:217-230, 405-417, 1956.

2. Mayow, J.: *Tractatus Quinque Medico-Physici,* Oxonii: e Theatro Sheldoniano, 1674.
3. Mayow, J.: *Medico-Physical Works,* Edinburgh: Alembic Club, 1907, translation of Mayow.[2]
4. Anon: An Account of Two Books, *Philos Trans* 9: 101-113, 1674.

Royal College of Physicians

Christopher Wren (1632-1723)

SIR CHRISTOPHER WREN, genius of architecture and one of the founders of British science, neither practiced medicine nor devoted any significant portion of his time to the medical sciences. Nevertheless, his contributions to anatomical drawing and experimental physiology have been firmly inscribed in the archives of medical history. Line drawings for Thomas Willis' *Cerebri anatome* and infusion experiments on a dog are highlights in this category. He assisted Scarburgh in anatomical experiments, prepared anatomical models of the muscles of the body, and designed an artificial eye, with the humors accurately and dioptrically made.

Christopher came of an honorable family; his father was dean of Windsor and chaplain to Charles I. Because of the boy's tender health, he was privately tutored before studying at Westminster School and later at Wadham College, Oxford.[1] In the meantime, he had shown his inventive brilliance, having devised a pneumatic engine and a farm implement for planting corn. More than fifty inventions have been credited to Wren. Devices of his imaginative mind include a reflecting dial, a meteorological barometer, planetarium for illumination of the moon and planets in a dark room, a perpetual motion apparatus, a device for writing in the dark, and probable ways for making potable water at sea.[2]

Wren was appointed professor of astronomy at Gresham College, London, in 1657, followed shortly by a summons from Whitehall to assist in planning the reconstruction of St. Paul's Cathedral.[3] Political intrigue and jealousy delayed plans for restoration, until the great fire of 1666 left the cathedral in ruins. Urgency and bold planning resulted in the rebuilding of one of the greatest churches of the Western world. Although Wren was first consulted about St. Paul's as a young man, it was not until he was seventy-nine years of age that the highest stone of the lantern was placed on the cupola, thus signaling the completion of his assigned task. In the interim, he designed more than fifty churches in London, the Palace of Charles II at Greenwich, additions to Windsor Castle, the Royal Exchange, the Temple Bar, the Doric column which commemorated the fire, the College of Physicians building in Warwick Lane, long since destroyed, and the first permanent structure, known as the Main building, at the College of William and Mary at Williamsburg, Va. This last name was later changed to the Sir Christopher Wren Building.

Wren was commissioned by Willis to prepare the anatomical drawings for the *Cerebri Anatome,* now a collector's item of the 17th century. His skill in line drawing complemented the anatomical perspicuity of Thomas Willis. In experimental physiology, the *Philosophical Transactions* for 1665 recounts the report of Wren's observations on intravenous infusion. Wren was ably assisted in the experiments by Robert Boyle, who prepared a suitable piece of apparatus for the infusion.[4]

To joyn all these circumstances together, 'Tis notorious, that at least six years since (a good while before it was heard off, that any one did pretend to have so much as thought of it) the Learned and Igenious Dr. *Christopher Wren* did propose in the *University* of *Oxford* (where he now is the Worthy Savilian Professor of *Astron-*

omy, and where very many Curious Persons are ready to attest this relation) to that Noble Benefactor to Experimental Philosophy, Mr. *Robert Boyle,* Dr. *Wilkins,* and other deserving Persons, That he thought, he could easily contrive a Way to conveigh any liquid thing immediately into the Mass of Blood; *videl:* By making Ligatures on the Veines, and then opening them on the side of the Ligature towards the Heart, and by putting into them slender Syringes or Quills, fastened to Bladders (in the manner of Clysterpipes) containing the matter to be injected; performing that Operation upon pretty big and lean doggs, that the Vessels might be large enough and easily accessible.

This proposition being made, M. *Boyle* soon gave order for an *Apparatus,* to put it to Experiment; wherein at several times, upon several Doggs, *Opium* & the Infusion of *Crocus Metallorum* were injected into that part of the hind-legs of those Animals whence the larger Vessels, that carry the Blood, are most easily to be taken hold of: whereof the success was, that the *Opium,* being soon circulated into the Brain, did within a short time stupify, though not kill the Dog; but a large Dose of the *Crocus Metallorum,* made an other Dog Vomit up Life and all.

Wren died in his ninety-first year and was buried in a vault in St. Paul's. No architect of the modern world has left so great a heritage to the design of public buildings, and, although not medically trained, will be remembered as a contributor to pictorial anatomy and experimental physiology.

1. "Sir Christopher Wren," in *The Dictionary of National Biography,* vol 21, L. Stephen, and Sir S. Lee, ed., 1917, pp 995-1009.
2. Wren, C.: *Parentalia, or Memoirs of the Wrens,* London: S. Wren, 1750.
3. Tillotson, J.: *Lives of Eminent Men,* London: T. Holmes, n.d.
4. Boyle, R.: An Account of the Rise and Attempts, of a Way to conveigh Liquors immediately into the Mass of Blood, *Philos Trans,* 1665, pp 128-131.

Frederik Ruysch (1638-1731)

FREDERIK RUYSCH, outstanding prosector of his time, was born at The Hague, son of the secretary of the States General of Holland.[1] He became a pharmacist prior to studying medicine at Leyden, where he took the doctor's degree in 1664, presenting a dissertation on pleurisy. He then returned to The Hague to begin the practice of medicine. Shortly after, during an epidemic of plague, he was charged by the State with the care of the afflicted in his community.

Composite by G. Bako

The assignment was effectively carried out. However, practice alone would have left a void in his intellectual life if he had not pursued his interests in anatomical dissection and the pathogenesis of physiological functions. Ruysch was rewarded in 1665 with the discovery of valves in the lymphatics and the call to Amsterdam to the chair of anatomy. In 1672, the chair of midwifery was added and, in 1695, forensic medicine. Late in his career (1727) he was elected a fellow of the Royal Society of London and the Academy of Sciences of Paris.

In spite of or because of these several academic responsibilities, Ruysch continued his investigations in comparative and human anatomy in addition to his practice. Improvement in the techniques of others for the injection and permanent visualization of blood vessels in anatomical specimens was his greatest contribution; however, he dissected plants with the same precision as specimens from the animal kingdom. The injection process, kept secret unto his death, consisted of installation of a colored preservative into the smallest blood vessels, producing a lifelike appearance in regional tissues as well as in intact cadavers. In the application of the technique, he extended the existing knowledge of bronchial arteries, vascularity of the brain, vascular plexuses of the heart, and structure of the tunica vasculosa of the eye. The preparation of the multitude of specimens is assumed charitably to have been so laborious that time did not permit any reference to the contributions of others. This apology was offered to offset the criticism that Ruysch claimed discoveries which were not original.

The number of specimens and the popular appeal of his bountifully stocked and beautifully displayed museum gained the attention of Peter the Great, who, in 1717, purchased the collection and removed it to St. Petersburg. False reports of misfortune to the collection in transit to Russia at that time as well as in World War II, more than two centuries later, have been slow to be quashed. Mann has recently confirmed the preservation of more than 900 specimens of the collection in the Kunstkammer of Peter the Great in the Leningrad Academy of Science.[2] Subsequently, Ruysch established another anatomical museum with specimens as well-prepared and as numerous as the original collection. This was acquired eventually by the University of Wittenberg.

In addition to his treatises on anatomy, based on his extensive dissections, Ruysch published a text on practical observations in medicine and surgery.[3] A description of caries of the ribs from a huge aneurysm of the aorta is excerpted below, from the translation by W. H. Wilder, Jr.[4]

Just as sweat coming through the pores of the skin is so acrid in some that undergarments, even shirts, very shortly take on an odor from it, so the humours show the same trait when the true ribs become carious simply from an aneurysm of the ascending aorta. Twenty-two years ago I dissected the body of a man who for a long time had had in the chest an aneurysm of such great size that it equalled the head of a new born child, with a strong pulsation that smote the hand applied to the chest. When we opened the body we found an aneurysm in the great ascending artery one digit from the heart. . . . By the growth of this aneurysm the ribs were not only

forced apart from each other, but, as we found, so corroded that they were lacking in great part, and what did remain could easily be resolved into a paste by rubbing with the fingers. When many years ago I related this case to the celebrated Van der Schagen, Doctor of Medicine, who was then alive, he told me that he also had seen caries of the ribs caused by pectoral aneurysm. It might indeed me more easily wondered at than explained how an enclosed aneurysm (that seems much like a dilated artery) can so corrode the ribs, if the following case had not come my way.

1. Pettigrew, T. J.: "Frederic Ruysch, M.D. F.R.S.," in *Medical Portrait Gallery*, London: Fisher, Son, & Co., 1840, vol 1, pp 1-4.
2. Mann G.: The Anatomical Collections of Frederik Ruysch at Leningrad, *Bull Cleveland Med Libr* 11:10-13 (Jan) 1964.
3. Ruysch, F.: *Centuria of Anatomico-Surgical Observations* (L), Amsterdam: H. & T. Boom, 1691.
4. Long, E. R. (ed.): "Frederik Ruysch (1638-1731)," in *Selected Readings in Pathology*, W. H. Wilder, Jr. (trans.), Springfield, Ill. Charles C Thomas, 1929.

Composite by G. Bako

Jan Swammerdam (1637-1680)

JAN SWAMMERDAM, one of the great natural scientists of the 17th century, was born in Amsterdam, the son of an apothecary and student of natural history who had amassed an assortment of insects, plants, fossils, and miscellanea.[1] The expanse of the colonial empire of the Netherlands at that time fostered the formation of private collections while the paternal hobby became the professional pursuit of Jan. After he was instructed in Latin and in Greek but forced to delay his higher education because of poor health, he followed the proper course for a natural scientist and studied medicine at Leyden. There he enjoyed the instruction of Silvius de la Boe, professor of medicine, formed a lasting friendship with Nicholas Steno and introduced the method of injection in the preparation of anatomical specimens.

About 1665, Swammerdam visited several parts of France seeking to overcome a chronic illness, a malady which continued to handicap him periodically throughout his relatively short professional career. He returned to Holland, continued the study of anatomy and medicine and graduated two years later. In his inaugural thesis on respiration, he describes the medico-legal fact that fetal lungs will float if respiration has taken place. By this time, Swammerdam had observed red corpuscles in the circulating blood and valves in the lymphatics of the frog but published neither finding until many years later.

Contrary to the wishes of his father, Swammerdam did not engage in the practice of medicine but continued the collection and anatomical investigation of lower forms of life—particularly insects. He assembled and classified more than 3000 species of insects which can be readily identified today because of his skill in sketching them for the monograph. Boerhaave stated that all the ages from the commencement of natural history to his time had produced nothing comparable to his *General History of Insects*.[2]

Swammerdam anticipated Galvani's frog experiment with the nerve fibers of an exposed muscle bound with a silver wire and brought in contact with a brass loop. Contraction of the isolated muscle followed. Although the work was done while a student at Leyden, it was not published until the assembly of his work and the preparation of Boerhaave's biography many years later.[3]

EXPERIMENT TO DEMONSTRATE CONTRACTION OF FROG MUSCLE

Another very delicate and useful experiment may be made, if one of the largest muscles be separated from the thigh of a Frog, and, together with its adherent nerve, prepared in such a manner as to remain unhurt.

We very clearly find also by experiments, that the motion produced in the muscle by irritating the nerve, is always propagated out of the larger into the smaller branches, and goes afterwards continually descending. The nerves designed for the senses are circumstanced in quite different manner; for in these, the sensitive motions, doubtless, tend upwards. In order to contract any muscle, it is necessary that its nerve be irritated in the region above the muscle, or at its insertion into it; since the motion never tends upwards, but always downwards. . . .

If, instead of the heart, we should chuse to make use of some other muscle, we may proceed in the manner represented in the eighth figure, where the glass siphon, Tab. XLIX. Fig. VIII, *a,* contains within its hollow the muscle, *b,* and the nerve hanging from the muscle is fastened, without being cut or bruised to a slender twisted silver wire, *cc,* that runs at the other end, an eye made in a piece of brass wire, soldered to the embolus or piston of the siphon, *d.* Things being thus made ready, a drop of water, *e,* must be let into the slender tube of the siphon by a very fine funnel. Now, if after this, the silver wire be cautiously drawn with a leisurely hand *f* through the ring or eye of the brass wire, till the nerve is irritated by the compression, it must by this means undergo, the muscle will contract.

Swammerdam renounced his science in his prime when he came under the spell of a fanatical religious sectarian, was disinherited by his father, and wasted by disease. In the frenzy he came to regard scientific research as worldly and giving himself up to religious contemplation he destroyed some of his experimental communications and manuscripts before they were published.

1. Duncan, J.: *Memoir of Swammerdam, Introduction of Entomology,* The Naturalists Library, London: Bohn, 1860, pp 17-58.

2. Swammerdam, J.: *General History of Insects* (L), 2 parts, Utrecht (sic): M. van Dreunen, 1669.

3. Swammerdam, J.: *The Book of Nature; or the History of Insects* (L), translated from Dutch and Latin originally by T. Elloyd. Revised and improved by notes from Reanmur and others, by John Hill, MD, London: 1758.

Richard Lower (1631-1691)

RICHARD LOWER, pupil and research associate of Thomas Willis, was born at Tremeere near Bodmin, Cornwall; Richard was educated at Westminster School, where he obtained a scholarship to Christ Church, Oxford. In succession he qualified for his degrees, the AB and the AM, and in 1665 the MD. For a number of years his destiny in the study of medicine and in research in anatomy, especially of the nervous system, was interwoven with that of Willis, whom he followed eventually to London. There Lower established a practice, was elected to Fellowship in the Royal Society in 1667, and to the Royal College of Physicians in 1675. His medical writing began at Oxford, where he published a defense of Willis' work on fevers and in turn was credited with assisting in the preparation of De cerebro. Although Lower's later contributions are associated with London, his identity with the remarkable group of natural scientists of Oxford, notably Willis, Black, Boyle, and Wren, was assured.

The treatise in Latin on the form and function of the heart, Tractatus de corde, which appeared in 1669, contained the first important experimental study of the organ after Harvey.[1] A second edition in 1670 included, as an appendix, an unrelated but important observation, a refutation of the theory of the formation of nasal secretions from the central nervous system. It has been held by Hippocrates, supported by Galen, and not disproved in the intervening years, that nasal secretions were excreted through the cribriform plate from the brain. Lower showed by observation that catarrh is not a product of the brain.[2]

The wife of a certain citizen of London, aged 30, healthy and active enough previously, became very dejected and melancholy during the last three years of her life, suffered from breathlessness on the least exertion, had a small and often an intermittent pulse, and complained almost continuously of attacks of pain and of great physical discomfort . . . in the precordium. . . . When the body was opened no abnormalities at all were visible among the abdominal viscera. While examining the other organs, however, we discovered a pathological condition of the heart, to which we may rightly attribute the cause of all her troubles. The thorax was opened and the lungs were healthy enough; the pericardium, however, had become closely attached all over to the whole surface of the heart, so that it could only with difficulty be separated from it. Further, this membrane had become thick, opaque, and hard, instead of being thin and transparent, as it should naturally have been. Hence, as there was no space for the free movement of the heart, and no fluid for moistening its surface, it is little wonder that she complained all the time of these ills. Further, as the diaphragm is always attached to the pericardium in man, when the heart itself was also united to . . . the pericardium, the diaphragm must of necessity have carried the heart down with it at every inspiration, and during that time must have held up and suppressed its movement. So the observed intermission of the pulse succeeded regularly at every inspiration.

The color of the blood, the subject of the second portion of the subtitle of Tractatus, dealt with the dark venous blood and the bright arterial blood. With in vivo and in vitro experiments, Lower showed that the blue venous blood became bright in color following passage through the lungs, suggesting that the blood absorbed from the air a chemical substance necessary for life and that the pulmonary circulation was a vital function of the body rather than merely nutrient vessels to the lung. A simple in vitro experiment showed the affinity of venous blood for oxygen.[3]

Further, that this red colour is entirely due to the penetration of particles of air into the blood, is quite clear from the fact that, while the blood becomes red throughout its mass in the lungs (because the air diffuses in them through all the particles of blood, and hence becomes more thoroughly mixed with the blood), when venous blood is received into . . . a vessel, the surface and uppermost part of it takes on this scarlet colour through exposure to the air. If this is removed with a knife, the part lying next below will soon change to the same colour through similar contact with the air.

Indeed, if the cake of blood is turned over after remaining stationary for a long while, its outer and uppermost layer takes on the red colour in a short space of time (provided the blood is still fresh). It is a matter of common knowledge that venous blood becomes completely red when received into a dish and shaken up for a long time to cause a thorough penetration of air into it.

On this account it is extremely probable that the blood takes in air in its course through the lungs, and owes its bright colour entirely to the admixture of air. Moreover, after the air has in large measure left the blood again within the body and the parenchyma of the viscera, and has transpired through the pores of the body, it is equally consistent with the reason that the venous blood, which has lost its air, should forthwith appear darker and blacker.

One of Lower's most remarkable experiments was the direct transfusion of blood from the artery of the donor through a quill cannula into the jugular vein of the recipient. The first attempt suggested by the experiments of Christopher Wren in injecting poisons into veins, was performed at Oxford in 1665. The intention of the experiment was to exploit the procedure as a means of treating disease in man, but before this was realized by Lower, Denys in Paris performed the first human transfusion. The transfusion from animal to animal by Lower was communicated by Robert Boyle to the Royal Society in 1666, and the transfusion from a sheep to a man was communicated by Edmund King one year later. Each appeared in the *Philosophical Transactions*.[4,5]

First, Take up the *Carotidal* Artery of the Dog or other Animal, whose Bloud is to be transfused into another of the same or a different kind, and separate it from the Nerve of the *Eight pair*, and lay it bare above an inch. Then make a strong Ligature on the *upper* part of the Artery, not to be untied again: but an inch below, *videl.* towards the Heart, make another Ligature of a *running* knot, which may be loosen'd or fastned as there shall be occasion. Having made these two knots, draw two threds under the Artery between the two Ligatures; and then open the Artery, and put in a Quill, and tie the Artery upon the Quill very fast by those two threds, and stop the Quill with a stick. After this, make bare the *Jugular* Vein in the other Dog about an inch and a half long; and at each end make a Ligature with a running knot, and in the space betwixt the two running knots drawn under the Vein two threds, as in the other: then make an Incision in the Vein, and put into it two Quills, one into the *descendent* part of the Vein, to receive the bloud from the other Dog, and carry it to the Heart: and the other Quill put into the other part of the *Jugular* Vein, which comes from the Head (out of which, the second Dogs own bloud must run into Dishes.)

All things being thus prepar'd, tie the Dogs on their sides towards one another so conveniently, that the Quill may go into each other, (for the Dogs necks cannot be brought so near, but that you must put two or three several Quills more into the first two, to convey the bloud from one to another.) After that, unstop the Quill that goes down into the first Dog's *Jugular* Vein, and the other quill coming out of the other Dog's Artery; and by the help of two or three other Quills, put into each other, according as there shall be occasion, insert them into one another. Then slip the running knots, and immediately the bloud runs through the Quills, as through an Artery, very impetuously. And immediately, as the bloud runs into the Dog, unstop the other Quill, coming out of the *upper* part of his *Jugular* Vein (a Ligature being first made about his Neck, or else his other *Jugular* Vein being compress'd by ones Finger;) and let his own bloud run out at the same time into Dishes.

Then take out both the Quills out of the Dogs *Jugular* Vein, and tye the running knot fast, and cut the Vein asunder. . . . This done, sow up the skin and dis-mis him, and the Dog will leap from the Table and shake himself, and run away, as if nothing ailed him.

The Experiment of Transfusion of Blood into an *humane* Veine was made by Us in this manner. Having prepared the *Carotid* Artery in a young Sheep, we inserted a Silver-Pipe into the Quills to let the Blood run through it into a Poringer, and in the space of almost a *minut,* about 12. ounces of the Sheeps-bloud ran through the Pipe into the Poringer; which was somewhat to direct us in the quantity of Bloud now to be Transfus'd into the Man. Which done when we came to prepare the *Veine* in the Man's Arme. . . . And, having open'd the Veine in the Man's Arme, with as much ease as in the common way of Venae-section, we let thence run out 6 or 7 ounces of Blood. Then we planted our silver-pipe into the said Incision, and inserted Quils between the two Pipes already advanced in the two subjects, to convey the *Arteriall* bloud from the Sheep into the Veine of the Man. . . . And as to the quantity of Blood receiv'd into the Man's Veine, we Judge, there was about 9, or 10. ounces.

The Man *after* this operation, as well as *in* it, found himself very well, and hath given in his own Narrative under his own hand, enlarging more upon the benefit, he thinks he hath received by it, than we think fit to own as yet. He urged us to have the Experiment repeated upon him within three or four dayes after this; but it was thought advisable, to put it off somewhat longer.

Lower was a most successful practitioner in London, possibly the leading physician in his generation, but, as a confirmed Whig, he suffered badly by the political alliance. With the ascension of James II following the death of Charles II, his court appointment was lost, many of his patients left him, and he retired to Cornwall. He left 1,000 £ to St. Bartholomew's Hospital in his will. Two epitaphs on Lower remain, presenting diverse opinions of the essence of his spirit.[3] The lines are reproduced from the *Elegy* a flattering commentary.[6]

An
ELEGY
ON THE
Death of that Learned and Famous PHYSICIAN
Dr. RICHARD LOWER

Unhappy Age! That must at last resign
A Soul so great, and so Adorn'd as thine:
Adorn'd with all that former Times could shew;
All that the Ancients taught, or Moderns knew.
When the learn'd WILLIS dy'd, he did impart
His utmost Skill to thy capacious Heart.
Full well he knew, there was no other Shrine
So fit to keep his Treasure in, as thine.
So the Old Seer did to his Son dispense,
A double Portion of Prophetick Sense,
When in his fiery Chair he mounted hence.
WILLIS Expiring, joy'd in Thee, to find
He'd such a Legacy for Human kind.
A Legacy more valuable far,
Than both the *Indies* and their Riches are.
They cannot to our Days one Minute give;
But Thousands by thy powerful Art still live.
And live thou wilt in them, till Time shall be
Quite swallow'd up in vast Eternity.
How many Millons did thy Art restore?
Just to the Rich, and Tender to the Poor:
In Consults serious, in Debating sound;

Free in Advice, in Judgment most profound.
Thy Friendship Courted equal with thy Art,
Unenvy'd Greatness, and diffusive Heart;
None ever did with more Success embrace
The Peoples Wishes, and the Prince's Grace.
Oh had kind Heaven, e'er thou from hence wer't hurl'd,
Been pleas'd to lend Thee longer to the World!
What lasting Monuments had'st thou design'd
Both to relieve and to support Mankind,
When our wise King thy Worth and Parts had try'd,
And found Thee fit for Armies to provide?
Then gave Thee leave his Bounties to dispense,
Best for thy Countries Honour, and thy Prince.
And Reader, now would'st thou his Equal know;
Go follow him, for there's none left below;
Go, follow to that Blessed Place Above,
Where all your Admiration will be LOVE.

1. Lower, R.: *Tractatus de Corde*, London: J. Allestry, 1669.

2. Lower, R.: *De Catarrhis, 1672*, facsimile reproduction, R. Hunter, and I. Macalpine (trans.), London: Dawsons, 1963.

3. Lower, R.: *Tractatus de Corde, in Gunther*, R. T.: *Early Science in Oxford*, vol 9, K. J. Franklin (trans.), Oxford, 1932.

4. Lower, R.: The Method Observed in Transfusing the Blood out of One Live Animal Into Another, *Philos Trans* 1:353-358, 1666.

5. Lower, R.: An Account of the Experiment of Transfusion Practiced Upon a Man in London, *Philos Trans* 2:557-564, 1667.

6. Anon: *An Elegy on the Death of that Learned and Famous Physician Dr. Richard Lower*, London: E. Reyner, 1691.

Giovanni Maria Lancisi
(1654-1720)

LANCISI, THE FOREMOST ITALIAN PHYSICIAN of his time, left a rich heritage in professional service to three popes, the publication of the anatomical plates of Eustachius, engineering recommendations for the drainage of swamp lands in the environs of Rome to control fevers, and sundry communications in epidemiology and clinical medicine, particularly cardiovascular disease. Giovanni, born in Rome of middle-class parents, pursued theology for a time but later diverted his attention to the natural sciences, studying anatomy, chemistry, and botany at the Collegio de Sapienza. He received his doctor's degree at the age of 18, was appointed professor of anatomy at the Collegio at the age of 30, and professor of the theory and practice of medicine at the age of 43, a position held until his death. In the meantime, Innocent XI appointed him papal physician as did his successor, Innocent XII; Clement XI commissioned him to investigate the pathogenesis of sudden death in Rome and the painting of the anatomical plates of Eustachius which had lain fallow in the Papal Library for 162 years.[1]

Lancisi prepared three major treatises and several minor ones. He proposed a relatively satisfactory classification of aneurysm (hypertrophy and dilatation) of the heart, enumerating the underlying factors:

heredity, mechanical obstruction, calcified or incompetent valves, calcification of a large vessel, palpitation, nervous disorders, chronic catarrh, and asthma. It is possible that palpitation and nervousness refer to symptoms of hyperthyroidism and that chronic catarrh and asthma include bronchiectasis and emphysema. He described acute and chronic valvulitis, pulsating cervical veins with dilatation of the right side of the heart, and a positive venous pulse. Lancisi anticipated Auenbrugger in the significance of percussion of the precordial area in the diagnosis of cardiac enlargement.

His compendium on motion of the heart and aneurysm, *De motu cordis et aneurysmatibus* was published eight years after his death. The portion of the volume on aneurysms was translated and published by the Sydenham Society in 1844[2] and more recently by Wright.[3] The discussion of tertiary syphilis and especially luetic aneurysms is given in chap 2, vol 2, proposition XXXII, "on the mode of formation, the causes and symptoms of a syphilitic aneurism."[2]

As an acrid fluid, distilling from the aneurismal cyst or sac, may penetrate as far as the bones or ligaments, which it may gradually corrode, and wear away; so, on the contrary, it may sometimes happen that the lymph, abounding in syphilitic humours, may, first of all, give rise to congestion in the bones and ligaments; but by and by, having become more acrid, and settling in the external coat of the artery, it may begin to corrode, and thus to dilate it into an aneurism; which being produced both by compression and erosion, is much worse than the others, . . . Marcus Aurelius Severinus had also stated, in his treatise "De Novissima Observatione Abscessus," that aneurisms arise from a syphilitic cachexy.

A venereal aneurism may be known not only by the suspicious connexion and the appearance of syphilitic infection in other parts of the body, by which it has been preceded, . . .

Aortic stenosis with cardiac dilatation was described clearly in proposition LIII, "Treats of a bony induration that affects the arteries and valves of the heart, and which is often found in those who have died of aneurism."[2]

There are very many instances of the arteries and valves having become converted into a bony matter in those who have laboured under aneurism of the heart.

We likewise have seen in the body of the most illustrious Johannes Baptista Palaggi, a canon of St. Peter in the Vatican, that of the valves at the orifice of the aorta one was osseous and two were cartilaginous, in consequence of which the passage of the blood into that artery was very much impeded.

The description of cardiac failure and auricular fibrillation is given in proposition L, "Aneurisms of the heart and of the larger vessels happen very easily, in consequence of the continued action of the repercussed blood."[2]

. . . but the freedom of the passage of the blood from the ventricles into the arteries, or from the larger trunks of these into their branches is interfered with, on which account the pulse is always, in cases of palpitation, small, irregular, and often intermitting, but never large, full and regular.

Lancisi's reputation as a brilliant clinician and investigator, trained in the correlation of clinical findings with postmortem examination, contributed to his receiving the assignment from Clement XI to study the causes of sudden death in Rome. In accepting the doctrine of the iatromechanical school, he gives a simple and helpful classification, ie, suffocation from disturbances of the respiratory passage, syncope from failure of the heart and blood vessels, and apoplexy from disturbances in the central nervous system. Acute pulmonary edema and traumatic pneumothorax were listed as causes of death in the first category; cerebrovascular disease and injury to the head in the third category. Sudden death from disturbance of the heart and large blood vessels was based upon a physiological approach with failure of structure, obstruction of blood flow, or diminution of the propelling force.[4]

Next we should speak of diseases of the heart and large arteries which are speedily fatal. All of these, no matter how many are named, come to this, that they stop the intrinsic motion of the heart and bring about a fatal syncope. Three things, however, must be considered necessary to life in connection with the heart: first, harmonious structure of both the heart and the large

arteries, secondly, freedom of the passages, and thirdly the moving power, which is called the pulsive faculty. Certainly from any one of these sources grave abnormalities may easily arise, which can promptly kill.

Lancisi described epidemics of influenza, of cattle plague, and of malaria fever. In the discussion of swamp fevers, he accepted the doctrine of miasmas but displayed a remarkable insight into the pathogenesis of contagion. Lancisi drew the obvious conclusion that swamps which harbored noxious matter should be eradicated. Although lacking experimental proof he gave a strikingly modern interpretation of transmission of malaria by the culex mosquito and speculated on the possible presence of subliminal organisms in the blood. The natural history of the mosquito was described from the larval form, with mention of the possibility that the mosquito might infect water and might deposit noxious matter under the skin, and that the proboscis as well as the feces might harbor disease-producing material.[1,5]

Furthermore, no controversy can surely arise among professional men concerning the harmful effect which the insects of the swamps inflict upon us by mixing their noxious juices with their saliva and gastro-intestinal fluids. For, as I have shown above at length, their proboscis is always wet, and, as all their viscera are full of deleterious liquids, it is not possible that the juices rolling down with food and liquids into the stomach, are not there mixed with our ferments, and thus damage is inflicted upon us as is done by unhealthy food.

Here, then, is the question; namely, if in the small wounds, which are opened by the insects in the surface of the body, they always inject their salivary juices, which are harmful to our nature, and if they also deposit their ova.

The question arises whether amongst the animated effluvia of marshes there are some (organisms) more minute than the rest, which are carried to the blood-vessels, there to be multiplied in a manner detrimental (to the host); and what is the difference between the true plague and these other grave pestilences?

Furthermore, I would take the rôle of a seer and not of a philosopher if, without experiments, I should dare to affirm that in camp fevers of this sort the worms penetrate and ascend to the blood-vessels. For it would be necessary (in order to establish this) for those who suffer from marsh fever to have this very blood let, which medical practice would scarcely allow, and then, by means of the microscope, to diligently examine such insects, if there be any. So far we have not been able to do this.

1. Foote, J.: Giovanni Maria Lancisi (1654-1720) *Int Clinic* 2:292-308, 1917.
2. Erichsen, J. E.: "Lancisi," in *Observations on Aneurism,* London: Sydenham Society, 1844.
3. Lancisi, J. M.: *De Aneurysmatibus,* W. C. Wright, trans., New York: MacMillan Company, 1952.
4. Lancisi, J. M.: *De Subitaneis Mortibus,* Rome: F. Buagni, 1707, in *Selected Readings in Pathology,* W. H. Wilder, Jr., trans., E. R. Long. ed., Springfield, Ill: Charles C Thomas, 1929.
5. Lancisi, J. M.: De Noxiis Paludum Effluviis eorumque Remediis, Tournes, in Ronand Ross and the Prevention of Malaria Fever, W. C. Gorgas, and F. H. Garrison, trans., *Sci Monthly* 3:133-150, 1916.

Composite by G. Bako

François Mauriceau (1637-1709)

To all my dear Brethren, the Sworn Master-Chirurgeons of the City of Paris.

GENTLEMEN,

Wanting a firm and solid Prop for the weakness of my Conceptions, I will imitate the generality of Authors, who choose the protection of some credible Persons, under whose Names to publish their Works to the World: But I'le not follow the custom of those who dedicate them for the most part to Persons wholly ignorant of the Matter treated on, from no other Inducement but a mercenary Recompence. This (*Gentlemen*) obligeth me to address my self to you (as to the only fit Judges of it) and to offer you the first Fruits of my Labours, which might run the hazard of being gnawed by the Worm of Envy, if not put into your hands to protect. I offer it you, in acknowledgement of the Honour you did me, when some time since you received me into your famous Company; and to acquit my self of the Obligation I owed you: for being a Member of your Body, all my pains ought to be for you. . . . I thought to discharge my self intirely of my Duty, you will not judg amiss, my publishing this Book to the World, which I present you; in which I endeavour to demonstrate exactly the means of remedying many Indispositions of Women with Child and in Child-bed, with an exact Method of well-practising the Art of Midwifery, being perswaded that it may be very profitable to young Chirurgeons living in the Country, where but very few sufficiently instructed in all things necessary to be known, can be met with; I have also the rather undertaken this, that Midwives may find in it what they ought to know, to enable them the better to exercise their Art, and undergo the Examination.

This incomplete "Epistle Dedicatory" was extracted from Hugh Chamberlen's[1] 1683 translation of Mauriceau's outstanding treatise on midwifery, which served as a guide for European accoucheurs for generations. The translator was a member of the Chamberlen clan, who kept secret for generations the knowledge of delivery forceps.

Mauriceau was born in Paris and, although not a graduate in medicine, was a sworn master-surgeon of Saint-Côme. Having acquired an intimate knowledge of anatomy and physiology, he was the dominant obstetrician of Paris and practiced in the maternity wards of Hôtel Dïeu. The treatise appeared first in 1668, was followed by a number of editions, and subsequently was translated into German, Dutch, Italian, Latin, and Flemish, as well as English. Many of the errors and prejudices of the ancients, notably those of Hippocrates and Galen, and those more immediate to his time were perpetuated; others were rejected on evidence from his researches and experiences. The treatise is divided into three books preceded by a chapter on the anatomy of the generative organs of the female, "An Anatomical Treatise of the Parts of a

Woman Destined to Generation." The French editions are illustrated with seven engravings prepared from copper plates. The legends and reference to Figure 5 mention by name the first time in modern writing "la fourchette," the posterior commissure of the labia majora, and "la fosse naviculaire," the portion of the vestibule of the vagina immediately posterior to the vaginal orifice. The first book discusses the diseases and disposition of a woman with child; the second book, natural and unnatural labors; and the third, the care of mother and child following delivery. In 1694, to the 4th edition, 283 aphorisms on pregnancy and the puerperium are appended.[2]

Mauriceau accepted the doctrine that impregnation occurs in the uterus through the mixture of male and female semen, regarded the ovarian ligaments as ducts for the transmission of the products of the ovary into the uterus, considered the lochia as an unnatural secretion, and believed that the uterus in pregnancy was distended, similar to the urinary bladder, without increasing its muscle mass. On the other hand, he enlarged upon the management of footling presentation, mentioned earlier by Guillemeau. Later the technique was refined by Smellie, Viet, and others—hence the term, Mauriceau-Smellie-Viet maneuver. He presented a detailed analysis of the mechanism of labor, introduced the practice of delivering patients in bed rather than on a birth stool, described the management of placenta praevia, and gave an early account of prevention of congenital syphilis by antileutic treatment during pregnancy. He denied the separation of the pubic bones during labor and, in support of the argument, reported that his patients were ambulatory immediately following delivery. He disapproved of Cesarean section of the living woman but considered it lawful and necessary if the mother was dead. He favored immediate repair of a lacerated perineum and concluded his treatise with a chapter on the choice of a good wet nurse. In Book I, he suggests a procedure for determination of tubal patency in an examination for infertility.[1]

If a Woman doth not conceive, and you are desirous to know whether she is capable, or no; wrap her close round with clothes, and put a perfume under her: and if she perceive the scent to pass through her body to her nose and mouth, be assured (saith he) it is not her fault she is barren.

The initial portion of the section on breech delivery, "To deliver a Woman when the Child comes footling," is excerpted from Chamberlen.[1]

As soon then as 'tis known the Child comes thus, and the Womb is open enough to admit the Chirurgeons Hand into it, or else by anointing the Passages with Oil or Hogs grease, to endeavour to dilate by little and little, using to this purpose his Fingers, spreading them one from the other after they are together entered, and continuing so to do, 'til it be sufficiently dilated; then, having his Nails well pared, and no Rings on his Fingers, his Hands well anointed with Oil or fresh Butter, as also the Woman placed after the manner as we have already often directed, let him gently introduce his Hand into the entry of the Womb, where finding the Child's foot, let him draw it forth in that posture.

As soon then as the Chirurgeon hath found both the Child's Feet, he may draw them forth . . . till the Hips be come forth: the whilst let him observe to wrap the parts in a single Napkin . . . which being done, he may take hold under the Hips so to draw it forth, to the beginning of the Breast, and then let him on both sides with his hand bring down the Arms along the Child's Body, which he may than easily find, and be careful that the Belly and Face be downwards, lest being upwards, the Head be stopt by the Chin over the Share-bone, wherefore if it be not so, he must turn it to that posture . . . and having brought it to the Shoulders, let him lose no time, (desiring the Woman at the same time to bear down) that so in drawing the Head at that instant may take its place, and not be stopt in the passage.

The critical passage on delivery of the head, first incorporated in Mauriceau's 2nd edition, is translated by Speert as follows.[3]

But while some other person will pull unskillfully on the infant's body, holding it by both feet or above the knees, the Surgeon will disengage the head gradually from the bones of the pelvis. This he will do gently sliding one or two fingers of his left hand into the infant's mouth, in order to release the chin first, and with his right hand he will grasp the back of the infant's neck, above the shoulders, with the help of one of the fingers of his left hand placed in the infant's mouth, as I have just said, to disengage the chin; for it is chiefly this part that causes the head to be held up in the pelvis, out of which one cannot extract it until the chin is completely disengaged.

Rapid delivery was recommended for the management of placenta praevia and toxemia of pregnancy with convulsions. In the chapter on flooding Mauriceau mentioned the death of his young sister from delayed evacuation of the uterus during exsanguination from the misplaced placenta.[1]

But if the Flooding proceeds from the separation of the after-burthen from the Womb, as my Sisters was, all these things are to little purpose; and the best expedient is to deliver the Woman as soon as may be, tho she were but three or four Months gone with Child, or less.

OF FLOODINGS OR CONVULSIONS IN LABOUR.

The best Expedient and safest Remedy for Mother and Child in this case, who are both in great danger, is to deliver the Woman presently without any delay, fetching the Child away by the feet, at what time soever of the Woman's being with Child, whether at full reckoning or no.

In the care of the infant, Mauriceau followed the practice of swaddling handed down from the ancients, under the mistaken belief that an infant would develop a distorted frame unless the body were molded by tight bandaging immediately following birth.[1]

. . . let his Arms and Legs be wrapped in his Bed, and stretched strait out and swathed to keep them so, viz. his Arms along his Sides, and his Legs equally both together, with a little of the Bed between them, that so they may not be galled by rubbing one another; after all this, the Head must be kept steady & streight, with a Stay fastned on each side the Blanket, and then wrap the Child up in Mantles or Blankets to keep it warm. He must be thus swadled, to give his little Body a streight Figure, which is most decent and convenient for a Man, and to accustom him to keep upon the Feet, for else he would go upon all four, as most other Animals do.

1. Mauriceau, F.: *The Diseases of Women With Child, and in Child-bed* (Fr), Paris: l'Auteur, 1668, translated by H. Chamberlen, ed 2, London: J. Darby, 1683.

2. Mauriceau, F.: *Observations on the Diseases of the Pregnant Female* (With Aphorisms) (Fr), ed 4, Paris: L. d'Houry, 1694.

3. Speert, H.: Obstetric-Gynecologic Eponyms, François Mauriceau and His Maneuver in Breech Delivery, *Obstet Gynec* 9:371-376 (March) 1957.

Composite by G. Bako

Raymond de Vieussens
(1641-1715)

VIEUSSENS, the son of a lieutenant colonel in the French army, was born in Vieussens, a small village in Rouergue.[1] Without financial support he provided for his own education, studying philosophy at Rhodez and medicine at Montpellier, until graduation in 1671. Both before and after graduation he displayed great interest in anatomical dissection. After appointment as physician to the hospital of Saint Eloy in Montpellier, Vieussens utilized his time to great advantage in the morgue. His first great work, a compendium of the anatomy and some physiology of the nervous system, adequately illustrated and based upon 500 anatomical dissections of postmortem material, was published in 1685. The *Neurographia universalis,*[2] prepared in Latin, provided the most complete description of the brain and spinal cord to appear in the 17th century. Vieussens showed that the spinal cord was a functionally independent structure and not merely a prolongation of the central nervous system. This provided the first correct description of the centrum ovale, the central white matter of the cerebrum, as seen when a horizontal section is cut at the level of the dorsal border of the corpus callosum. On the other hand, his poorly written physiological discussions contained only trivia. The excellent reception of the 250-page treatise, however, brought him membership in the Academy of Sciences in Paris and Fellowship in the Royal Society of London.

Meanwhile, having acquired a reputation as a skilled clinician, in 1688, Vieussens was called to Paris to attend the royal family and was honored by a pension granted by Louis XIV. Upon the death of Mme. de Montpensier, cousin of the king, in 1693, Vieussens returned to Montpellier and to his duties at the hospital of Saint Eloy. There he continued his anatomical investigations, clinical practice, and service on the faculty as professor of medicine. While in Paris, he became intrigued with the observations on the chemistry of body fluids and dabbled in fermentation and acids in the blood. His scientific contributions during these years though unimportant were followed by his most interesting studies on the form and function of the cardiovascular system.

During the year of his death, Vieussens' treatise on the heart appeared, prepared also in Latin.[3] A discussion of the pericardium and its diseases comprises the first chapter. He then presents his general findings on the heart, nerves, coronary veins, arteries, etc: most are well illustrated, including the foramina, the openings of the small cardiac veins into the right atrium, the valve at the junction of the great cardiac vein, the coronary sinus, and the small veins of the heart which drain into the anterior and posterior surfaces of the right ventricle and open directly into the right atrium. In this work, interlaced with hypothetical speculations, Vieussens presented the clinical and pathological findings of one patient suffering from aortic insufficiency and another from mitral stenosis. The former patient, an epileptic approximately 35 years of age afflicted with orthopnea, showed pallor and the characteristic water-hammer pulse, findings later associated with Corrigan's name.

At postmortem, the aortic cusps were found to be incompetent and the aorta bony. Extended excerpts of each of these have been translated.[3]

After having remarked the sunkenness of his eyes, the puffiness, & the pallor of his face, I examined his pulse, which appeared to be very full, very fast, very hard, unequal, & so strong the artery of the first one & then the other arm, struck the ends of my fingers just as a cord would have done which was very tightly drawn & violently shaken. The pulse of this patient, the like of which I had never seen and do not hope to again, persuaded me that he was suffering from a violent palpitation of the Heart. I was not deceived, for having questioned him upon this fact, he told me for a long time he had not been able to sleep comfortably, neither on one nor on the other side, nor indeed upon his back, if his head were not very high, because the strong beating of his heart prevented it; & he added that when he reclined on one or the other side, & particularly on the left side, it seemed to him as if one struck on his ribs with a hammer.

My prognosis proved correct; for the patient died in three days: I opened his body, I found a polyp [thrombus] in the right auricle; the left ventricle was extraordinarily dilated; the walls of the trunk of the aorta appeared to me very thick, very hard, & like cartilage; the semilunar valves are markedly stretched & cut off at their tips: all these cuts which bore some resemblance to the teeth of a saw, were in fact osseous. The walls of the trunk of the aorta had become very thick, hard, & like cartilage, the lymph which the blood of the canals of the Heart, to which they were closely attached, furnished for nourishment, had no longer a free flow.

Equally clear was Vieussens' clinical description of the terminal symptoms and the postmortem findings in a patient with mitral stenosis. This patient, also seen on the service at the hospital of Saint Eloy in 1705, had been an apothecary who was troubled with shortness of breath, anasarca, ashen lips, and sunken eyes. His pulse was small, weak, and irregular.[3]

. . . I examined his condition; he was lying on his bed, his head quite high; his respiration seemed to me very difficult, his Heart was working with a very violent palpitation; his pulse appeared very small, feeble & quite unequal, his lips were the color of lead and his eyes sunken; & his legs & his hips were swollen; & rather cold than hot. . . . I opened his body on the morrow . . . the sternum having been separated from the ribs and thrown back above, we saw that the entire cavity of the chest was filled with a yellow serous fluid. . . . I removed the Heart with the trunks of the blood-vessels from the cavity of the chest, in order to examine all of their parts; its size was so extraordinary, that it approached that of a beef's Heart: the coronary veins & all of their branches were very much dilated; the cavities of the right ventricle & the right auricle were very large.

After having examined well the trunk of the pulmonary vein, I opened the left ventricle, & I discovered here first that which I have just pointed out: namely, that the substance of the mitral valves has became bony, & that it had very markedly diminished, & indeed changed the natural appearance of its lumen: I observed in the second place that the bundles of the columnae carneae which formed the sides of the fossas of this ventricle, had lost, some of them, much of their natural size, because they did not receive as much blood as they had been accustomed to receive before the mitral valves were changed into a bony structure, & others not receiving any at all, had become pale, & had taken the form of small tendinous ligaments very little like those of the mitral valve.

The lumen of the left ventricle being markedly narrowed, & its margin having lost all of its natural suppleness, blood could no more enter freely & as abundantly as it should have into the cavity of this ventricle: so that in the beginning the circulation was impaired, it commenced to dilate extraordinarily the pulmonary vein, because the blood remained too long & accumulated in too large an amount . . . & consequently . . . interfered with the free entrance of air or prevented it from leaving freely; that is why the patient always breathed with a great deal of difficulty.

1. "Raymond Vieussens," in Bayle and Thillaye: *Medical Biography* (Fr.), Paris: A. Delahays, 1855.

2. Vieussens, R.: *Universal Neurology* (L), Lyon, France: J. Certe, 1685.

3. Vieussens, R.: *New Treatise on the Structure of the Heart and on the Causes of Spontaneous Heart Beat* (Fr), Toulouse, France: J. Guillemette, 1715, excerpt translated in Major, R.: *Classic Descriptions of Disease,* Springfield, Ill: C. C Thomas, 1932.

Daniel LeClerc (1652-1728)

THE FIRST MAJOR TREATISE on medical history in modern times has been attributed to Daniel LeClerc, whose monographic work began with a descriptive critique of ancient medicine and continued into the 17th century. LeClerc was born in Geneva, the son of a physician, studied in Montpellier and in Paris, and in 1670 received the MD degree in Valencia.[1] He returned to Geneva to begin the practice of medicine, but his

Composite by G. Bako

greatest energies were expended in scholarship and composition. The first edition of his monumental history of medicine was published in 1696. This dealt at length with the ancients through Hippocrates and Galen but included a refutation of the extravagances of Paracelsus.[2] Subsequent editions brought the work into his contemporary times.

A monograph on helminthology, prepared in Latin and translated into English, and an illustrated work on anatomy, co-authored with Manget, also prepared in Latin,[3] were other commendable works. Early in the 18th century LeClerc added politics to his activities and in 1702 became counselor of state, continuing in this position until his death.

The first edition of his history was published in French. This was translated into English by Drs. Drake and Baden under the title *The History of Physick etc. . . . with additional notes and sculptures.* The following is excerpted from the admonition To The Reader by the translators.[2]

Mr. Le Clerc is the first that has given us a distinct view of the state of Physick in the fabulous Ages of the world. He has taken exact care to settle the age of the several reputed Inventers of it, and from a confusion of Traditions, absurd, fabulous or uncertain, so judiciously to extricate the truth, as with a great measure of certainty to deliver to us no contemptible account of the growth, and encrease of Physick during those dark times. As his light encreased his prospect clears up, and the second Book gives us a succinct, but a well digested account of the Progress of the Science, under the management and cultivation of the Philosophers, till the time of *Hippocrates,* whose Reputation and Abilities grew to such a heighth, as to overtop and obscure all that went before him and even to cast a damp and a cloud upon the Merits of all that have succeeded him for so many Ages to this day.

The Author's Preface follows **immediately and contains the following.²**

I shall not amuse my self with the several uses that may be made of the History of Physick, the title alone sufficiently shows, what is to be expected. I shall only take notice, that one may see, (as 'twere) with the cast [of] an Eye by means of this History the principal Reasonings, and most considerable Experiences that have been found out from the beginning of the World, either for the prevention or cure of Diseases. The Books which Physicians daily write are filled with their own proper Experiences; or their particular Reasonings; or those of others; to which, if they approve 'em, they endeavour to give a new turn; but we seldom see there, those that are not for their Palate; or at least we are not permitted to see the fairest side of 'em.

Tis not so with this History, which is obliged to penetrate into the very soul of every age, and every Author; to relate faithfully and impartially the thoughts of all, and to maintain every one in his right, not giving to the Moderns what belongs to the Ancients, nor bestowing upon these latter what is due to, the former; leaving everybody at liberty to make reflections for himself upon the matters of Fact as they stand related.

In the substance of the book the following excerpts from Asclepius and Hippocrates are taken.²

There are yet some Medals of *Esculapius* remaining, on which he is stampt a full length, with the *Pallium* after the Greek fashion, which exposes the body naked to the view from the Girdle upwards, leaning upon a Staff. In others he has a *Cock* at his feet, to insinuate that a Physician ought to be vigilant. In some others we find an *Owlet,* to shew that a Physician ought to be as *clear-sighted,* and *ready* in the *Night* as the Day for the service of their Patients.

The *Serpent* was so dear to *Esculapius,* that his usual appearance was under that Shape. In that

he came to free *Rome* from the Plague, in its three hundred and fiftieth year. *The Romans,* says *Aurelius Victor, sent ten Deputies to* Epidaurus *by the advice of the Oracle, to bring the God Esculapius* to Rome. *The chief of them was* O. Ogulnius.

Hippocrates makes it appear in most of his Writings, that he acknowledges a *general principle,* which he called *nature,* to which he ascrib'd a mighty power. *Nature is of it self sufficient to every animal, and that in all respects. She performs every thing that is necessary to them, without needing the least instruction from any one how to do it.*

He affirms elsewhere, *that it is the faculty which gives nourishment, preservation and growth to all things.*

The manner wherein nature acts, or its most sensible administration by the means of the faculties, according to him consists on one side in *attracting* what is good and agreeable to each species, and in *retaining, preparing,* or *changing* it, and on the other side in *rejecting* whatever is superfluous or hurtful, after she has separated it from the good. The Physick of *Hippocrates* generally turns upon this hinge.

Concerning the Writings of this Ancient Physician, here are three things chiefly to be observ'd. First, The esteem they have always met with. Secondly, The distinction between those Writings which are legitimate, and those that are superstitious. Thirdly, His Language and Stile.

Subsequent revisions and editions of his great treatise appeared in the immediate following years, the latest in 1729, but were not translated into English.⁴ LeClerc questioned the ancients by subjecting their speculations to scientific methods that were being introduced or that were replacing the pseudo-scientific speculation exemplified by Paracelsus. The writings of the past were critically analyzed in relation to contemporary experiences, the only basis for scientific objectivity. His history of medicine was undertaken in a painstaking and scholarly fashion and remains as a major contribution to medical thought of his time.

1. Gautier, L.: *Geneva Medicine to the End of the 18th Century* (Fr), Geneve: J. Jullien, Georg & Co., 1906.
2. LeClerc, D.: *The History of Physick* (Fr), translated by Drake and Baden, 411 pp, London: D. Brown, 1699.
3. Leclerc, D., and Manget, I.: *Bibliotheca Anatomica, Medica, Chirurgica,* 3 vols, Saboy, 1711-1714.
4. LeClerc, D.: *The History of Medicine,* A. La Haye, I. van de Kloot, 1729.

Walter Harris (1647-1732)

WALTER HARRIS' most noteworthy contribution to medicine is a treatise on diseases of childhood first printed nearly 300 years ago. In the introduction to a discourse on the prophylactic management of acute gouty arthritis, he discussed the advantage of a physician's concentrating on one disease. In addition, he prepared various other medical and surgical dissertations.[1] Harris was born in Gloucester, attended Winchester school, and graduated from Oxford in the arts, and from Bourges in medicine. He came to Oxford a Protestant but left it a Papist, continuing in this faith until the Roman Catholics were expelled from London in 1678. A sincere apology for rejecting this belief is offered in *A Farewell to Popery: in a Letter to Dr. Nicholas, Vice-Chancellor of Oxford, and Warden of New-College, from W.H.M.D. lately Fellow of the same College. Shewing, The true Motives that withdrew him to the Romish Religion, and the reasons of his Return to the Church of England: Concluding with some short Reflections concerning the Great Duty of Charity.*[2]

Harris settled in London for practice, received the MD degree at Cambridge in 1679, and was elected a Fellow of the College of Physicians in 1682. He held several of the important posts in the College, including that of censor, Harveian lecturer, treasurer, counselor, and finally Lumleian lecturer from 1710 until his death.[3] Harris attended Queen Mary in her last illness, when the differential diagnosis included measles and smallpox. Subsequently he was appointed physician-in-ordinary to His Majesty, William III, who bade him accompany him on the campaign to Holland. While on the Continent, *De morbis acutis infantum,* Harris' first medical treatise, was composed in halting Latin prose. It was published in Amsterdam in 1698. Several translations appeared, including one in English, entitled *A Full View of All the Diseases Incident to Children.*[4] His biographers credit him with considerable vanity; he was a name-dropper in his writings and rarely failed to mention the rank of notable patients under his care. An example is the anecdote concerning Sydenham.[4]

As some Years ago, in Conversation with that most accomplished Physician Dr. *Sydenham,* I took Occasion to mention the Success I had met with in those Diseases, which are commonly the most fatal to Infants: That great Man was very curious to inform himself of my Method in a Branch of the Practice, which was hitherto so lame, and which (to say no worse) the most eminent in the Profession were not yet perfectly acquainted with. Upon which I very frankly laid before him a View of the Practice, which I had found the most successful. He, after having duly examined and put it to the Trial, was so far from disapproving of it, that he recommended it from his own experience, and . . . in the great Humanity of his Heart expressed himself to me in the following Terms: "I never flatter any one, and I say it without any Compliment, you are the first I ever envied. It is my sincere Opinion, that this little Book may be of greater Service to Mankind than all I ever wrote." This I do not repeat out of Vanity, or to answer any selfish Purpose; but from a kind of secret Impulse, I know not how. For what is empty Praise, or the Breath of popular Applause to an old Man like me? or of what Use is unmerited Fame to one who must shortly bid adieu to the Vanities of this World?

I am sensible that this Province of Physick, which I propose to treat of, has hitherto been very carelessly cultivated, or rather entirely neglected. And indeed no Wonder, since Children, when indisposed, especially such as are yet in the State of Infancy, afford no Light to the Physician towards forming any tolerable Diagnosis of their Disease; but what can very hardly be gathered from their peevish Whinings, and a Crossness, which it is not always easy to discover the Meaning of. Upon which Account several very celebrated Physicians have oftener than once honestly acknowledged to me, it was with the greatest Reluctance, and almost without the smallest Hopes of Success, that they went to visit those tender Patients, especially such as were lately come into the World. Certain it is, there is nothing more to be wished for in the Science of Physick, however deficient it still appears in some of its Parts, than a successful Method of treating the Diseases of Infants.

The etiology of childhood diseases was attributed generally to acidosis. Alkalis, substances high in calcium salts, were given to rid the body of the abnormal elements.[4]

The antecedent and more distant Causes of the Diseases of Infants, however numerous or various they may be, all center, at last, in one immediate Cause, *viz.* In an Acid prevailing through the whole Habit.

But there are other Medicines of a perfectly mild Nature, which efficaciously absorb any prevalent Acidity, subdue any preternatural Commotions in the Humours, and perform the Function of Anodynes both effectually and safely. Such are, Crabs Eyes and Claws, Oyster-shells, Cockle-shells, Bone of the Cuttle-Fish, Egg-shells, Chalk, Coral, Coralline, Pearls, Mother of Pearl, both Kinds of Bezoar, burnt Harts Horn, burnt Ivory, Bone of a Stag's Heart, Shavings of Hartshorn, and of that of the Unicorn, Bole Armeniack, sealed Earth, Blood Stone, &c.

The introduction to the chapter on gout, in his *Pharmacologia Anti-Empirica: Or A Rational Discourse of Remedies both Chymical and Galenical,* justified the concentration by a physician upon one disease. In detailing the clinical aspects of gout, Harris emphasized the prevention of acute attacks, rejected a rigid diet in mangement, and noted the higher incidence among men of intellect.[5]

That it was a Custom *heretofore, for* Physicians *to apply themselves more* particularly *to* One Disease. *That this* Custom *was not so absurd, as may at first be imagined. How the* Genius *and* Opportunities *of men do lie different ways. That* Reputation, *is procured by* Artifices *as well as* Merit. *That the* wisest *men have had but a mean opinion of their own* Knowledg. *A more* particular Application *of the* Author *to the* Cure *of the* Gout, *why no hindrance to his other performances. This his* Particular Application *vindicated.* A Hearty Profession *of the* Author *hereupon. The* Gout *described, and distinguished from a* Fitt. *The* Cure *of the Gout, and the* Cure *of the* Fitt, *to be differently managed. . . . The* Cure *of the* Gout *properly* Prophylactik. *How that is to be* managed. . . . . *Whither* Bacchus *and* Venus *be the common* Causes *of it. . . . The preceding opinion, as to* Wine *and* Women, *proved unjust and uncharitable. The* Cure *by* Diet *examined. Some instances in favour of* Diet *afterwards* answered. *That those who are subject to the* Gout, *are seldom men of* Common Understandings.

To be plain, I have for some years past applied my mind more *particularly* to unriddle the *Nature,* and, as much as lies in my small power, to *perfectionate* the *Cure* of that *Opprobrium* to most *Physicians,* the *Gout.* The *Gout* is an habitual, or long-contracted Disposition of nature to throw off offensive humours upon the Joynts, as often as upon any remarkable irregularity, or a gradual collection of such matter as is like to

prove injurious to the Stomach. . . . Now a man may have a *Gouty Disposition* of body, even when he is quite free from any *Actual Fitt.*

And now for the *Rationality* of that vulgar opinion, that *Wine,* and *Women* are the *adequate* and most *general Cause* of the *Gout,* it is very Censorious, uncharitable, injurious, and improbable. I do not doubt but it is in some the *True,* and *main Cause,* but in abundance of others has a very *small* if *any share* in its production.

Therefore the true *Prophylactick Cure* of the *Gout* must be so adapted to most people, as to let them live in great measure as they did before, and not to make a *Baby* of a *man* of *Sense,* and feed him nothing but *Milk* and *Spoon-meats.*

In his fading years of life, Harris queried the mysteries of the universe and the insignificance of healing by man in comparison with the phenomena of the unknown,[4] a sentiment voiced by Ambroise Paré more than a century earlier.

I wou'd have all such to remember, that Nature is the true Physician, and we who bear that Title are only her Servants. They might with the same Grace complain, that we are sent naked into the World, that Nature is content with little, and that it is the Business of Art to imitate Nature as much as possible.

1. "Walter Harris," in *Dictionary of National Biography,* vol 9, L. Steven, and S. Lee, ed., Oxford: University Press, 1959-1960.

2. Harris, W.: *A Farewell to Popery,* London: W. Kettilby, 1679.

3. Harris, W.: *Dissertationes Medicae & Chirurgicae Habitae in Amphitheatro Collegii Regalis,* London: G. & J. Innvs. 1725.

4. *A Full View of All the Diseases Incident to Children.* J. Armstrong , trans. (?). London: A. Millar, 1742.

5. Harris, W.: *Pharmacologia Anti-Empirica: Or A Rational Discourse of Remedies both Chymical and Galenical,* London: R. Chiswell, 1683.

Bodlein Library, Oxford

William Musgrave (1655-1721)

WILLIAM MUSGRAVE, one of the several English physicians whose contributions as an antiquarian surpassed his medical writings, was born in Nettlecombe, in the county of Somerset.[1] He received his early training at Winchester College and in 1675 matriculated at New College, Oxford. Except for one session at Leyden in physic, he remained in Oxford and was admitted bachelor of civil law in 1682. Before taking a degree in medicine, however, he moved to London, distinuished himself by his knowlede of natural philosophy as well as physic, was elected a Fellow of the Royal Society, served as their secretary, and edited several volumes of their *Philosophical Transactions*. Returning to Oxford in 1685, he practiced for several years and received the MD degree in 1689. He was admitted a candidate to the College of Physicians in London in 1690; meanwhile, he had settled in Exeter, to enter upon 30 years of successful practice.

In 1703, Musgrave's treatise in Latin, *The Symptoms of Arthritis*,[2] received meritorious acclaim. Musgrave's antiquarian investigations, however, judged to be his greatest work, led to his discoveries in the ancient communities of the Belgae in southern Britain. The 4-volume treatise received a special commendation from the King. He also prepared a dissertation on the goddess of health, with descriptions and illustrations of her symbols, temples, coins, statutes, and inscriptions. Before his death,

Musgrave requested to be buried outside the city because he considered cemeteries unwholesome for the living.

The treatise on arthritis contains a number of case histories, examples of secondary or symptomatic arthritis associated with asthma, scurvy, fevers, or lues venerea. One patient suffering from arthritis following chronic bronchitis may have been a case of pulmonary osteoarthropathy. He described arthritis associated with psoriasis, arthritis in a man with a urethral discharge, and a case of Poitou colic, years later to be identified as Devonshire colic associated with excessive ingestion of lead. Podagra is mentioned repeatedly. However, there is no readily recognized case of gouty arthritis except for an example of arthritis and renal colic, possibly a urate calculus in a patient with gout. Half a century later Warner quotes extensively from *De arthritide* in his monograph devoted to gout, a reflection of the reputation Musgrave enjoyed for so long a time.[3]

1. Munk, W.: *The Roll of the Royal College of Physicians of London*, London: Royal College 1878, pp 486-490.
2. Musgrave, W.: *De Arthritide Symptomatica Dissertatio*, Exeter: Farley, 1703.
3. Warner, F.: *A Full and Plain Account of the Gout*, ed 2, London: T. Cadell, 1768.

George Ernst Stahl (1660-1734)

GEORGE STAHL, natural philosopher and physician, advanced a system of medicine and a theory of chemistry, each of which commanded varying degrees of respect for a significant span of years. Stahl was born at Ansbach, Bavaria, became a doctor of medicine at Jena, served as personal physician to Duke Johann Ernst of Saxe-Weimar, and held the chair of medicine at Halle for more than 20 years. In 1715, he was called to Berlin as court physician to Frederick Wilhelm I; in addition, he presided at the Prussian Medical College until his death.

Stahl's system of medicine was based upon the *anima*.[1] The concept of life which became effective through motion and physical activity was advanced to counteract the prevailing concept of dualism, ie, the spirit and the body, the mechanistic philosophy

Composite by G. Bako

of Descartes. According to Stahl, motion which was synonymous with life was integrated with the soul or nature. The integration resisted stress and disease through maintenance of equilibrium. *Anima* was something apart from the material, but was the basis of integrated action of the biological system. All biological processes were endowed with a purpose and thereby resisted decay. An example is the rise in temperature and increase in pulse rate following infection, a series of movements emanating from the *anima* to return the organism to its normal state.

Stahl was a successful practitioner of medicine, carrying along his theory of living matter. Nature, or the *anima,* should be dominant in treatment as well as in pathogenesis. Thus, he prescribed phlebotomy, purgatives, emetics, diaphoretics, and other mild agents supported by assistance of Nature. He doubted the efficacy of opium and rejected cinchona bark because it was excessively potent and, when misused, led to dropsy. In believing that the *anima* was capable of exerting control over body func-

tions, it was easy to assume that something happened below the level of consciousness which bore some resemblance to the subconscious of contemporary psychiatry. He did not develop a doctrine which might serve as a foundation for psychiatry, but some have suggested that his thinking related emotion to vital activity.

While Stahl's concept of the *anima* prob-*ably* contributed to progress in medicine, his popularization of the phlogiston theory was a deterrent to progress in chemistry for almost a century.[2] His explanation of combustion, which emerged as a part of a generalized theory, gained wide acceptance and became the central doctrine of chemistry of his time.[3] It embraced inorganic compounds but overlooked organic reagents. According to the phlogiston theory, an inflammable principle left a metal and escaped into space during combustion and conversion to the calx (oxide in contemporary terminology). The nature of phlogiston, since it was an elementary principle, could be determined only from its effects. Stahl also postulated that phlogiston was given off in the oxidation of a metal. Lavoisier, more than a generation later, showed that instead of something being lost, oxygen was added. Stahl must have assumed that phlogiston was weightless since he overlooked the quantitative fact of gain in weight.

1. Stahl GE: *Theory of Medicine* (L). Halle, lit Orphanotrophei, 1708.

2. Rappaport R.: Rouelle and Stahl—the phlogistic revolution in France. *Chymia* 7:73-102, 1961.

3. Stahl GE: *Philosophical Principles of Universal Chemistry.* P. Shaw (trans), London: J Osborn & T Longman, 1730.

Antonio Maria Valsalva
(1666-1723)

ANTONIO MARIA VALSALVA, pupil of Malpighi and teacher of Morgagni, contributed handsomely to the knowledge of anatomy and physiology of the ear.[1] Born of a noble family in Imola, Italy, a village to the east of Bologna, he studied philosophy and mathematics and later medicine in its university. There he was attracted particularly to Malpighi, and inherited his great interest in dissection. In 1687, after Valsalva received the doctorate in medicine and philosophy, he was accepted in the registry of doctors of Bologna for the practice of medicine and surgery. Although Valsalva became a skillful practitioner, he found his greatest passion in experimental physiology and anatomical dissection. He is credited with 1,000 dissections. In 1697, Valsalva succeeded Malpighi in the chair of anatomy and, in 1705, became the public professor in the subject. By then his reputation rested in part on the appearance of his great book on the anatomy of the human ear—a treatise accepted for decades as the standard reference work.

Valsalva was the first to subdivide the ear into its internal, middle, and external parts. He described and named the Eustachian tube; studied the function of the labyrinth, the semicircular canals, and the form of the tympanic cavity; outlined the external auditory canal and the muscles of the external ear; described the incisuras, identified the sebaceous glands of the ear lobe; and associated the preauricular lymph node with the lymphatic system. He dissected the auditory apparatus of the fetus and identified the sinuses posterior to the semilunar valves of the aorta, now known as the sinuses of Valsalva. He was one of the first to examine the tympanic membrane in the living and postulated one cause of deafness from the isolated finding of ossified ossicles in a cadaver.

The name of Valsalva is traditionally associated with a readily reproducible maneuver, a phenomenon of interest to the physiologist as well as to the clinician. If the Eustachian tubes are patent, a forcible expiratory effort, with nose and mouth closed, produces increased pressure on the tympanic membranes. Valsalva employed the principles of this procedure for expulsion of foreign bodies from the ear, treatment of deafness, and especially for drainage of pus from the middle ear. He was in error, however, in attributing the usual source of middle ear suppuration to a primary focus in the cranial cavity. This error was corrected later by Morgagni.

The knowledge surrounding the Valsalva maneuver has been expanded and its usefulness extended in the intervening years. With an increase of pressure in the nasopharynx and thorax, the return of blood to the heart is momentarily reduced and the veins in the neck become engorged. The maneuver is of practical value to the otologist in testing the patency of the Eustachian tubes and the mobility of the tympanic membrane, of value to the radiologist in inflating the hypopharynx, and to the internist in determining the degree of expansion of a collapsed lung after pneumothorax. The procedure was described as follows.[2]

Thus (in order to offer one of many proofs) if someone would instill a medicinal fluid into the tympanic cavity or in the area of an ulcer or in the outer portion of the auditory meatus and if now, with mouth and nose closed, an attempt is made to compress the air, fluid would flow copiously from the auditory meatus. I recommend this for a prompt evacuation of a suppurative lesion since this may be remedial for the illness which might not occur by itself. We have seen illnesses benefit when from these foramina the unnatural excretions of the brain can be diverted to the outside either by way of the wound, or by way of the nares, or through the auditory meatus. However, many more benefits may be derived from the physician's knowledge of these functions.

Valsalva, a tireless investigator of human form and function, introduced rational therapy into the practice of otolaryngology. His great compassion caused him to urge the unchaining of the insane who had been treated as criminals. He was elected a member of the Royal Society of London at the same time as his pupil, Morgagni, also a student of morbid anatomy, who assembled and published posthumously the anatomical works of his teacher, in two volumes.[3]

1. Castiglioni, A.: *A History of Medicine*, ed 2, E. B. Krumbhaar (trans.-ed.), New York: A. A. Knopf, 1947.
2. Valsalva, A. M.: *The Human Ear* (L), Bononiae: C. Pisarri, 1704.
3. Morgagni, G. B.: *Works of Valsalva* (L), 2 vol, Venice: F. Pitteri, 1740.

ferred to Gonville and Caius College, Cambridge, because of its reputation for medical instruction, and graduated bachelor of medicine in 1687. This was followed by

Composite by G. Bako

Thomas Dover (1662-1742)

THOMAS DOVER—physician and swashbuckler—is equally famous for the compounding of Dover's powder, and the rescuing of Alexander Selkirk (the original Robinson Crusoe) from an island off the coast of Chile. The retriever of Selkirk was an English physician of Bristol, who, having established a fine practice and reputation, could not resist the opportunity to contribute funds and to participate in a privateering enterprise against Spanish New World strongholds. This remarkable man of medicine, dubbed "Doctor Quicksilver," was born in a village in the Cotswold hills of Warwickshire of a family which established the Cotswold Games. He matriculated in Magdalen Hall, Oxford, receiving his AB degree in 1684. Two years later he trans-

study and training in London with Thomas Sydenham, where he contracted smallpox and was treated by the English Hippocrates.[1]

Whilst I lived with Dr. *Sydenham,* I had my self the Small Pox, and fell ill on Twelfth-Day. In the Beginning I lost twenty-two Ounces of Blood; He gave me a vomit; but I find, by Experience, Purging much better. I went abroad, by his Direction, till I was blind, and then took to my Bed. I had no Fire allow'd in my Room, my Windows were constantly open, my Bed-Clothes were order'd to be laid no higher than my Waist. He made me take twelve Bottles of small Beer, acidulated with Spirit of Vitriol, every twenty-four Hours.

The period in Dover's life from the time he returned to his home community after studying under Sydenham until his removal to Bristol, about 1696, remains obscure. Greeted, however, by a typhus epidemic that struck the port city soon after his arrival, he later not only describes the scourge but also breaks the silence about his own activities.[1]

> About thirty-seven Years since, this Fever raged much in *Bristol,* so that I visited from twenty-five to thirty Patients a Day for a considerable Time, besides their poor Children taken into their Workhouse, when I engaged my self, for the Encouragement of so good and charitable an Undertaking, to find them Physick, and give them Advice at my own Expense and Trouble, for the two first Years. All these poor Children in general had this Fever, yet no more than one died of the whole Number, which was near two hundred.

Bristol, in the 18th century, was a popular watering spot. It was also an international port of trade next in importance to London in all of Britain. Ships put in at Bristol as a port-of-call or a home harbor for legitimate commerce or privateering. The opportunities for observation of good and bad features of long sea voyages were commonplace experiences for Bristol folk but were not taken so casually by Dover. When imperial rivalry with the French and Spanish jeopardized English trade during the war of the Spanish Succession, the island kindom struggled with all available means to retain its prestige. Dover could not resist the adventure of privateering in the attempt to drive the Spaniards to cover and free the seas for English trade. Having contributed financially, Dover was placed third in command of a two-ship expedition under Captain Woodes Rogers and made second captain of the *Duke.*

The privateers crossed the Atlantic to the coast of Brazil, reached the Pacific around Cape Horn, and held to the west coast of South America, looking for Spanish prizes. After the long sea voyage, with the crew suffering from poor food and privation, some incapacitated by scurvy, the vessels reached what is now known as Ma's a Tierra, one of the Juan Fernandez islands. Dover led a small party ashore and found a man clothed in goatskin, who had been left on the island more than four years earlier after a quarrel with his captain of the ship Cinque-ports. Alexander Selkirk of Largo, Ayrshire county, Scotland, had

chosen to remain on the island in preference to continuing in what he charged was an unseaworthy vessel.[2]

> He had with him his clothes and bedding, with a firelock and some powder and bullets, some tobacco, a knife, a kettle, a bible, with some other books, and his mathematical instruments. He diverted himself and provided for his sustenance as well as he could; but had much ado to bear up against melancholy for the first eight months. . . . He built himself two huts of pimento trees, thatched with long grass, and lined with goat-skins, killing goats as he needed them with his gun, so long as his powder lasted, which was only about a pound at first. When that was all spent, he procured fire by rubbing two sticks of pimento wood together. He slept in his larger hut, and cooked his victuals in the smaller, which was at some distance, and employed himself in reading, praying, and singing psalms, so that he said he was a better Christian during his solitude than he had ever been before, or than, as he was afraid, he should ever be again.

The commander, recognizing Selkirk's previous marine training, made him mate of the *Duke,* which continued its plundering of the Spanish coast. The next incident was a foray against Guayaquil, Ecuador, led by Dover. Proceeding farther to the coast of Lower California, the ships continued to plunder, then crossed the Pacific, touching several remote islands, and returned with Selkirk to Bristol by way of Cape Town after more than three years on the seas. The first edition of Defoe's *Robinson Crusoe* appeared in 1719, eight years after the return of the privateers to England.

A decade after Dover's return, he qualified for the Licentiate of the Royal College of Physicians in London and practiced in London for the remainder of his active years. The first edition of *The Ancient Physician's Legacy to His Country,* Dover's most famous medical treatise, was published in 1732. The monograph was not profound scientifically as judged by 18th century standards; rather it may be described best as little more than the "housewive's medical friend." It did not pretend to be a scientific text for students or physicians; in fact, it contained bitter diatribes against the apothecaries and the practitioners of his day. Subsequent editions contained appendices of testimonials, glowing tributes to his compound of opium and ipecac and to the therapeutic efficacy of quicksilver in hysteria, scurvy, kidney stone, worms, colic, asthma, intestinal obstruction, and other complaints.[3] The prescription, identified as "Dover's powder," was in the second portion of the section on therapy in the chapter on "Gout," the first malady to be discussed in the popular treatise. Dover was free to admit that his success in the treatment of gouty arthritis was remarkable, either by the use of Dover's powder or metallic mercury.[4]

The preface to the *Physician's Legacy* begins as an apology.[1]

I have spent the greatest Part of my Life without the least Thought of becoming an Author; and if it should be ask'd What makes me now appear in Print: I answer, That I have acquired in Physick, by my long Study and Practice, what I conceive may be for the common Benefit of Mankind; and therefore I publish my Observations.

Authors, for the most Part, follow one another, and deviate but little from the common Track. This Method I shall in no wise pursue; my Design being to set down only such Things as have occurred to me from the Practice and Experience of *Forty-nine* Years.

This has various Names, according to the Parts affected: 'Tis term'd *Podagra* when in the Foot, *Chiragra* when in the Hand, *Gonegra* when in the knee, *Sciatica* when in the Hip.

The clinical description of gout makes no contribution to the natural history of the disease and in no way compares with the excellent description by his teacher, Sydenham. The composition of the famous remedy for the cure of gout and other afflictions, Dover's powder, was classified as an "easy sudorific."[1]

Take Opium one Ounce, Salt-Petre and Tartar vitriolated, each four Ounces, Ipocacuana one Ounce, Liquorish one Ounce. Put the Salt-Petre and Tartar into a red-hot Mortar, stirring them with a Spoon till they have done flaming. . . . Then powder them very fine; after that slice in your Opium; grind these to a Powder, and then mix the other Powders with these. Dose from forty to sixty or seventy Grains in a Glass of White-Wine Posset, going to Bed. . . . Covering up warm, and drinking a Quart or three Pints of the Posset-Drink while sweating.

In two or three Hours, at farthest, the Patient will be perfectly free from Pain; and though

before not able to put one Foot to the Ground, 'tis very much if he cannot walk the next Day. When it is taken, keep your Bed till next Day Noon. This remedy may be taken once a Week, or once a Month.

If 40 to 60 or 70 grains of this 10% compound of opium were taken, it is little wonder that the patient experienced relief from pain. One must also raise the question as to whether or not this dosage might produce addiction.

A testimonial by a grateful patient to the value of quicksilver in relieving distress from gouty arthritis constitutes one of the appendices in the 1733 edition.[1]

I had the Gout in my Stomach and Bowels for a considerable Time, insomuch that I had two Physicians with me for six Weeks: They gave me all the heating Medicines they could contrive or think of; but all to no Purpose; so that at the last, I was brought to extreme Faintings and Cold Sweats that I wetted a Pair of Sheets in an Hour.

A very worthy neighboring Gentleman hearing of my miserable Condition, came to see me, and perswaded me to take two Ounces of Quicksilver; which I accordingly did, and found Relief thereby in four Hours Time, and in three Days all the gouty Matters were thrown down into my Feet. Upon which I persisted in taking of Quicksilver; and have ever since enjoy'd a good State of Health, which is for near two Years in Space. *I am,*

> Sir,
> *Your humble Servant,*
> Harvey

The worthlessness of metallic mercury as a therapeutic agent was exposed by Daniel Turner (p. 184) in a condemnation of the *Physician's Legacy*. Since metallic mercury is a biologically inert substance, it has no effect except as an intestinal lubricant.[5]

One Gentleman says, he had found it in his Shoes, in one of which his Servant taking it off, shewed it him; in some it slips away with a *Crepitus;* Esq; *Grosvenor*, with whose Case I am to acquaint you presently, told me, that perceiving himself wet, he would at some times put his Hand up to the *Anus,* and bring out a little mass of the Quicksilver in the Palm thereof: I once observed several little Globules on the Floor of a publick Room at a Tavern, and asking the Drawer how it came there, he told me there were two Gentlemen who came constantly in a Morning, with their little Bottles of Quicksilver, which having swallowed they smoaked their Pipes, and took each a Gill of Wine. He could not tell, he said, but that some of it might be scattered out of the Bottles, tho' I rather believed from their Backsides. Thus it is doubtless the Case of many, who thinking the Remedy is working Miracles in the Blood, might find it in their Breeches, or on the Ground, if they mist it in the Close-stool. I have heard a pleasant Story of a mercurial Lady, who in Dancing at a publick Assembly, happened to let go some Particles of Quicksilver she had taken in the Morning, which shining on the Floor in the midst of so great an Illumination, like so many little *Brilliants,* there were several stooping down to take them up; but finding themselves deceived, it afforded Matter for much Laughter among the Gentlemen, and Blushing among the Ladies, especially she that was most concerned; for the Cry went through the Room, that some Lady had scattered her Diamonds.

The combination of an emetic and a potent sudorific, the active ingredients of Dover's famous prescription, remains in current pharmacopeias.

1. Dover, T.: *The Ancient Physician's Legacy to his Country,* 5th ed, London: A. Bettesworth, and C. Hitch, 1733.
2. Kerr, R.: *A General History and Collection of Voyages and Travel,* vol 10, Edinburgh: William Blackwood, and London: T. Cadell, 1824.
3. Strong, L. A. G.: *Dr. Quicksilver, 1660-1742, The Life and Times of Thomas Dover, M.D.,* London: Andrew Melrose, 1955.
4. Anon: *A Treatise on Mercury: Shewing, The Danger of Taking it crude for all Manner of Disorders, after the present Fashion, from its Nature, its Manner of Operating in the Human Body, and Facts, with some Remarks on the Antient Physician's Legacy,* 2nd ed, London: J. Roberts, 1733.
5. Turner, D.: *The Ancient Physician's Legacy Impartially Surveyed,* London: John Clarke, 1733.

Hermann Boerhaave
(1668-1738)

HERMANN BOERHAAVE was born in Voorhout, a few miles from Leyden, Holland, during the final hours of 1668. In his days of prime professional maturity, he was the leading physician of Europe. Not since Galen, had a clinician achieved such a wide reputation as a teacher. He did not choose to affiliate with the Eclectic Sect but selected from all sects what he judged good and serviceable. He systematized medical knowledge and clarified and expounded medical theory, while his contributions to the art of medicine were beyond measure, through teaching and exemplary performance in the

Los Angeles County Medical Library

care of the sick. His interests included philosophy, theology, chemistry, botany, physic, and clinical medicine.[1] His father, a scholarly clergyman, took special care that his son would be skilled in Latin, Greek, Hebrew, and Chaldean literature, and hoped that he would succeed him in the Church. Hermann was an apt pupil and before adolescence translated Latin and composed in it. In later years his linguistic capability embraced English, Latin, French, German, and Dutch, as well as a reading ability in Italian and Spanish. After two years at the public school in Leyden, Boerhaave was admitted to the University at the age of 16, Proficiency in logic, natural philosophy, metaphysics, and ethics was rapidly acquired, and in due time he could "publicly maintain disputations in them."[2] With limited monetary means, and to support continuing higher education, he acted as a tutor to families of substance.

The degree of doctor of philosophy was received in 1690. The inaugural dissertation refuted the doctrines of Spinoza, Hobbes, and Epicurus. Although it was his original intention to follow the professional path of his father, he became diverted and began the study of medicine. Richardson attributes some of this interest to an indolent ulcer that appeared on his thigh at the age of 12.[2] This persisted for several years and was cured ultimately by a mixture of salt and wine (or brine) and urine. The works of Vesalius, Fallopius, and Bartholinus formed the basis of his early medical education, supplemented by courses in anatomy and dissection. Hippocrates and Sydenham were the preferred clinical texts. Presumably these studies were not all-absorbing, since considerable time was given to botany and chemistry. The degree, doctor of physic, was awarded in 1693 by the University of Harderwijk, situated in a small coastal town on the Zuider Zee. The inaugural dissertation described the excretions during illness. In 1701, Boerhaave was appointed lecturer in medicine.

Sylvius, who preceded Boerhaave as professor of medicine at Leyden, introduced a system of bedside teaching that was carried on by his successor.[3]

When followed by his pupils, he approached the bedside of a patient, he assumed the air of one who is entirely ignorant of the nature of that person's malady, of the accompanying symptoms, and of the treatment which was being carried out. Then he began to ask first one and then another of the students a great variety of questions respecting the case that was under consideration,—questions which at first seemed to have been propounded in a haphazard fashion, but which in reality were so cleverly formulated as to elicit from the class all the information needed for the making of a correct diagnosis, while leaving on the minds of the students, the impression that they, and not the professor, had worked out the problem to a successful result.

Boerhaave soon dazzled his contemporaries.[2] Flattering offers of professorships from other universities were received. Patients sought his consultation from as far away as China. Czar Peter is reported to have spent the night on a barge near Boerhaave's home for a 2-hour conversation the following morning. William III, hereditary prince of the Netherlands, tapped him for the position of court physician at The Hague. The University at Groningen offered him the chair of medicine. He declined each

offer and remained at Leyden, to teach and to practice. In 1709, he accepted a professorship at the University in medicine, chemistry, and botany but was forced to vacate the chair prematurely because of his gouty affliction. Before doing so, however, he served two interrupted terms as rector of the University.

Not only was Boerhaave famous as an internist but also he was extremely popular as a citizen of Leyden. On one occasion, after he had been confined for several months to his home because of recurring attacks of acute gouty arthritis, the citizens of the city planned a public celebration for his recovery. On two subsequent occasions, in 1727 and again in 1729, he relapsed into prolonged bouts of acute articular gout.

Boerhaave's lectures were illustrated by the application of revered and new concepts of basic science. Physiological functions as well as the phenomena of morbidity were explained, according to the laws of physics, mathematics, and chemistry. An oration in 1718 laid the foundation for his *Elements of Chemistry,* a volume that went through many editions and one of the most popular books on the subject for more than a century. He described rupture of the esophagus, dilatation of the heart, and suffocation from a fatty tumor of the chest. The site of pleurisy was judged to be exclusively in the pleura. The spread of smallpox by contagion was recognized. His aphorisms are not easily understood, when compared with those of Hippocrates.[4] Thus, no. 21:

DISTEMPERS OF THE SOLID SIMPLE FIBRE.

21. Those parts (which being separated from the Fluid contained in the Vessels, are applied and sticking to each other by the Strength of the living Body, and make the least Fibre) are the least, the simplest, earthy and hardly changeable from or by vertue of any Cause, which are found in our living Bodies.

Twenty-nine aphorisms are devoted to gout, probably derived from personal experience. No. 1255 states:

Which when undisturb'd it doth run its own natural Stage, is usually the Companion of People past the middle Age, of the Male Sex, Men of acute and deep Sense, that exercise the same much, and protract their Studies late in the Night;

Such as we live voluptuously, and at Night drink great quantities of Wine or spirituous Liquors: Such as have been addicted to Venery in their younger and unripe Years; large, broad and full habited Men; Such as are too much addicted to Acids, cool their sweaty Feet too suddenly; sweat in wet Stockings or Shoes; hence such as do hunt or ride much in cold weather; such as have it from their Parents, or lie much with gouty People.

No. 1259 is quite apt today:

The Place which it (gout) commonly first and regularly invades, is always the Foot, and chiefly those Parts of the same through which the Liquids flow the most difficultly; as the Periosteum, Tendons, Nerves, Membranes, Ligaments; such as are the remotest from the Heart, and the most pressed and pinch'd.

Gibbs suggests that Johnson translated from the Latin the first 8 sheets of Boerhaave's *Elementa Chemiae*.[5] This was a remarkable document. It contains a drawing of the first thermometer constructed by Fahrenheit and one designed for taking body temperature. The basis of modern organic chemistry was described, including the identification of urea:[2]

. . . in saline globes of a particular kind that are perfectly distinct from every other salt, not foetid, not alkaline, but very evanescent, the native salt of urine.

Probably less appreciated was his interest in botany. He developed a large herbarium, a physic garden, with plants from many parts of the world. Pupils were attracted by Boerhaave to the study of botany as they were to medicine. Included in the former was the great Linnaeus, whose friendship with Boerhaave was loyal and firm.

Boerhaave was an early riser and regularly devoted many hours to study. He was fond of music, played the violin, sang, and conducted a concert at home once a week during the winter. After one discipline had been mastered, another was attempted. He added "physick to divinity, chymistry to the mathematicks, and anatomy to botany."[5] He lectured in Latin extempore and firmly established the value of bedside teaching. He died at the age of 70, the most influential physician of the 18th century.[6]

Samuel Johnson, in *The Life of Boerhaave,* wrote:[7]

Thus died Boerhaave, a man formed by nature for great designs, and guided by religion in the exertion of his abilities. He was of a robust and athletick constitution of body, so hardened by early severities, and wholesome fatigue, that he was insensible of any sharpness of air, or inclemency of weather.

1. Pettigrew, T. J.: "Hermann Boerhaave, M.D., F.R.S.," in *Medical Portrait Gallery: Biographical Memoirs,* vol III, London: Whittaker & Co., 1840.
2. Richardson, B. W.: *Disciples of Aesculapius,* vol I, New York: E P. Dutton & Co., 1901.
3. Buck, A. H.: *The Growth of Medicine from the Earliest Times to About 1800,* New Haven, Conn.: Yale University Press, 1917.
4. *Boerhaave's Aphorisms: Concerning the Knowledge and Cure of Diseases,* London: William and John Innys, 1724.
5. Gibbs, F. W.: Dr. Johnson's First Published Work? *Ambix* 8:24 (Feb) 1960.
6. King, L. S.: *The Medical World of the Eighteenth Century,* Chicago: University of Chicago Press, 1958.
7. Black, D. A. K.: Johnson on Boerhaave, *Med Hist* 3:325 (Oct)1959.

Samuel Garth (1661-1718)

SAMUEL GARTH, clever and fashionable physician in London, left no medical manuscripts, but his doggerel verse attests to literary accomplishments which justified his membership in the Kit-Kat Club. The scanty information regarding his professional and private life was brought up to date by Harvey Cushing early in this century.[1] It is known that Garth lived in Covent Garden, London, was in demand as a practicing physician, typified the upper-class man of his day, and grew rich in practice. Under George I he was knighted and became physician-in-ordinary to the King and physician-general to the army.

Garth was born in the West Riding of Yorkshire, was schooled at Ingleton, and entered Peterhouse in Cambridge, where he graduated AB in 1679 and AM in 1648. After studying medicine at Leyden he received the MD degree from Cambridge in 1691 and then settled in London. Two years later he was elected a Fellow of the Royal College of Physicians and was honored as the Gulstonian laureate in 1694 and the Harveian laureate in 1697. The second lecture, a panegyric on William III, prepared in Latin, was ordered

Royal College of Physicians

by the president and censors to be printed shortly after delivery. The address concluded with a proposal for the establishment of a dispensary where the poor could obtain medical advice and prescriptions— the practice of a lucrative art without lucre. The majority of the Fellows of the College, favoring the proposal, contested bitterly the objections of the minority who were in league with the apothecaries and were unwilling to participate in charitable out-patient service. In support of the commendable plan, Garth composed *The Dispensary: A Poem,* which satirized the apothecaries and their allies in the College.

One of Garth's notable displays of benevolence was the provision for a gentlemen's burial for John Dryden, who died in 1700 in neglected circumstances. Garth raised a subscription to defray the expense of the funeral and to inter the remains in Westminster Abbey. Through an appeal to the censors of the College of Physicians,

services were held in public and a burial cortege from the College to Westminster Abbey restored the great poet to his deserved honor.

Garth's reputation among all classes in London was described by Sir Richard Steele in 1715 in the "Dedication" of *The Lover*.[2]

> Sir, as soon as I thought of making the *Lover* a Present to one of my Friends, I resolved, without farther distracting my Choice, to send it *To the Best-natured Man.* You are so universally known for this Character, that an Epistle so directed would find its Way to You without your Name, and I believe no Body but You yourself would deliver such a Superscription to any other Person.
>
> As this is Your natural Bent, I cannot but congratulate to You the singular Felicity that your Profession is so agreeable to your Temper. For what Condition is more desirable than a constant Impulse to relieve the Distressed, and a Capacity to administer that Relief? When the sick Man hangs his Eye on that of his Physician, how pleasing must it be to speak Comfort to his Anguish, to raise in him the first Motions of Hope, to lead him into a Persuasion that he shall return to the Company of his Friends, the Care of his Family, and all the Blessings of Being?
>
> The Manner in which You practise this heavenly Faculty of aiding human Life, is according to the Liberality of Science, and demonstrates that your Heart is more set upon doing Good than growing Rich.

The concluding paragraph in the Harveian Oration, delivered by Garth at the age of 36, identified him as a Whig and a senior spokesman in the battle for a dispensary. In 1687, the censors of the College of Physicians issued an edict "requiring all the fellows, candidates, and licentiates, to give gratuitous advice to the neighbouring poor," as determined by the clergy. The plan was opposed by the apothecaries, who not only filled prescriptions but gave advice and wrote prescriptions, and thus were in competition with the physicians. In this enterprise the apothecaries were classed as quacks for several reasons, including the exorbitant fees they charged. Repeated efforts to enforce the edict by the College were unsuccessful because of opposition from within, as well as from without. Garth summarized the affairs as of 1697, pleading for support of the dispensary and unity in the College.[3]

I propound unto you the example of the best and most learned President, and of many others of this Society who are here present; For they share with others in their Calamities and Necessities. They have provided a Repositorie well furnished with Druggs for the help of the Poor. If therefore so great Pietie, so much Charitie may be of force to move you, if not in other things, yet in this I beseech you be conformable; unless things [to] be come to this passe, that our keenest enemies are to be found at home. If Statutes, if Solemn Oaths are vain names, yet how ever 'tis your Interest as Fellowes of this Colledge, [lest] that they learn not to contemn your Authoritie, who ought to obey you, but that the Priviledges you have received from your Ancestors, may be left by you to Posterity. [Again] Therefore I earnestly intreat you to return again to unitie and concord; so all differences amongst us being buried, we may joyntly seek the advantage of our Societie.

The Dispensary: A Poem in Six Canto's was circulated first in manuscript form and was printed a few weeks later, followed by a second and a third edition within a year. Subsequent revised editions appeared, the last in 1807. The mock-heroic poem describes a Homeric struggle between the physicians and the apothecaries. The dedication of the third edition to Anthony Henley discloses Garth's skill in composition and warmth of character; one of the concluding verses of the sixth canto is an example of his poetic skill.[4]

TO
ANTHONY HENLEY ESQ;

A Man of your Character can no more Prevent a Dedication, than he wou'd Encourage one; for Merit, like a Virgin's Blushes, is still most discover'd when it labours most to be conceal'd. 'Tis hard, to think well of you, shou'd be but Justice, and to tell you so, shou'd be an Offence: Thus rather than violate your Modesty, I must be wanting to your other Virtues; and to gratifie One good Quality, do wrong to a Thousand. The World generally measures our Esteem by the Ardour of our Pretences; and will scarce believe that so much Zeal in the Heart, can be consistent with so much Faintness in the Expressions; but when They reflect on your Readiness to do Good, and your Industry to hide it; on your Passion to oblige, and your Pain to hear it own'd; They'll conclude, that Acknowledgments wou'd be Ungrateful to a Person who even seems to receive the Obligations he confers.

But tho' I shou'd persuade my self to be silent upon all Occasions; those more Polite Arts, which,

till of late, have Languish'd and Decay'd, wou'd appear under their present Advantages, and own you for one of their generous Restorers: Insomuch, that Sculpture now Breaths, Panting Speaks, Musick Ravishes; and as you help to refine Our Taste, you distinguish your Own. Your Approbation of this Poem, is the only Exception to the Opinion the World has of your Judgment, that ought to rellish nothing so much, as what you write your self: But you are resolv'd to forget to be a Critick, by remembering you are a Friend. To say more, wou'd be uneasie to you, and to say less wou'd be unjust in

Your Humble Servant.

Wou'd but *Apollo* some great Bard inspire
With sacred veh'mence of Poetick Fire;
To celebrate in Song that God-like Power,
Which did the labouring Universe restore;
Fair *Albion's* Cliffs wou'd Eccho to the Strain,
And praise the Arm that Conquer'd to regain
The Earth's repose, and Empire o'er the Main.
  Still may th'immortal Man his Cares repeat,
To make his Blessings endless as they're great:
Whilst *Malice* and *Ingratitude* confess
They've strove for Ruin long without success.

The Kit-Kat Club, a group of the most distinguished British—statesmen, poets, soldiers, patriots, and those of royal blood—accepted Garth as the only physician on their roster. The club was dubbed from the contraction of the names of the pastry cook, Christopher, or Kit, and his tavern near Temple Bar, At the Sign of the Cat and the Fiddle. Although Garth was censored for his love of pleasure, a biographer found it easier to excuse than to defend him.[5]

He was likewise made Physician in Ordinary to the King, and Physician-General to the army. As his known services procured him a great interest with those in power, so his humanity and good nature inclined him to make use of that interest rather for the support and encouragement of men of letters who had merit, than for the advancement of his own fortune, his views in that respect having been always very moderate. He lived with the Great in that degree of esteem and independency, and with all that freedom which became a man possessed of superior genius, and the most valuable talents. He was not so haughty as to be above being obliged, and he had a fund of gratitude and good sense, which induced as well as enabled him to oblige them in return.

  1. Cushing, H.: Dr. Garth: the Kit-Kat Poet, *Bull Johns Hopkins Hosp* 17:1-17, 1906.
  2. Steele, R.: *The Lover*, London: J. Tonson, 1715.

3. Garth, S.: The Harveian Oration (L), *Aedibus Collegii Regalis Med Lond*, Sept 17, 1697, pp 4-16. Ellis, F. H., trans. Garth's Harveian Oration *J. Hist Med* 18: 8-19, 1963.

4. Garth, S.: *The Dispensary: A Poem In Six Canto's*, ed 3, London: J. Nutt, 1699.

5. *Biographica Britannica: or, the Lives of the Most eminent Persons Who have flourished in Great Britain and Ireland*, vol 3, London: W. Innys, 1750.

The whole art of gaming, where there is anything of hazard, is to calculate, in dubious cases, on which side there are most chances; and the principles here laid down would enable anyone, even in the midst of the game, to make a sufficiently accurate conjecture.

But gaming was not the only reason for his interest in mathematics. In the early days of medical practice, he published *An Essay on the Usefulness of Mathematical Learnin, in a Letter from a Gentleman in the City to his Friend in Oxford.* Several reasons were advanced for the help offered by mathematics in a small book sometimes attributed to Martin Strong.[2]

First, the Mathematicks make the Mind attentive to the objects, which it considers. . . . The second advantage, which the Mind reaps from *Mathematical* knowledge, is a habit of *clear, demonstrative,* and *methodical* Reasoning. . . . Thirdly, *Mathematical* knowledge adds a manly vigour to the Mind, frees it from *prejudice, credulity,* and *superstition.*

At the age of 29, Arbuthnot took his degree in medicine at St. Andrews and began the practice of medicine in London. His name was spelled with two "t's" in the signature of his voluminous correspondence at St. Andrews, but only one "t" was used on the title page of his books.[3] The one "t" is the older form of the name. Not long after he took up medicine in London, he became firmly established as a man of letters and a man of physic. He was appointed a member of the committee of the Royal Society, consisting of Sir Isaac Newton, Sir Christopher Wren, and others, to supervise the publications of the Astronomer Royal. He was also a member of a committee to adjudicate the dispute between Leibnitz and Newton as to which one discovered the method of fluxions. Newton was judged the discoverer. Another honor and responsibility was the appointment as Physician Extraordinary to Queen Anne, the Queen with gout, in consideration of his ministrations to Prince George of Denmark, who had been taken suddenly ill at Epsom. As one reviews the writings of the court physician, there seems little doubt that his fame as a satirist excelled any basic contributions to medical science. The essay, published in

Composite by G. Bako

John Arbuthnot (1667-1735)

JOHN ARBUTHNOT, physician to Queen Anne, was as well known in the literary world for his satire and wit as he was in London for his medical skill. John was born in 1667 near Bervie on the coast of Scotland. His father, the Jacobite Episcopalian clergyman of Arbuthnott, lost his parish because he would not embrace Presbyterianism in the revolution of 1688. When his father died shortly after, John moved to London, lectured in mathematics, and employed the applied science at the gaming table. The translation from Latin to English of Huygens' essay, "Of the Laws of Chance," was assumed to be the work of Arbuthnot. An especially enlightened statement in the preface noted that[1]

1733 on the effects of air on human bodies, is somewhat difficult to evaluate. The following passage is illustrative of the frustration in interpretation.[4]

From the flaccid state of the Lungs of Animals that die *in Vacuo,* it seems evident that the Lungs do not expand themselves upon the Exsuction of the Air, consequently the Air is suck'd out or escapes through the Blood-Vessels of the Lungs; else, if retain'd, it would expand and swell them; if the Air has a free Egress through the Coats of the Vessels of the Lungs, it may have a free Ingress. On the other hand, Attempts to force Air into Blood-Vessels of the Lungs by the Windpipe, have prov'd unsuccessful, and the Lungs of Animals that die *in Vacuo,* afterwards swell in the Air-pump. Things may happen in a live animal, which will not succeed in a dead one. Air will pass through any Membrane, when moist. The quick Restoration of the Balance of Air within and without Human Bodies, shows that there is a free Communication; and it is probable that it is so in the Lungs, as well as in other Parts of the Body.

Together with Jonathan Swift and Alexander Pope, members of the famous Scribblers Club, a combined satire on pedantry in the manner of Cervantes was planned, "On the Abuse of Human Learning in Every Branch." Arbuthnot was to lend his knowledge of science, and, masquerading as Martinus Scriblerus,[1]

He attempted to find out specifics for all the passions; and as other physicians throw their patients into sweats, vomits, purgations &c., he cast them into love, hatred, hope, fear, joy, grief, &c. And indeed the great irregularity of the passions in the English nation was the chief motive that induced him to apply his whole studies, while he continued among us, to the diseases of the mind.

To this purpose he directed, in the first place, his late acquired skill in anatomy. He considered virtues and vices as certain habits which proceed from the natural formation and structure of particular parts of the body.

Firstly. He observed, that the soul and body mutually operate upon each other, and therefore if you deprive the mind of the outward instruments whereby she usually expresseth that passion, you will in time abate the passion itself, in like manner as castration abates lust.

Fourthly. That a muscle may be strengthened or weakened by weakening or strengthening the force of its antagonist. These things premised, he took notice.

That complaisance, humility, assent, approbation, and civility, were expressed by nodding the head and bowing the body forward; on the contrary, dissent, dislike, refusal, pride, and arrogance, were marked by tossing the head, and bending the body backwards. . . . Now he observed that complaisant and civil people had the flexors of the head very strong; but in the proud and insolent there was a great overbalance of strength in the extensors of the neck and muscles of the back, whence they perform with great facility the motion of tossing, but with great difficulty that of bowing, and therefore have justly acquired the title of stiff-necked. In order to reduce such persons to a just balance, he judged that the pair of muscles called *recti interni,* the mastoidal, with other flexors of the head, neck, and body must be strengthened; their antagonists, the *splenii complexi,* and the extensors of the spine weakened: for which purpose nature herself seems to have directed mankind to correct this muscular immorality by tying such fellows neck and heels.

Arbuthnot was the first to typify the English male as "John Bull." The essay, published in 1712, was entitled, "Law is a Bottomless Pit, Exemplify'd in the Case of the Lord Strutt, John Bull, Nicholas Frog, and Lewis Baboon, who spent all they had in a Law Suit." The tale was a satire on the War of the Spanish Succession. Lord Strutt was the late king of Spain; Nicholas Frog, the Dutchman; Lewis Baboon, the French king. Although there is some question regarding authorship, the consensus is that Arbuthnot was solely responsible for this colloquial gem.

Lord Chesterfield, literary associate and patient, stated that,[5]

Dr. Arbuthnot was both my physician and my friend, and in both those capacities I justly placed the utmost confidence in him.

Without any of the craft, he had all the skill of his profession, which he exerted with the most care and pleasure upon those unfortunate patients, who could not give him a fee.

To great and various erudition, he joined an infinite fund of wit and humour, to which his friends Pope and Swift were more obliged, than they have acknowledged themselves to be.

His imagination was almost inexhaustible, and whatever subject he treated, or was consulted upon, he immediately overflowed with all that it could possibly produce.

He indulged his palate to excess, I might have said to gluttony, which gave him a gross plethoric habit of body, that was the cause of his death.

Arbuthnot died a devout Christian. His will, composed in 1733 and activated by the court in 1735, begins:[1]

I John Arbuthnott Doctor of Physick thus make my last Will and Testament. I recommend my Soul to its merciful Creator hoping to be saved by the merits of Jesus Christ, and that I may be found in him not having on my own Righteousness but his which is of faith.

1. Aitken, G. A.: *The Life and Works of John Arbuthnot*, Oxford: Clarendon Press, 1892.

2. Anonymous: *An Essay on the Usefulness of Mathematical Learning, in a Letter from a Gentleman in the City of his Friend in Oxford,* 2nd ed., Oxford: L. Lichfield, 1721.

3. Men of the British School: John Arbuthnott, M.D., F.R.S., Our Great Ones of the Past, *Med Times Gaz* 34: 494 (Nov 15) 1856; 523 (Nov 22) 1856.

4. Arbuthnot, J.: *An Essay Concerning the Effects of Air on Human Bodies,* London: J. Tonson, 1733.

5. *Letters of Philip Dormer Stanhope, Lord Chesterfield,* vol 2, Lord Mahon, ed., London: Richard Bentley, 1847, p 446.

George Cheyne (1671-1743)

I WAS BORN OF HEALTHY PARENTS, in the *Prime* of their Days, but dispos'd to *Corpulence,* by the whole Race of one Side of my Family. I passed my Youth in close Study, and almost constant Application to the *abstracted Sciences,* (wherein my chief Pleasure consisted) and consequently in great *Temperance* and a *sedentary Life;* yet not so much but that I sometimes kept *Holiday,* diverted myself with the Works of *Imagination,* and roused *Nature* by agreeable Company and *good Cheer.*

Upon my coming to *London,* I all of a sudden changed my whole Manner of Living; I found the *Bottle-Companions,* the *younger Gentry,* and *Free-livers,* to be the most easy of Access, and most quickly susceptible of *Friendship* and *Acquaintance;* nothing being necessary for that Purpose, but to be able to *Eat* lustily, and swallow down much *Liquor;* and being naturally of a large Size, a chearful Temper, and tolerable lively *Imagination;* and having, in my Country Retirement, laid in Store of *Ideas* and *Facts;* by these Qualifications I soon became caressed by them, and grew daily in *Bulk* and in *Friendship* with these gay Gentlemen and their Acquaintances.

The paragraphs above introducing Cheyne's autobiography[1] appeared first in his treatise on *The English Malady;*[2] they are representative of his literary style, superior to that of any of his contributions to medical science. His writing skill was recognized by his contemporories as at least not inferior to his medical skill in the practice of his profession. Cheyne, a native of Methlick, Aberdeen, Scotland, excelled in his early studies in mathematics and natural philosophy. This superior intelligence led his parents to consider a career in the church for their son. However, his choice of Edinburgh for advanced studies quickly dispelled any ecclesiastical intentions. Here he came under the influence of Archibald Pitcairn, a member of the faculty, a leading physician of Scotland, a learned scholar, and a writer of considerable talent. Since Cheyne's mathematical skills were for the most part consonant with the iatro-mechanical or mathematical school of medicine recommended by Pitcairn, a firm relationship developed between pupil and mentor. His one exception to complete acceptance of the theory of a mechanical basis for all physiological functions was Cheyne's interpretation of a force, in addition to a mechanical pump and conduits of varying sizes, necessary to explain the circulation of blood.

Cheyne became a Fellow of the College of Physicians of Edinburgh, and, although he lived in Scotland for the first three decades of his life, references in letters and published material indicate he was known in London for his talents in mathematics, narration, and practical medicine. In 1701, he was elected, in absentia, to the Royal Society. At the time Edinburgh did not grant degrees in medicine; therefore, he sought his MD degree from Aberdeen, without residence. The following year he moved to London, acknowledged his active membership in the Royal Society, and published *A New Theory of Acute and Slow Continued Fevers,* the first of his two medical treatises. Neither this monograph nor his essay on gout advanced the science of medicine appreciably. His other works, except for the treatise on geometry, appear to have been prepared primarily for lay reading. Much of the commonplace advice was based upon his own hypochondriasis, his perpetual struggle with corpulence—he weighed, by his own measure, 440 pounds at one time—and his moderately distressing gouty arthritis.

Cheyne's style, easy and fluid, excessively repetitive within each volume and from volume to volume, proved pleasant to read, nevertheless. His contemporaries must have held a similar opinion since the books went into several editions, and with translations into foreign languages. The text on abstracted geometry and algebra (integral calculus), appearing in 1703, was followed in 1705 by his work, *Philosophical Principles of Natural Religion,* a strange mixture of mathematics and theology. Before his pen was dry, he had prepared eight major tracts and had written a vast number of letters; those to the Countess of Huntingdon and Samuel Richardson have been reprinted recently as separate collections. Cheyne's first venture into print is described in his autobiography as follows.[1]

The first Time I adventured in Print, was on the Account of my great Master and generous Friend, Dr. *Pitcairn.* He thought himself ill-used by some of his Brethren of the Profession, who then were at intestine War on the Subject of *Fevers;* and fancied the handsomest Way to bring them down, was to exhibit a more specious Account of this Disease, than any of them had shewn. His Business then in the Practice of Physick was so great, as not to allow him sufficient Time for such a Work. Two others therefore, with myself, were joined to manage the Affair: In which he was to cut and carve, and to add the practical Part. My Province was the Theory. I was very young in the Profession, and

living in the Country. But in a few Days I brought in my Part finished, as it now appears, under the Title of *The New Theory of Fevers.*

Cheyne's chronic ill health provided clinical data for his popular expositions as well as for his essay on gout, which extended to 40 pages in the discussion of *The English Malady.* Troubled with dyspnea, lethargy, and fatigue from obesity, he took the water cure at Bath in 1725, adhered to a milk and vegetable diet, and lost considerable weight, but not his nervous indigestion. Before, as well as after, coming to London, where his many profligate habits may have contributed to his nervous indigestion and hypochondriasis, he noted that:[2]

. . . upon the slightest *Excesses,* I always found slippery Bowels, or a Spitting to be the *Crise;* whence afterwards, on *Reflection,* I concluded, that my *Glands* were naturally *lax,* and my *Solids feeble;* in which Opinion I was confirmed, by an early *Shakeing* of my *Hands,* and a Disposition to be easily ruffled on a *Surprize.*

For one Year I went on tolerably well, tho' as it were *jumbled* and *turbid,* and neither so *clear* in my Faculties, nor so *gay* in Temper: But next Autumn I was suddenly seized with a *vertiginous Paroxysm,* so extreamly frightful and terrible, as to approach near to a *Fit* of an *Apoplexy,* and I was forced in it to lay hold on the Posts of my Bed, for fear of tumbling out, as I apprehended. After immediate *Bleeding* and *Vomiting* (whereby its Violence was abated) . . . I found . . . some small Returns of my *Vertigo* . . . but by Degrees it turned to a constant violent *Head-ach, Giddiness, Lowness, Anxiety* and *Terror,* so that I went about like a *Malefactor* condemn'd, or one who expected every Moment to be crushed by a *ponderous* Instrument of Death, hanging over his Head.

While I was thus (as I have said) forsaken by my *Holiday* Friends, and my Body was, as it were, melting away like a *Snow-ball* in Summer, being dejected, *melancholy,* and much confin'd at home, by my Course of *mineral* Medicines, and Country Retirement, I had a long Season for undisturbed *Meditation* and *Reflection.*

I am heartily ashamed, and humbly beg Pardon of my *polite* and *delicate* Readers (if any such should deign to look into this low *Tattle,* contrary to my Intention.) I know how *indecent* and *shocking Egotism* is, and for an *Author* to make himself the Subject of his Words or Works, especially in so tedious and circumstantiated a *Detail:* . . . and I have, on that Account, written *this* in a plain *narrative* Stile, with the fewest Terms of Art possible, without supposing my

Reader, or shewing *myself,* to have look'd ever into a *physical* Book before; thinking this *Manner Stile* might be most instructive.

Observations Concerning the Nature and Due Method of Treating the Gout was the vehicle for the disclosure of Cheyne's iatromechanical theory of gout, in which he attributed the disease to the accumulation of tartarous and urinous salts from quantities of rich animal foods and drink. The joints were affected most because here the vessels were compressed by the prominence of bony structures. Water was recommended for its diuretic action, meats were condemned for their richness, and opiates were prescribed only as a last resort for the control of pain.[3]

The Cause of an acquir'd *Gout* in the first Person, or in those born of sound Parents, seems to me, to be the Abundance of Tartarous, Urinous, or other Salts, introduc'd into the Blood by the Food. . . . These Salts receiv'd in abundance, but Neither sufficiently broke by the Digestive Powers, nor driven out of the Habit by due Exercise; but by their Plenty and Nearness, uniting in greater Clusters, must necessarily form Obstructions, and give Pain, when, by the Force of the Circulation, they are thrust through narrower and stiffer small Vessels.

Water is the universal Dissolvent of Salts of all sorts; and being replenish'd with the spicy, bitter and active Parts of other Bodies, strengthens the Stomach and Bowels; breaks and dissolves the Salts; cleanses the insides of the Vessels from the Foulness that constantly adheres to them, and carries it out of the Body, by increas'd Perspiration and Urine.

In the general, it is the safest side, not to administer any kind of *Opiats* in the Fits; because they constantly pall the Appetite and leave a Nauseating, and perhaps a Reaching on the Stomach, the readiest way to bring the *Gout* there. But in Extremities, when the Patient has been many Days without Rest, and the Pain becomes intolerable, all other Means failing, or equally dangerous, *Opiats* may be so qualify'd, and their mischievous Effects so bridl'd, by joining spicy, nervous and Stomach Medicines to them, that they may become an excellent Remedy.

Cheyne's interpretation of philosophy was disclosed in the preface of his *Essay on Regimen,* prepared in his later years. He came to London to seek a career, the city was kind to him. It provided his neurasthenic and hypochondriacal personality with food and drink to excess. The reaction was an austere regimen to which he returned from time to time with benefit. Although he sought the "cure" at fashionable bathing spas, he always returned to London, where his patients and friends lived, among them the most notable of the day: Samuel Johnson, John Wesley, David Hume, Alexander Pope, and Richard Tennison. In spite of real or imaginary handicaps, Cheyne never abandoned his philosophy of living expressed in a style that seems so admirable. As a physician he accepted physic as a part of philosophy, which helps explain his addressing his remarks to the laity as well as to the profession.[4]

True Philosophy *is the* Science *of living the most happily, through the whole* Period *of our Existence, the Nature of things will permit;* Physic *is but one Branch of this* Philosophy, *and regards but one part of our Composition, and but for a small* Period *of our Duration.* True Philosophy *takes in the whole Extent of our Being, from its most distant Beginning, to its most advanced* Stages, *possible or conceivable. True Physic is that only which directs how the Body may be preserved the most* healthful, *the intellectual Organs depending on the Body the most acute, the* Senses *the most perfect, and the* Limbs *the most active; not for a while only, and by Fits and Starts, but uniformly, as long as* they *were made to last, and as the original* Frame and Texture *will permit.*

1. Cheyne, G.: *Dr. Cheyne's Account of Himself and of His Writings,* ed 2, London: J. Wilford, 1743.
2. Cheyne, G.: *The English Malady: or a Treatise of Nervous Diseases of All Kinds,* London: G. Strahan, 1733.
3. Cheyne, G.: *Observations Concerning the Nature and Due Method of Treating the Gout,* London: G. Strahan, 1720.
4. Cheyne, G.: *An Essay on Regimen. Together With Five Discourses, Medical, Moral, and Philosophical,* London: C. Rivington, 1740.

Composite by G. Bako

John Radcliffe (1650-1714)

ALTHOUGH JOHN RADCLIFFE made no significant literary or scientific contributions to medicine, his philanthropic gifts to Oxford and London will continue throughout the centuries. He came of humble origin, rose to an enviable position in English medicine as physician to the royal family, and undoubtedly was the first physician of London in his day. Born in a house in the market place at Wakefield in Yorkshire, he attended Wakefield grammar school, and at the age of 15 was admitted to the University College, Oxford.[1] He studied the classics and graduated AB in 1669. Either because a fellowship was not available or because of his irascible personality, he transferred to Lincoln College in Oxford and received the AM degree in 1672. He concentrated on medical subjects, receiving the bachelor of physick in 1675, and began the practice of medicine in Oxford. The doctor of physick degree was awarded in 1682, as Grand Compounder, which implied a modest holding at least in land or estates.

Radcliffe gave little heed to conventional practice and boasted that his medical equipment consisted of nothing more than a few phials, a skeleton, and an herbal. But he possessed a keen intellect, was shrewd in his professional and business activities, and had an ebullient personality that attracted as well as repelled. Patients eagerly sought his advice; and, during the epidemic of smallpox, he advised fresh air, good ventilation, and daylight, contrary to the then current practice. His art and skill in practice fanned his ambition, and a transfer to London was inevitable, where he found many opportunities for practice. Success succeeds, and soon he became recognized as the heir-apparent to the position held by Richard Lower, the leading physician of London. Radcliffe became the first bearer of the gold-headed cane; when he retired from practice, the cane was passed on to Richard Mead.[2] It would have taken more than good fortune to have dampened his spontaneous wit or his ready temper or change his religious beliefs. In rejecting an appeal from Mr. Walker of University College, Oxford, to accept the Roman Catholic faith, Radcliffe replied in a letter.[1]

The Advantages you propose to me, may be very great, for all that I know: God Almighty can do very much, and so can the King, but you'll pardon me, if I cease to speak like a Physician for once, and with an Air of Gravity, am very apprehensive that I may anger the one, in being too complaisant to the other. You cannot call this pinning my Faith to any Man's Sleeve; those that know me, are too well appriz'd of a quite contrary Tendency. As I never flatter'd a Man my self, so 'tis my firm Resolution never to be wheedled out of my real Sentiments; which are, that since it has been my good Fortune to be educated according to the Usage of the Church of England, establish'd by Law, I shall never make my self so unhappy as to shame my Teachers and Instructors, by departing from what I have imbib'd from them.

Yet though I shall never be brought over to confide in your Doctrines, no one breathing can have a greater Esteem for your Conversation, by Letter, or Word of Mouth, than, Sir, Your most affectionate and faithful servant, John Radcliffe.

Within a reasonable time after his move to London, Radcliffe was appointed physician to Princess Anne of Denmark, accepted a fellowship in the Royal College of Physicians, and, in giving a window for the chapel at University College, Oxford, began a series of financial benefactions for which he is best remembered. William III rewarded his services to the Earl of Portland and the Earl of Rochford with a handsome purse and the offer for him to become his personal physician. However, Radcliffe declined the commission, using as an excuse the demands required of private practice. He was offered next a baronetcy. This too was declined on the plea of having no progeny to inherit the title. It is noteworthy that, having rejected all offers of royal appointments, he continued to treat the immediate and distant members of the royal family, although not always with respect or reserve. One famous error is recorded. When Queen Mary II was suffering from smallpox, Radcliffe misdiagnosed the malady as measles and gave a dire prognosis.

He was disappointed in at least one love affair and never married. The expected child of his bride-to-be was in need of a last name, and in the letter to the prosperous father of his prospective bride he wrote:[1]

Mrs. Mary is a very deserving Gentlewoman; but, you must pardon me, if I think her by no Means fit to be my Wife, since she is another Man's already, or ought to be. . . . I shall ever take Pride in being among the Number of your Friends, who am, Sir, Your most obedient Servant.

Radcliffe's financial, as well as professional interests, led him to invest in several tracts and to sustain heavy losses in other business ventures; nevertheless, his prosperity increased. He served as a member of parliament from 1690-1695 and again in 1713. He was a delightful letter-writer, although not a contributor to the medical literature. However, a number of his prescriptions were published in *Pharmacopoeia Radcliffiana*, printed in 1716.[3]

Radcliffe's magnanimity, sometimes anonymous, appears in retrospect to have been as sound and thoughtful as was his skill in accumulating great wealth. He gave money for distribution among the poor nonjuring clergy to support them in their refusal to swear allegiance to the King and Queen, and, under a fictitious name, contributed to the propagation of the gospel abroad. He left his estate in Yorkshire to the University College, Oxford, for two traveling fellowships and for the purchase of perpetual advowsons for the members of the college. The Radcliffe Library, the Radcliffe Infirmary, and the Observatory were built with funds that he donated to Oxford.[4] In London, he contributed to the building fund of the Royal College of Physicians and gave monies to St. Bartholomew's Hospital, where he was governor, "for mending the diet of the patients, and for the purchase of linen."

Radcliffe suffered from gout, although little more than mention is made of this in his letters or by his biographers. One may assume that he was only mildly afflicted. He was buried in St. Mary's Church, Oxford. A true copy of his will is a long, detailed, and carefully prepared document. Friends, relatives, and servants were remembered by a legacy. The portion regarding the library is as follows:[1]

And will, that my Executors pay forty thousand Pounds in the Term of ten Years, by yearly Payments of four thousand Pounds, the first Payment thereof to begin, and be made after the Decease of my two Sisters, for the building a Library in Oxon, and the purchasing the Houses, the House, between S. Mary's and the Schools in Cat-Street, where I intend the Library to be built; and when the said Library is built, I give one hundred and fifty Pounds per Annum, for ever, to the Library-Keeper thereof, for the Time being; and one hundred Pounds a Year, per Annum, for ever, for buying Books for the same Library.

1. *Some Memoirs of the Life of John Radcliffe, M.D.,* 2nd ed, London: E. Curll, 1715.
2. Macmichael, W.: *The Gold-Headed Cane,* 2nd ed, London: J. Murray, 1828.
3. Radcliffe, J.: *Pharmacopoeia Radcliffiana,* 2nd ed, London: Rivington, 1716.
4. Nias, J. B.: *Dr. John Radcliffe,* Oxford: Clarendon Press, 1918.

Composite by G. Bako

Sir Hans Sloane (1660-1753)

HANS SLOANE, whose collection of plants, minerals, coins, medals, prints, pictures, manuscripts, and books formed the nucleus of the British Museum, was born at Kille-leagh, County Down in the north of Ireland.[1] Of Scotch extraction, his father, receiver-general of taxes, was the leader of the colony of Scots who settled in Ulster. Sloane's inclination for natural history and subsequently medicine was strengthened by a sound education; however, a bout of hemoptysis from pulmonary tuberculosis at 16 years of age interrupted his regular course of study for three years. He studied medicine in Paris and Montpellier and took the degree of doctor of medicine in the University of Orange-Nassau in 1683. The following year Sloane yielded to the attractions of London and was befriended, tutored, and made a member of the household by Sydenham. One year later he was elected a Fellow of the Royal Society.

In 1687, Sloane was created a Fellow of the College of Physicians, but, instead of entering practice, his love of natural science led him to accompany the Duke of Albemarle, then governor of Jamaica, to the West Indies. He remained 15 months as physician to the Duke and consultant to the natives. Before returning to London, Sloane collected several hundred species of plants from the islands of Madeira, Barbados, Nieves, and St. Christopher. He settled in practice in Bloomsbury Square, was immediately successful, and served on the staff of Christ's Hospital for many years. Several hospitals in London received his philanthropy while alive as well as legacies in his will. Another unselfish act was the presentation to the Society of the Apothecaries, in 1722, of his rich botanical garden in Chelsea. In 1693, Sloane was elected secretary of the Royal Society and, on the death of Sir Isaac Newton in 1727, was chosen president, the first physician to be so honored. The post was held until 1741; meanwhile, he revived the publication of their *Philosophical Transactions* and supervised the publication until 1712. Sloane held similarly important offices in the Royal College of Physicians, including the presidency from 1719 to 1735 and censor during 1705, 1709, and 1715. He was responsible for a number of scientific contributions to the Philosophical Society and prepared three monographs. A catalog of plants from Jamaica written in Latin, was followed by a two-volume treatise on his voyage to the West Indies and other islands. His major medical treatise on sore eyes, esteemed by his contemporaries, is of historical interest only today.[2]

Sloane's enviable reputation in practice led to his appointment as consultant to Queen Anne and, on the accession of George I, commission as physician-general to the army. He favored inoculation against smallpox, having so treated members of the Royal family. A gregarious Londoner, Sloane held open house once a week for his learned friends. In 1716, he was created a baronet, the first physician to be knighted, and, for his benefaction to the Bodleian Library in Oxford, he was created doctor of medicine in 1701. Outside of England, Sloane's reputation was recognized by his election to foreign membership in the

French Academy of Sciences, the Imperial Academy of St. Petersburg, and the Royal Academy of Madrid.

Undoubtedly, the founding of the British Museum was the greatest of all of Sloane's philanthropic efforts and contributions. He seems to have been a born collector, and accumulated, because of interest and financial capacity, remarkable number of volumes. The size of ˙the collection may be judged from its appraised value, £80,000 in 1753, when it was accepted by the British Parliament for a permanent museum. The collection has grown tremendously since it was opened in 1759 and has become one of the greatest exhibition halls of the world; meanwhile, the Sloane manuscripts in the rare book room remain one of the principal sources of 17th century medical history in England.

1. Munk, W.: *The Roll of the Royal College of Physicians of London*, ed 2, London: Royal College of Physicians, 1878, vol 1, pp 460-467.
2. Sloane, H.: *An Account of a Most Efficacious Medicine for Soreness, Weakness, and Several Other Distempers of the Eyes*, London: D. Browne, 1745.

Edmond Halley (1656-1742)

EDMOND (EDMUND) HALLEY, usually remembered for his many contributions to theoretical and applied astronomy and especially for the prediction of the return of one heavenly body every 76 years, Halley's comet, ranked next to Sir Isaac Newton as the leading English scientist of his day. Halley was born in London, into a family of comfortable circumstances. He attended St. Paul's school and Queen's College, Oxford, was outstanding in classics, as well as in the natural sciences, but showed particular interest in and capacity for mathematics and astronomy.[1] Considerable time abroad in study and investigation contributed to his remarkable success in the identification and the charting of the movement of the planets and the stars. In 1703, Halley was appointed professor of geometry at Oxford; in 1713, he succeeded Sir Hans Sloane as secretary to the Royal Society, and in 1721

was appointed astronomer to the King. A prolific writer, he was a heavy contributor to the *Philosophical Transactions* of the Royal Society and its editor for several years.[2]

Composite by G. Bako

Halley's only diversion into medical subjects was sufficiently noteworthy and timely to place him among the first and the best of vital statisticians. The mortality and birth tables of Breslau, Silesia, communicated to the Royal Society by Mr. Justell for the five years 1687-1691, provided the raw data. From these Halley prepared revised tables and drew critical deductions. He proceeded to calculate the sum total of persons of all ages in the city of Breslau, the proportion of men able to bear arms, the vitality in all ages, and the probability of death of a person of any age. The significance of the life table as a computation instrument found less appeal among vital statisticians than among actuarians, particularly in the financing of assurance programs, through pricing of annuities and calculating premiums.[3] An excerpt from Halley's lasting contribution follows.[4]

The first use hereof is to shew the Proportion of *Men* able to bear *Arms* in any *Multitude,* which are those between 18 and 56, rather than 16 and 60; the one being generally too weak to bear the *Fatigues* of *War* and the Weight of *Arms,* and the other too crasie and infirm from *Age,* notwithstanding particular Instances to the contrary. . . . At least one half thereof are Males, or 9027: So that the whole Force this City can raise of *Fencible Men,* as the *Scotch* call them, is about 9000, or 9/34, or somewhat more than a quarter of the *Number of Souls,* which may perhaps pass for a Rule for all other places.

The *Second Use* of this Table is to shew the differing degrees of *Mortality,* or rather *Vitality* in all *Ages;* for if the number of Persons of any *Age* remaining after one year, be divided by the difference between that and the number of the Age proposed, it shews the *odds* that there is, that a Person of that Age does not die in a *Year.*

Use III. But if it be enquired at what number of *Years,* it is an even Lay that a Person of any *Age* shall die, this Table readily performs it:

Use IV. By what has been said, the *Price of Insurance* upon *Lives* ought to be regulated, and the difference is discovered between the *price* of ensuring the *Life* of a *Man* of 20 and 50, for Example: it being 100 to 1 that a Man of 20 dies not in a year, and but 38 to 1 for a Man of 50 Years of Age.

Use V. On this depends the Valuation of *Annuities* upon *Lives;* for it is plain that the *Purchaser* ought to pay for only such a part of the value of the *Annuity,* as he has Chances that he is living; and this ought to be computed yearly, and the Sum of all those yearly Values being added together, will amount to the value of the *Annuity* for the *Life* of the Person proposed.

1. Fontenelle, M.: The Elegy of Dr. Halley, *Gentleman's Magazine* 17:455-458; 503-507, 1747.

2. MacPike, E. F.: *Dr. Edmond Halley,* London: Taylor and Francis, Ltd., 1939.

3. Greenwood, M.: *Medical Statistics from Graunt to Farr,* Cambridge: University Press, 1948.

4. Halley, E.: An Estimate of the Degrees of the Mortality to Mankind, drawn from curious Tables of the Births and Funerals at the City of Breslau, with an Attempt to ascertain the Price of Annuities upon Lives, *Philos Trans* 17:596-610, 1694.

Daniel Turner (1667-1740)

DANIEL TURNER, recipient of the first medical diploma granted by an American school, was born in London. There he spent an extremely active professional life, practicing the art and writing on diverse subjects.[1] Without benefit of a degree he be-

came a member of the Barber-Surgeon's Company, pursuing the practice of surgery until he became disenchanted with his membership. Upon the payment of a fine of

Composite by G. Bako

£50, he was disfranchised. A few months later he was allowed to appear before the Royal College of Physicians of London and was approved subsequently as a licentiate of that body. His sentiments and gratitude to the President and Censors of the College for this opportunity to shift allegiance are expressed in the Epistle Dedicatory of his monograph, *De morbis cutaneis.* The text, one of the first treatises in English devoted to cutaneous disorders, appeared first in 1714 and enjoyed several editions; the fifth and last was published in 1736. The chapter discussions were supported by brief case reports, notably on herpes naevi, relaxed skin and perspiration, and an extensive list of topical and general remedies. Turner's cerate, a mixture of calamine, wax, and olive oil, was listed in the *National Formulary* through the 1919 edition. Turner's dedication, which conveys to the reader his style of composition follows.[2]

When, after the customary Examinations at the Censor's Board, You were pleas'd to think me qualify'd for that weighty Province of Medicinal Prescription, and honour'd me with the College *Diploma* for a Licentiate's Privilege; having lately quitted the Hurry of Business in a Branch of the same Profession, I had Time to look over some scatter'd Memoirs which I had taken of certain remarkable Occurrences, and to reduce them into some better Order; which when I had digested and Fitted the Best I could for the Press, I had no Need to deliberate where I should present them, since by Duty, as well as Interest, they were intirely Yours.

It was my Duty to offer (I cannot say my first Fruits from the Press, having been often there before, but) the first I publish'd since I came among You, by which I might convince You (whatever may be the Fate of the Performance) that You have given that Privilege to no idle, and I hope, no useless Person.

It was my Interest to sue for Your Protection, which being granted, and the said Performance honour'd with Your *Imprimatur,* its Access may be the easier to the Men of Art, who will find as the Author has not been asham'd to venture it abroad, so neither have You the learned President, nor Ye the learned Censors of Our renowned College, disdain'd to countenance its Passage: Be that however as it will, yet is He still the same, I mean

(Most honour'd President,
And much honour'd Censors)
Your much obliged
And very humble Servant,

DANIEL TURNER

Turner's first monograph, the *Apologia chyrurgica,* appeared in 1695. The long subtitle disclosed the design to expose the various quacks of his time:[3] "A Vindication of the Noble Art of Chyrurgery, FROM the gross Abuses offer'd thereunto by *Mountebanks, Quacks, Barbers, Pretending Bone-setters,* with other Ignorant Undertakers, WHEREIN Their Fraudulent Practices are plainly detected by several remarkable Observations, their Fair Promises prov'd Fictions, their Administrations pernicious, their Confident Pretences injurious and destructive to the Welfare of the People." Other extended tracts included *Syphilis,* in two parts; *The Art of Surgery,* in two volumes; *A Discourse Concerning Fevers; Aphrodisiacus,* a summary of ancient works on venereal diseases; *The Ancient Physician's Legacy Impartially Surveyed;* and *The Force of the Mother's Imagination upon the Foetus in Utero.*

The events surrounding Turner's honorary degree of doctor of medicine, the first conferred in the English colonies in North America, have been delightfully described by Lane.[1] In 18th century England, the Royal College of Physicians of London restricted fellowships, in most instances, to graduates of Oxford or Cambridge; whereas licensure was granted to physicians with foreign degrees upon examination, without which they could not legally practice in London. While practicing in London as a surgeon, Turner possessed no medical degree. When he became a licentiate of the College, a partial attempt to correct the deficiency and remove any apprehension was accomplished through negotiations for an honorary degree. Turner sought help from Jeremiah Dummer, appointee of the general court of Connecticut as agent for Connecticut in London. In anticipation of a favorable reception, Turner, in 1722, bestowed on the College of the Academy of Yale his portrait and a number of medical and nonmedical books, including treatises on anatomy, theology, natural history, and his own texts and, beseeching in turn: "If your worships consider me worthy of the doctoral degree of Yale Academy and have the diploma sent to me, I shall receive it not only as a sign of your gratitude, but I shall consider it an honour as much as though it had been conferred by another university, though of greater note." Following receipt of the several items, his degree was granted by Yale on Sept 11, 1723. Turner's letter as well as several of the books remain in the rare archives of the historical library at Yale Medical School.

1. Lane, J. E.: Daniel Turner and the First Degree of Doctor of Medicine Conferred in the English Colonies of North America by Yale College in 1723, *Ann Med Hist* 2:367-380 (Dec) 1919.

2. Turner, D.: *De Morbis Cutaneis. A Treatise of Diseases Incident to the Skin,* London: R. Bonwicke, 1714.

3. Turner, D.: *Apologia Chyrurgica,* London: J. Whitlock, 1695.

Composite by G. Bako

Richard Mead (1673-1754)

RICHARD MEAD received from Radcliffe the gold-headed cane, a symbol of excellence in 17th and 18th century London medicine. However, the two recipients possessed quite opposite personalities.[1] Mead was born the eleventh child of a Nonconformist minister of Stepney, Middlesex, whose private means provided excellent tutorial education for his children. Having acquired facility in languages and a good classical education, Richard followed his father into voluntary exile in Holland, spent three years at Utrecht, and extended his knowledge of classical literature and antiquities. At the age of 19 he entered Leyden as a student of medicine. Archibald Pitcairn, then a member of the faculty, supported the iatromechanical school and taught the practice of physic; whereas Boerhaave, later Leyden's most renowned physician, was a young graduate. Mead traveled in various parts of Europe and graduated MD from Padua in 1695. Although lacking a license from the College of Physicians, Mead began the practice of medicine in 1696 in the parental home in Stepney.

This legal deficiency proved no barrier to his professional progress, and shortly afterwards he prepared an experimental disser-

tation entitled *A Mechanical Account of Poisons* (1702). He himself tasted the venom of deadly vipers and also injected it into the veins of animals, without fatal consequences. This was described in a new edition of *The Medical Works of Richard Mead*.[2]

> We resolved to end our poison-inquiries by tasting the venomous liquor. Accordingly, having diluted a quantity of it with a very little warm water, several of us ventured to put some of it upon the tip of our tongues. We all agreed, that it tasted very sharp and fiery, as if the tongue had been struck through with something scalding or burning. This sensation went not off in two or three hours: and one gentleman, who would not be satisfied without trying a large drop undiluted, found his tongue swelled with a little inflammation, and the soreness lasted two days. But neither his nor our boldness was attended with any ill consequence.

An abstract of this study was published in the *Philosophical Transactions,* which was followed by his election to the Royal Society in 1703. In the same year, he communicated to the Royal Society an account of Bonomo's discovery in 1687 of the scabies mite, which had not been accepted in England as a pathogenic agent. This is excerpted as follows.[3]

> Having frequently observed that the Poor Women when their Children are troubled with the *Itch,* do with the point of a Pin pull out of the Scabby Skin little Bladders of Water, and crack them like Fleas upon their Nails; and that the Scabby Slaves in the *Bagno* at *Leghorne* do often practice this Mutual Kindness upon one another; it came into my Mind to examine what these *Bladders* might really be.
>
> I quickly found an *Itchy* person, and asking him where he felt the greatest and most acute *Itching,* he pointed to a great many little *Pustles* not yet Scabb'd over, of which picking out one with a very fine Needle, and squeezing from it a thin Water, I took out a very small white *Globule,* scarcely discernible: Observing this with a Microscope, I found it to be a very minute Living Creature, in shape resembling a Tortoise, of whitish colour, a little dark upon the Back, with some thin and long Hairs, of nimble motion, with six Feet, a sharp Head, with two little Horns at the end of the Snout.
>
> With great earnestness I examined whether or no these Animalcules laid Eggs, and after many enquiries, at last by good Fortune while I was drawing the Figure of one of 'em by a Micro-

scope, from the hinder part I saw drop a very small and scarcely visible white Egg, almost Transparent, and oblong.

I oftentimes found these Eggs afterwards, from which no doubt these Creatures are generated, as all others are, that is, from a Male and Female, tho I have not yet been able by any difference of Figure to distinguish the Sex of these Animals.

Mead was subsequently elected physician to St. Thomas' Hospital and was responsible for the teaching of anatomy; but not until 1707 was his medical degree from Padua acknowledged by Oxford, which granted him the MD, prerequisite for admission to the College of Physicians. This recognition was somewhat overdue, and by then Mead had acquired a large practice and had taken over Radcliffe's house in Bloomsbury Square.

Among his patients were members of the Royal family. The most famous was Queen Anne, who was seen shortly before her death; John Radcliffe, because of acute exacerbation of gout, was unable to attend her. Mead predicted the outcome but did not voice his findings immediately. He attended Charles II, Sir Isaac Newton in his last illness, and was a friend of many of the worthies of his day, including Hans Sloane, Pope, Freind, Halley, Garth, and Arbuthnot. He was reported to have earned much, spent much, and given away much following the pattern of Radcliffe. Politically, Mead was a Whig, but there is only one story of his entering politics. This was to intercede with Walpole for Freind, who had been committed to the Tower.

Mead accepted the theory of spread of the plague by contagion, advocated quarantine, and, at the request of the Prince of Wales, inoculated seven criminals with smallpox lymph. Their recovery insured greater confidence in the safety of the practice. Following this event the children in the Royal family were so protected. Late in life he published his *Discourse on the Small-Pox and Measles.* This included a history of inoculation, reputedly an invention of the Circeans to protect the beauty of the young women who were sold as slaves to neighboring people.[4]

The custom of inoculating, or transferring the Small-Pox from an infected person to one that is sound, has prevailed among us for some years. This matter has drawn our physicians into parties; some approving, and others disapproving this new practice. I shall therefore freely interpose my opinion in the case.

Our nature is so formed, that although we are always inclined to avoid whatsoever may be hurtful; yet, when any evil is to be undergone, which can only be suffered once, this we are impatient to go through, even with a certain boldness; with this view, that the remainder of life may be passed without the uneasiness which arises from the continual apprehension of its coming upon us.

It having therefore been found by experience, that no body was seized with the Small-Pox a second time, and that scarce one in a thousand escaped having it once; men began to consult how the disease might be communicated; it manifestly appearing to be contagious, and it was obvious to conjecture, that the seeds of that contagion lay hidden in the pustules.

Mead's collection of manuscripts, books, coins, antiquities, and treasures of art was one of the largest of his time. Scholars and artists were kept in his pay, who in turn labored for the benefit of the public, while the museum was open to students of the arts. He returned to the public in monies and compassion a portion of what he had received from patients. A liberal contributor to the Foundling Hospital, he is reported to have induced Mr. Guy, the bookseller, to contribute to the beginning of the hospital which bears the name of the benefactor. During a full professional life, Mead maintained a deep interest in literary labours as expressed in his biography, prepared in his retiring years, as the preface to *Medica Sacra*—a treatise planned to account on natural grounds for the diseases mentioned in the Scriptures.[5]

My declining years having in a great measure released me from those medical fatigues, in which, for the public good, (at least as I hope), I have been employed about fifty years, I have determined to pass the short remains of life in such a sort of leisure, as may prove neither disagreeable to myself, nor useless to others. For good men are of opinion, that we must give an account even of our idle hours, and therefore thought it necessary, that they should be always well spent.

Having from my earliest childhood entertained a strong passion for learning, after I had chosen the art of medicine for my profession, I still never intermitted my literary studies; to which I had recourse, from time to time, as to refreshments, strengthening me in my daily labours, and charming my cares.

1. Maty, M.: *Authentic Memoirs of the Life of Richard Mead, M.D.*, London: J. Whiston & B. White, 1755.

2. Mead, R.: *A Mechanical Account of Poisons*, London: R. South, 1702, in *The Medical Works of Richard Mead, M.D.*, Edinburgh: A Donaldson & C. Elliot, 1775.

3. Mead, R.: An Abstract of part of a Letter from Dr. Bonomo to Signior Redi, containing some Observations concerning the Worms of Humane Bodies, *Philos Trans* 23:1296-1299, 1703.

4. Mead, R.: *A Discourse on Small-pox and Measles* (L), London: J. Brindley, 1747, translated in *The Medical Works of Richard Mead, M.D.*, Edinburgh: A. Donaldson & C. Elliot, 1775.

5. Mead, R.: *Medica Sacra* (L), London: J. Brindley, 1749, translated in *The Medical Works of Richard Mead, M.D.*, Edinburgh: A. Donaldson & C. Elliott, 1775.

Composite by G. Bako

Stephen Hales (1677-1761)

THE REVEREND DOCTOR STEPHEN HALES remained active as the "perpetual curate" of Teddington, Middlesex, from 1709, the year of his appointment, until his death in 1761.[1] To medical and physiological scientists, this ordained minister is best known for his contributions to the dynamics of the circulation, particularly for the first quantitative measurement of the systemic blood pressure. He is equally well known to botanists for original discoveries in their field. Toward the close of his life, he concerned himself with the practical and social aspects of science and became involved in such diverse activities as the passage of the Gin Act of 1736, a trusteeship for founding the colony of Georgia, and the effective ventilation of jails and slave ships.[2]

Stephen was born in 1677 at Bekesbourne, Kent. Little is known about his life and education prior to his entry into Corpus Christi College, Cambridge, at age 19. At Cambridge, he was firmly grounded in Newtonian physics and astronomy. While there he met William Stukeley, an enthusiastic young naturalist several years his junior, and soon began to participate in Stukeley's biological exploitations, dissections, and experiments. Gradually, he began to design experiments of his own: a method for preparing a lead cast of the bronchial tree and an astronomical model to illustrate the planets. He received his bachelor of arts at 25, his master of arts the next year, his bachelor of divinity in 1711 and became a Fellow of the Royal Society in 1717. At 56, he became doctor of divinity (Oxford).

Although Hales never forsook duties in his little parish, St. Mary's-in-the-Meadows, the microcosm of his theology suffers when compared with the macrocosm of his natural science. His botanical experiments on the movement of sap in plants and trees were reported in brief to the Royal Society in 1719 and were published in full in *Vegetable Staticks* in 1727. To perform these experiments, he had to devise new techniques for the quantitative study of the absorption of water by the roots and the transpiration from the leaves of plants and trees. He also succeeded in measuring the propulsive force of the sap in the stem, i.e., the root pressure. Although carbon dioxide (fixed air) was not yet identified, Hales suspected that atmospheric gases supplied substance to plants through the leaves and bark. By placing marks on the young shoots near the joints, he measured the growth of the stems. The identifying marks separated during growth, without changing their original distance from the joints. This same approach was also used to identify the segment of growth of long bones in chicks.

The better-known contributions, dealing with the hemodynamics of the central and the peripheral circulation, were described in *Haemastaticks,* published in 1733. These critical investigations were started at least 20 years before publication. This monograph was consolidated with *Vegetable Staticks* and appeared as *Statical Essays* dated the same year.[3] The first circulatory experiments were performed on dogs; later a horse, a lamb, and other animals served as experimental subjects. A glass tube, a satisfactory manometer, was attached to an artery of the experimental animal. The connecting piece between manometer and blood vessel was the windpipe of a goose. Blood pressure was measured directly from the height of the blood in the tube.[3]

Then laying bare the left Carotid Artery, I fixed to it towards the Heart and the Brass Pipe, and to that the Wind-Pipe of a Goose; to the other End of which a Glass Tube was fixed, which was twelve Feet nine Inches long. The Design of using the Wind-Pipe was by its Pliancy to prevent the Inconveniences that might happen when the Mare struggled; if the Tube had been immediately fixed to the Artery, without the Intervention of this pliant Pipe.

There had been lost before the Tube was fixed to the Artery, about seventy cubick Inches of Blood. The Blood rose in the Tube in the same manner as in the Case of the two former Horses, till it reached to nine Feet six Inches Height. I then took away the Tube from the Artery, and let out by Measure sixty cubick Inches of Blood, and then immediately replaced the Tube to see how high the Blood would rise in it after each Evacuation; this was repeated several times, till the Mare expired, as follows, viz.

The volume of the ventricle was determined by casting with wax.[3]

So that this Piece of Wax thus formed, may reasonably be taken to be nearly commensurate to the Quantity of Blood received into this Ventricle at each *Diastole,* and is thence propelled into the *Aorta* at the subsequent *Systoles.*

The multiplication of the ventricular volume and the pulse rate gave the cardiac output.

Hales' studies on peripheral resistance carried out on the dog concerned the perfusion of water at body temperature through the descending aorta. The volume of flow was measured as the perfusing fluid escaped through a cut in the intestine. Continuing the experiment, he followed the mesenteric vessels and severed them, progressing toward the aorta. The resistance was maximum the farthest removed from the large vessel. Also he observed that the combined cross section of the branches beyond a bifurcation was greater than the cross section of the parent trunk central to the branching.[3]

I Slit open with a Pair of Scissors, from end to end, the Guts of a Dog, on that side which was opposite to the Insertion of the mesenterick Arteries and Veins; and having fixed a Tube 4½ Feet high to the descending *Aorta* a little below the Heart, I poured blood warm Water thro' a Funnel into the Tube, which descended thence into the *Aorta,* with a Force equal to that, with which the Blood is there impelled by the Heart: This Water passed off thro' the Orifices of innumerable small capillary Vessels, which were cut asunder thro' the whole Length of the slit Gut. But notwithstanding it was impelled with a Force equal to that of the arterial Blood in a live Dog, yet it did not spout out in little distinct Streams, but only seemed to ouze out at the very fine Orifices of the Arteries, in the same manner as the Blood does from the capillary Arteries of a muscle cut transversely.

But the Resistance which the Blood meets with in those capillary Passages, may be greatly varied, either by the different Degrees of the Viscidity or Fluidity of the Blood, or by the several Degrees of Constriction or Relaxation of those fine Vessels.

And as the State of the Blood or Bloodvessels are in these Respects continually varying from divers Causes, as Motion, Rest, Food, Evacuations, Heat, Cold, &c. so as probably never to be exactly the same, any two Minutes, during the whole Life of an Animal; so nature has wisely provided, that a considerable Variation in these, shall not greatly disturb the healthy State of the Animal.

Variations in peripheral vascular resistance were measured by observing the effect of heat and brandy.[3]

4. I first poured in seven Pots full of warm Water, the first of which passed off in fifty two Seconds, and the remaining six, gradually in less time, to the last which passed in forty six seconds.

5. Then, I poured in five Pots of Common Brandy, or unrectify'd Spirits of Malt, the first of which was 68" in passing, the last 72".

6. Then I poured in a Pot of warm Water which was 54" in passing.

7. Hence we see that Brandy contracts the fine capillary Arteries of the Guts, and that Water soon relaxes them again, by diluting and carrying off the spiritous Part of Brandy, which as it is well known, not only contracts the Coats of the Blood-vessels, but also thickens the Blood and Humours, both which Effects contribute to the sudden Heating of the Blood, by much increasing thereby its Friction in the contracted capillary Vessels.

Thus, Hales introduced quantitative measurement into the study of the circulation, progressing from the simple measurement of blood pressure to the more complex circulatory interplay of pressure, flow, and resistance.[4]

The practical and social aspects of his scientific studies came to the fore in the sixth decade of his life. They are typified by his inventions for the improvement of ventilation of jails, ships, and hospitals. For example, he used large bellows operated manually or by a windmill, to improve the ventilation in crowded quarters. Although it is difficult to determine whether lives were saved by these devices, they surely provided more tolerable living conditions.

Hales received the Copley Medal of the Royal Society in 1739 for his relatively unimportant experiments on the solubility of urinary tract stones.[3] Although observations in natural science were the primary interest of Parson Hales, he did not fail to discuss theology when offered the opportunity. He delivered the annual Croonian sermon for the Royal College of Physicians at the age of 70, reaffirming his dedication to his vocation, even though he is best remembered for his avocational contributions.

1. Clark Kennedy, A. E.: *Stephen Hales, D.D., F.R.S.,* London: Cambridge University Press, 1929.

2. Krafka, J., Jr.: Stephen Hales and the Founding of Georgia, *J Med Ass Georgia* 33:149-50 (May) 1944.

3. Hales, S.: *Statical Essays: Containing Haemastaticks; or, An Account of Some Hydraulick and Hydrostatical Experiments Made on the Blood and Blood-Vessels of Animals,* vol. 2, London: W. Innys and R. Manby, 1733.

4. Burchell, H. B.: Stephen Hales, September 17, 1677- January 4, 1761, editorial, *Circulation* 23:1-6 (Jan) 1961.

Giovanni Battista Morgagni (1682-1771)

MORGAGNI was born in Romagna, not far from the birthsite of Malpighi, his academic godfather. At Bologna, Morgagni studied with Albertini, who correlated dyspnea with heart disease and with Valsalva, who described the anatomy of the ear and the maneuver that bears his name. Also, Morgagni assisted Valsalva in the anatomical amphitheater, before and after graduation. Although Morgagni's reputation in current times is associated principally with anatomy and pathology, he manifested great interest in physiological experiments, and was recognized as a skillful clinician in consultation.

After study at Padua and medical practice at Forli, Morgagni was elected, at the age of 29, to the chair of theoretical medicine at Padua. Four years later, he was elevated by the senate at Venice to the professorship of anatomy, which he held for nearly 60 years. In this position he demonstrated his great talents as a scholar, teacher, physician, philosopher, medical historian, and pathologist as well as the less desirable traits of arrogance and egotism.[1] He blended scholarship in literature and medicine, was an acquaintance of several popes, and a physician to Clement XIII, before the latter became pontiff in Rome.[2]

Giovanni Battista (John Baptist) Morgagni began his scientific composition with the publishing of *Adversaria Anatomica* at the age of 24.[3] His great work, *The Seats and Causes of Diseases, Investigated by Anat-*

omy (*De sedibus et causis morborum per anatomen indagatis*), composed in the Latin of Cicero, rather than the late Latin of his day, summarized a lifetime study of clinical observations and of pathological anatomy. It was published when Morgagni was 79. Frequent references were made in *De sedibus* to comparative pathology of animals. He usually attributed pathogenesis and morbid states in man to mechanical disturbance, although his discussion of selected infectious diseases shows some recognition of a contagious etiology. The treatise established the organ concept of disease, gave some hint that disease was localized within the cells of the body, and placed pathological anatomy firmly in the medical sciences as a major discipline. It is the only one of his several comprehensive texts that has been translated into English; many of his letters and lesser manuscripts have never been published.

The study developed from a series of letters written to a young physician who sought counsel from the master. Morgagni dispatched the letters privately, but revised, edited, and eventually incorporated them into a system of pathological anatomy, the culmination of more than 50 years of clinical and postmortem observations. A recent reprinting of the translation by Benjamin Alexander of the 1769 edition, three beautifully prepared and bound volumes, makes it easy for one to peruse the writing of this great pathological anatomist. Paul Klemperer prepared the preface and introduction and a fresh translation of five letters to professional colleagues. The introduction is especially helpful in interpreting the pathology of Morgagni with those who preceded and with those who followed him.[4]

Morgagni sought to correlate physical findings and the clinical course of the disease with anticipated structural alterations. The discussions, however, gave little evidence of insight into the pathogenesis of specific diseases. He was the first to describe cerebral gummata and the first to show that intracranial suppuration may be associated with a discharge from the ear. He was one of the first to describe structural changes of the cardiac valves, syphilitic aneurysm,

acute yellow atrophy of the liver, tuberculosis of the kidney, and heart block (Stokes-Adams disease). The clinical features of pneumonia were identified with solidification of the lungs, the Morgagnian cataract was described, and the hypothesis of Valsalva that the cerebral lesion in apoplexy is on the opposite side from the resulting paralysis was substantiated. Kelley lists 24 eponyms of Morgagni.[5] Familiar to many physicians are the crypts of Morgagni in the lower rectum, the foramen of Morgagni between the sternal and costal attachments of the diaphragm, Morgagni's tubercle—the olfactory bulb, and Morgagni's disease—endocranial hyperostosis.

It is hazardous to select a few characteristic passages or to provide brief quotes from three huge tomes of rambling observations. In volume 1, Morgagni reported a case of angina pectoris observed in 1707. In letter III, a case of mitral stenosis is presented. Morgagni probably described tuberculous meningitis at about the time Whytt traced the clinical course of this morbid process (book I, letter I, article 1, 3). The observations by Morgagni were reported second hand from a case history by Valsalva.[4]

2. A boy of thirteen years of age, of a ready wit, whose brother and sister died of a consumption, having himself labour'd under an inflammation of the left lobe of the lungs the year before, was seiz'd with a pain in his head over his eyes: his eyes were also painful, and troubled with a viscid defluxion. The day following he became delirious; his eyes were fix'd on those about him; and he threw up a little tough phlegm. Then on a sudden, he was seiz'd with convulsions; after which he fell into a kind of lethargy: yet was frequently rous'd by convulsions, attended with difficult respiration. At length he died. . . . Having saw'd open the skull, the dura mater was found ting'd with a cineritious colour, along the sides of the blood vessels. And when the dura mater was torn away from the crista galli, a little sanious serum burst forth.

Cerebral gummata were described (book I, letter I, article 14).[4]

. . . . another woman, . . . Being first affected with the lues venerea, and after that with a fever, join'd to severe pains of the head and delirium, she died of this complication of disorders in the hospital at Padua. . . . the dura mater, where it lay nearest to the upper and middle region of the lateral sinus on the right side, was much thicken'd, and perfectly coalesc'd with the pia mater, and even with the substance of the brain: the meninges and brain were in that part also semi-putrid, and glar'd with a very disagreeable colour, which was compos'd of a yellowish, mix'd with an ash like hue, especially in the cortical part of the cerebrum.

Among diseases of the thorax, Morgagni described a 50-year-old man who spat blood at times and, under sudden exertion, became apneic, and within half an hour died from a ruptured aortic aneurysm (book II, letter XXVI, article 3).[4]

The left cavity of the thorax was found quite full of blood, the greater part of which had coagulated. This blood had burst forth from the great artery that was eroded at the part where, being about to descend to the vertebrae, it is inflected. For in that place, being dilated into an aneurism, it had hollow'd out the corresponding vertebrae; and where these were hollow'd out, there the artery seem'd to be consum'd.

A description of cardiac failure in mitral stenosis was given (book II, letter XXVI, article 33).[4]

33. This old man was, to appearance, about sixty years of age, and had three months before been in the hospital, complaining of a difficulty of breathing, and spitting up an ill condition'd matter. Having been in the country lately, about the beginning of March, in the year 1742, and having been expos'd to a cold wind, upon his return home again, he was seiz'd in the night with a very great difficulty of breathing. Wherefore, being brought into the same hospital again, in the morning, and sitting a little time by the fireside, while they were warming his bed, he had scarcely laid himself down therein, but he instantly died.

The thorax, therefore, immediately cut into, and the sternum being taken away, the lungs appear'd to be so turgid as to fill up the whole cavities; . . . There was, in both cavities of the thorax, a considerable quantity of water, not turbid, but of the colour of urine; which kind of water, also, was found in the pericardium in somewhat larger quantities than it is generally . . . the [left] ventricle . . . seem'd to be wider than natural, and the mitral valves to be hard and thick; and all the semilunar valves had their edges hard, white, and what is more than all the rest, becomes so much thicken'd as to equal a line and a half of the inch of bologna in thickness.

Morgagni reported on another observation from Valsalva's series, acute yellow atrophy of the liver as it appeared in a young male (book III, letter XXXVII, article 2).[4]

2. A young priest was seiz'd with the jaundice, a little after a kind of perturbation of mind: this disorder was also attended with a pain at the region of the stomach, and a vomiting, by means of which he threw up both his food, and his medicines, frequently. . . . The physician did not observe any fever, till the close of the third day: at which time it discover'd itself with great violence, with a delirium, and convulsions of such a nature, that the patient was oblig'd to gnaw every thing with his teeth, and by his great strugglings almost overcame the strength of those who were about him: besides these, he was troubled with a vomiting of a darkish-coloured matter. . . . He died on the beginning of the fifth day.

The belly being open'd, the liver was found to be flaccid, and inclining to a palish colour: in the gall-bladder was a darkish bile.

Throughout the *Seats and Causes of Disease,* reference is made to the *Sepulchretum* of Bonet, studies of Benivieni, Boerhaave, Stenzelius, Trombelli, Caelius Aurelianus, Donatus, Bellini, Galen, Hippocrates, and Pliny, as well as those of Valsalva his teacher. Frequently the case reports as translated tell a good clinical story, in a pleasing discursive style so characteristic of Morgagni, rather than in the stilted phrases of a textbook of medicine. The description of hepatization in lobar pneumonia, predicted antemortem is typical (book I, letter XXI, article 27).[4]

27. A virgin of two-and-forty years of age, who had, every winter, been subject to a violent cough . . . was seiz'd, in the night, with a fever, with which she first shivered, and was cold through her whole body, and after that grew hot. After an interval of twenty-four hours, a pain on one side of the breast was added to the fever, together with a difficulty of breathing, a cough quite dry, and a rather hard pulse. . . . In the progress of the disease, the pain shifted from one side of the breast to the opposite part. There was a sense of weight within the thorax . . . on the beginning of the seventh day she died. When I had heard this relation, I said, in dependence upon those appearances, that I had always found after the chief of such kind of symptoms, "Come, let the body be dissected; this will be certainly found

to be the nature of the disease, that the lungs shall appear to have the substance of the liver."

Podagra was not overlooked by Morgagni. In the section entitled "Treats of the Gout, and other Pains of the Joints," he deplored the lack of postmortem material for study (book IV, letter LVII, article 1).[4]

As the gout is generally a disorder of the rich, and very seldom of the poor; and the carcases of the latter, not of the former, are deliver'd to anatomists; or as, if at any time the bodies of the rich are to be open'd, the viscera only are subjected to examination, for the most part, and scarcely ever the limbs; it happens from hence, that observations which properly relate to the gout, are far more rare in the books of anatomists, than those of a great number of other diseases.

1. King, L. S.: *The Medical World of the Eighteenth Century*, Chicago: Univ of Chicago Press, 1958.
2. Jarcho, S.: Giovanni Battista Morgagni: His Interests, Ideas and Achievements, *Bull Hist Med* 22:503-527, 1948.
3. Morgagni, G. B.: *Adversaria Anatomica*, 6 parts, pt 1, Bologna, 1706.
4. Morgagni, G. B.: *De Sedibus et Causis Morborum per Anatomen Indagatis*, 1761, B. Alexander, trans., London: A. Millar, 1769, reprinted, New York: Hafner Publishing Co., 1960.
5. Giovanni Battista Morgagni, *Med Classics* 4:629-749 (March) 1940.

Lorenz Heister (1683-1758)

LORENZ HEISTER, one of the founders of scientific surgery, was born in Frankfurt-am-Main. His father, an innkeeper, enjoyed preferred rights in this electoral city of the Holy Roman Empire at the time of the escape of European Christendom from Moslem influence. Heister attended the Latin School; there he displayed exceptional intelligence, a proficiency in music and painting, and a zeal for the study of humanities including the classics, mathematics, philosophy, and history, as well as French, English, and Dutch. In his 19th year he began the study of medicine at the University of Giessen and became an intimate in the household of Moeller, the anatomist and physician, whom he assisted with demon-

strations on the cadaver and on visits to the sick. In the years 1706-1708, Heister attended the public lectures of Rau, assisted the great anatomist, Ruysch, in Amsterdam,

Composite by G. Bako

and studied under Albinus, Sr., and Boerhaave in Leyden. His doctoral thesis, *De tunica choroidea oculi,* in support of his degree granted by the University of Hardewyk in 1708, refuted the belief that the choroid is a continuation of the membranes of the brain. Heister restudied the eye in later years, confirming the lens as the locus for cataracts.

Both before and after taking the MD degree, Heister visited the Dutch camp in Brabant, Flanders, to observe the practice of the English, Dutch, and German surgeons who were serving in the war between the French and the Dutch. Following a brief residence in Amsterdam, where he practiced physic and surgery and taught anatomy and surgery in German, Latin, and English, he was called to the chair of anatomy and surgery in Altorf, near Nürnberg. In preparation for the major assignment, he spent several months in Britain visiting Cambridge, Oxford, and London, assimilating their advances in the practice of physic.

Heister's *Surgery,* published during his sojourn in Altorf, reveals both his knowledge of what had been written in the past and his familiarity with contemporary European work.[1] It is one of the first encyclopedic treatises on the subject and is profusely illustrated with copper-plate engravings of instruments and operative procedures, prepared under his direction. The first edition appeared in 1718 and was widely read and followed. It was revised, updated, and translated into English, French, Spanish, Italian, and Dutch. The description of the motives for its preparation and the selection of German when Latin was customary for scholarly texts was omitted initially but was included in subsequent editions, which bear a modified title and expanded contents.[2]

In this Station [Altorf] I was under a Necessity of teaching publickly, among the other Parts of *Physic,* that most ancient, necessary, and useful Branch of it which we call *Surgery,* and which I had before taught privately during the two preceding Winters in *Holland;* but in doing this I was much perplexed for want of a convenient Manual, or compendious System of the Art, to assist and inform those Learners who attended my Lectures. To our want of such a *Compendium* I also attributed the general Ignorance and Insufficiency of the young Surgeons and Students in this Branch of *Physic,* which at that time universally prevailed, through *Germany* especially. And from the same Cause the Generality of our Surgeons, being unequal to the more difficult Operations, were content with being able to cure a slight Wound, open a Vein or Abscess, or at most to set a Fracture, and reduce a Luxation; leaving those Disorders and Operations which required the greatest Skill to the Management of daring Quacks and itinerant Operators, with which *Germany* at that time swarmed.

These were chiefly the Motives that first induced me to attempt the Composition of a Chirurgical System, to be subservient to my own Lectures and Auditors; in doing which I endeavoured to take in all the more useful Part both of our ancient and modern Writers in every Branch of Surgery, rejecting what appeared useless or obsolete, and comparing or correcting the whole, conformably to my own Experience, and what I had seen in the Practice of the Art under many of the most skilful Surgeons and Physicians.

These my first Labours I wrote originally in *Latin,* in which Language they were also delivered to my Hearers, and permitted to be *transcribed* by them; but considering the immense Fatigue that this Method of obtaining it gave the Student, with the Great Loss of Time, which he might have otherwise employed to more Advantage, I was at length determined to *publish* it in *Latin,* in the Manner I had then composed it. But considering the Ignorance of our *German* Surgeons, at that time of Day, as well in the Latin Tongue, as in their own Profession, it being chiefly composed and intended for them, I now judged it would be more useful to print the Book in our native *German;* that then both the learned, and ignorant of the *Latin,* might have the same Benefit of it. Accordingly I translated and sent it to the Press in the Year 1717, and in the Year following, 1718, it was published as my *Surgery* in Quarto at *Norimberg,* being illustrated with Copper-Plates exhibiting the best Instruments, &c. And from this time it is that we have had better or more expert Surgeons in *Germany* than before; many of which have since often declared to me, that they had drawn most of their Knowledge from my Surgery.

The *Surgery* was divided into three parts: the first, entitled Of Wounds, Fractures, Luxations, Tumors, and Ulcers, of all Kinds; the second, Of the several Operations performed on all Parts of the Body; and the third, Of the several Bandages applied in all Operations and Disorders. Heister advised control of the hemorrhage first, dressing the wound after removal of foreign matter. He recommended prompt thawing of frozen parts and attributed the fatal action of low environmental temperatures to the contraction of small blood vessels. In the treatment of breast cancer, he noted the futility of surgery if the axillary glands were involved. Hematothorax was treated by paracentesis low on the chest wall; progressive removal of ascitic fluid on successive days was advised. Hydrocele was differentiated from enlargement of the scrotum in anasarca. He described a spinal brace and an apparatus for whole blood transfusion, although there is no record he attempted a transfusion in humans. Finally, he condemned the preparation of texts of surgery by physicians with limited experience, as well as by surgeons with no background in anatomy.

The following descriptions of an external intestinal fistula, tracheotomy for suffocation, and a case for placenta praevia are excerpts from the German edition of 1739.[2]

Where any Part of the Intestine is carried away, the Case seems to be plainly desperate; it was therefore wonderful that Persons thus wounded did not all die upon the Spot, or in the Operation of making the Sutures, till *Hildanus, Blegny, Dionis, Palsynus, Jo. Maur. Hoffman, Schacher, Vater, Cheselden,* and others, observed that the Lips of Intestines so wounded would sometimes quite unexpectedly adhere to the Wound in the Abdomen, and therefore there seemed to be no reason why we should not take this Hint from Nature. Whenever therefore a Surgeon is called to a Case of this Kind, after he has diligently examined the State of the upper Part of the Intestine, which has suffered a Loss of Substance, he should stitch it to the external Wound: For by this Means the Patient may not only be saved from instant Death, but there have been Instances where the wounded Intestine has been so far healed, that the Faeces, which used to be voided *per Anum,* have been voided by the Wound in the Abdomen; which, from the Necessity of wearing a Tin or Silver Pipe, or keeping Cloaths constantly upon the Part to receive the Excrement, may seem to be very troublesome; but it is surely far better to part with one of the Conveniences of Life, than to part with Life itself: Besides, the Excrements that are voided by this Passage, are not altogether so offensive, as those that are voided *per Anum.*

OF BRONCHOTOMY, LARYNGOTOMY, OR TRACHEOTOMY.

By all these Names is intended an Opening or Incision made in the *Aspera Arteria* or Windpipe; which is necessary in many Cases, and especially in (1) a violent Quinsey, to prevent Suffocation from the great Inflammation or Tumor of the Parts: (2) When a Bean, Pea, Plumb, or Cherrystone, or some such Bodies are slipt into the Trachea, and seem to threaten Suffocation: (3) And lastly, this Operation may be practised upon People that have been lately drowned, and are not yet entirely suffocated, for by dividing the Trachea and inflating Air into the Lungs of such Persons several have been recovered.

III. When repeated Bleeding and the Use of proper Medicines take no Effect in a Quinsey, his Operation may be necessary to prevent the Patient from being suffocated. . . . Then the Surgeon makes an Incision with his Scalpell between two of the annular Cartilages, or else, as I have sometimes seen, by dividing one of the Cartilages in the Middle, at the same time; after which he may easily introduce a small round or flat Tube of Silver or Lead.

Of profuse Haemorrhages or Floodings of the Uterus in Women with Child.

Sometimes Women with Child, especially those who are near their Time, have a more or less copious Discharge of Blood from the Uterus, which is different from the Menses, because it happens in Women who are pregnant. . . . but very often in the last Months the Haemorrhage proceeds from a total or partial Separation of the Placenta, occasioned by some external Violence, as a Fall, Leap, Blow, &c. or from too great a Redundancy of Blood, to which some of the Moderns add an Adhesion of the Placenta to the Mouth of the Uterus, which separates when that Part relaxes itself at the Time of Delivery, so that the more the *Os Uteri* is dilated, the greater Separation is made of the placenta; and consequently a greater Haemorrhage follows, which is sometimes so profuse as greatly to weaken the Mother, if not to endanger her Life, and if the Foetus be not timely extracted with the Hand before fainting Fits, &c. come on, both it and the Mother cannot long survive.

At Altorf, Heister was as successful a practitioner as a teacher and became one of the most sought-after physicians in central Europe. He carried on an extensive correspondence with learned men of many countries and was offered professional chairs at the universities of Göttingen, Kiel, and Rostock. Shortly after the completion of his *Compendium Anatomicum,*[3] a companion text to his *Surgery,* he accepted the post at the Julian University in Helmstadt. The *Compendium,* also highly regarded, appeared in Latin and modern tongues and was revised many times. It was the universally accepted anatomical reference work for more than a century and contains illustrations of Heister's diverticulum, the sinus of the jugular vein, and Heister's fold or valve, a spiral valve of the cystic duct. In addition to these two great works, he prepared treatises on ophthalmology, the practice of physic, and botany. One of the early descriptions of the postmortem findings in a case of appendicitis was described in his *Medical, Chirurgical and Anatomical Cases and Observations,* published in Rostock near the close of his career.[4]

When I dissected the body of a criminal in November 1711 in the public anatomical theater at Altdorf, I found the small intestine reddened and inflamed in many places; even the smallest vessels were so filled with blood that they looked like they had been injected with red wax according to Ruysch's method. But when I wanted to show the observers the true condition of the large intestine, I found the appendix of the caecum to be unusually black and adherent to the peritoneum. When I attempted to separate it by gentle pulling, the membranes of the appendix broke, even though the corpse was still quite fresh, and disclosed 2 or 3 tablespoonsful of pus. This observation proves that inflammation, suppuration, and swelling can occur in the vermiform appendix as in any other part of the body, but at times the signs may be very mild; thus, when pain and burning are found in the area of the appendix, a physician should pay attention to the symptoms. The patient, during life, must have suffered from pain, but I was not able to learn about it. In this case the usual anti-inflammatory agents would have been appropriate, as well as other therapy. Enemas with softening and dispersing medicants like Malua, Althea, and Chamille-tea, brewed with milk, should have been given, since these agents could disperse inflammation or bring about a rupture of the abscess into the lumen of the large intestine, partially by the action of heat and partially by their softening and dissolving properties; then the suppuration could pass into the colon and the patient would have been saved. Otherwise, if the abscess were to discharged into the body cavity, it could and would cause death.

Heister sought to make practical surgery a handmaiden in the diagnosis and treatment of many diseases. He developed a botanical garden for materia medica and raised the school of surgery at Helmstadt to a position of rank, attracting students from many countries. His 38 years at Helmstadt formed the great days of the university, which declined after his retirement and was disbanded in 1809. Special honors for Heister included membership in the Imperial Academy of Naturalists and the Royal Societies of London and Berlin.

1. Heister, L.: *Surgery, in Which All that Belongs to Wounds, after the Newest and Latest Art* (Ger), 2d ed, Nürnberg: J. Hoffmanns, 1724.
2. Heister, L.: *A General System of Surgery,* translated into English from the Latin, 3rd ed, London: W. Innys, 1748.
3. Heister, L.: *Compendium of Anatomy* (L), Altorf and Nürnberg: Kohl & Adolph, 1719.
4. Heister, L.: *Medical Chirurgical and Anatomical Cases and Observations* (Ger), Rostock, Germany: J. C. Koppe, 1753, except translated by Z. Danilevicius.

National Library of Medicine

Jean Astruc (1684-1766)

JEAN ASTRUC, one of the learned men of France in the 18th century, shared scholarship and interest in the humanities with almost every segment of the medical sciences. He was born at Sauve in Languedoc shortly after his father, a Protestant minister, accepted Catholicism; leaving the ministry to practice law, he tutored his children during their early years of education.[1] Jean, a precocious and brilliant son, received the AM deree from the University of Montpellier at the age of 16 and the MD at the age of 19. He taught anatomy for a time at Toulouse, served as professor of medicine at Montpellier, and finally advanced to Paris in 1728 where, in proper time, he was named to the chair of medicine at the Collège Royal. Montpellier, however, was not forgotten and, while teaching in Paris, he wrote the best extant history of the school at Montpellier—an example of his many scholarly achievements. Natural history, the antiquities, and the *Bible* were especially singled out in the humanities for attention by Astruc. Since Latin was the language of the scholars, many of his treatises were prepared in Latin, and the best were translated and made available in English not long after their early publication. He continued to write up to the time of his death on subjects, which included, in addition to those already noted, anatomy, physiology, psychology, pathology, therapeutics, gynecology, neurology, and pediatrics. His first major medical publication was a discourse on venereal diseases in which he recognized the contagious pathogenesis and infectious etiology generally of such maladies but failed to distinguish between syphilis and gonorrhea. It was published in 1736 and was translated into English the following year. He contended that venereal disease was introduced into Europe from America.[2]

In the *Neapolitan,* or rather in the *Spanish* army there were not a few of the Soldiers, who returning from the *Indies,* either in the first voyage with *Christopher Columbus* in the month of *March* 1493, or in the second with *Antonio de Torrez* in the beginning of the year 1494, or in the third with *Pedro de Margo* at the end of the same year, were as yet infected with the *Venereal Disease,* or at least had contracted it in *Spain,* after it had been brought by others into *Europe.* And therefore it is by no means strange, that many of the *Neapolitans* should be infected with the same Distemper, as they served under the same colors and conversed with the same wenches, who followed the Camp.

We have seen in the foregoing Chapter that the *Venereal Disease* in *Europe* is propagated solely by contagion. There are therefore convey'd from the diseas'd into the sound, certain seeds of morbifick matter, which being introduc'd into a sound body in the smallest quantity and by *indiscernible* ways, and gradually increasing in bulk, form and efficacy, sooner or later are able to infect and corrupt the whole mass of humours.

This method of propagation is not peculiar to the *Venereal Disease,* but common to all other contagious distempers. So the Small-pox may be communicated by taking a small portion of corrupted matter out of pustules, and instilling it into an incision made in the skin; the Plague, by matter flowing out of the bubos and dropt into a wound made in any animal; the itch or tetters, by the ichor discharg'd from a diseased skin and adhering to a sound one; the *hydrophobia* by the admission of the *saliva* of a mad Dog into the part that is bitten; the indisposition occasion'd by the *Tarantula,* by the humour which that Spider conveys by its bite into the skin, as by so many ferments peculiar to each Disease.

Although never trained in obstetrics and never having served as an accoucheur, Astruc prepared a handbook, *The Art of Midwifery.* In the Preface he notes that:[3]

I declare here, in the very front of this work, that I have never practiced midwifery: though I undertake, nevertheless, to teach the art of delivery. As this may, consequently, appear paradoxical, it demands some explanation.
I was appointed, by the Faculty of Medicine at Paris, in the year 1745, to give to the midwives, and their pupils, a course of lectures on midwifery; which was then intended to be established in the physic schools; and which has been since continued. I complied, without hesitation, with the request of the faculty; though I had only then that general knowledge of the subject, which every physician, who has a due regard to his profession, ought to have in all branches of the medicinal art; even though he does not, nor ever intends to practice. This course was not, however, to be given, till six months afterwards and I took the advantage of that interval, to read, or study, all the treatises in the art of midwifery, which have appeared for the last thirty years, either in Latin or French. I found, in almost all of them, matters, that were just, useful, important, and deserving of approbation.

In the *Treatise on All the Diseases Incident to Children,* one of Astruc's frequently quoted passages concerns hydrocephalus.[4]

An *Hydrocephalus* in general signifies a collection of water in the head, of which there are four sorts, according to several observations. Of these, two are contained in the cavity of the cranium, and two on the outside. . . . Of the internal dropsies of the head, the first is seated betwixt the cranium and dura mater. The second is, betwixt the dura and pia mater, or in the circumvolutions of the brain, or in its ventricles, which last is the most frequent of all.

The soon-to-be famous *Conjectures on the Sources of the Book of Genesis,*[5] though unsigned, belonged to Astruc and was largely responsible for his reputation as the modern critic and authority on the *Bible.* He advanced convincing evidence that Moses had used at least two separate documents in the account of the creation. In one chapter, the creator is named Elohim; whereas later the contemporary name of Jehovah is used. The descriptions differ somewhat in detail and in style. There is no satisfactory explanation for Astruc's failing to accept credit for this startling revelation on an ancient critical document, having achieved stature in many areas of learning.

1. Doe, J.: Jean Astruc (1684-1766): A Biographical and Bibliographical Study, *J Hist Med* 15:184-197, 1960.
2. Astruc, J.: *A Treatise of the Venereal Disease* (L), W. Barrowby, trans., London: W. Innys, and R. Manby, 1737.
3. Astruc, J.: *The Art of Midwifery Reduced to Principles*, London: J. Nourse, 1767.
4. Astruc, J.: *A General and Compleat Treatise on All the Diseases Incident to Children*, London: J. Nourse, 1746.
5. Anonymous: *Conjectures sur les Memoires Originaux*, Bruxelles: Fricx, 1753.

William Cheselden (1688-1752)

WILLIAM CHESELDEN, preceptor of John Hunter, was born in 1688 in Somerby in Leicestershire, only a short walk from the Roman encampment at Burrow-on-the Hill.[1] His first communication to the Royal Society, dispatched at the age of 24, described the skeletal remains recovered from a Roman urn. Cheselden's family were well-to-do graziers. Pre-medical education embraced classical Greek and Latin; medical education included apprenticeship at the age of 15 to Wilkes, surgeon of Leicester, and, successively, he became a pupil of William Cowper, anatomist, and James Ferne, surgeon and lithotomist to St. Thomas' Hospital. Formal education was completed, and an academic career began with admission to membership in the Company of Barber-Surgeons. Lecturing on anatomy, started at the age of 22, was followed in three years by the publication of the *Anatomy of the Human Body*. A syllabus for the lectures, prepared in Latin, was included as an appendix in the early editions of the *Anatomy*. The text, composed in English, contrary to the custom of his day, which preferred Latin, established Cheselden as the first regular and recognized teacher of anatomy in London. It was designed as a student's handbook and, being well illustrated, enjoyed an enviable reputation for almost a century. Several editions were published in America. In the preface to the fourth edition, he notes:[2]

I have pretty much neglected the Minutiae in ANATOMY: Nor have I been very particular about those things which cannot be understood without being seen, and being seen need little description; but have endeavoured to be more explicit about those which are of greatest use in PHILOSOPHY, PHYSIC and SURGERY.

The treatise went beyond descriptive structure; it included several discussions on physiology. Especially significant was the rejection of the mechanical pathogenesis of digestion. Cheselden concluded that putrefraction and degradation, through saliva and other digestive fluids, were dominant; whereas mechanical action was only contributory.[2]

The manner in which digestion is performed has been a matter of great controversy . . . the moderns more generally attribute it to the muscular force of the stomach; . . . And this is as certain as that action and reaction are the same; that the abdominal muscles and the diaphragm, compress the stomach with no greater force than they do the liver and all other parts contained in the abdomen; and that the Foetus in Utero, and all the Viscera in the Abdomen, receive much more of this force, during the time of gestation; and yet neither the Foetus, nor any other contained part, is digested by that force; . . . Therefore . . . it appears to me that our digestion is performed by a Menstruum which is chiefly

Saliva, assisted by the action of the stomach, and the abdominal muscles, and by that principle of corruption which is in all dead bodies.

Osteographia, or the Anatomy of the Bones, a specially printed folio and the first volume of a comprehensive atlas of anatomy, was profusely illustrated and dedicated to Queen Caroline, who appointed him to the Court in 1727. The first pages of *Osteographia* contain beautifully executed drawings of skeletons of animals in action. Included are the buck, bear, water tortoise, man-tyger, crocodile, eagle, weasel, armadillo, ostrich, sparrow, swan, and mole. The drawings were prepared by the author and his artists, with the help of a camera obscura. In the charge to the reader in the introduction, Cheselden noted that:[3]

There are no more [copies] printed in English than three hundred, and one hundred prints are taken off designed for a latin or french edition, which being finished, the plates shall be destroyed that the price of the book may never sink in the possession of the subscribers.

After an unusually long period of waiting for a secure hospital appointment, he was received at St. Thomas' Hospital as surgeon at the age of 30, succeeding his teacher, Mr. Ferne. The practice of surgery by Cheselden was based upon his excellent knowledge of anatomy, exemplified by the procedure for extraction of large bladder stones. Historically, the "high operation," the suprapubic approach, was preferred.[4] This approach was abandoned by Cheselden in favor of the lateral route, which remained in vogue for more than a century. The lateral operation, patterned after the procedure of Rau of Leyden and Jacques of Paris, could be completed in less than 60 seconds.[2]

This operation I do in the following manner. I tie the patient, as for the greater Apparatus, but lay him upon a blanket several doubles upon an horizontal table three foot high, or a little more, with his head only raised. I first make as long an incision as I well can, beginning near the place where the old operation ends, and cutting down between the Musculus Accelerator Urinae, and Erector Penis, and by the side of the Intestinum Rectum: I then feel for the staff, and cut upon

it the length of the prostate gland strait on to the bladder, holding down the gut all the while with one or two fingers of my left hand. The rest of this operation is the same as in the old way: But in this way there being often cut small vessels, I always tie them with a ligature, passed under them by the help of a crooked needle.

From the bladder, Cheselden proceeded to the study of the eye and the ear. The sight of a young man stricken with congenital blindness was restored by couching with a specially designed knife useful in cataract extraction. An artificial pupil was devised.[5]

When he first saw, he was so far from making any Judgment about Distances, that he thought all Objects whatever touch'd his Eyes, (as he express'd it) as what he felt, did his Skin; and thought no Objects so agreeable as those which were smooth and regular . . . but having too many Objects to learn at once, he forgot many of them; and (as he said) at first he learn'd to know, and again forgot a thousand Things in a Day. One Particular only (tho' it may appear trifling) I will relate; Having often forgot which was the Cat, and which the Dog, he was asham'd to ask; but catching the Cat (which he knew by feeling) he was observ'd to look at her stedfastly, and then letting her down, said, So Puss! I shall know you another Time. Before he was couch'd, he expected little Advantage from Seeing, worth undergoing an Operation for, except reading and writing; for he said, He thought, he could have no more Pleasure in walking abroad than he had in the Garden; which he could do safely and readily. And even Blindness he observ'd, had this Advantage, that he could go any where in the Dark much better than those who can see; and after he had seen, he did not soon lose this Quality; nor desire a Light to go about the House in the Night.

By then, Cheselden's reputation was established with the commoners and at Court, and he was appointed to the Westminster Infirmary and, later, to the newly formed St. George's Hospital. But fame in court suffered badly, and when the Queen developed a strangulated umbilical hernia from which she died in 1737, his counsel as court physician was not sought. The cause of his fall from favor has been attributed to the release of a criminal, who had been reprieved, at his request, in anticipation of an experiment on the ear drum. Cheselden previously had noted from dissection that perforation of the drum did not necessarily result in deafness. He wished to substantiate the premise that the tympanum was not critical for hearing in man.[2]

. . . . I have seen a man smoak a whole pipe of tobacco out through his ears, which must go from the mouth, through the Eustachian tube, and through the Tympanum, yet this man heard perfectly well. These cases occasioned me to break the Tympanum in both ears of a dog, and it did not destroy his hearing, but for some time he received strong sounds with great horror.

A significant change in surgical responsibilities occurred at the age of 49, without a documented motive.[6] After more than two decades of a successful surgical practice and rewarding teaching responsibilities, Cheselden accepted the post of surgeon at Chelsea Hospital (for Veterans). This has been interpreted as a regressive move for the leading surgeon in Britain. In 1745, he was a prime instigator in the separation of the surgeons from the Barber's Company. The surgeons moved to a new Surgeon's Hall in the Old Bailey, where Cheselden served as Senior Warden; whereas the barbers remained in the old hall as the Barbers' Company.

The respect Cheselden enjoyed as the master surgeon in his days of great glory has been expressed in a poem in the *Gentlemen's Magazine*, 1732.[7]

> The work was in a moment done,
> If possible, without a groan:
> So swift thy hand, I could not feel
> The progress of the cutting steel.
> Aeneas could not less endure,
> Tho' Venus did attend the Cure:
> Not her soft touch, nor hand divine,
> Perform'd more tenderly than thine;
> When by her help Iapis own'd,
> The barbed arrow left the wound.
> For quicker e'en than sense, or thought,
> The latent ill view was brought;
> And I behold with ravish'd eyes,
> The cause of all my agonies.
>
> And above all the race of men,
> I'll bless my GOD for Cheselden.

1. Cope, Z.: *William Cheselden, 1688-1752* Edinburgh and London: E. & S. Livingstone Ltd., 1953.
2. Cheselden, W.: *Anatomy of the Human Body*, 4th ed., London: W. Bowyer, 1730.
3. Cheselden, W.: *Osteographia, or the Anatomy of the Bones*, London; no publisher indicated, but probably the author, an elephant folio sold by subscription, 1733.
4. Cheselden, W.: *A Treatise on the High Operation for the Stone*, London: J. Osborn, 1723.
5. Cheselden, W.: An account of Some Observations Made by a Young Gentleman, Who Was Born Blind, or Lost His Sight So Early, That He had no Remembrance or Ever Having Seen, and Was Couch'd Between 13 and 14 Years of Age, *Philos Trans* 34:447-450, 1728.
6. Men of the British School: William Cheselden, *Med Times Gaz* 34:421-425 (Oct 25) 1856.
7. Yeo, R.: The Grateful Patient, *Gentlemen's Magazine* 2:769 (May) 1732.

National Library of Medicine

John Freke (1688-1756)

THE FIRST CURATOR of the pathological museum of St. Bartholomew's Hospital, London, was charged, among his minor responsibilities, with arranging the calculi in the counting house for exchange with patients upon payment of their surgeon's bills. John Freke, the son of a clergyman, was in his late thirties at the time of this commission, having served a long apprenticeship under Mr. Richard Blundell, and practiced surgery under a diploma from the Barber-Surgeons' Company.[1] He was a prominent and successful surgeon of London during the first half of the 18th century, a period of relative peace following civil unrest and before the wars with France and America. In medicine and surgery Freke described a case of myositis ossificans, couched the eyes of the poor at St. Bartholomew's, devised an instrument for the reduction of dislocations of the shoulder joint, recognized the significance of lymphatic spread of carcinoma of the breast, described the proper treatment for empyema, and was familiar with clinical gout from personal experience. Having been licensed by the Barber-Surgeons and having received an MD degree, he participated in the achievement of a notable goal in medical licensure with the separation of the surgeons from the barbers and the approval, by Parliament and the Crown, of the Company of Surgeons in 1745.

Freke was a patron of the arts and a social acquaintance of several of the leading citizens of London. He spoke his thoughts on art so that the painter Hogarth would hear; led Henry Fielding, author of *Tom Jones,* to take note of his imaginative philosophizing in this notorious novel; and was friendly with Richard Mead, William Cheselden, and Sir Hans Sloane. Near the close of his career, Freke prepared treatises on fire, electricity, and magnetism, which are primarily of historical interest. The description of myositis ossificans progressiva, one of the first in contemporary times, appeared as a short letter to the Royal Society several years after Freke had been elected a Fellow.[2]

GENTLEMEN,

I Would not have troubled you with this Account of a Case which came to my Inspection Yesterday at *St. Bartholomew's* Hospital, had I ever seen the same before in my Practice. I know it may be said to come under the Denomination of an *Exostosis,* but as all others that I have seen, which have been very many, arose upon some particular Parts, and have not been found to proceed from a general Dissolution of the Bones, as this hath, I think fit to submit it to your Consideration. The Case is as follows: Yesterday there came a Boy of a healthy Look, and about Fourteen Years old, to ask of us at the Hospital, what should be done to cure him of many large Swellings on his Back, which began about Three Years since, and have continued to grow as large on many Parts as a Peny-loaf. particularly on the Left Side: They arise from all the *Verterbrae* of

the Neck, and reach down to the *Os Sacrum;* they likewise arise from every Rib of his Body, and joining together in all Parts of his Back, as the Ramifications of Coral do, they make, as it were, a fixed bony Pair of Bodice. If this be found worthy of your Thoughts, it will afford a Pleasure to,

GENTLEMEN,
Your most humble Servant,
John Freke.

Salisbury-Court
April 15, 1736.

It is to be observed that he had no other Symptom of the Rickets on any Joint of his Limbs.

Drainage of the pleural cavity in the treatment of empyema was probably Freke's best contribution to clinical surgery. This was described in the *Essay on the Art of Healing.* Although others had favored delay in operation until the purulent process had pointed, Freke recommended paracentesis as soon as the affected side was distended and breath sounds altered.[3]

. . . . as most Authors recommend to the Surgeon not to open them till some thin Point offers itself to the Touch, it gives me the Occasion of treating of this Disease.

The best method of doing this Operation is to divide the Skin with the intercostal Muscles near to the *Pleura;* and that I chuse to push thro' with my Finger for Safety. When I have discharged the Matter, I keep the Wound open by a *Canula* large enough to discharge such glutinous Matter with small Sloughs through it, as are often separate from the Lobes of the Lungs: For I believe these Abscesses, when they are quite in the Cavity, generally proceed from the Lungs; and probably the *Empyema,* which appears inflamed outwardly, and comes to a Point, arises from a Pleurisy, or an Inflammation only of the *Pleura;* although it may distend itself largely inward at some times.

The home treatment of a simple tendon sheath ganglion and the substitution of a gouty typhus for blackboard chalk are items of curiosity.

A *Ganglion* is a Tumor arising from a strained Tendon. Those of the Wrist are more subject to this Disease than any others of the Limbs.

It may often be cured by Accident, when, by a Knock, or greater Strain than the Membrane will bear, its Texture is so alter'd, that thereupon this Fluid perspires quite away.

Now, though this Disease [gout] generally begins in the Joint, it sometimes conveys itself, from the same Cause, down into the *Sinovia* lodged in the *Vagina* of the Tendons. And this may account for the difficult Motion of the Muscles, as well as for the burning Pain in the Joints from the Gout. Nor does it end here, when it becomes habitual to the Patient: A small Accident of a common Cold produces it.

. . . in this Disease, and the Stone, it strays out of its natural Bounds: and that in the Gout it forms within the *Ligamentum Bursale,* at first, a chalky Matter, and at length it produces Chalk, with which a Person may write with as with common Chalk.

The resection of local metastases in the lymphatic and regional lymph nodes was advised in the chapter on carcinoma of the breast.[3]

. . . . I seldom take off a cancerous Breast but I look for some black Spots in the Glands of it; and I scarce ever fail to find them appear like a Drop of Ink, sometimes only in one Gland, sometimes in divers Parts of the Breast.

Whatever this Poison is which occasions a *Cancer,* it is a very deadly one, but yet not so fatal as to have the Cure of it always despair'd of: For it is frequently local, and then Extirpation will cure it. The Difficulty of its Cure proceeds from its Uncertainty of being come at; because, when the Operator thinks he has extirpated the Whole, some distant unperceiv'd Glands, from the Communication of their Ducts with the former, have render'd the Cure incomplete.

For 30 years the destinies of John Freke and St. Bartholomew's Hospital were inseparable. In the early years of association, he was appointed assistant-surgeon and curator of the anatomical and pathological specimens, was placed in charge of the eye cases among the poor, and, at the age of 41, was made surgeon of the hospital and then senior surgeon, having previously been elected a governor. A great deal of the 18th century rebuilding of the hospital took place during his professional and administrative tenure. Freke was buried beside his wife in the churchyard of St. Bartholomew-the-less.

1. Chalstrey, J.: The Life and Works of John Freke (1688-1756), *St. Bartholomew's Hosp J* 61:85-89 (March); 108-112 (April) 1957.

2. Freke, J.: *A Letter from Mr. John Freke,* F.R.S. Surgeon to St. Bartholomew's Hospital, *Philos Trans* 41: 369-370, 1743.

3. Freke, J.: *An Essay on the Art of Healing,* London: W. Innys, 1748.

Swedenborg Foundation

Emanuel Swedenborg (1688-1772)

EMANUEL SWEDENBORG, better known for his writings in theosophy than in science, was born "Swedberg," in Stockholm; however, he spent the greater portion of his early life in Uppsala, where his father, a Lutheran bishop, lived in comfortable circumstances.[1] Even as a youth his mind was engaged in contemplation of God, salvation, and the spiritual ills of man. After attending the university at Uppsala, where he concentrated on mathematics and mining, he began the first of several extended tours of England and the Continent, studying the natural sciences, conducting experiments, and making acquaintances with the learned men of his day. His imaginative mind at various times in his life dealt with such practical subjects as the construction of submarines, airplanes, mercury air pumps, hydraulic engines, machine guns, and canals; crystallography; shifting coastlines; improvement in mining and smelting of ores; and the determination of longitude from observations of the moon.[2]

In 1715, he returned to Sweden, devoted his time largely to scientific rather than religious matters, and founded *Daedalus hy-*

perboreus, a journal for mathematics and philosophy. In due time he was appointed by the King to the Board of Mines, first as extraordinary assessor and later as ordinary assessor. In 1719, his family was ennobled by Queen Ulrica Eleanora, and the name was changed from Swedberg to Swedenborg.

Swedenborg's treatise, *Principia,* the first volume of his *Opera philosophica et mineralia,* which appeared in 1734, speculated on cosmic evolution, advancing "the nebular hypothesis," a theory later made familiar by Laplace. He anticipated the modern molecular theory of magnetism as well as the concept of the atom, called by him the first elementary particle. He wrote abundantly on scientific matters in this period of his life and was equally prolific when he changed emphasis and moved on to theosophy. Discussions of neurology, neurophysiology, psychology, and the seat of the soul provided continuity in the transition. In 1747, he resigned his position with the Board of Mines to settle in London.

Swedenborg's contributions in the medical sciences, prepared in Latin, lay unnoticed in the library of the Swedish Royal Academy of Sciences until the 1880's, when Tafel translated into English the four-volume treatise, *The Brain.*[3] Included in this monograph were observations on cortical localization, the somatotropic arrangement of the motor cortex, references to integrative action of the nervous system, the significance of the pituitary gland, the formation of cerebrospinal fluid, and a pronouncement on what is now known as the neuron theory. The cerebral cortex, the intermediary between the sensory receptors and the soul, conditions the faculties unique to man such as imagination, judgment, will, and the source of motor volition.[3]

The cerebrum is the common bond connecting the organs of sense of the body with the sensories of the soul; for all fibres after having passed through the brain terminate in the cortical substances.

On this account the cerebrum is called the *common or general sensory;* for all the generals belonging to sense are proper to the cerebrum; consequently, as is the order and government, so

is the copula and uniting medium which conveys the modes of the body to the soul. For it is the office of the cerebrum [to provide] that the internal sensations shall flourish, and, as behooves in a regular system, that they shall live harmoniously among one another; and therefore it is its office to provide that the inmost senses shall be able to perceive, think, judge, and will, thus to contemplate ends, or to see whether a thing be true or false, and to insert it among its analytical conclusions. Upon the cerebrum therefore depend the faculties of remembering, imagining, craving, desiring, willing, etc.

The cortical substance of the frontal lobe, or the "anterior province of the cerebrum," was recognized by Swedenborg as the center of the intellect, concerned with memory and the seat of the subconscious. It was divided structurally into three lobes for innervation of the skeletal muscles in the reverse anatomical order.[3]

. . . . consequently it is the determiner of the will and the desires of the mind into ends having respect to the election of good and evil, and into ultimate acts. Wherefore *the cerebrum is the general voluntary organ of motion.*

The cerebrum acts the part of a *regulating organ* not only of the inmost sensories, where the intellect resides, but also *of the internal sight and its memory and recollection;* of that faculty, namely, which presents to the intellect material ideas for discussion, in order that hence they may exist abstractedly from material terms.
. . . the muscles and actions which are in the ultimates of the body or in the soles of the feet depend more immediately upon the highest parts; upon the middle lobe the muscles which belong to the abdomen and thorax, and upon the third lobe those which belong to the face and head; for they seem to correspond to one another in an inverse ratio.
Here also is a lesser faculty of expansion, consequently a lesser faculty of changing its states; the changes producing thoughts. It cannot, indeed, be denied that sensations reach even thither, yet our mind does not become conscious of them to the same degree as it does in the anterior part of the cerebrum, in the very courts.

Selected deductions were made for experimental observations supported by pathological findings. One example was the effect on the determination of the will in disease.[3]

. . . . for if the cerebrum is either inflamed, or obstructed, or flaccid, or injured otherwise, the intellectual faculty is unsettled.

The pituitary gland, the "arch-gland" of Swedenborg, was recognized as possessing special function in body economy, two centuries before contemporary endocrinology. Also, he extended the observations of Willis on the formation of cerebrospinal fluid by the fourth ventricle.[3]

Wherefore the pituitary gland deserves to be called the arch-gland. This appellation it also deserves on this ground, that it devotes its whole force to the transmission of the genuine liquids of the brain in the interiors, and also in the exteriors, of its body, notwithstanding both being so well closed up; but chiefly, on this ground, that it receives the whole spirit of the brain, and communicates it to the blood, to which it thereby imparts a special quality, upon which quality, compared with its quantity, depends the life of the whole of its kingdom. And further, on this ground, that all the members of the brain, and also those of the dura mater, their planes, axes and centres, and the very bones of the cranium itself have respect to that gland as to their final terminus; and since it repels the *pituita* of the brain, rather than carries it abroad, it may deservedly be styled the arch-gland.

This fourth ventricle, on account of the actuality of motion which it secures for the circumjacent members of the encephalon, supplies also a noble and most highly gifted juice impregnated with spirit to the roots of the nerves, and hands it over for distribution to the medulla oblongata, and especially to the spinal marrow. This choicest serum and defecated lymph, which is expressed from the tender shoots and villi of the vertebral artery between the laminae and inmost folds of the cerebellum, and which enters thence into the fibrillous interstices of its medulla, cannot escape or be discharged by any other way than by that of the medullary stems into the subjacent ventricle, or into that cavity which is intercepted and closed up by the peduncles; for there is no other egress.

In the *Economy of the Animal Kingdom,* Swedenborg described the blood flow of the myocardium through the Thebesian vessels.[4]

. . . . let us, by induction from what we have stated, yet still with experience at our side, ascertain how the blood is carried downwards from the lacunae, through these ducts into the muscular substance of the heart, and how it is carried downwards into the coronary vessels. One thing is evident, that there are ducts leading into the muscular substance of the heart, and which we shall call *Immissaries* [Thebesian-capillary system]; that there are also ducts leading from the muscular substance into the coronary vessels, and

which we shall call *Emissaries* [coronary venules and arterioles?]; and that there are ducts leading immediately from the lacunae into the coronary vessels, and from these back into the lacunae, and which we may call *Commissaries* [Thebesian-arterial, Thebesian-venous anastomses].

Swedenborg's transition from neurophysiology to spiritual science was essentially complete in 1745. His zealous devotion to meditation and philosophical writing influenced the lives of many spiritual leaders for more than two centuries. The *Doctrine of the New Church,* originally published in Latin in Amsterdam in 1769, was translated and published in London after his death. It rejected a faith in three Gods offering:[5]

I. That there is One God, in Whom is a Divine Trinity, and that He is the Lord Jesus Christ.
II. That saving Faith is to believe in Him.
III. That Evils ought to be shunned, because they are of the Devil and from the Devil.
IV. That Good Works ought to be done, because they are of God and from God.
V. And that they ought to be done by Man as of himself, but with a Belief, that they are from the Lord operating in him and by him.

Swedenborg died in London and was buried adjacent to a small Swedish church. The Swedenborgians, the religious sect based on the belief that Swedenborg had witnessed the last judgment, was founded after the death of their leader.

1. Rodgers, R. R.: Swedenborg, the Philosopher and Theologian, *Trans Int Swedenborg Congr.* 1910, pp 269-284.
2. Ramström, M.: *Emanuel Swedenborg's Investigations in Natural Science,* Uppsala, Sweden: University of Uppsala, 1910.
3. Swedenborg, E.: *The Brain,* R. L. Tafel, (trans.-ed.), London: J. Spiers, vol 1, 1882; vol 2, 1887.
4. Swedenborg, E.: *Oeconomia Regni Animalis,* A. Clissold (trans.), Boston, 1868, in Pratt, F. H.: Swedenborg on the Thebesian Blood Flow of the Heart, *Ann Med Hist* 4:434-439, 1932.
5. Swedenborg, E.: *A Brief Exposition of the Doctrine of the New Church* (L), London: R. Hindmarsh, 1789.

Composite by G. Bako

John Huxham (1692-1768)

JOHN HUXHAM, born at Totnes, Devonshire, was orphaned early in life and, being entrusted to a nonconformist minister as guardian, he was sent to the dissenting Academy at Exeter.[1] At the age of 17 he entered Leyden to study under Boerhaave, but his inconsiderable inheritance was exhausted before the required three years of study, and he turned to Rheims, where he graduated MD in 1717. After beginning the practice of medicine in the town of his birth, he moved to Plymouth, where greater opportunities enabled him to develop an enviable practice and to achieve great fame. Initially, however, finding the practice among the dissenters little challenge to his talents, he found it advantageous to accept the Church of England. Though he bore himself in public with some ostentation, affecting a gold-headed cane and taking a servant with him on sick calls, he did possess great dignity, and his intellectual capabilities were rewarded by his election to the Royal Society and by the award of the Copley medal.

Huxham's contributions to medical posterity may be attributed to his respect for Hippocrates, whom he read in the original; the acceptance of Boerhaave as the outstanding teacher of his time; and adherence to the precepts of Sydenham, a student of the sick from direct observation. From this triple legacy came a succession of remarkable writings, chiefly on clinical subjects observed in his practice. Several of his earlier communications were published in the *Philosophical Transactions. Observations on the Air and Epidemic Diseases* was his first monograph, published in 1731; a short dissertation on the Devonshire colic was appended in subsequent editions. Huxham's best work, *An Essay on Fevers,* was published first in 1739. In a later edition of this monograph, *A Dissertation on a Malignant Ulcerous Sore Throat* was appended. One of his last reports, pertinent observations on scurvy, which appeared first in a lay publication, was incorporated as a second appendix to the work on fevers. In each of the discussions of morbid processes, Huxham gave full attention to treatment, including his best-known preparation, Huxham's tincture, in which the potent principle was cinchona bark. The essay on fevers differentiated the etiology and clinical manifestations of the slow nervous fever (typhoid) from the putrid malignant fever (typhus). The long insidious onset, fatigue, vertigo, anorexia, fever, difficulty in breathing, diarrhea, delirium, and death in a period of three weeks identifies several features of typhoid fever; whereas a violent onset, higher fever, headache, nausea, vomiting, and a florid, petechial rash suggests typhus fever.[2]

I Cannot conclude this Essay on Fevers, without taking Notice of the very great Difference there is between the *putrid malignant,* and the *slow nervous Fever;* the Want of which Distinction, I am fully persuaded, hath been often productive of no small Errors in Practice, as they resemble one another in some Respects, tho' very essentially different in others.

Now as these two Fevers have a very different Origin, they cannot but shew their Effects in different Symptoms, and require a very different Method of Cure.

I Begin with a Description of the slow nervous Fever, which hath been very exactly taken from too many, who have fallen Victims to this insidious and dangerous Enemy.

The Patient at first grows somewhat listless and feels slight Chills and Shudders, with uncertain Flushes of Heat, and a Kind of Weariness all over, like what is felt after great Fatigue: This is always attended with a Sort of Heaviness and Dejection of Spirit, and more or less of a Load, Pain or Giddiness of the Head; a *Nausea* and Disrelish of every Thing soon follows, without any considerable Thirst, but frequently with urging to Vomit, tho' little but insipid Phlegm is brought up.

The Head grows more heavy, or giddy, the Heats greater, the Pulse quicker but weak, with an oppressive Kind of Breathing.

In this Condition the Patient often continues for five or six Days, with a heavy pale sunk Countenance, seeming not very sick, and yet far from being well.

The Pulse, during all this Time, is quick, weak and unequal, sometimes fluttering, and sometimes for a few Minutes slow, nay intermitting.

Frequently profuse Sweats, pour forth all at once about the ninth, or twelfth Day, commonly coldish and clammy on the Extremities: oftentimes very thin Stools are discharged.

The Delirium now ends in a profound *Coma,* and that soon in eternal Sleep.—The Stools, Urine, and Tears run off involuntarily, and denounce a speedy Dissolution, as the vast Tremblings and Twitching of the Nerves and Tendons are Preludes to a general Convulsion, which at once snaps off the Thread of Life.—In one or other of these Ways are the Sick carried off, after having languished on for fourteen, eighteen, or twenty Days; nay, sometimes much longer.

Let us next take a View of the putrid, malignant, or pestilential, petechial Fevers, and then proceed to offer some few Directions as to the Method of Cure.

In general however these Fevers attack with much more Violence than the slow nervous, the *Rigors,* if any, are greater (sometimes they are very great) the Heats much sharper and permanent, yet at first sudden, transient and remittent: The Pulse more tense or hard, but commonly quick and small, though sometimes slow and seemingly regular for a Time, and then fluttering and unequal.—The Head-ach, Giddiness, *Nausea* and *Vomiting* are much more considerable, even from the very Beginning.

When black, livid, dun, or greenish Spots appear, no one doubts of the Malignity; the more florid however the Spots are, the less is to be feared: it is a good Sign, when the black, or violet *Petechiae* become of a brighter Colour.

Huxham's description of diphtheritic throat was blemished only by the inclusion of selected features of the angina of scarlet fever, especially generalized desquamation. The report proceeds from a recounting of the internal systemic symptoms of the malignant ulcerous sore throat epidemic in 1752. The identifying passage describes the membrane in the pharynx and the obstruction to the air passages.[2]

The attack of this Disease was very different in different Persons.—Sometimes a Rigor, with some Fulness and Soreness of the Throat, and painful Stiffness of the Neck, were the very first Symptoms complained of.—Sometimes alternate Chills and Heats, with some Degree of Head-ach, Giddiness, or Drowsiness, ushered in the Distemper.

Some few Hours after the Seizure, and sometimes contemporary with it, a Swelling and Soreness of the Throat was perceived, and the Tonsils became very tumid and inflamed, and many times the parotid and maxillary Glands swelled very much, and very suddenly, even at the very Beginning; sometimes so much as even to threaten Strangulation. The Fauces also very soon appeared of a high florid Red, or rather of a bright Crimson Colour, very shining and glossy; and most commonly on the *Uvula, Tonsils, Velum Palatinum,* and back Part of the *Pharynx,* several whitish, or Ash-coloured Spots appeared scattered up and down, which oftentimes encreased very fast, and soon covered one or both the Tonsils, Uvula, &c: these in Event proved the *Sloughs* of superficial Ulcers (which sometimes however eat very deep into the Parts).

The Breathing became much more difficult, with a Kind of a *rattling Stertor,* as if the Patient was actually strangling, the Voice being exceeding hoarse and hollow, exactly resembling that from *venereal Ulcers in the Fauces;* this Noise in Speaking and Breathing was so peculiar, that any Person in the least conversant with the Disease might easily know it by this odd Noise; from whence indeed the *Spanish Physicians* gave it the Name of *Garotillo,* expressing the Noise such make as are strangling with a Rope.

Most commonly the *Angina* came on before the *Exanthemata,* but many times the cuticular Eruption appeared before the Sore-Throat, and was sometimes very considerable, though there was little, or no Pain in the Fauces; on the contrary, a very severe Angina seized some Patients that had no Manner of Eruption, and yet, even in these Cases, a very great Itching and Desquamation of the Skin sometimes ensued.

Huxham's homeland, Devonshire, was an endemic center for lead intoxication, and the malady had already acquired the provincial name when he described his clinical experience and the incidence of gout therewith. He erroneously attributed the noxious agent to a native ingredient of apples and cider rather than to the lead pipes used in the processing. It remained for George Baker a few years later to identify the causative agent. The symptom triad in lead poisoning—abdominal colic, constipation, and palsy—and, in some patients, encephalopathy and gouty arthritis, were documented by Huxham as follows.[3]

In the Beginning of Autumn, 1724, a Disorder exceedingly epidemical spread itself over all the County of *Devon*, amongst the Populace especially, and those who were not very elegant and careful in their Diet.

This Disease began its Attack by an excessively tormenting Pain in the Stomach, and epigastric Region, with an unequal, weak Pulse, . . . Things continuing in this State for a Day or two, the Belly became extreamly bound, neither answering to the most drastic Purges, or sharpest Clysters, the latter coming off without Wind or Stool; the former being soon vomited.

Thus was the first Stage of the Disease; but the Tragedy was not yet over, nor this the End of the Calamity, for though the terrible Griping and Pain of the Belly might have ceased a little . . . a most excruciating Pain now seized the whole Spine of the Back, most violent between the Shoulder-Blades; thence soon affecting the Arms it fixed chiefly in the Articulations, and altogether destroyed the Motion of the Hands— nor were the Legs and Thighs much less tormented.

Some, but very few, after having been long and greatly afflicted with this Disease, were seized with Epileptic-Fits, and died of it.

If I am not greatly mistaken the Cause of this Epidemic was very manifest, to wit, such an incredible Quantity of Apples as we had that Year. Apples in one Form, or another, were in all their Diet; Cyder (I should rather call it Must) was all their Drink; for this being cheaper than the smallest Beer, indeed almost as easily procured as Water, and yet far more grateful, the joyful Populace drank abundantly, ignorant of the future ill Consequence.

. . . nor are there any where so many, even amongst the very common People, as in the County of *Devon*, most famous for Cyder, that are afflicted with the Gout—And it is reasonable to believe that the Frequency of the Disease, in both Counties, is owing to the large and long continued Use of vinous Liquors, that very greatly abound with Tartar; such as the *Moselle* and *French* Wines, and our Cyder; for, since the Use of them hath much prevailed, the Gout hath been far more frequent than heretofore.

Although Huxham was not the first to attribute preventive and healing properties to green vegetables and citrus fruits, a passage on this subject has genuine merit. A method for preserving the health of seamen on long cruises and voyages with selected items of diet supported the observations made at least two centuries earlier.[2]

I have known more than a thousand Men put ashore sick out of one single Squadron, after a three Months Cruise, most of them highly scorbutic; besides many that died in the Voyage. The Fleet returns to its Port; fresh Air, wholesome Liquor, fresh Provisions, especially proper Fruits and Herbage, soon purify the Blood and Juices of the Sick, and restore their Health.

Physicians well know, that the most effectual Method of correcting an alcalescent Acrimony of the Blood, and of preventing the further Advances of Putrefaction in the Humors, is by vegetable and mineral Acids; the former of which are much the safest, and may be given in Draughts, the other only by Drops.

Now it is also well known, that a vegetable acescent Diet and Regimen, fresh Air, fresh Provisions, subacid and vinous Drinks, are its certain and speedy Cure, when not very far advanced. Apples, Oranges, and Lemons, alone, have been often known to do surprising Things in the Cure of very deplorable scorbutic Cases, that arose from bad Provisions, bad Water, &c. in long Voyages.

1. "John Huxham, M.D.," in *Dictionary of National Biography*, vol 10, L. Stephen, and S. Lee, ed., Oxford: University Press, 1891-1892.

2. Huxham, J.: *An Essay on Fevers*, London: J. Hinton, 1757.

3. Huxham, J.: "A Short Dissertation on the Devonshire Colic," in *Observation on the Air and Epidemic Diseases*, London: J. Hinton, 1759.

Composite by G. Bako

Cadwallader Colden
(1688-1776)

ALTHOUGH CADWALLADER COLDEN spent most of his professional days in political activities, many of his writings reflect a continuing interest in selected medical matters. Colden was born in Ireland of Scottish parents and was destined to follow his father in the ministry. However, upon completion of his studies for the baccalaureate in Edinburgh in 1705, he yielded to a stronger urge and turned to medicine.[1] After three years of study of anatomy, chemistry, and botany in London, he came to Philadelphia in 1710, where he practiced medicine and carried on a mercantile business.

In 1718, Colden was persuaded by Robert Hunter, governor of New York Colony, to enter upon a public career, first as surveyor-general. In 1721, he was appointed to the Governor's Council and, in 1760, finally yielding to repeated pressures, he became lieutenant-governor and presiding officer of the Assembly of the Colony. Colden's writings—extensive, diffuse, and frequently speculative—display a remarkable versatility of interests, embracing history, applied mathematics, moral and materialistic philosophy, a new method of printing, astronomy, physics, botany, and clinical medicine. His personal correspondence was equally prolific, including exchanges with Linnaeus, Robert Whytt, Benjamin Franklin, John Fothergill, Samuel Johnson, and other worthies of his time.

Selected biographical statements concerning Colden, have been investigated and found in error by Jarcho, medical historian and recognized authority on Colden's works, and have been corrected.[2] Jarcho has also compiled an extensive bibliography, which begins with the nine volumes of letters and papers collected by the New York Historical Society.[3] The ninth volume contains the continuation of Colden's *History of the Five Indian Nations,* observations collected during his tour as surveyor-general in upper New York state and based largely upon French source material. In the pursuit of his botanical interests, Colden followed the Linnaean system and classified approximately 300 specimens. The data were published in 1743 in the *Acta Societatis Regiae Scientarum Upsaliensis.*

Most of Colden's writings in medicine concern fevers, and probably include scarlet fever, diphtheria, malaria, typhoid, yaws, syphilis, smallpox, as well as yellow fever prevalent in the Colony. Climate in relation to disease, treatment of cancer, and the medical properties of tar-water were afforded special attention. Much of his discussion is not based upon extensive clinical experience, but reflects the state of medical knowledge in the 18th century as viewed by a iatrochemist.

Always loyal to the British Crown, Colden chose to enforce the Stamp Act in 1764 and was burned in effigy during one of the riots. Of greater pragmatic value was his proposal, among other sanitary reforms, for the construction of drains at public expense. In 1760, he recommended an examination of a candidate's fitness to practice medicine and surgery in the city of New York, the first Colony to pass such an act. It is excerpted as follows:[4]

Whereas many ignorant and unskillful Persons in Physick and Surgery, in order to gain a Subsistence, do take upon themselves to administer Physick, and practice Surgery in the City of *New-York,* to the endangering of the Lives and Limbs of their Patients; and many poor and ignorant Persons inhabiting the said City, who have been persuaded to become their Patients have been great Sufferers thereby: For preventing such Abuses for the future . . .

I. BE IT ENACTED *by his Honour the Lieutenant Governor, the Council, and the General Assembly, and it is hereby Enacted by the Authority of the same,* That from and after the Publication of this Act no Person whatsoever shall practice as a Physician or surgeon in the said City of *New-York* before he shall first have been examined in Physick or Surgery, and approved of and admitted by one of His Majesty's Council, the Judges of the Supreme Court, the King's Attorney-General, and the Mayor of the City of *New-York* . . . taking to their Assistance for such Examination, such proper Person or Persons as they in their discretion shall think fit . . . shall give . . . a Testimonial of his Examination and Admission . . . without such Testimonial as aforesaid, he shall for every such Offense, forfeit the sum of *Five Pounds,* . . .

1. Stookey, B.: *A History of Colonial Medical Education,* Springfield, Ill: Charles C Thomas, 1962.
2. Jarcho, S.: Biographical and Bibliographical Notes on Cadwallader Colden, *Bull Hist Med* 32:322-334 (July-Aug) 1958.
3. Colden, C.: *Letters and Papers,* 9 vol, New York: New York Historical Society Collections for the years 1917-1935, 1918-1937.
4. "An Act to regulate the Practice of Physick and Surgery in the City of New-York, Pass'd the 10th June, 1760, Published According to an Act of the General Assembly," in *Laws of New-York from The Year 1691 to 1773 Inclusive,* New York: H. Gaine, 1774, vol 1.

Bernhard Siegfried Albinus (1697-1770)

THE DELICATE DELINEATION of muscles and bones of the human body by Albinus, German by birth and Dutch by adoption, was a preeminent contribution to anatomy in the 18th century. Albinus was born at Frankfurt-on-the Oder, but in 1702 his father accepted the chair of medicine at Leyden. Thus, most of the youth's formal education was in the Dutch school, where his teachers included Boerhaave, Rau, and Ruysch.[1] Also, a short time was spent in Paris with

Winslow and Senac. As a precocious professor he was recalled to Leyden to succeed Rau in the chair of anatomy and surgery and was given the doctorate without examination or inaugural dissertation. Before the

National Library of Medicine

age of 25, Albinus had replaced his father as professor of anatomy; in 1745, he was appointed to the chair of therapeutics and subsequently twice served as Rector of the university. Meanwhile, a younger brother, Christian Bernhard Albinus, became professor of medicine in the University of Utrecht. Albinus edited the works of Harvey, Vesalius, Fabricius ab Aquapendente, and the long-lost plates of Eustachius, recruiting the best artistic talent and providing superior direction in the preparation of figures to render them attractive and without compromise with nature. From his monographs on descriptive anatomy come two eponymic muscles—the scalenus medius and the risorius, a triangular-shaped muscle passing from the side of the nose to the nasal labial furrow.[2]

For more than 50 years Bernhard Siegfried Albinus adorned the University of Leyden and gave new direction to a school of human anatomy, incorporating thoroughness in detail and perspective exactness in anatomic representation. His graphic portrayal contrasted with the anatomy of Peter

Camper, compatriot and competitor, who favored geometric design over perspective illustration. In this endeavor, Albinus was fortunate in having the services of artist and engraver, Jan Wandelaer, who had been trained in anatomic illustration by Ruysch. The diligent research pursued in the preparation of the anatomic drawings was described in the preface to the first volume of his *Academicarum Annotationum,* an eight-volume treatise on anatomy, physiology, psychology, pathology, zoography, and phytography.[3]

To reproduce, not free hand (according to the view), as is customary, but from actual measure: to reproduce what the best in nature displays: to reproduce, not as the demonstrators of anatomy generally do, by merely placing before the eyes of the artist what they have uncovered, but by collecting (data) from one body after another, and making a composite according to rule so that the actual truth will be displayed. . . . Then it does not suffice, though this, to be sure, is something, to search the body and reveal its composition like a carpenter dismantling a house with care, but just as the architect knows the structure through and through; in the same way we must thoroughly acquaint ourselves with the construction of the body. . . . I have commendation for that art which expresses nature fully. Those who know admit that it is no easy task to imitate nature: the less you neglect this, the better you will serve the interests of those for whom you imitate.

And not a single picture has been drawn free hand. All have been measured, brought down to scale, either from an indeterminate distance, as the architects do, a method which has been followed in most cases, or from a distance of forty feet through diopters which corresponds to an indeterminate distance in such cases, as for example, the pictures of the skeletons, upon which finally, as upon a ground plan, the mucles have been drawn in. Where the skeletons were not large enough the muscles have been measured from an indeterminate distance, and finally reproduced, somewhat shortened as the distance from the center required. The tiny bones of the ear the artist measured with a very small and perfect compass, the points of which were particularly sharp.

Several of the plates are signed by the artist Wandelaer; companion drawings are unsigned. The drawings, which are embellished with ornaments and landscape, are delicately shaded, without sacrifice of anatomic accuracy. A stone wall, a statue, cher-ubs, a tomb, a stream, buildings, a flower garden, and a rhinoceros are portrayed, giving dimensional perspective. In paying respects to Wandelaer, who began to assist him in 1723, Albinus rewards the artist with abundant praise.[4]

He has reproduced everything with truth and accuracy and with a marvelous refinement of skill. He has reproduced all the smallest details and what is most difficult, the very appearance, in so far as that art could. Still better is the fact that he draws beautifully and, what is even more important, draws the pictures on copper after the objects themselves. These pictures, moreover, of the bones of the embryo, he has cut after the little bones themselves. For this reason not only have the engravings not been reduced at all, as is the case with those that are cut after a picture, but these pictures are far finer than those, since none can sketch as well as such an artist can cut with the objects themselves for his model. He has reproduced everything under my guidance and nothing that he had not first thoroughly understood.

1. Choulant, L.: *Geschichte und Bibliographie der Anatomischen Abbildung,* Leipzig: R. Weigel, 1852. Frank, M. (trans.): *History and Bibliography of Anatomic Illustration,* rev. ed, New York: Hafner Publishing Co., 1962, pp. 276-283.
2. Albinus, B. S.: *Historia Musculorum Hominis,* Leyden: T. Haak & H. Mulhovium, 1734.
3. Albinus, B. S.: *Academicarum Annotationum,* 8 vol, Leyden: J. & H. Verbeek, 1754-1768, in Choulant,[1] M. Frank (trans.), p 277.
4. Albinus, B. S.: *Icones Ossium Foetus Humani,* Leyden: J. & H. Verbeek, 1737, in Choulant,[1] M. Frank (trans.), p 278.

William Hogarth (1697-1764)

HOGARTH'S APPRAISAL of physicians and medical practice in 18th century London is reflected in a number of his skillful caricatures and satirical engravings. Born at Ship Court, Old Bailey, London, into an unauspicious schoolmaster's family, William was apprenticed to a silversmith who taught him the art of engraving. Later he studied oil painting under Sir James Thornhill in the academy at Covent Garden. This training and the resultant capacity for expression was exploited in the preparation of many of his engravings, which were made from oil paintings or sketches. The discerning eye of

Hogarth captured fine and subtle details in the exposure of the weaknesses of mind and body, as well as levity and quackery of physicians.[1]

Tate Gallery

A perusal of the titles of Hogarth's single and serial engravings leaves no doubt of his intent in their composition.[2] In "The Harlot's Progress," a six-member series published in 1732, a country girl is enticed by a procuress, becomes the mistress of a man of wealth, regresses (or progresses) to become a common prostitute, is sent to a reformatory, and finally dies in poverty and ignorance. The fifth plate portrays two quack physicians arguing over the efficacy of their respective medicines and methods of treatment while the patient, unattended, dies. "Marriage à-la-Mode" (1745), a series of six plates, depicts another view of an impostor practicing medicine. Plate 3, a "Scene in the Quack Doctor's Office," portrays a room filled with drugs, surgical instruments, a skull, skeleton, stuffed crocodile, and other props, to impress the patient. The Viscount, protesting the failure of the physician's medicines to cure his young protégée, finds no sympathy from the unconcerned quack and his procuress assist-

ant. Nobleman and harlot received similar treatment from Hogarth's quack physicians.

In 1736, "The Undertaker's Arms or a Consultation of Physicians" was produced.[3] Hogarth not only designed the engraving, but also executed it, displaying a detailed knowledge of heraldry in the curious coat of arms consisting of fifteen faces. Twelve physicians of doubtful reputation were included. Each carries a gold-headed cane, while one contemplates, with mock erudition, a urinal. The upper third of the painting or coat of arms contains three recognizable contemporary physicians, of whom at least two were charlatans. Possibly the central figure is Sir Hans Sloane, physician, founder of the British Museum, and political enemy of the artist. The ironic motto for this shield of "quack-heads," physicians or undertakers as the case may be, is *Et Plurima Mortis Imago,* "And the manifold image of death."

One of the last engravings in which Hogarth included physicians was the fourth plate of the "Four Stages of Cruelty," published in 1751. The scene is a dissecting amphitheater believed to be a fair reproduction of the anatomical theater of the Royal College of Physicians of London.[4] In this series a boy wearing the badge of St. Giles' Charity School is first seen torturing a dog, while companions, rich and poor, torment other small animals. The second plate depicts the boy, now a coachman, beating his fallen horse, while his passengers decry only their inconvenience and discomfort. Next, having seduced and enticed a young girl to steal from her mistress, the rake kills her, but is caught after the act by an angry mob. A moral message by Hogarth complements each engraving in the gruesome progression. "Cruelty in Perfection," the third of the series, carries the self-evident reminder.[5]

To lawless LOVE when once betray'd,
  Soon CRIME to CRIME succeeds:
At length beguil'd to THEFT, the MAID
  By her BEGUILER bleeds.

Yet learn, seducing MAN 'nor NIGHT,
  With all its sable CLOUD,
Can screen the guilty DEED from SIGHT:
  Foul MURDER cries aloud.

The gaping WOUNDS and blood-stained STEEL,
  Now shock his trembling SOUL:
But Oh! what PANGS his BREAST must feel,
  When DEATH his KNELL shall toll.

Finally, the villain lies dead in the dissecting room, executed by a decree of the courts. Two skeletons on either side of the picture, "The Reward of Cruelty," point to the Physician's crest (a hand feeling a pulse) on the president's chair, while the president and colleagues observe a thorough, somewhat repulsive, dissection of the reprobate. At the time of the engraving, the president of the Surgeons Company was Mr. John Freke, a friend of Hogarth, indicating that this, the most gruesome of Hogarth's engravings, was designed to expose the moral depravity of the times, not to attack anatomical dissection or physicians.[4]

Behold the VILLAIN's dire disgrace,
  Not DEATH itself can end.
He finds no peaceful BURIAL-PLACE,
  His breathless CORSE, no friend.

Torn from the ROOT, that wicked TONGUE,
  Which daily swore and curst!
Those EYEBALLS, from their SOCKETS wrung,
  That glow'd with lawless LUST!

His HEART, expos'd to prying EYES,
  To PITY has no CLAIM;
But, dreadful, from his BONE shall rise,
  His MONUMENT of SHAME.

Despite many critical prints, Hogarth was a friend of the physician. Three engravings of medical significance neither expose their weaknesses nor depict them as quacks and charlatans; the "Good Samaritan" and the "Pool of Bethesda," large pictures which hang in the stairwell of St. Bartholomew's Hospital, were given to the hospital by Hogarth. He, in turn, was appointed a member of the Board of Governors. Also, the Foundling Hospital, established by sea captain Thomas Coram, cherishes a coat of arms executed by the artist. After the granting of the Royal Charter in 1739, Hogarth served as Governor of the hospital.

Austin Dobson, one of Hogarth's biographers, believed that his achievements as an engraver and painter were responsible for his unique position among English artists. However, Dobson continued:[1]

It is as a pictorial chronicler of life and manners, as a satirist and humorist upon canvas, that he makes his chief claim upon posterity. His skill in seizing upon the ridiculous and the fantastic was only equalled by his power of rendering the tragic and the terrible. And it was not given to him to see unerringly and to select unfalteringly, but to this was added a rare and special faculty for narrative by action. Other artists have succeeded in single scenes of humorous *genre*, or in isolated effects of passion and horror; but none has combined both with such signal ability, and carried them from one canvas to another with such assured dexterity, as this dramatist of the brush. To take some social blot, some burning fashionable vice, and hold it up sternly to "hard hearts"; to imagine it vividly, and body it forth with all the resources of unshrinking realism; to tear away its conventional trappings; to probe it to the quick, and lay its secret shameful workings to their inevitable end; to play upon it with inexhaustible ingenuity; with the keenest and happiest humour; to decorate it with the utmost profuseness of fanciful accessory and suggestive detail; to be conscious at the gravest how the grotesque in life elbows the pathetic, and the strange grating laugh of Mephistopheles is heard through the sorriest story:—these were his gifts, and this was his vocation, a vocation in which he has never yet been rivalled.

1. Dobson, A.: *William Hogarth*, New York: Dodd, Mead and Company, 1891.
2. Trusler, J.: *The Works of William Hogarth*, London: Jones and Co., 1833.
3. Gwyn, N. B.: Interpretation of the Hogarth Print "The Arms of the Company of Undertakers," *Bull Hist Med* 8:115-127, 1940.
4. Le Fanu, W. R.: The Reward of Cruelty, *Ann Roy Coll Surg Engl* 21:390-394, 1957.
5. *The Works of William Hogarth*, vol I, with an introduction by J. Lafarge, Philadelphia: G. Barrie & Son, 1900; type faces in *The Works of William Hogarth from the Original Plates Restored by James Heath*, London: Baldwin and Cradock, nd.

William Smellie (1697-1763)

THE REJECTION OF SUPERSTITION and the mystery of delivery, the introduction of anatomically-designed instruments as standard items in obstetrical practice, and the acceptance of the physician as the trained accoucheur are the critical contributions of William Smellie, the foremost obstetrician of the 18th century in England. William was born in Lanarkshire, Scotland, the birthplace of the Hunters and Cullen, at a time when the country was impoverished but slowly recovering from bitter religious strife. His grammar school days, in which he concentrated upon the study of Latin, French,

Composite by G. Bako

and mathematics, must have been happy ones since he bequeathed to the school library at Lanark his nonmedical books and pamphlets, "nine English Floots with the thick quarto gilt Music Book" and two hundred pounds of sterling for repairing the building.[1] Following an apprenticeship in Glasgow, Smellie began the practice of medicine at Lanark. About 1733, he became a member of the Faculty of Physicians and Surgeons of Glasgow, but the extent of his teaching responsibilities remains obscure. The University granted him the MD degree in 1745.

Smellie is described as rawboned, sympathetic, kind, and understanding; coming from a small country community, he did not display the supercilious refinement and the undisguised social graces frequently associated with "fashionable" city folk. He was fond of music, and, although the practice of medicine and particularly midwifery gave little incentive or time for cultural development in the arts and humanities, he

acquired some skill as an artist, even to the extent of composing a self-portrait. During his practice in Lanark, he read extensively, was a precise observer, and kept elaborate notes on his interesting and important cases. Subsequently, these were published in a three-volume treatise on midwifery. The first edition, bearing the date 1752, appeared at the peak of his professional career.[2] After nearly two decades of country practice, he traveled to Paris to study obstetrics with Grégoire, noted for his use of manikins in instruction. Disappointed in Grégoire, Smellie departed for London with a conviction that a major portion of his professional time should be dedicated to teaching and the practice of obstetrics in an urban community.

Mechanical aids as a prelude to practical application were devised by Smellie as early as 1743. A manikin was fabricated from the bones of a human pelvis, appropriate padding added, and the whole covered with leather. The puppet fetus was of natural size, while the abdominal contents simulated normal structures. The model was designed so that the mock-up cervix could be dilated, simulating labor, and the head of the fetus moulded under pressure. Because of imaginative capacity and extensive clinical experience, and obstetric fame now within Smellie's grasp, his services were sought by rich and indigent alike. Not only were the needy of London delivered in their homes or hovels without charge as part of his instructional demonstrations, but also his pupils contributed to a common fund planned for special assistance to the poor. In spite of his popularity as a teacher (William Hunter was one of his most famous pupils), no record mentions his teaching or his visiting any of the lying-in hospitals of London, even those founded during the period of his residence, ending in 1759.[3]

Due to superstition, backed by centuries of tradition, the female accoucheur usually, but the male midwife always, was expected to deliver a child under the bed coverings. Direct inspection of the pudendum during delivery was condemned. In order to circumvent this prejudice, a pair of forceps, made of wood to avoid the clinking of metal on manipulation, was designed. There was a similar taboo in vogue against the use of any obstetrical aid. This has been attributed to the high incidence of injury inflicted when applied by the unskilled. Smellie was conservative in his indications for the use of instruments and recommended them in only a small percentage of patients. The significant advance in design of Smellie's forceps was the double curvature, a cephalic as well as a pelvic contour, reported simultaneously (1751) by Levret in Paris. The application of a steel lock to the double curvature made this the prototype of the current instrument. The length of the blade for better grip on the head was another but less significant modification introduced by Smellie.[2]

Being properly seated, I introduced my right hand up the left side of the vagina, till my fingers reached the left side of the child's face; then with my left hand I insinuated a blade of the forceps up to that part. As I withdrew my right hand to make more room, I slipped the blade farther, that the end of it might reach as high as the upper part of the child's head; then I moved it towards the left groin of the patient, that the blade might be over the left ear, which was at that part; the part of the blade that was bent to one side was to the pubes; and the convex part was backwards, to suit the concavity of the sacrum.

My left hand was next introduced up the right side, betwixt the sacrum and ischium, and along on the inside of my hand the other blade in the same cautious manner, over the right ear; having locked them together, I introduced a finger of my left hand into the child's mouth, to keep the face from turning upwards; then pulling the handles of the instrument with my right, and increasing the force, I brought down the forehead past the narrow part of the pelvis; and turning it backwards to the concavity of the sacrum, brought the head through the os externum, by pulling upwards over the pubes, to prevent a laceration of the perineum.

There was a small impression made by the forceps on the scalp, which dispersed soon after: the child was strong and healthy; and, although I used a good deal of force, the mother recovered without any uncommon complaints.

Six years were spent in preparing the first volume of his treatise, a general discussion of normal and abnormal obstetrics.[2] The second and third volumes were largely case histories. The third volume was begun in retirement and was completed postmortem

by his friend Tobias Smollett. The set of anatomical tables (1754) was prepared as a companion volume to the treatise.[4] Many of the illustrations were drawn by Camper, a pupil of Smellie's from Holland. The three-volume monograph as well as the anatomical tables went through several editions. Section 5 of the first chapter of volume I, entitled the "Mechanism of Parturition," describes the correct passage of the head through the pelvis. This was the first time the term was used and is judged Smellie's greatest contribution to normal obstetrics. It had been assumed up to that time that the head presented with the occiput turned toward the front of the mother's pelvis. For the first time the correct position and progress of the head in the passage through the birth canal in normal delivery were described. It was clear that in the majority of deliveries the widest diameter of the head should pass through the widest portion of the pelvis.[2]

This, therefore, is the manner of its progression. When the head first presents itself at the brim of the pelvis, the fore-head is to one side, and the hind-head to the other, and sometimes it is placed diagonal in the cavity: thus the widest part of the head is turned to the widest part of the pelvis, and the narrow part of the head from ear to ear applied to the narrow part of the pelvis, between the pubes and the sacrum.

The head, being squeezed along, the vertex descends to the lower part of the ischium, where the pelvis becoming narrower at the sides, the wide part of the head can proceed no farther in the same line of direction: but the ischium being much lower than the os pubis, the hind-head is forced in below this last bone, where there is less resistance. The fore-head then turns into the hollow at the lower end of the sacrum, and now again the narrow part of the head is turned to the narrow part of the pelvis. . . . The os pubis being only two inches deep, the vertex and hind-head rise upward from below it; the fore-head presses back the coccyx; and the head rising upward by degrees, comes out with a half-round turn from below the share-bone: the wide part of the head now being betwixt the os pubis and the coccyx, which, being pushed backwards, opens the widest space below, and allows the fore-head to rise up also with a half-round turn from the under part of the os externum.

Smellie extended our knowledge of the gravid uterus and was responsible for the introduction of scientific observations into obstetrical practice in England. He was the first to measure and determine the shape of a pelvis and the dimensions and shape of the fetal head. Through thoughtful contemplation and conservative imagination, he visualized the proper path of the fetal head through the birth canal, correcting the misconception of centuries. He was the first to rotate the head with forceps and one of the first to describe a rachitic pelvis. Although Smellie designed forceps that remain as the prototype, he believed that labor for most mothers should be allowed to proceed without mechanical interference and thereby proposed sensible criteria for the use of forceps. Despite this caution, he was bitterly criticized by a few of his contemporaries, possibly through jealousy or more likely through inexperience in their use.

1. Johnstone, R. W.: *William Smellie*, Edinburgh: E. & S. Livingstone Ltd, 1952.
2. McClintock, A. H.: *Smellie's Treatise on the Theory and Practice of Midwifery*, London: The New Sydenham Society, vol 1-3, 1876-78.
3. Cianfrani, T.: *A Short History of Obstetrics and Gynecology*, Springfield, Ill: Charles C Thomas, 1960.
4. Smellie, W.: *A Set of Anatomical Tables, with Explanations,* annotated by A. Hamilton, Worcester, Mass: I. Thomas, 1793.

Paul Gottlieb Werlhof (1699-1767)

PAUL GOTTLIEB WERLHOF, severely afflicted with gouty arthritis since his early 30's, provided one of the first descriptions of purpura haemorrhagica. He was born in Helmstedt, Germany, the son of a professor of law at the University.[1] A remarkable youth interested in natural sciences and language, he began the study of medicine at the University at the age of 17. His favorite teachers, Meibohm and Heister, directed his interests particularly to anatomical dissection and pathological observations. Werlhof finished his formal training in 1721, practiced for two years in Peine, near Hiedesheim, and in 1723 received the MD degree from Helmstedt, with a Latin disser-

tation, *Use and Abuse of Medicines.* Seeking greater opportunities, he moved to Hanover, where he attracted a large local clientele as well as patients from other coun-

Composite by G. Bako

tries. His clinical skill and fluency in English, French, and Swedish led to his counsel being sought by the royal families of England, Denmark, Braunschweig, Cologne, and Bonn.

Subsequently, Werlhof declined attractive offers from several universities and in Hanover built his reputation upon medical experience and extensive writings, usually in Latin. These included a dissertation on intermittent fevers, another on variola and anthrax, and a two-volume treatise on medicine. His greatest contribution was the description of purpura haemorrhagica or thrombocytopenic purpura (Werlhof's disease), a short communication published in 1735,[2] and reprinted posthumously in a three-volume work.[3]

An adult girl, robust, without manifest cause, was attacked recently, towards the period of her menses with a sudden severe hemorrhage from the nose, with bright but foul blood escaping together with a bloody vomiting of a very thick extremely black blood. Immediately there appeared about the neck & on the arms, spots partly black, partly violaceus or purple, such as are often seen in malignant smallpox. The sudden loss of strength, & the sufficient singular sufficient characteristics of this *spotted hemorrhagic disease* being known to me, of which indeed there is only little discussion in medical writings, we forbade venesection. I gave the first day acid remedies & largely nitric, which while they did not help, but enduring continually both hemorrhages from the nose & indeed by vomiting, weakness & chilliness of the extremities, with a small & most rapid pulse, a more efficient aid was needed; moreover the number of the spots increasing & surrounding completely both of the eyes, the back of the nose & the skin around the mouth & chin, with a livid black color, like marked from bruises. I gave twice hourly in any mixture desired half a drachm of Peruvian bark, adding alternately liquid laudanum of Sydenham four drops. The same day the bleeding from the nose gradually stopped, the vomiting became less, & the next day ceased; no lesions recurred; the spots daily, at the same time with a livid appearance assumed first a very ruddy then a pale color, and disappeared the seventh day, so that also the pulse now recovered the normal character of its beat, her strength was nearly restored to its normal state, although the menses do not appear at the proper time, which is by no means unusual following hemorrhages.

1. Rohlfs, H.: *Medical Classics of Germany* (Ger), Stuttgart, Germany: F. Enke, 1875.
2. Werlhof, P. F.: *Medical and Philological Discussion of Smallpox and Anthrax* (L), Hanover, Germany: N. Foersteri, 1735, in Major, R. H. (trans.): *Classic Descriptions of Disease*, Springfield, Ill: C. C Thomas, 1932.
3. Werlhof, P. G.: *Medical Works* (L), 3 vol, Hanover, Germany: Helwingiorum, 1775-1776.

Gerhard Van Swieten (1700-1772)

THE INITIAL PLANS and their effective implementation for the great school of clinical medicine in Vienna in the mid-18th century were largely the responsibility of Gerhard Van Swieten, a Dutchman who had been persuaded to come to Austria by Empress Maria Theresa. Van Swieten was born in Leyden of steadfast Catholic parents.[1] He received his first instruction in the town's classical school and graduated with honors, being notably proficient in Latin and Greek. At 16 he went to Louvain, where he studied law, modern languages, and the natural sciences, meanwhile demonstrating excep-

tional industry, a prodigious memory, skill in speed writing, and brilliance in diverse disciplines. He returned to Leyden at 18 to begin the study of medicine, particularly

under Boerhaave, the best-known member of the faculty, who was then 50 years of age and enjoying notable fame. A mutual friendship and admiration for Boerhaave enabled Van Swieten to profit maximally from the teaching of the master; in turn, Boerhaave judged Van Swieten the most promising of his many pupils. The MD degree was granted in 1725; his inaugural thesis, prepared in Latin, discussed the structure of arteries. Although the Netherlands was predominantly Protestant and Van Swieten was a devout Catholic, he chose to remain in Leyden to practice, teach, and continue auditing and recording the lectures of Boerhaave so that patients, pupils, and physicians would benefit.

Van Swieten made the most of his opportunities with Boerhaave, but the excessive labors and his extreme loyalty to his profession left him little time to pursue research and to prepare his own scientific contributions. Be this as it may, in due course, it would have been natural for him to don the mantle of Boerhaave at the University and the leading chair in the medical faculty. Two factors intervened. A Catholic professor in a Protestant community might have been tolerated but not encouraged nor welcomed. More important was the invitation from Maria Theresa to come to Vienna as court physician and to instill new life into the university. It was suffering from domination by the Jesuits, who supported the colleges of theology and law at the expense of philosophy and medicine. The Viennese faculty lacked chemical laboratories; a botanical garden for the teaching of materia medica had not been provided; anatomical dissection was not included in the curriculum; bedside teaching was not practiced in the clinic, and the few professors were underpaid. Yet more serious was the resistance of the faculty to accept higher standards of pedagogy.

Van Swieten honored the invitation from Vienna at the age of 45 and promptly began his medical lectures in the amphitheater attached to the court library, of which he had been appointed director. The first year he discussed physiology and the structure of the body, using anatomical preparations brought from Leyden. The second-year lectures were devoted to pathology, the pathogenesis of disease, and treatment. The period was also used as an opportunity to survey the inherent attributes and deficiencies of the university. In proper time his recommendations for fundamental change were submitted to the Empress, who recognized the value of his suggestions and subsequently supported the measures for reform. The authority for granting licensure and professional appointments was removed from the Jesuits and given to the State. The chiefs of the departments served as personal representatives of the monarch.

Van Swieten, the first member of the new faculty, became president of the school. Adequate facilities for the study of anatomy and chemistry were provided, and, by 1754, clinical instruction at the bedside was begun under Anton De Haen, also of Leyden, a pupil of Boerhaave and friend of Van Swieten. Jaus and Leber were appointed professors of surgery, Gasser was called to the chair of anatomy, and Stoerck to pharmacology. In addition to reform in medicine, Van Swieten opened the library to the public and, in the philosophical faculty, established new chairs in mathematics, astronomy, physics, chemistry, and the several branches of natural history.

The ability to speak Latin, Greek, French, German, Italian, Spanish, and English, in addition to his native Dutch, enabled Van Swieten to be current in scientific thought throughout Europe; however, in Vienna as in Leyden, there was little time left for scientific labors after consultations and assigned duties were completed. Nevertheless, he continued the compilation and periodic publication of his *Commentaries*,[2] composed a treatise in 1758 on the *Diseases Incident to Armies*,[3] and prepared a study of *Constitutional Factors in Epidemics,* published posthumously. Brief communications included a discussion of aphasia, bladder stone, the paralytic type of rabies, and the use of corrosive sublimate in the treatment of syphilis. The *Commentaries Upon the Aphorisms of Herman Boerhaave,* written originally in Latin, was translated into Dutch, Spanish, French, German, and English. The first volume appeared in 1741 and the last in 1772. The English translations, which were published between 1741 and 1773, embrace 18 volumes. Van Swieten began each inquiry with observations from clinical experience and developed the argument with theoretical considerations. His critical judgment and simplification of the prevailing thoughts are worthy of emulation. The treatise on gout, which covers 242 pages, serves as an example.

Either by question or commentary, Van Swieten discussed the term "gout," rejected by some in favor of the term "arthritis." He mentioned mental stress as a precipitating factor and the healthy state of the afflicted between paroxysms, and realized that the cure extended beyond relief from acute pain.[2]

This baleful, this inauspicious term, the gout, is however, in a more peculiar manner offensive to the generality of patients, who, for the first time, lie under the pangs of this disorder, well knowing how highly the brotherhood divert themselves at the expense of a new fellow-sufferer. But as the term *arthritis,* arthritick pains, is in general less displeasing; most sick people, even physicians too, conceal the gout under this appellation, till the return of a regular fit puts it beyond all manner of uncertainty. This, in reality, is the more excusable, as physicians of the first eminence have, in the same manner, ranked the gout as a species under the general term *arthritis*.

Sitting up late at study. How much this contributes to bring on the gout, has also been shown. I knew an eminent mathematician, to whom this disease was hereditary, who, though he lived with great sobriety and chastity, yet, by long and constant application to the solution of a difficult problem, brought on a sudden fit of this distemper; for it had always, before this, has been very regular, and generally, at stated periods, used to pay him a visit twice a year.

For gouty people, during the whole interval between each paroxysm, believe themselves to be in very good health; nay, even when they have sometimes gone to bed very well, not in the least suspecting an attack, the cruel pain has waked them in the middle of the night, as hath been already observed; whence, it was concluded, that the more immediate cause of the gout resided in the most subtile and finest of the solid and fluid parts of the body.

To alleviate the pain, is not properly to cure the gout, seeing the pain always abates of itself, the fits going off when all the morbid matter is entirely dissipated. But the true cure of the gout is when there are no more returns of the distemper.

Van Swieten enjoyed at all times the confidence of Maria Theresa, was elevated to the baronetcy, and was made director of the Army Medical Service. Following this era, during which Boerhaave's doctrines of clinical observation and therapeutic principles were so thoroughly integrated into the Viennese medical school, it is reasonable to believe that the principles persisted and formed the substance of the second great school of medicine developed a century later.

1. Gerster, A. G.: The Life and Times of Gerhardt Van Swieten, *Johns Hopkins Hosp Bull* 20:161-168 (June) 1909.

2. Van Swieten, G.: *The Commentaries Upon the Aphorisms of Dr. Herman Boerhaave*, vol 13, London: R. Horsfield and T. Longman, 1765.

3. Van Swieten, G.: *The Diseases Incident to Armies With the Method of Cure*, Philadelphia: R. Bell, 1776.

William Hillary (1700-1763)

WILLIAM HILLARY, physician and meteorologist, collected a significant mass of weather data in England and the West Indies, but from these observations he drew general conclusions only and avoided unscientific or fanciful deductions. In his practice he followed the teachings of Hippocrates, Sydenham, and Boerhaave and, in his *Inquiry into the Means of Improving Medical Knowledge,* lauded them for their[1]

. . . . accurate Observations, judicious Experiments, *assisted by* just inductive Reasoning, *conformable to* Nature, *that all* medicinal Knowledge *has been obtained, and all the Discoveries and Improvements therein have been made; and it is by the same Methods only, that it must and can be yet further improved, and brought to greater Perfection.*

It is well known, that many fine Hypotheses, and pleasing plausible Theories, *on various Diseases, have been invented and formed in various Ages, and especially within this last Century; Such of them as are perfectly consistent with* Truth, *and comformable to* Nature, *let us embrace, and strictly follow them; and such as are imperfect, yet have some Congruity with Nature and Truth, let us endeavour to improve and perfect them; but such as are only hypothetical, let us entirely reject them: And I sincerely wish, that the Number of the first were more than they are; let us therefore endeavour to add to and increase them, by producing more such as really are so.*

Having thus spent some leisure Hours in collecting this Account of the Methods and Means by which all medical Knowledge has been obtained and improved, and carefully remarked those Methods which have hindered the Progress of its Improvement, I laid it aside, purposing to leave it as a posthumous Tract; but some Persons of Distinction and Learning, happening by chance to see it, were pleased to think it contained some Things which are both new, and would be useful, especially to young Physicians, as it might both instruct and prevent their falling into the Empirical Method of Practice, now so much in fashion; therefore they desired that I would publish it now; wherefore I now comply with their Request.

Hillary was born in London, studied at Leyden as a pupil of Boerhaave, and graduated MD in 1722, presenting a dissertation on intermittent fevers. He practiced at Ripon, Bath, London, and Bridgetown, Barbados, British West Indies. At Bridgetown he was consulted by George Washington, who had accompanied his ill stepbrother Lawrence Washington from Virginia to the warmer climate, in the hopes that this would rid him of his pulmonary tuberculosis.[2] Following Hillary's return to London, he published his *Observations on the Changes of the Air and the Concomitant Epidemical Diseases, in the Island of Barbados.* The first edition appeared in 1759. An American reprint, with notes by Benjamin Rush, was published in Philadelphia in 1811. This treatise contains his clinical observations on lead intoxication, tropical sprue, and infectious hepatitis. Although no mention was made of the pathogenic agent in lead intoxication, Ramazzini had noted similar symptoms, and Devonshire colic had been described previously. The several symptoms of lead intoxication noted by Hillary leave little doubt of the malady. These include acute epigastric pain, obstipation, benumbed sensation of the extremities, stupor, convulsions, and sometimes a fatal ending. The description was provided in the chapter entitled "Of the Dry Gripes, or Dry Belly-Ache."[3]

It generally seizes the Patient with an acute Pain at the Pit of the Stomach, which extends itself down with griping Pains to the Bowels, which are soon after much distended with Wind, with frequent Reachings to vomit, which sometimes bring up small Quantities of Bile and Phlegm. An obstinate Costiveness, yet sometimes attended with a Tenesmus, and the Bowels seem to the Patient as if they were drawn up towards the Back, at other times they are drawn into hard Lumps, or hard Rolls, which are plainly perceptible to the Hand on the Belly, by strong convulsive Spasms: And sometimes the Coats of the Intestines seem to be contracted and drawn up from the Anus, and down from the Pilorus, . . . The pulse is generally low, though often a little quicker from the acute Pain, but no Fever, nor any Symptoms of an Inflammation of the Parts affected, . . . And when the Pain in the Bowels has continued long, and at last begins to abate, a Pain in the Shoulder-points, and adjoining Muscles, comes on, with an unusual Sensation and Tingling along the spinal Marrow; which soon after extends itself from thence to the Nerves of the Arms and Legs, and they become weak, and that Weakness increases till those extreme Parts become paralytic, with a total Loss of Motion, though a benumbed Sensation often remains.
The subtle Cause of this Disease, is sometimes carried by a sudden Metastasis of it to the Brain,

and produces a Stupor, or a Delirium; and soon after the whole nervous System is so affected, as to produce strong Convulsions, which too often are followed By death.

In the discussion of tropical sprue, Hillary found it to be endemial and confined to the wet tropics. Symptoms or findings included intermittency, gastrointestinal involvement from the lips to the anus, diarrhea, ptyalism, glossitis, aphthous lesions of the buccal mucosa, denuding of the lingual papillae, dehydration, weight loss, malnutrition, and depression.[3]

And I shall begin with the Description of a Disease, which I think I may safely say is new, and has never yet been described by any Author, neither Ancient nor Modern, not even by any of the *Arabian Physicians;* most of whom lived and practised in the hot Countries of *Persia, Syria, Arabia, and AEgypt;* but of late years is become endemial and frequent in Barbadoes, and the other West-India Islands.
The Patient who labours under this Disease, usually first complains of an uneasy Sensation, or slight burning Heat about the Cardia, or upper Mouth of the Stomach; which comes slowly on, and gradually increases, and rises up the *Oesophagus* into the Mouth, without any Fever, or the least feverish Heat, or much Pain attending it.
Soon after this burning Heat, little small Pustulae, or Pimples, filled with a clear acrid Lymph, no bigger than a Pin's Head begin to rise; generally first on the End and Sides of the Tongue, which gradually increase in Number, not in Magnitude, and slowly spread under the Tongue, and sometimes to the Palate and Roof of the Mouth, and the Inside of the Lips; and soon after the thin Skin which covers those Pustulae, slips off, and the Tongue looks red and a little inflamed, though not swelled, yet is almost raw like a Piece of raw Flesh, and is so tender and sore, that the Patient can eat no Food but what is soft and smooth, nor drink any thing that is vinous, spirituous, or the least pungent, without acute Pain; so that some suffer much from the want of proper Food. In some a Ptyalisme comes on, and continues a long time, which is so far from being of any Service, or giving any Relief to the Patient, that on the contrary it drains and exhausts the Fluids of the Body, and greatly wastes and sinks them.
. . . This generally continues but a little time before a Diarrhoea comes on, and continues a longer and shorter time in different Patients, and sometimes for a longer or shorter time in the same Person, and in some it continues for many Weeks; and in all it greatly wastes their Flesh and Strength, and sinks their Spirits very much. . . .

Some chance time, though but seldom, after the Disease has continued a long time, it affects all the *Primae Viae* from the Lips to the Anus at the same time and excoriates the last.

The reference to catarrhal jaundice or infectious hepatitis was brief, mentioning age incidence, anorexia, and the benign nature.[3]

The Jaundice which seized Children, chiefly from three to seven or eight Years of Age, usually came on with an Indisposition to play, and an Indolence to Motion, a Loss of Appetite, white costive Stools, a small dull Pain at the Region of the Liver; some were a little feverish, but none had any Symptoms of an Inflammation of the Liver, or of the biliary Ducts; others had no feverish Heat, but they all had a considerable degree of Yellowness in their Skin and their Eyes.

This uncommon Jaundice was generally carried off by gentle opening Catharticks, and a few saponaceous Medicines, with a few gentle, easy Stomachics to restore the Appetite after.

1. Hillary, W.: *An Inquiry into the Means of Improving Medical Knowledge*, London: C. Hitch, and L. Hawes, 1761.

2. *The Daily Journal of Major George Washington in 1751-2, Kept While on a Tour from Virginia to the Island of Barbadoes.* J. M. Toner, ed., Albany, NY: J. Munsell's Sons, Publishers, 1892.

3. Hillary, W.: *Observations on the Changes of the Air and the Concomitant Epidemical Diseases in the Island of Barbados*, London: C. Hitch, and L. Hawes, 1759.

Nils Rosén von Rosenstein (1706-1773)

NILS (NICHOLAS) ROSÉN was born near Gothenburg, the son of an Army chaplain, while his mother came from a family of clergymen.[1] He attended the Gymnasium in Gothenburg, studied theology at Lund, and began the study of medicine in Uppsala with Stobaeus. Before he took his MD degree at Harderwijk, Holland, in 1731, where he defended his inaugural thesis, *The Description of the History of Disease,* he had spent varying periods of time in several of the medical centers in Germany, France, Belgium, and Holland. One of his brothers, Eberhard, became professor of medicine at Lund University and was subsequently

knighted and took the name Rosenblad. Nils became professor of medicine at Uppsala, was ennobled in 1762, and took the name Rosenstein.

Medical Historical Museum, Stockholm

Following graduation Rosén returned to Uppsala, taught practical medicine and anatomy, and published in 1738 his *Compendium Anatomicum* in Stockholm.[2] At the age of 29, he received the first of many honors; he was appointed physician to King Frederick I of Sweden, having treated him successfully for stone. In 1740, Rosén was appointed professor of natural history at Uppsala, sharing outstanding faculty appointments with Carl von Linné, professor of medicine. The two positions were exchanged a year later by mutual consent and to mutual advantage; meanwhile, each contributed to the great renown of the university as a center of learning. Rosén was an eminently popular teacher—eloquent in the lecture hall and skilled at the bedside. In 1745, he was appointed "Archiater" physician-in-chief of the teaching hospital and in 1757 was given the Royal Order of the North Star. Posthumously the Academy struck a medal in his honor.

Rosén discussed a variety of medical subjects. Several were published in the almanacs of the Swedish Academy of Sciences, founded in 1739, of which he was a sponsor. The report of a case of *Hyoscyamus* poisoning and its mydriatic effect has been noted by his biographers as worthy of mention. His lasting contribution was his book on *Diseases of Children,* published first in 1753. This was recognized as a fundamental work of great value in the development of pediatrics as a discipline of general medicine. The book passed through several Swedish editions and was translated into English, French, German, Dutch, Danish, Italian, and Hungarian. An English edition, published in London in 1776, was a translation by Sparrman from the Swedish edition of 1771. The book was sectioned into symptoms or diseases and contained primarily contemporary observations. Under smallpox, he described what is obviously varicella, which carries a low mortality in contrast to true smallpox. The description of scarlet fever was based on his experiences in the Swedish epidemic of 1741 and included the reference to anasarca in association with bloody urine. Causal identification of these specific findings with kidney disease had not then been recognized. In his remarks on whooping cough, Rosén approached the concept of bacterial infection as closely as anyone prior to Pasteur. A novel procedure for extraction of worms was described. Excerpts from each of these sections follow.[3]

OF THE SMALL-POX

From this we find the small-pox to be a contagious distemper, affecting only those who have not had it before, and in whose fluids there is a disposition to receive the infection. Thence we justly conclude, that the poison of the small-pox is not bred in the air, neither propagated by that element; and that a village or town might be preserved from the small-pox, if the same precautions were taken against that disease, as against the plague. Nay, a whole kingdom would always be freed from the small-pox, if all those who have not yet been infected, were inoculated at a time: their clothes which they had used during the disease, ought to be buried in the earth, and the infection should likewise be prevented in the same manner as in the plague.

The warthy or stony, and the chrystalline or watery small-pox, break out within 24 hours, and disappear within five, or at most six days. The eruptions of the former sort are hard as stones, and may leave some scars after them; the latter resemble clear water-bladders. Before breaking out, they are attended with anxiety in some persons; but after the eruption, the evil is generally over. A lady 48 years old, became affected with both these sorts at once, accompanied with so great an uneasiness and anxiety, even after the eruption, that every one present took it to be the true small-pox. The report would certainly have spread, that she was affected with the small-pox

for the second time, had not I myself, together with several other physicians, seen and known the disease. The same is perhaps the case with all those, who are said to have had the small-pox twice, or several times; therefore physicians ought not to assert any thing, but what they have seen themselves.

ON THE SCARLET FEVER

But others. . . . began to look low-spirited between the eighteenth and twenty-second days, when the disease was supposed to be quite cured; and they complained of weakness: just at which time, first the face and then the body began to swell, as in a dropsy (anasarca); and upon this came on a fever, anxiety, uneasiness, oppression, and asthma. Very little was discharged, and it is said to have been bloody in some patients, or appeared as water in which fresh meat has been washed. Several children have been lost in this *stadium* at *Stockholm* in the year 1763, that is to say, such as did not follow advice, or asked it too late.

ON THE HOOPING COUGH OR CHINCOUGH

It is likewise observable that the hooping-cough always appears as an epidemical disease. I think its nature is easily to be understood, since I have many times plainly perceived it to be contagious, and that it infects only such children who have not yet had it. Therefore it infects in the same manner as the measles or small-pox. I knew the hooping-cough conveyed from a patient to two other children in a different house by means of an emissary. I have even myself carried it from one house to another undesignedly.

A person who has once had the hooping-cough is as secure from the danger of catching that disorder again as those who had had the small-pox and measles are with regard to those respective diseases. During my practice I never found or heard of any one who has been infected with the hooping-cough more than once.

The true cause of this disease must be some heterogeneous matter or seed which has a multiplicative power, as is the case with smallpox. . . . Whether this multiplicative *miasma* be a kind of insects, I cannot affirm with any certainty; however, we find that it is communicated by infection, and that a part of it is attracted by the breath down into the lungs.

ON WORMS

The *ascarides* are often expelled by eating raw carrots, or drinking birch-juice, or by sucking the juice of the young bark of fir, till one gets a looseness: also by tying a string to a piece of fresh pork, introducing it into the *intestinum rectum*, and pulling it out again after a little time; for a number of these worms then always follow. This must be done repeatedly, changing the pork at each time, in order to evacuate them all. One may likewise eradicate them with clysters of tepid milk and a little salt, or with our common mineral waters and salt; likewise with a clyster of a drachm of fine sugar and an equal portion of rats-dung, well rubbed together, and mixed with tepid milk (not boiled), to be injected five or six nights running.

But the most efficacious remedy is a clyster of tobacco-smoke.

1. Lindfors, A. O.: In Memory of Nils Rosén von Rosenstein (Swed), *Acta Soc Med Upsal* 11:113-129, 1905-1906.

2. Rosén, N.: *Compendium Anatomicum* (Swed), Stockholm: B. G. Schneiders, 1738.

3. von Rosenstein, N. R.: *Diseases of Children and Their Remedies* (Swed), Stockholm: Wenneberg and Nordstrom, 1771, translated by A. Sparrman, London: T. Cadell, 1776.

Carolus Linnaeus (1707-1778)

CARL VON LINNÉ is better known for his binomial nomenclature in natural science than for his contributions in the teaching or practice of medicine. The familiar "L" in botany refers to the binomial names of plants in his *Species plantarum* (1753). This classification of plants was based upon characteristics derived from the sexual organs of the flower, the stamens and pistils. Since the design of classification emphasized the identifying features of the flower at the expense of the whole plant, the taxonomic system was not ideal but extremely useful. It dominated European botany for a century.

Linnaeus came of peasant stock; his father, an amateur botanist, was a pastor of extremely modest means and desired that his son follow him into theology. Linnaeus, on the other hand, came to believe that the Lord had chosen him to study the natural sciences and, through Divine Grace, to explore the phenomena of nature more intensely than anyone who had preceded him.[1] Before he turned to his earthly destiny as a naturalist, however, he began the study of medicine and allied disciplines. Boerhaave's *Institutiones medicae* was one of the treasured books read in preparation for university studies at Lund. A few years later, when Linnaeus was in Holland for his degree, a warm friendship ripened with this great clinician of Leyden.[2] Linnaeus transferred to Uppsala after a year at Lund primarily to study medicine, subsequently his serious profession for years, but never for a moment lost his absorbing interest in botany. Thus the avocation of the father became the preoccupation of the son. Friends and family were impressed with the young student's knowledge of plants. Rudbeck, professor of botany at Uppsala, was the teacher who furthered this interest. It was not long before Linnaeus was working in the botanic garden, cataloging and classifying the large collection. A profound attraction for botany along the road to a doctorate in medicine would not be suppressed. Linnaeus was appointed adjunct lecturer on natural history and taught mineralogy and physiology in addition.

At the age of 24, Linnaeus served as a naturalist at large in Lapland on an expedition sanctioned and modestly supported by the Academy of Sciences at Uppsala. Lapland was then regarded as a strange and mysterious country, not only in Sweden but elsewhere in Europe as well. The hardships and adventures in Lapland, shared by two Lap companions, were much to his liking. It proved to be an extremely profitable scientific expedition, resulting in the preparation of *Flora Lapponica* and a story of the life and customs of the Laps, entitled *Iter Lapponicum.*[3]

At the age of 28, lacking a degree in medicine, necessary at that time to anyone who wished to claim any standing as a botanist, Linnaeus traveled to Holland and the University of Harderwijk, near Leyden. The doctorate of medicine was not granted in Sweden at that time. Upon payment of a fee, then required, and the submission of a thesis on intermittent fevers, based on his geographical and medical observations in Sweden, the degree was granted. The pathogenesis of intermittent fevers was attributed to the drinking of loamy water. This concept was consistent with the mechanistic-iatrophysical view of natural phenomena advocated by Boerhaave. Linnaeus assumed that particles of loam in the water found their way into the blood stream and obstructed the small vessels, with subsequent fever and sweating.

Next in importance to his desire for a medical degree came his intense longing to meet Boerhaave. After some days delay the meeting quickly convinced Boerhaave of an unusual industry and intelligence in Linnaeus. Thus comradeship began under favorable auspices. As the years passed and plans were made for Linnaeus to return to Sweden, Boerhaave strongly urged him to remain in Holland and to continue his career there.

Another outstanding compatriot in Holland, John Frederick Gronovius,[1] physicist and botanist, immediately recognized the significance of the *Systema naturae* and arranged for its publication at his own expense. An introduction was arranged with wealthy George Clifford, one-time burgomaster of Amsterdam, director of the Dutch East India Company, and owner of an excellent botanical garden. Linnaeus, placed in charge of the garden, lived and studied for two years without concern for finances. These were some of his most productive years. The *Systema naturae*, which included a classification of minerals and animals, was printed first in 1735; it went through many editions. Linnaeus published more than a dozen treatises of great scientific importance while in Holland. With these came an in-

ternational reputation. Before returning to Sweden, he visited Oxford and London. Particularly noteworthy was the letter of introduction by Boerhaave to Sir Hans Sloane, founder of the British Museum. Back in Stockholm, an initial period of medical practice, which began slowly but later led to the highest recognition as the Queen's physician, was followed by scientific acclaim and election as the first president of the Swedish Royal Academy of Science. He was made a Knight of the Polar Star and assumed the name Carl von Linné. He became Sweden's first morbid anatomist, after receiving official permission to carry out postmortem examinations. Other allied medical interests included chemistry, physiology, pharmacology, and surgery.

The second great reform in botany by Linnaeus was the binomial nomenclature. Previously there had been little uniformity in assigning names to plants. He eliminated multiple terms and used a maximum of two, the first identifying the genus, the second, the species. A professorship in Uppsala was offered, accepted in 1741, and held until his death in 1778. His first appointment was to the chair of physic and anatomy. This was exchanged later with Rosén, the professor of botany. Having contributed to the classification of plants, minerals, shells, and animals, Linnaeus turned to classification of disease. *Genera morborum,* published in 1759, was one of his important medical manuscripts.[4] Diseases were divided into classes, orders, and species, similarly to classification of plants. The first three classes of disease were characterized by fever, followed by pain, mental aberrations, motor disturbances, evacuations, discharges, deformities, and external palpable changes. Edema, fractures, hernia, tumors, and dermatologic conditions were included in this class. Unrelated to nosology was Linnaeus' description of aphasia, rediscovered by Viets.[5] Personal afflictions included gout and urinary calculus. The wood-strawberry was believed to be a specific in treatment.

Although Linnaeus lived a century before Pasteur and Koch, he believed that certain diseases—dysentery, whooping cough, small-

pox, syphilis, leprosy, and consumption—
were contagious and were associated with
the entrance of small animals into the body.[4]
While these could not be seen or described
by Linnaeus, there was:

. . . . in the spread of infectious diseases a similarity to the mode of reproduction and increase
of many animals, especially insects. The smaller
an animal, the more numerous and rapid its
progeny; hence it is not difficult to conceive that
some of these minute organisms by their excessively rapid multiplication may in a short time
totally fill, as it were, the whole body.

The name of Linnaeus not only was a
beacon in the natural sciences, but also is
perpetuated by the Linnaean Society of London and Linnaeus collection of natural objects in the British Museum, a proper accolade to a physician whose greatest scientific
contributions were made not in medicine
but in botany.[6]

1. Buckman, T. R.: *A Catalog of an Exhibition Com-
memorating the 250th Anniversary of the Birth of Carolus
Linnaeus,* Lawrence, Kan.: University of Kansas Libraries,
1957.
2. Lindeboom, G. A.: Linnaeus and Boerhaave, *Janus*
46:264, 1957.
3. Jackson, B. D.: *Linnaeus,* London: H. F. & G.
Witherby, 1923.
4. Hunt, J. H.: Charles Linnaeus, M.D., *Med Libr
Hist J* 5:173, 1907.
5. Viets, H. R.: Aphasia As Described by **Linnaeus**
and As Painted by Ribera, *Bull Hist Med* 13:328, 1943.
6. Goerke, H.: *Carl von Linné,* Wissenschaftliche
Verlasgesellschaft, Stuttgart: 1966.

Thomas Cadwalader (1708-1779)

THOMAS CADWALADER, second only to Benjamin Franklin as a leading citizen of Philadelphia in the 18th century, was the son of
a Welshman who came to America with
William Penn on his second voyage. Cadwalader attended the Friends' Public School
in Philadelphia and Rev. William Tennant's
academy at Bensalem, Bucks County, before being apprenticed for two years to his
uncle, Dr. Evan Jones.[1] His medical training was continued in Europe; there he
studied anatomy and dissection under Ches-

elden and may have attended courses at the
University of Rheims, France, for a short
time. When Cadwalader returned to Phila-
dephia in 1730, he brought with him his
European training, but no medical degree,
as this was not a prerequisite to practice in

his day. With his personal charm and a good
family name, he soon rose to eminence as a
leader in medicine and an outstanding citizen. He supported Kearsley, Zachary, and
Bond in advocating inoculation against the
smallpox and, filling a critical void in the
medical training available in Philadelphia,
offered a series of dissections for interested
students. William Shippen, Sr. attended the
demonstrations as did Cadwalader's nephew,
John Jones, who later became professor of
surgery upon the founding of King's College, New York City, in 1767.

Although Cadwalader seemed destined to
practice and reside in Philadelphia, his marriage in 1738 to the daughter of a land
owner in Trenton township, New Jersey, induced him to move to his father-in-law's
estate. Although maintaining ties with Philadelphia, he did not return to Pennsylvania
permanently until 1750. Meanwhile, he
published one of the earliest medical treatises and a report on one of the first autopsies in America. The two contributions appeared in a volume from Benjamin Franklin's press, with the preface indicating his

residence as "New-Jersey, Trenton, March 25, 1745." The original manuscript was prepared with two possible prefaces and is treasured as one of the rare documents in the Library of the College of Physicians of Philadelphia. The volume, entitled *An Essay on the West-India Dry-Gripes: with the Method of Preventing and Curing that Cruel Distemper. To which is added, an Extraordinary Case in Physick,* included three case reports and detailed procedures for management of the "iliac passion." Cadwalader's discussion of the malady, associated with drinking of rum distilled in lead utensils, gave no suggestion that the base metal was the pathogenic agent. Nevertheless, the presentation was comprehensive and described encephalopathy, peripheral paralysis, constipation, and abdominal pain—features of lead intoxication.[2]

The *European* Physicians give an Account of a Disease similar to the *Dry-Gripes,* calling it *Cholica Pictonum,* because most frequent at *Poictiers.* They are both attended with excessive griping Pains in the Pit of the Stomach and Bowels, which are much distended with Wind; violent and frequent Reachings to vomit, sometimes bringing up small Quantities of bilious Matter; at other times there is a Sensation, as if the Bowels were drawn together by Ropes; great Costiveness, and frequently a continual Inclination to go to Stool without vomiting any Thing.

The Intestines are drawn up towards the Back with almost continual convulsive Twitches. The Pains are frequently so sharp, that the Patient will fall on the Floor, and cry out violently in the greatest Agony.

The Alcaline Acrimony impacted on the Stomach and Intestines, is so great in many Cases, as to communicate its malign Influence to the whole nervous System, causing violent Convulsions, which are very dangerous Symptoms; tho' I have known many recover after having a Number of them. But if the excessive Pain continues any considerable Time, the *Peristaltic* Motion of the Intestines becomes inverted, and the *Iliac Passion* ensues.

This sore Malady usually degenerates into the Palsy, and a Deprivation of all Sort of Motion in the Hands and Feet.

The essay, "An Extraordinary Case in Physick," which concluded the publication, has proved to be of greater medical significance. The case was one of the earliest examples in contemporary literature of massive decalcification of the skeletal structures. The 40-year-old patient, who suffered from "diabetes" and severe bone pain, was bedridden within two years and died four years after the onset of symptoms, having lost 17 inches in height. Cadwalader performed the autopsy and described generalized softening of the bones, concluding with a retrospective suggestion that an "alcaline regimen" might have prevented calcium loss. In the absence of chemical or metabolic data, the possibility that the patient was suffering from osteitis fibrosa cystica generalisata has been suggested by Edward C. Reifenstein, Jr. The report contains the following facts.[2]

The Wife of one *B.S.* who had been a healthy, lively Woman, and the Mother of two Children, was seized, in the Year 1738, with a *Diabetes,* and the usual Symptoms, *viz.* a frequent and copious Discharge by Urine, a gradual Wasting of the Body, a Hectic Fever, with a quick, low Pulse, Thirst, great Pains in her Shoulders, Back and Limbs, and Loss of Appetite. She continued in this Manner two Years, notwithstanding the Use of Medicines usually prescribed in such Cases, but much emaciated. She was then attacked with an *Intermitting Fever,* which soon left her; and after this the *Diabetes* gradually decreased; so that in a few Months she was intirely free from that Disorder; but the Pains in her Limbs still continued. She recovered her Appetite very well, breathed freely, and her *Hectic Fever* was very much lessened, tho' she sometimes had Excaberaions of the same. About the Beginning of Winter, 1740, she had such a Weakness and Pain in her Limbs, as to confine her to Bed altogether; and in a few Months afterwards the Bones in her Legs and Arms felt somewhat soft to the Touch, and were so pliable, as to be bent into a Curve; nay, for several Months before her Death, they were as limber as a Rag, and would bend any way with less Difficulty than the muscular Parts of a healthy Person's Leg, without the Interposition of the Bones.

The 12th of *April,* 1742, she died, being then near the Age of Forty; and, having the Consent of her Friends, I had the Curiosity to Examine the Body. Upon raising the *Cutis,* I found the *Membrana Adiposa* much thicker than I expected in a Person so much emaciated; the *Sternum* and Ribs, with their Cartilages, very soft; and all the cartilaginous Productions of the *Ribs* on the Left-side doubled over one another.

She had Appearances of several *Anchyloses* formed in the small Joynts, *viz. Carpal* and *Metacarpal* Bones &c. which had been without Motion for several Months; but upon laying them open, I found they were only like a thin Shell. The cartilaginous *Epiphyses* of the Bones were intirely dissolved, and no Part of the Heads remaining, but an Outside, not thicker than an Eggshell. Upon making Incisions in her Legs and Arms of five or six Inches long, I found the outer *Laminae* of the Bones soft, and perfectly membranous, about the Thickness of the *Peritonaeum;* and containing (instead of a boney Substance) a Fluid of the Consistence of Honey when thick, and of a reddish Colour, but not at all disagreeable to the Smell. There was, however, an Appearance of Bones near the Joynts of her Legs and Arms, tho' in part dissolved; but what remained was very soft, and full of large Holes, like a Honeycomb. The Bones of the Head yielded easily to the Pressure of my Finger.

Quaere. Whether a corrosive, *acid* State of the Fluids, might not have been the Cause of this uncommon Dissolution of the Bones? For had it been an *alcaline* Acrimony, I am of Opinion, those Fluids, long extravasated, would have arrived to a great Degree of Putrefaction, and consequenty must have been extremely offensive to the Smell, as is usual in other Cases proceeding from such a Cause.

Supposing therefore a corrosive, *acid* State of the Fluids, to have been the proximate Cause; *Quaere,* Whether an *alcaline* Regimen, timely pursued, would not have been the most likely Method to have succeeded in this poor Woman's Case?

In addition to the practice of medicine, Cadwalader's interests included financial and moral support of many worthwhile enterprises. He joined Franklin in 1731 in founding the Library Company of Philadelphia and served several terms as director. In 1751, he pledged moneys to the proposed Pennsylvania Hospital and was appointed on a committee of four members to assist the staff in consultation on extraordinary cases while caring for the sick in the hospital's temporary facilities. When the permanent building was opened for patients in 1756, Cadwalader enjoyed a senior staff position until his death. An unusual resolution by the visiting physicians directed the application of any fees derived from their hospital services to the establishment of a medical library for the students in training. He began his trusteeship with the University of Pennsylvania in 1751 when it was an academy, was a member of the committee which received the charter of the College of Philadelphia in 1755, and became a trustee of the College of Philadelphia at the time of the founding of the medical depart-

ment in 1765. He was a founding member of the Philadelphia Medical Society, organized in 1765, and continued his interest when this organization merged with the American Society for Promoting Useful Knowledge; in turn, he held office when the American Society merged with the American Philosophical Society. Cadwalader served from 1751 to 1776 on the City Council of Philadelphia and, displaying his ardent patriotism, served with the Provincial Councils for military defense. When fighting began, he contributed a substantial amount of money in lieu of active duty for a physician of his age. One of Cadwalader's last assignments in the War was to assist General Prescott, then a prisoner of the Continental Army, who, in turn, had befriended Cadwalader's son following his capture by the British.

1. Middleton, W. S.: Thomas Cadwalader and His Essay, *Ann Med Hist* 3:101-113, 1941.

2. Cadwalader, T.: *An Essay on the West-India Dry-Gripes; with the Method of Preventing and Curing that Cruel Distemper, To which is added, an Extraordinary Case in Physick,* Philadelphia: B. Franklin, 1745

Benjamin Hoadly (1706-1757)

BENJAMIN HOADLY, justly famous for his impact on the progress of medicine in the 18th century, left only a faint residuum, however. He was born in London, the son of a bishop. He attended Corpus Christi College at the University of Cambridge, and graduated MD in 1727 and MD in 1728, having been elected a Fellow of the Royal Society in the interim. Hoadly settled in London and served Royalty as well as the laity. As a Fellow of the College of Physicians, he delivered the Gulstonian lectures in 1737 and the Harveian oration in 1742, each a pedestrian effort. Of greater significance was his appointment as physician to the King's family in 1742, and then to the Prince of Wales.[1]

Hoadly was fond of the stage, which led him to compose two comedies. *The Suspicious Husband,* characterized at the time as Hoadly's "profligate pantomime," was intimately associated with David Garrick, theater manager, producer, and writer, who wrote the prologue and assumed the role of Ranger on the stage. The comedy received favorable press notices, and the concluding remarks about Ranger the rake were as follows.[2]

> The rake is a lively portrait of that character in life; his errors arise from the want of reflection. A lively imagination, with a great flow of spirits, hurries him into all the follies of the town; but there is not the least shadow of wickedness or dishonour in any of his actions: he avoids both with the same care that he would a precipice. . . . He does, in truth, survive the loss of his monkey, but is never tolerable company after.

1. Stephen, L., and Lee, S. (eds.): Benjamin Hoadly, M.D., in *Dictionary of National Biography*, London: Oxford University Press, 1917.
2. Hoadly, B.: The Suspicious Husband: A Comedy in Five Acts, in *The British Drama*, London: Jones & Co., 1824, vol 1, pp 488-510.

Tobias Smollett (1721-1771)

SMOLLETT, born at Dalquhurn in Dumbartonshire, Scotland, and christened Tobias George, was never more than a mediocre physician, but he achieved enviable fame as a satirical novelist in 18th century London.[1] Smollett's father, a cultivated man with a weak and petulant disposition, died when Tobias was an infant. His mother, with a sense of humor and a passion for cards, witnessed his classical education at Dumbarton Grammar School received through the generosity of his grandfather. At this early age his creative capacity became evident when he demonstrated a propensity for satirical verse at the expense of his schoolmates. In 1736, Smollett enrolled in Glasgow University, giving attention first to Latin and Greek and later to medical subjects. In the interim, to support his interest in medicine, he was apprenticed to John Gordon; however, the contract was voided in 1739 after the death of his grandfather and consequent termination of financial support. William Hunter, who was studying medicine in Glasgow at the time, accepted his friendship, which continued in London and into his declining days, as manifested by advance of funds for Smollett's subsistence. In appreciation, Smollett directed in his will that his body be added to Hunter's anatomical collection.

In early maturity Smollett left Scotland and set out for London with his first satirical composition entitled, *The Regicide,* a tragedy based upon the murder of James I. Unable to find a proper sponsor for his play and lacking other means of livelihood, Smollett obtained an appointment as naval surgeon. He subsequently sailed on the *Cumberland* with the fleet and engaged in the assault against Cartagena in the West Indies. Following cessation of hostilities he settled for a time in Jamaica and there fell in love with the daughter of an English planter who brought a substantial dowry to the marriage several years later. Upon his return to London, he removed his name from the naval books and, in 1744, set up a surgical practice in Downing Street. Here Smollett vacillated for a decade between satire and practice, seemingly favoring composition, but struggling nevertheless to succeed in medicine. Meanwhile, he prepared the most spontaneous and best remembered of his poems, "The Tears of Scotland," written in 1746 in indignation at the crushing of the Highland rebellion.[2]

Mourn, hapless Caledonia, mourn
Thy banish'd peace, thy laurels torn!
Thy sons, for valour long renown'd,
Lie slaughter'd on their native ground;
Thy hospitable roofs no more
Invite the stranger to the door;
In smoky ruins sunk they lie,
The monuments of cruelty.

Failing in practice, Smollett moved to less expensive quarters and finally settled in Chelsea, which remained his home until he left England for the last time in 1769. The apparent final effort in medicine was the procurement of the degree of MD in 1750, from Marischal College, Aberdeen, upon payment of appropriate fees and the publication of *An Essay on the External Use of Water*. He had previously communicated to William Smellie a description of separation of the pubic bone immediately preceding delivery, which was included in his *Treatise on Midwifery*. Smollett also assisted Smellie in the third edition of *Midwifery*. But the fame and notoriety of his creative writing prevailed, and, except for an occasional reference to medicine in his novels, he abandoned himself to tavern life, coffee-house society, and his substantial circle of Scottish friends.

Although Smollett's reputation was based upon his novels, which contained disguised, as well as overt, autobiographical passages, his literary endeavors were not limited to self-revelation. Among his achievements were numerous book reviews, an extensive history of England, a translation of *Don Quixote,* and a 38-volume translation of Voltaire. A few poems and a travelogue of France and Italy complete the list. His novels were essentially loosely connected vignettes, short stories, and character sketches—an art he developed to a high degree. Ruthless characterizations of sinners, scoundrels, libertines, and courtesans punctuate the novels, especially in his three great works, *The Adventures of Roderick Random, The Adventures of Peregrine Pickle,* and *The Adventures of Ferdinand Count Fatham,* published between 1748 and 1753. In *Roderick Random,* Smollett described his first journey from Scotland to London, and, from his experiences in the West Indies

campaign, he exposed the deplorable conditions of hospital ships. He ridiculed the unsavory conventions of apothecaries, surgeons, and physicians, who, while feuding with each other, failed to give heed to the public welfare, as illustrated in *Count Fathom.* The satirical excerpt centers on the practitioners but includes others in practice or those who assist.[3]

In his researches, he found that the great world was wholly engrossed by a few practitioners who had arrived at the summit of their reputation, consequently were no longer obliged to cultivate those arts by which they rose; and that the rest of the business was parcelled out into small inclosures, occupied by different groupes of personages, male and female, who stood in rings, and tossed the ball from one to another, there being in each department two sets, the individuals of which relieved one another occasionally. Every knot was composed of a waiting-woman, nurse, apothecary, surgeon and physician, and, sometimes, a midwife was admitted into the partie; and in this manner the farce was commonly performed.

The conditions of the spas portrayed in their sorriest light, either the springs for drinking or the waters for bathing, were described in *The Expedition of Humphrey Clinker.* His firsthand information was obtained at Bath, where he had attempted to establish himself as a physician following the extended disenchantment with London practice.[4]

Two days ago, I went into the King's bath, by the advice of our friend Ch——, in order to clear the strainer of the skin, for the benefit of a free perspiration; and the first object that saluted my eye, was a child full of scrofulous ulcers, carried in the arms of one of the guides, under the very noses of the bathers. I was so shocked at the sight, that I retired immediately with indignation and disgust. Suppose the matter of those ulcers, floating on the water, comes in contact with my skin, when the pores are all open, I would ask you what must be the consequence?

But I am now as much afraid of drinking as of bathing for, after a long conversation with the doctor, about the construction of the pump and cistern, it is very far from being clear with me, that the patients in the Pump Room don't swallow the scourings of the bathers. I can't help suspecting that there is, or may be, some regurgitation from the bath into the cistern of the pump. In that case, what a delicate beverage is every day quaffed by the drinkers! medicated with the sweat, and dirt, and dandruff, and the abominable discharges of various kinds, from twenty different diseased bodies parboiling in the kettle below. In order to avoid this filthy composition, I had recourse to the spring that supplies the private baths on the Abbey Green; but I at once perceived something extraordinary in the taste and smell: and, upon inquiry, I find that the Roman baths in this quarter were found covered by an old burying-ground belonging to the abbey; through which, in all probability, the water drains in its passage: so that as we drink the decoction of living bodies at the Pump Room, we swallow the strainings of rotten bones and carcasses at the private bath.

Through satire with wide popular appeal, Smollett sought reform in mid-18th century London. His creative gift in composition and full range of expression rank him as one of the great Scottish novelists. Many of his passages have been described as indelicate; if they were lewd or immoral, it was because the people whom he was describing were guilty of social misconduct. In his description of people and places, he had a remarkable capacity for exactness of detail, and whether irreligious or pagan by personal faith, his desire for reform was paramount. Although Smollett can be described as a moderately prolific writer, a bibliography of critiques and censures of his works include more than 300 references,[5] not inappropriate for one only slightly less gifted than Henry Fielding or James Boswell in the London of David Hume, David Garrick, John Wilkes, and Lord Chesterfield.

1. Anderson, R.: *The Life of Tobias Smollett, M.D.*, Edinburgh: Mundell & Son, 1800.
2. Buck, H. S.: *Smollett as Poet*, New Haven, Conn: Yale University Press, 1927.
3. Smollett, T. G.: *The Adventures of Ferdinand Count Fathom*, London: Hutchinson & Co., 1753.
4. Smollett, T. G.: *The Expedition of Humphry Clinker*, London: Hutchinson & Co., 1771.
5. Cordasco, F.: *Smollett Criticism, 1770-1924: a Bibliography, Enumerative and Annotative*, Brooklyn: Long Island University Press, 1948.

Albrecht von Haller (1708-1777)

ALBRECHT VON HALLER was one of the most prolific medical writers of all time. He was born into a patrician family in Bern, Switzerland, whose members held positions of state. In carrying on this tradition in later life, Haller was appointed "Magistrate Without Portfolio" in his native city.

One of the requirements for matriculation in secondary schools was the composition of an original essay in Latin. Being a child prodigy, Albrecht chose a more difficult task—the essay was prepared in faultless Greek. He was skilled in yet another language, the Chaldean of the ancient Semitic tribes of the Tigris and Euphrates. But language was only the means for more complete expression; it was not the goal. Other areas of accomplishment included poetry, botany, philosophy, physiology, anatomy, clinical medicine, historical science, and biography. While in school he assembled a biography of more than 2,000 persons.

Chronic illness as a child, the loss of his mother, then the death of his father might have proved serious handicaps. However, the personality that emerged from such physical and emotional hardships reflected the resilience of his character and the brilliance of his intellect as a patent extrovert. He is described as a gay, adventurous young fellow while in residence at the University of Tübingen, where the study of medicine was begun, and later in Paris, where he defied the law in obtaining bodies for anatomic dissection.[1]

At Tübingen, at the age of 15, Haller exposed the fallacious theory of his teacher, Professor Coschwitz, who contended that the lingual vein was a salivary duct. The biologic function of the structure was disclosed through wax injections. Following this scientific exposé, he proceeded to Leyden for his MD degree and studied under Boerhaave and Albinus. For a short time he was a pupil of the mathematical wizard, Bernouilli. Haller was equal to the masterful instruction of these outstanding scientists. England was the next country visited. Friendships were made with members of the royal family, with Swift, Addison, and other men of letters and with scientists, which included William Cheselden and Sir Hans Sloane.

Haller returned to Bern to begin the practice of medicine for a livelihood, but not to the exclusion of botanizing, composing poetry, beginning his experimental studies on irritability of muscle, and carrying on a voluminous correspondence with a loyal friend, Johannes Gessner of Zurich. Haller's concept of irritability and sensibility marked the beginning of modern physiology. The English physician, Glisson, described the muscles' capacity to contract as *"irritabilitas."* The Bern physician, by a series of experiments, deduced that contractility of muscle is an integral function of the fibers. Sensibility, on the other hand, depended on the presence of nerves. Thus, function was identified specifically with structure.

At the age of 27, Haller was offered the chair of medicine, anatomy, surgery, and botany at the new University of Göttingen, which had been created by King George II of England, Duke of Hanover. Seventeen years were spent in the university near the Harz mountains. These were productive years for the young medical scientist, especially in botany, anatomy, writing, and

clinical medicine. It is hazardous to select only two excerpts from as prolific a writer as Haller. However, his discussion of aneurisms, from a monograph on diseases of the aorta and vena cava, seems appropriate in retrospect.[2]

1. Aneurisms of the aorta, near the heart, are no longer of rare occurrence; nevertheless, I am persuaded that I shall not do anything that is displeasing to well-informed medical men, if I relate two cases that have lately occurred, which I saw when the bodies were dissected, and both of which are observations of interest.

2. The first was that of a woman, whose case Wincklerus has related. In her aorta, where it is attached to the heart, had become so enlarged as to attain a circumference of five inches and two lines. In this dilated part, which was bounded by those vertebrae that were near the vessel, there was considerable ulceration, the internal membrane of the artery being everywhere changed into projecting floating tufts, and being torn and rugged. . . . The valves of the aorta were partly indurated, and partly studded with knobs of a stony hardness. The other valves situated in the heart were healthy and natural.

In the second patient, an aneurism of the arch of the aorta was described:

5. On cutting into the tumour, the nature of which we did not well understand, there was found a large quantity of grumous blood about the centre of the artery. A great part of it was collected not so much into coagula as into broad laminae, scarcely a line in thickness; these were tough, pale, resembling membrane, but softer, and were free and floating, being indeed distinct polypi. Lastly, as the coats of the aorta appeared to be five or six lines in thickness, we found that a new accessory membrane growing from the tumour had adhered to its internal tunic, and might easily have been taken for a part of it. It was white, pulpy, and lamellated, being partly of a membraneous character and partly composed of a kind of cruor, but it everywhere adhered equally to the internal coat of the artery. In the artery itself there were found many white hard scales, appearing as if full of pus, such as we have just described.

9. On inquiring into the progress and formation of these very serious diseases, it is not at all improbable that the aneurism has arisen from the large number of osseous scales which did not admit of dilatation, and which were formed of the concretion of a yellow humour. These offer such an obstacle to the heart, that it being, during life, excited to overcome this resistance, gradually distends the artery very forcibly, thus giving rise to an aneurismal sac.

After 17 years in Göttingen, Haller's love for his homeland became irresistible, and he returned to Switzerland in the face of attractive offers to remain. The ensuing years were spent in unremitting toil in the library, surrounded by members of his family, friends, and associates who had been pressed into service to assist in incredible tasks of writing and editing. By count, several hundred books, manuscripts, monographs, scientific notices, poems, and letters were prepared in this stupendous program.

Before leaving Göttingen, Haller had edited and published Boerhaave's *Institutiones rei medicae* in six volumes; his own *Icones anatomicae* in eight parts, seven volues of miscellaneous anatomical papers, a textbook of physiology, and a volume of botanical papers; and was the founder and principal contributor to the famous *Göttinge Gelehrte Zeitung*.[3] After returning to Bern, he continued his interests in the *Zeitung* as a contributor and editor. He edited seven volumes of medical classics and a monograph on surgery (although he never performed an operation). His critical edition of Hippocrates covered eight volumes and the *Natural History of the Native Plants of Switzerland* three volumes. The *Elements of Human Physiology* extended over eight volumes and was finished in 1766.

1. Buess, H.: Albrecht Von Haller and His 'Elementa Physiologiae' as the Beginning of Pathological Physiology, *Med Hist* 3:124 (April) 1959.

2. "Haller," in *Observations on Aneurism*, trans, and ed. J. E. Erichsen, London: Sydenham Society, 1844.

3. Bay, J. C.: Albrecht Von Haller: Medical Encyclopedist, *Bull Med Libr Ass* 48:393 (Oct.) 1960.

Peter Camper (1722-1789)

PETER CAMPER, anatomist, anthropologist, illustrator, physician, and surgeon, was born in Leyden, where he was quick to benefit from an abundant intellectual and material family heritage. His grandfather was a physician; whereas his father was at one time a clergyman in the Dutch East Indies. Florent Camper amassed much wealth, took philosophy and the arts seriously, and enjoyed the

friendship of learned people in the community, including Boerhaave.[1] Peter was diligent and bright and easily excelled his classmates in scholarship. He learned the

Royal College of Physicians

art of design and painting from the De Moores (father and son), an accomplishment which served him well in his anatomical drawings. Before his twelfth birthday he was accepted at Leyden University, where he studied the classics, medicine, and the natural sciences. The degrees of doctor of philosophy and doctor of medicine were granted at the age of 24. Another example of Camper's span of talents was fluency in speech and with pen in Latin, French, English, and German. In later years, when his children were abroad, he corresponded with them in the language of the country they were visiting.

Camper practiced for a time in Leyden, but his feet were restless. He visited England for postgraduate study, which included matriculation in the Painters' Academy of London and Smellie's course on midwifery. When not on tour he maintained professional contact by correspondence with notable physicians, especially those in England, France, Germany, and Switzerland.

While enroute from Paris to Geneva, at the age of 27, Camper was notified of his appointment in philosophy to the faculty at Franeker University in the Dutch province of Friesland. The chairs of medicine and surgery were added to that of philosophy shortly after. The illustrations for Smellie's famous book on midwifery were probably prepared by Camper when he revisited England in 1752. In 1757, he was appointed professor at the University of Groningen, where his assignment included surgery, botany, anatomy, and medicine. His last trip to England was made in 1785 when he visited John Hunter, Joshua Reynolds, Cavendish, and other members of the Royal Society to which he had been elected as a young scientist. Upon retirement from academic and clinical medicine, Camper was nominated a member of the State Council and was welcomed by nobility and royalty.

Although Camper's interest in the graphic arts was largely expressed in studies on anatomy and pathology, he sketched zoological objects, landscapes, people, and artifacts of Greek antiquity. He painted in oil and pastels, made etchings, and was skilled in line drawings. His illustrations in anatomy were architecturally correct; he did not follow the school of Vesalius, those of his teacher Albinus, nor others who adhered to laws of perspective. A two-volume treatise on the relationship between anatomy and the art of drawing, painting, and statuary was translated into English by Cogan in 1794. The following excerpt discloses his appraisal of painting.[2]

The art of painting was, in times the most remote, not only valued as a passing, but as a very important art. Aristotle informs us, that the Greeks made it an essential part of their education; and that it was universally expected of the children of richer citizens, that they should be able to criticise the works of their renowned artists with judgment, and be qualified to furnish their own mansions with taste and elegance.

Their laudable example was once imitated with zeal and success by the inhabitants of this country. In almost every town the citizens of distinction were educated in some knowledge of the arts. We must now lament the change that has taken place in most of the towns which were once the residence of celebrated artists. Your city alone shews itself to be the patron of this amiable sister of poetry; and its fostering care not only promises every advantage to rising youth, but inspires a spirit of emulation in the bosom of artists themselves, that has been productive of works which reflect an honour upon the country at large.

Most of Camper's scientific treatises were published in Dutch, but a few appeared in Latin. Selected items were translated into French, German, and English. In anatomy, he described what are labelled as "Camper's fascia," "Camper's chiasma tendinum," and the "processus vaginalis testis." The following excerpt is from his minor writings, which was translated into German in 1785.[3]

The peritoneum or intestinal lining forms a round opening just where the processus vaginalis takes its course outward. In monkeys (or apes) and dogs one can pass a quill through that opening; in horses two fingers will easily get through. Along that opening the peritoneum runs outward in a thin neck through the abdominal rings, and it then forms an oblong sack or passage which becomes progressively wider and which surrounds the spermatic ducts and the whole testicle. The spermatic ducts are located within this double membrane and are dangling in the passage, like the bowels in the doubled peritoneum which is called *mesenterium*. The testicle and the epididymis are free, that is to say, they have no special membrane, as we find it in healthy people.

In obstetrics, in addition to illustrating Smellie's book, Camper prepared a five-volume reference work between 1751 and 1765, was an early advocate of natural expulsion of the placenta, and replaced caesarean section with symphysiotomy, having practiced the operation on sacrificed pigs. In orthopedics, he prepared a monograph on the patella and the olecranon and discussed congenital dislocation of the hip. He improved the procedure of cutting for bladder stone, advocated inoculation, and lectuured on legal medicine. In ophthalmology, his monograph on vision, written in Latin, has recently appeared in facsimile, with an English translation.[4]

Vision, the subject of this dissertation, is the perception of an object, which is outside the eye, transferred by light: therefore there are generally three things required, viz., an object, light and an eye and necessarily the conjunction of this latter with the soul.

The object can be anything, solid or fluid, opaque or pellucid, the surface of which deflects so much light towards the eye as is sufficient to form an image *in fundo oculi;* there can be no doubt of this, whether we see wood, a metal glass, water or similar things.

The second requisite for vision is some light, especially of the sun, the moon or candles, for the electric phosphor or similar materials do not illuminate the objects sufficiently vividly. Light, which must be regarded as *causa efficiens,* comes from the single points of the objects along straight lines and expands in all directions. These points are called "radiant points." This extremely subtle and pure fluid has also other precious qualities necessary for vision. We suppose that these are known and demonstrated. Therefore we will add nothing about dioptrics.

The third requisite is an eye, well built and very freely connected with the soul. The eyes of dead people have the same structure and there are the same images as in the living eye; but there is no sensation.

In comparative anatomy, Camper discussed the air spaces in bird bones, the hearing of fishes, the croaking of frogs, the air movement in blow fishes, and the control of epizootic diseases.[5] Thorough dissections were made on the rhinoceros, the orangoutang, and the elephant. He compared the vocal apparatus of the orangoutang and man and explained the inability of the former to articulate.

In describing the facial angle and Camper's line, he helped to create the science of anthropology.[5,6]

After I had studied (the skulls from) many nations I thought that I had found what constitutes the pertinent differences between them, not only in the protruding upper jaw, but also in the breadth of the face and the quadrangle to the lower jaw. And this difference is confirmed by a considerable number of skulls which I have brought together or have drawn at random.

When I was given the head of a Kalmuck in addition to that of a Negro (which I possessed) and when I compared them with a *European* head, and, then, put the head of a monkey next to both of them, I noticed that a line drawn from the forehead to the upper eyelid indicated the differences between these nations. . . . I arranged some of these faces in a horizontal line, and, in addition, I drew the facial line under various positions of an angle. If I let the face line incline forwards, I found an antique face. If I let the line fall backwards, I found a Negro face. If I

inclined it even more backwards, the line resulted in (the face of an) ape, a dog, or a woodcock. This explains the first principle of my doctrine.

1. Biographical Sketch of Camper, *Edinburgh Med Surg J* 3:257-262, 1807.

2. *The Works of the Late Professor Camper, on the Connexion Between the Science of Anatomy and the Arts of Drawing, Painting, Statuary,* T. Cogan, trans., London: C. Dilly, 1794.

3. Camper, P.: *Minor Writings,* trans. into German by J. F. M. Herbell, Leipzig: S. L. Crusius, 1785, excerpt trans by F. Sternthal.

4. Camper, P.: *Optical Dissertation on Vision,* 1746, G. Ten Doeschate, trans., Nieuwkoop: B. De Graaf, 1962.

5. Kaplan, E. B.: *Peter Camper 1722-1789, Bull Hosp Joint Dis* 17:371-385, 1956.

6. Camper, P.: *On the Natural Differences of Facial Features in Man of Different Ages and in Different Parts of the World,* A. G. Camper, ed., trans. into German by S. T. Sömmering, Berlin: Voss, 1792, excerpt trans by F. Sternthal.

James Lind (1716-1794)

JAMES LIND, pioneer surgeon of the British Navy, was born in Edinburgh, Scotland, into an upper middle class family.[1] He received a classical education and, at the age of 15, became apprenticed to George Langlands, a Fellow of the College of Surgeons of Edinburgh. No noteworthy events are recorded in the succeeding years, until 1739, when he entered the British Navy as a surgeon's mate. The assignment occurred during the prime period of England's global colonization and expansion of world trade. In England's mission of great destiny, a navy was indispensable, but the seafarers of the 18th century were beleaguered by pestilence, scurvy, and foul quarters. Britain could not have ruled the waves without radical reform in naval hygiene. It was Lind, more than any other medical officer on land or sea, who, when confronted with the evils of life on ships, was able to make practical suggestions for the abatement, and especially the prevention and cure, of scurvy. The measures advocated by Lind, based upon firsthand observation during a decade of service, led to a reform in the health of the sailors unequaled in any period of naval history.

In 1748, Lind returned to the University of Edinburgh, where he graduated MD, presenting a thesis in Latin on the local lesions of venereal disease. He remained to practice in Edinburgh for the following decade, was elected a Fellow of the College of Physicians of Edinburgh, and composed two of his master monographs. *A Treatise of the Scurvy* was published in 1753; *An Essay on the Most Effectual Means of Preserving the Health of Seamen in the Royal Navy* appeared in 1757. His third, and last, monograph, *An Essay on Diseases Incidental to Europeans in Hot Climates,* was published in 1768, while he was serving as physician to the Naval Hospital at Haslar, an appointment that he held from 1758 until 1783.

Many of Lind's important contributions, which so greatly improved the health and living conditions of seamen, were not original in the true sense of the word; nevertheless, the influence of his writings was profound. Both the clinical findings in scorbutic patients and the value of fruits and vegetables in treatment had been recognized prior to Lind's essay on scurvy, but it was he who emphasized the remedial properties of fresh provisions and proposed practical means of providing antiscorbutic items in the daily rations during long sea voyages. In the preface to the first edition of the treatise on scurvy, Lind noted:[2]

Armies have been supposed to lose more of their men by sickness, than by the sword. But this observation has been much more verified in our fleets and squadrons; where the scurvy alone, during the last war, proved a more destructive enemy, and cut off more valuable lives, than the united efforts of the French *and* Spanish *arms.*

The first indication of the approach of this disease, is generally a change of colour in the face, from the natural and usual look, to a pale and bloated complexion; with a listlessness to action, or an aversion to any sort of exercise.

Their gums soon after become itchy, swell, and are apt to bleed upon the gentlest friction. . . . They are subject not only to a bleeding from the gums, but prone to fall into haemorrhages from other parts of the body.

Their skin at this time feels dry, . . . And, when examined, it is found covered with several reddish, bluish, or rather black and livid spots, equal with the surface of the skin, resembling an extravasation under it, as it were from a bruise.

Many have a swelling of their legs; . . . with this difference only in some, that it does not so easily yield to the finger, and preserves the impression of it longer afterwards than a true oedema.

The antiscorbutic items listed by Lind included green vegetables, sauerkraut, onions, wine, and especially cider; but his great emphasis was upon the juice of lemons and oranges, the means of preserving them for use at sea, and their value in treatment.[2]

As oranges and lemons are liable to spoil, and cannot be procured at every port, nor at all seasons in equal plenty; and it may be inconvenient to take on board such large quantities as are necessary in ships for their preservation from this and other diseases; the next thing to be proposed, is the method of preserving their virtues entire for years in a convenient and small bulk.

Two dozen of good oranges, weighing five pounds four ounces, will yield one pound nine ounces and a half of depurated juice; and when evaporated, there will remain about five ounces of the *rob* or extract; which in bulk will be equal to less than three ounces of water. So that thus the acid, and virtues of twelve dozen of lemons or oranges, may be put into a quart-bottle, and preserved for several years.

Although Lind's treatise concerning prevention and treatment of scurvy was published in 1753 and went through several editions, the recommendations did not become regulation in the Royal Navy until the year following his death, and only then through the efforts of Sir Gilbert Blane.

Proceedings from the investigation of scurvy to contagion (only slightly less critical in morbidity among seamen), Lind presented his recommendations for prevention of contagious diseases, particularly jail distemper (typhus fever) and malaria, among the impressed landsmen. A quarantine ship, a bath, clean clothes, and clean bedding, with physical examinations before assignment to a ship, seem self-evident precautionary measures. The enlarged third edition of *Health of Seamen,* 1779, states:[3]

The most effectual preservative against this infection, during a press, would, perhaps, be to appoint a ship for receiving all ragged and suspected persons, before they are admitted into the receiving guardship. This ship should be furnished with slops [seamen's clothes], shirts, bedding, and all the necessary articles of seamen's apparel; with soap, tubs, and proper conveniences for bathing, and with a room upon deck for fumigating of clothes. Every suspecting person, whether imprest at sea, or on shore, should be first put on board of her; their stay in her, however, should be short, as soon as they are stripped of their rags, well washed and cleaned, they should be supplied with new cloaths and bedding, and be sent on board the receiving guardships.

If the nature of the service would permit, whenever the dysentery, or other infectious disease, especially a malignant and petechial, or what is called the *Jail* fever, are apprehended, the most proper place for the sick in warm weather, or in a hot climate, is under the *Forecastle.* They might there be sufficiently defended from the rain or damps, by having canvas hung around them, or a partition made with boards; and by this means all the parts of the ship below would be kept sweet, clean and wholesome.

For further security, frequent fumigation is also requisite, as a necessary means for the more certain purification of the tainted air. The fumes of camphorated vinegar, of nitre, of pitch, tar, and the like, will be found servicable. But what I would chiefly advise, is to burn two or three times a day, in different parts of the ship, a small quantity of wetted gun-powder, secured in a proper vessel.

This would provide ventilation two or three times a day to rid the quarters of the products of fumigation.

For prevention of malarial fever, Lind recommended a regular ration of extract of cinchona, Peruvian bark containing quinine.

The means, by which particular persons may best defend themselves against contagion, are next to be considered. A glass of the bark-bitter [cinchona-quinine] taken once or twice a day, will be found an excellent prevention.

Lind's process for preparing fresh water from sea water was described in his *An Essay on Diseases Incidental to Europeans in Hot Climates.*[4]

In the year 1761, I was so fortunate as to discover, that the steam arising from boiling sea water was perfectly fresh, and that sea water, simply distilled, without the addition of any ingredient, afforded a water as pure and wholesome as that obtained from the best springs. I found, after a series of experiments, that the steam arising from sea water, while boiling, did not contain any perceptible salt or bitumen; that it was sufficient to cool this steam in order to have good water.
The distillation may be carried on, when fuel is plenty, by having nothing but the sea water put into the pot: but, when fuel is scarce, to save that article as much as possible, it may be carried on by applying the still-head to the pot in which the provisions are boiling; the distilled water will be equally good, whether the water in which the provisions are boiled be fresh or salt, only it will have received a slight flavour from the particular article boiled.

Any neglect of James Lind by physicians, nutrititionists, or the University of Edinburgh in the decades following his critical observations was compensated for by the bicentenary celebration of his *Treatise of the Scurvy.* In 1953, the Nutrition Society of Great Britain sponsored a symposium at the University of Edinburgh and published a special number of the *Proceedings* of the Society in Lind's honor,[5] while Stewart and Guthrie reprinted a facsimile of the first edition of his *Treatise.*[6]

1. Roddis, L. H.: *James Lind, Founder of Nautical Medicine,* New York: H. Schuman, 1950.
2. Lind, J.: *A Treatise of the Scurvy,* Edinburgh, Sands, Murray, and Cochran, 1753.
3. Lind, J.: *An Essay on the Most Effectual Means of Preserving the Health of Seamen in the Royal Navy,* London: J. Murray, 1779.
4. Lind, J.: *An Essay on Diseases Incidental to Europeans in Hot Climates,* ed 4, London: J. Murray, 1788.
5. Ingleby-MacKenzie, A.: James Lind, Lind Bicentenary Symposium, *Proc Nutr Soc* 12:233-236, 1953.
6. Stewart, C. P., and Guthrie, D. (eds.): *Lind's Treatise on Scurvy,* Edinburgh: University Press, 1953.

National Maritime Museum

Captain James Cook (1728-1779)

JAMES COOK, famous world circumnavigator, provided his crew with fresh fruit and vegetables to prevent scurvy during long sea voyages, confirmation of the observations of James Lind a few years earlier. Cook's grandfather was a Scots elder; his father, a common husbandman of Yorkshire, provided James with an average secondary education.[1] He went to work at the age of 13, to sea four years later, and although a naval officer during a long period of warfare by England, he engaged in only one minor military operation. In 1759, Cook was appointed master of the *Mercury* and sailed for North America; there he surveyed the St. Lawrence River channel. In 1768, he became First Lieutenant in command of the *Endeavour,* a scientific mission sponsored by the Royal Society. The expedition made astronomical surveys, collected botanical specimens, and engaged in other activities concerned with exploration.

Cook's observations on antiscorbutic foods were recorded during his second major expedition, in command of the *Resolution.* Joseph Banks, a member of the Royal Society and fellow traveler, persuaded Cook to describe his antiscorbutic measures, an important feature of a policy of general hygiene on ships. His report, published in the *Transactions* of the Society in 1776, addressed to Sir John Pringle and contains the following:[2]

As many gentlemen have expressed some surprize at the uncommon good state of health which the crew of the *Resolution,* under my command, experienced during her late voyage; I take the liberty to communicate to you the methods that were taken to obtain that end. Much was owing to the extraordinary attention given by the Admiralty, in causing such articles to be put on board. as either by experience or conjecture were judged to tend most to preserve the health of seamen.

We had on board a large quantity of Malt, of which was made sweet-wort, and given (not only to those men who had manifest symptoms of the scurvy, but to such also as were, from circumstances, judged to be most liable to that disorder) from one to two or three pints in the day to each man, or in such proportion as the surgeon thought necessary; which sometimes amounted to three quarts in the twenty-four hours.

Sour Krout, of which we had also a large provision. is not only a wholesome vegetable food, but, in my judgment, highly antiscorbutic, and spoils not by keeping. A pound of it was served to each man, when at sea, twice a week, or oftener when it is thought necessary.

Further, we were provided with Rob of lemons and oranges; which the surgeon found useful in several cases.

These. Sir. were the methods. under the care of Providence, by which the *Resolution* performed a voyage of three years and eighteen days, through all the climates from 52° North to 71° South. with the loss of one man only by disease, and who died of a complicated and lingering illness. without any mixture of scurvy.

1. Muir, J. R.: *The Life and Achievements of Captain James Cook,* London: Blackie & Son, Ltd., 1939.
2. Cook, J.: The Method taken for preserving the Health of the Crew of His Majesty's Ship the *Resolution* during her late Voyage round the World, *Philos Trans* 66:402-406, 1776.

Francis Home (1719-1813)

FRANCIS HOME was born in Berwickshire, Scotland, the son of an advocate. He is recognized as a forerunner of the experimental approach to medicine, not to be firmly established in England until a century later. Home's early training in medicine came through an apprenticeship to Rattray, a practitioner in Edinburgh. At the age of 23, without having qualified for the MD degree, he was appointed military surgeon to a British regiment. He served on the Continent during the campaigns of the Austrian Succession and remained with the English forces until peace was signed in 1748. Meanwhile, he exploited the seven years of intermittent warfare for professional advancement. In Flanders, Home studied at Leyden, still under the influence of Boerhaave, where he absorbed the spirit of critical clinical observation at the bedside. He systematically tabulated the epidemiological findings among the troops of the epidemic fever in 1847, studied an epizootic of glanders among the cavalry mounts, and insisted upon the boiling of drinking water as one of his regimental orders for the prevention of epidemic disease. After mustering out, Home continued his medical studies and received the doctorate at the University of Edinburgh in 1750. He defended his dissertation, prepared in Latin, with the declaration of the belief in precise observation and comprehensive acquisition of scientific knowledge in the practice of medicine.

Entering into practice in Edinburgh and sharing his time between teaching and investigation, Home rapidly achieved deserved recognition. He became a Fellow of the Royal College of Physicians of Edinburgh and was appointed professor of materia medica in 1768, the first to hold this title. He served as physician to the Royal Infirmary, where he taught clinical medicine, and later was designated one of His Majesty's Physicians for Scotland. In addition to his abiding medical interests, Home explored selected problems in agriculture and industry. He was an authority on bleaching, receiving a gold medal for his essay, *The Principles of Agriculture and Vegetation,* and later held the first professorship in agriculture at the university.

Home was responsible for several brief communications and a number of important monographs. One of his first contributions, prepared while an apprentice, was based on the survival of earthworms in Spa waters versus ordinary spring waters. He entertained the possibility of an anthelmintic ingredient in the mineral water. Two of his books were essentially guides to therapy, directly related to his teaching of materia medica. The three monographs usually quoted by his biographers are: *Medical Facts and Experiments*[2]; the treatise on croup[3]; and *Clinical Experiments, Histories, and Dissections.*[4] Although Home was convinced of the discovery of a new disease reported in his monograph on croup, he was mistakenly merely emphasizing one manifestation of a condition already described—the development of laryngeal and tracheal involvement in diphtheria. In the preface to *Clinical Experiments,* the advantages to teacher and pupil of acquiring experience in clinical medicine and experimental therapy in a hospital rather than the home were discussed. Home judged this feature, unhampered by regulations and controlled only by the conscience of the physician, an important distinction between civilized and barbarian nations.[4]

Besides the pleasure which arises in a benevolent mind from the contemplation of the relief which hospitals afford, these charitable institutions amply repay the expence which the public bestows on them, by promoting the study and practice of medicine.

The student has there an opportunity of seeing a variety of diseases, without much loss of time; and becomes a skilful practitioner, before he claims, as a physician, the confidence of his fellow-citizens.

The physician finds many advantages there for the improvement of his art. The patients, with whom he meets, have seldom contributed to debilitate their constitutions; their complaints originate from the body, and but rarely from the mind; their theories and caprices are not so troublesome to him as those of people in higher life; they have seldom undergone a long course of medicine; and their diet is under absolute control.

Nothing hinders the physician from following his own reason and experience in the cure, and he is responsible to his own conscience alone. He can try different and new methods of cure, provided he has a probability of success, and proceeds with proper caution.

Home's capitalization of the experimental method in his continuing search for new facts was exemplified in his observations on the composition of urine from diabetic patients, the unusual appearance of coagulated blood drawn from patients with different types of fevers, and on his successful inoculation against measles. He noted the ineffectiveness of quinine or Peruvian bark on nonmalarial febrile patients who threw up a sizy (buffy) coat in the blood from suppuration and leukocytosis. His study of measles innoculation, believed to be his most enterprising experimental work, was designed to duplicate the success of smallpox vaccination by using against measles an attenuated substance from afflicted children. During the florid period he selected droplets from the lungs or skin desquamate. Finding these ineffective in prophylaxis, he obtained blood for transfer at the peak of fever. This intuitive judgment received scientific confirmation two centuries later when viremia in measles was shown to exist for a short time only at the stage of infection. Home reported his results in 12 children. After in-

oculation an eruption considered characteristic of the disease appeared in ten. One of the older children who failed to develop an exanthem gave a history of measles.[2]

Considering how destructive this disease is, in some seasons; considering how many die, even in the mildest epidemical constitution; considering how it hurts the lungs and eyes; I thought I should do no small service to mankind, if I could render this disease more mild and safe, in the same way as the Turks have taught us to mitigate the small-pox. I suspected strongly, that the cough, often so harassing, even in the mildest kind, was produced by receiving the infection mostly by the lungs; and I hoped that this symptom would abate considerably, if I could find a method of communicating the infection by the skin alone.

But there was not matter to be had from the measles. . . . I then applied directly to the magazine of all epidemic diseases, the blood.

As the measly matter behooved to be but a small proportion of the whole mass, I chused to make use of the blood, when it contained the morbific matter in the highest state of acrimony. In that situation the blood seemed to me to be, the next day after the turn of the measles . . . the cause of the inflammations which happened then, and afterwards. I therefore ordered a very superficial incision to be made amongst the thickest of the measles, and the blood which came slowly away was received upon some cotton.

What I had most to fear, was a deficiency of morbillous matter; and therefore, it was plain, that the sooner it was applied, and the more close it was kept, the better chance it had to succeed. An incision in each arm, as is done in the small-pox, was giving it a greater opportunity to take place. . . . I have always let it remain three days in the wound. I have kept exactly to all these circumstances, finding that the observance of them was attended with success.

Under an uncertainty, whether I was able to produce this disease, I made trial, and found it succeed.

The blood of a measly patient taken in the manner before described, contains a sufficient quantity of the morbific matter, to produce, by some fermentative power natural to it, the measles.

It appears that the inoculated measles are a much milder disease than the natural. . . . Inoculation appears to weaken the force of all diseases.

The majority of investigators who subsequently attempted to confirm Home's results met with failure, although a few successes were reported. Mass inoculation was not justified until recently, when attenuated measles virus vaccine was shown to be safe and effective. Meanwhile Enders, who was successful in cultivating measles virus in the laboratory, supports the minority opinion that full credit for success should be given Home for his early attempts.[1]

1. Enders, J. F.: Francis Home and His Experimental Approach to Medicine, *Bull Hist Med* 38:101-112 (March-April) 1964.

2. Home, F.: *Medical Facts and Experiments*, London: A. Millar, 1759.

3. Home, F.: *An Enquiry Into the Nature, Cause, and Cure of the Croup*, Edinburgh: A. Kincaid & J. Bell, 1765.

4. Home, F.: *Clinical Experiments, Histories, and Dissections*, Edinburgh: W. Creech, 1780.

Royal College of Physicians

William Heberden (1710-1801)

WILLIAM HEBERDEN, the elder, the outstanding physician of London in the mid-18th century, shared the medical glories of Britain with William Cullen, a contemporary in Scotland. Heberden has been described as a gentle physician with a brilliant intellect, a genius for clinical observation, a meticulous and prodigious notetaker, and one endowed with an unaffected modesty in the acquisition of knowledge and the display of scholarship.[1] In the last category he was an intimate of many of the classical writers and scholars of his time, and by means of his deep interest and evident talent in Greek and Hebrew literature, he provided the classicists with substantial assistance. Two eponyms, Heberden's asthma and Heberden's nodes attest to his professional industry, the former a significant clinical observation, the latter a minor contribution. At the age of 14, Heberden was accepted as a student at St. John's College, Cambridge, where he remained on as a Fellow and later a candidate for the MD degree. After a decade in Cambridge lecturing on materia medica interspersed with the practice of medicine, he returned to London, the city of his birth, for a rich and productive professional career. The Royal College of Physicians recognized his genius early, and at the age of 40 he had been appointed Gulstonian and Croonian lecturer and Harveian orator.

Noteworthy circumstances surrounded the postmortem examination of Heberden's first case of angina pectoris (Heberden's asthma), albeit he was not the first to describe *dolor pectoris*. The memoirs of the Earl of Clarendon, published in 1632, contain one of the first descriptions of this symptom complex. More than a century later, a physician, unidentified by name, recognized the symptoms of angina in himself and requested Heberden to conduct an autopsy upon his death. The physician died not long after, and in fulfillment of his wish, a postmortem examination was performed. Although the pathological changes now recognized as intimate to the pathogenesis of angina pectoris were not described in the protocol, Heberden judged the conclusions to be of value because they excluded a number of etiologic possibilities. There is even serious doubt as to whether the coronary vessels were examined.[2] The initial deficiencies were subsequently corrected. In a report to the Royal College of Physicians in London, July 21, 1768, Heberden noted:[3]

There is a disorder of the breast, marked with strong and peculiar symptoms, considerable for the kind of danger belonging to it, and not extremely rare, of which I do not recollect any mention among medical authors. The seat of it, and sense of strangling and anxiety with which it is attended, may make it not improperly be called Angina pectoris.

Those, who are afflicted with it, are seized, while they are walking, and more particularly when they walk soon after eating, with a painful and most disagreeable sensation in the breast, which seems as if it would take their life away, if it were to increase or to continue: the moment they stand still, all this uneasiness vanishes.

I have observed something like this affection of the breast in one woman who was paralytic, and have heard one or two young men complain of it in a slight degree; but all the rest, whom I have seen, who are at least twenty, were men, and almost all above fifty years old, and most of them with a short neck, and inclining to be fat.

When I first took notice of this distemper, and could find no satisfaction from books, I consulted an able physician of long experience, who told me that he had known several ill of it, and that all of them had died suddenly. This observation I have reason to think is generally true of such patients, having known six of those, for whom I had been consulted, die in this manner; and more perhaps may have experienced the same death, which I had no opportunity of knowing. But though the natural tendency of this illness be to kill the patients suddenly, yet unless it have a power of preserving a person from all other ails, it will easily be believed, that some of those, who are afflicted with it, may die in a different manner, since this disorder will last, as I have known it more than once, near twenty years, and most usually attacks only those who are above fifty years of age.

The pulse is, at least sometimes, not disturbed by this pain, and consequently the heart is not affected by it; which I have had an opportunity of knowing by feeling the pulse, during the paroxysm; but I have never had it in my power to see any one opened, who had died of it; the sudden death of the patients adding so much to the common difficulties of making such an enquiry, that most of those, with whose cases I had been acquainted, were buried, before I had heard that they were dead.

Four years later before the College of Physicians, Heberden read a letter from Dr. Wall, in which calcification of the aortic valves was observed in the postmortem examination of a patient who had suffered from angina pectoris.[4]

A few days ago, I was permitted to inspect the body of a person who died of the disorder which you have described in No vi. Vol. II. of the Medical Transactions, and named the *angina pectoris*. As this is the only opportunity I have ever had of enquiring into the cause of that complaint; and as you yourself acknowledge that you never saw anyone opened, who had died of this disease, I hope the following account, im-

perfect as it is, will not be entirely unacceptable to you or the College. . . . the pain under the sternum constantly extended itself on each side across the breast in the direction of the pectoral muscle, and affected one, or commonly both arms, exactly in the place where the muscle is inserted into the os humeri.

Upon examining the heart, no part appeared diseased, till we opened the left ventricle; and there, the semilunar valves, placed at the origin of the aorta, were found to be perfectly ossified. From this instant this rigidity in the valves first began, the circulation through the heart, and consequently through the lungs, was in some degree impeded.

The *Commentaries* of Heberden, written in Latin and published by William Heberden, the younger, in 1802, the year following his father's death, extend to 102 short chapters. They were based upon the rich clinical experience of a discerning practitioner, who followed the best of the classic writers in describing sickness and disease. Heberden did not indulge in speculation. He was concerned principally with factual documentation of morbid findings. The result is a series of elegant descriptions of disease before the introduction of the stethoscope into physical examination, the use of the clinical thermometer at the bedside, biochemical determination in the laboratory, or the use of the microscope in the study of morbid tissues. Cinchona was his favorite drug in the treatment of fever. One chapter described severe afflictions of the throat, scarlet fever, diphtheria, and streptococcal pharyngitis. A significant decrease in incidence of diphtheria after adolescence was recognized. In a discussion of arthritis, the distinction between gout, rheumatoid arthritis, and osteoarthritis was not always definitive. His brief comments on the hypertrophic nodes observed on the peripheral phalangeal joints of the finger are currently valid, with some qualification.[5]

DIGITORUM NODI

What are these little hard knobs, about the size of a small pea, which are frequently seen upon the fingers, particularly a little below the top, near the joint? They have no connexion with the gout, being found in persons who never had it: they continue for life; and being hardly ever attended by pain, or disposed to become sores, are rather unsightly, than inconvenient, though they must be of some little hindrance to the free use of the fingers.

On the other hand, confusion between the tophi of gouty arthritis and the hypertropic nodes of osteoarthritis crept into Heberden's writings. This is not particularly surprising; the differentiation may not be resolved in each instance from clinical examination in contemporary medical practice. The failure of osteoarthritic nodes to develop before puberty was contrasted with the appearance of "violent" rheumatism in the young. Acute rheumatic fever following pharyngitis was reported. Although Heberden advanced no clear identification of chorea as a cerebral manifestation of acute rheumatic fever, an excellent account was given of the development of acute arthritis of the knee which may precede a bout of St. Vitus' dance. Heberden described anaphylactoid purpura and purpureae maculae some time before similar observations were reported by Willan, Schönlein, and Henoch.

The association of renal stones and urinary tract infection was mentioned by Heberden. His interest in renal calculi was well-known and probably was responsible for Benjamin Franklin's seeking his counsel on his bladder stone. Franklin and Heberden also collaborated on a pamphlet recounting the success of inoculation for smallpox in America and England.[6] The then current belief that scabies was caused by a parasite was not accepted by Heberden. Sulfur was recommended as a specific remedy for this cutaneous malady. He rejected the assumption that diabetes was caused by a dysfunction of the kidneys, although the distinction between diabetes mellitus and insipidus had been suggested but not clearly made at that time. The fecundity of consumptive women was noted. Night blindness or nyctalopia was described. The bradycardia of jaundice, bile in the tears of jaundiced patients, and chills following biliary colic were observed. Smallpox and chickenpox were judged to be specific and unrelated maladies. Heberden's *Essay on Mithridatium and Theriaca* was one of the first measures in the crusade to castigate these mysterious agents that had been in the pharmacopeia since Mithridates Eupator the Great (133-63 BC).[2]

Heberden's *Commentaries* received the honor of being the last important medical treatise in England originally prepared in Latin. Heberden died at the beginning of the 19th century, having rejected the appointment as physician to Queen Charlotte, wife of George III, because it would have interfered with his mission in the bedside study of disease and the careful recording of clinical findings. His system of accumulation of a corpus of clinical material, excluding unconfirmed inferences from the past or from a priori authority, was an outstanding contribution to medical science. He copied not from other books but from the revelations of the natural history of disease. He followed the "Analytical or Inductive Method which Harvey practised, which Bacon taught, and by which Newton attained his marvellous results."[7]

1. Macmichael, W.: *Lives of British Physicians*, London: John Murray, 1830.

2. Rolleston, H.: The Two Heberdens, *Ann Med Hist* 5:409-427 (Sept.); 5:566-583 (Nov.) 1933.

3. Heberden, W.: Some Account of a Disorder of the Breast, *Med Trans* 2:59-67, 1786.

4. A Letter from Dr. Wall to Dr. Heberden, on the same Subject, *Med Trans* 3:12-24, 1785.

5. Heberden, W.: *Commentaries on The History and Cure of Diseases*, London: T. Payne, 1802.

6. Franklin, B., and Heberden, W.: *Some Account of the Success of Inoculation for the Small-pox in England and America*, London: W. Strahn, 1759.

7. Buller, A. C.: *The Life and Works of Heberden*, London: Bradbury, Agnew, & Co., 1879.

William Cadogan (1711-1797)

IN LONDON IN THE 18TH CENTURY when gin drinking, infanticide, and illegitimacy were condoned, if not accepted, as contemporory mores, infant mortality was as high as 50 per cent. The opulent social life of a few in contrast to the poverty of many encouraged wanton neglect of a significant percentage of infants born either within wedlock or without. If the babe lived through delivery, the odds were against survival in the following years. The establishment of the Foundling Hospital in London was one of the first attempts in London to correct this deplorable situation. Thomas Coram (1668-1751), a seafarer and shipmaster, has been considered the prime mover in the founding of the hospital.

Cadogan was born either in London or in southeast Wales, probably the latter, according to Rendle-Short.[1] He attended Oriel College, Oxford, as a servitor, a third-class student who performed domestic tasks in return for financial assistance from the college. In addition, he studied physic at Leyden while Boerhaave was in his retiring years. After the MD was granted at the age of 25, Cadogan began the practice of medicine in the prosperous port of Bristol and became associated with the Bristol Infirmary. An examination by the bishop of the diocese was sufficient at that time for a license to practice beyond the urban limits of London. His pediatric contributions include the common-sense handling of infants and inoculation for smallpox by friction instead of by incision. After the application of a blister plaster, lint, impregnated with the contents of a smallpox pustule, was applied. Immunity usually developed.

The treatise on the handling of infants, published in 1748, was entitled *An Essay upon Nursing and the Management of Children*. The pamphlet is believed to have been prepared at the request of one of the governors of the hospital, although there is some uncertainty whether this was an original contribution of Cadogan. Conyers, a physician and governor of the Foundling Hospital, asserted that some of the views expressed by Cadogan had been taken from his (Conyer's) inaugural dissertation prepared 20 years earlier. This is probably less important than the success of Cadogan in convincing the authorities of the hospital to accept the recommendations advanced. The essay begins as if it were prepared on request.[2]

You perceive, Sir, by the Hints I have already dropp'd, what I am going to complain of is, that children in general are over-cloath'd and over-fed, and fed and cloath'd improperly. To these Causes I impute almost all their Diseases. But to be a little more explicit. The first great Mistake is, that they think a new-born Infant cannot be kept too warm; from this Prejudice they load and bind it with Flannels, Wrappers, Swaths, Stays, &c. . . . which all together are almost equal to its own Weight. . . . But what is worse than this, at the End of the Month, if things go on apparently well, this Hot-bed Plant is sent out into the Country, to be rear'd in a leaky House, that lets in Wind and Rain from every Quarter. Is it any Wonder the Child never thrives afterwards? . . . There are many Instances both ancient and modern of Infants exposed and deserted, that have lived several days. . . . These instances may serve to shew, that Nature has made Children able to bear even great Hardships, before they are made weak and sickly by their mistaken Nurses. But besides the Mischief arising from the Weight and Heat of these

Swaddling-cloaths, they are put on so tight, and the Child is so cramp'd by them, that its Bowels have not Room, nor the Limbs any Liberty, to act and exert themselves in the free easy manner they ought.

The feeding of Children properly is of much greater Importance to them than their Cloathing. . . . When a Child is first born, there seems to be no Provision at all made for it: for the Mother's Milk seldom comes 'till the third Day; so that, according to Nature, a Child would be left a Day and a half, or two Days, without any Food; . . . However extraordinary this might appear, I am sure it is better it were not fed at all; for it sleeps almost the Whole Time, and when the Milk is ready for it, would be hungry, and suck with more Eagerness; which is often necessary, for it seldom comes freely at first. At least It would prevail thus far, that the Child be not awaked out of its Sleep to be fed, as is commonly done.

Cadogan's gouty troubles were first reported while he was in military service in the war against Spain. Cadogan and John Hunter were appointed to the hospital ship which put in at Lisbon to care for the wounded. Shortly after docking, Cadogan became critically ill with dysentery followed by the initial and severe attack of acute gouty arthritis.[1] Convalescence was so prolonged that he sought release from duty; whereupon he returned to London to practice. A decade later his treatise on gout based upon personal observation was published.[3] It went through a number of editions and was republished for its historical value as recently as 1925 in the United States.[4] Gout, a popular disease in England during the 18th century, was caricatured by the laity and discussed in a number of monographs by physicians. Undoubtedly, many instances of joint disease were misdiagnosed as gout. There is no question, however, that is was a prevalent malady, but probably no more prevalent in England in the 18th century than in America today. Cadogan denied that gout was hereditary, seasonal, or curable. Temperance was recommended in treatment, not abstinence from spirits or proteins. A common-sense policy of management was in order.[3]

He [the gouty patient] must never lose sight of the three great principles of health and long life, Activity, Temperance, and Peace of Mind. With these ever in view, he may eat and drink of every thing the earth produces, but his diet must be plain, simple, solid and tender, or in proportion to his consumption; he must eat but of one thing or two at most at a meal, and this will soon bring him to be satisfied with about half his usual quantity.

Although the book was widely read the admonitions were not necessarily accepted. Cadogan was abused out of proportion to an objective appraisal.[5] "The Doctor Dissected or Willy Cadogan" is an example.[4]

The Town are half mad (you have heard without
  doubt)
For a book that is called *Dissertation on Gout,*
The author, to Styx, in a sulphurous flame,
They'd waft, and extirpate the breed and the
  name:
But, lest the poor wight, shou'd oblivion lie snug
  in,
Without further preface—tis *Willy Cadogan.*

David Garrick, sufferer from gout[6] and friend of Cadogan's daughter, interpreted the principles literally and replied:[4]

. . . . I cannot quit Peck and Booze.—What's Life without sack and sugar! . . . A Dr. Cadogan has written a pamphlet lately upon ye Gout, it is much admired and has certainly Its merit—I was frightened with it for a Week; but as Sin will outpull repentance when there are passions and palates, I have postponed the Dr's Regimen till my wife and I are tete a tete, and so make ye mortifications as compleat as her father Confessor would prescribe to her in Lent.

Cadogan received honors from Oxford and Cambridge universities, but his greatest honors were the reverence for his doctrine of common-sense care of the child, and, for a physician afflicted with gout, common-sense recommendations to his patients similarly afflicted.

1. Rendle-Short, J.: William Cadogan, Eighteenth-Century Physician, *Bull Hist Med* 4:288-309 (Oct) 1960.
2. Cadogan, W.: *An Essay upon Nursing and the Management of Children,* London: J. Roberts, 1748.
3. Cadogan, W.: *A Dissertation on the Gout,* 5th ed, London: J. Dodsley, 1771.
4. Ruhräh, J.: *William Cadogan [His Essay on Gout],* New York: Paul B. Hoeber, Inc., 1925.
5. Shebbeare, J.: *A Candid Enquiry into the Merits of Doctor* Cadogan's *Dissertation on the Gout,* London: S. Hooper, 1773.
6. *Some Unpublished Correspondence of David Garrick,* G. P. Baker, ed. Boston: Houghton Mifflin & Co., 1907.

William Cullen (1710-1790)

WILLIAM CULLEN, 18th century nosographer, and one of the most famous physicians in Britain in his time, seems to have risen to his greatest height as an inspiring teacher of students from many parts. He was born in Hamilton, Lanarkshire, Scotland, into a large family in rather humble circumstances.[1] His early education was gained at the local grammar school where a prodigious memory was soon recognized. This was followed by student days at the University of Glasgow and an apprenticeship to Mr. Paisley, a member of the rudimentary faculty of Physicians and Surgeons of Glasgow. In his late teens, Cullen served as a surgeon on a merchant ship plying between England and the West Indies, and as an apothecary's assistant in London. He chose Shotts, the home of Matthew Baillie, as the initial community to continue his reading in philosophy and general literature, and to pursue a sporadic practice for financial gain.

Preparation for the degree of doctor of medicine was begun in Edinburgh, the only university in Scotland with an organized program of medical teaching under a faculty of medicine. Monro *Primus,* professor of anatomy, was the best-known member of the faculty. While in Edinburgh, Cullen was

an active member of the students' medical society, which became the Royal Medical Society, encouraging, rather than suppressing, youthful physicians. He returned to Hamilton, land of his nativity, and for the second time began a clinical practice, treating the indigent and the prosperous without discrimination. Cullen became acquainted with William Hunter through friendship with the Duke of Hamilton and gave some thought for a time to a joint partnership. This was not consummated, as Hunter was attracted to London, while Cullen remained in the north and achieved an early ambition by receiving the doctorate of medicine from Glasgow in 1740. Thereupon he settled in the university town, probably with the hope of lecturing in medicine, or even starting a medical school.

Although Glasgow claimed no organized medical college at that time, medical lectures were delivered regularly at the university. In 1746, arrangements were made for Cullen to deliver a course of instruction on the theory and practice of physic. This assignment was one of the first steps in the founding of the school of medicine in the University of Glasgow. The lectures included sessions in chemistry, botany, and materia medica. A notable feature was the rejection of Latin and selection of English; for communication. The use of the vernacular contributed to the lessening of the esteem of the ancients, whose writings were recorded in Latin or Greek, and constituted the first body of reference information in English. In 1751, Cullen was appointed by the King professor of medicine in Glasgow, although he continued his interest in general chemistry, agricultural chemistry, and botany. He popularized chemistry as a liberal science and persuaded the university to build a chemical laboratory for the use of teachers and students. He used diagrams to illustrate problems in chemistry and emphasized the natural influences in chemical processes.

As a teacher, Cullen continued to be a diligent student, frequently surpassing his pupils in industry. The teacher-pupil relationship was exemplary. Fees were sometimes refused, a precedent in that era. Although his pupils did not approach his intellectual stature, they were accepted as social equals. One must assume that Cullen's lectures, delivered from notes only, were stimulating, interesting, and rewarding; otherwise he would not have attracted pupils from at home and abroad, who in turn achieved fame and success in subsequent years. From America came Benjamin Rush, John Morgan, William Shippen, Jr., James McClurg, and Samuel Bard; from France came Pinel, and locally came Joseph Black.

In 1755, at the age of 44, Cullen severed his academic affiliations in Glasgow and returned to Edinburgh, where he remained for the following three decades and under whose genius it became the leading medical school in Europe. By then, Monro *Secundus* occupied the chair of anatomy. Lectures in chemistry and clinical medicine were conducted by Cullen at the Royal Infirmary. Subsequently, he was appointed to the chair of the institutes of the theory of medicine (physiology). Not until he was 63, however, did Cullen become the sole professor of medicine, a post which he occupied for the next 16 years, and relinquished only shortly before his death.

An orderly mind and the desire to document his lectures in outline stimulated Cullen to compile an 18th century version of a system of medicine, *Synopsis nosologicae methodicae* (1769), a classification of disease. Although admittedly incomplete and inexact, this was an improvement over the classification of his predecessors, including Boerhaave of Leyden, Sauvages of Montpellier, Linnaeus of Uppsala, and Vogel of Göttingen.[2] The nosology attracted the attention of Benjamin Franklin.[3] Four classes of disease were distinguished: *pyrexias, neuroses* (a term he used first), *cachexias,* and *local diseases.* The last-named class was omitted in the first edition but added subsequently. In the development of his system of medicine, he reduced the number of classes, which were then divided into orders and the orders into genera.

The orders in the class of pyrexias included (1) generalized fever, (2) localized inflammation, and (3) hemorrhages. The discussion of fever was an interesting con-

tribution. Spasm of the vessel was held responsible for pyrexia, which progressed from the cold stage to the fever and finally to the sweat. The physiological description of fever and chills comprised peripheral vasoconstriction, vasodilation, and sweating. Cullen spoke of many contagions and believed that for each specific contagious fever a specific contagion was responsible. Inflammation differed from fever; it was local rather than systemic.

In dealing with neuroses, mania and melancholia were included in the fourth group, defined as a disorder of intellectual function. Basic to Cullen's psychiatric exposition was his neurophysiological theory that the brain was an active organ which produced a hypothetical nervous fluid. The amount of nervous fluid in the body determined the amount of nervous energy available, which, in turn, reflected the healthy or morbid state of the entire body. The theory was largely physiological and mechanistic. The brain could affect or be affected by other organs of the body. Stimulation of the peripheral nervous system as well as commonly-experienced emotions could increase the total nervous energy and lead to mania. The treatment of mania by restraint or chastisement reflected the practice of the time.

In *A Treatise of the Materia Medica,* published in 1789, only a few years after Withering had published his essays on digitalis, Cullen noted: [4]

The powers of this plant as a diuretic are now ascertained by numberless experiments, but upon what sort of operation these powers depend, I am at a loss to explain. Whether it be by a specific stimulus applied to the kidneys, or by a general operation upon the system, which particularly affects the kidneys, does not appear very clearly. With respect to this I could wish to lay down here rules for the proper management of this medicine; but I will not attempt it, because I can direct my reader to a more proper means of instruction by referring him to the treatise of my very ingenious and learned friend Withering on this subject, which is a treatise in many persons hands, and, in my opinion, should be in the hands of every practitioner of physic.

In the *Practice of Physic,* Cullen devoted 35 pages to gout, a personal affliction which developed in early maturity. The current concept that gout affects the wise was advanced.[2]

> . . . . it is alleged, that it more frequently attacks the wise than the foolish. Indeed it would require a good deal of discussion to settle the precise state of this fact, or to say how far it is applicable; but this subject is more curious than useful.

The familiar renal involvement in gouty persons and the incidence of renal disease in gouty families were expressed as follows:[2]

> In most persons who have laboured under the gout for many years, a nephritic affection comes on, and discovers itself by all the symptoms which usually attend calculous concretions in the kidney.
> This also may be observed, that children of gouty or nephritic parents commonly inherit one or the other of these diseases, but whatever may have been the principal disease of the parent, some of the children have the one, and some the other. In some of them the nephritic affection occurs alone without any gout supervening; and this happens to be frequently the case of the female offspring of gouty persons.

Cullen accepted the current belief that gout developed because of plethora and excessive vigor. Initially he followed the treatment in vogue, abstentious living and a nonprotein diet. No mention was made of colchicum, although this had been described as an anti-gout remedy for several centuries. After a period of temperate living, Cullen suffered increasing incapacity from gout and completely reversed his dietary practices. He avoided fish and vegetables, relied upon animal food, and accepted the joy provided by wine.[5]

> It is therefore a diet of a middle nature that is to be chosen; and milk is precisely of this kind, as containing both animal and vegetable matter. With respect to drink, fermented liquors are useful only when they are joined with animal food.

Cullen considered the human body to be an animated organ, regulated by laws for the promotion of general health and with a mechanism for correction of deviations and deficiencies through a preestablished relation between the internal and external environment. He administered one drug at a

time and did not believe in polypharmacy. The production of edema from large evacuations of blood was described, either from spontaneous hemorrhage or therapeutic bloodletting.[4]

> . . . . these evacuations, by abstracting a large proportion of red globules and gluten, which are the principal means of retaining serum in the red vessels, allow the serum to run off more readily by the exhalents; and hence dropsies have been frequently the consequence of such evacuations.

In the discussion of dropsies, anascara, and hydrothorax, Cullen noted that:[5]

> . . . . thereby dropsy . . . as frequently occurring, and that is intemperance in the use of intoxicating liquors; from whence it is that drunkards of all kinds, and especially dram-drinkers, are affected with this disease.

William Cullen, graduate of Glasgow, teacher, and a member of the distinguished faculty in Edinburgh, made no lasting contributions to medicine as measured by a significant discovery or a critical clinical observation. His contributions were in other areas of human advancement. He was a notable nosographer, was highly regarded as a consultant, and particularly respected as a teacher. His monographs remained as standard texts in medicine for more than a century. He received many honors including membership in the Royal Society of London, Royal Society of Medicine of Paris, and the American Philosophical Society of Philadelphia. And lastly, Cullen was a member of that distinguished coterie of intellectuals afflicted with familial gout.

1. Thomson, J.: *An Account of the Life, Lectures, and Writings of William Cullen, M.D.* vol. 1, Edinburgh and London: William Blackwood and Sons, 1832; vol 2, 1859.
2. Cullen, W.: *The Works of William Cullen, M.D.*, J. Thomson, ed., vol 1, 2, Edinburgh: William Blackwood, 1827.
3. Franklin, B.: *The Writings of Benjamin Franklin*, A. H. Smyth, ed., New York: Macmillan & Company, 1906, vol 6, pp. 100-101.
4. Cullen, W.: *A Treatise of the Materia Medica*, vol 1, 2, Dublin: Luke White, 1789.
5. Cullen, W.: *First Lines of the Practice of Physic*, vol 1, Edinburgh: William Creech, 1778; vol 4, Edinburgh: C. Elliot, 1784.

Robert Whytt (1714-1766)

ROBERT WHYTT, the predecessor of William Cullen in the chair of medicine at Edinburgh, is less well known, but his contributions to clinical medicine and particularly to the pathogenesis of reflex action place him firmly among the foremost physicians of Edinburgh in the 18th century. His clear description of tuberculosis meningitis, his explanation of the sentient (sensitivity) principle in involuntary action, and the significance of emotions in the natural history of organic diseases easily offset his mistaken emphasis on the value of lime-water in the treatment of urinary tract concretions. Whytt (pronounced White) was born four years after Cullen. His father, a member of the Scottish bar and proprietor of the estate of Bennochie, died six months before Robert was born. His mother died when he was six years old. He must have been blessed with wise and good guardians who made it possible for him to obtain an excellent education. Following graduation with a master of arts degree from St. Andrews in 1730, he spent the next four years studying medicine at Edinburgh, concentrating in anatomy

under Monro *Primus*. He then went to London, became a pupil of Cheselden, and walked the wards of the city hospitals. After London, he made his pilgrimage to the Continent, spent time in Paris at La Charité and Hôtel Dieu, and in Leyden audited the lectures of Albinus, who was in his mid-maturity and those of Boerhaave, who was in his retiring years.[1]

Whytt took the degree of medicine at Rheims in 1736. Rheims, though seldom mentioned among the great schools of France, enjoyed a short term of popularity with the physicians of Edinburgh, several of whom graduated MD from this school in the 18th century. Whytt received a second MD degree from St. Andrews and became a licentiate of the Royal College of Physicians of Edinburgh. He presented both degrees for fellowship in the College in 1738 and immediately began practice. At the age of 33, he was appointed professor of the theory of medicine at Edinburgh and held the chair until his death in 1766. Cullen did not succeed to the post until seven years later. In 1752, Whytt was elected a fellow of the Royal Society of London and in 1761 was appointed physician to the king of Scotland.

Before succeeding to the chair in Edinburgh, Whytt published a treatise on the use of alicant soap and lime-water in the treatment of urinary tract calculi. Since bladder stones were encountered frequently in the practice of his time, effective measures for preventing or dissolving the concretions appealed greatly. Whytt, by his chemical studies, exploited the possibilities of the secret formula developed by Mrs. Joanna Stephens, which had been purchased by the British government and which consisted of calcined egg-shells, soap, and aromatic bitters. The therapeutic value of lime-water was attributed to a peculiar property of the solvent, when used as a bladder irrigant, rather than to its alkaline reaction. It is possible that large quantities of an alkaline fluid might have caused some inhibition of formation of uric acid stones; whereas a high fluid intake in persons who had previously been on a low fluid intake might have brought slight benefit. Probably the most enduring consequence of the lime-water misconception was the attention given to the subject by Joseph Black, who, in searching for a solvent for stones a decade later, discovered "fixed air" or carbon dioxide.

In the chair of medicine, Whytt devoted much time to physiological investigation. The *Essay on the Vital and Other Involuntary Motions of Animals* is primarily concerned with reflex action, his best contribution to scientific medicine.[2] It was published in 1751 and presented the concept of a sentient principle which received the afferent stimulus and dispatched the efferent response in involuntary motions. Descartes, Robert Boyle, and Stephen Hales had previously discussed reflex action, which knowledge was extended by Whytt, who demonstrated in physiological experiments that only a small segment of the spinal cord was necessary for reflex action. Reflex function was shown to depend neither upon the integrity of the brain nor upon the intact and entire spinal cord. This physiological explanation was quite contrary to the rational, conscious soul concept advanced by Stahl. Whytt also localized the reflex action of the pupil (Whytt's reflex), noting the afferent pathway in the optic nerve and the efferent pathway in the third nerve. Also, he suggested that persistent dilatation of the pupil could be produced by compression of the optic thalamus.[3]

From this case it seems probable that the dilatation of the pupil soon after the coming on of the *coma,* was owing to the compression of the *thlamami nervorum opticorum,* by the water collected in the brain, which rendered the *retina* insensible of the *stimulus* of light.

This presentation of sensibility and irritability, which could be demonstrated by a number of involuntary actions, brought a rebuke from von Haller, who contended that irritability of a muscle was independent of nervous influence and sensation. Whytt remained firm in his conviction that muscular contraction was under nervous control. One of the best illustrations of the sentient principle is the rhythm of the heart.[2]

How far the mind is really concerned in the motion of the heart, may easily appear from what has been already in the preceding Sections; where, if I mistake not, it has been shewn beyond doubt, that the contraction of the heart is owing to the returning venous blood acting as a *stimulus* upon it; and made highly probable, both from reason and analogy, that a *stimulus* excites our muscles into motion, only as they are animated by a sentient principle. Whence it must follow, that the alternate contractions of the heart are in no other sense owing to the irritation of the returning blood, than as the mind or sentient principle is, by this, excited to increase the action of the nerves upon its fibres.

This doctrine of the alternate motion of the heart as proceeding from the power of the mind, excited into action by the *stimulus* of the returning venous blood admitted into its cavities, is greatly strengthened by the account we have given of the alternate motions of respiration, of the contractions of the muscles of the internal ear and of the pupil. These we have clearly shewn to proceed from the mind, as affected by a *stimulus,* and to be altogether inexplicable upon principles merely mechanical.

The mind, therefore, in carrying on the vital and other involuntary motions, does not act as a rational, but as a sentient principle; which, without reasoning upon the matter, is as certainly determined by an ungrateful sensation or *stimulus,* affecting the organs, to exert its power, in bringing about these motions, as is a balance, while, from mechanical laws, it preponderates on that side where the greatest weight prevails.

Whytt's neurophysiological discussions were complemented by clinical observations on nervousness, hypochondriasis, and hysteria. The extent that emotional factors penetrate into or become an integral factor in the pathogenesis of clinical disorders, not usually classified primarily nervous, is exemplary and modern.[4]

The disorders which are the subject of the following Observations, have been treated of by authors, under the names of Flatulent, Spasmodic, Hypochrondriac or Hysteric. Of late, they have also got the name of NERVOUS; which appellation having been commonly given to many symptoms seemingly different, and very obscure in their nature, has often made it be said that Physicians have bestowed the character of *nervous* on all those disorders whose nature and causes they were ignorant of. To wipe off this reproach, and, at the same time, to throw some light on nervous, hypochrondriac and hysteric complaints, is the design of the following Observations; which are also intended to shew, how far the principles laid down in my Essay on the vital and other involuntary Motions of Animals, may be of use in explaining the nature of several diseases, and consequently, in leading to the most proper method of cure.

Since, in almost every disease, the nerves suffer more or less, and there are very few disorders which may not in a large sense be called *nervous*, it might be thought that a treatise on nervous diseases should comprehend almost all the complaints to which the human body is liable.

The monograph on tuberculosis meningitis, published posthumously by his son with the title *Observations on the Dropsy in the Brain,* has been adjudged his most important clinicopathological study. The natural history of the disease was divided into three stages according to the pulse rate, alternating from rapid to slow to rapid.[5]

Children who have water in the ventricles of the brain begin to have many of the following symptoms, four, five, or six weeks, and in some cases much longer, before their death.

At first they lose their appetite and spirits; they look pale, and fall away in flesh; they have always a quick pulse, and some degree of fever.

While the feverishness continues or increases, they lose their appetite more and more; . . . They are thirsty, and frequently vomit once or twice in a day, or once in two days. They complain of a pain in the crown of their head, or in the forehead above their eyes. . . . Their spirits being low, they incline mostly to lie in bed, altho' they are often more disposed to watching than to sleep. They cannot easily bear the light, and complain when a candle is brought before their eyes.

I date the beginning of the second stage from the time the pulse, from being quick but regular, becomes slow and irregular. This sometimes happens about three weeks, often a fortnight or less, before the death of the patient.

During the second stage, most of the symptoms mentioned in the first continue. The sick are then unable to sit up, tho' generally they sleep little, till towards the end of this period, when they begin to grow drowsy. They moan heavily, yet cannot tell what ails them. Their eyes are often turned towards their nose, or they squint outwards, and sometimes they complain of seeing objects double. Some, towards the end of this stage, grow delirious, and cry out in a wild manner, as if they were much frightened.

In the third stage, the patient, who before was little disposed to sleep, becomes then drowsy and comatose. When roused, he utters only a few incoherent words, and appears to be insensible. The beginning of the *coma* is uncertain; it is often

about the end of the second stage before the pulse grows quicker for the second time.

Frequently one eye-lid loses its motion, and afterwards the other becomes also paralytic.

In this stage, the patients are sometimes observed to be constantly raising one of their hands to their head; and are generally troubled with convulsions of the muscles of the arms, legs, or face, as well as with a *subsultus tendinum*.

Upon opening the heads of ten of those patients from whom I have collected the symptoms above mentioned, I found in all of them a clear thin fluid in the anterior ventricles of the brain, immediately below the *corpus callosum*. There was frequently the same kind of liquor in the third and fourth ventricles; but whether this is always the case, I cannot say, as I had not attended sufficiently to this circumstance.

1. Seller, W.: Memoir of the Life and Writings of Robert Whytt, M.D., *Trans Roy Soc Edinburgh* 23:99-131, 1864.

2. Whytt, R.: *An Essay on the Vital and Other Involuntary Motions of Animals*, 2nd ed, Edinburgh: J. Balfour, 1763.

3. Whytt, R.: *The Works of Robert Whytt, M.D.*, published by his son, Edinburgh: J. Balfour, 1768.

4. Whytt, R.: *Observations on the Nature, Causes, and Cure of Those Disorders Which Have Been Commonly Called Nervous, Hypochrondiac, or Hysteric*, Edinburgh: J. Balfour, 1765.

5. Whytt, R.: *Observations on the Dropsy in the Brain*, Edinburgh: J. Balfour, 1768.

Royal College of Physicians

John Fothergill (1712-1780)

JOHN FOTHERGILL was born in Yorkshire to a family of devout Quakers. His father, also John Fothergill, had visited the American colonies several times in the service of his faith. Though principally concerned with the Pennsylvania Quakers, on a side trip to Virginia the elder Fothergill attended a council with Justice Lawrence Washington, the grandfather of George.

Upon the early death of John's mother, his maternal uncle Thomas Hough became responsible for his upbringing and early education. At the old Grammar School at Sedburgh, John acquired some knowledge of Greek and the complete mastery of Latin. This proficiency enabled him to transcribe a lecture in Latin into this language and to take notes on lectures in English, also in Latin, then to compare them with the original text. However, before he matriculated, he was apprenticed for six years to Benjamin Bartlett, a Quaker apothecary.[1]

The youth, who was destined at a future time to become one of the first physicians of the age, soon afforded such instances of superior sagacity, as induced his intelligent master to permit him, at an early period, to visit and prescribe for his patients; and this he did with so much approbation, that his contemporaries in that neighbourhood have always spoken, in terms of respectful recollection, of his assiduity and practical success.

At the age of 22, John entered the University of Edinburgh after a three days' journey by horse from Yorkshire. As a Dissenter, the universities of England were closed to him and he found no available funds for higher education on the Continent. Edinburgh was no second choice, however. Although a young institution, it was destined to be the outstanding medical school in the British Isles under the leadership of a number of remarkable Scottish physicians trained by Boerhaave of Leyden. Many prominent teachers comprised the faculty; Monro *primus* led the register. Fothergill received his MD degree in two years. St. Thomas' Hospital in London was selected for further training, followed by a tour of the Continent, with a stopover in Leyden.

In 1740, at the age of 28, Fothergill settled in London as a practicing physician, a dedicated Quaker, an extremely kind and gentle person. Since his reputation as a clinician spread rapidly, soon the days were crowded with patients, and with vocational as well as avocational activities. The latter included botany, conchology, entomology, philanthropy, and a manifest interest in the American colonies. In 1748, two years after he was admitted as a licentiate of the Royal College of Physicians, his 72-page treatise on sore throat was published. The first description of diphtheria is attributed to Aretaeus of Cappadocia in the 2nd century; several case reports were published in Spain during the 17th century. However, Fothergill gave full credit to others, and made no claim for absolute priority. Because the terminal phase of the disease resembled the Spanish style of execution by strangling, it was called "morbus suffocans" or "garotillo" on the Iberian peninsula. Almost a century after Fothergill, Bretonneau of Tours segregated diphtheretic pharyngitis as a separate entity, but not until 1883 was the specific etiologic organism identified by Klebs.

In the preface to *An Account of the Sore Throat Attended with Ulcers: A Disease Which Hath of Late Years Appeared in This City, and the Parts Adjacent,* the seriousness of the affliction was recognized.[2]

A simple inflammation on the tonsils, or of other parts about the fauces, from its frequently happening without any considerable hazard attending it, is commonly looked upon as a troublesome, rather than a dangerous disease. . . . But a disease hath of late years appeared in this city . . . is of a very different nature from the common one . . . a disease almost certainly fatal. 'Tis said, that a similar, if not the same disease hath long been in some of our American Colonies, and the West-India Islands. . . . pain or soreness in the throat, with a stiffness of the neck, an uneasiness on moving it . . . and frequently in breathing also, with a disagreeable fetid smell and taste. On inspection, the uvula, the tonsils, pharynx, and the whole fauces, appeared of a remarkably florid red colour, like that attending an erysipelas.

If the attack was violent, they had an extreme difficulty in breathing, and also in swallowing; with a kind of compressive pain and straitness of the breast and back, a redness of the whole face and neck, great heat of all the parts affected, deprivation of the voice, an unquenchable thirst, and the patient seemingly in danger of being choaked.

The neck and throat soon after began to swell externally; the tumour was of a soft aedematous kind, and increased in magnitude as the disease advanced. . . . About the fourth day this tumour was generally grown very large, and the white places in the fauces began to turn black; a putrid corrosive sanies was discharged by the mouth and nostrils; the breath grew extremely offensive; respiration, if hitherto not much affected, now became difficult, and the patient expired in a very short time.

The second stage is that wherein the white sloughs begin to appear, which is a step towards a gangrenous colliquation. . . . the cause of this tendency is a putrid virus, or miasma sui generis, introduced into the habit by contagion; principally by means of the breath of the person affected.

Although the description of diphtheritic pharyngitis is Fothergill's most remarkable contribution to clinical medicine, less well known, but equally important, is an excellent discussion of calcification of the coronary arteries in a patient who suffered from symptoms of angina pectoris. The communication appeared only a short time after Heberden's paper on this subject. Heberden's clinical description was published in 1772, but the postmortem observations did not appear in print until 1785. The second of two postmortem examinations of Fothergill's patients suffering from angina pectoris was performed by John Hunter, who noted that[3]

The heart to external appearances was also sound; but, upon examination, I found that its substance was paler than common, more of a ligamentous consistence, and in many parts of the left ventricle it was become almost white and hard, having just the appearance of a beginning ossification.

The *valvulae mitrales* had a vast number of such appearances in them, and were less pliant than in the natural state; but did not appear to be unfit for use.

The semilunar valves of the aorta were thicker than common, but very readily filled the area of the artery.

The aorta had several small ossifications on it, and several white parts, which are generally the beginning of ossifications, and which were similar to those found in the heart and *valves*.

The two coronary arteries, from their origins to many of their ramifications upon the heart, were become one piece of bone.

The scar-like appearance of the heart very likely was due to a previous myocardial infarction. Booth concluded that Fothergill had suspected the myocardial pathogenesis of angina pectoris, and that it was he who suggested to Hunter the careful inspection of the coronaries for this possibility.

Fothergill discussed a number of diverse clinical phenomena. Tic douloureux was distinguished from other painful afflictions of the face and teeth. Only adequate amounts of opium gave relief. The routine use of opiates in gout, however, was to be avoided. Although Fothergill was not the first to describe lead intoxication in his "Observations on Disorders to Which Painters in Water-Colours are Exposed," he recounted the triad of colic, constipation, and feebleness of hand (wristdrop). The recovery of a miner who was resuscitated by mouth-to-mouth insufflation was described in 1745.

Fothergill recommended this rediscovered procedure in sudden accidental death, especially by drowning, suffocation, lightning, or hanging. The establishment of a bureau of vital statistics for the registration of births, burials, and marriages was proposed by Fothergill in 1754. Although the Bills of Mortality, designed for this purpose, had been in existence in London for a century and a half, the entries were imperfect and the causes of death inaccurate.

Because London could not provide him with sufficient land or variety of plants, Fothergill's expanding interest in botany led him to acquire an estate in Essex. With the assistance of world travelers, including several sea captains, he obtained trees, herbs, and plants from many countries. Initially the estate comprised 30 acres. The horticultural collection was surpassed only by the royal gardens at Kew. Naturalists were induced to botanize the virgin lands of North America and West Africa. In 1773, one well-equipped expedition explored the coast of Carolina and Georgia, and areas later to become the states of Florida, Alabama, and Tennessee. The arboretum contained an orange tree, a tea tree, a strawberry bush, bamboo cane, a cinnamon tree, ginseng, and the starry anise. Fifteen gardeners were employed to nurse the collection, while as many as four artists prepared drawings on vellum of the blooms.

Fothergill's multifaceted interest in the American colonies, and especially the Quaker colony, was kept active by prolific correspondence. He was an avowed abolitionist and gave serious thought to the establishment of a settlement in Africa for freed Negroes. The Philadelphia Quakers, however, failed to support the project, and, after due consideration, it was their decision that "the Negroes should live together with whites in a mixed community." Benjamin Franklin was one of his warmest colonial friends. He and Fothergill expended great energies and worked unceasingly to avert the War of Independence. Franklin also sought medical counsel from Fothergill, but there is no mention by Fothergill or his biographers of Franklin's bladder stone. William Heberden apparently was the

London consultant for this complication of gout. Fothergill's great devotion to America was reflected in his presentation of 18 anatomical illustrations and three cases of models to the Pennsylvania Hospital, in the expectation that a medical school would be organized in conjunction with the hospital. This became a fact in 1765. John Morgan, the first professor of medicine in America, and William Shippen, professor of anatomy and surgery, were members of the original faculty. Each had studied under the Hunters in London. Fothergill played a minor part in the founding of Harvard Medical School. Benjamin Waterhouse, the son of a first cousin, was born in America, and studied in London with Fothergill and later in Edinburgh and Leyden before returning to Massachusetts to become the first professor of physic.

Fothergill was elected a member of the American Philosophical Society, the oldest cultural society in North America, in 1770. America claims a number of Fothergilliana.[4] A Gilbert Stuart portrait is in possession of the Pennsylvania Academy of Fine Arts in Philadelphia. His gold-headed cane and a number of manuscripts and letters are in various repositories in the Quaker city. Fothergill died in London at the age of 68 from urinary obstruction due to prostatic hypertrophy.

1. Lettsom, J. C.: *Some Account of the Late John Fothergill, M.D.*, London: C. Dilly, 1783.
2. Fothergill, J.: *An Account of the Sore Throat Attended with Ulcers*, London: C. Davis, 1748.
3. Fothergill, J.: Further Account of the Angina Pectoris, *Med Obs Inq* vol 252.
4. Macmichael, W.: *Lives of British Physicians*, London: John Murray, 1830.

Percivall Pott (1714-1788)

PERCIVALL POTT, son of a scrivener, and outstanding surgeon of St. Bartholomew's Hospital London, was born on Threadneedle Street, during one of the most exciting periods of English medicine. This was the era when the surgeons finally broke with the barbers. His father died when Percivall was an infant, and he was educated by the patronage of Dr. Wilcox, Bishop of Rochester, a distant relative of his mother. After private school and while in his mid-teens, he was apprenticed to Edward Nourse, one

of the senior surgeons at St. Bartholomew's Hospital. In this assignment and for several years thereafter, he prepared the dissections for Nourse's anatomical lectures, acquired the habit of accurate sketching of specimens, and learned the rational treatment of disease and the proper techniques for surgical operations. At the age of 22, Percival was admitted into the "Freedom of the Company of the Barber-Surgeons," which entitled him to practice by virtue of the "Great Diploma."[1] He "toke the livery of the Barber-Surgeons' Company" three years later[2] and at the age of 30 was appointed assistant surgeon at Bart's.

A fracture of the leg in 1756, which required long convalescence, provided the leisure time to prepare his first manuscript, *A Treatise on Ruptures*. The description of congenital hernia was published two years after a similar report by Albrecht von Haller and shortly after the Hunters became interested in the subject. Pott was accused by the Hunters of scientific larceny, although it is believed that he was unaware of either of these works. During the next quarter cen-

tury he published scarcely a dozen manuscripts, each on a different subject. Lacrimal fistula, fistula in ano, carcinoma of the scrotum in chimney sweeps, hydrocele, and head injuries were described in his writings. The three best-known contributions are on fractures, caries of the spine, and puffy tumor (osteomyelitis of the calvarium secondary to frontal sinusitis or an extradural abscess). The discussion on fractures and dislocations included a common fracture of the lower leg, which may or may not have been the lesion that he suffered early in his professional career. The description of the physiology or function of the ankle and the pathological findings is the origin of the eponym, Pott's fracture.[3]

Whoever will take a view of the leg of a skeleton, will see that although the fibula be a very small and slender bone, and very inconsiderable in strength, when compared with the tibia, yet the support of the lower joint of that limb (the ancle) depends so much on this slender bone, that without it the body would not be upheld, nor locomotion performed, without hazard of dislocation every moment. The lower extremity of this bone, which descends considerably below that end of the tibia, is very strong and inelastic ligaments firmly connected with the last-named bone, and with the astragalus, or that bone of the tarsus which is principally concerned in forming the joint of the ancle. This lower extremity of the fibula has, in its posterior part, a superficial sulcus for the lodgement and passage of the tendons of the peronei muscles, which are here tied down by strong ligamentous capsulae, and have their action so determined from this point or angle, that the smallest degree of variation from it, in consequence of external force, must necessarily have considerable effect on the motions they are designed to execute, and consequently distort the foot.

If the tibia and fibula be both broken, they are both generally displaced in such manner, that the inferior extremity, or that connected with the foot, is drawn under that part of the fractured bone which is connected with the knee; making by this means a deformed, unequal tumefaction in the fractured part, and rendering the broken limb shorter than it ought to be, or than its fellow. And this is generally the case, let the fracture be in what part of the leg it may.

If either of these be perverted or prevented, so that the former bone is forced from its just and perpendicular position on the astragalus; or if it be separated by violence from its connexion with the latter, the joint of the ancle will suffer a partial dislocation internally; which partial dislocation cannot happen without not only a considerable extension, or perhaps laceration of the bursal ligament of the joint, which is lax and weak, but a laceration of those strong tendinous ligaments, which connect the lower end of the tibia with the astragalus and os calcis, and which constitute in great measure the ligamentous strength of the joint of the ancle.

Caries of the spine, Pott's disease, the second eponym, had been described by Hippocrates and Galen. The aphorism by Hippocrates on gibbosity has been assumed to refer to psoas abscess, communicating with the spine, usually tuberculous in nature. In 1779, David presented a case report, with clinical findings highly suggestive of tuberculosis of the spine with suppuration.[4] Pott did not recognize the tuberculous etiology but described the deformity and its sequelae and, in following the teachings of Hippocrates, recommended drainage in treatment. The monograph was entiled *Remarks on That Kind of Palsy of the Lower Limbs Which Is Frequently Found to Accompany a Curvature of the Spine, and Is Supposed to Be Caused by It,* etc.[5]

The disease of which I mean to speak, is generally called a palsy, as it consists in a total or partial abolition of the power of using, and sometimes of even moving the lower limbs, in consequence, as is generally supposed, of a curvature of some part of the spine.

When it affects a child who is old enough to have already walked, and who has been able to walk, the loss of the use of his legs is gradual, though in general not very slow. He at first complains of being very soon tired, is languid, listless, and unwilling to move much, or at all briskly; in no great length of time after this he may be observed frequently to trip, and stumble, although there be no impediment in his way; and whenever he attempts to move briskly, he finds that his legs involuntarily cross each other, by which he is frequently thrown down, and that without stumbling; upon endeavouring to stand still and erect, without support, even for a few minutes, his knees give way and bend forward. When the distemper is a little farther advanced, it will be found that he cannot, without much difficulty and deliberation, direct either of his feet precisely to any exact point; and very soon after this, both thighs and legs lose a good deal of their natural sensibility, and become perfectly useless for all the purposes of locomotion . . . and do also lose much of their natural sensibility, but notwithstanding this, they have neither the flabby feel, which a truly paralytick limb has, nor have

they that seeming looseness at the joints, nor that total incapacity of resistance, which allows the latter to be twisted in almost all directions.

When a naturally weak infant is the subject, and the curvature is in the vertebrae of the back, it is not infrequently productive of additional deformity, by gradually rendering the whole back what is commonly called humped; and by alterations which all the bones of the thorax sometimes undergo, in consequence of the flexure and weakness of the spine, by which such persons are justly said to be shortened in their stature; My next patient was a tall thin man, about thirty-five years old, . . . he could with difficulty go about the room with the help of a pair of crutches, but he could neither rise from his chair, nor get his crutches without the assistance of another person, nor could he without them walk at all.

I made a seton on each side of the curve, which was in his back, about the middle, and having given his wife directions how to dress them, I called on him once in three or four days. At the end of six weeks he had recovered the due degree of sensation in his limbs, and found much less necessity for the use of his crutches.

Although not an eponym, his description of cancer of the scrotum in chimney sweeps and recommended treatment is a classic in industrial medicine, the first example of a specific neoplasm related to a specific occupation.[3]

The disease, in these people, seems to derive its origin from a lodgement of soot in the rugae of the scrotum, and at first not to be a disease of the habit. . . . The scrotum is no vital organ, nor can the loss of a part of it ever be attended with any the smallest degree of inconvenience; and if a life can be preserved by the removal of all that portion that is distempered, it will be a very good and easy composition.

In his prime years of practice, Pott was the fashionable surgeon of London. He lived in Lincoln's Inn Fields and enjoyed such prominent persons for patients as David Garrick and Samuel Johnson. However, Garrick, who suffered from "Gout, Herpes and Stone,"[2] failed to benefit from the consultant's recommendations, received reluctantly. The first member of the new school of surgeons in London in the 18th century was noted for his contributions to surgical teaching, surgical writing and surgical practice. After Pott came the Hunters, especially John, anatomist and experimental surgeon, who was Pott's most famous English pupil. Pott instituted humane treatment of the surgically sick before the use of ether and chloroform in anesthesia. He rejected cautery as a cruel invention and insisted that bandages be soft and light, not bulky and tight. His scientific compositions were clear and meaningful, his patients sometimes famous but always receiving the best treatment possible in the judgment of this remarkable surgeon.

1. Horder, T. J.: *Life and Works of Percivall Pott*, St *Bartholomew's Hosp Rep* 30:163-187, 1894.
2. Lloyd, G. M.: *Life and Works of Percivall Pott*, St *Bartholomew's Hosp Rep* 66:291-336, 1933.
3. Earle, J.: *Chirurgical Works of Percivall Pott, F.R.S.*, vol. 1, 2, Philadelphia: James Webster, 1819.
4. David, J. P.: *Dissertation on the Effects of Movement and Rest on Surgical Conditions*, Paris: Veuve Vallat-la-Chapelle, 1779.
5. Pott, P.: *Remarks on That Kind of Palsy of the Lower Limbs Which is Frequently Found to Accompany a Curvature of the Spine, and Is Supposed to Be Caused by It, Together with Its Method of Cure. To Which Are Added Observations on the Necessity and Propriety of Amputation in Certain Cases and Under Certain Circumstances*, London: Johnson, 1779.

William Hunter (1718-1783)

WILLIAM HUNTER, ten years older than his brother John, and of a contrary temperament, was born in Lanarkshire in the environs of Glasgow on the family estate, Long Calderwood.[1] The family was large, some were tubercular, others were gouty, but the stock was outstanding, and means were available for proper education of each of the children. At the age of 14, William began his studies at the University of Glasgow, where he remained five years and acquired the reputation of a good scholar. Following the wishes of his father, he had intended to train for duties in the Scottish church; however, uncertainty in subscribing to the tenets of the Presbytery caused him to turn to anatomy and medicine. The desire was consummated during a three-year apprenticeship (described by Hunter as the happiest years of his life) in the home of William Cullen, who was then practicing at Hamilton. At the age of 22, Hunter attended

the classes of Alexander Monro; thereafter he continued his medical studies in London, residing first with William Smellie, one of the leading obstetricians of London, and later with James Douglas, anatomist and

obstetrician (Douglas' pouch), whom he served as a dissector. He was also accepted as a surgeon's pupil at St. George's Hospital, meanwhile acquiring clinical experience and developing his skill and furthering his interest in anatomical dissection. In 1743, he communicated an important work to the Royal Society on structure and diseases of the articulating cartilages.

At the age of 28, Hunter had his first opportunity to lecture on the operations of surgery and bandaging, in which he incorporated anatomy, to a society of navy surgeons. In the following year he was admitted a member of the Corporation of Surgeons. A tour of the Continent was then undertaken, where he visited, among several, Albinus of Leyden, who displayed his outstanding anatomical dissections. Hunter subsequently returned to London to practice and to teach surgery and midwifery and to begin the assembly of his museum, which grew rapidly in size and scope. He was appointed surgeon accoucheur in the Middlesex Hospital in 1748 and to the British Lying-In Hospital in 1749. Thus, at the age of 31, he was accepted as the leading anatomist in London. Meanwhile, he accepted his brother's offer who, motivated by the greater opportunities of the urban community, wished to come to London and to assist in dissection. John's manners were rough and coarse, in contrast to William's cultured and polite instincts—ample reason for the development of a schism a decade later.

In 1750, William obtained the degree of doctor of medicine from the University of Glasgow. He was admitted a licentiate of the Royal College of Physicians in 1756, and soon after was elected a member of the Society of Physicians, which later became the Medical Society of London. Meanwhile, he sought disfranchisement by the Surgeon's Corporation and affiliated with the Physicians' College without formally receiving permission from the surgeons. As the unrivaled obstetrician of London, he was consulted, in 1762, by Queen Charlotte, to whom he was appointed Physician Extraordinary two years later. In 1767, Hunter was elected a Fellow of the Royal Society; the following year he was appointed the first professor of anatomy to the newly-founded Royal Academy. Respected by laity and profession alike for his clinical skill and inquisitive mind, the only deficiency seemed to be adequate quarters for practice and facilities for teaching and the housing of his growing anatomical collection. The need was not satisfied until 1770, when he had built in Great Windmill Street a house with a lecture amphitheater, a dissecting room, and a large museum—William Hunter's School of Anatomy. Here he lived as a bachelor for the remainder of his life, and as an inspired teacher taught the future anatomists and surgeons of the era.

Hunter was not an especially prolific writer, but his communications to the *Philosophical Transactions* and to the *Medical Observations and Inquiries* displayed his varied interests which included aneurysms, old dislocations of the shoulder, history of anatomy, aspiration of ovarian cyst, avoid-ance of forceps in delivery, the round ligament of the uterus (Hunter's ligament), the linea alba, the tubules of the testis, the ducts of the lachrymal gland, the origin and function of the lacteal and lymphatic vessels, anatomical characteristics of the symphysis pubis, rejection of symphysiotomy, forensic features of death of bastard children, malformations of the heart, and venereal diseases. The selected excerpts seem inadequate when judged in the light of his great accomplishments. In a disputation with Monro *secundus* of Edinburgh, Hunter showed his controversial nature, particularly when his claims of priority in the anatomy of the tubules of the testes and the function of the lymphatics were questioned. The concluding remarks in the Introduction to this polemic follow.[2]

But what I thought the great fault of the performance, was the open violation of truth and candour. How far I had reason for taking such offence, the reader will judge. The original dispute between us is about *facts* and *dates,* and does not allow of quibble or evasion. One of us must be in the right, the other must be in the wrong. Therefore, what relates to the injection of the *tubuli testis,* and to the use of the lymphatic vessels, must be historical, and must be supported by sufficient vouchers. That circumstance has rendered the first part of this work more tedious than I could have wished. The latter part, I flatter myself, will be found both more entertaining, and more useful as it is interspersed with many curious experiments and observations, particularly on the subject of absorption, and on the state of the *testis* in the *foetus,* which were made, and communicated to me, by my brother.

If the world should think that I ought to have published this defence sooner, I beg they may recollect that when my friends first engaged me in it, I only promised to do it *with proper authority.* It required a good deal of time, and I had little to spare: the subject was unpleasant, and therefore I was very seldom in the humour to take it up: Dr. Monro's performance did not hurt me with my friends, and I was less solicitous what others might think of me: no person could suffer by the delay, but myself: and, as I well know that I could make every thing very clear, I thought it of no consequence whether I appealed to the public a little sooner or later.

Hunter's anatomical research and his anatomical drawings of the human gravid uterus stand as his greatest work.[3] It was printed in Latin and English in parallel columns. Many of the dissections were prepared jointly with John Hunter. The majority of the 34 copper engravings, which have never been surpassed, were prepared by Rymsdyck; they have remained great examples of art as well as superb anatomical drawings. Several of the illustrations of the uterus and foetus throughout gestation and the relationship of the placenta to the uterus were presented life-size. The task represented 30 years of difficult, painstaking work.

In 1794, following his death, the companion piece, *An Anatomical Description of the Human Gravid Uterus and Its Contents,* was edited and assembled for publication by Matthew Baillie, Hunter's nephew. In this, Hunter demonstrated the two fold nature of the circulation of the placenta and described the decidua as hypertrophied endometrium instead of the residue of inflammation.[4]

The outer surface [of the placenta] which adheres to the womb, and is therefore naturally convex, is rough, tender in its substance, commonly covered with blood, lightly subdivided into smaller constituent lobes, and, to a common observer, seems to have no apparent blood vessels, at least none of any considerable size.

Its internal surface, naturally more or less concave, is glossy, hard or compact in its texture, and beautifully marked with the ramifications of the umbilical vessels. The navel string, which produces these branching vessels, is inserted sometimes into the very centre, but more commonly a little nearer the edge, and often into the very edge of the placenta, In at least four different cases, I have seen the navel string terminate on the inside of the membranes, at the distance of five or six inches from the placenta. In all these cases the umbilical vessels parted from one another even to considerable distances in their course upon the membranes, and came to the edge and inner surface of the placenta at different places, even at the opposite parts. The termination or insertion of the navel string, wherever it happens to be, makes the centre of ramification for the large vessels on the internal surface of the placenta.

Commonly there is only one centre; but in those cases where a navel string attaches itself to the membranes, there are just so many centres of ramification as there are trunks of large arteries or veins coming separately to the edge of the placenta. The internal surface of the placenta is covered with the membranes amnion and chorion,

and the external with the decidua; of which hereafter.

The decidua resembles a good deal in its appearance, as well as in its mode of formation, the lamina of coagulable lymph which is formed by inflamed surfaces. Both membranes are of a yellowish white colour; both are tender, pulpy, and vascular. The lamina of coagulable lymph is formed by an inflamed membrane; the uterus before the decidua is formed becomes much more vascular, so as to change into a state somewhat analogous to inflammation. The points of comparison, however, between those two membranes reach no farther. The lamina of coagulable lymph is gradually changed into the membrane of adhesion, which resembles exactly the common cellular membrane of the body; but the decidua continues throughout a peculiar membrane.

In summary, remarks on the retroverted uterus, the first to use this term, in an address to the Medical Society, Hunter emphasized the comparative frequency of the condition and contradicted the assumption of some that the condition scarcely existed. The prophylactic correction of the misplacement was described as follows:[5]

The growing bulk of the *uterus* in the first months of pregnancy, before it rises above the brim of the *pelvis,* has a natural tendency to produce micturition, dysury, and suppression of urine. The particular form and state of the *pelvis,* in many instances, may contribute much to such complaints, and even to the *retroversion* itself, in various degrees. I say, *various degrees;* because I am convinced, by the cases which I have seen, as well as by the nature of the parts concerned, that, in different cases of that kind, the axis of the *uterus* is thrown into different directions.

If the causes of the complaint exist in a less degree, which is most commonly the case, especially when accompanied with favourable postures and motions of the body, and if the patient takes pains to keep the bladder tolerably empty, nature will recover herself, and go on in her usual course.

But, when the contraries happen, the *uterus,* increasing daily in bulk, will, at length, be so jammed in the *pelvis,* as to bring the patient into a very painful and hazardous situation; being kept down by the descended bladder, which rises over it, and urged frequently and powerfully downwards by the efforts of the patient, it is pressed against the *parietes,* and especially the lower parts of the *pelvis;* where those *parietes,* are bony, it is restrained to the cavity of the *pelvis,* but where fleshy and yielding, it swells outwards and forms projections which fix it almost immovably in that situation. In this distressing state, the *uterus* may be, 1. Fully retroverted; or 2. Half retroverted; or 3. So far in its natural state, that the orifice of the *uterus* shall be downwards.

With regard to the treatment of the disease, experience, as well as I can judge, has only confirmed what was at first proposed. I have been told, indeed, that the rertoverted *uterus* would of itself recover its natural situation, if, by the constant and proper use of the catheter, the bladder were but kept moderately empty. In many, perhaps, it might be so. And yet, I think, where it can be done with ease, (and in most instances it may) it would be better to put an end at once to pain and danger, by replacing the *uterus*. Practitioners know both how painful and how dangerous the situation of a patient is, whose urine cannot pass but through the catheter; and when it is sometimes so very difficult to insinuate the catheter, that even expert operators fail; and that, in most of those cases, the patient is liable to be without help at the proper times, and to be thereby exposed to, perhaps, an irreparable mischief.

All of Hunter's energies were devoted to his teaching, his museum, and his patients. It is to his great credit that he trained his brother John, Matthew Baillie, William Hewson, and W. C. Cruikshank. In addition to a vast collection of anatomical specimens, the museum contained coins, medals, minerals, shells, manuscripts, and Latin and Greek texts.[6] By his will, the museum was left to three trustees, with stewardship to Matthew Baillie for 30 years, when it was to become the permanent possession of the University of Glasgow. The size and importance approached that of John Hunter's museum in the Royal College of Surgeons of London. Shortly before death, Hunter was elected a foreign associate of the Royal Medical Society of Paris and the Academy of Science of Paris. His health began to fail while still in his prime due to acute attacks of familial gout, notwithstanding his frugal manner of living and simple tastes. The complaints of severe headache and nausea in his terminal illness suggest renal insufficiency as a complication of the metabolic disorder.

1. Fox, R. H.: *William Hunter, Anatomist, Physician, Obstetrician, (1718-1783)*, London: H. K. Lewis, 1901.

2. Hunter, W.: *Medical Commentaries, Part I. Containing a Plain and Direct Answer to Professor Monro, jun.*, London: A. Hamilton, 1762.

3. Hunter, W.: *The Anatomy of the Human Gravid Uterus*, Birmingham, England: J. Baskerville, 1774.

4. Hunter, W.: *An Anatomical Description of the Human Gravid Uterus and Its Contents*, London: J. Johnson, 1794.

5. Hunter, W.: Summary Remarks on the Retroverted Uterus, *Med Obs Inq* 2:388-393, 1762.

6. Marshall, A. J., and Burton, J. A. G. (compilers): *Catalogue of the Pathological Preparations of Dr. William Hunter, Sir William Macewen, Professor John H. Teacher, Professor J. A. G. Burton*, Glasgow: University of Glasgow, 1962.

John Hunter (1728-1793)

JOHN HUNTER, younger brother of William Hunter, teacher of Edward Jenner, and urologic consultant to Benjamin Franklin, was one of the greatest surgeons, if not the greatest, England has produced. The Junior Hunter, famous for the admonition "Don't think, try; be patient, be accurate . . .," was born in Long Calderwood, seven miles from Glasgow, the youngest of ten children. His father was a retired grain merchant, his mother the daughter of a "maltster."[1]

Just as Francis Bacon was judged the most learned Englishman of the 17th century, John Hunter deserves a similar accolade as the leading surgeon and medical scientist in the 18th century. If one pursues this comparison, Hunter was the greatest experimental surgeon of his era, just as Claude Bernard was the greatest experimental physiologist in the following century.

His brother William's sense of responsibility brought John to London to study and later to teach anatomy and to practice surgery. It was necessary in those days to socialize with the "resurrection-men" who obtained bodies for the dissecting room. Such socialization was profitable since it provided Hunter with valuable material, otherwise difficult to obtain because of the existing laws against dissection. John devoted his waking hours to anatomical dissection and, because of his interest and skill, was advanced to the post of demonstrator only one year after he had bade farewell to Long Calderwood. In 1751, John Hunter became a surgeon's pupil at St. Bartholomew's Hospital, where Percivall Pott was the leading surgeon. Three years later he transferred his allegiance to St. George's Hospital where he served as surgeon for more than 25 years. Two months at Oxford, a tour of military duty with the fleet during the war with Spain, and he was back in London at the age of 35. London claimed him for the remainder of his natural life.

The abrogation of John's allegiance to his older brother is a mystery and remains a sad commentary upon the lives of these great men of medicine.[1] The brothers were united in their attacks against the Monros and Percivall Pott over the discovery of the lacrimal ducts in man, the discovery of the seminiferous tubules, and the description of congenital hernias. The last-named subject belonged to neither group but probably to Albrecht von Haller. The individual claim of William and John over the anatomy of the placenta was a breaking point of professional association which became public knowledge in 1780. So bitter was the dispute that the Royal Society refused to publish their polemics in the transactions. William Hunter died in 1783 at the age of 64, two weeks after a bad attack of acute gout. His oft-quoted death-bed words were: "If I had the strength to hold a pen, I would write how pleasant and easy a thing it is to die." Gout is a familial malady and did not

spare John. It is not recorded what sympathy he gave Benjamin Franklin, a fellow sufferer from this malady, but the record is clear that Hunter was called in consultation by William Heberden to attend the Minister Plenipotentiary from the United States while he was suffering from the distress of a large bladder stone.

The Hunterian collection of specimens had been begun before John left Long Calderwood; the fame of the collection is associated with the museum in London. A small tract of land only a few miles from London was acquired for the site of Hunter's laboratory and museum. It was as much a circus and a menagerie as an assemblage of anatomical dissections. The live specimens included leopards, snakes, bats, buffaloes, a jackal, a zebra, and an ostrich. The two most famous skeletons were the rorqual (bone-whale of the genus *Balaenoptera*) and the Irish giant Byrne or O'Brien. When the Irish giant was nearing his death, Hunter arranged with his own henchman, Howison, to stalk O'Brien. The giant countered by contracting with the undertaker to arrange for a watch over the bier day and night until a lead coffin was fashioned. The coffin was to be taken to sea and cast overboard. Howison was successful in carrying out his charge from Hunter, however, by offering a most attractive bribe so that he could snatch the body and take it to the anatomist-surgeon. Hunter rapidly dismembered the remains and later reassembled the skeleton. The brown color that is evident today was caused by the rapidity with which it was necessary for Hunter to discharge this task. The amount of the bribe is reputed to be 500 pounds sterling—a fabulous sum in 1783. Harvey Cushing was permitted to examine the skull in 1909 and determined that the contour of the sella turcica established beyond doubt that the giant suffered from acromegaly. The inhabitants of Littlebridge, the *heimat* of O'Brien, attributed his size to the supernatural influence of the place where his parents, both of normal dimensions, supposedly conceived him atop a high haystack.[2]

John Hunter's estate, Earl's Court House, was to be sold on his death. The collection was offered first to the English government, then to a foreign government, and was finally sold at auction. The government was in no mood to spend money lavishly at that time, and it was not until 15 years after Hunter's death that 15,000 pounds were appropriated for the purchase of the collection. The museum became the property of the Royal College of Surgeons in 1800. The last move was to Lincoln's Inn Fields. A significant portion of the structures and specimens was destroyed in 1941 during the bombing of London, first by a high explosive shell, later by incendiary bombs.

Hunter died on the same day and on the same hour that Marie Antoinette, Queen of France, was beheaded, October 16, 1793. His antemortem request for a postmortem examination was respected. This was followed by burial in St. Martin's-in-the-Fields. His widow could not afford the fees for a vault in Westminster Abbey. The coffin was not transferred to the Abbey until 1859. The portrait of John Hunter, painted by Sir Joshua Reynolds, remains in the College of Surgeons collection, faded but recognizable. The zinc etching by William Sharp in the flyleaf of Stephen Paget's life of Hunter[1] is excellent.

The description of the technique for the surgical treatment of a popliteal aneurysm was recorded by his brother-in-law. It consisted of a single ligature of the artery at a distance high in the healthy tissues.[3]

From these considerations, suggested by the accident of the artery giving way, which happened several times to Mr. Hunter, he proposed, in performing this operation, that the artery should be taken up at some distance from the diseased part, so as to diminish the risk of haemorrhage, and admit of the artery being more readily secured, should any such accident happen. The force of the circulation being thus taken off from the aneurismal sac, the cause of the disease would, in Mr. Hunter's opinion, be removed; and he thought it highly probable that if the parts were left to themselves, the sac, with the coagulated blood contained in it, might be absorbed, and the whole of the tumour removed by the actions of the animal oeconomy, which would consequently render any opening into the sac unnecessary.

In the pre-Pasteur era of Hunter's day, venereal diseases were thought to be due to a single agent. To test this assumption he inoculated himself with the discharge from a patient with gonorrhea, who in addition and unknown to Hunter, suffered from syphilis as well. When Hunter contracted syphilis he maintained that the two diseases were caused by a single pathogen. The studies were described in a monograph on the venereal disease, a standard text for generations. Unfortunately, the weight of his authority impeded progress in the understanding of venereal diseases for some time.[4]

To ascertain several facts relative to the venereal disease, the following experiments were made. They were begun in May 1767.

Two punctures were made on the penis with a lancet dipped in venereal matter from a gonorrhoea; one puncture was on the glans, the other on the prepuce.

This was on a Friday; on the Sunday following there was a teasing itching in those parts, which lasted till the Tuesday following. In the mean time, these parts being often examined, there seemed to be a greater redness and moisture than usual, which was imputed to the parts being rubbed.

The above case is only uncommon in the mode of contracting the disease, and the particular views with which some parts of the treatment were directed; but as it was meant to prove many things which though not uncommon, are yet not attended to, attention was paid to all the circumstances. It proves many things, and opens a field for further conjectures.

It proves, first, that matter from a gonorrhoea will produce chancres.

Hunter speculated on the probability of achieving fertilization by artificial insemination, described the thermoregulatory mechanism of the hedgehog, and interested Edward Jenner in devising a test for color blindness. The Hunterian museum is probably John's best-known contribution to posterity. The Hunterian Orations, established in 1814 and given biannually in this century, perpetuate his many contributions to science and to medicine specifically. Stephen Paget concludes one chapter: "He brought surgery into closer touch with science. Contrast him with Ambroise Paré, a surgeon in some ways like himself, shrewd, observant, ahead of his age; the achievements of Paré, side by side with those of Hunter, are like child's play in comparison with the serious affairs of men; Paré advanced the art of surgery, but Hunter taught the science of it."

1. Paget, S.: *John Hunter: Man of Science and Surgeon, 1728-1793, With an Introduction by Sir James Paget,* London: T. Fisher Unwin, 1897.

2. Kobler, J.: *The Reluctant Surgeon: Biography of John Hunter, Medical Genius and Great Inquirer of Johnson's England,* Garden City, N. Y., Doubleday & Company, Inc., 1960.

3. Home, E.: An Account of Mr. Hunter's Method of Performing the Operation for the Popliteal Aneurism, *London Med J* 7:391-406 1786.

4. Hunter, J.: *A Treatise on the Venereal Disease,* London, 1786.

official founding of the medical school. The need for study of human anatomy had been recognized in the community two centuries earlier, through an action of the surgeons

Alexander Monro, Secundus

Alexander Monro, Tertius
National Library of Medicine

Alexander Monro, Primus

The Monros of Edinburgh

AN UNBROKEN LINE OF SUCCESSION for 126 years is a record for a family dynasty in academic medicine. Nor is there any substantial evidence to cast suspicion upon the wisdom of such nepotism during the glorious era of Edinburgh medicine.[1] Drs. Alexander Monro, *Primus, Secundus,* and *Tertius,* Professors of Anatomy and Surgery during the 18th and 19th centuries, made secure the fame of the Edinburgh school. The dynasty began, in fact, in 1712 when John Monro, father of Monro *Primus* and an army surgeon, became President of the Edinburgh College of Surgeons 14 years before the official founding of the medical school. The need for study of human anatomy had been recognized in the community two centuries earlier, through an action of the surgeons and barbers in their charter, dated 1505, which assured them the body of a condemned man once a year for dissection. In the interim, the study of botany was added, with the botanical garden for an outdoor laboratory of materia medica. Coming closer and closer to actuality, an anatomical amphitheatre for dissection was built by the

Surgeons in 1697, and Robert Elliot was appointed the first Professor of Anatomy in 1705. In 1726, the medical school became an official institution of learning, after this prolonged period of preparation, by the creation of a Faculty of Medicine in the University of Edinburgh.

Monro *Primus* is credited as the true founder of the school of medicine in Edinburgh, although his father gave strong moral support and his teachers, Cheselden of London and Boerhaave of Leyden, undoubtedly provided a substantial impetus. The President and Fellows of the College of Physicians and the city surgeons of Edinburgh were invited to the convocation lecture, which was based upon Monro's anatomical collection. The recently-appointed professor had neglected to bring his lecture notes and was forced to talk extemporaneously. But the job was well done, and the lecture was judged worthy of the new incumbent. His formal induction into the Chair of Anatomy took place in 1720. An infirmary was built by volunteer labor in 1741. Initially it contained 228 beds. The first major addition, a surgical annex, was opened in 1832. It was here that Lister began his study of the antiseptic method which was to revolutionize surgery.

More than 55 essays on a wide range of medical subjects were prepared by Monro, and a method of teaching anatomy which was accepted for more than a century came into existence.[2]

He began (his lectures) with the history of Anatomy, giving a regular account of the most remarkable anatomists from the earliest times up to his own time, mentioning their different improvements and discoveries, the dates of the times in which they were made, and the different claims of authors to the honour of particular discoveries. The minds of his pupils thus prepared, he proceeds to the study of Osteology, beginning with the bones in general, then passing to each particular bone, demonstrating its parts, structure, uses, and diseases to which it is liable. From the study of the skeleton he moved to the muscles, the abdominal and thoracic viscera, the brain, the nerves, the blood-vessels, taking the anatomy first of each part, and next the structure and diseases of each part.

The anatomical dissections by Monro *Primus* were prepared with meticulous care. An excursion into physiology covered the nutrition of the fetus. Scientists were undecided at that time whether the fetus was nourished exclusively through the umbilical cord or received nourishment from the embryonic fluid by the mouth as well. Monro concluded that the umbilical cord provided the entire nourishment. The effect of disease on various organs was explored. Surgical operations upon cadavers were performed; the proper application of bandages to patients was studied. A journal of case studies was kept, and each Saturday morning in the operating amphitheatre, Monro would tender an account of the patients treated during the preceding week. His best-known work was a discussion of osteology. Monro assisted in forming the Royal Society of Edinburgh and was elected a Fellow of the Royal Society of London. Also, the Royal Academy of Surgery of Paris awarded him a diploma. Nonmedical honors included a directorship of the Bank of Scotland and appointment as Justice of the Peace and Commissioner of High Roads.

Alexander *Secundus* was true to the faith entrusted in him by his father and was judged the most brilliant of the Monros. He received the MD degree at Edinburgh in 1755. Later he studied with Hunter in London, Albinus in Leyden, and Meckel, grandfather of Johann Friedrich, in Berlin. By 1783 pupils from America included John Morgan, William Shippen, and Benjamin Rush.[3]

. . . . this seminary of medical education frequented yearly by three or four hundred students, many of whom came from the most distant corners of his Majesty's dominions; and to see it arrive at a degree of reputation far beyond his most sanguine hopes, being equalled by few, and inferior to none, in Europe.

The foundation of future observations on the lymphatics of the testis and seminal vesicles in animals was revealed in Monro's inaugural dissertation. This was illustrated with 5 engravings; in one, the trunks of the lymphatics from the testis and the neighboring parts were sharply outlined by injection.[4] The lymphatics were described as a

. . . . distinct system of vessels, having no immediate connection with the arteries and veins, but arising in small branches from all cavities and cells of the body into which fluids are thrown, and stating that their use was to absorb the whole or the thinner parts of these fluids, and to restore them to the general circulation.

Monro *Secundus* was parsimonious in regard to his time. He was as industrious near the end of his life as he was at the beginning of his career. He was not one to deliver a series of stereotyped lectures but was continually improving them. His most famous discoveries were the foramen (of Monro) and an incomplete description of the lymphatic system. Like his father, he was the acknowledged medical figure of his day in Edinburgh. The Royal Academies of Paris, Berlin, Madrid, and Moscow honored him. The charms of the comic as well as the tragic muse were enjoyed. He loved his garden and was[4]

. . . . an agreeable companion over a social glass. . . . . Without transgressing the bounds of the most strict sobriety, he afforded us demonstrative evidence of the exhilarating power of wine.

The final steps of nepotism, Alexander Monro, *Tertius,* also an Edinburgh graduate, was less fortunate than his ancestors. The line was beginning to weaken. He begot 12 children, but none was prepared to pursue the traditional profession of the family.[5] The third Monro graduated with the MD degree in 1797 and assumed a professorship in the University in 1808 after the resignation of his father. He continued to teach until 1846. A number of writings were prepared, based largely upon a recapitulation of the contributions of others. The first and second Monros, primarily anatomists and teachers of surgery, resisted the establishment of a competing Chair in Surgery. Monro *Tertius* was less successful. The Royal commission corrected this deficiency, which had already been started with a Professorship of Clinical Surgery in 1803.

1. Guthrie, D.: The Three Alexander Monros, *J Roy Coll Surg Edinburgh* 2:24-34 (Sept.) 1956.
2. Richardson, B. W.: "Alexander Monro, M.D., F.R.S," in *The Asclepiad,* Vol. VII, London: Longmans, Green, and Company, 1890, pp. 49-67.

3. Monro, A.: *The Works of Alexander Monro, M.D.,* Edinburgh: Charles Elliot, 1781.
4. Duncan, A.: *An Account of the Life, Writings, and Character of the late Dr. Alexander Monro Secundus,* Delivered as the Harveian Oration at Edinburgh for the Year 1818, National Library of Medicine Pamphlet, Vol. 5523, 1818.
5. Wright-St. Clair, R. E.: *Doctors Monro: A Medical Saga,* 190 pp, London: Wellcome Historical Medical Library, 1964.

Composite by G. Bako

S. A. Tissot (1728-1797)

SIMON-ANDRÉ-DAVID TISSOT was born in Waatlande, Switzerland, studied medicine in Geneva and Montpellier, and graduated MD in 1749.[1] He settled in Lausanne, where his time was divided between practice and writing. In 1766, Tissot rose to the professorship of medicine in the college. His medical monographs include discussions on smallpox and inoculation, epilepsy, nervous diseases, catalepsy and migraine, and bilious fevers. The English titles to his popular treatises, which held great appeal and were translated into several languages, are: *On the Disorders of People of Fashion; On*

Diseases Incidental to Literary and Sedentary Persons; On Onanism: or, A Treatise Upon the Disorders Produced by Masturbation: or, The Effects of Secret and Excessive Venery; and a family medical guide, *Advice to the People in General, with Regard to Their Health.* In the discussion of diseases incidental to literary and sedentary persons, he mentioned the influence of cerebration upon digestion and described a patient of Van Swieten who had suffered an acute attack of gout following "the application of the mind."[2]

Daily observation proves the force of the mind's action upon the stomach; and this, every man has an opportunity of experiencing in himself; for the more intensely any man thinks, and the more strongly he exerts the reflecting powers of the mind, his more slowly and with the greater difficulty, *coeteris paribus,* does he digest what he eats; and, on the other hand, the freer a man's mind is from reflexion, the more readily and the better he digests.

The night air is so unfavourable to study, that the celebrated Van Swieten knew a gouty man, in whom the slightest application of mind, and even the reading of a letter after sun-set, occasioned a fit of the gout.

In his treatise on onanism, Tissot describes dire physical and mental effects of masturbation and of secret and excessive venery. Male and female were equally culpable; several examples of gout were attributed to the practice. The following case report is illustrative of general disaster.[3]

L.D.—was by profession a watchmaker; he had lived prudently, and had enjoyed a good state of health, till he was about seventeen years of age; at this period he gave himself up to masturbation, which he repeated every day, sometimes even to the third time, and the ejaculation was always preceded and followed by a slight insensibility. . . . A year had not elapsed, before he began to feel a great weakness after every act: . . . and the repetition of his crime became every day more frequent, till such time as he was in a state which gave no reason to apprehend his death.

Every one, who addicts himself to this odious and criminal habit, is not so cruelly punished: but there are none who are not in some degree afflicted. . . . The ills, which I have the most frequently seen, are, first, a total disorder of the stomach. . . . Secondly, a weakness in the organs of respiration, from which follow dry coughs, almost always hoarseness, weakness of the voice, and shortness of breath upon the least extraordinary exercise.

Tissot's counsel to country folk unable to obtain medical assistance was his greatest prepared contribution. He accepted the axiom that Nature cures disease and that the mildest, simplest, and least hazardous remedies would best assist Her. In the preface he advanced the purpose of filling the obvious void.[4]

Unfeignedly affected with the unhappy Situation of the poor Sick in Country Places in Switzerland, where they are lost from a Scarcity of the best Assistance, and from a fatal Superfluity of the worst, my sole Purpose in writing this Treatise has been to serve, and to comfort them. I had intended it only for a small Extent of Country, with a moderate Number of Inhabitants; and was greatly surprized to find, that within five or six Months after its Publication, it was become one of the most extensively published Books in Europe.
. . . . that it was my original Purpose to oppose the Errors incurred in Country Places, in the Treatment of acute Diseases; and to display the best Method of conducting such, as do not admit of waiting for the Arrival of distant Succour; or of removing the Patients to Cities, or large Towns . . . but then there are both Time and Convenience to convey the Patients within the Reach of better Advice; or for procuring them the Attendance of the best Advisers, at their own Places of Residence.

Tissot left Lausanne for three years to serve as professor in Pavia; during his sojourn in Italy he enjoyed an audience with Pope Pius VI. He was a friend of von Haller, a corresponding member of the Royal Society of London, a member of the Medical and Philosophical Society of Basel, a member of the Oeconomical Society of Bern, and a member of the Society of Experimental Physiology of Rotterdam.

1. Bayle, A. L., and Thillaye, J.: "S.A.D. Tissot," in *Medical Biographies* (Fr), Paris: A. Delahays, 1855, vol 2, pp 532-534.
2. Tissot, S. A.: *Three Essays* (Fr), F. B. Lee; M. Danes; and A. Hume (trans.), Dublin: J. Williams, 1772.
3. Tissot, S. A.: *Onanism* (Fr), A. Hume (trans.), London: J. Pridden, 1766.
4. Tissot, S. A.: *Advice to the People in General, with Regard to Their Health* (Fr), J. Kirkpatrick (trans.), London: T. Becket & P. A. De Hondt, 1765.

Composite by G. Bako

John Redman (1722-1808)

JOHN REDMAN, preceptor of Morgan, Rush, and others, and the first president of the College of Physicians of Philadelphia, waged a relentless campaign in support of inoculation against smallpox in the generation preceding Jenner's observations on the value of cowpox vaccine. Following an apprenticeship with Mr. John Kearsley, Redman practiced in Bermuda for several years. Subsequently, he pursued postgraduate work in Edinburgh with Monroe *primus,* in London at Guy's Hospital, and in Paris where he attended lectures and dissections. At the age of 26, the MD, with honors, was granted by the University of Leyden upon receipt of the inaugural dissertation "De abortu," composed in Latin and dedicated to William Allen and John Kearsley.[1]

Redman returned to Philadelphia, one of the best educated physicians in America in the 18th century, to practice surgery and midwifery as a staff member of the Pennsylvania Hospital. His delicate health, however, proved a major handicap, and he found the pursuit of physic more acceptable. His practice was based upon the tenets of Sydenham, while his principles in medical management closely followed the teaching of Boerhaave, whose fame in Leyden lingered during Redman's student days in Holland. He purged, bled, and administered mercury liberally, believing that stronger medicines were necessary, especially for the treatment of the sick in the Colonies than for comparable maladies in Europe.

The defense of inoculation against smallpox was printed in 1760 as a letter. It was prepared to counter the sentiment against inoculation, since many believed prevention to be as hazardous and debilitating as the disease. Although the identification is not absolute, the initials "J.R." at the end are believed to be those of John Redman. The introductory paragraphs remove the prevailing secrecy of preparation for inoculation and provide quantitative directions for the purge, containing calomel, sulfur, and antimony, and the proper time for bleeding. The letter concludes with a challenge.[2]

As I had used my own Method to some Scores of Patients, before I was informed of theirs, and with at least equal Success, I have seen no Reason yet to alter it. If you see fit to communicate this to any of your Friends here or abroad, or to the Public, and by that Means the important Affair of Inoculation may be promoted, it will give me much Pleasure, and for which I desire no greater Reward, than that they would communicate as freely as they receive. . . . I took my Hints chiefly from Boerhaave and Hillary, and should have before this Time made them more public, but I wanted to confirm them by a proper Number of Observations in my own Practice, and also was in Hopes some of those, who declared themselves possessed of a grand Secret, would have been generous enough to divulge it for the Benefit of Mankind; not knowing till lately how much better it might be than my Method above specified. But I have not failed to communicate it freely, where I had a proper Opportunity, and by that Means there are some practising it in different Parts of this and other Provinces, with amazing Success on great Numbers. Please to accept this as a Token of the sincere Regards of

Your much obliged Friend, and humble Servant,

J.R.

The letter is followed by an uninitialed postscript, almost as long as the letter, which provides a more interesting example of Redman's medical prose.[2]

If any Thing I have said may contribute to the general Good of Mankind, or the Credit of the Profession, or prompt any to make public their Improvements in Inoculation, &c. I have obtained my End. . . . Recollect, how when you have come to inoculate a Child, the distressed Parent has met you bathed in Tears, dreading the Hand that is to sow the Seeds of Disease (so often fatal) in the Flesh of her tender Infant, shewing by her Aspect that nothing but absolute Necessity, and the almost certain Persuasion of Success, could have prevailed on her to do what her Conscience hardly allows. See with what Anxiety and Care she overcomes her own Tenderness, in forcing down the Antidote, and implicity follows every Direction that has a Promise of Success annexed. And when the pretty Babe begins to feel the dreaded Poison operate, how does every Look, every Word, every Action call on you for Comfort. But when the eruptive Fever is finished, and the promised Hopes confirmed, by a kindly Eruption of so few Pustules, that neither Life, Health, or Beauty are in Danger, but especially when the happy Crisis is performed, and the last well adapted Dose is administered, how does her Eyes and Tongue meet you with Gratitude, looking on you, under Providence, as the Preserver of her beloved Infant, now blessing the Hand and Heart she once thought almost cruel.

By the age of 40, Redman was finally established in Philadelphia medicine. Although he never accepted more than two apprentices at a time, the selection was unexcelled for his day and included John Morgan, founder of the first medical school in North America; Benjamin Rush and William Shippen, clinicians of eminence; Caspar Wistar, the anatomist; and John Redman Coxe, his grandson and founder of medical journalism in Pennsylvania. By the age of 50, Redman had passed his peak of performance and was reconciled to a slackening of pace, precipitated by a long bout of rheumatism and a subdiaphragmatic abscess which ruptured into the bronchial tree. However, his spirit of service and the respect that he enjoyed from students, apprentices, and patients remained. He gave liberally to the poor, enjoyed an enviable reputation for his ministrations at the bedside, and displayed an exemplary compassion for the ill. Redman served as a consulant to the Pennsylvania Hospital, as a trustee of the College of New Jersey (Princeton) and the College of Philadelphia, which became the University of Penn-

sylvania later in the century.[3] He was not a prolific writer. In addition to his graduation thesis and a few letters,[4] the only scientific contribution was a description of the yellow fever epidemic of 1762; it was based upon his notes that formed an address to the College of Physicians in 1793, at the time of a subsequent epidemic, and was published in 1865 by the college. This reflects the best scientific management of a mortal malady two centuries ago.[5]

Thus, gentlemen, have I endeavoured to give you a concise and plain narrative of the disease then imported and prevailing among us, and our generall mode of treating it, in the best manner I could from recollection, without attempting to theorize upon it. But a plain inference from our manner of encountering it is, that whatever might be the specific quality of the morbid cause, its effects were a stagnation and corruption of the bile and the contents of all the abdominal glands, dissolving the blood and other fluids, and thereby depraving and debilitating all the functions of life, and rendering them unfit and unable to preserve it, and that our chief curative intentions were to discharge the morbid matter as fast as possible, first by the prima via, and then by the pores of the skin and urinary passages, at the same time using such medicines as tended to correct any acrimony in the fluids, resist their effects, and strengthen the whole habit for their expulsion, and with such kind of nutriment as was adapted to the same purpose, or to restore strength to the debilitated powers after the disease was terminated.

A man of integrity, whose manners were old-fashioned for this time, Redman was a devout Christian, unashamed of his faith. He served as elder in the Presbyterian Church, which must have soothed his sorrows caused by the death of two sons in infancy, and the fleeing of his elder daughter, wife of Daniel Coxe, one of the King's counselors, to England during the War of Independence. Her subsequent return to America did not occur until shortly before the death of her parents.

1. Redman, J.: *Dissertatio Medica Inauguralis de Abortu*, Leyden, 1748.
2. Correspondence, *Penn Gaz*, July 3, 1760.
3. Coxe, J. R.: Memoirs of the Life and Character of John Redman, M.D. *Phila Med Museum* 5:49-56, 1808.
4. Middleton, W. S.: John Redman, *Ann Med Hist* 8: 213-223, 1926.
5. Redman, J.: *An Account of the Yellow Fever*, Philadelphia: College of Physicians, 1865.

Composite by G. Bako

John Morgan (1735-1789)

JOHN MORGAN, the principal physician in the founding of the first medical school in the colonies, the American Philosophical Society, and the College of Physicians of Philadelphia, should also be remembered for his critical document on medical education and medical practice, and for his efforts to implement an inadequate medical department in the Revolutionary Army. Each endeavor was notable and successful, except for the military appointment.

The Morgans of Philadelphia were affluent Quakers; Evan, father of John, owed his prosperity to real estate and iron.[1] Young Morgan attended the Nottingham School under the classical scholar, Reverend Mr. Finley, and, through industry and ability, qualified in advanced standing for the Academy and the College of Philadelphia. His studies in liberal arts were complemented by a six-year apprenticeship with Dr. John Redman, the last year being spent as apothecary to the Pennsylvania Hospital; there he learned the favorite prescriptions of many of the physicians of Philadelphia. The bachelor of arts degree was

granted with the first graduating class of 1757. Immediately following graduation Morgan served the British with distinction in the French and Indian War, acquiring firsthand knowledge of military medicine and surgery and valuable experience for his tour of duty as surgeon-general in the War of the Revolution.

A long preceptorship, practice in compounding at the apothecary shop, and service with the troops seemed to have been sufficient for him to enter medical practice in civilian life. Before accepting this responsibility, however, Morgan spent five years with several of the great masters of medicine in Europe. A family friendship with Benjamin Franklin gave him easy access to prominent professional and lay persons in London and on the Continent. He learned anatomical dissection from the Hunters in London and clinical medicine from Cullen and the Monros in Edinburgh. Morgan graduated MD from Edinburgh in 1763, presenting a thesis in Latin on pus formation *De puopoiesi,* which advanced the theory that purulence began in the blood vessels. Building on the warm friendship with Cullen, and having established a reputation as a medical scientist, Morgan studied anatomy under Sue in Paris, then visited Switzerland and Italy. He enjoyed an audience with the Pope in Rome, with Morgagni in Padua, and with Voltaire in France. Superior medical training and a wide acquaintanceship with persons of influence made him a logical candidate for outstanding Continental honors, which included licentiate of the Royal College of Physicians of Edinburgh and London, Fellow in the Royal Society of London, member of the Belles-Lettres Society of Rome, and associate in the Royal Academy of Surgery in Paris.

Communication with America had been maintained while Morgan was in Europe. When he returned in 1765, he brought his memorable document on medical education, *A Discourse Upon the Institution of Medical Schools in America,* a plea for an institution of formal medical training in Philadelphia, heavily influenced by the Edinburgh system. Having given lectures in anatomy since 1762, William Shippen, Jr., found it was natural for him to join Morgan in planning the program. Shippen was less well trained than Morgan and quite different in personality, but the joint leadership prevailed in the formative years. Later, however, as a schism grew, suspicion and hatred separated the two physicians who had so much in common academically.

The reception of the proposals by the Board of Trustees of the College of Philadelphia (which was incorporated as the University of Pennsylvania in 1791) resulted in the election of Morgan as professor of the theory and practice of physic on May 3, 1765. Later in the month he delivered his *Discourse* as the Inaugural Address at the commencement of the College. The medical school of the College of Philadelphia began instruction on Nov 14, 1765, with a course on anatomy given by Shippen. Morgan's lectures, later published as *Materia Medica with Some Useful Observations on Medicine and the Proper Manner of Conducting the Study of Physic,* began the following week. The development of the motif by Morgan does not follow in sequence, and in selecting excerpts for this essay, the preparation for medicine is followed by a discussion of the establishment of a medical library and of professional practice by physicians, surgeons, and apothecaries, returning finally to the "Preface," in which he discussed the need of leisure time for professors to prepare lectures, and the separation of professional fees from the cost of dispensing of drugs.[2]

It will not be improper however to observe here, that young men ought to come well prepared for the study of Medicine, by having their minds enriched with all the aids they can receive from the languages, and the liberal arts. Latin and Greek are very necessary to be known by a Physician. The latter contains the rich original treasures of ancient medical science, and of the first parents of the healing arts. The former contains all the wealth of more modern literature. It is the vehicle of knowledge in which the learned men of every nation in Europe choose to convey their sentiments, and communicate their discoveries to the world.

The establishment of a medical library in this college would prove another benefit to students,

and tend likewise to influence their resort hither. Proper means may possibly be suggested to accomplish this, without any great additional charge to the college. . . . Perhaps the physicians of Philadelphia, touched with generous sentiments of regard for the rising generation and the manifest advantages accruing to the college thereby, would spare some useful books, or contribute somewhat as a foundation on which we might begin.

Whilst Medicine from the greatness of its object, the preservation of the species, is one of the most useful subjects of knowledge to a state, and at the same time one of the most expensive and difficult; we must regret that the very different employment of a Physician, Surgeon, and Apothecary, should be promiscuously followed by any one man, however great his abilities. They certainly require very different talents.

If Physic, Surgery, and Pharmacy were in different hands, practitioners would then enjoy much more satisfaction in practice. They would commonly be less burdened with an over hurry of business, and have an opportunity of studying the cases of the sick at more leisure. Would not this tend to the more speedy relief of diseases and the perfection of medical science, as every Physician would have more time by study, observation, and experience united, to cultivate that knowledge which is the only foundation of practice?

The paying of a physician for attendance and the apothecary for his Medicines apart, is certainly the most eligible mode of practice, both to patient and practitioner. The apothecary, then, who is not obliged to spend his time in visiting patients, can afford to make up medicines at a reasonable price and it is as desirable as just in itself that patients should allow fees for attendance—whatever it may be thought to deserve.

They ought to know what it is they really pay for their medicine and what for medical advice and attendance.

The next notable event in Morgan's life, a display of patriotism which ended in temporary disgrace, took place in 1775. He was appointed by the Continental Congress to fill a recent vacancy and reported to General George Washington in Cambridge as director-general and physician in chief to the General Hospital of the Army. The medical department was disorganized, irresponsible, and grossly inadequate in supplies and funds. Morgan's knowledge of troops in the field, his ability to organize, and his standing in the profession should have allowed him to accomplish many needed reforms, to provide military hospitals for the sick, sanitary measures for the combatant, and medical care for the wounded. The intrigues, promulgated by many but particularly by Shippen, threatened substantial accomplishments and led to his dismissal by Congress early in 1777. The act was anticipated, inasmuch as Morgan had prepared his *Vindication* in rebuttal to charges against his administrative actions. The well prepared defense discloses the sad state of all major features of the medical department under the War Office. In the prefatory remarks in the "Prolegomenon," he begins:[3]

That a mean and *invidious* set of men have looked upon my elevation . . . with an *evil eye,* and long have been concerting *my removal,* is a matter of which I have too substantial proof to doubt: That the unwearied pains I have taken to support economy, regularity and order, so far as they had been introduced into the department, before it came under my management; to introduce, recommend and inforce them, where wanting; and to oppose and reform abuses that were creeping, or had already crept into it, from the infancy of the service, were the root of the enmity which sprung up against my proceedings, are no less certain.

Morgan returned to Philadelphia in 1779 to receive his vindication from Congress, but his great years were ended. He did not resume his previous assignments at the medical school and, in 1783, resigned his senior medical post at the Pennsylvania Hospital. The failure to claim the position of leadership in Philadelphia can be attributed in part to his mistreatment by Congress, coupled with ill health. His personal papers were destroyed during the war and the two documents referred to above remain his only published communications of note. Minor publications include *Four Dissertations, on the Reciprocal Advantages of a Perpetual Union Between Great-Britain and Her American Colonies,*[4] *A Recommendation of Inoculation, According to Baron Dimsdale's Method,*[5] and a description for the preparation of anatomical specimens by corrosion. Morgan's reputation as an eminent Philadelphian and a preeminent physician and teacher in the society of learned men of medicine remains firm through the scholarly efforts of the recent full-scale biography by Bell.[1]

1. Bell, W. J., Jr.: *John Morgan: Continental Doctor,* Philadelphia: University of Pennsylvania Press, 1965.
2. Morgan, J.: *A Discourse Upon the Institution of Medical Schools in America,* Philadelphia: W. Bradford, 1965.
3. Morgan, J.: *A Vindication of His Public Character in the Station of Director-General of the Military Hospitals, and Physician in Chief to the American Army,* Boston, Powars & Willis, 1777.
4. Morgan, J.: *Four Dissertations, on the Reciprocal Advantages of a Perpetual Union Between Great-Britain and Her American Colonies,* Philadelphia: W. & T. Bradford, 1766.
5. Morgan, J.: *A Recommendation of Inoculation According to Baron Dimsdale's Method,* Boston: J. Gill, 1776.

Ephraim McDowell (1771-1830)

EPHRAIM McDOWELL, frontier physician endowed with resolute courage and a sturdy body, was the first to achieve success in removing a large ovarian cyst. Others had aspirated the cystic contents for alleviation of symptoms, but any gain was temporary and a cure was possible only by complete extirpation of the diseased tissue. McDowell excised a large ovarion cyst, followed the patient through an uneventful convalescence, and was outlived by the patient by a score of years. The operation was performed in 1809 in McDowell's office in Danville, Ky., the community to which he came with his parents as a child.

Ephraim was born in Augusta County, later named Rockbridge County, in Virginia, of Samuel and Mary McClung McDowell. The McDowell ancestors had migrated from Scotland by way of Northern Ireland.[1] Samuel McDowell was successively a member of the general assembly of Virginia, a colonel of the militia during the Revolutionary War, and a judge of a court of common law in Kentucky. In the new state he was an influential citizen and comfortable financially.[2] After early schooling in Kentucky, Ephraim returned to Virginia to serve an apprenticeship with Dr. Alexander Humphreys of Staunton, a loyal alumnus of the medical school in Edinburgh. Humphreys continued the tradition of Edinburgh in apprenticeship and taught anatomy and surgery by dissection rather than by placing full faith in books. Ephraim, with the Scottish blood of his ancestors, followed the example set by his teacher, chose Edinburgh for formal medical training, and arrived during the 1792-93 session. Instead of following the recommended curriculum of medical lectures, he studied chemistry, enrolled in a private course with John Bell, and left Edinburgh without the MD degree. This deficiency did not deter him from a rich professional career in the Ohio River Valley, begun at the age of 24. When well established in practice in Danville, he married Sarah Shelby, daughter of the first governor of Kentucky. Six children were born to this union.

It was necessary in the frontier for the physician to make long rides on horseback to visit the sick. At that time, chloroform and ether as general anesthetics had not yet been discovered; antisepsis and the concept of bacterial pathogenesis of diseases were further in the future. The bladder had been explored for the removal of stones, caesarean section had been performed successfully, but surgical entrance into the abdominal cavity was considered an invitation to disaster. The first ovariotomy in recorded history was performed on Mrs. Jane Todd Crawford, after McDowell had been in practice 14 years. The operation was repeated in 1813 and again in 1816. McDowell rode on horseback to visit Mrs. Crawford, who, at the age of 47, had thought herself pregnant. The inclination of the tumor to one side and an empty uterus at vaginal examination convinced McDowell that it must be an enlarged ovarion cyst.[3]

Having never seen so large a substance extracted, nor heard of an attempt, or success attending any operation, such as this required, I gave to the unhappy woman information of her dangerous situation. She appeared willing to undergo an experiment, which I promised to perform if she would come to Danville, (the town where I live) a distance of sixty miles from her place of residence. This appeared almost impracticable by any,, even the most favourable conveyance, though she performed the journey in a few days on horseback. With the assistance of my nephew and colleague, James M'Dowell, MD, I commenced the operation, which was concluded as follows: Having placed her on a table of the ordinary height, on her back, and removed all her dressing which might in any way impede the operation, I made an incision about three inches from the musculus rectus abdominis, on the left side, continuing the same nine inches in length, parallel with the fibres of the above named muscle, extending into the cavity of the abdomen, the parietes of which were a good deal contused, which we ascribed to the resting of the tumor on the horn of the saddle during her journey. The tumor then appeared full in view, but was so large that we could not take it away entire. We put a strong ligature around the fallopian tube near to the uterus; we then cut open the tumor, which was the ovarium and fimbrious part of the fallopian tube very much enlarged. We took out fifteen pounds of a dirty, gelatinous looking substance. After which we cut through the fallopian tube, and extracted the sack, which weighed seven pounds and one half. As soon as the external opening was made, the intestines rushed out upon the table; and so completely was the abdomen filled by the tumor, that they could not be replaced during the operation, which was terminated in about twenty-five minutes. We then turned her upon her left side, so as to permit the blood to escape; after which we closed the external opening with the interrupted suture, leaving out, at the lower end of the incision, the ligature which surrounded the fallopian tube. Between every two stitches we put a strip of adhesive plaster, which, by keeping the parts in contact, hastened the healing of the incision. . . . In five days I visited her, and much to my astonishment found her engaged in making up her bed. I gave her particular caution for the future; and in twenty-five days, she returned home as she came, in good health, which she continues to enjoy.

The operation was a notable achievement, but McDowell was neither an eager nor a prolific writer. Only two scientific communications were published. The account of his first three cases appeared eight years after the operation on Mrs. Crawford. The manuscript was sent first to John Bell, who was away from Scotland at the time. It was passed on, by default, to Bell''s assistant, John Lizars. Another copy of the report was forwarded to Philip Physick in Philadelphia, who failed to acknowledge its receipt. On the third try it was reviewed and accepted for publication in 1817 by Thomas C. James, Professor of Midwifery of Philadelphia, and editor of the *Eclectic Repertory and Analytical Review, Medical and Philosophical*. The first communication was followed by a second one in 1819, with a description of two additional cases. McDowell took this opportunity to respond to some of the bitter criticisms that had been directed against him for the risk that he had taken and for the conclusions drawn from the advantages of surgical extirpation over aspiration.[4] Neither report was widely read, and the operative procedure received slow reception by the medical profession. Even in America, Nathan Smith of Vermont performed a similar operation in 1821, ignorant of the earlier achievements of the Kentuckian.

Ephraim McDowell was recognized as the outstanding general surgeon west of the Atlantic seaboard. His operative skill was based upon a sound knowledge of anatomy and a benevolence for those who needed his help. It is believed that he performed thirteen ovariotomies, with eight recoveries, plus a number of lithotomies and herniotomies. He removed a stone from James K. Polk, later President of the United States. He was officially recognized by the Medical Society of Philadelphia in 1807 with a diploma and by the University of Maryland with an honorary MD degree in 1825. A monument was erected to him in Danville in 1879, and a commemorative stamp was issued by the United States Postal Department in December, 1959.

1. Gross, S. D.: *Lives of Eminent American Physicians and Surgeons of the Nineteenth Century*, Philadelphia: Lindsay & Blakiston, 1861, pp 207-230.

2. Horine, E. F.: The Stagesetting for Ephraim McDowell, 1771-1830, *Bull Hist Med* 24:149-160 (March-April) 1950.

3. McDowell, E.: Three Cases of Extirpation of Diseased Ovaria, *Electric Repertory, & Analyt Rev* 7:242-244, 1817.

4. McDowell, E.: Observations on Diseased Ovaria, *Eclectric Repertory, & Analyt Rev* 9:546-553, 1819.

Los Angeles County Medical Library

Thomas Percival (1740-1804)

THE CODE OF ETHICS adopted by the American Medical Association in 1847 was attributed officially to Thomas Percival of Manchester, who, in 1803, published his *Medical Ethics; or, a Code of Institutes and Precepts, Adapted to the Professional Conduct of Physicians and Surgeons*.[1] Although the AMA Code was revised several times and the format changed in the following century, the rules of ethical conduct of the physician remain those postulated by the English codist.

Percival was born near Warrington, Lancashire. His parents died when he was young, and his early care and educational guidance was assumed by his eldest sister; however, his maturing interests in medicine were directed both by the legacy and library of his father's brother, a practicing physician.[2] As a dissenter, Percival was expelled from Oxford and Cambridge; thus, after training in Warrington, he proceeded to the University of Edinburgh for the study of physic. After spending a year in London, where he was elected a Fellow of the Royal Society, he completed his medical studies at Leyden and took the degree at the age of 24, presenting a thesis in Latin, *De frigore,* a philosophical and experimental study of cold.

Percival practiced for two years in his home town and then moved to Manchester; there he soon made a reputation by contributing medical, philosophical, and experimental essays to various periodicals, introducing cod liver oil into the practice of medicine, serving as staff physician to the Manchester Infirmary, and participating in the founding of the Literary and Philosophical Society of that city. A scholar in science, literature, and ethics, he added to each area of intellectual activity, to wit, his *Philosophical, Medical, and Experimental Essays,*[3] a book of tales for children entitled *A Father's Instructions,*[4] and the Medical *Ethics.*[1] In the overlapping fields of social conscience such as urban responsibility, vital statistics, and environmental health, he was responsible for the establishment of accurate and detailed bills of mortality in Manchester; he also crusaded for proper sanitation, advocated the establishment of public baths and cleanliness in lodging houses, and defined a healthy environment for factory workers.

The first volume of *Essays Medical and Experimental*[5] appeared in 1767, offering a learned discussion entitled "The Empiric; or, Arguments Against the Use of Theory and Reasoning in Physic," and countering in a second essay with the unveiled title "The Dogmatic; or, Arguments for the Use of Theory and Reasoning in Physic." Percival equated empiricism with dogmatism, meanwhile extracting the best from each philosophy. In support of the empiricist, Percival came to his defense as follows.[5]

It is evident then that THEORY is absurd and fallacious, always useless, and often in the highest degree pernicious. The annals of medicine afford the most striking proof, that it hath in all ages been the bane and disgrace of the healing art. And as it favours the indolence, flatters the vanity, and gratifies the curiosity of man, ever inquisitive after causes, I fear the passion for it will not be easily suppressed amongst the professors of medicine. The invention of an hypothesis is a work of no difficulty to a lively imagination; and the fiction by its tinsel glitter, never fails to dazzle the ignorant and vulgar. But to watch with close attention the operations of nature, to treasure up a store of useful facts, to learn by accurate observations the diagnostics of diseases, and by unbiased experience, the true method of cure, requires unwearied labour, assiduity, and patience, at the same time that it admits of no pompous display of wit or knowledge.

But he [the dogmatist] is not wedded to systems, nor anxiously bent upon explaining every phenomenon which occurs in the animal frame. He diligently avails himself indeed of all the assistances with which philosophy furnishes the healing art; but sensible of its imperfection, he ingenuously acknowledges that in diseases there are numberless anomalous symptoms, that the operation of medicines is often irregular and uncertain, and that even in the healthy body there are many appearances, which are inexplicable to the wisest and most experienced of the faculty. But where his theory is deficient, his practice is proportionately more cautious and reserved. If experience fails him, he calls in analogy to his aid; and judges it better to pursue a doubtful path, than to stand still in uncertainty and suspense. In the most intricate cases, however, he is not totally without a clue: Reason and philosophy are his guides; and under such direction, there is at least a probability that he will not mistake his course. And by thus treading occasionally in unbeaten tracks, he enlarges the boundaries of science in general, and adds new discoveries to the art of medicine. In a word, the Rationalist has every advantage which the Empiric can boast, from reading, observation, and practice, accompanied with superior knowledge, understanding, and judgment.

One of Percival's most delightful literary efforts was prepared for reading to his children as he sought leisure in the intimate bonds of his family. This small book was entitled *A Father's Instructions; Consisting of Moral Tales, Fables, and Reflections. Designed to Promote the Love of Virtue, a Taste for Knowledge, and an Early Acquaintance With the Works of Nature.* The narrations were designed to ". . . refine the feelings of the heart, and to inspire the mind with the love of moral excellence . . . to awaken curiosity, to excite the spirit of in-quiry . . . to promote a more early ac-quaintance with the use of words and idi-oms."[4] The fable selected for this essay concerned the governing of passions by rea-son and introduced a contemporary Ameri-can and correspondent of Percival's, then well known to London.[4]

Sophron and Alexis had frequently heard Euphronius mention the experiment of stilling the waves with oil, made by his friend Doctor Franklin. They were impatient to repeat it; and a brisk wind proving favourable to the trial, they hastened, one evening, to a sheet of water in the pleasure grounds of Eugenio, near Hart-Hill. The oil was scattered upon the pool, and spread itself instantly on all sides, calming the whole surface of the water, and reflecting the most beautiful colours. Elated with success, the youth returned to Euphronius, to inquire the cause of such a wonderful appearance. He informed them that the wind blowing upon water which is covered with a coat of oil, slides over the surface of it, and produces no friction that can raise a wave. But this curious philosophical fact, said he, suggests a most important moral reflection. When you suffer yourselves to be ruffled by pas-sion, your minds resemble the *puddle in a storm*. But reason, if you hearken to her voice, will then, like oil poured upon the water, calm the turbu-lence within you, and restore you to serenity and peace.

Achieving higher and higher goals, Per-cival's last and best work was his *Medical Ethics,* which appeared first in a private edi-tion in 1794, entitled *Medical Jurispru-dence.* It was circulated, criticized, and amended. The more familiar term was chosen for the first public edition of 1803. A second edition with annotations was pub-lished in 1827; the third edition appeared in 1849, after the AMA Code had been adopted. The 1803 edition covered 114 pages plus appendix; the contents were pre-sented in four sections. The first discussed professional conduct relative to hospitals; then in succession followed professional conduct in private or general practice, con-duct of physicians to apothecaries, conclud-ing with professional duties which require a knowledge of law. Several of the provisions have been described by Leake as procedures of etiquette among professionals.[2] Others re-flect the moral fiber deep within the physi-cian's mind (soul), the responsible indi-vidual who keeps in trust the health and welfare of his patients, holding in confidence secrets and always aware of the goal of practice—the restoration of the physical and mental well-being of his patients.

The following excerpts are illustrative, individually comprehensive, and exemplary only of the unabridged *Code.* They mention expression of tenderness by the physician, respect for feelings and emotions of pa-tients, discrimination between medical and surgical patients, need of consultation, avoidance of gloomy prognosis, treatment of clergymen gratis, avoidance of quack medicine and secret remedies, collection of fees from affluent patients, and compilation of accurate clinical records. If one were to compare the present AMA Code,[6] the source would be readily apparent.[1]

I. HOSPITAL PHYSICIANS and SURGEONS should minister to the sick, with due impressions of the importance of their office, reflecting that the ease, the health, and the lives of those committed to their charge depend on their skill, attention and fidelity. They should study, also, in their de-portment, so to unite *tenderness* with *steadiness,* and *condescension* with *authority,* as to inspire the minds of their patients with gratitude, respect and confidence.

III. The *feelings* and *emotions* of the patients, under critical circumstances, require to be known and to be attended to, no less than the symptoms of their diseases. . . . Even the *prejudices* of the sick are not to be contemned, or opposed with harshness.

XI. A proper *discrimination* being established in all hospitals between the *medical* and *chirurgi-cal* cases, it should be faithfully adhered to, by the physicians and surgeons, on the admission of patients.

XVIII. The harmonious intercourse, which has been recommended to the gentlemen of the faculty, will naturally produce *frequent consulta-tions,* viz. of the physicians on medical cases, of the surgeons on chirurgical cases.

Chapter II, III. A physician should not be forward to make gloomy prognostications; be-cause they savour of empiricism, by magnifying the importance of his services in the treatment or cure of the disease. But he should not fail, on proper occasions, to give to the friends of the patient, timely notice of danger, when it really occurs, and even to the patient himself, if absolutely necessary.

VI. In large and opulent towns, the *distinction* between the *provinces* of *physic* and *surgery* should be steadily maintained.

XVIII. Clergymen, who experience the *res augusta domi,* should be visited gratuitously by the faculty.

XXI. The use of *quack medicines* should be discouraged by the faculty, as disgraceful to the profession, injurious to the health, and often destructive even of life.

XXII. No physician or surgeon should dispense a secret *nostrum,* whether it be his invention, or exclusive property.

XXV. A wealthy physician should not give advice *gratis* to the affluent; because it is an injury to his professional brethren. The office of physician can never be supported but as a lucrative one; and it is defrauding, in some degree, the common funds for its support, when fees are dispensed with, which might justly be claimed.

XXVIII. At the close of every interesting and important case, especially when it hath terminated fatally, a physician should trace back, in calm reflection, all the steps which he had taken in the treatment of it. This review of the origin, progress, and conclusion of the malady; of the whole curative plan pursued; and of the particular operation of the several remedies employed, as well as of the doses and periods of time in which they were administered, will furnish the most authentic documents, on which individual experience can be formed.

1. Percival, T.: *Medical Ethics; or, a Code of Institutes and Precepts, Adapted to the Professional Conduct of Physicians and Surgeons,* Manchester: S. Russell, 1803.

2. Leake, C. D.: *Percival's Medical Ethics,* Baltimore: Williams & Wilkins, 1927.

3. Percival, T.: *Philosophical, Medical, and Experimental Essays,* London: J. Johnson, 1776.

4. Percival, T.: *A Father's Instructions; Consisting of Moral Tales, Fables, and Reflections,* London: W. Osborne, T. Griffin, and H. and G. Mozley, 1798.

5. Percival, T.: *Essays Medical and Experimental,* London: J. Johnson, 1767.

6. "Principles of Medical Ethics," in *Opinions and Reports, 1964,* JUDICIAL COUNCIL, Chicago: American Medical Association, 1964.

Joseph Black (1728-1799)

THE MODERN DOCTRINE OF THE EXCHANGE OF GASES in respiration began with the discovery of oxygen by Scheele, Priestley, and Lavoisier, and the rediscovery of carbon dioxide by Joseph Black. Although these contributions are chemical in nature, each scientist, except Scheele, had received medical training. Black, in addition to his contributions to chemistry and medicine, is credited with major discoveries in physics, especially for his discussions of "specific heat," "capacity for heat," and "latent heat."

Joseph Black, of Scottish descent, was born at Bordeaux, France, in 1728, where

National Library of Medicine

his father, a native of Belfast, was a wine merchant.[1] Joseph spent some years in school in Ireland, then attended Glasgow University, and studied under Cullen. Black went to Edinburgh in 1750 for his medical studies. It was there that, as a medical student, while pondering the origin of kidney stones, he began his investigations on limestone and quicklime. The degree of medicine was taken in 1754. His thesis, prepared in Latin, on magnesia and the acid produced by food in the stomach, presaged the discovery of carbon dioxide.[2] The observations were clarified in the celebrated work, *Experiments upon Magnesia Alba, Quicklime, and Other Alcaline Substances.*[3] In 1756, Black succeeded Cullen at Glasgow, where he remained for ten years; when Cullen was appointed professor of medicine at Edinburgh, Black assumed the professorship of chemistry.

The phlogiston theory of Stahl had been accepted for a century without serious challenge, until the 1770's. Black's observations have been interpreted as the first step in the rejection of the then current explanation of oxidation and the proposal of the valid interpretation. Black reported that, when ordinary or mild lime was burned to form caustic lime, fixed air (carbon dioxide) escaped, with the resulting mass weighing less. He also stated that calcium carbonate is formed when fixed air is passed through a clear solution of lime water. Caustic lime, when combined with carbonic acid gas, forms mild lime. A short time later **Black** discovered that this particular type of air is present in the expired air of man and is also formed when charcoal is burned. He had rediscovered the *gas sylvestre* of van Helmont, whose observations had been made a hundred years earlier. Although fixed air was not particularly toxic, it was physiologically irrespirable.[4]

Quicklime, therefore, does not attract the air that is usually contained in common water, nor does it attract the whole of the mass of atmospherical air, as I have already observed.

I gave it the name of Fixed Air, for the reasons already mentioned, a term which was then common to denote any elastic matter, capable of entering into the composition of bodies, and of being condensed in them to a solid concrete state, by its chemical attraction for some of their constituent parts.

I fully intend to make their air [fixed air], and some other elastic fluids which frequently occur, the subject of serious study. . . . I had discovered that this particular kind of air, attracted by alkaline substances, is deadly to all animals that breath[e] it by the mouth and nostrils together; but that if the nostrils were kept shut, I was led to think that it might be breathed with safety. I found, for example, that when sparrows died in it in ten or eleven seconds, they would live in it for three or four minutes when the nostrils were shut by melted suet. And I convinced myself, that the change produced on wholesome air by breathing it, consisted chiefly, if not solely, in the conversion of part of it into fixed air. For I found, that by blowing through a pipe into lime-water, or a solution of caustic alkali, the lime was precipitated, and the alkali was rendered mild.

Black also discovered that "fixed air" escaped during fermentation.[4]

van Helmont says, that the *dunste,* or deadly vapour of burning charcoal, is the same gas silvestre; but this was also a random conjecture. He does not even say that it extinguishes flame; yet this was known to the chemists of his day. I had now the certain means of deciding the question, since, if the same, it must be fixed air. I made several indistinct experiments as soon as the conjecture occurred to my thoughts, but they were with little contrivance or accuracy. In the evening of the same day that I discovered that it was fixed air that escaped from fermenting liquors, I made an experiment which satisfied me. Unfixing the nozzle of a pair of chamber-bellows, I put a bit of charcoal, just red hot, into the wide end of it, and then quickly putting it into its place again, I plunged the pipe to the bottom of a phial, and forced the air very slowly through the charcoal, so as to maintain its combustion, but not produce a heat too suddenly for the phial to bear. When I judged that the air of the phial was completely vitiated, I poured lime-water into it, and had the pleasure of seeing it become milky in a moment.

I now admired van Helmont's sagacity, or his fortunate conjecture; and, for some years, I took it for granted that all those vapours formed in liquids in the vinous fermentation which extinguish flame, and are destructive of animal life, without irritating the lungs, or giving warning by their corrosive nature, are the gas silvestre of van Helmont, or fixed air.

In 1763, Black noted that, in the melting of ice, more heat was lost than was indicated by a thermometer and that, on the condensation of steam, an unexpected proportion of heat became apparent. The interpretations of the mechanism of these phenomena led to the discovery of latent heat or the absorption of heat when matter passed from solid to liquid and from the liquid to the gaseous state. The heat, having no appreciable effect on the surroundings, could not be recorded by a thermometer. A full account of this discovery was discussed in his lectures and was referred to in the communication published in the *Philosophical Transactions* for 1775.[5]

The third great discovery of Black was that which has been called the doctrine of "specific heat," but which he termed the "capacity" of bodies for heat. Different bodies contain different quantities of heat in the same volume or weight; furthermore, different quantities of heat are required to raise different bodies to the same sensible temperature. These doctrines of latent and specific heat are vital to the interpretation of combustion, calcination of metals, and respiration of animals, which, in the following two decades, Lavoisier deduced from the experiments of Priestley and Scheele upon oxygen, and of Cavendish on hydrogen.

Although Black studied medicine, the excursion into this discipline received scant notice in his biographies. It is natural that a chemist interested in alkaline salts would show some concern for bladder stones, a common affliction of his day. He speculated on the pathogenesis of stone formation and described means for ridding the body of bladder calculi.

Adam Smith, a close friend of Black's and author of *Wealth of Nations,* said, he "had less nonsense in his head than any man living."[6] Black remained in Edinburgh until his death in 1799—a physician and teacher whose observations in chemistry and physics contributed mightily to an understanding of the phenomena of vital gases and the mechanism of respiration.

1. Ramsay, W.: *The Life and Letters of Joseph Black,* London: Constable & Co., Ltd., 1918.

2. Black, J.: *Dissertatio Medica Inauguralis, De Humore Acido a Cibis Orto, et Magnesia Alba,* communicated by L. Dobbin, C. Brown, trans., *J Chem Educ* 12: 225-228 (May); 268-273 (June) 1935.

3. Black, J.: *Experiments upon Magnesia Alba, Quicklime, and Some Other Alcaline Substances,* Edinburgh: William Creech, 1782.

4. Black, J.: *Lectures on the Elements of Chemistry, Delivered in the University of Edinburgh,* vol II, Edinburgh: Mundell & Son, 1803.

5. Black, J.: The Supposed Effect of Boiling upon Water, in Disposing It To Freeze More Readily, Ascertained by Experiments, *Philos Trans London* 65:124-128, 1775.

6. Farber, E.: "Joseph Black," in *Great Chemists,* New York: Interscience Publishers, 1961, chap 16.

Joseph Priestley (1733-1804)

JOSEPH PRIESTLEY was born in 1733 a few miles from Leeds in Yorkshire, and died in exile in Northumberland, Pa., in 1804.[1] He isolated oxygen but did not "discover" it because of his bondage to the phlogiston doctrine. First honors went to Lavoisier by default. However, Priestley's investigations

in respiration constituted basic advances in general physiology, although he was neither a physician nor a physiologist. Like Stephen Hales, who measured the blood pressure in

Composite by G. Bako

a horse, Priestley's interests in physiology were avocational. Theology was the vocation of each, with one notable difference. Priestley moved from parish to parish bettering his position each time; whereas Hales remained a perpetual curate in one parish. Priestley was neither a University man nor an avowed scientist, but gained most of his livelihood as a minister, supplemented by royalties from his writing and assistance from his friends for scientific research.

There were two determining forces in Priestley's childhood that were evident throughout his active years. After Joseph's mother died when he was six years old, his father's sister took him into her home. The aunt was a Dissenter; her home was a haven for the dissenting clergy. (Priestley remained in the minority and spoke from the pulpit as a heterodox minister.) In grammar school, he made commendable progress in Latin, Greek, Hebrew, French, Italian, German and acquired some knowledge of

Chaldean, Syriac, and Arabic languages. He was a prolific reader and a prolific writer; most of his compositions dealt with theology, natural philosophy, and metaphysics.[2] Scientific presentations included a history of electricity, with original experiments which attracted world-wide interest, a history of optics, and diverse experiments in chemistry. Of particular interest to physicians are his observations on different kinds of air.

Priestley began his investigations in natural philosophy at Nantwich, Cheshire, in 1758. Finances were modest, insufficient possibly for medical training, but sufficient to permit him the acquisition of a few instruments for the critical studies on experimental philosophy. He received early recognition for his scientific accomplishments; Edinburgh awarded his an honorary LLD in 1764, and the Royal Society elected him a Fellow in 1766. From 1761 to 1767 he taught at one of the most influential dissenting schools in England, Warrington Academy. The years at Warrington were noteworthy, for he introduced the teaching of modern history and political science to pupils who would devote their lives to political and civic activities rather than to a learned profession. The next appointment was a position at the chapel in Leeds, which carried an adequate salary for the support of his family. It was here that he conducted his experiments on the restoration, by vegetation, of air deficient in oxygen. In the *Philosophical Transactions* for 1772 (but according to Guerlac,[3] not published until 1773), Priestley discussed different kinds of air. He described his photosynthesis experiments as follows:[4]

It is well known that flame cannot subsist long without change of air, so that the common air is necessary to it, except in the case of substances, into the composition of which nitre enters; for these will burn *in vacuo,* in fixed air, or even under water. . . . The quantity of air which even a small flame requires to keep it burning is prodigious. It is generally said, that an ordinary candle consumes, as it is called, about a gallon in a minute. Considering this amazing consumption of air, by fires of all kinds, volcano's, &c. it becomes a great object of philosophical inquiry, to ascertain what change is made in the constitution of the air by flame, and to discover what

provision there is in nature for remedying the injury which the atmosphere receives by this means.

. . . . I flatter myself that I have accidentally hit upon a method of restoring air which has been injured by the burning of candles, and that I have discovered at least one of the restoratives which nature employs for this purpose. It is vegetation.

One might have imagined that, since common air is necessary to vegetable, as well as to animal life, both plants and animals had affected it in the same manner, and I own I had that expectation, when I first put a sprig of mint into a glass-jar, standing inverted in a vessel of water; but when it had continued growing there for some months, I found that the air would neither extinguish a candle, nor was it at all inconvenient to a mouse, which I put into it.

The plant was not affected any otherwise than was the necessary consequence of its confined situation; for plants growing in several other kinds of air, were all affected in the very same manner.

Finding that candles burn very well in air which plants had grown a long time, and having had some reason to think, that there was something attending vegetation, which restored air that had been injured by respiration, I thought it was possible that the same process might also restore the air that had been injured by the burning of candles.

Accordingly, on the 17th of August, 1771, I put a sprig of mint into a quantity of air, in which a wax candle had burned out, and found that, on the 27th of the same month, another candle had burned perfectly well in it.

Three years later, Priestley announced the recovery of depholgisticated air (oxygen) from the heating of mercuric oxide. The oxide was placed in a retort, heated with a burning glass, and the released gas collected. He wrote:[5]

But the most remarkable of all the kinds of air that I have produced by this process is, one that is five or six times better than common air, for the purpose of respiration, inflammation, and, I believe, every other use of common atmospherical air. As I think I have sufficiently proved, that the fitness of air for respiration depends upon its capacity to receive the *phlogiston* exhaled from the lungs, this species may not improperly be called *dephlogisticated air.* This species of air I first produced from *mercurius calcinatus per se,* then from the red precipitate of mercury, and now from red lead. A candle burned in this air with an amazing strength of flame; and a bit of red hot wood crackled and burned with a prodigious rapidity, exhibiting an appearance something like that of iron glowing with a white heat, and throwing out sparks in all directions. But to complete the proof of the superior quality of this air, I introduced a mouse into it; and in a quantity in which, had it been in common air, it would have died in about a quarter of an hour, it lived at two different times, a whole hour, and was taken out quite vigorous.

Oxygen had been isolated in these experiments, but Priestley failed to appreciate the importance of the observation. Being a firm adherent to the phlogiston theory, he interpreted the findings as a Stahlist. Common air was believed to support combustion in proportion to its ability to absorb phlogiston; as it became saturated with phlogiston, combustion in it would cease. The new air Priestley recovered from mercuric oxide supported combustion much more effectively than did the common air. It was, therefore, considered wholly dephlogisticated. Lavoisier, not bound by the phlogiston theory, emphasized a different pattern of interpretation which led to today's explanation of the role of oxygen in combustion.

A number of other gases were studied by Priestley.[6] Included were nitrous oxide, chloric, sulfurous, and fluor acid, and ammoniacal gas. He investigated the crystalline compound of sulfuric acid with the vapors of nitrous acid, the reaction of oxygen and metals, combustion, respiration of lower and higher animals, putrefaction, and the relation between animal and vegetable kingdoms.

In 1791, Priestley's meeting-house, home, and laboratory in Birmingham were destroyed by rioters, who resorted to widespread and repetitive violence to express contempt for his sympathy with the arms of the French Revolution. The library and many unpublished manuscripts were burned; his experimental apparatus was demolished. Priestley escaped to London as a fugitive under an assumed name. Although a Fellow of the Royal Society, he was not accepted by society members, and therefore ceased to attend their meetings and discontinued reporting to them his scientific observations. His sons, disgusted with the persecution of their father, came to America, hopeful that he would follow. Priestley left

England in 1794 and was welcomed in the new land with an offer of a professorship of chemistry in the College of Philadelphia. Being relatively independent financially by now, he did not seek the appointment but settled in Northumberland, Pa., where residence was maintained until his death. Possibly his selection of a quiet and secluded spot was wise, since hospitality in America was at a low ebb during the presidency of John Adams. At one time, Priestley was threatened with deportation, but when Thomas Jefferson became president, Priestley's residency in the states was assured.

Joseph Priestley, theologian and natural philosopher, is described as a kindly man, who did not deserve the bitterness and strife to which he was subjected throughout his professional years. He probably would have discovered oxygen had he not stubbornly held to the phlogiston theory and refused to accept the significance of his critical experiments. It is noteworthy that he was almost driven out of England because of his heterodox teaching, and fled, not to the Continent, but to Pennsylvania, the home state of his friend and scientific colleague, Benjamin Franklin.[7]

1. Thomson, T.: Biographical Account of Joseph Priestley, LL.D., F.R.S., Annals of Philosophy; or Magazine of Chemistry, Mineralogy, Mechanics, Natural History, Agriculture, and the Arts 1:81-98 (Feb) 1813.
2. Schofield, R. E.: Scientific Background of Joseph Priestley, Ann Sci 13:148-163 (Sept) 1957.
3. Guerlac, H.: Priestley's First Papers on Gases, J Hist Med 12:1-12 (Jan) 1957.
4. Priestley, J.: Observations on Different Kinds of Air, Philos Trans 62: 147, 1772.
5. Priestley, J.: An Account of Further Discoveries in Air, Philos Trans 1:384-390, 1775.
6. Henry, W.: "Joseph Priestley," in Great Chemists, E. Farber, ed., New York: Interscience Publishers, 1961.
7. Smyth, A. H.: The Writings of Benjamin Franklin, vol. 6, New York: MacMillan Co., 1906.

Antoine Laurent Lavoisier (1734-1794)

ANTOINE LAURENT LAVOISIER began the chemical revolution contemporaneously with the American Revolution and was himself finished by the French revolutionists on the guillotine five years after Bastille Day. The events that were associated with our Independence seems much closer in history than does the rejection of the phlogiston theory and the replacement by Lavoisier of the sci-

entific basis of specific chemical elements of combustion and the interchange of gases in the lungs. Lavoisier was born in Paris and studied at the Collège Mazarin, where he gained a prize for rhetoric in general competition. His literary ambitions were complemented by interests in law, mathematics, botany, geology, chemistry, anatomy, and meteorology. Studies in anatomy and chemistry led him into speculation on respiration later in life, while an interest in meteorology was pursued intermittently until his death.

At the age of 25, Lavoisier entered the *Ferme,* a band of financiers who, for a fee, enjoyed the privilege of collecting the national taxes in France. This association was a contributing factor in his conviction and death by the guillotine with other members of the organization in the early years of the French revolution.

The elements of matter propounded by Aristotle—earth, air, fire and water, with transmutability of matter—formed the basis of Medieval and Renaissance chemistry, *chemeia.* With the dominance of the Arabs, it acquired the name *al-kimia* which subse-

quently became *alchemy,* with the waning of Arabic prestige.[1] Paracelsus reduced the number of elements to three—salt, sulfur, and mercury—in his search for chemical medicines. These three principles, unlike their present-day counterparts, resembled these substances only in their general properties. This reduction was a partial break from tradition, but thoroughly unscientific according to modern concepts of chemistry. The theories of Aristotle and Paracelsus were, in turn, rejected by Becher and Stahl, who substituted the phlogiston theory.

In the 1770's, Lavoisier, not satisfied with the current theories, reinvestigated the gain in weight of metals on oxidation and noted that a quantitative relationship could be established by the combination of one-fifth of atmospheric air.[3] This portion is active in combustion and respiration, while the remaining four fifths (later identified as nitrogen) is inactive. A note depsited with the secretary of the French Academy in 1772 recounts:[1]

About eight days ago I discovered that sulphur, in burning, far from losing weight, on the contrary gains it; that is to say that from a *livre* of sulphur one can obtain much more than a *livre* of vitrolic acid, making allowance for the humidity of the air; it is the same with phosphorus; this increase of weight arises from a prodigious quantity of air that is fixed during the combustion and combines with the vapours.

This discovery, which I have established by experiments that I regard as decisive, has led me to think that what is observed in the combustion of sulphur and phosphorus may well take place in the case of all substances that gain in weight by combustion and calcination.

In 1774, Joseph Priestley isolated oxygen and attempted to fit his observation into the phlogiston cycle. Stubbornly he clung to this idea. Lavoisier, on the other hand, chose a more rational explanation and appreciated that this new gas was a substance absorbed during oxidation. He was not aware at that time that nearly 150 years earlier Jean Rey had explained the increase in weight of metals on calcination, an observation that had remained unrecognized in the intervening decades.

Lavoisier's new chemistry was slowly accepted. There were many who clung to the old theory, and not until a much later time was the correct concept firmly established. With the announcement of the new chemistry, it was necessary to devise a new nomenclature. No longer were "earth," "air," "fire," and "water" sufficient. There was need to separate acids from alkalis and the light metals from the heavy metals; vital air became "oxygen"; inflammable gas became "hydrogen"; "phlogisticated air," "azote" (Gr. *a*, not + *zoe*, life). Charcoal, sulfur, and phosphorus became "radicals" of acids. The salts of sulfuric and sulfurous acids were called "sulfates" and "sulfites." Fixed air became "carbonic acid gas." The compounds of metals with oxygen were "oxides." The earth became "*silice*." The new system of nomenclature based upon the chemistry of Lavoisier listed 33 elements. The basic names have been retained with but few exceptions, although the number has been tripled in the intervening years with the evolution of the periodic table based upon electrical charges.

From chemistry Lavoisier proceeded to physiology and respiration. Usually he worked with his wife, who kept the experimental notes and helped to write the reports.[4]

Does it not then follow, from all these facts, that this pure species of air has the property of combining with the blood, and that this combination constitutes its red colour. But whichever of these two opinions we embrace, whether that the respirable portion of the air combines with the blood, or that it is changed into fixed air in passing through the lungs; or lastly, as I am inclined to believe, that both these effects take place in the act of respiration, we may, from facts alone, consider as proved.

First that respiration acts only on the portion of pure or defloglisticated air (oxygen), contained in the atmosphere; that the residium or mephitic part (nitrogen) is merely passive medium which enters into the lungs and departs from them nearly in the same state, without change or alteration.

Thirdly, that, in like manner, if an animal be confined in a given quantity of air, it will perish as soon as it has absorbed, or converted into fixed air (carbon dioxide), the major part of the respirable portion of air, and the remainder is reduced to a mephitic state.

Lavoisier was beheaded at the age of 51, long before his scientific researches were completed. His enemies, who included scientists and politicians, bitterly denounced him and refused to come to his aid. Prior to his trial the counter-revolutionaries were removed from the roster of the Society of Medicine and the Academy of Medicine. Subsequently, the Academy was suppressed and financially embarrassed. The *Ferme* suffered a similar fate from the National Assembly. A seal was placed on Lavoisier's home, and he was cast into prison. After a most unfair trial he was taken to the Place de la Révolution, and on May 8, 1794, was beheaded with 31 other prisoners, following his father-in-law to the guillotine.

1. McKie, D.: *Antoine Lavoisier: Father of Modern Chemistry*, Philadelphia: J. B. Lippincott Company, 1936.
2. Conant, J. B.: *On Understanding Science*, New Haven, Conn.: Yale University Press, 1947.
3. Lavoisier, A.: *Essays on the Effects Produced by Various Processes on Atmospheric Air*, trans. T. Henry, Warrington, England: W. Eyres, 1783.
4. *Selected Readings in the History of Physiology*, ed. J. F. Fulton, Sprinfigeld, Ill.: Charles C Thomas, 1930.

Joseph Louis Gay-Lussac (1778-1850)

JOSEPH LOUIS GAY-LUSSAC, one of the great scholars and natural scientists of France, is best-known for his theoretical and practical studies of the behavior of gases— the laws of Gay-Lussac. He was born at Saint Leonard in the province of Limousin in south central France. His grandfather was a physician and his father a prosecutor for the king and a judge at Point de Noblac. Gay-Lussac was readily recognized as a brilliant pupil, and, upon his return from the Mediterranean campaign of Napoleon, Berthollet, aware of his brilliance, chose him without hesitation for a laboratory assistant. Gay-Lussac must have disappointed his mentor, since he failed to confirm several of the theoretical assumptions of Berthollet, just as at a later time he discovered the faulty technique in the experimental observations of von Humboldt on the constituents of atmospheric air.

Although Gay-Lussac made the most of his observations on the ground near sea level, he did collect some of his data in the mountains, ascending in a Montoglofiere fire balloon, once with Biot, and later solo, to the greatest height then reached by man in

Composite by G. Bako

order to study magnetic inclinations and the physical characteristics of atmospheric gases.[1] The record-breaking ascent to 23,000 feet was made in 1804. The temperature decrement was found to be disproportional to the altitude; the greater the elevation, the greater the decrement in environmental temperature. An accelerated diminution in the amount of moisture in the air, as determined by the hygrometer during ascent, was another critical observation. During the trip he experienced tachycardia and tachypnea as well as extreme dryness of the throat.

In a study of Volta's eudiometer, presented before the Academy of Sciences in 1805, von Humboldt and Gay-Lussac expressed the concept, later developed by Gay-Lussac into his law of simple volume relations, that oxygen and hydrogen combine to form water in the exact proportion of 100 volumes of oxygen to 200 volumes of hydrogen.[2] The joint observations on the intensity of the inclination of magnetic forces

in the mountain expeditions in France, Switzerland, Italy, and Germany appeared as the first presentation in the first volume of Berthollet's erudite scientific journal, *Mémoires de Physique et de Chimie, de la Société D'Arcueil*.[3] The second volume of the *Mémoires,* published in 1809, contains an extensive discussion of the combination of gases first mentioned in 1805. The studies were contemporary with Dalton in England, whose work was unknown to Gay-Lussac at that time.[4]

. . . . the combinations of gaseous substances always proceed in the simplest manner and if we use the unit system of terms with one as the base, the union is one and one, one and two, and two and three. These volume relations are not seen in solid or liquid substances, and when we consider weight, it is further evidence that only in the gaseous state are substances placed in the same relationship and follow regular laws. . . . The apparent contractions in volume which gases undergo in combination also have simple relationships with the volume of each of them, a property particular to gases.

The free expansion of gases, particularly of carbon dioxide, oxygen, atmospheric air, and hydrogen, was compared. Six conclusions were deduced from these investigations.[5]

1st. When a gas is made to occupy an empty space, the heat set free is not due to the traces of air which can be supposed to have been present.
2d. If we join two equal spaces, one empty, the other full of a gas, the thermometric changes which take place in each are the same.
3d. For the same gas, these temperature-changes are proportional to the changes in density which are experienced.
4th. These temperature-changes are not the same for all gases. They are greater the smaller the specific gravities.
5th. The capacities of the same gas for heat diminish with the density, the volume being the same.
6th. The capacities of gases for heat, for equal volumes, are greater the smaller the specific gravities.

In addition to his work with gases, Gay-Lussac discovered boron from the decomposition of boracic acid; he invented a portable siphon barometer and made other notable contributions to meteorology. After the discovery of sodium and potassium in 1807, he became interested in large-scale production of the new elements and succeeded in obtaining far greater yields than those given by a colossal battery put at the disposal of the École Polytechnique by Emperor Napoleon. He proposed that iodine, discovered by Courtois, be given this name because of the violet color of its vapor. He also noted the analogy between iodine, chlorine, and sulfur, and gave an exact analysis of the acid present in Prussian blue, naming it "hydrocyanic acid." To replace the old method of cupellation, Gay-Lussac discovered a new process of analyzing alloys of silver and copper. The hazards of chemical research were intimately known; in an experiment on the preparation of potassium, he suffered burns on the face and was blinded temporarily.

The literary style of Gay-Lussac is simple and easy to follow. Fluency in Italian, English, and German contributed to the quality of his lectures, which were precise and serious, with overtones of the mathematical spirit acquired from student days at the Polytechnique School. When Berthollet died in 1822, he willed to Gay-Lussac, his most illustrious pupil, his sword and uniform as Peer of France, signifying the passing on of the mantle of theoretical and applied chemistry and physics.

1. Arago, F.: Eulogy on Gay-Lussac, *Ann Rep Smithsonian Inst*, 1877, pp 138-172.

2. De Humboldt, A., and Gay-Lussac, J.: Experiences of the Eudiometer and the Proportion of the Principal Constituents of the Atmosphere, *J Physique* 60, 1805.

3. De Humboldt, A., and Gay-Lussac, J.: The Intensity of Inclination of Magnetic Force in France, Switzerland, Italy, and Germany, excerpts translated by F. Stennthal, *Mem Physique Chim Soc D'Arcueil* 1:1-22, 1807.

4. Gay-Lussac, J.: The Combination Gases, the One with the Other (Fr), excerpts translated by F. Stennthal. *Mem Physique Chim Soc D'Arcueil* 2:207-234, 1809.

5. Gay-Lussac, J.: *The Free Expansion of Gases*, J. S. Ames, trans-ed., New York and London: Harper & Brothers, 1898, pp 3-13.

Composite by G. Bako

Jons Jacob Berzelius (1779-1848)

IN THE TRANSITION OF SCIENTIFIC THOUGHT from alchemy to chemistry, Jons Berzelius dominated chemistry in the first half of the 19th century. Despite his remoteness in Sweden, he managed to maintain social contact and to exchange scientific findings with eminent contemporaries in neighboring countries and to their envy make singular advances in chemistry with apparent ease. The son of a school principal in Linköping, Berzelius was born in 1779 at Wäfversunda, where his family spent their vacations. At the death of his parents before his tenth birthday, he thereafter lived with stepparents and relatives in modest circumstances.[1] An early interest in the natural sciences led him into medicine, and, with the help of a medical scholarship and tutoring, he qualified for and received, with distinction, the MD degree at Uppsala. His graduation thesis discussed galvanic current apparatus and electrical stimulation in organic bodies. Having completed his studies, Berzelius served in the Lying-In House and the Serafim Hospital of Stockholm, and received an appointment at the school of surgery in Stockholm. This training, in addition to a few years of practice before receiving his degree, constituted his practical experience in medicine. However, he wrote in depth on medical education, periodically left the general chemistry laboratory to study the elements of urine quantitatively, and near the close of his career prepared an unimportant monograph on the kidneys and urine.

In 1806, Berzelius received his first salaried academic appointment. With the reorganization of the medical schools in Stockholm in 1810, he was appointed to the chair of chemistry and pharmacy in the Karoline Institute. Discovery followed discovery, beginning in 1803 with the identification of cerium, a study carried out with Hisinger, mine operator and practical chemist. Berzelius rapidly matured professionally, and in 1808 was elected a member of the Academy of Sciences and its president in 1810. Meanwhile, he had begun a lifelong exchange of scientific information by letter or mutual communion with chemists in other countries, marked particularly by extended visits in Paris with Berthollet and in London with Sir Humphry Davy, with Wollaston, who first identified uric acid crystals in gouty tophi, with Thomas Young, decipherer of the Rosetta stone, and with Alexander Marcet, lecturer in chemistry at Guy's Hospital. His laboratory in Stockholm was exceedingly popular, and a list of his students between 1811 and 1841 included many of the great chemists and mineralogists of Europe: Gmelin, professor of chemistry at Tübingen; the Roses of Berlin; Gustav Magnus, professor of physics and technology in Berlin; and Wöhler, synthesizer of urea and professor of chemistry at Göttingen. Another of his well-known admirers was William MacMichael, a practicing physician in London, who prepared one of the literary gems of medicine, *The Gold-Headed Cane*.

One of Berzelius' great contributions in chemistry was the consideration and development of analytical evidence in support of Dalton's atomic hypothesis, which led to the identification of seven new metals not previously isolated. In expanding and supporting the atomic theory, Berzelius gave chemistry its alphabet, vocabulary, and nomenclature.[2] Following the Latin, the symbols for the elements were established: natrium, Na for sodium; kalium K for potassium; O for oxygen; and H for hydrogen, etc. With oxygen as a reference element and its atomic weight arbitrarily set at 100, he prepared a preliminary table of atomic weights in 1814, followed by an expanded table a few years later. A contemporary chemist, Thomas Thomson, wrote in 1813 on the choice of oxygen as a reference element, saying:[3]

Before we can draw up a table of the relative weights of the atoms of bodies, we must fix upon some one whose atom shall be represented by unity. Mr. Dalton has made choice of hydrogen for that purpose, because it is the lightest of all known bodies. Sir Humphry Davy has followed his example; but he has doubled the weight of an atom of oxygen, and consequently of all other bodies, by the arbitrary supposition that water is composed of two atoms of hydrogen and one of oxygen. Dr. Wollaston and Professor Berzelius have both proposed the atom of oxygen as the most convenient unit: nor can there be any hesitation in embracing their plan. Oxygen is in fact the substance by means of which the weight of the atoms of almost all other bodies is determined. It enters into a much greater number of combinations than any other known body; hence the great advantage attending a convenient number for that body to the practical chemist.

To the twenty-odd chemicals known in Lavoisier's day, Berzelius added cerium (1803), selenium (1817), silicon (1823), zirconium (1824), titanium (1825), and thorium (1828).[4] In addition, he exploited such garden-variety laboratory items as the blowpipe, and introduced rubber tubing into laboratory apparatus and filter paper into analytical chemistry.

Berzelius' earlier experiments in electrochemistry led to the development (c 1811) of the dualistic or electrochemical theory. Again with Hisinger, the behavior of electrolytes was studied, with the observation that acids, bases, and salts decomposed in solutions exposed to the current from a voltaic pile. Hydrogen and metals were liberated at the negative pole; whereas oxygen was liberated at the positive pole. In *An Attempt to Establish a Pure Scientific Sys-*

tem of Mineralogy, Berzelius commented that:[5]

. . . . every combination of two or more oxides possesses the nature of a salt, i.e., has its acid. And, if we suppose this combination decomposed by the galvanic battery, the first will be collected round the positive pole, and the second round the negative. Hence in every mineral composed of oxidised bodies, whether of an earthy or saline nature, we must seek for the electro-negative and electro-positive ingredients; and after the nature and qualities of these are found, a critical application of the chemical theory will tell us what the fossil in question is.

With a rapidly-expanding science, publication and dissemination of data from Berzelius' laboratory and others were inevitable. His *Handbook of Chemistry,* first published in 1808, later was revised and translated into French and German. A comprehensive review of chemistry, the *Jahres Bericht,* appeared first in 1822. Although Berzelius' greatest contributions were made in theoretical and practical chemistry, an interest in medicine and medical education reappeared periodically. Only a few years before his death he assisted in plans for medical instruction at the Karoline Institute. In his 1840 autobiography, prepared in fulfillment of membership requirements of the Academy of Sciences, Berzelius commented on medical education.[1]

I attempted therein to establish the incontroverted position that a school of medicine cannot produce practically qualified physicians without one or more large hospitals. The faculties of our universities, located in small cities, neither had nor could have large hospitals. The study of practical medicine without long practice in the sick-house becomes merely a reading of lessons. In this manner I had become a doctor of medicine and well knew how one, under such circumstances, although provided with good certificates of examination, nevertheless is but little qualified at the sick-bed. Stockholm, with its many hospitals, is the only place in Sweden, where a medical school can be maintained.

1. Berzelius, J. J.: *Autobiographical Notes,* O. Larsell, trans, Baltimore: Williams & Wilkins Company, 1934.
2. Thomson, T.: Outline of Dr. Berzelius's Nomenclature, *Ann Philos* 3:450-455, 1814.
3. Thomson, T.: On the Daltonian Theory of Definite Proportions in Chemical Combinations, *Ann Philos* 2:32-52, 1813.
4. Muspratt, S.: The Biography of Baron Berzelius, MD, PhD, *Lancet* 1:492-497, 1851.

5. Berzelius, J. J.: *An Attempt to Establish a Pure Scientific System of Minerology,* J. Black, trans., London: R. Baldwin, 1814.

Johann Friedrich Meckel (1724-1774)

J. F. MECKEL, THE ELDER, born in Wetzlar, Germany, studied medicine at Göttingen and later at the University of Berlin.[1] After qualifying in 1748 for the MD degree at Göttingen, he returned to Berlin, became prosector in anatomy, and taught obstetrics at the Charité. In 1751, he obtained the rank of professor of anatomy, botany, and obstetrics but devoted most of his time to anatomical studies. Several of his scientific communications were prepared in Latin or German; others were translated from the Latin into French and appeared in the *Memoirs of the Academy of Science of Berlin* between 1749 and 1765. Meckel's treatment of the visceral branches of the veins and lymphatics, prepared shortly before death, was his last but one of his most important contributions. The description of the sphenopalatine ganglion (Meckel's ganglion), published in Latin, was included in his inaugural dissertation; the description of the recess in the dura (Meckel's recess), the lodgement for the Gasserian ganglion, and a case report of coarctation of the aorta, associated with hypertrophy of the heart, appeared in the *Memoirs*. The sphenopalatine ganglion was traced as follows.[2]

The branches unite at an acute angle posteriorly and from the Vidian nerve which is composed of these branches and the fibers of the intercostal nerve which passes through the carotid canal and unites with the branches of the fifth nerve.

The sum of these branches forms a large ganglion which is quite similar because of its branches and configuration to the ganglia of the intercostal nerves in the chest and in the abdomen.

The Vidian nerve in its initial course becomes the second branch of the superior maxillary nerve and is called the palatine branch. Having its origin in the superior maxillary nerve, behind the nasal artery, it descends to the pterygopalatine fossa and divides into three smaller branches, of which the anterior one is larger and the two others are smaller. All of these descend through three separate pterygopalatine canals, the anterior, posterior, and exterior canals, and supply the palate.

The description of coarctation of the aorta in a young girl was illustrated with an anterior and posterior view of the enlarged heart. The patient suffered from palpitation, tremors, delayed menarche, depression, and syncope. Treatment included wine, purges, emmenagogues, and phlebotomy. The postmortem performed by Meckel made no mention of collateral circulation; the chambers and veins were reported to be distended in contrast to narrowing of the aorta and the contiguous smaller arteries. Excerpts of the translation by Jarcho, which conclude with a series of mathematical calculations, are as follows:[3]

In his beautiful and useful book on the movement of the heart and on aneurysms, the famous Lancisi, a very accurate writer, undertook to present all the causes of aneurysm and dilatation of the heart which might be called *contra naturam*. He omitted one cause, which perhaps neither he nor any other author had ever seen and which nevertheless is able, almost alone, to cause enlargement of the whole heart. This cause is the aorta, when it is unnaturally narrow.

Some time ago, among the large number of cadavers with which our anatomical theater is so plentifully supplied . . . we had the body of an

eighteen year old girl. . . Since childhood the patient had been very choleric . . . From time to time she had been tormented by palpitation of the heart and by oppressions, which were followed by general trembling of the limbs . . . Her pulse was always fluttery and the oppression and palpitation tortured her without respite. . . . After four weeks in bed during which she had continual palpitation and extreme respiratory difficulty she died in a state of suffocation.

I dissected the cadaver myself. While injecting the arteries I found that all the branches of the aorta, and this vessel itself during its descent through the abdomen, were astonishingly narrow. When I opened the thorax the relative size of the aorta was even smaller, since the heart, which I had been intending to fill with an injection of wax, and which I therefore examined very carefully, occupied almost the whole left half of the small chest. . . . As for the aorta . . . it was so narrow that its diameter was smaller by half than that of the pulmonary artery, which it should have exceeded or at least equalled in calibre. The entire heart was extraordinarily dilated and its apex had an obtuse contour because of the ventricles, which were expanded up to that point.

From this it follows that the pulmonary artery and veins carry one and a half times more blood than the aorta received from the left ventricle. This is a sufficient explanation of all the troubles which the poor patient suffered during her life.

The medical dynasty was carried on by his son, Philipp Friedrich Theodor, born in Berlin in 1756, who also studied at Göttingen and graduated from Strasburg in 1777. At the age of 23, he accepted a call as professor of anatomy and surgery in Halle. He was best known as an obstetrician and established a private Accoucheur Institut in Halle. Also, he was a favorite obstetrician of Russian nobility. Within 48 hours after he died, dissection and preparation of his skeleton, with 13 thoracic vertebrae, was begun. Eventually it was placed on display in a glass case in the department of anatomy. His oldest son, in turn, named Johann Friedrich, was called Meckel "The Younger."

1. Dezeimeris: Meckel, J. F. (Fr), *Biog Med* 2:489-490, 1855.

2. Meckel, J. F.: *Anatomical Physiological Treatise on the Fifth Facial Nerve* (L), Göttingen: A. Vandenhoeck, 1749, excerpt translated by Z. Danilevicius.

3. Meckel, J. F.: Physiological and Anatomical Observations of Extraordinary Dilatation of the Heart, With Contraction of the Aorta (Fr), *Mem Acad Sci Berlin*, presented 1750, published in 1752, pp 163-182, in Jarcho, S. (trans.): Coarctation of the Aorta, *Amer J Cardiol* 7:844-852, 1961.

Johann Friedrich Meckel, The Younger (1781-1833)

JOHANN FRIEDRICH MECKEL, the greatest comparative anatomist in Germany prior to Johannes Müller, is recognized as the most renowned of the scientific Meckel dynasty. His grandfather, Meckel the Elder, served as professor of anatomy, physic, and obstetrics of the University of Berlin; whereas the father of Meckel the Younger, Philipp Friedrich Theodor, served as professor of anatomy, surgery, and obstetrics at Halle. P. F. T. Meckel's two sons were August Albert, professor of anatomy and forensic medicine at Berne, who died prematurely, and Johann Friedrich.

Meckel the Younger studied medicine at Halle and Göttingen and graduated MD from Halle in 1802.[1] His doctoral dissertation, prepared in Latin, *De cordis conditionibus abnormibus,* discussed congenital abnormalities of the heart.[2] After a long study tour, which included visits to Würzburg, Vienna, Paris, and other medical centers, he returned to his alma mater in 1805. Meckel submitted an inaugural dissertation for academic standing which extended the observations on teratology presented in the doctoral thesis. That same year he returned to Paris, studied with Cuvier and Hum-

boldt, and became so impressed with Cuvier's five volumes of *Lessons in Comparative Anatomy* that he began a translation of the work which was finally published in 1810. Meckel went from Paris to Italy; as Napoleon swept through Europe, he returned to Halle to find the conqueror occupying the family home. By 1808, conditions were quiet again, and he succeeded to the chair of anatomy, pathological anatomy, surgery, and obstetrics vacated earlier by his father.

An intensive investigator and prolific writer, Meckel explored in great depth human anatomy, pathology, embryology, and especially comparative anatomy. His inductive conclusions, drawn from experimental observations, anticipated Darwin. His reasoning led him to assert that the development of the individual organism proceeds according to general laws which are valid for the entire animal kingdom, and that during its development higher animal life passes through the stages of life which have preceded it. His observations were recorded both in brief and long communications to scientific periodicals and in single and multiple volume treatises which commanded great respect. In addition to his graduation and inaugural theses, he prepared in Latin two monographs on congenital abnormalities, a four-volume series of anatomical-pathological tables, and a translation from the Latin of Soemmering's *Lymphatic System* (1828). He edited Reil's *Archives,* successor to *Deutsches Archiv für Physiologie* from 1815-1833, and from 1826-1832 was editor of the *Archiv für Anatomie und Physiologie.* One or more volumes of each of his five encyclopedic treatises on anatomy and pathology were published in his native tongue during a relatively short period of time, beginning at the age of 27. The first carried a most comprehensive title, *Human and Comparative Anatomy and Physiology* (1806).[3] A two-volume text, entitled *Comparative Anatomy* (1808-1811),[4] was followed by his *Handbook of Pathological Anatomy* also in two volumes (1812-1816),[5] and his *Handbook of Human Anatomy* (1815-1820).[6] *The System of Comparative Anatomy* was published in six volumes between 1821 and 1831.[7] Several of the texts were translated into foreign languages; his *Handbook of Human Anatomy,* translated into French by Jourdan and Breschet, in turn was translated from the French by Doane and was published in Philadelphia in three volumes in 1832.[8]

Two eponymic terms are associated with Meckel. Meckel's cartilage is the first branchial cartilage; Meckel's diverticulum appears as a residuum of the embryonic union between the gut and the yolk sac, the vitellointestinal duct, a few centimeters proximal to the ileocecal valve. The vestigial organ persists in approximately two per cent of humans and may produce clinical symptoms at the site of diverticulitis or the site of bleeding within the intestinal tract. Recognition of the diverticulum was not original with Meckel. Others had noted it before, but his elaboration and detailed description of its embryonic development have fixed his name to the structure.[9]

One type of intestinal appendage is composed not of all layers of the intestinal tract, but only of the peritoneum, the vascular layer, and the epithelium; the fibers of the muscular layer diverge at their base and soon disappear. These appendages can be observed in the esophagus, stomach, duodenum, the small and the large intestine. Most often several will occur in the individual.

Another type of appendage has quite a different structure. . . . Usually, only one is present. It appears at a specific site in the ileum and the wall contains each of the several layers of the intestinal tract.

These diverticula arise from the communication between the umbilical sac (yolk sac) and the intestinal lumen. Usually the yolk stalk separates from the intestines and closes, so that the gut forms a cyindrical tube throughout its length. The lumen of the yolk stalk, which usually is within the mesentery, closes parallel to the opposing intestinal wall. If this fails to occur, and if the smaller or larger portion of the umbilical stalk remains attached to the intestinal canal, it develops into an intestinal appendage and remains throughout life, since it becomes vestigial only at a specific stage of development.

The proof that the diverticulum is a residuum of the communication between the intestinal canal and the umbilical stalk rests in the findings which I have observed in three stillborn, full-term fetuses.

In the past two years, I have observed it seven times [in the cadaver] and always it arises from the ileum. In adults it is approximately four feet from the cecum; in the newborn it is one foot from the cecum.

The intestinal appendage has been found only in animals that develop a tunica erythroides or a yolk sac.

1. Beneke, R.: *Johann Friedrich Meckel the Younger* (Ger), Halle: M. Niemeyer, 1934.
2. Meckel, J. F.: *The Abnormal Structures of the Heart* (L), Halle: Batheanis, 1802.
3. Meckel, J. F.: *Human and Comparative Anatomy and Physiology* (Ger), Halle: Hemmerde & Schwetschke, 1806.
4. Meckel, J. F.: *Comparative Anatomy* (Ger), 2 vol, Leipzig: C. H. Reclam, 1808-1811.
5. Meckel, J. F.: *Handbok of Pathological Anatomy* (Ger), 2 vol, Leipzig: C. H. Reclam, 1812-1816.
6. Meckel, J. F.: *Handbook of Human Anatomy* (Ger), 4 vol, Halle & Berlin, 1815-1820.
7. Meckel, J. F.: *System of Comparative Anatomy* (Ger), 6 vol, Halle: Renger, 1821-1831.
8. Meckel, J. F.: *Manual of General, Descriptive, and Pathological Anatomy,* 3 vol, translated from the French by A. S. Doane, Philadelphia: Carey & Lea, 1832.
9. Meckel, J. F.: *The Diverticula of the Gastrointestinal Tract* (Ger), Arch Physiol 9:421-453, 1809, excerpt translated by Z. Danilevicius.

Composite by Bako

Kaspar Friedrich Wolff
(1733-1794)

K. F. WOLFF produced, at the age of 26, a treatise entitled *Theoria generationis* which formed the basis of the germ-layer theory of embryonic development and thereby refuted the preformation hypothesis espoused especially by Haller. Wolff was born in

Berlin, the son of a master tailor. Little is known of his early education until 1753 when he entered the Medico-Chirurgicum College in Berlin (later the Kaiser-Wilhelm Academy for military surgeons).[1] Being dissatisfied with the limited training in the institution, he continued in science at the University of Halle, where he added philosophy and botany to his embryologic and medical interests. In 1759, Wolff gained the doctor of medicine degree upon presentation of the famous dissertation on epigenesis. This was prepared in Latin, an Aristotelian concept of embryonic growth, which is recognized as the outstanding contribution in the field between the work of Malpighi in the 17th century and von Baer in the 19th century. In 1761, Wolff was called to Breslau to conduct lectures for medical officers assigned to this area. They were immediately successful, and, having been advanced to full-time status, he served in this post until the Declaration of Peace.

Wolff returned to Berlin and the Medico-Chirurgicum College in 1763 and continued his scientific studies in embryology, a subject which attracted little interest at that time among natural scientists. After a series of difficult incidents with the faculty, he obtained permission to deliver private lectures in logic, theory, physiology, and pathology. These also proved to be outstanding, although they failed to gain him a desirable post on the staff. Instead, his reputation, in 1766, induced Catherine the Great to offer him the professorship of anatomy and physiology in the Russian Academy of Sciences in St. Petersburg. Here he continued in a quiet, modest fashion his ceaseless endeavors to explain cell differentiation in plants and animals.

Notable among these researches were the observations on the formation of the intestinal tract in the chick, an extension of his theories presented in his doctoral dissertation, and a series of contributions on the fibers of the myocardium. In his *Theory of Generation (Reproduction),* self-illustrated and translated into German five years after its preparation, Wolff showed that the organs of plants and animals develop from undifferentiated tissue. He postulated that this could not be a simple process of ex-

pansion of infinitely minute preformed elements, as proposed by Haller, but was predetermined growth from amorphous, undifferentiated substance, ie epigenesis. Wolff showed that organs and systems, similar to cellular metamorphosis in the development of plants, emerge from homogeneous tissue that originally provides no clue as to its ultimate fate. Although his experiments and hypotheses effectively refuted the preformation theory, and the epigenesis theory was eventually modified significantly, his explanation of embryologic development excerpted below was closer rather than farther from the facts validated by subsequent investigators.[2]

From the theory of epigenesis we deduce that the parts of the body have not pre-existed but that they were formed gradually. This does not happen through an accumulation of small particles, or through any type of fermentation, or due to mechanical causes, or through the action of the soul. The basis for the development of the parts is present; they are structured in such a manner that it is easy to recognize that these are not yet fully developed but are only rudiments which later will be transformed into the differentiated structures of the body.

Established in St. Petersburg, Wolff improved his laboratory techniques and continued his investigations of epigenesis as a mature scientist. He wisely chose to study the intestinal tract of the chick embryo. Haller had erroneously assumed that the embryo was preformed because of the intimate connection of the yolk in the area of the gut. Wolff, on the contrary, rejected this explanation and set about to provide scientific proof in support of his position. With convincing evidence he described the formation of the gut and thereby provided the most telling arguments for epigenesis. The following translated excerpts were prepared in German by J. F. Meckel The Younger, in 1812 from the original Latin treatise of 1769.[2]

The false amnion is only a vesicle but if observed from the lower surface of the vascular area it appears as a closed sac or a tube lying on the upper sheath. The appearance depends on the changes during development. The tube is flat, elongated, indented on both sides and the middle, wider and round at its upper end, narrow and sharp at its lower end. Its lateral walls run parallel; the right, which is turned toward the right side observed from below the vascular area, is slightly concave, the left side is slightly convex. This shape corresponds to the embryo at this moment of development. In fact, the false amnion represents the outline of the embryo so that the vesicle seems to be bulging more and more with the growth of the body and follows the formation of its parts with the changes in the position of the embryo. . . . The upper portion of the amnion corresponds to the head, the lower portion to the tail, the right border corresponds to the abdomen, the left border to the back.

Near the end of the third day the false amnion is almost completely developed. It contains other parts which may be identified anatomically: the depression for the stomach, the cleavage of the false amnion, and its lower opening. . . . The lower sheath of the vascular area, as much as it is in contact with the vesicle, forms the layer from which the intestinal canal develops. A canal is formed from an undifferentiated flat membrane, so that the stomach depression is the beginning of the stomach, the cleavage is the beginning of the middle or the primary gut, and the lower opening becomes the precursor of the colon.

Since the stomach opening at this time remains open, the embryo is open along its entire anterior surface, except for its upper part, which lies above the stomach depression. This part then turns into a tube which is closed at the upper end but remains open in its lower end and eventually forms the stomach. The extension of the tube above is not the chest cavity; it seems more likely that it is the precursor of the esophagus.

Wolff's name is attached to three embryonic structures: the Wolffian ridge, a longitudinal ridge on either side of the embryonic mesentery in which the Wolffian body, the mesonephros, develops, and the Wolffian duct, the mesonephric duct, which remains as the male urethra. Descriptions of each are excepted as follows.[3]

The cellular substance, which becomes visible first on the third day on the anterior surface of the spine [Wolffian ridge], and which proceeds into the allantois on the fourth and fifth day is the first structural evidence of the transformation into the shape of kidneys. This substance exists in one undivided body [Wolffian body] at the site of the kidneys; at this time liquid which later becomes urine is enclosed [Wolffian duct], which appears in this form as early as the third day.

The kidneys begin as a single body. Urine-like fluid in minimal quantity is enclosed in a minimal mass of tissue; it is elaborated from the material within the egg, in a similar manner as later in the adult, and the urine is filtered out when the animal begins to take nourishment and excrete the urine from its already formed parts.

By the continuous formation and transit of the liquid, vessels begin to develop, many in the form of complicated loops, to form eventually the internal structure of the kidney. At first, the kidneys extend into ureters which are initially a structureless mass and appear as one structure through which the urine is passed and from which then the other vessels or ducts are formed. There is no doubt that the uriniferous ducts, renal pelvis, and the ureters are formed by the flow of the urine in the same manner as the blood vessels are formed by pressure from circulating blood.

Interwoven with Wolff's penetrating study of generation was his belief in the "vitalism" of Stahl, the ill-defined force responsible for the development of plants and animals, which he mentioned in the opening chapter of his *Theory*. Equipped with a microscope of low magnification only, Wolff saw the globules (cells), of which plants and animals are structured, assimilate food, grow, and reproduce. In plants, differentiation produces the stem, leaves, and stamen; whereas in the animal body the primitive cells are the precursors of the heart, blood vessels, limbs, alimentary canal, kidney, etc. Plant growth results from organization of cells in the stem which process spreads peripherally to the branches. Nutrition to the vital parts is provided by sap in plants and blood in animals through a vital force, which Wolff called *vis essentialis*. This phenomenon operates through counter forces, attracts substances that are beneficial for development, and rejects the worthless. Subsequently, sap flows through organized channels not previously existing in plants and blood in animals through vessels. As noted above, in the case of the kidney, the liquid excreta is expelled by the essential force into a mass of preexisting, but unorganized substance, the mesonephros, which subsequently becomes the lumen of the uriniferous tubules and the ureters.

1. Wunschmann, G.: Kaspar Friedrich Wolff (Ger), *Allg Deutsche Biog* 44:41-43, 1898.

2. Wolff, C. F.: *The Formation of the Intestinal Canal in a Hatched Chick* (Ger), J. F. Meckel (trans.), Halle: Germany, 1812, excerpts translated by Z. Danilevicius.

3. Wolff, C. F.: *Theory of Generation* (L), Halae and Salam, lit. Hendelianis, 1759, and *Theory of Generation* (Ger), Berlin: F. W. Birnstiel, 1764, excerpt translated by Z. Danilevicius.

Abbe Lazzaro Spallanzani (1729-1799)

SPALLANZANI, a brilliant investigator in geology, biology, and experimental physiology, advanced fundamental precepts that are retained in contemporary achievements. Although he was not a physician, his contributions in the medical sciences exerted a great influence on the practice of medicine. If any one scientist is entitled to the glory associated with the appellation, "founder of experimental physiology," Spallanzani is probably most worthy.[1] He was born in Scandiano, a small community in northern Italy. His father practiced law and hoped that the son would follow in this profession. However, as a law student at the University of Bologna, his cousin, Laura Bassi, Professor of Physics, turned his interests toward natural science. Earlier, Spallanzani had attended the Jesuit College at Reggio, where he was ordained a priest. His interest in the humanities in the early academic years equaled his curiosity for scientific subjects in later years. On one assignment he taught Greek and Philosophy. His capacity for composition in Latin and French was outstanding.[2]

The microscope, a new tool in biologic research, enabled Spallanzani to study the Infusoria. A long controversy with Needham in England and Buffon in France prompted a series of essays which rejected the then current theories of spontaneous generation—prophetic of the discoveries of Pasteur and others. The low magnification of the microscope permitted Spallanzani to delve no deeper than the Infusoria. Their mortality, nutrition, the effect of noxious substances in their environment, and the capacity for regeneration were investigated. Vessels with eleven kinds of seeds were hermetically sealed and were heated for various periods of time. One group of microorganisms which he called animalcula of the higher class, the protozoa, were destroyed with little heating. Those of the lower class, bacteria, were more resistant.[3]

We are therefore induced to believe, that those animalcula originate from germs there included, which, for a certain time, withstand the effects of heat, but at length yield under it; and, since animalcula of the higher classes only exist when the heat is less intense, we must imagine they are much sooner affected by it, than those of the lower classes. Whence we should conclude, that this multitude of the superior animalcula, seen in the infusions of open vessels, exposed not only to the heat of boiling water, but to the flame of a blowpipe, appears there, not because their germs have withstood so great a degree of heat, but because new germs come to the infusions, after cessation of the heat.

The studies on Infusoria attracted wide interest and a professional chair at the University of Pavia. Other investigations included the regeneration of extremities and appendages of earthworms, frogs, salamanders, lizards, and snails (feelers). In 1768, regeneration of the spinal cord in experiments on the lizard was described. More than a century later, these observations were exploited by Morgan, Loeb, and others. Another important revelation was the necessity of spermatic fluid for fertilization of the ovum. Artificial fertilization of amphibian ova and of the silkworm was successful. He failed, however, to appreciate the critical nature of spermatozoa in spermatic fluid, the particulate matter having been described by Hamm in 1677.

Spallanzani's physiological studies on gaseous exchange followed, by two centuries later, Leonardo da Vinci's statement: "No animal can live in an atmosphere where a flame does not burn." Lavoisier had observed that gaseous exchange of oxygen and carbon dioxide occurred in the lungs. Spallanzani considered the transfer a natural manifestation of all tissues, even in animals that had not developed teleologically a pulmonary apparatus. The discovery of white blood cells was attributed to Spallanzani by Franchini. Such credit is not universally accorded.

His studies concerning the digestive power of saliva and gastric juice led to an argument with John Hunter. Spallanzani differentiated the mechanical function of the muscular coats of the stomach from the mucosa which elaborated digestive juices. He studied the process in birds, reptiles, and dogs and offered definite evidence that juices were active agents. They were endowed with antiseptic properties quite different from fermentation or putrefaction. The solvent property of gastric juice acting *in vitro* was demonstrated, but the acid character was unrecognized. It remained for John Young (1803), an American physiologist, to make this observation. Other physiologic studies concerned the cardiac force and rhythm transmitted to the great vessels and the independent contractility of the arteries. Spallanzani was the first to observe that, in the chick embryo, blood passes from the arteries to the veins through capillaries. His experiments on the bat proved that this animal was only slightly dependent upon vision, and its deficiency in visual purple was presumably related to disuse.

Turning from physiology to geology and marine biology Spallanzani established a laboratory at Marseilles and another at Porto Venere for the study of marine fauna. He described new species of marine fireflies and revealed that the depths of the sea were phosphorescent. The biology of electrically charged crampfish in its reproduction by ovulation received his attention. The maintenance of the sexual posture in the frog

as a spinal reflex after decapitation was demonstrated. Clinical investigations during his travels about Europe included goiter and endemic cretinism. He rejected a flattering offer from Padua to occupy a chair in that famous university. While enjoying the privileges as a guest of the Venetian Embassy in Istanbul (Constantinople), he pursued scientific investigations in the architectural properties of the mosques and the temples. A copper mine was discovered on the island of Calki and an iron mine on the island of the Leaders. Upon returning to Italy, he inspected a number of volcanoes and studied the composition of the vapors and lava.

The complexities of scientific investigation prevent a contemporary scientist from delving into and exploiting as many natural phenomena as Spallanzani. Truly he was a great scientist who left a profound impact upon medicine and the medical sciences. He was a clear writer with an easy style, void of any rhetorical embroidery. He was not a hermit in his laboratory but, enjoyed public appearances and traveled widely among the universities and laboratories in Europe. In the courtyard of the University of Pavia, a monument to Spalanzani attests to the stature afforded him by this learned institution.

1. Franchini, G.: Lazzaro Spallanzani (1729-1799), *Ann Med Hist* 2:56-62 (Jan.) 1930.
2. Tortonese, E.: Spallanzani, Founder of Experimental physiology, *Endeavour* 7:92-96, 1948.
3. Spallanzani, L.: "Tracts on the Nature of Animals and Vegetables," 2 vol, Modena, *Soc tipografica*, 1776, translated in Brock, T. D.: *Milestones in Microbiology*, Prentice-Hall, Englewood Cliffs, NJ, 1961.

Aloysio Luigi Galvani
(1737-1798)

ALOYSIO OR LUIGI GALVANI, who showed little preference for either given name, was born in Bologna. There he was associated with its university for an academic lifetime. Among others attracted to the great center of science were Malpighi, Valsalva, and Morgagni who, in the generation preceding Galvani, fostered a notable reputation for the university and for themselves. Galvani likewise, by his accomplishments in recognizing the significance of animal electricity, joined his predecessors in enhancing the fame of Bologna and attaining personal recognition.[1] Early in life Galvani evidenced some interest in entering the Church; however, he chose medicine, and after appropriate study and preparation of a doctoral thesis discussing formation and development of the skeletal structure, he obtained his medical degree in 1762. An interest in form and function was carried into his practice of surgery and obstetrics; indeed, it won for him a minor post in the departments of anatomy (and physiology) and custodianship of the Anatomical Museum at the University of Bologna.

Galvani attended the sick as his principal means of livelihood and gave public lectures, neither elegant nor especially inspiring. Nevertheless, on his acceptance of the professor's chair at Bologna, his keen interest in experimental physiology produced remarkable results. A variety of subjects felt the impact of his researches although many investigations were not published until long after their completion. Such reluctance delayed critical perusal and adequate evaluation by his contemporaries. Studies chosen to report included the action of opiates on the nerves of the frog, the structure of the ear, physiology of hearing in birds, comparative anatomy of the urinary tract, and his most noted observations on tissue irritability, which were described in a dissertation published in 1772 and which became known as Galvanism. Although the description is obscure and ambiguous in parts, leading some to raise doubts regarding Galvani's full appreciation of his critical observations, the nerve-muscle preparation of the frog as the experimental model provided a significant step toward the discovery of a new biological principle. The treatise, *De viribus electricitatis in motu musculari commentarius,* was published in the Bologna proceedings in a volume with an imprimatur of March 27, 1791.[2] The work was translated into German in 1793, and two English translations appeared simultaneously in 1953.[3,4]

In the midst of Galvani's experiments on muscular contraction on the frog, Benjamin Franklin was experimenting with atmospheric electricity and enjoying the fame from his monograph on electrical action. Moreover, Galvani's animal electricity, detected from observations near a static machine and confirmed by exposure to atmospheric electricity, led him to a third observation, the discovery of a phenomenon soon to be known as galvanic current, a specific form of energy exchange based on electric current generated from the contact of two dissimilar metals. The term has since been carried into manufacturing, in which galvanization relates to electroplating a thick coating of zinc over iron or steel to protect against rust.

Galvani's observations on the nerve-muscle preparation of the frog have been judged elementary by some, since he presented few experimental data and failed to understand the principles of electrostatic induction. Nevertheless, he provided a basic experiment for Volta, who had earlier described the condensing electroscope and the electrophorus and who, eight years later, designed a device which became known as the Voltaic pile or battery. The 55-page communication by Galvani to the Bologna Institute of Arts and Sciences in 1791, *Commentary on the Effect of Electricity on Muscular Motion,* describes his initial findings on the nerve-muscle preparation of the frog. In 1780, while engaged in studying the exposed nerve-muscle preparation near a static electricity machine, one of Galvani's assistants accidentally touched the crural nerve with a scalpel at the same time a spark was drawn from the static machine. The muscles of the frog's leg convulsed. A series of experiments with the nerve-muscle preparation followed.

Galvani produced similar convulsive contractions when the nerve and muscle were joined by a metallic arc formed of two metals. Carrying the experiment out-of-doors, he attached an insulated iron wire from the ridge of his house to the nerve of the freshly-prepared frog on a table at ground level. Another wire joined the muscle group to the water in the well. Each time lightning flashed, the muscle convulsed. Even in calm weather atmospheric electricity was detected by faint twitchings of the muscles. A crucial experiment involved the suspension of the frog preparation from an iron lattice by a brass hook through the spinal marrow.

This provided another type of conducting arc, and, when the leg brushed the iron grill, the muscles responded. Galvani attributed the electricity to a specific property of living tissue and believed he had discovered the vital nervous fluid. He likened the nerve-muscle preparation to a Leyden jar, in which the muscles were the reservoirs of this peculiar electricity; whereas the nerves were conductors. The following excerpts are from Green's translation of the *Commentary,*[3] one of the important components in the surge of Galvanic literature during the past generation. A bibliography of his commentaries and the translation and publication of his diary are other noteworthy contributions.[1]

I dissected and prepared a frog . . . and placed it on a table, on which was an electrical machine . . . widely removed from its conductor and separated by no brief interval. When by chance one of those who were assisting me gently touched the point of a scalpel to the medial crural nerves . . . of this frog, immediately all the muscles of the limbs seemed to be so contracted that they appeared to have fallen into violent tonic convulsions. But another of the assistants, who was on hand when I did electrical experiments, seemed to observe that the same things occurred whenever a spark was discharged from the conductor of the machine.

Aroused by the novelty of the circumstance, we resolved to test it in various ways, and to experiment . . . since the scalpel had a bone handle, when the same handle was held by the hand, even though a spark was produced, no movements resulted, but they did ensue, if the fingers touched either the metallic blade or the iron nails securing the blade of the scalpel.

Now, since dry bones possess a non-conductile, but the metallic blade and the iron nails a conductile nature, we came into this suspicion, that perhaps it happened that when we held the bony handle with our fingers, then all access was cut off from the electric current, in whatever way it was acting on the frog, but that it was afforded when we touched the blade or the nails communicating therewith.

The effects of stormy atmospheric electricity having been tested, my heart burned with desire to test also the power of peaceful, everyday electricity.

Wherefore, since I had sometimes seen prepared frogs placed in iron gratings which surround a certain hanging garden of my house, equipped also with bronze hooks in their spinal cord, fall into the customary contractions, not only when the sky was lightning, but also sometimes when it was quiet and serene, I thought these contractions derived their origin from the changes which sometimes occur in atmospheric electricity. . . . Finally, weary with vain expectation I began to press the bronze hooks, whereby their spinal cords were fixed, against the iron gratings, to see whether by this kind of device they excited muscular contractions, and in various states of the atmosphere, and of electricity whatever variety and mutation they presented; not infrequently, indeed, I observed contractions, but bearing no relation to varied state of atmosphere or of electricity.

But when I had transported the animal into a closed chamber and placed him on an iron surface, and had begun to press against it the hook fixed in his spinal cord, behold the same contractions and the same motions! Likewise continuously, I tried using other metals, in other places, other houses and days; and the same result.

Two members of Galvani's family on his experimental team aided him in the defense of his thesis against Volta and other antagonists. Lucia, his wife, attractive, learned, and daughter of Domenico Galeazzi, Galvani's teacher of anatomy, was an effective collaborator in the laboratory. His nephew, Giovanni Aldini, an electrical scientist in his own right and professor of physics at Bologna, sparred effectively with Volta, who had initially accepted Galvani's interpretations but later repudiated them. Aldini carried on the study of animal electricity, edited some of his uncle's original work during the latter's saddened final years, and continued writing after Galvani's death. Galvani himself seemed less disturbed by the scientific polemics than by the death of his wife and the decree by Napoleon whereby officers of the state were required to swear an oath of allegiance to the new constitution. Galvani refused, having already pledged his life to the old constitution. He was deprived temporarily of his university position and was reinstated only posthumously, a regrettable finale for a great medical scientist who recognized, but inadequately appreciated, his discovery of animal electricity.

1. Fulton, J. F., and Cushing, H.: A Bibliographical Study of the Galvani and the Aldini Writings on Animal Electricity, *Ann Sci* 1:239-268 (July) 1936.

2. Galvani, A. L.: De Viribus Electricitatis in Motu Musculari Commentarius, *Bonon Sci Art Inst Acad* 7:363-418, 1791.

3. Galvani, A. L.: *Commentary on the Effect of Electricity on Muscular Motion*, R. Green (trans.), Cambridge, Mass: E. Licht, 1953.

4. Galvani, A. L.: *Commentary on the Effects of Electricity on Muscular Motion*, M. G. Foley (trans.), Norwalk, Conn: Burndy Library, 1953.

5. *Unpublished Memoirs and Experiments of Luigi Galvani* (Ital), Bologna: L. Capelli, 1937.

Biblioteca Nazionale, Milan

Domenico Cotugno
(1736-1822)

DOMENICO COTUGNO (Dominicus Cotunnius), practitioner to the people and the Royal house and professor of anatomy at the University of Naples, was born into a family of humble means in Ruvo, southern Italy.[1] He received his early education from the Jesuits. At the age of 17, under the sponsorship of the feudal lord of the Cotugno family, Domenico attended the University of Naples where each of his major contributions was made in the years immediately following. For the sake of his education, he underwent a great physical and economic struggle and endured a temporary period of critical illness contracted while serving as resident physician in the Neapolitan Hospital for Incurables. Subsequently, having received doctorate degrees in philosophy and physic, and secure in his interest in medicine and his improved health, he taught surgery and began his research and practice.

In anatomy, Cotugno gave particular attention to the petrous portion of the temporal bone, describing his findings in *De aquaeductibus auris humanae internae*.[2] The profusely illustrated volume, first published in 1760, identified the aqueduct of the inner ear (the canal of Cotunnius), the columns in the osseous spiral lamina of the cochlea (Cotunnius' columns), and the nasopalatine nerve, observed concomitantly with Scarpa. Cotugno also confirmed the presence of fluid in the labyrinth of the semicircular canals, first described in 1742 by Pyl, who discussed its role in the transmission of sound. His second great work, *De ischiade nervosa commentarius*, appeared in 1764. In it he described albumin in the urine in a patient with acute nephritis and also the cerebrospinal fluid as observed in anatomical dissection. Cotugno's profound appreciation to the patrons and governors of the hospital for the responsibilities assigned at so young an age is expressed in the preface.[3]

For I remember that from the time in which you nominated me to the office of Physician of your hospital (during the space of ten years) you have omitted no opportunity of laying on me additional obligations. But above all, I now, and ever shall remember your great kindness towards me, in appointing me, when I was scarce three-and-twenty years old, to that important province of reading lectures in the Royal Academy, to a select number of pupils in Surgery; a study that draws such multitudes to the hospital. Since, before me, no one was ever appointed by you, except a man distinguished above others for his learning; and since I, who was so young, was preferred before many famous men to this important trust, it is a sufficient indication of the notice you was [sic] pleased to take, not of my abilities, but my diligence and assiduity; in which I strove not to be outdone by any one.

In the section on coagulability of body fluids a thermolabile substance in the urine of a young soldier with rapidly developing anasarca was noted. Although Dekker of Leyden, in 1694, had observed the effect of heat and acetic acid on singular urines, Cotugno's findings of albuminuria in a case of acute nephritis are worthy of excerpting.[3]

I will begin with the urine, which is supposed in general not to be coagulable, and yet, in some experiments, which I shall mention by and by, I have observed it acquire a coagulum.

17. There was a soldier of about eight-and-twenty years of age, who, for a great part of the summer, was stationed at the swamps of Bajae. About the end of August he was seized with a quotidian intermittent fever, and on the fifth day

he had a wonderful eruption of intercutaneous water. About the beginning of September he was sent to the hospital of incurables, and put under my care. At this time, besides an enormous watery tumor over his whole body, he laboured under a quotidian fever: the dropsy, under the attacks of the fever, seemed to encrease every day.

Now, therefore, I resolved to try what *Cream of Tartar* would do, as I had often found before that it provoked urine without any great acceleration of the pulse. I began to give him the quantity of half an ounce in the morning, every day, dissolved in a considerable quantity of the decoction of Germander. The quantity was so encreased by this remedy, that the patient voided every night ten or twelve pints of high-coloured urine. But as the patient himself confessed what he drank was much less in quantity, it is beyond a doubt that this prodigious quantity of urine was drawn off, in a great measure, from those waters which caused the dropsy. Although the decreasing tumour manifested this plainly, I yet thought proper, by placing the urine over a fire, to prove it experimentally; for, as I knew that the intercutaneous water, which I had observed in the bodies of such as died of the dropsy, contained a coagulable matter, I was induced to hope, that, if the patient had voided any such water by urine, the coagulable matter, which abounded there, would be shewn by the fire. This was proved, experimentally, to be as I imagined; for, on placing two pints of the urine over the fire, when one half was evaporated, the other formed itself into a white mass, like the soft white of an egg when boiled.

In the first portion of the treatise, Cotugno differentiated the principal species of sciatica—one of the first contemporary descriptions. Fixation of pain in the hip identified the first type, arthritic sciatica; whereas radiation down the leg identified the second type, nervous sciatica (Cotugno's disease). The latter was further divided into anterior and posterior radiation. Little progress has been made in determining the pathogenesis of the disturbance in the intervening centuries.[3]

8. If therefore the seat of this Posterior Nervous Sciatica is in the Ischiadic Nerve, it remains to enquire, what cause begets this affection of the nerve, and what part of the nerve it invests, and whence derived. For it seems to be an acrid and irritating matter, which lying on the nerve, preys on the stamina, and gives rise to the pain. Nor can it be doubted that this matter occupies the cavities of the nervous Stamina, as they are full of a humour which they receive from the brain, and which cannot be acrid when

the fountain is uncorrupt. Therefore it seems to pass between the nervous Stamina, and to be contained in the celluar Vaginae that enclose them. From whence this matter is derived, seems no easy question to be resolved.

In the same chapter Cotugno discusses the fluid within the dura mater of the brain and spinal cord. The failure of anatomists to observe the fluid was attributed to its escape in the common practice of decapitation in carrying out the death penalty in criminals, or to the "preposterous" technique of dissection. When the brain was dissected in the intact body, cerebrospinal fluid was present and had not been replaced by air, nor was the space collapsed. In testing its coagulability, Cotugno found it low in albumin since it evaporated without a residuum when when placed over a fire.[3]

This tube of the Dura Mater is not so large as to touch the surrounding enclosure of the spine on all sides, nor so narrow as to embrace the included marrow closely: but it is somewhat distant from the hollow of the spine, chiefly backwards towards the seat of the spinal *Apophyses,* and is separated from the *Ambitus* of the enclosed marrow by a considerable space. These two spaces, when a man is in health, are not empty, but each is filled with a matter peculiar to itself; for all that space, which is between the Dura Mater and the enclosure of the hollow of the spine, is always filled with a cellular kind of substance, replete with a soft and fluid kind of fat; in the room of this, in consumptive persons there is a mucid *vapour,* and a true mucus in dropsical persons, and in foetuses suffocated in difficult labours, a sanguineous *vapour.* But, also, all that space which is between the Vagina of the Dura Mater, and the spinal marrow, is always found to be filled, not as some eminent men imagine (because the fact is as yet immersed in obscurity) by the marrow itself, which is more full in living, than in dead subjects, nor by a thick vapour; but with water, like that which the Pericardium contains about the heart; or such as fills the hollows of the ventricles of the brain, the labyrinth of the ear, or other cavities of the body, which are impervious to the air.

10. This water, which fills the tube of the Dura Mater even to the *Os sacrum,* does not entirely enclose the spinal marrow, but even abounds in the cavity of the skull, and fills all the spaces which are between the brain and the *ambitus* of the Dura Mater.

11. The reason that anatomists have never yet observed this collection of water about the brain, and in the spine, is owing to the common preposterous method of dissecting; for, when they are about to examine the brain, they commonly cut off the head from the neck; by this means the tube of the Dura Mater, which descends by the spine of the neck, being cut through, all the water that is collected about the brain, and the spinal marrow, flows out, and is foolishly lost; so that, when the skull is opened, all the spaces between the brain and the Dura Mater, which were before filled with water, are now found empty; and deceive the anatomist with the appearance of empty cavities, which, perhaps, some dissipable vapour filled.

Cotugno provided a good pathological description of pustules in smallpox, and, during the 1764 typhus-typhoid epidemic in Naples, he observed intestinal ulcers which were reported by Sarcone. He advocated measures for the prevention and spread of pulmonary tuberculosis and was one of the first to formulate a theory on the physiology of hearing. In the midst of these highly productive years and just after reaching the age of 30, Cotugno was chosen professor of surgery and anatomy. Shortly before receiving his professorial appointment, he made a leisurely pilgrimage to counsel with Morgagni, visiting private and public libraries along the way. During the impoverished years of medical study, Cotugno was granted the unusual privilege of using the hospital library. He was a collector as well as admirer of books and owned a remarkable private library at his death. Many of the items were bequeathed to the National Library in Naples; the poor of the hospital where he spent his formative years received a substantial endowment.

1. Viets, H. R.: Domenico Cotugno: His Description of the Cerebrospinal Fluid, *Bull Hist Med* 3:701-738 (Nov) 1935.

2. Cotugno, D.: *The Aqueduct of the Human Internal Ear* (L), Vienna: R. Graeffer, 1774.

3. Cotugno, D.: *Treatise on the Nervous Sciatica or Nervous Hip Gout* (L), Naples: Simonios Brothers, 1764.

Antonio Scarpa (1752-1832)

ANTONIO SCARPA, best known for Scarpa's triangle, one of his lesser contributions. He was a learned man of great industry, however, born in poverty in the Venetian village of Mott di Livenza and dying in Pavia, leaving a great legacy.[1] Brilliant and precocious, he was taught by his uncle, a priest, until the age of 15, when he entered the University of Padua as a student in medicine, becoming the assistant and later personal secretary of the aging Morgagni. An interest in pathological anatomy, precise

National Library of Medicine

procedures of investigation, and other commendable attributes may be traced to the tutelage and influence of his academic master. He preferred Latin as the language of scientific communication, written and spoken. During a full life, Scarpa left valuable contributions in otolaryngology, orthopedics, ophthalmology, neuroanatomy, and general surgery.

At the age of 20, Scarpa was appointed professor of anatomy and clinical surgery at the University of Modena, where he began his extraordinary career of teaching, investigation, and literary composition. While in his early 30's, he was called to the chair of anatomy at the University of Pavia, with the promise of a new laboratory, an anatomical amphitheater, a museum, and other facilities for the revitalization of the school of medicine. At various times he visited medical centers in Paris and London, for his tyranny and his temper often made absences from Italy not only feasible but also desirable.

One of Scarpa's first treatises on the anatomy and physiology of the ear, *De*

structura fenestrae rotundae auris, appeared in 1772.[2] The membrane attached to the round window was identified as the second tympanum and was recognized as the transmitting organ between the tympanic membrane and the inner ear. The investigations on the auditory and olfactory nerves were published in 1789.[3] *Anatomicae disquisitiones* provides the initial description of the membranous labyrinth, the aqua labyrinthi, and the recognition and definition of the channels of the semicircular canals. The fluid was later known as liquor scarpae. Scarpa described the naso-palatine nerve, the roots of the olfactory nerve in the brain, the structure of the olfactory area, and cubitodigital neuralgia (Weir Mitchell's causalgia). His contributions were particularly remarkable when it is realized that Pavia was a community of less than 20,000 persons and the hospital wards contained fewer than 300 beds.

The physiology of the heart and surgery of blood vessels were other subjects of study. The cardiac nerves were found to be independent of central nervous origins. The sympathetic nerves that supplied the muscle bundles were described in a treatise which appeared in 1794 and which enjoyed several editions. In the discussion of the ligature of the principal arteries of the extremities, partial closure of the vessel, followed by a period of waiting, was recommended. The final step was intraluminal closure.[4]

This process of union between the two opposite internal parietes of the inflamed artery, kept in mutual contact, does not differ essentially from that of the re-union of a simple wound, nor materially from that where reciprocal and firm adhesion is formed between *similar* parts inflamed and closely applied to each other: whether this be effected merely by the inosculation of vessels, or by means of the organisable coagulable lymph, or by both of these modes of union conjoined.

In describing the development of an aneurism of the thoracic and abdominal aorta, Scarpa attributed the primary pathogenesis to dissolution and separation of the inner coats of the vessel followed by dilation of the enveloping membranes.[5]

1. It is a great error, if I may be permitted to say so, although one which has been for a long

time introduced into medicine, to suppose, that the aneurism at the curvature, or in the trunk of the aorta, produced by a violent and sudden exertion of the whole body, or of the heart in particular, and preceded by a congenital relaxation of a certain portion of this artery, or by some internal morbid cause, capable of weakening its coats, ought always to be considered as a tumour formed by the distention or dilatation of the proper coats of the artery itself, that is, of its internal and fibrous coats. In opposition to this doctrine, which has been generally adopted in the schools, there is nothing in all pathology, which, in my opinion, can be more easily demonstrated than the contrary, or that the aneurism at the curvature, or in the thoracic or abdominal trunk of the aorta, is not produced by a dilatation, but by a corrosion and rupture of the proper coats of the aorta, and consequently by the effusion of arterial blood under the cellular sheath, or any other membrane which covers externally the injured artery.

In a treatise on congenital clubfeet of children—one of the early monographs in orthopedics—Scarpa based his manipulative correction upon anatomical and functional principles.[6]

18. In consequence of what has been stated with regard to the particular manner of contortion round their lesser axis of the greater part of the bones of the tarsus, in the *congenital club foot turned* inwards, and with regard to the want of equilibrium between the muscular powers moving the foot, as well as of their tendons and ligaments, the indications of cure of this deformity will be: 1. To cause an insensible and gradual turning of the *os naviculare, cuboides,* and *os calcis,* and with these the *cuneiform* and *metatarsal* bones in a contrary direction to that which the deformity has produced, and, consequently, to bring back the fore-part of the foot into its proper and natural direction with the tibia. 2. To substitute for the deficiency of the activity of the external ligaments of the foot, but more particularly of the *peronei* muscles, an artificial force, capable not only of counterbalancing that of the tense internal ligaments, and of the shortened *tibiales* muscles, but likewise of overcoming it, and of causing, by means of this artificial force, the external margin of the foot to remain, to use the expression, as it were, suspended upon the ground. 3. As soon as the equilibrium between the muscles of the tibia and fibula is restored, to promote, by means of the combined action of these two classes of muscles, the direct flexion of the foot upon the tibia, so that, as soon as the great tension of the tendo Achilles, and of the muscles of the calf of the leg, is overcome, the posterior tuberosity of the *os calcis* may be depressed, and brought into a proper direction with

the sole of the foot, and that the foot may thus regain its aptitude for performing the motions of flexion and extension.

The monograph on disorders of the eye was published in 1801[7] and was followed by translations into French, German, Dutch, and English. The cataract was treated by depression as opposed to extraction. Scarpa described also the procedure for treatment of staphyloma, instruction for making an artificial pupil, and the surgical treatment of dropsy of the eyeball.

In his *Treatise on Hernia,* Scarpa differentiated between inguinal and femoral hernias, described the sliding hernia of the inguinal canal, and was the first to suggest a means for correcting strangulation without entering the scrotal sac. Thus, he disclosed an accurate knowledge of the correct nature of the lesion.[8]

34. The scrotal hernia formed by the caecum with the appendix vermiformis, and the beginning of the colon, being always large, presents appearances in the act of operating which may lead to error, and especially it might be thought, that these intestines were on the outside of the hernial sac, or unprovided with a membranous sac formed by the descent of the peritoneum. If any one skilled in anatomy will reflect a little on this transposition of parts, and recollect, that the caecum with the beginning of the colon in the right ileo-lumbar region, is not entirely inclosed within the great sac of the peritoneum, and that a portion of these intestines, sunk in the cellular substance on the right side, is absolutely without the great abdominal membranous sac, he will immediately discover, that in a scrotal hernia of such a description, a portion of the caecum and of the beginning of the colon, will be found included and contained in the hernial sac, while another portion of the same intestines will be necessarily without the sac, and lying denuded in the cellular substance which accompanies the descent of the peritoneum in the hernia.

But supposing, that a large and inveterate hernia formed by the caecum is actually affected by strangulation, so that the operation is absolutely necessary for freeing the patient from so dangerous an accident, the surgeon will prepare for it, guided by the reflection that the protruded viscera, on account of their particular connexion with the hernial sac, are not susceptible of being completely returned into the abdomen. On which account, there not being the smallest suspicion of gangrene, and knowing likewise that in this case, as in all those of large and old scrotal hernia [sic], the neck of the hernial sac is never the immediate cause of strangulation, the surgeon having divided the common integuments, will lay bare the inguinal ring, and will divide it from [the dermal aspect] without his hand unsupported, taking care not to wound the subjacent neck of the hernial sac, in such a manner as to set the protruded viscera at liberty, without exposing them to the contact of the air, and by gentle pressure on the tumor he will make the accumulated feces and flatus as much as possible to return the protruded viscera.

Scarpa's triangle, an area bordered by the inguinal ligament and the superficial muscles of the thigh, was described in the report of an operation for a popliteal aneurism.[5]

The surgeon pressing with his fore-finger, will explore the course of the *superficial* femoral artery, from the crural arch downwards, and when he comes to the place where he does not feel any more, or very confusedly, the vibration of the *superficial* femoral artery, he will there fix with his eye the inferior angle or extremity of the incision which he proposes to make for bringing this artery into view. This lower angle of the incision to be made will fall nearly on the internal margin of the sartorius muscle, just where this muscle crosses the course of the *superficial* femoral artery, and at the apex of the triangle formed by the convergence of the adductor *secundus* and vastus *internus* muscles of the thigh. A little more than three inches above the place pointed out, the surgeon will begin the incision of the integuments and cellular substance with the convex-edged bistoury, and will carry the incision along the thigh, in a slightly oblique line from without inwards, following the course of the femoral artery as far as the point fixed with the eye, or to the apex of the triangle formed by the intersection of the two just mentioned muscles, and where this vertex is crossed by the sartorius muscle.

Since Scarpa was endowed with indefatigable industry, his accomplishments of one-half a century in medicine were surpassed by few. In a review of his contributions, one soon reaches the assumption that he approached the stature in medical sciences in Italy attained by a few countrymen, notably Malpighi, Morgagni, and Vesalius. Whether because of his brilliant mind, or in spite of his many accomplishments, Scarpa was ruthless in his dealings with others and was feared or hated by some. He never married, but he apparently sired several sons, for whom he assumed some responsibility. Honors included for-

eign membership in the Royal Society of London and the Royal Academy of Sciences in Paris, and the Cross of the Legion of Honor bestowed by Napoleon, inadequate as honors are for such a brilliant anatomist and surgeon.

1. Monti, A.: *Antonio Scarpa*, F. L. Loria, trans., New York: Vigo Press, 1957.
2. Scarpa, A.: *De Structura Fenestrae Rotundae Auris et de Tympano Secundario Anatomicae Observationes,* Mutinae: 1772.
3. Scarpa, A.: *Anatomicae Disquisitiones de Auditu et Alfactu,* Ticini: P. Galeatii, 1789.
4. Scarpa, A.: *A Treatise on Aneurism,* J. H. Wishart, trans., Edinburgh: Stirling and Slade, 1819.
5. Scarpa, A.: *A Treatise on the Anatomy, Pathology, and Surgical Treatment of Aneurism,* J. H. Wishart, trans., Edingurgh: Mundell, Doig & Stevenson, 1808.
6. Scarpa, A.: *A Memoir on the Congenital Club Feet of Children,* J. H. Wishart, trans., Edinburgh: A. Constable and Company, 1818.
7. Scarpa, A.: *A Treatise on the Principal Diseases of the Eyes,* 2nd ed, J. Briggs, trans., London: T. Cadell and W. Davies, 1818.
8. Scarpa, A.: *A Treatise on Hernia,* J. H. Wishart, trans., Edinburgh: T. Bryce & Co., 1814.

Jacob Anton Helm (1761-1831)

ALTHOUGH WILLIAM BEAUMONT is usually credited with the first experimental studies of gastric digestion from direct observation of the contents of the human stomach, a Viennese physician, Jacob (Jakob) Helm, a generation earlier, recorded the first critical clinical and experimental findings in a woman with a hole in her stomach. Helm was born in a suburb of Vienna, became later the father of three sons, one of whom entered law, the other two medicine. He was a warm, sympathetic, and unpretentious general practitioner who taught obstetrics at the University of Vienna, was physician to the Pensions-Institut für Witwen und Waisen, a charitable society for widows and orphans of physicians, and served as superintendent of another charitable institution, Stumpfe'sche Stiftung für Mediziner.[1]

Helm's main claim to renown in the history of medicine is a protocol of direct observations on the physiological response of the gastric mucosa to mechanical stimulation and his thorough investigations of the digestion in the human stomach. Scant attention was given to Helm and his experimental studies in the immediate subsequent period in Europe; whereas Beaumont made no mention of his predecessor's work in his monograph published in 1833. One exception was a reference by Benjamin Waterhouse of Boston in a public lecture on the evils of tobacco.[2] The initial report by Helm appeared in a family almanac in 1801.[3] This was followed in 1803 by a communication in book form.[4] No visual studies were reported of the response of the lining of the stomach; however, there were chemical studies on the aspirated gastric juice, investigations on the effect of mechanical stimulation of the gastric mucosa, the speed of digestion of various foods, and the delayed digestion following irrigation of the stomach.[3]

A patient's history in an almanac—Pfui!—this does not belong here. Many of our readers will think and say so, without considering that we speak of the stomach (an organ, which, even if one does not assume it to be the seat of the soul as some philosophers state, is regarded by many as the index of bourgeois happiness) which arouses a very special interest.

Theresia Perzin, 56 years old, from Braitenwaida in northern Austria, the wife of a straw cutter, mother of 7 children, suffered for 18 years from attacks of vomiting, abdominal pains and from an external inflammation of the abdominal wall, without consulting a doctor. The mass in the abdominal wall finally burst and, through an infected fistula, came food and liquid that had been swallowed. The fistula communicated with the inside of the stomach. This was evident from touch. It was possible to insert a finger into the stomach and feel the pulsations of the aorta. During this maneuver, the patient felt neither pain nor revulsion.

With the aggravation of symptoms the unlucky woman finally sought relief from the General Hospital of Vienna in 1798. Of all foods, nothing gave her less pain than sauerkraut, sour vegetable roots, and salads. If she felt uncomfortable after such a meal, she drew the offending food out through the opening of her stomach with her fingers. Then she flushed out her stomach with drinking water; this relieved her and the appetite returned.

I had her come back to Vienna in November 1800, partly to observe this remarkable case more closely, partly to show her to some of my colleagues who did not believe my story. In Vienna she was seen by many and was shown to the young doctors and surgeons during all public medical lectures.

I repeated the experiment with milk and noticed that it always turned sour and coagulated. The sole exception was immediately after the patient had flushed her stomach; the milk which she drank immediately after did not coagulate for some time, presumably for the lack of gastric juice. That could be hastened always by stimulating the inner surface of her stomach with the finger.

Further experiments showed that of the different kinds of milk, donkey's milk took the longest to coagulate. Cow's milk did not immediately as did goat's milk and human milk. Among the different food, meat was digested quickest; also cheese and eggs. All vegetables took longer.

The patient, who was observed over a period of five years, died in 1802. In his book, Helm referred to physiological and pharmacological observations on digestion by Spallanzani and Gosse as well as control experiments on himself and a Mr. Ziriak Siebeler. He also noted that the temperature of the fundus of the stomach was greater than that of the mouth or axilla and demonstrated the practicability of feeding a patient for periods of time through an artificial opening in the stomach wall.[4]

During a five-year period, during which I studied the patient, I made the following observations:

Injection of a solution of one grain of tartar emetic dissolved in an ounce of water into the stomach made the patient uneasy within five minutes, with a burning pain. Since she was emaciated, the worm-like movements of the stomach were visible through the abdominal wall. To relieve the pain, the stomach was washed repeatedly with water and milk; one-half hour later she was relieved. Three hours later there were four watery bowel movements.

I made the experiment of feeding the patient through the opening. Every four hours I brought small amounts of different kinds of food into the opening of the stomach, and the patient felt neither hunger nor thirst. After 14 hours, she felt dryness of the mouth and the throat, which disappeared as soon as she rinsed her mouth with water. In this way she felt excellent for 36 hours.

Even though thorough chewing of foods is good for digestion, the patient digested very well the food which was inserted directly into the stomach. Pastour Koppauer, whom I mentioned above, assured me that the patient later on repeatedly used this way of feeding herself by inserting the food into the opening directly, because it was more comfortable for her and she did not have to change the bandages as often as before. In order to observe the digestion of different kinds of foods, ie, to see how digestion starts, which foods are digested most easily, and how the digestion of my patient differs from that of healthy people, I repeated the experimentations of Spallanzani and Gosse.

1. Kisch, B.: Jacob Helm's Observations and Experiments on Human Digestion, *J Hist Med* 9:311-328, 1954.

2. Waterhouse, B.: *Cautions to Young Persons Concerning Health,* Cambridge: University Press, 1805.

3. Helm, J.: History of an Otherwise Healthy Person with a Hole in the Stomach Which Can Be Seen from the Outside (Ger), *Gesundheits Taschenbuch,* Vienna: K. Schaumburg, 1801, pp 241-245, excerpt translated by E. Longar.

4. Helm, J.: *Two Case Histories* (Ger), Vienna: *Camesinaischen Buchhandlung,* 1803, excerpt translated by E. Longar.

William Charles Wells (1757-1817)

WILLIAM CHARLES WELLS, born at Charleston, South Carolina, rose to fame in London as a natural scientist and an acute clinical observer, and lived a life of notable and diverse adventures and fortunes. His parents were born near Glasgow, Scotland; his father was an untalented bookbinder, newspaper man, and an uncompromising Colonial Tory.[1] After the parents emigrated to America, their son completed his grammar school training in Dumfries, Scotland, and spent one year in the lower classes at the University of Edinburgh. Returning to Charleston, Wells pursued a three-year apprenticeship with Dr. Alexander Garden, the community's prominent physician, who retained a scholarly interest in zoology and botany.

In 1775, shortly after the Revolution broke out in New England, Tory sympathies drew father and son back to Great Britain; there William Charles devoted three years to formal medical studies at Edinburgh. He passed the preparatory trials for the MD degree but did not graduate at that time. His training was continued in London, where he attended lectures of William Hunter and took instruction in practical anatomy. Subsequently, he was accepted as surgeon's pupil at St. Bartholomew's Hos-

pital. Early in 1779, Wells served with a Scottish regiment in Holland but gave up the commission after a year because of an irascible temper and dissatisfaction with his commanding officer. During three months spent in Leyden, he prepared his inaugural thesis on the subject of cold, "a paltry affair." He then proceeded to Edinburgh, and in 1780 received the degree of doctor of medicine. Wells returned to Charleston while the English troops were still on foreign soil. Upon their evacuation of Charleston in 1782, he moved to St. Augustine, Florida, and set up a printing press which he had brought with him. He began the publication of a weekly newspaper and in his leisure time performed in a repertory theater. Following preliminary peace negotiations, Wells returned to Charleston but soon was arrested for his Tory sentiments (published or expressed verbally) and his brother's debts. He spent a few weeks in prison but not in repentance.

Wells's wanderings ceased in 1784. He arrived in London to spend the remainder of his life, except for a short holiday in 1785 in Paris, in scientific endeavors and a financially disappointing practice of medicine. Even as a bachelor, he barely subsisted with hospital appointments. This difficult life was counterbalanced by the friendship and backing of Matthew Baillie, David Pitcairn, and a number of other London notables.

Wells was admitted a licentiate of the College of Physicians in 1788 but was not advanced to Fellow at the time he judged it his due. He was appointed physician to the Finsbury Dispensary in 1789, assistant physician to St. Thomas' Hospital in 1795, and full physician in 1800. Fellowship in the Royal Society of London came to him in 1793, and, in 1816, he received their Rumford medal for his original investigations on the formation of evening dew, which were simply planned but eminently fruitful.

During this portion of his career, Wells made his major scientific contributions and clinical observations. In ophthalmology, he discussed single vision with two eyes, hyperopia, the effects of belladonna on the refractive point of the eye, and consensual pupillary reaction. General medical discourses included erysipelas, tetanus, pulmonary consumption, and the two observations excerpted below. One of his last essays, the difference in the color and form between the white and Negro races of men,[2] was highly regarded by Charles Darwin and was mentioned in the latter's *Origin of Species* as follows.[3]

In this paper he [Wells] distinctly recognizes the principle of natural selection, and this is the first recognition which has been indicated; but he applies it only to the races of man, and to certain characters alone. . . . He observes, firstly, that all animals tend to vary in some degree, and, secondly, that agriculturists improve their domesticated animals by selection; and then, he adds, but what is done in this latter case "by art, seems to be done with equal efficiency, though more slowly, by nature, in the formation of varieties of mankind, fitted for the country which they inhabit."

Wells's essay on dew[4] was published shortly before his death. He described his evening observations collected under considerable physical handicap, having suffered his first attack of apoplexy more than a decade earlier. Working in the garden of a friend in Surrey with small thermometers, metal plates, watchglasses, and pledgets of wool and swansdown, Wells showed that dew as well as hoarfrost is the result of decreased temperature of ground substances, which had lost heat by radiation consequent to the setting of the sun under a clear sky. Most bodies radiate heat with a subsequent decrement in temperature, but at night the sun cannot make up the deficit. Poor conductors of heat, such as grass, radiate heat more rapidly, are more quickly cooled below the dew point of the atmosphere, and are most susceptible to formation of dew.

Two clinical observations by Wells are also valuable. Irrespective of chronological priority, his recognition of cardiac complications in acute rheumatic fever proved to be a notable report for the Society for the Improvement of Medical and Chirurgical Knowledge. Wells introduced his communication on rheumatic valvular heart disease with a reference to David Pitcairn's observations of 1788. These were published in 1797 in the second edition of Baillie's *Morbid Anatomy*. Wells added 14 examples to the literature, described rheumatic nodules in one case and liver enlargement and pericarditis, postmortem, in another. Excerpts of case reports of three of his young patients are as follows.[5]

Mr. T. M. came from Scotland in April, 1798, to reside in Berkshire, being then in his eighteenth year. He was of a fair complexion, short stature, and a habit rather full than muscular. From the age of nine years he had been every year attacked with acute rheumatism. Four of the attacks had been very severe, each of them confining him to bed for several weeks; the others seldom kept him at home longer than a week, though the redness, swelling, and pain of the joints did not leave him for two or three weeks more.
I began to suspect, that this disease might be rheumatism of the heart, of which I knew nothing, except what I had learned from Dr. Baillie's publication. I carried him therefore to Dr. Pitcairn, who confirmed my conjecture, and was fearful that he would not recover.

Martha Clifton, aged nearly fifteen years, was admitted into St. Thomas' Hospital, on the 18th of February, 1802, after labouring under acute rheumatism about sixteen days. Her pulse was small, but the heart struck the ribs with such force, that its beats could be reckoned by applying the hand to the right side of the chest.
Many of the tendons of the superficial muscles in this patient were studded with numerous small hard tumours, an appearance I have observed only in one other person, a thin and feeble man forty-one years old, who also laboured under rheumatism.

I visited Miss A. L. for the first time, on the 17th of September, 1806, at her father's house in Surrey, distant about eight miles from London. She was sixteen years old, tall, and thin, and had never menstruated.
In the beginning of August, shortly after remaining some time in a cold cellar, she was seized with pains, swelling, and redness of her joints, and fever. These symptoms lasted only ten days.
The whole of the internal surface of the pericardium was attached to the heart, by means of two distinct layers of solid matter, each having the thickness of a shilling; the outer resembled coagulated blood, while the inner was whitish, and sufficiently tenacious to permit its being torn. The surface of the heart was also inflamed, and, from the right auricle to the apex, black; its substance was flaccid, and appeared to be enlarged. About a pint of bloody serum was found in each cavity of the chest. A considerable quantity of fluid, slightly red, was likewise found

in the abdomen. The right lobe of the liver was enlarged, and much inflammed, and on its concave surface, black.

The second of Wells's bedside observations, made 15 years before Richard Bright's remarkable monograph, was the detection of albuminous urine in patients with anascara. Albumin was identified in 78 urines obtained from a total of 130 patients afflicted with dropsy unrelated to scarlet fever. Although postmortem observations in some cases showed significant alterations of the kidney, Wells recognized no specific cause-and-effect relationship between anatomical changes in the kidney and albuminuria.[6]

I have examined by means of one, or other, or both, of the tests which have been mentioned, the urine of one hundred and thirty persons, affected with dropsy from other causes than scarlet fever, of whom ninety-five were males, and thirty-five females; and have found serum in that of seventy-eight, sixty of whom were males and eighteen females.

In about a third of the cases in which serum was detected in the urine, its quantity was small, the bulk of the coagulum produced by heat and nitrous acid, after remaining undisturbed twenty-four hours, being only from one-tenth to one-fortieth of that of the urine, which contained it. . . . In the remaining cases with serous urine, amounting to about half of the whole number, all the distinguishable intermediate quantities of coagulated matter were formed in that fluid by heat and nitrous acid.

I shall now mention what was seen in the body of another person, a soldier, forty-seven years old, who had likewise died dropsical, and in whose urine a considerable quantity of serum had been present.

The kidnies were much harder than they usually are. Their cortical part was thickened and changed in its structure, from the deposition of coagulable lymph, and there was a small quantity of pus in the pelvis of one of them. I do not conclude, however, from these appearances, and those which were found in the former case, that the kidneys are always diseased, when the urine in dropsy contains much serum. The morbid appearances in the kidnies might be altogether unconnected with the morbid secretion.

1. Wells, W. C.: *A Memoir of the Life of William Charles Wells,* London: A Constable & Co. Edinburgh, 1818.

2. Wells, W. C.: *An Account of a Female of the White Race of Mankind, Part of Whose Skin Resembles That of a Negro,* London: A. Constable & Co. Edinburgh, 1818.

3. Darwin, C.: *The Origin of Species,* New York: D. Appleton & Co., 1896, vol 1.

4. Wells, W. C.: *An Essay on Dew, and Several Appearances Connected With It,* London: Taylor & Hessey, 1814.

5. Wells, W. C.: On Rheumatism of the Heart, *Trans Soc Improv Med Chir Knowl* 3:373-424, 1812.

6. Wells, W. C.: On the Presence of Red Matter and Serum of Blood in the Urine of Dropsy, Which Has Not Originated From Scarlet Fever, *Trans Soc Improv Med Chir Knowl* 3:194-257, 1812.

National Library of Medicine

William Beaumont (1785-1853)

No MORE FAMOUS DOCTOR-PATIENT RELATIONSHIP is recorded in medical or lay literature than William Beaumont's medical and surgical care of Alexis St. Martin, implemented by sympathetic and charitable ministrations to this French Canadian voyageur. Alexis, in return, and through practical appreciation, permitted intermittently for almost a decade a unique series of direct observations on his gastric juice and the physiological phenomena of digestion. Beaumont was born in Lebanon, Connecticut, in 1785, whereas his patient, Alexis Bidagan dit St. Martin, was born at Berthier, Lower Canada, now the Province of Quebec, near Montreal, Canada. The precise date of St. Martin's birth remains *sub judice*. Beaumont's clinical notes (1822) merely state that he cared for an 18-year-old. Whittaker,[1] a long time student of St. Martin and Beaumont, believes the correct date to be April 18, 1794, which would make St. Martin a decade older than Beaumont. A parish record for Berthier lists an Alexis St. Martin born in 1794.[2] There is some suspicion, however, that this person subsequently died and that the famous patient was born in 1803 or 1804.

In the winter of 1806-07, Beaumont left home, tried farming for a time in Champlain, New York, taught school, and read medicine, until 1810, when he became apprenticed to Dr. Benamin Chandler of St. Alban's, Vermont. Two years were devoted to professional apprenticeship, which included note taking, reading medical texts from Chandler's library, and occasionally dissection and a postmortem examination.[3] Beaumont became licensed in 1812 by the Third Medical Society of the State of Vermont to practice physic and surgery. He then joined the expanding US Army during the campaigns of the second war with Britain. His diary in the war years proved him to be an ambitious and industrious military surgeon. So strong was the appeal of the Army that he returned to service after a period of civilian practice following the peace of 1815. In 1820, he was commissioned post surgeon by President Monroe and was ordered to duty at Fort Mackinac, Michigan Territory.

In 1822, Beaumont, the only surgeon on the island, was called to treat a young voyageur and trapper, an employee of the American Fur Company, who had lingered in the crowded quarters of the basement of the company's retail store at Michilimackinac. A shotgun was fired; the muzzle was less than a yard away from St. Martin. The full charge of buckshot entered posteriorly on the left lateral flank, shot away a portion of the abdominal wall, and fractured and splintered the 5th and 6th ribs, exposing the lower portion of the left lung and the diaphragm, and leaving a perforation in the anterior wall of the stomach.

Beaumont was summoned from the fort, a short distance away, and arrived minutes later. He cleaned the wound, removed some of the foreign matter, including bits of clothing and a part of the charge, applied a poultice, and rendered a grave prognosis.[4]

In this dilemma I considered any attempt to save his life entirely useless. But as I had ever considered it a duty to use every means in my power to preserve life when called to administer relief, I proceeded to cleanse the wound and give it a superficial dressing, not believing it possible for him to survive twenty minutes.

The wound might have been mortal to many, but St. Martin did not go into irreversible shock and did not develop an overwhelming infection. He endured, in a surprising fashion, weeks of sloughing and healing of the lacerated tissue and months of slow convalescence, without inanition or malnutrition.

During the first days after the accident, firm dressings were necessary to keep the contents of the stomach from spewing through the performation. After the fourth week, the aperture was closed, but not sealed, by partial inversion. Access to the cavity could be made readily by inserting a finger. In spite of the exposure of the gastric mucosa to the exterior, Beaumont records not the slightest nausea. By the fourth week, St. Martin's appetite returned and digestion became regular.

Eighteen months after the accident, a small fold appeared, composed of the coats of the stomach, filling the aperture and acting as a natural valve in retaining food and drink in the hollow viscus.[4]

This valvular formation adapted itself to the accidental orifice, so as completely to prevent the efflux of the gastric contents when the stomach was full, but was easily depressed with the finger.

The initial studies by Beaumont on the physiology of the stomach were begun at Fort Mackinac three years after the accident. By then, Beaumont had assumed financial and professional responsibility for St. Martin. The civil authorities had abandoned their charge after 18 months, and St. Martin, sometimes willingly, sometimes only after firm persuasion by the army surgeon, participated in the experimental studies for board, room, and a very modest honorarium. The second series of experiments was performed in 1829 at Fort Crawford, Prairie du Chien, Wis, on the upper Mississippi; the third series, in 1832, at Washington, DC; and the fourth series, in 1833, in Plattsburgh, New York. In Washington, St. Martin was appointed sergeant in the US Army. When he left Beaumont in 1833, the studies were terminated. Beaumont was never able to induce the sergeant to return to the laboratory, in spite of the promise of a tour to Europe, where St. Martin's fame was secure. The trapper died in Canada, and was buried in an unmarked grave, eight feet deep. Elaborate precautions were taken by friends and family to prevent posthumous examination. William Osler's attempt to secure the stomach for the Army Medical Museum was unsuccessful.[3] In 1960, the granddaughter of St. Martin. (in her 80's) revealed to the local priest and to the Canadian Physiological Society the site of the grave in the churchyard at St. Thomas de Joliette, a village about 40 miles northeast of Montreal.[2] On June 9, 1962, a memorial plaque was placed on the wall of the church near the presumed site of the grave.

No special medical tools or instruments were used by Beaumont in his physiological studies. The observations were made primarily with eyes, nose, taste buds, hands, a magnifying lens, and a Fahrenheit thermometer. Gastric juice, pure and mixed with food, could be recovered from the fistula with ease. When the juice was siphoned from the fasting stomach, it was essentially clear, almost odorless, and slightly acid to taste. Beaumont's monograph, entitled *Experiments and Observations on the Gastric Juice and the Physiology of Digestion,* was published first by Allen in Plattsburgh in 1833. Several editions appeared in the following years, with translations into German and French. Facts were presented, but the reader was left to draw deductions and conclusions.[4]

I make no claim to originality in my opinions, as it respects the existence and operation of the gastric juice. My experiments confirm the doctrines (with some modifications) taught by SPALLANZINI, and many of the most enlightened physiological writers. They are experiments made in the true spirit of enquiry, suggested by the very extraordinary case which gave me an opportunity of making them. I had no particular hypothesis to support; and I have therefore honestly recorded the result of each experiment exactly as it occurred.

I submit a body of facts which cannot be invalidated. My opinions may be doubted, or approved, according as they conflict or agree with the opinions of each individual who may read them; but their worth will be best determined by the foundation on which they rest—the incontrovertible facts.

The technique employed and the imaginative skill in planning the experiments were highly productive.[4]

Mode of extracting the Gastric Juice.—The usual method of extracting the gastric juice, for experiment, is by placing the subject on his right side, depressing the valve within the aperture, introducing a gum-elastic tube, of the size of a large quill, five or six inches into the stomach, and then turning him on the left side, until the orifice becomes dependent. . . . The quantity of fluid ordinarily obtained is from four drachms to one and a half or two ounces, varying with the circumstances and condition of the stomach. Its extraction is generally attended by that peculiar sensation at the pit of the stomach, termed sinking, with some degree of faintness, which renders it necessary to stop the operation.

On laying him horizontally on his back, pressing the hand upon the hepatic region, agitating a little, and at the same time turning him to the left side, bright yellow bile appears to flow freely through the pylorus, and passes out through the tube.

Vegetables are generally slower of digestion than meat and farinaceous substances, though they sometimes pass out of the stomach before them, in an undigested state.

It would be a task of great difficulty to designate the exact kind of diet that would, if generally adopted, be the most conducive to health and longevity. A considerable variety seems to be necessary to man, in a state of civilization. This want of variety is induced by long habit, which it would probably be unsafe to break through. Whether man was originally carnivorous or granivorous, is a question which we cannot solve, and perhaps it is not worth the attempt; at present he is both, and with his present mode of existence we have to do.

The *quantity* of aliment is probably of more importance than the *quality,* to ensure health. The system requires much less than is generally supplied to it.

Beaumont's concept of hunger was based upon dilatation of the gastric vessels, which, when they emptied themselves of fluid, caused the hunger pain to disappear.[4]

It is, therefore, inferred from the pain, (and no one, it is believed, will deny that *hunger* is a painful sensation, whatever may be his opinion of *appetite*) that vessels of some kind are distended; and it is demonstrated, I think, in some of the following experiments, that these are the gastric vessels. On applying aliment to the internal coat of the stomach, which, in health, is merely lubricated with mucus, innumerable minute papillae, the orifices, undoubtedly, of the gastric vessels, immediately throw out a quantity of the fluid, which mixes with the food. . . . It is certain, that at the introduction of every meal, or on the application of alimentary stimulus to the internal coat of the stomach, a very large secretion of a fluid, which has repeatedly been ascertained to be an alimentary solvent, immediately takes place; and that when the stomach is destitute of food or some other irritating substance, no such secretion can be found in it.

This sensation [thirst] is felt in the mouth and fauces. Like hunger, it is a kind provision of nature, designed to remind men and animals of the necessity, not of replenishing the wasting solids of the system, but of diluting the fluids that are carrying on these processes. . . . I apprehend a remote cause of this sensation may be found in the viscidity of the blood, which requires a liquid to render it more fluid, and more susceptible of introduction into the capillaries and secreting surfaces.

These are the preliminary steps in the process of digestion [mastication, insalivation, and deglutition]. The comparative importance of these processes has been elevated or depressed, according to the preponderance which each of them may have received from the opinions of the different physiologists who have made them subjects of observation. As man and animals are constituted, they are all absolutely necessary to the digestion of food. But in an abstract point of view, disconnected as a means of introducing ingestae into the stomach, I believe I hazard nothing in saying that they may be considered as perfectly non-essential to chymification. If the *materia alimentaria* could be introduced into the stomach in a finely divided state, the operations of mastication, insalivation and deglutition, would not be necessary.

The effect of emotional influence was illustrated in experiment 34:[4]

Another circumstance or two, may also, have contributed to interrupt the progress of digestion, such as anger and impatience, which were manifested by the subject, during this experiment.

The importance of Beaumont's observations to experimental physiology and, in particular, physiology of digestion was that they formed a basis for studies by well-known physiologists at home and abroad, such as Carlson, Cannon, Pavlov, Müller, and Bernard. The experimental findings soon were quoted in texts and treatises in America and in Europe, giving Beaumont full credit for the original observations. At the eighth International Physiological Congress, held in Boston in 1929, Beaumont's book was reprinted and presented to each member of the Congress as a souvenir of one of America's great contributions to physiology.

Whittaker has listed the communities in the United States and Canada that have honored Beaumont.[1] The memorial monument dedicated in 1900 by the Michigan State Medical Society is located facing the parade grounds in restored Fort Mackinac, looking out over the straits. The Beaumont Medical Club, with headquarters in the Cushing Medical Library at Yale University, is interested in acquiring the birthplace of Beaumont in Lebanon, Connecticut. The William Beaumont Memorial Committee of the St. Louis Medical Society, where Beaumont practiced following separation from the service, conducts an annual pilgrimage to his grave in Bellefontaine Cemetery. Manuscripts, letters, and books of Beaumont were collected by George Dock and were given to Washington University Library by Beaumont's granddaughter.[2] The American Fur Company's retail store in Mackinac Island, Michigan, where Alexis was injured, has been restored by the Michigan State Medical Society as the Beaumont Memorial. It was presented to the people of the State of Michigan to be administered by the Mackinac Island Park Commission as a national medical shrine. In Prairie du Chien, Wisconsin, the Beaumont Museum on the site of the restored hospital, a unit of Fort Crawford II, was dedicated in 1960 by the Wisconsin State Medical Society. This is but one unit of the Wisconsin Museum of Medical Progress established by the Charitable, Educational and Scientific Foundation of the State Medical Society and operated by the State Historical Society of Wisconsin. At the Beaumont and Medical History Room of the Wayne County Medical Society in Detroit are portraits and a collection of Beaumontiana. At the Old Fort Howard Museum in Green Bay, Wisconsin, are Beaumont's desks, office furniture, and books. At the University of Chicago Library are correspondence and other memorabilia of Beaumont—Army physician and experimental physiologist—whose curiosity and compassion for the injury to a fur trapper's stomach provide the stimulus to explore the secrets of digestion in man.

1. Whittaker, A. H.: Centers of Beaumont Interest, *J Mich Med Soc* 58:742-750 (May) 1959.

2. Bensley, E. H.: Alexis St. Martin, *J Mich Med Soc* 58:738-741 (May) 1959.

3. Myer, J. S.: *Life and Letters of Dr. William Beaumont*, St. Louis: C. V. Mosby Co., 1912.

4. Beaumont, W.: *Experiments and Observations on the Gastric Juice and the Physiology of Digestion*, Plattsburgh, NY: F. P. Allen, 1833.

Sir George Baker (1722-1809)

GEORGE BAKER, son of the vicar of Modbury, Devonshire, made his important scientific contribution by describing the pathogenesis of the disease endemic in his home county. He began his general education at Eton and continued in King's College, Cambridge, where he received the AB in 1745, the AM in 1749, and the MD in 1756.[1] After a period of practice at Stamford, he sought the greater opportunities offered in London. There he soon was recognized as an accomplished practitioner. A profound scholar, Baker enjoyed a long and distinguished association with the Royal College of Physicians, qualifying as a Fellow in 1757. He was censor for four years, Harveian orator in 1761, and served as president nine times. Equally important honors included Fellowship in the Royal Society, physician-in-ordinary to the Queen and to King George III, and a baronetcy in 1776. As an active Latin scholar, he prepared in Latin his Harveian oration, his Cambridge thesis on diseases of animals and their relation to man, a treatise on epidemic dysentery in London,

the Preface to the London *Pharmacopoeia* of 1788, and nonmedical, occasional verse.

The discovery of the pathogenesis of Devonshire colic, for which Baker is best

Composite by Bako

known, was presented in a lucid scientific treatise. From documented historical aspects of the disease, he deduced that Devonshire colic was similar to clinical lead intoxication. The recovery of significant quantities of lead from Devonshire cider concluded the proof. Baker quoted from ancient medical texts, which described colic and paralysis following exposure to lead, and agreed with others that painter's colic, dry gripes of the West Indies, and the colic of Poitou were provincial terms for the same malady. The colic was indigenous to Baker's native Devonshire, where its incidence exceeded that in neighboring counties—particularly Hereford, Gloucester, and Worcester. Reviewing the hospital records of Exeter hospital, he reported that the diagnosis of colic was made in 285 cases between 1762 and 1767. The link between the noxious agent and deposition of lead in the tissues implicated cider, which absorbed lead from the grinding troughs, the calking in the presses, the conduits, or from other uses of the heavy metal in manufacture. The recovery of lead from the cider of Devonshire, but not from the Herefordshire presses, was described in Baker's initial contribution on the subject. He concluded with a prophylactic recommendation for removal of the offending agent and thereby for prevention of the calamity.[2]

It seems therefore not to have been without sufficient foundation, that I have for some time suspected, that the cause of this Colic is not to be sought for in the pure Cyder; but in some, either fraudulent, or accidental, adulteration.

According to my information, eighty Patients, under the effects of the Devonshire colic, were admitted into the Bath-hospital in the course of the last year. . . . the proportion of such Patients from Devonshire, to that from the counties of Hereford, Gloucester, and Worcester, is generally as eight to one.

Were the *apparatus* for making cyder the same in all the cyder-counties, it would appear very remarkable, that the inhabitants of one county should experience such terrible effects from the use of this liquor, while those of the other counties drink it with impunity. But, if we inquire into the method of making cyder in the county of Devon, we shall be able to conjecture with some degree of probability, what it is that occasions such a difference. The large circular trough, in which the apples are ground, is generally composed of several pieces of moor-stones, cramped together with iron, some melted Lead being poured into the interstices.

It is likewise common, in several parts of the county, either to line the cyder-presses entirely with Lead, in order to prevent their leaking; or to make a border of Lead quite round the press, in order to receive the juice of the apples, and to convey it into a vessel, made of wood or stone, placed underneath. And in many other places, where these methods are not used, it is common to nail sheet-lead over any cracks or joints in the presses; and likewise to convey the juice of the apples from the presses in leaden pipes. Moreover I am informed, that it is the practice of some Farmers, in managing their weak cyder, made early in the year, before the apples are ripe, to put a leaden weight into the casks, in order to prevent the liquor from growing sour.

EXPERIMENT V.

In order to leave the matter entirely without doubt, an extract from 18 common quart bottles of Devonshire cyder (first strained through a cloth) which had been in my cellar more than three months, was prepared. This extract, being assayed with black flux, a quantity of Lead, weighing four grains and an half, was found at the bottom of the crucible. These experiments were made in October 1766.

May not I presume to hope, that the present discovery of a poison, which has for many years exerted its virulent effects on the inhabitants of Devonshire, incorporated with their daily liquor, unobserved, and unsuspected, may be esteemed by those, who have power, and who have opportunities to remove the source of so much mischief, to be an object worthy of their most serious attention? I have long lamented, that a County, which is distinguished by some peculiar blessings, should likewise be distinguished by a peculiar calamity, as it were in consequence of its fertility.

1. Munk, W.: "Sir George Baker, Bart., M.D.," in *The Roll of the Royal College of Physicians of London*, ed 2, London: Royal College of Physicians, 1878, vol 2, pp 213-218.

2. Baker, G.: *An Essay Concerning the Cause of the Endemial Colic of Devonshire*, London: J. Hughs, 1767.

Composite by G. Bako

John Howard (1726[27]-1790)

JOHN HOWARD, prison reformer of England, gave a fortune to accumulate data in support of his private mission to eradicate the wretched conditions in prisons, hospitals, and lazarettos and to prevent the plague in such institutions. He was born near London at Enfield or Hackney; there is uncertainty regarding his birth year as well as birth-place.[1] His father, a Protestant dissenter who engaged in the upholstery and carpet business, died when his son was just beginning an upper-class education. He had only partially fulfilled the wish of his father—that he serve an apprenticeship to a wholesale grocer—when he obtained a release from his identure and toured the Continent. In 1756, on a visit to Portugal as a passenger on the Lisbon packet, Howard was captured by a French privateer, was imprisoned in France, and suffered great privations. He was first held captive without food or water for almost two days and then was cast into a dungeon at Brest.[2]

In the castle at Brest, I lay six nights upon straw; and observing how cruelly my countrymen were used there, and at Morlaix, whither I was carried next; during the two months I was at Carhaix upon parole, I corresponded with the English prisoners at Brest, Morlaix, and Dinnan: at the last of those towns were several of our ship's crew, and my servant. I had sufficient evidence of their being treated with such barbarity, that many hundreds had perished; and that thirty-six were buried in a hole at Dinnan in one day. When I came to England, still on parole, I made known to the commissioners of sick and wounded seamen the sundry particulars: which gained their attention, and thanks.

This loathsome experience did not lead immediately to an attempt to reform, the action for which Howard was most famous. Rather he took up residence on his property at Cardington, Bedfordshire, erected model cottages, suffered at least one violent fit of gout, was elected a Fellow of the Royal Society, and composed three unimportant manuscripts on meteorology, which were published in the Society's *Philosophical Transactions*.

With the appointment as high sheriff of Bedford, Howard began his career as a prison reformer. This assignment entailed the systematic inspection of prisons, lazarettos, and other institutions of incarceration in Great Britain, Ireland, and many of the Continental countries as far east as Smyrna, Constantinople, and selected cities in Russia. Howard was concerned especially with the filthy conditions of primitive existence in the English penal houses, and with

the nefarious practices of the gaolers who permitted torture of the inmates, exacted "garnish" from them, and provided little or no food for sustenance, little or no water for drinking or washing, and scant medical care for social and epidemic diseases.

Throughout Howard's travels and tours a great mass of statistics he accumulated from firsthand observation. In 1777, he published the first edition of his remarkable treatise *The State of the Prisons in England and Wales, with Preliminary Observations, and an Account of Some Foreign Prisons and Hospitals*.[2] He was assisted in the preparation by Dr. Price. The printing was done in a near-by shop. At Howard's suggestion, the price of the treatise was set at a low figure so that the cost would be no deterrent; in addition, copies were widely distributed gratis. It was translated into several foreign languages, and with each revision, new data were added. The great reforms which he envisioned were accomplished in large part through an aroused citizenry and appropriate legislation before his death.

Having prepared the first modern, detailed document on prisons of the 18th century, Howard turned his attention to the lazarettos on the Continent. They provided better quarantine quarters for the protection of their people against the plague than those found in English ports. The lazarettos were land-based houses of confinement for passengers sailing from plague-infested ports or for those stricken with contagion while at sea; the crews of the infested ships were quarantined on the boats. Howard's *An Account of the Principal Lazarettos in Europe* was as detailed, port by port, as his observations on prisons, but with greater emphasis on the contagiousness of the plague than on gaol fever.[3]

Though there are various points in which the answerers of the preceding questions disagree, yet it is with pleasure I observe that they all in the most explicit manner concur in representing the plague as a *contagious* disease, communicated by near approach to, or actual contact with infected persons or things. This is a fact of the greatest importance to be established, as all the proposed means of prevention by cutting off communication with the sources of infection, must depend upon it: it is a fact too, which one would suppose after such manifold and repeated experience, no one would now call in question.

On Howard's last tour of Europe, which included southern Russia, he was stricken with a fever in Kherson. At his death he had expended most of his fortune in the improvement of public houses of confinement and hospitals. It is especially noteworthy that throughout it all he shunned honors and accolades for his reforms. Posthumously he could not prevent the construction of a pyramid over his grave or the dedication of a statute in St. Paul's Cathedral, executed by Bacon.

1. Aikin, J.: *A View of the Character and Public Services of the Late John Howard, Esq.*, London: J. Johnson, 1792.
2. Howard, J.: *The State of the Prisons in England and Wales*, 4th ed, London: J. Johnson, C. Dilly, and T. Cadell, 1792.
3. Howard, J.: *An Account of the Principal Lazarettos in Europe*, Warrington: W. Eyres, 1789.

Matthew Dobson (1735?-1784)

MATTHEW DOBSON, born in Yorkshire, was the son a Nonconformist minister and had planned at one time to follow his father's profession.[1] When he decided upon medicine, he entered the University of Edinburgh and graduated in 1756 upon presentation of a dissertation on menstruation. Dobson commenced practice in Liverpool, served on the staff of the Liverpool Infirmary, and in 1770, was advanced to physician, a position held for a decade until ill health forced him to retire to Bath, where he died.

The uncertainty regarding Dobson's birth date is consistent with the lack of information concerning many details of his personal and public life. He has been described as a natural philosopher, an experimental physiologist, and a skilled clinical observer. *A Medical Commentary on Fixed Air* (carbon dioxide), dedicated to William Cullen, was the only subject that received monographic treatment. His experiments on physiological stress experienced by humans at critical high temperature and observations on the petrifying properties of water at Matlock

were communicated through Dr. Fothergill to the Royal Society of London, of which each was a member, and were published in their *Philosophical Transactions*. Dobson's clinical studies, which included the treatment of internal hydrocephalus with large doses of mercury salts, appeared in *Medical Observations and Inquiries*, the organ of Society of Physicians in London. Dobson's most important work was his observations and experiments on patients with diabetes mellitus. He described the extraction of a sweet substance from the urine and serum of one patient, a 33-year-old male, who was afflicted with clinical diabetes mellitus. The symptoms currently recognized as characteristic included polydipsia, polyphagia, polyuria, weight loss, dry skin, and paroxysmal fever. He described five experiments and concluded with eight observations and queries. In these, he sensed the metabolic defect in discussing etiology and suggested an enhanced assimilation of nutrients by the body in treatment. The report was communicated by Dr. Fothergill; excerpts follow.[2]

EXPERIMENT II.

Eight ounces of blood taken from the arm of this patient, exhibited, after standing a proper time, the following appearances. . . . The *serum* was opaque, and much resembled common cheese whey; it was sweetish, but I thought not so sweet as the urine.

EXPERIMENT V.

Two quarts of this urine were, by a gentle heat, evaporated to dryness, under the inspection of Mr. Poole, apothecary to the hospital, and Mr. Walthall, one of the house apprentices. There remained, after the evaporation, a white cake which . . . was granulated, and broke easily between the fingers; it smelled sweet like brown sugar, neither could it, by the taste, be distinguished from sugar, except that the sweetness left a slight sense of coolness on the palate.

These experiments suggest the following:

OBSERVATIONS AND QUERIES.

1. That the fluid which was separated by the kidneys of this patient, had very little of the nature or sensible qualities of urine, but contained a substance which readily passed through the vinous, acetous, and putrefactive fermentations.

3. It appears from Experiment V. that a considerable quantity of saccharine matter passed off by the kidneys, in this case of diabetes, and probably does so in every instance of this dis-

ease, where the urine has a sweet taste. From Experiment II. it further appears, that this saccharine matter was not formed in the secretory organ, but previously existed in the serum of the blood.

5. This idea of the disease, also, well explains its emaciating effects, from so large a proportion of the alimentary matter being draw off by the kidneys, before it is perfectly assimilated, and applied to the purposes of nutrition. The *diabetes* proves, in some cases, a very rapid consumption; I have known it terminate fatally in less than five weeks. In others, it becomes a chronic complaint.

8. This idea of the nature of the *diabetes,* suggests more clearly and explicitly the method of cure. For if it is a disease of the system in general, if it is to be considered as a species of imperfect digestion and assimilation, the obvious indication of cure are, to strengthen the digestive powers, to promote a due sanguification, and establish a perfect assimilation through the whole oeconomy.

1. Williams, O. T.: Matthew Dobson, Physician to the Liverpool Infirmary, 1770-1780: One Who Extended the Confines of Knowledge, *Liverpool Medicochir J* 32: 245-254, 1912.

2. Dobson, M.: Experiments and Observations on the Urine in a Diabetes, *Med Obs Inq* 5:298-316, 1776.

ied and lived with John Hunter, attended the anatomical lectures of William Hunter, and enrolled as a pupil at Guy's and St. Thomas' hospitals. When John Hunter went abroad with the army one year later, Hew-

Composite by G. Bako

William Hewson (1739-1774)

WITH AN INQUISITIVE MIND and the effective use of the experimental tools available two centuries ago, William Hewson made several observations of fundamental significance in physiology and clinical medicine. He recommended paracentesis of air for correction of pneumothorax, proved the existence of lymphatics in birds, fishes, and amphibia, isolated coagulable lymph (fibrinogen) from the blood, and defined several of the physical properties of the erythrocyte in man and animals. These successes, produced in a professional span shorter than a decade, were terminated by his death at the age of 35.

William was born at Hexham, Northumberland, in 1739, the son of a surgeon and apothecary. He attended Hexham grammar school, pursued an apprenticeship with his father, completed a period of study with Mr. Lambert, surgeon of Newcastle, and went to London at the age of 20. There he stud-

son served in his place in the preparation of anatomical demonstrations and provided assistance, when needed, in William Hunter's lectures. The assignment was scientifically and financially profitable.[1]

Since William Hunter readily appreciated the industry and skills of Hewson, he offered him a partnership, upon the condition that he would study with Monro *secundus,* anatomist and surgeon of Edinburgh. Hewson accepted the offer, spent a year in Edinburgh, and returned to London to share both income and lectures with Hunter. The partnership permitted Hewson to practice, as well as to spend considerable time in experimental physiology. He performed a remarkable number of experiments on rabbits, dogs, fowl, birds, fishes, and amphibia, studied the physical characteristics of blood collected during phlebotomy of the sick or at the abattoir, and, in less than ten years, submitted important scientific contributions to the *Philosophical Transactions.* The partnership served each well, so long as Hewson remained a bachelor, but it was disrupted when, in 1770, Hewson married a young friend of Benjamin Franklin.

Hewson's first important communication discussed the proper means of treating traumatic pneumothorax. The study was prompted by the high mortality from the then current treatment. As a result of experimental studies on rabbits and dogs, Hewson concluded that provision for the escape of air from the pleural cavity at a designated site would alleviate symptoms and foster recovery.[2]

Although the operation of the paracentesis thoracis is advisable in most cases where air is contained in the cavity of the chest; yet some may be so complicated with other injuries, that the operation, though in itself proper, may yet be unsuccessful. But this remark may be unnecessary here, as the same may be made of every chirurgical operation; and as men of experience will be cautious how they attribute to the remedy that want of success which may be owing to another cause.

When the operation becomes necessary, the best place for performing it, if the disease is on the right side, will be on the fore-part of the chest, between the fifth and sixth ribs; for there the integuments are thin, and, in the case of air, no depending drain is required. But, if the disease is on the left side, it will be more advisable to make the opening between the seventh and eighth, or eighth and ninth ribs, that we may be sure of avoiding the pericardium. With regard to the size of the wound, it may be proper to observe, that as large penetrating wounds of the chest are inconvenient on account of the air's entering by the aperture in such a quantity as to prevent the expansion of the lungs, a small wound will therefore be eligible, and especially as the fluid requires not a large vent for its discharge. Lastly, as to the manner of performing the operation, I should thinks it more advisable to do it with a knife, by a cautious dissection, than by the more coarse and hazardous method, the thrusting in a trocar.

This recommendation drew the first of two bitter tirades from Monro, who claimed that his former pupil had, by recommending incision with a scalpel rather than by permitting air to escape with a trocar, made no contribution and had done little but share the glory of Monro's original observation. Monro accused Hewson of stealing the idea received from his student days in Edinburgh. Having taken few notes, the defendant could not produce documentary evidence to refute the argument, but he denied the accusation and concluded that, although he might have coveted fame, he was not ruthless in its acquisition.

The observations on the lymphatic system of lower animals constituted Hewson's best work, one of a series of communications which appeared in *Philosophical Transactions* and which were later collected in volumes entitled *Experimental Inquiries*. More than a century earlier (1622) Aselli had discovered lacteals, but the relationship of the lymphatic system to the physiology and economy of the body was disputed. There were some scientists who believed that the fluid in the lymphatics was only a condensate. Hewson settled the issue in a series of experiments conducted in 1768, on the coast of Sussex. He showed that lymphatic vessels are absorbent vessels and that the lacteals and the lymphatics are integrated in serving an important function in life.[3]

Having been so fortunate, in a series of experiments made with that view, as to trace out the lymphatic system in birds, I have ventured to offer the following account of it to you, in order to be presented, if you think proper, to the Royal Society; and, I flatter myself, this discovery will be looked upon as some acquisition to physiology.

This system in birds differs most from that in quadrupeds in the following particulars. 1st, In the chyle being transparent, and colourless. 2dly, In there being no visible lymphatic glands, neither in the course of the lacteals, nor in that of the lymphatics of the *abdomen,* nor near the thoracic ducts. 3dly, In the several parts of this system in birds being more frequently enlarged, or varicose, than in quadrupeds.

Mr. Hewson begs leave to add, that since the above paper on the lymphatic system in birds was put into the hands of the secretary of the Royal Society, he has discovered the same system in fish; and has likewise been so fortunate as to procure a Turtle, whose lymphatic system he has traced out, and has got delineated. An account of those dissections, with the fingers, he intends soon to have the honour of laying before the Society.

This study was responsible for his election shortly after to the Royal Society and for his receiving the Copley medal. The medal was awarded first to Benjamin Franklin, Hewson's dedicatee in the second portion of the *Experimental Inquiries*. The animosity between Hewson and Monro flared once more when Hewson was accused of failing to acknowledge similar conclusions by Monro on the lymphatic system. The award by the Royal Society may be taken as firm evidence that, in their judgment, honor for the integration and the function in animal economy of the lymphatics was rightfully due Hewson. A logical step in Hewson's reasoning concerned the fluid in the lymphatic system, which was found to be coagulable and similar to the coagulable lymph in other body fluids, exemplified by serum and the buffy coat of whole blood allowed to settle in a cool environment.

In 1770, as a Fellow of the Royal Society, Hewson personally presented his remarks on coagulable lymph, now identified as fibrinogen.[4]

It is well known, that the *crassamentum* [clot] consists of two parts, of which one gives it solidity, and is by some called the fibrous part of the blood, or the gluten, but by others with more propriety termed the *coagulable lymph;* and of another, which gives the red colour to the blood, and is called the red globules. These two parts can be separated by washing the *crassamentum* in water, the red particles dissolving in the water, whilst the coagulable lymph remains solid. That it is the coagulable lymph which by its becoming solid gives firmness to the *crassamentum,* is proved by agitating fresh blood with a stick, so as to collect this coagulable lymph on the stick, in which case the rest of the blood remains fluid.

Although the coagulable lymph so readily becomes solid when exposed to the air, yet whilst it circulates it is far from being solid: it has indeed been supposed to be fibrous, even whilst moving in the blood-vessels, but erroneously.

It is this coagulable lymph which forms the inflammatory crust, or *buff* as it is called. It likewise forms *polypi* of the heart [postmortem clots], and sometimes fills up the cavities of aneurisms, and plugs up the extremities of divided arteries. It is supposed, by its becoming solid in the body, to occasion obstructions and inflammations; and even mortifications, from the exposition to cold, have been attributed to its coagulation. In a word, this lymph is supposed to have so great a share in the cause of several diseases, that it would be desirable to ascertain what brings on that coagulation, either in the body or out of it.

The effects of salts on the physical characteristics of the red blood cells in animals and man, their tendency to rouleau formation, and their fragility and osmolarity as a function of the salt concentration were studied by Hewson and reported in the *Philosophical Transactions.*[5]

The red particles of the blood in the human subject have, since the time of Leeuwenhoeck, been so generally allowed to be spherical, that in almost all books of physiology they are denominated red globules. A few authors, however, have at different times doubted whether they were spheres, and amongst the rest Father de la Torré whose curious observations, together with his glasses, were presented to the Royal Society, Anno 1766. As I flatter myself that I have made some new observations on these particles, I shall do myself the honour of communicating them to the Society.

It is a curious and important fact, that these particles are found so generally through the animal kingdom; that is, they are found in the human species, in all quadrupeds, in all birds, in all amphibious animals, and in all fish, in which animals they are red, and colour the blood. The blood even of insects contains particles similar in shape to those of the blood of more perfect animals, but differing in colour. In water insects, as lobsters and shrimps, these particles are white; in some land insects, as the caterpillar and the grasshopper they appear of a faint green, when in the vessels as I am persuaded from experiments. I have seen them in an insect no bigger than a pin's head, and suspect they exist almost universally through the animal kingdom.

These particles of the blood, improperly called globules, are in reality flat bodies. Leeuwenhoeck and others have allowed, that in fish and in the *amphibia* they are flat and elliptical; but in the human subject and in quadrupeds almost all microscopial observers have agreed in their being spherical.

If then they really be not globular but flat, and if water so readily alter their shape, whence is it that the serum has the property of preserving them in that form which seems so necessary, because it is so general through the animal creation?

It is principally by the salts of the serum that this effect is produced, as is provided by adding a small quantity of any neutral salt to water, when the water is no longer capable of dissolving those particles, nor does it alter their shape, when the salts is used in a certain proportion.

EXPERIMENT III. If a saturated solution of any of the common neutral salts be mixed with fresh blood, and the globules (as they have been called, but which for the future I shall call flat vesicles) be then examined in a microscope, the salt will be found to have contracted or shriveled the vesicles, so that they appear quite solid, the vesicular substance being closely applied all round the central piece.

Hewson had not reached professional maturity when he was stricken with bacteremia, occasioned by a wound he received during a postmortem dissection. Following his death, his wife and children were invited to the United States by Benjamin Franklin. She accepted and settled in Bristol, Pennsylvania, where her eldest son, William, established a medical practice. Her second son, Thomas Tickell Hewson, became a distinguished practitioner in Philadelphia and served as president of the College of Physicians of Philadelphia and professor of comparative anatomy at the University of Pennsylvania. One of his sons, in turn, Addinell Hewson, carried on the medical tradition, while Addinell Hewson, Jr., was associated with the anatomy departments of Jefferson Medical College and the University of Pennsylvania.[6]

1. Lettersom, J. C.: Memoirs of the Late William Hewson, *Trans Med Soc Lond* 1:51-63, 1810.
2. Gulliver, G.: The Works of William Hewson, F.R.S., London: The Sydenham Society, 1846.
3. Hewson, W.: An Account of the Lymphatic System in Birds, *Philos Trans* 58:217-226, 1769.
4. Hewson, W.: Experiments on the Blood, with Some Remarks on Its Morbid Appearances, *Philos Trans* 60:368-413, 1771.
5. Hewson, W.: On the Figure and Composition of the Red Particles of the Blood, Commonly Called the Red Globules, *Philos Trans* 63:303-323, 1773.
6. Bailey, G. H.: William Hewson, F.R.S. (1739-1774): An Account of His Life and Work, *Ann Med Hist* 5:2091224 (Sept) 1923.

John Coakley Lettsom
(1744-1815)

LITTLE JOST VAN DYKE, a tiny island near Tortola in the British Virgin Islands, was the birthsite (1744) of John Coakley Lettsome, who prepared an original account of alcoholism, one of the first manuscripts on this addiction. John's father, Quaker and planter, sent his son, at the age of 7, to London for his education and medical career. As a member of the Society of Friends, John enrolled in the Quaker School at Penketh but was not eligible to attend Oxford or Cambridge; at 16, he was apprenticed to Sutcliff, a Quaker surgeon-apothecary and

classical scholar at Settle, Yorkshire. In accepting the apprenticeship he agreed that[1] "he his master well and faithfully shall serve; his secrets shall keep; taverns he shall

not haunt; at dice, card tables, bowls, or any other unlawful game he shall not play." The apprentice, in turn, shall be taught "the art, trade, mystery and occupation of an apothecary."

In school, Lettsom attracted the attention of Samuel Fothergill, Quaker preacher and brother of John Fothergill, one of the leading physicians in London. Lettsom continued his training with John Fothergill at St. Thomas' Hospital; however, his funds were limited and the fees for an extended series of lectures were not within his means. Learning was restricted largely to pragmatic medicine at the bedside. It was his habit to make early morning rounds, jotting down impressions of the diagnosis and treatment, for comparison with judgments of the visiting staff at formal rounds later in the day.[2]

I was compelled to learn at the bed of sickness. Here I saw nature, and learnt my art without the leading-strings of professors. I acquired an early habit of behaving with kindness to the sick, and having known want, I knew how to sympathize with distress.

When his funds were exhausted, Lettsom returned to the Virgin Islands and began the practice of medicine. Meanwhile, his father had died and left only a few slaves and a small tract of land. Lettsom freed the slaves, parceled his land, and gave them tools to cultivate the crop. After a few months he had acquired sufficient income to return to Edinburgh, where he studied for a time with Cullen, and then to Leyden, where he received the MD degree in 1769. The graduation thesis criticized the avowed merits of tea, a forewarning of the treatise on addiction to alcohol. The general decrease in the strength of the English was attributed to tea drinking.[3]

Our Bodies have lost that strength, we admire in our ancestors, and became enervated, and liable to more diseases; and those depending upon relaxation and debility are now endemic. Hence that frequency of Hysterics in both Sexes, the Hypochondriasis, Palsy, Cachexy, Dropsy &c.

Notwithstanding what has been advanc'd I wou'd by no means conclude that Tea is the sole cause of all these complaints; for luxury of every kind, to please the palate, has almost everywhere extended its influence, & even enter'd our Kitchens and Cellars, and contributed its share in the production of those diseases with which we labour. Under this head the frequent use of spirituous liquors stands foremost.

Lettsom visited Paris and select health resorts on the Continent before returning to London to marry a lady of financial substance and to establish a medical practice. Shortly after receiving Licentiateship in the Royal College of Physicians, he founded the General Dispensary, an outpatient clinic. This move inaugurated a new era in the treatment of the poor of London. It was a revival of ambulatory care of patients exemplified first by Hippocrates. Outpatient care had scarcely existed in previous generations in London. This deficiency was but one example of unhealthful conditions for rich and poor, even as measured by 18th century standards. Poverty, thievery, gin drinking, contagion, and filth were rampant. Such a deplorable environment could not have escaped the attention of many enlightened citizens and, in turn, caused them to consider correction and reform. The Quakers especially put thoughts into action. The General Dispensary was one of the notable objectives. Senior physicians treated the poor in the clinic, and if the patients were too sick to attend, they were treated at home. Another feature and benefit of the outpatient clinic was the opportunity for training young physicians. In this venture, the dispensaries entered into competition for students' fees with the teaching hospitals.

Lettsom's description of chronic alcoholism, which was published in the *Memoirs of the Medical Society of London,* has been acclaimed his best clinical treatise.[4]

Persons who have indulged themselves in hard-drinking, gradually lose a relish for solid food, or if the appetite is not so far vitiated, as totally to obliterate this natural propensity, it is usually in search of high seasoned and salted substances, which neither contribute to wholesome nourishment, nor to avert the increasing *dyspepsia.*

The *First* I shall notice, as being generally less painful, though equally permanent, are the symptoms more especially attendant on persons who have, early in life, habituated themselves to drink freely of wine of various kinds, . . . Punch-drinkers, likewise, have been liable to similar complaints. The first appearance of disease is a slight degree of *dyspepsia,* which at length is succeeded by *gastrodynia:* . . . . For several years in this unhappy state, the patient drags on a life, rendered now and then more supportable, either by renewed potations, or repeated exsputations, till at length the bodily and mental powers become impaired: the object grows emaciated, the whole body shrinks; neither *anasarca* nor dropsy appear, though the countenance looks sallow; the region of the liver is not enlarged, but this *viscus* seems less than natural.

At this time, if an ascites, or fatal jaundice, do not terminate existence, the legs shrink, are swarthy-coloured like the rest of the body, and somtimes *petechiae* appear and disappear for many months; the extremities feel sore to the touch, and upon scratching them, exude blood: the thighs likewise shrink, but the body, and particularly about the hepatic region, enlarges, and the hardness of the liver may be frequently traced: the face is nearly copper-coloured, is emaciated, sometimes with little suppurations, which dry and turn scaly; the breath smells like rotten apples, and the *morbus niger,* or vomitings of a fluid like that of coffee-grounds, snatch the patient from complicated misery.

The persons liable to these symptoms [the female sex], have been those of delicate habits, who have endeavoured to overcome the nervous debility, by the aid of spirits: . . . the relief, however, being temporary, to keep up their effects, frequent access is had to the same delusion, till at length what was taken by compulsion, gains attachment, and a little drop of brandy, or gin and water, become as necessary as food; the female sex, from natural delicacy, acquire this custom by slow degrees, and the poison being admitted in small doses, is slow in its operations, but not less painful in its effects.

I would not, however, infer, that every spirit-drinker acquires the symptoms of disease above related, or that other diseases do not more frequently succeed this dangerous habit; hepatic affections, of various kinds, it is well known, usually result from intemperance, and dropsies often succeed: . . . . There is something in spirituous liquors, so injurious to the human frame, that too much attention cannot be paid in discouraging the use of them . . . and it is from the most decided conviction of the inquiry, that I would guard every person from beginning with even a little drop of this fascinating poison, which once admitted, is seldom, if ever, afterwards overcome.

Lettsom is closely identified with two societies. The Medical Society of London, founded in 1773 by Lettsom and others, commemorates his name with Fothergill's in the Lettsomian and Fothergillian lectureships. The Royal Humane Society, founded the following year, was dedicated to the rescue of persons apparently drowned. The recommended procedures for resuscitation included artificial respiration plus stimulation of the large bowel by tobacco smoke blown into the rectum through a bellows. Although Lettsom was opposed to tobacco in any form, lifesaving or not, this maneuver was not rescinded by the Humane Society until a few years before Lettsom died. He was active in prison reform, promoted a summer camp for poor children, and founded the Royal Sea-Bathing Hospital at Margate, a forerunner of the open air sanatorium, recommended for the sick and the convalescent a century later. Lettsom sponsored smallpox inoculation before Jenner's observations on cowpox. After accepting the merits of Jenner's discovery, he provided Benjamin Waterhouse of Boston and others with dried lymph for vaccination. Most of his writings, prolific correspondence, and scientific contributions were prepared in his carriage while making house calls or visiting hospitals. The subjects of his communications included effects of bad air, treatment and cure of fevers, and chlorosis in boarding schools.

Lettsom's marriage to a woman of financial substance has been judged by some to have been one of convenience; husband and wife lived ten miles apart. He wrote that he continued to love his wife dearly because he saw her so seldom. The combination of a wealthy wife and a profitable practice provided financial security. Money was not hoarded, however. He gave sometimes wisely, sometimes unwisely, to charitable causes and indigent patients. Nor were his charities bestowed only in his native land. Harvard, Dartmouth, Dickinson, and Bowdoin colleges were recipients of gifts, books, and specimens of natural history. Pennsylvania Hospital sought his advice in the selection of books for the medical library and, in turn, received suggestions and volumes from his own library.[5] The College of Physicians of Philadelphia elected him a Fellow, and Harvard College honored him with a Doctor of Laws. Lettsom died in 1815 of a streptococcal infection acquired in a postmortem examination.

Lettsom clung to the simple Quaker dress, a symbol of affection for man, manifested by handsome philanthropy for the poor and social reform for all. But surely the love of medicine practiced in the outpatient dispensary and expressed in one of his letters gave him the greatest satisfaction.[2]

. . . . this is the highest and most divine profession, that can engage human intellect. I have attended eighty-two thousand patients, and what can equal the dignity of having so many lives intrusted to your decision;—What more divine, than to soothe the afflicted, and soften agony! What more sublime than to restore to life the victim of disease! I envy not the prince on the throne, nor the sultan in his haram, whilst I enjoy the confidence of the sick chamber, and the blessings of the restored. I love my profession, perhaps too much. It loves me, and I have no objection to die in the chamber of malady, provided I can mitigate it in a fellow creature,—and so every other physician would, I doubt not, reason.

1. Abraham, J. J.: *Lettsom: His Life, Times, Friends and Descendants,* London: William Heinemann, Ltd., 1933.

2. Pettigrew, T. J.: *Memoirs of the Life and Writings of the Late John Coakley Lettsom*, vol 1, 2, 3, London: Longman, Hurst, Rees, Orme, & Brown, 1817.

3. Trent, J. C.: John Coakley Lettsom, *Bull Hist Med* 22:528-542, 1948.

4. Lettsom, J. C.: *Some Remarks on the Effects of Lignum Quassiae Amarae*, *Mem Med Soc London* 1:128-165, 1787.

Composite by G. Bako

William C. Cruikshank
(1745-1800)

WILLIAM CUMBERLAND CRUIKSHANK, assistant to William Hunter and physician to Samuel Johnson, was born in Edinburgh, the son of an examiner of the Excise.[1] William, originally intending to enter the clergy, was educated at Edinburgh and Glasgow universities, where his outstanding scholarship drew immediate attention. Excellence in classical and modern languages enabled him to coach his classmates and act as preceptor in families of distinction; meanwhile a strong propensity for anatomy and physic led him from the church into medicine. After graduating AM at Glasgow in 1767, he was apprenticed in surgery and pharmacy until 1771, when Hunter brought him to London as assistant in the Windmill Street school. Cruikshank applied himself to dissection with great industry, gave demonstrations in the anatomical theater, occasionally replaced Hunter in lectures, and offered his consultative services to rich and poor alike. He was an able substitute for Hunter on the rostrum, delighting the pupils with his clarity and erudition. At all times he zealously allocated each hour and even every minute to activities certain to contribute to his professional advancement either in the school, private practice, or his standing among the literary figures of the day. Hunter's approval of Cruikshank led to a partnership and to a beneficiary in his will after his nephew, Matthew Baillie, for the anatomical museum. Upon Cruikshank's death, the collection was to pass to its permanent home in Glasgow. Cruikshank received an honorary degree of doctor of physic from the University of Glasgow and was admitted a Fellow of the Royal Society shortly before he died from apoplexy.

Although Cruikshank trained in anatomy and surgery, his investigations were physiologically oriented, and results were described in a limited number of published contributions. His discussion of the lymphatics, the absorbent system in the body, is regarded as the most noteworthy communication. He investigated, without benefit of the microscope, the reunion and regeneration of divided nerves, demonstrated the expiration of carbon dioxide by the skin, and followed the migration of the impregnated ova of rabbits. An essay on the cure of abscesses and the treatment of wounds and ulcers, and remarks on the absorption of calomel from the mucous lining of the mouth were lesser contributions.

In 1776, John Hunter communicated to the Royal Society, a report not published until 19 years later, Cruikshank's experiments on the regeneration of the par vagum and intercostal nerves of dogs. The divided nerves were inspected at varying time intervals for gross evidence of regeneration. Cruikshank interpreted the reparative changes about the nerve trunks as evidence of nerve regeneration, although the follow-up period was several months short of time sufficient to allow physiological resumption of nerve transmission.[2]

EXPERIMENT I.

January 24th, 1776, I divided, in a dog, one nerve of the par vagum, with the intercostal, on the right side. The symptoms, consequent to the operation, were heaviness, and slight inflammation of the right eye; breathing with a kind of struggle, as if something stuck in his throat, which he wanted to get up; sullenness, and a disposition to keep quiet: the pulse did not seem affected, nor had he lost his voice in the least. The unfavourable symptoms did not continue above a day or two; and on the eighth day he was in very high spirits, and seemed perfectly to have recovered.

EXPERIMENT II.

February 3d, I cut out a portion of the two nerves of the opposite side, in the same dog; the piece might be about an inch long. . . . The seventh day after this second operation, he was found dead, at a considerable distance from his bed. . . . The divided nerves of the right side were united by a substance of the same colour as nerve, but not fibrous; and the extremities formed by the division were still distinguished by swelling, rounded in form of ganglions. The same appearance had taken place, with respect to the nerves of the left side; though the divided extremities seemed to have been full two inches apart; the uniting substance was more bloody than that of the other side. . . . As I found the nerves regenerated, a circumstance never hitherto observed, it occurred to me, that it might be objected to the reasoning, that the two first nerves were doing their office, before the two last were divided.

Experiments on the Insensible Perspiration of the Human Body was published first in 1779 and was republished, with additions and corrections, in a monograph of 1795. After a detailed description of the structure of the skin, Cruikshank answered his own questions as to whether or not there was some substance in insensible perspiration, other than the watery vapor, which spoiled atmospheric air; whether an affinity existed between the vapor of insensible perspiration and the expired vapor from the lungs and whether activity influenced the rate of insensible loss. His hand or foot was inserted into a wide-mouth glass jar, the neck was sealed about the limb, and the transpirate collected for one hour. The presence of moisture and fixed air (carbon dioxide), which gave a positive test for carbonic acid in lime water, demonstrated the loss of this compound from the skin to the atmosphere.[3]

THE SKIN ITSELF

Was given to man not only for feeling, in a general sense, but for perspiration, absorption, and particularly for *touch,* in which he excels all other animals, and which resides, principally, in the *tips of the fingers.* He was intended for examining, reasoning, forming a judgment, and acting accordingly;—he was fitted by this sense to examine accurately the properties of surrounding bodies, not capable of being examined by his other senses. This, among other reasons, was one why he was made erect, that the points of his fingers should not be made callous, or less sensible *by walking on them.*

EXPERIMENT I.

About ten in the morning. . . . feeling perfectly well, I washed and dried my hands, and introduced my right hand into a clean empty bottle. . . . After keeping my hand in this situation an hour, I found I had collected a teaspoonful of transparent and perfectly insipid fluid. This fluid I poured into the scale of a balance, which had in its opposite scale a weight, equal to the weight of a bit of dry sponge. With this sponge I absorbed the remaining fluid in the bottle, and put it into the scale with the former fluid. The fluid I had thus collected weighed thirty grains. This experiment I repeated several times, and in general with the same effect.

EXPERIMENT II.

I repeated the foregoing experiment some hours after walking gently in open air; at the end of the hour, the collected fluid weighed forty-eight grains. This experiment also was repeated with the same effect. From this I inferred, that the insensible perspiration was increased two-thirds nearly, during exercise; the whole surface of my skin lost in this hour six ounces; and at that rate, in twenty-four hours, would have lost twelve pounds. Hard working people, very probably, lose still more.

EXPERIMENT VIII.

I repeated experiment first, and threw the fluid so collected into lime-water; it produced no change in it. I threw some lime-water into the bottle where my hand had remained an hour; after some agitation the lime-water became faintly turbid.

The first edition of *The Anatomy of the Absorbing Vessels of the Human Body,* published in 1786, described the form and function of the lymphatic system. The work, originally undertaken at Hunter's suggestion, gives an extended history of the lacteals and lymphatics, noting particularly that Aselli had traced the lacteals in the mesentery of the dog but had never acknowledged having seen them in the human. Cruikshank described the minute structure of the lacteals and the lymphatics, included the lymphatic glands as part of the absorbing system, gave the first comprehensive anatomical description, and traced the channels throughout the body. To him, the lymphatic system was much more than channels for the transport of chyle from the intestines to the blood stream.[4]

Now the lymphatics are not only branches of the same trunk, as Dr. Hunter observed, but there is such a connection between them, such an anastomosis, that the fluids absorbed by the lacteals are in part transmitted to the lymphatics, and through them, at last, conveyed into the blood. A very remarkable instance of this kind I demonstrated at a lecture in Windmill Street, about two years ago. The lymphatics of the diaphragm were seen turgid with chyle, which they had received from the lacteals, some of which were passing that way, towards the subclavian veins. A stronger proof that lymphatics are absorbents, is, that whenever fluids are extravasated on surfaces, or into cavities, or whenever such fluids preternaturally distend their reservoirs, the lymphatics belonging to these surfaces and cavities are found full of the same fluid.

I have said, that these vessels carry fluids into the blood-vessels, and there is no fluid in the body which they do not occasionally carry into them; but those which more peculiarly belong to them, are the chyle and lymph.

Another general observation I wish also to premise is, that independent of those absorbents which accompany the arteries, and which are usually one on each side, there is on the extremities a set of cutaneous absorbents, accompanying the major trunks of the cutaneous veins, as the saphena major and minor, in the lower extremity; the basilic and cephalic veins, in the upper extremity. There is also on the viscera commonly a superficial and a deep-seated set; the first run by themselves, on the surfaces of the viscera; the second accompany the principal blood-vessels of the viscera, and ramify in the same manner. This distinction takes place even amongst the absorbents of the intestines themselves.

The experimental observations on the passage of impregnated ova through the fallopian tube of the rabbit were communicated by Everard Home to the Royal Society shortly before Cruikshank was elected to Fellowship. In the beginning of the summer of 1778, and at the end of his team lectures, Cruikshank was introduced by William Hunter to the keeper of a rabbit warren in Chelsea. The animals were provided at Hunter's expense, and a total of 29 experiments were reported. The uterus and tubes of each animal were inspected in periods from two hours to three weeks following insemination. Gross inspection of the fallopian tubes of the rabbit the third day after impregnation found several ova in the tubes near their end, but none in the uterus. Under the microscope the ova appeared to have three coats. After three and one-half days, ova were found first in the uterus. In addition to the crucial chronological observations, conclusions and clinical relevance were discussed.[5]

Accordingly he [Hunter] carried me to Chelsea, introduced me to a man who kept a rabbit warren, and desired him to let me have as many rabbits as I pleased. I made the experiments; and shall now lay a copy of my journal, then made, before this Society.

Experiment II.

I opened a female rabbit two hours after she received the male.

Experiment III.

I opened another female rabbit the third day after impregnation: that she was impregnated I could have no doubt, . . . but though I examined the fallopian tubes in the sunshine, and with great care, I could not find any ova, neither in them nor in the horns of the uterus.

Experiment XXIV.

Opened another at three days and a half: ovaria had the appearance as if the ova had not yet gone out; however, many of them were found in the uterus, and many in the tubes; I got about six; others were lost, from the great difficulty in slitting up the fallopian tubes without bruising the ova with the fingers or with the point of scissars; there were eight or nine *corpora lutea* in one ovarium, and two only in the other; on the side of the two I only found one ovum, but twice as large as those on the other side.

General Conclusions

5thly. The ovum comes into the uterus on the fourth day.

6thly. De Graaf did not see the foetus till the tenth day; I saw it on the eighth.

7thly. These experiments explain what is seen in the human female.

C. The ovum sometimes misses the fallopian tube, falls into the abdomen, and forms the extra-uterine foetus; this sometimes grows to its full size, labour pains come on at the ninth month, the child may then be taken out alive by the Caesarean section; or, dying and wasting, but not putrefying, may remain without much inconviency to the mother for many years.

D. The ovum, although it has gone some way down the fallopian tube, may be arrested in its course and become stationary, and form what is called the fallopian tube case. A remarkable case of this kind is given by Dr. HUNTER, in his book on the gravid uterus, where the tube burst, and the mother bled to death.

1. William Cruikshank, Esq., Obituary, *Ann Med* 4-5: 497-503, 1801.
2. Cruikshank, W. C.: Experiments on the Nerves, Particularly on Their Reproduction; and on the Spinal Marrow of Living Animals, *Philos Trans* 85:177-189, 1795.
3. Cruikshank, W. C.: *Experiments on the Insensible Perspiration of the Human Body, shewing its Affinity to Respiration,* London: G. Nicol, 1795.
4. Cruikshank, W. C.: *The Anatomy of the Absorbing Vessels of the Human Body,* London: G. Nicol, 1786.
5. Cruikshank, W. C.: Experiments in Which, on the Third Day After Impregnation, the Ovo of Rabbits Were Found in the Fallopian Tubes, and on the Fourth Day After Impregnation in the Uterus Itself; With the First Appearances of the Foetus, *Philos Trans* 87:197-214, 1797.

Sir Henry Halford (1766-1844)

THE INTEREST OF MOST PHYSICIANS in death terminates with the conviction that the best possible care has been rendered the patient or that a postmortem examination has been performed in order that the living may benefit from the dead. Sir Henry Halford, born Henry Vaughan, was an exception.[1] His interest in death extended from an inquiry into the death of eminent persons of modern times and illustrious persons of antiquity, to an account of the opening of the tomb of Charles I more than 160 years after he had been beheaded.

Henry Vaughan was the second son of a successful physician of Leicester. He attended Rugby and Christ Church, Oxford, receiving his AB in 1788 and MD in 1791. In the meantime, he attended three winter sessions at Edinburgh and, when not in the pursuit of formal education, assisted his father in the care of the sick. Late in 1792

Vaughan settled in London for the practice of medicine, having borrowed funds to carry him over a lean period. He was elected physician to Middlesex Hospital in

Royal College of Physicians

1793, the same year he was admitted a candidate of the College of Physicians.

Any apprehension that he might have felt for a slow start in practice was scarcely warranted, since a classical education, family connections, Oxford associates, and proper introduction into London society provided a firm base for a notable position among the aristocracy, civil and royal. Within a year, and before he was 27 years of age, Halford was appointed physician extraordinary to the King. By 1800, having married a lady of rank and fashion and having developed an extensive private practice, he gave up his hospital appointment. Upon the death of his mother's cousin, Sir Charles Halford, he fell heir to a large legacy, changed his name by an act of Parliament from Vaughan to Halford, and was created a baronet by George III in recognition of his services. Following Matthew Baillie's death in 1823, Halford was acknowledged to be the leading physician of London and attended a total of four sovereigns—George

III, George IV, William IV, and Queen Victoria.

Halford's observations at the opening of the tomb of King Charles I were described in his *Essays and Orations,* delivered at a session of the Royal College of Physicians when he was president of the College. The tomb was opened in 1813, having been discovered in the vault of King Henry VIII at Windsor. A square opening was made in the upper part of the lead lid. The head was exposed, found to be detached from the torso, and was removed from the coffin for closed inspection.[2]

On holding up the head, to examine the place of separation from the body, the muscles of the neck had evidently retracted themselves considerably; and the fourth cervical vertebra was found to be cut through its substance transversely, leaving the surfaces of the divided portions perfectly smooth and even, an appearance which could have been produced only by a heavy blow, inflicted with a very sharp instrument, and which furnished the last proof wanting to identify King Charles the First.

The first ten essays in the volume that preceded the recounting of this mobid procedure are not remarkable scientifically but are to be judged typical of a sound clinician and therapist, who knew less of pathology and physical examination of the sick than of the attributes identified with an appealing and exemplary bedside manner. The subjects included climacteric disease, tic douloureux, insanity, and gout. In discussing the management of gout, great reliance was placed upon the value of *Colchicum* (colchicine) in the treatment of the acute attack.[2]

With regard to the remedies for Gout, my dependence is placed upon the Colchicum. Under the common circumstances of an attack of Gout in the extremities, I do not use it immediately, but wait a day or two, until the malady shall have fixed itself. I then direct the wine of the root, prepared according to the directions of the Pharmacopoeia; and I do not hesitate to declare, that I have not known a single instance of any untoward effect from it. It often cures the disease without any manifest increase of any of the excretions.

It has been objected to the Colchicum that it produces a temporary good effect only, and that

the Gout is apt to recur when treated with this medicine after a shorter interval than usual. Be it so for arguments sake—yet surely the weight of three or four attacks of the disease, of three or four days' continuance each, not more, is hardly to be compared with the pressure of a six weeks' painful confinement in the spring, and one of equal duration at the latter end of the year, as was the case before the value of this remedy was known.

Sir Henry's interests in the sick room led him to a discussion of medical ethics, including how much to tell the patient stricken with a fatal malady.[2]

And here you will forgive me, perhaps, if I presume to state what appears to me to be the conduct proper to be observed by a physician in withholding, or making his patient acquainted with, his opinion of the probable issue of a malady manifesting mortal symptoms. I own I think it my first duty to protect his life by all practicable means, and to interpose myself between him and everything which may possibly aggravate his danger. And unless I shall have found him averse from doing what was necessary in aid of my remedies, from a want of a proper sense of his perilous situation, I forbear to step out of the bounds of my province in order to offer any advice which is not necessary to promote his cure. At the same time, I think it indispensable to let his friends know the danger of his case, the instant I discover it. An arrangement of his worldly affairs, in which the comfort or unhappiness of those who are to come after him is involved, may be necessary; and a suggestion of his danger, by which the accomplishment of this object is to be obtained, naturally induces a contemplation of his more important spiritual concerns, a careful review of his past life, and such sincere sorrow and contrition for what he has done amiss, as justifies our humble hope of his pardon and acceptance hereafter. If friends can do these good offices at a proper time, and under the suggestions of the physician, it is far better that they should undertake them than the medical adviser. They do so without destroying his hopes, for the patient will still believe that he has an appeal to his physician beyond their fears; whereas, if the physician lay open his danger to him, however delicately he may do this, he runs a risk of appearing to pronounce a sentence of condemnation to death, against which there is no appeal—*no hope;* and, *on that account,* what is most awful to think of, perhaps the sick man's repentance may be less available.

1. Munk, W.: *The Life of Sir Henry Halford, Bart,* London: Longmans, Green and Co., 1895.
2. Halford, H.: *Essays and Orations,* London: J. Murray, 1833.

Royal College of Physicians

Thomas M. Winterbottom
(1766-1859)

THOMAS WINTERBOTTOM, who provided one of the early descriptions of African sleeping sickness, was born in South Shields, England, son of a physician.[1] He studied first at Edinburgh about 1790, where he received the AM degree and completed his training at Glasgow for the MD degree in 1792. His medical dissertation on diseases of the puerperium was prepared in Latin. Following graduation, Winterbottom was appointed physician to the colony of Sierra Leone in West Africa and served for more than four years. On his return, he entered general practice with his father; there he gained the esteem of his patients, acquired a commendable reputation, and accumulated considerable wealth. The experiences in Sierra Leone provided material for two scientific treatises. The first, published in 1802, contained general medical advice for navigators and settlers in equatorial climates; the second, a two-volume

account of the health and disease of the native Africans, was published in 1803. In the first volume of this work, he considered general subjects such as meteorology, agriculture, diet, dress, noise of crickets at night, amusements, polygamy, trade, religion, burials, and superstition. The second volume was devoted to empirical medicine and contained sections or chapters on fever, venereal diseases, elephantiasis, worms, gout, snake bite, dirt eating, large bellies, circumcision, and lethargy. The last is one of the earliest accounts in English of sleeping sickness from trypanosome infestation, noting especially the appearance of glandular tumors before the development of lethargy.[2]

The Africans are very subject to a species of lethargy, which they are much afraid of, as it proves fatal in every instance. The Timmanees call it márree, or, 'nluoi, and the Bulloms, nagónloe, or kadeera: it is called the Soosoos, kee kóllee kondee, or sleepy sickness, and by the Mandingos, seeoyúncaree, a word of similar import. This disease is very frequent in the Foola country, and it is said to be much more common in the interior parts of the country than upon the sea coast. Children are very rarely, or never, affected with this complaint, nor is it more common among slaves than among free people, though it is asserted that the slaves from Benin are very subject to it. At the commencement of the disease, the patient has commonly a ravenous appetite, eating twice the quantity of food he was accustomed to take when in health, and becoming very fat. When the disease has continued some time, the appetite declines, and the patient gradually wastes away. Squinting occurs sometimes, though very seldom, in this disease, and in some rare instances the patient is carried off in convulsions. Small glandular tumors are sometimes observed in the neck a little before the commencement of this complaint, though probably depending rather upon accidental circumstances than upon the disease itself. Slave traders, however, appear to consider these tumors as a symptom indicating a disposition to lethargy, and they either never buy such slaves, or get quit of them as soon as they observe any such appearances. The disposition to sleep is so strong, as scarcely to leave a sufficient respite for the taking of food; even the repeated application of a whip, a remedy which has been frequently used, is hardly sufficient to keep the poor wretch awake. The repeated application of blisters and of setons has been employed by European surgeons without avail, as the disease, under every mode of treatment, usually proves fatal within three or four months. The natives are totally at a loss to what cause this complaint ought to be attributed; sweating is the only means they make use of, or from which they hope for any success: this is never tried but in incipient cases, for when the disease has been of any continuance they think it in vain to make the attempt. The root of a grass, called by the Soosoos kallee, and the dried leaves of a plant, called in Soosoo fingka, are boiled for some time in water, in an iron pot; when this is removed from the fire, the patient is seated over it, and is covered over with cotton cloths, a process which never fails to excite a copious perspiration. This mode of cure is repeated two or three times a day, and is persisted in for a considerable length of time, until the disease be carried off, or appears to be gaining ground. No internal medicines are given in the complaint.

Winterbottom retired from practice at 56, with a comfortable fortune, and devoted the latter years of his life to scholarship, language, extended tours of the Continent, and philanthropy. His principal published writings during this period were a series of communications, the first, was entitled "Thoughts on Quarantine and Contagion," appeared in the *Edinburgh Medical and Surgical Journal,* 1828-1829.

1. Thomas M. Winterbottom, M.D., Obituary, *Lancet* 2:76-77, (July 16) 1859.
2. Winterbottom, T.: *An Account of the Native Africans in the Neighborhood of Sierra Leone,* vol 2, London: J. Hatchard & J. Mawman, 1803.

Gaspard-Laurent Bayle (1744-1816)

G.-L. BAYLE, who gave the best description of his time of the varieties of tubercular infection, was born into a well-to-do family in the mountain village of Vernet of Haute-Provence. As a youth he was interested in natural biology, but, plagued with indecision, he ventured first into theology, then law, and finally medicine. The introduction to the latter at Montpellier was prompted by an unhappy turn of political events in which he was involved in his community. Subsequently, Bayle returned to Paris and, in 1801, received the degree of doctor of medicine.[1] The late matriculation in medicine was soon outweighed by his industry and talents in teaching on the wards and in the morgue and in clinical management of internal diseases. In 1807, he was appointed to the staff of Charité and the following year physician to the royal household and the royal infirmary.

Composite by G. Bako

Bayle's *Researches on Pulmonary Phthisis,* published in 1810, was an outstanding clinical-pathological contribution and influenced the physicians of his generation and particularly his friend and colleague Laennec. Bayle taught correctly that tuberculosis was a specific disease entity and not a morbid process degeneration or descended from a preceding malady. He observed that tubercles might develop before symptoms appeared, recognized cavity formation as a complication of pulmonary consumption, and described several forms of tubercular infection. These included acute miliary tuberculosis, tubercular laryngitis, lymphadenitis, enteritis, and tuberculosis of the ovaries. His monograph, which was published first in French, was translated in 1815 by Barrow of Liverpool. The Preface proceeds from Barrow's concept of the general character of phthisis to Bayle's definition of the denominations of the species.[2]

The generic character of Phthisis may be drawn from the symptoms, or from the nature and seat of the disorder.

It is evidently necessary to unite the two characters of which we have been speaking. In fact the cough, wasting, hectic fever, and purulent expectoration, are the effects of the disorganization of the lungs. These symptoms shew that this disorganization is advanced; but the disease is no less real in its commencement, and the essential character is even then applicable. Besides, this disease may exist without presenting the union of symptoms named *Pathognomonic*. Authors have remarked that different persons have died of Phthisis, who have never shewn manifest signs of it; thus persons have been seen to die, who were in a state of hectic fever and marasmus, without cough or expectoration, where numberless tubercles were found in the lungs, and what is more inconceivable, large ulcers. The same injury of the lungs has been found in other persons, of whom some appear to have had only excessive diarrhoea, and to have died of inanition alone.

FIRST SPECIES—TUBERCULAR PHTHISIS

This, the most common species of all, is often simple. . . . The lungs then present tubercles either encysted or not encysted. . . . The tubercles vary in size from a millet seed to that of a chestnut. Miliary tubercles are commonly excessively numerous. As to the others, they are so much the fewer the larger they are, and sometimes two or three only are to be found.

The large number of dissections performed by Bayle as a staff physician at Hôpital de la Charité and as a member of the Society of the Faculty of Medicine of Paris provided the protocols for a remarkable variety of tubercular cases. Each account of a case presented a clinical résumé, the gross postmortem findings, and a summary of reflections. Bayle's descriptions of tubercles of the bladder, mesentery, and intestines have been selected for excerpting.[2]

The bladder adhered very intimately to the anterior surface of the womb. Its internal membrane had a deep brown red colour; it was covered with tubercles pretty much crowded together, of a miliary or lenticular size, and whitish internally.
REFLECTIONS.—We see that this girl died in an attack of intermittent fever. The pains she perceived in the belly proceeded from the disease of the ovarium, or of the peritonaeum, or its duplications. It is astonishing that there should be no pain in the bladder, which, as we have seen, was so much injured.

The exterior of the body presented the *embonpoint* and freshness of youth; the lungs were free, voluminous, hard like liver in their whole extent, and contained heavy and large tubercular masses not encysted, most of them of the size of small walnuts, others of the size of nuts, and some smaller. . . . but there were in the mesentery, glands nearly tubercular throughout, and as large as almonds.

Ulcerations of the intestines are very frequent in putrid and in malignant fevers: they render the disorder more serious, but do not prevent the cure of it; and when these fevers do not terminate fatally, the ulcerations cicatrise.

Bayle died at the early age of 42—whether from tuberculosis or not—the record is not clear. It would not be surprising had he fallen a victim to the disease that attracted a deep interest, in view of the repeated exposure in the morgue to tubercular lesions. There are only 17 items in his bibliography. The inaugural dissertation on nosology was his first;[3] a two-volume posthumous treatise on cancer, prepared by his nephew, was his last.[4]

1. Deleuze, J. P. F.: *Biography of M. Bayle,* Paris: A. Belin, 1816.
2. Bayle, G.-L.: *Researches on Pulmonary Phthisis,* Paris: Gabon, 1810, W. Barrow, trans., Liverpool: G. F. Harris' Widow and Brothers, 1815.
3. Bayle G.-L.: *Reflections on Nosology* (Fr), Paris: Boiste, Gabon, 1802.
4. Bayle, G.-L.: *Treatise on Cancer* (Fr), Paris: M. Gautret, 1833-1839.

Carl Wilhelm Scheele (1732-1786)

C. W. SCHEELE, the greatest organic chemist of his time and possibly of all times, spent all of his professional years as a practicing apothecary. He was born in Stralsund, Sweden, into a family of German descent.[1] His father was a brewer and broker with limited resources, but he provided private schooling followed by Gymnasium training. Scheele was attracted to chemistry early in life and, at the age of 14, began an apprenticeship in Gothenburg in an apothecary shop, the only route at that time to the profession. In addition to fulfilling the duties of an apprentice, Scheele read the best chemical works available, including those of Lemery, Stahl, and Kunkel. Also, he repeated with crude and simple equipment selected experiments of the recognized masters.

Scheele's apothecary work was continued in succession in Malmö and Stockholm;

Composite by G. Bako

while in Uppsala in 1770, he was appointed director of laboratory work in a pharmacy. This assignment permitted him to carry on his chemical experiments and to establish scientific liaison with Bergman, professor of chemistry in the University, and Gahn, a noted mineralogist. His final five years were spent in charge of the pharmacy in Köping; there he was sorely troubled with intractable gouty arthritis, a malady to which he made a great chemical contribution.

Scheele's fruitful investigations embraced inorganic, organic, and physical chemistry. Even though the phlogiston theory of combustion prevailed, his remarkable powers of observation and keen discernment overcame the concept which had been an obstacle for almost a century to an understanding of oxidation and reduction. Many of his studies were communicated to the Royal Academy of Science, Stockholm, and through translation became readily available in German, French, and English. His greatest monograph, *Chemical Treatise on Air and Fire*,[2] was written in Swedish in 1775, trans-

lated into German, published in 1777, and translated into English three years later. The last edition of Scheele's collected works, translated into English from which the excerpts in this biography were taken, appeared in 1931. His discoveries on the nature of combustion were conducted independently and paralleled those of Priestley, who anticipated him in the discovery of oxygen, calling it "dephlogisticated air."

Although it had been accepted since the speculations of Aristotle and Galen that air was an element and indivisible, Scheele determined in simple but ingenious experiments that air is composed of two gases in the approximate ratio of three to one. Eventually breaking from the phlogiston theory, Scheele retained the term in the *Treatise* and assumed heat and light to be combinations of oxygen and phlogiston, each in different proportions. Oxygen was isolated during the ignition of red oxide of mercury, silver carbonate, magnesium nitrate, and potassium nitrate. The gas was recognized by him to be odorless and tasteless, and essential to respiration and in the germination of seeds. Two of Scheele's experiments were translated as follows.[3]

First Experiment. I mixed so much concentrated oil of vitriol with finely powdered manganese that it became a stiff magma. I distilled this mixture from a small retort on the open fire. In place of a receiver I made use of a bladder, empty of air, and in order that the vapours which might pass over should not attack the bladder, I poured into it some milk of lime. As soon as the bottom of the retort became red-hot, an air passed over which gradually expanded the bladder. This air had all the properties of a pure fire air.

Second Experiment. When I distilled two parts of finely pulverised manganese with one part of the phosphoric acid from urine in the same way as is indicated in the preceding paragraph, I likewise obtained fire air.

A summary of many of Scheele's original observations in inorganic and organic chemistry was enumerated by Dobbin in the translator's introduction to *The Collected Papers of Carl Wilhelm Scheele*.[3]

These include the independent discovery of oxygen and the discovery of chlorine and of barium compounds; also the observations of the solubility of manganous carbonate in water containing dissolved carbon dioxide, of the dark colour of precipitated manganous hydroxide as due to the air dissolved in the solutions employed; of the formation of manganate and permanganate; of the effect of manganese dioxide in removing the green colour, due to iron, from ordinary bottle glass; of the production of mercuric cyanide in solution by boiling a mixture of Prussian blue and mercuric oxide with water; of the liberation of hydrogen by the interaction of iron with water only; of the varying effects of the different parts of the solar spectrum on silver chloride; of the different effects produced by the exposure to direct sunlight of two thermometers, otherwise similar but of which the one contained red-coloured and the other colourless spirit; and of the absorption of gases by charcoal.

Amongst numerous observations by Scheele which are of analytical importance, there are those concerned with the recognition of dissolved oxygen in water by means of ferrous sulphate and potassium carbonate; of hydrocyanic acid in admixture with air by suspending in the air for some time a paper strip which has been moistened successively with ferrous sulphate and alkali-metal hydroxide solutions, and afterwards treating the strip with hydrochloric acid; of the presence of manganese in plant ash by fusing the ash with potassium nitrate; and of uric acid in calculus by heating the latter with nitric acid.

In the discovery of uric acid, the initial observations were made on a collection of bladder calculi, which were pulverized and their properties studied with various physical and chemical agents. The previously unknown concrete or calculus acid was found in all urines and in higher concentration in the sick than in the healthy.[4]

Pure water dissolves the calculus completely, but much water is required for this. When five ounces of water are poured upon eight grains of finely powdered calculus, and boiled for a short time, it is dissolved. The solution makes tincture of litmus red, and does not precipitate lime water. When it cools, the greater part of the calculus separates from it in the form of fine crystals.

Finally, I have found some calculus dissolved in all urine, even in that of children. When four *kannes* of clear and fresh urine are evaporated till only two ounces of it remain, a fine powder is deposited on cooling, a part of which adheres firmly to the glass vessel. It is dissolved quite easily, without heat, by a few drops of caustic lye and possesses besides all the properties of calculus. The sediment which deposits itself like brick-dust in the urine of those who have the ague, is of the same nature.

In accordance with the experiments cited, all urine thus contains, besides the previously known substances (which are sal ammoniac, common salt, digestive salt, Glauber's salt, microcosmic salt, perlate salt, and an oily extract), a previously unknown concrete acid, or calculus, and animal earth. It is remarkable that the urine of sick persons is more acid and contains more animal earth than that of the healthy.

Scheele led a simple life completely absorbed in his chemical studies. His genius was recognized at home and abroad, but always he preferred to be known as an "apothecary" and so signed his documents. When he was 32 years of age, he was elected to the Swedish Academy of Science and received a life annuity in recognition of his work. Several unaccepted offers to study and teach came from abroad, as well as membership in the Society of Naturalists in Berlin in 1778 and the Academy of Sciences of Turin in 1780. Monuments in Scheele's honor have been erected in Stockholm and Köping; his country and international learned societies have honored him posthumously.

1. Urdang, G.: *Carl Wilhelm Scheele, A Pictorial Biography*, Madison, Wis: American Institute of the History of Pharmacy, 1958.
2. Scheele, C. W.: *Chemical Treatise on Air and Fire* (Ger), Upsala and Leipzig: M. Swederus, 1777.
3. Dobbin, L.: *The Collected Papers of Carl Wilhelm Scheele*, London: G. Bell & Sons, Ltd., 1931.
4. Scheele, K.: Investigations of Bladder Stones (Swed), *Kongl Vetenskaps Acad Handl* 37:327-332, 1776.

Sir Charles Blagden (1748-1820)

THE SCIENTIFIC ACCOMPLISHMENTS OF CHARLES BLAGDEN, denied public school and college education, centered about the stability of body temperature in man in the heat, and the thermolabile property of water in the cold. Blagden was born in the village of Wooten-under-Edge, Gloucestershire. In 1768, through his own efforts, he acquired sufficient preliminary education to begin the study of medicine at the University of Edinburgh.[1] Three years later he received the MD degree, presenting a discussion on the etiology of apoplexy for his thesis. Without any record of having practiced medicine, he entered the military service at the outbreak of war with the American Colonies in 1776, and served as surgeon with

National Library of Medicine

the British army. Blagden returned to Plymouth approximately three years later, where he practiced for a limited period only. Natural philosophy, dialogues with notable scholars, and international travel mainly occupied his attention throughout the remainder of his life. In his final years he spent a portion of each year in France. He died suddenly of apoplexy while visiting his friend and confidant, Berthollet, and was buried in French soil.

Blagden enoyed an extended friendship with Sir Joseph Banks, president of the Royal Society of London, and served as its secretary from 1784 to 1797. During this time he exploited the opportunity of meeting the most distinguished English and European scientists of his time. In 1782, he was accepted as assistant to the celebrated chemist, Cavendish, who settled an annuity of considerable size on him with the understanding that he would "give up medicine and devote his time to philosophy." In this commitment he proved to be a methodical investigator and an accurate writer, communicating each of his major and many of his minor observations to the Royal So-

ciety for publication in their *Philosophical Transactions*. His experimental observations on the importance of perspiration in the dissipation of body heat and protection by clothes against conduction and radiation from surrounding air during exposure in a superheated chamber were conducted in 1774; Blagden and associates acted as experimental subjects. A rapid increase in pulse rate, with minimal increments in body temperature and excreted urine, was recorded when the environmental temperature was 200 F or higher. An ancillary observation, the significance of which was not discussed, concerned the dissipation of heat in a dog, in contrast to man, through panting and excessive salivation. A brief reference to the therapeutic value of the hot room in treatment of systemic disease concluded the presentation. Excerpts from the successive communications follow.[2]

About the middle of January, several gentlemen and myself received an invitation from Dr. GOERGE FORDYCE, to observe the effects of air heated to a much higher degree than it was formerly thought any living creature could bear. We all rejoiced at the opportunity of being convinced, by our own experience, of the wonderful power with which the animal body is endued, of resisting an heat vastly greater than its own temperature; and our curiosity was not a little excited to observe the circumstances attending this remarkable power.

Soon afterwards Dr. SOLANDER entered the room alone, and saw the thermometer at 210°; but, during three minutes that he staid there, it sunk to 196°. Another time, he found it almost five minutes before the heat was lessened from 210° to 196°. . . . The air heated to these high degrees felt unpleasantly hot, but was very bearable. . . . Our respiration was not at all affected; it became neither quick nor laborious; the only difference was a want of that refreshing sensation which accompanies a full inspiration of cool air. . . . But the most striking effects proceeded from our power of preserving our natural temperature. . . . Upon touching my side it felt cold like a corpse; and yet the actual heat of my body, tried under my tongue, and by applying closely the thermometer to my skin, was 98°, about a degree higher than its ordinary temperature.

These experiments, therefore, prove in the clearest manner, that the body has a power of destroying heat. . . . But it was only a small part of our bodies that exerted the power of destroying heat with such a violent effort as seems necessary at first sight. Our clothes, contrived to guard us from cold, guarded us from the heat on the same principles.

My pulse, counted as soon as I came into the cool air, for the uneasy feeling rendered me incapable of examining it in the room, was found to beat at the rate of 144 pulsations in a minute, which is more than double its ordinary quickness.

In the present case it appears beyond all doubt, that the living powers were very much assisted by the perspiration, that cooling evaporation which is a further provision of nature for enabling animals to support great heats. Had we been provided with a proper balance, it would undoubtedly have rendered the experiment more complete to have taken the exact weight of my body at going into, and coming out of, the room; as from the quantity lost some estimate might be formed of the share which the perspiration had in keeping the body cool.

. . . . We subjected a bitch weighing thirty-two pounds, to the following experiment. When the thermometer had risen to 220°, the animal was shut up in the heated room, inclosed in a basket, that its feet might be defended from the scorching of the floor, and with a piece of paper before its head and breast to intercept the direct heat of the cockle. In about ten minutes it began to pant and hold out its tongue, which symptoms continued till the end of the experiment, without ever becoming more violent than they are usually observed in dogs after exercise in hot weather; and the animal was so little affected during the whole time, as to shew signs of pleasure whenever we approached the basket. After the experiment had continued half an hour, when the thermometer has risen to 236°, we opened the basket, and found the bottom of it very wet with *saliva*.

The heated room will, I hope, in time become a very useful instrument in the hands of the physician. Hitherto the necessary experiments have not been made to direct its application with a sufficient degree of certainty. However, we can already perceive a foundation for some distinctions in the use of this uncommon remedy. Should the object in view be to produce a profuse perspiration, a dry heat acting on the naked body would most effectually answer that purpose. The histories of dropsies and some other diseases, supposed to have been cured by such means, are well known to every physician.

Other subjects discussed by Blagden include the effects of lightning, the congelation of mercury, fiery meteors, the tides at Naples, temperature of the water in the Gulf Stream, and recovering the legibility of ancient inks and decayed writings. His experiments on the cooling of water below its freezing point and the effects of various substances in lowering the point of the congelation of water rank in significance with his observations on evaporation. In discussing supercooling, he discovered that distilled water might be supercooled to 23 F before ice is formed,[3] and determined the degree of depression of the freezing point of water with the addition of dissolved substances beginning with common salt.[4] Similar experiments were performed with niter, sal ammoniac, Rochelle salt, magnesium sulphate, copper sulphate, and white vitriol. His general conclusion was that salt lowers the freezing point of water in the simple inverse ratio of the proportion which water bears to it in the solution. This has since become known as Blagden's law.

The well-known property of water, that under different circumstances it will bear to be cooled several degrees below its freezing point without congealing, . . . I began with endeavouring to determine, whether this property belongs to it as pure water, or depends upon extraneous admixtures. For that purpose I poured some clean distilled water into a common tumbler glass, till it reached two or three inches above the bottom, and then set the glass in a frigorific mixture, made with snow and common salt. This was the method I used in most of the following experiments, sometimes employing ice instead of snow, substituting a glass jar or cylinder instead of a tumbler, and filling the vessel to a greater or less height above the bottom. I found that, in the frigoric mixture, the distilled water readily sunk many degrees below 32°, still continuing fluid; and by repeating the experiment with care, I several times cooled it to 24°, 23°½, and even almost to 23°. . . . I put some of the same distilled water over the fire to boil, in a clean silver vessel, and kept it in violent ebullition for a considerable time. In a few minutes after it had been taken off the fire, and before it was nearly cold, I set it in the frigorific mixture after the usual manner; when, instead of freezing more readily, it bore to be cooled two degrees lower than I had ever been able to reduce the unboiled water, not congealing till the thermometer in it had sunk to 21°.

But here a further circumstance came to be considered. It is well known, that such substances, uniting with water, have a power of lowering its point of congelation a greater or less number of degrees, according to the nature and quantity of the substance employed. The first object, therefore, was to determine in what manner the property of bearing to be cooled would be affected with regard to that new point of congelation. For this purpose I made many experiments with several different substances, which it would be too long to relate in detail, but the principal were [sic] as follows.

Having dissolved in distilled water as much common salt as lowered its freezing point to 28°, I cooled it to 18°½ before it congealed. Another solution of the same salt, whose freezing point was 16°, bore to be cooled to 9°, and a stronger solution, whose freezing point was 13°½, cooled to 5° before it shot.

My first object of investigation was the ratio according to which equal additions of the same substance depress the freezing point. I began with common salt; and in order to avoid as much as possible a fallacy in the experiments, because the ordinary salt is never pure, and often not perfectly neutral, I chose some clean salt, in fair crystals, which is sold in London under the name of Borrowstounness pure salt. This salt I dissolved in distilled water, in various proportions, and found the corresponding points of congelation to be as is expressed in the annexed table; where the first column indicates the number of parts and decimals of water to one part of the salt, and the second column shews the freezing point found by the experiment. It appeared clearly, on comparing the proportions of water to salt, with the coresponding number of degrees which the freezing point was reduced below 32°, that the effect of the salt was nearly in a simple ratio; namely, that if the addition of a *tenth* part of salt to the water sunk the freezing point about 11 degrees, or to 21°, it would be depressed double that quantity, or to 10° nearly, when a *fifth* part of the salt was dissolved in water.

1. Getman, F. H.: Sir Charles Blagden, F. R. S., *Osiris* 3:69-87, 1938.
2. Blagden, C.: Experiments and Observations in an Heated Room, *Philos Trans* 65:111-123, 484-494, 1775.
3. Blagden, C.: Experiments on the Cooling of Water Below Its Freezing Point, *Philos Trans* 78:125-146, 1788.
4. Blagden, C.: Experiments on the Effect of Various Substances in Lowering the Point of Congelation of Water, *Philos Trans* 78:277-12, 1788.

John Bell (1763-1820)

BELL, BRILLIANT, SKILLFUL, AND SCHOLARLY, a proponent of surgical anatomy, was born in Edinburgh when his father was 59 years old. He received excellent early training at home, and continued his education at the High School.[1] Upon the advice of his father, Bell was apprenticed for five years to Alexander Wood, an eminent surgeon, and attended the lectures of Cullen, Black,

and the second Monro at the University of Edinburgh. He presented to the faculty a doctoral thesis in Latin on malignant fever. Following a short study tour of Russia and northern Europe, he returned to Edinburgh

National Library of Medicine

in 1786 and was admitted a Fellow of the Royal College of Surgeons of Edinburgh.

Although a member of the College and thereby entitled to staff privileges at the Royal Infirmary, Bell was never appointed a member of the University faculty. Instead, in 1790, he built his own lecture amphitheatre adjacent to Surgeon's Hall and gave outstanding lectures on midwifery, anatomy, and surgery, and developed an extensive private practice. His anatomical lectures were based upon practical surgery, while surgical pathology was introduced whenever appropriate. The attraction of a large following of pupils posed an academic threat to the University's singular reputation, particularly at the expense of Monro, who lacked the oratorical fluency of his former student. Standing in competition with the University teachers, Bell suffered a serious blow to his prestige in 1800 when he was excluded from the Infirmary during its reorganization by Gregory, professor of medicine. Also, he was attacked by Gregory with placards, pamplets, and a volume of accusations published under the pseudonym "Jonathan Dawplucker." After a delay of

10 years, Bell published his reply in his *Letters on Professional Character and Manners; on the Education of a Surgeon and the Duties and Qualifications of a Physician: Addressed to James Gregory, M.D.* In this scathing rebuttal Bell gives us an example of his skill in nonmedical composition, his ability to hold his ground in an argument, as well as restraint in acting slowly rather than hastily.[2]

> The task I have undertaken is painful, but it is a duty to my much injured profession, and I have one great consolation ever present to my mind, that I am not wounding the reputation of a good, nor the peace of an innocent man: I endeavour to repress the aggressions of a priviliged and powerful assailant, daring in calumny, and indifferent to all the decencies and properties of polished life: to repel his malice, only after the unanimous voice of my profession has declared it such as has never been known, and should not be endured.
>
> It is ever to be lamented, that Dr. James Gregory, Professor of Practice in the most celebrated seminary of education that has grown up in modern times; the son of a respected Father, and the companion, from his early years, of many able and liberal men; trained from his youth in the best parts of learning; the appointed defender of his profession, and of its morals; should descend from the dignity of his station, to enmities and calumnies plainly connected with his interests, and should so entirely fail in the virtues of generosity, truth, and candour, as to make his way of life a theme for all tongues,—a lesson for all ages.
>
> That Dr. James Gregory has traduced my professional and moral reputation, is most true: It is the most trivial perhaps of his offences, that which the public will the most easily pardon, and which I was inclined, from pride and conscious rectitude, to pass in silence. Seven years have elapsed, and more, since he sought to ruin my good name, and concluded a defamatory quarto of five hundred and thirteen pages with this memorable warning to the inhabitants of this my native city,—"Any man, if himself or his family were sick, should as soon think of calling in a mad dog, as Mr. John Bell, or any who held the principles he professes." My principles, my feelings, my professional talents, and my integrity, may easily find more partial judges than Dr. Gregory: If I have made any uncharitable conclusion concerning his, it is one which conveys a compliment to his prudence. He wrote, published, distributed, this memorable and calumnious essay on my poor talents, not merely for the gratification of his own malicious propensities, but for the behoof of those who could reward them.

Bell was a prodigious worker, a student of Latin and Greek, a musician, an artist, a scholar and an author of outstanding treatises in anatomy and surgery as well as monographs and shorter communications on the practice of his art. The first volume of *The Anatomy of the Human Body* appeared in 1793; volumes 2 and 3 appeared in subsequent years. In 1794, he designed and engraved the illustrations on *Bones, Muscles and Joints* to accompany volume 1; in 1801, *Engravings of the Arteries,* as a companion to the second volume. In 1795, Bell published *Discourses on the Nature and Cure of Wounds,* in which he discussed the desirability of healing by first intention, a break from contemporary practice. Between 1801 and 1807, his 3-volume treatise, *The Principles of Surgery,* appeared.[4] With each series his younger brother Charles assisted in or was responsible for subsequent editions. Because Bell practiced and taught sound principles for the handling of specific and general wounds, portions from his 1795 *Discourses* will be excerpted, followed by passages on the anatomy and surgery of the vasular system, with which he was particularly concerned. Discourse I, "On Procuring Adhesions," in the text *Nature and Cure of Wounds* expressed Bell's thoughts on healing by first intention.[3]

> When a modern surgeon allows himself to talk about the "mundifying, incarning, and cicatrizing of wounds, or directs how to fill the wound up with good and sound flesh, and keep it to a fair and even level with the adjacent skin," he but proclaims his own ignorance of the properties of the living body. Perhaps he talks this language idly, and in mere compliance with the usual forms of speaking; but if he has seriously any such notion of the business and duties of a surgeon, there is much reason to fear, lest he should both teach and practise imaginary cures; which far from incarning or cicatrizing wounds, will rather interfere with the regular process of nature. It is an old, but it is a becoming and modest thought, that in our profession, we are but as the ministers of nature: and indeed the surgeon, still more than the physician, achieves nothing by his own immediate power, but does all his services by observing and managing the properties of the living body; where the living principle is so strong and active in every part, that by the energy alone, it regenerates the lost substance, or re-unites in a more immediate way, the more simple wounds.

Bell demonstrated the effectiveness of collateral circulation and found it thoroughly adequate to handle the blood supply when the main trunk was ligated. Thus, he justified ligation above the superior gluteal artery in the treatment of aneurysm, a procedure described in volume 2 of his *Principles of Surgery*. A leech-catcher fell as he was stepping out of a boat, and a long pair of scissors used in the trade pierced his hip over the sciatic notch, where the great iliac artery emerges from the pelvis. The artery was impaled with the point of the scissors, and, whether from hemorrhage, fright, or pain, the patient fainted. The attending surgeon experienced little difficulty in stopping the hemorrhage, and the skin subsequently healed at the point of entrance. The vessel continued to ooze internally, however, and six weeks later the patient presented with a huge tumor of the buttock and a cold, useless leg. After preliminary inspection and consultation, extensive surgery was performed, without benefit of inhalation anesthesia.[4]

There was little doubt of this being a great aneurism, but there was a possibility of its being a vast abscess; and it was resolved in consultation that the patient should be carried into the operation room; that a small incision should be made; that the skin being cut, the bag itself should be just touched with the point of a lancet; if found to contain matter, it should be fully opened; but if blood, then it was to be considered as an aneurism of so particular a kind, as to entitle us to call for a full consultation. . . . The knife was struck into it, and large clots of very firm black blood rolled out; for such was the tenseness of the tumor, that it began to emit the clots in this way, the moment it was punctured. There was one thing further desirable, that before we put the patient to bed, we should understand the case so far as to be able to report to the consultation, whether the artery was absolutely open, and whether it was the great artery of the hip.

This was done at one o'clock, and at four the consultation met, and the operation was performed. And in my notes, I find two steps of the operation chiefly marked:—First, That upon our opening the tumor fully with an incision of eight inches long, and turning out the great clots, the blood was thrown out with a whishing noise, and with such impetus, that the assistants were covered with it, and in a moment twenty hands were about the tumor, and the bag was filled with sponges, and cloths of all kinds, which had no better effect than the cloths which, in any accident, the friends in great confusion wrap around a wounded arm.

Secondly, Seeing, in this critical moment, that if he was to be saved, it was to be only by a sudden stroke, I ran the bistory upwards and downwards, and at once made my incision two foot in length. . . . The assistants laid aside the edges of this prodigious sac, and sought out the several smaller sponges which had been thrust in, and the sac being deliberately cleaned, and its edges held aside, I kept the fore-finger of my left hand steady upon the artery, passed one of the largest needles round under my fore-finger, so as to surround the artery: one of my friends tied the ligature, and then lifting the point of my finger, it was distinctly seen, that it was the posterior iliac artery,— that the artery had been cut fairly across, and had bled with open mouth— that it was cut and tied exactly where it turns over the bone.

He was cured of this great wound in less than seven months, although his cure was protracted by the foul suppuration of such a sac, and by the exfoliation of the ilium and sacrum.

Dr. Farquharson, who succeeded me in the charge of the hospital, has just informed me, of this man having called upon him after his return from England, walking stoutly, and in good health.

Although Bell retired from teaching when he lost his Infirmary appointment, he remained in active practice until 1816. In that year he was thrown from a horse and seems never to have completely recovered. The following year he sought restitution in Italy but was never confident he would find it. He turned for a time from surgery to art, architecture, and travel; upon his death Bell left a volume of notes on paintings, statuary, and human life. Bishop Sandford assembled the documents and published *Observations on Italy* posthumously.

1. Struthers, J.: *Historical Sketch of the Edinburgh Anatomical School*, Edinburgh: Maclachlan & Stewart, 1867, pp 37-44.
2. Bell, J.: *Letters on Professional Character and Manners*, Edinburgh: J. Moir, 1810.
3. Bell, J.: *Discourses on the Nature and Cure of Wounds*, Edinburgh: Bell & Bradfute, 1795.
4. Bell, J.: *The Principles of Surgery*, 3 vol, Edinburgh and London: T. Cadell & W. Davies, 1801-1808.

National Library of Medicine

John Abernethy (1764-1831)

ALTHOUGH JOHN ABERNETHY, heir apparent in London of John Hunter, was acclaimed by his contemporaries and immediate followers as a great teacher of surgery, the evidence from perusal of his writings warrants a slightly lower position in the scale of greatness. One explanation for this partial paradox may be the difficulty in documenting his contributions to medical science.

John, born of Scottish-Irish parents, was not particularly outstanding in his early schooling. When the boy was 15, Charles Blicke, surgeon of St. Bartholomew's Hospital, received him as an apprentice after he abandoned the thoughts of a legal career and acceded to the wishes of his father. Abernethy attended the lectures of Blizard, and the private series by Hunter, the usual practice at that time, at the London Hospital. When Percivall Pott retired as senior surgeon, Blicke was advanced, and, in turn, the position of assistant surgeon, without salary, was filled by Abernethy. This position, which permitted teaching to private pupils, was held by Abernethy for 28 years.[1]

It was customary for the staff members to lecture at home or in a private amphitheater prior to the founding of the medical school. The announcement of Abernethy's series of anatomical lectures appeared in *The Times* for 1788. A few years later the need for a hospital amphitheater was satisfied by the construction of a lecture theater at Bart's. One of the initial lecturers in the new facility, and very likely a strong advocate of the construction of the theater, was Abernethy, who has been identified as one of the founders of St. Bartholomew's Medical School. He was elected to the Royal Society at the age of 32; after 28 years as assistant surgeon, he advanced to senior grade.[2] The appointment was the excuse for publishing a pamphlet on the evils attending the prolonged tenure of office by senior surgeons. At the age of 60, he had hoped to follow his own advice, but the Governors persuaded him to remain on for three additional years.

Abernethy was an extremely popular and forceful lecturer, making frequent reference to comparative anatomy and morbid states in an extemporaneous style of discourse, in contrast to stereotyped lectures. He was a renowned storyteller as well as a purveyor of experiences in anatomy and surgery. When he resorted to overt histrionics, it was to emphasize a point rather than to attract special attention. As a successful practicing surgeon in London, he cared for the rich and the poor, but not alike. He favored the poor on the wards because they had no choice in consultants. The rich, on the other hand, if they did not savor his medical advice, could afford and were privileged to seek other medical help. He was short-tempered, sometimes harsh, and sometimes rude. At other times he was most kind, a "family" man and a friend of man. His social deficiencies may have reflected a desire to accomplish as much and to see as many patients as possible within the allotted time, or he may have so disliked private practice that his eagerness to get back to the hospital and teaching created an unfavorable impression.

One of Abernethy's early scientific contributions described the drainage of a lumbar abscess. A means was devised for evacuating the suppuration without admission of air. The anaerobic technique proved superior to the then current practice of wide exposure, with ample opportunity for secondary infection. The respiration of the skin was studied by immersing the hand in an inverted jar of mercury. The gas recovered above the mercury disclosed a positive test for carbon dioxide when passed through lime water. The residual gas consisted of nitrogen. Removal of a femoral aneurism below Poupart's ligament followed and extended the technique of Hunter. The reciprocal effect of irritability of the central nervous system and the secretions of the stomach and bowel was described:[3] "We cannot reasonably expect tranquility of the nervous system whilst there is disorder of the digestive organs."

Abernethy was deeply interested in the discovery of the principles of medicine and surgery and the constitutional origin and constitutional treatment of local diseases (surgical diseases).[4] He was one of the first to ligate the external iliac artery for aneurism. One of his cases, frequently used as reference by his biographers, was a 40-year-old female, somewhat addicted to drinking to excess, with a large femoral aneurism.[3]

She was quite incapable of using the least exercise, or of sitting upright; and even in bed she suffered continual pain, which was much aggravated during the pulsation of the aneurism. The pain was so violent as to preclude sleep. . . . An incision, about three inches in length, was made through the integuments of the abdomen, beginning just above Poupart's ligament. . . . Having thus made room for the admission of my finger, I put it down upon the artery, felt its pulsation, and gently insinuated it beneath the vessel; and then, with the aneurismal needle, passed under it two moderately thick ligatures, carrying them upwards and downwards, as far as the detachment of the artery permitted, and tying them as firmly as I could. I next divided the artery in the interval, but much nearer to the lower ligature than to the upper one. Two days later the skin temperature of both feet was similar. On the fourth post-operative day the vessel escaped from the lower ligature but the patient overcame this untrained exit and continued to improve. . . . The wound healed like a healthy wound; and was nearly closed in a month after the operation.

Abernethy fared no better with Wakley, of the *Lancet,* than did Sir Astley Cooper earlier. The lectures were printed verbatim, which irritated Abernethy, who had intended to publish them in book form. After the lectures were pirated and published in the *Lancet,* he confessed:[1]

I believe I can't prevent it, but it is very disagreeable to me, and at least it shall never be done with my sanction. If the hireling of *The Lancet* is present, I demand that he will step forward, and I shall be glad to return him his money. Perhaps I am wrong in supposing that he will come forward here publicly, but if he will not, there is a private room in the house, and a servant will return him his money, or I shall be glad to do so at my own house. God forbid, gentlemen, that I should wish to keep back from you any knowledge that I can be able to afford, or that you should not have an opportunity of reaping the full benefit of it. Take the substance of what I say, you are perfectly welcome to it— you have paid for it—it is yours; but I do protest that I think no one has a right to publish it to the world: I do not like it; and certainly, he shall never have my sanction in so doing.

Subsequently, Abernethy applied to the Court of Chancery for an injunction to restrain continuation of piracy. To which Wakley replied:[5]

. . . . it appears that Mr. Abernethy's notion of law is, that it can alter the past as well as the future. He may possibly have vanity enough to suppose that we shall *reprint* his lectures. On this point his mind may be perfectly at ease; our pages have been already obscured with his hypothetical nonsense during six tedious months, and when we read the proof of the last paragraph we felt relieved, as we formerly stated, of a most intolerable *incubus.*

1. Thornton, J. L.: *John Abernethy: A Biography,* London: Simpkin Marshall Ltd., 1953.
2. Macilwain, G.: *Memoirs of John Abernethy,* New York: Harper & Brothers, 1853.
3. Abernethy, J.: *Surgical Observations on the Constitutional Origin and Treatment of Local Diseases and on Aneurisms,* 8th ed, London: Longman, Hurst, Rees, Orme, Brown, and Greene, 1825.
4. Bettany, G. T.: *Eminent Doctors,* vol 1, 2nd ed, London: John Hogg, 1885.
5. More "Hole and Corner" Doings, editorial, *Lancet* 7:225 (May 28) 1825.

Sir Astley Paston Cooper
(1768-1841)

AMONG THE GREAT MEDICAL PERSONALI-TIES of Guy's in the first half of the 19th century, who were responsible for the flowering of medicine in London, the surgeons were outnumbered heavily by the physicians. Bright, Addison, and Hodgkin are the best known of the latter. On the surgical roster Astley Cooper enjoyed an enviable position that was never seriously threatened. Hale-White repeated the generally accepted appraisal a century ago of notable persons in London.[1] "The two best-known men in London were George the Fourth and Sir Astley Cooper."

The Cooper family was well educated, well-to-do, and highly respected. Medicine was a rightful inheritance to Astley. His paternal grandfather was a surgeon in Norwich; Uncle William, a surgeon at Guy's Hospital. The father, a Doctor of Divinity and wrangler, was a stern disciplinarian in the Church and at home. The mother, a lady of property and a writer of semi-religious novels before her marriage, raised her chil-dren in the fashion of East Anglia. The children were put out to nurse. In his mature years, Sir Astley expressed strong disapproval of this practice.[2]

A female of luxury and refinement is often in this respect a worse mother than the inhabitant of the meanest hovel, who nurses her children, and brings them up healthy under privations and bodily exertions to obtain subsistence, which might almost excuse her refusal.

The frequent sight of the child, watching it at the breast, the repeated calls for attention, the dawn of each attack of disease, and the cause of its little cries are constantly begetting feelings of affection, which a mother who does not suckle seldom feels in an equal degree, when she allows the care of her child to devolve upon another, and suffers her maternal feelings to give place to indolence or caprice, on the empty calls of a fashionable and luxurious life.

At the age of 11, according to several of his biographers, Astley was faced with a surgical emergency. The son of his wet nurse suffered a laceration of the femoral artery. The bleeding was not stopped until Astley applied a tourniquet above the severed vessel. There is no evidence from any other yarn of his youth that presaged the professional or academic stature he attained ultimately. On the contrary, he was a mischievous boy, the village prankster, and a practical joker. A modest knowledge of English grammar and history was gained from his mother and an ordinary acquaintance with the Latin and Greek classics from his father. Although he never professed to be a scholar, and, according to the then current standards surely was not, fundamentals of grammar, construction, diction, and etymology acquired from his parents were naturally of great assistance throughout his prolific professional life.

When Astley was 16, Uncle William, surgeon at Guy's, brought him to London, where he was to remain until retirement. St. Thomas' and Guy's Hospitals, which were on opposite sides of St. Thomas' Street, constituted the medical school of the United Borough Hospitals. Although it would have been natural for Astley to live with Uncle William, he chose rather Henry Cline, surgeon to St. Thomas' Hospital and lecturer on anatomy. Cline was a liberal, sympathetic to the French Revolution, and held opinions on religion and politics quite opposite to those of Astley's parents. Shortly after taking up residence in London, Cooper was nominated for membership in the Guy's Hospital Physical Society, a proper medical organization. Jenner had given in London his first account of vaccination, and Hunter had presented his communication on ligature of the popliteal artery for aneurysm before this body.

In the course of the winter session, Cooper transferred his traineeship from his uncle to Cline and continued under the latter's tutelage in subsequent winter sessions. After 2 years in London, the third was spent in Edinburgh. There is no indication from his writing or the comments of others that he fully appreciated the educational opportunities in this famous medical center. At least, there are no scientific contributions that can be traced directly to the influence of Cullen, Black, or Fyfe. In Edinburgh, Cooper was elected a member of the Royal Society of Medicine, attended the meetings regularly, and was allowed to participate in the debates. It can be established, however, that in this educational community, skill was acquired in the systematic arrangement of his thoughts and the merits of the application of such skill in the documentation of a patient's illness.

On the return to London, the lectures of John Hunter were audited; a deep interest in dissection and anatomy was maintained. In 1789 at the age of 21, Cooper was appointed demonstrator in anatomy at St. Thomas'. This was followed in 2 years by a joint lectureship with Cline in anatomy and surgery, which provided the first earned income. It seemed appropriate, therefore, to powder his hair, color his cheeks, wear a wig, and consider marriage.[3] His wife brought a dowry of 14,000 £—a sufficient sum to subjugate any serious worries over the need for a private practice. Time was thus provided for dissection, study, and teaching. Even the night of the wedding found him delivering a lecture at the hospital. Prior to Cooper's review of the curriculum, lectures in anatomy and surgery were presented together. It was Cooper's opinion that they would best accomplish

the respective purposes if they were separated. Thereafter, Cline discussed anatomy, his pupil, surgery.

Honeymooning abroad was delayed until summer, when Paris was in the midst of the Revolution. Politics were as interesting as medicine to Cooper. Meetings of the National Assembly were attended. The harangues of Danton, Marat, and Robespierre, as well as the lectures of Desault and Chopart, held great appeal. Contrariwise, no mention was made in the biographical sketches of any particular interest in the great clinicians of Paris of that day.

On Cooper's return to London, dissection and teaching were continued at St. Thomas', and for 3 years he held the lectureship in anatomy at the Surgeons' Hall. Each day was full; it began with dissection at the hospital before breakfast, and dissecting and lecturing through the morning and again in the evening. As if dissection in London were not sufficient, a dissecting room at his summer home in Gadesbridge permitted uninterrupted activity while away from London. Cooper did not engage in private practice until 1795; then it was not his primary goal. Devotion to dissection was paramount. Cooper succeeded Uncle William as surgeon to Guy's in 1800 at the age of 32.

In 1821, advice was sought regarding a wen on the scalp of George the Fourth.[2] The king requested that there might be no hurry during surgery, and he bore the operation well. As a reward for his professional services, Cooper was made a baronet.

The next morning when I went, the King was on sofa,— his great toe was red with gout,—and his head had lost its soreness, and all its unpleasant feelings. From this time the wound healed in the most favourable manner.

At a later time, Astley recounted an incident of his King and gout.

He suffered much from rheumatism and gout, but the colchicum relieved him.
One morning, when he had rheumatism in his hip, and there was a doubt about the propriety of giving colchicum, he said, "Gentlemen, I have borne your half-measures long enough to please you—now I will please myself, and take colchicum."

The report concludes with a satisfactory symptomatic result.

Although Cooper had invested his personal funds in the construction of the lecture amphitheater and the anatomical museum at St. Thomas', the authorities did not appoint him to the senior post when this became vacant upon the retirement of Cline. This deficiency and other items contributed to the disassociation of the United Borough Hospitals of Thomas' and Guy's. In 1825, Guy's went on its own and organized a separate medical school.

Sir Astley Cooper was a fine teacher, a refreshing writer, a great technical surgeon, a skillful diagnostician, and a highly respected master of medicine. However, he was not a profound investigator; his major advances were clinical and technical. Ligation of vessels in humans was preceded by similar studies in animals. The abdominal aorta was ligated above its bifurcation for an aneurysm of the common iliac. One patient survived 18 years after ligation of the external iliac artery. Amputation at the hip joint by Cooper was one of the first operations of this type in modern surgery.

His writings encompassed hernia, fractures, dislocations, diseases of the breast, the testis, and the thymus. Many of the lectures were published in the *Lancet*. In the first issue of this journal, the editor, Thomas Wakley, published a lecture prepared from longhand notes, without permission from Cooper. A bitter controversy followed. Wakley reported the inaugural lecture as follows:[4]

SURGICAL LECTURES.

Theatre, St. Thomas's Hospital, Wednesday Evening, October 1, 1823. At half-past seven this theatre was crowded in every part, upwards of four hundred students of the most respectable appearance being present.

About eight o'clock, Sir Astley Cooper arrived, and was received with the most enthusiastic applause; which having ceased, this distinguished surgeon commenced his discourse by observing,— That, while it is the province of the physician to attend to internal disease, it is the duty of the Surgeon to attend to those that are external; to perform operations for the removal of diseased parts; and to know how to regulate the system by the use of medicine, when local diseases are produced by constitutional derangement. Surgery is usually divided into the principles and practice. The first are learned from obser-

vations on the living when diseased, by dissection of the dead, and by experiments upon living animals. Our deductions from these sources furnish us with the means of knowing a malady by its symptoms, the alteration of structure in a part when diseased, and the various ways in which *Nature* attempts the reparative process, both in external and internal parts. A man who has seen much of morbid preparations, possesses great advantages; but his anatomical knowledge cannot be perfect unless he has frequently seen and assisted in the dissection of the human body. In the surgical science · hypothesis should be entirely discarded, and sound theory, derived from actual observation and experience, alone encouraged. The first is an ignis fatuus which is sure to mislead; the last a polar star, a never-failing guide. Experiments on living animals have been found of the greatest utility in directing us to a knowledge of the means by which Nature acts in the reparation of injuries, and in the restoration of lost parts. Thus the method she would adopt in uniting a fracture in the bone of a dog, will show you the manner in which union of a fractured bone would be effected in man; the secretion of ossific matter by the blood-vessels being in each case precisely the same.

Cooper enjoyed many honors. These included membership in the Institute of France, officer status in the Legion of Honour, a fellowship in the Royal Society of Göttingen, and kudos from the Netherlands, Russia, Heidelberg, New Orleans, Palermo, and Mexico. Oxford and Edinburgh awarded him honorary doctorates in law. He was twice president of the Royal College of Surgeons.

Richard Bright attended him during his fatal illness in 1841. In keeping with a premortem request, a postmortem examination was performed. The examination confirmed the satisfactory repair of a hernia and revealed healed phthisis, hypertrophy of the heart, and granular kidneys. The protocol was published in *Guy's Hospital Reports* in 1841,[5] in the same issue with an account of three of Cooper's cases—a fitting memorial to a great surgeon of England of the early 19th century.

1. Hale-White, W.: *Great Doctors of the Nineteenth Century*, London: Edward Arnold & Co., 1935.
2. Cooper, B. B.: *The Life of Sir Astley Cooper, Bart.*, vol I, II, London: John W. Parker 1843.
3. Bettany, G. T.: *Eminent Doctors: Their Lives and Their Work*, London: John Hogg, 1885.
4. Surgical Lectures, *Lancet* 1:1-9, 3rd ed, 1823-24.
5. History of The Last Illness of Sir Astley Cooper, and Examination of the Body After Death, *Guy's Hosp Rep*, vol 6 (April) 1841.

Abraham Colles (1773-1843)

COLLES IS REMEMBERED FOR HIS ANATOMICAL DESCRIPTION of the perineal fascia, the diagnosis and treatment of fracture of the wrist, and clinical observations on syphilis. Born a few miles from Kilkenny in southeastern Ireland into a well-to-do family who operated a marble quarry, Abraham entered Trinity College, Dublin, at the age of 17. Since Irish medicine had not reached its zenith and did not until a generation later, Edinburgh, one of the great centers for medical education, was selected for graduate training. Colles spent two sessions at Edinburgh and was rewarded by the MD degree at the conclusion.

Any aspiring surgeon in the early 19th century, endowed with energy and ambition, most surely would have chosen Sir Astley Cooper in London for postgraduate study. Colles was no exception. After a few months in the anatomical laboratory with Cooper, he returned to Dublin and was recognized to be the outstanding surgeon in Ireland for more than 30 years. A significant portion of this time was served as professor of anatomy and surgery at the university. His reputation as a teacher attracted a great number of students to the university and to his classes, which increased tenfold during his tenure as a professor. He did more than any other surgeon to enhance the stature of his specialty in Dublin at a time when it did not compare favorably with the practice of physic.

In Colles' most fruitful years, surgery had recently emerged from bondage with the barbers. There were few satisfactory treatises of surgical anatomy. Suppuration was respected as "laudable pus," anesthesia was limited to opiates and spirits, means for combating surgical shock were unknown, and diagnostic tools did not extend beyond the five senses of man. Although Colles was not a brilliant surgeon, he was an indefatigable worker, ever willing to practice the best surgery possible on the basis of his knowledge of regional anatomy. He deplored the emphasis upon systemic anatomy and preferred to consider the region, rather than the system, in the management of morbid states. Meanwhile, he was aware of the need to document his observations and deductions for contemporary fellows and future generations. His incomplete monograph, *Treatise on Surgical Anatomy,* published in 1811, contributed to the correction of this deficiency.

One may speculate that Colles' clarity of teaching compared favorably with his clarity of writing. Outstanding in this category is the description of the fracture of the radius, which probably had been observed by others but had not been described as a surgical entity. Several decades elapsed before the significance of Colles' observations was generally appreciated and incorporated in the then current texts.[1]

The posterior surface of the limb presents a considerable deformity; for a depression is seen in the fore-arm, about an inch and a half above the end of this bone, while a considerable swelling occupies the wrist and metacarpus.

On viewing the anterior surface of the limb, we observe a considerable fulness, as if caused by the flexor tendons being thrown forwards. This fulness extends upwards to about one-third of the length of the fore-arm, and terminates below at the upper edge of the annular ligament of the wrist.

On the posterior surface, he will discover by the touch that the swelling on the wrist, and metacarpus, is not caused entirely by an effusion. . . . When he moves his fingers along the anterior surface of the radius, he finds it more full and prominent than is natural; a similar examination of the posterior surface of this bone, induces him to think that a depression is felt about an inch and half above its carpal extremity.

He now expects to find satisfactory proofs of a fracture of the radius at this spot. For this purpose, he attempts to move the broken pieces of the bone in opposite directions; but, although the patient is by this examination subjected to considerable pain, yet neither crepitus nor a yielding of the bone at the seat of fracture, nor any other positive evidence of the existence of such an injury is thereby obtained.

If the surgeon lock his hand in that of the patient's, and make extension, even with a moderate force, he restores the limb to its natural form, but the distortion of the limb instantly returns on the extension being removed.

Let the surgeon apply the fingers of one hand to the seat of the suspected fracture, and, locking the other hand in that of the patient, make a moderate extension, until he observes the limb restored to its natural form. As soon as this is effected, let him move the patient's hand backward and forward; and he will, at every such attempt, be sensible of a yielding of the fractured ends of the bone, and this to such a degree as must remove all doubt from his mind.

It is obvious that, in the treatment of this fracture, our attention should be principally directed to guard against the carpal end of the radius being drawn backwards. For this purpose, while assistants hold the limb in a middle state between pronation and supination, let a thick and firm compress be applied transversely on the anterior surface of the limb, at the seat of fracture, taking care that it shall not press on the ulna; let this be bound on firmly with a roller, and then let a tin spint, formed to the shape of the arm, be applied to both its anterior and posterior surfaces.

The anatomy of the perineum (Colles' fascia and Colles' space) was described in his *Treatise*.[2] The lucid deductions concerning the extravasation of urine into the perineal space lead one to believe that the dissections were made on fresh postmortem material or on relatively fresh bodies stolen from the grave. Dry specimens of the cadaver are most unsatisfactory for identification of these structures. (The Anatomy Act, which legalized dissection of human bodies, was not passed until 1832.)

Raise the skin of the perineum, extending the dissection beyond the tubera ischii to the thighs. This exposes to view a strong fascia, which on dissection, will be found to cover the entire space of the perineum, and to blend itself with the structure of the scrotum. This fascia, although on a superficial view it appears continuous with the fascia of the muscles of the thigh, will yet be found, on closer examination, to attach itself very firmly to the rami of the ischium and pubis. The texture and connexions of this fascia will serve to explain many of those phenomena attendant on the effusion of urine into the perineum, by rupture or ulceration of the posterior part of the canal of the urethra.

In general, then, we find that the urine having caused some tumefaction in perineo, passes on into the scrotum. Here meeting with only a very feeble resistance from the lax texture of this part, it quickly distends it to a very considerable size. In some instances the mischief does not extend further, for suppuration takes place in the scrotum, and a quantity of very hard fetid fluid, composed of urine and pus, is discharged as soon as the abscess spontaneously bursts, or is opened by the surgeon. In other cases, the effused urine continues its progress until it arrives at the pubis.

The observations on the contagion of syphilis, which were made before the discovery of the spirochete or the Wassermann reaction, reflect Colles' interest in general medicine.[3]

I have never seen or heard of a single instance in which a syphilitic infant, (although its mouth be ulcerated,) suckled by its own mother, had produced ulceration of her breasts; whereas very few instances have occurred where a syphilitic infant had not infected a strange hired wet nurse, and who had been previously in good health.

The apparent immunity of the mother most likely was related to a preexisting infection, which made her resistant to reinfection by the infant.

Colles' bibliography was limited to scarcely more than a dozen contributions between 1797 (the year he received his degree at Edinburgh) and the lectures on the theory and practice of surgery published in 1844, the year following his death. Colles' ligament is a portion of the aponeurosis of the external oblique muscle, extending from Poupart's ligament to the linea alba—the reflected inguinal ligament or triangular fascia. Lesser contributions in surgery include a discussion of the conservative management of depressed fractures of the skull, ligation of the subclavian artery for aneurysm, lithotomy, early surgical intervention for strangulated hernia, and the treatment of hydrocele through the installation of a mixture of port wine and water or a mixture of brandy and zinc sulfate.

Colles was a modest man and, in spite of his reputation and well-recognized surgical accomplishments, he twice refused a baronetcy.[4] This refusal may have been motivated by the failure to have this honor extended earlier in his career. He preferred not to be a late choice and offered as an excuse the inconvenience to his children of accepting a hereditary title.

The period of the great days of the Irish school of medicine was relatively short. It seems idle speculation to attribute one or a series of facts to this golden era. Physicians and surgeons had practiced in Dublin before, as well as after, those golden days of the 19th century, without attaining the heights of Colles in surgery or of Graves, Stokes, and Corrigan in internal medicine.

1. Colles, A.: On the Fracture of the Carpal Extremity of the Radius, *Edinburgh Med Surg J* 10:182-186, 1814.

2. Colles, A.: "Anatomy of the Perineum," in *A Treatise on Surgical Aanatomy*, Dublin: Gilbert and Hodges, 1811, pp 174-180.

3. Abraham Colles, *Med Classics* 4:1027-1078 (June) 1940.

4. *Selections from the Works of Abraham Colles*, R. McDonnell, ed., London: The New Sydenham Society, 1881.

Sir Benjamin Collins Brodie (1783-1862)

THE MANTLE OF THE SENIOR SURGEON of London was passed from Sir Astley Cooper to Benjamin C. Brodie, sergeant-surgeon to the queen and to two kings. Brodie was born at Winterslow in Wiltshire, the son of a parish rector, who was responsible for the early education of his children, particularly in the Greek and Latin languages.[1] At the age of 18, Brodie went to London, where he studied anatomy under Abernethy at St. Bartholomew's Hospital, dissected with Wilson in the Great Windmill Street School of Medicine, and became a pupil of Sir Everard Home, borther-in-law of John Hunter and surgeon at St. George's Hospital. He was a sensitive youth who accepted the study of surgery upon his father's suggestion, although he might have done equally well in law or business. Under Home, Brodie made excellent progress and was given more than the usual responsibility in dissection, in conducting of physio-

Composite by G. Bako

logical experiments, and in the care of the patients of Home and Wilson. For more than 35 years he served at St. George's Hospital, resigning the post of surgeon at the age of 57. After retirement from active staff duties, he continued to practice and contribute to the literature at frequent intervals.

Brodie was elected to the Royal Society at an early age and was one of the few practitioners to become president of England's best known scientific institution. The Croonian Lecture in 1810 described the independent action of the heart and circulation if respiration was maintained after separation of the spinal cord from the brain. The following year he discussed the toxic effects of alcohol, nicotine, woorara (carare), and other poisons. He noted that when woorara was applied to a wound it entered the circulation, leading to apparent death, but in some instances if respiration was maintained artificially the animal recovered. In 1811, the production of animal heat was described, and, in 1814, Brodie submitted to the royal Society for publication in the *Philosophical Transactions* his observations on suppression of the secretions of the stomach after severance of the vagus nerve. Artificial conditions were established to test this hypothesis. It had been ascertained that dogs, poisoned by arsenic, secreted large quantities of mucus and fluid from the membranes of the stomach and intestines.[2]

In an inquiry which I had formerly instituted, respecting the functions of the stomach, I divided these nerves [*par vagum*] in the neck of a dog, for the purpose of ascertaining the influence which they possess on the secretion of the gastric juice.
. . . . we may conclude that the suppression of the secretions in all of them was to be attributed solely to the division of the nerves: and all the facts which have been stated sufficiently demonstrate, that the secretions of the stomach and intestines are very much under the control of the nervous system.

The period of physiological investigation was followed by Brodie's noteworthy contributions in surgery and pathological anatomy, in the capacity of a physician-surgeon rather than of an operating surgeon. Diseases of the bones and joints were of particular interest and were described in his monograph entitled *Pathological and Surgical Observations on Diseases of the Joints*.[3] Several of the eponyms identified with Brodie refer to the articular system. Brodie's abscess is the best known. Although the pathogenesis occasionally was attributed to tuberculosis, especially when it appeared in the head of the tibia, there was only one reference to scrofula in association with the several cases of bone abscess described by Brodie between 1828 and 1845. The first reference to a tibial osteomyelitis appeared in a clinical lecture entitled "Trephining the Tibia."[4]

There is another disease of the tibia requiring the trephine, I mean an abscess in its centre without external opening, which may remain for many years, and render the patient's life completely miserable.
The first thing which particularly drew my attention to what I have now mentioned, was the case of a gentleman, who applied to me with an enlargement of the lower extremity of the tibia. The pain was excruciating, and at times he had such violent attacks of it as to confine him to his room for months together. When I saw him he had been suffering in this way, at intervals, for thirteen or fourteen years, and he declared to me that his life was completely miserable. . . . On dissection of the limb, we discovered in the tibia, about half an inch above the ankle-joint, a cavity about the size of a walnut, which contained discoloured pus; whilst the cancellated structure around it had been converted into hard and almost solid bone.

It struck me when I saw the issue of this case, that should a similar one occur to me again, I would open the abscess with the trephine, and such an opportunity did occur. The patient pointed to a particular spot as the centre of the agonizing pain which he suffered, and here I divided the periosteum and peeled it off. I then applied the trephine as deeply as the instrument would go, and took away a circular piece of bone. Soft bony matter only was exposed, but on breaking it up with the elevator, I thought I saw some yellow fluid. I broke up still more of the bone, and opened into a distinct abscess, from which issued about a couple of drachms of pus. I took away bone enough to leave a ready exit for the matter. The gentleman was free from pain that night, except what belonged to the operation, and has never suffered any pain since. I saw him a fortnight ago, when the wound was nearly healed, and the patient going to the country.

The account of chronic abscess of the tibia in three patients and treatment by local drainage in two, published in the *Medico-Chirurgical Transactions* of 1832, is usually mentioned as the original source of the description of Brodie's abscess.[5] The reference to a scrofulous etiology of bone or joint disease was made in the same year, without mention of aspiration.[6]

SCROFULOUS AFFECTION OF THE ANKLE-JOINT.—There are at present two cases of this nature in the hospital under the care of Mr. Brodie. The earlier treatment consisted of rest in the horizontal posture, and poultices to the part. . . . These remedies have scarcely yet been persevered in for a sufficient length of time for a decided opinion to be pronounced upon their effects; but Mr. Brodie is of opinion, that in most of these cases (ulceration of the cartilages from chronic inflammation of the bones) surgeons have relied too much upon local applications.

In addition to extensive writing on bone and joint disease, Brodie described an operation for fistula in ano, treated varicose veins by severing the vessel above and below the varicosity, observed the physiological changes in digestion following ligation of the common duct, prepared treatises on urology and the action of local nervous afflictions, and reported on chronic cystic mastitis, Brodie's tumor follow:[7]

The first perceptible indication of the disease is a globular tumor imbedded in the glandular structure of the breast, and to a certain extent moveable underneath the skin. Sometimes there is only one such tumor; at other times there are two or three, or many more. The examination of the breast in the living person does not enable you to determine the exact number which exists, as it is only where they have attained a certain magnitude that they are perceptible through the skin. In most instances the disease is confined to one breast, though it is by no means very uncommon for both breasts to be similarly affected.
I have never known the disease to occur previously to the age of puberty, nor after the middle period of life: and if I am not much mistaken, it is more common in single than in married women.
The disease, in its early stages, causes no suffering, and may remain for years, or for the whole of the patient's life, without advancing farther, and under these circumstances, no harm can possibly arise from delay.

In 1819, Brodie was appointed professor of comparative anatomy and physiology at the Royal College of Surgeons and attended George IV, assisting in an operation for the removal of a tumor of the scalp. When William IV ascended to the throne, Brodie was appointed surgeon major and two years later a baronet. He became the first surgeon of London on the retirement of Cooper in 1828 and served as president of the Royal College of Surgeons of London. He continued to practice until his vision failed at the age of 75, and he is thought to have died of a sarcoma of the shoulder. His love of hospital practice and clinical surgery is summarized in a quotation from his autobiography.[1]

During these thirty-two years the hospital, as far as my profession was concerned, was the greatest object of interest that I possessed. Except during the brief intervals of my absence from London, it rarely happened that I was not some time during the day within its walls. I was indebted to the opportunities which it afforded me for the best part of the knowledge which I had been able to attain. It had rendered my professional life one of agreeable study, instead of one of mechanical and irksome drudgery. Some of my happiest hours were those during which I was occupied in the wards, with my pupils around me, answering their inquiries, explaining the cases to them at the bedside of the patients, informing them as to the grounds on which I formed my diagnosis, and my reasons for the treatment which I employed, and not concealing from them my oversights and errors; and all this to kind and willing and only too partial listeners. My intercourse with the students, and, I may add, with the patients also, was always to me a source of real gratification; and even now (many years afterwards) these scenes are often renewed to me at night, and events of which I have no recollection when awake come before me in my dreams.

1. Brodie, B. C.: *Autobiography of the Late Sir Benjamin C. Brodie,* London: Longman, Green, Longman, Roberts, & Green, 1865.
2. Brodie B. C.: Experiments and Observations on the Influence of the Nerves of the Eighth Pair on the Secretions of the Stomach, *Trans Roy Soc* pt 1:102-106, 1814.
3. Brodie, B. C.: *Pathological and Surgical Observations on Diseases of the Joints,* Philadelphia: B. Warner, 1821.
4. Brodie, B. C.: Abstract of a Clinical Lecture on Trephining the Tibia, *London Med Gaz* 2:70-74, 1828.
5. Brodie, B. C.: An Account of Some Cases of Chronic Abscess of the Tibia, *Medicochir Trans* 17:239-249, 1832.
6. Clinical Remarks by Mr. Brodie, *Lancet* 1:168-170, 1833.
7. Brodie, B. C.: Lecture on Sero-Cystic Tumors of the Breast, *London Med Gaz* 1:808-814, 1840.

Guillaume Dupuytren (1777-1835)

DUPUYTREN, who, through fair means or base intrigue, rose from poverty and obscurity to wealth and international fame as the leading surgeon of Paris in the early part of the 19th century, left an indelible imprint on the science and art of his profession. He was born in Pierre-Buffière, a small village of the district of Haute Vienne in west central France. His father was a lawyer of small means and his teacher in elementary subjects. He was enrolled in the Collège of La Marche, as a result of a chance meeting with and a favorable impression upon a brother of the principal of the school. Dupuytren's remarkable characteristics were apparent to his superiors in his early youth, although there is no record of his brilliance as a scholar at that time. He abandoned higher learning for a brief period at the age of 16, but, upon the firm direction of his father, returned to Paris to prepare for a career in surgery. He studied anatomy with Boyer at the Charité, attended the clinical lectures of Pinel at Salpêtrière, and those of Cuvier at Garden du Plante. His father could provide little financial assistance, and Dupuytren lived a miserable existence in the pursuit of higher learning until the age of 18, when he secured the appointment as prosector at Ecole de Santi. Not until his early 20's, however, was he free from want and able to live in even modest circumstances.

Dupuytren conducted a course of formal instruction in anatomy at the age of 23; although his lectures lacked organization and academic sophistication, he compensated with a profound knowledge of structure, combined with skill in dissection. Having mastered anatomy, he turned to pathology, and in 1803 offered a course in pathology, which attracted Laennec as pupil and assistant, the year following the death of Bichat, whose untimely summons undoubtedly eliminated a bitter rival in Dupuytren's career. An appointment at the Hôtel Dieu at the age of 27, under the chief surgeon, Pelletan, led to a contentious struggle between an eager youth with overweening ambitions and an elderly chief who was conservative and complacent. Only the removal of Pelletan in 1814 and the elevation of Dupuytren to his position closed this phase of intransigent strife.

During his rise to surgical eminence in Paris, when Parisian surgery exerted a greater influence on this discipline in America and Europe than in any subsequent period, Dupuytren was cold, ruthless, and ambitious, with little regard for subordinates, associates, or superiors. Yet he possessed unusual talents and despised nothing so much as mediocrity. His goal was clear. Nothing was to prevent its achievement. With a solid foundation in anatomy and pathology, he demonstrated outstanding ability in the diagnosis of disease and surgical management of appropriate patients. At the bedside, he sensed the cause of a patient's problems with no more than a sentence or two of inquiry and possessed a memory pattern for past medical events that permitted instant retrieval, to the amazement of his students.

For almost 30 years Dupuytren reigned supreme at Hôtel Dieu. The morning visit began at 6 a.m. Students and staff followed the master, listening to a clinical monologue. Usually he was sympathetic to the patients but showed little warmth for the members of the professional entourage. His statements were to be accepted without question; his surgical wisdom was never to be disputed. Nothing was to disturb the aura of omnipotence. It was hardly an example of vainglory, however, since Dupuytren was a genius, in his way, and a superbly gifted surgeon. The tabulations of his surgical contributions comprise a remarkable memorabile. The bibliography in *Medical Classics,* which lists the contributions from his clinical lectures, covers 31 pages.[1] The majority of the communications were prepared by assistants and were published in French medical or surgical journals. A few were translated by his pupils and published in England and Scotland. Only a small percentage were composed by the chief. His *Leçons orales de clinique chirurgicale* was translated and reprinted in New York in 1833 as *Clinical Lectures on Surgery.* In England, the Sydenham Society translated and reported his studies on injuries and diseases of the bone. It is practical to enumerate only a few areas within surgical purview that benefited from his wisdom and skill.

His discussion of the fracture of the lower portion of the fibula, Dupuytren's fracture, was excerpted by a pupil from a clinical lecture delivered at Hôtel Dieu in 1832. The communication refers to the contributions of Pott, David, Charles Bell, and others on the subject, together with the pathogenesis, diagnosis, signs, complications, and management advanced by Dupuytren.[2]

Reduction. There is no reduction, said M. Dupuytren, which can be accomplished more easily than that of fractures of the fibula attended with dislocation of the foot, when we have discovered the mode of overcoming the resistance of the muscles. The obstacles arising from this resistance, have exercised the talents of surgeons from Hippocrates to our days. In order to attain this, we have merely to flex the leg on the thigh, and distract the attention of the patient. The muscles soon lose their tension, the resistance ceases as if by enchantment, and the parts resume their natural situation and relations almost without effort.

Mode of keeping the parts reduced. It is evident that the position which rendered the reduc-

tion of the fracture so easy, by relaxing the muscles, is also the first mode to be used to keep the parts reduced. But we can imagine it would be imprudent thus to leave a fractured limb to itself, and that the bones must be kept together by a dressing until the callus has formed and become solid. This dressing should be modified more or less, according to the kind of dislocation attending the fracture.

A cushion, a splint, and two bandages compose all which M. Dupuytren has used so successfully for more than twenty-five years, in fracture of the fibula attended with dislocation inward.

Of two hundred and seven patients treated by M. Dupuytren's method, two hundred and two have been cured; five only have died, three from symptoms dependent on the disease, and two from complications independent of it.

All have recovered the free use of the motions of the foot; in one only was an ankylosis of this with the leg.

Dupuytren's contracture, fibrosis of the palmar fascia, had been described by Sir Astley Cooper, but Dupuytren ignored this prior study in a communication, transcribed by Paillard and Marx, that describes the clinical findings and surgical correction.[3]

Individuals pre-disposed to the affection we are describing, observe that it is more difficult to extend the fingers of the affected hand: the ring finger soon contracts; the retraction occurs first in the first phalanx, the others follow the motion; in proportion as the disease advances, the ring finger flexes more and more; at this period, the flexion of the two adjacent fingers is well marked. At this stage of the disease, there is no nodosity before and around the cord presented by the palmar face of the ring finger. Its last two phalanges are straight and movable. The first is flexed at nearly a right angle, and is movable on the metacarpus. In this state the most powerful efforts are insufficient to extend it. At first view, we should be led to think the skin diseased; but dissection proves the cutaneous envelope to be unaffected. On touching the palmar face of the ring finger, we feel a very tense cord. The summit of this cord is directed towards the first phalanx; we can trace it to the upper extremity of the palm of the hand. In flexing the finger it almost disappears. On attempting to extend the fingers, the tendon of the palmaris longus is moved, and this motion extends to the upper part of the palmar aponeurosis; the continuity of these two parts explains their simultaneous action. . . . the articulations were in their normal state; the bones were neither swelled nor uneven; they were not in the least affected, either externally or internally: there was no perceptible change in the inclination of the articular surfaces, nor alteration in the external ligaments, nor anklyosis:

the synovial sheaths, the cartilages, the synovia, were perfectly unchanged. Hence it was natural to conclude, that the commencement of the disease was in the unusual tension of the palmar aponeurosis, and that this tension arose from a contusion of the aponeurosis, in consequence of the too violent or too long continued action of a hard body upon the palm of the hand.

The hand of the patient being fixed firmly, he [Dupuytren] commenced by making a transverse incision ten lines long, opposite the metacarpophalangean articulation of the ring finger: the bistoury first divided the skin, next the palmar aponeurosis, with a distinct crackling. The incision terminated, the ring finger became straight, and could be extended almost as easily as in the natural state.

An account of tying of the subclavian artery was communicated to the *Edinburgh Medical and Surgical Journal* in 1819 by a correspondent.[4]

This day, Dupuytren, surgeon of this hospital, tied the subclavian artery of the left side, just as it emerges from behind the anterior scalenus, in a case of false aneurism of the axillary artery, in a man of thirty-seven years, of an excellent and robust constitution. He was a soldier, and seven years ago, in a charge of cavalry, received a thrust of a sword from behind, which opened the axillary artery. He lost much blood, but the flow was stopped by the dressing, and the wound healed in three weeks. A false aneurism gradually came on, and has continued to increase, slowly at first, but for some time past more quickly. The tumour now distends the axilla enormously, distends the pectoral, raises up the clavicle, and is about the size of a child's head. . . . He was operated upon in bed to avoid the annoyance caused by the noise of those in the amphitheatre who do not see. Dupuytren made his incision about three-fourths of an inch above the clavicle, beginning close at the outer edge of the sternomastoid, a small part of which was cut. . . . Having isolated the artery from the nerves, he tied the ligature round it, and brought the lips together. . . . The operation lasted one hour and a quarter, but he was extremely cautious. . . . Every thing went on well, and about the sixth day the tumour began sensibly to diminish. About the fifteenth day the ligature came away; and on the 27th of March, when I last saw the wound, it was nearly healed.

Another successful vascular operation was ligation of the external iliac artery. Ligation was recommended in place of amputation for fractures of the extremities complicated by aneurysm. Wryneck was corrected by subcutaneous section of the sternocleidomastoid muscle; complete resection of the lower jaw was accomplished. An enterotome was devised for treating artificial anus; vaginitis in maidens was a malady of particular interest. Goiter was treated by a seton; nervousness and delirium were described. Although Dupuytren usually was correct in his surgical opinions, his views on the pathogenesis of right iliac fossa inflammation were not supported by contemporary and succeeding surgeons. Dupuytren was incorrect in his statement that the caecum is usually the site of inflammation [acute appendicitis].[5]

There are few physicians or surgeons in the history of medicine whose character seems as cynical and jealous and whose path to preeminence is strewn with such grim austerity as Dupuytren's. He faced poverty early in life; indigence persisted during the first years of medical training, changing to affluence during a long period of lucrative surgical practice. Dupuytren was highly successful as a teacher, but he never enjoyed the warm sympathy of students or associates frequently given to outstanding teachers. He enjoyed few professional or social friends. It was his wish to stand alone, impressing patients, pupils, and surgeons from near and far with his diagnostic acumen on the wards and his great skill in the surgical amphitheater. He rose through rugged competition to be known as the "Brigand of Hôtel Dieu." Dupuytren permitted no surgical rivals in Paris, at a time when Parisian medicine and surgery were strong, outstanding, and internationally renowned.

1. Guillaume Dupuytren, *Med Classics* 4:87-172 (Oct) 1939.
2. Dupuytren, G.: "Of Fractures of the Lower Extremity of the Fibula, and Luxations of the Foot," in *Clinical Lectures on Surgery*, A. S. Doane, trans., New York: Collins & Hannay, Publishers, 1833, pp 160-197.
3. Paillard, A., and Marx, M.: "Permanent Retraction of the Fingers," in *Clinical Lectures on Surgery*, A. S. Doane, trans., New York: Collins & Hannay, Publishers, 1833, pp 14-25.
4. Combe, A.: Account of the Tying of the Subclavian Artery, by M. Dupuytren, *Edinburgh Med Surg J* 15: 476 (July) 1819.
5. Paillard, A.: Abscess in the Small Pelvis, by Baron Dupuytren, *Rev Med* 1:367-8, 1829.

Composite by G. Bako

Benjamin Travers (1783-1858)

BENJAMIN TRAVERS was one of the first surgeons of England who, having pursued anatomy in a masterly fashion in preparation for general surgery, chose to consecrate his most productive years to the physiology and morbidity of the eye. Travers was born in Cheapside, the second of ten children in an affluent family in the sugar-baking (refining) business.[1] After receiving a classical education at the grammar school of Cheshunt, Hertforshire, he was tutored until he entered his father's business at the age of 16. This excursion into trade was brief since he profoundly disliked commerce. He then turned to medicine, where his interests and talents received fitting rewards. Travers became the first pupil of Sir Astley Cooper, studying under and assisting his teacher at Guy's Hospital. The earlier attendance of his father at Cooper's lectures, a custom of the day for enlightened laity, seems an adequate explanation for the son's selection of a master.

Travers rose rapidly in London surgery. Admitted a member of the College of Surgeons in 1806, he spent the following winter session at Edinburgh; upon his return to London, was appointed demonstrator of anatomy at Guy's Hospital. His first senior appointment, offered in 1810, was as surgeon to the London Infirmary for Diseases of the Eye, later renamed Moorefields Ophthalmic Hospital. In accepting this assignment Travers proved a bulwark against quacks and charlatans of the day who, though entrenched, were totally unqualified to handle diseases of vision. He was elected a Fellow of the Royal Society in 1813 and surgeon to St. Thomas' Hospital in 1815. The warm friendship between Travers and Cooper was evidenced by a series of joint lectures at Guy's Hospital, but especially by his taking possession of Cooper's home in 1816. Politically, Travers was a loyal supporter of the Whig predilections of his family and an organization man in London surgery.

Travers' writings—clear, unostentatious, and scholarly—were published in his 30's, culminating in the outstanding monograph on the eye in 1820. An appreciable slackening in his scientific work appeared in mid-maturity, due in part to an affliction described as "palpitation of the heart." He published several articles on general surgery before and after his best-known treatise. These communications included such subjects as the process of nature in repairing injuries of the intestines,[2] the treatment of an aneurysm of the orbit by ligature of the common carotid artery, excision of the clavicle for a tumor, a revival of the concept of "constitutional irritation,"[3] a discussion of wounds and ligatures of the veins, and a text on phymosis and paraphymosis. Several of the communications in general medicine and surgery and on the eye appeared in the *Transactions* of the Medical and Chirurgical Society of London, a society which honored Travers as president in 1828. *A Synopsis of the Diseases of the Eye,* one of the earliest systematic treatises in English on ophthalmology, is elegantly written, with five colored plates of excellent quality and design. The contents were founded on the author's clinical experience and were documented with his case reports. His position in ophthalmology was clearly stated in the "Preface."[4]

In this country, I believe no one before myself, who designed to practise general surgery, ventured to give more than a customary attention to the diseases of the eye. A fear of being disqualified in public opinion, by a reputation acquired in these, for the treatment of other diseases, was a motive, however groundless, sufficient to deter surgeons from the cultivation of a large and legitimate field of observation and practice.

It was with a public avowal of the sentiments so well-expressed . . . that I accepted the situation of Surgeon to the Eye Infirmary, in the year 1810; from these I have never swerved.

Part I contains the anatomical and physiological descriptions of the eye and its appendages. The second part discusses pathology and concludes with treatment. Glaucoma is passed over lightly, although it was recognized as a distinct disease for centuries. Its confusion with cataract is described under "Organic Amaurosis." Later in the book, the treatment of iritis with mercury is given. Travers reasoned that it would prove useful because of beneficial action in lues, another disturbance of inflammation of serous membranes. The following excerpts describe glaucoma and treatment of iritis.[4]

A diffused turbidity or milkiness, apparently of the vitreous humor, strikingly observable when contrasted with the jetty brightness of a healthy eye. It is little more than the healthy appearance of the humors in the eye of the horse. This state, which the antients termed glaucoma, is very often mistaken for incipient cataract; and I have known it called a black cataract, and the operation of extracting the transparent lens performed. It appears deep-seated, diffused, and of uniform density; and in examining some such cases at long intervals, I have not found the appearance to vary. The lens remains transparent. . . . The vision is in general defective in a much greater degree than the visible opacity explains; and this, combined with the depth of the opacity, a dilated and sluggish pupil, and some other symptoms of amaurosis, makes for the opinion that it belongs to the latter class.

On the treatment of deep-seated inflammation, whether affecting the choroid or iris, . . . I have now and then found that the incipient inflammation, where it has extended from the conjunctiva, yields to a copious venesection, and two or three brisk doses of calomel and rhubarb, followed up by the infusion of senna; but, generally speaking, the system must be made to feel the influence of mercury before the disease is permanently subdued.

But if any two facts are well established in modern medicine, I apprehend they are these:— first, the power of mercury to arrest acute membranous inflammation, both prior to and after the effusion of adhesive matter; and second, its power rapidly to remove, by an excitement of the absorbing system peculiar to itself, the newly effused adhesive matter.

A case of an arterial-venous aneurism with anastomosis in the orbit, cured by ligation of the common carotid artery, was reported in the second volume of the *Medico-Chirurgical Transactions*. A 34-year-old, healthy woman, several months pregnant in 1804, sensed a painful sudden snap on the left side of her forehead followed by a copious effusion into the substance of the eyelids. For some days previously she had complained of a constant noise resembling the blowing of a pair of bellows and of severe pain in the head, which had increased so that she was unable to raise her head from the pillow. Examination revealed a swelling of the orbit, protrusion of the globe, a circumscribed tumor upon the infraorbitary ridge, and a softer diffuse swelling above the tendon of the orbicularis palpebrarum. The lower tumor conveyed, by sight and touch, the pulse of the larger arteries; the upper tumor produced a strong vibratory thrill.[5]

Upon applying my thumb to the trunk of the common carotid, I found the pulsation cease altogether, and the whiz of the little swelling was rendered so exceedingly faint, that it was difficult to determine whether it continued or not.

Being satisfied of the growth of the disease; . . . I proceeded to the operation on Tuesday the 23rd of May, 1809. An incision, about two inches and a half in length, was commenced. . . . Through this opening, which was of very small extent, a curved eye probe, carrying a stout round ligature, was passed beneath the artery, care being taken to exclude the nerve. The probe being cut away, the ligatures were drawn apart from each other, the lower being tied at the lowermost point of the denudation of the artery, the upper at the highest. They were about one fourth of an inch distant; and whilst they were tightened, the division of the internal coat of the vessel could be distinctly felt.

The patient, before she quitted the table, observed that the pain was numbed, and that the noise in her head had entirely ceased.

May, 1811.—Mrs. Stoffell is looking florid and healthy. Of the disease, a knob of the size of a large pea over the inner angle of the eye is the only vestige that remains.

Travers' association with the Royal College of Surgeons of London was long and distinguished. He filled each of the important offices, serving two terms as president. His Hunterian Oration was extolled for its excellence. Upon formation of the queen's medical establishment, he was appointed one of her surgeons-extraordinary, afterwards becoming surgeon-in-ordinary to the prince consort and serjeant-surgeon.

1. Dunn, P.: Benjamin Travers, F.R.S., *Brit J. Ophthal* 1:273-281, 1917.
2. Travers, B.: *An Inquiry into the Process of Nature in Repairing Injuries of the Intestines,* London: Longman, Hurst, Rees, Orme, and Brown, 1812.
3. Travers, B.: *An Inquiry Concerning That Disturbed State of the Vital Functions Usually Documented Constitutional Irritation,* London: Longman, Rees, Orme, Brown, and Green, 1826.
4. Travers, B.: *A Symposium of the Diseases of the Eye and Their Treatment,* ed 2, London; Longman, Hurst, Rees, Orme, and Brown, 1821.
5. Travers, B.: A Case of Aneurism by Anastomosis in the Orbit, *Medicochir Trans* 2:1-16, 1811.

Composite by G. Bako

Alexander Philip Wilson Philip (1770-1851)

ALEXANDER PHILIP WILSON, Scottish physician and physiologist, was born at Sheethall near Glasgow. In 1811, he changed his surname from Wilson to Philip by Royal License when he succeeded to the chieftainship of his clan on the death of his paternal grandmother, Susannah Wilson. He received his primary education at the Edinburgh High School and, when he was 12, was placed in the hands of William Cullen for his higher education.[1] Wilson proceeded in the preparation for medicine to the University of Edinburgh. The doctorate was bestowed in 1792 upon presentation of a thesis, entitled *De Dyspepsia,* prepared in Latin. He received his final training in London at St. George's Hospital and attended the lectures of Matthew Baillie, who befriended him later in some of his bitter polemics with distinguished medical scientists.

Wilson returned to Edinburgh in 1794 and through most of his professional life shared time in his waking hours between physiological studies in lower animals, extensive writing, private lectures presented without academic aegis, and a successful clinical practice. His writing proclivity was evident shortly after graduation when he published a small monograph on urinary gravel. However, he was better known for his clinical writings on diet and digestion. In 1795, Wilson was admitted a Fellow of the Royal College of Physicians of Edinburgh; but, by 1799, because of failing health or other unidentified reasons, he abandoned Edinburgh in what seemed to have been a favorable environment for practice and investigation. Wilson settled first in Winchester and a short time later transferred his activities to Worcester. There he found himself in the midst of a medical-surgical feud in which he took the side of the doctors of physic. Dissension finally led to his resignation from the staff of the Worcester General Infirmary in 1818 and departure for London two years later.

Wilson's first major composition, *A Treatise on Febrile Diseases,* in four volumes, was dedicated to Matthew Baillie. This went through four editions, an American printing, and translation into German and French. The contents were largely speculative, with a few case reports, and retrospectively seem to contain little of interest. His writings continued at an ever-quickening pace during his Worcester tenure. However, in contrast to the verbose speculative discussions on clinical subjects lacking style and frequently difficult to understand, he turned to experimental physiology and published a number of contributions in the *Philosophical Transactions*. The experimental data were derived from a series of physiological studies pursued after 1812 with the assistance of Charles Hastings, apothecary house-surgeon. The relationship between the cardiovascular and the nervous system was investigated. Rabbits and frogs served as experimental animals, and the critical observations of the capillary circulation were made under the microscope. Wilson Philip believed that the heart and blood vessels were capable of acting independently of the brain and spinal cord as others had presumed or shown. Furthermore, he also believed that the nervous system could be the source for either acceleration or inhibition of the heart and blood vessels as a result of stimuli applied to the nervous system, and that the blood vessels possessed a propulsive power which was independent of that of the heart.[2]

As it is now generally admitted by physiologists, as appears from the report just laid before the reader, that the heart is capable of performing its functions after the brain is removed, the first question which presents itself is, how far does the power of this organ depend on the influence of the spinal marrow.

Exp. 1. A rabbit was deprived of sensation and voluntary power by a blow on the occiput. When the rabbit is killed in this way, the respiration immediately ceases; but the action of the heart and the circulation continue, and may be supported for a considerable length of time by artificial respiration. The spinal marrow was laid bare from the occiput to the beginning of the dorsal vertebrae. The chest was then opened, and the heart found beating regularly, and with considerable force. The spinal marrow, as far as it had been laid bare, was now wholly removed, but without in the least affecting the action of the heart. . . . The skull was then opened, and the whole of the brain removed, so that no part of the nervous system remained above the dorsal vertebrae, but without any abatement of the action of the heart, which still continued to be more or less powerful.

We are now to inquire whether the action of the vessels of circulation is also independent of the brain and spinal marrow.

The following experiments, and some others which I shall have occasion to relate, were made on the capillaries of the frog, which, from the extent and transparency of the web of its hind feet, and from its great tenacity of life, appeared the best subject for such experiments.

Exp. 12. A strong ligature was thrown round the neck of a frog, and the head cut off without any loss of blood; much loss of blood immediately destroys the circulation in the extremities. The spinal marrow was then destroyed by a wire. On bringing the web of one of the hind legs before the miscroscope, I found the circulation in it vigorous for many minutes, and in all respects resembling that in the web of a healthy frog.

Does it not seem a necessary inference, from the experiments related in this chapter, that the action of the heart and vessels of circulation depends on a power inherent in themselves, and having no direct dependence on the nervous system?

Exp. 14. A rabbit was deprived of sensation and voluntary motion by a blow on the occiput, the action of the heart supported by artificial respiration, and the brain and cervical part of the spinal marrow laid bare. The thorax was now opened, and the action of the heart, which beat with strength and regularity, observed. Spirit of wine was then applied to the spinal marrow, and a greatly increased action of the heart was the consequence. It was afterwards applied to the brain with the same effect. The increase of motion was immediate and decided in both cases.

Exp. 15. The foregoing experiment was repeated, with the difference, that the whole of the spinal marrow was laid bare. The motion of the heart was nearly, if not quite, as much influenced by the stimulus to the dorsal, as to the cervical portion of the spinal marrow; but it was very little influenced by its application to the lumbar portion.

Exp. 16. In this experiment, only that part of the brain which occupies the anterior part of the head was laid bare. The rabbit in other respects was prepared in the same way as in the preceding experiments. The spirit of wine applied to this part of the brain, produced as decided an effect on the motion of the heart as in those experiments. The spirit of wine was washed off, and a watery solution, first of opium, then of tobacco, applied, with the effect of an increase, but a much less increase of the heart's action than arose from the spirit of wine. . . . The first effect of both was soon succeeded by a more languid action of the heart than that which preceded their application to the brain. This effect was greatest, and came on soonest when the tobacco was used, and we always, for we frequently repeated the experiment, saw an evident increase in the action of the heart when we washed off the tobacco. We could also perceive this, though in a less degree, when the opium was washed off. Little or none of this debilitating effect was observed when the spirit of wine was used.

What are the simple results of the experiments related in this and the preceding chapter? The first set prove, that the power of the heart and vessels of circulation is independent of the brain and spinal marrow, for we find that the functions of the former organs continue after the latter are destroyed or removed, and that their removal is not attended with any immediate effect on the motions of the heart and vessels.

Another interesting series of experiments concerned the value of galvanism in man for derangements of the nervous system and for asthma. The following account also describes the placebo effect (using control observations) on the same patient without use of a current.[3]

I have employed galvanism in many cases of habitual asthma, and almost uniformly with relief.

The galvanism was applied in the following manner. Two thin plates of metal about two or three inches in diameter, dipped in water, were applied, one to the nape of the neck, the other to the pit of the stomach, or rather lower. The wires from the different ends of the trough were brought into contact with these plates, and as observed above, as great a galvanic power maintained, as the patient could bear without complaint. . . . The relief seemed much the same, whether the positive wire was applied to the nape of the neck, or the pit of the stomach.

I wished to try, if the impression on the mind, in the employment of galvanism, had any share in the relief obtained from it. I found, that by scratching the skin with the sharp end of a wire, I could produce a sensation so similar to that excited by galvanism, that those who had most frequently been subjected to this influence were deceived by it. By these means, and arranging the trough pieces of metal &c. as usual, I deceived several who had formerly received relief from galvanism, and also several who had not yet used it. All of them said that they experienced no relief from what I did. Without allowing them to rise, I substituted for this process the real application of galvanism, merely by immersing in the trough one end of the wire with which I had scratched the nape of the neck, the wire at the pit of the stomach having been all the time applied as usual by the patient himself. Before the application of the galvanism had been continued as long as the previous process, they all said they were relieved.

In London, Philip continued to write, to feud, and to enjoy great success in the management of dyspeptic patients. In 1820, he was admitted a licentiate of the Royal College of Physicians in London; in 1826, a Fellow of the Royal Society; and in 1834, a Fellow of the Royal College of Physicians. More than a dozen of his contributions were accepted for publication in the *Philosophical Transactions*. In 1835, Philip delivered the Gulstonian lectures on *The more obscure Affections of the Brain, on which the Nature and Successful Treatment of many Chronic Diseases depend*. This was a rambling, confused, diffuse work ignored by the editor of *Lancet*.

By 1842, Philip had retired from practice and published his last work, *A Treatise on Protracted Indigestion and Its Consequences*. Shortly after, he suddenly disappeared from London, having been suspected of injudicious financial dealings, and went to live in Bologna in order to escape imprisonment. His name ceased to appear on the registry of the Royal Society in 1850 and on the roll of the Royal College of Physicians in 1851. He is assumed to have died in poverty.

1. McMenemey, W. H.: Alexander Philip(s) Wilson Philip (1770-1847) Physiologist and Physician, *J Hist Med* 13:289-328, 1958.

2. Philip, A. P. W.: *An Experimental Inquiry Into the Laws of the Vital Functions*, London: T. & G. Underwood, 1817.

3. Philip, A. P. W.: On the Effects of Galvanism in Restoring the Due Action of the Lungs, *Philos Trans* 107: 22-31, 1817.

Daniel Merrem (1790-1859)

DANIEL KARL THEODOR MERREM was born in Duisburg, Germany, the son of the professor of public finance and general science in the university.[1] Subsequently, the family moved to Marburg, where his father occupied a similar post on the faculty. There Daniel continued his education and in 1810 received the MD degree in surgery and obstetrics from the university. His inaugural dissertation presented at the time describes his notable contribution on experimental surgery in animals.[2] Following graduation he traveled extensively in central Europe, visiting scientific centers and establishing scientific contacts. In 1812, Merrem was appointed general staff surgeon in the Westphalian Army Corps, concerned with administration of sanitary measures in the field and with the organization of field aid stations. He participated in the Russian campaign, returned to Germany after Napoleon's retreat, was appointed director of the military hospital of Halberstadt, and progressively held more responsible posts in medical-military affairs in northern and in southern Germany. In 1816, Merrem was assigned to the medical college of Cologne, became medical advisor to the government, and was responsible for the organization of regional medical facilities. A year later he was placed in charge of the midwives' school in Cologne, in 1827 was appointed to the editorial board of the *Deutsche Zeitschrift für Geburtskunde,* and in 1842 gained a senior post in the governing hierarchy.

Merrem's great contribution was his experimental work on pylorectomy described in the third chapter of his inaugural dissertation, entitled *Extirpation of the Pylorus.* The incentive has been attributed to C. F. Michaelis, who spent some time with the Hessian troops in America during the Revolutionary War. Upon his return to Germany, Michaelis served as professor of surgery at the University of Marburg while Merrem was a student. This association has been well documented by Temkin, who has also translated the critical features of the first protocol by Merrem. The pylorectomy on the dog, who lived for 23 days, is described as follows.[3]

On November 15, 1809, in the presence of my fellow students and friends. . . . I made an incision into the skin on the right side below the false ribs where the stomach passes into the duodenum. This was done on a black Pomeranian dog after the hair had been shaved. . . . After the muscles had been cautiously dissected and the peritoneum opened, I inserted the index finger of my left hand and over it enlarged the upper and lower ends of the wound to the length of three inches. A prolapsed part of the duodenum and jejunum together with the smaller omentum was immediately placed back in their natural position. Then I separated the pylorus from the small omentum and a part of the duodenum from the mesentery. . . . Afterwards I extirpated the pylorus by twice applying the

scissors so that I removed a part approximately three lines long from the stomach and duodenum.

At the same moment both injured parts contracted with such force that with their edges turned backwards they formed two sphincters impeding all access. Therefore I drove in three needles, equidistant from one another, half an inch from the ventricular edge, and, at the same distance, I pushed them through the internal surface of the duodenum to its external surface.

1. Obituary, *Allg med Central-Zeitung* 26:695, 1859.
2. Merrem, D. C. T.: *Observations on Experimental Surgery in Animals* (L), Giessiae: Tashe et Mueller, 1810.
3. Temkin, O.: Merrem's Youthful Dream. The Early History of Experimental Pylorectomy, *Bull Hist Med* 31: 29-43, 1957.

Composite by G. Bako

John Jones (1729-1791)

JOHN JONES, lithotomist of New York and Philadelphia, and one of five petitioners for the founding of a medical school under the aegis of King's College, occupied the chair of surgery upon approval of the petition; in keeping with the honor of such a post, he prepared the first text on surgery in America.[1] Jones was born in Jamaica, Long Island, of Welsh Quaker stock and was privately schooled in Manhattan. At the age of 18, he was apprenticed to Thomas Cadwalader for three years. Formal medical training was not then available in the Colonies; therefore, Jones proceeded to London, where he attended the lectures of William Hunter and followed the work of Percival Pott in St. Bartholomew's Hospital. He continued his learning in Paris, received the MD degree from the University of Rheims, and concluded his European pilgrimage at Leyden and Edinburgh.

The practice of surgery and obstetrics, begun by Jones in New York some years later, was interrupted by military service during the French and Indian War. As the outstanding surgeon in New York, he might be expected to agitate in favor of a medical school. Therefore, his appointment as professor of surgery in the medical school of King's College is not surprising. The rather long title of his chair is recorded as "The Theory of Chirurgery with a Course of Operations upon the Human Body."[2] A copy of the introductory lecture, delivered at the opening of King's College Medical School in 1769, is treasured by the College of Physicians of Philadelphia. His sound advice on the practice of surgery elaborated upon the advantages of careful observation complementing experimental studies.[3]

What method ought surgeons to follow, in order to give the highest degree of perfection to their art?

Is it from that experience which is acquir'd from practice alone, wee are to expect this perfection? . . . if that had been the case, the art, wou'd many ages ago, have been at its height.

But there is another source of improvement, equally essential to the perfecting our art, & perhaps with more difficulty acquir'd, than that wee obtain from practice alone.

Observation, & Physical experiments, which form the only basis of surgery, have then, two different objects.

Observation regards the sensible qualities of bodies, the course of diseases, their Phenomena, with the effects which result from the process of the art. Physical experiments, unravel the structure & uses of the parts; the composition of mix'd bodies, the properties of those fluids which circulate in the vessels, the nature of aliments, & the action of medicines . . . yet, these so necessary helps, do not conduct us separately, to the hidden truths, which may serve to enrich our art.

Observation improves our experiments, & experiments influence our observations; . . . they mutually assist each other, & are like lights united, for the dissipation of obscurity.

Shortly before the Revolutionary War, Jones went again to London, this time to seek relief from bronchial asthma. The climate is believed to have improved his health, and he returned to his teaching, writing, and practice. In 1775, he published the first American text on surgery, entitled *Plain Concise Practical Remarks on the Treatment of Wounds and Fractures*. A second edition appeared the following year in Philadelphia. This was not a system of surgery, but a series of essays on trauma and its complications and sensible counsel on the practice of surgery.[4]

HENCE it will appear very evident, how necessary it is for the student in Surgery, to make himself thoroughly acquainted with most of those branches of medicine, which are requisite to form an accomplished Physician.

BESIDES a competent acquaintance with the learned languages, which are to lay the foundation of every other acquisition; he must possess an accurate knowledge of the structure of the human body, acquired not only by attending anatomical lectures, but by frequent dissections of dead bodies with his own hands.—This practice cannot be too warmly recommended to the students in Surgery: It is from this source, and a knowledge in hydraulics, they must derive any adequate notions of the animal economy or physiology. Chymistry and Materia Medica are very necessary to a right understanding of pharmacy or composition.—To these should be added some progress in the mathematics and mechanics, which I will venture to assert may be applied with much more utility and safety to the science of Surgery, than Physic. But there must be a happiness, as well as art, to complete the character of the great Surgeon.

Jones had long sensed the need for a general hospital in New York and, together with Samuel Bard, had voiced this objective at the opening of King's College in 1769. A charter was granted to New York Hospital in 1771, and, when Jones was in London the next year, he collected money and bought supplies for the hospital upon direction of the board of governors. The first building destroyed by fire, was not rebuilt and in service until 1791.

John Jones served for a time in the state senate, left New York City when the British took possession, and campaigned as assistant surgeon in the Tenth Massachusetts Regiment. He continued in military service until 1781. Before his resignation from the Continental Army, he resumed the practice of surgery in Philadelphia and succeeded John Redman on the staff at the Pennsylvania Hospital. Jones was a founding member of the College of Physicians of Philadelphia and for several years was the first vice president.

Benjamin Franklin and George Washington were his two most famous patients. Washington outlived Jones, and it was in the President's home that the physician was stricken. Franklin, who for many years had been troubled with a large bladder stone associated with his gout, was attended by Jones in his last illness. The account by Jones of Franklin's terminal events was published in the *Pennsylvania Gazette* for Wednesday, April 21, 1790, together with Congressional proceedings signed by George Washington, President, and Thomas Jefferson, Secretary of State. The medical report was as follows.[5]

The stone, with which he had been afflicted for several years, had for the last twelve months confined him chiefly to his bed; and during the extreme painful paroxysms, he was obliged to take large doses of laudanum to mitigate his torture—still, in the intervals of pain, he not only amused himself with reading and conversing chearfully with his family and a few friends, who visited him, but was often employed in doing business of a public as well as private nature, with various persons, who waited on him for that purpose; and in every instance displayed, not only that readiness and disposition of doing good, which was the distinguishing characteristic of his life, but the fullest and clearest possession of his uncommon mental abilities; and not unfrequently indulged himself in those *Jeux D'esprit* and entertaining anecdotes, which were the delight of all who heard him.

About sixteen days before his death, he was seized with a feverish indisposition, without any particular symptoms attending it till the third or fourth day, when he complained of a pain in his left breast, which increased till it became extremely acute, attended with a cough and laborious breathing. During this state, when the severity of his pains sometimes drew forth a groan of complaint, he would observe—that he was afraid he did not bear them as he ought—acknowledged his grateful sense of the many blessings he had received from that Supreme Being, who had raised him, from small and low beginnings, to such high rank and consideration among men— and made no doubt his present afflictions were

kindly intended to wean him from a world, in which he was no longer fit to act the part assigned him. In this frame of body and mind he continued till five days before his death, when his pain and difficulty of breathing entirely left him, and his family were flattering themselves with the hopes of his recovery, when an imposthumation, which had formed itself in his lungs, suddenly burst, and discharged a great quantity of matter, which he continued to throw up while he had sufficient strength to do it, but, as that failed, the organs of respiration became gradually oppressed—a calm lethargic state succeeded—and on the 17th instant, about eleven o'clock at night, he quietly expired, closing a long and useful life of eighty-four years and three months.

1. Thacher, J.: *American Medical Biography*, Boston: Richardson & Lord, 1828.

2. Stookey, B.: *A History of Colonial Medical Education*, Springfield, Ill.: Charles C Thomas, Publisher, 1962.

3. McDaniel, W. B., II: John Jones, Introductory Lecture to His Course in Surgery (1769), King's College, Printed from the Author's Manuscript, *Tran Coll Physicians Phila* 8:180-190, 1940-1941.

4. Jones, J.: *Plain Concise Practical Remarks on the Treatment of Wounds and Fractures*, New York: J. Holt, 1775.

5. Jones, J.: A Short Account of Doctor Franklin's Last Illness, by his Attending Physician, *Penn Gaz*, April 21, 1790.

Benjamin Rush (1745-1813)

A RUSH MONUMENT COMMITTEE of the American Medical Association was appointed in 1884 to raise funds for a suitable memorial. The campaign was a fizzle according to the committee report published in 1890.[1]

Benjamin Rush to be commemorated as the greatest physician America has ever produced . . . your committee have felt confident that among that number (100,000 physician members) there would be at least forty thousand, who would spontaneously· contribute one dollar each toward the erection of a monument. . . . Alas! At the end of five years, their Treasurer reports that he has only received the first thousand of that forty on which they had so confidently counted.

It was hoped that the House of Delegates Resolution No. 34 introduced on June 13, 1960, for study of a shrine for American Medicine in Philadelphia, would not meet a similar fate. If a shrine to medicine is established in Philadelphia, it will commemorate among many, Benjamin Rush, patriot, humanitarian, abolitionist, teacher, military surgeon, physician to the indigent, founder

of liberal arts colleges, and a proponent of a new theory of disease, who shared honors with Benjamin Franklin as great Philadelphians of the 18th century.

Rush, a pious man interested in public affairs although not a politician, was born of English Quaker ancestry on December 24, 1745, on a plantation near Philadelphia. Some will remember him as a member of the Continental Congress and a signer of the Declaration of Independence whose name appears on this document just above Benjamin Franklin's. Rush's father, a gunsmith, died when his son was only six. His mother, in order to educate the children, opened a grocery shop in Philadelphia and sold liquors, among other items. The success of her commercial venture is confirmed by the fact that she educated her children in proper style. Benjamin attended a country school in Nottingham, Md.; after preliminary examinations he was admitted to the junior class at the College of New Jersey (Princeton) at the age of 15. The AB degree was granted 18 months later. Dr. Finley, the headmaster of Nottingham School,

has been credited with diverting Rush from law and toward the natural sciences.[2]

On what slight circumstances do our destinies in life seem to depend! . . . . There were periods in my life in which I regretted the choice I had made of the profession of medicine, and once, after I was thirty years of age, I made preparations for beginning the study of the law. But providence overruled my intentions by an event to be mentioned hereafter. I now rejoice that I followed Dr. Finley's advice. I have seen the hand of heaven clearly in it.

In preparation for formal medical education, Rush was apprenticed to John Redman, the leading physician of Philadelphia. Rush prepared and compounded medicines, visited the sick, performed the office duties of a nurse, and was in charge of the books and the accounts. Boerhaave's lectures in physiology and pathology and Sydenham's works on clinical medicine were read in the evenings. There was also an opportunity to attend the lectures of Shippen and Morgan in anatomy and materia medica at the Medical School of the College of Philadelphia.

It may not be amiss to mention here that before I began the study of medicine, I had an uncommon aversion from seeing such sights as are connected with its practice. But a little time and habit soon wore away all that degree of sensibility which is painful, and enabled me to see and even assist with composure in performing the most severe operations in surgery.

In 1766, at the age of 21, Rush sailed for Liverpool and Edinburgh. Cullen was the outstanding professor in Edinburgh. The years abroad were considered to be "the most important in their influence upon my character and conduct of any period of my life." Leisure time in the summer was spent in attaining proficiency in mathematics, Latin, and the Romance languages. Following graduation in 1768, Rush traveled to London and then to Paris. William Hunter, John Fothergill, and George Fordyce were outstanding teachers and physicians in London. Johnson, Goldsmith, and Boswell were leaders in the humanities. Benjamin Franklin took a particular interest in Rush and introduced him to a number of prominent citizens. His days at Paris were spent sightseeing and visiting the Hôtel de la Charité and Hôtel Dieu.[3]

The return to Philadelphia found him beginning the practice of medicine and seeking the professorship of chemistry in the College of Philadelphia. This appointment completed the medical faculty of the first medical school established in the 13 colonies. In 1791, the College of Philadelphia merged with the University of the State of Pennsylvania. The University of Pennsylvania was born. Rush was appointed professor of the Institutes of Medicine and Clinical Practice in the new school. His teaching and practice was the subject of acrimonious debate, bitter criticism, and serious skepticism by his fellow physicians as well as by the public press.[4] Rush's teaching reflected the medical philosophy of Cullen, who had rejected the humoral theory of physiology and pathology and replaced it with a theory of balance and counterbalance. This was modified by John Brown (Brunonian theory) to include stimuli acting upon the excitability of the body. When the stimuli are strengthened, the disease is sthenic; when the stimuli are weak, asthenia appears. Rush believed that all disease is related to debility, which may be either direct from insufficiency of stimulation or indirect from the after-effects of excess stimulation. This theory was regarded as heresy in Philadelphia.

Between 1769 and 1775, Rush led a "life of constant labor and self-denial."[2] The poor were treated in the morning; the evenings were devoted to study. His lectures in the Medical School were widely acclaimed and attracted a large following. Calomel and the lancet were recommended for several maladies, including yellow fever. When he was stricken with yellow fever, he submitted to such treatment. In the early years of practice, Rush complained that his services as a consultant were not in great demand. This he attributed to his advanced theories of pathogenesis and treatment of disease. He limited his materia medica to 15 or 20 items and stripped medicine of some of its mystery by refusing to write prescriptions in Latin and condemning the practice of publishing inaugural dissertations in a dead language. He was instrumental in establishing the Philadelphia Dispensary,

although it reduced the number of his patients by one-fourth.

The first public assignment was membership in the Provincial Conference in 1776. The following year he succeeded Morgan as Surgeon-General of the Middle Department of the Continental Army. Revolutionary troops had suffered greatly; it was estimated that the morbidity and mortality was fivefold that of the British casualties. This appalling situation was attributed to a number of items; included were overcrowding, depletion of hospital stores, lack of discipline, and the delegation of authority to the Director-General of the hospital rather than to the Surgeon-General. The belief was current that "9 out of 10 who die under our hands perish with fevers *caught* in our hospitals." Old disorders were prolonged and new ones contracted. A letter addressed to Congress in protest proved ineffectual. He prepared a bitter letter to General George Washington, resigned from the Army, and moved to Princeton while the British troops occupied Philadelphia and did not return until the British had retired.

Rush assisted in founding the schools now known as Franklin and Marshall College in Lancaster, and Dickinson College in Carlisle. He recommended the abolition of capital punishment, favored the restriction of the use of alcohol and tobacco, was active in founding a Bible Society, and wrote extensively on moral and philosophical themes. Of thirteen children, three became physicians. His most famous son was Richard, one-time Secretary of the Treasury of the United States.

Benjamin Rush was the first American to discuss cholera infantum and focal infection in the teeth. He urged the study of veterinary medicine and was the first physician in this country to achieve a general literary reputation. His letters were collected by Butterfield and, when published, filled two thick volumes.[5] Interested in psychiatry and especially dreams, he recounted a number in his autobiography. His treatise on diseases of the mind was the first comprehensive discussion in America on mental illness. Its influence was profound for several decades.[6] In his later years, Rush was disturbed to discover that his practice was dwindling. New patients did not appear; former patients had died or sought consultation from other physicians. Since the state of his finances required outside income, he applied, with 40 other candidates, for the position of Treasurer of the United States Mint. He was successful and held the appointment from 1799 until his death in 1813, when his son succeeded him.

1. Report of the Rush Monument Committee, Association News, *JAMA* 14:620 (April 26) 1890.
2. Rush, B.: *The Autobiography of Benjamin Rush,* edited by G. W. Corner, Princeton, N.J.: Princeton University Press, 1948.
3. Pepper, W.: Benjamin Rush, *JAMA* 14:593 (April 26) 1890.
4. Packard, F. R.: "Benjamin Rush," in Kelly, H. A., and Burrage, W. L.: *American Medical Biographics,* Baltimore: Norman, Remington Company, 1920, p. 1007.
5. *Letters of Benjamin Rush,* edited by L. H. Butterfield, Princeton, N.J.: Princeton University Press, 1951.
6. Rush, B.: *Medical Inquiries and Observations upon the Diseases of the Mind,* Philadelphia: Kimber and Richardson, 1812.

Samuel Bard (1742-1821)

SAMUEL BARD, founder or cofounder of several eleemosynary institutions in New York City, was born in Philadelphia where his father, John Bard, was practicing medicine.[1] Ancestors on both his father's and mother's side were Huguenots who had fled France; his mother's forebears settled in Hyde Park on the Hudson River; his father's forebears took up residence along the Delaware River below Philadelphia. When Samuel was four years of age, the family moved to New York. There his father established an excellent practice, was recognized in the best social circles, and provided his children with superior educational opportunities for his time. At the age of 17, Samuel entered King's College (later Columbia University), followed the classical course, and, upon graduation in 1761, left for Europe on a British square-rigger to begin his formal instruction in medicine. The journey was made during the unrest between England and France, and the ship was captured by a French frigate. Bard was held prisoner in Bayonne Castle for several months but was

liberated through the efforts of Benjamin Franklin, a friend of the family.

With proper letters of introduction, Bard continued to London, where he became ac-

New York Academy of Medicine

quainted with John Fothergill, William Hunter, Mackenzie, and others. He was admitted as an assistant at St. Thomas' Hospital and received private instruction from Alexander Russell. Six months later he proceeded to the University of Edinburgh during the great days of medical education in Scotland when Whytt, Cullen, Hope, and the Monros, *Primus* and *Secundus,* adorned the faculty. Fellow students included John Morgan, Thomas Percival, and Haygarth Bard displayed great industry and intellectual activity and in his third year won a medal in botany. He took the MD degree in 1765, upon defense of his thesis composed in Latin, *De veribus opii.* He had studied the effects of opium *in vivo,* using himself and his roommate as experimental subjects. A few months of duty as a pupil at Guy's and St. Thomas' Hospitals in London concluded his foreign study.

Bard entered practice in New York with his father in the summer of 1766, devoting himself to internal medicine, midwifery, and the planning of a medical school. For three years he received no share of the professional income from the combined practice so that he might repay the paternal debt for his European education. A proposal that had been in his father's thoughts for some time became a high-priority project; the first medical school in Manhattan, the medical school of King's College, was established. Bard, with five associates, formed the faculty which began instruction in medicine on Nov 2, 1767. The assignments were: Samuel Clossy in anatomy, Peter Middleton in physiology and pathology, John Jones in surgery, James Smith in chemistry and materia medica, John V. B. Tennent in midwifery, and Bard in theory and practice of physic.[2] An honorary MD degree was given to Bard the following year in recognition of his services; the first earned degree, the bachelor of medicine, was conferred at the Commencement in 1769, several months after a similar award by the University of Pennsylvania. The following year King's College bestowed the first earned MD degree in America.

Bard was associated with the medical faculty of King's College or its successors for 40 years. From 1767 to 1775, he held the chair of physic; from 1792 to 1804, he was dean of the medical faculty, Columbia College; from 1787 to 1804, he held a trusteeship of Columbia College; and from 1811 to 1820, he held the presidency of the College of Physicians and Surgeons in the City of New York, a name which persists for the medical department of Columbia University.

Bard's discourse on the duties of a physician was delivered before the president and governors of King's College at the commencement held on the 16th of May, 1769. The address, subtitled "As Advice to those GENTLEMEN who then received the First MEDICAL DEGREES conferred by that UNIVERSITY," implored the graduates to continue as perpetual students in practice. It also contained suggestions for a public hospital to receive the indigent sick and to benefit the afflicted of every rank.[3]

Do not therefore imagine, that from this Time your Studies are to cease; so far from it, you are to be considered as but just entering upon them; and unless your whole Lives, are one continued Series of Application and Improvement, you will fall short of your Duty. . . . In a Profession then, like that you have embraced, where the Object is of so great Importance as the Life of a Man; you are accountable even for the Errors of Ignorance, unless you have embraced every Opportunity of obtaining Knowledge.

In your Behaviour to the Sick, remember always that your Patient is the Object of the tenderest Affection, to some one, or perhaps to many about him; it is therefore your Duty, not only to endeavour to preserve his Life, but to avoid wounding the Sensibility of a tender Parent, a distressed Wife, or an affectionate Child. Let your Carriage be humane and attentive, be interested in his Welfare, and shew your Apprehension of his Danger, rather by your Assiduity to relieve, than by any harsh or brutal Expressions of it. On the other hand, never buoy up a dying Man with groundless Expectations of Recovery, this is at best a good natured and humane Deception, but too often it arises from the baser Motives of Lucre and Avarice.

I cannot however help regretting, the very frequent Opportunities you will meet with, particularly in this Place, of exercising your Humanity upon such Occasions; owing to the want of a proper Asylum, for such unhappy and real Objects of Charity, it is truly a reproach, that a City like this, should want a public Hospital, one of the most useful and necessary charitable Institutions that can possibly be imagined.

Nor would the good Effects of an Hospital be wholly confined to the Poor, they would extend to every Rank, and greatly contribute to the Safety and Welfare of the whole Community.

Nor is the Scheme of a Public Hospital I believe so impracticable, as at first sight it may appear to be. There are Numbers in this Place I am sure (was a Subscription once set on foot, upon an extensive and generous Plan) whose Fortunes enable them, and whose Benevolence would prompt them, liberally to contribute to so useful an Institution; it wants but a Prime Mover, whose Authority would give Weight to the Undertaking, and whose Zeal and Industry, would promote it.

Bard was as instrumental in founding a hospital as a medical school. With the support of his father, Peter Middleton, and John Jones, the final draft of a hospital charter was approved in 1771. Two years later the New York State legislature gave financial support to the plan and appropriated £800 annually from an excise on spirits, to continue for 20 years. The cornerstone of the New York Hospital was laid in the fall of 1773; however, before the building was completed it was partially destroyed by fire and, when rebuilt, served as a military hospital. It did not receive civilian patients until 1791. At that time Bard was a member of the visiting staff and served until retirement.

The rising tension between the Colonies and England had a great effect upon Bard's activities for almost a decade. Since his sympathy leaned heavily toward the Mother Country because of his education in Britain, he interrupted his New York practice in July, 1776, and left for Hyde Park, where his family had gone before him. After temporary residence in Shrewsbury, New Jersey, and an unsuccessful venture in the manufacture of salt, he returned to Manhattan to resume practice. However, not until the summer of 1884, with the restoration of peace, were times conducive to his return to full duties as teacher, practitioner, and influential citizen. In the latter capacities he knew Alexander Hamilton, Aaron Burr, and George Washington, on whom he incised a deep-seated carbuncle on the left thigh shortly after the President's inauguration. Bard moved into partial retirement in 1794, when he resumed residence in Hyde Park. Thereafter, he travelled back and forth in his teaching, administrative, and medical duties. In 1795, he entered into partnership with David Hosack, but, upon being stricken with yellow fever during the epidemic of 1798, he retired completely from practice, continuing only his administrative work with the medical school.

Bard prepared two important monographs on medicine and one on sheep raising. In the dual role of a self-taught veterinarian and authority on breeding and care of sheep, he published in retirement a handbook entitled *A Guide for Young Shepherds,* assembled from writings of others and confirmed by his experiences. Also in retirement he prepared *A Compendium of the Theory and Practice of Midwifery,* which was intended largely for students and midwives. The work was revised five times following the first edition in 1807. More important than each of these was his treatise on diphtheria, published in 1771, entitled *An Enquiry into the Nature, Cause and Cure of the Angina Suffocativa, or, Sore Throat Distemper, as it is commonly called by the inhabitants of this City and Colony.* The monograph, which was translated into French in 1810 and was excerpted by Bretonneau, contained excellent passages of the clinical and postmortem findings of the epidemic malady.[4]

And the first symptoms, in most instances, were a slightly inflamed and watry eye, a bloated and livid countenance, with a few red eruptions here and there upon the face, and in one case a small ulcer in the nose, whence oosed an ichor so sharp as to inflame and erode the upper lip. At the same time, or very soon after, such as could speak, complained of an uneasy sensation in the throat, but without any great soreness or pain. Upon examining it, the tonsils *or almonds,* appeared swelled and slightly inflamed, with a few white specks upon them, which, in some, increased so as to cover them all over with one general slough, and in a few the swelling was so great, as almost to close up the passage of the throat; but this, altho' a frequent symptom, did not invariably attend the disease; and some had all the other symptoms without it.

These symptoms, with a slight fever at night, continued in some for five or six days, without alarming their friends; in others a difficulty of breathing came on within twenty-four hours, especially in the time of sleep, and was often suddenly encreased to so great a degree as to threaten immediate suffocation.

These symptoms continued for one, two, or three days. By that time it was usual for them to be greatly increased in such as died; and the patients, though commonly somewhat comatous from the beginning, now become much more so; yet even when the disorder was at the worst, they retained their senses, and would give distinct answers, when spoken to; although on being left to themselves, they lay for the most part in a lethargic situation, only raising up now and then to receive their drink.

The second dissection I attended, was of a child about seven years old, who had had all the symptoms with which this disease is commonly attended, except that in this case the glands of the throat, and upper parts of the wind pipe, were found entirely free from any complaint, and the disease seemed to be confined to the trachea only, which was lined with this tough mucus, inspissated so as to resemble a membrane: We could trace it into the larger divisions of the trachea, and it was evident that the smallest branches were obstructed by it, for it was very observable, that upon opening the breast the lungs did not collapse as much as is usual, but remained distended, and felt remarkably firm and heavy, as if they were stuffed with the same mucus.

Bard's interest in medical education began with his advocating a full liberal arts course for pre-medical students and a proposal that the State legislature appropriate money for scholarships for medical students from each county. At a time when medical practice needed direction and control, Bard, as president of the Dutchess County Medical Society, urged his provincial body to set an example for New York State, as well as others, in regulating the practice of physicians in their respective counties. In scientific and cultural areas, Bard supported Hosack in his botanical project, the Elgin Garden, and assisted in the establishment of the American Academy of Arts, the New York City Library, and the New York Dispensary. He was an honorary member of the New York Historical Society; Princeton University awarded him the LLD degree in 1816, and the College of Physicians of Philadelphia conferred honorary membership in 1811. The name of Bard is perpetuated at Columbia-Presbyterian Hospital Medical Center in uptown New York City, in Bard Hall, a resident home for medical students, and the Bard Professorship of the Practice of Medicine on the faculty of the College of Physicians and Surgeons.

    1. Langstaff, J. B.: *Doctor Bard of Hyde Park,* New York: E. P. Dutton & Co., Inc., 1942.
    2. Stookey, B.: *A History of Colonial Medical Education,* Springfield, Ill: C. C Thomas, 1962.
    3. Bard, S.: *A Discourse Upon the Duties of a Physician,* New York: A. & J. Robertson, 1769.
    4. Bard, S.: *An Enquiry into the Nature, Cause and Cure of the Angina Suffocativa,* New York: S. Inslee, & A. Carr, 1771.

Richard Bayley (1745-1801)

DURING RICHARD BAYLEY'S brief tenure as health officer to the port of the City of New York he prepared two treatises, *An Account of the Epidemic Fever* as well as *Letters from the Health-Office, Submitted to the Common Council.* They reveal an interest in infection and contagion first manifest in a discussion of croup early in his medical career. He was born in Fairfield, Connecticut, to English and French parents, studied medicine with Dr. Charlton in New York and for two years was a pupil of William Hunter in London.[1] He returned to New

Composite by G. Bako

York in 1772 to commence practice. There the first case of angina trachealis, described in his discussion of croup, came under his supervision. The 4-year-old boy was bled, a large blister was applied to the throat, and calomel and antiseptics were administered, but the patient died within 36 hours from the first fit of strangulation. A young patient with similar distress but dissimilar findings on examination was observed subsequently.[2]

In the succeeding month just such another exit happened, where early applications were made, and where the patient had every advantage which could be derived from medicine adapted to the *received opinion,* of the nature of this disease— on examination, the child's fauces were covered with an ash-coloured mucus of very little consistence, which, by applying the smallest force, could easily be removed: the *pendulous palate* when dismantled, appeared enlarged and of *livid colour*; the fauces, when uncovered, seemed as if its vessels had been much distended with blood: when the wind-pipe was opened, there was found, diffused through its whole length, and entering the

Bronchia, a membrane of a whitish colour, of such tenacity as to require a considerable force to pull it asunder; after entering the Bronchia it changed its consistency and became a glary mucus.

Shortly after this dissection I was called in consultation with Dr. Van Vleck to visit a child, which he informed me had been attacked three days before with the *putrid sore-throat*: the complaint had made great progress; the ulcers were large, and increased during a free use of the most powerful antiseptics.

The parents obligingly permitted the child to be examined: The tonsils were totally destroyed, and the fauces were one continued ulcer; the pendulous palate was changed to a mere suspended slough, though the larynx and aspera arteria were free from every appearance of disease.

Reflecting on these two cases, Bayley was convinced they were two distinct diseases, differentiating between membranous croup (diphtheria) and angina trachealis (putrid sorethroat). The observations were first published in Richter's *Chirurgische Bibliothek* as a verbal communication to Michaelis, surgeon to the Hessian troups,[3] and were reprinted in English in 1781 as a letter to William Hunter. Subsequent observers believe the clear description of the tenacious membrane was the description of an accompaniment of diphtheria; whereas the putrid ulcers suggested streptococcal pharyngitis.

Bayley was a Loyalist, and, following a revisit to England, he returned to America in 1776 as surgeon in the English Army under General Howe. When the British troops took possession of Newport, Rhode Island, he served as hospital surgeon at the post but later resigned and resumed practice in New York. He was a recognized leader in the profession, gaining a respected reputation in practice, particularly for the study and treatment of contagious diseases. In 1787, his lectures on anatomy were begun, and, in 1792, he served on the faculty of Columbia College as professor of anatomy; meanwhile, he sponsored his son-in-law, Wright Post, as professor of surgery. During Post's absence in London Bayley occupied both chairs, but, when Post returned, a switch was made and Bayley resumed teaching his favorite subject, surgery. An interest in public health administration

was evidenced by the fact that he organized the New York Dispensary and also accepted the position of health physician to the port of New York. *An Account of the Epidemic Fever Which Prevailed in the City of New-York During Part of the Summer and Fall of 1795,* which Bayley prepared while serving as health officer, differentiated infection from contagion. Sound conclusions were advanced a century before Pasteur's bacteriologic observations.[4]

It will have been perceived before this, that we have been somewhat solicitous to establish a distinction between diseases which are *infectious,* and those which are *contagious.* By contagion we understand something *peculiar* and *specific,* possessing properties *essentially* different from anything else. Thus the contagion of the small-pox, the measles, &c. Those diseases do not require the concurrence of certain causes to render them contagious; they are so under *all* circumstances. But other diseases may, or may *not* be *infectious,* according to the conditional state in which they are placed.

In the *Letters from the Health-Office, Submitted to the Common Council, of the City of New-York,* Bayley included several of his communications to Governor John Jay and others to the Mayor of the city. They help portray the widespread prevalence of filth and pestilence in New York, concentrated in but not exclusive to the river docks, which, according to Bayley, were the major contributing cause to the development of yellow fever (epidemic fever).[5]

Before I undertake to account for the origin of the Fever which made its appearance in this city in June last, I must be permitted to revert to certain facts and opinions contained in a work which I furnished to the Public on the subject of a similar Fever, which prevailed more generally in this city, during part of the Summer and Autumn of 1795.

In that publication it was stated, that the fever was first observed in the neighborhood of Fitch's wharf in Water-street, and that it gradually extended from thence, in different ways, but more particularly in the direction of the prevailing winds. In the month of April of this year, I had frequent occasion to visit the White-hall:—The stench which already issued from the dock, was highly offensive:—and on enquiring, I found that the matter which had been employed to make the new ground, consisted chiefly of the dirt which had been accumulating in the streets during the winter season; and that, besides dogs, cats, hogs, &c. there had been actually two horses buried in the rubbish, which had died in the spring, in a small hovel, erected on the margin of this nuisance.

The malignant fever of the last summer and autumn, tho' for a time very alarming, . . . prevailed in the White-hall and Moore-streets, and in Water and Front streets . . . but did not cause alarm till about the middle of July, from which time to 1st of November, the number attacked with it was about 247, of which there died sixty-seven; of this last number seven or eight died at Bellevue or Bedlow's Island, and are included in the return of deaths from thence.

Bayley proposed state quarantine laws for ships arriving at the port of New York, founded the lazaretto on Bedloe's Island, and instituted reform so the sick on board would be removed to adequate quarters in the quarantine hospital on land. In the pursuit of his duties, he contracted "ship fever" (typhus) from passengers or crew of an Irish emigrant ship and died seven days later. New York City lost a successful practitioner and an enlightened health officer for the principal port for European immigrants on their way to seek employment in industry or to cultivate the soil in a rapidly expanding America.

1. Thacher, J.: "Richard Bayley," in *American Medical Biography*, Boston: Richardson & Lord, 1828.

2. Bayley, R.: *Cases of the Angina Trachealis, With the Mode of Cure, in a Letter to William Hunter, M.D. &c.&c.*, New York: H. Gaine, 1781.

3. Letter from H. D. Michaelis, *Chir Bibliothek* 5:734-746, 1779.

4. Bayley, R.: *An Account of the Epidemic Fever Which Prevailed in the City of New-York, During Part of the Summer and Fall of 1795*, New York: T. and J. Swords, 1796.

5. Bayley, R.: *Letters From the Health-Office, Submitted to the Common Council, of the City of New-York*, New York: J. Furman, 1798.

David Hosack (1769-1835)

JUST AS EVERY GENERATION PRODUCES PHYSISCANS both wise and skillful, so, early in the 19th century, the leading practitioner of the city of New York, David Hosack, furnishes us with another example of the ideal physician. His father, born in Scotland, and

an artillery officer under General Jeffrey Amherst, was wounded at the retaking of Louisburgh. David was consecutively a pupil of McWhorter in the Academy in Newark, New Jersey, and of Wilson in the Academy

Composite by G. Bako

in Hackensack, where he studied Latin and Greek. After beginning higher education at Columbia College and finding unemployed hours, he tutored with Richard Bayley in surgery. The final year of college spent at Princeton, earned him the AB at the age of twenty. He returned to New York City to resume his medical studies and attended lectures on anatomy, physiology, chemistry, physic, and midwifery. He then proceeded to Philadelphia, where Shippen, Rush, Kuhn, Wistar, and others were teaching; there Hosack received the degree of doctor of medicine from the University of Pennsylvania. The inaugural dissertation dealt with cholera morbus. After practicing for short periods in Princeton and New York City, he felt the need for European postgraduate experience. Two years spent in Edinburgh and London resulted in a liberal exposure to men of letters, learned theologians, and distinguished citizens of each community. Botany was especially alluring as an allied medical science, an interest which proved to be particularly helpful upon return to the States. In the first year of practice in New York, he attracted a few private pupils—the beginning of a rapid rise to prominence. The following year Hosack was appointed professor of botany in Columbia College. Subsequently, he became associated with Samuel Bard, foremost physician at the time, who upon retirement bequeathed a large and attractive clientele to him. During the several epidemics of yellow fever, Hosack accepted pathogenesis by contagion and supported mild treatment for the afflicted in contrast to others who recommended bleeding and purging. He himself was stricken but recovered without incident.

Instruction in elocution aided him in his multiple and productive teaching assignments and in presenting lucid lectures, documented with detailed case histories. Since one of the measures of devotion to teaching is the encouragement given to the young, it is not surprising that pupils came from near and distant points to study under him.

He was fond of adopting protégés in adolescence and directing them toward medicine or the medical sciences. He served on the staff of New York Hospital, and filled, in succession, the chairs of materia medica in Columbia College, surgery and midwifery at the College of Physicians and Surgeons, and the theory and practice of physic and clinical medicine.

His first major scientific treatise, presenting his concept of vision, was prepared in London, transmitted to the Royal Society, and published in their *Transactions*. Accommodation of the eye was attributed to the action of the external muscles. Because the action of the iris was limited, the lens was thought not to possess accommodative powers. Although his concepts were not supported by subsequent investigators, Hosack was elected a member of the Royal Society at that time.

In discussing the cause of disease, he maintained that the body was judged to be no more, or less, than the sum of its organic and functional parts. Hosack summarized this concept as follows.[1]

The principles of the practice of medicine should invariably be deduced from the structure of the body and the cause of disease. Principles are but the assemblage and classification of facts, and are the only safeguards to practice, as has been well observed by Rush. The plan to be pursued in studying the theory and practice of medicine will be:

1st. The structure of the human frame, more especially the various functions it performs in health, including those that appertain to the mind.

2d. The natural functions of the system; the causes of disease, whether inherent in the body, or produced by the operation of external agents; the influence of climate, soil, clothing, food, sleep, and exercise, both bodily and mental; the passions of the mind; the functions peculiar to the sexes; the various trades and occupations; as also the sensible and adventitious qualities of the atmosphere in the production of endemic and epidemic diseases.

3d. How far the functions of the constitution extend their influence, in overcoming or preventing disease, as ascribed to it by the ancients and some moderns, under the term of *"vis medicatrix naturae."*

Hosack's home was warm with hospitality, radiant with refinement, and pleasant as an assembly place for distinguished New Yorkers. These included DeWitt Clinton, John Marshall, Fenimore Cooper, Washington Irving, Alexander Hamilton, and Aaron Burr, men of the post-Revolutionary times. He was one of the attending physicians in 1804 at the Burr-Hamilton duel. As a connoisseur of the fine arts, Hosack carried on a large correspondence with prominent literary and scientific persons in this country and abroad and promoted the arts, sciences, and literary tastes of the community.

In teaching and the practice of medicine, Hosack was punctual and industrious; when his counsel was sought as a consultant, he treated his fellow physicians with respect. Although primarily a professor of physic, he was competent in surgery, served at the Almshouse Hospital, and was one of the first in America to ligate the femoral artery for aneurysm and to treat hydrocele by injection. Upon being appointed to the chair of surgery at the opening of the College of Physicians and Surgeons, his introductory lecture, entitled "Surgery of the Ancients," contained his translations from Greek and Latin.

His son, Alexander E. Hosack, followed his father into medicine, and the son's widow presented Hosack Hall to the New York Academy of Medicine in 1889 as a memorial. David Hosack was partly responsible for the founding of Bellevue Hospital and became one of the four faculty members of the short-lived Rutgers Medical College. With his pupil and later partner, John W. Francis, the *American Medical and Philosophical Register* was established and published for four years. His major writings included *Essays on Various Subjects of Medical Science*,[2] in three volumes, and *A System of Practical Nosology*,[3] while his *Lectures on the Theory and Practice of Physic*,[4] delivered at the College of Physicians and Surgeons, was issued posthumously.

Hosack gave liberally to scientific and benevolent institutions. He was awarded an LLD by Princton, to which he bequeathed his extensive mineralogy collection. An early interest in botany reappeared in maturity in his founding the Elgin Botanic Garden, named after the birthplace of his father, opposite the cathedral at 50th Street and 5th Avenue.[5] The garden later was sold to the state and subsequently was acquired by Columbia University. A genus of plants was named for him, as were various species of *Hosackia* found in the Southwest.

1. *Lives of Eminent American Physicians and Surgeons,* S. D. Gross, ed., Philadelphia: Lindsay & Blakiston, 1861.
2. Hosack, D.: *Essays on Various Subjects of Medical Science,* 3 vol, New York: J. Seymour, 1824.
3. Hosack, D.: *A System of Practical Nosology,* New York: C. S. Van Winkle, 1818.
4. Hosack, D.: *Lectures on the Theory and Practice of Physic,* Philadelphia: H. Hooker, 1838.
5. Brown, A.: *The Elgin Botanic Garden,* Lancaster, Pa: New Era Printing Company, 1908.

John Redman Coxe (1773-1864)

JOHN REDMAN COXE, petulant professor at the University of Pennsylvania, was born in Trenton, New Jersey, and was raised by his physician grandfather, the distinguished John Redman of Philadelphia.[1] After attending lower school in London, young Coxe finished his classical studies in Edinburgh, where he attended hospitals and studied botany and natural history during the summer. In 1789, he returned to London and completed courses in anatomy and chemistry at the London Hospital. In his 17th year, Coxe

began the study of practical medicine under Benjamin Rush in Philadelphia and continued with him until the MD degree was received in 1794 from the University of Pennsylvania.

Composite by G. Bako

During the yellow fever epidemic of 1793, Coxe assisted Rush in caring each day for as many as 50 patients stricken with the disease. Following graduation he went abroad again, served as house-pupil for one year in the London Hospital, and later studied in the hospitals and clinics of Edinburgh and Paris.

At the age of 24, Coxe settled in Philadelphia, where he divided his professional efforts among practice, teaching, and writing. In practice he was an early advocate of vaccination. At the University he taught chemistry and later materia medica until his dismissal in 1835 led to a vehement public refutation. His first important published document, appearing in 1802, contained his *Practical Observations on Vaccination,* as well as the experience of the vaccination of himself and his son Edward Jenner Coxe, then 23 days old. This report helped to counteract the prejudice against vaccination and to foster confidence in its preventive value. Although Jenner had published his experimental observations in 1798 and Waterhouse of Boston had advocated the practice in 1800, suspicion of the procedure prevailed. Coxe noted:[2]

I shall here conclude with a short remark on the still existing prejudices of many against inoculation generally, under a false impression that, as all diseases are in the hands of the ALMIGHTY, it is a species of impiety to tempt him, by thus usurping his prerogative in producing a disease, which probably might have been escaped! But should not all who argue thus, to act consistently, refuse medical assistance in every instance? Does not accepting a dose of physic from the hands of a Physician, argue the same impiety, inasmuch, as without such aid, health may be restored by the blessing of PROVIDENCE? But the fact is, the error consists in blindly refusing to employ the means which are placed in our power, to remove the evils to which we are exposed.—That same bounteous CREATOR who has provided us with food necessary to our existence, has likewise supplied those medicines which are administered to our relief in a state of disease; and has given reason to man, to enable him to distinguish what may benefit, from what may injure him. Inoculation then should be viewed as a medicine, disagreeable in itself, yet administered to escape a greater evil.—In the same light ought we to view, and to prefer, this new species of inoculation; as it possesses every advantage, exempt from the disadvantages, of that dreadful disease the Smallpox.

In 1809, Coxe was appointed professor of chemistry at the University of Pennsylvania and served in this post until 1818, when he transferred to the chair of materia medica and pharmacy. As early as 1792, before receiving his degree, he assisted in the formation of the Chemical Society in Philadelphia and was elected by his fellow students to lecture on the subject. Coxe instructed prospective pharmacists on materia medica and pharmacy, and, as a founder of the Philadelphia College of Pharmacy in 1822, he is regarded as the father of pharmacy in Philadelphia. In that era most physicians compounded their own prescriptions, partly because pharmacies were scarce and partly from a desire to exercise closer control over the preparation and dispensing of chemicals and botanicals. Coxe introduced the jalap plant into the United States and devised the compound syrup of squill, de-

scribed in the *United States Pharmacopeia* and generally known as Coxe's hive syrup.

In the lecture hall Coxe was a clumsy demonstrator and a dull teacher. In fact, his conservative philosophy and uninspiring lectures drove the students to protest and the Trustees of the University to act. This led to dismissal from his professorship in 1835. Coxe resorted to the public press to refute the charges against him, but to no avail. In an attempt to answer academic accusations, he composed a detailed brief, more typical of a rebuttal in court for a criminal charge. The introductory sentences in the preface disclosed his skill in composition and are excerpted more for this reason than as an example of injustice.[3]

I PRESENT the following statement to the public, with extreme reluctance and pain. For nearly forty-five years I have been employed in the practice and study of medicine, and in teaching it to others, in the city of Philadelphia; and at the close of this period, myself and my family have been held up to derision, for my alleged incompetency to discharge the duties of the Chair of Materia Medica, which I have held for more than fifteen years of that time. No one of common sensibility, can be supposed to present to the public, a statement which records such a result, without extreme pain. But I have a duty, public and private, to perform; and I mean to perform it. I have suffered, and still do suffer from unmerited persecution and contumely; from the gross and scandalous violence of young men, the pupils of the Medical School, to whom its governors have seen fit to yield; and from the insidious artifices of older men, who have been willing to sacrifice me, even at the expense of the character of the University; but no sense of suffering shall deter me from exposing the injustice with which I have been treated. I executed the duties of my station with what I supposed to be general approbation, until it was deemed expedient by some members of the Medical Faculty to supply my place with such as might better suit their views.

I arraign the Medical Faculty of the University for their connivance at this act of scandalous indecorum and resistance to collegiate authority. Of this at least they have been guilty. The Professors may say that they did not stimulate it, and such as choose may believe them; but they had, everyone knows that they had, the undoubted means to repress the disorder, and they would not use them. The charge of which they stand convicted, is, that they approved of the rebellion and violence, however disgraceful to the college, it served their turn. They approved it, and in conscience and common sense it was their act, because they would not repress it when they might. Theirs was the outrage, without the merit of openly assuming its responsibility, and some of them may have occasion to recollect the precedent hereafter.

Coxe achieved his greatest success in medical writing and medical journalism; he was responsible for an exceptionally high percentage of the medical literature published in Philadelphia in his time. *The Medical Museum,* a quarterly periodical, was published under his aegis between 1804 and 1811, and was followed by service as editor of the *Emporium of Arts and Sciences* for the five volumes published in 1812 and 1813. *The American Dispensatory,* which followed closely Duncan's second edition of the *Edinburgh New Dispensatory* appeared first in 1806 and went through nine editions. In 1808, he published *The Philadelphia Medical Dictionary,* which was revised in 1817. His first critique entitled *An Inquiry Into the Claims of William Harvey,* appeared in 1829; in 1846, *The Writings of Hippocrates and Galen* was issued; and after a decade in retirement he published his *Essays on Recognition of Friends in Another World.*

By faith, Coxe was an Episcopalian and was active as a vestryman. He served as physician of the Pennsylvania Hospital and member of the Board of Trustees of the University of Pennsylvania; in addition, he was a member of the Philosophical Society of Philadelphia, the Batavian Society of Sciences at Harlem, the Royal Medical Society of London, and the Royal Society of Sciences of Copenhagen. His scholarship included proficiency in nine languages. His library, one of the largest private collections in the country, was sold at auction after his death.

1. Coxe, M. C.: A Biographical Sketch of John Redman Coxe, M.D., and John Redman, M.D., *Univ Penn Med Bull* 20:294-301, 1908.

2. Coxe, J. R., *Practical Observations on Vaccination: or Inoculation for the Cow-Pock,* Philadelphia: J. Humphreys, 1802.

3. Coxe, J. R.: *An Appeal to the Medical Public From the Proceedings of the Trustees of the University of Pennsylvania, Vacating the Chair of Materia Medica and Pharmacy,* Philadelphia: J. R. Coxe, 1835.

Composite by G. Bako

James Thacher (1754-1844)

JAMES THACHER, a native of Barnstable, Massachusetts, a physician of Plymouth, and a prolific writer, prepared an *American Medical Biography,* one of the first textbooks on the practice of medicine in America, several treatises on a variety of subjects, and a diary of his experiences during the Revolutionary War.[1] His father, a farmer, and unable to give him the proper education of his time, apprenticed his son at the age of 16 to Abner Hersey, the leading practitioner of Barnstable. Following five years of practical medicine, Thacher seemed prepared to practice on his own; however, the events of 1775 stirred his patriotism, and, upon application to the medical board of the provincial congress, he was appointed surgeon's mate to the military hospital in Cambridge. Active duty embraced a number of assignments, including service in Whitcomb's regiment at Prospect Hill and later in Boston after the evacuation by the British, and participation in the retreat from Ticonderoga. In succession, he was assigned to the military hospital above Albany, served in the field with the First Virginia Regiment and then with the Massachusetts Regiment, spending a miserable winter (1779-1780) in New Jersey. He retired from the Army in 1783, having witnessed the surrender of Lord Cornwallis in Yorktown.

Thacher kept a careful diary while on military duty, which was not published until 1823. This describes the agonies of hunger, fatigue, cold, and inadequate clothing of the Continental soldiers in the field. Although untrained in composition, Thacher's diary was well prepared and remains an important historical document. The *Military Journal* began in January 1775, with remarks on rights and liberties for the Colonies that should never bore freemen.[2]

MILITARY JOURNAL.—1775

January.—At the precise period when my medical studies and education are completed, . . . and I am contemplating the commencement of a new career in life, I find our country about to be involved in all the horrors of a civil war. A series of arbitrary and oppressive measures, on the part of the mother country, has long been advancing to that awful crisis, when an appeal to the power of the sword becomes inevitable. The event of this mighty struggle is to decide an affair of infinite magnitude, not merely as it respects the present generation, but as it will affect the welfare and happiness of unborn millions. The great fundamental principle, in the present controversy, is the right which is claimed by the Parliament of Great Britain, to exercise dominion, as the only supreme, and uncontrollable legislative power over all the American Colonies. "Can they make laws to bind the colonies in all cases whatever; levy taxes on them without their consent; dispose of the revenues, thus raised, without their control; . . . divert the usual channels of justice; deprive the colonists of trial by a jury of their countrymen; in short, break down the barriers which their forefathers have erected against arbitrary power, and enforce their edicts by fleets and armies?" . . . "The people of these colonies consider themselves as British subjects, entitled to all the rights and privileges of Freemen. It is inseparately essential to the freedom of a people, and the undoubted right of Englishmen, that no taxes be imposed on them but with their own consent, given personally or by their representatives." . . . All acts of Parliament therefore, for raising a revenue in America, are considered as depriving us of our property, without our consent, and consequently as a palpable infringement of our ancient rights and privileges. They are unconsitutional and arbitrary laws, subversive of the liberties and privileges secured to us by our royal charters.

It is not consistent with the principles which actuate the American people, ever tamely to submit to such a degrading system of government; not however from a want of loyalty to our king, . . . but it is an innate love of liberty, and our just rights, that impels us to the arduous struggle. In no country, it is asserted, is the love of liberty more deeply rooted, or the knowledge of the rights inherent to freemen more generally diffused, or better understood, than among the British American Colonies. Our religious and political privileges are derived from our virtuous fathers; they were inhaled with our earliest breath; and are, and will I trust ever be, implanted and cherished in the bosom of the present and future generations. These are the prevalent sentiments in New England at this eventful crisis.

The practice of civilian medicine was begun in Plymouth in 1784, where Thacher soon became the leading practitioner and medical tutor, recognized for his skill in each pursuit, but especially for his medical writing. The first edition of his *American Modern Practice: or, a Simple Method of Prevention and Cure of Diseases* was published in 1817. The introduction is an important historical document, for it includes a résumé of ancient medicine, pertinent details of 17 medical schools then in operation in the Colonies, and reference to several of the 20 medical societies, the 12 medical periodicals, and more than 200 hospitals that had been established in America in a little more than half a century.[3]

AMONG the various sciences and literary pursuits of life, there is no more pre-eminently important than that which is emphatically styled the healing art; that which brings health and joy to mankind. It is an inestimable blessing, bestowed in mercy, to counterpoise the frail condition of our nature, and to meliorate or remedy the miseries which result from the indulgence of our vicious propensities. It assuages the anguish of corporeal disease, and soothes that keen mental distress, which overwhelms the faculties of the soul.

The *American Medical Biography* of 1828 contains the biographies of 168 physicians, including Zabdiel Boylston, Joseph Warren, and John Warren of Boston; Cadwallader Colden, Samuel Bard, and James Tilton of New York; and John Morgan, John Redman, Benjamin Rush, William

Shippen, Adam Kuhn, and Caspar Wistar of Philadelphia.[4] The plan of presentation was retained in subsequent expanded editions or successors: the last, prepared by Kelly and Burrage in 1928, entitled *Dictionary of American Medical Biography*, includes 2,049 sketches.[5]

Less important treatises were his *Observations on Hydrophobia* (1812), *The American New Dispensary* (1810), *History of the Town of Plymouth* (1832), *The American Orchardist* (1822), *A Practical Treatise on the Management of Bees* (1829), and *An Essay on Demonology, Ghosts and Apparitions* (1831). In the last essay Thacher offered a sound description of the superstitious mind and an interesting reflection upon quackery, composed in delightful style for one with little opportunity for formal education in grammar and English.[6]

Such is the constitution of the human mind, that it never attains to perfection; it is constantly susceptible of erroneous impressions and perverse propensities. The faculties of the soul are bound in thraldom by superstition, and the intellect, under its influence, is scarcely capable of reflecting on its divine origin, its nobleness and dignity. The mind that is imbued with a superstitious temperament, is liable to incessant torment, and is prepared to inflict the most atrocious evils on mankind; even murder, suicide, and merciless persecution, have proceeded from, and been sanctioned by a superstitious spirit. It is this, in its most appalling aspect, which impels the heathen to a life of mutilation and perpetual pain and torment of body, which degrades the understanding below that of a brute.

Notwithstanding that in all the medical institutions in the United States, the most judicious energetic measures have been adopted to prevent the evils of quackery, there are ignorant and unprincipled impostors, who set at defiance all learning and theoretical knowledge, and practise the vilest acts and deceptions, sporting with the health and lives of their fellow-men without remorse. Such miscreants are too frequently encouraged by the heedless multitude, who, delighting in marvellous and magical airs, readily yield themselves dupes to the grossest absurdities.

1. Viets, H. R.: James Thacher and His Influence on American Medicine, *Virginia Med Monthly*, Aug 1949, pp 384-399.
2. Thacher, J.: *A Military Journal During the American Revolutionary War*, Boston: Richardson & Lord, 1823.
3. Thacher, J.: *American Modern Practice: or, a Simple Method of Prevention and Cure of Diseases*, Boston: E. Read, 1817.
4. Thacher, J.: *American Medical Biography*, Boston: Richardson & Lord and Cottons & Barnard, 1828.
5. Kelly, H. A., and Burrage, W. L.: *Dictionary of American Medical Biography*, New York: D. Appleton and Co., 1928.
6. Thacher, J.: *An Essay on Demonology, Ghosts and Apparitions*, Boston: Carter and Hendee, 1831.

Composite by G. Bako

William Shippen, Jr.
(1736-1808)

THERE ARE THREE SOURCE ITEMS worthy of reference in a narrative of the ambitions, accomplishments, and heartaches of William Shippen, Jr., distinguished as the first professor of anatomy in the first medical school founded in the American colonies at Philadelphia. He is also identified with the College of Physicians of Philadelphia, of which he was a cofounder (1787) and, in his last years, its president. Caspar Wistar, who followed Shippen in the chair of anatomy, delivered Shippen's eulogium before the College in 1809.[1] The second document is a two-part article, by W. S. Middleton, published in 1932.[2] The most recent of the basic contributions is Shippen's diary edited by Betsy Copping Corner.[3]

Wistar's eulogy is factual, but filled with quaint expressions, the epitome of genteel discourse a century and a half ago. Middleton's account is particularly valuable for its documentation of the founding of the medical school, and of Shippen's misadventures while serving with the Continental Army; whereas Mrs. Corner presents, along with biographical data, a carefully annotated transcription of Shippen's student diary, prepared in London, 1759-1760, and a translation, by George W. Corner, of Shippen's Edinburgh inaugural dissertation (1761), entitled *De placentae cum utero nexu*. The dissertation, judged to be an unimportant contribution in obstetrics, is the only scientific publication attributed to Shippen.

His father, William Shippen, Sr., a Philadelphian, studied medicine as an apprentice under Jorn Kearsley, Sr., and went directly into practice. He achieved a high reputation as a physician in Pennsylvania and New Jersey. He was one of the founders of the College of New Jersey (Princeton), donated handsome sums to the institution, and was a trustee of the College of Philadelphia, and for many years physician to the Pennsylvania Hospital.

His son, William, Jr., attended the West Nottingham Academy kept by the Rev. Samuel Finley, in which John Morgan and Benjamin Rush also studied. William, Jr. received the AB degree from the College of New Jersey in 1754. As valedictorian of his class, he displayed great elocutionary talent. After three years of apprenticeship to his father, young William was sent to Europe for study in London and Edinburgh. While in London, he lodged with John Hunter.[3] A hastily written diary mirrors his life in that city and includes details of study with the celebrated Hunters.

His working days in London were devoted to the dissecting room or observations in the hospitals. In free time he loved to attend theatrical performances and saw Garrick in *Macbeth* and other plays. Before leaving London, Shippen met Dr. John Fothergill, who later presented a series of anatomical crayon drawings and models to the Pennsylvania Hospital and proposed him as a candidate for the professorship of anatomy. Although anatomy seems to have had the greatest appeal during the early years in London, he walked the wards at St. Thomas', St. George's, and St. Bartholomew's hospitals, and audited lectures in midwifery by MacKenzie.[1]

After London, Shippen went to Edinburgh for the MD degree. In so doing, he was following the policy of acquiring practical experience based upon a solid anatomical foundation from the Hunters before entering upon the theory of medicine at Edinburgh under William Cullen and Monro *Secundus*. Paris was the last medical center visited before returning to America in 1762. By then, Shippen was qualified to teach anatomy and to practice midwifery, pursuits relatively new in America and free of competition. Nor were there many physicians practicing in Philadelphia who had received the MD degree from any of the European schools. Shippen began his lectures in anatomy to students of medicine and to selected gentlemen. There were only 12 pupils in the first class, but the number increased rapidly in subsequent years. In the spring of 1765, John Morgan, who had long been interested in the founding of a medical school in Philadelphia, proposed to the trustees of the College of Philadelphia the establishment of a medical school in connection with the college. He was subsequently made professor of the theory and practice of medicine. Shippen, professor of anatomy and surgery, received the second appointment. The other charter professorships were held by Adam Kuhn and Benjamin Rush. Shippen was immediately successful in teaching.[1]

He went through the substance of each preceding lecture by interrogation, instead of recapitulation, thus fixing the attention of the students—and his manner was so happy, that this grave process proceeded like a piece of amusement. His irony of a delicate kind, and so blended with good humor, that he could repress forwardness, and take notice of negligence, so as to admonish his class without too much exposing the defaulter.

In midwifery, Shippen enjoyed similar success. Lectures in midwifery, begun in 1765, constituted the first systematic obstetrical instruction in America. He admitted women as well as men to the lectures but seized the leadership from the female midwives.[1]

Confessed as it now is, that the important process of parturition ought to be superintended by persons whose professional knowledge will enable them to decide confidently, and to act promptly when the case requires it, still in Philadelphia, at this time, there were very few occasions where medical men were employed for this purpose in the first instance. It was only when something very important was to be done, that they were resorted to—and, very often, when too late.

Two great disappointments befell Shippen; one occurred in the armed services, the other at home. In 1776, he was appointed chief physician to the Flying Camp of 10,-000 men, and later placed in charge of the entire hospital service of the Continental Army west of the Hudson River. John Morgan, Director-General of the Medical Service of the Army, was responsible for the territory east of the Hudson. Thus began a series of differences which led to estrangement and an open breach. Morgan was dismissed in 1777 following reorganization of the medical department; whereas Shippen was elevated to the supreme command of the medical department. Not long after, he was accused of appropriating military funds and medical supplies, was court-martialed, acquitted, but came before the tribunal a second time. He resigned after the second trial and, although not truly cleared, returned to Philadelphia and accepted the professorship of anatomy, surgery, and midwifery at the medical school. His second tribulation was the death of his son, who had been given every educational opportunity including 4 years in Europe. He died in his early 30's after a long period of ill health. Deep sorrow led to solemn introspection, and "he now read and thought much on the subject of universal restoration, and finally adopted that belief, with great confidence."[1]

1. Wistar, C.: *Eulogium on Doctor William Shippen; Delivered Before the College of Physicians of Philadelphia, March, 1809*, Philadelphia: T. Dobson & Son, 1818; reprinted with minor changes, *Philadelphia J. Med Phys Sci* 5:173-188, 1822.

2. Middleton, W. S.: William Shippen, Junior, *Ann Med Hist* n.s. 4:440-452, 538-549, 1932.

3. Corner, B. C.: *William Shippen, Jr.: Pioneer in American Medical Education*, Philadelphia: American Philosophical Society, 1951.

Composite by G. Bako

Caspar Wistar (1761-1818)

CASPAR WISTAR, whose maternal ancestors were English and paternal ancestors German, was brought up in the Society of Friends in Philadelphia. He is probably best remembered for the Wistar Institute of Anatomy and Biology.[1] Caspar attended the Penn Charter School founded by William Penn; when he had completed his classical education, he began the study of medicine under John Redman, assisted John Jones in his practice while this physician was temporarily absent from New York during the occupation by the British troops, and attended the lectures of Drs. Morgan, Shippen, Rush, and Kuhn. Wistar received the degree of bachelor of medicine from the University in 1782. In keeping with the tradition at that time of ambitious young physicians in the States to seek further training in Europe, he spent a year in London and a somewhat longer time in Edinburgh. Here he was a favorite of William Cullen. The MD degree was conferred by the University in 1786, with the thesis *De animo demisso,* a philosophical discussion of mind and matter, dedicated to Benjamin Franklin and William Cullen.

Wistar returned to Philadelphia and served as physician to the Philadelphia Dispensary following its establishment in 1787. From 1793 to 1810 he was physician to the Pennsylvania Hospital. He was largely instrumental in uniting, in 1791, the medical departments of the University of Pennsylvania and the College of Philadelphia, which received a new charter in 1783. Wistar became an adjunct professor to Shippen in anatomy, midwifery, and surgery in the University of Pennsylvania. Subsequently, surgery and midwifery were separated from anatomy, and, in 1808, upon the death of Shippen, Wistar was made professor of anatomy.

Wistar's publications were limited; his best work was *A System of Anatomy for the Use of Students of Medicine* published in two volumes (1811-1814).[2] The text was the first comprehensive treatise on the subject prepared by an American and published in this country. The treatise reflects his knowledge of anatomy and physiology, best displayed in his lectures to the students. Wistar's other writings include scattered unimportant scientific contributions, except for the study of the development of the ethmoid and spenoid bones and their attachments. The most appeared in the *Transactions of the American Philosophical Society.*

Wistar's contemporary biographers paid greatest attention to his scholarly talents in the classroom. His lectures, prepared with diligence and skill, were delivered with admirable fluency. His reputation as a practitioner was based upon prolonged questioning and meticulous management of the afflicted. As an unselfish physician and friend, Wistar cared for the ill during the yellow fever epidemic of 1793. In 1809, he founded the Society for the Promotion of Vaccination, and succeeded Benjamin Rush as president of the Society for the Abolition of Slavery. In 1787, he was elected to the American Philosophical Society, was one of its most active members, and, in 1815, succeeded Thomas Jefferson as its

president, serving in this office for three years.

Wistar's gregariousness was widely known from his social evenings. He kept open house or provided regular entertainment for students, members of the Philosophical Society, visiting scientists, from near or far, and a host of others. Wishing to perpetuate the tradition of the open houses, his associates formed the Wistar Association designed to sponsor the "Wistar parties."[3]

Another illustration of his wide interests included an honor accorded him by Thomas Nuttall, a personal friend and distinguished botanist. The flowering vine with its drooping clusters, *Wisteria speciosa,* was named by Nuttall and was dedicated to Caspar Wistar; the spelling was changed later to "Wistaria" to identify properly the honoree.[4]

After his death, Wistar's family presented his large anatomical collection to the University of Pennsylvania for an anatomical museum. The collection was enhanced by the anatomical specimens prepared by his successor, William E. Horner, and for several years was known as the Wistar and Horner Museum. In 1892, it was recognized as the Wistar Institute of Anatomy and Biology. This was modestly endowed by a great-nephew, Gen Isaac Jones Wistar, as an independent instiution and is housed in a separate structure within the University of Pennsylvania complex.

1. Morris, C.: "Caspar Wistar," in Gross, S.D. (ed.): *Lives of Eminent American Physicians and Surgeons,* Philadelphia: Lindsay & Blakiston, 1861, pp. 116-138.

2. Wistar, C.: *A System of Anatomy for the Use of Students of Medicine,* 2 vol, Philadelphia: T. Dobson, 1811-1814.

3. Carson, H. L.: *The Centenary of the Wistar Party,* Philadelphia: Wistar Association, 1918.

4. Fernald, M. L.: *Gray's Manual of Botany,* New York: American Book Co., 1950.

Philip Syng Physick (1768-1837)

THE NAME OF THIS PHILADELPHIA PHYSI-CIAN is intriguing, but would have been more so had he been a professor of physic rather than a professor of surgery. Philip was born of a distinguished Philadelphia family.[1] On his mother's side were silver-smiths; his grandfather's artisanship was responsible for the silver stand which held the ink for the final composition of the Declaration of Independence and the Constitution. Philip's father, Edmund Physick, was keeper of the Pennsylvania Great Seal and in the post-Revolution days was manager for the Penn family in America.[2]

Philip attended undergraduate college at the University of Pennsylvania, and soon after began the study of medicine under Adam Kuhn, graduating AM at the age of 20. Following graduation, Philip traveled to London with his father, became an apprentice to John Hunter in the dissecting room, and attended the classes of William Hunter in the Great Windmill Street School of Anatomy. Physick was appointed house surgeon to St. George's Hospital at the end of the year of apprenticeship. He received a diploma from the Royal College of Surgeons of London and then went to Edinburgh for further study. There has been speculation as to the cause of this transfer from London to Edinburgh, since each city enjoyed an enviable distinction as a remarkable medical center in Europe. Evidence indicates that a warm social and professional attachment had developed between Physick and Hunter, and there was little to choose between London and Edinburgh. Indeed, Hunter had urged Physick to remain in London as his assistant. The thesis, submitted in 1792 for fulfillment of requirements for the MD degree, discussed apoplexy; it was composed in Latin and was dedicated to John Hunter.

With the intellectual security of having studied in Europe and with a European degree in hand, Physick began the practice of surgery in Philadelphia. This venture was interrupted by several periods of ill health. Infirmities included yellow fever, an attack of typhoid fever (or typhus), renal colic, and myocardial failure. During a bout with yellow fever, Physick was convinced that bleeding and purging, as recommended by Benjamin Rush, personal friend and personal physician, were responsible for his recovery.[3] In 1794, Physick was elected to the staff of the Pennsylvania Hospital and the Philadelphia Almshouse. He was professor of surgery at the University of Pennsylvania from 1805 to 1819 and then professor of anatomy until 1831. The establishment of the chair of surgery was the final step in separating surgery from anatomy. The physiological principles of surgery, expounded by John Hunter, were carried by Physick into practice and teaching. For this he became recognized as the Father of American Surgery.[4] His assignment at the university was strengthened by a petition from the students who wanted to hear more from this conservative lecturer. Physick confined his lectures to those subjects with which he had actual experience. Samuel Gross noted that "As a surgeon . . . he never spilled a drop of blood uselessly or, as a teacher ever wasted a word." Physick's interest in medical education prompted Thomas Jefferson to seek his advice in planning for the "anatomical school" at the University of Virginia.

The writings of Physick were primarily descriptions of a technical device or a preliminary report of a new or modified surgical instrument. One might assume that the technical artistry of his silversmith grandfather aided him in the design and modification of surgical equipment. He revised, for example, Desault's splint for fractures of the thigh. In some instances, his patients were bled to the critical point of exsanguination to promote relaxation in reducing difficult fractures. Physick introduced absorbent ligatures of kid and buckskin[5] and was successful in treating ununited fractures of the humerus without open surgery.[6] A seton was threaded through the affected area, which led to inflammation, a foreign body reaction, and stimulation of new bone formation. A forceps and a curved needle were fashioned for ligaturing an artery.[7] Physick devised an operation for artificial anus,[8] and improved the lithotomy instruments. He designed a catheter and bougie in one instrument, a dental forceps, a double cannula for snaring tonsils, an instrument for hemorrhoidectomy, and a procedure for enucleation of the lens in treatment of cataracts. One of Physick's most famous patients was Chief Justice John Marshall. After Physick had retired from active practice, he was consulted by Marshall, then aged 76, because of painful bladder stones. The operation was successful, and Marshall survived for several years.[9]

The name of Physick in the practice of medicine could not go long without becoming a victim of doggerel rhymes or satire. The following verse is taken from "The Court of Session Garland," published by T. G. Stevenson, Edinburgh, 1839.[10]

Sing Physic! Sing Physic! for Philip Syng Physick
Is dubbed Dr. Phil for his wonderful skill;
Each sick phiz he'll physic, he'll cure every phthisic,
Their lips fill with Physic, with potion and pill.

Syng Physick for fees seeks the sick man to physic,
But unsought hopes the fee of his physics and skill;

So ne'er let Phil Physick or physic the fee seek
Nor the sick man be fee-sick of Physic and Phil.

Let physick sing Philip, for Philip Syng Physick
From plain Philip Physick is dubbed Dr. Phil,
Sing Syng then, each patient, while Philip shall physic,
And Physick shall fillip with potion and pill.

That Apollo the god is of physic and song,
Each school-boy I think, will readily follow;
Then since to his name the same arts do belong,
Be Philip Syng Physick our Magnus Apollo.

Garrison seems to underrate Physick and could discover little of consequence in his writings.[11] However, in judging Physick as a professor of surgery in the 19th century, I estimate his accomplishments as well as inventive ingenuity to be highly commendable. To have trained under the Hunters of London, been offered as assistantship with John Hunter, to have received a doctorate at Edinburgh, and to have been one of the first teachers of surgery in one of the foremost medical schools in America is worthy of note.

1. Randolph, J.: A Memoir on the Life and Character of Philip Syng Physick, M.D., Philadelphia: T. K. & P. G. Collins, 1839.

2. Agnew, L. R. C., and Sheldon, G. F.: Philip Syng Physick (1768-1837): "The Father of American Surgery," J Med Educ 35:541-549 (June) 1960.

3. Sheldon, G. F.: Rush and Physick: An Important Medical Friendship, Trans Coll Physicians Phila 29:28-38 (July) 1961.

4. Bell, J.: "Philip Syng Physick," in Lives of Eminent American Physicians and Surgeons of the Nineteenth Century, S. D. Gross, ed., Philadelphia: Lindsay and Blakiston, 1861.

5, Physick, P.: Absorbable Ligatures, Eclectic Repertory 6:389, 1816.

6. Physick, P.: The Use of the Seton in Ununited Fractures, Med Repository 1:127, 1804.

7. Physick, P.: Description of a Forceps, Amer J Med Sci 2:116-117, 1828.

8. Physick, P.: Extracts from an Account of a Case, in Which a New and Peculiar Operation for Artificial Anus Was Performed, Philadelphia: J Med Phys Sci 13:199-202, 1826.

9. Randall, A.: Philip Syng Physick's Last Major Operation, Ann Med Hist 9:133-141 (March) 1937.

10. Rogers, F. B.: Witty Verses About Dr. Philip Syng Physick, Composed by Friends in 1792, Phila Med 54:933-942 (Aug. 29), 1958.

11. Garrison, F. H.: An Introduction to the History of Medicine, 4th ed, Philadelpha: W. B. Saunders Co., 1929.

John Conrad Otto (1774-1844)

JOHN CONRAD OTTO brought the first definitive account of hemophilia to the attention of physicians in America and Europe although descriptions of familial bleeders were contained in the writings of the ancients. Otto was born near Woodbury, New Jersey, into a family of physicians of Swiss-German stock. While his father served in the Revolutionary War, his grandfather attended the American Army at the encampment at Valley Forge and was in charge of the hospital during the tragic winter of 1778.[1] Otto graduated AB from the College of New Jersey (Princeton) at the age of 18 and was apprenticed to Benjamin Rush the following spring. In 1796, he graduated MD from the University of Pennsylvania, presenting an inaugural essay on epilepsy.

Otto, closely affiliated with Rush, began the practice of medicine in Philadelphia and was physician to the Dispensary, the Orphan Asylum, and the Magdalen Asylum. He succeeded Rush as attending physician at the Pennsylvania Hospital in 1813. Like Rush, he had extensive experience with epidemic yellow fever and in 1798, suffered

himself from the disease. He was also afflicted periodically with acute attacks of gouty arthritis. Otto served admirably, in 1832, as chairman of a committee to control the cholera epidemic in Philadelphia. During the later years of his service at the Pennsylvania Hospital, which attracted students from various parts of the country, he was in charge of the medical wards.

Otto is described by his biographers as a practitioner of sound medical judgment, endowed with a deep sense of responsibility and displaying tenderness and humane regard for his patients. On his teaching rounds personal attention was given and pertinent inquiries were made to patients in an unaffected, although impressive, manner, meanwhile addressing himself to the students upon the significant aspects of each case. Otto was neither brilliant nor imaginative in scientific accomplishments and lacked critical scrutiny in his published comments on therapy. Fortunately his contributions to the literature were limited, for, in each instance, his recommendations for management were not confirmed by others. He returned to the study of epilepsy a quarter of a century following his inaugural essay, and in one patient attributed to anthelmintics a four-year period of freedom from symptoms. The use of calomel and opium until salivation developed was reported to be helpful in several forms of chronic rheumatism; in hemophilia, the disease for which he is best remembered, he reported benefit from sodium sulfate. Such deficiencies should be counterbalanced by his clinical description of fatal bleeding, termed "hemophilia" by Schönlein a quarter of a century later.

Krumbhaar documented an excellent history of hemophilia noting that in the *Talmud* (about 200 AD) circumcision of a child was forbidden when the procedure had proved fatal successively in two brothers.[2] He then listed subsequent examples of familial fatal bleeding and concluded with the 1894 reference to J. Homer Wright, who demonstrated impaired coagulability of the blood in hemophilia. Otto's rather complete description was a notable contribution to recognition of this condition as a specific entity. The account appeared in the *Medical Repository* of 1803. A Mrs. Smith from New Hampshire transmitted the bleeding tendency successively to her male descendants over a period of eight decades. Although females are exempt, they are capable of transmitting it to their male children. Only the essential clinical features were presented; the remainder of the report was devoted to therapy and a personal communication from Benjamin Rush. The clinical features were described as follows.[3]

About seventy or eighty years ago, a woman by the name of Smith, settled in the vicinity of Plymouth, New Hampshire, and transmitted the following idiosyncrasy to her descendants. It is one, she observed, to which her family is unfortunately subject, and had been the source not only of great solicitude, but frequently the cause of death. If the least scratch is made on the skin of some of them, as mortal a hemorrahagy will eventually ensue as if the largest wound is inflicted.

A few years since the sulphate of soda was accidentally found to be completely curative of the hemorrhages I have described. An ordinary purging dose, administered two or three days in succession, generally stops them; and by a more frequent repetition, is certain of producing this effect.

It is a surprising circumstance that the males only are subject to this strange affection, and that all of them are not liable to it. Some persons, who are curious, suppose they can distinguish the bleeders (for this is the name given to them) even in infancy; but as yet the characteristic marks are not ascertained sufficiently definite. Although the females are exempt, they are still capable of transmitting it to their male children.

The persons subject to this hemorrhagic disposition are remarkably healthy, and, when indisposed, they do not differ in their complaints, except in this particular, from their neighbors. No age is exempt, nor does any one appear to be particularly liable to it. The situation of their residence is not favourable to scorbutic affections or disease in general. They live, like the inhabitants of the country, upon solid and nutritious food, and when arrived to manhood, are athletic, of florid complexions, and extremely irascible.

1. Parrish, I.: Biographical Memoir of John C. Otto, M.D., *Trans Coll Physicians Phila* 1:305-318, 1845.
2. Krumbhaar, E. B.: John Conrad Otto and the Recognition of Hemophilia, *Bull Johns Hopkins Hosp* 46:123-140, 1930.
3. Otto, J. C.: An Account of an Hemorrhagic Disposition Existing in Certain Families, *Med Repository* 6:1-4, 1803.

Library College of Physicians, Philadelphia

Nathaniel Chapman (1780-1853)

NATHANIEL CHAPMAN, first president of the American Medical Association, was born at Summer Hill, Fairfax County, Virginia, on the banks of the Potomac, into a family of means.[1] He received his early education at the Classical Academy of Alexandria, founded by George Washington. At the age of 15, Nathaniel began his apprenticeship in medicine. He read first with John Weems of Georgetown, Maryland, and later with Dick of Alexandria, Virginia, who was often called by George Washington and stood at his bedside in death. By then Chapman had shown a fondness for literature and displayed poetic talents evidenced by paraphrasing selected odes of Horace. In 1797, he began formal medical training in the medical school of the University of Pennsylvania and became a private pupil of Benjamin Rush. He studied the classics as well as read medicine and completed the regular course of study by 1801 and graduated with honors.

Chapman's inaugural essay concerned hydrophobia, a subject suggested by Rush to bolster his own theory of disease. Chapman also prepared a companion thesis on the sympathetic connections of the stomach with the other regions of the body, a concept to which he returned in later years. He left for Europe immediately after graduation and spent the first year as a private pupil of Abernethy in London, followed by two years in Edinburgh, the mecca for medical studies at that time. While in Edinburgh, he was soon recognized for his delightful personality, sparkling wit, gay and jovial mood, and his outstanding social charms.

Returning to Philadelphia in 1804, Chapman almost immediately became a favorite with the upper classes of society and established firm associations with the academic community. His initial venture was a private course of lectures in obstetrics and an alliance with T. C. James, who, in 1810, was appointed professor of midwifery in the University. In 1813, following the death of Benjamin Rush and the reorganization of faculty and curriculum, Chapman was appointed professor of materia medica. His lectures on this subject were afterward incorporated in his *Elements of Therapeutics and Materia Medica,*[2] judged to be one of the excellent treatises in the English langauge on this subject at the time of publication.

In 1816, Chapman's appointment to the chair of the theory and practice of medicine and clinical medicine, for more than a third of a century, led to distinction and finally a national reputation.

A deliberate and emphatic lecturer, Chapman was thoroughly in command of the situation and displayed a great erudition, drawing examples from his large experience and enlivening dull subjects with a pun or an anecdote. His theory of medicine, expounded immediately before the discovery of the cellular composition of body tissue and the pathogenesis of bacteria and living organisms in the cause of disease, hardly outlived his time. However, Chapman recognized the difference in structure and function in tissues and organs and diversity of pathological conditions and restored the classification of diseases discarded by Rush. In management, he was conservative and an ardent phlebotomist, even recommending bloodletting in hemorrhaging patients.

In 1817, Chapman established the Medical Institute of Philadelphia, one of the first postgraduate medical schools in America; there he conducted courses for 20 years. In 1820, he founded the *Philadelphia Journal of the Medical and Physical Sciences,* several years later to be changed to the *American Journal of the Medical Sciences.* Many of his contributions appeared in this journal. He was also responsible for several monographs and reports of varying lengths. In 1847, Chapman was elected the first President of the American Medical Association, and when he took office at their first meeting in 1848, he spoke as follows:[3]

Believe me, gentlemen, that I feel extremely gratified in meeting you on this occasion, and I cannot forbear to tender to you my respectful salutations. Taking the liveliest interest in the great cause in which we are all embarked, I greet you with a welcome, warm, cordial, and sincere.

This assemblage presents a spectacle of moral grandeur delightful to contemplate. Few of the kind have I ever witnessed more imposing in its aspect, and certainly none inspired by purer motives, or having views of a wider range of beneficence. The profession to which we belong, once venerated on account of its antiquity,—its various and profound science—its elegant literature—its polite accomplishments—its virtues,—has become corrupt, and degenerate, to the forfeiture of its social position, and with it, of the homage it formerly received spontaneously and universally. Do not suppose that I comprise the whole profession in this reprobation. There are numerous members of it, who still retain the qualities by which it was formerly distinguished. It may, indeed, be affirmed, that never in its history has it exhibited so many claims to respect as at this very moment. With the present century the spirit of philosophy began to be infused into it, creative of real and substantial improvements in its theories and modes of practice, raising it from a low and conjectural art, to a place among the legitimate sciences, by which great good is already attained, and further benefit of inestimable value promised to suffering humanity. Nor have its disciples among us lingered behind in the career of reform and general advancement. Yet the preceding averment of the deterioration of the profession in some of its features, cannot be denied. The truth of it, indeed, is everywhere recognized and proclaimed. Complaints, at first heard only in the murmurs of discontent, are now so loud, distinct, and potential, as not to be disregarded or admit of further postponement. The commission which accredits you to this Association sufficiently attests the tone of professional sentiment on the subject. Does it not declare the fact, that the profession is environed by difficulties and dangers, arising mainly from the too ready admixture into it of individuals unworthy of the association, either by intellectual culture, or moral discipline, by whom it is abased? and are you not imperatively instructed to purify its taints and abuses, and restore it to its former elevation and dignity?

1. Richman, I.: *The Brightest Ornament: A Biography of Nathaniel Chapman, M.D.*, Bellefonte, Pa: Pennsylvania Heritage, Inc., 1967.
2. Chapman, N.: *Discourses on the Elements of Therapeutics and Materia Medica*, 2 vol, Philadelphia: J. Webster, 1817-1819.
3. Chapman, N.: Minutes of the First Annual Meeting of the American Medical Association, *Trans Amer Med Assoc* 1:7-9, 1848.

Stubbins H. Ffirth (1784-1820)

THE CONTRIBUTIONS OF STUBBINS H. FFIRTH to the pathogenesis of yellow fever more than a century and a half ago are exemplary. Stubbins was born in Salem, New Jersey, and conducted experiments on the epidemiology of yellow fever while pursuing his medical training at the University of Pennsylvania. The critical events in the thesis entitled, *A Treatise on Malignant Fever; with an Attempt to Prove Its Non-Contagious Nature,* were presented for graduation in 1804.[1] Ffirth described his inability to transmit yellow fever to animals or to himself through injection, ingestion, inhalation, or subcutaneous instillation of excreta from the afflicted. The dissertation is introduced by a chronological history of malignant fever in North America, and complements the investigations of Cathrall on dogs, cats, and fowl also carried out in Philadelphia a few years earlier. The studies by Ffirth were designed to discover the nature, properties, and qualities of the black vomit from patients with yellow fever.

From his analytical study of yellow fever epidemics, Ffirth was convinced of the difference in the contagiousness of yellow fever from that of measles, lues, smallpox, and other selected afflictions. He noted that only a small percentage of the population were affected in a yellow fever epidemic, and that those in immediate contact with the sick or the dying did not necessarily contract the disease. This led him to study the "noncontagiousness of yellow fever." Fifteen experiments were described, in which animals and human volunteers received black vomit or blood from the afflicted. Although the experiments were properly conducted and the data were sound, yellow fever could not be transmitted under the conditions of Ffirth's experiments.[1]

Ex. II. A small sized cat was confined in a room, and kept without food; at the end of three days, I gave her three ounces of the black vomit, which she ate with avidity; the same quantity was given her daily for five days, without her evincing any signs of disease; the discharges were of a dark colour.

Ex. III. Having made a large incision into the back of a dog, and dissected the skin off from the cellular membrane and muscles, thereby forming a cavity, into which I poured one dram of fresh black vomit, (obtained from a patient in the city hospital, who was in the last agonies which precede dissolution) and drawing the skin together, kept it in that situation by means of the dry suture; a pledget of lint was applied over this, and a bandage passed round the abdomen and over the part. The dog was confined, and prevented from irritating his back by rubbing it; the incision healed by the first intention, the black vomit was absorbed, and he continued perfectly healthy.

Ex. VI. On the 4th of October, 1802, I made an incision in my left arm, mid way between the elbow and wrist, so as to draw a few drops of blood; into the incision I introduced some fresh black vomit, a slight degree of inflammation ensued, which entirely subsided in three days, and the wound healed up very readily.

Ex. VII. Four days after the above experiment, having obtained some fresh black vomit, I made a considerable incision in my right arm, into which I introduced five drops of it; having closed the sides of the wound, and applied an adhesive plaster over it, with a bandage round the arm it was left so for two days, when upon examination it appeared, that no more inflammation had taken place than would have occurred had not the black vomit been introduced: The wound healed up in a few days without any difficulty, and without the formation of pus.

Ex. IX. Two drops of fresh black vomit were dropped into my right eye; it felt a little uneasy for about a minute, but produced no pain or inflammation; I have frequently had cold water to produce the same effect.

Ex. XIII. After repeating the two last experiments several times, and with precisely the same results, I took half an ounce of the black vomit immediately after it was ejected from a patient, and diluting it with an ounce and a half of water, swallowed it; the taste was very slightly acid; as I felt no mental anxiety of uneasiness, I could attend particularly to my sensations.

Ex. XIV. The serum of the blood drawn from a patient in the first or inflammatory stage of the malignant fever, was taken, and four drops of it inserted in my left leg; the wound was closed, and retained so by the dry suture; a slight degree of inflammation was produced, and the wound healed up in a few days. This experiment was frequently repeated with precisely the same consequence. It was also swallowed in considerable quantities without producing the least effect.

Ffirth was skilled in programming his experiments, in preparing the protocols, and in formulating conclusions for publication. The preface to the treatise reveals his skill in composition and style of presentation.

TO THE
INHABITANTS OF PHILADELPHIA

FELLOW CITIZENS,

YOU who have felt, who have seen, and who have trembled at the dire progress of a malignant epidemic, spreading its baneful influence, its rapid progress, and its march characterized by disorder, dismay, desolation and death; who, by your fear and forebodings, have accelerated the advances thereof, hastened its termination, and added force to its malignancy, can alone judge whether this work, which is intended to obviate those evils, be worthy of your patronage. To you I commit it; if you think it is worthy thereof, (as on the basis of its own merit let it stand,) cherish it; but if not, let it immediately descend to the tomb of oblivion, which ultimately awaits all the productions of man.

With sentiments of high consideration,
I remain your fellow citizen,
S. FFIRTH

The studies were not graciously received by those interested in the pathogenesis of diseases; more attention seemed to be focused on the esthetics of the experiments. The reviewer in the *Philadelphia Medical Museum* gave a fair analysis of the communication but considered one of the experiments to be as unnecessary as it was disgusting.[2] Ffirth replied as follows:[3]

You are pleased to say the experiment was "disgusting," as well as "unnecessary:"—to a belle or petite-maitre, it certainly would be extremely so; but to a person anxious for the investigation of truth, nothing having a tendency thereto, or in any way to elucidate the subject, ought to be considered as such; every thing which has this object in view ought to be encouraged. Such reflections are of no use, they will neither prevent the advances of science in a mind ardent in the investigation of physical causes, nor will they accelerate the progress of the experimenter. It is my opinion, it is the opinion of the most learned and best men, that the progress of science tends to the extension of human happiness; every thing therefore having a relation to this, whether it be disgusting or not, is laudable.

Proceeding to sea immediately after graduation, Ffirth spent several years touring the world and, from his observations, submitted essays to the *Medical Repository* of New York on American and Asiatic fevers as well as a short monograph on tetanus from patients seen in Charleston, SC. During the voyage from Philadelphia to Batavia, Java, he described diseases which occurred on shipboard; an account is also given of the unhealthfulness of Batavia, in which he again discussed the noncontagious nature of yellow fever. These, along with an article on the use of nitric acid in hepatitis, were published in the *Philadelphia Medical Museum*.

Ffirth eventually settled in Charleston and pursued a busy practice, aiding rich and poor alike. There are no other scientific publications to his credit during his practice in Charleston. He died in 1820, and the inscription on his tombstone in Old Dorchester Churchyard reads as follows: "As a Physician he was eminent in his profession, had an extensive practice, was prompt and ready at every call, whether proceeding from the poor or the rich, as thousands can testify." His studies on yellow fever attracted little attention for almost a century until Finlay, Reed, and others built upon his fundamental observations.[4]

1. Ffirth, S.: *A Treatise on Malignant Fever; with an Attempt to Prove Its Non-Contagious Nature*, Philadelphia: B. Graves, 1804.

2. An Inaugural Dissertation, New Publications, *Phila Med Museum* 1:114-120, 1805.

3. Ffirth, S.: Letter to the Editor, in Answer to a Review of His Thesis on "Malignant Fever," *Phila Med Museum* 3:xxxv-xl, 1807.

4. Peller, S.: Walter Reed, C. Finlay, and Their Predecessors Around 1800, *Bull Hist Med* 33:195-211 (May-June) 1959.

Composite by G. Bako

Valentine Mott (1785-1865)

VALENTINE MOTT, leading surgeon of New York in the 19th century, achieved his fame, among several accomplishments, for the application of ligatures to many of the great vessels. Mott was born in Glen Cove, Long Island; his father was a physician; his family were Quakers.[1] At the age of 19, Mott was apprenticed to kinsman Valentine Seaman, surgeon to the New York Hospital. At the age of 21, he obtained his medical degree from the Medical Department at Columbia College; as a "Citizen of the State of New-York, and President of the American Aesculapian Society," he presented the inaugural dissertation, entitled *The Chemical and Medical Properties of Statice Limonium*,[2] a plant with astringent properties sometimes used in the treatment of diarrhea and hemorrhoids.

Mott went to Europe for two years to continue postgraduate instruction, and there he was attracted to Sir Astley Cooper, then approaching the zenith of his career. The deficiency in Mott's education caused by the scarcity of cadavers for dissection in America was corrected under the tutelage of Cooper. From London, Mott went to Edinburgh, while plans to spend time in Paris were suspended because political unrest created an unfavorable climate for study. Returning to New York in 1809, Mott opened an office and, with permission of the authorities of Columbia College, gave private lectures and demonstrations in the anatomy quarters of the school. Two years later he was appointed professor of surgery, a position he held until 1813, when the Columbia Medical School united with the College of Physicians and Surgeons.

In 1826, the Board of Regents of the State of New York enacted certain resolutions considered detrimental to the faculty, enjoying resigned as a body. Wishing to continue teaching and enjoying the reputation afforded faculty members, the abdicants soon incorporated under the auspices of Rutgers Medical College of New Brunswick, New Jersey, and, by an arrangement that remains unexplained, affiliated for a short period of time with the Geneva College of Western New York. The Rutgers School, situated in Manhattan, was forced to close on account of technical illegalities in its power of conferring degrees. In 1831, Mott returned to the College of Physicians and Surgeons, with appointment as professor of operative surgery with surgical and pathological anatomy—a position he occupied until failing health caused him to abandon practice and teaching in 1834. For six years he traveled for business and pleasure, visiting clinics in London, Ireland, Scotland, and western Europe. In Berlin he was especially attracted to Dieffenbach and von Graefe. In Paris he was received by Baron Larrey and Velpeau and, using Paris as a base, extended his visits to the major cities of the Middle East. In Europe he was entertained by royalty, and in Constantinople he removed a tumor from the head of the reigning sultan.[3]

Before returning to New York in 1841, Mott was appointed professor of surgery and surgical anatomy and president of the faculty of the University of the City of New York. Resigning this post in 1850, he again visited Europe. Upon return he became professor emeritus in the College of Physicians and Surgeons, remaining active in teaching up to the time of his death. While moving from one academic post to another, Mott was recognized as an outstanding teacher and a skillful, ambidextrous, and considerate surgeon, with a modest number of recorded contributions. Most of his operations were performed in the generation before the introduction of ether for anesthesia, in which deep surgery, the environment for vascular ligation, required intimate knowledge of surgical anatomy, great confidence in planning, and speed in execution. In the introductory paragraph in his essay on "Pain and Anaesthetics," prepared for the United States Sanitary Commission, Mott discussed the fear of pain and the use of opium and alcohol from his experiences in the pre-ether era.[4]

Among the many improvements which characterize modern surgery, one of the most invaluable is the introduction of Anaesthetics. That we should be enabled safely and conveniently to place the human system in such a state, that the most painful operations may be performed without consciousness, is to have secured to man immunity from what he most dreads; for most men fear pain even more than death.

If we examine these doctrines [relief from pain] carefully, we shall find that they are in fact not essentially new. The principles on which they are founded have been long recognised *in the use of narcotics*. I was in the habit of giving opiates freely before the introduction of anaesthetics, both before and after operations; and now, after over fifty years of experience, I still retain them in my confidence.

Alcoholic stimulants are also well known to exercise a limited anaesthetic power. Men in a condition of complete intoxication are sometimes unconscious of the injuries they receive, and formerly some surgeons were in the habit of benumbing the sensibility of the patient, and sometimes I fear their own, by copious draughts of spirituous liquors.

But there is another reason for employing anaesthetics which must not be forgotten. *The insensibility of the patient is a great convenience to the surgeon.*

How often, when operating in some deep, dark wound, along the course of some great vein, with thin walls, alternately distended and flaccid with the vital current—how often have I dreaded that some unfortunate struggle of the patient would deviate the knife a little from its proper course, and that I, who fain would be the deliverer, should involuntarily become the executioner, seeing my patient perish in my hands by the most appalling form of death! Had he been insensible, I should have felt no alarm.

It was with such limited means of providing anesthesia that Mott, in 1818, ligated the innominate artery two inches above the heart in the treatment of a subclavian aneurysm. The patient, a 57-year-old seaman, fell upon his right arm, shoulder, and the back of his head, which led in a few days to pain and inflammation of the affected parts. In spite of antiphlogistic treatment, neither subsidence of pain nor restoration of function was accomplished; after proper consultation and statement of probability of success to the patient, an attempt was made to ligate the innominate artery, with a presumptive diagnosis of traumatic aneurysm.[5]

On the 7th I directed a consultation of my colleagues to be called, consisting of Drs. Post, Kissam and Stevens. I now stated to them that I wished to perform an operation which would enable me to pass a ligature around the subclavian artery, before it passes through the scaleni muscles, or the arteria innominata, if the size of the tumour should prevent the accomplishment of the former. This I was permitted to do, provided the patient should assent, after a candid and fair representation was made to him of the probable termination of his disease; and that the operation, though uncertain, gave him some chance, and, as we thought, the only one of his life.

Dr. Post, at my request, communicated with him privately on this subject, and after a full explanation of the nature of the case, my patient requested to have any operation performed which promised him a chance for his life, saying that in his present state he was truly wretched. . . . I commenced my incision upon the tumour, just above the clavicle, and carried it close to this bone and the upper end of the sternum, and terminated it immediately over the trachea; making it in extent about three inches.

With this appearance of disease in the subclavian artery, it only remained for me either to pass the ligature around the arteria innominata, or abandon my patient. Although I very well know, that this artery had never been taken up for any condition of aneurisms, or ever performed as a surgical operation, yet with the approbation of my friends, and reposing great confidence in the resources of the system, when aided by the noblest efforts of scientific surgery, I resolved upon the operation.

After fairly denuding the artery upon its upper surface, I very cautiously, with the handle of a scalpel, separated the cellular substance from the sides of it, so as to avoid wounding the pleura. A round silken ligature was now readily passed around it, and the artery was tied about half an inch below the bifurcation.

Immediately after the ligature was drawn tight, the tumour was reduced in size about one third, and the course of the clavicle could be distinctly felt.

Ten minutes after the operation the pulse is regular, and not the least variation can be perceived; it beats 69 strokes in a minute; the patient says is perfectly comfortable, and has no new or unnatural sensation.

Since the patient lived 28 days following surgery, it can be assumed the operative technique was effective. It was not until 1864 that Smyth of New Orleans reported a permanent cure. Mott, in the meantime, had successfully ligated, in a series of patients, the common iliac at its origin, the carotid for subclavian aneurysm, the carotid for anastomosing aneurysm in a three-month-old infant, the external iliac for a femoral aneurysm, the right subclavian, both carotids simultaneously, the right internal iliac, and the innominate artery. In addition to vascular surgery he excised the right portion of the lower jaw after tying the carotid artery, amputated the leg at the hip joint, excised the left clavicle for osteosarcoma, and removed a large fibrous growth from the nostril by dividing the nasal and maxillary bones. Several of his biographers summarize his operations during his long career as 1,000 amputations, 150 excisions for bladder stones, and ligation of 40 large arteries.

Mott assembled a library and a surgical and pathological museum which were given to the medical profession. He was one of the founders of the New York Academy of Medicine, delivered the first scientific communication on the treatment of ununited fractures at the meeting on March 3, 1847, and twice served as its president. Orderly and humble in his domestic habits, he spent his evenings reading in his library, writing, or conversing with his friends. Mott was made an Honorary Fellow of the Kings and Queens College of Physicians of Ireland. The University of Edinburgh conferred on him the honorary degree of MD; the University of the State of New York, the LLD degree; while the College of Physicians and Surgeons of Columbia honors him with the Valentine Mott Professorship of Surgery in the faculty. As a friend and correspondent of Abraham Lincoln, he bore the shock of the President's death heavily and died 10 days later.

1. Gross, S. D.: *Memoir of Valentine Mott, M.D., L.L.D.,* New York: D. Appleton & Co., 1968.
2. Mott, V.: *An Experimental Inquiry Into the Chemical and Medical Properties of the Statice Limonium of Linnaeus,* New York: T. & F. Swords, 1806.
3. Mott, V.: *Travels in Europe and the East,* New York: Harper & Brothers, 1842.
4. Mott, V.: "Pain and Anesthetics," in *Military, Medical and Surgical Essays Prepared for the United States Sanitary Commission 1862-1864,* Washington, DC, 1865.
5. Mott, V.: Reflections on Securing in a Ligature the Arteria Innominata, *Med Surg Register* 1:9-54, 1818.

Composite by G. Bako

Joseph Warren III (1741-1775)

JOSEPH WARREN, one of the first of the distinguished line of medical Warrens of Boston and Roxbury, was killed in the battle of Breeds Hill (Bunker Hill) at the age of 34. He was born on a farm stocked with apple trees (Warren Russet), cattle, and a yoke of oxen. He pursued the tradition of the intellectually elite of New England at Roxbury Latin School, where the classical languages and literature were emphasized, and entered Harvard College at the age of 14. Following graduation, Warren served a term as a teacher in Roxbury Latin School, while qualifying for a master's degree at Harvard. One of the requirements for the higher degree was a thesis.[1] Warren defended his thesis from notes; no formal dissertation remains in the archives of Harvard College according to Cary.[2]

If an American colonial wished to receive formal instruction in medicine in the mid-18th century, it was necessary to travel to England or to the Continent. The University of Pennsylvania Medical School was not founded until 1766, and Harvard Medical School was not organized until 1782. As an effective substitute for planned instruction, Warren was apprenticed to James Lloyd, who had studied under William Cheselden, was an acquaintance of the Hunters of England, and "kept a genteel equipage and commanded a more respectable circle of practice than any other of the physicians of his day."[3] Five years were spent with Lloyd on rounds and in the apothecary shop, at the sacrifice of instruction in anatomy and dissection. At the age of 22, Warren began the practice of medicine in Boston, then a metropolis of 16,000 or 18,000, during the smallpox epidemic. Although smallpox inoculation had accomplished much in England in reducing the incidence of this scourge, there were few advocates of such protection in America. Cotton Mather and Zabdiel Boylston led the crusade. Warren belonged to this small band, and as the epidemic reached serious proportions, his energies were completely consumed in treating the sick and inoculating the well at the smallpox hospital at Castle William. Accommodations were provided for almost 500 patients during the eight-months' epidemic of 1763. Once the epidemic was clearly on the wane, Warren returned to Boston, where, in less than a decade, he became one of the best of the medical profession in colonial Massachusetts. Although there are no classic descriptions of medicine or surgery attributed to Warren, he was a highly successful teacher. Classes in anatomy, surgery, and general medicine were held in his home. Probably his most famous student was his brother John Warren, one of the great surgeons of the late 18th century and the single most important figure in the founding of Harvard Medical School.

Had Joseph confined his attention to medicine, he might well have occupied a position similar to his brother's. The burning fire of patriotism, however, diverted more and more of his energies and talents, and in the final months of life, medicine was abandoned for the crusade of liberty. The Stamp Act, the Townshend Revenue Acts, and his "true patriot" letters of the 1760's gave him an opportunity as leader of the Liberal party to appeal for popular support. As tension rose, street fighting between the townspeople and the British troops led to the Boston Massacre of 1770. The Boston Tea Party of 1773, another act of agitation, revealed the strength of the opposition to laws passed without Colonial approval. Warren's devotion to the Revolutionary crusade was augmented by well-known compatriots including Paul Revere, Samuel Adams, and John Hancock. Warren appeared more and more in the center of political activity and contributed heavily to shaping the policy of the Bay Colony, although he held no government post until 1774. Warren directed the opposition during the Liberty incident, which led to the stationing of troops in Boston, and was influential in ousting Governor Francis Bernard from the colony and in the prosecution of Captain Preston after the Boston Massacre. He was the leader of the committee of safety, President of the Provincial Congress which pledged the American colonies to resist political oppression with an armed militia, and designer of the Suffolk Resolves calling for interruption of commerce with Britain, if necessary. The adoption of the Resolves by the Continental Congress led the English authorities to declare that Massachusetts was in a state of rebellion.

As April, 1775, approached, Warren organized the resistance in Massachusetts to counter the British forces under the command of Thomas Gage. He sent the warning to Lexington by Paul Revere on April 18th that the British were leaving Boston, probably to capture the supply depot at Concord. He participated in the skirmish in Lexington and became the semiofficial commander-in-chief of the Bay Colony militia. The Provincial Congress appointed him Major General of the armed forces on June 14th; troops were recruited and the support of the loyal was enlisted in the cause of freedom. The fortification of Bunker Hill was begun on June 15th. Before this was complete the British attacked; Prescott and Warren were heavily outnumbered and staged a strategic withdrawal. During this maneuver, the general was hit by a bullet and probably died instantly.

Joseph Warren began his professional life as a physician and a teacher. The transition to politician and patriot seemed natural. He was probably considered by some of his countrymen a revolutionary in the derogatory sense of the term. His actions, however, placed him in the van as a leader for freedom, exemplary of many of the New Englanders of the 18th century. He believed in nationalism, home rule, and independence from the political shackles of the Old World.

1. Warren J.: *An omnes Morbi oriantur ab Obstructionibus. Negat Respondens Josephus Warren,* MS Book of Theses and Quaestiones, Harvard College Archives.

2. Cary, J.: *Joseph Warren, Physician, Politician, Patriot,* Urbana, Ill.: University of Illinois Press, 1961.

3. Frothingham, R.: *Life and Times of Joseph Warren,* Boston: Little, Brown and Company, 1865.

John Warren (1753-1815)

JOHN WARREN, Revolutionary surgeon and practitioner in Salem and Boston, was influential in the founding of Harvard Medical School, where he lectured for over 30 years. Warren was born on a farm in Roxbury, Massachusetts, attended the local grammar school (which later became the Roxbury Latin School), and entered Harvard College at the age of 14.[1] He maintained himself by his own efforts, was proficient in the classics, and showing a proclivity for anatomy, took the lead in forming a students' association for the study of the subject. Having received the AB degree in 1771, he entered the office of his brother, Dr. Joseph Warren, as an apprentice, studying his preceptor's limited medical library, assisting in the dispensing of medicines, and

attending him in the office and on house visits. After two years of such study, he chose Salem as a site for practice, believing that Boston was abundantly supplied with

Composite by G. Bako

physicians. He gained the confidence of Dr. Holyoke, the leading practitioner of Salem, and was soon engaged in an extensive practice which continued until the critical political events of 1775.

Imbued with a deep sense of patriotism, Warren joined Pickering's militia as a private in support of the garrison at Lexington but missed the April 19th engagement with the British. Two months later he went to the scene of the Battle of Bunker Hill, having heard the rumor that his brother, then General Joseph Warren, had been wounded or killed in the assault. While searching for his brother, he crossed toward the enemy position and received a bayonet wound from the British sentry. As the Revolutionary War settled into extended combat and periodic campaigns, Warren was commissioned major general and assigned by General Washington to the Military Hospital in Cambridge. There he served as senior surgeon during the uneasy months of preparedness by the Colonies and until May, 1776, when the hospital was moved to Long Island. Warren continued to care for the wounded and share the hardships of the Continental Army through the spring of 1777. He then returned to head the military hospital in Boston and remained to the close of the war.

In 1780, Warren gave his first series of lectures in anatomy in the military hospital, located adjacent to the area where the Massachusetts General Hospital now stands. The lectures were conducted with secrecy because public prejudice against dissection remained strong. The following year he was bolder and gave open lectures to a few Harvard College students, President Joseph Willard of Harvard, members of the Harvard Corporation, and others. The time was propitious, the setting favorable, and in the fall of 1782, the Corporation voted to establish a medical school modeled after Warren's suggestions. Warren himself was appointed to fill the chair of anatomy and surgery, one of the proposed professorships. Although he was largely dependent for financial support upon student fees from his lectures and demonstrations, an endowment had been started in 1772; Dr. Ezekiel Hersey, of Hingham, bequeathed £1,000 to support a professor of anatomy and surgery at the College. The appointment of Warren was followed by that of Benjamin Waterhouse as professor of the theory and practice of physic, and Aaron Dexter as professor of chemistry and materia medica. In 1786, Warren was awarded the honorary degrees AM and MD; in 1791, his professorship was changed to Hersey professor of anatomy and surgery in recognition of the early bequest.

The year 1780 was important for Warren in other phases of medicine and left little doubt that he was, or soon would be, a leading practitioner in Boston. In May he assembled a group of physicians at the Green-Dragon Tavern in Boston to organize the Boston Medical Society, which survived for a decade, with the intention of designing a code of medical fees to counteract the critical depreciation of the Continental currency. In 1781, he was one of 31 who petitioned the Massachusetts House of Representatives for a charter to form the Massachusetts Medical Society. He served this organization in varying positions, including the presidential chair from 1804 until his death. Warren actively supported the Massachusetts Humane Society, founded in 1780 for resuscitation of the drowned, and served as its second president. He was a member of the American Academy of Arts and Sciences and, in the first volume of the *Memoirs,* published one of his few medical communications, "A History of a Large Tumour, in the Region of the Abdomen, Containing Hair." In 1778, Warren and associates formed a partnership for the establishment of a hospital near Boston for inoculation against smallpox and the treatment of patients afflicted with the disease. The hospital was indispensable during the epidemic of 1792. Yellow fever was another medical scourge in Boston, and, during the epidemic in 1798, Warren attended an incredible number of patients and conducted postmortem examinations on many of the fatal cases.

Warren's biography by his son reflects the political and social period of his life and describes him as cheerful in disposition, impulsive in his decisions, affectionate, generous, kind, and endowed with an acute perception and with strong sympathies. As a teacher he inspired enthusiasm in his pupils who came to him in numbers, was skillful in surgical procedures, and evidenced sound clinical judgment. He wasted no time on home visits, applying himself to the case immediately on arrival and departing with equal dispatch.

Warren's longest prepared communication was his query into the merits of mercury in the practice of medicine, particularly in febrile diseases.[2] A shorter but more interesting document appeared in the first volume of the *New England Journal of Medicine and Surgery.* This discussed angina pectoris, a disease from which he suffered. After reviewing the contributions of several before him, with particular reference to ossification of the coronary arteries, he notes:[3]

Whether any particular mode of derangement is connected with Angina Pectoris in the relation of cause and effect, must be discovered by dissections and faithful reports of morbid appearances in the dead body. A number of such reports sufficient for this purpose does not, as yet, seem to have been made. It has been seldom that the physician, after having witnessed the form of the paroxysms, has had it in his power to compare them with his discoveries after death. Some of the earliest observers had no suspicion of ossification in the coronary arteries. Dr. Jenner, in particular, mentions a case of dissection, in which the examination of them was not thought of; and a modern author has even doubted whether organic affection was concerned in producing the symptoms, or whether they were any thing more than a mere spasm of the heart.

It seems appropriate for the leading 18th century surgeon of Boston, a Revolutionary patriot accustomed to lecturing before medical students, to deliver the oration on July 4, 1783, the anniversary of the Declaration of Independence. In this speech, reputedly the first July 4th oration, he said:[4]

The constitution, or frame of government, in a republican State, is circumscribed by barriers, which the ambitious or designing cannot easily remove, without giving the alarm to those whose privileges might be infringed by the innovation; but that the principles of administration may be grossly corrupted, that the people may be abused and enslaved under the best of constitutions, is a truth to which the annals of the world may be adduced to bear a melancholy attestation.
A general prevalence of that love for our country, which teaches us to esteem it glorious to die in her defence, is the only means of perpetuating the enjoyment of that liberty and security, for the support of which all government was originally intended.

1. Warren, E.: *The Life of John Warren, M.D.*, Boston: Noyes, Holmes, & Co., 1874.
2. Warren, J.: *View of the Mercurial Practice in Febrile Diseases,* Boston: T. B. Wait & Co., 1813.
3. Warren, J.: Remarks on Angina Pectoris, *New Eng J Med Surg* 1:1-11, 1812.
4. Warren, J.: *An Oration, Delivered July 4th, at the Request of the Inhabitants of the Town of* Boston; *in Celebration of the Anniversary of American Independence,* Boston, Commonwealth of Massachusetts: J. Gill, 1783.

John Collins Warren (1778-1856)

JOHN COLLINS WARREN, the eldest son of Dr. John Warren, was identified with Boston and Boston medicine throughout his life. Although he was primarily a surgeon, he served internal medicine well and cherished several non-medical interests. His

early education was under the care of his Public Latin school, where he excelled scholastically and was honored as the valedictory Laureate.[1] He matriculated in Harvard

Countway Medical Library

College and, in 1797, was Latin valedictorian of his class and president of the Hasty Pudding Club of which he had been one of the founders.

Warren did not immediately pursue higher education. His father intended him for a business career, but, finding no suitable opening in a countinghouse following graduation, he was allowed to spend a dilettante year learning French. After another year as apprentice in his father's office, Warren, then 21, sailed for Europe and studied under the best medical teachers of his day. These included William Cooper and Astley Cooper of Guy's Hospital, London; John and Charles Bell, Hope, and Monro *Secundus* at Edinburgh; and Dubois at the Hospice de l'École de Médecine in Paris.

Having received an honorary MD degree from St. Andrew's University, Scotland, in the fall of 1802, Warren returned to Boston and entered into partnership with his father. He assisted an anatomical dissection and began his own private lectures in anatomy and physiology. In 1809, he was appointed adjunct-professor of anatomy and surgery at Harvard Medical School. Upon the death of his father in 1815, Warren became Hersey Professor of the same subjects, a position held until 1847, when he was named professor emeritus. From 1816 to 1819 he served as dean of the school and was awarded an honorary MD degree by Harvard at the conclusion of this assignment.

The Massachusetts General Hospital was Warren's second educational affiliation. When the Harvard Medical School moved from Cambridge to Boston in 1810, efforts were already under way to provide for an associated teaching hospital and an asylum for the indigent. As early as 1810, Warren, together with James Jackson, Hersey Professor of the Theory and Practice of Physic, solicited funds from wealthy citizens of the community to build such a structure. When the hospital was opened for patients in 1821, Jackson and Warren shared the honors as chiefs of the respective clinical services. At the time Warren took over the surgical service he was in delicate health, yet he arose early in the morning, spent the day at professional activities and his evenings (even after midnight) at his books and his writings. In the organization and conduct of the surgical staff, Warren was noted for his attention to detail. On the contrary, the house staff, called "house pupils" at that time, were given little responsibility, were addressed as "Mister," and were not allowed to use the doctor's title during their tenure, a pattern of servitude which persisted for more than a century.

The third notable contribution by Warren to medical education was the establishment of the *New England Journal of Medicine and Surgery* in 1812. The initiating committee included Jackson, Gorham, Bigelow, and Channing. In 1828, the publication merged with the *Medical Intelligencer* and took the name *Boston Medical and Surgical Journal*. Warren was a regular contributor, with case reports and general communications. His work in surgery, largely done before the demonstration of ether, was extensive in scope, imaginative in design, and skillful in execution. He was one of the first surgeons in America to operate on a strangulated hernia, to pattern his vascular surgery after his European teachers, extract cataracts with remarkable success, and to excise tumors, diseased bone, and morbid extremities. A detailed description of his work on growths, entitled *Surgical Operations on Tumors,* appeared in a monograph in 1837. An appendix to his biography lists many of his important surgical operations.[1]

One of Warren's greatest days was October 16, 1846, when he allowed William Morton to administer ether by inhalation to a young patient while he removed a tumor from the neck. Thereafter his preference for ether over chloroform in inhalation anesthesia was clearly stated. An excerpt from his small monograph, published in 1848, describes his interest and use of ether since he first entered practice, almost half a century earlier.[2]

Many years have elapsed since I myself used ethereal inhalation to relieve the distress attending the last stage of pulmonary inflammation. So long ago as the year 1805, it was applied for this purpose, in the case of a gentleman of distinction in the city, very frequently since, and particularly in the year 1812, to a member of my family, who experienced from it great relief, and still lives, to give testimony to its effects. The manner in which it was applied was by moistening a handkerchief and placing it near the face of the patient.

A new era has opened to the operating surgeon! His visitations on the most delicate parts are performed, not only without the agonizing screams he has been accustomed to hear, but sometimes with a state of perfect insensibility, and occasionally even with the expression of pleasure on the part of the patient. Who could have imagined that drawing the knife over the delicate skin of the face might produce a sensation of unmixed delight! that the turning and twisting of instruments in the most sensitive bladder might be accompanied by a beautiful dream! that the contorting of anchylosed joints should co-exist with a celestial vision! If Ambrose Paré, and Louis, and Desault, and Cheselden, and Hunter, and Cooper, could see what our eyes daily witness, how would they long to come among us, and perform their exploits once more!

Warren's outstanding surgical contribution, the operation for the cure of the natural fissure of the soft palate without benefit of general anesthesia, was described as follows:[3]

The patient was a healthy young woman of sixteen. She was induced to apply for an operation, in consequence of the impracticability of distinctly articulating her words, so that her speech was offensive from its guttural tones, and not intelligible to those unaccustomed to it.

The patient being well supported and secured, a piece of wood an inch wide, a little curved at the end, with a handle to be held by an assistant, was placed between the molar teeth on one side, to keep the mouth open. A sharp-pointed curved bistoury was thrust through the top of the palate, above the angle of the fissure, and carried down on one edge of the fissure to its extremity. The same was done on the opposite side, thus cutting out a piece in the form of the letter V, including about a line from each edge. Next a hook with an eye in its extremity . . . armed with a triple thread of strong silk, was passed doubled into the mouth, through the fissure and behind the palate. The palate was pierced by it, at one-third of the length of the fissure from the upper angle of the wound, so as to include about three lines of the edge of the soft palate. The eye with the ligature being seen, the latter was seized by a common hook and drawn out. The eyed hook was then drawn back, turned behind the palate, and the other edge transfixed in a similar manner. A second and a third stitch were passed in the same manner, the third being as near as possible to the lower end of the fissure. Then seizing the upper ligature, I found no difficulty in tying it with my fingers, without the aid of a serve-noeud. The others were tied in the same manner, and the knots placed on one side of the wound, in order to prevent their pressing into the fissure. On drawing the third ligature I had the satisfaction to see the whole fissure closed.

The patient was exhausted by the operation, but soon revived. . . . About two years subsequent to the operation I saw her, and found she swallowed perfectly, spoke very well, and was daily improving.

Warren was active in the early years of the American Medical Association and served as President in 1850. His Presidential Address, given in Cincinnati, was an uninspiring, unimportant presentation. Beyond the practice of medicine he was an inveterate crusader against alcoholic beverages, an active member of the Society of Natural History, a member of the Society for the Study of Natural Philosophy, and coeditor of the monthly *Anthology,* sponsored by a society which later became the Boston Athenaeum. Warren assembled an anatomical museum which later was given to Harvard and persists as the Warren Museum in the Harvard Medical School. His interest in paleontology and comparative anatomy was climaxed by the purchase of a mastodon, which remained in Boston until his death. It was subsequently sold by his heirs to J. Pierpont Morgan, who donated it to the American Museum of Natural History, New York city. Warren's final years were sustained with peace and serenity. As a physician and natural scientist, he was always eager to help others as well as himself in the acquisition of knowledge. This is illustrated in a letter to his son that a postmortem be performed and his skeleton be placed on exhibition.[1]

LETTER TO HIS SON.

To be opened after my Death, and before the Funeral.

The final and principal object of writing this letter is this, which regards the disposition of my mortal remains after the spirit has quitted them. The arrangement I wish is the following, subject to any peculiar circumstances of season, &c:—

1. Let the body be injected with arsenic after death, *soon.*

2. The funeral solemnities to take place in St. Paul's Church, in the full and proper form of the church-service.

3. The body afterwards to be removed to the Medical College; examined or dissected, according to circumstances. Any morbid parts to be carefully preserved; and particular attention is to be paid to the heart, spleen, and prostate gland.

4. The bones to be carefully preserved, whitened, articulated, and placed in the lecture-room of the Medical College, near my bust; affording, as I hope, a lesson useful, at the same time, to mortality and science.

I earnestly request that you and my family will lay aside any natural feeling of opposition to this my last request; considering that it is for the interest of humanity, and for mine and their honor.

Finally, I take leave of you in the hope of our meeting again, and enjoying the society of our blessed friends who have gone before.

Affectionately,

JOHN C. WARREN

Boston, July 14, 1842.

1. Warren, E.: *The Life of John Collins Warren, M.D.,* *Compiled Chiefly From His Autobiography and Journals,* 2 vol, Boston: Ticknor and Fields, 1860.

2. Warren, J. C.: *Etherization; With Surgical Remarks,* Boston: W. D. Ticknor & Co., 1848.

3. Warren, J. C.: On an Operation for the Cure of Natural Fissure of the Soft Palate, *Amer J. Med Sci* 3:1-3, 1828.

Dartmouth College Alumni Archives

Nathan Smith (1762-1829)

THE FIRST PHYSICIAN OF NEW ENGLAND a century and a half ago had no rivals in the dissemination of American medicine. Nathan Smith was a combination of frontier physician and progressive teacher, who gathered more medical schools and medical courses into his protectorate than his nearest competitor, Daniel Drake, counterpart in the Ohio River Valley. A definite biography of Nathan Smith and his contributions has not yet been prepared. He has not suffered, however, from lack of biographical documentation, and Oliver S. Hayward especially has written extensively in current medical literature on the various aspects of Smith's professional life and interests.[1]

Little is known of his childhood and early education beyond the fact that he was born in Rehoboth, Massachusetts, of steadfast New England ancestry, and that his family later moved to a farm in Chester, Vermont. At the age of 21, he became attracted to medicine through contacts with Dr. Josiah Goodhue, who encouraged him first to study the classics with the Reverend Mr. Whiting of Rockingham, Vermont; subsequently, Smith became an apprentice of Dr. Goodhue's.

Nathan Smith served as physician's apprentice for three years, assisting in the medical and surgical practice and reading the available medical texts. Thus trained in the tradition of his time and without benefit of a college or medical degree, he began the practice in Cornish, New Hampshire, at the age of 25. He soon discovered that such training was entirely inadequate. Neither a profitable practice nor the respect of the community was sufficient compensation for the lack of formal training or the shortcomings of medical education in the New England states, obvious defects which commanded his devotion, industry, and thought in the years immediately following. Smith abandoned practice, enrolled in Harvard College, and became one of the first students to receive formal instruction in the recently formed Institute of Medicine. The faculty was proud to boast a total staff of three: John Warren, Aaron Dexter, and Benjamin Waterhouse. The Bachelor of Medicine was granted Smith at the age of 28, the fifth student in the third class at the school. The MD was given later to all living holders of the BM degree.

Smith then returned to Cornish to practice and to marry Elizabeth Chase, daughter of General Jonathan Chase. Cornish was not far from Dartmouth College, destined to be the site for the second medical college in the New England states. Plans for construction of the school and a professorship of the theory and practice of medicine were discussed with President Wheelock. During a temporary delay in the approval of the program, Smith seized the opportunity to pursue postgraduate training in Britain, and, at the age of 34, he sailed for Glasgow and on to Edinburgh, where Monro *Secundus* instructed in anatomy and Black dominated in chemistry. But since Edinburgh's great days were on the wane, Smith, disappointed in the instruction, moved on to London. He soon found a friend in Lettsom and perhaps attended some of the lectures at the Windmill Street School. Upon Smith's return to America, in addition to resuming practice and tutoring, he began the first course of medical lectures at Dartmouth College. The following year he was appointed professor of anatomy, surgery, and physic. A bonus from Dartmouth College was provided on the condition that he move from Cornish to Hanover. The first medical building was erected at Dartmouth from a $3,450 grant by the New Hampshire legislature and a personal contribution of $1,200 from Smith, later paid by the state. His adroitness in persuading the state of New Hampshire to supply the funds without direct supervision of the school was a notable feat. He made similar arrangements with the legislatures of Vermont, Maine, and Connecticut.

Not to be outstripped by Dartmouth, Yale University at New Haven, the University of Vermont at Burlington, and Bowdoin College in Maine sought his counsel and services in founding medical departments. For several years, Smith was responsible for courses and lectures in each of the three schools, believing that each state should support a medical school. In substance, Nathan Smith was essentially the medical school faculty for 16 years at Dartmouth and was largely responsible for the courses in the theory and practice of physic, surgery, obstetrics, and anatomy there. For the next 16 years he headed the faculty at Yale.

In the midst of private practice and teaching, he found time for medical writing and the preparation of several notable contributions. His best discussed typhoid fever, called both "Typhous" and "Typhus," but the clinical description leaves little doubt that the disease was typhoid fever. It was clearly differentiated from typhus, accurately identified by Gerhard a few years later, although no postmortem findings

were given to support this presumption. It was fortunate that his series was confined to patients suffering only from typhoid fever. The monograph was subsequently published, with Yale College as the only academic affiliation. Specific mention was made of the contagious pathogenesis, dicrotic pulse, gastro-intestinal bleeding, peculiar odor of the afflicted, and reduction of body temperature by means of cold baths.[2]

That the Typhus Fever is contagious is a fact so evident to those who have seen much of the disease, and who have paid attention to the subject, that I should have spared myself the trouble of saying any thing with regard to it, did I not know that there are some physicians in this country, who still dispute the point; one, which I think can be as fully demonstrated, as that the measles, small-pox, and other diseases universally allowed to be contagious, are so.
The pulse is generally rather easily compressed, and when the disease is severe, has often a peculiar, undulating stroke, or a second small beat following each full one.
Haemorrhage is not an uncommon symptom in this disease. In a majority of instances in which it takes place, it arises from the intestines, not infrequently from the nose, and more rarely from the kidneys.
There is a remarkable odour arising from a person affected by this disease, so peculiar that I feel assured that upon entering a room, blindfolded, where a person had been confined for some length of time, I should be able to distinguish it from all other febrile affections.—
But the most effectual method of reducing the temperature of the body is by the use of cold water, which may be taken internally, or applied externally. When persons, sick of this disease, desire cold water to drink, it should never be denied them—they should be allowed to drink *ad libitum*. The quantity of heat abstracted from the body by the water which they will drink, however, is but small, and except in cases where, by its influence on the stomach, it produces perspiration, its effects are very trifling.
The only effectual method of cooling the body, in these cases, is by the use of cold water applied externally; by this means we can lessen the heat to any degree we please. Different physicians have adopted different modes of making the application. Some advise to take a patient out of bed, pour buckets of water upon him, and then to replace him again; while others prefer sponging him with cold water. We have cases, where cold water would be of service, in which our patients are too much reduced to be taken out of bed and placed in a sitting posture without injury. In these cases a different management will be neces-

sary. The method, which I have adopted, is to turn down the bed-clothes and to dash from a pint to a gallon of water on the patient's head, face and body, so as to wet both the bed and body linen thoroughly.

Smith wrote extensively on amputations and described the removal of an ovarian tumor, possibly unaware that Ephraim McDowell had preceded him in this operative procedure by a few years. In the operation for lithotomy he used the lateral approach, a wide incision, and the gorget, invented by Physick of Philadelphia. He was one of the first to perform staphylorrhaphy in America. Osteomyelitis of the bone, with early removal of the sequestra, is a clear and classical account, published the year before Brodie performed his first operation on an abscessed tibia.[3]

When the disease has not extended over the whole circumference of the bone, that is, when only a portion of one side of the bone is affected, the dead portion may be removed, if the operation be thought necessary, at any time after the dead bone is detached, which is generally in no very great length of time. This can be ascertained by the sound it gives on rapping it with a probe, or any other instrument, and more certainly by pressing directly upon it with the end of the probe, for sometimes we can perceive that the sequestra is moved by the pressure. When this cannot be perceived, if, when you fix the end of the probe directly on the dead portion of bone, you make considerable pressure upon it, and the patient complains of pain, you may be certain that the bone is detached, as such pressure will otherwise cause no sensation, for they are granulations which have started from the edges of the living bone that are hurt by the pressure. In such cases the dead bone had better be removed early, otherwise a new bony structure will be formed over the sequestra, which may make it necessary to remove some portion of the former with the saw, which would be avoided by a timely operation.

Of all Nathan Smith's attributes it is believed this his skill in handling patients deserves priority, when so little specifically could be done for disease. He displayed a keen, inquisitive mind and a highly retentive memory, from which he could recall examples from his clinical practice that helped him in consultation and in correctly diagnosing disease. He engaged in little philosophical speculation and was inter-

ested only in practical results. An undaunted moral courage in major decisions stood him in good stead, but he was ever mindful of the need for kindness and sympathy in telling the harsh facts to the immedicable patient. As a fitting climax to his career and as a tribute to a father, each of Nathan Smith's four sons carried on the medical tradition.[4]

1. Hayward, O. S.: Dr. Nathan Smth (1762-1829)—American Pioneer, *New Eng J Med* 261:489-494, 1959.
2. Smith, N.: *A Practical Essay on Typhous Fever*, New York: E. Bliss, and E. White, 1824.
3. Smith, N.: Observations on the Pathology and Treatment of Necrosis, *Phila Monthly J Med Surg* 1:11-19, 68-75, 1827.
4. Smith, E. A.: *The Life and Letters of Nathan Smith, M.B., M.D.*, New Haven: Yale University Press, 1914.

Composite by G. Bako

Daniel Drake (1785-1852)

DANIEL DRAKE, the dominant physician in the Ohio River Valley in the 19th century, was born near Plainfield, New Jersey, in 1785.[1] Three years later, his father, endowed with meager material possessions but with the spirit of a rugged pioneer, crossed the Alleghenies, transferred the family to a flatboat on the Ohio River, and followed the current to Maysville, Kentucky. It was customary on the river to fasten several boats together for safety purposes. Dr. William Goforth, Drake's preceptor in medicine in later years, was on another portion of the New Jersey convoy. The Drake family settled on 38 acres of land, their portion of a 1,400 acre tract a few miles from the village of Washington. Log cabins without windows were built. Drake's early education bears a striking resemblance to that of Abraham Lincoln's. He read whatever books were available; these included the *Bible, Aesop's Fables, Pilgrim's Progress,* and *Franklin's Life.* He attended school when he could be spared from clearing the forest and assisting with the farm chores.

After a decade of practice near Maysville, Goforth moved to Cincinnati, where Drake followed him in 1800 at the age of 15. The population of Cincinnati, a booming frontier town, comprised 750 settlers. Drake's father paid Goforth $400 to apprentice his son for the study of medicine. The pupil was vaccinated by the teacher not long after his arrival, one of the first to be vaccinated in the West. This was within 2 years after Jenner had published his "Inquiry into the Cow Pox." Goforth, an avid naturalist, together with Drake, studied the remains of the mastodon at the Bigbone Lick deposits in Kentucky.

In 1805, Goforth inscribed in longhand a diploma for Drake, the first medical degree issued west of the Alleghenies.[2]

I do hereby certify that Daniel Drake has pursued under my direction for four years, the study of Physic, Surgery, and Midwifery. From his good Abilities and marked Attention to the Prosecution of his studies, I am fully convinced that he is well qualified to practice in those branches.

Although authorized to practice medicine, Drake sought further training at the University of Pennsylvania. His fees for the study of physic with Benjamin Rush were $20 and for surgery under Philip Syng Physick, physician to President Polk, were $10. The term of instruction at Philadelphia lasted 5 months only. Drake then re-turned to the Ohio River Valley, opened an office in May's Lick, Kentucky, and one year later took over Goforth's practice in Cincinnati. One of his patients was William H. Harrison, later President of the United States.

One of the first scientific contributions that Drake published (1810) was a pamphlet entitled "Notices Concerning Cincinnati, Its Topography, Climate and Diseases." The geological and social survey of Cincinnati and its environs was expanded into a book in 1815, *Natural and Statistical View or Picture of Cincinnati and the Miami County, Illustrated by Maps, with an Appendix Containing Observations on the Late Earthquakes, the Aurora Borealis and Southwest Winds.*[3] His masterpiece, prepared late in life, the second volume of which was not published until after his death, was entitled: *A Systematic Treatise, Historical, Etiological, and Practical, on the Principal Diseases of the Interior Valleys of North America, as They Appear in the Caucasian, African, Indian, and Esquimaux Varieties of Its Population.*[4] This work covered 1,900 pages. The geologic, hydrographic, topographic, climatic, social, medical, and physiologic conditions of the Mississippi Valley were considered. At the 1850 meeting in Cincinnati, the Standing Committee on Medical Literature of the American Medical Association reported on the volume as follows:[5]

This volume which contains nearly nine hundred pages, is taken up with the medical topography, the climate, the manners of the inhabitants, and to the autumnal fevers of this vast region. Owing to the late period of its publication, the Committee have been unable to examine the treatise thoroughly, and they might, therefore, rest contented with a bare announcement of its existence. But they are reluctant to do so, since even a superficial inspection of the work has convinced them that it belongs to the very highest rank of our medical literature, and may very probably come to be regarded as the most valuable original work yet published in America. It is certainly unrivalled in the amount and variety of its materials; its style is perspicuous, correct, and elevated; and it appears to have been elaborated with great industry and care. Its distinguished author has raised a durable monument to his own name, and to the medical reputation, not only of the Great Valley, but of the greater Union.

As was frequently the custom in early pioneer days, a physician owned the drug store as a sideline. "D. Drake & Co., Drugs and Medicines" featured a soda fountain and dispensed hardware and groceries as well as Dover's powder, Glauber's salt, and Peruvian bark. He was particularly interested in the study of typhoid fever, malaria, cholera, and yellow fever—diseases prevalent in the interior valley.

The Western Museum Society was one of Drake's civic interests. He personally solicited funds for its endowment and support. Although not a member of any church until late in life, he encouraged the construction of the first Episcopal church in Cincinnati; he started a Library Society, a Debating Society, a School of Literature and Arts, and the first Public Library. Drake was one of the founder trustees of Lancaster Seminary, which later became the Cincinnati College, whose medical faculty he organized.

Drake practiced for more than a decade with no more authority than the certificate issued by Goforth. He did not have an MD degree. This deficiency, together with a great urge to teach, prompted him to study a second time in Philadelphia in order to complete his formal training. After this had been completed, he accepted the professorship at the Transylvania University in 1817. This move to Lexington was prophetic of a commuting career between Lexington, Cincinnati, Philadelphia, and Louisville.

Transylvania, in Lexington, Kentucky, "The Athens of the West" and the first medical school in the Middle West, was founded in 1799. Drake was fickle in his academic interests and returned to Cincinnati to begin plans for the formation of a medical school. The result was the Medical College of Ohio, which received its charter in 1819. Drake lectured on the Theory and Practice of Medicine for only three years. The relatively short tenure was precipitated by dismissal upon a two-thirds vote of the faculty. The other two members of the faculty voted for dismissal. Drake returned once more to Transylvania University, be-

came dean of the school in 1825, but resigned after a short tour of duty. In 1827, he founded the Cincinnati Eye Infirmary and started the *Western Journal of Medical and Physical Sciences*. He was appointed Professor of Medicine in Jefferson Medical College in Philadelphia in 1830, but remained only long enough to recruit personnel for the new medical school proposed by the trustees of Miami University, a land-grant school, which was planned for Cincinnati.

The Medical College of Ohio, suspicious of competition, appointed Drake Professor of Clinical Medicine and offered his recruits from Philadelphia various positions on the faculty. These included Willard Parker, late Professor of Surgery at Columbia University College of Physicians and Surgeons, and Samuel D. Gross of Philadelphia, Professor of Pathological Anatomy. Tenure was short once more, however, and in 1835 the Medical Department of Cincinnati College—the third medical school started by Drake—was in the process of formation. It was in operation only four years. The Cincinnati College Hospital with which his eye infirmary was merged closed in February, 1839. However, the Commercial Hospital founded in 1821 by Drake and later controlled by the Trustees of the Medical College of Ohio is in existence as the Cincinnati General Hospital.

In 1839, Drake moved to Louisville for a professorship in the Louisville Medical Institute. During the following 10 years, he taught, practiced medicine, and wrote his monumental treatise on the interior valley. He then returned to Ohio Medical College, followed by a second tour of duty in Louisville, and finally to Ohio Medical College in Cincinnati where he died.

Twenty medical schools were established in Cincinnati between 1819 and 1893. The only one remaining is the Cincinnati University Medical School, a merger of the Medical College of Ohio and the Miami Medical College—the two schools founded by Drake.

Drake's introductory lectures to his classes were stirring appeals for industry and dedication, spurning temporal pleasures.

The following excerpts were delivered in 1844.[1]

The love of pleasure and the love of science may coexist, but cannot be indulged at the same time; though in fact they are seldom united. A student should draw his pleasures from the discovery of truth, and find his amusements in the beauties and wonders of nature. He should seek for recreation, not debauchery. The former invigorates the mind, the latter enervates it. Study and recreation, properly alternated, bring out the glorius results of rich and powerful thought, original conception and elevated design; dissipation wastes the whole, perverts the moral taste and impoverishes the intellect.

The case of a student who comes to the school with idle habits, is not hopeless; but he who goes from it without their being corrected, is incurable, and should be banished from the ranks of our noble profession.

William Pepper, in eulogizing Drake,[6] stated:

To Drake, it was the gift of nature, the power of expressing in pure and flowing and brilliant language the lofty ideals, the clear thoughts, the graceful fancies of his ardent nature and his powerful mind.

1. Horine, E. F.: *Daniel Drake (1785-1852) Pioneer Physician of the Midwest,* Philadelphia: University of Pennsylvania Press, 1961.
2. Vance, C. A.: Dr. Daniel Drake, *Kentucky Med J* 46:445-453 (Nov.) 1948.
3. Drake, D.: *Natural and Statistical View, or Picture of Cincinnati and the Miami County, Illustrated by Maps, With an Appendix Containing Observations on "The Late Earthquakes, the Aurora Borealis and Southwest Winds,"* Cincinnati: Looker & Wallace, 1815.
4. Drake, D.: *A Systematic Treatise, Historical, Etiological, and Practical, on the Principal Diseases of the Interior Valley of North America, as They Appear in the Caucasian, African, Indian, and Esquimaux Varieties of Its Population,* Cincinnati: W. B. Smith, 1850.
5. Minutes of the Third Annual Meeting of the American Medical Association, *Trans Amer Med Assoc* 3:166, 1850.
6. Pepper, W.: Daniel Drake: Or Then and Now, *JAMA* 25:429-436 (Sept. 14) 1895.

David Ramsay (1749-1815)

DAVID RAMSAY, trained as a practitioner of the art of physic, achieved greatest recognition, however, as an ardent patriot and an accomplished historian. He was born in Lancaster County, Pennsylvania, of Irish stock. His farmer-father, aware of the advantages of higher education, lived to see these expectations fulfilled in the professional accomplisments of each of his sons.

Composite by G. Bako

Following graduation from the College of New Jersey (Princeton), the eldest became a minister, the second son a lawyer, and then came David. This precocious child was so far advanced as to be able to tutor his seniors. Before entering Princeton, with advanced standing at the age of 14, he had served for a year as assistant tutor at Carlisle Academy. After the AB was granted in 1765, Ramsay tutored for two more years before continuing his training.

He gained his medical education at the College of Pennsylvania, later chartered by the state as the University of Pennsylvania, where Bond, Shippen, Morgan, and especially Rush were members of the faculty. Ramsay graduated bachelor of physic in 1772 and, in 1780, received the degree of doctor of medicine upon submission of a thesis. In 1786, Yale recognized his accomplishments by awarding him the honorary MD degree. Following a year of practice in

Maryland, and upon the recommendation of Rush, Ramsay moved to Charleston, South Carolina, in 1773. His letter of recommendation documented his great abilities, talents, universal knowledge, strength of memory and imagination, and fine judgment.

Upon settling in Charleston Ramsay rapidly acquired eminence in the practice of physic and a reputation for experience in the study of yellow fever, a disease prevalent in the community at that time. Over and above these accomplishments, he proved to be a zealous advocate of independence during the Revolutionary War, became deeply involved in political activities, and began a second career, this in American history. His political ventures, more commanding than party politics, included membership in the House of Representatives of South Carolina and the Continental Congress and, in the absence of John Hancock, service for a year as President pro tempore of the United States Congress. As a member of the Continental Army, Ramsay participated in the siege of Savannah and, in 1780, was exiled with a number of other prominent citizens to St. Augustine for nearly a year.

Ramsay's austere personal habits and indefatigable industry were disclosed in his dissertation on the means of preserving health in Charleston and the adjacent lowlands. Indeed only by effectively utilizing every waking hour was he able to carry on two professions.[2]

The coolest period of the day is a little before sun rising. This naturally proves a temptation to spend those precious moments in sleep. If this is indulged, the body lies immersed in the air which has been fouled by its perspiration through the night, and in a situation which tends to relax it nearly as much as if it was in a vapor bath. . . . The cool morning air acts like the cold bath in invigorating the body, and has an advantage over it by being inhaled and applied to the vitals. In another view of this subject, it may be added, that a man who rises early will comparatively add seven years of the best time for study and business to a life of sixty-five.

One should mention two medical brochures before listing his works on American history. His *Sketch of the Soil, Climate, Weather, and Diseases of South Carolina* discusses the weather records for a decade near the close of the 18th century and at the beginning of the 19th century, he published *A Review of the Improvements, Progress and State of Medicine in the XVIIIth Century.* The following excerpts are illustrative of his elegant style, with judicious selection of plain simple words in describing the progress of medicine.[3]

Millions of the human race have lived and died without ever having seen such a day as the present. . . . No one, who now hears me, will ever see the like again. . . . On this singular day, of which only one occurs in the life of man, it is decent and proper to make a pause, and look back on that important division of time, which yesterday was completely and for ever closed. It was, therefore, wisely resolved by our society, to appoint of its members to introduce the new century, by recapitulating what had been done by, and for our profession, in the old.

While the great and striking improvements made by our predecessors, in the healing art, are passing in review before us, the advantages which have resulted from their labours, cannot fail of enkindling in our breasts a holy ambition to imitate their glorious example, by perfecting what they have left undone.

The following are Ramsay's major historical contributions: *The History of the Revolution of South-Carolina,* 2 volumes (1785); *History of South Carolina From Its First Settlement in 1670 to the Year 1808,* 2 volumes (1809); *The History of the American Revolution,* 2 volumes (1789); *The Life of George Washington,* ed 2 (1811); *A History of the United States to the Year 1808,* 3 volumes (1816-1817); and *Universal History Americanized,* 12 volumes (1819), published posthumously. In these monumental historical endeavors Ramsay was sometimes lax in allocating full credit to the source for each passage used. It may not be surprising, then, that professional historians charged him with plagiarism for his heavy reliance upon the British *Annual Register* in preparing *The History of the American Revolution.* More than a century later in *The American Historical Review* an attempt was made to besmirch his reputation as a Colonial historian. The best example advanced in this communication leaves considerable doubt that the charge was justified. Since the *Annual Reg-*

ister was an official document and public property, the charge of plagiarism seems to be a minor rather than a major charge. The quotations are as follows.[4]

Annual Register, 1775, p. 10, c. 1-2.
The people of America at this time, with respect to political opinions, might in general be divided into two great classes. Of these one was for rushing headlong into the greatest extremities. . . . The other, if less numerous, was not less respectable and though more moderate was perhaps equally firm. . . .

Ramsay, I. 125. The inhabitants of the colonies at this time with regard to political opinions might be divided into three classes; of these one was for rushing precipitately into extremities. . . . Another party equally respectable, both as to character, property and patriotism, was more moderate but not less firm. . . . A third class disapproved of what was generally going on. . . . All these latter classes for the most part lay still, while the friends of liberty acted with spirit.

A friend of Washington, Jefferson, Madison, and other statesmen, Ramsay was recognized as one of the great patriots of colonial times. His life ended abruptly when he was shot in the back with a horse pistol by a lunatic, a defendant in court on a charge of insanity. Ramsay had given medical testimony against him.[5]

1. Hayne, R. Y.: Biographical Memoir of David Ramsay, M.D., *Analectic Mag* 6:204-224, 1815.
2. Ramsay, D.: *Dissertation on the Means of Preserving Health, in Charleston, and the Adjacent Low Country,* Charleston, SC: Markland & Melver, 1790.
3. Ramsay, D.: *A Review of the Improvements, Progress and State of Medicine in the XVIIIth Century,* Charleston, SC: W. P. Young, 1801.
4. Libby, O. G.: Ramsay as a Plagiarist, *Amer Hist Rev* 7:697-703, 1902.
5. Waring, J. I.: *A History of Medicine in South Carolina 1670-1825,* Charleston, SC: South Carolina Medical Associaton, 1964.

Lemuel Hopkins (1750-1801)

LEMUEL HOPKINS, physician and popular satirist, was born near Waterbury, Connecticut, the son of a well-to-do farmer of sturdy Colonial stock.[1] The children worked the land but were provided a sound primary education. Lemuel's training in medicine was gained as an apprentice to Dr. Jared Potter of Wallingford and Dr. Seth Bird of Litchfield, where about 1776 he began his practice. By 1784, Yale recognized his repu-

Composite by G. Bako

tation and outstanding traits and conferred on him the honorary degree of AM. At about this time Hopkins moved to Hartford; there he remained until death from tuberculosis.

Hopkins, an eminent practitioner, displayed a keen mind, an unusual memory, and an outspoken distaste for quackery. He was one of the founders of the Connecticut Medical Society and an honorary member of the Massachusetts Medical Society. The family tendency toward consumption focused his attention on the disease; and, as he became a recognized authority on tuberculosis, he was in great demand as a consultant. His regimen of treatment of diseases was in advance of the time, especially his recommendation of fresh air, wholesome food, and exercise for tuberculosis as well as for other fevers.[2] The original manuscript on tuberculosis has been destroyed, but a transcription remains.

Equally notable were Hopkins' satirical contributions to the Hartford Wits, a literary group that cultivated poetry after the Revolution. Among the contributors, attracting wide attention, were John Trumbull, Joel Barlow, David Humphreys, and Lemuel Hopkins. They composed, among several items, *The Anarchiad: a Poem on the Restoration of Chaos and Substantial Night,* a political satire.[3] Hopkins had his hand in others; whereas his "Epitaph on a Patient Killed by a Cancer Quack" exposed the charlatans who claimed cancer could be cured by secret remedies. Excerpts are as follows:[4]

Here lies a fool flat on his back,
The victim of a Cancer Quack;
Who lost his money and his life,
By plaister, caustic, and by knife.
The case was this—a pimple rose,
South-east a little of his nose;
Which daily reden'd and grew bigger,
As too much drinking gave it vigour:
A score of gossips soon ensure
Full three score diff'rent modes of cure:
But yet the full-fed pimple still
Defied all petticoated skill;
When fortune led him to peruse
A hand-bill in the weekly news;
Sign'd by six fools of diff'rent sorts,
All cur'd of cancers made of warts;
Who recommend, with due submission,
This cancer-monger as magician;
Fear wing'd his flight to find the quack,
And prove his cancer-curing knack;
But on his way he found another,
A second advertising brother.

This doctor view'd, with moony eyes
And scowl'd up face, the pimple's size;
Then christen'd it in solemn answer,
And cried, "This pimple's name is CANCER."
"But courage, friend, I see you're pale,
"My sweating plaisters never fail;
"I've sweated hundreds out with ease,
"With roots as long as maple trees;
"And never fail'd in all my trials—
"Behold these samples here in vials!
"Preserv'd to shew my wond'rous merits,
"Just as my liver is—in spirits."

"Courage, 'tis done," the doctor cried,
And quick th' incision knife applied:
That with three cuts made such a hole,
Out flew the patient's tortur'd soul!

Go, readers, gentle, eke and simple,
If you have wart, or corn, or pimple;
To quack infallible apply;

Here's room enough for you to lie.
His skill triumphant still prevails,
For DEATH's a cure that never fails.

1. Thacher, J.: "Dr. Lemuel Hopkins," in *American Medical Biography,* Boston: Richardson & Lord & Cottons & Barnard, 1828, vol 1, pp. 298-304.

2. Steiner, W. R.: Dr. Lemuel Hopkins, One of the Celebrated Hartford Wits, and a Forgotten, Distinguished American Student of Tuberculosis, *Bull Hopkins Hosp* 21:16-27, 1910.

3. Humphreys, D., et al: *The Anarchiad: a New England Poem,* New Haven, Conn: T. H. Pease, 1861.

4. Hopkins, L.: Epitaph on a Patient Killed by a Cancer Quack, *American Poems,* Litchfield, Conn: Collier and Buel, 1793, vol 1, pp 137-139.

Composite by G. Bako

William Thornton (1761-1828)

THE STORY OF THE PROFESSIONAL CAREER of William Thornton tells of a physician with many talents who failed to give the practice of medicine an opportunity to develop.[1] He was born of English Quaker parents on Jost van Dyke island in the British West Indies and at the age of five was sent to Lancaster to be with his grandparents. At the age of 16, he began an apprenticeship in medicine, which was followed by three years at the University of Edinburgh. Lacking full credit he qualified for the MD degree at the University of Aberdeen in 1784. Thornton had intended to practice medicine in the West Indies but after hospital experience at St. Bartholomew's in London and an extended tour of the Continent, he was attracted to America and, in 1788, obtained citizenship in the state of Delaware. With a Quaker background he was further attracted to Philadelphia, where he established residence and social contacts with Thomas Jefferson, Benjamin Franklin, and Benjamin Rush.

Thornton's first professional conquest was the prize in competition for the Ionic design of the quarters for the Library Company of Philadelphia. This was gained in 1789 without formal training in architecture, nothing more than a critical perusal of related books on the subject in the stacks and an ability to sketch. His next and greatest success in architecture was the National Capitol in Washington. Although he was living in the West Indies at the time of announcement of request for plans, he succeeded in postponing the deadline for final plans and when his revised design was reviewed, he was awarded in 1792 the $500 prize and a building lot in the capital city. George Washington was especially pleased with Thornton's plans which required extensive further revision for structural execution.[2] Modifications were carried out under the direction of Hallet, French contender for the prize, an appointee as consulting architect. Thornton could not be retained, because he lacked professional training. In 1794, Thornton was appointed to the Board of Commissioners and succeeded Hallet as architect. The building as finally constructed contained the wings according to Thornton's plans and a compromised central Rotunda.

Thornton remained in Washington in the employment of the government as superintendent of the newly-formed Patent Office and held this post until his death. In the meantime, at the request of Thomas Jefferson, he designed Pavilion VII at the University of Virginia in Charlottesville and

several homes in Washington, especially the Octagon, the temporary home of President Madison after the burning of the White House in 1814. His official duties in the Patent Office were peculiarly suited to him. Together with John Fitch, who had made a boat propelled by steam reach a speed of eight miles per hour as early as 1788, he foresaw the advantages of steam power almost three decades before Fulton's successful run on the Hudson River.[1] During the capture of Washington by the British in 1814 the Patent Office was saved from destruction by Thornton's direct intervention. Also, Thornton was an artist, loved horse racing, composed poetry, recommended colonization of Africa by the slaves in America, was sympathetic to the liberation of South America, proposed a canal between the Atlantic and the Pacific in Panama, and was a breeder of racing horses and merino sheep.

Thornton's only composition of medical interest is an essay on teaching the deaf to speak, which Alexander Graham Bell believed to be the first published work on the subject. This appeared in the *Transactions of the American Philosophical Society,* of which Thornton was a member.[4]

The difficulties under which those have laboured, who have attempted to teach the surd, and consequently dumb to speak, have prevented many from engaging in a labour that can scarcely be exceeded in utility; for some of those to whom nature has denied particular faculties have in other respects been the boast of the human species; and whoever supplies the defects of formation, and gives to man the means of surmounting natural impediments, must be considered as a benefactor. There have been many successful attempts in diverse nations, to procure to the deaf and dumb the modes of acquiring and communicating ideas.—The methods however are slow and imperfect.—The written and spoken languages are so different, that they become to such pupils two distinct studies.

The more I resolve in my mind this subject, the more I am astonished that even the most improved nations have neglected so important a matter as that of correcting their language; I know of none, not even the Italian, that is not replete with absurdity; and I shall endeavour to shew the facility with which the deaf might be taught to speak, if proper attention were once paid to this important point.

I have attempted to shew that in the English language there are thirty characters, and must suppose a dictionary according to this scheme of the alphabet, upon which I mean to build.

1. Clarke, A. C.: Doctor and Mrs. William Thornton, *Records of the Columbia Historical Society,* 18:144-208, Washington, D.C., 1915.

2. Kimball, S., and Bennett, W.: William Thornton and the Design of the United States Capitol, in *Art Studies: Medieval Renaissance and Modern;* Edited by Members of the Departments of the Fine Arts at Harvard and Princeton Universities, 4 vol, Cambridge, Mass.: Harvard University Press, 1923, vol 1, pp 76-92.

3. Bell, M.: *Dr. William Thornton and his Essay on "Teaching the Deaf, or Surd, and Consequently Dumb, to Speak,"* 1793, pp 228-230.

Composite by G. Bako

John Peter Mettauer (1787-1875)

JOHN P. METTAUER, son of an Alsatian surgeon who came to America under Rochambeau, subsequently settled near Farmville in Prince Edward County, Virginia. Young Mettauer began his education in the secondary schools followed by higher learning in the college of Hampden-Sydney. In 1807, he began the study of medicine at the University of Pennsylvania.[1] Shippen, Rush, Wistar, and Physick were members of the faculty which awarded him the MD degree in 1809. Mettauer returned to Prince Edward County to practice and to remain until his death, except for duty in the War of 1812 and a short period of time spent as professor of surgery at Washington Medical College, Baltimore.

Mettauer, a bold, original, and resourceful surgeon, attracted patients from many parts of the United States to his provincial practice and country hospital. His operations, numbered in the hundreds, included cataract, stricture of the urethra, staphylorrhaphy, extirpation of the parotid, ligation of the carotid artery, resection of the superior maxilla, lithotomy, and cleft palate. Many were performed before the discovery of ether for anesthesia; most with instruments made by himself or under his direction. Apart from gynecology and surgery Mettauer is believed to have recognized typhus fever as a distinct disease from typhoid fever before Louis and Gerhart. Although he practiced bleeding and purging, he appreciated the pathological state now identified as shock, which he called a "traumatic irritation," and realized that lithotomy or any surgical procedure in its presence associated with significant loss of blood might be fatal.

Mettauer was a ceaseless writer. In addition to many contributions appearing in local or national medical journals, he left unpublished at his death more than 3,000 manuscript pages for a text on surgery. His interest in medical education extended beyond the instruction of apprentices. In 1837, Mettauer organized the Prince Edward Medical Institute at Prince Edward Courthouse and remained as the only member of the faculty responsible for the teaching of preclinical and clinical subjects until 1847; it then became the Medical Department of Randolph-Macon College with an expanded faculty to include his two older sons. The school exercised the power of conferring degrees until it closed in 1855.

Mettauer's gynecologic procedures were probably his best-known operations. In 1833, he reported a case of parturient laceration of the rectovaginal septum with the employment of metallic sutures. In 1838, Mettauer treated successfully a vesico-vabinal fistula later reported in the *Boston Medical and Surgical Journal.*[2]

Sir,—In my last letter to you, I am not certain whether I informed you that I had succeeded in relieving a case of vesico-vaginal fistula of most unpromising character. If I have not made such intimation to you, I will now state, that I operated in August, 1838. The opening had existed three years, was fully as large as half a dollar, and had, at the time I treated it, a large fungous growth protruding from the mucous membrane of the bladder through it, which greatly embarrassed the operation. I was enabled to gain admission to the fistulous opening through a hollow conoidal speculum of proper size and length; through it the operation was executed. The margins at the opening were denuded with curved scissors, using hooks to draw out the portions to be removed. In closing the opening, I employed an instrument similar to the one I constructed for cleft palate, for introducing the ligatures from the vesical surface, and the leaden wire was used as the means of suture. Only one operation was required. Six sutures were introduced; and it was only necessary to tighten them once after the operation. In three weeks the wires were removed, and a firm and perfect union was found to have taken place between the edges of the opening. A short silver tube was kept constantly in the urethra for four weeks. The patient, at the date of this note, is well—nearly two years since the operation was performed.

I should think my case the first one successfully treated in this country, as it preceded Dr. Hayward's nearly a year.

In personal life Mettauer was exclusive in his habits, admitting few persons to intimacy. He showed great capacity for work, almost into his terminal days, and was tireless in the pursuit of the many phases of a country doctor a century ago, except for attendance at religious services. He was tall and immediately recognized by a stovepipe hat worn at all times, including appearances in court. He was married four times and sired three daughters and three sons; all of the latter followed their father in his profession.

1. Rucker, P.: Dr. John Peter Mettauer; An Early Southern Gynecologist, *Ann Med Hist* 10:36-46, 1938.
2. Mettauer, J. P., Vesico-vaginal Fistula, *Boston Med Surg J* 22:154-155, 1840.

Composite by G. Bako

William E. Horner (1793-1853)

W. E. HORNER, native of Warrenton, Virginia, and successor sequentially to Philip Syng Physick, John Syng Dorsey, Caspar Wistar, and William Shippen in the chair of anatomy at the University of Pennsylvania, prepared the first treatise in America on pathological anatomy. His father, a merchant of modest means, provided academy schooling at Warrenton and Dumfries under a classical scholar, the Rev. Charles O'Neill, and an apprenticeship with Dr. John Spence for three years.[1] At the age of 19, Horner entered the University of Pennsylvania; the following year he was commissioned as surgeon's mate and served in the Niagara frontier at the head of Lake Erie, attending the wounded from the battles of Chippewa, Bridgewater, Black Rock, and Fort Erie. A furlough granted through the winter enabled him to complete his work at Pennsylvania, and in the spring of 1814 he received the MD degree. After release from the service, he began general practice in Warrenton but soon was attracted to Philadelphia, with the expectation of greater opportunities.

Frail of constitution and aware of his limitations, Horner sought emotional outlets in his books and studies, which enhanced an average intellect and an unimaginative mind. Because of an interest in teaching in the medical school, Caspar Wistar appointed him dissector in anatomy, followed in time as demonstrator to John Syng Dorsey and assistant to Philip Syng Physick. By 1819, Horner was adjunct professor of anatomy and in 1831 was elected head of the department, one of the outstanding chairs in the preclinical departments in America. Meanwhile, he continued the private practice of surgery and was appointed dean of the Medical School, a post he held for more than 30 years.

Horner's contributions to the medical literature included three monographs, several anatomical descriptions, and a number of case reports in the *American Journal of the Medical Sciences.* The description of the tensor tarsi, a muscle in the lachrymal apparatus which bears his name, appeared in the *Philadelphia Journal of the Medical and Physical Sciences,* then edited by Nathaniel Chapman, first President of the American Medical Association. Other minor anatomical advances included a description of the cartilages at the bronchial subdivisions, a comparative study of the axillary sweat glands of the Caucasian and Negro races, and investigations on the musculature of the rectum and the fibroelastic submucous membrane of the larynx which he called the "Phonetic or Vocal Membrane." Horner's dissection of the larchrymal apparatus of sheep led to the discovery of the small muscle of the internal commissure of the eyelid (muscle of Horner), which resulted from a search for the explanation of the constant application of the puncta lachrymalia to the surface of the eye. Not satisfied with his investigations in the sheep, he laid open the orbit of a human subject, noting[2]:

I . . . forthwith had the pleasure of finding a small muscle, which from its position and connexions, seemed well adapted to supply the defect in the known mechanism of the lachrymal passages.

The muscle alluded to, lies on the posterior face of the lachrymal ducts and sac. It is oblong, being in the adult about three lines broad and six lines long. It arises from the posterior superior part of the os unguis just in advance of the vertical suture between the os planum and the os unguis.

The existence of this muscle being fully established by observations which every anatomist can readily verify, it will be extremely useful to ascertain its agency on the motion of the eyelids, and its influence in conducting, or in assisting to conduct, the tears from the ball of the eye to the nose. It appears to be clear, from its origin and insertion, that its contraction in a moderate degree will tend to apply the puncta lachrymalia to the ball of the eye, and is therefore so far efficient in regulating the lachrymal passages, by keeping the puncta immersed in the tears that accumulate at the internal commissure of the eyelids.

Horner's first text, a handbook for dissection entitled *Lessons in Practical Anatomy, for the Use of Dissectors,* unimportant but prophetic, was followed by his *Special Anatomy and Histology,* which appeared in two volumes in 1826, followed three years later with *A Treatise on Pathological Anatomy.* The contents of the latter follow the traditional discussions of the standard texts on the subject by European authors. Inflammation, with its sequelae in the mucous and serous membranes and connective tissue, was assigned the pathogenic factors in most diseases. Many postmortem protocols were presented. In the "Introduction," Horner identifies the position of pathological anatomy in the training of a physician.[3]

Without pathological anatomy it is very possible for a physician to be fully instructed in the literature of his profession, to be versed in the theories of all the celebrated teachers from Hippocrates to the present time, to have an intellect perfectly sound in the processes of induction, to be continually exercising his judgement and skill in the treatment of diseases; yet if he has not accurately depicted on his mind, the morbid lesions which are going on in the system, it is impossible to exercise his calling as a science, and as has been pithily observed, he will have seen many patients, but no diseases. Execute dissections, and a new horizon is unfolded to view: the darkness which hung over his path becomes a brilliant and a shining light; the uncertainty which attended his steps is converted into assurance; the mistakes of prognostic which compromitted his character, are converted into the prophecies of a superior intelligence. Such is the difference between the practical and the speculative physician; between the man whose studies have been chastened by a continued reference to the evidence of dissections, and one who has resisted or neglected them.

Medical problems as well as surgical practice occupied Horner's time. During the cholera epidemic of 1832, he was placed in charge of the municipal hospital on Dock Street and served as prescribing physician at the Alms House Hospital on Spruce Street. Experience derived from these assignments was augmented in 1834 by a return of cholera in his private practice and among the inmates of the Alms House, which had then been transferred to the new building in Blockley Township. More than 200 cases of cholera, including hospital and private practice, were under his immediate care. Microscopic study of the stools and intestinal lesions postmortem convinced him that the rice water appearance of the feces followed the desquamation of the epithelium of the intestines. He summarized the morbid anatomical characteristics of the alimentary canal in cholera as follows:[4]

First.—A copious vesicular eruption, entirely distinct from the tumefaction of villi, muciparous follicles or glands, and which pervades the whole canal.

Second.—A lining membrane of coagulated lymph, which exists in the small intestines at least, if not in the stomach and colon also, and resembles in texture and mode of adhesion the membrane of croup.

Third.—Vascular derangements and phenomena which are confined almost exclusively, if not entirely so, to the venous system.

Fourth.—An exfoliation of the epidermic and venous lining of the alimentary canal, whereby the extremities of the venous system are denuded, and left patulous.

Horner spent a year on the Continent in 1821 and subsequently returned there in 1848, lingering with Rokitansky in Vienna and visiting hospitals and anatomical museums in England, France, and Germany. An injury to his head in his late twenties left him with attacks of vertigo and headache and periods of despondency. In later years he was troubled with attacks of dyspnea, pulmonary edema, and terminally with dropsy. Whether there was any relation between a feeble body and despondency is questionable, but his biographers mention his tendency to introspection and moral conscience as a habitual state of mind. Always a deeply religious man, Horner changed from the Episcopalian faith to Catholicism after study and meditation. He served his new religion as a communicant as well as physician and surgeon to the newly-built

St. Joseph's Hospital. One of the reasons advanced for his conversion was the utter abandonment of self by the priests and nuns caring for the cholera patients during the epidemics. While others shunned the afflicted in the gloom of pestilence, Horner was aware that the members of the holy orders cared for the sick and looked to Heaven for their reward.

1. Jackson, S.: *A Discourse Commemorative of the Late William E. Horner, M.D.*, Philadelphia: T. K. & P. G. Collins, 1853.
2. Horner, W. E.: Description of a Small Muscle at the Internal Commissure of the Eyelids, *Phila J Med Phys Sci* 8:70-80, 1824.
3. Horner, W. E.: *A Treatise on Pathological Anatomy*, Philadelphia: Carey, Lea & Carey, 1829.
4. Horner, W. E.: On the Anatomical Characters of Asiatic Cholera, With Remarks on the Structure of the Mucous Coat of the Alimentary Canal, *Amer J Med Sci* 16:58-295, 1835.

Composite by G. Bako

George McClellan (1796-1847)

GEORGE McCLELLAN, bright and capricious surgeon of Philadelphia, was born in Woodstock, Connecticut, of rugged Scottish stock.[1] His father was principal of the Woodstock Academy, where he obtained his early education, with attention to mathematics, Greek, and Latin. McClellan was admitted to Yale College in advanced standing, graduating AB in 1816. There he formed a close friendship with Professor Silliman, who interested him in the natural sciences. Following graduation he was apprenticed to Thomas Hubbard of Pomfret, later professor of surgery at the medical school in New Haven. McClellan continued his medical training at the University of Pennsylvania as a pupil of John Syng Dorsey, professor of anatomy and materia medica. The MD degree was granted in 1819, upon presentation of a thesis, entitled *Surgical Anatomy of Arteries*. Meanwhile his service for one year as undergraduate resident at the Philadelphia Almshouse provided him the opportunity to spend many hours in the morgue, examining and dissecting the dead and developing his operative techniques for common as well as unusual operations.

McClellan opened an office in Philadelphia for the practice of medicine and surgery, gave private lectures in anatomy and surgery, and built a reputation as a bold and skillful ophthalmic and general surgeon. He also founded an institution for the diseases of the eye and ear. Abandoning this project four years later, McClellan led a small group of less competent associates in founding Jefferson Medical College, the medical department of Jefferson College at Canonsburg, Pennsylvania, under the control of Scottish Presbyterians. After the school received a charter from the legislature in 1825, the following year McClellan took over the chair of surgery.

The establishment of a second medical school in Philadelphia was widely condemned, and many of his opponents never forgave him. However, the school was successful and provided healthy competition to the Pennsylvania faculty. In spite of attracting a large number of students, adverse conditions developed; for reasons never publicly stated, the Board of Trustees declared all the professional chairs vacant and refused to reappoint McClellan. He countered, however, by obtaining a charter for the medical department of Pennsylvania College, an affiliate of the school of the same name at Gettysburg, Pennsylvania. The first

course of lectures was begun in November, 1839, and, because of several factors including financial difficulties, the lectures were terminated in the spring of 1843. This proved his last attempt to establish a medical institution, for he passed the remaining years of his life in active practice.

McClellan's skill in dissection and operative surgery fostered from his earlier days at the Almshouse led to his recognized leadership in American surgery. He developed a number of unusual procedures, notably, ligation of the innominate artery, dissection of the clavicle and scapula, dissection of one or more ribs, and extirpation of the parotid gland. The latter was performed on eleven patients with one death. The operations were performed without benefit of ether or chloroform anesthesia and were described in his *Principles and Practice of Surgery*, an unimportant text incomplete at his death. It was published later by his son. In the initial section, entitled "The Immediate Effects of Injuries Upon the System," the discussion of shock was commendable. Excerpts are as follows.[2]

The more immediate effects of injuries, and of all other influences which produce similar results upon the animal fabric, are unquestionably communicated through the medium of the nervous system. The contents of the blood-vessels disturb the actions of life only when they are contaminated by the admission of morbid, or irritating, or poisonous materials; and then it is a question whether the results are not dependent on a final impression upon some portion of the cerebral or spinal apparatus. The vessels are everywhere, in a great degree, subordinate to the nerves.

The first result of a local injury upon the living parts, is a more or less appreciable disturbance of their functions in an outward, or, if we may use the expression, in a centrifugal direction from the nervous centres. . . . Many patients are not made aware of an injury by any feeling of its consequences on the system. Local inconveniences in the same way occur without any suffering of the constitution.

But it more frequently happens that the direct as well as ultimate impression of an injury is propagated towards the great nervous centres. Whenever a painful sensation is experienced, the nervous current must have been centripetal—for a divided sentient filament can never be irritated by an impression on its remote extremity. Every pain felt in the injured part must be the result of a reflexion from the sensorium through the affected nervous filaments; and the sympathetic distant sensations, as well as muscular spasms, which are so often experienced after wounds, can only be referred to the reflex actions of the spinal cord.

Shocks are, however, generally propagated more extensively throughout the system, and become the evidences of what the old surgeons used to call constitutional alarm. In very severe cases the same effects are produced as occur in concussions of the brain. After terrible falls and injuries upon the trunk or extremities, the abolition of sense and motion and of circulating power, is as complete as when the force is directly communicated to the head. It must not be supposed, however, that such cases are always the result of cerebral injury. The passage of heavy bodies, like large timbers or millstones, across the lower extremities, has produced the same condition of things, although no suspicion of a concussion of the brain could have been entertained.

But this extension of the force of a shock is distributed in a great diversity of modes as well as intensity in different cases. The circulating or respiratory organs will be most deranged in one case, the cerebral in another, and the digestive or urinary in a third. In the less intense forms there is nothing but a paleness or languor, and universal sense of coldness, sometimes attended with tremors and fright, and hurried respiration. In a severer grade there will be a small, intermitting or tremulous pulse, irregular or sighing respiration, shivering or rigors, with imperfect apprehension and incoherency of mind, vomiting and convulsions frequently supervening. In a still graver form, the patient will be either delirious or comatose, with involuntary discharges and a cold clammy sweat; and in the highest grades, such as have been termed overwhelming shocks, he will present the appearance of extreme and protracted syncope.

McClellan was not a prolific writer and apparently found little interest in this phase of academic medicine. However, he was capable of clear thinking and concise composition on financial as well as clinical matters, as judged by the excerpts from his valedictory address, delivered in 1836 to the graduates of the Jefferson Medical College.[3]

But it is natural that you should look for a support, nay, even for a great superfluity of emolument from the exercise of so onerous and self-denying a profession as ours. Although it is easy to talk of disinterestedness and of a zeal for the public welfare, still I presume it will be hard to point out any one among you, who has not some reference in his calculations to the degree of remuneration he is to receive for the long and expensive course of preparation he has undergone, and for the life of severe and unremitting labour he is to lead.

In regard to the best mode of cultivating your profession, I shall have time to say but a few words. Recollect what I have so often, and so constantly urged on your attention, respecting the rules of inductive science. Be always governed by the observation of symptoms, and not by the imaginary causes of them. The whole science of nature consists in the classification of phenomena. We can do but very little in the way of theory, and nothing in the way of hypothesis. Be content, I beg of you, to follow the dictates of common sense, in all cases, and under all circumstances. Be satisfied with the opinions you can form, from a plain and careful examination of the indications which nature holds up to your view; and reject all inquiry into the secret and definable causes of life and disease.

But the wealth you may acquire from the most brilliant success, will be nothing; the reputation which you may hope to gain, throughout the whole civilized globe, by a long life of industry and genius, will be nothing; in comparison with the heart-cheering satisfaction which you will experience, in being conscious of your *usefulness*. You will serve the deepest interests of humanity.

The brilliancy mentioned initially is documented by his incorporation into his current experiences the results of his speed reading, the stimulus provided his associates and students, his penetrating and rapid analysis of clinical problems, and the early age of professional maturity. Within the span of years allotted, McClellan lived many decades as judged by the accomplishments of others.

1. Gross, S. D.: *Lives of Eminent American Physicians and Surgeons,* Philadelphia: Lindsay & Blakiston, 1861.
2. McClellan, G.: *Principles and Practice of Surgery,* Philadelphia: Grigg, Elliot & Co., 1848.
3. McClellan, G.: *Valedictory Address Delivered to the Graduates of the Jefferson Medical College, March, 1836,* Philadelphia: W. S. Martien, 1836.

Thomas Young (1773-1829)

THE ENGLISH LEONARDO DA VINCI, Thomas Young, a humanist endowed with the intellect of a genius, dealt in depth with a great number of scientific matters, including the practice of medicine, the theory of color vision, and the mechanism of ocular accommodation. Thomas was born in Milverton, England, the eldest of ten children of a Quaker and a substantial property owner.[1] Evidence of the son's precocity was readily apparent, since he learned to read at the age of two and began the study of Latin at the age of six. Greek, mathematics, and natural philosophy were then pursued, followed by studies in philosophy including Hebrew, Chaldean, Syriac, and Persian. At the age of 13, he wrote a comprehensive analysis of the Greek schools of philosophy and was recognized as a classical tutor when only 14, having added French, Italian, and Spanish to his repertory.[2]

Upon the advice of Dr. Richard Brocklesby, a maternal great uncle, Thomas was persuaded to enter medicine. He took up residence in London in 1792 and attended the lectures of Matthew Baillie, William Cruikshank, and John Hunter. He studied for a time at St. Bartholomew's Hospital and, in the following year, prepared a treatise on accommodation, an outstanding contribution to the science of optics. The communication was presented to the Royal Society of London, was published in the *Philosophical Transactions,* and was held to be a contributing factor in Young's election to this body shortly after. After two years in medicine and languages at the University of Edinburgh, he later studied at Göttingen, where he was made doctor of physic upon presentation of a thesis, "De corporis humani viribus conservatricibus."

The death of Brocklesby provided Young with financial independence and a home in London, where he had begun the practice of medicine at the age of 26. He shared time and intellectual energy in medicine with studies and lectures on sound and light and other nonmedical subjects. In spite of great talents and interest in academic pursuits and formal scholarship, Young held only one professorship, that of natural philosophy at the Royal Institution, and this for two years only. Under natural philosophy he discussed mechanics—theoretical and practical, hydrostatics, hydrodynamics, acoustics, optics, astronomy, theory of time, properties of matter, cohesion, electricity, magnetism, theory of heat, and climatology. Critical investigations in physics in later years led to the introduction of the physical concepts of modules of elasticity, "energy," and "work done," and their proportionality. Heat was regarded as molecular vibrations of particles larger than those of light. His lectures were reputed to embrace one of the greatest systems of natural philosophy ever present. They were precise and accurate, hence frequently considered dull by listeners. Abstruse and difficult subjects were discussed and, like da Vinci, Young displayed a prophetic insight into many matters.

Rigorous habits of work enabled him to accomplish so much. He rose an hour earlier than his classmates in summer and retired an hour or more later in winter. His philosophy of intellectual industry and intellectual leisure was defined while a student.[3]

Leisure and application are the great requisites for improving the mind: leisure is useless without application; but application with a very little leisure may produce very material benefit. If you are careful of your vacant minutes, you may advance yourselves more than many do who have every convenience afforded them.

In order to test the accuracy of his idioms and syntax, Young wrote in whatever language he was studying at any specific period. When he read in French or Italian, annotations were made in the respective tongue. His diary and thesis were prepared in Latin. Study notes were written in Latin, and the reference treatises were translated from Latin into English. His writings were laconic and remarkably clear, but the material presented presumed knowledge and understanding by the reader equal to that of the writer. Thus, his published communications, like his lectures, were considered cumbersome and prosaic by those of inferior training and intellect.

The deciphering of the Rosetta stone was the most spectacular of his investigations in philology. Fifteen years after the discovery of this remarkable stone tablet, attempts to decipher the hieroglyphics had been only partially successful. On the other hand, the first crucial steps toward decipherment had been taken by Young three years after the task was undertaken. The decree of the priests was carved on the tablet in three scripts: Egyptian hieroglyphic or sacred, Egyptian demotic or enchorial, and Greek. The name "Ptolemy" was recognized by Young, who unraveled the phonetic character of the hierglyphs in the royal rings. From the name he deciphered the hieroglyphs, now translated *p, t, l, m, y, s* and gave to them the assigned values *p, t, ole, m, i, os,* and from other portions, *f.* Thus, the phonetic character of Egyptian writing was exposed. So great was Young's interest in Egyptian hieroglyphic literature and antiquities, he was engaged in the preparation of an Egyptian dictionary up to his death.

Young was elected a Fellow of the College of Physicians in 1809, having received first a BM, and in 1808 the MD at Cambridge. He was on the staff and lectured at Middlesex Hospital and St. George's Hos-

pital, until he retired from practice in 1814. Young was not a particularly popular physician. Perhaps he was too discerning a scientist to inspire faith in his patients. However, any lack of confidence in his medical judgment was undeserved. In the study of disease and evaluation of medical literature, he was highly competent. His practical and historical treatise on *Consumptive Diseases* was thoroughly comprehensive and unusual in that it reflected upon significant items of ancient and modern medicine. *An Introduction to Medical Literature, Including a System of Practical Nosology* was published shortly before he retired from practice.[4] It broke from the tradition of Cullen and followed the botanical system of Linnaeus. The Croonian lectures in 1808 discussed the function of the heart and arteries and the regulation of the flow of blood through the body.

Young accepted several government responsibilities. He participated in a study of the risks associated with the proposed introduction of illuminating gas in London, and was a member of a commission for ascertaining the length of the second's pendulum and for the establishment of the imperial gallon of ten pounds of water. He received a mandate to prepare the calculations of the Nautical Almanack, submitted a report on marine architecture, served on the Board of Longitude, was appointed inspector of calculations to the Palladium Insurance Company, and published several communications that dealt with probabilities in life insurance.

His observations on the physiology of vision, presented before the Royal Society while a student in London, gave full credit to those who preceded him, and particularly to Descartes, who assumed that contraction and elongation of the lens was responsible for accommodation. One year after the following excerpts were published, it was demonstrated by Sir Everard Home and the optician, Ramsden, that no part of the lens is muscular.[5]

It is well known that the eye, when not acted upon by any exertion of the mind, conveys a distinct impression of those objects only which are situated at a certain distance from itself; that this distance is different in different persons, and that the eye can, by the volition of the mind, be accommodated to view other objects at a much less distance: but how this accommodation is effected, has long been a matter of dispute, and has not yet been satisfactorily explained.

From these considerations, and from the observation of Dr. Porterfield, that those who have been couched have no longer the power of accommodating the eye to different distances, I had concluded that the rays of light, emitted by objects at a small distance, could only be brought to foci on the retina by a nearer approach of the crystalline to a spherical form; and I could imagine no other power capable of producing this change than a muscularity of a part, or the whole, or its capsule.

The statement of the theory of color vision (later modified and called the Young-Helmholtz theory), appeared in the *Philosophical Transactions of the Royal Society* of 1802.[6] According to Young, the retina contained three types of cones. When stimulated by light, the sensations of red, green, and blue were elicited. Color blindness, on the other hand, was due to a failure of one or more structures to respond to normal stimuli.

. . . . It was long an established opinion, that heat consists in vibrations of the particles of bodies, and is capable of being transmitted by undulations through an apparent vacuum.

Let us suppose that these vibrations are less frequent than those of light; all bodies therefore are liable to permanent vibrations slower than those of light; and indeed almost all are liable to luminous vibrations, either when in a state of ignition, or in the circumstances of solar phosphori; but much less easily, and in a much less degree, than to the vibrations of heat. It will follow from these suppositions, that the more frequent luminous undulations will be more retarded than the less frequent; and consequently, that blue light will be more refrangible than red, and radiant heat least of all.

In discussing the mechanism of the eye, Young gave the first description of the measurement of astigmatism, a table of optical constants of the eye, and the description of an improved optometer.[7]

. . . . I shall then enumerate some dioptrical propositions subservient to my purposes, and describe an instrument for readily ascertaining the focal distance of the eye. On these foundations, I shall investigate the dimensions and re-fractive powers of the human eye in its quiescent state; and the form and magnitude of the picture which is delineated on the retina.

Young did not understand or fully comprehend that astigmatism could be present in the cornea as well as in the lens, nor did he suggest correction by a cylindrical lens. Helmholtz summarized the stature of the contributions of the greatest natural philosopher in England, next to Newton, and the most erudite physician·in his generation.[1]

He was one of the most clearsighted men who have ever lived, but he had the misfortune to be too greatly superior in sagacity to his contemporaries. They gazed at him with astonishment, but could not always follow the bold flights of his intellect, and thus a multitude of his most important ideas lay buried and forgotten in the great tomes of the Royal Society of London, till a later generation in tardy advance remade his discoveries and convinced itself of the accuracy and force of his inferences.

1. "Thomas Young," in *The Dictionary of National Biography*, vol 21, Oxford: University Press, 1917, pp 1308-1314.
2. Peacock, G.: *Life of Thomas Young, M.D., F.R.S.*, London: J. Murray, 1855.
3. Pettigrew, T. J.: *Biographical Memoirs of the Most Celebrated Physicians and Surgeons*, vol 4, London: Whittaker & Co., 1840.
4. Young, T.: *An Introduction to Medical Literature, Including a System of Practical Nosology*, London: B. R. Howlett, 1813.
5. Young, T.: Observations on Vision, Communicated by Richard Brocklesby, *Philos Trans* 83:169-181, 1793.
6. Young, T.: The Bakerian Lecture. On the Theory of Light and Colours, *Philos Trans* 91:12-48, 1802.
7. Young, T.: The Bakerian Lecture. On the Mechanism of the Eye, *Philos Trans* 91:23-88, 1801.

Peter Mark Roget (1779-1869)

PETER M. ROGET, physician, educator, and scholar, was born in London, son of John Roget, native of Geneva and at the time pastor of the French Protestant Church, a Swiss parish.[1] Peter received his early education in Kensington, where he was partial to mathematical studies. He completed his higher education at Edinburgh, obtaining the degree of doctor of medicine before his 20th year. He returned to London to study under Baillie, Cruikshank, Willan, Heberden, Abernethy, and others. After a series of varied professional activities on the Continent and in England, in his 26th year he was appointed physician to the infirmary at Manchester, successor to Thomas Percival.

Composite by G. Bako

He gave a course of lectures and demonstrations on anatomy and physiology and in due time became one of the founders of the Manchester Medical School, a successful venture.

Four years after his appointment Roget left Manchester and established himself in London. He was admitted a licentiate of the College of Physicians and gave a popular course on animal physiology at the Russell Institution. Later he lectured on the practice of physic at the anatomical school on Great Windmill Street and for several years was responsible for the teaching of comparative physiology at the Royal Institution. Meanwhile, Roget was chosen one of the secretaries of the Medico-Chirurgical Society of London and for a dozen years edited their *Transactions*. His design of a new slide rule procured his election in 1815 to Fellowship in the Royal Society.

After the establishment of the school of medicine in Aldersgate Street in 1826, Ro-

get undertook an extended course of lectures on physiology subsequently published. In 1827, he was appointed senior secretary of the Royal Society and in 1831 Fellow of the Royal College of Physicians of London. His Gulstonian lectures to the College discussed "The Laws of Sensation and Perception." In 1834, Roget was nominated to the new chair of physiology in the Royal Institution and for three years delivered the Fullerian lectures. An even greater contemporary honor was the selection of Roget as one of the contributors to the Bridgewater Treatises. These were established "to enforce the great truths of Natural Theology, by adducing those evidences of the power, wisdom, and goodness of God which are manifested in the living creation."[2] Roget advanced his evidence in support of natural theology a generation before Charles Darwin published his *Origin of Species* and later *The Descent of Man*. He speculated that the changes and modifications of living creatures from the common type are found usually to be exquisitely adapted to their various destinations and circumstances. The recognition of a common type was proposed as an argument in favor of the existence of a Creator. The modifications for the adaption of the archetype to new conditions was as clear a proof of design as could be afforded by an entirely new structure for each class of living creatures. Nature appeared to Roget to have kept in view a type or standard in spite of innumerable modifications rendered necessary for survival of each species. He wrote:[2]

. . . . unity of design and identity of operation pervade the whole nature; and they clearly point to one Great and only Cause of all things, arrayed in the attributes of infinite power, wisdom, and benevolence, whose mighty works extend throughout the boundless regions of space, and whose comprehensive plans embrace eternity. Thus we find that each new form which arises, in following the ascending scale of creation, retains a strong affinity to that which had preceded it, and also tends to impress its own features on those which immediately succeed: and thus their specific differences result merely from the different extent and direction given to those organic developements; those of inferior races proceeding to a certain point only, and there stopping; while in beings of a higher rank they advance farther, and lead to all the observed diversities of conformation and endowments.

Roget's boldness of conception, simple exposition of natural phenomena, and purity of style made this, with but one exception, his most famous composition. Other works included monographs on medical subjects, sections in encyclopedias, medical and general, and contributions on natural philosophy to the *Edinburgh Review,* the *Philosophical Transactions,* and the *Annals of Philosophy,* and the *Parliamentary Review.*

Roget held the office of censor of the Royal College of Physicians, was a member of the Senate of the University of London, chairman of the Medical Faculty, and examiner in comparative anatomy and physiology at the University of London, a Fellow of several scientific bodies, and a member of literary and philosophical societies in England, Europe, and America.

Roget retired from practice in the beginning of his seventh decade and united his efforts in compiling his *Thesarus of English Words and Phrases Classified and Arranged so as to Facilitate the Expression of Ideas and Assist in Literary Composition.* The value of such a volume entered his thoughts as a young physician in Manchester, half a century earlier. The preface to the first edition of the *Thesaurus* (treasury) is given in its entirety.[3]

It is now nearly fifty years since I first projected a system of verbal classification similar to that on which the present work is founded. Conceiving that such a compilation might help to supply my own deficiencies, I had, in the year 1805, completed a classed catalog of words on a small scale, but on the same principle, and nearly in the same form, as the Thesaurus now published. I had often during that long interval found this little collection, scanty and imperfect as it was, of much use to me in literary composition and often contemplated its extension and improvement; but a sense of the magnitude of the task, amidst a multitude of other avocations, deterred me from the attempt. Since my retirement from the duties of Secretary of the Royal Society, however, finding myself possessed of more leisure, and believing that a repertory of which I had myself experienced the advantage might, when amplified, prove useful to others, I resolved to embark in an undertaking which, for the last three or four years, has given me incessant occupation, and has, indeed, imposed

upon me an amount of labor very much greater than I had anticipated. Notwithstanding all the pains I have bestowed on its execution, I am fully aware of its numerous deficiencies and imperfections, and of its falling far short of the degree of excellence that might be attained. But, in a work of this nature, where perfection is placed at so great a distance. I have thought it best to limit my ambition to that moderate share of merit which it may claim in its present form; trusting to the indulgence of those for whose benefit it is intended, and to the candor of critics who, while they find it easy to detect faults, can at the same time duly appreciate difficulties.

The success and popularity of the volume is attested to by the knowledge that Roget was engaged in preparing the 20th edition of the work at the time of his death, while a remarkable number of editions, revisions, and translations have appeared in the intervening century.

1. Pettigrew, T. J.: "Peter Mark Roget, M.D., F.R.S.," in *Biographical Memoirs of the Most Celebrated Physicians, Surgeons, etc.,* London: Whittaker & Co., 1840, vol 4, pp 1-16.

2. Roget, P. M.: *Animal and Vegetable Physiology, Considered With Reference to Natural Theology,* 2 vol, London: W. Pickering, 1834.

3. Roget, P. M.: *Thesaurus of English Words and Phrases,* London: Longman, Brown, Green & Longmans, 1852.

James Copland (1791-1870)

JAMES COPLAND, editor and sole compiler of a monumental compendium of medicine upon which his fame rests, was born in the Orkneys, surrounded by the rugged grandeur of Nature. His family subsequently moved to Lerwick, one of the Shetland Islands, where he received his early schooling with the parish clergymen. In his 16th year his father took him to Edinburgh: there he attended the literature, mathematics and philosophy classes at the University in anticipation of entering the Church. After four years of higher education, Copland lost interest in the ministry, since such a course offered him no new field of research: instead he began the study of medicine. His graduation thesis, composed in Latin and presented for the MD degree in

1815, advanced the doctrine that the origin of inflammation resided in lesions of the nerves supplying the capillary vessels. Having gained particular attention from his teachers with his brilliance, he was encour-

Composite by G. Bako

aged to go to London with the intention of setting up a medical practice. However, because the appropriate departments of the London hospitals suffered in comparison with Edinburgh institutions, his thoughts turned to a surgical practice.

Before resuming residence in London, Copland observed the practice of medicine in France and Germany for two years. In 1820, with his wandering over, he became a licentiate of the Royal College of Physicians and a member of the London Medical Society. Lacking hospital connection, he helped found the South London Dispensary for the poor, subsequently named the Royal Infirmary for the Diseases of Children. Copland later was appointed lecturer on medicine at Middlesex Hospital Medical School. As during his first attempts at practice, the few consultants and meager fees forced him to seek gainful employment in writing. The *Quarterly Journal of Foreign Medicine* and the *London Medical and Physical Journal* accepted his literary work

initially; in 1822, he assumed the editorship of the *London Medical Repository,* serving in this capacity for five years. In 1824, Copland revised Richerand's *Elements of Physiology.* The reviews were more controversial than critical, but his thinking and writing attracted notable attention. He was elected a Fellow of the Royal Society in 1833, and was selected as Gulstonian lecturer (1838), Croonian lecturer (1844, 1845, 1846), Lumleian lecturer (1854 and 1855), and Harveian orator (1857).

Copland wrote more on medicine than did most Fellows of the Royal College of Physicians. Three short treatises were entitled *The Forms, Complications, Causes, Prevention and Treatment of Consumption and Bronchitis, Of the Causes, Nature, and Treatment of Palsy and Apoplexy,* and *On the Drainage and Sewage of London.* His great work, however, was *A Dictionary of Practical Medicine.* The first volume appeared in 1832. The concluding portions appeared 28 years later. The total comprised more than 3,500 pages, two columns each, of small type. It was translated into German, and one edition was printed in the United States. Much of the composition was done throughout the evening and into the early hours of the following morning. The *Dictionary* was an extraordinary labor, which involved extensive reading and not always too critical selection of information from ancient and contemporary works. Most diseases known at that time were presented in amazing detail and included sections on definition, history, clinical findings, pathogenesis, prognosis, physiology, pathology, and treatment. The discussion on gout, a disease from which he suffered, was approximately 30 pages long; the only serious complication, gouty nephritis, may have been responsible for his death which came 12 years after completion of his work. The descriptive title is illustrative of the comprehensive undertaking.[2] *A Dictionary of Practical Medicine. Comprising General Pathology, the Nature and Treatment of Diseases, Morbid Structures, and the Disorders Especially Incidental to Climates, to the Sex, and to the Different Epochs of Life, With Numerous Prescriptions for the Medicines*

Recommended; A Classification of Diseases According to Pathological Principles; A Copious Bibliography, With References; and An Appendix of Approved Formulae. The Whole Forming a Library of Pathology and Practical Medicine and a Digest of Medical Literature.

The comments in the Book Review section of the *Lancet* upon the appearance of Part X of the Dictionary in 1845, are sufficiently laudatory to warrant repetition.[3]

REMARKS of the kind are very trite, but we are forced to repeat, with the appearance of every part of this immense work, that viewed as a mere effort of labour, it is one of the most extraordinary, that has ever appeared in the medical literature of this country, as a single-handed production. Dr. Copland has proved himself a paladin of the pen; when his dictionary has reached its full proportions, for which a few more parts will suffice, it will indeed be an intellectual pyramid. Looking at the thickset page with its double columns, and diamond type, the multitudinous references, and copious bibliography, any one accustomed to literary labour must feel astounded at its being the work of one man. It could only have been wrought out by unwearied and pains-taking application, and the most careful husbandry of time. In one of the early parts of the work, in the article on the Eye, we get an insight into the time it has taken the learned artificer to produce his work, he says:—"I have continued, for many years, to read or write from eight o'clock in the evening till two or three in the morning." Six or seven hours nightly, spent by the mass in pleasure, idleness, or sleep. This is truly spending the midnight oil; nothing but the hardiest *physique* could have stood against such a perpetual moil and left the worker hale and strong, as we believe is the fortunate lot of Dr. Copland.

1. Munk, W.: *The Roll of the Royal College of Physicians of London,* ed 2, London: Royal College of Physicians, 1878, vol 3, pp. 218-222.

2. Copland, J.: *A Dictionary of Practical Medicine,* London: Longman, Brown, Green, Longmans, & Roberts, 1832-1858.

3. *A Dictionary of Practical Medicine,* reviews, *Lancet* 2:453, 1845.

National Library of Medicine

Thomas Wakley (1795-1862)

THOMAS WAKLEY (pronounced Wakely) was born in Devon, England; his body was interred in the catacombs of Kensal Green Cemetery (London's greatest outdoor museum). The fame of Wakley is specifically identified with the founding and direction of the British Journal *Lancet.* Equally famous, even notorious, are his polemics and documented crusadings,[1] obviously on the side of right and justice. Wakley was only 28 years of age when he published the first issue of *Lancet.* For 40 years thereafter, as a protagonist of worthy causes in the lay, as well as in the medical press, he found himself in conflict with his professional peers and also the civil courts. Except for the leniency of the libel laws a century ago, he might have spent a great deal of his time in jail or in bankruptcy. But the few verdicts that were rendered against him failed to dampen his enthusiasm or stay his zeal.

He was not adept at clever "politicking" and made no pretense of discretion in discussion. Struggling to improve facilities for students seeking a medical education, he assailed the barriers erected against the young London physicians who sought a staff appointment in a teaching hospital. Many of the reforms advocated by the battling surgeon were closely connected with the social changes of the Industrial Revolution. In the judgment of Charles W. Brook[2] Wakley was the most important member of the British medical profession in the 19th century. "Lord Lister was a mere pygmy by the side of Thomas Wakley."

Medicine in England, at the beginning of the 19th century was composed of three classes of practitioners, the physicians, the surgeons, and the apothecaries. The physicians were the social gentry, learned in the classics, members of the Royal College of Physicians, and devoted to a strict ethical code, patterned after the precepts of Hippocrates. They were graduates of Oxford or Cambridge, schools that did not admit Roman Catholics or Dissenters. The surgeons were in the final stages of metamorphosis from a craft to a profession.[2]

The Royal College of Surgeons of London had recently been transferred from a City livery company into a chartered corporation and its leading members were devoting more of their time to the practice of pure mdicine rather than that of operative surgery.

Social distinction between surgeons and physicians has largely disappeared although the custom of recognizing a surgeon as "Mister," a master of the craft, persists. The third category of practice, the apothecaries, were the dispensers of pills and liquids. Thomas Wakley, choosing to be a surgeon, came to London just after the battle of Waterloo and "walked" St. Thomas' and Guy's United Hospitals. Sir Astley Cooper was the dominant personality in the hospitals when Wakley was appointed. An allowance of 80£ per year to cover all expenses, including 20£ for hospital tuition fees, was provided by his father. Wakley walked to Devonshire on his annual holiday, for he had no travel allowance. Membership in the Royal College of Surgeons was granted him two years later, in 1817.

Wakley's first encounter with the civil courts involved a fire in his new home, which had been provided by his father-in-law. The insurance company charged him with arson. Wakley won this first fight. Presumably it sharpened his legal wits, and his appearance in court was a repetitive affair during the remainder of his professional days.

The transition in his professional life from surgery to journalism occurred on Sunday, October 5, 1823, with the publication of the first issue of *Lancet*. Editorial assistants of Wakley included a free-lance writer and two members of the Royal College of Surgeons. There was plenty of variety in the first issue of the *Lancet,* which was published for a sixpence, and contained thirty-six pages. A lecture by Sir Astley Cooper occupied the place of honour.[2]

There were reports of cases of clinical interest and of operations that had fatal terminations. An excellent article, 'The Composition of Quack Medicines,' gave the results of an analysis of Dalby's Carminative, Daffy's Elixir, and Spelbury's Antiscorbutic Drops. There were dramatic criticisms and a political article, probably inspired or written by Cobbett, in which the younger Pitt was accused of having been 'the political coxcomb, running after wild impracticable schemes, regardless of everything but the gratification of his own senseless, remorseless and petty ambitions.' Robert Southey, the Poet Laureate, was referred to as 'sack-hunting hypocritical rhymer.' Wakley had always been a chess enthusiast, and for a short time there was a weekly article, 'The Chess Table.' This had to be discontinued owing to pressure of space, but it is an interesting fact that the *Lancet* was the journal which inaugurated the practice of publishing chess problems and reports of games of chess. Another excellent feature, undoubtedly inspired by Lawrence, and early incorporated in the *Lancet,* was a special section titled 'Foreign Department,' in which new methods of treatment and accounts of operations were reported.

The biography by Brook is a recounting of Wakley's recurring war on hospitals, war on the professional colleges, war on quacks, war against his fellow practitioners. One example will illustrate the last-named. He characterized the leading hospital surgeons as "Bats and Corruptionists" and published detailed accounts of their surgical failures.[2]

If the enemies of a free medical press, if the corruptionists of our hospitals—if the despicable Bats and Aberdeen Dubs, who disgrace medical society—cannot distinguish between forbearance from fear, and forbearance arising from pity for the fallen, we will soon teach them a lesson, which they will not forget to the last hour of their filthy existence.

The fruits of the corrupt system that prevails at our public hospitals, are seen in the numerous cases of ignorance and incompetency on the part of hospital functionaries, which have been recorded in public journals, though these, it must be admitted, are few indeed, compared with those which have actually occurred.

Ten years after Wakley had founded the *Lancet* he carried his argumentative skills to the House of Commons. In Parliament he attacked the Poor Law Amendment Act. He championed the cause of the Tolpuddle Martyrs, sought repeal of the Newspaper Stamp Act, and legislation in favor of opening museums and art galleries on Sunday. He supported the claim of Ireland for self-government and fought against the long tenure of the copyright law. His appointment to the House of Lords was considered but never consummated. Five years before his health began to fail because of active pulmonary tuberculosis, he had arranged for his two sons to share responsibility for the publishing of *Lancet*. The transfer became complete prior to his death.

Wakley was born a farmer's son; he was trained to be a surgeon. Most of his professional years were spent as a crusading medical editor; he was a "do-it-yourself" barrister. His heritage to British medicine was great.

1. Sprigge, S. S.: *Life and Times of Thomas Wakley*, London, Longmans, Green & Company, 1897.
2. Brook, C. W.: *Battling Surgeon*, Glasgow, Strickland Press, 1945.

John Brown (1810-1882)

JOHN BROWN, contemporary and counterpart of O. W. Holmes of Boston and S. W. Mitchell of Philadelphia, was Edinburgh's outstanding medical littérateur. The short story, "Rab and His Friends," Brown's masterpiece, was presented initially as an address to the townsfolk of his native community, who did not realize at the time its inherent worth as a warm narrative built around an unremarkable event in the daily

Composite by G. Bako

practice of medicine.[1] The remarks prepared by Brown in longhand were revised, expanded, and published in 1858 in the first volume (series) of his *Horae Subsecivae*.[1] This intriguing title, freely translated as "spare hours" or "leisure hours," was selected for the three-volume collection of essays and short stories that reflect his gentle culture, compassion for human and animal emotions, and great skill as a literary composer. The second volume appeared in 1861 and the third in 1882.[2] Two of his lesser-known essays are "Marjory Fleming," the story of a young girl stricken with meningitis, and "Locke and Sydenham," a discourse on medical education.

His primary objectives in preparation of *Horae Subsecivae* were stated in the initial volume.

I. To give my vote for going back to the old mainly intellectual and literary culture of the days of Sydenham, Arbuthnot, and Gregory; when a physician fed, enlarged, and quickened his entire nature; when he lived in the world of letters as a free-holder, and reverenced the ancients, while, at the same time, he pushed on among his fellows, and lived in the present, believing that his profession and his patients need not suffer, though his *horae subsecivae* were devoted occasionally to miscellaneous thinking and reading, and to a course of what is elsewhere called "fine confused feeding," or though, as his Gaelic historian says of Rob Roy at his bye hours, he be "a man of incoherent transactions." As I have said, system is not always method, much less progress.

II. That the study in himself and others of the human understanding, its modes and laws as objective realities, and his gaining that power over mental action in himself and others, which alone comes from knowledge at first-hand, is one which every physician should not only begin in youth, but continue all his life long, and which in fact all men of sense and original thought do make, though it may lie in their minds, as it were, unformed and without a tongue.

Brown was born at Biggar in Lanarkshire, the son of a Biblical scholar and a Secession Minister, who was largely responsible for his son's education up to the age of 12.[3] At that time, the family moved to Edinburgh, where John entered a classical school. This was followed by matriculation in arts and literature at the University of Edinburgh, leading to the study of medicine. He accepted the convention of his time, and, in addition to taking formal courses at the university, he served an apprenticeship under James Syme, who later became professor of surgery at Edinburgh.

He graduated in medicine from Edinburgh in 1833 and immediately began the practice of medicine, remaining in Edinburgh, practicing and writing throughout his life. He became a Fellow of the Royal College of Physicians of Edinburgh in 1847 and for a time served as their librarian. The original manuscript of "Rab and His Friends" now rests in the library of the College, through the efforts of William Osler. The honorary degree of LLD was conferred by the University of Edinburgh in 1874 for his literary accomplishments rather than for his activities in the medical sciences. Brown was responsible for no laboratory investigations and published no scientific contributions. On the other hand, he offered sound advice to young physicians and disclosed an enviable understanding of the value of bedside medicine.[4]

Give more attention to steady common observation, the old Hippocratic ακριβεια, exactness, literal accuracy, precision, niceness of sense; what Sydenham calls the natural history of disease. *Symptoms* are universally available; they are the voice of nature: *signs* by which I mean more artificial and refined means of scrutiny—the stethoscope, the microscope, etc.—are not always within the power of every man, and with all their help, are additions, not substitutes. Besides, the best natural and unassisted observer, the man bred in the constant practice of keen, discriminating insight—is the best man for all instrumental niceties.

Brown enjoyed a wide circle of friends—human and animal. His patients appreciated his compassionate understanding of their physical and emotional troubles, while his professional confreres in literature, including Ruskin, Thackeray, O. W. Holmes, and Samuel Clemens, held him in noble esteem.[5] His love for dogs was deep, and he became an authority on breeding and pedigrees. In the rapidly receding years of his life, he was afflicted with melancholia, partially withdrew from society, and only shortly before his death did he appear to shake off the morbid affliction and present once more a cheerful and sparkling character.

The incident described in "Rab and His Friends" occurred in 1830 while Brown was acting dispenser, clerk, and assistant at Minto House Hospital, the infirmary of James Syme. James Noble brought his wife, Ailie, suffering from a breast tumor, to consult Syme. Rab, the dog, followed his master and mistress to the hospital and was allowed in the operating room during the removal of the breast which was described as "hard as stone." The patient walked to and from the operating room. The operation was swiftly performed without benefit of any soporific, as described by Brown.[1]

The operating theatre is crowded; much talk and fun, and all the cordiality and stir of youth. The sugeon with his staff of assistants is there. In comes Ailie: one look at her quiets and abates the eager students. That beautiful old woman is too much for them; they sit down, and are dumb, and gaze at her. These rough boys feel the power of her presence. She walks in quickly, but without haste; dressed in her mutch, her neckerchief, her white dimity shortgown, her black bombazeen petticoat, showing her white worsted stockings and her carpet-shoes. Behind her was

James, with Rab. James sat down in the distance, and took that huge and noble head between his knees. Rab looked perplexed and dangerous; for ever cocking his ear and dropping it as fast.

Ailie stepped up on a seat and laid herself on the table, as her friend the surgeon told her; arranged herself, gave a rapid look at James, shut her eyes, rested herself on me, and took my hand. The operation was at once begun; it was necessarily slow; and chloroform—one of God's best gifts to his suffering children—was then unknown. The surgeon did his work. The pale face showed its pain, but was still and silent. Rab's soul was working within him; he saw that something strange was going on,—blood flowing from his mistress, and she suffering; his ragged ear was up, and importunate; he growled and gave now and then a sharp impatient yelp; he would have liked to have done something to that man. But James had him firm, and gave him a glower from time to time, and an intimation of a possible kick:—all the better for James, it kept his eye and his mind off Ailie.

It is over: she is dressed, steps gently and decently down from the table, looks for James; then, turning to the surgeon and the students, she curtsies,—and in a low, clear voice, begs their pardon if she has behaved ill. The students—all of us—wept like children; the surgeon happed her up carefully,—and, resting on James and me, Ailie went to her room, Rab following. We put her to bed. James took off his heavy shoes, crammed with tackets, heel-capt and toe-capt and put them carefully under the table, saying, "Maister John, I'm for nane o' yer strynge nurse bodies for Ailie. I'll be her nurse and on my stockin' soles I'll gang about as canny as pussy." And so he did; and handy and clever, and swift and tender as any woman, was that horny-handed, snell, peremptory little man. Everything she got he gave her: he seldom slept; and often I saw his small shrewd eyes out of the darkness, fixed on her. As before, they spoke little.

1. Brown, J.: *Horae Subsecivae, Locke and Sydenham with Other Occasional Papers*, Edinburgh: T. Constable, 1858.

2. Brown, J.: *Horae Subsecivae*, 3 vol; Edinburgh: D. Douglas, 1882.

3. Brown, J. T.: *Dr. John Brown, A Biography and a Criticism*, London: A. and C. Black, 1903.

4. Peddie, A.: Obituary, John Brown, *Edinburgh Med J* 27 (pt II): 1131-1137, 1882.

5. *Letters of Dr. John Brown*, J. Brown and D. W. Forrest, ed, London: A. and C. Black, 1907.

Composite by G. Bako

Samuel D. Gross (1805-1884)

THE PROFESSIONAL PATH of the farm boy of sturdy Pennsylvania-Dutch heritage to the prime position of eminence in American surgery in the 19th century has been recounted many times. The biographers of Samuel D. Gross concur that he displayed a strong but gentle personality—sensitive and tender in the care of the sick—and enjoyed the respect and the devotion of his pupils. Samuel was born near Easton, Pennsylvania, on a rich and fertile farm and early in life developed a wholesome interest in plants, trees, and flowers. In the environs of his birth and within the confines of his home, Pennsylvania-Dutch rather than English was the language of communication. Medicine as a career was selected early in life, and, at the age of 17, he began an apprenticeship in the office of a country physician. Discouraged by this first venture he tried a second physician, with no greater success. The explanation was self-evident: his elementary education in a log schoolhouse was inadequate for a preceptorship. To correct the deficiency Gross enrolled in the Wilkes-Barre Academy, followed by classical studies in a school in the Bowery of New York. He then returned to Easton for tutoring in Latin and Greek and completed his preparatory education at Lawrenceville High School in New Jersey.[1]

At the age of 19, Gross resumed the study of medicine in the office of J. K. Swift, where he spent a year, until ill health forced him to abandon his studies. These were resumed in the fall of 1826 as a full-time student at Jefferson Medical College under the tutelage of George McClellan, professor of surgery and founder of the college. Gross graduated in 1828 in a class of 27 and opened an office for the practice of medicine at the corner of Fifth and Library streets. Since patients were few, most of the hours were devoted to the translation of French and German medical texts into English. The financial rewards were so meager that, after 18 months of indigence, Gross returned to Easton, where living expenses were less and opportunities for a young physician were somewhat greater. He purchased a home, built a small laboratory in the rear for animal experiments and for dissection of animals and cadavers, and resumed practice.

The spring of 1833 was particularly significant. He sought and was successful in an appointment as demonstrator of anatomy in the Ohio Medical College at Cincinnati. The decision required a change in residence and an equally greater change from the life of a family practitioner, with a deep and manifest interest in the medical sciences, to a career of teaching, consulting, and medical writing. Two years later he advanced to the chair of pathological anatomy in the newly organized Cincinnati Medical College, founded by Daniel Drake. In this capacity, Gross delivered the first comprehensive course of lectures on pathological anatomy in the United States. Not long after, and influenced by the decline of the Cincinnati Medical College, he moved to Louisville Medical Institute (afterward the University of Louisville) and, in so doing, followed Daniel Drake. Gross remained at Louisville as professor of surgery for 16 years, with the exception of a few months spent as a member of the faculty of the University of the City of New York. After 23 years in the Ohio River Valley, he returned to his alma mater as professor of surgery. The chair was occupied until he was 77, only two years before his death.

There was no lapse in writing during a long and prolific career.[2] Gross's first literary efforts were translations of European books, made while practicing in Easton. Thereafter, his writings were original scientific contributions. In Cincinnati and Louisville, he prepared the *Elements of Pathological Anatomy,* published in 1839, the first systematic treatise on this subect in the United States. The two volumes were heavily illustrated with woodcuts and colored engravings. The second edition[3] was highly regarded by Rudolf Virchow, eminent German scientist, who publicly acknowledged the importance of it. The treatise incorporated the newer contributions of experimental and morphologic pathology as interpreted by a pragmatic and skillful surgeon and teacher. Lesser contributions by Gross included *The Anatomy, Physiology, and Diseases of the Bones and Joints* (1830); *An Experimental and Critical Inquiry into the Nature and Treatment of Wounds of the Intestines* (1843); *A Practical Treatise on the Diseases, Injuries, and Malformations of the Urinary Bladder, the Prostate Gland, and the Urethra* (1851); and *A Practical Treatise on Foreign Bodies in the Air-Passages* (1854). An interest in medical history complemented his contributions in the medical sciences.[4] He wrote on the history of Kentucky and prepared a number of medical biographies.

As a sympathetic scientist in the selected use of animals in the experimental laboratory, Gross stated his views on antivivisection.[2]

I have sacrificed for experimental purposes nearly one hundred dogs, and, if I were not thoroughly satisfied that the objects had been most laudable, I should consider myself as a most cruel, heartless man, deserving of the severest condemnation. The results of my experiments will, I am sure, eventually receive that attention to which their importance so justly entitles them. The experiments of Jones on hemorrhage, of Smith and Travers on wounds of the intestines, of Magendie and Charles Bell on the functions of the nerves, and of hundreds of physicians upon the action of medicines upon the human frame, have shed an immense flood of light upon the healing art, putting to flight the mawkish sentimentality of the societies for the prevention of cruelty to animals, which have made so much ado about this matter.

While in Philadelphia, Gross prepared a two-volume system of surgery, profusely illustrated, in which the qualifications of a surgeon as he interpreted them are clearly stated.[5]

Qualifications of a Surgeon.—The performance of operations presupposes the possession of certain qualities on the part of the surgeon. It is not every man that can become an operator, even presuming that he has the requisite knowledge of anatomy and of the use of instruments. . . . Courage, like poetry, has often been said to be a gift of nature, and nothing is, perhaps, more true; but it is equally certain that a timid man, by attention to his education, and by constant practice, become, in the end, a good operator. . . . Celsus, long ago, happily defined the qualities which constitute a good operator. He should possess, says the illustrious Roman, a firm and steady hand, a keen eye, and the most unflinching courage, which can disregard alike the sight of blood and the cries of the patient.

But the above are not the only qualities, important though they be, which should be possessed by an operator. If he is not honest in his purposes, or scrupulously determined, in every case, to act only with an eye single to the benefit of his patient, and the glory of his profession, he is not worthy of the name which he bears, or fit for the discharge of the solemn duties which he assumes. In a word, such an operator is not to be trusted; for he will be certain, whenever opportunity offers, to employ the knife rather for the temporary eclât which may follow its use, than for the good of the individual whom he unnecessarily tortures. . . . Such men, of whom there are, even yet, unfortunately, too many in our profession, deserve the name of knivesmen and knaves rather than of surgeons and honest men.

Gross was an organization man, a regular attendant at the annual meetings of the American Medical Association, and its 20th president. He delivered the presidential address at the Washington session in 1868. The first item dealt with the *Transactions of the American Medical Association,* the forerunner of *J A M A.* Several recommendations, if approved,[6] "would greatly reduce the bulk of the volumes, and proportionately diminish the expense of publication, would impart a more literary and scientific tone to our labors, meet the approbation of enlightened physicians, and tend to exalt the character of the Association as a great national institution." He failed to follow his advice for brevity and submitted a 137-page report on surgical operations in malignant diseases for publication in the *Transactions.* Additional evidence of an interest in society organizations was the active role he played in the formation of the American Surgical Association and the Philadelphia Pathological Association. Two medical journals, the *Louisville Medical Review* and the *North American Medico-Chirurgical Review,* were founded by Gross and T. G. Richardson. During the Civil War, he was a surgical consultant for the Surgeon General of the Union Army and prepared a small handbook on military medicine.

Early in his career, Gross disclosed his concern for American medical literature and, in order to correct the deficiency, submitted three resolutions to the American Medical Association.[7]

Resolved, That this Association earnestly and respectfully recommend, first, the universal adoption, whenever practicable, by our schools, of American works as text-books for their pupils; secondly, the discontinuance of the practice of editing foreign writings; thirdly, a more independent course of the medical periodical press towards foreign productions, and a more liberal one towards American; and, fourthly, a better and more efficient employment of the facts which are continually furnished by our public institutions for the elucidation of the nature of diseases and accidents, and, indirectly, for the formation of an original, a vigorous, and an independent national medical literature.

Samuel D. Gross was favored with honorary degrees from Oxford, Cambridge, Edinburgh, and the University of Pennsylvania. His statue rests in the grounds of the Army Medical Museum. These are a few of the singular glories accorded a farm boy from the Pennsylvania-Dutch country. Through dedication to medicine, he realized the inadequacies of his early education and premature apprenticeships, corrected each in turn, and at the peak of his career was a prolific writer, the composer of the first text in America on pathological anatomy, and the leading surgeon of America. The concluding remarks in his Inaugural Address, delivered at the opening session of his first year as professor of surgery at the Jefferson Medical College, would have been appropriate at any period of his life.[8]

Whatever of life, and of health, and of strength remains to me, I hereby, in the presence of Almighty God and of this large essemblage, dedicate to the cause of my Alma Mater, to the interests of Medical Science and to good of my fellow-creatures.

1. *Autobiography of Samuel D. Gross, MD, with Sketches of His Contemporaries,* edited by his sons, Philadelphia: G. Barrie, 1887.

2. Hays, I. M.: A Memoir of Samuel D. Gross, *Amer J Med Sci* 175:293-308(July) 1884.

3. Gross, S. D.: *Elements of Pathological Anatomy,* 2nd ed, Philadelphia: E. Barrington & G. D. Haswell, 1945.

4. Gross, S. D.: *History of American Medical Literature from 1776 to the Present Time,* Philadelphia: Collins, 1876.

5. Gross, S. D.: *A System of Surgery,* Philadelphia: Blanchard and Lea, 1859.

6. Gross, S. D.: Address, *Trans Amer Med Assn* 19:57-74, 1868.

7. Gross, S. D.: Report on the Causes Which Impede the Progress of American Medical Literature, *Trans Amer Med Assn* 9:399-362, 1856.

8. Gross, S. D.: *An Inaugural Address,* Philadelphia: J. M. Wilson, 1856.

Sir Samuel Wilks (1824-1911)

THE MEMOIRS OF SIR SAMUEL WILKS is an excellent account of a great number of clinical and physiological contributions to medicine during the 19th century.[1] It is part autobiographical, part biographical. Since he was an acquaintance or associate of many of the leaders of London medicine of the 19th century, it is to be expected that the urban physicians received proportionately greater biographical attention. Wilks, endowed with a warm but strong personality, was associated with Guy's Hospital throughout his professional career, and as editor of *Guy's Hospital Reports,* he did much to establish firmly the diseases described by Bright, Addison, Gull, Hodgkin, Paget, and others.

At the age of 16, with the avowed intent of becoming a general practitioner, Wilks was apprenticed to their family's doctor. A fee was given for the apprenticeship, which involved preparation of medicines, vaccinat-

ing, bleeding, and extraction of teeth. The following year a course in anatomy was pursued at Guy's. The University of London granted him the BM degree in 1848 and the

Composite by G. Bako

MD degree, with the gold medal, in 1850. Meanwhile, Wilks began the practice of medicine and became a member and later a Fellow of the Royal College of Physicians. His first appointment to the teaching staff of Guy's was in 1856. A decade later he was advanced to full physician, accepting the post held by Gull. Subsequently, he was appointed physician to the Duke of Connaught, elected a Fellow of the Royal Society, honored by Edinburgh with an LLD degree, created a baronet by the Crown, and Physician-Extraordinary to Queen Victoria. The new Guy's Hospital, with Bright, Hodgkin, Gull, and Addison on the staff, was the mid-century center for meticulous clinical examination and detailed tabulation of clinical and pathological findings. Wilks played an important part in the activities of the Clinical Report Society, founded especially for students. He lectured on pathology and was curator of the museum, a post held previously by Thomas Hodgkin. In 1859, his lectures on pathological anatomy were assembled in a treatise "Lectures on Pathological Anatomy Delivered at Guy's Hospital During the Summer Sessions, 1857-1858," a major contribution to the foundation of scientific pathology in the 19th century.[2] A decade of lecturing on the products of the death house was fine preparation for the course of systematic lectures on general medicine. Also, his treatise on *Diseases of the Nervous System* was a compilation of the individual contributions that had appeared in *Guy's Hospital Reports*.

A number of diseases benefited from Wilks' keen powers of observation as a postmortem prosecutor. Dissecting room warts (*verrucae necrogenicae*), the cutaneous tuberculosis of Laennec, were described.[3] He was one of the first to delve deeply into the visceral manifestations of syphilis, which included the central nervous system, aortic aneurysm and gummatous involvement of the liver, lung, larynx, and bone. Previously, syphilis had been held to be an external malady. A patient who died from syphilis was examined postmortem by Wilks: "This will ever be remembered by me as bringing with it one of my chief honours."

Thirty years after Thomas Hodgkin disclosed his findings in the communication, *On Some Morbid Appearances of the Absorbent Glands and Spleen,* Wilks rediscovered the entity. Immediately he was credited with having made an original observation. However, Wilks was quick to correct this false supposition and gave full credit to Hodgkin—thus, the beginning of the use of the term "Hodgkin's disease." Necrosis of the lower jaw from phosphorus poisoning, which developed in lucifer matchmakers, was discussed in 1846. The "phossy jaw" became so serious an industrial hazard in the manufacture of matches that an act of Parliament was necessary for the substitution of white phosphorus. Wilks was one of the first to draw attention to alcoholic paraplegia, and he gave the first description of *lineae atrophicae*.[4] A decade before Marie described acromegaly, an example of this malady was reported by Wilks.[1] A 28-year-old female was referred to Wilks in 1869 by the oculist who discovered no intrinsic eye disease and attributed the dysfunction to a cerebral malady. Complete loss of vision of the left eye, partial loss in the right eye, and moderate exophthalmos were observed. The patient had been amenorrheic for 6 years.

The skin was thickened, distorting all her features, so as to give her a truly hideous expression, the nose being enlarged as well as the lips, and ears prominent somewhat like those of a negress. The hands were very large and the fingers like sausages. . . . This change had been coming on for about six years. . . . I learned that she died . . . about six years after I first saw her.

Skepticism had been expressed on the intimate association of morbid changes in the suprarenal capsules and the clinical symptoms described by Addison, now identified as chronic adrenal insufficiency. Wilks strongly supported the concept of pathogenesis advanced by Addison.[5]

Several years having now elapsed since the publication of Addison's treatise on "Diseases of the Supra-renal Capsules," a fitting opportunity would seem to have arrived to undertake an examination of the additional facts which have in the meantime been collected, in order to discover whether they tend to strengthen or to weaken his conclusions. I may say at once, that my own observations entirely uphold his argument; and the cases, therefore, which I shall bring forward, will be found to substantiate (I consider), beyond disputation, his original facts.

It may be said, I think, with truth, that Addison's views have by no means received the support of the profession at large; but this scepticism, as far as I can judge from the circumstances which have induced it, can carry no important weight against their ultimate reception; for, when it is remembered that all true and valuable discoveries require a long time to strike root, and that a hasty and general acceptance of a novelty is to be regarded in the light of a bad omen as to its truthfulness, this hesitation only shows that long observation and study are necessary to place this, like all other new doctrines, on a sure and stable foundation.

In 1856, "lardaceous waxy" or amyloid disease was attributed to syphilis or chronic disease of the bone.[1] Wilks collected over 100 cases of amyloid disease which was usually observed in patients suffering from protracted caries or necrosis of the bone, tubercular or luetic in etiology. In 1869, several years before Paget's description of osteitis deformans, Wilks reported a case under the name of "osteoporosis." An acquired curvature and a great increase in the size of all the bones were noted, "so that he had when standing, more the appearance of ape than of a man, and the skull also was much hypertrophied."[1] Not finding any periostitis at postmortem examination, Wilks preferred the name "osteoporosis deformans." He also reported typhlitis or perityphlitis (which in later years was accepted as appendicitis), bacterial endocarditis (*arterial pyaemia*), and adherent pericarditis. He supported Bright's concept of kidney disease, assembled a series of cases and prepared an essay for the Physical Society in 1845. This won the competition.

In acute cases the water was discoloured, was albuminous, and the patient had dropsy, and after death the kidneys would be found large and pale, whereas in the chronic cases there was no definite history of a commencement, there might be no dropsy, and after death the kidney would be found shrunken and granular.

Although the Boswell of Guy's may not have enjoyed quite such fame as came to his biographees, Wilks was an esteemed physician, a notable morbid anatomist, and a loyal historian of the maladies described by Gull, Hodgkin, Addison, Paget, Bright, and other London physicians of the mid-19th century.

1. Wilks, S.: *Biographical Reminiscences of Sir Samuel Wilks*, London: Adlard & Son, 1911.
2. Obituary: Sir Samuel Wilks, Bart., M.D., F.R.S., *Brit Med J*, 1384-90 (Nov. 18) 1911.
3. Wilks, S.: Description of Some New Wax Models Lately Added to the Museum: Disease of the Skin Produced by Post-mortem Examinations, or Verruca Necrogenica, *Guy's Hosp Rep* 8:263-265, 1862.
4. Wilks, S.: Description of Some New Wax Models Illustrating a Peculiar Atrophy of the Skin, *Guy's Hosp Rep* 7:297-301, 1861.
5. Wilks, S.: On Disease of the Supra-renal Capsules; or, Morbus Addisonii, *Guy's Hosp Rep* 8:1-63, 1862.

Benjamin Richardson
(1828-1896)

THE CAREER OF BENJAMIN W. RICHARDSON embraced a temperance crusade, compositions in biography, poetry, and play and novel writing, and substantial professional contributions on physiology, pharmacology, pathology, internal medicine, anesthesia, epidemiology, sanitation, public health, and dental hygiene. The varied interests exemplify the belief that a capable physician with a well-trained mind may spread his influence into one or more nonmedical areas of human interest and concern.

Richardson was born at Somerby in Rutland, was privately schooled, and was apprenticed in succession to several practitioners before he qualified at the University of Glasgow at the age of 22.[1] Four years later he became a master of arts and doctor of medicine at the University of St. Andrews and won the Fothergillian medal for his essay "Diseases of the Foetus in Utero." During the preparation of this composition, he was accepted into the fellowship of the literary club in Covent Garden, whose members included Thackeray, George Cruik-shank, caricaturist, and Mark Lemon, founder and first editor of *Punch*. Richardson became affiliated with the Grosvenor Place Medical School adjoining St. George's Hospital, was appointed lecturer on medical jurisprudence, and later lecturer in physiology, a post which he held until the school closed in 1865, having merged with St. George's Hospital.

Richardson seemed to be always busy writing. A complete bibliography is appended to the biography by MacNalty.[1] The final draft for his *Vita Medica*, a philosophy of life and the universe as well as an autobiography, was completed only hours before death.[2] One of his best essays, an oration delivered at the 83rd anniversary of the Medical Society of London, discussed the vocation of the medical scholar.[3]

By the general term "Scholar," I for one understand, not the mere classic grubbing out and retaining an immense vocabulary of words from languages called somewhat improperly *dead*; . . . but the man who tries to grasp the meaning of the universe in which he dwells, past and present, as one great whole— . . . the man who reads a language in everything—in the rushing torrent, in the murmur of the summer breeze, in the accents of his fellow-men, wherever and however pronounced;—who acknowledges in his own senses a unity of purpose and of principle;—who comprehends this nature and its truths so far, that to him the rustling of the forest leaf and the volley of the thunder-cloud are equal wonders;—who, putting full faith in the innate powers of intellect, foreshadows the time when matter shall be the absolute servant of mind, and who believes that such knowledge as tends to accomplish this great end is the goal to which the eye and the step of the learned should be constantly directed.

With this estimate of scholastic duties before him, the true scholar marches on his way. Then, in whatever path of science or knowledge he may be thrown, its requirements become more clear, its objects more widely comprehended, its study more liberal and impressive. . . . Then, if in his thoughts and tasks any new idea, any new observation flits across his mind, he rests not until he has tested its truth, not only by examining into it as an isolated something, but by finding whether it is compatible with nature altogether, and is attuned to the harmony of the world.

In laboratory and clinical medicine Richardson advanced his theory of coagulation of blood, studied the action of drugs, especially amyl nitrite, and became an authority on anesthetics and artificial respiration. As a by-product of his researches on carbon compounds, he pursued enthusiastically, the physiological and pathological effects of alcohol and the evils of tobacco. His treatise, *The Temperance Lesson Book, a Series of Short Lessons on Alcohol and Its Action on the Body, Designed for Reading in Schools and Families*, clearly stated his interpretation of the baneful effects, unsupported by physiological or clinical evidence.[4]

In short, in whatever way alcohol acts on the body, whether it acts slowly and by successive states, or rapidly, so as to produce all its evil action in one sharp charge, it acts as a reducer of the powers of life. Never let this lesson be forgotten in thinking of the effects of strong drink, that the drink is strong only to destroy; that it never by any possibility adds strength to those who take it, and that to resort to it for the sake of getting strength from it is like seeking strength in exhausting and tiring exercises.

Several of Richardson's tracts were published under the direction of the Committee of General Literature and Education, Appointed by the Society for Promoting Christian Knowledge. Exercise, physical as well as mental, was discussed frequently. Although an advocate of cycling in his later years, in his youth he manifested little interest in cricket or athletic contests. In the *Manuals of Health, on Health and Occupation,* selected chapters are entitled "Health of the Different Classes of the Occupied," "Injuries From Dusts," "Injuries From Contact With Soluble Chemical Compounds," "Injuries From Noxious Vapours," "Hours for Work," "Clothing and Work," and "Cleanliness and Work."[5] At the 1875 Brighton Meeting of the Social Science Association, Richardson projected the Utopian city of Hygeia, offering a novel but practical design almost a century ago for the control of air pollution, the detritus from the burning of coal.[6]

The most radical changes in the houses of our city are in the chimneys, the roofs, the kitchens, and their adjoining offices. The chimneys, arranged after the manner proposed by Mr. Spencer Wells, are all connected with central shafts, into which the smoke is drawn, and, after being passed through a gas furnace to destroy the free carbon, is discharged colourless into the open air. The city, therefore, at the expense of a small smoke rate, is free of raised chimneys and of the intolerable nuisance of smoke.

The 11 volumes of *The Asclepiad,* founded and written presumably by Richardson, contain the curriculum vitae of 44 eminent medical scientists or natural philosophers.[7] These are extended, well-prepared biographies and excellent reference sources, especially for the personalities and humanistic traits of the subjects. Also presented are narratives on such varied subjects as "Morphia Habitués and Their Treatment," "Maintenance of Life in a Factitious Atmosphere," "Felicity as a Sanitary Research," and "Homeless and Nomadic Populations: Their Sanitary Condition and Inspection." Many of the biographies were revised and reprinted in the posthumous volume *Disciples of Aesculapius,* compiled by his daughter and published in 1901.[8]

Academic honors included Fellowship in the Royal College of Physicians of London, Croonian lecturer, Fellowship in the Royal Society, an LLD from the University of St. Andrews, honorary membership in the American Philosophical Society, and one notable civic honor, knighthood in 1893. Richardson founded two medical periodicals, the *Journal of Public Health and Sanitary Review* and the *Social Science Review.* Neither survived long. His three poems were entitled "The Arsenic Wreath," "Anacaona," and "Balthaser's Lament"; his three plays were *A Day with Cromwell, The Blacksmith of Antwerp,* and *The Mask of Fame.*

Richardson advocated painless death for unwanted domestic animals, and in the initial chapter of *Diseases of Modern Life,* prepared in his literary prime, the following was uttered regarding transition of man from natural life to natural death—true euthanasia.[9]

By the strict law of Nature a man should die as unconscious of his death as of his birth.

Subjected at birth to what would be, in the after conscious state, an ordeal to which the most cruel of deaths were not possibly more severe, he sleeps through the process, and only upon the subsequent awakening feels the impressions, painful or pleasant, of the world into which he is delivered. In this instance the perfect law is fulfilled, because the carrying of it out is retained by Nature herself: human free-will and the caprice that springs from it have no influence.

By the hand of Nature death were equally a painless portion. The cycle of life completed, the living being sleeps into death when Nature has her way.

This purely painless process, this descent by oblivious trance into oblivion, this natural physical death, is the true Euthanasia; .... Euthanasia is the sequel of health, the happy death engrafted on the perfect life.

1. MacNalty, A. S.: *A Biography of Sir Benjamin Ward Richardson,* London: Harvey & Blythe Ltd., 1950.
2. Richardson, B. W.: *Vita Medica: Chapters of Medical Life and Work,* London: Longmans, Green, & Co., 1897.
3. Richardson, B. W.: *The Vocation of the Medical Scholar: Being the Oration Delivered at the Eighty-Third Anniversary of the Medical Society of London,* London: T. Richards, 1856.
4. Richardson, B. W.: *The Temperance Lesson Book,* London: W. Tweedie & Co., 1878.
5. Richardson, B. W.: *Manuals of Health, on Health and Occupation,* London: Society for Promoting Christian Knowledge, 1879.
6. Richardson, B. W.: *Hygeia, a City of Health,* London: Macmillan & Co., 1876.
7. Richardson, B. W.: *The Asclepiad,* London: Longmans, Green, & Co., 1884-1895.
8. Richardson, B. W., *Disciples of Aesculapius,* New York: E. P. Dutton & Co., 1901.
9. Richardson, B. W.: *Diseases of Modern Life,* New York: Bermingham & Co., 1882.

Silas Weir Mitchell (1829-1914)

NEITHER OF THE TWO MOST PROLIFIC WRITERS of psychiatric novels in the 19th century was an orthodox psychiatrist. Oliver W. Holmes, a family practitioner, occupied the Chair of Anatomy at Harvard Medical School; S. Weir Mitchell, 20 years his junior, began his medical career as a neurologist in Philadelphia.[1] Scientific inquiry into mental phenomena, enhanced by enduring devotion to the practice of medicine, was a characteristic of each.

The world of the sick-bed explains in a measure some of the things that are strange in daily life.[2]

Although the designation "prudish" might be too harsh, Mitchell reflected his puritanical Philadelphia background in actions and writing. Attendance at Sunday school and church was habitual; games on Sunday and card playing at all times were considered evil by his parents. Mitchell was conservative in his approach to the subject of sex. Correspondence during his postgraduate days in Paris gave no indication that he was lured by the French fleshpots, and his behavior toward women as reflected

in the characters of his novels was genteel and restrained. He was freer in his scientific presentations of taboo subjects and in novels prepared for lay reading than in his presentations before lay audiences. In a talk at Radcliffe College, he confessed:[3]

It is impossible to speak frankly as to certain matters. I never could, and never will, lecture medically to women. And so I must talk as best I can, and you must read unspoken wisdom between the lines.

Lest there be any question about the propriety of his novels, it is clear that they were fit reading for young ladies. His books were never banned in Boston.

The brief biographical sketch of Mitchell and a detailed discussion of his novels by Rein credits two sources for valuable material. A number of unpublished documents were provided by Mitchell's granddaughter, Sarah Worthington Macdonough. The Historical Society of Pennsylvania and the Library of the College of Physicians of Philadelphia were equally cooperative. The latter is a remarkable library in my experience, with an impressive number of bound volumes of uncommon and difficult-to-obtain medical periodicals. Not far from the College of Physicians, on Walnut Street, is a plaque which reads:

On this spot stood
  The House of
S. Weir Mitchell
  Physician. Physiologist.
  Poet. Man of Letters.

He taught the use of rest for the nervous
He created "Hugh Wynne"
He pictured for us "The Red City" in which
He lived & Laboured from 1829 until 1914.

  Erected by Franklin Inn of which
he was a founder & first president.

I could not discover the reason for Mitchell's rejection of his first name, Silas, and the preference for Weir. Silas was a Biblical prophet, and there must have been some good reason for Mitchell's lack of affection for this man or name. Mitchell entered the University of Pennsylvania at the age of 15, but adjustment to higher learning came slowly; disorderly conduct and poor scholarship at first were black marks against his academic record. By graduation, however, he had become a leader in his class. He finished Jefferson Medical College in 1850 at the age of 21. This was followed by postgraduate training in Paris, where he came under the influence of Claude Bernard, the premier physiologist in Europe. Bernard was interested in hysteria at that time, a subject of great concern to Mitchell in subsequent years. Upon his return to Philadelphia, he continued to devote several hours each day to laboratory investigation. The first extensive study concerned the venom of rattlesnakes and was published by the Smithsonian Institution in 1860.

When the Civil War interrupted peacetime pursuits, he accepted a part-time assignment in the Army in order to concentrate his energies on nerve injuries and phantom pain in stumps of arms or legs. Surgeon General Hammond, aware of Mitchell's interest in the physiology and pathology of nervous tissue, established a special hospital for nervous diseases, with Mitchell in charge. He studied the epileptics, palsied, and chorea patients who were dispatched to the center. This resulted in a major treatise which was published in 1864, entitled *Gunshot Wounds and Other Injuries of Nerves.* Also, experience during the war undoubtedly contributed background material for a novel *In War Time,* which, however, was not published until 1884. Rein assumes that Mitchell's experience during the war led him from physiological to psychiatric observations. But there was never the same interest manifested in organic disease in subsequent years as in psychological and psychiatric phenomena. The transition was apparent in the character of "George Dedlow."

The lead communication in a 1908 issue of *JAMA* is an address by Mitchell before the American Neurological Association, in which he begins:

I have asked the privilege of speaking to this representative body of physicians in regard to rest treatment and psychotherapy.[4]

An English physician of distinction believed Mitchell's contributions to be "the greatest practical advance in medicine made in the last twenty-five years." Mitchell was certainly not a particularly modest man. He is reputed to have held that

. . . . to be a truly successful man, one must have risen to the top of one's profession, to have written a successful novel and to have killed a king salmon.

He had done all three.

Mitchell's practical therapy of bedrest was widely accepted in subsequent generations. Contributions on the injuries to nerves and the consequences, and a description of ascending neuritis are his. The treatment of neuritis by cold, the effect of meteorologic changes upon the amputation stump, causalgia, and erythromelalgia were discussed in his writings. He described the structual changes of the nervous tissue of stumps and the hallucinations of the amputee in the last chapter of his monograph on *Injuries of Nerves and Their Consequences* (1872). Of himself he wrote:

I was inclined to gloomy prognostications, and this weakened my capacity to do good. And yet I was a conscientious man, and eager to do what was right. I have, however, observed that sanguine men, or men who deliberately and constantly predict relief or cure, are best. If failure comes, it explains itself, or may be explained. I knew once a foxy old country doctor, who said to me, "Hide your indecisions; tell folks they will get well; tell their friends your doubts afterwards." This may be one way of practising a profession; it was not mine.[3]

A number of psychiatric novels appeared between 1897 and the year of his death, 1914. *Hugh Wynne* was a best seller. Rein considers *In War Time,* a tale of Revolutionary days, Mitchell's best contribution. Some of his characters as described in the volume entitled *Characteristics*[5] were as gruesome as those portrayed by Charles Addams:

There is a nice story in that big book on Brazil; it is the only thing I got out of it. It will answer to kill your large talk. An ancient Indian convert of the Jesuits, at Para, was sick to death, and being asked by the good padre what delicacies he would like to comfort him on his way to purgatory, said, "I should like the tender hand of a Tapuya boy, well broiled."

Other characters were alcoholics, with varying degrees of affliction. The "couch-loving invalid," reminiscent of Victorian hypo-chondriasis, was portrayed by several characters. Some suffered from a split personality; a few characters became insane. Several doctors were included in the novels; none was autobiographical. His friend Owen Wister concluded that:

The tone of his books is a lesson and a tonic for an age that is sick and weak with literary perverts.

1. Rein, D. M.: S. *Weir Mitchell as a Psychiatric Novelist*, New York: International Universities Press, Inc., 1952.

2. Mitchell, S. W.: *Doctor and Patient*, 3d ed. Philadelphia: J. B. Lippincott Company, 1889.

3. Mitchell, S. W.: *Circumstance*, New York: The Century Company, 1901.

4. Mitchell, S. W.: The Treatment by Rest, Seclusion, Etc., in Relation to Psychotherapy, *JAMA* 50: 2033-2037 (June 20) 1908.

5. Mitchell, S. W.: *Characteristics*, New York: the Century Company, 1892.

John Shaw Billings (1883-1913)

A PECULIAR INGREDIENT IN THE ENVIRON-MENT of the state of Indiana that spawns litterateurs and lexicographers such as Lew Wallace, George Ade, Booth Tarkington, James W. Riley, and the adopted son, Kin Hubbard, must contribute to the brilliant reputation of the writers of the Hoosier state. To this list should be added John Shaw Billings, military surgeon, planner of hospitals, and lexicographer who established the world's greatest medical library and was Superintendent-in-Chief of the New York Public Library as his last great achievement in the world of books.

Billings was born in 1838, in Cotton Township, Switzerland County, Indiana.[1] The family moved first to Rhode Island but returned to the Midwest and settled in the village of Allensville on the road from Rising Sun to Vevay. His father served as postmaster, shoemaker, and keeper of the crossroads country store. Billings was avid for knowledge and, with the help of a dictionary, studied Latin and Greek before he

embarked upon his higher education. At graduation with an AB from Miami University he stood second in his class scholastically and delivered the Latin salutatory.[1]

In the fall of 1858, Billings enrolled for the 2-year medical course in Miami Medi-

Composite by G. Bako

cal College (later the Medical College of Ohio—the 10th medical school founded in this country). He was self-supporting during this time. The term consisted of five months of instruction; the second year was a repetition of the first. He did not attend the lectures regularly but preferred to spend his time in the dissecting room and in the clinics. In preparation for his graduation thesis, he explored the medical libraries in Cincinnati, Philadelphia, Washington, and elsewhere to assemble all available data regarding the surgical treatment of epilepsy. Although the accumulation of the reference material and the compilation of the dissertation was a "melancholy duty," the influence of this duty upon his professional career was clear. It brought home to him the realization that the United States could not boast of an adequate medical library. If one wished to pursue an exhaustive study of a medical subject, it was necessary to consult a library in Europe. Following graduation he remained as Demonstrator of Anatomy. Tickets for his course were available for $6; the professor's tickets were $105. Hospital advantages were reported to be "unsurpassed."

At the outbreak of the War between the States, Billings answered the appeal for volunteers and appeared before the examining board for admission to the medical corps of the United States Army. He rose from First Lieutenant in 1862 to Lieutenant Colonel in 1894. Upon reporting for duty, he was equipped with three items that none of the other surgeons possessed: a set of clinical thermometers, a straight and curved one; a hypodermic syringe; and a Symes staff for urethral stricturotomy. The syringe and the Symes staff were used extensively, the clinical thermometers less so. While a field surgeon with the Army of the Potomac under General Hooker, Billings operated extensively and cared for the wounded at Chancellorsville and Gettysburg. Other engagements included Spottsylvania Court House and the assault on Petersburg. He served under Grant at the Battle of the Wilderness. Frequently he cared for the sick or operated within range of the Reb batteries, but was never injured.

The collection of material for the three-volume medical and surgical history of the War was begun upon assignment to the Surgeon General's office in Washington in 1864. He remained on continuous duty until he retired at his own request in 1895. The first decade in Washington was uninspiring. He was placed in charge of the Veterans Reserve Corps in matters that concerned contract physicians, accounting of property, and disbursing of accounts. In his reports to the Surgeon General, he discussed the state of the barracks and hospitals of the regular Army and the hygiene of the enlisted men. He believed that the enlisted men were "the best-fed and the worst-housed army in the world." The pavilion type of hospital was recommended. One report noted that:

Our military system is, or should be, organized on the theory that it is to act as a nucleus and organizing power for the force to be called into existence in time of war. When a war breaks out we must have large hospitals; if these are to be efficient they must be thoroughly organized. The knowledge of this organization is best obtained by practising it previously on a small scale.

This philosophy prevailed during the Spanish-American War and the First and Second World Wars. Billings recommended jet showers or bathing tubs, a 25% excess food ration, and abundance of ice for the Southern posts, lime juice to be a part of the rations for scouts and expeditions, and canned tomatoes to be issued if fresh vegetables were not available. Since an army travels on its belly, the chief cook should be a permanent detail, with extra pay, and should be prepared for duty by instruction in a school for cooks.

Billings became interested in national public health and active in the affairs of the American Public Health Association, of which he was President in 1880. As an officer of the National Board of Health, he proposed that all American cities and towns of 5,000 or more inhabitants be subjected to a survey of sanitation. He suspected the infectious nature of yellow fever and noted that many people agreed with the farmer that "yellow fever can't go anywhere unless yer tote it!"

As a consulting designer for medical schools, his advice was sought early by the Trustees of the Johns Hopkins Fund, who, in 1876, selected him as the medical adviser to the architect. A 2-story pavilion-type building, a dispensary for out-patients, clinical instruction on the wards and in the out-patient department, and emphasis upon beside teaching were recommended. The need for integration of the medical school and the university teaching hospital was noted. According to Billings, the hospital had a triple mission—in promoting charity, education, and science.[2] A system of records and an annual volume of reports similar to Guy's Hospital were recommended. Billings was instrumental in the appointment of Welch as Professor of Pathology and Osler as Physician-in-Chief. The interview with Osler in Philadelphia lasted only a few minutes. Billings lectured on the history of medicine at Hopkins for a number of years. Also he participated in planning the buildings of the Barnes Hospital (Soldiers' Home, Washington, DC), the Army Medical Library and Museum, the Laboratory of Hygiene and the William Pepper Laboratory of Clinical Medicine of the University of Pennsylvania. One of his last consulting responsibilities concerned the plans for the Peter Bent Brigham Hospital in Boston.

The need for a national medical library and catalog was high on his priority list for a number of years. At the close of the War between the States, the medical library of the Surgeon General comprised 1,365 volumes. A year later, the catalog listed 2,253 volumes. The increase was related to $80,000 in funds that had been turned in from the Army hospitals at the close of the war. Between 1865 and 1887, the books were kept in the Army medical museum—the old Ford's theater in which Lincoln had been assassinated. By 1873, the library contained approximately 25,000 volumes, and the catalog had grown to 3 volumes. The *Specimen Fasciculus* was published in 1876. The style and arrangement followed the *Index Catalogue*. Appropriations were then made by Congress. The first volume of the *Index Catalogue* comprising 888 pages was published in 1880. This was a notable year in the development of medical literature for the United States. Dr. Robert Fletcher of Bristol, England, who helped with the *Index Catalogue,* carried on simultaneously the preparation of the *Index Medicus* listing of the current medical literature. The first series of the *Index Medicus* comprised 21 volumes. Its course was a stormy one, and not until 1903, with Fletcher as Editor-in-Chief, was it placed upon a firm basis. The first series of the *Index Catalogue* was published over a period of 16 years.

Billings' crowning triumph was the development of the New York Public Library. He retired from the Surgeon General's Office in 1895 to assume the duties of Professor of Hygiene at the University of Pennsylvania. This assignment was brief, however, and scarcely had he begun than he was offered the position as chief executive of the New York Public Library. The cornerstone of the Library was laid in 1902; the Library was opened in 1911. Two years later Billings died and was buried in Arlington Cemetery.

What is the status of the projects that Billings started? The New York Public Library and the Johns Hopkins Hospital need no statements to document their attainments. The *Index Catalogue* of the Library of the Surgeon General's office is now in its fifth series. Volume I of this series was published in 1959; the remaining 2 volumes will be published this year. The annual *Catalog of the National Library of Medicine,* which was started in 1948, lists books, theses, and pamphlets received by the National Library, listed by author and subject with complete information for cataloguing. The *Index Medicus,* which had such a stormy career in the earlier years, was replaced by the *Quarterly Cumulative Index Medicus.* This fell behind during the Second World War and never caught up. Through the cooperation of the National Library of Medicine, the American Medical Association published the first annual volumes of the *Cumulated Index Medicus.* The 1969 (Vol 10) *Cumulated Index Medicus* contains literature citations to more than 224,000 articles from the biomedical literature.

1. Garrison, F. H.: *John Shaw Billings: a Memoir,* New York: G. P. Putnam's Sons, 1915.
2. Rogers, F. B.: *Selected Papers of John Shaw Billings,* Chicago: Med Lib Assn, 1965.

Sir Norman Moore (1847-1922)

NORMAN MOORE, who occupied important offices in two of the most respected medical institutions in London—St. Bartholomew's Hospital and the Royal College of Physicians—was born at Higher Broughton in Lancashire. He was the only son of a barrister, a descendant of an Ulster family and a graduate of Trinity College in Dublin, from whom he inherited a taste for literature. Norman was educated at Castle School, Lancaster; Owens College, Manchester; and St. Catharine's College, Cambridge. Having graduated AB from Cambridge, he entered St. Bartholomew's in 1869, served as house physician (1872-

Composite by G. Bako

1874), and, in time, returned to Cambridge, taking the BM and AM degrees and finally the MD in 1876.[1] While at Cambridge he satisfied the basic course requirements in science and medicine; however, he was attracted to literature and in his private associations turned to those professing the arts.

Moore was admitted a member of the Royal College of Physicians in 1873 and the following year was appointed casualty physician at St. Bartholomew's Hospital and warden of the Hospital School. Living in for an unusually long period, he knew the resident students intimately, lectured to them on comparative anatomy, pathology, and clinical medicine, and commanded great respect for his kindly nature and admirable qualities of leadership. He was a clear and emphatic teacher. His presentations were scattered with witty historical citations, and pertinent references to his clinical experiences in the morgue and at the bedside.

Moore's veneration for the past and clarity in presenting his thoughts brought him multiple assignments for the *Dictionary of National Biography*. He assembled more than 450 biographies, chiefly of physicians and surgeons: he initially reviewed all readily available items in the bibliography of his splendid *History of St. Bartholomew's Hospital*, on which he worked unremittingly for 30 years. Together with Stephen Paget, Moore prepared a history of *The Royal Medical and Chirurgical Society of London* (1905). Through his influence the Fitz-Patrick lectures in the history of medicine were established at the College of Physicians, and, as Linacre lecturer at Cambridge in 1913, he discussed the contributions of physicians to English political history. *The History of St. Bartholomew's Hospital*, which established a standard of excellence for histories of illustrious hospitals, contained the following introductory paragraph in the Preface.[2]

The history of St. Bartholomew's Hospital from its foundation in 1123 to the present day is a part of the history of England which has never before been written at length, and which I have endeavoured to set forth in this book. Such a work must enter upon many separate parts of historical study besides that dealing with transactions within the hospital walls. The city of London and its inhabitants, the social life of successive periods, particular events in the reigns of our kings, the organization of the several parts of the profession of medicine, the growth of medical education, the increase of medical knowledge, the lives of a long series of men concerned in the practice and teaching of medicine—all these and many subjects of less extent form natural parts of this history.

In performing his various offices Moore served the Royal College of Physicians as loyally as he served the hospital. He delivered the Bradshaw lecture (1889), the Lumleian lectures (1909), and the Harvey oration (1901); for seven years he was the Harveian librarian; he represented the College on the General Medical Council for two decades, and from 1918 until his death was president of the College.

Moore's clinical teaching was founded on a triple base: consideration for the patient, study of the signs and symptoms of the presenting malady, and a precise statement of the findings and conclusions. In the Introduction to the inaugural lecture for his formal course on the principles and practice of medicine, delivered 20 years after he began his house residency, he confessed his great devotion to the revered hospital, identified exemplary performances in the pursuit of learning, and documented pertinent political and medical events in English history.[3]

During these twenty years this hospital has been the place of my study, and what I propose to-day is to explain to you how I can best help you to attain a knowedge of medicine in this place. It is impossible not to feel some pride in being a teacher of medicine in such a hospital as this, where for more than seven centuries and a half the original purpose of our honoured founder Rahere has been carried out with ever-increasing efficiency. It is no inconsiderable honour to teach in a seat of medical practice and learning older than any college in either university, a foundation more venerable than nearly every institution of this ancient city. Our hospital was already flourishing when Henry Fitz-Elwin, the first mayor, began to preside over the citizens of London. Magna Carta is, according to Sir William Blackstone, the earliest extant statute of the realm, and at the date of its first draft our doors had been open to the sick for more than ninety years. Patients had been admitted and discharged here for 140 years before the first Parliament—with knights, citizens, and burgesses—was elected. Our wards have received the subjects of every English dynasty since the Conquest. The antiquity of St. Bartholomew's Hospital is, however, but a small part of its glory. The greatest consists in the vast numbers of the sick poor whom it has relieved, and in the large additions to medical knowledge which have been made within its walls. I need hardly remind you that it was whilst he was in charge of this hospital that Harvey laboriously worked out his discovery of the circulation of the blood.
My own opinion is that the principles and practice of medicine, like every scientific subject, or indeed every subject, must be taught in the closest relation to the actual facts on which the statements of the lecturer are based. . . . I shall try as far as possible, with the aid of the medical registrar, to let you know what cases illustrative of my lectures are in the wards, so that you may go round with the physicians and see them. A further part of your observation I shall direct to the post-mortem room and to our fine pathological museum.
You will find your medical reading much easier and more interesting if you can spare time now and then to read a page or two in other books than your textbook. After its primary object of making a man ready to observe, the true use of reading in medicine is to make him think. The difference between perfect and imperfect knowledge is not so much in the facts known as in the way they are treated by the mind. Perfect knowledge is that which has been thought over; imperfect knowledge that which has only been remembered. This is particularly noticeable in medicine, where a few observations well thought over will make a man far more useful than the mental retention of abstracts of hundreds of books.

Norman Moore was a bibliophile and antiquarian, a delightful and spirited teacher, and a sound physician who despised dogmatism. Although he wrote on many clinical subjects, he will not be remembered as well in this area as for his contributions to the other intellectual fields. He was elected Fellow of the Royal College of Physicians of Ireland in 1912, was created a baronet in 1919, served as a trustee of the British Museum, and received an honorary LLD from Cambridge the following year. Although he lived his life in England, he retained a love for the Irish, as evidenced by an essay, *The History of Medicine in Ireland,* founded on an examination of some manuscripts in the British Museum; in addition, Moore provided a translation of an Irish grammar and a translation of an Irish text, *Loss of the Crown of Loegaire Lurc.* Born a Protestant, he accepted the Roman Catholic faith many years before his death.

1. Chaplin, A.: Sir Norman Moore, obituary, *Brit. Med J* 2:1148-1150 (Dec 9) 1922.
2. Moore, N.: *The History of St. Bartholomew's Hospital,* 2 vol, London: C. A. Pearson, 1918.
3. Moore, N.: *The Principles and Practice of Medicine,* London: Adlard & Son, 1893.

Sir William Hale-White (1857-1949)

THE WRITING CAREER OF WILLIAM HALE-White began with the preparation of medical histories and summaries of a series of cases for the *Transactions of the Pathological Society of London.* It culminated half a century later in the publication of *Great Doctors of the Nineteenth Century,* biographical essays of selected British physicians by Sir William Hale-White. (The hyphen was added after his father's death.) Born in London, the son of a clerk in the admiralty

Composite by G. Bako

who was himself well known as a novelist under the nom de plume Mark Rutherford, William entered Guy's Hospital as a medical student at 17 and obtained his MB at 22 from the University of London.[1] Returning to Guy's Hospital, he served as house physician, later as demonstrator of anatomy, and at the early age of 33 became a full physician.

Hale-White's contributions to the medical sciences covered a great number of subjects. They began with anatomy and physiology, continued through pathological anatomy and clinical medicine, and concluded with materia medica and therapeutics. In 1935, he assembled his *Great Doctors of the Nineteenth Century*,[2] completing, with a literary flourish, *Keats as Doctor and Patient*.[3] *Materia Medica, Pharmacy, Pharmacology and Therapeutics*, Hale-White's most popular text, appeared first in 1892.[4] The treatise went through 28 editions in two generations and outshone similar efforts for more than a quarter of a century. In the

interim, he published *A Text-Book of General Therapeutics*,[5] was a regular contributor to *Guy's Hospital Reports*, and served as one of the editors from 1886 to 1893.

The *Quarterly Journal of Medicine*, founded in 1907, was his most influential clinical periodical. This was sponsored by the Association of Physicians of Great Britain and Ireland, and was supported by William Osler, A. E. Garrod, H. D. Rolleston, and others. Hale-White was treasurer of the Association and editor of the *Journal*. During World War I, he served as chairman of Queen Mary's Royal Naval Hospital, Southend, and in 1919 was appointed Knight of the British Empire. He was awarded an honorary MD degree from Dublin and LLD from Edinburgh. Following the war he showed a great interest in the Royal Society of Medicine and for several years edited the *Proceedings*.

Hale-White's students knew him as a kindly teacher, his patients as a sympathetic physician, and his associates as a consultant with diverse interests in clinical medicine. He was called by Osler to his bedside in his terminal illness—two outstanding clinicians uncertain of the affliction of the elder. Nonprofessional activities included golf, bridge, photography, and foreign travel. An example of Hale-White's style in clinical reporting is taken from the concluding paragraph of his *Common Affections of the Liver*.[6]

It is quite common to meet with persons said to suffer from "a torpid liver" or from "an attack of liver," or a well-educated man will be content with saying he knows what is the matter with himself, and he tells his doctor "he has a liver." The symptoms of this condition are a feeling of distension, or of a weight in the upper part of the abdomen, together with flatulence, constipation, and the usual symptoms of dyspepsia. Depression of spirits and headache are common. There is no evidence that these symptoms are due to disease of the liver; probably they are caused by some gastro-intestinal catarrh, the result of over-eating, and if a slight tint of jaundice is present, this may well be owing to a mild catarrh of the bile ducts caused by the spread of duodenal catarrh. The motions are often a little pale, but it is rash to assume from this that the liver is primarily at fault; sometimes this colour of the faeces is due to bubbles of gas, resulting from excessive carbo-hydrate fermentation. The condition is readily cured by plain simple diet, and by some simple aperient such as calomel.

1. Campbell, M.: Sir William Hale-White, *Guy's Hosp Rep* 98:1-17, 1949.

2. Hale-White, W.: *Great Doctors of the Nineteenth Century*, London: E. Arnold & Co., 1935.

3. Hale-White, W.: *Keats As Doctor and Patient*, London: Oxford University Press, 1938.

4. White, H. W.: *Materia Medica, Pharmacy, Pharmacology and Therapeutics*, Philadelphia: P. Blakiston, Son & Co., 1892.

5. White, W. H.: *A Text-Book of General Therapeutics*, London: MacMillan and Co., 1889.

6. White, H. W.: *Common Affections of the Liver*, London: J. Nisbet & Co., Limited, 1908.

Composite by G. Bako

Sir John Pringle (1707-1782)

JOHN PRINGLE, one of the early exponents of humane treatment of soldiers and penal inmates, was born in the county of Roxburgh, Scotland, into a family of baronets and scholars. He was privately tutored for a time, but at an early age was sent to the University of St. Andrew's, where his uncle, Francis Pringle, was professor of Greek. At the age of 21, John entered the University of Edinburgh, planning for a career in commerce, and a year later went to Amsterdam for further training and practical experience in business. While there he came under the influence of Boerhaave of Leyden, changed his goal in life to medicine, and received his MD from Leyden in 1730. Studies were continued at Paris before he returned to Edinburgh for the practice of medicine and, as an additional responsibility, the joint professorship of moral philosophy in the University. The contributions of Bacon were stressed in his lectures on ethics.

At the age of 35, Pringle was commissioned a surgeon to the British forces on the Continent, who were allied with the soldiers of Empress Maria Teresa in the struggle against France. The inhumanity to which prisoners of war and the wounded on both sides were subjected was shocking and readily apparent to Pringle. In an attempt to allay these deplorable conditions, a convention was drafted and signed by representatives of the English, French, and Austrian commanders. This forerunner of the demilitarization of Red Cross hospitals insured prompt exchange or ransom of prisoners of war and the declaration of neutrality for military hospitals. The agreement, petitioned by Pringle, was described in his *Observations on the Diseases of the Army*. The first printing was prepared in London in 1752 and remained popular through several editions. The following excerpt is from the first American edition, edited with notes by Benamin Rush, Pringle's correspondent in Philadelphia.[1]

But the earl of Stair, my illustrious patron, being sensible of this hardship, when the army was encamped, at Aschaffenburg, proposed to the Duke de Noailles (of whose humanity he was well assured) that the hospitals on both sides should be considered as sanctuaries for the sick, and mutually protected. This was readily agreed to by the French general, who took the first opportunity to show a particular regard to his engagement. For when our hospital was at Feckenheim, a village upon the Maine, at a distance from the camp, the Duke de Noailles having occasion to send a detachment to another village upon the opposite bank, and apprehending that this might alarm our sick, he sent to acquaint them, that as he knew the British hospital was there, he had given express orders to his troops not to disturb them. This agreement was strictly observed on both sides during that campaign.

Pringle remained on the Continent during a major portion of the assignment, returning to London in 1748; meanwhile, he had resigned his professorship in Edinburgh. In 1758, he was admitted a licentiate of the Royal College of Physicians of London, was made a baronet in 1766, and in 1774 was appointed physician to the King. His positions brought him honors in scientific circles as well as in professional practice. He served as president of the Royal Society, participated in the annual awards of the Copley medal for scientific research, and was chosen successor to Linnaeus as one of the eight foreign members elected to the Academy of Sciences in Paris. The address delivered at the anniversary meeting of the Royal Society in 1776 described the observations of Captain Cook in preventing disease, especially scurvy, among mariners.[2]

The logical extension of Pringle's interest in the unfortunate in battle and those stricken with scurvy at sea was a crusade for cleanliness, adequate ventilation, and good hygiene in the galleys on ships and in civilian jails. His observations on the nature and cure of hospital and jail fevers were described in a letter to Mead, physician to His Majesty. Pringle provided a clinical description of typhus fever and attributed it to filth, crowding, and utter lack of hygiene.[3]

And upon this account, jayls and military hospitals, are most obnoxious to this kind of pestilential infection; as the first are kept in a constant state of filth and impurity; and the last are so much filled with the poisonous *effluvia* of sores, mortifications, dysenteric and other putrid excrements.

Some preserve their senses, allowing for a confusion and, *stupor* through the whole course of the disease till recovery; few keep them till death. They rarely sleep, and at all times look like men pensive or in deep thought rather than a fever. The face is late in acquiring either a ghastly or a very morbid look. The confusion of the head often rises to a *delirium,* especially at night, but rarely turns to rage, or to those high flights of imagination frequent in other fevers. It is likewise more common to observe in a *tremor* than a *subsultus tendinum;* or if that symptom seizes them, it is in a less degree than in inflammatory fevers. All along as the pulse sinks, the *stupor* or *delirium,* and *tremor* increase; and in proportion to its rising the head and spirits are relieved. Frequently from the first beginning the patient is dull of hearing, and at last grows almost deaf.

There are certain spots which are the frequent but not inseparable attendants of the fever, in its worst state. These are less usual on the first breaking out in hospitals; but when the air becomes more corrupted, the spots are common. They are of the petechial kind, of an obscure red colour, paler than the measles, not raised above the skin, of no regular shape, but confluent. . . . These petechiae are very irregular, sometimes appearing as early as the fourth or fifth day, and at other times as late as the fourteenth. They are not at all crucial, nor are they reckoned among the mortal signs, as they only concur with other circumstances to argue more danger. The nearer these spots approach to a purple colour, the more ominous they are, tho' not absolutely mortal.

1. Pringle, J.: *Observations on the Diseases of the Army,* 1st American ed, with notes by B. Rush, Philadelphia: E. Earle, 1810.

2. Pringle, J.: *A Discourse upon Some Late Improvements of the Means for Preserving the Health of Mariners,* London: Royal Society, 1776.

3. Pringle, J.: *Observations on the Nature and Cure of Hospital and Jayl-Fevers,* London: A. Miller, and D. Wilson, 1750.

Composite by G. Bako

James Tilton (1745-1822)

FROM A FULL TOUR OF DUTY in the Revolutionary War, James Tilton assembled, into one of the first American treatises on military medicine, experience in military hospitals and knowledge on the presention and cure of diseases incidental to the Army. Tilton was born in the county of Kent, Delaware, then one of the counties in the province of Pennsylvania. He engaged in classical learning at Knottingham Academy under the direction of the Reverend Doctor Samuel Finley, later president of Princeton College.[1] The study of medicine was commenced as an apprentice to Dr. Ridgely of Dover and was continued in the medical department of the College of Philadelphia. Tilton received the BM in 1768, the only medical degree conferred by the College from 1768 until 1771, when it conferred the MD on each of the four members of the first class. His inaugural dissertation on dropsy was submitted in Latin in 1771 to fulfill the requirements for the doctorate.

Tilton practiced in Dover until 1776 when he abandoned a civilian living, joined the Delaware regiment, and cared for the wounded in the battles of Long Island and White Plains. His talents and accomplishments brought his name to the attention of higher authority; consequently, on assignment from the hospital department of the Army, he directed the hospitals at Princeton, Trenton, and New Windsor, and inspected the military hospitals at Bethlehem, Reading, Manheim, Lancaster, and Newport. The state of patients and conditions was deplorable in each installation; quarters were overcrowded and filthy; food and housekeeping supplies inadequate to a critical degree; and the gross lack of sanitary facilities spawned jail fever (typhus), dysentery, and intractable diarrhea. The effects of the abominable environment were greater scourges to the sick and wounded than were gunfire and the sword to the soldier in the field. Tilton's experiments with hospital huts during the winter of 1779-1780 to better the lot of the casualties are described in his manual on military hospitals.[2]

It would be shocking to humanity to relate the history of our general hospital, in the years 1777 and 1778, when it swallowed up at least one half of our army, owing to a fatal tendency in the system to throw all the sick of the army into the general hospital; whence crowds, infection and consequent mortality too affecting to mention. I doubt not but humanity at first dictated the ample provision made for the sick in general hospitals, but we should learn, from experience, to contract our plan into greater simplicity; and to make it the *interest,* as well as the duty of all concerned in curing the sick to send as few as possible to the general hospital.

And to give some idea of the mortality of their hospital, one of the surgeons asked me if I were acquainted with that fine volunteer regiment of Virginia, commanded, I think, by Col. Gibson. I answered I know it only by reputation. He then went on to say that forty of that regiment had come to their hospital, and then asked me how many I supposed would ever join the regiment? I guessed a third or a fourth part. He declared solemnly that not three would ever return, that one man had joined his regiment; that another was convalescent and might possibly recover; but that the only remaining one besides, was in the last stage of the colliquative flux and must soon die. I was obliged to acknowledge the hospital at Bethlehem had been more fatal than that at Princeton.

After the siege of the British in Virginia, the capture of Yorktown, and the surrender of Cornwallis, Tilton returned to Dover to resume a full and active practice. He served one term (1783-1785) in the Continental Congress and several terms as a member of the state legislature. Looking forward in his 60's to retirement to a country home in the hills adoining Wilmington, he added horticulture and agriculture to his interests. In such a pleasant state of living, he witnessed resumption of minor hostilities with the British in 1812. Possibly in hopes of preventing a recurrence of the wretched hospital conditions for the wounded, he published for the first time his Revolutionary experiences and recommendations therefrom in 1813. The volume was dedicated to Gen John Armstrong, Secretary of War, and surely contributed to his being offered and promptly accepting the position of Physician and Surgeon General of the Army. His first tour of inspection included the hospital facilities in the northern frontier extending from Lake Erie to Lake Champlain. Little change was apparent from the conditions of hospitals a quarter of a century earlier.

Extended duties in the field were curtailed by the development of a malignant lesion on his knee and subsequent amputation of the leg at the thigh. Tilton continued to hold office until the post was abolished in 1815 by an act of Congress, but not before his efforts to improve the hospital and field care of the soldier were successful. *Regulations for the Medical Department* was published as a part of a general order issued from the War Office establishing *Regulations for the Army of the United States* in December, 1814. The orders defined the duties of hospital surgeons, mates, stewards, wardmasters, regimental surgeons, post surgeons, and apothecary general.[3] The excerpts from his military manual are illustrative of the evidence submitted in support of personal and contact cleanliness, proper clothing, mess-prepared food, a mind subservient to health, avoidance of hospital infection, and use of a well ventilated Indian-type hut.[2]

Cleanliness is essential in all conditions of life, but especially to soldiers. Without the necessary cautions on this score, an army is literally poisoned, and dwindles into insignificance. Officers, therefore, should be very solicitous to protect their men, as well as themselves, from the dreadful effects of filth and nastiness. . . . Bathing should be encouraged in warm weather, with this caution however, that the men should remain no longer in the water than is necessary to make their skins clean. That the camp may be kept free from excrementitious filth of every kind, a penalty should be annexed to dropping any thing of this kind within the bounds of the encampment.

The regular muster of clothing is of immense consequence to an army. Before the introduction of this measure, our army was kept bare and naked, by multitudes of soldiers selling their clothes for drink and otherwise wasting them.

Diet is another article of immense consequence to a soldier. The ordinary ration is sufficient if well managed. The soldiers ought to eat in messes; and it would be of importance if an old well educated soldier could be associated in every mess. An old soldier would make good and wholesome foods of materials that a young recruit would spoil, in such a manner, as hardly to be fit to eat.

Not only the body, but the mind of a soldier should also be trained, in subserviency to health. The influence of the mind upon the body is astonishing.

The cardinal point or principle to be observed in the direction of all hospitals, is to avoid infection.

In such cases [cold climates and winter seasons], the best hospital I have ever contrived was upon the plan of an Indian hut. The fire was built in the midst of the ward, without any chimney, and the smoke circulating round about, passed off thro' an opening about four inches wide in the ridge of the roof. The common surface of the earth served for the floor. The patients laid with their heads to the wall round about, and their feet were all turned to the fire. The wards thus completely ventilated. . . . This was the expedient I employed in the hard winter of '70. '79, '80, when the army was hutted near Morris Town, and I was well satisfied with the experiment.

1. Thacher, J.: "James Tilton," in *American Medical Biography*, vol 1, Boston: Richardson & Lord and Cottons & Barnard, 1828.

2. Tilton, J.: *Economical Observations on Military Hospitals; and the Prevention and Cure of Diseases Incident to an Army*, Wilmington, Del: J. Wilson, 1813.

3. Brown, H. E.: *The Medical Department of the United States Army from 1775 to 1873*, Washington, DC: Surgeon General's Office, 1873.

National Library of Medicine

Dominique Jean Larrey
(1766-1842)

MODERN MILITARY MEDICINE began with Napoleon's surgeon, D. J. Larrey, whose imagination in planning for the health of the soldier and practical skill in the care of the wounded on the field and in the hospital equaled the genius and strategy of his Commander-in-Chief.[1] Larrey's special talents were utilized by Napoleon in planning for a campaign, while in the execution of his plans. Larrey earned the respect of the soldiers for his courage, humane care, and surgical skill. He participated in each of Napoleon's campaigns, in most of the battles, and in many of the engagements. On the field, he attended first the wounded who were in greatest need, irrespective of rank or grade. The design and use of "flying ambulances," and descriptions of early amputation, frostbite, trench foot, the contagious nature of Egyptian ophthalmia, and amputation of limbs affected with tetanus are examples of his fine contributions to military medicine included in his *Memoirs*.[2] The four-volume treatise on his military career was published consecutively between 1812 and 1817 and was available shortly after in a two-volume English translation.

Larrey, not content with the immediate effects of his medical and surgical ability, shared his activities in the field with pedagogy. He was constantly on the search for opportunities to teach, and conducted tutorial classes whenever the opportunity presented. The only formal teaching post was professor at the École de Médecine Militaire at Val-de-Grâce.

Larrey was born in the village of Baudéan in the Pyrenees. Orphaned at the age of 13, he was placed in the charge of his uncle, chief surgeon in Toulouse, under whose care he remained until the age of 20, studying medicine. Although handicapped by extreme poverty, Larrey completed formal surgical study in Paris, was successful in competition for the post of assistant naval surgeon, and at the age of 21 served as ship's surgeon on a vessel sailing for Newfoundland. While waiting for the departure from Brest, he gave lectures on anatomy and surgery to the physicians in the community and prepared himself broadly for future contingencies. He visited the galley slaves, inspected arsenals and shipyards, sought information about the climate of Newfoundland, its influence on visitors, and details of the health, character, and interests of the inhabitants. Although the frigate was a strong ship for the sea, a violent storm made Larrey critically ill. He describes the agony of intractable seasickness.[2]

The nutrition of the body is suspended, because nothing can be retained on the stomach; emaciation ensues and increases. The faculties of the mind suffer in common with the organs of animal life, and this charge takes place to such a degree, that instead of dreading death, as in the commencement of the disease, their suffering is so intolerable, that they desire it; and as I have seen, attempt to commit suicide.

Upon return to the Continent in the midst of the Revolution, Larrey resigned his naval commission and continued his study at Hôtel Royal des Invalides and at Hôtel Dieu with Desault, celebrated surgeon of Paris. By now Larrey was fully prepared as a medical officer, and when war broke out in 1792, he was attached to the Army of the Rhine with the rank of surgeon-major. Triage and first-aid were performed in the combat zone; whereas the critically wounded were dispatched to the rear in the "flying ambulance," sharply different from the then current practice of slow evacuation.[2]

I now first discovered the inconveniences to which we were subjected in moving our *ambulances,* or military hospitals. The military regulations required that they should always be one league distant from the army. The wounded were left on the field, until after the engagement, and were then collected at a convenient spot, to which the *ambulances* repaired as speedily as possible; but the number of wagons interposed between them and the army, and many other difficulties so retarded their progress, that they never arrived in less than twenty-four or thirty-six hours, so that most of the wounded died for want of assistance. . . . This suggested to me the idea of constructing an *ambulance* in such a manner that it might afford a ready conveyance for the wounded during the battle.

At Limbourg, our advanced guard had a brisk engagement with that of the king of Prussia. The remoteness of our *ambulances* deprived the wounded of the requisite attention. . . . We found it impossible to bring off our wounded, who fell into the power of the enemy. This misfortune induced me to propose to the general, and to the commissary-general, who felt great solicitude for these unfortunate men, the plan of an ambulance, calculated to follow the advanced guard in the same manner as the flying artillery. My proposition was accepted, and I was authorized to construct a carriage, which I called the *flying ambulance.*

At the age of 28, Larrey was appointed chief surgeon of the army intended for Corsica and was ordered to report to Toulon. This was the first meeting with Bonaparte, three years his junior and commander of an artillery brigade. The campaigns of Egypt and Syria, begun in 1798, were especially appealing to Larrey.[2]

Little did I think, when I received the order of government to repair to Toulon, for the Mediterranean expedition, that I was destined to follow the French army, under the command of general Bonaparte, into the richest and most interesting country in the world.

The great preparations which were made for the embarkation of this army, and the presence of a chief so justly celebrated, who was to command it, announced the importance of the expedition. Zealous to merit the confidence of the government, I made every effort to fulfill its intentions, as chief surgeon to a body of thirty thousand choice troops.

An order was issued to the health officers connected with this expedition, to procure assistants, and every article necessary for their respective service. It was incumbent on me to perform the first part of my duty in a very short time.

Consequently, I wrote to the medical schools of Montpellier and Toulouse, requesting them to send me, with the least possible delay, a specified number of intelligent surgeons, who would be capable of supporting the fatigues of a long and laborious campaign.

My invitation was scarcely published in the schools, when all expressed a desire to partake our dangers and our glory. A hundred and eight surgeons, comprising those in the divisions departing for Italy, were embodied under my orders at the period of embarkation, exclusive of the surgeons of the different corps of the army.

On my arrival at Cairo, I organized the surgical staff, and in the principal hospital I established a school of practical surgery, for the instruction of the young surgeons of the army. I carefully superintended the treatment of the wounded, and of those affected with diseases of the eyes, for the ophthalmia had already appeared.—This was at the period of the overflowing of the Nile.

The therapeutic value of maggots in management of wounds was noted in the report of the campaign in Syria.[2]

During the progress of suppuration, the patients were only troubled by worms or larvae of the blue flies common in Syria.

The hatching of the eggs, which these flies constantly deposit in the wounds or dressings, was assisted by the heat of the weather, and by the quality of the dressings, which were of cotton, which alone could be procured in this country.

The presence of these insects in the wounds, appeared to accelerate their suppuration; but they caused a disagreeable pruritis, and obliged us to dress them three or four times a day.

Although these insects were troublesome, they expedited the healing of the wounds by shortening the work of nature, and causing the sloughs to fall off.

In the description of the Austrian campaign, early amputation was recommended for critically injured extremities.[2]

With my flying *ambulance* I followed the movements of the guards till the decisive moment, and we dressed the wounded on the ground as fast as they were brought up: . . . The majority of whom being severely wounded by cannon or other shot required important operations. Here the necessity of immediate amputation was most evidently confirmed. And I do not hesitate to say, that without it a large portion of our wounded must have perished within twenty-four hours.

According to my plan [for amputation of the hip-joint] I first applied a ligature on the femoral artery; after this the vessels were tied, and the operation completed in fifteen seconds without loss of blood, and both these men immediately became calm and one of them fell asleep.

I am of the opinion, that if this operation were instantly performed by an expert surgeon, when the wound required it, as in these two cases, it would succeed as well as amputation of the shoulder-joint. But few successful cases of which were formerly recorded.

In each of these instances the patient died within a few hours; on the other hand, amputation of the shoulder-joint was successful, and there are two recorded instances of amputation at the hip-joint with survival.

The winter retreat from Moscow of the demoralized troops led to frostbite and trench foot, insults more devastating than artillery shells or rifle fire.

A copious fall of sleet on the morning of the tenth, was the precursor of the thaw which took place the next day, and continued for some time. There were immediately a number of the soldiers of the guard and of the line, who complained of acute pains in the feet, torpour, heaviness, and a disagreeable pricking in the extremities, which were slightly swelled, and of a dark red. In some I perceived a slight redness about the base of the toes, and on the upper surface of the foot: in others the toes had lost their sensibility, heat and motion, and were black, and in a manner dried. They all assured me that they felt no symptoms of pain during the period of severe cold which they were obliged to support in *bivouac.* . . . Then they first felt a painful pricking in the feet, that was succeeded by numbness, stiffness, immobility, and weight, with a sensation of cold at the same time, but it was not severe. They who were able to go into the town, or to the fire of the *bivouac* to warm themselves, were most affected: fortunately the greatest number followed the advice of my colleagues and myself. We directed them to rub the parts immediately with snow, and afterwards with camphorated brandy, which prevented gangrene in those cases where it had not already taken place.

The chief surgeon was wounded three times, the last in the battle of Waterloo, where he was left for dead. However, Larrey regained consciousness and tried to escape, but he was captured by the Prussians and sentenced to be shot. His recognition by a former pupil saved his life, and he was

brought before Field Marshal Blücher, whose son's life had been saved by Larrey in a previous engagement. Blücher gave Larrey his life and safe passage to a neutral country. At the battle of Wagram, Larrey was made Baron on the field by Napoleon. In his will, Napoleon bequeathed Larrey 100,-000 francs, but at another time paid him a tribute greater than a monetary reward. He referred to him as "the most virtuous man that I have ever known," in recognition of his many accomplishments in bettering the welfare of the troops and the introduction of skillful and expeditious management of the wounded.

No nation accepted the truth of Larrey's organizational concepts until America was well into the Civil War. Larrey's teachings were completely ignored by the British in the Crimea; on the other hand, Pirogoff, in the Russian army, tried to put some of them into effect. At the beginning of the Civil War, the Union army had only two ambulances and they were in the Quartermaster Department. It was not until the Sanitary Commission had insisted upon the appointment of Dr. William A. Hammond as Surgeon General that the situation changed; then, at his instigation and because of the organizational ability of Jonathan Letterman, the medical organization for battlefield care and evacuation, so well demonstrated by Larrey, was instituted. It was not until the battle of Antietam that the wounded were removed from the battlefield on the same day of the battle.

1. Da Costa, J. C.: Baron Larrey: a Sketch, *Bull Johns Hopkins Hosp* 17:195-215 (July) 1906.
2. Larrey, D. J.: *Memoirs of Military Surgery, and Campaigns of the French Armies*, R. W. Hall, trans., Baltimore: J. Cushing, 1814.

Sir James McGrigor (1771-1858)

JAMES McGRIGOR, "Father" of the Royal Army Medical Corps, was born at Cromdale in the Scottish Highlands. He was educated at the grammar school at Aberdeen, where he graduated with the first prize.[1] He proceeded to Marischal College and received the AM in 1788. By then James had decided on medicine and commenced its study under Dr. French, reading texts and attending lectures at the Royal Infirmary.

Composite by G. Bako

After three years he began formal medical training at Edinburgh but did not qualify at that time for the MD degree. In 1793, McGrigor went to London, attended lectures in anatomy, and began general practice. His basic urge, however, was for military life; upon the outbreak of the war with France, his father purchased an army assignment for him in an Irish corps. The unit became famous later as the 88th Regiment or the Connaught Rangers.

McGrigor saw foreign service in Grenada and St. Vincent in the West Indies, India, Ceylon, and Egypt. In 1804, he returned with his regiment to England, received the MD degree at Marischal College, and, with this background and experience in the field, brought knowledge and understanding of administration as well as patient care to the military hospitals at home. He was assigned deputy inspector-general of hospitals in the northern district and introduced a system of detailed clinical case records and their periodic review by attending physicians. His next assignment was to the southwest district which included Portsmouth, the embarkation port, and a large general hospital

on the Isle of Wight, the depot for recruiting by all regiments.

Throughout his foreign duty McGrigor gained extensive experience in handling epidemic diseases, sometimes related to indigenous lack of sanitation on foreign soil or at sea, at other times caused by lack of appreciation of necessary medical measures by those in command. Major epidemics in which he was involved included plague, yellow fever, ophthalmia, typhus fever, guinea worm, hepatitis, and dysentery.[2] Whether in England or on foreign duty, McGrigor's understanding of the problems of the sick and an outstanding capacity for medical administration were highly productive. His interest in inducing the military hierarchy to provide the best possible medical care for the troops is described as follows.[1]

It is not only in the sense of humanity, but in that of a sound policy and real economy, that the state should provide able medical and surgical advice for the soldier when sick or wounded. I look upon it to be an implied part of the compact of citizens with the State, that, whoever enters the service of his country as a soldier to fight its battles, should be provided with the same quality of medical aid, when sick or wounded, which he enjoyed when a citizen.

McGrigor seems equally sound in establishing procedures for proper bedside instruction for the mutual benefit of patient and physician. His systems of medical reports and returns from all military stations formed the basis of the *Statistical Returns of the Health of the Army,* perpetuated in the annual reports of the Army Medical Department. His case work-ups were proposed as follows.[1]

In the York district I commenced a practice, which I ever after perservered in, and found it of the greatest advantage. In my inspection of the hospital of each corps, accompanied by its medical officers, I examined each patient's history, the medical officer reading the particulars of the case at the patient's bed side, and the treatment hitherto pursued; I then questioned the patient, generally approving of what had been done; but suggesting what might occur to me as to further treatment. On the evening of the day on which I inspected an hospital, all the hospital books were sent to my inn, where I examined them, making note of my remarks. These remarks I subsequently embodied in a letter to the surgeon, when I did not fail to advert to whatever I had indicated on former instructions, if it appeared to have been unattended to; and in this letter I referred to different authors on the diseases which were prevalent, or in which diseases the surgeon appeared not to have been successful. These letters, marked private, and always couched in friendly terms, had, but with few exceptions, the best effects.

In 1812, McGrigor was appointed chief of the medical staff under Lord Wellington in the Peninsular War and performed with great skill and ingenuity under tremendous difficulties. The Army took the field with a sick list of almost 5,000 soldiers. At the conclusion of 20 consecutive days of marching, the enemy was defeated with minimal loss of manpower—the ranks having been maintained with recruits from the convalescents. Upon return to England, McGrigor was knighted and pensioned from the service. Because England was soon at war again, the retirement was short; in 1815, he was appointed director general of the medical department with the relative rank of major general and was present at the Battle of Waterloo. He retired permanently in 1851.

McGrigor founded a library and a museum of natural history and pathological anatomy collected from specimens under his command, at Fort Pit, Chatham, later removed to Netley Hospital. In 1816, he started the Army Medical Friendly Society for the relief of widows and in 1820 the Army Medical Benevolent Society for assisting the orphans of medical officers. At all times in the years between wars, McGrigor searched for improvements in the station of army medical officers, gave great attention to the selection of men for foreign service, and was sympathetic to the problems of young and immature soldiers.

McGrigor was elected a Fellow of the Royal Society of London in 1816, received an honorary LLD from Edinburgh, and served as rector of the University of Aberdeen in 1826, 1827, and again in 1841. He was a Fellow of the College of Physicians of London and of Edinburgh, honorary physician to the Queen, and in 1850 became a Knight Commander of the Bath.

1. McGrigor, J.: *The Autobiography and Services of Sir James McGrigor, Bart.*, London: Longman, Green, Longman, & Roberts, 1861.

2. McGrigor, J.: *Medical Sketches of the Expedition to Egypt from India*, London: J. Murray, 1804.

George James Guthrie
(1785-1856)

ALTHOUGH G. J. GUTHRIE was the outstanding military surgeon in England in his time, he was never appointed to the highest post, Inspector General of its army hospitals.[1] He was born in London, where his father was engaged in the manufacture of emplastrum lythargyri and other surgical supplies, providing a substantial income. Guthrie was educated in boyhood by a French tutor, but misfortune in the family business forced him to prepare for his life's work independently. At 13 years of age, he was apprenticed to the medical profession; two years later he was appointed an assistant at York (military) Hospital. This was followed by qualification as a diplomate of the Royal College of Surgeons and appointment as assistant surgeon to the 29th Regiment, which served in Canada from 1802 to 1807. Since no military activity during this sojourn abroad is reported, it is assumed that his assignment was uneventful. In contrast, however, his tour of duty in Spain as surgeon of his regiment, where he served a major portion of the time until 1814, was arduous but rewarding. Guthrie, who assumed medical responsibility of the wounded in a number of important battles, gained thereby the confidence of the Duke of Wellington. On one occasion he was placed in charge of 3,000 wounded: several times he himself was a casualty from battle wounds or campaign fever. His acts of bravery and use of phenomenal logistics in evacuation and transportation of the wounded demonstrated his superiority. The practice of long incisions for the treatment of erysipelas proved an important surgical procedure introduced during the long campaign.

Guthrie was relieved of his military duties in 1814 and placed on half-pay. Subsequently, he returned to London, resumed the study of anatomy and surgery at Windmill Street, and attended the lectures of Mr. Abernethy at St. Bartholomew's Hospital. After the battle of Waterloo he returned to the Continent, extracted a ball from a soldier's bladder, and performed two remarkable operations—one, an amputation of the hip in a French soldier[2] and the other on a private in the German Legion whose peroneal artery was ligated.[3] The patients from the battlefront were sent eventually to the York Hospital, where Guthrie was assigned two wards.

Francois de Gay, private in the 45th regiment of French infantry, was wounded . . . by a musket ball, which entered behind, fractured the neck of the femur, and made its exit anteriorly, about four inches below the groin. . . . The wounds being cleansed, and the thigh placed in proper position, he remained until the 7th, when the operation of amputation at the hip-joint was considered advisable. This operation was performed by Mr. Guthrie at two o'clock of the 7th; nineteen days after the injury. His [patient's] pulse was 120; and a considerable deviation was observed by Dr. Hennen and Mr. Collier, between the pulse at the wrist and at the groin, at the termination of the operation; his spirits good; he lost about twenty-four ounces of blood; was immediately put to bed, and had an anodyne draught. In the evening his pulse was only 108; had lemonade for common drink.

19th. Health improving; the stump and bedsore look healthy. Was visited by the Baron Larrey, who had been wounded and taken prisoner by the Prussians. . . . he was brought to England by Mr. Campbell, and sent to the York Hospital, where the remaining sore healed without inconvenience. . . . He is capable of walking as much as three miles at a time, the wooden leg which he has attached to his body being thrown forwards by an exertion of the muscles of the trunk. He is in very good health, not quite so fat as when in England, talks of getting married, and is not, as the French express it, "*sage.*"

The subject of my operation, Henry Vigarelie, a private in the German legion, was wounded on the 18th of June . . . by a musket ball which entered the right leg immediately behind and below the inner head of the tibia, inclining downwards, and under or before a part of the soleus and gastrocnemius muscles, and coming out through them four inches and three quarters below the head of the fibula, nearly in the middle, but towards the side of the calf of the leg.

Having gone to Brussels after the battle of Waterloo, with the view of obtaining additional support to some opinions I had advanced in military surgery, this man was shewn to me by my friends, Messrs. Campbell and Hill, surgeons to the forces, under whose care he was, and who were desirous of avoiding an amputation, if possible, although the site of the wound, and the uncertainty of the vessel wounded, as it bled from both openings, rendered it doubtful.

On passing the finger into the outer opening, and pressing it against the fibula, a sort of small aneurismal tumour could be felt under it, and the haemorrhage ceased, indicating that the peroneal artery was in all probability the only vessel wounded.

In this case there was, in addition to the wound of the artery, a quantity of blood between the muscles, which in gunshot wounds accompanied by inflammation is always a dangerous occurrence.

The man being laid on his face with the calf of the leg uppermost, I made an incision near seven inches in length in the axis of the limb, taking the shot-hole nearly as a central point, and carried it by successive strokes through the gastrocnemius and soleus muscles towards the peroneal artery.

I made a transverse incision outwards from the shot-hole to the edge of the fibula, which enabled me to turn back two little flaps, and gave greater facility in the use of my instruments. I could now pass a tenaculum under the spot from whence the blood came, which I raised a little with it, but could not distinctly see the wounded artery in the altered state of parts so as to secure it separately. I therefore passed a small needle, bearing two threads, a sufficient distance above the tenaculum, to induce me to believe it was in sound parts, but including very little in the ligature, when the haemorrhage ceased: another was passed in the same manner below, and the tenaculum withdrawn.

The man is now in York Hospital at Chelsea, and walks about without appearing lame, although he cannot do so for any great distance.

Guthrie remained in military medicine for two years and, in 1816, sponsored the formation of an infirmary for diseases of the eye. Although his best-known book, *On Gun-shot Wounds of the Extremities,* was first published in 1815, his writings throughout a long professional career included *A Treatise on the Operations for the Formation of an Artificial Pupil, Lectures on the Operative Surgery of the Eye, On the Diseases and Injuries of the Arteries, Anatomy and Surgery of Herniae, On the Anatomy and Diseases of the Urinary and Sexual Organs, Clinical Lectures on Compound Fractures of the Extremities, On Injuries of the Head Affecting the Brain,* and *On Wounds and Injuries of the Abdomen and the Pelvis.* He gave lectures on surgery gratis to all officers of the Army, Navy, and East India Company for nearly 30 years. Guthrie served on the staff of the Westminster Hospital, the outgrowth of the Infirmary for Diseases of the Eye, and resigned only in 1843 so that his son, an assistant surgeon, might succeed him. He served longer than usual in various capacities with the Royal College of Surgeons, was three times its president, and professor of anatomy and surgery from 1828 to 1831, delivered the Hunterian Oration in 1830, and was elected to membership in the Royal Society in 1827.

The influence of Guthrie's writings on military medicine and surgery extended to the United States, with the Sanitary Commission in 1861 publishing his *Directions to Army Surgeons on the Field of Battle.* The document detailed 34 precepts or procedures for the Union forces advanced by the English military surgeon.[4]

1. Bettany, G. T.: "George James Guthrie," in *The Dictionary of National Biography,* vol 8, Oxford: University Press, 1959-1960.

2. Guthrie, G. J.: *A Treatise on Gun-Shot Wounds, on Injuries of Nerves, and on Wounds of the Extremities,* ed 2, London: Burgess & Hill, 1820.

3. Guthrie, G. J.: Case of a Wound on the Peroneal Artery, Successfully Treated by Ligature, *Mediochir Trans* 7:330-337, 1816.

Guthrie, G. J.: *Directions to Army Surgeons on the Field of Battle,* US Sanitary Commission, No. 14, ed 2, New York, 1861, pp 1-9.

Composite by G. Bako

Joseph Lovell (1788-1836)

JOSEPH LOVELL was born in Boston, the son of a patriot with the grade of major in the Continental Army during the Revolutionary War. His grandfather was a leading member of the "Sons of Liberty," a Whig organization, and a member of the Continental Congress from 1777 to 1782.[1] Joseph gained his early education in Boston and graduated in 1807 from Harvard College. He began the study of medicine as an apprentice to William Ingalls and graduated from Harvard Medical School in 1811 with the first class to receive the MD. Graduates previously had been awarded the BM. In 1812, Lovell volunteered for service with the 9th Infantry. Shortly after, he was detached from his regiment and placed in command of the general hospital in Burlington, Vermont, designed to service troops protecting the frontier in the War of 1812. Lovell was soon recognized as a skilled practitioner in the management of the sick and a competent hospital administrator. His efficient efforts provided a model installation for other military hospitals. He established a system of regular reports of the census and medical state of the hospitalized soldiers, instituted a practice of frequent washing of the walls and floors of the structure, provided fresh air to rooms and wards, segregated infectious and contagious diseases from surgical cases, and provided a separate ward for patients with venereal and skin diseases.

In 1814, Lovell was advanced in the service to full hospital surgeon and was assigned responsibilities for establishing a general hospital for 1,100 patients at Williamsville, NY. When the United States Army was reorganized four years later and a medical department incorporated in the structure, Lovell received the appointment as surgeon general—a new position in the tables of organization. He continued in office until his death. One of his early tasks was the revision of the Medical Regulations, the basis for subsequent modifications. One of his last acts—a collection of books, formed the basis of the army medical library. At all times Lovell championed the side of the medical officers and the medical department in the pursuit of good medical care, and sought to attract capable physicians to replace the indolent and inefficient officers.

In addition to Lovell's outstanding accomplishments in the practice of his profession and administrative ability, he encouraged William Beaumont's physiological studies on Alexis St. Martin; furthermore, he ordered all medical officers to submit quarterly reports of weather for their relevance to disease—the historical beginning of the government weather bureau. Beaumont, retired from the army after the War of 1812, reentered it in 1819 at the request of Lovell. In 1824, he submitted his initial studies on Alexis St. Martin to the surgeon general for his critique.[2] In turn, Lovell encouraged Beaumont to submit his experimental findings for publication and procured several reference books on digestion for Beaumont's perusal. In 1832, when Beaumont was assigned to Washington and took St. Martin along, Lovell further en-couraged Beaumont to seek chemical advice from American and European scientists—evidence of the mutual respect held by these military surgeons.

The first publication on meteorology by the medical department of the Army appeared in 1826.[3] Prepared under the direction of the surgeon general, it began with observations collected during 1822. As early as 1817, however, Lovell had included reference to meteorologic data in his report as the chief medical officer of the Northern Department, which were later to be incorporated in the official regulations.[4]

To this end he should not only keep a prescription book containing a daily account of the symptoms and circumstances of each patient in every important case, the medicines prescribed, and the result of his practice; but also one, in which should be stated everything directed relative to the diet and regimen. . . . The surgeon should also keep a diary of the weather; noting in it whatever may be supposed to produce or vary the forms of disease. By a reference to these, the surgeon in his quarterly reports, instead of a mere list of names usually made out by the steward, would be enabled to give such an account of the diseases that had occurred, their causes and his treatment, as would be the best possible criterion not only of his medical abilities, but also of his industry and attention to duty. And besides this, an abstract of these reports would soon enable the surgeon at headquarters to furnish what is much wanted at present, and what can only be effectually supplied in this way, viz.: a system of medical police and army practice suited to the diseases incident to the troops at the several posts in the division; and at the same time of suggesting such means of preventing these complaints, as the experience of the different surgeons may have found most beneficial, under different circumstances of time and place.

1. Phalen, J. M.: Chiefs of the Medical Department United States Army, 1775-1940, *Army Med Bull* 52:27-32, 1940.
2. Brodman, E.: Scientific and Editorial Relationship Between Joseph Lovell and William Beaumont, *Bull Hist Med* 38:127-132, 1964.
3. *Meteorological Register for the Years 1822-1825 Inclusive, From Observations Made by the Surgeons of the Army at the Military Posts of the United States; Prepared Under the Direction of Joseph Lovell, M.D., Surgeon-General of the U.S. Army*, US War Dept, 1826.

Composite by G. Bako

William Hey (1736-1819)

WILLIAM HEY was born at Pudsey near Leeds, Yorkshire, England, the son of a respectable tradesman noted for his scrupulous honesty and ramrod integrity. His maternal grandfather and great-grandfather were surgeon and physician respectively.[1] The good judgment of his mother greatly influenced the character of the large family. At the age of four in an accident with a penknife young Hey lost the sight of his right eye; however, he retained excellent acuity in the left eye, even late in life performing the details of surgical practice without the aid of a corrective lens. At seven he was enrolled in an academy near Wakefield, where he was instructed in the classics, natural philosophy, and the French language. At 14 he complied with the wishes of his parents and was apprenticed to surgeon-apothecary Dawson in Leeds; he remained there until 1757, when he went to London to complete his medical education. During the first winter Hey spent long hours in the dissecting room and subsequently became a pupil of Bromfield in surgery, Don-

ald Monro in medicine, and MacKenzie in midwifery at St. George's Hospital.

Having completed his formal training, Hey returned to Leeds, set up practice, and without delay acquired a reputation as a surgeon. The lack of facilities for hospital care at Leeds prompted him to promote a program to correct the deficiency. In 1771, he witnessed the opening of Leeds Infirmary for the admittance of patients. Hey was appointed senior surgeon at the Infirmary, a position held from 1773 to 1812. In the meantime he formed a close friendship with Joseph Priestely, who then lived at Leeds and who sponsored his Fellowship in the Royal Society of London approved in 1775. Hey was president of Leeds Literary and Philosophical Society in 1783, and was twice mayor of the city. He loved music, was a profoundly religious man, and a strong Methodist until 1781, when he joined the Church of England and wrote *Tracts and Essays, Moral and Theological, Including a Defence of the Doctrines of the Divinity of Christ, and of the Atonement.* During his mayorality his severe denouncement of profanity and vice led the population to burn him in effigy. Hey suffered a series of family tragedies; three sons, two daughters, and a daughter-in-law died from pulmonary tuberculosis.

Hey was an excellent surgical operator and, as a member of the Royal College of Surgeons of London, late in life gave courses in anatomy on the bodies of executed criminals at Leeds Infirmary. He introduced significant improvements in the treatment of hernia, cataract, and dislocations; suggested amputation of the foot distal to the tarsometatarsal joint; described and named the growth, "fungus hematodes;" and offered convincing evidence of the transmission of venereal disease to the fetus in utero.

In addition to Hey's religious tracts he contributed several manuscripts on structural anomalies to the *Philosophical Transactions* and wrote a monograph, *Practical Observations in Surgery,* first published in 1803. His two most important contributions to clinical surgery appeared in this volume.[2] The description of the types of scrotal hernia in infants began with deductions from the autopsy findings of an 18-months-old child.

I found that the tunica vaginalis was continued up to the abdominal ring, and inclosed the hernial sac, adhering to that sac by a loose cellular substance, from the ring to within half an inch of its extremity. The fibres of the cremaster muscle were evident upon the outside of the exterior sac, or tunica vaginalis. The interior or true hernial sac was a production of the peritoneum as usual, and contained only the caecum or head of the colon. . . . Having removed the proper hernial sac, I examined the posterior part of the exterior sac, and found it connected with the spermatic vessels in the same manner as the *tunica vaginalis* is, when the testis has descended into the scrotum. An additional proof, that the exterior sac was the *tunica vaginalis.*

From all these circumstances it is evident, that this hernia differed both from the common scrotal rupture, in which the hernial sac lies on the outside of the tunica vaginalis; and also from the *hernia congenita,* where the prolapsed part comes into contact with the testicle, having no other hernial sac besides the tunica vaginalis.

To understand the cause of the hernial sac being in contact with the testicle, and surrounded by the tunica vaginalis, it is necessary to consider the manner in which this coat of the testicle is originally formed.

In the foetus a process of the peritoneum is brought down, through the ring of the external oblique muscle of the abdomen, by the testicle as it descends into the scrotum; which process forms an oblong bag communicating with the cavity of the abdomen, by an aperture in its upper part. This aperture is intirely closed, at, or soon after, birth. The upper part of the bag then gradually contracts itself, till the communication between that portion of it which includes the superior and greater part of the spermatic chord, and the lower part of the bag, which includes the testicle and a small share of the chord, is obliterated. The lower part of the process or bag retains its membranous appearance, and is called *tunica vaginalis testis propria;* while the upper part becomes an irregular cellular substance, without any sensible cavity, diffused amongst the spermatic vessels, and connecting them together.

In the hernia which I am describing, the intestine was protruded after the aperture in the abdomen was closed; and therefore the peritoneum was carried down along with the intestine, and formed the hernial sac. It is evident also, that the hernia must have been produced while the original tunica vaginalis remained in the form of a bag as high as the abdominal ring; on which account that tunic would receive the

hernial sac with its included intestine, and permit the sac to come into contact with the testicle. The proper hernial sac, remaining constantly in its prolapsed state, contracted an adhesion to the original process of the peritoneum which surrounded it, except at its inferior extremity: there the external surface of the hernial sac was smooth and shining, as the interior surface of the tunica vaginalis is in its natural state.

This kind of scrotal hernia may, therefore, not improperly be called *hernia infantilis,* as it can only exist when the rupture is formed while the parts retain the state peculiar to early infancy.

The scrotal hernia may be divided into three species, the specific difference of which arises from the state of the tunica vaginalis at the time of the descent. 1. If the abdominal aperture of this process is open when the intestine or omentum is protruded, the rupture is then called *hernia congenita.* 2. If the upper part of the process remains open, but the abdominal aperture is closed, and is capable of resisting the force of the protruding part, the hernia then becomes of that species which I have now described, the *hernia infantilis.* 3. If the cavity of the upper part of the process is obliterated, and the septum is formed a little above the testicle, as in the adult state; the hernial sac then descends on the outside of the tunica vaginalis, and forms the most common species of scrotal rupture, which may with propriety be called *hernia virilis.*

In the same treatise Hey discussed the factors involved in internal derangement of the knee that follows minor trauma.[2]

The disease is, indeed, now and then removed, as suddenly as it is produced, by the natural motions of the joint, without surgical assistance; but it may remain for weeks or months, and will then become a serious misfortune, as it causes a considerable degree of lameness. I am not acquainted with any author who has described either the disease or the remedy; I shall, therefore, give such a description as my own experience has furnished me.

The leg is readily bent or extended by the hands of the surgeon, and without pain to the patient; at most, the degree of uneasiness caused by this flexion and extension is trifling. But the patient himself cannot freely bend, nor perfectly extend the limb in walking; but is compelled to walk with an invariable and small degree of flexion. Though the patient is obliged to keep the leg thus stiff in walking; yet in sitting down the affected joint will move like the other.

The complaint which I have described may be brought on, I apprehend, by any such alteration in the state of the joint, as will prevent the condyles of the os femoris from moving truly in the hollow formed by the semilunar cartilages and articular depressions of the tibia. An unequal tension of the lateral, or cross ligaments of the joint, or some slight derangement of the semi-lunar cartilages, may probably be sufficient to bring on the complaint. When the disorder is the effect of contusion, it is most likely that the lateral ligament on one side of the joint may be rendered somewhat more rigid than usual, and hereby prevent that equable motion of the condyles of the os femoris, which is necessary for walking with firmness.

1. Bell, B.: The Life, Character, and Writings of William Hey of Leeds: A Discourse Delivered at the Annual Meeting of the Harveian Society, Edinburgh, April 12, 1867, *Edinburgh Med J* 12:1061-1080, 1867.
2. Hey, W.: *Practical Observations in Surgery*, London: T. Cadell, Jun., & W. Davies, 1803.

Royal College of Physicians

Edward Jenner (1749-1823)

WE LACK CONCLUSIVE EVIDENCE of the prevalence of smallpox in ancient times.[1] Bishop Marius of Avenches is credited with the initial use of the scientific term *variola* in AD 570. Smallpox very likely was the malady noted by Bishop Gregory of Tours in AD 582 when he wrote of an epidemic disease that began with fever and backache followed by a pustular eruption. The attempted differentiation between smallpox and measles has been attributed to Rhazes in the 9th century and to Avicenna in the 10th. At the time of Edward Jenner, it was estimated that every 10th person in Europe died from smallpox. In some epidemics as much as half the population died of this disease. An epidemic in Iceland early in the 18th century was fatal to nearly 40% of the population. In Europe, lifetime prevalence was estimated to be as high as 80%. In London during the 1760 decade, there were 24,234 deaths from smallpox and 234,412 deaths from all causes. The population of London at that time was approximately 650,000. Thus, approximately 4% of the entire population died from smallpox during this decade. Ninety percent of the cases were in children under 10 years of age. These data are recounted to emphasize the devastation wrought by smallpox among the unvaccinated. Smallpox continues to be epidemic as well as endemic in many countries. As recently as 1938 in Hong Kong, more than 800 cases were admitted to the smallpox hospital. At the peak of the epidemic, 192 deaths were recorded among 236 cases.[1]

Prior to vaccination with cowpox virus, smallpox inoculation provided protection. The introducttion of smallpox inoculation into England has been attributed to the wife of the British Ambassador to Turkey, Lady Mary Wortley Montagu. This practice had been followed in the Orient since ancient times. The inoculation of pus from a vesicle or a pustule from a patient with smallpox into the skin of a well person resulted usually in a modified attack of smallpox. In some instances the illness was as severe as the natural affliction. The ideal time to obtain the inoculum was reputed to be on the 12th or 13th day after the onset of symptoms. The pustules were evacuated manually. The inoculum was saved and incubated at body temperature if not needed immediately. The skin of the inoculee was scarified with a needle on one or several areas of the body. Small amounts of the inoculum were introduced into the needle pricks. Zabdiel Boylston was thought to be the first to use inoculation in North America. His son and two slaves were successfully inoculated in 1721. Benjamin Franklin supported the procedure and, together with William Heberden, the London physician, published a pamphlet on this subject in 1759. Franklin noted that introduction of inoculation reduced the fatality in smallpox from 17% to less than 1%.[2]

Edward Jenner, born in the vicarage in Berkeley, Gloucestershire, a country physician and writer of verse, was an apprentice and pupil of John Hunter for several years. Hunter was able to encourage Jenner's curiosity about natural phenomena, such as the habits of cuckoos, the migration of birds, the hibernation of the hedgehog, and distemper in dogs. They were a famous pair of doctors and maintained a lively correspondence for many years after Jenner forsook London and assumed a country practice in Berkeley. Jenner had discussed with Hunter the observation that dairymaids who were exposed to an eruptive fever of the teats and udders of cows were protected against smallpox. Cowpox, spread through dairy herds by the hands of the milkers, was a benign but highly contagious malady and was usually ignored by the dairymen. The lesions first appeared as small red papules. A transition to blisters, with clear fluid, was followed by turbidity and scabbing. The dairymaids, because of the chance vaccination against smallpox, were the envy of the ladies not similarly protected.

Jenner's first publication (1798) *An Inquiry into the Causes and Effects of the Variolae Vaccinae* was based upon his experimental observations begun in 1788. The study comprised 23 cases. He used the word *virus* in the general sense of a disease-producing agent. The restricted use of the term which included the causative agents of smallpox and cowpox did not become current until a century later. Jenner advanced three contentions that were subsequently proved to be incorrect. He affirmed that (a) the virus must be acquired from the cow after its passage through the horse, (b) only the true virus provides protection against smallpox, and (c) protection is permanent. The introduction to the treatise is excerpted as follows:[3]

There is a disease to which the Horse, from his state of domestication, is frequently subject. The Farriers have termed it *the Grease*. It is an inflammation and swelling of the heel, from which issues matter possessing properties of a very peculiar kind, which seems capable of generating a disease in the Human Body (after it has undergone the modification which I shall presently speak of), which bears so strong a resemblance to the Small Pox, that I think it highly probable it may be the source of that disease.

In this Dairy Country a great number of Cows are kept, and the office of milking is performed indiscriminately by Men and Maid Servants. One of the former having been appointed to apply dressings to the heels of a Horse affected with *the Grease,* and not paying due attention to cleanliness, incautiously bears his part in milking the Cows, with some particles of the infectious matter adhering to his fingers. When this is the case, it commonly happens that a disease is communicated to the Cows, and from the Cows to the Dairy-maids, which spreads through the farm until most of the cattle and domestics feels its unpleasant consequences. This disease has obtained the name of Cow Pox. It appears on the nipples of the Cows in the form of irregular pustules. . . . The animals become indisposed, and the secretion of milk is much lessened. Inflamed spots now begin to appear on different parts of the hands of the domestics employed in milking, and sometimes on the wrists, which quickly run on to suppuration, first assuming the appearance of the small vesications produced by a burn. Most commonly they appear about the joints of the fingers, and at their extremities; but whatever parts are affected, if the situation will admit, these superficial suppurations put on a circular form, with their edges more elevated than their centre, and of a colour distantly approaching to blue. Absorption takes place, and tumours appear in each axilla. The system becomes affected—the pulse is quickened; and shiverings, with general lassitude and pains about the loins and limbs, with vomiting, come on. The head is painful, and the patient is now and then even affected with delirium. These symptoms, varying in their degrees of violence, generally continue from one day to three or four, leaving ulcerated sores about the hands, which, from the sensibility of the parts, are very troublesome, and commonly heal slowly, frequently becoming phagedenic, like those from whence they sprung. The lips, nostrils, eyelids, and other parts of the body, are sometimes affected with sores; but these evidently arise from their being heedlessly rubbed or scratched with the patient's infected fingers. No eruptions on the skin have followed the decline of the feverish symptoms in any instance that has come under my inspection, one only excepted, and in this case a very few appeared on the arms: they were very minute, of a vivid red colour, and soon died away without advancing to maturation; so that I cannot determine whether they had any connection with the preceding symptoms.

Thus the disease makes its progress from the Horse to the nipple of the Cow, and from the Cow to the Human Subject.

Morbid matter of various kinds, when absorbed into the system, may produce effects in some degree similar; but what renders the Cow-pox virus so extremely singular, is, that the person who has been thus affected is for ever after secure from the infection of the Small Pox, neither exposure to the variolous effluvia, nor the insertion of the matter into the skin, producing this distemper.

In support of so extraordinary a fact, I shall lay before my Reader a great number of instances.

Jenner did not claim priority for the observations. An equally important contribution was the dissemination of information to the profession and to the public. In this program he was a vigorous pamphleteer and letter writer, eager to discuss the subject or to defend his position.[4] Also, he demonstrated his appreciation for James Phipps, his first vaccinated subject, when he built a cottage for him and planted the roses in the garden with his own hands.

Just as the smallpox virus was recovered and stored for future use, so cowpox virus was preserved. Sometimes it was transmitted great distances. Pieces of silk or linen thread, soaked in material from the cowpox vesicle, were placed in glass vials and sealed.

Benjamin Waterhouse of Harvard, introduced vaccination into the United States. Some of the vaccine forwarded by Jenner to Waterhouse was transhipped to Thomas Jefferson, who vaccinated not only his family but also his friends, neighbors, and servants. Waterhouse attempted to benefit financially from vaccination and to acquire a monopoly of the source and use of the smallpox vaccine.

One of the patients (Case IV) displayed a reaction that has been judged retrospectively as an early description of anaphylaxis.[3]

Mary Barge, of Woodford, in this parish, was inoculated with variolous matter in the year 1791. An efflorescence of a palish red colour soon appeared about the parts where the matter was inserted, and spread itself rather extensively, but died away in a few days without producing any variolous symptoms. She has since been repeatedly employed as a nurse to Small-pox patients, without experiencing any ill consequences. This woman had the Cow Pox when she lived in the service of a Farmer in this parish thirty-one years before.

It is remarkable that variolous matter, when the system is disposed to reject it, should excite inflammation on the part to which it is applied more speedily than when it produces the Small Pox. Indeed it becomes almost a criterion by which we can determine whether the infection will be received or not. It seems as if a change, which endures through life, had been produced in the action, or disposition to action, in the vessels of the skin; and it is remarkable too, that whether this change has been effected by the Small Pox, or the Cow Pox, that the disposition to sudden cuticular inflammation is the same on the application of variolous matter.

In 1805, Napoleon ordered all French soldiers who had not contracted smallpox to be vaccinated. Napoleon also ordered a medal struck to commemorate the discovery of vaccination, and at Jenner's request released English prisoners captured during the war between France and England. Initially, the Parliament granted Jenner 10,000 pounds and later 20,000 pounds in recognition of his discovery and as reimbursement for the time devoted to the public good at the expense of his private practice.

Although Jenner began the practice of medicine at the age of 23, he was not granted an MD degree from St. Andrew's University until 20 years later. In 1788, he was elected a Fellow of the Royal Society, while the honorary degree of Doctor of Medicine was given him by Oxford at the age of 64. He suffered an apoplectic attack at the age of 71 but lived for 3 more years. The government offered the family a burial plot in Westminster Abbey, but the expense of a public funeral prevented acceptance of the offer. Burial in Berkeley in the churchyard near his home was selected.

Smallpox vaccination probably saved more lives than any other medical discovery or public health measure. Jenner introduced into medical science an entirely new concept of preventive medicine—the production of a *forme fruste* affliction as a means of inciting immunity from a dread morbid process.

1. Wilkinson, P. B.: *Variations on a Theme by Sydenham: Small-pox,* Bristol, England: John Wright and Sons, Ltd., 1959.

2. Franklin, B.: *Some Account of the Success of Inoculation for the Small-pox in England and America,* London: W. Strahan, 1759.

3. Jenner, E.: *An Inquiry into the Causes and Effects of the Variolae Vaccine,* London: Sampson Low, 1798.

4. LeFanu, W. R.: *A Bio-Bibliography of Edward Jenner,* Philadelphia: J. B. Lippincott Company, 1951.

Boston Medical Library

Benjamin Waterhouse (1754-1846)

BENJAMIN WATERHOUSE, Hersey professor of the theory and practice of physic at Harvard, introduced vaccination against smallpox into the United States, demonstrating its value on his own children. He was the first professor of medicine at Harvard, the first to give a course of lectures on natural history at Rhode Island College (Brown) in Providence, founder of the botanical garden at Cambridge, and curator of the collection of minerals at Harvard.[1] Benjamin was born in Newport, RI, the son of a tanner and cabinet maker, who later became a judge of the Court of Common Pleas. His mother was the niece of John Fothergill, one of the outstanding physicians of a remarkable period in London medicine. At the age of 16, Waterhouse was apprenticed to

John Halliburton, a physician in Newport, with whom he spent six years in the first stage of medical training. Gilbert Stuart, portrait painter of Newport, was one of his close schoolmates whose friendship continued in good times and bad, and especially when Stuart was having difficulties seeking clients and commissions in London.[2]

Waterhouse sailed to England in April, 1775, on the last ship allowed by the British to leave Boston and remained abroad until 1782. He lived and studied with his relative, Fothergill, walked the wards at Guy's and St. Thomas' hospitals, and audited the lectures of John Hunter in anatomy and those of James Fergusson in experimental philosophy. John Coakley Lettsom, John Haygarth, and Joseph Priestley were other friends in the medical sciences. Following an arrangement made by Fothergill, Waterhouse studied at Edinburgh with William Cullen and Monro *Secundus.* Leyden, then the popular medical school in Europe, was next on the itinerary where he received the MD degree in 1780. Waterhouse remained in Leyden after graduation, studying history and law. Thus, his European years of study included several nonmedical disciplines and provided the opportunities for nonmedical acquaintances, who included John Adams, John Quincy Adams, and Benjamin Franklin, America's first citizen in Europe.

After seven years in Europe, Waterhouse began the practice of medicine in Newport at the age of 28. Experiences such as these, supplemented by broad interests in the natural sciences and the humanities, left no doubt that he was one of the best educated physicians to return to America. Within a year he was invited by Harvard College to take the chair of medicine (theory and practice of physic) as one of three members of the faculty of the prospective medical school, sharing honors and responsibilities with John Warren of Boston, professor of anatomy and surgery, and Aaron Dexter, professor of chemistry. The school lacked clinical facilities for teaching and had no funds for faculty salaries. The rules stated, however, that the professor of theory and practice should:[3]

. . . teach the students by directing and superintending, as much as may be, their private studies; lecturing of the diseases of the human body, and taking such of them as are qualified to visit their patients; making proper observations on the nature of the diseases and the peculiar circumstances attending them, and their method of cure; and, whenever the professors be desired by any other gentlemen of the Faculty to visit their patients in difficult and uncommon cases, they shall use their endeavors to introduce with them their pupils who are properly qualified.

The interest shown by Waterhouse, who lived and practiced in Cambridge, in clinical medicine was remittent. Frequently his ideas and actions were criticized by the laity and the profession, and finally in 1812 he was relieved of his professorship. According to O. W. Holmes,[3] "The good people of Cambridge listened to his learned talk when they were well, and sent for one of the other two doctors when they were sick. He probably liked to write and talk about medicine better than to practise it."

Any deficiency in clinical practice was compensated by his crusade for vaccination against smallpox—its greatest advocate in America. His interest in vaccination began in the fall of 1798 when John Coakley Lettson informed him of the value of cowpox inoculation. The information was supported by a copy of Jenner's *An Inquiry into the Causes and Effects of the Variolae Vaccinae* (1798). The presentation copy has been retrieved and now is in the rare book collection of the Boston Medical Library. Waterhouse recognized the importance of Jenner's observations and immediately made plans for the dispatch of a supply of the vaccine matter to convince the skeptics of its merits. In June, 1800, he obtained a small supply from Haygarth of Bath, England, and proceeded to conduct the first American experiment on smallpox vaccination. The report carried a long title of a detailed description of his clinical experience:[4] *A Prospect of Exterminating the Small-Pox: Being the History of the Variolae Vaccinae, or Kine-Pox, Commonly Called the Cow-Pox; As It Has Appeared in England: With an Account of a Series of Inoculations Performed for the Kine-Pox, in Massachusetts.*

In the beginning of the year 1799, I received from my friend Dr. LETTSOM of London, a copy of Dr. EDWARD JENNER'S *"Inquiry into the causes and effects of the* VARIOLAE VACCINE, *or Cow-Pox"*; a disease totally unknown in this quarter of the world. On perusing this work, I was struck with the unspeakable advantages that might accrue to this country, and indeed to the human race at large, from the discovery of a mild distemper that would ever after secure the constitution from that terrible scourge, the small-pox.

As the ordinary mode of communicating even medical discoveries in this country is by newspapers, I drew up the following account of the *cowpox*, which was printed in the *Columbian Centinel*, March 12th, 1799.

This *variolae vaccine* or *cow-pox*, is very readily communicated to those who milk cows infected with it. This malady appears first on the teats of the cows in the form of irregular pustles or pocks. They are commonly of a palish blue, somewhat approaching to livid, and surrounded by an erysipelatous inflammation, resembling the St. Anthony's fire. These pustles, unless timely remedied, degenerate into those ragged ulcers known by the surgeons under the name of *phagedenic*. The cows soon become sick, and the secretion of milk is lessened, but I never heard of one dying with it. Those who milk cows thus affected, seldom or ever fail catching the distemper, *if there be cracks, wounds, or abrasions in the hands*. That is to say, *they are inoculated*.

But what makes this newly discovered disease so very curious, and so extremely important is, that every person thus affected, is EVER AFTER SECURED FROM THE ORDINARY SMALL-POX, *let him be ever so much exposed to the effluvium of it, or let ever so much ripe matter be inserted in the skin by inoculation*. In other words—a person who has undergone the *local* disease and *specific fever* occasioned by the cowpox infection, *is thereby rendered ever after unsusceptible of the small pox*. It is worthy of remark that the infection of the cow-pox can be conveyed to the human species by the ordinary mode of inoculation. And it is observed, that there is no difference in the effects of the matter taken from the cow, and of the matter generated successively in the second, third, fourth or fifth human creature.

Such are the outlines of a mild disease, the knowledge of which may lead to consequences of the utmost importance to the whole human race, no less indeed than that of *superseding, if not extinguishing, the terrible scourge, the small-pox.*

This publication shared the fate of most others on new discoveries. A few received it as a very important discovery, highly interesting to humanity, some doubted it; others observed that wise and prudent conduct, which allows them to condemn or applaud, as the event might prove;

while a greater number absolutely ridiculed it as one of those medical whims which arise to-day and to-morrow are no more.

Under a serious impression of effecting a public benefit, and conceiving it, moreover, a duty in my official situation in this University, I sent to England for some of the *vaccine* or *cow-pox matter* for trial. After several fruitless attempts, I obtained some by a short passage from Bristol, and with it I inoculated all the younger part of my family.

The first of my children that I inoculated, was a boy of five years old, named DANIEL OLIVER WATERHOUSE. I made a slight incision in the usual place for inoculation in the arm, inserted a small portion of the infected thread, and covered it with a sticking-plaster. . . . The sore in the arm proceeded exactly as Drs. JENNER and WOODVILLE described, and appeared to the eye very like the second plate in Dr. JENNER's elegant publication.

The inoculated part in this boy, was surrounded by an efflorescence which extended from his shoulder to his elbow, which made it necessary to apply some remedies to lessen it; but the "symptoms," as they are called, scarcely drew him from his play more than an hour or two; and he went through the disease in so light a manner, as hardly ever to express any marks of peevishness.

Satisfied with the appearance and symptoms in this boy, I inoculated another of three years of age, with matter taken from his brother's arm, for he had no pustles on his body. He likewise went through the disease in a perfect and very satisfactory manner. This child pursued his amusements with as little interruption as his brother. Then I inoculated a servant boy of about 12 years of age, with some of the infected thread from England.

From a full maturated pustle in my little boy of three years old, I inoculated his infant sister, already weaned, of one year. At the same time, and from the same pustle, I inoculated its nursery maid. They both went through the disease with equal regularity.

Thomas Jefferson, then President of the United States, was deeply impressed with these vaccination studies and requested that some active virus be sent to Monticello for his family.[5]

Washington, Dec. 25, 1800.
Sir,

I received last night, and have read with great satisfaction, your pamphlet on the subject of the kine-pock, and pray you to accept my thanks for the communication of it.

I had before attended to your publications on the subject in the newspapers, and took much interest in the result of the experiments you were making. Every friend of humanity must look with pleasure on this discovery, by which one evil more is withdrawn from the condition of man; and must contemplate the possibility, that future improvements and discoveries may still more and more lessen the catalogue of evils. In this line of proceeding you deserve well of your country; and I pray you accept my portion of the tribute due to you, and assurances of high consideration and respect, with which I am, Sir,

Your most obedient, humble servant,
Thomas Jefferson
(Copy)
Dr. Waterhouse, Cambridge.

There were skeptics in America as well as in England, and not until 1802 was Waterhouse successful, through the support of James Jackson, in persuading the Board of Health of Boston to conduct a public experiment. The results were conclusive, and the enlightened physicians, citizens, and public health officials accepted the experimental studies. Waterhouse then turned to the purity of the virus. Harm had come to some persons who assumed they had been vaccinated but had been subjected to impotent material; others had been exposed to lymph serums contaminated with pathogenic bacteria, or had been inoculated with material from pustules of small-pox which produced a modified type of the disease and provided partial protection.

In 1807, President Jefferson appointed Waterhouse physician to the Marine Hospital at Charlestown, Mass, in recognition of his contributions to vaccination. But his enemies did not remain idle, and openly or secretly they attacked the crusader, his motives, and his character. He was relieved of his lectureship in natural history at Harvard and his position as curator of the mineralogy collection. The great blow came in 1812 when the Harvard corporation removed him from the chair of medicine.

As professor of the theory and practice of physic, Waterhouse was less interested in clinical medicine than in other subjects. His monograph on whooping cough[6] and a treatise on botany[7] should be mentioned but are not to be equated with his studies on vaccination. One of his popular treatises was entitled *Cautions to Young Persons Concerning Health, in a Public Lecture Delivered at the Close of the Medical*

Course in the Chapel at Cambridge, November 20, 1804; Containing the General Doctrine of Dyspepsia and Chronic Diseases; Shewing the Evil Tendency of the Use of Tobacco upon Young Persons; More Especially the Pernicious Effects of Smoking Cigars, with Observations on the Use of Ardent and Vinous Spirits.[8]

I am entirely convinced, that smoking and chewing injures ultimately the hearing, smell, taste, and teeth. "Good teeth," says Hipprocates, "conduce to long life"; because he, who does not masticate his food properly, and mix it thoroughly with a due portion of saliva, will find his digestion fail; and this failure will gradually open the avenues to death.

The practice of smoking is productive of indolence; and tends to confirm the lazy in their laziness. Instead of exercising in the open air, as formerly, you sit down before large fires and smoke tobacco.

Benjamin Waterhouse was better known as a liberal thinker, a Quaker, a strong advocate of vaccination, and a lecturer in the natural sciences than as a bedside teacher of clinical disease. He died in Cambridge having commanded greater respect abroad than at home for his accomplishments.

1. Welch, W. M.: The Jenner of America, *Proc Phila Co Med Soc* 7:172-201, 1885.
2. Benjamin Waterhouse and Gilbert Stuart, editorial, *New Engl J Med* 267:624-625 (Sept 20), 675-677 (Sept 27) 1962.
3. Harrington, T. F.: *The Harvard Medical School,1782-1906*, vol. 1, privately printed, 1905.
4. Waterhouse, B.: *A Prospect of Exterminating the Small Pox*, pt I, Cambridge, Mass: W. Hilliard, 1800.
5. Waterhouse, B.: *A Prospect of Exterminating the Small Pox*, pt II, Cambridge, Mass: W. Hilliard, 1802.
6. Waterhouse, B.: *An Essay Concerning Tussis Convulsiva, or, Whooping Cough*, Boston: Munroe and Francis, 1822.
7. Waterhouse, B.: *The Botanist. Being the Botanical Part of a Course of Lectures on Natural History*, Boston: J. T. Buckingham, 1811.
8. Waterhouse, B.: *Cautions to Young Persons Concerning Health*, 5th ed, Cambridge: University Press, 1822.

Matthew Baillie (1761-1823)

MATTHEW BAILLIE, wise clinician and industrious morbid anatomist, was born on October 27, 1761, at the Manse of Shots, in the county of Lanark, Scotland. His father, the Reverend James Baillie, professor of divinity in the University of Glasgow, died shortly before Matthew began his medical education under William Hunter. His

Royal College of Physicians

mother, Dorothea Hunter, was a sister of William and John Hunter. The influence of the distinguished physicians on the nephew in the decision of law vs theology vs medicine most likely was the determining factor.

At the University of Glasgow, Matthew's courses included Greek, Latin, logic, and moral physiology. Classical education was continued at Balliol, Oxford, for one year, and then he went to London to study with William Hunter.[1]

In no department of life do men rise to eminence who have gone through a severe course of study and elaborate preparation; for, whatever be the difference in the original capacities of individuals, it is the cultivation of the mind alone which elevates to distinction.

Early in life Baillie began the cultivation of his mind which contributed to his professional fame and scientific attainment in later years.[1]

Men sow the seeds of their future reputation, perhaps, at a much earlier period than is usually supposed, and the latter years of life are occupied merely in digesting and arranging what was in earlier years impressed. . . . Experience is too apt to be confounded with observation, and in contemplating the life of Doctor Baillie, it is evident that all he did for medical science, was accompished before he had reached his fortieth year.

In the will of Hunter, the anatomical museum, the house in Windmill Street, and 100 pounds per year were bequeathed to Baillie. According to Wardrop, his uncle advanced an interesting explanation for not leaving a larger amount.[1]

That it was his intention to leave him but little money, as he had derived too much pleasure from making his own fortune to deprive him of doing the same.

The beginning of the accumulation of medical knowledge and the clinical reputation of Baillie may be traced to the dissecting room of the Hunterian Museum. Every opportunity to examine morbid tissues were exploited. Accurate clinical notes were kept and correlated with pathological findings. A knowledge of pathological anatomy in the 19th century was as vital to the practice of general medicine (internal medcine) as was anatomy to the practice of surgery. However, the pathological laboratory almost cost him his life. On one occasion, a laceration on the hand from a dissecting knife was responsible for a nearly fatal septicemia.

In 1787, Baillie was appointed physician to St. George's Hospital; 2 years later at the age of 29, he received his degree at Oxford and became a Fellow of the College of Physicians of London. The first edition of his greatest contribution, *The Morbid Anatomy of Some of the Most Important Parts of the Human Body,*[2] was published in his 35th year. The simplicity of style and clarity of expression contributed to its popularity and great usefulness. Subsequent editions included clinical symptoms and were illustrated with copperplates by Mr. William Clift, the famulus of William Hunter. Prior to the publication of this volume, dissertations on pathological anatomy were scat-

tered throughout the medical literature. Baillie was responsible for the systematic documentation of the subject. The orderly discussion of morbid anatomy may be compared with the systematic tabulation by Osler of morbid states a century later.

Baillie proceeded from an exposition of the morbid anatomy of the heart and lungs, to the neck, the abdominal cavity, and the genitourinary tract. He concluded with the brain. The joints, spinal cord, peripheral nervous system, and special senses were not described. A number of clinicopathological deductions appear valid a century and a half later. Selected excerpts are illustrative:[2]

Asymptomatic Gall-stone:

While gall-stones remain in the gall-bladder, and no attempt is made towards their passing through the ductus cysticus, and ductus communis choledochus, very little inconvenience is commonly produced by them. It frequently happens that gall-stones are found in the gall-bladder after death, where there was not the least suspicion of their existence during life.

Relative Incidence of Carcinoma in Small and Large Intestine:

Schirrhus (cancer of the intestine) is a disease which takes place much more commonly in the great than in the small intestines . . . is to be found much more frequently at the sigmoid flexure of the colon, or in the rectum, than any where else. . . . At first there is but little pain in the part affected . . . the stools . . . are sometimes besmeared with mucus, pus, and blood. . . . In advanced stages of the disease, the countenance is sallow, the strength is much impaired, the body is much emaciated, and the constitution at length altogether sinks.

Angina Pectoris and Calcification of the Coronary Arteries:

Ossification of the Coronary Arteries would seem to produce, or to be intimately connected with, the Symptoms which constitute *Angina Pectoris.* These consist of a pain which shoots from the middle of the sternum across the left breast, and passes down the left arm, to near the elbow.

Hepatization of the lungs:

The lungs are sometimes converted into a solid substance very much resembling the liver. . . . I am inclined to believe that it has been produced by a widely extended inflammation.

Ascites in Cirrhosis of the Liver:

When there is a scirrhous liver accompanying the dropsy (ascites), the water is commonly of a yellowish or greenish colour. . . . In some cases too, the spleen has been found to be enlarged and hard.

Dermoid of the Ovary:

The ovaria are sometimes converted into a fatty substance, intermixed with long Hair and Teeth, which is surrounded by a capsule consisting of a white strong membrane (dermoid). The hairs are most of them loose in the fatty substance, but many of them also adhere on the inside of the capsule. . . . This production could not possibly, under such circumstances, have any connexion with impregnation; and if it occurs without it in one part of the body, there can be no good reason why it may not also take place without impregnation in another part. These productions are much more frequent in the ovaria than any where else, probably because the process which forms them bears some analogy to generation, in which the ovaria are materially concerned.

Except for personal and professional correspondence, Baillie's scientific writings ceased at the age of 36, with the appearance of the second edition of *Morbid Anatomy*. He resigned his appointment at St. George's Hospital and discontinued his anatomical lectures. The remainder of his life was devoted to the private practice of medicine. He accepted the gold-headed cane from Pitcairn and enjoyed a phenomenal practice:

I consider it not only a professional, but a moral duty, to meet punctually my professional brethren of all ranks. My equals have a right to such a mark of my respect, and I would shudder at the apprehension of lessening a junior practitioner in the eyes of his patient, by not keeping an appointment with him.

In the practice of medicine, Baillie showed no favoritism between rich and poor. He was reputed to have been as devoted to the care of the indigent as to the care of the King, acting in his official capacity as physician extraordinary to George III.

1. Wardrop, J.: *Works of Matthew Baillie, M.D.,* London: Longman, Hurst, Rees, Orme, Brown, and Green, 1825.
2. Baillie, M.: *The Morbid Anatomy of Some of the Most Important Parts of the Human Body,* 2nd ed., Walpole, N. H.: G. W. Nichols, 1808.

Composite by G. Bako

Richard Powell (1767-1834)

RICHARD POWELL, born at Thame, Oxfordshire, received his early education at Winchester College, and at Oxford took the AB, AM, and BM degrees, concluding with the MD in 1795.[1] He came to London for clinical training at St. Bartholomew's Hospital, where he remained to teach and to practice, making notable contributions to understanding the pathogenesis or delineation of facial palsy, tuberculous meningitis, pituitary tumor, and other clinical conditions. He translated the only 19th century edition of the *London Pharmacopoeia* from Latin to English. Admitted a Fellow of the Royal College of Physicians in 1796, he delivered the Gulstonian lectures in the year 1799, entitled *Observations on the Bile and Its Diseases, and on the Oeconomy of the Liver.* This is an excellent discourse on the anatomy and physiology of the liver and biliary passages; he describes asymptomatic stones in the bladder and common duct and the asymptomatic passage of large stones through a fistula between the gallbladder and the colon.[2]

In by far the greater number of examinations in which I have seen biliary concretions, their presence had not been suspected during the life of the patient, so little peculiar derangement had they produced. They have sometimes, but very rarely, occasioned ulceration of the inner coat of the bladder, and given birth to the train of symptoms which must necessarily attend such a case; but it may be stated generally that, during their continuance there, they are harmless, and that much inconvenience only attends upon the accident of their being carried from thence into the narrower ducts, whose cavity must be distended for their passage, if they are of any size.

The symptoms which arise will be best described by taking the most violent cases, which are not commonly met with, and allowing in the opposite extreme for the passage of the concretion without the attendance of a single symptom, and in intermediate ones for every possible variation in degree.

Concretions have occasionally been passed, of the nature of which there cannot be a doubt; but which, from their size, never could have passed through the gall ducts. I have seen single pieces of such, which were more than an inch in their diameter, and three inches in length; these then must be supposed to have passed directly from the bladder to the colon, by a previous adhesion, and subsequent union of the two cavities, as happens in many cases of abscesses of internal parts.

In 1801, Powell succeeded Richard Budd as physician at St. Bartholomew's Hospital, where he delivered special lectures on the theory and practice of medicine and was responsible for courses in chemistry and materia medica. In the Royal College he was censor for several years, Harveian orator in 1808, and Lumleian lecturer from 1811 to 1822. He aided John Abernethy in founding the Medical and Philosophical Society, afterwards named the Abernethian Society, which was organized for the reading of medical and scientific papers, their discussion, and the maintenance of a library.

In the fifth volume of the *Medical Transactions* of the Royal College of Physicians, Powell described several afflictions of the peripheral or central nervous system, with selected autopsy findings. The case histories of three patients with acute dysfunction of the facial nerve were presented more than two decades before the published report by Charles Bell on this subject. An excerpt of the clinical record of the third patient, whose symptoms developed following exposure to wind and cold and who recovered within ten days, is given below.[3]

A gentleman had suffered for some time from rheumatic pains which often shifted their situation, but had chiefly affected the muscles of his chest. I considered him as convalescent, when he again called upon me in a state of considerable alarm, and informed me, that on the day before, one of his friends had observed his face to be somewhat drawn to the left side, and that in the course of the night, the affection had very much increased in its degree. He had then lost all power over the relaxed side of the face, and was even obliged to take drink with some caution and management into the opposite side of the mouth. There was no pain nor numbness, nor loss of sensibility in the relaxed part, nor was there any affection of the sight or want of contractility in the pupil of the eye. I could not in this so manifestly, as in the former cases, connect the disease with its cause. He had come to town from Highgate in the morning of the day, when the affection was first noticed: it was cold and windy, and the window next to the affected side was open the whole of the way; but he did not consider this exposure of consequence enough to excite his particular notice, or as any thing out of the way of his ordinary habits. When I saw him again at the distance of ten days, he had perfectly recovered.

In the same volume of the Transactions for 1815, Powell reported under the title, *Some Cases, Illustrative of the Pathology of the Brain,* both a patient with tuberculous meningitis who suffered from severe headache, opisthotonos, failing vision, and stupor, and also a soldier afflicted with a pituitary tumor who complained of intractable headache and progressive loss of vision.[4]

A. P., aged 23, was under my care, in St. Bartholomew's Hospital, for 27 days before her dissolution, which took place January 31, 1810. It appeared that her illness had commenced about three months before. . . . Since that period she had suffered frequent hysterical fits . . . her complaint was wholly referred to the head, where she complained of excessive pain. . . . Her sight was imperfect and misty. Her eyes were full and starting, and their pupils dilated . . . but they contracted when a strong light was applied. . . . In the night of the 12th of January, she was attacked, without any previous notice, with a sort of fit, under which she was described to have been totally insensible for about an hour, whilst her head and neck were drawn backwards, and rendered stiff and immovable. Her speech was wholly lost on the following morning, but in the course of the two following days, she gradually acquired the power of expressing herself, and still complained of violent pain in the head. Her sight became less and less perfect; the pupils, which at first had been dilated and indolent, ceased to be at all affected by light. . . . and after the 22d she fell into a state of permanent stupor, from which, for the two next days, she could be roused so as to answer questions without any difficulty, and at such times she always complained of the violence of the pain in her head. Her strength gradually diminished until her death on the 31st.

On examining the head, all the membranes appeared to be much more loaded with blood than natural. The convolutions of the brain were rather flattened, and in three places upon the surface of the right hemisphere, there were hardened spots of about an inch diameter. These constituted a part of the same number of considerable tubercles which extended into the medullary substance of the brain.

Mr. L. was by birth a Peruvian, and had served several years in the Spanish army in Europe. . . . About two years before his death, he was attacked by very severe pains in his head, for which no permanent relief was obtained, but by degrees they subsided, leaving behind them a constant sensation of tightness across the middle of the forehead, and a feeling of want of room within the skull. Nearly six or eight months after the first attack, while sitting in one of the theatres at Paris, he was sensible of a sudden diminution of the sight of the right eye, and this defect increased until the power of vision on that side was completely lost. The sight of the left eye then became impaired in the same manner, and as the affection of this eye advanced, the other recovered a small power of vision, but in the progress of the disorder he became completely blind. . . . After death, the head was examined by Mr. Brodie. . . . The pituitary gland, which is situated below the optic nerve, was converted into a pulpy structure, about five or six times the usual bulk of the gland; and the sella turcica, which contains it, had become enlarged in the same proportion. . . . The fibres of the optic nerve were seen expanded, and almost destroyed, on the side of the tumour.

Other contributions to clinical medicine singled out by Powell's biographers included descriptions of subdural hematoma, septic meningitis following necrosis of the mastoid bone, hydrophobia, and painful affections of the alimentary tract. As a member of the Board of Commissioners for Licensing and Inspecting Madhouses, he published, in 1813, his "Observations Upon the Comparative Prevalence of Insanity, at Different Periods." Probably his greatest service to the practice of medicine was the English translation of the 1809 Latin edition of the

London Pharmacopoeia, which he had helped revise.[5] Although not all the ridiculous, unsavory, or disgusting excerpts were deleted, his edition was a vast improvement over the first edition of 1618. Finally, for his hospital alma mater, he gave some attention to the history of St. Bartholomew's and published the text of Rahere's charter to Hagno, the deed of 1137 granted by the Prior and Convent of St. Bartholomew.[6]

1. Moore, N.: *The History of St. Bartholomew's Hospital,* vol 2, London: C. A. Pearson Ltd., 1918, pp 550-551.

2. Powell, R.: *Observations on the Bile and Its Diseases, and on the Oeconomy of the Liver,* London: F. and C. Rivington, 1800.

3. Powell, R.: Observations Upon Some Cases of Paralytic Affection, *Med Trans* 5:96-108, 1815.

4. Powell, R.: Some Cases, Illustrative of the Pathology of the Brain, *Med Trans* 5:198-256, 1815.

5. Powell, R.: *The Pharmacopoeia of the Royal College of Physicians of London, MDCCCIX, Translated Into English,* ed 2, London: Longman, Hurst, Rees, and Orme, 1809.

6. Powell, R.: An Account of Two Seals Attached to a Deed of the Twelfth Century, Granted by the Prior and Convent of St Bartholomew, in Smithfield, *Archaeologia* (Society of Antiquaries of London) 19:49-55, 1821.

Philippe Pinel (1745-1826)

PINEL, one of the first of the modern school of alienists to study in depth the reactions of the mentally disturbed, was also one of the first to promote a humane regimen of treatment for the institutionalized insane. Although his unshackling of the unfortunate was a dramatic and widely acclaimed program, his formulation of a nosology of disease, based upon accurate observation and accurate description, and a rational regimen of management are equally noteworthy. Pinel was born at St. André in the département du Tarn and attended the Collège des Doctrinaires at Lavaur, where he concentrated on ancient and contemporary logic and philosophy. Intending at one time to enter the priesthood, he turned from the humanities to science and medicine; however, he effectively integrated a diversity of interests in the practice of psychiatry. The medical degree was taken at Toulouse in 1773, followed by further studies in anatomy and physiology at Montpellier and the selection of Paris as a permanent home at the age of 33.[1] He lived modestly in the Latin Quarter, engaging in tutoring mathematics, translating texts such as Cullen's *In-*

stitutes of Medicine, editing, writing, and other scholarly pursuits.

Pinel's career as a skillful reformer achieved its first triumph in 1793, when he was nominated Director of Bicêtre, the Parisian institution for insane men. Two years later he was called to Salpêtrière, where the female insane were confined, and served as professor of internal pathology and director of the hospital. The management of the maniacal and conditions during commitment were similar. They were clothed in vermin-infested rags, bound with rope or chains, and lived on a bed of straw in fetid stone cells without light, heat, ventilation, or sanitary facilities. Pinel's compassion for the sordid victims was expressed by his initial appearance before the committee for public safety, urging removal of the shackles and correction of the deplorable conditions. Without having received full authority and presumably on an experimental basis, he removed the chains from a few of the male patients at Bicêtre shortly after his appointment. The released were easier to manage, not more difficult as some had predicted. Release from bondage was followed by

transfer to a humane and hygienic environment. Some were assigned work in the fields and, when indicated, were treated with quieting and gentle drugs or occupational therapy.

Although the removal of the fetters was spectacular and humane and has lost none of its dramatic appeal over a century and a half, Pinel's study of the mentally sick was penetrating and productive. Refusing to accept metaphysical abstractions, and choosing instead to base his conclusions on observations and empirical deductions, he set an example for Bichat, Louis, Corvisart, and Laennec, men of stature who followed him in Parisian medicine. Pinel's first major scientific effort, *Nosographie Philosophique,* published in 1798, discredited work by hypothesis, advocating instead an analytical method for the study and classification of disease—clearly a scientific method for medical investigation. Not long after, Pinel prepared his *Treatise on Insanity,* a monograph outlining a general method for studying the insane.[2]

Nothing has more contributed to the rapid improvement of modern natural history, than the spirit of minute and accurate observation which has distinguished its votaries. The habit of analytical investigation, thus adopted, has induced an accuracy of expression and a propriety of classification, which have themselves, in no small degree, contributed to the advancement of natural knowledge. . . . On my entrance upon the duties of that hospital [Bicêtre], every thing presented to me the appearance of chaos and confusion. Some of my unfortunate patients laboured under the horrors of a most gloomy and desponding melancholy. Others were furious, and subject to the influence of a perpetual delirium. Some appeared to possess a correct judgement upon most subjects, but were occasionally agitated by violent sallies of maniacal fury; while those of another class were sunk into a state of stupid idiotism and imbecility. Symptoms so different, and all comprehended under the general title of insanity, required, on my part, much study and discrimination; . . . From systems of nosology, I had little assistance to expect; since the arbitrary distributions of Sauvages and Cullen were better calculated to impress the conviction of their insufficiency than to simplify my labour, I, therefore, resolved to adopt that method of investigation which has invariably succeeded in all the departments of natural history, viz. to notice successively every fact, without any other object than that of collecting materials for future use; and to endeavour, as far as possible, to divest myself of the influence, both of my own prepossessions and the authority of others. With this view, I first of all took a general statement of the symptoms of my patients. To ascertain their characteristic peculiarities, the above survey was followed by cautions and repeated examinations into the condition of individuals. All our new cases were entered at great length upon the journals of the house. Due attention was paid to the changes of the seasons and the weather, and their respective influences upon the patients were minutely noticed. Having a peculiar attachment for the more general method of descriptive history, I did not confine myself to any exclusive mode of arranging my observations, nor to any one system of nosography. The facts which I have thus collected are now submitted to the consideration of the public, in the form of a regular treatise.

Having studied the conscious faculties of the afflicted—their memory, judgment, intelligence, will, and passions—Pinel defined five categories of mental derangements in the first edition of the *Treatise:* (1) melancholia, or delirium, (2) mania without delirium, (3) mania with delirium, (4) dementia, or the abolition of the thinking faculty, and (5) idiotism, or obliteration of the intellectual faculties and affections.[3] Although this nosology has long since become obsolete, current nomenclature is strikingly similar and includes as counterparts to Pinel's classifications: (1) depression, (2) psychopathic personality, (3) manic psychosis, (4) schizophrenic psychosis, and (5) mental deficiency.

Pinel's observations on mania with delirium are frequently mentioned as currently valid.[2]

We may very justly admire the writings of Mr. Locke, without admitting his authority upon subjects not necessarily connected with his enquiries. On resuming at Bicêtre my researches into this disorder, I thought, with the above author, that it was inseparable from delirium; and, I was not a little surprised to find many maniacs who at no period gave evidence of any lesion of the understanding, but who were under the dominion of instinctive and abstract fury, as if the active faculties alone sustained the injury.

Pinel's contributions on the insane fall into three categories which follow in logical sequence; firstly, he released them from their bonds; second, they were studied intensively

and their diagnosis classified; and finally, a rational regimen was prescribed. Medicines were withheld at times to judge the clinical status—improvement or regression; at all times, the patient was encouraged and reassured with a hopeful prognosis.

Pinel was elected a Fellow of the Academy of Science, honored as Chevalier of the Legion of Honor, and appointed consulting physician to Napoleon. The appointment as personal physician to the Emperor was refused, possibly because he preferred to concentrate on teaching, study, and practice, caring less for popular adulation. A large statute stands on the grounds of Salpêtrière in honor of the physician who developed a nosology of psychiatry and who changed an asylum into a hospital and brought psychiatry closer to the practice of general medicine.

1. Mackness, J.: *The Moral Aspects of Medical Life,* London: J. Churchill, 1846.
2. Pinel, P.: *A Treatise on Insanity,* D. D. Davis, trans., Sheffield: W. Todd, 1806; republished by Hafner Publishing Company, New York, 1962.
3. Pinel P.: *Medical-Philosophical Treatise on Mental Disease,* 2nd ed, Paris: J. A. Brosson, 1809, excerpt translated by Z. Danilevicius.

James Parkinson (1755-1824)

JAMES PARKINSON, son of an apothecary and surgeon, was born in 1755 in Shoreditch, London.[1] Little is known of his school days according to the excellent biography by McMenemey,[1] but from Parkinson's small book, *The Hospital Pupil,* it may be assumed that his instruction included Latin, Greek, natural philosophy, and shorthand, subjects recommended by Parkinson early in the 19th century as proper basic tools for a physician. He studied and assisted his father, and very likely took over the paternal practice before his father died in 1784. The following year, Parkinson attended John Hunter's lectures on surgery and recorded them in shorthand. They were transcribed and published, in turn, by his son half a century later.

In the closing years of the 18th century, Parkinson's interests were divided successfully between social reform and the practice of medicine. The critical events associated with the French and American revolutions and the social scandals of the times provided the English reformers with ample motives for action and rational grounds for agitation in support of equity in the law. Although there is no record of Parkinson's having taken an active part in riots or public demonstrations, he was a member of two of the dining clubs dedicated to reform, the Society for Constitutional Information and the influential London Corresponding Society. As a militant pamphleteer, he argued for revolution without bloodshed, restoration of the rights and prerogatives of the disenfranchised, equitable levying of taxes, amendment of the poor laws which imposed prison sentence for the indigent who sought employment in other parishes, abolition of the game laws which permitted hunting by the rich on the lands of the poor, but not vice versa, and proper remuneration of the clergy from the vast revenues of the bishops. He was hailed before Pitt and the Privy Council and stood his ground staunchly. His less polemical writings dealt with advice on sports, preservation of health, self-medication, and hints for the improvement of trusses. Sundays he spent opening new Sunday schools for the poor.

Parkinson's little-known medical monograph, *Observations on the Nature and Cure of Gout,* published in 1805, contains one statement of then current interest.[2]

When we view in a person who has been long subject to this disease, the prodigious quantity of this matter [uric acid] which has been separated from the system, forming almost all the smaller joints of the hands into white, and apparently cretaceous nodules, we are naturally led to the opinion, that the blood must have been preternaturally charged with this matter, or with the principles of which it is formed.

Leeches were recommended in the treatment of acute gouty arthritis. There is no explanation for the subsidence of chronic tophi through the daily administration of soda, an agent with minimal effect upon the urinary excretion of uric acid. Parkinson observed, nevertheless, that the use of soda in doses of 5 to 15 grains a day caused a[2]

. . . gradual diminution, and finally the complete removal of such tumours [subcutaneous tophi] as have existed for several months, have been thus procured; whilst those which have existed for some years have been so much reduced, as to allow of considerable motion in joints which had become nearly immoveable.

The monograph on shaking palsy, an illness that had received prior attention from Galen, Sylvius (Franciscus de la Boë), Juncker, Cullen, and others, was Parkinson's best-known medical contribution to paralysis agitans (Parkinson's disease). The distinctive feature of the essay, published in 1817 by this diligent practitioner, was the remarkably complete clinical description. A single postmortem examination suggested swelling of the medulla as a possible link to the ailment, but no further efforts were made for morphologic investigation. He regretted the lack of interest by the pathologists and even hinted that a prime motive of his treatise was to help counter the prevailing laggardness. There is one reference only to the possibility of an infectious pathogenesis. Lumbago developed in one patient several years before the onset of neurological symptoms.

Parkinson's communication described the insidious onset and the development of anterior flexion of the thorax as the disease progressed, accelerated gait, drooling, and tremulous motion of the limbs while awake and asleep. No mention was made of the mask-like face (Parkinson's facies), an eponym that came into medical literature after his death.[3]

So slight and nearly imperceptible are the first inroads of this malady, and so extremely slow is its progress, that it rarely happens, that the patient can form any recollection of the precise period of its commencement. The first symptoms perceived are, a slight sense of weakness, with a proneness to trembling in some particular part; . . . but most commonly in one of the hands and arms.

After a few more months the patient is found to be less strict than usual in preserving an upright posture; this being most observable whilst walking, but sometimes whilst sitting or standing.

Hitherto the patient will have experienced but little inconvenience; and befriended by the strong influence of habitual endurance, would perhaps seldom think of his being the subject of disease, except when reminded of it by the unsteadiness of his hand, whilst writing or employing himself in any nicer kind of manipulation. But as the disease proceeds, similar employments are accomplished with considerable difficulty, the hand failing to answer with exactness to the dictates of the will. Walking becomes a task which cannot be performed without considerable attention. The legs are not raised to that height, or with that promptitude which the will directs, so that the utmost care is necessary to prevent frequent falls. As time and the disease proceed, difficulties increase: writing can now be hardly at all accomplished; . . . Whilst at meals the fork not being duly directed frequently fails to raise the morsel from the plate: which, when seized, is with much difficulty conveyed to the mouth.

The propensity to lean forward [in walking] becomes invincible, and the patient is thereby forced to step on the toes and fore part of the feet, whilst the upper part of the body is thrown so far forward as to render it difficult to avoid falling on the face . . . being, at the same time, irresistibly impelled to take much quicker and shorter steps, and thereby to adopt unwillingly a running pace. In some cases it is found necessary entirely to substitute running for walking.

In this stage, the sleep becomes much disturbed. The tremulous motion of the limbs occur during sleep, and augment until they awaken the patient, and frequently with much agitation and alarm. The power of conveying the food to the mouth is at length so much impeded that he is obliged to consent to be fed by others. . . . As the disease proceeds towards its last stage, the trunk is almost permanently bowed, the muscular power is more decidedly diminished, and the tremulous agitation becomes violent. The patient walks now with great difficulty, and unable any longer to support himself with his stick, he dares not venture on this exercise, unless assisted by an attendant, who walking backwards before him, prevents his falling forwards, by the pressure of his hands against the fore part of his shoulders. His words are now scarcely intelligible; and he is not only no longer able to feed himsef, but when the food is conveyed to the mouth, so much are the actions of the muscles of the tongue, pharynx, &c. impeded by impaired action and perpetual agitation, that the food is with difficulty retained in the mouth until masticated; and then as difficultly swallowed. Now also, from the same cause, another very unpleasant circumstance occurs: the saliva fails of being directed to the back part of the fauces, and hence is continually draining from the mouth, mixed with the particles of food, which he is no longer able to clear from the inside of the mouth.

As the debility increases and the influence of the will over the muscles fades away, the tremulous agitation becomes more vehement. It now seldom leaves him for a moment; but even when exhausted nature siezes a small portion of sleep, the motion becomes so violent as not only to shake the bed-hangings, but even the floor and sashes of the room. The chin is now almost immoveably bent down upon the sternum. The slops with which he is attempted to be fed, with the saliva, are continually trickling from the mouth. The power of articulation is lost. The urine and faeces are passed involuntarily; and at the last, constant sleepiness, with slight delirium, and other marks of extreme exhaustion, announce the wished-for release.

The medical profession tends to resent the attachment of an eponym to an illness. However, since the time-honored names "paralysis agitans" and "shaking palsy" are false and unscientific (because not only physicians but the afflicted know that paralysis is not a finding in this disease), it seems better to retain the eponym "Parkinson," than to accept scientific frauds. Furthermore, the name "Parkinson's disease" is now strongly entrenched in the literature. "Perhaps in time to come a suitable scientific term will be found to replace the eponym."[4]

The description of a case of appendicitis with perforation preceded that of Fitz by half a century. This was observed in a 5-year-old boy, who, two days before death, was stricken with vomiting and great prostration. The abdomen[5]

. . . became very hard and painful upon being pressed; his countenance pale and sunken, his pulse hardly perceptible. Death, preceeded [sic] by extreme restlessness and delirium, took place within twenty-four hours.

Upon examination [postmortem] the whole surface of the peritoneum was found inflamed, and covered with a thin coat of coagulable lymph; and slight adhesions had taken place between the peritoneum covering the viscera, and the parities of the abdomen. The viscera independent of the inflammation of the peritoneal covering, appeared in a perfectly healthy state, excepting the appendix vermiformis of the caecum. No diseased appearance was seen in this part near to the caecum; but an inch of its extremity was considerably enlarged and thickened, its internal surface ulcerated, and an opening from ulceration, which would have admitted a crow quill, was found at the commencement of the diseased part, about the middle of the appendix, through which it appeared that a thin dark-colored and highly fetid fluid, had escaped into the cavity of the abdomen.

The interests of Parkinson in natural philosophy were expressed in texts on chemistry, geology, and oryctology. The first edition of his inorganic and physiological chemistry appeared in 1799, followed in 1801 by an American edition.[6] Oryctology is described by Parkinson as[7]

. . . the science which enquires into the nature, origin, and formation of those bodies which possess the figures, markings, or structure of vegetables or animals, whilst their substance evinces their having been preserved through many ages, by certain changes effected in subaqueous or subterranean situations.

The substances of which these bodies are formed being generally of a mineral nature, the term *FOSSILS* is applied to them, as declaratory of their having been *dug* from subterranean situations.

1. McMenemey, W. H., in *James Parkinson (1755-1824): A Bicentenary Volume of Papers Dealing with Parkinson's Disease, Incorporating the Original "Essay on the Shaking Palsy,"* M. Critchley, ed., London: Macmillan & Co. 1955.

2. Parkinson, J.: *Observations on the Nature and Cure of Gout; on Nodes of the Joints; and on the Influence of Certain Articles of Diet, in Gout, Rheumatism, and Gravel,* London: H. D. Symonds, 1805.

3. Parkinson, J.: *An Essay on the Shaking Palsy,* London: Sherwood, Neely, and Jones, 1817.

4. Doshay, L. J.: Parkinson's Disease, *JAMA* 174:1962 (Dec. 10) 1960.

5. Parkinson, J.: Case of Diseased Appendix Vermiformis, *Medicochir Trans* 3:57, 1812.

6. Parkinson, J.: *The Chemical Pocket-Book,* Philadelphia: J. Humyhreys, 1802.

7. Parkinson, J.: *Outlines of Oryctology: An Introduction to the Study of Fossil Organic Remains,* London: Sherwood, Neely, and Jones, 1822.

Charles Bell (1774-1842)

SIR CHARLES BELL, impeccable dresser and discerning dissector, was Edinburgh's great contribution to neurology.[1] His discoveries[2]

on the functions of the nervous system is the most important fact which science owes to the physiologists of Great Britian, since the doctrine of Harvey on the circulation of the blood.

Charles was the youngest of four brothers in a family that included several ministers. His father and both grandfathers were clergymen. The paternal grandfather preached the sermon on the death of William III before the General Assembly of the Church of Scotland. Charles' older brother

was the celebrated surgeon, John Bell. The other brothers were outstanding lawyers. According to Bell he was a self-taught stu-

National Library of Medicine

dent, except for the help and devotion of his mother. His formal education was not neglected entirely, however. His biographers refer to his attendance at the Edinburgh High School. Possibly the greatest skills that he developed through maternal instruction were sketching, drawing, painting, and etching. This avocation served him well throughout his professional years in illustrating the medical works of his brother and his own.

Charles was born in 1774; his father died when he was only 5. Financial vicissitudes plus his mediocrity as a student caused him to question during adolescence the possibility of a professional career. His brother, John, however, 11 years his senior, came to his aid and induced him to enroll in the University of Edinburgh. This was the most decisive moment. Two years later a career in medicine was uppermost in his mind, and even before graduation he published his *System of Dissections*. He was elected to Fellowship in the Royal College of Surgeons to Edinburgh and received an appointment at the Royal Infirmary at the age of 25. Since the practice of medicine occupied only a small portion of his time, he devoted most of his energies to drawing and sketching pathologic specimens and to the preparation of them in wax. Dissension and jealousy between the senior and junior members of the Royal Infirmary resulted in the failure of Charles and John to be reappointed to the staff. Charles was not even permitted to attend the postmortem examinations or to sketch the pathologic specimens. It is rather sad that petty bitterness kept the greatest neurologist of Edinburgh from an appointment to the local hospital. Most surely he would have adorned Edinburgh if Infirmary privileges had been extended to him. The fates of Scotland turned against him, however, and he was off to London.

London held special attraction, although Scotsmen were not particularly welcome in the city in the 18th century. Staff privileges at Westminster Hospital, the logical institution, were denied him. He was able to enlist the support of few physicians capable of implementing his professional desires. It seemed best, therefore, to develop his own facilities for medical instruction. In 1806, a lecture hall, consultation rooms, and living quarters were constructed in Leicester Square. His first consultation fee was not received until after he had practiced for more than a year.

However, success was not a remote realization. His fame spread with the popularity of his lectures and his two-volume "System of Operative Surgery" published in (1807-1809).[3] Medical students, medical writers, and medical illustrators soon discovered his stimulating and attractive personality. At the age of 38 he was offered a partnership in the Great Windmill Street Medical School, which had been founded a generation earlier by brother Scotsmen, John and William Hunter. His anatomic and pathologic collection was placed temporarily in the great museum. Admittance to the Royal College of Surgeons of London and to the staff of the Middlesex Hospital followed. He was appointed professor of anatomy in the Royal College at the age of 50. Not long after, royalty took official recognition of his talents. George IV decreed him the recipient of the annual medal in science. He was knighted by William IV.

In the interim he crossed the Channel and cared for casualties at the Battle of Waterloo in a tour of duty as a military surgeon.

Bell's greatest contributions concerned the cranial and spinal nerves. Although he does not hold undisputed credit for the clear differentiation of the motor and sensory pathways of the spinal nerves he reported as follows in a small pamphlet privately printed in 1811 entitled: Idea of a new anatomy of the brain; submitted for the observation of his friends.[4]

On laying bare the roots of the spinal nerves, I found that I could cut across the posterior fasciculus of nerves, which took its origin from the posterior portion of the spinal marrow without convulsing the muscles of the back; but that on touching the anterior fasciculus with the point of the knife, the muscles of the back were immediately convulsed.

Bell was 38 when this manuscript was published. Bell's law relates to this phenomenon. Convincing proof of the diverse functions of the posterior and anterior roots was provided by Magendie upon a litter of puppies a decade later and was confirmed by Johannes Müller a decade after Magendie. The latter made no mention of Bell's original work. His studies of the motor and sensory functions of the seventh facial nerve is probably best associated with the eponymic malady, Bell's palsy (facial nerve paralysis). The lesion is unilateral; the muscles of expression are paralyzed for voluntary, emotional, and associated movements. The eyebrow droops, and the wrinkles of the brow are absent. The palpebral fissure is widened, owing to paralyses of the orbicularis oculi. The patient is unable to retract the angle of the mouth or to purse the lips, as in whistling. Displacement of the mouth causes deviation of the tongue to the sound side when it is protruded.[5]

The respiratory nerve of the face [portio dura of the seventh], emerging through the stylomastoid foramen, divides into many branches, and these diverging, spread to all the side of the face. First, a branch is sent to the muscles of the outward ear; another is sent, under the angle of the jaw, to the muscles of the throat. The principal nerve then passes through the parotid gland and comes upon the face. Here the branches continue to scatter, to go upwards upon the temple, and downwards upon the side of the neck, forming on the neck a superficial plexus. The principal branches, however, go forward to the muscles of the forehead and eyelids; a branch called superior facial is sent to the muscles of the cheek and the side of the nose; while an inferior facial branch is given to the angle of the mouth and the muscles which concentrate there. We have proofs equal to experiments, that in the human face the actions of the muscles which produce smiling and laughing, are a consequence of the influence of this respiratory nerve. A man had the trunk of the respiratory nerve of the face injured by a suppuration, which took place anterior to the ear, and through which the nerve passed in its course to the face. It was observed that, in smiling and laughing, his mouth was drawn in a very remarkable manner to the opposite side. The attempt to whistle was attended with a ludicrous distortion of the lips; when he took snuff and sneezed, the side where the suppuration had affected the nerve remained placid, while the opposite side exhibited the usual distortion.

He concluded that ocular strabismus should be correctable by severing the nerves to the intact muscle responsible for deviation. This was tested experimentally on a monkey. Bell's phenomenon is an outward and upward rolling of the eyeball in an attempt to close the eye, which occurs on the affected side in Bell's palsy. Bell's nerve is otherwise known as the long thoracic nerve, the external respiratory nerve.

Returning to Edinburgh after 32 years in London, Bell held the professorship of surgery at the University of Edinburgh, until he died of a coronary thrombosis in 1842 at the age of 68. A portrait in the National Gallery shows him dressed in a white waistcoat and a green jacket, with his hair short and without powder—"a true dandy." One of his wife's letters noted that he "dressed himself young."

It is reported that either a native or an adopted medical son of Edinburgh never loses his love for the city on the Firth of Forth. Surely this legend held true for Bell. In spite of his popularity as a teacher, his skill as a clinician, and his brilliance as an investigator in neuroanatomy, he was not at home in London in the accepted interpretation of this term. He wrote to his brother George, professor of law at the University of Edinburgh:[1]

London is a place to live in, but not to die in. My comfort has ever been a labour for some great purpose, and my great object of study has been attained. There is but one place where I can hope to fulfill the object of my scientific labour, and that is Edinburgh.

1. Gordon-Taylor, G., and Walls, E. W.: *Sir Charles Bell: His Life and Times*, Edinburgh: E. & S. Livingstone, Ltd., 1958.
2. Pichot, A.: *The Life and Labours of Sir Charles Bell*, London: Richard Bentley, 1860.
3. Bell, C.: *System of Operative Surgery, Founded in the Basis of Anatomy*, vol 1-2, London: Longman, Hurst, Rees, & Orme, 1807-1809.
4. Bell, C.: An Idea of a New Anatomy of the Brain; Submitted for the Observation of His Friends, London: Strahan & Preston, 1811, In Fulton, J., *Selected Readings in the History of Physiology*, ed 2, Springfield, Ill: C. C Thomas, 1966.
5. Bell, C.: *On the nerves; giving an account of some experiments on their structure and functions, which lead to a new arrangement of the system*, Philos Trans 111:398-424, 1821.

François Magendie
(1783-1855)

THE BELL-MAGENDIE CONTROVERSY, regarding priority of the differentiation of sensory and motor function of peripheral nerves, appears to have aroused deeper sentiments among medical historians and friends than among the individuals directly concerned.[1]

The second member of the Scots-French doublet was a leader of the brilliant school of Parisian physiology and medicine in the 19th century. The time was a critical period of French history near the end of the French Revolution and during the formative years of the establishment of the French Republic. Magendie's writings reflect little of the turbulent political passions. He appears to have been completely absorbed in physiologic investigations, teaching, and clinical medicine.

From the document signed by the Empress Marie Louise (in the absence of Napoleon from Paris) exempting Magendie from military service, it is learned that François was born in Bordeaux in 1783. His mother, a Parisian, intimated that her social rank was somewhat above that of her surgeon-husband. She was in poor health and died shortly after the family moved to Paris, when François was 8 years of age. The lack of maternal guidance and incentive to formal education was readily evident. François was unable to read and write until after his 10th birthday. The educational gap was rapidly closed in the initial teenage years, and, at the age of 14, he won the grand prize in his class for an essay on the rights of man and the constitution. Two years later he began the study of medicine as a pupil of Citizen Boyer.

Late in the 18th century, the universities in France had suffered severely under imperial edicts, and for several years, classes, instruction, and prescribed courses were abandoned. A laissez-faire philosophy of higher education soon became so unsatisfactory that, in 1794, provisions were made for the reactivation of schools in the three medical centers of pre-revolutionary days: Paris, Montpellier, and Strasbourg. Boyer was affiliated with the Collège de France and taught at Hôtel Dieu and Charité. Boyer was quick to recognize the capacities of François who became his favorite pupil and prosector in anatomy. The period of apprenticeship was short, and soon the pupil was conducting classes in anatomy and dissection. Such a precedent had been set by Bichat a decade earlier, who held classes as he was learning anatomy. Bichat's brilliant career was in the zenith, and he had advanced to senior surgeonship at Hôtel Dieu when Magendie began his studies under Boyer.

When Magendie became self-supporting, meager though the support, and the apprentice-instruction role was proceeding satisfactorily, he turned to the classics momentarily. Then followed a successful competitive examination for internship at the hospital Saint Louis at the age of 19, and finally in 1808, the clinical examination for Doctor of Medicine. The final step for Magendie was the preparation of a thesis and its defense before the faculty. "The Uses of the Soft Palate, with Some Remarks on the Cartilage of the Ribs" was the title. It was dedicated to his father. The granting of the MD degree coincided with the founding of the present Paris Faculty of Medicine, in which Magendie was to accept the senior post in later years. His private lectures in anatomy were continued and expanded to include selected subjects in operative surgery. Although Magendie had considered entering the field of surgery in preference to medicine or physiology, this idea was abandoned in 1813. It is not certain whether Dupuytren was influential in this decision because of apprehension lest he have a strong competitor in Paris. The basis for the decision seems unimportant; Magendie would have advanced medical science, irrespective. During the next three decades, Magendie appeared on numerous occasions before the Paris Academy of Sciences to describe his experimental studies in medicine and physiology. These communications covered a variety of subjects without attaining any consummate generalizations.

The beginning of experimental pharmacology has been attributed to Magendie. Having procured crude preparations of strychnine from Java, the site of action of the poison was investigated. He concluded that convulsions from strychnine intoxication were produced by the active agent being carried by the blood stream to the spinal cord. Others had contended that poisons from the gastrointestinal tract were transported by the lymphatics. Another experiment is currently familiar. Crossed circulation of two dogs was successful technically, but the pharmacologic results were inconclusive. The reason was the insufficient time allowed for the poison to be transported from the donor through the artificial circulation to the recipient. Another research concerned the actions of emetics.[2] It was concluded that the mechanism for vomiting was located centrally and the diaphragm, the principal target organ. The stomach, which was found to be a passive viscus, regurgitated its contents through the spasmodic action of the diaphragm. In the dog, the stomach was replaced by a pig's bladder filled with dye. Emesis followed the intravenous administration of a concentrate of tartar emetic. The mechanism of vomiting, as revealed by Magendie, remains valid except for the failure to include relaxation of the cardia and constriction of the pylorus. Magendie assumed that the action of the stomach followed the diaphragm.

Magendie's textbook of physiology, *The Precis,* was completed in 1816 and maintained an enviable position as a physiology text for several decades. It was translated into German and English. An American edition, *Lectures on Blood and on the Changes Which It Undergoes During Disease,* appeared in 1839.[3] The subjects covered by Magendie included the special sense organs and their functions, digestion, circulation, respiration, secretion, and reproduction. Studies in pharmacology and his interest in clinical medicine contributed to the preparation of a formulary similar to *Useful Drugs* of this generation. The handbook contained many new drugs, their pharmacologic action, dose, and mode of administration. Magendie, meanwhile, continued his lectures and his studies. He did not enjoy a senior appointment on the medical faculty nor an appointment with tenure in any of the Parisian hospitals. It was not until 1826, at the age of 43, that he was proposed as a substitute physician at the Salpétrière. He was elected to the Academy of Sciences at the age of 38. He was twice rebuffed in a desire to hold the Chair of Medicine at the Collège, occupied first by Hallé, later by Laennec. At the age of 47, he was appointed to the Chair of Medicine at the Collège de France and became the chief physician at Hôtel Dieu.

In 1822, Magendie's studies on a litter of puppies confirmed Bell's preliminary investigations on the function of anterior and posterior nerve roots and crowned his scientific career.[4]

For a long time I had wished to perform the experiment of cutting the anterior and posterior roots of the nerves arising from the spinal cord of an animal . . . then before my eyes the anterior roots of the lumbar and sacral pairs, and, raising them up successfully on the blade of a pair of small scissors, I cut them on one side. . . . I reunited the wound by means of a suture through the skin and observed the animal. . . . It was insensitive to pricks and to the strongest compression . . . but soon, to my great surprise, I saw it move perceptibly. although sensibility was always entirely absent. . . . I began to regard it as probable that the posterior roots of the spinal nerves might have different functions from the anterior roots, and that they were particularly designed for sensibility.

As in the preceding experiments, I made the section on only one side (anterior roots). . . . The results were not doubtful; the member was completely immovable and flaccid, although it preserved an unequivocable sensibility. . . . It is sufficient for me to be able to affirm to-day, as positive, that the anterior and posterior roots of the nerves which arise from the cord have different functions; that the posterior appear to be more particularly devoted to sensibility, while the anterior appear more especially associated with movement.

Eponyms include Magendie's foramen, a median aperture in the membranous roof of the fourth ventricle which connects the fourth ventricle with the subarachnoid space;[5] the Bell-Magendie law of sensory and motor function of nerves; Magendie's solution (morphine sulfate); and Magendie's spaces, lymph spaces between the pia and arachnoid corresponding to the principal sulci of the brain. Although Magendie contributed to a number of scientific periodicals, he is closely identified with the *Journal de physiologie expérimentale,* whose name was changed to *Journal de physiologie expérimentale et pathologique.* He regarded physiology as the best basic training for the practice of medicine. As editor of the *Journal de physiologie,* he systematically verified all experiments submitted for publication. Contributors were requested to transmit manuscripts one month in advance so that the experiment might be verified before sending on the manuscript to the printer. Magendie's *Journal* ceased publication in 1831.[6]

In 1845 he retired from full-time academic life, with Claude Bernard assuming the mantle at Collège de France. He continued his lectures until 1852, but he appeared less frequently at the sessions of the Academy of Sciences.

1. Temkin, O.: Philosophical Background of Magendie's Physiology, *Bull Hist Med* 20:10 (June) 1946.

2. *On Vomiting.* Being the Account of a Memoir of M. Magendie on Vomiting, read to the Imperial Institute of France on the 1st of March, 1813, *Ann Philos* 1:429-438 (June) 1813.

3. Magendie, F.: *Lectures on the Blood and on the Changes Which It Undergoes During Disease,* Philadelphia: Haswell, Barrington, and Haswell, 1939.

4. Magendie, R.: Experiments on the Function of the Roots of the Spinal Nerves (Fr), *J Physiol exp Path* 2:276-279, 1822, translated by Dawson, P. M.: A Biography of Francois Magendie, *Med Libr Hist J* 4:45, 198, 292, 364, 1906; 5-24, 1907.

5. Magendie, F.: *Clinical and Physiological Researches on Cerebro-Spinal Fluid* (Fr), 1 vol & Atlas, Paris: Mequignon-Marvis, 1842.

6. Olmsted, J. M. D.: *Francois Magendie,* New York: Schuman's, 1944.

Italian, Hungarian, Serbian, Lithuanian, and Danish. Such a recounting is indeed remarkable even in his day, when familiarity with several languages was an accepted prerequisite in academic circles. Henry J.

Composite by G. Bako

Johannes Evangelista Purkyně (1787-1869)

THE COUCHING OF CRITICAL SCIENTIFIC CONTRIBUTIONS in an obscure language is an unusual phenomenon in the Western world. Dissemination to many is the usual happier fate. The discoveries of Johannes Evangelista Purkyně, one of the founders of modern physiology and pharmacology, belong in the restricted category. In some instances the observations published in Czech were overlooked for almost a century. Purkyně was born in 1787, in Libochovice, Bohemia—old Austro-Hungary. Czechoslovakia was not constituted until the Treaty of Versailles. The passionate nationalism of the Czechs, apparent more than a century before their independence, was supported by Purkyně.

Although Czech was Purkyně's native tongue, he was skilled in German and Latin, and his linguistic talents included French, English, Russian, Polish, Greek,

John, the most recent biographer of Purkyně, discovered that the family name was spelled nine different ways in the literature.[1] It is pronounced Poor'-keyn-ie in Czech. In America the pronunciation is Per-kin'-je or Per'-kin-je. Purkinje is the phonetic approximation in German of the Czech derivation.

Born of poor parents, he spent the second decade of life in the monasteries of the Piarist Order. But a monastic life was not for him; final vows in the Piarist order were not taken. The scholastic environment, however, stimulated his interest in philosophy, which was apparent when he entered Charles University in Prague with the expressed desire to concentrate in this field. Interest was shifted subsequently to medicine and the formal study begun at the age of 25. Purkyně served as an assistant in anatomy and physiology following graduation from the University. He was appointed to the Chair of Physiology at the University of Breslau at the age of 36.

During the 27 years in Breslau, Purkyně pursued as remarkable a series of investigations in diversified fields closely or remotely related to physiology as any investigator in the history of medical science. He rejected the theoretical speculations of his predecessors in planning the course in physiology. The lectures were based upon demonstrations and the recounting of human and animal experiments. This was accomplished under great handicap. Monies for such demonstrations were not provided in the budget, and the Dean of the College, Professor Otto, was unable to fill the void. Laboratory space and laboratory equipment were lacking. Nine years were required to obtain a microscope. Eventually a laboratory was constructed in his home, with provision for animals for experimental studies. This was supplanted by a Physiological Institute, the first such institute in the history of contemporary physiology. Physiology, as interpreted by Purkyně, included anthropology, anatomy, history, embryology, mechanics, biochemistry, psychology, experimental physiology, applied physiology, and general physiology. Purkyně built a microtome, was one of the first investigators to use Canada balsam and, with his new microscope, explored the field of histology and embryology.

The success of his lectures and the brilliance of his scientific attainments during his productive years may be imposingly documented in inverse proportion to the obstacles that were overcome along the way. Personal tragedy compounded his struggle. He did not marry until he was 40. Two daughters died of scarlet fever; his wife died of meningitis. Purkyně was left with two infant sons at the peak of his professional career.

Purkyně's images (Sanson images) and Purkyně's phenomenon are eponymic terms that refer to the physiology of the eye. Thau, in collecting material for his biography of Purkyně, noted that some of the master's contributions in ophthalmoscopy had lain fallow and unappreciated until they were discovered by Heidenhain in 1887 and translated into English.[2] Purkyně measured the curvature of the anterior surface of the cornea and both surfaces of the lens, essential physical data for the formation of the image of an external object on the retina. Discovery of the eye mirror by Helmholtz

several decades later was based upon Purkyne's original observations excerpted as follows:[2]

But I also had a chance to see the interior of the eye where the vitreous body is located. . . . I examined the eye of a dog in order to learn about the nature of the shine . . . until I discovered that the light is reflected from the hollow surface of the lens into the eye and then returned. When the experiment was immediately repeated with human beings the same phenomenon occurred. . . . Being still uncertain about the location of the reflected light, I constructed an artificial eye, which I filled with water, either clear or tubid to some degree, and the light shining through revealed both the background and the nature of the fluid. . . . Thus, from now on practically no membrane or liquid content of the eye will escape the properly reflected light or the scrutinizing eye, and if practitioners, spurning the painstaking inquiry of physiologists, will not disdain or fear this (method), they will find it useful in ocular diagnosis.

A drop of oil on the skin and a bright light were employed in the study of the capillary network.[4] This observation was not explored until a century later. The Purkyně cell is a large branching neuron that comprises the middle layer of the cerebellar cortex; the Purkyně fibers in the heart are probably more familiar to the physician. The Purkyně network is a reticulation of immature muscle fibers in the subendocardial tissue of the ventricles. The structure of bone, cartilage, blood vessels, and the ducts of the sweat glands were described. The Purkyně vesicle, the germinal vesicle discovered in the chicken egg in 1825, was a major contribution to the cellular theory. The "little particles" or "little granules" in animal and plant tissues most surely were nuclear and cellular structures. Schwann capitalized on these and the observations of others in the following years in the development of the new concept of form and structure of living matter.

The majority of the great discoveries of Purkyně were made in his home laboratory during periods of great adversity. A simple spirometer was designed for the quantitative measurement of air. The kinesiscope, the kinesimeter, and the kinematograph originated with Purkyně. A hearing aid based upon conduction through bone was constructed. A paper on the psychology of dreams attested to his interest in psychological manifestations. The dark-field microscope, methods of intra-vital staining, and photomicrographs were proof of his genius in histology and microscopy technique. He employed the acetic acid technique of Burdach for the study of nervous tissue and identified the sympathetic nerve fibers about the vessels of the dura.[3]

My observations shew that especially near the oblique sinus and in the membrane of tentorium to the base of the skull, a very rich net-work of nervous fibres is spread out, which, when moistened with acetic acid, becomes distinctly visible to the naked eye or by a weak magnifying power. If we examine in this manner all the points of the dura mater, we must come to the conclusion that the largest collections of the nerves are to be found close to the anterior, middle, and posterior arteries, where they enter this membrane, and it is not very difficult to trace them running with the arteries back to their origin in the sympathetic system.

He described finger- and toe-printing (dactyloscopy) 75 years before Francis Galton made it a useful tool in identification.[4]

Our attention is now attracted by the remarkable disposition and flexures of the contiguous rugae and sulci in the inner part of the hand and foot, especially in the terminal phalanges of the fingers. In general, indeed, some mention of them occurs in every physiological or anatomical epitome. But in an organ of such great importance as the human hand, which serves not only for movements of many different types but also for the sense of touch, every inquiry, however minute, brings to light some worthwhile information. After innumerable observations, I have found nine important varieties of patterns of rugae and sulci serving for touch on the palmar surface of the terminal phalanges of the fingers. I present these nine, though the lines of demarcation between types are often obscure; the figures will explain them.

The term "protoplasm" was introduced by Purkyně. Continuous ciliary movement was studied in collaboration with his pupil, Valentin. Its significance and its independence of nervous control or muscular influence was recognized. He studied gastric secretion and observed that the secretion of hydrochloric acid by the gastric glands is under nervous control. The digestive properties of acidulated pancreatic juice were demonstrated. The significance of eugenics for humanity was appreciated. The flicker phenomenon in digitalis intoxication and the pharmacology of belladonna, camphor, and oil of nutmeg upon the gastrointestinal tract were studied, with Purkyně as the experimental subject. Extracurricular duties included founding and editing the *Journal of Natural History, Ziva,* and election to the Senate following retirement from the University.

1. John, H. J.: *Jan Evangelista Purkyne,* Philadelphia: American Philosophical Society, 1959.
2. Thau, W.: Purkyne: A Pioneer in Ophthalmoscopy, *Arch Ophthal* 27:299 (Feb) 1942.
3. Purkyne, J. H.: Microscopic-Neurologic Observations, *Muller's Arch Anat Physiol Med* 281-295, 1845, W. W. Gull (trans.) *London Med Gaz* 1:1066-1069, 1156-1159, 1845.
4. Purkyne, J. H.: External Physiological Examination of the Integumentary System (L), Breslau: Habilitation Dissertation, 1823, H. Cummins and R. Kennedy (trans.) *J. Amer Inst Crim Law Criminol* 31:343-356, 1941.

Marshall Hall (1790-1857)

MARSHALL HALL, an Edinburgh graduate, a Nottinghamshire practitioner, and a London consultant, was responsible for several fundamental contributions in neurology, medicine, and physiology without being honored with a major hospital appointment. His father, cotton spinner and ingenious chemist in the textile industry, was one of the first to use chlorine in the bleaching of fabrics. It seemed reasonable for Marshall to choose Edinburgh for medicine; it was recognized as the leading medical school in Britain in the early 19th century. Ward visits were conducted daily in the hospital by physicians and surgeons who shared responsibilities with the resident physician or "clinical clerk." Such a policy had been firmly established in Edinburgh a generation before it was adopted by London hospitals.

Following graduation, Hall was appointed resident physician at the Royal Infirmary for a 2-year period. He left Edinburgh in

1814 with a fine reputation, undoubtedly related to an outstanding series of contributions on the "Principles of Diagnosis." These were expanded shortly after into a remarkable text on diagnosis.[1] After the

Composite by G. Bako

customary tour on the Continent, the circuit including the medical schools in Paris, Berlin, and Göttingen, Hall returned to Nottinghamshire for a decade of practice as a provincial physician. The final professional move to London, possibly because of the influence of Matthew Baillie, was motivated by the yearning for greater opportunities as a consultant, just as he had been attracted to Edinburgh for medical training as a youth.

The *Memoirs of Marshall Hall* was prepared by his widow and published 4 years after his death.[2] "May we not hope that the ennobling one afforded by the life of Marshall Hall may not be without its good effect." The notable contributions to medicine recounted by Green on the centenary of Hall's death include the physiological changes accompanying hemorrhage, reflex action,[3] and observations on the pre- and postcapillary vessels of the arterial and venous systems. Observations on the hiber-

nation of mammals and amphibians and participation in the founding of the British Medical Association were recorded as lesser achievements.

His *Researches, Chiefly Relative to the Morbid and Curative Effects of Loss of Blood,*[2] presents several astute observations on bloodletting:

A rule by which the detraction of too much or of too little blood is equally avoided. The patient is placed sitting perfectly upright looking upwards, the arm being previously prepared, the blood is allowed to flow from a *free* opening to incipient syncope. If there be inflammation, and youth, and strength, there is great tolerance of loss of blood, and much blood flows before syncope is induced; this is precisely what is required in such cases. If, instead of inflammation, there be only irritation, there is early syncope from the flow of blood, and the vital fluid is economized, the just and proper quantity still, however, being taken.

The studies on the reflex action were received with greater acclaim on the Continent than at home. The aphorism of the prophet was exemplified once more. In England, Hall was "the object of obloquy, and denounced as the propagator of absurd and idle theories." It had been previously determined that the brain was not essential for reflex action. The observation by Hall was accidental.

. . . whilst examining the pneumonic circulation in the Triton. . . . It was during the course of this investigation that I was struck with the fact which led to the discovery of the Spinal System.

The decapitated triton lay on the table. I divided it between the anterior and posterior extremities, and I separated the tail. I now touched the external integument with the point of a needle; it moved with energy, assuming various curvilinear forms! What was the nature of this phenomenon? I had not touched a muscle; I had not touched a muscular nerve; I had not touched the spinal marrow. I had touched a cutaneous nerve. That the influence of this touch was exerted through the spinal marrow was demonstrated by the fact that the phenomenon ceased when the spinal marrow was destroyed. It was obvious that the same influence was reflected along the muscular nerve to the muscles, for the phenomenon again ceased when these nerves were divided. And thus we had the most perfect evidence of a reflex, or diastaltic, or diacentric action.

The first publication of this discovery appeared in the *Proceedings of the Committee of Science of the Zoological Society,* from a paper given in 1832.[2] The views were expanded in a communication to the Royal Society and were published in the *Philosophical Transactions* the following year.[3] This paper was translated and published in Müller's *Archiv für Anatomie, Physiologie und Wissenschaftliche Medicin.*[4] In 1837, a second paper on the subject was presented to the Royal Society but was rejected by the Council and not placed in the record. In spite of pleas by the author, the observations and the communications were not accepted by contemporary British scientists— a reflection, according to Green, of the sad general state of the Royal Society at that time.

An unsigned biographical sketch of Hall published in the *Lancet* in 1850 probably reflects the appraisal of Thomas Wakley, the editor.[5]

... the most important of all Dr. Marshall Hall's discoveries; that which will henceforth rank him with Harvey in the field of science and experiment, because, like Harvey, he has, by inductive reasoning, clearly developed A NEW SYSTEM— a system all-important in itself, and almost equally so in relation to the other systems of the animal frame. On this splendid discovery—this solid basis—Dr. Marshall Hall's future fame will rest, and descend to posterity.

Wakley continued, with the gratuitous remarks:

How much does our profession owe to an independent medical press—and how much, not infrequently, is owed to opposition itself! ... but we have likewise always predicted that such opposition would weigh as nothing in the balance against the triumphant establishment of the great FACTS and TRUTHS advanced by these two eminent men (Hall and Dr. Robert Lee). But without a truly independent medical press, these truths could not have been so boldly advanced nor so widely disseminated; and we have often heard Dr. Hall express his deep sense of obligation to THE LANCET, in coming to his aid on the side of truth and justice.

In 1831, Hall's observations on the circulation of blood were published.[2]

I proposed to trace the anatomy and physiology of the vessels placed between the last terminations of the arteries and the first beginnings of the veins more distinctly than had been done before. I chose the batrachia as the subjects of my experiments, and traced, under the microscope, the circulation of the minute vessels placed intermediately between the arteries and veins, both in regard to their anatomy and their anatomy and physiology.

I soon discovered that these vessels are not only extremely minute and *capillary,* but totally distinct, both from the artery whence they arise, and the vein whither they tend. The characteristic of the artery is to divide continually into minuter branches; whilst that of the vein is to unite continually into larger trunks.

Two types of hibernation were recognized in a comprehensive study of the effect of varying degrees of cold upon the dormouse, hedgehog, and the bat.[6]

In the sleep of the hybernating animal, the respiration is more or less impaired: if the animal be placed in circumstances which best admit of observation, the acts of respiration will be found to have greatly diminished; ... if its temperature be taken by the thermometer, it will be found to be many degrees lower than that of the animal in its active state; if it be deprived of atmospheric air, it is not immediately incommoded or injured. ... There is an important distinction between true hybernation and torpor from cold (hypothermia). ... Severe cold, like all other causes of pain, rouses the hybernating animal from its lethargy; and, if continued, induces the state of torpor.

The above recounting of critical observations in comparative physiology was prepared by a practicing physician more than a century ago. Hall was a prolific writer and a wise observer in a number of areas. Between 1812 and 1857 he published more than 100 scientific contributions, which included studies on the eye, the larynx, the puerperal state, diseases of women, the action of ergot and strychnine, a new operation for naevus, esophageal vomiting, tetanus, spasmodic tic, on the influence of the mind on the body, the ethics of animal experimentation, epilepsy, asphyxia, artificial respiration for drowning, and the disposal of sewage in London. Nonmedical subjects included a dissertation on slavery in the United States following an extensive tour of this country and several letters to the editor of the London *Times.* According to Riese,[7]

... for the first time in the history of neurology, the concept of the reflex arc was adopted, the basic mechanism of nervous disease, and this makes Marshall Hall the Father of Modern Neurology, although as a neurophysiologist, he had his predecessors.

1. Hall, M.: *On Diagnosis,* London: Longman, Hurst, Rees, Orme, and Brown, 1817.
2. Hall, C.: *Memoirs of Marshall Hall,* London: Richard Bentley, 1861.
3. Hall, M.: Reflex Function of the Medulla Oblongata and Medulla Spinalis, *Phil Trans Roy Soc London,* 1833, p. 635.
4. Green, J. H. S.: Marshall Hall (1790-1857): A Biographical Study, *Med Hist* 2:120 (April) 1958.
5. Biographical Sketch of Marshall Hall, M.D., F.R.S., editorial, *Lancet* 2:120, 1850.
6. Hall, M.: On Hybernation, *Phil Trans Roy Soc London,* 1832, p. 335.
7. Riese, W.: History and Principles of Classification of Nervous Diseases, *Bull Hist Med* 18:483 (Dec.) 1945.

Composite by G. Bako

John Haygarth (1740-1827)

JOHN HAYGARTH, born at Garsdale, Yorkshire, was educated at Sedbergh School, where he became one of the select pupils of John Dawson, physician and mathematician.[1] An interest in the systematic study of quantitative data may have led him to compile vital statistics in support of a program planned to prevent the spread of febrile contagion and the establishment of the Society for Promoting General Inoculation in the Prevention of Smallpox in Chester. After graduating BM at St. John's College, Cambridge, Haygarth studied in Edinburgh and London and returned to Chester in 1767 as a practicing physician. Besides Dawson, John Fothergill of London, who was in the habit of spending his summer holidays in Chester, was the second friend and professional confidant whose influence on Haygarth was profound.

Haygarth's scientific studies began with his meticulous documenting of the clinical data of patients under his care. The case records of symptoms, clinical course, and remedies applied were prepared in Latin in order to retain their confidential nature. As early as 1774, his quantitative data justified the segregation of wards for fever patients; whereas in his *Inquiry,* published in 1784, more than a decade before Jenner's observation on the cowpox, he discussed the unequivocal progress of the Society against smallpox and advanced logical arguments for isolation of patients in a campaign for prevention. His critical findings, of which several remain valid nearly two centuries later, were clearly stated.[2]

Before this society commenced, half as many children under ten years old, died of the Smallpox, in Chester, as of all other diseases. It is, beyond all comparison, the most mortal Pestilence that has visited this island for more than a century past. Your proceedings have clearly proved, that it is medically possible to exterminate this Pestilence. You have seen, not only the medical principles, but the practical rules so firmly built, on the foundation of facts, that they can never be shaken by any temporary or local prejudice.

II. The Small-pox was never known, since its original commencement, to be produced by any other cause than infection.

VI. Persons, liable to the Small-pox, are infected by breathing the air, impregnated with variolous miasms: Either (I) very near a patient in the distemper, from about the time that the eruption has appeared, 'till the last scab is dropt off the body; or (II) very near the variolous poison, in a recent state; or (III) that has been close shut up, ever since it was recent.

VII. Clothes, furniture, food, &c. exposed to the variolous miasms, never, or very rarely become infectious.

IX. Consequently, the Small-pox may be prevented, by keeping Persons, liable to the distemper, from approaching within the infectious distance of the variolous poison, till it can be destroyed.

Haygarth practiced in Chester until 1798, when he moved to Bath and continued his crusade. The communication detailing the rules for prevention of spread of the infection to the noninfected infirmary patients was read to the Literary and Philosophical Society of Bath and was based upon his experience with the fever wards of the Chester Infirmary.[3] The number of patients ill of fever at the Infirmary before the enforced isolation averaged approximately 44 patients per month for three 8-month periods each. This number decreased to fewer than three patients per month after construction of the fever wards.[3]

Rules for the Fever Wards; to prevent the Infection of other Patients in the Chester Infirmary.
I. Fresh water and coals are to be brought up to the Fever Wards every morning and other necessaries on ringing a bell.
II. No Fever patients, nor their nurses, are suffered to go into other parts of the house. No other patient is allowed to visit the Fever Wards; nor any stranger, unless accompanied by the apothecary or his assistant.
III. Every patient, on admission, is to change his infectious for clean linen; the face and hands are to be washed clean with warm water, and the lower extremities fomented.
IV. All discharges from the patients are to be taken out of the ward as soon as possible.
VII. Blankets, and other bed and body clothes, are to be exposed to the open and fresh air for some hours, before they are used by another patient.
VIII. All the bed clothes of the Fever Wards are to be marked Fever Ward, and all the knives, forks, pots, cups, and other utensils, are to be of a peculiar colour, lest they be inadvertently taken among other patients.
X. No patient can be suffered to wear, nor any acquaintance to take away, any linen unwashed, nor other clothes, till they have been long exposed to the fresh air.

With dissemination of Jenner's discovery of the value of the cowpox lymph, Haygarth turned to the study of acute rheumatic fever, chronic arthritis, and the preparation of the *London Pharmacopoeia*. Although he gave an acceptable description

of the clinical findings of acute rheumatic fever, including an inciting pharyngitis, tachycardia, leukocytosis, good prognosis, and pulmonary involvement, he did not clearly differentiate between nodosity of the joints in rheumatoid arthritis and osteoarthritis.[4]

VII

Hence it is manifest that this Fever [acute rheumatic fever] is most frequent in the five cold months of December, January, February, March, and April, . . . no part of the year is exempt from this malady.

X

Hence we learn that persons who have been previously affected with the acute or chronical Rheumatism, the Gout, or sore throat, especially the first, are most liable to suffer attacks of this disease, and ought therefore to be particularly careful to avoid exposure to cold and moisture.

XVI

Out of 93 cases only 5 had a pulse below 72 in a minute; the most frequent number was from 84 to 107, comprehending 47 being a full half of these patients; however in 29, being near one-third, the pulse had a greater frequency, from 108 to 130.

XVII

In 31 cases the blood had an inflammatory crust [buffy coat], which in some was very dense.
Hence it appears that 23 out of 25 patients ill of the acute Rheumatism were restored to health in one month.
No. 17. A young lady of 16, who had for ten years been subject to wandering pains, was attacked by a Rheumatick Fever, with pain and swelling of her hands, feet, &c.; shortness of breath; vomiting of food and drink. . . . On the 10th day of the Fever, and 5th inclusive after I saw her, the swelling of the hands receded; her breath became shorter, with a cough and spitting of blood, which soon terminated fatally. The rheumatick inflammation seems here to have been translated from the joints to the lungs.

In specific reference to nodosity of the joints, a portion of the description suggests osteoarthritis; other comments suggest rheumatoid arthritis; whereas either possibility is clearly differentiated from gout.[4]

IX. This disease has hitherto passed under the name of Gout or Rheumatism, or perhaps has been most commonly called Rheumatick Gout. But as several advantages would result from a separation of this disorder from others with which it has been confounded, I have ventured to call it the *Nodosity of the Joints.* Under this application, as a distinct *Genus,* it will become a more direct object of medical attention.

The Nodes appear most nearly to resemble Gout. Both of them are attended with pain and swelling of the joints: but they differ essentially in many distinguishable circumstances. 1. In the Gout, the skin and other integuments are generally inflamed with pain which is often acute, soreness to the touch, redness and swelling of the soft parts, but in no respect like the hardness of bone. 2. The Gout attacks the patient in paroxysms of a few days, weeks, or months, and has complete intermissions at first for years, but afterwards for shorter periods. 3. The Gout attacks men much more frequently than women.

These Nodes are clearly distinguishable from Acute Rheumatism, because they are not attended with Fever. The tumour of the joints is much harder, more durable, and less painful in the former than the latter disease.

I do not recollect that in cases of Nodes, any notice is taken of that pink-coloured sediment in the urine [uric acid], which appears in Gout, or in Acute Rheumatism.

1. Elliott, J.: A Medical Pioneer: John Haygarth of Chester, *Brit Med J* 1:235-242 (Feb 1) 1913.
2. Haygarth, J.: *An Inquiry How to Prevent the Smallpox, and Proceedings of a Society,* Chester: J. Monk, 1784.
3. Haygarth, J.: *A Letter to Dr. Percival, on the Prevention of Infectious Fevers,* Bath: R. Cruttwell, 1801.
4. Haygarth, J.: *A Clinical History of Diseases,* 1. *A Clinical History of the Acute Rheumatism.* 2. *A Clinical History of the Nodosity of the Joints,* Bath: R. Cruttwell, 1805.

Johann Peter Frank
(1745-1821)

JOHANN PETER FRANK, considered by many to be the founder of modern public health, was born in Rotalben near Zweibrucken into a large family of German and French descent.[1] His professional life was spent in writing, teaching, and practice in this chronological order; meanwhile, his influence spread among several university centers in Europe. While his father wished him to follow a trade, his mother hoped that his life would be spent in the Roman Catholic Church and directed his elementary education to the latter goal. He studied first at the Piarist Latin School in Rastadt and later at the Jesuit School in Bocken-

heim, Lorraine. Johann was encouraged to develop his soprano voice and to study music. A frail constitution was aggravated by quartan fever as a boy and gouty arthritis in his later years.

Composite by G. Bako

Frank's higher education, begun in Metz in 1761, continued the following year in Pont-à-Mousson, where he was attracted especially to physics. With the degree of philosophy at the age of 18 he began the study of medicine at Heidelberg. After two years of study and discouraged by the unprogressive medical curriculum, he completed his training with a final year at the University of Strassburg. In 1766, in Heidelberg, Frank in defending his multiphasic thesis included a discussion of the clinical management of juvenile appendicitis and condemnation of the opponents of smallpox inoculation. This interest in such practical matters as clinical medicine, to be sure, was included in his professional repertory. However, his great work embraced a much more ambitious program.

Encouraged by an older brother, Frank took a French degree at Pont-à-Mousson in order to qualify for medical practice at Bitsch, Lorraine. Unable to enjoy stability of residence, however, he moved from place to place in his mature years as he had during his education. After two years at

Bitsch, he returned to Baden, Germany, to practice. By then, his mind was bent on the preparation of an encyclopedic treatise of public health: the immediate subsequent events merely strengthened these interests. The loss of his wife from puerperal fever within one year of marriage and the death of the child a few months later turned his attention to the study of obstetrics and midwifery in relation to public health. Frank was appointed director of the Midwives Association in Baden and was commissioned by the court at Rastadt to investigate an epidemic of typhus fever in Gernsbach. Later he was appointed court and garrison physician and in 1772, served as town and country physician in Bruchsal. Since Frank was placed in charge of the military hospital and the home for the sick-poor, his clinical experience was enhanced. The following year he was appointed physician to the Prince-Bishop of Speyer who supported him in his health reform measures; among these was the founding of a school of obstetrics in which Frank was an active faculty member.

In 1779, the first volume of his encyclopedic *System einer vollständigen medizinischen Polizey* appeared.[2] More than a decade had been spent in preparation and several years in finding a publisher. Any literal translation into English of "medizinischen Polizey," *Medical Police,* remains unsatisfactory. "Preventive medicine," "public and private hygiene," policed medicine," "governmental medicine," and "state medicine" have been suggested, but each has serious deficiencies in relation to Frank's concept of his mission. "Public health by decree" seems the best interpretation, but this too is inadequate. Sound as were his recommendations, his concept of public and private health measures lawfully enacted and enforced by public officials is only partially fulfilled two centuries later. He introduced the subject with a discussion of the necessity of political action during the maturation of civilization.[3]

The internal security of the State is the aim of my general science of police [hygiene]. An important part thereof is the science which will enable us to further the health of human beings living in society and of those animals they need to assist them in their labours and for their entertainment, acting in accordance with definite principles; consequently we must promote the welfare of the population by means which will enable persons cheerfully and for lengthy periods to enjoy the advantages which social life can offer them without suffering unduly from the vicissitudes and the variations to which social life cannot fail to expose them as soon as they have resolved to tame the wildness of nature and to renounce certain advantages which in no department were so overwhelming as under the rude and strenuous conditions of human beings before they became artificialised.

By 1788, when the fourth volume of the encyclopedic work was published, Frank's teaching and writing had commanded the attention of several university centers, and, almost simultaneously, he received offers from the University of Mainz to serve as professor of physiology and preventive medicine and from Göttingen and Pavia, as professor of clinical medicine. Although he was a Catholic, he rejected the offer from Mainz and chose Göttingen, the famous Protestant university. Moving there in 1784, he made regular ward rounds and delivered lectures on general and special physiology, pathology, and therapeutics. The work was arduous and left him little time for writing or promotion of his program of national health reform. Since the post in Pavia had remained unoccupied following Tissot's retirement, Frank accepted it after one year at Göttingen. The change in languages was no problem, inasmuch as he possessed varying degrees of fluency in Italian, English, and Dutch as well as Latin, German, and French.

At Pavia, Frank administered the hospital, taught in the medical school, and eventually was promoted to the post of director-general of all medical affairs in Austrian Lombardy and in the duchy of Mantua. One of his first chores was upgrading the medical faculty. He established new professional chairs, elevated the standards of the practice of midwifery, and founded a museum of pathological anatomy, a new surgical clinic, and an apothecary school. Students of internal medicine were directed to attend the surgical lectures and vice versa. Recognized widely as an expert in the construction of hospitals and clinics he found his professional advice was sought beyond the environs of Pavia.

During this period, the first volume of his treatment of diseases of man *De curandis hominum morbis epitome* appeared. In addition to expanding it into six volumes and translating it into several languages Frank published the first volume of his *Delectus opusculorum medicorum* etc., a collection of clinical lectures and case reports. Twelve volumes appeared between 1785 and 1793. However, disheartened by the interfaculty feuds and bickering at Pavia in 1795, he accepted the offer of the directorship of the Allgemeines Krankenhaus in Vienna and a professorship in the University.

In Vienna Frank reorganized the staff, had a new postmortem room built, complemented by a museum of pathological anatomy, and increased the beds available for clinical instruction. In 1800, an epidemic of smallpox gave Frank an excellent opportunity to inoculate with Jenner's new material. The following year the government issued a decree recommending inoculation generally—one of the few examples of implementation of Frank's work. After nine years in Vienna his popularity waned. As anti-Frank intrigue increased, he sought solace in Russia. One year at the University of Vilna was sufficient, followed by an appointment in St. Petersburg as physician-in-ordinary to the Czar and director of the Medico-Surgical Academy.

Troubled by gout and waning energies, Frank sought easement from administrative duties for his pressing literary labors. Rejecting a request from Napoleon to live in Paris as his physician, he retired to Freiburg to complete the fifth volume of his *System*. In 1811, weary of Freiburg as he had wearied of other places, Frank returned to Vienna, resumed a large clinical practice, prepared his sixth volume, and remained in the Austrian capital until his death.

The subjects discussed in his *System* are markedly diverse. Frank judged it the duty of the Establishment to carry out the needed reforms in the prevention of disease and maintenance of sound health and hygiene.

The subject headings in the eight sections, prepared in Latin and translated into French as well as German,[2] but not into English, include: population problems, comprehensive vital statistics, control of prostitution, longevity, health of school children, family size, premarital sex education, hygiene in the home, taxation of bachelors, harmful effects of celibacy among priests and soldiers, hazardous sports, contamination of beer and wine by improper storage, poisoning of fish in polluted water, potable drinking water, suitable clothing for pregnant women, infant and maternal welfare, limitation of the responsibility of midwives, protection and care of illegitimate children, selection of wet nurses, spread of disease by travelers, value of outdoor exercise, disposal of sewage and garbage, inspection of food, proper diet, and control of adulterated food. This listing is but a sample of the entire contents.

Essentially unrelated to his great efforts in the advancement of public hygiene, Frank was a sound clinician; he was a consultant in demand and an enlightened therapist. In his six-volume treatise on *The Treatment of Diseases of Man,* he presented discussions of a variety of conditions including a tangential discussion of diabetes insipidus under the heading of the general group of diabetes, which to him differed from diabetes mellitus only in the absence of sugar in the urine. Pertinent excerpts containing an interesting speculation on pathogenesis follow.[4]

The subdivisions of diabetes depend on the quality and external modifications of the excreted urine which may at times be insipid, clear as water, at other times as sweet as honey.

Physicians of olden times did not know about abnormal quality of urine excreted by diabetic patients. Generally, even though I and other observers have occasionally seen cases of completely insipid urine without a trace of sweetness, in most cases the pale, serous, and clear urine had honey-like or sugar-line taste; at times it may have the peculiar sweetness similar to the taste of sap which flows in the spring from birch trees.

The main illness becomes worse if diarrhea sets in—I have seen this in one case of diabetes insipidus—but, on some occasions, as other observers have maintained, the polyuria may subside with benefit to the patient.

Diabetes, which I call insipidus, or the false diabetes, is difficult to explain, but it is impossible that in some cases a moderate quantity of sugar-containing chylus seeps into the blood and that it is assimilated at a higher rate than in diabetic patients in whom the chylus appears in the urine.

1. Frank, J. P.: *Biography of Dr. Johann Peter Frank Written by Himself* (Ger), Vienna: K. Schaumburg & Co., 1802, trans G. Rosen, *J Hist Med* 3:11-46, 279-314, 1948.
2. Frank, J. P.: *System of Comprehensive Medical Police* (Ger), Mannheim, Tubingen, Wien, 1779-1827.
3. Sigerist, H. E.: *The Great Doctors,* New York: Doubleday & Co., Inc., 1958.
4. Frank, J. P.: *The Treatment of Diseases of Man* (Ger), bk 5, Berlin: G. Fincke, 1830, excerpt translated by Z. Danilevicius.

Composite by G. Bako

John Brown (1735-1788)

THE BRUNONIAN THEORY OF MEDICINE, a mixture of good and bad concepts, was developed by John Brown during his suffering and convalescence from an attack of gouty arthritis. The new doctrine enoyed its peak of popularity in the latter part of the 18th century but was not rejected finally until long after Brown's death. Meanwhile,

it had generated much controversy and had gained converts and equally vehement antagonists. The University of Göttingen was one of the last strongholds of the cult, the disappointing and delusive theory having been shown by von Helmholtz to be contrary to the natural laws of chemistry and physics.

John was born of humble parents in the parish of Buncle in Berwickshire, Scotland. His father was a day-laborer and in religious devotion followed the teachings of the seceders, the Whigs of Scotland. Furthermore, he was determined that his son would receive a good religious education and arranged for formal teaching at a younger age than usual. By the age of five when his father died, John had read almost all of the "Old Testament."[1] Tutored by the Latin scholar Cruikshank of the Dunse grammar school, he soon advanced to the head of the class. Meanwhile, endowed with a prodigious mind and a photographic memory, he could repeat long passages verbatim after a single reading. His body was as strong as his mind, as reflected in skill at wrestling and boxing. But, in spite of his brilliance and diversified interests, he was removed from school to learn the weaver's trade. John soon rejected the shuttle and the loom, and at the age of 13 was allowed to return to school where he became a pupil-teacher.

At the age of 18, Brown departed for Edinburgh to attend lectures in philosophy and divinity, supporting himself by tutoring students in Greek and Latin. The serious study of medicine was undertaken at the age of 24 at the feet of Cullen and the Monros, of the distinguished Edinburgh faculty. He especially enjoyed the intimacy of the Cullen family and, in turn, was charged with supervising the education of their children. Brown's fluency in Latin was appreciated by Cullen and was sought by the students for the composition of their inaugural dissertations. This splendid state of friendship with Cullen dissolved as Brown developed his new theory of medicine, which was in conflict with Cullen and his disciples. Thus, Edinburgh seemed closed to Brown for a degree, and in 1779 he took the MD from St. Andrew's. Although demonstrating talents and great capacity in pedagogy, he was never elected to an academic post. Nevertheless, he became a member of the students' Royal Medical Society of Edinburgh and served as president in 1776. By then his new theory of medicine, later described in his *Elementa medicinae* and composed in pure Latin style, had been graciously received by some and disputed by others. The appraisal by one reviewer, his eldest son, 25 years after the publication of the controversial treatise, disclosed that the work was intended by the author: [2]

... to exhibit the outlines of a system for some years taught at Edinburgh, and which, it was fondly imagined, was to effectuate a complete revolution in the principles, as well as in the practice, of medicine.
In spite of the most liberal and persevering opposition, in spite of faction, persecution, and inquisitorial authority, it has, we are told, found its way into every part of the world where literature and science prevail. Every where, but especially on the continent, it has gained numerous proselytes and warm friends.

Brown became bolder as the result of his newly-gained popularity, and, as the schism with Cullen widened, he composed two rebuttals that were critical of the current teaching at Edinburgh. *Observations on the Present System of Spasm as taught in the University of Edinburgh* (1787) was purported to be an exposé of Cullen's misapprehensions in his critique of the *Elementa Medicinae*. Also, *An Inquiry into the State of Medicine, on the Principles of Inductive Philosophy* (1782), appeared under the nom de plume of Robert Jones. William Cullen Brown believed, as did others, that the author was the senior Brown.[1] *A Treatise on the Gout* was an unfinished manuscript, in which Brown fell into theorizing that a common affiliation existed between gout and a great number of unrelated diseases.

To further complicate a complicated life, Brown incurred heavy debts, had a large family to support, and in 1786 chose London over Edinburgh where he tutored in his home and developed a small private practice. Also, he drank too much wine and consumed too much opium in the attempt to control the pain of his acute gouty ar-

thritis. The first attack appeared when Brown was 35. Having been intemperate in food and wine for several months, leading to the first attack, the pendulum swung full range, and he pursued an abstemious regimen. A second attack of gout was treated also by abstention, without substantial effect upon the articular distress. The paradoxical result gave rise to his considering that the pathogenesis related to indirect debility rather than to an excess of vigor. He returned to a high-protein diet and was liberal with wine and opium. Proceeding from this personal experience, a theory of medicine was developed and diseases were segregated into "sthenic" and "asthenic" groups. The weaknesses of former methods were exposed and a number of cures proposed. Living tissues were believed to be inherently endowed with excitability, a reinterpretation of Haller's irritability. The excitability resided in the nervous system and in the muscles, and thereby was evenly distributed throughout the body. The reaction of stimulation and excitability led to excitement. The quality of the stimulant was unimportant; it was the quality that was determinative.

The brunonian theory may be illustrated by excerpts from his discussion on gout, a malady assigned to the asthenic group.[3]

Of the Gout of weakened Persons.
DCXIII. The gout of weakened persons, which is an increased degree of the gout of strong persons, is that asthenia, in which the inflammation runs out to greater length, and at last, does not form at all; and the general affection increases in violence, in obstinacy, and, at last, attains its highest degree; exhibiting, towards the end of the disease, almost all the symptoms of debility, every form of asthenia, and sometimes by a false resemblance, counterfeiting synocha.

DCXV. For the cure of them all, abstinence, fatigue, evacuations, acids, and acescents, cold, directly and indirectly debilitating passions, the debility arising from exertion of the intellectual function, and impurity of air, must be avoided. The cure of every one of them must be stimulant. When each of them is but slight, beef soup and similar rich ones, which act partly by dilution, partly by a nourishing and stimulant operation, in the weak state of the stomach, and by supporting the system, and afterwards, when the strength is so far recovered, solid animal food, and moderately diluted drink, which, at last, confirm the strength, are sufficient. In a higher degree of violence of any of them, while the soups should still be continued, at the same time pure strong drink should be administered. And when the violence of any case baffles this whole form of stimulus, recourse must be had to musk, volatile alkali, camphor, aether, and opium.

John Brown, the Paracelsus of Scotland and a student of Edinburgh, was a hard-drinking opium user and suffered with gout. He proposed the brunonian theory of excitability, which dominated medicine for more than a quarter of a century before its inherent fallacy was exposed. Brown was a talented teacher but never held a senior academic post; he disseminated his theory through public lectures, tutees, and books, of which the most famous was *Elementa Medicinae*.

1. Brown, W. C.: The Works of Dr. John Brown, 3 vol, London: J. Johnson, 1804.
2. The Works of Dr. John Brown, *Edinburgh Med Surg J* 1:357-375, 1805.
3. Brown, J.: *The Elements of Medicine; or, a Translation of the Elementa Medicinae Brunonis*, Philadelphia: T. Dobson, 1795.

F. J. V. Broussais (1772-1838)

FRANCOIS JOSEPH VICTOR BROUSSAIS, a stormy medical figure in early 19th century France, was born at St. Malo, son of a Breton physician to be later killed by the Royalists. Following exposure to medicine as an apprentice in his father's practice, he served in combat as a sergeant in the Republican Army.[1] In 1792, he studied in the hospital of St. Malo and gained experience as a naval surgeon against the British in government vessels as well as with privateers. Broussais went to Paris in 1800 and in 1803 received the MD degree, working under Bichat, Corvisart, and Pinel. He then spent three years campaigning with Napoleon's forces. During these years he was developing, without experimental evidence, his theory of disease. After the fall of the Emperor in 1814, Broussais returned to Paris and joined the medical faculty at the mili-

tary hospital at Val-de-Grâce. In 1831, he became professor of general pathology and therapeutics in the Paris Faculty of Medicine. By this time, his unscientific pathological concepts had been generally rejected.

Composite by G. Bako

Broussais' theory of medicine, described as medical physiology, appeared first in monographic form in 1808 and attracted erudite followers as well as violent antagonists. Broussais lambasted the concept of disease entities and advanced the belief that particular diseases, even those with well defined pathological changes, represented nothing more than degrees of irritation from excitation or stimulation. Irritation gave rise to inflammation, whose primary site in most diseases was in the gastrointestinal tract. Tuberculosis, syphilis, acute fevers, and cancer were nonspecific conditions and little more than varied tissue responses to localized irritation. As an atheist Broussais denied Nature's healing powers and sought to abort sickness by stringent measures, employing powerful antiphlogistics, disseminated leeching, and debilitating regimens, which deprived patients of vital nourishment and strength.

Broussais' popularity waned after a generation of broadsides and polemics. His theories gave way to the initial phases of scientific medicine exemplified by Corvisart, Laennec, Louis, etc. An English translation by Hays and Griffith of Broussais' *Principles of Physiological Medicine* appeared in 1832. The exposition of his theory which encompasses the exanthemata is excerpted as follows:[2]

Active morbid congestion being always the companion of super-excitation or super-irritation, it suffices to name this last to be understood in developing the progress of diseases: we may even, to be more brief, content ourselves with the word irritation, provided the same signification is attached to it as to these two preceding expressions; but the epithet morbid must always be understood.

The long-protracted use of excitants of all kinds almost always terminates by elevating the sensibility of the mucous membranes to a degree which renders the functions of the organs very painful. As the stomach is, of all the viscera, that which is most exposed to super-stimulations, it is also this viscus that furnishes the most frequent examples of this vicious exaltation of sensibility.

Intense irritations of all organs are constantly transmitted to the stomach from their very commencement; hence results loss of appetite, alteration of the colour of the tongue and of its mucus: if the irritation received by the stomach attains to the degree of inflammation, symptoms of gastritis appear, and as then the brain is always more irritated, it develops in a higher degree the sympathies which are proper to it and may even become inflamed.

No extra-cerebral inflammation can produce mania without the concurrence of inflammation of the stomach and small intestines; and the liver in this case is affected only secondarily.

All the *essential* fevers of authors are referrible to simple or complicated gastro-enteritis.

It is by an acute gastro-enteritis, the primary effect of the contagious virus, that small-pox makes its first appearance. Cutaneous inflammation replaces the gastro-enteritis, and puts an end to it when the pustules are few in number.

Rubeola and scarlatina commence with gastro-enteritis, and by an acute catarrhal inflammation of the eyes, schneiderian membrane, throat or bronchiae.

1. Bayle and Thillaye: "Francois-Joseph-Victor Broussais" (Fr), in *Biographie Medicale*, vol 2, Paris: A. Delahays, 1855, pp. 875-882.

2. Broussais, F. J. V.: *Principles of Physiological Medicine in the Form of Propositions* (Fr), I. Hays, and R. E. Griffith (trans.), Philadelphia: Carey & Lea, 1832.

Composite by G. Bako

Robert E. Watt (1774-1819)

ROBERT WATT, physician and biographer, was born in the parish of Stewarton, Ayrshire, Scotland, on a farm near the family of Robert Burns, who were also engaged in living off the soil.[1] Robert Watt left school at the age of 12 and served at times as a plowboy, stone-dyker, road builder, and cabinet maker. Even when engaged in manual labor he found time to read and contemplate good books. In 1793, having been tutored each morning in Greek and Latin by a schoolmaster in Stewarton, he entered Glasgow University and won a prize for excellence in Greek. In 1795, he attended Edinburgh University and studied moral and natural philosophy, pointing toward the ministry. But learning was not exclusively in the humanities; some time was spent in an anatomy class, and he finished with a small prize for an essay on "Regeneration." By 1799, Watt, having studied sufficient medical subjects, abandoned thoughts of a career in the church and qualified as a licentiate with the Faculty of Physicians and Surgeons of Glasgow. He then set up practice near Glasgow, in Paisley (famous for the cashmere pattern of weaving), and began a medical-literary career.

The first major work by Watt, *Cases of Diabetes, Consumption . . . with Observations on the History and Treatment of Diseases in General,* was published in 1808. By then he had been appointed a member of the Faculty of Physicians and Surgeons on the basis of his clinical experience and reputation. Without further study, he received the degree of MD in 1810 from King's College, Aberdeen, and resumed practice in Glasgow. Sensing the need for a list of the best authors and titles on the practice of medicine, he published, in 1812, a catalog of 1,066 medical books for the use of students attending lectures. The catalog, rare in the first edition, was reprinted in facsimile in 1950.[2] In the preface in his address to medical students, Watt noted:

In prosecuting the study of Medicine, you are no doubt actuated by a laudable ambition to rise to eminence in that profession. Besides, the personal considerations of an honest frame and a handsome income, you have the pride of upholding the dignity of a science which, amid all the revolutions of society, has obtained the confidence and the esteem of mankind. Trusting that such are your motives, I shall attempt to direct your views to that path by which you may most successfully reach the objects of your pursuit.

These men, whose respectability and wealth you admire, obtained not the enviable situation they now hold, because they wished to be rich and respectable; but because they loved their profession with ardour and pursued it with zeal. The envy and spite of disappointed rivals may tell you otherwise; but depend upon it, that the industry which arises from a love of your profession, is the TRUE path, I may almost say the ONLY path, which leads to respectability.

In every age and in every Sect in Medicine you will find many useful authors. Observe their facts, however lightly you may esteem their reasoning. In all cases, where it is practicable, acquire information at first hand. Scrutinize with accuracy, and form your own judgment. It is this frame of mind, this faculty of discrimination, which distinguishes the man of genius from the dull imitator, the dogmatist, and the empyric.

The following year Watt published his *Treatise on the History, Nature, and Treatment of Chincough.*[3] He discussed the derivation of the term and in the appendix concluded with an epidemiological observation on the incidence of smallpox and measles. From a review of the registers in the burying grounds, he observed a marked increase in measles and a decline in smallpox following the wide practice of vaccination with cowpox.

This disease has been known by a great variety of names. In Britain it has been promiscuously denominated the Hooping cough, the Kink-cough, and the Chincough. The first of these terms, I believe, is the one most generally employed, though perhaps, the most exceptionable of the three.

It has been termed Hooping cough, because the patient, during the fit of coughing, produces a peculiar sound, or what has been denominated a *hoop,* in drawing in his breath.

The term Kink-cough is mostly confined to Scotland. It is derived from the circumstance, that the cough returns in paroxysms. The first part of the term is a Scotch word, synonymous with fit or paroxysm, and is not applied to coughing alone; but to some other involuntary or convulsive motions, and particularly such as produce noise.

The word Chincough is the ancient English expression for the disease, . . . Dr. Johnson thinks, that the first part of the term may probably come from the Dutch word *kinckin,* which signifies to pant.

Another derivation is given, which appears to be still more ridiculous, . . . The disease is supposed to consist chiefly in an affection of the spine. The spine consisting of several parts joined to one another, like so many links, has been supposed to resemble a chain. Hence we are told, that the disease ought to be, and was originally termed *Chain*-cough; but by a corruption of language, it has come to be spelled and pronounced Chincough.

The Latin terms for Chincough are still more numerous than the English. From the celebrated Sydenham we have *Pertussis,* . . . From the illustrious Willis we have *Tussis Convulsiva;* from Hoffman *Tussis Convulsiva* sive *Ferina.* From others we have *Tussis Clangosa, Tussis Perennis, Tussis Amphimerina, Tussis Suffocativa, Tussis Puerilis, Tussiculosa,* &c.

The first thing which strikes the mind on surveying the preceding Table, is the vast diminution in the proportion of deaths by the Small Pox; a reduction from 19.55 to 3.90; but the increase in the subsequent column is still more remarkable, an increase from .95 to 10.76. In the Small Pox we have the deaths reduced to nearly a fifth of what they were five years ago; in the same period, the deaths by Measles have increased more than eleven times.

In 1814, Watt was elected president of the Faculty of Physicians and Surgeons and physician to the Royal Infirmary of Glasgow; from 1816 to 1817 he was president of the Glasgow Philosophical Society. Upon completion of the term of office, he withdrew from practice, retired to a suburb of Glasgow, and devoted the remaining years of his life to the preparation of *Bibliotheca Britannica,* a monumental bibliography of Greek, Latin, and English classics, art, and science, comparable in this country in medicine to the *Surgeon General's Catalog,* which appeared half a century later. Only a few pages of *Bibliotheca Britannica* went to the printers before Watt's death, but the basic work was Watt's. The manuscript was left in a state of readiness and was published in Edinburgh in 1824. The first two volumes listed the authors; the second two volumes, the subjects, with cross-reference to the first volumes. The work is still a useful library tool for general international literature published prior to 1819. The slips of paper, the basis of the original manuscript, remained in the possession of Watt's daughter and, at her death in 1864, were found in two large sacks. Following discovery, they were bound in 69 volumes and were acquired by the Paisley Public Library.

In the charge to subscribers of Volume 1, dateline Glasgow, April 14th, 1819, representatives of the university, the church, and the city of Glasgow reported certain vital statistics in the preparation.[4]

> The Author, we understand, devoted the greater part of the last twenty years of his life, to the collection and arrangement of the necessary materials; and, of these *the whole* has been copied *thrice,* and some parts of them even *six and seven times.* During the last four years, his son has been engaged, under the direction of his father, in forwarding and completing the work; and, from the experience which he has thus had, as well as in other respects, we have no doubt of his qualifications for perfecting what yet remains to be done, in adding the new publications which may make their appearance during the progress of the work through the press.
>
> It is with sincere satisfaction we thus state our conviction, that this important work is not likely to suffer from the decease of its Author— and it is, at the same time, our earnest desire and hope, that his bereaved family may reap, both in credit and emolument, the fruits of the courage which projected, and the industry which completed, a publication, which we are satisfied, will, on several accounts, form a very valuable acquisition to the Literary World.

1. Finlayson, J.: *An Account of the Life and Works of Dr. Robert Watt, Author of the 'Bibliotheca Britannica,'* London: Smith, Elder & Co., 1897.

2. Cordasco, F.: *A Bibliography of Robert Watt, M.D., Author of the Bibliotheca Britannica,* New York: W. F. Kelleher, 1950.

3. Watt, R.: *Treatise on the History, Nature, and Treatment of Chincough,* Glascow: J. Smith & Son, 1813.

4. Watt, R.: *Bibliotheca Britannica; or a General Index to British and Foreign Literature,* Edinburgh: A. Constable & Co., 1824.

Composite by G. Bako

Thomas Joseph Pettigrew
(1791-1865)

T. J. PETTIGREW claimed no fundamental contributions in the basic sciences or clinical medicine, but, because of his reputation as a medical biographer and renown as an antiquarian, he is one of the better-known English physicians of the 19th century. The Medical Portrait Gallery contains plump biographies of 68 celebrated physicians and surgeons, including his own.[1] In addition, he prepared the critical data on more than 500 physicians and surgeons for Rose's *Biographical Dictionary.*

Thomas was born in Fleet Street, London, the son and grandson of naval surgeons, was educated at a private school, and began dissection and the study of anatomy with William Hilliard, a surgeon. At the age of 14, he temporarily abandoned formal schooling to assist his father in the care of the inmates of the workhouse and the poor of a large parish. A passion for anatomy found expression in the examination of those who died in the workhouse where no restriction was placed upon postmortem inquiry. He advanced in the study of anatomy and clinical medicine in the private anatomy school of John Taunton, skilled practitioner and unlettered surgeon of the City and Finsbury Dispensaries and founder of the City of London Truss Society. Visiting the sick for Pettigrew began at 6 AM, followed by lectures in such diverse subjects as anatomy, physiology, surgery, medicine, materia medica, chemistry, and midwifery. Private patients were seen in the United Borough Hospitals of St. Thomas' and Guy's.

In proper time, Pettigrew completed his preparatory training, began the practice of medicine, and, as one of his first clinical assignments, assisted in the establishment of a dispensary for diseases of children, which became the Royal Infirmary for Diseases of Children in Waterloo Road. Subsequently, he resigned this position, was elected surgeon to the Asylum for Female Orphans, and became affiliated with the West London Infirmary, the forerunner of the Charing Cross Hospital. Here he was responsible for a course on anatomy and physiology and lectures in surgery and practical medicine. He was also interested in comparative anatomy, particularly in preparation of the medical section of the *Encyclopedia Metropolitana,* projected by his friend Samuel Taylor Coleridge. Somewhat removed from teaching and clinical practice were the postmortem examinations of the animals that died at the Exeter Change Menagerie. At one time, his dissecting room was filled with an extraordinary collection of dead mammals—a lion, a tiger, a leopard, a bear, and a monkey. Medical jurisprudence was another neglected subject not intimately related to clinical medicine at that time, according to Pettigrew. The anniversary oration at the Medical Society of London was delivered by Pettigrew on this thesis in 1819.

Pettigrew's interest in writing and literature may be traced to his study of Greek, Latin, and philosophy and to the formal duties imposed upon him as an officer of the Medical Society of London, The City Philosophical Society, and the Philosophical Society of London. His first medical communication, *Views of the Basis of the Brain and Cranium, accompanied with Outlines, and a Dissertation on the Origins of the Nerves, interspersed with Surgical Observations,* was published at the age of 18, followed by his election to membership in the Royal College of Surgeons. Fellowship in the Royal Society was offered him more than a decade later. As one of the secretaries and later registrar of the Medical Society, it was necessary for Pettigrew to record minutes of the discussions, conduct the domestic correspondence, edit the transactions, and assist the members in their researches. At the age of 17, he prepared the first lecture to the City Philosophical Society. The topic of insanity was chosen for personal reasons; the discourse was prepared after extensive investigation in the archives. Pettigrew had suffered from poor health, nervousness, and severe headaches, and he feared dire consequences. The Philosophical Society of London also was addressed by Pettigrew at its first meeting, with his subject entitled, "On the Objects of Science and Literature and the Advantages Arising from the Establishment of Philosophical Societies." *Memoirs of the Life and Writings of the Late John Coakley Lettsom,* in three volumes, was his most comprehensive biography.[2]

The Duke and Duchess of Kent made Pettigrew their surgeon, and, in turn, he vaccinated their daughter, later Queen Victoria, with lymph obtained from one of the grandchildren of Dr. Lettsom. Following the death of the Duke of Kent, his brother, the Duke of Sussex, continued the royal appointment and, in addition, that of cataloguer of the library in Kensington Palace. The bibliographic assignment was accepted, although Pettigrew's family was growing and his practice was demanding more of his time. Plans were prepared for segregating the books and publishing a catalogue. Volume 1 of *Bibliotheca Sussexiana* appeared in two parts. Part 1 listed the theological manuscripts, numbering 12 Greek, 148 Latin, 51 Hebrew, and 86 miscellaneous copies of the *Old* or *New Testament*. Short biographical sketches of the authors or transcribers were included in the catalogue. The second part of volume 1 described many of the theological books, many set in letterpress type. It is ironical that Pettigrew, still lacking a doctoral degree in medicine, received the doctorate of philosophy from the University of Göttingen for his literary scholarship rather than for his medical contributions. Turning from teaching, practice, and the preparation of medical biographies to antiquarianism, he prepared a treatise, *A History of Egyptian Mummies*,[3] was a founder of the British Archeological Association, and contributed regularly to their periodical. In spite of the great interest in Egyptian archeology, Pettigrew never visited Egypt but accumulated his knowledge from reading, conversing with Egyptologists, and unwrapping mummies in England.[4]

In his autobiography Pettigrew gives his views on a literary career, complementary to teaching and practicing.[1]

I know an impression prevails that it is impossible for a man who devotes his attention to literary subjects, or the various branches of general science, to become a skillful practitioner. I have particularly noticed this subject in my Memoir of the late Dr. Thomas Young, who justly ranks as one of the most brilliant contributors to the annals of science and literature. I am fully aware that my own professional practice in private life has been more limited than might otherwise have been the case, had my attention to literature and general science been less than it has been. Wealth, however, with me has always been, and I trust will ever continue to be, a secondary consideration. I have never placed it in competition with reputation or the pleasures which result from the exercise of intellectual pursuits; and if I have not been overwhelmed by professional labours, I have at least had it in my power to cultivate learning, and to associate with many of those whose names adorn the pages of our literature and science. The opportunities that have offered to me in this respect have not been neglected, and I have the happiness to rank among my friends a large number of the most distinguished in literature, art, and science. The respect entertained for me by these, constitutes one of my chiefest sources of delight; but it is in the bosom of my family, where I happily find that which is paramount to every thing else, and in attending to the education of my children, I feel that I am best following out the destiny of my nature.

1. Pettigrew, T. J.: *Biographical Memoirs of the Most Celebrated Physicians and Surgeons,* 4 vol, London: Whittaker & Co., 1840.
2. Pettigrew, T. J.: *Memoirs of the Life and Writings of the Late John Coakley Lettsom,* 3 col, London: Nichols, Son, and Bentley, 1817.
3. Pettigrew, T. J.: *A History of Egyptian Mummies,* London: Longman, Rees, Orme, Brown, Green, and Longman, 1834.
4. Pettigrew, T. J.: *Chronicles of the Tombs,* London: H. G. Bohn, 1857.

Composite by G. Bako

Pierre Bretonneau (1778-1862)

PIERRE-FIDELE BRETONNEAU, physician of Tours, believed to have been the first to identify specific features of diphtheria and typhoid fever, completed a successful tracheotomy in a child with diphtheritic croup nearly a century and a half ago, and advanced the doctrine of specificity of disease before the general acknowledgement of the germ theory of infectious maladies. Bretonneau was born at St. Georges-sur-Cher into a family that claimed 15 practitioners of the healing arts in nine generations.[1] Although he did not learn to read until he was nine years of age, he acquired from his father a taste for natural history and medicine. Selecting the latter for a career, Pierre began the study of medicine at the age of 17 at the École de Santé in Paris, where his fellow student included Dupuytren and Bayle.

Before Bretonneau had completed three years of study, ill health and a prolonged convalescence at home forced him to interrupt his work. While at home he was exposed to the gracious life of Mme. Dupin, the châtelaine of Chenonceaux, once one of the most beautiful and wittiest women of her day, then an old lady but in full command of her faculties. She taught Bretonneau Italian and English, the art of conversation, and drawing room affectations. After her death in 1799, he completed his medical studies in Paris, passed some of his examinations in brilliant style, but failed in botany, a favorite subject. Without a doctorate he returned to Chenonceaux to practice, served as sanitary officer, and pursued several avocations including instrument making, chemistry, horticulture, drawing, painting, and bee-keeping. He forged his own cataract needles, designed capillary tubes for storing vaccine lymph, and constructed thermometers and barometers for friends. In practice his reputation spread rapidly, which in turn brought his talents to the attention of influential citizens of Tours; consequently, they encouraged him to become chief of medicine in their hospital. To meet this challenge he completed the requirements for the doctorate in Paris and was awarded the degree in 1814.

At the age of 37, Bretonneau changed from provincial practitioner to teacher of bedside medicine, peripatetic clinician in the morgue, and compiler of pertinent clinical-pathological observations on diphtheritis and dothienenteritis. The teaching and the care of the sick at Tours was an integrated assignment. Hospital visits began at 6 AM. Bretonneau was unhurried in his clinical examination of the patients with infectious diseases in whom he was particularly interested. He practiced an informal Socratic method of teaching, sometimes continuing from the hospital wards into his botanical garden. Detailed clinical reports, correlating clinical observations with findings in the morgue, were prepared in longhand. The worth of his instruction may be appraised by the accomplishments of two of his pupils, Velpeau and Trousseau, who became outstanding physicians in their maturity and to whom Bretonneau owed much for their respect and loyalty.

The two diseases in which he was most interested appeared periodically in epidemic form in the communities where he practiced and taught. He was in Chenonceaux during the typhoid epidemics of 1802 and 1812. From the hospital at Tours he witnessed the typhoid epidemic of 1819 and the 1818-1820 epidemic of malignant sore throat. In each instance the high mortality and required postmortem study of the dead provided abundant pathological specimens.

As a result of his clinical-pathological studies of malignant croup, two communications were presented in 1821 to the Royal Academy of Medicine in Paris. He proposed the name diphtheritis (diphthérite) from the Greek meaning leathery skin; however, the term was changed later to diphtheria (diphthérie) at the suggestion of Velpeau and others. The reports were not published until 1826.[2] A free translation of the 1826 communication was prepared by the New Sydenham Society in 1859[3]; while Major, in *Classic Descriptions of Disease,* follows the original more closely.[4] Several excerpts from Major are followed by a single paragraph from Semple.

1. The communication which I have the honor of submitting to the judgment of the Academy, is based on a collection of observations upon special inflammations of the mucous membranes. All of the work tends to prove that many of the inflammatory lesions of the mucous membranes have been confused, also that the variations of the same affection have often been mistaken for different diseases.

2. The inflammations of the mucous membranes show just as varied characteristics as cutaneous inflammations, whose classification has tested the talent of the nosographers. The exudation which accompanies them presents itself some marked differences, sometimes it is a thin fluid, . . . At other times it is a membraneous substance closely adherent, or indeed, a membraneous film, simply attached.

3. Far from entering into these distinctions and insisting upon the difference of the inflammatory processes of the mucous membranes, I undertake now to prove the evidence of facts that scorbutic gangrene of the gums, croup and malignant angina are nothing but a single and identical type of inflammation. These facts which are assembled from numerous researches of

pathological anatomy, have been noted and collected, during the course of an epidemic, which raged in Tours from 1818 until 1820, and they have been collected either in the town, with a population of twenty-odd thousand, or at the hospital, where the number of patients varied from one hundred and twenty to four hundred.

5. Sixty autopsies have been made in the course of the epidemic. If the examination of viscera, which during life showed no signs of disease, has been occasionally neglected, at least, the state of digestive tract and the air passages have been studied with great care.

6. I am led to carry my researches upon the bodies of those who have shown particularly the characteristic symptoms of croup, or those of malignant angina, either where there was no attempt to arrest the progress of the disease, or when it has been vainly combatted by active and opposing medications. I have been able to follow, in a large number of subjects, the varied modifications of the disease until its perfect cure obtained under the influence of special, general, or local treatment. One hundred and thirty soldiers and twenty individuals, of every age, have shown diverse variations pellicular chronic, or scorbutic gangrene, limited to the mouth, or extending to the larynx and not differing in the latter case from gangrenous angina.

As it is impossible to apply to a special inflammation which is so well-marked, any one of the improper names which have been given to each of its varieties, let it be permitted me to designate this phlegmasia by the name of Diphthérite, derived from διφθερα, pellis, exuvium, vestis coriacea whence comes διφθερoω, corio obtego.

A case description, communicated to the Academy in July 1825, presents a child, aged four, critically ill from diphtheritic croup who was subjected to tracheotomy, a procedure previously performed successfully by Bretonneau on animals. A curved silver cannula was inserted on the seventh day of the disease when the patient was in critical respiratory difficulty. By the fourth day after insertion, improvement was sufficient to permit temporary withdrawal of the cannula for cleaning. On the 11th day after the operation, the cannula was removed and not replaced.[2]

Seventh day: at 4 A.M., after two hours of sleep, dry cough, wheezing inspirations; the lips and the body became purple; crying and alternating spells of convulsive cough were followed by expectoration of membrane-like tenacious masses. Imminent danger forced me to prepare for tra-

cheotomy. . . . The bluish pallor of the face, which indicates progressing asphyxia, did not permit delay.

On the basis of experience from animal experiments, with successful tracheotomy, I modified the operation in this instance.

I proportioned the size of the canula to the size of the trachea; and in order to make it easier to insert and to maintain I designed it cylindrical, slightly flattened and curved along its length, and beveled at an angle at each end.

The head was held back by an aid in a fashion to force forward the deep portion of the neck . . . the incision, made along a perviously marked line, extended from the inferior border of the thyroid to the suprasternal fossa. Five rings of the trachea were divided and a curved silver canula was placed in the airway. Respiration became calm, easier, and the oozing of blood gradually ceased.

The canula was held in place by a twisted string, tied around the neck and passing between the rings protruding at the orifice.

Immediately after the dressing was applied, the child asked for a drink and lifted the glass to the lips with own hands.

A second tube, closely adapted to the canula, which can be removed and cleaned with ease, helps to avoid the inconvenience of displacement of the canula which, although not painful, caused considerable discomfort. I had this second tube prepared by a skillful craftsman, but it was too late to be of any use in this patient.

Bretonneau's studies on typhoid fever were published in 1826 by Trousseau. Bretonneau assumed responsibility of authorship in his address to the Academy in 1829, the same year Louis differentiated typhoid from typhus and gave it its present name. Louis made no reference to Bretonneau's earlier observations and overlooked the role of contagion in the disease. Trousseau's communication contains the substance of Bretonneau's conclusions supporting the specificity of dothienenteritis (typhoid), determined on the basis of clinical-pathological findings.[5]

The long and useful work of Dr. Bretonneau has finally cleared up this question. Since 1813 he has collected a large number of cases in his civil practice, as in the hospital at Tours, at whose head his merits have placed him.

He has been led to distinguish a disease, the seat of which appears to be exclusively in the glands of Peyer and Brunner, which one finds in the jejunum, ileum and large intestine. He has given this affection the name of dothi[e]nenteritis (from δοθιην-button, postule, furuncle; and εντεοον-intestine). He has indicated the relationships, traced the symptoms and described with precision, the appearance of the disease, which changes on successive days. He has stressed so well, all of the essentials of the diagnosis, that few of his pupils, or of the great number of those who have had knowledge of his researches and ideas, cannot [but] distinguish perfectly well in most cases, from all other forms, this form of enteritis which is so common. . . . if one visualizes that his disease is just as common and no less murderous than smallpox, measles and scarlet fever, that few people go to the end of their life without having experienced its attack, that it enjoys, as well as the cutaneous inflammation, which I am going to decribe, the singular character of affecting an individual only once during life, and perhap of a contagious nature that it is nothing else than *febris putrid genuina*.

I would not feel that we had completed the picture of pathological alterations peculiar to the inflammation, some of whose characteristics I have just described, if I did not briefly indicate the point of the election of the dothi[e]nenteritic eruption. Dr. Bretonneau and after him all of his pupils, who at Tours or Paris or in the army, have carried on researches upon dothi[e]nenteritis, have always noted that the last position of the ileum was constantly involved, that the dothi[e]-nenteritis inflammation would not occupy more than three, six, or ten inches of the small intestine. These were the third, sixth or tenth last inches of the ileum, that the eruption was invariably more confluent when one examined the internal membrane close to the ileo-caecal valve: that the stomach, the duodenum, the first part of the jejunum, has never shown any papillary inflammation in dothi[e]nenteritis, that in the large intestine the eruptive dothi[e]nenteritis inflammation was more confluent as it approached nearer the cecum; that never, in this disease, had spontaneous perforation taken place, elsewhere than in the center of a gland of Brunner or of an ulcerated gland of Peyer.

Without doubt it would have been better to have let M. Bretonneau himself, publish his ideas on dothi[e]nenteritis; this physician has traced with more clearness the picture of the changes which follow this important disease. But it is important, both for the glory of my Master, and for science, to present a glimpse of the important work, to which he has placed his hand. This conscientious practitioner, who believes it would be false to the principles of his profession, if he would establish a law, which was not for him, the expression of the entire truth, carries on each day new researches, adds to them, compares them, and enriches them with new facts and waits before submitting his work to the judgment of the public, until he, himself, judges it worthy of being presented.

In spite of his world-wide renown gained during 23 years on the hospital staff at Tours, his lack of acceptance by the local practitioners led to his resignation in his prime. In order to substantiate his conclusions and to refute the scoffing by professional associates at his postmortem deductions, he resorted to the exhuming of the recent dead to obtain evidence supporting his contention that the pathological findings of the sick at home were similar to those of the sick in the hospital. At the age of 60, he studied Greek better to search the ancient manuscripts on infectious diseases and, as a result, found in his opinion what he considered to be the first description of diphtheria by Aretius. He was wildly eccentric in his habits of eating and sleeping and marriage. His first wife, a companion of Mme. Dupin, was 25 years his senior, while his second wife was a young girl, aged 18, whom, in spite of the protests of his friends, he married at the age of 78. He was not embarrassed when he fell asleep in the midst of conversation or in consultation and immediately upon awakening resumed the thread of conversation. He disliked useless discussion, was reluctant to participate in formal consultations, and showed little respect for wishes of others. Bretonneau cared little for money, never pressed the matter of fees, and was generous to the poor—another feature of a singular combination of characteristics of a French physician of note.

1. Triaire, P.: *Bretonneau et ses Correspondants*, Paris: F. Alcan, 1892.

2. Bretonneau, P. F.: *Special Inflammations of the Mucous Membranes, and in Particular Diphtheria, or Pellicular Inflammation* (Fr), Paris: Crevot, 1826, excerpts translated by Z. Danilevicius.

3. Semple, R. H.: *Memoirs on Diphtheria. From the Writings of Bretonneau*, etc., London: The New Sydenham Society, 1859.

4. Major, R. H.: *Classic Descriptions of Disease*, ed 3, Springfield, Ill.: C. C Thomas, 1945, pp 157-161, 182-184.

5. Trousseau, M.: Concerning the Disease to Which M. Bretonneau . . . Has Given the name of Dothi[e]nenteritis (Fr), *Arch Gen Med* 10:67-78, 169-216, 1826, translated in Major.[4]

Composite by G. Bako

John Keats (1795-1821)

JOHN KEATS, Frederick von Schiller, and Oliver Goldsmith are examples of illustrious poets who chose a career in medicine before they deviated to another professional path. Exposure to 18th or early 19th century literature probably began in college for most of us. A few were exposed at home to Keats and Shelley in days when reading from the Bible before breakfast, reading from the masterpieces of the literary geniuses during library hours, or even serious dinner conversation of contributions to *Harper's Weekly or Atlantic Monthly* were proper. Almost every physician has read Gray's "Elegy Written in a Country Churchyard." Not all have understood the implications. Possibly the "beatnik" of the 18th century could have interpreted word, phrase, and paragraph correctly, or incorrectly, depending on his obtuseness, but interpreted it, nevertheless.

Walter A. Wells[1] has described the medical findings of the events leading to the death of John Keats, one of the greatest 19th century poets, but has made no pretense of interpreting his poetry. The Aesculapian poet died at the age of 25. He had spent a greater amount of precious time in his apprenticeship as an apothecary and

practicing physician than was allotted to him in the fulfillment of his burning desire to compose metric verse—either that which rhymed or that which conveyed to the reader a new thought, an inspiration, or his elucidation and interpretation of truth by means of blank verse. At the age of 20 years Keats wrote:

> O for ten years, that I may overwhelm
> Myself in poesy; so I may do the deed
> That my own soul has to itself decreed.

Keats became an apprentice apothecary-surgeon at the age of 17 and acquired practical medical experience in this apprenticeship for four years. After two years of observing, he was permitted to practice as a medical assistant. This was followed by the equivalent of an internship at the Borough School of Medicine, an affiliation of Guy's and St. Thomas' hospitals. The editor of the *Lancet* for many years, Thomas Wakley, was a fellow novitiate. They studied under the intellectual tutelage of Sir Astley Cooper. This famous English surgeon was so impressed with Keats that he arranged to have him live with Cooper's cousin George Cooper. Other attending physicians besides Sir Astley Cooper at Guy's Hospital at that time were Richard Bright, Thomas Addison, and Thomas Hodgkin. But all was not serious with Keats! On one of the blank pages of a chemistry textbook he wrote,

> Give me woman, wine and snuff
> Until I cry, 'Hold, Enough.'
> You may do so *sans* objection
> Until the Day of Resurrection.

Another classmate was John W. Webster, subsequently the professor of chemistry at Harvard College and later murderer of George Parkman, benefactor of Harvard College and donor of the building site for Harvard Medical School (formerly called The Massachusetts Medical College) in 1846.

More than five years of medical training and medical practice were sufficient for Keats. At the age of 23 he turned from medicine to poetry and permissible passion. At least three burning loves have been described. The deep emotional desires may have been related to his overwhelming illness, pulmonary tuberculosis. Other patients afflicted with this malady have experienced an insatiable sexual urge. Several of Keats' family had died of tuberculosis before Keats succumbed. During the last months of his life his money was spent, his love affairs were past history, and, in spite of his multiple adversities, his greatest poems, "Endymion" and "Hyperion," were produced. Security need not be indispensable for intellectual fecundity.

1. Wells, W. A.: Doctor's Life of John Keats, New York, Vantage Press, Inc., 1959.

William Withering
(1741-1799)

DIGITALIS, one of the most useful drugs in the practice of medicine and one of the few naturally-occurring substances with a specific action, is derived from the foxglove. Although William Withering is closely associated with the scientific introduction of the active principle of the digitalis plant into clinical medicine, the botanical had been used empirically by herbalists for an unrecorded period of time in the treatment of epilepsy and healing of wounds, and as an expectorant. Digitalis derives its name from the foxglove blossoms, folk's-glove (fairies' glove), or ladies' thimbles. Because of this resemblance, Fuchs, a German physician and botanist, gave the plant its scientific name, digitalis, in 1542. A number of potent cardiac glycosides have been isolated from the plant. These include digitalin, digitoxin, digitonin, gitalin, and the lanatosides.

William Withering, the physician, was a man of many talents.[1] His contributions in botany rank just below his skill and fame as a practitioner. He was an able mineralogist, chemist, musician, and meteorologist. William was born in a family of physicians. His maternal grandfather had delivered Samuel Johnson. His father was a successful physician at Wellington in Shropshire. William's early education was upper class, which included the classical languages, mathematics, geography, and history. In this pursuit he was an average student and gave no indication in his premedical years of the stature that was awaiting him in maturity. At the age of 21, he entered the University of Edinburgh, a school that had great appeal for a number of English students in the 18th and 19th centuries.

Several influences may be traced to the Edinburgh days. Withering's interest in botany in subsequent years most assuredly was related to John Hope. He also became a golfer and learned to play the Scottish national instrument, the bagpipes. Withering graduated from Edinburgh with the degree of "Doctor of Physic" at the age of 25. His inaugural dissertation was prepared in Latin and concerned streptococcal laryngitis. Although Withering was proficient in Latin, his attitude towards this and other languages was rather neutral. Following graduation he established a practice in Stafford, not far from Wellington. During the earlier years, this practice permitted him leisure time for nonclinical activities, particularly botany. This was strengthened by his attraction to one of his lady patients who was interested in flower painting; their mutual attraction resulted in marriage. On house calls and during his spare time, he collected specimens for his herbarium and for his bride-to-be.

Withering's first major scientific contribution was in botany, not medicine. In 1776, he published a monograph on the flora of the British Isles entitled, *A Botani-*

cal Arrangement of All the Vegetables Naturally Growing in Great Britain with Descriptions of the Genera and Species According to Linnaeus. Osler indicated that this treatise was the standard reference work in botany for many years in Britain. Withering designed a microscope specifically for the study of botanical specimens. This instrument was described in the first edition of the *Encyclopedia Britannica.* Other interest included analyses of mineral water from spas and watering places, the solubility of salts, Peruvian bark, and urinary calculi. The discovery of native barium carbonate (witherite) and the description of baryta as a test for sulfates were noteworthy scientific accomplishments.

Although Withering had a wife, a home, and a satisfactory practice in Stafford, he was receptive to an offer from Erasmus Darwin of Birmingham of greater clinical opportunities. The grandfather of Charles Darwin sponsored Withering in Birmingham, where his practice expanded rapidly. Within a short time, his services as a consultant had wide appeal. He joined the select Lunar Society, an organization which met at the homes of the members, usually once a month in the full of the moon. The members included James Watt, the inventor of the steam engine; Josiah Wedgwood, the pottery manufacturer; Dr. Small, one-time professor of Natural Philosophy at William and Mary College, Williamsburg, Virginia; Baskerville, the printer; and Joseph Priestley, the discoverer of oxygen. A popular guest at one of the meetings was Benjamin Franklin. Franklin also consulted Withering by letter regarding the treatment of his urinary calculi, related no doubt to Franklin's gouty arthritis.

Withering began the use of foxglove in the treatment of dropsy in 1775, the year before he moved to Birmingham. He describes the evidence to support such clinical trial: [3]

In the year 1775 my opinion was asked concerning a family recipe for the cure of dropsy. I was told that it had long been kept a secret by an old woman in Shropshire who had sometimes made cures after the more regular practitioners had failed. I was informed also that the effects produced were violent vomiting and purging; for

the diuretic effects seemed to have been overlooked. This medicine was composed of twenty or more different herbs; but it was not very difficult for one conversant in these subjects to perceive that the active herb could be no other than foxglove.

A decoction of foxglove was used initially. This was replaced by an infusion, and later the simplest preparation which remains today a standard item—dried leaves of the foxglove. The leaves were gathered just before the blossoming of the plant. The midrib was removed; the leaf blade only was used. The dosage recommended is valid in current therapy, 1 or 2 grains, twice a day. Withering recognized that slow digitalization required several days.

Equally important was his appreciation of, and caution against digitalis toxicity. Digitalization was effective until evidence of its action upon "the kidneys, the stomach, the pulse, or the bowels" was apparent; then it was to be stopped. The discussion of digitalis intoxication ranks with the recognition of the value of this agent in cardiac failure. [3]

I have lately been told that a person in the neighborhood of Warwick possesses a famous family recipe for the dropsy, in which the Foxglove is the active medicine, and a lady from the western part of Yorkshire assures me that the people in her county often cure themselves of dropsical complaints by taking Foxglove tea. In confirmation of this I recollect about two years ago being desired to visit a travelling Yorkshire tradesman. I found him incessantly vomiting, his vision indistinct, his pulse 40 in a minute. On enquiry it came out that his wife had stewed a large handfull of green Foxglove leaves in half a pint of water and given him the liquor which he drank at a draught, in order to cure him of an asthmatic affection. This good woman knew the medicine of her county, but not the dose of it, for her husband narrowly escaped with his life.

Digitalis was included in the Edinburgh *Pharmacopoeia* in 1783, although no published announcement by Withering was made until his monograph in 1785. This was prompted as much by his desire to caution the medical profession against digitalis intoxication as to acquaint them with his clinical experience. One associate who urged him to publish his findings was Fowler of Fowler's solution fame, the first to study systematically the value of arsenic in the practice of medicine. Digitalis intoxication as described by Withering was associated with vomiting, purging, confused vision (objects appearing green or yellow), slow pulse (35 or less per minute), cold sweat, convulsions, syncope, and death. Any one of the symptoms might appear individually and should be interpreted as overdosage, at which time the drug was to be discontinued.[3]

Let the medicine therefore be given in the doses, and at the intervals mentioned above:— let it be continued until it either acts on the kidneys, the stomach, the pulse, or the bowels; let it be stopped upon the first appearance of any one of these effects, and I will maintain that the patient will not suffer from its exhibition, nor the practitioner be disappointed in any reasonable expectation.

For the last 15 years of his life, Withering was incapacitated intermittently by a chronic cough, bronchiectasis, hemoptysis, and other evidence of pulmonary tuberculosis. He was buried in a vault at Edgbaston Church. The Foxglove adorns the commemorative tablet in the church and shares honors with the emblem of Aesculapius. A pun composed at his death, repeated in a number of his biographical sketches, is worthy of repetition: "The flower of English medicine is Withering."

1. Cushny, A. R.: William Withering, *Proc Roy Soc Med* 8:85-94, 1915.
2. Roddis, L. H.: William Withering and the Introduction of Digitalis into Medical Practice, *Ann Med Hist* 8:93-112 (March) 185-201 (May) 1936.
3. Withering, W.: *An Account of the Foxglove, and Some of its Medical Uses: with Practical Remarks on Dropsy and Other Diseases,* Birmingham: M. Swinney, 1785.

Joseph Leopold Auenbrugger (1722-1809)

AUENBRUGGER, born at Gratz in Styria, Austria, the son of an innkeeper, studied medicine at the University of Vienna, a pupil of Van Swieten. During his affiliation with the Spanish Hospital in Vienna, he became intrigued with the variation in percussion notes over different areas of the chest. He sensed the possibility of interpreting clinical findings, antemortem, in terms of structural changes in the sick at the time

National Library of Medicine

in history when observations of the pulse and respiration were the principal tools of examination of patients suffering from diseases of the chest. Nor did percussion require more complicated devices. The fingers and the ears of the physician were the only requirements for this new technique. Knowledge of sound and acoustics, an interest in music, and his familiarity with the significance of the tapping of wine barrels in his father's inn, helped Auenbrugger develop the science of percussion. An empty barrel or a normal chest gave a resonant sound on percussion. A barrel filled with wine or the pleural cavity with an effusion gave forth a different percussion note. He was also able to outline the size of the heart in the healthy or diseased state.

Seven years were required to develop the methods, check on autopsies, and experiment on cadavers at the Spanish Hospital and prepare the treatise which was published in Latin in 1761. Auenbrugger used only 1200 words to state the purpose of his communication and the interpretation of his experimental findings. This short tome elicited some praise but more criticism. The unpopularity of his discoveries was responsible for his forced resignation from the hospital and his assumption of full-time practice in Vienna.

Almost 50 years elapsed before clinicians accepted his method of examination and used it in clinical diagnosis and treatment. The French, led by Corvisart, physician to Napoleon I and the outstanding medical leader in France at that time, were the first to accept the new technique. The original treatise was revised and expanded by Corvisart into a volume of more than 400 pages supplemented by his personal observations. Auenbrugger died in 1809, only a few months after Corvisart's translation was published. The introduction of percussion into England was delayed until after the translation into English by Forbes and publication in 1824. Auenbrugger published other contributions in medicine and at least one libretto, to Salieri's opera "The Chimney Sweep."

There were 14 brief sections in the Observations by Auenbrugger. The natural sounds of the chest and the method of percussion were included in the first two Observations. In the third, fourth, and fifth Observations he discussed the changes produced by acute or chronic disease. Emphysema, pericardial effusion, and aneurysm of the heart (dilatation and hypertrophy) were described, as well as rupture of the pleura, and scirrhous lesions of the lungs.

The thorax of a healthy person sounds, when struck. . . . The sound thus elicited from the healthy chest resembles the stifled sound of a drum covered with a thick woolen cloth or other envelope. . . . The sound is more distinct in the lean, and proportionately duller in the robust; in very fat persons it is almost lost.

The thorax ought to be struck, slowly and gently, with the points of the fingers, brought close together and at the same time extended. . . . During the application of percussion the patient is first to go on breathing in the natural manner, and then is to hold his breath after a full inspiration. The difference of sound during inspiration, expiration, and the retention of the breath, is important in fixing our diagnosis.

For I have learned from much experience that diseases of the worst description may exist within the chest, unmarked by any symptoms, and undiscoverable by any other means than percussion alone.

Auenbrugger, endowed with great clinical capacity, introduced into clinical medicine one of the important techniques of examination. He was forced to resign his position in the hospital because of the controversy raised by his startling discovery. Even Van Swieten was skeptical of the value in diagnosis. Thereafter, Auenbrugger devoted himself to the practice of medicine and the enjoyment of music in the golden splendor of Vienna late in the 18th and early in the 19th centuries. Earlier he had found favor with Empress Maria Theresa and Emperor Joseph raised him to noble rank in 1784.

1. Auenbrugger, L.: *New Observations on Percussion of the Chest* (L), Vindobonae, J. T. Trattner, 1761.

2. Sigerist, H. E.: *On Percussion of the Chest, Being a Translation of Auenbrugger's Original Treatise Entitled,* "Inventum Novum ex Percussione Thoracis Humani, ut Signo Abstrusos Interni Pectoris Morbos Detegendi," (Vienna, 1761) by John Forbes, (London, 1824), Baltimore: The Johns Hopkins Press, 1936.

3. Neuberger, M.: Leopold Auenbrugger's *Inventum Novum Facsimile of the Original Publications with translation in French, English and German* (Ger), Vienna and Leipzig, Safar, 1922.

Composite by G. Bako

Jean-Nicholas Corvisart
(1755-1821)

CORVISART, physician to Napoleon and rediscoverer of Auenbrugger's studies on percussion, published one of the first treatises on heart disease in modern medicine, 150 years ago. Born in the village of Dricourt, then a part of Champagne but now in the Department of Ardennes, he was not particularly gifted in his early schooling. A professed interest in medicine and attendance at medical clinics in the Paris hospitals appeared only after he began the study of law. This preference for medicine angered his father, who refused to continue financial support. Without funds or friends, Corvisart obtained employment, shelter, and training at Hôtel Dieu, the oldest hospital in Paris. In return for services as a male nurse, he received bed and board and an opportunity to continue medical training.

It is easy to believe that Corvisart's talents were soon recognized, and he became a favorite pupil of A. Antoine Louis and Petit, but especially of Desault and Desbois de Rochefort.[1] Corvisart finished school, the youngest in his class but the first in scholarship. In 1785, at the age of 30, the degree of Doctor-regent was awarded by the Paris Faculty of Medicine. His doctoral discourse contrasted the pleasures of medical study with the disappointments in medical practice. In seeking a postgraduate hospital appointment, Corvisart was rejected by the director of the new Necker Hospital because of his refusal to wear a powdered wig. In 1788, he was appointed physician to the Charité Hospital, and in 1797 accepted the professorship of medicine at the Collège de France, where his great skill as a teacher insured him professional success.

Corvisart's most famous patient was Napoleon Bonaparte when he was First Consul. With the formation of the first Empire, the Emperor appointed Corvisart his personal physician and chief physician to the court and to the Empress. Napoleon, with more than the average interest in morbid states and quick to pose medical questions, had greater faith in his physician than in the practice of medicine generally. Napoleon suffered at least two significant illnesses which responded to Corvisart's clinical skill. On one occasion the Emperor was stricken with what has been interpreted as bronchial pneumonia. Later, following his triumphal entry into Vienna in 1809, the Emperor suffered a neurodermatitis on the nape of the neck. In each instance, when summoned to his side, Corvisart offered wise counsel. As personal physician to the royal house, Corvisart received an annual salary of 30,000 francs, and was created a baron and an officer of the Legion of Honor. He was bold enough to advise the Emperor against marriage to Marie-Louise, and to advise the Empress against following Napoleon to Elba. Corvisart retired from active practice following Napoleon's abdication.

The manner of bedside teaching, in the style of Sydenham, for which the Paris School of Medicine was famous for a century, was described in the first issue of the first volume of the *New England Journal of Medicine and Surgery* in 1812.[2]

Although the subject of diseases of the heart has been heretofore ably treated, especially by Senac and Morgagni, yet very much remained to be learnt when Corvisart took it up. . . . While the anatomy of the heart and the uses of its various parts have been as well, or perhaps better understood than those of any other organ, its diseases have passed comparatively unobserved; and even while many great men, and great medical men too, have been suffering and sinking under the ravages of those diseases.

Pupils of Corvisart at the bedside and in the morgue included Bretonneau, Bouillaud, Dupuytren, Bichat, Bayle, and Laennec. His teaching at the Charité, more than that of any other contemporary, made this a famous center of clinical instruction. The translation into French of Auenbrugger's masterpiece on percussion of the chest happened more than 40 years after the first edition of Auenbrugger was published. Corvisart's rediscovery of the significance of percussion was complemented by the observations of his pupil Laennec on auscultation. The value of Auenbrugger's discovery was discussed in his *Aphorisms,* which were translated into English and appeared in an American edition.[3]

Percussion of the thorax is the best touchstone which we possess to enable us to recognize many of the diseases of that cavity or to clarify our knowledge of such a lesion It allows one to estimate the size of the heart, the condition of the lungs, the presence of plural effusions, the location of a purulent collection of abscess (vomica), of a tumor.

Corvisart's most famous work, *An Essay on the Organic Diseases and Lesions of the Heart and Great Vessels,* appeared in collaboration with Horeau and was translated by Gates into English. The contributions to clinical cardiology and the correlation of clinical-pathological features of heart disease signaled a notable advance in postgraduate education. Cardiac hypertrophy (Corvisart's disease) was distinguished from cardiac dilatation; the facies of cardiac failure (Corvisart's facies) was described. Three types of pericarditis were recognized as well as the dyspnea of effort and the thrill felt in mitral stenosis upon palpation of the precordium.[4]

The cartilaginous or osseous induration of the orifices of the auricles and ventricles, of the mitral and tricuspid valves, of the aortic and pulmonary semi-lunar valves, and the vegetations, growing upon either the ventricular or arterial valves, tend principally to produce a more or less complete constriction of the orifices affected.

When these constrictions exist, the circulation is embarrassed, and its phenomena singularly perverted. By observing the disorder of the circulation, the practitioner may find, in the living man, I should presume, certain signs of this species of affection.

The obscurity, involving the signs of the constrictions of the right orifices, is not entirely dissipated, when it is requisite to recognize the imperfect obliteration of the left auricle and ventricle. Beside the general signs of the diseases of the heart, which are ever found in this case as in the first, because an aneurismal [hypertrophy] complication generally obtains, some particular signs manifest the affections in question.

Of the preceding number of symptoms is a peculiar rushing like water, difficult to be described, sensible to the hand applied over the precordial region, a rushing which proceeds, apparently, from the embarrassment which the blood undergoes in passing through an opening which is no longer proportioned to the quantity of fluid which it ought to discharge.

In a discussion of the physical signs of aortic aneurysm, Corvisart noted:[4]

The principal effect from the presence of these [aneurysmal] tumors, which prevails uniformly, is the difficult respiration, the inevitable consequence of the permanent compression and sanguineous engorgement of the pulmonary organs.

An other analogous effect, but which determines phenomena more appropriate to the disease is the compression of the inferior portion of the trachea, which produces a rattling, a peculiarly well known hissing, and which perfectly indicates that a part of this aerial tube is intercepted by the pressure of some supernatural body.

The leading symptoms which then appeared, were the bloatedness of the countenance more evident on the right side than on the left, the face of a violet color, the elevation of the left parietes of the thorax, the infiltration of the extremities, extreme difficulty of respiration, which was high, frequent, short and hissing; the inspirations never appeared to be perfectly made; the thorax when struck did not sound in the least on the middle and superior part of the left side. By laying the hand over, and even above the region of the heart, we felt a trembling, and a rushing which exhibited to the touch what is felt by applying the hand over the thorax of the dying who have the rattle. The patient could neither lie in bed, nor take a moment's rest.

One may often ascribe to the presence of a similar tumor the inequality of the pulse in both arms, the debility, and even the insensibility of the pulsations of the left radial artery, for example, united with the force and evolution of the pulsations of the same artery on the right side.

Jean Nicolas Corvisart des Marets, professor in the Collège de France in Paris, formulated a system of clinical instruction which epitomized the fine attributes of the French school of medicine. He was a meticulous observer of the sick at the bedside and correlated his findings on physical diagnosis with anatomical changes postmortem. He rose to fame with Napoleon and, as Napoleon's physician, retired from active practice of medicine when the Emperor abdicated. Corvisart died after a series of strokes a few months after his most famous patient died in St. Helena.

1. Beeson, B. B.: Corvisart, His Life and Works, *Ann Med Hist* 2:297-307, 1930.
2. Anon.: Critique on Corvisart, J. N.: *An Essay on the Organic Diseases and Lesions of the Heart and Great Vessels*, article 7, *New Eng J Med* 1:292-301, 1812.
3. McDonald, A. L.: The Aphorisms of Corvisart, *Ann Med Hist* 1:374-387 (July) 1939.
4. Corvisart, J. N.: *An Essay on the Organic Diseases and Lesions of the Heart and Great Vessels*, J. Gates (trans.), Boston: Bradford & Reed, 1812.

Caleb Hillier Parry
(1755-1822)

CALEB HILLIER PARRY was an outstanding example of a fashionable physician practicing sound medicine in a community without a medical school, nevertheless making noteworthy contributions and composing several remarkable medical monographs. Parry's description of exophthalmic goiter, published in 1825, preceded the reports of Graves (1835), von Basedow (1840), and Stokes (1854), but followed those of Flajani (1802), Demours (1821), and Scarpa (1821). Although the report by Parry was not published until 1825, the first case was observed originally in 1786, more than a decade before Flajani's report. Osler called the affliction "Parry's disease," acknowledging the priority. Equally significant were the clinical description and pathological obser-

vations on angina pectoris subsequent to the communications of Morgagni, Heberden, Fothergill, Wall, Percival, and Black. Parry also described the clinical manifes-

Composite by G. Bako

tations of tetanus, rabies, dilatation of the colon, and the arterial pulse.

Parry, of Welsh stock, was the son of a nonconformist minister, attended lower school with Edward Jenner and the Dissenters' Academy at Warrington, and came under the influence of William Cullen at Edinburgh, where he matriculated in medicine, at the age of 18. After a period of study in London, he returned to Edinburgh for his MD degree. While in Edinburgh, he was elected president of the Medical Society and later obtained a royal charter for the unique students' organization, the Royal Medical Society of Edinburgh. The inaugural dissertation concerned rabies, a subject discussed in depth in later years. At the age of 24, Parry entered into medical practice at Bath, where residence was retained until his death. Hospital appointments at Bath included the Casualty and the Puerperal Charity, which later was merged with the Bath City Infirmary to form the Royal United Hospital.

A description of eight cases of exophthalmic goiter, "Enlargement of the Thyroid Gland in Connection with Enlargement or Palpitation of the Heart," and five cases of "Bronchocele, with Affections of the Head," appeared in 1825. Nothing of significance was omitted among the symptoms and clinical findings, which included tachycardia, palpitation, exophthalmos, localized or diffuse thyroid swelling, tachypnea, dyspnea, irregular menses, insomnia, nervousness, night sweats, irregular pulse, gastrointestinal irritability, edema, and concentrated urine. Digitalis was prescribed for the cardiac aberrations. There were no males in the first group and only one in the series of bronchoceles.

Enlargement of the thyroid gland in connection with enlargement or palpitation of the heart was described.[2]

There is one malady which I have in five cases seen coincident with what appeared to be enlargement of the heart, and which, so far as I know, has not been noticed, in that connection, by medical writers. The malady to which I allude is enlargement of the thyroid gland.

The first case of this coincidence which I witnessed was that of Grace B., a married woman, aged thirty-seven, in the month of August, 1786. Six years before this period she caught cold lying-in, and for a month suffered under a very acute rheumatic fever; subsequently to which, she became subject to more or less of palpitation of the heart, very much augmented by bodily exercise, and gradually increasing in force and frequency till my attendance, when it was so vehement, that each systole of the heart shook the whole thorax. Her pulse was 156 in a minute, very full and hard, alike in both wrists, irregular as to strength, and intermitting at least once in six beats. She had no cough, tendency to fainting, or blueness of the skin, but had twice or thrice been seized in the night with a sense of constriction and difficulty of breathing, which was attended with a spitting of a small quantity of blood. She described herself also as having frequent and violent stitches of pain about the lower part of the sternum.

About three months after lying-in, while she was suckling her child, a lump of about the size of a walnut was perceived on the right side of her neck. This continued to enlarge till the period of my attendance, when it occupied both sides of her neck, so as to have reached an enormous size, projecting forwards before the margin of the lower jaw. The part swelled was the thyroid gland. The carotid arteries on each side were greatly distended; the eyes were protruded from their sockets, and the countenance exhibited an appearance of agitation and distress, especially on any muscular exertion, which I have rarely seen equalled. She suffered no pain in her head, but was frequenty affected with giddiness.

For three weeks she had . . . oedematous swelling of her legs and thighs, attended with very deficient urine, which was high coloured, and deposited a sediment. Until the commencement of the anasarcous swellings, she had long suffered night sweats, which totally disappeared as the swellings occurred. She was frequently sick in the morning, and often threw up fluid tinged with bile. . . . For the last four months her menses had been irregular as to intervals, and defective in quantity and colour. Bowels usually lax, and more especially so for the last weeks.

Case 2 was a 21-year-old girl who was:[2]

. . . thrown out of a wheel chair in coming fast down hill, 28th of April last, and very much frightened, though not much hurt. From this time she has been subject to palpitation of the heart, and various nervous affections. About a fortnight after this period she began to observe a swelling of the thyroid gland, which has since varied at different times, so as to be once or twice nearly gone. It is now swelled on both sides, but more especially the right, without pain or soreness on pressure. The pulsation of the carotids is very strong and full on both sides.

On the 25th, she was ordered to take thrice a day a teaspoonful of a mixture of Tincture of Digitalis thirty drops, Syrup of Squills an ounce and a half.

Case 5 was a 40-year-old female who had:[2]

. . . a very quick pulse, with great shortness and difficulty of breathing, and frequent cough, attended with copious expectoration. She had also an extremely large swelling of the thyroid gland on each side of the neck, with a considerable dilatation of the carotid arteries.

My attendance on the three last patients having occurred at the same time, first suggested to me the notion of some connection between the malady of the heart and the bronchocele [thyroid].

Patient 6 complained of globus hystericus, insomnia, and apprehension of impending death, symptoms sometimes reported in hyperthyroidism.

In summarizing the five cases of bronchocele with affections of the head, Parry attributed the swelling of the thyroid to a reservoir of blood.[2]

. . . the coincidence is so frequent and remarkable, that one can scarcely avoid suspecting that the thyroid gland, of which no use whatever has hitherto been hinted at by physiologists, is intended in part to serve as a diverticulum in order to avert from the brain a part of the blood, which, urged with too great force by various causes, might disorder or destroy the functions of that important organ.

Parry's treatise of 167 pages on syncope anginosa, published in 1799, gave full credit to Heberden and Jenner for earlier descriptions of the malady.[3]

More than thirty years have now elapsed since Dr. HEBERDEN published a description of a disease highly alarming as to its consequences, and till then, as it should seem, unnoticed among physicians. One of the leading symptoms of this disease being a sort of undescribable anguish across the breast, he assumed that symptom as the foundation of a name, and called the disease Angina Pectoris.

It was generally admitted that many of the cases, which are vulgarly called asthma, originated, through different media, from diseases of that organ; and it was suggested by Dr. JENNER, that the Angina Pectoris arose from some morbid change in the structure of the heart, which change was probably ossification, or some similar disease, of the coronary arteries.

Persons affected with this disease are said to be usually turned of fifty years of age. This however is not universally true, as appears from the authors to whom I have referred; and I have lately seen a very clearly marked example of the Angina Pectoris, in which the age of the patient scarcely exceeded forty years. The disease generally attacks persons of the male sex; and, of them, those who are inclined to corpulency.

The first symptom is an uneasy sensation, which has been variously denominated a stricture, an anxiety, or a pain, extending generally from about the middle of the sternum across the left breast, and, in certain stages of the disorder usually stretching into the left arm a little above the elbow.

During the fit the pulse sinks in a greater degree; the face and extremities become pale, and bathed in a cold sweat, and for a while, perhaps, the patient is deprived of the powers of sense and voluntary motion.

Parry also provided material from his own cases:

In the *Elements of Pathology and Therapeutics,* published in 1815, Parry described an acute attack of gout following aphthae in the mouth and throat, and in mumps, swelling of the breasts in females and swelling of the testes in males.[4] The monograph, *Cases of Tetanus; and Rabies Contagiosa, or Canine Hydrophobia,* was dedicated to Edward Jenner and signed "My dear and oldest friend." Several years earlier Jenner had dedicated his treatise on cowpox to Parry. The brochure of Parry's was prepared to distinguish hydrophobia from similar serious maladies. The initial wound in tetanus was described.[5]

A person, in apparently sound health, shall receive a wound, or some other injury, usually in the extremities. This wound shall be extremely slight, as the mere prick of a thorn in one finger; or, if more violent, shall proceed in the most favourable way towards recovery; when, on a sudden, in some instances within a few hours, the patient shall be seized with a stiffness of certain muscles, which shall vary in force at different times, and even occasionally, and for a short time, cease. . . . When the spasms affect the temporal and masseter muscles, as is usually the case, the lower jaw is more or less rigidly drawn upwards against the upper jaw, and that modification of the disease is produced which is called Trismus, or locked jaw.

Parry was a meticulous observer of clinical findings and described his personal difficulties with a bladder stone and gouty arthritis.[2]

For a fortnight after I had begun to go out, which was on the 16th of January, 1811, after erysipelas faciei with acute fever, the passage of a nephritic calculus with great pain and black urine for a week, and the successive appearance of inflammatory gout in my left patella, left foot, left wrist, and right foot, had confined me to the house, and chiefly to my bed for twenty-six days.

Hemiatrophy and hemiplegia were described in a 28-year-old female who:[2]

. . . thirteen or fourteen years ago, when at school, was rather suddenly seized with some degree of hemiplegia of the left side, accompanied with transient confusion of intellects. The exact state of the original symptoms it is now impossible to ascertain. It is certain, however, that she has at various times been affected with headaches, and that from the period of the attack the left side of the face began to grow more thin than the right, and the eye to become less prominent, and therefore to appearance smaller. That, however, which is most extraordinary is, that, from the same period, her hair on the upper part of the left side of her head, which was before of a dark brown colour, began to grow white, and is now so to a considerable extent, without the mixture of a single brown hair.

Parry's most original contribution, according to Rolleston,[1] was the inquiry into the nature and cause of arterial pulse.[6] His philosophy of clinical inquiry, complemented by observations in the postmortem room, is summarized in the introduction to the discussion on syncope anginosa:[3]

But when I consider that truth is the sole foundation of moral and religious virtue, and therefore of happiness, my regard to personal delicacy is lost in the more general and greater obligation of publick utility. In reality, it is of little importance who is the discoverer of truths, however valuable. To mankind it suffices that the truth is actually known, and the good obtained.

1. Rolleston, H.: Caleb Hillier Parry, M.D., F.R.S., *Ann Med Hist* 7:205-215, 1925.
2. Parry. C. H.: *Collections from the Unpublished Medical Writings of the Late Caleb Hillier Parry,* vol. 1, 2, London: Underwoods, 1825.
3. Parry, C. H.: *An Inquiry into the Symptoms and Causes of the Syncope Anginosa, Commonly Called Angina Pectoris,* Bath, England: R. Cruttwell, 1799.
4. Parry, C. H.: *Elements of Pathology and Therapeutics, Being the Outlines of a Work,* Bath, England: R. Cruttwell, 1815.
5. Parry, C. H.: *Cases of Tetanus; and Rabies Contagiosa, or Canine Hydrophobia,* Bath, England: R. Cruttwell, 1814.
6. Parry, C. H.: *An Experimental Inquiry into the Nature, Cause, and Varieties of the Arterial Pulse; and into Certain Other Properties of the Larger Arteries, in Animals with Warm Blood,* Bath, England: R. Cruttwell, 1816.

James Carson (1772-1843)

JAMES CARSON, who began his professional career as a minister of the Church of Scotland, turned to the study of physiology in his mid-twenties and received the MD degree from Edinburgh in 1799.[1] His graduation thesis discusses the circulation of blood, and indicates, as early as 1799, the focus of his investigations with their significant contributions while gaining a livelihood in practice in Liverpool.[2] Carson's

Composite by G. Bako

curiosity about the physical characteristics and purpose of the elasticity of the lungs led him to attribute to this phenomenon the venous return of blood to the heart. The same curiosity led to the practical demonstration of the value of pneumothorax in the treatment of pulmonary diseases. First at Edinburgh and later at Glasgow, Carson was a candidate for a professorship of medicine for which his talents and training qualified him; however, he was unsuccessful in each quest and remained in practice until ill health forced him to retire to Malta, where he died from cholera.

Harvey taught that the pulsations of the heart were sufficient to explain the movement of blood in the greater and lesser circulation, the vis-a-tergo concept. Carson was unwilling to attribute to the heart and the large arteries the sole responsibility for the return of venous blood in the greater circuit. Rather, he employed his knowledge and interest in physical sciences to assign to the lungs a major portion of this physiological task, and proved by hydrodynamic experiments that the return in the venae cavae was largely a function of the elasticity of the lungs. He observed that pulsation of the blood was absent following the opening of a peripheral vein, and that the superior and inferior vena cavae were poorly aligned architecturally if propagation of the impulses was centripetal. In aspects of cardiopulmonary physiology, he expressed belief that diastole is a passive rather than an active process, that systole is initiated by the inrush of blood during diastole, that the lungs are brought under the influence of atmospheric pressure at the onset of respiration following delivery, and that the lungs collapse if the seal of the pleural space is compromised. The assumption that the negative pressure in the pleural cavity and the elasticity of the pulmonary parenchyma enhance the return of venous blood to the heart—a persistently valid physiological concept—was supported by measurements of negative pressure in bullocks, sheep, dogs, and cats.[3]

In a Treatise which I published a few years ago on the motion of the Blood and the mechanism of Respiration, it was contended, that a cause essential to the performance of these functions, had escaped the notice of physiologists. This cause was stated to be the elasticity or resilience of the lungs. The resilient property of the substance of the lungs had indeed been admitted by all anatomists and physiologists; and it is commonly demonstrated in the lecture room, that, if a piece of the substance of the lungs be cut out and stretched, it will recover its former dimensions when released from the extending power. But though the existence of this property had been universally admitted, no physiologist had attempted, as far as I know, to explain the means by which nature had contrived to render it subservient to the purposes of life.

In the Inquiry into the causes of the motion of the blood, it was contended, that the elastic substance of the lungs, in consequence of the degree to which that substance was stretched in the living body, generated a permanent power of great extent, and that this power was employed by nature to circulate the blood, and to carry on the process of respiration.

The cause of the successive contractions of the diaphragm, in those cases at least in which the will is not concerned, seems to admit of the following explanation. A permanent and invariable load is sustained by its lower surface. By this load the relaxed muscular fibres become stretched to a degree which at length becomes painful and stimulating. To relieve itself from this irksome burden, the diaphragm is roused to contraction; but this contractile power, agreeably to the laws of muscularity, is soon exhausted, and falling into a quiescent state, allows the painful and stimulating distension of the relaxed fibres of the diaphragm to be again renewed. From the irksomeness of this condition it relieves itself by a fresh contraction.

In a similar and equally effective manner, the elasticity of the lungs will be found to influence the movements ·of the heart and the motion of the blood.

At the same time, Carson was conducting related physiological experiments on animals to determine the harmful effects as opposed to the value of pneumothorax in the treatment of pulmonary tuberculosis and other chronic infections of the lungs. The first pneumothorax recommended by Carson was performed by a surgical colleague in 1822 in Liverpool. Pleural adhesions thwarted the attempted collapse and the patient died a few months later. He seized advantage of this experience to advise a direct approach to the surgical management of a lung abscess, but this procedure also failed when the incision fell short of reaching the infected area. Carson's reasoning for producing collapse and putting at rest infected pulmonary tissue follows.[4]

In the case of the collapse of a single lung the impunity is no doubt secured by the tenseness of the mediastinum, or membrane which is placed vertically in the middle of the chest, between the lungs; and which, after the collapsing of one lung, by the admission of the external air into contact with its surface, secures to the other lung nearly its own proportion of the cavity of the chest, and protects it from being materially impeded in the performance of its functions.

Our next object is to consider the effects which the collapse of a single lung, or of both lungs in succession, is likely to produce in some of the diseases of the chest.

Lesions in the structure, and abscesses in the substance of the lungs, are known to be less frequently healed than the same affections in, I believe, any other part of the body; and when they occur, as they do most frequently, to lead to the most deplorable consequences. The peculiar obstinacy observable in the cure of injuries of the lungs, has generally been attributed to the constant motions, and different degrees of distension to which these organs are subjected in the process of respiration.

The chief cause of the peculiar obstinacy observed in the healing of injuries of the lungs arises, in my opinion, from the state in which the substance of these organs is held in the living system. It has been proved that the substance of the lungs is powerfully elastic, and that in the living system it is at all times on the stretch.

It is evident that if one of the lungs were reduced to a state of collapse, both the causes supposed to give a peculiarly unfavourable character to affections of the lungs, would so far as this lung is concerned be destroyed. For in this situation the diseased part would be placed in a quiescent state, receiving little or no disturbance from the movements of respiration which would be performed solely by the other lung.

We have seen that one of the lungs of an animal may be reduced to a state of collapse, without the life of the animal being brought into danger. It not unfrequently and in the early stages perhaps generally happens, that the deplorable disease termed consumption has its seat in one lung only; and, when this occurs, there is little difficulty in general in ascertaining to what lung it belongs.

The means we possess of reducing this lung to a state of collapse, or of divesting it for a time of its peculiar functions are equally simple and safe. In those cases in which the disease is placed in one of the lungs only, the remedy would appear to be simple, safe and complete.

1. Lord Cohen of Birkenhead: James Carson, M.D., F.R.S., of Liverpool, *Med Hist* 7:1-12 (Jan) 1963.

2. Carson, J.: *An Inquiry into the Causes of the Motion of the Blood*, Liverpool: F. B. Wright, 1815.

3. Carson, J.: On the Elasticity of the Lungs, *Philos Trans*, 1820, pp 29-44.

4. Carson, J.: *Essays, Physiological and Practical*, Liverpool: F. B. Wright, 1820.

R. T. Laennec (1781-1826)

A CYLINDER OF PAPER, three quires thick, was the first stethoscope used by Rene-Theophile-Hyacinthe Laennec in his examination of a patient's chest in the Necker Hospital in Paris.[1] This remarkable contribution to the diagnosis of disease was conceived at the age of 35 during his first year of service in the hospital (1816). Prior to Laennec, the examination of the chest utilized palpation, ausculation by direct application of the examining ear to the thorax,

and the recently-described method of percussion by Auenbrugger. The hollow paper cylinder was replaced later by a stethoscope of wood, concave on the examining end

and fabricated of two closely-fitted sections, so that it could be used as a short instrument or a long one. A flexible stethoscope was suggested by Dr. N. P. Comins in 1828 and by Dr. C. J. B. Williams in 1829. An improvement in the binaural design has been attributed to Dr. George Cammann of New York City (circa 1851).[2] The stethoscope as an examining tool was first mentioned in the catalogue of Harvard Medical School in 1868-69, although Henry Ingersoll Bowditch had published his book on the stethoscope several years earlier.

Laennec, born in 1781 in lower Brittany, was 5 years of age when his mother died of tuberculosis. He was placed initially in the charge of his uncle, a curé, and later in the charge of another uncle, a professor of medicine at the University of Nantes. He completed his formal medical education in Paris, the center of medicine in Europe, during the stirring days of the Revolution and enjoyed the friendship and guidance of Corvisart, the physician of Napoleon I. Loyal to his pupil and sensing a great medical future for him, Corvisart furthered his career at every opportunity. Bichat and Dupuytren were also on the faculty. During the last three years of formal medical training, Laennec prepared meticulous histories on more than 400 cases. He was honored with the first two prizes in medicine and surgery.

Early in his career his proficiency in composition won him the position of chief editor of the *Journal De Medecine* for five years. He assumed this responsibility immediately following graduation at the age of 23. A prolific writer, in these fruitful years he prepared several monographs. The outstanding contributions in his pre-stethoscope days were in pathological anatomy.[2] He showed great interest in diseases of the chest, identified the diagnostic significance of cardiac and pulmonary sounds, differentiated bronchiectasis, pneumothorax, hemorrhagic pleurisy, pulmonary gangrene, infarct and emphysema, discussed the significance of tubercles of the pulmonary parenchyma, and described a specific form of cirrhosis of the liver.

The correlation of clinical observations of the patient with postmortem findings, i.e., the case system of teaching, was emphasized. Following his appointment as visiting physician at the Necker Hospital, he insisted that his students keep meticulous notes after each examination of the patient as well as to follow closely the course of the disease. Laennec, appointed to the chair of medicine in the Collège de France at the age of 41, succeeded his teacher, Corvisart, as full professor of medicine the following year. Laennec died three years later at the age of 45. The stethoscope (Gr. *stethos* chest, *skopein* to examine) was given this name by Laennec, although he referred to his invention usually as a baton or a cylinder. Several types of rales were described as well as pectoriloquy, egophony, succussion, cavernous breathing, and the metallic tinkle; each was an important sign in the examination of the thorax before the introduction of roentgenography into clinical medicine.[2]

The first instrument which I used was a cylindrical roll of paper about one foot in length, made of three sheets of coarse paper, wound tightly, held by glue and smoothed at each end by a file. Since this roll consisted of a few layers only, it had a conduit of only 3 to 4 mm. in diameter. . . . The hollow center was indispensable for detection of respiratory sounds. Such a simple instrument is the best device for heart sounds. It is sufficient in examining respirations merely to listen for râles.

Substances of medium density such as wood and cane are preferable. . . . As a consequence, I used a wooden cylinder 16 mm. in diameter, one foot in length, with a lumen of approximately .25 inch in diameter, and connected at one end to a bell about 1½ inch in size. . . . At first I did not feel it was necessary to give a name to such a simple instrument. Since others felt differently I created several names, each of them improper, such as sonometer, pectoriloque, pectoriloquie, thoraciloque, medical cornet, etc. Finally I called it "stethoscope" which I thought best expressed the principle of its use. We hoped it can be applied to other uses aside from exploration of the chest.

Excerpts from his postmortem observations on pulmonary tuberculosis, the disease from which Laennec suffered, correctly interprets the development of cavities and the description of tubercles of the lung.[2] The following translation is excerpted from Hale-White.[3]

The cavities producing pectoriloquy are those vulgarly known as *ulcers of the lung*. They are not, as was long supposed, and is still believed by the majority of medical practitioners, an outcome of inflammation and suppuration of the pulmonary tissue. The recent advances in pathological anatomy have proved beyond all manner of doubt that these cavities are due to the softening and subsequent evacuation of a peculiar kind of accidental information which modern anatomists have specially designated by the name *tubercle*, formerly applied without distinction to any sort of unnatural protuberance or tumour. The presence of tubercles in the lung is the cause, and constitutes the peculiar anatomical characteristic of pulmonary phthisis.

The cavities produced by tubercle differ essentially from an ulcer, inasmuch as this spreads by eating into the tissue in which it is formed, whereas the first are produced by the spontaneous destruction of accidental formations which have pushed aside and compressed the pulmonary tissue, but not destroyed it, and have no tendency to increase at its expense.

Laennec is best known among internists for his description of the condition now known as atrophic cirrhosis of the liver or Laennec's cirrhosis. The following report appeared in an autopsy protocol in the (1826) edition of the treatise.[2]

The liver, reduced to one-third of its ordinary volume, was clearly seen in the area which it normally occupies; its external surface, granular and wrinkled, had a grayish-green appearance. When cut, it seemed to be composed of a multitude of small round or oval lobules; the size varied from a grain of mustard to a grain of hemp. Between these lobules, no normal liver tissue could be seen; their color was brownish or reddish-yellow. In areas they seemed almost green. The remaining tissue presented a sensation of small pieces of soft leather.
Footnote: This structure was similar to a number of conditions wnich we call *scirrhous*. I would like to name it *cirrhosis* because of its color. Its development in the liver is one of the common causes of ascites and when cirrhosis develops, normal liver tissue is reduced and as happened in this patient, it disappears entirely; also in all of the cases, a liver which becomes cirrhotic will lose rather than increase its volume.

1. Laennec, R. T. H.: *A Treatise on the Diseases of the Chest and on Mediate Auscultation*, translated from the latest French edition by J. Forbes Underwood, London, 1821.

2. Laennec, R. T. H.: *A Treatise on the Diseases of the Chest and on Mediate Auscultation (Fr)*, Brosson & Chaudé, Paris, 1819, excerpts translated by Z. Danilevicius.

3. Laennec, R. T. H.: *A Treatise on the Diseases of the Chest and on Mediate Auscultation*, translated from the 1st edition by Sir Wm. Hale-White, Medical Classics Series, London, 1923.

P. C. A. Louis (1787-1872)

PIERRE-CHARLES ALEXANDRE LOUIS (angle of Louis—the angle between the manubrium and the body of the sternum), successor to Laennec as the leading clinician in Paris in the early 19th century, disseminated the beneficence of French medicine beyond the provincial borders and particularly to the medical centers of the Eastern seaboard of the United States. Louis was born in Aï on the Marne, the son of a vineyard keeper. After starting the study of law, he found this profession not to his liking, switched to medicine, studied at Rheims, and completed his preparation for a medical career at Paris. He graduated at

the age of 27 in 1813, six years before Laennec described the stethoscope in auscultatory examination of the chest. Louis returned to Aï, undecided on the locale for

Los Angeles County Medical Library

the practice of medicine. A friend, on a visit to the family home, suggested that Louis accompany him on an official mission to Russia. The acceptance of this offer, implemented by a diploma which gave him license in Russia, enabled Louis to pursue a peripatetic practice in this adopted land.

Louis traveled from city to city in Russia for three years before settling in Odessa. Practice here was terminated by a distressing clinical experience with diphtheria among children. The high mortality from diphtheria prompted Louis to seek additional study in Paris, particularly in childhood diseases. He accepted an appointment at La Charité under his associate and pupil, Chomel, and for six years gave undivided attention in the wards and in the death house to the end-result of the fatal maladies. A prodigious notetaker, Louis used the accumulated data as the basis for several medical monographs. Clinical therapeutics and pathological observations were treated statistically—one of Louis' great contributions to clinical medicine. He was particularly concerned with the circumstances surrounding the onset of the disease, early and late symptoms, and the natural history with postmortem changes.[1]

When this had been done, the analysis of the cases becomes possible, and has not, in fact, many great difficulties. We can very soon see, by running through one of the columns of these last tables, how many times one symptom has occurred in a certain number of persons, at what period it commenced, when it ceased, how often it was slight, and how often severe.

After more than six years of concentration on the sick and the dead, low funds made it impossible for Louis to remain in Paris. Consequently, he retired for a year in Brussels to study his statistical findings in preparation for publication.

Two treatises especially contributed to Louis' fame as a clinician, whose bedside teaching was enhanced immeasurably by accurate postmortem studies. The study of tuberculosis was first published in 1825.[2]

Bayle established as many species of Phthisis as there exist organic lesions of the lungs capable, according to his views, of producing death as a consequence of their development: he admitted a tuberculous, a granular, a cancerous, a melanic, a calculous and an ulcerous phthisis. Laennec maintains, on the contrary, that there is but one species of phthisis—the tuberculous; in other words, but one single organic lesion of the lungs capable of destroying life by inducing physical wasting in all its stages, together with the series of symptoms characteristic of phthisis. I have now devoted myself for upwards of twenty years, with more or less assiduity, to clinical observation, and during this period I have not met with a single instance of an individual, dying phthisical, whose lungs did not present, as their chief morbid change, a greater or less number of tuberculous cavities, tubercles, or semi-transparent gray granulations. My observations consequently confirm those of Laennec, and I agree with him in recognizing tubercles in the lungs as the anatomical character of phthisis.

The monograph enjoyed a number of editions, including translations into English and German. From this intensive study came Louis' law: tuberculosis usually begins in the left lung, and a tuberculous lesion in any part of the body probably is a dissemination from the primary site. After the clinical investigations, Louis deliberated

on its epidemiological control and social aspects. He concluded with a plea for the organized study of tuberculosis by groups of physicians, and commented on the fact, or fancy, of a change in libido with tuberculosis.[2]

I have in several instances, made inquiry of phthisical patients respecting the state of their amative propensities, and in every instance these have appeared to me to have failed in proportion to the loss of strength, the general uneasiness, and the other symptoms,—very much in the same manner as in individuals affected with any other kind of chronic ailment and enfeebled to a similar amount. However, where the tuberculous affection has as yet made but slight progress, and but slight diminution of strength has taken place, though sufficient to prevent the patient from following his usual avocations, it may be that some of them experience stronger sexual desires than in the state of perfect health. This would be easily explained as an effect of idleness, the most favourable condition for the play of imagination in such matters.

Fate was unkind in his family life; an only son died of tuberculosis at the age of 18 years. Still interested in fevers, he joined an expedition to investigate the yellow fever epidemic at Gibraltar in 1828. The monograph describing the findings appeared first in English in 1839.[3] It was not published in French until later.

But the most remarkable lesion of the liver, was the alteration of its color . . . the liver being sometimes of the color of fresh butter, sometimes of a straw color, sometimes of the color of coffee and milk, sometimes a yellowish gum color, or a mustard color, or, finally, sometimes an orange or pistachio color.

Louis is probably best known for his clinical-pathological description of typhoid fever. This was prepared in 1829 in two volumes from data based upon notes collected in the preceding years. He compared 138 cases of fevers with gastroenteric symptoms, morbid states classed as typhoid (or typhus) fever, with a control group several times this size. Although it remained for Gerhard, his pupil from Philadelphia, to differentiate clearly typhus from typhoid fever, the pathological changes in the intestines were distinctive. Peyer's patches were involved without exception in 50 autopsy cases accumulated from the series of patients with gastroenteric fever.[4]

The elliptical patches of the ileum were more or less seriously changed in structure in all the patients, in the last two or eight feet of the canal.

This was found in the same patients in very different degrees, in different parts, being most severe in those patches which were nearest the caecum, and the least so, in those farthest from the large intestine.

In the intervals between these diseased patches were scarcely ever found any in a perfectly healthy state, which seems to indicate, as I have remarked previously, that their alterations went on in a gradual manner from the caecum to the duodenum, and did not commence simultaneously in all the places between these two spots.

Finally, at a greater or less distance from the caecum, the patches had ulcerations upon them, some superficial or just commencing, with an imperfect destruction of the mucous membrane; others deeper, with entire destruction of this membrane.

The submucous cellular tissue, which composed the surface of the ulcerations, was in many of them very nearly in the same state as in the patches which were not ulcerated, and it had not lost any of its substance, whilst, in those nearer the caecum, it was destroyed to a depth and extent which varied on the different patches, and the muscular coat, when exposed, was more or less red and thickened, its fibres being very distinct. In some cases they were to a certain extent destroyed, and the peritoneum being ruptured, a perforation of the canal was the consequence.

The condition of the mesenteric glands therefore, in these two groups of patients, was in exact relation with the condition of elliptical patches of the ileum, so that in those cases in which the patches were but slightly, or not at all ulcerated, these glands contained no pus; and when the ulceration was more marked, the disease of older date, pus began to appear and absolutely existed in many cases.

The spleen was three, four and five times as large as usual, in seventeen of the forty-six patients whose histories we study.

This softening [of the spleen] existed in different degrees in three quarters of the cases.

Louis' numerical treatment of disease led him astray in the consideration of the merits of bloodletting versus use of other measures in dealing with lobar pneumonia. In a series of 29 previously healthy adults,

only four died ($<$14%). Recoveries included those who had been bled one or more times, usually to the point of faintness.[5]

The influence of Louis on the leaders of medicine in the United States seems as remarkable as his research on fevers. In 1897, Osler prepared a partial list of the American students in Paris between 1830-1840 who had studied with Louis.[6] These included James Jackson, Jr., O. W. Holmes, George C. Shattuck, Jr., J. C. Warren, and J. M. Warren, from Boston; Abraham Dubois and Valentine Mott, Sr., from New York; George W. Norris, W. W. Gerhard, Casper W. Pennock, Alfred Stille, and William Pepper, Sr., from Philadelphia; and others from Baltimore, Charleston, and Virginia. An inscription on a photograph sent to one of his favorite American pupils, H. I. Bowditch, expressed his philosophy of life: [7]

There is something rarer than the spirit of discernment; it is the need of truth; that state of the soul which does not allow us to stop in any scientific labors at what is only probable, but compels us to continue our researches until we have arrived at evidence.

1. Louis, P. C. A.: "Memoir on the Proper Method of Examining a Patient and of Arriving at Facts of a General Nature," H. I. Bowditch, trans., in *Medical and Surgical Monographs*, Philadelphia: A. Waldie, 1838, pp 149-187.
2. Louis, P. C. A.: *Researches on Phthisis*, 2nd ed, London: Sydenham Society, 1844.
3. Louis, P. C. A.: *Anatomical, Parthological and Therapeutic Researches on the Yellow Fever of Gibraltar of 1828*, G. C. Shattuck, Jr., Trans., Boston: Little and Brown, 1839.
4. Louis, P. C. A.: *Anatomical, Pathological and Therapeutic Researches upon the Disease Known under the Name of Gastro-Enterite, Putrid, Adynamic, Ataxic or Typhoid Fever, etc.*, vol 1, H. I. Bowditch, trans., Boston: Isaac R. Butts, 1836.
5. Louis, P. C. A.: *Researchs on the Effect of Bloodletting in Some Inflammatory Diseases, and on the Influence of Tartarized Antimony and Vesication in Pneumonitis*, C. G. Putnam, trans., Boston: Hilliard, Gray & Company, 1836.
6. Osler, W.: Influence of Louis on American Medicine *Bull Johns Hopkins Hosp* 8: 161-167 (Aug-Sept) 1897.
7. Middleton, W. S.: Biographic History of Physical Diagnosis, *Ann Med Hist* 6:426-451, 1924.

John Cheyne (1777-1836)

JOHN CHEYNE OF DUBLIN, not to be confused with George Cheyne of London (1671-1743), who described hypochondriasis—"the English malady," is the senior partner in the Cheyne-Stokes respiration syndrome. Several of his ancestors had practiced medicine in or near Edinburgh. Education in grammar school, supplemented by tutoring under a clergyman of the Episcopal Church of Scotland, was disappointing. "Both master and pupil had more relish for idle talk than for Homer or Virgil."[1] In his 13th year, John began to attend the poor among his father's practice. The assignment was "to ascertain that they were supplied with medicines, to bleed them, to dress their wounds, and report upon their condition"—surely a remarkably young age to begin the practice of medicine and to assume major responsibilities in the care of the sick. Before John became 16, the auditing of medical lectures at the University of Edinburgh complemented his clinical training. Association with medical students several years his senior at the boarding house left no doubt in his mind that he was as qualified as they to prepare for the doctorate examination. Such confidence, plus the assistance of Mr. Candlish,

a celebrated "grinder," enabled Cheyne to pass without difficulty. The medical degree was granted at the age of 18.

In the following four years, Cheyne served as surgeon in the headquarters of the Royal Regiment of Artillery. Since this was not too strenuous a professional life, ample leisure time was spent in[1]

. . . shooting, playing billiards, reading such books as the circulating library supplied, and in complete dissipation. He studied nothing but the manners of his superiors, and learnt nothing but ease and propriety of behaviour.

The first tour of duty was in Scotland, the second in Ireland. Apparently four years of such sophisticated parasitism was sufficint, for he returned to Scotland and began to study medicine anew. While serving at the Ordnance Hospital in Leith Fort near Edinburgh, he accepted an assistantship to his father. This second tour of duty, however, found him undertaking a critical and serious study of disease among his father's patients. Detailed notes were kept of the clinical course of each grave malady, and, when the patient died, a "necroscopic examination" was performed.

It was natural that the clinical studies should center about the maladies most prevalent in the community. Clinical experience was gained through observations, reading the best monographs on the subject, and the study of carefully assembled notes. For the second time it became evident that Cheyne was a shrewd and calculating fellow who hoped to profit by a study of the basis for success of others, particularly those physicians who enjoyed great stature in the medical profession. Cheyne appreciated also that it was something easier to achieve success than it was to retain it. Respect from one's colleagues was judged as important as respect from one's patients. Friendship with Sir Charles Bell was a rewarding experience. Although Bell was only a few years older, the great capacity and industry of the neurophysiologist exerted a favorable influence upon Cheyne. In 1801, when Cheyne was 24, the essay on "Cynanche Trachealis, or Croup" was published.[2] Not long after, he prepared a manuscript on "Bowel Complaints . . ." illustrated with color plates from drawings by Charles Bell.

The lure of Ireland or possibly the hope that Dublin would be a more profitable city than Edinburgh attracted Cheyne in 1809. The physicians in the Irish metropolis followed the Cullen school and relied upon symptoms at the expense of pathology. The practice of general medicine was largely in the control of the surgeons. These concepts so contrary to the training of Cheyne, led him to take steps to alter them. Private practice was rather slow in Dublin; meanwhile, a notable contribution on acute hydrocephalus was prepared, inscribed to Charles Bell. Subsequently, he was elected to the staff at Meath Hospital, which claimed Graves and Stokes a generation later. These and other physicians were responsible for the fame and fortune of the new school of Irish medicine in Dublin. In 1813, Cheyne was elected professor of medicine at the College of Surgery and lectured in military medicine and surgery. In 1815, he was appointed physician to the House of Industry Hospitals, where, in cooperation with Perceval, a School of Clinical Medicine and a Museum of Morbid Anatomy were established.[3] The House of Industry accommodated more than 70 patients, usually with acute maladies and especially "fevers." The hospital also contained[1]

. . . separate cells for lunatics; a large asylum for destitute children; and in an immense number of paupers, with bodies in every stage of disorganization.

Cheyne was such a meticulous note taker that the accumulation of records demanded an outlet and led to the publication of the *Dublin Hospital Reports*. Five volumes, published between 1817 and 1830,[2] included manuscripts contributed by Cheyne on the subject of epidemic fevers, dysentery, melena, jaundice of the newborn, fatal erethism of the stomach, and incipient phthisis. The discussion of "A Case of Apoplexy, in Which the Fleshy Part of the Heart Was Converted into Fat,"[4] recounted the undulating breathing identified today as Cheyne-Stokes respiration. Strangely enough no one of these three bibliographies con-

sulted,[1-3] which were prepared prior to 1888, mentions this manuscript that was published in the *Dublin Hospital Reports* in 1818. The case of a 60-year-old male who suffered several attacks of acute gouty arthritis in his feet was described. A few days before death[4]

. . . a horse-radish bath was ordered, in consequence of some slight demonstration of gout. . . . The only peculiarity in the last period of his illness, which lasted eight or nine days, was in the state of the respiration: For several days his breathing was irregular; it would entirely cease for a quarter of a minute, then it would become perceptible, though very low, then by degrees it became heaving and quick, and then it would gradually cease again: this revolution in the state of his breathing occupied about a minute, during which there were about thirty acts of respiration.

By the time of Cheyne's death in 1836 at the age of 59, the leadership of the Dublin School now rested on the shoulders of Graves and Stokes. The directions for his burial were specific and plain.[5]

I would have no tolling of bells, if it can be avoided. The ringers may have an order for bread, to the amount usually given upon such occasions; if they get money they will spend it in the ale-house. . . . My funeral must be as inexpensive as possible: let there be no attempt at a funeral sermon. . . . My decease may be announced in the Irish newspapers in the following words. . . . Not one word more; no panegyric.

1. Pettigrew, T. J.: *Memoir of John Cheyne, M.D., F.R.S.E., M.R.I.A.*, London: Whittaker & Co., 1839.
2. John Cheyne, *Med Times & Gaz* 14:17-20 (Jan 3); 41-43 (Jan 10); 69-70 (Jan 17) 1857.
3. Ormsby, L. H.: *Medical History of the Meath Hospital* Dublin: Fannin & Co., 1888.
4. Cheyne, J.: A Case of Apoplexy, in Which the Fleshy Part of the Heart Was Converted into Fat, *Dublin Hosp Rep* 2:216-223, 1818.
5. Cheyne, J.: *Essays on Partial Derangement of the Mind*, Dublin: William Curry, Jun. & Co., 1843.

Composite by G. Bako

Joseph Hodgson (1788-1869)

JOSEPH HODGSON, an able surgeon of the clinical school but sometimes reluctant to accept changes in practice, was, nevertheless, a highly successful consultant. He is best known by historians for the preparation of *A Treatise on the Diseases of Arteries and Veins, Containing the Pathology and Treatment of Aneurisms and Wounded Arteries.*[1] Hodgson was born at Penrith, Cumberland, the son of a Birmingham merchant, and was educated at King Edward VI's grammar school.[2] After serving an apprenticeship to Mr. Freer, he became, through an uncle's generosity, a pupil at St. Bartholomew's Hospital; there he observed several of the cases described in his monograph. He obtained the diploma of the College of Surgeons of London in 1811 and commenced practice, supplementing an inadequate income by taking pupils and editing the *London Medical Review*. In 1815, his famous monograph appeared, accompanied by a companion piece, *Engravings,* illustrating the test.[3] Disappointment in London and faulty health caused him to return

to Birmingham, where he spent the major portion of his medical years.

Hodgson took an important part in founding the Birmingham Eye Infirmary in 1824 and served as surgeon to the General Dispensary and to the General Hospital in Birmingham. Gaining a reputation especially for lithotomy, he developed an extensive and profitable practice. He cut "eighty-six patients for stone, and lost only four." Returning to London in 1849, Hodgson accepted a number of responsibilities in national medical societies in addition to reestablishing a city practice; he served on the Council of the College of Surgeons, Examiner in Surgery to London University, member and president of both the Royal College of Surgeons and the Royal Medical and Chirurgical Society, a Fellow of the Royal Society, and Hunterian orator in 1855. In practice Hodgson was meticulous in examination, discerning in diagnosis, but somewhat gloomy when offering a prognosis. As a medical advisor to the Peel family, he attended Sir Robert Peel in his last illness.

The *Treatise on the Diseases of the Arteries* contained important passages on the pathogenesis of aneurysms, particularly aortic aneurysms. He documented the morbid appearance of the coats of arteries and compared the effects of medical and surgical treatment. He reported that the most frequent site of aortic aneurysm was the ascending portion in the arch, noting that the dilatation commenced with deterioration of the internal and middle coat and bulging of the external coat. Also, he indicated that ulceration was rarely observed within the artery which had not undergone morbid change. Excerpts from the preface and contents follow.[1]

My principal objects have been to examine the various morbid appearances that are met with in the coats of arteries; to trace the pathology of aneurism; to investigate the processes by which the spontaneous cure of this disease is sometimes accomplished; to compare these processes with the effects of medical and surgical treatment; and, from the result of these inquiries, to deduce the principles which regulate the treatment of this disease. I have also been desirous of collecting and arranging observations relating to the improvements which have recently been made in the different operations for aneurism, so as to form an historical, as well as practical account of these important subjects.

The changes which arteries undergo in consequence of accident or disease, are referrible [sic] to the peculiar textures which enter into their composition. Arteries, like most other parts of the animal body, are composed of blood vessels, nerves, and absorbents, which render them liable to the same morbid alterations, and endow them with the same powers of reparation, as soft parts in general. Thus, the coats of arteries inflame and pass through all the stages of adhesion, suppuration, or gangrene, in the same manner as the skin, a gland, or a muscle.

NOTWITHSTANDING the attention which has been given to this branch of pathology, there exists much uncertainty as to the nature of the parts which form an aneurism sac. The question is simply this: Does aneurism ever consist in a general or partial dilatation of all the coats of an artery, or is it constantly produced by the destruction of all or most of these coats, and the formation of a sac by the influx of the blood into the sheath of the vessel and surrounding parts? The controversies which have existed upon this subject appear to have arisen from a reluctance to admit the possibility of more than one cause in the production of the same effect, and from an adherence to opinions deduced from very imperfect observations.

A great proportion of the aneurismal sacs which I have had an opportunity of examining, were unquestionably formed in the manner which Scarpa has described, namely, by a destruction of the internal and middle coats of the artery, and the expansion of the external or cellular coat into a sac. The cellular coat at length gives way, and the sheath of the artery and the surrounding parts form the boundary of the tumour. When the internal and middle coats of an artery are divided, and air or water is injected into the vessel, the external coat bulges very considerably, and constitutes a small aneurism sac. . . . I have frequently repeated the experiment by dividing the internal and middle coats of different arteries by the application of a ligature, which being removed, and the vessel forcibly inflated, the external coat has always exhibited a sufficient degree of dilatation to prove that it is more liable to yield and to be expanded into a sac, than to be ruptured by the impulse of the circulating blood. It appears therefore that when the internal and middle coats are destroyed, the sac is in the first instance formed by an expansion of the external coat of the artery: as the distention advances this membrane gradually gives way; the sheath of the vessel then restrains the effusion, and yielding in its turn, the surrounding parts, whatever may be their texture, form the

walls of the extravasation. Ulceration, as I have already observed, is rarely met with in the coats of an artery which have not undergone some previous morbid alteration. It, however, frequently takes place in arteries the coats of which contain atheromatous or calcareous depositions.

1. Hodgson, J.: *A Treatise on the Diseases of Arteries and Veins,* London: T. Underwood, 1815.
2. Anon: Joseph Hodgson, Esq., F.R.S., obituary, *Lancet* 1:243-244, 1869.
3. Hodgson, J.: *Engravings Intended to Illustrate Some of the Diseases of Arteries,* London: T. Underwood, 1815.

Johann Lucas Schonlein (1793-1864)

JOHANN LUCAS SCHÖNLEIN and Johannes Müller were the leaders in Germany of scientific medicine and bedside medicine, respectively, during the first half of the 19th century. Müller was a prolific writer who commanded respect from his students and associates because of his warm personality and scientific accomplishments in the laboratory. Schönlein, on the other hand, wrote little and wielded his greatest influence at the bedside and in the clinic.[1]

Schönlein, the son of a ropemaker, was born in Bamberg and received his first serious exposure to learning at Landshut, well known for its school of natural philosophy and brunonianism. He took the MD degree at Würzburg in 1816, where eight years later he became professor of medicine. He was a liberal politically and was dismissed from his post on this pretext in 1832. The following year he was called to Zurich, where he remained for six years. After the sojourn in Switzerland, he accepted his third and last academic post as professor of medicine at the University of Berlin. Here he established a medical clinic in the modern pattern of instruction, employed new methods of clinical examination and diagnosis, and abandoned Latin for German as the language of communication. Auscultation and percussion were practiced, blood was examined chemically, urine was examined microscopically, and the presumptive diagnosis confirmed or rejected by postmortem examination. This new science of clinical medicine (natural science) represented a sharp cleavage from the school of natural philosophy and was particularly appealing to his students. He described for the first time fine rales in pneumonia, the metallic tinkle in pneumothorax, and the ausculatory murmur over the femoral artery in aortic insufficiency, and introduced the terms "typhus abdominalis," "typhus exanthematicus," and "hemophilia."

Schönlein's outstanding reputation, acquired first in Würzburg, followed him to Zurich, where students and patients in increasing numbers sought his tutelage or counsel. It was here that the only scientific manuscripts prepared by his own hand were composed. One described the urinary excretion of triple phosphates in typhoid fever; another communication announced the recovery in the scalp of a filiform parasite belonging to the order, *Hyphomycetes,* subsequently named *Trichophyton [Achorion] schoenleini.* The former was an unimportant observation, the latter, an important clinical finding which supported the infectious pathogenesis of disease and particularly the pathogenesis of a parasitic invader. The description of favus was a contribution of only 23 lines and appeared in Müller's *Archiv.*[2]

You know *Bassi's* beautiful discovery of the true nature of muscardine [parasitic fungus]. I believe this fact to be the greatest interest to pathogenesis, though for all I know no physician has so far found it worth an investigation. For this reason I had sent to me from Milan a great number of silkworms that had muscardine. My experiments then did not only confirm the reports of *Bassi and Audouin,* but yielded a few other not altogether unimportant results; and this fact, in its turn, reminded me of my theory which stated that some impetigos are of a vegetable nature. This view was strongly supported by Unger's excellent paper on exanthemas of vegetable origin. Since I happened to have a few cases of porrigo lupinosa [favus] at the hospital, I began a careful investigation, and the first experiments left no doubt about the fungus character of those so-called pustules. I enclose a microscopic illustration of a pustle. Simultaneously, I am sending a few porrigo pustules which I shelled out from the top layer of the corium of a patient.

Peliosis rheumatica, or Schönlein's disease, was redescribed by his pupil Henoch and remains in contemporary medicine as the eponym Schöenlein-Henoch disease, a triad of arthralgia, abdominal pain, and a purpuric rash. Schönlein differentiated the purpura from Werlhof's disease (idiopathic thrombocytopenic purpura) by the absence of purpura in the mouth, absence of hemorrhages (in contrast to purpura), the character of the exanthema, the association with articular symptoms, the absence of nervous symptoms, and a favorable prognosis. The clinical findings were assembled in his treatise, *General and Special Pathology and Therapy,* published by his students.[3]

The patients have either suffered earlier from rheumatism or rheumatic symptoms appear in the same time, gently periodic sticking pains in the joints (in the ankles and in the knees, seldom in the hand and shoulder joints), which are oedematous, swollen and very painful when moved; the characteristic spots of the disease appear in the majority of cases first on the extremities and particularly on the lower ones (seldom the upper ones), and here only up to the knee. The spots are small, the size of a lentil, a millet seed, bright red, not elevated above the skin, disappearing on pressure of the finger; they become gradually a dirty brown, yellowish, the skin over the spots appears somewhat branny, the eruption comes by fits and starts, often thoughout several weeks. Every slight change in temperature, for instance going around in a room that is a little cooled off, can produce a new eruption. The disease appears usually with fever; the fever has a remitting type. Towards evening the appearances are most marked; in the morning there is a letting-up of the signs.

Although Schönlein's years in Zurich were rewarding professionally, he considered himself more a foreigner than an adopted son, and, when the opportunity came to return to Germany and to direct the clinic in Berlin, it was readily accepted. Meanwhile, he had declined a similar post in Berne and the honor as physician-in-ordinary to the court of the Belgians. By then the popular concepts of the natural philosophy school at Landshut had lost favor, and his teaching of clinical medicine based upon observation and repetitive experience was thoroughly integrated in the school of natural history, the basis of modern physical diagnosis in the examination of the patient.

1. Virchow, R.: *Gedächtnissrede auf Joh. Lucas Schönlein*, Berlin: A. Hirschwald, 1865.
2. Schönlein, J. L.: On the Pathogenesis of Impetigos, *Anat Physiol Wissenschaft Med.* 1839, p. 82, excerpt translated by F. Sternthal.
3. Schönlein, J. L.: "Peliosis Rheumatica," in *Allgemeine und specielle Pathologie und Therapie*, 3rd ed, vol 3, Herisau, Switzerland: Literatur-Comptoir, 1837, pp 48-49, trans. in Major, R. H.: *Classic Descriptions of Disease*, Springfield, Ill: Charles C Thomas, 1932, p 177.

Robert Gooch (1784-1830)

ROBERT GOOCH OF LONDON, an outstanding physician of his time, was born at Yarmouth, Norfolk, the son of a sea captain.[1] In spite of his failure to enjoy the advantages of a classical education, his intellectual endowment and industry were exploited maximally. At 15 he was apprenticed to surgeon-apothecary Borrett. Through a chance friendship with a blind Mr. Harley, he acquired, while reading aloud and up-

holding his part in nightly dialogue, a taste for literature, philosophy, and abstract reasoning. Formal studies in medicine were begun at Edinburgh; where he graduated MD in 1807, presenting in Latin an inaugural dissertation on rickets. The following winter

Composite by G. Bako

Gooch studied anatomy and surgery at the Borough hospitals in London, tutored under Astley Cooper, and, in 1808, began general practice at Croydon.

Following the death from consumption of his wife and later his only child, Gooch came to London; there he practiced until his early death at the age of 45, also presumed to be from tuberculosis. The move to London was not a thoughtless transition, for he had established a professional and literary reputation by contributing to the *London Medical Review* and was soon admitted a licentiate of the College of Physicians. He chose to become an accoucheur and accepted appointments to the Westminster Lying-In Hospital and the City of London Lying-In Hospital; Gooch also served as joint lecturer on midwifery at St. Bartholomew's Hospital. The appointments provided unusual opportunities for professional experience, and he soon gained fame as a male midwife and consultant in the diseases of women; while his remarkable intellect compensated for periods of physical infirmity.

Two major treatises were composed by Gooch. *An Account of Some of the Most Important Diseases Peculiar to Women* appeared first in 1829.[2] The leading text in his day, it was reprinted by the New Sydenham Society with a prefatory essay by Robert Ferguson. Probably his greatest literary accolade was the appointment as librarian to the King, the first medical officer to serve in this position. Gooch's *Lectures on Practical Midwifery,* delivered at St. Bartholomew's Hospital, appeared in 1831. Three of his best published contributions discussed puerperal insanity, spread of puerperal fever, and the Anatomy Act. A discussion of puerperal insanity, with case studies and a grim prognosis, which was read at the College of Physicians in 1819, contained the following passages.[3]

It is well known that some women, who are perfectly sane at all other times, become deranged after delivery, and that this form of the disease is called puerperal insanity. My situation gives me more than the common opportunities of seeing it, and though I am unable to make any important additions to our knowledge of the subject, I have witnessed some things which seem to me to deserve relation: these I will venture to describe, together with what I have observed about the causes, progress, and treatment, of this distressing malady.

The most common time for it to begin is a few days, or a few weeks, after delivery; sometimes it happens after several months, during nursing, or soon after weaning; I have seen it at the commencement of pregnancy, and it is said sometimes to arise at the commencement of labour.

The approach of the disease is announced by symptoms which excite little apprehension, because they so often occur without any such termination; the pulse is quick without any manifest cause, the nights are restless, and the temper is sharp; soon, however, there is an indescribable hurry, and peculiarity of manner, which a watchful and experienced observer and those accustomed to the patient will notice her conduct and language become wild and incoherent, and at length she becomes decidedly maniacal; it is fortunate if she does not attempt her life before the nature of the malady is discovered.

In a committee report, *The Doctrine of Contagion in the Plague,* which appeared in 1826 Gooch displays familiarity with the spread of puerperal fever some time before Holmes and Semmelweis began the collection of epidemiologic data which led to preventive measures and control of infection. In an unsigned report, believed to be a contribution by Gooch, the communication contains the following.[4]

Lying-in women are subject to a disease called puerperal fever. In general it is of unfrequent occurrence, and out of large numbers scarcely one suffers from it. There are times, however, when this disease rages like an epidemic, and is very fatal. At these times circumstances occur which create a strong suspicion that the disorder may be communicated by a medical attendant or nurse from one lying-in woman to another. We give the following out of many authentic instances. A surgeon practising midwifery in a populous town, opened the body of a woman who died of puerperal fever, and thereby contracted an offensive smell in his clothes: nevertheless, surgeon-like, he continued to wear them, and to visit and deliver his patients in them. The first woman whom he attended after the dissection, was seized with, and died of, the same disease—the same happened to the second and the third. At length he was struck with the suspicion that puerperal fever might be contagious, and that he was carrying it from patient to patient in his offensive clothes;—he burnt them, and not another of his patients was affected.

A powerful plea in support of the Anatomy Act for the lawful supply of suitable material for dissection, basic in the training of anatomist and surgeon, was concluded as follows.[5]

In the mean time, to the framers of the bill, aided by competent advisers, we leave the details of its provisions, begging them to carry this at least in their minds—that there are only three plans from which to select: one, to prohibit the study of anatomy altogether, and cause surgery to relapse into the infancy of the art; another, to support the breed of resurrection-men, plunder graves, and, after all, supply the nation with half-informed anatomists and unskillful surgeons; the last is to give up unclaimed bodies to the schools of anatomy, by which resurrection-men would be abolished, the buried lie quietly in their graves, and the nation be supplied with an ample stock of expert anatomists and dexterous surgeons. The legislature and the nation must take their choice; and, should they unfortunately select one of the two former, they cannot in reason complain of, and ought not in justice to punish, that professional ignorance which is the inevitable consequence of either of those measures.

1. Munk, W.: *The Roll of the Royal College of Physicians of London,* ed 2, 1878, vol 3, pp 100-105.

2. Gooch, R.: *An Account of Some of the Most Important Diseases Peculiar to Women,* London: J. Murray, 1829.

3. Gooch, R.: Observations on Puerperal Insanity, *Med Trans* 6:263-324, 1820.

4. Gooch, R.: The Progress of Opinions on the Subject of Contagion, *Quart Rev* 33:218-257, 1826.

5. Gooch, R.: A Bill for Presenting the Unlawful Disinterment of Human Bodies, and for Regulating Schools of Anatomy, *Quart Rev* 42:1-17, 1830.

Composite by G. Bako

James Blundell (1790-1877)

JAMES BLUNDELL, proponent of physiological concepts, teacher of the conservative practice of obstetrics, and one of the first to practice blood transfusion in humans, was an eccentric physician of Guy's Hospital. Little is known of Blundell's early life beyond the cursory details provided by Pettigrew[1] in his *Medical Portrait Gallery.* He notes that Blundell was born in London and received an excellent classical education under Rev. Thomas Thomason.

Blundell's medical education began at the United Southwark Hospitals, where he studied anatomy and surgery under Sir Astley Cooper and midwifery and physiology with his maternal uncle, Dr. John Haighton, a dominant influence in his professional career. His medical studies continued at Edinburgh, and, upon presentation of a thesis prepared in Latin discussing the senses for music and hearing, he received the MD degree in 1813. Returning to London, he began his academic career with lectures on midwifery under Haighton, to which he added shortly thereafter a course in physiology. He was admitted a licentiate of the Royal College of Physicians in 1818; and in the same year succeeded his uncle as lecturer in the united schools of St. Thomas' and Guy's hospitals.

Blundell's experimental work was initiated and completed within a decade. His important physiological contributions, investigations of surgical management of the pelvic organs, and introduction into clinical practice of the transfusion of whole blood have been attributed to his intimacy with Haighton. Practicing vivisection, Blundell refuted the arguments of the opposition and maintained that gains from physiological knowledge justified the experimental exposure of animals in the laboratory. The importance of blood transfusion was offered as an example which carried direct implications from the dog to man. From the laboratory facilities at Guy's Hospital, he presented in 1818 his findings associated with the transfusion of whole blood, by means of the syringe, in a series of dogs.[2] The benefits of rapid execution of the procedure to prevent coagulation of blood, the importance of avoiding the introduction of air into the recipient's veins, and the incompatibility of heterologous donors were discussed.

Although the possibility of transfusing whole blood from human to human had been discussed in the literature for centuries, Blundell made the hypothesis a reality. He completed four successful transfusions out of slightly more than twice this number. As he pursued his experimental trials in dogs, he performed, with a syringe, the first transfusion in humans in 1818.[2]

Complicated instruments were described subsequently. One device named an "Impellor" provided blood under pressure to the recipient; the Gravitator, a gravity feed apparatus, was described in the *Lancet* in 1829. The indications for transfusion included postpartum hemorrhage, extreme malnutrition, puerperal fever, cancer of the pylorus, ruptured uterus, and hydrophobia. Since each of his patients was critically ill at the time of decision, it is impossible to discover from the clinical notes whether a transfusion reaction appeared as a complication in any. Excerpts from the *Lancet* report follow.[3]

In the present state of our knowledge respecting the operation, although it has not been clearly shown to have proved fatal in any one instance, yet not to mention possible, though unknown risks, inflammation of the arm has certainly been produced by it on one or two occasions; and therefore seems right, as the operation now stands, to confine transfusion to the first class of cases only, namely, those in which there seems to be no hope for the patient, unless blood can be thrown into the veins.

The object of the Gravitator is, to give help in this last extremity, by transmitting the blood in a regulated stream from one individual to another, with as little exposure as may be to air, cold, and inanimate surface; ordinary venesection being the only operation performed on the person who emits the blood; and the insertion of a small tube into the vein usually laid open in bleeding, being all the operation which it is necessary to execute on the person who receives it.

Although the description of the instrument must appear complex, its use is simple; in truth, when the transfusion is once begun, the operator has little to do; his principal cares are—first, to see that the cup never empties itself entirely, otherwise air might be carried down along with the blood. Secondly, to make sure that blood which issues by dribbling, from the arm of the person who supplies it, may not be admitted into the receiver, as its fitness for use is doubtful. Thirdly, to watch the accumulation of blood in the receiver, and to prevent its rise above the prescribed level; and, lastly, to observe with attention the countenance of the patient, and to guard, as before stated, against an overcharge of the heart. *This latter cause is of great importance.*

Blundell's experimental investigations of the response of the peritoneum of animals to surgical interference held considerable interest because of the possibilities for surgical advances generally and for obstetrics and gynecology specifically. He accumulated convincing evidence that the abdomen was surgically approachable. Proceeding to implement these observations in humans, he gained experience in correcting intraperitoneal rupture of the bladder, relieving intestinal intussusception by passing the folds of the small bowel through the fingers after a small abdominal incision, dividing the Fallopian tubes at Caesarean operation to prevent further pregnancy, and alleviating severe dysmenorrhea by removal of healthy ovaries.

In his obstetrical practice and teaching, Blundell urged against unnecessary interference, differentiated between placenta previa and accidental hemorrhage, advised late interference only in breech presentation, was cautious in employing forceps, and treated eclampsia by venesection, emetics, and purgatives. Vaginal or abdominal hysterectomy was recommended for cancer of the cervix. His lectures in physiology and midwifery appeared in the *Lancet* against his wishes but in accordance with a policy practiced by Wakley, the editor. His treatise, entitled *Researches Physiological and Pathological, Instituted Principally with a View to Improvement of Medical and Surgical Practice,* was prepared as three essays.[4] The second on generation in rabbits proved that semen must have access to the rudiments for reproduction, and that the corpus luteum develops unrelated to pregnancy. His *Lectures on Midwifery,* assembled as a text in 1832,[5] was followed by a larger volume on *The Principles and Practice of Obstetricy,* edited by Castle,[6] which was superseded in 1837 by his *Observations on Some of the More Important Diseases of Women,* also edited by Castle.[7] This text was popular as judged by its several revisions and editions, including printings outside of Great Britain.

Blundell was admitted a Fellow of the Royal College of Physicians in 1838, two years after he retired from Guy's Hospital in an irreconcilable dispute with the administration. The loss to Guy's and to future pupils who might have benefited from his research and teaching was great. He retired from these pursuits to full-time practice and eccentric hours of work. He arose at midday, saw patients in his office at home throughout the afternoon, and spent the evening making house calls in his carriage, which was fitted with illumination so that he could read between calls. Blundell's secondary retirement, this time from practice while in his late fifties, enabled him to devote his leisure to literary pursuits, especially the study of Greek.

1. Pettigrew, T. J.: *Biographical Memoirs of the Most Celebrated Physicians, Surgeons, etc., Medical Portrait Gallery,* vol 1, London: Fisher, Son, & Co., 1840.
2. Blundell, J.: Experiments on the Transfusion of Blood by the Syringe, *Medicochir Trans* 9:56-92, 1818.
3. Blundell, J.: Observations of Transfusion of Blood, *Lancet* 2:321-324, 1829.
4. Blundell, J.: *Researches Physiological and Pathological,* London: E. Cox & Son, 1824.
5. Blundell, J.: *Lectures on Midwifery and the Diseases of Women and Children,* London: Field & Bull, 1832.
6. Blundell, J.: *The Principles and Practice of Obstetricy,* T. Castle (ed.), Washington: D. Green, 1834.
7. Blundell, J.: *Observations on Some of the More Important Diseases of Women,* T. Castle (ed.), London: E. Cox, 1837.

National Library of Medicine

John Bostock The Younger (1773-1846)

JOHN BOSTOCK was the only child of Dr. and Mrs. John Bostock of Liverpool.[1] He was educated at the University of Edinburgh, received the MD degree in 1798 and returned to his native city. There he settled in practice, was elected one of the physicians to the General Dispensary, and remained until 1817. He then moved to London and abandoned the practice of medicine, to engage in the study of chemistry, physiology, and general science.

In spite of his excellent exposure to distinguished scientists in Edinburgh, Liverpool, and London, perusal of his curriculum vitae leaves little doubt that he fell short of career expectations. The clinical description of hay fever, from which he suffered, was the exception. His bitter and irresponsible remarks published in 1810 on the new edition of the *London Pharmacopoeia,* which had been prepared by the London College of Physicians, had little impact upon contemporary medical practice. The suggestions for nomenclature, in which he advocated the use of long chemical or botanical terms instead of easily identifiable names, have long since been forgotten. Red precipitate of lead, readily recognized in the profession, was termed by Bostock *Oxidum hydrargyri rubrum per acidum nitricum.* If his recommendations had prevailed, the *Pharmacopoeia* today would be scarcely understood except by the organic chemist, and many generic names and all brand names would be disallowed. He prepared varied contributions to the *Annals of Philosophy,* the *Medico-Chirurgical Transactions,* and the *Edinburgh Medical Journal,* as well as various chapters for Forbes, Tweedie, and Conolly's *Cyclopedia of Practical Medicine,* and Todd's *Cyclopedia of Anatomy and Physiology.* Monographs included *An Essay on Respiration* (1804), *An Account of the History and Present State of Galvinism* [sic] (1818), and *A Sketch of the History of Medicine, From Its Origin to the Commencement of the Nineteenth Century* (1835). From 1824 through 1827, he published three volumes of *An Elementary System of Physiology,* judged a superficial treatise of his day.

Only Bostock's description of hay fever deserves rereading for its scientific contents a century and a half later. His first communication in 1819 on the matter was a case report of a patient suffering from inflammation of the eyes and chest. In 1828, he summarized his findings on 28 cases, proposed the name "catarrhus aestivus," and acknowledged that Heberden and others had mentioned features of the malady in earlier and briefer communications. Proper credit is due Bostock, however, because he described the seasonal symptoms of the syndrome—inflammation and watering of the eyes, fullness of the head, congestion of the nasal passages alternating with rhinorrhea, sneezing, and shortness of breath. His symptoms began at the age of eight; he found benefit from exposure to fresh cool air. The concluding excerpt was prepared from the 1828 report;[2] the other passages are excerpted from the 1819 communication.[3]

About the beginning or middle of June in every year the following symptoms make their appearance, with a greater or less degree of violence. A sensation of heat and fulness is experienced in the eyes, first along the edges of the lids, and especially in the inner angles, but after some time over the whole of the ball. At the commencement the external appearance of the eye is little affected, except that there is a slight degree of redness and a discharge of tears. This state gradually increases, until the sensation becomes converted into what may be characterized as a combination of the most acute itching and smarting, accompanied with a feeling of small points striking upon or darting into the ball, at the same time that the eyes become extremely inflamed, and discharge very copiously a thick mucous fluid. This state of the eyes comes on in paroxysms, at uncertain intervals, from about the second week in June to the middle of July. The eyes are seldom quite well for the whole of this period, but the violent paroxysms never occur more than two or three times daily, lasting an hour or two each time; but with respect to their frequency and duration there is the greatest uncertainty.

After this state of the eyes has subsided for a week or ten tays, a general fulness is experienced in the head, and particularly about the fore part; to this succeeds irriation of the nose, producing sneezing, which occurs in fits of extreme violence, coming on at uncertain intervals. To the sneezings are added a farther sensation of tightness of the chest, and a difficulty of breathing, with a general irritation of the fauces and trachea. There is no absolute pain in any part of the chest, but a feeling of want of room to receive the air necessary for respiration, a huskiness of the voice, and an incapactity of speaking aloud for any time without inconvenience.

With respect to what is termed the exciting cause of the disease, since the attention of the public has been turned to the subject, an idea has very generally prevailed, that it is produced by the effluvium from new hay, and it has hence obtained the popular name of the hay-fever. As it is extremely important to ascertain the truth of this opinion, I have made it the subject of distinct observation, as far as regards my own person, and by minutely attending to the accession of the symptoms, for a number of successive seasons, in relation to this supposed cause, I think myself fully warranted in asserting, that in my own case the effluvium from hay has no connection with the disease.

Bostock served on the committee of the Fever Hospital, was active as a member or an administrator in the Medico-Chirurgical Society, the Royal Society, the Royal Society of Literature, and the Geological, Linnaean, Zoological, Horticultural, and Astronomical societies of London. He held membership in the Royal Academy of Medicine of France, and was honorary member of the Literary and Philosophical Society of New York. Although he had long withdrawn from the practice of medicine, as late as 1834 he evinced interest in this subject by a brochure, entitled, "Outlines of a Plan for the Future Regulation of the Medical Profession," a proposal to ensure a supply of competent practitioners and to promote the dignity of the profession.

1. Pettigrew, T. J.: "John Bostock, M.D. F.R.S.," In *Biographical Memoirs of the Most Celebrated Physicians, Surgeons, etc.*, London: Whittaker & Co., 1839, pp 1-20.
2. Bostock, J.: Of the Catarrhus Aestivus, or Summer Catarrh, *Medicochir Trans* 14:437-446, 1828.
3. Bostock, J.: Case of a Periodical Affection of the Eyes and Chest, *Medicochir Trans* 10:161-165, 1819.

Los Angeles County Medical Library

Marie Francois Xavier Bichat
(1771-1802)

XAVIER BICHAT, a brilliant man of medicine, interposed his interpretations of tissue structure between the organ pathology of Morgagni and the cellular pathology of Virchow. In a remarkably short time in the medical world, Bichat established the significance of tissues in the study of anatomy and pathology.

Born at Thoirette, he early showed proficiency in the Latin language, mathematics, and physics. His father, a doctor of medicine at the University of Montpellier, gave him instruction in medicine and surgery; this was followed by anatomical instructions at Lyons under surgeon Petit. The Revolution forced Bichat to seek refuge in Paris; there, as a part, he sat at the feet of Desault and other lecturers at Hôtel Dieu.[1]

During the early days in Paris, an epochal event in the classroom mentioned by most of his biographers occurred. It was customary for an assigned pupil to present to the abstractors, as a review for the class, a summary of the lecture of the preceding day. Bichat's opportunity came when the tardiness of the assigned pupil gave Bichat the opportunity to make an impromptu but brilliant presentation. This incident caught Desault's attention, and he then befriended Bichat and took him into his home as an adopted son and professional associate. He was apprenticed to his master at rounds, at operations, and in his literary labors. Upon Desault's sudden death in 1795, the tragedy became a stimulus rather than a deterrent to his pupil's activities and reputation.

Bichat became a teacher at the age of 26, giving informal demonstrations to a small class and simultaneously developing his system of structure and function. His success rapidly forced him to seek larger quarters for demonstrations in dissection and experiments in physiology. The days passed in teaching, investigation, and a limited practice; whereas late hours at night were spent in medical cogitation, planning, and drafting. Within a period of five years, his medical studies at Hôtel Dieu provided sufficient data to lead to four major publications: *A Treatise on the Membranes, Physiological Researches on Life and Death, General Anatomy Applied to Physiology and Medicine,* and *Pathological Anatomy,* a posthumous volume prepared by Béclard from Bichat's last course of lectures. Excerpts from three of these works follow.

Without benefit of the microscope Bichat founded the science of histology—the study of tissues. He used to advantage, however, his special senses, a capacity for deduction, and available procedures for analyzing the components of the body, including dissection, putrefaction, desiccation, maceration, boiling, and chemical action. The analysis was supported by pertinent animal experiments and critical surgical observations, leading to an understanding of the integration of function and structure. According to Bichat an organ was made up of several tissues; whereas disease might induce pathological change in one tissue only. Thus, in a malady of the heart, the endocardium might be involved while the myocardium remained sound, or the pleura might escape even though the parenchyma of the lung would be seriously affected.

Bichat identified three simple membranous tissues: mucous membranes, serous membranes, and fibrous membranes. The superior resistance to inflammation by mucous membranes over serous membranes was recognized. Their nature, quality, and reaction under normal and pathological stimuli were other differences of the simple membranes.[1]

7. In thus classing the membranes we may, I believe, refer them to two general divisions, simple and compound. I call those, simple membranes, which are not connected by any direct relations of organization, with the parts contiguous; a compound membrane is formed of two or three of the preceding, and often unites characters very dissimilar.

8. We may distribute the simple membranes into three general classes; the first comprises the *mucous* membranes, so named from the fluid which habitually moistens their unconnected surface, and which is furnished by the small glands inherent in their structure. They line all the hollow organs which communicate exteriorly by different openings through the skin; such are the cavities of the mouth, the oesophagus, the stomach, the intestines, the bladder, the womb, the nasal fossae, all the excretory ducts, etc. In the second class are found the *serous* membranes, also characterized by the lymphatic fluid, which incessantly lubricates them, and which, being separated from the mass of blood by exhalation, differs in this from the preceding fluid, which escapes from the blood by secretion.

Here belong the pericardium, pleura, peritoneum, the tunica vaginalis, the arachnoides, the synovial membrane of the joints, that of the groove of the tendons, etc.

The third and last class comprehends the *fibrous* membranes; these, not moistened by any fluid, are thus named from their texture, composed of a white fibre, analogous to that of the tendons, and to which are referred the periosteum, the duramater, the sclerotica, the envelope of the corpora cavernosa, the aponeuroses, the articular capsules, the tendinous sheaths, etc.

Bichat's *General Anatomy* was prepared in three volumes. The title page notes his affiliation at Hôtel Dieu as physician and professor of anatomy and physiology. A significant portion of the first volume was devoted to general observations, deductions from physiological experiments, and postmortem observations. A vitalistic doctrine of the characteristics of living bodies was prepared and physiological phenomena referred to these functions. As the thesis was developed, examples were given of the relation of tissues to disease of organs and the varied susceptibility of textures to afflictions.[2]

Observe the itch, herpes, cancer, venereal disease, &c. when they have ceased to be local affections, they spread themselves universally; they alternately attack different textures, according to the relation which they have with the organic sensibility of these textures. But it is almost always separately that they attack them; an organ is never as a whole influenced by them in all its parts. What do I say? If two of these diseases exist at the same time, one seizes upon one texture, the other upon a different one of the same organ.

Let us not, however, exaggerate this independence of the textures of the organs in diseases, lest experience should contradict us. We shall see that the cellular system is oftentimes a medium of communication, not only from one texture to another in the same organ, but from one organ to a neighboring one. . . . Observe phthisis, exhibiting in the beginning some small tubercles in the pulmonary texture, at length invading oftentimes the pleura, the bronchial membrane, &c. How little soever you may examine bodies with a view to the same chronic disease, and at different periods, you will be convinced of the truth of this assertion, viz. that a texture being at first affected in an organ, communicates its affection gradually to others, and that you will be deceived in judging of the primitive seat of the disease, if you attempt to determine it from the parts found affected at the time of the examination.

Although Bichat's works proceeded from histology and physiology to general anatomy and pathological anatomy, there is continuous interweaving of his thoughts on each of the medical sciences. He was also concerned with practical clinical matters of the doctor in his labors. Diseases as well as physicians were divided into two groups. In the preliminary discourse of his last session on pathological anatomy, he mentions the goals in practice, the response to disease of the general system in contrast to the response of an organ, and the value of the postmortem examination.[3]

Medicine has two general objects in view; first, the knowledge of diseases, and second, their cure. Under this last relation there are few diseases submitted to the empire of medicine, and it is only to the former that we refer pathological anatomy.

Disease may be divided into two classes: those which affect the general system, and those which attack only one organ in particular. The first do not come under the cognizance of pathological anatomy. All the diverse kinds of fevers produce a general derangement, although, oftentimes no organ be particularly injured. The knowledge of general diseases differs essentially from that of organic diseases: for the former, observation is sufficient; in the latter, on the contrary, we have besides observation, *postmortem examination.*

It is well known into how many errors we have fallen, so long as we had confined ourselves to the simple observation of symptoms. Let us take for example consumption. It has been considered as an *essential malady,* before we had recourse to post-mortem examination; since, it has been shown that marasmus was only a consecutive symptomatic malady of the affection of an organ. Jaundice has been for a long time considered by practitioners as an *essential malady;* post-mortem examination has also proved that this affection, thought primitive, was in reality only consecutive to diverse alterations of the liver, of which it is always the symptom.

We may distinguish two classes of physicians; those who have only observed, and those who to observation have added post-mortem examination. The former are very numerous; the latter are confined to a very small number, and are only to be met with in the last century.

Only a few medical scientists have been able to compress into a few years of maturity the quantity of investigation, teaching, and writing of a Bichat. In one specific domain, postmortem examination, accomplishments include more than 600 autopsies in less than a year. One wonders whether he enjoyed any leisure moments.

1. Bichat, X.: *A Treatise on the Membranes,* J. G. Coffin (trans.), Boston: Cummings and Hilliard, 1813.

2. Bichat, X., *General Anatomy, Applied to Physiology and Medicine,* 3 vol, G. Hayward (trans.), Boston: Richardson and Lord, 1822.

3. Béclard, P. A.: *Pathological Anatomy. The Last Course of Xavier Bichat,* J. Togno (trans), Philadelphia: J. Grigg, 1827.

Composite by G. Bako

Robert Willan (1757-?)

ROBERT WILLAN, of Quaker stock, was the founder of modern dermatology in England. Together with Thomas Bateman, pupil and devoted associate, he established the classification and description of dermatologic disorders on a firm basis that was widely accepted for generations.[1] Willan was born near Sedbergh, Yorkshire, in 1757, the son of a practitioner of medicine. His biographers noted that he was a favorite pupil and was advanced into the classes of his seniors, where he maintained his status by the excellence of his lessons and exercises.[2] "He became ultimately an accomplished classical scholar, and was deemed to excel his master in his critical knowledge of Greek." Formal medical education was completed at Edinburgh at the age of 23. Following postgraduate training in London and a short period of private practice at Darlington, Willan acceded to the inducement of John Fothergill and settled in London in 1782, where he remained throughout his professional career. One propitious incident is related to his fine scholarship. Although the examination for licensure in the Royal College of Physicians was conducted in Latin, Willan addressed the censors at the conclusion with phrases of praise in Greek. In the professional years, his study of antiquities was continued, especially in the study of primeval Greek and in the review of epidemic and contagious diseases in the early centuries of the Christian era.

Willan began visiting and lecturing at the Public Dispensary; later he added the Finsbury Dispensary. The initial lectures covering the principles and practice of medicine were dismal failures, even though they were carefully prepared and were based upon case histories recorded in "neat Latin style."[2] The students preferred the large teaching hospitals of London to the small and less attractive dispensaries. After this unsuccessful pedagogic venture, he changed from formal lecturing to informal bedside teaching. This proved to be a wise decision since it greatly aided the development of the discipline of cutaneous disorders and carried the Public Dispensary to the mythical designation as the "Cradle of Dermatology in England."

Willan's classification of dermatologic disorders reckoned with and correlated Greek, Latin, and Arabic terms. The general plan of the presentation and description had been communicated to the Medical Society of London in 1785, and in 1790, he was awarded the Fothergillian Gold Medal. Of the six medalists in the history of this award, Edward Jenner was so honored for his contributions to smallpox. By 1808, Willan had largely completed the first volume in the proposed definitive series.[3] His death in 1812 interrupted the project, which was completed by Bateman.[4] A number of other subjects were treated by Willan in his lifetime. Public health, antiquarianism, the ministry of Jesus Christ, and the intemperate use of spirituous liquors are not usually associated with a teacher of bedside medicine. Clinical subjects included chorea, obstruction of the bowels, anascara, and scarlet fever.

The description by Willan of the disorders of the integument was clear and precise, and the qualifying terms were chosen with skill and imagination. Eight orders of cutaneous diseases were defined: I, Papulae; II, Squamae; III, Exanthemata; IV, Bullae; V, Pustulae; VI, Vesiculae; VII, Tubercula; VIII, Maculae. Bateman extended this list to include four additional classes.

Sutherland, in a detailed study of the publishing of the *Description and Treatment of Cutaneous Diseases,* recounts the serial appearance of the several portions, a common practice at that time.[5] The first portion (order 1) appeared in 1798, with orders 2, 3, and 4 in the following years. Volume 1, the only volume finished by Willan, was dated 1808, and was composed of the 1798, 1801, 1805, and 1808 portions, which were bound at the discretion of the subscribers. Originals of the first three portions are available in the rare book collection of the College of Physicians Library, Philadelphia. In the introduction, Willan outlined the motif of his treatise:[6]

1. To fix the sense of the terms employed, by proper definitions.
2. To constitute general divisions or orders of the diseases, from leading and peculiar circumstances in their appearance: to arrange them into their distinct genera, and to describe at large their specific forms, or varieties.
3. To classify and give names to such as have not been hitherto sufficiently distinguished.
4. To specify the mode of treatment for each disease.

Although not an uncompromising therapeutic nihilist, Willan expressed little faith in drugs; rather, placed emphasis upon bathing and cleanliness as proper prophylaxis for skin troubles, particularly against occupational dermatoses.

The original descriptions of cutaneous diseases have been judged to be of greater value than his classification. He described psoriasis, ichthyosis, sycosis, pityriasis versicolor, lupus, erythema nodosum, pemphigus, impetigo, several forms of dermatitis in the general category of eczema, Henoch's purpura with visceral symptoms, and herpes iris. It seems appropriate to reproduce in this essay excerpts from Willan's descriptions of psoriasis, ichthyosis, erythema nodosum, and pemphigus. In the discussion of one of the "Scaly Diseases of the Skin," Willan noted, on psoriasis:[3]

The second Order of Cutaneous Diseases includes those affections which are characterized by an appearance of Scales, arising from a morbid state of the cuticle [psoriasis], as specified in the second Definition.
1. The LEPRA VULGARIS at first exhibits small, distinct elevations of the cuticle, which are redish and shining, but never contain any fluid. Their

surface, when examined through a magnifying glass, appears tense and smooth; within twenty-four hours, however, thin white scales form on their tops.

This species of Lepra sometimes appears first at the elbow, or on the fore arm, but more generally about the knee. In the latter case, the primary patch forms immediately below the patella. Within a few weeks, several other scaly circles appear along the fore parts of the leg and thigh, increasing by degrees till they come nearly into contact. . . .

1. The scaly patches are generally situated where the bone is nearest the surface, as, along the shin, about the elbow, and upon the ulna in the forearm; on the scalp, and along the spine, os ilium, and shoulder-blades. They rarely appear on the calf of the leg, on the fleshy part of the arm and thigh, or within the flexures of the joints.

2. The Lepra almost constantly affects both sides, appearing at each elbow or at each knee about the same time, and extending from thence along the limbs, in a smiilar manner.

3. Though fresh patches arise, from time to time, in different situations, there is no alteration in the state of the parts first affected, as happens in some other cutaneous diseases.

4. The incrustation of the scalp encroaches a little on the forehead and temples: but I have never yet observed any of the scaly patches on the cheeks, or chin, on the nose, or near the eye-brows.

Willan described ichthyosis, as excerpted from the 1801 copy:[6]

The characteristic of ICHTHYOSIS is a permanently harsh, dry, scaly, and, in some cases, almost horny texture of the integuments of the body, unconnected with internal disorder. Psoriasis, and Lepra differ from this affection in being but partially diffused, and in having deciduous scales.

The arrangement, and distribution of the scales in Ichthyosis are peculiar. Above and below the olecranon on the arm, . . . and in a similar situation with respect to the patella on the thigh and leg, they are small, rounded, prominent or papillary, and of a black colour. . . . There is usually, in this complaint a dryness, and roughness of the soles of the feet; sometimes a thickened, and brittle state of the skin in the palms of the hands, with large painful fissures, and on the face an appearance of scurf rather than of scales.

On erythema nodosum, Willan noted:[3]

6. In the ERYTHEMA NODOSUM, many of the red patches are large and rounded: The central parts of them are very gradually elevated, and on the sixth or seventh day, form hard and painful protuberances, which are often taken for imposthumes, but from the seventh to the tenth they constantly soften and subside, without ulceration.

The Erythema nodosum usually affects the fore part of the legs. I have only seen it in females, most of whom were servants. It is preceded by irregular shiverings, nausea, head-ache, and fretfulness, with a quick unequal pulse, and a whitish fur on the tongue. These symptoms continue for a week, or more, but they usually abate on the appearance of the Erythema.

The description of pemphigus (Pompholyx diutinus-Pemphigus vegetans) was noteworthy.[3]

2. The POMPHOLYX DIUTINUS is a tedious and painful disorder, chiefly affecting persons of a debilitated constitution, and particularly severe in those who are of an advanced age. It commences with numerous bullae or vesications on the face and arms, and is diffused, by a gradual progression, to the neck and breasts, and round the body, to the groins, thighs, and legs, and sometimes to the tongue, fauces, and the inside of the cheeks . . . within twenty-four hours they are of the size of a pea, and perfectly transparent, but if permitted to dilate, they afterwards become as large as a walnut, sometimes assuming a yellowish hue. If the fluid be discharged from any of them by a small orifice, they are again filled with lymph during the succeeding night. When the vesications are rubbed off, or otherwise removed prematurely, the excoriated surface is extremely sore and inflamed, and does not heal for a considerable time. . . . In some cases under my own observation, it continued two months, in others three, or four, or even five months, so that the whole number of bullae amounted to several thousands. After a cessation of some weeks, or months, the eruption frequently returned again, and proceeded in the same manner as before.

Willan is described as a benevolent and kindly physician, sympathetic in the sickroom, friendly in conversation with associates, and interested in the indigent of London. He deplored the miserable living conditions, the high incidence of contagious diseases, especially pulmonary tuberculosis, and furthered the opportunities for correction through promotion of public health. Technical improvements were recommended in the manufacture of white lead to protect against lead intoxication. A treatise, praised by Jenner, was prepared on inoculation against smallpox. The establishment of a recovery or fever hospital for patients with pulmonary disease was urged, in spite of vigorous protests lest the hospital spread contagion rather than check it. However, the institute opened in 1802, and Willan was appointed a senior physician on the staff.[7]

> The good effects of all these applications are often superseded by the miserable accommodations of the poor, with respect to bedding, and by a total neglect of ventilation in their narrow, crowded dwellings. It will scarcely appear credible, though it is precisely true, that persons of the lowest class do not put clean sheets on their beds three times a year; that, even where no sheets are used, they never wash or scour their blankets and coverlets, nor renew them till they are no longer tenable . . . lastly, that from three to eight individuals, of different ages, often sleep in the same bed; there being, in general, but one room, and one bed, for each family. But where is a remedy we found for so many evils?—Hospitals are either barred against the entrance of contagious diseases, or, if leave of entrance be obtained, it generally comes when the patient is incapable of being removed, . . . Let Houses of Recovery be established in open, airy situations, at some distance from other buildings, but adjoining to different districts of the metropolis.

A woodcut of Willan is on the cover of each issue of the *British Journal of Dermatology,* a measure of the esteem in which he is held today. The founder of modern dermatology in Britain was succeeded by his equally famous pupil, Thomas Bateman, who continued with the preparation and publication of the system of cutaneous diseases, the standard text in dermatology for more than a generation. At least seven editions, with printings in America and translations into French, German, and Italian, appeared. Willan will be remembered as a physician with an uncompromising sympathy for the sick and the indigent and a broad clinical interest strengthened by a background in the classical languages, basic in the pursuit of scholarly medicine.

1. Lane, J. E.: Robert Willan, *Arch Derm (Chic)* 13:737-760 (June) 1926.
2. Bateman, T.: Biographical Memoir of the Late Dr. Willan, *Edinburgh Med Surg J* 8:502-512 (Oct.) 1812.
3. Willan, R.: *On Cutaneous Diseases,* vol. 1, London: J. Johnson, 1808.
4. Bateman, T.: *A Practical Synopsis of Cutaneous Diseases,* 2nd ed. London: Longman, Hurst, Rees, Orme, and Brown, 1813.
5. Sutherland, F. M.: Willan's Cutaneous Diseases, *J Hist Med* 13:92-94 (Jan.) 1958.
6. Willan, R.: *Description and Treatment of Cutaneous Diseases,* London: J. Johnson, 1801.
7. Willan, R.: *Reports on the Diseases of London,* London: R. Phillips, 1801.

National Library of Medicine

Jean Louis Alibert (1768-1837)

JEAN LOUIS ALIBERT inherited wards of medical derelicts at the Hôpital St. Louis as his first major professional assignment; in so doing, he was blessed with a golden opportunity for the study and classification of one of the largest groups of diseases in the hospital—those affecting the skin. The design of a "tree" of descriptive dermatology, unique lectures in the garden of St. Louis, and the tutelage of his star pupil, Biett, are notable accomplishments. Each contributed to the well-earned designation, "the Father of Parisian Dermatology and the Founder of the French School of Cutaneous Diseases."[1]

Alibert was born in 1768 in Villefranche-de-Rouergue, where his parents were important persons of the community. He decided to enter the priesthood, was accepted in the school conducted by the Fathers of the Christian Doctrine, and passed his novitiate at Toulouse. However, his resolve to teach upon returning home was summarily interrupted by the Revolution and the dispersal of all religious orders. At the age of 25, his manifest interest thwarted, he turned to Paris, where fame and fortune came to him after a period of indecision and uncertainty. The study of medicine was not begun until the age of 27; the friendships and influence of Roussel and Cabanis have been held responsible for the selection. A thesis on pernicious intermittent fevers, submitted for the MD degree, was dedicated to his favorite medical teacher, Philippe Pinel.[2] It was highly regarded and was published in several editions and translated into several languages.

Within two years after graduation, Alibert was appointed adjunct physician to Hôpital St. Louis followed by full staff membership. At the turn of the century, this hospital had been set aside by law for the reflux from Hôtel Dieu of patients with chronic disorders, since the physicians of the latter institution were primarily interested in acute problems. Although St. Louis was singled out as an institution for chronic diseases, a broad definition of the term was accepted. In practice, patients unwanted by other hospitals filled the wards. This included a preponderance of individuals with cutaneous maladies. The beds were occupied with sufferers from scurvy, glandular adenopathy, leprosy, the eczemas, cutaneous ulcers, cutaneous syphilis, and cutaneous tuberculosis. A physician of lesser stature might have fled to another hospital or accepted the assignment with resignation and failed to take full advantage of the unusual opportunity to bring order into the existing dermatologic chaos.

In formulating a descriptive system of cutaneous disease, Alibert brought fame to St. Louis as the pre-eminent hospital for dermatology in France, which has continued as a hospital exclusively for skin diseases. Alibert's classification, which he called *Nosologie Naturelle,* was patterned after the Linnaean concept of classification of the animal and vegetable kingdoms into order,

genera, and species. Alibert carried the analogy so far as to construct a tree with branches—a tree of dermatoses. His classification suffered by comparison with that of Willan, his contemporary in England, whose classification was based on the characteristics of the primary lesion. However, Alibert was responsible for several excellent clinical descriptions and the coining of terms that persist in current use. "Syphilid," "dermatosis," "keloid," and "dermatolysis" were included in Alibert's nosology. Both Willan and Alibert employed colored sketches to illustrate the cutaneous lesions. Alibert's lectures at St. Louis Hospital, his outlet for educational histrionics, were given in the garden of the hospital, weather permitting. He made dermatology a fascinating subject, emphasizing his points with similes and metaphors. The principles of practice of the French school of medicine were followed. Detailed and precise case histories were recorded; materia medica and therapeutics were discussed for each case. His fame attracted not only pupils and patients of the bourgoisie, but he also was the personal physician of Louis XVIII and Charles X. In 1823, the King appointed him professor of materia medica and therapeutics, since a chair of dermatology had not been founded.

Alibert's descriptions of keloid,[3] mycosis fungoides,[4] and pustule d' Aleppo (cutaneous leishmaniasis) are cited as notable contributions.[5]

A keloid is a fleshlike excrescence, sometimes oval, sometimes oblong, of pink color, and interspersed with whitish lines that are separated from each other. The keloid is absolutely adherent as if it were encased in the skin, and it transforms the color of the skin in the elevated places. It resembles the form of a scar resulting from severe burns, and sometimes it produces small elongations that are divided into branches. They somewhat resemble the feet of a crawfish, and this justifies the name I believe proper to be given to this truly extraordinary tumor.

The keloids I observed formed flat and compact tumors that were elevated at the edges and a little depressed towards the center. The latter condition was particularly true if they had an oval shape, and they protruded by one or two lines above the level of the teguments. The tumors were shiny, a bit wrinkled, and hard and resistant to touch. They had a very red color, and on their surface one could see a great number of small veins that were filled with a sanguine liquid. Their edges, however, had a much less intense color. If one compressed the keloid, it became momentarily white under the (pressure from the) fingers. The epidermis of the irritated part sometimes transformed itself into small scales. In certain cases I saw keloids of a cylindrical form; they looked as though they were encased in the interior of the skin. . . . Surgeons have sometimes excised those strange tumors. When examined after operation, they proved to have fibrous tissue that was tight, whitish, crossed and intertwined, like the glandular body of a breast.

These nodules [mycosis fungoides] generally affect the face, and successively the arms, the lower extremities, etc. In time one sees them soften, open, and produce a thick gummy pus with a greenish color. This results in virulent ulcers; the liquid which flows from them is so acrimonious that it produces eschars on the skin.

Two periods can be distinguished, therefore, in the course and deveopment of Pian fongoïde. In the first period of its existence the growths are so hard and renitent that one would hardly suspect an approaching suppuration. But in the second period the skin which covers them opens, and each tubercle becomes a fetid ulcer; as decomposition progresses, these tubercles take on a greenish black color or a very dark violaceous tint. One can picture them as fruits rotting on the stem that bears them.

The pustles of Pian fongoïde resemble warts, for the most part, when they begin to develop; later they enlarge, taking the form of mushrooms, and spread out in great numbers over the surface of the body. There eventually comes a time when almost the whole cutaneous surface is covered.

After some months the tumors collapse and shrink; the withered and dried skin is so insensible that it may sometimes be cut with the scissors without the patients feeling the least painful sensation. The latter fall little by little into a state of emaciation that weakens them to the extreme; they end up succumbing, or leading a miserable life for many years.

. . . there is another form of eruption which is no less strange and about which I should like my readers to learn. It is the disease usually called endemic pyrophlyctide [oriental sore or cutaneous leishmaniasis], according to my classification, and commonly known as Aleppo boil.

This pustular eruption occurs in foreigners as well as in natives; it appears in all parts of the human body, and it is in the different places in the tegumental structure that make the disease more inconvenient and more painful.

It usually starts with a pink point that rises and that, during its development, becomes ever more red. This point is painful when pressed, and it is covered with small white and scaly membranes which detach themselves successively.

Towards the third month the surface becomes covered with ridges which on their edges transform themselves into a crust of a barnacle-like shape. Also, a liquid, at first rather limpid, is seen to gush from the top, and it soils the laundry with a characteristic yellow color. Towards the sixth month the crust detaches itself and makes visible a purulent and fetid wound. The crust rapidly forms itself again, and from its edges it lets escape the periodic secretion of the ulcer which by then has all its force. One may expect that on 5 or 6 occasions the crusts will fall off, and this happens every three weeks. Eventually, the tumor declines until it is completely healed.

Concerning the cause for this extraordinary boil, it is supposed to be found in the water that fertilizes the gardens of Aleppo and feeds its fountains.

This, then, was the course of the disease commonly known as pustula of Aleppo. This disease is absolutely the same as the one known by the name of Baghdad boil and Ispahan boil. For in those two cities one can always notice people who have this desolating disease. By its characteristics it obviously belongs to the group of pyrophlyctics, according to my classification, and it is one of the eczematous dermatoses.

Scientific bodies throughout Europe honored Alibert with membership; he received the Order of St. Michael, became an officer of the Legion of Honor, was the founder of the Academy of Medicine, and was created a baron by the King.

His glory was dimmed by the preference of his brilliant pupil Biett for Willan's classification. Biett, upon his return home from London after studying under Willan, chose Willan's system of classification, which had greatly impressed him, rather than Alibert's nosology. In a vigorous and full professional career, this seems to be the only disheartening event for the Father of French Dermatology, who originally had decided to serve the church but took up medicine as a second choice. It is evident that medicine gained and the church lost. He died in 1837 of carcinoma of the stomach. The autopsy was performed by Cruveilhier.

1. Brodier, L.: J. L. Alibert, Médicin de l'hôpital Saint-Louis, 1768-1837, Paris: A Maloine & Sons, 1923.

2. Alibert, J. L.: Traité des Fièvres Pernicieuses Intermittentes, Paris: Crapart, Caille, & Ravier, 1804.

3. Alibert, J. L.: Remarks on Keloids, L. Woods, trans., Universel Sci Med 2:207-216, 1816.

4. Shelley, W. B., and Crissey, J. T.: "Mycosis Fungoides," in *Classics in Clinical Dermatology*, Springfield, Ill.: Charles C Thomas, Publisher, 1953.

5. Alibert, J. L.: On Endemic Pyrophlyctide, or Aleppo Pustula, (Fr) *Rev Med Franc* 3:62-68, 1829, excerpt translated by F. Sternthal.

Thomas Bateman (1778-1821)

THOMAS BATEMAN, son of a successful surgeon, was born in Whitby, in Yorkshire and followed the professional path of his teacher and colleague, Robert Willan.[1] The association of Bateman and Willan in the two major treatises on cutaneous diseases is so intimate that it is hazardous to attempt to disentangle and to identfy correctly the scientific accomplishments of each.[2,3] Bateman, before his death in 1821, and while still in mid-maturity, repented of his impiety and reaffirmed his belief in Christ in deep devotion. Such an emotional experience surely is not unique in medical practice but rarely is recorded in extant biographies.

The early days and schooling of Bateman were unremarkable, sometimes lackadaisical. The study of Latin was begun at the age of six. At the age of 16, he was apprenticed to an apothecary, meanwhile, being tutored in French, mathematics, and mineralogy. Full-time devotion to medical studies was assumed in 1797, at the age of 19, at the Windmill Street School of Anatomy in London, where Baillie and Cruikshank were lecturers. Time was also found to attend exercises at St. George's Hospital. An MD degree was granted in 1801 after 3 years of study at Edinburgh and the submission of a thesis on petechial hemorrhage. He returned to London for the practice of medicine, having completed a highly profitable period of training, in proper sequence i.e., apprenticeship in Yorkshire, anatomy and practical experience in London, and theoretical medicine in Edinburgh.

Bateman's attention to cutaneous disorders has been attributed to his awareness of the void in general and specific information on diseases of the integument, his habitual fondness for inquiry into morbidity marked by external characteristics, and a deep interest in the accumulation of valid clinical data and their arrangement in logical order. Since Willan was the leading student in London of cutaneous diseases, Bateman's attraction was a logical consequence. He enrolled as a pupil of Willan at the Public Dispensary and in 1804 was appointed physician to the Fever Institution, later renamed Fever Hospital. A year later he became a licentiate of the Royal College of Physicians. At the age of 27, Bateman had completed a course of instruction without compromise, had qualified for practice in London, and had selected the leading hospitals, dispensary, and dermatologist for professional alliance. Thereafter, his mind was never idle nor his desire to document his clinical findings unrequited. His industry was profound and unceasing. Minutes were precious and not to be wasted, irrespective of the time of day.[1]

His pen was always in his hand the moment he came downstairs in the morning. His papers and books were on the table during the short interval which elapsed before he breakfasted. And again at dinner-time, the little space that intervened between his return home and his dinner being put upon the table, was employed in the same way, unless indeed it was given to the organ. . . . In his daily rounds at the Dispensary he was equally careful not to waste time, taking every short cut, and not disdaining to contrive how to save even a few steps, since all these savings in the aggregate procured him a little more time.

Although Bateman attracted a large and lucrative clinical practice, considerable time was allocated to medical editing and medical writing. Together with Duncan and Reeve, he established the *Edinburgh Medical and Surgical Journal* in 1805, which continues as the *Edinburgh Medical Journal*. His best-known scientific writings are *A Practical Synopsis of Cutaneous Diseases*,[3] and the *Delineations of Cutaneous Diseases*.[2] Each book represents a revision and amplification of the descriptive and illustrative studies of dermatologic disorders started by Willan in 1798, but which were still incomplete upon Willan's death in 1812. Bateman's *Synopsis* was translated into French, German, and Italian; it was also a favorite of the Emperor of Russia, who welcomed subsequent contributions from Bateman's pen. Garrison attributes the original description of three skin conditions to Bateman: molluscum contagiosum, lichen urticatus (papular urticaria), and ecthyma, which are excerpted, as well as the reckoning of visceral symptoms of purpura haemorrhagica,[3] first described by Werlhof in 1735.

2. The PURPURA *haemorrhagica* . . . is considerably more severe; the petechiae are often of a larger size, and are interspersed with vibices and ecchymoses, or livid stripes and patches, resembling the marks left by the strokes of a whip, or by violent bruises. They commonly appear first on the legs, and at uncertain periods afterwards, on the thighs, arms, and trunk of the body; . . .

The same state of the habit which gives rise to these effusions under the cuticle, produces likewise copious discharges of blood, especially from the internal parts, which are defenced by more delicate coverings.

This singular disease is often preceded for some weeks by great lassitude, faintness, and pains in the limbs, which render the patients incapable of any exertion; but, not unfrequently, it appears suddenly, in the midst of apparent good health. It is always accompanied with extreme debility and depression of spirits: the pulse is commonly feeble, and sometimes quickened; and heat, flushing, perspiration, and other symptoms of slight febrile irritation, recurring like the paroxysms of hectic, occasionally attend. In some patients, deep-seated pains have been felt about the praecordia, and in the chest, loins, or abdomen; and in others a considerable cough has accompanied the complaint, or a tumour and tension of the epigastrium and hypochondria, with tenderness on pressure, and a constipated or irregular state of bowels.

The three descriptions original with Bateman are as follows:[3]

Since the second edition was printed, a patient was sent to me . . . affected with a singular species of molluscum, which appears to be communicable by contact. . . . The face and neck of this young woman were thickly studded with round prominent tubercles, of various sizes, from that of a large pin's head to that of a small bean, which were hard, smooth, and shining on their surface, with a slight degree of transparency, and nearly of the colour of the skin. . . . The progress of their growth was very slow: for the first tubercle had appeared on the chin a twelvemonth ago, and only a few of them had attained a large size.

She ascribed the origin of this disease to contact with the face of a child, whom she nursed, on which a large tubercle of the same sort existed; on a subsequent visit she informed me, that two other children of the same family were disfigured by similar tubercles; . . . the parents believed that the first child had received the eruption from a servant, on whose face it was observed.

7. There is scarcely any limit to the varieties of these papular affections: but I have observed one form, which is so uniform in its character, as to be entitled to notice here. It may be called Lichen *urticatus;* as its first appearance is in irregular, inflamed wheals, so closely resembling the spots excited by the bites of bugs or gnats, as almost to deceive the observer. The inflammation, however, subsides in a day or two, leaving small, elevated, itching papulae. While the first wheals are thus terminating, new ones continue to appear in succession, until the whole body and limbs are spotted. . . . This eruption is peculiar to children: . . . Both the wheals and the papulae are accompanied with intense itching, which is exceedingly severe in the night.

The ECZEMA is characterized by an eruption of small vesicles, on various parts of the skin, usually set close or crowded together, with little or no inflammation round their bases, and unattended by fever. It is not contagious.

Bateman's *Delineations of Cutaneous Diseases,* published in 1817, completed the series of engravings initiated by Dr. Willan.[2] Several illustrations were prepared *de novo* by Bateman; others were retouched from Willan's original plates. *Delineations* is an illustrated atlas designed to be used in conjunction with the *Synopsis.* Priority was given on the title page of *Delineations* to Bateman's title, "Librarian of the Medical and Chirurgical Society of London," followed by "Honorary Member of the Literary and Philosophical Society of New York," and, lastly "Physician to the Public Dispensary, and to the London House of Recovery."

Studies on statistics and fever complemented Bateman's dermatologic accomplishments. Vital statistics and clinical comments on fevers collected over a decade were analyzed and published in his *Reports on the Diseases of London, and the State of the Weather from 1804 to 1816.* They constitute an important document on the history of epidemics. Two cases of retinitis and anascara following scarlatina were described, very likely complications of acute glomerular nephritis.[4]

In one of these an unusual circumstance occurred, which appears worthy to be noticed. The fever had left the patient (a boy of 12 years) five weeks before I saw him. He was in a state of debility, with slight anasarca of the lower limbs, and some accumulation of water in the scrotum . . . a dull appearance of the eyes led me to examine them, and I found that, although the pupils were not greatly dilated, and contracted on the approach of a candle, yet he was totally insensible to its light, when within three inches of his face: In short, he was quite blind. . . . His sight was partially restored on the next day, and perfectly on the day following.

Bateman wrote with great fluency. In the preparation of the assigned chapters in Rees' *Cyclopaedia;*[1]

. . . he was in the habit of noting down on a scrap of paper the heads into which he thought of dividing his subject, then reading all the books upon it which he had occasion to consult, after which he arranged in his mind all he proposed to say, so that when he began to write he considered his labour done. He wrote, indeed, as fast as his pen could move, and with so little necessity of correction or interlineation, that his first copy always went to press.

Critical illness befell Bateman in 1821, and, as his life began to ebb, he confessed, as published by an anonymous friend in a memoir to Bateman.[5]

"But all these sufferings are a just punishment for my long scepticism, and neglect of God and religion." This led to a conversation, in the course of which he observed, that medical men were very generally sceptical; and that the mischief arose from what he considered a natural tendency of some of their studies to lead to materialism. For two or three days he shewed increasing interest in the subject of religion; and I read to him continually the Scriptures, and other books which seemed to me best calculated to give him the information he thirsted for. When I went into his room a few mornings after, he said, "It is quite impossible to describe to you the change which has taken place in my mind: I feel as if a new world was opened to me, and all the interests and pursuits of *this* have faded into nothing in comparison with it." . . . He often expressed in the strongest terms, and with many tears, his deep repentance, and his abhorrence of himself for his former sinful life and rebellion against God; but he seemed to have from the first so clear a view of the all-sufficiency of the Saviour's atonement, and of the Christian scheme of salvation, as freed him at once from that distrust of forgiveness which is so apt to afflict persons at the first sight of their sins, and of the purity and holiness of Him.

1. Anon. (attributed to Rumsey, J.): *Some account of the Life and Character of the Late Thomas Bateman,* 2nd ed, London: Longman, Reese, Orme, Brown, and Green, 1827.

2. Bateman, T.: *Delineations of Cutaneous Diseases; Exhibiting the Characteristic Appearances of the Principal Genera and Species, Comprised in the Classification of the Late Dr. Willan; and Completing the Series of Engravings Begun by that Author,* London: Longman, Hurst, Rees, Orme, and Brown, 1817.

3. Bateman, T.: *A Practical Synopsis of Cutaneous Diseases According to the Arrangement of Dr. Willan, Exhibiting a Concise View of the Diagnostic Symptoms and the Method of Treatment,* 5th ed. London: Longman, Hurst, Rees, Orme, and Brown, 1819.

4. Bateman, T.: *Reports on the Diseases of London, and the State of the Weather from 1804 to 1816; Including Practical Remarks on the Causes and Treatment of the Former; and Preceded by a Historical View of the State of Health and Disease in the Metropolis in Past Times,* London: Longman, Hurst, Rees, Orme, and Brown, 1819.

5. Anon.: *A Brief Memoir of the Late Thomas Bateman, M.D.,* 6th ed. London: J. Butterworth & Son, 1822.

Composite by G. Bako

Pierre-François Rayer
(1793-1867)

RAYER OF PARIS is better known among dermatologists for his *Treatise on Diseases of the Skin,* which contains excellent early descriptions of several cutaneous maladies, than to internists for his monograph on *Diseases of the Kidney.* In comparative medicine, however, he was at his best in a discussion of the contagiousness of farcy, a variant of glanders. Rayer was born at Saint Sylvain, studied medicine, and served his internship in the French capital. His doctoral thesis was devoted to the history of pathological anatomy, an indication of a broad interest in the medical sciences and in a subject that was to form the basis of his contributions to dermatology. He was associated first with Saint Antoine Hospital, but he moved on to Charité, where the affiliation was mutually agreeable and long-lasting. His well-deserved academic appointments, however, were not above political intrigue. Rayer was elected to the Academy of Medicine at the age of 30 and the Academy of Sciences some years later. He served as dean of the Faculty of the Paris Medical School and professor of comparative medicine for only two years, but was physician to King Louis Philippe and Louis Napoleon for a longer period of time.

The first edition of Rayer's two-volume text on the skin appeared while he was on service at Saint Antoine. The second edition, accompanied by an atlas, was translated by Willis into English and was published in 1835.[1] The first American edition appeared in 1845. The classification of skin diseases followed that of Willan of London but contained several original descriptions and preceded Hebra in stressing pathology. Rayer's classification was not elaborate. Four groups of diseases were recognized: (1) those spread by contagion, (2) those of external origin, (3) those of internal origin with external manifestations, and (4) the congenital dermatoses. Also, he has been credited with early descriptions of eczema and adenoma sebaceum. Shelley and Crissey selected excerpts from his descriptions of ecthyma, pityriasis labrum, and lingua nigra.[2] Since his contributions, outside of cutaneous disorders, are less well known, appropriate selections will be noted at this time. These include a description of gouty kidney, recovery of anthrax bacilli from the blood of a sheep, and the contagiousness of farcy. One of the earlier descriptions of the gouty kidney is given in the three-volume *Treatise on Diseases of the Kidney*. Rayer noted the frequent delayed development of symptoms, the varying incidence of urate deposits in the parenchyma, and the tendency for urate gravel to concentrate in the renal calyces and not in the cortex.[3]

479. The symptoms that herald the various lesions of the kidneys during life vary with each case and with the extent of lesions. It is apparent that a certain quantity of uric acid gravel may be deposited in the cortical substance of the kidney without causing any lumbar pain, or without pain radiating along the course of the ureters, . . . however, if gravel or the calculus lodges in a ureter and obstructs its lumen, colic will appear and the urine will show albumin or blood corpuscles; usually the spells abate as soon as the gravel or the calculus passes to the outside. In other instances, patients suffer severe pain in the lumbar region bilaterally with radiation into the testicle on the affected side.

Anthrax bacilli were recognized in the blood of a sheep following inoculation from an infected animal.[4]

The blood, examined microscopically, was similar to the blood from sheep affected with anthrax which served as the donor of blood from the spleen for inoculation. The corpuscles, instead of retaining their shape, agglutinated in irregular masses; also there were small filiform bodies approximately twice as long as corpuscles of blood. These small bodies did not show any spontaneous movement.

Rayer's best contribution to comparative medicine was a 100-page monograph on the contagiousness of farcy, the cutaneous form of glanders. The subject was introduced with an excellent historical review, followed by a report of the death of Prost, a groom who suffered from glanders contracted from a horse. Fluid recovered antemortem from the pustules was inoculated into the nose, conjunctiva, shoulder, buttock, and groin of a mare.[5]

On the 1st and 2nd day there were no appreciable changes on the inoculated parts.
At seven p.m. of the 3rd day a round circumscribed swelling was visible at the punctures on the right buttock; in the center of the swelling there was a depression corresponding to each puncture; painful tumefaction appeared on the left shoulder at the site of punctures . . . near the punctures on the left nostril the skin was swollen; there was serious discharge from the nares.

During the following days the illness progressed and on the 9th day after the inoculation the animal was sacrificed, having presented the characteristic symptoms and findings of acute glanders. The following day I submitted to the Academy several postmortem specimens.

The following sequence may be recounted: Prost slept in a stable near a horse ill with glanders. A few days after the death of the animal, Prost fell ill with a fatal disease, characterized by pustular eruptions of the skin, the nasal and pharyngeal cavities, by ecchymosis and gangrenous lesions below the ear, on the chin, on the feet, by small abscesses in the lungs, by an abscess below the shoulder and in the muscles, and by symptoms generally classed as "typhoid." The diverse lesions and phenomena have been observed in patients who have been accidentally inoculated with the disease. I believe that the findings and alterations in the horse with the cutaneous form of glanders (farcy) are the same as in acute glanders and that the two forms can appear together, as observed by competent veterinarians.

Finally, since the fluid from the bullae and the pustles on Prost, inoculated into the nostrils of a healthy horse, transmitted glanders, I conclude with the conviction that Prost contracted glanders.

1. Rayer, P.: *A Theoretical and Practical Treatise on the Diseases of the Skin,* R. Willis, trans., London: J. B. Baillière, 1835.

2. Shelley, W. B., and Crissey, J. T.: *Classics in Clinical Dermatology,* Springfield, Ill: Charles C Thomas, 1953.

3. Rayer, P.: *Treatise on Diseases of the Kidney* (Fr), Paris: J. B. Baillière, 1840, excerpt translated by Z. Danilevicius.

4. Rayer, P.: Inoculation of the Blood of the Sheep (Fr), *C R Soc Biol (Par)* 2:141-144, 1850, excerpt translated by Z. Danilevicius.

5. Rayer, P.: Glanders and Farcy in Man (Fr), *Mem Acad Roy Med* 16:625-662, 807-871, 1837, excerpt translated by Z. Danilevicius.

Alphée Cazenave (1795-1877)

PIERRE LOUIS ALPHÉE CAZENAVE OF PARIS, pupil of Biett, founded the first journal devoted to diseases of the skin and syphilis—*Annales des Maladies de la Peau et de la Syphilis* (1843-1852). The *Annales* published a number of dermatologic communications by Cazenave based upon clinical observations in the wards of the Hospital of Saint Louis, while he was professor on the faculty of medicine in Paris. In 1828, Cazenave and Schedel collabo-

rated on a textbook of medicine, *Handbook of Diseases of the Skin,* which dealt largely with the clinical lectures of Biett.[1] The interest of Cazenave in cutaneous diseases

National Library of Medicine

was disclosed early in his career; his doctoral thesis discussed dermatologic problems in general medicine. His name is associated particularly with chronic lupus erythematosus and with pemphigus foliaceus.

The term "lupus erythematosus" did not appear in the communications early in the 19th century, and there is no record that Biett himself published a description of lupus. Albert, in 1825, had distinguished between three types of dartre rougeante (later regarded as identical with lupus by Cazenave and Schedel), namely: 1) the idiopathic type, 2) the scrofulous type, and 3) the venereal type. Cazenave stated that Biett identified three types: 1) lupus destroying the surface, 2) lupus causing deep destruction, and 3) lupus associated with hypertrophy of the skin. Lupus erythematosus probably is included in type 1. There are passages in Cazenave's description of lupus that are similar to those in the 1851-1852 communication, in which lupus erythematosus was first described as an entity.[2] More than 25 pages in the *Handbook* are devoted to lupus. The following excerpt probably describes discoid lupus.[1]

Under some circumstances lupus manifests itself by a purplish-blue erythema on areas of the face, particularly on top of the nose, which may be swollen for several months.

The skin becomes thinner by rarely perceptible stages and appears as a cicatrix without having shown any preceding tubercles, ulcers or other lesions except for a vivid hue, and occasional slight desquamation, . . . the redness disappears on digital pressure; the patient has no pain except after palpation. When the progress of the disease stops, the redness disappears; the minimal exfoliations cease, while the skin remains thin and shiny.

The patient with lupus enjoys fairly good health; only menstruation, in women, seems to be disturbed occasionally, particularly if lupus spreads.

The term "lupus erythematosus" by Cazenave appears first in the general discussion of lupus in the *Annales* for 1850-1851.[3] However, a publication issued one year before describes a clinical conference held by Cazenave in which the expression lupus erythematosus is used. The communication apparently prepared by someone who attended the conference was signed only with the initial Z.[4]

That which characterizes lupus, in general, is its onset particularly during late childhood, and rarely after adolescence: an important characteristic which should be an aid in diagnosis in order to differentiate lupus from certain forms that share with it a great similarity, but which affect adults, 25 to 30 years of age, only.

At the onset, lupus erythematosus may be identified by its urticarial, or better erythematous, plaques, particularly of the erythema pernio or chilblain type. But the persistence of the plaques of lupus, their purplish color, the small number, occasionally the unification of the spots, and their exclusive location will suffice to be a warning until the appearance of shiny, thick skin, the desquamation, and finally the scars will leave no doubt.

In the communication, Cazenave described a case from his clinic of a 38-year-old male, which might be interpreted as an example of systemic lupus erythematosus. The suggestion that the disease was systemic has been assumed from the discussion, reported by the scribe, which follows the clinical record.[3]

The eruption with which he is at present affected dates from 1841; it appeared without appreciable cause, and began with red spots, without elevation, without itching, the spots occupying at times the cheeks and at other times the ears, and which disappeared readily under the influence of a soft diet and tisanes. . . . The spots which are present on the hands date only from last year and appeared a short time before his admission.

At the present time the following symptoms are observed: an erythema, light pink in color, disappearing on digital pressure and reappearing immediately on release, which occupies the superciliary arches, both cheeks, the entire external surface of the nose, the eyelids (the edge alone on the right is unaffected), with an injection of their mucous surfaces which is quite marked, the free edge of the lips, the ears, and the hair line.

This disease, which Biett indicated under the name *érythème centrifuge,* is a variety of lupus.

Without going into the general considerations of lupus, M. Cazenave felt it necessary to present several considerations on this curious variety which he calls *lupus erythematosus.*

Lupus erythematosus has an almost exclusive predilection for the face; it localizes especially on the nose in women; in men, on the contrary, it is more frequent on the cheeks. It may, moreover, extend to the chin, the forehead, to the edges of the scalp, and sometimes to the scalp itself. One finds it rarely in other places, perhaps on the neck and hands. . . . Thus, it may be determined by the influence of cold, and also by the direct effect of a hot fire; it is also especially frequent in persons with a fine skin, women, and individuals exposed by occupation to great heat, as blacksmiths and cooks. One finds it also in messengers and coachmen, and it then appears to result from the direct action of the air.

The description of pemphigus foliaceus, a cutaneous malady, which seems to have been ignored prior to Cazenave, appeared in the first volume of the first year of the *Annales.*[5]

The present illness had already existed for 4 years. It was ushered in, according to the patient, by an erysipelas of the face which spread to the chest, and then involved successively the entire surface of the body. These erysipelatous plaques were then, from the beginning the seat of the blisters of pemphigus. However that may be, for a long time the face, the abdomen, and the medial part of the thighs were continually the seat of large irregular elevations of the epidermis containing a serosity which was very limpid at first, but which soon became reddish. The eruption appeared usually without pain; the bullae, which were at first quite full and quite distended, ruptured or were lacerated by the least movement of the patient, and left more or less completely exposed a surface which became less and less red, and less and less painful. New ones formed daily; little by little the lesions became more crowded, the bullae became less confluent; they formed less perfectly; they were less regular; still later, finally, they appeared as uneven, soft, scarcely elevated lesions lifting the epidermis in an almost insensible manner: the liquid flowed with difficulty and dried in place, producing a kind of crust which after a certain time formed into a general encasement with an entirely distinctive appearance . . . she emitted a characteristic nauseating odor, and finally, she had a constant fever that increased in the evening.

1. Cazenave, A., and Schedel, H. E.: "Lupus," in *Handbook of Diseases of the Skin*, Paris: Béchet, 1828, pp 384-410, excerpt translated by H. Frey.
2. Cazenave, A.: Lupus, *Ann Malad Peau Syph* 4:225-228 (June) 1852, excerpt translated by H. Frey.
3. Cazenave, A.: Lupus Erythémateaux, *Ann Malad Peau Syph* 3:297-299 (June) 1851, in Shelley, W. B., and Crissey, J. T.: *Classics in Clinical Dermatology*, Springfield, Ill.: Charles C Thomas, 1953.
4. Z.: Formes du lupus et son traitement, *Lancette francaise, Gazette des Hôpitaux* 23:354 [July] 1850.
5. Cazenave, A.: Pemphigus Chronique Général; Forme Rare de Pemphigus Foliacé, *Ann Malad Peau Syph* 1:208-210, 1844, in Shelley, W. B., and Crissey, J. T.: *Classics in Clinical Dermatology*, Springfield, Ill.: Charles C Thomas, 1953.

Jean Baptiste Bouillaud (1796-1881)

J. B. BOUILLAUD, born near Angoulême, France, of poor parents, rose to become one of the outstanding clinical teachers in his time at the University of Paris.[1] In his youth he distinguished himself at the Angoulême lysée, and, with the financial and moral support of his uncle, a surgeon major in the French army, he began the study of medicine in Paris. However, troubled political affairs during the march of the Allies on Paris interrupted this study; subsequently, he served in a Hussar regiment upon Napoleon's return from Elba. His medical work at the University was not resumed until after the battle of Waterloo. The poverty of his material possessions even into maturity, was compensated for, however,

by the excellence of his teachers. Bouillaud studied surgery under Dupuytren, medicine under Broussais, cardiology under Corvisart, and experimental physiology under

National Library of Medicine

Magendie. In 1818, he became an intern in the Hospitals of Paris and, in 1823, received the MD degree after presenting a thesis on the diagnosis of aneurysms of the aorta.

Following graduation, Bouillaud became an intern at the Hôpital Cochin under Bertin, whom he assisted in the preparation of a two-volume treatise on the *Maladies of the Heart* (1824). The Academy of Medicine accepted him into membership in 1825, and a year later the University granted him professional status. In 1831, he advanced to professor of clinical medicine and was appointed to the staff of Hôpital de la Pitié and later to the staff of la Charité. His most notable pupils included Velpeau, Cornil, and Potain. Bouillaud's monograph, *A Clinical Treatise on the Maladies of the Heart*,[2] was published in 1835 and two years later was translated into English. By this time his thrèe most important scientific contributions had been described; however, his academic and clinical activities continued without interruption throughout his active years, resulted in a tremendous bibliography of books and shorter communications.

Departing temporarily from clinical cardiology early in his career, Bouillaud distinguished between external and internal language, and, impressed with Gall's studies on cerebral localization, he deduced from his pathological material that speech disorders were associated with lesions of the frontal lobe. His contributions on localization, incompletely stated in 1825, were not generally accepted until revised in 1861 by Aubertin, his son-in-law.[3]

The several preceding cases prove that the organs of speech are under the control of the anterior lobes of the brain. We had established by experiment and by observation that: (1) paralysis of these organs, independent of other parts of the body, was found in cases with extensive lesions of the anterior lobes; that such paralysis and loss of speech were not complete when the lesions in the anterior lobes were minimal; (2) the free exercise of speech persisted when the brain was altered in other areas but not in the anterior lobes.

General Conclusions:

(5) The loss of speech depends both on the failure of words and on the muscular movements which compose speech, which may be a similar phenomenon; the first depends on a lesion of the grey substance; the second on a lesion of the white substance of the anterior lobes.

(6) The loss of speech does not include movements of the tongue, considered to be the organ of prehension, mastication and deglutition of food; nor does it include the loss of taste; the supposition that the nervous center of the tongue has three distinct sources of control is consistent with triple innervation of the tissues of the tongue.

In studying the functions of the cerebellum, Bouillaud concluded, by relating clinical-pathological findings and experimental work, that this organ influenced coordinated movements and equilibrium.[4]

In examining the clinical facts and comparing them with experiments on animals, I was able to prove that the cerebellum is a nervous center which controls diverse acts of standing, of maintaining the equilibrium, and of locomotion—in brief, the cerebellum coordinates the functions which help the animal stand and walk upright and move from one place to another.

If we compare the clinical findings with the observations in laboratory animals whose cerebellum has been injured, inflamed, or cauterized, the similarity of the changes is impressive. The

hyperflexion of the head, the hysteriform seizures, general agitation, oscillation of the pupils, fixation of the eyes—each of these symptoms has been reproduced in my experimental research on the cerebellum. This is an admirable example of the accord between experimental physiology, pathology, and clinical findings.

In his clinical and pathological work on the heart, in which he made accurate physical measurements, Bouillaud attributed great significance to auscultatory findings. Preparation of an account of congenital heart disease led to the sequential association of acute rheumatic fever and pancarditis, and the description in health and disease of the lining membrane of the heart, to which he gave the name *endocardium.* Physical signs which he first recognized included chlorosis and other anemias as possible causes of a systolic heart murmur, a venous pulse over the jugular vein associated with an incompetent triscuspid valve, weak pulsations caused by extrasystoles from a fibrillating heart, friction rub and retraction of the pericardial region in adhesive pericarditis, and gallop rhythm and the agony of terminal mitral stenosis.

Bouillaud was not the first to associate endocarditis and pericarditis with acute inflammatory rheumatism; David Pitcairn, Edward Jenner, W. C. Wells, and probably others had commented casually on this subject. The comprehensive understanding and statistical evaluation of Bouillaud's series stand in marked contrast to the incomplete reports of single cases by his predecessors. He noted that acute rheumatic pericarditis was rarely fatal, and that the threat to health developed later from valvular deformity and chronic endocarditis. The association was discussed originally in his treatise on the heart, which was followed shortly thereafter by his *New Researches on Acute Articular Rheumatism in General and Especially on the Law of Coincidence of Pericarditis and Endocarditis With This Disease.* He reported 92 observations based upon his excellent diagnostic acumen and supported by postmortem findings. In 17 patients an attack of acute articular rheumatism preceded the development of pericarditis, and in 14 patients an attack of endocarditis preceded it. Thus, one third of the cases had a recognizable history of acute rheumatic fever; possibly others in which this item was not recorded in the anamnesis might also have suffered.[5]

The newest and most curious point of view of these researches is, without doubt, the discovery of coincidence of inflammation of the sero-fibrous internal and external tissues of the heart (*rheumatismal* endocarditis and pericarditis) with acute articular rheumatism. In auscultating the sounds of the heart in some individuals still labouring under, or convalescing from, acute articular rheumatism, I was not a little surprised to hear a strong, file, saw, or bellows sound (*bruit de râpe, de scie ou de soufflet*), such as I had often met with in chronic or organic induration of the valves, with contraction of the orifices of the heart. . . . Many of them were for the first time affected with articular rheumatism, and had hitherto enjoyed the most perfect health. . . . I soon discovered that an acute affection of the heart, in cases of acute articular rheumatism associated with violent fever, was not a simple accident, a rare, or as it were fortuitous complication, but in truth the most usual accompaniment of this disease.

It is demonstrated by these calculations that inflammation of the pericardium and of the endocardium has coincided with an articular rheumatism in a third of the cases. But we are far from asserting, that in the remaining two thirds there did not exist articular rheumatism. In fact, many of these cases are deficient in etiological details; and it appears probable enough, that amongst these last a certain number belonged also to the list of rheumatic pericarditis and endocarditis.

Bouillaud's concept of the endocardium as a membrane susceptible to inflammation was presented 35 years after Bichat's *Treatise on Membranes,* one of the great expositions of modern anatomy and pathology. Three periods of anatomic alterations of the endocardium in pathological regression were described by Bouillaud as follows: the first period, sanguinary congestion, softening, and ulceration or suppuration; the second period, organization of secreted products or fibrinous concretions; and the third period, cartilaginous, osseous, or calcareous induration of the endocardium and of the valves, with or without narrowing of the orifices of the heart. The following excerpts are from the second period.[2]

When endocarditis does not terminate in prompt resolution, if it is prolonged a considerable time (fifteen, twenty, thirty days or more), the inflamed tissues are more or less thickened, and the plastic part of the products abnormally secreted by these tissues pass from an amorphous state into a state of organization. Then, according to accidents of position, of configuration or of composition of the organizable matter, one encounters either vegetations or granulations, either cellulo-fibrinous adhesions or fibrinous or serofibrinous layers, and so forth.

The vegetations or granulations have remarkable predilection for the valves and particularly for their free border. Also, one finds them in certain cases on the internal surface of the cavities of the heart and especially the auricles. . . . They have been divided by M. Laënnec into two divisions: globular vegetations and verrucous vegetations The first appear to us more exactly described as albuminous or fibrinous granulations. The expression "verrucous" is happily chosen, for the vegetations or excrescences to which they apply resemble warts. One may thus designate them under the denomination of "cornified" or "cartilaginous" vegetations or excrescences.

The albuminous or fibrinous vegetations . . . have appeared to me to be analogous to those which are sometimes found on the surface of the chronically inflamed pleura, the pericardium or the peritoneum.

The verrucous vegetations, very analogous to venereal warts, are held and implanted so firmly, and are rooted with such tenacity, that they may almost be said to form an identity with the tissue to which they are attached. The tissue of these vegetations is, as it were, cornified; it makes a noise under the instrument which divides it like fibrocartilage.

It is rare that these vegetations of the valves or of the internal wall of the heart exist alone; usually, as our observations show, they are accompanied by a fibrocartilaginous or calcareous induration of the valves. However this may be, however they are multiplied, confluent, grouped like cabbage flowers, they give rise to a narrowing of the orifices to which are adapted the valves which they overload and whose movements they impede; the existence of this peculiar type of narrowing is an important circumstance to note.

Other writings by Bouillaud include monographs on cholera, varieties of hermaphrodism, encephalitis, venous obstruction and dropsy, diagnosis and cure of cancer, vitalism in the organism, influence of doctrine and pathological systems on therapy, philosophy of clinical medicine, and a five-volume treatise on medical nosography. As an extremely successful practitioner he was consulted by patients throughout Europe, attended Napoleon III, cared for Dupuytren in his terminal illness, and, following a premortem request, performed the autopsy. As a reactionary therapeutist, he used blood-letting as one of his favorite tools, and was critical of the salicylate treatment of rheumatism introduced by Sée in 1877— the second specific agent in the treatment of joint disease. Also, he initially refused to accept the findings of Pasteur but recognized the value of this research later.

Bouillaud was elected a member of the Chamber of Deputies for Angoulême in 1840, became dean of the Faculty of Medicine in 1848, and president of the Academy of Medicine in 1862, an organization which found him one of the most industrious discussers, though many times tactless and arrogant. He retired from his professorial chair in 1864 and served as president of the first International Medical Congress in Paris in 1867; the following year he was made commander of the Legion of Honor.

1. Bergeron, J.: Biography (Fr), *Bull Acad Med* 18:810-838, 1887.

2. Bouillaud, J. B.: *A Clinical Treatise on the Maladies of the Heart* (Fr), 2 vol, Paris: J.-B. Baillière, 1835, in Willius, F. A., and Keys, T. E., E. Hausner (trans.): *Cardiac Classics*, St. Louis: C. V. Mosby Co., 1941, pp 446-455.

3. Bouillaud, J. B.: Clinical Studies to Demonstrate That Loss of Speech Corresponds With Lesions of the Anterior Lobes of the Brain, and to Confirm Gall's Opinion on the Seat of Articulate Language (Fr), *Arch Gen Med* 8:25-45, 1825, excerpt translated by Z. Danilevicius.

4. Bouillaud, J. B.: Clinical Studies Tending to Refute Gall's Opinion on the Function of the Cerebellum and to Prove That This Organ Coordinates Equilibrium and Ability to Stand and Walk (Fr), *Arch Gen Med* 15:225-247, 1827, excerpt translated by Z. Danilevicius.

5. Bouillaud, J. B.: *New Researches on Acute Articular Rheumatism* (Fr), Paris: J.-B. Baillière, 1836, translated by J. Kitchen, Philadelphia: Haswell, Barrington, & Haswell, 1837.

William Prout (1785-1850)

WILLIAM PROUT, physician and natural scientist, was born at Horton, Gloucestershire, where his family had farmed for several generations.[1] The first and major portion of his professional career was devoted to evaluation of experimental observations and projection of theoretical deductions in analytical chemistry, which reflected his out-

standing intellectual endowments; his remaining years were spent in the successful practice of physic. Prout's name is associated with two important works: the unitary

Composited by G. Bako

hypothesis of atomic numbers, ie, the chemical elements possess atomic weights which are multiples or fractions of the atomic weight of hydrogen; and, as a recognized authority on the analysis of organic and inorganic substances, the discovery of hydrochloric acid in the gastric juice of animals and man.

Prout's early education sporadic and inadequate ceased first at the age of 13. Four years later an awakening interest in mechanics, mathematics, and music led him to attend Turner's private academy in Wiltshire; here he sought to make amends for his deficiencies in traditional learning and to acquire the fundamentals of Latin and Greek. After a second lapse of study, he spent two years at the classical seminary of the Rev. Thomas Jones at Redland, Bristol. Handicapped by meager resources, he assisted in the instruction of the younger students in return for his tuition. At the age of 23, Prout entered the University of Edinburgh, since Oxford and Cambridge were closed to students of his social status. Upon presentation of an uninspiring thesis on intermittent fevers, the MD degree was granted in 1811.

Following graduation, Prout was attracted to London, where he walked the wards of the hospitals of St. Thomas' and Guy's, came to know Sir Astley Cooper, was admitted licentiate of the Royal College of Physicians in 1812, and subsequently set up practice just off the Strand in a house that served as home, lecture hall, quarters for scientific speculation, and laboratory for his investigations in physiology and analytical chemistry. By 1813, his research had become sufficiently productive to warrant public reporting. In Thomas Thomson's *Annals of Philosophy*, Prout described the diurnal variation of carbon dioxide, observed with the aid of an analytical spirometer, during experiments in which he himself was the subject. Records of the effect of exercise, food, and drink disclosed variations which were attributed incorrectly to daylight and darkness.

Two years later an anonymous communication appeared in the *Annals of Philosophy*, "On the Relations Between the Specific Gravities of Bodies in Their Gaseous State and the Weights of Their Atoms." The anonymity was broken by Thomson six months later, and authorship was admitted by Prout immediately thereafter. The calculations of the relative densities of the elements, provided by others and available in the literature, formed the substance of Prout's theory—his most important contribution to natural science. Prout failed to clarify some of the terms used, such as volume, atom, and molecule; however, the relation between the atomic weights of the elements, setting hydrogen as unity, became known as Prout's hypothesis: "the atomic weights of all the elements are exact multiples of the atomic weight of hydrogen or half that of hydrogen."[2]

The author of the following essay submits it to the public with the greatest diffidence; for though he has taken the utmost pains to arrive at the truth, yet he has not that confidence in his abilities as an experimentalist as to induce him to dictate to others far superior to himself in chemical acquirements and fame. He trusts, however, that its importance will be seen, and that some one will undertake to examine it, and thus verify or refute its conclusions. If these should be proved erroneous, still new facts may be brought to light, or old ones better established, by the investigation; but if they should be verified, a new and interesting light will be thrown upon the whole science of chemistry.

It will perhaps be necessary to premise that the observations about to be offered are chiefly founded on the doctrine of volumes as first generalized by M. Gay-Lussac; and which, as far as the author is aware at least, is now universally admitted by chemists. Hence the sp. gr. of hydrogen will be found to be .0694, atmospheric air being 1.0000. It will be also observed that the sp. gr. of oxygen as obtained above is just 16 times that of hydrogen as now ascertained, and the sp. gr. of azote just 14 times.

Table III.—This table likewise exhibits some striking examples of the coincidence above noticed. Indeed, I had often observed the near approach to round numbers of many of the weights of the atoms, before I was led to investigate the subject. Dr. Thompson appears also to have made the same remark. It is also worthy of observation, that the three magnetic metals, as noticed by Dr. Thomson, have the same weight, which is exactly double that of azote. Substances in general of the same weight appear to combine readily, and somewhat resemble one another in their nature.

On a general review of the tables, we may notice,

1. That all the elementary numbers, hydrogen being considered as 1, are divisible by 4, except carbon, azote, and barytium, and these are divisible by 2, appearing therefore to indicate that they are modified by a higher number than that of unity or hydrogen. Is the other number 16, or oxygen? And are all substances compounded of these two elements?

An an analytical chemist of biological matter, Prout devised many of his precision instruments and procedures. He discovered that the excreta of a boa constrictor was almost pure uric acid, and gave considerable attention to renal and vesical calculi and gravel, and to the constituents of urine in health and disease. Having isolated a relatively pure sample of urea from urine, he used the atomic weight values previously described to calculate the proportional number of 37.5.[3] This was accepted by Wöhler in his investigations on the synthesis of urea a decade later. With Wollason, Prout gave the name "pupuric acid" to the ammonium salt of uric acid, a scientific contribution which prompted his election to the Royal

Society in 1819. Prout's first and only important monograph was published in 1821; the first edition was titled *An Inquiry Into the Nature and Treatment of Gravel, Calculus, and Other Diseases Connected With a Deranged Operation of the Urinary Organs.* The term "diabetes" was interjected into the title in the second and subsequent editions, including the last London edition, the 5th, of 1848. Two American editions and two German translations were published also. In the chapter on diabetes, Prout restricted the definition and mentioned diet in management.[4]

I would recommend that the term be restricted to those affections in which the urine is *saccharine.* Hence, I would define diabetes to be a disease in which a saccharine state of the urine is the characteristic symptom.

It seems to be generally admitted that animal diet has a tendency to diminish the quantity of urine; but whether it really improves its quality, we are not at present enabled to state.

Prout's theoretical considerations and experimental observations on digestion, which antedated and anticipated important contributions by Liebig, led to his discovery of hydrocholic acid in gastric juice. He traced the steps of blood formation from foods, beginning with digestion in the stomach, continuing through chymification in the intestine, chylification in the lacteals, and concluding with sanguification in the blood vessels. In examining the content of the rabbit's stomach, the acid reaction of the food mass with litmus paper was noted, and, on chemical analysis, traces of alkaline chloride and other substances were detected. The initial report of free hydrochloric acid was brief: data from six experiments were presented in evidence. The communication in the *Philosophical Transactions* of the Royal Society is excerpted as follows:[5]

THAT a free, or at least an unsaturated acid usually exists in the stomachs of animals, and is in some manner connected with the important process of digestion, seems to have been the general opinion of physiologists till the time of SPALLANZANI. This illustrious philosopher concluded, from his numerous experiments, that the gastric fluids, when in a perfectly natural state, are neither acid nor alkaline. Even SPALLANZANI, however, admitted that the contents of the stomach are very generally acid; and this accords not only wtih my own observation, but with that, I believe, of almost every individual who has made any experiments on the subject.

The object of the present communication is to show, that the acid in question is the *muriatic acid,* and that the salts usually met with in the stomach, are the alkaline muriates. As to the origin and use of these principles, as well as the occasional appearance of other acids, &c. in the stomach, I reserve what I have to say on these subjects till a future opportunity, and shall merely remark at present, that the facts now adduced seem to be intimately connected, not only with the physiology and pathology of the digestive process, but with other important animal functions.

These results then seem to demonstrate, that free, or at least unsaturated muriatic acid in no small quantity exists in the stomach of these animals during the digestive process; and I have ascertained, in a general manner, that the same is the case in the stomach of the hare, the horse, the calf, and the dog. I have also uniformly found free muriatic acid in great abundance in the acid fluid ejected from the human stomach in severe cases of dyspepsia, as the following examples show.

For his analytical investigation of simple alimentary substances, Prout was awarded the Copley medal in 1827. After 15 years of highly productive scientific investigation, conducted without benefit of hospital or medical school laboratory facilities, an increasing deafness led to withdrawal from scientific intercourse. He began to let major advances by others, both in Britain and on the Continent, pass him by. Except for revision of his texts, he deserted research in favor of full-time practice. Prout was elected a Fellow of the Royal College of Physicians in 1829 and was honored as Gulstonian lecturer for 1831. His series of addresses, entitled "The Application of Chemistry to Physiology, Pathology, and Practice," summarized those aspects of his investigations previously reported. In 1834, he was charged with the preparation of the eighth Bridgewater Treatise which he entitled *The Chemistry, Meteorology, and the Function of Digestion, Considered With Reference to Natural Theology.* Portions of this work appeared in revisions of his last and less important monograph, *On the Nature and Treatment of Stomach and Urinary Diseases.* In the first book of his

treatise, he enunciated the principles of behavior of gases, now recognized as Avo-
gadro's law; whereas in the third book he
divided foodstuffs into saccharinous, oleaginous, and albuminous categories.

1. Brock, W. H.: The Life and Work of William Prout,
Med Hist 9:101-126 (April) 1965.
2. Anonymous (Prout, W.): On the Relation Between the
Specific Gravities of Bodies in Their Gaseous State and
the Weights of Their Atoms, *Ann Philos* 6:321-330 (Nov)
1815.
3. Prout, W.: Observations on the Nature of Some of the
Proximate Principles of the Urine, *Medicochir Trans* 8:526-
549, 1817.
4. Prout, W.: *An Inquiry Into the Nature and Treatment of Gravel, Calculus, and Other Diseases Connected
With a Deranged Operation of the Urinary Organs,* London: Baldwin, Cradock & Joy, 1821.
5. Prout, W.: On the Nature of the Acid and Saline
Matters Usually Existing in the Stomachs of Animals,
Philos Trans 114:45-49, 1824.

Composite by G. Bako

Jean Cruveilhier (1791-1874)

JEAN CRUVEILHIER, pupil of Dupuytren and
first occupant of the chair of pathological
anatomy in Paris, prepared two major treatises on this subject, combining his clinical
experiences at the bedside with extensive
observations from the autopsy table. He
was born at Limoges, France, in the post-
revolutionary days of poverty and strife; his
father, an army surgeon, favored medicine
over holy orders for his son.[1] Jean reluctantly accepted medicine as his calling and

only on the second attempt received the
MD degree from the University of Paris. He
began the practice of general medicine in
his home town, but, in 1823, upon the recommendation of Dupuytren, Cruveilhier
was offered the professorship of operative
medicine at Montpellier. However, this position failed to satisfy him, and just as he
was prepared to abandon academic life and
return to practice, the chair of descriptive
anatomy in Paris became vacant unexpectedly. He accepted the professorship,
but in time advanced to occupy for 30 years
the newly created professorship of pathological anatomy endowed by Dupuytren.
Cruveilhier's *Pathological Anatomy of the
Human Body* appeared in two volumes. The
first, 1829-1835, gives la Salpêtrière as the
hospital affiliation; the second, 1835-1842,
lists la Charité. The contents of this great
work were beautifully illustrated and provided excellent descriptions of gross pathology. In addition to holding a senior faculty
post, Cruveilhier was a consultant in great
demand, who was able to complement pathology with clinical practice, exploiting
each discipline with knowledge of the other.

The misery in the poorly staffed, frequently filthy, hospitals, fostered by the
poverty of the people, afforded great opportunities for observation by the clinical-pathological anatomist—greater in comparison
than for the personal practitioner who at
that time lacked diagnostic aids and specific
therapeutic agents. Phlebitis, peptic ulcer,
and progressive muscular atrophy are three
of several notable clinicopathological discussions by Cruveilhier, excerpts of which
are included here. The study of inflammation and infection from the abundant material available led him to a false belief that
phlebitis and pyemia were intimately related,
and to the false conclusion that phlebitis
dominated all pathology.[2]

In a way phlebitis dominates all pathology. It
is the tie which unites the blind and almost instinctive humoralism of the ancients with the
rational humoralism of the moderns.
Phlebitis belongs to both surgery and medicine.
We find a *traumatic phlebitis* and a *non-trau-
matic or spontaneous phlebitis.* The death of
the largest number of those who succumb to
wounds and surgical operations is the result of
phlebitis.

The first effect of all phlebitis is the coagulation of the bood and its adherence to the walls of the vessel. . . . I have frequently produced it in my experiments on living animals, either by introducing a wooden splint into the veins, or by the injection of some chemically irritating substance.

In the first volume of the *Pathological Anatomy,* Cruveilhier had already identified inflammation of the pulmonary artery with localized consolidation of the lungs and phlebitis, noting that the pulmonary changes are a frequent complication of a surgical operation and that efforts should be made to prevent this dire complication.[3]

From the general considerations on which I wrote above it follows: first, that lobular pneumonia is the most frequent change following wounds and surgical operations; second, this lobular pneumonia is nothing but a capillary phlebitis; third, this capillary phlebitis always coincides with some phlebitis more or less distant giving rise to pus; . . . fifth, the practitioner must concentrate all his efforts on this primitive phlebitis; prevent it, if possible, limit it, if it has already declared itself.

The differential pathological findings in peptic ulcer (la maladie de Cruveilhier) were discussed in relation to clinical symptoms. In the section on diseases of the stomach, Cruveilhier reported his findings on benign gastric ulcer, differentiating it from cancer symptomatically and structurally, with perforation and hemorrhage as complications.[4]

I. Anatomically considered, the simple chronic ulcer of the stomach consists of a spontaneous loss of substance, ordinarily circular, with the margins cut perpendicularly, the bottom gashed and thick and of variable dimensions. Almost always single, the ulcer is situated most commonly either on the small curvature or upon the posterior wall of the stomach . . . it excavates deeply; and if helpful adhesions do not oppose, sooner or later the stomach is perforated and the contents are scattered throughout the peritoneal cavity.
III. Simple ulcer of the stomach does not present other than a gross resemblance to cancerous ulcer with which however it has always been confused. The base of it does not show any of the characterisitcs of either a hard cancer or a soft cancer, one does not find the circumscribed hypertrophy which practically always accompanies cancer and which has been taken so often for a cancerous degeneration itself. The

best proof, however, that these ulcerations are not cancerous is their curability by a very simple treatment, ineffectual in internal cancer as well as in external cancer.
The principal symptoms are the following: loss of appetite or bizarre appetite, insurmountable distress, difficult digestion, nausea or heavy pains in the epigastrium, and sometimes epigastric pain extremely sharp during the process of digestion or indeed when there is no food in the stomach. The epigastric pain, or rather the xyphoid or substernal pain, is referred sometimes to a corresponding place on the spine, and I have seen many patients complain more of a spinal point than of an epigastric point of tenderness. The more or less rapid loss of weight, constipation, nausea, vomiting after the digestion of food, finally the hemorrhagic or black vomiting, are the ensemble of symptoms which individuals affected with simple ulcers of the stomach present.
VI. Pathological anatomy accounts fully for the bloody and black vomiting which often accompanies ulcer of the stomach: . . . as the blood remains a longer or shorter time in the stomach, and is in contact with the acid of the gastric juice, it becomes a black color or the color of soot which had been noted by all observers.

Progressive muscular atrophy of the Aran-Duchenne type (Cruveilhier's palsy) was described in a communication published in 1852-1853. Two cases were mentioned, with postmortem findings. The absence of changes in the spinal cord and peripheral nerves stood in contrast to the extensive muscular atrophy. The findings in Cruveilhier's second case were subsequently used by Aran and Duchenne to enrich their communication on the subject.[5]

The first observation that I made on gradual paralysis due to muscular atrophy was in 1832. It was a lady, 40 years old, a widow of a general, a woman very remarkable because of her spirit as well as her lovely constitution.
I found her affected with a generalized paralysis, the upper extremities affected more than the lower extremities. The muscles had undergone a remarkable atrophy, especially of the hands, palms, and muscles of the shoulders and deltoids. . . . Her face had lost some of its expression. Articulation was low, monotonous, and incomplete. But the fact that attracted my attention most was that, in spite of all these profound alterations in muscular function and motility, her sensitivity had been preserved in the affected parts of the body. The organs of touch as well as the organs of sense remained exquisitely sensitive, and she had complete preservation of her intellectual faculties.

I diagnosed this case as one of general muscular paralysis due to a lesion of the spinal cord, the origin of paralysis in the anterior of the spinal cord. . . .

It was only at the Charité Hospital that I found again a case of gradual paralysis of the body with conservation of intellect and sensitivity.

Adolph Legrand, a 28-year-old shepherd, was brought to the Charité Hospital and placed under my service. His condition was as follows:

General muscular atrophy of the muscles of the trunk and the muscles of the upper and lower extremities. . . . The face was without expression, and gave the appearance of a baby. The only muscle of the face partially preserved was the orbicular muscle of the eye lids. Even this contracted incompletely, since the patient was not able to close his eyes completely.

Autopsy showed no abnormalities of the brain or spinal cord, the same as in the previous case. Thus, this being the second time the source of the paralysis of the muscles was traced to the cerebral-spinal tract, I assumed it was necessary to search for the cause either in the nerves to the muscles or in the muscles themselves. . . . in my course given in the summer of 1848, I was able to present the primary or idiopathic muscular atrophy as the cause of a particular form of paralysis; also, Mr. Duchenne was able to present to the Institute during the 1849 commencement a memorandum entitled: *Muscular Atrophy with Fatty Degeneration*, admitting that it was the autopsy, results of which I had communicated to him, that gave him the understanding of the pathologic anatomy of this condition. It was also because of the desire to determine the organic nature of this paralysis that enabled Mr. Aran in 1850 to collaborate with his excellent work under the title of *Progressive Muscular Atrophy*, with a description of a great number of facts of the same kind, observed at the Charité Hospital; he had received the communication about the findings of the autopsy, which I described, from Mr. Duchenne.

In the concluding excerpt, on the structural changes in gout, Cruveilhier moved from clear deductions concerning the familial transmission of the tendency to urate concretions, augmented output of urates in the urine, and the supposition that articular deposits of urates appear first on the cartilage. The discussion was documented by excellent illustrations of urate incrustations.[6]

. . . the affinity between gravel, the concretions in the bladder, and gout is recognized, as is the interchange in the same patient or in members of the same family of the patient with gout. The heredity of gout has been understood to a certain degree, because no disease is transmitted from generation to generation so easily as is the disposition to gout or excretion of urates.

It is clear from the facts described that the urates are more often deposited not in the cartilage or in the synovia surrounding them, but rather on the free surface . . . of the cartilage, as well as outside of the synovia, in the free cellular tissue surrounding a joint, in the fatty tissue, along the ligaments and tendons, in the thickness of the muscles, under the aponeuroses, on the periosteum, in the synovial tendon-sheaths, in the subcutaneous sheaths, and even to the marrow of the bone—in short, in all parts concerned with locomotion.

1. Béclard, J.: *Notices and Biographies from the Academy of Medicine*, Paris: G. Masson, 1878.
2. Cruveilhier, J.: "Phlebitis," in *Dictionaire de médecine et de chirurgie pratiques*, new ed, Brussels: Th. Le Jeune, 1837, translated in Long, E. R.: *Selected Readings in Pathology*, Springfield, Ill: Charles C Thomas, 1929.
3. Cruveilhier, J.: *Pathological Anatomy of the Human Body*, Paris: J. B. Baillière, vol 1, 1829-1835; vol 2, 1835-1842, translated in Long, E. R.: *Selected Readings in Pathology*, Springfield, Ill: Charles C Thomas, 1929.
4. Cruveilhier, J.: *Pathological Anatomy of the Human Body*, vol 1, Paris: J. B. Baillière, 1829-1835, translated in Major, R. H.: *Classic Descriptions of Disease*, Springfield, Ill: Charles C Thomas, 1945.
5. Cruveilhier, J.: Progressive Muscular Paraylsis with Atrophy (Fr), *Bull Acad Nat Med (Par)* 18:490-502, 546-583, 1852-1853, excerpt translated by Z. Danilevicius.
6. Cruveilhier, J.: *Pathological Anatomy of the Human Body* (Fr), vol 1, Paris, J. B. Baillière, 1829-1835, excerpt translated by Z. Danilevicius.

Composite by G. Bako

Karl Ernst von Baer
(1792-1876)

BAER, doctor of medicine without a practice, shifted his interest from gross anatomy to comparative anatomy, but made his greatest contribution in embryology. He described the notochord, advanced the hypothesis of the germ layer, recognized the similarity of the early stages of embryonic development in related species, and was the first to identify the mammalian ovum. He was born near Piep, Estland (Estonia), was taught reading and writing by a governess, mathematics and mathematical geography by a private tutor in languages, and music, general science, and botany by a part-time general practitioner.[1] Baer began his study of medicine at the recently founded University of Dorpat, Estonia, over the wishes of his parents who preferred one of the German schools. Satisfied with the MD degree received at the age of 22 but not with the clinical training, he turned to Vienna, only to discover that he possessed a feeble interest in bedside medicine. Whereupon he literally wandered over the hills to Würzburg, where Döllinger was directing the research and teaching in anatomy and embryology. The embryology of the chick was Baer's assignment. Within a year he was invited to Königsberg as prosector in

anatomy. However, before accepting this appointment, Baer spent the winter in Berlin, still undecided whether he should practice medicine. With the appointment two years later as professor extraordinary, his life work in the anatomical sciences was settled, and the need to practice for a living vanished.

The ovum in the graafian vesicle of the dog was recognized by Baer in the laboratory of Königsberg in 1827. The discovery was anticipated since he was convinced that the egg was responsible for the embryo. This assumption was contrary to the belief of Haller, who postulated that the embryo existed in an amorphous state in the graafian follicle and the structure appeared only after the uterus was reached. Baer's discovery was described in a letter to the Imperial Academy of Sciences of St. Petersburg, to which he had been elected a corresponding member. It was prepared simultaneously in Latin and in German, and was published in Leipzig in 1827. The communication is an enthusiastic description of the histology and physiology of the embryo, with mention of the contributions of Cruikshank, Prévost, Dumas, Wolff, and his one-time scientific associate, Pander. Each had approached the discovery, but no one had made it.[2]

Led on more by inquisitiveness than by the hope of seeing the ovules in the ovaries with the naked eye through all the coverings of the Graafian vesicles, I opened a vesicle, of which, as I said, I had raised the top with the edge of a scalpel—so clearly did I see it distinguished from the surrounding mucous—and placed it under the microscope. I was astounded when I saw an ovule, already recognized from the tubes, so plainly that a blind man could scarcely deny it. It is truly remarkable and astonishing that a thing so persistently and constantly sought and in all compendia of physiology considered as inextricable, could be put before the eyes with such facility.

Conclusions

Every animal which springs from the coition of male and female is developed from an ovum, and none from a simple, formative liquid.

The male semen acts through the membrane of the ovum, which is pervious by no foramen, and in the ovum it acts first on certain innate parts of the ovum.

All development proceeds from the center to the periphery. Therefore the central parts are formed before the periphery.

The same method of development occurs in all vertebrate animals, beginning at the spine.

In this critical communication Baer made reference to germ-layers, suggested stages of development, and observed the first rudiment of the dorsal spine, later called the *chorda dorsalis* or notochord. Each of the structures was better defined and identified in a two-volume treatise, *Embryology of Animals*, the first volume appearing in 1828 and the second in 1837. The germ-layer theory espoused by Baer included four layers, which were revised downward by Remak into the ectoderm, the endoderm, and the mesoderm. The skin and nervous system arose from the ectoderm; the notochord, the lining of the gastrointestinal tract, and the digestive organs from the endoderm; and the muscular, skeletal, and excretory systems from the mesoderm.[3]

The first effect of impregnation is the progressive separation of the germ (ovum), the yolk and the membrane of the yolk, when the germ begins to increase in size. During the first hours the germ separates from the yolk, but adheres to the yolk membrane. . . . The elevation of the germ-layer (Pander's kernel of the chick-embryo) follows the yolk-membrane, but it does not come completely clear of it, but takes some of the yolk-substance with it. Soon the center of this elevation is separated by a small amount of fluid from the center of the germ. The germ becomes thinner and firmer, and looks more like a sheet.
With the thickening of the germ the process of division into two layers begins: into the upper, thinner, and firmer membrane-like layer, and the lower, thicker, more granulous and more friable layer. . . . The beginning of the separation probably corresponds with the first stage following impregnation. It is noticeable at the twelfth hour, if the germ is carefully dissected under the microscope.
For better understanding I divided the development of the chick embryo into three periods according to the stages of circulation. The first period lasts about two days, until the primary circulation is fully developed. The second period lasts as long as the circulation through the vessels of the yolk sac continues; that is three days, until the vessels of the urinary sac are developed and begin to share in the circulation. The third period lasts until birth or until the pulmonary circulation appears. The fourth period begins with life outside the egg.
In the development of the skeletal tissue, an accumulation of the dark granules is seen, corresponding to the axis of the embryo. The granules form a chain, the *spine-chain* (chorda dorsalis).

As these important contributions were nearing completion, Baer was troubled with inadequate financial support for his researches and publications. He had hoped for an academic post in Estonia or in a prominent German university. A third choice was an appointment in the Academy of Petersburg, which he finally accepted in 1834. Ample funds for construction and research were made available, more time was planned for research, and St. Petersburg was near his homeland. However, his brilliant observations in embryology were never systematically expanded. On the contrary, the study of embryonic develpment was substantially abandoned. The remaining years were devoted to the study of physical geography and anthropology, subjects taught by his tutor in Dorpat. Baer traveled, became a recognized Russian geographer, and accepted assignments for the government fisheries—but his great work was over. He taught and lived in Russia until his death.

1. von Baer, K. E.: *Life and Letters* (Ger), Braunschweig: F. Vieweg and Son, 1886.
2. von Baer, K. E.: On the Genesis of the Ovum of Mammals and of Man (L), Leipzig: L. Voss, 1827; trans. by C. D. O'Malley, *Isis* 47:117-153, 1956.
3. Baer, K. E.: *Embryology of Animals* (Ger), 2 vol, Königsberg: G. Bornträger, 1828 and 1837, excerpt translated by Z. Danilevicius.

National Library of Medicine

Ernst Heinrich Weber
(1795-1878)

ERNST HEINRICH WEBER applied physical principles to the investigation of physiological problems, which in turn led to major contributions in defining the function of the central and peripheral nerves and the dynamics of the circulation. Weber was born and attended grammar school in Wittenberg, where his father was professor of theology. After attending the Fürstenschule at Meissen, he returned to Wittenberg in his 16th year to begin university studies.[1] When the town came under Prussian control in the political campaigns of 1813 and 1814, the university was placed beyond the confines; there Weber received the MD degree in 1815, qualifying in comparative anatomy after submitting an inaugural dissertation entitled *Comparative Anatomy of the Sympathetic Nerves.*[2] Three teachers especially influenced his academic development: Chladni, a family friend to whom a monograph was later dedicated, the anatomist Rosenmüller, and the physicist Gilbert.[3] Although Weber began the practice of medicine in Leipzig, he never abandoned his physiological investigations; when offered professional status in the department of anatomy at the university, he accepted the full-time appointment and entered into research and teaching. In 1821, he succeeded Rosenmüller as ordinary professor of human anatomy and, after Kuhn's death, as-

sumed responsibility for the chair of physiology as well. In this field his important contributions were made.

Ernest Heinrich acted as preceptor for his younger brothers Wilhelm and Eduard. He and Wilhelm jointly began investigating the physics of wave motion in bodies of water and the pulse wave in animals. The circular path of particulate matter near the surface of lakes was observed to contrast with motion of immersed minutiae which described ellipses, the horizontal axes of which were longer than the vertical. The movements of water and mercury were compared in a related study. Waves were discovered to move with equal rapidity on the surface; whereas the rapidity increased with the depth of the liquid. These findings were exploited in the interpretation, in 1825, of pulse wave propagation which exceeded the flow of blood.[3]

The flow of blood, even though it is remarkably fast, proceeds much slower than the pulse.

The pulse is a sudden *expansion of the arteries caused by the pressure of the contained blood. Blood pressure increases each time a fresh quantity of blood is expelled from the ventricle of the heart into the arteries already filled.* . . . The blood within the arteries not only exerts pressure on the walls in the direction of flow, but in all axes. Thus the arteries are affected not only by longitudinal flow but by lateral pressure. . . . Extension of the axis as well as the diameter of the arteries increases the intraarterial space so as to receive the quantity of blood expelled by the heart before the space is vacated by the blood proceeding into the capillaries and veins.

The tactile illusion, identified with Weber, was described in 1834.[3] When compass points are kept equidistant and applied to the skin at random with equal pressure over a similar surface with varying sensitivity, the subject experiences a converging sensation when the probes pass from an area of increased sensitivity to one of decreased sensitivity, and the reverse when they pass from areas of diminished to greater sensitivity. The illusion involves not only differences in responsiveness of the sense organs, but perception of movement on the skin, relative localization of the two moving probes, and estimation of intervening distance.

Weber was the first to show that a "common sensation," such as pain or fatigue, may be analyzed into its visceral and muscular components, which in turn can be differentiated from tactile sensation. This concept was expanded by Fechner in one of his contributions to experimental psychophysics. Measurements were applied by Weber to sensations of pain, heat, and pressure, leading to the generalization known as Weber's law, ie, the increase in stimulus necessary to produce the smallest perceptible increase in sensation bears a constant ratio to the strength of the stimulus already acting. Also, a quantitated stimulus is less perceptible when added to a larger rather than a smaller one; or, when the sensation increases in arithmetic progression, the stimulus must increase by geometric progression.

Continuing his study of fluid velocity, Weber compared the transit of lymphocytes in the lymph vessels of the frog with the velocity of red blood corpuscles. The blood cells were judged to move at a speed 20 times faster than "lymph cells" in lymph spaces.[4]

Investigation shows the [lymph] space is separated from the lumen of the blood vessel by a wall, even though this wall is not [always] visible. Because the flat blood corpuscles never enter this transparent space, one sees only occasionally a round lymph cell moving. . . . These lymph-granules move slowly and from time to time remain stationary, while the blood corpuscles move with great speed. If this transparent space were not separated by the vessel wall from the blood stream, the flat blood cells would move towards the lymph granules and mix.

I believe the lymph bodies move at least 10 to 20 times slower than the blood cells. Their movement is so slow that, with the help of a glass micrometer installed in the ocular of the microscope, one can evaluate their size even when they are moving.

Wilhelm, who had earlier collaborated with Ernst on waves, advanced to the professorship of physics at Göttingen, prepared an atlas of the earth's magnetism in 1840, and constructed the first electromagnetic telegraph in 1853. Brother Eduard Friedrich, however, remained at Leipzig and, in 1845, described the inhibitory action of the

vagus nerve on the heart rate in a joint communication with Ernst to a scientific congress in Naples.[5] While the Webers justly receive credit for observing the effects of vagal stimulation in several animals and for recognizing their implications in man, an effect by the vagus on the heart rate had been recognized centuries before.[6] In the original communication the Webers believed bilateral stimulation of the vagi was needed to decrease the heart rate, an observation not subsequently confirmed. Other investigators showed that stimulation of either vagus was sufficient to produce inhibition. Slowing of the heart rate was produced initially by connecting one pole of an electromagnet to a frog's nose and the other pole to the mid-region of the spinal cord; thus, the pathway initiating the action of the vagus was traced. A translation of the communication which disclosed an inhibitory center within the central nervous system appeared in Italian and is available from Fulton as follows.[5]

THE EXPERIMENTS OF EDWARD AND ERNEST HENRY WEBER BY WHICH IT IS PROVED THAT WHEN STIMULATED WITH A ROTARY ELECTROMAGNETIC APPARATUS THE VAGUS NERVES SLOW DOWN AND, TO A CONSIDERABLE EXTENT, INTERRUPT THE HEART-BEAT

I. If the medulla oblongata of a frog or the ends of the isolated vagus nerves are excited by the rotation of a fairly strong electromagnetic machine, the heart suddenly stops beating, but at the end of excitation begins after a short interval to beat again: at first slowly and weakly, then gradually more strongly and more frequently until finally the original beat observed before excitation is restored.

II. The rotation of a less powerful instrument slows down and weakens the heart-beat. The heart, whose beat is by this means interrupted, is not contracted as in a tetanic convulsion, but remains relaxed and has a flat appearance.

III. The excitation of the vagus nerve on one side only does not change the heart-beat.

1. Ludwig, C. F. W.: *Address in Memory of Ernst Heinrich Weber* (Ger), Leipzig: von Veit & Co., 1878.
2. Weber, E. H.: *Comparative Anatomy of the Sympathetic Nerves* (L), Leipzig: C. H. Reclam, 1817.
3. Weber, E. H.: *Comments on Anatomy and Physiology* (L), Leipzig: C. F. Koehler, 1834.
4. Weber, E. H.: Microscopic Observations on the Movement of Lymphocytes (Ger), *Arch Anat Physiol*, 1837, pp 267-272, excerpt translated by Z. Danilevicius.

5. Weber, E. F., and Weber, E. H.: Experiments Which Prove That the Vagus Nerves When Stimulated by a Rotary Electromagnet Inhibit and to a Considerable Extent Interrupt the Heart Beat (It), *Ann Univ Med* 20:227-228, 1845, translated in Fulton, J. F.: *Selected Readings in the History of Physiology*, Springfield, Ill: C. C Thomas, 1930, pp. 276-278.

6. Hoff, H. E.: Vagal Stimulation Before the Webers, *Ann Med Hist* 8:138-144, 1936.

Museum for Medical History, Stockholm

Anders Adolf Retzius
(1796-1860)

ADOLF RETZIUS, father and son of outstanding scholars, was born in the university town of Lund, Sweden. After completing the usual courses of secondary learning, he entered the university at Lund; there he was attracted especially to the teachings of Florman, professor of anatomy, and to those of his father, professor of natural history and chemistry, Anders Jahan Retzius.[1] In 1816, Adolf spent a year at the University of Copenhagen and came under the influence of the Danish anatomist, Jacobsson; he then returned to Lund, where he received the MD degree in 1819. His doctoral thesis, dedicated to Jacobsson, discussed the anatomy of the chondropterygious fishes and described

his discovery of the suprarenal gland in Elasmobranchs.

While still an undergraduate Retzius instructed in the veterinary department of the Royal Military Academy in Karlberg; in 1821, he served on the staff of the Veterinary Institute of Stockholm, and two years later he was appointed professor of veterinary science. There he matured rapidly and was appointed to the chair of human anatomy and physiology at the Caroline Institute of Medicine and Surgery. Both positions were held until 1840 when he transferred all of his activities to the Institute, actively participated in its reorganization, subsequently served as its Rector, and remained on the staff until his death.

Although Retzius practiced neither medicine nor surgery, he was a skillful technician, interested in clinical problems, and conducted experimental studies on the ligaturing of arteries and the effect of vagotomy on the digestive system. He discussed the mechanism of the semilunar valves, the function of the transverse vertebral processes in man and animals, and the microscopic anatomy of the liver. Among his outstanding zoological achievements, he discovered a number of previously unrecognized morphologic features of the hag fish, sometimes duplicating or complementing the work of his close friend, Johannes Müller. In association with Billings, Retzius identified the ciliary ganglion of the horse, advanced our knowledge of the sphenopalatine ganglion, studied the respiratory system of birds and reptiles, contributed to the histology of teeth, and described the pyloric region of the stomach.

Retzius' vision began to fail in the early 1840's, and he was no longer able to continue microscopic work. He turned then to anthropology and topographical anatomy. He delineated the gastric canal along the lesser curvature of the stomach and contributed to the descriptive morphology of the brain. His identification of the extraperitoneal cavity in the ventral body wall and the vesical cavity above the pubis which is remembered in the literature as the cave of Retzius. This structure provides surgical access to the bladder without entering the peritoneal cavity.[2]

I call this structure (apparatus)—the capsular pelvio-prostatic ligament. The thin membrane covering the urinary bladder, often described as a layer of pelvic fascia which externally ends in the *arcus tendineus* as described by Santesson, continues from the lower portion of the bladder onto the prostate and below. When this layer reaches the prostate it is thickened and adherent to the gland. The anterior part of the *levatores ani* lies close to the sides of this capsule without a fascia of its own. The capsule is thinnest at the posterior surface of the prostate and extends between the prostate and the rectum, continues underneath the prostate, covers the posterior aspect of the urethral musculature with the enclosed Cowper's glands, extends laterally to the ascending *rami of the os ischii* and there is attached. Between these attachments it spreads as a thick membrane below and posterior to the *bubus urethrae* and ends in an acute angle at the *ligamentum triangulare*. On the sides of the prostate, where the capsulur ligament is thickest, it extends outwardly and attaches at the opposing *rami of the ischia* and to the public bones. The sides of the capsule are spread like a tent and, after leaving the prostate, cover the *plexi venosi pudendales* with the adjacent arteries and nerves. The insertion on the lateral edges of the pelvis extends from the horizontal branches of *os pubis* to the vicinity of *tubera ischiadica*. The anterior edges of these lateral wings create the aponeurotic part of the *ligamenta pubo-prostatica (pubo-vesicalia)*; the posterior edges from the *rami of the os ischii* to cover the urethral muscles; together with the muscles they form two thick borders; similar to the corners of a quadrangular tent, and then join the posterior portion.

Between these borders *(ligamenta pubo-vesicalia)* lies a deep empty space [cave] which engulfs, as mentioned above, the venous plexuses extending over both urethra and prostate *(plexus pubicus impar)*.

Retzius' final work, a classification of subdivisions of the human race based on anthropological measurements of cranial and cephalic indices, contrasted with the prevailing classification prepared by Blumenbach based on skin, color and geographic habitat. A comparison of the ratio of head breadth to head length separated European males into two groups. The dolichocephalic were long-headed and the brachycephalic were round-headed. These were further subdivided into the orthognathic and prognathic groups of each head type. The initial contribution was published in Sweden.[3] Three years later it was translated into German. In 1860, Retzius pre-pared a summary communication for the Smithsonian Institute in America, with a description of the skull forms based upon his measurements. The following excerpts are noteworthy.[4]

Towards the north we find on the Atlantic coast, both of the United States and Canada, a predominance of the dolichocephalic form among the tribes, that is to say, who pass under the general name of redskins, as the Algonquins and Iroquois. The same result may be definitely arrived at by a study of the delineations given by Morton of Cherokees, Chippeways, Miamies, Oneidas, Hurons, Pottawatomies, Cayugas, (particularly remarkable,) Cotonays or Blackfeet, &c.

To these facts it must be added that the Esquimaux, who extend also to the eastern coast, belong equally to the dolichocephalae, though holding an altogether special place among them.

A Swedish geometer, M. Hellenberg, who resided long in Ohio, learnedly defends the opinion maintained by many others, that the Indians of North America are descended from the tribes of Israel, alleging that their features are essentially Jewish, that McKenzie saw the Chippeways practice circumcision, &c. . . . In view of the developments of modern geology respecting the rise and subsidence of vast tracts of land, there would seem to be nothing absurd in admitting that America was once united with Africa or Asia, and obscure traditions to this effect are said still to exist among the American Indians. The compression of the top of the head among the Indians of Oregon (Flat-heads) has no doubt sprung from their proximity to the Esquimaux, whose heads are full and large. The frontal compression (Huanchas, Caribs) seems to have been designed to render the head more dolichocephalic, and was exclusively practiced by dolichocephalae, for whom I propose, in analogy with the term used by Dr. Latham, as mentioned above, the name of *American Semites*.

Retzius, a devoted popular teacher, attracted students from Uppsala and from Lund even though the Caroline Institute had not then been granted a charter for awarding higher academic degrees. He displayed a wide interest in nature, wrote on horticulture, sanitation, and water supplies, introduced osteology and comparative anatomy into the medical curriculum, and several new plants into Sweden. Retzius was elected to the Royal Academy of Science in 1826, served as their president in 1845, and became an honorary or corresponding Fellow of many foreign societies. His scientific friends included luminaries such as Bischoff, Liebig, Berzelius, Rudolph Wagner, Johannes Müller, von Baer, and Purkyně, whom he visited during his periodic foreign travels. Some of his greatest accomplishments were the contributions to the position of distinction now enjoyed by the Caroline Institute of Medicine and Surgery.

1. Wilson, C.: Obituary Notice of Professor Anders A. Retzius, Foreign Corresponding Member of the Medico-Chirurgical Society of Edinburgh, *Edinburgh Med J* 6:777-783 (March) 1861.

2. Retzius, A.: The Pelvio-Prostatic Ligament or the Apparatus by Which the Urinary Bladder, Prostate, and Urethra Are Affixed to the Lower Pelvic Outlet (Ger), *Arch Anat Physiol (Wiss Med)*, 1849, pp 182-190, excerpt translated by Z. Danilevicius.

3. Retzius, A.: On the Form of the Nordic Skull (Swed), *Forhandl Skand Naturforsk*, July 1842, pp 157-201, and *Arch Anat Physiol (Wiss Med)*, 1845, pp 84-129.

4. Retzius, A.: Present State of Ethnology in Relation to the Form of the Human Skull, *Annual Report of the Board of Regents of the Smithsonian Institution*, Washington: T. H. Ford, 1860.

Composite by G. Bako

Theodor Schwann (1810-1882)

THE PIOUS THEODOR SCHWANN and the sea lawyer Matthias Jacob Schleiden, contemporary German scientists, were foremost in the select coterie of investigators who re-vealed the cellular structure of living matter. Schleiden, after studying law and medicine, was professor of botany successively at Jena, Dorpat, and Frankfort-on-Main. In 1838, he postulated that plant tissues are composed of groups of cells. He believed erroneously that they originated spontaneously from the cytoplast (nucleus). Schwann, reasoning from Schleiden's hypothesis that if plants were composed of cells, concluded that animal tissues should have a similar structural unit. Schwann, who was dining one day with Schleiden, only a few years his senior, reported: [1]

The discoveries of Schleiden made us more accurately acquainted with the process of development in the cells of plants. This process contained sufficient characteristic data to render a comparison of the animal cells in reference to a similar principle of development practicable. In this sense I compared the cells of cartilage and of the chorda dorsalis with vegetable cells, and found the most complete accordance. The discovery, upon which my inquiry was based, immediately lay in the perception of the principle contained in the proposition, that two elementary particles, physiologically different, may be developed in the same manner. For it follows, from the foregoing, that if we maintain the accordance of two kinds of cells in this sense, we are compelled to assume the same principle of development for all elementary particles, however dissimilar they may be, because the distinction between the other particles and a cell differs only in degree from that which exists between two cells; so also the principle of development in the latter can only then be similar, when it repeats itself in the rest of the elementary particles. I therefore quickly asserted this position also, so soon as I was convinced of the accordance between the cells of cartilage and those of plants in this sense.

In 1838, the cell theory was advanced; in 1839, the investigations on the structure of plants and animals were published. The manuscript was submitted to the Archbishop of Malines for ecclesiastical approval before publication. The studies exerted a profound effect upon the new disciplines of histology and physiology. The cell is a structural unit of life. Without the concept of the cell, Darwin might have failed to appreciate the significance of growth and change. The physiological capacities of different cells are obvious. Physical activity stems from muscular contraction. Hormones are secreted by another type of cell. Digestion occurs through still another physiological cellular function. Cells of the brain are responsible for thought and initiation of nervous stimuli. Schwann described the stripped muscle in the upper portion of the esophagus in 1837 and the sheath of the axis cylinder of nerves in 1838. He was the first to investigate the laws of muscular contraction by physical and mathematical methods and to demonstrate that the tension of a contracting muscle varies with its length. Du Bois-Reymond and others expanded these fundamental studies in later years.

Schwann is best known for his concept of the form and function of cells. The word "protoplasm" was not used by him. Purkyně is responsible for this principle. Schwann attributed the growth of cells to the capacity for nutrition and compared molecular arrangement of the colloid compartments to the molecular structure of crystals. He searched for cell structure in vegetable and animal tissue and concluded:[1]

ALTHOUGH plants present so great a variety of external form, yet they are no less remarkable for the simplicity of their internal structure. This extraordinary diversity in figure is produced solely by different modes of junction of simple elementary structures, which, though they present various modifications, are yet throughout essentially the same, namely, *cells*. The entire class of the Cellular plants consists only of cells; many of them are formed solely of homogeneous cells strung together, some of even a single cell.

Animals, which present a much greater variety of external form than is found in the vegetable kingdom, exhibit also, and especially the higher classes in the perfectly-developed condition, a much more complex structure in their individual tissues. How broad is the distinction between a muscle and a nerve, between the latter and cellular tissue, (which agrees only in name with that of plants,) or elastic or horny tissue, and so on. When, however, we turn to the history of the development of these tissues, it appears, that all their manifold forms originate likewise only from cells, indeed from cells which are entirely analogous to those of vegetables, and which exhibit the most remarkable accordance with them in some of the vital phenomena which they manifest.

As with many critical advances in the medical sciences, no one investigation or the deliberations of one investigator could be documented as unique and singularly responsible for the cell theory. Malpighi (1661), Brown (1831), Purkyně (1834), Valentin (1835), Schulze 1836), Müller 1836), Donné (1837), Henle (1837), Vogel (1838) and undoubtedly others participated in the development of modern physiology, histology, and pathology. The first half of the 19th century was propitious, however, for the correlation and confirmation of experimental studies which established the previously unsubstantiated speculations concerning the cell and thereby firmly entrenched the cell theory.

Schwann was born in 1810 near Düsseldorf.[2] Great mechanical skill and capacity for fabrication of physical instruments were inherited from his father, a jeweler and printer. This skill proved helpful in laboratory experiments throughout his professional career. The parents, devout Catholics, enrolled their son initially in the Jesuit College in Cologne. An ecclesiastical life seemed imminent when theology was included in the curriculum at the University of Bonn, the school selected after Cologne. While in Bonn he came under the influence of Johannes Müller, Professor of Anatomy and one of the great 19th century German scientists. The MD degree was granted in 1834 at the University of Berlin. The inaugural dissertation, submitted at graduation, discussed oxygen need and other phases of respiration in the development of the chick embryo. By then, Müller had accepted the professorship of anatomy at Berlin. Schwann served as an assistant in experimental physiology under Müller for the first 5 postgraduate years. A lifetime of scientific investigations was completed by Schwann in this short span; four major discoveries were reported. Although his academic career was just beginning, his great scientific accomplishments were completed before he was 29 years of age. Pepsin was discovered in 1836. The capacity of an enzyme to convert nondiffusable albumens into peptones was the beginning of modern gastrointestinal physiology. The organic nature of yeast and the production of alcohol by fermentation was reported shortly after. Schwann devised convincing experiments to support the theory that particulate matter in the air, living material responsible for fermentation and putrefaction, could be destroyed by heating. This observation was another link in the chain of evidence against the doctrine of spontaneous generation. These and other experiments convinced Schwann that[3]

. . . putrefaction may be explained as the development of spores which consume organic substances as food and thereby bring about the decomposition which constitutes putrefaction.

The Schwann cell, whose cytoplasm enfolds myelinated and nonmyelinated nerve fibers, has been studied in recent years by a number of investigators who have utilized the electron microscope and modern techniques of tissue culture, with rewarding results. The cells have a separate existence and are not syncytial. Furthermore, cytoplasmic discontinuity has been demonstrated, with tiny filaments separating the nerve fiber from the cell wall.

Schwann was appointed professor first at the Catholic University of Louvain, Belgium, in 1839 at the age of 29. Nine years later he occupied the chair of anatomy at Liége, where he remained until his death at the age of 72. He was a bachelor, a man of simple tastes, and a retiring disposition. He was not gregarious either nationally nor internationally. He traveled little and preferred his small circle of close friends and students. As a Fellow of the Royal Society of London, he received the Copley Medal of the Society in 1845. He was offered professorial positions at Breslau, Würzburg, Munich, and Giessen, but he remained in Belgium and lectured in an adopted tongue. Many scientists contributed to the cellular theory of plant and animal tissue, but no one name deserves greater acclaim than that of Theodor Schwann.

1. Schwann, T.: *Microscopical Researches into the Srtucture and Growth of Plants and Animals* (Ger), Berlin, 1839, H. Smith (trans.) London: Sydenham Society, 1847.

2. Waterman, R.: *Theodor Schwann: His Life and Work*, Dusseldorf: L. Schwann, 1960.

3. Doetsch, R. N.: "Theodor Schwann, 1810 to 1882," *Microbiology*, New Brunswick, NJ: Rutgers University Press, 1960.

National Library of Medicine

Herbert Mayo (1796-1852)

HERBERT MAYO, pupil of Sir Charles Bell, was a contender with him for honors in the identification of the functions of the branches of the fifth and seventh nerves and the description of reflex action.[1] Mayo was born in London, where his father was physician-in-ordinary to the Prince of Wales and physician to the Middlesex Hospital. Herbert, in turn, entered Middlesex as a surgical pupil in 1814. After completing his training with Bell one year later, Mayo studied at Leyden, and in 1818 presented his graduation thesis for the MD degree in Latin on *The Urethra and Its Strictures*. He returned to Middlesex Hospital as house surgeon, was elected a member of the Royal College of Surgeons in 1819, and began a fruitful career of practice, teaching, and investigation. From 1827 to 1842, he served the hospital as surgeon and promoted the establishment of the Middlesex Hospital Medical School, which opened its doors in 1836.

Mayo lectured in anatomy in the Great Windmill Street school, illustrating his remarks with delightful and helpful diagrams.

He served as professor of anatomy and surgery to the Royal College of Surgeons in 1828 and 1829, in 1830 was appointed professor of anatomy at King's College; he was advanced to the professorship of physiology and pathological anatomy in 1836. Other professional honors included Fellowship in the Royal Society in 1828 and, upon their reorganization in 1843, one of the original 300 Fellowships in the Royal College of Surgeons. Mayo was a recognized scholar, well versed in 18th century history and literature. His affliction from crippling gouty arthritis compelled him gradually to restrict his activities and forced him into early retirement.

Mayo's medical writings included major treatises and short communications. Monographs were prepared on the nervous system, syphilis, disease of the rectum, human pathology, the organs of digestion, the philosophy of living, the value of hydrotherapy, which he practiced in the management of his crippling arthritis, and, fascinated with mesmerism, he wrote on popular superstitions. In his *Introductory Lecture to the Medical Classes in King's College* in 1834, Mayo described the transition in the preceding decades of the schools of medicine from proprietary practice to scholarly status.[2]

Till within the last ten or fifteen years the schools of medicine in London had not risen above the character of private tuition. The anatomical theatre and museum had used to belong to the lecturer, who held and disposed of them as his private property. The student about to attend lectures, made himself the pupil, not of a school, but of this or that individual, of whose competency to teach he surrendered his right to judge, on becoming his pupil. At the present the lecturer, in the larger and better schools, holds his office on a different tenure. His appointment is not obtained by purchase or inheritance: he is elected on the presumption that he is thoroughly qualified for his professorship, for the proper discharge of the duties of which he is answerable to public opinion, to those who appointed him, to those whom he undertakes to instruct.

In the first volume of his *Anatomical and Physiological Commentaries,* which appeared in 1822, Mayo presented his arguments and physiological studies on the ass, in which he differentiated motor power from sensory response of the roots of the fifth nerve. Charles Bell, who had investigated the subject in the preceding year, failed to provide the definitive evidence deduced by Mayo and by Magendie. In the section entitled "Experiments to Determine the Influence of the Portio Dura [Motor] of the Seventh, and of the Facial Branches of the Fifth Pair of Nerves," Mayo contrasted his experimental evidence with Bell's conclusions. In allocation of credit, Whewell, of Trinity College, Cambridge, after a careful review of all evidence stated his belief: "I should wish to describe the discovery as having been 'made by Sir Charles Bell, Mr. Mayo, and M. Magendie; the two latter physiologists having corrected and completed the researches of the former.' "[3] Mayo noted that[4]

I infer, from the [my] preceding experiments, that in the ass, the portio dura is a simple nerve of voluntary motion; and that the frontal, infra-orbital, and inferior maxillary, are nerves of sensation only, to which office, that branch of the fifth which joins the portio dura probably contributes: and from the preceding anatomical details, that other branches of the third division of the fifth, are voluntary nerves to the pterygoid, the masseter, the temporal, and buccinator muscles.

I was induced to perform the preceding experiments on reading an essay by Mr. Bell [*Philosophical Transactions of the Royal Society of London* 111:398-424, 1821], in which a novel view of the functions of certain nerves is propounded; resting in part upon experiments in great measure similar to those above narrated, but differing materially in their results. As nothing is so prejudicial to the interests of science, as the temporary adoption of an unsound theory, I shall hazard a few remarks upon that of Mr. Bell.

Mr. Bell observes that "the nerves of the spine, the tenth, or suboccipital nerve, and the fifth or trigeminus of the system of Willis . . . are all muscular nerves, ordering the voluntary movements of the frame; that they are all exquisitely sensible; and the source of the common sensibility of the surface of the body; and that when accurately represented on paper, they are seen to pervade every part."

On the other hand, Mr. Bell observes that the par vagum, the portio dura, the spinal accessory, the phrenic, and the posterior thoracic, are "respiratory nerves;" that is to say, "they connect the internal organs of respiration with the sensibilities of remote parts, and with the respiratory muscles, and are distinguished from those, of which we have been speaking, by many circumstances."

I shall endeavour to show, that the preceding distinction is not founded on correct observation, and that in truth the nerves, which Mr. Bell terms "respiratory," do not differ in any important respect, as a class, from those, with which he contrasts them.

2. The portio dura of the seventh is proved, by the experiments which I have detailed, to be a common nerve of voluntary motion: if it be divided, the muscles, which receive branches from it, are completely paralysed.

Having stated these facts, I leave it to the reader to decide whether they are consistent with, or subversive of, Mr. Bell's theory of "Symmetrical and Respiratory Nerves," and proceed to give an account of his experiments.

These consist in the division of the portio dura on one side of the head in different animals, and of the division of the infraorbital nerves on both sides.

"An ass being tied and thrown, the superior maxillary branch of the fifth nerve was exposed. Touching this nerve gave acute pain. It was divided, but no change took place in the motion of the nostril: the cartilages continued to expand regularly in time with the other parts, which combine in the act of respiration, *but the side of the lip was observed to hang low, and it was dragged to the other side.* The same branch of the fifth was divided on the opposite side, and the animal let loose. He could no longer pick up his corn: *the power of elevating and projecting the lip, as in gathering food, was lost.* To open the lips, the animal pressed the mouth against the ground, and at length licked the oats from the ground with his tongue."

The first statement, printed in italics, is contrary to my own observation; the second, a theoretical account of the fact that the animal did not elevate and project its lip. This fact was noticed in my own experiments, but appeared to me from the first equally consistent with the hypothesis, that the lip had merely lost its sensibility.

A description of reflex action is the second important neurophysiological phenomenon that concerned Bell and Magendie as well as Mayo. In Part II of Mayo's *Anatomical and Physiological Commentaries,* he clarified the concept somewhat vaguely introduced into neurophysiology by his teacher. Using the ass, dog, cat, and pigeon, Mayo discovered that a stimulus propagated along a sensory nerve to the corresponding motor nerve, through the intervention of that part only of the central nervous system which is mutually attached, induced the

muscle to respond. This concept, described concurrently by Magendie, was expressed by Mayo as follows.[4]

On the one hand, it is clear that an influence, independent of the will, occasionally throws voluntary muscles into action, as appears in tetanus and other spasmodic disorders; and is shown remarkably in the physiological experiment of irritating the skin on the lower extremities, after the division of the spinal chord in the back, when the occurrence of action limited to the muscles of the inferior extremities, evinces that a connection exists, independently of the will, between sentient surfaces and the action of voluntary muscles. I have varied this experiment by dividing the spinal chord at once in the neck and in the back, upon which three unconnected nervous centres exist; and the division of the skin in either part (and especially at the soles of the feet, in the two hinder portions) produces a convulsive action of muscles in that part alone.

1. Mayo, C. H.: Herbert Mayo, *Dictionary of National Biography,* Oxford: University Press, 1960, vol 13, pp 172-173.

2. Mayo, H.: *An Introductory Lecture to the Medical Classes in King's College, London,* London: Burgess & Hill, 1834.

3. Whewell, W.: History of Discoveries in the Nervous System, *London Med Gaz* 1:525-528 (Dec 11) 1837.

4. Mayo, H.: *Anatomical and Physiological Commentaries,* 2 parts, London: T. & G. Underwood, 1822-1823.

Prosper Menière (1799-1862)

THE DESCRIPTION OF THE AFFLICTION characterized by sudden attacks of vertigo, tinnitus, nausea, and unilateral deafness was the last and most important medical contribution by Prosper Menière. Born at Angers in southwest France, the son of a tradesman, he received his early education in the Lyceè; there he was recognized as a brilliant student in the classics and the sciences.[1] In 1819, he continued his medical studies at the Hôtel Dieu in Paris, served as assistant to Baron Dupuytren, received a gold medal in 1826, and the MD in 1828.

In 1832, Menière was appointed assistant professor on the faculty of medicine; however, his Paris career was interrupted first by the government of King Louis Philippe in collaboration with the Duchesse de Berry, whose son was a pretender to the throne. Later he was sent on a mission to control the spread of cholera in the departments of Aude and Haute-Taronne. For these services he received the chevalier of

Composite by G. Bako

the Legion of Honor. Failing to obtain the professorship of medicine and hygiene at the university, in 1838 he secured the appointment of physician-in-chief in the Institute for Deaf-mutes, where most of his professional activities were pursued in otolaryngology. Meanwhile he married Mlle. Becquerel, a member of the Becquerel family which included Antoine, a co-discoverer of radioactivity. Their son Emile also achieved fame in otolaryngology and succeeded his father at the Institute.

Menière complemented his training in medicine with an abiding interest in the intellectual life of Paris. He was a lifelong scholar in the Greek and Latin classics, a favorite in government circles, and an intimate of Balzac, Victor Hugo, and other men of letters. His knowledge of anatomy, recognized skill and outstanding powers of accurate observation in clinical medicine, and persistence in seeking the seat of diseases led him to identify the correct site of the symptom-complex later associated with his name.

Capitalizing on the experimental results by Flourens in animals, Menière disassoci-

ated vertigo, tinnitus, nausea, and, usually, unilateral deafness from involvement of the central nervous system and placed the lesion in the labyrinth. Although several others—anatomists, physiologists, neurologists, and otologists—had skirted the knowledge of the etiology and had contributed to the understanding of the pathogenesis, the clinical clue for Menière was the finding of a "reddish" exudate in the semicircular canals of a young girl stricken with the triad of acute symptoms. Although periodic attempts have been made in the intervening century to attribute the symptoms to hemorrhage into the semicircular canals, it is generally agreed that the pathophysiology remains undefined.

The four contributions published by Menière on the symptom-complex, all in 1861, have been translated by Atkinson.[2] The excerpts below were taken from his revised draft of the presentation before the Imperial Academy of Medicine in January 1861.[3]

There has come to my attention for some long time now a certain number of patients presenting a group of symptoms which are always the same, symptoms apparently serious, giving the impression of an organic lesion of the most distressing kind, recurring from time to time over weeks, months, years, then disappearing suddenly and presenting as a result common to them all the abolition of a special sense.

A healthy young man would experience suddenly, without apparent cause, vertigo, nausea, vomiting; a condition of indescribable distress drained his strength; his face, pale and bathed with sweat, proclaimed approaching collapse. Often even, the patient, feeling himself swaying, stunned, has fallen to the ground and been unable to rise again; lying on his back he could not open his eyes without seeing the objects around him whirling in space; the slighest movement of the head increased the vertigo and nausea; vomiting started again as soon as the patient tried to change his position. . . . They arose during periods of perfect health; their duration was short, but their character was such that the doctors called to attend him believed that they were dealing with a cerebral congestion and prescribed treatment in accordance with this view of the cause.

I had frequent opportunity to observe similar facts, I set myself with curiosity to determine their true signficance, and circumstances arose so favorable to this inquiry that I was led to consider this association of cerebral and auditory lesions as a single disease.

I believed myself sufficiently justified in considering these phenomena, so severe and so distressing, as no more than the symptomatic expression of a lesion of a special apparatus, compatible with the preservation of general health, and in fact many patients, after having been a prey to attacks of this nature for months and years, had seen them disappear little by little and leave no trace behind them.

May one, on the basis of a single case, establish an essential correlation between the vertigo, the deafness and a lesion of the semicircular canals? We should not have the temerity to reply in the affirmative to this question if we had no other support for this point of view; but in the light of the experiments of M. Flourens on section of these canals, taking account of the disturbances of function which arise from these artificial lesions, and above all of the gyrations of the animals, one feels inclined to think that the symptoms which appear in man and which consist of vertigo, nausea, syncope, which are accompanied by head noises and which result in deafness, depend upon a disturbance which has its seat in that part of the labyrinth of which we have spoken.

We will summarize this work in the following propositions:

1. An auditory apparatus hitherto perfectly healthy can become suddenly the site of disturbances of function consisting of noises of varying nature, continuous or intermittent, and these noises are soon accompanied by a diminution of hearing of greater or lesser degree.

2. These disturbances of function which have their origin in the internal auditory apparatus can give rise to attacks reputedly of cerebral origin, such as vertigo, dizziness, uncertain gait, staggering and falling, and are furthermore accompanied by nausea, vomiting and syncope.

3. These attacks, which are of an intermittent nature, are rapidly followed by deafness of more and more severe degree, and often the hearing is suddenly and completely abolished.

4. All the evidence indicates that the organic lesion which produces these disturbances of function is situated in the semicircular canals.

1. Stothers, H. H.: Prosper Menière: The Centenary of an Eponym, *Ann Otol* 70:319-336 (June) 1961.

2. Atkinson, M.: Menière's Original Papers, *Acta Otolaryng*, suppl 162, pp 7-77, 1961.

3. Menière, P.: A Report on Lesions of the Inner Ear Giving Rise to Symptoms of Cerebral Congestion of Apoplectic Type, *Gaz Med Paris* 16:597-601, 1861.

Composite by G. Bako

Moritz Heinrich Romberg (1795-1873)

ROMBERG, author of the first nosology of diseases of the nervous system, was born in Meningen, capital of the former Duchy of Saxe-Meiningen and since 1946 just inside the border of East Germany. Throughout the treatise, treatment was systematized; whereas in the section on tabes dorsalis, ataxia in patients with central nervous system syphilis—Romberg's sign—was described. Romberg's inaugural dissertation, presented in 1817 for graduation from the University of Berlin, discussed achondroplasia (congenital rickets, rachitide congenita),[1] a subject to which he never returned in his writing. After formal education he remained in Berlin and in proper time became professor of medicine and director of the Royal Polyclinic Institute of Friedrich Wilhelm University. His *Lehrbuch der Nervenkrankheiten,* which emphasized the significance of physiological principles in interpreting neurological function, appeared first in 1840. An English translation in 1853 sponsored by the Sydenham Society contained the preface to the first and second editions. In the preface to the first edition, Romberg was critical of the failure of his predecessors to prepare a work on nervous disorders worthy of this segment of clinical science, reaffirming the criticism voiced by

Charles Bell a decade earlier in his *Nervous System*. Romberg wrote:[2]

The blame lies in a measure with the distinguished members of our profession who have been deterred by a fear that pathological investigations would fail to cope with the advanced state of physiological inquiry; in others, the fault is to be attributed to that mental indolence, which gives the preference to the easy path of tradition, and with foolish scepticism rejects everything that is new. But in no department of pathology has physiology exerted so great an influence, no where has free research achieved so glorious a victory over dull, traditional routine, as in the doctrine of Nervous Diseases. The present work, the fruit of twenty years of research, is intended to afford evidence of this fact. I feel assured of the existence of numerous defects and errors, as I know that it will only serve as a stage of transition to more perfect works; but the foundation upon which it has been constructed is not to be shaken, as it is *the physiological principle;* this is based upon the unchangeable functions of the animal economy.

The nosology of Romberg followed Cullen''s doctrine of neurosis: dysfunction of sensibility and dysfunction of motion. In classifying disturbances of motion and sensation, Romberg was also following the delineations of Whytt, published a century earlier. Each dysfunction was subdivided. Hyperesthesia and anesthesia, the subdivision of the neuroses of sensibility, are concepts that remain in current use; whereas hyperkineses (spasms) and akineses (paralyses) were neuroses of motion. Although the two volumes contained more than 100 chapters, only a few disease entities were specifically segregated and discussed. Facial hemiatrophy sometimes is identified as Romberg's disease. Ciliary neuralgia was presented as a neurosis of sensibility; whereas ataxia in syphilis of the central nervous system was presented as a neurosis of motility.[2]

The spinal cord viewed as a central organ, not only serves as an agent for the mutual transmission of stimuli, but also as a source of nervous power, of the principle of motor and sensory tension, by which the continuance and vigour of motion and sensation is secured, and a general stimulus for the entire organism provided. The disease, which is characterised by a diminution of this power, is termed tabes dorsalis.

Early in the disease we find the sense of touch and the muscular sense diminished, while the sensibility of the skin is unaltered in reference to the temperature and painful impressions. . . . The gait begins to be insecure, and the patient attempts to improve it by making a greater effort of the will; as he does not feel the tread to be firm, he puts down his heels with greater force. From the commencement of the disease the indidual keeps his eyes on his feet to prevent his movements from becoming still more unsteady. If he is ordered to close his eyes while in the erect posture, he at once commences to totter and swing from side to side; the insecurity of his gait also exhibits itself more in the dark. Painful sensations of different kinds almost invariably accompany the affection; the most common in a sense of constriction, which proceeds from the dorsal or lumbar vertebrae, encircles the trunk like a hoop, and not unfrequently renders breathing laborious. Several of my patients have described this sensation as particularly troublesome during sleep, causing them suddenly to start up and scream out. . . . The necessity of employing his eyes becomes more and more urgent; if he closes his eyes, even while sitting, his body begins to sway to and fro; . . . Even when the optic nerve was not implicated, I have repeatedly found a change in the pupils of one or both eyes, consisting in a contraction with loss of motion, which in one case, that of a man aged 45, attained to such a height that the pupils were reduced to the size of a pin's head.
Although the post-mortem records of this disease may present considerable variations, they almost without exception show the existence of partial atrophy of the spinal cord; the lumbar portion and the nerves given off from it are the parts generally affected.

Ciliary neuralgia, episodic pain of the orbit or periorbital area sometimes associated with migraine, which commanded its own chapter in the *Handbook*, was summarized as follows:[2]

Painful sensation in the eye, which are generally confined to one side, and are excited or increased by rays of light and by visual efforts, are the characteristic symptoms of this affection. In the higher degrees photophobia is present; this is therefore the term generally applied to the affection. The patient avoids solar and artificial light, as the bulb of the eye becomes painful when exposed to their influence, and the eyelids contract painfully. The pupil is contracted. The pain not unfrequently extends over the head and face. The eye generally weeps and becomes red. These symptoms occur in paroxysms, of a uniform or irregular character, and isolated or combined with facial neuralgia and hemicrania.

These phenomena have been attributed to an affection of the optic nerve, though unjustly, as this nerve is incapable of receiving any other impression but that of light and colour, and its hyperaesthesia is manifested exclusively by luminous phenomena, as its anaesthetic conditions show themselves by an inability to perceive light and colour. The optic nerve has nothing to do with the tactile sensation of the luminous rays; the possibility of a doubt on this subject is removed by the observation, that amaurotic individuals may suffer from photophobia. The disturbance in the functions of the optic nerve occurring in ciliary neuralgia, proves the close relation that exists between the sensory nerve of the organ of sight and the special nerve of vision.

In the preface to the second edition, Romberg had not forgotten Bell but confessed that the hope expressed earlier for the future of neurology had been only partially fulfilled.[2]

The study of nervous diseases, which some persons have refused to acknowledge as anything but the manifestation of other morbid processes, has been declared a fruitless research, and in some schools has been almost interdicted. . . . To guard against greater debasement, we must enter anew upon the path which the master-mind of Charles Bell, the Harvey of our century, has opened to us.
Let our guide be the analysis of observation, not the cavilling spirit which even attacks the solid basis of physiological laws, such as the law of eccentrical phenomena, or the law prohibiting one nerve from acting for another,—but that purifying criticism which lays bare defects, and mercilessly eradicates fallacies and untruths.

The nosology of Romberg was slowly abandoned, as specific neurological and neuromuscular entities were recognized and the pathogenesis of some revealed. Since his physiological principles that were the basis for classification were sound and his treatise was the first modern compendium of nervous diseases, it seems proper that he be remembered by at least one eponymic term in clinical neurology. "Romberg's sign" has been the one retained by common usage.

1. Romberg, M. H.: *Inaugural Dissertation on Congenital Rickets,* (Ger) Berlin: Karl August Platen, 1817.
2. Romberg, M. H.: *A Manual of the Nervous Diseases of Man,* (Ger) H. Sieveking, trans-ed., London: Sydenham Society, 1853.

Composite by G. Bako

Anson Jones (1798-1858)

ANSON JONES was a capable country doctor as judged by the standards of his day, but his contributions to the flowering of frontier Texas were largely political rather than scientific. Jones was born on a scrubby farm near Great Barrington, Massachusetts, the 13th among 14 siblings.[1] He inherited little from his family beyond tolerance for poverty and indebtedness and the knowledge that any betterment of his indigence must come from his own initiative. During his drab New England upbringing, he attended a country school when not needed for the farm chores. However, young Jones showed sufficient interest in learning to acquire some familiarity with English literature and a smattering of Greek, Latin, and mathematics.[2] His basic education was over after one term at Lenox academy. When the family disbanded upon his mother's death, he was left to act on his wits except for their advice.[3]

A zeal for reading attracted Jones to printing. Such a prospective livelihood was favorably received by his brothers. On the other hand, his father and his sisters won him over to medicine, a study which was begun reluctantly, first as an apprentice to

Dr. Sheldon of Litchfield, Connecticut, and later to Dr. Hull of Utica. Each assignment was interrupted by teaching school in order to keep him relatively free from debt. Preliminary medical training was completed in the fall of 1820, when he appeared before the Board of Censors of the Medical Society of Oneida County, New York, was examined, and received a license to practice physic and surgery.

The authorization proved to be of little practical value, for it failed to bring Jones patients when he opened his office at Bainbridge, Chenango County, New York, or when he ventured into pharmacy in Norwich. He met with similar failure after a few months in Philadelphia. Upon learning of an opportunity for practice in South America that required an American physician, he sailed for Caracas, Venezuela. Two years later Jones had liquidated his debts and accumulated a comfortable reserve. The favorable financial state allowed him to return to Philadelphia; there he realized the importance of theoretical studies in medicine, and enrolled for a term in Jefferson Medical College. In 1827, he was called to defend his thesis on ophthalmia and, being successful, received the doctor of medicine degree. Practice was resumed once more and, sensing the need to attract patients, Jones developed strong bonds of fellowship among members of the Masonic Lodge and Order of Odd Fellows. Although such activities were energy consuming and socially rewarding, they failed to help him professionally, and again his practice faltered.

By 1832, Jones's savings depleted once more and his practice a great disappointment, he sailed for New Orleans and entered a mercantile partnership. The time was inopportune, however; an epidemic of cholera and yellow fever had disrupted the community. To add to his miseries he contracted yellow fever and was invalided for several months. Disheartened, he turned to gambling and drinking but subsequently overcame these vices and in 1833 boarded a ship that took him along the coast of Texas, then under Mexican sovereignty.

Jones was attracted to Brazoria on the Brazos River, since the community needed a physician. Although he soon developed an extensive practice, stirring political events at that time commanded increasing attention from many. Skirmish after skirmish took place between the armed Mexicans and the Texas settlers. When a provisional government was formed in the fall of 1835, with Sam Houston as major general of the frontier forces, Jones, a duly elected representative from Brazoria to the "Consultation," joined the revolutionaries. In 1836, before the senseless slaughter at the Alamo, the provisional Texas government declared independence from Mexico while hostilities continued. Jones served as regimental surgeon and later assistant surgeon general and medical purveyor of the Army, a title changed later to apothecary-general. Following the battle of San Jacinto on April 21, 1836, when Houston defeated the Mexican army and captured Santa Anna, the Republic of Texas was established. Jones was elected a member of their Second Congress in September 1837. By then his medical career was essentially over. Although a neophyte in politics, he represented the new Republic in Washington for three years. When recalled to serve in the Texas Senate, he rose to become presiding officer and, in 1841, Secretary of State.

In 1844, Jones succeeded Sam Houston as the President of Texas and after suffrage by the Republic and two-thirds vote of the Senate of the United States, the Republic became the 28th state of the Union. Jones retired to his plantation on the Brazos River named "Barrington" in honor of his birthplace. In 1858, he ran for a seat in the United States Senate, his last political venture. His defeat was overwhelming, and, in a state of depression in the city of Houston early in 1858, he took his own life.

1. Gambrell, H.: *Anson Jones, the Last President of Texas*, Garden City, NY: Doubleday & Co., Inc., 1948.

2. Clark, T. W.: The Downs and Ups of Anson Jones, M.D., *J. Hist Med* 3:95-104, 1948.

3. Jones, A.: *Republic of Texas*, New York: D. Appleton & Co., 1859.

Composite by G. Bako

George Bodington (1799-1882)

GEORGE BODINGTON, descendant of an old Warwickshire family, was one of the first to recommend country air, a nutritious diet, sedation, and domiciliary care for those stricken with tuberculosis.[1] After attending Magdalen College School at Oxford, he was apprenticed at the age of 17 for two years to a surgeon in the market town of Atherstone. Two years later he went to London, where he became a student at St. Bartholomew's Hospital and, in 1825, a licentiate of the Society of Apothecaries. These qualifications were sufficient for practice at this time. After a short stay in Birmingham, he cared for the sick in the neighboring villages of Erdington and Sutton Coldfield. During this period, Bodington became a licentiate of the Royal College of Physicians in Edinburgh and received an MD degree from the University of Erlangen.

In 1836, having acquired limited experience in his common-sense management of tuberculosis, Bodington became proprietor of Driffold House Asylum at Sutton Coldfield, with accommodations for 20 victims of insanity. Four years later he sold his practice but retained supervision of the asylum and converted a residence into a sanitarium in the neighboring village of Maney for patients suffering from tuberculosis. Bodington continued institutional practice until late in life, although public affairs claimed some of his time and efforts. He served as Warden of the Royal Borough of Sutton Coldfield for two terms and was one of its most active members and magistrates, albeit unsuccessful as a conservative in election for the parliamentary seat at Birmingham.

Bodington's scientific contributions were limited. He discussed a case of Asiatic cholera, published in *Lancet,* prepared a small pamphlet on the influence of climate, and in 1840 published his *An Essay on the Treatment and Cure of Pulmonary Consumption.*[2] He reasoned that if out-of-door occupations rendered persons less susceptible to pulmonary tuberculosis, the advantages of an open air environment with supplementary measures would benefit the afflicted. Recognizing that selected features of his recommendations for management of patients with consumption had been practiced for centuries, he was one of the first physicians of his time to break from current procedures of blood letting, drugging, confinement, and prohibition of cool fresh air, and to substantiate his practical management with patients who showed substantial benefit. Bodington's reported series was restricted to six patients with one death, a commendable nine-year record. Limited exercise was permitted during convalescence, and out-of-door employment was advised when the patient was cured. In breaking from traditional means of management, his views were not generally accepted; on the contrary, they were attacked privately and publicly in such a devastating manner that he abandoned subsequently this phase of practice and confined his attention to the insane. However, his theoretical considerations and the demonstrated merit of them prevailed, and before his death a number of sanatoria were established. One of the first tubercular sanatoria in the United States was founded by Trudeau in Saranac Lake in the Adirondacks in upper New York State in 1884. Pertinent paragraphs from Bodington's report follow.[2]

I should recommend to one thus consuming away, under the influence of this *wasting disease,* a nutritious diet of mild, fresh animal, and farinaceous food, aided by the stimulus of a proper quantity of wine, having regard to the general state and condition of the patient.

. . . I have taken for the purpose a house in every respect adapted, and near to my own residence, for the reception of patients of this class, who may be desirous, or who are recommended to remove from their homes for the benefit of change of air, etc. It is presumed that, as the situation is very superior in point of dryness, mildness, and purity of air, the advantages to be derived from systemic arrangements with regard to exercise, diet, and general treatment . . . and it is hoped that this plan may meet the approbation of the medical profession, and prove beneficial to many afflicted or threatened with the first symptoms of this direful disease in this neighbourhood or elsewhere. Farmers, shepherds, ploughmen, etc., are rarely liable to consumption, living constantly in the open air; whilst the inhabitants of the towns, and persons living much in close rooms, or whose occupations confine them many hours within doors, are its victims: The habits of these latter ought, in the treatment of the disease, to be made to resemble as much as possible those of the former class, as respects air and exercise, in order to effect a cure.

Tuberculous matter is often found deposited upon sound lungs, where it has been rendered harmless, by a vigorous state of nutrition, and the sanguiferous system; but let individuals thus affected be exposed to the causes of innutrition, and there are but too many, by which the muscular and sanguiferous systems lose their tone and become weakened, and you have removed the barriers to the progress of consumption.

In order then to restore a consumptive patient, it will be necessary especially to attend to the following matters. We shall find first of all a rapid and weak pulse, ranging from 120 to 140 beats in a minute, clearly indicating a deficient supply of blood, and the heart and arteries irritable in proportion to this deficiency. This condition must be met at once, not by the means termed "antiphlogistic," but with frequent supplies, in moderate quantities, of nourishing diet and wine; a glass of good Sherry or Madeira in the forenoon, with an egg, another glass of wine after dinner, fresh meat for dinner, some nourishing food for supper, such as sago, or boiled milk, according to the taste and digestive powers of the patient. This will be supplying means to rectify the morbid condition of the nutritive functions, and to allay the irritability of the heart and arteries. I have generally succeeded in the course of a few days, or perhaps a week, in reducing the pulse from 130 to 140 down to 90, by means of this diet, and by a systematic use of sedative medicines, and other means. The whole nervous system is unduly excited, or affected in some way we know not

how to express or understand, from our limited knowledge of it, when under the influence of this disease, and neither can nutrition be effected, or the muscular system recover strength, or the vessels be filled with a due supply of the vital fluid, unless that nervous disorder be allayed and soothed, or rendered more in accordance with a healthy condition. The plan to obtain this object is, to give alternative doses of sedatives, and also direct or full ones. The former consist of moderate doses given at intervals throughout the day, with the view of allaying the general nervous excitement. The direct or full dose is given at bed-time, to allay coughing and procure sleep. Aconite, henbane, or the salts of morphia may be used. I have preferred generally the hydrochlorate of morphine: A sufficient dose to procure a whole night's repose should be given every night.

1. George Bodington, MD, Erlangen, LRCP Ed, obituary, *Lancet* 1:416 (March 11) 1882.
2. Bodington, G: *An Essay on the Treatment and Cure of Pulmonary Consumption*, London: Longman, Orme, Brown, Green, & Longmans, 1840, in *Selected Essays and Monographs*, London: New Sydenham Society, 1901.

Los Angeles County Medical Library

Alfred Velpeau (1795-1867)

ALFRED ARMAND LOUIS MARIE VELPEAU is an example of a member of the profession who, motivated by tremendous energy, achieved extraordinary clinical goals with scarcely any elementary education and without superior intellectual endowments. He was born in Breche, a small village in the department of Indre-et-Loire, the son of a poor blacksmith, and seemed destined to follow the family trade.[1] He learned to read by concentrating on the religious tracts of the church and a few veterinary texts acquired by his father. Alfred attended a curate's school for a few months in his 20th year; without further education an interested physician arranged for him, under the shelter of a gentleman of Tours, to prepare for the post of Health Officer in that community.

In this pursuit Velpeau made the rounds of the hospital and the dissecting room under Bretonneau, the most distinguished physician of Tours. Although the usual fees for study were canceled because of his impoverished state, he subsisted on a miserable diet and enjoyed no social life. He was further handicapped by an extremely limited knowledge of the French language and even less of Latin. After 15 months he received the diploma of a sanitary officer but continued the study of medicine and served as first "interne" at the l'Hôpital de Tours. In time he was advanced to first assistant to Bretonneau, and in this capacity attended to the private patients of his chief and occasionally collected a well-earned fee to augment his diet of bread and cheese. Velpeau's clinical zeal and exceptional capacity for learning was generally appreciated and especially so by Bretonneau, who, in 1820, sent him to Paris for further study under the aegis of Jules Cloquet.

At the end of the year he won the prize in anatomy and physiology; the next year he was elected assistant in anatomy. Velpeau's success seemed assured in spite of harassing poverty, and, in competition, he qualified for extern in l'Hôpital St. Louis. In 1823, his thesis on general medical subjects was presented to the Faculty of Medicine of Paris who granted the MD degree. The following year he was appointed professor agrégé. Meanwhile he had begun the preparation for publication of brief scientific contributions and the two-volume *Treatise of Surgical Anatomy,* which appeared in 1825.[2] This was followed by the two-volume *The Elementary Treatise on the Art of Mid-*

wifery in 1829[3] and the *New Elements of Operative Surgery* in three volumes in 1832.[4] These encyclopedic works represented only a portion of his prolific composition during his most active decade. They were important treatises, were widely read, and although frequently uncritical, were translated into English shortly after their appearance in French.

In 1828, Velpeau became surgeon to the Central Bureau but failed in competition at the university, first for the chair of external pathology and two years later for the professorship of obstetrics. Finally, in 1835, having served as surgeon to the hospital of Saint-Antoine, la Pitié, and la Charité, he won the chair of clinical surgery which embraced midwifery, anatomy, and pathological and operative surgery. The Academy of Medicine honored him with membership in 1833 and the Academy of Sciences, in 1843. In addition to the enrichment of the clinical literature, Velpeau presented lucid and detailed lectures, became a skilled technical operator, and was in great demand as a consultant.

Short communications to the French medical literature include discussions of surgical management of aneurysms, diseases of the uterus, laryngopharyngeal fistula, the lymphatic system, tumors of the skin, puerperal convulsions, purulent infections, version of the fetus, treatment of hemmorhage, amputation of the jaw and wrist, and neurectomy of the maxillofacial nerve. Eponymic terms include: Velpeau's hernia, femoral hernia external to the great vessels, and Velpeau's bandage, designed to support the arm in luxation or fracture of the clavicle. This was described and illustrated in the second edition of his operative surgery.[4]

I have designed a bandage from a long strip of fabric which is suitable in sternoclavicular luxations, for which I had originally created this type of bandage, also in achromioclavicular luxations, in fractures of the clavicle, in fractures of the acromion, in fractures of the scapula, and even in fractures of the neck of the humerus. To prepare this bandage one should procure a narrow strip of fabric about 30 to 38 feet long. The end is placed in the axilla of the healthy side or on the back. It is then applied diagonally across the back and over the shoulder to the clavicle of the injured side. The affected hand is placed on the acromion of the healthy shoulder. In this manner the elbow is lifted to approximately the tip of the sternum and the injured shoulder is forced upward toward the back by the action of the humerus and toward the outside; the humerus now rests on the side of the chest and acts as a lever both directly and through the movement of the chest. While an assistant holds the arm and forearm in place the surgeon places the bandage on the anterior surface of the arm, slightly toward the outside and underneath the elbow and then carries the bandage through the axilla on the healthy side and back, in front and on the level of the axilla. This is repeated three or four times, creating diagonal loops which obliquely cover the injured clavicle, the upper part of the chest, and the upper-outer part of the arm. In order to fix the bandage on the injured shoulder it is brought horizontally over the posterior surface of the chest, then wound over the outer surface of the arm across the elbow, and across the forearm. These circular slings are applied until the hand resting on the healthy shoulder and the shoulder itself remain the only parts of the chest that are not covered. The bandaging is finished by applying a few more diagonal slings and by adding a number of horizontal circular slings.

A second roll of bandage, well-soaked in starch, is applied in the same fashion over the first one making this bandage immoveable in which the elbow rests without effort and incapable of being dislodged. . . . I use little padding; at times a roll may be placed in the supraclavicular space almost directly in front of the sternum, or in some cases in front of the acromion, depending upon which anatomical point more pressure is to be applied. To avoid chafing of the skin it is desirable to place two layers of linen between the chest and the arm; it may also be useful, but not important, to place a wedge of material in the axilla as Desault does in cases of fracture of the neck of the humerus.

Velpeau's description of hyperplastic fibrocystic disease of the breast appeared in his final and best monographic work in 1854, entitled *A Treatise on Diseases of the Breast and Mammary Region*. Clinical experiences with more than 2,000 cases were presented. Several were included from his earliest hospital days at Tours. Several types of cysts are discussed, of which the majority currently are considered to be variants only of mammary dysplasia. They appear chiefly in the final decade of reproductive life but may not be recognized until after the menopause. The tract was translated into English, from which the following excerpts on serous cysts were taken.[5]

10. CYSTS OF THE MAMMARY REGION.—Hardly any description has been given of fluid tumours, except that of A. Cooper and Dr. Warren, under the title of *hydatids of the breast*. Nevertheless, I have met with a considerable number of varieties of cysts in this situation, all very different from hydatids. Without mentioning the galactoceles just described, I have to speak of serosanguineous, mucilaginous, and sero-mucous cysts. Sebaceous cysts also may be developed here, so as to simulate other kinds of tumours.

Serous cysts of the breast generally arise, without evident cause. . . . Their exciting cause is frequently unknown, and this depends, no doubt, on the circumstance, that as they are unattended with pain, they are in the first instance perceived only by chance, at a period when their growth is pretty well advanced, and the patients are generally quite unable to point out in what locality they first arose.

Left to themselves, these serous cysts would be compatible with perfect health, were it possible to arrest their progress, and if their existence were not the cause of incessant uneasiness in the patient's mind. As they undergo no malignant degeneration, their prognosis is neither more nor less serious than that of a common hydrocele. They may distress the patient, by their size or weight, and produce mechanical alteration in the neighbouring parts or organs; but, in their own nature, they are destitute of any real danger.

Consequently, they may be left to themselves, if the patient has no pain, and is sensible enough not to feel uneasy, or, if she has great dread of such measures as would effectually get rid of them. In the treatment of these, we may without hesitation employ the same operation as for hydrocele. Others, also unilocular, have such thick and dense walls that fluctuation is always doubtful, and the volume of the tumour depends more on the tissue of the cyst than on the fluid in its cavity. The diagnosis is consequently rendered so difficult, that, before the operation, the surgeon is often in doubt whether the tumour arise from a cyst or from a solid growth. . . . It is thus of primary importance to distinguish accurately the kind of cyst we are called upon to treat.

1. Béclard, J.: "M. Velpeau" (Fr), in *Notices and Portraits, Obituaries from the Academy of Medicine*, Paris: G. Masson, 1878, pp 167-196.
2. Velpeau, A. A. L. M.: *A Treatise on Surgical Anatomy* (Fr), 2 vol, Paris: Crevot, 1825-1826, translated by Sterling, J. W.: New York: S. Wood & Sons, 1830.
3. Velpeau, A. A. L. M.: *An Elementary Treatise on Midwifery* (Fr), Paris: J. B. Baillière, 2 vol, 1829, translated by Meigs, C. D.: Philadelphia: J. Grigg, 1831.
4. Velpeau, A. A. L. M.: *New Elements of Operative Surgery* (Fr), Paris: J. B. Baillière, 1832, ed 2, 1839, excerpt translated by Z. Danilevicius.
5. Velpeau, A. A. L. M.: *A Treatise on the Diseases of the Breast and Mammary Region* (Fr), Paris: V. Masson, 1854, translated by Henry, M.: London: Sydenham Society, 1856.

Robert Liston (1794-1847)

ROBERT LISTON, who performed the first major operation in London under ether anesthesia, spent all but a few months of his career practicing bold surgery without benefit of anesthetic drugs. Liston was born in the manse of Ecclesmachan Linlithgowshire, the eldest child of the minister of the parish.[1] He was educated chiefly by his father and, at the age of 14, entered the University of Edinburgh, where he promptly excelled in Latin. At the age of 16, he became assistant to Dr. John Barclay, who in his lectures on anatomy and physiology, passed on to his pupils respect and appreciation for good surgery. Liston began his hospital training at the Royal Infirmary of Edinburgh, then continued under the Blizards at the London Hospital, and under Abernethy at St. Bartholomew's Hospital. He returned to Edinburgh and, by the age of 24, was a member of the Royal College of Surgeons of England and the Edinburgh College of Surgeons.

In his home city he allied himself in anatomical lectures with his cousin, James Syme, only a few years his junior, gaining a great reputation as teacher and operating surgeon. But Liston was not at peace with the authorities of the Royal Infirmary. He was accused of enticing and then operating upon patients who were denied surgery at the Infirmary; as a consequence, his staff privileges were revoked for five years. The ban was removed in 1827, with appointment to a senior surgical post. In the University, however, the professorship of clinical surgery was awarded to Syme. The sting was soothed the following year when he was offered a similar position in the newly-founded University of London Hospital; this was accepted and thereafter Liston never returned to private professional practice. In London he was elected a Fellow of the Royal Society and was honored by membership in the council of the Royal College of Surgeons and by appointment to the Court of Examiners.

Liston was not a scientific surgeon; rather, his reputation was gained through great knowledge of anatomy, deep dedication to teaching, and most important, complete self-assurance, dexterity, and speed in major surgical interventions. In Edinburgh his text *Elements of Surgery*[2] was published in three parts; his *Practical Surgery* was prepared in London however.[3] The second and third London editions of *Practical Surgery* were republished in Philadelphia, with notes and illustrations by George W. Norris.[4] In the "Preface" to the *Elements of Surgery*, Liston admits there are hazards in operative procedures, but affirms meanwhile a belief in the surgeon's capacity to be of greater help to the patient in need of surgery than any conservative course. The first except emphasizes the importance of anatomy and experience in surgery;[2] the second, concern for the emotions of the patient;[2] and the third, the need for courageous action, from the "Introduction" to *Practical Surgery*.[3]

To treat surgical diseases as they ought to be treated, the practitioner must be thoroughly acquainted with the healthy and morbid structure; he must also have a mind vigorous and firm from nature, well instructed in the best precedents, and matured by observation.

It is only from experience, directed and aided by previous study, that accuracy of diagnosis and celerity of decision can be acquired. Besides knowing in what manner to proceed, the Surgeon must know well wherefore he acts, and also the precise time at which he should interfere. With knowledge and confidence derived from experience, he will perform such operations as are indispensable for the removal of pain and deformity, or for the preservation of life, with calmness and facility—with safety to his patient, and satisfaction to those who assist in, or witness, his proceedings.

It is of the utmost importance to attend to the state of the patient's mind and feelings. He ought not be kept in suspense, but encouraged and assured; and his apprehensions must be allayed. If this cannot be effected—if he is dejected and despondent—talks of the great risk, and of the certainty of his dying, it is better that the operation be abandoned, or at least delayed. If, on the contrary, he is confident in the resources of his constitution, and in the ability of his attendant, and looks forward to the advantage to be derived from his own fortitude, then should there be no delay.

Were the recommendations given above better followed, we should have presented to us fewer of those scenes shocking to humanity, which have been so well described by one of the most interesting writers on surgery; the operators are represented as agitated, miserable, trembling, hesitating in the midst of difficulties, feeling in the wound for things the position of which they had not understood, turning round to their friends for that support which should come from within, holding consultations amidst the cries of the patient, or even retiring to consult about his case whilst he was bleeding, in great pain, and awful expectation.

A description of amputation at the hip joint, in the period immediately preceding the discovery of ether for anesthesia, is indeed graphic.[2]

Amputation at the *hip-joint* is deservedly ranked amongst the most formidable operations in surgery. It ought, therefore, never to be performed but as a last and necessitous resource for the salvation of life. . . . The patient is placed recumbent on a firm table, his nates resting on, or rather projecting a little over the front edge. The sound limb is separated from the one to be removed, and held aside by an assistant. Or it is secured to the foot of the table by a towel, the necessity for an additional assistant being thus done away with, and more freedom in his movement afforded to the operator. . . . The other limb is supported by an experienced and intelligent assistant, who understands, and is able to perform, the movements to facilitate the different steps of the operation. The compression is intrusted also to an experienced and steady assistant, who, standing by the patient's side, presses firmly with one or both thumbs on the femoral artery, where it passes over the pubes; and in this more than in any other operation, should the pressure be delayed till the instant of incision, for otherwise the blood lost *in* the limb will be immense. Transfixion, by a knife proportioned in size to the dimensions of the limb, is made horizontally, the instrument being passed in a somewhat semicircular direction, so as to include as much of the soft parts as possible; an anterior flap is made by cutting downwards. During the passage of the knife across the joint, the assistant rotates the limb a little so as to facilitate the bringing of the instrument out with its point well inwards; in the left limb the rotation will be inwards, in the right outwards. After formation of the flap, the assistant abducts forcibly, and presses downwards; the joint is opened, the round ligament cut, the capsule divided, and the blade of the knife placed behind the head of the bone and the large trochanter; the posterior flap is then made rapidly. After transfixion for the superior flap, and when the sawing motion downwards has advanced but a little way, the compressing assistant shifts his hands into the incision immediately behind the back of the knife, and so obtains a firm grasp of the femoral previously to its division. He retains this hold, at the same time retracting the flap, during the rest of the operation. As soon as the limb has been separated, the surgeon secures the vessels on the posterior flap, partly by his fingers, partly by compression with a large sponge, and ligatures are applied as quickly as possible. The femoral is secured last, for, as long as the assistant retains his hold, haemorrhage from it is not to be dreaded. Thus, when both surgeon and assistants are quick and cool, the operation may be completed with the loss of much less blood than might be expected.

A few years after this treatise was prepared, the *Lancet* published Liston's letter describing his success with the use of inhaled ether in amputation of the thigh. Liston noted that the anesthetic agent was "a fine thing for operating surgeons," surely a most modest appraisal of an anesthetic drug, announced to the world only a short time previously.[5]

Clifford Street,
Dec. 21, 1846.

My DEAR SIR,—I tried the ether inhalation to-day in a case of amputation of the thigh, and in another requiring evulsion of both sides of the great toe-nail, one of the most painful operations in surgery, and with the most perfect and satisfactory results.

It is a very great matter to be able thus to destroy sensibility to such an extent, and without, apparently, any bad result. It is a fine thing for operating surgeons, and I thank you most sincerely for the early information you were so kind as to give me of it.

Yours, faithfully,
ROBERT LISTON.

Other noteworthy items mentioned by Liston's biographers include a monograph on inguinal and femoral hernia, which appeared in 1819;[6] several communications to the *Edinburgh Medical and Surgical Journal* on surgical subjects; descriptions of a laryngeal mirror and a shoe for club foot; devices for reducing dislocations and for crushing and cutting for stone; plastic operations on the nose, and excision of the upper jaw. Liston died from a ruptured aneurysm of the arch of the aorta, having complained of constriction in the larynx and difficulty in swallowing.

1. Stephen, L., and Lee, S. (eds.): "Robert Liston," in *The Dictionary of National Biography,* Oxford: University Press, 1917.

2. Liston, R.: *Elements of Surgery,* London: Longman, Rees, Orme, Brown, Green, and Longman, 1831.

3. Liston, R.: *Practical Surgery,* London: J. Churchill, 1837.

4. Liston, R.: *Practical Surgery,* 2nd American, from the 3rd London edition with additional notes and illustrations, by G. W. Norris, Philadelphia: Thomas, Cowperthwait & Co., 1842.

5. Liston, R.: Letter to the Editor, *Lancet* 1:8, 1847.

6. Liston, R.: *Memoir on the Formation and Connexions of the Crural Arch, and Other Parts Concerned in Inguinal and Femoral Hernia,* Edinburgh: P. Hill & Co., 1819.

James Syme (1799-1870)

JAMES SYME, surgeon in ordinary to the Queen of Scotland, professor of clinical surgery in the University of Edinburgh, and senior attending surgeon in the Royal Infirmary, occupied an enviable station in Edinburgh during the first half of the 19th century.[1] He was born on Princes Street, Edinburgh, into a family of wealth and position. His father had been a Writer to the Signet. James's preliminary education was gained at the local schools, where he

showed, at an early age, an interest in chemistry and developed a solvent for India rubber. Syme sent a communication on the new substance to Dr. Thomson, dated

March 5, 1818, which was published in the *Annals of Philosophy.*[2]

As coal tar in every respect bears the strongest resemblance to petroleum, it occurred to me that by distilling it a fluid might be procured which, like naphtha, should have the property of dissolving caoutchouc, and that in this way I should procure a solvent free from the objections to which the known solvents of that remarkable substance are all more or less liable.

Syme studied at the University of Edinburgh, concentrating in anatomy as a pupil of John Barclay, followed by an assistantship to Robert Liston as demonstrator in the dissecting room. In 1820, without receiving an MD degree, he was appointed superintendent of the Edinburgh Fever Hospital and the following year was elected a member of the London College of Surgeons. After visiting Paris for further training in anatomy and surgery, by 1823 Syme had gained sufficient experience and knowledge to change from pupil to teacher status. Upon the retirement of Liston and the payment of an annuity to his former tutor, he began a regular course of lectures on anatomy, but abandoned them shortly after in preference for surgery. About this time, the ignition of his smoldering quarrels with Liston resulted in his failure to receive a surgical appointment to the Royal Infirmary. He countered with the establishment of a private surgical hospital, Minto House. Here his pupil John Brown described, in *Rab and His Friends,* the personality of the dog Rab and the operation for carcinoma of the breast on Rab's mistress.

In 1833, the Crown appointed Syme professor of clinical surgery in Edinburgh University and, for the first time, he received an appointment at the Royal Infirmary. The following year, when Liston proceeded to London as professor of clinical surgery in University College, Syme succeeded to the London chair but, after a few months, returned to his recently abandoned post in the Royal Infirmary.

Syme's surgical skill antedated his academic advancement and, at the age of only 24 years, he performed the first amputation at the hip joint in Scotland, with Liston as his assistant. In 1827, he removed the mandible for an osteosarcoma and shortly after excised the upper jaw for the first time in Great Britain. Amputation at the ankle joint, Syme's amputation, was performed on a 16-year-old male suffering from osteomyelitis of the foot.[3]

As the disease extended beyond the limits of Chopart's operation, it would have been necessary, in accordance with ordinary practice, to remove the leg below the knee, but as the ankle-joint seemed to be sound, I resolved to perform disarticulation there. With this view, I cut across the integuments of the instep in a curved direction, with the convexity towards the toes, and then across the sole of the foot, so that the incisions were nearly opposite to each other. The disarticulation being then readily completed, the malleolar projections were removed by means of cutting pliers.

Techniques for surgery of the shoulder joint, elbow joint, and knee joint were described in a monograph, *Treatise on the Excision of Diseased Joints,* published in 1831.[4] The *Transactions of the Royal Society of Edinburgh* contained a discussion on experimental pathology concerning the capacity of the periosteum to form osseous tissue.[5]

This property was first attributed to the periosteum by DUHAMEL, just 100 years ago. Having been engaged in the study of vegetable physiology, and more particularly the formation of wood, he imagined that there might be an analogy between the inner layer of the bark and the periosteum, and that as the former hardens in successive layers so as to constitute the wood, the latter might suffer a corresponding conversion into bone.

This observation led to a very careful dissection of the parts concerned; and they are now before the Society. It will be seen that the tibia had died very nearly from end to end, and that the new shell enclosing it has been formed in the periosteum. The new osseous substance may be observed at some parts in the form of small distinct scales.

At other parts it looked as if it had originally consisted of separate portions, and been composed by their union.

But, with the view of making the matter still more clear, I performed the following experiments. I exposed the radius of a dog, and removed an inch and three-quarters of it together with the periosteum. At the same time I exposed the radius of the other leg, and removed a corresponding portion *without* the periosteum, which was carefully detached from it and left quite entire, except where slit open in front. Six weeks afterwards the dog was killed, and the bones examined. In the one from which a portion had been taken together with the periosteum, the extremities were found extended toward each other in a conical form, with a great deficiency of bone between them, and in its place merely a small band of tough ligamentous texture. In the other, where the periosteum had been allowed to remain, there was a compact mass of bone not only occupying the space left by the portion removed, but rather exceeding it.

As advancements were made in surgery, Syme was ready to accept and eager to put them to the test. Only a short time following the announcement from Boston of the value of ether in inducing general anesthesia, Syme performed, with benefit of ether, the removal of a large fibrous tumor of the breast, amputation at the shoulder joint for osteosarcoma of the humerus, excision of the shoulder joint including the head of the humerus and the glenoid cavity, amputation of the foot, and excision of tumors of the scrotum and the jaw.

Syme never earned a medical degree but was awarded honorary degrees by the universities of Dublin, Bonn, and Oxford. He was a great teacher of surgery, a surgeon in wide demand, and one who developed sound principles based upon the anatomy and experimental pathology that were available a century or more ago. He was a prolific writer, a regular contributor to the Edinburgh journals, and an initial contributor to the first issue of the *British Medical Journal* on the antiseptic methods advanced by his son-in-law Lister. Syme published a discussion on medical reform and a number of texts and treatises in surgery, including *Principles of Surgery, On Diseases of the Rectum, On Stricture of the Urethra and Fistula in Perineo, Observations in Clinical Surgery,* and *Excision of the Scapula.* In turn, his son-in-law described his character and achievements as a surgeon as follows.[6]

As a practical surgeon, Mr. Syme presented a remarkable combination of qualities; and we have not known whether to admire most the soundness of his pathological knowledge; his skill in diagnosis, resembling intuition, though in reality the result of acute and accurate observation and laborious experience, well stored and methodised; the rapidity and soundness of his judgment; his fertility in resources as an operator, combined with simplicity of the means employed; his skill and celerity of execution; his fearless courage; or the singleness of purpose with which all his proceedings were directed to the good of his patients.

The hostility which he excited in a few was greatly outweighed by the friendship which he inspired in the many. Rarely is it granted to any one to attach to himself the enduring love and admiration of so large a number of his fellow-men. This was due not only to his perfect genuineness of character, which could not fail to gain respect even from those who differed from him, but also to another quality, as essential as truthfulness to a good surgeon— a most warm heart, a true love for his fellow-creatures, and a generous appreciation of sterling merit in whatever form it might present itself. Mr. Syme, in short, besides being a surgical genius of the highest order, was a perfect gentleman and a good as well as a great man.

1. Paterson, R.: *Memorials of the Life of James Syme,* Edinburgh: Edmondston and Douglas, 1874.

2. Syme, J.: *On a Substance from Coal Tar, Ann Philos* 12:112-113, 1818.

3. Syme, J.: Amputation at the Ankle-Joint, *London Edinburgh Mo Jo* 26:93-96, 1843.

4. Syme, J.: *Treatise on the Excision of Diseased Joints,* Edinburgh: A. Black, 1831.

5. Syme, J.: On the Power of the Periosteum to Form New Bone; *Trans Roy Soc Edinburgh* 14:158-163, 1840.

6. Lister, J.: James Syme, *Scotsman,* June 28, 1870.

Francis Rynd (1801-1861)

FRANCIS RYND, one of the first to practice infiltration of nerve trunks by subcutaneous injection, was born in Dublin and studied at Trinity College.[1] He received his early education at Meath Hospital, complemented by an apprenticeship to Sir Philip Crampton. Rynd is described as a perfect gentleman, passionately fond of hunting, a fashionable dresser, and a favorite with the ladies. Cultivating a society practice, he numbered most of the nobility of Ireland as his patients. He courted the good will and appreciation of the public and his pupils rather than his professional colleagues.

Rynd's initial description of the infiltration of an analgesic solution in the treatment of neuralgia was published in 1845 in the *Dublin Medical Press.* He described the experimental use in two patients from the Meath Hospital, County of Dublin. Fifteen years later he had extended his observations and success to a larger number of patients. His first case was reported as follows.[2]

Margaret Cox, aetat. 59, of spare habit, was admitted into hospital, May 18, 1844, complaining of acute pain over the entire of left side of face, particularly in the supraorbital region, shooting into the eye, along the branches of the portio dura in the cheek, along the gums of both upper and lower jaw, much increased in this situation by shutting the mouth and pressing her teeth close together, and occasionally darting to the opposite side of the face and to the top and back of her head.

On the 3rd of June a solution of fifteen grains of acetate of morphia, dissolved in one drachm of creosote, was introduced to the supra-orbital nerve, and along the course of the temporal, malar, and buccal nerves, by four punctures of an instrument made for the purpose. In the space of a minute all pain (except that caused by the operation, which was very slight) had ceased, and she slept better that night than she had for months. After the interval of a week she had slight return of pain in the gums of both upper and under jaw. The fluid was again introduced by two punctures made in the gum of each jaw, and the pain disappeared. After this the pain did not recur, and she was detained in hospital for some weeks, during which time her health improved, her sleep was restored, and she became quite a happy looking person. She left the hospital on the 1st of August in high spirits, and promised to return if she ever felt the slighest pain again. We conclude she continues well, for we have not heard from her since.

1. Ormsby, L.: *Medical History of the Meath Hospital and County Dublin Infirmary,* Dublin: Fannin & Co., 1888.
2. Rynd, F.: Neuralgia—Introduction of Fluid to the Nerve, *Dublin Med Press* 13:167-168, 1845.

Composite by G. Bako

Willard Parker (1800-1884)

WILLARD PARKER, recognized as the leading New York City surgeon in the mid-19th century, was born in the village of Lindeborough, Hillsborough County, NH, into a farming family. He was raised in Chelmsford [now Lowell], Massachusetts, and, after teaching in a district school to prepare himself scholastically and financially for higher education, he entered Harvard College, from which he received the AB degree in 1826. Although he planned initially for the ministry, a chance observation of John C. Warren's surgical skill turned him to medicine and the Harvard Medical School.[1] After practical training as an intern at the Chelsea Marine Hospital, Parker graduated MD from Harvard in 1830. The same year he was appointed professor of anatomy in the Vermont Medical College at Woodstock, Vermont, there dividing his time with the Berkshire County Medical College at Pittsfield, Massachusetts. He taught two terms as professor of anatomy at Geneva Medical College, Geneva, New York, and, in 1836-1837, one term as professor of surgery at Cincinnati Medical College, where he was closely associated with Samuel D. Gross. Before accepting a permanent post, Parker went abroad and spent a short time in London; however, the greater portion of the year was spent in Paris, where he walked the wards of the great hospitals, studyîng with Chomel, Louis, and other leading clinicians of the day.

Upon returning to the United States, Parker accepted the chair of surgery, later entitled "principles and practice of surgery and surgical pathology", in the College of Physicians and Surgeons in New York. For 30 years he adorned the position as well as other institutional affiliations, including Bellevue, St. Luke's, Roosevelt, Mt. Sinai, and New York hospitals. In 1845, he supported James R. Wood in reorganizing the Alms House at Bellevue Hospital Center. A founder of the New York Academy of Medicine, Parker served as its president and, while associated with the Academy, supported reform in the Board of Health and recommended the establishment of a hospital for infectious diseases.

Parker's scientific contributions were limited. Several short case reports and a posthumous monograph reviewing approximately 400 cases of cancer of the female breast were published. He reported the ligation of the subclavian artery for aneurysm on five patients, described the management of intractable cystitis by cystotomy, and performed the first successful operation in modern times upon an abscessed appendix. The lateral operation on the bladder for persistent cystitis was described in 1851, in a patient with disseminated tuberculosis which ended fatally. A follow-up report in 1867 disclosed no further opportunity to test the expediency of this operation, although a communication from an associate in Nashville, Tennessee, described a successful result. The initial communication was presented by Stephen Smith, assistant surgeon in Bellevue Hospital.[2]

As medication had failed to cure, and the condition of the patient was daily deteriorating, Dr. Parker resolved to perform the lateral operation upon the bladder. The object in view was to open a channel by which the urine could drain off as fast as secreted, and thus afford to the bladder *rest,* the first essential indication in the treatment of inflammation.

An operation for an abscess of the vermiform appendix was performed in 1843, before Hancock of London had successfully operated on a patient similarly affected. Parker recognized the folly of waiting for gross suppuration, suggesting instead that as soon as signs of localization of the inflammatory process appeared, an incision be made over the appendix, avoiding the peritoneum. Although the first operation was performed in 1843, the series of four cases was not published until 1867.[3]

In 1843, I was called in consultation to visit Dr. T., of Brooklyn. He had been confined to bed for some weeks, suffering from pain in the bowels, constipation, disturbance of system, fever, tenderness in right inguinal region, etc. On examination, I found a swelling in the neighborhood of the iliac fossa, in which questionable fluctuation existed. An opening of exploration was made, which justified a free incision. I accordingly cut down into, and excavated the contents of the abscess; with the pus, a little concretion, the size of a raisin-seed, came out. In a short time the patient recovered, and is living now, in good health.

Reasoning thus, I had convinced myself of the practability of an operation, in cases of abscess of the appendix vermiformis. Of its safety there could be no doubt, for there was no danger in the division of those structures through which the incision would pass. That it was perfectly justifiable, I had no doubt, for, taking into consideration the two possibilities of any case, I could find no reason why the operation should not be performed. The first of these, was where the diagnosis had been clearly made out. This has been sufficiently dwelt upon in the foregoing paragraphs. The second, was in those cases in which there was doubt as to the diagnosis. If no abscess had already formed, in case one should be in process of formation, an external opening would tend to make it point in a safe direction. And even if no abscess should form, a free incision would relieve tension, thus adding to the comfort of the patient, and in no way prejudicing his safety. One other question remained. Would the operation be successful in bringing about a cure? Judging from the result of the three cases reported above, an affirmative answer seemed certain; for these recorded, because in each one nature had provided for an external discharge of the contents of the abscess, and what nature had provided for in these three, an operation would provide for in all cases.

Parker was a physician of deep religious conviction who although not an abstainer, counseled against intemperance and served as president of the Inebriate Asylum of Binghampton, New York. When the Metropolitan Board of Health was created in New York in 1866, he was appointed one of the commissioners. His clinical teaching was widely acclaimed, and he was noted for his encouragement and courtesy to pupils and younger members of the profession. The vitality of his personality was apparent and was complemented by a capacity for clarity in presentation. In general medical problems as well as in surgery, Parker was in demand as a sympathetic consultant and wise physician. He possessed an admirable surgical technique, being ambidextrous with surgical instruments. His diagnostic acumen was based more upon his clinical experience than on reference to the experience of others as recounted in texts and journals. In spite of an apparent lack of interest in books, he held a number of works of the ancients in his large library, which was given to the Medical Society of the County of Kings in Brooklyn.[4] He was honored with the LLD from Princeton College in 1870; however, the greatest tribute was in the naming of the Willard Parker Hospital, Infectious Diseases, the hospital established in the year of his death and which he first promoted. It served as the hospital for contagious diseases in New York City until 1955. Parker was buried in New Canaan, Connecticut, where he had a summer residence and farm for many years.

1. Harrington, T. F.: *The Harvard Medical School,* vol 2, New York: Lewis Publishing Co., 1905, pp 735-738.

2. Parker, W.: Cystitis; Lateral Operation on the Bladder, Death; Tuberculous Kidney, *New York J Med* 7:83-86, 1851.

3. Parker, W.: An Operation for Abscess of the Appendix Vermiformis Caeci, *Med Rec* 2: 25-27, 1867.

4. Warbasse, J. P.: Willard Parker and His Medical Library, *Long Island Med J* 1:122-124, 1907.

Composite by G. Bako

Joseph Pancoast (1805-1882)

JOSEPH PANCOAST, descendant of a family which came from England with William Penn, was born in Burlington, New Jersey. He completed his medical education and a long professional career in Philadelphia, earned the MD degree at the University of Pennsylvania in 1828, and soon thereafter entered the Philadelphia Hospital as resident physician.[1] By 1831, he had begun the practice of surgery and added instruction in practical anatomy and surgery to his duties. Pancoast was elected physician to the Philadelphia Hospital (Blockley) in 1835 and, from 1838 to 1845, served as visiting surgeon; from 1854 to 1864 he attended the Pennsylvania Hospital. Meanwhile, in 1838, the Board of Trustees of Jefferson Medical College elected him to the vacancy created by the retirement of George McClellan, professor of surgery. From 1841 until 1874, he held the chair of general, descriptive and

surgical anatomy, retiring as emeritus professor of anatomy.

One of the leading surgeons of Philadelphia in his time, Pancoast was recognized as an operator with great skill, a medical writer of renown, a painter of considerable talent, and a most enlightening and popular teacher of living tissue, ie, surgical anatomy. In addition, he was a regular contributor to the *American Journal of the Medical Sciences,* the *American Medical Intelligencer* and the *Medical Examiner,* in which he described his surgical experiences and presented his case studies in detail. Pancoast was one of the first American surgeons to devise a plastic operation for exstrophy of the bladder by replacing the missing anterior vesicle wall with reconstructed abdominal flaps. Other successful procedures included needling for soft and mixed cataracts, thoracentesis for empyema, tenotomy for strabismus, application of an abdominal tourniquet to compress the lower portion of the aorta for amputation at the hip joint, reconstruction of the eyebrow, severing the trunks of the second and third division of the fifth pair of nerves as they emerge at the base of the skull for tic douloureux, and surgical relief of contraction of the muscles of the face.

His medical writing began with a translation from the Latin of Lobstein, bearing the English title, *Treatise on the Structure, Functions and Diseases of the Human Sympathetic Nerve.*[2] He was responsible for three editions of Wistar and Horner's *System of Anatomy* and for four editions of Quain and Wilson's *Anatomical Plates.* His greatest literary achievement was his own *A Treatise on Operative Surgery,* of which the first edition was published in 1844 and the third and last in 1852.[3] Containing 80 plates prepared from stone lithographs by S. Ceichowski and others, the treatise was described as neither a manual nor a complete reference work, but was the best on operative surgery in the English language and proved invaluable for the student and practicing surgeon. Pancoast was a member of the American Philosophical Society and a Fellow of the College of Physicians of Philadelphia. Several of his introductory and valedictory lectures or addresses to the students of Jefferson Medical College were published privately; one of his best was his *A Lecture Introductory to the Course of Surgery,* given in 1839. The appraisal of the status of medical science 125 years ago is not unlike current expression of optimism.[4]

So rapid and so constant has the communication been for a long period between all parts of the civilized world, that almost every novelty in medical and surgical science, whether originating in this country, or in Europe, or India, or even in Egypt, that ancient seat of learning, has been tested by numerous observers in this city, and under such various opportunities for observation, that its proper value has become generally known.—In fact, the whole medical world seems to be actuated by one great gigantic mind, which is steadily engaged in urging science onward, till it appears about to reach the utmost degree of perfection of which it is susceptible. To keep up with this advancing march of our profession to combine and arrange the general results of medical experience, and to dress them up with the aid of what advantages their own observations in public and private practice may afford, is the pleasing task of your instructors.

1. Joseph Pancoast, obituary, *Boston Med Surg J* 106:260 (March 16) 1882.
2. Lobstein, J. F.: *A Treatise on the Structure, Functions and Diseases of the Human Sympathetic Nerve,* Paris, 1823, J. Pancoast (trans.), Philadelphia: J. G. Auner, 1831.
3. Pancoast, J.: *A Treatise on Operative Surgery,* Philadelphia: Carey and Hart, 1844.
4. Pancoast, J.: *A Lecture Introductory to the Course of Surgery, in the Jefferson Medical College, of Philadelphia, for the Session of 1839-1840,* Philadelphia: W. F. Geddes, 1839.

Joseph-Francois Malgaigne (1806-1865)

J. F. MALGAIGNE, of humble stock with meager material resources, rose to become one of the great scholars in the history of surgery. He was born at Charmes in the department of the Vosges; his father, practicing physician and health officer of the community, would have been satisfied if his son had followed his own career. Ambition and industry, however, led Joseph-Francois to seek higher goals, and, motivated by inspired teaching in his early years,

National Library of Medicine

he began the study of medicine in Nancy at the age of 15. Four years later he had finished his courses, assumed the duties of sanitation officer of Nancy, had written several plays, and had prepared several contributions for the local press. Malgaigne continued his medicine in one of the Schools of Practice in Paris and gained necessary employment for a livelihood as secretary to a savant, M. le Marquis de Villeneuve. He profited immensely from this intimate experience, wherein he was able to develop his literary tastes, gain additional instruction in the classics, and to enhance his oratorical skills. These and other data we learn from the uninspired biography prepared by his son-in-law.[1]

At the age of 21, Malgaigne, prepared for clinical medicine and enriched in literature, was appointed extern in the Hospitals of Paris. There at the conclusion of the year he won a prize for his thesis *A New Theory of the Human Voice.* Hard pressed for finances he entered the Val-de-Grâce military school of surgery, where once more he won several honors. In 1830, he presented his first major treatise, *A New Theory of Vision;* in 1831, upon presentation of a thesis,

The Paradoxes of the Theory and Practice of Medicine, in which he recommended instruction in history and literature to medical students, he received the degree of doctor of medicine. He then spent a few months with an ambulance corps in the war between Poland and Russia. When this mission was abandoned, Malgaigne returned to Paris to practice and teach in his alma mater and subsequently to be associated with St. Louis Hospital and la Charité. He became professeur agrégé in 1835, a member of the Academy of Medicine in 1846, but not until 1850 did he win the chair of operative surgery. Malgaigne was a skillful technician, the first surgeon in France to use ether for general anesthesia, and an advocate of the statistical method for determining the results of surgery. Ill health forced his premature retirement three years before his death, which followed a stroke.

Malgaigne's writings covered a wide range of subjects, prepared in an attractive style and with seemingly little effort. They were scientific, scholarly, and reflected his classical training and genius for exposition. In 1840, he founded the *Journal de Chirurgie,* which in 1847 became the *Revue medico-chirurgicale de Paris* under his editorship. He was well schooled in Latin and Greek and became self-taught in Hebrew in order to comprehend the early books of the Bible. However, he left unfinished at his death a history of medicine in the *Bible.* Published tracts beyond the practice of surgery include *Letters on the History of Surgery, Anatomy and Physiology of Homeric Times, Greek Medicine Before Hippocrates,* and a translation in modern French of the 5th edition of *The Works of Ambroise Paré.*[2] The last work was published in three volumes. The Introduction, a brief history of Western surgery, has been recently translated by Hamby. This provides the following excerpts from the Preface which explains Malgaigne's attraction for the history of surgery.[3]

The history of science, too long neglected among us, begins finally to enjoy a deserved favor. Less subject to systematizing than internal medicine, surgery especially risked enclosing itself within the narrow limits of a single school and of a single epoch, requiring it to arouse itself to draw together to a common end the works of all centuries and times, in a word, to light the route to best insure arriving there.

But if many minds turn avidly toward these new studies, some let themselves be obstructed. At present in the three faculties of France, we have not a single chair that teaches its students the origins and the development of the art; not a work, especially for surgery, that serves to fill this gap in instruction.

I have now developed the project, not of a history of surgery, for history, as complete as imaginable, does not represent the objects themselves but only the impression gained by the historian. For each great epoch, I want to reproduce completely, either by original text or by accurate translations, works of the most remarkable writers and to add, in notes or in special introductions, the observations and doctrines of lesser ones. Thus, for the ancients, to the surgery of Hippocrates and Celsus would be added that of Galen, of Aëtius, of Paul of Aegina, etc. Albucasis would be the example of Arabian surgery, complemented by extracts from Rhazes, Ali-Abbas, and Avicenna. To Guy de Chauliac I would attach the Arabists; to Ambroise Paré, all the surgeons of the fifteenth and sixteenth centuries.

For me Ambroise Paré is not an isolated surgeon; he is the chief representative of an entire era, and I have wanted to show him with his whole era. Guy de Chauliac is equally the most brilliant expression of the time of the Arabists; it is against his surgical efforts, progress, and even his errors that I have posed those of Ambroise Paré.

Malgaigne prepared three major treatises on the practice of surgery. In 1834, a *Manual of Operative Surgery* appeared; in 1838, a two-volume treatise, *Surgical Anatomy and Experimental Surgery* was published; and, in 1847-1855, a two-volume *Treatise on Fractures and Luxations* appeared. The first and third texts were translated into English and were printed in Philadelphia. His discussion of the double vertical fracture of the pelvis which was noted as an original contribution by him appeared in *Fractures* and is excerpted as follows.[4]

Under this name I shall describe a form of multiple fracture of the pelvis, distinguished from all others by a species of regularity, and meriting besides special attention in the triple aspect of diagnosis, prognosis and treatment. It is a combination of two vertical fractures, separating at one side of the pelvis a middle fragment comprising the hip-joint; according as this fragment is carried upward or inward, the femur follows its movements, and hence result changes in the length and direction of the limb which have often misled practitioners.

Of these two fractures the anterior is almost constantly seated in the horizontal and descending rami of the pubis, separating this bone from the ilium and ischium; the posterior is always back of the cotyloid cavity, and generally in the ilium.

The causes are most frequently direct, such as falling from a height upon the hip, crushing of the pelvis between two carriages, a wheel passing over the hip, the kick of a horse, etc. These are exactly such forms of violence as those by which the crista ilii is broken; and we sometimes see this fracture combined with the two others. It is presumed however that to fracture the pelvis from top to bottom, the shock should fall lower down and more full, and should bear chiefly upon the great trochanter.

The first phenomena of this fracture are pain, contusion and its consequent swelling, and impairment or loss of motion in the lower extremity. Generally the foot is more or less everted.

The diagnosis is quite easy when we can readily feel the middle fragment moving under our fingers; otherwise the rarity of the fracture may put us off the right track; and hence mistakes in diagnosis are not unfrequent.

To sum up, it is necessary first to ascertain the exact relations of the fragments; if there is really shortening, to make extension on the leg, and counter-extension from the axillae; but it must be seen that the fragment goes properly into its place.

Reduction being made as completely as possible, it is to be kept up until consolidation is accomplished, that is to say, for at least forty-five or fifty days.

1. Pilastre, E.: *Malgaigne (1806-1865) Study of His Life and His Ideas From His Writings, From His Familiar Works and Particular Memoirs* (Fr), Paris: F. Alcan, 1905.

2. Paré, A.: *Complete Works of Ambroise Paré* (Fr), 3 vol, J. F. Malgaigne (ed.) Paris: J.-B. Bailliere, 1840-1841.

3. Hamby, W. B. (trans.-ed) *Surgery and Ambroise Paré by J. F. Malgaigne*, Norman: University of Oklahoma Press, 1965.

4. Malgaigne, J.: *Treatise on Fractures and Luxations* (Fr), 2 vol, Paris: J.-B. Bailliere, 1847-1855.

Nikolai Ivanovich Pirogoff (1810-1881)

THE DIVERSE ACCOMPLISHMENTS of Russian-born but German-educated Pirogoff firmly support the judgment of his biographers, who recognized him as the outstanding 19th century surgeon of his native country. Born in Moscow into a large family with an unstable fortune, Pirogoff gained his early education initially at home and later in a private school.[1] At 14, he registered in the Faculty of Medicine of the University of Moscow and three years later was awarded the MD degree.[2] Because of low academic standards compared to other European schools, he gained additional training at the newly-founded University of Dorpat in Esthonia. Dorpat, strongly influenced by German science and pedagogy, performed a unique mission; the school was designed to provide basic training, by European standards, for prospective professors of Russian faculties. In addition, the professor-students soon acquired polish in an established school, with a preference for German institutions because of their excellent intrinsic stature.

At Dorpat, Pirogoff was occupied with anatomical dissection, having been exposed to anatomical lectures only at Moscow. He performed experiments on laboratory animals involving ligations of blood vessels and composed his first scientific dissertation in Latin, a discussion of experimental ligation of the abdominal aorta. Pirogoff's tour of study in Dorpat was prolonged five years by the French Revolution, and after receiving a second doctorate of medicine in 1833 he pursued postgraduate work at the universities of Berlin and Göttingen.

Academic achievement came rapidly and brought him, at the age of 26, appointment as professor of surgery at Dorpat; there he remained for almost five years, practicing his art in the community and lecturing to his students on the theory and practice of clinical surgery and on surgical and pathological anatomy. It was here Pirogoff began collecting material for his monograph on regional anatomy, perfecting the technique of sectioning frozen cadavers with a saw, a chisel, and a hammer. His long training and comprehensive exposure to German science increased his awareness of the serious educational deficiencies in his country and, in turn, challenged him to institute reforms. Pirogoff's final faculty move, to the Medico-Surgical Academy at St. Petersburg, was made at the age of 30, with the understanding that a hospital clinic would complement the chair of surgery. The post was held until he resigned in disgust at the age of 46; Pirogoff then departed for Vishnia, where he built a second career in education although he never abandoned medicine and surgery. As late as 1876 he was in the midst of a cholera epidemic during which he performed several hundred autopsies on victims of the affliction.

An intense interest, thorough competency, and deep devotion to the art and practice of clinical surgery were strong allies in Pirogoff's achievements. While building the department in St. Petersburg, he remained conversant with advances in Western medicine through persistent contact with the outstanding medical scientists in America and in Europe, especially those in Italy, France, and Germany. Thus, only a few months after the published report from Boston describing the use of ether for surgical anesthesia, Pirogoff introduced the procedure in the handling of those wounded in the Caucasus military campaign. His patronage of military surgery was further extended in the Crimean War, in which he served as surgeon general, planned a corps of female nurses in cooperation with the Grand Duchess Helena Pavlovna, and thereby created a prototype of the Red Cross. Extraordinary efforts were made to better the care of the Russian sick and wounded in military hospitals and to enforce the criteria established by Florence Nightingale among the English forces.

Pirogoff's frustration with the intrigue in the military hierarchy and its complete lack of concern for social reform led him to resign and to turn from military medicine and academic surgery to become an administrative pedagogue. He held the directorship of education in the South for five years and then was placed in charge of the selection of candidates for professional positions in Russian universities. This assignment required considerable travel, especially to Germany and France, where he visited universities having Russian candidates in residence. On one such visit to Heidelberg, Germany, he counseled the wounded Garibaldi.

Pirogoff's scientific contributions were prepared with equal facility in Latin, Russian, German, or French. His inaugural dissertation on ligation of the aorta and his *Atlas of Topographical Anatomy,* prepared in four parts with 220 plates, were composed in Latin.[2] In 1847, he published his *Practical and Physiological Researches on Etherization* in French, describing therein operations on patients and experimental studies on animals and healthy persons.[3] Pirogoff first used ether by inhalation only to replace it with ether vapor given rectally, a recommendation reported simultaneously with Dupuy in Paris. Pirogoff's *Fundamentals of General Military Surgery* was prepared in German and was translated into Russian.[4] Medical achievements on the battlefield and in the military hospital were premised on sound administration and prevention of further morbidity as well as on the best scientific medicine then available. This included classification of injuries and early triage of patients, enforcement of measures to avoid cross infection, ether anesthesia, conservative management of wounds, and introduction of plaster of paris for casts.

The osteoplastic elongation of the bones of the leg during amputation of the foot, one of Pirogoff's most noted surgical contributions, was described in the *Russian Journal of Military Medicine* for 1854. As with many surgeons, in designing new procedures, he built upon the experience of others but described for the first time a technique which gave a satisfactory restitution for an inadequate foot.[5]

I begin the incision immediately in front of the external malleolus, carrying the incision downward towards the plantar surface, then across the sole and finally vertically upward to the internal malleolus, where, keeping anterior to the malleolus, I complete the incision by a second incision curved toward the distal end of the foot across the instep; in doing this, at the same time I incise the soft tissues to the calcaneal bone. The second or anterior part of the incision is made in front of the ankle as a semi-circle directed distally and connecting at the malleoli the vertical incision across the lower part of the foot. In this second incision all the tissues are separated to the bone; then the joint is opened anteriorly, the lateral ligaments are cut and the tarsus is shelled out. A small amputation file is placed immediately behind the head of the tarsus, on the calcaneal bone at the supporting ligament, and the calcaneal bone is divided by the saw following the first or the lower part of the incision through the soft tissues. Finally I dissect the soft anterior flap from each malleolus and amputate the lower part of each malleolus at their lowest portion.

I have used this method on three of my patients: twice on boys, aged 12 and 13 respectively, and once on a youth, 19 years of age. All recovered uneventfully, and two are able to walk without crutches, even without a walking stick, and without any cosmetic defect. These three cases incontestably prove the following:

(1) The tuberosity of the calcaneal bone remaining in the posterior flap can extend to the end of the bones of the leg, and by this the leg is lengthened by at least 1⅓ inches and it can serve as the most important point of weight bearing since it is almost on the same plane with the sole of the healthy foot.

Pirogoff received many honors at home and from abroad. A monument was dedicated to him in Moscow, and an anatomical museum was named for him in St. Petersburg. By order of the government of the USSR, his last home in the village of Shere-metka (Vishnia) was declared an historical shrine in 1944. His memoirs, which were prepared in retirement and published in German following his death, contain the following sentiments in the preface.[6]

From the earliest years of my life, science constituted my ideal. Truth, which is at the basis of science, became my highest aim, toward the accomplishment of which I have always striven. Science has raised me above the masses; science has taught me to love truth; and science has contributed to the development in me of the sacred idea of duty and obligation. Nothing can cleanse the soul of emptiness like science.

1. Halperin, G.: Nikolai Ivanovich Pirogov, *Bull Hist Med* 30:347-355, 1956.
2. *Memoirs, N. I. Pirogoff: Letters and Reminiscences from Sevastopol* (Russ), Academy of Sciences of the USSR, Scientific Popular Series, Publishing House of the Academy of Sciences, 1950.
3. Pirogoff, N. I.: *Practical and Physiological Researches on Etherization* (Fr), St. Petersbourg, F. Bellizard, 1847.
4. Pirogoff, N. I.: *Fundamentals of General Military Surgery* (Ger), Leipzig: F. C. W. Vogel, 1864.
5. Pirogoff, N. I.: Osteoplastic Elongation of the Bones of the Leg in Amputation of the Foot (Russ), *Voyenno Med J* 63:83-100, 1854, excerpt translated by Z. Danilevicius.
6. Pirogow, N. I.: *Diary of an Old Physician* (Ger), Stuttgart: J. G. Cotta, 1894, excerpt translated in Halperin.[1]

Sir William Fergusson (1808-1877)

WILLIAM FERGUSSON, practical surgeon of Edinburgh, might have preferred to remain in the North; however, the preeminence of the slightly older James Syme in Scotland caused Ferguson to choose London. He attended Lochmaben grammar school near his birthplace, Prestonpans, East Lothian, Scotland, followed by high school and university work at Edinburgh.[1] At the age of 15 he served as an apprentice in a law office, but after two years of drudgery and discontent, he changed to medicine, becoming the pupil of anatomist Robert Knox. The spell of the dissecting room led to the reward of assistant demonstrator to Knox. In these incredibly large classes his skill as a prosector in anatomy won him signal recognition. He became a licentiate of the Edinburgh College of Surgeons at 19 and a Fellow one year later. Continuing the professional ascent, he was elected surgeon to the Royal Dispensary in Edinburgh and in 1836, surgeon to the Royal Infirmary, the

surgical bastion of James Syme, where Fergusson became a strong contender for surgical supremacy. Meanwhile, his marriage to an heiress insured a financially comfortable life. At the relatively early age of 32, he accepted the professorship of surgery at King's College and the surgeoncy at King's College Hospital, London, where he remained until retirement.

Fergusson was a strong advocate of "conservative" and "preservative" surgery, applying it especially to his notable operations for harelip, cleft palate, lithotomy, excision of the head of the femur, removal of the scapula, and removal of the knee joint. The principles were based upon surgical anatomy as outlined in the introduction to *A System of Practical Surgery,* prepared shortly after his residence in London.[2]

The inseparable connexion between Practical Surgery and Surgical Anatomy, induces me so to associate these two subjects in the following pages, that I may be enabled to give full scope and effect to those objects and intentions, which influence me in undertaking the arrangement and elucidation of what I have ventured to term "A System of Practical Surgery."

The term Surgical Anatomy is used to express the relative position of the different textures and organs of the human frame, as the surgeon finds them in the treatment of the diseases and accidents which belong to his department of the profession. The term is usually understood as applicable to the parts in their normal state; but this by no means gives a sufficiently comprehensive idea of what the practical surgeon implies by Surgical Anatomy. In addition to a knowledge of relative position, it may be said that no one can possess a thorough knowledge of Surgical Anatomy who is not conversant with the various alterations effected by disease or accident, in the appearance, shape, and size, as also with the differences in relative position, occasioned by disease, in or near any portion of the body.

Fergusson's second and last important treatise, published not long before retirement, contains in the second lecture his philosophy of the preservation of parts.[3]

Amongst various characteristics of modern surgery, I shall now venture to draw special attention to a field in which I have myself been a humble labourer. To save life and limb is a grand feat; it may be said to be the highest reach in surgery.

I believe it to be a common opinion, that when a piece of bone is bare, or a joint grates, there is no probability of recovery in the part, and that amputation is the proper course. This, however, is a great error; for bare bone is covered again in many instances, and a joint may still be so far restored that there may be a certain amount of motion in it, or if not, there may still be a cessation of disease, with a useful member. Even when bone is dead nature causes a separation, and thus leads the way to its removal, either by spontaneous evolution, or by the hands of the surgeon; so that a limb may be retained with much of its original appearance.

These things are so thoroughly understood by most well-educated men of the day, that it may seem strange to allude to them; yet my own experience has told me that fingers and thumbs— ay, even large limbs—are frequently sacrificed, when a little waiting and judicious management might bring about a result far more creditable to surgery and advantageous to the patient.

It would indeed be arrogation were I to affect being the first in such a field of practice. In the paper referred to, I showed how others had been before me; and it may be truly said that all surgery is conservative, its grand object being to save limb and life. Yet the phrase was new in surgery, and was used in a particular sense, which it is partly my object to explain in this lecture. It is, indeed, with feelings of pride that I see and hear it used so familiarly. It is now a part of our common nomenclature; it is often in the mouths of those who know not its origin; it is used by military practitioners as well as civil; it has become familiar in our provinces and colonies, and has resounded even from the antipodes.

In operating for the cleft palate, Fergusson practiced careful dissection and free division of the levator palati muscles preparatory to apposing the edges of the soft cleft. "Fergusson's incision" was planned to conserve the normal features and prevent gross disfiguration in resection of tumors of the face.[3]

The inferences which I drew were, that if the palato-glossus, palato-pharyngeus, and levator palati on each side were divided, the soft flaps would thereafter, for a long time, be so relaxed that in all probability the mesial line of adaptation would be so little disturbed that union would take place. The tensor palati I considered would have little disturbing influence, nor did I put much importance on that of the palato-glossus. My impression was, that the action of the levator palati and palato-pharyngeus, particularly that part in the posterior pillar of the fauces, was likely to prove detrimental and, in accordance with the somewhat novel and already popular practice of myotomy and tenotomy in other directions, I recommended division of these muscles as an adjunct to the ordinary operation for cleft palate.

After all my experience and repeated trials, I have latterly formed a strong opinion that the features of the face may be better preserved than as yet by the generality of surgeons; and my anxiety to impress these views is certainly not the least object of this lecture. First, I consider that many tumours of the upper jaw may be summarily removed without cutting the lips or cheek at all; and next, should more space be needful, it may be gained at less cost of feature than has generally been supposed. In dealing with the upper lip for removal of tumors of the upper jaw, I greatly object to any other incision than one in the mesial line, which must be run into one, or both nostrils if required.

As if to compensate for never having qualified for an academic degree in medicine, Fergusson received appointments and honors commensurate with his tutorial and surgical skill. The College of Surgeons of London made him a member when he took up residence in the city and elected him president in 1870 and Hunterian Orator in 1871. He was appointed surgeon-in-ordinary to

Prince Albert in 1849, surgeon-extraordinary to the Queen in 1855, a baronet in 1866, and sergeant-surgeon in 1867. The kudos seemed complete with election to the Royal Society, selection as the president of the British Medical Association, and bestowing of an honorary LLD from Edinburgh.

Fergusson was a social and hospitable person, but reticent and uninspiring as a lecturer. His speed in surgery was facilitated by many instruments of his own design; cutting for the stone was a momentary procedure. An expert in carpentry and metal work, an enthusiastic fly fisherman, and a good violinist with a flair for dancing Scottish reels, he was more brilliant in technical skill than in surgical philosophy.

1. "Sir William Fergusson," in *Plarr's Lives of the Fellows of the Royal College of Surgeons of England*, revised by Sir D. Power, Bristol: J. Wright & Sons. Ltd., 1930.
2. Fergusson, W.: *A System of Practical Surgery*, Philadelphia: Lea and Blanchard, 1843.
3. Fergusson, W.: *Lectures on the Progress of Anatomy and Surgery During the Present Century*, London: J. Churchill and Sons, 1867.

Thomas Blizard Curling
(1811-1888)

THOMAS BLIZARD CURLING, consulting surgeon to the London Hospital for many years, was born in Tavistock Place, London; his father was Secretary to the Commissioners of Customs.[1] Thomas' primary education was gained at Manor House, Cheswick, and at the early age of 21, without an MD degree, he obtained appointment as assistant surgeon to the London Hospital through the recommendation and influence of his uncle, Sir William Blizard. This post was held until 1849 when he advanced to surgeon, a position he filled until 1869. Curling stayed in London for a few years following retirement from the Hospital, but before the age of 60 he left practice to live in Brighton. He died in Cannes, France.

The opportunities associated with the London Hospital and Medical School gave Curling a rich and varied experience for the study of clinical matters and description of pathological findings. He was a meticulous worker who compensated for a lack of brilliancy by scrupulous exactitude in his work.

Composite by G. Bako

The rewards of industry and good connections were evident: he was elected a Fellow of the Royal Society while still an assistant surgeon, and he served the University of London as examiner in surgery and the College of Surgeons as council member and later as president. Curling's writings, prepared from observations in the wards and the morgue, did not contain hypothetical theories or ill-proved hypotheses. Among his works were a prize winning *Essay on Tetanus,* a lengthy discussion of *Atrophy of Bone, A Practical Treatise on the Diseases of the Testis, and of the Spermatic Cord and Scrotum,* and two monographs, the first, entitled *Observations on the Diseases of the Rectum,* and another, *Diseases of the Intestines.* None of these is as important historically as is his description of the symptoms of cretinism in two cases of athyreosis and the finding of ulcers of the duodendum following extensive burns.

The description of two cases of total absence of thyroid tissue appeared in 1850 in the outlet for most of his case reports, the *Medico-Chirurgical Transactions.* Although cretinism had been known since antiquity and had been observed in goitrous regions and thereby was associated with hypertrophy of the thyroid, Curling took the opposing view of pathogenesis. He suggested that the absence of the thyroid was responsible for specific systemic symptoms and findings, more than two decades before Gull described his observations of the malady later known as myxedema. Curling's first case was a young girl, ten years of age, the second an infant, aged six months. The findings included inhibited growth, disproportionately large limbs, idiocy, thick tongue, and aphasia.[2]

The imperfect state of our knowledge of the office of the thyroid body, and the assistance often derived from facts, even of a negative character, in physiological investigations, independently of other circumstances of interest, lead me to consider the two following cases deserving of record.

Case I.—In July 1849, Dr. Little invited me to see a case of what he considered *cretinism,* at the Idiot Asylum at Highgate; and to examine some swellings at the sides of the neck, the nature of which were doubtful, but which had been suspected to be enlargements either of the lobes of the thyroid body, or of the lymphatic glands. The inmate was a female child, of stunted growth, ten years of age, and a native of Lancashire. She measured two feet six inches in height. Her body was thick, and her limbs disproportionately large and long. The dorsal surface of the body and limbs was hairy. The head was heavy looking, the forehead flat, and the fontanelles unclosed. The countenance had a marked and very unpleasant idiotic expression. The mouth was large, and the tongue thick and protuberant. . . . The child had very little power of locomotion; but could manage to walk from chair to chair with a little assistance. She had no power of speech. She was able to recognise her parents, and evinced some manifestations of the exercise of the will.

The body was examined twenty-four hours after death by Mr. Callaway, who has favoured me with the following particulars. The body was much emaciated. The swellings in the neck were much less in size than what they had been prior to her illness. They were composed of fat, and occupied the posterior triangle of either side of the neck, dipping downwards behind the clavicles, and filling the axillae. . . . There was not the slightest trace of a thyroid body.

I am not acquainted with any case on record in which a deficiency of the thyroid gland has been observed in the human body. . . . In countries where cretinism and bronchocele prevail, it was long supposed, that there was some connection between the defective condition of the brain, and the hypertrophy of the thyroid. Pathologists have recently been inclined to view the coincidence of these two affections as accidental, or as having no direct relation. In the foregoing cases we have examples of a directly opposite condition, viz., a defective brain, or cretinism, combined with an entire absence of the thyroid, which may be regarded as tending to confirm the more modern opinion respecting the connection between cretinism and bronchocele.

In 1842, Curling presented his findings *On Acute Ulceration of the Duodenum in Cases of Burn* to the Royal Medical and Chirurgical Society. Four cases of extensive thermal injury had come under his observation. In addition, two protocols were furnished by associates, and a final four had been culled from the literature. The majority were children or young persons who had a negative past history for gastrointestinal symptoms. The first case is illustrative.

In no part of the alimentary canal are the diseases to which it is liable, so obscure, both in their origin and diagnosis, as in the duodenum; and as the following cases of ulceration of this portion of the small intestines in connection with burns, may be interesting, as tending to throw some light on its pathology, and to awaken attention to a source of danger in these accidents not generally suspected.

CASE I.

Extensive burn.—Ulceration of the Duodenum.—Fatal haematemesis.

M.A. Fox, a girl aged 11, was brought to the London Hospital May 9th, 1841, on account of a severe burn on the chest and both arms, the skin of which was extensively destroyed. She had apparently been going on tolerably well until the 27th instant, when I was summoned to the case in consequence of the occurrence of profuse haematemesis. She afterwards repeatedly ejected blood from the mouth, and also passed some by stool, and notwithstanding the remedies employed, expired in fifteen hours after first vomiting blood.

The body was examined on the following day. The surface was pale and exsanguineous. The heart and lungs were healthy, but nearly devoid of blood. The stomach was sound, and contained a quantity of dark grumous blood. In the duodenum, at the distance of an inch from the pylorus, there was a circular ulcer about half an inch in diameter, and its edges slightly elevated, which had extended through all the coats of the intestine, the bottom of the ulcer being formed by the glandular substance of the pancreas, which was closely united to the duodenum at that part. The open mouth of a considerable-sized vessel could be distinctly seen at the base of the ulcer, apparently on the surface of the pancreas. There was no further disease of the intestinal canal, but it contained a good deal of dark-coloured blood mixed with the faeces.

One of Curling's teaching responsibilities was the offering of formal counsel to students. His *Introductory Address,* delivered in the fall of 1846, discloses his concern for the proper ingredients in the study as well as the practice of medicine.[4]

Ours is a learned and a liberal profession. It is said to be a learned profession in virtue of the scientific attainments and cultivated minds of its more enlightened members; and it is regarded as a liberal profession, in right of those general accomplishments, moral qualities, and honourable feelings, which entitle the possessor of them to the character and designation of a *gentleman.* You must maintain that character, and I sincerely trust that you have all come here determined and well prepared to do so; that you have received a sound preliminary education, such an education as cannot fail to form a most valuable introduction to your medical studies, and a solid foundation for professional success. A good general education is very necessary for all intended for the learned professions, but is of essential importance to those destined for the study of medicine, which embraces so many and such varied subjects and pursuits. I need scarcely remark, that no one can be qualified to commence his studies here, who does not possess a competent knowledge of the Latin and Greek languages.

A knowledge of the two modern languages, French and German, is also desirable, I may say indispensable, to enable you to keep pace with the rapid march of medical science, and to avail yourselves of the numerous improvements made in the celebrated universities and schools on the continent. There is, however, no language a thorough knowledge of which is so essential, and which the student of medicine should be so careful not to neglect as his own, which he is constantly employing in the varied intercourse and correspondence of a busy professional life.

1. Sieveking, E. H.: President's Address, *Mediocochir Trans* 72:1-5, 1889.

2. Curling, T. B.: Two Cases of Absence of the Thyroid Body, *Medicochir Trans* 33:303-306, 1850.

3. Curling, T. B.: On Acute Ulceration of the Duodenum, in Cases of Burn, *Medicochir Trans* 7:260-281, 1842.
4. Curling, T. B.: *The Introductory Address Delivered at the London Hospital School of Medicine*, London: Gilbert & Rivington, 1846.

Composite by G. Bako

Bernhard von Langenbeck
(1810-1887)

BERNHARD RUDOLF CONRAD LANGENBECK, recognized forerunner of central European surgical progress in the mid-19th century, was born in the village of Padingbüttel, where the Weser empties into the North Sea.[1] His father, a clergyman and teacher, provided his early education, intended to lead ultimately to the ministry. However, an early interest in biology and dissection turned him toward medicine and he entered the University of Göttingen in 1830, under the watchful eye of his uncle, Conrad J. M. Langenbeck, professor of surgery and anatomy. Langenbeck received his doctorate with honors in 1834, upon presentation of an inaugural dissertation on the structure of the retina. A Blummback honorarium provided him a two-year period of postdoctoral study in clinics of his choice. He went to Belgium and to Paris but was particularly fortunate in London; there he audited the sessions of the Medico-Chirurgical Society and became friendly with prominent surgeons, including Sir Benjamin Brodie and especially Sir Astley Cooper, who displayed an intimate interest in the German student.

Langenbeck's personal characteristics, professional skills, and, particularly, his talents for instruction in operative surgery on the cadaver, marked him as a surgeon destined to academic ascendancy. It is not surprising to find him appointed privatdocent (physiology and pathological anatomy) on his return to Göttingen, subsequently professor of pathological anatomy at the age of 30, and the following year professor of surgery in Kiel. This assignment was interrupted by service in the army, the first of four tours of military duty. Langenbeck participated in each of the Schleswig-Holstein Wars, in the war with Austria in 1866, and in the Franco-Prussian War of 1870. He was appointed general staff surgeon of the army in 1842, general physician of the Prussian Army headquarters in 1864, and, finally, to the permanent post in peacetime as surgeon-general of the army, rising to the grade of lieutenant general in 1882.

During the Franco-Prussian War, Langenbeck conducted classes in military surgery, performed a number of subperiosteal resections which decreased the need for amputation, and perfected the ambulance system of evacuation in the field. His military experiences were assembled in a treatise published in 1874.[2] A combination of extensive field duty and a deep personal awareness of the need for providing humane care for the sick and wounded in war led to his promotion of the International Red Cross. He insisted on the absolute neutrality of military hospitals, was a founding member and constant advisor of the German Red Cross, and, in 1884, served as president of the Geneva International Convention.

In civilian life Langenbeck accepted, in 1848, the professorship of surgery in the University of Berlin, having rejected proposals from other German Universities. One of central Europe's great university clinics had claimed the brilliant prize among contemporary young surgeons to fill a vacancy created by the sudden death of Dieffenbach. Langenbach and Berlin were mutually satisfied, and, during his 34-year tenure, he built the surgical clinic into an institution of repute, meanwhile enjoying great popularity as a teacher, general respect as a consultant, and enviable recognition as a dextrous operator. He sponsored the founding of the German Surgical Society and the *Archiv für Chirurgie* and served as president of the Berlin Medical Society and the German Surgical Congress. Langenbeck prepared a series of lectures which were sufficiently valuable to be assembled and published posthumously.[3]

The training and development of pupils was the best proof of his professional attainments. Notable surgeons who studied with Langenbeck included Billroth, von Bergmann, Gurlt, Krönlein, Trendelenburg, and Lücke. The surgical school of Langenbeck emphasized physiological and anatomical knowledge in operative techniques, the value of microscopic investigation, and respect for wound infection. His overall contributions to German surgery are more important than specific experimental contributions. In the laboratory, Langenbeck directed studies on the development of injured bone and regeneration of tissue; in the amphitheater, he displayed new techniques for joint and plastic surgery. For treating fractures he advocated immediate fixation by firm dressings. One of his early contributions to medical science was given credit by Israel, retrospectively, with the inclusion of some of his 1845 sketches of material recovered from a case of actinomycosis of the vertebral column.[4]

When I showed to Privy Medical Councillor von Langenbeck the pus and the fungi, he recalled that in 1845 in Kiel he had observed a similar case of vertebral caries with abscesses. He was so kind as to allow me to publish the history [of this case] with illustrations prepared by him.

Inspection of the drawings is sufficient to conclude that they are identical to the ones I had observed. What von Langenbeck called "cylindrical bodies having peculiar light-breaking power" corresponded to my "pear-shaped or bat-shaped bodies." It is also clear that the budding and lengthwise cleavage of these bodies is identical to the forms that I had seen.

The first report of the splitting of the hard palate for correction of cleft palate was presented at a meeting of the Berlin Medical Society in 1861 and was followed by extended discussions later in the year.[5]

This patient, a boy aged 14, was born with a hare-lip on the left and a total cleft of soft and hard palate and with a cleft in the left alveolar process. The operation for hare-lip was performed soon after birth, but was unsuccessful, and only a second operation performed during the second year of life healed properly. On February 6 of this year [1861] Dr. Langenbeck united the split parts of the soft palate by suturing. On May 11 of this year, Dr. Langenbeck performed uranoplasty in the following manner: Close to the edges of the flap, the mucosa and the periosteum of the hard palate were incised to the bone with a large blade, uncovering the edges of the cleft. With a raspatory, the mucosa of the palate was separated, together with the periosteum, and was freed from the bone on both sides. Two flaps, formed in this manner, were united anteriorly at the gumline below the alveolar process. The posterior portion of the flaps extended into the soft palate which was separated from the posterior edge of the hard palate. The free edges of these flaps were united in the midline with five silk sutures; the whole palate was closed to the incisors. The separation of the mucosa of the palate together with the periosteum can be carried out by tedious and careful dissection without additional injury. . . . When the sutures were removed between the 8th and 14th post-operative day, the healing throughout the length of the suture had been achieved by first intention. The reconstructed palate differs from the normal only by a small scar through the length of the palate and by a slight deformation at the tip of the uvula.

Subperiosteal resection is probably Langenbeck's best remembered contribution to operative technique. The procedure had fallen into disfavor from the failure of previous surgeons to appreciate the mechanism of muscle and tendinous attachments and their lack of proper understanding of joint function. Some patients subjected to improper subperiosteal resection would have retained more useful function if an amputation had been performed instead of resection. Although the implementation of functional restoration of the wounded in battle was difficult for some, Lanbenbeck had observed it to be so effective as to allow a front-line officer to return to active duty and a soldier with a resected foot to wear regular shoes in subsequent mountaineering.[2]

. . . the choice of method is less important than careful performance of the procedure. The surgeon who performs a subperiosteal resection must avoid, in shoulder and elbow resection, the misuse of the periosteal elevator, and thereby prevent tears and bruises which delay healing. . . . The term "subperiosteal resection" implies maintenance of the proximity of muscles and tendinous insertion at the periosteum of the diaphyses. The advantage of this method is prevention of luxation of the joint at the completion of resection; the ends of the resected bones are not pulled apart by the attachment of the muscles but are held together by the supporting structures.

1. von Bergmann, E.: *Memorial to Bernhard von Langenbeck* (Ger), Berlin: A. Hirschwald, 1888.
2. von Langenbeck, B.: *Surgical Observations From the War* (Ger), Berlin: A Hirschwald, 1874, excerpt translated by Z. Danilevicius.
3. Gluck, T.: *Lectures in Operative Surgery by Dr. Bernhard von Langenbeck* (Ger), Berlin: A. Hirschwald, 1888.
4. Israel, J.: Recent Observations on the Mycosis of Man (Ger), *Arch Path Anat* 74: 15-53, 1878, excerpt translated by Z. Danilevicius.
5. van Langenbeck, B.: New Method for Splitting the Hard Palate (Ger), *Deutsch Klin* 12:231-232, 1861, excerpt translated by Z. Danilevicius.

National Library of Medicine

Henry Jacob Bigelow (1818-1890)

HENRY J. BIGELOW, grandson of a clergyman, and son of Jacob Bigelow, physician of Boston and the second professor of materia medica at Harvard Medical School, was the leading surgeon of New England in his time.[1] He prepared at the Boston Latin School, graduated from Harvard College in 1837, and received the MD from Harvard in 1841. In training, he attended the lectures of O. W. Holmes, visiting professor at Dartmouth, and served as housepupil at the Massachusetts General Hospital. Following graduation Bigelow continued the pursuit of knowledge in Europe and studied with P. C. A. Louis in Paris and with James Paget in London. Not until 1844 did he take up practice in Boston and become closely allied with the surgical service at the Massachusetts General Hospital and the department of surgery at the Harvard Medical School. An interest in pathological anatomy as a foundation subject for clinical research was disclosed in an essay on orthopedic surgery, which won first place in competition for the Boylston Prize for 1844. Although the prize essay was entitled "Manual of Orthopedic Surgery," strabismus, stammering, and other nonorthopedic subjects were mentioned.

The 1840's were particularly important years in Boston, and on October 16, 1846, Bigelow witnessed the first administration of ether by Morton. The clinical events were described to the members of the American Academy of Arts and Sciences on November 3, repeated a few days later before the Boston Society for Medical Improvement, and published in the *Boston Medical and Surgical Journal* for November 18, 1846. Although Bigelow deserves credit neither for the anesthesia nor for the surgery, his sense of significance of the event is noteworthy. Appropriately, the presentation concludes with a discussion of the privileges and responsibilities of a physician who holds the destiny of a discovery in medical science in his grasp.[2]

On the 16th of Oct., 1846, an operation was performed at the hospital, upon a patient who had inhaled a preparation administered by Dr. Morton, a dentist of this city, with the alleged intention of producing insensibility to pain. Dr. Morton was understood to have extracted teeth under similar circumstances, without the knowledge of the patient. The present operation was performed by Dr. Warren and though comparatively slight, involved an incision near the lower jaw of some inches in extent. During the operation the patient muttered, as in a semiconscious state, and afterwards stated that the pain was considerable, though mitigated; in his own words, as though the skin had been scratched with a hoe.

I will add, in conclusion, a few remarks upon the actual position of this invention as regards the public.

No one will deny that he who benefits the world should receive from it an equivalent. The only question is, of what nature shall the equivalent be? Shall it be vountarily ceded by the world, or levied upon it? For various reasons, discoveries in high science have been usually rewarded indirectly by fame, honor, position, and occasionally, in other countries, by funds appropriated for the purpose. Discoveries in medical science, whose domain approaches so nearly that of philanthropy, have been generally ranked with them; and many will assent with reluctance to the propriety of restricting by letters patent the use of an agent capable of mitigating human suffering.

We understand, already, that the proprietor ceded its use to the Mass. General Hospital, and that his intentions are extremely liberal with regard to the medical profession generally, and that so soon as necessary arrangements can be made for publicity of the process, great facilities will be offered to those who are disposed to avail themselves of what now promises to be one of the important discoveries of the age.

Following this critical communication, Bibelow returned enthusiastically to the study of pathologic anatomy and orthopedics, paying particular attention to dislocations and the hip joint. He was one of the first in America to excise the head of the femur and devised a method for reducing dorsal dislocation of the hip without the aid of pulleys, the procedure in vogue at that time. The resection, performed with a chain saw, was described in the *American Journal of the Medical Sciences* in 1852.[3] The patient, a boy of ten, died 12 days after surgery. Although reduction had been described by others, Bigelow re-emphasized the importance of flexion of the hip in order to relax the accessory component of the Y ligament of the capsule. He described the Y ligament, a triangular band with a thin central portion, which gives the appearance of an inverted Y and which is attached by its apex to the anterior inferior iliac spine and acetabular margin, and by its base to the intertrochanteric line of the femur, in the control of the head of the femur during and after dislocation. This control was exploited in directing the displaced head of the femur to follow the .same route into the socket that it had traveled during dislocation.[4]

The ilio-femoral ligament, known also as the ligament of Bertin [and later the Y ligament of Bigelow], has been usually described as reinforcing the capsule by a single fibrous band extending from the inferior iliac spine to the inner extremity of the anterior intertrochanteric line, and playing no very important part in health or injury. This ligament is more or less adherent to the acetabular prominence and to the neck of the femur.

The divergent branches of the Y ligament are sometimes well developed, with scarcely any intervening membrane. In other cases the intermediate tissue is thicker, and requires to be slit or removal before the bands are distinctly defined; and sometimes the whole triangle is of nearly uniform thickness.

The Y ligament is of remarkable tenacity and strength, being at some points, when well developed, nearly a quarter of an inch in thickness, and forming an unyielding suspensory band, by which the femur, when in a state of extension, as in walking, is forcibly retained in its socket.

When the patient lies upon his back, especially if etherized, the dislocated limb gravitates, and the Y ligament becomes more and more tense as the limb approaches nearer and nearer to a state of complete extension. If, now, as is here maintained, the chief obstacle to reduction of the luxated hip is found in this ligament: it follows that the method taught by Sir Astley Cooper, the weight of whose unquestioned authority has unfortunately availed to give it currency during many years, is based upon an erroneous conception of the nature of difficulty to be encountered. By that method the limb is placed as nearly as may be in the axis of the body, thus rendering the Y ligament tense and inviting its maximum of resistance before traction is made. Hence the necessity for pulleys, the tendency of which is undoubtedly to elongate, or partly detach, at its femoral insertion, this powerful ligamentous band, at great sacrifice of mechanical force, with proportionate violence to the neighboring tissues and uncertainty as to the result. By the flexion method, which dates from a remote antiquity, the Y ligament is relaxed, its resistance annulled, and reduction often accomplished with surprising facility.

One of Bigelow's last contributions was the recommendation of lithotrity at a single operation, in contrast to multiple procedures then in vogue for removal of vesicular calculi. Stones were first crushed, the bladder flushed with water through a large urethral tube, and the debris extracted in a single sitting.[5]

Under favourable circumstances, such an operation, lasting a few minutes, is not only simple, but safe. Yet the fact that it is not always so could not fail to arrest the attention of surgeons. It may happen that during the succeeding night the patient has a chill: not the chill of so-called "urethral fever," which some times follows the mere passage of a bougie, and which is of little consequence; but one accompanied or followed by other symptoms, such as tenderness of the region of the bladder, a quickened pulse, and the frequent and painful passage of urine. . . . The surgeon vainly waits for a favourable moment to repeat his operation [in the two-stage procedure]; it becomes too evident that the patient is seriously ill, and it is quite within the range of possibilities that in the course of days or weeks he may quietly succumb.

While many years ago I had not unfrequently prolonged lithotrity to ten or fifteen minutes, and longer, it is only within two years that I have aimed at the evacuation of a considerable stone during a single sitting; and although long experience will perhaps be necessary to determine precisely what cases are unfavourable to such an operation, there can now be no question that it is practicable to remove at once a far greater quantity of debris than has hitherto been considered possible.

In teaching, Bigelow has been described as terse and epigrammatic; his ambidexterity made him an exceptional draftsman. He was chairman of the medical faculty when Charles W. Eliot, upon becoming president of Harvard University, proposed certain changes in the medical school curriculum. He sought to place the school upon a sound financial and educational basis equal to the departments in the University. No longer should it be a proprietary school, acting with benefit of the prestige but removed

from the constraining influence of a parent body. Bigelow's resistance to educational progress was counterbalanced by his many contributions to clinical surgery and a working interest in music and art as manifested by his service as one of the first trustees of the Boston Museum of Fine Arts and as a regular subscriber to the Boston Symphony Orchestra.

1. A Memoir of Henry Jacob Bigelow, Boston: Little, Brown, and Company, 1900.
2. Bigelow, H. J.: Insensibility During Surgical Operations Produced by Inhalation, Boston Med Surg J 35:309-317, 1847.
3. Bigelow, H. J.: Resection of the Head of a Femur, Amer J Med Sci 24:90,1852.
4. Bigelow, H. J.: The Mechanism of Dislocation and Fracture of the Hip, Philadelphia: H. C. Lea, 1869.
5. Bigelow, H. J.: Lithotrity by a Single Operation, Amer J Med Sci 75:117-134, 1878.

Composite by G. Bako

Carl Thiersch (1822-1895)

CARL THIERSCH, descendant of gifted ancestors, interested equally in the sciences and the humanities, carried on the traditional pursuits during his own productive life. He was born in Munich, where his father, a well-known humanist and lay leader in the church, held the professorship of classics in the university and presidency of the Academy of Science.[1] Carl's older brother was a theologian, his younger brother a well-known painter. Following graduation from the Gymnasium, he began the study of medicine in Munich; there he came under the influence of Stromeyer, professor of surgery. Later Berlin, Vienna, and Paris were on his study circuit which led, in 1848, to the MD degree, received from Munich upon presentation of a dissertation on materia medica.

Thiersch's immediate association with the Munich faculty as prosector provided an opportunity particularly to increase his knowledge of pathological anatomy. The following year he qualified as privatdocent, presenting an inaugural thesis on pyemia and, in 1853, achieved professorial status. At the unusually early age of 32, Thiersch was called to Erlangen as professor of surgery. He remained there until 1867, when he accepted the professorship at Leipzig. This assignment extended beyond the supervision of students, patients, and research, to include the design of new teaching hospital facilities. Jacob's hospital was constructed in barracks style, based upon knowledge gained from recent advances in the epidemiologic study of bacterial infection and the recognition of the importance of antisepsis by cleanliness and ventilation. The development of the surgical clinic and of the surgical department was an equally laudable goal. Thiersch had hoped that his clinic would rival the medical clinic under Wunderlich, while the department of surgery would equal that of physiology under Carl Ludwig.

Thiersch operated and taught as a general surgeon, but he was especially competent as a plastic surgeon of the head and neck and showed particular concern for the patients on the children's wards. His bibliography covers a wide range of subjects, medical and surgical, which include the contagious features of cholera, the histogenesis of cancer and especially epithelial cancer, phosphorus necrosis of the jaw, operative treatment of hypospadias and epispadias, the use of salicylic acid as an antiseptic, resection of the elbow, pseudoarthritis deformans, mycotic infection of the skin, resection of the trigeminal nerve for intractable neural-

gia, pyonephrosis, and the significance of Koch's discoveries. He prepared several monographs; his best was entitled *Epithelial Cancer of the Skin*[2] and was followed in significance by *Clinical Studies of Lister's Management of Wounds and on the Substitution of Salicylic Acid for Carbolic Acid.* The latter was translated by G. Whitley and was published in 1877 by the New Sydenham Society. The treatise on epithelial carcinoma advanced the belief, based upon his investigations and interest in embryology, that the malignant cells came from other cells and were not derived from connective tissue as Virchow had assumed.

The work for which Thiersch was most famous was the preparation of thin skin grafts founded upon his earlier microscopic investigations of granulation tissue. A limb prior to amputation was seeded periodically with transplants, which were studied microscopically for evidence of repair following amputation.[3]

I chose this case for transplanting small portions of skin at regular intervals during the three weeks prior to surgery. The last sections of skin were transplanted 18 hours before amputation. In order not to complicate the experiment I used only one modification, i.e., I transplanted rectangular pieces of skin, 1 cm. in diameter, after removing the fatty subcutaneous tissue.

Following amputation the limb was injected with Gerlach's media, and the skin fixed. . . . The thin sections were stained by various techniques; the observations may be summarized as follows.

(1) The grafts take in the absence of a layer of structureless subcutaneous tissue.

(2) The transplant takes because of the development of blood vessels which appear after 18 hours; union occurs because of intercellular ducts which are filled with blood between the vessels of the granulation tissue and the transplant.

(3) The vessels of the transplant undergo secondary changes and become similar in structure to the vessels of the granulation tissue.

(4) Sometimes the patch does not take in its full thickness; only the lower layer adjacent to connective tissue takes; the upper layers may be sloughed. The lower layer contains sweat-glands (epithelium).

It is evident that the transplant may be supplied adequately with vessels from the granulation tissue 18 hours after transplantation. This is proof that circulation has been established. Before the second week the vessels of the skin are enlarged, crenated, and branched; that it, they assume an embryonic appearance. Normal structure appears in the third and fourth weeks when several types of vessels may be seen, those that have completely and those that have assumed only partially a normal appearance.

Skin transplantation serves two purposes: either it hastens the healing of an otherwise slowly granulating surface, or it complements natural scarring if spontaneous healing has ceased.

In 1850, Thiersch served under Stromeyer as a volunteer in the 2nd Schleswig-Holstein War and was consulting general to the 12th Army Corps in the Franco-Prussian War of 1870-1871. In this assignment he exploited the knowledge gained a decade earlier by surgeons in the Civil War in America. His biographers note his warm personality, which was reflected in his treatment of pupils and patients on the wards and in the operating amphitheater, and his lectures, which were presented with brevity, clarity, and understanding of the fundamentals of normal and pathological tissue. He possessed a delicate understanding of truth, was an accurate observer, while his scientific works show great maturity. Thiersch lived a life of good common sense, had a fine appreciation of humor, and loved to repeat good as well as shady jokes. He described himself as an anatomist who had strayed into surgery.

1. Thiersch, J.: *Carl Thiersch—His Life* (Ger), Leipzig: J. A. Barth, 1922.

2. Thiersch, C.: *Epithelial Cancer of the Skin* (Ger), 1 vol and atlas, Leipzig: W. Engelmann, 1865.

3. Thiersch, C.: The Finer Anatomical Changes of Healing and Granulation of the Skin (Ger), *Verh Deutsch Ges Chir* 3:69-75, 1874, excerpt translated by Z. Danilevicius.

Sir William Morrant Baker
(1839-1896)

W. MORRANT BAKER, son of a solicitor in Andover, England, served his apprenticeship to Mr. Payne and entered St. Bartholomew's Hospital, where he attracted the attention of his superiors by his industry

and scholarship.[1] Baker was accepted by Sir James Paget as an assistant in his private practice. In 1864, he became a Fellow of the Royal College of Surgeons and the following year demonstrator of anatomy and physiology at "Barts." His most notable

Composite by G. Bako

general writing, the edition of Kirkes's *Physiology*, carried his name through several editions until 1885. In the meantime advancing through the surgical chairs at the hospital in 1882 he was appointed surgeon. Because of ill health in 1892, Baker was elected governor of the hospital and retired from private practice.

In addition to his service at St. Bartholomew's Hospital, Baker held a staff appointment at Evelina Hospital for Sick Children, was examiner in general anatomy and physiology at the Royal College of Surgeons of England, and examiner in surgery for the universities of London and Durham. In his early years at St. Bartholomew's Hospital, Baker observed a series of cases of synovial cysts of the knee joint and, in 1877, published the first of two communications in their *Hospital Reports*. These investigations led to the eponymic description, "Baker cysts." The cysts had developed rapidly in some patients, associated with clinical osteo-arthritis, rheumatoid arthritis, or tabetic arthropathy; they appeared to arise in the popliteal space and tended to migrate to-ward the calf. The following features were presented in the initial report.[2]

1. That in cases of effusion into the knee-joint, and especially in those in which the primary disease is osteo-arthritis, the fluid secreted may make its way out of the joint, and form by distension of neighbouring parts a synovial cyst of large or small size.

2. That the synovial cyst so produced may occupy (a) the popliteal space and upper part of the calf of the leg, or may (b) be evident in the calf of the leg only, projecting most, as a rule, on the inner aspect of the leg, or (c) may be perceptible only at the upper and inner part of the leg as a small defined swelling, not approaching within three or four inches of any part of the knee-joint.

3. That however large the synovial cyst may be, fluctuation may not be communicable from it to the interior of the knee-joint; but the ab-scence of such fluctuation must not be taken to contra-indicate the existence of a connection between the joint and the cyst.

4. That the synovial cyst may be expected to disappear after a longer or shorter period, with-out leaving traces of its existence, even on dissection of the limb.

5. That the cyst should not be punctured or otherwise subjected to operation, unless there appear strong reasons for so doing; inasmuch as interference may lead to acute inflammation and suppuration of the knee-joint.

6. That most often the disease in the knee-joint will be found to have begun some time before the appearance of the secondary synovial cyst; but sometimes the patient's attention may be first drawn to the latter, or the cyst may seem for a long period the more important part of the disease.

Several years later Baker added six cases to the series and extended the involved sites to other major joints.[3]

1. That abnormal synovial cysts may be formed in connection, not only with the knee, but in connection with the shoulder, the elbow, the wrist, the hip, and the ankle joints.

2. That the manner of formation of these synovial cysts probably resembles that which has been proved to occur in connection with the knee-joint, namely, that the synovial fluid on reaching a certain amount of tension by accumulation within the joint, finds its way out in the direction of least resistance, either by the channel by which some normal bursa com-municates with the joint, or, in the absence of

any such channel, by forming first a hernia of the synovial membrane. In both cases, should the tension continue, or increase, the fluid at length escapes from the sac, and its boundaries are then formed only by the muscles and other tissues between and amongst which it accumu-lates.

Baker was also credited in the literature with the initial description of erythema ser-pens, usually called "erysipeloid of Rosen-bach," following the latter's communication in 1887. The condition is not associated with constitutional symptoms and was be-lieved to be associated with the introduction of foreign matter at the initial site. Ex-cerpts are as follows.[4]

The disease to which I venture to draw atten-tion, and to call by the name *Erythema Serpens,* must be tolerably familiar to all who have seen many cases in minor surgery; but, although a trivial complaint, certain aspects are often presented by it which may render it not a little difficult to be diagnosed.

The disease generally comes under notice in the following manner:—A patient complains of pain in the hand or fingers, and from the ap-parent distress, often mental as well as bodily, it would seem as if there must be some serious local affection.

The disease looks like a mild 'erythema' of some kind or other. There is an inflammatory blush, but not quite an ordinary blush. . . . It is in blotches or patches—here pink, fading into the natural skin colour; there a large part of the integment (sic) quite unaffected. It affects especially the region of the finger-joints and knuckles.

The pain is described as very considerable, as tingling or burning, and shooting, and for the most part in the hand or fingers only; but some patients describe it as also shooting up the arm. . . . This freedom from marked affec-tion of the lymphatics is one distinctive feature of the disease.

The constitutional disturbance is not great, but it is frequently, as before observed, large in proportion to the apparent local inflamma-tion.

The history of the disease is nearly always that a few days or a week before, sometimes even a fortnight or more, the hand or a finger sustained some slight injury, commonly a scratch. But if the part be examined, instead of finding at the seat of injury some explanation of the erythema in the form of a pustule or small ulcer or the like, all that can be dis-cerned is the scar—if so tiny a mark can be called by the name—of a little scratch or abra-sion.

1. Obituary, William Morrant Baker, *Brit Med J* 2:1169-1170 (Oct 17) 1896.

2. Baker, W. M.: On the Formation of Synovial Cysts in the Leg in Connection With Disease of the Knee-Joint, *St Bart Hosp Rep* 13:245-261, 1877.

3. Baker, W. M.: The Formation of Abnormal Synovial Cysts in Connection With the Joints, *St Bart Hosp Rep* 21:177-190, 1885.

4. Baker, W. M.: Erythema Serpens, *St Bart Hosp Rep* 9:198-211, 1873.

Composite by G. Bako

Sir William Jenner (1815-1898)

WILLIAM JENNER, physician to Queen Victoria, was born at Chatham, England, and received his early schooling at the dockyard town of Rochester, where Charles Dickens had spent his early years.[1] Jenner began his medical education at the University of London followed by an apprenticeship in Regent's Park. He became a licentiate of the Society of Apothecaries in 1837 and a member of the Royal College of Surgeons of England shortly after. He immediately started general practice and later served as surgeon-accoucheur to the Royal Maternity Charity. However, in 1844, the year Jenner graduated doctor of medicine at the university, he changed his professional course. After four years of study of pathology, he was elected a member of the Royal College of Physicians and in 1849 was appointed professor of pathologic anatomy at University College. When the Hospital for Sick Children was established (1852), Jenner was appointed its first physician and in 1853 was elected assistant physician to the London Fever Hospital. In 1861, he became physician extraordinary to Queen Victoria and the following year physician-in-ordinary to the Prince of Wales. Jenner attended the prince consort in 1861 during his fatal illness from typhoid fever as well as the Prince of Wales from the same affliction ten years later.

Jenner, a leading consultant in London and a skilled bedside teacher, attracted an unusually large number of clinical clerks, house physicians, and patients. He demanded precision in the preparation of clinical notes and was quick to point out deficiencies. From 1863 to 1872 he held the chair of the principles and practice of medicine at University College and in 1864 was elected Fellow of the Royal Society.

During his service at the Fever Hospital, Jenner began a systematic clinical-pathological investigation of the differentiation of typhus and typhoid fever based upon a careful review of more than 1,000 cases. The pathological study of 66 fatal examples confirmed the differential conclusions of Louis, Gerhard, and others.[2] The significant clinical findings included age, duration of the prodromal period, onset of acute symptoms, the time of appearance and characteristics of the cutaneous reaction, and varied symptoms of the overt sickness; the pathological differentiation was based upon the absence or involvement of Peyer's patches.

Jenner prepared monographs on *Diphtheria, Its Symptoms and Treatment; Lectures and Essays on Fevers and Diphtheria;* and *Clinical Lectures and Essays on Rickets, Tuberculosis, Abdominal Tumors, and Other Subjects.* In the address delivered before the British Medical Association in 1869, he presented his thoughts on bedside teaching and medical education and referred to progress in medicine as he judged it a century ago when therapeutic nihilism was in vogue.[3]

. . . in fact to all advances in Medicine as a practical science, it must be remembered that it is rarely—very rarely, if ever—that any great discovery, any great step forward has been the direct result of the labours of a single man. All but invariably it has resulted from the successive labours of many men. . . . It is to the experience of the mass of the profession that we look for the final establishment of doctrine and of rules of practice.

Those points have been to me of the greatest practical service when teaching the student at the bed-side. It is clinical teaching that brings most closely home to a physician the importance of every advance in our practical knowledge.

Keeping in view then those practical aims and objects for which medicine is esteemed by the public, viz., its power to prevent disease, to cure disease, to prolong life, to alleviate suffering, I feel that I have said enough amply to prove the truth of my assertion, that the progress of medicine as an art during the past twenty-five years has been second to that of no other science. While the present advanced state of medical education—the perfection of the means of physical research—the many new centres of knowledge being established in our colonial empire and in America—the widely diffused acquaintance of the profession with modern languages—the rapidity with which knowledge spreads—the confirmation, correction, or refutation which follows so quickly on the publication of novelties—the great ability, the absence of prejudice, the untiring energy, and the truthfulness exhibited by the younger workers in the field of our science, render me hopeful that the next quarter of a century will be distinguished by far greater progress than has the last, great though that be.

Jenner attended his Queen for more than three decades and in 1868 was created a baronet. He served the Royal College of Physicians with equal devotion. He delivered the Gulstonian lectures in 1853, became councillor and censor, was Harveian orator in 1876, and president for seven years beginning in 1881. Oxford awarded him the honorary DCL, and Cambridge and Edinburgh an honorary LLD.

1. Sir William Jenner, obituary, *Lancet* 2:1674-1676 (Dec 17) 1898.

2. Jenner, W.: On Typhoid and Typhus Fevers, *Monthly J Med Sci* 9:663-680 (April) 1849.

3. Jenner, W.: *The Practical Medicine of Today*, London: H. K. Lewis, 1869.

Johannes Müller (1801-1858)

JOHANNES MÜLLER, professor at the University of Berlin in anatomy, physiology, and pathology, was one of the leaders of the 19th century school of physiology in Germany. He was born in Coblenz into a shoemaker's family, was educated in the faith of the Roman Catholic Church in a stormy period of European history, and at 10 years of age, entered a venerable Latin seminary of the Jesuits.[1] Proficiency in Latin and Greek, skill in mathematics, and a self-developed interest in biology and zoology were forces which contributed to his turning from a life in the church to the medical sciences. After serving for a year as a volunteer in the army, in 1819 Müller began his higher education at the University of Bonn. The study of respiration of the fetus based upon experimental observations, which won him a prize in competition, was an early example of his abiding curiosity in the unraveling of physiological phenomena. He graduated MD from Bonn in 1822, presenting an inaugural thesis on the laws of motion. He then proceeded to Berlin to pass the state examination for a physician's license. While in Berlin, Müller made the acquaintance of Rudolphi, physiologist at the university, who spoke for recognition of the importance of anatomy in physiological investigation.

Müller returned to Bonn and established himself in private practice. He was impressed, nevertheless, with opportunities for the full-time professional pursuit of anatomy and the need to strengthen the union between natural philosophy and experimental physiology. In this endeavor, he became privatdocent on the faculty, took up the study of the sense organs and the nervous system, prepared a communication in Latin on the minute structure and anatomy of glands throughout the animal kingdom, and resolved a controversy between the adherents of Malpighi and Ruysch over the structure of glands. It was soon apparent that practice was not Müller's basic interest. Rather, he chose the academic road, where advancement was rapid and productive for him. Only three years after he received senior professorial status at Bonn, he applied for and was successful in obtaining the prized professorship of anatomy, physiology, and pathology vacated by Rudolphi upon retirement in Berlin. Müller remained in Berlin (meanwhile ignoring solicitations from other universities), until he resigned in 1848 while serving as rector of the university. He went into retirement, plagued by despondency and failing health. Because he died ten years later on his appointed day, the evidence suggests suicide. This act is partially understandable. In spite of his complete acceptance of experimental science, he was a dreamy mystic and proponent of the vitalistic theory, believing in the existence of a dynamic force insusceptible to mechanical or physical measurement.

Müller's interpretation of physiology, which exerted a profound influence on scientific medicine, was all-inclusive and embraced biology, comparative anatomy, chemistry, psychology, pathology, zoology, paleontology, and embryology. The number of scientific areas explored was surpassed only by the quantity and quality of his communications to scientific periodicals or prepared as monographs or texts. Several were translated into English for wider dissemination and easier accessibility. If Müller lacked one attribute in academic life, it was the charm of an engaging lecturer. The deficiency was minor, however; as if to compensate, his scientific "inspiration" profoundly influenced a number of brilliant pupils who were trained by him to reason

as natural scientists. The list of followers includes Brücke, Du Bois Reymond, Helmholtz, Kölliker, Henle, and especially Schwann, who enunciated the cellular theory, and Virchow, the father of cellular pathology.

The first volume of Müller's most famous treatise, *The Handbook of Human Physiology,*[2] appeared in 1834 and was translated into English in 1837. He summarized important advances in preceding decades and rendered current each subject, with integration of contributions made by chemistry and physical instruments. Consequently, physiology emerged under his leadership as a specific discipline among the medical sciences. Seizing every method of observation and utilizing mathematics and physics to investigate the intellect and the senses, he entertained the conviction that physiological investigation must exploit psychological understanding in interpreting mind and the soul. Although his law of specific nerve energies was propounded first at Bonn in 1826, his *Physiology* included a mature presentation of his conclusions.[2]

If the nerves are mere passive conductors of the impressions of light, sonorous vibrations, and odours, how does it happen that the nerve which perceives odours is sensible to this kind of impressions only, and to no others, while by another nerve odours are not perceived: that the nerve which is sensible to the matter of light, or the luminous oscillations, is insensible to the vibrations of sonorous bodies; that the auditory nerve is not sensible to light, nor the nerve of taste to odours; while, to the common sensitive nerve, the vibrations of bodies give the sensation, not of sound, but merely of tremours? These considerations have induced physiologists to ascribe to the individual nerves of the senses a special sensibility to certain impressions, by which they are supposed to be rendered conductors of certain qualities of bodies, and not of others.

A consideration of such facts could not but lead to the inference that the special susceptibility of nerves for certain impressions is not a satisfactory theory, and that the nerves of the senses are not mere passive conductors, but that each peculiar nerve of sense has special powers or qualities which the exciting causes merely render manifest.

Sensation, therefore, consists in the communication of the sensorium, not of the quality or state of the external body, but of the condition of the nerves themselves, excited by the external cause.

Müller supplied experimental proof in the frog for the Bell-Magendie doctrine of the function of spinal nerves, to wit: anterior roots carry centrifugal fibers and the posterior roots carry centripetal fibers. The correct experimental procedure was selected by Müller to support his physiological experience and intuitive judgment.[3]

The presence of sensory and motor nerves in the same trunk is one of the most important phenomenon in physiology. Charles Bell was the first to suggest that the posterior roots of a ganglion of the spinal nerves have only sensory functions and the anterior roots have only motor function, and that the fibers of these roots supply the skin and the muscles from one nerve tract.

Frogs seem best suited for the experiments; they withstand the exposure of the spinal canal, the nerves remain sensitive for very long periods, and the thick nerve roots of the lower extremities run a protracted and separate course in the spinal canal before they unite into larger trunks.

In each repetitive experiment we come to the conviction that irritation of the posterior root fails to produce the slighest contraction in the lower extremities. The same can be shown for the posterior roots that supply the upper extremities.

On the other hand, at the slighest stimulation of the anterior roots, the muscles twitch and contract. When the roots are separated from the spinal cord, any irritation produces energetic twitching.

The results of these experiments leave no doubt that Bell's law is valid and correct.

Another study in anatomy and physiology led to the discovery, in selecting amphibians, of four distinct hearts of the lymphatic system. The pulsating organs were encountered in the quest for frog lymph for demonstration to students. Posterior lymphatic hearts were identified first.[4]

These are most easily found in the frog, but they exist also in the toad, the salamander, and the green lizard; probably in all amphibia, the naked as well as those provided with scales. The organ is double, and, in the frog, lies on each side, behind the articulation of the os femoris, near the anus, in the regio ischiadica. . . . The organ lies immediately under the skin. Its regular contractions may be seen more distinctly when this is removed. The arteries and

vena ischiadica, the largest vessels in the thigh, run immediately underneath the organ, but the motion of the blood in these vessels has no influence upon it. The contractions are neither synchronous with the motions of the heart, nor with those of the lungs. . . . They [contractions] continue after the removal of the heart. . . . The pulsations of the two organs, on the right and left sides, sometimes alternate at irregular intervals.

The anterior lymphatic hearts lie on each side, upon the great processus transversus of the third vertebra. . . . They are round in shape and connected with the contiguous vein. The fluid which is discharged into the vein is colourless.

In physiological chemistry, Müller isolated chondrin and gluten. In zoology, he studied the amphioxus, the starfish, sea cucumbers, and sharks; he became a paleontologist and studied fossil fishes, mammalia, echinites, and snails. In embryology, the paramesonephric duct (Müller's duct) was discovered by him in the developing chick. Müller's law of the eccentric projection of sensations from the peripheral sense organs to other nerve terminals, a theory of color contrast, and his work on strabismus and a comprehension of binocular vision represent borderline subjects between neurology and ophthalmology. An explanation of the color sensations (pressure-phosphenes), produced by pressure on the retina, was described in *Physiology of Sight of Men and Animals.*[5]

When pressure is applied with the finger tips to the lateral areas of the closed eyes, light rings appear in the periphery of the darkened field of vision. Lateral pressure on the right eye produces a light ring in the periphery on the medial side, and the lateral pressure on the left eye produces a light ring on the medial side of the field of vision. If the pressure is applied to the medial sides of either eye, the light rings appear again at the extreme periphery of the field of vision.

We conclude from these experiments that the retina of either eye is identical and forms one and the same subjective organ of vision; all parts lying in a certain meridian and at a certain distance from the central point of the eye are identical with the corresponding parts of the retina of the opposite eye, lying in the same meridian and at the same distance from the central point of the retina of that eye.

In demonstrating the harmony which existed between the pathological and the embryonic development of tumors, Müller was one of the first to employ the microscope. Until his time, the prevailing view considered cancer to be a general disease and the tumor a local manifestation. Müller showed that the cancer consisted of a growth of abnormal cells. He began a program of tumor identity, but death prevented its completion.[6]

According to Schwann, all the tissues in the embryo are formed from cells, which are themselves developed from nuclei; growth being the result of fresh formations of cells, which afterwards undergo transformation into other tissues. These observations led the author to examine morbid growths very carefully; both those in which no cells had hitherto been discovered, and also such as were known to present a cellular structure with a view to determine the presence of nuclei in the walls, or within the interior of the cells; while the author further hoped to verify the truth of that principle which Schwann has laid down. By employing a high magnifying power, cells were observed in many morbid growths in which they were not previously known to exist, as in collonema, in many varieties of carcinoma, and in enchondroma. In most growths presenting a cellular structure, with the exception of cholesteatoma and cellular polypi, the nuclei of the cells were discovered, situated either in their walls or in their interior: in many instances, too, young cells were formed within older ones, as was the case in sarcoma, enchondroma, carcinoma, and collonema. Thus, then, as might have been anticipated, did the examination of morbid structures confirm Schwann's observations touching the development and growth of healthy tissues.

Whether the carcinomatous diathesis be peculiar and distinct from all others, or whether, under certain circumstances, any other structure may pass into the state of carcinoma, still the same question presents itself;—is there any other characteristic of carcinomatous growths than such as are derived from their minute structure, or from the process of their development? The solution of this question must always be the grand problem in the anatomy of morbid growths. The examination of numerous specimens of carcinoma has taught the author that they are, indeed, possessed of certain peculiar anatomical characters, which may serve to identify them; and, further, that these characters are distinguishable, on making a section of the growth, either by the naked eye, or at any rate by the aid of a common magnifying glass.

In 1834, Müller founded the *Archiv für Anatomie, Physiologie und Wissenshaftliche Medicin,* later known as *Müller's Archiv.*

He was a member of almost all scientific bodies in Germany and of many foreign societies, including the Philosophical Society of Philadelphia and the American Academy of Arts and Sciences of Boston. He received the Copley medal of the Royal Society of London and was honored by the kings of Prussia, Sweden, Bavaria, and Sardinia.

1. Virchow, R.: *Elogy of Johannes Müller* (Ger), Berlin: A. Hirschwald, 1858, translated by A. M. Adam, *Edinburgh Med J* 4:452-463; 527-544 (July) 1858.
2. Müller, J.: *Handbook of Human Physiology* (Ger), Coblenz: J. Holscher, 1834-1840, translated by W. Baly, London: Taylor & Walton, 1837.
3. Müller, J.: Confirmation of Bell's Law (Ger), *Notiz Geb Natur Heilk* 30:113-122, 1831.
4. Müller, J.: On the Existence of Four Distinct Hearts, Having Regular Pulsations, Connected With the Lymphatic System, in Certain Amphibious Animals (Ger), *Philos Trans,* pt 1, pp 89-94, 1833.
5. Müller, J.: *Physiology of Sight of Men and Animals* (Ger), Leipzig: K. Knobloch, 1826.
6. Müller, J.: *On the Nature and Structural Characteristics of Cancer* (Ger), Berlin: G. Reimer, 1838, translated by C. West, London: Sherwood, Gilbert, & Piper, 1840.

Composite by G. Bako

Justus von Liebig (1803-1873)

ONE OF THE BEST EXAMPLES of medicine's debt to chemistry is the compendium of contributions by Justus von Liebig. At the end of the 18th century and into the early part of the following century, chemistry in Germany was a poor second to other countries in Europe. Berzelius in Stockholm and Gay-Lussac in Paris were not then threatened by scientific competition in Germany, a country destined to lead in chemistry a generation later. One of the first of many brilliant chemists in this new era was Liebig of Darmstadt.[1] Early in life he displayed a great interest in chemistry. Justus' father, a dealer in drugs and dyes, could not provide his son with the then current beneficent educational training beyond the Gymnasium. Any deficiency in his early education, however, proved no serious handcap to a remarkable career in agricultural chemistry, organic chemistry, and physiological chemistry. By his 14th year he had read all the chemical journals in the Darmstadt library and had repeated most of the chemical experiments within his means.

At 15, Justus became a pharmacist's apprentice but was not satisfied with the prospect of such a career. He abandoned pharmacy, and after a brief period of preparation for higher learning, enrolled first in the University of Bonn and later studied at Erlangen, where he received the PHD degree. His first scientific publication concerned the investigation of silver fulminate, an explosive formed by dissolving silver in nitric acid and reacting the silver nitrate with alcohol. The appeal of the Parisian school of chemistry under Gay-Lussac could not be resisted permanently, and although refused admission initially, the presentation of his observations on silver fulminate to the French Academy of Sciences won the praise of many. Alexander von Humboldt was helpful in persuading Gay-Lussac to take on the young German student.

Liebig's studies in Paris were made possible through a traveling stipend granted by the Grand Duke of Hesse-Darmstadt. The productive researches in Gay-Lussac's laboratory were recognized by German royalty; and, in 1824, at the age of 21, Grand Duke Ludwig appointed Liebig professor extraordinary of chemistry at the University of Giessen—on the banks of the Lahn. There were few chairs of chemistry in Germany at that time, and the appointment was accepted with a twofold purpose. Not only did this provide an opportunity to expand and continue his chemical investigations, it also enabled him to establish an educational laboratory for interested and qualified students from all parts of Europe. The successes in each enterprise were vital forces in the inception of modern chemistry in Germany.

There was no branch of chemistry that did not enjoy the fruits of Liebig's labors. An earnestness of purpose, an infectious enthusiasm, and a superior intellect assured him the attainment of a remarkable professional career. Scientific literature was enriched by his writings, as was the daily press by his letters to the editor. The studies in agricultural chemistry provided an effective rebuttal to the Malthusian economists.[2] The increasing scarcity of food could be corrected if man understood the chemistry of plants and soil. Liebig postulated that the inorganic constituents of plants, which remain as ash when ignited, are essential to agriculture. If the soil is repeatedly depleted, without replenishment, the crops eventually suffer. This concept is self-evident in current agronomy, but Liebig established the relationship on a firm scientific basis. It seemed reasonable to him that minerals should be returned to the soil by artificial fertilizers.[3]

In organic chemistry, chloral and chloroform were discovered, and new concepts of nutrition and metabolism (*Stoffwechsel*) of higher animals and man were advanced. Chloroform was discovered simultaneously with Guthrie in America and Soubeiran in France.

His researches in physiological chemistry concerned carbohydrates and fats, and the degradation of proteins and purines to urea, uric acid, and hippuric acid. Liebig advanced the hypothesis that plants are capable of assimilating inorganic compounds, carbonic acid, and nitrogenous substances and building complex compounds from them, which in turn, are the substances essential to man and animals. These were divided into the *nitrogenous* substances, which serve in the formation of blood and the structural elements of the body, and the *non-nitrogenous* substances, the fats and the carbohydrates, which provide fuel for the body. Liebig judged it unnecessary to speculate on the mechanism of nervous activity or to accept Stahl's "vitalism" theory of life. Quantitatively, metabolism could be accounted for on the basis of chemical activity.

The reciprocal conversion of carbohydrates and fats was proposed. The quantity of fat in pigs and geese, subsisting entirely on grain and plants, could be attributed best to this phenomenon. Also, when bees were fed exclusively on sugar, they produced normal amounts of wax. A joint project with Wöhler, who synthesized urea (1828), revealed that allantoin was a degradation product of uric acid. Liebig established the formula for creatine and examined its products of decomposition, creatinine, sarcosine, and other substances in the juice of flesh. He devised a formula for infant feeding as a substitute for breast milk after analysis of the latter substance. Liebig's meat extract was designed as a general nutrient.

At the stage in the history of the development of the chemical understanding of living cells, when Liebig found so much to be done, it is not surprising to find errors in interpretation.[4] He was convinced that vitalism was false and that biological processes could be explained by chemical reactions. For this reason, he refused to believe that fermentation and putrefaction were caused by living organisms. Because of this bias, the experiments of Pasteur were rejected, and a heated controversy developed between these two great men. Although the investigations of Pasteur eventually led to the development of the concept of the germ theory of disease, Liebig's opposition to Pasteur may have delayed this development. However, Liebig's extensive and eminent contributions to physiological chemistry more than compensate for any errors in reasoning on fermentation and putrefaction.

In his 60th year, almost a century ago, Liebig composed his biography in longhand, only portions of which are extant. It concludes with the following:[5]

Mistakes were made, not in the facts, but in the deductions about organic reactions; we were the first pioneers in unknown regions, and the difficulties in the way of keeping on the right path were sometimes insuperable.

Now, when the paths of research are beaten roads, it is a much easier matter; but all the wonderful discoveries which recent times have brought forth were then our own dreams, whose realizations we surely and without doubt anticipated.

1. Obituary Notices of Fellows Deceased: Justus Liebig, *Proc Roy Soc London* 24:xxvii-xxxvii (Nov. 18-April 27) 1875-76.

2. Hofmann, A. W.: *The Faraday Lecture for 1875: The Life Work of Liebig,* London: Macmillan and Co., 1876.

3. von Liebig, J.: *Die organische Chemie in ihrer Anwendung auf Physiologie und Pathologie,* Braunschweig: F. Vieweg, 1842.

4. *Milestones in Microbiology,* trans. and ed. T. Brock, Englewood Cliffs, N. J.: Prentice-Hall Inc., 1961.

5. "Justice von Liebig: An Autobiographical Sketch," in *Annual Report of the Board of Regents of the Smithsonian Institution,* Washington: Government Printing Office, 1893.

Composite by G. Bako

Carl von Rokitansky (1804-1878)

ROKITANSKY, premier pathologist of the "Allgemeines Krankenhaus," is the recognized leader of the triad of medical scientists, the illustrious "Dreigestirn," who were born in Bohemia, and were largely responsible for the revival of Vienna as the great medical center of the world in the mid-19th century. The other members were Joseph Skoda (Skoda's resonance), chief of the medical clinic, and Ferdinand von Hebra, dermatologist of renown.

Through Rokitansky's efforts, Emperor Joseph II decreed that all who died in the general hospital would be subject to a post-mortem examination. This edict permitted Rokitansky to be responsible for more than 60,000 autopsies; many of this number were performed with his own hands. No one before or since probably has had the opportunity for such extensive experience in the deathhouse. Although he never practiced medicine, and made few contributions to the pathogenesis of disease as a logical step from pathological revelations to bedside medicine, his descriptive classification of structural changes exerted a profound influence on clinical medicine.

Rokitansky was born in Königgrätz, Bohemia,[1] and studied medicine first at Prague and then Vienna, where he received his MD degree at the age of 24. He went directly to the pathology laboratory and remained there throughout his professional career. Although he succeeded Wagner in 1832 as director of the Pathological Institute and was advanced to full professorship at the age of 30, Rokitansky was self-taught at the necropsy table; he was guided neither by his predecessor nor by any other teacher.

The advances in pathology, begun in the late 18th century and early in the 19th century, were attributed largely to the schools in London and Paris. The French school, particularly under Bichat, and the English school under the Hunters and Baillie emphasized pathological anatomy; the Viennese, on the other hand, emphasized anatomical pathology. In developing a philosophy of anatomical pathology, Rokitansky displayed obvious shortcomings, and encountered distressing difficulties when his thoughts left the postmortem amphitheater and he began to speculate on the humoral cause of disease. A strange doctrine of "crases" and "dyscrases" was proposed in the first volume of *A Manual of Pathological Anatomy*.[2] In spite of the bizarre speculations, that covered a few pages only, the *Manual* proved to be an outstanding treatise.

Humoral pathology is simply a requirement of common practical sense; and it has always held a place in medical science, although the limits of its domain have, no doubt, been variously circumscribed or interpreted at different times. Of late years it has met with a new basis and support in morbid anatomy, which, in the inadequacy of its discoveries in the solids to account for disease and death, has been compelled to seek for an extension of its boundary through a direct examination of the blood itself.

This fanciful theory was bitterly criticized as a "monstrous anachronism" by Virchow, professor of pathology in Berlin, and 17 years Rokitansky's junior, who was exploring the doctrine of cellular pathology. Rokitansky had no scientific data to support his humoral theory and chose to abandon it in later editions of his treatise. The incorporation of microscopic descriptions was another modification that appeared in subsequent editions.

Rokitansky was appointed dean of the medical faculty in 1849, and the following year, rector of the University. He was an outstanding teacher and attracted students from near and far to the pathological amphitheater. More than a decade was devoted to collecting material for his studies on the defects of the septum of the heart.[3] The monograph on disease of the arteries, published in 1852, was probably his greatest contribution to his chosen field of endeavor.[4]

He was the first to differentiate lobar and lobular pneumonia.[2]

f. Inflammation of the Lungs (Pneumoniae).—Pathologists are in the habit of recognising only one form of pneumonia. It is true that this is by far the most frequent form; but even in regard to this there are several points in which we cannot agree with the accepted view. We may provisionally and very briefly remark that the evidence of its croupous nature will be the more manifest in proportion to the epidemic constitution and the special cause of the disease, the rapidity of its course, the degree of its intensity, etc. We shall treat of this, the most common form of pneumonia, under the designation of:—

1. *Croupous Pneumonia.*—The course of this disease is divided, as is well known, into three stages which have received the names of *inflammatory engorgement, hepatisation,* and *purulent infiltration.* We shall first consider the case in which a whole lung, or at least a whole lobe, is affected.

Pneumonia, according to its variety, attacks, as we have already described, the whole of one of the larger divisions of the lung, that is to say, a whole lobe, or a great part of one, and it is then termed *lobar*.

Or it attacks only smaller portions of the lungs, a number of individual lobules or single aggregations of lobules, between which we find the parenchyma in a comparatively normal state. It is then termed *lobular pneumonia*.

In discussing the development of emphysema, Rokitansky noted that:[2]

It presents many varieties in degree and extent. By degree, we refer to the extent of the dilatation of the pulmonary cells; it must, however, be remarked, that in emphysema of long standing, we always simultaneously find several degrees of dilatation, and that it is only during the commencement of the disease that the dilatation is observed to be uniform. The pulmonary cells may be dilated to the side of a millet-seed or pin's head, or to that of a hemp-seed, a pea, or even a bean, and in proportion to the size which they attain, they deviate the more from their original shape. At first the disease is a genuine, simple dilatation of the cells, and when the cell-walls become to a certain extent thickened and rigid, it may be regarded as an active dilatation of the cells somewhat analogous to hypertrophy of the lungs. In higher degrees, on the contrary, the dilated cells unite to form a larger space, their walls becoming atrophied by the pressure they exert on one another.

Acute yellow atrophy of the liver was described.[2]

This affection is characterised by the saturated yellow colour, owing to a diffusion of bile throughout the tissue, by extreme flabbiness and pulpiness, loss of the granular texture, extreme rapidity in the reduction of size, which chiefly affects the vertical diameter, and consequently induces a flattening of the liver. It occurs chiefly in the early years of life, during puberty, and in the prime; it is remarkable for the rapid course it runs, for extreme tenderness of the liver, nervous attacks, and jaundice; it terminates fatally with febrile symptoms of a disorganized state of the blood, irritation of the brain.

The first pathological description of spondylolisthesis is attributed to Rokitansky.[5]

There are cases in which the lordotic protrusion of the lumbar parts of the vertebral column into the pelvis is produced in a different manner, and in which the tilting of the pelvis not only is not increased, but on the contrary, is greatly diminished.

The first sacral vertebra is unusually low, and takes up by means of two inward-facing, slightly concave articular surfaces, anteriorly and posteriorly to the synchondrosis sacro-iliaca, two articular processes originating from the lower lateral portion of the last lumbar vertebra, in such a manner, that the latter appears wedged into the sacrum. At the same time, the very much inclined connecting surface of the aforementioned sacral vertebra has the effect that it deeply protrudes into the pelvis.

Rokitansky detected bacteria in lesions of malignant endocarditis and described the sinuses of the gallbladder—Rokitansky-Aschoff sinuses—herniations of the gallbladder mucosa into subjacent layers. Acute dilatation of the stomach was recognized as were pulmonary complications of typhoid fever.

Patent ductus arteriosus was classified as a congenital lesion.[2]

On Dilatations of the Ductus Botalli.—The dilatations which in rare cases are observed in the Ductus arteriosus, in every period of life, from the earliest infancy, are simple, and not dependent upon any alteration of texture in the coats of the vessel. They are occasioned by a deficient involution of the duct after birth.

As a teacher, Rokitansky was jovial and highly respected by his students. He was responsible for the imperial decree incorporating pathological anatomy into the medical curriculum. The fame of Vienna as the center of medical learning in the mid-19th century may be traced directly to Rokitansky and his clinical colleagues, natives of Bohemia. He brought the clinician to the autopsy table so that they could learn of their triumphs and their failures in the diagnosis at the bedside. Anatomical lesions were classified and related, when possible, to symptoms observed clinically. Anatomical pathology, as propounded by Rokitansky, revealed the natural history of the morbid process, the progress of the clinical course of disease consonant with the structural changes.

1. Rokitansky, C.: *Autobiography and Inaugural Address* (Ger), ed. E Lesky, Vienna: Hermann Böhlaus Nachf., 1960.

2. Rokitansky, C.: *A Manual of Pathological Atonomy,* Vol. 1-4, London: The Sydenham Society, 1849-1854.

3. Rokitansky, C.: *Defects of the Valves of the Heart* (Ger), Vienna, 1875.

4. Rokitansky, C.: *Diseases of the Arteries* (Ger), Vienna, 1852.

5. Rokitansky, C.: Studies on Curvature of the Vertebral Column (Ger), *Med Jahr Osterr* 19:202, 1889.

Joseph Hyrtl (1810-1894)

JOSEPH HYRTL, distinguished professor of anatomy at the University of Vienna, was not known for a multitude of discoveries in what proved to be a fertile period for new observations from the dissecting amphitheater; rather, he was recognized for his capacity and charm as a lecturer, skill as a prosector, proficiency in preparation of handbooks of anatomy, and scholarly monographs on medical and anatomical philology.

Hyrtl was born into a family of modest means in the Hungarian village of Eisenstadt, but received his education in Vienna, in the Gymnasium and the medical school of the University.[1] An interest in comparative anatomy led to his appointment as prosector, and, although still a student, he taught anatomy to practitioners in the community who came for instruction. His inaugural thesis, prepared in Latin and presented in 1835, was entitled *Antiquitates anatomicae rariores*. Hyrtl remained in Vienna as prosector for two years after his graduation, leaving at 26 years of age to accept a call to Prague as professor of anatomy. This position he held until 1845 when,

reluctantly, he returned to Vienna to accept a similar post at his alma mater. One of his initial accomplishments in this position was the publication of his first text and one of his best known works, *Handbook of Human Anatomy*. This remarkable tract of anatomical structure and function contained no illustrations, inasmuch as he had provided his students with appropriate line drawings or shaded sketches at each lecture. Also, his anatomical lectures were recognized as histrionic masterpieces, with items of nomenclature, history, surgery, and physiology interwoven in the exposition. The introduction to the first edition, which was written in a clear descriptive style, contained the following thoughts.[2]

> I chose to prepare this text on anatomy in order to present my students with a concise statement of the current views, to acquaint them with the spirit of science and to illustrate its progress, and also to offer suggestions on the value of anatomy in medical practice. Anatomical compendia of the size of this treatise are not meant to enrich the science. Their goal is to acquaint the reader with the field and to prepare him for more intensive investigation in the abundant anatomical literature.
>
> Where useful, I have included some practical notes and suggestions which are important to the young physician and which he can understand without special knowledge of diseases. I know from my own experience as a medical student that I would have liked to have had some of the reasons why the study of anatomy was necessary and important. If any of my readers finds this deviation from strictly anatomical tasks unpleasant, he is completely free to skip these paragraphs.
>
> My goal for this book was completeness and brevity. Clarity is not always a result of many words and I'll wager that the students for whom this book was written will not criticize it specifically for its brevity.

The desire to write persisted and the following year Hyrtl published a *Handbook of Topographical Anatomy,* one of the first treatises in German on the subject.[3] It enjoyed several editions and was translated into several languages. A manual of dissection (1860) and his corrosion anatomy (1873) complete the list of texts for teacher and student of topographic and regional anatomy. The development and expansion of the Anatomical Museum was another major assignment. As his success approached that of William Hunter's great institution of comparative anatomy in London, political strife at the mid-century gravely interfered with the continued progress; not until the late 1850's was Hyrtl again able to give undivided attention to the museum. Primarily through his efforts, it reached the goal he had envisioned.

Hyrtl's contributions from the dissecting room concerned the osseous and vascular systems. His communications included descriptions of the distribution of blood vessels in birds and amphibians, the variations in distribution of the veins in man, the portal vein of the adrenal capsule, the function of the cartilage of the knee, and the mechanics of the hip joint. During his investigation on non-vascular hearts, a bitter polemic developed with Brücke, professor of physiology. Although Hyrtl's assertions concerning the origin of the coronary arteries and their filling in the cardiac cycle were proved and his beliefs justified he developed a morose spirit, never quite restored. In a comparative study of the anatomy of the ear, he described the epitympanic recess, "Hyrtl's recess," a lodging for the head of the malleus and a greater part of the incus.[4]

In a *Phoca vitulina* [seal] recently examined I found a new muscle of the incus which has not been reported previously. This muscle lies not in the cavity of the middle ear where the other muscles of the ossicles are located, but it is found in the recess containing the head of the malleus and the body of the incus; this recess is inequally developed in various species of animals and in some of them it is much larger than in *Phoca*.

Hyrtl resigned from his professorship after 30 years and retired to his villa at Perchtoldsdorf in the environs of Vienna. The retirement, slightly earlier than statutory, was motivated by failing vision and faculty friction. Nonetheless, Hyrtl's mind was not idle, and a lifelong interest in anatomy was directed toward the derivation of anatomical terms. *Arabic and Hebraic in Anatomy*[5] was a philological exercise in the meaning and origin of contemporary nomenclature, preceded by a general treatise on the contradictions, misnomers, and

grammatical errors in anatomical terminology which began as follows: [6]

It has often been said that the science of anatomy is an arbitrary language which adheres to no principles. During the last century, the natural scientists revised their terminology but the anatomists did not. They were so completely engrossed in the tasks of their discipline that they found no time; or perhaps they did not consider it necessary to subject their terminology to rigorous criticism and to replace the outdated, erroneous, and contradictory terms.

Out of respect for antiquity we continue to tolerate the anatomical terms inherited from Greek and Roman physicians. These terms are based upon the physiological concepts of our forefathers—for example, *Arteria, Parenchyma, Anastomosis, Aponeurosis, Glandula pinealis, Cardia, Bronchus, Torcular*—concepts which have changed so long ago that the terms no longer make sense.

My intention is only to point out the need for reform to those who will make the effort to review this text. I hope they will not deny me the credit for having done the preparatory work, for identifying where need of improvement lies. The purification of anatomical terminology would inevitably stimulate revision of medical language in general. The language of medicine suffers even more grievously than that of anatomy. There are fanciful names not only for the diseases themselves but for many of the signs and symptoms.

In the isolation of my retirement I can no longer deal with my former scientific discipline. Thus, I turned to the words of Horatio, "cadentque, quae nunc sunt in honore vocabula" (let the names be forgotten which now are being honored).

At the age of 75, Hyrtl concluded his anatomical narratives which were based upon a review of obsolete anatomical terms in the German language. The following excerpts from the introduction give every evidence of his retention of skill in composition and the scholarly pursuit of literary research.[7]

When I exchanged the life of a professor for country retirement ten years ago, I was not able to separate myself from anatomy in the days of my old age because I felt that my whole life belonged to this science. I was accustomed to hard work, and at the age of 75 I did not feel ready to let my hands rest in my lap watching the sand in the hourglass run out. In order to enjoy blessed country leisure with proper dignity among the ruins of the castle at Perchtoldsdorf, where I make a home in common with the owls of the palace of Athena and the ravens of justice, I began collecting all German anatomy texts that have emerged since the invention of the press. I wanted to determine what the Germans thought and wrote on the subject of anatomy over the span of many centuries. I . . . was well compensated by the rich, remarkable, although sometimes obtuse, language in which these books were written. I wrote down thousands of words that I had not known before; from these I selected the most interesting ones, especially those whose meaning I was able to understand only from the context.

The University of Vienna was grateful to Hyrtl for his academic achievements and decreed him honorary Rector for the 500th anniversary celebration in 1864. Hyrtl, in turn, always gave of his best without stint to his pupils, associates, and profession. In quite another area of benefaction, financial donations to social endeavors increased during his retirement. Amounts of money, substantial for an anatomy professor or even a philanthropist, were given to an orphans' home, a boarding school, and a church, while deserving students in medicine received endowments to complete their formal training.

1. Miller, W. S.; Joseph Hyrtl: Anatomist, *Bull Soc Med Hist* 3:96-108, 1923-1925.
2. Hyrtl, J.: *Handbook of Human Anatomy* (Ger), Prag: F. Ehrlich, 1846, excerpt translated by Z. Danilevicius.
3. Hyrtl, J.: *Handbook of Topographical Anatomy* (Ger), 2 vol, Wien: W. Braumüller, 1847, excerpt translated by Z. Danilevicius.
4. Hyrtl, J.: Comparative Anatomy of the Middle Ear (Ger), *Denkschr Akad Wiss* 1:29-37, 1850, excerpt translated by Z. Danilevicius.
5. Hyrtl, J.: *Arabic and Hebraic in Anatomy* (Ger), Wien: W. Braumüller, 1879, excerpt translated by Z. Danilevicius.
6. Hyrtl, J.: *History and Criticism of the Present Language of Anatomy* (Ger), Wien: W. Braumüller, 1880, excerpt translated by Z. Danilevicius.
7. Hyrtl, J.: *The Old German Technical Terms of Anatomy* (Ger), Wien: W. Braumüller, 1884, excerpt translated by Z. Danilevicius.

Robert Remak (1815-1865)

BRILLIANT SCIENTIFIC ACHIEVEMENTS and deep-seated frustrations of a Polish Jew in Prussian Berlin in the first half of the 19th century were the warp and woof of the life of Robert Remak. He was born in the ghetto of Posen, a town turned over to Prussia after the fall of Napoleon I. His father ran a cigar store and sold lottery tickets.[1] Robert received a good Gymnasium education and graduated at the age of 18, with honors, which entitled him to attend any school of higher learning in Germany. He made a wise scholastic choice in the University of Berlin, one of the youngest in Germany and especially noted for its research and teaching in the biological and medical sciences. Johannes Müller, who had only recently (1833) been offered the chair of anatomy and physiology, in turn, attracted such pupils as Schwann, Henle, Du Bois Reymond, Helmholtz, Kölliker, Virchow, Haeckel, Meissner, and Auerbach. Ehrenberg was a member of the faculty and was shortly joined (1840) by Schönlein. Remak soon set a pattern of excellence in the study of the form and function of the nervous system for contemporaries and teachers to admire and, in some instances, to envy. His interests included neural histology first, and later embryology and electrotherapy. When thwarted because of his religion in the quest for a teaching position in the basic sciences, Remak turned to Schönlein's Medical Clinic. As a practicing physician he became one of the founders of modern galvanotherapy, made important contributions to our knowledge of ascending and descending neuritis, and discussed inflammation of the ganglia in the production of peripheral paralysis. But his most important and lasting contributions to modern medicine were his investigations in the field of neurology, cytology, and embryology.

The first observations on the minute structure of the nervous system were derived with the help of Müller's private microscope and were described in Müller's *Archiv* and in Foriep's journal in 1836, while he was still a medical student. Remak came up for the degree of doctor of medicine and surgery, cum laude, in 1838, with an inaugural dissertation in Latin—*Anatomical and Microscopic Observations on the Structure of the Nervous System*.[2] He described for the first time the axis cylinder and the nonmedullated nerve fibers (Remak's fibers), and provided documentary evidence in support of the relationship between ganglionic cells and nerve fibers. His doctoral thesis, which summarized these discoveries, was dedicated not to any of his German colleagues or teachers but to De Bentkowski, the son of a Polish professor in Warsaw. The origin of the nerve fiber from the ganglion cell in the autonomic nervous system, which he called the "organic nervous system," was described as follows.[1]

But one thing that is unquestionably most important with respect to the nature of the ganglionic cells. . . . *The organic fibers originate from the substance of the nucleated globules itself.* In spite of the fact that this observation is difficult and requires great dexterity in preparation as well as observation, it is so well founded that it already would not be possible to doubt it. . . . *The sympathetic ganglion has to be regarded as the real center of the organic nervous system.*

The function of the organic nervous system (today known as the autonomic nervous system) was elaborated on by Remak in 1840. He postulated that the differences in the structure of the organic nerve fibers and other nerves corresponded to a difference in their function. The motor and sensory nerves originate from the central nervous system (Remak's animal nervous system) the organic nerve fibers originate in the ganglionic cells of the peripheral ganglia. This basic discovery and his own experiments led Remak to the recognition that the physiological function of the organic nerves was concerned with all involuntary muscle movement, with secretion, and possibly with the skin. These observations were published first in 1838 in a Polish periodical in his native tongue under the title, "o budowie nerwow i zwojow nerwowych" (on the structure of nerves and nerve plexuses).

Remak continued the philosophical-scientific inquiry on organic nerve fibers and speculated on the possibility of involuntary organic reflexes. In 1840, he discovered ganglia in many organs with involuntary muscles like the bladder and, in 1844, in the heart (Remak's ganglia).[3]

The organic nerves are connected with the function of the organs of blood circulation (the heart, blood vessels, lungs, spleen), with the chylopoietic and uropoietic organs (the stomach, intestinal canal, liver, pancreas, the bladder,

kidneys), and with the secretory membranes (the mucous membranes, serous membranes, and probably also with the skin). Also, the function of all these organs is dependent upon the influence of organic nerve fibers.

Because the liver has no quantity of involuntary muscles, but a rich supply of organic nerves, it is concluded that the liver secretion depends also on these nerves. The hypothesis drawn from these facts is that, via organic nerve fibers, each secretory organ receives impulses to perform its secretory function. . . . We come, however, to the unusual conclusion that the function of the involuntary muscles of absorption and of the secretion of glands and some secretory membranes is influenced by organic nerves. It does not cease entirely after elimination of these nerves.

We have learned that the heart is influenced by peripheral ganglia and that the organic fibers which emanate from these ganglia can stimulate its contraction.

Remak continued his fundamental investigations in Müller's laboratory, with no official academic status. It is not surprising for a physician, so thwarted, to turn to private practice, which he pursued through the remainder of his life, always seeking but never achieving full academic status in Berlin. For many years he had taught privately in his home; later he was appointed an assistant by Schönlein, and in 1847 finally admitted as privatdocent to the teaching staff of the Berlin Medical Faculty. Only in 1859, after the faculty had recommended him several times for this honor, did he attain professional status.

In 1845, Remak published his *Diagnostic and Pathogenetic Investigations,* dedicating the treatise to Schönlein. His only academic by-line in the preface was "practicing physician and surgeon in Berlin." In this book he described the causative agents of favus and named the fungus *Achorion schönleini,* taking no credit for the discovery, but attributing it to his chief. Remak experimentally produced favus on his own skin.[4]

Since the contagiousness of the fungus causing favus disease is a reality and often observed in children's hospitals; since furthermore Fuchs has noticed that favus is easier contracted by normal skin than by injured tissue; therefore I placed several small pieces of crust with English adhesive tape on the back of my left lower arm. After a few days the crusts fell away, without leaving a trace, since the tape had dried out. I considered the experiment a failure, and resumed washing the arm with soap and water. But after 14 days, during which I have bathed several times in the river, I noticed a strong itching on one of the inoculation areas. I found a dark red spot the size of a vest button, covered with epidermis scales, similar to psoriasis. The skin was thickened and hardened. In the center of the red patch a small eruption appeared, with fresh pus. About 3 weeks after its first appearance, I removed the crust and the pus in order to be rid of the troublesome itching, and found at the bottom a white caseous body which contained only favus fungus.

Continuing a deep interest in microscopic morphology, Remak confirmed and extended the observations of Baer, introduced the three-layer concept in embryology, and noted that the skin and nervous system are formed from the ectoderm, that the notochord and the lining membrane of the digestive canal and of the digestive organs arise from the entoderm, and that the muscular, skeletal, and excretory systems arise from the mesoderm.

Remak's contribution to the cell theory seems as important as that of Schwann. He rejected spontaneous generation of cells and proved that each cell is a product of another cell and that the growth of new tissue must come from existing cells.[5]

> The results are closely related to pathology as well as to physiology. It can hardly be disputed any more that the cells of pathological tissue are only variants of the normal embryonic cells and it is not likely that they should possess the capacity of extra-cellular development. . . . I dare to express the theory that pathological tissue, not less than normal tissue, is not formed by an extra-cellular cytoblastema, but is derived from or produced by normal tissue of the organism.

1. Kisch, B.: Forgotten Leaders in Modern Medicine, *Trans Amer Philos Soc* 44:227-297, 1954.

2. Remak, R.: *Observationes Anatomicae et Microscopicae de Systematis Nervosi Structura*, thesis, Berlin, 1838.

3. Remak, R.: The Physiological Significance of the Organic Nervous System, *Mschr med* 3:225-265, 1840, excerpt translated by Z. Danilevicius.

4. Remak, R.: *Diagnostic and Pathogenetic Investigations* (Ger), Berlin: A. Hirschwald, 1845, excerpt translated by E. Longar.

5. Muller, J.: Extracellular Development of Animal Cells (Ger), *Arch Anat Physiol*, 1852, pp 47-57, excerpt translated by E. Longar.

Composite by G. Bako

Ludwig Traube (1818-1876)

LUDWIG TRAUBE struggled against seemingly overwhelming odds in becoming the outstanding clinical figure in experimental pathology during the middle 19th century in Germany. Ludwig, the son of a wine broker, was born in Ratibor into a large Jewish family.[1] He was tutored initially and then attended the Gymnasium at Ratibor until the age of 17, when at the urging of his father he began the study of medicine at the University of Breslau. There he showed particular interest in the old languages, mathematics, and philosophy. Traube was attracted above all others to Johannes Purkyně, the Bohemian physiologist and the outstanding member of the faculty. Two years later he continued his studies at the University of Berlin, where Johannes Müller held a similar position on the faculty and a similar appeal for Traube. At this stage in his training, he was acutely aware of the mediocre state of medical education in Germany and turned to the writings of Magendie and Laennec, the leaders of the French school of medicine. The former was famous for his belief that pathology was essentially a disturbance of physiology; whereas the latter rediscovered and introduced auscultation and percussion in the routine clinical examination of the chest.

Before Traube could receive full recognition in the teaching circles of Berlin, radical changes were needed. Following the political revolution of 1846-1848, which removed the anti-Semitic strictures and reformed University hospital appointments, Traube was appointed privatdocent at the University of Berlin. This allowed him to lecture on auscultation and percussion and was followed by an assistantship to Schönlein in the chest clinic at Charité. He was advanced to director of the chest division at Charité in 1853, assistant professor in 1857, and finally full professor in 1872.

Although Traube did not live to complete his academic tenure, he enjoyed a quarter of a century of increasingly productive work as an investigator, teacher, and clinical consultant. During this time, he declined professorial appointments in Heidelberg, Breslau, and Zurich. Undoubtedly these were difficult to reject, but Berlin held the greatest appeal as the center for scientific medicine. His physiological studies were collected and published in 1871 in volume 1, *Gesammelte Beiträge zur Pathologie und Physiologie.* Volume 2 contained many of his clinical studies; volume 3 was published posthumously, together with other clinical items from his *Tagebuch,* by his nephew, Fraenkel.

One physiological study and three clinical reports are excerpted in this essay. Other important contributions discuss suffocation, the pathology of fever, effects of digitalis and other drugs in the mangement of heart disease, use of thermometry in clinical medicine, and the protocol of a ruptured appendix, with complications. In 1865, Traube described the rhythmic variations in the tone of the vasoconstrictor center (Traube-Hering waves). The tracings appear as slow, rhythmic waves on the blood pressure record when animals are poisoned with curare so as to arrest respiration or when the blood is deficient in oxygen or charged with carbon dioxide. The aberrant waves are attributed to variations in response to the vasomotor center in the medulla.[2]

Traube received the MD degree from the University of Berlin in 1840, upon presentation of a dissertation entitled *Physiological and Pathological Specimens.* Before passing his state examination in 1841, he spent nearly a year in Vienna with Skoda in clinical medicine and with Rokitansky in pathological anatomy. He practiced medicine for sustenance upon return to Berlin, although he found pathological and physiological investigation of clinical conditions more alluring. However, clinical material was indispensable to his goal, and the Charité, the only public hospital in Berlin, was under the control of the military. In order to overcome the obstacle, he became an assistant to Natorp, an army physician on the staff. Even this benefit was largely nullified by a regulation prepared subsequently, which prohibited student examination of patients in Charité. Furthermore, Traube was a Jew, a victim of prevailing anti-Semitism aggravated by petty jealousies of his talents in the school and in the hospital. As if to prepare for a final onslaught, he revisited Vienna in 1843 for further work with his former teachers. He then settled in Berlin, imbued with a nihilistic doctrine in therapy but maintaining faith in the value of experimental work and its application to clinical problems.

Traube's attention to clinical details, as recorded in his *Tagebuch,* was as precise as the protocols in his physiological experiments and postmortem examinations. It is understandable then why his ward rounds and prepared lectures were so popular with students and practitioners alike. They were searching for a leader to bring to Germany the clinical advances enjoyed by Viennese and Parisian physicians. As one phase of such leadership, he established, together with Reinhardt and Virchow in 1846, a journal for experimental studies, entitled *Beitrage für Experimentale Pathologie und Physiologie.* The venture was abandoned after two issues, to be replaced the following year by the respected *Archiv für pathologische Anatomie und Physiologie und für klinische Medizin,* edited by Reinhardt and Virchow and later known as *Virchow's Archiv.* These publications contained many of the communications identifying the transition period in Germany into the new clinical medicine founded upon experimental studies.

When artificial respiration is discontinued in an animal paralyzed by worara and with both vagi cut, the increment in aortic blood-pressure may approach the original value. This increase may persist two or three minutes while the record usually assumes the form of a curve with wide wave-like undulations despite the fact that the animal is quiet and passive movements of the chest have ceased. The number of these undulations may increase to 7/minute, and the height of the curve may exceed 40 mm. The upward and downward portions are equally long and steep. The pulse-frequency remains unchanged.

The second phenomenon, the increase in blood pressure following CO_2 inhalation, is caused by the stimulation of the motor nerves of the heart. . . . Since the center of vasomotor activity rests in the medulla oblongata the periodic response appears under the influence of excess carbon dioxide. Carbon dioxide stimulates the vasomotor center and the vessels into periodic contraction and relaxation.

Traube's description of pulsus alternans is his most quoted contribution.[3]

In my experiments on animals I have for years been acquainted with a type of pulse, which I have named "pulsus bigeminus."

The nature of the pulsus bigeminus may be said to be this: following every two pulses which originate in the aorta, a longer pause ensues. This phenomenon is differentiated from the pulsus dicroticus by the fact that in the latter there is only one contraction of the heart for every two beats of the pulse, while in pulsus bigeminus there are two contractions of the heart, which follow one another rapidly and are separated from the preceding and succeeding contractions by a longer pause. For every two beats of the pulsus dicroticus there occur, as in the normal pulse, only two heart tones, while in pulsus bigeminus four heart tones are audible.

The following case, which came under my observation toward the close of last year, demonstrates a variation of the pulsus bigeminus; I designate it with the name of "pulsus alternans." It has certain features in common with the pulsus bigeminus in that the normal rhythm is not replaced by an arrhythmia but by a new extraordinary rhythm in which two consecutive pulses are in closer approximation to one another: it involves a succession of high and low pulses, in such a manner that a low pulse regularly follows a high pulse and this low pulse is separated from the ensuing high pulse by a shorter pause than that between it and the preceding high pulse.

An important monograph published in 1856 discussed the association between left ventricular hypertrophy and the kidney. Traube reported renal lesions caused by passive congestion of cardiac origin; his deductions were less critical than Bright's in attributing hypertension and subsequent hypertrophy of the heart to regressive structural changes in the kidney.[4]

The shrinking of the renal parenchyma has, therefore, two-fold consequences. It will act, first, by decreasing the blood volume which flows out in a given time from the arterial system into the venous system. It will, secondly, act by decreasing the amount of liquid which at the same time is removed from the arterial system as urinary secretion. As a result of both these conditions, particularly because of the latter, as is clear from what has just been stated, the mean pressure of the arterial system must increase. Consequently again, an increase in resistances is produced which oppose the emptying of the left ventricle.

Fraentzel, Traube's assistant at Charité, reported on a patient, afflicted with pneumonic consolidation and fibroserous exudate in the pericardium who exhibited [Traube's] semilunar space, an area on the chest wall over which it is possible to percuss the resonance of gastric air-bubble in the stomach.[5]

The percussion note on the left anterior chest was dulled as well as over the entire left side and onto the upper part of the back. In the lower part of the back it was completely dull. The "half-moon space" was still preserved but markedly smaller.

Why was the semilunar space diminished and why was vocal fremitus decreased? An area of tympanic percussion on the left thorax has been known for a long time. Investigation of this subject was undertaken recently by Prof. Traube. The results of this investigation may be summarized as follows:

a) The above mentioned area of tympanic dullness is shaped like a "half-moon": below, its border is the rim of the rib cage, above, it is limited by a bow-like line with its concavity pointed downward.

b) This half-moon space begins anteriorly below the 5th or 6th rib and extends along the edge of the thorax and posteriorly to the anterior end of the 9th or 10th rib.

c) Its greatest width approaches 3 to 3½ inches.

d) Percussion over this area differs not only in its tympanic character but also by its loudness in comparison with percussion over the area of normal lung.

e) When the lung expands during deep inspiration, the half-moon space becomes smaller and thus shows that the lung is capable of expanding.

f) A considerable increase of the semilunar space is usually a sign of immobility of the lower edge of the lung and serves as an indicator of scarring.

g) In the presence of pleural effusion the half-moon space may disappear and the beginning of reabsorption will be heralded by its reappearance; the progress of recovery will be best determined by the increase of the half-moon space.

h) During pneumonic infiltration of the entire left lung the half-moon remains either intact or only slightly narrowed.

Traube's struggle for status in the medical world is a story of intermittent frustration and achievement. He was deeply devoted to his science, frequently tactless in his criticism, sometimes unsociable, and jealous of those more successful. Despite these difficulties Traube was recognized as a skillful teacher, highly regarded by his pupils, always searching for sound explanations of clinical phenomena that could be supported or disproved through physiological experiments. His mind was uncluttered with speculative interpretations. He died from coronary sclerosis and congestive heart failure, following repeated attacks of angina pectoris only two months after his wife's death.

1. Leyden, E.: Biography of Ludwig Traube (Ger), *Charité-Ann* 2:767-800. 1877.

2. Traube, L.: The Periodic Activity of the Vasomotor Nervous System (Ger), *Zbl Med Wiss* 3:881-885, excerpt translated by Z. Danilevicius.

3. Traube, L.: The Case of Pulsus Bigeminus, Including Remarks on the Enlargement of the Liver in Valvular Insufficiency and on Acute Atrophy of the Liver (Ger), *Klin Wschr* 9: 185-188, 221-224, 1872, translated in Willius, F. A., and Keys, T. E.: *Classics of Cardiology*, vol 2, New York: H. Schuman, Inc., 1941.

4. Traube, L.: *The Interdependence of Heart and Kidney Disease* (Ger), Berlin: A. Hirschwald, 1856, excerpt translated in Fishman, A. P., and Richards, D. W., *Circulation of the Blood*, New York: Oxford University Press, 1964, p 496.

5. Fraentzel: Left Lung in Its Total Extent of Grey Hepatinization, Fibroserous Exudate in the Pericardium. Observations on the Half-Moon Space Shape and Vocal Fremitus (Ger), *Klin Wschr* 5: 509-511, 1868, excerpt translated by Z. Danilevicius.

Composite by G. Bako

Armand Trousseau (1801-1867

ARMAND TROUSSEAU, master expositor of clinical medicine in composition, in the clinic, and at the bedside, entered medicine after a short professorship in rhetoric. He was born in Tours, the capital of Old Gaul, where his father, a provincial boarding school keeper, had been improverished by the Napoleonic Wars.[1] Trousseau received his primary education at the lyceums of Orleans and Lyons and, at the age of 20, served on the faculty at the college of Chateauroux. His mind was turned to medicine by Bretonneau, leading physician of Tours, with whom he studied for three years in the Touraine Hospital. After receiving the MD degree at the University of Paris in 1825, Trousseau interned at the state asylum of Charenton. Subsequently, he continued the study of pathology at the veterinary school at Alfort, received professorial status in 1827, and prepared a text on veterinary surgery the following year. Later, under government direction, he investigated a diphtheria epidemic in the Sologne and accompanied Louis and Chervin on a yellow fever survey at Gibraltar, where he contracted the fever in a mild form.

Following formal medical training Trousseau longed to return to Tours to practice, but, upon the insistence and urging of Bretonneau, he entered competition in Paris and won. However, he spurned Parisian social life and declined to have his name proposed for the Academy of Medicine until he was certain in 1856 of his acceptance. He received his hospital appointment with the Central Bureau in 1831 and served successively at Hôtel Dieu, at St. Marguerite (renamed Hôpital Trousseau), at Necker, and at St. Antoine. From 1833 to 1848 Trousseau was coeditor with LeBaudy and Gouraud of the *Journal of Medical and Surgical Information*. In 1839, he was advanced to the chair of therapeutics in the university. There the wide recognition of the exceptional quality of his lectures led to the highest academic appointment as professor of clinical medicine and physician to Hôtel Dieu in 1852. He abandoned this post shortly before his death from carcinoma of the stomach, and returned to the department of therapeutics.

Trousseau neither discovered nor described in detail a new disease in the usual sense of the expression and was no peer of the German clinicians of his time in the advancement of scientific medicine. On the other hand, the enticing spirit of his personality, the brilliance of his lectures at Hôtel Dieu, and the clarity of his descriptions of clinical-pathological findings went unchallenged in the French school of clinical medicine in the mid-19th century. He shared with Velpeau the distinction of being the most talented pupil of Bretonneau and, in turn, attracted many followers to his service, including Da Costa of Philadelphia.

Trousseau's career may be divided into two portions, each concluding with a monumental treatise. As professor of therapeutics, he took his cue from Bretonneau and succeeded in expanding the limited means of management, largely bloodletting and purging, to include the rational use of herbs and chemicals, conservative abstinence from use of potent substances in some diseases, local surgical intervention in others; in substance, Trousseau led the therapeutic renaissance in French medicine. He was one of the first in Paris to perform a tracheotomy

in diphtheritic croup and popularized thoracentesis for pleural emphysema and exudative pleurisy. Several of his best agents were received from Bretonneau. The use of iron in the anemia of goiter and chlorosis was recommended; he revived the use of quinine in malarial fever and cod liver oil in rickets. The first edition of his *Therapeutics* was published with Pidoux as co-author in two volumes between 1836-1839.[2] The ninth edition appeared in 1875-1877. It was translated into English, Spanish, and Italian; the translation by Lincoln of the ninth edition was published in New York in 1880.[3] A comprehensive history of each agent or procedure introduced each section.

Trousseau's clinical lectures, which were rivaled only by those of Charcôt at Salpêtrière, first appeared in print in 1861.[4] They went through several editions in translation and were published in English by the New Sydenham Society. Especially notable contributions include the concept of aphasia as a deficiency of speech and thought, a description of cutaneous diphtheria, hemochromatosis, and infantile tetany. His presentations of unusual nervous diseases were guided by the elocution and clinical acumen of Duchenne. The eponymic term, Addison's disease, was assigned by him to chronic adrenal insufficiency.

Trousseau's report of cutaneous diphtheria,[5] which he probably observed during his first government assignment, has been translated by Shelley and Crissey. Excerpts from his description of infantile tetany,[6] produced by pressure over the nerve trunks or large vessels of the extremities (Trousseau's sign), now known to be associated with the disturbance of the electrolytes of body fluids, and a casual reference to bronzing of the skin in a patient with sugar diabetes, an enlarged liver and normal adrenals, probably a case of hemochromatosis, are provided from the English translation.[7]

It is not uncommon to see the complaint [tetany] in children, and even in infants from 1 to 2 years old; and you may recollect seeing a very remarkable case, that of a little girl 21 months old.

Of these pathological conditions, *diarrhoea*, especially when abundant and chronic, is the one which exerts the most striking influence.

The person has a sensation of tingling in the hands and feet, and then feels some hesitation, some impediment in the movements of his fingers and toes, which are not as free as usual. Tonic convulsions then set in, the affected limbs become stiff, and the will cannot completely overcome this stiffness. . . . The involuntary contraction increases, becomes painful, and is exactly like a cramp to which the patient compares it besides.

In the upper limbs, the thumb is forcibly and violently adducted; the fingers are pressed closely together, and semi-flexed over the thumb in consequence of the flexion of the metacarpophalangeal articulation; and the palm of the hand being made hollow by the approximation of its outer and inner margins, the hand assumes a conical shape, or better the shape which the accoucheur gives to it when introducing it into the vagina.

In the lower limbs, the toes are bent down towards the sole, and press against one another, while the big toe turns in under them, and the sole becomes hollowed out in the same manner as the hand. The dorsum of the foot is strongly arched, and the heel pulled up by the contracted muscles at the back of the leg, while the leg itself and the thigh are in a state of extension. The contractions may affect the upper and lower limbs simultaneously, or alternately; or they may be confined to one of them. So long as the attack is not over, the paroxysms may be reproduced at will . . . by simply *compressing the affected parts, either in the direction of their principal nerve-trunk, or over their bloody vessels, so as to impede the venous or arterial circulation.*

I discovered this influence of pressure by chance. I was present when a woman suffering from contractions was being bled from the arm at the Necker Hospital, and I saw a paroxysm return in the hand on the same side when the bandage was applied round the arm.

There are also cases [saccharine diabetes] in which temporary glucosuria appears consecutively to irritation affecting directly the liver. . . . Similar cases would perhaps have been more frequently recorded, had the attention of physicians been more directed to the relation between diabetes and diseases of the liver.

Notwithstanding the ravenous appetite, and the perfect digestion of the food, nutrition is badly accomplished, the nutritive functions being perverted by the diseaese; and consequently, diabetic patients rapidly lose flesh, and wasting of the body inevitably leads them to the tomb. This occurred in the case of a man aged 28, whom you have very recently seen in bed 3 of St. Agnes's ward.

Two years ago, this man was thrown out of work, and reduced to be a deliverer of newspapers. He was thus jaded, and without the means of restoring the waste of the body by adequate alimentation. . . . His step was tottering, his look expressionless, his countenance sad, and his tongue dry and rough. . . . His liver was enlarged, and very hard: it extended three finger breadths below the false ribs, and occupied the epigastric region: it was neither hobnailed nor painful.

It is right to add, that from the time this man came into the hospital, I was struck by the almost bronzed appearance of his countenance, and the blackish colour of his penis.

At the autopsy, we did not find any morbid state of the suprarenal capsules. . . . It was otherwise with the liver, which was at least twice its normal volume: the length of the right lobe was nineteen centimeters: the left lobe, which extended to the spleen, was twenty centimeters in length: and the total length of the liver was thirty-four centimeters. . . . There was well-marked cirrhosis; but the cirrhosis was hypertrophic.

1. Lasègue, C.: Eulogy of Professor Trousseau (Fr), *Arch Gen Med* 2:359-375, 1869.

2. Trousseau, A., and Pidoux, H.: *Traite de Therapeutique* (Fr), 2 vol, Paris: Bechet Jeune, 1836-1839.

3. Trousseau, A., and Pidoux, H.: *Treatise on Therapeutics*, New York: W. Wood & Co., 1880, translated by D. F. Lincoln.

4. Trousseau, A.: *Clinique Medicale de l'Hotel-Dieu de Paris* (Fr), 2 vol, J.-B. Bailliere, 1861.

5. Trousseau, A.: Cutaneous Diphtheria (Fr), *Arch Gen Med* 23:383-402, 1830, in Shelley, W., and Crissey, J.: *Classics in Clinical Dermatology*, Springfield, Ill: C. C Thomas, 1948.

6. Trousseau, A.: *Lectures on Clinical Medicine*, London: The New Sydenham Society, 1868, translated by P. V. Bazire.

7. Trousseau, A.: *Lectures on Clinical Medicine*, London: The New Sydenham Society, 1870, translated by J. R. Cormack.

Royal College of Physicians

Golding Bird (1814-1854)

GOLDING BIRD, physician of repute, lecturer on natural philosophy, electrical therapist, and clinical chemist, was a frequent contributor to the medical journals of London on these subjects of special interest. He took pride in rescuing the use of galvanic stimulation from the quacks and prepared a monograph on urinary deposits. Bird was born at Downham Market, Norfolk, began his instruction in the home of a clergyman, and continued in an ill-selected private school in London, where he busied himself during off-school hours with chemistry and botany. The young student gave instruction voluntarily to his classmates, to the displeasure of the headmaster.[1] His boyhood was over at 14 when he became apprenticed to apothecary William Pretty and later was accepted as a pupil at Guy's Hospital. Here Bird attracted the attention of Thomas Addison, whose friendship and respect were honored in the dedication of his monograph on urinary deposits. Another of his teachers, Sir Astley Cooper, exploited Bird's knowledge of the elements in the preparation of the chemical

discussion for a treatise on diseases of the breast.

The examinations at Apothecaries' Hall were passed by Bird with honors, but medical practice in London was pursued with little enthusiasm. However, his aims were unswerving and to best realize them, he petitioned successfully St. Andrews, for the MD degree. One of Bird's first assignments at Guy's was a series of lectures in natural philosophy and medical botany, which formed the basis of his *Elements of Natural Philosophy*, first published in 1839. He was elected assistant physician in 1843 and held this post until a year before his premature death at 39 from the complications of aortic regurgitation. An attack of acute rheumatic fever followed by chronic valvular heart disease impaired his physical activity, but not his scientific curiosity or professional industry. He was elected a Fellow of the Royal College of Physicians in 1845, where he lectured in materia medica, and the following year was made a Fellow of the Royal Society.

In addition to varied assignments at Guy's Hospital in natural philosophy and clinical pathology, Bird showed an early interest in electricity and the galvanic cell.

A communication in *Guy's Hospital Reports* contained many case reports of patients with hysterical paralysis who benefited remarkably from galvanic stimulation. One is described as follows.[2]

CASE 29—*Hysteric Paralysis of the Lower Half of the Body.*

JANE GOULDER, aged 15, a florid-looking girl, admitted into the hospital on October 6th. Six months ago she suffered from what was presumed to be an injury to the ancle, as she appeared to have lost all power over it; but a week afterwards, after an hysteric attack, she became completely paraplegic, having lost all power, whether of sensation or motion, over her lower extremities. At the time of her admission, she had slight return of power, being able to move her toes. She menstruates regularly, but with pain. Shocks were ordered to be passed from the sacrum to the toes daily.

Oct. 18. No remains of paralysis. She has recovered complete power over the lower extremities, and is capable of walking nearly as well as ever. Sensation has completely returned.

23. Presented, cured.

The chemical analysis of the urine and the investigation of urinary deposits were significant features of medical practice and medical science in the 19th century.[3] However, with the passage of time and the development of instruments that permit greater refinement, this significance has become almost obsolete. Oxaluria, Bird's disease, is an example. An increase in the quantity of oxalates in the urine of "nervous" patients was reported as a new and clinically helpful finding.[4]

... I have, in the extensive field of experience in public practice at my command, carried on these researches on a large scale, and have examined microscopically the urine in many hundreds of cases of various diseases. The result of this investigation has been the discovery of the comparative frequency of oxalate of lime in the urine in fine and well-defined octahedral crystals, and of the connection between the occurrence of this substance and the existence of certain definite ailments, all characterized by great nervous irritability.

Bird, a pious man, took an interest in the religious milieu of medical students and became one of the founders of the London Christian Medical Association. The following commentary, which might well have been included in his obituary, was prepared during his terminal illness.[5]

Dr. Golding Bird has the felicity and the profit of enjoying a name as well known as that of any other member of the corps of physicians. The profession marvel at him, the public gossip about him, the sick pine for his opinion, and the sound jot down his name in a corner of their note-books as a ready reference in the hour of nature's trial. If the medical attendant, sitting at the bedside during the progress of a doubtful case, mutter an unintelligible monosyllable in his patient's ear, an inquiring glance, accompanying the name of Golding Bird, is the prompt solution of the enigma. The fever-stricken, the palsied, the gouty, and the hypped, experience alike at one or other period in the progress of their maladies, some irregularity of the renal secretion, and forthwith apply to the oracle in Russell Square for the mystical utterance that shall clarify the "fons et origo mali," and remove their sufferings and their fears. He is the magician of the fountain, the water-sprite, that comes upon the stage at the crisis of fate to punish the evil genius, and dispense blessings abroad. The usual honorarium will at any time "call this spirit from the vasty deep," and win his beneficent influences.

1. Anon.: The Late Dr. Golding Bird. *Assoc Med J* 105 (n.s.): 1-6, 1855.
2. Bird, G.: Report on the Value of Electricity, as a Remedial Agent in the Treatment of Diseases, *Guy's Hosp Rep* 6:84-120, 1841.
3. Bird, G.: *Observations on Urinary Concretion and Deposits,* London: J. Churchill, 1842.
4. Bird, G.: Researches into the Nature of Certain Frequent Forms of Disease Characterized by the Presence of Oxalate of Lime in the Urine, *Lond Med Gaz* 2:637-643, 749-754, 793-799, 1842.
5. Bird, George: Golding Bird, M.D., *Med Circ Gen Med Adv* 1:230-231, 1852.

Composite by G. Bako

John Hughes Bennett (1812-1875)

JOHN HUGHES BENNETT was born in London and received his early education at the Grammar and Mount Radford Schools at Exeter.[1] His mother, an intelligent cultured woman, spent an unusual amount of time with her son, nurturing his literary and artistic tastes and instructing him in elocution and histrionics. Traveling on the Continent, especially in France, they spent many hours together before he began the study of medicine. In 1829, Bennett became apprenticed to Sedgwick, a surgeon at Maidstone; in 1833, he began formal training in medicine at the University of Edinburgh.

Lacking friends, but with a well-prepared mind and a zeal for medicine, Bennett promptly acquired a reputation as an industrious student of anatomy, physiology, and pathology. A ready discusser in the scientific sessions of the Royal Medical Society, he found participation in polemics sharpened his debating skill and enhanced his knowledge in the medical sciences. The highest scholastic honors were decreed in 1837 when he received the MD degree, with the recommendation of James Syme for his surgical thesis, and with the blessing of Charles Bell for his Inaugural Dissertation on the *Physiology and Pathology of the Brain.* Two postgraduate years were spent in France and a similar period in selected German clinics. In each country Bennett benefited from advanced methods of clinical instruction; his sojourn in France was particularly profitable in that he acquired proficiency in microscopy and the bedside teaching of medicine.

Returning to Edinburgh in 1841, Bennett instituted a series of lectures on histology which emphasized the importance of the microscope. Subsequently, he developed the course of instruction into a series of exercises on the practical teaching of physiology and pathology and organized a private museum of gross pathology to complement his microscopic collection. In 1848, he was elected to the chair of the Institutes of Medicine and was held responsible for the lectures on clinical medicine. His qualifications for the post included an excellent background and understanding of physiology, pathology, and management of disease, capacity for delivering outstanding lectures from the podium, and skill in promoting a close liaison between pupil and teacher at the bedside. This led to a pattern of performance in which the student participated maximally in the examination of the patient in the comprehensive survey of the case.

Bennett was a frequent contributor to medical periodicals. In 1846, he took over the editorship and became owner of the *London and Edinburgh Monthly Journal of Medical Sciences.* A few months later this journal amalgamated with the *Northern Journal of Medicine,* which in turn was sold and later reacquired. His obituary in the *British Medical Journal* lists more than 100 contributions to the literature and seven treatises in addition to his inaugural dissertation.[2] His *Clinical Lectures on the Principles and Practice of Medicine,* which passed through five British and six United States editions, as well as translations into French, Russian, and Hindu,

proved to be his most popular treatise and typified his greatest accomplishments. Among Bennett's many case reports and scientific communications, his biographers note particularly his discovery of an *Aspergillus* in the sputum during life and in the lung postmortem of a patient seen at the Royal Infirmary; a long dissertation on the benefits of cod liver oil in the treatment of gout, rheumatism, and scrofula; and, on the basis of statistical evaluations, the rejection of mercury and bleeding for uncomplicated pneumonia. The clinical and pathological findings in a case of leukemia, with hypertrophy of the spleen and liver, was recognized as an unusual observation. However, no thought was given to the possibility that the morbid processes were part of a hematologic disorder, although Bennett later used the term "Leucocythamia." The initial report appeared at essentially the same time as the description by Virchow of a case of "white blood."[3]

The very remarkable case about to be related derives unusual interest from its similitude in almost every respect to the one just recorded by Dr. Craigie. Although the most evident lesion during life was enlargement of the spleen, I agree with him in thinking that the immediate cause of death was owing to the presence of purulent matter in the blood, notwithstanding the absence of any recent inflammation, or collection of pus in the tissues.

The blood throughout the body much changed. . . . The red portion was of a brick-red colour; it did not present the dark purple smooth and glossy appearance of a healthy coagulum, but was dull and somewhat granular on section, and when squeezed readily broke down into a grumous pulp. The yellow portion was of a light yellow colour, opaque and dull, in no way resembling the gelatinous appearance of a healthy decolorized clot. When squeezed out of the veins as was sometimes accidentally done where they were divided, it resembled thick creamy pus.

The *spleen* also enormously enlarged with simple hypertrophy. It was of a spindle shape, largest in the centre, tapering towards the extremities. It weighed seven pounds twelve ounces. It measured in length fourteen inches; in breadth, at its widest part, seven inches; and in thickness, four and a-half inches. Toward its anterior surface was a yellow firm exudation, about an inch deep, and three inches long. The peritoneum, also covering a portion of its anterior surface, was thickened, opaque, and dense over a portion about the size of the hand.

The *lymphatic glands* were every where much enlarged. In the groin they formed a large cluster, some being nearly the size of a small hen's-egg, and several being that of a walnut. The axillary glands were similarly affected.

MICROSCOPIC EXAMINATION.—The yellow coagulum of the blood was composed of coagulated fibrin in filaments, intermixed with numerous pus corpuscles, which could be readily squeezed out from it when pressed between glasses.

Bennett, suffering from occasional attacks of gouty arthritis, spent his three final winters in the south of France. The removal of a bladder stone was followed by complications and death. Analysis showed the stone to be composed of lithic acid, a characteristic finding for a sufferer of gout. Postmortem examination showed an extradural tumor on the right and flattening of the cerebral convolutions.

1. M'Kendrick, J. G.: John Hughes Bennett, obituary, *Edinburgh Med J* 21:466-474 (Nov) 1875.
2. Anon: John Hughes Bennett, M.D., F.R.S.E., obituary, *Brit Med J* 2:473-478 (Oct 9) 1875.
3. Bennett, J. H.: Case of Hypertrophy of the Spleen and Liver, in Which Death Took Place From Suppuration of the Blood, *Edinburgh Med Surg* 64:413-423, 1845.
4. Bennett, J. H.: Case of Cerebral Tumour, *Brit Med J* 1:988-989 (May 16) 1885.

Gabriel Gustav Valentin
(1810-1883)

GUSTAV VALENTIN, son of a Jewish goldsmith of Breslau, displayed an encyclopedic knowledge and was endowed with an enviable retentive memory.[1] He is recognized as one of a small coterie of experimental physiologists in central Europe in the 19th century who participated in the evolutionary development of experimental physiology as a basic discipline. He attended first a private school and, at the age of 11, entered the Maria Magdalena Gymnasium in Breslau, where he pursued general as well as Talmudic studies. At the age of 18, Valentin entered the University of Breslau for the study of medicine and natural science. Here he came under the influence of Purkyně, founder of the laboratory for experimental physiology.

When Valentin graduated from the medical faculty in 1832, his scholarly thesis in Latin displayed his great zeal for experimental

physiology in the discussion of the embryonic development of muscle tissue. Valentin, ineligible for an academic appointment at a Prussian university because he was a Jew, began the practice of medicine. He was allowed, however, to continue his research in

Composite by G. Bako

Purkyně's laboratory and subsequently gained an appointment at the University of Bern.

Early in his career Valentin utilized the microscope to investigate the ramifications of the nerve-muscle endings, recognized the distinction between cells and fibers in nervous tissue but failed to appreciate their functional unity, described the nucleolus within the nucleus, and reported on the development of the eye of vertebrates and the artificial production of freaks in the chick embryo. He coauthored with Purkyně and Pappenheim studies on the histology of the mucous membrane of the stomach, and with Purkyně contributed to the understanding of the function of ciliary epithelium. This work, which according to Purkyně was primarily Valentin's, related embryology and general physiology to comparative embryology and comparative physiology. The Academy of Sciences of France awarded him their gold medal for the cilial study in 1835. Excerpts of the preliminary report published in *Müller's Archiv*, antedating the monograph prepared in Latin one year later as follow:[2]

> Last spring one of us observed with the microscope at autopsy obvious motion about the axis in small portions of mucosa of the oviducts in rabbits which had been impregnated three days earlier. The other confirmed this phenomenon and recognized it immediately as a shimmering movement such as light on water. Therefore we investigated the entire oviduct and sex organs and concluded that these movements are always present but that they appear with different intensity in different areas. They are most marked in the tubes, less so in the horns, even less in parts of the uterus. The most rapid movements are in the mouth of the oviducts. We next investigated animals not in gestation and found similar movements.
>
> The shimmering movements are confined to the respiratory tract and the female sex organs in mammals, birds and mature amphibia. Not a trace of shimmering was observed in the entire gastrointestinal tract in vertebrates. In amphibia, snakes, salamanders, birds, and mammals, shimmering movement throughout the entire mucosa of the oviducts in the impregnated as well as in the normal may be observed. This is also true for the mucosa of the respiratory tract from the largest to the smallest segments that can be investigated. The larynx and the mucous lining of the mouth and nose show no trace of the phenomenon.
>
> Since the movements occur along the whole surface of the mucosa it is necessary to use a strong lens. According to our observations, the shimmering is caused by cilia which should not be misinterpreted in the female genitalia or the respiratory organs as anything else.

In 1835, Valentin was invited by the German University of Dorpat to join its faculty on the condition that he be baptized. He rejected this offer as well as one from Königsberg but shortly after accepted the professorship of physiology, anatomy, and botany at the University of Bern, where he lectured in French as well as German. He lost his Prussian citizenship when he moved to Bern but in 1850 became a naturalized Swiss. He remained in Bern throughout his professional days, rejecting offers from the universities of Tübingen, Utrecht, Marburg, Brussels, and Lüttich.

One of Valentin's ventures was the publishing of the quarterly *Repertorium für Anatomie und Physiologie*, media for his investigations, a review of the current literature, and a critical appraisal of the work of other scientists. The *Repertorium* was discontinued in 1840 when he transferred his abstracting responsibilities to Cannstatt's *Jahresberichte* and published many of his own investigations in *Müller's Archiv*. Other major writings included a *Handbook on Comparative Embryology*[3] (1835), a *Handbook of Physiology of Man*[4] (1844), and the *Fundamentals of Human Physiology* (1846), which went through several editions and was translated into Dutch and English.

Upon coming to Bern, Valentin was allowed to choose his field for investigation. He studied hibernation and the spermatozoa of the bear, the heraldic animal of the city; selected aspects of parasitology and marine life to produce a monograph on echinodermata and another on the electric eel; developed the use of polarized light; discovered the pancreatic diastase; and detected lithium in the body.[5] Although physics and mathematics were fundamental tools in these investigations, he showed a compassion for clinical implications as illustrated by his work on the accelerator effect of the sympathetic nerve on the heart, the constrictor effect of nervous stimulation on blood vessels and lymphatic vessels; and identification of myohemoglobin as the coloring substance in muscle, rather than the presence of hemoglobin from the red cells in the vascular channels.

Valentin, rich in his international associates, included among them von Humboldt, Anders Retzius, Corti, Müller, Remak, and C. Vogt. Honors included a degree from the University of Bern and membership in many scientific societies. He was appointed dean of the faculty at Bern but never served as rector. Temperamentally Valentin was an obstinate man, and instigator of scientific polemics, suspicious of scientific criticism, and jealous of his reputation. He was quick to criticize his closest associates who might be either his teachers, peers, or pupils. However, he lost his scientific arguments with Müller and Remak.

1. Kisch, B.: Forgotten Leaders in Modern Medicine, *Trans Amer Philos Soc* 44:142-192, 1954.

2. Purkinje, J., and Valentin, G.: Further Observations on Ciliary Movement (Ger), *Arch Anat Physiol (Wiss Med)*, 1834, pp 391-400, excerpts translated by E. Longar.

3. Valentin, G.: "History of the Development of the Human Ovum," in *Handbook on Comparative Embryology*

(Ger), Berlin: A. Rücker, 1835, translated and abstracted by M. Barry, *Edinburgh Med Surg J* 45:393-423, 1836.

4. Valentin, G.: *Handbook of Physiology of Man* (Ger), 2 vol, Braunschweig: F. Bieweg & Sohn, 1844.

5. Hintzsche, E.: *Gabriel Gustav Valentin (1810-1883)* (Ger), Bern: P. Haupt, 1953.

Friedrich Gustave Jacob Henle (1809-1885)

IF A CONTEMPORARY INVESTIGATOR in the medical sciences is sufficiently talented and ultimately so fortunate as to be credited with one major scientific contribution, this is a fair allotment. On the other hand, a century ago, the laboratory was so fertile a field for investigation that it was possible for a medical scientist to be accountable for divers discoveries of great significance, meanwhile living a well-rounded life as determined by interest and participation in the arts and humanities. Jacob Henle was such an individual. He was judged the greatest histologist of his day and one of the great anatomists of all eras.[1]

Henle was born in 1809 of Jewish parents who renounced Judaism a decade later. The community of his birth was Fürth near Nürnberg, Germany; the period, one of deep political unrest. Henle was richly endowed intellectually; his parents were eager to germinate his intellectual potentialities. Such an environment was propitious for maximum exploitation of anatomical and physiologic researches. His father was a successful merchant and, typical of many cultured persons of central Europe, was interested in music and the arts. Like father, like son—Jacob became an accomplished violinist, violoncellist, and flutist. At one stage of his education, music was all absorbing. The move of the family from Mainz to Coblenz contributed to the abandonment of a career in music. Henle came under the influence of Johannes Müller, the prince of anatomy, at the University of Bonn. Müller, a leader of the new movement in scientific research in Germany—particularly in physiology and the physiologic concepts which were constructed upon anatomic principles—siphoned Henle's talents to medicine. One of the first assignments from Müller was the preparation of the illustrations for the professor's book on glands (Müller's glands). This provided the pupil with an unusual opportunity to display his knowledge of anatomy with the stylus and the brush. A misstep as a student at the university was affiliation with the Burschenschaft, a society with avowed liberal tenets. It sought German unity, political freedom, and a constitutional government. While a member of the society, he suffered a wound in the left cheek in a friendly duel. More important was the blight in subsequent years in the minds of certain state officials in his having been associated with a society that was considered so far left as to be stigmatized as revolutionary.

In keeping with the then current practice of showing no favoritism between universities, Henle studied for a time at Heidelberg, but returned to Bonn and received his MD degree at the age of 23. Two years later when Müller was appointed professor of anatomy and physiology at the University of Berlin, Henle had already preceded him to the capital city and was serving as prosector for the anatomical museum. The following year he applied for the position of privatdocent. This application was delayed by a 26-day prison sentence imposed as a result of his previous association with the Burschenschaft. Some time later, he was sentenced to incarceration for 6 years in a forest camp and deprivation of state office. He probably would have been compelled to serve this sentence had not some of his friends, particularly Alexander von Humboldt (Humboldt Current), intervened. The years in Berlin with Müller were extremely fruitful. Henle had acquired an international reputation in his early 30's through his brilliant publications in anatomy and histology. This led to a call as professor of anatomy and physiology from Zürich, Switzerland, the land of liberty in Europe in the 19th century. The School of Rational Medicine was founded as well as the *Journal of Rational Medicine*, with Carl von Pfeufer as co-editor. The next move was to Heidelberg as professor of anatomy. About this time, he was intrigued by the possibility of emigrating to America. I question whether he would have made the contributions to medical science in America in the pre-Civil War days that were his by remaining in Germany. The government of Baden honored him with the *Hofrat*, a distinguished decoration. The last move was to Göttingen, where he lived out his life as professor of anatomy and taught, among others, Robert Koch.

It is apparent from his biographies that Henle abounded in social graces. He loved the theater and found time to organize musical and theatrical circles. He was gregarious and friendly, an expert dancer and horseback rider; his home was a center for artists. At one time he was in love with the daughter of Felix Mendelssohn. After being thrice thwarted in serious love affairs, he married a beautiful girl, Elise, from a lower social stratum. Any deficiency in social charm was corrected prior to marriage under the skillful tutelage of Henle's sister. The partnership was severed subsequently in Zürich, where Elise died. But their devotion was not forgotten. It was the basis for a novel, a play, and verse—so widely known and tragic was their fate.

Henle's scientific contributions began with his inaugural dissertation for the Doctorate in Medicine. This was not based upon a review of the literature, as was customary for many students, but was a report of original dissections and a description of the embryology of the eye. In later years, he returned to the studies on the eye and described the fibers, the construction, and development of the lens, and the physiology of the lachrymal canal. More than a dozen eponymic terms are attributed to Henle. These include the trachoma glands of Henle (small tubular glands in the deep folds of the conjunctiva), Henle's elastic membrane (a fenestrated layer between the outer and middle tunics of certain arteries), Henle's membrane (the lamina basalis chorioideae), Henle's fenestrated membrane (a subendothelial fibroelastic fenestrated layer in the intima of an artery), Henle's stratum nerveum (thin fibrous layer outside of the sheath of Schwann), Henle's warts, Henle's layer (of the hair follicle), Henle's spine, Henle's fissures, Henle's ligament (between the sheaths of the rectus muscle and the transverse abdominal muscle), Henle's ampula, the canal of Henle (a portion of the uriniferous tubule), Henle's cells (in seminiferous tubules), Henle's fibrin, Henle's internal cremaster (fibres of the gubernaculum testis), and Henle's sphincter (of the prostatic urethra). The Henle tubule of the loop of Henle of the kidney, already noted as the canal of Henle, is the best-remembered eponym.[2]

In examining the anatomical characteristics of the medulla of the kidney we discovered a new type of canaliculi which do not enter the open urinary tubules but end at the cortex, constantly decreasing in number in the direction of the papillae. . . . Each pair of tubules forms a horseshoe loop which penetrates deep into the medulla from the cortex.

The tiny tubules of the medulla have coarse, granular epithelium in the pyramid and clear columnar epithelium deeper in the medulla, while the tip of the loop contains clear and cylindrical epithelial cells and the ends of the loop-like tubules closer to the cortical substance are composed of coarse and granular epithelium.

Possibly Henle's greatest anatomical work concerned the concept of the epithelial tissues of the body. It was not pure chance that all free surfaces of the body and inner surfaces of the tubes, canals, and cavities were lined with epithelium. The cells of the superficial layers of epithelium were larger than the nonvascular cells in the deeper strata. Henle demonstrated that the vibrating cilia are superimposed upon structures that represent modified epithelium. This revelation was an important building block for the cellular theory as developed by Schleiden and Schwann. Simultaneously with Purkyně, he described the structure of hepatic cells. Henle's explanation of metastasis in neoplastic disease was the forerunner of the cellular pathology of Virchow. The presence of smooth muscle in the middle coats of the small arteries was fundamental to the theory of vasomotor action. A rational explanation of fever contributed to the germ theory of infection. Living organisms were thought to be the cause of infection and contagious diseases and to be invisible because they were so like normal structure. The essay "Von den Miasmen und Kontagien" was based upon deductions only and contained no experimental data in support of his concepts that subsequently were found to be sound. The use of dyes by Koch 3 decades later in the staining of bacterial organisms confirmed Henle's theory.[3]

The contagious agent is a substance which in the course of a disease is excreted by the sick organism— I do not say produced in the diseased body, as one usually expresses it—and which communicated to healthy individuals, produces the same disease in them.

The contagions are divided into the transient and the fixed. The latter are communicated by direct contact, the former through the atmosphere. The fixed contagions may be transmitted or inoculated by means of matter which has been taken from the sick organism, the transient ones cannot be transmitted.

It is easy to prove that contagions and miasmas actually multiply within the diseased organisms. An atom of pox poison can produce a rash over the entire body . . . is again capable of infecting a new organism, etc.: whether this can proceed indefinitely is still doubtful. The contagious matter, however, does not multiply only in the entire body during the course of the contagious disease, but also locally.

I will now adduce the reasons which prove that the matter of the contagions is not only organic, but also animate, indeed endowed with individual life, and that it stands in the relation of a parasitic organism to the diseased body.

The ability to multiply by assimilating foreign materials is known to us only in living organic beings. No dead chemical substance, not even an organic one, multiplies at the expense of any other; when brought together, they always enter into combinations from which the original quantities of the materials acting upon each other may again be separated.

Fermentation is considered proof of the contrary, and it is assumed that during fermentation the ferment reproduces itself, since the smallest quantity of the latter suffices to maintain fermentation in the largest quantities of the fermentable fluids, as long as there is sugar to be converted into alcohol and carbonic acid can escape.

The disease begins with the entrance of the parasitic organisms or their germs. The entrance occurs only in mucous membranes, as far as they are accessible from without, or in injured places of the external skin, and indeed, often in sharply defined regions, according to the species of the parasites.

In addition to founding a scientific journal, Henle was a prolific writer. He composed 3 large treatises illustrated with many of his own drawings. In Zürich *The Handbook of General Anatomy* was composed; in Heidelberg he completed *The Handbook of Rational Pathology;* and in Göttingen the monumental work, *Handbook of Systematic Anatomy* together with an *Atlas* was prepared. The last major contribution was a monograph on the "Growth of the Human Nail and the Horsehoof."

Henle died in Göttingen at the age of 76, having refused the professorial chair in Berlin in the interim. He preferred to remain in the delightful university community at the foot of the Harz Mountains, which was appealing also to Coleridge, Longfellow, Edward Everett, and Bismarck. There were no railroads or industry in Göttingen when Henle accepted the professorship. A monument on the edge of town to Gauss and Weber honors the inventors in 1833 of the electromagnetic telegraph. There is also a statue to Wohler, the chemist, the synthesizer of urea and the discoverer of aluminum. In the city square, the goose-girl fountain by Nissen is pointed out to tourists. In recent times, Nobel Laureates who taught at Göttingen include Windaus, Planck, and Butenandt. The Anatomy Institute of Henle (Theatrium Anatomican) at Göttingen became the Physiologic Institute early in this century. Its director was Hermann Rein, who did so much to recapture the leadership in physiology for Germany between the two World Wars.

1. Robinson, V.: *Life of Jacob Henle*, New York: Medical Life Company, 1921.

2. Henle, F. G. J.: *Anatomy of the Kidney* (Ger), *Akad Wissensch* 10:223-254, Göttingen: 1862, except translated by Z. Danilevicius.

3. Henle, F. G. J.: *Miasmata and Contagia* (Ger), *Path Untersuch*, Berlin, 1840, pp 1-82, translated by Rosen, G.: *Bull Inst Hist Med* 6:907-983, 1938.

Composite by G. Bako

Claude Bernard (1813-1878)

CLAUDE BERNARD and Louis Pasteur, contemporaries in French medicine, have suffered quite different fates posthumously. Bernard, who defined the rules and procedures for experimental medicine, is credited with significant advances in carbohydrate metabolism, the sympathetic nervous system, and anesthesia. Beyond this, the essence of his accomplishments appears misty—he is almost a mythical figure. Hollywood has not glorified him in a *cordon bleu* motion picture. The spiritual aura of Pasteur, on the other hand, is familiar to almost every child in grammar school. His immediate contributions were immeasurably greater than those of Bernard, but his scientific horizon was convergent rather than divergent. Claude Bernard was the spirit of experimental medicine. His philosophical scientific models are interwoven in the basic elements of contemporary clinical investigation.

Bernard was born in the village of Saint Julien, Department of the Rhone, near Villefranche.[1] His father, a vineyard keeper, was unsuccessful financially and found it necessary to teach school in the village to augment a meagre income. Classes were held in the home; school buildings were lacking. At the age of 8, Claude's instruction was entrusted to the village curé. The avowed purpose was concentration in Latin. Instruction was continued in the Jesuit College of Villefranche and included Greek, arithmetic, and geometry. Natural science and modern languages were largely omitted. His scholastic performance was unimpressive. Especially apparent was a dislike for reading which seemed to be a waste of good time. At the age of 18, Claude was apprenticed to a pharmacist since the family could no longer continue full-time schooling. The chores as a pharmacist-apprentice included the delivery of drugs to a veterinary school. It is reasonable to suspect that such exposure awakened an interest in animal experimentation and, possibly, experimental medicine.

There is no evidence that documents a latent desire for playwriting, until the ennui of the pharmacy regressed to boredom. The first of the two plays composed initially, published in 1833, proved to be a mild success. The plot of the second was developed around King John in an historical tragedy. In Bernard's efforts to stage the production in Paris, he obtained an introduction to Girardin, famous drama critic and professor of literature at the Sorbonne. Girardin read the manuscript, and unimpressed, said, "You have worked in a pharmacy; therefore you can study medicine. You lack the temperament for a dramatic author."[1] Thus, at the age of 21, Bernard abandoned literature as a potential career and entered the medical school in Paris.

Under continued financial harassment, Bernard soon sought substantial support by tutoring in a girls' school. Even at this stage of formal learning, Bernard appears as an average medical student—unhurried in the acquisition of the fundamentals of anatomy, theoretical and practical. But anatomy was a critical discipline for an experimental physiologist. Structure and form proved indispensable for the development of the germinating new natural science, the physiology of animals and man. This in turn was the esoteric reality of medical science, the 19th century's contribution to the growth of clinical medicine.

In a competitive examination for internship, Bernard's performance was barely passing. The turning point in his career may have occurred with the appointment to Magendie's service at Hotel Dieu. This distinguished teacher and investigator was quick to recognize his pupil's talents and assigned Bernard to neurophysiological problems. The first manuscript outlined the anatomy of the chorda tympani nerve and its relation to facial paralysis. His thesis for the MD degree at the Collège de France concerned gastric juice and its role in nutrition. Bernard remained in the experimental laboratory following graduation and never practiced medicine.

It is often said of great men that they "lived before their time." This presumably implies that their thinking was in advance of their contemporaries and that their contributions provided a basis for subsequent development of an area of science or learning. Bernard explored the field of experimental medicine "before his time." The investigations concerned physiology; the art of experimentation embraced the concepts advanced. The investigator, in the development of a speculative possibility or an appealing reflection, challenges Nature for an answer. The experiment is planned on a working hypothesis; the observations are recorded without bias.[2]

. . . from the point of view of the art of investigation, observation and experiment should be considered only as *facts* brought out by investigators, and we have added that methods of investigation do not differentiate the men who observe from the men who experiment. Where then, you will ask, is the difference between observers and experimenters? It is here: we give the name observer to the man who applies methods of investigation, whether simple or complex, to the study of phenomena which he does not vary and which he therefore gathers as nature offers them. We give the name experimenter to the man who applies methods of investigation, whether simple or complex, so as to make natural phenomena vary, or so as to alter them with some purpose or other, and to make them present themselves in circumstances or conditions in which nature does not show them. In this sense, observation is investigation of a natural phenomenon, and experiment is investigation of a phenomenon altered by the investigator.

In 1844 at the age of 31, Bernard competed for the position of assistant professor of anatomy and physiology in order to devote his entire energies to experimental physiology.

By then a private laboratory had been built, directly opposite the site of Dr. Guillotin's experimental work-shop. These were difficult years, but also the most productive scientifically. Bernard's first substantial academic appointment came in 1847 as a substitute lecturer to Magendie at the Collège de France. In his lecture he stated:[1]

The scientific medicine which it is my duty to teach you does not exist. The only thing to do is to lay the foundations upon which future generations may build, to create the physiology upon which this science may later be established.

Bernard's treatise, *An Introduction to the Study of Experimental Medicine*, published in 1865, reported the cumulative thoughts of his abundant scientific career.[2] Meanwhile, his communications appeared in the publications of the Academy of Sciences and in the *Archives Générales de Médicine*. He was a charter member of the Société de Biologie. By the age of 38, he had won, on 3 successive occasions, the prize in experimental physiology as well as the Red Ribbon of the Legion of Honor for investigations on digestion and the pancreas. Magendie had much to do with selecting the medalist. The origin of sugar in the animal body was included in the studies on digestion. Bernard had previously shown that the injection of cane sugar into the vein of a dog was followed by the spilling of sugar in the urine. On the other hand, if the cane sugar had been exposed to gastric juice prior to injection, the urine remained sugar-free. The glycogenic function of the liver was revealed by a series of precisely-planned experiments. It was generally accepted that sugar was continuously present in the blood of animals, irrespective of the type of food eaten or the interval following the last meal. Sugar was also detected in the hepatic vein. Bernard concluded that[3]

. . . 2. the formation of this sugar takes place in the liver, and that it is independent of a sweet or starchy alimentation. 3. That this formation of sugar in the liver begins to operate in the animal before birth, and consequently before the direct ingestion of foodstuffs. . . . In diabetics, it is known that the sugar disappears from the urine in the last period of the life; it disappears equally from the liver, because the liver of a diabetic which I had occasion to examine in this connection contained no sugar.

Continuing his experimental studies on carbohydrate metabolism, Bernard observed that a puncture (piqûre) of the floor of the fourth ventricle of the brain in dogs produced diabetes temporarily. This observation was made quite by chance. He reasoned that liver glucose was under the influence of the vagi and that severance of the vagi would interrupt the elaboration of sugar from the liver. Contrariwise, stimulation of the vagi would produce increased formation of sugar. The experiment was negative. The next step was to enhance stimulation by means of a wound in the brain at the point of emergence of a nerve. The brain was punctured near the exit of the vagus nerve. The first rabbit showed glycosuria. A number of failures followed the first positive finding. Fortune favored the area selected for puncture in the first experiment. In another series, severing the vagi and puncturing the brain produced the same glycosuria as if the vagi were intact. The original premise was false. It was apparent that sympathetic nerves rather than the vagi were responsible for the glycosuria. His brief report on the diabetic dog is as follows:[4]

Mr. Claude Bernard had already demonstrated to this Society that by puncturing a definite area in the fourth ventricle of rabbits these animals can be rendered diabetic. This remarkable experiment had not been performed by him on other animals. Today he reported to the Society that he repeated the experiment on a dog and that the experiment was a complete success. The urine examined before the experiment did not contain any sugar; twenty minutes after the puncture (the fourth ventricle) it contained an appreciable amount of sugar. Otherwise all the elements of urine, such as urea and phosphates, remained unchanged.

Extension of the studies on pancreatic juice and its role in digestion demonstrated that[5]

... pancreatic fluid is intended, to the exclusion of all other intestinal fluids, to modify in a special manner, or, said in another way, to digest the neutral fat material contained in the food, and to permit in this manner their later absorption by the chyliferous vessels.

Prior to this observation, digestion was believed to be complete by the time the bolus had left the stomach. Other studies included the toxic effects of curare and carbon monoxide, the function of the brain, production

of heat in asphyxia, vasomotor nerves of the salivary glands, exophthalmos, catalepsy, innervation of the kidney, anesthesia and asphyxia, defoliation of beets, and alcoholic fermentation. Bernard noted that cutting the sympathetic nerve in the neck causes an increase of temperature on the ipsilateral side of the face. This contribution was judged worthy of his fourth and last prize in experimental physiology by the Academy of Sciences. Shortly after, he was appointed chairman of the committee for awarding prizes— most likely an act of good judgment by the Academy to promote wider distribution of this honor. In 1854, a chair of general physiology in the Faculty of Sciences at the Sorbonne was created. The following year, upon the death of Magendie, he succeeded to the Professorship of Medicine at the Collège de France, the most coveted post in the medical sciences in France. Napoleon III built a fine laboratory for him at the Sorbonne and another at the Museum de History Naturelle (1868). He was appointed a senator in 1869 by Imperial decree.

Bernard's married life was not tranquil. He was an avowed vivisectionist; whereas his wife supported the French equivalent of the Society for the Prevention of Cruelty to Animals. A decree of separation was finally granted in 1870.

His health began to fail not long after, which has been attributed unjustly to the unsanitary condition of the experimental laboratory at the Collège. Attacks of pyelonephritis which began in 1860 left him in poor health. No scientific contributions comparable to the earlier studies were produced after that. The field of experimental medicine and experimental physiology, to which he gave so much for so many years, continued to benefit from the product of his brilliant mind posthumously. The year following his death, his technique of cardiac catheterization on dogs was published.[6]

But the most interesting point to us is the study of the heart by means of catheterization, that is to say, by the introduction of catheters in the great vessels that we advance until they get into the heart. . . . It is quite easy to arrive at the right heart. To this effect we introduce a catheter in the jugular vein, entering directly into the heart. . . . It is more difficult to get into the left heart.

Bernard clearly was a great scientist, far in advance of his time. His scientific contributions, theoretical and practical, form the philosophical and methodological basis for clinical medicine today, a century after Bernard firmly established them.

1. Olmsted, J. M. D.: *Claude Bernard: Physiologist,* New York and London: Harper & Brothers, Publishers, 1938.
2. Bernard, C.: *An Introduction to the Study of Experimental Medicine,* H. C. Greene (trans.) New York: The Macmillan Company, 1927.
3. Bernard, C.: *The Origin of Sugar in the Animal Body, Arch gén Med* 18:303-319, series 4, 1848, translated in *Med Classics* 3:567-580 (Jan), 1939.
4. Bernard, C.: *Experimental Diabetes in a Dog, Compt Rend Soc Biol* 1:60, 1850, excerpt translated by Z. Danilevicius.
5. Bernard, C.: *Pancreatic Juice and Its Role in the Phenomenon of Digestion, Arch gén Med* 19:60-81, series 4, 1894, translated in *Med Classics* 3:600-617 (Jan), 1939.
6. Bernard, C.: *Leçons de Physiologie Operatoire,* pp 277-286, Paris: 1879, Ballière, (trans.), Buzzi, A.: *Claude Bernard on Cardiac Catheterization, Amer J Cardiol* 4:405 (Sept), 1959.

National Library of Medicine

Carl Ludwig (1816-1895)

CARL FREDERICK WILHELM LUDWIG'S influence on 19th century physiological thought, directly through his scientific contributions and indirectly through his pupils, was remarkable. This preceptor to a multitude was born in Witzenhausen on the Weser near Kassel. His father, an officer in the Napoleonic wars, disabled in service, was rewarded with a civilian post in Hanau. After finishing at the Gymnasium, Ludwig attended the University of Marburg, where he suffered facial wounds in dueling and temporarily lost his academic standing as a result of unacceptable political activities. After interim courses at Erlangen and Bamburg, he returned to Marburg in 1839 and received the doctor's degree.[1] He became prosector in anatomy under Fick and the following year was admitted to the faculty, offering a dissertation on the mechanism of renal secretion.[2] Ludwig changed academic titles and university professorships several times over a period of 25 years. He advanced with each new appointment, maintaining throughout a flow of brilliant contributions to a grand mosaic of general physiology. He was first a professor of comparative anatomy at Marburg in 1846, three years later, professor of anatomy and physiology at Zürich. In 1855, he was called to Vienna as professor of physiology and zoology at the academy for army physicians, the Josephinum; a decade later he succeeded Ernst Weber in Leipzig, becoming professor of physiology and director of the projected Physiological Institute.

In retrospect, Ludwig's career seems meticulously planned. His training in anatomy provided indispensable knowledge of structure for the investigation of physiological phenomena, which proved useful in refutation to the then prevailing vitalistic doctrines. He rejected the existence of a mystical vital force at the command of a whimsical power and gave witness to the new knowledge which respected only chemical and physical laws, measurable and reproducible. In the introduction to the second edition (1858) of his *Textbook of Human Physiology,*[3] his thoughts were introduced as follows.

The problem of scientific physiology is to determine the functions of the animal body and deduce them as a necessity from its elementary conditions.

Whenever the body of an animal is subdivided to its ultimate parts, one always finally arrives at a limited number of chemical atoms, and upon phenomena which are explainable on the assumption of a light ether and electricity. One draws the conclusion in harmony with this observation, that all forms of activity arising in the animal body must be a result of the simple attractions and repulsions which would be observed on the coming together of those elementary objects. This conclusion would be unassailable, if it were possible to show with mathematical accuracy, that the elementary conditions were so arranged in the animal body with respect to direction, time and quantity, that all of the phenomena of living and dead organisms must necessarily flow from their interaction. This conception, as is well known, is not the traditional; it is the one among the newer, which, as especially opposed to the vitalistic, has been named the physical. The view, aside from all details, finds its justification in the irrefutable demand of logic, that a cause shall underlie every result, and further in the soundest rule of every experimental science, that one draws only on absolutely necessary grounds of explanation.

An example of Ludwig's aversion to philosophical speculation appears in his thesis on the formation of urine, which followed immediately upon the formulation of the Bowman-Heidenhain theory. However, he countered with a physical theory. Although Bowman assumed the kidney secreted urine by the vital activity of the cells, Ludwig held that formation of urine was initiated by hydrostatic pressure in the glomerulus, that proteins were retained by a partially permeable glomerular membrane, and that the remaining constituents of the plasma were concentrated in the tubules by the diffusion of most of the water returned to the blood through endosmosis. This mechanical explanation is only historically interesting now, and Ludwig soon abandoned absorption in the tubules as a simple diffusion process and accepted differential absorption. Selected conclusions in his treatise of 1843 follow.[2]

... when concentrated blood flows past the glomerulus, it creates a strong endosmosis, and the quantity of fluid in the tubule further decreases.

The quantity and the concentration of urine increase when the amount of waste material and salts (to be excreted by the kidney) increases in the blood; for example: with the action of diuretics, sugar diuresis, etc.

In the presence of intensive endosmosis—since actually only the degree of concentration is important— any quantity of urine will contain relatively less urea when the content of other materials in the normal urine increases; or, when the urine is concentrated without containing sufficient amounts of urea; the tubules are soon filled with urine and because of this are emptied quickly. Thus, an additional supply of exogenous fluid will be needed to remove successively the remaining quantity of urea.

The development of new instruments and mechanical devices for the testing of hypotheses and the formulation of physiological laws was as important to the physiologist in the 19th century as was the microscope to the histologist in the previous century. In 1846, Ludwig introduced the graphic method to physiologists already known to meteorologists and physicists. He devised a kymographion in Marburg to study the relation between respiratory movements and arterial blood pressure. A U-shaped manometer tube, partly filled with mercury, was connected to an artery to record simultaneously the vital signs. The device was described as follows:[4]

In order to obtain reliable pressure readings under all circumstances and in order to be able to register the duration and the time sequence of various pressure measurements, the following method with Poiseuille's manometer can be used. A rod-like float is placed on the mercury column. A stylus is attached to the upper portion of the float which registers continuously on the smooth surface over which it glides with the movement of the float. The height of the curves expresses the oscillations of the blood pressure. The width of the curves depends on time and the speed of the recording surface of the stylus.

The stylus writes on a sheet of smooth vellum paper, tightly fixed to a copper cylinder which turns with a constant speed by a clock mechanism, pulled by a weight, the speed of which is regulated by a rotating pendulum.

The mercury pump, designed by his pupil Setschenow according to Ludwig's suggestions, was one of the early devices to quantitate blood gases. The principle of the Torricellian vacuum was used as in the Van Slyke blood-gas analyzer. The communication, which carried only Setschenow's name and describes quantitative measurements of oxygen and carbon dioxide in the blood, was reported from Moscow and is an example of the complete scientific unselfishness, displayed by Ludwig throughout his life, permitting and encouraging full credit to his associates and pupils. In some instances, as in the latter communication, credit to Ludwig and his laboratory was confined to a few words. The acknowledgement by Setschenow and selected conclusions are as follows:[5]

I proposed to Professor Ludwig the Toricellian vacuum as the principle of the apparatus, since with this principle the vacuum can be readily spent and easily re-formed. The next apparatus was prepared according to this principle and followed the several details of Professor Ludwig's instructions.

A summary of the second contribution shows:

(1) At this stage of asphyxia [of the experimental animal] when the fifth nerve is insensitive but the respiratory movements and the heart beat persist, the blood contains no oxygen which may be removed by boiling or by the vacuum.

(3) The free carbon dioxide of the normal arterial blood, which can be removed by heating or by vacuum, has been found to be three to four times in excess of what had been previously assumed. The large quantity of extractable carbon dioxide in the blood, when compared with the small quantity in the air, clearly shows that the carbon dioxide can readily leave the blood for expiration from the lungs.

(c) in the blood of suffocated animals the amount of free carbon dioxide is larger, but not in direct relation to the decrease of oxygen. The reason for this can be found in the loss of gases from the blood as well as in the fact that a portion of the oxygen is used for purposes other than the formation of carbon dioxide.

A third instrument for physiological investigation was the stromuhr, a device for measurement of blood flow. The first apparatus was based upon gross displacement of a liquid, recorded visually. The current device for electronic measurement of blood flow through vessels had its beginning in Ludwig's laboratory directed by Dogiel, who studied blood flow in isolated organs and the output of the heart in animals.[6]

For our purpose an instrument designed by Professor C. Ludwig proved most helpful; and since the practical application of this apparatus had not yet been tested, I took on this assignment in Leipzig.

The principle of the new method depends on gauging the stream—to use the terminology of hydroengineers. The total volume of blood flow is determined by the fluid which flows through a vessel during the experiment. A short vertical glass receptacle with a sphere at each end is inserted into the artery. The portion of glass receptacle towards the heart is filled with purified olive oil; the other portion, directed towards the capillaries, is filled with defibrinated blood. . . . Since the capacity of each receptacle is known and the time needed to propel the oil from the first sphere into the second one is measurable, it is possible to calculate the amount of blood which passes through the artery in a given period.

Noll's studies on lymph formation (1850) is another example of an excellent contribution from Ludwig's laboratory, which acknowledged the influence of the chief without listing him as an author. The principal factor in the formation of lymph was assumed to be the hydrostatic pressure of blood in the capillaries. Ludwig summarized the physicochemical theory of formation of lymph in his text of 1858, relying upon his careful analysis of the query and precise methods of attack.[3]

The blood contained in the vessels tends to equalize its pressure and its chemical constitution with the extravascular fluids, which are separated from it by nothing more than the permeable bloodvessel walls. If, for example, the quantity of blood in the vessels has increased, the mean blood pressure is also increased and at once a portion of blood is driven into the tissues by filtration. A similar result follows the alteration of composition of the blood by absorption of food or by increased excretion by the kidneys, blood, or skin, or when the composition of the tissue fluids is altered from increased metabolic changes in the tissues. In the latter instance, the changes in the lymph are produced by processes of diffusion.

The richness of Ludwig's endeavors over an unusually long scientific career was achieved through his skillful division of labor and judicious assignment of research projects, consistent with his estimate of each pupil's ability and performance. Also, indispensable for the preparation of experimental or demonstrative apparatus in the laboratory was his first technical assistant, Salfamoser (or Salvenmoser), haughty but capable.

A recounting of Ludwig's major physiological contributions should include investigation of experimental ventricular fibrillation, the innervation of the salivary glands, the depressor nerve of the heart, the effect of the spinal cord on blood flow, the vasomotor center in the medulla, digestion of proteids, measurement of pressure in capillaries, the circulation of organs by injection of the vessels, fatigue and recovery of muscle, nonfatigue of nerves, absorption of various substances from the alimentary tract, transfusion of blood, the coagulation of blood, lactic acid in blood and other tissues, the ganglionic cells in the intra-auricular septum, analysis of the first heart sound, and the study of the lymphatics by injection.

There are some who believe that a listing of his pupils, even incomplete, reflects greater glory upon the life of Ludwig than a recounting of his scientific investigations. No medical scientist attracted so many earnest scholars who later became treachers, heads of departments, or directors of institutes in Europe and in America as did Carl Ludwig in his time. His biographers recognize more than 250 students who benefited from a longer or a shorter sojourn in his laboratory, which included from Europe: Mosso, Noll, Goll, Holmgren, Brunton, Bohr, de Cyon, Czermak, Burdon-Sanderson, Kronecker, Luciani, Tigerstedt, Johansson, Hammerstein, Loven, Gaskell, Horsley, Waller, von Frey, and Hufner; from America came Chittenden, Lombard, Mall, Bowditch, Minot, Welch and Abel.

1. Lombard, W. P.: The Life and Work of Carl Ludwig, *Science* 44:363-375, 1916.

2. Ludwig, C.: *The Mechanism of Urine Secretion* (Ger), Marburg: N. G. Elwert, 1843, excerpt translated by Z. Danilevicius.

3. Ludwig, C.: *Textbook of Human Physiology* (Ger), ed 2, Leipzig: C. F. Winter, 1858, in Fishman, A. P., and Richards, D. W.: (trans.) *Circulation of the Blood*, New York: Oxford University Press, 1964, p 390.

4. Ludwig, C.: The Influence of Respiratory Movements on Blood Flow in the Aorta (Ger), *Arch Anat Physiol Wiss Med*, 1847, pp 242-302, excerpt translated by Z. Danilevicius.

5. Setschenow, J.: Gas Exchange of the Blood (Ger), *Z Rationelle Med* 10:101-127, 1861, excerpt translated by Z. Danilevicius.

6. Dogiel, J.: The Measurement of Circulating Blood Volume (Ger), *Arb Physiol Anstalt Leipzig* 2:196-271, excerpt translated by Z. Danilevicius.

Emil Du Bois Reymond
(1818-1896)

EMIL DU BOIS REYMOND devoted his scientific energies to the study of animal electricity and, in his waning years, to a philosophic interpretation of life. The eminent German physiologist, pupil and successor to Johannes Müller, was born in Berlin and there attended primary school and the French College.[1] At the age of 11 he accompanied his parents to Switzerland, where he continued his education at the College of Neuchatel. At the age of 18 he returned to Germany and enrolled in the University of Berlin, which remained his university of preference, except for one term at Bonn. An initial interest in theology was superseded by a strong attraction to chemistry, natural philosophy, mathematics, and geology. After fulfilling the requirements for a degree in medicine, he accepted an assistantship under Müller, pro-

fessor of physiology, comparative anatomy and embryology. Upon Müller's death in 1858, Du Bois Reymond succeeded to the chair of physiology, contributing his brilliance to the illustrious faculty, meanwhile

Composite by G. Bako

developing a segment of physiology at a propitious time in the advance of science.

A singleness of purpose was maintained by Du Bois Reymond in a long series of perceptive researches, beginning with the charge by Müller to investigate the source of the "frog-current" of Nobili. He interpreted and built upon the electrophysiology of Volta and Galvani, effectively holding his own with the Italian physiologist Matteucci. Each studied muscle contraction of the nerve-muscle preparation of the frog when the nerve was placed on an injured spot of a second muscle. He confirmed Galvani's theory that animals have an electricity peculiar to themselves, which he called "Animal Electricity," and demonstrated the great affinity of nervous tissue for this force. He showed that contracting muscle undergoes chemical alteration and muscle and nerves undergo alteration of their electromotive properties during physiological activity. Du Bois Reymond's preliminary communication of 1843 on the frog-current and the electromotor fish was introduced as follows:[2]

(1) When the head and feet of a freshly killed and skinned frog are connected with a conduction bridge and no additional force applied, the instrument for measuring current inserted into the bridge registers a current proceeding from the animal's head toward his feet. A current of almost identical intensity and in the identical direction is registered when the indifferent conduction bridge touches the feet and the pelvis of a galvanic preparation. Between the thighs and shins of the frog, one can detect a current in the same pedal direction but of considerably less intensity.

Critical new devices as well as new scientific terms needed to pursue these researches were provided. They included unpolarizable electrodes; the Du Bois Reymond inductorium, a special type of induction coil in which the primary circuit remains unbroken; and the Du Bois Reymond key, an electrical apparatus of four terminals arranged in connecting pairs, with a movable switch of high conductivity so designed that, when the switch forms a bridge between the two pairs (ie, is closed), a portion of the circuit is shorted. He discovered and explained the "currents of rest," which diminish with muscular contraction, calling "negative fluctuation" the action potential. He assumed these currents were produced by "electromotive molecules," a prismatic arrangement in series, unbroken circuits being maintained because the units were moist conductors. He showed that a tetanized muscle yields an acid reaction; whereas a resting muscle is alkaline. The Du Bois Reymond law of stimulation states that effective stimulation with a constant current depends not upon the intensity but upon the rapidity of its variation or upon maximum variations in unit time. To study transmission of the impulse in nerve-muscle preparations, he constructed a galvanometer sufficiently sensitive to disclose electrical phenomena in a nerve. He then demonstrated centripetal transmission in motor nerves and centrifugal transmission in sensory nerves. The following excerpts are from his work on *Animal Electricity*,[3] prepared by C. E. Morgan, a devoted American pupil who studied in his laboratory for several years. The first is a translation from Du Bois Reymond's "Preliminary Abstract," the second, a summary interpretation of electrotonus.[4]

1. Currents, in all respects similar to the so-called frog-current, may be observed in any limb of any ani-

mal, whether warm or cold blooded. These currents in some limbs are directed upwards, as in the frog's legs, in others downwards. They are of different intensity in different limbs; but their intensity and direction are always the same in the same limb of different individuals of the same species. 2. The electromotive action on which these currents depend does not arise from the contact of heterogeneous tissues, as Volta supposed, for the different tissues—nerve, muscle, and tendon—in an electric point of view, are quite homogeneous. 3. These currents are produced by the muscles. If any undissected muscle of any animal be brought into the circuit longitudinally, it generally exhibits an electromotive action, the direction of which depends on the position of the muscle on the galvanometer-circuit, according to the law which will be immediately stated. Thus, the current might be a downward, or it might be an upward one. The current of a whole limb is nothing but the resultant of the partial currents which are engendered by each muscle of the limb; and the frog-current as well as the similar currents observed in other animals, are thus simply reduced to a *general muscular current.*

. . . *when the direction of the galvanic current in the nerve coincides* with the current of the latter itself, there *is an increase in the deflection of the needle;* whereas, in the *contrary case, there is a decrease.*

Now, as will presently be seen, these effects are not due to the invasion of the galvanometer by the battery-current, but to a new electromotive state developed in a portion of the nerve by the agency of this constant galvanic current, and hence styled Electrotonus by Du Bois Reymond.

. . . all the phenomena of Electrotonus are readily explained on the assumption that: *When any portion of the length of a nerve is traversed by any extraneous electrical current besides its own peculiar current action, a new electromotive action takes place in every part of that nerve having the same direction as the exciting current itself, and this new action, therefore, adds itself to the latter in the nerve-half in which both currents have the same direction, and subtracts itself from it in the other half in which they have contrary courses; so that the algebraic sum of the two is smaller in amount than that of the primitive nerve-current, which finally appears by itself when symmetrical points of the longitudinal section are applied to the deriving cushions.*

Du Bois Reymond, fluent in English, French, and Italian, an international physiologist and friend of the royal court, was honored by foreign and local scientific bodies and especially by the state in the construction of an Institute of Physiology, dedicated in 1877. He served as secretary of the Berlin Academy of Science and as president of both the Physical Society and the Physiological Society. Many years were spent on the editorial staff of the *Archiv für Anatomie, Physiologie, und Wissensch. Medicine,* which continued after 1877 as the *Archiv für Anatomie und Physiologie*. His several responsibilities outside the laboratory, including Rector of the University, gave him an opportunity to expand his philosophy of life and to express his thoughts in addresses and published communications. The preparation of biographical essays of permanent historical value, especially that on Voltaire, revealed an extensive knowledge of French literature. In *The Seven World Problems*, published in commemoration of Leibnitz' birthday, he considered in depth the existence of matter and force and advanced a mechanistic theory of biology in opposition to vitalism, a popular concept of his time.[5]

The primary origin of life in itself has nothing to do with consciousness, but is a question only of the arrangement of atoms and molecules and of the production of certain movements.

If this is conceded, it is permissible to ask if it is not still more worthy of the creative Almighty to avoid even that single intervention by means of established laws, and to endow matter from the beginning with the power of originating life under suitable conditions. There is no reason for denying this view, but with its acceptance the possibility of a mechanical origin of life is conceded, and we have only to consider whether the matter which can thus mechanically compose itself into a living condition always existed, or whether, as Leibnitz thought, it was created by God.

We may count and distinguish seven of these difficulties, of which I call those transcendental which appear insurmountable when we come to meet them in considering the ascending development of nature.

The first difficulty is the existence of matter and force, and is in itself transcendental.

The second difficulty is the origin of motion. We see motion arise and cease; we can conceive matter at rest, and motion appears to be something causal to it. It does not satisfy our demand for a causal agency to think of matter evenly distributed in illimitable space and at rest for endless time. Unless we admit a supernatural impulse, a sufficient occasion for the first motion is lacking. Or, if we imagine matter as in motion from eternity, we give up the elucidation of the point. I regard the difficulty as transcendent.

The third difficulty is the origin of life. As I have often said, I see no ground for considering this difficulty transcendent. When matter has once begun to move, worlds may originate; under suitable conditions, which we can as little imitate as we can those under which a multitude of inorganic processes take place, the peculiar condition of the dynamic balance of matter which we call life may also be produced. If we admit a supernatural act, one such act, creating the animated matter, is enough.

Three lectures were given in Cologne, tracing man from the primordial period, or "Age

of Unconscious Inferences," to modern time, and concluding with recommendations concerning Prussian Gymnasium education in the struggle against the progress of Americanization.[6]

Without scientific observation, experiment, and sound theory, no enduring progress can be made in the useful arts. Such progress necessarily depends on conscious utilization of natural forces observed in their orderly workings. Of this, on the whole, the ancients had no idea.

What now can check modern civilization? What lightnings can ever shatter this tower of Babel? It makes one dizzy to think of what mankind is destined to be a hundred, a thousand, ten thousand, a hundred thousand or more years hence. What is there to which it may not attain? As it nowadays, mole-like, works its way through mountain-chains and under the ocean, why may it not at some future time imitate the flight of the bird? And, as it has solved the enigmas of mechanics, why should it not solve also the enigmas of mind?

Du Bois Reymond exercised a powerful influence on physiology, especially electrophysiology, and German scientific thought.[7] His erudite lectures were prepared with great care and were delivered with precision. Enjoying the hospitality of the royal family, he was also respected by his students and honored by his contemporaries. Endowed with Huguenot stock and half French by education, he was as pro-French as was possible for a distinguished German scientist and philosopher.

1. Stirling, W.: The Last of a Brilliant Quartette of Physiologists—E. Du Bois Reymond (Professor of Physiology in Berlin), *Med Chron* 6:241-250, 1896-1897.

2. Du Bois Reymond, E.: Preliminary Communication on the Investigation of the So-called Frog-Current and the Electromotor Fish (Ger), *Ann Physik Chem* 58:1-30, 1843, excerpt, pp 1-4, translated by Z. Danilevicius.

3. Du Bois Reymond, E.: *Investigation in Animal Electricity*, 3 vol, Berlin: G. Reimer, 1848-1884.

4. Morgan, C. E.: *Electro-Physiology and Therapeutics*, New York: W. Wood & Co., 1868.

5. Du Bois Reymond, E.: *The Seven World-Problems*, Berlin: Berlin Academy of Science, 1881, translated in *Popular Sci Monthly* 20:433-447, 1881-1882.

6. Du Bois Reymond, E.: *History of Culture and Science*, Leipzig: Von Veit & Co., 1878, in *Popular Sci Monthly* 13:257-275, 385-396, 529-539, J. Fitzgerald (trans.), 1878.

7. Boruttau, H.: *Emile Du Bois Reymond* (Ger) Vienna: Rikola, 1922.

National Library of Medicine

Sir William Bowman (1816-1892)

THE HISTOLOGIST ASSOCIATES BOWMAN with a description of striated muscle, the physiologist with the functioning unit of the kidney, while the ophthalomologist thinks of Bowman as the leading ophthalmic surgeon of the mid-19th century in England. Bowman's father was banker, botanist, and geologist; his mother, artist and painter of flowers. Bowman's paternal inheritance included a capacity for accurate observation of natural phenomena; the maternal inheritance found expression in the illustrating of experimental findings. At the age of 10, William enrolled in Hazelwood School, an extraordinary institution disciplined by a constitution and a code of laws prepared by the students, who were also responsible for their enforcement. One of the instructors was Rowland Hill, son of the founder and advocate of the penny postage stamp.

At the age of 16, Bowman left school and was apprenticed for 5 years to Hodgson, Quaker surgeon to the general hospital in Birmingham. Anatomy, physiology, and clinical medicine were studied. The description of morbid processes was begun at this early age. Several essays were read before the assembly of the Birmingham Medical Students' Debating Society. The following year a report on an influenza epidemic was prepared. Other student essays discussed hemorrhage from exter-

nal injury and spinal paraplegia. At the age of 21, equipped with a fine background of fundamental medical training and supplemented by extensive clinical experience, Bowman enrolled in King's College. He was admitted a member of the College of Surgeons two years later. Meanwhile, he had toured Europe with Sir Francis Galton, visiting medical centers in Austria, Germany, and the Low Counties.

His ability as an illustrator of medical phenomena was effectively utilized by his teachers in the preparation of clinical tests. *The Physiological Anatomy and Physiology of Man*[1] was co-authored with Todd, Professor of Physiology, General and Morbid Anatomy, in the medical department of King's College. More important was the contribution to the first edition of the *Cyclopaedia of Anatomy and Physiology* (1839-1859) by Todd. Bowman was assigned the sections on the microscopic structure of the skin, sense organs, nerves, mucous membranes, selected internal organs, and external structures such as muscle, bone, and cartilage. Bowman resorted to rewarding research in preparation of this work. Maceration and teasing were employed for the study of striated muscle. There was no microtome, differential straining, or high-powered magnification. Muscle fibers from mammals, birds, reptiles, fish, and insects were examined under the microscope. The primitive fasciculus, composed of fibrillae which, in turn, were made of elongated polygonal masses of "sarcous elements," was described. It was noted that the "elements" were united on the ends and the sides so as to constitute fibrillae and discs. The cell nucleus and the delicate sarcolemma were recognized. This brilliant work on striated muscle led to his election as Fellow of the Royal Society at the age of 25. The histologist owes much to Bowman for these observations.

The following year the Royal Medal of the Royal Society was awarded for his studies on the structure of the Malpghian body and for deductions concerning the circulation to the kidney.[2] Maluf has discussed in detail the morphology and function of the kidney that preceded Bowman's observations and conclusions.[3] Malpighi described the glomerulus but had not recognized the nephron as a functioning unit. Bowman, on the other hand, differentiated the basement membrane of the epithelium of the renal tubule from the membrane that enfolds the glomerulus. As described by Bowman:[4]

> . . . the circulation through the kidney may be stated to be as follows:—All the blood of the renal artery (with the exception of a small quantity distributed to the capsule, surrounding fat, and the coats of larger vessels) enters the capillary tufts of the Malpighian bodies; thence it passes into the capillary plexus surrounding the uriniferous tubes, and it finally leaves the organ through the branches of the renal vein.
>
> It would indeed be difficult to conceive a disposition of parts more calculated to favour the escape of water from the blood, than that of the Malpighian body. A large artery breaks up in a very direct manner into a number of minute branches, each of which suddenly opens into an assemblage of vessels of far greater aggregate capacity than itself, and from which there is but one narrow exit. Hence must arise a very abrupt retardation in the velocity of the current of blood. . . . Why is so wonderful an apparatus placed at the extremity of each uriniferous tube, if not to furnish water, to aid in the separation and solution of the urinous products from the epithelium of the tube?
>
> This abundance of water is apparently intended to serve chiefly as a menstruum for the proximate principles and salts which this secretion contains, and which, speaking generally, are far less soluble than those of any other animal product.

Thus, the physiologist is indebted to Bowman for observations on the morphology and the physiology of the nephron.

Maturing rapidly scientifically but growing old slowly, Bowman was appointed to the staff of Moorfield's Eye Hospital at the age of 30. A few years later, after the death of John Dalrymple, he succeeded to the post as chief ophthalmic surgeon. His contributions thereafter were restricted to clinical and histologic ophthalmology. It was not long before he became the outstanding ophthalmologist in London; patients were referred to him from many countries. He was a fine operator and ideally suited for operations on the eye. Meanwhile, his continuing interest in histology was reflected in precise observations on the insertion of the recti into the sclera. He described the corneal structure, with particular attention to the corneal tubes and the anterior elastic lamina, known today as Bowman's tubes and Bowman's muscle. Discovery of the "muscularity of the ciliary body, ie, the ciliary muscle" simultaneously with Bruecke,[5] was another notable contribution

to ophthalmology. He employed needles in the treatment of the detached retina. Scientific observations from other lands were promptly accepted. Bowman became skilled in the use of the ophthalmoscope, shortly after it had been emended by Helmholtz. The value of iridectomy and of Von Graefe's treatment of acute glaucoma was recognized. He advocated extraction of cataract by a traction instrument after iridectomy, a method used successfully by ophthalmologists on the Continent. Still in use are Bowman's lacrimal probes for dilating the lacrimal passages.

In 1876, Bowman reached the 60-year age limit for surgeons at Moorfield's Hospital and was obliged to retire from this position. Gradually, he limited his private practice; and at the age of 70, he abandoned it, but remained available to those who sought consultation. His last years were spent on his country estate near Dorking, in the south of England. He assumed leadership in several scientific societies, for which, because of his reputation and experience, he was the logical choice. In 1880, he presided over the ophthalmological section of the British Medical Association at Cambridge University and received (with Donders who was also present) the honorary degree of LLD. During the following year as chairman of the ophthalmological section of the International Medical Congress at London he received great acclaim from the entire membership. That same year the Ophthalmological Society of the United Congresses was organized, and again Bowman was chosen to head this organization. He encouraged every important endeavor, conducted the programs with great efficiency, contributed generously toward the cost of maintenance, and established a comprehensive library.

In 1883, the British Ophthalmological Society established the Bowman Lectures, held yearly under its auspices, in recognition of his outstanding position in ophthalmology and in general medicine and as evidence of the great service rendered to the Society as its first president. The following year he was made a baronet, an appropriate honor to a physician from central England whose contributions to histology, physiology, and ophthalmology remain untarnished now, 125 years later.

1. Todd, R. B., and Bowman, W.: *The Physiological Anatomy and Physiology of Man*, London J. W. Parker, 1845-59.

2. Davis, B. T.: William Bowman, *Queen's Med Magazine* 52:82-89 (June) 1960.

3. Maluf, N. S. R.: The Centenary of Bowman's Exposition of the Renal Unit (1842-1942), *Ann Med Hist* 4:427-449 (Nov.) 1942.

4. Bowman, W.: On the Structure and Use of the Malpighian Bodies of the Kidney, with Observations on the Circulation Through That Gland, *Phil Trans Roy Soc London*, Part I, pp. 57-80, 1842.

Hale-White, W.: *Great Doctors of the Nineteenth Century*, London: Edward Arnold & Co., 1935.

National Library of Medicine

Rudolf Heidenhain (1834-1897)

RUDOLF PETER HEINRICH HEIDENHAIN, professor of physiology at Breslau for many years, was born in Marienwerder, Germany, into a Prussian medical family.[1] His father and five younger brothers were physicians; Rudolf achieved the greatest fame. He studied medicine initially in Berlin, where he worked before and after graduation with Du Bois Reymond; he continued his training at Königsberg and concluded study at Halle, where he was a student of Volkmann. His inaugural dissertation, prepared in Latin and presented for graduation in 1854 at Berlin, discussed the innervation of the heart. Following graduation he worked in the private laboratory of Du Bois Reymond on nerve muscle physiology. In 1857, he presented a thesis on blood volume to the faculty in Halle to qualify as privatdocent. Two years later he accepted the chair of physiology and histology in Breslau and held the post until death.

Heidenhain's physiological contributions appeared first (1856) in his *Physiologische Studien*, which was later expanded into *Studien des physiologischen Institutes zu Breslau* (1861–1868). When Pflüger's *Archiv* was founded in 1868 this was the outlet for reports of his investigations and those of his pupils. Of the scientific subjects explored by Heidenhain, glandular secretion was the central theme. Other subjects, many developing a conjoint histological, chemical, and traditional physiological approach, included a justification for vivisection in experimental physiology, the action of drugs, spinal reflexes, innervation of blood vessels, structure of the pancreas, stimulation of sensory nerves on blood pressure, hypnotism or animal magnetism (translated in 1888 by Wooldridge into English), a monograph dedicated to Du Bois Reymond on mechanical stimulation, and evolution of heat and energy exchange of the active muscle during a single twitch and during tetanus.

The phenomenon of secretion was assumed by Heidenhain to be the result of cellular activity rather than physical forces. In pursuing this concept he opposed the filtration theory of the formation of lymph and urine advanced by Ludwig and presumed that lymph was formed through the activity of capillary walls as secretory organs and bodies called "lymphogogues" by him. Also, his outstanding work with Neisser on urinary secretion, taking advantage of indigo-carmine staining of kidney cells, led to the conclusion that inorganic salts in tubular urine were the secretory products of the glomerulus; whereas urea and uric acid were added through activity of the tubular cells. Finally, he studied the secretion of the salivary glands, pancreas, breast, and stomach.

In the case of the secretion of the gastric mucosa, he identified two cell types (in addition to the mucous secretory cells), the chief or central cell and the parietal or border cell.

For these experimental conclusions he prepared an isolated gastric pouch with an external fistula, later made famous by one of his pupils, Ivan Pavlov, familiarly known as the Pavlov pouch, but also as the Heidenhain-Pavlov pouch. Following the ingestion of food, Heidenhain showed that cells increased in size and after several hours returned to the fasting state.[2]

The formation of pepsin in the pylorus glands is still being disputed despite numerous evidence, particularly by Ebstein and Grutzner. The reasons for this opposition more often than not appear to be based upon preference for the old, ingrained theories, rather than objective judgment of new and proven facts. One of the most excellent publications dealing with these problems is by Klemensiewicz in Rollet's Laboratory. This investigator had the bold idea to isolate the pyloric part of the stomach in a manner similar to Thiry's isolation of loops of the small intestine. . . . Unfortunately, none of these dogs survived more than 72 hours postoperatively, the majority died even sooner.

When Klemensiewicz concluded from these experiments that the pylorus glands without doubt participate in the formation of pepsin, his opponents advanced their last and rather improbable argument: The mucosa of the pylorus normally was covered with a very thick layer of mucus, in and upon which pepsin secreted by the fundus was retained. This mucus was only gradually secreted, the period of observation was too short for a complete cleansing of the surface of the artificial pylorus pouch; therefore, Klemensiewicz after all only had obtained pepsin of the fundus.

Attempts were made by Klemensiewicz to keep the dogs alive after creation of the pyloric fistula to invalidate the above argument. Where Klemensiewicz failed, I was successful in three out of six cases by using Lister's antiseptic method.

The above observations, one of them over a period of 10 weeks, I feel should remove the last doubts regarding the formation of pepsin in the pylorus glands and should finally arbitrate the drawn-out dispute in which particularly Grützner was forced to participate for such a long time.[2]

Heidenhain's theory of urine formation was intermediary between the views of Bowman and Ludwig and the "modern" theory of Cushny. In subsequent decades the filtration-reabsorption theory has been repeatedly challenged but its fundamental tenets usually accepted. Serious doubt has again risen as to whether some of the solutes may not appear in bladder urine through secretion by tubular cells and not exclusively by glomerular filtration from hydrostatic pressure. No one questions the observation that foreign substances are transported from adjacent blood vessels into the lumen of the tubule. Excerpts of his doctrine of kidney function follow.[3]

Furthermore, an excretion of *indigo blue* took place in the strictest meaning of the word "excretion." Being present in the blood in a relatively small amount, the indigo blue is found in such quantities in the lumen of the tubule that even the superficial appearance of the kidney is blue-black, whereas the other areas have only a faint pale-blue coloring. This means that storage of the dye from the blood that flows through the organ has been transferred into the tubule. Excretion could not be demonstrated more clearly than by microscopic examination. There can be no doubt that segments of the uriniferous tubules participated in excretion.

The dye does not pass through the *malpighian* capsules. Not the slightest trace of the coloring matter is found there, though the closely adjacent convoluted tubules are filled. This result cannot be explained on the basis of *Ludwig's* pressure hypothesis, according to which all substances entering the urine are excreted through the glomerulus.

As the fluid is filtered through the *malpighian* capsules and descends through the canaliculi and the loops of *Henle* into the collecting tubules, it receives more and more solid particles. The more concentrated the solution the more indigo soda is present.

In this report I have so far avoided a question although it is a futile one for now. It is the following: What physical and chemical processes mediate excretion of indigo soda in the excreting epithelia? So long as the expression "the life of the cell" is merely a designation for a sum of unknown physical and chemical processes, we cannot hope for a more precise definition of the activity of an excreting cell. The following considerations represent only suggestions for further exploration.

The means by which the cells receive and discharge the pigment remains a question about which there is no hypothesis. The problem has advanced as far as that of the other glands, but not a step further. We know from the gastric glands that they collect chlorides from the lymph and after reduction, eliminate free acid. The same is true of the urinary tubules inasmuch as they absorb pigment and salts from their epithelium and eliminate them. The driving forces are unknown in either case.

1. Fuchs, S.: Rudolf Heidenhain, *Wien Klin Wschr* 10: 968-971, 1897.
2. Heidenhain, R.: Pepsin Formation in the Pyloric Glands, *Arch Ges Physiol* 18:169171, 1878; translated by P. W. Herron, *Surg Gynec Obstet* 110:123-125 (Jan) 1960.
3. Heindenhain, R.: Experiments on the Phenomenon of Urine Excretion, *Arch Ges Physiol Mensch Tiere* 9:1-27, 1874; excerpt translated by F. Sternthal.

Composite by G. Bako

Thomas Laycock (1812-1876)

THOMAS LAYCOCK, unwelcome professor at the University of Edinburgh, was born at Witherly, Yorkshire, into a Wesleyan clergyman's family. Educated at the Wesleyan Academy and the University college of London, he subsequently studied medicine under Louis, Lisfranc, and Velpeau in Paris, and served three years as the resident medical officer of York County Hospital before receiving the MD degree summa cum laude from Göttingen in 1839.[1] Returning to practice in York, he acquired a reputation as a skillful physician; in time, he was appointed physician to the York Dispensary and lecturer in medicine in the York Medical School. In 1855, when the chair of medicine at Edinburgh became vacant, his fame as a profound thinker, medical scientist, and a prolific writer significantly aided his candidacy. Eight contestants engaged in a bitter struggle for the post, and in spite of his selection by the Edinburgh Town Council, he was accepted neither by the public nor by the profession. Beset by strong antagonism and ill health, he continued his medical, philosophical, and psychological writing without interruption until

his death after affliction with pulmonary tuberculosis. During the progress of the disease, he had undergone amputation of his left leg for tuberculous arthritis of the knee.

While practicing in York, Laycock showed unusual curiosity in vital statistics and public health. He inquired into the state of sanitation and hygiene and presented his findings to the *Dublin Medical Press*, a frequent outlet for his contributions from York, including communications on political and forensic medicine, the morbidity and mortality of York, and statistics on the laboring class.[2] To the *British and Foreign Medical Review*, he submitted manuscripts on the problem of population and subsistence, the interment of the dead in England, the vital statistics of England, and the public hygiene of Great Britain.

Laycock's philosophical observations, for which he is best remembered, led him to the generalization that the entire nervous system functions on the reflex pattern, a concept which later formed the synthesis of nervous functions proposed by Pavlov, Sherrington, and Freud. Previously, the reflex concept had been advanced as an explanation of lower nervous functions, especially the spinal reflex. Laycock assumed that the ganglia within the cranium were continuations of the spinal cord and that their reactions were regulated by external agencies similar to those governing the functions of the spinal ganglia and their analogues in lower animals. Also, the reflex arc, which included transmittal to the cerebrum, at times associated with conscious ideas, led to peripheral motor activity. Laycock concluded in his psychological assumptions that[3] . . .

Four years have elapsed since I published my opinion, supported by such arguments as I could then state, that the brain, although the organ of consciousness, was subject to the laws of reflex action, and that in this respect it did not differ from the other ganglia of the nervous system. I was led to this opinion by the general principle, that the ganglia within the cranium being a continuation of the spinal cord, must necessarily be regulated as to their reaction on external agencies by laws identical with those governing the functions of the spinal ganglia and their analogues in the lower animals. And I was confirmed in this opinion by finding, after the investigation and collocation of known facts, that observations and arguments like those satisfactorily adduced in proof of the existence of the reflex function of the spinal ganglia, may be brought forward in proof that the cerebral ganglia have similar endowments.

We must consider then each half of the encephalon as consisting of two tracts of cortical, and two of medullary substance; the medullary associating ideas and combining muscular movements; the cortical, conducting impressions to the gray matter, giving rise to sensation and perception, and thence to the muscles, exciting motion. That impressions received by the sensitive nerves excite trains of ideas is generally acknowledged, and that the ideas constituting these trains have a connexion with the elementary constitution of the brain is clearly inferrible from the numerous observations recorded, in which the memory has been only partially abolished. The law of unity of type and function in animals, applied in the preceding pages to the function of the cerebrospinal axis in man, has shown . . . that the transition of structure and function is gradual, . . . The automatic acts pass insensibly into the reflex, the reflex into the instinctive, the instinctive are *quasi* emotional, the emotional are intellectual.

In his two-volume monograph, *Mind and Brain*, Laycock developed a systematic exposition of the general laws of existence and life, concluding with the functions of the brain. All the phenomena and processes of mental activity in consciousness were believed to have their homologues in nature; furthermore, natural laws associated with human awakeness were considered to be attained through a long and eventful evolutionary process. His work was basically an introduction to the study of medical psychology, stressing recognition and treatment of mental disorders. His principles of teleology or mental dynamics were developed in a law of design, and ideas were considered as causes not only of life and thought but of all features of creation.[4]

Having thus established a system of general principles, the Author proceeds to apply them in succession to the general laws of Life and Organisation, or Biology; to the development of a scientific Cerebral Psychology; and to the first principles of a Mental Physiology and Organology. By this method the reader is thus first led up to the great general laws of all phenomena over which mind, considered as an ordering force, dominates; and thence downwards, through the great laws of the archetypal development and physiological change, to the derivative, special, and ever-varying phenomena of consciousness and life. In examining the latter, the Author has more fully developed that great law of unconscious functional activity of the brain as the organ of consciousness— which he was the first to demonstrate.

Laycock entered into his duties at Edinburgh as professor of the practice of medicine and of clinical medicine. The title was expanded later to include lecturer on medical psychology and mental diseases, reflecting his great interest in psychology and metaphysics. The incumbent's recognized duties included the presentation of a suitable course of instruction for students and, by investigations and writings, extension of his personal reputation and that of the university. He succeeded less well in the first provision. The students preferred dogmatic lectures to help prepare for the examinations; Laycock preferred the abstract and presented a broad view of medical science, hoping students would gain knowledge by independent reading, without professional prodding. He was most successful in this hope with John Hughlings Jackson, who became the great contemporary theorist in clinical neurology in London a generation later. The introduction to Laycock's first lecture in his monograph, *The Principles and Methods of Medical Observation and Research for the Use of Advanced Students and Junior Practitioners*, begins with sound admonition for the acquisition of clinical experience.[5]

We are met to-day that we may study and practise medicine together at the bedside of the sick. These pursuits are of singular importance to us all. To you, clinical study is the culmination of your academic career, and upon the habits you now form, and the doctrines you now imbibe, much of your success and happiness in the practice of your future profession will depend. To me, clinical teaching and practice involve a grave responsibility; for to guide you rightly in your studies, as well by precept as by example, is to ensure, so far as I am concerned, that your career shall be successful and happy, and therewith human suffering largely alleviated, and the profession of medicine advanced.

First, however, let us understand what is implied in the phrase professional skill and tact. Skill implies both knowledge and experience; tact, quickness in applying that knowledge at the bedside, and ability to secure as well as direct the most appropriate treatment. With a ready appreciation of the essential points in the case before you, there must be a decisive opinion of what is needed, and prompt action upon the opinion. In a few words, it may be said that the sagacious practitioner determines quickly and clearly what ought to be done, what can be done, and how what can be done may be accomplished. Much of this skill and tact can be acquired in no other way than by familiarity with disease. The judgment and the senses must both have a practical training at the bedside.

Without it, indeed, science or learning is of little avail. Just as surgical dexterity can only be attained by practice of the art of surgery, so the medical dexterity known as tact can only be acquired by the practice of the art of medicine.

The subjects of Laycock's clinical communications included such varied matters as pathological physiology, special pathology, materia medica, clinical surgery, orthopedic surgery, hematology, medical meteorology, neurology, medical ethics, pathological anatomy, dietetics, medical diagnosis, and gynecology.[6] Some of the monographs not already mentioned include *An Essay on Hysteria* (1840), *Religio Medicorum, a Critical Essay on Medical Ethics* (1855), *The Social and Political Relations of Drunkenness* (1857), *A Treatise on the Nervous Diseases of Women* (1840), *Clinical Inquiries into the Influence of the Nervous System and of Diathetic Tissue Changes on the Production and Treatment of Dropsies* (1866), *A Syllabus of Lectures and Causes of Fever* (1861), and *Etiological Nosology of Diseases of the Skin* (1862).

Honors included fellowship in the Royal Society, Edinburgh, fellowship in the Royal College of Physicians of Edinburgh, and Physician in Ordinary to the Queen of Scotland.

1. Macleod, K.: Laycock, *Caled Med J* 7:339-352, 1907-1908.
2. Laycock, T.: *Report on the State of York,* York, 1844.
3. Laycock, T.: On the Reflex Function of the Brain, *Brit For Med Rev* 19:298-311, 1845.
4. Laycock, T.: *Mind and Brain,* 2 vol, ed 2, New York: D. Appleton & Co., 1869.
5. Laycock, T.: *The Principles and Methods of Medical Observation and Research,* ed 2, Edinburgh: Maclachlan & Stewart, 1864.
6. Laycock, T.: *A Chrononological Catalogue of the Essays, Reviews, and Treatises in the Various Departments of the Theory and Practice of Medicine,* York: W. Sotheran, 1855.

John Tyndall (1820-1893)

CONTRIBUTIONS OF THE FUNDAMENTAL SCIENTIFIC DISCIPLINES, physics, chemistry, and mathematics, to progress in medicine have provided impregnable support to medical research for centuries. No better example of this liaison can be adduced than that of a

hundred years ago associated especially with the names of Koch, Pasteur, and the less well known Cohn and Tyndall. Each made major contributions to the understanding of the new science of bacteriology by experiments pro-

Composite by G. Bako

found in concept but relatively simple in execution. Brilliant thinking preceded experimental testing of the hypotheses in the laboratory. Only Koch was trained as a physician.

John Tyndall was born at Leighlin Bridge, County Carlow, one of the smallest counties in eastern Ireland, south of Dublin. He studied physics at the University of Marburg in Germany, was elected a member of the Royal Society of London at the age of 32 and appointed professor of natural philosophy at the Royal Institution two years later. This meteoric rise to a position of eminence in science in England is another example of general appreciation of the intellectual potentialities of a strong individual early in his professional career. Tyndall delivered a series of lectures on heat, sound, and light in the United States in 1872 and 1873. He gave the profits from this tour, which by judicious investment amounted to more than $30,000, to a fund for the advancement of science in America.[1]

Tyndall's most notable achievements in the medical sciences were summarized in his *Essays on the Floating Matter of the Air in Relation to Putrefaction and Infection* published in 1881. He was a contemporary of Pasteur and it was at this time that the latter was investigating the bacteriologic pathogenesis of anthrax, septicemia, rabies, and cholera. Tyndall offered convincing proof of the fallacy of spontaneous generation, but he was not content to pursue his studies and let the medical scientists discover their potential value. He extended himself to acquaint physicians with the significance of his basic observations. The University of Tübingen awarded him an honorary doctorate of medicine in appreciation of his contributions to the health field.

A long treatise on *The Optical Deportment of the Atmosphere in Relation to the Phenomena of Putrefaction and Infection* was presented to the Royal Society of London in 1876.[2]

I at that time found that London air, which is always thick with motes, and also with matter too fine to be described as motes, after it had been filtered by passing it through densely packed cotton-wool, or calcined by passing it through a red-hot platinum-tube containing a bundle of red-hot platinum wires, or by carefully leading it over the top of a spirit-lamp flame, showed, when examined by a concentrated luminous beam, no trace of mechanically suspended matter.

The purely gaseous portion of our atmosphere was thus shown to be incompetent to scatter light.

I subsequently found that to render the air thus optically pure, it was only necessary to leave it to itself for a sufficient time in a closed chamber, or in a suitably closed vessel.

It was concluded that the power of scattering light and the power of producing life in the atmosphere were interwoven. Urine was used in one of Tyndall's experiments. Empty test tubes were heated in a closed box to destroy the atmospheric bacteria. Air that entered was filtered to remove the germ-laden dust particles. When a concentrated beam of light, which passed through the box at intervals, revealed that the air was "optically empty" (Tyndall Effect), the tubes were filled with urine through a pipette. The liquid was boiled and allowed to cool. After the tubes had been heated, the air was tested with a beam of light; the tubes were examined with

the naked eye. The tubes were clear, the air was clear, no motes were present, and no putrefaction had occurred. On the other hand, a control set of test tubes containing urine were heated but were exposed to room air. These tubes became turbid and were found to be swarming with bacteria. This epoch-making experiment contributed to the general rejection of the concept of spontaneous generation.

. . . It would be simply monstrous to conclude that they had been "spontaneously generated."

This reasoning applies word for word to the development of *Bacteria* from that floating matter which the electric beam reveals in the air, and in the absence of which no Bacterial life has been generated. I cannot see a flaw in the reasoning; and it is so simple as to render it unlikely that the notion of Bacterial life developed from dead dust can ever gain currency among the members of the medical profession.

Tyndall described the inhibition of bacterial growth by a blanket of *Penicillium* half a century before others capitalized on its potentiality for treatment of bacterial invasion of humans.[2]

The mutton in the study gathered over it a thick blanket of *Penicillium*. On the 13th it had assumed a light brown colour, "as if by a faint admixture of clay;" but the infusion became transparent. The "clay" here was the slime of dormant or dead *Bacteria*, the cause of their quiescence being the blanket of *Penicillium*. I found no active life in this tube, while all the others swarmed with *Bacteria*.

In presenting his findings Tyndall, the physicist, introduces a pithy comment on scientific observation and intellectual perception.[2]

For the right interpretation of scientific evidence, something more than mere sharpness of observation is requisite, very keen sight being perfectly compatible with very weak insight. I was therefore careful to have my infusions inspected by biologists, not only trained in the niceties of the microscope, but versed in all the processes of scientific reasoning.

1. Tyndall, L. C.: "John Tyndall," in *The Dictionary of National Biography*, vol 19, Oxford: University Press, 1959-1960, pp 1358-1363.

2. The Optical Deportment of the Atmosphere in Relation to the Phenomena of Putrefaction and Infection, *Philos Trans* 166:27-74, 1876.

Hermann von Helmholtz
(1821-1894)

HERMANN LUDWIG FERDINAND HELMHOLTZ was born in Potsdam at the beginning of the era of "The Flowering of Medical Science," in central Europe. His mother was a direct descendant of William Penn, his father a teacher in the Gymnasium. Although his father was not able financially to provide for an extended private education, he gave in its place an appreciation of poetry, a desire to study the Greek classics, and exposure to the metaphysics of Kant and Fichte. In his mature years, Helmholtz sponsored a scientific philosophy in German universities to counteract the prevailing metaphysical idealism.

Hermann, a sickly child, spent a considerable portion of his early years as an invalid. After overcoming childhood infirmities, he sought a free education in medicine at the Royal Medico-Chirurgical Friedrich Wilhelm Institute of Berlin University. The courses were complemented by clinical instruction at the Charité Hospital.[1]

My own original inclination was toward physics; external circumstances compelled me to commence the study of medicine, which was made possible to me by the liberal arrangements of this Institution. It had, however, been the custom of a former time to combine the study of medicine with that of the Natural Sciences, and whatever in this was compulsory I must consider fortunate; not merely that I entered medicine at a time in which any one who was even moderately at home in physical considerations found a fruitful virgin soil for cultivation; but I consider the study of medicine to have been that training which preached more impressively and more convincingly than any other could have done, the everlasting principles of all scientific work; principles which are so simple and yet are ever forgotten again; so clear and yet always hidden by a deceptive veil.

Education by the state was provided on the condition that the applicant pledge 10 years of service in the army. Following graduation at the age of 21, Helmholtz began the fulfillment of his contract as a surgeon in the Red Hussar's Regiment. But it was not the usual tour of duty of an army surgeon; a laboratory was constructed in the barracks at Potsdam, and a productive scientific career begun. Until his death, half a century later, he pursued a fabulous career of investigation which embraced a number of specifically medical and generally scientific subjects. Physics, physiology, pathology, anatomy, thermodynamics, ophthalmology, hydrodynamics, acoustics, nerve energy, color vision, and clinical medicine—each discipline benefited from his fertile mind. Nor was his interest confined to the natural sciences. The "Mathematical Monogram", by Bernoulli and the poetry of Goethe were studied with equal zeal.

In 1847, at the age of 26, Helmholtz presented his theoretical conclusions to the Physical Society of Berlin on the conservation of energy,[2] the first law of thermodynamics. The controversy over "vitalism" had not been resolved at that time, and Stahl's interpretation of a vital soul or force, in addition to the physical and chemical energies of organs, was acceptable to many. Justus von Leibig posed the question:[3] "Are the mechanical energy and heat produced by an organism entirely the product of its own metabolism?" Helmholtz answered the query in the affirmative and proved the thesis that mechanical energy cannot be produced in nature without an equal expenditure of energy. Nor is there loss of energy in the universe. "Nature as a whole possesses a store of energy which cannot in any wise be added to or subtracted from."

Shortly after this observation, Clausius and Lord Kelvin formulated the second law of thermodynamics. This was extended by Willard Gibbs of Yale, one of Helmholtz.

pupils, to include all physical and chemical phenomena. Thereafter, the philosophy of vitalism was slowly relegated to oblivion. The publication of this communication prompted Alexander von Humboldt and Johannes Müller, one of Helmholtz' teachers in Berlin, to obtain a release from his army commitment in order to devote all of his energies to scientific studies. At the age of 29, Helmholtz was appointed professor of physiology at Königsberg, at 35, professor of physiology in Bonn, and a few years later, to a similar post in Heidelberg. At the age of 50, he returned to Berlin as professor of physics and remained in that city until his death.

His studies on the measurement of the speed of transmission of the nerve impulse were started at Königsberg. The gastrocnemius muscle and sciatic nerve of the frog were used.[4]

It goes without saying that the time that the nervous excitation takes to traverse the nerve cannot depend on the magnitude of the load on the muscle, nor upon the height to which this load is lifted. . . . I have been able to establish that in stimulating alternately the upper and the lower portions of the nerve, the contraction begins a little later in the first case than in the second. The delay is manifest in the greater impulsion impressed on the needle of the galvanometer in the first case; and the proof that it does not derive from any other cause than the longer pathway to travel in the nerve, is that its duration was constant for the same individual, whatever weight was suspended from the muscle. . . . Here finally are the figures of my experiments. The distance between the points stimulated on the nerve being 50 to 60 millimeters, the nervous excitation took 0.0014 to 0.0020 seconds to traverse this distance.

The mean of these observations is approximately 30 meters a second, a currently accepted value.

Although Helmholtz never practiced ophthalmology or otolaryngology, he manifested great interest in the physiology and examination of the eye and ear. The invention of the ophthalmoscope for use in ophthalmology and clinical medicine (1851) was comparable in significance to the observations on the conservation of energy in the physical sciences. The ophthalmoscope permitted the physician, for the first time, to view the retina in health and disease.[5] His model consisted of several plates of glass laid one upon another. Later a rotary disc containing several small lenses was

affixed to the instrument by Rekoss, but the principle of the ophthalmoscope, irrespective of modification of design, remains today as Helmholtz conceived it. The modern instrument consists of a concave mirror or prism, which concentrates the light directed through the pupil and illuminates the retina or other parts of the eye. The physician views the object through a small hole in the center. A magnifying lens is interposed between the mirror and the target in indirect ophthalmoscopy.

Variations in the curvature of the lens were measured by the ophthalmometer. The mechanism of accommodation was investigated as were the index of refraction of the lens and other optical constants of the eye. His *Handbook of Physiological Optics*, published in three parts between 1856 and 1867, constituted one of the great contributions to medicine of the 19th century.[6] He turned from the eye to the ear and investigated acoustics. The manner in which different sounds excite the cochlea, the difference in tone qualities, scales in music, and the action of the tympanum and ossicles of the middle ear were studied.

As professor of physics in Berlin, most of Helmholtz' efforts were devoted to the study of matter in motion. The motion of liquids was compared with the electromagnetic action of electric currents. He believed that chemical atoms are, in their ultimate, electrical in nature. The concept of valence of modern chemistry is based upon this phenomenon. Helmholtz' mathematical interpretation of Maxwell's theory—that light is another form of electromagnetic wave—stimulated his associate Hertz to conduct experiments which later made possible the development of the wireless.

Four eponyms identify Helmholtz. Helmholtz' ligament is that portion of the anterior ligament of the malleus, which is attached to the greater tympanic spine. Helmholtz' theory of sound perception assumes that each basilar fiber responds sympathetically to a definite tone and stimulates the hair cells of Corti's organ, which rest upon the fiber. The nerve impulse from this stimulation of the hair cells is carried to the brain. Helmholtz' lines are those normal to the plane of the axis of rotation of the eye. Helmholtz' chess-board is a hyperbolic chess-board, a useful optic device.

1. von Helmholtz, H.: On Thought in Medicine, *Bull Hist Med* 6:123 (Feb.) 1938.

2. von Helmholtz, H. L. F.: *On the Conservation of Energy* (Ger), Berlin: G. Reimer, 1847.

3. Crombie, A. C.: Helmholtz, *Sci Amer* 198:94 (March) 1958, pp. 95 and 196.

4. Hoff, H. E., and Geddes, L. A.: Ballistics and the Instrumentation of Physiology: Velocity of the Projectile and of the Nerve Impulse, *J Hist Med* 15:143 (April) 1960.

5. von Helmholtz, H.: *Description of an Eye Mirror for Examination of the Retina in the Living Eye* (Ger), Berlin, 1851.

6. von Helmholtz, H.: *Handbook of Physiological Optics* (Ger), Leipzig: Voss, 1867.

Composite by G. Bako

Felix Hoppe-Seyler (1825-1895)

ERNST FELIX EMANUEL HOPPE was born in Freiburg-in-Thuringen, occupied the first chair of physiological chemistry in Germany, and directed the first institute devoted to this subject, which he distinguished, but did not divorce, from organic chemistry, physiology, and pathology. The hyphenated surname was acquired in maturity (1864) from the husband of his eldest sister, Doctor Seyler, who sheltered him when he was orphaned. His mother died when he was six and his father, a pastor, three years later. For a considerable time Hoppe lived under Spartan austerity at an orphan asylum, where he was introduced to chemistry by the institution's apothecary. His

higher education began with matriculation in the University of Halle and continued in Leipzig; there he attended the lectures of the Weber brothers in physics, physiology, and anatomy, Erdmann's classes in organic chemistry, and Lehmann's in physiological chemistry. The doctorate in medicine was granted in 1850 by the University of Berlin upon presentation of the graduation thesis, entitled *On the Structure of Cartilage and Chondrin*. His presentation was so promising that it attracted the attention of the great Virchow, who subsequently counseled him in his career.

In the following years Hoppe was uncertain about his professional planning; he studied obstetrics in Prague, pursued general practice in Berlin, and taught anatomy in Greifswald. Nothing seemed satisfying, and emigration to America was considered. However, he was dissuaded from this venture by Virchow and returned once more to Berlin to assist in Virchow's laboratory. In 1860, he accepted the professorship of chemistry in the University. His investigations in physiological chemistry were becoming fruitful, his originality and skill in research were recognized, and consequently pupils in substantial numbers were attracted to his laboratory. Subsequently he left Berlin, accepted the chair of applied chemistry at Tubingen, assumed the name of Hoppe-Seyler, and took charge of a laboratory with only primitive facilities. But spirit and productivity more than compensated for inadequate arrangements for work; students came to him in greater numbers than ever. The final University step was the assumption of the chair of physiological chemistry in Strassburg.

Hoppe-Seyler was the 19th century epitome of the brilliant German professor and a natural scientist with many interests. Possessed of a highly imaginative mind, he was an excellent investigator, a stimulating teacher, a prolific writer, a competent administrator, and a lover of mountains and walking. His *Handbook of Physiological and Pathological Chemical Analysis* was a standard text and went through several editions, as did his four-volume *Textbook of Physiological Chemistry*, the great work of his time. His biochemical and general chemical investigations embraced botany, mineralogy, geology, general chemistry, and physical diagnosis. The spectroscope served him in the study of chlorophyll and the pigments of blood, urine, and bile. Analyses of dentine showed it to be similar to apatite, and dentine enamel of fossils and living animals was found to be identical in chemical composition. Cholesterol and lecithin were isolated from red blood cells; the term "proteids" was introduced. Hoppe-Seyler studied the oxidation and reduction reactions in transudates, in cells, and in fermentation. Interpreting the critical sequelae upon man's return to atmospheric pressure after working in compressed air, he attributed the symptoms to the escape of gases dissolved in the blood under pressure. In investigating osmolarity of urine, he noted that, although urine may have a greater osmotic pressure than blood, a hyperosmotic state cannot be attained by endosmosis.

Some consider Hoppe-Seyler's greatest scientific contribution to be the definition of the chemical and physiological characteristics of hemoglobin and its derivatives during their biological mission in living processes —especially in relation to blood gas transport during the respiratory cycle. He was the first to assign the term "hemoglobin" to the pigment and to differentiate oxygenated from reduced hemoglobin in spectrum analysis. He showed that oxygen is released by hemoglobin in the molecular, not the atomic, form and that hemin is the hydrochlorate of hematin.[2]

The crystals, which are easily separated from the blood of some rodents by the addition of water and from dog's blood by the addition of water and alcohol, contain the chromogens. . . . The crystals are water soluble; at a temperature of 5°C the saturated solution of dog blood crystals contains 2 grams of dry chromogen in 100 ml of fluid. To avoid any confusion, I named the chromogen *hematoglobin* or *hemoglobin*. This material consists primarily of the contents of the red blood cells of humans and dogs. . . . There is no other chromogen in the blood of man, dogs, oxen, sheep, guinea pigs, rats, muskrats, mice, hedgehogs, geese, doves, roosters, frogs, vipers, turtles, and other vertebrates.

If a solution of hemoglobin is freed of O_2 by a stream of CO_2 or by the process of decomposition, its light refraction brings the sun spectrum almost to Frauenhofer's band C. If the solution is shaken with air, the absorption of light moves from band C into the neighborhood of band D with considerable translucence. This part of the spectrum is of high intensity, and the range from A to C is of low light intensity;

this explains the bright color and the translucency of arterial blood as compared with the dark venous blood.

Hemoglobin is converted into hematin and globulin by the action of acids such as acetic acid. The same conversion occurs rapidly when hemoglobin is treated with strong alkali, but much slower when it is treated with ammonia.

Continuing the investigations of hemoglobin, Hoppe-Seyler quantitated the volume of oxygen bound to hemoglobin, contrasted the affinity of hemoglobin for oxygen and carbon monoxide, derived the chemical formula of hematin, and estimated the molecular weight of hemoglobin. Although his values have been revised significantly, they represent commendable achievements a century ago.[2]

The bright red color of the blood crystals from dog or goose blood depends on the oxygen content of the blood cells. Even though the oxygen content of the crystals, or the amount of oxygen which can be removed by heating in a vacuum, is even smaller than that of the dry crystals, still, as long as they are not decomposed, all of the crystals contain some loosely bound oxygen. From an amorphous mass of crystals containing 100 gm of dry hemoglobin one can obtain 63.6 ml of oxygen. The same quantity of dried crystals contains about 58.4 ml of oxygen. One hundred grams of hemoglobin dried at a temperature of 0°C and then pulverized would contain 41.1 ml of oxygen.

Beautiful crystals can be obtained from the carbon monoxide treated blood of dogs and geese. Similar crystals are obtained from solutions of blood crystals exposed to carbon monoxide. The structure of these crystals is the same as that of hemoglobin crystals which contain oxygen. The color is specific for blood containing carbon monoxide. These crystals are more stable than the crystals without oxygen. . . . The crystals formed with an admixture of carbon monoxide release very little of the carbon monoxide when heated in a vacuum to a temperature up to 100°C. . . . It is calculated that 100 gm of dry hemoglobin would produce 13.4 ml of carbon monoxide under such conditions. At 0° temperature and a pressure of 76 cm essentially the same amount of carbon monoxide was recovered.

The composition of hemin is $C_{48}H_{51}N_6Fe_3O_9$, hydrochloride (HCl). This formula requires 3.64% of chlorine, a quantity which corresponds with the above findings. Hemin is a well crystallized chemical substance and it is possible to calculate molecular weight of hemoglobin since it breaks down into hemin. It is possible to do the same with globulin. This can be done if it is certain that one molecule of hemoglobin produces one molecule of globulin. The molecular weight of hemin according to the above formula is 975.5 and the molecular weight of hematin is 939; thus hemoglobin should have a molecular weight of 18,665 and globulin of approximately 17,726.

If we compare the above formula of hematin with the one Stadeler developed from his studies on bile pigments, and which is supposed to represent bilirubin, we can obtain this simple equation:

$$2(C_{48}H_{51}N_6Fe_3O_9) + 3 \ H_2O =$$
Hematin
$$6(C_{16}H_{18}N_2O_3) + 3 \ Fe_2O$$
Bilirubin

Substituting hydrogen for iron, one molecule of hematin would correspond to three molecules of bilirubin.

As Hoppe-Seyler approached the end of his academic tenure, the new Institute for Physiological Chemistry of the Kaiser Wilhelm University, Strassburg, was dedicated. This Institute culminated his vision of a laboratory in which others could conduct research as he had done in the less adequate facilities provided him. The spread of his scientific influence was weighty and broad; physiological chemistry became a new discipline in the medical sciences largely through his efforts. In order to be certain of an ever-ready medium for dissemination of new observations, he founded the *Zeitschrift für physiologische Chemie*, *Hoppe-Seyler's Zeitschrift*, which was published from 1877 to 1895 under his jurisdiction and continued until 1917. His address at the opening of the Institute covered the development of physiological chemistry and included the following remarks, italicized by him for emphasis.[3]

. . . all these considerations must bring us to the conviction *that definite fundamental chemical formations and changes are common to all living beings, and that the life-processes common to them all, especially their growth through formation of their own substance and their propagation without limit under conditions peculiar to them, must be formed in the presence of those chemical constituents; that also in the further processes of change, often appearing so different in the different classes, orders, and families of animals and plants, many processes can take place according to a conformable fundamental type; and that finally in the life-processes of man these parallels are again found, whose simplest manifestation we, perhaps, follow with the least difficulty in the lowest organisms.*

1. Baumann, E., and Kossel, A.: To the Memory of Felix Hoppe-Seyler (Ger), *Hoppe Seyler Z Physiol Chem* 21:1-61, 1895-1896.
2. Hoppe-Seyler, F.: The Chemical and Optical Activity of Hemoglobin (Ger), *Arch Path Anat* 29:233-235, 597-600, 1864, excerpts translated by Z. Danilevicius.
3. Hoppe-Seyler, F.: *On the Development of Physiological Chemistry and Its Significance for Medicine* (Ger), Strassburg: K. J. Trübner, 1884, translated in *New York Med J* 440:169-171; 197-199, 1884.

Composite by G. Backo

Adolph Fick (1829-1901)

ADOLPH FICK, one of the exemplary physiologists in central Europe in the 19th century, was born in Kassel, Germany, the son of a construction engineer.[1] After attending the local Gymnasium, in 1847 he began his higher education at the University of Marburg; there his oldest brother, Ludwig, was professor of anatomy and his older brother, Heinrich, who later became professor of Roman law at the University of Zurich, was privatdocent in law. More important than the patronage of either of his brothers, however, was the influence of Carl Ludwig, then privatdocent in anatomy and physiology. Fick showed great interest in mathematics and analytic mechanics and, by the age of 21, had published his first investigation, a study of the dynamics of the muscles of the thigh. A mutual interest in physiological research and great respect for Ludwig's intellectual accomplishments formed a social and academic friendship that persisted for a lifetime.

In the fall of 1849, Fick transferred his work to Berlin, where he attended the clinical lectures of Langenbeck, Romberg, and Schönlein and studied with Müller, Helmholtz, and

Du Bois Reymond. He returned to Marburg to receive the MD degree in 1851, presenting an inaugural disseration on the optic tract. After spending a short time with his brother in the anatomical laboratory, Fick was called to Zurich by Ludwig to serve as prosector; in 1861, when Ludwig was called to Vienna, Fick succeeded to the chair of anatomy and physiology. In 1868, he accepted a similar post at Würzburg, which he held for 31 years. Fick's work paralleled Ludwig's; each devised instruments for quantitative measurement of physiological phenomena which led to major advances, each by his own skill, intellect, and productive capacity.

One of Fick's first contributions was the exposition of the law of diffusion of liquids. He advanced the general concept that diffusion was proportional to the concentration gradient, developed from Fourier's theory of heat equilibrium. In 1856, he published his first monograph, entitled *Medical Physics*.[2] The work included detailed descriptions of improved laboratory devices for quantitative measurement of physiological functions, a discussion of the mixing of gases in the lungs, measurements of carbon dioxide output, calculation of the work output of the heart, an approximation of the heat economy and heat output in disease, discussions of the dynamics of the circulation, and accommodation of the eyes. Having a special interest in the physiology of muscular contraction, Fick investigated the mechanics of muscular movement and disproved Liebig's theory that energy for muscular exercise is derived exclusively from protein foods.

The measurement of isometric and isotonic muscular contraction was pursued with delicate instruments which retained their practical value for almost a century. Studying skeletal and heart muscle, he calculated expenditure of energy and development of heat during muscle contraction, concluding that chemical energy is directly transferred to mechanical energy, but that muscle is susceptible to thermodynamic interpretation. Other studies embraced neurophysiology and especially the function of the critical sense organs. He introduced the aneroid manometer for the determination of blood pressure, devised a myotonograph, the cosine lever, a tonometer for measuring ocular pressure, and improved the plethysmograph and the thermopile.

The calculation of cardiac output by measuring gas exchange in the lungs is probably Fick's best-known contribution to human physiology. Fick's principle, proposed without benefit of laboratory confirmation, has remained one of the most important fundamental concepts in the study of cardiopulmonary function in man and higher animals. He used the determined arteriovenous (A-V) difference of pulmonary gases for the dog and the total carbon dioxide output (or oxygen uptake) for man. Fick reasoned that if the total oxygen absorbed per minute were divided by the uptake of oxygen by the blood, per unit of blood flow, the arteriovenous oxygen difference would provide the total blood flow through the lungs or through the heart. Such a principle would also apply for comparable measurements of carbon dioxide output and carbon dioxide arteriovenous differences of any other gas, native or foreign, not altered in the cardiopulmonary circuit. This simple physiological concept of blood flow and transport of respiratory gases was presented in 1870. The tenet was nothing more than the expression of the dilution principle for measurement of blood flow in vivo, ie, the faster the blood flow, the less oxygen taken up per unit of moving blood. It remains the basis of many of the accepted methods for measuring cardiac output, the movement of foreign gases, and blood flow through the kidney and the liver by clearance techniques. The entire communication, one of the briefest and one of the most important in the study of human physiology, was presented by an intermediary.[3]

Herr Fick had a contribution on the measurement of the amount of blood ejected by the ventricle of the heart with each systole, a quantity the knowledge of which is certainly of great importance. Varying opinions have been expressed on this. While Thomas Young estimated the quantity at about 45 cc., most estimates in modern textbooks, supported by the views of Volkmann and Vierordt, run much higher, up to 180 cc. It is surprising that no one has arrived at the following procedure by which this important value is available by direct determination, at least in animals. One measures how much oxygen an animal absorbs from the air in a given time, and how much CO_2 it gives off. One takes during this time a sample of arterial and a sample of venous blood; in both samples oxygen content and CO_2 content are measured. The difference of oxygen content gives the amount of oxygen each cubic centimeter of blood takes up in its passage through the lungs; and as one knows how much total oxygen has been taken up in given time, one can calculate how many cubic centimeters of blood have passed through the lungs in this time, or if one divides by the number of heartbeats during this time, how many cubic centimeters of blood are ejected with each beat. The corresponding calculation with CO_2 quantities gives a determination of the same value, which provides a control for the other calculation.

Since for the demonstration of this method two gas pumps are needed, your reporter unfortunately is not in a position to communicate experimental data. He will only give, therefore, a calculation of blood flow in man according to this method, based on more or less arbitrary data. According to the experiments of Scheffer in Ludwig's laboratory, dog's arterial blood contains 0.146 cc. oxygen per cc. (measured at 0°C. and 1 atm. pressure); 1 cc. of venous blood contains 0.0905 cc. oxygen. Each cc. of blood therefore takes up 0.0555 cc. oxygen in its passage through the lungs. Let us assume the same in man. Assume, further, that a man absorbs in 24 hours 833 grams of oxygen. This will occupy a space of 433,200 cc. at 0°C. and 1 atm. pressure. According to this 5 cc. of oxygen would be absorbed by the lungs of a man each second. In order to effect this absorption, 5 /0.0555 cc. of blood must perfuse the lungs per second, that is, 90 cc. Assuming, finally, 7 systoles in 6 seconds, each systole would then eject 77 cc. of blood.

In addition to *Medical Physics*, Fick's monographs include *Compendium of Physiology*, which appeared between 1860 and 1890; *Researches on Muscular Activity*, 1867; *Handbook of Anatomy and Physiology of the Sense Organs*, 1862; and *Circulation of Blood*, 1872. In his later years he added philosophy to his writing.

Fick was several times dean of the College of Medicine at Würzburg and onetime rector of the University. When offered the Bavarian Order of the Crown, he refused because of his democratic convictions. Also, he was an uncompromising crusader against the use of alcoholic beverages. The scientific academies of Berlin, Munich, Stockholm, and Uppsala placed his name on their rosters, and the College of Philosophy at Leipzig University awarded him the honory degree of doctor of philosophy.

1. Voit, C.: Adolf Fick (Ger), obituary, *Sitzung Math-Physik Classe* 32:277-287, 1902, translated by E. Longar.

2. Fick, A.: *Medical Physics* (Ger), Braunschweig: F. Vieweg & Son, 1856.

3. Fick, A.: The Measurement of Cardiac Ventricular output (Ger), *Phys Med Ges* 16:XVI, 1870, translated in Fishman, A. P., and Richards, D. W. (eds.): *Circulation of the Blood, Men and Ideas,* New York: Oxford University Press, 1964.

Countway Medical Library, Boston

John C. Dalton, Jr. (1825-1889)

JOHN CALL DALTON, JR., the first professor of physiology in America, was born in Chelmsford, Massachusetts, into a family claiming a number of physicians in its lineage including his father. Young Dalton entered Harvard College at the age of 15, demonstrated outstanding scholastic leadership, and graduated AB in 1844.[1] In his second year at Harvard Medical School, he served as house-pupil at the Massachusetts General Hospital, where he witnessed the administration of ether by Morton. Hinckley's retrospective painting of the historic event shows the red-headed medical student among the distinguished gathering of senior physicians and surgeons, which included H. J. Bigelow and J. C. Warren. Dalton received the MD degree in 1847 and remained in Boston for three years, apportioning his time in the cholera hospital and investigating the clinical and pathologic aspects of the malady during a severe epidemic. In the report to the city of Boston on the several features of the devastating infection, prepared at the close of the epidemic, he was a major contributor and the principal illustrator.[2]

One result of this exposure to investigative medicine was the urge to study in Paris with Claude Bernard, who had recently achieved fame as the exponent of the new field of experimental medicine and who was in the midst of investigating the glycogenic function of the liver. Upon returning to America after one year in Paris, Dalton made no attempt to practice medicine but instead devoted his time to the study of physiological phenomena. Also, he prepared an essay, entitled "On the Corpus Luteum of Menstruation and Pregnancy," which, following submission in competition to the American Medical Association, received the attention of the faculty at the University of Buffalo School of Medicine and resulted in the offer to Dalton of a professorship in physiology. In accepting the offer, in 1851, he became the first professor to occupy such a chair in America; physiology had been taught formerly as a joint enterprise with anatomy, chemistry, or pathology. With the freedom to plan his course and unhampered by ties to other disciplines, Dalton introduced the experimental method as practiced by Claude Bernard. In place of didactic lectures Dalton demonstrated selected mechanisms of physiological function. He was aided in this venture by the recent discovery of ether for anesthesia and was able to conduct painless demonstrations on experimental animals, thereby providing illustrative exercises in the laboratory and living exhibits in the classroom.

Dalton remained in Buffalo for two years, then acknowledged a call to the Vermont Medical College at Woodstock, for a similar period of time. In addition, during the winter term (1854-1855) he presented a series of lectures at the College of Physicians and Surgeons in New York. In 1855, he moved to Manhattan, where he was appointed professor of physiology and microscopic anatomy. Subsequently the anatomy portion of the assignment was dropped. From 1859 to 1861, Dal-

ton also taught physiology at the Long Island College Hospital. At the outbreak of the Civil War, he went south with the Seventh Regiment from New York and, until 1864, served in the medical corps of the volunteer army as a brigade surgeon. At the end of the war, Dalton resumed his peacetime duties as professor of physiology, a post which he held without interruption until shortly before the age of 60, when he was advanced to the presidency of the College of Physicians and Surgeons. He remained in this post until death from kidney trouble.

Dalton is credited with no notable discovery in physiology; on the other hand, just as he was the first professor of physiology, he also composed the first major text on the subject in America and prepared other worthwhile treatises or monographs. The contents of his *Physiology*, reflecting his careful analysis of contemporary information, were supported by animal experiments.[3] Undergraduate studies in the classics developed into an interest in medical history, which resulted in the preparation of his *Doctrines of the Circulation*[4] and an extended presentation before the New York Academy of Medicine on *Galen and Paracelsus*. A discussion of the experimental method in medical science formed the basis of the Cartwright lectures on Galvani, Buffon, Bonnet, and Sir Charles Bell.[5] Even in retirement he continued to write and prepared a 3-volume compendium, entitled *Topographical Anatomy of the Brain*,[6] profusely illustrated with his pen drawings.

In the preparation of *A Treatise on Human Physiology*, published in 1859, Dalton appears as the first native teacher of the subject, with the self-evident conviction that an American physiologist, equal to a German or a Frenchman, has the talent for the development of his special field of medical science. His physiology text went through seven editions during his lifetime and established an enviable reputation for him in less than one quarter of a century. To complement the professional treatise he prepared a popular discussion for domestic use, *A Treatise on Physiology and Hygiene; for Schools, Families, and Colleges*. In his introductory address to the College of Physicians and Surgeons in 1859, when student and professor were contemplating their future in the school for the first time, he noted his respect for the medical profession as follows.[7]

There is probably but little occasion for me to speak of the worth and dignity of the medical profession. If you were not already sensible of these, you would not have chosen it for the occupation of your lives. Still it may not be out of place here to say that further acquaintance with it will not disappoint the expectations you have formed. I do not know any profession whose members are more thoroughly and sincerely attached to it than the medical;—there are few where they are so much so. We sometimes, it is true, hear medical men complain . . . [but] they forget, for the time, that the Profession of Medicine has a duration in the past and a security in the future, that raise it above the level of temporary disaster, and protect it equally from the passing attacks of ignorance and dishonesty. And whatever may be said of the practice of medicine by the disappointed or the over-sensitive, all will agree that its study, as a worthy pursuit for vigorous and cultivated minds, has no superior in the whole field of knowledge, open to human investigation.

One of Dalton's great services to the medical sciences was his crusade for the legal utilization of animals in the experimental laboratory and his effective resistance in preventing antivivisectionists from legislating against it. In 1866, he presented a long brief to the New York Academy of Medicine, outlining the advantages derived from animal experiments throughout medical history.[8] No other procedure for the advancement of physiology was available at the time. Each objection that the experiments were cruel and unnecessary and produced invalid conclusions was refuted effectively. He displayed caution in explaining the significance of results from animals of different species but noted that each important discovery in physiology has been deduced from experiments on living animals or man. Included were: the earliest observations of Galen that arteries as well as veins contained blood; the demonstration by Harvey of the motion of blood through the heart and vascular system; experiments on respiration by Boyle, Mayow, Priestley, and Black; transfusion of blood by Boyle and Lower; artificial respiration by Robert Hooke; digestion by William Beaumont; study of the nervous system by Bell and Magendie; the operation for aneurysm by John Hunter; and the regeneration of

periosteum by DuHamel, Hunter, and others. In the monograph of 1875, entitled *Experimentation on Animals as a Means of Knowledge in Physiology, Pathology, and Practical Medicine*, he noted as follows:[9]

The charge of inhumanity, as brought against the practice of experimentation on animals, seems to ignore in great measure the motive and object of such investigations. Cruelty is the wanton destruction of life or infliction of pain, either for the gratification of a morbid ferocity, or for an unthinking amusement which disregards the suffering it may cause. Neither of these faults can be charged upon scientific investigation. Its object is solely the acquisition of a kind of knowledge which has been shown to be inferior to none in its importance for the welfare of mankind. It is also at the farthest possible remove from a careless or trifling occupation. Scientific knowledge is simply a knowledge which is definite and precise, which has been attained by known means, and which is capable of verification by repeated trials. It is a laborious pursuit, requiring care, industry, exactitude, and perseverance.

It is a universal conviction that animal life is properly to be sacrificed whenever it may be necessary for the welfare of mankind. Nothing is more essential to this welfare, than the preservation of health and the relief or cure of disease. If we slaughter our cattle for their beef and hides, musk-deer for their perfume, the cochineal insect for its carmine, and Spanish flies for the materials of a blister, there can be no doubt that any useful knowledge in medicine or surgery is abundantly worth the lives of the animals destroyed to obtain it.

Dalton lived a simple, unpretentious life. As a quiet scholar, endowed with a teaching instinct and devoted to the laboratory and his library, he was a bachelor throughout. He took an active part in the affairs of the New York Academy of Medicine, serving as vice president for several terms, and was an active member of local, state, and national medical bodies. Although not a practitioner of medicine, he maintained a lively interest in the affairs of the profession, typical of a professor in the basic sciences a century ago.

1. Harrington, T. F.: *The Harvard Medical School, a History, Narrative and Documentary*, vol 2, New York: Lewis Publishing Co., 1905, pp 886-901.

2. *Report of the City Physician on the Cholera Hospital*, Boston, Dec, 1849 (City Document No. 66).

3. Dalton, J. C.: *A Treatise on Human Physiology: Designed for the Use of Students and Practitioners of Medicine*, Philadelphia: Blanchard & Lea, 1859.

4. Dalton, J. C.: *Doctrines of the Circulation. A History of Physiological Opinion and Discovery, in Regard to the Circulation of the Blood*, Philadelphia: H. C. Lea's Son & Co., 1884.

5. Dalton, J. C.: *The Experimental Method in Medical Science*, New York: G. P. Putnam's Sons, 1882.

6. Dalton, J. C.: *Topographical Anatomy of the Brain*, Philadelphia: Lea Brothers & Co., 1885.

7. Dalton, J. C.: *Introductory Address, Delivered at the College of Physicians and Surgeons, New York. October 16, 1885*, New York: J. J. Schroeder, 1855.

8. Dalton, J. C.: Vivisection: What It Is, and What It Has Accomplished, *Bull New York Acad Med*, 1867, pp 1-40.

9. Dalton, J. C.: *Experimentation on Animals, as a Means of Knowledge in Physiology, Pathology, and Practical Medicine*, New York: F. W. Christern, 1875.

Composite by G. Bako

Moritz Schiff (1823-1896)

MORITZ SCHIFF, who displayed a great diversity of interests in the comprehensive exploration of biological phenomena, was born in Frankfurt-am-Main. He received his early education in the Senckenberg Institute in Frankfurt, studied medicine at Heidelberg and Berlin, and received the MD degree at Göttingen in 1844.[1] Professing little concern for the practice of medicine, his early scientific training attracted him to zoology and particularly ornithology.

In 1845, Schiff proceeded to Paris to study in the Museum des Jardins des Plantes when Magendie and Longet were carrying on their investigations in neurophysiology. From this work came a monograph on the flora of South America. In 1847, Schiff returned to Frankfurt and was appointed director of the

ornithologic department of the Zoological Museum. When the time came for academic recognition, his participation as a military surgeon on the side of the revolutionaries in 1848 made him unacceptable to German universities. He was denied, therefore, qualification as privatdocent in zoology by the University of Göttingen, with the excuse that his teaching would be dangerous to the students. An academic career, however, was not denied him, and, in 1854, he was appointed professor of comparative anatomy in the University of Bern. He held this post until 1863, when he was called to the chair of physiology in the Institute of Advanced Studies at Florence, Italy. Eventually he encountered serious hostility because of his vivisection policies and practice, and, in 1876, made his final move to the University of Geneva, also as professor of physiology; there he remained until his death.

Although many of Schiff's contributions may be classed as neurophysiologic, they overlapped into the cardiovascular, metabolic, gastrointestinal, and endocrine areas. His bibliography is extensive, his contributions are many—typical of the outstanding natural scientists of his time in Central Europe. Only selected items will be noted in this essay. In 1849, Schiff found evidence to suspect the motor function of the vagus nerve, a forerunner of the discovery of the accelerating fibers a generation later. Following sectioning of the spinal cord, he postulated the existence of a site in the higher centers for control of vasomotor fibers. Vasodilation of small vessels of the tongue of experimental animals, after section of the lingual and hypoglossal nerves, was detected in physiological experiments and confirmed grossly postmortem. The tongue was a suitable experimental organ since visual comparison could be made between changes in vascular supply of the paralyzed and intact side.[2]

In some of the animals [with severed hypoglossal nerve] the lingual nerve on the same side was severed also; within ten minutes, at times even earlier, the paralyzed side became redder than the control and the increased redness persisted. Looking only at the paralyzed side, the redness was not conspicuous but was easily detectable when compared with the normal side.

In a few of the animals with a severed lingual nerve, I interrupted also the hypoglossus nerve and the redness suddenly appeared on the paralyzed side, spreading smoothly and intensively to the midline, precisely the same as in the previous experiments.

I concluded from these experiments that the tonus of the small vessels of the tongue depends on the hypoglossus as well as the lingual nerve; this is based not only on each nerve supplying the blood vessels of the various areas which they innervate, but in a manner compatible with the influence of both nerves on all the smaller vessels of the same area. Thus, the activity of one nerve can modify the activity of the other if the other is paralyzed, showing that the distribution of vasomotor activity of both nerves is identical.

Vasomotor nerves of the extremities were similarly studied and identified.[3]

If the roots of the nerves that control voluntary movements of the anterior extremities are interrupted at the spinal cord, only the paw and lower quarter of the foreleg become warmer and persistent dilatation of vessels in the interdigital membrane becomes visible.

If the fourth and fifth anterior thoracic roots of the spinal cord are severed in the dog, cat, or rabbit, the thoracic skin and the entire limb become hot. Even the paw and the lower part of the foreleg are warmer than on the opposite side.

The paw as well as the leg has a dual source of neurovascular supply. One portion originates in the brachial plexus; it begins with the last cervical root and includes the first two dorsal roots. These branches combine to form the trunk of the axillary plexus.

Another portion originates from the third through the sixth dorsal roots; this portion combines with the nerves that supply the upper leg and forms the superior thoracic sympathetic branch before supplying the upper part of the extremity or the subclavicular region.

In order to alter the temperature of the foreleg and the adjoining skin it is necessary to sever either the roots of the posterior thoracic nerves of the brachial plexus or the communicating fibers between the trunks originating from these roots and between the sympathetic ganglia, or the interganglionic fibers of sympathetic nerves between the first and second thoracic ganglia, or the first thoracic ganglion and the lower cervical ganglion.

Schiff's experimental work on the endocrine glands and metabolic disorders concerned particularly the thyroid and the artificial induction of diabetes mellitus. Following excision of the thyroid, he reproduced several of the symptoms of myxedema and, on the contrary, attempted to prevent systemic deterioration in dogs by aberrant transplants. The sugar-forming capacity of the liver in frogs rendered diabetic by Bernard's puncture of the floor of the fourth ventricle was described as follows:[4]

The experiments of Bernard have taught us that in higher animals, an injury to a specific site in the central nervous system produces diabetes, but the origin of the urinary sugar produced with this procedure has not been discovered.

The sugar-producing activity of the liver was eliminated by removing the liver or ligating its vessels following Bernard's puncture. Since this operation cannot be performed on higher animals, the frog was selected.

The essential experiments showed that sugar which appeared in the urine after the puncture was produced in the liver. After a few hours (2 to 5 hours) sugar could be found in the urine of all frogs; following this the liver was temporarily extracted through an abdominal incision and a ligature was placed around the vessels. In one half of the experimental animals the ligature was removed subsequently; in the other half it was tightened so that the circulation was completely occluded; the liver was replaced in the abdominal cavity and the incision closed. Animals whose liver was ligated showed sugar in the urine for not more than three hours and in small amounts only; as soon as the blood lost the sugar which it held at the time of operation, it then disappeared from the urine.

Schiff prepared several monographs; one on the physiology of the nervous system, another on muscle and nerve physiology, and a two-volume treatise on the physiology of digestion are especially noteworthy. Each of his earlier contributions and many of his later ones were published in German medical periodicals in his native tongue. While he was in Florence, his communications were prepared in Italian, while in Geneva, much of his work appeared in French. From 1862 on he served as co-editor of the *Schweizerische Zeitschrift für Heilkunde*. Not all of his findings were confirmed by others; at times he speculated beyond the experimental data and subsequently rescinded some of his theoretical speculations. However, his natural philosophy was experimentally based in an era when experimental physiology was just being recognized as the new tool for significant advances in understanding of physiologic phenomena.

1. Biedl, A.: Moritz Schiff (Ger), *Wien Klin Wschr* 9:1007-1010, 1896.

2. Schiff, M.: Influence of Nerves on the Vessels of the Tongue (Ger), *Arch Physiol Heilk* 12:377-391, 1853, excerpt translated by Z. Danilevicius.

3. Schiff, M.: Vasomotor Nerves of the Forelegs (Fr), *Proc Acad Sci* 55:425-427, 1862, excerpt translated by Z. Danilevicius.

4. Schiff, M.: The Formation of Sugar in the Liver and the Influence of the Nervous System on the Cause of Diabetes (Ger), Z. Danilevicius (trans.), *Nachr Georg-Augusts Univ*, 1856, pp 243-247.

Composite by G. Bako

Paul Bert (1833-1886)

PAUL BERT, pupil of Claude Bernard and a political activist, was born at Auxerre, France, and received his early education in the Department of Yonne.[1] He first became interested in engineering, then the study of law, and passed his examinations; but before entering the bar, Bert turned his attention to anatomy and physiology. He obtained the doctorate of medicine in 1863 from the Faculty of Medicine of Paris. His thesis on animal grafting attracted the attention of Bernard, a senior examiner at the time, in whose laboratory he became an assistant. In 1866, Bert was admitted as a doctor of natural science and for several years taught zoology in Bordeaux; in 1869, he was named professor of physiology, as Bernard's successor in the Faculty of Sciences. During the terminal years of the Second Empire, Bert demonstrated his uncompromising Republicanism and began to exert himself in political affairs; meanwhile his great work on barometric pressure was maturing rapidly.

At this time, a Dr. Jourdanet, wealthy patron of the sciences, with experience in the observation of differences in physiological responses in the highlands of Mexico, provided funds for a decompression chamber for the experimental study of diminished barometric pressure of varying oxygen content.

An initial interest in the pathogenesis of acute mountain sickness later included the response of balloonists during ascent to critically high altitudes and the reaction by deep sea divers and caisson workers upon return to atmospheric pressure. Most of the experimental work was carried out during the early 1870's, summarized in a report, and translated into English in 1877[2]—a prelude to an extensive monograph on barometric pressure, published the following year, and translated into English in 1943.[3]

The varying affinity of hemoglobin for oxygen, displayed by the oxygen dissociation curves, was not defined until many years later. However, the fundamental reactions of barometric pressure, as measured by partial pressure of oxygen in man and animal described by Bert from his experimental observations, remain valid. All of his studies were essentially experiments in oxygen deprivation; although he was thoroughly familiar with long-term acclimatization effects in man and animals, he carried out no experimental studies among natives or temporary residents at high altitudes for comparison of their response with others living under normal barometric pressure.

Bert offered convincing proof that barometric pressure acts on human beings only by diminishing the tension of oxygen in the air and that the effects of diminution of pressure may be combated by the respiration of air sufficiently rich in oxygen to maintain the tension of the gas at sea level. For these experiments, which laid the foundation for aviation physiology almost a century later, the Academy of Sciences bestowed upon him the grand biennial award of 20,000 francs.

A summary of Bert's work begins with a description of the symptoms of acute mountain sickness (diminished oxygen), based upon a review of the literature and supplemented by his personal experiments.[2]

As every one knows, in proportion as we ascend from the sea-level, the barometric pressure diminishes at the rate of about one centimetre per 100 metres of vertical ascent.

Such modifications of pressure cannot be endured with impunity by the human organism.

[There is], first, a sense of fatigue out of proportion to the amount of walking or of work performed. The legs appear to become leaden, and one feels a weakness in the knees. Then the breath becomes short, difficult, labored; the pulse is quickened; the heart-beats occur isolatedly, and reverberate in the head. Next come singing in the ears, dimness of sight, and vertigo. The general sense of *malaise*, the feebleness, become such that the traveler must rest, else he will fall to the ground. Simultaneously there occur other symptoms having their seat in the digestive organs, such as nausea and vomiting. These various symptoms, taken together, constitute mountain-sickness (*mal des montagnes*), which bears a resemblance to sea-sickness.

When they first appear, a few moments rest suffices to banish them; this instantaneous restoration of strength and vigor sharply distinguishes mountain-sickness from ordinary fatigue. But at greater elevations, where graver symptoms appear, such as bleeding from the nose or from the lungs, repose cannot bring back the condition of perfect health, though it always affords some relief. Travelers agree in saying that a person on horseback suffers far less than one on foot.

This is the reason why aeronauts are attacked much later than those who ascend the mountain-side. I need not detail here the long series of experiments which have led me to conclude that the symptoms following diminished pressure, whether slowly or rapidly applied, are simply the result of a diminution of the oxygen in the blood; in a word, that they are nothing but a sort of asphyxia in the midst of the "pure and invigorating mountain-air."

Still I may repeat here an experiment which can be performed wherever we have a pneumatic apparatus; this experiment clearly proves that the lessening of the barometric pressure is of no account, mechanically, in the production of the phenomena. These are the result rather of chemicophysical action, the blood not being sufficiently charged with oxygen.

We place a sparrow in the pneumatic bell-glass. . . . When the manometer shows only 30 centimetres' pressure in the bell-glass, the bird gives pretty serious evidence of suffering; at 20 centimetres it totters, reels, and falls upon its side; at 18 centimetres it struggles violently, and would die in a few seconds, were I to leave it in this situation. So I quickly . . . introduce into the bell-glass not air, but oxygen. . . . At once the bird becomes himself again. I let it breathe a little while, and again I diminish the pressure. . . ; we reach a pressure much less than before, and yet the life of the bird is plainly not at all endangered. If I were to admit oxygen once again, I might diminish the pressure still more.

Hence it appears that it is not the lowering of mechanical pressure that produces the symptoms, but the low tension of the oxygen of the dilated air, which low tension prevents the oxygen from entering the blood in sufficient quantity.

Bert confirmed, with human experiments, the physiological responses in animals placed in a double air chamber of sheet iron. He carried a bag of oxygen into the chamber and showed that the cardiac acceleration during reduction of pressure could be reversed by inhalation of oxygen. Upon reducing the chamber pressure to simulate the height of the Himalayas, and at the same time maintaining sea-level oxygen tension, he showed no sense of discomfort was experienced.

Comparable studies on the effects of increased atmospheric pressure in the search for a physiological understanding of difficulties during decompression in submarine divers and in caisson workers suffering from bends followed. It had been recognized that compression as high as five atmospheres produced no symptoms immediately. Trouble began during decompression and was largely attributed to the escape of dissolved nitrogen in body tissues.

But how does decompression act? Very simply indeed. Here in this glass jar is a rat subjected to ten atmospheres. I now turn a cock, and in a moment bring the animal back to normal pressure; he turns around two or three times and drops dead. Were I to make an autopsy now, I should find the heart and the great vessels full of gas; . . . This gas is nitrogen with a little carbonic acid.

The process is as follows: The animal by breathing compressed air charges its blood with air in the proportions indicated by physical law; on the normal pressure being restored, the gases with which it was supersaturated pass into the free state. It is like drawing the cork of a bottle of beer. The oxygen combines on the spot, but the nitrogen is at once set free, and carries with it carbonic acid in becoming disengaged.

Almost from the beginning of his famous experimental studies, Bert devoted a considerable portion of his energy to public service. He became the Secretary-General of the prefecture of the Yonne in 1870, was chosen deputy in 1874, and took his seat on the Extreme Left. He strongly opposed the pretensions of the clergy to control the education of the young, and made alarming exposures of the abuses in the teaching and the texts. The clericals, considering him an avowed enemy, looked with great disfavor on his appointment in 1881 as Minister of Public Instruction and Worship. He succeeded in having a bill passed in the Chamber in 1884 to secularize the schools by appointing lay teachers in place of friars and nuns. Early in the year of his death, Bert was appointed Governor-General of Tonquin, French Indochina, and Minister-General of the Court of Anam for the French government. He carried out his civil duties in his new position, encouraged the development of science in the new French dependency, and favored a national library at Hanoi and public libraries in the principal towns. He refused to accommodate himself to the rigors of the humid tropical environment and succumbed to dysentery. In addition to his monograph, *Barometric Pressure*, he published a review of works on anatomy and physiology, notes on comparative anatomy and physiology, lessons in zoology, and his parliamentary addresses.

1. Sketch of Paul Bert, *Popular Sci Monthly* 33:401-407, 1888.
2. Bert, P.: Atmospheric Pressure and Life (Fr), *Rev Sci*, J. Fitzgerald (trans.), *Popular Sci Monthly* 11:316-329, 1877.
3. Bert, P.: *Barometric Pressure; Researches in Experimental Physiology*, (Fr), Paris: G. Masson, 1878, M. A. Hitchcock, and F. A.: Hitchock (trans.), Columbus, Ohio: College Book Co., 1943.

National Library of Medicine

Carl von Voit (1831-1908)

CARL VON VOIT, native of Amberg, Bavaria, carried on the tradition of metabolic research begun by his preceptor, Pettenkofer, and passed it in turn to Rubner, his most illustrious pupil. Voit's father, a well-known architect, August Voit, was responsible for the design of the glass palace in Munich.[1] After completing Gymnasium studies in Amberg during the troubled political times of 1848, Voit began the study of medicine in the University of Munich; there he showed an interest in the other natural sciences and particularly in botany. Before he returned to Munich to complete his medical training, he continued his education at Würzburg, where von Kölliker, Leydig, Virchow, and others were on the faculty. In 1854, he presented his dissertation for the MD degree on the distribution of nitrogen in the animal organism.

Following graduation, Voit spent a year in Wöhlers' laboratory in Göttingen and, returning to Munich, was appointed assistant by Bischoff in the Physiological Institute in 1856. Advancing rapidly from privatdocent in physiology in 1857, Voit became professor and director of the Physiological Institute in 1863. In 1865, he received membership in the Bavarian Academy of Science, the same year that he founded with Pettenkofer and Buhl and the *Zeitschrift für Biologie*. He was granted the title of Royal Privy Councillor in 1893.

Voit's important works, usually pursued jointly, were concerned with nutrition and metabolism for which his skill in designing laboratory equipment and devising chemical procedures proved highly valuable. One of the best examples is the Pettenkofer-Voit respiration chamber built by Pettenkofer for the study of respiratory exchange in normal man and in "metabolic" diseases, notably leukemia and diabetes mellitus. From the carbon dioxide content of expired air and the nitrogen content of urine, they estimated the kinds of substances metabolized and their oxygen equivalents and thereby established the dependency of oxygen uptake and utilization of nutrients as well as the exchange of oxygen and carbon dioxide.

Voit found early in his metabolic studies that living processes, although interdependent, were not directly proportional to the oxygen supply and that the metabolism of tissues, as measured by the exchange of vital gases, altered the oxygen and carbon dioxide content of the blood, which in turn regulated respiration. Another example of cooperative effort was the confirmation by Rubner of the validity of the law of conservation of energy in the animal body. Utilizing the data from the animal calorimeter and building upon the earlier work of Pettenkofer and Voit, Rubner found that the quantity of heat given off by the dog to the calorimeter equaled the amount calculated from metabolic activity.

Employing the respiration chamber for the investigation of the interaction of carbohydrates, fats, and proteins, Voit and associates discovered the conversion of carbohydrate to fat and a portion of the protein ingested to carbohydate.[2] It was learned that protein and fat were called upon for energy in starvation, while at rest less fat was consumed, especially during sleep, and that more fat was metabolized during exercise. In the dog, an exclusive protein diet was adequate; if fat was added, most of this was deposited as fat, and carbohydrates were burned, irrespective of the quantity and, similarly to fat, protected the body against fat loss. Voit's law of nitrogen metabolism stated that the nitrogen in the food was equivalent to the sum of the nitrogen in the urine and in the feces. No metabolic nitrogen was found in the respiratory gases. The study of the nutrition of proteins established that a carnivorous animal could be brought into "nitrogen equilibrium" if the experiment were adequately controlled. After the ingestion of an excessive quantity of nitrogenous foods, a portion, called by him "circulating protein," is retained temporarily. This is gradually eliminated from the cells upon reduction of the high-protein intake. He feuded with Liebig over the source of fuel for muscle activity. Liebig assigned this function to proteins. Voit could find no evidence from his investigations to support this premise.

The following translation by Lusk from Voit's summary of his metabolic investigations is mainly of historic interest but significant in that they point toward the importance of the cell in the phenomenon of living matter.[3]

The unknown causes of metabolism are found in the cells of the organism. The mass of these cells and their power to decompose materials determine the metabolism. It is absolutely proved that protein fed to the cells is the easiest of all the foodstuffs to be destroyed, next carbohydrates, and lastly fat. The metabolism continues in the cells until their power to metabolize is exhausted.

The metabolism of the different foodstuffs varies with the quality and quantity of the food. Proteid alone may burn, or little proteid and much carbohydrates and fat. I have determined the amount of the metabolism of the various foodstuffs under the most varied conditions.

All the functions of metabolism are derived from the processes in the cells. In a given condition of the cells, available proteid may be used exclusively if enough be furnished them. If the power of the cells to metabolize is not exhausted by the proteid furnished, then carbohydrates and fats are destroyed up to the limit of the ability of the cells to do so.

From this use of materials arise physical results, such as work, heat, electricity, which we can express in heat units. This is the power derived from metabolism.

It is possible to approach the subject in the reverse order, that is, to study the energy production (Kraftwechsel) and to draw conclusions regarding the metabolism (Stoffwechsel). It is perfectly possible to say the requirement of energy in the body or the production of the heat necessary to cover heat loss, or for energy to do work, are controlling factors over the metabolism; since on cooling the body or on working correspondingly more matter is destroyed. But one must not conclude that the loss of body heat or muscular work are the immediate causes of this increased metabolism.

The requirement for energy cannot possibly be the cause of metabolism, any more than the requirement for gold will put it in one's pocket. Hence the production of energy has a very definite upper limit, which is afforded by the ability of the cells to metabolize. If the cells will metabolize no more, then further increase of work ceases even in the presence of direst necessity; and this is also the case with the heat production, even though it were very necessary, and we were likely to freeze.

Voit's several monographs include *The Law of Protein in Nutrition* (1860); *The Animal Organism* (1863); *The Investigations of Food in Public Establishments* (1877); *Handbook of Metabolism and Nutrition* (1881); *Investigation of the Influence of Sodium Chloride, Coffee and Muscular Activity on Metabolism* (1860); *The Distinction Between Animal and Vegetable*

Nutrients (1869); and *The Development of the Study of the Source of Muscle Energy and Nutrition over a Quarter of a Century* (1870). He rarely attended national or international scientific meetings or congresses. His contact with the outside world was largely through the *Zeitschrift für Biologie.* Locally, Voit was a dominant force in the Munich faculty, and chose a member of his department, Otto Frank, as his successor. His pupils included Atwater, Cathcart, Lusk, Prausnitz, and others.

1. Frank, O.: In Memoriam Carl von Voit (Ger), *Z Biol* 51: I-XXIV, 1908.
2. Pettenkofer, M., and Voit, C.: Investigations on Respiration (Ger), *Ann Chem Pharm,* suppl 2, pp 52-70, 1862-1863.
3. Voit, C.: Isodynamic Equilibrium (Ger), *Muench Med Wschr* 49:233-235, 1902, in Lusk, G. (trans.): *The Elements of the Science of Nutrition,* Philadelphia: W. B. Sanders Co., 1906.

Hugo Kronecker (1839-1914)

KARL HUGO KRONECKER, one of the leading physiologists in the 19th century, was born in Liegnitz, Prussia, into a well-to-do family with scholarly interests.[1] His father

was a merchant, his older brother, Leopold, a celebrated mathematician. After completing his general education at the Gymnasium in Liegnitz, Hugo studied medicine in Berlin and later at Heidelberg; there he came under the influence of Helmholtz and Wundt. He received the MD degree from Berlin in 1863 and presented his inaugural dissertation on muscle fatigue, for him a subject of enduring interest. Intending to pursue the practice of medicine, he shared his time as an assistant to Traube in medicine with studies in physiological chemistry under Kühne. Kronecker's training was interrupted temporarily by a pulmonary infection, and, following advice to seek a warmer climate, he selected Pisa, Italy. Here he acquired proficiency in Italian, to complement his fluency in French and English. Upon recovering his health, he served in the Franco-Prussian War and received the Iron Cross for bravery.

Probably the most important appointment in Kronecker's investigative career came in 1868 when he entered Karl Ludwig's Institute in Leipzig, a brilliant center for students of physiology from many countries. In 1876, Kronecker was called to Berlin as head of the experimental physiology division in the Institute recently organized by Du Bois Reymond. Seven years later, he accepted the professorship of physiology at the University of Bern and held this post until his death.

As director of the Institute in Bern, which he preferred to call the "Hallerianum" for Albrecht von Haller, Kronecker emulated Ludwig in attracting a notable coterie of students; meanwhile he expanded his international contacts. The creation of new laboratory procedures and the design of new pieces of physiological apparatus were probably his greatest contributions to teaching and investigation. He was a prime mover in establishing the Marey Institute in Paris, an international establishment for the repository and demonstration of new physiological techniques. His sliding induction coil became a standard laboratory item for young and seasoned students. Kronecker invented the frog-heart manometer and a perfusion cannula, and directed von Basch in the first sphygmomanometric studies on human beings; however, his name was not included as an author in the publication.

Following Bowditch, Kronecker extended the observation on the "staircase" effect and the all-or-none principle of cardiac muscle. Also, he showed the impossibility of tetanizing cardiac muscle. His observations on the refractory period preceded those of Marey, one of his important contributions to the physiology of muscular contraction.[2]

The cooler the heart, the slower its motion, and the decreased frequency of its beats, if they appear. If the contractions of the heart are induced at intervals longer than the corresponding duration of one cycle, even weak stimuli may produce regular contractions; however, if a strong stimulus *is applied to the heart before the regular cycle is ended, the stimulus produces no response.*

To determine the length of the recovery period which the heart needs between two beats one can either determine the interval between the stimuli which effectively provoke contractions of the heart and correspond to the regular rhythm of the heart, or one may apply stimuli at such a rapid rate that only those stimuli provoke a contraction which fall immediately after the cycle ends.

Another noted contribution was the study with Meltzer, in the rabbit and dog, of swallowing and esophageal contractions with a balloon. The rate of transmission of the esophageal contractions and the absence of antiperistalsis activity, with regurgitation of air, are summarized as follows:[3]

The observations and experiments with rabbits have proved to us that the cardia belongs to the complex of deglutition. The cardia participates in the series of contractions with each swallow; it contracts even when it is separated from the esophagus.

Our experiments have shown that the mechanism of esophageal movement is associated with adjoining groups of ganglia; the first receives the stimulus from the sensory nerve and transmits it in a regular fashion to the other ganglia. The ganglia are interconnected but they communicate with the outside only by transmission of the stimulus firstly to the uppermost ganglion. However, each ganglion is connected directly to the motor nerves of the corresponding segment of the esophagus. The stimulus travels rapidly within each ganglion but slowly from one ganglion to another; the more caudad, the slower the propagation of the stimulus.

After each regurgitation of air, the motion of the esophagus is the same as during swallowing except that the two upper segments in swallowing do not participate.

Similar events were demonstrated in dogs whose esophagus had been exposed. When a few attempts at swallowing were produced by stimulation of the laryngeal nerves, the stomach of the dog was soon filled with air and the slightest motion forced the air to regurgitate into the esophagus. A progression downward of contractions could be noted even though there was no attempt at swallowing.

It is evident that regurgitation of air is followed by a peristaltic mechanism and is not associated with antiperistalsis.

Also, we observed the sequence of events during a series of stimuli to swallow. It seemed likely that the rate of contractions might change. A study of two rapidly successive attempts to swallow was needed. What happens if one swallow is followed by another in less than six seconds? What happens when the esophagus is still contracted at one point? Would the second bolus follow the first one with the same speed or would it remain stationary above the cardia where each bolus is stopped when the cardia is contracted?

Our questions were answered in a surprising manner.

(1) When the balloon was placed in the first segment of the esophagus and when the animal was made to swallow two or more times in succession less than 1-2 seconds apart, the contraction appeared only after the second swallow. When the balloon was placed in the middle of the esophagus, the swallows could be spread as far apart as three seconds without producing the contraction sooner than after the last swallow. After the third swallow, the intervals could have been increased to 5-6 seconds without producing a contraction earlier than after the last swallow.

From this we can conclude that each attempt at swallowing produces an inhibition which lies in a centrally located center.

Another of Kronecker's international interests was mountains and high-altitude sickness. A colleague of Italian physiologist, Mosso, he supported the establishment of an international institute for the study of physiology of high altitudes on Monte Rosa in the Italian Alps. A number of clinical observations on acute symptoms associated with altitude were made; some were attributed incorrectly to diminution of circulation of blood through the pulmonary vessels. Other international interests led him to organize, with Michael Foster, an International Congress of Physiology, which met first in London in 1881. During his presidency in 1888, the third International Congress met in Bern. The National Academy of Sciences (American), the Royal Society of London, as well as several central European scientific bodies honored him with membership. Kronecker received a number of honorary degrees, including the LLD from the universities of Glasgow, Aberdeen, St. Andrew's, and Edinburgh and the DSC from Cambridge.

1. Meltzer, S. J.: Professor Hugo Kronecker, obituary, *Science* 40:441-444, 1914.

2. Kronecker, H.: Characteristics of Heart Muscle Action (Ger), *Beitr Anat Physiol,* Oct 15, 1874, pp 173-204, Leipzig: F. C. W. Vogel, excerpt translated by Z. Danilevicius.

3. Kronecker, H., and Meltzer, S.: The Swallowing Mechanism, Its Stimulation and Inhibition (Ger), *Arch Anat Physiol Abt,* suppl-vol, pp 328-362, 1883, excerpt translated by Z. Danilevicius.

Composite by G. Bako

Sir Michael Foster (1836-1907)

MICHAEL FOSTER, preceptor of natural scientists, editor of the *Journal of Physiology,* and creator of the Cambridge school of physiology, was the son of an English surgeon at Huntingdon, a hamlet on the sedgy Ouse. Michael attended the Huntingdon grammar school and at the age of thirteen proceeded to University College School, London.[1] He received the AB at the age of 18, with a university scholarship in the classics, while on the playing field he served as captain of the cricket team. Remaining on at the University College in medicine, he received gold medals in anatomy, physiology, and chemistry, took the MB in 1858, and the MD the following year. Meanwhile, he came under the influence of William Sharpey, professor of anatomy and physiology.

Since Foster was trained for a career in clinical medicine, not physiology, he began the practice of medicine with his father at Huntingdon. Six years later his destiny changed, when Sharpey called him to University College to design a course in practical physiology. The venture was successful, and, within two years, he was advanced to the professorship, soon after succeeding Huxley as Fullerian professor of physiology at the Royal Institution.

In academic circles, Foster was better known for his accomplishments as a teacher and for a greater capacity to lead disciples into the research laboratory than for the completion of critical investigations. On the other hand, shortly after accepting the responsibilities in London, he studied the esophagus of the frog and determined the effect of hypothermia on the contraction of the frog's muscles. In observing the actions of the heart of the snail, Foster found that the force of each beat was directly proportional to the distension of the cardiac cavities during the preceding systole, and that any part of the heart separated from the remainder of the myocardium would beat rhythmically.[1] The conclusion was self-evident: the myocardial pulsations could not be the result of any localized nervous stimulation but were the inherent and peculiar property of general cardiac tissue.

In 1870, Foster left London for Cambridge where, upon the recommendation of Huxley, he was appointed to the newly created position of praelector of physiology at Trinity College. Thirteen years later he was advanced to professor of physiology. The highly productive years, in which the program in general physiology developed and matured, continued for more than three decades. In this mission at Cambridge, he shared honors with John S. Burdon-Sanderson, Waynflete professor of physiology at Oxford, a competent but less well known teacher. The two were largely responsible for the founding and development of the companion schools of general physiology in England in the last quarter of the 19th century.

When Foster accepted the Cambridge assignment, the lecture hall and the physiology laboratory were combined into a single room, with shabby and wretched experimental equipment. Immediate steps were taken to correct this deficiency, since it was Foster's belief that the student of physiology should complement the formal lectures with laboratory exercises. Furthermore, not only should the student observe and perform experimental studies, but also he should be encouraged to carry on a small research project under tutorial guidance. Simple experimental apparatus was a vital component of such a plan and, at that time, was not readily available or available only in unsuitable design and quantity in Cambridge for this bold venture. As a friend who possessed both wealth and a scientifically-oriented mind, Dew-Smith founded the Cambridge Instrument Company, a unique facility that was not formed primarily for profit. Many of the pieces of equipment necessary for laboratory or classroom demonstration or in research study, were made available by this company in single units or in small lots. The *Journal of Physiology* was the second venture in the master plan of Foster. The *Journal,* founded in 1878 with a strong editorial board, included three members from America, and the financial blessing of Dew-Smith. Foster continued as the critical editor until he passed the mantle on to Langley in 1894.

Foster was enviably successful in recruiting pupils, who, in turn, became professors either of general physiology or of related subjects.[2] Included were Langley, his successor as professor of physiology at Trinity; Balfour, founder of the new science of comparative embryology; Vines, professor of botany at Oxford; Gaskell, professor of physiology; Liversidge, professor of chemistry; Marshall, professor of zoology; Martin, professor of biology at Johns Hopkins University; Sherrington, professor of physiology at Liverpool and Oxford; Head, professor of neurology at Cambridge; Adami, professor of physiology at Queens Medical School, Kingston, Ontario; and Sidgwick, animal morphologist at Cambridge.

English was the proper language of the medical scientist according to Foster, who was an active promoter of the Royal Society Catalogue of Scientific Papers and the International Catalogue of Scientific Papers. In composition, he developed a free style which was fast moving and pleasant to read. The following advice was offered for those ambitious to prepare a popular book.[3]

> Never write a text book; if it is a failure it is time thrown away and worse than wasted; if it is a success, it is a millstone around your neck for the rest of your life.

Several outstanding books were published by Foster, individually or in conjunction with his associates. Together with Burdon-Sanderson, Brunton, and Klein, he prepared a *Text-Book for the Physiological Laboratory;* with Balfour, *The Elements of Embryology;* and with Langley, *A Course of Elementary Practical Physiology.* His best-known treatise, *Text Book of Physiology,* first published in 1877, was accepted as the oustanding text in physiology of its time.[4] A number of editions were published and translated into several languages. A popular brochure for the young scientist was entitled, *A Science Primer on Physiology.* His *History of Physiology During the Sixteenth, Seventeenth,* and *Eighteenth Centuries* was delivered as the Lane Lectures at San Francisco in 1900. In the introduction to "Claude Bernard: a Lecture," which preceded by two decades Foster's full-length biography, he said:[5]

> GENTLEMEN,—It has long been a heavy burden on my conscience that, while you are receiving your instruction in physiology here, you are told but little of the history of science— that your attention is only rarely and incidentally called to the various steps by which we have reached our present outlook. I fear that

such historical statements as do reach you are sadly limited to the controversies of the last decennium.

Foster was elected a Fellow of the Royal Society in 1872 and one of the general secretaries. In 1881, he succeeded Huxley as biological secretary, an office that he held for more than 20 years. The founding of the Physiological Society in 1875 was directly related to his efforts, and he and Kronecker were the prime movers in organizing the International Congress of Physiologists, which continues as the outstanding international assemblage for physiologists. Honorary degrees from Oxford, Glasgow, St. Andrews, Dublin, and Montreal were conferred upon him. Foster devoted a great deal of leisure time to and wrote extensively on horticulture, gardening, and the growing of irises. He was created Knight Commander of the Bath in 1899 and in the following year was elected to Parliament, representing the University of London. After serving for a time, he transferred to the liberal side, and, as secretary of the Royal Society, was helpful in establishing an intimate working relationship between this body and the government. He served on various Royal Commissions, that on vaccination in 1889, on the disposal of sewage in 1898, and on tuberculosis in 1901. A philosophy of instruction—practical and sound in principle —which was Foster's basis for a lasting influence in the development of modern physiology, was ably described by Gaskell.[6]

Foster held very strong views as to the proper method of teaching physiology to students at the beginning of their medical study. He held it to be a mistake to demonstrate during the lecture, and insisted that practical work, carried on by the student himself, illustrative of the facts on which the lecture was based, must immediately follow the lecture. The physiology of each organ must be dealt with as a whole in lecture, and the practical work must be so arranged as to bring home to the student all the points of each lecture. The student must not feel that the lectures and demonstrations have no relationship, but that they complement each other and form a whole. His ideal laboratory would be of sufficient size to provide every student with his own working place, both in the histological and in the chemical department at the same time. He also—and this was one of the great reasons of his success—encouraged his pupils at the very

earliest moment to engage in some original research, and then persuaded them to give a few lectures of an advanced character upon the subject on which they were working; for, as he said, there is no way of discovering the gaps in your knowledge of a subject better than lecturing on it. In this way he associated with himself a band of younger workers engaged in research, who gave the advanced teaching to the students, thus allowing him to confine himself to the introductory course.

1. Langley, J. N.: Sir Michael Foster. In Memoriam, *J Physiol* 35:233-246, 1906-07.
2. Garrison, F. H.: Sir Michael Foster and the Cambridge School of Physiologists, *Maryland Med J* 58:105-118 (May) 1915.
3. Rolleston, H. D.: *The Cambridge Medical School, A Biographical History,* Cambridge: University Press, 1932.
4. Foster, M.: *A Text Book of Physiology,* 5th ed, London: Macmillan and Co., 1891.
5. Foster, M.: Claude Bernard: A Lecture, *Brit Med J* 1:519-521 (April 13) 1878.
6. Gaskell, W. H.: Sir Michael Foster, 1836-1907, *Proc Roy Soc Lond* 80:71-81 (Dec) 1908.

Composite by G. Bako

Willy Kühne (1837-1900)

WILLY KÜHNE, student of F. Wöhler, R. Wagner, W. E. Weber, J. Henle, C. G. Lehmann, R. Virchow, C. Bernard, C. Ludwig, E. Brücke, Du Bois Reymond, and Hoppe-Seyler, equaled the stature of his teachers during an enviable career in scientific medicine. Kühne, born in Hamburg, studied first and last at Göttingen, where he took the degree of doctor of philosophy at the age of 19, having attended universities in Berlin, Paris, and Vienna in the interim.[1] His inaugural thesis on artificial diabetes in the frog was inspired by Bernard's epochal contribution on experimental diabetes. Other early communications by Kühne discussed icterus, the formation of hippuric acid from benzoic acid, the chemical constituents of bile, urinary excretion of hemoglobin, and the physical and physiological characteristics of muscle.

In 1861, Kühne was invited by Virchow to join the Pathological Institute at the University of Berlin as chemical assistant and successor to Hoppe-Seyler. His brilliant work won him unusual recognition for so young an investigator. The following year the degree of MD was conferred *honoris causa* by the University.

In 1868, Kühne accepted a call to Amsterdam to the chair of physiology, and three years later succeeded Helmholtz at Heidelberg. By then his reputation attracted from Europe and America students who came to explore one or more of three great fields of physiological inquiry then occupying his laboratory—form and function of muscle, response of the retina, and the chemistry of digestion.

An initial interest in the histological appearance of the end-organ of motor nerves in muscle and the chemistry of muscular contraction, begun in the laboratory of Du Bois Reymond, proved most fruitful. The passage of a continuous current through a living muscle fiber produced a wave of contraction proceeding from the positive toward the negative pole (Kühne or Porret's phenomenon). With the use of chemical stimuli in the sartorius muscle of the frog, devoid of nerve fibers for several millimeters, it was found that independent excitability unrelated to nervous stimulation produced a varied response under different chemical stimuli. He defined the physicochemical characteristics of the contractile properties of the muscle substance from warm-blooded and cold-blooded animals. The coagulation of muscle

in rigor mortis was compared to the formation of fibrin from the blood plasma, as excerpted below.[2]

> As I have shown in an earlier publication, rigor mortis appears independently of the muscle fibers when the coagulable substance comes in contact with certain other fluids having been expressed from the sarcolemma. Either dilute rugar water or a weak salt solution is satisfactory; 0.7 to 1% solution of sodium chloride is best. The mixture coagulates as readily as blood plasma; while the greater the coagulability the less the rigor previously.
>
> A muscle once in rigor at a temperature of 40 C, in oil, mercury, or water, cannot be restored by the action of any physiological factor; once the liquid is coagulated it does not clear. A fresh responsive muscle once heated to 40 C has lost its excitability; the gelling produced at 40 C is similar to the rigor mortis in that circulating blood cannot restore it.

The term "muscle spindle," introduced in the title of another of Kühne's earlier communications, is currently in use; however, considerable advance has been made in understanding the function of the unit. The histological structure in voluntary muscle was judged to be a specialized sensory organ of finely striated muscle fibers, provided with many nuclei, enclosed in a fibrous sheath, and innervated by a motor nerve. His description, profusely illustrated, of the unit activated by passively produced tension as a component of the proprioceptive system, has extended the significance of the complex.[3]

> The muscle spindle consists of varying degrees of thickening of the muscle-fiber, containing large, clear, translucent foamy nuclei. . . . Usually two nerve-fibers enter each muscle spindle which branch from the nerve in a fork-like fashion. . . . That these nerve-fibers enter the muscle can be demonstrated in the well developed sheath of the larger nerves. . . . The nerve sheath consists of layers rich in nuclei which are evident as it crosses over to the also nuclei-rich sheath of the muscle spindle.

Investigations on the chemistry of the retina were begun in Heidelberg shortly after the observations of Boll in 1876 that the retina of some vertebrates is colored during life because of a purple substance but loses the color under the influence of light rays or at death. Kühne was quick to implicate "visual purple" or "rhodopsin," indigenous to the outer segments of the rods of the retina, as a photochemical agent in the development of his theory of vision. Thus, the first step in the response of the rods to light consists of photochemical decomposition of visual purple, which in turn stimulates the nerve endings, thereby transforming light waves into nerve stimuli. Almost a century later it was shown that vitamin A is concerned in the resynthesis of visual purple. Kühne also succeeded in obtaining optograms, an image fixed on the retina by the photochemical action of light on visual purple. The light-insensitive pigments or chromophanes, the stable colors, were found to respond quite differently from visual purple.[4]

If the photo-chemical processes which take place in the retina separated from the eye, are taken as representing those which are going on in the living eye, the visual purple may be conceived of as continually being destroyed by the act of seeing, and by some process or other being as continually renewed; and indeed Boll has expressed some such view as this. The oculist led by experience would immediately seek for the process of regeneration in the nourishment brought by the circulating blood; for this is a favourite way of accounting for most of these kinds of events. In the case in point, however, the matter is far less complicated.

That which restores the visual purple is something nearer to hand, and cannot, in a frog's eye at all events, depend on the constant renewal of the blood, since an eye, when taken out and opened, exhibits the same apparent indifference to light as when connected with the whole body and the nutritive currents. If therefore we are correct in supposing the sensitive purple to be continually restored, the regeneration must proceed from something lying behind or on the rods, that is, from the retinal epithelium or from the choroid. Something must be there which either prevents the purple becoming lost, or re-creates it. The idea at once suggested itself that the mere pigment as pigment had something to do with the matter, because a more intense action of light is to be expected if the retina, which usually only receives light from the front, is in addition lighted from behind, as is the case when it is spread out upon a white surface, instead of lying in its natural condition upon a velvety black ground.

After I had discovered that the changeability of the purple of living and dead retinas was dependent only on light, I said to myself that it must be possible in the extirpated eye to discover after the removal of the object the well-known images which the dioptric apparatus throws upon the fundus.

In face of the wonderfully complete knowledge concerning the dioptrics of the eye, which, thanks to the conspicuous ability of the inquirers of present and past times, we now possess, I have little more to say concerning the small inverted retinal image, than that I have always attempted to bring it into view as sharply as possible before I attempted to fix it on the retina.

In one of Kühne's first communications from Virchow's Institute, he traced the disintegration of the proteid molecule through several stages and isolated leucine and tyrosin in crystalline form. He devised methods for separating the albumoses from the peptones, used the term "enzyme" first in 1876, and gave the name "trypsin" to the proteolytic enzyme in the pancreas. Kühne was the first to study the changes seen under the microscope in the living, secreting, gland cells of the pancreas. In addition, he saw and recognized the difference between the active and resting gland cells in the living state before they had been altered by reagents. The identification of trypsin and leucine is excerpted as follows:[5]

The snow-white non-transparent sediment of pancreatic residue [prepared by chemical extraction] gradually fuses into a resin-like mass and can be washed even with water and remains unsoluble. When incompletely washed, so much enzyme— which I shall call trypsin—adheres to it that in a warm room it melts on a filter and forms a peptone-mush containing tyrosine and leucine. When washed thoroughly it has no digestive activity, especially when diluted in 1% soda and precipitated by acetic acid once more. The solution separated from the residue and precipitated by alcohol provides purer trypsin-containing mass.

With his striking personality, Kühne lived the life of a great physiologist whose work touched many disciplines. His methods of research were simple but were programmed by a brilliant seeker for truth. He made his own illustrations for publication from his microscopic work and loved art as a connoisseur. From 1883 until 1900, Kühne was editor, with Carl Voit, of the *Zeitschrift für Biologie*. His monograph on physiological chemistry, first published in 1868, was the standard text for German physiologists.[6] There are no recorded honors in the usual interpretation except the Croonian lectures for the Royal Society of London in 1888.

1. Voit, C: Willy Kühne (Ger), *Sitzung Math-Physik Classe* 32:249-262, 1902.

2. Du Bois Reymond, E.: Communication by W. Kühne on the Coagulable Substance of Muscle (Ger), *Mschr Akad Wiss Berlin,* July 1859, pp 493-497, excerpt translated by Z. Danilevicius.

3. Kühne, W.: The Muscle Spindle (Ger), *Arch path Anat* 28:528-538, 1863, excerpt translated by Z. Danilevicius.

4. Kühne, W.: *On the Photochemistry of the Retina and on Visual Purple,* M. Foster (ed.), London: Macmillan & Co., 1878.

5. Kühne, W.: On Trypsin (Enzyme of the Pancreas) (Ger), *Verh naturh-med Ver Heidelberg* 1:194-198, 233-236, 1874-1875, excerpt translated by Z. Danilevicius.

6. Kühne, W.: *Handbook of Physiological Chemistry* (Ger), Leipzig, Germany: W. Engelmann, 1868.

Composite by G. Bako

Asa Gray (1810-1888)

ASA GRAY, doctor of medicine who contributed to the development of the theory of evolution presented in Darwin's *The Origin of Species*, was born in Sauquoit Valley, Oneida County, New York, where his father had set up a tannery and a shoe shop.[1] Beginning his formal education at the age of three, Asa was schooled in Latin and Greek before he entered Fairfield, New York, Academy at the age of 15. James Hadley, professor of materia medica and chemistry in the medical department, who also gave

instruction in the academy, aroused his interest in botany. In 1829, Gray entered the College of Physicians and Surgeons of the Western District of New York, Fairfield, the medical department of the academy, and received his MD degree in 1831. The sessions in the medical school were relatively brief, and Gray found time to study with several physicians in the neighborhood of Sauquoit. However, he never practiced medicine and never came closer to medicine than instructing in chemistry, mineralogy, and botany in Bartlett's High school in Utica, New York, where he taught for a portion of each year until 1835.

The first record of Gray's having given a regular course of lectures in botany was stated in the circular of Fairfield Medical School dated January, 1832.[2] "Asa Gray, M.D., will give a course of lectures and practical illustrations on botany, to commence [in June] and continue the same time with the lectures on chemistry [six weeks]. Fee, $4.00." For the next few years Gray botanized in England and America, wrote extensively, and, in 1842, moved to Cambridge, Mass., to fill the newly-endowed chair of Fisher Professorship of Natural History at Harvard College and director of the botanical gardens.

From then on his full attention was given to lecturing, collecting, and writing, and he soon became recognized as the foremost botanist in America. A score of years later he built the modest botanical garden into the Gray Herbarium, with at least 200,000 specimens and a library of more than 2,200 volumes. Of Gray's many monographs on botany the following deserve particular mention: the *Flora of North America*, the *Elements of Botany,* and *Manual of the Botany of the Northern United States.* He had carried on an extensive correspondence with Charles Darwin for several years, who relied heavily on scientific data collected by Gray on the descriptions of plants then living and those of the more distant past for his *The Origin of Species* (1859).[3]

Gray was a fellow or correspondent of the principal continental scientific academies and served as president and corresponding secretary of the American Association for the Advancement of Science. He was elected a foreign member of the Linnaean and the Royal Societies of London and was awarded the LLD by Oxford and Edinburgh, the DSC by Cambridge, and the AM and the LLD by Harvard. Three different genera and a number of floral species as well as a peak in Colorado on the Continental Divide were named to honor him.

1. Farlow, W. G.: "Memoir of Asa Gray 1810-1888," in *National Academy of Sciences: Biographical Memoirs,* Washington: National Academy of Sciences, 1895, vol 3, pp 163-175.

2. "Asa Gray," in *Proceedings of the American Academy of Arts and Sciences,* Boston: University Press: John Wilson & Son, 1888, vol 15, pp 321-343.

3. Gray, A.: *Darwiniana,* A. H. Dupree (ed.), Cambridge, Mass: The Belknap Press of Harvard University, 1963.

Composite by G. Bako

Joseph Leidy (1823-1891)

JOSEPH LEIDY, biologist, paleontologist, Civil War surgeon, and the foremost anatomist of his time, was highly successful in reconciling, without compromise, avid interests in the natural and the medical sciences. Joseph was born in Philadelphia, the son of a pros-

perous hatmaker, of German parentage. At the age of ten he was sent to the Classical Academy and studied English, Latin, and Greek. Even as a youth his pursuit of learning was broad, and, in addition to the humanities, he developed an insatiable interest in the minerals, plants, and animals found along the banks of the Schuylkill and the Wissahickon. Furthermore, he was so adept at sketching and drawing that his father suggested a career based on these talents. His step-mother, also his aunt, however, favored the sciences and prevailed. Leidy obtained the MD degree at the University of Pennsylvania in 1844, with the thesis entitled, "The Comparative Anatomy of the Eye of Vertebrated Animals." He served for a short time as assistant in the chemical laboratory, then engaged in the practice of medicine for a few months, but abandoned this for the teaching of anatomy. His destiny lay with the natural sciences and laboratory investigation, rather than with the practice of medicine.[1] Because of an inquisitive mind and a skilled hand in illustrating the disclosures of the microscope, notable contributions were made in parasitology, helminthology, and medical zoology.

Leidy held the chair of anatomy at the University of Pennsylvania from 1853 until his death 38 years later. During this time he was also professor of zoology and comparative anatomy, sharing his teaching talent and investigative genius with the medical school and with the University's department of Liberal Arts. He served his country as a surgeon during the war between the states, and for 15 years was professor of natural history at Swarthmore, while continuing his work at the University of Pennsylvania.

The father of paleontology in America was a member of the Academy of Natural Sciences of Philadelphia and a prolific contributor to its *Proceedings.* He published more than 550 communications during his scientific career. One of his noteworthy treatises was *On the Fossil Horse of America,* the presentation of convincing evidence that the horse once lived in America and became extinct in the pre-Columbian era. His first communciation appeared in the *Proceedings of the Natural History Society* of

Boston for 1845, "On the Existence of the Sack of the Dart and of the Dart in Several Species of North America Pneumonobranchiate Mollusks." The bibliography concluded with "Notice of Some Entozoa."[2] In the *Ancient Fauna of Nebraska*, Leidy reported on the fossil remains of the sabretoothed tiger, and described two species of rhinoceros that inhabited the prairie of what is now Nebraska. His study also included a description of walrus fossils, which supported the idea that the walrus had migrated from the North during the glacial epoch. Another earlier work, *A Flora and Fauna Within Living Animals*, advanced the theory of natural selection, anticipating Darwin by several years.[3]

The study of the earth's crust teaches us that very many species of plants and animals became extinct at successive periods, while other races originated to occupy their places. This probably was the result, in many cases, of a change in exterior conditions incompatible with the life of certain species, and favorable to the primitive production of others.

Leidy's *Elementary Treatise on Human Anatomy*, a standard text for generations, contained almost 400 illustrations, many of his own composition.[4] Latin terms were analyzed; root stems and synonyms were given in the footnotes—a helpful device in presenting a readable brochure to students. The table of contents of the *Fresh Water Rhizopods of North America*, his greatest achievement in the natural sciences, lists in small type more than two pages of the simplest form of animal life, freshwater rhizopods as they occur from the Atlantic border to an altitude of 10,000 ft in the Rocky Mountains. The illustrations, done in chromolithography, were also prepared by the author. His interest in the microscope, which was becoming firmly established as an indispensable tool in the laboratory, is well expressed in the introduction to the treatise.[5]

The revelations of the microscope are perhaps not exceeded in importance by those of the telescope. While exciting our curiosity, our wonder and admiration, they have proved of infinite service in advancing our knowledge of things around us. The present work, founded on such revelations, I have attempted to prepare in a manner to render it easy of comprehension, with the view of promoting and encouraging a taste for microscopic investigations.

I think it worth while to embrace the opportunity of informing students that microscopic observations, such as those which form the basis of the present work, do not require elaborate and high-priced instruments.

Leidy was first to describe *Trichina spiralis* in the hog, a parasite first recognized by Owen, Paget, and Hilton in the cadavers of humans.[6]

Dr. Leidy stated that he had lately detected the existence of an Entozoon in the superficial part of the extensor muscles of the thigh of a hog. The Entozoon is a minute, coiled worm, contained in a cyst.

The Entozoon he supposes to be the Trichina spiralis, heretofore considered as peculiar to the human species. He could perceive no distinction between it and the specimens of T. spiralis which he had met with in several human subjects in the dissecting rooms, where it had also been observed by others, since the attention of the scientific public had been directed to it by Mr. Hilton and Prof. Owen.

The studies in the tranplantation of tumor tissue in frogs were presented at the session of the Academy of Natural Sciences, June 17, 1861, following a contribution on helminthology.[7]

Dr. Leidy stated he had repeated the experiment of introducing cancerous matter beneath the integument of a frog, which was first announced to the Academy, May 6th, [1851]. This frog, still living, Dr. L. exhibited to the members, and by an incision through the integument, presented to view the fragment of cancer which had been introduced, and which had not only formed a vascular attachment to the integument, but for one half itself was of a fine red color from the net-work of capillaries which had become developed within it.

Dr. L. observed, the experiment not only proved the independent vitality of tissues, which was generally admitted, but also rendered it exceedingly probable that cancer was inoculable, for, as in the experiments, the cancerous fragments continued to live when introduced into cold-blooded animals, they would probably not only continue to live when introduced into warm-blooded animals, but would grow or increase in size.

The presence of flora in the intestines was considered to be a normal phenomenon and indispensable to animal life.[8]

From the opinion so frequently expressed that contagious diseases and some others might have their origin and reproductive character through the agency of cryptogamic spores, . . . I was led to reflect upon the possibility of plants of this description existing in healthy animals, as a natural condition; or, at least, apparently so, as in the case of entozoa. Upon considering that the conditions essential to vegetable growth were the same as those indispensable to animal life, I felt convinced that entophyta would be found in healthy living animals, as well, and probably as frequently, as entozoa. . . . I will give but a short description, for the purpose of establishing priority, and propose giving a more detailed account of them, with figures, in the second volume of the Journal.

The hookworm of humans was found in the cat and was believed to be the cause of pernicious anemia.[9]

The specimens, however, exhibit the same structure of the mouth as is described in the A. [Ancylostomum] duodenale of man. Beneath the upper lip are four strong recurved hooks and within the lower lip a pair of hooks. The finding of this parasite in the cat in this country renders it probable that it may also infest man with it, and is probably one of the previously unrecognized causes of pernicious anaemia. The occurrence of the same parasite in the cat is also of interest, as heretofore it has only been noticed in man.

Leidy was one of the most celebrated and bemedalled physicians of Philadelphia and acknowledged active or honorary membership in many learned societies in diverse parts of the world. Throughout his life he displayed those sturdy qualities of vigor and discipline so common among his German antecedents. He was modest and retiring but richly endowed mentally, a foremost anatomist, but an even greater authority on paleontology. Charles S. Minot of Boston included Leidy in the four masters of natural science in the United States in the 19th century. Louis Agassiz, Spencer F. Baird, and James D. Dana completed the quartet.[1] The Leidy Medal of the Academy of Natural Sciences of Philadelphia, established in 1923, is awarded triennially, while the American Association of Anatomists struck a bronze medallion for Leidy in 1938. A column in the Luray caverns of Virginia and two peaks in the western mountains of this country also do him honor. The Snake River expedition of 1872 gave the name Mount Leidy to a peak in Teton County, Wyoming, 10,315 feet in elevation; whereas Leidy Peak,

12,013 feet at the bench mark, is on the crest of the High Uintas on the border of Daggett and Uintah counties, Utah.

1. Middleton, W. S.: Joseph Leidy, Scientists, *Ann Med Hist* 5:100-112 (June) 1923.
2. Chapman, H. C.: Memoir of Joseph Leidy, MD, LLD, *Proc Acad Nat Sci*, pp 342-388 1891.
3. Leidy, J.: A Flora and Fauna Within Living Animals, *Smithsonian Contributions to Knowledge* 5:2-56, 1853.
4. Leidy, J.: *An Elementary Treatise on Human Anatomy*, Philadelphia: J. B. Lippincott & Co., 1861.
5. Leidy, J.: Fresh-Water Rhizopods of North America, *Rep US Geological Survey of Territories*, Dept of Interior, vol 12, 1879, pp 1-321.
6. Leidy, J.: On an Entozoon from the Thigh of a Hog, Trichina spiralis? *Proc Acad Nat Sci* 3:107-108, 1846-47.
7. Leidy, J.: Contributions to Helminthology, *Proc Acad Nat Sci* 5:212, 1850-51.
8. Leidy, J.: On the Existence of Entophyta in Healthy Animals, as a Natural Condition, *Proc Acad Nat Sci* 4:225-233, 1848-49.
9. Leidy, J.: Remarks on Parasites and Scorpions, *Trans Coll Physicians Phila* 8:441-442, 1886.

Composite by G. Bako

Oswald Schmiedeberg
(1838-1921)

O. SCHMIEDEBERG, successful reformer of experimental pharmacology, was born in Kurland, Germany, the son of a forester. Schmiedeberg spent his youth in Dorpat, where he attended the Gymnasium. He received his medical training from the University faculty, which included as members K. Schmidt in chemistry, F. Bidder in physiology, and R. Buchheim, director of the little-known Pharmacology Institute.[1] In 1866, Schmiedeberg presented his inaugural thesis, *Determination and Concentration of Chloroform in the Blood*, and received the MD degree. He assisted Buchheim until 1869, when his chief was called to Giessen, and he was advanced to the professorship of pharmacology, dietetics, and the history of medicine. Sensing the importance of the physiologic approach to drug investigation in man and animals for the advancement of basic and practical pharmacology, he spent a year in Leipzig with Carl Ludwig. Here he studied the pharmacologic action of nicotine and atropine on the heart of the frog and the dog, one of his most important scientific contributions. Schmiedeberg published a monograph with R. Koppe on the alkaloids of poisonous mushrooms. In 1872, he was called to Strasbourg to the recently-founded university; there he built an institute recognized as the most important center for experimental pharmacology in Europe, comparable in stature to similar great institutes in Germany devoted to one of the other medical sciences.

Schmiedeberg attracted a remarkable number of students throughout his long and productive career and enriched the pharmacologic literature, as well as establishing with Böhm, Klebs, and Naunyn the *Archiv für experimentelle Pathologie und Pharmakologie*. This was subsequently identified in conversational pharmacology as Schmiedeberg's *Archiv*. Schmiedeberg's name was carried on the masthead as professor of pharmacology from Baden-Baden after retirement from Strassburg and was not removed until his death. He received honorary degrees from Edinburgh and Bologna, and membership in the Academy of Medicine of Paris and the Ecclesiastical Academy of Science of Rome. In 1883, the first edition of his *Fundamentals of Drugs* appeared.[2] This was translated into English by Dixson in 1887, under the author's supervision, and was published in Edinburgh. The title of the fourth edition (1902) was changed to *Fun-*

damentals of Pharmacology and was revised in 1906, 1909, and 1913, evidence of its reputation as the basic treatise for his generation of pharmacologists.

Schmiedeberg's influence in developing theoretical medicine in Germany through pupils and published reports or monographs encompassed such diverse subjects as heavy metals and their effect on the organism, identification and naming of glycuronic acid, selected aspects of carbohydrate metabolism, the synthesis of hippuric acid by the kidney, the identification of sinistrin and histozyme, investigation of ferratin and digitalis compounds, the chemical composition of cartilage, the dietetic value of wines, diuretics, nucleic acid, chicory, methyl alcohol poisoning, mucoid, mucin and chondroitin metabolism, collagen, and amyloid. Excerpts from the initial studies of the effect of muscarin and atropine on the frog's heart are given below.[3]

Experiments performed with Koppe on Muscarin poisoning have shown among other features that the smallest amounts of the poison produced standstill in diastole without decreasing irritability. Cardiac arrest persists if countermeasures are not taken. Only a small fraction of a milligram of atropine, if injected subcutaneously, can completely abolish cardiac arrest in animals and nullify the effect of additional quantities of Muscarin. The action of small doses of atropine on the heart is apparent since neither electrical stimulation of the vagus nor stimulation of the venous sinus can produce cessation or slowing of the heart rate, and conduction fibers which respond to electrical stimulation are paralyzed by this poison. We conclude that Muscarin is an antagonist; it stimulates the structures that are paralyzed by atropine and which otherwise would lead to diastolic cardiac arrest if excited.

The stimulating action of nicotine on the endings of the vagus appears only when small amounts of the poison are applied. Immediately after the injection of ⅛ to ⅓ mg, the heart rate begins to decrease and soon reaches diastolic standstill which persists not longer than 60 or 90 seconds, when pulsations appear and soon reach the same frequency as before the injection. If traces of atropine are administered to the animal before the application of nicotine, cardiac arrest does not appear; after small doses the rate is unchanged; after larger doses, gradual slowing of the heart rate appears, as without the administration of atropine.

If Muscarin is administered to an animal after nicotine, which blocks the inhibiting action of the vagus, cardiac arrest appears even following the strongest electrical stimulation, and persists for a considerable time, but again, it can be interrupted by atropine.

In a comprehensive discussion of the digitalin group of botanicals, Schmiedeberg described neriin, oleandrin, and neriantin.[4] Following a short historical review of the therapeutic value of digitalis and the digitalein group, he listed more than a dozen compounds including antiarin, helleborein, thevetin, digitoxin, strophanthin, apocynin, scillain, adonidin, oleandrin, digitalein, apocynein, convallamarin, erythrophleine, phyrnin, and other substances not belonging to the digitalis group but endowed with a similar action. The physiologic and pharmacologic actions of drugs that are members of the group are summarized as follows.[2]

A number of non-nitrogenous botanicals, which mainly belong to the glucosides, act in so uniform a manner upon the heart of many animals, irrespective of quantitative differences, that each of the agents seems, with reference to this action, quite similar.

The action of these substances consists almost exclusively in a peculiar alteration of the elasticity of the cardiac muscle, without at first modifying the contractility of it. The immediate effect of this alteration is the increase of the volume of the pulse, with prolongation of diastole. At this stage of the action of digitalis, the absolute capacity of the heart experiences neither an increase nor a decrease. On the other hand, the quantity of blood which, at this time, is propelled into the aorta is greater than before, not only at every beat, but even in a given unit of time, although the rate may have diminished. These active substances, therefore, produce better filling of the arteries, as a reflection of the relative efficiency of the heart. As a result, the blood-pressure increases, irrespective of its previous level, such as very low in deep chloral narcosis. Together with an increase of pressure, which we can prove indirectly in man, the pulse slows, dependent upon stimulation of the inhibitory mechanism of the heart, partly through vagus action and partly through local effects. This slowing is absent if the inhibitory apparatus has been paralysed by atropine previously, a paralysis which shows no effect upon the increase of pressure.

Of these actions, the first stage—that is, the rise of blood-pressure, and the usually concurrent slowing of the pulse—can be brought about in man, and maintained for a long time, by small doses, without threat to life. Essential therapeutic benefit can be ascribed to the blood-pressure-

elevating property and to especially the slowing of the pulse, upon which so much stress is laid in the use of digitalis; they are either the results of the high arterial pressure, or appear as the inflammatory process at the point of suppuration as little more than disturbing factors.

If these agents result in improved filling of the arteries and subsequent rise of arterial pressure in the healthy and the sick, then the indication for rational employment follows.

1. Meyer, H. H.: The Contributions of Schmiedeberg (Ger), *Arch Exp Path* 92:III-XVII, 1922.
2. Schmiedeberg, O.: *Fundamentals of Drugs* (Ger), Leipzig: F. C. W. Vogel, 1883.
3. Schmiedeberg, O.: Investigations of Poisons on the Frog's Heart (Ger), *Arb Physiol Anst* 5:41-52, 1871, excerpt translated by Z. Danilevicius.
4. Schmiedeberg, O.: The Pharmacology of the Digitalius (Ger), *Arch Exp Path* 16:149-187, 1883.

Composite by G. Bako

Alfred Stillé (1813-1900)

AMONG THE GALAXY OF PHYSICIANS during the mid-19th century in Philadelphia, Alfred Stillé was one of William Osler's favorite academic ancestors.[1] Stillé prepared the first important general pathology textbook in America, was responsible for a two-volume treatise on therapeutics and materia medica, and wrote several monographs on specific maladies. He was born in Philadelphia, where he received his undergraduate and graduate training; however, his attendance for a few months in the undergraduate school at Yale College was terminated by participation in the "conic sections" rebellion.[1] The MD degree, bestowed in 1836, was the last of three degrees granted him by the University of Pennsylvania. While a house physician at "Blockley," later incorporated as the Philadelphia General Hospital, Stillé came under the influence of W. W. Gerhard, who differentiated typhoid from typhus fever and who taught and practiced the statistical medicine of Louis of Paris.

The contagiousness of Louis' scholarship spread to Gerhard, and, in turn, to Stillé, who went to Europe to continue his postgraduate studies; a portion of his time was spent with the great Parisian teacher. Upon completion of his European training, Stillé served as visiting physician to St. Joseph's Hospital, presenting simultaneously a series of lectures on pathology and the practice of medicine for the Philadelphia Association for Medical Instruction. In 1854, he was appointed to the chair of the practice of medicine at the Pennsylvania Medical College, and later succeeded William Pepper as professor of the theory and practice of medicine in the University of Pennsylvania.

The *Elements of General Pathology*, published in 1848, was designed by Stillé to correct the dearth of works in the field.[2] However, the goal was only partially achieved. The discussion dealt largely with symptoms of disease and speculative etiology. Only a small portion of the text was devoted to general morbid anatomy. He was more successful in extending Gerhard's observations in the differentiation of typhus and typhoid fever, and in recounting clinical findings in epidemic meningitis, the latter based on a review of 120 cases at the Philadelphia Hospital.[3] His monographs on yellow fever (1879) and particularly that on cholera (1885) discussed contagious etiology but largely overlooked the revolution in bacterial pathogenesis that was spreading rapidly at that time. As an instructor, Stillé has been described as a proper teacher whose lectures were perfectly polished literary essays, but didactic and without illustrative clinical material and not particularly inspiring.

Stillé was a Fellow of the College of Physicians of Philadelphia, its president in 1883, and one of the creators of the Philadelphia Pathological Society. In the field of organized medicine, he was one of the founders of the American Medical Association, having been a member of the committee to establish the National Medical Association of 1846 and one of the two secretaries when the Committee, in 1847, "resolved itself into the 'American Medical Association'." His presidential address, an extremely involved dissertation, delivered in 1871 on the 25th anniversary of the founding, dealt at length with medical education and especially the acceptance of women into medical schools.[4]

Another disease has become epidemic. "The woman question" in relation to medicine is only one of the forms in which the *pestis muliebris* vexes the world. In other shapes it attacks the bar, wriggles into the jury box, and clearly means to mount upon the bench; it strives, thus far in vain, to serve at the altar and thunder from the pulpit; it raves at political meetings, harangues in the lecture-room, infects the masses with its poison, and even pierces the triple brass that surrounds the politician's heart.

To the vulgar apprehension, nothing seems more natural than that women should be physicians, for is not nursing the chief agent in the cure of disease, and who so fit a nurse as woman! The logic is worthy of its subject, and is of the sort in which Eve's daughters excel.

The remarks made by Stillé in 1884, as judged by William Osler, reveal him as a gentle and sensitive physician and set forth the ideals which guided him in teaching and practice.[5]

I . . . have devoted whatever knowledge and skill I possessed to the simple, if difficult, task of knowing and curing diseases. I have striven, in season, and perhaps out of season, to impress upon you that medicine is, first of all, an art, but an art that can only be successfully practised when the physician is able to recognize the individual diseases he must meet with in practice, and distinguish from one another those which are similar in appearance, but unlike in nature.

. . . it is quite as necessary for the physician to know when to abstain from the use of medicine as it is for him to prescribe when medication is necessary; that he must, as far as possible, see the end of a disease from its beginning; that he must never forget that medical art has a far higher range and aim than the prescription of drugs or even of food and hygienic means, and that when neither of these avails to ward off the fatal ending, it is still no small portion of his art to rid his patient's path of thorns if he cannot make it bloom with roses.

1. Osler, W.: Memoir of Alfred Stillé M.D., *Trans Coll Physicians Phila* 24:lviii-lxxi, 1902.
2. Stillé, A.: *Elements of General Pathology: A Practical Treatise on the Causes, Form, Symptoms, and Results of Disease,* Philadelphia: Lindsay and Blakiston, 1848.
3. Stillé, A.: *Epidemic Meningitis, or Cererbo-Spinal Meningitis,* Philadelphia: Lindsay and Blakiston, 1867.
4. Stillé, A.: Address of the President, *Trans Amer Med Assoc* 22:75-98, 1871.
5. Stillé, A.: An Address Delivered to the Medical Classes of the University of Pennsylvania, *Med News* 44:433-438, 1884.

Composite by G. Bako

Peter Redfern (1821-1912)

SOME OF THE EARLIEST EXPERIMENTS on the pathological changes of articular cartilage were pursued by Peter Redfern, outstanding anatomist and practitioner of Scotland and Ireland. Redfern, born in Chesterfield, Derbyshire, received a major portion of his education in Scotland. Following current custom his apprenticeship to a physician allowed him not only to study disease but to carry out surgical procedures. The experience gained and reputation acquired led to the premature termination of the apprenticeship; whereupon Redfern began formal training in Edinburgh and won prizes in medicine, surgery, and midwifery. He continued training at London University, graduating

MB in 1844 and three years later receiving the MD degree. In each instance he gained a gold medal in medicine. Meanwhile, he became a member of the Royal College of Surgeons in England and in 1851 was admitted to Fellowship.

In 1845, Redfern was appointed lecturer in anatomy and physiology in Aberdeen and in 1860 was called to the new Queens College in Belfast as the first professor of anatomy and physiology. In addition to his teaching assignments he guided the authorities in the construction of dissecting rooms, a museum, lecture rooms, and amphitheaters, basic to the formation of a faculty of medicine. By 1865 the initial quarters had been expanded to handle the increased number of students attracted to the school. Redfern stressed the importance of anatomy as the fundamental subject for medical practice and in their training inspired his pupils to complete dedication. He prepared his lectures with great care and demanded similar excellence from his students.

For nearly half a century Redfern was an examiner for medical degrees in the universities of Aberdeen, London, and Queens University in Belfast. He was awarded the honorary DSC by his faculty, became a corresponding member of the Society of Biology, Paris, and an honorary member of the Royal Academy of Medicine of Belgium. His studies on articular cartilage were carried out in Aberdeen, with specimens from patients from the Royal Infirmary, from several afflicted with chronic rheumatism, and from dogs following surgical interference. The articular cartilage of the patella or the condyle of the femur was exposed in experimental animals, and periodic observations were made through the unhealed incisions. The animals were encouraged to remain ambulatory since they showed no evidence of painful disability. Redfern noted that repair was effected by generation of fibrous tissue or calcification; and that cartilage, unlike bone, showed no tendency to repair itself by proliferation of its cells. He summarized his findings as follows.[2]

The general result of these researches, appears in the strongest manner confirmatory of the conclusions previously drawn from the examination of the human articular cartilages, and to be of importance in demonstrating:—

1st. That the changes of structure which result from the most varied injuries, are of similar character in all cartilages.

2nd. That these changes invariably affect both the cells and intercellular substance.

3rd. That the only explanation of the nature of such changes which can be given is, that they depend upon an increased and anormal nutrition of the texture.

4th. That uncomplicated lesions of cartilage, especially such as have been artificially induced in the lower animals, manifest a very decided tendency to spontaneous cure by the production of fibrous tissue, or by calcification of the whole cartilage left after the injury.

5th. That the fibrous tissue, which heals up breaches in the texture of cartilage, contains both the white and yellow fibrous elements, the former being produced by an actual conversion of the hyaline substance into it and the latter by elongation of the discharged corpuscles of diseased cells into nuclear fibres.

6th. That diseased action arising from circumscribed destruction of the articular cartilages of the lower animals evinces no tendency to extend to the remaining parts of these textures, nor to involve other structures and lead to serious disease of the joint.

1. Peter Redfern, M.D., obituary, *Brit Med J* 1:51-52 (Jan 4) 1913.

2. Redfern, P.: Experimental Researches on the Nature of the Changes which May Be Induced by Operations on the Cartilages of the Lower Animals, in Illustration of the Process of Anormal Nutrition in Such Textures, *Monthly J Med Sci* 10:214-231 (March) 1850.

Oliver Wendell Holmes (1809-1894)

OLIVER WENDELL HOLMES was born in Cambridge, Massachusetts, beyond Harvard Yard, the present site of the Littauer School of Public Administration. His father, a minister and a childless widower, was 46 and his mother 41 when the future physician was born.[1] The volumes of good literature on the family shelves—Dryden, Pope, Goldsmith, Milton, and others—exerted sound influences on young Holmes and probably attracted him to verse and poesy at an early age. Dr. Benjamin Waterhouse, initial incumbent of the Professorship of the Theory and Practice of Physic at Harvard, and introducer of smallpox vaccination into America, was a neighbor and a frequent visitor. He vaccinated the young man. In grammar school, Holmes was moderately

Boston Medical Library

studious and especially fond of reading. One year at Andover Academy was followed by Harvard College, which he entered at the age of 16. The daily routine at college began with prayers before breakfast, recitations and study throughout the morning and afternoon, except for a few minutes for exercise after lunch, evening prayers, supper, and an 8:00 P.M. curfew.

Interest in the classics and good literature seems, in retrospect, to have been much greater a century ago than currently apparent, even in schools that emphasize the value of the best in scholarship. Holmes prepared for medical school by studying chemistry and mineralogy. Meanwhile, his manifest interest in verse and poetry was apparent. Initially he published his contributions unsigned; as he became older and bolder, they were signed with a capital "H." He was appointed class poet in his last year in school. "Old Ironsides," an argument against dismantling the *Constitution*, was composed shortly after graduation. "The Last Leaf," possibly a picture of the aging Waterhouse, was published the following year.

After attending Harvard Law School for a year, he then turned to medicine. The Harvard Medical School was situated in the environs of the Massachusetts General Hospital, with the Charles River flowing under the western portion of the frame building supported by piles. During his second year at medical school, the Massachusetts Anatomy Act legalized the dissection of the human body and thereby eliminated body snatching. John Warren, Professor of Anatomy and Surgery at Harvard Medical School, a predecessor of Holmes, was probably not unaware of this practice. Five subjects were taught in medical school: theory and practice of medicine, anatomy and surgery, obstetrics and medical jurisprudence, chemistry, and materia medica. Although the achromatic microscope and the stethoscope had been invented, neither item was emphasized routinely in instruction when Holmes was a student. Holmes had much to do with the introduction into the curriculum of the use of both the stethoscope and the microscope a decade later. Attendance at lectures was required during the short winter terms. The major portion of the academic year was spent as an apprentice to a general practitioner.

Throughout these years, as in later life, Holmes continued to write for literary periodicals. The breakfast-table conversations were begun in 1831.[2] After two years at Harvard he went to Paris, a popular diversion a century ago, to study with Pierre Ch. A. Louis, the leading teacher of medicine in France. The voyage from New York to Portsmouth, England, by packet required 24 or more days. Louis conducted daily rounds at La Pitié. Gerhard, the Jacksons, and the Shattucks helped to spread the influence and precepts of Louis to America. The master was strong in opposition to the ineffective therapy of his day and insisted that the practice of medicine should be based upon pathological anatomy. An inner circle of students of Louis formed the Société Médicale d'Observation. Other teachers in

the Paris school included Biett, Alibert, Dupuytren, Velpeau, and Bouillaud.

Holmes did not seek his doctorate in Paris; rather he returned to Boston, submitted an essay on "Acute Pericarditis," and appeared before the faculty for a final examination at the age of 27. His interest in writing continued; he lectured on the lyceum circuit and wrote for a number of magazines. Harvard honored him as the Phi Beta Kappa poet. He was the winner of the Boylston medical prize for his dissertation on "Direct Exploration," based upon the techniques of percussion, described by Auenbrugger, and auscultation by Laennec.

At the age of 38, he accepted an appointment at Harvard Medical School and served for 35 years. He taught physiology and pathology and listened to recitations in anatomy. His bachelor days were soon to be over:

I have several very nice young women in my eye, and it is by no means impossible that another summer or so may see my name among the hymeneal victims.

The favorite was Amelia Lee Jackson, niece of Dr. James Jackson and cousin of Dr. James Jackson, Jr. Before he married, however, he accepted the post of Professor of Anatomy at Dartmouth Medical School. This appointment required only 14 weeks in residence each academic year. While on the faculty at Hanover for two years, he was requested to prepare a poem for the Phi Beta Kappa chapter. Longfellow had been their poet in 1837 and Ralph Waldo Emerson their orator in 1838. With such distinguished predecessors, it would have been difficult to refuse the honor.

Throughout this period his interests in the practice of medicine and teaching were shared with literary exertions. His best known clinical contribution, "The Contagiousness of Puerperal Fever," based upon the statistical method he had learned from Louis, was presented originally to the Boston Society for Medical Improvement on February 13, 1843.[3] Although not an obstetrician, he gathered his facts from practitioners and concluded that the disease could be conveyed to the nonafflicted from the sick or from the morgue unless the hands of the midwife or surgeon were cleansed and clothes were changed after previous contact with the living or dead. The deductions of Semmelweis on puerperal fever in hospitals were conceived simultaneously. The premise and the first four recommendations for prevention of the spread of the dread disease are as follows:[4]

In collecting, enforcing and adding to the evidence accumulated upon this most serious subject, I would not be understood to imply that there exists a doubt in the mind of any well-informed member of the medical profession as to the fact that puerperal fever is sometimes communicated from one person to another, both directly and indirectly.

1. A physician holding himself in readiness to attend cases of midwifery, should never take any active part in the post-mortem examination of cases of puerperal fever.

2. If a physician is present at such autopsies, he should use thorough ablution, change every article of dress, and allow twenty-four hours or more to elapse before attending to any case of midwifery. It may be well to extend the same caution to cases of simple peritonitis.

3. Similar precautions should be taken after the autopsy or surgical treatment of cases of erysipelas, if the physician is obliged to unite such offices with his obstetrical duties, which is in the highest degree inexpedient.

4. On the occurrence of a single case of puerperal fever in his practice, the physician is bound to consider the next female he attends in labor, unless some weeks, at least, have elapsed, as in danger of being infected by him and it is his duty to take every precaution to diminish her risk of disease and death.

The appointment of Holmes as Parkman Professor of Anatomy and Physiology in 1847 followed the retirement of John Collins Warren. The professorship carried no salary; Holmes' income from teaching was limited to fees paid by students. Reorganization of the medical school increased the number of the faculty and the subjects taught to seven, when the new term began in 1847.

The Harvard Medical School was in that respect in line with the resolutions passed in May by the newly-founded American Medical Association.

Holmes gave up private practice at the age of 40 and devoted his efforts to writing and lecturing. As his essays were bound in book form, he included the subtitle "Everyman his own Boswell." In addition to essays, poems, and verse, he wrote three anti-Calvinist "medical" novels, *Elsie Venner* (1861), *The Guardian Angel* (1867), and *A Moral Antipathy* (1885). Oberndorf[5] considers Holmes a precursor of Freud. Just as S. Weir Mitchell based his psychiatric novels upon his clinical experience, Holmes presented the psychiatric problems with which he had firsthand information. The autocrat of the breakfast table, the professor of anatomy and physiology, who wrote so eloquently on the contagiousness of puerperal fever, made one other contribution of great importance. He sired Oliver Wendell Holmes, Jr., an Associate Justice of the Supreme Court of the United States from 1902 to 1932.

1. Tilton, E. M.: *Amiable Autocrat,* New York: Henry Schuman, Inc., 1947.

2. Howe, M. A. D.: *Holmes of the Breakfast-Table,* New York: Oxford University Press, 1939.

3. Viets, H. R.: A Mind Prepared: Oliver Wendell Holmes and "The Contagiousness of Puerperal Fever," 1843, *Bull Med Libr Ass* 31:319 (Oct.) 1943.

4. Holmes, O. W.: The Contagiousness of Puerperal Fever, *N Engl Quart J Med* 1:503-530, 1842-1843.

5. Oberndorf, C. P.: *The Psychiatric Novels of Oliver Wendell Holmes,* New York: Columbia University Press, 1946.

Composite by G. Bako

James Young Simpson (1811-1870)

THE SEVENTH SON of a baker of Bathgate, Scotland, James Young Simpson introduced inhalation anesthesia into obstetrical practice. His father, having failed as a brewer and a distiller, turned to the bakery trade to support a large family. The brothers and sister must have had some premonition of the eminence of the youngest brother. As manifest proof of Scottish "togetherness," they sacrificed that James might receive education and training in preparation for his ultimate destiny as the leading obstetrician in Great Britain.[1] At the age of 14, James journeyed a few miles to Edinburgh, where he began his university studies, principally in the humanities. But he lodged with pre-medical students from Bathgate, with the usual result. He continued on at Edinburgh and at the age of 19 qualified as a member of the Royal College of Surgeons. With little more than the basic stipulations satisfied, it was possible and customary to begin the practice of medicine. However, an application for the post of ship's surgeon, as well as for a local practice on the Clyde, was rejected. There appeared no choice but to return to the university, where the MD degree was conferred in 1832. The graduation thesis concerned "Death from Inflammation" ("De causa mortis in quibusdam inflammationibus proxima").[2]

The thesis was highly regarded by Professor Thomson of the department of pathology, who offered him an assistant's post. Thomson has been given full credit for pointing out the advantages of obstetrical medicine to the young surgeon. In 1833, Simpson joined the Royal Medical Society of Edinburgh and, upon assumption of duties as president 3 years later, delivered his inaugural dissertation on "Diseases of the Placenta." He attended lectures on midwifery, acted as house surgeon in the Lying-In Hospital, and devoted more and more of his practice time to obstetrics. At the age of 27 he began extramural lectures on obstetrics.

The following year found him waging an active campaign for succession to the Chair of Midwifery at Edinburgh, soon to be vacated. At that time, an appointment to a professorship was sought by the candidate; the Chair did not seek the man. Testimonials were prepared, printed at the expense of the applicant, and widely distributed in order to win the confidence of the electors, the 33 members of the Edinburgh Town Council. Simpson's election expenses were reported to be from £300 to £500. The vote was 17 to 16 in favor of Simpson. The honor of the post, plus a rapidly expanding private practice, made him a busier and busier physician. It was his custom to sleep not more than 4 or 5 hours each night. Reading, writing, and avocational duties were pursued with an industry that was truly remarkable. There were no allotted hours for leisure reading and writing; time was snatched between deliveries and at odd moments in the carriage while traveling between school, office, and the sick at home. But industry fosters industry. In spite of a tireless life, books were read, articles were written, and significant contributions to medicine were made.

In the years before Simpson had risen to academic heights in midwifery, he had been keenly aware of the importance of dulling the senses during childbirth. Mesmerism had been tried without success. When the fabulous tales had reached Scotland of the anesthetic effect of sulfuric ether in allaying pain, he was quick to explore the possibilities of this volatile agent in his practice. On Jan. 19, 1847, Simpson reported a clinical trial, with the reservation that the compound was irritating to the bronchial tree and the gastrointestinal tract. The likelihood that other compounds might be superior prompted a series of experimental trials with a number of chemical agents supplied by the chemist. Simpson and his friends were the experimental subjects. One of the agents was chloroform. Simpson was the first to inhale the vapor (Nov. 4, 1847) in his experimental series, the day following the trial of chloroform by Matthews Duncan and his colleagues. As the experiment was extended to others, it was observed that[2]

Immediately an unwonted hilarity seized the party; they became bright eyed, very happy and very loquacious, expatiating on the delicious aroma of the new fluid. The conversation was of unusual intelligence and quite charmed the listeners—some ladies of the family and a naval officer, brother-in-law of Dr. Simpson.

No time was lost in testing the validity of the experiment in the delivery room and the surgical amphitheater. A few days later chloroform was used for general anesthesia, as well as for labor pains.[3]

In this, her second confinement, pains supervened a fortnight before the full time. Three hours and a half after they commenced, and ere the first stage of the labour was completed, I placed her under the influence of the chloroform, by moistening, with half a teaspoonful of the liquid, a pocket handkerchief, rolled up into a funnel shape, and with the broad or open end of the funnel placed over her mouth and nostrils. In consequence of the evaporation of the fluid it was once more renewed in about ten or twelve minutes. The child was expelled in about twenty-five minutes after the inhalation was begun. The mother subsequently remained longer soporose than commonly happens after ether. . . . She then turned round and observed to me that she had "enjoyed a very comfortable sleep, and indeed required it, as she was so tired, but would now be more able for the work before her."

The clinical trial with chloroform was a success, but the need to suppress the pains of labor was not universally accepted by physicians or patients. There were some who believed that women should tolerate parturition without benefit of sedation or anesthesia. It was necessary for Simpson to carry on a vigorous campaign to counteract the opposition. Meanwhile, he did not rest on his new-found glory in pharmacology but devised a procedure for hemostasis called "acupressure." This was an ingenious method of passing a thin sharp needle through the tissues and around an artery and thereby compressing the vessel, without producing devitalization of tissue, an inevitable result with the then current procedure of ligaturing. Simpson was interested in leprosy and the contagion of cholera and smallpox. He devised the uterine sound,[4] introduced iron wire sutures, recommended version for a deformed pelvis, and advocated the pavilion-type hospital.[5] His lectures were extremely popular; frequently there was standing room only. He fought against the homeopathists, as he did against those who opposed the introduction of anesthesia into the delivery room. He traveled widely in Ireland and on the Continent for pleasure and for professional enlightenment. Medical societies in Europe and America made him an honorary member. He was appointed Physician in Scotland to the Queen, and knighted. Oxford University awarded him the doctor of civil law, while the citizens bestowed on him the Freedom of the City of Edinburgh. The use of chloroform in the delivery of Queen Victoria in 1853 represented acceptance of anesthesia during childbirth and, in particular, recognition of chloroform which Simpson had introduced into obstetrical practice. Simpson's death at the age of 59 led to one of the largest funerals ever held in Scotland. The university, the stock exchange, and all commercial activities were suspended.

1. Simpson, E. B.: "Sir James Y. Simpson," in *Famous Scots Series*, Edinburgh and London: Oliphant Anderson and Ferrier, 1896.
2. *Edinburgh Med J* (entire issue) 6:482-560 (June) 1911.
3. Simpson, J. Y.: On a New Anesthetic Agent, More Efficient Than Sulfuric Ether, *Lancet* 2:549-550, 1847.
4. Simpson, J. Y.: Contributions to the Pathology and Treatment of Diseases of the Uterus, London and Edinburgh: *Monthly J Med Sci* 3:702-715, 1843.
5. Gordon, H. L.: *Sir James Young Simpson and Chloroform*, London: T. Fisher Unwin, 1897.

Composite by G. Bako

James Marion Sims (1813-1883)

J. MARION SIMS, one of the great American surgeons, was born in Lancaster County, South Carolina, into a family of modest means. Through his remarkable mental endowment and great manual dexterity, he became a general surgeon of wide repute and a gynecologist of international fame. Sims attended medical lectures for a time at the Medical College of South Carolina (Charleston Medical College) in Charleston, and after additional training at the Jefferson Medical College in Philadelphia began the practice of medicine in 1835. For more than a dozen years practice was shared between his native state and Alabama, interspersed by service in the Seminole War and one expedition against the Creek Indians.

A notable incident befell one of his female patients in Alabama. The woman incurred a retroversion of the uterus in a fall from a horse. Digital examination of the vagina, with the patient in the quadruped position, led to the prompt correction of the displacement, accompanied by a sudden, and audible, rush of the air into the vagina. It was apparent to Sims that the knee-chest position allowed the uterus to move ventral-

cephalad and the vagina to balloon with air. The inspiration from this consultation proved to be the first step in the procedure for the correction of a vesicovaginal fistula (Sims' operation).[1] The persistence of a vesicovaginal fistula, a frequent complication of childbirth, particularly among the indigent in whom delivery was accomplished without the aid of instruments or anesthesia, was a distressing sociomedical problem. Other causes for the fistula included the prolonged retention of a vaginal pessary, an indolent ulcer, a calculus, or other foreign bodies in the bladder.

In describing the operation, which had been performed a number of times before 1852, Sims did not overlook the good results obtained in exceptional instances in America or Europe. The basic criteria for Sims' excellent record included proper positioning of the patient, the use of a specially designed speculum, devised from a bent silver spoon, silver wire sutures, and a catheter for constant bladder drainage.[1]

In order to obtain a correct view of the vaginal canal, I place the patient upon a table about 2½ by 4 feet, on her knees, with the nates elevated, and the head and shoulders depressed. The knees must be separated some 6 to 8 inches, the thighs at about right angles with the table, and the clothing all thoroughly loosened so that there shall be no compression of the abdominal parietes. An assistant on each side lays a hand in the fold between the glutei muscles and the thigh, the ends of the fingers extending quite to the labia majora; then, by simultaneously pulling the nates upwards and outwards, the os externum opens, the pelvic and adominal viscera all gravitate towards the epigastric region, the atmosphere enters the vagina, and there, pressing was a weight of 14 lbs. upon the square inch, soon stretches this canal out to its utmost limits, affording an easy view of the os tincae, fistula, &c. To facilitate the exhibition of the parts, the assistant on the right side of the patient introduces into the vagina the lever speculum . . . and then, by lifting the perineum, stretching the sphincter, and raising up the recto-vaginal septum, it is as easy to view the whole vagina canal as it is to examine the fauces by turning a mouth widely open, up to a strong light.

The duck-billed speculum was designed to[1]

. . . reflect a strong light down on the vaginovesical septum, the seat of fistula. Its breadth . . . is about ⅞ths of an inch, widening a little as it approaches the end, making it somewhat in the shape of a ducks' bill. The handle is made strong and unyielding, because a considerable degree of leverage has to be exercised by it.

Subsequently, Sims discovered that the left lateral position (Sims' position) was as effective for vaginal examinations as the knee-chest position.[1]

These simple instruments, with this position and a good light, are all that are necessary for obtaining an accurate view of the parts. If the vagina and outlet are ordinarily capacious, a good strong northern light, of a clear day, from a large solitary window, is all-sufficient. But if this canal has been narrowed by cicatrices after extensive sloughs, or from other causes, then sunlight is absolutely necessary for every stage of the operation from first to last. For this purpose, a small table is placed near a window admitting the sunlight. An assistant, sitting by, adjusts on the table a glass . . . some eight or ten inches in diameter, so as to throw the rays of light into the vagina, which, passing to the right of the operator, and striking the concave surface of the bright speculum, are reflected down on the anterior vaginal paries, making everything perfectly distinct.

The edges of the fistulous opening were then scarified with a sharp pointed knife.

Suturing with silk was thoroughly unsatisfactory. The tendency to infection and slough with use of unsterile silk presented formidable hazards. In order to correct this deficiency, Sims close narrow, silver wire and a shotted or twisted suture (Sims' suture).[1]

This suture is far preferable to anything before suggested for the purpose. Its introduction dates from June 1849, since which time I have had comparatively little trouble in the treatment of the great majority of cases of vesico-vaginal fistula. Properly applied, this suture never ulcerates out, having always to be removed by means of scissors, hooks, and forceps. It may be allowed to remain intact for six, eight, or ten days, or even longer.

The final step in the operation was the insertion of a double-curved silver, indwelling catheter.[1]

When well fitted to the case, it can be worn with great ease to the patient; and never turns, nor slips out, it matters not whether she lies on the back or side. It is perfectly self-retaining, being held in the bladder by an internal pressure against th symphysis pubis, and by an external pressure on the outer end exerted by the labia overlapping it, and hiding it entirely from view.

The year following publication of the description of this operation Sims moved to New York and continued his gynecologic surgery. He was responsible for the organization of the Woman's Hospital of the State of New York, where a temporary structure was occupied in 1855. It was moved to 50th Street and Lexington Avenue and later to Morningside Heights. His pen was not idle during these days. He wrote on a variety of subjects, mainly gynecologic; other communications were concerned with surgery of the head, neck, or abdomen. He described Sims' depressor, a loop of stout wire used in depressing the anterior vaginal wall for direct examination, and an operative technique for gallbladder disease, with cleansing of the peritoneal cavity. The procedure for amputating the cervix uteri,[2] the description of vaginismus,[3] and a method for treating trismus nascentium were judged outstanding contributions.

An extremely successful surgical practice was continued in New York until 1861. After the outbreak of the Civil War and because of divided loyalties, Sims journeyed to the British Isles and the Continent to practice and to teach postgraduate students. Nor was his social life compromised as a foreigner. He enjoyed the hospitality of Emperor Napoleon and cared for the Duchess of Hamilton and Empress Eugénie. One of the first European publications by Sims (*Lancet*, 1865) discussed painful menstruation. Both the *Lancet* and the *British Medical Journal* accepted his manuscripts during the next 15 years. His last European communication, "The Treatment of Syphilis," was published by the *British Medical Journal* in 1883.

After the close of the Civil War, Sims returned to New York, but the attraction for Europe and the smell of battle proved irresistible. Frequent visits were made to the Continent, and at the outbreak of the Franco-Prussian War in 1870, he organized and became surgeon-in-chief of the Anglo-American Ambulance Corps. After the battle of Sedan, the French conferred upon him the order of Commander of the Legion of Honour.

His presidential address before the annual meeting of the American Medical Association in 1876 discussed medical education, medical ethics, and the eradication of syphilis.[4] The cause of death of President Garfield, a victim of an assassin's bullet on July 2, 1881, was described by Sims, one of the surgical consultants. The ball fractured the first lumbar vertebra.[5]

> The President died of septic infection of the blood. It was blood poisoning, whether called pyaemia or septicaemia.
> Without the wound of the vertebrae, it would have been impossible for him to die. With it, it was impossible for him to live.

A statue to J. Marion Sims, erected by his friends, was placed originally in Bryant Park. Later it was moved to a spot opposite the New York Academy of Medicine on 103rd Street. The life of Sims is an American saga of a poor boy from the South who preferred the North and became the founder of modern gynecologic surgery in America.[6] He was described as a kindly physician, dignified and graceful in his professional conduct, but sweet and boyish when removed from the professional responsibilities of an urban environment.

1. Sims, J. M.: On the Treatment of Vesico-Vaginal Fistula, *Amer J Med Sci* 23:59-82 (Jan.) 1852.
2. Sims, J. M.: Amputation of the Cervix Uteri, *Trans New York Med Soc*, pp. 367-371, 1861.
3. Sims, J. M.: On Vaginismus, *Trans Obstet Soc Lond* 3:356-367, 1862.
4. Address of J. Marion Sims, M.D., *Trans AMA* 27:91-111, 1876.
5. Sims, J. M.: Surgical Treatment of President Garfield, *North Amer Rev* 133:594-601, 1881.
6. Sims, J. M.: *The Story of My Life*, New York: D. Appleton and Company, 1884.

Ignaz Phillip Semmelweis (1818-1865)

THE INSISTENCE OF THE GREEKS upon cleanliness in physical contacts between patient and physician might be conceived as the introduction of asepsis into medicine. But not until the latter part of the 18th century were infection and contagion under suspicion in the etiology of puerperal fever. White of Manchester observed that the in-

Composite by G. Bako

cidence of puerperal fever varied greatly among communities or segments of the population and inferred that this might be related to exogenous matter carried by midwives. Gordon of Aberdeen, in 1795, stated dogmatically that contact or communication between a patient with puerperal sepsis and a healthy parturient female was hazardous. Collins of the Dublin Lying-In Hospital instituted chlorine disinfection of the hands to suppress the dread malady. These and other clinical observations were corroborative evidence for O. W. Holmes. Obstetrics was not one of his many accomplishments. Although the concept of the contagiousness of puerperal sepsis was clearly expounded by Holmes, at the same time Semmelweis, the obstetrician, was gathering clinical data in the Allgemeines Krankenhaus in Vienna to prove the hypothesis.

Ignaz Philipp Semmelweis, a true scientist, dedicated, logical, and determined, sought academic freedom in Vienna in order to substantiate a theory, which when implemented, saved more parturients than any drug or other procedure.[1] Before this was realized, however, Semmelweis was subjected to an ordeal by fire, was rejected by the Chief of the obstetrical service, Professor

Klein, at the peak of his professional attainments, and died in an insane asylum at the age of 47.

Semmelweis was born in Buda across the river from Pest(h). Budapest was not a united city until 1872. Although Semmelweis is best known for his scientific contributions as a Viennese, his parents were not Austrian; they were Magyars. His father, a merchant, wanted his son to be a lawyer. Semmelweis studied for 2 years at the University of Pest before traveling to Vienna to pursue a career in law but soon changed to medicine. The MD degree was granted at the age of 26. The record is unclear as to the incipiency of the first profound interest in obstetrics. Few scientific communications were prepared by Semmelweis; he left no autobiography.[2] The probability of a pre-graduate interest in midwifery arises from a signed declaration of his intent to leave Vienna if granted a Master of Midwifery. The mastership was granted 6 months later. Johann Chiari, assistant in the obstetric clinic, befriended Semmelweis and called his attention to the postmortem examination of a patient who had died following removal of fibroids of the uterus. The pathological examination revealed structural changes identical with puerperal fever. While waiting for an appointment as assistant in the First Obstetric Clinic at the Allgemeines Krankenhaus, he studied as a volunteer in the clinic and was regular in his attendance in the morgue through the encouragement of Rokitansky, professor of pathological anatomy.

The segregation of the obstetrical cases into a First and Second Division provided an unusual opportunity for clinical observations of puerperal fever. Beginning in 1840, medical students were assigned to the First Division; the midwives were assigned to the Second Division. The students and assistants moved freely from the morgue, with victims of puerperal fever, to the wards. On the other hand, midwives were not allowed to attend the postmortem examinations or examine the cadavers. There was no opportunity for them to carry infection from the death house to the obstetrical patients. Semmelweis tabulated and compared the morbidity on the two Divisions. Between 1841 and 1846 there were almost 2,000 deaths among 20,000 cases in the First Division; in the Second Division there were less than 700 deaths in a slightly smaller number of cases admitted. The comparable percentages were 9.9 and 3.4. In 1846, the mortality was 11.4% in the First Division and 2.7% in the Second Division. Semmelweis reasoned that the differences were related to the spread of infection and contagion from the afflicted to the noninfected or from residua of the examination in the morgue of the cases that had died from sepsis and carried to the patients in the wards. The conclusions were obvious. For reasons not entirely clear, Semmelweis neither published his results nor presented his observations before any organized medical society at that time. Hebra, the Chief of the Dermatology Clinic, was the first to describe the critical statistical observations. As Editor of the *Journal of the Medical Society of Vienna*, he reported in 1847 that:[1]

The Editor of this Journal feels it is his duty to communicate to the medical profession, in view of the prevalence of puerperal fever in all lying-in hospitals, the following observations made by Dr. Semmelweis. . . . By daily visits to an institution of pathology and anatomy Dr. Semmelweis had learnt what were the injurious influences which were produced by filthy and putrid fluids upon even unwounded portions of the body of individuals engaged in postmortem examinations. These observations aroused in him the thought, that perhaps in lying-in hospitals the pregnant and parturient patients might be inoculated by the accoucheur himself, and the puerperal fever was in most cases nothing else than cadaveric infection.

In order to test this thesis, each student or assistant on the First Obstetric Clinic was required to wash his hands in an aqueous solution of chloride of lime before making an examination of a pregnant woman. The decrease in infection following the acceptance of this mandate was striking.

During the year 1848, the first 12 months in which chlorine disinfection was diligently practiced, the mortality in the First Division was, for the first time in many years, slightly less than the mortality in the Second Division. There were several months in which no deaths occurred. Two additional observations strengthened Semmelweis' belief in the validity of his hypothesis. In selected instances, puerperal sepsis had been traced from infections in the hospital other than parturient patients or from the death house; sepsis similar to childbed fever had appeared in nonparturient patients. A suppurated knee was found to be the source of infection in one instance. Professor Kolletschka, Professor of Medical Jurisprudence, in performing a postmortem examination, received a puncture wound of the finger. He died of a pathological process that resembled puerperal sepsis.

Note had been taken of these observations in the *Medico-Chirurgical Transactions of London*, the London *Lancet*, and the *American Journal of Medical Sciences* before Semmelweis chose to make his first presentation in 1850 to the medical profession on puerperal fever. The manuscript was published in abstract form and then only after urging by Skoda, Director of the Chest Division at the Allgemeines Krankenhaus. The medical profession was divided in its response to this new concept. His friends Hebra, Skoda, and Rokitansky were enthusiastic. His chief, Klein, refused to accept the correlation. Scanzoni of Prague, Meigs of Philadelphia, and Denham of Ireland were sympathetic to Klein.

Hungary and Austria at that time were in as great a turmoil as was Semmelweis in his mission on puerperal fever. Buda and Pest had been subjected to a state of siege for several years. Semmelweis fought with his brothers in the war against Austria in 1848. It is believed that this action may have contributed in some small degree to his failure to be appointed privatdocent of Midwifery at the Allgemeines Krankenhaus. He rereturned to Hungary reluctantly, thwarted in his academic ambitions, to accept Directorship of the Obstetrical Division of the St. Rochus Hospital at Pest. The medical school was in a sorry state and not conducive to clinical investigation. It gave him an opportunity, however, to prepare his one and only major treatise on the subject, "The Etiology, Concept, and Prophylaxis of Childbed Fever." This was published in 1861 in German when he was 42 years of age. After waiting almost a decade and a half, he prepared 543 printed pages which documented his observations that he had begun to collect in 1844.[3] There are many tables in the re-

port; it is repetitious and lacks characteristic style. A concise report would have been more effective. Excerpts follow but not in sequence.[4]

In the statement of the concept of childbed fever, we have expressed our conviction that all childbed fever, no single case excepted, is due to the absorption of a decomposed animal-organic matter. We have maintained that this decomposed animal-organic matter, which causes childbed fever on absorption, in the majority of cases is introduced into the patient from without, and that in only very few cases does the decomposed animal-organic matter originate within the individual affected.

Childbed fever is not a contagious disease but is communicable from an ill puerpera to a healthy one by means of a decomposed animal-organic matter.

But childbed fever cannot be carried from a puerpera ill with childbed fever to a healthy one, if a decomposed animal-organic matter is not transferred from one to the other. For example, a puerpera is seriously ill with puerperal fever; if the puerperal fever appears in a form which is not due to the implantation of a decomposed matter from without, then this childbed fever is not communicable to a healthy puerpera; but if childbed fever appears in a form which is due to the implantation of a decomposed matter from without, then this childbed fever is communicable to a healthy puerpera; e.g. a puerpera is ill with puerperal fever; it is septic endometritis, there are serious metastases present, and from this puerpera, childbed fever can be communicated to a healthy puerpera.

Thus childbed fever is caused not only by cadaveric particles clinging to the hand, but also by ichorous discharges originating in living organisms; for that reason, the hands of the examiner must be cleansed with chlorine water, not only after handling cadavers, but likewise after examining patients, wherein the hands may be contaminated by ichor, before proceeding to the examination of a second individual.

Afterwards, when examinations were made with clean hands as the result of the chlorine washings, the deaths ceased among those patients who had a prolonged first stage and the protracted first stage became as little dangerous, as it had been previously in the Second Division.

At the age of 38, Semmelweis married a girl 20 years his junior. There is every indication that it was a happy marriage until his tragic death 9 years later. He was taken to a lunatic asylum in Vienna by friends. One of the examining physicians discovered an injury to the finger of the right hand which probably had occurred during one of his last postmortem examinations. Cellulitis spread; he succumbed to septicemia within a fortnight after he had left Pest, from a variant of the disease which his professional life had been dedicted to eradicate.

1. Sinclair, W. J.: *Semmelweis: His Life and His Doctrine,* Manchester, England: Manchester University Press, 1909..
2. Murphy, F. P.: Ignaz Philipp Semmelweis (1818-1865): An Annotated Bibliography, *Bull Hist Med* 20:653-707 (Dec.) 1946.
3. Lesky, E.: Ignaz Philipp Semmelweis and the Vienna Medical School (Ger), Vienna: Bohlaus, 1964.
4. Semmelweis, I. P.: Etiology, Concept and Prophylaxis of Childbed Fever (Ger), Pest, Wien & Leipzig, C. A. Hartleben, 1861, translated in *Med Classics* 5:339-715, 1941.

Carl S. F. Crede (1819-1892)

CARL SIGMUND FRANZ CREDE was the founder of the gynecologic clinic at the Charité Hospital, Berlin; a proponent of gentle, external manipulation for expulsion of the placenta; and an advocate of silver nitrate instillation for prevention of ophthalmia neonatorum. He received his medical education in his native Berlin except for a semester spent at Heidelberg.[1] Carl's father, of French lineage, occupied a high position in the University of Berlin as head of the Department of Public Worship and Public Instruction. The MD degree was granted Credé in 1842 with the presentation of an inaugural thesis, entitled *De omphaloprotosi*. After a period of travel and study, he became an assistant in Busch's clinic and in 1850 qualified as privatdocent. Two years later he was appointed director of the Berlin School for Mid-wives and chief of the lying-in department of the Charité. In 1856, Credé succeeded Jörg as professor of midwifery in Leipzig, where, as in Berlin, he established an outpatient department for obstetric and gynecologic cases. He held the post until he retired in 1887 because of failing health from cancer of the prostate.

Credé's venture into published communications was consummated by the appearance in 1853 and 1854 of his "Clinical Lectures on Midwifery," in which he recommended a procedure for the management of the third stage of labor to be later identified with his name. From 1853 to 1869 he shared, with Busch, Ritgen, and Siebold, senior editorial responsibilities for the *Monatsschrift für Geburtskunde und Frauenkrankheiten.* When the *Monatsschrift* ceased publication and was replaced by the *Archiv für Gynaekologie,* Credé initially shared the editorial responsibilities; however, in 1881, he became sole editor. His contributions exemplified conciseness of presentation and clarity of expression; his text for midwives went through several editions and was translated into English. As successful in teaching as in writing, Credé was responsible for the training of a number of leading obstetricians. In this pursuit he stressed the significance of proper delivery as the best means of avoiding subsequent gynecologic surgery.

Credé's technique for the management of the third stage of labor (fifth by his count) was predicated on abstinence from internal interference in favor of external pressure for expression of the placenta. Not only did he appreciate the dangers from infection which accompanied the manual invasion of the vagina and uterus, but also other reasons equally valid. Although the concept was not new (the Old Calabar people [Nigeria] included a description of the management of the third stage of labor by external manipulation as did Hippocrates in his aphorism No. 1255), Credé reintroduced the procedure into modern obstetrical practice. His recommendations are as follows:[2]

In order not to prolong the anxiety for the parturient in the last stage of delivery, as well as to allow the physician to return to his other professional responsibilities, it is expedient and justifiable to hasten the slow course of nature. . . . One single energetic contraction of the uterus quickly ends the procedure. I have succeeded in innumerable cases, without exception, no matter how sluggish the labor, to produce an artificial and strong contraction one-quarter to one-half an hour after delivery of the infant by first a gentle then increasingly stronger massage of the fundus and body of the uterus through the abdominal wall. As soon as the contraction reaches its peak, I envelope the entire uterus with my hand so that the fundus lies in the palm of the hand and the five fingers spread over the sides of the body, exerting a gentle pressure. I can detect the placenta under my grasp slipping out of the uterus, in fact, this usually occurs with such force that the placenta protrudes beyond the external genitalia at once; at the least, the placenta moves to the lower portion of the vagina. . . . The uterus remains contracted with little danger of hemorrhage, since involution of the uterus cannot occur during regular contractions; albeit this is possible with the traditional method of expulsion of the placenta, irrespective of the care with which this is performed.

At the same time, the general support and strengthening of the parturient, who as a rule is exhausted, is to be attended to; the uterus is examined repeatedly through the abdominal wall and gently stimulated to contract; one continues in this manner even if the placenta has delivered and the parturient has entered the puerperium.

The first report of Credé's observations on prophylaxis against gonorrheal ophthalmia of the newborn appeared in 1881. Later he contrasted the data from the years 1874 to 1880, a period without a prophylactic agent with a shorter period when a solution of silver nitrate was employed. The incidence of ophthalmia ranged from 9.2% to 13.6% in the control period. With the routine instillation of silver nitrate in the subsequent four years, only one or two cases per annum appeared among 1,160 infants. With the widespread introduction of silver nitrate solution in the eyes of the infant immediately upon delivery, blindness has been prevented in an untold number of newborns. Credé's procedure was described in 1884 as follows.[3]

. . . all the sebaceous matter clinging to the eye-lids was removed. Then on the table where the child is swathed *before* clothes are put on the child, each eye is opened by means of two fingers, *a single drop of a 2 percent solution of silver nitrate hanging on a little glass rod* is brought close to the cornea until it touches it, and is dropped on the middle of it. *There is no further care given to the eyes.* Especially in the next 24 to 36 hours, in case a slight reddening or swelling of the lid with secretion of mucus should follow, the instillation *should not be repeated.*

In the Leipzig Lying-In Hospital, the instillations were made by the head-midwife alone, mostly without the supervision of a doctor; only one student-midwife can be useful to the extent that she delicately draws apart a little the child's eye-lids with one finger of her hand. By means of this assistance all the students are trained, and soon can carry out the process all by themselves.

1. Leopold, G.: Carl Sigmund Franz Credé (Ger), *Arch Gynaek* 42:193-213, 1892.

2. Credé, C. S. F.: Technique of Delivery (Ger), *Klin Vorträge Geburtsh* 1:579-603, 1853, excerpt translated by M. Borgwardt.

3. Credé, C. S. F.: *Prophylaxis of the Inflammation of the Eye of the Newborn* (Ger), Berlin: A. Hirschwald, 1884, in Thomas, H. (trans): *Classical Contributions of Obstetrics and Gynecology*, Springfield, Ill: C. C Thomas, 1935, pp 70-73.

John Braxton Hicks (1823-1897)

J. BRAXTON HICKS, an unpretentious physician, a great teacher of obstetrics and gynecology, and a devoted parishioner of the Church of England, was born at Rye in Sussex, the son of a one-time banker and chairman of the bench of county magistrates.[1] For three years, Braxton Hicks was a private pupil of the Reverend J. O. Zillwood of Compton Rectory. Subsequently he was apprenticed to a medical practitioner in his home town, and at the age of 18 entered Guy's Hospital as a medical student. His brilliant scholarship was quickly recognized, and in proper time he took prizes in anatomy, materia medica, practical chemistry, and botany, and won a medal in sports for double sculling. The degree of bachelor of medicine at the London University was granted in 1847, with honors in each subject plus a gold medal in materia medica. Soon afterwards he qualified for the diplomas of the Royal College of Surgeons and the Apothecaries Society and in 1851 was granted the MD degree. While acquiring an enviable record in medical sciences, Hicks studied mosses, algae, and insects, related areas of scholarship partially responsible for

National Library of Medicine

election to the Royal Society at a relatively early age. Unrelated subjects of special interest included Oriental china and Wedgwood ware.

Hicks spent several years in general medicine in Tottenham in partnership with W. Moon. In 1859, he left general practice and accepted the post of assistant obstetric physician at Guy's Hospital, where he remained until the compulsory retirement age of 60. Although he was appointed consulting physician at retirement, this did not satisfy so ambitious and talented a person. After several years without a hospital appointment, Hicks returned to an active teaching post— that of obstetric physician at St. Mary's Hospital—but never forgetting that he was a Guy's man. At various times, he served as examiner in obstetric medicine at the University of London, physician to the Royal Maternity Charity, and physician to the Royal Hospital for Women and Children in Waterloo Road.[1]

A communication on a new method of version in abnormal labor, which combined internal and external manipulation, was published in the *Lancet*.[2] The significance of the Braxton Hicks maneuver must have been sensed by the discoverer, since he preferred to publish the description so that it could be studied and critically analyzed before submitting his definitive conclusions to the Obstetrical Society for open discussion. Later contributions concerned the state of the uterus in obstructed labor, a physiological interpretation of the contractions of the uterus throughout pregnancy, extrauterine fetation, suppression of menses, uterine polypi, proliferous cysts of the ovary, treatment of malignant disease, and the failure of the recovery of kyestein (kiestine—an amorphous substance thought to be present only in the urine during pregnancy) to survive its expectation as a pregnancy test.

The version of the fetus in abnormal labor was not an original concept of Hicks. In a full-length discussion of the subject prepared three years after the preliminary communication, he gave credit to several of his predecessors. The majority had used either external pressure on the abdomen or internal pressure through the introduction of the hand or the arm into the uterus. The ineffectiveness of the external version and the obvious disadvantages in introducing the hand into the uterus were overcome by the Hicks maneuver. The improved procedure enabled the accoucheur to produce cephalic or podalic version, partial or complete, as soon as the os uteri was dilated to admit one or two fingers. Abnormal presentation could be rectified and complete version performed. This procedure was helpful when early intervention was indicated, but could be lifesaving in the management of placenta praevia when staunching the hemorrhage was an emergency requirement. Once the fetus acted as a plug in the cervical canal, it was possible for the uterus to dilate gradually and permit successful delivery. Cephalopelvic disproportion, malpresentation, and sometimes eclampsia also responded to turning of the fetus. In recent decades improved management has minimized the need for the procedure in any abnormal delivery.

Hicks's communication on bipolar version includes the following description.[2]

The method I have found successful, and very easy of application, is conducted thus:—We will suppose the simplest condition, a case where the uterus is passive, membranes unbroken, the liquor amnii plentiful, the os uteri expanded sufficiently to detect the presentation, which is cephalic, and in the first or fourth position (occiput to left side); the patient is in the ordinary position, the trunk curved forwards as much as possible, to relax the abdominal muscles. Introduce the left hand, with the usual precautions, into the vagina, so far as to fairly touch the foetal head, even should it recede an inch. (This generally requires the whole hand.) Having passed one or two fingers (if only one, let it be the middle finger) within the cervix, and resting them on the head, place the *right* hand on the *left* side of the breech at the fundus uteri, . . . Employ gentle pressure and slight impulsive movements on the fundus towards the right side, and simultaneously on the head towards the left iliac fossa. In a very short time it will be found that the head is rising and at the same time the breech is descending. The shoulder is now felt by the hand in place of the head, . . . it in like manner is pushed to the left, and at the same time the breech is depressed to the right iliac fossa. The foetus is now transverse; the knee will be opposite the os, and, the membranes being ruptured, it can be seized, . . . and brought into the vagina.

Having now the labour at command, the case must be treated according to the circumstances which called for turning. In obedience to the law above stated, when the foetus is placed transversely, a slight impulse will determine the final position of the head. When the leg is seized, therefore, it is advisable to place the right hand beneath the head in its new position on the left side, and gently press it towards the fundus. The same law renders it very easy to convert the cephalic, shoulder, neck, or even natural transverse, into a breech case. In either of these conditions it is merely necessary to push up the head, and, removing the left hand from the vagina without bringing down the knee or foot, place it on the breech in the right iliac fossa, so as to depress it into the cavity of the pelvis. No extra force should be used, for it will be found to obey a very "gentle persuasion." Indeed, the change is completed sometimes spontaneously, and the foot is at hand before it is expected. The breech now presenting, it is advisable to retain it till labour is fairly set in, by a firm bandage placed externally, and, should it be required, a pad on either side of the fundus. It should now be treated as an ordinary pelvic presentation.

A practical consideration of the fluctuating activity of the uterus in obstructive labor was advanced by Hicks following critical clinical observation. There were two eventualities in which the contractions ceased to be rhythmical, having been vigorous and normal.[3]

Now, when hard labour-pains have existed some time and we find the rhythmical action has subsided, we have one of two conditions, the discrimination of which is very important as a guide to our proper treatment.

The first and simplest form is well known, and is that in which the uterus is simply quiescent, resting passively for a time while the nervous power is being, so to speak, collected; after a time the uterus begins to act and the labour is accomplished. Now, in this case there is no rise of the pulse; generally, on the contrary, it is weak and feeble, nor are there any untoward symptoms but langour and possibly some faintness. In these the reflection function is deficient, and its action sluggish, and, therefore, the demand on the constitution to supply nerve force is proportionately small.

How can we further distinguish this class? Place the hand on the uterus externally, and through the abdominal walls it will easily be detected that the uterine walls are lax and flabby, the foetus readily detected within it floating about with ease.

So long as this condition lasts it will very rarely be found that we have any change from the natural condition of the patient, consequently but little, if any, cause of anxiety, nor generally for manipulative interference.

The second form of subsidence of the pains is, as already indicated, of the opposite character. The uterus becomes gradually irritated, so that although some of the pains still occur at irregular intervals, the uterus is really in more action than before, tightly compressing the child, falling into the inequalities of its form, whereby the foetus is prevented from escaping, every indentation of the uterus forming as it were a ledge past which it is difficult to draw the child or to pass the hand if we desire to turn.

When this condition, more frequent than generally supposed, and not infrequent in primiparae, has once been fairly established, it is rare that the rhythmical pains ever occur with such force as to expel the foetus; as a rule the continuous action remains, and sooner or later symptoms set in, telling one of the necessity for interference.

Evidence to support the belief that contractions of the uterus appear early in pregnancy and persist through delivery was presented to the Obstetrical Society in 1871, the year of Hicks's presidency.[4]

But after many years' constant observation, I have ascertained it to be a fact that the uterus possesses the power and habit of spontaneously contracting and relaxing from a very early period of pregnancy, as early, indeed, as it is possible to recognise the difference of consistence—that is, from about the third month.

In a general way the pregnant woman is not conscious of these contractions of the uterus, but sometimes she will remark that she has a tumour in her lower abdomen, thinking it a constant thing; but another will observe that she has a swelling sometimes, but which vanishes at other times. But occasionally it happens that the uterus is more than usually sensitive, and that the contractions are accompanied by pain; and then on examination it is found that each pain she complains of is coincident with a contraction.

Hicks was described as a mild-mannered man, unpretentious, but an erudite source of information on a great variety of subjects. He had wide interests in nature, was fond of art and architecture, and brilliant in intellect.

1. Cullingworth, C. J.: "A Short Notice of the Life and Work of the Late J. Braxton Hicks," in *Selected Essays and Monographs*, London: New Sydenham Society, 1901, pp 93-105.
2. Hicks, J. B.: On a New Method of Version in Abnormal Labour, *Lancet* 2:28-30 (July 14) 1860.
3. Hicks, J. B.: On the Condition of the Uterus in Obstructed Labour; and an Inquiry as to What Is Intended by the Terms "Cessation of Labour Pains," "Powerless Labour," and "Exhaustion," *Trans Obstet Soc Lond* 9:207-239, 1868.
4. Hicks, J. B.: On the Contractions of the Uterus Throughout Pregnancy: Their Physiological Effects and Their Value in the Diagnosis of Pregnancy, *Trans Obstet Soc Lond* 13:216-231, 1872.

Robert Lawson Tait (1854-1899)

ROBERT LAWSON TAIT, who had dropped the forename by the time he began his medical writing, was born in Edinburgh. Although his contributions were made while at Birmingham, England, he is characterized by his biographers as a rugged, indefatigable son of Scotland. He received his undergraduate and medical education at the University of Edinburgh without coming up for a degree. The deficiency was no handicap to the brilliant pupil of J. Y. Simpson, and at an early age Tait was admitted as a member of the Royal College of Surgeons of Edinburgh.[1] In 1867, he was appointed house-surgeon to the Wakefield hospital, where, during a three-year tenure, he performed bold surgery in the abdomen, including an

ovariotomy. Tait moved to Birmingham in 1870, became a leading surgical and civic figure in the community, and, within a year, was appointed surgeon to the newly-founded

National Library of Medicine

Hospital for Diseases of Women. An appointment of mutual good, it provided the Scottish gynecologist with patients and facilities in the maturation of a rich career in teaching, writing, and advancing the art of abdominal surgery. His medical thinking was exemplary of his times except for a failure to embrace Listerism, the new doctrine of antisepsis.

Tait was one of the great ovariotomists of his day and, in spite of any claim of priority, actually his first ovariotomy was performed on July 29, 1868, for cause unknown, "when Mr. Tait was only 23 years of age."[2] His description of ovariectomy for extra-ovarian dysfunction, one of the first in English, appeared in 1879.[3]

I have removed the ovaries for the arrest of haemorrhage in cases of myoma three times, in all three with a fatal result. The dates were August 1st, 1872; December 26th, 1873; and March 14th, 1874. It will thus be seen that this operation was performed in England five days after it was first performed in Germany, and sixteen days before it was performed by Dr. Battey. The facts of my cases, but not the details or the dates, were published some time ago.

In such matters, I do not think priority to be a matter of the slightest importance; but the facts of the history of this operation seem to me to favour the general objection to attaching individual names to operations. That this operation will prove a great addition to surgery I have no doubt. With our improved methods of operating, I believe that at least two, possibly all three, of my cases would recover now, if I had them over again.

The outcome of Tait's management of his first case of extrauterine pregnancy at the time of rupture, in which the uterus and appendages were removed, was as disheartening a decade later as were the first ovariotomies. The patient never regained consciousness after the operation. However, a few weeks later, in 1883, the operation was performed successfully.[4]

... I desire to place on record this, the first series, as I believe, of cases of extrauterine pregnancy operated upon at the time of rupture; that is, from the tenth to the thirteenth weeks. ... I have been unfortunate enough to see a large number of them, five or six and twenty, and of late I have been encouraged by my success in other abdominal diseases to try what surgery could do in these cases.

For this treatment, of course the difficulty was the diagnosis, but as I have now completely adopted the principle of always opening the abdomen when I find a patient in danger with abdominal symptoms, this barrier no longer exists. The diagnosis is, however, not so very difficult after all, for in many cases the existence of pregnancy has been suspected before the rupture occurred.

On March 1st, 1883, I saw, with Dr. Page of Solihull, a patient who had not been pregnant for many years, in whom there was a fixed mass in the pelvis, and whose menstruation had been arrested for about three months. She had a high pulse and an exalted temperature and great pain. I advised abdominal section, and found the abdomen full of clot. The right Fallopian tube was ruptured, and from it a placenta was protruding. I tied the tube and removed it. I searched for, but could not find the foetus, and I suppose it got amongst the folds of intestine and there was absorbed. Certainly it has not since been seen. The patient made a very protracted convalescence, but she is now perfectly well.

These cases all confirm the view of the pathology of extrauterine pregnancy, which I advanced many years ago, that in origin it is always tubal, and that its varieties depend merely on the direction in which rupture occurs. These results also confirm the soundness of the policy of interfering early in such cases, for four out of the five have been easily and completely cured of one of the most formidable conditions of pregnancy.

Another first for Tait in England was the amputation of the uterus for placenta previa following caesarian section, an extension of Porro's proposal. The matter was discussed by Tait in "An Address on the Surgical Aspect of Impacted Labour."[5]

In the old Caesarean Section, no matter whether applied to the living or the dead mother, the uterus was not removed. ... It used to be a byword in Scotland that the operation was never successful unless it was performed by a cow, an allusion to the fact that in cases in which accidentally a cow had ripped open a pregnant uterus, several recoveries had taken place, whereas hardly a patient was known to have recovered even when the operation was performed by a special surgeon.

Only one other suggestion I am disposed to lay before my obstetric brethren for the further extension of this operation, that is, the case of placenta praevia, a condition which is one of the most fatal that can affect a parturient woman. ... If I had to deal with a case of complete placenta praevia from the beginning of labour, and could carry out what I believe would be the ideal of surgical treatment of this condition, I should amputate the pregnant uterus. I should thereby save the child with certainty. I should relieve the mother with perfect safety from death by haemorrhage; and, by removing all the tissues in which large suppurating venous sinuses were present, I believe I should relieve her with almost equal certainty from the secondary risks.

Other operations performed by Tait early in the history of modern abdominal surgery included the removal of an ovary for chronic infection, hysterectomy for myomas, cholecystotomy, hepatotomy, the excision of a pyosalpinx and hydrosalpinx, and a flap-splitting operation for repair of the perineum.

One major misjudgment in a brilliant gynecologic career was skepticism regarding Lister's precepts of antisepsis. Tait compensated adequately by insisting upon maximum cleanliness of the patient, the operators, and instruments through the use of soap and hot water, concluding abdominal surgery with a cleansing of the peritoneal cavity with warm saline solution. With this scrupulous technique, he achieved a record of asepsis as impressive as that of the advocates of the carbolic acid spray.

In 1887, Tait was appointed professor of gynaecology at Queen's College, a department later transferred to Mason College and subsequently to the University of Birmingham. His several published monographs or texts included *Diseases of Women*, later expanded into *Diseases of Women and Abdominal Surgery, The Pathology and Treatment of Diseases of the Ovaries* (the Bevin Hastings Essay for 1873), *General Summary of Conclusions from One Thousand Cases of Abdominal Section, An Essay on Hospital Mortality*, and *Lectures on Ectopic Pregnancy and Haematocele*.

The bold surgeon with a vital personality and a rugged physique was one of the founders of the British Gynaecological Society. Recognition from America included an honorary fellowship in the American Gynecological Society and the American Association of Obstetricians and Gynecologists, the MD degree (*honoris causa*) conferred by the University of the State of New York and the College of Physicians and Surgeons of St. Louis, and the LLD by Union College of Albany.

1. McKay, W. J. S.: *Lawson Tait, His Life and Work*, London: Baillière, Tindall and Cox, 1922.
2. Obituary, Lawson Tait, *Brit Med J* 1:1561-1564, 1899.
3. Tait, L.: Removal of Normal Ovaries, *Brit Med J* 1:813-814, 1879.
4. Tait, L.: Five Cases of Extra-Uterine Pregnancy Operated Upon at the Time of Rupture, *Brit Med J* 1:1250-1251, 1884.
5. Tait, L.: An Address on the Surgical Aspect of Impacted Labour, *Brit Med J* 1:657-661, 1890.

Friedrich Trendelenburg
(1844-1924)

FRIEDRICH TRENDELENBURG, an adroit technical surgeon whose procedures were based upon physiological fundamentals, was born in Berlin, the son of a professor of philosophy at the University.[1] He received his early education at home, his mother tutoring him in English and his father in Latin and mathematics. After attending a boys' school in Berlin, he spent a year in Glasgow with his family, studying anatomy, embryology, and physics. His medical education was continued at the University of Berlin, where he studied under Traube and von Langenbeck and received the degree in medicine at the age of 22. The Military Hospital in Gorlitz

Composite by G. Bako

provided him with his first clinical responsibilities, and, after submitting his inaugural thesis in Latin on *Ancient Indian Surgery,* he became first assistant to von Langenbeck. Six years later he was placed in charge of a surgical ward at the Friedrichschain Hospital in Berlin. At the age of 31 Trendelenburg was given professorial status at the University of Rostock, at the age of 38 he was called to the University of Bonn, and at the age of 51 to the University of Leipzig.

Trendelenburg's many substantial studies include communications on injuries of bones and joints, stricture of the esophagus, exstrophy of the bladder, vesicovaginal fistula, puerperal pyemia, varicose veins, thrombophebitis, plastic repair of the ureter for hydronephrosis, and a physical finding (Trendelenburg's sign) for instability of the hip from dislocation, fracture of the femoral neck, or paralysis of the gluteus medius muscle; if a patient stands on the affected leg, the pelvis drops toward the opposite leg.

In a long discussion of vesicovaginal fistula, the elevated pelvic position for operations within the abdominal cavity—Trendelenburg's position—was described. Although the inversion of patients for surgical management of strangulated hernia, bladder stones, and other pelvic problems had been practiced since early times, the eponymic designation is credited to Trendelenburg. Willy Meyer, his pupil, reported employment of the position in the Bonn Clinic in 1885, which was followed by Trendelenburg's communication in 1890. The elevated pelvic position was particularly useful in successful surgical correction of vesicovaginal fistula, since air was sucked from the vagina through the fistula and into the bladder by creation of a negative intrapelvic pressure; the bladder was thereby exposed for adequate plastic repair. The elevated position was also recommended for other gynecological operations including panhysterectomy, supravaginal amputation of the uterus, and total extirpation of the myomatous uterus, and for general surgical procedures in the pelvis or lower abdomen such as tubercular stricture of the small bowel, internal incarceration of a hollow viscus, and lithotomy. In the early years of its use, Trendelenburg accomplished the pelvic elevation by directing an attendant to stand beyond the operating table with the knees of the patient backward over the attendant's shoulders. The improved technique was described as follows.[2]

If one places the body of a patient on the operating table in such a way that the symphysis pubis forms the highest point of the trunk and the long axis of the trunk forms an angle of at least 45 degrees with the horizontal, then the various organs, especially the liver, spleen and mesentery fall into the concavity of the diaphragm by virtue of their weight. The intestine follows and falls out of the true pelvis as far as the atmospheric pressure will permit. In the case of thin individuals and relaxed recti muscles in deep narcosis, the anterior wall of the abdomen in the hypogastric region in this way exerts a truly sucking effect on the pelvic cavity, so that in the latter region a deep space is formed.

The advantages of the elevated position of the pelvis are likewise of value in all gynecological operations in the pelvic cavity, and I believe that whoever has once removed a myomatous uterus or an adherent ovarian cyst in this way will not readily make up his mind to return to the old procedure.

In the same communication Trendelenburg described a plastic replacement of the ureter in hydronephrosis.[2]

Probably the elevated pelvic position could be used to advantage also in an operation which I undertook several years ago on a case of hydronephrosis, and which had for its purpose the correction of the cause of the formation of the hydronephrosis, namely, the abnormally high and valve-like insertion of the ureter into the kidney pelvis.

The cyst is punctured with the trocar at about a hands-breadth's distance from the ureter and emptied as far as possible. Thereupon the anterior wall is split downward from the same spot in order to free it, and the orifice of the ureter is sought for in the interior of the cyst thus opened. Then the ureter and the cyst wall are slit downward from the orifice throughout the entire extent of the tumor and the wound edges of the slit ureter firmly sutured to the wound edges of the cyst wall. Thus the opening is transferred to the lowest segment of the tumor.

Also while he was in Bonn, Trendelenburg's operation, ligation of the great saphenous vein for varicosities of the leg, was described. Particularly noteworthy was the design of the test to determine the integrity of the venous system of the lower extremities. Incompetence of the valve of the deep saphenous vein is suggested by a positive test.[3]

A very simple experiment will prove the correctness of this view. One lays the patient flat again, raises the leg to the perpendicular, lets all the blood flow out of the saphenous field and compresses the trunk of the saphenous with the finger at a spot where it is definitely recognizable. Now one lets the patient come down from the cot cautiously, without removing the compressing finger from the saphenous. We see that the whole saphenous vein now remains empty at first on standing. Not until the lapse of a quarter to a half a minute does one see the varicosities in the leg gradually begin to fill with blood again. The fullness, however, is not nearly so tense as it previously was, as long as pressure on the trunk persists.

A most dramatic procedure was related by Trendelenburg in 1908 from the Leipzig Clinic—an unsuccessful removal of an embolism of the pulmonary artery by direct surgical exposure. Having determined experimentally in animals the brief period of time the pulmonary artery tolerated compression, a technique for man was developed on a cadaver. Major steps included exposure of the pericardium through resection of the second rib adjacent to the sternum, identification of the aorta and the pulmonary artery, clamping of the aorta, and extraction of the embolus with a pair of forceps. An elapsed time of 45 seconds was allowed for the crucial action. Excerpts of the unsuccessful first attempt are given below. Two cases treated later in the same year survived several hours. It remained for his pupil, Kirschner, in 1924, to accomplish the feat.[4]

This concerns a 70-year-old deaf woman who fractured the neck of the femur six days previously. In the evening, one half hour after her bed had been changed, the patient suddenly collapsed, sweat profusely, and groaned in great anxiety. Three minutes later she lost consciousness; the pupils were widely dilated, the face was pale, the lips and tongue were livid, and the jugular veins were distended. The breathing was rapid, deep, and labored, pulse was imperceptible, the heart tones were not heard. The operation began 18 minutes after the symptoms set in. . . . Dark blood seeped from the small arteries. The pulmonary artery and the aorta were bulging without any evidence of pulsation.

The condition of the patient corresponded with the condition of an animal whose pulmonary artery has been clamped, leaving only a small opening; there was a severe drop in blood pressure, disappearance of the pulse, with continued breathing. In animals, when the compression of the pulmonary artery is relieved, the pulse and the blood pressure return to normal. Thus it might be expected that a patient with an embolism would also rapidly regain normal blood circulation and normal blood pressure. and would also become conscious again after the embolus has been removed.

This case shows that in a hospital there is sufficient time to begin an operation if the instruments are ready. . . . The operation, even though it was more difficult due to the old adhesions between the lung and the pleura, required only five minutes until the pulmonary artery was incised.

As a guest of the Section on Surgery and Anatomy at the 57th Annual Session of the American Medical Association in 1906, Trendelenburg chose to discuss the surgical treatment of puerperal sepsis and thrombosis of the pelvic veins. Also mentioned was the likelihood of benefit following ligation of the inferior vena cava.[5]

In 1901 I tied off the right internal iliac, the branches of which were all filled with thrombus in a woman of 35, who presented a chronic pyemia which came on six weeks after abortion and was

marked by very severe chills. Four and one-half weeks later these returned after having ceased entirely after operation, and then the right ovarian vein was also tied off. The fever then rapidly subsided, and after incising a metastatic abscess which subsequently developed recovery was complete.

It is known, however, that even in the presence of a thrombus in the vena cava spontaneous recovery may follow and that complete obliteration of the lumen of the vein may be succeeded by the development of a sufficiently extensive collateral circulation. It would seem feasible, therefore, in thrombosis of the vena cava, to ligate even this vessel above the site of the process and thus stop the progress of the latter.

1. Körte, W.: In Memory of Friedrich Trendelenburg (Ger), obituary, *Arch Klin Chir* 134:I-VI, 1925.

2. Trendelenburg, F.: Operations for Vesico-Vaginal Fistula and the Elevated Pelvic Position for Operations Within the Abdominal Cavity (Ger), *Samml Klin Vorträge* 355:3373-3392, 1890, translated in *Med Classics* 4:964-988, 1940.

3. Trendelenburg, F.: Ligation of the Great Saphenous Vein in Varicose Veins of the Leg (Ger), *Beitr Klin Chir* 7:195-210, 1891, translated in *Med Classics* 4:1008-1023, 1940.

4. Trendelenburg, F.: The Operative Management of Embolism of the Pulmonary Artery (Ger), *Arch Klin Chir* 86:686-700, 1908, excerpts translated by Z. Danilevicius.

5. Trendelenburg, F.: A Review of Surgical Progress, *JAMA* 47:81-83, 1906.

Composite by G. Bako

Friedrich von Esmarch
(1823-1908)

JOHANN FREIDRICH AUGUST VON ESMARCH was born in 1823, the son of a medical practitioner at Tönning, Schleswig-Holstein, at the time when the province was struggling for freedom from Denmark. Friedrich studied medicine at Göttingen and later at Kiel. His first teaching appointment was assistant to von Langenbeck, Chief of the Surgical Clinic at the University of Kiel, before he took the MD degree, and there he remained throughout his surgical career. In 1854, he was appointed director of the Surgical Clinic and three years later became professor, succeeding Stromeyer, who, in turn, had succeeded von Langenbeck. Esmarch's first marriage was to Stromeyer's daughter; his second at the age of 50 was to the princess of Schleswig-Holstein, an aunt of the German empress. The grace and comfort of the upper class, Old World society prevailed in his home, but, in spite of the noble marriage, it lacked the glittering splendor usually associated with royalty.[1]

Esmarch began the practice of surgery during the insurrection against Denmark; he helped organize resistance groups, partici-

pated in the battles of 1848-1850, and on one occasion was held prisoner for several weeks. In 1866, he was placed in charge of the surgical department of the Berlin barracks on Tempelhof field. From 1868 through 1871, he was active in the wars with Austria and France, while in 1871 he served as Surgeon General of the army. His many contributions to surgical procedures and medical management were based largely upon his military experiences, but were applied whenever possible to civilian practice and teaching. The pavilion system of military hospital construction, which had been developed in America during the Civil War a decade earlier, was advocated by Esmarch upon the suggestion of Rudolf Virchow. He prepared a number of monographs and scientific communications dealing with theoretical and practical surgery. A discussion of chronic inflammation of the joints[2] and the value of early resection after gunshot wounds reflected his imaginative mind. The bloodless operation by means of the Esmarch bandage, the introduction of first-aid on the battlefield and in civilian life, and the establishment of Samaritan schools were his chief accomplishments. The Lister method of treatment was introduced on his hospital service shortly after the announcement by the originator. Consistent with the motives of other great military surgeons, he accepted his service responsibilities with skill and imagination, displayed deep concern for the wounded, and devised means for immediate and subsequent medical management. A first-aid pack was provided for each soldier, with proper instructions for its use.

The excessive loss of blood during surgery of the extremities prompted the development of the bloodless technique for the mutilated in battle. The description and design for application of the Esmarch bandage was published in 1873. It was advised for surgery of the extremities and the male genitalia. An illustrative case from his civilian practice described an operation of the lower extremities for bilateral osteomyelitis.[3]

. . . we wrap the legs tightly from the toes to above the knees, with elastic bandages made from woven rubber, forcing the blood out of the vessels of the limb by an even compression. Then we apply rubber tubing tightly, four or five times around the upper thigh at the point where the bandage stops and connect one end of the tubing to the other by a hook and a copper chain. The rubber tubing compresses all soft parts in such a manner that not one drop of blood can enter the parts below it. It is better than a tourniquet because it can be used on any point of the limb irrespective of the position of the artery. In this simple manner you are able to control the blood flow completely, even with muscular or fat patients.

When we remove the bandage . . . you can see that both legs below the rubber hose look like the legs of a corpse, and contrast in their pale color with the rosy color of the remainder of the body surface. You will observe too that we operate on them as if they were a corpse.

Following the operation we remove slowly the encircling rubber tubing. You observe how the pale skin of the feet reddens slowly, first in patches, then evenly all over and eventually shows a darker red than the body. . . . The patient has lost no more than a teaspoonful of blood! Now observe the patient sleeping quietly. He has the same red cheeks as before the operation, his pulse is strong and regular and I can assure you he will make a quicker recovery from this than if we had done his necrotomy in the usual way.

In the handbook, *Early Aid in Injuries and Accidents*, translated by Princess Christian and published in Philadelphia, Esmarch explained the fundamentals of emergency treatment. The proposed suggestions were to be of help before the physician arrived, not to replace professional management.[4]

Though I have invited you here to teach you how to render the first aid to the injured, I do not in the least aim at rendering a doctor's services unnecessary; on the contrary, I hope to convince you how important the immediate help of a doctor is in most cases. What I wish to do is to enable you to give the *right kind of aid* before the doctor arrives —without which, irreparable injury might be done, and perhaps even a valuable life be lost.

When I look back on my career as a surgeon, I can with truth say that many and many are the times I have deplored that so very few people know how to render the first aid to those who have suddenly met with some injury. This specially applies to the field of battle: of the thousands who have flocked thither in their desire to help, so few have understood how to render aid.

But my remark equally applies to the circumstances of daily life. How many there are every year who die a miserable death, and who might have been saved by prompt aid, had any one been near who knew how to give it.

The Samaritan letters were written and the Samaritan classes formed to teach and to disseminate first-aid information throughout Germany. The movement was highly successful, and at the most prosperous period of the program there was scarcely a hamlet or a rural district without a branch of the association.

You may perhaps know that in forming these classes I am following the example of the English order of St. John of Jerusalem, which for the last five years has established in England the same kind of schools or classes under the direction of the best surgeons.

As a member of the Red Cross Society, I have originated this school. There are many among you who have already done service in time of war, and many who, in the event of another war, would be ready to do so again. In these lectures I shall constantly have to refer to the battle-field. I hope and trust that, under the protection of the Red Cross, similar Samaritan Schools may arise all over Germany, and prove of much service in times alike of peace and war.

Esmarch has been adjudged an excellent surgical teacher, who did much to improve the immediate management of the wounded in battle, the evacuation of the wounded, and their proper care in military hospitals.[5] The experiences of war served him well in civilian practice and made him one of the leading surgeons of Germany in the latter half of the 19th century, worthy of the "von" bestowed upon him by his emperor.

1. Zobeltitz, H.: *A Day in the House of Friedrich von Esmarch on His Seventieth Birthday*, B. Skeete, trans., *Med Mag* 2:9-21 (July) 1893.

2. Esmarch, F.: *Chronic Inflammation of the Joints* (Ger), Kiel: Schwers', 1866.

3. Esmarch, F.: The Art of the Bloodless Operation (Ger), *Sammlung Klin Vorträge* 58:373-384, 1873, excerpt translated by E. Longar.

4. Esmarch, F.: *Early Aid in Injuries and Accidents,* H. R. H. Princess Christian, trans., Philadelphia: Henry C. Lea's Son & Co., 1883.

5. Esmarch, F.: First-Aid on the Battlefield (Ger), Kiel: Schwers', 1869.

National Library of Medicine

Theodor Billroth (1829-1894)

CHRISTIAN ALBERT THEODOR BILLROTH was a medical educator of great vision, a scholar of great depth, and a musician of appreciable talent.[1] Born of Swedish stock in the Prussian community of Bergen on the island of Ruegen in the Baltic Sea, Theodor was Austrian by adoption, and Viennese in spirit. Although many of the great physicians of England and Scotland came of clerical families, a majority of the great physicians of Austria and Germany were the sons of merchants, natural scientists, or lawyers. Billroth was the exception; his father, a minister, died of pulmonary tuberculosis, leaving a wife and a young family. Pulmonary tuberculosis reappeared in Billroth's children; two daughters died from this disease.

Theodor was an average student scholastically. Through help of friends at the University of Greifswald and in deference to the wishes of his mother, he enrolled as a student of medicine at the age of 19; however, it has been suggested by his biographers that a career in music was preferred. Medical training was completed at the University of Göttingen, a school with an outstanding faculty in the sciences and a brilliant department of music. Hence, he came under the influence of a reasonable number of scientific and clinical persons, meanwhile furthering his latent love for music.

After graduation and the fulfillment of his military duties, Billroth received employment in the private clinic of von Graefe. Then followed in succession a disappointing period of private practice, offset by a prized appointment in the Langenbeck Clinic. There he began his prolific career in surgery. In 1856, he was appointed privatdocent, lecturing in pathological anatomy, general and special surgery, and operative technique. Operative surgery was his professional preference, and in this field he was considered to rank only with the best.

The dawn broke in 1860. At the age of 31, Billroth was offered and accepted the professorship of surgery in the University of Zurich. The seven years in Switzerland were pleasant—professionally and culturally. He performed as a guest conductor for the symphony orchestra and frequently contributed musical items to the daily newspaper. He joined a stringed quartet of university professors and began an interesting and lasting friendship with Johannes Brahms. With Langenbeck and Gurlt, the propensity for editorial expression led to the founding of the *Archiv für klinische Chirurgie* during his first year at Zurich. The handbook, *General Surgical Pathology and Therapeutics*, the first of several monographs, was published in 1863. An American edition appeared in 1872.[2]

At the age of 38, Billroth accepted the call to Vienna as professor of surgery in a faculty composed of Rokitansky, Brucke, Hebra, Skoda, and Appolzer. Undoubtedly the position was reluctantly offered by the Viennese since Billroth was born a Prussian, and it probably was reluctantly accepted by Billroth; at that time Vienna was a none-too-friendly community for Prussians so soon after the defeat of the Austrians in the battle of Sadowa. But Billroth was the brilliant young surgeon of Europe, and Vienna was the medical center of the Western world. It was an inevitable appointment and insured an inexhaustible supply of patients who were more apt to come from afar than nearby. In due time, a love for the Austrian capital and the appreciation of the opportunities for the development of a new school of surgery were so strong that he remained in Vienna until the end of his days.

Billroth was an early riser and an individual of great industry. Whether he suffered from insomnia or not is immaterial; he required only a few hours of bed rest each night. The days were spent in teaching, developing techniques in the laboratory, operating, and consulting. The evenings were devoted to the enjoyment of music—at the opera or at home—topped off by reading or writing before his usual late bedtime. Sound principles of surgery were emphasized on rounds, in the lecture amphitheater, and in the laboratory.[3] The exceptions concerned surgical bacteriology and antisepsis. He was slow to accept the new concepts of bacterial etiology of surgical complications. One of the first major contributions to surgical technique was the resection of the esophagus through the cervical route in a mongrel—one example proving that he tested his theories in animals preparatory to corrective procedures on man.[4]

On April 21, 1870, under chloroform anesthesia, a huge yellow dog had his esophagus deeply exposed on the left side. The latter was disconnected from its origin to the extent of 2 inches; this was done with the aid of a finger and a scalpel handle. The esophagus then was cut transversely in toto, and 1½ inches of it were completely severed. The lower end was joined to the skin of the lower edge of the wound by two sutures, in order to facilitate the insertion of the pharyngeal sound for artificial feeding. The food put into the sound consisted exclusively of milk. On April 26 it became possible to insert a soft pharyngeal sound from above through the mouth into the stomach if one helped with the finger. . . . After the wound healed the dog was able to eat meat, potatoes, etc. and to gulp his food. He was in a good state of nourishment. We were careful to avoid giving him bones.

I killed the dog with cyanide of potassium on July 26. The specimen . . . shows that my assumption of a healing process had been correct . . . there was a simple, annular and very faint scar, hardly half a line in width, which had remained amenable to dilatation.

On the strength of the above mentioned facts, I would feel justified to perform resection of the esophagus in a suitable case on man.

A total laryngectomy was carried out in 1873 on a 36-year-old male, following the technique used by Czerny on dogs. The natural organ infiltrated with tumor was removed in two stages and was replaced by an artificial larynx, which served the patient well until a recurrence of new growth the following year. The procedure was performed only after a physiological study in dogs showed that swallowing was possible after surgical removal of the larynx.[5]

The human larynx has no function other than to produce a sound of a particular timbre. That sound, amplified by resonance in the pharyngeal, buccal, and nasal cavities, becomes language by use of articulation. It was, therefore, clear from the beginning that all that was needed was an apparatus which by expiration would allow a sound to be produced similar to that of the human voice, in pitch and timbre; and that this sound could be used for articulation.

Such a device would be a modified reed-pipe. The question was only *where should such a sound-producing apparatus be placed and should the sound be directed into the pharyngeal and buccal cavities, or into the latter only.* . . . Czerny had already used the first method when he inserted a T-shaped cannula, provided with a metal tongue, into his dogs and attached a ball valve that blocked the expiration stream at the throat and forced the former into the pharyngeal cavity. However incomplete *Czerny's* experiments may have been in animals, they made me . . . determined to use the same method in man, by imitating the natural situation. The patient was able to *talk so loudly with a clear voice that even in a large hospital room* he could be understood. His reading rendition (of a text) could be understood *as far away as the farthest corners of the room.* The only differences from the normal voice were that *his voice was monotonous, it had another timbre, and the effort of talking must have been much greater.*

Pyloric resection was performed in 1881, after Billroth had shown that gastric juices would not digest the suture line or inhibit healing of the opposing ends. Success with the first gastric resection (Billroth I) gave him false hope. Fate sometimes is fickle with the great as with the mediocre. Subsequent failures prompted Billroth to leave the stomach and duodenum as a blind pouch and to anastomose the wall of the stomach to the jejunum (Billroth II). The description of the first pyloric resection is as follows.[6]

The motile tumor was located above and a little to the right of the umbilicus, and it seemed to have the volume of a medium-sized apple. A transverse incision above the tumor was made through the thin abdominal wall. The tumor turned out to be partly nodular, partly infiltrating carcinoma of the pylorus which extended beyond the lower third of the stomach. The adhesions with the omentum and the colon transversum were separated as well as the greater and lesser omentum. All the vessels were ligated before they were cut; there was a minimal loss of blood. The tumor was taken out of the abdomen and placed on the abdominal wall. The stomach was cut 1 cm beyond the infiltrated section; first cutting only posteriorly, then through the duodenum. An attempt at approximating the incised ends showed that union was possible. Six sutures were placed through the edges of the wound. Another incision was made through the stomach, obliquely from above, always at a distance of 1 cm from the infiltrated part of the stomach wall. The oblique stomach wound was sutured from below to above until the opening was only large enough to fit the duodenum. The tumor was excised from the duodenum in its entirety 1 cm beyond the infiltration. An incision was made parallel to the one in the stomach.

Including the slowly administered anesthesia, the operation lasted 1½ hours. The patient complained of no weakness, no vomiting and no pain after the operation. During the first 24 hours ice only was given per os, then peptone enemas containing wine. On the following day a tablespoon of sour milk was given first every hour, then every thirty minutes.

Billroth was attentive to details of pre- and postoperative patient care. Body temperatures were taken regularly following surgery. He was one of the first to apply statistics to the evaluation of surgical data. A rigid follow-up system provided a record of successes and failures, which was used as a basis for discussing the surgical results with his pupils. This discipline was routine, without embarrassment or shame, but rather with the purpose of searching for the cause of the errors and devising means for correction.

The number of pupils trained by Billroth spread his surgical influence throughout central Europe, and his suggestions were in demand when an academic vacancy arose. Absolon has listed 9 first generation and 35 second generation pupils in a communication that contains a comprehensive biography of the inner circle.[1] In the first category are Winiwarter of Liege, von Czerny and Narath of Heidelberg, Gussenbauer of Prague and Vienna, von Eiselsberg and Gersuny of Vienna, von Mikulicz-Radecki of Breslau, von Hacker of Graz, and Wölfler of Prague.

The social and professional friendship begun in Zurich with Brahms was continued in Vienna, where, in his drawing room, Brahms' chamber music was played for the first time. Haenslich, music critic and professor of music at the University, was another loyal friend in the arts. The great surgeon was in the midst of the preparation of a treatise on rhythm and the influence of music on the organism when death ended his avocation.

Billroth's only scientific misjudgment may be forgiven if not forgotten. In studying infection and bacteria, he believed there was only one species of coccus, which had the capacity to change under different environmental conditions into other cocci or to bacteria. Such a false concept was reviewed in his monograph published in 1874, *Cocco-Bacteria Septica*. The findings of Lister on the importance of antisepsis were not accepted by Billroth for almost a decade after they were well known and accepted by many.

A discussion of Billroth's philosophy of medical education was published in Geneva in 1879, translated by Welch, and published in English in 1924. A number of statements made more than three-quarters of a century ago remain applicable.[7]

Culture is always an aristocratic thing. The physician, the school-teacher, the lawyer, the clergyman should be the best men of their village, of their city, of the circles in which they move. In order to be so they must have the super-power that comes with knowledge and skill, and this is acquired only through the hard work of study, and even more through the cultivation of the inner urge to study.

All courses ought, as a matter of fact, to be permeated by the historical spirit. That would foster interest not merely in general historical interpretations, but in special historical research, to a greater extent than courses in the history of medicine can ever do. But that the latter courses could by skillful correlation and combination with the history of civilization, both general and national, be made most attractive, I cannot doubt; in fact, I should like to take such a course even now.

It would seem unnecessary to waste words in defense of the intellectual, disciplinary value of the study of the Latin and Greek languages, or of the pedagogic importance of the classical historians of antiquity and the classic poets. A like degree of elasticity of thought can be attained by no other method of preparation, nor is there any other subject matter so well suited to fill the minds of boys and young men with exalted ideals and beautiful concepts, as the history and literature of the ancient world.

1. Absolon, K. B.: The Surgical School of Theodor Billroth, *Surgery* 50:697-715, 1961.

2. Billroth, T.: *General Surgical Pathology and Therapeutics,* New York: D. Appleton and Company, 1872.

3. Billroth, T.: *Lectures on Surgical Pathology and Therapeutics,* vol 1, London: New Sydenham Society, 1877.

4. Billroth, T.: Resection of the Esophagus (Ger), *Arch Klin Chir* 13:65-69, 1872, excerpt translated by F. Sternthal.

5. Gussenbauer, C.: The First Laryngectomy of Man Performed by Billroth (Ger), *Arch Klin Chir* 17:343-356, 1874, excerpt translated by F. Sternthal.

6. Billroth, T.: Open Letter to Dr. L. W. Wittelshöfer, Resection of the Pylorus (Ger), *Wien Med Wschr* 31:161-165, 1881, excerpt translated by F. Sternthal.

7. Billroth, T.: *The Medical Sciences in the German Universities, A Study in the History of Civilization,* W. H. Welch, trans., New York: Macmillan Company, 1924.

Composite by G. Bako

Augustus Volney Waller (1816-1870)

AUGUSTUS WALLER, whose name is associated with the regressive changes in severed nerves, was born on a farm in Kent, England. However, he spent most of his childhood with his family in the south of France.[1] Upon the death of his father, when Augustus was only 14 years of age, he returned to England, eventually living and studying under Dr. William Lambe, a practicing vegetarian. Waller began the study of medicine in Paris and, in 1840, obtained the degree of doctor of medicine, presenting a graduation thesis entitled *Percussion Médiate.* The following year he was admitted a licentiate by the Society of Apothecaries in London and, in 1842, entered into general medical practice in Kensington, England.

Waller soon acquired a substantial following; however, a desire for original investigation drew him into experimental work and, after presenting two important studies to the *Philosophical Transactions* of the Royal Society, he was elected to Fellowship. Wishing to abandon practice and to devote his life to science, later in the year he left England for Bonn, Germany. Here Waller became an associate of J. L. Budge, who provided suitable facilities for his scientific work. This opportunity proved highly rewarding for five years until he transferred his experimental work to Flourens' laboratory at the Jardin des Plantes in Paris. There his investigations were interrupted by a debilitating fever which invalided him for two years. Recovering his health in England, Waller accepted the professorship of physiology at Queen's College, Birmingham, and, in 1858, became physician in their teaching hospital. Because of incipient heart disease he retired shortly after and moved to Bruges, Belgium. In 1868, having survived critical illness a second time, he resumed the practice of medicine in Geneva until his death, which was attributed to angina pectoris.

Waller's physiological investigations were confined to the nervous system and complemented the work of Claude Bernard, Brown-Séquard, and Budge. His first communication to the Royal Society was an account of the diapedesis from the capillaries of circulating white cells, which confirmed the observations of Thomas Addison and others. The second report, submitted in the fall of 1849 and read three months later, described experiments on the section of the glossopharyngeal and hypoglossal nerves of the frog—one phase of a series of studies describing alterations in the form and function of nerves consequent to transection. The characteristic features of the peripheral degeneration, later called "Wallerian degeneration," marked the beginning of a new hypothesis from which it was inferred that the nerve cells nourished the nerve fibers. Waller reported as follows:[2]

. . . it is my intention at present to describe various alterations, as seen under the microscope, which take place in the structure of the same nerves after their continuity with the brain has been interrupted by section. The innervation of the frog's tongue is, as I have already shown, derived from two pairs of nerves, one arising from the brain, and traversing a foremen in the posterior part of the cranium, accompanied by the pneumogastric nerve. This pair corresponds to the glossopharyngeal in Man. . . . The other pair arises from the anterior part of the spinal marrow, traverses the first cervical foramen, and constitutes the first cervical pair of nerves. Following the example of Burdach, I regard this pair as corresponding to the hypoglossal in Man, and shall apply that term to it.

For the purpose of avoiding this loss of life, I adopt the plan of dividing the glossopharyngeal on one side only of the tongue, and I find that it has the desired effect of preserving the life of the animal, while we can observe the same alterations on the corresponding side, as well as when both nerves are divided. Another advantage found in the division of a single nerve is, that on the uninjured side we have constantly at hand a means of comparison by which we can judge with certainty respecting any alterations that may be produced in the divided nerve.

The first effects of section of a glossopharyngeal nerve at the throat, are decreased power of moving the tongue, diminished sensibility, generally very slight on the divided side, and symptoms indicative of some disturbance of the nutritive functions. The diminution of motor power is very slight, as is evident by the almost molecular tremor which still exists in any part irritated, and by the capability of retracting the tongue. The loss of sensation, which is also very slight, arises from the section of a few sensitive filaments contained in the glossopharyngeal nerve, and are distributed principally about the tubercular extremities.

Generally, at the end of the third and fourth day, we detect the first alteration by a slightly turbid or coagulated appearance of the medulla. . . . About five or six days after section, the alteration of the nerve-tubes in the papillae has become much more distinct, by a kind of coagulation or curdling of the medulla into particles of various sizes.

About the twentieth day the medullary particles are completely reduced to a granular state. . . . They are still contained in the tubular membrane, which is but very faintly distinguished, probably from the loss of the medulla and from atrophy of its tissue.

When the hypoglossal nerves are divided at their exit from the spine, all movements of the throat and tongue are abolished, and the process of respiration entirely at an end. The tongue may be drawn from the mouth remaining completely inert,

pinching or cutting causing no appearance of pain. Hence, we may conclude that this nerve is of a mixed nature, containing sensorial as well as motor filaments.

During the four first days, after section of the hypoglossal nerve, no change is observed in its structure. . . . After twelve or fifteen days many of the single tubules have ceased to be visible, their granular medulla having been removed by absorption. The branches contain masses of amorphous medulla.

At present we have restricted our observations to the alterations which take place in the ramifications originating from two trunks, but we cannot suppose that this is a local phenomenon. . . . It is impossible not to anticipate results from the application of this inquiry to the different nerves of the animal system.

Together with Budge, Waller demonstrated the pathway of the pupillary dilator fibers. They noted incomplete degeneration of the peripheral portion of the nerve upon severance of the vagosympathetic trunk of a dog. The intact fibers were identified with the sympathetic trunk and were traced to the first and second thoracic segments of the spinal cord. When this region of the cord was stimulated in the intact animal, the pupil was dilated but, when the cervical portion of the sympathetic trunk was divided unilaterally, stimulation no longer dilated the pupil. They named the center the "ciliospinal" center. In 1852, they were awarded the Monthyon Prize by the Paris Academy of Sciences for this work which is excerpted.[3]

This experiment demonstrates the motor activity of the cervical sympathetic nerve and explains the basis of the contraction of the pupil following section, a fact demonstrated by Petit in 1712 but unappreciated.

We exposed the spinal cord of a rabbit from the lower dorsal region to the upper part of the neck. By applying galvanic current to the center of the exposed portion, the dilatation of the pupils occurred as promptly as in other experiments. The portion of the cord displaying this property is limited to the segment between the first cervical vertebra and the sixth dorsal, inclusive. To indicate precisely the portion of the cord that acts on the pupil, we will call it the *cilio-spinal* or *central cilio-spinal region*. Beyond the limits that we have indicated, the application of galvanic current to the cord produced no effect on the pupils.

When the cilio-spinal region is transversally severed at different levels, parts separated from the center, at or below the level of the articulation of the second and third dorsal vertebrae, have lost their influence on the pupils; on the contrary, all central portions continue to respond. If the entire cilio-spinal portion is removed, and if the electrodes are applied at different points, only those points that have the power to dilate the pupil are situated at the junction between the second and third dorsal nerves. The effect on this area is so clearly delimited that, when the electrodes are displaced by 1 mm, the effect on the pupils immediately disappears. Galvanic current was applied on the same animal, below the last cervical ganglion and the lower point at which the pupil was affected was marked by a ligature. Post-mortem dissection showed that the branch that acted on the eye came from the second dorsal pair.

In 1856, the Parisian Academy conferred upon Waller the Monthyon Prize for the second time. Subsequently, a medal was awarded by the Royal Society of London for his studies on nerve degeneration. In 1870, he delivered the Croonian lecture before the Royal Society, in which he described his investigations on the functions of the pneumogastric and sympathetic nerves.

1. Obituary, *Proc Roy Soc* 20:xi-xiii, 1872.
2. Waller, A.: Experiments on the Section of the Glossopharyngeal and Hypoglossal Nerves of the Frog, and Observations of the Alterations Produced Thereby in the Structure of Their Primitive Fibres, *Philos Trans* 140:423-429, 1850.
3. Waller, A., and Budge, J. L.: Researches on the Nervous System (Fr), *C R Acad Sci* 33:370-374 (Oct 6); 606-611 (Dec 1) 1851, excerpt translated by Z. Danilevicius.

Albert von Kölliker (1817-1905)

RUDOLF ALBERT VON KÖLLIKER, native of Zürich and investigator of multiple natural phenomena, was associated with the medical faculty of the University of Würzburg for more than 50 years.[1] After attending the local Gymnasium, he studied geology, zoology, and natural philosophy under outstanding professors at the University of Zürich. Proceeding to medical school at Bonn and subsequently to Berlin, he studied comparative and pathological anatomy under Johannes Müller, and normal histology under Jacob Henle. Kölliker then returned to Zürich in 1841 for the degree of doctor of philosophy. A few months later he took the MD degree in Heidelberg without an oral examination, presenting a thesis on the de-

velopment of *Chironomus* and *Donacia*. Kölliker's contributions dealing with gross and microscopic form and function in lower forms of life as well as in man came at a

Composite by G. Bako

propitious time in the history of scientific development; the elaboration of the cell theory of Schleiden and Schwann immediately preceded the completion of his formal education.

In 1841, the year after Henle came to Zürich as professor of anatomy and histology, the scientific liaison which began in Berlin was reestablished, with Kölliker serving as assistant. Then began his periodic visits to scientific centers in Europe and Great Britain for study, intellectual exchange, and maintenance or improvement of his fluency in foreign languages. In Naples and Sicily he collaborated with Carl Nägeli on investigations of aquatic life, including the Amphioxus and Cephalopoda. At other times his study of marine forms included Alcyonaria, polyps, mollusks, Amphitrites, and various fishes. In 1844, when Henle moved to Heidelberg, Kölliker, then only 27 years of age, was appointed professor of physiology and comparative anatomy. He was called to Würzburg as professor for physiology in 1847. When the chair of anatomy became vacant two years later, he became head of the two Institutes. The dual assignment persisted until physiology was separated from anatomy in 1864, at which time his teaching and research were largely devoted to the revelations of the microscope. He retired upon completion of his tenure in 1897 but was provided laboratory space and lectured until 1901.

The whole animal kingdom was Kölliker's field of study. He taught and made important contributions in microscopic anatomy, comparative anatomy, embryology, biology, and physiology, and was largely responsible for developing the discipline of comparative anatomy of the nervous system.

Kölliker was the first to isolate smooth muscle, showed that contraction of muscle produces an electric current, studied the emission of light by eels, demonstrated the relation of the nerve cell to the medullated nerve fiber, and studied the action of curare. In his monograph on comparative embryology, the relation of the vertebrate notochord to the adult skull and spine was defined.[2] An interest in comparative anatomy provided a sound scientific basis upon which he critically examined the Darwinian theory. After the discovery of the x-rays, he appropriately called them Röentgen rays. Eponymic terms include Kölliker's dental crest, the incisor portion of the developing maxilla, Kölliker's membrane, the reticular lamina of the cochlea, and Kölliker's nucleus, the medial nucleus of the thalamus. His first major text, *Manual of Human Histology* (Microscopical Anatomy)[3] was translated subsequently into English and French. With each new edition he added discussions of recent advances so that the text remained the standard reference treatise for decades. The last edition appeared in three volumes between 1889 and 1899. In 1849, with Siebold, Kölliker founded the *Zeitschrift für Wissenschaftliche Zoologie* and served as its editor for half a century.

It would be inexpedient to excerpt portions from each of his published contributions. The number in this essay will be restricted to three and will be presented in succession: the description of nerve endings in Pacinian bodies in the palm of the hand and sole of the foot, the origin and development of spermatozoa, and the pathogenesis of the intracellular substance of connective tissue. The initial description of his findings in Pacinian bodies appeared from Zürich in 1844[4] and was discussed in length in his *Manual*. The following is from the American edition of this text.[5]

One kind, only, of termination of the spinal nerves, is still to be noticed here,—that in the *Pacinian bodies*. The small bodies, so named by Henle and myself ("Ueber die Pacin, Körperchen des Menschen und der Thiere," Zürich, 1844), were first accurately described by the Italian Pacini ("Nuovi organi scoperti nel corpo umano," Pistoja, 1840), especially in the nerves of the palm of the hand and sole of the foot, and in fact, as Langer of Vienna afterwards showed, had been previously noticed by A. Vater (J. G. Lehmann, "De consensu partium corp. hum.," Vitembergae, 1741), although their nature had not been recognized. Each body presents a rounded peduncle, formed from the continuation of its lamellae, and connected with a nervous twig, and in which a dark nerve-fibre, 0.006–0.068 of a line (in the Cat, 0.0044–0.0077 of a line) thick, runs to the Pacinian body. This fibre enters the central cavity from the peduncle, where it becomes 0.006 of a line wide and 0.004 of a line thick, pale, non-medullated, almost like an axis-cylinder, and terminates in the upper part of the cavity, in a free, slightly granular tubercle, the extremity being frequently bifid or trifid.

In 1841, Kölliker demonstrated that the spermatozoa are not extraneous bodies as had been suspected but originate in the testicular cells and migrate to fertilize the ovum. The findings comprised a substantial monograph prepared before he had completed his formal education.[6]

In order for copulation to be fruitful, the spermatic fluid or more precisely speaking, the spermatozoa which constitute the essential ingredient must come into direct contact with the ovum.

Spermatozoa develop either in or from cells which are formed in the testes during sexual maturity and possibly during sexual excitement. The development follows the same course as the development of alimentary parts, but different from the development of animals from eggs.

Spermatozoa vary little in different species of animals, even though the differences between these animals are remarkable. Almost always the form of the spermatozoa is either identical or similar in the families and classes of the same species. Each kind of animal has only one type of spermatozoa.

It is impossible to prove that spermatozoa are able to multiply by themselves.

The movements of the spermatozoa are related to the procreative ability of the spermatic fluid. Usually movement starts only after copulation within the female genital organs, or in the medium surrounding the ova.

Spermatozoa are organic elementary components.

It has been proved that all the psychic and physical life of the male animal is expressed in its spermatic fluid and in its spermatozoa.

In discussing the origin of the intracellular substance of connective tissue,[7] Kölliker left unanswered questions which still remain without solution—the mechanism of the fibrillar formation and the nature and site of the homogeneous ground substance.[3]

The connective tissue is invariably developed from cells, and, in fact, from fusiform or stellate vesicles, which become united into long fibres or networks, and often break up into fibrils before their union. The mode in which this takes place is not yet quite made out, but it is most probable that the cells, as they elongate, change with their membrane and contents, into a homogeneous softish mass, which subsequently breaks up into a bundle of fine fibrils and some intermediate substance. The development of the homogeneous connective tissue has as yet been little investigated, but it would seem, like the other, to proceed from a fusion of rounded or elongated cells, which are perhaps united by an intermediate substance, in which the metamorphic process has only gone as far as the development of a homogeneous mass, has not attained the stage of fibrillation. The bundles of the connective tissue, when once formed, grow in length and thickness like the elastic fibres, until they have attained the size which they possess in the adult; however, there arise subsequently, in many places, additional elements, which are combined with the original ones.

In the Croonian lecture delivered to the Royal Society in London in 1862, Kölliker discussed nerve endings in the muscle of the frog. He served one term as Rector of his university, was ennobled with the highest Bavarian order, and received the Order of Merit from Prussia. The title of "Excellence" by the Bavarian government honored him on his 80th birthday. Kölliker met the problems of his job and the liaison with associates and students in a charming manner; he was a great teacher and an academic leader with a warm heart.

1. Kölliker, A.: *Recollections From My Life* (Ger), Leipzig: W. Engelmann, 1899.

2. Kölliker, A.: *Embryology of Man and Higher Animals* (Ger), Leipzig: W. Engelmann, 1861.

3. Kölliker, A.: *Manual of Human Histology* (Ger), Leipzig: W. Engelmann, 1852, G. Bush, and T. Huxley, (trans.), London: New Sydenham Society, 1853-1854.

4. Henle, J., and Kölliker, A.: The Pacinian Bodies in the Nerves of Men and Animals (Ger), *Virchow Arch Path Anat* 10:1-40, 1844.

5. Kölliker, A.: *A Manual of Human Microscopical Anatomy* (Ger), G. Bush, and T. Huxley, (trans.), Philadelphia: Lippincott, Grambo & Co., 1854.

6. Kölliker, A.: *Treatise on Sexual Relations and Movement of Spermatozoa in Vertebrates* (Ger), Berlin: W. Logier, 1841, excerpts translated by Z. Danilevicius.

7. Kölliker, A.: Recent Investigations of the Development of Connective Tissue (Ger), *Würz Naturwiss Z* 1:141-170, 1861.

Rudolph Virchow (1821-1902)

RUDOLPH LUDWIG KARL VIRCHOW, the "Father of Modern Pathology," gave the principal credit for the advances in medicine during 2,000 years to recorded contributions in gross or microscopic anatomy. Through his cellular pathology, he introduced a new concept of disease in the mid-19th century, which in a few years was strengthened but also overshadowed by discoveries in bacteriology and chemistry; they, in turn, led to an enlightened interpretation of the etiology and pathogenesis of disease. Disease to Virchow, as interpreted also by his predecessors, was an altered form of physiology, not necessarily the result of an insult from the environment. If this was correct, disease could be thwarted by changing or restoring the altered form and function. Health could be retrieved by driving out the cause of the disease rather than the disease itself.[1] The most recent investigative devices for the study of cellular components represent a throwback to Virchow's concepts of a century ago and confirm his theories.[2]

The history of medicine teaches us, if we will only take a somewhat comprehensive survey of it, that at all times permanent advances have been marked by anatomical innovations, and that every more important epoch has been directly ushered in by a series of important discoveries concerning the structure of the body. So it was in those old times, when the observations of the Alexandrian school, based for the first time upon the anatomy of man, prepared the way for the system of Galen; so it was, too, in the Middle Ages, when Vesalius laid the foundations of anatomy, and therewith began the real reformation of medicine; so, lastly, was it at the commencement of this century, when Bichat developed the principles of general anatomy. What Schwann, however, has done for histology, has as yet been but in a very slight degree built up and developed for pathology, and it may be said that nothing has penetrated less deeply into the minds of all than the cell-theory in its intimate connection with pathology.

Virchow was born in Schivelbein, rural Pomerania, a land currently under Communist domination in East Germany.[3] His graduation thesis from the Gymnasium, entitled, "A Life Filled with Toil and Work Is Not a Burden, But a Blessing," was prophetic of his industry for almost six decades. He graduated in Berlin in 1843 and served as prosector and assistant to Froriep at the Charité Hospital. At the age of 26, Virchow and Reinhardt founded the *Archiv für pathologische Anatomie und Physiologie und für klinische Medicin*, the famous Virchow's *Archiv*. When Reinhardt died in 1852, Virchow assumed full direction. The *Archiv*, published through 169 volumes, was highly regarded by medical scientists for a lifetime, and provided an outlet for the theoretical and experimental studies on cellular pathology.

Virchow's professional studies were interrupted temporarily by his sympathy for the democratic revolution and participation in the 1848 uprising in Berlin. More fruitful was his participation in a government mission to investigate an epidemic of typhus among the weavers of Upper Silesia. Shocked by the pestilence, the famine, and indigence of the peasants he recommended public subsidy for

suitable sanitation, a necessary ingredient of any plan for improvement. The Prussian government respected his scientific conclusions, but were suspicious of his liberal political thoughts. A mutual decision was reached the following year when Virchow was relieved of his prosectorship at the Charité to accept the chair of pathological anatomy at Würzburg in a more tolerant intellectual environment. After seven years in Würzburg, he returned to Berlin as professor of pathology and director of the Pathological Institute.

The fundamental concepts of Virchow's physiological and pathological histology were published in 1858 in *Cellular Pathology*, a compilation of lectures given to practitioners immediately following his return. Virchow advanced the concept that the cell, the basic component of tissue and organ, reproduces other cells; whereas in disease the cell is altered in structure and molecular nature.[2]

. . . the cell is really the ultimate morphological element in which there is any manifestation of life, and that we must not transfer the seat of real action to any point beyond the cell. . . . But I think that we must look upon this as certain, that, however much of the more delicate interchange of matter, which takes place within a cell, may not concern the material structure as a whole, yet the real action does proceed from the structure as such, and that the living element only maintains its activity as long as it really presents itself to us as an independent whole.

It is only when we adhere to this view of the matter, when we separate from the cell all that has been added to it by and after-development, that we obtain a simple, homogeneous, extremely monotonous structure, recurring with extraordinary constancy in living organisms. But just this very constancy forms the best criterion of our having before us in this structure one of those really elementary bodies, to be built up of which is eminently characteristic of every living thing —without the pre-existence of which no living forms arise, and to which the continuance and the maintenance of life is intimately attached.

At the present time, neither fibres, nor globules, nor elementary granules, can be looked upon as histological starting-points. As long as living elements were conceived to be produced out of parts previously destitute of shape, such as formative fluids, or matters (*plastic matter, blastema, cytoblastema*), any one of the above views could of course be entertained, but it is in this very particular that the revolution which the last few years have brought with them has been the most marked. Even in pathology we can now go so far as to establish, as a general principle, *that no development of any kind begins* de novo, *and consequently as to reject the theory of equivocal* (spontaneous) *generation just as much in the history of the development of individual parts as we do in that of entire organisms.* . . .

Where a cell arises, there a cell must have previously existed (*omnis cellula e cellula*). just as an animal can spring only from an animal, a plant only from a plant.

Virchow, fearless in supporting scientifically sound conclusions, although the scientific data were sometimes less than adequate, was equally fearless in attacking an unproved assumption. He exposed Rokitansky's theory of "crases" and "discrases" and denied Cruveilhier's theory that phlebitis dominates the whole pathology. In turn, he was rebuked for failing to accept the views of Koch and Behring on toxins and antitoxins and was slow to accept the new theories in bacteriology and immunology. Virchow encouraged his pupil Cohnheim to disprove his (Virchow's) previously advanced hypothesis that blood cells do not migrate from the capillaries in inflammation. Although Virchow never practiced medicine, he was keenly interested in clinical problems, effectively bridged the division between pathological anatomy and clinical practice, clearly defined the ideal physician, and was firm in his conviction that the achievements of scientific medicine must be the basis of the performance of the physician.[3]

It is no longer necessary today to write that scientific medicine is also the best foundation for medical practice. It is sufficient to point out how completely even the external character of medical practice has changed in the last thirty years. Scientific methods have been introduced everywhere into practice. The diagnosis and prognosis of the physician are based on the experience of the pathological anatomist and the physiologist. Therapeutic doctrine has become biological and thereby experimental science. Concepts of healing processes are no longer separated from those of physiological regulatory processes. Even surgical practice has been altered to its foundations, not by the empiricism of war, but in a much more radical manner by means of a completely theoretically constructed therapy.

Scientific medicine is compounded of two integrated parts—pathology, which delivers, or is supposed to deliver, information about the altered conditions and altered physiological phenomena, and therapy, which seeks out the means of restoring or maintaining normal conditions.

Thus practical medicine is never the same thing as scientific medicine, but, even in the hands of the greatest master, rather an application of it. The scientific practitioner, however, distinguishes himself from the routinier and the medical opportunist by making the achievements of scientific medicine his own so that they form the basis of his performance and he serves neither the idol of accustomed routine nor that of chance.

The number of notable clinical and pathological subjects discussed in Virchow's writings is remarkable. These included the distinction between pyemia and septicemia. Leukemia was described as "white blood" in 1845,[4] simultaneously with Bennett. Virchow described the lymphatic sheaths of the cerebral arteries, identified leucine and tyrosine in the pancreas removed postmortem, and gave the first modern description of neuroglia. He investigated trichinosis and mycotic infection of the lungs, studied the clinical features of "lupus tuberculosis," leontiasis ossea, hematoma of the dura mater, and spina bifida occulta, described amyloid degeneration of the kidney, and introduced new pathological concepts such as agenesia, heterotopia, and ochronosis. He identified rheumatic gout as "arthritis deformans," a distinct entity not to be confused with familial gouty arthritis. A new concept of embolism was advanced in 1846 in a discussion on occlusion of the pulmonary arteries.[5]

Against these quite hypothetical assumptions I believe the following conclusion can be derived from the facts:

The primary occurrence of old, long antemortem clots (fibrin plugs) in the pulmonary artery, where obviously the obstruction of the artery precedes the surrounding changes in the parenchyma, or is independent thereof, is, in relation to the original site of the clotting, always secondary. These plugs arise from any part of the vascular system preceding the lung in the circulation, that is, in the veins or the right heart and are brought to the pulmonary artery through the blood stream. I consider the following facts proof of this statement:

As often as I have found plugs in the pulmonary artery I have always been able to demonstrate plugs also in the venous system leading thereto (the portal system of course does not, while the right heart does, belong to this system) and I consider the occurrence of the former a sure sign that old blood clots are to be found in some part of the venous system.

A monograph on the ancient skulls of America, prepared in 1892, was one of Virchow's contributions to anthropology. One chapter, "Flathead von Oregon," discussed a skull recovered from the Columbia River valley.[6] As an archeologist he dug with Henry Schliemann at Troy, who wrote:[7]

I have finally to mention the great authority of Professor Rudolph Virchow, who assisted me in my excavations at Hissarlik, from the 4th of April till the 4th of May, 1879, and who energetically opposes the Troy-

Bounarbashi theory, and enthusiastically declares in favor of the identity of Hissarlik with the Homeric Troy.

Virchow joined the Prussian Lower House in 1862 and served as a member of the Reichstag from 1880 until 1893. Many honors at home and abroad were tendered him. Virchow Institute and the Virchow Hospital in Berlin bore his name.

1. Ackerknecht, E. H.: *Rudolph Virchow, Doctor, Statesman, Anthropologist,* Madison: University of Wisconsin Press, 1953.
2. Virchow, R.: *Cellular Pathology as Based upon Physiological and Pathological Histology,* F. Chance, trans., New York: R. M. DeWitt, 1860.
3. Rather, L. J.: *Disease, Life, and Man, Selected Essays by Rudolph Virchow,* Stanford: Stanford University Press, 1958.
4. Virchow, R.: White Blood, *Neue Notizen* 33:152-156 (Jan-March) 1845.
5. Virchow, R.: "On Occlusion of the Pulmonary Arteries," from *Collected Papers in Medical Science,* Frankfurt, Main: Meidinger Son & Co., 1856, in Long, E. R.: *Selected Readings in Pathology,* Springfield, Ill: Charles C Thomas, 1929.
6. Virchow, R.: "Flathead from Oregon," in *Crania Ethnica Americana,* Berlin: A. Asher & Co., 1892, excerpt translated by F. Sternthal.
7. Schliemann, H.: *Ilios, the City and Country of the Trojans,* New York: Harper & Brothers, 1881.

Charles Rouget (1824-1904)

CHARLES-MARIE-BENJAMIN ROUGET, son of a distinguished military surgeon who served under Baron Jean-Dominique Larrey, was born at Gisors, France.[1] Charles pursued his general studies at the Collège Sainte-Barbé, completed his formal medical courses in the university in Paris, and went on with his clinical training at Hotel Dieu. He stood in competition for a post in Paris, but, finding no vacancy, in 1860 he accepted the chair of physiology at Montpellier. Rouget served with distinction until 1878, when, following the death of Claude Bernard, a new chair of general physiology was created for Rouget at the Museum of Natural History in Paris. Again he served with distinction from 1879 to 1893. An excellent teacher, highly industrious, he made his best contributions in correlating physiology and microscopic structure. Utilizing a special technique in photography, he gained a high degree of magnification of muscle fibers of vertebrates. Similar detailed observations were carried out on the contractile cells of the capillaries of tadpoles and frogs. The studies were presented to the

Nouvelles Archives du Muséum d'Histoire Naturelle, Paris

anatomical section of the Academy of Sciences in 1874 but did not receive the attention which they deserved until the resurgence of interest by Vimptrup, Krogh, and others more than a generation later. The initial report[2] was translated by Fulton, from which the following excerpts were taken.[3]

Further research into the development of blood vessels, conducted since the early spring on the larvae of amphibians, proves beyond doubt the contractility of cells with ramified protoplasmic elongations which I observed last year in the blood vessels of the hyaloid membrane of an adult frog.

Indeed, identical cells in larvae constitute a so-called "adventitial" wall in arterial, venous and true capillaries. This wall being merely a continuation of the muscular walls of the arteries and veins, it follows that the whole blood vascular system, from the heart to the capillaries inclusive, is surrounded by a contractile wall.

The blood vessels of the dorsal fin of amphibian larvae—which, according to a commonly accepted error which I shared myself till last year, have the complete structure of primitive capillaries, *i.e.* one membrane only of parietal (endothelial) cells—should be, according to my most recent observations, classed not only from a functional but also from a structural point of view, into arteries, veins and a network of capillary vessels.

The first contractile cells which make their appearance in a recently-formed blood vessel, do not proceed either from the primitive vascular cells (endothelial) . . . or from the cells of the surrounding connective tissue. On the contrary I have often observed that in young vessels, as yet lacking a contractile tunic, the ameboid cells spread their elongations over their walls, . . . of connective or adventitial tissue.

The observations were extended and reported later.[4]

Five years ago I communicated to the Academy the first results of my observations on the contractility of the blood vessels of the dorsal fin of tadpoles. All these vessels are contractile and they do not owe this property to the endothelium—which, as I have shown, is entirely made up of cells of naked vacuolar protoplasm—but rather to a network of ramified contractile cells, whose existence I previously established for the first time in the capillaries of the hyaloid membrane of adult frogs. Even during contraction crenations are visible on the edge of the capillaries, which correspond to refracted annular strictures bearing here and there globular projecting nuclei, fairly far apart from each other. These constricting bands and nuclei are part of the contractile cells and their ramified protoplasmic elongations, the earliest embryonic form of the fusiform muscle cells of the vessels, developing from them in successive divisions.

Without contractility the capillaries would not be able to rid themselves of the blood which they contain

1. Grehant, N.: obituary, *Nouv Arch Muséum Hist Nat* 6:iii-xii, 1904.

2. Rouget, C.: Note on the Development of the Contractile Walls of Blood Vessels (Fr), *C R Acad Sci (Paris)* 79:559-562, 1874.

3. Fulton, J. F.: *Selected Readings in the History of Physiology,* Springfield, Ill: Charles C Thomas, Publisher, 1930, pp 94-100.

4. Rouget, C.: The Contractility of Blood Capillaries (Fr), *C R Acad Sci (Paris)* 88:916-918, 1879.

Leopold Auerbach (1828-1897)

LEOPOLD AUERBACH, born of gifted and successful parents in Breslau, the capital of German Silesia, made important contributions in microscopic anatomy without benefit of customary laboratory facilities or academic support.[1] Auerbach, raised in the Jewish ghetto, lived through a lessening of anti-Semitic oppression, but the stigma of discrimination colored all major decisions of his life. He received his early education in reading and writ-

Composite by G. Bako

ing from private tutors and at the age of 10 was admitted to the Elizabeth Gymnasium. He was an average student without evidence of brilliance. However, at the age of 13, in keeping with the custom of his day, he became an apprentice in business. A year later, being dissatisfied with the prospects of a commercial career, he resumed his studies at the Royal Catholic Gymnasium and, at 16, began the study of medicine at the University of Breslau. His graduation certificate, issued two years later and signed by J. E. Purkyně as Dean, makes special mention of his proficiency in Latin and Greek, his knowledge of German literature, and his mastery of the French language.

Auerbach's medical studies were continued at the University of Berlin, which was then enjoying great popularity with an outstanding faculty, including Müller, Remak, Romberg, Schönlein, Traube, and Virchow. He was accompanied to Berlin by Ferdinand Cohn, also of Breslau, with whom he shared living quarters and the excitement of the Revolution of 1848. Auerbach was especially fortunate in his laboratory studies, for he owned a microscope, an essential instrument in the field of investigation. He received the doctor of medicine degree from the University early in 1849. His thesis, prepared in Latin and dedicated to his parents, was entitled *Critical Studies on Nervous Stimuli*. This discussed the influence of a changing temperature as an irritant for nerve conduction rather than the application of heat or cold, just as a change in intensity of current or of voltage, in contrast to a steady electric current, induces nerve action.

Since academic posts were scarcely attainable for a Jew, Auerbach returned to Breslau, entered general practice with special emphasis on neurology, and pursued his microscopical studies as a vocation in his home. Without benefit of a university affiliation or laboratory space, within a few years he published a communication on the neuropsychiatric functions of lower animals. This was followed by a treatise on amebas, with the first proof that this type of organism was unicellular.[2] The next and one of the most important events in his life culminated in 1862 with the publication of his research of the preceding years on the discovery of a ganglionic plexus of the intestines of vertebrates, which he called the "plexus myentericus." The account of what continues to be known as Auerbach's plexus was published privately as a small pamphlet and was abstracted shortly after in the *Proceedings* of the Schlesian Society. He announced that he had found, in addition to the layer of nerve fibers and ganglion cells in the submucosa of the intestines (later known as Meissner's plexus), another plexus of nerve fibers interspersed with ganglion cells between the muscular layers of birds and mammals. Initially the plexus was identified throughout the intestinal canal from the pylorus to the rectum, and later found in the stomach also, a continuous syncytium between the circular and the longitudinal muscles. Where the colon lacked longitudinal muscle, the plexus lay immediately beneath the peritoneum.[3]

It is evident that the nerve fibers which terminate in the muscle layer of the intestine are intended to initiate the contractions. It has been known for some time that the peculiar character of the peristaltic movement of the bowel is caused by involuntary action and is independent of the cerebrospinal centres. Also, the successive and slowly propagating stimulus from each point of the bowel through its length in either direction is a function of the nerves and ganglia of the muscle layer which I have discovered.

It is possible that the network with the ganglia of the submucosa is intimate to the mucosa and participates in its function both for the contraction of the muscle layers as well as for certain trophic and vegetative functions. Since the vegetative function of the mucosa is minimal, the main function of the nerve network is the peristaltic contraction of the muscularis. Because of the physiological implications of the location of the network within the muscle layers, I will name the gut-muscle-network the Plexus myentericus.

The significance of Auerbach's discovery brought him recognition the following year by the University of Breslau as privatdocent upon submission of a special thesis, *The Muscular Stomach of Birds*. However, the appointment was without salary, laboratory space, technical or secretarial assistance. It gave him no more than the opportunity to conduct a series of lectures, with the approval of the head of the department and the faculty. Among his other contributions to microscopical research was the confirmation of the postulate, advanced 20 years earlier by Remak, that the blood capillaries and small lymph vessels consisted of flat epithelium-like cells, each with a nucleus.[4] This discovery was made independently and simultaneously by Eberth in Würzburg and by Aeby in Berne. In 1874, Auerbach summarized his investigations which had been under way for several years on the fertilized egg.[5] Working with nematodes, he studied the nuclei in the process of division of the egg, upon which modern knowledge of fertilization was developed. Although he observed the fusion of two nuclei in the fertilized egg, he was unaware that they were the nucleus of the ovum and the spermatozoon.

In 1866, during the German struggle for national unity, Auerbach was lazaret-physician in Breslau. In 1872, he was invited to Berlin to receive a professional title; this, too, was essentially honorary and carried few academic responsibilities. As if to compensate for his frustrations in faculty appointments, he lived to see his eldest son, Felix, called to a professorship in physics in the University of Jena, and his youngest son, Frederick, receive his PHD summa cum laude in physical chemistry from the University of Breslau and for many years serve as commissioner of the Federal Health Office in Berlin. Remarkably, in spite of the time-consuming demands of general practice, his brilliant and active mind found opportunity to write slightly fewer than 50 scientific communications, mainly in microscopical research.

1. Kisch, B.: Forgotten Leaders in Modern Medicine: Valentin, Gruby, Rebak, Auerbach, *Amer Philos Soc* 44:297-430 (June) 1854.

2. Auerbach, L.: Unicellularity of the Amoeba (Ger), Z *Wiss Zool* 7:365-430, 1956.

3. Auerbach, L.: *The Myenteric Plexus* (Ger), Breslau: E. Morgenstern, 1862, excerpt translated by E. Longar.

4. Auerbach, L.: Investigations of Lymph and Capillary Vessels (Ger), *Arch path Anat* 33:340-394, 1865.

5. Auerbach, L.: *Organology Studies* (Ger), vol 1, 2, Breslau: E. Morgenstern, 1874.

Wilhelm His, Sr. (1831-1904)

WILHELM HIS, SR. may not be as well known to American physicians as is his son and namesake, who described the bundle of His, but his critical study of the origin of tissues and the gross and microscopic study of the development of cells mark him as one of the leaders in the basic medical sciences in the 19th century. His contributions were con-

temporary and complementary to those of Henle and von Kölliker on microscopic findings in healthy mature tissue and to those of Virchow on the evolution of the fundamental concepts of cellular pathology.

Wilhelm was born in Basel, Switzerland, of well-to-do parents who, consistent with their Old World ideals of individual and state, believed that service to the community, a good education, simplicity in living, clarity in thinking, and a serious motive in life were basic principles of living.[1] He began his medical studies in Basel and continued at Bern, discovering that the intrinsic nature of a teacher may be more important than the subject taught. Later he was attracted to Berlin for the study of anatomy with Johannes Müller and embryology with Remak; next, to Würzburg with Virchow and von Kölliker, followed by further study at Prague and Vienna. The circle was completed upon his return to Basel for the MD degree, which was granted with honors. Already he had demonstrated his skill in research and, while a student with Virchow, had explored the histology of the cornea.

The three years after graduation were divided between laboratory investigation and intellectual peregrinations among the outstanding medical centers in Europe. Returning once more to Basel and the University, he began lecturing on histology. When the chair of anatomy became vacant, he was selected to the senior post at the age of 26. Then followed a distinguished series of scientific communications in embryology and histology. The studies on the structure of the thymus, lymph glands, and lymphatic channels were reported in the immediately following years; some of the contributions were illustrated with line drawings by the author. One of his finest contributions, a treatise on the tissue layers and spaces of the body, appeared in 1865.[2] A monograph on the embryology of the chick appeared three years later. He left Basel in 1872 for Leipzig, where, as professor of anatomy, he joined Carl Ludwig, then professor of physiology. He continued to prosper scientifically and intellectually, and for this illustrious professor the Institute of Anatomy was designed. In the years between 1880 and 1885, a monograph in three parts on the anatomy of the human embryo, beginning with the stage of 2-2.5 cm length, was published.[3] One example of his philosophy of natural science is disclosed in a letter to Mr. John Murray on the principles of animal morphology. The description related to the development of the salmon embryo which, surrounded by the yoke sac, was formed from the segmented germ without any increase in volume. The phenomenon was accomplished by displacement of its masses.[4]

Embryology and morphology cannot proceed independently of all reference to the general laws of matter,—to the laws of physics and of mechanics. This proposition would, perhaps, seem indisputable to every natural •philosopher; but, in morphological schools, there are very few who are disposed to adopt it with all its consequences.

In the laboratory and in the classroom, technical and visual aids were developed for effective instruction and investigation. Prototypes of the microtome and wax histologic models of His are in current use. An early design of a microtome for the preparation of thick serial sections of the embryo was published while His was in Basel.[5] Large-scale teaching models were prepared—after the method of Born—from wax plates. The His-Steger models, a subsequent refinement, were essential ingredients of a first-rate embryologic study collection in the teaching of histogenesis. In the maturing years of embryology and histology, new terms were needed and a scientific approach to terminology indispensable. Once more it was His who accepted leadership. He was instrumental in founding the Anatomische Gesellschraft, which was charged with formulating a uniform nomenclature and reducing the number of acceptable anatomical terms.[6] His, Krause, and Waldeyer were members of the special editing committee which suggested terms for the BNA, "Basel Nomina Anatomica." This was a final great step in classification and formulation of terms, first apparent to His at Basel when he recognized the need for a scientifically-designed terminology, specifically for embryology. Less successful were his plans for an international institute for the study of the brain. As an editor, His was one of the founders of the *Archiv für Anthropolgie* and the *Zeitschrift für Anatomie und Entwicklungsgeschichte*. Shortly after, the latter peri-

orical merged with the Müller—du Bois-Reymond *Archiv*, with His and Wilhelm Braune assuming responsibility for the anatomical division.

Franklin P. Mall, an intimate friend and scientific admirer of His, summarized his life and scientific contributions at a distance, concluding that:[1]

Through His, another milestone has been set for anatomy. Through him the great mother science has given birth to a new science, histogenesis. His career is marked by a monument of neurological research which is unique. His's life was that of the ideal scholar. During youth he was strengthened through his own efforts, directed by great masters. During middle age, he won many victories for anatomy, improving the science in all its parts. In old age, he completed and rounded up his work, leaving a great legacy to his survivors, no small part of which consists of wise plans for future work.

1. Mall, F. P.: William His, His Relations to Institutions of Learning, *Amer J Anat* 4:139-161, 1904-1905.
2. His, W.: *On the Tissues and Spaces of the Body* (Ger), Basel: Schweighauser, 1865.
3. His, D.: *Anatomy of the Human Embryo* (Ger), 3 pt and atlas, Leipzig: F. C. W. Vogel, 1880-1885.
4. His, W.: On the Principles of Animal Morphology, Letter to Mr. John Murray, *Proc Roy Soc Edinburgh* 15:287-298 (April 2) 1888.
5. His, W.: Description of a Microtome (Ger), *Arch Mikroskop Anat* 6:229-232, 1870.
6. His, W.: *Anatomical Nomenclature* (Ger), Leipzig: Veit & Co., 1895.

Ernest Haeckel (1834-1919)

IN GERMANY, ERNST HAECKEL supported the theory of evolution and the descent of man advanced by Darwin as did Asa Gray in America and Thomas Huxley in England. Haeckel, a generation younger than Darwin, combined a remarkable capacity for accurate observation of form and structure, a receptive intellect for grasping generalities, an imaginative mind for biological speculation, and an inherent talent for clear exposition. These qualities proved indispensable as a defender of the theory of transmutation of species, at a time when biologists were content with description and classification and when it was generally accepted that class, order, genus, and species maintained identity from the origin of the universe.

Haeckel was born in Potsdam and studied at the universities of Würzburg, Berlin, and Vienna, where he received the MD degree.[1] He was a pupil of the best medical scientists of

Composite by G. Bako

his time, including Kölliker, Leydig, Virchow, and Müller. He stayed on in Vienna, attending the clinics of Oppolzer, Skoda, and Hebra, and, having passed his examination, returned to Berlin to practice. But his writing skill and spirit were not in his work; he abandoned practice and went to Italy to study the *Radiolaria*. These simple components of the sea comprised his first major scientific interest in an ascent to heights attained by few among the great biologists in Germany during the 19th century. While Haeckel was still in Italy, Darwin disclosed to the world his theory of evolution, followed by the publication in 1859 of the *Origin of Species*. Darwin's theory found a receptive friend in Haeckel, who prepared his monograph on the *Radiolaria* from a Darwinian standpoint. In the meantime (1861), he was appointed privatdocent at the University of Jena, a university famed for tolerance in individual thinking. Haeckel remained on its faculty throughout his academic tenure, despite enticing offers from other universities. In 1865, he was advanced to a professorship in zoology.

Haeckel's *General Morphology*[2] ranks as one of the great books in biology, presenting the practical application of the hypothesis of evolution. The biogenetic law, which carries Haeckel's name, asserts that ontogeny, the life history of the individual organism, recapitulates phylogeny, the evolutionary changes through which the species passes, in attaining its present structure. The two-layered gastrula was conceived as the ancestral form of multicellular animals, his now outmoded gastraea theory.[3] After fertilization, the ovum of all multicellular animals develops a primitive germinal structure consisting of two layers of cells and a primitive mouth, the gastrula stage. The organs of the body develop into the adult forms from this primitive structure.

Haeckel's philosophy of creation was expressed in many of his writings, but, because of the number, the opportunities for various interpretations exposed him to unsympathetic critics as well as to warm supporters. He seemed able to reconcile crass materialism with souls in cells, which led some to judge his Monism as hardly any philosophy at all. The understanding of life and the universe to Haeckel embraced the Nature of the realist-scientist, the Cosmos of the idealist-philosopher, and the Creator of the pious believer.[4]

At the onset, I am entirely at one with him as to that unifying conception of nature as a whole which we designate in a single word as Monism. By this we unambiguously express our conviction that there lives "one spirit in all things" and that the whole cognisable world is constituted, and has been developed, in accordance with one common fundamental law. We emphasize by it, in particular, the essential unity of inorganic and organic nature, the latter having been evolved from the former only at a relatively late period. We cannot draw a sharp line of distinction between these two great divisions of nature, any more than we can recognize an absolute distinction between the animal and the vegetable kingdom, or between the lower animals and man. Similarly, we regard the whole of human knowledge as a structural unity; in this sphere we refuse to accept the distinction usually drawn between the natural and the spiritual. The latter is only a part of the former (or *vice versa*); both are one. Our monistic view of the worlds belongs, therefore, to that group of philosophical systems which from other points of view have been designated also as mechanical or as pantheistic.

Haeckel's *General Morphology* was followed by his *Natural History of Creation* and in 1874 by a monograph, *The Evolution of*

Man.[5] He made biology and zoology understandable, through a clear and unencumbered style, especially evident in the later editions of his works, and supported by a logical hypothesis of development and evolution. It was necessary for Haeckel to be a standard-bearer if he expected his views to be heard and to be accepted. Reticence and modesty would not have helped him champion the Darwinian theory of evolution as exemplified by his deep insight into biology, beginning with the *Radiolaria* and ending with *homo sapiens*.

1. Bolsche, W.: *Haeckel, His Life and Work*, J. McCabe, trans., London: T. F. Unwin, 1906.

2. Haeckel, E.: *General Morphology of the Organism* (Ger), Berlin: G. Reimer, 1866.

3. Haeckel, E.: The Gastraea Theorie (Ger), *Jenaische Z Naturwiss* 8:1-55, 1874.

4. Haeckel, E.: *Monism as Connecting Religion and Science, the Confession of Faith of a Man of Science*, J. Gilchrist, trans., London: A. & C. Black, 1895.

5. Haeckel, E.: *Anthropogeny or the Evolution of Man*, Leipzig: W. Engelmann, 1874, republished by D. Appleton, New York, 1886.

Friedrich von Recklinghausen (1833-1910)

HISTORICALLY, VON RECKLINGHAUSEN'S NAME is associated with neurofibromatosis[1] and lymph canaliculi. His name is also associated with a condition now recognized as hyperparathyroidism, in the description of which he inadvertently described another disease (polyostotic fibrous dysplasia), with which his name did not become associated. One of the foremost German pathologists in the 19th century, Friedrich Daniel von Recklinghausen was born in Gütersloh, Westphalia, and studied medicine in the universities of Bonn, Würzburg, and Berlin. He gained the doctor's degree in Berlin in 1855, defending his inaugural thesis on the theories of pyemia, prepared in Latin. Following graduation, he devoted himself to pathological anatomy with Virchow, and, except for periods of study and research in Vienna, Rome, and Paris, he remained in Berlin until 1864.

Without passing through the usual academic steps, Recklinghausen was appointed professor of pathological anatomy in Königs-

Composite by G. Bako

berg in 1864. After a few months he accepted a similar post in Würzburg. Finally, in 1872, he was appointed professor of general pathology and pathological anatomy at Strassburg. Here he was instrumental in assembling an outstanding faculty as the model for its time. In 1877, he served his university as rector, but in 1884 he rejected a call to succeed Cohnheim in Leipzig, preferring to remain in Strassburg.

Recklinghausen published several important contributions from Virchow's laboratory. *The Lymph Vessels and Their Significance in Connective Tissue*[2] was his first monograph and has been adjudged to be one of his best. Silver salt stains were developed for the demonstration of lymph spaces communicating with lymphatics. Other noteworthy studies, as determined by his biographer and pupil, Chiari,[1] include the ameboid motion of specific cells and their identity with leukocytes in inflammation, phagocytosis, the relationship between metastatic inflammatory foci and bacterial masses in the blood vessels, basophilic mast cells in the blood, disturbances of circulation and nutrition, rickets and osteomalacia, microphotography, myomas of the uterus as a source of bleeding, spina bifida, significance of the uterus and fallopian tubes, theories of vision, function of the retina, tubercles in the myocardium, hemorrhagic infarcts of the kidney, and the three subjects excerpted in this essay. Many of his contributions were published in the *Archiv für Experimentelle Pathologie und Pharmakologie*, which he founded with Naunyn in 1873 and served as coeditor.

In 1889, von Recklinghausen gave hemochromatosis, the disease described by Trousseau in 1865, its present name. The brief report was made to the section on general pathology and pathological anatomy chaired by Virchow. It was recorded by Neumann as follows:[3]

On Hemochromatosis.

After his attention had been attracted by an unusual case, Dr. v. Recklinghausen examined a number of cadavers looking for the unusual pigment that he had found in the case; this pigment was "hemofuscin" which he was usually able to identify. It is characterized by its color and very fine granular amorphous appearance, and gives a negative iron reaction. The pigment is found in the cells of smooth muscle, in blood and lymph vessels, lymph glands, in the liver (apart from other pigment), and in the pancreas, but it is almost never found in the kidney. It has not been found in striated muscle, but occasionally in vessels supplying the muscle. In well developed cases it is easily recognizable on microscopic examination; it gives the organs a peculiar discoloration, and accentuates the lymph vessels especially. Recently it is considered to have been derived from the degeneration of blood. v. Recklinghausen believes that this pigment is originally transported in a soluble state and that the cells, which contain it, behave toward it as chromophilic cells. He does not believe that the prototype of the pigment is hemosiderin.

von Recklinghausen's name is most appropriately associated with the condition identified with multiple neurofibrous pigmented tumors developing along the course of cutaneous nerves, often in segmental patterns, and associated with nevi. Morbidity involves somatic and autonomic elements and not infrequently central nervous tissue. The tumors are prone to malignancy and to recurrence after surgical removal. "Axillary freckling" and numerous pale yellow-brown macules in the skin, café au lait spots, as large as 15 cm in diameter, may develop in the skin. These spots may be distinguished microscopically

from the pigmented areas of polyostotic fibrous dysplasia by the presence of giant pigment granules in malpighian cells or melanocytes or both in the café au lait macules and in uninvolved skin. Accompanying bone lesions in neurofibromatosis consist of whorls of fibrous tissue and subperiosteum bone cysts. Excerpts from the report of his second case, translated by Long, are as follows:[4]

His [a 47-year-old-male] most striking abnormality consisted of innumerable tumors, running close to a thousand altogether, in the outer skin layer. Herr Lacquer (who referred the patient) recalled bringing this case of multiple fibromas to my attention at the medical society meeting where I presented my first case two and a half years ago. As to the history of these tumors, the patient could only report that he had had them as long as he could remember, that they had become apparent soon after his attack of purpura, and that they had increased markedly after his fifteenth year. Information as to the first growth of these tumors came from his mother; she had not told him if he had been born with them.

The skin of the face, particularly the sides of the cheeks, which had little beard, was covered with small flat tumors averaging half the size of a pea, which extended in similar nodular form up to the skin of the forehead. There were small nodules even close to the point of the nose at the lower margin of the nasal septum, and also at the margin of the left eyelid. The ears, however, were uninvolved. . . . On the crown of the head there was an especially large, firm nodule, the size of a cherry, with a partial stalk, in which the painful tension already noted concentrated.

On the neck and trunk the nodules were distributed in a manner rather similar to that in case I, i.e., in the middle parts of the back and sides of the abdomen. They were most numerous on the loins and sides. . . . Larger, prominent tumors, like half or three-quarters spheres, were widely distributed; there was an apple-sized nodule on the right shoulder blade below its spine, and one on the left, near its lower angle. . . . The palms of the hands and soles of the feet were quite free from nodules, up to the base of the ball of the right thumb, where a flat, disc-like nodule lay, extending into the deeper tissue.

The middle sized and larger nodules stood out from the rest of the skin chiefly through a delicate, sometimes dark and sometimes light, rosy coloring like the hue of the skin in the new-born; the coloring was determined first by distinct, fine blood vessels in the covering skin and secondly by an increase in transparency. It was this color tone, also, which called attention to deep-lying tumors, especially over both pectorals, which were moveable but cohered closely to the unraised skin of the reddish patches.

My interest turned understandably to the externally palpable peripheral nerve trunks, and since the subcutaneous tissue was thin and distinctly poor in fat, I was soon able clearly to recognize thickenings of these in their gross distribution. The left supraorbital nerve, from the incisura to the middle of the forehead, was palpable as a nodular cord, about as thick as the quill of a pigeon feather, while on the right side there was no definite thickening of the trunk. On each side, along the large vessels of the neck several elongated bodies were felt, which I believed corresponded with the vagus nerves, although admittedly lymph nodes could not be excluded.

Without appreciating the difference, von Recklinghausen described one case of osteitis fibrosa generalisata (primary hyperparathyroidism) and two cases of polyostotic fibrous dysplasia, or Albright's syndrome, in his monograph, entitled *Fibrous or Deforming Osteitis, Osteomalacia, and Osteoplastic Carcinosis.* This communication has further complicated eponymic terminology. Currently, generalized osteitis fibrosa is a multiworded description for primary hyperparathyroidism, and the terms may be used interchangeably without need of introducing von Recklinghausen's name. And to further clarify rather than complicate this bizarre condition without a recognized etiology, polyostotic fibrous dysplasia or osteitis fibrosa disseminata, with cutaneous pigmentation and sexual precocity in females, is identified currently as Albright's syndrome.[5] Excerpts of the extended report and discussion of Case V, most likely a case of polyostotic fibrous dysplasia, follow.[6]

Case V.

Disseminated Deforming Osteitis with Tumors and Cysts.

My own observations are similar to a case presented by Virchow at the Berlin Congress of Natural Science, 1886, which I cite accordingly:

Generalized hyperostosis of the skeleton together with formation of cysts; extensive hyperostosis of the skull; hyperostosis and curvature of the femora and of the right humerus; other bones are spongy, especially the upper ribs; the malformations are not caused by fractures; hard bone, spongy bone, large fibrocartilaginous islands, and huge cysts are present in the bone marrow.

At the Heidelberg Congress of 1889 I presented the following observations which agree with Virchow's and identified the condition as "tumor producing osteitis deformans."

The patient was a 66-year-old female. I found marked flexion of the hips and the knees; genu valgum, so much so on the left that the left knee was displaced and markedly above the right. Both femora were curved like a shepherd's staff; the summit of the curvature was 120 mm above the head of the femur. . . . The left tibia and fibula were soft, curved and thinned. A cross section of the right tibia, which had a normal form and structure and was 330 mm long, showed

three cysts within the marrow; the largest, 120 mm from the upper end, was 35 mm long. . . . Even the largest cyst was just contained within the marrow. All three showed a smooth fibroid wall adjacent to the usual fatty marrow.

The tumor [in the fibula] is for the most part filled with a white, fluid substance and edematous connective tissue without cysts. . . . A fat cyst, in the form of a bowling pin, 25 mm in dimension, imbedded half in the white substance, is present in the femur; it contains a brownish gluey mass.

The bones of the left foot are normal except for a fibrous mass in the neck of the metatarsus near the end of its marrow cavity, a thickened plaque in the center of the right calcaneus, and a small 7 mm cyst in the phalanx. . . . The pelvis is distorted; the right is higher than the left. The tuber ischii is curved outward on the right so as to form a trough into the socket. There is marked kyphos of the upper spine and slight curvature of the lower spine to the right. The sternum is bent forward and contains a fibrotic plaque 40 mm long.

The skull is distorted. The seams are difficult to recognize but generally the structure is thin, while the right half of the occiput is markedly thickened. . . . Because of the bony involvement, particularly of the calvarium, the huge tumor-like thickening of the femora, the extensive deformities which appear so regularly that they could not possibly be caused by multiple fractures, although multiple incomplete fractures have not been excluded, I believe the findings can be attributed to deforming osteitis.

The pathological structure of the fibromatous cysts, especially the bone but also the connective tissue, gives an impression of being mature and completely developed. Microscopically little osteoid tissue devoid of calcium is found, while the soft tissue is seldom young and rich in cells. On the contrary, it is poor in cells and mainly fibrous tissue; the wall of the cyst resembles old, fibrinous, sclerotic, connective tissue so that we may regard this process as a stationary state which was reached years ago.

In support of this theory of maturity are the great hardness, the density, and the compact composition of even the thin shell of the tumor, sometimes with holes which obviously have not been preformed, but have developed during the illness. We must date the illness to the earlier decades of life.

von Recklinghausen, a prime component in the development of pathological anatomy as a medical science, attracted investigators to his department from many countries. His pathological anatomy was based on knowledge of embryology and intimate details of the stages of maturation of tissue. He was unusually adept in the preparation and delivery of lectures in the amphitheater as well as in commanding attention of small groups in informal laboratory exercises. Although he participated in investigation and welcomed each advance in knowledge, von Recklinghausen failed to appreciate the significance of bacteriologic investigations or the opportunities offered by recently-developed experimental methods.

1. Chiari, H.: Friedrich Daniel v. Recklinghausen, (Ger), *Verh Deutsch Path Ges* 15:478-488, 1912.

2. von Recklinghausen, F.: *The Lymph Vessels and Their Significance in Connective Tissue* (Ger), Berlin: A. Hirschwald, 1862.

3. von Recklinghausen, F.: Hemochromatosis (Ger), *Klin Wschr* 26:925, 1889, translated by Z. Danilevicius.

4. von Recklinghausen, F.: *Multiple Fibromas of the Skin and Multiple Neuromas* (Ger), Berlin: A. Hirschwald, 1882, in Long, E. R. (trans): *Selected Readings in Pathology*, ed 2, Springfield, Ill: C. C Thomas, 1961.

5. Albright, F., and Reifenstein, Jr., E. C.: *The Parathyroid Glands and Metabolic Bone Disease*, Baltimore: Williams & Wilkins Co., 1948.

6. von Recklinghausen, F.: "The Fibrous or Deforming Osteitis, Osteomalacia, and Osteoplastic Carcinosis in their Proper Significance" (Ger), in *Festschrift for Rudolf Virchow*, Berlin: G. Reimer, 1891, excerpt translated by E. Longar.

Julius Cohnheim (1839-1884)

JULIUS FRIEDRICH COHNHEIM, successor to Virchow and his most apt pupil, was born in Demmin, Pomerania, in northern Prussia.[1] He received his gymnasium training at Prenzlau and, overcoming the handicap of family and financial misfortunes, began the study of medicine at the University of Berlin at the age of 17. Because his father was forced to flee to Australia, his early training was the responsibility of his mother who, in turn, depended upon him for support. Cohnheim interrupted his medical education in Berlin to study with von Kölliker in Würzburg and to audit a term at Greifswald. Returning to Berlin he prepared his doctoral thesis under the direction of Virchow at the Pathological Institute of the Charité Hospital, one of the great intellectual centers of medicine in Europe. Von Recklinghausen and Klebs were Virchow's assistants who, together with Traube, professor of medicine, undoubtedly offered great inspiration to Cohnheim. The dissertation, submitted in 1861, concerned inflammation of serous membranes, a subject which benefited greatly from Cohnheim's continued contributions in subsequent years.

Between the receipt of the doctorate in medicine and his first professional appointment, Cohnheim was occupied with implementing a modest research program at Virchow's Institute. He also engaged in a limited medical practice to support his mother and served as surgeon with the Prussian Army in the German-Danish War of 1864. However, the time at the Institute was most productive; many of his important contributions to experimental and structural pathology were reported during this period. These included the introduction of fresh frozen tissue for microscopy, researches on the structure of striped muscle fiber, investigation of sugar-forming ferments, investigation with silver stains of nerve endings in muscle, delineation with gold salts of sensory nerve endings in the cornea, experimental inoculation of the cornea with tuberculous matter, and descriptions of pathological findings in tuberculosis of the choroid, pseudoleukemia, sarcoma of the fibula, multiple exostosis, and fatal trichinosis. In 1868, Cohnheim was called to Kiel as professor of pathology, remaining until 1872 when he left to occupy a similar post at Breslau. He went to the University of Leipzig in 1878; there he remained until his death from complications of severe chronic gouty arthritis.

At Kiel, Cohnheim resumed study of the circulation, which had been interrupted by a brief period with Ludwig; from him he learned techniques for the particular field of investigation. He offered convincing evidence that coronary arteries were, in fact, end arteries, wrote his monograph on the critical investigation of embolic phenomena,[2] and described an example of paradoxical embolism from the deep leg veins shortly after a similar case of a thrombus from the auricle was reported by Litten. The translation by McKee of Cohnheim's *Lectures on General Pathology*, published by the New Sydenham Society, describes a patient with extensive thrombosis of the veins of the lower extremity and a fatal embolus to the middle cerebral vessel.[3]

Where the transport of the embolus appears to take place in opposition to anatomical laws, there are usually, as though to prove the rule, anomalies in the distribution of the vessels or in the heart. Thus I had quite lately an opportunity of observing a case of recent fatal embolism of one of the mid. cerebrals in a woman thirty-five years of age, where the valves of the heart, aorta ascendens, in short all the arteries from which an embolus might have been conveyed, were absolutely intact, while on the other hand an extensive thrombosis had occurred in the veins of the lower extremity. I had not, as you may suppose, at first the remotest idea of connecting the two conditions, till on more carefully inspecting the heart I discovered a *foramen ovale* so large that I could easily pass three fingers through it.

Cohnheim's six years at Breslau were marked by two important events. In 1875, Robert Koch, then a country practitioner, arrived on a special mission with cultures of anthrax bacilli for demonstration to microbiologist Ferdinand Julius Cohn. Cohnheim, a deeply-interested observer, was immediately impressed and continued with greater incentive his work on the bacilli of cholera and tuberculosis. Secondly, he founded a Pathological Institute and, as its chief, attracted many students and assistants who enabled him to extend the investigative work far beyond that possible for a scientist working alone. Cohnheim suffered increasingly at Breslau from attacks of gouty arthritis, which in subsequent years seemed to resist all treatment. In his lectures on general pathology, the pathogenesis of increased uric acid concentration in the blood of gouty patients was discussed: the intake of foods of high-protein content and the role of disturbance of the

secretory activity of the kidney in the pathogenesis were placed in proper perspective.[3]

. . . since, about the beginning of this century, it became known that uric acid forms the chief constituent of the gouty deposits, and that the blood of the gouty is abnormally rich in this body, the theory was soon started that incomplete oxidation of the albuminates taken in excess is the cause of the increased production of uric acid. The theory has been repeated by one writer after another up to the present day, although its weak points are apparent enough . . . we, pathological anatomists, have from year to year opportunities, even in this part 'of the country where gout is not very frequent, of examining the bodies of persons who, though they lived in the most needy circumstances, have a more or less large number of joints abundantly incrusted with most typical urates. . . . Taking everything into account, I hold it to be not certainly made out that the excessive supply of albuminates has any essential influence on the production of uric acid.

For that the kidneys are invariably and from the start diseased in the gouty is a perfectly arbitrary assumption; on the contrary, the urine continues to be for years absolutely normal in the intervals between the attacks.

Cohnheim's deep interest in inflammation was a recurring curiosity, but, despite unquestioned admiration for Virchow, his conclusions differed from those of his chief. Virchow's theory of inflammation was based upon an assumption of the nonmigration of blood cells to the inflammatory site. He considered leukocytes in situ to have stemmed from the adjacent connective tissue. Cohnheim, on the other hand, proved that the essential feature of inflammation involved the diapedesis of leukocytes through the capillary walls by their attraction to the site of injury. The theory—without blood vessels, no inflamation is possible—had been approached by William Addison in the Goulstonian lectures in 1859, but Cohnheim produced the first convincing experimental evidence. His initial communication appeared in 1867,[4] while he was working in Virchow's laboratory at Berlin. A decade later his findings on inflammation were presented in his formal lectures.[3] The first excerpt is translated from the earlier communication, the others are taken from his lectures.

. . . the so-called pus cells in the inflamed cornea are colorless blood corpuscles, which forced their way out of the blood vessels into the cornea. . . . The white blood cells that have left the blood vessel gradually move away from the blood vessel and their place is immediately taken by cells which newly migrate out of the vessel.

There is no inflammation without the participation of blood vessels.

During the last few years several theories have been suggested with the view of explaining the manner in which the colourless cells, which received the name of *exudation-* or *pus-corpuscles*, enter the inflammatory effusion; but with a minute exposition of these you will be glad to dispense, now that we have succeeded in directly observing the passage of the colourless corpuscles from the interior of the vessels into the tissue of the vicinity. We now know, not merely that the pus-corpuscles perfectly agree in form and characters with the colourless blood-corpuscles—a point to which Virchow had long ago more than once emphatically directed attention—but *that they are nothing more or less than extravasated white corpuscles.* . . . But altogether apart from this, it seems to me that the enormous production of pus-corpuscles will be decidedly easier of comprehension if we be permitted to regard the whole organism as concerned in it, and not merely that portion in which the inflammation has been established. No one surely will suppose that all the pus-corpuscles produced in the course of a phlegmonous inflammation were already present in the blood at the commencement of the process. On the contrary, it is beyond doubt that, even under perfectly normal conditions, new colourless corpuscles are being constantly supplied to the blood to replace those that have been used up; and in inflammation it would only be a question of an abnormally increased formation, and supply, of colourless cells. . . . Yet there is much in favour of the view that the same organs, on which very probably the formation of lymph-corpuscles is physiologically incumbent, receive greater calls on their activity in inflammation. At least, nothing is more usual than for the *lymphatic glands* in the neighbourhood of an inflamed part to be more or less swollen; and even the *spleen* is found, in many of the more extensive inflammations, in a condition of pronounced hyperplasia.

Cohnheim's rich scientific career was shortened by intractable gouty arthritis, and his final years were severely compromised by the affliction. For long periods he was confined to home or spa, chairridden or bedridden. The postmortem examination showed granular kidneys with urate deposits and massive hypertrophy of the heart, although the joints inspected were free of urate deposits.

1. Wagner, E.: *Collected Works of Julius Cohnheim* (Ger), Berlin: A. Hirschwald, 1885.
2. Cohnheim, J.: *Investigations of the Embolic Process* (Ger), Berlin: A. Hirschwald, 1872.
3. Cohnheim, J.: *Lectures on General Pathology* (Ger), A. B. McKee (trans.), London: New Sydenham Society, 1889-1890.
4. Cohnheim, J.: Inflammation and Suppuration (Ger), *Arch Path Anat* 40:1-79, excerpts translated by Z. Danilevicius.

Andre-Victor Cornil (1837-1908)

A. V. CORNIL, Parisian clinician and organ pathologist, was born in Cusset (Allier), the son of an established physician.[1] He received his higher education at the University of Paris, became intern of the city hospitals in 1860, and in 1865 received the degree of doctor of medicine. Experienced in the latest pathological techniques, Cornil became chief of the clinic at Hotel Dieu in 1867, two years later professor agrégé on the faculty of medicine, and subsequently physician to the hospitals of Paris. When Charcot retired in 1882, Cornil rightfully succeeded to the professorship of pathological anatomy.

Together with Ranvier, an inseparable coworker and equally ambitious pathologist, they designed a private histologic laboratory. As Cornil's reputation grew, his requirements for space increased. Eventually adequate laboratory facilities were provided in conjunction with the clinic at Hotel Dieu, where he investigated a remarkable number of pathological-clinical subjects. Many of the contributions were presented without collaboration; others were prepared with the cooperation of distinguished associates of his time, enhanced by self-prepared line drawings and water colors.

One of his best works was a two-volume manual of pathological histology in three parts (1869-1876) coauthored with Ranvier.[2] It was translated into English in 1880. In 1885, with Babes of Budapest, Cornil prepared a monograph on the participation of bacteria in the anatomy and histology of infectious diseases. His work on the pathology of the kidney, based on research pursued with Brault over a period of 30 years, was described in two monographs. A communication on the parasite of leprosy, prepared with assistance from Suchard, was translated and published by the New Sydenham Society.

Other subjects described by Cornil included public hygiene, medical-legal testimony, cancer, epithelial tumors, melanosis, syphilis, pulmonary tuberculosis, malignant polps of the stomach, and salpingitis. A considerable time before routinely recommended biopsies, he realized the potential value of the procedure and was accustomed to examine fresh material as soon as he received it from the surgeon.

Two of Cornil's reports on articular disease —a description of juvenile rheumatoid arthritis and structural changes observed postmortem in the joints and kidneys of a case of gouty arthritis with peripheral evidence of rheumatoid arthritis—were prepared while an intern. In describing the renal and articular changes associated with the deposition of sodium urate in gouty patients, Cornil gave a detailed report of the findings in an 84-year-old woman suffering from chronic tophaceous gout. Symptoms had begun almost 50 years earlier. On examination, advanced changes caused by rheumatoid arthritis of the peripheral joints, with ulnar deviation, flexion deformity, and subluxation, were apparent. The gross examination revealed extensive urate deposition on and into the cartilage of the small and large joints, ligaments, and tendons. The observations were described as follows.[3]

The joints of the extremities, with the exception of the hips, showed massive deposits of sodium urate or deeply imbedded on the surface of the cartilage. The ligaments and tendons near the joints were infiltrated with small chalky concretions. The phalanges were fixed in flexion and abduction. Because of subluxation of the proximal heads of phalanges, the heads of the metacarpals had become dislodged and were displaced subcutaneously.

With high magnification (200X) of the urates in the articular cartilages the irregular masses showed fine, long crystals, pointing toward the cells of the articular surface. Urates within the cartilage cells were amorphous and formed a circular or oval opaque mass around which crystalline needles radiated into intercellular structureless cartilage. On the serous surfaces, particularly about the cartilages of the knee, small, chalky deposits were seen. . . . On the addition of acetic acid, the masses of crystals of uric acid dissolved. Great numbers of chalky deposits of similar structure and composition were found in the subserous cellular tissue, in the ligaments, in the tendons of the muscles, in the neurilemma of the digital nerves, in the subcutaneous connective tissue, in the deep layers of the skin, and in the fibrous periarticular tissues.

Examination of the kidney (magnification 20 to 300X) showed the arterial walls to be thickened. No area escaped urate deposition.

We have shown that (1) in a number of gouty patients (due to irritation produced by the passage of large quantities of urates through the kidney) albumin appears in the urine irregularly and in small quantity and may be accompanied by edema; (2) these findings are consistent with renal pathology, at times quite advanced, which represents chronic albuminous nephritis (parenchymatous nephritis) or chronic atrophy of the parenchyma with swelling of the fibrous elements and of the arterial walls (interstitial nephritis or gouty kidney of Todd). These lesions independently have little in common with gout; (3) the two alterations in the kidney structure that should be properly ascribed to gout are (a) uric acid deposits or gouty nephritis of Rayer and; (b) sodium urate deposits characteristic of gout and identical to similar deposits in the joints.

A patient with juvenile rheumatoid arthritis, from Charcot's service at Salpetrière, was a 29-year-old girl whose articular symptoms had begun at the age of 12. They recurred periodically as acute episodes of pain, swelling, redness, and heat; by the age of 18 chronic changes had developed. Upon examination during the terminal admission, she complained of excruciating pain and showed extensive flexion deformities of the fingers which were positioned in abduction as well as pallor of the skin, except for redness about affected joints. Death was attributed to cardiac failure. Postmortem examination revealed massive enlargement of the heart and pericardium, fibrinous pericarditis, but no evidence of endocarditis or atrophic kidneys, considered by Cornil characteristic of advanced Bright's disease.[4]

The right knee was firmly ankylosed. The patella was attached to the femoral condyles by thick, fibrous tissue. The epiphysis was rarified, friable, and consisted of a thin layer of bone and an oily yellow marrow. The articular surface of the left knee showed velvet-like abnormal tissue; the swollen and fissured cartilage simulated the surface of a sponge; the cartilage had almost disappeared from the femoral condyle and was replaced with an uneven and a partially eroded bony surface. The phalangeal articulations showed less drastic changes although the bone was denuded of cartilage, and deformations similar to those of rheumatic arthritis were present; the synovial membranes were inflamed and rough. The changes were typical of chronic articular rheumatism, pericarditis, pleurisy, and Bright's disease. It is clear that renal involvement and pericarditis were caused by the same chronic rheumatic process.

Cornil was a member of the Society of Biology of Paris, from 1874 to 1882 served as editor of the *Journal of Practical Medicine and Pharmacology*, and in 1884 became a member of the Academy of Medicine. Early in his career, political activities, and especially the great Republican movement, dominated his emotions and claimed a portion of his time. In 1870, Cornil was appointed prefect in the department of his birthplace and, in 1877, was elected to the Chamber of Deputies, where he served until 1882. In 1885, he was elected senator from Allier, holding the position until 1903. Cornil died from pulmonary tuberculosis, probably contracted from exposure to tubercle bacilli at postmortem dissections. Following his death, Verlet designed a bas relief of him which was unveiled in Cusset. He is shown as the central figure before a postmortem slab surrounded by associates and pupils.

1. Letulle, M.: Professor Cornil (1837-1908) (Fr), *Rev Sci* (Paris) 49:40-44, 1911.

2. Cornil, V., and Ranvier, L.: Manual of Histologic Pathology (Fr), 3 pt, Paris: Germer Bailliere & Co., 1869-1876, Shakespeare, E. O., and Simes, J. H. C. (trans.): *A Manual of Pathological Histology*, Philadelphia: Henry C. Lea, 1880.

3. Charcot, J. M., and Cornil, V.: Study of the Anatomical Changes in Gout (Fr), *C R Soc Biol* 5:139-163, 1864, excerpt translated by Z. Danilevicius.

4. Cornil, V.: Pathological Findings in Chronic Articular Rheumatism (Fr), *C R Soc Biol* 4th series. 1:3-25, 1864, excerpt translated by Z. Danilevicius.

Library of the College of Physicians, Philadelphia

Sir Jonathan Hutchinson (1828-1913)

THE QUANTITY AND QUALITY OF MEDICAL COMPOSITION by Jonathan Hutchinson attest to the industry and scientific integrity of one of Britain's best. Jonathan was born in Selby, Yorkshire, into a Quaker family; his father was a successful merchant in flax. A Quaker governess was largely responsible for his early education, which was followed by an apprenticeship, begun at the age of 17, under Caleb Williams, Quaker surgeon and Quaker preacher. After three years at the school of medicine at York, Jonathan left for London and St. Bartholomew's Hospital, where he studed under James Paget, and in due time became president of the Abernethian Society, a discussion group of medical students. Having procured the License of the Society of Apothecaries and membership in the Royal College of Surgeons of England, Hutchinson returned to York for graduate hospital experience at the County Hospital. The final professional move was back to London, for visiting service at the Hospital for Diseases of the Chest, for experience in diseases of the eye at

Moorfields, and diseases of the skin at Black-friars. His chief post was surgeon to the London Hospital, where he became assistant surgeon in 1860.

Hutchinson's first medical manuscript was published in the *Medical Times and Gazette* at the age of 24. It was an unsigned description of gonorrheal and luetic iritis. This, a single communication, was published the first year in London: two communications were published the second year; and six in the third—a reflection of an accelerated tempo that persisted until the 1900's. During the last decade of the 19th century, Hutchinson was responsible for one volume per year of the *Archives of Surgery*, 300 to 400 pages per volume, and a similar number of printed pages in medical periodicals. The variety of subjects discussed betrayed an encyclopedic interest in medicine, which included internal medicine, surgery, ophthalmology, dermatology, pathology, syphilology, and neurology. Since specialization came later in England than on the Continent, it was not unusual for a "surgeon" to display deep interest in more than one area of clinical medicine or medical science.

In 1858, at the age of 30, the effects of congenital syphilis on the development of teeth (Hutchinson's teeth) were reported in a 7-page communication to the Pathological Society of London.[1]

For a considerable time past, I have been in the habit of recognising in a certain very peculiar development of the permanent teeth an indication that their possessor had in infancy suffered from hereditary syphilis. . . . Most of the cases taken, were those of patients attending at the Royal Ophthalmic Hospital, on account of chronic interstitial keratitis, an affection which is, I believe, almost always a result of inherited syphilis. Their ages varied from twenty-eight years to five years. In all a clear history of syphilis was established, either by the free confession of the patient's parents, or by the account given of symptoms of undoubted character during infancy.

That there is a peculiar condition of the teeth, which results from the influence of hereditary syphilis, and that the most frequent features of this condition are the following:—a. Smallness.—The teeth stand apart with interspaces, and are rounded and peggy in form instead of flat. *b. Notching.*—They usually exhibit in their border a broad shallow notch, or at times, two or three (serrated). Owing to their softness; these teeth rapidly wear away, and this notching is thus often obliterated, but when markedly present, it is one of the most decisive conditions. *d. Colour.*—Instead of the clear, smooth, white exterior of good teeth, they present a dirty greyish surface, totally destitute of polish and rarely smooth. No amount of cleaning will materially alter this feature which owes its existence, I believe, to the great deficiency of enamel. *e. Wearing down.*—As before observed their softness from deficiency of enamel renders them liable to premature wearing down. The teeth of a syphilitic patient not twenty, will often be ground down as much as those of a very old person should be, and this in cases in which there is no pecularity as to position, such as the front teeth meeting in the bite. *f.* The signs mentioned apply almost exclusively to the incisors and canines, and in fact the grinders are usually altered in a very much less degree.

The triad of deformed incisor teeth, interstitial keratitis, and deafness was described in a series of communications published in the Royal London *Ophthalmic Hospital Reports.*[2]

My objects in the following essay are—

I. To give a more detailed account, than has yet been attempted, of the form of acute iritis, occasionally met with in syphilitic infants.

II. To shew that acute iritis as a consequence of hereditary syphilis is not so very rare as it has been thought, and that it now and then occurs at periods subsequent to infancy.

III. To endeavour to prove that the form of kerato-iritis met with in young persons, and formerly known as "aquocapsulitis," is, in the majority of instances, of specific origin.

IV. To endeavour to prove that the disease known as "Chronic corneitis," "Interstitial corneitis," "Strumous corneitis," is almost always a direct result of inherited syphilis.

V. To illustrate the connexion with hereditary taint, of some of the cases of deposit in or upon the retina or choroid, hitherto classed as "scrofulous."

Chronic Interstitial Keratitis usually commences as a diffuse haziness in the centre of the cornea of one eye. There is at this stage no ulceration and exceedingly slight evidence of the congestion of any tunic. The patient, however, almost always complains of some irritability of the eye, as well as of dim sight. If looked at carefully, the dots of haze are seen in the structure of the cornea itself, and not on either surface; they are also separate from each other like so many microscopic masses of fog. In the course of a few weeks, or it may be more rapidly, the whole cornea, excepting a band near its margin, has become densely opaque by the spreading and confluence of these interstitial opacities. Still, however, the greater density of certain parts,—centres, as it were, of the disease,—is clearly perceptible. At this stage, the comparison to ground glass is very appropriate, and there is almost always a zone of sclerotic congestion, and more or less intolerance of light and pain around the orbit.

My reasons for believing that this disease is dependent upon an inherited syphilitic taint are the following:—

That in almost all cases the subjects of it present a *very peculiar physiognomy*, of which a coarse flabby skin, pits and scars on the face and forehead, cicatrices of old fissures at the angles of the mouth, a sunken bridge to the nose, and a set of permanent teeth peculiar for their smallness, bad colour, and vertically notched edges, are the most striking. Several of the cases described suffered from otorrhoea, with unilateral deafness.

While on the staff of the Blackfriars' Hospital, for diseases of the skin, Hutchinson founded the New Sydenham Society (with the dissolution of the Sydenham Society), described a number of dermatologic conditions, and prepared the *Atlas of Skin Diseases*.[4] His original descriptions included bullous eruptions produced by potassium iodide, melanotic whitlow, the cutaneous nodules and papules of Hutchinson-Boeck's disease (sarcoidosis), and varicella gangrenosa.[3]

I have tried to prove that it is possible for the eruption of varicella in isolated cases and in connection with idiosyncracy on the part of the patient, to assume a very severe type, becoming bullous, petechial, or even gangrenous. In these gangrenous forms there is much constitutional disturbance, and death may result.

Respecting my own case I do not think that there can be any reasonable doubt. The child was in excellent health, was successfully vaccinated, and was affected seven days afterwards by a general eruption which was taken for smallpox. This eruption became gangrenous, and the child died of exhaustion on the twenty-first day.

Several types of lupus were recognized: lupus verrucosus, nevus lupus (acquired cutaneous angioma or angioma serpiginosum), and lupus lymphaticus (lymphangioma circumscriptum).[4]

I will say that the name lupus is applicable to a chronic inflammation of the skin, attended by a cell-growth in the deeper layers, which spreads slowly at its edge, and thus involves adjacent parts, which inevitably disorganises the parts attacked, and always, after cure, leaves a scar. It is by this tendency to leave a scar that we separate lupus from psoriasis, for after the cure of the latter the skin is left quite sound.

The more common forms of erythematosus lupus are met with, however, not in children, but in young or middle-aged adults, and are attended by much less peculiar conditions. Usually the disease begins on the nose, and a red, slightly roughened patch is produced on the middle of that organ; next, two symmetrical red patches are seen on the cheeks (seldom continuous first with that on the nose), and after a time patches occur in both ears. The tendency to symmetry is very remarkable, and I must beg your especial attention to

the fact that the patches are independent, and not continuous.

References to gout embrace tooth-grinding, gouty seborrhea of the ear, and the "hot-eye" (gouty iritis). No one of these associations is recognized currently by physicians interested in gout and gouty arthritis.[5]

A gentleman, named W., consulted me on account of attacks of irritability, first of one eye, and then of the other. The eye would become a little red, and feel as if he had sand in it. The attacks would usually last from two to four days, but they recurred very frequently, and were a source of much annoyance. He had made his own diagnosis before coming to me, and remarked, "I never knew what they meant until, a year ago, I had an attack of gout in the great toe." . . . He inherited gout strongly on both sides. Having noticed the identity of name, I asked him if he was a relative of a certain Dr. W., whose eyes I had treated for gouty iritis more than twenty years ago. "Yes," he said. "I am his first cousin, and there is the same inheritance in both of us." In the latter case, the patient, then a young man, lost one eye from recurrent attacks of iritis, and had much damage to the other. His case is given in the series which I have published, illustrating the peculiar form of destructive iritis which goes with hereditary gout. Thus the two cases support each other, and afford strong evidence: firstly, as to the connection, with inheritance of gout-tendencies, of the destructive form of iritis; and, secondly, with personal proclivity to gout of the "hot eye."

Hutchinson recognized the spontaneous tendency to recovery in patients with Graves' disease.[6]

One of the most remarkable features in the clinical history of Graves' disease is its spontaneous tendency to recovery, and the patient's freedom from all risk of relapse when once recovery is established.

He presented an example of temporal arteritis.[7]

The "red streaks" proved, on examination, to be his temporal arteries, which on both sides were found to be inflamed and swollen. The streaks extended from the temporal region almost to the middle of the scalp, and several branches of each artery could be distinctly traced. The conditions were nearly symmetrical. . . . We appear to have in this case an unquestionable example of an arteritis which spread along the affected vessels, causing swelling of their external coats and adjacent cellular tissue with congestion of the overlying skin, and which resulted very quickly in occlusion of the vessels. It is not proved that there was any thrombosis; it is indeed, certain that in the first stage there was not. I am not able to state whether the final stage of plugging occurred suddenly or not.

Hutchinson was appointed professor of surgery at the Royal College of Surgeons at the age of 51. He was elected a Fellow of the Royal Society and later president of the Royal College of Surgeons. Knighthood was conferred on him at the age of 80.[8]

1. Hutchinson, J.: Report on the Effects of Infantile Syphilis in Marring the Development of the Teeth, *Trans Path Soc Lond* 9:449-456, 1858.

2. Hutchinson, J.: On the Different Forms of Inflammation of the Eye Consequent on Inherited Syphilis, *Ophthal Hosp Rep* 1:191-203; 216-224, 1857-58-59; ibid 2:54-105; 258-283, 1859-60.

3. Hutchinson, J.: On Gangrenous Eruptions in Connection with Vaccination and Chicken-pox, *Medicochir Trans* 65:1-11, 1882.

4. Hutchinson, J.: Lupus Erythematosus, *Med Times* 1:1 (Jan. 4) 1879.

5. Hutchinson, J.: Illustrations of Exceptional Symptoms and Examples of Rare Forms of Disease, *Brit Med J* 1:1018 (May 29) 1886.

6. Hutchinson, J.: "Diseases of the Nervous System: On Recovery from Graves' Disease (Exophthalmic Goitre)," in *Archives of Surgery*, vol. 1, London: J. & A. Churchill, 1890.

7. Hutchinson, J.: "Case of Arteritis of the Temporal Arteries," in *Archives of Surgery*, vol. 1, London: J. & A. Churchill, 1890.

8. Hutchinson, H.: *Jonathan Hutchinson: Life and Letters*, London: William Heinemann, Ltd., 1946.

Albrecht von Graefe (1828-1870)

FREDRICK WILHELM ERNST ALBRECHT VON GRAEFE, the son of an important German surgeon, Carl Ferdinand von Graefe, was born into a family of social standing and affluence. Endowed with a fine intellect, he benefited handsomely from private tutoring at home, supplemented by preparatory education at the French gymnasium in Berlin.[1] The study of logic and philosophy preceded medical instruction at the University of Berlin, which claimed a remarkable faculty including Johannes Müller, Virchow, von Brücke, Du Bois Reymond, Remak, and Schlemm in the basic sciences, and Traube, Dieffenbach, Romberg, and Schönlein in the clinical sciences. Graefe received the doctor's degree in 1847 upon presentation of a thesis based upon original experiments, *De bromo ejusque praecipuis praeparatis*. Postgraduate experience was gained with von Jaksch and Arlt in Prague, with Ricord, Trousseau, and Claude Bernard in Paris, with Rokitansky, von Brücke, Oppolzer, and Hebra in Vienna, and

with Bowman and Critchett in London. This list, including the faculty in Berlin, contained the medical elite of Europe in the mid-19th century. Thus, it is not surprising that by 1850

Graefe felt sufficiently prepared to return to his native city, where he was determined to specialize in ophthalmology. Without benefit of a university affiliation, he began a small clinic which grew in less than a decade into an international center for ophthalmologic research and clinical ophthalmology. Larger quarters, needed within two years, contained a clinic and a hospital, in which rich and poor were treated with equal care and attention. Although Graefe qualified as privatdocent in surgery and ophthalmology at the University of Berlin, he was not appointed head of the department until 1866. By that time he had founded the *Archiv für Ophthalmologie* as an outlet for his contributions, had attracted students and patients from diverse areas of the world, had contributed to the knowledge of the physiology of the eye, had enhanced the understanding of the eye in systemic disease, and had improved the surgical treatment of ophthalmologic conditions. In substance, von Graefe had achieved international fame in ophthalmology.

In selecting noteworthy clinical and surgical contributions for excerpting, iridectomy for treatment of glaucoma, the pathogenesis of embolism of the central retinal artery, von Graefe's sign in thyrotoxicosis, and the description of conical cornea seem most pertinent. Other contributions include early recognition of the value of the Helmholtz ophthalmoscope, the deduction that optic nerve paralysis is the result of inflammation of the optic nerve, the association between increased intracranial pressure from a cerebral tumor and choked disc, the pathogenesis and surgical correction of strabismus, as well as descriptions of diphtheritic conjunctivitis, sympathetic ophthalmia, detachment of the retina, intraocular tumors, and choroidal tubercles.[2]

Von Graefe's important work on iridectomy in glaucoma, suggesting that symptoms are caused by an increase in intraocular pressure, was reported in 1857, and was translated and reprinted by the New Sydenham Society in 1859.[3]

Now when I compared the general appearance of this glaucomatous inflammation with that of other internal inflammations, for example, of the common irido-choroiditis, it seemed to me that all the characteristic symptoms tended to one point—*increase of the intra-ocular pressure.*

The hardness of the glaucomatous globe has been remarked from the earliest periods of ophthalmology. Since no change in the sclerotic, capable of explaining the altered resistance of the globe, can be justly admitted, it must be founded on the more complete filling of the globe with fluid.

Supported by these facts and considerations, I considered myself perfectly justified in performing iridectomy in glaucoma; for I knew the favorable action of the operation on the condition of the choroid in regard to its circulation; and everything seemed to favour the opinion that the operation probably possessed a physiological, and certainly, in many cases, a therapeutical pressure-diminishing action. The first trials were extremely uncertain, for I had no fixed principles, either in regard to the choice of cases or the manner of making the trial. I first employed this method in June, 1856, and from that time have continued it, especially in the cases which I have already described as acute glaucoma.

An account of an embolism of the central artery of the retina was presented in 1859. The patient, a stable-hand, injured on the thorax, developed shortness of breath, fatigue, and hemoptysis. More than two months following the injury, the patient complained of a mist before his right eye. Ophthalmic examination showed marked narrowing of the vessels.[4]

One day while working in the stable, the patient noticed that a mist developed before his right eye. He shut his left eye to test this phenomenon. First he was able to see all objects but diffused, as through a colored cloud. Then his area of vision contracted rapidly and within minutes all light sensation had gone from his right eye. All that remained was a pattern of subjectively "seen" colors, which increased with movement and varied greatly.

Upon examination of the patient, an absolute blindness in the right eye was present, with no quantitative sensitivity to light. Pressure failed to produce fire circles, the pupil was completely unresponsive to light in the right eye but contracted sympathetically when the left pupil was exposed to light or to accommodation. The external examination of the eye was otherwise normal.

During the examination with the ophthalmic mirror, I was surprised to observe changes that I had never seen previously in a case of recent blindness. I found the refractive media clear, the optic disc pale, and the vessels reduced to a minimum. The main arterial vessels beyond the disc in the retina appeared as small channels whose branches became correspondingly smaller and smaller. . . . Under such circumstances were we justified in making a diagnosis of an embolism of the central artery of the retina? In the examination, ample evidence was found for such a condition. An alteration of the aortic valves suggested an acute endocarditis; the change in the right eye could be explained only by an obstruction in the lumen of the artery.

Von Graefe's observations on paralysis of the ocular muscles led him to appreciate the significance of the lag of the upper lid in hyperthyroidism, an important clinical finding in thyrotoxicosis, von Graefe's sign. The findings, distinct from exophthalmos, were reported in the *Deutsche Klinik* in 1864, during a discussion of Basedow's disease.[5]

1. Mr. *v. Graefe: Concerning Basedow's Disease.*— As is well known, the protrusion of the eyeball is one of the most important symptoms of Basedow's disease: Indeed, this, with the abnormally rapid heart rate and the strumous swelling of the neck, forms the characteristic symptom complex. In this exophthalmic protrusion, *the pressing forward of the axis* has been emphasized too much and not enough attention has been paid to another symptom, which has value in its earlier phases and mild degrees of illness. This consists in the *disturbed relationship between the movement of the lid and the elevation and sinking of the level of vision.*

Another proof that this symptom is not dependent upon the exophthalmos, consists in the fact that it may disappear in the course of Basedow's disease, either spontaneously or as the result of treatment, while the exophthalmos itself persists. . . . Therefore it is obviously to be considered as a peculiar *disturbance in the innervation of muscles of the lid.*

Von Graefe's first case of conical cornea, with surgical management, was described in 1854. However, he devised a more satisfactory method of treatment, the results of which were published later.[6]

The anomaly of the cornea, which presents finite and characteristic symptoms from the beginning, is usually described as conical deformity. Speaking precisely, the normally gently ellipsoid dome-like curvature of the cornea becomes more and more hyperbolloid; its tip usually remains in the center of the cornea. When the anomaly becomes more advanced, the profile identifies the lesion.

In the advanced cases the profile is sufficient for a diagnosis; in others, if functional complaints are noted, the lesion can be diagnosed by observing the corneal reflexes. The Helmholtz ophthalmometer, which is most helpful in measuring the corneal curvature, is of little value in the diagnosis of keratoconus; rather, it is more useful in the determination of the geometrical form of the corneal dome and in detecting small changes during treatment.

The abnormal curvature of the cornea presents several signs when the anterior chamber and iris are illuminated. . . . There is an opacity at the tip of the keratoconus; early it suggests a grayish cloud, later it persists as a whitish-gray lesion.

In patients with keratoconus, we find the highest degree of irregular astigmatism, while no successful optical correction exists.

Since medical treatment is not available, except for atropine applications during the initial stages to decrease the pressure in the anterior chamber, surgical intervention remains. A small section of corneal substance is excised from the tip of the cornea with a fine, narrow knife. (The knife should not pierce the cornea; no perforation should result, only in a thinning-out.) . . . When this small flap of corneal tissue is raised with a pupillary forceps, its length is extended to about ½ mm; it is then lifted and detached. The following day the base of the incision is cauterized and the procedure repeated every three to six days. If a yellowish glistening infiltration is produced, and the pericorneal reaction is only moderate, the effect is sufficient and nothing else need be done except to use atropine drops. When the inflammatory reaction has subsided and a scar has developed, the center of the cornea contracts, becomes thicker; the opaque scar decreases and as the corneal dome approaches its normal shape, the vision improves.

Von Graefe's work habits may have contributed to his early death from pulmonary tuberculosis. He required less sleep than others and went to bed either late at night or the following morning. Between early rising and late morning, his time was spent in his office, reading and preparing material for clinical presentation or scientific communications, examination of patients, discussion of cases scheduled for surgery, hospital rounds, or consultations away from the office. In the afternoon he operated frequently but leisurely, usually with pupils in attendance. The evening hours were devoted to additional consultations and evening rounds at the hospital. Sunday afternoon was a partial holiday spent with his family. Each autumn a long vacation was planned, usually in Heidelberg or Würzburg, but occasionally in Switzerland.

1. Michaelis, E.: *Albrecht von Graefe, His Life and Work* (Ger), Berlin: G. Reimer, 1877.

2. Perera, C. A.: Albrecht von Graefe, Founder of Modern Ophthalmology, *Arch Ophthal* 14:742-772, 1935.

3. von Graefe, A.: Iridectomy for Glaucoma and the Glaucomatous Process, *Arch Ophthal* 3:456-555, 1857, in *Selected Monographs,* T. Windsor (trans.), London: New Sydenham Society, 1859, p 287.

4. von Graefe, A.: Embolism of the Central Retinal Artery (Ger), *Arch Ophthal* 5:136-157, 1859, excerpt translated by E. Longar.

5. von Graefe, A.: Basedow's Disease, *Deutsch Klin* 16:158-159, 1864, translated in Major, R. M.: *Classic Descriptions of Disease,* Springfield, Ill: Charles C Thomas, 1939, pp 245-246.

6. von Graefe, A.: Corneal Conus (Ger), *Klin Wschr* 5:241-244, 249-254, 1868, excerpts translated by Z. Danilevicius.

Johann Friedrich Horner (1831-1886)

FRIEDRICH HORNER, whose name is associated with the clinical syndrome that follows unilateral interruption of the cervical sympathetic fibers, was born in Zürich, where his father was a practicing physician.[1] Horner, delicate of body but strong of mind, was schooled in the classics, mathematics, and natural history. Upon completion of his country's compulsory military training in 1849, he matriculated in the University of Zürich and went on into medicine; there he gained high scholastic honors, particularly in anatomy and physiology under Carl Ludwig and in botany under Oswald Heer. Sorrow came to the family during this time, for within a few months his parents and brother died of unrelated conditions. He received the MD degree in 1854, presenting a thesis on the curvature of the spine. His postgraduate work was begun in Vienna, where he took courses with Oppolzer, Skoda, and Hebra. This was followed by an assistantship under Graefe, Breslau ophthalmologist,

Composite by G. Bako

who exerted a great influence on Horner's professional career. His "travel years" were concluded with a few months spent in Paris in the eye clinic of Desmarres.

Horner returned to Zürich in 1856 and began medical practice. He gave private lectures on ophthalmologic subjects and subsequently passed the examination for docent. In 1862, he was appointed adjunct professor of ophthalmology at the University and director of the ophthalmology clinic and, in 1873, became full professor. He continued in active practice, teaching, and research until his death.

Although the eponymic syndrome was described by Horner in 1869, the association of specific functions of the eye or adjacent tissue with stimuli conducted by the cervical sympathetic was recognized experimentally more than a century earlier. Horner unwittingly overlooked these reports in his discussion. In 1727, Francois Pourfour du Petit published in the *Historie de l'Academie Royale des Sciences* of Paris his findings following severance of the vagosympathetic nerve in dogs. Depression of the globe, diminished convexity of the cornea, narrowing of the palpebral fissure, injection of the conjunctiva, and relaxation of the nictitating membrane were observed. An appraisal of the experimental studies, confirming or expanding this work, was presented by Fulton. He included the observation by Claude Bernard, which led to the use of a dual eponym in France— the Claude Bernard-Horner syndrome.[2] Fulton also mentioned the clinical report by Hare in 1838, describing a case of a rapidly growing tumor arising on the left side of the neck, producing symptoms of compression of the brachial plexus.[3]

"In addition to the foregoing symptoms, the pupil of the left eye became contracted; and the levator palpebrae ceased to perform its office." At necropsy, a hard irregular carcinoma had involved all the nerves and blood vessels on the left side of the neck. The phrenic and lower cervical ganglions of the sympathetic were also involved. The connection of the tumor with paralysis of the arm was considered obvious by Hare, but the "paralysis of the levator palpebrae which receives a branch from the third pair . . . cannot . . . be referred to any *direct* communication between the structural disease and these several affections, but rather they must be regarded as an instance of that remote sympathy which is found to exist between distant parts of the same individual, and is most frequently displayed in a person of nervous temperament."

A similar clinical correlation was reported by Mitchell, Morehouse, and Keen in 1863 of a Civil War soldier who received a full blast of gunshot in the right side of his neck. The following findings as observed several weeks after the injury were reported as follows:[4]

The pupil of the right eye is very small, that of the left eye unusually large. There is a slight but very distinct ptosis of the right eye, and its outer angle appears as though it were dropped a little lower than the inner angle. . . . The conjunctiva of the right eye is somewhat redder than that of the left and the pupil of the right eye is a little deformed. . . . It [face] became distinctly flushed on the right side only, and pale on the left. . . . Was this a case of wound or injury of the cervical sympathetic nerve? Had the peculiar phenomena been observed from the date of the wound, such a conclusion would have been irresistible. It is scarcely less than this even under the present circumstances.

The failure of Horner to refer to these cases has been attributed charitably to the limited exchange of scientific information at that time. Thus, it is not surprising that Horner believed he had made an original clinical observation in a 40-year-old peasant woman who had noted a slight drooping of the right eyelid six weeks after her last confinement. The pathogenesis of the paralysis of the cervical sympathetic on the right was not discussed, nor was a satisfactory follow-up study reported.[5]

The upper lid covers the right cornea to the upper edge of the pupil; the lid is not loose or wrinkled but somewhat sunken into the orbit and is still capable of movement. . . . The upper convex furrows on the right side of the forehead indicate that the frontalis muscle is working as a substitute (for the levator palpebrae superioris).

The pupil of the right eye is considerably more constricted than that of the left, but reacts to light; the globe has sunk inward very slightly and repeated determinations showed that it was somewhat less firm than the left. Both eyes . . . have normal visual acuity.

During the clinical discussion of the case, the right side of her face became red and warm, the color and heat increasing in intensity under our observation, while the left side remained pale and cool. The right side seemed turgid and rounded, the left more sunken and angular; the one perfectly dry, the other moist. The boundary of the redness and warmth was exactly in the midline.

The patient thereupon told us that the right side had never perspired, and that the flushed feeling, and also the ptosis, had only developed in the course of the last year. The redness of the right side of the forehead and cheek was said to be present in the evening as a rule but was also brought on more or less markedly at other times by any emotion.

The sensation in both cheeks was exactly the same. This investigation thus proves the integrity of the sensory trigeminal nerves, transitory paralysis of the vasomotor fibers in the right trigeminal area; higher initial temperature on the right side with slowly rising (temperature) curve.

Two points necessitate the conclusion that the vasomotor disturbance involves not only the trigeminal area, but also that of the fibers of the cervical sympathetic: first, the slight but distinct variation in temperature in the axillae, secondly, and more important, the small size of the right pupil.

Let us now turn to the question of the causation of the ptosis. I believe that nobody who had seen all the foregoing symptoms, would be surprised at my considering this ptosis, which comes on gradually but remains incomplete, to be a paralysis of the musculus palpebrae superioris supplied by the sympathetic nerve (H. Müller, Harling), and the appearance of the upper lid as part and parcel of the whole symptom-complex.

Horner wrote extensively about the eye. His clinical presentations, many of which appeared in Zehender's *Klinische Monatsblatter für Augenheilkunde*, discussed glaucoma, cataracts, tumors of the eye, herpes of the cornea, retinal findings in Bright's disease, coloboma, pterygium, strabismus, sympathetic inflammation, and congenital myopia. His chapter on diseases of the eye in childhood in Gerhardt's *Handbook of Pediatrics* was another noteworthy contribution. Endowed with excellent general medical knowledge, Horner pointed out the ocular manifestations of general disease at every opportunity. He attracted patients and pupils from great distances. At his death in midprofessional maturity, he was recognized as a member of the group of clinical scientists who had contributed to the maturation of ophthalmology in central Europe in the midportion of the 19th century.

1. Landolt, E.: *Dr J. F. Horner, An Autobiography* (Ger), Frauenfeld: J. Huber, 1887.
2. Fulton, J. F.: Horner and the Syndrome of Paralysis of the Cervical Sympathetic, *Arch Surg* (Chicago) 18:2025-2039, 1929.
3. Hare, E. S.: Tumor Involving Certain Nerves, *London Med Gaz* 1:16-18, 1839.
4. Mitchell, S. W.; Morehouse, G. R.; and Keen, W. W.: *Gunshot Wounds and Other Injuries of Nerves*, Philadelphia: J. B. Lippincott & Co., 1864.
5. Horner, F.: A Form of Ptosis (Ger), *Klin Mbl Augenheilk* 7:193-198, 1869, translated in Fulton.[2]

Argyll Robertson (1837-1909)

DOUGLAS MORAY COOPER LAMB ARGYLL ROBERTSON, lecturer in physiology, experimental pharmacologist, and ophthalmic surgeon, was born in Edinburgh, the son of John Argyll Robertson, surgeon and lecturer in the medical school.[1] The three supernumerary given names were discovered only in his obituaries; scientific communications were signed "D. Argyll Robertson." The familiar eponym is compressed conveniently to "Argyll Robertson pupil." Robertson received his undergraduate and a portion of his medical training at the University of Edinburgh; the remainder was taken at St. Andrews, where the MD degree was granted at the age of 20. After a year as house surgeon in the

Royal Infirmary, he studied ophthalmology under von Arlt in Prague and von Graefe in Berlin. Ophthalmology and Edinburgh seemed the logical choices for discipline and domicile. Each benefited from Robertson's many

Composite by G. Bako

contributions during a highly successful professional career. He was ophthalmic surgeon to the Royal Infirmary, lecturer in physiology, and instructor on diseases of the eye in a voluntary course at the University of Edinburgh. As the singular ophthalmic surgeon in Scotland in his day, he held elective and appointed positions, which included honorary surgeon-oculist to Queen Victoria in Scotland and to King Edward VII, president of the Royal College of Surgeons in Edinburgh, president of the Ophthalmological Society of the United Kingdom, and LLD *honoris causa*, University of Edinburgh.

Robertson's fifty-odd scientific communications were devoted almost exclusively to the physiology and morbidity of the eye. Lupus of the eyelid, etiology of glaucoma, melanotic tumor, diphtheritic ophthalmia, sympathetic ophthalmia, retinitis pigmentosa, hypertrophy of the lacrimal gland, senile entropion, hydrophthalmos, asteroid hyalitis, pulsating exophthalmos, *Loa loa* beneath the conjunctiva, and microphthalmos are examples of his lesser contributions. The pharmacology of the active principle of the Calabar bean on the eye, the action of belladonna on the iris, and the action of light on the pupil in central nervous system syphilis are his best-known contributions.

The studies on the extract of the Calabar bean (*Physostigma venenosum*) were motivated by a clinical need for an agent capable of constricting the pupil and counteracting the effects of atropine.[2]

For more than a year past I have recognized the numerous advantages that would flow from the discovery of a substance which, when applied to the conjunctiva, should produce effects exactly opposite to those well known to result from belladonna or atropine; which should stimulate the muscle of accommodation and the sphincter pupillae as the above-named remedies paralyze them. . . . These investigations were, however, productive of no satisfactory results, until my friend Dr. Fraser informed me that he had seen contraction of the pupil result from the local application of an extract of the ordeal bean of Calabar. . . . With some difficulty I got a few Calabar beans, and . . . prepared from them three extracts of varying strengths.

With these solutions, I then proceeded to perform the following experiments, . . .

Experiment 1.—On the 17th of January, I carefully examined the condition of my eyes, and found that with both my sight was normal. . . .

These points having been determined, I introduced a drop of the weakest extract of the Calabar bean into my left eye, . . .

At 12:30, or 20 minutes after the introduction of the extract, a marked alteration in the size of the pupils was observable; the left pupil being only 1 line in diameter, while the right measured fully two lines.

On the following morning, there was still an appreciable difference in the size of the pupils, and vision with the left eye was still slightly affected; but the symptoms gradually subsided, and in the afternoon completely disappeared.

These experiments prove that the local application of the Calabar bean to the eye induces,—*first*, A condition of short-sightedness. . . . And, *second*, It occasions contraction of the pupil, and sympathetically dilatation of the pupil of the other eye. We further observe that atropine possesses the power of counteracting its effects, and, *vice versa*, that it is capable of overcoming the effects produced by atropine. . . . I am inclined to believe that the contraction of the pupil is due to increased action of the sphincter pupillae, and this chiefly on the ground that the other effects produced by the Calabar bean can only be explained by an induced contraction of the ciliary muscle—the muscle of accommodation; and as the sphincter pupillae and ciliary muscle are both supplied by the ciliary nerves, I think the most feasible explanation of the action of the Calabar bean on the eye is to regard it as a stimulant to the ciliary nerves.

This significant observation was made at the age of 26, shortly after Robertson began practice in Edinburgh. A few years later, the ocular symptoms and the action of belladonna on the iris in a patient with spinal disease were described in his favorite medical periodical, the *Edinburgh Medical Journal*. The patient, 59 years of age, afflicted with central nervous system syphilis, admitted of an unsteady gait, particularly in the dark. The ocular response—the Argyll Robertson pupil—was described.[3]

I could not observe any contraction of either pupil under the influence of light, but, on accommodating the eyes for a near object, both pupils contracted.

On first seeing the patient I was struck with the extreme contraction of the pupils, and having previously had one case of myosis apparently dependent on spinal disease under my own care, and seen several such cases while attending Professor Remak's clinique in Berlin, I was led to suspect the dependence of this symptom on a spinal cause—a suspicion which the history of the case verified. . . . The iris in the mammalia, as is now universally admitted, contains two sets of nonstriated muscular fibres, the one arranged circularly at its pupillary margin, the other radiating from these circular fibres to the ciliary ligament. By the first the pupil is contracted; it is generally termed the sphincter pupillae muscle, and is under the influence of the motor oculi nerve. By the second the pupil is dilated; it is usually termed the dilator pupillae muscle, and is under the influence of nervous filaments passing from the spinal cord through the cervical sympathetic to the eye. These fibres are usually termed sympathetic, but I incline to consider them true spinal nerves.

Robertson continued, modestly, with reference to Romberg's observation that the pupil was contracted in tabes dorsalis. He also admitted that a similar finding had been observed by Trousseau in progressive locomotor ataxy, and mentioned the observations of Duchenne, Radcliffe, and von Carion, each of whom observed contraction of the pupil in spinal disease.

Four examples of spinal myosis were reported by Robertson.[4]

These four cases serve well to illustrate the connexion between certain eye-symptoms and a diseased condition of the spinal cord. In all of them there was marked contraction of the pupil, which differed from myosis due to other causes, in that the pupil was insensible to light, but contracted still further during the act of accommodation for near objects, while strong solutions of atropine only induced a medium dilatation of the pupil. In three of the cases a slight degree of atrophy of the optic nerves existed, as was evinced by a shallow excavation and lighter colour of the optic disc. . . . In all of them the retina was thoroughly sensitive to light, and in all of them the ciliary branches of the third pair were healthy and active (as was shown by the further contraction of the pupil during the act of accommodation, which can only be referred to these nerves). But in all there were symptoms of spinal disease, and in all myosis due to paralysis of the ciliospinal nerves.

Robertson was a tall, handsome physician, an athlete eager for competition in golf, shooting, archery, or curling. Scotland's national pastime was his favorite sport, and he played frequently on the links at St. Andrews. Nor did he forsake golf late in life; a home near a golf course was selected on retirement to the Isle of Jersey. He enjoyed travel as well as ophthalmology and, only a few years before his death, circled the globe by way of India and Japan. A friendship with the Thakur of Gondal, India, led to a second and last visit to India where he died at the age of 72. A fine sense of humor, Robertson must have appreciated the witticism that it is "far better to be an Argyll Robertson pupil than to have one."

1. Douglas Moray Cooper Lamb Argyll Robertson, obituary, *Ophthalmoscope* 7:135-141 (Feb 1) 1909.

2. Robertson, D. A.: On the Calabar Bean as a New Agent in Ophthalmic Medicine, *Edinburgh Med J* 93:815-820 (March) 1863.

3. Robertson, D. A.: On an Interesting Series of Eye-Symptoms in a Case of Spinal Disease, with Remarks on the Action of Belladonna on the Iris, etc., *Edinburgh Med J* 14:696-708 (Feb) 1869.

4. Robertson, D. A.: Four Cases of Spinal Myosis; with Remarks on the Action of Light on the Pupil, *Edinburgh Med J* 15:487-493 (Dec) 1869.

Edward Nettleship (1845-1913)

EDWARD NETTLESHIP, in the period between a brief career in veterinary surgery and the professional days when he was primarily concerned with ophthalmology, described the dermatologic findings in a case of urticaria pigmentosa. Nettleship was born at Kettering, Northamptonshire, into a distinguished family headed by Henry John Nettleship, well-known solicitor.[1] His early education was gained at the Kettering grammar school and as an amateur naturalist in the woods and fields. He received his higher education at the Royal Agricultural College in Cirencester and at the Royal Veterinary College while he attended medical courses at King's College and

Composite by G. Bako

the London Hospital. In 1867, Nettleship obtained the diploma of membership in the Royal College of Veterinary Surgery and the diploma of licentiate of the Society of Apothecaries. He served for a year as professor of veterinary surgery at Cirencester College and in 1868 qualified as Member in the Royal College of Surgeons and two years later as Fellow.

By then, Nettleship had begun to favor ophthalmology and became a star pupil of Jonathan Hutchinson at the London Hospital and later at Moorfield's Eye Hospital. Here he served as curator of the museum and librarian. Nettleship's first staff appointment was at the South London Ophthalmic Hospital (Royal Eye Hospital). His two most important posts were lecturer in ophthalmology and ophthalmic surgeon at St. Thomas's Hospital and surgeon to Moorfield's Hospital. For three years, beginning in 1888, he was Dean of the medical school at St. Thomas's

Hospital. He was a founding member of the Ophthalmological Society of the United Kingdom and was president for two years.

The formation of the section of ophthalmology of the Royal Society of Medicine was largely a function of his activities.

Early in his career Nettleship described an unnamed dermatologic condition, later called urticaria pigmentosa, one of the rare forms of urticaria in a two-year-old child.[2]

HOSPITAL FOR DISEASES OF SKIN, BLACKFRIARS.
I.—Chronic Urticaria, Leaving Brown Stains: Nearly Two Years' Duration.
(Reported by Mr. Nettleship.)

EMILIE P., aged 2 years, living at Blackheath Hill, was admitted at the Hospital for Skin Diseases on July 27th, 1869. She was the subject of chronic urticaria; and the eruption was peculiar, in leaving stains of a light brown colour, their tint being very like that of chloasma, for which the disease might easily have been mistaken at first glance. She had light hair and a very fair complexion. The mother says that the child "has never suffered from any illness since her birth"; and she is in excellent health. There was no history of urticaria in other members of the family. The present eruption began when she was three months old, and she has never been free from it since. The mother's account is, that the spots began as "white lumps like the sting of a nettle"; these itch severely, and, on subsiding, leave the curious brownish stains above noticed. The rash, on admission, thickly covered the neck and trunk, the extremities being more sparsely affected. There were no spots on the face, but a few brown stains of former wheals at the margin of the scalp on the forehead. There were no *red* wheals, but some slightly raised patches of light brown colour with slight congestion, and some stains of former wheals. The true nature of the raised patches was proved by their centres turning nearly white when the skin was stretched. The wheals are of uniform size, and about as large as threepennypieces. It was noticed that a scratch with the fingernail produced, in a few minutes, an ordinary urticaria wheal, with white centre and red edges; and, at a subsequent occasion, a number of recent patches of elevated and erythematous skin were observed; these had not yet become brown. When the child first came, there was little or no evidence of scratching; but, several weeks afterwards, it is noted that, "in addition to the urticaria, there are scratched papules, like those of prurigo; no lice can, however, be found." At her last attendance, five weeks from admission, she was in much the same condition as at first, excepting the pruriginous spots.

We do not find any mention of a similar condition in our standard works. The patient is still attending, and can be seen by any one interested in it.

Nettleship conducted his demanding private practice from his office on Wimpole Street; yet he found time for the preparation of many communications on clinical ophthalmology, medical and surgical. He prepared a students' textbook on diseases of the eye of which five editions were published.[3] He was a mediocre lecturer in the classroom and a mediocre surgeon in the operating amphitheater. At the height of his professional career, he retired from practice. Upon his departure from London in 1902, Nettleship enjoyed the appreciation expressed by his pupils and colleagues in the establishment of a triennial award for the encouragement of scientific ophthalmic work. The move to Hindhead, Surrey, where he had spent weekends and holidays for many years, was the beginning of a new career. The last decade of his life was given over to important investigations in the hereditary diseases of the eye. His work on congenital night blindness traced the disease in 1,800 persons over 10 generations.[4] The pedigrees of families afflicted with congenital cataracts, lamellar and discoid cataracts, and retinitis pigmentosa were also described. The importance of these researches on heredity was recognized by his election in 1912 to Fellowship in the Royal Society. At his death he had just completed a study of albinism together with Karl Pearson and C. H. Usher.

1. Lawford, J. B.: Edward Nettleship, F.R.S., F.R.C.S. 1845-1913, *Brit J Ophthal* 7:1-9, 1923.
2. Nettleship, E.: Chronic Urticaria, Leaving Brown Stains, *Brit Med J* 2:323 (Sept 18) 1869.
3. Nettleship, E.: *The Student's Guide to Diseases of the Eye*, ed 2, London: J. & A. Churchill, 1882.
4. Nettleship, E.: A History of Congenital Stationary Night-Blindness in Nine Consecutive Generations, *Trans Ophthal Soc UK* 27:269, 293, 1907.

Hugh Owens Thomas
(1834-1891)

UNDERSTANDING THE VIRTUE OF A CURVED HEEL for improvement in defections of gait and posture is but one example of Thomas' application of anatomy and physiology to the practice of orthopedics. Such contributions as the Thomas posterior or hip splint for immobilization of the hip, the Thomas knee splint for immobilization of this structure, the Thomas caliper for ambulating patients,

Thomas' sign for diagnosis of disease of the hip, the Thomas wrench, the behavioral correction of dislocations of the ankle joint and hip, and reduction of Pott's fracture of the ankle remain currently in favor.

Composite by G. Bako

Thomas was born in Bodedern, Anglesey in Wales, while his mother was on a visit to her parents.[1] His father, following the bonesetter trade of his ancestors, had set up practice in Liverpool. After excellent early schooling, Thomas was apprenticed for four years to his uncle, Dr. Owen Roberts, of St. Asaph, Wales. He then spent two years at the University of Edinburgh and a final year walking the wards in Paris hospitals and at University College, London. At the age of 23, he qualified for membership in the Royal College of Surgeons of England.

Thomas returned to Liverpool the following year and, after joining his father in practice for a brief period, went on his own, setting up an office and a workshop in the busiest quarter of town. Both the location of the office and the hope offered the afflicted appealed especially to the dock men who came to him with fractures and dislocations. A knowledge of anatomy and physiology in the investigation of each case and shrewd application, when indicated, placed Thomas far in advance of the bone-setters of his day. He had expert knowledge of proper splints designed in his workshop and recognized the value of progress notes. In proper time, according to his judgment, he published his scientific results, selecting his own printer. Thomas held no major hospital appointments nor any professorship in a medical school; rather he devoted his time and efforts to medical practice and his workshop. Although ether had been discovered before he returned to Liverpool and the antiseptic principles of Lister were advanced, such aids in orthopedic surgery seemed less important to Thomas than the proper application of forms and splints designed in his workshop.

In 1867, Thomas published in the *Lancet* a brief communication on the treatment of ununited fractures; in 1873, he described the use of silver ligatures for compound fractures of the mandible; and, in 1875, he published his text on *Diseases of the Hip, Knee, and Ankle Joints*.[2] A facsimile copy of the second edition has recently been published.[3] Subsequent scientific contributions appeared from 1883 to 1890 in pamphlet form, privately printed, and for relatively private distribution, in a series of annual volumes entitled *Contributions to Surgery and Medicine*.[4]

Thomas' mechanical skill, designed to implement his principles of orthopedic practice, is exemplified in the discussions of immobilization of the hip and in management of fracture of the femur. Thomas maintained that extension alone was not sufficient; it was essential that the joint or limb should have adequate support to maintain correct alignment and to withstand the muscular and tendonous forces acting upon the affected part.[2]

I assert that a fractured thigh, if treated by extension only, would be accompanied with vastly more muscular irritability than if the same case was placed in a modern appliance, in which the limb was immoveably in the strict meaning of the term fixation. Then we should not have the slightest muscular excitement. Traction is a very inefficient sedative in joint disease, as well as in fractures, compared with the effect of the immobility modern surgical appliances place at our disposal, while I admit that extension is one of the indispensable aids in the treatment of certain fractures, though of secondary value compared with an immobility that places the limb at perfect ease.

14.—If the hip appliance be not so fitted as to remain continuously behind the trunk, it will not give any ease from pain, or benefit the joint in any way; so, to avoid pain, and eversion or inversion of the thigh, the upright portions of the hip appliance must be fitted so as to remain uninterruptedly close to the posterior superior spine below the crest of the external ilium of the side affected, and over the prominence of the buttock, and not to rotate towards the diseased side; moreover, it is essential not to interrupt for a moment the first stage of the treatment in hip disease.

In reduction of dislocation of the hip, Thomas fixed the pelvis to the ground by a looped towel passing over the patient's groin and under the arch of the operator's foot. With the towel in the groin, the flexed knee of the patient was drawn over the surgeon's thigh, who, grasping the patient's leg, continued to flex the knee and used the leg as a lever to apply stress on the fixed point. With this maneuver the operator was able to apply force and meanwhile was free to flex, abduct, or to extend the limb without interruption of the application of force.

The use of hyperemia for ununited fractures was recommended by Thomas some years before the principle was proposed by Bier. Thomas believed that constriction above and below an ununited fracture would lead to irritation, tissue unrest, and increased efforts toward repair. This recommendation was a corollary to his insistence upon rest for diseases of the intestinal tract, given monographic treatment in his *Contributions*.[4]

Thomas was the oldest of five brothers who all became qualified surgeons. Although he attracted a large following of disciples, his nephew, Sir Robert Jones, an outstanding orthopedic surgeon in the United Kingdom, was probably the best-known member of the family. Personally, Thomas was eccentric and took delight in riding in his carriage on the streets of Liverpool wearing a dark oversized greatcoat, a cap pulled over one eye, and tremendous gauntlet gloves—a "Dickens character in everyday life."[5]

1. Aitken, D. M.: *Hugh Owen Thomas, His Principles and Practice*, London: Oxford University Press, 1935.
2. Thomas, H. O.: *Diseases of the Hip, Knee, and Ankle Joints, With Their Deformities, Treated by a New and Efficient Method*, Liverpool: T. Dobb & Co., 1875.
3. Thomas, H. O.: *Diseases of the Hip, Knee and Ankle Joints*, facsimile of ed 2, Boston: Little, Brown & Co., 1962.
4. Thomas, H. O.: *Contributions to Surgery and Medicine*, 8 parts, London: H. K. Lewis, 1883-1890.
5. Watson, F.: *Hugh Owen Thomas, a Personal Study*, London: Oxford University Press, 1934.

Composite by G. Bako

Julius Wolff (1836-1902)

JULIUS WOLFF, experimental orthopedic surgeon born in West Prussia, attended the University of Berlin, where Langenbeck, Johannes Müller, Henoch, and Frerichs were on the faculty. At the suggestion of Langenbeck, he studied the natural and aberrant formation of bone in animals, the substance of his doctoral thesis presented in 1860.[1] Wolff began the practice of orthopedic surgery in Berlin, but continued his investigations into the form and function of bone on his own initiative, fostered a University affiliation, and, in 1868, became privatdocent in the department of surgery. Later Wolff was advanced to professorial status; in 1890, he was appointed director of the University Clinic for Orthopaedic Surgery which he had established, and in 1899 was advanced to geheimrat. Earlier in his career he saw military service in the campaigns of 1864, 1866, and 1870-1871.

Wolff was not the first to consider bone as living tissue, but he focused attention on the assumption that its external appearance and internal structure changed with alteration of function. He showed that increased stress led to increased compactness of interstitial substance, while decreased pressure led to loss of matrix. He proved that the structural result of traction was similar to the action of pressure; it strengthened bone. In fractures, ankylosis, and rickets, increased bone formation developed on the concave side of the deformation where the stress was greatest; on the convex side, however, where there was lessened pressure, bone atrophied. The axiom, later identified as Wolff's law, evolved from these studies. It has been stated in various forms including the following:

> If a normal bone is used in a new way its structure and form will change to meet its new function; . . . if normal function returns to a deformed bone, that bone will rearrange its architecture to its former shape and structure.

The usually accepted translation follows.[2]

> Every change in the form and the function of a bone or of their function alone, is followed by certain definite changes in their internal architecture, and equally definite secondary alterations in their external conformation, in accordance with mathematical laws.

John B. Murphy of Chicago found a simpler expression.[2] "The amount of growth in a bone depends upon the need for it."

In concentrating upon osteology Wolff overlooked faulty use or inefficiency of contiguous muscle groups. Nor was he concerned with the role played by osteoblasts in bone transformation, the elements of the skeleton which resist the forces to which the structure is exposed. He visualized bone as a plastic substance responding to stresses and strains according to mathematically predictable laws, and, when bone is deformed, the internal structure may be markedly changed.[3] The structural changes follow the alteration of the static function so that the deformation becomes adapted to its new function or structural position. Knock knee or genu valgum was cited as an example. This deformity was attributed to the deflection of the normal lines of pressure which keep the lower limbs apart and was amenable to surgery. Clubfoot, on the other hand, was handled by step wire splinting and restoration of the static load distribution without open surgery. Congenital dislocation of the hip was treated also by his technique of "functional orthopedics."

After Wolff had concentrated upon bones and joints early in his career, he incorporated plastic surgery and, based upon extensive experimental studies, transposed portions of resected bone. Also he was a recognized authority on surgical correction of harelip and cleft palate and was successful in performing laryngectomy and thyroidectomy.

1. Hoffa, A.: Julius Wolff (Ger), *Munchen Med Wschr* 49:532-534, 1902.
2. Keith, A.: *Menders of the Maimed*, London: H. Frowde, Hodder & Stoughton, 1919, pp 277-289.
3. Wolff, J.: *The Law of the Transformation of Bone* (Ger), Berlin: A. Hirschwald, 1892.

Los Angeles County Medical Library

Adam Politzer (1835-1920)

ADAM POLITZER, the first professor of otology at the University of Vienna, was born in Alberti, Hungary, the son of a prosperous Jewish merchant.[1] Politzer showed an unusual interest in diseases of the ear while preparing for a medical career at the university; there Skoda, Rokitansky, Oppolzer, Ludwig, and other notable teachers and investigators were members of the faculty. While at the Physiological Institute directed by Ludwig, and before completing his medical studies, Politzer described the innervation of the intrinsic muscles of the ear and the variations in air pressure on the tympanic cavity. After receiving his doctorate in medicine and surgery in 1859, Politzer left Vienna to continue his studies on the anatomy, physiology, and pathology of the organs of hearing with Kölliker and Tröltsch in Würzburg, with Helmholtz in Heidelberg, with Claude Bernard and Prosper Ménière in Paris, and with Toynbee in London. Returning to Vienna in 1861, he was appointed docent in otology. In 1864, together with Tröltsch and Schwartze, Politzer founded the *Archiv für Ohrenheilkunde*. He reached professorial status in 1870, and shortly thereafter was appointed co-chief of the ear clinic recently established in the Allgemeines Krankenhaus. In 1902, he became hofrat professor and in 1907 was retired as professor emeritus.

Having access to the nearly limitless clinical and postmortem material in one of the largest teaching hospitals in central Europe, Politzer made noteworthy contributions in teaching, patient care, investigation, and writing. During his academic years he helped to make Vienna, above all others in the Western World, the recognized center for medical study, especially in the specialties for graduate students. An additional advantage in attracting students from many countries was his fluency in Hungarian, German, English, French, and Italian. Just as pupils came to him from many lands, so patients seeking help from otologic distress came to consult him. Sympathetic and kind to students and patients alike, he bore the hallmark of an outstanding clinician. His delicate touch in the examination and treatment of the ill was equally advantageous in his handling of anatomical specimens and drafting graphic illustrations. This appreciation of the esthetic was evident also in one of his hobbies: he was a connoisseur and a notable collector of etchings and paintings.

In 1865, Politzer's atlas of the tympanic membrane appeared, with colored illustrations prepared from his own preliminary sketches obtained by indirect illumination. The small treatise was translated into English by Mathewson and Newton, the first of several of his works which were thereby made readily available.[2] Judged to be his most important work, *A Text-book of the Diseases of the Ear*[3] appeared in 1878; the fifth edition, the last prepared by Politzer, appeared in 1908. As he approached academic retirement, he was drawn to historical matters; the first volume of his *History of Otolaryngology* was published in 1907, the second in 1913. Other contributions during his active years included a pneumatic device for inflating the middle ear,[4] improvement in tuning-fork tests, use of the otoscope in the diagnosis of seromucous exudate in the tympanic cavity, and investigations in the pathological anatomy of cholesteatoma, congenital deafness, and labyrinthitis. A description of otosclerosis was presented to the First Pan-American Medical Congress in 1893 in a communication entitled, "On a Peculiar Affection of the Labyrinthine Capsule as a Frequent Cause of Deafness."[5]

The following are the histological changes observed in the microscopical sections made from the specimens: The parts surrounding the oval window are transformed into a uniform mass of newly formed osseous tissue. The normal articulations between the stapes and oval window have entirely disappeared. The plate of the stapes is frequently thickened, even to five or six times the normal size. The ossificatory changes begin in the bony labyrinth capsule and extend toward the oval window and the plate of the stapes, sometimes even toward the cochlea and the vestibulum. Sometimes the ossificatory changes only produce partial ossification of the stapedio-vestibular articulation, so that in the same section we find one portion of the articulation ossified and another still membranous. This partial anchylosis explains why the hearing power for a loud voice is still retained in some cases. The newly formed osseous tissue stains more deeply with carmine, and this difference in color enables us to distinguish the pathological tissue from the normal, even with the naked eye. The number of bone corpuscles is usually increased, the lacunar and medullary spaces are generally larger and contain fibrillar tissue, cells, blood-vessels, osteoblasts, and osteoclasts. It may be well to assume that the changes are due to a primary inflammatory process in the labyrinth capsule, producing a formation of new and young osseous tissue, which successively replaces the normal bone, and by extension toward the stapes and other contiguous parts finally causes the important functional changes due to anchylosis of the stapes. These conditions represent one form of progressive deafness.

Politzer left to the otologic fraternity a legacy of clinical accomplishments, a pattern of industry and an example of the dignity of work. His library was bequeathed to his university, while his remarkable collection of histologic and pathologic preparations and illustrations of his own dissections, drawn by pen or pencil, was divided among the Allgemeines Krankenhaus, the University of Budapest, and the Library of the College of Physicians of Philadelphia; in the latter place his series of tympanic membranes are on permanent display in the Mütter Museum. a remarkable collection of nineteenth century normal and pathologic specimens.

1. Alexander, G.: Adam Politzer, *Wien Klin Wschr* 20:1260-1262, 1907.

2. Politzer, A.: *The Membrana Tympani in Health and Disease* (Ger), Vienna: W. Braumuller, 1865, A. Mathewson, and H. G. Newton (trans.), New York: W. Wood & Co., 1869.

3. Politzer, A.: *A Text-book of the Diseases of the Ear* (Ger), 2 vol, Stuttgart: F. Enke, 1878-1882, J. P. Cassells (trans.), Philadelphia: H. C. Lea's Son & Co., 1883.

4. Politzer, A.: Treatment of Diseases of Middle Ear by Inflation (Ger), *Allg Wien Med Ztg* 1:235-236, 260, 1863.

5. Politzer, A.: On a Peculiar Affection of the Labyrinthine Capsule as a Frequent Cause of Deafness, *Trans 1st Panamer Med Congr*, 1893 (pt 3), 1895, pp 1607-1608.

Sir Morell Mackenzie
(1837-1892)

MORELL MACKENZIE was born at Leytonstone, Essex, the eldest son of the surgeon Stephen Mackenzie, and was recognized in his generation as the leading laryngologist of England.[1] He was educated at Dr. Greig's school in Walthamstow and served as a clerk in the Union Assurance Office for a short time before he began the study of medicine at the London Hospital College. After he qualified for membership in the Royal College of Surgeons in 1858, he began postgraduate study in Paris and continued in Vienna, and especially in Budapest, Hungary, where he was instructed by Czermack in the use of the recently-invented laryngoscope. Mackenzie graduated bachelor of medicine from London University in 1861, and a year later, doctor of medicine. Thereafter he established himself as a specialist in diseases of the throat. In succession he won the Jacksonian prize of the Royal College of Surgeons for an essay, "The Pathology of the Larynx," and founded the Hospital for Diseases of the Throat,

Golden Square. He was appointed assistant physician at the London Hospital in 1866 and full physician in 1873.

Mackenzie is rightfully recognized as the founder of modern laryngology in England,

National Library of Medicine

and although he lectured at London Hospital Medical School and prepared long treatises on the subject, he devoted most of his time to private and consultation practice. His best-known text, in two volumes, *A Manual of Diseases of the Throat and Nose*,[2] which appeared in 1880 and 1884, described the fruits of an extremely active life. His description of the laryngeal mirror illustrated with excellent woodcuts appeared in 1865. It began with a résumé of the history of the laryngoscope and was supported by his new methods of examination of the larynx. One of his outstanding technical devices for better visualization and maneuvering of laryngeal instruments was achieved by advancing to a right angle the wide curve of German design.

Mackenzie modified the laryngeal guillotine of Philip Syng Physic, popularized tonsillectomy, and applied the terms abductor and adductor to the paired set of intrinsic muscles of the larynx. An analysis of 100 consecutive cases of tumors was published in 1870 in a monograph entitled "The Larynx." In 1877, he and Wolfenden founded the *Journal of Laryngology* and the following year established the British Rhinolaryngology Association. This merged with the London Laryngology Association in 1907, and became the section of laryngology of the Royal Society of Medicine.

Mackenzie's international reputation led to his being called in consultation in the prime of his career to attend Crown Prince Frederick (later Emperor Frederick III), who suffered from symptoms highly suggestive of cancer of the larynx. Mackenzie was opposed to the surgical regimen as recommended by Frederick's countrymen until a biopsy and microscopic examination of the tissue removed had been performed. After the lesion had been sampled, Virchow reported no malignant cells. In retrospect the tissue very likely was inadequate for so dogmatic a conclusion. Nevertheless, Mackenzie allowed this relatively new technique to overrule his clinical judgment. A few months later when the correct diagnosis became apparent, a palliative tracheotomy was performed but the Emperor died shortly thereafter. In the meantime, Mackenzie's services were recognized with the title of knight bachelor, and he was decorated by the Emperor with the grand cross of the Hohenzollern order. Although Mackenzie held the confidence of the Royal family even after the death of the Emperor, he suffered badly in the hands of the German surgeons for the presumptive incorrect diagnosis. He replied to local and foreign criticism with an ill-advised and angry vindication entitled *The Fatal Illness of Frederick the Noble*. During the heat of the argument he was censored informally by his colleagues and officially by the Royal College of Surgeons and the British Medical Association. He summarized and justified his judgment as follows upon his resignation from the College.[3]

Consoling Reflections.—In looking back on this sad case there are one or two matters which will always be a source of deep satisfaction to me: one is that through the mild and painless operations performed by myself the dangerous methods recommended by Gerhardt and von Bergmann were prevented, and that I thereby not only prolonged the life of the Emperor, but also saved him much suffering. The other point which affords me some consolation is that I was able to prevent His Majesty suffering any actual pain during the long course of his distressing complaint. Even in February, when he was put to so much trouble and inconvenience, when he passed weary days and sleepless nights, whilst von Bergmann and Bramann were in charge of the case after the performance of tracheotomy, the Emperor experienced no actual pain.

1. Haweis, H. R.: Sir Morell Mackenzie, Physician and Operator: A Memoir Compiled From Private Papers and Personal Reminiscences, London: W. H. Allen & Co., Ltd., 1893.

2. Mackenzie, M.: A Manual of Diseases of the Throat and Nose, Including the Pharynx, Larynx, Trachea, Oesophagus, Nose, and Naso-pharynx, London: J. & A. Churchill, 1880 and 1884, vol 1 and 2.

3. Mackenzie, M.: The Fatal Illness of Frederick the Noble, London: Sampson Low, Marston, Searle & Rivington, 1888.

Nathan Smith Davis (1817-1904)

N. S. DAVIS, whose notable accomplishments in medical education and organized medicine extended over one-half century, was born in a log house near Greene, Chenango County, New York, into a pioneer rural family.[1] Although a major portion of his early childhood was given to the farm which his father had homesteaded, Davis attended the village school, and then for a six months' term, the Cazenovia Seminary in Madison County; there he studied English, Latin, chemistry, natural philosophy, and algebra. Without benefit of additional instruction, young Nathan began an apprenticeship in practice in 1834 with Dr. Daniel Clark, of Smithville Flats and continued in the office of Dr. Thomas Jackson of Binghamton, New York. In the meantime, he attended three courses of lectures at the College of Physicians and Surgeons of Western New York at Fairfield, from which he graduated in 1837, three years before the school was disbanded. His thesis, entitled Animal Temperatures, which refuted the prevailing belief that carbon and oxygen combined in the lungs, was one of four selected by the faculty to be read at commencement.

Davis' first postgraduate months, spent in general practice in Vienna, New York, were unappealing. He moved to Binghamton, a somewhat larger community, where his practice developed rapidly; however, it was not so demanding that he could not include regular reading in the natural sciences, classical literature, political economy, and medical jurisprudence, thus providing an opportunity to develop his brilliant and active mind. It was also in Binghamton that Davis displayed his first interest in medical society affairs and began working to improve the standards of medical education, a task later associated with organized medicine on a national scale. He was appointed a delegate to the Broome County Medical Society, served as secretary of the Society from 1841 to 1843, and sometime later was chosen a delegate to the New York State Medical Society, serving until 1846. His initial efforts to improve the quality, expand the quantity of medical education, and strengthen licensure in New York were made known to his associates in 1844, with the hope that other states would follow. His persistence led to the calling of a medical convention in 1846, the predecessor of the American Medical Association. This and other achievements, was responsible for the family's move to New York City in 1847.

Upon beginning practice in Manhattan, Davis began medical editing and instruction to medical students. He was placed in charge of the dissecting rooms of the College of Physicians and Surgeons of Columbia University, taught medical jurisprudence and practical anatomy, and was assistant editor and later editor of the *Annalist*, a semimonthly medical journal. After spending little more than two years in New York, Davis was offered the chair of physiology and general pathology at Rush Medical College. Traveling by railroad, stage, canal boat, and packet, he reached Chicago, which at that time lacked a general hospital for the sick, a general medical society, and a general sewage system. Once he was in the midst of the medical problems of the frontier his perceptive mind recognized the serious deficiencies. By personal and direct efforts, he was largely responsible for a generation of unrest in Chicago medicine which, however, resulted ultimately in great gains.

Davis' lectures began at Rush in October of 1849; the following year his academic title was changed to professor of pathology, practice of medicine and clinical medicine. Before substantial progress was made in improving the curriculum of the school, Davis and a small band of disappointed faculty members resigned in 1859 to found a new medical school, the Medical Department of Lind University. Financial difficulties plagued this venture; the faculty reorganized again in 1864 under the name of Chicago Medical College, with Davis as the president. In 1870, this newly-founded school, under Davis as dean, became the medical department of Northwestern University. The name was changed in 1891 and has continued as the Northwestern University Medical School. Throughout his period of association with Northwestern University, Davis, as a member of the first Board of Trustees, was an imaginative planner for medical school progress and was responsible for many of the advances in medical education that identified the school as a leader in 19th century Midwest medicine.

Mercy Hospital, the first public hospital in Chicago, was the next institution to benefit from Davis and his long-range plans. The hospital was started in 1850 as the Illinois General Hospital of the Great Lakes. To it Davis gave generously of his time—visiting on the wards, teaching medical students, and serving as senior physician on the professional staff, a position held until his death. Meanwhile, his office practice was conducted on a methodical basis; most problems were handled quickly but graciously; whereas the difficult-to-diagnose patients were studied and examined without haste. Continuing to display his zeal for progress in medical practice, he gave strong support to the establishment of the Illinois Medical Society and the Chicago Medical Society. Other worthwhile activities included charter membership in the Illinois State Microscopical Society and the Chicago Academy of Sciences, patron of the Chicago Historical Society, participation in the organization of the Union College of Law as the law department of the [former] University of Chicago and Northwestern University, and one of the founders of the Washingtonian Home.

Medical editing was yet another area of medical industry which Davis resumed shortly after he came to Chicago. He was editor of the *Chicago Medical Journal* from 1855 to 1859, and, as founder of the *Chicago Medical Examiner* in 1860, he served as editor until it merged with the *Chicago Medical Journal* in 1873. At other times he held editorial positions with the *Northwestern Medical and Surgical Journal*, the *Eclectic Journal of Education and Literary Review*, and the *American Medical Temperance Quarterly*. More significant than each of these, however, was his intimate relation with the *Journal of the American Medical Association*.

The proposal for a weekly medical journal to replace the annual volume of the *Transactions* was first suggested by Dr. Samuel D. Gross of Philadelphia at the Annual Meeting of the American Medical Association held in 1870. This was not acted upon until more than a decade later when a resolution offered by Davis was adopted in 1882 at the Annual Meeting in St. Paul. Davis resigned as a Trustee, was chosen editor of *JAMA*, first issue of which appeared on the 14th of July, 1883. He reluctantly retired from the post five years later because of ceaseless demands from his teaching, private practice, and multiple civic interests, including the abolition of alcoholic beverages and social and sanitary reform.

The events surrounding the founding of the American Medical Association include another of Davis' great efforts. Although not the first to suggest the need for a national medical association, he was the first to have his resolutions implemented. At the annual meeting of the Medical Society of the State of New York in Albany in 1844, Davis offered a series of resolutions designed to raise the standards of general education for students preparing for the study of medicine, to extend the period of medical instruction, and to grant licenses for the practice of medicine by state boards independent of the medical colleges. The resolutions were held over until the meeting in 1845 when they were taken from the table, favorably received, and approved as follows:[2]

WHEREAS, it is believed that a National Convention would be conducive to the elevation of the standard of medical education in the United States; and whereas, there is no mode of accomplishing so desirable an object without concert of action on the part of the medical colleges, societies, and institutions of all the States, therefore,

Resolved, That the New York State Medical Society earnestly recommends a National Convention of delegates from medical societies and colleges in the whole Union, to convene in the city of New York, on the first Tuesday in May, in the year 1846, for the purpose of adopting some concerted action on the subject set forth in the foregoing preamble.

Resolved, That a committee of three be appointed to carry the foregoing resolution into effect.

At the meeting of the National Medical Convention on May 5, 1846, held pursuant to the call of the New York State Medical Society, preliminary matters were handled, and, in addition to the appointment of a committee whose duty it was to report at the next annual meeting to be held in Philadelphia in 1847, the following resolutions were approved.[3]

1st. Resolved, That it is expedient for the Medical Profession of the United States, to institute a National Medical Association, . . .

4th. Resolved, That it is desirable that a uniform and elevated standard of requirements for the degree of M.D., should be adopted by all the Medical Schools in the United States, . . .

5th. Resolved, That it is desirable that young men before being received as students of Medicine, should have acquired a suitable preliminary education; . . .

6th. Resolved, That it is expedient that the Medical Profession in the United States should be governed by the same code of Medical Ethics, . . .

The last official preparatory action occurred on May 5, 1847, when approximately 250 delegates from 22 of the 26 states then constituting the United States, representing more than 40 medical societies and 28 medical schools, assembled in Philadelphia in the con-

fines of the Academy of Natural Sciences. One delegate was allowed to each regularly organized medical society for every ten resident members, and each medical school faculty was allotted two delegates. The duly constituted committees reported on the constitution and by-laws and the code of ethics. Subsequently, the convention resolved itself into the American Medical Association, which recommended a slate of officers including Dr. Nathaniel Chapman of Philadelphia for president. After members were appointed to the several standing committees, as required by the constitution, it was agreed to hold the next Annual Meeting in Baltimore on the first Tuesday in May, 1848—the first announced meeting of the American Medical Association. The deliberations and scientific reports were recorded annually in the *Transactions*, which were published until 1882; then *The Journal of the American Medical Association* became the official medium. During this time Davis maintained an intimate working relationship with the American Medical Association, missed few of its regular meetings, and served in 1865 as the elected President during the Annual Session held in the State House in Boston.

Davis was a total abstainer and an unremitting crusader against alcohol. He preached temperance to his medical students, served as president of the American Medical Temperance Association in 1901, and was an active supporter of the Washingtonian Home for Inebriates in Chicago. In his presidential address to the Temperance Association, published as the lead communication in *JAMA*, his thoughts were summarized as follows.[4]

That the daily or habitual use of alcoholic drinks, even in moderate doses, not only impairs both health and morals and leads to slow tissue degenerations, but also so impairs the metabolic and nutritive processes as to render the individual more liable to attacks of all acute infectious diseases, and more liable to die when attacked, has been fully demonstrated not only in the laboratory of the scientists, but also in every field of human labor and in every variety of climate.

That the alcohol, as it exists in fermented and distilled liquors, is a positive protoplasmic poison, directly impairing every natural structure and function of the living body in proportion to the quantity used, and the length of time its use is continued, is proved by the results of every experimental investigation concerning it, instituted by eminent scientific men, both in this country and Europe.

Their verdict is abundantly confirmed by the history and condition of the inmates of every asylum for the poor, the feeble-minded, the epileptics, the insane and the inebriates; those of every reformatory and prison; by the records of every police and criminal court; and by the details of every well-kept registry of vital statistics. As concerns danger to human life, every intelligent reader of the public press knows that the ordinary use of alcoholic liquors by persons claiming to be in health, is the direct cause of more suicides, homicides and murders every month, than is produced by all the other poisons known to toxicologists in a year.

Davis displayed tireless energy and capitalized on every moment of his waking hours. He had a large consulting practice among the less fortunate as well as among the well-to-do, with fees in proportion to ability to pay. His portrait shows the face of a serious man, with penetrating eyes and a ruff of neck whiskers. Many of his communications on clinical medicine appeared in current medical periodicals, and included the *Transactions* and *The Journal of the American Medical Association*. In addition to the monograph already noted, he published *A Textbook on Agriculture* (1848), *History of Medical Education and Institutions in the United States* (1851), *Clinical Lectures on Various Important Diseases* (1873), *Lectures on the Principles and Practice of Medicine* (1884), and *The History of Medicine, With the Code of Ethics* (1903). Davis was equally interested and equally competent in practice, teaching, writing, promoting and founding institutions; undoubtedly he was the most important physician in Chicago medicine in the 19th century.

1. Danforth, I. N.: *The Life of Nathan Smith Davis,* Chicago: Cleveland Press, 1907.
2. Davis, N. S.: *History of the American Medical Association,* Philadelphia: Lippincott, Grambo & Co., 1855.
3. *Proceedings of the National Medical Conventions, held in New York, May, 1846, and in Philadelphia, May, 1847,* Philadelphia: T. K. & P. G. Collins, 1847.
4. Davis, N. S.: Poverty and Degeneracy: Their Cause, Prevention and Cure, *JAMA* 37:1-3 (July 6) 1901.

National Library of Medicine

Sir Francis Galton (1822-1911)

FRANCIS GALTON was born in Birmingham, England, into a Quaker family of fortune and great ability in real estate, business, and professional pursuits. After a classical education, Francis studied medicine in the Birmingham General Hospital and completed a year of formal training at King's College, London.[1] At the age of 18, he abandoned medicine and entered Trinity College, Cambridge; there he showed an interest in meteorology, geography, fingerprinting, and psychology, but especially in mathematics, the first indication of devotion to a subject fundamental to his lifetime contributions in statistics and heredity. He received an ordinary degree at Cambridge and did not apply for honors.

After graduation, and finding himself in comfortable circumstances, Galton was free to pursue scientific interests, wherever they led. He first achieved a reputation as an explorer and geographer, taking an ambitious voyage into southwest equatorial Africa through uncharted country largely unknown to the civilized world. His exploration was described in *Tropical South Africa* (1853), followed by a useful handbook, *The Art of Travel* (1855).[2] Largely on the basis of these works, Galton was elected a Fellow of the Royal Society, to which he gave liberally of his time in council activities. In connection with his experiences in Africa, he discussed adroitness in the bush in terms of speed of pursuer and pursued as follows.[3]

THE RUSH OF AN ENRAGED ANIMAL is far more easily avoided than is usually supposed. The way the Spanish bull-fighters play with the bull, is well known; any man can avoid a mere headlong charge. . . . The speed of an ordinary horse is not more than 24 miles an hour; now even the fastest wild beast is unable to catch an ordinary horse, except by crawling unobserved to his side, and springing upon him; therefore I am convinced that the rush of no wild beast exceeds 24 miles an hour, or three times the speed of a man. . . . It is perfectly easy for a person who is cool, to avoid an animal by dodging to one side or another of a bush. Few animals turn, if the rush be unsuccessful. The buffalo is an exception; he regularly hunts a man, and is therefore peculiarly dangerous. Unthinking persons talk of the fearful rapidity of a lion's or tiger's spring. It is not rapid at all; it is a slow movement, as must be evident from the following consideration. No wild animal can leap ten yards, and they all make a high trajectory in their leaps. Now think of the speed of a ball thrown or rather pitched, with just sufficient force to be caught by a person ten yards off; it is a mere nothing. The catcher can play with it as he likes; he has even time to turn after it, if thrown wide. But the speed of a springing animal is undeniably the same as that of a ball, thrown so as to make a flight of equal length and height in the air. The corollary to all this is that if charged, you must keep cool and watchful, and your chance of escape is far greater than nonsportsmen would imagine.

From geography, Galton turned to meteorology and, in 1863, published *Meteorographica*, a treatise on mapping the weather. He was one of the first to note the importance of anticyclones and the clockwise circulation of air about a high pressure center in the northern hemisphere. This formed a basis of weather forecasting which has not become obsolete a century later.

Only in his late forties, at an age when his associates were in their prime of intellectual achievement, was Galton beginning to take seriously the statistical tabulation of human attributes and the investigation of the laws of heredity. In this area his best work was done and a great reputation subsequently gained. Several reasons have been offered for his de-

layed entry into the science in which his best-known accomplishments were made. He loved out-of-door sports, suffered from periods of ill health, and, as a wealthy country gentleman, worked only when he chose.

A growing interest in heredity was related to the publication of the *Origin of Species*, by Charles Darwin, a cousin of his mother. Galton's *Hereditary Genius*, a compilation of biographical data of men of eminence, appeared in 1869. He observed that superior mental ability recurred in families, sometimes in a specific form, such as in the sciences, law, arts, business. The proportion of descendants of stature in families exceeded that expected by mathematical chance. His conclusions, based largely upon statistical data, disregarded in such persons opportunities for education, socioeconomic status, and scholarly influence of eminent friends and relatives. Galton included in his review men of renown—judges, statesmen, English peers, commanders, litterateurs, scientists, poets, musicians, painters, clergymen, as well as oarsmen and wrestlers. The comparative worth of different races and influences that affected the natural ability of nations concluded the monograph. In the preface he states:[4]

I began by thinking over the dispositions and achievements of my contemporaries at school, at college, and in after life, and was surprised to find how frequently ability seemed to go by descent. Then I made a cursory examination into the kindred of about four hundred illustrious men of all periods of history, and the results were such, in my own opinion, as completely to establish the theory that genius was hereditary, under limitations that required to be investigated. Thereupon I set to work to gather a large amount of carefully selected biographical data.

The theory of hereditary genius, though usually scouted, has been advocated by a few writers in past as well as in modern times. But I may claim to be the first to treat the subject in a statistical manner, to arrive at numerical results, and to introduce the "law of deviation from an average" into discussions on heredity.

A study of lesser importance concerned the impression of fingers, which came from his anthropometric laboratory established at the International Health Exhibition of 1884–1885. The program was designed to collect statistics on sensory acuteness, height, weight, and other physical measurements of large numbers of people. It proved to be the predecessor of the biometric laboratory at University College, London. In the investigative process Galton confirmed earlier observations of others on the permanence of finger marking and prepared a dictionary of personal identity. He pointed out their value in identifying criminals in his *Finger Prints*. The study was statistical, dealing with the frequency of the several kinds of patterns, and, on the basis of binomial calculation, Galton concluded that the prints of the ten digits of no two persons were identical.[5]

The palms of the hands and the soles of the feet are covered with two totally distinct classes of marks. The most conspicuous are the creases or folds of the skin which interest the followers of palmistry, but which are no more significant to others than the creases in old clothes; they show the lines of most frequent flexure, and nothing more.

The least conspicuous marks, but the most numerous by far, are the so-called papillary ridges; they form the subject of the present book.

But the value to honest men is always great of being able to identify offenders, whether they be merely deserters or formerly convicted criminals, and the method of finger prints is shown to be applicable to that purpose. . . . But whenever two suspected duplicates of measurements, bodily marks, photographs and finger prints have to be compared, the lineations of the finger prints would give an incomparably more trustworthy answer to the question, whether or no the suspicion of their referring to the same person was justified, than all the rest put together.

The statistical law of ancestral heredity, mentioned initially in his monograph on *Natural Inheritance* (1889), embodied the generally recognized share of parents and grandparents and more remote ancestors in bisexual descent.[6]

The law to be verified may seem at first sight too artificial to be true, but a closer examination shows that prejudice arising from the cursory impression is unfounded. This subject will be alluded to again, in the meantime the law shall be stated. It is that the two parents contribute between them on the average one-half, or (0.5) of the total heritage of the offspring; the four grandparents, one-quarter, or $(0.5)^2$; the eight-grandparents, one-eighth, or $(0.5)^3$, and so on. Thus the sum of the ancestral contributions is expressed by the series $\{(0.5) + (0.5)^2 + (0.5)^3, \text{etc.}\}$, which, being equal to 1, accounts for the whole heritage.

It should be noted that nothing in this statistical law contradicts the generally accepted view that the chief, if not the sole, line of descent runs from germ to germ and not from person to person. The person may be accepted on the whole as a fair representative of the germ, and, being so, the statistical laws which apply

to the persons would apply to the germs also, though with less precision in individual cases. Now this law is strictly consonant with the observed binary subdivisions of the germ cells, and the concomitant extrusion and loss of one-half of the several contributions from each of the two parents to the germ-cell of the offspring.

Galton's investigation required greater knowledge of the fundamentals of statistics than he possessed; therefore, it remained for others, particularly his most famous pupil Karl Pearson, author of a four-volume work entitled *The Life, Letters and Labours of Francis Galton*,[3] to complete the development of statistical methods which have remained valid and useful. In this area, Galton showed that the degree of relationship between any pair of individuals may be calculated from a numerical factor, termed the "correlation." The method was applied to variations in physical qualities, such as stature and head length, and head length and head breadth.

Galton, who was consulting editor to *Biometrika*, coined the term, "eugenics," founded eugenic societies, and established a eugenics laboratory.[7]

The word "Eugenics" was coined and used by me in my book *Human Faculty*, published as long ago as 1883. . . . In it I emphasized the essential brotherhood of mankind, heredity being to my mind a very real thing; also the belief that we are born to act, and not wait for help like able-bodied idlers, whining for doles.

In his will, Galton established a foundation for a chair of eugenics in the University of London; its first occupant was Karl Pearson. Many honors were received, including medals from the English and French Geographical Societies, the Huxley medal of the Anthropological Institute, the Darwin and Copley medals of the Royal Society, the Darwin-Wallace medal of the Linnaean Society, honorary DCL from Oxford and DSC from Cambridge. He was knighted two years before his death.

1. Galton, F.: *Memories of My Life*, New York: E. P. Dutton & Co., 1909.
2. Galton, F.: *The Art of Travel*, London: J. Murray, 1855.
3. Pearson, K.: *The Life, Letters and Labours of Francis Galton*, 4 vol, Cambridge: University Press, 1924.
4. Galton, F.: *Hereditary Genius*, London: MacMillan & Co., 1869.
5. Galton, F.: *Finger Prints*, London: MacMillan & Co., 1892.

6. Galton, F.: The Average Contribution of Each Several Ancestor to Total Heritage of the Offspring, *Proc Roy Soc Lond* 61:401-413, 1897.

7. Galton, F.: *Probability, the Foundation of Eugenics,* Oxford: Clarendon Press, 1907.

Composite by G. Bako

John Chapman (1822-1894)

JOHN CHAPMAN, popular socialite in Victorian England (especially among economic and political reformers before he took medicine seriously), was born in Nottingham, the son of a chemist. Nor were his contributions in the practice of medicine or medical writing commensurate with his works as publisher and editor or with his eminence among the advanced writers and philosophers of the times as appraised by Poynter.[1] Most of Chapman's youth was spent at the village of Ruddington before he was apprenticed to a watchmaker of Worksop. This venture soon lost its appeal, and he sought asylum with his eldest brother studying medicine in Edinburgh; the latter subsequently provided money and supplies to set him up as a watchmaker and optician in Adelaide, Australia. Chapman was not destined for business in small wares, however, and he returned to train for medicine first in St. Bartholomew's Hospital and later in Paris.

By 1843, Chapman described himself as a "surgeon"; but his practice in London must have failed to thrive, for he found time to prepare a manuscript on human nature and a discussion of the divine institution of reward and punishment, which was presented for publication to John Green of Newgate Street. Green was less interested in publishing the book than in selling the business to the young practitioner. With financial help from his wife, Chapman took over Green's established business and, at the age of 22, became a publisher for his own and other books. Pursuing a dominant interest in the literary world, he became editor and owner of the *Westminster Review* seven years later. Meanwhile, he leased a large house at 142 Strand, where office and private living quarters were combined with a social center and hotel accommodations for American and English literary greats.

Ralph Waldo Emerson was one of the first Americans to enjoy Chapman's hospitality while negotiating for the publication of an English edition of his poems. Other transients from America included Horace Greeley, W. C. Bryant, and G. P. Putnam. English writers who gathered at Chapman's home included Dickens, Thackeray, Carlyle, J. S. Mill, Browning, Herbert Spencer, George Combe, G. H. Lewes, and especially Mary Ann Evans. Later she took the pen name of George Eliot and became an associate in his publishing work and editorial affairs and an intimate in his notorious promiscuity. Endowed with great literary capacity, George Eliot developed from an unsophisticated country girl into the most famous Englishwoman of her day, largely through Chapman's attention. She prepared a number of essays for his *Westminster Review* and, in 1854, granted him publication rights to the translation of *The Essence of Christianity by Ludwig Feuerbach*, the only book which carries her legal name.[2]

By his early thirties, Chapman had approached the zenith of his influence as an entrepreneur of scholars and publisher of the works of rebellious philosophers and litterateurs. Thereupon he took up medicine seriously, attended lectures at University College and King's College, pursued clinical work at St. George's Hospital, and, in 1857, upon the payment of a fee, procured the MD degree from St. Andrew's University. Later in the same year, Chapman became a licentiate of the Royal College of Physicians and, in three years, a member of the Royal College of Surgeons. Even before he resumed his medical training, he had published his aversion to medical despotism in the *Westminster Review*, a tirade against restriction of the personal liberties of the physician as incited by the proposed legislation on medical reform.[3]

Between the belief in the divine right of kings and the recognition of the sovereignty of the individual, is an interval so vast, that mankind takes ages to traverse it. In the mean time, every government conceives itself commissioned to regulate the private life of its citizens, and does not hesitate, for the sake of achieving a doubtful and even temporary benefit, to sacrifice permanently their personal freedom. In curing one malady, statesmen, as well as doctors, too often cause another; and still oftener their remedial attempts, while inflicting great suffering, fail of their object altogether. But, despite the lessons of experience, a profound belief in the might and efficacy of legislation is everywhere cherished. No sooner does an evil show itself, than we exclaim, "Why does not the Government put it down?" Education, opinions, creeds, conduct, must all be regulated by statute. So provident is Parliament, even now, for our individual welfare, that it strives to secure it for us in the next world as well as in the present, and upholds a costly hierarchy to guard us from eternal perdition.

Chapman's exhortations of extreme liberalism and crusades for reform in the mid-1880's seem moderate in today's forum on control of medical practice. This is illustrated in his *The Medical Institutions of the United Kingdom*, prepared after passage of the Medical Act of 1858. He advanced the argument, well documented historically, of the evils of over-legislation. He appealed to the public, to the Ministry, and to Parliament to become familiar with the medical organizations and the practice of medicine in the United Kingdom; they would then appreciate the need for enlightened legislation that would replace the Medical Act of 1858, judged to be a "heavy chain on the otherwise free life of the professional body."

In April, 1856, we expressed at length our objections to the *forcible* constitution of any central council whatever as a governmental organ for exercising supreme

jurisdiction over the profession of surgery and medicine, and recommended the simple expedient of severing the connexion of all medical bodies with the State.

What is really wanted is less, not more, Government interference; the possibility of vigorous activity, not the petrifying influence of another Act of Parliament prescribing rules and regulations for the conduct of a body of men who, as a profession, are the most scientific in the Kingdom, and who, in respect to medical education, being infinitely better qualified to determine from time to time what is needful than Parliament ever can be, ought to be ashamed either to ask or to accept its help. No educational scheme adopted in any particular year, or by any one Medical Corporation, or even Medical Council, can long satisfy an eminently progressive body like that of the medical profession.

. . . complete separation of the medical profession from the State, is the one which has our entire and earnest support. We firmly believe that it is open to no well-grounded objections, that indirectly it would cause the complete removal of all the evils of which the Profession has long and rightly complained, that it would result in the spontaneous organization of the Medical Body in a manner far more perfect than has ever yet been exemplified, or than is ever possible by governmental agency, and that, as a result of these organic changes, the public would be supplied with medical men better qualified for the performance of the duties devolving upon them, than is possible either under the present system, or under any of the others which we have passed in review.

Similar "liberal" views were expressed in Chapman's monograph on *Medical Charity: Its Abuses and How to Remedy Them*.[5]

But there are two kinds of charity: one seeing clearly into the character and conditions of its objects, the other blind; one wise, the other foolish; one beneficent, the other injurious. Clairvoyant, wise and beneficent charity raises its objects, . . . calls forth in them a spirit of independence; but blind, foolish, and injurious charity, even while temporarily benefiting its recipients, permanently degrades them: not perceiving the real nature of its applicants, it gives to those who are not really in need, and those who may be needing only temporary help, it . . . gives to those who clamour most, and neglects those who, being too modest or too feeble to make themselves heard amid the crowd of competitors for its favours, suffer in silence; it discourages thrift and prudence; it induces habits of carelessness, improvidence, and helplessness; and it both generates and fosters that spirit of dependence which is the chief source of pauperism in this country.

Medical pauperism, as we have now described it, certainly prevails in the metropolis and in all the large towns of Great Britain on an immense scale; and the question arises, Does this special kind of pauperism tend to induce complete pauperism on a scale sufficiently large to cause any appreciable rise in the poor-rates? It may perhaps be impossible to present absolutely indisputable proofs that it does, but facts and considerations bearing on the subject compel every one, we believe, who gives due attention to it to conclude that the habit of receiving gratuitous medical relief and that of receiving parish relief stand to each other, in a vast number of instances, in the relation of cause and effect.

All physicians and surgeons of dispensaries and of the out-patient departments of hospitals cannot fail to be impressed with the striking change in the demeanour of many patients who have become habitual recipients of medical charity. When they apply for it on the first occasion they evince shame and compunction, apologize for coming to the hospital or dispensary at all, and in some cases, indeed, give satisfactory proofs that they have maintained their independence as long as they could; but when once they have experienced how easy it is to get medical advice and medicine without paying for either, and when they find in the waiting-room many persons whose positions in life are similar to their own, their views respecting medical charity are modified: they begin to think themselves quite proper objects of it, and soon, instead of the hesitating diffidence and apologetic manner which they manifested when applying for gratuitous relief in the first instance, they evince a comfortable self-assurance and consciousness of being entitled to the medical aid they ask for, which could scarcely be more pronounced if they had paid a guinea on the occasion of each visit. It is readily conceivable that they who have become habitual recipients of medical charity, and have thus deadened their feelings of independence, are easily tempted to take the further step of applying for parochial charity also.

Although Chapman will never be remembered for any significant discoveries in clinical medicine or fundamental science, he was no dilettante. He published more than a dozen monographs on clinical medicine or medical subjects and, as a practicing physician, attempted to explain disease upon carefully considered fundamental principles of the new physiology. The fact that his speculations proved false and his theories could not be confirmed seems less important a century later than his recognition, well documented today, of the psychological features of organic disease and the presumption that the physician should be a psychologist and a moral philosopher to be of maximum help to his patients. His interest in applying the new physiology of Claude Bernard and Brown-Sequard led to his theory of control of the circulation to the spinal area of the blood in different parts of the body by application of heat or cold by means of a long rubber bag (Chapman's bag). This theoretical concept of the pathogenesis and treatment of disease was recommended by him especially for seasickness, diabetes,

cholera, diarrhea, and epilepsy. He speculated as follows:[6]

I have discovered that a controlling power over the circulation of the blood in the brain, in the spinal cord, in the ganglia of the sympathetic nervous system, and, through the agency of these nervous centres, also in every other organ of the body, can be exercised by means of cold and heat applied to different parts of the back. In this manner the reflex excitability, or excito-motor power of the spinal cord, and the contractile force of the arteries in all parts of the body can be immediately modified.

In order to lessen the excito-motor power of the spinal cord only, I apply ice in an india-rubber bag about two inches wide along that part of the spinal column containing the part of the cord on which I wish to act. On the same principle, the vitality of the spinal cord may be increased by applying hot water and ice alternately, each in an india-rubber bag, if very energetic action be required; if less vigorous action be necessary, I apply ice, or iced water only, using it several times a day, for a short time on each occasion, with a long interval between each application.

Chapman left London for Paris in 1874, where he continued to practice medicine, largely confined to the English colony. Five years later he took on a second wife, having long since been emotionally separated from his first wife. His home continued to be a center for radicals—English, American, and French. Approximately a year before his death he was hit by a taxicab and suffered injuries which contributed to his death. His remains were buried in Highgate Cemetery, London, adjacent to George Eliot's grave.

1. Poynter, F.: John Chapman (1821-1894) Publisher, Physician, and Medical Reformer, *J Hist Med* 1:1-22, 1950.

2. Haight, G.: *George Eliot and John Chapman, With Chapman's Diaries*, New Haven, Conn: Yale University Press, 1940.

3. Chapman, J.: Medical Despotism, *Westminster Rev* 65:530-562, 1856.

4. Chapman, J.: *The Medical Institutions of the United Kingdom: A History Exemplifying the Evils of Over-Legislation*, London: J. Churchill & Sons, 1870, reprinted from *Med Mirror*, 1869-1870, no. 7-13.

5. Chapman, J.: *Medical Charity: Its Abuses, and How to Remedy Them*, London: Trüber & Co., 1874.

6. Chapman, J.: A New Method of Treating Disease by Controlling the Circulation of the Blood in Different Parts of the Body, *Med Times Gaz* 2:60-62 (July 18) 1863.

Composite by G. Bako

Arthur Conan Doyle (1859-1930)

ARTHUR CONAN DOYLE, physician, novelist, athlete, soldier, historian, and spiritualist, will be remembered primarily for his recounting of the detective exploits of Sherlock Holmes. This is considered by some to be his self-portrait and Holmes is certainly one of the most famous characters in contemporary world literature. Doyle, born in Edinburgh, was raised in a large family of meager financial means. His ancestors came of Anglo-Norman stock and had lived in Ireland for several generations.[1] His grandfather was the great caricaturist, John Doyle; his uncle, Richard Doyle, designed the cover for *Punch;* while his father, a civil servant and an artist of rare talent, supplemented his income by painting and illustrating. Doyle's boyhood and elementary education exemplified Spartan austerity.

After a year in a Jesuit school of Vorarlberg, Austria, Doyle entered the University of Edinburgh as a medical student at the age of 17. He paid his tuition by serving as a practitioner's assistant when not in school, played on the university Rugby team, became a capable amateur boxer, and spent several months as ship's surgeon on a whaler in the Arctic. His talents for spinning tales were apparent even before graduation. He received a modest fee for his first short story "The Mystery of the Sassassa Valley," published in *Chambers' Journal.* Near the close of 1881, Doyle received the degree of bachelor of medicine from Edinburgh and, in 1885, the MD degree upon presentation of a thesis entitled, *On Vasomotor Influence in Tabes Dorsalis.*

After graduation, Doyle served as ship's surgeon to West Africa, followed by a miserable experience in attempting to establish a practice. Initially, he joined George Budd, a classmate whom he called "Cullingworth" in *The Stark Munro Letters,* in practice in Southsea (Plymouth) but later decided to practice independently in Portsmouth. Although the serious attempts to establish a practice were unrewarding and unexciting, complicated by the need to contribute to his parents' subsistence as well as his own, his nonmedical writing was not long in bringing him fame and funds. His concluding ventures in medicine included a visit to Koch's laboratory in Berlin, a few months of postgraduate study in Paris and Vienna, and a brief period of practice as an eye specialist. The final attempt at private practice proved unrewarding after three months, but by then his literary success was secure.

In 1887, Doyle introduced Sherlock Holmes and Dr. Watson to the public, patterning the detective activities of Holmes after Doyle's teacher, Dr. Joseph Bell, surgeon to the Edinburgh infirmary. Bell had pursued each clinical diagnosis as an adroit criminal investigator, speculating on occupation, heredity, character, etc., in addition to clinical symptoms.[2] Doyle's biographers also assume that he was inspired by Emile Gaboriau and M. Dupin, the latter Edgar Allen Poe's scientific sleuth. The final adventure of Sherlock Holmes appeared in 1927. The period of 40 years was interrupted by an unsuccessful attempt to close this series by killing Holmes, but not for long, since the public demanded more of his adventures, and he reappeared in one of Doyle's best detective stories, *The Hound of the Baskervilles.* The later tales, as viewed retrospectively, suffered in comparison with the earlier compositions, but the appeal to readers continued.

Holmes and Dr. Watson first met in *A Study in Scarlet*, when the two agreed to share a suite at 221B Baker Street. Watson's appraisal of Holmes began as follows.[2]

Sherlock Holmes—his limits

1. Knowledge of Literature.—Nil.
2. "   " Philosophy.—Nil.
3. "   " Astronomy.—Nil.
4. "   " Politics.—Feeble.
5. "   " Botany.—Variable.
   Well up in belladonna, opium, and poisons generally. Knows nothing of practical gardening.
6. Knowledge of Geology.—Practical, but limited. Tells at a glance different soils from each other. After walks has shown me splashes upon his trousers, and told me by their colour and consistence in what part of London he had received them.
7. Knowledge of Chemistry.—Profound.
8. "   " Anatomy.—Accurate, but unsystematic.
9. "   " Sensational Literature.—Immense. He appears to know every detail of every horror perpetrated in the century.
10. Plays the violin well.
11. Is an expert singlestick player, boxer, and swordsman.
12. Has a good practical knowledge of British law.
    When I had got so far in my list I threw it into the fire in despair. "If I can only find what the fellow is driving at by reconciling all these accomplishments, and discovering a calling which needs them all," I said to myself, "I may as well give up the attempt at once."

The tools placed in Holmes's hands were middle 19th century instruments, a magnifying glass, a tape measure, a hunting crop, a revolver, and a double-billed cap. Doyle's deductive reasoning was thoroughly practical and world famous. The Egyptian and pre-Communist Chinese police used his works for instruction, and the Federal Bureau of Investigation of the United States incorporated his methods for detection of crime. Although his success as a detective story writer might have satisfied the less gifted, he confessed his desire to be recognized as an historian of military affairs in preference.

Doyle was more than a military buff. He served as a correspondent in several campaigns, was recognized as a ballistics expert, and planned and organized the British Volunteer System, the forerunner of the Homeguard. He served as a war correspondent with Kitchener's engagements in Egypt in 1896 and participated in the South African rebellion as a senior physician of the Langman Field Hospital. His book, *The Great Boer War*, which went through 16 editions, is the authoritative history of the campaign. He also prepared a brochure, "The Cause and Conduct of the War in South Africa," which was designed to counteract the criticism of the British in their expeditionary operations. With the outbreak of World War I, Doyle organized the first volunteer force in Sussex and joined the ranks as a private. He received recognition from his government later for his talents and performance and was permitted roving reconnaissance of the French and Italian fronts. After a armistice, he prepared a six-volume compendium, *History of the British Campaign in France and Flanders*, but the public failed to accord him distinguished historian status.

Through many of his writings he utilized his background of medicine, discussing such diverse subjects as angina pectoris, typhoid fever, fracture of the skull, psychiatric manifestations, epilepsy, opium and cocaine addiction, hypertension, stroke, genetics, tuberculosis, and poisoning by gases or chemicals. In the first short story "Behind the Times" in his *Round the Red Lamp* he gives a description of his family doctor, accoucheur to his mother.[3]

He has the healing touch—that magnetic thing which defies explanation or analysis, but which is a very evident fact none the less. His mere presence leaves the patient with more hopefulness and vitality. The sight of disease affects him as dust does a careful housewife. It makes him angry and impatient. "Tut, tut, this will never do!" he cries, as he takes over a new case. He would shoo death out of the room as though he were an intrusive hen. But when the intruder refuses to be dislodged, when the blood moves more slowly and the eyes grow dimmer, then it is that Dr. Winter is of more avail than all the drugs in his surgery. Dying folk cling to his hand as if the presence of his bulk and vigour gives them more courage to face the change; and that kindly, wind-beaten face has been the last earthly impression which many a sufferer has carried into the unknown.

Doyle was knighted in 1902 and received an honorary degree from Edinburgh in 1905. As a humanitarian he supported those who had suffered injustice, whether at home or in the Belgian Congo. Following World War I, his interest in spiritualism sent him on a lecture tour of England and America and the writing of several books. He wrote a few plays, while several novels were adapted for the legitimate theater or for motion pictures. *The Story of Waterloo*, his best play, lacked the appeal of the adventures of Sherlock Holmes. His two volumes of poems *Songs of Action* and *Songs of the Road* were better received. Doyle's style of writing was straightforward and clean, without tricks of composition or intrusions of nosology. His skill in composition and love for writing overshadowed what might have been a successful career in medicine and produced one of the most widely read and most successful novelists of this century. His literary output exceeded 70 books. Doyle was a man of many interests, successful in most, a romantic novelist who lived a romantic life.

1. Carr, J. D.: *The Life of Sir Arthur Conan Doyle*, New York: Harper & Brothers, 1949.
2. Doyle, A. C.: *The Complete Sherlock Holmes*, Garden City, N. Y.: Doubleday & Co., Inc., 1930.
3. Doyle, A. C.: *Round the Red Lamp. Being Facts and Fancies of Medical Life*, London: Methuen & Co., 1894.

William Somerset Maugham (1874-1965)

W. SOMERSET MAUGHAM, judged by some critics to be the most successful of the coterie of 20th century novelists trained in medicine (shared honors with A. J. Cronin and A. C. Doyle), was born in Paris, the son of a solicitor to the British Embassy. His paternal ancestors were Celts who had emigrated from Ireland to the Lake district of England and had become gentlemen farmers and government officials. Maugham's mother also was well born, but died from tuberculosis when her son was only eight.[1] Following his mother's death, he was taken out of the French school he was attending and was tutored in English. After two years of instruction, and his father's death, he came for several years under the charge of an uncle, the Reverend Henry Maugham, vicar of All Saints' Church in Whitstable, Kent. During the interminably long interlude at the vicarage, he completed his primary education in the King's School in Canterbury, spent two winters for his health on the French Riviera, and audited courses

for an academic year at the University of Heidelberg. This was the most miserable period of his life prior to his declining years. It was the period, also, when a growing love for literature provided the setting for a number of his later writings.

Composite by G. Bako

Maugham was small of stature, afflicted with poor health, shy to a critical degree, and stammered badly. He rebelled against the religious dogma of his adopted household and longed for the happiness and freedom of his youth in France. By the time of his return from Germany, he had settled upon writing as a career but was reluctant to admit this in the vicarage. Instead he chose medicine and entered St. Thomas' Medical School in 1892. By then he had gained release from the bondage of his home, had forsaken the "narrow" creeds of Anglicanism, and had acquired a lust for travel and an amoral philosophy.

In medical school, Maugham used his spare time for reading English and European literature and making notes for development later into stories and plays. Life in the Lambeth slums showed him the depths of misery and despair; the hospital outpatient department provided a plethora of physical and emotional misery. While an extern in the obstetrical service, he delivered more than 50 infants and drafted his first novel, *Liza of Lambeth*.[2] This was published in 1897, the year that he became a member of the Royal College of Surgeons, a licentiate of the Royal College of Physicians, and the succession to a substantial legacy from his uncle. *Liza of Lambeth* described the terminal months of a factory girl, a sympathetic and light study of a short and happy love affair, and an appraisal of the slums without resentment. A lack of interest in the practice of medicine, if he ever showed any, and the success of this novel established his professional future.

Having settled in a flat in London, he devoted the following decade largely to writing of novels, but published a few short stories. His first play, *Lady Frederick*, became an immediate success in 1907. With his reputation and income assured, he wrote as he pleased, short or long plays, more than 25 in all, which were so popular that in one season he had four plays running at one time in London. But with success there came a change in his writings from the sympathy and humor displayed in *Liza* to cynicism or contempt, which brought out the weaknesses and sometimes the worst in his characters, as illustrated in *Of Human Bondage*.[3] This appeared in 1915, a revision of an earlier manuscript, *The Artistic Temperament of Stephen Carey*. It was admittedly autobiographical of his life in the vicarage, the story of a cripple with physical and emotional weaknesses. The British critics were neutral, and the sale was modest until Theodore Dreiser's review in the *New York Nation* called the attention of the literary world to its greatness. Scarcely appreciated at home, it was "discovered" in America.

With the outbreak of World War I, Maugham served for a few months with a Red Cross ambulance unit in France, followed by an assignment in Switzerland as a British intelligence agent; there his knowledge of French, German, and Italian was most helpful. In the fall of 1917, he was sent on a mission to Russia in an attempt to persuade her to stay in the war against Germany; while in the winter of 1917, he was confined to a tuberculosis sanitarium in Scotland. Meanwhile, Maugham continued his composition, and, with each new experience, wrote plays or novels with its respective background. After the war he toured the South Seas, collecting material that was used in several of his short stories, particularly the seduction of a missionary by Miss Sadie Thompson, which became a popular stage production, *Rain*, and later was the basis for a motion picture.

Maugham continued to write plays until 1933. In 1928, he acquired a villa at Cap Ferrat on the French Riviera, where he lived after World War II. With the fall of France in 1940, he resided on the South Carolina estate of Nelson Doubleday, his publisher. He enjoyed social sports, bridge, and modern paintings. In 1962, his collection of paintings was sold at auction, bringing him more than $1,500,000. These funds were held in a trust for struggling or impoverished writers. Although Maugham disclaimed that his *The Summing Up*, published in 1938, was an undisguised autobiography, it is filled with personal experiences, many times the repetition of experiences of his own life which he had incorporated into his many works. He describes his reasons for the book as follows.[1]

I write this book to disembarrass my soul of certain notions that have hovered about in it too long for my comfort. I do not seek to persuade anybody. I am devoid of the pedagogic instinct and when I know a thing never feel in myself the desire to impart it to others. I do not much care if people agree with me. Of course I think I am right, otherwise I should not think as I do, and they are wrong, but it does not offend me that they should be wrong. Nor does it greatly disturb me to discover that my judgment is at variance with that of the majority. I have a certain confidence in my instinct.

Maugham was honored by France with the appointment of Commander of the Legion of Honour, and Companion of Honour, a Fellow of the Library of Congress, and a Fellow of the Royal Society of Literature. Honorary doctorates of literature were granted by Oxford and Toulouse Universities. On his 80th birthday he was feted at the Garrick Club in London with a dinner, the fourth member to be so honored. Predecessors were Dickens, Trollope, and Thackeray. He was a nonbeliever in religion and a nonconformist in contemporary morals.

1. Maugham, W. S.: *The Summing Up,* New York: Doubleday, Doran & Co., Inc., 1938.

2. Maugham, W. S.: *Liza of Lambeth,* London: F. Unwin, 1897.

3. Maugham, W. S.: *Of Human Bondage,* New York: G. H. Doran Co., 1915.

Composite by G. Bako

Lemuel Shattuck (1793-1859)

LEMUEL SHATTUCK, foremost advocate in America of the need for community and state appreciation of knowledge and action in the broad domain of environmental health, was born in Ashby, Massachusetts, into a Puritan family. He had no opportunity for public school instruction and in most matters was self-taught, through the judicious use of moments for appropriate reading.[1] In this fashion he achieved considerable erudition and followed the teaching profession for several years, serving in Troy, Albany, and Detroit. He then settled in Concord, Massachusetts, where he shared his hours and efforts between running a general store and more teaching. The first evidence of an interest in civic responsibility was felt by the town officials who were urged to organize the public schools, to account properly for public school funds, and to formulate and adopt a code of school regulations. This led eventually to the passage of measures in the state of Massachusetts which required all schools to prepare annual reports.

In 1833, Shattuck moved to Boston and engaged in the business of book publishing, book selling, and writing. A *History of the Town of Concord,* which was published in 1835, displayed his interest in genealogy as well as pointed out the then current serious deficiencies in the recording of births, marriages, and deaths. This was the first substantial evidence that Shattuck was interested in statistics, a subject that became paramount in his later public health measures. At the age of 46, he retired from business and spent the remainder of his life in public service. He prepared a number of monographs on public health, most of them as a private citizen without professional assistance or political support; however, he served on the Boston City Council and in the state legislature. His contributions included "Vital Statistics of Boston," 1841; *Report to the Committee of the City Council,* 1846; "Contributions to the Vital Statistics of the State of New York," 1850; *Bills of Mortality, 1810–1849, City of Boston with an Essay on the Vital Statistics of Boston from 1810 to 1831,* 1893; a genealogy of his own family; and a long letter to Jonathan Preston on the water supply of Boston.

A *Complete System of Family Registration,* with recommendations for registering births, marriages, and deaths in Massachusetts was prepared in 1841. The recommendations, supported by the American Academy of Arts and Sciences and the counselors of the Massachusetts Medical Society, were accepted by the legislature and became a model for other states. The significance of the health of the Commonwealth was documented in a letter to the Secretary of State in 1845.[2]

Let the facts which the Registry System proposes to collect concerning Births, Deaths and Marriages, and the circumstances which attend them, be collected, digested, arranged, published and diffused annually, and their effects on the living energies of the people would be incalculable. They would be an annual lesson on the laws of human life in their operation among ourselves—a kind of *Practical Physiology* taught in all our towns and at our firesides—and hence, far more instructive and impressive than any derived from books. They would teach our people how to understand human life, and how to improve, prolong and make it happy.

We are not a theorist—an experimentalist. We have no sympathy with the opinions of some modern reformers, who seem to be governed by theories founded on uncertain, partial data, or vague conjecture. We are a statist—a dealer in facts. We wish to ascertain the laws of human life, developed by the natural constitution of our bodies, as they actually exist under the influences that surround them, and to learn how far they may be favorably modified and improved. This can only be done by an accurate knowledge of the facts that are daily occurring among us. These matters are important to the physician to aid him in curing the sick, but far more important to the people to aid them in *learning how to live without being sick;* and they deserve the serious consideration of all persons in this Commonwealth.

As the militant proponent of public health measures in his county, Shattuck was chairman of the state commission to prepare a sanitary survey of Massachusetts. The communication, probably written entirely by Shattuck and published in 1850, was entitled *Report of a General Plan for the Promotion of Public and Personal Health, Devised and Recommended by the Commissioners Appointed Under a Resolve of the Legislature of Massachusetts, Relating to a Sanitary Survey of the State.*[3] The document exceeded 500 printed pages and traced the history of public health measures from classical Greece and Rome to his contemporary times. It was of substantial practical value and presented a variety of subjects such as recommendations for local and state boards of health, sanitary rules and regulations, annual reports of boards of health, atmospheric observations, causes of disease and death, planning of new towns, regulation of public buildings, overcrowding of lodgings, abatement of nuisances, inquest on dead bodies, and adulterated foods and drugs. It is not surprising that the committee recommended its adoption on the grounds that it was useful, charitable, and moral and because progress demanded it. Massachusetts, however, was not then ready for the layman's recommendations, and a decade elapsed after Shattuck's death before the Massachusetts State Board of Health, one of the first in the United States, was created. As if to make some amends nearly a century later, the Commonwealth of Massachusetts dedicated the Lemuel Shattuck Hospital for Chronic Diseases to honor the memory of the self-educated statistician who contributed greatly to the public health movement in the 19th century.

1. Walker, M. E. M.: *Pioneers of Public Health,* Edinburgh: Oliver and Boyd, 1930.

2. Shattuck, L.: "Letter to the Secretary of State on the Registration of Births, Marriages and Deaths in Massachusetts," Boston, 1845.

3. Shattuck, L., Banks, Jr., N. P., and Abbott, J.: *Report of a General Plan for the Promotion of Public and Personal Health,* Boston: Dutton and Wentworth, 1850.

Composite by G. Bako

Sir Edwin Chadwick (1800-1890)

EDWIN CHADWICK, the most articulate and effective reformer in 19th century London, was born at Longsight, near Manchester.[1] His father, versatile and well known for a remarkable character, taught botany and music to John Dalton and in later years emigrated to the United States to continue a career in journalism. Young Chadwick was educated in local private schools until the age of ten. He then moved with his parents to London and there was tutored in French, Italian, Spanish, and the classical languages. As he approached the age of 15 he was placed in a barrister's office, was admitted to the Society of the Inner Temple in 1823, and became barrister-at-law of the Inner Temple in 1830. While reading for the bar, he too pursued journalism for gain; in 1828, he prepared topical essays for the *Morning Herald, West-*

minster Review, and the *London Review*. One of his first commentaries, published in the *Westminster Review*, dealt with life assurance, brought him unusual attention, and led subsequently to the development of a theme later labelled the "sanitary idea." He advanced strong arguments for general availability of potable water, adequate disposal of waste, and provision of habitable living conditions for the poor of England similar to those enjoyed by the rich.

Chadwick's intellectual associates fostered his zeal for reform, particularly John S. Mill, with whom he debated morals and metaphysics, and Jeremy Bentham, believer in the greatest happiness for the greatest number. He rejected a proposed annuity from Bentham for the propagation of Bentham's philosophy, but compromised by accepting a legacy and a part of his library. As an intimate of several physicians, Chadwick profited from discussion of current medical doctrines and aspects of disease, which proved useful in his crusade to improve a socially inadequate environment. While struggling for achievement in the dual schools of law and journalism, and before attracting public recognition as a reformer, Chadwick developed habits of tremendous industry and methods of seeking out unrecorded data. Forthright expression, coupled with his inborn arrogance, marked him as outstanding during the mid-19th century when social and sanitary reform desperately needed active vigorous support.

Summarizing the calculations from empiric observations and inductions in the life insurance study, Chadwick devised the first principles of causes for ill health and rejected the wide assumption of fate as the cause. While hesitating about his ultimate future but busily investigating fever dens and other retreats for human misery, he received and accepted, in 1832, the offer of asistant commissioner on the English Poor-Law Commission. The Commission was charged by the government to inquire into the obsolete poor law system known as the Act for the Relief of the Poor. This system had been codified in 1601 and was forced upon the legislature at that time. During his year as assistant to the Commission, Chadwick displayed his usual great strength for work, capacity for detail, excel-

lent memory for facts and figures, and originality in devising ideas for correction. Although he was appointed chief commissioner one year later, with increased authority for recommendation and direction, he continued the on-site investigations and collection of data which assured him a strong position in the support of his proposals. When the Poor-Law Amendment Act became official in 1834, it contained his regulations for implementation. Also, he served as paid secretary of the first Poor-Law Board appointed under the Act.

While the new law was criticized by some as an act of tyranny, others believed the measure saved the country from perpetuation of great social ills, if not from social revolution. Mr. Gladstone called it the greatest reform of the 19th century. The original Act separated each parish from all others so that the poor were divided and were helpless in any attempt to correct their adverse state. Chadwick urged the formation of large administrative areas under the supervision of qualified and responsible paid officials elected by the representatives of the people. As the Board began to function, he proposed the separation of the destitute into several classes. Indigent children were to be placed in healthful and well-ordered industrial schools in which they could be fed, clothed, educated, and taught a useful trade. The aged were to be housed and cared for in almshouses where they could pass their remaining days in comfort. The blind, the deaf, the idiotic, and the sick were to be placed in appropriate institutions, supervised, and their peculiar requirements satisfied. Juvenile delinquency was counteracted by organized instruction of underprivileged children in morals, religion, and industry.

Chadwick was also a member of a commission investigating the employment of children in factories. He drafted a report which recommended the limitation to six hours of work per day for children under 13 years of age. This led to the passage of the Ten Hours Act and the establishment of the half-time system of education. Working children were required to attend school, supervised by qualified teachers, for at least three hours each day. In another area of concern, Chadwick, in 1833, gave evidence on drunkenness to a committee of the House of Commons. He reasoned that if healthy recreation were available for the masses, if coffee taverns were substituted for gin mills, and if restriction were placed upon traffic in hard liquors, the incidence of intemperance would dwindle. He insisted that railroad men be paid weekly instead of at long intervals, which provided substantial sums of money for periodic intemperance and debauchery. Although he held management in factories responsible for accidents from faulty construction or from machiney, a law to achieve this was not passed until 1898.

In 1838, following a severe epidemic in the London East End, an appeal by officials to the Poor-Law Board instigated a Medical Commission of Inquiry. Disclosure of the shameful condition of the water supply, inadequate sewage disposal, and the attendant potential threats to health led in due time to correction. Although it was not a part of the Poor-Law reformation, Chadwick sponsored a bill to provide for the registration by the state and not by the church of all births, marriages, and deaths. If such could be accomplished, statistics of great epidemics, fatal diseases, accidents, violent deaths, and infantile mortality would be available. Chadwick proposed an annual census and recommended William Farr for the office of Registrar General, which the latter held from 1838 to 1880. An appeal for an efficient constabulary in the counties, similar to Sir Robert Peel's London police ("Bobbies"), became a fact in 1838. He advocated the principle of removal of the favorable climate for crime, rather than apprehension of the criminal after the act. He wrote at length on interment of the dead and favored a national system for burial, the establishment of cemeteries in each town, and in some communities the establishment of a crematorium.

In 1846, the Poor-Law Commission was dissolved, partially as a result of the dissension between Chadwick and his commissioners. However, when the first Board of Health was established in London in 1848, he was appointed to the Board and named a member of the Consolidated Commission of Sewers. In 1854, the Board of Health, although it was never formally dissolved, merged into the local government board in association with the Poor-Law Administration. This marked the end of Chadwick's official life. He retired on a pension of £1000 a year; however, he soon became concerned with the sanitary condition of the soldiers in the Crimea and urged the dispatch of sanitary commissioners at the time Florence Nightingale was organizing her nursing service. Chadwick ran for Parliament twice but was never elected. Meanwhile, he continued his writings, which have been summarized in two volumes by Richardson, entitled *The Health of Nations.*[2] These are long, extended summaries of longer original communications. Brevity was never one of Chadwick's virtues. As a public figure and one of the great sanitarians of all times, he received many private and public denunciations and few public rewards. The exception was the order of Commander of the Bath, of which he was one of the first selected for purely civil as distinguished from military service.

1. Lewis, R. A.: *Edwin Chadwick and the Public Health Movement 1832-1854,* London: Longmans, Green & Co., 1952.
2. Richardson, B. W.: *The Health of Nations. A Review of the Works of Edwin Chadwick,* 2 vol, London: Longmans, Green & Co., 1887.

Philippe Ricord (1800-1889)

PHILIPPE RICORD, illustrious, whimsical, and anecdotal student of clinical syphilis, was born in Baltimore to Gallic parents, who escaped arrest by coming to America as political refugees near the end of the French Revolution.[1] Philippe attended the Economical School in New York established for French refugee children. Upon graduation, he turned for support to odd jobs, and subsequently traveled with his nature-scientist brother, gathering botanical and zoological specimens. Upon direction of Baron Hyde du Neuville, the recently appointed Ambassador to the United States, the Ricord brothers collected specimens for the Natural Science Museum of France and helped transport them to Paris. By then Philippe was 20 and entered the Academy of Val-de-Grâce to begin study under the Faculty of Medicine. This selection was not surprising; his grandfather was a physician in Marseilles. Philippe assisted Dupuytren at Hotel Dieu and Lisfranc in the Hopital de la Pitié. Upon submission of his inaugural thesis, *Diverses Propositions de Chirurgie*, he received his MD degree in 1826. Lacking means to remain in Paris, he chose general practice away from the city, but

Composite by G. Bako

returned two years later to be attached first as surgeon to the Hopital de la Pitié and, in 1831, to the Hopital du Midi, at that time reserved for the treatment of venereal affections in the male.

Ricord soon acquired an international reputation through his captivating lectures, experimental studies of inoculation of the venereal virus, and clinical judgment of the ambulatory and bedridden. The identification of syphilis and gonorrhea as distinct diseases deviated from the respected teaching of John Hunter, who had not differentiated the venereal entities. By repeating Hunter's experiment of inoculation, Ricord identified the specific pathogenesis of the virus, separating virulent syphilis from nonvirulent blennorrhagia (gonorrhea) and dividing the clinical manifestations of lues into the three stages currently acceptable more than a century later—primary, secondary, and tertiary. These pertinent clinical deductions were presented in a monograph published in Paris in 1838 and translated into English in 1842.[2]

Hence, according to the opponents of inoculation, must we not admit that when the pus of an ulcer pro-

duces certain symptoms constant in their form and development, and which present certain characteristic conditions, the ulcer, whose pus has been inoculated, was a chancre, and consequently that the necessary character, without which an ulcer cannot be called chancre, is to furnish a pus capable of being inoculated under the given conditions?

To most persons, who will examine with unprejudiced minds, it must be clear from the study of the phenomena of general contagion, and, as I have before said, from the constant and regular connexions between cause and effect, that the syphilitic diseases are ascribable to a specific agent or deleterious principle, which is only to be considered an entity in the same degree as the peculiar principle of hydrophobia, the venom of the viper, the specific cause of the small pox, &c. &c. &c.

Now, the incontestable existence of the venereal virus is proved by a peculiar property of a distinct morbid secretion, and therefore the pus furnished by certain syphilitic affections has the constant and regular property of reproducing a pus similar to itself.

I. A venereal affection already cured, or still existing at any period of its duration, does not prevent others being contracted, and the number of successive infections cannot be limited.

II. An individual actually infected, and under the influence only of primary symptoms in one region, never sees symptoms similar to the first developed in other parts of his system, except by a new contagion from contact with the pus of the first, or communicated by another individual.

III. Secondary symptoms, or general infection, never prevent the patient from contracting other primary affections.

IV. The frequency of constitutional syphilis bears no direct ratio to the number of primary symptoms developed at one time.

Do not the observations of former times combine with daily experience to corroborate the experiment of Hunter, which prove that one infection does not prevent a second; not only in the development of symptoms different in form and principle, but also of those which are owing to a cause of the same nature? Do we not often see patients who have a blenorrhoea contract a chancre by other sexual intercourse; or who have at first a chancre, and are attacked with gonorrhoea, after a new coition? I should think no candid person would attempt to deny so well known a fact. But the manner in which the symptoms following the first are produced, might be contested. Those who think there cannot be a primary infection without general symptoms, look upon all those which follow as in consequence of a first symptom, without the necessity of a new contagion. Thus they attribute distinct diseases, contracted at different times, to the same cause.

The most common means of propagating syphilis, is undoubtedly that by the sexual organs in the intercourse between the sexes; because the virus generally has its seat in these organs, and because they are always moist, and the epidermis which covers them is delicate and thin, the organs remain in contact, and friction renders absorption more easy. The organs of the mouth are often the propagators of the contagion by a lascivious kiss, by the application of the lips or tongue to some part of the mucous membrane, by suction of the breasts, and especially in suckling. If the mouth of an infant can infect a nurse, the breast of a nurse can infect a child.

We confess our incredulity as to contagion by means of a seat of a privy or a chamber-pot, which no one had used for several hours; or a sponge not used since the previous day.

4. The symptoms of constitutional syphilis are not the consequence of blenorrhoea. In all the cases in which authors mention that it was an antecedent, the frequency of which precisely corresponds with that of masked chancres. (chancres larvés,) the diagnosis was not correct; the diseased surfaces not having been examined.

INOCULATION DISTINGUISHES PRIMARY FROM SECONDARY SYMPTOMS

My clinical observations have led me to the following classification of the symptoms of syphilis.

1. *Primary symptom*, (*accident primitif*), chancre from the direct action of the virus which it produces, and by means of which it propagates itself by contagion from a diseased to a healthy individual.

2. *Successive symptoms*, (*accidents successifs*), or those which arise from contiguity of tissue, or by simple extension of the first local symptom, as new chancres; simple inflammatory, or virulent abscesses, or simple or virulent adenitis, &c.

3. *Secondary symptoms*, or symptoms of general infection, in which the virus has undergone a modification and produced the *syphilitic temperament;* symptoms appearing on the skin, the mucous membranes, the eyes, testicles, &c., and seldom happening before the first two weeks of the duration of the primary affection, chancre; but generally after the fourth, sixth, eighth, or even much later; not capable of inoculating.

4. *Tertiary symptoms* (*accidents tertiaires*), occurring at indefinite periods, but generally long after the cessation of the primary affection; not appearing in most subjects until after secondary symptoms have occurred, . . . Under the head of tertiary affections, we must place nodes, deep seated tubercles, tubercles of the cellular tissue, periostoses, exostoses, caries, necrosis, syphilitic tubercles of the brain.

Ricord's writings encompassed all facets of clinical and pathological aspects of syphilis and other venereal maladies. His *Clinique Iconographique*[3] contained 50 superbly prepared colored plates, characterizing a remarkable clinical experience at the Hopital du Midi and depicting a multitude of chancres variously disseminated on primary and secondary sex organs of each sex, including vaginal, uterine, and urethral chancres. He discussed at length gonorrhea in women and epididymitis in men and accepted the value of silver nitrate for the treatment of gonorrheal ophthalmia shortly after its introduc-

tion. His discussion of hereditary syphilis is an enlightened scientific approach.[4]

In order that a child, the offspring of healthy parents, should be at all infected, after it has existed more or less time in utero, the mother must, by direct inoculation, become affected with an indurated chancre, and all its consequences; then the foetus may inherit the diathesis of the mother. The latter might perhaps transmit the diathesis to a first foetus by means of a second germ (the first being quite healthy), in a case of super-foetation; but even under these circumstances it would be still by the instrumentality of the mother that this first foetus would become contaminated. It is therefore evident that the mother, in order to infect her child, must have upon herself a secondary syphilitic affection, either acquired whilst the foetus is in utero, or before that event.

Ricord was honored at home and abroad. He served as president of the Academy of Medicine and was promoted to the dignity of the Commander and Grand Officer of the Legion of Honour of France. At the age of 60, he retired from his hospital service to devote his time to an extensive private practice. This was interrupted during the siege of Paris when he served as ambulance physician on the battlefield. His clinical counsel was in great demand, but the nature of the ailments dictated that several waiting rooms be provided in his house for the reception of different categories of patients. He was generous in arranging for settlement of fees, and those who could not afford to pay and who were in need were doubly helped. Fond of the humanities, he maintained a private collection of sculptures and paintings, and, as a practitioner of Crouy-sur-Ourcq, he composed a poem in three cantos. In addition, he prepared an epitaph in the French verse style used specifically for the purpose. His criticism of Liebig's artificial milk, an alexandrine quatrain here freely translated, was presented at a meeting of the French Academy of Medicine prior to a speech by Depaul in criticism of Liebig.[5]

Liebig prefers his milk for our children,
And it seems to agree with young Teutons by test,
But Depaul instructs us that children of France,
Are much better when kept on the milk of the breast.

1. Monod, C.: Eulogy of Philippe Ricord, *Bull Mem Soc Chir Par* 18:22-42, 1892.

2. Ricord, P.: *A Practical Treatise of Venereal Diseases* (Fr), Paris: Rouvier and Le Bouvier, 1838, English translation, New York: P. Gordon, 1842.

3. Ricord, P.: *Clinique Iconographique de L'Hôpital des Vénériens*, Paris: Rouvier, 1851.

4. Ricord, P.: *Lectures on Venereal and Other Diseases Arising From Sexual Intercourse*, reported and translated by V. de Meric, Philadelphia: Barrington & G. D. Haswell, 1849.

5. Chereau, A.: *Dictionary of Physician-Poets of France*, (Fr), Paris: A. Delahaye, 1874.

Composite by G. Bako

William Farr (1807-1883)

WILLIAM FARR, founder of the English system of vital statistics, was born at Kenley in Shropshire. His parents, of humble circumstances, permitted his adoption in infancy by a wealthy and benevolent squire, Joseph Pryce. He assisted the elderly guardian in his affairs of commerce, meanwhile educating himself without benefit of formal instruction.[1] At the age of 19, Farr turned to medicine, studying with Dr. Webster of Shrewsbury and, as dresser, assisting Mr. Sutton at the Shrewsbury Infirmary. In 1829, supported by a legacy from his adopted father, he continued his studies at Hotel Dieu, La Charité, and La Pitié in Paris. Dupuytren in surgery, Louis in medical statistics, Andral in hygiene, and Gay-Lussac in chemistry were brilliant lights on the highly reputable faculty at that time. A great interest in and talent for medical statistics and hygiene led to his appointment in the Registrar-General's office.

Before returning to England, however, Farr toured Switzerland and collected a series of measurements of the vertical and horizontal dimensions of the heads of the cretinous natives. He later studied at University College, London, and in 1832 became a licentiate of the Apothecary Society. This was his only earned document in the medical sciences. For several years he subsisted on a diffident private practice and paltry returns from medical writing and lecturing on what he called "hygiology." It was not until 1838 that Farr achieved a full-time assignment as compiler of abstracts in the office of the Registrar-General and was thereby able to devote his undivided energies to medical and vital tabu-law data. His excellent chapter, "Vital Statistics," published in McCulloch's *A Statistical Account of the British Empire* in 1837, was a contributing factor in this critical step in his career. Vital statistics, which included health, sickness, disease, and death, according to Farr, was designed:[2]

To exhibit the sanatory state of the British population as accurately as existing materials permit, we shall severally examine the mortality, the sickness, the endemics, the prevailing forms of disease, and the various ways in which, at all ages, its successive generations perish.

Man's existence may terminate at any instant between 0 and 100 years; it may be a constant process of disease, or remain uninterrupted by a day's sickness. On opening a watch, or any piece of mechanism, and observing the state of its springs, chains, or wheels, it is not difficult to foresee how long its movements will continue; but no one, contemplating a solitary individual of the human species, and ignorant of the secret sources of his life, as well as of the many conjunctures of external circumstances in which he may be placed, can foretell the period when some mortal derangement will occur in his organisation, what diseases he will encounter, how long he will suffer, or the hour when his sufferings and his existence will end. The same uncertainty is extended in the popular thought to families, nations, and mankind, considered in collective masses; but observation proves that generations succeed each other, develope their energies, are afflicted with sickness, and waste in the procession of their life, according to fixed laws; that the mortality and sickness of a people are constant in the same circumstances, or only revolve through a prescribed cycle, varying as the causes favourable or unfavourable to health preponderate.

For 40 years Farr's lucid annotations on vital statistics enlivened the *Annual Reports of the Registrar-General of Births, Deaths, and*

Marriages. The *Reports*, presented with literary skill, comprise a statistical history of the people of England, combined with critical evaluation of the data and technical deductions. They provide delightful reading and betray little of the dullness sometimes characteristic of comprehensive tabular data. In the first report he appreciated the need for scientific terminology and a statistical nosology, noting that:[3]

> Each disease has in many instances been denoted by three or four terms, and each term has been applied to as many different diseases; vague, inconvenient names have been employed, or complications have been registered instead of primary diseases. The nomenclature is of as much importance in this department of inquiry, as weights and measures in the physical sciences, and should be settled without delay.

> The diseases proving fatal in childhood, manhood, and old age, are not the same: for this reason, to determine the peculiar diseases—the nature of the dangers—we have to encounter at different periods of life, becomes a most important problem. Very few statistical observations exist in which the deaths from each disease, at different ages, are enumerated.[4]

Farr's law of epidemics, deduced from his statistical tabulation of the incidence of small-pox, assumed a skewed bell shape.[1]

> It appears probable, however, that small-pox increases at an accelerated and then a retarded rate; that it declines first at a slightly accelerated, then at a rapidly accelerated, and lastly at a retarded rate, until the disease attains the minimum intensity and remains stationary.

Although vital statistics of the civilian population was Farr's great interest, the breadth of his curiosity was remarkable. He wrote or prepared reports on a great number of subjects including life tables for insurance purposes, army medical statistics, water supply, uniformity of weights and measures, international coinage, direct taxation, population density, and the mortality of lunatics. Farr remained in the Registrar-General's office until he retired in 1879, an underpaid and overworked subordinate, never having been appointed to the top post. On the other hand, his talents and achievements in sanitation and preventive medicine did not go unrecognized. He was elected a Fellow of the Royal Society, received an honorary degree from Oxford and the Gold Medal of the British Medical Association, and became a Commander of the Order of the Bath and a Corresponding Member of the Institute of France. Farr's projection of public health in 1837 remained unaltered in 1875.[4]

How the people of England live is one of the most important questions that can be considered; and how —of what causes, and at what ages—they die is scarcely of less account; for it is the complement of the primary question teaching men how to live a longer, healthier, and happier life.

1. *Vital Statistics: A Memorial Volume of Selections from Reports and Writings of William Farr, M.D., D.C.L., C.B., F.R.S.,* London: E. Stanford, 1885.
2. McCulloch, J. R.: *A Statistical Account of the British Empire,* London: C. Knight and Co., 1837.
3. "Letter to the Registrar-General, from William Farr, Esq." in *First Annual Report of the Registrar-General,* London: W. Clowes and Sons, 1839, pp 86-118.

Library of the College of Physicians, Philadelphia

W. W. Gerhard (1809-1872)

WILLIAM WOOD GERHARD, the most distinguished pupil of Louis, the great Parisian clinician of the 19th century, bested his teacher in the clear differentiation of typhus and typhoid fever. Previously, the diverse manifestations had been described and the afflicted treated as typhoid fever victims, without discrimination. Gerhard was born in Philadelphia, received his undergraduate training at nearby Dickinson College, founded by Benjamin Rush and others, and in 1830 obtained his doctorate in medicine at the University of Pennsylvania. His graduation thesis, which discussed endermic medication, was published in the *North American Medical and Surgical Journal*.[1] Devotion to the community, a characteristic of loyal Philadelphians, was interrupted by residence elsewhere on one occasion only—a two-year period of postgraduate study in Paris, the medical center of the world at that time. Although Chomel, Andral, Piorry, and others were judged to be excellent teachers in Paris and offered courses sought by Gerhard, the ultimate desire was private instruction with P-C-A Louis. The arrangement was consummated through a polite note accompanied by a handsome pecuniary offer.[2]

Gerhard followed the numerical or statistical approach of his teacher in the study of fevers. He collected a mass of clinical notes from adults and children, which formed the basis of his remarkable contributions during the decade following his return to Philadelphia. Associates of Gerhard who studied under Louis at that time were Pennock of Philadelphia and James Jackson, Jr., of Boston, the former co-author with Gerhard of the treatise on the Asiatic cholera epidemic of 1831-32.[3] Other studies published from his detailed clinical-pathological observations in Paris included pneumonia[4] and tuberculous meningitis in children,[5] and smallpox.[6]

Upon return to Philadelphia, Gerhard was appointed resident physician at the Philadelphia Hospital, known at that time as Old Blockley. He held a staff appointment until 1868, with an overlapping appointment in the department of the Institutes of Medicine at the University of Pennsylvania. Gerhard's studies on fevers, begun under Louis, were continued and were supplemented by the opportunity to investigate the typhus epidemic of 1836 in Philadelphia. The clinical-pathological contribution for which he was most famous, the dissertation on typhus fever, was published in 1837 at the age of 28.[7] The disease was studied at the bedside and in the death house by a perceptive and highly inquisitive mind.

The master monograph on fevers by Louis published in 1829, in which the name "typhoid" (Gr. *typhos*, stupor *eidos*, resemblance) was first used, did not differentiate typhoid from typhus fever. Neither the English nor the Parisian physicians recognized them as distinct entities. The involvement of Peyer's patches was assumed to be an incidental finding in typhus fever. The year that Gerhard's studies appeared in his hometown medical periodical, the *American Journal of the Medical Sciences*, he suffered a severe attack of typhoid fever which undoubtedly handicapped one so active physically and mentally.

In studying the clinical features of typhoid fever, Gerhard noted that the slow pulse and intestinal symptoms, typical in typhoid fever, were absent in typhus fever. The cutaneous eruption of typhus fever and the rose spots of typhoid fever were clearly distinct and unrelated manifestations. The communication of 1837 was documented by a number of case reports.[7]

During a residence of two or three years in Paris, I had studied with great care the pathology and treatment of the disease usually termed, in the French hospitals, typhoid fever or typhoid affection. There is another designation for it, founded on its anatomical characters, and therefore, more directly in accordance with modern medical nomenclature; it is dothinenteritis. This variety of fever, which is identical with the disease termed typhus mitior or nervous fever, is frequent at Paris, and is almost the only fever which can be said to be endemic there.

These fevers were the only ones known at Paris for some years past; but in 1813-14, there occurred a severe epidemic fever, characterized by extreme prostration and strongly marked cerebral symptoms. . . . Louis and Chomel are inclined to consider it as identical with the prevailing dothinenteritis, but their opinion is probably erroneous, and the disease, as far as we know, should be classed amongst the forms of continued fever, distinguished by the terms typhus, typhus gravior, petechial or spotted fever, &c.

Having once established the complete identity of a fever which is so common at Paris and so well described, with a similar affection, not unfrequently met with at Philadelphia, I examined the pathological phenomena of our remittent and intermittent fevers of the severe malignant character. . . . In all these fevers, the glands of Peyer as well as the other intestinal follicles, were found perfectly healthy; the large intestine was occasionally but not constantly diseased, while the stomach, and to a still greater degree the liver and spleen were invariably found in a morbid condition.

There is a marked difference between the petechial eruption and the rose-coloured spots of typhoid fever. In typhoid fever the eruption is rare, very seldom extending beyond the abdomen and thorax; whereas in the epidemic typhus, the eruption is almost always general, extending to the limbs as well as the trunk.

Thus, the triple lesion of the glands of Peyer, mesenteric glands and spleen, constituting the anatomical characteristic of the dothinenteritis or typhoid fever, although sought for with the greatest care, evidently did not exist in the epidemic typhus.

The fact that the morbid changes pathognomonic of dothinenteritis, are not met with in the typhus fever, would of itself seem conclusive that the two diseases are no more identical than pneumonia and pleurisy.

At the same time that Gerhard was collecting his series of cases, Shattuck of Boston, Perry of Glasgow, and Lombard of Geneva were similarly engaged and reached similar conclusions. Osler is credited with assigning priority to Gerhard for the typhus-typhoid differentiation, although undoubtedly others in preceding decades or even in preceding generations had some appreciation of the clinical and pathological characteristics of these maladies, alike in name but dissimilar in many respects.

The intrinsic worth of a careful clinical examination of a patient with the five senses of man, as propounded by Louis, was recognized and practiced by Gerhard. Physical diagnosis became an indispensable adjunct in the recognition and management of morbid states. Two books were prepared by Gerhard on the diagnosis and treatment of diseases of the chest, the second published in 1842. By then his contributions to medical literature ceased. The bout of typhoid fever in 1837 and a period of ill health in 1844 ended the fruitful years of research and writing. The last 20 years of his life were devoted to teaching and practice as the leading clinician of Philadelphia.

1. Gerhard, W. W.: Observations on the Endermic Application of Medicines, *N Amer Med & Surg J* 9:392-402; 10:145-160, 1830.

2. Stewardson, T.: Biographical Memoir of William W. Gerhard, *Trans Coll Physicians Philadelphia* 4:473-481 (Jan.-Feb.) 1874.

3. Pennock, C. W., and Gerhard, W. W.: *Observations on the Cholera of Paris*, Philadelphia: J. R. A. Skerrett, 1832.

4. Gerhard, W. W.: On the Pneumonia of Children, *Amer J Med Sci* 14:328-346 (Aug.) 1834; 15:87-106 (Nov.) 1834.

5. Gerhard, W. D.: Cerebral Affections of Children, *Amer J Med Sci* 13:313-359 (Feb.) 1833; 14:99-111 (May) 1834.

6. Gerhard, W. W.: Cases of Small-Pox, with Fatal Termination, Observed at the Hôpital des Enfans Malades of Paris, *Amer J Med Sci* 11:368-408 (Feb.) 1833.

7. Gerhard, W. W.: On the Typhus Fever Which Occurred at Philadelphia in the Spring and Summer of 1836, *Amer J Med Sci* 18:289-322 (Feb.) 1837; 20:289-322 (Aug.) 1837.

Composite by G. Bako

William Budd (1811-1880)

TWENTY-FIVE YEARS before *Salmonella typhosa* was identified as the pathogenic agent in typhoid fever, country practitioner William Budd, by inductive reasoning, had clearly defined the epidemiology of one of the great scourges in modern medicine. Although the recommendations of Budd were strenuously opposed by some, when accepted and practiced, they provided an effective control of the contagion. William was born in 1811 in North Tawton, Devonshire, into a family of physicians of great talent. He studied medicine in London, Edinburgh, and Paris (four years), and survived a bout of typhoid fever, the disease that commanded his great interest throughout his medical career. In 1838, the University of Edinburgh conferred the doctorate degree on Budd, as well as a gold medal for an essay on acute rheumatism.[1] Not long after, while on duty as a naval surgeon, he was stricken with typhoid fever from which he almost died. He resigned his commission on the hospital ship, returned to North Tawton to assist his father in country practice, and began his studies in field epidemiology that encompassed a number of contagious diseases of man and animals. At the age of 32, Budd moved to Bristol, where he was associated with St. Peter's Hospital, the Bristol Royal Infirmary, and the Bristol medical school. His knowledge of French and German enabled him to be informed on current medical advances on the Continent, although living some distance from the great teaching hospitals in London.

Budd contributed frequently but not prolifically to the medical journals. Meanwhile he pursued critical epidemiologic investigations, which led subsequently to his election to the Royal Society. The contagion of the zymotic diseases, rinderpest (cattle plague), and variola ovina (smallpox of sheep) as well as scarlet fever, yellow fever, and phthisis in man were investigated. To John Snow belongs the credit for recognizing the dissemination of cholera by drinking water; to Budd belongs the credit for proving that, by disinfecting the alvine discharges and isolation of the sick, the pollution of the water could be prevented and typhoid fever held in check. Budd's contributions in the literature reveal a delightful style of composition as well as a prophecy of a microbiologic agent.[2]

There are few things in which the people of this country have a deeper concern than in knowing the real truth in what relates to the mode in which this fatal disorder [typhoid fever] is disseminated amongst them. Every year, on an average, some twenty thousaid British souls perish miserably by it, and disasters, which, occurring in the army of the Crimea, made the nation shudder, occur annually in the peaceful, working, army at home, without giving the nation a thought.

It is humiliating to think that issues such as these should be contingent on the powers of an agent so low in the scale of created things, that the mildew which springs up on decaying wood must be considered high in comparison. To know how these powers take effect, in what way they grow to such a height, and to learn therefrom, perchance, by what means their operation may be defeated, are problems in which human happiness is deeply interested. Perhaps there are few battles to be fought in which a successful issue depends so closely as here on a real knowledge of the enemy.

Although Budd began the study of the origin and transmission of typhoid fever in North Tawton in 1839, definitive conclusions that this was a self-propagated disease were not stated in print until 1856, and then in the midst of powerful opposition to the contagion theory.[3]

This species of fever has two fundamental characteristics. The first is, that it is an essentially contagious disorder; the second, that by far the most virulent part of the specific poison by which the contagion takes effect is contained in the diarrhoeal discharges which issue from the diseased and *exanthematous* bowel.

His best known treatise, *Typhoid Fever: Its Nature, Mode of Spreading, and Prevention*, which summarized the findings of a fruitful career, was published in 1873. The conclusions in the monograph, valid today except for contamination of air, attest to his clear thinking.[4]

1. That typhoid fever is, in its essence, a contagious, or self-propagating fever, and is a member of the great natural family of contagious fevers, of which smallpox may be taken to be the type.

2. That the living body of the infected man is the soil in which the specific poison, which is the cause of the fever, breeds and multiplies.

3. That the reproduction of this poison in the infected body, and the disturbance attaching to it constitute the fever.

4. That this reproduction is the same in kind as that of which we have, in small-pox, ocular demonstration.

5. That the disease of the intestine, which is its distinctive anatomical mark, is the specific eruption of the fever, and bears the same pathological relation to it which the small-pox eruption bears to small-pox.

6. That, as might have been anticipated from this view, the contagious matter by which the fever is propagated is cast off, chiefly, in the discharges from the diseased intestine.

7. That as a necessary result, sewers and the cloacae which, under existing sanitary arrangements, are the common receptacles of these discharges are, also, the principal instruments in the transmission of the contagion; and, consequently, that, in many instances, the infected sewer, and not the infected man, appears as if it were the primary source of the specific poison.

8. That once cast off by the intestine this poison may communicate the fever to other persons in two principal ways—either by contaminating the drinking water, or by infecting the air.

9. That, as an inevitable consequence of the impalpable minuteness of the contagious unit, and the many invisible and untraceable ways in which it is transmitted, cases must be constantly occurring, exactly as in the other contagious fevers, whose linear descent cannot be followed, and which spring up, therefore, under the semblance of spontaneous origin.

10. That the occurrence of such cases obviously constitutes no proof, whatever, that this fever ever does arise spontaneously.

11. That the exceeding specialty of the conditions attaching to the reproduction of the specific poison in the living body itself, as well as the facts relating to the geographical distribution, past and present, of this and

the other contagious fevers, constitute evidence as strong as such evidence can ever be, that none of these fevers originate spontaneously, but are propagated solely by the law of continuous succession.

And, lastly—to crown the whole induction, by a practical test—That by destroying the infective power of the intestinal discharges, by strong chemicals, or otherwise, the spread of the fever may be entirely prevented, and that by repeating this process in every fresh case as it arises, the disease may in time be finally extinguished.

1. "William Budd," in *The Dictionary of National Biography*, vol 3, London: Oxford Univ. Press, 1959-60.

2. Budd, W.: On Intestinal Fever: Its Mode of Propagation, *Lancet* 2:694-695 (Dec 27) 1856.

3. Budd, W.: On the Fever at the Clergy Orphan Asylum, *Lancet* 2:617-619 (Dec 6) 1856.

4. Budd, W.: *Typhoid Fever: Its Nature, Mode of Spreading, and Prevention,* London: Longmans, Green, and Co., 1873.

Composite by G. Bako

John Snow (1813-1858)

JOHN SNOW, epidemiologist, pharmacologist, anesthetist, and physician, celibate and crusader against alcohol, seems as pure as his name. As the perceptive epidemiologist of the cholera epidemics in London and Newcastle in the mid-19th century, he was the first to provide experimental data in support of the water-borne theory of the spread of the pathogenic agent. The demonstration of the anesthetic properties of ether and chloroform enabled him to display his talents in quite another field of medical science. With the pursuit of a systematic pharmacological study of volatile anesthetic drugs and with the information gained, he became the foremost anesthetist in London.

Snow was born in York in 1813, the son of a farmer. In private school, it is reported that he was eager to learn and was especially fond of mathematics. At the age of 14, he became a pupil of William Hardcastle, surgeon at Newcastle-on-Tyne, and studied at the Newcastle Infirmary. Before he had completed his training as a surgeon's apprentice, he became a vegetarian and a prohibitionist. Having accepted this way of life, he remained a vigilant crusader in the following years. His first experience with cholera was in the 1831 epidemic in Newcastle. It began or was first recognized during the Polish-Russian War, and moved westward across Europe, over to Britain, and eventually spread to a number of countries throughout the world. More than 20,000 persons died in Britain during the epidemic.

Snow was not a particularly social fellow; rather, he preferred books, laboratory experiments, and bodily exercise. Reserved, clever, and considered by some to be a little peculiar, he was not too proud to ask for a translation in the library when the original treatise was unclear.[1] Furthermore, he was a faithful member of the Westminster Medical Society, a body which gave particular encouragement to young members of the profession who were eager to present a scientific essay or engage in a debate. In 1838, at the age of 25, Snow qualified for membership in the Royal College of Surgeons of England. His formal education was completed in 1844, at the age of 31, and he passed the MD examination at the University of London.

Epidemiology and anesthesia shared Snow's attention while he was building a practice in London. His contributions to epidemiology were not as extensive possibly as those in anesthesia, but were judged by several to be more significant. Cholera epidemics provided the source data for his observations in field epidemiology, which are fundamental and were made some time before the investigations of Pasteur and Koch in microbiology. The concept of the spread of cholera remains valid, although micropathogenic agents were not identified until decades later. Snow reasoned that, since the initial symptoms of cholera usually indicated primary affliction of the alimentary tract, the pathogenic agent gained entrance into the body via the stomach.[2]

There is sufficient evidence also, I believe, in the following pages, to prove the mode of communication of cholera here explained.
The instances in which minute quantities of the ejections and dejections of cholera patients must be swallowed are sufficiently numerous to account for the spread of the disease; and on examination it is found to spread most where the facilities for this mode of communication are greatest.

First-hand experience was obtained in an outbreak of cholera which occurred near the intersection of Cambridge and Broad streets, Golden Square, London, in 1854. In a period of 10 days, more than 500 fatal cases were reported. The number would have been considerably greater had not a large percentage of the population fled the city. Snow's epidemiologic studies concentrated on the contamination of the water from the street pump.

I suspected some contamination of the water of the much-frequented street-pump in Broad Street. . . . I requested permission, therefore, to take a list, at the General Register Office, of the deaths from cholera, registered during the week end . . . which was kindly granted. Eighty-nine deaths from cholera were registered, during the week.
On proceeding to the spot, I found that nearly all the deaths had taken place within a short distance of the pump. . . . The result of the inquiry then was, that there had been no particular outbreak or increase of cholera, in this part of London, except among the persons who were in the habit of drinking the water of the above-mentioned pump-well. I had an interview with the Board of Guardians of St. James's Parish, on the evening of Thursday, 7th September, and represented the above circumstances to them. In consequence of what I said, the handle of the pump was removed on the following day.

Before pursuing the epochal investigations in the spread of cholera, Snow did not ignore the opportunities in the newly discovered anesthetic agents in the 1840's. One of his first communications before the medical society described a device for treatment of asphyxia and the resuscitation of the newly born.[3] The instrument was based on the principle of a pulmotor, which had been invented by a Mr. Read of Regent Circus. Snow assumed that the stimulus for the first respiration in the newborn was similar to that for others; that is to say, it arose from inadequate oxygen pressure. Also, he speculated that the pulsive action of the blood was partially related to the capillaries, since the action of the heart was not sufficient to propel the blood throughout the circuit.

While Snow was waiting for his practice to expand, the discovery of ether for anesthesia was announced to the world. With a background and interest in respiration and asphyxia, it seems natural for this manifest curiosity to have led him into experimental studies on the pharmacology of anesthetic agents and the use of ether in the practice of anesthesia. A few of the experimental studies dealt with ether. Chloroform, on the other hand, benefited most from his investigations. The design of an improved inhaler, supplemented by experimental studies on anesthesia, placed Snow in the advanced anesthesia coterie in London.

The uncertain reputation of ether, plus the desire of the English to be somewhat different from the Americans, has been held responsible for the preference of Syme and Simpson, especially, for chloroform. However, neither physician was endowed with the capacity or displayed any consuming desire to investigate chloroform in the laboratory. Snow filled the void. The physical and pharmacological properties of a number of volatile agents were studied. The boiling point, the percentage of mixture of the experimental substance with air, and the quantity required by inhalation for insensibility were included in the physical studies. The pharmacological aspects included the minimal lethal dose in animals and mode of death, whether by cardiac or respiratory failure. However, extensive precautions were taken to prevent unnecessary suffering in animals; they were not used thoughtlessly in experiments. The effect of the agents on man concluded the investigation. Snow was invariably the experimental subject in this phase.

Snow administered chloroform to the young and the old. By 1857, this agent had been given to 186 infants under one year of age; two were only 8 and 10 days old. At the other extreme, chloroform was administered to several patients over 75 years of age and to one as old as 90 years.[3] The precipitation of a fit of epilepsy with chloroform was observed in the susceptible. Neither menstruation nor pregnancy was judged to be a contraindication if there was need for anethesia. No ill-effects were observed in patients with pulmonary tuberculosis. Skillful administration of anesthesia permitted the surgeon to operate on patients with heart disease. Even with anesthesia, however, surgery was for the swift. Readministration of chloroform was recommended, "if the operation lasts more than a minute or two."[4]

When the surgeon is cutting in the neighbourhood of important parts, it is desirable to prevent any sign of sensibility, and to keep repeating the chloroform so as to keep up the coma, without, however, causing embarrassment of the breathing, or wide dilatation of the pupil. In the greater number of operations, however, it is better to wait till there is some sign of sensibility, such as a slight cry or tendency to flinch, before the inhalation is resumed; and then a few inspirations of well diluted vapour make the patient quiet again.

The records of 50 fatal cases of inhalation, including postmortem examinations when performed, assembled from the hospitals in England and Scotland, were reviewed critically. The deaths in several of the cases upon review were judged to be unrelated to the anesthetic agent, in others to an overdose of the agent, with cardiac arrest. In Case 44, mouth-to-mouth respiration was practiced.

Mr. Bowman commenced practising artificial breathing, by the application of his own mouth to that of the patient. By this means, the chest was made to fill very completely, and the process was kept up almost without intermission for from five to eight minutes. During the first three or four minutes after the alarm began, the patient continued at times to make slight sighing efforts at voluntary inspiration, and the case was not thought, by those looking on, to be by any means hopeless. At length, however, these finally ceased, and from that time it was apparent that the man was dead.

The extent of Snow's anesthetic practice was remarkable. Although the incidence data for each of the surgical procedures were not recorded, he reported that:[4]

I have notes of 49 cases of amputation of the thigh in which I have administered chloroform. . . . I have notes of 31 cases in which I have administered chloroform during this amputation (of the leg). . . . I have memoranda of 197 cases of necrosis in which I have given chloroform. . . . I have notes of 147 operations for hare-lip, for which I have given chloroform. . . . I have notes of nineteen cases in which I have administered chloroform during this operation (division of the sensory nerves of the face. . . . I have, however, administered chloroform fifty-three times during the extraction of cataract. . . . I have notes of 867 cases in which I have administered chloroform during extraction of teeth. . . . I have memoranda of twenty-seven cases in which I have administered chloroform during the removal of a testicle, generally for malignant disease; and six cases in which I have administered it for amputation of the penis, always for malignant disease.

Whether studying an epidemic of cholera or extending the information on anesthesia, Snow remained an excellent practitioner of medicine. Completely devoted to his patients, he was willing to forego a fee when the patient was unable to pay. His life was rather selfish in that he never married and his hours were not troubled by the responsibilities of a home or family. He died at the age of 45, having suffered from hematemesis several times in the years preceding his death. The terminal event was preceded by left hemiparesis.

1. Richardson, B. W.: *Disciples of Aesculapius*, vol. 1, New York: E. P. Dutton & Co., 1901.
2. Snow, J.: *On the Mode of Communication of Cholera*, 2d ed., London: John Churchill, 1855.
3. Snow, J.: On Asphyxia, and on the Still-born, *London Med Gaz* 1:222-227, 1842.
4. Snow, J.: *On Chloroform and Other Anesthetics*, B. W. Richardson, ed., London: John Churchill, 1858.

Sulpice Antoine Fauvel
(1813-1884)

SULPICE A. FAUVEL, born in Paris and educated at the University of Paris, made one important contribution to cardiology. However, he devoted his scientific efforts primarily to the study of contagious diseases. He received his doctor's degree in 1840 upon the presentation of a thesis on capillary bronchitis, purulent and pseudomembranous catarrh of infants.[1] Sometime later Fauvel was appointed clinic chief at Hôtel Dieu, where he continued his studies on the epidemiology of scurvy and typhoid fever. When the Institute for Public Health in the Levant was organized, he was called to Constantinople in a senior position; one year later he was appointed a member of the Imperial Council of the Ottoman Empire. In 1849, Fauvel accepted the professorship of pathology at the school of medicine in Constantinople. Remaining in the Near East for almost two decades, he devoted his time largely to public health administration and epidemiologic field studies of cholera, plague, yellow fever, and typhus.

In 1851, Fauvel presented his findings and recommendations for control of the plague to the International Sanitary Congress in Paris. These proposals led to a series of reforms in the European quarantine system. During the Crimean War he inspected military hospitals, studied an epidemic of plague in Bulgaria, and investigated the spread of cholera in the French army. From these experiences he published a treatise on his mission to Bulgaria, a medical history of the Crimean War, and a study of typhus among field soldiers. In 1856, Fauvel founded the *Gazette Médicale d'Orient* and, in collaboration with the military surgeons of the allied armies, organized the Imperial Medical Society in Constantinople. Subsequently he succeeded to its presidency.

Several of Fauvel's theories on the cause and control of epidemic disease did not meet general acceptance; however, he was widely respected for his observations, and especially for his proposals regarding quarantine of overland and maritime travelers from the East. His views on quarantine and control of epidemics were summarized in 1869 before the Academy of Medicine when he spoke as follows:[2]

On the question of knowledge to what degree we are being menaced by the new invasion of cholera, France is presently endangered by three active foci from which cholera could be easily imported. . . . It is not necessary to expect that the enemy is at our doorstep ready to occupy us and it is fruitless to oppose this enemy by disorganized and ineffective measures; our foresight goes farther, we can prevent the danger, we can act upon the primary focus of the disease, we can stop the march of the epidemic from the Orient by blocking all routes it could follow in entering Europe.

In 1843, Fauvel published a contribution on the auscultatory signs in mitral stenosis, for which he is better remembered in clinical medicine than for his activities in public health. Following an historical introduction and reference to the work of Gendrin, he described an abnormal bruit in five patients observed at Hôtel Dieu between 25 and 50 years of age suffering from mitral stenosis. Two showed no insufficiency; the third case showed evidence of mitral insufficiency and aortic stenosis. The findings in each instance were consistent with a clinical diagnosis of rheumatic valvular heart disease. Excerpts from the postmortem examination in one case confirmed the clinical suspicion of mitral stenosis as follows.[3]

Many times I have been able to demonstrate the fact already pointed out by M. Gendrin, that, in certain cases, the abnormal bruit precedes the shock of the heart: but I did not then attach any great importance to it.

This year my attention was particularly attracted by a patient in whom this phenomenon existed with certain remarkable characteristics. It was a man of 25, who presented all the signs of an organic affection of the heart, because of which he had been dismissed from military service. He entered the Hôtel Dieu the 16th day of June, because of an acute articular rheumatism of moderate intensity. In the precordial region, besides a forceful impulse and a considerable area of dullness, one heard an *intense rasping murmur (bruit de râpe), preceding the first sound, finishing with it,* having its maximum intensity at the apex of the heart and to the left. The patient was dismissed cured of his rheumatism the fifteenth of July.

Soon chance favored me to such an extent that, in a very short space of time, four new cases have just come one after the other, to fix my attention and anew because of a repetition of the same stethoscopic signs.

I shall content myself with extracting from these observations that which is relative to the subject.

OBSERVATION I—AURICULO-VENTRICULAR
STENOSIS WITHOUT INSUFFICIENCY

A woman named Logrogue, aged 50 years, grocer, was admitted to the Hôtel Dieu, Saint-Bernard hall, the 19th of September 1842.

On admission it was noted that besides the complications resulting from a cerebral lesion, there was an elevation coinciding with the forceful heave in the precordial region. Percussion showed a dullness of about eight to ten centimeters.

On auscultation there was made out a rasping murmur *quite loud, having its maximum intensity at the level of the fifth rib, to the left of the nipple. This abnor-*

mal sound began during the silence which follows the second normal sound, and finishes at the moment when one hears the first sound, the abnormal sound becomes faint as one passes to the right or towards the base of the heart. The beats show some intermittence. The pulse was small, irregular. There was no edema of the extremities.

Autopsy showed a *stenosis of the left auriculo-ventricular orifice allowing scarcely the introduction of the tip of the fore-finger.* The narrowing was due to a yellowish deposit of the fibro-cartilagenous consistence placed in the substance of the mitral valve, and to warty-like concretions adherent to its auricular service. The chorda tendinae and the free margin of the valve had retained their suppleness and their normal length, in such a manner that there was no insufficiency. The walls of the ventricle were a little hypertrophied, without notable increase in size of the cavity. The other orifices were normal.

This observation, in which I regret the absence of certain anatomical details, is important, since it shows that in a marked stenosis of the auriculo-ventricular orifice there is present an abnormal sound, of such nature that it commences shortly after the middle of the long silence, and finishes at the instant when the first sound was heard. This fact has all the more value, since it was not possible to explain it by any lesion than a stenosis.

In conclusion, I conclude from the facts presented in this communication, that an abnormal pre-systolic murmur, localized towards the apex of the heart, in the present state of the science, is the most probable stethoscopic sign of a stenosis of the left auriculo-ventricular orifice. I do not say the certain sign: for the small number of cases upon which this conclusion is based, does not allow us to regard this conclusion as other than provisional, and requiring confirmation by new observations.

Returning to Paris in 1866, Fauvel was appointed General Inspector of the Health Service for France, an appointment held until a few months before his death. He was a member of the Academy of Medicine and served as its vice-president. Fauvel represented France at two International Sanitary Congresses; the first met in Constantinople in 1866 and the second in Vienna in 1874.

1. Fauvel, S.: *Investigations of Capillary Bronchitis, Purulent and Pseudomembranous (Suffocating Catarrh, Bronchial Croup) in Infants* (Fr), thesis, University of Paris, 1840.

2. Bergeron, M.: Obituary of Mr. Fauvel (Fr), *Bull Acad Med* 13:1607-1617, 1884, excerpt translated by Z. Danilevicius.

3. Fauvel, S.: The Stethoscopic Signs of Narrowing of the Left Auriculo-Ventricular Orifice of the Heart (Fr), *Arch Gen Med* 1:1-16, 1843, in Major, R. H. (trans.): *Classic Descriptions of Disease*, Springfield, Ill: C. C Thomas, 1932, pp 348-350.

Composite by G. Bako

Sir John Simon (1816-1904)

A PROFOUND INFLUENCE upon education and legislation in England in the areas usually identified as intimate to preventive medicine has been attributed to the first Medical Officer of Health of the City of London, John Simon. A native son and physician of London, he displayed little evidence of an interest in public health until mid-maturity, a decade after accepting an appointment as Demonstrator of Anatomy at King's College. John, christened at St. Olave's Church, where Pepys worshipped, prepared for higher education at Dr. Burney's school in Greenwich and subsequently spent a year studying in Prussia. Upon his return to London in 1833, he was apprenticed for six years, for the "usual fee of 500 guineas," to Joseph Henry Green, surgeon to St. Thomas' Hospital and professor of surgery in the Royal College of Surgeons and at King's College. At the age of 24, having achieved membership in the Royal College, Simon qualified as senior assistant surgeon at King's College Hospital. In 1847, he accepted the lectureship in anatomical pathology and, with it, ward responsibilities at St. Thomas'.

In spite of this excellent preparation and training in anatomy and clinical surgery and without manifest premonition, according to his biographers, Simon turned to public health. This was a new discipline in the medical sciences, endowed with great opportunities for contribution in urban sanitation, slum clearance, and mass inoculation against smallpox. This transition in socioscientific interest should not seem surprising for a physician of great vision. The time was propitious for correction of many of the sociomedical evils. The Public Health Act of 1848 had been prepared largely through the efforts of Sir Edwin Chadwick, one of the first designers of modern public health activities. William Farr of the General Registry Office, another pioneer in this domain, collected and published critical statistical data on disease and death. Building upon the accomplishments, concepts, and collected data of Chadwick, Farr, Snow, Budd, and others, it was apparent to Simon that contagion, poverty, and filth required corrective legislation for effective control. Simon accepted the challenge, and in 1848 became the first Medical Officer of Health of the City of London.[1] From this post he was transferred in 1855 to Medical Officer to the General Board of Health. The Board was abolished in 1858, but its functions were assumed by the newly constituted Medical Department of the Privy Council. Simon remained as Medical Officer to the new department, and when its functions were in turn transferred to the local government board, he served until his retirement in 1876.[2] During all this period he was a member of the staff of St. Thomas' Hospital, as pathologist and later as surgeon.

A great mass of data, collected while he was medical officer, on overcrowding, inadequate ventilation, general filth, lack of drainage, contaminated water supplies, as well as proposals for correction, is preserved in two thick volumes of general reports.[3] Causes of death in London were presented regularly by Simon to the City Council. The great threat to health from dumping the city sewage into the tidal Thames, as well as the medical hazards of cesspools, was evident. Housing was deplorable, tenements were filthy, overcrowding was common, and control of contagion, particularly cholera, malaria, and typhoid, became an almost impossible goal. Butchering was carried out under foul, wretched circumstances in the abattoirs. There was an endless number of accidental or criminal deaths from poisoning or other preventable calamities. Nutritional deficiencies were prevalent. Time was long overdue, not only for medical reform but also for common sense correction of many of the social ills. The serious deficiencies in supply of water is one example from the *Public Health Reports* of 1887.[3]

I am sure that I do not exaggerate the sanitary importance of water, when I affirm that its unrestricted supply is the first essential of decency, of comfort, and of health; that no civilization of the poorer classes can exist without it; and that any limitation to its use in the metropolis is a barrier, which must maintain thousands in a state of the most unwholesome filth and degradation.

In the City of London the supply of water is but a fraction of what it should be. Thousands of the population have no supply of it to the houses where they dwell. For their possession of this first necessary of social life, such persons wholly depend on their power of attending at some fixed hour of the day, pail in hand, beside the nearest standcock; where, with their neighbours, they wait their turn—sometimes not without a struggle, during the tedious dribbling of a single small pipe. Sometimes there is a partial improvement on this plan; a group of houses will have a butt or cistern for the common use of some scores of inmates, who thus are saved the necessity of waiting at a standcock, but who still remain most insufficiently supplied with water. Next in the scale of improvement we find water-pipes laid on to the houses; but the water is turned on only a few hours in the week, so that all who care to be adequately supplied with it must be provided with very spacious receptacles.

I consider the system of intermittent water-supply to be radically bad; not only because it is a system of stint in what ought to be lavishly bestowed, but also because of the necessity which it creates that large and extensive receptacles should be provided, and because of the liability to contamination incurred by water which has to be retained, often during a considerable period. In inspecting the courts and alleys of the City, one constantly sees butts, for the reception of water, either public, or in the open yards of the houses, or sometimes in their cellars; and these butts, dirty, mouldering, and coverless; receiving soot and all other impurities from the air; absorbing stench from the adjacent cesspool; inviting filth from insects, vermin, sparrows, cats, and children; their contents often augmented through a rain water-pipe by the washings of the roof, and every hour becoming fustier and more offensive.

Simon was knighted in 1887, at Queen Victoria's Jubilee, having received in the preceding years honorary degrees from the universities of Oxford, Cambridge, Edinburgh, and Dublin. He served as president of the Royal College of Surgeons in 1878.[4] He was recognized as a linguist, a student of Oriental literature, and a friend of artists, philosophers, and writers. The latter category included Thackeray, Tennyson, and Ruskin. His *English Sanitary Institutions* of 1890 reviewed the history of sanitation.[5] Public Health measures were traced from the earliest times through the development of their political and social relations. The discourse is in delightfully light style, and contains outstanding examples of good composition as well as excellent discussions of sanitary science, political, economic, sociologic, religious, and scientific aspects of this new discipline.

The obituary notice in the London *Times* at his death at the age of 88 described Simon as[6]

> The master of sanitary science, the organizer, and for years the official head of a system of public health preservation which is without equal in the world, the philosopher whose teaching has saved the lives of hundreds of thousands of our people, whose name is a household word wherever preventive medicine is studied, and whose writings form the classical literature of the subject to which much of his life has been devoted.

1. "Simon, Sir John (1816-1904)," in *Plarr's Lives of the Fellows of the Royal College of Surgeons of England*, vol. II, Bristol, England: John Wright & Sons Ltd., 1930.
2. Obituary, Sir John Simon, *Brit Med J* 2:265-267 (July 30) 1904.
3. Simon, J.: *Public Health Reports*, London: J. & A. Churchill, vol. I, II, 1887.
4. Simon, J.: *Personal Recollections of Sir John Simon, K.C.B.*, privately printed,, 1898.
5. Simon, J.: *English Sanitary Institutions*, London: Cassell & Co., Ltd., 1890.
6. Death of Sir John Simon, *The Times*, Mon., July 25, 1904, p. 6.

Max von Pettenkofer (1818-1901)

PROGRESS IN PUBLIC HYGIENE in the first portion of the 19th century faltered in Germany, in comparison with England, until Pettenkofer, chemist and physiologist, successfully convinced the citizenry and the state of the practical importance of this aspect of living. Max Pettenkofer was born in Lichtenheim, Bavaria, into a family impoverished because of size and lack of material resources.[1] Formal learning began with an apprentice-

ship under his uncle, a court apothecary. He continued his education at the University of Munich, where he concentrated in chemistry and mineralogy and qualified for

National Library of Medicine

the MD degree. While yet a student, Pettenkofer published one communication on the chemical identification of arsenic and another on the qualitative separation of arsenic from antimony. But he was restless and uncertain; he tried acting on the stage for a time and wrote a volume of sonnets before receiving the professional degree.

Subsequently, he undertook postgraduate studies in chemistry at Würzburg, where he identified hippuric acid in the urine and described the qualitative test for bile salts—the Pettenkofer test.[2] During postgraduate work with von Liebig at Giessen, he discovered creatinin. However, Pettenkofer, finding himself unemployable in the medical sciences, sought work as a metallurgist in the Royal Mint. Pursuing an earlier interest in metallurgy he designed a new assay method for gold and silver. In 1847, he was called to Munich as professor of medical chemistry, a newly created position. The assignment was interpreted literally, as he moved toward the area of public health, building on a foundation of experimental physiology, physiological chemistry, and epidemiology. One of his first students was Carl von Voit, whose name is associated with his teacher in the Pettenkofer-Voit respiration apparatus. The amounts of carbohydrates and fat consumed by the body at rest were determined. The Pettenkofer method for determination of carbon dioxide in air and water was a useful procedure in the related field of energy metabolism.[3] Voit continued to study the physiology of respiration; whereas Pettenkofer moved, by gradual stages, into experimental hygiene.

Pettenkofer's first objective was achieved in 1865, when the Bavarian government sanctioned a department of hygiene at the University of Munich. The second objective, facilities for experimental research and instruction of students, was fulfilled in 1879 by the construction of the Institute of Hygiene. The lectures given by Pettenkofer at the Institute disclosed his breadth and depth of interest in hygiene. They included diet, sanitary regulations, sewage disposal, handling of food, ventilation, botanicals in the home and out-of-doors, water supply, burial of the dead, substances poisonous to man, medical statistics, clothing, lighting, and heating. The laboratory investigations complementing the lectures included, among many subjects, the manufacture of illuminating gas from wood, development of a new procedure for the production of building cement, compounding of an amalgam for dental fillings, and restoration of oil paintings. Pettenkofer founded two scientific periodicals: the *Zeitschrift für Biologie*, co-edited with Voit in 1865, and the *Archives für Hygiene* in 1883.

Pettenkofer was a thoroughly practical administrator and, in the furthering of his program in private and public health, found the use of vital statistics valuable. Much of the scientific data upon which public health matured came from his laboratory. A need for active support from the citizenry in implementing his program was recognized, sought, and subsequently exploited upon approval by the community. An example was the construction of sewers in Munich, with the virtual elimination of typhoid fever.[4] On the other hand, his concept of multiple factors in the etiology of bacterial disease led him slightly astray and in direct conflict with Koch regarding the pathogenesis of cholera. Koch attributed cholera specifically to the *Vibrio comma;* Pettenkofer placed less significance upon a "germ" as the offending microbiologic agent and advanced the hypothesis that the disease was caused by a combination of factors: soil contaminated with decaying material and a toxic substance interacting with the specific agent (a ferment) in a susceptible environment. This theory is not so bizarre as it appears on casual review, since it is currently recognized that infestation of a host by bacterial invasion or contact does not invariably lead to clinical symptoms associated with overt infection. A previous exposure, with development of titratable immunity, is not always a confirmable explanation of escape from infection. A number of factors probably contribute to susceptibility to infection and individual affliction by an epidemic malady. Pettenkofer noted in cholera that:[5]

> In my opinion four conditions are essential in order to bring about an epidemic of cholera:
> 1. A specific germ (or ferment).
> 2. Certain local conditions.
> 3. Certain seasonal conditions.
> 4. Certain individual conditions.

I have not investigated the nature of the cholera germ as disseminated by human intercourse. I have only taken for granted that it exists in the intestinal discharges of persons coming from infected places. My own investigations have been chiefly confined to the second and third before-mentioned conditions. Hitherto I have considered the human subject only so far as he is the bearer of the infecting matter of cholera or of the germ of this matter; and have with facts contended against the pure contagionists, who declare that the infecting matter is produced by a process of multiplication within the bodies of those affected by the disease. My chief proofs of this have always lain in simple *facts* (independent of any theory) as to the spread of cholera over large districts. There are certainly *places* enjoying complete immunity from cholera, also *periods* of immunity. The development of epidemics, and the immunity of many places, is totally inexplicable, by the simple assumption of contagion from person to person. Observe the spread of epidemics along the course of railways and other ways of inter-communication. Nor are they to be explained by certain individual disposition of person (food, drinks, domestic arrangements, age, position, &c); but the circumstances require, besides these, the existence of local and seasonal aiding causes, which have to be assumed.

Are these in immediate relation to the cholera germ itself, or to the individual disposition? Facts speak in favour of the first opinion only. 1. Persons from an un-affected place going to an affected one, are attacked quite as numerously and as soon as the persons who constantly reside in these places. 2. Cases are on record where a person from an infected district conveys (in a way not clearly ascertained) infecting matter in a place enjoying complete immunity from cholera; and there, by means of his limited amount of infecting matter, infects a few persons who themselves had never been subject to the local conditions of an infected place, and therefore could not have had their individual disposi-tion altered by it. Facts imperiously demand that we should consider that the "seasonal" and "local" con-ditions are intimately connected with the cholera germ, although they may, in addition be in a condition to act on the predisposition also.

Pettenkofer was given personal nobility, then hereditary nobility. In 1896, the title "Excellency" was conferred upon him and the following year the gold Harben Medal of the British Institute of Public Health. Meanwhile, the city of Munich supported their distin-guished sanitary scientist and contributed bountifully to the Pettenkofer Foundation for Hygienic Investigation. It seems a paradox for one who valued health and hygiene so highly that he killed himself at the age of 83 with a shot from a revolver. In one of his popular lectures delivered in 1873, he sum-marized his concept of health.[6]

Every one in this world wishes to be healthy, for life without health is a torment, a torture, from which all wish to be released, even—if there is no other way left —be renouncing life, through death. . . . Health and sickness, like strength and weakness, are not simple, sharply defined conditions, but very complex, highly involved and relative conditions, with no sharp border-lines. No one is abolutely or completely healthy, and no one is absolutely sick; every one is in such a condi-tion only more or less. We measure the degree of health and sickness by the amount of disturbance that our physical condition causes in our ability to perform our usual tasks.

Since the value of our life depends on what we ac-complish, and our accomplishments depend on our ability to work, the value of health to each individual is obvious. Today, however, I would like to draw your attention particularly to the fact that each individual derives advantage, not only from his own health but just as much, and sometimes even more, from the health of other people, of his fellowmen.

1. Hume, E. E.: *Max von Pettenkofer*, New York: P. B. Hoeber, Inc, 1927.

2. Pettenkofer, M.: A New Reaction of Bile and Carbo-hydrate (Ger), *Ann Chem Pharm* 52:90-96, 1844.

3. Pettenkofer, M.: A Method of Detecting Carbon Dioxide in the Air (Ger), *J Prakt Chem* 85:165-184, 1862.

4. Pettenkofer, M.: *The Canal or Sewer System in Munich* (Ger), Munich: H. Manz, 1869.

5. Pettenkofer, M.: Causes of Cholera, *Med Press Cir*, p 405 (May 12) 1869.

6. Pettenkofer, M.: The Value of Health to a City, H. E. Sigerist, trans., *Bul Hist Med* 10:473-613, 1941.

Medical Museum of History, Stockholm

Peter Ludvig Panum
(1820-1885)

P. L. PANUM, who made notable observations on the contagion of measles before receiving his doctorate, was the son of a military sur-geon at Ronne on the island Bornholm, off the coast of Sweden.[1] After the family moved to Rendsburg, Schleswig-Holstein, he began his university studies at the University of Kiel and later matriculated in medicine at the Uni-versity of Copenhagen, qualifying for the de-gree in 1845. The following year his hospital training was interrupted when the govern-ment Medical Board, having observed his talents for investigation, sent the young phy-sician as epidemiologist on a special mission to the Faeroe Islands to investigate a violent epidemic of measles. The report of this mis-sion marked Panum not only as an outstand-ing inquirer into the customs and habits of a remote civilization, but especially as an in-quirer into the contagious spread of measles.[2] His next assignment was at the University of Berlin. There he made the acquaintance of

Virchow, who persuaded him to publish an abstract of his full-length document in the first volume of the newly established *Archiv für pathologische Anatomie und Physiologie und für klinische Medicin*.[3]

Continuing his hospital training in Copenhagen in his preparation for medicine, Panum took part in the Danish-German war as a surgeon in the Danish navy. In 1850, he again was sent by his government—this time to Bandholm on the island of Laaland to investigate one of the first of minor cholera epidemics in Denmark. After presenting his dissertation on fibrin and receiving the MD degree from the University of Copenhagen, Panum spent two years in graduate work, studying at Würzburg, Leipzig, and Paris, where his teachers included von Kölliker, Lehmann, and Claude Bernard. His fame preceded his return to Denmark. He was appointed to the professorship of physiology, medical chemistry, and general pathology at the University of Kiel, accepting simultaneously an assignment to establish suitable laboratory facilities. This double appointment was brief, inasmuch as political events in Schleswig-Holstein were so distracting that he accepted a call to Copenhagen as professor of physiology. He held this post until a rupture of the myocardium caused his death just before the statutory age of retirement.

The majority of Panum's scientific contributions, which included work in epidemiology, hygiene, public health, metabolism, nutrition, bacteriology, embryology, physiology, pathology, and optics, were published in Danish.[2] Several communications were published in German or were translated into German from the Danish; whereas a few appeared in English in abstract or in full translation. Panum prepared several small texts and a series of communications on the history of medicine and physiology in Denmark, and was Copenhagen's medical ambassador to the principal medical schools in Europe and a crusader against the antivivisectionists. His executive ability and diplomatic skill were recognized by his serving as president of the Eighth International Medical Congress in Copenhagen in 1884. Establishing a liaison between Scandinavian medical scientists and those of other countries was another personal mission, necessary because their languages, and especially Danish, were relatively unfamiliar in scientific circles abroad.

A favorable opportunity for investigation of the epidemiological features of measles on the Faeroes was directly related to the geographic isolation and peculiar topography, which limited social intercourse among the inhabitants of the several villages. The Faeroese, fearful of the spread of contagious diseases, were, in general, meticulous in recounting events relating to afflicted persons. Such documentation enhanced the speed of data collection, in addition to authenticating the intercourse between contacts and others. In the pursuit of his epidemiological assignment on measles, Panum was aware of and commented on the spread of syphilis, heart disease, rheumatic fever, chronic bronchitis, cutaneous diseases, hysteria, pipe-smoking by women, longevity, and influenza. He found little or no typhoid, typhus, tuberculosis, cancer, Bright's disease, scarlet fever, or whooping cough among the Faeroese. The social customs and religious superstitions were discussed; their eating habits were critically analyzed. Respiratory distress was attributed to living in smoke-filled huts. Excerpts on the natural history or contagion of measles from Gafafer's translation of the German abstract follow.[3]

On the Faroe Islands which lie between the Shetlands and Iceland there raged, from April to October of 1846, an epidemic of measles which attacked more than 6000 of the 7782 inhabitants. This almost unexampled spread of an epidemic in which there was no selection of a particular age group was due to the fact that there had been no recognizable outbreak of measles since 1781, a period of 65 years. The following circumstances will serve to explain these extraordinary phenomena. The Faroese are not only isolated geographically but for centuries they have been isolated from the rest of the world commercially. . . . Because of this unnatural isolation, the inhabitants are visited rarely by epidemic diseases and hence on the average their lives are prolonged.

The inhabited islands, seventeen in number, are so separated by fjords, some of which are very dangerous, that the inhabitants of one island with their very limited knowledge of the world, often think of themselves as an independent people. . . . Perhaps the only time when one sees people from different villages gathered together in larger numbers is when they trade their products for necessities at one of the marts, or when a general call is heard by the men to assemble by hundreds to catch *Grind* [large, dolphin-like animal]. This isolation of the detached villages and their inhabitants means, furthermore, that every contact with the inhabitants of other places is known to every one and what is extraordinary, it is often recorded on the calendar, and thus after the passage of time is remembered by all.

The first village that I reached on my travels was Tjörnevig on Nordströmö on July 2 where 80 of the 100 inhabitants were affected with measles. On June 4, 10 men of Tjörnevig in a boat took part in a *grind* catch in Westmannhavn and exactly 14 days later, that is on June 18, the eruption appeared in all 10 men after feeling ill for 2–4 days and after they had suffered from cough and aching of the eyes.

This experience gave rise to the supposition that the contagium of measles causes no visible effects for a more or less long time, ordinarily 10–12 days, after it is received by the organism, since the early catarrhal stage began only after the passing of this time and the eruption appeared first on the 14th day following the reception of the infecting matter. If this supposition were confirmed, then the observation that the second and third series of attacks each followed after an interval of about 14 days, would make it probable that measles has its greatest infectivity during the stage of eruption and efflorescence and not as is generally said during desquamation.

The rule: That the contagium of measles may not cause disease phenomena for some time after its introduction into the organism, and then only after an indefinite prodromal period, according to my observations always on the 13th or 14th day after exposure, was proved constant to me in a significant series of accurate observations.

As a consequence we may say, at least, that measles is not infective so long as the contagium is latent . . . it is certain *that measles is very infectious during eruption and efflorescence, whereas the capacity to infect remains doubtful in the prodromal as well as in the desquamation period.* I arrived at the conclusion, however, that *there is no relation at all between cowpox and measles, and that they may develop at the same time in the same individual.* I am, therefore, inclined to admit, *that those cases in which measles occurred twice in the same individual are founded on an erroneous diagnosis, or, at least are very rare.*

There can be no doubt, however, that isolation is the most dependable means to check the spread of measles. The experience pointing toward the purely contagious nature of measles rather than the miasmatic was paid for so dearly on the Faroes that the people must without any hesitation believe with us that at least in private practice it is correct to think of measles not as a miasmatic or miasmatic-contagious disease, but as a contagious one.

The original report, 74 pages in length, was abstracted to 20 pages and contained the following observations in summary, which contributes to our contemporary understanding of measles and the epidemiology of infectious disease: clinical symptoms do not develop until days after exposure to the contagion, the rash appears regularly on the 13th or 14th day after exposure, it is contagious only during eruption and efflorescence, there is no relation between cowpox and measles, the disease does not occur twice in the same person, it is not miasmic-borne but purely contagious, and isolation is the most certain means of arresting progress of its epidemic nature.

1. Gafafer, W. M.: Bibliographical Biography of Peter Ludvig Panum (1820-1885), Epidemiologist and Physiologist, *Bull Inst Hist Med* 2:259-280, 1934.

2. Panum, P. L.: Observations Made During the Measles Epidemic on the Faroe Islands in the Year 1846, *Bibl Laeger* 1:270-344, 1847, translated in *Med Classics* 3:803-886, 1939.

3. Panum, P. L.: Remarks on the Contagion of Measles, abstract of Panum,[2] *Arch Path Anat* 1:492-512, 1847, translated by W. M. Gafafer, *Isis* 24:90-101, 1935-1936.

National Library of Medicine

Louis Pasteur (1822-1895)

No MEDICAL SCIENTIST'S NAME is more familiar to the profession and the laity than that of Louis Pasteur. His contributions, planned and pursued with simplicity, established the causal relationship of microorganisms to several industrial problems indigenous to France, and later to infectious diseases in animals and man. They have proved to be the keystone of contemporary microbiology.

Pasteur, born at Dole, Jura, was the son of a tanner and a retired sergeant from Napoleon's army.[1] His patient but undistinguished industry as a youth centered on sketching for a period until an interest in science brought him greater attention. After receiving the AB degree at Besançon, he continued his higher education in Paris at the École Normale and later at the Sorbonne. Here, attracted by the lectures of Dumas, the brilliant chemist and senator, he began to follow a lifelong interest in the physical sciences.

Pasteur began teaching reluctantly while still a student; in 1848, the next year after receipt of the PHD degree at École Normale, he was appointed professor of physics at the Lyceum at Dijon. In one of his initial investigations in the laboratory with crystals and dimorphous substances he first recognized the nonuniformity of the crystals of tartaric acid and paratartaric acid (racemic), as well as their salts. He discovered that crystals of ordinary tartaric salts in solution caused polarized light to deviate to the right; whereas crystals of paratartaric salts caused the light to deviate to the left. From these observations, Pasteur reasoned that dissymmetry of form corresponded to molecular dissymmetry and advanced the concept that synthesis by living organisms was basically responsible for substances with optical activity. This work was continued at Strasbourg when he joined their faculty in 1852 as adjuvant professor of chemistry. By then his discoveries had attracted the commendation of the Royal Society of London, which, in 1856 awarded him their Rumford medal.

Following the habit of French scientists of frequent periodic reporting of most of his research, Pasteur presented brief and sometimes scarcely related portions of his investigations eventually to be developed into an integrated module. However, in none of his writings can one discern as clearly as has become self-evident retrospectively the doctrine destined to form the foundation of modern bacteriology.

In 1854, Pasteur was called by the Faculty of Sciences of the newly-formed school at Lille to become dean and professor of chemistry. There, centering his attention on the study of fermentation, he confirmed the observations of Schwann and Cagniard de La-

tour that viable yeast cells are essential for the production of alcohol, and carbonic acid for the fermentation of sugar. However, he found that microorganisms other than yeast cells, by the production of butyric and lactic acid, were responsible for souring of wine, milk, and other substances. These studies constituted the initial phases in the refutation of the widely held, but scientifically untenable, position of Liebig who rejected the theory that living organisms participate in fermentation, and attributed the phenomenon to a "vital force." In 1860, the Académie des Sciences conferred the prize in experimental physiology on Pasteur for these studies. Among several other features in the phenomenon, its anaerobic properties and the small quantity of ferment required to convert a large quantity of sugar were particularly noteworthy.[2]

It is possible to observe in ordinary lactic acid fermentation, on top of the sediment of chalk and nitrogenous material, a gray substance which occurs at the surface of this deposit. Under microscopic examination it can be barely distinguished from the casein, disintegrating gluten, etc. so that nothing indicates that it may be a special material, nor that it has arisen during the fermentation. Nevertheless, it is this substance which plays the principal role in the fermentation. Its appearance is similar to that of the beer yeast when it is studied *en masse* and squeezed or pressed. Under the microscope it is seen to form tiny globules or small objects which are very short, isolated or in groups of irregular masses. These globules are much smaller than those of beer yeasts and move actively by Brownian movement. If washed with a large amount of water by decantation, then diluted into a solution of pure sugar, they immediately begin to make acid, but quite slowly, since acid inhibits significantly their action on sugar. . . . Only a small amount of this yeast is needed to convert a large amount of sugar. This fermentation is preferably carried out in the absence of air, since it is inhibited by plants or by parasitic infusoria.

In providing convincing proof against the doctrine of spontaneous generation, Pasteur demonstrated that organized bodies are native to man's environment and that living matter, in infusions previously sterilized by heat, originates only from extant living substances in suspension in the atmosphere.[3]

The greatest interest of this method is that it proves without doubt that the origin of life, in infusions which have been boiled, arises uniquely from the solid particles which are suspended in the air. Gas, various fluids, electricity, magnetism, ozone, things known or things unknown—there is absolutely nothing in ordi-

nary atmospheric air which brings about the phenomenon of putrefaction or fermentation in the liquids which we have studied except these solid particles. . . .

The experiments of the preceding chapters can be
summarized in the following double proposition:

1. There exist continually in the air organized bodies
which cannot be distinguished from true germs of the
organisms of infusions.

2. In the case that these bodies, and the amorphous
debris associated with them, are inseminated into a
liquid which has been subjected to boiling and which
would have remained unaltered in previously heated
air if the insemination had not taken place, the same
beings appear in the liquid as those which develop
when the liquid is exposed to the open air.

In 1857, Pasteur was recalled to Paris to
direct the scientific studies of the École
Normale, an institution handicapped by an
ailing faculty and grossly inadequate physical
facilities. In 1862, he was elected to the
Académie des Sciences; in 1863, he served as
profesor of geology and chemistry at the
École des Beaux Arts; and from 1867 to 1899
as professor of chemistry at the Sorbonne,
pursuing meanwhile productive fundamental
investigations. These concerned especially the
making of vinegar, spoilage of French wines,
upgrading of French beer, and diseases of
silkworms. Approaching each industrial problem with meager specific knowledge and little
intimate experience, but endowed with a desire to help his country and its people, his investigations were valuable in each instance.

Pasteur taught vinegar makers that the development of the indispensable film on the
liquor can be hastened by seeding with living
ferments. The solution for the winemakers'
difficulties lay in providing partial heat sterilization, with a temperature between 55 and
60 C. This process, now known as pasteuriza-
tion, was applied subsequently to other perish-
able fluids and foods and especially to milk.
Sought by the Minister of Agriculture supported by Dumas to combat a scourge in the
silk industry, Pasteur found that silkworms
were dying either from pébrine, an hereditary
parasitic infestation, or from a bacterial infection of intestinal origin. Gaining knowledge of the source of the trouble, he saved the
industry. The results of these investigations
and their extension into animal pathology led
to his investigations on infectious diseases of
animals and man.

In the midst of these labors and while only
46 years of age, Pasteur was stricken with
hemiplegia. A series of small fits impaired his
speech but not his mind. He continued his
work during convalescence and slowly regained the use of his paralyzed limbs. An uneasiness in his walk and a weakness in his left
arm were the only permanent residua. As his
fundamental investigations were coming
closer and closer to clinical medicine and to
the pathogenesis of infectious diseases, he developed greater interest in the phenomenon
of immunity than in taxonomic bacteriology.
Nevertheless, he confirmed the findings of
Davaine and Koch on the pathogenesis of
anthrax, identified *Staphylococcus pyogenes*
in boils, and *Streptococcus pyogenes* in puerperal fever.

One of the first reports of international interest in the clinical application of Pasteur's
work was the use of carbolic acid by Lister of
Edinburgh for prevention of the suppuration
frequently following surgical intervention. In
comparative microbiology, Pasteur's observations on inoculation for chicken cholera
disclosed the survival of some fowl following
exposure to a highly virulent bacilli, while a
chance discovery showed that pathogenic
properties may be attenuated or heightened
by successive passages through appropriate
animals. The critical observation disclosed
that immunity had been induced by injection
of cultures which had lost their virulence by
design.[4]

In examining the animals which have not died during this study on virulence, it can be seen that they
have been sick from the same disease which has killed
the other animals, since one can find in their muscles
the same tiny organism in large numbers. If we consider that in general acute diseases do not ordinarily
recur, it may be asked if this disease, which exists without killing the animals, would not be able to hinder
the recovery from the fatal disease. But, if we inoculate these chickens which have not died, with a virus
which is highly virulent to fresh chickens, one which
has not been in contact with air, and which is able to
kill 100 times out of 100, we find that it no longer kills,
and that it never is able to develop. Evidently, we have
discovered a virus-vaccine for fowl cholera. . . . Indeed, if one studies the virulence of a culture every 15
days for a number of months, it is easy to show that
there is a gradual diminution in virulence, and each
virus can be considered as a vaccine for the virus above
it. Here is therefore the idea of a vaccine, well known
in medicine since Jenner, but which reveals itself in
very new conditions in a microscopic organism.

Pasteur's triumph over rabies, his last great scientific work, is a prime example of his ability to begin an investigation with plausible hypotheses and progress, in spite of apparently insurmountable obstacles, to a clear, conceptual victory. The transmission of rabies through the bite of a mad dog pointed to an infectious agent and warranted the study of saliva of rabid dogs for the recovery and identification of the specific substance. Systematic efforts failed, however, nor was transmission by saliva reliable. Whereupon Pasteur, acting on the suggestion that the disease is primarily a central nervous system malady, inoculated successfully brain tissue from a rabid dog into the central nervous system of a healthy animal. With this achievement he proceeded in painstaking studies to immunize dogs and subsequently humans. He described these investigations as follows.[5]

After making almost innumerable experiments, I have discovered a prophylactic method which is practical and prompt, and which has already in dogs afforded me results sufficiently numerous, certain, and successful, to warrant my having confidence in its general applicability to all animals, and even to man himself.

This method depends essentially on the following facts:

The inoculation of the infective spinal cord of a dog suffering from ordinary rabies, under the dura mater of a rabbit, always produces rabies after a period of incubation having a mean duration of about fifteen days.

If, by the above method of inoculation, the virus of the first rabbit is passed into a second, and that of the second into a third, and so on, in series, a more and more striking tendency is soon manifested towards a diminution of the duration of the incubation period of rabies in the rabbits successively inoculated.

After passing twenty or twenty-five times from rabbit to rabbit, inoculation periods of eight days are met with, and continue for another interval, during which the virus is passed twenty or twenty-five times from rabbit to rabbit. Then an incubation period of seven days is reached, which is encountered with striking regularity throughout a new series extending as far as the ninetieth animal.

Experiments of this class, begun in November, 1882, have now lasted for three years without any break in the continuity of the series, and without our ever being obliged to have recourse to any other virus than that of the rabbits successively dead of rabies. Consequently, nothing is easier than to have constantly at our disposal, over considerable intervals of time, a virus of rabies, quite pure, and always quite or very nearly identical.

Through the years Pasteur attracted such outstanding pupils and associates as Metchnikoff, Roux, Yersin, Calmette, Chantemesse, Chamberland, and others. Equally significant was the opening of the Pasteur Institute in 1888, a monument built by public subscription and international contributions for living quarters and laboratory facilities; however, by then he was no longer able to direct the program. Pasteur was not faultless; he made many mistakes and advanced unsubstantiated premises, but his contributions to medicine and mankind are triumphal marks of a great scientist.

1. Vallery-Radot, R.: *The Life of Pasteur* (Fr), R. L. Devonshire (trans.), Garden City, NY: Doubleday, Page & Co., 1924.
2. Pasteur, L.: On Lactic Acid Fermentation (Fr), *C R Acad Sci (Paris)* 45:913-916, 1857, in Brock, T. D. (trans.-ed.): *Milestones in Microbiology*, Englewood Cliffs, NJ: Prentice-Hall, Inc., 1961.
3. Pasteur, L.: On the Doctrine of Spontaneous Generation (Fr), *Ann Sci Nat Zool (Paris)* 16:5-98, 1861, in Brock, T. D. (trans.-ed): *Milestones in Microbiology*, Englewood Cliffs, NJ: Prentice-Hall, Inc., 1961.
4. Pasteur, L.: The Vaccine-Virus of Fowl Cholera and Anthrax (Fr), *C R Congr Agron*, Versailles, June 1881, pp 151-162, in Brock, T. D. (trans.-ed): *Milestones in Microbiology*, Englewood Cliffs, NJ: Prentice-Hall, Inc., 1961.
5. Pasteur, L.: Prevention of Rabies After Exposure (Fr), *C R Acad Sci (Paris)* 101:764-785, 1885, in Metchnikoff, E.: *The Founders of Modern Medicine*, D. Berger (trans), New York: Walden Publications, 1939.

Los Angeles County Medical Library

Elie Metchnikoff (1845-1916)

ELIE [ILIA-ELIJAH] METCHNIKOFF, one of the world's great biologists, was born on an estate near Kharkoff in a remote part of Little Russia. In the last months of his life his wife prepared an intimate but objective biography[1] from dictation of his recollections. Midway through his life he advanced his hypothesis of phagocytosis for which he is best remembered. Building upon this work he energetically studied immunologic phenomena. Also, he demonstrated that bacteriolysis, or Pfeiffer's phenomenon, can occur in vitro, and with Roux he inoculated apes with the spirochete of syphilis.

Metchnikoff showed an early interest in natural history, entered the Kharkoff Lycée at the age of 11, and completed a four-year course at Kharkoff University in two years. Dissatisfied with the reactionary scientists and mediocre education in Russia, he spent four years out of the country, studying at the universities of Giessen, Munich, and Göttingen. Before returning home he investigated Mediterranean fauna on the shores of Naples, an enterprise to which he returned on several occasions. Supported by a combination of exposure to the stringent education provided in Germany and experience in investigation, he began an academic career with minor appointments at Odessa and St. Petersburg, advancing in 1872 to the professorship of zoology at the University of Odessa. After a decade of formal teaching he began serving as director of the Municipal Bacteriology Laboratory in Odessa, an interim assignment held until 1888. He then accepted Pasteur's invitation to head a department in the newly-founded Pasteur Institute in Paris. Here he spent the remainder of his life as one of the brilliant investigators who attracted a school of devoted pupils and made the Institute one of the great scientific centers of the world. With a frail body and a capricious eyesight, Metchnikoff was emotional, impulsive and melancholic by nature, but generous and unselfish in his dealings with others.

Although Metchnikoff's practical investigations concerned bacteriology, immunology, and pathology, he approached his problems as a zoologist concerned with unicellular life. In 1865, one of his first documented studies was reported from Giessen—the discovery of intracellular digestion in a small flatworm. The research proved to be a precursor of the concept promulgated almost two decades later that the essence of inflammation in invertebrates and in vertebrates is the response of particular cells to destroy, to devitalize, or to engulf foreign objects. Although Virchow's cellular theory of pathology had been maturing for a quarter of a century, inflammation was still judged to be an acute vascular response, and the participation by fixed connective tissue cells or migrant special cells was overlooked.

Metchnikoff considered bacteria to be potential food for the phagocyte, even though some invaders might resist ingestion by multiplication; whereas others would devise means eventually to destroy the host. Thus, digestion and defense were essential and indistinguishable ingredients of Metchnikoff's theory of phagocytosis and inflammation. In the lower Metazoa, defense and digestion were interchangeable attributes of the same type of cell although functional differentiation was not excluded. With development of germinal layers in higher animals, the mesoderm would take over both functions. When specialized mechanisms for secreting enzymes replaced intracellular digestion, the mesoderm retained its powers of defense. In higher animals and in man, the functions of defense resided in further differentiated cells, such as leukocytes of the blood, endothelium cells of capillaries, and the large cells of lymphoid tissue. According to Metchnikoff, throughout the entire scale of invertebrate and vertebrate life, phagocytosis was the basic characteristic of inflammation, recognizable before the vascular system appeared in the animal kingdom.

The greatest scientific event in Metchnikoff's life, his earliest awakening to the concept of phagocytosis, took place at the marine biological laboratory in Messina, during one of his periods of absence from Russia, and was described as follows:[1]

I was resting from the shock of the events which provoked my resignation from the University and indulging enthusiastically in researches in the splendid setting of the Straits of Messina.

One day when the whole family had gone to a circus to see some extraordinary performing apes, I remained alone with my microscope, observing the life in the mobile cells of a transparent star-fish larva, when a new thought suddenly flashed across my brain. It struck me that similar cells might serve in the defense of the organism against intruders. Feeling that there was in this something of surpassing interest, I felt so excited that I began striding up and down the room and even went to the seashore in order to collect my thoughts.

I said to myself that, if my supposition was true, a splinter introduced into the body of a star-fish larva, devoid of blood-vessels or of a nervous system, should soon be surrounded by mobile cells as is to be observed in a man who runs a splinter into his finger. This was no sooner said than done.

There was a small garden to our dwelling, in which we had a few days previously organised a "Christmas tree" for the children on a little tangerine tree; I fetched from it a few rose thorns and introduced them at once under the skin of some beautiful star-fish larvae as transparent as water. . . . Very early the next morning I ascertained that it had fully succeeded.

That experiment formed the basis of the phagocyte theory, to the development of which I devoted the next twenty-five years of my life.

While still in Messina, a visit from Virchow offered Metchnikoff an opportunity to explain his hypothesis. He was urged to proceed with caution because of the current belief that the leukocytes, instead of destroying bacteria, furnished them a favorable media for growth; having ingested the bacteria, leukocytes might carry them to other parts of the body and so spread the disease. Undeterred,

he made plans to return to Russia but interrupted his journey to consult with Claus, professor of zoology at Vienna. In searching with Claus for a Greek term for devouring cells, "phagocyte" was suggested. The first public communication on phagocytosis was presented in the fall of 1883 before a congress of physicians and natural scientists at Odessa. The communication, entitled "On the Mesodermal Phagocytes of Certain Vertebrates," was subsequently translated and is widely quoted. Excerpts from a recent translation follow.[2]

Recently, I used the name *phagocytes* to describe various cells capable of accepting and digesting solid nutrients. The nature of phagocytosis is best demonstrated in the mesoderm, where a great number of ameboid cells are found, which devour foreign bodies as well as dead or at least weakened elements of their own body. This ability of white blood cells is well documented in pathology, although it was not admitted that the incorporation of foreign objects represented food intake or that the decomposition of the ingested substances (such as the red blood cells) implied digestion. The results seen in invertebrates and especially the evidence that ameboid mesodermal cells of *Spongia* play an important role in digestion, similar to that seen in *Bipinnaria*, *Phyllirhoe*, etc., where these cells eventually function as digestive organs, lead to the conclusion that in the mesodermal cells of vertebrates also, an intracellular ingestion occurs.

To determine whether the phagocytes of vertebrates are also able to devour harmful bacteria, I created an artificial septicemia in frogs by injecting subcutaneously some foetid blood. The white blood cells of the infected animals contained motile and immotile bacteria, enclosed in vacuoles. I found many of the pathogenic bacteria in the phagocytes of the spleen, which corroborates the accepted theory held by many pathologists that the white blood cells, containing unsoluble or scarcely soluble materials, usually transport them to the spleen.

Having reflected upon the phenomenon of phagocytosis, he moved logically into the study of immunity. But in so doing, Metchnikoff came into conflict with the German school of humoralists, who explained the mechanism of immunity by the changes which occurred in the body fluids following a successful encounter with an infectious agent. The fact of phagocytosis was not accepted, rather its significance was belittled. Metchnikoff showed the presence of phagocytes and the occurrence of phagolysis to be essential to the reaction, which did not develop in body fluid poor in these cells. In his monograph,

Immunity in Infective Diseases, published from the Pasteur Institute in French in 1901, the practical aspects of immunity intimately connected with theoretical considerations of cellular response were emphasized. In the development of the current understanding of cellular immunity, previous exposure or immunization against a virulent microbiologic invader is assumed to have activated mechanisms which enhance the protective effectiveness of the inflammatory reaction. Acquired immunity is similar to natural resistance; however, antibodies themselves possess neither bactericidal nor bacteriostatic power. They merely sensitize the bacteria to phagocytosis or attack by complement-like agents. Thus we return to Metchnikoff's original hypothesis of identifying resistance to infection with the ability of the leukocytes to check or destroy infectious agents.

Although valid in principle, Metchnikoff's theory of inflammatory response is an oversimplification, known to operate in a limited number of infections, but is adequately qualified to accept both cellular and humoral components in the adaptive responses. Increased knowledge has made us aware of antibodies, complement, and various antimicrobial substances of tissues and body fluids. Nervous and chemical influences, known to control the behavior of the vascular bed, determine the composition of the fluid and regulate the hydrogen ion concentration of the microenvironment. Metchnikoff's concept of the refractory state and display of immunity is excerpted as follows:[2]

As soon as he is born, man becomes the habitat of a very rich microbial flora. The skin, the mucous membranes, and the gastrointestinal contents become stocked with such a flora, but a very small number of these microorganisms have up to the present been recognised or described. The buccal cavity, the stomach, the intestines and the genital organs offer a feeding ground for Bacteria and inferior Fungi of various kinds. For long it was thought that in healthy individuals all these micro-organisms were inoffensive and sometimes even useful. It was supposed that when an infective malady was set up a specific pathogenic micro-organism was added to the benign flora. Exact bacteriological researches have, however, clearly demonstrated that as a matter of fact the varied vegetation in healthy persons often includes representatives of noxious species of bacteria. Besides the diphtheria bacillus and the cholera vibrio, which have repeatedly been found in the virulent form in perfectly healthy individuals, it has been demonstrated that certain pathogenic micro-organisms, e.g., the *Pneumococcus*, staphylococci, streptococci and the *Bacillus coli*, are always, or almost constantly, found among the microbial flora of healthy persons.

This observation has necessarily led to the conclusion that in addition to the micro-organism there exists a secondary cause of infective diseases—a predisposition, or absence of immunity. An individual in whom one of the above-mentioned pathogenic species is present, manifests a permanent or transitory refractory state as regards this specific organism. As soon however as the cause of this immunity ceases to act, the micro-organism gets the upper hand and sets up the specific disease.

It is unnecessary to multiply the number of such examples; they demonstrate in the clearest fashion that, in addition to the causes of disease which come from the outer world and which are represented by the micro-organisms, there are yet other causes which lie within the organism itself. When these internal factors are powerless to prevent the development of the morbific germs, a disease is set up; when, on the other hand, they resist the invasion of the micro-organisms properly, the organism is in a refractory condition and exhibits immunity.

After joining the Pasteur Institute, Metchnikoff wrote with increasing optimism. Having twice attempted suicide in the 1870's and 1880's, he prepared a monograph, in 1903, on *The Nature of Man, Studies in Optimistic Philosophy*, which included sorties into many scientific and general matters. Later an inquiry into the mechanism of eventual dissolution of humans led him wrongly to associate arteriosclerosis with intestinal intoxication and to treat his own physiological intestinal putrefaction by ingesting sour-milk products. His rich rewards for investigations of inflammation and immunity included the Nobel Prize in Medicine shared with Paul Ehrlich in 1908. Honorary degrees were received from the University of Cambridge and the Military Medical Association of St. Petersburg; medals or corresponding membership were granted by many learned societies in Europe and America, notably, from London, the Copley medal of the Royal Society, and the Albert medal of the Royal Society of Arts. Metchnikoff was an active writer, and in addition to works already mentioned, he prepared several monographs which were translated into English. Even as he wrote in his optimistic period, he pondered over the ultimate futility of life and the sureness of death, with the hope for a more rewarding destiny because of his contributions to science.[4]

As soon as the goal of life has been seen clearly, luxury ceases to be true happiness as it hinders the making perfect of the normal cycle of human life. Young people, instead of abandoning themselves to all the pleasures because they have nothing before them but a sad prospect of morbid old age and death, ought to make ready for physiological old age and natural death. The apprenticeship certainly will be long. In our time the years of study already last much longer than occurred even a century ago. As the body of knowledge grows greater, the time to acquire it will become prolonged, but this period of preparation will serve as the prelude to ripe maturity and ideal old age.

Old age is repulsive at present, because it is an old age devoid of its true meaning, full of egoism, narrowness of view, incapacity and malignancy. The physiological old age of the future assuredly will be very different. . . . Old age, at present practically a useless burden on the community, will become a period of work valuable to the community. As the old man will no longer be subject to loss of memory or to intellectual weakness, he will be able to apply his great experience to the most complicated and the most delicate parts of the social life.

1. Metchnikoff, O.: *Life of Elie Metchnikoff*, London: Constable & Co., 1921.

2. Metchnikoff, E.: On the Mesodermal Phagocytes of Certain Vertebrates (Ger), *Biol Central* 3:560-565, 1883, excerpt translated by Z. Danilevicius.

3. Metchnikoff, E.: *Immunity in Infective Diseases* (Fr), 1901, F. G. Binnie (trans.), Cambridge: University Press, 1907.

4. Metchnikoff, E.: *The Nature of Man, Studies in Optimistic Philosophy* (Fr), 1903, P. C. Mitchell (trans.), New York: G. P. Putnam's Sons, 1903.

Lord Lister (1827-1912)

THE TWO GREAT CONTRIBUTIONS TO SURGERY in the 19th century were anesthesia and antisepsis. In each instance, the achievements were based upon the effective employment of chemical agents—examples of medicine's debt to chemistry. Joseph Lister, advocate of antisepsis, was born only five years after Pasteur, whose studies on putrefaction and fermentation constituted basic observations for the surgeon to develop. The data on fermentation of wine had a practical application in the reduction in mortality from infection in the surgical wards.

Joseph was born in London of Quaker parents. His father, a wine merchant, was interested in optics and the development of the achromatic lens.[1] Joseph studied French, German, and the classics in a private preparatory school. Oxford and Cambridge might well have been selected for his arts training,

but neither university was open to Quakers; all students were required to take an oath supporting the articles of the Episcopalian faith. Subsequently, Lister renounced the Quaker faith and became an Episcopalian before his marriage to the daughter of his chief, James Syme, the leading surgeon of Scotland.

Money was not a problem in Lister's education. His father had the financial means to insure a comfortable education. At the age of 21, he began his medical studies at the University College, London; three years later he obtained the MD degree and a Fellowship in the Royal College of Surgeons. At the suggestion of Sharpey, a Scot who was the first to hold the chair of physiology at University College, London, Lister moved to Edinburgh and through friendship for Sharpey, was invited to assist Syme, professor of surgery, in private and hospital practice. This required the composition of clinical notes and performance of menial chores. At the age of 27, Lister's appointment as house surgeon to Syme, placed him in charge of the clinical management of patients and selection of those who required operative surgery. When the post of Regius Professor of Surgery at the University of Glasgow became vacant, Lister applied and was appointed (1860). The principles of antisepsis in surgery were developed in the following years. In 1869, Lister's father-in-law died, and Lister was appointed professor of clinical surgery at Edinburgh and surgeon to the Royal Infirmary. Thereafter, Lister's efforts were concentrated on the spread of the doctrine of antisepsis to the Continent, which was more receptive than was the medical profession in England and Scotland.

In the mid-1860's, Pasteur's studies on fermentation and putrefraction proved to be the prelude to the concept that suppuration and disease are due to living organisms—the germ theory postulated by Koch a decade later. It is reported that, in 1865, Thomas Anderson, professor of chemistry at Glasgow, called Lister's attention to Pasteur's observations. Pasteur had conceived of three ways for combating bacterial invasion: by heat, by filtering, and by destruction with chemicals. Neither heat nor filtering could be used in the prevention or management of suppuration in the patient. This left, then, destruction by chemicals. Although carbolic acid had been recognized as a powerful antiseptic by Lemaire and others, the experimental results were disappointing. There is one other background item that was useful to Lister in the selection of carbolic acid as a bactericidal agent. Known also as German creosote, carbolic acid had been used to disinfect sewage at Carlisle. Although the value of phenol in the prevention and management of infection in the principle of antiseptic surgery is Lister's best-remembered contribution, he preferred to be identified with the conception of a new broad principle in control of surgical infection. He stressed principle rather than the use of any one specific chemical compound.

In 1867, Lister published the first series of cases on the virtue of carbolic acid in the management of compound fractures. Of the 11 consecutive cases, one required amputation, and another died of secondary hemorrhage several months later. The remaining 9 recovered, a remarkable percentage in that era. Case no. 3 illustrates the success of antisepsis:[2]

John H., aged twenty-one, a moulder in an iron foundry, was admitted on May 19th, 1866, with compound fracture of the left leg. . . . Dr. A. Cameron, my house-surgeon, finding, on manipulating the limb, that bubbles escaped along with the blood, implying that air had been introduced during the movements of the leg as the patient was being carried to the infirmary, thought it best that I should see the case, which I did at three P.M., three hours and a half after the accident. In order to expel the air I squeezed out as much as I could of the clotted and fluid blood which lay accumulated beneath the skin, and then applied a bit of lint dipped in carbolic acid slightly larger than the wound, and over this a piece of sheet tin about four inches square. Finally the limb was placed in pasteboard splints, resting on its outer side with the knee bent. . . . A hot fomentation also was applied over the inner aspect of the leg, the crust being protected by the tin. . . . The fomentation was changed night and morning, and gave great comfort to patient, and once a day carbolic acid was applied lightly to the crust.

At the close of the third week the application of carbolic acid to the crust was discontinued, and the original internal pasteboard splint padded with cotton was again employed instead of the tin and fomentation.

At the expiration of six weeks from the receipt of the injury the fragments were found firmly united in good position, just as if the fracture had been a simple one, though the cicatrisation of the rather extensive sore was not complete till a later period.

Although chemically pure carbolic acid was used in this patient, it was soon discovered to be too powerful and too toxic. Various solutions, strengths, and means of application were tried subsequently. Carbolized putty, mixtures of paraffin and olive oil, shellac, and various styles of dressing were tested. The device for spraying carbolic acid in the operating room brought ridicule from some of Lister's scientific colleagues. The spray was used by Lister from 1871 until 1887. After he demonstrated that wound suppuration could be reduced or prevented by the antiseptic, the importance of clean surgical hands, clean instruments, and a clean operating room were logical steps in development. Previously, surgeons were terrified of entering articular spaces; however, Lister operated successfully upon the ankle and wrist without fear of complicating infection.[3]

To save a human hand from amputation, and restore its usefulness, is an object well worthy of any labour involved in it. When caries affects the shoulder or the elbow, the limb is preserved by excision of the diseased joint, and the brilliant success of these operations naturally suggested a similar procedure for the wrist.

My last case, that of E. P.———, aged thirteen, a strumous girl, whose right wrist was excised on the 27th of November, 1864, for caries limited to the lower and outer part of the carpus and the base of the second metacarpal bone, which appeared to be affected with tubercular deposit. The hand had been useless for a year, but is now already useful as well as sound and of perfect shape, with better movements than in any former case at the same stage.

Antisepsis was not the only subject that benefited from Lister's imaginative mind. The Croonian Lecture, delivered in 1863, summarized his conclusions on the coagulation of blood. The hypothesis that coagulation was related to liberation of ammonia was rejected; rather it was shown to depend upon vascular injury plus contact with foreign matter. The studies on coagulation were carried out concurrently with the experiments on inflammation and suppuration. In 1873, Lister identified the organism causing the natural souring of milk, *Bacterium lactis*, as he called it. He used the then-current bacteriologic tools, a calibrated microsyringe, and suitable culture media.[4]

We see, therefore, from the facts which I have adduced, that the souring of milk, instead of being—as might naturally supposed *a priori* from seeing it occur constantly in all milk brought from a dairy—an inherent property of the liquid, is a change which, whether is boiled milk or unboiled, requires the introduction of something from without, and that something a scarce article, both in air and in water, except in dairies. Indeed, even in a dairy, though it exists in all the milk in the pans, it does not necessarily follow that it is the most frequent ferment in the air.

But not only were the results of this experiment in harmony with the view that the *Bacterium lactis* was the real fermentative agent: they would, as I believe, afford indisputable evidence of the truth of the theory, provided it should turn out, as former experience made me feel sure would be the case, that every glass which had curdled contained the bacterium, and that every one which remained fluid contained none.

Lister was also concerned with the high incidence of dire complications from surgical sutures and explored a number of possibilities, including carbolized silk.[5] The first experiment with sterilized ligatures was performed in 1867. The vessel of a horse was ligated with unwaxed purse silk prepared by soaking it in carbolic acid. Several weeks later the horse died and the ligature was examined. The ligature was intact and was surrounded by fibrous tissue. Later, sterilized ligatures were used for the management of a femoral aneurysm. Although the patient made an uneventful recovery, she died several months later from rupture of an abdominal aortic aneurysm. Evidence of irritation of the femoral vessel from the silk was apparent. This finding prompted Lister to try catgut (kit, a fiddle + gut, intestine) ligatures prepared from sheep intestines. The preparation of the gut with chromic solutions was subjected to experimental trial in an effort to procure a more desirable suture.

Lister was invited to fill the chair of surgery at Kings College Hospital, London, in 1877. He returned to the city, an object of criticism and skepticism, sometimes overt hostility. The antiseptic principles of carbolic acid had been accepted abroad but not at home. Several of the leading surgeons of London, and especially Sir James Paget, considered the Lister doctrine useless.

Lister did not retire from practice until 1896. Meanwhile, he had received more honors than any other 19th century surgeon, and fame at last came to him at home. He was the recipient of the Order of Merit and the Copley medal of the Royal Society, and the first physician to be raised to the peerage. He succeeded Lord Kelvin as president of the Royal Society. He reasoned with Queen Victoria in favor of vivisection and against legislative interference.

Lord Lister was tall, stately, and in manner somewhat serious but always kindly, and a Quaker in action and thought. He was not a particularly brilliant lecturer or an outstanding technical surgeon. His contributions to bacteriology and his principles of antiseptic surgery, however, made him the greatest of all English surgeons. Although his methods are no longer used in the operating amphitheater, his principles remain sound.

1. Guthrie, D.: *Lord Lister, His Life and Doctrine,* Baltimore: Williams and Wilkins Company, 1949.
2. Lister, J.: On a New Method of Treating Compound Fracture, Abscess, etc., *Lancet* 1:328 (March 16) 1867.
3. Lister, J.: On Excision of the Wrist for Caries, *Lancet* 1:308-312 (March 25); 362-364 (April 8) 1865.
4. Lister, J.: On Lactic Fermentation, *Trans Path Soc Lond* 29:425-467, 1878.
5. Lister, J.: President's Address, *Trans Clin Soc Lond* 14:xliii-lxiii, 1881.

Composite by G. Bako

Edwin Klebs (1834-1913)

THEODOR ALBRECHT EDWIN KLEBS, a native of Königsberg and contemporary of Pasteur and Koch enjoyed an unrivaled experience in pathological anatomy and gained scientific rewards equal to other great European bacteriologists.[1] Klebs studied medicine in Königsberg with Rathke, Helmholtz, and others, and in 1855 proceeded to Würzburg, where Kölliker and Virchow were teaching. He traveled to Berlin the following year; there he presented his dissertation in Latin on types of tuberculosis which affect the intestines, part of a general subject to command his investigative interests throughout his life. After practicing for a short time in Königsberg, Klebs was appointed privatdocent in general pathology and assistant in the Physiological Institute under Wittich. In 1861, he became assistant to Virchow in Berlin; there he published his studies on paraffin embedding and designed solid media for bacterial culture.[2] Early in 1866, he was appointed professor of pathology in Bern and held in succession the chairs of pathology (pathological anatomy) at Würzburg (1872), Prague (1873), and Zürich (1882). During these years he prepared his *Handbook on Pathological Anatomy*, which was followed by his comprehensive *Treatise on*

General Pathology. Klebs was responsible for the establishment of two scientific periodicals, the *Archiv für Experimentelle Pathologie und Pharmakologie*, started in 1873, and *Die Prager Medicinische Wochenschrift*, begun in 1876. In the Franco-Prussian war, 1870-1871, Klebs pursued one of the first comprehensive studies of pathology and bacteriology of war wounds in the military hospital in Karlsruhe. Although he regarded the different forms of bacteria as essentially the same organism, his studies furnished the basis for important future investigations on suppuration in battle casualties.

In 1883, in Zürich, shortly after accepting the Swiss post, Klebs described the isolation of a specific bacillus from the membrane of patients with laryngeal croup. Although the *Corynebacterium diphtheriae* was shown to be the pathogenic microorganism, it was Löffler, the following year, who satisfied Koch's postulates for diphtheria and dissociated the human type from bovine and avian varieties. In the 1883 presentation, Klebs described the pathological findings in the brain, kidney, heart, liver, and lungs. The bacillus, found to be similar in size to the tubercle bacillus, was reported as follows:[3]

I have examined carefully the microorganisms, produced pure cultures of them, and through one of my students, Graham Brown, I proved that there is no difficulty in transferring the microorganisms to the cornea. It seemed therefore justified to consider these microorganisms to be the cause of diphtheria . . . the only microorganism.

I termed them *Microsporon diphtheriticum*, which produces linear or globular micrococci during development.

In the highest magnification . . . these appear as short and narrow rods in the superficial layers of the membrane as if imbedded in gelatine. . . . The rods are uniformly long, narrow, and usually smaller than tubercle bacilli. A considerable number have spores; one spore is at both ends of each rod.

The findings in bacillary diphtheria may be summarized as follows: (1) The fibrinous exudation on the tonsil shows a marked tendency to extend to the trachea; (2) A constant finding is a specific form of bacillus (rods) in the diseased membrane composed of epithelial elements, fibrinous exudate, and vascular lesions; (3) Pyrexia is associated with extension of the membranous exudate; when this stage subsides, fever recurs only in the presence of septic complications; (4) Interstitial inflammation of internal organs (pneumonia, myocarditis, neuritis, albuminuria, nephritis) depends less on the spread of the infectious organisms than on a vascular disorder; (5) Necrosis of the membrane with septic complications and sometimes death occurs even when the diphtheritic process has subsided.

The process which was formerly termed "croup", namely, fibrinous exudate which could be ascribed to atmospheric influences as it occurs only in isolated cases, may no longer be considered simple inflammation when it becomes endemic and spreads by contagion. Based on microscopic findings it must be considered an infectious disease.

Similar findings were made on the typhoid (typhus) bacillus in a series of 22 cases studied postmortem in Zürich beginning in 1879, the year before Eberth's observations. *Salmonella typhi* is currently classed by *Bergy's Manual of Determinative Bacteriology* under Division I, *Protophyta;* Class II, *Schizomycetes;* Tribe V, *Salmonelleae;* Genus IX, *Salmonella;* 4, *Salmonella typhosa.* Klebs reported as follows.[4]

Additional studies showed that rod and spindle forms are regularly found in abdominal typhus [typhoid]. Often they are found in the areas immediately before necrosis appears.

Judged from the cases examined since the beginning of last year, the following hypothesis is justified: in all examined cases of abdominal typhus we were successful in finding one and the same form of schistomycetes [bacillus] in new and advanced lesions, often in sufficient quantities to fill the tissue spaces. The characteristic elements consist of rods and spindles, the latter as long as 80 μ and as wide as 0.5 to 0.6 μ. The cytoplasm is homogenous with a slight gloss; only rarely could we discover smaller bacteria which would indicate potential formation of spores.

The third observation, preceding either of the above-mentioned contributions, was his recognition of a spirillar organism in syphilitic lesions and the inoculation of apes to produce experimental syphilis 30 years before Schaudinn discovered the *Spirochaeta pallida* (*Treponema pallidum*). In human syphilitic lesions, Klebs found "helicomonads," slender motile rods, 0.5 μ wide and 5 μ long, which produced pathological changes in animals after cultivation on a special media.[5]

Experimentation beginning in 1875, in the attempt to innoculate syphilis into animals, suggested that none of the usual animals (dogs, goats, rabbits, guinea-pigs, and apes), would develop the same process as in man, *except for apes.* Apes could be inoculated successfully.

The first inoculation performed on apes was on the 27th of July, 1877. Prof. Pick extirpated an induration from the labia minora of a syphilitic woman. A lentil-sized portion of the lesion was implanted into the scrotum of the male Capuchin ape.

It is concluded that:

(1) Syphilis of man can be inoculated in animals by implanting portions of a syphilitic lesion. Apes and rabbits develop lesions of syphilis similar to those found in man.

(2) In human syphilitic lesions peculiar mycotic organisms can be found which, when cultured *in vitro,* assume characteristic forms called helicomonads.

(3) By transferring these bodies into animals susceptible to syphilis one can produce lesions and disease similar to the syphilis of man and identical with the inoculation-syphilis of animals.

Although a student and friend of Virchow, Klebs failed to subscribe to his preceptor's emphasis on postmortem findings, advancing instead the premise that the study of pathogens was as important in understanding infection as the end-result of tissues affected. He produced endocarditis by mechanical instrumentation and bacterial agents, and published a monograph on gigantism in 1884, two years before Pierre Marie's communication on acromegaly and the pituitary body. During his early days in Bern, Klebs noticed that tuberculosis was prevalent among the highlanders who relied heavily upon milk and milk products for food. This observation led him to suspect, before Koch's observations, that milk was a probable carrier of tuberculosis. A final example of a continuing interest in tuberculosis was the unsuccessful attempt to treat human tuberculosis with bacilli from cold-blooded animals.

In spite of so many important and varied investigations, Kleb's restless temperament kept him from carrying to a logical conclusion many of his studies in pathology. His treatise with Tommasi-Crudeli on the pathogenesis of malaria is an example of incompleteness and unsubstantiated assumptions. They wrongly inferred that the "bacillus malaria" was responsible for the affliction. This work, however, was translated by the Sydenham Society in appreciation of the importance of Kleb's approach to the pathological study of infectious diseases. The belief that endemic cretinism was caused by a microorganism was his most serious error.

As Klebs approached retirement, his mercurial temperament brought him to America. He first assumed charge of a sanatorium in Asheville, North Carolina; in 1896, he served as professor of pathological anatomy at Rush Medical College in Chicago and later as director of the pathological laboratory of its postgraduate medical school. In 1900, he returned to Germany, first to a private laboratory in Hanover and, in succession, worked at a small laboratory at the Pathological Institute in Berlin, lived a few years in Lausanne, and died in Bern. Klebs was a fluent, forceful speaker and an untiring investigator in the laboratory and at the bedside. His pupils included scientists from Germany, England, America, and Japan.

1. Haberling, W.: "Klebs, Edwin," in *Biographisches Lexikon* (Ger), vol 3, Munich: Urban & Schwarzenberg, 1962, pp 539-540.
2. Klebs, T. A. E.: The Embedding Methods: a Contribution to Microscopic Technique (Ger), *Arch Mikr Anat* 5:164-166, 1869.
3. Klebs, T. A. E.: Diptheria (Ger), *Verh Congr Inner Med* 2:139-154, 1883, excerpt translated by Z. Danilevicius.
4. Klebs, T. A. E.: Ileotyphus, a Schistomycosis (Ger), *Arch Exp Path Pharm* 12:231-236, 1880, excerpt translated by Z. Danilevicius.
5. Klebs, T. A. E.: The Contagion of Syphilis, an Experimental Study (Ger), *Arch Exp Path Pharm* 10:161-218, 1879, excerpt translated by Z. Danilevicius.

Composite by G. Bako

Carlos Juan Finlay (1833-1915)

FINLAY'S INQUIRIES into the spread of yellow fever, a tropical and subtropical endemic disease manifested by pyrexia, jaundice, albuminuria, and hematemesis, began in a logical fashion with the study of the environment. Shortly after graduation from medical school, he broke new ground for the agents of dissemination by implicating, from deductive speculation, the *Culex* mosquito as the vector. This search continued through his close liaison with the Yellow Fever Commission of Reed and associates in 1902 and was climaxed by greater recognition posthumously for his contributions than he had received during his productive years.

Carlos was born to a French mother in the city of Puerto Principe (now Camagüey) in Cuba, where his Scottish father was a practicing physician and coffee grower.[1] His early schooling was begun under a paternal aunt who had moved to Cuba and was continued at Havre, France. However, it was interrupted by an attack of chorea, which caused him to return home and left him with a residual stammer. Finlay returned to Europe in 1848, but unsettled conditions in France caused him to favor London; later he spent a year in Mentz on the Rhine and finally returned to Rouen, France. Illness again struck before he qualified for a liberal arts degree, and, in 1851, he returned to Cuba to recover from an attack of typhoid fever. Lacking an AB degree and failing, therefore, to qualify for medical study at the University of Havana, he turned to Jefferson Medical College, Philadelphia, where he graduated MD in 1855.

In Philadelphia, Finlay came under the influence of Drs. John Kearsly Mitchell, and his son, S. Weir Mitchell. The former was an early proponent of the germ theory of disease; the latter, Finlay's preceptor, encouraged him to practice in New York City following graduation. Finlay's sentiments lay in Cuba; however, he did not finally settle in Havana to pursue his profession until 1865. In the interim, he lived for a time in Lima, Peru, and also studied in the hospital clinics in Paris.

Finlay's first reference in the scientific literature to yellow fever (black vomit) appeared in 1872 in a discussion of the alkalinity of the air judged to be favorable to propagation of the disease. Nearly a decade later he prepared his two most important communications. As a special delegate from Puerto Rico and Cuba to the International Sanitary Conference held in Washington, D. C., on February 18, 1881, he advanced an hypothesis without mentioning a specific vector.[2]

It is my personal opinion that three conditions are necessary in order that the propagation of yellow fever shall take place:

1. The presence of a previous case of yellow fever within certain limits of time, counting back from the moment that we are considering.
2. The presence of a person apt to contract the disease.
3. The presence of an agent entirely independent for its existence both of the disease and of the sick man, but which is necessary in order that the disease shall be conveyed from the yellow-fever patient to a healthy individual.

Undoubtedly Finlay carried strong convictions in support of the theory of transmission by the mosquito; inasmuch as only six months later, during the August 14th session of the Royal Academy of Medical, Physical and Natural Sciences of Cuba, he presented a communication entitled, "The Mosquito Hypothetically Considered as the Agent of Transmission of Yellow Fever."[3] The meteorologic variations known to influence the development of yellow fever were reviewed, and the ecology of two of the common mosquitoes in Cuba was compared. Finlay implicated as the vector the *Culex*, later known as *Stegomyia fasciatus*, and currently as the *Aedes aegypti*. He discussed the peculiarity of the anatomical parts of the *Culex* favorable for biting, advanced the conditions for the propagation of yellow fever, speculated on inoculation for immunity, and proposed means for eventual control of the disease.[3]

Three conditions will, therefore, be necessary in order that yellow fever may be propagated: 1. The existence of a yellow fever patient into whose capillaries the mosquito is able to drive its sting and to impregnate it with the virulent particles, at an appropriate stage of the disease. 2. That the life of the mosquito be spared after its bite upon the patient until it has a chance of biting the person in whom the disease is to be reproduced. 3. The coincidence that some of the persons whom the same mosquito happens to bite thereafter shall be susceptible of contracting the disease.

CONCLUSIONS

2. Inasmuch as the mouth-parts of the mosquito are very well adapted to retain particles that may be in suspension in the liquids absorbed by that insect, it cannot be denied that there is a possibility that said mosquito should retain upon the setae of its sting some of the virulent particles contained in a diseased blood, and may inoculate them to the persons whom it afterwards chances to bite.

3. The direct experiments undertaken to decide whether the mosquito is able to transmit yellow fever in the above stated manner, have been limited to five attempted inoculations, with a single bite, . . . From which results it must be inferred that the inoculation with a single bite is insufficient to produce the severe forms of yellow fever, and that a final decision as to the efficacy of such inoculations must be deferred until opportunity is found for experimenting under absolutely decisive conditions, outside of the epidemic zone.

4. Should it be finally proven that the mosquito-inoculation not only reproduces the yellow fever, but that it constitutes the regular process through which the disease is propagated, the conditions of existence and of development for that dipterous insect would account for the anomalies hitherto observed in the propagation of yellow fever, and while we might, on the one hand, have the means of preventing the disease from spreading, non-immunes might at the same time be protected through a mild inoculation.

Finlay continued the practice of medicine in Havana as well as his experimental studies and inquiries into the transmission of yellow fever. In 1886, he prepared an interim report regarding inoculation but admitted the failure to transmit the disease within a reasonably short time by a mosquito which had previously bitten a patient. Finlay did not know, as Carter showed a decade later, that 12 days is the optimum time for the digestion of infected blood by the mosquito before successful transmission to a nonimmune suspect. Finlay's experimental procedures and almost successful observations follow.[4]

For the purpose of carrying into effect this novel inoculation, my plan has been to catch a female mosquito while in the act of stinging and before it has filled, by inverting an empty phial or test-tube over it and closing the mouth of the phial with a plug of cotton-wool. The insect is thus in readiness to renew its bite as soon as it has become accustomed to its place of confinement. . . . The captive is then taken to a confirmed case of yellow fever, and the tube being inverted and the cotton plug carefully removed over the bare surface of the patient's arm or hand, the insect is allowed to fill at leisure with the tainted blood, and the plug reinserted. After this blood has been digested, generally between the second and fourth day, the mosquito is applied in the same manner to the arm of a subject liable to the disease, and then allowed again to fill itself completely.

These requisites, so difficult to be obtained by one whose leisure hours, in the midst of an active professional life, are necessarily limited, will account for the small number of my experiments, some twenty-four individuals only having been inoculated by me since June, 1881. Of this number only one has died of yellow fever; he had been inoculated in November, 1883, without any visible result, and was attacked, after severe exposure, in June, 1884, with a malignant form of yellow fever.

The history and etiology of yellow fever exclude from our consideration, as possible agents of transmission, other blood-sucking insects, such as fleas, etc., the habits and geographical distribution of which in no wise agree with the course of that disease; whereas, a careful study of the habits and natural history of the mosquito shows a remarkable agreement with the circumstances that favor or impede the transmission of yellow fever. . . . From these considerations . . . it is to be inferred that these insects are the habitual agents of its transmission.

Finlay's final part in the yellow fever investigation was to offer Walter Reed and members of his Commission *Culex* larvae for the experimental transmission, illustrated in the painting reproduced many times in his honor. The Commission confirmed, in 1900, Finlay's postulates of 1881. In a speech read at the meeting of the American Public Health Association in Indianapolis, Reed recognized Finlay's help.[5]

We here desire to express our sincere thanks to Dr. Finlay, who accorded us a most courteous interview and has gladly placed at our disposal his several publications relating to yellow fever, during the past 19 years; and also for ova of the variety of mosquito with which he had made his several inoculations.

With the mosquitoes thus obtained we have been able to conduct our experiments. Specimens of this mosquito forwarded to Mr. L. A. Howard, Entomologist, Department of Agriculture, Washington, D. C., were kindly identified as *Culex fasciatus*, Fabr.

The mosquito serves as the intermediate host for the parasite of yellow fever, and it is highly probable that the disease is only propagated through the bite of this insect.

Following the outbreak of the Spanish American War, Finlay, who was then 65 years of age, served in the field throughout the Santiago campaign as acting assistant surgeon in the United States Army. Later, during the American occupation of Cuba, he assisted in the sanitary department of Havana and, from 1902 to 1908, functioned as chief sanitary officer. Finlay's medical writings,

largely devoted to yellow fever, included communications on filariasis, trichinosis, exophthalmic goiter, tetanus of the newborn, cholera, leprosy, and beriberi. He spoke English, French and German, as well as Spanish; mathematics, chess, and philology were his hobbies. Jefferson Medical College, Finlay's medical alma mater, awarded him the honorary degree of doctor of science in 1902. Other honors included fellowship in the College of Physicians of Philadelphia, the Mary Kingsley medal of the Liverpool School of Tropical Medicine, and the decoration of officer of the Legion of Honor conferred on him by the French government. A statue was erected in his honor in Finlay Square in Havana, and the state of Pennsylvania declared a Finlay Day, Sept. 22, 1955, upon presentation of a marble bust to Jefferson Medical College by the Cuban Minister of Health. In 1959, a brochure was prepared to accompany his nomination to the Hall of Fame for Great Americans at New York University.[6] These seem appropriate honors for a practicing physician who pursued independently the transmission of yellow fever, identified the vector, and stood in the vanguard of preventive health in attempting to inoculate against the malady. He proposed sound procedures for the control of a disseminated endemic disease, proved after his time to be caused by a small virus.

1. Finlay, C. E.: *Carlos Finlay and Yellow Fever,* New York: Oxford University Press, 1940.

2. Finlay, C. J.: "Transmission of Yellow Fever," in *International Sanitary Conference of Washington, Proceedings,* Protocol No. 7, Feb 18, 1881, p 119.

3. Finlay, C. J.: The Mosquito Hypothetically Considered as the Agent of Transmission of Yellow Fever (Sp), *An Acad Ceinc Med Habana* 18:147-169, 1881, translated in *Med Classics* 2:590-612, 1938.

4. Finlay, C. J.: Yellow Fever: Its Transmission by Means of the Culex Mosquito, *Amer J Med Sci* 92:395-409, 1886.

5. Reed, W.: The Etiology of Yellow Fever, a Preliminary Note, *Phila Med J* 6:790-796, 1900.

6. *Booklet on Sanitation History: Dr. Carlos J. Finlay and the "Hall of Fame" of New York,* Havana: Ministry of Sanitation and Hospital's Assistance, 1959.

Robert Koch (1843-1910)

THE TUBERCLE BACILLUS was implicated in 1882 by Koch as the etiologic agent responsible for tuberculosis. The postulates, probably his best remembered contribution to the concept of infection and disease, were not published until two years later. Koch developed bacteriologic techniques when none existed and thereby exposed the mysteries of infection. The logical conclusions deriving from his contributions typify the brilliance of his scientific reasoning. This bursting flower of bacteriology was attracting the attention of many scientists and focusing it upon this productive new area in medicine. To be sure, tuberculosis had been studied intensively for a long time, but the chain of evidence between identification of the suspected organism and reproduction of disease in animals had not hitherto been completed.

When this void in scientific knowledge became apparent, Koch endeavored to fill it by developing a new type of culture medium based upon the solidification of gelatin; potato slices were another fertile medium. Sections of tissue from lymph nodes, lungs, and joints from human beings affected with tuberculosis revealed the suspected organism as did infected tissue from rabbits, guinea pigs, cat-

tle, and other animals. The characteristic bacterium was identified in each instance. But this was not sufficient. The transmission from culture to susceptible animals or from infected animals to susceptible animals was convincing but not conclusive. The four postulates suggested in part by Henle in 1840 could not be fulfilled at that time. Progress in bacteriology and medical microbiology was quite impossible without first bringing order to the confusion that dominated the beginning of the bacteriologic era. For this reason the postulates of Koch were by necessity rigid.[1]

(1) The organism, germ, should always be found microscopically in the bodies of animals having the disease and in that disease only; it should occur in such numbers, and be distributed in such a manner as to explain the lesions of the disease; (2) the germ should be obtained from the diseased animal and grown outside the body; (3) the inoculation of these germs, in pure cultures, freed by successive transplantations from the smallest particle of matter taken from the original animal, should produce the same disease in a susceptible animal; (4) the germs should be found in the diseased areas so produced in the animal.

King,[2] has expressed the currently prevailing sentiments against the zealous interpretation of these postulates and suggests that Koch did not intend them to be rigid and dogmatic. It is appreciated that the first postulate especially, requiring the isolation of pathogens from the sick only, is too rigid. Many pathogens such as streptococci, staphylococci, and diptheria are found in normal individuals. It is believed, however, that the postulates served a highly purposeful function during the maturation days of infectious disease.

Koch was born at Clausthal on the western slope of the Harz Mountains in Central Germany, famous for their singing canaries. There were 13 children in the family. Black bread, buttermilk, and legumes were the staple foods. White bread was served only on Sunday; meat was provided only twice a week.

Koch studied medicine in the nearby University of Göttingen, where he graduated at the age of 19. He accepted an internship at the general hospital in Hamburg and entered the private practice of medicine immediately after. He practiced in several communities but was not particularly successful financially in his early years. Before and after the Franco-

Prussian War, in which he served as a field surgeon, he practiced medicine in Eastern Germany. Upon his return to the village of Wollstein in Posen after the war, he built a small laboratory in his office for the pursuit of his avocation which later was to be all-consuming. The light microscope was not a new tool, but it had not been exploited in the new discipline, bacteriology. With the aid of a microtome, a homemade incubator, and a relatively simple microscope, Koch began his study of algae. Later he switched to pathogenic organisms. Anthrax, which was devastating the herds of cattle and flocks of sheep in Europe, was next in his field of interest in natural science. Ten years of silence, filled with arduous investigation, preceded his announcement of the discovery of the anthrax bacillus as the cause of anthrax. He continued to support himself in private practice. The discovery of the anthrax bacillus was announced to a group of professors at Breslau in 1876. Julius Cohnheim, who was in the group, stated: "It leaves nothing more to be proved. I regard it as the greatest discovery ever made with bacteria and I believe that this is not the last time that this young Robert Koch will surprise and shame us by the brilliancy of his investigations."[2] The discovery was reported as follows:[2]

Since the discovery of rod-shaped bodies in the blood of animals dying of anthrax, there had been much effort directed to attempts to prove that these rod-shaped bodies are responsible for the transmissability of this disease as well as for the sporadic appearance of it.

The lack of proof of the direct transmission of the anthrax disease in man and animals is due to the ability of the bacteria to remain alive for a long time in dry conditions and to be transmitted through the air by insects and the like. It seems here that the mode of transmission of anthrax has been explained.

Since I have had the opportunity several times of examining animals which had died of anthrax, I performed a series of experiments which would clear up the uncertainties in the etiology of anthrax. As I will show later, the blood, which contains only rods, keeps its ability to induce anthrax on inoculation only a few weeks in the dry state, and only a few days when moist. How is it possible then for an organism which is so easily destroyed to maintain itself as a dormant contagium for a year in soil and throughout the winter? If bacteria are really the cause of anthrax, then we must hypothesize that they can go through a change in life history and assume a condition which will be resistant to alternate drying and moisture. What is more likely, and what has already been indicated by

Prof. Cohn is that the bacteria can form spores which possess the ability to reform bacteria after a long or short resting period.

All of my experiments were designed to discover this developmental stage of the anthrax bacterium. After many unsuccessful experiments, I was finally able to reach this goal, and thus to find a basis for the etiology of anthrax.

It is helpful in visualizing the significance of Koch's observations to appreciate the background of public health and bacteriology in the final quarter of the last century. During this critical scientific period, the organisms responsible for anthrax, gonorrhea, relapsing fever, leprosy, pneumonia, typhoid fever, glanders, and malaria were discovered. However, the germ theory at that time presupposed that the organism was not an infestation—it was little more than a parasite. As a part of the individual it shared the essence of life with the host. The possibility of an organism being cultured outside the body or modified on artificial media was a concept original with Pasteur. The significance of the sterilization of milk and the filtration of public water supplies was not appreciated. Isolated facts were recognized, but separate parts of the puzzle had not yet been integrated into a sound theory of infection. The prevention of disease, either through public health measures or inoculation, was still a hazy concept.

In 1880, eight years after he had returned to Wollstein, he received an offer to join the Imperial Health Office in Berlin, with the opportunity to devote himself exclusively to bacteriology. Another of his most important discoveries was the causative agent of Asiatic cholera, *Vibrio comma*, made in 1883.

The announcement by Koch of the cause of tuberculosis was made before the Berlin Physiological Society on March 24, 1882. Approximately two weeks later, on the morning of April 3, the news reached America. The announcement appeared in the *London Times* on April 2 and the *New York World* the next day. The initial communication contained the following:[4]

On the basis of my extensive observations, I consider it as proven that in all tuberculous conditions of man and animals there exists a characteristic bacterium which I have designated as the tubercle bacillus, which had specific properties which allow it to be distinguished from all other microorganisms.

From this correlation between the presence of tuberculous conditions and bacilli, it does not necessarily follow that these phenomena are causally related. However, a high degree of probability for this causal relationship might be inferred from the observation that the bacilli are generally most frequent when the tuberculous process is developing or progressing, and that they disappear when the disease becomes quiescent.

In order to prove that tuberculosis is brought about through the penetration of the bacilli, and is a definite parasitic disease brought about by the growth and reproduction of these same bacilli, the bacilli must be isolated from the body, and cultured so long in pure culture, that they are freed from any diseased production of the animal organism which may still be adhering to the bacilli. After this, the isolated bacilli must bring about the transfer of the disease to other animals, and cause the same disease picture which can be brought about through the inoculation of healthy animals with naturally developing tubercle materials.

All of these facts taken together lead to the conclusion that the bacilli which are present in the tuberculous substances not only accompany the tuberculosis process, but are the cause of it. In the bacillus we have, therefore, the actual tubercle virus.

Koch's contribution to the knowledge of immunity in tuberculosis seems to be almost as important as his contributions to the bacteriology of this disease. Koch found that a previously-infected guinea pig produces accelerated response to reinoculation of tubercle bacilli; the resultant inflammation and ulceration of the injected area may be regarded as a purposeful reaction to stop the invading organisms. This observation—the famous Koch phenomenon—might also explain the fundamental mechanisms involved in the adult type of tuberculosis. The self-destruction seems to be an exaggerated but basically teleologic mechanism for cleansing the invaded area of bacilli. Koch also was the discoverer of tuberculin. This discovery had consequences beyond the field of tuberculosis: the tuberculin reaction—or delayed type of hypersensitivity—is now recognized as a fundamental immune reaction, playing an important role in many diseases.

It is most exciting to trace the history of the discovery of Koch's phenomenon and tuberculin. At the 10th International Congress of Medicine (Berlin, 1890), Koch announced that he had discovered a substance which could cure tuberculosis. The nature of the curative substance was not mentioned. The name "tuberculin" was used for the first time in a communication in 1891. This included also the method of tuberculin production. It is understandable that the announcement of a cure for tuberculosis by a famous scientist provoked enormous excitement over the world. Thousands of patients rushed to Berlin to search for help (one of these patients was an English girl accompanied by her uncle, Dr. Joseph Lister). Being mainly interested in the idea of curing tuberculosis with tuberculin, Koch described in only a few sentences what is now known as Koch's phenomenon, apparently considering it as an observation of minor importance. However, the treatment of tuberculous patients with tuberculin (at least in the way it was practiced in those days) proved to be a disaster and one of the most dreadful mistakes in the history of medicine. In contrast, the Koch phenomenon (now frequently defined as a local inflammatory reaction following injection of tuberculin into the skin of animals and human beings previously exposed to the tubercle bacilli) proved to be a useful diagnostic tool and belongs among the more important medical discoveries.

Koch refused a call to a professorship at the University of Leipzig in 1885. Instead he became head of the New Hygienic Institute and professor of hygiene at the University of Berlin. J. R. Petri (culture dish), F. A. J. Löffler (diphtheria bacillus), R. F. J. Pfeiffer (Pfeiffer's bacillus), W. Hesse and his wife (agar), P. Ehrlich ("606"), E. A. von Behring (diphtheria antitoxin), S. Kitasato (bubonic plague bacillus), and others worked in the new laboratory. Koch, in cooperation with Flügge, founded the *Journal of Hygiene*. His last assignment, head of the Institute for Infectious Disease, in 1891, rededicated later as the Koch Institute, permitted the professor to return part time to clinical medicine.

It may not be surprising to learn that so brilliant a mind sometimes encounters certain difficulties in sociologic adjustment. At no time in his career did Koch climb the academic ladder characteristic of professors in Germany in his day. In academic circles he was considered an outsider.

Koch studied infectious diseases in many lands during the last 15 years of his life. These included the bubonic plague in India, cattle plague in South Africa, tsetse disease in West Africa, and malaria in the East Indies. His Nobel prize oration, delivered in 1905, was on the subject of his great interest, tuberculosis. Three years later when he came to New York, he was elected an honorary member of the Academy of Medicine at a dinner given in his honor. Andrew Carnegie presented him with a gift of 500,000 marks for the Koch Foundation in Berlin. In reply he stated:[1]

> Were I to review everything that has been said in my praise, and also to take into consideration the great distinction conferred by you upon me, I must necessarily ask myself, am I really entitled to such homage? . . . But I have done nothing else than what you are doing every day. I have worked as hard as I could and have fulfilled my duty and obligations. . . . We have achieved all we could in our fight against tuberculosis. We have come to a point where we hardly hope for more success. The idea of building sanitoria will not accomplish much; . . . We must make new researches. Such researches will become possible in the Robert Koch Institute in Berlin, a foundation which Andrew Carnegie has so munificently endowed. In this Institute investigation will be made which will open new fields, new theories, new modes and possibilities of fighting the old enemy, tuberculosis. It will be an international affair, benefitting all mankind.

The new researches of which Koch spoke did not reach fruition until recently. The cause of tuberculosis was discovered by the bacteriologist 75 years ago. Effective management was not achieved until the labors of the soil chemist and the organic chemist produced antituberculosis drugs only a few years ago.

1. Brown, L.: Robert Koch (1843-1970), An American Tribute, Ann Med Hist 7:99 (March); 292 (May); 385 (July) 1935.
2. King, L. S.: Dr. Koch's Postulates, J Hist Med 7: 350 (Autumn) 1952.
3. Koch, R.: The Etiology of Anthrax, Beitr Biol Pflanzen 2:277-310, 1876, translated in Brock, T. D.: Milestones in Microbiology, Prentice Hall, Englewood Cliffs, 1961.
4. Koch, R.: The Etiology of Tuberculosis, Berlin Klin Wschr 19:221-230, 1882, translated in Brock, T. D.: Milestones in Microbiology, Prentice Hall, Englewood Cliffs, 1961.

Hansen (1841-1912)

GERHARD HENRIK ARMAUER HANSEN of Bergen, Norway, devoted his professional life to several aspects of leprosy, which included its epidemiology, etiology, prevention, and institutional management.[1] Born into a large family of meager resources, he taught in a girls' school, was an avowed agnostic, and ex-

pressed grave concern over the religious teaching to which he was exposed. These fears for the adverse effects of the lag of religion in its acceptance of "the new science" are expressed

Composite by G. Bako

in his autobiography, prepared in the late years of his life, and subsequently translated into halting English.[2]

Hansen, a brilliant student and inherently industrious, was accustomed to rise at 5:30 a.m. to begin the most productive hours of the day, from 6 to 8 a.m. When he joined the staff of the hospital for leprosy (Lungegard Hospital), Danielssen, the physician in charge who later became his father-in-law, and who was co-author with Boeck of a monograph on leprosy, held that the etiology of the affliction was either humoral or hereditary but surely not contagious. This conclusion was supported by the failure to transmit the supposed contagion to animals or to himself through direct inoculations of morbid tissue. On the other hand, Hansen's suspicion of the infectious nature of leprosy was supported by meticulous statistical and epidemiological studies of its incidence in several communities in Norway and the highly significant finding of "small staff-like bodies, much resembling bacteria," in leprous nodules.

Leprosy was frequently encountered in Norway in the middle of the 19th century, with the incidence in some communities reported to be as high as one in one thousand. Thus, it was not difficult for anyone interested in epidemiology to accumulate adequate vital statistics on the morbid process. Although leprosy appeared in families, it could be traced to contact, and the epidemiological conclusions did not support a hereditary etiology. Although 1873 usually is given as the year of "discovery of the bacilli," as early as 1869 "large brown elements" were identified in leprous nodules.[3] In 1874, Hansen communicated his observations and assumptions on the etiology of leprosy to the Medical Society of Christiania (Oslo).[4]

I have now produced what, according to the extent of my investigations, I have been able to collect in the way of information as to the occurrence of leprosy here in this country, and its conditions, and I have endeavored to point out those things which appear to me to be influential for the guidance of our judgment. Even if I have not been able to furnish any decisive proof in any direction, I think that I have pointed out a number of phenomena in the occurrence of the disease which find a natural explanation by supposing contation, but which, on the contrary, must remain unexplained under the supposition of heredity. Leprosy will thus, according to my conception, come into the category of specific diseases which are contagious, but, like specific diseases in general, are not transmitted by inheritance.

But if leprosy is a specific and contagious disease we might, perhaps, expect to find that, like syphilis, it is also transmissible to the offspring. That such is the case can neither be denied nor affirmed. There are some observations of leprosy in so early an age, in the first and second year of children born of leprous parents, that they might be supposed, by reason of the slow development of this disease, to have got the disease while in the uterus. But the cases are so extremely rare, and the leprous parents who have children are so many, that it is not probable. Most of the children who have leprosy are over five years of age, and it seems, indeed, reasonable to suppose that they have contracted the disease after birth.

While leprosy may be thus indirectly proved to be a specific disease by demonstrating its contagiousness, it would, of course, be the best if a direct proof could be given. I will briefly mention what seems to indicate, that such proof is, perhaps, attainable. There are to be found in every leprous tubercle extirpated from a living individual—and I have examined a great number of them—small staff-like bodies, much resembling bacteria, lying within the cells; not in all, but in many of them. . . . It is worthy of notice, however, that the large brown elements found in all leprous proliferations in advanced stages, of which I have in 1869 already given engravings, republished in 'Leprous Diseases of the Eye', by O. B. Bull and G. A. Hansen, bear a striking likeness to bacteria in certain states of development.

The 1873, communication by Bull and Hansen referred to the usual staining property of the foreign bodies.[5]

The elements in the softened part are almost exclusively brown and brownish yellow bodies of extremely different form and size (Fig. 13 shows such elements taken from cutaneous tubers, corresponding perfectly to those which are found in the Cornea, and not there only, but also in other leprously affected parts of the eye, in the spleen, liver, lymphatic glands, testicles and nerves, as result of regressive metamorphosis of the elements). Not seldom there occur also large Myeloplaque-like cells, with contents of even or patchy brown color. Like other regressive elements the contents of these cells cannot be colored with carmine.

Since the *Mycobacterium leprae* are as difficult to stain, because of their acid-fastness, as the tubercle bacillus discovered by Koch in 1882, identification of the brown nodules in stained microscopic sections was delayed until the development of a suitable histologic technique. This deficiency was corrected by Neisser of Breslau, who came to Bergen in 1879, studied the morbid tissue supplied by Hansen, and was shortly successful in staining the foreign bodies and identifying them as masses of bacilli. This discovery by Neisser in no measure detracts from Hansen's fundamental observations. In 1880, Hansen assigned the name *"Bacillus leprae"* to the organism, now classified as *Myco leprae*.

As early as 1874, Hansen failed to infect rabbits and cats with leprous tissue. Efforts to transmit the disease to animals or to cultivate the organism artificially have remained fruitless until recent years, when Shepard was successful in carrying on repeated passage infections in the foot-pad of the mouse. The organism for the induced lesion has not been cultivated, but an antigen has been recovered which suggests specificity of the infection.[6] According to current epidemiological concepts of the transmission of the disease in humans, prolonged and intimate contact is necessary, exemplified by a mother nursing, bathing, and otherwise caring for her offspring, with contact over a period of years.

Hansen was a student of zoology and displayed more than casual interest in marine fauna. He defended the evolution theory propounded by Darwin at a time when the cause was unpopular, particularly because of its supposed antireligious context. In later years, he was active in civic promotion and legislative efforts to control and, hopefully, to eradicate leprosy. Isolation in hospitals for patients and residence under conditions approved by the hygiene board were enforced by a statute of 1877. Husband and wife were not separated, except under extraordinary circumstances. Scant attention was given by Hansen to specific therapeutic agents. He made casual mention only of chaulmoogra oil, which had been used for centuries in the East, but was not introduced into Western medicine until the middle of the 19th century. Currently, the diaminodiphenyl sulfones are preferred by most leprologists, although no specific agent is recognized as curative.

The statistically planned epidemiological studies by Hansen and the unhurried microscopic investigations of leprosy advanced the presumptive evidence that the rods in the leprous nodules were the pathogenic offenders, the first contagious agent held responsible for a chronic disease. Although the conclusive proof remains concealed, this assumption was advanced nearly a century ago. The infection has not been transmitted to animals except as noted above, the bacilli resist culturing in the laboratory, and vaccination against infection has been ineffective. Leprosy remains an enigma.

1. Kobro, I.: Gerhard Henrik Armauer Hansen, *Ann Med Hist* 7:127-132, 1925.

2. Hansen, G. A.: *Memoirs and Contemplations* (N), Dr. Pearson, trans., Kristiania: H. Aschehoug & Co., 1910.

3. Hansen, G. H. A.: Forelöbige Bidrag til Spedalskhedens Karakteristik (Preliminary Contributions to Characterization of Leprosy) (N), *Nord Med Ark* I: No. 13, 1-12, 1869.

4. Hansen, G. A.: On the Etiology of Leprosy (N), *Nord mag Laeger* 9: no. 3, 1874, trans, *Brit Foreign Medicochir Rev* 55:459-489, 1875.

5. Bull, O. B., and Hansen, G. A.: *The Leprous Diseases of the Eye, with 6 Colored Plates* (N), Christiania: Albert Cammermeyer, 1873.

6. Shepard, C. C.: The Experimental Disease That Follows the Injection of Human Leprosy Bacilli into Foot-Pads of Mice, *J Exp Med* 112:445-454 (Sept 1) 1960.

Composite by G. Bako

Sir Patrick Manson (1884-1922)

PATRICK MANSON was born near Aberdeen, Scotland, into a family of considerable means. His father, a laird (landowner) of Fingask and manager of the local branch of the British Linen Bank at Old Meldrum, was able to provide his son the proper schooling of that time. Patrick, fond of carpentry, hunting, and mechanics, terminated his early education at the age of 15 and became an apprentice in the ironworks of his mother's relatives. While in this heavy industry, he acquired a curvature of the spine and flaccid paralysis of the right arm. The need to rest several hours each day caused him to abandon mechanics and engineering. During this enforced leisure he read natural history and developed an interest in medicine. He entered the University of Aberdeen in 1860 and complemented his studies at Edinburgh University during the summer. Following the granting of the MB and CM degrees by Aberdeen, he was appointed assistant medical officer at the Durham Lunatic Asylum. The experimental observations gathered from the examinations at the asylum formed the corpus of his MD thesis entitled "A Peculiar Affection of the Internal Carotid Artery in Connexion with Diseases of the Brain." Interest in asylum work was soon satiated, and he obtained the appointment as medical officer to the Chinese Imperial Maritime Customs in Formosa. While in this post he suffered his first attack of gout, a malady which recurred intermittently throughout his life.

Manson remained in the Far East—first at Formosa, then Amoy, and later Hong Kong —until the age of 45. Professional activities were divided between medicine, surgery, and original investigations in parasitology, a discipline vaguely defined and scarcely recognized as a professional pursuit a half century ago. Private practice provided a substantial income for this avocational interest, the study of subliminal organisms. Many of his scientific endeavors were described in the reports of the Chinese Imperial Maritime Customs. Even though Manson had received no special training in laboratory investigation, a microscope and a few accessory items were sufficient tools to begin a series of remarkable investigations on *Trichophyton, Filaria, Sparganum, Schistosoma, Trypanosoma,* and the malaria parasites. In these investigations, Manson introduced the concept of transmission of infection by arthropods, which permitted a new understanding of disease.

One of his first encounters with a tropical disease was a case of beriberi, masquerading as heart disease, which etiologic relationship was not recognized until several years later.[1]

One day I was called to see a Chinese clerk employed in a European firm. . . . I found the patient sitting propped up in a chair, short of breath, dropsical from head to foot, with a cardiac bruit, irregular tumbling action of the heart, and complaining of a feeling of distress in his chest. As there was no albumin in his urine, and there was a loud bruit with manifest disturbance of the heart, I felt convinced it was a case of heart disease, and, from other circumstances in the case, one which treatment would benefit. . . . Next day I went to see the lad expecting to find an improvement. I thought as I passed the door that there was a strange hush about the house. I entered what was my patient's room. On the bed, covered with a blanket, there was something long and rounded and still, which explained the hush I had noticed.

In 1879, Manson trod on the periphery of another significant observation, without appreciating its significance. After his successful study of the cause of filariasis, he searched for parasites in "leper-juice" or lymph from leprous nodules. Rod-like bodies were discovered which most probably were the causative bacilli. They were described and identified the same year by Hansen.

Manson's most important medical contribution was the culmination of a search for the intermediate host for *Filaria*. The *Filaria* embryos had been recognized in the blood of a human by Lewis in 1872. The parent worm was discovered in 1876 by Bancroft of Brisbane (*Filaria bancrofti*). The incidence of filariasis in infested areas might be as high as 50% of the population, with most of the affected in apparent good health, despite the persistence of parasites in the blood. In others, with clinical symptoms, parasites could not be recovered. Manson speculated that the parasites might appear in the peripheral blood intermittently, diurnally or nocturnally. Arrangements were made, therefore, to examine patients periodically through a 24-hour period.[2]

You will find that it [*Filaria*] is present in enormous numbers—perhaps three or four hundred per drop— at midnight, that it is practically absent at midday; that it begins to put in an appearance about six or seven in the evening, gradually increasing in numbers up to about midnight and gradually decreasing in numbers up to about seven or eight in the morning, and that it is almost entirely absent from eight or nine a.m., till about six or seven p.m.

A postmortem examination in a case of suicide disclosed the migration site of the *Filaria* from the peripheral circulation. The examination revealed no *Filaria* in the blood, liver, or the spleen. On the other hand, in blood expressed from the lungs, there were thousands in each drop. The diurnal migration provided the clue for the next step in identifying a supposed vector.[2]

The abstracting agency must be a blood-eater or blood-sucker of nocturnal habits, and that it operates through the skin. Further, this blood-sucker of nocturnal habits must have a geographical range corresponding to that of the filaria—that is to say, be indigenous to the tropics and subtropics.

The common tropical mosquito, *Culex fatigans*, which had not been fed previously on patients with filariasis, was placed under a mosquito net that covered an infected person. The next morning the mosquito was retrieved, fed on fresh bananas for a time, and examined. Microscopic sections revealed the *Filaria* in the mosquito's stomach and in the thoracic muscles. The life cycle between man and mosquito was exposed.

In 1880, Manson discovered, quite by chance, the lung fluke, *Paragonimus westermani*, the cause of endemic hemoptysis.[2]

> On one occasion I was consulted by a Chinaman, a petty mandarin, about an eruption between his fingers, to wit, the itch. While I was engaged in examining his hands my patient began to cough. He hawked up, and, after the manner of his race, incontinentally expectorated the result of his efforts on to my study carpet. I observed that the expectorated material was red and viscid; and so, instead of reproaching him for spitting on my carpet, requested him to repeat the cough and this time to deposit the sputum in a watchglass. He very obligingly did so. My forbearance was rewarded. On placing a little of the rusty sputum under the microscope I found it to be loaded with little brown operculated bodies, manifestly the ova of a parasite.

A number of other notable accomplishments were Manson's, either pursued while in the Far East or after his return to London. These included a description of *Sparganum mansoni*, the larval stage of *Filaria loa*, the eggs of *Schistosoma mansoni*, *Trypanosoma gambiense*, the fungus *Trichophyton mansoni*, and a clinical description of tinea imbricata and tropical sprue.

After his return to London, Manson encouraged Ross, who was practicing in Bombay at that time, to investigate the mosquito as an intermediary host for malaria. The correspondence between the parasitologists during the years 1895–97 was prodigious. Ross, who was awarded the Nobel prize for identification of the dapple-winged mosquito, the *Anopheles*, as the carrier of the malarial parasite, refused to share the honor with Manson. He asserted that "The work was done by me alone, with Manson's occasional advice, it is true, but *not* by his instructions, as frequently pretended."

Manson provided the major impetus in the establishment of two medical schools. The Hong Kong Medical College opened its classrooms in 1887. Sun Yat Sen, one of the great men of modern China, was one of the first graduates of the school. Several years later Manson befriended his former student, in London, a fugitive from the Chinese government. The London School of Tropical Medicine, the second educational venture, was founded in 1899 in connection with the Albert Dock Hospital and under the aegis of the Seamen's Hospital Society. Later the hospital merged with the London School of Hygiene under a charter granted to the London School of Hygiene and Tropical Medicine. Manson was alone responsible for founding the Royal Society of Tropical Medicine and the section of tropical medicine in the British Medical Association.

Honors in abundance came to the expert on filariasis. The universities of Aberdeen, London, Oxford, Cambridge, and Hong Kong esteemed his remarkable contributions. Honorary membership in a number of distinguished medical societies was decreed. He delivered the Lane Lectures at Cooper Medical College in San Francisco in 1905.[3] He was a medalist of several learned societies.

Manson's gout, which he had endured since the age of 27, continued to plague him as it had Sydenham a century and a half before. Did gout contribute to his outstanding personality, his warmth of character, and kindliness as a physician and investigator? One can only speculate.

1. Manson-Bahr, P. H.: *The Life and Work of Sir Patrick Manson*, London, Toronto, Melbourne, and Sydney: Cassell and Company, Ltd. 1927.
2. Manson, P.: *Lectures on Tropical Diseases: The Lane Lectures for 1905*, Chicago: W. T. Keener & Co., 1905.
3. Manson-Bahr, P. H.: The Malaria Story, *Proc Roy Soc Med* 54:91-100 (Feb.) 1961.

Sir Ronald Ross (1857-1932)

SIR RONALD ROSS, poet, novelist, musician, scientist, and reluctant physician, was awarded the Nobel prize in medicine in 1902 for his contributions to the pathogenesis of malaria, the climax of a professional career, wavering between literature and science. Ross was born in the Himalayan Mountains of India, the son of the commander of the British forces on the Northwest frontier. As an obedient son of Scottish lineage, he enrolled at St. Bartholomew's Hospital at the age of 17.[1]

> I wished to be an artist, but my father was opposed to this. I wished also to enter the Army or Navy; but my father had set his heart upon my joining the medical profession and, finally, the Indian Medical Service, which was then well paid and possessed many good appointments; and, as I was a dreamy boy not too well inclined towards uninteresting mental exertion, I resigned myself to this scheme, especially because it would give me experience of life in India, with shoot-

ing and riding, and also a knowledge of biology and considerable leisure for any other hobbies I might have a mind for. But I had no predilection at all for medicine and, like most youths, felt disposed to look down upon it.

Composite by G. Bako

Norman Moore, the warden of St. Bartholomew's Hospital Medical School, considered it unnecessary for Ross to attend Oxford or Cambridge for a liberal arts education before matriculating in medicine. The judgment to leapfrog undergraduate instruction permitted Ross to enter immediately upon the study of anatomy and physiology. He graduated five years later, having spent at least one summer holiday on a camping trip, which revealed to him the joys to be gained from the out-of-doors:

> Give back to me, O time-forgetting Nature,
> The days of my boyhood;
> Give back to me those golden days of summer-time,
> To wisdom so wasted but wasted not to life.

As a man of letters, he had this to say about books after he had finished his medical training.[2]

It is not too much to say that the whole fabric of our civilisation is based upon books, which hand down to one generation the experience of former ones and knit together the past and present. To conceive their im-

portance, let us imagine the effect of a total destruction of them. The arts, the sciences would perish and history vanish, for the beginning of books was to mankind what the beginning of self-consciousness is to men, and literature is indeed the memory of humanity.

Do not take away this simple art of writing [books], and in a few years you and your children will return to those levels you now despise—your tillages untilled, your palaces rotting, your wharves unused, your engines rusted.

He had intended to accede to his father's wishes to enter the Indian medical service. The first step was the successful application for membership in the Royal College of Surgeons. The second step, the examination for the Indian medical service, was a failure. While waiting for a second attempt, Ross served as ship's surgeon on a vessel plying between London and New York. He was rewarded on the second attempt, and, for the following two decades, India served as the base for operations.

The first years in India were richly productive of verse and prose but idle ones medically. However, the scourge of malaria was ever apparent to Ross. It was estimated at the time that more than a million persons died from this disease in India each year.[1]

> In this, O Nature, yield I pray to me.
> I pace and pace, and think and think, and take
> The fever'd hands, and note down all I see,
> That some dim distant light may haply break.
>
> The painful faces ask, can we not cure?
> We answer, No, not yet; we seek the laws.
> O God, reveal thro' all this thing obscure
> The unseen, small, but million-murdering cause.

Ross returned to London in 1889 to study bacteriology and to become a diplomate in public health, a plan of study designed to insure a more productive second tour of duty. Malaria became the object of scientific interest, and for more than a decade was all-absorbing except for precious time allocated to music and the composition of poetry, prose, and dramettas.[2] The studies of malaria were built upon the identification of the malarial parasite by Nobel laureate Alphonse Laveran in 1880 with the guiding hand of Patrick Manson, the discoverer of the transmission of *Filaria bancrofti* by the *Culex* mosquito in 1879. It would seem that two such important observations might well have permitted the closing of the ring on the parasite-mosquito-host pathogenesis of malaria. Five years of relentless toil, however, were necessary before Ross revealed on Aug. 20, 1897, that he had discovered what had been the object of his search, the female form of the parasite in the stomach of the *Anopheles*.[3] The zygotes or sexual forms were found in the stomach. The sporoblasts or progeny were identified in the salivary glands. The parasites were present only in insects that had dined on the blood of persons infected with malaria. The critical observations were consummated with little more than makeshift laboratory tools that would be considered primitive by current standards. A dilapidated microscope, a cracked eyepiece, a few test tubes, bottles, slides, and cover slips seemed ill-matched to the importance of this great discovery. The identification of the zygotes through recognition of the melanin pigment in the *Anopheles* mosquito, was a twofold victory expressed by Ross:[1]

> This day designing God
>   Hath put into my hand
> A wondrous thing. And God
>   Be praised. At His command,
>
> I have found thy secret deeds
>   Oh million-murdering Death.
>
> I know that this little thing
>   A million men will save—
> Oh death where is thy sting?
>   Thy victory oh grave?

There were some doubts expressed at home and abroad over the validity of the observations, but Ross had rallied strong men in support of his conviction. They included Robert Koch, Sir William Osler, Patrick Manson, and Sir John Bland-Sutton.

Having completed the pathonomy of malaria, there remained the eradication of the disease, the modern scourge of man. Quinine, which had been discovered in Peru and found useful in the treatment of South American fevers, had been introduced into Europe by the Countess d'El Cinchon, wife of the Viceroy of Peru, shortly after Pizarro's conquest of this land in the early 16th century. Pelletier and Caventou extracted the alkaloid quinine from the bark in 1820. The drug remained the only specific for malaria until early in World War II. In anticipation of the interception of normal trade routes and the interruption of

the supply of quinine to the Allies, a large-scale program for the synthesis of antimalarials was begun. The drugs that came from these researchers have largely replaced quinine as agents of choice in the prophylaxis and treatment of malaria.

Ross was acutely aware of the pharmacologic properties of quinine and of the grossly inadequate supply in the world half a century ago, a quantity insufficient to produce any significant impact upon the incidence of the disease, particularly in the highly malarious countries. Since an adequate quantity of quinine for the prophylaxis or suppression of the disease was lacking, the alternative was eradication of the carrier. This is preventive medicine at its most effective site. Charting the campaign for control of the *Anopheles* was begun upon Ross' return to Great Britain in 1900, first at the newly formed Liverpool School of Tropical Medicine and finally at the Ross Institute in London. The latter was established in 1926 and subsequently became a unit of the Postgraduate Medical School of the University of London, the School of Hygiene and Tropical Medicine.

United States benefited especially from the discoveries. According to a letter prepared in 1914 from General W. G. Gorgas, the scientific observations of Ross contributed significantly to the building of the Panama Canal:[4]

As you are aware malaria was the great disease that incapacitated the working forces at Panama before our day. If we had known no more about the sanitation of Malaria than the French did, I do not think that we could have done any better than they did. Your discovery that the mosquito transferred the malarial parasite from man to man has enabled us at Panama to hold in check this disease, to eradicate it almost entirely from most points on the Isthmus where our forces were engaged.

It seems to me not extreme, therefore, to say that it was your discovery of this fact that enabled us to build the Canal at the Isthmus of Panama.

Sir Ronald Ross, who completed the *Anopheles-Plasmodium*-man cycle, was reluctant to enter medicine, but having done so, made a notable contribution to the greatest morbid hazard of mankind.

1. Ross, R.: *Memoirs, with a Full Account of the Great Malaria Problem and Its Solution*, London: John Murray, 1923.

2. Megroz, R. L.: *Ronald Ross, Discoverer and Creator*, London: George Allen & Unwin, 1931.

3. Ross, R.: On Some Peculiar Pigmented Cells Found in Two Mosquitos Fed on Malarial Blood, *Brit Med J*, pp. 1786-1789 (Dec 18) 1897.

4. Pitfield, R. L.: Sir Ronald Ross Number, *Med Life* (May) 1930.

Composite by G. Bako

William H. Welch (1850-1934)

WILLIAM HENRY WELCH, teacher, pathologist, bacteriologist, editor, and founder of the first public health school as well as the first institute of medical history in this country, was the architect of contemporary medical education in America. Welch was born into a family of country doctors in Norfolk, Connecticut.[1] His mother died when he was an infant and his early upbringing was largely entrusted to his grandmother. At 12 he attended the Winchester Institute and graduated from Yale shortly after his 20th birthday. For a year at Norwich, New York, he pursued his original intention of teaching Latin and Greek. The following year Welch spent as an apprentice to his father before he was attracted once more to Yale. This time he chose the Sheffield Scientific School, where laboratory work was possible in a scholastic environment. He then entered the College of Physicians and Surgeons, from which he graduated in 1875, with a brilliant record.

Welch's first academic post was a pathology appointment at Bellevue Hospital, where he met Abraham Jacobi and listened to his great tales of medical science in central Europe. At the same time the possibility of a chair of pathology was beginning to ferment in his thoughts. Welch was sufficiently bold to hope that Johns Hopkins University, in the planning stage, might be receptive to his ambitions. In preparation for this or an undetermined post in the United States, Welch wisely planned his postgraduate years in Europe. He studied histology under Waldeyer, pathology under von Recklinghausen, and physiological chemistry under Hoppe-Seyler, and audited lectures in medicine by von Leyden at Strasbourg. Then followed work in Leipzig in the pathological laboratory of Wagner and the physiology laboratory of Carl Ludwig, and in Breslau, where he studied edema of the lungs with the experimental pathologist, Julius Cohnheim.

Early in 1878, Welch returned to New York. Failing to obtain an appointment at the College of Physicians and Surgeons, he turned to Bellevue Hospital, where, in cramped quarters in the hospital, with a few microscopes, six students to instruct, pathological material to study, and literature to review, his design was beginning to be realized. The financial returns from these endeavors were so minimal that he engaged in limited private practice, did private tutoring, and composed for medical texts. Welch struggled in this fashion for a projected but fleeting goal, until his patience and perserverance were rewarded in 1884—he was offered and accepted the professorship of pathology at Johns Hopkins University. His next decision was to return to Germany and study the emerging subject, bacteriology, concluding this tour in the laboratory of Robert Koch, the master of this science in the Western World. In the fall of 1885, Welch was given working space in Martin's biological laboratory in Baltimore; the following year on the Johns Hopkins Hospital grounds he had his own quarters which provided room for combined investigations in pathological anatomy, bacteriology, and experimental pathology. Inasmuch as neither the hospital nor the medical school was open for patients or medical students until several years later, Welch offered instruction and research opportunities only to graduates in medicine or advanced students. Subsequently, Welch's working quarters, the "Pathological," became the center for research, teaching, and medical science at Hopkins for more than a quarter of a century. Many of his pupils in time became department heads or dedicated teachers in medical schools throughout the land.

At the 25th anniversary of Welch's graduation from medical school (1900), he expressed his thoughts about his formative years in pathology.[2]

When Dr. Prudden and I first started our small laboratories in New York, he at the College of Physicians and Surgeons, and I at the Bellevue Hospital Medical College, the outlook was not encouraging for a young man to select pathology for his career. The contrast between then and now in this respect is indeed a striking one. To-day, pathology is everywhere recognized as a subject of fundamental importance in medical education and is represented in our best medical schools by a full professorship; at least a dozen good pathological laboratories, equipped not only for teaching but also for research, have been founded; many of our best hospitals have established clinical and pathological laboratories; fellowships and assistantships afford opportunity for the thorough training and advancement of those who wish to follow pathology as their career; special workers with suitable preliminary education are attracted to undertake original studies in our pathological laboratories; students are beginning to realize the benefits of a year or more spent in pathological work after their graduation, as a foundation for future success in practical medicine, surgery, or the specialties; and as a result of all these activities the contributions to pathology from our American laboratories take rank with those from the best European laboratories. While we realize that we are only at the beginning of better things and that far more remains to be accomplished than has been attained, nevertheless, the progress of pathology in America during these twenty-five years has surely been most encouraging.

Welch's written contributions were divided among experimental work, medical education, the history of medicine, and nonscientific matters. For more than a decade embolism and thrombosis were major objects of study. Three outstanding investigations which combined histologic pathology, experimental pathology, and bacteriology were reported in 1892. He discovered the *Staphylococcus epidermis albus* and its relation to skin infection, a gas-producing bacillus, and simultaneously with von Behring, the lesions produced by diphtheria toxins. In one of the early communications to the *Bulletin of the Johns Hopkins Hospital*, he described findings in a bricklayer suffering from a luetic aneurysm who died from a gas-producing bacillus. The organism was recovered in pure culture throughout the blood vessels of the body. The offender was an obligate anaerobe which, following intravenous injection, was capable of forming gas in the experimental animal, demonstrable after sacrifice. The pathological findings in the patient, the staining characteristics of the organism, and the naming of the organism later classified as Welch's bacillus—*Clostridium welchii*—were described as follows:[3]

Before making the usual incisions into the abdomen and thorax, a number of veins and arteries, including the jugular, femoral and brachial veins, superficial veins of abdominal wall, femoral and temporal arteries, are carefully exposed by small suitable incisions through the skin covering them, and the presence of gas-bubbles is determined in all of them without opening them. The presence of gas in the subcutaneous connective tissue of the neck is also determined by incision. The gas burns with a pale bluish, almost colorless flame, a slight explosive sound being heard at the moment of ignition.

In the sections the bacilli stain readily with all of the ordinary aniline dyes (methylene-blue, gentian-violet, fuchsine) and stain well even with haematoxylin. They stain excellently by Gram's method, retaining the color after the nuclei have been decolorized. Their length averages one-half to two-thirds the diameter of the red blood corpuscles seen on the same sections, and their thickness is perhaps a little greater than that of anthrax bacilli, from which they are especially distinguished by not occurring in long chains.

In endeavoring to select a name suitable for the bacillus described in this article we have thought of several designations, . . . Upon the whole we prefer the first name, bacillus aerogenes capsulatus. The presence of a capsule does not appear to be constant, but it is common and forms a characteristic feature of the morphology of the bacillus.

The histological lesions produced by the toxalbumin of diphtheria in guinea pigs, rabbits, and kittens were reported by Welch and his pupil and biographer, Simon Flexner, then a fellow in pathology. The preliminary communication on experimental diphtheria led to the following conclusions.[4]

It may be considered as established now that the toxic products and not the bacilli themselves invade the tissues in diphtheria. This fact would at once suggest that the general lesions (those produced at a distance from the seat of inoculation in animals, and the situation of the local process in human beings) were the effects of the soluble poison diffused through the body. Hence, it was desirable to demonstrate this assumption experimentally; and it is not unimportant to know that the lesions in the tissues produced by the bacilli and the toxic principle on the one hand, and the toxic principle alone on the other, are in perfect correspondence with each other. And, moreover, it would seem not to be superfluous to emphasize the occurrence of definite focal lesions in the tissues of the body, produced by a soluble poison circulating in the blood.

Scarcely had Welch begun to see the unfolding of his plans for the pathological laboratory than he was assigned, in recognition of his wisdom and talent, the selection of other senior members of the medical faculty in a university environment. The appointment by President Gilman of Osler in medicine, Halsted in surgery, and Kelly in gynecology followed the advice offered by counselor Welch. He assisted in determining the conditions under which clinical departments were to be directed in close liaison with the university hospital. The full-time system of medicine for the clinical departments was soon called the "Hopkins System," which criteria embraced direction of research, walking the wards, as well as limited availability for private consultation. However, the opportunities for clinical practice were so restricted that any fees accrued necessarily reverted to the medical school. Medical education stimulated by Welch and others was to advance in the United States and compete with, or surpass, European schools. Research laboratories were to be established and directed by the chiefs of the clinical departments, ever mindful that the purpose of medical education was to train practitioners of medicine and surgery. His attempt to establish full-time university chairs in the clinical departments was only partially successful in Baltimore. The loss of Osler to Oxford in 1905 was related to the latter's unwillingness to give up private practice in keeping with the Hopkins' concept. This entailed undivided attention to teaching, research, and administration, with limited consultation privileges, but formed the basis for practically all progressive American medical education and medical reorganization in recent decades. Welch summarized these thoughts in an address delivered at the convocation exercises of the University of Chicago in 1907.[5]

The historical and the proper home of the medical school is the university, of which it should be an integral part co-ordinate with the other faculties.

In manifold ways the environment of a university is that best adapted to the teaching and the advancement of medicine. The medical school needs the ideals of the university in maintaining the dignity of its high calling, in laying a broad foundation for professional study, in applying correct educational principles in the arrangement of the curriculum and in methods of instruction, in assigning the proper place and share to the scientific and the practical studies, in giving due emphasis to both the teaching and the investigating sides of its work, in stimulating productive research, and in determining what shall be the qualifications of its teachers and of the recipients of its degree. Most invigorating is the contact of medical teachers and investigators with workers in those sciences on which medicine is dependent—chemistry, physics and biology.

In order to place the clinical side of medical instruction on the same satisfactory foundation as that of laboratory teaching, two reforms are especially needed in most of our medical schools.

The first is that the heads of the principal clinical departments, particularly the medical and the surgical, should devote their main energies and time to their hospital work and to teaching and investigating without the necessity of seeking their livelihood in a busy outside practice and without allowing such practice to become their chief professional occupation.

The other reform is the introduction of the system of practical training of students in the hospital, which I have indicated, and with it the foundation and support of teaching and investigating laboratories connected with the clinics, to which I have already referred, necessitating the possession of a hospital by the medical school or the establishment of such relations with outside hospitals as will make possible these conditions.

Welch, a careful writer and meticulous editor, was largely responsible for the founding of the *Bulletin of the Johns Hopkins Hospital*, and the early volumes published much of the work from his pathological laboratory. He was also founder and editor of the *Journal of Experimental Medicine* and only when he found too little time to fulfill the editorial assignment to his satisfaction was the journal transferred to the Rockefeller Institute for Medical Research. The *American Journal of Hygiene* was the third scientific periodical to be established under his aegis.

As a senior statesman for American medicine, Welch recognized the need for two additional components for an integrated medical school for 20th century medicine. With the support of the Rockefeller Foundation and through the direction of the International Health Board, he was largely responsible for adding a School of Hygiene and Public Health at the Johns Hopkins University and became its first director. His last years in Baltimore were spent in the organization of the Institute of the History of Medicine, which was opened in 1929, also under his charge.

The honors that came to Welch were well deserved by the Dean of American Medicine, as well as the one-time dean of the Johns Hopkins School of Medicine. He served at various times as president of the Board of Scientific Directors of the Rockefeller Institute for Medical Research, president of the National Academy of Sciences, the American Medical Association, the Association of American Physicians, the American Association for the Advancement of Science, the Association of Pathologists and Bacteriologists, and chairman of the Executive Committee of the Carnegie Institution of Washington. Honorary degrees from many of the great universities of this country and decorations and medals from foreign governments were proffered him. After serving as consultant to the Surgeon General of the Army in World War I, he retired from the Reserve Corps with the rank of major general. Although Welch never married, there is no record of unrequited love, albeit he was affectionately known by many as "Popsy." His pleasures beyond his great contributions to medicine included warm friendship in great measure for students and associates, tolerance for all, a love of good food and cigars, sunbathing at the shore, and proper care of his mild gout. His concluding remarks upon retirement from the president's chair of the American Association for the Advancement of Science are appropriate for concluding this biographical essay of a natural scientist of many talents and many interests.[6]

It is well that the sciences of nature hold out attractions to so many different types of mind, for the edifice of science is built of material which must be drawn from many sources. A quarry opened in the interest of one enriches all of these sciences. The deeper we can lay the foundations and penetrate into the nature of things, the closer are the workers drawn together, the

clearer becomes their community of purpose, and the more significant to the welfare of mankind the upbuilding of natural knowledge.

1. Flexner, S., and Flexner, J. T.: *William Henry Welch and the Heroic Age of American Medicine*, New York: Viking Press, 1941.
2. Welch, W. H.: Address, Twenty-Fifth Anniversary of Dr. Welch's Graduation, *Bull Johns Hopkins Hosp* 11:135-137, 1900.
3. Welch, W. H., and Nuttall, G. H. F.: A Gas-Producing Bacillus (Bacillus Aerogenes Capsulatus, Nov. Spec.) Capable of Rapid Development in the Blood-Vessels After Death, *Bull Johns Hopkins Hosp* 3:81-91, 1892.
4. Welch, W. H., and Flexner, S.: The Histological Lesions Produced by the Tox-Albumen of Diphtheria, *Bull Johns Hopkins Hosp* 3:17-18, 1892.
5. Welch, W. H.: Medicine and the University, *JAMA* 50:1-7, 1908.
6. Welch, W. H.: The Interdependence of Medicine and Other Sciences of Nature, *Science* 27:49-64, 1908.

Composite by G. Bako

Friedrich Loeffler (1852-1915)

FRIEDRICH AUGUST JOHANNES LOEFFLER was born at Frankfurt-am-Oder. While associated with the Universities of Greifswald and of Berlin, he became one of the outstanding investigators of microorganisms and immunology in the great days of these disciplines in central Europe.[1] His initial exposure to medicine and military service came through his father, who, as a senior army surgeon, reached the rank of general with the title of professor at the Kaiser Wilhelm Academy for Military Medicine in Berlin. Friedrich's early education, gained at Marburg and the Royal French College in Berlin, was followed by the study of medicine at Würzburg. Completion of his training was interrupted by the Franco-Prussian War, in which he served as a hospital assistant. The MD degree was granted in 1874 by the Kaiser Wilhelm Academy. The following year he was stationed in Hanover and later in Pottsdam, where he practiced medicine while functioning as sanitary officer. In 1879, shortly after his transfer to the newly established Imperial Health Department in Berlin, he became associated with Robert Koch, who turned his interest to bacteriologic investigation.

Loeffler gained faculty status in the University of Berlin in 1886. Two years later he was called to Greifswald, and, having served as rector of the University between 1903 and 1907, he returned to Berlin as director of the Robert Koch Institute of Infectious Diseases. With the outbreak of World War I, he returned to military service as consultant to the military hospitals with the rank of surgeon general, but died a few months later. In editorial pursuits, together with Uhlworm and Leuckart in 1887, he founded the *Centralblatt für Bakteriologie und Parasitenkunde;* working alone, he began a monumental history of bacteriology. Only a small portion of the projected whole was finished at his death.[2]

Loeffler is best known for his satisfying the postulates of Koch in the investigation of the etiology of diphtheria. Earlier he had discovered the causative agent in glanders; later he isolated the bacteria of swine erysipelas and *Salmonella typhimurium* and, together with Frosch, found that the infectious agent of foot and mouth disease passed through filters which retained bacteria. This led to his use of the now obsolete term, "filterable virus," as well as to inoculation against the affliction. Loeffler's interest in the health of the people was apparent in his studies on milk hygiene, sewage disposal, bacteriology of water, and examination of fecal material.

The history of clinical diphtheria as recounted by Loeffler[3] began with a description of its prevalence in ancient times in Egypt and the Middle East. Not until 1883, when Klebs presented his findings, however, was a specific bacillus associated with the false membrane in the pharynx. The following year Loeffler satisfied the three postulates of pathogenesis. First, the organism was identified in its characteristic site in the characteristic lesion. Secondly, the organism was isolated and survived reculturing. Thirdly, the inoculation of the pure culture reproduced the disease experimentally. An alkaline solution of highly concentrated methylene blue was selected for staining. Twenty-seven cases of serious sore throat were investigated. Five cases of scarlatina pharyngitis were included. The typical clinical cases of diphtheria elaborated a thick false membrane from which the bacteria were isolated. Below the conglomerates of various types of bacteria, the bacilli of Klebs, *Corynebacterium diphtheriae*, were arranged in characteristic small groups. Koch's nutrient jelly, used as the culture medium, gave pure strains of a chain-forming micrococcus but was unsatisfactory for the bacillus under suspicion. On the other hand, when coagulated blood serum was incorporated into the nutrient media, pure colonies of bacilli were isolated. The organisms were nonmotile, pleomorphic, and specifically identifiable by the deeper staining at each pole. Following experimental inoculation rats and mice enjoyed immunity, although guinea pigs, rabbits, and small birds were readily infected.[4] By 1888, Roux and Yersin had defined diphtheria toxin; in 1890, von Behring had produced an antitoxin, but not until 1923, when Ramon discovered that the *toxin* could be altered, was the first diphtheria *toxoid* available for disseminated immunization. A condensed version of the long report was freely translated and published by the New Sydenham Society. Excerpts communicated in the third person follow.[5]

Loeffler was thus induced to apply the more accurate methods of Koch to the elucidation of the questions as to the significance of the various organisms found in diphtheria, and as to their efficacy in propagating the disease in animals.

In the second class of cases the bacilli first described by Klebs are present. These bacilli occur exclusively in those typical cases which are characterized by a thick false membrane extending over the mucous membrane of the fauces, larynx, and trachea, the mucous membrane being traversed by enormously dilated vessels. Below the masses of bacteria of different kinds which cover the surface, among which may be the streptococcus before referred to, Klebs' bacilli are found arranged in little groups. They become intensely stained with methylene blue.

Material for cultivation was selected from four typical cases in children aged 5, 6, 8 and 9 years, the membrane being taken on the second day of the disease before any treatment had been begun. The false membrane, which was in all cases firmly adherent, was seized with forceps, and a portion removed and cut with the freezing microtome. . . . It was from the deeper part that the material was taken for cultivation in all the cases, and that identical organisms were obtained from all the patients was proved both by their morphological and their biological characteristics.

Inoculation experiments were made on mice, rats, guinea-pigs, rabbits, monkeys, pigeons, hens and smaller birds, and the behaviour of the bacilli towards the various species is a matter of great interest. The modes of infection tried consisted of subcutaneous inoculation, inoculation on the wounded or unharmed mucous membrane and inhalation.

When inoculations were made through the skin or mucous membrane the following results were obtained: rats and mice enjoy complete immunity, while guinea-pigs fall easy victims; . . . Pigeons also are susceptible, and hens behave similarily, but hens and pigeons are not as susceptible as the small birds and cannot be infected through an uninjured mucous membrane. Rabbits do not give such uniform results as the preceding; it would appear from the experiments of Loeffler that death is due in their case to the mechanical effects of the false membrane caused by infection, and that a chemical poison is not developed in the blood, as in the case of guinea-pigs.

In 1882, Loeffler and Schütz cultivated a bacillus from nodules in the lungs and spleen of a horse which had suffered from glanders.[6] A month later a small quantity of the fourth generation of cultured organisms was inoculated on the mucous membrane of the nose and shoulders of an apparently healthy horse. Clinical symptoms appeared within eight days after inoculation and, on sacrifice, bacilli were isolated from nodules in the internal organs. The experiment was repeated and the findings confirmed.[5]

In accordance with Koch's method of cultivation for the bacillus of tubercle, a number of small particles, carefully selected from glanders nodules taken from the lungs and spleen of a horse which had suffered from glanders, were placed, on the 14th of September, in a series of sterilized test tubes containing the blood serum of a horse or sheep. During the first two days no changes were observed on the inoculated surface of the serum. On the third day however numerous transparent droplets which had formed in places on the surface of the serum were observed in the majority of the test tubes. . . . Similar droplets were found in almost all the test tubes inoculated with

glanders material, and always contained the one kind of bacterium. Such being the case, one was naturally induced to test these bacilli as to their causal relation with glanders by inoculation of healthy animals susceptible to the disease. When a successful result was obtained the cultures were further continued through four generations for one month, in order that the objection might not be raised that particles of the original material were present in the vaccinating fluid. On the 14th of October, a small quantity of this fourth cultivation, consisting only of the above described bacilli, was inoculated on the mucous membrane of the nose, and on the two shoulders of an old and apparently healthy horse. In forty-eight hours the animal began to show signs of high fever. At the inoculated spots deep ulcers developed, from which knotted lymphatic cords extended to the nearest lymphatic glands, so that in about eight days after the inoculation the horse exhibited the pronounced clinical appearance of glanders.

The post-mortem was surprising. . . . The fresh glanders material taken from the animal was employed for new cultures. Transparent drops similar to the previous culture developed in three days and contained only the above described bacilli. The same bacilli were found after treatment with methylene blue from the fresh glanders products taken from the dead horse. During November the fresh organs from another horse suffering from glanders were examined, and the same transparent drops containing bacilli were successfully cultivated from the glanders nodules present in the liver. Again on the 1st of December, in a fourth case, cultures were successfully made from fresh glanders nodules, and the result was in all cases the same.

Loeffler's studies on the bacterium of mouse typhoid, *Sal typhimurium*, prompted the Greek government to enlist his services in the eradication of the field mouse plague in Thessaly, one of the first field trials of microbiological warfare on animals pests.[7] The pilot experiment was successful and should have served as a model for extended trials, but several factors intervened including local resentment and subsequent realization that the pathogenicity of the organism is not confined to the field mouse.

1. Abel, R.: Friedrich Loeffler, obituary, (Ger), *Cbl Bakt* 76:241-245, 1915.

2. Loeffler, F.: *Lectures on the Historical Development of the Study of Bacteriology* (Ger), Leipzig: F. C. W. Vogel, 1887.

3. Nuttall, G. H. F., and Graham-Smith, G. S.: *The Bacteriology of Diphtheria*, Cambridge: University Press, 1908.

4. Loeffler, F.: Investigations of the Significance of the Microorganism in the Development of Diphtheria in Man (Ger), *Mitt Gesundh* 2:421-499, 1884.

5. Cheyne, W. W. (Ed.): *Recent Essays by Various Authors on Bacteria in Relation to Disease*, London: New Sydenham Society, 1886.

6. Struck, Dr.: Preliminary Report of the Studies of the Imperial Sanitary Institute Which Led to the Discovery of the Bacillus of Glanders (Ger), *Deutsch Med Wschr* 8:707-708, 1882.

7. Loeffler, F.: The Field Mouse Infestation in Thessaly and the Attempts to Eradicate It With the Typhic Murium Bacillus (Ger), *Cbl Bakt* 12:1-17, 1892.

Composite by G. Bako

Martinus Willem Beijerinck
(1851-1931)

THE TWO GREAT MICROBIOLOGISTS OF HOL-
LAND, Leeuwenhoek and Beijerinck, lived two centuries apart. The one magnified sub-liminal life with a primitive microscope; the other recognized the ultrafilterability of vi-ruses and the role of microbes in natural processes, which provided one of the founda-tion principles for the ecologic concepts that contribute so strongly to our present under-standing of disease. Beijerinck was born in Amsterdam, the son of a tobacconist, into a family of good culture but modest resources at that time, due to his father's failure in busi-ness ventures. But the economic environment was no deterrent to the development of Beij-erinck's interest in the natural sciences, ini-tially in botany. When Martinus was 15, the Dutch Society of Agriculture recognized this interest with the award of a silver medal for an outstanding essay.[1] At 18, he entered the Polytechnic Institute at Delft and finished his training as a "Chemical Engineer" in 1872. He returned to his botany in Leyden but abandoned this pursuit for a lectureship in botany, physiology, and physics at the Agri-cultural School at Warffum. After that he re-sumed his studies at Leyden.

The doctorate from this University in 1877 was consummated by submission of a disser-tation on plant galls, a subject overlapping botany and microbiology. His researches and teachings, prolific and productive, were con-tinued in an academic environment (Agricul-tural High School at Wageninger) until 1885, when he joined the research staff at the Yeast and Spirits Works in Delft. The Board of Directors allowed him to perform pure scien-tific investigation, besides his routine tasks. Delft claimed him throughout the remainder of his professional career. Leaving industry at the age of 44, he became a full-time profes-sor at the Polytechnic School and cultivated maximally a broad interest in the natural sci-ences, including general chemistry, soil chem-istry, colloid chemistry, agricultural chemis-try, parasitology, bacteriology, microbiology, and virology.

The horticulturist is especially attracted to Beijerinck's studies on the formation of nod-ules on the roots of leguminous plants and the contagious nature of gummosis. The bacteri-ologist is attracted to his studies on the sulfur-oxidizing, sulfate-reducing, and nitrogen-fixing bacteria; whereas the medical scientist may remember him for the discovery of the mosaic virus of tobacco plants. While em-ployed in the Yeast and Spirits Works, he pro-duced gummosis in an apparently healthy peach tree by inserting gum, contaminated with spores of fungi from a diseased tree, under the bark of the healthy specimen.[2] The fungus was later identified as a new species and classified as *Coryneum beijerinckii*. It was postulated that *C. beijerinckii* excreted a fer-ment which altered the cell wall and formed gum. As the enzyme diffused beyond the im-mediate confines of the fungus growth, the disease was transmitted into healthy areas, without the presence of the original parasite.

The isolation of *Bacillus radicicola* offered experimental proof that this bacterium was responsible for the formation of the nodules on the roots of leguminous plants. On the other hand, Beijerinck was not convinced that the fixation of nitrogen was caused exclusively by the plant or by the bacterium. Others accepted the challenge and offered irrefutable proof in favor of the bacterium. In 1894, Beijerinck described the *Spirillum desulfuricans* (*Vibrio desulfuricans*), a bacterium responsible for the conversion of sulfates into sulfides. This practical observation was motivated by the desire to remove calcium sulfate from the canal water used in the steam boilers in the yeast factory. He concluded that the causative organism was anaerobic and thrived only in media with low concentrations of simple organic compounds. Also, excellent work was done on the sulfur-oxidizing bacteria which he called *Thiobacillus*.[3]

The studies on the tobacco mosaic virus, which were begun in the industrial laboratory, did not appear to be particularly important at that time. Although the contagious nature of the disease was suspected, Beijerinck did not produce experimental evidence until more than a decade later.[2] Meanwhile, Iwanowski was successful in 1892 in passing mosaic virus through an ultramicroscopic filter. The report by Beijerinck in 1898 left no doubt that the agent responsible for transmitting the disease to healthy plants passed through the filter, leaving all visible particles in the residuum. The principle was capable of reproduction, diffused through agar gel, and was destroyed on heating to 90° C.

It was identified specifically as the "*contagium vivum fluidum*." The term "virus" was used several times in the report by Beijerinck, who offered experimental proof that the contagium multiplied only in tissues in which cell division took place. Viability was not lost by desiccation at low temperatures or by precipitation with alcohol from the aqueous solution. Thus, the characteristic properties of all viruses were postulated. Other microbiologic interests of Beijerinck included researches on bacterial heredity, luminous bacteria, fermentation, yeast, algae, biological purification of the air, and the assimilative powers of the chromatophores of diatoms.

In accepting the Leeuwenhoek medal, named in honor of the first Delft microbacteriologist, Beijerinck mentioned his contribution in extending ecology to the pathogenesis of human disease, one of a group of natural scientists to whom medicine is indebted deeply. He replied:[4]

I am happy to note that the way in which I approach microbiology has the approval of the best judges. This approach can be concisely stated as the study of microbial ecology, i.e., of the relation between environmental conditions and the special forms of life corresponding to them.

In an experimental sense the ecological approach to microbiology consists of two complementary phases which give rise to the endless number of experiments. On the one hand it leads to investigating the conditions for the development of organisms that have for some reason or other, perhaps fortuitously, come to our attention; on the other hand, to the discovery of living organisms that appear under predetermined conditions, either because they alone can develop, or because they are the more fit and win out over their competitors.

1. Bulloch, W.: Martinus Willem Beijerinck, Obituary, *Proc Roy Soc Lond* 109:i-iii (Jan) 1932.
2. Van Iterson, Jr., G.; Den Dooren De Jong, L. E.; and Kluyver, A. J.: *Martinus Willem Beijerinck, His Life and His Work*, The Hague: Martinus Nijhoff, 1940.
3. Waksman, S. A.: Martinus Willem Beijerinck, *Sci Monthly* 33:285-288 (July-Dec) 1931.
4. Van Niel, C. B.: The "Delft School" and the Rise of General Microbiology, *Bacteriol Rev* 13:161-174 (Sept) 1949.

Bernhard Bang (1848-1932)

BERNHARD LAURITS FREDERIK BANG, credited with the discovery of the pathogenic agent of contagious abortion, was born at Soro on the Danish island of Sealand, into a family of distinguished ancestry.[1] His father, headmaster of the academy at Soro and a scholar in Latin and Greek, collected a large classical library. Bernhard acquired proficiency in these languages as well as fluency in English, French, and German, valuable adjuncts in the pursuit of his scientific goals. He proceeded through orthodox medical training in Copenhagen, finding the rapidly developing disciplines of microbiology and pathological anatomy of particular interest. After graduating bachelor of medicine in 1872, he spent the two following years studying veterinary science. Presumably his mind was set on the investigation of epizootic diseases; however, when there were no immediate openings on the faculty

National Library of Medicine

at the Veterinary College he was forced to hesitate once more. After a few months in Strasbourg with von Recklinghausen he returned to medicine as house officer in pathology at the Copenhagen City Hospital for three years. The next step, resident physician on the medical wards, permitted time for a modest private practice. In 1880, Bang submitted the dissertation, *Observations and Studies on Fatal Embolism and Thrombosis in the Pulmonary Arteries*, for the degree of doctor of medicine.

Having failed in competition for an appointment as chief of the medical service in a community hospital, Bang was offered the double responsibility of assistant in obstetrics and surgery and director of the ambulatory clinic at the Royal Veterinary-Agriculture College in Copenhagen. There he devoted the remainder of his professional years to research, teaching, and practice and was recognized as the outstanding scientist on the faculty, attracting students from many countries. Following the prototype of a professor of medicine, rounds were made each morning,

with his students, on the sick animals, correlating environment and exposure with morbidity; in the afternoon his time was spent in the laboratory or in the lecture hall. Full academic status was reached in 1887 when he was appointed professor of pathological anatomy in the Veterinary College, a post created for him.

In his studies of contagious abortion and tuberculosis in cattle, Bang utilized the newer knowledge in bacteriology and pathological anatomy, having learned the techniques from Salomonsen, teacher of bacteriology in the medical school. Bang's 1897 communication on the abortion bacillus summarized previous investigations, which had recognized the contagious nature without identifying a causative organism. Nocard had approached the solution, but no one had been successful in isolating a causative microorganism. Bang and his pupil Stribolt described a gram-negative bacillus recovered from the uterus of a pregnant cow with premonitory symptoms of abortion, cultured a partially anaerobic organism, and produced abortion in pregnant cows, thereby fulfilling the postulates of Koch. A similar organism was also isolated from mummified fetuses preserved from cases of missed abortion. With these incontrovertible data, Bang advocated the isolation of infected cattle to reduce and eventually eradicate the contagion. However, he did not recognize the infectious nature for man, first demonstrated in 1918 by Dr. Alice Evans, who noted the close relationship between various *Brucella* organisms, *Br abortus*, *Br melitensis*, and *Br suis*. The organism studied by Bang in cattle was later known as Bang's bacillus and the disease in cattle, Bang's disease.[2]

As soon as we had placed before ourselves the task of discovering the cause of epizootic abortion, it became evident that we must obtain a pregnant cow from a herd suffering from the disease, and indeed we required such a cow already showing the signs of impending abortion. In this we easily succeeded . . . we purchased . . . a five-year-old cow, which . . . had shown the well-known premonitory symptoms of abortion. The cow was there and then slaughtered under Mr. Stribolt's directions, and . . . the genital organs . . . removed.

. . . when the mucous membrane was divided we saw *between that and the foetal envelopes an abundant odourless exudate*.

The examination of a cover-glass preparation made from the yellowish exudate and stained with Loeffler's methylene-blue immediately showed the presence of a very small bacterium, apparently in pure culture.

This discovery indicates that *epizootic abortion ought to be regarded as a specific uterine catarrh, determined by a definite species of bacterium.*

The next object in our investigation of the disease, namely, to cultivate the bacterium which we had found in a state of purity, and to furnish evidence that it constituted one definite species, was very easily accomplished by making cultures in test tubes containing serum-gelatine-agar.

By both these experiments we have furnished the complete proof that the bacillus discovered by us is the cause of epizootic abortion. They also prove that the mere depositon of the bacilli in the vagina can produce the disease.

Bang's studies on tuberculosis in cows were published only three years after Koch's announcement of the isolation of the tubercle bacillus. In his research Bang recovered the organism from the milk of tuberculous cows, was one of the first to demonstrate the value of heating milk to kill the bacillus, carried out multiple tests on the value of tuberculin-testing in cattle, and devised a means for preventing the spread of bovine tuberculosis. He recommended tuberculin-testing of all animals and separation of nonreactors. After Bang discovered that newborn calves did not react to tuberculin and concluded that tuberculosis in the young was usually acquired by contact with tuberculous mothers, the calves of affected cows were removed from their mother after birth and were fed with milk from uninfected udders. In the initial stages of testing, he discovered that in one herd the majority of the adult cattle were apparently healthy but positive reactors; whereas other herds were essentially free of reactors. This observation substantiated his belief that tuberculosis was a contagious disease spread by intimate contact. Bang further recommended that nonreacting animals should be retested with tuberculin semiannually and any positive reactors transferred to the appropriate group. With this design for eradication, the nonreacting herd would increase, meanwhile allowing the reactors to serve usefully for production of milk and for calving. As the cows in the latter group died or were slaughtered,

the herd would eventually be rendered tuberculous-free.[3]

In order to avoid infection we must not allow healthy animals to live with cattle affected with open tuberculosis, and we must not feed them on raw tuberculous milk or milk-products.

It was a knowledge of all these circumstances that led me in 1892 to make attempts gradually to change a tuberculous herd of cattle into a healthy one. My plan was above all conservative. I hoped to be able to prove that it was possible to produce a new tubercle-free herd by rearing the calves, even such born of cows infected with tuberculosis, when they were separated as soon as possible from the infected stable and were protected against infection through the milk. And I hoped to accelerate the formation of a new healthy herd by testing the old herd with tuberculin and separating the non-reacting animals carefully from the reacting ones.

The first farm on which my method was assayed (Thurebylille in Seeland) had 208 head of cattle. 131 of the animals reacted, i.e. about 80 percent of the adults, about 40 per cent of the steers and heifers and 46 per cent of the calves. The non-reacting animals were separated from the reacting by dividing the large stable by means of a solid wooden partition-wall, and connected with the partition for non-reacting animals were smaller compartments for the calves. Calves born of reacting cows were removed from the infected stable immediately after birth; the first day I gave them their mothers colostrum, later either raw milk from healthy cows or boiled milk (or milk heated sufficiently to destroy tubercle bacilli). As I clearly saw that there was a danger that tubercle bacilli from the reacting animals might be introduced into the healthy section when both sections lived in the same farm, I decided that the healthy herd should be tested with tuberculin twice a year (on other farms it was often done only once a year) in order to separate as soon as practically possible the lately infected animals from the healthy ones and place them with the reacting ones. There were two sets of stable hands, one for each of the two divisions, and the two parts of the herd were kept apart when grazing as well as in the stable.

The practicability of the plan was soon proved, as the calves which were born in the infected division of reacting parents were nearly all found to be healthy (very few being born tuberculous) and remained so.

In 1890, one other bacteriologic discovery was made by Bang—isolation of the necrosing bacillus in swine.[4] He made two trips to the United States, giving a special lecture at the Sixth International Congress on Tuberculosis in 1908 and a special lecture at Cornell University in 1928. He received high Danish orders and held honorary degrees from the universities of Vienna, Utrecht, Budapest, and Kristiana (Oslo).

1. Williams, T. F., and McKusick, V. A.: Bernhard Bang: Physician, Veterinarian, Scientist, *Bull Hist Med* 28:60-72, 1954.

2. Bang, B.: The Etiology of Epizootic Abortion, *Z Thiermed* 1:241-278, 1898, transated in Bang.[4]

3. Bang, B.: What are we to do for the Repression and Eradication of Tuberculosis in Cattle, International Congress on Cattle Breeding, 1923, translated in Bang.[4]

4. *Bernhard Bang, Selected Works*, Adsersen, V. (ed.): London: Oxford University Press, 1936.

Los Angeles County Medical Library

Emil Adolf von Behring (1854-1917)

EMIL VON BEHRING, discoverer of the class of biological products known as antitoxins, was born at Hansdorf in Deutsch-Eylau (West Prussia). He received his professional education at the Army Medical College in Berlin, qualified for the MD degree in 1878, and passed the state examination for the practice of medicine in 1880.[1] During his seven years of service as a squadron physician of the Prussian Army in the province of Posen, he became interested in the bactericidal property of iodoform and for one year at Bonn with Binz continued his studies on infection. Upon return to Berlin in 1888, he taught for one year in the Army Medical College. In 1890, having completed his military service, Behring received the appointment of first assistant at the Institute of Hygiene under Robert Koch. Here his outstanding investigations of immunity

to diphtheria and tetanus toxins was carried out. The title of professor was granted in 1893, and the following year he was called to the chair of hygiene at the University of Halle. In 1895, he was appointed professor and director of the Institute of Hygiene at Philipps University, Marburg.

In Marburg, Behring became associated with one and then a second commercial laboratory for the production of diphtheria and tetanus antitoxic sera. In addition, he developed vaccines for protection against several diseases, notably against bovine and human tuberculosis. The production of clinically potent antitoxic sera succeeded, but the failure of extension of the principles of immunization to the practical control of other diseases contrasts with his earlier contributions. In 1901, Behring was awarded the Nobel Prize for Medicine and, in 1903, received the title of Excellency from his government. He shared with Roux a 25,000-fr. prize of the Paris Academy of Medicine and was awarded individually a 50,000 franc prize by the Institute of France.

In the development of antitoxic sera, Behring extended the documented observations of others. Roux and Yersin showed that the detrimental effects of diphtheric bacilli may be reproduced in experimental animals by injection of a cell-free filtrate of toxin elaborated by the bacilli; Kitasato at the same time discovered the toxin of tetanus bacilli able to reproduce all of the symptoms of tetanus infection. Behring and Kitasato together demonstrated how the toxin of tetanus bacillus,[2] upon injection into experimental animals, resulted in the appearance of neutralizing substances in the serum with protective properties readily apparent clinically upon challenge. Immediately thereafter Behring did the same experiment with the toxin of the diphtheria bacillus with parallel results.[3] The phenomenon was attributed to the development of antitoxic bodies, an early example of an antibody produced in response to the stimulus by an antigen.

A quantity of toxin, considerably greater than the lethal dose in animals, could be rendered innocuous by the previous addition in vitro of antitoxin. The investigations also showed that antitoxic serum, when injected into normal subjects, creates passive immunity, a term used in contrast to active immunity to describe a condition which the animal develops following a series of treatments with small amounts of toxin. And lastly, antitoxin was found to be intrinsically curative as well as protective and, when administered at the proper time, was capable of preventing death. The development of immunity by antibodies against exogenous toxin was specific, and no cross immunization between tetanus and diphtheria toxin was demonstrated. Excerpts of each communication have been translated and selected as follows:[4]

In the studies which we have been carrying out for some time on diphtheria (von Behring) and tetanus (Kitasato), we have also considered questions of therapy and immunization. In both infectious diseases, we have been able to cure infected animals, as well as to pretreat healthy animals so that later they will not succumb to diphtheria or tetanus.

In what way the therapy and immunization have been obtained will only be stated here in enough detail to demonstrate the truth of the following sentence:

"The immunity of rabbits and mice, which have been immunized against tetanus, depends on the ability of the cell-free blood fluid to render harmless the toxic substance which the tetanus bacillus produces."

After many negative experiments, it was discovered that the blood of immune animals had the ability to neutralize the diphtheria toxin, and this discovery revealed the reason for the insensitivity of these animals to diphtheria. But it was only by applying this concept to tetanus that we were able to achieve results which, so far as we can tell, are completely conclusive.

The experiments to be outlined below show:

1. The blood of rabbits immune to tetanus has the ability to neutralize or destroy the tetanus toxin.

2. This property exists also in extravascular blood and in cell-free serum.

3. This property is so stable that it remains effective even in the body of other animals, so that it is possible, through blood or serum transfusions, to achieve an outstanding therapeutic effect.

4. The property which destroys tetanus toxin does not exist in the blood of animals which are not immune to tetanus, and when one incorporates tetanus toxin into nonimmune animals, the toxin can be still demonstrated in the blood and other body fluids of the animal, even after its death.

Although clinical trials satisfactory to current therapeutic criteria for efficacy were not reported, the value of diphtheria antitoxin for the management of the affliction in man was anticipated shortly after discovery. The first administration of diphtheric antitoxin serum was made in 1891 to a child in von Berg-

mann's clinic in Berlin. Behring concluded his therapeutic findings in 1893 as follows:[5]

The response to the disease can be segregated into three groups, each defined by the proper and sufficient use of the antitoxin serum.

I. Prevention of the disease, if the serum is administered before the appearance of symptoms.

II. Prevention of progression of the disease when it is apparent clinically.

III. Reversal of severe and advanced affliction leaving only a mild and benign illness.

Diphtheria antitoxin serum, following Ehrlich's work in standardization procedures, was widely used prior to 1923 at which time a suitable toxoid for prophylaxis (active immunization) was developed. Currently available diphtheria toxoid confers lasting immunity. Protection against tetanus, on the other hand, requires reinoculation at infrequent intervals with tetanus toxoid to insure adequate immunity. Although tetanus antitoxin is usually recommended for all cases of suspected tetanus infection, its value after the development of clinical symptoms is doubtful.

1. Kossel, H.: Emil von Behring, Klin Wschr 54:471, 1917.

2. Behring, E., and Kitasato, S.: Diphtheria Immunity and Tetanus Immunity in Animals (Ger), Deutsch Med Wschr 16:1113-1114, 1890.

3. Behring, E.: The Status of Diphtheria Immunity With Animals (Ger), Deutsch Med Wschr 16:1145-1148, 1890.

4. Brock, J. D.: Milestones in Microbiology, Englewood Cliffs, N. J.: Prentice-Hall, Inc., 1961.

5. Behring, E., and Boer, O.: The Value of Diphtheria Serum (Ger), Deutsch Med Wschr 19:415-418, 1893, excerpt translated by Z. Danilevicius.

William Thompson Sedgwick (1855-1921)

WILLIAM T. SEDGWICK, the architect of the theory and practice of public health and sanitary engineering in America, was associated throughout his professional years with the Massachusetts Institute of Technology. Born in West Hartford, Connecticut, he attended Hartford High School, showed a great interest in the natural sciences, and in 1877 graduated from the Sheffield Scientific School of Yale University.[1] Although he began the study of medicine, he shortly abandoned it for physiological chemistry under Chittenden at Yale. In 1879, Sedgwick accepted a fellowship in biology at Johns Hopkins University with Newell Martin, a student of Huxley's. The

Composite by G. Bako

PHD degree was granted in 1881. In 1883, he was called from Johns Hopkins University to the Massachusetts Institute of Technology by Francis Walker, whose brilliant service as president of the Institute envisioned the need for broad, technological instruction, including sanitary engineering. The initial appointment was in the department of biology and public health. This recounting of preparatory training and early academic duties seems scattered or even haphazard. On the other hand, each field of scientific exposure contributed subsequently to an integrated approach to the development of public health in its broadest concepts and specifically to the maturing field of sanitary science. The propositions upon which Sedgwick built his academic career and achieved his professional goals were ably expressed retrospectively, in the preface to his

Principles of Sanitary Science and the Public Health.[2]

The modern conception of disease as due to imperfection, misbehavior or disturbance of a physical mechanism depended for its development on an acquaintance with the physiology of the body and its microscopic structure which did not exist before the introduction, in the third decade, of the achromatic objective. The microscopical renaissance which began with this pregnant invention speedily led to discoveries of the first importance in the normal structure of organized bodies; disclosed in abnormal tissues the material ravages, and, in some cases, the parasitic origin of disease; brought into full view a flora and a funa hitherto unseen or only half seen; and, by the end of the fifth decade, was throwing a new and increasingly powerful light on the long-vexed question of the relation of ferments and fermentation to decomposition, putrefaction and disease. At the end of the sixth decade a new theory of infectious disease—the "germ" theory—had arisen, and in the hands of Pasteur, Lister and many others was already bearing fruit.

Standing on the threshold of the twentieth century, and surrounded by the innumerable municipal, medical, domestic, public and private sanitary safeguards which have already sprung from these discoveries so that, in spite of facilities for the spread of disease by the development of easy international transportation, such as the world has never before known, pestilences and plagues are no longer greatly dreaded, it is hard to realize that our not very remote ancestors regarded disease as an insoluble mystery, an inscrutable visitation of divine Providence, or as the penalty and consequence of sin. Under such beliefs there could be no sanitary science. But if disease be disturbance of a physical mechanism, and due to the fact that the mechanism is made of poor materials, or of good materials badly put together, or that it is badly operated, or that it is interfered with by unfavorable environmental conditions, it becomes easy to comprehend at least approximately the causes of diseases, and in many cases to remove or forestall them. It is precisely this which the science and art of hygiene seek to do, namely, to comprehend the nature of the human body and its diseases, in order as far as possible to prevent the latter. Hygiene is the science and art of the conservation and improvement of normal living, the prevention not merely of premature death but of abnormal life; and sanitary science, or hygiology, is simply the body of scientific doctrine, or the principles, underlying the sanitary arts.

Prior to Sedgwick's time, sanitary science had dealt largely with the opportunities offered by advances in chemistry. The emergence of microbiological agents in the pathogenesis of disease caused a shift of scientific inquiry, and Sedgwick, through his theoretical training and practical experience, was ideally qualified to lead the evolution, and thereby benefit large numbers of people in rural and in urban populations. It seems reasonable to us half a century later to expect that public water supplies will be free from contamination, that milk and other foodstuffs will be delivered to the consumer bacteriologically safe for consumption, and that industrial and human waste will be scientifically and hygienically disposed of. The optimum benefit from these obvious measures would be possible only through the cooperation of city and state governments, practicing physicians, and receptive citizens. Sedgwick knew well from long experience and close contact with political problems the importance of governmental action and responsibility at the local, state, and national levels.

Sedgwick never left his academic post but gave liberally of his time to community and state programs. When the Massachusetts State Board of Health was reorganized and the Lawrence Experiment Station established in 1888, he was appointed to the board as consulting biologist. One of his functions was the supervision of the municipal water filtration plant at Lawrence on the Merrimac River, the first scientifically designed plant in America to control pollution and to prevent disease. The city of Lawrence, downstream on the Merrimac, drew its water supply from the river which had been polluted by the alvine discharges of adjacent communities of New Hampshire and Massachusetts, which, in turn, caused epidemics and "endemic" outbreaks of typhoid fever.[2]

One of the common phrases of sanitary science, especially in popular discussions, is that which describes disease as "endemic" in certain localities. What is meant by the expression is that the disease appears to have, in the localities mentioned, a local and permanent residence. Expressions of this kind, however, at least when applied to infectious disease, have very little value. It was formerly said, for example, that typhoid fever was "endemic" in Lowell and Lawrence, by which was meant the obvious fact that it was always to be found there, with the added implication that there was something peculiar in the local conditions, such, for example, as a special soil, ground water, or other local condition, which made these cities an especially favorable dwelling-place for the disease. The fact was undoubtedly correct: typhoid fever was always or nearly always present; but the implication was incorrect. There was nothing in Lowell or Lawrence essentially different in respect to soil or people or any other particular (with one exception) from the conditions prevailing in Concord, Manchester, Nashua, or Haverhill, neighboring cities in the same valley. The one exception was the water supply, by which the germs of typhoid fever were distributed among the citizens. Once this element of infection was removed, the disease nearly disappeared, and ceased to be endemic. As a matter of fact, it had never been endemic, but was rather constantly epidemic.

Sedgwick was a teacher of teachers; instruction was planned to prepare students for a career either in medicine or in public health. He displayed a warm understanding of students and academic associates and was on friendly terms with craftsmen and artisans at home and at work.[3] In his lectures he discussed broad principles rather than exhibiting blind devotion to details. As a classical scholar, Sedgwick frequently used the Socratic method of teaching. Excerpts from the Bible, selected Greek classics, and literary gems of England's men of letters were readily available in his intellectual storeroom for use at an appropriate time.[1] He contributed to current scientific periodicals and prepared text with pleasing fluency. As a realist he found formal philosophy to be vague and inconclusive. He was curator of the Lowell Institute and president of the American Society of Naturalists, the American Public Health Association, and the New England Water Works Association. He was appointed a member of the Advisory Board of the United States Hygienic Laboratory, the predecessor of the National Institutes of Health of the United States Public Health Service.

William Thompson Sedgwick introduced biology, bacteriology, epidemiology, and engineering into the public health field and fused the pertinent features into a new discipline of sanitary science. At the conclusion of a long and productive career, the movement had been so successful, through individual efforts and wide acceptance of principles, that disease, formerly spread through contaminated milk, food, and water supply, had been reduced significantly. When contagion broke out, either from an epidemic or an endemic source, it was through negligence or technical failure in supply of food and fluid or the disposal of sewage.[4]

The foundations of prevention are, in fact, as broad as biology itself. Prevention, inhibition, interference with natural phenomena are all characteristic of life, and the less our submission to environment, the greater our interference, the more complete our control, the higher is our development—the more notable the progress of civilization.

1. Winslow, C.-E. A.: William Thompson Sedgwick, 1855-1921, *J Bact* 6-255-262, 1921.
2. Sedgwick, W. T.: *Principles of Sanitary Science and the Public Health,* New York: Macmillan Co., 1902.
3. Jordan, E. O.; Whipple, G. C.; and Winslow, C.-E. A.: *A Pioneer of Public Health: William Thompson Sedgwick,* New Haven, Conn., Yale University Press, 1924.
4. Sedgwick, W. T.: The Foundations of Prevention, *Bull Amer Acad Med* 11:692-704, 1910.

Countway Medical Library, Boston

Theobald Smith (1859-1934)

THE TWO AMERICANS who approached the meridian in bacteriology and microbiology in the last quarter of the 19th century were William H. Welch, of Johns Hopkins University, and Theobald Smith, one-time professor at Harvard Medical School. Welch, warm of heart and quickly responsive, was an inspiration for young scientists; Smith, although impersonal and critical, was even more an investigator to be emulated. Theobald Smith

was born in Albany, New York, in 1859, five years after his parents had immigrated from Germany. His father conducted a small tailoring shop in Albany; Theobald attended the Albany public schools. This was followed by an arts course at Cornell University, with financial support from a state scholarship won in competition. Biology and mathematics were his fields of concentration. The MD degree was received after two years of study at Albany Medical School, interrupted by a semester in the biological laboratory at Johns Hopkins University. Although Smith never used his medical training in the care of humans, his protocols of experimental and diseased animals, particularly of cattle, were as detailed and critical as those of a meticulous observer of clinical phenomena at the bedside.[1]

At the age of 25, Smith was appointed director of the Pathological Laboratory of the United States Bureau of Animal Industry, Washington, D. C. This assignment was due to chance and to two small pieces of histologic research carried out with Professor Gage of Cornell, Smith's cherished teacher and lifelong friend. The Bureau and Daniel F. Salmon, its chief, had been charged with the investigation of Texas cattle fever, an affliction which caused critical morbidity and high mortality among stock in the Southern states. The evidence that the severe anemia of Texas cattle fever was caused by an intracellular parasite transmitted by the tick is one of Smith's finest scientific achievements. Although Manson had already proved that filariasis was transmitted by mosquitoes, the experimental transmission of disease of man or lower animals through an intermediary host had not yet been accomplished. Smith furnished the final link in the chain of evidence by infecting healthy cattle with the offending parasite of Texas cattle fever, recovered from the host tick.

The studies on Texas cattle fever were summarized in a monograph published for the Bureau of Animal Industry by the Government Printing Office in 1893,[2] preceded by preliminary reports in 1889 and 1891. Smith did not ignore those who took the first steps. He credits Stiles with seeing the parasite in the red blood cell and Babes with "culturing" a diplococcus recovered from afflicted stock.

It was Smith and his colleagues, however, after years of toil and travail, who fulfilled the necessary criteria for the establishment of the pathogenesis of the disease and the effective control of a severe epizootic.

Smith was a field as well as a laboratory bacteriologist. He went into the corral and onto the range to pursue epidemiologic, clinical, and postmortem studies. The programing for the investigation of infected herds in North Carolina was similar to a clinical and epidemiologic study of human disease, but it was more readily handled because the disease could be studied in its natural host instead of in a foreign species. Sick cattle and well cattle, with and without the tick carriers of the parasite, were placed in assigned isolated enclosures. Examination of the acutely ill cattle revealed elevations of temperature, pulse, and respiration, loss of appetite, cessation of rumination and milk secretion, constipation, and hyperemia followed by pallor of the hide and mucous membranes. Involvement of the central nervous system was suggested by partial loss of vision, delirium, staggering, and swaying of the hind quarters. Examination of the urine showed protein and pigment, identified as degradation products of hemoglobin. Microscopic examination of the blood showed anemia as severe as 1 or 2 million cu mm, compared with the normal cattle count of 5 to 6 million cu mm. The critical observation was the identification of the parasite (*Piroplasma bigemina*, now classified as *Babesia bigemina*) in the red blood cells. The conclusions contained in the monograph summarized these fruitful years of research, set a standard for epidemiologic excellence, and exposed the potentialities for investigation of other insect-borne diseases, especially yellow fever, sleeping sickness, bubonic plague, and typhus.[2]

(1) Texas cattle fever is a disease of the blood, characterized by a destruction of red corpuscles. The symptoms are partly due to the anaemia produced; partly to the large amount of débris in the blood, which is excreted with difficulty, and which causes derangement of the organs occupied with its removal.
(2) The destruction of the red corpuscles is due to a microörganism or microparasite which lives within them. It belongs to the protozoa and passes through several distinct phases in the blood.
(3) Cattle from the permanently infected territory, though otherwise healthy, carry the microparasite of Texas fever in their blood.

(4) Texas fever may be produced in susceptible cattle by direct inoculation of blood containing the microparasite.
(5) Texas fever in nature is transmitted from cattle which come from the permanently infected territory to cattle outside of this territory by the cattle tick (*Boophilus bovis*).
(6) The infection is carried by the [transovarian passage through the] progeny of the ticks which matured on infected cattle, and is inoculated by them directly into the blood of susceptible cattle.
(7) Sick natives may be a source of infection (when ticks are present).

Less dramatic but equally significant were Smith's researches on human and bovine tubercle bacilli and the fatal epizootics of hogs. Koch had reported little difference between the bovine and the human type of tubercle bacilli in his original studies. Smith, on the other hand, who had become interested in tuberculosis as a medical student, demonstrated the morphologic and biologic characteristics of the two types. In the rabbit[3]

The human bacillus produced [experimentally] a slight eruption of small tubercle-like bodies, which did not present even microscopically the characters of true tubercles, while the bovine bacillus produced an exquisite case of pearly disease both in the thorax and abdomen, with the formation of large, grape-like masses in the chest.
In glycerin egg culture media: . . . the human bacilli grew from the start much more vigorously than the bovine bacilli.
The size of bovine bacilli in the various cultures was quite constant. . . . With the human bacilli the form was not so constant.
A summary of the three separate tests on cattle . . . in which twelve animals were used, shows that 6 animals were inoculated with human bacilli, 5 with bovine bacilli; 1 animal was inoculated with swine bacilli.
Of the sputum cases, 1 showed no disease, 2 showed very slight lesions; 3 showed only local lesions without dissemination.
Of the bovine cases, 2 died of generalized disease; 2 showed extensive lesions; 1 showed less extensive lesions.

There were at least three confusing diseases to which swine were susceptible, hog cholera, swine plague, and swine erysipelas. In a cooperative study with Salmon, Smith cultured a gram-negative, motile bacillus from cases of hog cholera and described characteristic parenchymatous changes in experimental animals.[4] The organism *Bacillus choleraesuis* was later named *Salmonella choleraesuis*.

The now commonly-employed immune reactions, demonstrating a specific relationship between a particular organism and a disease, were still unknown, and Smith and Salmon erred in thinking that they had isolated the specific causative agent of hog cholera. The confusion was not resolved until 1903 when de Schweinitz and Dorset, of the Bureau of Animal Industry, successfully transmitted a disease that proved by all tests to be hog cholera, by injecting bacteria-free filtrates from diseased animals into controls. *S. choleraesuis* proved to be a pathogenic secondary invader.

In 1895, when Smith was still in his thirties, he was called by Harvard to be the first incumbent of the endowed chair of comparative pathology, and by the Commonwealth of Massachusetts to be its director of the Antitoxin and Vaccine Laboratory. Here he demonstrated the immunization properties of toxin-antitoxin mixtures and improved the methods for the production of diphtheria toxin.[5]

The foregoing and earlier data taken together demonstrate that active immunity, lasting several years, can be produced in guinea pigs by the injection of toxin-antitoxin mixtures, which have no recognizable harmful effect either immediate or remote. They also show (what might have been anticipated) that, under the same conditions, mixtures which produce local lesions and which, therefore, contain an excess of toxin, produce a much higher degree of immunity than the neutral mixtures, and that an excess of antitoxin reduces the possibility of producing an active immunity, and may extinguish it altogether.

The dual nature of bacterial agglutinins was described in a contribution by Smith and Reagh, using various cultures including those of hog cholera bacillus.[6]

There exist agglutination relationships between the pathogenic groups of bacilli which ferment dextrose as given in the text. . . .
7. Of the pathogenic cultures examined, *B. icteroides* and the hog-cholera bacillus α on the one hand, and spermophile and guinea-pig disease α (and β) possess nearly identical agglutinative properties.
8. The typhoid bacillus shows slight agglutinative affinities with the group described under I [hog-cholera] above.

Smith planned for the manufacture and distribution of smallpox vaccine throughout the Commonwealth of Massachusetts, the first of the United States to provide safe vaccine, a policy already in effect in several European countries. Thus, his achievements in public health were practical demonstrations of the scope of interest of an academic microbiologist.

Passive immunization of guinea pigs in utero was discussed in a casual conversation with Paul Ehrlich. Smith described the hypersensitivity or anaphylaxis, which Ehrlich termed the "Theobald Smith Phenomenon."

At the age of 56, Smith made his third and last professional move when he accepted the directorship of the Department of Animal Diseases of the Rockefeller Institute for Medical Research at Princeton. His international reputation made him an easy target for named lectureships, honorary degrees, and association with distinguished scientific and academic bodies, inevitable kudos for a great American bacteriologist. The new post demanded less administration and allowed more time for investigation. One of the last studies at Princeton, in collaboration with R. B. Little, explored the pathogenesis of diarrhea in newborn calves.[7]

. . . it may be concluded that the function of the colostrum is essentially protective against miscellaneous bacteria which are harmless later on when the protective functions of the calf have begun to operate and accumulate energy. There appears to be no function inherent in colostrum which controls development or growth or which is essential to the starting of the mechanism of digestion, since calves not having had colostrum appear to do as well as the others when the infection has been overcome.

Smith was shy and restrained, never able to participate in an exchange of warmth with pupils, so characteristic of Welch; hence, his laboratory did not attract the large following of students that might have been his destiny. He was an industrious investigator; hard work to him was considered a privilege. He loved music and enjoyed his summer holidays on Silver Lake near Chocorua, New Hampshire, where his early interest as a naturalist began. His remarks made at retirement convey his philosophy of research.[8]

To those who have the urge to do research and who are prepared to give up most things in life eagerly pursued by the man in the street, discovery should come as an adventure rather than as the result of a logical process of thought. Sharp, prolonged thinking is necessary that we may keep on the chosen road but it does not itself necessarily lead to discovery. The investigator must be ready and on the spot when the light comes from whatever direction.

1. Clark, P. F.: Theobald Smith, Student of Disease (1859-1934), *J Hist Med* 14:490-514 (Oct) 1959.

2. Smith, T., and Kilborne, F. L.: *Investigations into the Nature, Causation, and Prevention of Southern Cattle Fever*, US Dept of Agriculture, Bureau of Animal Husbandry, 8th and 9th Annual Reports of the Years 1891-1892, 1893.

3. Smith, T.: A Comparative Study of Bovine Tubercle Bacilli and of Human Bacilli from Sputum, *J Exp Med* 3:451-511, 1898.

4. Salmon, D. E., and Smith, T.: The Bacterium of Swine-Plague, *Amer Mo Microscop J* 7:204-205 (Nov) 1886.

5. Smith, T.: Active Immunity Produced by So-Called Balanced or Neutral Mixtures of Diphtheria Toxin and Antitoxin, *J Exp Med* 11:241-256 (March 1) 1909.

6. Smith, T., and Reagh, A. L.: The Agglutination Affinities of Related Bacteria Parasitic in Different Hosts, *J Med Res* 9:270-300 (May) 1903.

7. Smith, T., and Little, R. B.: The Significance of Colostrum to the New-Born Calf, *J Exp Med* 36:181-198 (July 1) 1922.

8. Smith, T.: Letter to Dr. Krumbhaar, *J Bact* 27:19-20 (Jan) 1934.

Composite by G. Bako

Fernand Widal (1862-1929)

GEORGES FERNAND ISIDORE WIDAL was born at Dellys in Algiers, the son of a physician, then medical inspector of the army, and the nephew of Mathieu Hirtz, soon to be appointed Dean of the Faculty of Medicine at Strasbourg.[1] Widal studied medicine in Paris, where the tradition of bedside medicine was firmly established and was complemented by the recent surge in basic science, particularly from the discoveries of Louis Pasteur. Widal's studies were completed in the hospitals of Paris. He took his doctorate at the age of 26, presenting a thesis on the several clinical manifestations of streptococcal infection, which included puerperal phlebitis, endocarditis, and erysipelas. Continuing his academic ties, he was appointed to the professional group at the age of 32; at 48, he was appointed professor of internal pathology, and seven years later he succeeded to the chair of clinical medicine.

Widal's best-known contribution, the [Widal] agglutination test for typhoid fever, followed a concentrated investigation on the pathogenesis of the disease in cooperation with Chantemesse. Eberth's studies on the bacterial cause of the disease were confirmed in rats; those immunized by the parenteral injection of killed cultures of the offending organism remained healthy on challenge. The description of the agglutination test was presented to the Medical Society of the Hospitals of Paris in June, 1896.[2] The date carries some importance since others were approaching the discovery at the same time. Grüber, Durham, and Grünbaum, especially, were exploring the possibilities for a rapid and easily performed agglutination test before Widal described his procedure. An English communication by Widal appeared in *Lancet* not long after the preliminary report in Paris.[3]

On June 26th last I brought before the Medical Society of the Paris Hospitals a new method—to which I gave the term "sero-diagnosis"—by which typhoid fever could be recognised almost instantaneously by simply observing microscopically how the serum of a patient acted on a culture of Eberth's bacillus.

For ordinary daily practice I prefer the improvised process. I have shown that all that was necessary was to add a drop of serum or even a drop of blood taken from the tip of the finger of the patient to ten drops of a young culture in bouillon of typhoid fever bacilli, and to see almost immediately under the microscope the formation of "heaps" or agglomerations of bacilli, which often allows an almost instantaneous diagnosis of typhoid fever to be made.

Up to June 26th, 1896, the date of my first communication, the phenomenon of agglutination had been considered as a "reaction of immunity" appearing only in immunised animals. I was the first to show that it was indeed a "reaction of infection," that it appeared in man during the first days of the disease, and I thus arrived at the conception of sero-diagnosis and its implications.

Widal, a critical bedside student and teacher, relied on effective investigation in the clinical laboratory as an adjunct to diagnosis and treatment of a number of maladies. On the basis of altered function, he separated types of chronic nephritis, a disease which had been largely a pathological entity in the generation following Richard Bright. Edema was attributed to retention of sodium chloride; the concentration of blood urea was related to prognosis, and the significance of cells and casts in the urinary sediment was discussed. Pasteur Vallery-Radot, son-in-law of Pasteur, was a junior author in this presentation.[4]

The practical importance of the urea content of the serum of patients with chronic nephritis has been demonstrated. With the help of this simple test we can construct the clinical history of azotemia and can distinguish symptoms which are characteristic of chloride retention or arterial hypertension.

The urea content in the blood permits us to establish the prognosis in Bright's disease, which otherwise would be an unsolved problem.

No one should assume responsibility for treating a patient with chronic nephritis without having established the presence or absence of nitrogen retention. It would be better to omit the examination for albumin in the urine than to neglect the urea content in the blood.

The results are easy to interpret. As long as the serum urea does not exceed 50 mg/100 ml we are not dealing with [critical] azotemia. When urea is elevated to amounts between 50 mg and 100 mg one must determine whether the tendency is towards decrease or progression of azotemia. The critical level in a doubtful prognosis is 100 mg/100 ml. Prognosis in patients with chronic Bright's disease is as poor as in cancer patients, if the urea content exceeds 200 mg/100 ml.

In the investigation of anaphylaxis, which had been described by Richet, a fellow Parisian, Widal studied hemolytic anemias (the Hayem-Widal type) and paroxysmal hemoglobinuria produced by cold. Hemolytic (acholuric) jaundice and cytodiagnosis of exudates were discussed with distinction. In the report on anaphylaxis, urticaria, and hemolytic crisis, Widal compared paroxysmal hemoglobinuria induced by exposure to cold to the development of anaphylaxis from exposure to antigenic foreign proteins.[5]

The study of this unique hemolytic crisis is helpful in interpreting the clinical manifestations of anaphylaxis, for it seems to constitute one of the most constant and stable characteristics of the phenomenon. But one should not assume it to be the result of the toxicity of heterologous proteins introduced into blood. The investigators have demonstrated its existence during the course of paroxysmal hemoglobinuria, when it develops because of the unique action of cold. It can also follow the introduction of non-colloidal substances into the blood. If the crisis is observed in the course of anaphylaxis, it occurs because the shock is an expression of the same loss of balance in the physio-chemical equilibrium of plasma. It is a true "hemolytic shock" and can be called a "hemoclasic crisis."

Widal's school of clinical medicine at the Hopital Cochin in Paris attracted students and patients in large numbers. Each came to benefit from the professor's clinical knowledge and experience, and, in so doing, must have felt the warmth of the personality of the kindly physician. A Socratic teacher, he combined a zeal for investigation with clinical wisdom and experimental precision. He received the highest French scientific honor, membership in the "Institute," as well as the Grand Cross of the Legion of Honour, the highest French civilian honor. Widal contributed more than his share toward making medicine an exact science, and was always attentive to other disciplines which might offer something to clinical medicine.[1]

We should heed carefully the progress in all sciences. One observation recorded in a completely unfamiliar area may be of unexpected value to us. The clinician makes use of knowledge wherever he finds it. The sciences have nothing to lose by lending us their discoveries; their application to medicine can only accentuate their splendor. We never know what surprise awaits us tomorrow, and this is not the least of the charms of our science. But to physicians, the discovery which is especially welcome is that which enables us to better recognize diseases and which enables us to handle them more successfully. Medicine is the most exciting of all sciences because it deals with the problems of life and attempts to penetrate its mysteries. It would not be the noblest if it did not examine all discoveries for means to alleviate human suffering.

1. Joltrain, E.: "Fernand Widal, The Man, His Work, His School," in Les Urticaires (Fr), Paris: G. Doin & Co., 1930, excerpt translated by Z. Danilevicius.

2. Widal, F.: Sero-Diagnosis of Typhoid Fever (Fr), Bull Soc Med Hop Paris 13:561-566, 1896, excerpt translated by Z. Danilevicius.

3. Widal, F.: On the Sero-Diagnosis of Typhoid Fever, Lancet 2:1371-1372, 1896.

4. Widal, F., Weill, A., and Vallery-Radot, P.: Prognosis in Chronic Nephritis (Fr), Presse Med 22:407-411, 1914, excerpt translated by Z. Danilevicius.

5. Widal, F., et al: Anaphylactic Reactions in Urticaria: Initial Hemoclasic Crisis (Fr), Presse Med 22:117, 1914, excerpt translated by Z. Danilevicius.

Composite by G. Bako

August von Wassermann
(1866-1925)

AUGUST WASSERMANN, investigator and teacher whose name for many years was preeminent in the serologic test for syphilis, was born at Bamberg, Germany, the son of a court banker.[1] His medical studies were pursued in Erlangen, Vienna, Munich, and finally in Strasbourg, where he graduated MD in 1888. In 1891, he became an assistant to Robert Koch in the Institute for Infectious Diseases in Berlin; subsequently, he lectured in internal medicine and made ward visits at the Charité Hospital in conjunction with the Institute appointment. In 1898, Wassermann received professorial status at the University of Berlin. He was knighted in 1910 and received a full professorship the following year. But only in 1913, almost 25 years after he began his investigative career, was he placed in charge of his own program upon being appointed director of the new Kaiser Wilhelm Institute for Experimental Therapy in Dahlem.

Wassermann's productive work in the many phases of the fundamentals of immunity was carried over to the solution of practical clinical problems in diagnosis and treatment. As a pupil of Koch and a follower of Ehrlich, he displayed a great capacity for clarity as well as humor in the lecture hall and in organized medical circles. His scientific interests covered many subjects in the rapidly expanding field of immunology and therapy. The majority of his important investigations were coauthored. His early work on the immunology of cholera was carried out with Pfeiffer, and the fixation of tetanus toxin by nerve tissues was studied with Takaki. In collaboration with Ficker, he attempted to cultivate *Treponema pallidum;* with Schutze he pursued precipitation studies for detection of blood in forensic cases; with Proskauer he investigated the toxin of diphtheria bacilli; with Ostertag polyvalent vaccination; with Neisser and Sachs complement-fixation; and with Bruck complement-fixation with meningococci. Less successful were his efforts to devise serologic tests for tuberculosis and cancer and therapeutic agents for mouse tumors. His best-known monograph, *Immune Sera Haemolysins, Cytotoxins, and Precipitins,* a series of lectures given at the University of Berlin, was translated into English. Together with Kolle he edited the monumental *Handbook of Pathogenic Microorganisms.*

The first reliable procedure for the serodiagnosis of syphilis was devised by Wassermann and was reported as a brief communication in conjunction with Bruck, his assistant and Neisser of Breslau, head of the dermatology clinic, who supplied syphilitic tissue and syphilitic serum. Schucht, assistant to Neisser, not listed as coauthor, prepared the extracts.

The work of Wassermann and his colleagues was preceded by two fundamental discoveries in the field of experimental syphilology. In 1903, Metchnikoff and Roux succeeded in transferring syphilis to apes, and, in 1905, Schaudinn and Hoffmann identified the causative agent of syphilis, *T pallidum.* The serologic procedure that Wassermann, Neisser, and Bruck employed for studies on syphilis was the complement fixation test described by Bordet and Gengou in 1901. These investigators at the Pasteur Institute in Paris found that a complex formed by a bacterial antigen and its corresponding antibody to be capable of binding complement, a thermolabile component of normal mammalian sera. Binding of complement by the antigen-antibody complex could be conveniently demonstrated by adding to the mixture sheep erythrocytes combined with anti-sheep erythrocyte antibodies. Such erythrocytes would undergo lysis in the presence of free complement; accordingly, a lack of lysis indicates a positive reaction, ie. the binding of complement by the complex of bacterial antigen and the antibacterial antibody.

As with all serologic reactions, complement fixation procedures may be used for identification of either an antibody or an antigen. Identification of an antibody requires the use of a known antigen as a reagent. Positive reaction between such an antigen-reagent and a serum under investigation indicates that the serum indeed contains antibodies directed against this antigen. On the other hand, in order to identify an antigen, a serum containing known antibodies as a reagent is needed. Here, the positive reaction between antibody-reagent and the tested specimen would indicate that this specimen contains the antigen against which the antibody is directed.

The logical experimental design to pursue was to use the *T pallidum* antigen in order to detect antibodies in the serum of a patient suspected of syphilis, and in this way, establish the diagnosis. A culture of *T pallidum* on artificial media was not available, nor is it available now. For this reason, Wassermann and his colleagues used extracts of syphilitic lesions from apes and man as a source of antigen. It was anticipated that such extracts would contain antigens of *T pallidum* and accordingly would be suitable for detecting antibodies to this agent. Alternatively, they used sera from apes immunized with tissues from syphilitic patients as well as sera from apes and man suffering from known syphilitic infection as reagents to detect *T pallidum* antigens in extracts of presumably syphilitic lesions. In 1906, Wassermann and his colleagues summarized the results which they obtained in their experiments performed by means of the complement fixation tests.[2]

On one hand we can determine in vitro whether a human serum or animal immune serum contains antibodies specific for substances of the syphilitic agent and we will be able to quantitate these antibodies. On the other hand, in using the described reaction, it is possible to demonstrate whether a particular organ contains syphilitic substances.

The first part of this statement dealing with detection of antibodies in the syphilis serum may be considered as the very foundation of what is now known as the Wassermann test. On the other hand, the detection of antigens characteristic for syphilis in organs, with which Wassermann and his colleagues were equally preoccupied, was never developed into any meaningful procedure.

It is amazing that Wassermann and his collaborators obtained consistently negative results in their controls in which extracts of normal organs were used for demonstration of antibodies in syphilitic sera. A few years after Wassermann's original report, Landsteiner, Müller, and Pötzl in Vienna and Marie and Levaditi in Paris showed that the antigen acting in the Wassermann reaction was present in normal tissues of human and animal origin as a thermostable, ethanol-soluble component. Purification of this antigen was achieved by Pangborn of Albany, New York, who isolated cardiolipin, a phospholipid, from crude ethanol extracts.

From the historic perspective of 60 years, the Wassermann test may be considered as an incidental discovery since, instead of an intended test in which the antibody would combine with the *T pallidum* antigen, a test was elaborated in which the antibody acts upon a ubiquitous tissue antigen. The puzzle of the mechanism of the Wassermann reaction and the origin of the antibody detected in this test have attracted numerous investigators for several decades. The solution of this puzzle seems close but it has not yet been reached. The studies on cerebrospinal fluid follow.[3]

From 41 different lumbar fluids from paralytics, 32 showed, when mixed with the extract from luetic organs, a noticeable inhibition of hemolysis; when 0.2 to 0.1 ml of extract was used, there was a complete inhibition; the lumbar fluids alone did not inhibit the hemolysis. In 4 cases we observed incomplete inhibition, in 5 cases, no inhibition. These same lumbar fluids, when mixed with the extracts from the organs of a non-syphilitic foetus, produced no inhibition. We also tested 19 lumbar fluids from persons without syphilis and combined them with the extracts of syphilitic organs. No inhibition was observed in contrast to significant inhibition with the spinal fluids from paralytic patients. Therefore we can distinguish, at least according to the results of our experimental material up to this date (1906), and clearly separate by this reaction, the majority of the lumbar fluids of paralytics from the lumbar fluids of persons who did not suffer from lues or paresis.

Our investigations are not adequate to draw the conclusion that the paralysis is causally related to the lues and to which extent this is the case. In order to do so, investigations are needed of the reaction of the lumbar fluids of persons who have suffered from lues earlier, or are now in the florid state, but who have not developed paralysis or tabes, in addition to the investigation of a larger number of normal, ie, nonsyphilitic lumbar fluids.

1. Friedberger, E.: August v. Wassermann (Ger), *Z Immunitatsforsch* 43:i-xii, 1925.

2. Wassermann, A.; Neisser, A.; and Bruck, C.: The Diagnostic Reaction for Syphilis (Ger), *Deutsch Med Wschr* 32:745-746, 1906.

3. Wassermann, A., and Plaut, F.: The Presence of Syphilitic Antibodies in Cerebral Spinal Fluid of Paralytics (Ger), *Deutsch Med Wschr* 32:1769-1772, 1906, excerpt translated by E. Longar.

Composite by G. Bako

Charles Nicolle (1866-1936)

CHARLES NICOLLE, recipient of the Nobel Prize for his work on exanthematous typhus, was born in Rouen, capital of the ancient province of Normandy, the son of a practicing physician.[1] He received his medical education in Rouen and completed his internship in the hospitals of Paris in 1893. After teaching for a time in his alma mater, he studied in the Pasteur Institute of Paris under the direction of Metchnikoff and Roux. In 1902, he was appointed the first director of the Pasteur Institute of Tunis in North Africa and remained

at his post until his death 33 years later. Nicolle's investigations concentrated upon infectious diseases indigenous to the southern coast of the Mediterrean Sea; however, his laboratory attracted students from countries throughout Europe as well as from the United States. Within a relatively short time the scientific status and the bacteriologic research of the Institute in North Africa, guided by Nicolle and his associates, rivalled the parent Institute in Paris. Nicolle founded the *Archives of the Pasteur Institute of Tunis*, a provincial medium for their contributions, and, maintaining an excellent esprit de corps, he directed the Institute for more than a quarter of a century.

Although exanthematous typhus was the center of Nicolle's attentions, his diverse interests in general bacteriology, immunology, and the pathogenesis of infectious diseases included the discovery of toxoplasma, recognition of the filtrability of the trachoma virus, suggestion of the viral nature of influenza, an inquiry into the prophylactic value of convalescent serum in typhoid fever, studies on endemic relapsing fever, demonstration of the protective value in susceptible individuals of serum from patients convalescing from measles, identification of the body louse as the vector of epidemic typhus fever, and an unsuccessful attempt to prepare a therapeutic equine serum.

One of Nicolle's first discoveries in protozoology was culturing of *Leishmania tropica* (oriental sore) and reproduction of the disease by inoculation of the culture in the dog and monkey. As a joint contribution with Manceaux, the *Toxoplasma gondii*, a protozoan parasite in rodents, was described and named the same year it was demonstrated by Splendore in Brazil.[2] Several decades elapsed before the first proven human case of infestation, with symptoms, was recognized by Aldo Castellani in Ceylon.[2]

We have found in a North African rodent a parasite similar to *Leishmania*. . . . It is 5 to 5.5 microns in diameter. . . . The nucleus is a true nucleus, round and within the protoplasm, and consisting of loosely packed chromatin of small particles. The protozoa is a parasite of the white blood cell and of selected organs, especially the spleen and liver. If the identity with *Leishmania* would be proven, one must assume that leishmaniasis of rodents in Tunisia causes human skin lesions, the same as canine leishmaniasis in Tunis is associated with infant kala-azar. Provisionally, the new protozoa is designated *Leishmania gondi*.

Finally, it was recognized by Nicolle that the parasite was not *Leishmania*, but belonged to another genus of which it is the only known representative, *Toxoplasma gondii*.

The filtrability of a virus from trachoma lesions was demonstrated in 1912, several years after cytoplasmic inclusion bodies had been described by Halberstaedter and Prowazek. Although trachoma continues to be classified as a viral disease, it is now known to be caused by an obligate, intracellular microorganism of the psittacosis group. Nicolle was successful in reproducing granulomatous conjunctivitis in the monkey, the rabbit, and the chimpanzee, with characteristics similar to human infection. It was contagious throughout development and was spread by flies. After a period of incubation and without immediate inflammatory reaction, symptoms in the experimental animal appeared on the eighth day following exposure.[3]

After the incubation period, without secretion and without inflammatory reaction, granulations appeared on the 14th day, identical with those in man in the same primordial and elective site on the upper lids at the edge of the tarsal cartilage. The infection spread onto the neighboring areas in several weeks, affecting the lower lids, the angle and the caruncle, but always sparing the cornea.

The clinical picture became typical during the third or fourth week. After remaining stationary for approximately a fortnight, the lesions began to pale and recede; they disappeared on the parts which were affected last but persisted for a time in the area of predilection at the edge of the tarsal cartilage; towards the third month, the lesions disappeared without producing secretion and without leaving residuum.

The tears of patients are infectious when inoculated into excoriated conjunctiva; at times even simple contact with the mucous membrane leads to infection. This fact, together with extreme severity of trachoma, and its persistent contagiousness as shown in our previous experiments, points to the need for rigorous prophylaxis.

The Nobel Prize in Medicine and Physiology was awarded to Nicolle in 1928, on the 25th anniversary of his appointment as director of the Tunis Institute. The citation noted the successful transmission of exanthematous typhus fever to chimpanzees in the acute stages by the injection of a small amount of blood, as well as the transmission of the disease from monkey to monkey by the bite of the body louse. The experiments on two monkeys were described in 1909.[4]

Study of the recent epidemics of typhus which have raged in Regency, particularly at Tunis, Metlaoui and Redeyef (phosphate company of Gafsa) and on the Kerkennah Islands, have led us to consider an insect as the probable agent in transmission of the disease.

Typhus in upper Africa is a result of crowding and poverty; it rages among the people who are the poorest and the least respectful of hygienic measures; it is not contagious in a clean dwelling, or in the wards of a disciplined hospital. Therefore, only the insects of the dwelling, clothing and body can be suspected, lice, fleas and bedbugs. The appearance of typhus in the spring excludes mosquitoes, ticks, and stomox.

These observations were known to us when one of us succeeded in inoculating a chimpanzee with typhus and after passing it through the chimpanzee to a bonnet-macaque (*macacus sinicus*). Also since the beginning of our investigations, we have attempted the transmission of the disease from monkey to monkey by means of the *body louse*.

The general condition [of one experimental animal] was good until the 30th day, when depression appeared, the animal ate less, and did not resist restraint. Extreme agitation without an exception developed during the second febrile period. Violet discoloration of the lips was noted during the two terminal days. At autopsy, no lesion was apparent except for an irregular ulceration of the caecum covered with a diphtheroid exudate.

These experiments show that it is possible to transmit the typhus of the infected bonnet-macaque to another monkey, by the body louse. The application of this finding to the understanding of the etiology and the prophylaxis of the disease in man is noteworthy. Measures to combat typhus should have as their aim destruction of the parasites which live principally on the body, in the linens, and clothes of patients.

During a mission to Mexico, Nicolle distinguished a murine typhus transmitted by lice to rats from the historical typhus common to man. Experimental subjects immunized against one type were protected against challenge by the second type; whereas immunity in rats was conferred temporarily by inapparent typhus.[5]

We were successful in white rats with a new series of transfers of exanthematous virus. Two rats were inoculated in each experiment, using one guinea pig as a control. The inoculation was performed with the brain of a rat which had been inoculated at the same time as the guinea pig. The rat was sacrificed exactly at the time when the guinea pig was in the second or third day of febrile typhus or, in case the typhus in the guinea pig was either late or very mild, the rat was sacrificed on the 11th to the 13th day after inoculation. A second rat in each passage was observed for a period of 30 days and proved by the absence of any temperature elevation that the infection in the sacrificed rat had developed as in the second rat and was completely apyretic. The control guinea pig showed that the rat of the preceding transfer had been infected with typhus.

Even more than in the first series, we have observed the transformation of the apyretic or inapparent typhus into febrile typhus. The inapparent typhus thus seems to be nothing more than a type of the same exanthematic infection which has been observed in rats.

In another series of experiments we have shown that inapparent typhus, which is the only form of typhus in the rat, provides immunity, generally of short duration although it may persist several months.

Five rats which showed the inapparent typhus and were proven experimentally to have been infected, proved to be refractory to a second inoculation, after 4 months in three instances and after 6 months in two instances.

These results confirm our previous conclusion that the inapparent typhus leaves an immunity for several months. A procedure in man which would give immunity of approximately the same duration would probably suffice for the prophylaxis of typhus; admittedly, however, first degree resistance could not be enhanced by a subsequent inoculation.

Charles Nicolle was a philosopher, a poet, and a scholar in addition to his outstanding investigations in bacteriology and immunoloy. He received from his government the degree of Commander of the Legion of Honor. In 1920, he was named associate in the Academy of Medicine and correspondent to the Academy of Sciences; he received the Osiris Prize in 1927, and in 1932 was named professor in the College of France following Claude Bernard, Laennec, d'Arsonval, and other great French scientists.

1. Charles Nicolle 1866-1936 (Fr), obituary, *Ann Inst Pasteur (Paris)* 56:353-358, 1936.

2. Nicolle, C., and Manceaux, L.: An Infection From Leishman in Rodents (Fr), *C R Acad Sci (Paris)* 147:763-767, 1908, excerpts translated by Z. Danilevicius.

3. Nicolle, C.; Blaisot, L.; and Cuénod, A.: The Transmission of Trachoma to Apes. The Filtrability of the Virus (Fr), *C R Acad Sci (Paris)* 155-241-243, 1912, excerpt translated by Z. Danilevicius.

4. Nicolle, C.; Comte, C.; and Conseil, E.: Experimental Transmission of Typhus Exanthematicus by the Body Louse (Fr), *C R Acad Sci (Paris)* 149:486-489, 1909, translated in Major, T.: *Classic Description of Disease*, Springfield, Ill.: C C Thomas, 1932.

5. Nicolle, C.: A New Contribution to the Knowledge of Experimental Murine Typhus (Fr), *Arch Inst Pasteur Tunis* 15:267-275, 1926, excerpt translated by Z. Danilevicius.

Composite by G. Bako

Fritz Richard Schaudinn
(1871-1906)

SCHAUDINN was born in Roesiningken in East Prussia in 1871 and died in 1906, crowding into an investigative career of only a dozen years a tremendous number of significant contributions, particularly in protozoology. The discovery of the *Spirochaeta pallida* (*Treponema pallidum*) of syphilis was his great achievement. Although never actively associated with a medical institute his studies on amebic infestation, hookworm disease, and tertian malaria were of major clinical interest.[1]

Following upper-class schooling, Schaudinn entered the University of Berlin in 1890, with the intention of studying philology. However, his interest shifted to zoology in the university, and the doctorate in philosophy was granted, with a thesis on the description of a new species and a new genus of a marine *Foraminifera*. The demonstration that the two forms of the many-chambered marine organisms, those with a large and with a small embryonal chamber represented two stages in the life cycle of the organism and not two distinct genera, settled a long-standing controversy. Delineation of the life cycle of the protozoan was the pattern of investigation applied to other lower organisms. Included were the life histories of *Cyclospora*, the pathogenic agent of enteritis of the mole; a blood parasite of the lizard; three blood parasites of the owl. *Proteosoma, Halteridium,* and *Haemamoeba (Haemosporidia);* and a coccidian, a parasite of a centipede (*Lithobius*). The unity of each of the several species was clarified, as it was shown that they were merely stages of one life cycle. In England, Lister's investigations in protozoan morphology overlapped those of Schaudinn. Lister and Schaudinn independently and simultaneously showed that dimorphism in *Polustomella crispa* is part of the integral cycle—one form multiplying by flagellospore formation and alternating with the form which multiplies by the production of ameba-spores. Investigation of the life cycle of the newly discovered rhizopod *Trichosphoerium sieboldi* was very thorough, and little was left to be discovered by subsequent investigators.

Before Schaudinn's studies on *Entamoeba* (*Endamoeba*), there was considerable evidence to suggest that the *Entamoeba coli*, described by Loesch in 1875, was responsible for tropical dysentery. The identification of an ameba, not clearly distinguishable from *E coli* in the intestines of healthy persons raised considerable doubt as to the specific pathogenicity of this organism. It could have been only a normal inhabitant. Schaudinn recognized the difference between *E coli* and *E histolytica,* the latter the pathogenic agent for amebic dysentery. It was shown that the pathogenic ameba produced small encysted organisms, whose nuclei were derived from the chromidial network of the parent. In the reproduction of *E coli*, a single ameba encysts, forming two daughter nuclei from the original single nucleus.

In 1901, Schaudinn was assigned by the German government to the marine laboratory at Rovigno for the study of marine protozoa particularly. He saw the entrance of the malarial sporozoite into the red blood cell, the end stage of the sexual cycle in the mosquito and, of the merozoite, the end stage of the asexual cycle in man. The observations of Ross and of Grassi on the *Plasmodium vivax*, the cause of tertian malaria, were confirmed.[2] Two years before his death, Schaudinn was recalled to Berlin as director in the Imperial Health Office and was responsible for the newly established division for protozoology. His final years in the laboratory were the most rewarding to medical science. One of the first assignments was the investigation of the mode of entry into the body of the larva of *Ancylostomum duodenale* and the means of preventing such entry. Schaudinn's experiments on monkeys left no doubt that the larva of hookworm penetrated the normal skin, leading to intestinal infection.

In May, 1905, together with Hoffman, Schaudinn discovered the *Spirochaeta pallida* (*Treponema pallidum*) as the pathogenic agent in syphilis. Before the year ended, he described the morphology of the *Spirochaeta* organisms and established the new genus, *Treponema,* with characteristics different from other spirochaetae. Schaudinn also demonstrated the organism in vivo and in stained tissues.[3]

At the suggestion of the president of the Imperial Office of Health Dr. Köhler and in cooperation with Doctors E. Lesser, Neufeld, and Gonder, an investigation concerning the presence of micro-organisms in syphilitic disease was started. In this work, Schaudinn recovered organisms from the living subject as well as in stained preparations, organisms which must be considered as belonging to the family of the spirochete, a family which Schaudinn insists belongs to the protozoa. . . . The spirochete has been seen and isolated on the surface of open syphilitic lesions as well as in the depth of the tissues and in diseased glands.

Since the spirochetes of the syphilitic lesions are extraordinarily delicate, rapid moving, and active, and appear poorly under illumination, samples were taken directly from the lesion onto a glass slide.

For the proof of the spirochete in a stained slide, a smear was fixed as thin as possible from the same parts of the diseased tissue, and after drying in air, was placed in a solution of alcohol. The spirochetes took up the color with varying degrees of ease.

The professional career of Fritz Schaudinn was brief. However, he crowded into a period little longer than a decade many critical observations in protozoology, a branch of biology which was emerging from an inexact discipline into an exact science. Studies of the malarial parasite, *E histolytica,* and the larva of hookworm were of considerable clinical value. His greatest achievement was the recovery of the *T pallidum* from syphilitic lesions, of interest to the clinician, the microbiologist, and the practitioner of preventive medicine.

1. Schultz, O. T.: Fritz Schaudinn: A Review of His Work, *Johns Hopkins Hosp Bull* 19:169-173 (June) 1908.

2. Schaudinn, F.: Studies on Pathogenic Protozoa, II: *Plasmodium vivax*, (Grassi & Feletti), The Cause of Tertian Fever in Man, *Arb Kaiserlichen Gesundheitsamte* 19:169-250, 1903.

3. Schaudinn, F., and Hoffmann, E.: Preliminary Report on the Occurrence of Spirochetes in Syphilitic Sickness-Products and in Papillomas (Ger), *Arb Kaiserlichen Gesundheitsamte* 22:527-534, 1905, excerpt translated by E. Longar.

Composite by G. Bako

Hideyo Noguchi (1876-1928)

THERE ARE TWO ORIENTAL SCIENTISTS whose names appear repeatedly in medical contributions in America in the first quarter of the 20th century. H. Wu, collaborating biochemist with Otto Folin, was content to be the junior member in the description of the Folin-Wu procedures. Hideyo Noguchi, on the other hand, although deeply indebted to his American associates, was rather resentful of overt collaboration and, whenever possible, preferred to be identified without coauthors and avoided sharing scientific honors.

Hideyo was born in impoverished circumstances in 1876 in a small Japanese village.[1] He studied in the Kitasato Institute of Infectious Diseases in Tokyo, where, in 1899, he met Simon Flexner, professor of pathology at the University of Pennsylvania, who was on a tour of the Orient. A casual offer of hospitality by Flexner to come to America was taken seriously. Noguchi arrived in Philadelphia a few months later, began to work under Flexner, and while he later visited Japan, he never lived again in his native country.

The first decade of Noguchi's career in America was concerned largely with snake venoms. S. Weir Mitchell, who had been interested in the subject, obtained financial assistance that enabled Noguchi to continue studies then underway at the University of Pennsylvania on the immunologic responses of *Serpentes* poisons. These investigations led to the monograph *Snake Venoms*. The preface betrayed Noguchi's evaluation of his contributions.[2]

No single work in the English language exists at this time which treats of the facts of zoological, anatomical, physiological, and pathological features of venomous snakes, with particular reference to the properties of their venoms.

If the significance and number of Noguchi's contributions were plotted as a function of time, the curve would resemble the familiar bell shape. In the first decade of his career in America, snake venom was the principal subject for investigation. In the second decade, the peak period of his contributions, the spirochetes became the center of attention. In the interim, he accompanied Flexner to New York and the Rockefeller Institute for Medical Research, where the latter had been appointed director of the new institute. Noguchi soon rose to prominence, was appointed an associate in 1906 and a full member in 1914. In the declining decade as the curve regressed, trachoma, yellow fever, and Oroya fever were studied. Because of his diverse interests, Noguchi reminds one of a juggler keeping several platters in the air, simultaneously. He displayed tremendous industry—always a master craftsman in devices and techniques, but rarely a slave to procedure.

An attempt to cultivate the *Treponema pallidum* was Noguchi's first major project at the Rockefeller Institute. The experimental infection of primates by Metchnikoff and Roux, the discovery by Schaudinn and Hoffman of the *T pallidum* as the causative agent of syphilis, and the development of the serologic test by Wassermann in the immediately preceding years reflected interest in this subject at that time. Although Noguchi stated in his report of 1911 that he had grown the *T pallidum* in pure culture, he had merely extended the observations of Metchnikoff and Roux of successful animal inoculation.[3]

Unlike all previous investigators, who used syphilitic tissues directly from human cases, I have employed the spirochaetae—containing testicular tissue of rabbits which have been inoculated with human syphilitic material for the purpose of cultivating the pallidum. The rabbit testicle, when inoculated with human material rich in pallida, swells gradually after a fortnight's incubation period and reaches its maximum, as a rule, in from four to six weeks.

It may be pointed out that this is the first time that *Treponema pallidum* of Schaudinn has been proven beyond all doubt to have been obtained in pure culture.

Other spirochetes studied by Noguchi included *Borrelia gallinarum* (*Spirochaeta gallinarum*), *Bor refringens* (*S refringens*), *T mucosum*, *Bor kochii*, *Bor novyi* (*S novyi*), and *S obermeieri*, each obtained in pure culture. The demonstration of the *Treponema* as the pathogenic agent in the brain from cases with a clinical diagnosis of general paralysis has been judged one of his two best scientific contributions. A mass survey of slides, using the silver impregnation techniques, proved successful.[4]

In the present communication we wish to report the results of examinations for *Treponema pallidum* on seventy paretic brains. One of us (Noguchi) succeeded in finding the pallidum in twelve out of the seventy specimens.

The spirochaetae were found in all layers of the cortex with the exception of the outer, or neuroglia layer. One was located at the border of this layer, but not within it. A few were found subcortically. Careful search of the pia failed to reveal any of the organisms. In all instances they seemed to have wandered into the nerve tissue. They were not found in the vessel sheaths and seldom in close proximity to the larger vessels.

During the last decade of his life, Noguchi traveled to the southwestern desert of the United States to study trachoma, to Peru, where he observed examples of Oroya fever (Carrion's disease or verruga peruana), and to South America and Africa in the pursuit of the pathogenesis of yellow fever. Except for Oroya fever, subsequent events did not substantiate his initial optimistic expectations. He was convinced that the *Noguchia gran-*

ulosis (*Bacterium granulosis*)[5] was associated with the etiology of trachoma when, in fact, a virus has been found to be the offending agent.

No other microorganism obtained from the human cases of trachoma produces in animals effects comparable to those induced by *Bacterium granulosis*. In the absence, therefore, of indications to the contrary, we may consider that in *Bacterium granulosis* we have the inciting microorganism of trachoma in man and its equivalent, granular conjunctivitis in monkeys.

Prior to Noguchi's interest in Oroya fever, a Peruvian student, Carrion, had reported the contagion of a papule from a patient with verruga peruana, while Barton had described a bacillus, later named *Bartonella bacilliformis* by Strong, Tyzzer, and Sellards, from a case of Oroya fever. These are two stages of one morbid process. Oroya fever, associated with anemia, usually is mild but in some instances may be overwhelming and fatal. Verruga peruana, on the other hand, may develop after the subsidence of the hematologic manifestations, or it may develop without the preceding anemia. Cultivation of the infectious agent by Noguchi made it possible to establish the unitarian etiology of two apparently unrelated manifestations of the disease. This, with his other studies on the vector, phlebotomus, was another major contribution.[6]

The data obtained justify the conclusion that verruga peruana is caused by *B bacilliformis*. They also definitely establish the fact that the inoculation of blood or sanguineous exudate from lesions of verruga peruana is capable of inducing in susceptible individuals a severe febrile systemic infection, such as that to which Carrion succumbed. The designation "bartonellosis" is therefore the appropriate one for both forms of the infection.

Noguchi fared less well with yellow fever. His thinking and researches on the etiology of this affliction appeared to be the reflection of a harried mind in the hopes of making at least one final contribution in microbiology.

In Guayaquil, Ecuador, and later in neighboring countries, Noguchi isolated from patients with yellow fever an infectious agent closely resembling *Leptospira icterohaemorrhagiae* which he named *L icteroides*. Erroneously, he assumed this microorganism to be the cause of yellow fever. His apparent success was overshadowed by the obvious failure of others to repeat the work and the eventual demonstration that yellow fever is of viral origin. His most tragic mistake was a failure to protect himself against the disease. He contracted yellow fever while on a mission in Africa and died there in 1928.

1. Clark, P. F.: Hideyo Noguchi, 1876-1928, *Bull Hist Med* 33:1-20 (Jan-Feb) 1959.

2. Noguchi, H.: *Snake Venoms: An Investigation of Venomous Snakes with Special Reference to the Phenomena of Their Venoms*, Washington, D.C.: Carnegie Institution of Washington, 1909.

3. Noguchi, H.: A Method for the Pure Cultivation of Pathogenic Treponema Pallidum (Spirochaeta Pallida), *J Exp Med* 14:99-108 (July 1) 1911.

4. Noguchi, H., and Moore, J. W.: A Demonstration of Treponema pallidum in the Brain in Cases of General Paralysis, *J. Exp Med* 17:232-238 (Feb. 1) 1913.

5. Noguchi, H.: The Etiology of Trachoma, *J Exp Med* 48:1-52 (July 1) 1928.

6. Noguchi, H.: The Etiology of Verruga Peruana, *J Exp Med* 45:175-189, 1927.

Hans Zinsser (1878-1940)

THE BOOK, *As I Remember Him, The Biography of R. S.,*[1] is an undisguised autobiography of Hans Zinsser, natural philosopher, bacteriologist, poet, and a highly rational intellectual. He was not one who appeared to be a different person to different individuals; rather these attributes and accomplishments were intimately interwoven, continually seeking expression in words or deeds. Through his personality and presentation of outstanding texts on infection and bacteriology, he exerted a great and profound influence on his students in the classroom and his research associates in the laboratory at a time when these subjects were approaching professional maturity in America.

Hans was born in New York City, the first generation of German-born parents. His father was a successful chemist; his mother had been educated in a convent in the Black Forest. After being tutored at home, he spent a school year in Wiesbaden, Germany, and entered Columbia College, more interested in literature and poetry than in the natural sciences. In 1903, Zinsser received the AB degree, followed by the MD from the College of Physicians and Surgeons (Columbia University). After an internship at Roosevelt Hospital in New York City, he pursued private practice reluctantly for a few months, and, in time, accepted an appointment in the department of bacteriology at his alma mater. Within two years after beginning full-time teaching, he had prepared a *Text-book of Bacteriology,*[2] co-authored with Hiss, which proved to be the leading text on the subject for a full generation. Then followed, in succession, professorships in bacteriology and immunology at Stanford University, at the College of Physicians and Surgeons, and lastly at Harvard Medical School, the longest tour of duty, where for 17 years he occupied the Charles Wilder professorship, terminated only by his death. In 1914, *Infection and Resistance*, his second ambitious treatise, was published. It was identified as[3] "an exposition of the biological phenomena underlying the occurrence of infection and the recovery of the animal body from infectious disease."

Zinsser went to Serbia in 1915 with the American Red Cross Sanitary Commission under Richard P. Strong, which provided his first field contact with an epidemic of typhus fever. The typhus epidemic started on the Belgrade front in the fall, spreading from the army to the civilians. It was estimated that at least 150,000 persons were stricken, with a case fatality of 60 to 70%. Although the Red

Cross expedition was not welcomed by the Serbs, it was possible for the investigators to extend their knowledge of the clinical aspects of typhus and to begin the separation of fact from speculation, in understanding the bacteriology, the pathology, and the clinical manifestations of the malady.[4]

Nearly two decades later when his popular scientific "biography" appeared, *Rats, Lice and History*, Zinsser confessed that he could write "with the greatest enjoyment about Rickettsiae, leprosy, allergy, and syphilis," but the "dramatic episodes like war, epidemics, revolutions and riots," left him "pentied."[5] His treatment and studies on typhus, which offered him the greatest satisfaction in the laboratory and in the field, disclosed the basic characteristics of his personality. The epidemiology of typhus, the habits of the louse, and the culture of *Rickettsia* organisms were approached and investigated, and the results discussed as a natural philosopher.

Zinsser returned to Europe in 1917 with the American Expeditionary Forces as an expert in epidemiology and bacteriology. His war assignments were scarcely mentioned in conversation or in his autobiography, except for the treatise *The Sanitation of a Field Army*.[6] The silence on combat exploits stemmed not from a sense of modesty, but rather from an inability to comprehend man's hidden reason or overjustification for wanton destruction of life and property. On the other hand, he was ever ready to discuss the motivation of great men of the past and the influences of philosophers, scientists, and events. He was keenly aware of the rapid maturation of science in the Western world, particularly in America, and its relation to public health, preventive medicine, and the day-by-day practice of medicine by the personal physician. An attempt was sought to integrate science with philosophy—an attempt not understood by contemporary critics.[1]

They [critics] appeared to feel toward science somewhat as the Church did in the sixteenth century.

To R. S. this was confusing, since with his own profound distrust of mere fact accumulated without philosophical and aesthetic coördination, the philosopher and the great artist were to him the architects who must build the cultural edifice of the future, using science—among other things—as an indispensable part of their equipment. But he found among most of his friends little or no appreciation of the fact that the last forty years had witnessed an era of enlightenment in man's understanding both of nature and of himself which was not incomparable to the epic beginning with Galileo.

Zinsser was awarded the Distinguished Service Medal of the United States Army and later was decorated by Serbia and by France, with the Legion d'Honneur, of the rank of chevalier. During the years of uneasy peace between the two World Wars, he was concerned with the biologic and chemical integration of bacteriology and immunology and with the nature of antigens and antibodies and the mechanisms of their reaction. The *Rickettsia prowazeki* var *prowazeki* was cultured in his laboratory, the pathogenic agent in recrudescent louse-borne typhus, which is increasingly being called Brill-Zinsser disease. Interest in bacterial hypersensitivity related particularly to the tuberculin reaction. Independently, but simultaneously with Dochez and Avery, he studied the specific precipitable substances identified as polysaccharides in the blood and urine of patients with pneumonia. In discussing the allergic hypothesis of rheumatic fever, he advanced a generalization of first importance.

In the laboratory, Zinsser's intriguing speculations were always seeking the value of basic research in the prevention or treatment of diseases, illustrated by general principles of attack.[1]

There is in this profession, especially as it concerns itself with infectious diseases, a fascination which holds the spirit with feelings that are not exaggerated by the word "passion"; indeed, like the happiest personal passions, it feeds on the intimate daily association of long years and grows, like love, with an increasing familiarity that never becomes complete knowledge. For what can be more happily exciting than to study a disease in all its natural manifestations, isolate its cause, and subject this to precise scrutiny and analysis; to grow it apart from its host, study its manner of multiplication, its habits under artificial conditions, its changes, its possible toxic products; then to carry it back to the animal body and follow the processes by which it injures and kills; explore the details of the animal defenses, and pursue it again into the epidemic; examine its manner of conveyance from case to case, its relationship to water and food, animal carriers, insect vectors; its geographical, climatic, and seasonal distribution; the laws of its epidemic waves; and then, with all the weapons of the knowledge gained, to assist in its arrest and circumvention, even contribute to protection and possibly individual cure.

Hans Zinsser was found to be suffering from lymphatic leukemia two years before his death. The expression of his father, also a gentle agnostic, was handed down.[1]

He had no belief in God. He had no hope of immortality. And in these negations he did not weaken during the months of agony. If he shed a tear, it was for the sorrow of leaving us who loved him so deeply. He believed that man's immortality lies in the offspring of his body and mind, and wanted no consolation for what he accepted as the inevitable destiny of all living things.

Several of Zinsser's poems have been published in current literary periodicals, and his book of sonnets, *Spring, Summer; and Autumn*, was assembled following his death. In his last sonnet he confessed a merry association with those dear to him, even though his own prognosis was clear.[7]

Now is Death merciful. He calls me hence
Gently, with friendly soothing of my fears
Of ugly age and feeble impotence
And cruel disintegration of slow years.
Nor does he leap upon me unaware
Like some wild beast that hungers for its prey,
But gives me kindly warning to prepare
Before I go, to kiss your tears away.
How sweet the summer! And the autumn shone
Late warmth within our hearts as in the sky,
Ripening rich harvests that our love had sown.
How good that ere the winter comes, I die!
Then, ageless, in your heart I'll come to rest
Serene and proud as when you loved me best.

1. Zinsser, H.: *As I Remember Him, the Biography of R. S. Boston:* Little, Brown and Company, 1940.
2. Hiss, P. H., Jr., and Zinsser, H.: *A Text-book of Bacteriology,* New York: D. Appleton and Company, 1910.
3. Zinsser, H.: *Infection and Resistance,* New York: Macmillan Company, 1914.
4. Strong, R. P., et al: *Typhus Fever with Particular Reference to the Serbian Epidemic,* Cambridge: Harvard University Press, 1920.
5. Zinsser, H.: *Rats, Lice and History,* Boston: Little, Brown and Company, 1935.
6. Zinsser, H.: *The Sanitation of a Field Army,* 1919.
7. Zinsser, H.: *Spring, Summer and Autumn,* New York: Alfred A. Knopf, 1942.

Hans Reiter (1881-1969)

HANS CONRAD REITER, public and social hygienist, investigator of spirochetes, immunization, and vaccination against specific infections, was born in Leipzig, the son of an industrialist.[1] After attending the Gymnasium and studying medicine at Leipzig, Breslau, and Tübingen, he received the MD degree in 1906 upon presentation of an inaugural dissertation, entitled "Nephritis and Tuberculosis." He continued postgraduate training at

Composite by G. Bako

the Pasteur Institute in Paris, St. Mary's Hospital in London under Sir Almroth Wright, and the Institute of Hygiene at the University of Berlin. In 1913, Reiter was appointed privatdocent at the Institute of Hygiene in Königsberg, and, for a few months preceding World War I, he was Deputy Department Director at the Institute for Hygiene of the University of Berlin. With the outbreak of hostilities, he served in the German army on the Western Front, where he identified the causative organism in Weil's disease, his first important discovery. Later Reiter was transferred to the Balkan front with the First Hungarian army; there he cared for a young lieutenant who was suffering from a triad of symptoms, urethritis, conjunctivitis, and arthritis, to which Reiter's name was attached later.

Following the war, Reiter was appointed professor of hygiene at Rostock University and a section director of the Institute of Public Health, and in 1923 section director in the Kaiser Wilhelm Institute of Experimental Therapy in Berlin-Dahlem. In 1926, he became director of the health department of the state of Mecklenburg. When Adolph Hitler sought support for the National Socialist movement in the 1930's, one source was a group of university professors. Those ostensibly loyal to Hitler signed an oath of allegiance in 1932. Reiter was a member of the group and in return received appointments in the Nazi government. In 1933, he was appointed president of the health department in Berlin by Hindenburg and honorary professor of hygiene in the University of Berlin. The following year, at the instigation of the minister of Internal Affairs, he directed the Federation of Scientific Societies which assumed all functions of the dissolved National Health office. In 1935, he was appointed president of the Robert Koch Institute for Infectious Diseases and, from 1933 to 1945, represented Germany at the International Health Organization in Paris.

Reiter's extended interest in the spirochete led to a communication from his military experience on the etiology of one of the group of infectious maladies identified as Weil's disease. In the same month, Inada and colleagues in Japan described a leptospira in the blood of similarly afflicted patients. Hübener summarized the clinical and laboratory findings associated with the etiologic agent, *Leptospira icterohaemorrhagiae* as follows.[2]

Our investigations extend beyond the eight patients which we have reported and in which our transmission experiments produced positive results.

Weil's disease is an acute, noncontagious, infectious disease who causative agent belongs to the group of spirochaetae which can be transmitted to man through the bite of insects. Introduced into the blood stream, the spirochete affects internal organs and tissues simultaneously and produces specific toxic substances which cause systemic disease with typical fever and with predilection for the kidneys and the liver.

The case of urethritis, conjunctivitis, and arthritis, which was reported initially as a spirochetal infection (although the symptoms failed to respond to salvarsan), was also observed while Reiter was in military service. The polyarticular symptoms at various times in the natural history involved all of the large joints of the body as well as the sacroiliacs and the spine. The discharge from the urethra, with edema of the glans and prepuce, disclosed no gonococci. The eye symptoms included iritis and cyclitis. Within a year after

the preliminary report, Reiter retracted the spirochetal etiology. However, he continued to be interested in the clinical syndrome, adding more cases to his clinical experience and supplementing them by a surprisingly large number of cases reported in the literature. His initial report includes the following pertinent data.[3]

On Oct 14, 1916, Lt N was admitted to the reserve hospital with a history of becoming ill with abdominal cramps, diarrhea, and bloody stools on the 21st of Aug. A discharge from the urethra and purulent conjunctival catarrh developed on the 29th of Aug. Rheumatic complaints appeared the following day. On the 31st of Aug the patient was admitted to a field hospital.

The findings on admission included: a red urethral meatus, purulent urethral discharge, dysuria, intense injection of purulent secretion of the conjunctivae, edema of the eyelids, swelling of the right knee with no active movement possible, passive movement produced severe pain. On the 2nd of Sept the evening temperature exceeded 39 C; both knees were swollen and very painful, no active motion was possible, discharge was diminishing. On the 10th of Sept the urethral secretions contained no gonococci. The following day the left foot was swollen. On the 15th of Sept the right elbow and the left hand were swollen, and while the conjunctivitis had disappeared, minute corneal opacities remained. On the 18th of Sept it was necessary to feed the patient because of severe limitation of joint function.

On admission to the Reserve Hospital on Oct 14, many of the large and small joints of the extremities were markedly swollen, painful, and limited in motion, while passive motion produced severe pain. The spleen was easily palpable. The liver was not enlarged. The prepuce was edematous and swollen; the glans penis was covered with thick pus. Gonococci could not be recovered by prostatic massage. The temperature fluctuated between 37 C and 39 C associated with night sweats. On the 20th of Oct the conjunctiva were markedly swollen and red.

A pure culture of spirochaeta was obtained in the blood from venous puncture on the 21st of Oct. An injection of 0.3 gm of neosalvarsan was made on Nov 3 and Nov 6.

Characteristic of this disease, which I propose to call *spirochetosis arthritica*, is the course of fever which, if not influenced by aspirin, periodically fluctuated between 37 C in the morning and 39 C at night and is accompanied by regular night sweats. Outstanding clinical symptoms are the severe joint involvement, cystitis and conjunctivitis. For 13 weeks the clinical course remained unchanged, his condition was serious, patient being bedfast, debilitated, with decubiti, and completely unable to take care of himself, even needing assistance in eating. The skin was pale and the hemoglobin content was decreased to 60% to 70%. Salvarsan exerted no influence on the course of the illness.

Reiter's professional interests were shared between investigations in the laboratory and applied hygiene in the field. In seeking to preserve and strengthen the health of the people, he applied current biological, medical, and sociological advances in selected areas of Germany, and combined a shrewd evaluation of scientific knowledge with a practical understanding of what was reasonable and attainable. From the laboratory or the clinic he described the entoptic symptoms of digitalis intoxication, otherwise known as the "cornflower phenomenon," identified, named, and studied extensively the (Reiter) strain of the *Treponema pallidum* and developed a specific antigen for it, which led to his protein complement-fixation test for syphilis. Reiter's better-known monograph concerned vaccine diagnosis and vaccine treatment. He was honored with the Gold Doctoral Diploma of the University of Leipzig, the Robert Koch medal, the Great Medal of Honor of the Red Cross, and affiliate membership in the Royal Society of London.

1. Wiedel, P.: Biographical Sketch, Sixtieth Birthday (Ger), *Münch Med Wschr* 88:226-227, 1941.
2. Hübener, and Reiter, H., Etiology of Weil's Disease (Ger), *Deutsch Med Wschr* 42:131-133, 1916, excerpt translated by Z. Danilevicius.
3. Reiter, H.: A Previously Unknown Spirochetal Infection (Spirochetal Arthritis) (Ger), *Deutsch Med Wschr* 42: 1535-1536, 1916, excerpt translated by Z. Danilevicius.

John Gorrie (1803-1855)

THE DEVICES OF JOHN GORRIE, physician of Apalachicola, Florida, for ice making and cooling of air in the sickroom issued from his search for a means of reducing the incidence of malaria and yellow fever. Gorrie accepted the prevailing belief of his time that contagions were related to the miasma from swamps and low lands, and if air could be purified and cooled, the result would be salutary.

Little is known of Gorrie's youth and preparatory education beyond the fact that he was born and educated in Charleston, South Carolina, and, that after two years of study, he graduated MD in 1827 from the College of

Physicians and Surgeons of the Western District of the State of New York in Fairfield, a predecessor of the Buffalo Medical College. Significant voids in the biographical data of

Composite by G. Bako

Gorrie were partially corrected in 1897 by George H. Whiteside, of the Southern Ice Exchange,[1] and by Ruth Eugenie Mier, in a thesis for the degree of master of arts in 1938.[2] The record relates that Gorrie settled in the river town of Apalachicola, which soon became one of the principal ports on the Gulf of Mexico for shipping of cotton, but whose aquatic environment harbored malaria and yellow fever. While engaged in the practice of medicine, Gorrie held several civil offices as an outstanding physician-citizen-entrepreneur of the frontier community. Elective or appointed offices included membership on the City Council, postmaster, city treasurer, and intendant (mayor). His business ventures included an interest in a bank, real estate holdings, and part ownership in a company founded to manufacture his ice-making machine.

Gorrie's attack on malaria, almost 50 years before the mosquito was recognized as the parasitic vector, was premised on the belief that stagnant water from the marshes and decaying matter from the lowlands contributed to the baneful effect of the miasma. He urged that low places in the city be filled with rock or sand or be drained, and that the fever of the afflicted be soothed by cooled air. His cooling device was based upon the existing knowledge of air currents, the availability of natural ice, and floor and ceiling conduits for circulation. It was designed in the early 1840's and shortly after was cooling two rooms that had been set aside for the care of the sick in his home. However, not until 1855 was the apparatus described in a medical publication.[3]

Ice has three properties which eminently fit it for the purpose of refrigerative ventilation, viz.: it maintains a permanently low temperature, it is an energetic absorber of heat, and in the process of solution it renders a large portion of heat latent. As a means of producing change of temperature it is rendered by these properties quite as effective a motive power in causing an ingress of air, and hence a ventilation in a limited space, as a body heated as much above as it may be below the surrounding medium. Every particle introduced into a room of higher temperature than itself, acts as a cause of ventilation and refrigeration, more or less efficient, according as the difference of temperature between it and the general atmosphere is greater or less, or the position it occupies conforms with an advantageous use of the laws of nature brought into requisition. The absorbtion [sic] of heat from the air with which it comes in contact, condenses it and tends to form a vacuum which must be filled from the surrounding atmosphere. If placed in an elevated part of a room the increase of specific gravity which the absorption of heat, and consequent condensation imparts to the air, must cause it to descend; and if provision be made for the escape of this air at its lowest point of descent, a constant circulation of it may be maintained.

My whole process consists in, first, suspending an ornamental mantle vase, urn or basin, in which the ice is placed, by chains, like a lamp or chandelier, from the centre of, and close to the ceiling of a room. Next, over this vessel an opening is made in the ceiling from which a pipe is extended, between the ceiling and the floor above, to the chimney of the house. It is made to enter the chimney for an important auxiliary purpose, which will be presently explained; and through it and the pipe, instead of the doors and windows, all the air, as far as possible, required for respiration or the combustion of lights, ought to be received. As a free and unimpeded current of air must be allowed to pass through the room, so as to maintain thorough ventilation, and prevent the pernicious effects of the foetid exhalations arising from the human body and combustion, there must be, third, a similar but shorter pipe, with a self-acting adjustable valve, communicating with the interior of the room, on a level with its floor and the open air.

In such an arrangement, the external and fresh air is attracted through the first mentioned pipe to the upper part of the room, in consequence of the partial vacuum formed around the ice; and thence, after being cooled, it is dismissed in a diffused shower, like a cataract, to the floor, to be discharged by the lower pipe.

Since the air cooling principle depended upon natural ice, which was not always available in the summer, Gorrie set about to correct the deficiency by an ice making machine. The evidence is not thoroughly documented, but biographers Whiteside and Mier accept as highly probable his ability to make artificial ice by 1850. At least he applied for his first patent in 1849 and, finally, in 1851 was issued patent No. 8080. The description of the machine, based upon known physical principles of heat exchange, which accompanied the drawing of an ice machine, states that:[4]

It is a well-known law of nature that the condensation of air by compression is accompanied by the development of heat, while the absorption of heat from surrounding bodies, or the manifestation of the sensible effect, commonly called "cold," uniformly attends the expansion of air, and this is particularly marked when it is liberated from compression.

The nature of my invention consists in taking advantage of this law to convert water into ice artificially by absorbing its heat of liquefaction with expanding air. To obtain this effect in the most advantageous manner it is necessary to compress atmospheric air into a reservoir by means of a force-pump to one-eighth, one-tenth, or other convenient and suitable proportion of its ordinary volume. The power thus consumed in condensing the air is, to a considerable extent, recovered at the same time that the desired frigorific effect is produced by allowing the air to act with its expansive force upon the piston of an engine, which, by a connection with a beam or other contrivance common to both, helps to work the condensing-pump. This engine is constructed and arranged in the manner of a high-pressure steam-engine having cut-offs and working the steam expansively. When the air, cooled by its expansion, escapes from the engine, it is made to pass round a vessel containing the water to be converted into ice, or through a pipe for effecting refrigeration otherwise, the air while expanding in the engine being supplied with an uncongealable liquid whose heat it will absorb and which can in turn be used to absorb heat from water to be congealed. By this arrangement I accomplish my object with the least possible expenditure of mechanical force, and produce artificial refrigeration in greater quantity from atmospheric air than can be done by any known means.

Gorrie did not live to witness the general application either of his recommendation for the cooling of rooms or the manufacture of his ice making machine. Decades were to elapse before artificial ice was conveniently available, and almost a century passed before air conditioning became practical for hospital sickrooms, factories, offices, homes—wherever man lived and worked in temperate or tropical climate according to current standards of Western living. Honors to Gorrie were equally slow. In Apalachicola, in 1899, a monument was erected to Gorrie by the Southern Ice Exchange. The state of Florida dedicated his statue in Statuary Hall, Washington, DC, in 1914. Two public schools in Tampa and Jacksonville now carry his name, and the Gorrie Bridge dedicated in 1935 spans the Apalachicola River and Bay on Florida's Gulf Coast Highway.

1. Whiteside, G. H.: Dr. John Gorrie; *Ice and Refrig* 12:351-357, 1897.
2. Mier, R. E.: *John Gorrie, Florida Medical Pioneer and Harbinger of Air Conditioning*, thesis, John B. Stetson University, Deland, Fla. 1938.
3. Gorrie, G.: On the Nature of Malaria, and Prevention of Its Morbid Agency, *New Orleans Med Surg J* 11:616-634, 750-769, 1855.
4. J. Gorrie, Ice Machine, Patent No. 8080, US Dept of Commerce, May 6, 1851.

Florence Nightingale (1820-1910)

FLORENCE NIGHTINGALE is best remembered for her successful efforts to establish a nursing service for the British army during the Crimean War. However, other engagements in public welfare that were strengthened by her imaginative mind and persistent determination, although less well known, do not suffer in comparison. She was named for the city of her birth, Florence, Italy, where her parents had gone on one of their periodic visits to the Continent. Florence received her elementary schooling in the usual fundamental subjects, concentrating on the classics, from her father, a country gentleman of wealth and culture from Lea Hall, Derbyshire.[1] As a young girl she displayed an unusual interest in the sick and was accustomed to visit hospitals in her immediate environs as well as in London. Nursing then was a menial occupation, a haven for female drunkards and women of the street. It was not considered a suitable calling for an educated lady in high social standing.

Countway Medical Library, Boston

There were few training schools for nurses as we understand them today in operation on the Continent; England was even less well off. The continental schools usually were under the control and supervision of religious orders, Catholic or Protestant. Hence, in 1850, when Miss Nightingale sought training in nursing, she chose the best prospect in her judgment, the Institute of Protestant Deaconesses at Kaiserswerth, below Düsseldorf on the Rhine. Knowledge of the administration and operation of the training school program was as important to Miss Nightingale as the need for personal practical nursing experience. She remained in Kaiserswerth for an extensive tour of training and returned to England two years before the outbreak of the Crimean War. In 1853, Miss Nightingale was appointed superintendent of the Hospital for Invalid Gentlewomen in London.

The initial engagements in the Crimea exposed the deplorable lack of suitable food, hygiene, and sanitation in the British Army on the battlefield, as well as the neglect of the wounded and inadequate nursing of the sick.

The need for radical reform was self-evident, and Florence Nightingale, through her friendship with Sidney Herbert, secretary of war in London, was called upon for help in an area where she was best qualified to give it. Under her direction, a small group of nurses was recruited and proceeded to Turkey; the staff assembled consisted of representatives from the Roman Catholic Church, Sisters of Mercy of the Church of England, and nurses from St. John's Institute and several London hospitals.

The barracks hospital at Scutari, a makeshift structure grossly inadequate, infected, and filthy, was her assignment in the Crimea. It lacked a kitchen, plumbing, central heating, utensils, garments for the patients, soap, or towels. Most of the food was spoiled. One pint of water per patient was allotted for drinking and washing. Within a few months, Miss Nightingale and her associates transformed the barracks into a military hospital with clean wards, a laundry, a suitable kitchen, reading and recreation rooms, and a banking service for the soldiers to send money home. She established an enviable pattern in overcoming ancient regulations and substituted efficient administration and effectual nursing care. A phenomenal decrease in mortality followed. Although she remained in the theater of operation for more than two years and finally returned to England reluctantly, the transformation in the hospitals and nursing care of the wounded was accomplished rapidly through her expressed authority and demonstrated efficiency.

Upon her return, Miss Nightingale added the training of civilian nurses to her interests. The Nightingale School and Home for Nurses was established at St. Thomas' Hospital with monies provided by friends. The training school was planned to be a home as well as a training center. Suitable rooms were provided for the pupil nurses. The superintendent kept individual records on punctuality, personality, neatness, and ward management. Appropriate instruction was given by the resident medical staff and the visiting physicians. The training school at St. Thomas' not only served as a model for other schools, but its graduates also became heads of other schools in England and the United States. Miss Nightingale advocated the recording of vital statistics in the hospital, including admissions, discharges, and incidence of diseases and deaths.[2]

Turning her attention from the training school to the War Department, Florence Nightingale urged the establishment of an army medical school and reorganization of the medical department. Other recommendations included sanitary facilities in the barracks, a statistical department in headquarters, radical revision of the hospital regulations, and the graded promotion of the medical officers. She procured supporting background data for the undersecretary of war who, in turn, was successful in implementing the recommendations, even though it added substantially to the budget for defense.

Miss Nightingale was a prolific letter writer and composed several books and pamphlets on diverse subjects such as sanitation in India, the causes of famine, and the correction of indigency. Some communications were privately printed at her expense; others were published and enjoyed several editions and translations into foreign languages.[3] Her most famous monograph, *Notes on Nursing, What It Is and What It Is Not*, was published in 1859. The introductory paragraph states her philosophy of nursing.[4]

Shall we begin by taking it as a general principle— that all disease, at some period or other of its course, is more or less a reparative process, not necessarily accompanied with suffering: an effort of nature to remedy a process of poisoning or of decay, which has taken place weeks, months, sometimes years beforehand, unnoticed, the termination of the disease being then, while the antecedent process was going on, determined?

In watching diseases, both in private houses and in public hospitals, the thing which strikes the experienced observer most forcibly is this, that the symptoms or the sufferings generally considered to be inevitable and incident to the disease are very often not symptoms of the disease at all, but of something quite different—of the want of fresh air, or of light, or of warmth, or of quiet, or of cleanliness, or of punctuality and care in the administration of diet, of each or of all of these. And this quite as much in private as in hospital nursing.

The chapter, "Observation of the Sick," emphasizes the importance of this characteristic in the humanistic point of view.[4]

The most important practical lesson that can be given to nurses is to teach them what to observe— how to observe—what symptoms indicate improvement—what the reverse—which are of importance—

which are of none—which are the evidence of neglect—and of what kind of neglect.

All this is what ought to make part, and an essential part, of the training of every nurse. At present how few there are, either professional or unprofessional, who really know at all whether any sick person they may be with is better or worse.

Florence Nightingale spoke several languages, was fluent on philosophical questions, and at times betrayed evidence of being a mystic. Her allegiance to the Church of England began to subside as she became more closely associated with the Roman Catholic Church. Although she did not support the suffrage movement, she favored the emancipation of women. She never married, although she had several suitors. Miss Nightingale was the first woman to receive the Order of Merit and continually attempted to teach ladies to be nurses and nurses to be ladies, strong of character but gentle and kind to the sick. However, in her own affairs she was not always an exemplar of her profession. There were periods of depression, bitterness, and remorse in the early days of service; whereas later she was dogmatic and even ruthless, if need be, to gain an end.

The following letter, sent as a regret for not being able to attend the anniversary of the battle of Balaclava, is profoundly philosophical and expresses her thoughts on war and death.[3]

10, South Street,
Park Lane, W.
October 4th.

Dear Sir:

Though I am not able to be with you in presence, at your annual commemoration, yet my heart and soul are with you. How pleased I am, though ill, to be able to write a few lines to you. I thank you with all my heart for your kind thoughts to me. I wish I could say, as we thought a few days ago we might have said, that there would be peace. But still, as was once written about the advantages of persecution, we may write about the advantages of war, yet few men, and perhaps no women, have seen as much as I have of the horrors of war. But see those manly fellows in time of war, men not near the beasts, as sometimes we too sadly see in times of peace; see them not one taking a drop too much; not one gallivanting with the women; every one devoting, aye, even his life for his comrade, fetching his comrade off the field, without notice of praise from anyone, either in words or in print; and if killed in the attempt his name only goes down as "Killed in Battle"; always devoted, even to the death, as our Great Master and Friend, Jesus Christ was to His fellow men. Of, if such he was, we will not say, "Death

comes not untimely to him who is fit to die. The briefer life, the earlier immortality!" And who would keep him back? Not even his wife. My friends, survivors of Balaclava, I pledge you in this cup, not all of grief, but of living life, worth, perhaps, all the downy chairs we know of. Those who are gone are with us still, working with us for the good and right and the happiness of our fellow men.

Pray believe me, ever your faithful friend,

Florence Nightingale

To Mr. H. Herbert, President of the Balaclava Society (1899).

1. Woodham-Smith, C.: *Florence Nightingale, 1820-1910*, New York: McGraw-Hill Book Company, Inc., 1951.
2. Nightingale, F.: *Notes on Hospitals*, 3rd ed, London: Longman, Green, Longman, Roberts, and Green, 1863.
3. Bishop, W. J., and Goldie, S.: *A Bio-Bibliography of Florence Nightingale*, London: Dawsons of Pall Mall, 1962.
4. Nightingale, F.: *Notes on Nursing, What It Is and What It Is Not*, New York and London: D. Appleton and Company, 1929.

National Library of Medicine

William A. Hammond
(1828-1900)

THE STRUGGLE AGAINST MILITARY INTRIGUE by a versatile physician with a brilliant mind is amply documented in the professional life of Brig Gen William A. Hammond, Surgeon General of the United States Army. Hammond was born at Annapolis, Maryland, the son of a physician; he received his early education at Harrisburg, Pennsylvania, began the study of medicine at the age of 16, and graduated from the medical department of the University of the City of New York at the age of 20.[1] He worked for a year in the Pennsylvania Hospital, Philadelphia, and then qualified as an assistant surgeon in the United States Army. During the first tour of army duty, he served in various posts over the country, engaged in several campaigns against the Indians, but found sufficient time for the cultivation of academic friendships and the pursuit of botanical and physiological investigations. In a metabolic experiment the basis of one study, he served as both experimental subject and responsible investigator. The data were incorporated in a report in 1857, entitled "Experimental Researches Relative to the Nutritive Value and Physiological Effects of Albumen, Starch, and Gum When Singly and Exclusively Used as Foods," judged the prize essay of the American Medical Association for that year.

In 1860, Hammond resigned from the army and joined the faculty at the University of Maryland as professor of anatomy and physiology. When the outbreak of the war between the states interrupted this assignment shortly after, he returned to military service. His previous experience and broad scope of civilian and military medical knowledge set him apart as one destined for rapid promotion over those with longer experience but less competent. He organized and directed the Camden Street Hospital in Baltimore for reception and care of the wounded and was appointed medical inspector of camps and hospitals. In the spring of 1862, Hammond was appointed surgeon general of the Army, with the rank of brigadier general under Secretary of War Stanton. During the following months he pressed for an increase in the size of the medical corps, the construction of pavilion-type hospitals, improvement in field hospitalization, rapid evacuation of the wounded, and an orderly system of records and reports.

A proposal for an Army Medical Museum, recently renamed the Armed Forces Institute of Pathology, was initiated by Hammond in a circular dated May 21, 1862.[2]

As it is proposed to establish in Washington, an *Army Medical Museum*, officers are directed diligently to collect, and to forward to the office of the Surgeon General, all specimens of morbid anatomy, surgical or medical, which may be regarded as valuable; together with projectiles and foreign bodies removed, and such other matters as may prove of interest in the study of military medicine or surgery.

These objects should be accompanied by short explanatory notes.

Each specimen in the collection will have appended the name of the medical officer by whom it was prepared.

Two weeks later he directed the medical officers of the regular and volunteer services to forward to the Surgeon General's office topographical, sanitary, medical, and surgical reports for publication in the *Medical and Surgical History of the War of the Rebellion*. Other and more immediate contributions were the provision of a liberal supply of medical texts and journals to the medical corps and the recognition of the need for autonomy in conditions of military hospitals and autonomy in transportation of medical supplies. Later his other recommendations for the establishment of an Army Medical School, a permanent general army hospital in Washington, an ambulance corps, and a military medical laboratory were accepted. In spite of a tremendous day-by-day load of responsibilities in planning an efficient and rapidly-expanding medical department for the Union Army, Hammond found time to prepare *A Treatise on Hygiene with Special Reference to the Military Service*, several manuals for military surgeons, and his *Physiological Memoirs*, a compilation of essays on a variety of physiological and clinical subjects.

In spite of great accomplishments under stress and duress, his self assurance broke into tactless language and at times arrogant and inflexible behavior. He met his match in Secretary of War Stanton, who disapproved of many of his actions and decisions and who ordered an investigation of the Medical Department. Charged with irregularities in procurement of medical supplies, he found his powers as Surgeon General annulled and at a court martial, he was dismissed from the service in 1864. Before final action was taken by the court, an attempt to present his case to President A. Lincoln was rejected.[3] Fifteen years later he was vindicated by the Senate and House of Representatives of the United States and placed on the retired list of the

Army as surgeon general and brigadier general.

The temporary disgrace only slightly affected Hammond's professional and literary achievements. He borrowed money from friends, moved to New York City, and built an enviable reputation as a neurologist. In this capacity he served on the faculty of the College of Physicians and Surgeons of Columbia University, the Bellevue Hospital Medical College, and as professor of diseases of the mind and nervous system in the Medical Department of the University of the City of New York. He also served on the faculty of the University of Vermont School of Medicine for a summer session and helped found the Postgraduate Medical School of New York. Other activities included editorial responsibilities with the *Quarterly Journal of Physiological Medicine and Jurisprudence*, the *New York Medical Journal*, the *Journal of Nervous and Mental Diseases*, and the *Maryland and Virginia Medical Journal*. On his own he prepared treatises on insanity, spiritualism, sleep, wakefulness, and, most important, the first text in the United States on *Diseases of the Nervous System*, relying heavily on the lectures of Charcot.

Hammond was one of the founders of the New York Neurological Society and the American Neurological Society, serving as president of both organizations. He shared with S. Weir Mitchell the distinction of placing neurology in the United States as a proper specialty. He coined the term "athetosis" (from the Greek meaning "without fixed position"), postulating that the region responsible for athetoid movements would be found in the corpus striatum.[4] This assumption was proved correct several years later.

There is slight tremor of both upper extremities, but there is no paralysis of any part of his body. There are, however, involuntary grotesque muscular movements of the fingers and toes of the right side, and these are not those of simple flexion and extension, but of more complicated form. They occur, not only when he is awake, but also when he is asleep, and are only restrained by certain positions, and by extraordinary efforts of the will.

The phenomena indicate the implication of intracranial ganglia, and the upper part of the spinal cord. The analogies of the affection are with chorea and cerebro-spinal sclerosis, but it is clearly neither of these diseases. One probable seat of the morbid process is the corpus striatum.

In 1878, Hammond moved to Washington, opened a private sanitarium for nervous disorders, and continued his writing of novels begun in 1867. Though several were popular at the time, they were inferior to those of O. W. Holmes or S. W. Mitchell. His last, *The Son of Perdition*, a story of the Christ, made no attempt to justify the acts of God although it included Judas, Satan, Herod, Pontius Pilot, Mary Magdalene, Peter, and others as characters.

1. Pilcher, J. E.: The Surgeon Generals of the United States Army, *Milit Surg* 15:145-155, 1904.
2. Circular No. 2, Surgeon General's Office, United States Army, Washington City, 21, May, 1862.
3. Hammond, W. A.: *A Statement of the Causes Which Led to the Dismissal of Surgeon-General William A. Hammond From the Army; With a Review of the Evidence Adduced Before the Court*, New York, 1864.
4. Hammond, W. A.: *A Treatise on Diseases of the Nervous System*, New York: D. Appleton & Co., 1871.

Composite by G. Bako

George Miller Sternberg
(1838-1915)

GEORGE M. STERNBERG, bacteriologist and epidemiologist, of the U. S. Army Medical Corps, was born in Oswego County, New York, the son of a Lutheran minister and principal of the Hartwick Seminary.[1] At the age of 16 he concluded undergraduate education and began teaching school in New Germantown, New Jersey. Three years later he began the study of medicine under Dr. Horace Lathrop of Cooperstown, New York, and in succession attended the Buffalo School of Medicine in upstate New York and the College of Physicians and Surgeons in New York City. Sternberg practiced in Elizabeth City, New Jersey, until May, 1861, when he enlisted in the Federal army. His service in the field was brief, for he was captured at the battle of Bull Run, but he escaped shortly and served throughout the remainder of the war in various capacities in the Medical Corps. Following the war he chose the army as a career, rotated through a number of military posts, engaged in occasional Indian skirmishes, and eventually rose to be surgeon-general, during the Spanish-American War. Although the surgeon-general is charged by decree with the practical logistic problems of hygiene and medical care of troops in the barracks and in the field, Sternberg maintained a deep interest in basic bacteriology and immunonogy and experimental epidemiology.

Among Sternberg's first scientific communications were recommendations for management of the critical epidemics in the field, particularly yellow fever and malaria. For a quarter of a century, he paid particular attention to the pathogenesis and control of the former scourge. He published first on yellow fever poison in 1875. This interest was reaffirmed when he was with the Havana Yellow Fever Commission of the National Board of Health in 1879; consequently, he recommended the appointment of Walter Reed to the pathological laboratory at the Johns Hopkins University Hospital in preparation for his experimental studies on yellow fever in Cuba, and in 1900 organized the Yellow Fever Commission. This last endeavor was soon to implicate the mosquito of the genus *Stegomyia* as the vector in the transmission of the affliction.

Among Sternberg's writings, *A Manual of Bacteriology* appeared in 1892[2] and a monograph *Infection and Immunity*, the following decade.[3] Lesser monographs included *A Treatise on Asiatic Cholera, Sanitary Lessons of the War, Photomicrographs and How to Make Them*, and *Malaria and Malarial Diseases*. In the laboratory he was the first in the United States to photograph the tubercle bacillus and, more important, to identify the pneumococcus (concurrently with Louis Pasteur) as a normal inhabitant of the mouth, but pathogenic for rabbits. In isolating the organism, later named *Micrococcus pasteuri*, Sternberg showed that saliva, when injected into the subcutaneous spaces of a rabbit, produced a fatal septicemia; whereas a similar quantity of blood or urine failed to kill. A description of a capsule of the organism was also presented.[4]

(h) *Successive cultures in which but a small drop is taken each time to inoculate a fresh quantity of bouillon exclude the white and red blood corpuscles* (filtration-experiments have already shown the poison to be particulate) *as possible agents in the production of this virulence, and prove conclusively that the veritable cause is the presence of a micrococcus,* found first in the saliva, then in the serum from the connective tissue, and (usually) in the blood of the animal killed by the injection of saliva, and finally in each successive culture-fluid inoculated (in the first instance) with a small quantity of this serum or blood.

The most striking morphological difference between the micrococcus . . . is the aureole which surrounds the well-defined dark central portion in the latter figure.

While in the Surgeon-General's office, Sternberg supported the program which provided for a corps of female nurses for permanent Army hospitals and sponsored the founding of the Army Medical School. General Order No. 51, Adjutant General's Office, June 24, 1893, provided for a faculty and a course of instruction for four months each year. The first portion stated that:[5]

By direction of the Secretary of War, upon the recommendation of the Surgeon General of the Army, an Army Medical School will be established in the city of Washington for the purpose of instructing approved candidates for admission to the Medical Corps of the Army in their duties as medical officers.

Four professors will be selected from among the senior medical officers of the Army stationed in or near the city of Washington, and as many associate professors as may be required to give practical laboratory instruction in the methods of sanitary analyses, microscopical technique, clinical microscopy, bacteriology, urine analysis, &c.

Sternberg maintained a dedicated working interest in medical societies, especially the American Public Health Association, the Association of American Physicians, and the Association of American Medical Colleges.

He served as president of the American Medical Association, 1897–1898, but the Spanish-American War prevented his delivering the presidential address in person. The following excerpts are indicative of his general concern for the teaching and practice of medicine and are illustrative of trenchant matters then, similar to those three-quarters of a century later.[6]

Our Association, as the representative body of American physicians, will no doubt continue to increase in membership and in influence. The day is perhaps not far distant when no reputable physician will be willing to confess that he does not belong to the American Medical Association and when no progressive physician can afford to do without our JOURNAL. . . . I would not exclude a reputable physician from membership because the State, County or District Medical Society to which he belongs declines to adopt our code of ethics. If he, individually, is willing to be governed by the regulations made by this representative body I see no good reason for rejecting his application for membership.

There are those who still speak of us as "old school physicians," ignorant apparently of the fact that scientific medicine is to a great extent of very recent origin, and that all of the great discoveries in relation to the etiology, prevention and specific treatment of infectious diseases, and nearly all the improved methods and instrumental appliances for clinical diagnosis and surgical treatment have had their origin within the ranks of the regular profession. While, therefore, we still have with us some "old school doctors," who have fallen behind the procession, the profession as a whole has been moving forward with incredible activity upon the substantial basis of scientific research, and if we are to be characterized by any distinctive name, the only one applicable would be "*the new school of scientific medicine.*"

We must not fail to recognize, however, that the progress of knowledge has been so rapid that it is impossible for the busy practitioner to keep pace with it, and that even the requirement now generally adopted by our leading medical schools, for a four years' course of study, is inadequate for the attainment of such a degree of professional knowledge and practical skill in diagnosis and therapeutics as is desirable for one who intends to practice scientific medicine.

1. Sternberg, M. L.: *George Miller Sternberg, A Biography,* Chicago: American Medical Association, 1920.
2. Sternberg, G. M.: *A Manual of Bacteriology,* New York: William Wood & Company, 1892.
3. Sternberg, G. M.: *Infection and Immunity,* New York: G. P. Putnam's Sons, 1903.
4. Sternberg, G. M.: A Fatal Form of Septicaemia in the Rabbit, Produced by the Sub-cutaneous Injection of Human Saliva, *Stud Biol Lab Johns Hopkins Univ* 2:183-200, 1882.
5. General Order Order No. 51, Adjutant General's Office, June 24, 1893.
6. Sternberg, G. M.: The Address of the President, *JAMA* 30:1376-1380, 1898.

Composite by G. Bako

Walter Reed (1851-1902)

WALTER REED, director of the Yellow Fever Commission of the U.S. Army, produced conclusive evidence that the *Stegomyia fasciata*, classified now as *Aedes aegypti*, was the vector in the transmission of this dread disease, which took its toll in military campaigns as well as in civilian life.

Walter was born in Gloucester County, Virginia, the son of an itinerant Methodist minister. The family moved to Charlottesville, Virginia, on one of the pastoral assignments, where for three years the prodigy studied first in a private school, then in the academic department of the University, and finally in the medical department. The degree of doctor of medicine was granted to Reed in 1869 at the age of 17, the youngest graduate in the medical school up to that time. According to Bean,[1] it was less expensive for Reed to be trained in medicine than in the classics, although he showed greater interest in Latin, Greek, literature, and philosophy than in the natural sciences. Following graduation, Reed continued his medical training at Bellevue Hospital Medical College in New York and received the second doctorate of medicine. An internship at King's County Hospital, an appointment as inspector with the Brooklyn Board of Health, and a period of practice occupied the intervening years until he was commissioned first lieutenant, U.S. Army, in 1875. The initial military assignment was a post in Arizona, the only physician for soldiers and civilians in a limitless frontier. Just as his father was a circuit-riding minister, the young army surgeon was responsible for the medical care of the personnel on scattered military posts.

Reed did not mature early scientifically. His first medical communication was published in the *Boston Medical and Surgical Journal* at the age of 41. It discussed the contagiousness of erysipelas. Nor was Reed prolific with the pen; scarcely more than 30 scientific contributions were published before he died a decade later. Most of the manuscripts concerned bacteriology and parasitology, including studies on malaria, cholera, typhoid fever, and yellow fever.

In 1890, Reed was ordered to Baltimore, where William H. Welch, professor of bacteriology and pathology at Johns Hopkins University, accepted him in the laboratory. This permitted exposure to the latest thinking and modern methods of scientific research, at a time when Johns Hopkins was in one of its most productive periods. In 1893, Reed was ordered to duty in the Surgeon General's office in Washington as curator of the Army Medical Museum and professor of bacteriology and clinical microscopy in the newly organized Army Medical School, a postgraduate training unit. The promotion carried with it the title of full surgeon with the rank of major. After the outbreak of the Spanish-American War, he served as chairman of a committee to study the causation and modes of propagation of typhoid fever. Additional evidence was revealed supporting the spread of typhoid fever in camps by the common fly, vectors carrying the contagion to susceptible persons from infected patients, infected bedding, and infected waste.

Reed's last and most significant Army assignment was the delineation of the mode of transmission of yellow fever. This was accomplished by a bold but simple experiment. The observations left no doubt regarding the role of the mosquito in the transmission of yellow fever. Military and civilian persons had suffered badly in Cuba, and in spite of the successful efforts of William Gorgas, health officer of Havana, to clean up the city, the devastation from yellow fever continued. In planning the experiment, he reviewed the unsuccessful attempts of the past and defined the causes for failure.[2] In the 1880's, Carlos Finlay postulated transmission of the disease by the *Stegomyia fasciata*. Seventy-five years before Finlay, S. Ffirth presented an inaugural dissertation to the University of Pennsylvania on the noncontagious nature of yellow fever. His experiments, bloody, foul, and nauseating, disclosed that neither the vomit, bile, sweat, serum, or urine of patients terminally ill with yellow fever was contagious to man or experimental animals. And lastly, the observations of U.S. Marine Hospital surgeon Henry R. Carter, a graduate in engineering of the University of Virginia, proved helpful. Carter had observed that an interval of two or three weeks usually, lapsed between the appearance of the first and subsequent cases attributed to contagion. This corresponded to the latent period of incubation of the virus in the vector.[3]

The yellow fever commission arrived in Cuba early in the summer of 1900. Reed's associates were Drs. James Carroll, bacteriologist; Jessie W. Lazear, entomologist and bacteriologist; and Aristides Agramonte, pathologist, who was immune to yellow fever. Bacteriologic observations on the mortally stricken were studied first. The findings were discouragingly negative. Failing in this phase, the commission concentrated on a search for the vector. The observations of Ffirth were confirmed. The nurses and attendants of the yellow fever victims who came in close contact with fomites did not contract the disease. Through the cooperation of Carlos Finlay, eggs of the *Stegomyia fasciata* were provided for animal experimentation. However, since animals do not contract the disease, this preliminary study, likewise, was fruitless and abandoned in due time. There remained, then, the granting of permission from Governor General Leonard Wood for human studies. After this official act, Carroll exposed himself to the bite of an infected mosquito fed on yellow fever victims and then held captive during the critical incubation period. Carroll contracted yellow fever, the first victim in the study of experimental inoculation.

Account was also taken of the criterion that the mosquito must bite the afflicted and ingest the virus within the first few days of clinical manifestations.[4] Thus, the critical chronology —feeding the mosquito within the first 3 to 5 days of the disease and a minimum incubation period of 12 days in the mosquito—provided the data that extended Finlay's hypothesis to confirmation. Lazear was accidentally bitten not long after and died of yellow fever before the series of planned experiments was begun late in the fall.

The experimental design included the construction of two mosquito-proof buildings, procurement of army volunteers, and mosquitoes bred from the eggs provided by Finlay. Nonimmune volunteers were exposed to the bites of infected mosquitoes. The disease was contracted only by the volunteers who were bitten. The second significant experiment was the rejection of the belief that yellow fever was conveyed by fomites. Again, nonimmune volunteers were used. They slept in a dark and poorly vented mosquito-proof room furnished with soiled bedding and clothing. None became infected. The third and last experimental phase took place in a dwelling divided into halves by a mosquito-proof screen. On one side of the screen, the volunteer was exposed to the mosquito; the other side was mosquito-free. The volunteer, exposed to infected mosquitoes, contracted yellow fever in proper time; the others did not. The epidemiologic studies having provided convincing conclusions, there remained two laboratory aspects for the commission to study.

Yellow fever developed in experimental subjects following the subcutaneous injection of blood taken from patients in the first few days of their illness. Direct transfer showed that the agent was present in the blood and that the mosquito played a role similar to that of the *Anopheles* in the spread of malaria. Carroll studied the nature of the infectious agent in the laboratory by passing serum from yellow fever victims through a Berkefeld

filter. The ultrafiltrable nature of the virus was established.[5]

In view of these data, we believe we are justified in expressing the opinion that the source of infection in Case X must be attributed to the injection of blood drawn from Case VII, . . . and further, that the blood in Case VII contained the specific agent of yellow fever, which had, therefore, passed through the filter along with the filtrate with which this latter individual had been inoculated.

Shortly after the findings of the commission were revealed, Gorgas instituted appropriate measures in Cuba to control the mosquito, and thereby introduced an effective and enduring control of yellow fever. In retrospect, the study was one of the most brilliant in the history of military medicine. The conclusions contributed vitally to the protection of the workers on the Panama Canal and the cities of the United States throughout the South and the Atlantic seaboard, which had been regularly visited by yellow fever epidemics. These conclusions were summarized by Reed in an address before the Pan-American Congress in February, 1901.[6]

CONCLUSIONS.

1. The mosquito—C. fasciatus—serves as the intermediate host for the parasite of yellow fever.

2. Yellow fever is transmitted to the non-immune individual by means of the bite of the mosquito that has previously fed on the blood of those sick with this disease.

3. An interval of about twelve days or more after contamination appears to be necessary before the mosquito is capable of conveying the infection.

4. The bite of the mosquito at an earlier period after contamination does not appear to confer any immunity against a subsequent attack.

5. Yellow fever can also be experimentally produced by the subcutaneous injection of blood taken from the general circulation during the first and second days of this disease.

6. An attack of yellow fever, produced by the bite of the mosquito, confers immunity against the subsequent injection of the blood of an individual suffering from the non-experimental form of this disease.

7. The period of incubation in thirteen cases of experimental yellow fever has varied from forty-one hours to five days and seventeen hours.

8. Yellow fever is not conveyed by formites, and hence disinfection of articles of clothing, bedding, or merchandise, supposedly contaminated by contact with those sick with this disease, is unnecessary.

9. A house may be said to be infected with yellow fever only when there are present within its walls con-

taminated mosquitoes capable of conveying the parasite of this disease.

10. The spread of yellow fever can be most effectually controlled by measures directed to the destruction of mosquitoes and the protection of the sick against the bites of these insects.

Walter Reed lived little more than a year after the completion of the commission's work. He returned to Washington as professor of pathology and bacteriology at both the Army Medical School and Columbia Medical School, now George Washington Medical School. Late in 1902, he was stricken with acute appendicitis. It was not until 48 hours after the onset of clinical symptoms that professional counsel was sought. The abdomen was not explored until the lapse of an additional 48 hours. The periappendiceal abscess did not respond to treatment.[7]

The conclusions of the US Army yellow fever commission under Major Walter Reed had far-reaching effects on the affliction throughout the civilian and military populations of the world.[8] The simplicity of the experimental design is exemplary. The number of studies was small, but the planning, based upon previous knowledge, was critical, and the findings irrefutable. It is appropriate that the memory of the greatest military surgeon of the US Army be perpetuated in the Walter Reed Army Medical Center in Washington.

1. Bean, W. B.: Walter Reed, *Arch Intern Med (Chic)* 89:171-187 (Feb) 1952.

2. Reed, W., et al: Etiology of Yellow Fever: A Preliminary Note, *Philadelphia Med J* 6:790-796 (Oct 27) 1900.

3. Carter, H. R.: A Note on the Interval Between Infecting and Secondary Cases of Yellow Fever from the Records of Yellow Fever at Orwood and Taylor, Mississippi, in 1898, *New Orleans Med Surg J* 52:617-636, 1900.

4. Reed, W.; Carroll, J.; and Agramonte, A.: Experimental Yellow Fever, *Trans Ass Amer Physicians* 16:45-71, 1901.

5. Reed, W., and Carroll, J.: Etiology of Yellow Fever: Supplemental Note, *Amer Med* 3:301-305 (Feb 22) 1902.

6. Reed, W.; Carroll, J.; and Agramonte, A.: Etiology of Yellow Fever: An Additional Note, *JAMA* 36:431-440 (Feb 16) 1901.

7. White, C. S.: The Last Illness of Major Walter Reed, *Med Ann DC* 24:396-398 (Aug) 1955.

8. Kelly, H. A.: *Walter Reed and Yellow Fever,* New York City: McClure, Phillips & Co., 1906.

Composite by G. Bako

William Crawford Gorgas
(1854-1920)

THE BEST TRADITION OF APPLIED MEDICAL SCIENCE was exemplified by William Crawford Gorgas in his use of knowledge of the control of vector-borne disease during construction of the Panama Canal. Although yellow fever and malaria were the principal hazards, the general planning for the control of the tropical environment for the workmen was an epitome of excellence. Gorgas, born into the army, was the son of Maj Josiah Gorgas, who was assigned to the ordnance service in command of Mt. Vernon Arsenal near Mobile, Alabama; his mother was the daughter of a one-time governor of that state.[1] The elder Gorgas resigned his commission with the federal forces before the attack on Fort Sumter and served in the Confederate Army as chief of ordnance, rising to the grade of brigadier general. Young Gorgas sought an appointment to the United States Military Academy at West Point; failing, he entered the service through the medical department. He attended Bellevue Hospital Medical College, graduated in 1879, served an internship in Bellevue Hospital, and in 1880 was appointed assistant surgeon in the medical corps.

The first 20 years of Gorgas' service was the usual life of an army surgeon. Tours of duty included various forts in Texas, one in North Dakota, and an extended assignment at Fort Barrancas, Florida. While stationed at Fort Brown, Texas, he contracted a mild case of yellow fever and thereby acquired immunity to the disease. From Fort Barrancas he was transferred to the yellow fever camp at Sibony, near Havana. During the Spanish-American War, he was appointed chief sanitary officer in Havana under Gen Leonard Wood, military governor of Cuba. At that time yellow fever was epidemic among the natives, as well as among the American occupation forces.

Before the Walter Reed experiment, Gorgas was not convinced that yellow fever was a mosquito-borne disease as suggested by Carlos Finlay; rather, he attributed it to filth and environmental corruption and set about to cleanse the city. The sanitary measures were ineffective and the epidemic was not suppressed until the Yellow Fever Board furnished proof that the *Stegomyia* mosquito (*Aedes aegypti*) was the carrier, which led to destruction of the breeding places of the mosquito and isolation of the infected patients. Rigid enforcement of two critical measures resulted in a decrease in mortality from yellow fever in Havana from approximately 1,300 deaths in 1896 to fewer than 20 deaths in 1901.[2] The procedures were described as follows:[3]

These two methods of destroying yellow fever mosquitoes, namely, that of killing the grown mosquito in the neighborhood of every yellow-fever patient with a smudge and of looking after the wigglers in all rain-water deposits about the house, were steadily enforced during the year 1901. The results were better than we had dared to hope. Few cases occurred in which yellow fever spread from a case cared for in this way. Yellow fever rapidly decreased, and on September 28, 1901, the last case of yellow fever occurred in Habana, and since that time—now more than two years—not a single new case has developed in the City.

I think it is evident that the disappearance of yellow fever from Habana was due solely to this mosquito work. Remember that it was an every-day disease in Habana, and had been so for more than a hundred years.

In Habana, even now, a case or two of yellow fever comes in every month from Mexico and other infected regions which have a considerable trade with Habana. The ships are carefully inspected by the quarantine authorities, just as is done in our country.

If a person sick of yellow fever, or suspected yellow fever, is discovered, he is landed at the city wharf, in the heart of the business district, placed in an ambulance, carried to the yellow fever hospital, which is well within the city limits, and treated there. The only precaution taken is to see that Habana mosquitoes do not get an opportunity to bite him. The authorities at Habana thoroughly believe that if they can prevent mosquitoes from biting a yellow fever patient, the city will be entirely safe in handling him and taking care of him.

So successful was Gorgas in Cuba that he seemed the logical sanitarian to plan the epidemiologic ecology of the workers to be assigned shortly to the construction of the canal through the Isthmus of Panama. The French, beginning in 1880 under de Lesseps, had eventually admitted defeat on the Atlantic side of the Isthmus, due more to morbidity and mortality from disease than to any other single factor. In some months several hundred workers died. In retrospect, after his worst trials were over, Gorgas noted that:[4]

Our Army in Cuba during the Santiago campaign had during the last two months of our stay there a constant sick rate of over six hundred per thousand. Undoubtedly, the French rate approximated this during their period of active work [in Panama], and we can safely calculate that their constant sick rate was at least three hundred and thirty-three per thousand, or one-third their force.

Gorgas was transferred from Havana to Washington in 1902, visited the Suez Canal and the Isthmus of Panama, and, on the basis of his experience in Cuba, advanced his bold plan.[5]

The records of the French hospitals showed that they suffered from most of the diseases to which man is heir. But their excessive mortality was caused by yellow fever and malaria, but principally from malaria. While my plan contemplates a sanitary organization a good deal such as resulted so successful at Havana, it will, of course, have to be modified to some extent to meet the changed conditions at Panama. I would propose the ordinary health organization for the care of infectious and contagious diseases, such as we have in New York, or any other American city, and I think that there is no doubt that such diseases can be controlled as they are in New York or elsewhere. I feel confident of being able to eliminate yellow fever by the same methods that were so successfully adopted in Havana. But malaria, in my opinion, is the disease on which the success of our sanitary measures at Panama will depend. If we can control malaria, I feel very little anxiety about other diseases. If we do not control malaria our mortality is going to be heavy.

When construction was started by the United States in 1904, and for more than a year after, his advice for sanitary measures was ignored. Following an outbreak of yellow fever and through the intervention of President Theodore Roosevelt, Gorgas was elevated from chief sanitary officer to a member of the Panama Canal Commission, with full authority to enforce his sanitary regulations. Breeding places for mosquitoes were eliminated or controlled, cases of yellow fever segregated, and within six months yellow fever was on the wane. But administrative difficulties arose a second time; Goethals, becoming chief engineer in 1908, and contemptuous of Gorgas, transferred the medical department to the quartermaster corps. However, the sanitary measures were maintained; yellow fever did not return, and malaria was kept under control through the draining of swamps and the spreading of oil over the breeding places of mosquitoes.[6]

I am inclined to think that the advances made in recent years in tropical sanitation will have a much wider and more far-reaching effect than freeing Havana of yellow fever or enabling us to build the Panama Canal. I think the sanitarian can now show that any population coming into the tropics can protect itself against these two diseases by measures that are both simple and inexpensive; that with these two diseases eliminated, life in the tropics for the Anglo-Saxon will be more healthful than in the temperate zones; that gradually, within the next two or three centuries, tropical countries, which offer a much greater return for man's labor than do the temperate zones, will be settled up by the white races, and that again the centers of wealth, civilization and population will be in the tropics, as they were in the dawn of man's history, rather than in the temperate zones, as at present.

Before the canal was finished, the brilliant planning and execution of the control of contagious diseases and the sanitation and housing of the workers and families in hazardous areas had made Gorgas' name known to many throughout the world. In addition, the death rate in Panama from all diseases compared favorably with that of most American communities. In 1914, he was appointed Surgeon-General of the Army, with the rank of brigadier general. In the following year he was advanced to the grade of major general. Gorgas was responsible for the tremendous expansion of the medical corps during World War I, from a few hundred regular army officers to over 30,000 on active duty. He retired from the service at the statutory age, only a few weeks before the Armistice. Georgas served as president of the American Medical Association in 1908 and was the recipient of much kudos, including honorary degrees from the universities of Harvard, Brown, Pennsylvania, Johns Hopkins, and the University of the South. He was invited to inspect the Transvaal mines in South Africa and to make recommendations for the control of pneumonia among the workers, was advisor to the International Health Board of the newly-founded Rockefeller Foundation, and visited Central and South American countries, advising on the control of yellow fever. He was knighted by the King of England while on his deathbed in the Queen Alexandria Military Hospital, London. Fueral services were held in St. Paul's Cathedral.

In Panama City, the Gorgas Memorial Laboratory carries on his work as a living memorial. The laboratory was established in 1929 as the research unit of the Gorgas Memorial Institute of Tropical and Preventive Medicine, Inc. In 1963, a new research building was completed to provide additional facilities for the departments of bacteriology, parasitology, pathology, and vertebrate zoology.

1. Gibson, J. M.: *Physician to the World, the Life of General William C. Gorgas*, Durham, NC: Duke University Press, 1950.

2. Gorgas, W. C.: Mosquito Work in Havana, *Med Rec*, July 19, 1902.

3. Gorgas, W. C.: *A Few General Directions with Regard to Destroying Mosquitoes, Particularly the Yellow Fever Mosquito*, Washington, DC, Government Printing Office, 1904.

4. Gorgas, W. C.: *Sanitation in Panama*, New York and London: D. Appleton and Company, 1915.

5. Gorgas, W. C.: Report on the Isthmian Canal, *Engineer Rec*, New York, May 25, 1904.

6. Gorgas, W. C.: Sanitation in the Canal Zone, *JAMA* 49:6-8 (July 6) 1907.

Composite by G. Bako

Ferdinand Julius Cohn
(1828-1898)

FERDINAND COHN'S scientific accomplishments were closely interwoven with those of Louis Pasteur in the exposure of the fallacy of spontaneous generation and with those of Robert Koch in whose presence the anthrax bacillus was demonstrated. Cohn was born in Breslau and was educated at the University of Breslau. Because he was a Jew he was denied a higher degree and was compelled to finish his training at the more liberal University of Berlin, from which he graduated in 1849, presenting a thesis in Latin. He returned to Breslau, worked in the Physiological Institute under Purkyně, and was appointed professor of botany in 1859. He dreamed of an institute for plant physiology but he experienced great obstacles and the dream was not realized until many years later at approximately the same time he founded the *Beitrage Zur Biologie der Pflanzen.* Meanwhile he pursued his investigations on classification of bacteria and fungi and advanced concepts which are as modern today as a current textbook on the subject. He described the life cycle of several genera of algae and recognized early in the 1870's six genera of bacteria; *Micrococcus, Bacterium, Bacillus,*

Vibrio, Spirillum and *Spirochaete.* He identified the spores of *bacillus subtilis* and defended the theory of the unity of different genera of bacteria. Their identification as a living bridge between plants and animals constituted the first major stride in establishing bacteriology as a scientific discipline. Viruses were suspected but cultural methods and the electron microscope were not yet available to confirm their existence.

As a cryptogamic botanist, Cohn summarized his thoughts in an extensive treatise on bacteria published in 1872 before Koch had demonstrated the life history of the anthrax bacillus and before Pasteur discovered the staphylococcus pyogenes in boils and the streptococcus in puerperal septicemia, early events in the history of modern bacteriology. Excerpts from his 1873 treatise on bacteria in which he discusses epidemics, infectious origin of disease, and the flow of bacteria from outer space to the earth and vice versa are given:[2]

At last, in the most recent times, an unexpected knowledge of the secret life energies of bacteria has been revealed, through which they rule with demoniacal power over the weal and woe, and even over the life and death of man.

Probably with the increase of commerce the visitation of that scourge of God, the epidemic, has grown more frequent, in the last ten years, on man and animals. . . . Only too often the physician's skill and knowledge are exercised in vain to wrest the victim from the devastating power of these diseases, or to limit their course by rules of precaution. As various as are the different forms of disease, yet all epidemics, cholera, pestilence, typhus, diphtheria, variola, scarletina, hospital gangrene, epizootic, and the like, have certain features in common. These diseases originate nowhere of themselves, neither from internal nor external causes, but are introduced from another place where they have been prevalent, by means of a diseased person or through material which has been in contact with such: they spread only through contagion. . . . After a certain time of incubation, the disease breaks out through a powerful disturbance of the normal action of all the organs, from the brain to the digestive system; the diseased person appears as if he were under the influence of a poison which had penetrated into his blood; and as he himself is infected by the virus, he spreads it further by the breath, by the perspiration, by the excretions, even in the clothing or the washing.

All these facts make it in the highest degree probable that the already identified bacteria are in many diseases the conveyors and originators of infection, that they are the ferment of contagion. We have the firm conviction that to a more thorough and clearer knowledge of these facts will be joined the discovery of new methods by which to encounter the fearful enemy with better success than hitherto.

The development history of the bacteria allows us to think of another origin of life on the earth. We have calculated the weight of one bacterium at 0.000,000,-001,57 milligrammes; we know that these infinitely light little bodies are carried away through the evaporation of water, and float around in the air as little particles of sun dust, and with the dust again settle down; but they may be carried by the winds to unmeasurable distances, and also to extraordinary heights. It is more probable that these particles of fine dust are sometimes carried up by ascending currents of air, so far that they are deprived of the attraction of our planet, and reach space. . . . It is perhaps not impossible that an ascending particle of bacteria dust, which has floated for a long time in space, may reach the atmosphere of another world, and if it find there circumstances favorable to life, it multiplies. On the other hand, it is possible to think that a germ of *Bacterium*, or any other exceedingly small and simple form, from some other life-nourishing world, may have been moving about in space, and that such a germ, finally reaching our atmosphere, settled to the earth.

1. Kionka, H.: Ferdinand Cohn (Ger), *Deutsch Med Wschr* 24:482-483, 1898.

2. Cohn, F.: *Bacteria, the Smallest of Living Organisms* (Ger), Berlin: Lüder, 1872, translated by C. S. Dolley, Rochester, N. Y., 1881.

and muscles. Probably he is best remembered for the eponymic maladies, Duchenne's paralysis—bulbar or labiolingual paralysis—and spinal progressive muscular atrophy of Aran-Duchenne.[1]

Composite by G. Bako

G.-B.-A. Duchenne (1806-1875)

GUILLAUME-BENJAMIN-AMAND DUCHENNE, a distinguished member of the French school of medicine during its glorious days of the mid-19th century, never was honored with a hospital appointment nor occupied a professorial chair. Yet, he was an untiring student of clinical neurology and was recognized as one of the outstanding teachers in Paris. His father, a seafarer of Boulogne, had hoped that his son would follow this calling. However, the medical faculty in Paris composed of Bichat, Laennec, Louis, Magendie, Bernard, Dupuytren, and Cruveilhier had greater appeal, and Duchenne went to Paris, where he graduated from the medical school in 1831. His inaugural dissertation concerned burns. This was his last discussion of a surgical subject; the remainder of his life was dedicated to the practice of medicine and to the meticulous study of disorders associated with nerves

His accomplishments as a student were unimpressive. He was not marked as a brilliant member of the class and was not urged to stay on as an assistant following graduation. Rather, he returned to Boulogne and practiced for more than a decade among the fishermen and other seafarers. The death of his wife from puerperal infection, an unhappy remarriage, and a desire to pursue clinical research culminated in his return to Paris.[2] During an electropuncture on one of his patients with peripheral neuritis, the contraction of a single muscle fiber was observed. This led him to consult the meager literature sources in Boulogne on electricity and to built a machine for electrical stimulation of nerves and muscle. The concept of "localized electrisation" resulted. Thus, Duchenne came to Paris with a homemade Faradic induction coil and batteries to extend his observations to as many patients as the hospital of that great city provided.

Duchenne was avid for knowledge provided by the careful study and "localized electrisation" of patient after patient among the indigent. It is logical to assume that the recording of a meticulous history and the detailed physical examination, with its subsequent fruitful results, served as a fine example to the students who followed in his steps. It was not unusual for him to document the natural history of disease by following a patient from hospital to hospital. The failure to obtain a hospital assignment did not dampen his enthusiasm. He was physician-at-large throughout Paris. Certain advantages in such an unorthodox career were counterbalanced by the failure to control or supervise the postmortem examination of the patients whom he had followed. Furthermore, the jesting of the young physicians in the hospitals, similar to that of contemporary interns, as well as the coolness of the physicians-in-chief who accepted him with a patronizing air, did not hamper the enthusiasm of the neurologist who haunted the Parisian hospitals day after day. Ridicule and satire bothered him not at all. His alter ego, Trousseau, spoke on his behalf when necessary. Other outstanding men of medicine who have been thwarted in the desire for a specific hospital or academic appointment include Sir Charles Bell, Ignaz Semmelweis, and Jan Purkyně.

Ultimately, Duchenne became highly regarded as a clinical neurologist. His services were sought as a consultant, and his private practice was rewarding. In rebuttal to von Heine,[3] who described infantile paralysis as a spinal lesion and asserted that it should be regarded as atrophic myasthenia from inactivity, Duchenne was convinced that as profound a malady as infantile paralysis should be associated with a specific lesion, probably in the anterior horn cells of the spinal cord.

The new Sydenham Society of London translated, edited, and condensed his contributions on spinal progressive muscular atrophy in 1883:[4]

Progressive muscular atrophy attacks the upper limb, and destroys its muscles in an irregular fashion. It begins in such cases by attacking one after another the muscles of the thenar eminence, spreading from the superficial to the deep layer. As the abductor pollicis is wasted, its absence is marked by a depression, and by the attitude, during repose, of the first metacarpal bone, which lies too close to the second. . . . Depressions of the hypothenar eminence and interosscal

spaces next announce the atrophy of the muscles of those regions. The loss of the interossei muscles is shown by the clawlike attitude of the fingers during the extension of the hand.

The flexors of the elbow and the deltoid are the first to atrophy. . . . The triceps extensor cubiti is the last of the muscles of the upper limb to become affected. . . . The atrophy equally invades the lower limbs, but only when the muscles of the upper limbs and trunk are in great part destroyed.

The application of artificial respiration by faradization of the phrenic nerve to a patient who had attempted to asphyxiate himself was described:

I was about to excite artificial respiration through the phrenic nerves, when I saw that the rheophores had been forgotten. The danger being very urgent, I instantly applied the metallic extremity of one of the conductors of the induced current of my instrument (at its maximum, and with rapid intermissions) over the left nipple, and moved the other conductor about over the apex of the heart. After a few seconds, slow and weak respiratory movements appeared, and increased progressively in frequency and depth.

Duchenne died in Paris—a lonely man and scarcely appreciated by the profession, even though he towered above his contemporaries. Twenty years elapsed before a monument was erected to his memory in Salpêtrière, and he was given a proper accolade as one of the great clinical neurologists of France, sharing such an honor with Charcot and Marie.

1. Collins, J.: Duchenne of Boulogne, Med Rec 73:50-54 (Jan 11) 1908.
2. Bailey, P.: Personal communication.
3. Robinson, V.: "Guillaume-Benjamin-Amand Duchenne," in Pathfinders in Medicine, New York: Medical Life Press, 1929, pp 555-577.
4. Selections from the Clinical Works of Dr. Duchenne, translated, edited, and condensed by G. V. Poore, London: New Sydenham Society, 1883.

Charles-Édouard Brown-Séquard (1817-1894)

CHARLES-ÉDOUARD BROWN-SÉQUARD was an internationalist at birth. His nativity was the island of Mauritius in the Indian Ocean, at one time under French domination, but in 1817, an English possession. Charles-Édouard's father, from Ireland or Philadelphia (the record remains unclear), a captain in the

Merchant Marine, died before the birth of his son, leaving no estate. His mother was French. Elementary schooling was sought at the Pensionnat Singery, but formal education

was abandoned at the age of 15 to help with the family finances by clerking in the general store. The store served as the local bistro and a meeting place of poets, writers, and dramatists. The intellectual elite recognized Charles-Édouard's talented mind and gave him moral stimulus as well as financial backing for higher education in France.

Having passed the baccalaureate in letters in Paris, he enrolled in the École de Médecine. Earlier he was temporarily diverted by literary aspirations and made use of an introduction to Charles Nodier in the hope that a collection of manuscripts which included "plays, poems, pieces of light verse and philosophical bits" would be sold and thereby provide supplementary income.[1] The advice was discouraging. Medicine was the gainer and belles-lettres the loser. The immediate problem of finances was solved when his mother established a small boarding house in Paris for Mauritian students. A rigorous routine was maintained in study, which was followed throughout his professional career. By arising at 2 or 3 o'clock each morning, he accomplished the most serious intellectual work without interruption; 8 PM was curfew time.

Brown-Séquard's first experimental studies on gastric juice, conducted in Martin-Magron's laboratory, were published in the *Comptes rendus* (1844) of the Paris Academy of Sciences. Many of the investigations in subsequent years dealt with the nervous system and with the endocrine glands. The final researches and surely the most frustrating concerned physical rejuvenation. He prepared extracts of various endocrine glands, in the futile hope that senescence could be postponed or prevented.[2]

On the first of June I sent to the Society of Biology a communication, which was followed by several others, showing the remarkable effects produced on myself by the subcutaneous injection of a liquid obtained by the maceration on a mortar of the testicle of a dog or of a guinea pig to which one has added a little water.

... I concluded at that time that: "I hope that other physiologists of advanced age will repeat these experiments and will show whether the effects which I have obtained on myself depend on my personal idiosyncrasy or not."

Although his earlier years had been interspersed with obstacles and hardships, the period immediately following graduation was the most trying professionally and personally. He was miserably poor but determined to continue his investigations, meanwhile supporting himself by the practice of medicine. Since there were too many Browns in Paris, he added his mother's name and became legally Brown-Séquard. The experience of Magendie in the use of an electric current in the treatment of neurological ailments contributed to Brown-Séquard's interest in this specialty. Du Bois-Reymond had invented the induction coil and had described faradic stimulation. There is some confusion whether direct galvanic current or induced faradic current was employed in Brown-Séquard's neurological practice, but the conduction machine loaned by Rayer, a good friend and physician, provided faradic stimulation.

Three years after graduation, Brown-Séquard was elected a member of the Société philomathique. Claude Bernard and Magendie were fellow members. In competition with Bernard, Brown-Séquard submitted experimental data for the Montyon Prize of the Academy of Sciences. Bernard won the prize but Brown-Séquard was given a sum of money equal to the prize to defray the expenses of the experiments. This remarkable gesture of good faith helped support Brown-Séquard's studies in experimental neurology. In competition for academic posts in Paris, Claude Bernard, a few years his senior, had a decided advantage. Bernard was a Frenchman and an outstanding investigator. Brown-Séquard was a British subject and lacked the stability and the maturity of Bernard. Brown-Séquard chose then to come to the United States, although he knew little English. This skill was acquired on a slow boat across the Atlantic.

In 1849, the investigations on the transverse section of the spinal cord were summarized and the essential features of the Brown-Séquard syndrome enumerated. The sympton-complex involves loss of sensation below the lesion on the contralateral side of the body and increased sensation on the ipsilateral side. It was concluded that, if some sensory sensations are conveyed by the posterior columns of the cord, the majority are conveyed by other parts of the nervous pathways. These experiments were not accepted generally until several years later when Broca, best known for his work on aphasia, gave the weight of authority to the deductions.[3] Excerpts from these studies are presented below as well as those from his earlier work on stimulation of the cervical sympathetic:[4]

It seems absolutely certain, from the above facts and reasonings, that there is no decussation of the voluntary motor fibres of the trunk and limbs above the crossing of the pyramids. On the other hand, we have already shown, in a previous lecture, that there seems to be no decussation of these fibres in the spinal cord —i.e., below the crossing of the pyramids; to that we are led to admit that most if, if not all, the conductors of the orders of the will to muscles decussate at the lower part of the medulla oblongata, and that these conductors chiefly form the anterior pyramids, after their decussation. An interesting fact, in addition to those already mentioned, concerning these pyramids, is, that when a lesion exists at the place of decussation, it produces a paralysis in the two sides of the body, because it destroys fibres belonging to them both. This is a feature quite peculiar to this part of the cerebro-spinal axis.

From the preceding remarks, and from the facts and reasonings contained in our lectures (the third and seventh) on the decussation of the conductors of sensitive impressions, it results that, as regards anaesthesia and paralysis, three different groups of symptoms may be observed, according to the place of the alteration in a lateral half of the cerebro-spinal axis: 1st, above the decussation of the pyramids, a lesion on either the medulla oblongata, the pons Varolii, the crura cerebri, the optic thalami, the corpora striata, or the brain proper, if it produces anesthesia and paralysis, produces them both in the opposite side of the body; 2d, below the decussation in the pyramids, a lesion in the spinal cord produces paralysis in the same side, and anaesthesia in the opposite side; 3d, at the level of the decussation of the pyramids, and upon the decussating fibres, and also behind them, a lesion produces paralysis in both sides of the body, and anaesthesia only in the opposite side. So that *wherever the lesion, in a lateral half of the cerebro-spinal axis, may be—below, above, or at the level of the crossing of the pyramids—if it produces anaesthesia, it is in the opposite side; while paralysis, in these three cases, is either in the same or the opposite side, or in both sides.*

I have found that the remarkable phenomena which follow the section of the cervical part of the sympathetic, are mere consequences of the paralysis and therefore of the dilatation of the blood-vessels. The blood finding a larger way than usual, arrives there in greater quantity; therefore the nutrition is more active. Now the sensibility is increased because the vital properties of the nerves are augmented when their nutrition is augmented.

... I base my opinion in part on the following experiments: If galvanism is applied to the superior portion of the sympathetic after it has been cut in the neck, the vessels of the face and of the ear after a certain time begin to contract; their contraction increases slowly, but at last it is evident that they resume their normal condition, if they are not even smaller. Then the temperature and the sensibility diminish in the face and in the ear, and they become in the palsied side the same as in the sound side.

When the galvanic current ceases to act, the vessels begin to dilate again, and all the phenomena discovered by Dr. Bernard reappear.

In an American lecture tour begun in Philadelphia in 1852, Brown-Séquard discussed the fundamental concepts of the nerve fibers of the cervical sympathetic and their action upon the blood vessels of the head. These lectures, published in the *Philadelphia Medical Examiner*, were followed by other lectures in Boston and New York City. An attempt to practice medicine in New York City to solve financial problems was a miserable failure. Marriage to a niece of the first wife of Daniel Webster was more successful. At the Annual Meeting of the American Medical Association in Richmond, Va., in 1852, professional contacts were made with a number of physicians. Undoubtedly these contributed to an invitation two years later to accept the Professorship of the Institutes of Medicine and Medical Jurisprudence at the Medical College of Virginia. This academic safari was finished scarcely before it had begun. He was not especially popular—a verdict that is not surprising since he was opposed to slavery. His resignation was submitted at the end of the first term.

Brown-Séquard returned to Paris and received a warm reception by his associates in the Société de Biologie. In a small laboratory in the Rue Saint-Jacques, he began experiments on the endocrine glands. In 1856, he reported on the effects of the removal of the suprarenal bodies. He had discovered that removal of both adrenals was associated with muscle weakness, a feeble heart rate, a fall of body temperature, and death within a few hours. Blood from a healthy animal injected into the veins of an animal with bilateral extirpation was associated with additional hours of survival. The conclusion was clear; adrenals are essential to life, at least for mammals, and ablation leads to death more rapidly than does removal of both kidneys. He also reported death in animals with severe inflammation of the suprarenals.[5]

My studies following ablation of both suprarenal capsules show that: (1) Symptoms are the same in all species of animals in which I removed the suprarenal capsules; (2) Symptoms consist of severe weakness, varying difficulties in breathing, abnormal circulation, and development of convulsions, delirium, and coma.

I have established that the death after removal of the suprarenal capsules is not due to hemorrhage, peritonitis, nor to injury of organs adjacent to the suprarenal capsules.

Also, I have seen rabbits in whom the suprarenal glands were severely inflamed; this inflammation rapidly leads to death with similar symptoms seen following extirpation of the suprarenals.

CONCLUSIONS: (1) Death following removal of the suprarenal capsules could not be attributed exclusively or principally to any of the lesions which necessarily or accidentally accompany the operation; (2) Death is due excusively to the absence of suprarenal capsules i.e. due to the absence of their functions; (3) Since death follows the ablation of these organs in every instance and rapidly, it follows from this and from the previous statements that THE FUNCTION OF THE SUPRARENAL CAPSULES IS ESSENTIAL TO LIFE.

The major contributions of Brown-Séquard were made before the age of 40. At the peak of his professional career, he was in great demand as a lecturer. In addition, several medical schools offered him professorships, and he founded the *Journal de la Physiologie de l'Homme et des Animaux*. Lectureships in Dublin, Edinburgh, and Glasgow were accepted. In the last community, he was made a Fellow of the Faculty of Physicians and Surgeons and offered a chair at the university. By 1860, Brown-Séquard had abandoned medical practice in Paris in order to accept an appointment as physician at the National Hospital for the Paralysed and Epileptics in Queens Square, London. In 1861, the Royal Society's Croonian Lecture and the College of Physicians' Gulstonian Lecture were delivered by him.

The professorship of physiology and pathology of the nervous system at Harvard Medical School was offered in 1864, where a warm friendship was established with Louis Agassiz, the Swiss naturalist. After three years at Harvard, Brown-Séquard returned to Paris and joined the Faculty of Medicine as professor of experimental and comparative pathology. During the remaining years, he visited Paris, Dublin, London, Boston, and Washington. Finally at the age of 61, he was appointed to the coveted chair of experimental medicine at École de Médecine. But his period of great productivity was over; the post that held such attraction for so many years was almost an empty honor. He was buried in a cemetery on Montparnasse in 1894, the last of the three great physiologists of France—Magendie, Bernard, and Brown-Séquard—whose creative talents spanned the 19th century.

1. Olmsted, J. M. D.: *Charles-Édouard Brown-Séquard*, Baltimore: Johns Hopkins Press, 1946.

2. Brown-Séquard, C. E.: Experiment Demonstrating the Dynamogenic Power in Man of An Extract of the Testicles of Animals (Fr), *Arch Physiol norm path* 1:651-658, 5 ser, 1889.

3. Brown-Séquard, C. E.: *Course of Lectures on the Physiology and Pathology of the Central Nervous System*, Philadelphia: Collins, 1860, xii, 276 pp, 3 pl.

4. Brown-Séquard, C. E.: Experimental Researches Applied to Physiology and Pathology, *Med Exam* (Philadelphia) 8:481-504, 1852.

5. Brown-Séquard, C. E.: Experimental Studies on the Physiology and Pathology of the Adrenal Glands (Fr), *C R Acad Sci (Paris)* 43:422-425, 542-546, 1856, excerpt translated by Z. Danilevicius.

Jean-Martin Charcot (1825-1893)

THE BIOGRAPHY of J-M Charcot by Guillain[1] is as much a story of the Salpêtrière as it is of the clinical life of Charcot. This was inevitable; they were inseparable. Each was a strong pillar in the building of the edifice of the greatest century of Parisian medicine. Charcot shared honors with Dupuytren, Bichat, Corvisart, Bayle, Laennec, Magendie, Cruveilhier, Louis Pasteur, Claude Bernard, Duchenne of Boulogne, Broca, and Vulpian. "Charcot—Caesar of the Salpêtrière—entered neurology in its infancy and left it at its coming-of-age, largely nourished by his own contributions." The Salpêtrière was transformed from a prison and an asylum of unwanted womanhood into one of the great clinical centers of the world.

Jean-Martin Charcot was born in Paris on November 29, 1825. His father, aged 27 at Charcot's birth, was a carriage builder. His mother was not yet 17 years of age. Jean-Martin had one older and two younger brothers. The parents were neither poor nor wealthy; they were of modest means and able to provide adequately for the higher education of their children.[1]

We have very little information on Charcot's childhood; he himself did not leave any written documents related to this phase of his life. We do know, however, that from an early age he possessed a cold, taciturn personality and that he liked to be alone in order to read and to draw. The truism that childhood personality traits tend to persist throughout life seems especially applicable to the life of Charcot.

The scientific propensity and intellectual capacity of Charcot were recognized during his early student days. He was recommended for a house staff appointment, *l'Internat des Hôpitaux* (intern as opposed to extern), one year before the usual time. The Dean of the Faculty of Medicine of the University of Paris, Rayer, physician to Emperor Napoleon III, gave him strong support. It is of note that Rayer, a Protestant, was not permitted to qualify as a candidate for one of the senior professorships of the faculty during the French Restoration because of his religious faith. Charcot prepared at the Salpêtrière his doctoral thesis on the differential symptoms and lesions of gout and arthritis.

Charcot was appointed to the post of senior physician at the Salpêtrière in 1862 at the age of 37. He realized the tremendous opportunity for clinical study and investigation in a hospital with more than 5,000 patients afflicted with chronic diseases, especially diseases of the nervous system. Within 10 years the contributions of Charcot left no doubt that modern neurology had been born. During the war of 1870 he sent his family to London, but he himself remained in Paris to care for patients, particularly those stricken with typhoid fever and smallpox. Following his appointment as professor of pathologic anatomy in 1872, he lectured on diseases of the lungs, liver, kidneys, brain, and spinal cord. The chair of neurology was not created until 1882 when he was 56 years of age. He did not relinquish the chair until his death 11 years later from pulmonary edema associated with chronic aortitis and coronary occlusion. Charcot was always punctual; sometimes he kept an appointment a few minutes in advance of the prearranged time and expected the same punctuality from others. He expressed disdain for impressionistic art and preferred the Italian paintings of the Renaissance and the sculptors of ancient Greece. He drew and painted well himself. Shakespeare was his favorite author but he read and reread Greek and Latin classics.

As one enters the arched gateway of the Salpêtrière, the majestic dome dominates the hospital just as Charcot dominated the intellectual architecture. The hospital has been altered structurally very little since it was built 400 years ago. In both World Wars American military hospitals used the facilities. The modest structural changes over the centuries at the Salpêtrière have been accomplished without altering the architectural charm of the original buildings. The name Salpêtrière comes from saltpeter, the nitrate used in the manufacture of gunpowder. For many years gunpowder was stored on the right bank of the Seine behind the ramparts of the old city. By popular demand, and on the order of Louis XIII, the arsenal was relocated to a site on the left bank in 1565. It was outside the city limits of Paris at that time and was considered a safe spot for the Little Arsenal—la Salpêtrière. Two centuries later it became a women's asylum for beggars, the aged, the infirm, and the insane. The beggars remained until 1768. A few years later it was transformed into a hospital with an officially appointed medical and surgical staff. The establishment of a chair of clinical diseases of the nervous system in 1882 identified the hospital as one especially dedicated to the study and treatment of nervous diseases. A bronze statue of Charcot was cast and erected in the courtyard of the Salpêtrière by subscription of his pupils. A significant portion of the funds came from physicians outside France. The statue was removed by the Nazis during the occupation of Paris in 1942 and melted for the war machine. It has not been replaced.

Charcot inaugurated an out-patient department following his appointment as profession and limited his in-patient service to neurological patients. The clinical services were supplemented by a pathological laboratory and a routine laboratory equipped with microscopes, photographic instruments, and other items necessary for a well-rounded teaching and research service. He possessed the ideal trinity for the head of a department: he had a great passion for teaching; his clinical skill was of international repute; his dedication to research was well established. He was a great mimic in his clinics and classes. The distortion of the face in facial paralysis, the position of a hand in peripheral paralysis, or the rigidity of a patient with Parkinson's disease could be simulated by Charcot in order to stress a clinical point. A number of physicians of note studied under the professor at the Faculty of Medicine in Paris. These included C. Bouchard, Hanot, Pierre Marie, Bechterew, Raymond, Potain, Sachs, Freud and J. Babinski. Cardinal Mercier, professor at the University of Louvain, enrolled in Charcot's course in 1887.

Charcot's earlier studies were devoted to rheumatism, gout, and diseases of the aged. Later he became particularly interested in exophthalmic goiter and intermittent claudication. In 1863, in collaboration with his intern Cornil, he studied the anatomic lesions of joints and of the kidneys among patients suffering from gout. In 1864, for example, he discussed the significance of lead intoxication as an etiologic factor in gout.[2] "It seems if I am to agree with Garrod that the widespread use of lead in industry can, along with other predisposing causes, contribute to the etiology of gout, then I must also state that there is nothing to indicate that all the forms of gout result from the exclusive influence of lead intoxication."

Charcot's great contributions to neurology included studies on multiple sclerosis, amyotrophic lateral sclerosis (Charcot's disease), the tabetic arthropathies (Charcot's joints), cerebral localizations, spastic paralysis, aphasia, neuroses, and hysteria. The excerpts below are taken from early translations of his extended discussions of the triad of symptoms in disseminated sclerosis, intention tremor, nystagmus, and scanning speech,[3] and selected features of tabetic arthropathy.[4]

The *trembling* of which we speak *does not show itself except on the occasion of intentional movements of a certain extent; it ceases to exist when the muscles are left to complete repose.* Such is the phenomenon which I have been led to consider as one of the most important clinical characters of cerebro-spinal sclerosis in patches.

Nystagmus is a symptom of great diagnostic importance, since it is observed in nearly half of the cases. So far as I know, we meet with it only very exceptionally in ataxy. There is question, as you see, of little shocks which cause the two eyeballs to oscillate simultaneously from right to left, or inversely. There are cases in which the nystagmus is wanting so long as the look remains vague, without precise direction; but it manifests itself suddenly, in a manner more or less marked so soon as the patients are requested to fix their attention upon an object.

A symptom more frequent still than nystagmus (nearly almost constant in multilocular cerebrospinal sclerosis, since we find it mentioned twenty times in twenty-three cases which we have analyzed), is a *peculiar difficulty in articulation,* which you may study in our patient in its type of complete development.

The speech is slow, drawling, and now and again almost unintelligible. It seems as if the tongue had become "too thick," and the utterance recalls that of people somewhat inebriated. A more attentive study enables us to discover that the words are as if scanned: there is a pause between each syllable, and the latter are pronounced slowly. There is some hesitation in the articulation of the words; but, properly speaking, nothing resembling stammering. Certain consonants, *l, p,* and *g,* are, in particular, badly pronounced.

This arthropathy is developed at a *but slightly advanced period of the spinal disease,* and most commonly when its symptomatology is limited to the lightning pains. The incoordination, it is true, does not generally make its appearance when the arthropathy has occurred. Thus it has, as you observe, its place marked for it in the regular succession of the symptoms of locomotor ataxia.

The irritative lesions of the spinal cord, especially those which occupy the grey substance, react sometimes, you are aware, on the periphery, and determine various nutritive disorders, either in the skin or in the deeper parts, such as the muscles. The bones and articulations do not appear to escape this law. It follows that the arthropathies of locomotor ataxia would be, according to my judgment, one of the forms of these articular affections, developed under the more or less direct influence of a lesion of the spinal centre.

It is proper now, gentlemen, to examine what information is supplied us by pathological anatomy. Undoubtedly, in cases of old standing, when the articular surfaces, worn and deprived of cartilage, have continued to move on each other, the limbs being still made use of more or less imperfectly, the signs observed are those of dry arthritis: to wit, eburnation and deformation of the articular surfaces, deformation of the osseous extremities, bony burrs and stalactites, foreign bodies, &c.

Notwithstanding the anatomical characters which connect it more or less closely with the standard type of dry arthritis, the *arthropathy of ataxia* remains no less a distinct variety, because both of the originality of the symptomatic group which it presents, and of its evident relationship with locomotor ataxia, of which, as an epiphenomenon, it really forms a part.

1. Guillain, G.: *J.-M. Charcot, Paris:* Masson, 1955, edited and translated by P. Bailey, New York: Paul B. Hoeber, Inc., 1959.
2. Charcot, J., and Cornil, M. V.: Contributions to the Anatomical Changes in Gout, Especially the Gouty Kidney (Fr), *C R Soc Biol* 15:139, 1864.
3. Charcot, J.-M.: *Clinical Lectures on Diseases of the Nervous System,* Paris: 1872-1873, translated by T. Oliver, *Edinburgh Med J* 22:50-56, 117-125, 1876.
4. Charcot, J.-M.: *Clinical Lectures on Diseases of the Nervous System,* Paris: 1880, translated by G. Sigerson, London: The New Sydenham Society, 1881.

National Medical Library

Paul Broca (1824-1880)

PIERRE PAUL BROCA, whose name has been associated for more than a century with the localization of speech in the posterior portion of the third frontal convolution on the left, was born at Sainte-Foy-la-Grande (Gironde) into a Huguenot family.[1] After the usual schooling, he took the bachelor's degree at the age of 16, with high honors, in the Faculties of Literature and Science at the college of Sainte-Foy, then popular with the Protestant youth of France. He had intended to make a career in the military, based upon his talents in the physical sciences, but the death of his sister and only sibling altered his destiny. With the support of his father, a successful country practitioner who had served in the army in Spain under the first Napoleon, Broca entered the Faculty of

Medicine in Paris in 1842. There in succession he surpassed competition for the position of externe, interne, and finally interne laureate of the hospitals.

Continuing his academic advancement in Paris, Broca was appointed anatomy assistant in 1846 and prosector in 1848. The following year he received the MD degree, upon submission of a thesis on the spread of inflammation in relation to the dissemination of tumors. He won the title "Surgeon of the Hospitals," conducted independent researches, and contributed to the scientific literature, a practice he continued without interruption until he died. Initially his communications on anatomy, surgery, and pathology were published in clinical periodicals. Subjects discussed included clinical features of bone, cartilage, tumors, and aneurysms. The bulk of his scientific writing, however, concerned a variety of subjects which had some relevance to anthropology.

Broca's breadth of knowledge, his encompassing skills, and great erudition, won respect from his pupils in medicine, contemporaries in clinical surgery, and associates in anthropologic investigations. He served on the surgical staff of the hospitals of St. Antoine, la Pitié, des Cliniques, and Necker. During the war of 1870–1871, a major portion of his time was given to the surgical care of the wounded at Pitié. Broca was appointed assistant professor of surgery in 1853, and, in 1867, the Faculty of Medicine appointed him to the professorship of external pathology. This post was exchanged promptly for the chair of clinical surgery, which provided opportunities to exploit anthropology wherever his inquiring mind led him. Relieved of financial worries in an academic career through his marriage to the daughter of Dr. Lugol, a highly successful surgeon, he changed his goals in the pursuit of a dual professional career.

Broca's curiosity about anthropology and ethnology appeared at a relatively early age. As an anatomy assistant he was directed by the Prefect of the Seine to report on the skeletal remains in ancient burial grounds in Paris. The official report of his excavations, prepared after extensive reading of the anthropology literature, was included in the

first of his five-volume compendium, *Memoirs of Anthropology*.[2] In the same decade Broca formed an anthropological society to fill the void left by the Ethnological Society, which had exhausted its intellectual resources. With Broca as the acting secretary, the charter members, all young physicians, proposed a broad mission for their organization.

The society was designed to provide a forum for scientific communications on comparative anatomy, paleontology, linguistics, craniology, and ethnology as well as the more inclusive subjects of formal anthropology. After years of frustration and considerable maneuvering with the granting agencies of the government, the first meeting of the Society was held in 1859. The first volume of the *Bulletins de la Societe d'Anthropologie* was published later in the same year. Two years later Broca presented his case report on articulate speech.

Broca was not the first to advance the hypothesis of cerebral localization. Gibson[3] has identified ancient and contemporary observers, including Franz Joseph Gall, anatomist and phrenologist of Vienna; Marc Dax, general practitioner of Montpellier; Jean-Baptiste Bouillaud, Broca's teacher; and Ernest Auburtin, son-in-law of Bouillaud and a contemporary of Broca. Probably the greatest contribution prior to Broca's observations was published in 1825 by Bouillaud, later professor of clinical medicine at the Charité and Dean of the Faculty of Medicine. Boullaud assumed from his clinical-pathological studies that derangement or loss of speech was associated with a lesion of the frontal lobe and was dependent upon the ability to control the movements which form words in speech as well as to retain them in memory. Such a deficiency need not be accompanied by a dysfunction or disturbance of other cerebral functions. Bouillaud's contention was not generally accepted; in fact, it was either forgotten by many or was strongly opposed by a few, among them Cruveilhier, leading anatomist of Paris. The hypothesis of Bouillaud, fallow for a generation, was reintroduced into scientific communication before the Anthropological Society by his son-in-law, Auburtin, shortly before Broca's presentation.

The strength of Broca's argument rested with Laborgne, a patient at Bicêtre, who had been admitted first 21 years before his final illness. At the age of 30, Laborgne lost his ability to speak, and his only utterance was the monosyllable "tan" which came to be his nickname. Ten years following the onset of aphasia, slow paralysis of the right arm and the right leg developed. Weakness on the left side of the face appeared shortly before his terminal admission. At Broca's request he was examined by Auburtin for confirmation of the neurological findings. "Tan" died on April 17, 1861. The brain was hardened intact, without sectioning. The gross pathological findings were reported briefly by Broca in April 1861, before the Anthropological Society. In reconstructing the structural changes Broca assumed that degeneration of the cortex began in the left third frontal convolution which accounted for the loss of speech. As the lytic process extended to the left striate body, hemiplegia appeared. Broca referred to the neurological deficiency as "aphemia," a term criticized by Trousseau, who preferred "aphasia." Broca's concept of cerebral localization was opposed by some, especially by Hughlings Jackson in 1868, and, in the early 1900's, by Pierre Marie, who examined Tan's brain and redescribed the cerebral lesion. Marie emphasized the extensive damage in the temporal and parietal areas and contended that aphasia involved a loss of intellectual capacity necessary for the formulation of language and could not be localized as precisely. The more detailed report by Broca, translated by von Bonin, is excerpted as follows:[4]

The observations which I present to the Anatomical Society support the ideas of M. Bouillaud on the seat of the faculty of language. This question which is both physiological and pathological deserves more attention than most doctors have given it so far and the matter is sufficiently complicated and the subject sufficiently obscure so that it seems useful to make a few remarks before relating the facts which I have observed. . . . Without considering the language as a simple faculty depending on only one cerebral organ and without trying to circumscribe within a few millimeters the place of this organ, as did the school

of Gall, this professor has been led by the analysis of a large number of clinical facts, followed by autopsies, to state that certain lesions of the hemisphere abolish speech without destroying intelligence and that these lesions are always in the anterior lobes of the brain. From this he has concluded that there are somewhere in these lobes one or several convolutions, from whom depends one of the elements essential for the complex phenomenon of language.

There are cases where the general faculty of language persists unaltered, where the oratory apparatus is intact, where all muscles without exception, even those of voice and articulation follow volition and where nonetheless the cerebral lesion has abolished articulate language. This abolition of speech in individuals, who are neither paralyzed nor idiots, is a sufficiently important symptom so that it seems useful to designate it by a special name. I have given it the name Aphemia (a privativum $+ \phi\eta\mu\eta$, voice, I speak), for what is missing in these patients is only the faculty to articulate the words; they hear and understand all that is said to them, they have all their intelligence and they emit easily vocal sounds. They execute with their tongue and their lips movements larger and more energetic than would be necessary to articulate sounds, and nonetheless, the well-sensed response which they would like to make, becomes reduced to a very small number of articulate sounds. They are always the same and always arranged in the same way.

I thought that I should sum up in a few words this discussion to bring out the topical interest of the observation which I present today at the Anatomical Society. Without doubt the value of the facts depend not on the circumstances in which one observes them, but our impression depends, to a large extent, on these circumstances, and when a few days after having heard the argument of M. Auburtin, I found one morning on my service a dying patient who 21 years ago had lost the faculty of articulate language.

On the eleventh of April, 1861, to the general infirmary of the Bicêtre, to the service of surgery, was brought a man 51-years-old called Leborgne who had a diffused gangrenous cellulitis of the whole right inferior extremity, from the foot to the buttocks. To the questions which one addressed to him on the next day as to the origin of his disease he responded only by the monosyllable "tan," repeated twice in succession and accompanied by a gesture of the left hand. I tried to find out more about the antecedents of this man, who had been at Bicêtre for 21 years. I asked his attendants, his comrades on the ward, and those of his relatives who used to see him and here is the result of this inquiry.

Since his youth he was subject to epileptic attacks, but he could become a last-maker at which he worked until he was 31 years old. At that time he lost the ability to speak, and that is why he was admitted at the Hôspice of Bicêtre.

One could not find out whether this loss of speech came on slowly or fast, nor whether some other symptom accompanied the beginning of this affection.

When he arrived at Bicêtre he could not speak for 2 or 3 months. He was then quite healthy and intelligent and differed from a normal person only by the loss of articulate language. He came and went in the Hôspice where he was known under the name of "Tan." He understood all that was said to him. His hearing was actually very good. Whatever question one addressed to him, he always answered, "tan, tan," accompanied by varied gestures, by which he succeeded in expressing most of his ideas. If one did not understand his gestures, he usually got irate, and added to his vocabulary a gross swear word.

He had lost his speech for 10 years when a new symptom appeared. The muscles of the right arm began getting weak and ended by being completely paralyzed. Tan continued to walk without difficulty, but the paralysis gradually extended to the inferior right extremity, and after having trained the leg for some time the patient had resigned himself to stay in bed. About four years had elapsed, when the beginning of a paralysis of the arm set up. At this time the paralysis of the leg was sufficiently advanced to make standing absolutely impossible. Before he was brought to the infirmary Tan was in bed for almost seven years.

The two right extremities were completely paralyzed. The left one could be moved voluntarily, and although weak, could without hesitation execute all movements. Emission of urine and fecal matters was normal, but deglutition was difficult. Mastication, on the other hand was executed very well. The face did not deviate; however, in whistling, the left cheek appeared a little less inflated than the right, which indicated that the muscles of this side of the face were a little weak.

The patient died on April 17, at 11 o'clock a.m. Autopsy was performed as soon as possible, that is to say, after 24 hours. The temperature was a little elevated. The cadaver showed no signs of putrefaction. The brain was shown a few hours later in the Society of Anthropology, then put immediately into alcohol. This organ was so altered that one had to be very careful to preserve it. Only after two months and after several changes of the fluid, the piece began to harden. Today it is in perfect condition, and it has been deposited in the Musée Dupuytren under the number 55a of the nervous system.

To sum up, the destroyed organs are the following.

The small inferior marginal convolution of the temporal lobe, the small convolutions of the insula and the underlying part of the striate body, finally, in the frontal lobe, the inferior part of the transverse frontal, and the posterior part of those two great convolutions designated as the second and third frontal convolutions.

If one wanted to be more precise, one could remark that the third frontal convolution is the one which shows the greatest loss of substance, that it is not only cut transversely at the level of the anterior end of the Sylvian fissure, but is also completely destroyed in its posterior half, it alone has undergone a loss of substance, equal to about one-half of the total; that the second or middle frontal convolution, although deeply affected, still preserves its continuity in its innermost parts, and that, consequently, it is most likely in the third convolution that the disease began.

I have now only to add a few words to point out the consequences of this observation.

1. The aphemia, i.e., the loss of speech, before any other intellectual trouble and before any paralysis, was a consequence of a lesion of one of the frontal lobes of the brain.

2. Our observation confirms thus the opinion of M. Bouillaud who places in these lobes the seat of the faculty of articulate speech.

3. The observations which have so far been made, at least those accompanied by clear and precise anatomical description, are not numerous enough to consider as definitely demonstrated the localization of a particular faculty in a particular lobe, but one can consider it at least extremely probable.

Although the hypothesis of cerebral localization may have been Broca's best-known contribution to natural science, his best hours were spent in the anthropology laboratory or at the meetings of the Anthropological Society. By 1863, the society had grown and required a general secretary; Broca was appointed and served in this capacity until his death. The anthropology laboratory was assigned limited space in the Dupuytren Museum of the Faculty of Medicine. Broca conducted his dissections and measurements, especially of the cranium and brain, with the aid of instruments and essential laboratory tools, of which many were designed and manufactured under his direction. The *Memoirs* of the Society were published first in 1860, and in 1899, were combined with the *Bulletin* to receive communications from the society members. The *Revue d'Anthropologie,* a third publication of the Society, was founded by Broca in 1872, and appeared regularly until he died. In 1876, long after the idea was proposed by Broca, the Anthropological Institute was conditionally recognized by the Minister of Public Instruction as a cultural agency. It provided facilities for public lectures, practical instruction in anthropology, and a laboratory for research.

Although Broca's assignments and responsibilities in the Society and later in the Institute seem to have demanded full-time efforts and activities, he continued his surgical work in the hospital. A raconteur, a loyal and gracious friend, and an original and independent thinker, he believed in educating all women as the only effective means of educating the nation. Two of the greatest honors bestowed on Broca were his election in 1866 to the French Academy of Medicine and in the year of his death to a lifetime membership in the Senate of the French Republic, representing science. Although the Bouillaud-Broca concept is an oversimplification, and speech today is regarded as but one aspect of language, thinking, intelligence, and consciousness, and although disordered speech or loss of speech is an effect in varying degrees of the total personality, still Broca's contributions are noteworthy.

1. Pozzi, S.: Paul Broca (Fr), Rev d'Anthrop, 3:577-608, 1880.

2. Broca, P.: Memoires d'Anthropologie, 5 vol, Paris: C. Reinwald, 1871-1877.

3. Gibson, W. C.: Pioneers in Localization of Function in the Brain, JAMA 180:944-951 (June 16) 1962.

4. Broca, P.: Remarks on the Seat of the Faculty of Articulate Language, Followed by an Observation of Aphemia (Fr), Bull Soc Anat Par 6:330-357, 1861, Bull Soc Anthrop 2:235-238, 1861, in von Bonin, G. (trans.): The Cerebral Cortex, Springfield, Ill: C. C Thomas, 1960, pp 49-72.

John Hughlings Jackson
(1834-1911)

THE TWO-VOLUME COLLECTION of the "selected" writings of J. Hughlings Jackson, which totals slightly more than 1,000 pages,[1] is indicative of the stature of the great neurologist of the National Hospital, Queen Square, London, in the second half of the 19th century. Born in 1834 into a rugged Yorkshire farming family, he appears to have been indifferent to schooling in his early years. An apprenticeship to a local doctor and then a student career at York Medical School, followed by advanced instruction at St. Bartholomew's Hospital in

London, were unremarkable. In proper time, Jackson became certified as a physician and achieved membership in the Royal College of Surgeons of England. He returned to the York Dispensary as resident

National Portrait Gallery

medical officer and came under the influence of Thomas Laycock, an exceptional teacher interested in neurology, who shortly was appointed professor of clinical medicine at Edinburgh. At the age of 26, Jackson received the MD degree from St. Andrews, having moved to London in the interim. In the following years a deep interest in philosophy more than any other influence enhanced his many contributions to neurology. Initially, the attraction to philosophy was scarcely resistible, and the dual trophism, philosophy or medicine, was not readily resolved. Medicine and neurology were eventually the victors, but philosophy was always in the background.

Jackson accepted hospital and teaching facilities in London and especially enjoyed an intimate professional association with Jonathan Hutchinson, who provided intellectual intercourse and financial support through a joint enterprise in medical journalism. He also came under the influence of Brown-Séquard, the brilliant neurologist, one of the two founding physicians of the National Hospital. Since Jackson espoused the discipline of neurology as few had done, perhaps any influence that swayed him to the study of medicine was justified. Hutchinson, however, did not accept this conclusion and queried whether Jackson might have made a greater contribution to philosophy, had the decision been different.

Jackson was affiliated with three outstanding hospitals in his clinical career.[2] The National Hospital for the Paralysed and Epileptic in Queen Square, to which he was appointed full physician in 1867, provided a wealth of neurological material; Moorfield's Eye Hospital, a variety of ophthalmologic cases; and the London Hospital, general medical and surgical cases with neurological complications. Such opportunities were not neglected, the clinical cases were utilized maximally.

Several neurological concepts are identifield with Hughlings Jackson.[3] Jacksonian epilepsy, or Bravais-Jacksonian epilepsy, is characterized by unilateral spasm, sometimes progressing to become bilateral, with retention of consciousness. Bravais, a medical student in France, described hemiplegic epilepsy in his graduation thesis of 1827, four decades before Jackson's description. Jackson used the term "epileptic" for the grand mal and "epileptiform" for the Jacksonian fit; whereas Charcot popularized the eponymic term. Although the epileptic seizure associated with a local gross disturbance was probably simpler to comprehend than symptomatic epilepsy without recognizable organic cause, Jackson was interested in each type. Jackson's rule states: After epileptic attacks, simple nervous processes are more quickly recovered than are complex ones. Jackson's syndrome refers to unilateral palsy of the motor components of the 10th, 11th, and 12th nerves—also called "the syndrome of vago-accessory-hypoglossal paralysis."

Jackson probed deeply into the physiology and philosophy of the nervous system in his discussion of evolution and dissolution.[4] Herbert Spencer's doctrine of evolution was applied, but the doctrine was not subjected to experimental scrutiny. Three levels of evolution in the nervous system were recognized.

The lowest level included the spinal cord and basal ganglia. Involuntary movements, not muscles, came into action at this level. The middle level encompassed the motor convolutions and the central ganglia. Movements became increasingly complex, with increasing specialization. The automatism was less distinct and the mechanism less well organized. The highest level represented the prefrontal area where the fine adjustments of the organism to the environment were accomplished. An interplay functioned between each of the levels, with higher centers exercising inhibitory powers over the lower centers.

Jackson's contributions to disorders of speech are the most profound as well as the most difficult to comprehend. The following excerpts are intended to serve as a brief introduction only to his interpretation of the phenomenon.[1]

When a person "Talks" there are three things going on—speech, articulation and voice. Disease can separate them. Thus from disease of the larynx, or from paralysis of its nerves, we have loss of voice, but articulation and speech remain good. Again, in complete paralysis of the tongue, lips and palate, articulation is lost, but speech is not even impaired; the patient remains able to express himself in writing, which shows that he retains speech—internal speech—that he propositionises well. Lastly, in extensive disease in a certain region in one half of the brain (left half usually) there is loss of speech, internal and external, but the articulatory muscles move well.

Let us make a wider division. Using the term language, we make two divisions of it, intellectual and emotional. The patient, whom we call speechless (he is also defective in pantomime) has lost intellectual language and has not lost emotional language.

The term Aphasia has been given to affections of speech by Trousseau; it is used for defects as well as for loss of speech. I think the expression Affections of Speech (including defects and loss) is preferable. Neither term is very good, for there is, at least in many cases, more than loss of *speech;* pantomime is impaired; there is often a loss or defect in symbolising relations of things in any way. Dr. Hamilton proposes the term Asemasia, which seems a good one. He derives it "from α and σημαινω, an inability to indicate by signs or language." It is too late, I fear, to displace the word aphasia. Aphasia will be sometimes used as synonymous with affections of speech in this article.

We must at once say briefly what we mean by speech, in addition to what has been said by implication when excluding articulation, as this is popularly understood, and voice. To speak is not simply to utter words, it is to propositionise. A proposition is such a relation of words that it makes one new meaning; not by a mere addition of what we call the separate meanings of the several words; the terms in a proposition are modified by each other.

It is well to insist again that speech and words are psychical terms; words have of course anatomical substrata or bases as all other psychical states have. We must as carefully distinguish betwixt words and their physical bases, as we do betwixt colour and its physical basis; a psychical state is always accompanied by a physical state, but nevertheless the two things have distinct natures. Hence we must not say that the "memory of words" is a *function* of any part of the nervous system, for function is a physiological term. . . . Memory or any other psychical state arises *during* not *from*—if "from" implies continuity of a psychical state with a physical state—functioning of nervous arrangements, which functioning is a purely physical thing—a discharge of nervous elements representing some impressions and movements.

Let us divide roughly [affections of speech] into three degrees: (1) *Defect of Speech.*—The patient has a full vocabulary, but makes mistakes in words, as saying "orange" for "onion," "chair" for "table"; or he uses approximate or quasi-metaphorical expressions, as "Light the fire up there," for "Light the gas." "When the warm water comes the weather will go away," for "When the sun comes out the fog will go away." (2) *Loss of Speech*—The patient is practically speechless and his pantomime is impaired. (3) *Loss of Language*—Besides being speechless, he has altogether lost pantomime, and emotional language is deeply involved.

Jackson was a lonely man in private life, and enjoyed few close friends with his obvious peculiar personal habits.[5] It was difficult for him to be tranquil during a rail or carriage journey. He was easily bored and would leave after the first act of a play or depart from the table before the end of a dinner party. Reading habits were both commendable and deplorable—the volume of reading commendable, the manhandling of the books and periodicals deplorable. Instead of annotating and marking items of interest inoffensively, he would tear out pages, irrespective of whether the book was his own or on loan.

In the preparation of a manuscript, Jackson composed draft after draft, usually increasing the length each time and rarely compressing the contents. He was fearful of

making unwarranted claims and sought to protect against this fault by lengthy descriptions. His last paper was published in 1909, only two years before his death at the age of 77. Between 1861 and 1909, he had prepared more than 300 scientific communications.[1] Some of his opinions were changed as new data were discovered, but this did not detract from the value of the constructive hypotheses that guided neurologists and physiologists in his day. Many of them continue to point the way to further advances. So it is that Jackson, more than any other, deserves the title of the "Father of Modern Neurology."

1. *Selected Writings of John Hughlings Jackson*, J. Taylor, ed., vol. I, II, New York: Basic Books, Inc., 1958.
2. Critchley, M.: Hughlings Jackson, the Man; and the Early Days of the National Hospital, *Proc Roy Soc Med* 3:888-917 (June) 1939.
4. McEachern, D.: John Hughlings Jackson, *Arch Neurol Psych* 33:636-642 (March) 1935.
5. Broadbent, W.: Hughlings Jackson as a Pioneer in Nervous Physiology and Pathology, *Brain* 26:305-336, 1903.

Wilhelm Heinrich Erb
(1840-1921)

ERB'S PARALYSIS, a relatively uncommon malady, probably is the cause for most physicians remembering the neurologist from Heidelberg.[1] Erb's interest in clinical neurology, however, was broad and diversified and included many contributions beyond the localized lesion of the brachial plexus. A hypothesis for the etiology of tabes dorsalis, the descriptions of myotonia congenita and a juvenile form of progressive muscular atrophy, use of the term "tendon reflex," and studies on electrodiagnosis and electrotherapy are other accomplishments. Wilhelm was born in the Black Forest in Bavaria, the son of a forester.[2] As a peripatetic student, typical of the German system of higher education, university studies were begun at Heidelberg and continued at Erlangen. At the age of 24, he received his MD degree at Munich. He selected internal medicine initially as his field of interest, but diverted later to neuropathology and clinical neurology. After a short term as professor of medicine at Leipzig, Erb returned to Heidelberg for a full professional life in clinical neurology. He succeeded Friedreich as professor of neurology (medicine) in 1880 and held the chair until 1907.

Two manuscripts prepared early in his academic life discussed the development of red blood cells and the physiologic and therapeutic value of picric acid. Thereafter, his writings dealt largely with neurologic lesions. The two outstanding monographs prepared by him in clinical neurology were *Diseases of the Peripheral and Cerebrospinal Nerves* and the *Handbook of Diseases of the Spinal Cord and Medulla*. Although Erb matured professionally at a relatively young age, there was no cessation of clinical productivity until his waning years.

The lesion in the cervical branch of the upper brachial plexus (Erb-Duchenne paralysis), frequently resulting from traction during delivery or by gross abduction of the shoulder or head in adults, was described in 1873. The lesion involves the fifth and sixth cervical roots, thus sparing the small muscles of the hand supplied by lower spinal nerves.[1]

While looking through my case histories pertaining to peripheral paralysis, I found a number of cases dealing with paralysis of the upper extremities which were distinguished by an astonishing similarity of the groups of muscles affected; and these were forms of paralysis which were not exclusively localized in one of the main branches of the plexus brachialis, but in which, at the same time, some of the different branches of the plexus—except the ulnar nerve—were affected and always the same muscles paralyzed.

In all four cases without exception, the deltoid, the biceps and internal brachial were involved, often the supinator longus, sometimes the supinator brevis, and the areas supplied by the median nerve. This grouping of paralyzed muscles cannot be accidental, but must have an anatomical reason.

We must look for the lesion in the brachial plexus, or more likely in one of its several roots, specifically where the motor fibers for the above-named muscles are joined together and have not spread into different trunks. One must look for the injury at the neck in the supraclavicular space.

I am convinced by the inspection of resected specimens that the fifth and sixth cervical nerves especially take part in the forming of these branches of the brachial plexus which are of special interest. On the other hand, the ulnar nerve is not involved but is formed primarily, if not exclusively, from the lower roots of the plexus.

We find another group of similar cases on birth paralysis, which appears all too often in newborn infants and has been described by Duchenne. In such cases, which supposedly are caused by difficult births, if the arm is lying wrongly or if there is a long pulling of the doctor's fingers, inserted into the armpit of the child, the deltoid, biceps, and internal brachial, in addition to the infraspinatus, are paralyzed.

Erb was one of the first neurologists to utilize galvanic and induction currents in diagnosis and treatment. Subsequently events proved Erb to be too enthusiastic in his faith in electrotherapy.[3] On the other hand, electrodiagnosis has remained a useful device and in recent years has been complemented in the study and diagnosis of neuromuscular disorders by the electromyograph, the electronmicroscope, and microbiochemical techniques. The hypothesis that tabes dorsalis was a late manifestation of syphilis a number of years before the discovery of the *Treponema pallidum* or the Wassermann reaction was a contribution of greater significance.[4]

The etiology of tabes received little attention until the later 1870's. French investigators were A. Fournier (1875), Vulpian (1879), and Grasset (1879). In England it was chiefly Gowers (1878-

79), and in Germany, I took up the question of the importance of syphilis for tabes in 1879/1881. Although at first not at all convinced of this importance, my own investigations have taught me better.

The most important and most significant result of these investigations is doubtless the observation of the *predominating influence of syphilis in the etiology of tabes.*

Having been interested in this question for 13 years, I have examined a large number of patients with tabes (now more than 600) in this respect, and I have published my results repeatedly.

Briefly summarized, the results of my statistical studies of tabes in man reveal that 89% had been previously infected; more particularly, 63% stated that they had had secondary syphilis, and 26% had had a chancre infection (without subsequent generalized symptoms). It is almost certain that, among the 26% with chancre, there is a considerable number who must be counted as having had syphilis; for instance, all of those with indurated chancres, and the not insignificant number in whom mild symptoms of secondary syphilis were overlooked.

The juvenile form of progressive muscular atrophy (Erb's dystrophy) was described in 1884;[5] the studies on myotonia congenita were presented at the 500th anniversary (1886) of the University of Heidelberg. Other eponymic items include Erb-Charcot paralysis, syphilitic spastic spinal paralysis;[6] Erb's point, a landmark 2 or 3 cm above the clavicle and the posterior border of the sternomastoid at the level of the transverse process of the 6th cervical vertebra; Erb's sclerosis; Erb-Goldflam syndrome, myasthenia gravis pseudoparalytica; Erb's phenomenon, increased electric irritability of motor nerves in tetany; Erb-Westphal sign, absence of patellar tendon reflex in tabes; and Erb's myotonic relation in myotonia congenita (syphilitic meningomyelitis). The term "tendon reflex" was used in a contribution in 1875.[7]

For quite some time I have observed in healthy persons, but particularly in patients with lesions of the spinal cord, well developed reflexes in the quadriceps femoris which are readily and promptly elicited and which I deem worthy of some attention and practical evaluation. They can be produced by slight tapping of the tendon of the quadriceps above as well as below the patella, particularly from the region of the patellar ligament. These reflexes indicate an intimate and close reflex relationship between this tendon and the associated muscles.

I do not believe that this observation is entirely new to my colleagues in neurology; it is probable that the majority are familiar with this manifestation. Nevertheless, the literature is almost completely silent about this and similar facts, which certainly are not without interest. Quite recently I have gone over a large volume of the literature on the physiology and pathology of the spinal cord and I have found no unequivocal and adequate reports about it, unless the statements in question were just the ones that escaped me.

For this reason I believe that a brief mention of these tendon reflexes should be permissible, especially because they have proved to be a frequent and readily demonstrable manifestation which certainly must have some diagnostic importance that should not be underestimated; because they occur moreover, as a rule, with greater clearness and significance than do the skin reflexes, with which the tendon reflexes are not always in parallel, and finally because I have observed them in many tendons in addition to the quadriceps.

Erb has been described as a teacher whose expressions were simple and straightforward and who displayed warmth and compassion for his students and associates. He was a sound clinician and widely recognized as a fine consultant in clinical neurology. He was the co-editor of the *Deutsche Zeitschrift für Nervenheilkunde* and prepared the introductory communication in the first number of this journal (1891). When the Society of German Neurologists was founded, he was elected its first president. The indigent and the carriage trade were treated with equal interest and respect. In typical central European manner, holiday times were spent either tramping in the Black Forest or attending scientific meetings. On his 70th birthday he was honored with the unveiling of a bronze statue in the hospital grounds in Heidelberg, and a street in the city was named for him. Erb became the outstanding clinical neurologist of Germany in his time and was responsible for major contributions to the understanding of neuromuscular disorders.

1. Erb, W. H.: Localization of Paralysis in the Brachial Plexus (Ger), *Verh naturhis-med Verein, Heidelberg* 1:130-136, 1873-1877, excerpt translated by E. Longar.

2. Torkildsen, A., and Erickson, T.: Wilhelm Heinrich Erb, 1840-1921, *Arch Neurol Psychiat* 33:842-846 (April) 1935.

3. Erb, W. H.: Use of Electricity in Internal Medicine (Ger), *Samml Klin Vorträge*, no. 46, 1872, pp 351-388.

4. Erb, W. H.: Etiology of Tabes (Ger), *Samml Klin Vorträge*, no. 53, 2nd series, 1892, pp 515-542, excerpt translated by E. Sieweke and H. Frey.

5. Erb, W. H.: A Juvenile Form of Progressive Muscular Atrophy (Ger), *Deutsch Arch Klin Med* 34:467-519, 1884.

6. Erb, W. H.: An Uncommon Form of Spinal Paralysis (Ger), *Klin Wschr* 12:357-359 (June 28) 1875.

7. Erb, W. H.: Tendon Reflexes in Health and in Spinal Cord Disease (Ger), *Arch Psychiat Nervenkr* 5:792-802, excerpt translated by E. Sieweke.

Composite by G. Bako

Camillo Golgi (1843-1926)

GOLGI, neurohistologist, pathologist and malariologist, was born in Córtena, an Alpine village in the valley of Camonico, Italy, the son of a distinguished practitioner. He followed the family tradition and studied medicine in the medieval city of Pavia, where he ultimately returned as professor of histology. His thesis, presented for graduation in 1865, explored the pathogenesis of mental disorders and stressed the need for classification of such maladies on the basis of structural changes and etiological factors. Following graduation, Golgi became associated with the Ospedale di San Matteo in Pavia, worked with Lombroso in the psychiatric clinic, and spent some time in the Institute of General Pathology with Mantegazza and later with Bizzozero.

With the opportunities for investigation in Pavia so highly satisfactory, Golgi probably would have preferred to remain in Pavia had not financial circumstances forced him to accept a more profitable position. The post of chief resident physician and surgeon in a hospital for incurables in nearby Abbiategrasso, province of Milan, was offered and accepted in 1872, even though laboratory facilities were grossly inadequate and hardly comparable to the academic and scientific intercourse so accessible at Pavia. He continued his pathological studies in a home laboratory, working there when not on duty at the hospital. Under the intellectual stimulus of Lombroso and Bizzozero, and moved to action by the critical perusal of Virchow's *Cellular Pathology,* Golgi investigated the structure and function of the nervous system.[1] He was called to Pavia in 1875 as extraordinary professor of histology and, except for a few months as professor of anatomy at the University of Siena, remained in Pavia, active in its scholastic and civic life almost to the end. In 1881, he was appointed full professor of general pathology and histology, but not until his early sixties was he provided a well-equipped histological laboratory suitable for the work of an investigator of his intellectual capacity.

Golgi described the perivascular spaces of the brain and the endothelial origin of psammomas in reports from the pathological laboratory; whereas his first communication from the psychiatric clinic recounted the clinical and postmortem findings of a case of pellagra. In the study of normal nervous tissue, by a mordant staining technique in which potassium bichromate or osmic acid was used, Golgi showed that the neuroglia of the gray and white matter of the cerebellum consisted of various-sized cells. The final step was the silver impregnation, which provided a stark silhouetting of the two main types of nerve cells and their appendages against a translucent yellow background. Golgi's type I and type II cells were identified by this staining technique. Type I cell was a single long axis cylinder with branched protoplasmic processes. Type II, with a short axon and multiple branching dendrites, formed a fine meshed network.[2]

Finally, it seems that in the cerebral cortex (and probably in the gray substance of the nervous centers in general), there are placed two types of gangliar cells, viz.: first, gangliar cells . . . whose nervous prolongation gives out but few lateral elements and is directly transformed into the cylinder axis of a medullary nervous fibre; 2nd, gangliar cells . . . whose nervous prolongation, subdividing complicatedly, loses its individuality and takes part, *in toto,* in the formation of a nervous network, extending to all the strata of the gray substance.

Type I cells were assumed to be motor units and Type II sensory cells. The dendrites were believed to provide nutrition. Forel exposed the fallacy of this assumption shortly after its presentation. The impregnation technique was widely accepted and generally used in neuropathological investigations by him and Cajal especially, in the development of the neuron theory, which Golgi refused to accept.[2]

Upon the whole, then, the opinion of ancient and modern anatomists and physiologists, that the protoplasmic prologations directly conjoin, may be declared an hypothesis; it is not corroborated by direct observations, and the figures representing such connections, which we see even in some modern histologists, may be declared theoretic or schematic.

Notwithstanding this accord in the denial of anatomists, as a general law, it is necessary to take into account a few cases of direct connection between two nervous cells, which have been made the subject of special description, and which, from the authority of the describers, ought to be regarded as authentic. Such would be the cases of anatomosis between two cells described by *Wagner, Arnold, Beffer,* and some others.

The authenticity of these isolated cases is not at all contested, but such cases cannot be made the basis of general law; rather does the fact that, despite innumerable researches, there could be collected the very small number recorded, go to prove that these represent, rather than a general law, some rare exceptions, or which should be regarded as occurring under an exceptional law.

Golgi erred also in attributing significance to the rete nervosa diffusa, a composite of the collaterals of the type I axon and the whole of the type II axon. Before leaving Abbiategrasso in 1875, he wrote a final description of the structure of the olfactory bulb and offered proof of the intertwining of the olfactory fibers and the processes of the cells within the olfactory lamina. Descriptions of the musculotendinous end organ and the peripheral and central nerve fibers were reported. Late in the 1880's, Golgi's attention was directed to general pathology, and, by the maceration technique, he disclosed the course of uriniferous tubules and their relation to one another and to the glomerulus of the kidney. Only a few years after Laveran had found the malarial parasites in the blood, Golgi described the plasmodium of the quartan and the tertian fever and their nonsexual development. The estivoautumnal type of malaria was recognized as a separate entity. He discovered that the febrile paroxysm coincides with the segmentation or sporulation, which occurs at definite intervals for each species. The destruction of plasmodium by quinine provided a rational explanation for therapy.[3]

Regarding the coincidence of the maturation and segmentation of parasites with the onset of attacks, as seen in a series of observations, it seems worth pointing out that, in the severe episodes (which always coincide with the presence of abundant parasitic forms), segmentation, beginning a short time before the febrile onset (the onset of fever does not coincide with the onset of shivering), is prolonged for two or three hours of the febrile episode; in mild attacks, on the contrary, it seems that segmentation takes place first. These remarks correspond also to what is observed in quartan fever.

In tertian intermittent fever, the process of segmentation takes place in a way different from that observed in the quartan. And the differences are so sharp that, at least generally speaking, the finding of one form rather than another may be sufficient for differential diagnosis between the two clinical types of intermittent fever. . . . Besides, whereas in the quartan type the variations of the typical form that I have described and illustrated are absolutely exceptional; in the tertian several modes of segmentation are observed. So far I have been able to ascertain two types of segmentation.

In fact, it is possible to list the following differences:

1. The number of corpuscles resulting from segmentation: ordinarily this number is 15 to 20 per organism in tertian, but 6 to 12 in quartan fever.

2. Size of the corpuscles, which in the tertian is markedly smaller than in the quartan.

3. The apparently different constitution of the individual globules.

4. The important fact that, in the tertian form, the differentiation and elongation of the crown on the round body, the pigmented body that was described above, limited by a distinct wall, remains free.

Many of Golgi's contributions were published in the *Archivio per le Scienze Mediche* or the *Rivista sperimentale di freniatria,* were assembled into a monograph and translated into English by Workman.[2] His *Opera Omnia,* profusely and beautifully illustrated by the author, appeared in 1903.[4]

Golgi's fame attracted a number of students including Nansen, the Arctic explorer, Albert von Kölliker, Swiss histologist, and Negri, who described the intercellular bodies in rabies, "Negri bodies." Golgi was elected to honorary membership in scientific societies in Berlin, Leningrad, Vienna, and Paris and the American Neurological Association. He was awarded an honorary degree by Cambridge University, and made an Honorary Fellow of the Royal Society of Medicine of London. In 1906, he was awarded the Nobel Prize jointly with Cajal of Spain. He was twice rector of the University of Pavia and a member of the Royal Senate for several years. He has been described as austere, modest, and reserved, with a brilliant scientific intellect. Since his passion for research did not disappear with retirement, he retained contact with his laboratory and hospital into his octogenarian years.

1. Chorobski, J.: Camillo Golgi, 1843-1926, *Arch Neurol (Chic)* 33:163-170, 1935.

2. Golgi, C.: Studies on the Minute Anatomy of the Central Organs of the Nervous System, *Alienist Neurol* 4:236-269 (April) 1883.

3. Golgi, C.: The Evolution Cycle of the Malarial Parasites in Tertian Fever, *Arch Sci (Tor)* 13:173-196, 1889, excerpt translated by L. C. Raymond.

4. Golgi, C.: *Opera Omnia*, Milan: U. Hoepli, 1903.

Carl Weigert (1845-1904)

THE DISCOVERIES OF CARL WEIGERT on the superiority of aniline dyes in the staining of morbid tissues are more widely recognized than his investigations into the fundamental concepts of the response of tissues to insult and repair. This is partially related to his taciturn ruminations in seminars and reticence in disseminating his philisophy of morbidity. Carl was born in Münsterberg, Silesia, in the same district and a few years earlier than his cousin, Paul Ehrlich, organic chemist and inventor of the modern concept of immunity. Weigert studied medicine at the universities of Breslau and Berlin and came under the influence of such outstanding medical scientists as Cohn, Heidenhain,

Composite by G. Bako

Traube, and Virchow. Following graduation, he was assistant to Waldeyer in Breslau, and, after a tour of duty as regimental surgeon in the Franco-Prussian war, he returned once more to this community as assistant to Lebert in the Medical Clinic.[1]

One of Weigert's first significant contributions in microscopic pathology was made during the smallpox epidemic of 1871–72. The detection of bacteria and the description of morbid changes in the skin of the afflicted marked the beginning of his reflections upon the fundamentals of necrosis and repair. Furthermore, he was content with demonstrating for the first time bacteria in human tissue, and was not led into what might have been an obvious trap in concluding that the bacteria were the pathogenic agents.[2]

The following observations have been made on several bodies dead of smallpox. There was such a regularity of association between the bacteria and the skin infections which are common in smallpox that I feel justified in publishing the following report.

In the corium of the above-mentioned cases, I found hollow stems or their cross-sections which were like vessels, widened in parts, often branching; they had a diameter of 0.01 to 0.02 mm and were full of many little granules sharply outlined, showing completely the characteristics of the bacteria described by von Recklinghausen. These aggregations did not change in acetic acid, caustic soda, or glycerin, and showed such regular, sharply accentuated granules that it was not readily possible to confuse them with detritus. If I stained the anatomical sections in an ammoniacal carmin solution, in which even the intercellular substance of the connective tissue stained red, these hollow stems remained colorless. But if I treated the cross-sections later with hydrochloric acid in glycerin, then the substance between the granules assumed a red color, whereas the connecting tissue remained colorless except for the nucleus.

This observation from the medical clinic attracted the attention of Julius Cohnheim, director of the Institute of Pathology at Breslau, who offered Weigert the position of privatdocent and induced him to transfer his laboratory pursuits to the Institute. This was a critical decision for Weigert, since from then on he remained in the field of pathology and never returned to clinical medicine. There were two fruitful areas for pathological research then as today; ie, experimental and structural pathology. In contrast to Cohnheim, experimentation on laboratory animals held little appeal for Weigert, who preferred to expand the histologic study of human organs insulted by disease or injured by external forces.

When Cohnheim was invited to the chair of pathological anatomy at the University of Leipzig in 1878, he accepted upon the condition that Weigert accompany him. Since Cohnheim was severely afflicted with gout, many academic and routine responsibilities at the university were delegated to Weigert. After the death of Cohnheim in 1884, it would have been natural for Weigert to succeed to the post. Biographers are in general agreement that the failure of the faculty to select Weigert was largely the result of his being a Jew and, to a lesser extent, his lack of aggressiveness.[3] Weigert countered this disillusionment in academic life with serious thoughts of returning to clinical medicine. This goal was not pursued, however, and he accepted the directorship of the Senckenberg Institute for Pathological Anatomy in Frankfurt-am-Main, a good choice. Frankfurt provided an abundance of pathological material in its several hospitals as well as close association with Ehrlich and Edinger. Thus, a great histopathologist was permitted to continue the development of staining techniques and the investigation of the reaction of tissues to injury and repair. Weigert was not offered a university post in subsequent years and according to Rieder, did not appreciate the devious techniques frequently used in competition for a desirable university appointment.[4]

Weigert's vision and extraordinary capacity for analysis in solving technical problems in his search for fundamental laws were most appealing to those of similar intellect and industry. He was not a stimulating teacher for the student with average ability, training, and scientific imagination. Except for his first communication, which discussed the lesions in smallpox, there was no desire to hurry a manuscript. Even the smallpox study was expanded and re-evaluated, and a revision published several years after the initial report. This described the staining technique, by which, with the use of hematoxylin, carmine, and picric acid dyes, the epithelium, connective tissue, and skin were differentiated. A total of less than 100 scientific contributions were published, a relatively small number for a brillant German scientist. Not a dull person socially, he was considered a good spinner of yarns, sprinkled with wit but not with satire, and was an excellent ventriloquist and amateur mind reader.

A philosophical approach to disease, which led Weigert to propose and to elaborate upon fundamental principles in the search for general laws for morphologic phenomena, is illustrated in his *Historical Notes on Schiwa* (a light reference to a Hindu god of destruction). The doctrine and discovery of the process termed by Cohnheim "coagulation necrosis" was opposed to that advanced by Virchow, who believed that inflammatory growth followed external stimuli.[3]

My observations on the role of outer influences on the bioplastic processes reach back a long time. It was at the time of the great smallpox epidemic when I had a fine opportunity to investigate the smallpox eruption. I then found to my great astonishment that the primary affection in the skin lesion was not an irritation but a necrobiosis. Already then did I recognize that this necrosis, by virtue of its size and nature, gave a specificity to the process, in contradistinction to other phenomena in the skin lesion. It also became clear to me that I was on the approach to a general law; and already then, between 1871 and 1873, I repeatedly ventured the opinion in a small circle of friends, that the primary condition in a pathological process is the passive tissue injury and not the active cell proliferation. . . . I then set down the condition that in the study of pathological irritative phenomena one must seek for a primary necrobiosis upon which are based the special properties of the many varying pathological processes. My task now was to investigate my theory under varying pathological conditions. . . . Then, in 1880, with the support of these investigations to my theory, I attempted to bring it out in an intelligible form. I stated that the pathological tissue proliferation is entirely analogous to physiological regeneration or repair. I now sought to make physiological repair mechanically intelligible through the teaching that diminution of growth restraint influences both physiological and pathological repair.

A classification of glomerular nephritis, Bright's disease, proposed while he was teaching in Breslau, remains valid.[5]

1. In the first group belong those forms in which there is only a small cell proliferation in the connective tissue (acute nephritis). There are also hemorrhages. Clinically, there is oliguria, albuminuria, white and red blood cells, casts, many times edema, but no hypertrophy of the heart.
2. Subacute Forms (already described by me as chronic hemorrhagic nephritis). There is connective tissue proliferation in the interstices, in the Malpighian capsules, endarteritis obliterans, without shrinkage of the kidney. There are hemorrhages, hypertrophy of the heart, retinitis, uremia, edema, massive albuminuria with varying amounts of blood.
3. Chronic Forms. Marked contraction of the kidney with retention of a major portion of the parenchyma, also hypertrophy of the heart, etc. Varying degrees of edema, albuminuria, and urine volume.
4. Advanced Chronic Forms. Granular atrophy, marked shrinkage of the kidney with little remaining parenchyma, cardiac hypertrophy, etc. No edema. Polyuria with little albumin.

Weigert discussed the pathology of tuberculosis before and after the demonstration of the tubercle bacillus. He opened the rupture of a tubercle into the circulation in a case of miliary tuberculosis and was successful in finding intimal tubercles in pulmonary veins.[6] Even today his theory of pathogenesis is of value.

The report of a thymus tumor in a patient with myasthenia gravis was the first, according to Weigert, of such an association, with the suggestion that the tumor might be related to muscle function.[7]

At the autopsy of a case of myasthenia gravis, . . . we found a reddish looking mass, 5 cm long and wide and 3 cm thick, in the frontal mediastinum lying close to the upper part of the heart at the site of the thymus gland.
Microscopic investigation of the tumor revealed . . . tissue islands of small cells for the most part which seemed to lack protoplasm, . . . and which possessed only one nucleus rich in chromatin. These lymphatic cells make up the main part of the normal thymus. There also were a few so-called epithelioid collections, that were rich in protoplasm and that had a pale large center, which enclosed, in a few instances, some smaller cells (macrophages) such as are seen in the normal thymus. Finally there were the well-known cell mass aggregates like a pearly ball, the so-called Hassal forms, characteristic of the thymus gland.
It is safe to assume that such a quantity of foreign cells could not be without influence on muscle function. In what direction and on which function these influences act, whether biological-chemical or mechanic-circulatory, is uncertain. However, this case merits special interest since this is the first positive finding in muscles in a case diagnosed by experts as Erb's illness.

The Weigert stain, modified by Pal[8] and later called the Pal-Weigert stain, applied to the myelin sheath, and was based on the observation that nerve sheaths stain selectively with hematoxylin when fixed with chromic salts. Other significant stains for tissue were a rapid myelin sheath stain (1889), the fibrin stain (1887), the neuroglia stain (1890), and the elastic fiber stain (1898).[3] He perfected the procedure for celloidin embedding, originally described by Schiefferdecker in 1882.

Carl Weigert, a master of staining technique, is best remembered for his investigations in neurohistology. Less well known were his fine intellect and philosophy of pathological phenomena, which embraced the concept of repair of cells and tissues following injury. Weigert was never elected to a senior post in a university, but, although lesser minds received greater honors, his steadfast devotion through his scientific career was remarkable and rewarding and left a lasting impression in the medical sciences. His contributions provided some of the fundamentals for neurologists and neuropathologists in subsequent generations for the investigation of form and function of the nervous system.

1. Dunham, E. K., and Herter, C. A.: The Collected Works of Carl Weigert, *JAMA* 48:412-415 (Feb 2) 1907.

2. Weigert, C.: Bacteria in the Skin of Patients with Smallpox (Ger), *Cbl med Wiss* 9:609-611 (Sept) 1871, excerpt translated by F. Sternthal.

3. Morrison, H.: Carl Weigert, *Ann Med Hist* 6:163-177 (June) 1924.

4. *The Collected Works of Carl Weigert*, R. Rieder, ed., Berlin: J. Springer, 1906.

5. Weigert, C.: Bright's Disease from a Pathologic-Anatomic Viewpoint, *Samml Klin Vorträge* 162-163:1411-1460, 1879.

6. Weigert, C.: Tuberculosis of the Veins, *Arch path Anat* 88:307-379, 1882.

7. Weigert, C.: Pathologic-Anatomic Consideration of Erb's Disease (Myasthenia Gravis) (Ger), *Neurol Cbl* 20:597-601, 1901, excerpt translated by E. Longar.

8. Pal, J.: A Contribution to the Techniques of Nervous Tissue Staining, *Med Jahrb* 1:619-631, 1886.

Ramón y Cajal (1852-1934)

THE AUTOBIOGRAPHY OF DON SANTIAGO RAMÓN Y CAJAL, distinguished neurohistologist and the first natural scientist to capture the attention of the medical world for Spain after the decline of the Moorish domination in the West, has been translated by Craigie and begins as follows:[1]

I was born on the first of May, 1852, in Petilla de Aragon, a small town of Navarre, situated, by a strange geographical freak, in the center of the province of Zaragoza not far from Sos. The uncertainties of the medical profession took my father, Justo Ramón Casasús, a pure-blooded Aragonese, and a modest surgeon at the time, to the insignificant village which was my birthplace, and where I passed the first two years of my life.

My father was a man of great energy, an extraordinarily hard worker, and full of noble ambition. Depressed during the early years of his professional life because he had been unable, through lack of funds, to complete his medical studies, he resolved, when already established and supporting a family, to save enough to complete his academic career, even at the cost of great privations. This enabled him to substitute for the humble title of second-class surgeon the brilliant diploma of physician and surgeon.

Not only was Ramón senior successful in his medical ambitions, but also he loved to

National Library of Medicine

teach and probably had a greater influence on Ramón junior in his most formative years than did the village schoolteachers. The father was scarcely an orthodox pedagogue; he preferred a shepherd's cave in the Pyrenees Mountains as the classroom. At the age of six, the son was skilled in writing and possessed some knowledge of geography, mathematics, and French. Sketching and drawing, however, was the dominant outlet for expression, a skill that came to be of great value in subsequent years in the preparation of his neurohistologic manuscripts. But the path was rugged and the discouragements frequent during adolescence. Ramón, an impulsive youth, needed the discipline that appeared to be best obtained in a preparatory school. The Esculapian seminary was selected in a neighboring community, where emphasis was placed on memorizing

Latin grammar. The policies of the school were enforced by flogging and short rations. The results, however, were dismal. Don Santiago returned home and was apprenticed first to a barber, and later to a cobbler. He became so skillful with the last and hammer that the best bootmaker in town enticed him with the promise of "two reals (*ca.* 10¢) a day," and subsequently, if he fulfilled the expectations, "meals and clothing provided." Such interruptions in education were followed by the first overt interest in medicine. In collaboration with his father, skeletal remains were recovered from a nearby cemetery and the study of osteology begun in an abandoned granary.[2] In contrast to Ramón's distaste for memorizing Greek and Latin, he pursued avidly the study of the skeleton, augmented by a love for drawing and sketching.

Father and son then moved to Zaragoza, the father an interim professor at the University, the son a student of medicine. At the age of 21, when Don Santiago had qualified for the MD degree, his anatomical illustrations were so numerous and so well executed that publication of an anatomical atlas was considered. This was never accomplished, however, but many of the drawings were preserved. Next came a tour of duty with the Medical Corps of the Spanish Army, and an eight-month campaign at Lérida, followed by service in Cuba, a land rampant with malaria and dysentery. Cajal was severely afflicted throughout the Cuban tour of duty and returned to Spain in poor health. Three years later, he suffered a severe pulmonary hemorrhage, but this was the last clinical evidence of active tuberculosis. The University of Zaragoza, which had honored his father, appointed the son director of the Anatomical Museum. The facilities were meager, however, and in order to correct such deficiencies, a histologic laboratory was set up at home. The first scientific communication, "Experimental Observations on Inflammation in the Mesentery, the Cornea, and Cartilage," appeared in 1880, illustrated with lithographs prepared by the author. The second scientific contribution was entitled "Microscopic Observations upon the Nerve Endings in Voluntary Muscles."

In 1884, Don Santiago was called to the chair of anatomy at Valencia, where, due to the epidemic devastation of cholera, a portion of his energies was diverted to bacteriology and serology. Three years later at the age of 35, he turned to neurohistology and, as professor at Barcelona, began a series of brilliant studies that marked him as the greatest medical scientist of modern Spain. Communication with scientists of renown outside of Spain was limited. Few non-Spanish medical periodicals were available. The potentialities of neurohistology, through the Golgi (of Pavia) chrome-silver stain, were reportedly brought to his attention by Simarra, a neuropsychiatrist in Madrid. In attempting to duplicate the Golgi technique, Cajal soon discovered that it was too capricious to be reliable. Rather than reject the technique, however, he resolved to build upon it. In a relatively short time he made two major modifications. If embryonic tissue were used, the specimens would be stained before the development of the medullary sheaths. Secondly, double impregnation resulted in greater dependability. The combination of the improved chrome-silver stain and the microscope, with 800 magnification, produced phenomenal results.

The peak of Cajal's academic career was reached in 1892 with the appointment to the faculty in the University of Madrid. Recognition from other countries soon followed. The Croonian Lectures were given in London in French (1894) on the histology of the nervous system. The year following the cessation of the Spanish-American War, Clark University in Worcester, Mass—a pioneer school in psychology and geology—honored him by a lectureship on the anatomy of the brain. In 1926, the Spanish government built the Cajal Institute to support his investigations in neuroanatomy. However, he preferred his home laboratory but desired that his successors reap the benefits of the physical improvements. In 1906, he shared the Nobel Prize in medicine or physiology with Golgi.

Although Cajal was on the road to success, the nod of approval by the outstanding German histologists was extremely helpful. In 1889, Cajal was determined to convince the German society of anatomists of the significance of his histologic preparations. Membership in the society included His, Retzius, Kölliker, Waldeyer, and Schwalbe. Kölliker of the University of Würzburg was immediately impressed; with the support of the German school, fame was assured.

Cajal revealed that the lateral and terminal ramifications of every axis cylinder terminate in the gray substance, not by means of a diffuse network as Gerlach and Golgi had stated, but by means of free arborizations that assume various forms—such as pericellular basket works, creeping branches, or *boutons terminaux*. These ramifications were identified as intimately related to the body and dendrites of the nerve cells which establish contact or an articulation between the receptive protoplasm and the last radiculi of the neuraxons. Golgi was in error in asserting that the soma and the protoplasmic expansions constituting the cell segments contribute little more than a nutrient role. They participate in the chain of conduction of the nerve impulse. Having excluded continuity from nerve cell to nerve cell, he found it was necessary to postulate a new theory; ie, transmission of the nerve impulse by contact or induction.

For 40 years, Cajal was a zealous investigator and a prolific writer. He published more than 200 scientific papers and several major treatises. The *Texture of the Nervous System of Man and the Vertebrates* was published in three volumes. His crowning achievement was the monograph *Histology of the Nervous System*. Many of the passages are revealing and sound today.

Honorary degrees were conferred by Oxford and Cambridge. While in London as a house guest of Sir Charles Sherrington, he had brought along some bottles of tissue in order to continue his investigation at odd hours while visiting. He was awarded the Moscow prize at the International Congress of Medicine in Paris, 1900, and the Helmholtz Medal of the Royal Prussian Academy in 1904. The Spanish government, at different times, offered him the ministry of public instruction and the honorary position of life Senator. He declined the former position and accepted the latter.

Cajal was a humanist as well as a scientist.[3] He frequented the street cafés for a "diastole of rest" to prepare for a "systole of work." The aphorisms from his *Coffee-house Chatter* include:[4]

Grey matter abounds in countries with grey skies.
A woman venerates her parents, esteems her husband but adores only her sons.
Try to honor your children lest they dishonor you.
The saddest thing about old age is that its future is behind it.

Spain's great scientist and neurohistologist, the leader of modern scientific medicine on the Iberian peninsula, was as indebted to his father near the end of his life as he had been as a child.

He bequeathed to me his moral qualities to which I owe what I am; the religion of the sovereignty of the will, faith in hard work, the conviction that a spirit of steadfast and unrelenting determination is capable of moulding and integrating everything from the muscle to the brain, making good the deficiencies of Nature and even overcoming the misfortunes of character, the most niggardly and refractory phenomena of life. It was from him also that I acquired the commendable ambition to be something, and the resolution neither to consider any sacrifice too great for the realization of my aspirations nor ever to change my course for any secondary considerations.

1. Cajal, S. R.: *Recollections of My Life*, E. Horne Craigie, trans., Philadelphia: American Philosophical Society, 2 vol, 1937.
2. Penfield, W.: The Career of Ramón y Cajal, *Arch Neurol Psychiat* 16:213-220 (Aug) 1926.
3. Gibson, W. C.: Santiago Ramón y Cajal (1852-1934), *Ann Med Hist* 8:385-394 (Sept) 1936.
4. "Ramón y Cajal," editorial *JAMA* 103:1541-43 (Nov 17) 1934.

Sir William Gowers (1845-1915)

WILLIAM GOWERS, clinical neurologist and junior colleague of J. Hughlings Jackson, was one of the early staff members of the National Hospital for the Paralysed and Epileptic, Queen Square, London, the outstanding center for neurology for more than a century. William began his education at Christ Church School, Oxford, and in keeping with the custom of his generation, was apprenticed at the age of 16 to Dr. Thomas Simpson at Coggeshall in Essex.[1] His medical training was continued as pupil and secretary to Sir William Jenner, at University

Composite by G. Bako

College Hospital in London, the city of his birth. It is expected that Gowers received some special indoctrination into the study of neurology, since this subject was a discipline of significance at University College. The MB degree granted in 1869 with gold medals in botany, physiology, anatomy, and materia medica, and the MD the following year, also with a gold medal, are ample evidence of his high scholastic attainments. In 1870, Gowers was appointed medical registrar at the National Hospital and later promoted to the honorary staff as assistant physician. In the meantime, while holding a staff position at University College Hospital, he became professor of clinical medicine, and reached his peak in neurological accomplishments.

Beginning early in his professional life, Gowers developed skill in shorthand, developed a native talent in drawing and sketching for lectures, bedside notes and contributions to books and periodicals, and tried his hand at water colors but avoided

oils. He also founded and became the first president of an organization devoted to writing skills, strangely known as the Society of Medical Phonographers. The inaugural address, "Writing and Shortwriting in Relation to Medical Work," urged students to learn shorthand before beginning a medical career. As further evidence of pragmatic interest he designed a hemocytometer and a hemoglobinometer, unglamorous but useful medical tools. The fundamental change in the hemocytometer was the transfer of the etched squares (0.1 mm square) from the eyepiece to the floor of the cell of the glass chamber. The hemocytometer utilized the calorimetric principle and was calibrated against a solution of carmine and picrocarmine. The instrument was accepted as the standard until modified by Haldane early in the 1900's.[2]

I have arranged a modification of Hayem's instrument, in which the lateral divisions are ruled on the bottom of the cell, so that the instrument can be employed with any microscope, and its convenient use is thus greatly extended.

The hemocytometer was used in study of the value of inorganic iron in the treatment of anemia, an agent that had been discovered and rediscovered intermittently for centuries. Following the intake orally of iron salts, the concentration of red cells was increased as well as the concentration of hemoglobin in the cell.[2]

This case is of interest in several particulars. It shows what a rapid and regular augmentation in the number of the corpuscles may be effected by iron, and that this effect is produced with perfect efficiency, by the chloroxide of iron.

In a discussion of the state of the arteries in Bright's disease, one of his several dissertations on the value of the ophthalmoscope in general medicine, Gowers included several drawings by his own hand and a speculation over the pathogenesis of vascular changes.[3]

The change in the size of the arteries is frequently such as to be recognised at once; . . . The reduction in size may be so considerable, that even the primary branches of the central artery are so small that their double contour is recognised with difficulty, and it may be unrecognisable even by direct examination, the arteries being, as in the example I have to show, visible only as lines.

In the latter case the veins may be normal in size or may be smaller than natural.

There is, of course, nothing new in the fact that the retinal arteries are small in Bright's disease; it has long been remarked as a common feature in albuminuric retinitis, and it is shown plainly in the best illustrations of this change (as in those of Liebreich). But it is usually regarded as a consequence of the retinal change, and the points on which I would insist are that it occurs also quite independently of the retinal change, and stands commonly in direct relation to another condition—the blood-tension.

If the tension of the arterial blood and the arterial contraction occur in common proportion, they must stand in a causal relation to one another. But the blood-tension cannot be the cause of the arterial contraction . . . on the other hand, as the immediate effect of contraction of the arterioles must be an increase in the arterial blood-pressure, it is reasonable to conclude that such is the sequence of events in the phenomena under consideration; that, although the two phenomena may be in part the result of a common cause (altered state of the blood), the contraction of the arteries, seen in those of the retina and inferred to exist elsewhere, is, in part at least, the cause of the increased blood-tension.

The clarity and simplicity of Gowers' writings reflect not only careful preparation but also insight and understanding of anatomy, physiology, pathology, and clinical neurology. The steps in the creation of a communication for *Lancet* or the *British Medical Journal* began with the recognition of an important clinical-pathological feature, observed usually in more than one case and presented informally or formally in a teaching exercise. Several contributions would then be combined in a monograph in one of his several outstanding treatises, such as *Epilepsy and Other Chronic Convulsive Diseases,*[4] *A Manual of Diseases of the Nervous System,*[5] or *The Diagnosis of Diseases of the Spinal Cord.*[6] A complete bibliography is given by Critchley.[1] Scarcely a malady in the field of neurology escaped Gowers' critical attention. He wrote on syphilis of the central nervous system, facial paralysis, brain injury, vertigo, cerebral aneurysm, writer's cramp, chorea, pseudohypertrophic muscular paralysis, tabes dorsalis, optic neuritis, tetany, ocular palsy, paraplegia, birth palsies, syringomyelia, ascending myelitis, infantile paralysis, bulbar paralysis, lead palsy, caries

of the spine, myasthenia gravis, and migraine. A special case report described a tumor of the spinal cord. The diagnosis was suspected from clinical findings and confirmed surgically by Victor Horsley, the first time that surgery had been successful in a case of spinal tumor.[7] In general medicine, Gowers discussed cardiac murmurs, leukocythemia, mitral disease, hypertrophy of the heart with primary renal disease, syphilitic disease of the lungs, a peculiar form of albumin in the urine (possibly Bence Jones protein) and introduced the term "fibrositis." Gowers referred to the knee-jerk, without appreciating the fact that this would be a standard diagnostic maneuver in subsequent generations, and described a method for enhancing a sluggish knee-jerk.[6]

Curiously, Gowers' tract, his best-known eponymic reference—a description of ascending degeneration—contains a footnote decrying the use of eponymic terms.[6]

. . . in a spinal cord of which the lower extremity was crushed, a symmetrical area of slight ascending degeneration in the anterior part of the lateral columns, [was observed] in front of the pyramidal tracts. Of its possible significance I will speak presently.

. . . But if sensation is conducted in part in the lateral columns, it is certainly not in that portion of them which is occupied by the pyramidal tracts, because there may be no loss when these are completely degenerated. It is probably, therefore, in front of these. This is the situation in which I have found the ascending degeneration in the case of the crushed cord in which sensation was greatly impaired.

The direct pyramidal tract is also called the column of Türck; the postero-median column is called the column of Goll, and the postero-external column is called the column of Burdach. I have avoided the use of these terms. This system of nomenclature is full of inconvenience, increasing the difficulties of the student, and leading to frequent mistakes in scientific writings. There are very few observations in medicine regarding which it is not obvious that they would speedily have been made by some one other than the actual observer; that it was very much of an accident that they were made by certain individuals. Scientific nomenclature should be itself scientific, not founded upon accidents. However, anxious [as] we may be to honour individuals, we have no right to do so at the expense of the convenience of all future generations of learners.

Gowers was knighted on the occasion of the Diamond Jubilee of Queen Victoria in

1897. He had previously resigned his clinical appointment because of poor health but remained on as a consultant.

He was the recipient of many honors including membership in the American Neurological Society and the Russian Medical Society, and Lettsomian Lecturer, a lectureship within the gift of the Medical Society of London. He was awarded the Goulstonian Lectureship, which is given to the youngest of the newly appointed Fellows of the Royal College of Physicians, while his Fellowship in the Royal Society was probably the greatest accolade, especially for a medical man.

1. Critchley, M.: *Sir William Gowers, 1845-1915, A Biographical Appreciation*, London: William Heinemann, 1949.

2. Gowers, W. R.: Numeration of Blood Corpuscles, and the Effect of Iron and Phosphorus on the Blood, *Practitioner* 21:1-17 (July) 1878.

3. Growers, W. R.: State of the Arteries in Bright's Disease, *Brit Med J* 2:743-745 (Dec 9) 1876.

4. Gowers, W. R.: *Epilepsy and Other Chronic Convulsive Diseases*, London: J. & A. Churchill, 1881.

5. Gowers, W. R.: *A Manual of Diseases of the Nervous System*, 2nd ed, London: J. & A. Churchill, 1892.

6. Gowers, W. R.: *The Diagnosis of Diseases of the Spinal Cord*, 3rd ed, London: J. & A. Churchill, 1884.

7. Gowers, W. R., and Horsley, V.: A Case of Tumour of the Spinal Cord, *Medicochir Trans* 71:377-428, 1888.

James J. Putnam (1846-1918)

Composite by G. Bako

JAMES JACKSON PUTNAM, son of a physician and maternal grandson of James Jackson, was born in Boston, graduated from Harvard College, trained for medicine at Harvard Medical School, and served as house-pupil at the Massachusetts General Hospital.[1] Devoting two years to postgraduate work in Europe, he spent various lengths of time in Vienna, Leipzig, Paris, and London and was influenced especially by Rokitansky, Meynert, and Hughlings Jackson. On his return to Harvard, he was appointed lecturer on a novel, but practical, subject—the application of electricity in nervous diseases. Continuing to serve on the faculty, Jackson progressed to the professorship of diseases of the nervous system in 1893, and served until 1912 as Harvard's first professor of this subject. Exemplary of the firm ties between Harvard Medical School and the Massachusetts General Hospital, Putnam started a neurological clinic at the hospital and served as its chief from 1874 to 1909. Although an enviable goal was subsequently achieved, gains came slowly. Neither inspiring nor brilliant as a teacher, he drew little support for his clinic, and so was forced to seek space in his home for a neuropathological laboratory. But, as his reputation grew and his consulting practice increased, Putnam found himself in command of a neurological clinic of stature. Subsequently, he became one of the founders of the American Neurological Association and the Boston Society of Psychiatry and Neurology.

Putnam's communications in the 19th century, in contrast to his psychiatric briefs of the 20th century, were primarily devoted to general medicine and neurology and covered a wide range of subjects, relying upon physiological interpretation of pathogenesis whenever possible. In this mission he benefited from the mutual exchange of scientific thought with H. P. Bowditch, for many years professor of physiology at Harvard. Although on intimate terms with William Osler, he turned to his friends, William James and Josiah P. Royce, for the illumination of his analytical and philosophical mind. One of his first reports was a 24-page discussion of a case of circumscribed analgesia, published in 1875. This was followed by a succession of case reports and clinical discussions of diverse subjects, including adult poliomyelitis, neuritis associated with lead and arsenic poisoning, endocrine disorders, thyroidectomy for Graves' disease, myxedema, dysfunction of the basal ganglion, athetosis, epilepsy, spinal cord tumors, and cardiopulmonary murmurs.

In 1891, Putnam described systemic sclerosis accompanied by degeneration of the spinal cord.[2] He observed eight fatal cases with involvement of the posterior and lateral columns. Except for the reference to Lichtheim's association of cord changes with pernicious anemia, he overlooked any correlation of a blood dyscrasia with the neurological symptoms and pathological findings. One of Putnam's patients suffered from pallor and presented clinical symptoms highly suggestive of pernicious anemia, but no blood studies were reported. A decade later Putnam prepared a subsequent report in collaboration with Taylor. Although still unwilling to accept a specific causal relationship in each instance, the general conclusions were stated as follows:[3]

1. That a well-defined lesion of the nervous system particularly localized in the cord exists, which may for the present be termed simply "diffuse degeneration."

2. That no fundamental characteristics of the lesion have been found depending on different causes.

3. That anemic states have been shown at times to be a concomitant condition, but not necessarily a cause.

4. That the actual causes are still wholly obscure.

Before the end of the 19th century, Putnam disclosed in his writings a great curiosity for psychiatric treatment of neurasthenia, one step in his acceptance of the merits of Freudian psychiatry. Regarding mind and matter he remarked:[4]

In health there is a certain degree of co-ordination and mutual support between all the vast activities of the mind, binding them to the consciousness on the one hand and to the vital functions of the body on the other; . . . The healthy man feels himself a consistent character, and can predict what he will do, not only as regards those new exigencies which require logical thought, but also as regards those which depend upon the promptings of all the deeper-lying and subconscious processes with which his mind is stocked. His reactions to the various problems which present themselves are as prompt as the conditions of the case permit, and the attention of his consciousness is at liberty to devote itself, unembarrassed, to the interest of each new question as it arises.

In neurasthenia, and still more in hysteria, this harmony of action, tending to the furtherance of single interests of the individual, one after another, is more or less deeply impaired. The patient's consciousness is no longer permitted to focus itself exclusively upon the main object of his attention, but unrelated ideas and emotions intrude themselves, to the detriment of his flow of thought, just as floating opacities in the vitreous humor of the eye drift over and obscure the field of vision.

With a penetrating appreciation of Freud's teaching, Putnam's accepted the psychoanalytic movement as a great advance in medicine. He was responsible for inducing Freud to present his famous series of lectures at Clark University, Worcester, Mass, in 1909.[5] As the search for the causes of distressing mental symptoms was pursued, whether the pathogenic factors were related to the environment, habits, experiences of childhood, or expressed in inherited physical traits, Putnam was ready to apply psychoanalytic principles in the interpretation of etiology and discussion of treatment.[6]

The Freud method (to which the name of "psychoanalytic" has been given) . . . is an attempt to enable the patient to penetrate with tireless zeal, increasing skill and fearless honesty, upon the details of his own emotion, life and thought, in the belief that nothing becomes less sacred or fails to become less painful, through being clearly seen.

The psycho-analytic method does not indeed necessarily give us all that we may need for spiritual progress, but it prepares the way and opens a long path. It does not exclude the other mode of treatment, but supplements some of them and often render all of them unnecessary. If the slogan of the suggestive psychotherapeutics has been, "You can do better if you *try*," the distinctive slogan of this method is "You can do better when you *know*."

But when you know what? The answer has been already given, "When you know yourself." The symptoms of the psychoneuroses,—morbid fears, irresistible impulses to thoughts and acts, distressing doubts, nameless apprehensions,—and not these symptoms of illness alone, but also their congeners, selfishness, envy, suspicion and temptation to cruelty and prejudice such as have filled the world with misery, have been largely the outcome of self-ignorance, in the sense that in this ignorance, the deeper sources of which have been, until now, imperfectly defined and largely unsuspected, lies the secret of the occurrence of these evils. It is the removal of this ignorance and the implantation of the desire as well as the ability to see things as they are that constitutes the best and only radical treatment.

Not the Disease Only, But Also the Man, Putnam's 1899 Shattuck Lecture before the Massachusetts Medical Society, discussed a concept of physician and patient that is revived periodically. In the transition period from treating neurasthenia as a neurologist to the acceptance of the psychoanalytic movement, he stated:[7]

He [the physician] works of necessity with a threefold object in view: to cure his patient; to leave him better able to cure himself another time; and to establish systems of treatment that shall reflect sound and liberal views. He must of necessity come into close personal contact with his patient, and may therefore, through the powerful influence of his own personality, make him narrow or suspicious, or unduly dependent on rules and mysteries; or, on the other hand, more reasonable, more self-reliant, more liberal, a firmer believer in his own genius, and the supporter of simpler creeds. The opportunity for usefulness is an enormous one; for I hold that to rid a patient of a tormenting delusion and to increase his power of resistance against debasing habits and thoughts is quite the equivalent of a successful operation for a painful disease, and needs as much skill and preparation.

In the "Preface" to his *Human Motives,* prepared in 1915, Putnam expressed what may be interpreted as some of his innermost sentiments on motivations.[8]

I believe, on the other hand, that men are more strongly bound than they usually recognize, by a sense of obligations definable as "ideal." Whatever name one may choose for these ties, they are virtually religious in their nature, and the recognition of them often gives rise to a feeling of new birth. The sense of these obligations, even though unacknowledged or denied, makes itself felt through the host of lesser motives.
On the other hand, men are handicapped by passions, longings, personal ambitions, cravings for success and mastery, to a degree of which they are never wholly conscious. Not only a portion of men's acts but all of them derive some

coloring from these sources. The influences underlying them are not to be designated as bad, but as tendencies needing to be appreciated and utilized in the service of progress of the best sort.

As a resident of Boston, Putnam identified himself with the city's civic and charitable endeavors, helping the needy individual or cause, among them the then recently organized social service department of the Massachusetts General Hospital which cared for neurotics. Modest in thought and manner, almost to an affectation, he adhered to the highest ethical standards in social intercourse. Professional membership included the American Academy of Arts and Sciences, the Society of Mental Hygiene, and the Association of American Physicians. His identity with Boston and Harvard Medical School persists, with the endowed chair of neurology at the Boston City Hospital and the J. J. Putnam professorship of neurology of Harvard Medical School.

1. Taylor, E. W.: James Jackson Putnam: His Contributions to American Neurology, *Arch Neurol Psychiat* 3:307-314, 1920.
2. Putnam, J. J.: A Group of Cases of System Scleroses of the Spinal Cord, Associated With Diffuse Collateral Degeneration; Occurring in Enfeebled Persons Past Middle Life, and Especially in Women; Studied With Particular Reference to Etiology, *J Nerv Ment Dis* 16(ns):69-110, 1891.
3. Putnam, J. J., and Taylor, E. W.: Diffuse Degeneration of the Spinal Cord, *J Nerv Ment Dis* 28-74-101, 1901.
4. Putnam, J. J.: Remarks on the Physical Treatment of Neurasthenia, *Boston Med Surg J* 132:505-511, 1895.
5. Putnam, J. J.: Personal Impressions of Sigmund Freud and His Work, With Special Reference to His Recent Lectures at Clark University, *J Abnorm Psychol* 4:293-310 (Dec 1909-Jan 1910), 372-379 (Feb-March) 1910.
6. Putnam, J. J.: On the Etiology and Treatment of the Psychoneuroses, *Boston Med Surg J* 163:75-82, 1910.
7. Putnam, J. J.: Not the Disease Only, But Also the Man, *Boston Med Surg J* 141:53-57, 77-81, 1899.
8. Putnam, J. J.: *Human Motives,* Boston: Little, Brown, & Co., 1915.

National Library of Medicine

Joseph Jules Dejerine
(1849-1917)

J. J. DEJERINE, born in Geneva of French parents, arrived in Paris for his higher education in 1871 during the period of great turmoil.[1] He won the post of extern of the Paris hospitals in 1872, intern in 1874, and the MD degree and a silver medal in 1879, with a thesis on lesions of the nervous system in acute ascending paralysis. After appointment as chief of the clinic at Charité in 1879 and physician to the hospitals of Paris in 1882, he was advanced to academic standing (agrégé) in the university faculty in 1886 and physician to Bicêtre the following year. In 1895, Dejerine was appointed physician to Saltpêtrière; in 1901, he assumed the professorship of the history of medicine and surgery, transferring later to the chair of internal pathology. By then he had given much thought to psychiatry and became clinical professor of nervous diseases and head of the clinic at Saltpêtrière, succeeding Raymond.

As a fruitful investigator and prolific writer, Dejerine was an important contributor to French neurologic literature for 40 years. In teaching clinics his performance was outstanding. The explanation of symptoms and findings disclosed profound anatomical knowledge of the central and peripheral nervous system, while his management of patients was carried out with great understanding and sympathy.

Through Dejerine's professional years he was blessed with able scientific assistance, especially from his wife, Augusta Marie Klumpke, who was born in San Francisco, graduated in medicine in 1889, and served as the first female intern in the hospitals of Paris. She collaborated in research and writing, including their monumental work, *Anatomy of the Nervous System,*[2] and continued the investigations and writings after his death. The *Classification of Diseases of the Nervous System,* which appeared in Bouchard's *System of General Pathology* and served as a text for students for decades, was prepared solely by Dejerine.[3] The Goddard prize from the Anatomical Society of Paris was awarded him in 1879 for his researches on the lesions of diphtheritic paralysis. With Landouzy the Montyon prize by the Academy of Sciences was awarded in 1886 for investigations on progressive atrophic myopathy, and with André Thomas the Montyon prize in 1910 for work on diseases of the spine. In 1914, Dejerine delivered the Hughlings Jackson lecture before the Royal Society of London and received the Moxon medal for his discussion of radiculitis. In collaboration with Gauckler (1911), his bibliographer,[1] a monograph on functional manifestations and treatment of psychoneurosis was prepared.

Dejerine made several contributions to the subject of aphasia, was a pioneer in the study of localization of function in the brain, and showed that word blindness may develop from lesions of the supramarginal and angular gyri. He prepared several communications on Friedreich's disease and correlated clinical findings with the nature of the sclerosis. In the Dejerine-Lichtheim phenomenon seen in expressive aphasia, the patient is unable to speak but can indicate by a show of fingers the number of syllables in a word. With André Thomas he described olivopontocerebellar atrophy. Dejerine's radicular syndrome is characterized by radicular pain, sensory and motor disturbances, and sometimes by trophic changes. In a study of peripheral nerves, he discovered an example of peripheral tabes due to infection or intoxication, which could be distinguished postmortem from medullary tabes as he notes.[4]

The following observation is important, especially since currently more peripheral neuritis is being implicated in the pathogenesis of paralyses which had otherwise been attributed to affections of the spinal cord. Actually it is recognized that specific infections and specific intoxications can produce alterations of sensitivity and motor activity in the peripheral nervous system, as well as circulatory and trophic changes. These depend exclusively on lesions of the peripheral nerves. . . . Among the intoxications, alcohol and lead are the prime offenders against the peripheral nervous system; in a person under the influence of alcohol it is possible to observe various complexes of symptoms in which the cutaneous nerves or the motor nerves are involved. Also, it is possible to discover clinical findings indistinguishable from classical tabes. The patient under consideration was the usual type of ataxic, a morphine addict who was affected by subacute paralysis of the lower extremities which eventually approached totality. The autopsy findings showed no alteration of the spinal cord, none of the usual lesions of tabes, no lesions of either the gray or of the white fibers which could have explained the paralysis. Histological examination of the peripheral nerves of the lower extremities provided the explanation.

Posterior sclerosis was associated with leptomeningitis and atrophy of the corresponding nerve roots with lesions typical of recent neuritis. There was also evidence of neuritis of the anterior roots in the dorsolumbar area and neuritis of the nerves supplying the muscles as well as the cutaneous nerves. The anterior gray column was intact, as well as the fibers of the white matter of the cord and the spinal ganglia.

Hypertrophic progressive interstitial neuritis, Dejerine-Sottas disease, is a rare heredofamilial malady appearing in infancy and characterized by a collagenous degeneration of the endoneurium, with degeneration of the myelin sheaths and nerve fibers. The clinical findings suggest a polyneuritis, the nerve trunks of the extremities are palpably thickenend, and extensive weakness and atrophy of the distal muscles of the extremities decreasing centrally are observed. The extended report was based upon the findings in a brother and sister and subsequent post-

mortem examination of the sister, who had developed severe choreiform movements, abolition of the plantar reflex, nystagmus, ataxia, and kyphoscoliosis.[5]

A type of progressive muscular atrophy beginning in infancy in the muscles of the lower extremities subsequently affects, after a shorter or longer period of time, the muscles of the hands. When the atrophy reaches an advanced stage of development, which requires a number of years, the clinical findings include atrophy of the four extremities. Both feet appear in direct equine position or in equine varus position; the plantar concavity is exaggerated. The atrophy of the muscles of the feet and the calves diminishes centripetally. Later the hands with atrophic muscles are deformed and the arms are flexed at the elbow. Muscular atrophy is symmetrical, muscle weakness depends on the degree of atrophy, and tendon reflexes are abolished. The reaction of degeneration can be observed frequently. In the majority of cases, skin sensitivity is intact; atrophic changes of the skin are absent.

Autopsy disclosed hypertrophy of the nerve trunks and the medullary root with alteration in the posterior bundles of the spinal cord. Histological examination showed hypertrophic interstitial neuritis of the nerve trunks, diminishing in severity from the periphery and highly developed in the muscular and cutaneous nerves.

Each bundle of the mixed nerves is enveloped in a connective tissue sheath and the essential elements tend to degenerate. The myelin sheath disappears first and later the axis cylinder. This alteration is maximal at the peripheral end of the nerves of the extremities, especially of the lower extremities. It becomes less intense toward the proximal ends of the nerve trunks and skips the ganglions but involves the anterior and posterior roots.

Dejerine gave the name "atrophic myopathy" to a group of heredofamilial maladies of unknown origin in which he recognized two types, scapulohumeral and facioscapulohumeral. The disease may affect or be transmitted by either sex. The varied clinical findings in the several syndromes classified in this category reflect the muscles or groups that are primarily affected. The sigificant pathological findings are confined to the muscles. The Dejerine-Landouzy type of facioscapulohumeral myopathy leads to a mask-like expression; the eyes are imperfectly closed in sleep. The scapulohumeral type was described as follows:[6]

It has been demonstrated by us that, in the clinical as well as in pathological findings, a group of muscular atrophies represented by the muscular atrophy of the Duchenne type, in which the central and peripheral nervous system remains intact, may be distinguished from progressive myelopathic muscular atrophy. The *myopathic* atrophies have been called by us *progressive atrophic myopathy,* with two clinical types: the facio-scapulo-humeral type in which the face muscles and the limbs are atrophic and the scapulo-humeral type which spares the face. The latter is less common than the former; the face is not affected throughout the prolonged illness.

Recently, an autopsy was performed on a patient with scapulo-humeral myopathy who was followed for more than two years. The patient died at the age of 66. The onset was at 20 years of age. The atrophy involved shoulder, arm, and back muscles. Forearms and hands were spared to a great extent. Muscle atrophy of the anterior area of the thighs and the legs was present while the face was intact. Death was caused by pulmonary tuberculosis.

At autopsy the spinal cord, anterior roots, and motor nerves were intact. Simple atrophy of the muscles with marked multiplication of their nuclei was observed; in the severely atrophied muscles, interstitial lipomatosis was observed. The absence of symptoms in the face when the autopsy showed myopathy suggests that the scapulo-humeral type, as we have described it, exists, although less frequently than the facio-scapulo-humeral type.

With Roussy, Dejerine described the thalamic syndrome, the result of localized thalamic injury from vascular insufficiency. If the main trunk of the posterior cerebral artery is thrombosed, both the thalamus and the occipital lobe are affected, and the syndrome develops, together with homonymous hemianopsia. Findings on the contralateral side to the lesions include fleeting hemiparesis or hemiplegia, usually flaccid, impairment of superficial and loss of deep sensation, agonizing burning pain, and choreo-athetoid movements.[7]

The thalamic syndrome is characterized by:

(1) a mild hemiplegia which usually leaves no contractures and is quickly regressive,

(2) a persistent superficial organic hemianesthesia which may be replaced in some cases by cutaneous hyperesthesia but is always accompanied by marked and persistent disorder of deep sensitivity,

(3) light hemiataxia and more or less complete astereognosis. These three constant and important symptoms are usually accompanied by:

(4) intense pain on the hemiplegic side, persistent, paroxysmal, often intolerable, and unyielding to any analgesic.

(5) choreo-athetotic movements in the extremities of the paralyzed side.

Dejerine's interest in military service was apparent shortly after he arrived in Paris. As an active auxiliary member of the International Committee of the French Society of Aid to the Military Sick and Wounded, he received the Bronze Cross in 1871. An honorary commission in the French Territorial Army was granted him in 1911; while during World War I, he served on the neurology service in an Army hospital. He was awarded the chevalier of the Legion of Honor in 1898 and became an officer in 1913, each civilian class. In 1908, Dejerine was elected to the Academy of Medicine of France and was granted an honorary doctor's degree by the University of Geneva in 1909.

1. Gauckler, E.: *Professor J. Dejerine 1849-1917* (Fr), Paris: Masson & Co., 1922.

2. Dejerine, J., and Dejerine-Klumpke, A.: *Anatomy of the Nervous System* (Fr), Paris: Rueff & Co., 1895.

3. Dejerine, J.: *Classification of Diseases of the Nervous System* (Fr), Paris: Masson & Co., 1914.

4. Dejerine, J.: A Case of Paraplegia of the Peripheral Nerves in a Morphine Addict (Fr), *C R Soc Biol* 4:137-143, 1887, excerpt translated by Z. Danilevicius.

5. Dejerine, J., and Sottas, J.: Hypertrophy and Progressive Neuritis of Infancy (Fr), *C R Soc Biol* 5:63-96, 1893, excerpt translated by Z. Danilevicius.

6. Landouzy, L., and Dejerine, J.: A Study of Progressive Muscular Atrophy—Scapulo-humeral type (Fr), *C R Soo Biol* 3:478-481, 1886, excerpt translated by Z. Danilevicius.

7. Dejerine, J., and Roussy, G.: The Thalamic Syndrome (Fr), *Rev Neurol* 14:521-532, 1906, excerpt translated by Z. Danilevicius.

George Huntington (1850-1916)

GEORGE HUNTINGTON was not the first to describe what is currently recognized as adult hereditary chorea or Huntington's chorea. However, he is rightfully credited with a detailed recounting of the symptoms and especially the regression, leading eventually into dementia. Huntington was born in East Hampton, Long Island, in a community where the familial malady had been endemic for several generations among the English stock who had migrated from Suffolk, England, to Connecticut.[1] His father and grandfather were family physicians familiar with the malady from firsthand examples in their practice. Huntington received his early medical training at his

Composite by G. Bako

father's side but completed formal training at the College of Physicians and Surgeons of Columbia University, where he graduated at the age of 21. He practiced for a time with his father on Long Island, then moved to Palmyra, Ohio; however, the greater portion of his professional days was spent in Duchess County, New York.

George Huntington was the archetype of the personal physician—gentle of nature, highly regarded by his patients, an avid reader of medical journals, a lover of nature, and a clever artisan. His contribution on familial chorea, an excellent composition worthy of emulation, was his only written medical document. The discussion began with a summary of Sydenham's chorea, followed by the differential diagnosis of the hereditary type in adults. No mention was made of the incomplete descriptions that had appeared earlier, except for casual reference to Dr. Wood and to one patient in the Pennsylvania Hospital. Huntington's communication appeared in the Original Department of the *Medical and Surgical Reporter* of Philadelphia.[2]

The hereditary chorea, as I shall call it, is confined to certain and fortunately a *few* families, and has been transmitted to them, an heirloom from generations away back in the dim past. It is spoken of by those in whose veins the seeds of the disease are known to exist, with a kind of horror, and not at all alluded to except through dire necessity, when it is mentioned as *"that disorder."* It is attended generally by all the symptoms of common chorea, only in an aggravated degree, hardly ever manifesting itself until *adult* or *middle* life, and then coming on gradually but surely, increasing by degrees, and often occupying years in its development, until the hapless sufferer is but a quivering wreck of his former self.

There are three marked peculiarities in this disease . . .

1. Of its hereditary nature. When either or both the parents have shown manifestations of the disease, and more especially when these manifestations have been of a *serious* nature, one or more of the offspring almost invariably suffer from the disease, if they live to adult age.

2. The tendency to insanity, and sometimes that form of insanity which leads to suicide, is marked. . . . As the disease progresses the mind becomes more or less impaired, in many amounting to insanity, while in others mind and body both gradually fail until death relieves them of their sufferings.

3. Its third peculiarity is its coming on, at least as a grave disease, only in adult life. I do not know of a single case that has shown any marked signs of chorea before the age of thirty or forty years, while those who pass the fortieth year *without* symptoms of the disease, are seldom attacked. It begins as an ordinary chorea might begin, by the irregular and spasmodic action of certain muscles, as of the face, arms, etc. These movements gradually increase when muscles hitherto unaffected take on the spasmodic action, until every muscle in the body becomes affected (excepting the involuntary ones), and the poor patient presents a spectacle which is anything but pleasing to witness. I have never known a recovery or even an amelioration of symptoms in this form of chorea; when once it begins it clings to the bitter end. No treatment seems to be of any avail, and indeed nowadays its end is so well known to the sufferer and his friends, that medical advice is seldom sought. It seems at least to be one of the incurables.

The bibliography on adult hereditary chorea, 1841 to 1908, appeared in *Neurographs,* in a symposium number honoring Huntington.[3] The tribute was paid to the family physician of Duchess County, who fully described the symptoms observed in a series of cases of a malady recognized by his grandfather, Abel Huntington, and classified by his father, George Lee Huntington. In the *Festschrift,* William Osler was responsible for the "Historical Note," documenting the 1842 reference by C. O. Waters of Franklin, New York, to the disease in Dunglison's *Practice of Medicine,*[4] and referring to the report in *American Medical Times* of 1863 by Irving W. Lyon.[5] These cases were observed in Westchester County, New York. There was yet a third area, Wyoming County, Pennsylvania, where C. R. Gorman reported an endemic center of what possibly was hereditary chorea.[3] Such evidence exposes the weakness of any claim, ancient or contemporary, to a "first."

1. Stevenson, C. S.: A Biography of George Huntington, M.D., *Bull Inst Hist Med* 2:53-76, 1934.
2. Huntington, G.: On Chorea, *Med Surg Rep* 26:317-321, 1872.
3. Browning, W.: The Huntington Number, *Neurographs, a Series of Neurological Studies, Cases and Notes* 1:85-165, 1908.
4. Dunglison, R.: *Practice of Medicine,* Philadelphia: Lea and Blanchard, 1842, vol 2, pp 312-313.
5. Lyon, I. W.: Chronic Hereditary Chorea, *Amer Med Times* 7:289-290, 1863.

medicine, where he came under the influence of Charcot. He finished formal medical training in 1883, became chief of Charcot's clinic at Salpêtrière, and, in 1889, was advanced to professor agrégé. Subsequently, he

Composite by G. Bako

Pierre Marie (1853-1940)

PIERRE MARIE, favorite pupil of Charcot and the leading French neurologist in his maturity, is associated with the clinical finding of several maladies within as well as outside his chosen field. During a span of scarcely a dozen years, he described acromegaly, pulmonary hypertrophic osteoarthropathy, cerebellar heredo-ataxia, spondylitis rhizomelica, and, together with Charcot, peroneal muscular atrophy. Lesser contributions include a description of the tremor in hyperthyroidism, denunciation of the hypothesis of Broca regarding the site of language in the third left frontal convolution, arteriopathic findings in progressive lacunar disintegration, and an early description of hereditary cleidocranial dysostosis.

Marie was a Parisian by birth; his family were wealthy bourgeois.[1] He studied law at the bidding of his father but, after three years, was allowed to enter the faculty of

was assigned to the staff at Hospice de Bicêtre; there he developed an internationally famous neurological service. In 1907, Marie was elected to the chair of pathologic anatomy. However, not until the age of 65 did he succeed to the chair of neurology at Salpêtrière, which had been created for Charcot but was occupied by Raymond, Brissaud, and Dejerine in the interim.

At the age of 33, Marie described two cases of acromegaly and gave the entity its current name. His monograph included the description of the patients studied on Charcot's service and several from the literature. Reference was made to the reports by Saucerotte (1772), Alibert (1822), and especially to Henrot (1877), who, in his clinical notes on myxedema, described several of the features of acromegaly and at postmortem identified a pituitary tumor. The cases reported by Marie developed symptoms in their teens and at the time of examination showed fully developed somatic changes. The two conclusions by Marie given below are followed by excerpts from the clinical records.[2]

There is a disease characterized by hypertrophy of the feet, hands, and face. We intend to call it *acromegaly,* that is to say, a hypertrophy of the extremities (not that the extremities are the only affected parts during the course of the disease), but their increase in size is an initial phenomenon and is a characteristic feature.

Acromegaly is different from myxedema, from *Paget's disease* (osteitis deformans), and from Virchow's *leontiasis ossea.*

In the two cases that aroused our suspicion a considerable increase in the hands, the feet, and the head was observed.

In the first case the hands were so enlarged that when the patient was first seen by Charcot, they were the center of attention, although the patient complained only of a violent headache.

The entire hand had undergone an increase in volume, greater in the transverse than in the vertical place. This gives a characteristic stubbed appearance.

The fingers are huge, are round at the tips, and their volume is approximately equal to their length.

A similar description applies to the feet. They have undergone considerable hypertrophy with little deformation.

The soft parts of the extremities do not present disproportionate alteration. They have followed the skeleton in development and are in proportion.

The head is increased in part, particularly the *nasal, malar,* and *lower maxillary* bones. In each patient the maxillary region had increased in volume to such an extent that it protruded below the mandible which too was increased in length, height, and density.

The skull is affected. The frontal prominences protrude, and this, together with hypertrophy of the malar bones, exaggerates the depression that is formed by the anterior part of the temporal fossa.

The *sense organs* vary in the degree of disturbance. In the first patient there was some *deafness;* in the second *complete blindness.* The cause of this is not known. There was an obvious hypertrophy of the *tongue* in each patient.

The *vertebral column* shows an anterior curvature so that the patient had great difficulty in raising the head and kept, for this reason, the chin on the sternum.

The *clavicles, ribs, patellae,* and the *iliacs* also become increased in volume.

The fibro-cartilages tend to hypertrophy. The joints are not affected.

In the same year, in a discussion coauthored with Charcot, a particular form of hereditary progressive muscular atrophy was described. Symptoms began in the feet and legs and subsequently involved the hands. It was later known as peroneal atrophy of the Charcot-Marie-Tooth type. Excerpts are as follows:[3]

This form of muscular atrophy presents characteristics sufficiently definite to warrant a special description in the framework of nosology.

Among the findings in the five patients, the following observations are significant:

Observation I: At the age of 5 the first sign of weakness in the lower limbs appeared. The feet turned inward on walking. . . . The hands were not affected until the age of 7.

There is bilateral foot-drop with internal rotation.

The muscle mass of the lower legs is much reduced; the calf has disappeared.

Atrophy is evident in the thighs, but remains localized above the knee.

Both hands appear as claws. There is considerable flattening of the hypothenar eminence. The muscles of the forearms are mildly affected.

The upper parts of the thighs, hips, trunk, shoulders, and face do not show atrophy.

The patient arises from the floor without the characteristic movements of pseudo-hypertrophy.

There are fibrillary twitchings in the muscles of the forearm . . . and the thigh.

Observation II: *Standing erect* is difficult. The patient cannot stand motionless. In order to keep his equilibrium, he has to shuffle his feet constantly with an incessant and particular manner of stationary walking.

Because the patient cannot lift his feet on *walking* he uses the joints of his knees and hips, and *steps up* in a special manner. He crosses a room but only with difficulty and he tires easily.

The *vasomotor changes* are generally intense in the affected parts of the body, particularly in the lower limbs. In all of our patients, the feet and the legs had a bluish or reddish color with extensive mottling of the skin.

Spasms appear in almost all of our patients, and to a degree of frequency and intensity that the patients never fail to mention this. They appear preferentially in the thighs, especially as voluntary and vigorous movements.

Marie's graduation thesis in 1883 presented a review of special features of Basedow's disease and postulated a psychoneurotic pathogenesis. He mentioned albuminuria, paroxysmal diarrhea, angina pectoris, increased pigmentation, vitiligo, alopecia, and especially the tremor.[4]

Furthermore, Basedow's disease has one more characteristic, *a tremor,* which contributes a valuable argument to the discussion. In none of the 15 cases of Basedow's disease, typical or atypical, has this symptom been absent. It is regarded as an integral phenomenon of Basedow's disease.

It is different from the tremor in other diseases (paralysis agitans, senile tremor, general paralysis, alcoholism). It may be present in different muscles of the body; but often it is present only in the extremities, especially the upper extremities. Sometimes it is so pronounced as to make the extremities unfit for certain types of work (writing, sewing, etc.). In order to recognize it, the patient must extend his arms and spread the fingers. The rhythm of the tremor is rapid, particularly when compared with senile tremor or paralysis agitans. With a tambour, we found that the frequency of oscillations was 8½ per second, while in other patients there were only 5 or 6 oscillations per second.

Marie's description of pulmonary hypertrophic osteoarthropathy was a logical extension of his observations on acromegaly. In advanced cases, generalized hypertrophy, bony and soft tissue of the hands and feet, but not prognathism, were noted. Selected excerpts follow.[5]

In describing a clinical syndrome under the name of pulmonary hypertrophic osteoarthropathy, I have two motives: firstly, I wish to liberate the concept of acromegaly from being uselessly invaded by facts that do not belong. Secondly, I thought it would be worthwhile to have seemingly unrelated facts classified and to present an autonomous disease entity, with a secondary process that appears as an accident, as it were, in the course of a primary affection.

The affection proved identical in each of the observations. There is a similar increase in the volume of hands and feet with predominance in the terminal phalanges, hypertrophy and extreme curvature of the nails (drumstick fingers, hippocratic fingers). The same phenomena occur in the joints of the extremities with an absence of prognathism in the lower jaw.

The three segments of the hands must be studied separately; the fingers, the carpal-metacarpal region, and the wrist.

Of these three segments it is the fingers that have undergone the greatest change. The fingers assume the appearance of a drumstick or a bell-clapper; this is not observed in acromegaly, with the thumb. The nail at the extremity of the finger is deformed. It is considerably enlarged, and most of all, it is curved (hippocratic feature) so that in profile, it could be mistaken for the curved bill of a parrot.

The feet present the same characteristics as the hands but are less pronounced.

It remain to justify the term pulmonary in my expression: pulmonary hypertrophic osteoarthropathy.

The cycle of development is as follows: (1) a lesion of the respiratory system permits, probably under the influence of micro-organisms, the development of putrid or fermentative substances (bronchitis, pleurisy with or without empyema); (2) resorption and passage into the general circulation of these substances that were produced in the respiratory system; (3) action of these substances on certain parts of the bones and joints, thus causing the lesions of hypertrophic osteoarthropathy.

In 1886, Marie with Charcot had observed a patient with a fixed spinal column who presented similar findings but did not seem to be a valid example of Paget's osteitis deformans. Ten years later he encountered a second case, and, in 1898 after observing a third case, he reported his findings. He described and illustrated the typical gait, dorsal kyphosis, and flexion of the hips and knees. Reference to the 1884 report of Strümpell was included. Excerpts of the introduction are as follows:[6]

At the meeting of the Société Hôpitaux on February 11 of this year I presented two patients who had an affection, the symptoms of which were identical and interesting enough for calling them to the attention of clinicians. In the preliminary communication I emphasized the marked rigidity of the vertebral column and the more or less complete union of the coxofemoral and the scapulohumeral articulations. Because of this form of rachidial rigidity, I proposed to call the disease rhizomelica spondylitis, the word spondylitis indicating vertebral ankylosis and the rhizomelica derived from root and limb, that is to say: "that which affects the roots of the limbs."

In 1886 I had the opportunity to see the first case of the disease. My teacher, Charcot, was consulted by a patient who had a rigidity of the vertebral column. Knowing my interest in affections of the skeleton Charcot was kind enough to let me examine the patient. Because we were ignorant of the nature of the disease the result of the examination raised the doubt as to whether this constituted osteitis deformans (Paget's disease). I made notes on the patient at the time and preserved them in the expectation that I would encounter a second case. I waited ten years, and then I had the good luck, only a year later, to observe yet another case. This makes a total of three personal observations.

As early as the first edition of Strümpell's text on internal pathology (1884) he prepared the following lines: "As a remarkable affection there is a morbid state in which, progressively and painlessly, a complete ankylosis of the entire vertebral column and the two coxofemoral articulations takes place so that the head, the trunk, and the thigh are intimately coalesced and rigid throughout, whereas the other articulations preserve their normal mobility."

Pierre Marie was immensely popular in attracting students and patients from far and near to his neurology clinic. Patients who came to him with muscular, skeletal, as well as neurological problems were managed with equal understanding and compassion.

1. Bailey, P.: "Pierre Marie, 1853-1940," in Haymaker, W. (ed): *The Founders of Neurology*, Springfield, Ill: C. C Thomas, 1953.
2. Marie, P.: Two Cases of Acromegalia (Fr), *Rev Med (Paris)* 6:297-333, 1886, excerpt translated by F. Sternthal.
3. Charcot, J. M., and Marie, P.: A Particular Form of Progressive Muscular Atrophy, Often Familial (Fr), *Rev Med (Paris)* 6:97-138, 1886, excerpt translated by F. Sternthal.
4. Marie, P.: On the Nature and on Some of the Symptoms of Basedow's Disease (Fr), *Arch Neurol (Paris)* 6:79-85, 1883, excerpt translated by F. Sternthal.
5. Marie, P.: Pulmonary Hypertrophic Osteoarthropathy (Fr), *Rev Med (Paris)* 10:1-36, 1890, excerpt translated by F. Sternthal.
6. Marie, P.: Spondylitis Rhizomelica (Fr), *Rev Med (Pais)* 18:285-315, 1898, excerpt translated by S. Sternthal.

The initial recognition of Korsakov's work in scientific circles was based largely upon the description in his inaugural dissertation, prepared in Russian, of alcoholic polyneuri-

National Library of Medicine

Sergei Sergeivich Korsakov (1853-1900)

S. S. KORSAKOV, one of the great Russian psychiatrists, was born in Vladimir Province, known for its glass factory of which his father was an official.[1] After studying medicine at the University of Moscow, Korsakov was appointed physician to the Preobrazhenskii Hospital and served for several years in the clinic for nervous diseases. In 1887, he presented a thesis on alcoholic paralysis for the MD degree; the following year he was advanced to privatdocent and in 1892 became superintendent and professor in the new university psychiatric clinic. Korsakov's reputation was enhanced by his comprehensive understanding of psychiatry as a general medical discipline, by the establishment of the concept of paranoia, by the gentle handling of mentally deranged patients, and by his textbook on psychiatry, the standard treatise for students for a generation.

tis combined with distinctive mental symptoms. The observations were extended subsequently to include varying degrees of polyneuritis and mental disturbances of confusion, disorientation of time and place, and amnesia for recent events.[2] He labeled it "toxemic cerebropathia" or "psychosis polyneuritis." Although the currently accepted term "Korsakov's psychosis" was applied by Jolly, Korsakov gave priority to Magnus Huss for an earlier description of the condition. A German translation of Korsakov's summary experience with polyneuritic psychosis was published in 1889 and was translated into English in 1955. Excerpts from this translation are as follows:[3]

In two articles, one published in the *Vestnik Psichiatrii* in 1887, the other in *Yejenedelnaja Klinicheskaja* this year, I have described a special form of *psychic disorder* which occurs *in conjunction with multiple neuritis.*
. . . in many instances, after the first days of agitation a considerable confusion appears: the patient begins to mix words, he cannot speak coherently, and confuses facts. Day after day the confusion increases. The patient begins to tell

implausible stories about himself, tell of his unusual voyages, confuses old recollections with
recent events, is unaware of where he is and who
are the people around him. Sometimes in addition, there occur illusions of sight and hearing
which confuse the patient still further.
. . . almost always there is severe emaciation,
frequently there is persistent vomiting.
. . . in alcoholism, the disease frequently begins
with symptoms resembling delirium tremens and
then follow paralyses and characteristic disturbances of memory. If one adds to all the above
the fact that the same form of the disease is
observed in alcoholism, and also apparently after
poisoning with arsenic, lead, hydrogen disulphide,
carbon monoxide, ergot, spoiled corn, and so on,
then one sees that the causes which can evoke
this disease are very diverse.
. . . this is why I call this disease *toxemic
cerebropathy* (cerebropathis psychica toxemica).
One might also call it *psychosis polyneuritica,* but
using this designation one must remember that an
identical psychic disturbance may occur also in
cases in which the symptoms of multiple degenerative neuritis may be very slight or even
entirely wanting.

In the intervening years little has been
added to the characteristic clinical findings,
except for the appreciation that the disease
may arise from the lack of a specific nutritional factor rather than an excess of a tissue
toxin. Although Korsakov did not include
any description of structural changes in the
brain, the histologic features confined to the
walls and floor of the third ventricle are
believed to be only partially explored.

1. Katzenelbogen, S.: Sergei Sergeivich Korsakov (1853-
1900), in Haymaker, W. (ed.): *The Founders of
Neurology,* Springfield, Ill: Charles C Thomas, Publisher,
1953, pp 311-314.
2. Korsakov, S. S.: A Psychic Disturbance Associated
With Multiple Neuritis (Ger), *Allg Z Psychiat* 46:475-
485, 1890.
3. Victor, M., and Yakovlev, P. I.: S. S. Korsakoff's
Psychic Disorder in Conjunction With Peripheral Neuritis,
Neurology 5:394-406, 1955.

Constantin von Monakow
(1853-1930)

CONSTANTIN VON MONAKOW, one of the
founders as well as one of the most picturesque figures in modern neurology, was
born in Vologda, Russia, north of Moscow,
but received most of his education and car-

ried out his life work in central Europe. His
wealthy and educated father, Ivan von
Monakow, nobleman and czarist censor of
the press, came into disfavor and left Russia

Composite by G. Bako

in 1863. The family emigrated first to Dresden, then to Paris, and settled finally in
Zürich.[1] Meanwhile his mother had died
from tuberculosis, and, lacking maternal
guidance, Constantin allowed his self-developed interests to predominate. He displayed a remarkable memory, became
deeply religious, enjoyed music and the
theater, and preferred self-instruction to
formal education.

Although physics and chemistry held little
appeal for Monakow contrary to his father's
advice, he registered in the medical faculty
in Zürich in 1872. Before receiving the MD
degree and passing the state examination in
1877, he studied histology and embryology
with von Frey, physiology with Hermann,
and assisted Hitzig in the psychiatric clinic
of Burghölzli. But von Gudden of Munich
probably exercised the greatest influence on
his medical career in introducing him to the
microtome. This tool was utilized for sectioning of the brain following experimental
degeneration. The neurohistologic techniques for the study of atrophy or degenera-

tion of tracts and nuclei of the central nervous system formed the basis for Monakow's outstanding contributions in neurology in the following decades.

After a brief unsuccessful attempt at private practice, Monakow abandoned this and, in 1878, obtained an appointment as assistant physician in the asylum for the insane at St. Pirminsberg in the canton of St. Gall. The combination of clinical work in neurology and psychiatry with the experimental techniques of degeneration provided the most productive years of his life. He found the lateral geniculate body and the anterior quadrigeminate body reduced in size, while the remainder of the thalamus was intact in rabbits kept alive for one year after extirpation of the occipital lobe shortly after birth. Also, Monakow distinguished the degenerative changes of the ganglion cells of the nucleus from the secondary deterioration of the fibers of the optic tract, which followed destructive lesions of the optic nerve or enucleation of the eye. The origin of the optic nerve from the ganglion cells in the retina was thereby confirmed.

Encouraged by the operative approach to the investigation of the higher centers of the central nervous system, Monakow showed the thalamus to be composed of various nuclei, projected to specific areas of the cortex—a valid neurohistologic concept. He applied a similar technique in tracing the pathways to the brain and discovered that hemisection of the cephalad portion of the spinal cord caused disappearance of the large ganglion cells of the nucleus of Deiter, preliminary work to the recognition of the vestibulospinal tract. As a result of an experimental lesion of the parietal region in the cat, which involved the internal capsule, he observed secondary degeneration in the lateral and ventral nuclei of the thalamus as well as atrophy of the fillet, which he traced through the internal arcuate fibers and the crossover to the nuclei of the posterior columns and the nuclei of the contralateral posterior columns.

One of Monakow's last extirpation experiments at St. Pirminsberg involved the acoustic tract and the rubrospinal bundle. Ascending and descending changes followed a lesion of the lateral fillet. Secondary degeneration ascended to the ganglion of the posterior quadrigeminal body and descended in the dorsal part of the superior olive on the ipsilateral side of the striae acusticae and the mitre-formed cells of the contralateral acustic tubercule. He also observed degeneration of the lateral column of the spinal cord, later called the "rubrospinal bundle of von Monakow."

In 1885, Monakow went to Berlin, where he attended the clinics and lectures of Westphal, Oppenheim, Virchow, du Bois-Reymond, and especially Munk. Upon his return to Zürich he resumed the practice of neurology and founded a private research laboratory, later to become the anatomical institute for the study of the brain. It was incorporated within the University of Zürich complex in 1894 when he was appointed extraordinary professor in the university.

Monakow was recognized as a prodigious worker, an omnivorous reader, and a prolific writer. The first edition of his *Pathology of the Brain* appeared in Nothnagel's *Handbook* in 1897.[2] Several years later the text was revised and expanded. In 1906, he established his own journal, *Arbeiten aus dem Hirnanatomischen Institut in Zürich,* which appeared regularly until 1917 when it was recast as the *Schweizer Archiv für Neurologie und Psychiatrie.* Monakow continued as editor-in-chief until his death. His best-known monograph on the red nucleus, published in two parts, appeared in 1909-1910;[3] his studies on the localization in the brain were summarized in a monograph in 1914,[4] largely a description of human clinicopathological material.

In the development of his concept of the activity of higher centers, Monakow dissented from the prevailing belief of those who localized the functions of the cortex in circumscribed areas. He assumed that during the phylogenic development of the forebrain more and more powers of integration are achieved, and in diseases of the cortex those centers which are developed last are usually the first to deteriorate. This chronological concept was expanded in his work on aphasia and his theory of diaschisis, an attempt to explain extensive initial loss of function following sudden damage to the central nervous system. Damage to a center, according to his hypothesis, severed the constituent elements of functions and destroyed their integration. Restoration of the functions of the individual elements was reestablished chronologically.[2]

If several neurons are united as links in a chain and coordinated for a common function, after sudden insult to one or more of the neuron links the others are able to function only under modified conditions but seldom immediately after disruption of their structural organization. The lower order of affected neurons will be unable to respond until new combinations stimulate them to activity. They will remain permanently faulty, however, since the primary functional components have been destroyed, but some function may be maintained even at a deficit level. . . . One such acute phenomenon, which relates to shock but is not identical, represents a local struggle for functional survival, which I have named "diaschisis." This implies a separation of the units by the elimination of the directing force in the chain.

At the end of World War I and with concern for the effects in Russia of the Bolshevik Revolution of 1917, Monakow became deeply absorbed in religion as he was in his youth, to which he added his mature thinking in philosophy, ethics, morality, and psychology. It has been suggested he was searching for enlightenment and interpretation of the turmoil—physical, political, and emotional—through which the world was passing. One of the last of his later contributions translated into English, *The Emotions, Morality and the Brain,* appeared in 1925. The translators admitted the inadequacies of a literal translation from the German text. A concluding paragraph of his neurobiologic psychiatry is illustrative of his interpretive concept of the subject.[5]

In healthy and well brought up persons, in the sphere of the central nervous system, just as in the motor sphere, the inhibitive apparatus with reciprocal relation to the powerful stimulative apparatus is well developed and organized. These two apparatuses are always in condition to influence and complement each other, provided the equilibrium in one direction or the other has not been disturbed by poisons, pathological processes, disastrous emotional experiences, catastrophies, etc. It is also indisputable that what we call the purpose of life and morality is the result of a conflict between emotional factors acting in contrary directions (the worst vices and the highest virtues are found side by side "in our breasts").

The physiological basis of these elements is to be sought, not only in the collective activities of the structures of the nervous system, or in the cortex, *i.e.,* in the so-called "world of ideas," but also in the inner secretions which work in, and with, these structures, that is, they are to be sought also in the biochemical factors of the unconscious volition and the mysterious primitive mnemes.

1. Minkowski, M.: Constantin von Monakow 1853-1930 (Ger), *Schweiz Arch Neurol Psychiat* 27:1-63, 1931.
2. v. Monakow, C.: *Pathology of the Brain* (Ger), Vienna: A. Hölder, 1905, excerpt translated by Z. Danilevicius.
3. v. Monakow, C.: The Red Nucleus, the Central Gray Matter and the Hypothalamic Region in Man and Other Mammals (Ger), *Arb Hirnanat Inst Zurich* 3:51-267, 1909; 4:103-225, 1910.
4. v. Monakow, C.: *Localization of the Cerebrum and the Function and Structure of the Cortical Centers* (Ger), Wiesbaden: J. F. Bergmann, 1914.
5. v. Monakow, C.: *The Emotions, Morality and the Brain* (Ger), G. Barnes, and S. E. Jelliffe (trans.), Washington, DC: Nervous and Mental Disease Publishing Co., 1925.

Sir Charles Scott Sherrington (1857-1952)

THE INTEGRATIVE ACTION OF THE NERVOUS SYSTEM by Sir Charles Sherrington was published in 1906 as the Silliman Lectures at Yale University.[1] This discussion of the physiology of the nervous system has been required reading for students of neurology for half a century. It has not lost its stature as an epochal monograph, prepared by one of the leaders of the English school of physiology. Lord Cohen of Birkenhead has interpreted the concepts of neurophysiology and the philosophy of Charles Scott Sherrington in the Fourth Sherrington Lecture given in Liverpool.[2] The publication of selected writings of Sherrington, compiled by D. Denny-Brown, preceded by two decades the appearance of this small volume.[3]

Charles Scott Sherrington, born in London in 1857, was the son of a country doctor who practiced at Yarmouth. The father died in Charles' childhood. After a short time, his mother married Dr. Caleb Rose, Jr., of Ipswich. Dr. Rose was a classicist, an archaeologist, a geologist, and a lover of the arts as well as a practicing physician. It is reasonable to believe that the profession of his father and his stepfather exerted considerable influence in directing Sherrington's interest toward clinical medicine and clinical neurology, even though he was a neurophysiologist by training. Sherrington passed

his preliminary examination in general education at the Royal College of Surgeons of England and began his training at St. Thomas' Hospital in London. This was followed by a primary examination for membership in the Royal College of Surgeons. His medical education was interrupted for four years, spent studying physiology at Gonville & Caius College, Cambridge. Following this period, he continued his clinical studies and qualified as a physician, with a Bachelor of Medicine from Cambridge in 1885.

Sherrington's interest in the nervous system dates from his student days and continued till his death at the age of 95. As an experimental neurophysiologist he passed on to his pupils a great curiosity for the study of reflex action, decerebrate rigidity, and cortical localization. Harvey Cushing, one of his first pupils from the United States, spent a month with him when he was at Liverpool

in 1901. Cushing was critical of Sherrington following the visit:[4]

. . . As far as I can see, the reason why he is so much quoted is not that he has done especially big things, but that his predecessors have done them all so poorly before. It's a great surprise all through physiological work to find that practically all observations are open to dispute or various interpretations.

The year following his qualification as a physician his attention was diverted to pathology. One of the assignments was a medical mission to Spain, specifically to obtain postmortem material of victims of Asiatic cholera. During this tour of duty in Spain, his interest in the studies of Ramón y Cajal, the outstanding Spanish neurohistologist, began. A year later when cholera appeared in Italy, a second expedition took Sherrington to Venice and Puglia. After he had collected his cholera specimens, he sought the counsel of Virchow in Berlin. Because of an unsatisfactory experience in Virchow's laboratory he transferred his interest to Robert Koch. The studies with Koch postponed his return to England for a year. At the age of 34 he was appointed physician-superintendent at the Brown Institution of the University of London, an institution engaged in research in diseases of animals useful to man. His published contributions concerned leukocytes, specific gravity of the blood, and changes in the blood as a consequence of inflammation. Sherrington's years at Liverpool, between 1895 and 1913 as Professor of Physiology, probably were his most productive in neurophysiology. Each of the three areas of interest as noted above was pursued vigorously.

The significance of "reflex action" had been sensed by René Descartes in 1649. The blinking of the eyelids was conceived as an involuntary action with a mechanical basis. In 1686, Bohn of Leipzig, maintained that reflexes on decapitated frogs, such as withdrawing the limb on irritation, are entirely mechanical. Thomas Willis, professor of medicine at Oxford, popularized the concept of reflex action. The first systematic demonstration of reflexes, however, was given in 1751 by Whytt, who occupied the Chair of the Institutes of Medicine at Edinburgh. He noted that only a small section of the cord was necessary for reflex action. This was followed by the discoveries of Bell and Magendie in 1822-23 of the sensory functions of the dorsal nerve roots and the motor functions of the anterior roots. The neuro-histologists, Schleiden and Schwann and Waller identified the cell as a structural unit in nerve conduction.

It was against this background that Sherrington pursued his studies on the building blocks of the nervous system, the neurons, and their combination into reflex arcs, which he judged to be as basic to neurophysiology as atoms and molecules, respectively, are to chemistry and to physics.

The following excerpts are illustrative of his literary style in presentation as well as examples of the breadth of his investigative interests.

CORRELATION OF REFLEXES AND THE PRINCIPLE OF THE COMMON PATH[5]

The reflex arcs (of the synaptic system) converge in their course so as to impinge upon links possessed by whole varied groups in common—*common paths*. This arrangement culminates in the convergence of many separately arising arcs upon the efferent-root neurone. This neurone thus forms a final common path for many different reflex arcs and acts. It is responsive in various rhythm and intensity, and is relatively unfatigable. Of the different arcs which use it in common, each can do so exclusively in due succession, but *different* arcs cannot use it simultaneously. There is, therefore, interference between the actions of the arcs possessing the common path, some reflexes excluding others and producing inhibitory phenomena, some reflexes reinforcing others and producing phenomena of 'bahnung.' . . . We commonly hear a muscle—or other effector organ—spoken of as innervated by a certain nerve; it would be more correct as well as more luminous to speak of it as innervated by certain receptors; thus, the hip flexor, now by this piece of skin, now by that, by its own foot, by the opposite fore-foot, by the labyrinth, by its own muscle-spindles, by the eye, by the 'motor' cortex, &c. This temporal variability, wanting to the nerve-net system of medusoid and lower visseral life, in the *synaptic* system provides the organism with a mechanism for higher integration. It fits that system to synthesise from a mere collection of tissue and organ an individual animal. The animal mechanism is thus given solidarity by this principle which for each effector organ allows and regulates interchange of the arcs playing upon it, a principle which I would briefly term that of 'the interaction of reflexes about their common path.'

ON THE PROPRIOCEPTIVE SYSTEM, ESPECIALLY IN ITS REFLEX ASPECT[6]

The receptor organs, if one regards their distribution from a broad point of view, fall naturally into two great groups, as judged by their locus in the body. . . . The surface sheet is directly exposed to the environment, and is adapted to react to many of the factors composing that environment, these factors constituting stimuli. Bedded in the surface sheet are numbers of receptor cells, developed in adaptation to the stimuli delivered by environmental agencies. Many of the agencies by which the environment acts on the organism do not, however, penetrate to the mass of cells forming the organism's deeper parts. Thus various stimuli in the form of light and heat, and localised pressures, and chemical substances expend themselves as stimuli at the surface sheet, and do not penetrate into the depth of the organism. But the deep tissues, although devoid of receptors adapted to these surface-reaching stimuli, are, nevertheless, not unprovided with receptors. They have receptors of other kinds apparently specific to them. Some agencies act not only at the surface of the organism, but also through its mass. . . . The deep receptors appear to be very usually adapted to mechanical stimuli of certain kinds. Thus they seem adapted to react to the compressions and strains produced by muscles, and an important adequate agent for them seems to be mass acting in the modes of weight and inertia, involving mechanical pressures and mechanical stresses.

Returning to the receptor organs bedded in the deep tissues, and to the study of the reactions which they subserve, two characters attract attention as differentiating them from those of the surface field, whether extero-ceptive or intero-ceptive. Of these features, one is that the *stimuli* effective on the receptors of the deep field differ fundamentally from those operative on the receptors of either subdivision of the surface field. . . . Since in the deep field the stimuli to the receptors are delivered by the organism *itself* the deep receptors may be termed, *proprio-ceptors*, and the deep field a field of proprioception.

REFLEXES IN RESPONSE TO STRETCH (MYOTATIC REFLEXES)[7]

Familiar to those who work with the decerebrate preparation must be the observation that passive flexion of the characteristically extended knee is felt to evoke some development of or resistance of it against that passive movement. Examination by the myograph of this resistance formed the point of departure of the following observations.

In this same muscle the "knee jerk" is doubtless a reflex in response to a stretch; but it is a reaction whose brevity makes it perhaps the most twitch-like of all reflexes, whereas the reflex under consideration here is tetanic and prolonged. Patellar-clonus, likewise a reaction to stretch, resembles a spaced series of knee jerks and, wanting tetanic character, likewise differs from the reflex under consideration here. . . .

In the knee-extensor (decerebrate preparation) a stretch applied to the muscles evokes contraction in it. This is reflex and purely proprioceptive, its receptors lying in the fleshy region of the muscle.

Within limits, so long as the stretch increases, the reflex continues to increase. When augmentation of the stretch ceases, augmentation of the reflex contraction also ceases and the reflex usually declines, merging into long-lasting plateau-like contraction, which is maintained by the stretched-posture, consequent from the precurrent stretch-movement. Withdrawal of the stretch causes immediate cessation of this postural stretch contraction.

The reflex is readily diminished and annulled by reflex inhibition provoked from the sources recognized as regularly inhibitory for the knee-extensor. Under this inhibition, the muscle's reaction to stretch resembles indistinguishably in our records that yielded by the muscle after complete paralysis from severance of its motor nerve.

The honors that came to Sherrington at home and abroad attest to his pre-eminence. Two of the highest scientific honors, The Order of Merit and Knight Grand Cross Order of the British Empire, were granted by His Majesty's government. He shared the Nobel Prize for medicine with Adrian in 1932. Although he was not on the faculty at Cambridge University, he holds an honorary AM, MD, and DSC from this university as well as an appointment as Honorary Fellow of Gonville & Caius College, where he spent many happy days. Also he was awarded an honorary LLD by a number of universities in the western world. American pupils included Alexander Forbes, Derek Denny-Brown, Stanley Cobb, Howard Florey, John Fulton, William Gibson, Jr., Wilder Penfield, David Rioch, Henry Viets, and Lewis Weed.

1. Sherrington, C. S.: *The Integrative Action of the Nervous System*, New Haven: Yale University Press, 1906.

2. Lord Cohen of Birkenhead: *Sherrington: Physiologist, Philosopher and Poet (The Sherrington Lectures IV)*, Springfield, Ill: Charles C Thomas, Publisher, 1958.

3. *Selected Writings of Sir Charles Sherrington*, compiled and edited by D. Denny-Brown, London: Hamish Hamilton Medical Books, 1939.

4. Fulton, J. F.: *Harvey Cushing: A Biography*, Springfield, Ill: Charles C Thomas, Publisher, 1946.

5. Sherrington, C. S.: Correlation of Reflexes and the Principle of the Common Path, *Rept Brit Ass* 74:728-741, 1904.

6. Sherrington, C. S.: On the Proprioceptive System, Especially in Its Reflex Aspect, *Brain* 29:467-482, 1906.

7. Liddel, E. G. T. and Sherrington, C. S.: Reflexes in Response to Stretch (Myotatic Reflexes), *Proc Roy Soc* 86B:212-242, 1924.

Composite by G. Bako

Sigmund Freud (1856-1939)

SIGMUND FREUD, native of Freiberg, Moravia, and son of a wool merchant, was closely associated throughout his life with the culture and learning of Vienna during its greatest period in contemporary times. Freud was a brilliant student and led his class in scholarship in the Gymnasium. At the age of 17 he entered the University of Vienna and received the MD degree in 1881.[1] His particular skill in languages included French, English, Italian, Spanish, and Hebrew, and he showed especial interest in philosophy. Although his courses followed the medical curriculum, he leaned to biology. Before the age of 20 Freud began the first of his researches on marine life in Brücke's laboratory. Later he worked in Meynert's laboratory, where his investigations on the medulla were carried out and where, in 1884, he suggested the anesthetic possibilities of cocaine in ophthalmologic practice. However, the credit historically goes to the ophthalmologist Koller, for his initial studies.

In spite of Freud's great interest in research under the support and protection of an academic laboratory, economic necessity forced him to consider medical practice for subsistence. In preparation he spent three years in the General Hospital in Vienna, rotating through the departments of medicine, psychiatry, dermatology, and neurology. In 1885, Freud was appointed lecturer in neuropathology and began neurologic practice. Shortly after, he was advanced to privatdocent when his interest in the form and function of the nervous system—reflected in the publication later of two outstanding monographs on organic disease, *The Concept of Aphasia* (1891) and *Infantile Cerebral Paralysis* (1897)—gradually changed to a concern for psychiatric matters.

The transition into the second and major portion of Freud's career was gradual when viewed retrospectively. During this period he constructed a system of psychology to which he gave the name "psychoanalysis," the cornerstones of which were a dynamic unconscious, transference, resistance, and dream analysis. An early inciting interest is attributed to Breuer, his Viennese colleague and a few years his senior, who was using hypnosis in the study of the pathogenesis of hysterical symptoms. Breuer was partially successful in relieving hysterical symptoms in some patients by inducing them to recall the circumstances of origin under hypnosis, through mental catharsis, as illustrated by their most famous patient, Anna O.[2] With each recollection, some of her symptoms disappeared. In the midst of the extended friendship with Breuer, Freud gained from the university a travelling stipend for postgraduate study with Charcot. Although Freud remained but a few months in Paris, they became firm friends, and he agreed to translate Charcot's lectures into German. The assignment, with footnotes added, redounded to the credit of each.

Freud recognized the incompleteness of knowledge of the unconscious gained by hypnosis and the inability to hypnotize all patients. However, having accepted Charcot's premise that hysteria was an affection of the mind and not a disease of the nerves, he instituted "free association" on the couch, or catharsis. This approach, begun in 1892, an early phase of psychoanalysis, allowed him to interpret the revelations of the dynamic unconscious in the interplay of conscious mental operations. While Freud encouraged free association in analysis, he noted frequently that related dreams, apparently unmeaningful to the patient, assumed significance under joint discussion. His monograph, *Interpretation of Dreams,*[3] was adjudged by him to be his most important contribution. Unconscious ideas and thoughts appearing through devious channels, such as slips of the tongue, forgetting of proper names, mistakes in reading and writing, superstitious beliefs, etc., were described somewhat earlier.[4] The transference phenomenon, another feature, arose out of his analytic work, became and remains a treatment tool unique to psychoanalysis. During the development of the technique of encouraging free association on the couch, Freud realized that the analyst's personal and unconscious difficulties might subtly bias his interpretations; therefore, personal analysis was obligatory for complete objectivity. From this belief evolved the required analytic treatment for all analysts and many general psychiatrists.

Building upon the foundation stones of free association, dreams, and transference, the ideologic significance of sexuality, particularly infantile sexuality, assumed great importance to Freud.[5] The phenomenon of neurosis sometimes was believed to be associated with a recent sexual conflict, at other times with the effect of an early sexual experience; but there was "no neurosis without an infantile neurosis." The erotic element apparent in the neurosis did not always develop with narrow sexual implications, but in the broad sense of libido as "energy" directed toward an object. This included physical love, love for friends and parents, and self-love. The unconscious or the repressed was assumed to be a wish denied gratification by opposing forces; psychiatric symptoms were oblique and modified expressions of these drives.

Two main theoretical systems devised by Freud still persist. Topological theory identifies functions of the mind in relation to awareness or consciousness (unconscious, preconscious, conscious). Structural theory identifies allocated functions in forces (id, ego, superego) without reference to levels of awareness. This represents a modern dynamic open system in agreement with modern science.[6]

The psychoanalytic technique is a form of treatment, but Freud made no claim for its value in schizophrenia, only in neuroses. However, several of his patients in the early years of his study were probably schizophrenic by contemporary definition. In devising a new technique for the study of the mind, he postulated the existence of the "unconscious" and believed that it could be defined and understood as a system amenable to observation and experiment. He referred to psychoanalysis as "scientific" but advanced no proof in support. It is irrelevant whether or not the several aspects of psychoanalysis were discovered by Freud. The beginning of the concept probably goes back to the beginning of modern man. It was Freud, however, a brilliant innovator, who founded the analytic movement as an identifiable conceptual schema still believed by many to be useful in studying human behavior.

1. Jones, E.: *The Life and Work of Sigmund Freud,* 3 vol, New York: Basic Books, Inc., 1953.

2. Breuer, J., and Freud, S.: The Psychic Mechanism of Hysterical Phenomena (Ger), *Neurol Cbl* 12:4-47 1893, in *Selected Papers on Hysteria and Other Psychoneuroses,* A. A. Brill (trans.), New York: Journal of Nervous & Mental Disease Publishing Co., 1909.

3. Freud, S.: *Interpretation of Dream* (Ger), Leipzig and Vienna: F. Deuticke, 1911, A. A. Brill (trans.), New York: MacMillan & Co., 1913.

4. Freud, S.: *Psychopathology of Everyday Life* (Ger), Berlin: S. Karger, 1904, A. A. Brill (trans.), London: T. F. Unwin Ltd., 1914.

5. Freud, S.: *Three Contributions to the Sexual Theory* (Ger), Leipzig and Vienna: F. Deuticke, 1905, A. A. Brill (trans.), New York: Journal of Nervous & Mental Disease Publishing Co., 1910.

6. Freud, S.: *The Standard Edition of the Complete Psychological Works of Sigmund Freud,* 24 vol. J. Stachey (trans.), London: Hogarth Press & the Institute of Psychoanalysis, 1953.

Emil Kraepelin (1856-1926)

EMIL KRAEPELIN, pioneer in experimental psychiatry and the proponent of a systematic classification of serious disorders of the mind, was born in Neustrelitz in the district of Mecklenburg. His father was a civil servant; his brother, Karl, eight years his senior and later director of the Zoological Museum in Hamburg, introduced him to biology. At the age of 18, Emil began the study of medicine, taking courses in Leipzig and Würzburg. There initial exposure to psychiatry came through the study of psychology under Wundt and the preparation of a prize essay under Rinecker, entitled, "The Influence of Acute Illness in the Causation of Mental Disorders." In 1878, he received the MD degree in Würzburg and the following year, having joined Gudden in Munich, prepared a thesis, entitled *The Place of Psychology in Psychiatry.* Kraepelin also served for a time as assistant to Flechsig and in Erb's clinic in Leipzig. In 1884, he was appointed senior physician in Leubus and the next year director of the Treatment and Nursing Institute in Dresden.[1]

At the age of 30, Kraepelin's first major professional desire was fulfilled: He was called to the University of Dorpat as professor of psychiatry. His increasing reputation expanded the number of senior academic opportunities offered to him and led to his being called to the head of the department in Heidelberg four years later. During the 14-year period at Heidelberg, he achieved national and international standing. In 1904, Kraepelin accepted the directorship of the newly opened Psychiatric Clinic in Munich and the professorship of psychiatry at the University. The Munich Clinic developed into an establishment of excellence for others to emulate; care for the mentally sick was equated with investigation into the cause of mental illness and with the indoctrination of basic concepts into the students and associates attracted to the great complex for clinical psychiatry. Kraepelin was an excellent teacher but not an eloquent speaker. He relinquished the usual academic responsibilities at the age of 66 but spent his remaining years in Munich developing the German Institute for Psychiatric Research. This unit of the University, a Kaiser Wilhelm Institute, was constructed with financial assistance from the Rockefeller Foundation of New York, the first gift of this kind for research in Europe. It was dedicated almost two years after Kraepelin's death.

Kraepelin's great contribution to psychiatry was his nosology. Based upon critical severity of the clinical course and introspective evaluation of prognosis, he introduced and defined in understandable terms, "dementia praecox," "manic-depressive insanity," and "paranoia." He was a rigid disciplinarian in collecting clinical data and drawing sound deductions. Undisciplined speculation was not tolerated, and objectivity in drawing conclusions was demanded in his clinic. The discovery of findings reproducible from patient to patient furnished incontrovertible data for his nomenclature. Although Kraepelin came to appreciate that differences were partially related to expressions of the personality and were somewhat dependent upon age of onset, he rejected outright the psychoanalytic implications of deviations of infantile sexuality, whether inborn or acquired by experience. The main types of reaction identified by Kraepelin, with some overlapping symptoms, remain inviolate.

In the laboratory, Kraepelin encouraged psychological and psychiatric investigation but especially neuropathological undertakings. Alzheimer, Nissl, Spielmayer, and other leading scientists of his time were encouraged to conduct their histopathological investigation in his clinic. By combining the skill of an administrator with the love for clinical observation and the creative thinking of a practical investigator, he provided a training center for postgraduate students; their clinical work was integrated with their investigative program, without his unduly directing their thinking into his conceptual channels. Kraepelin applied the methods of experimental psychology he had learned from Wundt to his own laboratory problems, which encompassed study of the structural and functional effects of intoxicants on the central nervous system, the nature of sleep, and the results of fatigue on the body.

Although Kraepelin's pragmatic researches were less fruitful than his other endeavors, he was the undisputed leader in developing psychiatry into a scientific discipline, thereby rejecting metaphysical speculation. Reflecting a deep social conscience, he favored indeterminate punishment for criminal offenses and opposed capital punishment. He crusaded against the use of alcohol, created a museum of the barbarities inflicted on the insane, studied the mentality of primitive people and the prevalence of paresis and insanity in the tropics and wrote poems for private enjoyment. Kraepelin's *Compendium der Psychiatrie* appeared first in 1883, when he was only 27 years of age; it outlined the perceptive path he chose to pursue. His style of composition was unadorned but definitive, as illustrated in the following passage from the introduction to the first edition.[2]

Psychiatry . . . belongs in the realm of medical sciences and uses the means and methods of natural science in its investigation. But psychiatry holds a special position within the medical disciplines because the object of its study belongs to the unique area of human characteristics, to the area of the mental processes. Mental processes, conception, emotions, and desires all belong solely to the inner life of an individual; they are not open to direct objective observation but their occurrence can be deduced from certain external manifestations such as the manner of speech, gestures, and actions.

The mental manifestations are nothing else but "functions" of the brain; mental disorders are diffuse illnesses of the cerebral cortex. Accordingly, psychiatry is only a specially developed branch of neuropathology; its main goal is pathology of the cerebral cortex and as precise an understanding as possible of all the pathological changes of form and structure occurring in the cerebral cortex under the influence of various factors.

The association between the cerebral and mental functions still defies understanding physiologically; we know only that this relation exists and that apparently it is an orderly one. From this undeniable thought necessarily stems the demand that psychiatric research must be approached from two sides: the study of the physical basis of mental disorders and the study of mental processes by the means and methods of the empirical sciences. Only in this manner, only by the internal integration of brain pathology with "psychopathology" may we succeed in understanding the laws of the dynamic relationship between the somatic and mental disorders and thus gain profound understanding of the manifestations of mental illness.

The last completed edition, the ninth of his *Psychiatry* (1927), was expanded to four volumes and contains approximately tenfold the number of pages as the first edition. In the fifth edition, published in 1896, the deteriorating processes (dementia praecox, catatonias, and dementia paranoids) are classified together; whereas in the 1899 edition, and more so in the seventh edition of 1904, dementia praecox, manic depressive psychosis, and paranoia are clearly distinguishable as separate psychiatric entities. From the eighth edition (1909-1915), Barclay has translated the presentation of the endogenous dementias, dementia praecox. As with the other major disorders, Kraepelin presented early in the treatise, for the reader's orientation, his general thoughts on classification and identification of the insanities which frequently began in adolescence. The introduction begins as follows:[3]

A series of morbid pictures are here brought together under the term "endogenous dementias" merely for the purpose of preliminary inquiry. Their clinical relations are not yet clear, but they all display two peculiarities, that they are in the first place, so far as can be seen, not occasioned from without but arise from internal causes, and that secondly, at least in the great majority of cases, they lead to a more or less well-marked mental enfeeblement. It appears that this form of mental weakness, in spite of great differences in detail, exhibits many features in common with other forms of dementia, such as are known to us as the result of paralysis, senility or epilepsy. For this reason I have hitherto decribed under the one name, dementia praecox, the morbid pictures under consideration. Bleuler also has taken them together in his "group of schizophrenias," without trying to make a further division of this group. I consider it an open question whether the same morbid process is not after all the cause of the divergent forms, though differing in the point of attack and taking a varying course. It appears to me expedient at the present stage to separate out a number of these clinical pictures from the domain of dementia praecox, which in any case is very extensive. Nevertheless it is dementia praecox which we must take as the first division of the endogenous dementias to be reviewed.

Kraepelin's work, moving from general concepts to isolated experiences, is best illustrated in his discussion of the manic-depressive psychoses, also translated by Barclay.[4]

MANIC-DEPRESSIVE insanity, as it is to be described in this section, includes on the one hand the whole domain of so-called *periodic and circular insanity,* on the other hand *simple mania,* the greater part of the morbid states termed *melancholia* and also a not inconsiderable number of cases of *amentia* [confusional or delirious insanit]. Lastly, we include here certain slight and slightest colourings of *mood,* some of them periodic, some of them continuously morbid, which on the one hand are to be regarded as the rudiment of more severe disorders, on the other hand pass over without sharp boundary into the domain of *personal predisposition.* In the course of the years I have become more and more convinced that all the above-mentioned states only represent manifestations of a *single morbid process.* It is certainly possible that later a series of subordinate forms may be described, or even individual small groups again entirely separated off. But if this happens, then according to my view those symptoms will most certainly not be authoritative, which hitherto have usually been placed in the foreground.

What has brought me to this position is first the experience that notwithstanding manifold external differences certain *common fundamental features* yet recur in all the morbid states mentioned. Along with changing symptoms, which may appear temporarily or may be completely absent, we meet in all forms of manic-depressive insanity a quite definite, narrow group of disorders, though certainly of very varied character and composition. Without any one of them being absolutely characteristic of the malady, still in association they impress a uniform stamp on all the multiform clinical states.

Kraepelin was a man with simple tastes. He enjoyed his family, nature, music, and his work. He cared little for social amenities or honors and was not a gregarious person. One of his great pleasures was a second home on Lake Maggiore in northern Italy, confiscated when Italy was at war with Germany but returned to him after the armistice. He lost four of his children and his personal property during the postwar inflationary debacle in Germany. Age appeared to have little effect on any of his attributes or characteristics. Although his poems were not particularly noteworthy and were not published until after his death according to his caprice, the first two verses of the tribute to the waterfall, "Voringsfoss," near Hardanger in Norway, disclose his love of nature and his form of expression in verse.[5]

> Far to the east in glacier ice
> Lusty the young stream has its birth;
> Out from the crystal gates with mirth,
> Free in its life course from its rise.
>
> Merry is its play of youth;
> See it sparkle, bubble, foam—
> Dreams it darkly of a home,
> Striving toward a goal, in truth?

1. Weygandt, Emil Kraepelin (Ger), *Allg Z Psychiat* 85:443-458, 1927, excerpts translated by Z. Danilevicius.
2. Kraepelin, E.: *Compendium of Psychiatry* (Ger), Leipzig: A. Abel, 1883, excerpt translated by Z. Danilevicius.
3. Kraepelin, E.: "Dementia Praecox and Paraphrenia" (Ger), in Kraepelin,[2] ed 8 (Ger), R. M. Barclay (trans.): *Dementia Praecox and Paraphrenia*, Edinburgh: E. & S. Livingstone, 1919.
4. Kraepelin, E.: "Manic-Depressive Insanity and Paranoia" (Ger), ed 8 (Ger), R. M. Barclay (trans.): *Manic-Depressive Insanity and Paranoia*, Edinburgh: E. & S. Livingstone, 1921.
5. Kraepelin, E.: *Werden, Sein, Vergehen [Coming, Being, Going]* (Ger), Munich; J. F. Lehmanns, 1928, in Brink, L., and Jelliffe, S. E. (trans.): Emil Kraepelin, Psychiatrist and Poet, *J Nerv Ment Dis* 77:134-152, 274-282, 1933.

Composite by G. Bako

Joseph Babinski (1857-1932)

JOSEPH FRANCOIS FÉLIX BABINSKI left a description of the plantar reflex, as familiar an eponymic term to medical students and physicians as any. Babinski, of Polish parentage, was born in Paris, took his degree in medicine from the University of Paris, and remained loyal to the French capital throughout his professional career. Although his name will be forever associated with the plantar response, he was a prolific writer with interests in physiology, neurosurgery, medicine, endocrinology, psychiatry, and medical editing. As a pupil of Charcot, Cornil, and Vulpian, and an associate of Duchenne, Déjerine, and Pierre Marie, he carried the traditional stature of the Parisan physicians of the preceding era into the 20th century.

The first scientific contribution (1882) of Babinski concerned typhoid fever.[1] His graduation thesis on multiple sclerosis, published 3 years later, was an attempt to correlate pathological and clinical findings.[2] At the age of 30, he became Charcot's Chief of Clinic at Salpêtrière; shortly after, he was nominated Médecin aux Hôpitaux. After the death of Charcot in 1893, Babinsik was appointed director of the Neurological Clinic at La Pitié, where he remained until a few years before his death. Together with Brissaud, Pierre Marie, Déjerine, and others, he founded the Société de Neurologie de Paris, and for many years was editor of the *Revue Neurologique*.

The eponymic sign was reported first in 1896.[3] The description was brief and merely stated that the normal plantar response consists of flexion of the toes together with flexion of the ankle, knee, and hip; while in certain cases of "paralysis," the toes on the affected side, instead of flexing when the sole is stimulated, execute an extensor movement on the metatarsal. Two years later this description of the phenomenon of the toes was expanded to include the strength of the response, strength of the stimulus, comparative speed, and need for relaxation of the foot before stimulation.[4] Fanning of the outer toes, ignored in the initial description, was included in a communication published in 1903.[5]

In a preceding communication [(1)], I showed that the *reflex* abduction provoked by stimulating the sole of the foot, when it is marked, indicates a disturbance of the pyramidal system.

More recently observed facts have led me to think that such a lesion could also effect an *associated* abduction of the toes. To witness this phenomenon, the following conditions must be observed: the subject lies on his back, then, having crossed his arms across his chest, performs alternate movements of flexion and extension of the trunk over the pelvis, as in the research of the "combined movement of flexion of the trunk and of the thigh." While he performs these acts, the toes will spread apart.

The associated abduction of the toes seems to have a clinical significance of the same order as does the reflex abduction, but it must be noted that if these two types of movement sometimes coexist, one may also exist in the absence of the other.

Associated abduction of the toes is a rather rare phenomenon that seems to me to be more common to infantile hemiplegia than in that of the adult, more frequent in hemiparesis than in hemiplegia.

Our colleague, M. Dupre, has proposed to call abduction of the toes—whether it be caused by reflex or whether it manifests itself as an associated movement—*the fan sign*. This is a picturesque image that deserves to be retained, but inasmuch as it may be of value to specify the conditions under which this sign is produced, it would perhaps be preferable to content oneself with the term *abduction of the toes,* to which may be added, according to the circumstances, the words *reflex, associated,* or *reflex and associated.*

I have observed association abduction of the toes on the right side of a patient with a function spasm of the upper right extremity which manifested itself specifically as writer's cramp; simultaneously this woman presented on the right the phenomenon of combined flexion of the thigh and the trunk. This suggested to me an idea analogous to that which I had propagated relative to the pathogenesis of so-called mental torticollis, that is, that a functional spasm, at least in some cases, is perhaps dependent upon a perturbation of the pyramidal system. However, this is still only a hypothesis which needs verification.

The late John F. Fulton, experimental neurologist, medical historian, and biographer of Babinski, whose perceptive studies in the laboratory and in the study chair have explored in depth the extensor plantar response, revealed that this reflex was absent in the lower primates, monkeys and baboons, after destruction of the pyramidal pathways. On the other hand, the persistence of the reflex in the higher anthropoids including the chimpanzee, after lesions of the corticospinal system, offered convincing proof that the pyramidal system is dominant at this stage of evolution.[4]

Less well known is Babinski's critical analysis of cerebellar physiology and symptomatology and the introduction of the concept of "asynergia," an inability to execute complex motor functions which involve the integrated action of separate muscle groups. In cerebellar disease, with dissociation of movements, the onset is delayed (cerebellar catalepsy); but once initiated, the action is carried over beyond the initial intent, with overshooting (hypermetria). Babinski also described adiadochokinesia, an inability to perform rapid alternating movements.

As a clinical neurologist, Babinski was not particularly interested in postmortem examinations or laboratory investigations. It was at the bedside or in the clinic that he displayed a remarkable faculty for morbid neurology and general medicine. He was a meticulous observer of disease, searching for small as well as large deviations from the normal, checking and rechecking and correlating his clinical findings with concepts of pathogenesis. The Babinski-Nageotte syndrome refers to multiple medullary lesions of vascular origin, involving the pyramidal tract, medial lemniscus, restiform body and reticular structures.[6] Babinski and Carpentier, his pupil and associate, described the abolition of the pupillary response to light in cerebrospinal syphilis. One of his published interests in neurological surgery was a report on the first spinal cord tumor to be operated on in France. Shortly before Fröhlich described the adiposogenital syndrome in the male, Babinski recognized this condition in the female. He was interested in hysteria ("pithiatisme") and noted that superficial and deep reflexes persisted without alteration in susceptible persons. His methods in treating the war neuroses in World War I were reported to be rather harsh but extremely succeessful.

Although an outstanding neurologist in France, Babinski shared with Duchenne the dubious honor of holding no university position in Paris. However, he was richly rewarded with kudos at home and abroad, including an honorary membership in the American Neurological Association.

The Babinski sign is an example of simplicity of clinical definition. However, it has great diagnostic significance based upon recognized pathological aberrations. The physical stature of the author may be compared to the clinical eponym. He was a large man, formidable in appearance but simple in speech, whose depth of perception reflected a keen intellect that contributed so much to clinical neurology. Nor did Parkinsonism, with which he was afflicted in the retiring years of his life, obliterate the desire to further his professional achievements.

1. Fulton, J. F.: Joseph François Félix Babinski, *Arch Neurol Psychiat* 29:168-174 (Jan) 1933.

2. Babinski, J.: Étude anatomique et clinique sur la sclérose en plaques, Thèse de Paris, 1885.

3. Babinski J.: Sur le réflexe cutané plantaire dans certaines affections organiques du système nerveux central, *Compt rend Soc biol* 3:207, 1896.

4. Fulton, J. F., and Keller, A. D.: *The Sign of Babinski: A Study of the Evolution of Cortical Dominance in Primates*, Springfield, Ill.: Charles C Thomas, 1932.

5. Babinski, J.: Abduction of the Toes (Fr), *Rev Neurol* 11:728-729, 1205-1206, 1903 excerpt translated by Z. Danilevicius.

6. Babinski, J.: Hémiasynergie, Lateropulsion et Myosis Bulbaires avec Hémianesthésie et Hémiplégie Croisées, *Rev Neurol* 10:358-363, 1902.

Composite by G. Bako

Franz Nissl (1860-1919)

FRANZ NISSL, was born in Bavarian Frankenthal, the son of a gymnasium teacher. He devoted his professional days to the histology of the cerebral cortex and of other higher centers, with the persistent intent to identify microstructure with function in health and disease.[1] His intellectual endowment was apparent even in medical school, where he won a first prize at the University of Munich for his inaugural thesis, *Pathological Changes of the Nerve Cells of the Cerebral Cortex*. Not only a remarkable treatise, it also proved to be prophetic of his many subsequent contributions on the preparation and microscopic inspection of nervous tissue. The preferred combination for processing nervous tissue, prior to Nissl's investigations, was Müller's solution of dichromate and sulfate for hardening and carmine for staining. In their place Nissl used alcohol and aniline dye and later gained maximum delineation of cellular structure with the use of methylene or toluidine blue dye.

Nissl passed his state medical examination in 1885 and for three years assisted in Gudden's clinic in the district insane asylum in Munich. Recurring kidney trouble interrupted his studies; following convalescence he returned to work in the state institution at Blankenhain. In 1889, he was offered a position at the state asylum in Frankfurt where Alois Alzheimer, of French birth, shared his interest in neurohistologic investigation. The two benefited from mutual friendship and scientific collaboration— sometimes close, at other times remote— over a quarter of a century. The brilliant imagination of Nissl complemented the analytic observations of Alzheimer. In time, they accepted the realization that alteration of cerebral structure was not specific for cerebral disease as they postulated. In 1895, through the inducement of Kraepelin, Nissl moved to Heidelburg, where he combined teaching and consultative work with research. He was advanced to adjunct professor in 1901 and, from 1904 to 1918, served as professor of psychiatry and director of the clinic, succeeding Kraepelin. While in Heidelberg, he published a monograph on the neuron, favoring the nerve-net theory, and devised a procedure for quantitative measurement of albumin in spinal fluid. In 1918, he returned to Munich, again under the strong backing of Kraepelin, and was able to give his entire energies to scientific activities. Here, through animal experiments, he identified significant correlative functions between the thalamic nucleus and the cerebral cortex.

Nissl's method for investigating microscopic structure of the central nervous system by interruption of pathways or excision of cell clusters was described by a recorder as a résumé in the *Neurologisches Centralblatt* for 1894.[2]

Dr. Nissl's new method is based on the following: (1) Interruption of the nerve cell with the end-organ—the muscle of the epithelial sensory cell—in fully grown or half-grown animals causes retrograde atrophy of the nerve cells. (2) After the excision of a nerve cell center in the cerebrum regressive changes appear in the nearest directly dependent center; changes can appear in the neighboring center, once removed, only after several weeks. It is immaterial whether the center is removed surgically or the communication from the center is severed. (3) The regressive changes vary in different types of nerve cells: initially, swelling of the cell-body begins, with granular degeneration of the stainable contents of the cell-body. (4) It is inevitably noted that when the cells of the central system suffer damage and undergo regressive changes, the surrounding glia cells undergo progressive changes. . . . When any factor damages the specific elements of the central nervous system organ, cell or fiber, the surrounding glia cells react by succulent swelling of the cell-body and increased differentiation. Parts of the cell which did not previously stain before now absorb the dye; the maximum changes are marked by karyokinesis. Nissl's methylene blue solution makes the alterations immediately visible. . . . The slides shown by Nissl demonstrated with great clarity the dependence of the cells of the thalamus on the cerebral cortex.

In the same year Nissl published a three-part discourse, entitled *The So-Called Granules in Nerve Cells,* a communication illustrated with photomicrographs of cells from the motor horn of the spinal column, medulla, spinal ganglion, olfactory bulb, and Ammon's horn. The granular basophilic material surrounding the nucleus in the cytoplasm of nerve cells, stained with toluidine blue, was recognized by Nissl and has come to be known as Nissl's granules or Nissl's bodies. He concluded with an objection to labeling the granules as *basophilic* or *acidophilic,* according to their absorption of acid or basic stains, believing it ridiculous to identify chemical properties of intracellular substances when so little was known of the chemical composition of the cell.[3]

These portions of the cell which are visible should be described as formed or stainable, the invisible parts are not formed and not stainable; the formed elements or the components of the stainable part should be labeled according to their shape: "granules," "granular parts," "rows," "groups," or "cords" of one type or other; the larger particles within the cell substance may be called "bodies" and especially typical ones may be described as "spindles," "grains," or "needles." This will provide sufficient terms for the formed elements within the cell, without resorting to prejudice and without attributing more to the substance than is known.

Nissl's work on the cortical changes of general paresis was carried out in collaboration with Alzheimer, who jointly sought the explanation of pathologic findings in nervous tissue through study of tissue from the afflicted, as well as from animal experimentation, with observation of the structural alterations following administration of noxious substances. The massive treatise emphasized the value of comparing findings from neuropathologic microscopy of tissue from patients not considered mentally ill with tissue from those overtly afflicted. The gross and microscopic changes of general paresis, described by Nissl in his assigned section, included pachymeningitis, atrophy of the hemispheres, dilatation of the lateral ventricles, inflammatory changes in the cerebral cortex, perivascular collections of lymphocytes and plasma cells, degenerative changes, neurologic proliferations, and an increase in number of "rod cells."[4]

If each case of mental illness coming to autopsy would be examined by the methods described, and if the cortex of patients without mental illness would be examined and compared, the conclusion would be evident; not a single instance of mental illness, irrespective of type, would be lacking in pathological changes.

The findings in general paresis are: enormous thickening and cloudiness of the membranes of each hemisphere, especially those covering the frontal area; sharp limitation of the cloudiness at the occiput; external hydrocephalus with localized subpial collection of large amounts of fluid, marked atrophy of the hemisphere.

In a lecture given in 1899, I reported another type of cell which does not appear to stem from nervous tissue. This cell should not be confused with the proliferating cells of the blood vessel intima. It is characterized by a long cell body with an elongated rod-like nucleus; the body of these cells is not clearly defined and shows fibrils at either pole. The contents of these cells remain lighter than other cells and contain only a few stained granules clustered in lineal formation in the elongated nucleus. The cells are observed in the brain of paralytics, parallel to the structure of brain substance.

Paralysis involves two different but parallel histopathologic disease processes. The first shows diffuse inflammatory characteristics and is easily recognized. The second lacks characteristics of inflammation.

The question whether paralytic cortical disease is an inflammatory process should be answered in the affirmative. This conclusion is reached with the understanding that the word "inflammatory" means exclusively histopathologic processes, in which the progressive and regressive changes in the parenchyma are accompanied at the same time by participation of blood vessels in the form of an exudative process, and that lymphocytes and plasma cells, seen in paralytical cortical changes in the meninges are also present, the plasma cells migrating from the vascular channels.

Nissl never married, and never stopped work except for illness. As the designer of the discipline of pathologic anatomy of men-

tal diseases, he never abandoned the belief in the intellectual rewards of neurohistologic and neuropathologic investigation. He prepared a broad substructure for topographical cortical histology and cyto-architecture, leaving for interested investigators the interpretation of the relation of nerve cells, medullated fibers, and fibrils to each other and to surrounding structure under normal and disordered states. He showed that the deeper layers of the cortex show a close relation to deeper structures beneath them; whereas the upper layers are essentially independent.

1. Kraepelin, E.: Franz Nissl, *J Nerv Ment Dis* 51:207-215, 1920.
2. Nissl, F.: New Methods of Investigation of the Central Nervous System (Ger), *Neurol Cbl* 13:507-508, 1894, translated by Z. Danilevicius.
3. Nissl, F.: The So-Called Granules in Nerve Cells (Ger), *Neurol Cbl* 13:676-685, 781-789, 810-815, 1894, excerpts translated by Z. Danilevicius.
4. Nissl, F.: *Histological and Histopathological Studies of the Cerebral Cortex* (Ger), vol 1, Jena: G. Fischer, 1904, excerpts translated by Z. Danilevicius.

Composite by G. Bako

Sir Henry Head (1861-1940)

HENRY HEAD, experimental physiologist and clinical neurologist of London, was born of Quaker parents in Stoke Newington.[1] His father was an insurance broker of Lloyds, his mother a relative of Lord Lister. Henry was a boarder at Friends' School, Tottenham, where Ashford, the headmaster, awakened an interest in the natural sciences. At 13, he went to Charterhouse and again came under the influence of the science master. This time it was Poole who taught him biology and the fundamentals of physiology and gave him private instruction in gross dissection and preparation of tissue for microscopic examination. It seems logical that Cambridge should be next on the academic route, where Head qualified for a scholarship at Trinity College, and with Shipley and Sherrington as contemporary students and with Gaskell and Foster on the resident faculty. Head graduated AB with honors in the natural sciences tripos. Seeking postgraduate training on the Continent, he visited first the University of Halle, followed by Prague, at that time a German university, where Hering was pursuing critical investigations in physiology. Two years were spent with Hering; the experimental findings and theoretical deductions on the respiratory action of the vagus nerve were disclosed in a long treatise, "On the Regulation of Respiration."[2]

During normal breathing the activity of the vagi produces two results—firstly, the inspiratory activity of the centre is regulated by the constant inhibitions produced by the dilatation of the lungs, and secondly, the potential inspiratory energy of the centre is raised. Thus division of the vagi will also produce a twofold effect upon the breathing. In the first place the inspiratory activity of the centre is no longer checked by the dilatation of the lungs, and the inspirations therefore increase both in strength and duration. Now if this was the only effect produced by dividing the vagi the breathing would at once assume a regular form, characterised by strong inspirations of considerable duration, followed by complete expiratory pauses. If the vitality of the centre is lowered by an excessive dose of chloral this is actually the case, but, if the centre is in a presumably normal condition, the inspiratory contractions which immediately follow division of the vagi differ greatly from those which appear subsequently.

After more than two years in Prague, Head completed his courses in anatomy and physiology in Cambridge and his clinical work at University College Hospital, London. Also, a very brief time was spent at National Hospital, Queen Square, under Thomas Buzzard. The MB was granted by Cambridge in 1890, and the MD in 1892, upon submission of a thesis entitled, "On Disturbances of Sensation with Especial Reference to the Pain of Visceral Disease." The publication, in three parts, in the journal *Brain* included plates with diagrams of the dermatomes, which remain as standard reference figures.[3]

Thus I think that these facts tend to show that there is an intimate connection between the central connections for the sensory nerves of the viscera and the nerves which supply the sensation of pain, heat and cold, and also those which exert a trophic influence on the skin. I do not therefore think we shall be far wrong in assuming that the trophic nerves to the viscera bear a similar relation to the sensory sympathetic fibres as the trophic nerves to the skin bear to the fibres for pain.

Thus to sum up I think we may conclude that the central connections of the pain fibres from the skin and viscera are closely connected with one another. The central connections of the nerves for heat and cold, and for trophic disturbances in the skin must also be in somewhat close association, though probably not actually connected. On the other hand the nerves for touch from the skin (we do not know whether nerves for touch exist in the viscera) are widely separated centrally from those of pain.

Following completion of university and hospital training, Head selected general medicine at Victoria Park Hospital for Diseases of the Chest, although his investigations and writings were concerned with clinical neurology. The report on herpes zoster in collaboration with A. W. Campbell, pathologist to the County Asylum, Rainhill, noted that others had made reference to the alterations in the posterior root ganglion, but that the pathological lesions had never been clearly described.[4]

If the patient has died with the eruption still out upon his skin the affected ganglion will be found to be in a condition of profound inflammation. The interstitial tissue will be crowded with small round cells which stain deeply with methylene blue and other nuclear dyes. Here and there these inflammatory cells may be closely massed into clumps, and such foci may be scattered round the periphery and in the central tissue of the ganglion.

If these foci of inflammatory cells are examined in serial sections they will occasionally be found to be situated around extravasated blood which has undergone more or less change according to the length of time at which death has occurred after the first appearance of the eruption.

One of Head's best-known experiments was the surgical interruption of the radial and external cutaneous nerves in his left arm. The sacrifice and detailed study of recovery of sensations led to his recognition of two forms of superficial or cutaneous sensibilities. The terms "protopathic" and "epicritic" served a useful purpose for a time. He had not smoked for two years prior to the experiment, and no alcohol was taken during the eight months' period of observation.[5] The nerve was divided near the elbow, a small portion was excised, and the ends united with silk suture. The surgical interruption resulted in loss of cutaneous sensibility on the radial half of the forearm and the back of the hand, but without loss of deep sensibility. The observations were continued until restoration of superficial or cutaneous sensation.

The reflex functions of the spinal cord, a monographic treatise of aphasia,[6] and the termination of secondary paths of sensation in the optic thalamus were other contributions in neurology.

Quite apart from his clinical practice, Head was interested in art, literature, music, and human beings. He was an able literary critic, one of the best in London in his day, and a poet of stature. His book of poems, *Destroyers and Other Verses,* appeared in 1919. One of the best is from a series entitled "Songs of La Mouche" and is a sentimental rhyme.[7]

> My tender ways and laughter
>   Have gained me lovers twain.
> I flouted the one, but the other
>   I bitterly love again.
>
> One loved me for my great virtue;
>   I was sweet, and pure, and good.
> He worshipped in me incarnate,
>   Mysterious womanhood.
>
> To the other my soul lies open—
>   I never could play my part—
> He thinks that virtue's scarcely
>   The thing I've most at heart.

Henry Head was fluent in French and German, a facile and prolific writer, and editor of *Brain* from 1910 to 1925. He was an excellent and highly respected teacher and, although an outstanding clinical neurologist, was never officially associated with National Hospital, a logical institute for such a notable neurologist. The Royal College of Physicians elected him to membership in 1894 and the Royal Society to fellowship in 1898. He delivered the Gulstonian lecture of the Royal College of Physicians and the Croonian lectures of the Royal Society. The honor of knighthood was bestowed on him in 1927. There were no children born to his marriage, but his wife did much to compensate for an otherwise larger family circle. Head, a man of humility, with a fine intellect, bore the physical and psychological hardships of Parkinson's disease with which he was afflicted for more than 20 years before his death.

1. Brain, R.: Henry Head: The Man and His Ideas, *Brain* 84:561-569, 1961.

2. Head, H.: On the Regulation of Respiration, *J Physiol* 10:1-70, 279-290, 1889.

3. Head, H.: On Disturbances of Sensation with Especial Reference to the Pain of Disease, *Brain* 16:1-133, 1893; 17:339-480, 1894; 19:153-276, 1896.

4. Head, H., and Campbell, A. W.: The Pathology of Herpes Zoster and Its Bearing on Sensory Localisation, *Brain* 23:353-523, 1900.

5. Head, H.; Rivers, W. H. R.; and Sherren, J.: The Afferent Nervous System from a New Aspect, *Brain* 28:99-115, 1905.

6. Head, H.: *Aphasia and Kindred Disorders of Speech,* 2 vol, Cambridge: University Press, 1926.

7. Head, H.: *Destroyers and Other Verses,* Oxford: University Press, 1919.

Alois Alzheimer (1864-1915)

ALOIS ALZHEIMER, pathologist of the central nervous system, was born in Marktbreit, Bavaria, the son of a government officer.[1] After attending school in Aschaffenburg and Würzburg, Alzheimer studied medicine at the universities of Würzburg, Tübingen, and Berlin. He received the MD degree from Würzburg in 1887, upon the presentation of a thesis on the wax-producing glands of the ear based upon work carried out in von Kölliker's laboratory. Following his internship he served seven years as assistant in the Irrenanstalt in Frankfurt-am-Main; there he was joined in 1889 by Nissl, who led him into systematic research in brain pathology and then served for seven years as director of the asylum. In 1895, Nissl was called to Heidelberg by Kraepelin, Alzheimer following in 1902. One year later Alzheimer and

Composite by G. Bako

Kraepelin moved to Munich. In 1904, later than most academic aspirants, Alzheimer was appointed privatdocent, and, in 1908, professor and director of the large anatomical laboratory in the psychiatric clinic which rapidly became a highly regarded center for neuropathology. In 1912, Alzheimer was called to Breslau as professor and director of the Psychiatric and Neurologic Institute, a position combining research and clinical practice. He held this post until his lingering illness and premature death from heart failure and uremia. From 1910 until 1916 he was editor for psychiatry of the *Zeitschrift für die gesamte Neurologie und Psychiatrie*.

In collaboration, Nissl's remarkable imagination and abundance of ideas complemented Alzheimer's vivid reasoning and capacity for the development of histologic stains and meticulous histologic technique. Working together they produced lucid descriptions of normal and abnormal structure in the central nervous system. Their findings were described in a six-volume encyclopedia entitled *Histologic and Histopathologic Studies of the Cerebral Cortex*. Although the goal of precise correlation of abnormal structures with clinical entities in psychiatric and neurologic disorders was never realized, their work was a stride forward.[2] The majority of Alzheimer's scientific contributions were brief and were concerned mainly with neurohistology. The subjects included acute alcoholic delirium, Westphal-Strümpell pseudosclerosis, dementia praecox, differential diagnosis of brain tumors, progressive paralysis of the young, epilepsy, leutic meningomyelitis and encephalitis, gliosis, Huntington's chorea, general paresis, hysterical bulbar paralysis, and stains for neurologic changes. His descriptions of senile plaques of the brain (called Alzheimer's disease by Kraepelin) and arteriosclerotic atrophy of the brain are excerpted.

Although the clinical findings described by Pick and Alzheimer in presenile dementia are similar, the entities are distiguishable, postmortem. Either disease begins in mid-maturity. The clinical features of Alzheimer's disease include progressive loss of intellectual facilities, disturbance in speech, and defective memory. Terminally, there are complete loss of intellectual activity, mutism, expressionalist facies, and reduction to a vegetative status. Atrophy is observed in the frontal and temporal lobes, postmortem. Except for the motor cortex, on microscopic examination there is loss of cells in each of the cortical layers, with secondary gliosis, silver staining plaques, and neurofibrillar degeneration.[3]

The case had presented such varied symptoms that it defied classification under existing illnesses, and pathological findings were different from any process so far known. The woman, 51 years of age, showed as her first symptom a jealousy towards her husband. Soon she showed a rapidly increasing amnesia; she became lost in her own apartment, carried objects about aimlessly, hid them, sometimes believed she was to be murdered, and had spells of unrestrained screaming.

When committed to the institution, her behavior was dominated by total helplessness. She was confused as to time and place. Occasionally she remarked that she did not understand anything and did not know her way about. At times she was delirious, and carried parts of her bed around, called for her husband and daughter, and had auditory hallucinations. Often she screamed in a frightening voice for hours at a time.

Her walk was normal and unhampered, patellar reflexes were present, and the pupils reacted.

Mental deterioration progressed and she died 4½ years later. By then she showed little response, remained in bed with her legs drawn to her body, neglected herself, and, in spite of all nursing, developed decubitus.

The autopsy showed a diffusely atrophied brain. The larger vessels were arteriosclerotic. Histologic sections stained by the Dielschowsky silver method showed remarkable changes of the neurofibrillae. In place of a normal cell, one or several fibrillae were prominent by their thickness and ability to take on stain. Upon further investigation, other fibrillae, which ran parallel to each other, were altered in a similar fashion. The nucleus and the cell disintegrated; subsequently, only a mass of fibrillae showed the site of a ganglion cell.

Since the fibrillae will take up different stains, a chemical change must have taken place in the fibrillar substance. This may be the cause for their surviving the death of the cell. The change in the fibrillae is concomitant with the infiltration by an undetermined metabolic product in the ganglion cells. One fourth to one third of all ganglion cells disappeared completely, especially in the upper layers.

Over the entire brain, and especially in the upper layers, miliary centers appeared, which were caused by an unusual substance. It resisted staining but could be recognized nevertheless. The glia became fibrous, and many glia cells showed fatty deposits. There was no involvement of the vessels. Apparently we are dealing with an unidentified illness.

In a brief communication from his laboratory in the asylum in Frankfurt, Alzheimer described the changes typically observed in arteriosclerotic atrophy of the brain, which were believed to be distinguishable from senile and other degenerative processes. According to Alzheimer, the disease appeared usually in the fifth and sixth decades, with the patient exhibiting apoplexy, paralysis, sometimes euphoria, at other times depression, regression of reasoning, later loss of pupillary reflexes, increase of tendon reflexes, and loss of memory. Macroscopically, atrophy of the cortex and cystic widening of the vessel were characteristic. Microscopically, small aneurysms, capillary bleeding, thickening of the neuroglia, and loss of cells were reported.[4]

Histologic examination of cases belonging to this specific group has shown characteristics different from those of general paralysis. In all of the cases, severe arteriosclerotic changes in the vessels of the brain were noted as well as tissue degeneration, which most likely depends on the blood vessel changes. This disease is not common. It affects mostly persons 45 to 58 years of age and with marked arteriosclerosis.

The disease begins insidiously with mild weakness, headaches, dizziness, and sleeplessness. Later, severe irritability and loss of memory develop. Patients complain bitterly of their symptoms. At times the disease is associated with a sudden apoplectic attack followed by hemiplegia. Increasing loss of memory and progressive clouding of mind appear later, with sudden mood changes, fluctuating between mild euphoria and exaggerated hypochondriasis; terminally the disease leads to stupor and child-like behavior. The features differ from patients with general paralysis by apparent calmness, by an organized behavior pattern, and by general ability of reasoning.

The disturbance of the pupillary reaction usually appears later, but tremors, weakness of the legs, and increased tendon reflexes are the initial symptoms. Many patients exhibit hemiparesis which involves disturbance of speech and differs appreciably from hemiparesis in paralytic patients. In the last stage of the disease either deep apathetic idiocy or complete loss of memory appears, but otherwise the patient remains quiet and orderly.

Autopsy often demonstrates not only arteriosclerotic heart and blood vessel changes but arteriosclerotic degeneration of the kidneys. The microscopic picture of the brain is typical. The changes in the blood vessels are present even in the smallest branches. The pia is cloudy, the cortex is atrophic, the convolutions of the brain and the deeper layers contain yellow streaks corresponding to the areas of vessels. At times the area surrounding these streaks is markedly sclerotic. Around the vessels the naked eye can detect wide areas filled with liquid; this is especially characteristic around the basal ganglia and at the inner capsule. It is possible to extract long segments of vessels from the cystic dilatations. If (under the microscope) some hydrochloric acid is added to the segments of vessels, many carbonic acid bubbles appear. Microscopic examination shows the presence of many small aneurysms, hematomas around rapidly degenerating capillary vessels, focal enlargement of neuroglia, and accumulation of granular cells in the cortex. Where large numbers of granular cells have accumulated, focal softening of the brain may be seen.

Alzheimer had seen multifocal glial hypertrophy around the vessels of the inner capsule in one of the cases. He considered these cases to be one form of arteriosclerotic atrophy of the brain.

1. Gaupp, R.: Alois Alzheimer (Ger), obituary, *Munch Med Wschr* 63:195-196, 1916.

2. Alzheimer, A., and Nissl, F.: *Histologic and Histopathologic Studies of the Cerebral Cortex* (Ger), 6 vol, Jena: G. Fischer, 1904-1918.

3. Alzheimer, A.: A New Disease of the Cortex (Ger), *Allg Z Psychiat* 64:146-148, 1907, excerpt translated by Z. Danilevicius.

4. Alzheimer, A.: Arteriosclerotic Atrophy of the Brain (Ger), *Neurol Cbl* 13:765-768, 1894, excerpt translated by Z. Danilevicius.

National Medical Library

Sir Victor Horsley (1857-1916)

SIR VICTOR HORSLEY, the foremost neuro-surgeon of England, was a spiritual disciple of John Hunter, teacher and practitioner of surgery, and a pupil of Burdon-Sanderson, experimental physiologist. Horsley was born in Kensington, with a family heritage for music, painting, and medicine. Although an exceptional schoolboy at Cranbrook, only at University College, London, did his special talents appear. After he graduated MB and BS in 1881 as scholar in surgery and gold medalist, in 1884, Horsley was appointed professor-superintendent of the Brown Institution, where he carried out a series of investigations in three diverse fields of medical science—endocrinology, microbiology, and neurophysiology. As a member of a commission to study the relationship of myxedema and cretinism, he produced, by total thyroidectomy, clinical myxedema in

a monkey. As a member of the Royal Commission on Hydrophobia, Horsley studied the application of the Pasteur treatment for rabies; with Sharpey-Schafer and his brother-in-law Gotsch, he studied cerebral localization of the motor cortex. This diversity of interests in medical science and active participation in organized medicine continued, without interruption, until a few years before his untimely death on duty with the British Army during the Mesopotamian campaign in World War I. While still a young surgeon he was elected Fellow of the Royal Society, surgeon to the National Hospital for the Paralysed and Epileptic, Queen Square, and professor of pathology at University College. Medical literature was enriched by his prolific contributions which were prepared in a clear effortless style. Horsley was an ardent vivisectionist, a champion of women's suffrage, and a reformer who spoke and wrote of the evils of alcohol and tobacco. In a monograph on alcohol a number of statements of his convictions could not be supported by scientific evidence. During the reorganization of the British Medical Association, he was an active participant and filled several administrative posts. Honors included the Cameron Prize for therapeutics by the University of Edinburgh, Croonian Lecturer of the Royal Society, Fullerian Professor of the Royal Institution, Royal Medalist of the Royal Society, recipient of the Fothergillian Medal of the Medical Society, and ultimately knighthood.[1]

In 1880, Horsley communicated his observations on the function of the thyroid to the Royal Society through Michael Foster. Although the intimate relationship of goiter and cretinism had been recognized for centuries and excision of a goiter had been followed by symptoms of cretinism, Horsley was successful in producing myxedema in a monkey through extirpation of the thyroid. The description of the immediate postoperative period, with the animal experiencing tremors and tetany, suggests that the parathyroids were removed or were critically damaged during surgery. Subsequently, the animal became apathetic, the skin of the face and abdomen myxedematous, the salivary glands hypertrophic, and the blood depleted of red cells.[2]

Moreover, the symptoms of the disease termed Myxoedema by Dr. Ord, and ordinary cretinism are gradually developed.
The animal becomes gradually more and more imbecile and apathetic, sitting, at it does, huddled up and taking no notice of anything, in strong contrast to its customary vivacious state.
It exhibits swellings of the skin of the face, abdomen, &c., due to infiltration of the tissues by mucin.
The salivary glands become enormously hypertrophied, and the parotid gland, which normally secretes a watery, serous fluid, now takes up a muciparous function, and produces quantities of mucin.
This increase of function is interesting, as probably offering a clue for further investigation into the physiology of secretion.
The blood is profoundly changed: there is a decrease of red corpuscles, and a primary increase of the leucocytes, followed by a decrease, oligaemia thus resulting. Moreover, it contains mucin in proportions to the duration of life after the operation, and the serum albumin is diminished.
The temperature, slightly raised by the operation, becomes variable, and then after about twenty-five days, gradually sinks far below the normal, and the animal dies comatose.

The Brown Lectures, delivered a few weeks later, expanded the experimental observations and noted that superficial reflexes were diminished, blood pressure decreased, and hair became sparse.

In clinical surgery, Horsley's contributions were most spectacular, especially surgical treatment of head injuries, trigeminal neuralgia, and spinal injuries. He was ingenious in devising means for minimizing postoperative discomfort, was capable of a rapid technical procedure when indicated, but at other times was slow and painstaking. At all times he displayed a courageous optimism, coupled with sympathy for the sick and good rapport with students and house staff.

The protocols of ten consecutive cases of operation upon the cranial cavity and its contents were published in the *British Medical Journal* in 1887.[3] Prior to Horsley's time, trephining of the skull (which probably should have been classed as skull surgery, not brain surgery) was the extent of

interference by the general surgeon. In developing brain surgery into a technical discipline, Horsley recognized the importance of early diagnosis, developed bone wax for staying hemorrhage, and utilized Lister's practical concept of antisepsis, the use of chloroform for general anesthesia, and a healthy respect for nervous tissue. Of the lesions which he excised, two were tuberculomas, one a glioma, another an unidentified tumor, and the other a cyst or scar tissue following trauma. Only one of the patients died as an immediate consequence of surgery.[3]

Diagnosis of disease of the central nervous system means an intimate acquaintance with its physiology and pathology, and this we may hope to see widely generalised in spite of iniquitous opposition to scientific experiment and foolish ignorance, which, so to speak, boasts that it "does not believe in localisation." For the full advantage to be gained from operative procedure it is obvious that the disease must be attacked in an early stage. Nothing illustrates this fact more clearly than the very valuable paper published by Dr. Hale White in the last volume of the *Guy's Hospital Reports,* on the morbid anatomy of certain cerebral tumours. In this paper, Dr. Hale White gives some details from the *post-mortem* room concerning 100 cases of intracranial tumour, in which he demonstrates with facility that at about the period when a patient dies from such a cause, surgical interference in the majority of cases would be as powerless as medicine.
When, however, the nature of the malady and its seat are completely diagnosed, as in nine of the ten cases in the table appended to this note, the question assumes an entirely different aspect, as will, no doubt, be conceded on the perusal of the facts there given, from which it will be seen that, with one exception, No. 10, every patient was considerably benefited. After all, however, the proposition that what is wanted in these cases is earlier treatment scarcely needs proving, and so we may pass on to the real object of this note.
In conclusion, I think the details of the cases contained in the accompanying table show that the operation of exposing and removing considerable portions of the brain is not to be ranked among the "dangerous" procedures of surgery.

The removal of a tumor of the spinal cord was accomplished in 1887 on a 42-year-old male who had developed paraplegia. The medical history and correct preoperative diagnosis by W. R. Gowers was followed by surgical excision by Horsley, with complete rehabilitation of the patient.[4]

The development of complete paraplegia, which had taken place during the preceding four months, rendered the diagnosis, up to a certain point, a simple matter. The symptoms were those characteristic of a transverse lesion of the cord a little above the middle of the dorsal region. The gradual onset of the paralysis, the affection of one leg before the other, and the long-preceding signs of nerve irritation at the level of the lesion, made it practically certain that the spinal cord was damaged by compression and that the cause of the pressure was outside the cord itself.

An operation gave a chance, the only chance, of cure. If the tumour should turn out to be one that could not be extirpated, it was possible that the removal of an arch, or the division of nerve-roots passing into the growth, might lessen the sufferings of the patient.

On opening the dura mater I saw on the left side of the subdural cavity a round, dark, bluish mass about three millimetres in diameter, resting upon the left lateral column and posterior root-zone of the spinal cord. I recognised it at once to be the lower end of a new growth, and therefore quickly cut away the major part of the lamina next above.

This enabled me to see almost the whole extent of the tumour when the dura mater was divided. . . . I therefore made an incision through the pia matral sheath of the spinal cord, and then found that I could easily dissect the tumour from the surface of the cord, lifting it out of the deep bed which it had formed for itself in the lateral column of the cord.

The growth, on microscopical examination, was found to be fibromyxoma.

A year later the patient wrote that he was in excellent health and was able to work 16 hours a day, including standing and walking about.

Horsley summed up his philosophy of service to medicine.[1]

"Work, whether political or scientific, if done in the interests of the profession, brings with it not only the ample satisfaction of having contributed to social progress, but also earns constantly recurring grateful acknowledgement from those who happen to more directly benefit by what has been attained."

1. Obituary, Sir Victor Horsley, *Brit Med J* 2:162-167, 1910.

2. Horsley, V.: On the Function of the Thyroid Gland, *Proc Roy Soc Lond* 38:5-7, 1885.

3. Horsley, V.: Remarks on Ten Consecutive Cases of Operations upon the Brain and Cranial Cavity to Illustrate the Details and Safety of the Method Employed, *Brit Med J* 1:863-865, 1887.

4. Gowers, W. R., and Horsley, V.: A Case of Tumour of the Spinal Cord. Removal; Recovery, *Medicochir Trans* 71:377-428, 1888.

Countway Medical Library

Harvey Cushing (1869-1939)

HARVEY WILLIAM CUSHING was born in Cleveland into a family with a strong medical tradition and a heritage of personal concern for the sick.[1] Harvey completed his arts and sciences at Yale and his professional studies at Harvard Medical School, graduating in 1895 with the degrees of AM and MD. His housemanship was passed on the surgical service at the Massachusetts General Hospital, where his histories were embellished with line drawings of preoperative findings and lesions revealed during surgical exposure or at postmortem. The practice of surgical sketching persisted throughout his clinical years, adding charm and scientific substance to the hospital records. Cushing left Boston for Baltimore in 1896 to complete a four-year surgical residency at Johns Hopkins Hospital under W. S. Halsted. In that same institution, Cushing was equally responsive to Osler's literary skill and humanitarianism at the bedside.

After Hopkins, Cushing spent a year abroad visiting clinics and laboratories, stopping occasionally for periods of research and study. With Kronecker, in Berne, he engaged in a physiological investigation on intracranial pressure; with Sherrington, in Liverpool, he studied the motor cortex in apes. He returned to Halsted's staff and for more than ten years exemplified the Hopkins surgical tradition, which included absolute hemostasis, gentle handling of tissue, and use of many layers of fine silk for closure of wounds. As Cushing was rapidly maturing professionally, it is not surprising that he received several attractive offers to direct departments of surgery in several thriving medical schools. Each he rejected until the one of his choice appeared. In 1910, the President and Fellows of Harvard University dispatched an initial letter of intent which became official by mutual consent in 1912, with Cushing's acceptance of the Moseley professorship of surgery. In the same year the trustees of Peter Bent Brigham Hospital tendered him the post of surgeon-in-chief of the new hospital, whose staff was to be integrated into the Harvard Medical School faculty.

During four decades of aggressive professional activities, Cushing was accepted as the founder of contemporary neurosurgery, the outstanding neurosurgeon in the Western World, military surgeon, a dedicated scholar, collector of medical books, and the biographer of William Osler, for which he won the Pulitzer Prize in 1926.

An interest in the structure and physiology of the nervous system appeared during his resident years in Baltimore. In 1900, Cushing described a method of total extirpation of the gasserian ganglion for trigeminal neuralgia, the first of a long series of studies on the physiology and surgery of nervous tissue. In 1912, he published his first monograph, *The Pituitary Body and Its Disorders*,[2] followed in 1917 with a treatise on

Tumors of the Nervous Acusticus and the Syndrome of the Cerebellopontile Angle.[3] A monumental treatise on meningiomas appeared just before his death.[4] In 1932, he presented twelve cases of basophilic adenomas of the pituitary taken from the literature or from his own patients, including one described in the 1912 monograph. To this "polyglandular syndrome," the name Cushing's disease, or Cushing's syndrome, was promptly applied. Review of the histories, physical findings, laboratory studies, and operative findings showed many features in common. Cushing concluded that the basophilic cells of the anterior pituitary were responsible, either acting directly or through the adrenal gland on various target cells. Each of the significant details of basophilism was mentioned, but treatment was left to the future.[5]

The following features are characteristic of all cases: (1) A rapidly acquired, peculiarly disposed and usually painful *adiposity* (in one instance representing a 40 per cent gain in weight) confined to face, neck and trunk, the extremities being spared; (2) A tendency to become round shouldered (kyphotic) even to the point of measurable loss of height . . . associated with lumbo-spinal pains; (3) A sexual dystrophy shown by early *amenorrhoea* in the females and ultimate functional *impotence* in the males; (4) An alteration in normal hirsuties shown by a tendency to *hypertrichosis* of face and trunk in all the females as well as the preadolescent males . . . and possibly the reverse in the adult males; (5) A dusky or plethoric appearance of the skin with *purplish lineae atrophicae* particularly marked on the abdomen; (6) *Vascular hypertension,* present in all cases except Cases 4, 7 and 9, where no mention was made of blood-pressure; it varied from the highest recorded in Case 6 of 230/170 to the lowest in Case 11 of 178/100; (7) A tendency to *erythraemia,* a count exceeding five million having been present in five of the nine cases in which blood counts were recorded; (8) Variable *backaches, abdominal pains, fatigability* and ultimate extreme *weakness.*

Other features less consistently recorded included acrocyanosis, ecchymoses, dryness of the skin, polyphagia, polydipsia and polyuria, edema of the lower extremities, susceptibility to pulmonary infections, albuminuria, a sense of suffocation, difficulty in swallowing, insomnia, while the postmortem studies showed susceptibility to infections, hypertrophy of the cardiac ventricle, osteoporosis of the skeleton (most marked in the spine), a basophilic adenoma of the pituitary body, cortical hyperplasia of the suprarenal gland, senile ovaries and uterus in the female, and atrophy of the spermatogenous epithelium of the testes in the male.

. . . the establishment of a clinical syndrome and its cause must usually precede effective treatment, and if my belief that the disorder is an expression of pituitary basophilism should be substantiated by further studies elsewhere, the most effective treatment can be left for further experience.

Cushing's contributions to neurosurgical techniques include the development of the trans-sphenoidal approach for pituitary adenomas, introduction of the silver clip for occlusion of blood vessels, and the use of bone wax and fresh homologous muscle for the control of hemorrhage. His operations were never hurried, and the observer in the uncomfortable pipe stands at the "Brigham" found him as meticulous in placing the initial suture in the scalp as in probing nervous tissue deep in the cranial vault. Operations were timed by hours, not minutes. Following the operation, it was Cushing's custom to visit the patient frequently. Although adequately supervised by nurses and staff, the patients were his responsibility, which he shared at all times, but he never assigned to others full responsibility for their medical care. Some objected to his surgical despotism or professional tyranny, but his rigid standards of practice and the preoperative and postoperative care of the patient were fundamentals responsible for his outstanding clinical results.

His nonsurgical contributions included a series of lectures, *The Medical Career*,[6] his World War I experiences, *From a Surgeon's Journal*,[7] but most noteworthy of all was his Pulitzer Prize-winning *Life of Sir William Osler*.[8] Because of a perennial friendship with Sir William and Lady Osler, he was commissioned by the latter to prepare the biography following Sir William's death. The work was begun in 1920 and finished four years later. The Pulitzer Prize committee were not long in recognizing it as the biography of the year, which is also the best medical biography of our times.

Cushing's interest in the general practice of medicine (pursuing meanwhile one of the most technical subspecialties of surgery) is illustrated by his insistence upon seeing private patients in consultation and a refusal to accept a full-time system for the department of surgery at the Brigham Hospital. When offered a full-time, salaried position in 1915, he tendered his resignation (which was never accepted) rather than subscribe to a philosophy advocated by the University officials. A prearranged, but premature, retirement at the age of 63 forced his resignation at Harvard. However, he returned to Yale Medical School as professor of neurology and completed his academic life as director of studies in the History of Medicine at New Haven.

Cushing's concern for military surgery appeared first in 1906, when he received a commission in the reserve corps of the United States Army. A decade later, before the United States entered World War I, he did hospital duty for a few months with the British Expeditionary Forces. When the United States joined the Allies in 1917, he had already begun the organization of Base Hospital No. 5 (Harvard Unit). He went with it to France, served as its director, and later became neurosurgical consultant to the American Expeditionary Forces. For his military service he received the Distinguished Service Award, one laurel in a perpetual accolade throughout his life. At home and abroad he was invited to give named lectures, to accept honorary or full membership in distinguished societies, to receive recognition from foreign powers, and to wear the distinctive academic hoods of famous universities. As examples one can mention Cavendish Lecturer, London; foreign membership in the Medical Society of London; doctor of science, Yale University; doctor of laws, University of Cambridge; Officier, Légion d'Honneur, France; doctor of science, Harvard University; and doctor of science "honoris causa," Oxford University. In the minds of many the founding in 1937 of the Harvey Cushing Society for neurosurgeons was his most gratifying provincial crown.

Cushing was as liberal in giving as he was gracious in receiving. His last great benefaction to scholars was the promotion of the

Historical Library at Yale Medical School. The cornerstone of the Historical Library was laid in 1939; the building was dedicated in 1941. It treasures more than 25,000 volumes, one of the great historical medical libraries in the world. The number of volumes has more than doubled by gift or purchase since its formation. Harvey Cushing is perhaps the most notable 20th century medcal literary figure, meanwhile achieving status as an international neurosurgeon and a one-time proud leader in the faculty at Harvard Medical School.

1. Fulton, J. F.: *Harvey Cushing, a Biography*, Springfield, Ill: Charles C Thomas, 1946.
2. Cushing, H.: *The Pituitary Body and Its Disorders*, Philadelphia: J. B. Lippincott Company, 1912.
3. Cushing, H.: *Tumors of the Nervus Acusticus and the Syndrome of the Cerebellopontile Angle*, Philadelphia: W. B. Saunders Company, 1917.
4. Cushing, H., and Eisenhardt, L.: *Meningiomas. Their Classification, Regional Behaviour, Life History, and Surgical End Results*, Springfield, Ill: Charles C Thomas, 1938.
5. Cushing, H.: *Papers Relating to the Pituitary Body, Hypothalamus and Parasympathetic Nervous System*, Springfield, Ill: Charles C Thomas, 1932.
6. Cushing, H.: *The Medical Career*, Boston: Little, Brown and Company, 1940.
7. Cushing, H.: *From a Surgeon's Journal, 1915-1918*, Boston: Little, Brown and Company, 1936.
8. Cushing, H.: *The Life of Sir William Osler*, 2 vol, Oxford: Clarendon Press, 1925.

Antonio Egas Moniz (1874-1955)

ANTONIO CAETANO DE ABREU FREIRE was born at Avanca in northwestern Portugal. However, during his student days as a liberal pamphleteer he added the nom de plume Egas Moniz, an accolade to Egas Moniz de Ribadouro, the hero of the Portuguese resistance to the Moors in the 12th century.[1] In 1891, Moniz entered the old University of Coimbra, Portugal, and for more than 20 years lived in the cloisters first as a student and later as a teacher. He completed his medical training in 1899 but not before he had overcome indecision between a career in mathematics vs medicine. His inaugural thesis covered the structural changes in diphtheria. Following graduation, Moniz remained in Coimbra and, in 1902, received a faculty appointment in medicine (neurology) upon submission of a thesis on the

physiological pathology of sexual activity. By then he had recognized the need for professional concentration and chose neurology and ophthalmology, particularly the former,

Composite by G. Bako

a specialty which remained his primary interest throughout a brillant career.

Moniz described himself as a French neurologist, having studied in Bordeaux with Pitres; in Paris with Raymond, Pierre Marie, and Dejerine at La Salpêtrière, with Babinski at La Pitié; he also enjoyed close friendship with Sicard of the Necker Hospital. His troubles with gouty arthritis, which began before he had finished medical school, had imposed restrictions on his physical activities but not his intellectual accomplishments. In 1911, Moniz accepted the new professorship in neurology at the University of Lisbon, and together with Flores developed the opportunity to establish a neurology clinic at the hospital of Santa Marta. Moniz remained a member of the faculty of medicine until he retired in 1945. In the interim he stepped outside his clinical work and clinical investigations at times to assume responsibilities in the Dean's office.

A mere recounting of the phases of Moniz's many-sided life and work would not adequately describe the brilliance and accomplishments of one of the great physicians of Portgual. He was interested in sculpture and the arts, wrote a treatise on the history of playing cards, was a gourmet, a frustrated revolutionary, and at one time a political prisoner. He prepared several biographies, which included a life of John XXI, Petrus Hispanus, the only physician who became a pope. Moniz commanded the Portuguese legion in Madrid for a year, returned to Lisbon as Minister of Foreign Affairs, and represented his country at the Peace Conference at Versailles in 1918. During these political years he was nearly killed by a schizophrenic would-be assassin and refused to be a candidate for the presidency. His political life was concluded in 1922 when the opposition party came into power.

Although Moniz was a fruitful investigator and a prolific writer, his two best-known contributions, cerebral angiography and leukotomy, were not made until late maturity. Building upon the work of Dandy, who introduced gases into the ventricles for contrast visualization of the structures of the brain, and also the work of Jacoboeus and Schuster, who introduced oily substances into extravascular spaces, Moniz searched for a relatively nontoxic radiopaque substance, thoroughly miscible in the vascular transit through the central nervous system, which would pass through the capillaries into the extracapillary spaces, thereby avoiding the hazards of embolism. Following animal experimentation in rabbits and dogs and charting the normal vascular pattern in cadaver heads, he selected a solution of sodium iodide for in vivo intraarterial injection. The results of the first series of cases from the Rocha Cabral Institute of Scientific Research and the Neurology Clinic in Lisbon were presented before the Neurological Society of Paris and were summarized as follows:[2]

Ventriculography has already been helpful in locating the site of brain tumors. If we succeeded in visualizing the arterial tree of the brain, we should also be able to localize the brain tumor by identifying the alterations in the arterial arborization.

A tumor causes alterations in the position of the internal carotid and the Sylvian artery and probably modifies the vascular pattern of the anterior cerebral vessel; but of this we are not completely convinced. The most important feature is the ability to compare the specific findings with normal radiographic appearances.

It is possible to examine the brain radioarteriographically and to localize tumors by this procedure.

Following injection of the main carotid trunk it is not difficult to visualise separately the meningeal and the cerebral channels.

Since blood flows at approximately 10 meters per second, it is necessary to obtain rapid sucessive exposures. It would be helpful to have cinematographic pictures of the opaque substance in motion, so as not to lose visualization at any time. It would also be helpful to obtain stereographic pictures of the opaque substance in the arteries.

The technique now recommended is well tolerated by the patient and capable of giving satisfactory arterial encephalographic pictures. It consists of the following:

(1) Prepare the patient with one or two injections of morphine and atropine;

(2) Expose the internal carotid artery;

(3) Fix the patient's head on the photographic chassis to avoid movement;

(4) Enter the carotid artery without permitting blood to enter the syringe;

(5) Avoid the entrance of air into the closed system;

(6) Place a temporary ligature around the internal carotid artery with a forceps;

(7) Rapidly inject 5 or 6 cc's of sodium iodide (25%) solution;

(8) Prepare one or more x-rays as rapidly as possible, meanwhile continuing the injection;

(9) Release the temporary ligature.

A decade later, having given considerable thought to the influence of the higher centers on the control of emotional and physical life, Moniz listened with great interest to the report by Fulton and Jacobson on the "Interruption of Higher Pathways in Chimpanzees, Controlling Anxiety," presented at the International Neurological Congress in London in 1935. Moniz reasoned that, if the interruption of the pathways of the frontal lobe prevented the development of experimental neurosis and eliminated frustrations in animals, would it not be possible to relieve critical anxiety states in man by a similar procedure? Enlisting the aid of Lima, the neurosurgeon, he immediately put this hypothesis to test. He found that, among 20 patients who were treated by leukotomy, almost a third were clinically cured; a similar number showed improvement, and the remainder were unchanged. In Moniz's description of the first series of cases in 1936, which included patients suffering from acute depression, obsession neurosis, persecution mania, and schizophrenia, he credits with counsel and assistance Sobral Cid, professor of psychiatry and director of the Manicome Bombarda hospital, who later turned against him; Caucela de Abreau, professor of neurology; and Almeida Lima, professor of neurosurgery. For this work Moniz, together with Hess of Zürich, received the Nobel Prize in medicine or physiology in 1948.[3] Excerpts from the citation are as follows:[4]

The lines of thought along which Antonio Egas Moniz has advanced to the discovery of the prefrontal leucotomy refer primarily to the localization of certain psychic functions in the brain. It has long been known that the frontal lobes are of great importance for higher cerebral activity, especially in regard to the emotions, and that the destruction of the frontal lobes, by bullet wounds or brain tumours, lead to certain typical changes of the personality, primarily on the affective plane, but sometimes also affecting the intellect, especially highly integrated intellectual functions such as power of judgement, social adaptability, and the like. The American physiologist, Fulton, and his collaborators have proved by experiments on anthropoid apes that neuroses caused experimentally disappeared if the frontal lobes were removed and that it was impossible to cause experimental neuroses in animals deprived of their frontal lobes.

It occurred to Moniz that psychic morbid states accompanied by affective tension might be relieved by destroying the frontal lobes or their connections to other parts of the brain. On the basis of this idea Moniz gradually worked out an operative method whose purpose was to interrupt the lines of communication of the frontal lobes to the rest of the brain. Since these lines of communication run through the white matter, this operation was called frontal or prefrontal leucotomy. It was soon found that morbid conditions in which emotional tension was a dominating part of the pathological picture reacted very favorably to such operations.

The interesting observation has also been made that serious, bodily conditioned pain can be successfully treated through frontal leucotomy. As the operation does not touch any pain-communicating tracts, and the capacity of the patient to feel pain is unimpaired, the effect must be due to a change in the psychic experience of pain.

Anguish and anxiety due to pain and the affective tension which accompanies pain disappear. When asked, the patient admits that he feels pain, but he does not care about the pain; he has become indifferent to it. These observations of psychically normal persons, on whom leucotomy has been performed in order to remove pain, have contributed in a high degree to the clarification of the influence of leucotomy on the normal mental functions. Without doubt there are, after double-sided leucotomy, changes of personality of the same type as observed after the destruction of the frontal lobes through other causes. When it becomes a question of persons who are complete invalids because of sickness, this may be of small importance, while in other cases a very strict interpretation of indications is necessary. Frontal leucotomy, despite certain limitations of the operative method, must be considered one of the most important discoveries ever made in psychiatric therapy, because through its use a great number of suffering people and total invalids have recovered and have been socially rehabilitated.

The initial clinical results by Moniz in each category were followed by expansion of the series and elaboration of the techniques based upon sound concepts. With but little modification, contemporary cerebral angiography follows the procedures devised by Moniz. Until the introduction of tranquilizers, the psychosurgical approach to the management of selected individuals remained the only substantial therapy for a large group of affected persons or palliation in those suffering from intractable pain.

Moniz was a member of many scientific organizations including the Royal Academy of Sciences of Lisbon and the American Society of Neurology. He was an honorary member of the Section of Neurology of the Royal Society of Medicine, a commander of the Legion of Honor of France, and recipient of honorary degrees from the universities of Bordeaux, Toulouse, and Lyon.

1. Fernandes, H. J. de B.: "Egas Moniz," in Kolle, K. (ed.): *Great Neurologists* (Ger), Stuttgart: G. Thieme, 1956.

2. Moniz, E.: Arterial Encephalography and Its Significance in the Localization of Cerebral Tumors (Fr), *Rev Neurol (Paris)* 2:72-90, 1927, excerpt translated by Z. Danilevicius.

3. Moniz, E.: *Operative Attempts in the Treatment of Certain Psychoses* (Fr), Paris: Masson, 1936.

4. *Nobel Lectures, Physiology or Medicine, 1942-1962,* Amsterdam, London, New York: Elsevier Publishing Co., 1964.

National Library of Medicine

Sir Gordon Holmes (1876-1965)

GORDON MORGAN HOLMES, leading clinical neurologist of England, was born in Dublin and educated at Trinity College.[1] He graduated AB at 21, and, after studying two years in medicine, Holmes received the MB and won a medical traveling prize and the Stewart scholarship in mental and nervous diseases. He chose the neurological department of the Senckenberg Institute at Frankfurt-am-Main for postgraduate work in neuroanatomy and neurohistology under Edinger and Weigert.

On his return from the Continent, Holmes qualified as house-physician at the National Hospital for Nervous Diseases, Queen Square, London—the beginning of a lifelong association with the institution famous for postgraduate neurological training. In 1904, he was appointed pathologist and director of research at the hospital and from 1909 until 1941 served on the honorary consulting staff. Holmes was associated also with the Royal Ophthalmic Hospital (Moorfields) and with Charing Cross Hospital, without holding a teaching post in a medical school. The Royal College of Physicians of London elected him to membership in 1908.

During World War I Holmes served as consulting neurologist of the British Army, with the rank of lieutenant colonel. His experiences were described in the Gulstonian lectures, entitled *The Spinal Injuries of Warfare*. In 1922, he delivered the Croonian lecture on cerebellar diseases; in 1933, Holmes was elected a Fellow of the Royal Society, and in 1945 delivered the Ferrier lecture.

Holmes's great contributions were made in clinical neurology.[2] For many years, succeeding Head as editor of *Brain,* he exercised critical control over neurological literature in England. His best-known monograph was entitled *The Examination of the Nervous System.* Holmes's outstanding knowledge of the anatomy and physiology of the nervous system, the effective use of such knowledge in the interpretation of clinical disorders (albeit impatient with the concepts of contemporary psychiatry) made him the premier clinical neurologist in Great Britain in the first half of the 20th century. Especially noteworthy were the revision of identification of the sensory centers of the brain, refinement of understanding of cerebellar functions, and the extension of the significance of the thalamic syndrome.

Early in his professional life Holmes reported the findings in a case of virilism attributed to a suprarenal tumor in a 24-year-old female. Restoration of normal features followed its surgical removal. Although others had described adrenal virilism, Holmes was the first to document the natural history of the disease, in this instance during nine years of development to a state of maximal changes and a nine-year followup after removal of the benign tumor (measuring $17 \times 9.5 \times 14$ cm). The résumé of the clinical and pathological findings is as follows:[3]

The case here recorded is that of a young woman in whom a large slowly growing tumour of the cortex of the right suprarenal body was associated with changes in the sexual organs (atrophy of the uterus, overgrowth of clitoris), disturbances of the sexual functions (cessation of menstruation for nine years), alteration in the secondary sexual characters (growth of hair, atrophy of mammae, change in the distribution of fat, and masculine appearance in limbs), and psychical changes (loss of erotic feelings, lack of modesty), all of which symptoms disappeared within a relatively short time after the removal of the tumour and left the patient again an apparently normal woman.

The tumour appears to be the least atypical of any yet described, i.e., most like normal supra-renal cortex. This is consistent with the hypothesis that the epithelial cells were producing a large amount of internal secretion which presumably caused the extraordinary physiological changes present.

The gathering of innumerable details from the history, recognition of the significance of aberrant or normal responses from the physical findings, and their correlation for a summary pronouncement constituted the basis for Holmes's clinical reputation and skill. More than any other neurologist in this century, he was responsible for the modern technique of clinical examination of the nervous system. Macdonald Critchley, formerly director of the Institute at the National Hospital, Derek Denny-Brown of Boston, Wilder Penfield of Montreal, and Charles D. Aring of Cincinnati are examples of his pupils from England and America. Excerpts from the Price lecture at Queens University, Belfast, in his discussion of "The Evolution of Clinical Medicine as Illustrated by the History of Epilepsy" are representative of his belief in his pedagogy.[4]

In many instances recognition of the nature and origin of a morbid condition has developed suddenly as a result of careful clinical observation, as the distinction of typhus from enteric fever; by the demonstration of constant and characteristic anatomical changes associated with it; and, more critically, by the discovery of a specific causal factor, as the infecting organism of an infectious illness. Sometimes, however, it has been due to introduction of new methods of investigation, as the use of the electrocardiograph.

More frequently the differentiation of separate diseases as seen through the centuries has been a long and slow process which has been retarded by failure to follow the straight path in the maze of clinical experience, by misinterpretation of observations, and particularly by failure to observe accurately and correlate clinical symptoms with morbid anatomy. And as most symptoms are disturbances of function, diagnosis has had in many cases to follow in the wake of physiology.

But the history of medicine reveals another and even more serious obstacle to progress which must be impressed on the student, or rather post-graduate, of to-day: it is too faithful submission to authority and failure to reason independently from facts observed.

1. Penfield, W.: Sir Gordon Morgan Holmes, *J Neurol Sci* 5:185-190, 1967.

2. Walshe, F. M. R. (ed.): *Selected Papers of Sir Gordon Holmes*, London & New York: Macmillan & Co., 1956.

3. Holmes, G.: A Case of Virilism Associated With a Suprarenal Tumour: Recovery After Its Removal, *Quart J Med* 18:143-152 (Jan) 1925.

4. Holmes, G.: The Evolution of Clinical Medicine as Illustrated by the History of Epilepsy, *Brit Med J* 2:1-4 (July 6) 1946.

Composite by G. Bako

S. A. Kinnier Wilson (1878-1937)

SAMUEL ALEXANDER KINNIER WILSON was born at Cedarville, New Jersey, the only son of the Rev. James Kinnier Wilson of County Monaghan, Ireland.[1] At an early age, young Wilson, along with the family, returned to Great Britain, where he was educated at the University of Edinburgh, receiving the AM in 1897, MD in 1902, and the BSC in physiology with first class honors in 1903. After serving as house physician for one year at the Edinburgh Royal Infirmary, he studied in Paris for a similar period on a Carnegie fellowship, attending the clinics of Pierre Marie at the Bicêtre and Babinski at Pitié. After a brief visit to Leipzig, Wilson became resident medical officer at the National Hospital, Queen Square, London. There he began an association of 33 years with the institution for the study and treatment of disorders of the nervous system, in addition to his duties as house physician, the offices of registrar, pathologist, and honorary physician he held in succession; while on the teaching staff, J. Hughlings Jackson and Sir William Gowers each left his imprint on Wilson.

The monograph, entitled *Progressive Lenticular Degeneration: a Familial Nervous Disease Associated With Cirrhosis of the Liver,* Wilson's best known work, of more than 200 pages in *Brain, A Journal of Neurology* and included clinical, pathological, and physiological discussions. The manuscript was prepared to meet the University of Edinburgh's requirements for the degree of MD, which was granted with a gold medal for excellence. Following this publication, the eponym, Wilson's disease, first became synonymous with the entity in the German literature. Although Wilson's clinical reports were not the initial descriptions of the malady in contemporary neurological literature, he was one of the first to detect an intimate relationship between liver disease and regressive changes in the lenticular nuclei and also the relationship between dystonic movements and alterations in the structure of the putamen and the caudate nucleus. His contribution was more than an adequate description of a disease entity; it was the beginning of contemporary studies of the anatomy, physiology, and pathology of the structures which he identified in the "extrapyramidal system."

Four cases came from his personal experience; a greater number were excerpted from unpublished sources or from incomplete descriptions in the literature. Wilson noted that the disease developed in young patients and usually was fatal within five years after the onset. The clinical symptoms included involuntary movements, usually a bilateral tremor of both upper and lower extremities, the head and neck also being involved at times; an intention tremor; pronounced spasticity of the limbs and of the face; dysphagia and dysarthria; and sometimes spasmodic laughing and emotionalism. There was considerable difficulty in maintaining equilibrium, true paralysis was not

observed, and transitory mental symptoms might be present. Wilson failed to appreciate its hereditary features and overlooked the brown pigment at the corneal margin, now known as the Kayser-Fleischer ring. Selected clinical and pathological conclusions were reported by Wilson as follows:[2]

Chapter VIII.—Clinical Conclusions

(1) Progressive lenticular degeneration is a disease of the motor nervous system, occurring in young people and very often familial. It is not congenital or hereditary.

(2) It is progressive and fatal within a varying period; acute cases may last only a few months; one chronic case has as a maximum continued for seven years; the average duration of chronic cases is four years.

(3) It is characterized by a definite symptom-complex, whose chief features are: generalized tremor, dysarthria and dysphagia, muscular rigidity and hypertonicity, emaciation, spasmodic contractions, contractures, emotionalism. There are also certain mental symptoms, either transient and such as one sees in a toxic psychosis, but not severe, or more chronic, consisting in a general restriction of the mental horizon, and a certain facility or docility without delusions or hallucinations, and not necessarily as progressive as the somatic symptoms. The mental symptoms may be very slight and are sometimes absent.

(4) In pure cases the affection constitutes an extrapyramidal motor disease, for the reflexes are normal from the point of view of the function of the pyramidal tracts. . . .

(7) Although cirrhosis of the liver is constantly found in this affection, and is an essential feature of it, there are no signs of liver disease during life.

Pathological Conclusions

(1) The chief pathological feature of the disease is bilateral symmetrical degeneration of the putamen and globus pallidus, in particular the former. . . .

(4) A constant, essential, and in all probability primary feature of the pathology of the disease is cirrhosis of the liver, not syphilitic or alcoholic; it is multilobular or mixed in type, always pronounced, but presenting a varying pathological picture of necrosis, fatty degeneration, and regeneration.

Although none of his neurological contributions was so important as *Progressive Lenticular Degeneration,* Wilson was a regular contributor to the neurological literature in which he discussed epilepsy, narcolepsy, affectations of speech, aphasia, extrapyramidal motor changes following epidemic encephalitis lethargica, apraxia, pathological laughing and crying, and amytrophy of chronic lead poisoning. One of his initial literary efforts was the translation into English, in 1907, of the French monograph, *Tics and Their Treatment,* by Meige and Feindel. A two-volume treatise, *Neurology,* his greatest literary legacy to medicine, was largely finished at his death.[3] A. N. Bruce edited the unfinished copy and published it posthumously in 1940.

Wilson was elected to the honorary staff of the Westminster Hospital in 1912 but terminated this appointment in 1919 to affiliate with King's College Hospital as junior neurologist. In 1920, he founded and became first editor of the *Journal of Neurology and Psychopathology*. In 1925, he delivered the Croonian lectures of the Royal College of Physicians of London on "Disorders of Motility and Muscle Tone." A number of foreign academic honors were bestowed on him, including honorary membership in the American Neurological Association. In oral presentation Wilson was lucid and witty, a master of histrionics. In the laboratory he was skilled in histological examination but made no serious attempt to become involved in experimental work. Wilson's strength rested in his firm, perceptive, but scholarly, approach to unsolved clinical matters, while his brilliance as a teacher was supported by his worldwide attraction of students to his clinics.

1. Critchley, M.: "Samuel Alexander Kinnier Wilson," in *Dictionary of National Biography,* London: Oxford University Press, 1931-1940, pp 914-915.

2. Wilson, S. A. K.: Progressive Lenticular Degeneration, a Familial Nervous Disease Associated With Cirrhosis of the Liver, *Brain* 34:295-509 (March) 1912.

3. Wilson, S. A. K.: *Neurology,* 2 vol, A. N. Bruce (ed.), London: E. Arnold & Co., 1940.

Ernst Kretschmer (1888-1964)

ERNST KRETSCHMER, one of the leading German psychiatrists between the first and second World Wars, established his reputation on studies correlating body build and personality.[1] Since the beginning of recorded observations physicians had attributed variations in temperament with the short, stocky

habitus vs the thin, tall, delicate structure; whereas others, following Kretschmer's exposition of his flexible postulates on constitution, elaborated and rigidly defined body

Composite by G. Bako

types beyond his original or later revised concepts.

Kretschmer, proud of his ancestors, was born in Wustenrot in Swabia. His mother was the daughter of a physician and his father a Lutheran minister. He received his early education in a monastery, but upon entering his university studies in Tübingen, he decided against the ministry. In preparing for medicine he pursued a cultural background which included studies in literature, philosophy, and history. His doctorate in medicine was granted in 1913, and the following year he began a residency in psychiatry in the Neurological Clinic with Gaupp at Tübingen.

Kretschmer was taken into the medical corps of the German Wehrmacht upon the outbreak of World War I and was attached to a field hospital. Later he was placed in charge of a rehabilitation center for neurotic and emotionally disturbed soldiers, which provided him a wealth of experience. His clinical observations on conversion reactions following shell shock and paranoid reactions, associated with brain trauma, formed the basis of his monograph entitled *Hysteria, Reflex and Instinct*. This work was translated into English as were his other notable contributions.[2]

> How does it occur that the majority of hysterical pictures are at once expedient and biologically performed? Well then, if certain of the nucleus groups of hysteria can really be traced back to old instinctive mechanisms, why should they not be expedient? Do we not find advantageous adaptation to and defense against the external irritants of life in just such instinctive expediencies? And if then, a person seeks adaptation and defense against the external irritants of life and is unable to procure them through the usual paths of sensible deliberation and volitional activity, ought he not then regress with his strivings, first of all to those old pathways which are offered him by his hereditary instincts?
>
> One will almost hit upon the core of our present conception of hysteria when one states that *such psychogenic reaction-forms are predominately called hysterical, where a tendency to dissimulation makes use of reflex, instinctive, or otherwise biologically performed mechanisms.*

Kretschmer's most creative period was during his first tour of duty at Tübingen. His *Ideas of Reference in Oversensitive Personalities, a Contribution to the Theory of Paranoia,* in which he derived a multidimensional formulation of etiologic processes of paranoia from the interaction of body, environment, and personality, was published in 1918. The thoughts advanced were challenged, particularly by Kraepelin, but seemed to have withstood most of the criticism through the third edition published in 1950. His next and probably most famous contribution, *Body Structure and Character,*[3] was published in 1921 and commanded worldwide attention. His postulates and classification extended beyond the earlier attempts of others to formulate a constitutional anatomy. Subjected to criticism as were his other books, there is little doubt that his great capacity for exposition contributed to its international success. His classification of men was based upon the physical features of the face, skull, general physique, body surface, endocrine glands, and gastrointestinal tract. He early admitted the fact of aberrant types and did not attempt to classify each individual into one of the main categories. In his later years he considered these earlier studies as merely the beginning of deeper

probing into the reaction of morphological development. He kept working on his theory of types throughout life and incorporated advances as they seemed pertinent into the later revisions of his book, which had exceeded 20 editions at the time of his death.

Kretschmer talked about correlations but never subjected them to statistical analysis; rather he preferred insight and intuition. Schizophrenia and manic depressive insanity represented the extremes of personality dimensions which encompassed normal reactions. He displayed the enviable capacity of stating his hypotheses in a few highly descriptive and well-chosen terms. While one might fail to agree with his statements, there was never any doubt as to his intent. His types at the extremes were described briefly as follows:[3]

> In the mind of the man-in-the-street, the devil is usually lean and has a thin beard growing on a narrow chin, while the fat devil has a strain of good-natured stupidity. The intriguer has a hunchback and a slight cough. The old witch shows us a withered hawk-like face. Where there is brightness and jollity we see the fat knight Falstaff— red-nosed and with shining pate. The peasant woman with a sound knowledge of human nature is undersized, tubby, and stands with her arms akimbo. Saints look abnormally lanky, long-limbed, of penetrating vision, pale, and godly.
>
> But this is beside the point. Our investigations do not proceed from such general reflections, but from the special problem of psychiatry, and only eventually with a certain inner necessity, ever making wider circles, do they stretch out over the boundaries of that study into general Psychology and the realm of Biology. It seems advisable, in the presentation of the results of our inquiry, to choose the order in which they have appeared. On the psychological side, then, we have in the first place, the advantage of already possessing in the two great psycho-pathological types of manic-depressive or "circular" insanity and schizophrenia (demanding praecox), which have been distinguished by Kraepelin; something which is fairly tangible and with which we can set to work.
>
> As soon as we have worked out the corresponding physiological types by the aid of these psycho-pathological types, we shall see at once that these bodily types not only correspond to the two psycho-pathological types, but that they have far more extensive relations to widespread normal-psychological types of temperament; which, on their side again, have close psychological and hereditary connections with the psycho-pathological types from which we started.
>
> Investigation into the build of the body must be made an exact branch of medical science. For it

it one of the master-keys to the problem of the constitution—that is to say, to the fundamental question of medical and psychiatric and clinical work. Good isolated observations on the part of medical practitioners of the past do certainly exist: they remain unused. Belle-lettristic *apercus* of a physiognomical nature do not help us much forward. There is nothing for it: we must plod along the bitter, wearisome road of systematic verbal description and inventory of the whole of the outer body from head to foot; wherever possible, measuring it with calipers and tape-measures, photographing, and drawing. And not only must we do this in a few interesting cases, but we must take hundreds of observations, using every patient we can get hold of, and for each must we make out the same complete scheme. Above all, we must learn again to use our eyes, to see at a glance, and to observe without a microscope or a laboratory.

In the case of *circulars,* among a number of mixed and indefinite forms, we find a marked preponderance of the pyknic bodily type on the one hand, and a comparatively weak distribution of the classical asthenic, athletic, and dysplastic forms on the other.

In the case of *schizophrenes* on the contrary, among a number of heterogeneously mixed and indefinite forms we find a marked preponderance of asthenic, athletic, and dysplastic types (with their mixtures) on the one hand, and a surprisingly weak distribution of typical cases of the pyknic bodily types on the other.

Kretschmer's typological theories were carried into the consideration of "genius" among males, which was intended to appeal to psychiatrists and psychologists as well as to the intelligent lay public. He discussed the relationship to mental disturbances, believing that mental disease, especially borderline reactions, tends to appear among men of genius as reiterated in the cliché that genius is close to madness. The psychopathic component was believed to be other than an accident of biological structure and an indispensable ingredient for each type of genius. In advocating the mixture of nations, racial stocks, and classes, for the optimum environment for the development of genius, he found himself running counter to the unsupported postulates of the Nazis in the Third Reich. It is surprising that he escaped persecution throughout the period of Nazi domination in Germany.[4]

Consequently we shall give the name of genius to those men who are able to arouse permanently, and in the highest degree, that positive, scientifically-grounded feeling of worth and value, in a wide group of human beings. But we shall do so only in those cases where the value arises with psychological necessity, out of the special mental structure of the bringer of value, not where a stroke of luck or some coincidence of factors has thrown it into his lap.

Our exclusive task in this research then, is to reveal the natural laws at work in the person of the genius himself and the mechanism of inheritance which produces him. At the same time we shall endeavour to give a living picture, true to nature in all essentials, of creative personalities. And we believe that the tragic pathos of men of genius can be more profoundly comprehended through such a detached, truthful, scientific presentation, than by the usual, conventional picture with its over-emphasis, its touching-up and its insincere idealisation.

In 1926, Kretschmer was appointed director of the neurologic clinic and head of the department of neuropsychiatry at Marburg, a post he held for 20 years. His home on the slope of a mountain overlooking the town was a gathering place for psychiatrists and intellectuals from many parts of the world. After retirement from Marburg, he returned to Tübingen to continue work in the neurologic clinic and entered retirement a second time in 1959. Kretschmer was the guest of honor of Columbia University in 1929 at the inauguration of the New York State Psychiatric Institute. In 1949, he published *Psychotherapeutic Studies;* this showed that much could be accomplished in a dimension of new medical treatment, which passed by German psychiatry for almost a generation. Meanwhile, significant advances had been made in this field in America.

1. Kretschmer, E.: *Character and Memoirs* (Ger), Stuttgart, Germany: G. Thieme, 1963.

2. Kretschmer, E.: *Hysteria* (Ger), Leipzig: G. Thieme, 1923, translated by O. H. Boltz, New York and Washington: Nervous and Mental Disease Publishing Co., 1926.

3. Kretschmer, E.: *Body Structure and Character* (Ger), Berlin: J. Springer, 1921, translated by W. J. H. Sprott, London: Kegan Paul, Trench, Trubner & Co., Ltd., 1925.

4. Kretschmer, E.: *Genius of Man* (Ger), Berlin: J. Springer, 1929, translated by R. B. Cattell, London: Kegan Paul, Trench, Trubner & Co., Ltd., 1931.

National Library of Medicine

Sydney Ringer (1835-1910)

SYDNEY RINGER'S name is associated with a balanced physiological solution, which contains selected inorganic constituents simulating a protein-free filtrate of body fluid. Sydney was born in Norwich, England.[1] His father, a tradesman, died while his children were young, but this misfortune did not prevent two of his sons from acquiring a fortune in the Far East. Sydney was educated at private schools, served as an apprentice in Norwich, and, at the age of 19, entered University College, London, as a medical student. He continued the association with this institution throughout his professional career. He received the MB in 1860 and the MD three years later, serving meanwhile as resident medical officer.

In 1863, Ringer became a Member of the Royal College of Physicians and a Fellow in 1870. At University College he was appointed professor of materia medica, pharmacology, and therapeutics from 1862-1878, professor of the principles of practice of medicine until 1887, and Holme professor of clinical medicine until 1900. At the time of graduation Ringer was appointed assistant physician to University College Hospital, in 1866, became a full physician, and in 1900 retired as consulting physician. He also served for several years as assistant physician to the Great Ormond Street Children's Hospital.

Ringer pursued concomitantly a career in clinical medicine and another in the laboratory. He was preeminently successful as a consultant and bedside clinician, skilled in his powers of clinical observation, shrewd in the interpretation of symptoms, and eager to confirm his diagnoses in the postmortem room. Associated with clinical responsibilities of teaching pharmacology, he prepared the well-known *Handbook of Therapeutics,* the standard text of his time. The first edition in 1869 was followed by 13 revisions. Materia medica was deemphasized; instead the action of drugs and poisons on normal tissue was stressed, thereby placing clinical pharmacology on a sound practical basis.

However, Ringer is best remembered today for his laboratory investigations on the physiological action of selected crystalloids and, to a lesser extent, of colloids on the heart and skeletal muscle of the frog. Since University College lacked a pharmacological laboratory, space in the physiological laboratory was put at his disposal for experimental investigation. Although fully occupied in clinical work as judged by the standards of many physicians, Ringer allocated time to visit the laboratory in the morning before beginning his clinical chores and again late in the afternoon when the bulk of his responsibilites to patients had been satisfied.

Such industry bore fruit in a series of reports in the *Journal of Physiology* and, in 1885, by election to Fellowship in the Royal Society. The pharmacological study of drugs, poisons, and salts in the animal body comprised the majority of communications; clinical reports were in the minority. One of Ringer's earliest investigations, which proved to be a base for subsequent work, compared the action on the ventricle of the frog's heart of a solution of reconstituted dried blood and hydrates of soda, ammonia, and potash. The following was observed.[2]

In this paper I record some experiments on the action of soda, ammonia, and potash on the same structure [frog's heart]. . . . These experiments were made with Roy's tonometer. I tied the ventricle to the cannula by a ligature passed round the auriculo-ventricular groove, so that I experimented only with the ventricle.

I used dried bullock's blood dissolved in water so as to represent normal blood; to this solution I added saline solution in the proportion of one part of blood to two of saline. On this mixture I employed three ounces in each experiment.

Shortly after, Ringer discovered that the protein-free saline solution used for the artificial mixture contained minute traces of other inorganic substances. Balanced quantities of calcium and potassium salts contributed to the physiological milieu and made an excellent artificial fluid for the experimental study of circulation through the heart. Later, other solutions were designed for replacement of whole blood.[3]

I find that calcium, in the form of lime water, or bicarbonate of lime or chloride of calcium, even in minute doses produces the changes in the ventricular beat described in my former paper.

A small quantity of calcium bicarbonate or calcium chloride (of chloride 1 in 19,500 parts), added to saline solution with 1 part of potassium chloride in 10,000 parts, makes a good artificial circulating fluid and the ventricle will continue beating perfectly for more than four hours, with calcium bicarbonate.

But whilst calcium salts are necessary for the proper contraction of the heart, yet if unantagonized by potassium salts the beats would become so broad and the diastolic dilatation so prolonged that much fusion of the beats would occur and the ventricle would be thrown into a state of tetanus.

As the ventricle will continue to beat perfectly for hours without any sodium bicarbonate, it is evident that the normal trace is the result of the antagonizing action of calcium and potassium salts.

If these two salts are not present in the correct proportions then the trace becomes abnormal. If too little potassium is present, the contractions become broader &c. and there results fusion of the beats. If too much potassium is present, or too little lime salts, then the contraction of the ventricle is imperfect, and by increasing the quantity of potassium salt the beat becomes weaker and weaker till it stops.

As the heart will continue to beat quite normally for hours without albumen or haemoglobin, it is obvious that these substances are not immediately necessary for contraction, but of course they are necessary to reconstruct the tissues from the loss due to contractions.

I next tried the effect on the trace of substituting for blood mixture saline solution containing a calcium salt and potassium chloride.

I first employed the following mixture, 200 c.c. saline solution containing 20 c.c. calcium bicarbonate solution and 1.5 c.c. potassium chloride solution. On substituting this mixture for blood mixture the beats for a short time grew weaker, but soon recovered and became stronger than with blood mixture.

I next tested the effect of a mixture composed of 100 c.c. saline, 5 c.c. calcium chloride solution, 0.75 c.c. potassium chloride solution. I first took a trace with blood mixture and then replaced the blood with the above mixture.

The composition of Ringer's protein-free solution for fluid replacement, whose basic ingredients include salts of sodium, potassium, and calcium, has been modified in the intervening years. The concentration of the essential components remains as follows: sodium chloride, 0.86%; potassium chloride, 0.03%; and calcium chloride, 0.033%.

1. Starling, E. A.: Sydney Ringer, 1835-1910, *Proc Roy Soc Lond* 84:I-III, 1912.

2. Ringer, S.: Regarding the Action of Hydrate of Soda, Hydrate of Ammonia, and Hydrate of Potash on the Ventricle of the Frog's Heart, *J Physiol* 3:195-202, 1880-1882.

3. Ringer, S.: A Further Contribution Regarding the Influence of the Different Constituents of the Blood on the Contraction of the Heart, *J Physiol* 4:29-42, 1883.

Sir Thomas Lauder Brunton (1844-1916)

T. LAUDER BRUNTON, foremost pharmacologist of his time, spent more than 15 years preparing his *Text Book of Pharmacology, Therapeutics and Materia Medica*.[1] The treatise was founded upon physiological principles, the critical deductions were confirmed in his experimental laboratory, and the presentation carefully recast to satisfy his discriminating taste.

When Brunton was born at Bowden, Roxburghshire, his father, age 67, was a farmer of average means and his mother a housewife of 37.[2] Privately educated, he pursued his medical training at the University of Edinburgh, receiving the MB and CM with distinction in 1866; after serving as house physician in the Edinburgh Infirmary, he qualified for the BS degree. In 1868, he gained the gold medal for his thesis on digitalis, was granted the degree of MD, and won the Baxter Natural Science Scholarship, which permitted travel abroad. He studied successively with Brücke and Rosenthal in

Composite by G. Bako

Vienna, no particular professor in Berlin, Kühne in Amsterdam, and Ludwig in Leipzig. His formal medical training was completed in 1870 by attaining the degree of doctor of science from Edinburgh.

In preference to remaining in Edinburgh, Brunton was attracted by the opportunities offered in London and was not disappointed. Shortly after arrival, he was admitted to membership in the Royal College of Physicians and appointed lecturer on materia medica and pharmacology at the Middlesex Hospital. A year later he transferred to St. Bartholomew's Hospital, serving as casualty physician and continuing his lectures on materia medica. In time Brunton was promoted to assistant physician at the hospital and for 20 years remained in charge of outpatient medicine. However, not until 1895 was he advanced to senior status as physician. His staff duties included the execution of pharmacologic experiments in a cramped scullery, where he trained pupils and assistants, and delivered vigorous and imaginative lectures. An outstanding teacher, Brun-

ton was punctual to the second, able to organize existing knowledge and present it in the lecture hall to the delight as well as enlightenment of his listeners. This power was matched by his skill in consultative practice. Election to the Royal Society in 1874 brought appropriate recognition of his theoretical and practical experimental work on the physiology of digestion and secretion, the chemical constituents of the blood, and the physiological action of digitalis and mercury. Public recognition of his literary talents came with the editorship of the *Practitioner*. Fellowship in the Royal College of Physicians was conferred on him in 1876 and during the following years he was honored as the Lettsomian lecturer, the Gulstonian lecturer, the Croonian lecturer, and the Harveian orator. He served as examiner in materia medica and pharmacology in the universities of Edinburgh, Oxford, London, and Victoria University of Manchester. Foreign recognition included an honorary membership in the American Academy of Arts and Science, an associate fellowship in the College of Physicians of Philadelphia, and an honorary membership in the Imperial Military Academy of Medicine of St. Petersburg. Knighthood was conferred in 1900 and a barony in 1908.

Brunton's goal in the practice of medicine was the application of pharmacologic action to the correction of abnormal function for the restoration of health. In practice he recommended no empirical remedy without seeking to discover its mode of action, a trait early and admirably illustrated in his doctoral thesis describing the therapeutic and toxic doses of digitalis. He served as the experimental subject, studying the effects of the drug on his own output of urine and its constitutents under carefully controlled conditions of eating, sleeping, and exercising. He ingested a standard, weighed diet and measured total excreta. Although small doses of digitalis produced no measurable alteration in function, profuse diuresis followed toxic quantities. During the diuresis the absolute quantity of solids excreted in the urine increased, although their proportion to the total urinary output diminished. Brunton favored the hypothesis that the rise in blood pressure produced by digitalis was due in great measure to contraction of the arterioles and, to a lesser degree, to increased force of the heart action.[3] His findings on the diuretic action of digitalis were eventually published in the *Proceedings of the Royal Society of London,* in which he offered the explanation that digitalis probably stimulated the vasomotor nerves throughout the body, with the maximum effect on the kidney. The action, inconsistent and feeble, had recently been attributed to a direct depressant action in the renal tubule. Brunton's explanation follows.[4]

At present, it is generally assumed that the diuretic action of *Digitalis* is not caused by any specific influence of the drug upon the kidney, but is due exclusively to its power of increasing the blood-pressure in the arterial system.

If *Digitalis* acted as a diuretic only by raising the blood-pressure, the flow of urine should have been greatly increased immediately after the injection, and should have diminished with the fall of arterial tension. Instead of this the secretion was least when the blood-pressure was highest, and most copious when the tension had fallen below the normal.

The explanation we would offer of these phenomena is, that *Digitalis* probably stimulates the vaso-motor nerves generally, but affects those of the kidney more powerfully than those of other parts of the body. Thus, it causes a moderate contraction of the systemic vessels, and raises the blood-pressure in them, but, at the same time, produces excessive contraction of the renal vessels, so as to stop the circulation in the kidneys and arrest the secretion of urine.

As the action of the drug on the systemic vessels passes off they relax, and the blood-pressure falls; but the renal arteries probably dilate more quickly and to a greater extent than the others. Ths pressure of blood in the glomeruli may thus be increased above that normally present in them, although the tension in the arterial system generally may have fallen below the normal.

Brunton's suspicion of the function of enzymes and extracts of organs in vital processes of the body led him to suspect the actuality of a glycolytic enzyme in muscle, with possible therapeutic value in the correction of hyperglycemia in patients with diabetes mellitus. While studying with Kühne in the winter of 1868-1869, he became interested in ferment-yielding substances, and especially in a substance able to transform sugar into lactic acid. These thoughts lay dormant for more than a decade; then in 1874, he described clinical trials with raw meat in a series of lectures on diabetes mellitus.[5]

In view of these facts, we are, I think, justified in believing that the sugar which is present in the blood becomes converted by the aid of a ferment in the blood, muscles, and probably lungs also, into lactic acid and glycerine; and then undergoes combustion, thus sustaining the temperature of the body. Supposing, however, that this ferment is deficient, a greater or less proportion of the sugar will not undergo conversion into acid.

Several months ago, I attempted to increase the decomposition of sugar in diabetics by supplying the ferment which I supposed to be wanting. Since sugar is probably decomposed chiefly in the muscles, the ferment which splits it up is probably contained to a much greater extent in them than in any other part of the body. By giving the pat:ents raw meat, we may hope that the ferment contained in it will be absorbed from the intestine into the blood, and there act on the sugar. It is necessary that the meat be given raw, for the heat to which meat is exposed in cooking completely destroys all ferments. . . . Shortly after I began the treatment of one case, I learned from Dr. Duckworth that it had been tried empirically with complete success by the captain of a merchant vessel, who had prescribed for himself. In the cases treated in the hospital, however, no cure was effected, although in certain of them there was some temporary benefit.

The use of amyl nitrite in the treatment of angina pectoris is probably Brunton's best-known clinical contribution. As house physician in the Royal Infirmary in Edinburgh, he cared for a patient with aortic stenosis and insufficiency who suffered severe anginal pain. In interpreting the relief obtained by small phlebotomies, diminution in arterial tension was given full credit. Remembering some unpublished observations in animals by Gamgee on the hypotensive effect of amyl nitrite, Brunton tried the substance on his patient with angina. Relief was immediate and was attributed to depression of arterial tension rather than to enhanced blood flow through the coronary vessels. Nor is the explanation of the nitrite effect in coronary artery disease clearly defined a century later. Nitroglycerine may exert its beneficial action by dilation of the coronary vessels capable of responding; a peripheral arteriolar and venous dilatation may contribute, as well as some direct action on the myocardial muscle. Brunton reported his findings.[6]

During the past winter there has been in the clinical wards one case in which the anginal pain was very severe, lasting from an hour to an hour and a half, and recurred every night, generally between two and four A.M.; besides several others in whom the affection, though present, was less frequent and less severe. Digitalis, aconite, and lobelia inflata were given in the intervals, without producing any benefit; and brandy and other diffusible stimulants during the fit produced little or no relief. When chlorform was given so as to produce partial stupefaction, it relieved the pain for the time; but whenever the senses again became clear, the pain was as bad as before. Small bleedings of three or four ounces, whether by cupping or venesection, were, however, always beneficial; the pain being completely absent for one night after the operation, but generally returning on the second. As I believed the relief produced by the bleeding to be due to the diminution it occasioned in the arterial tension, it occurred to me that a substance which possesses the power of lessening it in such an eminent degree as nitrite of amyl would probably produce the same effect, and might be repeated as often as necessary without detriment to the patient's health. On application to my friend Dr. Gamgee, he kindly furnished me with a supply of pure nitrite which he himself had made; and on proceeding to try it in the wards, with the sanction of the visiting physician, Dr. J. Hughes Bennett, my hopes were completely fulfilled. On pouring from five to ten drops of the nitrite on a cloth and giving it to the patient to inhale, the physiological action took place in from thirty to sixty seconds; and simultaneously with the flushing of the face the pain completely disappeared, and generally did not return till its wonted time next night. Occasionally it began to return about five minutes after its first disappearance; but on giving a few drops more it again disappeared, and did not return.

Brunton was responsible for a remarkable number of monographs and comprehensive discussions in general medicine in addition to his internationally known text of pharmacology, which was translated into several foreign languages and revised several times. Whenever appropriate, his contributions to current periodicals sought to relate chemical structure to physiological action. His monographs included *Experimental Investigation of the Action of Medicines,* 1875; *On Disorders of Digestion, Their Consequences and Treatment,* 1886; *Lectures on the Action of Medicines,* 1897; *On Disorders of Assimilation, Digestion, etc.,* 1901; *Collected Papers on Circulation and Respiration, First Series,* 1907; *The Bible and Science,* 1881; *Therapeutics of the Circulation,* 1908; and *Collected Papers on Physical and Military Training,* 1887-1915. In the area of medical and national interest, he was a staunch proponent of physical well-being for all, but especially for the young; in advocating military training early in this century, he anticipated conflict a decade before the outbreak of World War I.

1. Brunton, T. L.: A Text-Book of Pharmacology, Therapeutics and Materia Medica, Philadelphia: Lea Brothers, 1885.
2. Power, D'A.: Sir Thomas Lauder Burton, F.R.S., obituary, St. Bart Hosp Rep 52:1-9, 1916.
3. Brunton, T. L.: On Digitalis With Some Observations on the Urine, London: J. Churchill & Sons, 1868.
4. Brunton, T. L., and Power, H.: On the Diuretic Action of Digitalis, Proc Roy Soc Lond 22:420-421, 1874.
5. Brunton, T. L.: Lectures on the Pathology and Treatment of Diabetes Mellitus, lecture 3, Brit Med J 1:221-224, 1874.
6. Brunton, T. L.: On the Use of Nitrite of Amyl in Angina Pectoris, Lancet 2:97-98, 1867.

Composite by G. Bako

William Murrell (1853-1912)

WILLIAM MURRELL, licentiate of the Society of Apothecaries and laureate of the Academy of Medicine of Paris, was another who recognized clinical benefits from the administration of nitroglycerin drops in the management of patients afflicted with angina pectoris. Murrell, born in London, the son of a barrister-in-law, was educated at Murray School in Wimbledon and at University College, London.[1] After training at the University College and Brompton hospitals, he served as demonstrator of physiology and Sharpey Physiological Scholar at University College Hospital. He qualified for membership in the Royal College of Surgeons of England in 1875, and membership in the Royal College of Physicians in 1877. The MD degree was granted by the University of Brussels in 1879. Murrell held several hospital appointments but served longest at Westminster, where he rose from registrar in 1877 to full physician two decades later. In the course of his career, he lectured on practical physiology, materia medica and therapeutics, clinical medicine, and medicine. Not only did he command respect in London for his scientific acumen in clinical pharmacology, but his reputation was recognized by appointments as an examiner for the universities of Edinburgh, Glasgow, and Aberdeen.

In advocating scientific thinking and teaching in pharmacology and toxicology, Murrell disclosed the influence of his physiology teacher, Sidney Ringer. He described laboratory experiments on animals and humans, and attempted wherever possible to identify the specific action of drugs, rather than considering them in general categories, as was customary. Even more serious was the failure of some physicians, from ignorance of toxicologic doses, to recognize the harmful effects of certain agents which, when ingested in excess, led to recognized or unrecognized evidence of iatrogenic poisoning. Murrell's contributions to medical literature included discussions of influenzal arthritis, osteomyelitis, pneumonia, anemia, syphilis, tuberculosis, leukemia, cirrhosis of the liver, Banti's disease, and diabetes mellitus. *A Manual of Pharmacology and Therapeutics* and *What to Do in Cases of Poisoning* were two of his best known monographs. The latter was eminently popular and ran through 11 editions. Another monograph exposed the evils of pseudomassage as practiced in shady establishments in London.

The best known contribution by Murrell, the use of nitroglycerin as a remedy for angina pectoris, appeared in *Lancet* in 1879. The transitory effects of small doses of nitroglycerin, which included subjective fullness of the head, quickening of the pulse, nausea, and constriction of the throat, had been known for some time and were described in the introduction to the communication. Administering to himself amyl nitrite by inhalation and nitroglycerin by ingestion, Murrell confirmed the recorded observations of others, and, utilizing instruments of precision, he completed a series of sphygmographic tracings. Nitroglycerin was found to produce a more persistent dicrotic pulse when relaxation and dicrotism were desired. His description following prophylactic periodic nitroglycerin administration to the last of three patients with angina pectoris follows.[2]

L. B.—, soap-maker, aged forty-two. Complains of pain in the chest on the left side, constant, but increased by movement, very severe at times, and occasionally so acute as to make him cry out; seems as if it would take his breath away; sometimes occurs between the shoulders as well, and not unfrequently runs down the left arm as far as the elbow. If walking, and the pain comes on, he has to stop, but only for a few seconds, and then goes on again. The pain is increased by stooping down, as in putting on his boots. Any movement, even turning in bed, will bring on the acute pain; but still he is never entirely free from it. He has it more or less all day, and acutely on moving. He has the very greatest difficulty in doing his work. Has been abstemious all his life; a smoker, but not comsuming more than half an ounce of tobacco a week. Has had gout thirty times or more during the last twelve years. Has had winter cough for about the same time. Never had these pains until this year. Has been gradually losing flesh for some months past. Physical signs those of emphysema; heart normal; no albumen in the urine. The patient was ordered a gentian-and-soda mixture, and this he took for a fortnight without the slightest benefit. The medicine, he said, did him more harm than good. The local application of belladona failed to afford relief. He was then given drop doses of the one per cent. nitro-glycerine solution in half an ounce of water four times a day. A week later he reported that he had felt relief on the first day, and had steadily improved ever since. He could stoop down without getting the old attacks, and could walk about almost as well as ever. He had not the slightest difficulty in taking the medicine. He remained under observation for some time longer, but there was no return of the pain.

1. Spencer, W. G.: William Murrell, M.D., F.R.C.P., *Westminster Hosp Rep* 18:11-15, 1911-1912.
2. Murrell, W.: Nitro-Glycerine as a Remedy for Angina Pectoris, *Lancet* 1:80-81, 113-115, 151-152, 225-227, 1879.

Bernhard Naunyn (1839-1925)

NAUNYN, son of a well-to-do Berlin burgomaster, was recognized as one of the great clinical teachers and investigators of metabolic phenomena in the latter part of the 19th century.[1] Sharing honors with Ehrlich as a brilliant pupil of Frerichs, Naunyn subsequently surpassed his professor in achievements attendant upon investigation in the biochemical and physiology laboratory of clinical mysteries that appeared at the bedside. In another context, Naunyn was a member of a notable cast of physicians who advanced German medicine from an 18th century discipline of natural philosophy into 19th century science, founded upon reproducible evidence gained in the experimental laboratory.

Naunyn's early educational performance was not particularly brilliant. This may have been attributed to a serious illness in childhood which was identified in his autobiography as hydrocephalus.[2] He did not learn to speak until the age of four and was forced to repeat several of his elementary subjects at school. An avid interest in literature developed as he matured, but he was moody and subject to fits of depression. After finishing gymnasium in 1858, Naunyn began his university training at Bonn, intending to prepare for the law. However, uninterested he shifted to physics and chemistry. In 1860, Naunyn returned to Berlin to begin the study of medicine in the university. Frerichs, Traube, and Langenbeck were the clinicians credited with the greatest influence on his scientific thinking; whereas Kant was his philosophical mentor. In 1862, he presented his inaugural thesis for the MD degree on the development of the taenia of the *Echinococcus hominis* in the dog. This was a 35-page document prepared in Latin from data based on experimental studies of the hydatid cysts in the canine liver.

After six months' army service, at the request of Frerichs, Naunyn was released and returned to the latter's clinic at Charité as an assistant. By 1867, having been advanced to docent, he fell into disfavor at the university. In succession, Naunyn cared for victims of a typhus epidemic in East Prussia and engaged in private practice. However, when a vacancy was declared at the University of Dorpat, he applied and in 1869 was placed in charge of the department of medicine in the Russian-sponsored German university. Two years later Naunyn accepted a similar post at Bern; in 1872 he went to Königsberg, and in 1888 succeeded Kussmaul at Strasbourg. He retired to Baden-Baden in 1904 as professor emeritus.

Although Naunyn's name is usually associated with the pathogenesis and treatment of diabetes mellitus, in which he established the hereditary nature and recognized the severity of infantile diabetes, his investigations contributed to the knowledge of the formation of gallstones, hematogenic and hepatogenic icterus, aphasia, the mechanism of the production of the systolic murmur in mitral insufficiency, the response of spinal fluid pressure to alterations of blood flow, the mechanism of fever, regeneration of nervous tissue, syphilis of the central nervous system, senile epilepsy, and the difference between exudates and transudates.

An inquiry into the distribution of cerebrospinal fluid pressure was described in 1881 in collaboration with Schreiber. They showed that the hydrostatic pressure in the ventricles of dogs was in equilibrium with the subarachnoid fluid in the spinal cord as low as the cauda equina. Also, a decrease in the blood flow through the carotids led to an alteration of the pulse, respiration, and blood pressure.[3]

On the basis of our knowledge of the anatomy of the subarachnoid space, Key, Retzius and other investigators showed that an elevation of pressure in the subarachnoid space low in the spinal cord continues to the base of the brain and into the ventricles. . . . If a glass cannula is inserted into the subarachnoid space at the filum terminale and if the roof of the fourth ventricle is uncovered by dissection, an elevation of pressure in the subarachnoid space by only 6 or 8 mm Hg produces a visible and palpable bulging of the pia at the roof of the fourth ventricle; also, it is possible to show that pressure with the finger on the roof of the fourth ventricle will cause an increase in the manometric pressure in the subarachnoid cannula at the filum terminale.

In differentiating between hepatogenic and hematogenic jaundice, one has assumed that in hematogenic jaundice the urine contained bilirubin but not bile acids. In 1869, Naunyn showed that, in the horse and the dog, bilirubin could be detected in the blood and in the urine during fasting when the gallbladder was discharging no bile into the intestinal tract. Also, in hematogenic jaundice, bile acids can be recovered in the urine when the bile ducts are patent—convincing evidence that bile in the blood may arise directly from the liver. Naunyn assumed from indirect studies that the degradation of hemoglobin to bilirubin takes place in the liver, not in the blood passing through it. This was confirmed in birds by Minkowski. Bilirubin was not formed, and icterus did not appear after removal of the liver.

In the investigation of the formation of gallstones, which held his attention into his retiring years, Naunyn proved that gallstones are formed mainly in the gallbladder, following incomplete drainage. In addition to sluggish action, sloughing of epithelial cells and other detritus may form a nidus. Sometimes invasion of the bile ducts by *Escherichia coli* or *Salmonella typhi* enhances the process; at other times, stones are formed without demonstrable infection. In still other instances, cholangitis in the intrahepatic ducts may be responsible for the development of small concretions excreted into the gallbladder, and they too may act as a nidus for concentric deposition of calcium bilirubin and cholesterol. The investigations were summarized in his monograph on the subject published in 1892.[4] Many of the stones in his collection were reproduced in the treatise from illustrations prepared by his wife.

Naunyn's early interest in diabetes mellitus began with the study of gluconeogenesis from carbohydrates and protein. He showed that the liver of animals stores more glycogen with administration of a carbohydrate diet plus an adequate amount of protein than with a high-fat diet. This counteracted the prevailing opinion of the supposed benefit of a high-protein diet in the treatment of diabetes mellitus. He coined the cliché "Fats burn only in the fire of the carbohydrates." Building upon the experiments of Stadelmann, Minkowski, and the workers in Schmiedeberg's laboratory, who studied the increased excretion of ammonia acetone and β-oxybutyric acid in patients suffering from severe diabetes, Naunyn introduced the term "acidosis."[5]

Diabetic acidosis (intoxication with acid), is caused by acetonuria and excretion of acetic acid, ammonia and calcium.

Investigation of the acid described by Stadelmann, who came to no definite conclusions, was continued by Minkowski who proved it to be oxybutyric acid. . . . Later, Stadelmann described *coma diabeticum* as the coma of acidosis. . . . The first evidence of acidosis is a positive Gerhardt's iron-chloride reaction. . . . Diabetic acidosis usually appears sooner or later in severe cases of diabetes with marked glycosuria. . . . Typical diabetic coma depends upon diabetic acidosis and . . . patients who develop a severe degree of acidosis usually die in diabetic coma.

With Klebs and Schmiedeberg, Naunyn founded, in 1872, the *Archiv für Experimentelle Pathologie und Pharmakologie* and in 1896, with Mikulicz, the *Mittheilugen aus den Grenzgebieten der Medizin und Chirurgie*. In the clinic he was contemptuous of those who looked upon medicine as a means of achieving security and fame. He addressed himself to his more able students and lived in close intellectual proximity with his pupils and assistants. At the bedside Naunyn recognized the importance of psychotherapy before it was known by this term. He did not spurn private consultation, but made no attempt to develop an extensive private practice. His great energies were devoted to furthering the understanding of diseases which could be studied with animals and quantitative chemical procedures at the bedside and in the experimental laboratory.

1. Müller, F.: Bernhard Naunyn (Ger), *Deutsch Arch Klin Med* 60:1-12, 1925.
2. Naunyn, B.: *Memories, Thoughts, and Convictions* (Ger), Munich, Germany: J. F. Bergmann, 1925.
3. Naunyn, B., and Schreiber, J.: Pressure on the Brain (Ger), *Arch Exp Path Pharm* 14:1-112, 1881.
4. Naunyn, B.: *A Treatise on Cholelithiasis* (Ber), Leipzig, Germany: F. C. W. Vogel, 1892, translated by A. E. Garrod, London: New Sydenham Society, 1896.
5. Naunyn, B.: *Diabetes Mellitus* (Ger), Vienna: A. Hölder, 1898.

Paul Langerhans (1847-1888)

PAUL WILHELM HEINRICH LANGERHANS, the son of a successful physician politically active in Berlin, received his gymnasium training in his home city. After spending a year at the University of Jena under Ernst Haeckel,[1] he returned to Berlin and studied medicine under Julius Cohnheim, W. Kühne, and Rudolph Virchow, the last a friend of the family. Before receiving his degree in 1869, he published two communications in Virchow's *Archiv* on the pathological anatomy of tactile corpuscles in the human skin. Langerhans' lasting fame, however, came from his inaugural dissertation on the cells of the pancreas.[2]

After graduation, Langerhans joined Virchow's laboratory staff in anticipation of an academic career, which was interrupted by travel through North Africa and Asia Minor. The Franco-Prussian War next commanded his attention. He served in a military hospital in Berlin and engaged in ambulance work at the front. After spending brief periods with Credé and Ludwig in Leipzig, Langerhans spent four years studying pathology in Freiburg. Promotion to a full

professorship was postponed by a recurrence of pulmonary tuberculosis. He searched for a cure in Italy and, failing to arrest the disease, sought shelter in Madeira. He recovered sufficiently to enter private practice

Composite by G. Bako

and to resume research and writing. The latter included his studies on leprosy and the spread of tubercle bacilli—as well as a tourist guide to Madeira. The respite from sickness was short, however, and he died of kidney infection.

Prior to the microscopic observations of Langerhans, the pancreas was regarded as an abdominal salivary gland. Claude Bernard had demonstrated that its external secretions participated in the digestion of carbohydrates, proteins, and fats, but no one had extended the microscopic observations beyond the external secretory cells and the excretory channels. Langerhans' experimental work on the new cells of the pancreas was mainly with rabbits although he subsequently included the glands of other animals. No observations were made on the human pancreas. He studied the structures in the fresh state following maceration and after injection of the pancreatic duct with a compound of glycerin and Berlin blue. His differentiation of nine types of cells, included the acinar cells, the epithelial duct cells, nerve, connective tissue, and vascular structure. But especially he noted a cell not previously described found in small groups in the parenchyma and not associated with any excretory channels. He began his dissertation with an apology and continued with the following excerpts.[3]

With regret, I must open my communication with the declaration that I cannot in any way put forth the conclusive results of a completed investigation. I can describe, at most, a few isolated observations which suggest a much more complicated structure of the organ investigated than hitherto accepted. The purpose of these lines can therefore at best only be to help draw greater attention to the pancreas than has hitherto been given to it by anatomists.

I mentioned above when describing the varied structure which the pancreas shows, when teased apart after being kept in Müller's solution, under (9) a cell form not yet closely described. This cell is a small irregularly-polygonal structure. Its cytoplasm is perfectly briliant and free of any granules, its nucleus distinct, round, and of moderate size. Its diameter is between 0.0096-0.012 mm. and that of its nucleus 0.0075-0.008 mm.

These cells lie together generally in considerable numbers scattered diffusely in the parenchyma of the gland. If one observes under low magnification, about system 4 of Hartnack, a pancreas which was kept two to three days in Müller's solution one notices regularly scattered through the gland rounded spots stained intensely yellow about the size of the field of vision with ocular 3. Under higher magnification these spots are seen to consist entirely of our cells. These are massed together in rounded groups distributed at regular distances in the parenchyma (in the old sense of the word). These masses show generally a diameter of 0.1-0.24 mm. and can be discerned without difficulty in the fragmented preparations of fresh glands, or those treated for a short time with iodized serum. They show then, as do all cells seen fresh, an entirely red appearance, but do not deviate in any way from the above description; their content shows also here a characteristic brilliance.

If the answer I was able to give above to the question as to the nature of the centro-acinar cells was unsatisfying and conditional, so unfortunately am I unable even to a greater degree to answer a similar question in regard to these cells.

More than 20 years later, Laguesse suggested the clusters were the seat of an internal secretion and named them "ilots de Langerhans."[4] This speculation, based on the work of several men, including Kühne and Lea, believed these cell-groups to have a rich blood supply and enjoy an intimate relation with the capillaries and nerves. Von Mering and Minkowski showed that the pancreas was endowed with an internal as well as an external secretion; whereas Banting, Best, and associates established the direct function of the cells of the "islands of Langerhans" in carbohydrate metabolism and their deficiency in the development of clinical diabetes mellitus.

1. Bardeleben, K.: Paul Langerhans (Ger), *Anat Anz* 3:850-851, 1888.
2. Langerhans, P.: *Communication on the Microscopic Anatomy of the Pancreas,* Inaugural-Dissertation (Ger), Berlin: G. Lange, 1869.
3. Langerhans, P.: Contributions to the Microscopic Anatomy of the Pancreas, H. Morrison (trans.), *Bull Inst Hist Med* 5:259-297, 1937.
4. Laguesse, E.: The Formation of the Islets of Langerhans in the Pancreas (Fr), *Soc Biol (Paris)* 14:819-820, 1893.

Josef von Mering (1849-1908)

JOSEF FRIEDRICH V. MERING, whose name is associated with Minkowski for their experimental studies following the extirpation of the pancreas in dogs, was born in Cologne, studied in Bonn and Greifswald, and finished his medical training at Strasbourg in 1873.[1] In his youth he commanded respect for unusual physical strength and ability for independent thinking. During the Franco-Prussian War he served a volunteer ambulance assistant, receiving the Bavarian military cross. Although v. Mering's senior professorial appointment was in the department of medicine at Halle, diverse branches of medicine attracted him in the postgraduate and intervening decades. After working in Hoppe-Seyler's laboratory in Strasbourg, he was assistant to Krafft-Ebing and later to Jolly in the psychiatry and neurology clinic. Assisting Frerichs in the medical clinic in Berlin in 1875, v. Mering investigated reducing substances in the urine of patients with diabetes mellitus; following this, he studied the absorption of sugar with Ludwig in Leipzig. He reported uptake of carbohydrates from the intestines by the blood but not by the lymph; also, the concentration of sugar in the blood was found to be rela-

Composite by G. Bako

tively constant, whether the subject was fasting or was given a mixed diet. Bonn and work with Zuntz was next on his postgraduate circuit. In 1878, he returned to Strasbourg, where he collaborated with Goltz in physiology, von Schmiedeberg in pharmacology, and Kussmaul in the medical clinic. Professorial status in forensic medicine was achieved at Strasbourg in 1886, while in 1889, with Minkowski, he performed the famous experiment in which extirpation of the pancreas resulted in massive glycosuria. In v. Mering's last years at Strasbourg, he was in charge of the clinic for laryngology and rhinology and became physician in the city prison. After rejecting offers of the professorship of pharmacology in Marburg and Greifswald, he accepted a call to Halle in 1890; there he taught internal medicine and laryngology and four years later became full professor in medicine.

Although an able investigator, v. Mering was not a prolific writer. His graduation dissertation discussed the chemistry of cartilage, and clinical subjects of study included the etiology of typhus, the chemistry of gouty arthritis, and the therapeutic value of mineral waters. A monograph on potassium chlorate, based upon toxicity studies in dogs and a review of the therapeutic literature for humans, was prepared from the Physiological Chemistry Institute under Hoppe-Seyler.

Investigations of chloral hydrate and tertiary alcohols, motivated by his clinical experience in psychiatry and neurology, led to the discovery of the hypnotic action of tertiary amyl alcohol. Continuing the investigation of the relation between chemical composition and sedation, v. Mering found that secondary alcohols had a greater pharmacologic effect than did primary alcohols, whereas tertiary alcohols surpassed both groups. Also, if ethyl groups were attached to the tertiary alcohol, the action was further enhanced. Culminating these investigations was the discovery, in collaboration with Emil Fischer, of the barbiturate class of hypnotics. Their studies concluded with a clinical evaluation of diethylacetylurea, diethylmalonylurea, and dipropylmalonylurea. The second compound was found most suitable for practical use because of its taste, solubility, and ease of synthesis. The name "veronal" was suggested, and the following doses were recommended.[2]

For simple insomnia 0.5 gram is generally sufficient. For insomnia which is accompanied by increased irritability the dose may be increased to 1 gram. For weaker people, e.g. women, 0.3 gram is often sufficient. In order to induce sleep doses of 0.3 to 0.5 to 0.75 to 1 gram are required. It is seldom necessary to give more than 1 gram.

The discovery, in 1886, of the development of experimental diabetes by means of phlorhizin (phloridzin) intoxication reflects v. Mering's continuing interest in carbohydrate metabolism. The experiments were carried out in Strasbourg, concomitant with experimental observations in patients in Kussmaul's clinic. Dogs poisoned with phosphorus to depress liver function showed glycosuria following phlorhizin administration. Other dogs were fasted, fed a meat diet, or fed only fat. The development of glycosuria followed phlorhizin administration in each experimental group. The pertinent findings were summarized as follows:[3]

Last year I discovered a compound capable of producing artificial diabetes. This substance sheds some light on diabetes mellitus and sugar production. It is phloridzin, a glycoside found in the root bark of apple and cherry trees. When given to geese, dogs, or guinea pigs, it produces large amounts of sugar in the urine. When 1 gm of this substance per kg of body weight is given orally to a dog, sugar appears in the urine in a few hours with a content as high as 10%. The quantity of sugar in the urine is unrelated to diet. The quantity is the same, whether the dog is fed for weeks with meat alone, or if he has been kept on carbohydrates. It is concluded that phloridzin does not increase the production of sugar, but that its action lies in reducing utilization by the body.

v. Mering's greatest contribution to experimental physiology and clinical medicine was the inducement of massive glycosuria following extirpation of the pancreas, a joint effort with Minkowski. The experimental extirpation was designed to study the general response of the organism. The development of massive glycosuria was an unanticipated finding, and, although it proved to be a most critical experiment in the history of the pathogenesis of diabetes mellitus, this significance was not immediately recognized. The possibilities for clinical understanding of diabetes mellitus were not developed, and only after the studies of Opie and others a decade later were the islands of Langerhans implicated in the pathogenesis of clinical diabetes. Excerpts from the report on the extirpation of the pancreas follow.[4]

After complete removal of the organ, the dogs became diabetic. It has not to do simply with a transient glycosuria, but a genuine *lasting diabetes mellitus,* which in every respect corresponds to the most severe form of this disease in man.

The appearance of such diabetes, after complete extirpation of the pancreas, comes *without exception,* unless the animals have died from the immediate effects of the operation.

The *excretion of sugar* began 4 to 6 hours after the operation, usually later, often not until the following day. The first portion of urine contained, as a rule, only very small traces of sugar, which could scarcely be estimated. After 24 to 48 hours, the excretion of sugar reached its height, climbed up from 5 to 11 per cent, without the animals having received any nourishment whatever.

The excreted sugar proved to be fermentable dextrorotatory glucose. The comparative estimation of the sugar content with a polariscope and titration with Fehling's solution, proved that no other type of sugar was present in the urine in any important amounts.

Besides the constant excretion of sugar, we also noted in the operative animals, all the other symptoms which appear in the severe form of diabetes mellitus in man.

Immediately after the extirpation of the pancreas, the dogs—unless they were affected with some complicated disease—showed an abnormal *hunger* and an abnormally increased *thirst.*

Corresponding to the increased amount of water taken in, there was also a marked *polyuria.*

In spite of the rich, yes, *excessive,* feeding, one notices an extraordinarily quick *emaciation* and a rapid *loss of strength.* In the third week after the operation, the muscle-weakness was already so far developed that the animal could not go any further.

Sooner or later, there appeared in certain cases, besides the sugar in the urine, also large quantities of *acetone diacetic acid,* and *oxybutyric acid,* those substances which are so frequently found in the urine in severe cases of diabetes mellitus.

The sugar content of the blood was very markedly increased. In one case, we found, on the sixth day after operation, 0.3%, with a urine sugar of 7.1%; in another case, on the 27th day after the removal of the pancreas, it was 1.46%, with a sugar excretion of 7.5% in the urine.

The *glycogen content of the organ was reduced* early down to minimal traces. In the first of the animals just mentioned, which, after feeding with meat and milk, was killed on the 6th day after the operation, we found in the liver a quantity that could not be estimated, in the muscles, still 0.24% glycogen. In the second dog, on the 27th day, with the same feeding, we found, both in the liver and in the muscles, only traces of glycogen that could not be estimated.

The diabetes continues until the death of the animal.

1. Winternitz, H., and Zuntz, N.: Josef von Mering, *Munch Med Wschr* 55:400-402, 1908, translated by E. Longar.

2. Fischer, E., and von Mering, J.: On a New Class of Soporifics, *Therap Gegenw* 44:97-101, 1903, translated in Shuster, L. (ed.): *Readings in Pharmacology,* Boston: Little, Brown & Co., 1963.

3. von Mering, J.: On Experimental Diabetes, *Verh Congr Inner Med,* 5th Congress, Wiesbaden: J. F. Bergman, 1886, excerpt translated by Z. Danilevicius.

4. von Mering, J., and Minkowski, O.: Diabetes Mellitus After Removal of the Pancreas, *Arch Exp Path Pharm* 26:371-387, 1890, translated in Major, R. H.: *Classic Descriptions of Disease,* Springfield, Ill: C. C Thomas, 1932.

Composite by G. Bako

Oskar Minkowski (1858-1931)

OSKAR MINKOWSKI, in collaboration with Joseph von Mering, removed the pancreas of a dog to determine the chances for survival following loss of an organ whose function was poorly understood. The animal recovered from the operation but developed massive glycosuria. However, the significance of this unexpected development was not wholly appreciated at the time, and subsequent investigation did not disclose the pathogenesis of the phenomenon or its possible clinical value.

Minkowski was born at Alexoten in the province of Kovno, Russia, attended Gymnasium at Königsberg, and studied medicine at Strasbourg and Freiburg. He received his doctor's degree under Naunyn at Königsberg, a school recognized for its singular advances in physics, chemistry, and physiology in the understanding of morbid processes. In 1888, when Naunyn was called to Strasbourg as Kussmaul's successor, Minkowski accompanied him. Not until 1900, later in life than for many, was Minkowski offered a department of medicine to direct, first at Cologne, then Griefswald, and finally at Breslau.

Minkowski's scientific work revolved about clinical chemistry interwoven with bedside teaching; in each area he was recognized by his peers as worthy of the general esteem which he enjoyed.[1] He sought practical findings from the experimental study of metabolic disorders. Many diseases came under his clinical scrutiny and formed the substance of communications in the literature. Monographs or extended discussions for handbooks were prepared on diabetes mellitus, diabetes insipidus, liver disease, gout, pathology of breathing, diseases of the pancreas, and the action of poison gases. One of his first and briefer communications reported the isolation of oxybutyric acid from the urine of patients with diabetes mellitus, the ketone acidosis in diabetic coma, and the value of treatment with soda bicarbonate.[2]

The relation of oxybutyric acid to the acetone-producing substance of the urine is of special interest in regard to the pathogenesis of diabetic coma.

Acetone is the substance found regularly in the urine of patients dying with symptoms of diabetic intoxication. This circumstance points to a definite relation between the above-mentioned symptoms and the occurrence of oxybutyric acid in the urine.

Two aspects seem to be of particular importance, both implicating acid intoxication in the above-mentioned clinical course:

(1) A conspicuous improvement after the administration of alkali and

(2) the sustained acid reaction of the urine in spite of continued administration of large amounts of sodium carbonate.

Fluctuations in the course of diabetic coma are frequent. . . . The subjective impression, however, definitely suggests an association between temporary improvement and the administration of alkali.

In 1887, Minkowski described a case of acromegaly, with quadrant defects in the visual field of each eye, and discussed enlargement of the pituitary observed previously by others.[3]

The field of vision of the left eye . . . showed a defect in the outer upper quadrant. There is a defect in the field of the right eye, also in the outer upper quadrant, extending to 15° from the point of fixation. . . . Ophthalmoscopic examination revealed normal eye-grounds with little difference between the right and the left eye.

. . . in all the autopsied and carefully examined cases, a striking enlargement of the hypophysis cerebri accompanied the hypertrophy of various internal organs. In the case of Henrot the hypophysis was the size of a small egg; an enormous enlargement of this organ was also noticed in the cases of Brigidi and of Fritsche and Klebs. This enlargement led to widening of the sella turcica and to a compression of the optical nerves, subsequently causing the disturbance of vision. In our ease also, the continuous enlargement of the hypophysis was responsible for the progressive decrease of visual acuity. . . . One specific condition, recently emphasized by Virchow, permits us to speculate that the enlargement of the hypophysis may be of importance in relation to the total process; this condition is the similarity of the tissue of this gland and the tissue of the thyroid gland which was recently ascribed a specific influence on trophic processes of the body.

The crucial experiment on the pancreas, with unexpected results, was performed in 1889 with von Mering while Minkowski was serving as assistant to Naunyn; it proved to be one of the two most important experimental observations in the history of the pathogenesis of sugar diabetes. Following the chance observation, neither investigator devoted his full attention to the subject; however, Minkowski conducted additional experiments to determine whether other injuries or lesions produced by the operation were responsible for the appearance of urinary sugar. His investigations left no doubt that the pancreas was implicated, but what part or by which cells remained for others to discover. When the organ was removed from its site, but left in vascular connection with the duodenum, the animal did not become diabetic. Nor did diabetes appear when the excretory ducts of the pancreas were ligated and separated from the duodenum or when the pancreas was only partially removed. Minkowski produced convincing evidence that only after total removal of the gland did glycosuria appear, followed subsequently by death of the animal. Although the 1890 report gives Minkowski a junior position to von Mering,[4] a communication from Minkowski to the Société des Naturalistes et Médecins de Strasbourg forwarded to *Semaine Médicale,* May 20, 1889, credits Minkowski with the announcement in scientific literature.[5]

M. Minkowski.—With the help of Mr. von Mering, I shall describe a series of experiments with complete extirpation of the pancreas in the dog, rabbit, and pigeon.

We determined that removal of this organ produces diabetes mellitus in all these animals. In the dog, diabetes appears from 10 to 15 hours after the operation and persists until the animal dies; it closely resembles a severe form of this illness in man. The animals operated on also showed polyphagia, polydipsia, and polyuria, so characteristic of diabetes; these symptoms were accompanied by considerable loss of weight and progressive wasting, in spite of an abundant intake of food. When an animal was deprived of food 24 hours before and for several days after the operation, it continued to excrete large quantities of sugar, at times up to 5% or 6%.

Considering all these conditions, sugar diabetes should be considered a direct result of extirpation of the pancreas. We employed an operative procedure which absolutely excluded any possibility of an injury to the ganglion of the solar plexus. Besides, autopsy of all the experimental animals which have died has not shown any important injury in the vicinity of the pancreas.

. . . these observations open a new avenue of experimental research on this disease by demonstrating the possibility of producing at will a true and permanent diabetes in certain animals. It is noteworthy that elimination of sugar following extirpation of the pancreas has been established in all experiments, in spite of the fact that the animal was receiving no nourishment. This important fact shows that we are dealing not only with abolishment of the pancreas as an important factor in the process of digestion, but rather that the removal of the pancreas also eliminates some complicated functions which this organ exercises on intermediary metabolism. After the extirpation of the pancreas the resorption of fats became somewhat impaired and the proteins did not seem to be better utilized by the organism than by a normal animal.

[Forwarded by] Dr. M. Muret
[Strasbourg correspondent]

Minkowski was one of Naunyn's brilliant pupils, a clinician of unusual intelligence, who used critical judgment at the bedside and in the experimental laboratory. His name remains topmost among those who contributed to the understanding of the pathogenesis of diabetes mellitus—one of the outstanding clinical chemists in the great days of German medicine in the generation prior to World War I.

1. Krehl, L.: Oscar Minkowski, obituary (Ger), *Arch Exp Path Pharm* 163:621-634, 1931-1932.
2. Minkowski, O.: The Occurrence of Oxybutyric Acid in the Urine of Patients With Diabetes Melitus (Ger), *Arch Exp Path Pharm* 18:35-48, 1884, excerpt translated by Z. Danilevicius.

3. Minkowski, O.: A Case of Acromegaly (Ger), *Klin Wschr* 24:371-374, 1887, excerpt translated by Z. Danilevicius.

4. von Mering, J., and Minkowski, O.: Diabetes Mellitus After Removal of the Pancreas (Ger), *Arch Exp Path Pharm* 26:371-387, 1890.

5. Minkowski, O.: Removal of the Pancreas and Experimental Diabetes, letter (Fr), *Sem Med* 9:175-176, 1889, translated by Z. Danilevicius.

National Library of Medicine

Carl von Noorden (1858-1944)

CARL HARKO HERMANN JOHANNES VON NOORDEN, noted investigator of diabetes mellitus, was born of Dutch-Rhenish parents in Bonn, a university town and the present capital of West Germany.[1] His father was a noted professor of history; two great-grandfathers were physicians. Carl began his higher education in the humanities and law at Tübingen but later changed to medicine. Subsequently he studied at the University of Freiburg and in 1881 received the MD degree from the University of Leipzig. Von Noorden's initial academic appointments were at the Physiological Institute in Kiel and in the department of internal medicine in the University of Giessen. In 1889, he was called to Berlin by Gerhard and promoted to professor in 1893. Continuing his peripatetics, the following year he was appointed director of the medical clinic of the municipal hospital in Frankfurt-am-Main and, in 1906, succeeded Nothnagel as professor of internal medicine in Vienna. He returned to Frankfurt in 1913 and, at the age of 70, chose Vienna once more, first as director of the Lainz Hospital and Research Institute and finally, in 1935, retired to private practice as a consultant.

Throughout his long career he was an excellent teacher and investigator and trained outstanding students such as Falta, Eppinger, and Rudinger. One of his first studies of interest retrospectively, entitled "Albuminuria in Healthy Males," was pursued in Giessen and was presented in qualification for privatdocent. Among 701 urine samples from healthy men, 84% of the total examined contained albumin. He concluded the following:[2]

Thus, albuminuria is quite often found in healthy individuals. The frequency of appearance is influenced by various circumstances such as rest, physical activity, mental activity, digestion, and cold baths.

Von Noorden's great interest in diet and metabolic diseases, particularly diabetes mellitus and carbohydrate metabolism, was implemented by the preparation of extended treatises in the field. In 1900, the first volume of his *Encyclopedia of the Pathology and Therapy of Diseases of Metabolism and Nutrition* was published in ten sections[3] and translated into English the following year.[4] Equally monumental was the *Handbook of Pathology of Metabolic Diseases,* in two volumes, published in 1906.[5] In his *Treatment of Diabetes Mellitus,*[6] he was one of the first to advocate weighed diets, especially the oatmeal diet, notably low in protein and total caloric content. In investigating the underlying disturbance of sugar metabolism he described the liver as the depot organ for glycogen storage, the conversion of blood sugar to glycogen, and the release of glycogen for energy use. The findings were summarized in lectures delivered at the New York Postgraduate Medical School in 1912 as follows:[7]

The control of sugar formation and its distribution takes place in the liver. The other organs

elaborate and consume sugar, but do not share in its production. The cells of the glands and still more those of the muscles, have a certain local controlling power, in so far as they are able, when there is over-production, to take up a small reserve of glycogen. It is left to the liver, however, to supply the organism in general with sugar. The following processes occur in the liver:
1. The taking up of carbohydrates streaming in from the intestinal canal through the portal vein.
2. Their conversion into glycogen, and perhaps into fat, when there is a great excess. As we have said, it is not certain whether the liver can form fat out of carbohydrates, or whether this is the only organ in which this process takes place.
3. When there is a very rapid and extensive supply of sugar to the liver, a portion escapes conversion into glycogen and this leads to hyperglycaemia and eventually to alimentary glycosuria.
4. Intra-hepatic decomposition of protein leads to sugar formation. The details of this chemical process are unknown. Perhaps it is more a stimulus to sugar formation which occurs, and not a direct conversion of the protein nuclei into sugar.
5. If the remaining materials, the available carbohydrates, and in the last resort, the protein nuclei, are insufficient for the needs of the moment, sugar is formed from fat.
6. A diastatic process by which the glycogen in the liver is re-converted into sugar. Glucose is formed, and leaves the liver by the hepatic vein.

Von Noorden was one of the acknowledged leading clinicians of central Europe in the early years of this contemporary era of medicine when the investigation of disturbed physiological function and aberrant biochemical processes contributed substantially to the understanding of the pathogenesis, diagnosis, and treatment of a great body of maladies loosely grouped as metabolic disturbances. Included by von Noorden in this category were obesity, nephritis, colitis, inanition, and gout as well as diabetes mellitus, each of which continues to present unsolved problems, particularly in pathogenesis.

1. Salomon, H.: Von Noorden and His Work (Ger), Ther Mschr 23:305-307, 1918.
2. von Noorden, C.: Albuminuria in Healthy Men (Ger), Deutsch Arch Klin Med 38:207-247, 1866, excerpt translated by Z. Danilevicius.
3. von Noorden, C.: Encyclopedia of the Pathology and Therapy of Diseases of Metabolism and Nutrition (Ger), Berlin: Verlag von August Hirschwald, 1900-1910.
4. von Noorden, C.: Metabolism and Practical Medicine, I. W. Hall (trans.) Chicago: W. T. Keener & Co., 1907.
5. von Noorden, C.: Handbook of Pathology and Metabolism (Ger), Berlin: Verlag von August Hirschwald, 1907.
6. von Noorden, C.: Diabetes and Its Treatment (Ger), Berlin: Verlag von August Hirschwald, 1895.
7. von Noorden, C.: New Aspects of Diabetes, Pathology and Treatment, New York: E. B. Treat & Co., 1912.

Composite by G. Bako

Max Rubner (1854-1932)

MAX RUBNER, Munich born and German trained, was one of the recognized leaders in the calorimetric study of energy exchange of the three principal foodstuffs. Rubner began his training in Carl Voit's laboratory in Munich, where the Pettenkofer-Voit appartus for quantitative evaluation of respired gases of humans and animals provided mathematical definition to the metabolism of nutrients.[1] While still a comparatively young investigator, Rubner moved to Marburg as professor of hygiene. There he built a self-registering calorimeter, quantitated the calories produced in animals, and measured the expired carbon dioxide and the nitrogen excreted in the urine and feces. This led to the law of constant heat sums, expressed by Hess, ie, in a chemical reaction the total heat evolved or absorbed is the same, irrespective of the pathway providing the end-products. In 1891, Rubner succeeded Robert Koch as professor of hygiene at the University of Berlin, followed by appointment to the chair of physiology, a position held until he was 70.

Rubner measured the varying influence of foods on metabolism and, to account for the difference among carbohydrates, fats, and proteins, introduced the term "specific dynamic action." He suggested standard caloric values for the principal foodstuffs, in reviewing the average composition of a mixed diet, and defined the law of surface area; that is to say, energy metabolism is proportional to the size and surface area of animals. The isodynamic law of Rubner states that the three groups of foods are interchangeable in metabolic economy in relation to their caloric equivalents.

The derivation of the isodynamic law followed respiration experiments on rabbits during prolonged fasting. After the animals had lost most of their body fat, an increase in protein metabolism suggested that the calories derived from protein replaced those previously derived from fat.[2]

(1) *The isodynamic substances and values.*
The results of the experiments can be summarized as follows:
(a) Fat ingested with food is isodynamic with the body-fat in equal amounts by weight. . . . The loss of body-fat ceased after feeding fat in exactly the same amounts by weight as the body had lost by metabolism. I conclude that the first and the second are isodynamic when taken in equal quantity. . . . The fat in food, if it is composed of the same type of fat found in the body, is easily transformed into body-fat.
(b) Lean meat is also isodynamic when taken in equal amounts with the proteins of the body which are lost from wasting because of an insufficient intake of protein.
I have already shown that during fasting, when the body-fat has been exhausted, the body protein is lost at a rate which corresponds to the caloric value of the previously combusted fat. Because the rate of combustion of protein can be established only on "food protein," the experiment proves that "body protein" could not have any noticeably different caloric value. Thus it is most probable that the building of the body protein from the food protein takes place without any appreciable storage of potential energy.
(c) Fats and carbohydrates have different caloric values when taken in equal amounts; on the average, 100 portions of fat correspond to 240 portions of carbohydrate.
(d) The isodynamic value of the replaceable protein and carbohydrates can be determined by the difference of the isodynamic values between the fat and the protein and between the fat and carbohydrates; in this manner we discovered that 100 parts of dry protein correspond to 113 parts of cane sugar or to 122 parts of glucose in their isodynamic values.

These experiments show the validity of caloric isodynamics in which, under the conditions outlined, the separate energies of the body are used very properly and interchangeably and without any loss to the body itself. The animal body uses all its energies most economically.

Rubner classified temperature regulation into physical (heat loss) and chemical (heat production). The law of surface area, which states that heat production of mammals is a function of the surface area, was derived from calorimetric studies. The concept was not immediately accepted as valid, and Rubner was obliged to defend it from time to time. The initial studies, conducted on dogs and other animals in the laboratory in Munich were described.[3]

The dissipation of energy by dogs is achieved by cooling under various environmental conditions. The principle of economical dissipation of energy follows that shown in the discussion of the isodynamic interchangeability of various foods. There is no doubt that this rule applies not only to the dog but to all warm blooded mammals. When one proceeds from species to species and examines them, the significance of the body surface to energy dissipation is apparent. . . . The differences between species are astonishing. The surface area of a rat compared to man shows a ratio of 287:1,540 or 100:536. . . . Thus the cells of a rat are more than five times as active under comparable conditions as are the cells of man.
Since the animal body can adjust its metabolism to hunger and rest, as well as dissipation of heat, it follows that there could be no specific type of metabolism of any warm blooded mammal regulated by the composition of its cells alone.

Rubner's "standard values" for foodstuffs have been used for more than one-half a century in determining the fuel value of a mixed diet. Introduced early in one of his communications on calorimetry, they are the contributions probably best remembered by physicians.[4]

The knowledge of correct values of food combustion helps us to calculate the changes in metabolism under various living conditions; this is especially necessary because some important questions could not be solved directly by calorimeters.

The values of heat created when a man uses the so-called mixed diet are as follows:

1 gm protein—   4.1 calories
1 gm fat—   9.3 calories
1 gm carbohydrates— 4.1 calories

In a search for an explanation of the extra heat production associated with the ingestion of food, especially protein, Rubner called the phenomenon "specific dynamic action." A preliminary report from a study on dogs was presented to the Bavarian Academy of Science in 1885.[5]

(3) Individual substances show a specific ability to stimulate the production of heat. Most heat is produced by the ingestion of excessive amounts of protein, much less by excess of carbohydrates, the least by fat; by the same token in the presence of excessive protein intake the body gains the least in weight, with carbohydrates somewhat more, and by additional fat the greatest. Thus, it is evident that the greatest danger exists in becoming overweight when food is rich in fat content.

The excerpts given describe experimental studies on the body calorimeter over a span of only a few years. However, Rubner was the recognized leader in the investigation of metabolism of foodstuffs well into the current century. He prepared several monographs on food and energy metabolism and, as late as 1928, contributed to a compendium on metabolism and energy exchange. Although a physiologist, his concern for socioeconomic matters in Germany in 1931 seems to parallel the profound interest of physicians in America in 1970. Rubner wrote in a letter to Graham Lusk, his lifelong friend in calorimetry:[1]

The price of labor [in Germany] is decreed by the unions and is held high and will be so held, even though it is one of the most important causes of unemployment.

Another factor which appears to me to be necessary is a reduction in the salaries of certain government officials.

There are, however, two most important ways of reducing expenditures: through changes in health insurance and in unemployment insurance. Health insurance has completely failed and leaves every door open for fraud. Since the establishment of health insurance the number of sick has increased threefold, which means that every one can get an illness certificate.

The unemployment insurance is at the moment no better than the health insurance. If every working man were allowed to accept work, even though at a lower wage than formerly, then we would be able to put a large number of workmen into industry. That, however, is impossible because no working man is allowed to accept less than the established wage, and no industry is allowed to pay less than the unions prescribe. To the unemployed and the recipients of charity all social elements must be added, such as the lazy, loafers, thieves, etc., which make between 2 and 3 per cent of the population of large cities.

Everything which has been set up for the welfare of the working classes has gone to the bad through misuse. One must seek other organizations. I believe that your American arrangement of simple insurance dependent on personal payment is a very good one. Any change with us could be brought about only with great difficulty. But it must be done in the interest of the working man himself, because the present administration of our form of insurance wastes enormous sums of money.

1. Lusk, G.: Contributions to the Science of Nutrition, a Tribute to the Life and Works of Max Rubner, *Science* 76:129-135, 1932.

2. Rubner, M.: The Calculated Values of the Principal Organic Foodstuffs in Animals (Ger), *Z Biol* 19:313-396, 1883, excerpt translated by Z. Danilevicius.

3. Rubner, M.: The Effect of Body Size on Food and Energy Metabolism (Ger), *Z Biol* 19:535-562, 1883, excerpt translated by Z. Danilevicius.

4. Rubner, M.: Calorimetric Investigations (Ger), *Z Biol* 3:337-410, 1885, excerpt translated by Z. Danilevicius.

5. Rubner, M.: Contributions to the Study of Energy Exchange (Ger), *Sitzung Math-Physik Classe* 15:452-461, 1886, excerpt translated by Z. Danilevicius.

Graham Lusk (1866-1932)

GRAHAM LUSK, founder of the science of nutrition in America, capitalized on the experimental procedures of Carl Voit and interpreted the contributions of Max Rubner in the energy transformation of foods. His discoveries were not so important as those of either of the German physiologists, but he was able by synthesis and interpretation of reported data to extend the new field of science to our country. Lusk was born in Bridgeport, Conn, the son of a physician who had studied physiology in Germany and based the practice of medicine and obstetrics on physiological principles.[1] Following graduation from the School of Mines at Columbia University, Graham Lusk spent four years in Munich, most of the time in the laboratory of Carl Voit, where he worked on problems of carbohydrate and protein metabolism. Upon returning to this country he accepted an appointment in the department of physiology at Yale; there he carried on

Composite by G. Bako

his work on phlorhizin diabetes in dogs and was soon advanced to a professorship. In 1898, he was called to the professorship of physiology at New York University in Bellevue Hospital Medical College, and in 1909 accepted a similar appointment at Cornell University Medical College, succeeding to the post held by Austin Flint, Jr.

From the University of Munich Lusk received a PHD in 1891, and in his inaugural thesis, abstracted in the *New York Medical Journal,* described the influence of carbohydrates in protein metabolism with particular reference to diabetes mellitus.[2]

. . . it is clear from the foregoing that all the constitutional changes in diabetes can be attributed to the non-destruction of the carbohydrates. The diabetic patient loses flesh because the albumin-protecting property of the burning carbohydrates is eliminated, and loses fat because an amount of fat is burned equivalent to the sugar burned in the healthy person, and he inhales the same amount of oxygen and exhales the same amount of carbonic acid as the normal man under similar conditions.

At Yale, Lusk's studies on phlorhizin diabetes began with the investigation of the sources of glucose in the body. He utilized the phlorhizin technique, discovered by Von Mehring, to depancreatize animals. Lusk observed that, in the glycosuria in dogs following the administration of phlorhizin, the D:N ratio was 3.75. Thus, a quarter of a century before the isolation of insulin, if the endocrine function of the pancreas was completely suppressed, it was found that 3.7 gm of dextrose was excreted in the urine for every gram of urinary nitrogen, and that the calories lost in urinary sugar in diabetes were replaced by the increased protein metabolism. Whether the diabetic dog was fasting or fed on meat only or on fat alone, or a combination of meat and fat, no more fat was burned than in the normal or fasting control animal.[3]

1. Frequent subcutaneous injections of phlorhizin in fasting dogs establish ultimately the ratio in the urine of Dextrose: Nitrogen: 3.75:1, which indicates a production of 60 grams of dextrose from 100 grams of proteid. Taking the faecal nitrogen into consideration, the amount of dextrose obtained from protein may be more accurately estimated at 58.7 per cent.
2. The proteid metabolism may increase above that in simple fasting to an extent as high even as 560 per cent.
3. Dextrose fed in phlorhizin diabetes is quantitatively eliminated. Levulose and galactose are not eliminated as such, but only in so far as they are converted into dextrose.
4. Feeding fat does not affect the ratio.
5. Feeding meat does not affect the ratio for the day, but the sugar from eaten proteid may be eliminated before the nitrogen belonging to it, on account of an early preliminary cleavage of the molecule.

The move to Cornell University Medical College was associated with the construction of a respiration calorimeter of the Atwater-Rosa-Benedict type used for both dogs and children. Later, as scientific director of the Russell Sage Institute of Pathology, a respiration calorimeter for adults was located near the medical wards at Bellevue Hospital. This enabled Lusk to supplement the observations on phlorhizin diabetes in animals with a study of patients with severe diabetes mellitus.

While still at Bellevue Medical College Lusk published the first edition of his famous monograph, *The Elements of the Science of Nutrition,* dedicated to Carl von Voit.[4] This was a standard text on the subject for a quarter of a century and emphasized his great interest in metabolism. The only deficiency related to his training was Lusk's lack of appreciation of the significance of vitamins. In the Harvey Lectures, he summarized the existing state of knowledge of metabolism half a century ago.[5]

In the acute form of diabetes mellitus in man, there is complete loss of power to burn dextrose, and one may infer from the similarity of the conditions to those of pancreatic diabetes that the tissues do not retain glycogen. It is evident that such an organism must exist at the expense of protein and fat. Within the cells of the living body, certain motions are maintained, which are manifest in such physical forms as heat, work and electricity. These material forces are not generated from nothing, but from an exact equivalent of potential energy resident in the materials burned in the body. The requirement of energy for the maintenance of the life of a man is fixed and definite and in general amounts to 32 large calories per kilogramme of body substance in starvation and to 35 calories per kilogramme when an average mixed diet is taken. The diabetic who can not burn dextrose is thrown on protein and fat as sources of his potential energy. Were this an uncomplicated situation a diabetic could doubtless imitate the habits of the Esquimo, who lives on oil and meat. But it happens unfortunately that a major portion of the ingested protein is convertible into sugar in the diabetic organism, and that this sugar which is carried away by the urine may contain by far the greater part of the potential energy of protein which is available for cell life. To compensate for this, the protein metabolism increases, but fat metabolism remains the mainstay of the life of the diabetic as it does in the fasting individual. In diabetes the protein metabolism is abnormal, and conditions varying in severity also arise in which the end-products of fat metabolism, such as beta-oxybutyric acid, aceto-acetic acid and acetone, do not burn, but accumulate within the organism, and are eliminated in the urine.

Lusk, a great teacher, gave unstintingly of his time to medical students and postgraduate students, and spoke in favor of the full-time system of clinical teachers and frankly on the importance of medical education in America.[6] He helped to found the Society for Experimental Biology and Medicine, the Harvey Society of New York, and the American Society of Biological Chemists. He held membership in a number of

American and foreign scientific bodies and received honorary degrees from Yale, the Unversity of Glasgow, and the University of Munich. He left a large number of pupils in academic medicine in America, especially E. F. DuBois, Francis W. Peabody, Frederick M. Allen, Joseph Aub, J. H. Means, D. P. Barr, W. S. McCann, R. L. Cecil, W. S. Ladd, and John R. Murlin.

1. DuBois, E. F.: *Biographical Memoir of Graham Lusk 1866-1932,* Washington: National Academy of Sciences, 1940, pp. 95-142.
2. Lusk, G.: Influence of the Carbohydrates on Proteid Catabolism, With Special Reference to Diabetes, *New York Med J* 54:628-630, 1891.
3. Reilly, F. H., Nolan, F. W., and Lusk, G.: Phlorhizin Diabetes in Dogs, *Amer J Physiol* 1:395-410, 1898.
4. Lusk, G.: *The Elements of the Science of Nutrition,* Philadelphia: W. B. Saunders Co., 1906.
5. Lusk, G.: *Metabolism in Diabetes,* the Harvey Lectures Delivered Under the Auspices of the Harvey Society of New York 1908-09, Philadelphia: J. B. Lippincott Co., 1910, pp 69-96.
6. Lusk, G.: Medical Education, a plea for the Development of Leaders, *JAMA* 52:1229-1230, 1909.

Eugene F. DuBois (1882-1959)

EUGENE F. DuBOIS, successively professor of medicine and of physiology, is usually identified with clinical calorimetry; in collaboration with Graham Lusk, he took full advantage of the respiration calorimeter in the study of man in health and in disease. DuBois was born of Huguenot stock on Staten Island, prepared at Milton Academy, Massachusetts, and finished his formal education at Harvard College.[1] During the summer holidays in his 16th year, he worked as a volunteer orderly at the Army Hospital at Camp Wyckoff, Montauk Point, Long Island; there a number of Spanish-American War soldiers were either convalescing or dying from typhoid fever or dysentery. This exposure to epidemic disease surely was ample cause for a latent interest in infection, the metabolic effects of fever, and the investigation of the heat regulatory mechanism of the body. The AB degree was earned in three years, with the humanities rather than the biological sciences as his field of concentration. Returning to New York, DuBois graduated MD from the College of Physicians and Surgeons at the age of 24, two years younger than many of his classmates.

Before beginning an internship at the Presbyterian Hospital in New York, then situated on 71st Street, DuBois studied pathology under Henke at the Charlotten-

National Library of Medicine

burger Krankenhaus in Berlin. A second postgraduate tour in Berlin followed his internship, at which time he turned to clinical investigation under Theodor Brugsch at the Charité Hospital. It is related that DuBois initially planned to study bacteriology at the Pasteur Institute in Paris, but, upon the suggestion of John Howland, professor of pediatrics at New York University and later at Johns Hopkins Medical School, he turned instead to the investigation of the physiological phenomena of energy metabolism in health and in disease.[1] In this endeavor he was one of the first clinical scientists in the United States to reap the benefits of extensive training in the basic disciplines, particularly physiology and biochemistry, in anticipation of a full-time teaching assignment in the clinical department. Such an enlightened program of preparation for academic medicine reached a small peak before World War I, subsided between the wars, but subsequently experienced an unprecedented resurgence.

At the Charité in Berlin, DuBois and Borden Veeder of Pennsylvania Medical School restored a Pettenkofer-Voit metabolism chamber in order to define the energy requirements in diabetes mellitus.[2] In the midst of these studies, Graham Lusk, professor of physiology at Cornell, visited Kraus's laboratory and learned of the American investigators—thus beginning the Lusk-DuBois scientific liaison. While others had assumed that the energy requirements in diabetes mellitus were unchanged from the normal, scientific support was lacking. The total energy requirements and the 24-hour carbon dioxide excretion of patients with diabetes were measured with the respiration chamber. The experimental observations were sound, but not until the two investigators returned to the United States and submitted the results to Lusk were the proper inferences drawn and a presentable manuscript drafted.

DuBois' first appointment in the pathology department at the Presbyterian Hospital gave neither the occasion nor incentive for research, for routine duties demanded his full attention. The second call came in 1913 after Lusk had persuaded the authorities to construct a respiration calorimeter in Bellevue Hospital adjacent to a small metabolism ward. The project was supported by the Russell Sage Institute of Pathology and complemented Lusk's calorimetric researches in animals. DuBois was appointed medical director, a research position which required a minimum of teaching, administration, and clinical practice. Nevertheless, from his light the beam spread far. An unusual group of teachers of medicine, who, in turn, became advocates of the value of basic investigation for clinical instruction, found the source. Included in the list of students were Francis W. Peabody, David P. Barr, James H. Means, Joseph C. Aub, Carl T. Wiggers, William S. McCann, John P. Peters, Soma Weiss, James D. Hardy, Samuel Z. Levine, and Edward Mason.

Both world wars interrupted DuBois' peacetime pursuits, and rapidly diverted his attention to practical matters of physiological stress and survival in combat. Gas warfare and ventilation in submarines were prime subjects for study in World War I.

Brave as well as industrious, DuBois was awarded the Navy Cross for heroism in protecting the crew of a damaged submarine from chlorine gas. He returned to the Medical Corps of the Navy during World War II, with the rank of captain, and was assigned to the unit studying deep-sea diving and aviation.

DuBois was 48 before he accepted the professorship of medicine at Cornell, in charge of the clinical service at Bellevue Hospital. In spite of an appointment in the department of medicine for several years, his limited clinical experience led him to seize the opportunity of this transition period between downtown and uptown Manhattan to study with Friedrich von Müller in Munich. Upon his return, the New York Hospital-Cornell Medical Center was nearing completion. He served as professor of medicine until 1941. At that time he returned to physiology, his first love, and occupied the chair best suited to him.

One of DuBois' clinical contributions was the recognition in 1926 of hyperparathyroidism in sea captain Charles Martell. The abnormal exchange of calcium and phosphorous in the captain was similar to findings reported by Collip of McGill following administration of parathyroid extract to animals. The assumption was the first example of a presumptive diagnosis of osteitis fibrosis cystica being offered on the basis of a suspected tumor of the parathyroid glands. Electrolyte balance studies by DuBois disclosed an elevated concentration of serum calcium, an increased output of calcium in the urine, and a decreased concentration of serum phosphorus. The patient was transferred to ward 4 at the Massachusetts General Hospital, where the calcium and phosphorous aberrations were confirmed and a surgical search was begun for a parathyroid tumor.[3] Six unsuccessful attempts were made before the hyperfunctioning gland was located deep in the chest. Meanwhile, unknown to the Boston and New York investigators, S. Mandl had removed a parathyroid tumor in a case of osteitis fibrosis cystica.

Our patient then presents a picture which agrees in its essentials with that produced by the excessive administration of parathyroid extract and opposite to that found in hypoparathyroidism. These considerations and the finding of parathyroid tumors in patients with osteomalacia and similar bone disturbances led us to the conclusion that the underlying basis for the osteitis fibrosa cystica in our subject was a hyperactivity of the parathyroid bodies.

It was obvious that a search for some abnormality of the parathyroid glands was the next step indicated. At the closing of our metabolism ward for the summer the patient was transferred to the care of Drs. Aub and Bauer at the Massachusetts General Hospital for further studies of his calcium metabolism and a consideration of the advisability of removing one of his parathyroid glands.

Academic honors for DuBois included the Lane lectureship at Stanford University, the presidency and the Kober medal of the Association of American Physicians, an honorary DSC degree from the University of Rochester, Harveian lectureship in New York, membership in the National Academy of Sciences, and the presidency of the American Society of Clinical Investigation. Only a short time before his death, DuBois was nominated for the John Phillips Memorial Prize of the American College of Physicians but was forced to decline because of failing health.

1. Aub, J. C.: "Eugene Floyd Dubois," in *Biographical Memoirs, Nat Acad Sci* 36:125-145, 1962.

2. Dubois, E. F., and Veeder, B. S.: The Total Energy Requirement in Diabetes Mellitus, *Arch Intern Med* 5:37-46, 1910.

3. Hannon, R. R., et al: A Case of Osteitis Fibrosa Cystica (Osteomalacia?) With Evidence of Hyperactivity of the Parathyroid Bodies. Metabolic Study I, *J Clin Invest* 8:215-227, 1930.

Sir Frederick Gowland Hopkins (1861-1947)

TO F. GOWLAND HOPKINS, self-taught chemist of Cambridge University, is due full credit for strengthening the stature of biochemistry in England and equating it with physiology. Hopkins was born at Eastbourne shortly after his parents had moved from London.[1] His father died while he was an infant, and his mother arranged for an education without a recognized plan or a purposeful goal; rather, learning was gained at a succession of unimportant elementary schools. This was followed by three years of training in conventional statistical methods, and at the age of 20, matriculation in tech-

Composite by G. Blako

nical chemistry at University College, London. Two years later Hopkins was offered a position in the chemical laboratory at Guy's Hospital, where he remained for five years. Then followed, in succession, medical instruction, research, and a teaching assignment, all at Guy's, concluding with the MB from the University of London at the age of 33. Hopkins served as president of the Royal Society, was a charter member of the Medical Research Committee which administered the first annual grant for public money to support research in England, and was honored with the Order of Merit and knighthood.

The moment of decision in an enviable career came in 1898 when, after more than 15 years at Guy's Hospital, Hopkins was invited by Michael Foster to join the staff at Cambridge University; there he was charged with the development of teaching and research in chemical physiology. Tutorial work at Emmanuel College supplemented a modest university stipend. Subsequent steps of academic progress included a fellowship

in Trinity College and prelectorship in biochemistry, the chair of biochemistry, and ultimately an appointment as the first Sir William Dunn professor at the newly-founded institute of biochemistry.

The first scientific communication by Hopkins—adolescent observations on the purple vapor ejected by the bombardier beetle—appeared in *The Entomologist* when he was 17. A decade later he published a note on the yellow pigment in butterflies, which disclosed an interest in biochemistry and especially intermediary metabolism. His noteworthy contributions to biochemistry came from the laboratory in Cambridge and included the identification of tryptophane, an amino acid constituent of most proteins; isolation and characterization of glutathione, which functions as a carrier of oxygen or acceptor of hydrogen, in tissue respiration; discovery of xanthine oxidase; and quantitative observations on the function of lactic acid in fatigued muscle.

Hopkins' discovery that saturation with ammonium chloride was essential for the precipitation of uric acid from body fluids was communicated to the *Journal of Pathology and Bacteriology* while he was a Gull research student.[2] The technique remained a standard laboratory procedure for many years and exemplified his lifelong interest in clinical application of practical laboratory findings. An excerpt from the report "On the Estimation of Uric Acid in Urine" follows.[2]

After using it [the process] continuously for more than a year, with a large number of normal and pathological urines, I am strengthened in my belief that it is a process of very great accuracy. By its means uric acid may be estimated with an error of less than 1 per cent; a degree of accuracy unattainable in the case of any of the other organic constituents of the urine.

In a study of protein hydrolysis and tryptic digestion, a chance observation by one of his advanced students led to the discovery of the tryptophane reaction. The isolation and identification of one of the essential amino acids marked the beginning of studies in the chemistry of nutrition which culminated in his sharing with Eijkman, in 1929, the Nobel Prize in biochemistry for the recognition that accessory food factors, vitamins, were needed for normal growth. Excerpts from his report on tryptophane[3] will be followed by a statement on accessory food factors, the introduction to a report on a series of studies summarized in lectures delivered at Guy's Hospital in 1909.[4]

For reasons which will be understood in the sequel the substance is to be obtained in greatest amount from the products of pancreatic digestion and may be separated with especial ease when casein is the proteid employed. The tryptic digestion products of casein have therefore been the chief source of material for the experimental work described in the present paper. We have obtained an identical product however from the tryptic digestion of crystalline egg albumin, and from serum proteids after hydrolysis with sulphuric acid.

The composition of the substance corresponds with the formula $C_{11}H_{12}N_2O_2$. It yields abundantly skatol and indol on heating and gives the pine-splinter reaction direct.

The substance yields also a red derivative with bromine, and is itself the hitherto unisolated tryptophane.

The experiments described in this paper confirm the work of others in showing that animals cannot grow when fed upon so-called "synthetic" dietaries consisting of mixtures of pure proteins, fats, carbohydrates, and salts. But they show further that a substance or substances present in normal foodstuffs (e.g. milk) can, when added to the dietary in astonishingly small amount, secure the utilization for growth of the protein and energy contained in such artificial mixtures.

The isolation of glutathione, a major contribution in the study of tissue respiration and intermediary metabolism, was reported in 1921. For several years his foresight led him to believe that the complex of chemical reactions, oxidations, and reductions catalyzed by intracellular enzymes would yield to the understanding of cellular metabolism. The compound contained an SH group, was readily and reversibly oxidizable to an S-S linkage, and was widely distributed in plants and animals. Hopkins believed it to be a dipeptide of glutamic acid and cystein. Several years later he proved it to be a tripeptide of glutamic acid, glycine, and cystein. He concludes the first report as follows:[5]

The substance is autoxidisable, and, owing to the changes in the sulphur group of its cysteïn

moiety from the sulphydryl to the disulphide condition and vice versa, it acts readily under varying conditions either as a hydrogen acceptor or an oxygen acceptor (hydrogen "donator"). It can be both reduced and oxidised under the influence of factors shown to be present in the tissues themselves.

Evidence is discussed which suggests that the substance has actual functions in the chemical dynamics of the cell.

In cooperation with W. M. Fletcher, Hopkins studied muscle metabolism, the importance of oxygen as a function of lactic acid disappearance, and the accumulation of lactic acid following muscular activity. Quantitative methods of analysis were devised and the deterioration of lactic acid halted in fresh tissue at selected stages. The quantitative techniques were then developed by Hill, Meyerhof, and others in the definition of the carbohydrate cycle and the description of the liberation of energy in muscle contraction. Although the observations of Fletcher and Hopkins have been overshadowed by subsequent studies on phosphorylated bases and their relation to muscle-protein myosin, the initial report is worthy of note.[6]

For a generation it has been recognised that there are means available within the body by which the acid products of muscular activity may be disposed of, and there is already a large body of well-known evidence which indicates that this disposal of acid products—whatever the site of it may be—is most efficient when the conditions for oxidative processes are most favourable, and that it is incomplete when these conditions are unfavourable.

From a fatigued muscle, placed in oxygen, there is a disappearance of lactic acid already formed. The course of this disappearance has been followed by successive estimations in similar groups of muscles exposed to oxygen for different time intervals: it proceeds at first rapidly, then more slowly, and in general reaches a level about one half of the original yield of the fatigued muscle.

Although F. Gowland Hopkins never pursued the practice of medicine, his exposure to the unsolved problems of medicine and to teachers and practitioners of medicine made him at ease with clinical matters. He was aware of the importance of basic medical sciences in the advancement of clinical medicine, as expressed in a report to the Society of Public Analysts, 30 years after he had left the speciality for the medical sciences.[7]

I wish very much to make a point here which, if it seems too remote at present from your practical interests, may be considered as in parentheses. The care of the body in sickness, with all the delicacies of human relationship which it involves, must remain always an entire and carefully guarded prerogative of the physician; but the innate respect of the public, and even of the non-medical scientific public, for the physician's calling has led to a somewhat illogical attitude, and has tended to make sacrosanct not only the calling of the physician, but the scientific material which he deals with. . . . While a large part of future scientific medical studies must always be carried out by men who, though medically qualified, have preferred the laboratory to practice, and whose special qualification, therefore, is that they have had personal touch with the problems offered by disease, yet in a middle region these must be joined in their work by men whose primary qualifications are non-medical— men who, saved from the long years of clinical study, are able to bring well-grounded laboratory knowledge and (I may add) a sufficient knowledge of the literature of pathology, which is open to all, to join their medically qualified *confrères* in attacking the huge problems which await solution.

1. Dale, H. H.: Frederick Gowland Hopkins (1861-1947), *Obit Notices Fellows Roy Soc* 6:115-145, 1948.
2. Hopkins, F. G.: On the Estimation of Uric Acid in Urine, *J. Path Bact* 1:451-459, 1893.
3. Hopkins, F. G., and Cole, S. W.: A Contribution to the Chemistry of Proteids, *J. Physiol* 27:418-428, 1901-1902.
4. Hopkins, F. G.: Feeding Experiments Illustrating the Importance of Accessory Factors in Normal Dietaries, *J Physiol* 44:425-453, 1912.
5. Hopkins, F. G.: XXXII. On an Autoxidisable Constituent of the Cell, *Biochem J* 15:286-305, 1921.
6. Fletcher, W. M., and Hopkins, F. G.: Lactic Acid in Amphibian Muscle, *J. Physiol* 35:247-303, 1906-1907.
7. Hopkins, F. G.: The Analyst and the Medical Man, *Analyst* 31:385-397, 1906.

Ludolf von Krehl (1861-1937)

LUDOLF KREHL, famous for his clinical contributions and especially for a treatise on pathologic physiology, was born in Leipzig, where his grandfather held a full professorship in theology, and his father in orientalism in the university.[1] He received his clinical training under H. Curschmann and L. Wagner and studied pathologic anatomy with Cohnheim. But it was probably Carl Ludwig, director of the Physiological Institute in Leipzig, then developing his interpretation of normal and abnormal function as natural processes, who was more influen-

Composite by G. Bako

tial than any of these. Krehl served as Ludwig's assistant; however, instead of accepting blindly his chief's point of view of biology, he formulated his own and acknowledged that the natural sciences embraced but a portion of the fundamentals of medical science. He thus became a great skeptic in his search for truth among natural phenomena. Krehl examined and reexamined, leaving with his students an intentional impression of uncertainty; persisting even after a thorough exploration of all paths leading to the conclusion. In such a Diogenean role he proved an excellent teacher in the amphitheater and at the bedside, an inspiration to his pupils, and an exemplary clinician in attendance upon the sick.

In 1892, Krehl answered the first of several academic calls and became chief of the Polyclinic in Jena. In turn, he was chief and professor of medicine at Marburg, Greifswald, and Tübingen, and successor to Naunyn in Strasbourg. At his final post in Heidelberg, he succeeded Erb in 1906 as professor of medicine and chief of the medical service in the university hospital. Krehl's great monograph, *Fundamentals of General Clinical Pathology,* was published in 1893.[2] Five years later the title was changed to *Pathological Physiology.*[3] This text went through many German editions and was translated into other languages, including the third edition which was translated into English in 1905;[4] the latter, in turn, went through three American revisions.

Early in Krehl's career, systematic investigations centered about the heart and included discussions of failure of the heart valves, idiopathic myocardial disease, coronary occlusion, the beer drinker's heart, and fatty degeneration of the heart muscle—studies which were based upon anatomy, physiology, and chemistry, each with relevance to specific clinical cases. The gitalin part of digitalis (Verodigen) and of strophanthin was introduced in his clinic, and the influence of digitalis on urine excretion was demonstrated. He studied hypertrophy of the individual auricles and ventricles and concluded that hypertrophy of one chamber does not necessarily induce hypertrophy of the others. In 1891, Krehl discussed idiopathic diseases of the myocardium founded upon a series of cases observed clinically and studied postmortem. Failure of the heart muscle and valvular insufficiency, in spite of hypertrophy, were attributed to interstitial myocarditis.[5]

Numerous structural abnormalities of the fibers and nuclei of heart muscle are found in varying degrees of degeneration: some are enlarged in length and in width, at times with increased ability to stain and at times with decreased ability. . . . We are inclined to attribute this to diffuse nucleus degeneration . . . which could not appear without affecting function. Irrespective of the explanation of the causal relation of enlargement of nuclei and of the decrease of striated substance, the alterations must affect the contractile substance of the muscle.

We found in these hearts that in typical cases of several types of idiopathic hypertrophy of the heart muscle failure is caused by anatomical disease of the tissues. . . . The disorders seen in a hypertrophic heart of this type (idiopathic) may be caused by myocarditis which may progress and lead to the death of the organ even then when all adverse influences have been eliminated, which undoubtedly affected the diseased heart.

In coronary disease Krehl pointed out several clinical-pathologic phenomena. He noted that survival was possible with asymptomatic, complete occlusion of an artery or of a large branch. Another type of coronary patient may die suddenly, without apparent pain and without terminal respiratory agony.[6]

In the first place, it is positively known that in man more or less complete occlusion of at least a portion of a branch of the first order, if not of an entire coronary artery,—for example, the ramus descendens anterior of the left coronary vessel,—is perfectly compatible with continuance of life. This we know from the fact that large infarcts of the heart, often of old standing, in a state of calcification and corresponding to the distribution of one of the above-mentioned vessels, are not infrequently seen at the autopsy table.

It is possible that the accident sometimes happens without any symptoms that the patient is aware of; he lives on and never suspects what an abyss he has escaped.

Finally, some patients fall dead at the instant when occlusion of the vessel takes place, either without presenting any special symptoms or immediately after the beginning of an attack of angina pectoris.

Why the clinical symptoms of occlusion of the coronary vessel are so different in different cases is not, in my opinion, as yet susceptible of explanation. I do not believe that the contractions of the heart cease because part of the organ no longer contracts. My reason for not believing this is that large portions of the heart-wall sometimes suffer structural as well as functional death without the activity of the organ being completely abolished, and, on the other hand, sudden death may occur solely as the result of stenosis at the orifice of a coronary vessel, without complete occlusion.

Studies on the pathogenesis of fever in infections, which began with a biologic interest in the heat regulation of man and in homothermic and poikilothermic animals, led to important contributions in the understanding of the therapy of typhoid fever. With Matthes, Krehl investigated the pyrogenic effect of degeneration products of pneumococci and the bacilli of diptheria, *Pseudomonas pyocyaneus* infection, anthrax, tuberculosis, and typhoid fever. Rabbits, guinea pigs, hens, doves, and, while in Tübingen, even crocodiles served as experimental animals. Rubner's calorimeter was employed for the determination of heat exchange.[7]

The fasting state of animals proved satisfactory for the production of fever with living microorganisms. The pyrogenic action of chemical substances originating from bacteria on fasting animals was as a rule equally satisfactory.

Three periods may be distinguished in the temperature curve: the time of its rise, its peak, and its fall. . . . The production of heat is calculated from the loss of heat, the average weight of the animal, the initial- and concluding-temperatures, and the specific temperature of the animal.

The various components of the curve of heat loss behave differently; the loss by conduction and by radiation to the surroundings is generally diminished, the loss by water evaporation is likewise usually less than normal, but at times it may be slightly increased.

When the fever reached its height, we observed, in a few instances, a rise in heat production. The greatest increase was 60% above normal, the least 7% above normal, the average was approximately 19% above normal.

The factors associated with the decline in temperature varied. Usually the production of heat was decreased; not only was it found to be less than during fever, but sometimes was less than normal. The organism sometimes gives off little heat; its temperature falls mainly because of decreased heating.

We must admit that fever without detectable increase in heat production can occur, even though this is unusual.

Krehl was a kind and humble teacher, an unassuming clinician, and a wise consultant who attracted many from all parts of Europe. His interest in investigation began with the patient, and a fundamental requirement of a lecture hall was a door wide enough to admit a bed patient for demonstration. His courage and convictions led him to support Freud, one of the first internists to do so. For his military service during World War I as consultant to the German Army, with the rank of major general, he received the Iron Cross First Class. Furthermore, the Ordre Pour le Mérite (nonmilitary class) and the Alderschild, the highest honor that could be awarded by the German Republic, were conferred upon him. He maintained a deep religious faith as a member of the Evangelical-Lutheran church and received from the University of Tübingen the honorary doctorate of theology in 1927. The following translation from the Introduction to volume 3 of his opus tripartitum, entitled *Origin, Critical Examination, and Treatment of Internal Diseases,* published in 1931, presents a summary of his philosophy of a concluding search for an understanding of diseases and an insight into the fundamentals of life.[8] His thoughts as a scientist, an investigator, and a practicing physician are expressed in describing the futile attempt to delineate all aspects of internal medicine as he believed he had accomplished in pathologic physiology.

My original plan was to describe the treatment of internal diseases according to the principles of pathologic physiology. I dreamed the dream which the great Magendie dreamed one hundred years ago. This dream was then unattained and today remains our unattainable ideal. With painful grief and mental agony, I came to recognize that such a goal is not possible. This forced me to reflect upon the capabilities of our present treatment which evolved as follows: only in a small fraction of the cases is the deliberation which guides us as physicians in the treatment of patients capable of correlation with the concept of pathologic physiology. We treat relatively few patients and then only a portion of the disorders of those treated based on biological knowledge of the natural processes, a logical sequence of the deliberations discussed in pathologic physiology. Much more frequently other forms of consideration come into question in treatment so that, therefore, this last part of my Opus tripartium does not represent as I had wished and hoped for half of my life a consequence, but a supplement of the pathologic physiology, a supplement, however, which for its part must have again certain reactions upon the concept of pathologic physiology. For, in the last analysis, my entire descriptive attempt is intended to serve the medical science, and medical science is unity of itself. All processes of life, as far as they influence pathology and medical science, will, therefore, be affected by interpretation and in more than one respect be specific.

1. Schenck, E. G.: Personal Communication.
2. Krehl, L.: *Fundamentals of General Clinical Pathology* (Ger), Leipzig: F. C. W. Vogel, 1893.
3. Krehl, L.: *Pathological Physiology* (Ger), Leipzig: F. C. W. Vogel, 1898.
4. Krehl, L.: *The Principles of Clinical Pathology* (Ger), A. W. Hewlett (trans.), Philadelphia: J. B. Lippincott Co., 1905.
5. Krehl, L.: Idiopathic Diseases of the Heart Muscle (Ger), *Deutsch Arch Klin Med* 48:414-431, 1891, excerpts translated by Z. Danilevicius.
6. Krehl, L.: "Diseases of the Myocardium and Nervous Diseases of the Heart," (Ger), in Nothnagel's Practice, *Diseases of the Heart,* translated under the editorial supervision of A. Stengel, Philadelphia: W. B. Saunders Co., 1908.
7. Krehl, L., and Matthes, M.: Increase of Body Temperature in Fever (Ger), *Arch Exp Path Pharm* 38:284-320, 1897, excerpts translated by Z. Danilevicius.
8. Krehl, L.: *Origin, Critical Examination and Treatof Internal Diseases* (Ger), Berlin: F. C. W. Vogel, 1931, excerpt translated by H. J. Mezger [one-time pupil].

Composite by G. Bako

Ludwig Aschoff (1866-1942)

CARL ALBERT LUDWIG ASCHOFF, son of a respected physician of Berlin, chose pathology as a lifetime pursuit shortly after he began the study of medicine at the University of Bonn.[1] He contined his training in Berlin, spent several months with von Recklinghausen at Strasbourg and, in 1889, received the MD degree from Bonn. In 1891, he served as assistant to von Recklinghausen. Two years later Aschoff accepted a similar position with Orth in Göttingen. The following year he was promoted to privatdocent and remained in Göttingen for a total of ten years. At the age of 37, Aschoff progressed to the chair of pathology at Marburg and, after four productive years, accepted the call to Freiburg. There he served as professor and director of the Pathological and Anatomical Institute until the age of 70. Upon reaching the statutory age, he was appointed director of the department of the history of medicine and continued in Freiburg with a new career in a discipline dormant up to this time.

Aschoff was a descriptive tissue pathologist, whose observations and deductions were derived from gross and microscopic study of tissue retrieved from morbid patients. He exemplified the industry, energy, scientific accomplishments, leadership, and warm-heartedness of a chief of an institute of medical sciences in the German tradition during the early decades of this century. He carried dueling scars as evidence of loyalties to the Burschenshaft of student days at Bonn. Catholic and international in his thoughts and actions, he made many of his contributions in collaboration with pupils from other countries who enjoyed liaison with the professor. If one foreign country is to be singled out, it was Japan which sent to Freiburg a proportionately greater share of students. His laboratory was so filled with foreign and national pupils as to limit per capita working space to only a few feet. Moreover, each student furnished his own slides, glassware, and microscope, and sometimes a microtome. This arrangement proved to be a decided improvement over the freezing microtome provided.

Aschoff's skill in the direction or execution of investigative work was matched by his exposition in the lecture hall. His academic responsibilities were complemented by hospitality in his home and four-season activities in the Black Forest. His first investigations at Göttingen dealt with thrombosis and appendicitis. At Marburg, his work with Tawara led to the description of the atrioventricular node (the Aschoff-Tawara node) of the conduction system of the mammalian heart; while the microscopic findings in the heart in rheumatic fever established his reputation. At Freiburg, he was particularly interested in atherosclerosis, gallstones and gallbladder disease, tuberculosis, gastric ulcers, scurvy, endocrinology, and especially vital staining, a precursor to his broad generalizations on the reticuloendothelial system.

The sinuses in the gallbladder first observed by Rokitansky in 1842, redescribed by Luschka in 1863 and by Aschoff in 1905, are now called Rokitansky-Aschoff sinuses. There are epithelial lined clefts within the mucosa of the gallbladder which penetrate the muscular coat.[2]

There are—and I consider this of extreme importance—crypts in the epithelium of the normal gallbladder which are not false and extend into the muscular layer and are in relation to the vessels passing through the muscularis. It is known that the muscularis of the gallbladder has small openings in many cases through which the vessels enter and leave. Usually the openings are narrow and contain connective tissue. But often the clefts are noticeably wider and the mucosa forms a deep invagination when the bladder is markedly contracted, which then transverses the entire muscularis and may extend to the border of the tunica fibrosa. These are the Luschka ducts which he almost always found.

Little attention has been paid to the possibility of the Luschka ducts which are normally present acting as a focus for the development of chole-lithiasis. . . . Rokitansky has called attention to gallstone formation in the small invaginating pockets.

Aschoff's studies of the heart in cases of acute rheumatic fever with valvular insufficiency led him to the identification of a specific lesion. In each of five cases he discovered microscopically a round or spindle-shaped nodule containing multinucleated giant cells, fibroblasts, and basophilic cells with irregular borders. The lesions were present in subcutaneous nodules, in joints and tendons, in the aorta and pleura, and scattered throughout the pericardium, endo-cardium, and myocardium, including the conduction system. They are rarely found in the lungs.[3]

These nodules were plentiful and clearly deline-ated in only two cases of recurrent endocarditis, but corresponded exactly in their location to the cellular growth in the other cases. They regularly occur in the neighborhood of small or medium-sized vessels, and most frequently were present in the vicinity of the adventitia. Or there existed simultaneously a disease of all the vascular layers, such as is described in arteritis nodosa. The aforementioned nodules are unusually small, mostly submiliary, and originate by the conglom-eration of large elements, with one or more abnormally large indented or polymorphic nuclei. The arrangement of the cells frequently occurs in the form of a fan or a rosette. The periphery is formed by the large nuclei, the center by the paler or colorless-appearing necrotic mass of confluent cell protoplasm. By cursory examina-tion, the fan formations slightly resemble the necrosis of gout with a peripheral cell mantle, as is so frequently observed in the gouty kidney. The rheumatic nodules are not to be confused with tubercles or foreign body cells with more uniformly former nuclei, but are of a configura-tion that more nearly resembles the larger nuclear elements in certain sarcomas or the infil-trations in pseudoleukemia. In all events, the nodules do not exclusively consist of such large nucleated cells, but also small and large lympho-cytes, and polymorphonuclear leucocytes force

themselves a short distance between the large cells of the periphery, or form a peripheral zone, and from there, irregular projections may extend far into the connective tissue partitions. In these richly cellular projections are found isolated cells with large nuclei, with all the transitions to a simple large leukocytoid element, which are even found in a normal manner in the neighborhood of the smallest vessels and appear very distinct in all inflammations. These leukocytoid elements are the large cells already described by Hayem and Romberg, the genesis of which, however, remains uncertain to them. From these large cells, which are the inflamed swollen adventitial cells of the vessels, the giant cell-like large nucleated element arises; these appear singly or are collected in nodules, and give the rheumatic cellular infiltra-tion its peculiar configuration. It may be further stated that the number of eosinophilic nucleated cells in these nodules is extremently small. While in the one case the structure of the nodule gives the impression of a fresh cellular infiltration, in another case a partial or complete fibrous re-placement of the nodule is evident.

As we have the large cell nodule formation only in rheumtic endocarditis, and never in the typhoid heart, diphtheria heart, *et cetera,* we believe it permissible to conclude that it is es-pecially characteristic of rheumatic myocarditis.

The concept of the reticuloendothelial system was based upon isolated observa-tions by others and developed by Aschoff from his studies on supravital staining. The term was coined in 1913 in collaboration with his assistant, Landau, and referred to mesenchymal cells, widely distributed throughout the body, which phagocytized small particles and coarse colloids. Although his generalization remains, the cells are neither endothelial nor do they elaborate reticulin fibers. This error arose from the fact that the cells line the sinuses of the liver, spleen, bone marrow, and lymph nodes and are found in close association. The de-scription, which appeared first in Germany, formed the basis of his Janeway lectures de-livered in New York city shortly after. This appeared in a compilation of addresses de-livered during his American tour, which in-cluded the Lane lectures in San Francisco, a Harvey lecture in New York, and the Osler lecture in Los Angeles. Excerpts are as follows:[4]

But I hope to be able to show you that we have already collected sufficient data to permit us to speak of a special system. At any rate, as the author of the name, I feel the responsibility of justifying the conception which it is intended to convey, and shall endeavor to present briefly my reasons for holding this view.

When Landau and I proposed, in 1913, to group together a special type of cells of wide distribution in the mammalian organism as a system of reticuloendothelial cells, we had reached this conclusion only from a large number of individual observations of previous investigators, the value and importance of which were forcibly impressed upon us by our own studies.

Intra vitam staining by lithium carmine, pyrrhol-blue, trypan-blue etc., results in the appearance of dye granules in certain cells of the connective-tissue series, in consequence of which these cells can be distinguished at once from most of the parenchymatous cells, from the ordinary blood cells, myeloid as well as lymphoid, from the lymphocytes of the lymph nodes, and from the plasma cells and mast cells. These granules are of variable size, and stain with varying degrees of intensity. Arranged according to the fineness and compactness of these granules, an ascending series of vitally staining mesenchymal elements can be tabulated as follows:

1. The *endothelial cells* of blood and lymph vessels. They take the dye only when the staining has been carried to an advanced degree and only in the form of the very finest granules.

2. The *fibrocytes* or ordinary connective-tissue cells. They store the dye in variable degree after sufficiently prolonged staining, also in the form of rather fine granules. They are more easily stained than the endothelial cells.

3. The *reticulum cells* of the splenic pulp, the cortical nodules and pulp cords of the lymph nodes, and ultimately of the remainder of the lymphoid apparatus. These cells readily take the dye and stain more deeply than the connective-tissue cells, but in the rapidity and intensity of the stain fall behind the members of the following groups.

4. The *reticulo-endothelial cells* of the sinuses of the lymph nodes, the blood sinuses of the spleen, the capillaries of the liver lobules (Kupffer's stellate cells), the capillaries of the bone marrow, the adrenal cortex, and the hypophysis.

5. The *histiocytes,* as we have designated the wandering cells of the connective tissue, the clasmatocytes of Ranvier, etc., to distinguish them from the cells that give rise to connective tissue (the fibroblasts or fibrocytes). These cells stain almost as readily as those of Group 4, especially when in a state of heightened activity.

6. The *splenocytes* and vitally staining *monocytes* (endothelial leucocytes, blood histiocytes) which have their origin from the histiocytes (Group 5) and the reticulo-endothelial cells (Group 4).

How should we group together these cells which are so closely interrelated? We proposed at the time to eliminate Groups 1 and 2, which stain either faintly or not at all, and which, as we

shall see, function differently from the other groups. These cells are also the least mobile and the most fixed.

On the other hand, it seemed desirable to combine under a single heading Groups 3 and 4, because of their common function of producing reticulum and of lining sinusoid blood and lymph spaces, and to call it the *reticulo-endothelial system.*

Aschoff prepared a *Handbook of Pathological Anatomy,* which reached its 8th edition in 1935. For several years he edited his predecessor's specialty journal at Freiburg, Ziegler's *Beiträge.* During World War I, he served as a pathologist in the field and studied especially gas gangrene and war wounds. The Nazi suppression of freedom of thought and speech during the 1930's in Germany was a great burden to bear as several members of the Freiburg faculty were forced to leave the Fatherland. One of his last acts in international medicine was the delivery of the Finlayson Memorial Lecture in Glasgow in 1938 on the history of circulation. At his death from bronchial asthma which had plagued him for years, Aschoff was one of the last of the German school of pathologists whose students, in turn, were to enjoy the new pathology which utilized the experimental tools of electromicroscopy, isotopes, histochemistry, fluorescent tracers, and programming for computer analysis.

1. Schmidt, M. B.: Ludwig Aschoff (Ger), *Zbl Allg Path* 80:1-5, 1942.

2. Aschoff, L.: Observations on the Pathological Anatomy of Cholelithiasis (Ger), *Verh Deutsch Ges Path* 9:41-48, 1905, excerpt translated by E. Longar.

3. Aschoff, L.: Myocarditis (Ger), *Verh Deutsch Ges Path* 8:46-53, 1904, translated in Willius, F. A., and Keys, T. E.: *Cardiac Classics,* St. Louis: C. V. Mosby Co., 1941.

4. Aschoff, L.: Reticulo-endothelial System (Ger), *Ergebn Inn Med Kinderheilk* 26:1-118, 1924, summarized in Aschoff, L.: *Lectures on Pathology,* New York: P. B. Hoeber, Inc., 1924.

Otto Folin (1867-1934)

OTTO KNUT OLOF FOLIN, Hamilton Kuhn professor of biological chemistry at Harvard Medical School, was born in Asheda in southern Sweden to a large, thrifty, but relatively poor, family.[1] His mother, upon whom the family depended for support, seems to have exerted the greatest effect upon her son. After qualifying for licensure in nursing and midwifery, she became the official midwife of a large district. When it came time

Countway Medical Library, Boston

for Otto to receive his schooling, his mother arranged for him to attend a private Lutheran school where his training emphasized mathematics and German. Preceded by two brothers and an aunt, he followed the immigrant path to America at the age of 15, and joined his brother Axel in Stillwater, Minn, a lumber town on the St. Croix River. There he attended a country school to learn English, supported himself with odd jobs, including that of night clerk in a hotel, and worked on the log boom or in the harvest fields in the summer. After six years, he met the requirements of the eight-year course in elementary schooling.

Folin became a naturalized citizen in 1890, graduated from high school at the age of 21, enrolled at the University of Minnesota, and, still supporting himself, received the BS degree in 1892. Science and especially the chemistry courses held particular interest. He also showed considerable proficiency in English for a foreign-born student, and, in his senior year, edited the school newspaper. For graduate work he attended the University of Chicago, choosing chemistry as his major and physiology

as his minor subject. Julius Stieglitz, an outstanding physical chemist and Folin's faculty advisor, was working at that time on molecular rearrangements in organic compounds. As a result, Folin worked for his doctoral thesis, *On Urethane,* which was published in the *American Chemical Journal.* However, Folin was not particularly interested in theoretical chemistry, nor had he the background knowledge needed to pursue the mechanism of such reactions discovered several years later by others.

In 1896, Folin returned to Europe, spending considerable time in Hammarsten's laboratory at the University of Uppsala and the remainder in Salkowski's laboratory in Berlin, where he began his analytical work in the field to which he made his greatest contributions. The following year, with Kossel at Marburg, he investigated the hydrolysis of proteins. In 1898, he was awarded the PHD degree by the University of Chicago. After employment for a short time in a commercial laboratory, he accepted an assistant professorship of chemistry at West Virginia University.

In 1900, Folin was offered the opportunity to plan, at McLean Insane Hospital in the suburbs of Boston, a biochemistry laboratory which was designed to study the excretion products of the mentally ill. There he became familiar with several of the natural scientists at Harvard Medical School. In order to pursue this study effectively, he found it necessary to devise micromethods for the determination of inorganic constituents of the urine, a program in which the Duboscq colorimeter was maximally exploited. Colorimetry was thereby introduced into routine clinical-chemical procedures. With the development of micromethods, Folin was able to study the end-products of intermediary metabolism and the concentration of the constituents of the blood in health and disease. While his studies on intermediary metabolism, particularly of proteins, did not result in great contributions to our understanding of this phase of living matter, his contributions to the micro or semimicro procedures for determination of blood constituents were of inestimable value in the clinical evaluation of disease processes. His large bibliography included inquiries into a variety of biochemical problems and analyses of organic and inorganic constituents of body fluids and excretory substances.

Folin's investigations were interrupted temporarily by surgery for a mixed tumor of the parotid gland on the left and the severance of the facial nerve during surgical removal. There was no recurrence of the tumor, but it left him with a permanent facial disfigurement. In 1907, he joined the faculty of Harvard Medical School as an associate professor of biological chemistry and two years later was promoted to full professor and chairman of the department, a position that he held until his death. Always a stimulating teacher and a highly regarded chief, Folin attracted a large coterie of graduate students to his laboratory.

A description of the preparation of the protein-free filtrate of blood, the base for his quantitative procedures for the concentration of uric acid, sugar, noprotein nitrogen, urea, creatine, and creatinine, was published in 1919. The introduction to "A System of Blood Analysis" by Folin and Wu contains the following.[2]

The main purpose of the research recorded in this paper has been to combine a number of different analytical procedures into a compact system of blood analysis, the starting point for which should be a protein-free blood filtrate suitable for the largest possible number of different determinations. It scarcely need be pointed out what a convenience and advantage it would be if one could take the whole of a sample of blood and at once prepare from it a protein-free blood filtrate suitable for the determination of all or nearly all the water-soluble constituents, non-protein nitrogen, urea, creatinine, creatine, uric acid, and sugar.

In connection with our work on the problem we have also had in mind the desirability of reducing as far as practicable the amount of blood filtrate to be used for each determination, for by means of such reduction the total usefulness of the filtrate is correspondingly increased. There is no hard and fast limit as to the extent to which this reduction can be carried. It is doubtful, however, whether it is sound analytical practice regularly to use the smallest possible amount of material for each determination; whether, for example, blood filtrates corresponding to only 0.1 cc. of blood should regularly be used for non-protein nitrogen determinations, because it

may sometimes be advantageous or necessary to take no more. In this paper we deal chiefly with a semi microchemical scale of work representing only a moderate reduction of the quantities ordinarily taken for colorimetric work with the 60 mm. Duboscq colorimeter.

Both lengthy and brief communications discuss the uric acid problem. The finding of an elevated uric acid concentration in a relative of a gouty patient was one of the earliest reports of asymptomatic hyperuricemia in a gouty family.[3] In another communication, Folin offered sound clinical advice on the interpretation of hyperuricemia in the differential diagnosis of gouty arthritis and other joint disorders.[4]

Since it is by no means excluded that the blood in diseases other than gout may not, occasionally at least, carry more than the normal amount of uric acid, the diagnosis of gout by means of uric acid determinations is by no means so simple or certain that numerous and serious blunders will not occur. In the course of several hundred uric acid determinations made on many different kinds of human blood during the past three years we have become convinced that even exact quantitative uric acid determinations are not by themselves an adequate protection against frequent mistakes in the differential diagnosis of gout and other joint diseases.

His Harvey lecture given in the 1919-1920 series dwelt on blood analyses and their application. He was a member of the National Academy of Sciences, a charter member of the American Society of Biological Chemists, and, in 1909, its third president.

He served for many years on the editorial board of the *Journal of Biological Chemistry;* his laboratory manual of biochemistry went through five editions. His pupils included W. R. Bloor, Langley Porter, Cyrus Fisk, W. Rappleye, H. Berglund, A. Svedberg, Harry Trimble, A. D. Marenzi, W. Denis, A. B. Macallum, S. Bliss, P. A. Shaffer, and H. Malmros. The honorary DSC degree was granted by Washington University and the University of Chicago and the honorary MD by the University of Lund, Sweden. His portrait hangs in the faculty room at Harvard Medical School.

1. Shaffer, P. A.: Otto Folin 1867-1934, in *Biographical Memoirs*, Washington DC: National Academy of Sciences 1951, vol 26, pp 47-82.

2. Folin, O., and Wu, H.: A System of Blood Analysis, *J Biol Chem* 38:81-110, 1919.

3. Folin, O., and Lyman, H.: On the Influence of Phenylquinolin Carbonic Acid (Atophan) on the Uric Acid Elimination, *J. Pharmacol Exp Ther* 4:539-546, 1912-1913.

4. Folin, O., and Denis, W.: The Diagnostic Value of Uric Acid Determinations in Blood, *Arch Intern Med* 16:33-37, 1915.

Composite by G. Bako

Sir Henry Dale (1875-1968)

HENRY HALLETT DALE, one of the most productive natural scientists in contemporary England, and endowed with extraordinary longevity, was exceptional also in never holding a senior academic post.[1] Dale was a Londoner by birth and, after early schooling in London and Cambridge, began his university studies in Cambridge in 1894. There he spent four years in undergraduate work and two years as Coutts-Trotter Student in Trinity College, a humanistic college with a centuries old scientific tradition in a University which at that time was one of the great centers for physiology in Europe. Included among the teachers and investigators were Michael Foster, W. H. Gaskell, and J. N. Langley. Begining with independent research on the galvanotactic and chemotactic attraction of infusoria, Dale's work reflects his exposure to highly competent and productive investigators of the involuntary or autonomic nervous system.

Dale returned to London in 1900 and completed his medical training at St. Bartholomew's Hospital. Two years later, when faced with the decision of further clinical work versus basic investigation, he chose the latter. Subsequently, he joined the department of physiology in University College under Starling and Bayliss, being supported first by the Lewes Studentship and later by a Sharpey Studentship. Near the end of the first studentship, he spent a few months in Paul Ehrlich's Institute in Frankfurt, described by Dale as only moderately rewarding.

In 1904, an unusual offer was made to Dale by the Wellcome Physiological Research Laboratory situated in Herne Hill, London, and sponsored by an industrial entrepreneur. The laboratory had its inception in 1880 when Henry S. Wellcome and Silas K. Burroughs, fellow Americans, established the pharmaceutical firm of Burroughs Wellcome & Company. Wellcome became sole proprietor of the business and, in 1894, set aside funds for the research institute. Little of scientific significance was produced in the laboratory until Dale accepted the appointment as director of research in 1904, albeit against the warning of well-meaning friends. Dale's desire for freedom to pursue basic research, unrelated to the development of pharmacologic products, was respected at all times. As an interested observer Wellcome suggested the investigation of ergot, an idea which, upon acceptance and pursuit, led directly or indirectly to each of Dale's major contributions in later years. These include his studies on the sympatholytic actions of ergotoxine, the oxytoxic actions of extracts of the neurohypophysis, the pharmacologic effects of the pressor amines, the relation of histamine to allergic reactions, and the chemical transmission of the nerve impulse by humoral agents.[2] After a decade with the Wellcome Laboratories, Dale transferred his activities to the National Institute for Medical Research in Hampstead, where he served first as member and from 1928 to 1942 as director. Continuing his research without any slackening of pace, he was Fullerian professor of chemistry and director of laboratories of the Royal Institution and a member of the Medical Research Council from 1942 to 1946; while in his "retirement" years his counsel on committees and programs kept his alert mind as active as in the decades of great investigative fervor.

Dale's research and scientific communications cover a wide range of subjects and identify him as one of the outstanding physiologists and pharmacologists of the first half of the 20th century. His broad interests made him cognizant of, or conversant with, the essential problems in most phases of experimental medicine. The planning of his research, collection of valid data, and contributions for publication disclose a remarkable clarity of mind, great intellectual curiosity, and contagious enthusiasm. An excellent teacher, Dale by example made his students familiar with proper patterns for the development of scientific thinking, the art of observation, and the technique of experimentation. A capacity to turn detailed laboratory drudgery into a delightful intellectual exercise was noteworthy. Each of the five contributions to the understanding of vital physiological or pathological processes noted above has been selected for reference because of its merit. The action on the uterus by the extract of posterior lobe of the pituitary of the ox, the oxytocic action of pituitrin, was resolved in a communication comparing the activity of pituitary and suprarenal extracts. Dale previously had demonstrated that sympathomimetic amines inhibited uterine tone and contractions in the nonpregnant cat but stimulated them in the pregnant cat. In the report on neurohypophysial extracts he noted:[3]

I regard it, then, as of great significance that in the uterus of the cat, as well as in that of the dog, the guinea-pig, the rat, and the rabbit, I have always observed, in all functional conditions, powerful tonic contraction as the effect of applying pituitary extract. . . . So little, in my experience, is the effect dependent on the condition of the uterus as regards oestrum or pregnancy, that the uterus of a virgin, half-grown cat responded to the pituitary extract by as marked a tonic contraction as was given by any of the numerous pregnant or multiparous organs examined.

It is clear from the foregoing that the characteristic action of extracts of the posterior lobe of the pituitary body is stimulation of plain muscle fibres. Different organs containing plain muscle show a varying sensitiveness of response to the extract, the arteries, the uterus and the spleen being conspicuously affected.

While Dale was still at the Wellcome Laboratories, the mechanism of anaphylactic shock was investigated, in collaboration with his brilliant young associate P. P. Laidlaw. The study of histamine, an amine derivative from histidine, disclosed a remarkable resemblance between its production of vital symptoms in different species and anaphylactic shock in the same species. The importance of capillary dilatation and capillary permeability as a clinical problem was noted, as well as the similarity of symptoms of anaphylactic shock in humans and histamine shock in animals; namely, sudden hypotension, bronchial spasm, respiratory impairment, and right heart failure.[4]

β-IMINAZOLYLETHYLAMINE [histamine] is the amine which is produced when carbon dioxide is split off from histidine. . . . The activity of β-iminazolylethylamine was discovered in the course of the investigation of ergot and its extracts by G. Barger and one of us, who attributed this structure to a base which they obtained, and which in minute doses produced tonic contraction of the uterus.

In rodents the effects are very different in the case of intravenous and of subcutaneous injection. In a rabbit of medium size an injection of two mgms. intravenously (ear-vein) caused marked prostration, the respiration becoming irregular and laboured and the heart-beat intermittent and feeble. . . . Death was apparently due, therefore, to right-sided heart-failure, associated with, but apparently not wholly dependent on, respiratory disturbance.

In large guinea-pigs, weighing 800-1,000 grams, injection of 0.5 mgms. into the external saphenous vein caused death in a few minutes. The immediate effect was a marked respiratory impediment, resulting in violent but largely ineffective inspiratory efforts, during which the lower ribs were drawn in. . . . Death was clearly due to asphyxia, evidently resulting from progressive obstruction to the respiration, sufficient in its early stages to prevent the exit of the air sucked into the lungs by the violent inspiratory spasms, and later becoming complete. The larger the initial dose, and, therefore, the earlier the obstruction became complete, the less pronounced the distension of the lungs. Such an effect could only be due to constriction of the bronchioles by spasm of their muscular coats, though the effect would be aided by increased bronchial secretion.

The plethysmographic results thus show clearly that the fall of arterial pressure is mainly due to a general vasodilatation, in which the arterioles of the kidney do not participate.

Concerning this vaso-dilator mechanism we know definitely only that it is localised at the periphery.

Near the end of World War I, A. N. Richards, of Philadelphia, joined Dale at the Lister Institute in London. The joint effort concerned the vasodilator action of histamine, which caused anaphylactic shock similar to traumatic shock from tissue injury on the battleground. The irreversible fall of blood pressure was found to be related to stagnation of blood in the dilated capillaries of the intestines and to concentration of blood in the large vessels from loss of fluid through the capillary walls. The experimental observations were made on the cat by use of the air-oncometer for viscera or the plethysmograph for the perfused limb. Selected conclusions were as follows:[5]

1. The vasodilator actions of histamine, adrenaline and acetylcholine are purely peripheral effects on the blood vessels, independent of the integrity of any nervous connexion. The blood vessels are usually rendered abnormally sensitive to these actions by complete degeneration of the nerve-supply.

5. We conclude that the vasodilator effect of histamine, and probably that of adrenaline, are due to relaxation of the tone of the capillaries, while that of acetyl-choline is due to action on arteries. Histamine has a constrictor effect on arteries; the better known vasoconstrictor effect of adrenaline probably involves both arteries and capillaries.

9. The possibility is considered that substances with histamine-like action are produced by activity or injury of the tissues.

The Nobel Prize in physiology for 1936 was shared by Dale with Otto Loewi for their related investigations on the chemical transmisson of the nerve impulse. The suggestion that transmission might be affected by the release of a specific chemical substance was first offered by T. R. Elliot in the physiology laboratory in Cambridge, in which Dale had assisted with a few experiments. A decade later Dale discovered the parasympathetic action of acetylcholine and its inhibition by small doses of atropine. Further development of the subject was interrupted by World War II. In 1921, Loewi demonstrated that the vagus nerve liberates an inhibitory substance, similar to acetylcholine, which retains its special property when transferred to another animal. These and other studies further implicated acetylcholine and in the Linnacre Lectures delivered at St. John's College, Cambridge, in 1934, Dale noted:[6]

The conception of the transmission of a nervous impulse across a synapse by the release of such a substance, and by the action of this substance as the direct stimulant of the ganglion cell, though it satisfies my own desire to bring the nicotine action of acetylcholine into the physiological picture, is not without its difficulties, and it will have to justify itself to win general acceptance. One thing is clear—namely, that when preganglionic impulses arrive in the ganglion acetylcholine is there released in such an amount that it not only may be but *must* stimulate the ganglion cells to their only known form of activity, in the output of impulses in the post-ganglionic fibres, corresponding to those which arrive in the preganglionic fibres.

As a pharmacologist, Dale made important contributions to therapeutics with his program on biological standardization. The need for biological assay of the posterior lobe extract of the pituitary body was apparent shortly after its discovery. When the supplies of neoarsphenamine were interrupted by World War I, manufacturers in Britain were not able to produce as potent a product as did the Germans, and the necessary standardization was arranged by Dale. Insulin was the third product that came under his scrutiny shortly after its discovery in Toronto. In the development of an international standardization program, the Health Committee of the League of Nations arranged a Second International Conference on Biological Standardization of Certain Remedies in Geneva in 1925, with Dale as its chairman. International standards were agreed upon by representatives of several countries for thyroid gland, ergot, digitalis, anthelmintics, and vitamins as well as the above preparations. A concluding study of vital clinical importance, in 1936, led to the use by Walker of physostgmine and later neostigmine for the control of symptoms of myasthenia gravis—another example of Dale's interest in humoral substances acting in health and disease.

The honors received by Dale are commensurate with his scientific contributions. He was a member of many English and foreign scientific organizations, was president of the Royal Society of England for five years (1940-1945), and received the Order of Merit from the King in 1944. He was a trustee of the British Museum and a fellow of the Royal College of Physicians, as well as being elected honorary or corresponding member of many foreign, scientific, scholarly societies. Honorary degrees were conferred by Innsbruck, Louvain, Liége, Brussels, Utrecht, Paris, Ghent, Graz, Toronto, Kingston, Edinburgh, Belfast, Cambridge, Dublin, Durham, Manchester, Oxford, Sheffield, London, Princeton, Western Ontario, McGill, and Leeds.

1. Dale, H. H.: Autobiographical Sketch, *Perspect Biol Med* 1:125-137 (winter) 1958.

2. Dale, H. H.: *Adventures in Physiology*, London: Pergamon Press, 1953.

3. Dale, H. H.: The Action of Extracts of the Pituitary Body, *Biochem J* 4:427-447, 1909.

4. Dale, H. H., and Laidlaw, P. P.: The Physiological Action of β-Iminazolylethylamine, *J Physiol* 41:318-344, 1910-1911.

5. Dale, H. H., and Richards, A. N.: The Vasodilator Action of Histamine and of Some Other Substances, *J Physiol* 52:110-165, 1918-1919.

6. Dale, H. H.: Chemical Transmission of the Effects of Nerve Impulses, *Brit Med J* 1:835-841 (May 12) 1934.

Otto Meyerhof (1884-1951)

OTTO MEYERHOF, Nobel laureate in physiology or medicine, was born in Hanover, Germany, the son of a merchant. He studied in Freiburg, Berlin, Strasbourg, and Heidelberg,[1] receiving the MD degree in 1909, with an inaugural thesis on psychological theory —the first of several contributions on abstract or psychological thinking. Following graduation, Meyerhof entered the medical clinic of Ludolf Krehl; there he first met Otto Warburg, biochemist of note who had a great influence in directing his research into natural phenomena. In the following years they collaborated (especially on the metabolism of sea-urchin eggs) at the

Composite by G. Bako

Marine Zoological Laboratory in Naples, an international meeting place for biologists.

In 1912, Meyerhof settled in Kiel as privatdocent, and subsequently began his biochemical and physiological investigations of muscular contraction. He extended the observations of Fletcher and Hopkins on the formation of lactic acid in the living cell and developed a comprehensive theory of the relation of lactic acid, glycogen, oxygen uptake, and heat and tension production in the conversion of chemical energy. A. V. Hill, meanwhile, was concerned with heat production during muscle activity and concluded that the heat involved was proportional to work performed; whereas a measurable portion of the total heat was evolved during recovery. Meyerhof showed that muscle glycogen is the precursor of lactic acid in the absence of oxygen, while in the presence of oxygen, only a portion of the lactic acid formed during anaerobic contraction is oxidized and a small remainder converted to carbon dioxide and water. This reaction furnishes energy to reconvert the remaining larger percentage of lactic acid to glycogen. In this research, Meyerhof confirmed and extended Pasteur's hypothesis, advanced half a century earlier, that fermentation or glycolysis metabolism in the absence of oxygen, may substitute for respiration.[2] For these and other studies on the cyclic character of energy transformation in the living cell, Meyerhof and Hill shared the Nobel Prize in physiology or medicine in 1923. The joint citation by the chairman of the Nobel committee of the Royal Caroline Institute concluded as follows:[3]

Professors Hill and Meyerhof. Your brilliant discoveries concerning the vital phenomena of muscles supplement each other in a most happy manner. It has given a special satisfaction to be able to reward these two series of discoveries at the same time, since it gives a clear expression of one of the ideas upon which the will of Alfred Nobel was founded, that is, the conception that the greatest cultural advances are independent of the splitting-up of mankind into contending nations. I also feel confident that you will be glad to know that the proposition which has led to this award of the Nobel Prize originated from a German scientist who, in spite of all difficulties and disasters, has clearly recognized the main object of Alfred Nobel.

In 1924, Meyerhof joined the Kaiser Wilhelm Institute in Berlin-Dahlem and extended his researches on the dynamics of muscle activity.[4] He studied enzymes and coenzymes of previously unknown intermediates—the initial work leading to a concept of the fundamental unity and similarity of metabolic processes in all living cells. Further understanding of the mechanism of glycolysis was based upon the discovery of phosphocreatine by Fiske and SubbaRow and by the Eggletons and the discovery of adenosine triphosphate (ATP), which was shown to yield energy for muscular contraction more directly than the production of lactic acid. Also, Lundsgaard of Copenhagen found that muscle poisoned with iodoacetic acid, contracts without producing lactic acid, but at the expense of phosphocreatine breakdown. Further observations in Meyerhof's laboratory showed that the breakdown of ATP precedes that of phosphocreatine and serves as the primary source of energy in muscular contraction. Thus, both lactic acid production and phosphocreatine breakdown participate indirectly in muscular contraction and provide for the resynthesis of ATP. It is now known that ATP participates widely in energy transfer in cells, with ability to be converted into mechanical, osmotic, or electrical work as well as into light.

In 1929, Meyerhof became chief of the department of physiology at the Institute of Medical Research in Heidelberg under the administrative direction of Krehl. For the first time facilities were provided commensurate with his investigative genius. Pupils from many countries, attracted by his laboratory, enjoyed his gracious hospitality, benefited from his intellectual brilliance, and appreciated his philosophy of science. Meyerhof, an authority on Goethe's scientific contributions early in his career, also wrote poetry and greatly loved painting and literature.

After the rise of the Nazis to power, Meyerhof was able to forestall persecution as a Jew; however, in 1938, he chose voluntary exile in Paris and continued his researches at the Institute of Biology and Physical Chemistry. After the invasion of France by the Germans in 1940, he was brought to the United States with the help of American friends and funds from the Rockefeller Foundation. Subsequently, Meyerhof was appointed research professor of physiological chemistry at the University of Pennsylvania and became an American citizen in 1946. In 1927, he received an honorary LLD degree from Edinburgh, in 1937, foreign membership in the Royal Society of London, and in 1949, membership in the National Academy of Sciences.

1. Nachmansohn, D.: Ochoa, S.; and Lipmann, F. A.: Otto Meyerhof: 1884-1951, *Science* 115:365-368 (April 4) 1952.
2. Meyerhof, O.: The Presence of Coferments in Muscle and Their Significance in Respiration (Ger) *Hoppe Seyler Z Physiol Chem* 101:165-175, 1918.
3. *Nobel Lectures Including Presentation Speeches and Laureates' Biographies, Physiology or Medicine 1922-1941*, New York: Elsevier Publishing Co., 1965.
4. Meyerhof, O.: *Chemical Dynamics of Life Phenomena*, Philadelphia: J. B. Lippincott Co., 1924.

Composite by G. Bako

Casimir Funk (1884-1967)

CASIMIR FUNK, discoverer of thiamine, the first vitamin to be isolated, was born in Warsaw, Poland, but spent the greater portion of his professional days first in England, then France, and finally in the United States.[1] As a child he was introduced to the fundamentals of biology and medicine by his parents; his father was a dermatologist; whereas his mother before marriage had cherished a desire to enter medicine. Thus, when Casimir left for higher education in the University of Geneva, his course was set on botany, zoology, and comparative anatomy. His studies were continued the following years in Bern, where he stayed for more than three years, attending lectures in chemistry, physics, zoology, and botany, and where he obtained the PHD in 1904. Funk was handicapped by a congenital dislocation of the hip. While his affluent parents sought professional counsel for its correction in several countries, he was exposed to various foreign cultures and languages. Spending considerable time in Germany and Austria, he became as fluent in German as in Polish; while in Switzerland he added French to his language accomplishments, and, finally, English was acquired through reading and social contacts.

In 1904, Funk set out for the Pasteur Institute in Paris to study biochemistry, then second only to bacteriology in importance to the Institute. The gaiety of Paris and the cultural amenities were as interesting as the hours spent in research and scientific advancement. He went to Berlin, in 1906, to spend a year with Emil Fischer, but it was Abderhalden, one of Fischer's brilliant assistants and a few years older than Funk, who accepted him as a research associate. In 1907, upon Abderhalden's recommendation, Funk obtained a position as biochemist at the Municipal Hospital in Wiesbaden; there he conducted his first studies on diets deficient in selected amino acids. A year later, Funk returned to Berlin to work again with Abderhalden, but, after disappointment, frustration, and a few months at the Charité Hospital, he left for the Lister Institute in London. An assignment from C. J. Martin, the director, to study the cause of beriberi, a disorder of great interest to the English because of their possessions in the Far East, was the incentive which led to Funk's critical studies on vitamins.

In Funk's initial investigations he pursued Martin's theory that beriberi developed from an amino acid deficiency. However, the isolation of the protein products in polished rice and in rice polishings and comparison of the effect of the two extracts on the pigeon, an animal which rapidly developed polyneuritis, led to negative results. After several weeks of intensive investigation, he was convinced that an unidentified factor present in rice polishings and absent in polished rice probably was neither a protein nor an amino acid but some other nitrogenous substance. As the chemical fractionation continued, an active antiberiberi substance was found, which was not a ferment, but a compound belonging to the "pyrimidines." By repeated recrystallization, a potent substance with a constant boiling point was obtained. For this work, Funk received the doctor of science degree from the University of London. The initial report, six pages long, which appeared in the *Journal of Physiology,* contained the following summary.[2]

(1) Polyneuritis of birds as shown by Eykman, Gryns, Fraser and Stanton, is due to the lack of an essential substance in the diet. The substance is only present in minute amounts, probably not

more than 1 grm. per kilo of rice.

(2) The substance which is absent in polished rice and is contained in rice-polishings is an organic base which is completely precipitated by phosphotungstic acid and by silver nitrate and baryta. It is partially precipitated by mercury chloride in alcoholic solution in the presence of choline and is not precipitated by platinum chloride in alcoholic solution.

Reasons for provisionally regarding the active substance as a body giving a crystalline nitrate which has the percentage composition of 55.63%C, 5.29%H and 7.68%N are adduced, but by the time the search had approached the final stages the material became exhausted; duplicate analyses could not be made and but few animal experiments performed.

The chemical nature of the curative substance could not be further investigated immediately but larger quantities of raw material are being worked up.

(3) The curative dose of the active substance is small; a quantity of substance which contains 4 mgr. of nitrogen cured pigeons.

The active substance is now known as thiamine, or vitamin B_1. Funk was convinced that more than one compound was present in rice polishings; from the same fractions which yielded thiamine he isolated another substance in crystalline form and showed it to be nicotinic acid (niacin). In a subsequent communication Funk coined the term "vitamine-fraction" for the substances he had investigated, believing that these were amine compounds necessary for life. The British preferred the term, "accessory food factors," but "vitamin" without the "e" has persisted. The term "vitamine-fraction" was used in the title and repeated in the conclusions of the second report.[3]

1. The vitamine-fraction from yeast had been separated into three substances: a substance of the formula $C_{24}H_{19}O_9N_5$, a substance of the formula $C_{29}H_{23}O_9N_5$ and what appears to be nicotinic acid (m-pyridine-carboxylic acid). The first substance mixed with nicotinic acid seems to be necessary for curing pigeons.

2. The vitamine-fraction from rice-polishings has up to the present been separated in two substances: one of the formula $C_{26}H_{20}O_9N_4$ and nicotinic acid. The results concerning their curative power will be published after the chemical investigation of all the fractions has been completed.

Funk's monograph, *Die Vitamine,* appeared from Wiesbaden in 1914.[4] The second German edition was translated into English eight years later. By then much of the fundamental work had been done upon vitamin B_1 in beriberi and its manifestations, vitamin C in scurvy, and vitamin D in rickets. He supported Goldberger in his belief that pellagra was a deficiency disease, noting that some nutritionists had observed the development of pellagra on a diet that was productive of beriberi but deficient in substances present in grain polishings.

Funk was as restless in maturity as he was early in life. An opening for a biochemist at the Cancer Hospital Research Institute in London in 1913 attracted him, but, in 1915 with the first World War one year old, he came to the United States and continued his research at Memorial Hospital and the Loomis Laboratory of Cornell Medical College. Between 1921 and 1923 he was an associate in the department of biochemistry at the College of Physicians and Surgeons, Columbia University. Then followed four years as a biochemist in Poland at the Warsaw School of Hygiene, which was aided by financial support from the International Health Board of the Rockefeller Foundation. Funk returned to the United States in 1927, having held full-time or part-time jobs with various chemical or pharmaceutical companies in France and the United States. He remained in industry for the rest of his professional days. While working in a pharmaceutical laboratory in Paris, he became interested in the sex hormones. Measuring the characteristics of the comb of the castrated cock, Funk and associates detected appreciable quantities of a male hormone in the urine from mature males, one of the earlier advances in the isolation of the sex hormones.[5]

In the course of the work we noticed that the male hormone (testiculin) shows chemical properties similar to those of estrin. For example, testiculin, like estrin, can be extracted from urine by means of chloroform.

Using urinary extracts, we find that the comb growth is proportional to the amount of hormone present. Changes in size of comb, in turgor and color are plainly noticeable after a few days of treatment.

Urine sample U.M.2, was obtained from men in the prime of life. The curves show how uniform is the effect of this extract on 3 different groups of animals. U.M.3 represents the urine from men of various ages, and U.M.4 from men between

50-70 years of age The variation in hormone content is quite evident.

1. Harow, B.: *Casimir Funk, Pioneer in Vitamins and Hormones,* New York: Dodd, Mead & Co., 1955.

2. Funk, G.: On the Chemical Nature of the Substance Which Cures Polyneuritis in Birds Induced by a Diet of Polished Rice, *J Physiol* 43:395-400, 1911-1912.

3. Funk, C.: Studies on Beri-beri: VII. Chemistry of the Vitamine-Fraction From Yeast and Rice-Polishings, *J Physiol* 46:173-179, 1913.

4. Funk, C.: *The Vitamines* (Ger), Wiesbaden: J. F. Bergmann, 1914, translated from 2nd German edition by H. E. Dubin, Baltimore: Wiliams & Wilkins Co., 1922.

5. Funk, C., and Harrow, B.: The Male Hormone: II., *Proc Soc Exp Biol Med* 26:569-570, 1929.

National Library of Medicine

Jay McLean (1890-1957)

JAY McLEAN, who as a second-year medical student isolated an anticoagulant substance which was later named heparin, seemed to have expended his intellectual energies early in his professional days. He encountered and overcame substantial obstacles in preparing for a medical career, but his scientific maturation was not commensurate with his initial and only success in laboratory investigation.

McLean was born in San Francisco into a physician's family.[1] His father died four years later; the earthquake and fire of 1906 destroyed the family home and ruined his stepfather's business. Lacking parental support, he turned to interim nonprofessional jobs while completing his basic education. After graduating from Lowell High School in San Francisco, McLean finished two years of undergraduate work at the Berkeley campus of the University of California. He then stopped school and worked for 15 months in a Mojave Desert gold mine. Returning to Berkeley for a third year, he gained a small financial reserve by working in the recorder's office with Robert Sproul, later president of the University of California. McLean also held part-time jobs in the college infirmary and in the museum of invertebrate zoology. He scrubbed the decks of ferry boats crossing San Francisco Bay and clerked in the railway mail cars between Oakland and Denver.

McLean graduated from the University of California with a BS degree in 1914, having completed first year medical school requirements except for organic chemistry. Financially indigent again, he worked in the oil fields for more than a year and in the fall of 1915 left for Johns Hopkins medical school. In spite of initial uncertainty regarding his qualifications for matriculation as a second year medical student, he became duly registered. However, instead of following the prescribed medical school course, he spent the year in the physiological laboratory of W. H. Howell, with the hope of basing his clinical accomplishments upon physiology rather than anatomy. His aim was a surgical career. Howell's primary research interest at that time was the study of thromboplastic substances, especially kephalin (cephalin), a crude extract of a powerful coagulant obtained from brain tissue.

McLean was assigned space in Howell's laboratory where other workers included Donald Hooker, Cecil Drinker, and Stanley Cobb; each was reluctant to accept him as a scientific colleague. He devoted seven days a week to the extraction and purification of the thromboplastic principle, using brain substance first, and later, extracts of heart called "cuorin" and extracts from liver called "heparphosphatide." As the ether-soluble and the alcohol-insoluble agents were refined, ample evidence of thromboplastic properties was obtained. However, an additional unknown biologic factor appeared in the semirefined substances as they were tested from time to time during storage. As the cephalin from the heart and liver deteriorated and gave up their thromboplastic activity, an anticoagulant property appeared in a serum-plasma mixture. The development and exploitation of this substance, discovered incidentally and named "heparin" in 1918, was left to Howell, his co-workers, and other investigators in America and Europe.[2]

McLean's communication, entitled "The Thromboplastic Action of Cephalin," mentioned in a single paragraph the properties of the relatively crude substance.[3]

The heparaphosphatid on the other hand when purified by many precipitations in alcohol at 60° has no thromboplastic action and in fact shows a marked power to inhibit the coagulation. The anticoagulating action of this phosphatid is being studied and will be reported upon later. Cuorin and heparphosphatid when dry have no odor, but when moist with warm alcohol have a characteristic odor common to both. It is possible that on further purification the heparphosphatid may be shown to be identical with cuorin.

Before receiving the MD degree from Johns Hopkins in 1919, McLean served for a short time in the medical corps of the French army during World War I. He continued his work on the thromboplastic action of cephalin at the John Herr Musser Department of Research Medicine, University of Pennsylvania, from which he received the MS in 1917. For three years he served as assistant surgeon and instructor in surgery at Johns Hopkins, and from 1922 to 1924 pursued postgraduate studies at Leipzig and Paris as a National Research Fellow. Later he was appointed instructor and fellow at the College of Physicians and Surgeons, Columbia University, lecturer in the New York Polyclinic Medical School, research surgeon at Memorial Hospital for Cancer and Allied Diseases, and director of the Bureau of Cancer Control of the District of Columbia, Department of Health. He then turned to radiology, becoming affiliated with the department of surgical research at Ohio State College of Medicine and the Grant Hospital,

Columbus, Ohio. McLean was certified by the American Board of Radiology in 1943. From 1949 to 1957, he was director of the Savannah, Ga, Tumor Clinic.

McLean lived to see purified heparin become an indispensable substance in the experimental laboratory and a critical agent in the extracorporeal circuit for hemodialysis and open-heart surgery; he witnessed the development of the coumarins and other anticoagulants in the management of vascular diseases. His goal in obtaining medical training at Johns Hopkins Medical School was realized, but his intellectual impact in developing surgery upon physiological principles was of little moment.

1. McLean, J.: The Discovery of Heparin, *Circulation* 19:75-78, 1959.

2. Howell, W. H., and Holt, L. E.: Two New Factors in Blood Coagulation—Heparin and Pro-antithrombin, *Amer J Physiol* 47:328-341, 1919.

3. McLean, J.: The Thromboplastic Action of Cephalin, *Amer J Physiol* 1:250-257, 1916.

Composite by G. Bako

Caesar Peter Moeller Boeck
(1845-1917)

CAESAR BOECK, who described the cutaneous lesions and their histologic structure of the condition sometimes identified as Besnier-Boeck-Schaumann disease, was born in

Lier, Norway.[1] He graduated in 1871 from Christiania Medical School (Oslo) and pursued general practice for several years, with a special interest in dermatology. In 1874, he spent a year on the Continent, mainly in dermatology clinics, and particularly in Vienna, where he attended the lectures of the aging Hebra. Upon returning to Oslo Boeck was assistant for three years in the dermatologic clinic of the Rikshospitalet and in 1889 was made chief of the clinic. He reached professorial rank at the University in 1895, became a full professor in 1896, dean of the faculty in 1907, and professor emeritus in 1915. Meanwhile, in 1880, he founded the journal that continues today as the *Tidsskrift for den Norske Laegeforening*.

Boeck, an industrious investigator, wrote on a number of dermatologic conditions, including the tuberculids, exanthema, necrotic acne, cutaneous leprosy, syphilis, pemphigus, and molluscum contagiosum. His essay in English on "The Nature of Lupus Erythematosus," attributing the disease to tuberculosis, was reprinted by the New Sydenham Society of London in 1900. His best-known work, entitled "Multiple Benign Sarkoid of the Skin," from which the term "sarcoidosis" stemmed, later modified by him to "benign, military lupoid," appeared simultaneously in Norwegian and English.

One of the first cases of the entity was observed by Jonathan Hutchinson in 1869 and described in 1875. Later he added 10 cases to his series. In 1889, Besnier examined a patient with the affliction, referred historically to the initial description by Hutchinson, but dissociated the two and called his case "lupus pernio" or a form of lupus erythematosus.[2] Microscopic investigation was not pursued by either physician. The next step in the nosology of the malady was the description by Boeck of enlargement of the axillary, femoral, and cubital lymph nodes and widely distributed cutaneous nodules, with depressed violaceous-colored centers. Two nodules were biopsied and studied microscopically; microorganisms were not discovered. Excerpts from Boeck's report follow.[3]

The skin affection here described is, so far as I am aware, not generally recognized. I have seen two cases in Norway; one in a female many years ago on whose case I have no notes, and the example which forms the subject of this paper.

Clinically, we find in the middle-aged [age 36], pale, thin man, groups of lymph nodes much swollen, and on examination a slight augmentation of the number of white corpuscles. At the same time there exists a widespread, somewhat symmetrical eruption, firm nodules of varying size, on head and extensor surfaces of trunk and extremities. They range in size from a hemp-seed to a bean, and the larger have irregular contours. They involve the whole skin, and are movable with it. . . . The color of the early nodules is bright red, becoming darker and finally yellowish or brown. Slight scaling occurs on older lesions. They show a tendency to peripheral spreading and central depression. . . . The nodules disappear finally leaving as a rule a loss of substance in the skin, which may be white on the face, yellow on the back, and darker at the periphery on the legs. Exudation, ulceration never take place. A papular eruption grouped like lichen planus was seen on the inside of the thigh. A tendency to develop at the site of old injury should be remembered. The symmetry is not such as is found in affections whose localization is evidently determined by central nerve influence. The disease seems to be benign, and disappears under arsenic or perhaps spontaneously.

The histology was also unique. The areas of new growth might be described as perivascular sarcomatoid tissue built up by excessively rapid proliferation of epithelioid connective-tissue cells in the perivascular lymph spaces, with little addition of other varieties. The tumor soon begins to degenerate, and the tissue is rarefied, showing a network of branched connective-tissue cells.

As a preliminary name for the clinical and histological type here described the term, "Multiple Benign Sarkoid" perhaps will not be found unsuitable.

Several years later Schaumann extended the clinical and pathological findings[4] and believed that his name also should be attached to the eponym, a suggestion followed by some. He demonstrated the diffuse character of the disease, involvement of the lungs, spleen, liver, bone, and bone marrow, and called attention to the negative tubercular reaction even though the lesions were similar to tuberculosis. Stressing the benign course of the disease, Schaumann suggested the term "benign granulomatosis" in distinction from malignant granulomas or Hodgkin's disease.

In 1940, Boeck's patient was readmitted to the Dermatology Clinic in Oslo at the age of 80 for symptoms later found to be associated with carcinoma of the kidney with metastases. There was no clinical evidence at that time of cutaneous lesions, nor did the postmortem examination reveal any systemic findings of sarcoidosis. Before death, however, the Kveim reaction was positive, Pirquet's reaction negative.[5] Such terminal observations are consistent with the benign character of the disease, and the positive skin reaction for tuberculosis is an interesting finding in relation to the immunologic resistance.

Boeck was a respected teacher in his school, a consultant in demand in his community, and a recognized investigator in international circles. Having achieved a reputation in the early description of sarcoidosis, he continued to write on the subject throughout the remainder of his professional life. The majority of his communications appeared in German periodicals; some appeared in Scandinavian or English journals. He regularly attended international meetings and, being well versed in German, French, and English, maintained communication with his contemporaries in England and central Europe by frequent visits and regular correspondence. He was an honorary member of the American Dermatological Association and, in 1911, was made Knight of the 1st Class of the Order of St. Olav.

1. Haavaldsen, J.: Caesar Boeck, *Derm Wschr* 65:763-765, 1917.

2. Besnier, E.: Lupus Pernio of the Face (Fr), *Ann Derm Syph* 10:333-336, 1889.

3. Boeck, C.: Multiple Benign Sarkoid of the Skin (Nor), *Norsk Mag Laegevidensk* 14:1321-1334, 1899; *J Cutan Genitourin Dis* 17:543-550 (Dec) 1899.

4. Schauman, J. N.: Study of Lupus Pernio and Its Association With Sarcoidosis and Tuberculosis (Fr), *Ann Derm Syph* 6:357-373, 1916-1917.

5. Danbolt, N.: Re-Examination of Caesar Boeck's First Patient With "Multiple Benign Sarcoid of the Skin," *Schweiz Med Wschr* 77:1149-1150, 1947.

Christian Fenger (1840-1902)

CHRISTIAN FENGER, pathologic anatomist and surgeon to the hospitals of Chicago, influenced the careers of many in their rise to professional stature, some to eminence and fame. Fenger was born in Jutland (Denmark) at Breininggaard, an old estate, for-

merly a monastery, named for the village of Breininge Sogn.[1] One of twelve children, Fenger received some schooling at home, then attended a private school for eight years. One year of engineering was completed in a polytechnic school before he followed the family tradition and turned to medicine at the University of Copenhagen. During his seven years of higher education, a portion of his support was gained through teaching in the high school and instructing medical and dental students. His pursuit of medicine was twice interrupted by war; the first time he served as assistant physician to a Danish battery corps at Assens, in the Schleswig-Holstein War; the second assignment in 1871 was to an ambulance unit in the Franco-Prussian War, where he studied endoscopy of gunshot wounds under a grant from the Royal Danish Ministry of War. Following the armistice pathologic anatomy and surgery were pursued in Vienna for a short time. Upon his return to Denmark, Fenger was appointed prosector to the Communehospital. His thesis on cancer of the stomach was presented for the degree of doctor of medicine in 1874.

A recurring zeal for pathologic anatomy was evidenced by his application for the

University professorship in this subject following the incumbent's death. Discouraged because the vacancy was filled without competition, Fenger went to Alexandria, Egypt, in 1875 as locum tenens for his brother, who took a leave of absence. Upon his brother's return, Christian was appointed to the Board of Health in Cairo, where at various times he investigated trachoma in children, an epizootic among horses and mules, and bilharziosis in the large military hospital. While in Egypt he witnessed the premiere of *Aida,* composed by Verdi for the celebration of the opening of the Suez Canal and in honor of the coming of Napoleon III. Hepatitis forced Fenger to leave Egypt on two occasions; following the second bout, he emigrated to America—a country that he had learned about from association with members of the American colony in Cairo.

Receiving no encouragement to settle in New York, Fenger started west and arrived in Chicago in the fall of 1877. The following excerpts, in his words, identify several professional achievements in the following decades. The short autobiography was prepared in anticipation of receiving the order of the Knight of Dannebrog from King Christian IX of Denmark.[1]

In the spring of 1878 I secured, by means of borrowed money, a place as physician to Cook County Hospital, and here I commenced to give lectures and demonstrations in pathologic anatomy, a science which was unknown to the physicians there.

In 1880 I became curator of the Rush Medical College museum; in 1884, Professor of Surgery in the College of Physicians and Surgeons, and Surgeon-in-Chief at the Passavant Hospital and the German Hospital, when these two hospitals were founded. In 1893 I assumed the professorship of surgery in the Chicago Medical College, later the Northwestern University Medical School, and became surgeon to the Hospital of the Sisters of Mercy. In 1899 I left this medical school in order to fill the chair of Professor of Surgery in Rush Medical College, in affiliation with the University of Chicago, with a surgical service in the Presbyterian Hospital. In 1894 the Norwegians in Chicago erected the Lutheran Tabitha Hospital, and I accepted the position of Surgeon-in-Chief.

The Collected Works of Christian Fenger include fewer than 100 communications, the majority being case reports or descriptions of operations which were submitted to regional or national medical periodicals. Although he spoke eleven languages, his English was faulty and his writing straightforward but unimaginative. In 1881, he described two patients with trichinosis on whom he performed biopsies of the gastrocnemius muscle and identified the infecting parasite.[2]

With a harpoon I took out of the right gastrocnemius muscle about a cubic millimeter of muscular tissue. On microscopic examination this was found to contain three living muscle trichinae, one of which was rolled up in a spiral and apparently about to become encapsulated. The two others were free. Whether the two latter were torn out of newly formed capsules, or were not yet encapsulated I was unable to determine. For the next two months the patient was very weak and pale. Muscular strength returned very slowly, so that it was not until March, more than three months after the inception of the disease, that he was able to walk about the whole day, and think of recommencing work, and even now, about five months after the infection with trichinae, he has not entirely regained his strength.

The description of the "Operation for the Relief of Valve-Formation and Stricture of the Ureter in Hydro- or Pyo-Nephrosis," one of his best surgical contributions, appeared in *The Journal of the American Medical Association.* Consistent with his practice, Fenger presented a thorough historical review of the subject, describing the various methods of others before offering his recommendations for plastic repair.[3]

Exploration of the ureter as to its permeability should be done from the renal wound by a long flexible silver probe (a uterine probe) or an elastic bougie, either olive pointed or not. If the bougie passes into the bladder, the examination is at an end.

A stricture in the ureter, if not too extensive, can be treated by a plastic operation on the plan of the Heinecke-Mikulicz operation for stenosis of the pylorus; namely, longitudinal division of the stricture and transverse union of the longitudinal wound. The method of operating for ureteral stricture seems to me preferable to resection of the strictured part of the ureter (Küster's operation) for the following reason: It is a more economical operation and preferable when the elongation of the ureter is not sufficient to permit the two cut ends of the ureter, after excision of the stricture, not only to come in contact but even to permit of closure and invagination without stretching.

Christian Fenger's influence on his students and associates has been praised by all who have written about him. The blond Norseman, who loved cigars, was blunt but gentle, displayed indefatigable energy, and enjoyed a superior reputation as a consultant. His clinics were prepared with scrupulous care and he obtained more pathologic information from a wound than several observers combined. He was probably a better morbid pathologist than a technical surgeon, but the evaluation is relative rather than absolute. Wherever he went—to the bedside, the operating room, the morgue, the laboratory, the library, or his home—he found great satisfaction and assurance in being a part of the times. A testimonal dinner on his 60th birthday was a memorable occasion in Chicago medicine and was attended by physicians and surgeons from many lands and many cities. Among pupils or those who felt his scholarly warmth were J. B. Herrick, J. B. Murphy, Nicholas Senn, William J. Mayo, Frank Billings, and Ludvig Hektoen.

1. The Collected Works of Christian Fenger, M.D., 2 vol, Philadelphia: W. B. Saunders Company, 1912.
2. Fenger, C.: Trichinosis—Report of Two Cases, Chicago Med Rev 3:208, 1881.
3. Fenger, C.: Operation for the Relief of Valve-Formation and Stricture of the Ureter in Hydro- or Pyo-Nephrosis, JAMA 22:335, 1894.

George Oliver (1841-1915)

GEORGE OLIVER, bedside practitioner and clinical physiologist, enhanced the study of disease with the design of laboratory apparatus for the quantitation of cardiovascular abnormalities. In addition, he suspected an interrelationship between the "ductless" glands and, together with Schafer, demonstrated a pressor substance in the extract of suprarenal tissue.

Oliver was born in Middleton-in-Teesdale, Durham, the son of a surgeon.[1] He was educated at Gainford School, Yorkshire, and prepared for medicine at University College and University College Hospital, London. He began his practice at Redcar and in 1873 qualified for the MD degree, gaining several honors including gold medals. William Sharpey, professor of anatomy and physiology at University College during Oliver's training, exerted a considerable influence on his receptive mind. This was manifest from his later work on the pressor substance as well as his earlier contributions to bedside medicine. Interwoven with an extensive practice of medicine as a general physician and consultant, he designed test papers impregnated with reagents for the study of urine,[2] and also devised several apparatuses: an improved urinometer for the estimation of specific gravity for small quantities of urine, a hematocytometer, a hemoglobinometer, an arteriometer for measuring the size of an artery, and a sphygmomanometer.

In 1875, Oliver moved to Harrogate; the following year he received membership in the Royal College of Physicians and in 1887 advanced to fellowship. His work in the physiology laboratory in University College under E. A. Schäfer, who later legalized his name to Sharpey-Schafer, resulted in a joint communication on a pressor substance from the suprarenal capsules which was called "adrenalin" by them. Their findings were published in the 1894 proceedings of the Physiological Society as a preliminary report.[3]

The suprarenal capsules yield to water (cold or hot), to alcohol or to glycerine a substance which exerts a most powerful action upon the blood vessels, upon the heart, and upon the skeletal muscles. These effects have been investigated upon the dog, cat, rabbit and frog. In the frog the solutions were injected into the dorsal lymph-sac, in the rabbit subcutaneously and into a vein, in the other animals into a vein. The alcohol extracts were first dried and the residue extracted with normal saline; the watery decoctions were made with normal saline, and the glycerine extracts were largely diluted with the same previous to injection. The doses employed have varied from a mere trace up to an amount or extract equivalent to 3 grains (0.2 gramme) of the fresh gland; in one or two instances we have given larger doses with the object of obtaining if possible a lethal result. The extracts used have been made from the suprarenals of the calf, sheep and dog. Exactly similar effects have been obtained in each case.

The effect upon the blood vessels is to cause extreme contraction of the arteries, so that the blood-pressure is enormously raised. This is most evident when the vagi are cut in order to obviate the inhibitory action upon the heart which otherwise occurs; it is also seen after section of the cervical cord. The blood-pressure may rise from 2 to 4 times above normal. This extreme contraction of the vessels is evidenced by the plethysmograph; section of the nerves going to the limb produces no difference in the result. The effect is therefore peripheral. This can also be shown in the frog with its nerve-centres destroyed, and through the blood vessels of which normal saline is allowed to circulate; if only a small quantity of suprarenal extract is added to the saline the flow almost entirely ceases.

The effect upon the skeletal muscles has been investigated in the frog.

We have noticed a slight effect to be produced upon the respiration, which may become shallower; but in the doses we have used the result was very slight when compared with the prodigious effects upon the heart and blood vessels which were obtained.

Oliver discussed his studies on blood and blood pressure in the Croonian lectures in 1896, which were expanded into a monograph on hemomanometry in 1906. In 1904, he established a trust to endow the Oliver-Sharpey lectureship in physiological research under the jurisdiction of the Royal College of Physicians. He was honored as the first recipient of the award. The tissue-lymph circulation was discussed. In his composition he wrote and rewrote each sentence until he was convinced that the message was clear and expressed his meaning in the fewest possible words. One of his great aims was to make medicine a more exact science.

1. Taylor, F.: George Oliver in *The Annual Address Delivered to the Royal College of Physicians*, London: J. Bale, Sons & Danielsson, Ltd., 1916, pp 27-29.
2. Oliver, G.: *On Bedside Urine Testing: Qualitative Albumen and Sugar*, London: H. K. Lewis, 1883.
3. Oliver, G., and Schäfer, E. A.: On the Physiological Action of Extract of the Suprarenal Capsules, *J Physiol (Lond)* 17:i-v, 1894.

Magnus Gustaf Retzius
(1842-1919)

GUSTAF RETZIUS, a man of many talents, was born in Stockholm into a family distinguished in science and the humanities.[1] His father especially, Anders Adolf Retzius, was judged by some to have made even greater contributions to mankind than the

son for his achievements in craniometry. The elder Retzius served as professor of anatomy of the Caroline Medico-Chirurgical Institute of Stockholm and was one of its chief "creators." Gustaf received his early education at the Stockholm Gymnasium and, at the age of 18, entered the University of Uppsala, where he began his medical training. This was supplemented by further studies at the Caroline Institute, and, in 1871, he qualified for the MD degree from the University of Lund, one of the two universities where students from the several Scandinavian institutions were accustomed to take doctorate examinations. (The second school was Uppsala.) By then Retzius had exhibited skill in composition and potential in investigation of natural phenomena. He collected, edited, and published, posthumously, his father's personal correspondence and contributions to ethnology, and began his own comprehensive research on the skulls of ancient Swedes. These anthropologic data were collated nearly four decades later and published as a monumental treatise.[2]

Retzius' first academic appointment was docent in anatomy made in 1871 at the Caroline Institute; in 1877, he was advanced to assistant professor of histology and, in 1888, to full professor. Retzius was as fortunate in choosing a mate as he had been blessed with cultured parents. His wife, the daughter of the founder of the *Stockholm Aftonbladet,* the leading newspaper of the community, endowed their union with sufficient funds to assure financial independence, which enabled him to publish his scientific writings according to his wishes. This marriage also brought him the opportunity to serve as editor-in-chief of the *Aftonbladet* for three years. He met the challenge in this mission and in addition to directing an outstanding newspaper, he published a series of biographical sketches of scientific persons, political essays, travel sketches, poems, and literary translations.

Few contemporaries exceeded the volume of the contributions made by Retzius in scientific endeavors. His published work included a two-volume monograph on the gross anatomy of the human brain;[3] a two-volume monograph on the morphology and histology of the organ of hearing of vertebrates;[4] 18 volumes of biological investigations which appeared between 1890 and 1914; and, as an admirer of Swedenborg and an associate of Axel Key, major studies on the anatomy of the nervous system. Retzius pursued critical investigations on spermatozoa and ova, described the flow of cerebral spinal fluid through the central nervous spaces into the general circulation, identified the brown striae in the enamel of teeth through injection experiments (striae of Retzius), and recognized what was later known as the gyrus of Retzius within the hippocampus. His scientific communications were published either in Swedish or in German, with equal skill in composition. When invited to London in 1908 to deliver the Croonian lecture before the Royal Society, and the following year to deliver the Huxley lecture before the Royal Anthropological Institute of Great Britain and Ireland, he proved equally proficient in English. Many of his monographs contained illustrations drawn by his own hand; some are illustrated with colored plates. The principles of the minute structure of the nervous system, especially the nerve endings, and the inability to identify any direct connection between the endings of the nerve fibers and selected sensory cells for hearing, taste, and smell are excerpted from the Croonian lecture.[4]

As regards the *olfactory* organ, it could be shown clearly and distinctly by the Golgian method that the olfactory cells of the mucous membrane send out a central process which makes its way into the glomeruli of the olfactory bulbs, and there copiously ramifies among the ramifications of one or more other axons proceeding from the central nerve-cells, forming with them the glomeruli.

The sensory cells of the olfactory organ are to be regarded as a species of *peripheral nerve-cells.* They must also be regarded as corresponding fundamentally to those bipolar cells in the skin of the invertebrata already mentioned above.

In 1881 to 1884 I had shown that in the maculae and cristae acusticae of *the auditory organs* the nerve-fibres enclose the lower ends of the hair cells by means of calyx-shaped extensions, and even send out fine fibrils that proceed in an upward direction on the surface of these cells. Here the matter proved more complicated, for by the Golgian method I succeeded in 1892 in proving definitely that the terminations of the auditory nerve come to an end with free ramifications among the hair cells, and, to some extent, find their way up to the surface of the epithelium.

It is in any case plain that sensory cells of the auditory organ (the hair cells) may in principle be compared with those of the gustatory organ. Their development makes manifest, too, that they do not send out any fibres which proceed towards the centre, but that the bipolar nerve-cells situated in the ganglion acusticum dispatch their peripheral processes to the sensory cells in the epithelium.

By reason of these circumstances, constituting as they do an essential difference, I here distinguish sensory cells such as those of the olfactory organ, which I call *primary,* from sensory cells such as those of the gustatory and auditory organs, which I call *secondary.* The former are, of course, a species of peripheral nerve-cells, the latter are not.

Retzius' work in anthropology, emulating his father, led him to equally important observations in the study of the Lapps in the north of Finland, a description of ancient Swedish skulls, and anthropometric measurements of Swedish army recruits. Select findings were presented in his Huxley lecture, in which he expressed great concern for the ultimate fate of the Teutonic race. Retzius advanced the view that the north European peoples had been slowly giving ground for thousands of years to the short, dark, brachycephalic race, which originated in Asia and had for a long time been dominant in central and southeastern Europe. He held the belief, unsupported by time, that the Nordic temperament was not adaptable to an industrial civilization.[5]

The merits and demerits of the two race branches are easily recognisable. As regards the North European race branch, the description fits the Scandinavian peoples excellently, both for prehistoric and present times. That is proved by the warlike venturesomeness and the piratical expeditions of the Normans and the Vikings of an earlier day, and also by the armed mercantile journeys of the Swedes and the Varangians to Russia and Byzantium in the ninth century, when they subjugated nations, founded kingdoms, and became soldiers of fortune for the sake of fighting, plundering, and carrying on trade in slaves.

There are still to be seen a good many traces of that national temperament in the Scandinavian peoples. For my own part, I have for a long time become more and more afraid that the racial element will not be found to be suited for the conditions brought about by the direction in which civilisation is developing. The North European race branch cannot properly adapt itself to the demands made upon it by industrialism. The brachycephalic individual of Middle Europe, on the other hand, seems to be far better suited for the demands of industrial life; he is satisfied with a little, is possessed of patience and endurance even when things are dull and dreary, and his work tiring and little remunerative; he is not so much addicted to expensive forms of recreation, but lays by money for his family and for old age. We have not as yet any statistics based upon anthropological research into the racial characters of industrial operatives, but, to judge by the information I have received privately, I should be inclined to conclude that wherever the two races are both available, it is the dark-haired, small statured brachycephali who are preponderatingly employed in industrial occupations.

There are two reasons for my stating these facts. First, in order to point out that there may lie in the circumstances to which I have called attention, a very real danger of the North European dolichocephalic race branch not being able to hold its own. Just as it has been ousted during the past thousand years from Germany and other countries in Central and Eastern Europe by the dark-haired small-statured brachycephali, it will probably have to yield place here too, and be reduced in numbers, perhaps by degrees disappear entirely out of the fatherland of its ancestors and itself, by reason of the ever-increasing might and power of industrialism with which it seems ill-fitted to cope successfully in the long run.

Retzius ventured forth several times into the land of literature. In the very year of graduation in medicine, he published a volume of sonnets which apparently had been in preparation during his training for practice. With his sister, he translated into his native tongue many of the poems of Robert Burns. He composed at least two cantatas—one in 1898 in honor of Jöns Jacob Berzelius, the other in 1907 on the occasion of the 200th anniversary of the birth of Linnaeus. An extensive traveler, he prepared several illustrated travelogues, including one on North America.

Retzius was a close friend of many outstanding, internationally known scientists, and was appropriately recognized by learned societies and organizations in Europe and North America. He was an honorary member of the Washington and Philadelphia Academies of Science; an honorary fellow of the Royal Anthropological Institute; one of the 18 members of the Swedish Academy which selects Nobel laureates for literature, and a member of the Swedish Academy of Science which selects Nobel laureates in physics and chemistry. Honorary degrees were conferred by the Universities of Uppsala (PHD), Bologna, Würzburg, Budapest, Cambridge, Geneva, and Harvard (JD). At the request of his wife, his brain was removed, preserved, and studied in the department of pathology at the Caroline Institute.

1. Larsell, O.: Gustaf Retzius, 1842-1919, Sci Monthly 10:559-569, 1920.
2. Retzius, G.: Prehistoric Skulls of Sweden (Swed), Stockholm: Aftonblat, 1900.
3. Retzius, G.: Brain of Man (Ger), Stockholm: P. A. Norstedt, 1896.
4. Retzius, G.: The Organs of Hearing of Vertebrates (Ger), 2 vol, Stockholm: Samson & Wallin, 1881-1884.
5. Retzius, G.: The Principles of the Minute Structure of the Nervous System as Revealed by Recent Investigations, Proc Roy Soc [Biol] 80:414-443, 1908.
6. Retzius, G.: The So-Called North European Race of Mankind. A Review of, and Views on, the Development of Some Anthropological Questions, J Roy Anthrop Inst 39: 277-313, 1909.

Composite by G. Bako

Ivar Sandström (1852-1889)

IVAR SANDSTRÖM, recorder in the department of anatomy at the University of Upsala, was the first to identify as specific structures the small bodies posterior to the lateral lobes of the thyroid and to give them their current name.[1] The description of the gross and microscopic appearance of the parathyroids was communicated to the *Upsala Journal of Science* in 1880, but the document remained untranslated into English in its entirety for more than 50 years.[2] Although the small bodies had been described earlier by Remak and Virchow, it was Sandström, before he had completed his medical training, who recognized these structures in man and animals as something distinct from lymph or accessory thyroid tissue.

The curriculum vitae of the discoverer is incomplete, but it is known that he was born in Stockholm, to the wife of the Secretary of Agriculture. He matriculated at the University of Uppsala, and his acdemic career in the department of anatomy of his alma mater came to an end in his late 30's. The single reference to Sandström's skill in teaching notes his preference for group micrography.

Sandström's initial observations on the previously undescribed structures deep in the neck were made in a dog; a superficial microscopic study showed the structures to be unlike those of neighboring tissues. Subsequent comparative observations were made in the cat, ox, horse, rabbit, and in 50 postmortem searches in man. It was usual to find two glands of varying sizes on either side. Having identified a specific new structure adjacent to the thyroid, he believed they were related embryologically to the larger organ. The description of the chief cells containing glycogen and arranged in columns or follicles, sometimes with "colloid," is current, as is the description of oxyphil cells, with a richly granular (acidophilic) cytoplasm. On the other hand, Sandström made no mention of the water-clear cells, predominant in adenomas. Also, the characterization of the parathyroid as an endocrine gland, the definition of its relation to calcium metabolism, and the pathogenesis of tetany following extirpation remained for others in subsequent decades to investigate. A complete English translation of Sandström's original contribution was prepared by Seipel and was published in the *Bulletin of the Institute of the History of Medicine*.[1]

About three years ago [1877] I found on the thyroid gland of a dog a small organ, hardly as big as a hemp seed, which was enclosed in the same connective tissue capsule as the thyroid, but could be distinguished therefrom by a lighter color. A superficial examination revealed an organ of a totally different structure from that of the thyroid, and with very rich vascularity.

So much the greater was my astonishment therefore when in the first individual examined I found on both sides at the inferior border of the thyroid gland an organ of the size of a small pea, which, judging from its exterior, did not appear to be a lymph gland, nor an accessory thyroid gland, and upon histological examination showed a rather peculiar structure. After several examinations not only was I convinced of the constancy of its appearance but I was also able to show that two such glands in most cases occur on each side. Since then my interest has been so predominantly centered on a deeper study of the structure and importance of these glands in man, that examinations of animals have been limited to dog, cat, rabbit, ox, and horse, and even there they have been rather scanty.

The glands show under low magnification a granulated substance wherein under higher magnification one can see the cells lying close to each other. If a very thin part of a slice from a preparation fixed in osmic acid or in Müller's solution is chosen for examination one will see the cells containing a rounded homogeneous nucleus of about the size of a red blood corpuscle and a small amount of a finely granulated protoplasm.

The cells very often contain fat drops, . . . sometimes in such quantity that they look like the cells undergoing fatty degeneration which are so frequently found in pathological conditions. . . . They do not get cloudy nor are they dissolved by acids, by volatile oils or by ether. This seems to prove that they do not consist of fat or mucous substance, but seem to have all the characteristics of a colloid. . . . Besides the protoplasm-poor cells described above, there is often another kind, with a far more abundant, richly granulated protoplasm. Such cells are assembled in smaller or larger groups, generally at the surface of the gland, sometimes in its interior, and are now and then more clearly delimited from each other.

Finally the glandular substance may be arranged in larger or smaller cell groups, totally separated from one another. . . . I want especially to point out that the existence of the cell clusters mentioned above, or as I from here on want to call them, the follicles, is by no means limited to the parts of the gland where the cell arrangement is reticular, but appears equally often on the surface of a gland where the parenchyma is more continuous.

In the whole preceding description of the structure of the gland, the cell clusters, the cell strands, or the continuous cell mass have been mentioned as entirely solid structures. This is far from being always the case.

Although both of the aforementioned kinds of glands could with equal reasons claim the name of accessory thyroid glands, a special name seems to be required for those which are the subject of this paper, both with regard to the essentially different structure and on account of the fact that this kind of gland is constant in its occurrence, while the other one is extremely variable. I therefore suggest the use of the name *Glandulae parathyreoideae;* a name in which the characteristic of being bye-glands to the thyroid is expressed.

1. Seipel, C. M.: An English Translation of Sandström's *Glandulae Parathyreoideae, Bull Inst Hist Med* 6:179-180, 1938.

2. Sandström, I.: On a New Gland in Man Several Mammals, *Uppsala Läkareförenings Förhandlingar* 15:441-471, 1879-1880, trans. by Seipel, C. M.: *Bull Inst Hist Med* 6:181-222, 1938.

Composite by G. Bako

George Sumner Huntington (1861-1927)

GEORGE S. HUNTINGTON, first full-time professor of anatomy in America and collector of specimens and books, preferred the laboratory to the lecture hall for instruction of medical students. He effected a change in the medical curriculum, based on the premise that anatomy could be taught best in small groups in the laboratory, utilizing embryology, comparative morphology, and comparative physiology of vertebrates.

Huntington descended from prominent New England parents, several of his ancestors served in state legislatures or the national Congress. His father, a successful businessman rose to the presidency of the Hartford Fire Insurance Company, was 66 at the time of George's birth, while his mother, a Sumner descendant and a second wife was only 30. The family of the Sumners included deacons, soldiers, and at least one physician, George Sumner, who received the MD degree from the University of Pennsylvania in 1817.[1]

George Sumner Huntinton was left fatherless in his first year. At the age of 10, his mother took him to Germany where he attended the gymnasium until age 16. There he received careful, methodical training in Greek and Latin. Returning to the United States, he entered Trinity College, Hartford, and graduated with honors in 1881, seventh in a class of 19. His relative class standing improved considerably at the College of Physicians and Surgeons, Columbia University, where he won two prizes and ranked second in a class of 125 at graduation.

After serving as a member of the Roosevelt Hospital house staff for two years, Huntington returned to the College of Physicians and Surgeons as assistant demonstrator of anatomy, meanwhile conducting private classes and assisting H. B. Sands in his private practice of surgery. Later he held appointments as visiting surgeon to Bellevue Hospital, junior assisting attending surgeon at the Roosevelt Hospital, and chief of the clinic of the surgical department of Vanderbilt Clinic. At the age of 28, he was appointed full-time professor of anatomy at his alma mater and for 35 years directed the department for undergraduate and graduate students, assembling throughout a vast collection of vertebrate anatomical specimens. The monumental task approached in size and scientific excellence the Hunterian Museum of Comparative and Human Anatomy of the Royal College of Surgeons in London. Huntington included in his collection examples of vertebrates of all classes and orders, some acquired from the New York Zoological Society of which he was prosector, others from menageries in this country, or from collectors throughout the world. Such a museum, according to Huntington, was a vital educational factor in basic preparation for medicine 50 years ago.[2]

The educational value of the modern morphological museum has of late years received such general recognition that we may well regard its position as established in the university system.

The establishment of a museum of vertebrate comparative anatomy, on lines designed to illustrate and demonstrate to the fullest extent possible the morphological truths embodied in the doctrines of evolution, heredity and descent . . . has been rapid and the results gratifying.

This display forms the guiding thread to the study of the individual forms—in respect to typical structures, *i.e.,* the fundamental anatomical characters of the mammal, bird, reptile, amphibian and fish are grouped together to afford a comprehensive view of the entire organism, from which starting point the detailed investigation of characteristic structures in their various modifications is to be followed through the series of species belonging to the *same class.*

In this sense the museum fulfills its highest functions, stimulating and directly promoting investigation and rendering such investigation fruitful and effective by contributing the series necessary for comparison and reference.

The museum at one time occupied four floors in the anatomy building when the college was located on 59th Street. In 1921, the majority of the items in the osteology collection were sent to the Smithsonian Institution, Washington, DC, where they remain in storage but are available for research.

Huntington was not a prolific writer, although he was an outstanding teacher of anatomy and a respected investigator. His first contribution to the scientific literature, three years after his professorial appointment, discussed *The Ileocolon of the Procyon Lotor and Allied Forms,* the cecum, and vermiform appendix. The text is illustrated with several hundred preparations of type forms of the ileocecal junction from fish through mammals, as well as the human cecum and appendix in many of their variations. In 1903, he published the monograph *Anatomy of the Human Peritoneum and Abdominal Cavity,* which described these structures in man. The following excerpt illustrates his desire to relate form and function from comparative studies.[3]

2. The observer will be impressed by the fact that representatives of all the main types of ileo-colic junction are found within a very limited zoological range, as within the confines of a single order. Examples of this are furnished by the Marsupialia and, to a lesser extent, by the Edentata. The members of these zoological groups, while united by certain common anatomical characters, such as the reproductive system and dentition, differ widely in habit and in the kind and quantity of the food normally taken. These differences in the method of nutrition have impressed their influence on the structure of the alimentary canal and have led to the evolution of varying and divergent types of ileo-colic junction. The study of this segment of the intestinal tract can therefore elucidate the mutual relationship of the vertebrate groups only to a limited degree and in special cases. On the other hand, it renders very clear the fundamental structural ground-plan common to all vertebrates and accentuates the

specialized modifications of this plan which develop in response to the physiological environment. Moreover, such a review serves to reveal the significance of rudimentary and vestigial structures, such as the human vermiform appendix and the serous and vascular folds connected with the same. Throughout the entire vertebrate series the alimentary canal is found to respond with great readiness in its structure to varying grades of functional demand.

One of Huntington's best contributions in embryology was the correct delineation of the development of the systemic lymphatic vessels. Early in this century some believed the lymphatic channels arose from veins; others saw evidence that the lymphatic system developed directly from the mesoderm. The latter concept was supported by Huntington.[4]

1. The entire extensive system of the *lymphatic vessels* of the adult, including the thoracic and right lymphatic ducts and their tributaries, is formed by the confluence of numerous perivenous and extra intimal intercellular mesodermal spaces, in the sense previously defined. These primary anlages of the future systemic lymphatic vessels are, from their inception, lined by a *lymphatic* vascular endothelium, which is *not* derived from the *haemal* vascular endothelium, but which develops independently of the same.

The lymphatic channels, formed by the subsequent confluence of these originally discrete and separate mesodermal spaces, follow in large part the embryonic veins closely, but they are neither derived from them, nor do they communicate with them, except at the definite points at which the rudimentary mammalian type of a lymphatico-venous heart is developed.

2. This structure develops, as the jugular lymph sac of the typical mammal, directly from the perivenous capillary reticulum of the early pre- and post-cardinal veins, adjacent to, and including, their point of confluence to form the duct of Cuvier.

George Huntington taught a remarkable number of students who later occupied principal chairs at the College of Physicians and Surgeons. Included were Hugh Auchincloss, George Draper, Kneeland Frantz, Adrian Lambert, Samuel W. Lambert, Eugene Pool, Fordyce B. St. John, Frederick Tilney, Frederick T. van Beuren, Jr., and Allen Whipple. Honors acquired by Huntington included DSC from Columbia, the LLD from Jefferson Medical College, and membership in the National Academy of Sciences. He was the American editor for the (British)

Journal of Anatomy and Physiology, editor of the *Anatomical Memoirs,* and associate editor of the *American Journal of Anatomy.* His books comprise a named collection in the Medical School Library at P & S, purchased by small gifts to the Alumni Association.

1. McClure, C. F. W.: George Sumner Huntington, *Amer J Anat* 39:355-377, 1927.
2. Huntington, G. S.: The Morphological Museum as an Educational Factor in the University System, *Science* 13:601-611, 1901.
3. Huntington, G. S.: *The Anatomy of the Human Peritoneum and Abdominal Cavity,* Philadelphia and New York: Lea Brothers & Co., 1903.
4. Huntington, G. S.: The Genetic Principles of the Development of the Systemic Lymphatic Vessels in the Mammalian Embryo, *Anat Rec* 4:399-424, 1910.

Eugene Lindsay Opie (1873-)

EUGENE L. OPIE is the son of Thomas Opie, one of the founders of the College of Physicians and Surgeons of Baltimore, and professor of obstetrics and gynecology in the school and dean of its faculty for 33 years. Eugene was born in 1873 in Staunton, Virginia, where his mother was spending the summer to escape the heat of the city. Opie attended public schools in Baltimore and in 1893 received his bachelor of arts degree from Johns Hopkins University.[1] After one year at the College of Physicians and Surgeons, he transferred to Johns Hopkins Medical School and in 1897 received the MD degree as a member of the first graduating class. Influenced particularly by William H. Welch, professor of pathology, and William S. Thayer, of the department of medicine, and with the aid of the microscope and laboratory animals, he became interested in the experimental study of disease. During the summer following his third year of medical school, Opie and his classmate, W. G. MacCallum, investigated the incidence, sexual conjugation, and other characteristics of malarial-like parasites in Baltimore birds; their findings were reported in the *Journal of Experimental Medicine* in 1898.[2] The investigation was detailed, carefully planned, precisely reported, and adequately illustrated—a pattern of performance which was continued through an unusually long professional career.

After one year as a house officer on the medical service at Johns Hopkins Hospital, Opie joined the pathology department under Welch, where he remained five years. During this time he completed the first and critical phase of possibly his most important contribution to experimental pathology and, indirectly, to clinical medicine: hyaline degeneration of the islands of Langerhans was recognized in the postmortem examination of patients with diabetes mellitus. In 1904, he joined the newly founded Rockefeller Institute for Medical Research in New York, where he continued his fundamental studies in experimental pathology, served as co-editor of their *Journal of Experimental Medicine,* and for three years was visiting pathologist to the Presbyterian Hospital. In 1910, Opie moved to St. Louis as professor of pathology at Washington University; in addition, he assumed the duties of dean of the faculty from 1912 to 1915. Except for military duty in World War I, Opie remained in St. Louis until 1923 when he was called to the University of Pennsylvania as professor of pathology and director of the Henry Phipps Institute for the Study, Treatment, and Prevention of Tuberculosis. His next move was to Cornell University Medical College as professor of pathology and

pathologist to the New York Hospital. From 1935 to 1938 Opie served as scientific director of the International Health Division of the Rockefeller Foundation, and in 1939 he went to China as visiting professor of pathology at Peiping Union Medical College. During the war years he renewed his affiliation with the Rockefeller Institute as guest investigator and supervised the Phipps Institute as acting director.

Throughout Opie's long career in experimental pathology, subjects for investigation included the mechanism of inflammation and exudation, especially enzymes and antienzymes in inflammatory humors: relation of antigen to antibodies in sensitized tissues, particularly in the Arthus phenomenon; eosinophilic granulation and its relation to bacterial infection, pneumonia, and influenza; natural and acquired immunity in tuberculosis; the influence of diet in protecting the liver against noxious agents; the relation of cytochondria in the liver to carcinogenesis; and the pathogenesis of dysfunction of the pancreas.[3] The pathological alterations in the pancreas of patients with diabetes mellitus centered about the islands of Langerhans, which had been identified and studied a generation earlier. Only two years following his house officer experience, Opie described the relation of interstitial pancreatitis to diabetes mellitus in a communication in the *Journal of Experimental Medicine.* He reported on structural changes in the islands in 16 patients with various clinical diagnoses. No disturbance of the islands was found in syphilitic pancreatitis; whereas two types of chronic interstitial inflammation were distinguished. In interlobular pancreatitis, the inflammatory process implicated the islands only when the sclerotic process reached a severe grade. In interacinar pancreatitis, however, a relationship was recognized between lesions of the islands and the clinical diagnosis of diabetes mellitus. The significant findings were reported independently and concomitantly by Ssobolew; selected conclusions by Opie follow.[4]

(*a*) In one of eleven cases of interlobular pancreatitis diabetes of mild intensity occurred. The sclerosis, which in this case followed obstruction of the ducts by calculi, was far advanced and affected the islands of Langerhans.

(*b*) In two of three cases of interacinar pancreatitis, diabetes was present. The third case was associated with a condition, haemochromatosis, which at a later stage is associated with diabetes, the result of pancreatic lesion.

(*c*). In a fourth case of diabetes, hyaline deposit between the capillaries and the parenchymatous cells had so completely altered the islands of Langerhans that they were no longer recognizable.

Opie's interest in tuberculosis, reflected in several communications prepared in his first academic post, and reaffirmed periodically throughout his bibliography,[5] made him a logical choice for the directorship of the laboratories of the Henry Phipps Institute. He found marked differences in tuberculous infection among afflicted families in which the disease was slowly transmitted from one generation to the next, in contrast to those who, having escaped exposure to tuberculosis in childhood, died of fulminating tuberculosis following exposure in adulthood. Extending his studies to foreign people, he discovered that natives born in China or on the island of Jamaica, who abandoned the country for urban life, and who had had no prior exposure to the tubercle bacillus and thereby lacked immunity, succumbed rapidly to the infection. Shortly after Ghon's work on primary forms of tuberculosis in children, Opie reported his findings and results—again from a series of postmortem examinations.[6]

The foregoing observations have shown that tuberculous infection is practically universal. Dissemination of the disease among adults is so widespread that readily recognizable tuberculous lesions have been found in all of fifty individuals above the age of 18 years. First infection in almost all of those who reach adult life occurs in childhood and has the characters of a first infection in animals since it tends to implicate regional lymphatic nodes. Koch showed that a second infection of an animal already tuberculous shows greater tendency to heal and does not extend to regional lymphatic nodes, and this observation has been confirmed by numerous observers. Apical tuberculosis usually exhibits the characters of a second infection, since it pursues a chronic course and is unaccompanied by tuberculosis of regional lymphatic nodes.

Tuberculosis of children does not select the apices of the lungs, is accompanied by massive tuberculosis of regional lymphatic nodes, and

exhibits the characters of tuberculosis in a freshly infected animal, whereas tuberculosis which occurs in the pulmonary apices of adults has the characters of a second infection. Almost all human beings are spontaneously "vaccinated" with tuberculosis before they reach adult life.

During World War I Opie "enlisted" in the United States Army on May 16, 1917. After a month in England as a "guest of the government," he was assigned to Base Hospital 21, British Expeditionary Forces, and later to the American Hospital, near Rouen in Normandy. The commission to study trench fever was his next assignment. At the request of Washington University Medical School, Opie was ordered to return to the United States on April 2, 1918. Six weeks later, at his request, he returned to the United States Army and was stationed at Camp Funston, Kansas, and Camp Pike, Arkansas, where he was placed in command of a commission for the study of pneumonia and influenza. His active duty ended Jan 21, 1919.

As a scientist of high intellectual integrity, Opie pursued experimental pathology in an exemplary fashion of introspective study, meticulous execution of the experiment, and critical compilation of the data, carried out in cooperation with, and not at the expense of, his students. He was an investigator of strong convictions who exerted a great influence upon a remarkable number of physicians, teachers, and scientists for more than 50 years. The roster, several of whom continue to occupy professional chairs in this country, includes D. M. Angevine, J. Aronson, F. G. Blake, R. L. Cecil, A. R. Dochez, E. F. Du Bois, J. Freund, J. Furth, G. Hass, T. Ingalls, J. G. Kidd, E. B. Krumbhaar, H. R. M. Landis, M. Lurie, F. M. McPhedran, J. Meakins, V. Menkin, and R. M. Moore. Opie's honors include the Gerhard and Trudeau medals in 1929, the Weber-Parkes medal and award of the Royal College of Physicians in 1945, the Banting medal in 1946, the Jessie Stevenson-Kovalenko medal of the National Academy of Sciences in 1959, the New York Academy's medal, and the Gold-Headed Cane of the American Association of Pathologists and Bacteriologists in 1960. He is the only scientist to have presented three Harvey lectures.

The first in 1910 discussed inflammation; during the 1928-1929 series, he described his studies on tuberculosis; while in 1954-1955 he reported on osmotic activity in relation to movement of water under normal and pathological conditions. The honorary degrees granted Opie include the DSC by Yale in 1930, and the LLD by Washington University in 1940 and by Johns Hopkins University in 1947.

1. Kidd, J. G.: Citation and Presentation of the Academy Medal to Eugene L. Opie, M.D., *Bull NY Acad Med* 36:228-234, 1960.
2. Opie, E. L.: On the Haemocytozoa of Birds, *J Exp Med* 3:79-101, 1898.
3. Opie, E. L.: *Disease of the Pancreas,* Philadelphia: J. B. Lippincott Co., 1903.
4. Opie, E. L.: On the Relation of Chronic Interstitial Pancreatitis to the Islands of Langerhans and to Diabetes Mellitus, *J Exp Med* 5:397-428, 1900-1901.
5. Publications of Eugene L. Opie from 1898 to 1941, *Arch Path* 34:7-11, 1942.
6. Opie, E. L.: Focal Pulmonary Tuberculosis of Children and Adults, *J Exp Med* 25:855-876, 1917.

Sir J. S. Burdon-Sanderson (1828-1905)

JOHN SCOTT BURDON-SANDERSON was born at Jesmond, near Newcastle-on-Tyne, into a distinguished family of considerable means. His father, Richard Burdon, took the additional surname of Sanderson upon his marriage to the daughter of Sir James Sanderson, Member of Parliament.[1] As a boy, J. S. Burdon-Sanderson was educated at home and was intended for the law. However, his strong interest in natural science attracted him to medicine, and he graduated MD from the University of Edinburgh in 1851, with the gold medal for his thesis on blood corpuscles. Proceeding to Paris for postgraduate work, he studied chemistry under Gerhardt and Wurtz and physiology under Claude Bernard. Two years later Burdon-Sanderson settled in London as a practicing physician and medical registrar of St. Mary's Hospital, Paddington; in 1856, he was appointed medical officer of health for Paddington. During his 11 years tenure, he instituted reforms for the control of contagious diseases, especially cattle plague and chol-

era, exposed the evils of food adulteration and unsanitary dwelling-houses, and saw remedial measures taken.

Burdon-Sanderson was elected a Fellow of the Royal Society and their Croonian lec-

Composite by G. Bako

turer in 1867; only to give up private practice and devote himself to scientific investigation in 1870. He was soon rewarded with the appointment of professor superintendent of the Brown Institution (University of London) and professor of practical physiology and histology at University College, London. In this post he succeeded Sir Michael Foster, and, in 1874, he succeeded William Sharpey as Jodrell professor of physiology at University College. Burdon-Sanderson became a fellow of the Royal College of Physicians in 1871 and Harveian orator at the College in 1878; in 1881, he was invited to Oxford as first Waynflete professor of physiology and fellow at Magdalen College. His academic career was climaxed in 1895, with the appointment as regius professor of medicine at Oxford. Many of his earlier investigations were carried out on the excitable cells of the *Drosera* plant. In a similar area Burdon-Sanderson explored the excitation of animal tissue and the action currents of the heart. Together with Page he established the basis of the present understanding of the nature of the T-wave with the rheotome and studied the order of excitation and the nature of the process in the heart of the frog.[2] They found that the excited parts of the ventricle were negative to every unexcited part during the excitation state and that this state propagated in all directions. Also, their measurements of the duration of the excitatory state in frogs showed that partial warming of the surface of the ventricles shortened the local duration of the phase in the warmed part. In another study they described a photographic procedure, utilizing the capillary electrometer for recording the electrical response of animals and plants—one of the best-known contributions from his laboratory.[3]

As the photographic records commented on in the preceding paragraphs confirm in every respect the conclusions of our former paper as to the nature of the electrical phenomena which accompany the excitatory process in the ventricle, it is unnecessary to set them forth again in full. It is sufficient to note that the photographs afford the strongest evidence in favour of the most important of those results namely (1) that the electrical excitatory change instead of lasting a fraction of a second as supposed by all previous observers (its maximum duration according to Engelmann being half a second) lasts at ordinary temperature about two seconds, and (2) that in all cases the character of the electrical variation may be satisfactorily explained as resulting from the time-relations of the electrical processes which have their seats at the two leading off electrodes during the period that the excited state of the ventricular tissue lasts.

Burdon-Sanderson was three times Croonian lecturer for the Royal Society, was created a Baronet in 1899, and received the honorary LLD from Edinburgh and the honorary DSC from Dublin. Although not a stimulating lecturer, he was recognized as a leader in the development of the experimental laboratory for physiological research and teaching.

1. F. G.: Sir John Scott Burdon-Sanderson, Bart. 1828-1905, *Proc Roy Soc [Biol]* 79:iii-xviii (Nov) 1907.
2. Burdon-Sanderson, J., and Page, F. J. M.: On the Time-Relations of the Excitatory Process in the Ventricle of the Heart of the Frog, *J Physiol* 2:384-435, 1879-1880.
3. Burdon-Sanderson, J., and Page, F. J. M.: On the Electrical Phenomena of the Excitatory Process in the Heart of the Frog and of the Tortoise, as Investigated Photographically, *J. Physiol* 4:327-338, 1883-1884.

Composite by G. Bako

Henry Pickering Bowditch (1840-1911)

HENRY PICKERING BOWDITCH of Boston entered medicine later than many of his age because of extended service with the Massachusetts Cavalry during the war between the states.[1] His grandfather was a well-known mathematician and navigator, his father a successful Boston merchant. Bowditch graduated from Harvard College in 1861 and, having decided on a scientific career, enrolled in the Lawrence Scientific School, an affiliate of Harvard. A few months later, however, he answered the call to arms, became a second lieutenant in the Massachusetts Cavalry, and saw action in several campaigns. In June, 1865, he was mustered out with the grade of major and returned to Lawrence Scientific School. He received the

AM from Harvard University in 1866 and the MD from Harvard Medical School in 1868.

During three years in Europe Bowditch attended the clinics of Charcot, Broca, and Louis. However, he was thwarted in not finding a laboratory spot for work under Brown-Séquard and turned to Claude Bernard and Ranvier. After a short stay in Bonn, he settled in Leipzig in the physiological laboratory of Carl Ludwig; there the training was commensurate with his outstanding talents. Bowditch married the daughter of a Leipzig banker before returning to Boston in 1871, where he received an appointment on the faculty of Harvard Medical School.

With the laboratory apparatus brought back from Germany, Bowditch built in the North Grove Street structure of Harvard Medical School the first physiology laboratory for students in the United States. The center attracted those whose interest extended beyond general physiology; experimental work in biology, pharmacology, pathology, psychology, surgery, and bacteriology was pursued as well. Although the laboratory was makeshift, cramped, and unattractive, it served for more than a decade until new quarters were built on Boylston Street. In 1876, Bowditch was advanced to full professorship. As a full-time member of the faculty and a confidant of Charles W. Eliot, president of Harvard, he was privy to the plans for the new medical school building on Boylston Street, where he served for a decade as dean in addition to his professorship. Four years before retirement the George Higginson chair of physiology was established, and Bowditch acceded to this post.

Bowditch's bibliography was modest when compared with contemporary natural scientists, especially German physiologists. His published work included investigations on the interference between accelerator and inhibitor nerves in the heart and variations of arterial blood pressure, the nervous control of blood vessels, the effect of the respiratory movements on the pulmonary circulation, the enforcement of the patella tendon reflex, the accuracy of sight and touch in estimating special relations, optical illusions relative to moving objects, the advantages of chloroform over ether in depressing vasomotor reflexes, the rate of growth of prepubescent youth, and the inability of the apex of the frog's heart to develop a spontaneous rhythm after being isolated from the base although remaining irritable to external stimuli. Two of his best-known physiological contributions on contractions of cardiac muscle were made in Ludwig's laboratory and were published in their *Contributions.* His work on the inexhaustibility of nerve conduction came from the laboratory on North Grove Street.

Bowditch was one of the organizers of the American Physiological Society established in 1887. As a regular contributor to the *Boston Medical and Surgical Journal,* he was responsible for the semiannual reports on the progress of physiology. In addition, he was an American editor for the *British Journal of Physiology,* a founder of the *American Journal of Physiology,* and a member of its first editorial board. Bowditch, an active member of the American branch of the Society for Psychical Research and a vigorous vivisectionist, appeared before the legislature opposing bills aimed at restrictions on activities of medical investigators.

Bowditch's important observations on cardiac muscle described the Treppe (staircase) effect of stimulation and response and the all-or-none principle of contraction. The phenomenon, generally true of all irritable tissue, was defined as the increasing vigor of response, to a repetitious constant stimulus, to a value characteristic of the tissue under study. The graphic record has some similarity to a staircase. Since the communication was prepared by Bowditch, his use of the term Treppe continues to be applied. First described by Bowditch, the phenomenon remains incompletely explained in contemporary physiology. The all-or-none law is identified as the contraction of muscle maximally and independent of the strength of stimulation or no contraction at all. The effect can be demonstrated in skeletal muscle as well as in cardiac muscle and applies to the passage of impulses along nerve trunks.

Résumés of each of these phenomena in the isolated frog's heart follow.[2]

If before beginning a series of succeeding stimulations of maximal strength, occurring at 4- to 6-second-intervals and of constantly equal intensity, the apex is in complete rest for several minutes, it will produce a sequence of contractions.

The first contraction, the smallest, occurs after an interval of some minutes. Each succeeding increase progresses in such a manner that with an increasing number of contractions the increment becomes smaller and smaller, and finally disappears; thereafter the contractions are of the same magnitude. Such a series of contractions might be called a *"flight of stairs."* The steps of different flights of stairs, derived from the same heart, vary in minimal and maximal height as well as in the number of "steps."

Initially it was discovered that the shape in which the "flight of stairs" appears is independent of the direction and strength of the induction current. Although this could have been predicted, since maximal stimulation was always applied, I am convinced by precise experiments that the size of the first contraction, the increase from one contraction to another, and the magnitude of the maximal contraction are independent of selected characteristics of stimulation.

The weakest induction current able to produce a contraction of the heart does not produce the smallest contraction; furthermore if the intensity of the current is increased to a maximum, the strongest stimuli do not produce the largest contractions. In our experiments the induction current either produced a contraction or was unable to do so; if a contraction followed, it was the largest contraction which could be produced under given circumstances, the strength of the current notwithstanding. Thus, it follows that the size of the contraction depends rather on the characteristics of the muscle-fibers alone. It is hardly necessary to elaborate on the importance of this observation.

Bowditch completed the proof of the indefatigability of nerve transmission, a subject which had been incompletely explored by others. He produced a functional nerve block with curare and obtained muscular twitching as long as four hours later. The conduction of the nerve impulse was compared to a telegraph wire or the passage of the current to light or electricity. These observations furnished the rationale for nerve block anesthesia introduced subsequently into surgery.[3]

A cat was etherized and the sciatic nerve divided near the sacrum.

The animal then received a dose of curare (0.007—0.01 gram), sufficient to prevent muscular contractions, and the irritation of the nerve was steadily maintained while the animal was kept alive by artificial respiration. In the course of 1½ to 2 hours the curare was so far eliminated that the stimulation of the nerve which previously has been without effect began to produce muscular twitches which, as the elimination of the drug progressed, became more frequent and more violent.

In some of the experiments a second dose of curare was given, when the muscle began to twitch and the experiment continued till the drug was a second time eliminated. In this way it was found that stimulation of the nerve lasting from 1½ to 4 hours . . . did not exhaust the nerve.

Physiologists have long been in the habit of comparing nerves to telegraph wires, since they seem to be indifferent conductors transmitting inpulses equally well in both directions.

It would appear from these experiments that the absence of fatigue in consequence of activity is another very interesting point of resemblance.

The leadership of Bowditch in medical education as dean was reflected in his extension of the course of study to four years and the establishment of a department of bacteriology under H. C. Ernst. When the facilities on Boylston street became inadequate, he initiated a movement in the faculty for new buildings and together with C. W. Eliot and J. C. Warren raised funds for construction of the quadrangle on Longwood Avenue. The ingredients of sound medical education foremost in his mind were as important and worthwhile nearly three quarters of a century ago as they are today. He emphasized practical experience, concentration of attention on one subject at a time, programming of examinations to test the student's permanent acquisition of useful medical knowledge, and differentiating between desirable and essential subjects for learning. As president for the American Congress of Physicians and Surgeons, at their meeting in Washington in 1900, his five conclusions on the subject were studied.[4]

1. It [medical school] will be connected with a university, but will be so far independent of university control that the faculty will practically decide all questions relating to methods of instruction and the personnel of the teaching-body.

2. It will offer advanced instruction in every department of medicine and will therefore necessarily adopt an elective system of some sort,

since the amount of instruction provided will be far more than any one student can follow.

3. The laboratory method of instruction will be greatly extended and students will be trained to get their knowledge, as far as possible, by the direct study of nature, but the didactic lecture, though reduced in importance, will not be displaced from its position as an educational agency.

4. The work of the students will probably be so arranged that their attention will be concentrated upon one principal subject at a time and these subjects will follow each other in a natural order.

5. Examinations will be so conducted as to afford a test of both the faithfulness with which a student performs his daily work and of his permanent acquisition of medical knowledge fitting him to practise his profession.

Bowditch was a practical professor in the laboratory and in the home. He invented several pieces of apparatus for scientific investigation, designed the Bowditch chair, also known as the Adirondack chair, was skillful at the lathe and at glass blowing, and a pioneer in composite photography. Unsophisticated in the arts, he was red-green color blind and lacked any appreciation of music. Outdoor life and outdoor activities, much to his liking, included skating, mountain climbing, and kite flying. Memberships included the National Academy of Sciences, the American Philosophical Society, and the Royal Society of Medicine. He was a member of the Boston School Committee and a trustee of the Boston Public Library. The University of Cambridge granted him the honorary doctor of science, while Edinburgh, Toronto, Pennsylvania, and Harvard made him doctor of laws. His final years were saddened by advanced paralysis agitans, which was partly responsible for his relinquishing his professorial post before the statutory age.

1. Cannon, W. B.: Henry Pickering Bowditch, *Mem Nat Acad Sci* 17:183-196, 1924.

2. Bowditch, H. P.: Stimulation of Muscle Fibers of the Heart (Ger), *Arb Physiol Anst Leipzig* 6:139-176, 1872.

3. Bowditch, H. P.: Note on the Nature of Nerve-Force, *J Physiol (Lond)* 6:133-135, 1885.

4. Bowditch, H. P.: The Medical School of the Future, *Phila Med J* 5:1011-1018 (May 5) 1900.

Composite by G. Bako

John Newport Langley
(1852-1925)

LANGLEY, professor of physiology at Cambridge Uiversity, was born in Newbury in 1852, the son of a private schoolmaster.[1] He received instruction first at home and then at Exeter grammar school, where he progressed to a sizarship. Formal education was climaxed by a scholarship at St. John's College, Cambridge, where he read mathematics and history in preparation for the Indian civil service. Upon coming under the influence of Sir Michael Foster, first professor of physiology at Cambridge and founder and editor of the *Journal of Physiology,* Langley changed to the natural sciences. The potential superior talents of Langley were recognized immediately, and experimental investigations on jaborandi (pilocarpine) were begun under Foster's direction before completion of his graduate training. The following year he served as demonstrator in physiology and was responsible for the supervision of the laboratory work. Langley's first published paper described the action of pilocarpine on the heart. The report was read before the Cambridge Philosophical Society and appeared in the *Proceedings* of the society for 1875. The *Proceedings* were particularly noteworthy, since they were the foreruner of the *Journal of Physiology* founded in 1878. Langley remained at Cambridge, rising through successive stages of responsibility, and eventually (1903) succeeded to Foster's post, the senior position in the physiology department. Elliot Smith, A. V. Hill, Joseph Barcroft, Gowland Hopkins, and Edgar Adrian were some of the famous students in his department.

A review of Langley's bibliography discloses an unabated interest in the function of the involuntary nervous system. During his first decade of physiological investigation, secretory action of glandular tissue and the belief in the existence of "trophic" nerve fibers to the salivary glands received major attention. The Heidenhain concept of glandular secretion postulated that the secreting cell is more granular than the resting cell. Langley's investigations revealed quite the reverse effect.[2] Through anatomical and functional studies, he demonstrated that secretory granules accumulate within the gland in the presecretory phase. With the onset of secretory activity, the cells discharge the zymogen granules, with a consequent marked reduction in number. The plethoric and the depleted phases of secretory function remain valid.

Langley moved from secretory cells to research into broader phases of the autonomic nervous system. Gaskell, an equally competent student in Foster's laboratory, had made great progress in explaining the action of the "visceral" nervous system, the small medullated efferent fibers. Although it was recognized that the cranial and sacral nerve trunks were antagonistic in relation to the function of the sympathetic fibers, a number of items remained unclear. Langley, using nicotine which paralyzed the nerve cells in the ganglia, produced experimental evidence that the sympathetic fibers, from the spinal origin to the distal target cells, were single units and that each ganglion formed the one and only relay station for the fibers.[3] At this time, he coined the terms "pre-ganglionic" and "post-ganglionic."[4]

Broadly speaking, the fibres issuing from any one ganglion are connected with nerve-cells in that ganglion, and with no other sympathetic nerve-cell. In some cases a certain number of such fibres are connected with nerve-cells, not in the ganglion from which they issue, but in the ganglion immediately above or below it. In the following statement these fibres, and those which may take the course of the white rami, are, for the sake of simplicity, left out of account.

The fibres, before and after they have joined nerve-cells, I shall call respectively pre-ganglionic or pre-cellular, and post-ganglionic or post-cellular.

Langley was firm in his conviction that the sympathetic ganglia were integrated parts of efferent pathways only and that the spread of conduction along the branched nerve explained the apparent reflex phenomenon of visceral pain by the mechanism of the axon reflex. The next step was the differentiation of structure and function of the autonomic nervous system into the sympathetic and parasympathetic systems. The term "autonomic" was selected to signify independence from the central nervous system. The term "para-sympathetic" was chosen in 1905 to identify the cranial and sacral outflows in contrast to the thoraco-lumbar nerves of the sympathetic system. The pathways were separated and identified by different responses to adrenalin, pilocarpine, and other drugs.[4]

Sympathetic nerves have no special relation to sympathies. But the chief objection to calling the whole autonomic system sympathetic is that it confuses instead of simplifying nomenclature.

At the time I introduced the term "autonomic" there were two points of view from which the innervation of unstriated muscle and glands were regarded. From one point of view these tissues were supplied with nerve fibres partly by cerebro-spinal nerves and partly by sympathetic nerves. From the other (that of Gaskell) they were supplied by one system, which anatomically was separated into three parts by the development of the nerves to the limbs. Neither of these seemed to me properly to express the conditions. The facts that the sympathetic innervated the whole body, whilst the cranial and sacral outflows innervated parts only, and that the sympathetic had, in general, opposite functional effects from those of the other autonomic nerves, indicated that the sympathetic was a system distinct from the rest. The part of the cranial outflow supplying the eye seemed clearly to be distinct from the rest of the cranial outflow. Further, the bulbar part of the cranial outflow and the sacral outflow seemed equally clearly to form one system innervating the alimentary canal and parts developmentally connected with it. I divided (1898) the autonomic system into tectal, bulbo-sacral, and sympathetic systems, and considered that each had a different developmental history.

The theory that there is some fundamental differences between the sympathetic and the rest of the autonomic system was much strengthened by the discovery that the effects produced by adrenaline were apparently confined to effects caused by stimulating sympathetic nerves. . . . Since other drugs caused effects more or less confined to those produced by stimulating tectal and bulbo sacral nerves, it was convenient to have a common name for these nerves, and I placed them together as the parasympathetic system (1905). The pharmacological relations of the nerve systems and some variations in the meaning attached to parasympathetic I discuss later.

The integration of the central nervous system and the autonomic pathways was largely unappreciated by Langley and Gaskell; it remained for Sherrington early in the 20th century to explain the association. A monographic treatment of the autonomic nervous system was planned for Langley's retiring years. Part I only was published.[4] The discussion is a fine example of precise treatment of a complicated subject, to which Langley contributed heavily.

The third great achievement by Langley was in scientific composition and physiological journalism, as reflected in the guidance given to the sophisticated and highly respected *Journal of Physiology* founded by Foster in 1878. Langley served first on the Editorial Board. In 1894, he paid off the outstanding debt, accepted the unsold stock, and became owner and editor. But Langley was no casual editor who discharged his duties in a perfunctory fashion. In addition to a great love for teaching, he was equally dedicated to the preparation of scientific communications. It was not unusual to recast an entire manuscript, irrespective of whether it was submitted by a novice or by an investigator with an established reputation. He had great capacity for revision and compression, and, when the manuscript was ready for publication, it represented a new and scientifically established contribution to knowledge, a clear narrative which contained no irrelevant or redundant data and a minimum of speculation. Undoubtedly, such a policy annoyed or even alienated a few contributors. But this is the inevitable fate of a dedicated editor.

Langley received many honors from scientific societies and universities during his career as teacher, investigator, and editor. He was elected a Fellow of the Royal Society at the age of 31 and received the Royal Medal of the Society a decade later. He was awarded the Baly medal of the Royal College of Physicians and the Andreas Retzius medal of the Swedish Society of Physicians.

Langley loved sports and participated in rowing, skating, lawn tennis, and cycling. He was a fine gardener, as was his predecessor, Foster. Work habits were highly productive, if not always exemplary. He resented unnecessary interruptions during contemplation and left no doubt regarding his distaste for squandering time in conferences or committee work. When he died in 1925, he should have had no regrets in having left physiology far richer and having established the preeminence of physiological composition as editor of the *Journal of Physiology*.

1. Fletcher, W. M.: John Newport Langley. In Memoriam, *J Physiol (Lond)* 61:1-27, 1926.
2. Langley, J. N.: On the Structure of Serous Glands in Rest and Activity, *Proc Roy Soc Lond* 29:377-82 (Nov 27) 1879.
3. Langley, J. N.: Preliminary Account of the Arrangement of the Sympathetic Nervous System, Based Chiefly on Observation upon Pilo-motor Nerves, *Proc Roy Soc Lond* 52:547-556 (Feb 9) 1893.
4. Langley, J. N.: *The Automatic Nervous System,* part I, Cambridge: W. Heffer & Sons Ltd., 1921.

John Alexander MacWilliam
(1857-1937)

JOHN A. MACWILLIAM, born in Culmill, Scotland, received his medical training at the University of Aberdeen. In 1880, he qualified for the degree of master of medicine and was awarded the John Murray medal for high scholastic standing.[1] Two years later he presented a thesis on the muscle fibers of the myocardium and diaphragm in various classes of animals and received the degree of doctor of medicine with honors. MacWilliam pursued postgraduate work at the University of Edinburgh and University College, London; he also studied under Carl Ludwig in Leipzig, where, with Bowditch of Harvard and Gaskell of Cambridge, the physiologic properties of heart muscle were the center of interest. Subsequently, MacWilliam, appointed demonstrator of physiology at University College, London, for four years, served on the medical staff of the Charing Cross Hospital Medical School and the London School of Medicine for Women. In 1886, he was appointed to the chair of physiology at the University of Aberdeen. There for more than 40 years he was recog-

nized as an exemplary teacher of physiology, gained respect for his lucid exposition of physiologic phenomena, became skillful in experimental research, and endeared himself to many by his warm personality.

Scarcely one year had passed at Aberdeen before MacWilliam extracted from a series of anesthetized animals, including the dog, cat, mouse, hedgehog, and fowl, his deductions on fibrillar contraction of the myocardium. He proved that the aberrant response was an intrinsic phenomenon caused by a lack of harmony during contraction and relaxation of the muscle fibres. It is not due to interference from or destruction of a coordinating nerve center but is produced by a rapid succession of intrinsic uncoordinated peristaltic contractions. He also defined the relation of the refractory period to the disturbance when a faradic current was applied to the muscle bundles. The significance of the observations was not generally appreciated until some time later. The tenets of the study were presented as section headings as follows:[2]

The state of arhythmic fibrillar contraction is essentially due to certain changes occurring within the ventricles themselves. It is not due to the passages of any abnormal nerve impulses to the ventricles from other parts, or to the interruption of any impulses normally transmitted to the ventricles and necessary for their normal co-ordinated action. The condition is not due to injury or irritation of the nerves that pass over the ventricles from the base of the heart.

The arhythmic fibrillar contraction is not necessarily dependent on the destruction or paralysis of a co-ordinating centre located in any particular part of the ventricles.

The state of arhythmic fibrillar contraction (delirium cordis &c) appears to be constituted by a rapid succession of inco-ordinated peristaltic contractions—a condition that can be brought about either (1) by the influence of certain depressing or paralysing agents upon the ventricular tissue, or (2) by the application of certain forms of stimulation to the ventricular tissue.

The movements excited by faradisation in the auricles and ventricles differ very markedly in their relation to the inhibitory influence of the vagus nerve. The fibrillar movement in the ventricles appears to be entirely unaffected by vagus stimulation; the fluttering movement of the auricles can be checked or arrested by the influence of the vagus.

Two years later in the *British Medical Journal* MacWilliam postulated on the mechanism of sudden death in selected instances of fibrillary contraction in man.[3]

It seems to me in the highest degree probable that a similar phenomenon occurs in the human heart, and that it is the mode of cardiac failure and the direct and immediate cause of death in many cases of sudden dissolution. It is strange indeed if the phenomenon of fibrillar contraction is never manifested in the human heart, in any of the various conditions of altered and disordered nutrition to which it is liable. For this phenomenon has been observed in all warm-blooded animals examined; it is, as far as I am aware, a universal feature in the behaviour of the mammalian heart.

In conclusion, admitting the possibility of sudden syncope from plugging or obstruction of some portion of the coronary system . . . moreover, there is reason to assume that, in a certain number of instances, where none of the above-mentioned causes are present in any marked or dangerous degree, a sudden, unexpected, and irretrievable cardiac failure may, even in the absence of any prominent exciting cause, present itself in the form of an abrupt onset of fibrillar contraction (ventricular delirium). The cardiac pump is thrown out of gear, and the last of its vital energy is dissipated in a violent and prolonged turmoil of fruitless activity in the ventricular walls.

The cardiovascular system of man and animals continued to attract MacWilliam's attention, which included special attention to the influence of chloroform on the cardiovascular system and an exhaustive study of blood pressure in man.[4] In 1916, he was elected a fellow of the Royal Society of London, and shortly after his retirement in 1927 he received the honorary degree of doctor of laws from his alma mater.

1. John Alexander MacWilliam, M.D., obituary, *Lancet* 1:236 (Jan 23) 1939.
2. MacWilliam, J. A.: Fibrillar Contraction of the Heart, *J Physiol* 8:296-310, 1887.
3. MacWilliam, J. A.: Cardiac Failure and Sudden Death, *Brit Med J* 1:6-8 (Jan 5) 1889.
4. MacWilliam, J. A.: Blood Pressures in Man Under Normal and Pathological Conditions, *Physiol Rev* 5:303-335, 1925.

Composite by G. Bako

Ivan Petrovitch Pavlov (1849-1936)

IVAN P. PAVLOV, son of a poor parish priest with liberal beliefs and a large family, was born in the ancient village of Riazan in central Russia. Subsequently becoming one of the brilliant natural scientists of Russia, he did more than any other physiologist to quash the Cartesian belief that body and soul were separate entities. Pavlov's early education was gained in the Church; but at the age of 21, he left the seminary, prepared in the medical sciences at the University of St. Petersburg, and in his third year received a gold medal for his investigations on the pancreatic nerves.[1]

In 1875, Pavlov began the study of medicine at the Medico-Chirurgical (Military-Medical) Academy and served part time as an assistant in the physiology laboratory of the Veterinary Institute. Late in 1879, he completed the medical curriculum, passed the state examinations, and became a licensed physician. Although Pavlov did not intend to practice medicine, he received the degree of doctor of medicine in 1883 after submitting a dissertation on the nerves of the heart. In the meantime he received a two-year research fellowship in Botkin's physiological laboratory and studied with Ludwig in Leipzig and Heidenhain in Breslau. In 1890, Pavlov was appointed professor of pharmacology in the Military-Medical Academy, a year later received an additional appointment in the physiology department, and, in 1895, gained the chair of physiology which he retained until his tenure expired in 1924.

Pavlov displayed a singleness of purpose, an insatiable desire for knowledge, and a dedication to seek out logical truths in the realms of theoretical and experimental physiology; he also possessed great surgical skill, uncanny powers of observation, an enviable capacity for lecturing, a remarkable memory, and a curiosity to challenge the best natural scientists of his time. Toward the cat and the dog, his experimental subjects, Pavlov showed the same respect throughout the operative and convalescent periods as the compassionate surgeon feels for the human patient.

Pavlov planned his now famous investigations on salivary and gastric secretion with a modified Heidenhain pouch, a chronic fistula, which allowed him to study "psychic secretion" in experimental animals without disturbing the physiological responses of normal digestion. Vagal innervation was preserved, and the pouch remained connected with the stomach through a column of undamaged tissue. Gastric digestion was observed and gastric juice was collected in the pouch, while the bulk of the stomach within the abdomen responded to normal stimuli. Pavlov's initial surgical procedure, later modified, was described in 1879 in lecture form and subsequently was translated into English.[2]

My method was as follows. It differs slightly from Heidenhain's. From the wall of the duodenum, an oval piece, containing the orifice of the pancreatic duct, is cut out, the bowel, the lumen of which is not appreciably narrowed, stitched up, and the isolated piece of intestine sewn (with the mucous membrane outwards) into the slit in the abdominal wall. The whole heals quickly; the operation, which requires no special skill, is only of short duration (about half an hour), and is well borne by the animals. After two weeks they are ready for observation.

. . . it is tolerably easy to maintain an animal for many months, or even years, in a fit condition for experiment without the necessity of adopting any other special precautions.

Pavlov wisely chose initially to remain an objective physiological observer and disregarded psychological implications in interpretation of his findings. When he recorded secretion of gastric (and salivary) juice in response to visual, auditory, or gustatory stimuli, he assumed that it followed a physiological plan as a reproducible reflex act. The study of psychic secretion, following sham feeding which depended upon reactions integrated at the level of cerebral cortex, was an obvious step in the investigation of conditioned or acquired reflexes, differentiating them from unconditioned or innate reflexes. Thus, he progressed from the study of the physiology of digestion to the physiology of the higher centers of the brain. Sham feeding was described as follows.[2]

In the year 1889, we (myself and Madam Schumow-Simanowski) performed the operation of oesophagotomy on a dog already possessing a gastric fistula; that is to say, we divided the gullet in the neck, and caused both its divided ends to heal separately into an angle of the skin incision. We thereby accomplished the complete anatomical separation of the cavities of the mouth and stomach. Dogs so operated upon recover perfectly with careful nursing, and live many years in the best of health. In feeding, their food must naturally be brought directly into the stomach. We have here before us a dog operated upon in the manner I have described in the first lecture. . . . The animal eats greedily, but the whole of the food swallowed, comes out again at the oesophageal opening in the neck. After feeding in this way (which for shortness we will henceforth name "sham feeding") for five minutes, perfectly pure gastric juice makes its appearance at the fistula. . . . The meaning of this experiment is clear. It is obvious that the effect of the feeding is transmitted by nervous channels to the gastric glands.

Consequently, in the sham feeding experiment, by the act of eating, the excitation of the nerves of the gastric glands depends upon a psychical factor which has here grown into a physiological one . . . the process may be said to be a complicated reflex act. . . . The material to be digested— the food—is only found outside the organism in the surrounding world. It is acquired not alone by the exercise of muscular force, but also by the intervention of higher functions, such as judgment, will, desire. Hence the simultaneous excitation of the different sense organs, of sight, of hearing, of smell and taste, is the first and strongest impulse towards the activity of the gastric glands.

Although Pavlov was trained as a physiologist and chose to remain a physiologist, his work on conditioned reflexes became more and more psychological, meanwhile being sensitive to possible clinical implications.[3] He explored the observable relationships between external stimuli and glandular secretion, which could be reproduced at will and systematically analyzed in a controlled laboratory environment. The concept of the conditioned reflex had been carefully explored and adequately supported experimentally at the time Pavlov received the Nobel prize in medicine in 1904. He described the difference between the unconditioned and the conditioned reflexes in salivary secretion, recognizing the fact that the conditioned response is based upon an unconditioned reflex as follows:[4]

The difference between the two reflexes is firstly that our old physiological reflex is constant, unconditioned, while the new reflex continually fluctuates and, hence, is *conditioned*. . . . In the unconditioned reflex those properties of the object act as stimuli with which the saliva is confronted physiologically, e.g., hardness, dryness, certain chemical properties; in the conditioned reflex, however, those properties of the object act as stimuli that in themselves have no direct relation at all with the physiological role of the saliva, e.g., colour, etc. These last properties appear here in some way as signals for the first. One is bound to regard their stimulating action as a further, more delicate adaption of the salivary glands to the phenomena in the external world. . . . Any phenomenon in the external world can be made a temporary signal of an object stimulating the salivary glands, if the stimulation of the oral mucous membrane by this object has been associated repeatedly once or several times with the action of the given external phenomenon on other sensitive body surfaces. . . . Each conditioned reflex, ie, stimulation through the signalling characteristics of the objects is based on an unconditioned reflex, that is, a stimulation through the essential characteristics of the object.

Pavlov, who directed most of his energies to the laboratory in his long life, won the veneration of a large number of scientists throughout the world and received many national and international honors. In his personal life he was a humble man of simple tastes, regular in habits, a lover of physical work as the best recreation from mental activity, and an abstainer from tobacco. He was liberal in his thinking but uncompromising with the Bolsheviks; meanwhile, he was recognized by them as one of their great

Russian scientists. He is remembered by the laity as the bearded laboratory man with the dog, whose salivary juice responded to the ringing of a bell or the quarter tones of a violin—a man who dreamed of a "Tower of Silence," the ideal environment for his animal experiments.

1. Babkin, B. P.: *Pavlov: A Biography*, Chicago: University of Chicago Press, 1949.
2. Pavlov, I. P.: *The Work of the Digestive Glands* (Russ), W. H. Thompson (trans.), London: Charles Griffin & Co., Ltd., 1902.
3. Pavlov, I. P.: *Lectures on Conditional Reflexes* (Russ), W. H. Gantt (trans.-ed.), New York: International Publishers, 1941.
4. Mörner, K. A. H.: "Ivan Petrovitch," and Pavlov, I. P.: "Physiology of Digestion," in *Physiology or Medicine, 1901-1921*, New York: Elsevier Publishing Co., 1967, p. 135-155.

Composite by G. Bako

Sir E. A. Sharpey-Schafer (1850-1935)

EDWARD ALBERT SCHAFER, pupil of William Sharpey, one of the outstanding British physiologists, was born at Hornsey, England, and received his intermediate education at Clewer House School, Windsor.[1] He continued at University College, London, and began his medical training at University College Hospital. Although his brothers and father were in business, Schafer chose a scientific career and justified this decision while a medical student by capturing prizes in zoology, anatomy, and physiology. A developing interest in research and teaching led to the award, in 1871, of a scholarship at University College to pursue basic problems. This work was begun under William Sharpey, for whom the scholarship was named, when he held the professorship of general anatomy and physiology. Sharpey was one of a distinguished small number who helped design "English physiology," at a time when France and Germany were leading in physiologic science.

Shapey's early influence over Schafer attracted him to histology as a physiologic discipline. (Late in life, Schafer's surname was extended to Sharpey-Schafer, after dropping the umlaut, a token legally executed for the great esteem and respect held by the pupil for his teacher.) Schäfer was appointed assistant professor of physiology in 1874 under Burdon-Sanderson and served as Fullerian professor at the Royal Institution from 1878 to 1881. When Burdon-Sanderson left for Oxford in 1883, Schafer was advanced to the Jodrell professorship. He was elected to the chair of physiology at the University of Edinburgh in 1899 and held the post until 1933, when he retired as emeritus professor, having completed an exceptional career in teaching and research over a period of 60 years.

Schafer's early interest in histology—interpreting form in relation to function in the experimental laboratory—was maintained throughout his life. Among his many outstanding contributions are excerpted the discovery of adrenalin, the active principle of the adrenal medulla, and the resuscitation of the drowned, the Schafer method. Other noteworthy investigations identified by his biographers include the delineation and function of nerves of the jellyfish, the absorption of fat by the villi of the small intestine, the dynamics of the pulmonary circulation, the contraction and innervation of the spleen, interpretation of muscular contraction, action of the intercostal muscles,

cerebral localization, photographic recording of the action of the frog's heart, effects of stimulation of the partial transection of the spinal cord, and effects of section of the vagus and cervical sympathetic nerves. He concluded one of his experiments on nerve function with surgical severance of a nerve in his arm.

The constriction of selected arterioles and elevation of blood pressure produced by the parenteral injection of a simple extract of the suprarenal gland was reported by Oliver and Schafer in 1894 to the Physiological Society of London. This proved to be one of the first studies in the investigation of internal secretions, later called hormones, when the field of endocrinology was developing. The preliminary communication was brief and contained the following description.[2]

The suprarenal capsules yield to water (cold or hot), to alcohol or to glycerine a substance which exerts a most powerful action upon the blood vessels, upon the heart, and upon the skeletal muscles. These effects have been investigated upon the dog, cat, rabbit and frog. In the frog the solutions were injected into the dorsal lymph-sac, in the rabbit subcutaneously and into a vein, in the other animals into a vein. The alcohol extracts were first dried and the residue extracted with normal saline; the watery decoctions were made with normal saline, and the glycerine extracts were largely diluted with the same previous to injection. The doses employed have varied from a mere trace up to an amount of extract equivalent to 3 grains (0.2 gramme) of the fresh gland; in one or two instances we have given larger doses with the object of obtaining if possible a lethal result. The extracts used have been made from the suprarenals of the calf, sheep and dog. Exactly similar effects have been obtained in each case.

The effect upon the blood vessels is to cause extreme contraction of the arteries, so that the blood-pressure is enormously raised. This is most evident when the vagi are cut in order to obviate the inhibitory action upon the heart which otherwise occurs; it is also seen after section of the cervical cord. The blood-pressure may rise from 2 to 4 times above normal. This extreme contraction of the vessels is evidenced by the plethysmograph; section of the nerves going to the limb produces no difference in the result. The effect is therefore peripheral. This can also be shown in the frog with its nerve-centres destroyed, and through the blood vessels of which normal saline is allowed to circulate; if only a small quantity of suprarenal extract is added to the saline the flow almost entirely ceases.

The effect upon the skeletal muscles has been investigated in the frog. The movements of a frog to which a hypodermic injection of extract of suprarenal capsule (equal to 1 to 2 grains of the fresh gland) have been given soon become slow, and after about half-an-hour the reflexes are very faint and almost abolished; the animal soon appears completely paralysed. The muscles however still contract on being stimulated, either directly or through the motor nerves, but the contractions are modified, the relaxation period being greatly prolonged, as with veratria poisoning. The period of latent stimulation is not greatly, if at all, lengthened. The fatigue curves were rapidly developed. The effect is not at all comparable to that produced by curare.

We have noticed a slight effect to be produced upon the respiration, which may become shallower; but in the doses we have used the result was very slight when compared with the prodigious effects upon the heart and blood vessels which were obtained.

The prone-pressure method of applying artificial respiration on persons following immersion was communicated, in 1903, to the Royal Society of Edinburgh, of which he was a member. Schafer showed that the respiratory exchange was significantly greater than with other methods then in vogue. The procedure was recommended by the Royal Life Saving Society of England, which awarded him their distinguished service medal in 1909, and was widely adopted by national and international life-saving agencies. The method was generally practiced until recent years when it was replaced by mouth-to-mouth resuscitation. Shafer's complete instructions follow.[3]

Immediately on removal from the water, place the patient face downwards on the ground with a folded coat under the lower part of the chest. Not a moment must be lost in removing clothing. *If respiration has ceased, artificial respiration is to be commenced at once; every instant of delay is serious.*

To effect artificial respiration put yourself athwart or on one side of the patient's body in a kneeling posture and facing his head. Place your hands flat over the lower part of the back (on the lowest ribs), one on each side, and gradually throw the weight of your body forward on to them so as to produce firm pressure—which must not be violent—upon the patient's chest. By this means the air (and water, if there is any) is driven out of the patient's lungs. Immediately thereafter raise your body slowly so as to remove the pressure, but leaving your hands in position. Repeat this forward and backward movement (pressure and relaxation of pressure) every

four or five seconds. In other words, sway your body slowly forward and backwards upon your arms twelve to fifteen times a minute, without any marked pause between the movements. This course must be pursued for at least half an hour, or until the natural respirations are resumed. If they are resumed and, as sometimes happens, again tend to fail, the process of artificial respiration must be again resorted to as before.

Whilst one person is carrying out artificial respiration in this way, others may, if there be opportunity, busy themselves with applying hot flannels to the body and limbs, and hot bottles to the feet; but no attempt should be made to remove the wet clothing or to give any restoratives by the mouth until natural breathing has recommenced.

Hypodermic injections of atropine sulphate (1/100th to 1/50th grain) and of supra-renal extract (either as adrenalin chloride or in any other form) may be used to assist recovery.

In addition to Schafer's voluminous investigations and reputation as an outstanding teacher, he assumed significant editorial responsibilities and prepared a full quota of texts and monographs. His first teaching manual, *A Course of Practical Histology,* appeared in 1877. This was replaced in 1885 by *The Essentials of Histology,* which was updated through the 17th edition over a period of 68 years, of which Schäfer was responsible for almost 50 years.[4] His most ambitious undertaking was the two-volume *Text-Book of Physiology* (1898-1900), with major sections prepared by leading physiologists of Great Britain, and which became the standard work of physiologic reference.[5] Also, he prepared part I of volume two of the eighth edition of Quain's *Anatomy,* which dealt with microscopic anatomy; and a monograph, *The Endocrine Organs,* published in 1916, based upon the Lane medical lectures delivered at Stanford University in 1913. He was founder of the *Quarterly Journal of Experimental Physiology,* chief editor or a member of the editorial board until his retirement in 1933, and a member of the editorial board of the *Journal of Physiology* for many years.

Schafer was elected to membership in the Royal Society at the early age of 28 and received their Copley medal in 1924, the highest honor awarded by the Society. He was knighted in 1913 and was the recipient of the following degrees and awards: LLD Aberdeen 1897, McGill 1908, St. Andrews

1911, Edinburgh 1933; DSc Trinity College, Dublin 1905, Cambridge 1914, Melbourne 1914, Oxford 1926, National University, Ireland 1933; MD Bern 1910, Gröningen 1914; DSc Méd Louvain 1930; and the Baly Medal of the Royal College of Physicians in 1897. Schafer was a member of the British Medical Association for more than half a century, and was president of the British Association for the Advancement of Science in 1912, the International Congress of Physiologists in 1923, and the Royal Society of Edinburgh in 1933.

Sharpey-Schafer was endowed with a keen sense of humor, but he could also quote the Bible as readily as a theology student; a kind and gentle person, he loved adults as well as children. He was an ardent golfer, championed the rights of women (particularly favoring their admission to the medical profession), and as a gregarious professor, took great delight in extending hospitality in his home.

1. "Sir Edward Albert Sharpey-Schafer 1850-1935," in *Obituary Notices of Fellows of the Royal Society*, London: Harrison & Sons, Ltd., 1932-1935, vol 1, pp 401-407.
2. Oliver, G., and Schafer, E. A.: *On the Physiological Action of Extract of the Suprarenal Capsules*, J Physiol 16:1-4, 1894.
3. Schafer, E. A.: Description of a Simple and Efficient Method of Performing Artificial Respiration in the Human Subject Especially in Cases of Drowning, *Medicochir Trans* 87:609-614, 1904.
4. Schafer, E. A.: *The Essentials of Histology*, Philadelphia: Lea Brothers & Co., 1885.
5. Schafer, E. A.: *Text-Book of Physiology*, 2 vol, Edinburgh and London: Y. J. Pentland, 1898.

John Scott Haldane (1860-1936)

J. S. HALDANE, fellow of New College and Reader in physiology, University of Oxford, is best known for his contributions in basic and applied physiology of respiration. He was also a natural philosopher and documented his meditations on the phenomenon of life with his experimental studies on the physiology of breathing.[1] An interest in gas exchange in the lungs led him to study the sensitivity of the respiratory center; also such clinicophysiological subjects as hazards of diving, submarine living, occupational dusts, gas warfare, and hygiene of mining;

and the strictly clinical subjects—use of tannic acid for burns, ill effects of high environmental temperatures, and hookworm infection causing anemia in miners.

Composite by G. Bako

Haldane was born in Edinburgh into a family with a rich heritage, which was further enriched by members of his generation.[2] He was educated at Edinburgh Academy, Edinburgh University, and Jena University, receiving the MD degree from Edinburgh. Although Haldane never practiced clinical medicine, his medical education served him well in problems that involved physiological stress or occupational disease, and supported his deductions from experimental physiology in man when others were content to draw critical conclusions exclusively from animal studies.

Following graduation, Haldane studied in Carnelley's laboratory at University College, Dundee, and in Salkowski's laboratory in Berlin. In 1887, he joined his uncle, Burdon-Sanderson, first professor of physiology at Oxford, and thereafter never left Oxford for an academic appointment elsewhere, although never achieving the goal of professor of physiology. An interest in the composition of air in homes and schools at Dundee was extended to the chemical response of the blood to carbon monoxide, the lethal constituent of "after damp" in colliery explosions. The appreciation of the affinity of carbon monoxide for hemoglobin, so strong as to drive out the loosely bound oxygen, provided the clue for a physiological means of treatment. The afflicted were removed to fresh air, where the reversible reaction—$HbCO + O_2 \leftrightarrows HbO_2 + CO$—became effective. But early in the investigation of respiratory gases special tools were needed, such as a device for the determination of carbon dioxide and oxygen. His first respiratory gas analyzer was described in 1898.[3] This was modified later, but the basic principle remains useful. The Haldane gas analyzer has been an indispensable item of laboratory equipment for respiratory physiologists for more than one-half a century; although it has been replaced in selected instances by more rapid procedures, it occupies an indispensable place in the calibration of more modern equipment.

In the same pursuit of experimental devices, Haldane discovered the property of ferricyanide in releasing oxygen from oxyhemoglobin in whole blood, the basis for the Van Slyke gas analyzer, a companion piece to the "Haldane" in the cardiopulmonary laboratory. Yet a third critical device in the respiratory studies was a sampler for determination of composition of alveolar air. Until very recent years the essentials in the determination of the "arterial point" on the oxygen dissociation curve involved the collection of a sample of alveolar air by Haldane's method, determination of the partial pressure of carbon dioxide in the Haldane gas analyzer, and construction of a family of oxygen and carbon dioxide dissociation curves by means of the Haldane and Van Slyke gas analyzers. The first step, collection of alveolar air, was described as follows:[4]

METHOD OF OBTAINING NORMAL ALEVEOLAR AIR

A piece of india-rubber tube was taken of about 1 inch diameter and 4 feet long. Into one end . . . was fitted a mouthpiece, the other being either left open or connected with a spirometer. About 2 or 3 inches from the mouthpiece a small hole was made, through which was inserted air-tight the tube of a gas-receiver. The gas-receiver was provided with a 3-way tap at the upper end, the lower end being either opened or closed by a tap. Before an experiment the receiver was filled with mercury if the lower end was open, or else completely exhausted.

The subject of the experiment sat in a comfortable position and breathed quite normally for some time. Just as a normal inspiration ended he then expired quickly and very deeply through the mouthpiece and instantly closed it with his tongue. The tap of the receiver was then turned and a sample of the air in the tube taken for analysis.

Among Haldane's great contributions to basic physiology were the investigations into the control of respiration, the participation of the vagus nerve, and the importance of partial pressure of carbon dioxide on the respiratory center under normal conditions with an adequate supply of oxygen. The true stimulus was originally thought to be the partial pressure of carbon dioxide carried by the arterial blood to the respiratory center in the medulla. This hypothesis identified a chemical substance acting upon the center, independent of nervous stimuli. Although it was shown later that the partial pressure of carbon dioxide was a direct function of the hydrogen ion concentration, the critical variable rather than the carbon dioxide, our current understanding of respiration is based upon Haldane's experiments and speculation. Contemporary investigations have verified the chemical control of respiration, but the chemoreceptors have not been identified nor has the respiratory center been localized.[4]

The experiments which have been detailed above indicate clearly that under normal conditions the regulation of the lung-ventilation depends on the pressure of CO_2 in the alveolar air. Even a very slight rise or fall in the alveolar CO_2 pressure causes a great increase or diminution in the lung-ventilation. Thus we found that a rise of 0.2% of an atmosphere in the alveolar CO_2 pressure was sufficient to double the ventilation of the lung alveoli. For each individual the normal alveolar CO_2 pressure appears to be an extraordinarily sharply defined physiological constant.

The relationship between the partial pressure of carbon dioxide and of oxygen in the exchange of blood gases were expressed by Haldane in the carbon dioxide dissociation curves for oxygenated and reduced blood, a logical deduction, since carbonic acid influences the position of the S-shaped oxygen dissociation curves. The carbon dioxide dissociation curves plotted by Haldane were complementary to the oxygen dissociation curves of Barcroft.[5]

(1) Under normal conditions the curve representing the relation between pressure of CO_2 and amount of CO_2 taken up by fresh defibrinated human blood is very definite and constant for the same individual, and does not differ much for different individuls. At 40 mm. pressure at CO_2 100 volumes of oxygenated human blood take up about 50 volumes of CO_2; and at about 80 mm. pressure 15 additional volumes are taken up.
(2) At a given pressure of CO_2 blood which has been deprived of oxygen takes up considerably more CO_2 than oxygenated blood. The oxygen (and the same is true for CO) thus tends to drive out CO_2 and this action depends on the saturation of the haemoglobin. A curve is given, showing the extent of this action with varying pressures of CO_2.

In 1911, Haldane led an Anglo-American expedition to the summit of Pike's Peak, Colorado, for the study of the physiological effects of high altitude and the mechanism of acclimatization. The experimental observations were interpreted by Haldane as confirming his belief in the active secretion of oxygen by the pulmonary alveolar epithelium. The fact of acclimatization and an increase in partial pressure of oxygen in arterial blood were falsely interpreted as proof of the capacity of the alveolar cells to secrete oxygen.[6]

(3) After acclimatisation the resting arterial oxygen pressure had risen to about 35 mm. of mercury above the alveolar oxygen pressure, whereas at or near sea-level the resting arterial oxygen pressure is no higher than the alveolar oxygen pressure. The raising of arterial oxygen pressure is attributable to secretory activity of the cells lining the lung alveoli, and is a most important factor in the acclimatisation. On breathing air rich in oxygen the secretory activity was rapidly diminished.

Throughout Haldane's abundant scientific career he spoke periodically on philosophy, rejected the mechanistic theory of life, and accepted vitalism since it appeared to satisfy his belief in the unity of an organism. Several of his statements, prepared half a century ago and before our present knowledge of the transmission of individual char-

acteristics through the genetic chains, remain valid.[1]

This assumption is surely one which taxes scientific imagination to the utmost, but let us make it. We have now to imagine the mechanism of reproduction and heredity . . . all the evidence points to the nuclear germ-plasm as the essential carrier of hereditary characters. We are thus compelled, on the mechanistic hypothesis, to attribute to the germ-plasm, or germinal nuclear substance, a structure so arranged that in presence of suitable pabulum and stimuli it produces the whole of the vast and definitely ordered assemblage of mechanisms existing in the adult organism.
When we trace each nuclear mechanism backwards we find ourselves obligated to admit that it has been formed by division from a pre-existing nuclear mechanism, and this from pre-existing nuclear mechanisms through millions of cell-generations. We are thus forced to the admission that the germ-plasm is not only a structure or mechanism of inconceivable complexity, but that this structure is capable of dividing itself to an absolutely indefinite extent and yet retaining its original structure.

Full academic honors never came to Haldane although he received honorary degrees from Edinburgh, Birmingham, Oxford, Leeds, Cambridge, Dublin, and Witwatersrand. He resigned his readership when Sherrington was appointed professor of physiology, but he continued to work in his private laboratory at his home in Oxford. He was elected a fellow of the Royal Society in 1897, received a Royal medal in 1916, and the Copley medal in 1934.[7] The Silliman lectures at Yale, his greatest academic accolade, which he had been invited to deliver, were postponed because of World War I and were not published until 1922.[8] This is one of the remarkable treatises in contemporary human physiology.

1. Haldane, J. S.: *Mechanism, Life and Personality*, London: J. Murray, 1914.
2. Priestley, J. G.: Prof. J. S. Haldane, C. H., F. R. S., obituary, *Nature* 137:566-569, 1936.
3. Haldane, J.: Some Improved Methods of Gas Analysis, *J Physiol* 2:465-480, 1897-1898.
4. Haldane, J. S.: and Priestley, J. G.: The Regulation of the Lung-Ventilation, *J Physiol* 32:225-266, 1905.
5. Christiansen, J.: Douglas, C. G.: and Haldane, J. S.: The Absorption and Dissociation of Carbon Dioxide by Human Blood, *J Physiol* 48:244-271, 1914.
6. Douglas, C. G., et al: VI. Physiological Observations Made at Pike's Peak, Colorado, *Philos Trans Royal Soc Lond* 203:185-310, 1913.

7. Douglas, C. G.: "John Scott Haldane, 1860-1936," in *Obituary Notices of Fellows of the Royal Society of London* 2:114-139, 1936-1938.

8. Haldane, J. S.: *Respiration,* New Haven, Conn: Yale University Press, 1922.

urea and sulfate in the formation of urine. Starling was especially gifted in composition and prepared such classical treatises as the Harveian oration entitled *The Wisdom of the Body,* the Oliver-Sharpey lectures entitled *The Feeding of Nations,* a popular text for students of physiology, and a brochure describing the action of alcohol on man.

Starling, born in London into a family of modest means, attended King's College School, where he studied divinity, mathematics, and modern and ancient languages. As a brilliant student he won a number of prizes and found no difficulty in entering Guy's Hospital Medical School; there he served as demonstrator in physiology and received the MB degree in 1889. In the meantime, he served in Kühne's laboratory at Heidelberg and recognized the advantages of the exposition of the medical sciences in German universities as compared with schools in England. In 1890, he accepted an appointment in Schäfer's laboratory at University College and began a scientific and social association with William Maddock Bayliss, one of the most respected and capable leaders of the English school of physiology. In proper time, Starling succeeded Schäfer as Jodrell professor of physiology.

Composite by G. Bako

Ernest H. Starling (1866-1927)

THE COMING OF AGE OF PHYSIOLOGY in England half a century ago may be credited to a relatively small number of experimental scientists whose contributions usually lacked clinical application; their investigations were pursued without promise of immediate or remote pertinence to the understanding of disease. However, Ernest Henry Starling, the exception, has been termed "The Clinician's Physiologist" although he was concerned largely with physiological studies. His inquiries into the action of the heart under stress and the mechanism of transfer of solutes and fluids in capillary-tissue exchange eventually led to the understanding of the pathogenesis of cardiac failure. Other physiological studies included the discovery of secretin, the pancreatic stimulant, and the measurement of the tubular secretion of

In selecting appropriate items to the credit to Starling, it is noteworthy that, before the age of 30, he had prepared his experimental observations on the absorption of fluids from connective tissue spaces and had measured directly the osmotic pressure of the serum proteins. Twenty-five years were to elapse before his concept of the regulation of capillary pressure was accepted through micro technique of manipulation and injection of viable capillaries. Starling wrote:[2]

In the limbs and connective tissues generally of the peripheral parts of the body, we have capillaries which are more or less impervious to proteids. As the blood passes under pressure through these capillaries, a certain amount of lymph is filtered through their walls, but in the process it loses the greater part of its proteids. We have therefore on one side of the capillary wall blood-plasma with 8% proteids, on the other side lymph containing 2 to 3% proteids. In this separation of proteid a certain amount of work must have been done, and if the proteids of serum are really analogous to the substance *X* of my illustration and possess an osmotic pressure, there must be a difference of osmotic pressure between intra- and extravascular fluids tending to a reabsorption of the latter. It becomes desirable to inquire whether the proteids of serum have any osmotic pressure and if so, what is the extent of this pressure.

The importance of these measurements lies in the fact that, although the osmotic pressure of the proteids of the plasma is so insignificant, it is of an order of magnitude comparable to that of the capillary pressures; and whereas capillary pressure determines transudation, the osmotic pressure of the proteids of the serum determines absorption. Moreover, if we leave the frictional resistance of the capillary wall to the passage of fluid through it out of account, the osmotic attraction of the serum for the extravascular fluid will be proportional to the force expended in the production of this latter, so that, at any given time, there must be a balance between the hydrostatic pressure of the blood in the capillaries and the osmotic attraction of the blood for the surrounding fluids. With increased capillary pressure there must be increased transudation, until equilibrium is established at a somewhat higher point, when there is a more dilute fluid in the tissue-spaces and therefore a higher absorbing force to balance the increased capillary pressure.

Since the capillary wall permits the passage of crystalloids from the blood, the effective osmotic pressure is exerted by the serum proteids in equilibrium with the hydrostatic pressure. In cardiac failure, when the hydrostatic pressure rises, transudation follows and edema develops—a fundamental concept advanced by Starling and supported by his observations on the law of the heart. The extracardiac phase of cardiac failure, discussed in the Arris and Gale lectures for 1896, was based upon these experimental observations and on Weber's concept of mean systemic pressure, ie, that pressure in any closed fluid-filled system is the direct function of the capacity of the system and the quantity of contained fluid. If a pump is introduced (the heart), pressure forward of the pump rises and that behind it falls. Starling dissected the mechanism of cardiac failure into four stages.[3]

Stage 1.—Heart-pump failure; fall of arterial pressure; rise of pressure in the venous trunks near the heart; fall of capillary pressures in the peripheral parts of the body, in the kidneys, and in the intestine; and absorption of fluid by blood vessels from intestines and peripheral tissues.

Stage 2.—Continued absorption from the alimentary canal with diminished excretion from the kidneys, and production of hydraemic plethora with rise of mean systemic pressure. This leads to Stage 3—rise of capillary pressure in all dependent parts of the body, capillaries injured by malnutrition, and excessive transudation, leading to dropsy. Stage 4.—The continued hydraemic plethora leads to ever-increasing over-filling of the heart cavities and to ultimate failure of the already incompetent heart.

Starling's law of the heart, probably his best-known physiological exposition, was defined more than a decade later. Developing and improving the heart-lung preparation described by Martin, he confirmed his prior deductions that cardiac output is not fixed but is proportional to input and that the pressure in the left side of the heart rises at the same rate as in the right side. The familiar Starling curves, plotting volume output on the abscissa and inflow pressure on the ordinate, were published in 1914 in the *Journal of Physiology*[4] immediately preceding the statement of the law.[5] The law was restated later in the Linacre lecture.[6]

The law of the heart is therefore the same as that of skeletal muscle, namely that the mechanical energy set free on passage from the resting to the contracted state depends on the area of "chemically active surface," *i.e.* on the length of the muscle fibres.

Now here are two conditions in which the work of the heart is increased and in which this organ adapts itself by increasing the chemical changes in its muscle at each contraction to the increased demands made upon it. It is evident that there is one factor which is common to both cases, and that is the increased volume of the heart when it begins to contract. So that we may make the following general statement. Within physiological limits the larger the volume of the heart, the greater are the energy of its contraction and the amount of chemical change at each contraction.

The studies on secretin, fundamental to the development of the current concept of hormones, were conducted in the laboratories at University College in cooperation with Bayliss, by then his brother-in-law. At that time the teaching followed Pavlov's interpretation of secretory activity of the digestive glands, then believed to be exclusively under nervous control. Bayliss and Starling demonstrated the physiological effectiveness of a chemical substance on a structurally denervated organ.[7]

1. The secretion of the pancreatic juice is normally evoked by the entrance of acid chyme into the duodenum, and is proportional to the amount of acid entering (Pawlow). This secretion does not depend on a nervous reflex, and occurs when all the nervous connections of the intestine are destroyed.
2. The contact of the acid with the epithelial cells of the duodenum causes in them the production of a body (secretin), which is absorbed from the cells by the blood-current, and is carried to the pancreas, where it acts as a specific stimulus to the pancreatic cells, exciting a secretion of pancreatic juice proportonal to the amount of secretin present.

The law of the intestine, a local reflex, was another significant contribution to the physiology of digestion. It was defined by Bayliss and Starling as follows:[8]

1. Two kinds of movements are to be distinguished in the small intestine, viz. the rhythmic pendulum movements, and the true peristaltic contraction.
2. The pendulum movements are due to rhythmic contractions affecting longitudinal and circular coats simultaneously. They recur about 10 or 12 times in the minute, and travel along the intestine at a rate of 2 to 5 cm. per second. They are myogenic in origin, and are probably propagated by means of the muscle fibres.
3. The peristaltic contractions are true coordinated reflexes, started by mechanical stimulation of the intestine, and carried out by the local nervous mechanism (Auerbach's plexus). They are independent of the connections of the gut with the central nervous system. They travel only in one direction, from above downwards, and are abolished on paralysing the local nervous apparatus by means of nicotin or cocaine.
4. The production of the true peristaltic wave is dependent on the unvarying response of the intestinal nervous mechanism to local stimulation, the *law of the intestine*. This law is as follows:— Local stimulation of the gut produces excitation above and inhibition below the excited spot. These effects are dependent on the activity of the local nervous mechanism.

In 1922, Starling resigned his professorship at University College and the following year was appointed Foulerton Research Professor at the Royal Society. His most notable postwar investigations extended his studies on renal function begun in Guy's Hospital a quarter of a century earlier. The isolated dog kidney was utilized to explain the integration of function with structure. It had long been accepted that glomerular filtrate was a protein-free filtrate of plasma. The function of the tubule in adding or subtracting to the glomerular filtrate in the preparation of bladder urine had not been defined for each solute. Starling and Verney poisoned the renal tubules in the isolated dog kidney and discovered that urea and sulfates normally are excreted by the tubular cells.[9]

It is clear from the results of these workers that the formation of the urine cannot be explained on the basis of filtration and reabsorption of a fluid of constant and invariable composition. Selective reabsorption or secretion, or both, must be called into play, and we have attempted to decide this question by experiments on the isolated organ.

In Table V, in which tubular function was partially eliminated by perfusing the kidney for two minutes with cyanided blood, . . . it is evident that the return to the normal circulation was accompanied by a marked fall in the total urea eliminated per unit of time. The temperature of the blood, the blood pressure and blood flow through the kidney remained constant before and after the cyanided blood was pumped through. We therefore feel justified in assuming that there was no change in the rate of glomerular filtration. This fall in the total urea eliminated can, then, be explained only on the assumption that this body is actively secreted into the glomerular filtrate by the tubular epithelium.

The clinician's physiologist spoke wisely and clearly on medical education. He encouraged scientific maturity in his pupils from America, the Continent, and his homeland. Many rose to the summit in academic circles. Equally important in the learning guild was the capacity to point out the deficiencies as he saw them in the training of physicians and physiologists in the English schools. He believed that training and prolonged exposure to the basic sciences were critical for the development of clinicians in private practice and of full-time members of clinical departments in the medical school. A similar movement was started in the United States in the 1920's and just now is reaching fruition in the majority of our medical schools.

1. Chapman, C. B.: Ernest Henry Starling, The Clinician's Physiologist, *Ann Intern Med* (suppl 2) 57:1-43, 1962.

2. Starling, E. H.: On the Absorption of Fluids From the Connective Tissue Spaces, *J Physiol* 19:312-326, 1895-1896.

3. Starling, E. H.: The Arris and Gale Lectures on the Physiological Factors Involved in the Causation of Dropsy, *Lancet* 1:1267-1270, 1331-1334, 1407-1410, 1896.

4. Patterson, S. W., and Starling, E. H.: On The Mechanical Factors Which Determine the Output of the Ventricles, *J Physiol* 48:357-379, 1914.

5. Patterson, S. W.; Piper, H.; and Starling, E. H.: The Regulation of the Heart Beat, *J Physiol* 48:465-513, 1914.

6. Starling, E. H.: *The Linacre Lecture on the Law of the Heart,* London: Longmans, Green and Co., 1918.

7. Bayliss, W. M., and Starling, E. H.: The Mechanism of Pancreatic Secretion, *J Physiol* 28:325-353, 1902.

8. Bayliss, W. M., and Starling, E. H.: The Movements and Innervation of the Small Intestine, *J Physiol* 24:99-143, 1899.

9. Starling, E. H., and Verney, E. B.: The Secretion of Urine as Studied on the Isolated Kidney, *Proc Roy Soc [Biol]* 97:321-363, 1924-1925.

Composite by G. Bako

Heinrich Ewald Hering, Jr.
(1866-1948)

HERING THE YOUNGER, of Prague and Cologne, enriched our understanding of cardiovascular function with the interpretation of the carotid sinus reflex, experimental studies on the independent action of auricles and ventricles, and the analysis of pulsus

irregularis perpetuus, later called "auricular fibrillation." He was born in Vienna, where his father E. Hering, the noted physiologist, was then in residence but who later taught at Leipzig. The son matriculated at the University of Prague, advanced into the faculty, and at the age of 36 was appointed professor of general and experimental pathology. Just before World War I, he accepted an invitation to become Director of the Institute of Pathologic Physiology at the University of Cologne.[1]

Hering's initial studies concerned the innervation of skeletal muscle. This led him to the study of the physiologic and pathologic function of the heart and great vessels and the correlation with clinical findings of the activity of the chambers of the heart and the pulse rate. Although an irregular pulse had been observed by the ancients, in 1903, Hering described, as a special irregularity, auricular fibrillation and called it "pulsus irregularis perpetuus." Its current designation was assigned by Sir James Mackenzie in 1908. The short and long periods of the irregular action of the heart were attributed to extra stimuli of myogenic origin. Hering noted that:[2]

The pulsus irregularis perpetuus which has not been analysed previously seems initially to escape any sound basis with the confusing short and long periods, weak and strong pulses. We find, however, after reflection and with the aid of experimental studies that such an analysis is now possible.

From the theortical standpoint cardiac arrhythmia consists of two types, and may result either from (A) an *abnormal behavior of the stimulus* or (B) an abnormal behavior of the *irritability of the heart* or selected portions or (C) when both (A and B) exist.

These types can be distinguished experimentally; but this has not been proved from *clinical* observations, since the human heart cannot be subjected to direct investigation, and deductions can be made only on the basis of certain symptoms.

The pulsus irregularis observed in *valvular heart diseases, coronary sclerosis,* and *myocardial diseases* is persistent and for that reason, I have called it pulsus irregularis perpetuus; furthermore, it is essentially the *same* whether the patient's heart beats *faster* or *slower,* as for example, after digitalis; it does not arise under the influence of respiration, and thus it is not identical with pulsus irregularis respiratorius.

All of these facts suggest that the pulsus irregularis perpetuus has its origin within the heart and is of *cardiac origin*. The fact alone that there is no respiratory arrhythmia indicates that the abnormally short as well as the abnormally long periods *do not result from the direct influence of the extra-cardial cardiac nerves;* thus there is no pulsus irregularis that would depend on the direct influence of the extracardiac nerves unless in combination with the influence of respiration.

Two years after these conclusions, Hering reported on the independent action of the auricles and ventricles in dogs following the surgical interruption of the bundle of His. He found in the experimental animals that:[3]

(1) The ventricles beat slower than the auricles, but the beat of both, different in rate, remains regular.

(2) The ventricles beat in an absolute dissociation from the auricles.

(3) The extrasystoles of the auricles do not produce any extrasystoles of the ventricles, and the extrasystoles of the ventricles do not produce extrasystoles of the auricles.

(4) Both the auricles and the ventricles beat automatically, which is proved by the fact that ventricular extrasystoles are not followed by a compensatory pause.

(5) Irritation of extracardiac nerves (vagus, accelerans) alters the strength and the rate of both the auricles and ventricles simultaneously, even though there is a complete dissociation.

While still in Prague, Hering became interested in the description by Czermak of the vagus pressure test—the slowing of the pulse rate following pressure over the carotid vessels. It had been accepted that the slowing came from the stimulation of the vague trunk. In 1923, in Cologne, he localized the origin of the reflex in the nerve endings in the region of the carotid bifurcation, the carotid sinus. This experiment was followed by the proof that stimulation of the carotid sinus in the dog caused bradycardia and hypotension even after the vagus was severed from the artery. The effects were abolished after the glossopharyngeal branch was cut. His clinical and experimental studies were summarized as follows.[4]

The hypothesis, accepted since 1866, that, during the vagus pressure test in patients, the heart is slowed from irritation of the fibers of the vagus was not proved by Czermak, nor is it probable that this can be proved at all.

Against this are the following: (1) We have demonstrated by experiments that a much stronger pressure to the exposed vagus than is possible to exert on humans has no corresponding effect on the heart rate in rabbits or dogs. (2) The carotid pressure experiment shows that in certain cases only a slight pressure on the carotid leads to vigorous response even though the pressure does not affect the vagus. These procedures suggest that in humans the heart-vagus effect—the so-called vagus pressure test—is produced by reflex action.

It seems incorrect to speak of a vagus pressure test as such. I suggest the term "Carotid Pressure Test," because (1) this term identifies the organ affected, from which the reaction arises, and which is subjected to pressure, and (2) in all probability the carotid sinus is the point of origin of the pressure reflex.

The response of the carotid sinus from internal change in pressure was further defined in his monograph, published in 1927.[5]

The reflexes are initiated not only by the pressure from the outside or by traction on the sinus, but also by pressure from within. This is evident from the following:

(1) A probe inserted into the carotid artery initiates the reflex as soon as the carotid sinus is irritated mechanically.

(2) A forceful flow of blood which increases pressure in the peripheral portion of the communis carotid artery, when both the external and the internal carotids are peripherally isolated from the carotid sinus, initiates the reflex.

(3) If the common carotids are opened again after previous closure, the oncoming blood irritates the carotid sinus through pressure from within, decreases the blood pressure and temporarily slows the heart rate.

1. Rihl, J.: H. E. Hering on His 70th Birthday (Ger), *Klin Wschr* 15:839, 1936.

2. Hering, H. E.: Analysis of Pulsus Irregularis Perpetuus (Ger), *Prag Med Wschr* 28:377-381, 1903, excerpt translated by Z. Danilevicius.

3. Hering, H. E.: Recent Studies on the Action of the Heart (Ger), *Prag Med Wschr* 30:192-193, 1905, excerpt translated by Z. Danilevicius.

4. Hering, H. E.: The Carotid Pressure Investigations (Ger), *Munch Med Wschr* 70:1287-1290, 1923.

5. Hering, H. E.: The Carotid Sinus Reflex on the Heart and Vessels (Ger), Dresden: T. Steinkopff, 1927, excerpt translated by Z. Danilevicius.

Composite by G. Bako

Walter Bradford Cannon
(1871-1945)

W. B. CANNON, physiologist of international fame, was born in Prairie du Chien, Wisconsin, near Fort Crawford, the site of William Beaumont's second series of observations on the gastric fistula of Alexis St. Martin.[1] After public schooling, Cannon attended Harvard College on a scholarship, graduating in 1896, summa cum laude. While in college he collaborated with C. B. Davenport, instructor in zoology, in research on the orientation of minute swimming organisms to a source of light, a study subsequently published in the *Journal of Physiology*. As a result of this experience and an early interest in biology traced to the writings of Thomas Huxley, his association with George H. Parker, and dissuasion by William James from wasting his time in philosophy, Cannon became attracted to scientific research. Proceeding to Harvard Medical School he received the MA degree at the completion of his first year in medicine for his extracurricular studies in Harvard College and began his investigations on the alimentary tract by indirect observations. He received the MD degree cum laude at Har-

vard in 1900 and immediately was appointed instructor of physiology. Cannon served as George Higginson professor of physiology from 1906 until retirement in 1942 as emeritus professor. However, he continued his biological investigations in the laboratories in the College where he began nearly 50 years earlier.

Many of Cannon's earlier communications described the movements of the gastrointestinal tract and the mechanics of digestion, perhaps his most famous series of researches. These studies, immediately fruitful, led to a serendipitous byproduct—the measurable physiological effects of emotion, the focal point of research for a generation. As a skilled technician with experimental animals, Cannon devoted time and effort before World War I to advocating humane use and proper care of experimental animals, an endeavor which included preparation of several *Defense of Research* pamphlets issued by the Bureau on Protection of Medical Research of the Council on Health and Public Instruction of the American Medical Association.

During the first World War he served with the Harvard Hospital Unit, initially with the British army and later with the American Expeditionary Forces, pursuing clinical and experimental work on traumatic shock. With the coming of peace Cannon expanded his interests in the physiology of the nervous system and, in turn, dealt in depth with the chemical mediation of the nerve impulse. Although Cannon was a laboratory worker, his concern for clinical matters recurred regularly. His bibliography, which contains an unusually large number of references, includes the following clinical subjects: "The Use of Clinic Records in Teaching Medicine," "Intracranial Pressure After Head Injuries," "The Responsibility of the General Practitioner for Freedom of Medical Research," "Reasons for Optimism in the Care of the Sick," and "Some Problems of Readjustment in Medical Practice." During World War II he served his country as chairman of the National Research Council Committee on Shock and Transfusion, and as advisor to the huge program of supply of blood and plasma for the armed forces.

Cannon's first and preliminary report of the movements of the alimentary canal, as visualized by Röntgen rays, was communicated to the American Physiological Society in May, 1897, by H. P. Bowditch, Cannon's predecessor at Harvard. A goose served as the first experimental subject, and in time was replaced by the cat. The movements of a bismuth meal in the stomach were described the following year in a long communication to the *American Journal of Physiology*. The addition of a small quantity of bismuth subnitrate to liquid food permitted study of the contractions of the gastric wall and the progress of the gastric contents in the restrained but intact animal. In the pursuit of this experimental program, the effect of emotions on gastrointestinal movements was discussed.[2]

The mixing of a small quantity of subnitrate of bismuth with the food allows not only the contractions of the gastric wall, but also the movements of the gastric contents to be seen with the Röntgen rays in the uninjured animal during normal digestion. An unsuspected nicety of mechanical action and a surprising sensitiveness to nervous conditions have thereby been disclosed. Within five minutes after a cat has finished a meal of bread, there is visible near the duodenal end of the antrum a slight annular contraction which moves peristaltically to the pylorus; this is followed by several waves recurring at regular intervals. Two or three minutes after the first movement is seen, very slight constrictions appear near the middle of the stomach, and, pressing deeper into the greater curvature, course slowly towards the pyloric end. As new regions enter into constriction, the fibres just previously contracted become relaxed, so that there is a true moving wave, with a trough between two crests. When a wave swings round the bend in the pyloric part the indentation made by it deepens; and as digestion goes on the antrum elongates and the constrictions running over it grow stronger, but, until the stomach is nearly empty, they do not entirely divided the cavity.

No amount of kneading or compression of the abdomen with the fingers, short of making the cat angry, would cause the waves to stop; so that the cat's movements, in themselves, were not the source of the inhibition. And since expressions of strong feeling on the part of the animal always accompanied cessation of the constriction-waves, the inhibition was probably due to nervous influences. It has long been common knowledge that violent emotions interfere with the digestive process, but that the gastric motor activities should manifest such extreme sensitiveness to nervous conditions is surprising.

The segmental migration of the bismuth meal was followed through the small bowel into the colon. The strong contraction of the circular fibers of the colon, described as rings (Cannon's rings), were noted.[3]

The contents of the large intestine progress farther and farther from the caecum; meanwhile new tonic constrictions appear which separate the contents into a series of globular masses. . . . Comparing tracings made at rather long intervals (forty-five minutes), I found that the rings disappear from the transverse colon and then are present with the waste material in the descending colon. Thus in the cat also these rings which seem with short observation to be remaining in one position are in reality moving slowly away from the caecum, pushing the hardening contents before them.

One of Cannon's most popular books, *Bodily Changes in Pain, Hunger, Fear and Rage,*[4] which appeared in 1915, described measurable primitive experiences common to both human beings and the lower animals. Emotional responses suggested dominance of sympathetic impulses. For example, fright in the cat, associated with an outpouring of adrenal secretions, caused dilatation of the pupils, tachycardia, erection of the hairs, and inhibition of alimentary movements. According to Cannon's teleological interpretation, the sudden liberation of adrenalin activated the preparatory measures for combat or flight. The theory was put to test in the laboratory with blood from a calm and an enraged cat perfusing an isolated strip of intestine. A preliminary report, published in *The Journal of the American Medical Association,* was followed by a detailed discussion a few weeks later.[5]

In order to test this suggestion the natural enmity between two laboratory animals, dog and cat, was utilized. The cat, fastened to a comfortable holder, was placed near a barking dog. Some cats showed almost no signs of fear; others, with scarcely a movement of defence, made the typical picture of fright. In favorable cases the excitement was continued for five or ten minutes, and, in a few instances, longer. Samples of blood were taken within a few minutes before and after the period.

Magnus showed, in 1905, that longitudinal intestinal muscle, contracting rhythmically, is characteristically inhibited by suprarenin, 1:20,000,000. Though this reaction has not hitherto been utilized as a biological signal for adrenal secretion. it possesses noteworthy advantages over the other methods.

Although blood obtained by cardiac puncture gave in some cases characteristic results by this method, blood from the inferior vena cava was so much more regular and differential in its effects that it alone was finally used. To obtain blood from the inferior cava above the opening of the adrenal vessels, the skin over the femoral in the groin was made anaesthetic with ethyl chloride; the vein was bared, cleaned, tied, and opened; and a small flexible catheter (2.4 mm. diameter), coated with vaseline inside and out, was introduced through the iliac into the cava to near the level of the sternal notch. . . . Since there was no sign of sensation when the catheter was slipped into the vein, it was possible to obtain "quiet blood," with only local anesthesia. . . . After the animal had been frightened, the procedure was repeated, and thus the "excited blood" was secured.

After the initial shortening, the strip, if in quiet blood, soon began to contract rhythmically and at the same time to lengthen more with each relaxation, until a fairly even base line appeared in the written record.

The strip was originally beating in blood which contained no demonstrable amount of adrenal secretion; that blood was replaced by blood from the adrenal veins, obtained after quick etherization. Relaxation occurred almost immediately. Then the beats were renewed in the former blood, and thereupon the strip was immersed in blood from the left renal vein, obtained from the same animal and under the same conditions with the adrenal blood. No relaxation occurred. This and other similar tests proved the reliability of the method.

In a series of communications prepared in 1918 for *The Journal of the American Medical Association* from the experience of a committee appointed by the Medical Research Committee of Great Britain on Wound Shock and Allied Conditions, Cannon and associates described acidosis, hypotention, concentration of hemoglobin "lost blood," and the respiratory and cardiac changes in traumatic shock in combat. He advanced new concepts of the pathogenesis and recommended the intravenous administration of a solution of gum acacia, a predecessor of current blood volume expanders, for emergency use.[6,7]

In discussing the blood changes in shock it will be desirable to distinguish between cases of severe or extreme shock, as seen at the casualty clearing station, and those of moderate character. . . . Roughly, the moderate cases had a systolic pressure over 90 mm. of mercury, and the severe cases not over 70 mm.

The first noteworthy characteristic of the blood in shock is a high capillary red count. . . . In all but eleven of the cases the count was 6 million corpuscles or higher, and in eight cases it was more than 7 million corpuscles. When hemorrhage as a complicating factor tending to reduce the blood count is considered, these high counts are striking. They indicate that in shock a concentration of the blood occurs, at least in the superficial capillaries.

Transfusion of blood naturally raises both the count and the hemoglobin reading. Injection of a gum solution leads to a dilution of the blood that may persist for some hours. Intravenous administration of a large amount (2 pints) of hypertonic salt solution may markedly reduce the hemoglobin content of the blood; a smaller amount (1 pint) in our experience has not had this effect. Injection of the salt solution reduces the capillary stasis.

Cases of low blood pressure due to shock, hemorrhage, or infection with the gas bacillus have a diminished supply of available alkali in the blood, that is, an acidosis.

Shocked men suffering after operation from extreme acidosis with "air hunger" can be quickly relieved of their distress by intravenous injection of a solution of sodium bicarbonate, and their blood pressure restored to normal.

No attempt is made to enumerate each of the many areas of interest and investigation in which Cannon excelled. He was humble and unassuming in the experimental laboratory, as well as skilled in the design and execution of early 20th century physiological techniques. In the classroom he was not a particularly stimulating teacher; however, in his long and distinguished career, he maintained an exemplary relationship with students, research fellows, and peers. He was as interested in teaching students and exposing them to research as in the problems under investigation in his laboratory. His handbook of laboratory instruction,[8] based upon the case system of study, was revised and reprinted a number of times. The laboratory exercises were designed for student or animal participation as experimental subjects. He travelled extensively and attracted to his laboratory students from around the world; his international friends seemed as numerous as those at home. Liberal in his political philosophy, Cannon was a friend of Russian scientists; he favored the oppressed during the Civil War in Spain, always being moved to sympathy and indignation by suffering and injustice.

Cannon received a great number of honors in America and abroad and was an honorary member of many learned societies in the scientific community. At various times he was Croonian lecturer at the Royal Society, London; Harvard exchange professor to France; Linacre lecturer at Cambridge University, England; Baly medalist, Royal College of Physicians, London; Kober medalist of the Association of American Physicians; Hughlings Jackson lecturer at McGill University; member of the Academy of Science of the USSR; and visiting professor to Peiping Union Medical School. The decoration of the Companion of the Bath of the British Empire and the Distinguished Service Medal were awarded for his contributions during World War I. Honorary degrees conferred on him included the DSC from Yale and Harvard; the LLD from Wittenberg, Boston University, and Washington University; and Doctor honoris causa from the universities of Liège, Strasbourg, Paris, and Madrid. His death due to leukemia was probably associated with early exposure to Röntgen rays, his first experimental tool so effectively used while a medical student.

From 1906 to 1908, Cannon served as secretary of the Section on Pathology and Physiology and a member of the Council of Physical Therapy of the American Medical Association. The Chairman's address of the section, presented at the annual meeting in 1908, contains several excellent passages on antivivisection, handling of laboratory animals, and noteworthy discussions of the complex relation between research and practice.[9]

This complexity of the relation between discoveries and practice has important bearings in the present discussion of the opposition to medical research. It is the certainty that we are still woefully ignorant of many of the problems of disease, and that every fragment of biologic knowledge may be useful in solving these problems—it is this certainty, and the sincere conviction that the service he performs is in the highest sense humane, that cause the medical investigator to oppose any attempt to check the freedom of investigation.

The scientific application of the experimental method has transformed the world of commerce and industry. The marvel of that transformation is a story that man tells with a just pride in his own achievement. The same sort of painstaking search for knowledge that gave man control of the forces of inorganic nature, has given him most of the control which he now has over the forces of organic nature. It was the method of experiment applied to animals that wrought the change from the empirical medicine of sixty years ago to such exactness of treatment as modern medicine can utilize. And just as the future growth in the physical world must wait further discoveries and new applications of knowledge, so in the realm of biology and medicine, the hope of progress must rest on a continuation of the method which has brought us thus far out of the darkness of the unknown—it must rest on the study of normal and pathologic processes that go on in living animals.

1. Cannon, W. B.: The Way of an Investigator, New York: W. W. Norton & Co., 1945.

2. Cannon, W. B.: The Movements of the Stomach Studied by Means of the Röntgen Rays, Amer J Physiol 1:359-382, 1898.

3. Cannon, W. B.: The Movements of the Intestines Studied by Means of the Röntgen Rays, Amer J Physiol 6:251-277 (Jan 1) 1902.

4. Cannon, W. B.: Bodily Changes in Pain, Hunger, Fear and Rage, New York: D. Appleton & Co., 1915.

5. Cannon, W. B., and de la Paz, D.: Emotional Stimulation of Adrenal Secretion, Amer J Physiol 28:64-70 (April 1) 1911.

6. Cannon, W. B.; Fraser, J.; and Hooper, A. N.: Some Alterations in Distribution and Character of Blood in Shock and Hemorrhage JAMA 70:526-531 (Feb 23) 1918.

7. Cannon, W. B.: Acidosis in Cases of Shock, Hemorrhage and Gas Infection, JAMA 70:531-535 (Feb 23) 1918.

8. Cannon, W. B.: A Laboratory Course in Physiology, Cambridge, Mass: Harvard University Press, 1910.

9. Cannon, W. B.: The Opposition to Medical Research, JAMA 51:635-640 (Aug 22) 1908.

Composite by G. Bako

Joseph Barcroft (1872-1947)

JOSEPH BARCROFT, Professor of Physiology at Cambridge, lived, studied, and taught in the Golden Age of Physiology in England. He was born in The Glen near Newry, County Down, near the Belfast-Dublin Road in Northern Ireland, beyond the Mourne Mountains. He so loved his ancestral home that he returned to it regularly throughout his professional career. His parents, well-to-do Quakers, made possible an excellent education. Franklin, in the biography of Barcroft,[1] described him as "precocious" because of the circumstances that surrounded his acceptance of the Bachelor of Science degree by London University at the age of 19. A dissertation entitled *An Investigation of the Gaseous Metabolism of the Salivary Glands* was one of the requirements for the Doctorate of Philosophy by Cambridge University.

A glittering array of British and international physiologists were his associates, teachers, or pupils. These included J. N. Langley, M. Foster, W. H. Gaskell, H. H. Dale, A. V. Hill, E. H. Starling, I. P. Pavlov, F. J. W. Roughton, J. S. Haldane, L. J. Henderson, W. B. Cannon, Ff. Roberts, B. A. Houssay, A. Krogh, C. S. Sherrington, E. A. Sharpey-Schafer, R. Margaria, A.

Mosso, and W. M. Bayliss. His chief interests were in the physiological effects of high altitudes and the study of hemoglobin as the carrier of oxygen in the blood. Barcroft's first high altitude expedition to Teneriffe at 11,000 feet in the Canary Islands was designed to investigate the effect of altitude upon the oxygen dissociation curve of man. Preliminary physiological studies at 7,000 feet on the ascent permitted partial acclimatization. The main camp was the Alta Vista Hut, located just below the summit. The observations collected on this expedition were described in Barcroft's first monograph entitled *The Respiratory Function of the Blood*.[2]

Early in this century the question of the mechanism of adjustment to high altitude or low oxygen pressure was unsettled. J. S. Haldane firmly believed that acclimatization was associated with active secretion of oxygen by the alveolar epithelium of the lungs. The body, which is capable of performing phenomenal tasks, might secrete oxygen under stress in order to maintain life. One of the arguments advanced by Haldane in support of this possibility was the fact that two English mountaineers, Mallory and Irvine, were able to ascend Mt. Everest to an altitude greater than 27,000 feet without the use of supplementary oxygen. Haldane concluded that such a phenomenon was achieved by active secretion of oxygen by the alveolar membrane. The studies at Teneriffe, followed by those at 15,000 feet at Monte Rosa on the border of the Swiss Alps between Switzerland and Italy, readily visible from the vicinity of the Matterhorn, supplied additional evidence against the active secretion of oxygen by the lungs.

The first World War diverted Barcroft's physiologic interests into the study and treatment of poisoning from war gases. He went to Boulogne to study the troops gassed in the second battle of Ypres in 1915. The oral administration of alkali, in the anticipation that it might counteract any retention of acid from gas inhalation, proved fruitless. On the basis of chamber experiments, attention was later directed to the use of oxygen in treatment, a more rational procedure. Another war project, involving the exploration of a highly theoretical offensive weapon, led Barcroft to volunteer to enter a chamber filled with a dilute mixture of hydrocyanic gas. The hazardous exposure won him a commendation from David Lloyd George, Prime Minister of England. In the years following the war, Barcroft designed a glass chamber in which it was possible to reduce the percentage of oxygen to approximate the partial pressure of air on a mountain peak. Further evidence was sought in refutation of the oxygen secretion theory. One phase of the experiment involved an arterial puncture, a rather unusual procedure in 1920. Once again, the professor was the experimental subject. This devotion to duty and willingness to participate as the experimental subject as well as the designer seems highly commendable.

Barcroft planned the Anglo-American Expedition to Cerro de Pasco in 1921. The members were J. C. Meakins, J. H. Doggart, A. V. Bock, A. C. Redfield, H. S. Forbes, C. A. Binger, and G. Harrop; each a Doctor of Medicine, as well as a student of human physiology, except for Redfield, Doggart, and the Director. Upon the completion of the expedition to Peru, Barcroft came to America and gave the Lowell Lectures in Boston and the Harvey Society Lecture in New York. His conclusions regarding the transfer of oxygen across the pulmonary membrane from alveolar air into circulating blood and factors of acclimatization to decreased oxygen pressures are as follows:[3]

A number of tests were made for the purpose of discovering whether the pressure of oxygen in the blood was or was not higher than that in the alveolar air. In all cases they were so nearly the same that we attribute the passage of gas through the pulmonary epithelium to diffusion.

There remain three principal factors which appear to have a positive influence in acclimatisation:—

(a) The increase in total ventilation, which usually raises the alveolar oxygen pressure 10 or 12 mm. higher than it would otherwise be.

(b) The rise in the oxygen dissociation curve, so that at any oxygen pressure the haemoglobin will take up more oxygen than before.

(c) The rise in the number of red corpuscles and correspondingly in the quantity of haemoglobin.

These three factors may be regarded at first as independent variables and an attempt made to appraise their relative importance. The attempt has necessitated an enquiry into the laws which govern diffusion in the lungs and the tissues. This enquiry makes it obvious that:—

(1) The colour of the blood in the lungs must be almost that of arterial blood, whilst the colour of blood in the tissue capillaries approach that of the venous blood which emerges from the tissue in question.

(2) An explanation is found for the fact that, at high altitudes, the arterial blood darkens when exercise is taken, whilst it does not do so to an appreciable extent at the sea-level.

Among several major contributions to monographic literature was a volume entitled *Features in the Architecture of Physiological Function.* He summarized his studies on the oxygen dissociation of hemoglobin followed by a discussion of investigations of the fetal circulation, especially in the goat. One of the clichés related to this volume was the statement by Sir John Rose Bradford that "The difference between physiology as taught now and in my youth is that now the student is given principles; then he was only given facts." Barcroft's studies on the embryo revealed that the chick fetus begins to breathe about 24 hours before it hatches on the 21st day. This is preceded by a rhythmic respiratory movement which makes its appearance normally 3 days before hatching. The earliest spontaneous movements of the neck and head muscles in 5- and 6-day-old chicks continue throughout incubation and seem to be the inception of the respiratory pattern.

In 1939, Barcroft described his studies on man entitled "A Radiographic Demonstration of the Circulation Through the Heart in the Adult and in the Foetus, and the Identification of the Ductus Arteriosus." The ductus had been identified in the cinéradiograph record, a procedure unique at that time but routine in contemporary diagnostic medicine. Because of this interest, he was presented an Honorary Fellowship in the Royal College of Obstetricians and Gynaecologists.[4]

The circulation of the blood through the heart of the adult and the foetus is demonstrated by the analysis of X-ray cinematographic films recording the passage of injections of radio-opaque media.

In the adult, the blood from both venae cavae is seen to pass through the right side of the heart and the pulmonary arteries to the lungs. On returning from the lungs the flow is seen to pass through the left side of the heart into the systemic circulation.

In the foetus, the whole of the superior caval blood is seen to pass into the right ventricle and out through the pulmonary valve into the pulmonary trunk; from this vessel it passes on the one hand into the pulmonary arteries and, on the other, *via* the ductus arteriosus, into the descending aorta. As the brachiocephalic artery leaves the aorta proximal to the entry of the ductus arteriosus, the superior caval blood does not pass to the coronary system, the head and fore-limbs. The inferior caval blood has a double course through the heart. The main part goes through the foramen ovale to the left auricle and ventricle, and passes out into the aorta and coronary and brachiocephalic arteries. Hence, the heart and brain are given preferential treatment with respect to the supply of oxygenated blood coming from the placenta. On the other hand, a minor part of the inferior caval blood passes with the superior caval flow into the right ventricle and out into the pulmonary arteries and, *via* the ductus arteriosus, into the descending aorta.

During World War II, nutrition was a primary problem, and Barcroft served as a member of the Food Council of the British Government. I visited him last in 1945 in his laboratory in Cambridge. An American physician in uniform in his laboratory was not unusual. He described some of his studies on the fetal circulation that he hoped to continue once the war was over and restrictions were removed. However, he did not live long enough to accomplish this goal among several. Notes were discovered at his deathbed that comprised the basis of an address to the Student Christian Movement. They were published later in the *Lancet* under the title "Christianity and Medicine." Although Joseph Barcroft was not a physician, his contributions to human physiology were many, his friendship for medicine was profound, and his association with physiologically-oriented physicians was extensive.

1. Franklin, K. J.: *Joseph Barcroft—1872-1947*, Oxford, England: Blackwell Scientific Publications Limited, 1953.
2. Barcroft, J.: *The Respiratory Function of the Blood*, Cambridge: University Press, 1914.
3. Barcroft, J. et al: Observations Upon the Effect of High Altitude on the Physiological Processes of the Human Body, Carried Out in the Peruvian Andes, Chiefly at Cerro de Pasco, *Philos Trans Roy Soc London* Series B, 211:351-454, 1923.
4. Barclay, A. E.; Barcroft, J.; Barron, D. H.; and Franklin, K. J.: A Radiographic Demonstration of the Circulation Through the Heart in the Adult and in the Foetus, and the Identification of the Ductus Arteriosus, *British J Radiol* 12:505-517, 1939.

Countway Medical Library

Lawrence Joseph Henderson
(1878-1942)

L. J. HENDERSON of Harvard University, endowed with remarkable perception and profound wisdom, cultivated in depth biochemistry, general physiology, philosophy, history of science, and sociology, which led to fundamental contributions in each sphere of intellectual activity. He was born in Lynn, Mass, and entered Harvard College at the age of 16. There he displayed a capacity for mathematics, physics, and general chemistry, and at all times enjoyed freedom of thought and self-determination characteristic of students in Cambridge. The study of physical chemistry led Henderson to thinking about acids and bases in biological solutions, which resulted in an essay submitted for the Bowdoin Prize on Arrhenius' theory of electrolytic dissociation. The AB degree was granted magna cum laude in 1898; he then proceeded to Harvard Medical School, where he continued his studies in physiological chemistry, since the College offered no formal courses in the subject. He satisfied the requirements for the MD degree, including the clinical subjects, without any intention of practicing medicine. Rather, his future in the basic sciences was rapidly unfolding, with a philosophical approach to a mechanistic interpretation of cosmic forces.

Spending several years with Hofmeister in Strasbourg, he shared a respect for German science with a high regard for the great minds and also for the famous vintages of France. He returned to Harvard University, served first as assistant professor of biological chemistry, then as professor of biological chemistry, and, from 1934 until his untimely death, held the Abbott and James Lawrence professorship of chemistry in the University.

Henderson was never a laboratory man; his investigations had their inception and consummation in the philosopher's chair with vital but simple tools—an imaginative mind, a slide rule, and a block of notepaper. There are few medical scientists who did so much with so few laboratory data. Nor is it possible to separate by time or subject matter his many areas of interest. From his pronouncements on acid-base equilibria, he offered an explanation and interpretation of biologic life in the earthly environment and a teleological explanation of nature. Henderson carried the basic concepts of interaction of variables, influenced by Willard Gibbs, into the study of blood and body fluids, concluding his contributions with a sociologic study of human actions illustrated by the doctor and patient as a social system.

Henderson's applications of physical chemistry, in explaining maintenance of neutrality in body fluids, appeared first in the German literature in 1909. Hasselbalch expanded upon the subject in 1911, and the summation remains as the famous Henderson-Hasselbalch equation. His concept of neutrality was concise and clear.[1]

It appears that acids whose ionization constant is nearly equal to the hydrogen ionization at neutrality, possess, with the help of their salts, a great capacity for preserving neutrality in simple solution, while other acids are in like concentration of relatively very little effect in this matter. Other things being equal, the greatest possible efficiency in preserving neutrality, on both sides of the neutral point, is possessed by that acid whose ionization constant is precisely equal to the hydrogen ionization of water divided by the degree of ionization of the salt. Clearly, then, the ionization constant of carbonic acid, 3×10^{-7}, and of the ion H_2PO_4, 2×10^{-7}, gives them nearly the greatest possible efficiency for preserving neutrality in simple solution.

The participation of weak acids and strong acids in biological economy with hydrogen-ion concentration, depending upon the ratio of carbonic acid to sodium bicarbonate, led to his recognition of the great capacity of carbonic acid to preserve neutrality in a aqueous solution. In a series of lectures delivered at the Lowell Institute in Boston in 1913, which were recast into his monograph, *The Fitness of the Environment, an Inquiry Into the Biological Significance of the Properties of Matter,* Henderson discussed the significance of oxygen, hydrogen, and carbon in a masterful presentation of the mutual relationship between the organism and the environment. Living organisms as complex physiochemical mechanisms and well regulated systems survive in an environment which is also physiochemically well regulated. The continuous interchange between organism and environment of matter, energy, water, carbonic acid, and their constituent elements, displays an extraordinary fitness.[2]

I. The fitness of the environment is one part of a reciprocal relationship of which the fitness of the organism is the other. This relationship is completely and perfectly reciprocal; the one fitness is not less important than the other, nor less invariably a constituent of a particular case of biological fitness; it is not less frequently evident in the characteristics of water, carbonic acid, and the compounds of carbon, hydrogen, and oxygen than is fitness from adaptation in the characteristics of the organism.

II. The fitness of the environment results from characteristics which constitute a series of maxima—unique or nearly unique properties of water, carbonic acid, the compounds of carbon, hydrogen, and oxygen and the ocean—so numerous, so varied, so nearly complete among all things which are concerned in the problem that together they form certainly the greatest possible fitness. No other environment consisting of primary constituents made up of other known elements, or lacking water and carbonic acid, could possess a like number of fit characteristics or such highly fit characteristics, or in any manner such great fitness to promote complexity, durability, and active metabolism in the organic mechanism which we call life.

Henderson's argument was continued in his essay, *The Order of Nature,* published in 1917, in which we find reliance upon the mathematical analysis of Willard Gibbs, who showed ours to be a world of systems as Newton had shown it to be a world of masses. However, no system can be independent or isolated from the rest of the world, and the stability of a system increases with the number of phases and with the number of restrictions. These principles were more fully exemplified in Henderson's description of the blood a decade later. But in *The Order of Nature,* the examination of the properties of hydrogen, carbon, and oxygen, with the possibility of a great diversity of phases and systems, led him logically to accept the teleological appearance of natural phenomena.[3]

Our scientific examination of the properties and activities of the three elements may now be made to serve its purpose. For it has led to results that can be used in answering the question of the origin of the teleological appearance of nature.

The ensemble of properties of the elements hydrogen, carbon, and oxygen, meet most of these specifications. They lead, as we have seen, to the presence of water and carbon dioxide in the atmosphere, and to the meteorological cycle. This cycle regulates the temperature of the globe more perfectly than it could be regulated by any other substances concerned in any other similar cycle. It produces an almost constant temperature in the ocean, as well as constancy of composition and of alkalinity. It mobilizes all over the earth great quantities of all the elements; it deposits them in great variety and inexhaustible profusion in the ocean; it comminutes and disperses all kinds of insoluble minerals, thereby diversifying the land; it causes water to penetrate and to remain in nearly all localities; and all of these processes are perfect or more extensive than they could be if a large number of different properties of water were not what they are. Thereby the greatest variety and quantity of structural material is accumulated. Meanwhile the conditions which make for durability of structures are also assured.

Out of all these substances, inorganic and organic alike, as a result of the properties of water and of carbon dioxide, the construction of an almost infinite diversity of phases and systems is possible. Natural phases and systems may both vary almost indefinitely in number and variety of components, in concentrations, and in configurations. They may be so constituted as to produce the most varied forms of activity. Like their components they may manifest the greatest diversity of properties, and their forms may include all the possible forms of life and of the mineral kingdom.

According to the theory of probabilities this connection between the properties of matter and the process of evolution cannot be due to mere contingency. Therefore, since the physicochemical functional relationship is not in question, there must be admitted a functional relationship of another kind, somewhat like that known to physiology. This functional relationship can only be described as teleological.

Henderson's long interest in the study of variables led him to apply nomography to the visual exposition of the interaction of acids and bases in blood and body fluids. The study of carbon dioxide and oxygen dissociation curves in animals and in man at rest and during exercise and with disease was a logical development from the biological interrelationship of these substances in nature. The physically unimpressive, but intellectually highly productive, laboratory at the Massachusetts General Hospital under A. V. Bock and D. B. Dill supplied the experimental data for the mathematical illustration of the interrelationship of the many variables of the blood during the respiratory cycle. According to Henderson's interpretation, mathematical treatment was always a first approximation, and the achievements imperfect. His Silliman lectures at Yale University in 1928, published as the monograph, *Blood, a Study in General Physiology,* was one of the great monographs in physiology of this century. He concluded the treatise in his usual modest mathematical-philosophical style.[4]

The elementary condition of the phenomena of life is a particular kind of physico-chemical system. . . . Although the greater part of this book has been devoted to the elucidation of the properties of this class of systems, a comprehensive and detailed description is as yet unattained.

There are many grounds for objecting to this statement. Some will still say that the elementary condition of the phenomena of life is the cell. Others will prefer a metaphysical definition. To the latter objectors it may be replied that the physiologist is seeking his own ends; to the former that this is but a question of means to those ends, and that for the present rational, mathematical, and physico-chemical studies of equilibria and stationary states in living organisms are fruitful of the results that he seeks.

In the mid-1920's a new complex of buildings of the Harvard Business School was constructed across the Charles River from Harvard Yard. This gave L J the opportunity to establish the Harvard Fatigue Laboratory, with the support of Dean Wallace B. Donham of the Business School and Dean David L. Edsall of the Medical School and others; he obtained the required funds from the Laura Spellman Rockefeller Foundation for equipping the laboratory and from the Rockefeller Foundation for its operation. To some this move was an enigma; but to L. J. himself it was an opportunity to explore another area of interest—the interrelationship of individuals—building upon Pareto's *Trattato di Sociologia Generale.* Pareto, an Italian sociologist trained in mathematics and physical science, made considerable progress in analyzing human motives. His social system was similar to a physicochemical system. The works of Pareto were translated into English and, under the aegis of Henderson, formed the basis for a seminar on Pareto sponsored by the department of sociology. This led to Henderson's last monograph, *Pareto's General Sociology, a Physiologist's Interpretation.*[5]

The central feature of Pareto's General Sociology is the construction of a similar conceptual scheme: the social system. This possesses many of the same logical advantages and limitations that are present in the physico-chemical system. Pareto's social system contains individuals; they are roughly analogous to Gibbs's components. It is heterogeneous (cf. Gibbs's phases), for the individuals are of different families, trades, and professions; they are associated with different institutions and are members of different economic and social classes. As Gibbs considers temperature, pressure, and concentrations, so Pareto considers sentiments, or, strictly speaking, the manifestations of sentiments in words and deeds, verbal elaborations, and the economic interests. Like Gibbs, Pareto excludes many factors that are important in special cases, but he too has demonstrated that he can do much within the limitations that he has chosen, and that such limitations are necessary.

In an address presented to the Association of American Physicians at the annual meeting in Atlantic City, Henderson discussed the patient and physician as a social system, disclosing an understanding of clinical medicine, even though he had never cared for a sick patient, and an understanding of human relationships, even though he had never formally professed this subject in academic life.[6]

I now state a proposition. According to this definition, a physician and a patient taken together make up a social system. They do so because they are two and because they have relations of mutual dependence. Also they are heterogeneous, they manifest sentiments, they have economic interests, they talk, reason, pretend to reason, and rationalize.

If physician and patient constitute a social system, it is almost a trivial one compared with the larger social system of which the patient is a permanent member and in which he lives. This system, indeed, makes up the greater part of the environment in which he *feels* that he lives. I suggest that it is impossible to understand any man as a person without knowledge of this environment and especially of what he thinks and feels it is; which may be a very different thing.

L J has been described as a "unique" figure in the Harvard Faculty as if this were inelegant or un-American. Many revered him for his encompassing wisdom. With but few exceptions, those who knew him realized the warmth of personality beneath a sophisticated exterior, the latter sometimes a conscious and even gently humorous pose. One might assume that a natural philosopher would be uninterested in organization, but in his case, quite the contrary. His academic responsibilities brought him to several notable achievements. A department of biological chemistry was established by him in the College, and a department of physical chemistry in the Medical School. At the Harvard Business School, the Fatigue Laboratory was his project, while the Society of Fellows in Harvard University, patterned after the Trinity Prize Fellowship in Cambridge, England, was the result of one of several assignments given him by A. Lawrence Lowell, then president of Harvard. In this society, a small group of Senior Fellows were selected from the faculty, and a larger number of Junior Fellows were appointed for a period of three years, these scholars being freed from teaching and allowed to develop their interests at their discretion. L J was the first chairman of the group, and, with his intimate knowledge of mathematics, biology, philosophy, literature, medicine, and sociology, he directed this select community of scholars in its formative years. Honors included the DSC from Harvard University and the University of Cambridge, and the LLD from the University of Pennsylvania; in addition, he was a member of the Legion of Honor of France, a member of the National Academy of Sciences, Lowell lecturer at Harvard, Silliman lecturer at Yale, Mills lecturer at the University of California, and Leyden lecturer at the University of Berlin.

1. Henderson, L. J.: Concerning the Relationship Between the Strength of Acids and Their Capacity to Preserve Neutrality, *Amer J Physiol* 21:173-190, 1908.
2. Henderson, L. J.: *The Fitness of the Environment, an Inquiry Into the Biological Significance of the Properties of Matter,* New York: Macmillan Co., 1913.
3. Henderson, L. J.: *The Order of Nature,* Cambridge: Harvard University Press, 1917.
4. Henderson, L. J.: *Blood, a Study in General Physiology,* New Haven: Yale University Press, 1928.
5. Henderson, L. J.: *Pareto's General Sociology, a Physiologist's Interpretation,* Cambridge: Harvard University Press, 1935.
6. Henderson, L. J.: The Practice of Medicine as Applied Sociology, *Trans Assoc Amer Physicians* 51:8-22, 1936.

Rudolf Magnus (1873-1927)

RUDOLF MAGNUS, whose scientific work for more than 20 years encompassed the whole realm of animal posture, was born in Brunswick, Germany. His father was a practitioner of law; his paternal grandfather and great-grandfather were practitioners of medicine; his maternal grandfather was the director of the Hamburg Library.[1] Magnus began the study of medicine at Heidelberg, and, before graduating MD magna cum laude in 1898, he studied in Berlin and Munich. His inaugural dissertation described the measurement of blood pressure with the sphygmograph, prepared under the aegis of W. Kühne, professor of physiology. Following graduation from Heidelberg, Magnus carried on his experimental studies at the Pharmacology Institute; there he was appointed assistant in pharmacology, advanced to privatdocent in 1900, and to professor of pharmacology in 1904. Gottlieb, the director of the Institute at the time, collaborated with Magnus in several of the communications on diuresis, water balance, and the pharmacology of the digitalis group of drugs. The formation of lymph, pharmacology of breathing, and the action of drugs on the intestines were other areas of interest in these early years of research.

National Library of Medicine

In 1900, Magnus made the first of a series of visits to Scotland and England for experimental investigation, scientific liaison, or formal presentations of his work. In Edinburgh he studied, with Schäfer, the diuretic action of pituitary extracts and innervation of the spleen. The next two out-of-country travels took him to Naples, where, in the biology station under the direction of Uexhüll, he investigated the ganglia of *Ciona intestinalis* and the pupillary reaction of the octopus. In 1905, at Cambridge with Langley, Magnus studied the effects of drugs on the movement of the intestines before and after section of the mesentery nerves. Meanwhile, in his laboratory, he showed that the degree of stretching of the intestinal muscle determines the direction of conduction of the stimulus and that it would retain many of its physiological characteristics if suspended without perfusion in a warm, oxygenated Locke-Ringer solution.

A visit to Liverpool in 1908 and intimate exposure to Sherrington's investigations on the action of the nervous system stimulated Magnus' fundamental researches on the physiological dissection of the mechanism of mammalian posture. Later in the year he accepted a call to the Dutch University of Utrecht, since no vacancies in senior posts in pharmacology appeared imminent in Germany. The professorship was combined with the directorship of Holland's first Institute of Pharmacology, an ancient structure designed originally as a pesthouse for smallpox victims. The first of his notable communications on reflex regulation of animal posture in relation to gravity, which described work done in Sherrington's laboratory, was summarized as follows:[2]

I have already shown that the altered posture of the limbs is a deciding influence in their reflexes. Generally speaking, extension initiates the development of flexor response, while previous abduction initiates the development of adduction and vice versa. This is true for the entire extremity as well as for a single joint. We found in the hind legs of the spinal dog that the influence exerted by the proximal joints is greater than that of the distal joints. The position of the hip exerts a greater influence, as far as the direction of the reflex movement of the limb is concerned, than that of the knee; but the latter is more powerful than the ankle. These phenomena are especially evident when studying the crossed reflexes.

Each type of afferent nerve we have investigated, namely the superficial and deep skin sensory as well as those from the tendon, periosteum, and muscle, transmits stimuli to the central nervous system according to the place and position of the reacting limb or part and provides the impetus to varied and often opposing reflexes. We have also shown that the phenomenon may be produced, not only by spatial relations of the limbs themselves, but in an altered reception by one part of the central nervous system—the spinal marrow. The altered place and position of an extremity produces an altered reception of the motor centers for a single muscle as well as for muscle groups whose capacity for stimulation is altered as well as its purpose—the signal for the performance. This regulation is very sensitive. These findings are of fundamental importance for our concept of the function of the central nervous system. We found that the spinal marrow reacts differently with each movement and reflects the position of the different parts as well as the entire body. This is one of the reasons why reflexes create the impression of complete efficiency and operation.

In 1912 and the following years, de Kleijn collaborated in the definition of neck and labyrinth reflexes in man influenced by the position of the head that participates in the muscular tonus of the extremities. The observations began with the examination of the tail reflexes of a spinal cat. Incidental lifting of the head of the supine animal produced a stretch tonus of the forefeet which persisted so long as the head was raised. This work was described in a communication entitled, "Muscle Tone of the Extremities on the Position of the Head."[3]

Several thousand observations later, it was evident that two reflex mechanisms are operating. Elevating the head in one position (45° above the horizontal) produces through the labyrinthine reflexes a maximal bilateral stretch-tonus of all four extremities which becomes minimal when the head is lowered below 45° above the horizontal. The position of the head in relation to the trunk has a more complicated influence. One must distinguish between turning, bending, lifting, and bowing of the head. Usually the mandible will be brought forward and the parietal area of the head bent backward. These tonic reflexes are controlled not only by the labyrinth but by the cervical nerves.
Both mechanisms can either work synergistically or against one another. These are tonic posture-reflexes and under certain conditions can be found also in humans with a brain disorder. These are known as the *Magnus-de Kleijn* reflexes which are sought during each neurological examination. Bilateral tonus of the extremities is controlled by one labyrinth. There are also unilateral labyrinthine reflexes which can be brought out by stimulation of muscles of the neck and trunk.
Also important are the posture reflexes of the head which are controlled by the labyrinth. Reflexes in a *mid-brain-animal* control the fixation of the position of the head in space under all conditions; also, there are labyrinthine reflexes controlling the position of the head in compensation for the movement of the eyes.

Magnus' investigations on composite body posture were described in approximately 150 reports. Many were published in *Pfleuger Archiv*. His monograph, *Körperstellung*,[4] which appeared in 1924, reviewed the work from his laboratory that had been in progress for a decade and one half. The subject was presented in a resumé as the Croonian lecture to the Royal Society of London in 1925 and for the Cameron Prize lectures at the University of Edinburgh the following year. The former appeared in the *Proceedings of the Royal Society*. Excerpts follow.[5]

Every movement starts from and ends in some posture, so that I think a discussion of "Animal Posture" falls well within the scope of the intention of Dr. William Croone, when he founded these annual Lectures to promote the study of "Muscular Motion." Before beginning I wish to emphasise how greatly I appreciate the honour of delivering before you this Lecture, and how I especially enjoy the pleasure of doing so with Sir Charles Sherrington in the Chair, who long ago took the trouble to introduce me to his beautiful methods of investigating the central nervous system, and to allow me an insight into his fruitful views on the function of nervous centres.

As it is impossible to consider the whole problem of posture in one short lecture, I propose to speak to you to-day on four partial problems, which are closely connected with each other, and which provided the starting points for investigations which have been carried out in my laboratory at Utrecht, with the aid of a great number of able collaborators. These partial problems are:—

1. *Reflex standing.*—In order to carry the weight of the body against the action of gravity, it is necessary that a certain set of muscles, the "standing muscles," should have by reflex action a certain degree of enduring tone, to prevent the body from falling down on the ground.

2. *Normal distribution of tone.*—In the living animal not only do these standing muscles possess one, but also the other muscles of the body, especially their antagonists, *i.e.,* the flexors. Between these two sets of muscles a certain balance of tone exists, so that neither set of muscles gets too much or too little tone.

3. *Attitude.*—The position of the different parts of the body must harmonise with each other; if one part of the body be displaced, the other parts also change in posture, so that different well-adapted attitudes, evoked by the first displacement, will result.

4. *Righting function.*—If by its own active movements or by some outside force the body of an animal is brought out of the normal resting posture, then a series of reflexes are evoked, by which the normal position is reached again.

The main *centres* for all these four functions are situated in close neighbourhood subcortically in the brain-stem. Their function is to compound the activity of the whole body musculature to what we call *"posture."* The lower centres for the muscles of the different parts of the body are arranged segmentally in the spinal cord; the higher centres in the brain-stem put them into combined action, and in this way govern the posture of the animal as a whole. We have here a very good example of what Sherrington has called the "integrative action of the nervous system." And integration is especially necessary in the case of posture, because nervous excitations arising from very different sense organs are flowing towards the postural centres in the brain-stem, and must be combined so that a harmonising effect will result.

Nervous impulses, which can influence posture arise: (1) From the labyrinths, a double sense-organ: the otoliths reacting to changes in position, the ampullae of the semicircular canals to accelerations; (2) from the proprioceptive sense-organs in muscles, joints and tendons; (3) from exteroceptive nerve endings of the body surface, chiefly from the pressure sense-organs, which are stimulated, if the body touches the ground; (4) from teleceptors, reacting to distance stimuli, such as the eye, the ear, the nose. In fact a very finely elaborated central apparatus is needed to combine and distribute all these afferent impulses, depending on and adapted to the always changing circumstances of environment.

Although most attention has been given in this essay to animal posture, Magnus' assignment at Utrecht was not in neurophysiology. Already he has shown the breadth of his intellect with the composition of a series of lectures on Goethe as a scientist; and, as professor of pharmacology, he directed his own as well as the investigations of others at the Institute in this discipline. His complete bibliography is appended to the *Lane Lectures on Experimental Pharmacology and Medicine,* which were to be delivered in San Francisco in 1928 at Stanford University Medical School. The final draft of the *Lectures* together with an introductory biography was made ready for the printer by H. H. Dale and was published in 1930.[6]

During World War I, Magnus held to his German loyalties. In spite of his academic residence in Holland, he served in the military hospitals attached to the German Army in 1915 and later organized research for protection against chemical warfare and the treatment of gassed victims. After the war he returned to Utrecht. There he played a major part in the establishment of the Royal Institute for Pharmacologic Research, designed for the development of chemical and biological standards in the drug industry. Most important was his planning for a new institute of pharmacologic research to replace his inadequate facility. The project received financial support from the Rockefeller Foundation of the United States but was not dedicated until shortly after his death in Switzerland. Other academic accolades included the Baly Medal of the Royal College of Physicians of London, and honorary fellowships in the American Society for Pharmacology and Experimental Therapeutics, the American Laryngological, Rhinological, and Otological Society, and in various scientific organizations in Holland, Germany, Austria, and Russia.

1. Winkler, C.: Rudolf Magnus (Ger), *Schweiz Arch Neurol Psychiat* 21:175-180, 1927, excerpt translated by Z. Danilevicius.

2. Magnus, R.: Regulation of Movement Through the Central Nervous System (Ger), *Pflueger Arch Ges Physiol* 130:219-252, 1909, excerpt translated by E. Longar.

3. Magnus, R., and de Kleijn, A.: Muscle Tone of the Extremities Dependent on the Position of the Head (Ger), *Pflueger Arch Ges Physiol* 145:455-548, 1912.

4. Magnus, R.: *Body Posture* (Ger), Berlin: J. Springer, 1924.

5. Magnus, R.: Cronian Lecture.—*Animal Posture, Proc Roy Soc [Biol]* 98:339-353 (Nov) 1925.

6. Magnus, R.: *Lane Lectures on Experimental Pharmacology and Medicine*, Palo Alto, Calif: Stanford University Press, 1930.

Composite by G. Bako

Robert Barany (1876-1936)

THE 1914 NOBEL PRIZE IN PHYSIOLOGY OR MEDICINE was awarded for contributions on vestibular function to a native son of Vienna, who had been captured and held prisoner of war by the Russians after the fall of the fortress of Premysl. Robert Barany received the MD degree from the University of Vienna in 1900, having written his inaugural thesis on rhythmical nystagmus. Following graduation he studied internal medicine with von Noorden at Frankfurt, psychology with Kraepelin at Heidelberg, and neurology and psychiatry with Pfi at Freiburg. Returning to Vienna, he served as an assistant to Politzer, a relatively young professor in the world-famous ear clinic. Barany there began investigations on vestibular nystagmus.[1]

Because of additional training in internal medicine and psychiatry, a curiosity for the pathogenesis of motor function, and clinical devotion to otology, Barany was able to define normal and abnormal responses of the semicircular canals to special stimuli. His methods of investigation, supported by theories which have persisted or have subsequently been proved, centered around the function of the labyrinth. Before the end of World War I, and through the intervention of Prince Carl of Sweden and G. Holmgren of Uppsala, Barany was released by the Russian forces and accepted an appointment in the faculty of the University of Uppsala. He joined the department of otolaryngology, became a Swedish citizen, and lived out his natural life in his adopted land. Although Barany is best known for the caloric test of vestibular function, the mechanism of past pointing and of hearing, the bipartition of the granular layer of the optic cortex, and cerebellar localization also benefited from his productive investigations.

Correlation of fragmentary knowledge of vestibular function, nystagmus, and physiological response to the irrigation of hot and cold water in the external ear canal led to the elaboration of the Barany caloric test in 1906. Schmiedekam, in 1868, had observed the sudden appearance of vertigo, nausea, and vomiting from introduction of cold water into the external auditory canal. Later Hensen, Baginsky, and others skirted the implications of this phenomenon, but it remained for Barany to quantitate temperatures of the irrigating fluid and directional nystagmus. He reasoned that, if the temperature was warmer or colder than the endolymph, a current was assumed to be set up, causing movement of the hairs of the ampullary hair cells which stimulated the nerves. The stimulus was transmitted to the vestibular nuclei and, in turn, to the centers that controlled movement of the eyes and the skeletal musculature. The resulting eye movement was nystagmus, consisting of a slow conjugated eye movement in one direction and a quick movement in the opposite direction. The direction of the nystagmus was denoted as that of the quick component and depended upon whether warm or cold water was used and upon the position of the head. The degree of response was indicated by the duration of the nystagmus or its intensity. A delay or a negative response was observed when the labyrinthine function was impaired or nonresponsive (Barany's sign). Executing the caloric test involved inserting rubber tubes into the acoustic meatus and connecting them with a rubber balloon filled with water.[2]

If the right ear was irrigated with water cooler than body temperature and with the head in an upright position, a predominantly rotatory nystagmus quick to the left was noticed, with a horizontal component. . . . Nystagmus could be produced in any ear that had an intact vestibular apparatus. . . . In patients who had undergone a radical ear operation the nystagmus appeared in 5 to 10 seconds, while in patients with intact eardrums nystagmus appeared in 45 to 90 seconds. If the irrigating fluid was warmer than body temperature, the direction of nystagmus was opposite to that produced when cold water was used. . . . If the irrigating water was at body temperature, there was no nystagmus or vertigo. . . . It is most probable that the cooling or warming of the labyrinthine contents causing convection currents and movements of endolymph was directly responsible for the findings.

The chair test, based upon counter rotation of the orbit, was another measure of vestibular function described during Barany's highly productive years in clinical investigation. The procedure required a rotating chair with a head rest designed so the head might be inclined forward 30° to bring the horizontal semicircular canals into the horizontal plane. A pair of spectacles fitted with opaque lenses eliminated physiological optical nystagmus resulting from the shifting visual fixation during the rotation of the chair.

With normal vestibular function, horizontal nystagmus to the left occurred of 10 to 34 seconds' duration when the chair was rotated to the right and abruptly stopped. A marked increase in systolic blood pressure or a fall in diastolic blood pressure after rotation nullified the test.[3]

By the term counter rotation is implied a peculiar noticeable movement of both eyeballs that appears when the head is tilted from a straight upright position toward a shoulder. The eyeballs do not remain fixed, but rotate in a circular orbit in the direction opposite to the movement of the head. Counter rotation may be temporary or persistent. I have measured the counter rotation for 20°, 40°, and 60°, right and left tilts. . . . Rotation is maximum in the first 20° of tilt and thereafter it decreases gradually. Counter rotation may be as great as 6½° in the first 20°; in the second 20°, it increases by about 1° to 6½°; and in the third 20°, it increases only by ½° to 5°. The first 20° of the right and left tilt is approximately 6.3°, the value is 5.1° during the second 20°, and is only 4.1° in the third 20°. . . . In normals the first 20° of tilt produces about ⅓ of counter rotation of the orbit, the second 20°, about ¼, and the third 20°, only ⅕ of it. In normal persons the difference varied from 0° to 3½° on the same day, in the patients (all of them had dizziness as the main symptom) the difference varied from 2° to 6°. The average was 1.4° in the normals and 4° in those with symptoms.

Barany's syndrome embraces unilateral deafess, vertigo, and pain in the occipital region. In his clinical investigations patients who suffered from migraine or inner ear infection showed on the affected side:[4]

. . . unilateral deafness, with the characteristic inner-ear lesion. Associated with the deafness we have attacks of dizziness of vestibular type, and varying in degree. Besides, and this is most important, there are sensitive pain areas, localized on the posterior part of the head on the diseased side. Very noticeable in the anamnesis is the statement of the patients that at times they hear very well and at other times very poorly, being almost deaf. From this anamnesis alone I have concluded in eight to nine consecutive cases, that the above-described pointing-system would be present, and have found it practically every time. As I have already explained, the spontaneous pointing-error may be due to a stimulation of the center toward which the finger deviates, or oftener to a paralysis of the antagonistic center, and takes place there by a relative over-balancing of the physiological tonus of one center by paralysis of the other.

Localization in the cerebellar cortex of areas of correlation for the vestibular apparatus, directional pointing, and the higher centers was approached experimentally on humans. One patient, whose dura covering the cerebellum was exposed during a mastoid operation, survived with only the skin covering the previously exposed dura. Later Barany was able, by chilling the dura and the underlying cortical tissue with ethyl chloride, to identify the center controlling the abduction of the right arm in the cerebellum.[5]

When this area was chilled, impairment of pointing to the left appeared and when nystagmus was produced to the left, the reaction to the right was absent in the right arm. Thus there are three centers on the surface of the cerebellar cortex: (1) immediately posterior to the internal meatus acousticus, controlling the movement of the wrist toward the center (2) immediately behind the ear, controlling the movement of the arm toward the center, and (3) 5 cm behind the external ear, controlling the movement of the arm toward the outside.

Barany's pointing test, an easily performed clinical procedure, is valid as a useful diagnostic aid in detecting disturbance of cerebellar function.[6]

I ask the patient to close his eyes and to extent his arm and to touch my finger held directly in front of him. . . . This is repeated and usually is successful in normal individuals, without any preceding practice with eyes open. Eventually, after missing the finger once or twice, a normal person can touch the finger with the eyes shut. When horizontal nystagmus to the left is produced, the patient misses my finger by past pointing to the right. Even with great effort he does not succeed in touching my finger, but constantly deviates by pointing far to the right. This reaction originates in the cerebellum and specifically in the ipsilateral hemisphere, and is constant and regular.

Although Viennese by birth and training, and probably always holding some hope for an academic recall to Austria, no place was found for Barany in the University faculty as he approached scientific maturity. Ample evidence of Sweden's pride is found in the honors bestowed on him, including the *Dr. med. honoris causa* from the Karolinska Institute (1924) and Commander of the Northern Star of the First Class (1927).

Such tributes were merited by Barany, one of the outstanding clinical neurophysiologists and otologists of all time.

1. Holmgren, G.: Robert Barany, 1876-1936, *Ann Otol* 45:593-595, 1936.
2. Barany, R.: Investigation of the Vestibular Apparatus and Nystagmus (Ger), *Mschr Ohrenheilk* 40:193-297, 1906; 41:477-526, 1907, excerpt translated by Z. Danilevicius.
3. Barany, R.: Counter Rotation in Persons with Normal Hearing, Patients with Diseases of the Ear and in Deaf-Mutes (Ger), *Arch Ohrenheilk* 68:1-30, 1906, excerpt translated by Z. Danilevicius.
4. Barany, R.: The Vestibular Apparatus and the Central Nervous System, L. T. DeSwarte, trans., *Laryngoscope* 22:81-89, 1912.
5. Barany, R.: Vestibular Apparatus and the Central Nervous System (Ger), *Deutsch Z Nervenheilk* 43:356-358, 1912, excerpt translated by Z. Danilevicius.
6. Barany, R.: Localization in the Cortex of the Cerebellum (Ger), *Deutsch Med Wschr* 39:637-642, 1913, excerpt translated by Z. Danilevicius.

Composite by G. Bako

August Krogh (1874-1949)

SCHACK AUGUST STEENBERG KROGH, born in Grenaa, Jutland, Denmark, achieved preeminence among contemporary medical scientists for his investigations of animal and human physiology. In his youth he manifested interest in the natural sciences and, upon entering the University of Copenhagen, began the study of medicine; however, he shifted to zoology and graduated in this subject in 1899.[1] For almost a decade in the department of physiology in the Copenhagen Medical School, he assisted Christian Bohr, whose interest in respiration and blood gas physiology left a lifetime impression on the pupil. No suitable academic post was vacant in the University; therefore, an associate professorship in zoophysiology was created for Krogh in 1908. Eight years later he advanced as professor to the university chair in the same subject, a post held until retirement in 1945. International recognition of Krogh's accomplishments led, in 1920, to the award of the Nobel Prize for Physiology or Medicine. This honor, however, caused no cessation in his contributions to the understanding of respiratory gases and their transport in animals and man. The interpretation of blood gases and their transport required the development of new techniques and precise tools of measurement for optimal exploitation, which, in turn, contributed to his recognition as a physiologist among and for physiologists.

It is not surprising that Krogh, while assistant to Bohr, became involved in the investigations in progress in Copenhagen. In 1904, as junior author following Bohr and Hasselbalch, he described the influence of carbon dioxide tension on the binding of oxygen by hemoglobin, later known as the "Bohr effect."[2]

The biological importance of the lessening influence of carbonic acid on the blood's ability to bind oxygen is great. In experiments with high carbonic acid pressures, no appreciable influence on the oxygen uptake of blood is recorded when the oxygen pressure is high as in the pulmonary blood. However, when blood reaches the tissues where the oxygen tension is low and the carbonic acid pressure is high, enhanced oxygen dissociation leads to increased utilization of oxygen.

While still under the influence of Bohr but completely independent of his scientific reasoning, Krogh first accepted, then rejected, his chief's assumption of the active secretion of oxygen by the alveolar membrane. Krogh and his wife, Marie, utilized the microtonometer of his invention for measuring gas pressures in the blood. When carbon monoxide was used as a foreign gas, no evidence of secretion of gas across the alveolar membrane was demonstrated.[3]

As the investigations set forth in detail in the preceding papers had given results, which lent no support to the theory of gas-secretion in the lungs, but were in complete accordance with a simple diffusion-hypothesis, it became necessary to see whether the conditions of gas-diffusion in the lungs were such, as to allow the necessary quantities to pass through at the tension-differences which could be found. In this case, and in this one only, the secretion-theory ought, in our opinion, to be abandoned.

The only gas, which is available for such experiments, is the carbonic oxide, which may be taken up in large quantities by the blood, and forms with the haemoglobin a compound processing a very low tension of dissociation. The principle of the determination is to measure the quantity of CO_2 which is absorbed from the air of the lungs during a given time and with a known difference of CO_2-tension between the alveolar air and the blood. By means of this quantity the absorption of CO_2 per mm tension-difference and per minute is calculated and represents the diffusion-constant for CO_2 of the lungs in the state examined.

Bohr has pointed out that, when the diffusion-constants are so large, it must follow from a simple diffusion-theory, that the arterial CO_2-tension should always be equal to the mean alveolar CO_2-tension. The quantity of CO_2 eliminated during rest (about 300^{ccm} per m) requires less than 1^{mm} tension-difference for its transport, and even during very heavy work the mean tension-difference cannot be more than about 3^{mm}. The final tension-difference between the blood and the alveolar air must therefore in any case be imperceptible. It will be shown in the subsequent paper that the equality postulated does in fact exist.

In 1912, Krogh, together with Lindhard, observed the blood flow through the lungs of man with a technique dependent on the inhalation of a foreign gas in the blood. Although the recorded values by this method were less than anticipated or derived by other techniques, the changes observed during muscular activity were of considerable physiological merit. Blood flow during rest was shown to be as low as 2.8 liters per minute depending upon the supply of venous blood to the right heart; whereas during muscular work a maximum of 21.6 liters per minute was observed. Athletic training was found to have a measurable influence on the circulation during activity, enhancing oxygen utilization and efficient action of the heart.[4]

In recognition of his anatomical and physiological studies on the "capillariomotor mechanism," Krogh was awarded the Nobel Prize in 1920. Until a few years prior to this, little time had been spent investigating the quantitative histology of the capillary system; rather, it was assumed the number of open capillaries in any tissue depended upon the blood pressure in the arterioles which supplied the capillaries. As the blood pressure increased, as in physical exercise, additional capillaries opened to accommodate the increased circulation. Krogh assumed that, if the capillaries responded only to the stimulus of blood pressure, the capillaries of any tissue must vary in their susceptibility to this stimulus. In testing this hypothesis experimentally Krogh detected that no one capillary or group of capillaries functioned continuously. The capillaries were constantly changing in caliber. After one capillary opened and received blood, it closed, while adjacent ones opened and provided new channels for gas exchange. Furthermore, he disproved the dependence of dilation upon arteriolar pressure. Mechanical, thermal, or chemical stimulation produced dilation of capillaries and arterioles, and under strong stimulation the effect spread to adjoining areas. In the change from rest to activity, the oxygen requirements determined the opening and closing of vascular channels for the diffusion of oxygen from blood to tissues. A full account of his researches on the capillaries constituted the Silliman Lectures delivered at Yale University in 1922, an epochal treatise in 20th century physiology.[5]

My own first contribution to the problem of capillary contractility was published in Danish in 1918, about a month after Dale and Richards' paper, and somewhat later appeared in the *British Journal of Physiology* (1919). It was undertaken to test the hypothesis of a regulation of the supply of blood to muscles through the opening and closing of individual capillaries. I found it possible to observe at least the superficial capillaries of muscles both in the frog and in mammals through a binocular microscope, using strong reflected light as a source of illumination. Resting muscles observed in this way are usually quite pale, and the microscope reveals only a few capillaries at fairly regular intervals. These capillaries are so narrow that red corpuscles can pass through only at a slow rate and with a change of form

from the ordinary flat discs to elongated sausages. When the muscle under observation is stimulated to contractions a large number of capillaries become visible and dilated, and the rate of circulation though them is greatly increased. When the stimulus has lasted only a few seconds the circulation returns in some minutes to the resting state; the capillaries become narrower and most of them are emptied completely, while a small number remain open. Since capillaries, even in a group fed by the same arteriole, do not all behave in the same way, the changes obviously cannot be due to arterial pressure changes.

Precision instruments designed by Krogh include a recording spirometer for the routine determination of the basal metabolism, a bicycle ergometer for the study of physical activity in man, precision pipets, respiration apparatus, and advanced micro devices for analysis. Although the application of Krogh's investigations centered on man, the experimental approach throughout his rich career embraced lower life as well, as suggested by his academic title. While still an undergraduate, he studied the hydrostatic mechanism of the *Corethra* larvae and devised methods for microscopic analysis of the gas contained in their air bladders. He examined the gas exchange in the frog and reported great variations in pulmonary respiration; whereas the skin respiration was a relatively constant function. At other times he determined the tidal air, vital capacity, and the total capacity of the larva of the water beetle, which breathes through a pair of functional spiracles in the terminal body segment. He measured the oxygen content of the tibial tracheae of grasshoppers, recorded the elevation of body temperature by muscular contraction of flying insects preparatory to flight, and studied the adaptation of tracheal respiration to aquatic existence.[6] Many of his studies on aquatic animals were reviewed in a monograph on the subject published in 1939, which contained a description, current with the times, of the active transport mechanism across membranes composed of cells.[7]

Permeability of cell surfaces and membranes. The problems of permeability in living organisms turn out to be extremely complicated. In what is usually called permeability we have to deal with the movements of molecules and ions in which the driving force is concentration gradients or, in the case of ions, electrical potentials, and when such movements take place across a protoplasmic surface that surface is *eo ipso* permeable. The rate of penetration can be measured and put in relation to the driving force, and if the concentration gradients or potentials are reversed the direction will also become reversed, while the same rate will obtain, provided the physicochemical properties of the membrane remain unaltered. In this sense protoplasmic surfaces are generally permeable to water, to dissolved gases, to a number of organic substances with which we are not here concerned, and sometimes also to ions.

In a number of cases, on the other hand, we have found special mechanisms by which ions, certain organic substances and sometimes even water are transported in one direction only and may be moved against gradients and potentials. It would be absurd to deny that in such cases the surfaces in question are permeable, but it would be just as absurd to put this "permeability" in the same category as the simple permeability defined above.

Krogh received many honors, including the LLD, was a foreign member of the Royal Society of England, gave the Croonian Lecture to the Society, and received the Seegen Prize of the Imperial Academy of Sciences of Vienna and the Baly Medal of the Royal College of Physicians of London. His practical side and medical interest was demonstrated by the successful introduction of insulin into Denmark and arranging for its manufacture shortly after its discovery in Canada. Following retirement, he continued his investigations at home in a basement laboratory provided by the Carlsberg and the Scandinavian Insulin Foundations. His laboratory for half a century was one of the most sought after by students of many disciplines from neighboring countries and abroad. His pupils have held or continue to occupy a remarkable number of senior academic chairs in diverse subjects in various countries. Considered by some as aloof and austere, Krogh was accepted by those who knew him as a kind supervisor, a perceptive scientist, and a staunch friend.

1. Liljestrand, G.: Obituary Notice. August Krogh. 1874-1949, *Acta Physiol Scand* 20:109-116, 1950.

2. Bohr, C.: Hasselbalch, K.; and Krogh, A.: The Biological Dependence of Carbon Dioxide Tension of the Blood on Oxygen Binding, *Scand Arch Physiol* 16:402-412, 1904, excerpt translated by Z. Danilevicius.

3. Krogh, A., and Krogh, M.: On the Rate of Diffusion of Carbonic Oxide Into the Lungs of Man, *Scand Arch Physiol* 23:236-247, 1910.

4. Krogh, A., and Lindhard, J.: Measurements of the Blood Flow Through the Lungs of Man, *Scand Arch Physiol* 27:100-125, 1912.

5. Krogh, A.: *The Anatomy and Physiology of Capillaries*, Silliman Memorial Lectures, New Haven: Yale University Press, 1924.

6. Krogh, A.: *The Comparative Physiology of Respiratory Mechanisms*, Philadelphia: University of Pennsylvania Press, 1941.

7. Krogh, A.: *Osmotic Regulation in Aquatic Animals*, Cambridge: University Press, 1939.

Composite by G. Bako

Hans Queckenstedt (1876-1918)

HANS HEINRICH GEORG QUECKENSTEDT, whose communication on the significance of the interruption of the free flow of cerebrospinal fluid led to eponymic identification, was born in Leipzig-Reudnitz into a schoolteacher's family of limited means.[1] His intellectual capacity, apparent in his early youth, was expressed in an attraction to physics, mathematics, and the natural sciences. Upon completion of his medical education at the University of Leipzig, and passing the state examination in 1900, Queckenstedt entered the service of Professor S. J. M. Ganser in the Municipal Hospital in Zwickau, known at that time as the Dresden Hospital for Mental Diseases. In 1904, the MD degree was awarded upon presentation of an inaugural dissertation on carcinosarcoma to the medical faculty of Leipzig.

Queckenstedt, an excellent clinician, devoted most of his energies to the management of the sick, first in the medical polyclinic in Heidelberg and later at the medical clinic in Rostock. Subsequently, he advanced to privatdocent and professor under Martius and there made his two most important scientific contributions. During World War I, Queckenstedt attended the German troops as consulting internist, and in the waning months of conflct he accepted his final academic appointment—physician-in-chief to the medical section of the City Hospital of Harburg, near Hamburg. While on military duty a few days before the Armistice, he was thrown from a horse and killed by a munitions truck.

The number of Queckenstedt's published communications is disproportionate to his intellectual talents: his doctoral thesis; his findings on iron metabolism in pernicious anemia; a series of observations on periostitis in typhoid fever; and, during the war years, observations on the dynamics and constituents of cerebrospinal fluid. Having observed the usual oscillations in the recording manometer during respiration, straining, and coughing, Queckenstedt's curiosity led to the investigation of the response following compression of the jugular veins. The failure of the column to rise in selected patients was attributed to obstruction of the subarachnoid space between the foramen magnum and the lumbar region. In 1916 his best-known communication contained the protocols of three patients who gave an aberrant response during the recording of cerebrospinal fluid pressure. At operation, an echinococcus infection of the lumbar vertebra was found to be responsible for obstruction in one patient; a sarcomatous angioma of the conus medullaris was discovered postmortem in the second; a cord tumor was suspected but not confirmed in the third. Excerpts of the communication describing the procedure subsequently known as the Queckenstedt test are as follows.[2]

Although numerous reports in recent years have discussed the properties of the spinal fluid with compression lesions of the cord, the physical behavior or mechanical response has been overlooked. No one has given any consideration to the design of a simple experiment which can furnish proof of a diminution in space at the site of compression, which would then permit recognition of the nature of the trouble.

Any diminution in space of the spinal canal is disproportionate to the increase in size of the pathological process because of the swelling of the cord. Before signs of compression appear, edema of the adjacent tissues develops as well as "edema of the fluid," i.e., an increase of the albumin content without an increase in number of cells.

The narrowed channel impedes movement of fluid with an increase in pressure above the compression site; the fluid ceases to flow caudally or at a decreased rate according to the degree of obstruction. The increment in pressure above the obstruction can be demonstrated by compression of the neck, either circumferentially or unilaterally which produces an increase in venous blood in the cranial cavity, with concomitant reduction in space for the cerebrospinal fluid. The increased fluid pressure immediately transmitted throughout the system normally can be demonstrated with a pressure manometer attached to a lumbar puncture needle. In lesions of the cord the manometric change is greatly retarded and the pressure below the lesion rises slowly. Sometimes prolonged compression about the neck is necessary to produce a detectable increase in the manometric reading. When the compression is released, the pressure in the manometer decreases slowly or not at all.

Certain precautions must be taken to insure proper recording of oscillations of the fluid. Normal transmission of pressure can be recognized readily by respiratory excursions, but especially on compression or coughing, when the rise is immediate and rapid.

The value of the procedure in diagnosis will be in direct ratio to the absence of characteristic signs and symptoms. It can confirm compression from any lesion of an intervertebral disc. This procedure is helpful in the diagnosis of tumors, and sometimes may be the deciding criterion. I strongly recommend the routine application of the test which should be carried out regularly with each lumbar puncture in any cross-sectional lesion of the cord. In cases with characteristic but isolated complaints which suggest a tumor, such as unilateral root pains, the diagnosis may be confirmed shortly after onset of symptoms.

This test does not distinguish between extramedullary and intramedullary tumors; at least not consistently. An intramedullary growth can produce the same alterations in pressure as an extramedullary growth, especially in the production of collateral edema.

Queckenstedt's second communication worthy of excerpting described the changes in patients suffering from polyneuritis and sciatica. An increased protein content was found in the fluid, with little or no increase in concentration of the cells. Others had observed an albuminocytologic dissociation in selected conditions; Queckenstedt summarized his findings in 42 patients suffering from acute infectious and chronic polyneuritis. In diphtheritic polyneuritis he reported:[3]

A total of ten cases of diphtheritic polyneuritis, varying in severity, was investigated. Attention was given to the cell count and the albumin content of the fluid; the latter was determined initially according to the Nissl method; later the Nonne-Apelt qualitative globulin reaction procedure was adopted. . . . An increase in cell count was not observed in any of the cases studied. Not more than 4 cells per cmm were found, even in instances with the greatest increase in albumin. In summary, no direct correlation with severity of the neurological changes was observed. *In the majority of cases of diphtheritic neuritis an increase of albumin in the lumbar fluid reached considerable proportions, associated with little or no increase in concentration of cells.*

1. Stender, A.: Concerning Queckenstedt and His Test, *J Neurosurg* 5:337-340, 1948.
2. Queckenstedt, H.: Diagnosis of Compression of the Spinal Cord (Ger), *Deutsch Z Nervenheilk* 55:325-333, 1916, excerpt translated by E. Longar.
3. Queckenstedt, H.: Changes in the Spinal Fluid in Peripheral Neuritis, Especially Polyneuritis and Sciatica (Ger), *Deutsch Z Nervenheilk* 57:316-329, 1917, excerpts translated by E. Longar.

Corneille Heymans (1892-1968)

CORNEILLE JEAN FRANCOIS HEYMANS was born in Ghent, Belgium, the son of J. F. Heymans, founder of the J. F. Heymans Institute of Pharmacology and Therapeutics, professor of pharmacology, and sometime rector of the University of Ghent. After his secondary education at the schools in Ghent, he pursued medical education at the University where, in 1920, he obtained the doctor's degree. Heymans subsequently studied with Gley in Paris, Arthur in Lausanne, Meyer in Vienna, Starling in London, and Wiggers in Cleveland. In 1922, he was appointed lecturer in pharmacodynamics at the

Composite by G. Bako

University of Ghent, and in 1930 succeeded his father as director of the Heymans Institute, professor of pharmacology, and head of the department of pharmacology, pharmacodynamics, and toxicology.

Heymans' investigations, strongly influenced by those of his father and frequently carried out jointly, centered around the physiology and pharmacology of respiration and circulation. The discovery of chemoreceptors situated in the cardio-aortic and the carotid sinus areas, the proprioceptive regulation of arterial blood pressure, and the regulation of respiration earned for him the Nobel Prize.[1] The studies of the respiratory reflexes transmitted by the vagus nerve incorporated a technique of the isolating head of a dog remaining responsive by perfusion of blood from another dog; whereas torso and extremities remained viable by artificial respiration. Only the vagi constituted natural communication between the head and the remainder of the body.

Heymans, in collaboration with a number of students and associates, studied the reflexes arising from the carotid sinus, shown by Hering in 1923 to be the site of a depressor reflex. They provided irrefutable evidence of the participation of chemical stimuli in the control of blood pressure and respiration. This work led to the hypothesis of four types of reflexes originating in the sinus area. Blood pressure, cardiac rhythm, and respiration could be modified by pressure changes in the sinus; these physiological functions could also be modified by variations in the chemical composition of the blood produced by an increase in carbon dioxide tension or by a decrease of oxygen content. Heymans' 1929 monograph on the subject contained the following summary data of the pathological role of the carotid sinus and of other sensitive zones.[2]

Résumé of the pathological role of the carotid sinus and of other vasosensitive zones.

Denervation of the vasosensitive zones provokes arterial hypertension and cardiac disturbance characterized by tachycardia, extrasystoles, and ventricular fibrillation.

Hypotension related to the carotid sinuses follows compression of the common carotids, creates similar cardiovascular abnormalities.

The diminution or suppression of the sensitivity of the carotid sinuses is followed by chronic arterial hypertension, acceleration of the heart rate, and intermittent extrasystoles, accompanied by anatomical-pathological changes in the suprarenal glands, dilatation of the heart, and vascular and renal sclerosis.

Reflex insufficiency of the carotid sinuses exposes the cerebral vessels to spikes of arterial pressure.

It is probable that in a man certain pathological states of hypertension, tachycardia, extrasystole, cerebral hemorrhage, vascular and renal sclerosis, all are due to an insufficiency, to a hypotonia, of the vasosensitive zones regulating the vasomotor tonus, the secretion of adrenalin, and the heart rate.

Depression of the sensitivity of the zones could have its origin either in vascular sclerosis of the carotid sinuses and of the aorta, or in the depression of vasosensitivity by specific pathological humoral substances.

In 1945, when Heymans responded with the Nobel lecture to the Prize for Physiology or Medicine, printed in Ghent in 1940, he discussed the role of vascular pressoreceptors and chemoreceptors in respiratory control, as determined by his isolated dog's head perfusion technique, with the following excerpts.[1]

In this lecture I am privileged to describe contributions which my laboratory has made to the study of a number of physiological, physiopathological and pharmacological mechanisms which act on and control the functioning of the respiratory centre and thereby affect pulmonary ventilation and pulmonary gas exchanges.

Thus, this group of experiments carried out between 1924 and 1927 showed *that arterial hypertension in the cardio-aortic vascular area inhibits the activity of the respiratory centre by a reflex mechanism, while arterial hypotension in the same area has a stimulatory reflex effect on the activity of the respiratory centre.*

Using the isolated and perfused head technique, we found that hypotension in the isolated cephalic circulation stimulates the respiratory centre, whereas hypertension in the same area produces respiratory inhibition to the point of apnea. We undertook to examine the mechanism of the interaction between cephalic blood pressure and the activity of the respiratory centre. . . . the carotid sinuses, i.e, the arterial regions located in the area where the common carotid artery bifurcates into internal and external carotids and occipital artery, contain receptors, as does the homologous cardio-aortic zone, who, by a reflex mechanism, act upon and regulate the activity of the cardio-vascular centres and of the respiratory centres.

A number of experimental procedures have enabled us to show that an increase in endovascular pressure in the carotid sinus produces an inhibition of the respiratory centre to the point of apnea, by a reflex arising from the pressoreceptors, and that hypotension in the carotid sinus produces reflex stimulation of the respiration.

The several experimental observations summarized above thus demonstrate that *variations in arterial blood pressure act on the respiratory centre by a reflex mechanism involving endovascular presso-receptors located in the cardio-aortic zone and in the carotid sinus.*

All these observations lead to the conclusion that variations in arterial blood pressure exert an effect on the respiratory centre and on the cardio-vascular centres exclusively by a reflex mechanism involving the aortic and carotid sinus centres. Variations in arterial blood pressure and cerebral blood flow, within physiopathological limits, exert no direct effect on the respiratory and cardio-vascular centres.

The various experimental findings summarized in this lecture have thus brought to light a new physiological, physiopathological, and pharmacological mechanism which, by regulating the activity of the respiratory centre through the vascular presso- and chemo-sensitive reflexes, establishes, thus, an even closer functional correlation between the blood circulation, the metabolism, and the pulmonary respiratory exchanges.

The honors showered on Heymans exceeded those of any other Belgian in the medical sciences and were surpassed by few, if any, throughout the world during his active years. He was a member or honorary member of a large number of leading scientific societies concerned with physiology and medicine in Europe and the Americas. Under the broad distinction of scientific awards he was named to many lectureships, including the Dunham Memorial Foundation at Harvard, the Hanna Foundation at Western Reserve, the Greensfelder Memorial at the University of Chicago, and Lecturer of the Punser Memorial Foundation at Trinity College, Dublin. Heymans was a prolific author and publisher and editor-in-chief of the *Archives Internationales de Pharmacodynamic et de Thérapie,* founded in 1895 by his father and Gley in Paris. He was Field Artillery Officer during the first World War, a student of the history of medicine, and an art connoisseur.

1. Heymans, C.: "The Part Played by Vascular Presso- and Chemo-Receptors in Respiratory Control," in *Nobel Lectures, Physiology or Medicine, 1922-1941,* Amsterdam, London, New York: Elsevier Publishing Co., 1965, pp 460-478.
2. Heymans, C.: *The Carotid sinus and Other Reflexogenic Vasosensitive Zones* (Fr), Paris: Press of French Universities, 1929, pp 100-108.

Emil Fischer (1852-1919)

AMONG THE BRILLIANT INVESTIGATORS in the universities and industrial research laboratories in Germany late in the 19th century, no scientist is worthy of greater accolade than Emil Fischer.[1] He was born in Euskirchen near Cologne into a well-to-do family of commerce. Emil joined his father's company after completing the Gymnasium in Bonn, but dislike for the business world was apparent and he turned to the natural sciences. He was first attracted to the study of physics at the University of Bonn, becoming enraptured with the lectures of Kekulé. Fischer's travel year was spent at the newly founded German University at Strasbourg; here he was influenced especially by Adolph von Baeyer, chemist and discerning critic of chemical research, who

Composite by G. Bako

turned him to organic chemistry and his destiny in science. The inaugural dissertation for the PHD at Strsbourg concerned fluorescein and orcinphthalein, organic dyes. Within a year Fischer had discovered phenylhydrazine, which proved to be a critical compound in the experimental synthesis of sugars, a basic compound in the osazone test for sugars, and an essential compound in the synthesis of antipyrine. Since phenylhydrazine possessed unusual organic affinity, it was possible to synthesize a large number of new compounds, including two important classes of organic substances—the aldehydes and the ketones. Before these several researches were completed, Fischer and his cousin Otto (the latter had collaborated in the study of dyestuffs, particularly the derivatives of triphenylmethane) joined Baeyer, who had by then been called to Munich.

Fischer qualified as privatdocent in 1878 and only a short time later was given professional tenure by the university and financial security by his father. His reputation was now secure. Although hardly 30 years of age, he had rejected an important position in industry and instead accepted the chair of chemistry at Erlangen. The University at Würzburg was next, followed by an offer from the University of Berlin to direct the department of chemistry, one of the prized academic posts in Germany. The relatively brief periods of residence prior to Berlin were offset by his long sojourn in the capital; there he continued his teaching and highly productive research, culminating in the dedication of the Kaiser Wilhelm Institute for Chemistry in Dahlem-Berlin just before the outbreak of World War I. Fischer was an inspiring teacher, and, as his fame and reputation spread, his laboratory became the focus for investigation in organic chemistry, attracting students from both hemispheres.

In Berlin, Fischer returned to the investigation of uric acid and related substances. He succeeded in synthesizing xanthine, hypoxanthine, adenine, and guanine, arranged them in a logical scheme of nosology, and gave them the name "purine" (from *purum uricum*), thus identifying the mother substance. An equally remarkable accomplishment was the study of the degradation and reconstitution of proteins. Many of the essential amino acids were synthesized and combined into long molecular chains, to which he gave the name "polypeptid(e)s." He was successful in combining 18 amino acids to form a compound of the highest molecular weight that had yet been made in the laboratory. These and other researches were responsible for his receiving the Nobel prize in chemistry in 1902.

Many of Fischer's important investigations were republished in three substantive volumes, segregated in subject matter, but pursued simultaneously. The studies on the purine group covered the years 1882 through 1906;[2] the researches on amino acids, polypeptides, and proteins were carried on from 1899 to 1906; whereas the work on carbohydrates and ferments was done during the years 1884 to 1908. The identification of uric acid as a trioxypurine, a significant historical step in the understanding of the metabolic aberration in gout,

was expressed in a communication published five years after he was called to Berlin.[2]

In discussing the structure of the purine group it is necessary to speak individually of some of the important compounds. At the same time it is necessary to repeat some of the complicated conclusions that led to the formulation of structure. In this I shall follow a systematic order that is natural and easy to understand. I shall start with the oxypurines, of which in the first place are

Trioxypurine or Uric Acid

The structure of uric acid itself has been described in detail as noted above. The same can be said of the synthesis of pseudo-uric acid and its conversion into trichloropurine by treating it with phosphoroxychloride. Later the methyl derivatives of uric acid will be discussed.

Veronal, discovered in 1903, is another compound of clinical interest, one of the first of the modern soporifics that preceded the barbiturates.[3]

It is apparent that diethylacetyl urea is similar to sulfonal [sulfonmethane] in hypnotic strength, also that dipropylmalonyl urea is four times as powerful, but has the disadvantage of a long after-effect.

Between these two preparations is diethylmalonyl urea which surpasses all soporifics that have been studied. If this compound is readily produced and has advantages of taste and solubility, it seems to be the best among the members of the new class. Because of its complicated chemical designations, the name *Veronal* is suggested.

In the investigation of simple and complex sugars, Fischer built upon the stereochemical contributions of Pasteur, investigated ferments (enzymes), and showed that their action was specific, as is a key to a lock. Many of the natural sugars, including *d*-glucose, *d*-mannose, and *d*-fructose, and their optical antipodes were synthesized and their structural formulas defined. Expanding the theoretical deductions of Van't Hoff and Le Bel, he brought into reality most of the optically active aldohexoses, synthesized the first methylglucoside, and clarified the structure of the glucosides.[4]

Throughout these inquries, Fisher made frequent and skilful use of enzymes, developing a technique which will offer invaluable guidance to subsequent investigators of vital changes. In 1894, having assembled a great variety of artificial carbohydrates, he studied their behaviour towards different families of yeast, drawing the fundamental conclusion that the fermentative enzyme is an asymmetric agent attacking only those molecules of which the configuration does not differ too widely from that of *d*-glucose. Applying this principle to the natural and artifical *d*-glucosides, he ranged these in two groups, the *a-d*-glucosides being hydrolysed by maltase and indifferent towards emulsin, the *β-d*-glucosides exhibiting converse behaviour. The *l*-glucosides, *d*-galactosides, arabinosides, xylosides, rhamnosides, and glucoheptosides were not affected by either enzyme, and the glucosidic relation of sucrose, maltose, and lactose was determined by similar means. It was the knowledge thus gained which led Fisher to represent enzyme-action by the analogy of a lock-and-key, and to conclude that disaccharides are fermented only as a consequence of preliminary hydrolysis.

1. Harrow, B.: Emil Fischer, *Science* 50:150-154, 1919.
2. Fischer, E.: *Investigations of the Purine Group (1882-1906)*, Berlin: J. Springer, 1907.
3. Fischer, E., and v. Mering, J.: A New Class of Soporifics, *Therap Gegenw* 44:97-101, 1903 (Ger), excerpt trans. by F. Sternthal.
4. Forster, M. O.: Emil Fischer, *Proc Roy Soc Lond* 98:l-lvii, 1921.

Jacobus H. Van't Hoff (1852-1911)

Composite by G. Bako

JACOBUS HENRICUS VAN'T HOFF, physical chemist and father of stereochemistry, advanced convincing evidence that the performance of gases, as illustrated by Boyle's law, could be applied equally well to solutions. The brilliant theoretical chemist was born in Rotterdam, the son of a physician and Shakespearean scholar.[1] After attending the University of Leyden, he studied organic chemistry with Kekulé at Bonn and with Wurtz in Paris, where Le Bel, with whom his name was associated in the development of the theory of stereochemistry, was also a graduate student. The doctorate of natural philosophy was granted at Utrecht in 1874. Auguste Comte, the French philosophical mathematician, and William Whewell, the English philosopher of inductive reasoning, were also credited by van't Hoff for the derivation of the concept of the tridimensional structure of organic compounds and the relationship between optical activity and chemical constitution.

The period was propitious for interpretation of chemical structure and optical activity. Pasteur, in 1861, had suspected a relationship, and, in considering two optically active isomers, one molecule was assumed to have an asymmetric structure but in mirror image. Influenced by the studies of Wislicenus on lactic acid, and simultaneously with Le Bel, van't Hoff showed that optical activity of two optically active isomers differed only in the sign of their rotation when an asymmetric carbon atom was present—the van't Hoff-Le Bel theory. The historical development of this concept and the proposition that it was valid appeared first in 1874.[2]

Van't Hoff was appointed docent in physics in the State Veterinary School at Utrecht in 1876 and two years later professor of chemistry, mineralogy, and geology in the University of Amsterdam. He studied the kinetics of chemical solutions and applied the laws of thermodynamics to chemical equilibrium and affinity. A study of the laws regulating chemical equilibrium in solution gradually revealed a fundamental analogy between gaseous pressure and osmotic pressure.[3]

The analogy between dilute solutions and gases immediately takes on a more quantitative form when we consider that in both cases a change of concentration has a similar influence on the pressure, the two magnitudes being in the two cases proportional to each other.

This proportionality, which for gases goes under the name of Boyle's Law, can be proved for osmotic pressure experimentally from known data, and also theoretically.

Theoretical Proof.—Although these experiments render the proportionality between osmotic pressure and concentration highly probable, the theoretical proof is a welcome addition, especially as it is almost self-evident. If we consider osmotic pressure to be of kinetic origin, that is, as arising from the impacts of dissolved molecules, we have to prove proportionality between the number of impacts in unit time and the number of impinging molecules in unit volume. The method of proof is thus exactly the same as that adopted for Boyle's Law in ideal gases. On the other hand if we see in osmotic pressure the effect of an attraction for water, its magnitude is obviously proportional to the number of attracting molecules in unit volume, with the proviso (which is fulfilled in sufficiently dilute solutions) that the dissolved molecules are without action on one another, and that each contributes on its own account a constant amount to this attractive action.

Van't Hoff remained in Amsterdam until 1896, moving then to a professorship at the University of Berlin. In 1901, he honored the University of Chicago at its decennial celebration with a series of lectures and, in turn, received the honorary LLD. In conferring the honor at the convocation ceremony, President Harper eulogized:[4]

JACOB HENRY VAN'T HOFF,

Professor of physical chemistry in the University of Berlin; investigator who has brought to bear upon chemical problems a keen and logical mind; endowed with speculative and imaginative powers of the highest order; founder of the theory explaining the space relations of atoms in molecules—a theory which is essential to a comprehension of the chemistry of organized and inorganized matter; master in the field of dynamic chemistry; investigator and brilliant discoverer in the domain of the modern theory of solutions— a theory which constitutes one of the greatest advances made by chemical science in the last quarter of a century: for these splendid and fertile achievements, by the authority of the Board of Trustees of the University of Chicago, upon nomination of the University Senate, I confer upon you the degree of Doctor of Laws of this University, with all the rights and privileges appertaining thereunto.

The same year van't Hoff received the Nobel prize in chemistry, and the Emperor of Germany conferred the Order of Merit on him. He was a co-founder with Wilhelm Ostwald of the *Zeitschrift für physikalische Chemie, Stoichiometrie und Verwandtschaftslehre.* Although professing no comprehensive knowledge of biological phenomena, the influence of van't Hoff's work extended beyond the confines of theoretical physical chemistry, for physiology and biology deal with osmotic pressure, dilute solutions, and other natural phenomena.

1. Cohen, E.: "Jacobus Henricus Van't Hoff," in *Great Chemists,* E. Farber; ed., New York: Interscience Publishers, New York: 1961.
2. Van't Hoff, J. H.: *Chemistry in Space,* J. E. Marsh, trans-ed., Oxford: Clarendon Press, 1891.
3. Van't Hoff, J. H.: Foundation of the Theory of Dilute Solutions. I. The Role of Osmotic Pressure in the Analogy Between Solutions and Gases, *Z Physikal Chemie* 1:481-508, 1887; trans., Alembic Club Reprints—No. 19, Edinburgh: Alembic Club, 1929.
4. Van't Hoff, J. H.: *Physical Chemistry in the Service of the Sciences,* vol 18, A. Smith, trans., London: W. Wesley and Son, 1902.

Paul Ehrlich (1854-1915)

THE STORY OF PAUL EHRLICH as related by Martha Marquardt[1] is replete with scientific accomplishments and amply documented with personal experiences of the internationally famous German physician. Although Ehrlich led an abundant life, he is best remembered for his development of the spirocheticide arsphenamine ("606", or Salvarsan). The side-chain theory, concepts of immunity, aversion to the possibility of auto-antibodies — *horror autotoxicus* — development of organic dyes with histologic specificity, and the ability to apply the fruits of scientific investigation to the diagnosis and treatment of disease reflect the masterworks of a brilliant mind.

Ehrlich was born in Upper Silesia in Eastern Germany in the beginning of the Golden Age of intellectual supremacy of German scientific thought, basic and applied. His father was a prosperous innkeeper. Latin and mathematics came easy in gymnasium, but he was an indifferent student. German composition was particularly difficult—especially letters to his parents. He overcame this adolescent deficiency and throughout his professional career was a prolific writer.

As a student at the new university at Strasbourg, he developed a great interest in chemical dyes, an interest that was never relegated to a position of secondary importance. Characteristic of the German student, he studied at several universities in the pursuit of higher education. On his second tour of duty at Breslau University, mast cells were described, revealed by his new staining technique. Robert Koch had just discovered the anthrax bacillus and had come to Breslau to discuss his findings. Ehrlich and Koch shared mutual interests for many years. The degree of doctor of medicine was granted Ehrlich by Leipzig University at the age of 24. His inaugural dissertation, a requisite for the degree of doctor, revealed his great curiosity about dyes and staining methods. During his lifetime the thesis remained unprinted, even untyped. The document was discovered after his death in the archives of the University of Leipzig but was not published until 1956.[2] Dr. Richard Koch, professor of medical history at the University of Frankfurt, described the dissertation as follows:[1]

It contains the germ of Ehrlich's entire lifework which culminated in the invention of Salvarsan. . . . It proves that Ehrlich, when leaving the University and before he even became a clinical assistant, was already on the way to becoming the creator of Chemotherapy. . . .

Ehrlich's next academic move was characteristic of an ambitious young physician in central Europe who sought a career in cloistered halls. He became a privatdozent and later oberarzt at the Second Medical Clinic of the Charité Hospital in Berlin. In spite of the last 37 years of his life spent in the research laboratory, he never lost a deep interest in clinical medicine. Still another characteristic of German professors, a love of strong Havana cigars, led him to smoke sometimes a box a day.

A notable example of his national and international repute even in his early years was the staining of the tubercle bacillus. Robert Koch announced the discovery of the bacillus at a meeting of the Physiological Society of Berlin in 1882. The following day, through an error committed by the cleaning woman in the laboratory, a stained slide of sputum from a patient with pulmonary tuberculosis was heated unintentionally on a small stove in Ehrlich's laboratory. The application of aniline dye and heat revealed the bacilli. This observation was immediately transmitted to Koch. Thus again in medical history did an accident trigger a great discovery.[2]

Only a few weeks ago Herr Regierungs-Rath Dr. Koch reported on his highly significant work on the etiology and on the bacillus of tuberculosis. There is now a general duty to evaluate this extension of our knowledge in its relationships to diagnosis and therapy. I have been working in this direction and believed that this subject must be reexamined in its diagnostic significance. The main results of my experiments concerning a particular modification of the method will be presented here. It seems to me that these results indicate a certain simplification in the diagnostic procedures and at the same time give clues to certain characteristics of the tubercle bacillus.

It is expedient to fix the proteins. . . . In actual practice, a more suitable procedure is to take the dried preparations with forceps and pass them three times through the flame of a Bunsen burner.

For the staining I use water-saturated aniline oil. . . . The differentiation of the tubercle bacilli proceeds only very slowly with vesuvin, so that it is necessary to use acid. I have used strong, even heroic, concentrations of acid. The most effective is to mix one volume official nitric acid and two volumes of water. Within a few seconds one can see the preparation fade under the acid treatment . . . one would see that everything had been decolorized except the bacteria, and they had remained intensely colored.

All of these cases which I examined were frank cases of Phthisis pulmonum. I examined in all 26 cases and in all of them the bacillus could be demonstrated.

The sudden death of his chief, Professor von Frerichs, the appointment of a new chief who failed to appreciate his talents, and the suspicion of pulmonary tuberculosis revealed by the staining of his own sputum caused Ehrlich to resign from the Charité Hospital. He departed with his bride to Egypt for two years of rest. At the request of Robert Koch, director of the new Institute for Infectious Diseases, he returned to Berlin, recovered emotionally and physically. Emil von Behring had recently discovered specific immune substances in the blood of animals (guinea pigs) which had recovered from infections with somewhat attenuated diphtheria bacilli. This was the beginning of the development of a potent antitoxin for clinical use. The results were disappointing, however, until Ehrlich set his mind to the problem and devised a quantitative method of measuring the therapeutic units of antitoxin.

This result was accomplished in the serum of horses after repeated inoculations. Antidiphtheritic serum, practical for general clinical use, was the result. His standard of measurement continues to be used in the preparation of this serum. Ehrlich, the first to recognize the existence of a fully antigenic but nonpoisonous form of diphtheria toxin, called this substance "toxoid." Toxoid, later artificially prepared by Ramon, was used for active immunization against diphtheria. These achievements contributed to his appointment as director of a small state laboratory for the investigation and control of serum in Steglitz, a suburb of Berlin. Three years later he moved to Frankfurt to develop, and later to direct, a new Institute for Experimental Therapy. Ehrlich is best known for his contributions to medical science and to the welfare of mankind during the remaining 16 years of life. This includes his basic work on the blood of goats, which revealed the existence of what we now call blood group antigens and blood group isoantibodies, a discovery made independent of, and simultaneously with that of Landsteiner, in man.

The side-chain theory advanced by Ehrlich was analogous to the side-chain theory of the benzene ring. The central nucleus was considered the basic element of life. The side-chain or receptor could react with substances necessary for life, with resultant good. If a nonvital substance reacted with the receptor, the participation by the nucleus or core in vital processes would be ineffective. The body, in its attempt to compensate, would produce more and more receptors, which would be cast off into tissue fluids as antibodies. The following excerpt is translated from his monograph "The Requirement of the Organs for Oxygen" where the concept was first advanced.[3]

Although I therefore believe also that a cell with an actively reducing protoplasm, such as one which forms indophenol white, does not oxidize foreign substances, obviously the same does not apply to compounds which enter into the composition of protoplasm, and are fixed by it in the manner of side-chains.

The antibodies were highly specific immunologically in relation to antigens. The *horror autotoxicus* concept was an outgrowth of the side-chain theory.

No living organism would be capable of producing—or would dare to produce if you wish—an antibody against constituents of its own body, for this would be incompatible with life. On the basis of the side-chain theory, the concept of *horror autotoxicus* seems logical indeed.

Ehrlich's theory of antibody formation was rejected by most scientists in the thirties. The main objection was directed against his assumption that a receptor (antibody) specific for every possible antigenic structure pre-exists in the normal organism. As a matter of fact, an unlimited number of possible synthetic antigens made this theory rather improbable. Ehrlich's theory was replaced by template theories, assuming that the antibody is synthetized under direct influence of antigens. However, interestingly enough, the most recent concepts of antibody formation (Jerne, Burnet, Lederberg, Talmadge) revert to the basic concept of Ehrlich. According to clonal selection, the antigen stimulates the multiplication of cells which by chance produce globulins corresponding to its (the antigen's) structure. These concepts resemble closely Ehrlich's hyperproduction of corresponding receptors.

The effectiveness of organic chemicals in the management of infections that defied the development of antitoxins lured him into the investigation of trypanosomiasis and syphilis. The experimental animal was incapable of developing antitoxins against these organisms; hence, he reasoned, the use of chemicals might be rewarding. The great organic chemical industry of Germany cooperated in these researches. Rats and mice were inoculated with trypanosomes and spirochetes. Ehrlich was supplied with many organic chemicals to determine, on a trial and error basis, the effectiveness in destroying the pathogens. The results were productive in each category. *Therapia sterilisans magna* (curing and healing with single large doses) in trypanosomiasis was demonstrated by the sterilization in mice following injections of trypan-red dye. Salvarsan ("606") was the arsenical selected as the most efficient agent against the spirochete in infected rats.[4]

In summarizing from a general point of view the results of the investigations which have been reported here, I should like to lay the main emphasis on the fact that it has been shown to be possible, by deliberately planned chemotherapeutic approach, to discover curative agents which act specifically and aetiologically against diseases due to protozoal infections, and especially against the spirilloses, and amongst these against syphilis in the first place.

Further evidence for the specificity of the action of dihydroxydiaminoarsenobenzene is the disappearance of the Wassermann reaction, which reaction must of course be regarded as indicative of a reaction of the organism to the constituents of the spirochaetes.

Because of the short time that has elapsed since the introduction of the "606"-therapy, and bearing in mind that, in the beginning, the doses given were scarcely adequate, it seems to me that the proper time has not yet arrived to go into the question of the permanence of the cure; this must be left to the future.

If we now ask ourselves what vistas are opened up by the new era of experimental research in syphilis, it is my opinion that emphasis must be laid on the fact that syphilis has now lost in every direction the special position in relation to most infectious diseases which it has occupied hitherto, and that it has joined the group of those infectious diseases for which we can to-day make an accurate diagnosis in their different stages (identification of spirochaetes and serum-diagnosis) and for which, above all, we have a method of exact, experimentally established treatment. While, on the one hand, the chance of achieving a permanent cure and of preventing the occurrence of metasyphilitic conditions have, of course, been immensely improved for the individual through the rapid and intensive spirillicidal action, there are presented, on the other hand, inestimable advantages, from an epidemiological point of view, for the fight against syphilis in its role as a racial pestilence.

Thus in syphilis, as in all infectious diseases, every improvement in the treatment of the individual is also of the greatest importance to the community.

Ehrlich enjoyed detective stories, especially those of A. Conan Doyle. He was a friend of many; his professional associates included Albert Neisser, K. Shiga, H. Noguchi, Henry H. Dale, Gustav Embden, Julius von Sachs, Julius Morgenroth, Emil von Dungern, Karl Weigert, Christian Herter (the founder of the *Journal of Biological Chemistry*), Reid Hunt, William H. Welch, Fritz Schaudinn, Carl H. Browning, Emil Fischer, and K. Herxheimer. Ehrlich was a "diagonal reader," interpreted by Marquardt as one who starts at the left upper corner of a newspaper page and, scanning over the print, ends at the lower right hand corner. The Nobel Prize was awarded Ehrlich at the age of 54. He shared this honor with Metchnikoff of the Pasteur Institute in Paris for their studies on immunity. Ehrlich died in Frankfurt/Main August, 1915, one year after the beginning of World War I. He lies beneath a marble slab from his native Silesia.

1. Marquardt, M.: *Paul Ehrlich, With an Introduction by Sir Henry Dale,* New York: Henry Schuman, 1951.

2. Ehrlich, P.: A Method for Staining the Tubercle Bacillus, *Deutsch Med Wschr* 8:269-270, 1882, translated in Brock, T. D.: Milestones in Microbiology, Englewood Cliffs, NJ: Prentice-Hall, Inc., 1961.

3. Ehrlich, P.: *The Requirement of the Organs for Oxygen,* Berlin: A. Hirschwald, 1885, translated in Collected Papers of Paul Ehrlich, edited by F. Himmelweit,

M. Marquardt, and H. Dale, London and New York: Pergamon Press, 1956.

4. Ehrlich, P.: *Closing Notes on Experimental Chemotherapy of Spirilloses*, Berlin: J. Springer, 1910, translated in Collected Papers of Paul Ehrlich, edited by F. Himmelweit, M. Marquardt, and H. Dale, London and New York: Pergamon Press, 1956.

Wilhelm Conrad von Röntgen (1845-1923)

THE RISE TO GREAT ACHIEVEMENT by a brilliant mind does not always follow a predictable pattern in experimental science. A theoretical mathematician may display unmistakable evidence of a genius as a child, the potential compositions of a great musician may be apparent before adolescence, but the greatness of an experimental scientist may remain undetected until maturity. At least the governing body of the University of Utrecht, The Netherlands, refused to matriculate Wilhelm Conrad Röntgen, whose contributions to physics and medicine were fundamental and profound.[1]

Röntgen was born in 1845 in Lennep, Germany, a village in Bergischen (Rhine province.) The parents were German, with a considerable infusion of Dutch background. His father was a textile merchant. Several of the ancestors were artisans and undoubtedly proud of their skills as a coppersmith, a weaver, or a cabinetmaker. The Röntgens moving to Holland forfeited their Prussian citizenship when Wilhelm was only three years old. A foolish prank committed in the Technical High School caused his dismissal and prevented his admission to the University of Utrecht when he became of age. After special tutoring he was permitted to audit courses in natural sciences, but not to be enrolled as a regular student.

Despite his seeming inability to adjust to the Dutch educational system, a friend advised him to enroll at the Swiss Federal Polytechnic School in Zürich, Switzerland. A combination of favorable circumstances resulted in the stiff entrance examinations being waived for Röntgen, who was two years older than the average student. This was a handicap, but not an unsurmountable obstacle. After three years' application to mathematics and various branches of mechanical engineering, he received a diploma at the age of 23. One year later he received from the University of Zürich the Doctorate of Philosophy, after having submitted his thesis "Studies on Gases." This was just a little more than a quarter of a century before he was awarded an honorary degree of Doctor of Medicine in recognition of his discovery of the x-ray.

Röntgen's first academic post was at the University of Würzburg in southern Germany. He accompanied his teacher, Professor Kundt from Zürich. The association continued when Kundt was called to the University of Strasbourg. Three additional interim appointments, professor of physics and mathematics at the Agricultural Academy at Hohenheim in Württemberg, associate professor of theoretical physics at the University of Strasbourg, and professor of physics at the Hessian University in Giessen, were accepted in rapid succession. At the age of 41 he was offered the chair of physics at the University of Jena and 2 years later a similar position at the University of Utrecht, the university that had refused him admission not too many years before. However, he declined both offers and chose to return to Würzburg, where he succeeded Kohlrausch, the great experimental physicist of his generation. The inner circle of the University of Würzburg was as gracious socially as it was brilliant scientifically. Members of the faculty included Kolliker the father of histology, Fick the physiologist who described the Fick principle, Stöhr the anatomist, Boveri the biologist, and Kunkel the pharmacologist.

The researches of Röntgen at this time were concerned with such subjects as the compressibility of liquids, the conduction of electrolytes, and the thermal coefficient of expansion. Röntgen was elected Rector of the University at the age of 49 and upon assuming the high office stated:[1]

> The university is a nursery of scientific research and mental education, a place for the cultivation of ideals for students as well as for teachers. Its significance as such is much greater than its practical value, and for this reason one should make an effort in filling vacant places to choose men who have distinguished themselves not only as teachers but as investigators and promoters of science; for every genuine scientist, whatever his field, who takes his task seriously, fundamentally follows purely ideal goals and is an idealist in the best sense of the word. . . . Only gradually has the conviction gained importance that the experiment is the most powerful and most reliable lever enabling us to extract secrets from nature, and that the experiment must constitute the final judgment as to whether a hypothesis should be retained or be discarded.

The experiments of the cathode ray were initiated with a Lenard tube in June, 1894, over a year before his great discovery of the x-ray was announced. These experiments dealt with emanations of the cathode tube which had been covered with tin foil. Fluorescence was detected upon a small screen painted with barium platinocyanide. The rays also fogged unexposed photographic plates. One of the subsequent steps was partially accidental. The imposition of the hand of Frau Röntgen between the Hittorf-Crookes tube and the photographic plate revealed the outline of the bones of the hand. In the initial published announcement on the new rays which he had already named x-rays he reported the following:[2]

> A discharge from a large induction coil is passed through a Hittorf's vacuum tube, or through a well-exhausted Crookes' or Lenard's tube. The tube is surrounded by a fairly close-fitting shield of black paper; it is then possible to see, in a completely darkened room, that paper covered on one side with barium platino-cyanide lights up with brilliant fluorescence when brought into the neighbourhood of the tube, whether the painted side or the other be turned towards the tube. The fluorescence is still visible at two metres distance. It is easy to show that the origin of the fluorescence lies within the vacuum tube.

> It is seen, therefore, that some agent is capable of penetrating black cardboard which is quite opaque to ultra-violet light, sunlight, or arc-light. It is readily shown that all bodies possess this same transparency, but in very varying degrees. For example, paper is very transparent; the fluorescent screen will light up when placed behind a book of a thousand pages; printer's ink offers no marked resistance. Thick blocks of wood are still transparent. Boards of pine two or three centimetres thick absorb only very little.

> The X-rays, which are not deflected by a magnet, cannot be regarded as kathode rays which have passed through the glass, for that passage cannot, according to Lenard, be the cause of the different deflection of the rays. Hence I conclude that the X-rays are not identical with the kathode rays, but are produced from the kathode rays at the glass surface of the tube.

> The rays are generated not only in glass. I have obtained them in an apparatus closed by an aluminium plate 2 mm. thick.

> The justification of the term "rays," applied to the phenomena, lies partly in the regular shadow pictures produced by the interposition of a more or less permeable body between the source and a photographic plate or fluorescent screen.

> I have observed and photographed many such shadow pictures. Thus, I have an outline of part of a door covered with lead paint; the image was produced by placing the discharge-tube on one side of the door, and the sensitive plate on the other. I have also a shadow of the bones of the hand.

The critical observations were made in November, 1895. On New Year's Day, 1896, Röntgen sent reprints of the communication to many of his colleagues. A few days later the newspapers announced the discovery. Cartoons on the subject appeared in *Punch* or *The London Charivari*, and other magazines. The discovery was announced in *Photography* in verse:

> The Roentgen Rays, the Roentgen Rays,
> What is this craze:
> The town's ablaze
> With the new phase
> Of x-ray's ways.
>
> I'm full of daze,
> Shock and amaze;
> For nowadays
> I hear they'll gaze
> Thro' cloak and gown and even stays,
> These naughty, naughty Roentgen Rays.

According to the best German tradition, Röntgen sought no patents and entered into no contracts for the manufacture of any diagnostic apparatus. An opposing view was expressed by Thomas Alva Edison of Menlo Park, N. J., who confirmed Röntgen's findings within weeks after the announcement in America:[1]

Professor Röntgen probably does not draw one dollar profit from his discovery. He belongs to those pure scientsts who study for pleasure and love to delve into the secrets of nature. After they have discovered something wonderful, someone else must come to look at it from the commercial point of view. This will also be the case with Röntgen's discovery. One must see how to use it and how to profit by it financially.

Industry was quick to sense the significance of Röntgen's observations, and within a few months the F. J. Pearson Manufacturing Company of St. Louis advertised a "portable x-ray apparatus for physicians, professors, photographers, and students . . . for the price of $15 net delivered in the United States with full guarantee." Edison built four portable machines that were displayed in the National Electrical Exposition in New York City in 1896.

Potential harm from the wide use of x-rays was recognized early, but the serious consequences were slow to be appreciated. In New York, Mr. Hawks, a demonstrator of roentgenography in Bloomingdale Brothers Department Store, suffered a severe cutaneous burn. The apparatus was operated continuously for two or three hours each day. Hawks first observed dryness of the skin and changes that resembled sunburn. The nails stopped growing, and atrophic

changes appeared on the exposed areas of the skin. In order to demonstrate the roentgenogram of the skull, he had placed his head close to the tube. The hair of the temples, eyebrows, and eyelashes reacted to the depilatory action.

1. Glasser, O.: *Wilhelm Conrad Röntgen and the Early History of the Roentgen Rays,* Berlin: Springer, 1931.
2. Röntgen, W. C.: On a New Kind of Rays, Sitzungsberichte der Würzburger Physik-medic. Gesellschaft 132-141, 1895, translated by A. Stanton, *Nature* 53:274-277, 1896.

Courtesy of Leon Kabakexis

André Bocage (1892-1953)

ANDRÉ BOCAGE, who was a physician primarily interested in diseases of the skin, gave some attention to the statistical error in counting blood cells, the dosage of staphylococcus toxoid in the treatment of furunculosis, the danger of suboccipital puncture, and the development of a transfusion syringe. On the other hand, history will salute him for his theory of stratigraphy and pragmatic approach to the development of tomography. This notable contribution was largely overlooked for a number of years, and a practical apparatus for lucid roentgenography of deep tissues was not available until the 1930's.

Bocage was born in Paris of parents who had come from Lorraine. He studied in Paris and served as a hospital intern at the local hospitals, until World War I interrupted his medical training. His practice of dermatology was interrupted by World War II. In 1914, Bocage was sent to the front as a battalion physician and sometime later, at his request, was assigned to a radiologic unit. It was here that he gave thought to the physical laws underlying the formation of a roentgenographic image of selected portions of soft tissues deep in the interior, in which surrounding tissue was blotted out and which image would be as clear as that of bony structure. Following the Armistice and his subsequent return to Paris, Bocage became an assistant to Pierre Marie, Weill, and others. He graduated MD with a thesis on the albuminous content of spinal fluid, which brought him the silver medal. He graduated third in his class and became senior resident on the clinical service of Widal. Later he was associated with St. Louis Hospital, and was appointed physician to the Welfare Center of Prefecture of the Seine and consultant in dermatosyphilology at the Pasteur Institute.

The theory of tomography is based on the countermotion of the x-ray tube and the film, while each moves at a fixed distance from the target tissue. The mechanical concept consisted of synchronizing the movement of the x-ray tube and film, which proceeded in opposite directions, so as to provide a single fixed plane of which each point would cast its shadow at the same point on the x-ray film. Although the concept was born in 1917, the first patent application was recorded on June 3, 1921, and was published on May 4, 1922, under the title "Procédé et dispositifs de radiographie sur plaque en mouvement."[2] However, Bocage received little encouragement, and no steps were taken to build a machine based upon this theoretical concept.

Three methods for the practical accomplishment were proposed in the patent application: 1. The Röentgen tube moves in a straight line in a plane parallel to the recording medium. 2. Instead of the Röentgen rays and the film moving simultaneously in parallel planes in straight lines, they move in circles, squares, crosses, or in Archimedean spirals. 3. The Röentgen rays and the film rotate on an axis which lies in the plane of the section to be projected instead of moving in parallel planes.

A few months after this patent application, Portes and Chausse applied for a French patent for deep Röentgen therapy based upon the second method. It remained for Vallebona, after an initial failure, to design a practical apparatus for tomography. The principle was further elaborated by Ziedses des Plantes at about the same time.[3] The patent of invention granted by the National Office of Industrial Property of the Republic of France was assigned No. 536,-464. The résumé from this public document is as follows.[2]

This is the invention of a method and device in radiography based on the five principles:

(1) Continuous motion of a photographic plate and an x-ray tube during exposure is necessary.

(2) In order to obtain exposure in one plane, a geometric law is employed to co-ordinate motion.

(3) Only one plane of the subject is x-rayed.

(4) Secondary rays are eliminated.

(5) The apparent diameter of the focus of the tube is reduced.

1. Hillemand, P.: André Bocage, obituary (Fr), *Presse Med* 61:1496 (Nov 14) 1953.

2. Bocage, A. E. M.: A Method and Device of Radiography on a Moving Plate, Republic of France, National Office of Industrial Property, Patent No. 536,464, applied June 3, 1921 (Fr), published May 4, 1922.

3. Andrews, J. R.: Planigraphy: I. Introduction and History, *Amer J Roentgenol* 36:575-587 (Nov) 1936.

Madam Curie (1867-1934)

MARIE SKLODOWSKI, born in Warsaw, and endowed with genes for genius, was largely responsible for the fundamental studies on elementary radium—a participant in the scientific revolution in physics and chemistry which began at the close of the 19th century. Her father was a mathematics and physics teacher in an undergraduate school, and her mother held a responsible post in a women's school.[1] Marie, precocious but not overbearing, finished her schooling at the age of 17, a beautiful young lady. With the

Composite by G. Bako

possibility of being denied matriculation at the University of Warsaw in Russian Poland of the 1880's, she seemed uncertain about her future and served as governess for a time. Meanwhile, she read scientific as well as other literature avidly and was keenly aware of the oppression of her Polish people under the Czarist tyranny which contributed to the impoverished state of the country and her family.

In 1891, Marie Skoldowski, strongly motivated for further training, went to Paris, where her older sister was already married. She enrolled for study at the Sorbonne and provided for her Spartan physical wants by assisting in a laboratory. With her intellectual brilliance, Marie received her master's degree in physics in 1893 and in mathematics the following year. After a vacation in Poland she returned to Paris to continue experimental studies in preparation for her doctorate in physics. By then, she had met

Pierre Curie, a physician's son and eight years older, a teacher in the municipal school in Paris, whose brilliance in physics complemented her work in chemistry. They were married in 1895.

From this scientific collaboration of husband and wife, came discoveries of great moment. Two important observations of others provided the base for their outstanding work. Roentgen had recently discovered x-rays, when he discovered the fogging of a photograph plate by emanations from the Crookes tube. Shortly after, Henri Becquerel noted a fluorescence from uranium ore which, unrelated to solar exposure, was soon found to ionize the air and discharge a gold leaf electroscope by rendering the surrounding air a conductor. At their request, these unusual properties of uranium salts were assigned the Curies for further investigation. Working in an abandoned shed as a makeshift laboratory they screened many substances and identified only thorium and uranium as possessing what they called "radioactivity." Furthermore, they found that pitchblende, an ore from which silver was extracted, showed radioactivity several times greater than did pure uranium. The conclusion seemed clear that some other substance more radioactive than uranium lay in the crude ore.

The Curies then obtained a ton of pitchblende from the mines in Bohemia and began the laborious analytical process of extracting and separating chemically each fraction for ionization. The measuring tools consisted of an ionization chamber and a piezoelectric quartz electrometer, which, in itself, was a discovery sufficient to assure renown to Pierre Curie. Repeated refinement revealed minute traces of intensely ionizing substances present in one fraction containing bismuth and barium. The first new element identified was called "polonium" after Marie's native country. The report was presented to the Academy of Sciences by Professor Becquerel in the physical-chemical section on July 18, 1898, in a communication entitled *New Radioactive Substance Contained in Pitchblende*.[2]

Investigation of the compounds of uranium and thorium proved that the ability to emit rays rendering air conductive and acting upon photographic plates is a specific characteristic of uranium and thorium. It is found in all compounds of these metals; the power of these emissions, generally not very strong, depends upon the content of the active metal. The physical state of the substances seems to be of secondary importance only. Experiments proved that a mixture of these substances acts according to the proportion of active ingredients and according to the adsorption by inert substances. The danger of impurities with unfavorable influence on phosphorescence or fluorescence do not exist. Very likely these minerals, with greater radioactivity than uranium or thorium, contain a new substance.

We have attempted to isolate the substance from pitchblende to confirm our supposition.

The chemical investigations were constantly monitored by the radioactivity of the products separated at each step. Each product was placed on the surface of a condenser and the conductivity acquired by the air was measured with the help of an electrometer and a piezoelectric quartz. This provided not only an indication of the presence but also of the quantity of radioactive substance.

The pitchblende which we analyzed was approximately two and one half times as active as uranium. We exposed the pitchblende to the action of acids and treated the solution with hydrogen sulfide. Uranium and thorium remained in solution. The following conclusions were reached:

Precipitated sulfates contained an extremely active substance together with lead, bismuth, copper, arsenic, and antimony.

The new substance is quite insoluble in sulfuric ammonia by which it can be separated from arsenic and antimony.

The sulfates which are insoluble in ammonium sulfate dissolve in nitric acid. Then by the action of sulfuric acid the active substance can be partially separated from lead. By a prolonged treatment of lead sulfate with sulfuric acid a considerable portion of the active substance together with lead sulfate is dissolved.

The active substance present in solution with bismuth and copper is completely precipitated by ammonia, and thus can be separated from copper.

Finally, the active element remains with bismuth.

Thus we believe that the substance separated from pitchblende contains a metal unknown until today which is similar to bismuth in its analytical characteristics. If its existence is confirmed, we propose to call it polonium, according to the name of the country of origin of one of us.

Its discovery will have depended solely upon the new methods of investigation which were made possible by the discovery of the Becquerel rays.

Further extraction showed that the fraction containing barium salts had even more powerful radioactive properties to which the name "radium" was given and, in this instance, Becquerel presented the report Dec 26, 1898, before the section on physics of the Academy of Sciences.[3]

During this research we have encountered a *second* strongly radioactive substance with different chemical characteristics. In effect, hydrogen sulfate precipitates polonium in an acid solution; its salts are soluble in acids but water precipitates is solutions; polonium is completely precipitated by ammonia.

The second new radioactive substance seems to possess the chemical characteristics of barium since it is not precipitated either by hydrogen sulfate or by sulfate of ammonia or by ammonia; its sulfate is insoluble in water or in acids; its carbonate is insoluble in water; its fluorate is soluble in water, but insoluble in concentrated hydrochloric acid or in alcohol. Finally, this substance has the readily recognizable spectrum of barium.

We believe, however, that this substance, even though it contains a considerable proportion of barium, represents mainly the new element, emits radioactivity, and has chemical characteristics similar to barium.

DeMarcay found bands in the spectrum of this substance unlike any other known element. The bands are difficult to identify when chlorate 60 times as active as uranium is used, but become clearly distinguishable when the chlorate is enriched by fractionation to an activity 900 times that of uranium. Intensity of this band increases parallel to the increase of radioactivity; this strongly indicates that radioactivity can be ascribed to our new substance.

Other reasons, enumerated below, led us to believe that the new radioactive substance contained a new element which we propose to call radium.

For four additional years the Curies were relegated to a makeshift laboratory, an abandoned shed with an earth floor in the school of physics, since the Sorbonne was unable to provide suitable facilities and the Nobel Prize had not yet been awarded them. In 1903, the results of Marie's work were presented to the Paris faculty as a thesis in partial fulfillment for the doctor of science degree. In the same year the team was presented with the Davy medal of the Royal Society of London, followed in a few months by the Nobel Prize, which was shared with Becquerel. In 1904, Mme. Curie was placed in charge of the laboratory department, while Pierre was appointed professor of physics in the University. From 1899 to

1904, the Curies, sometimes together, sometimes separately, or sometimes with one of their colleagues, prepared more than 30 communications on radium salts and radium rays, while radioactivity was promptly explored by many investigators in many countries.

After Pierre's accidental death in 1906, having been cut down by a dray in the streets of Paris, Marie was advanced to her late husband's post; there she continued her work on the chemistry of radium. The work was presented, together with A. Debierne's, to the Section of Radioactivity of the Academy of Sciences on Sept 5, 1910, entitled *Metallic Radium, a Short Communication*.[4] Excerpts from the 1911 citation for the Nobel Prize in Chemistry and the response are as follows.[5]

In 1903 the Academy of Sciences of Sweden had the honor to award to you and your husband the Nobel Prize for Physics in the discovery of significant features of spontaneous radioactivity. This year the Academy awards you the prize in chemistry for your eminent investigations in the discovery of radium and polonium, for your analysis and description of the characteristics of radium, for isolation of this element in the metallic state, and for your outstanding research of its compounds. This is the first time the prize has been awarded to a laureate who had received the prize once before. This is evidence of the importance our Academy attaches to your recent discoveries, and I invite you to receive the prize from the hands of his Majesty the King who has agreed to transmit it to you.

I thank the Academy of Sciences for the great honor which does not belong to me alone. During long years Pierre Curie and I dedicated all our time to research which led to the discovery of radium and of polonium. I believe that I interpret correctly the wish of the Academy in stating that the prize awarded to me also pays homage to the name of Pierre Curie.

The following interpretation of current concepts of radium and its nuclides has been prepared by Marshall Brucer, MD.

On today's Chart of the Nuclides, radium is just the fifth step in the decay of uranium-238 through 12 different elements to stable lead. The 1602-year radium-226 (which is the atomic number 88 nuclides they were really talking about in the early days) is the last long-lived material in this series. It remained radium-226 long enough to be chemically isolated and identified and

characterized in terms of the 1896 definition of "chemical identification."

Its half life was sufficiently short so that once it was even partially separated by the Curies it glowed in the dark. The energy had to come from someplace. Even the most conservative scientists did not have to be convinced that this this did not fit the 1896 definition of an element. Marie Curie had stumbled on a violation of the most sacred of scientific laws, the conservation of energy.

In mid-century, Maxwell (a mathematician) had nudged the foundations of physics. In the 1870's, Crookes (a chemist) began to shake the foundations with his tube. In the early 1890's, J. J. Thomson (a physicist) destroyed the concept of the atom as the smallest piece of matter; thus he destroyed the chemical definition of the atom. With a hundred years of hindsight we can see that the revolution had already started. But all of this was rigorous reasoning about punctilious experiments. Even these men did not realize their contumacy. By the separation of radium, Marie Curie, only a student, had demonstrated beyond doubt that 19th century science was wrong.

Radium was the symbol of the scientific revolution in physics and chemistry. Its role in medicine was then, and still is, largely empirical. The alpha rays were absorbed in even the thinnest containers. The beta rays were similar to the cathode rays in the Crookes tube. The gamma rays were much more penetrating than the X-rays. If the X-rays had a biological effect that could be used in medical therapy, then the "X-rays" from radium should also have a biological effect.

As soon (around 1905-1910) as radiotherapy began to look towards deep-seated tumors, radium had an advantage over the highest possible (for then) energies of X-rays. The biological effects of radiation on abnormal tissue, particularly tumors, was quickly exploited, but the accompanying biological effect on normal tissue was also recognized. The science of radiobiology did not start for another third of a century, but its earliest beginnings began almost immediately with the recognition that radiation, first X-ray then radium, was not innocuous.

Marie was refused election to the Academy of Sciences of Paris because of her sex; on the other hand, she declined many national and international honors. In 1910, at the first International Congress of Radiology in Brussels, she was honored with the association of her name with the unit of radium disintegration, the curie. She was gracious during her 1921 tour of America in accepting the Willard Gibbs Medal of the American Chemical Society and honorary degrees from the universities of Chicago, Yale,

Northwestern, Smith, Wellesley, Columbia, and the Woman's Medical College of Pennsylvania. A crowning victory must have been felt by Marie Curie when, six months before her death, her daughter and son-in-law, the Joliot-Curies, discovered artificial radioactivity in 1934, for which they received the Nobel Prize in 1935. The Radium Institute at the University of Paris, completed in 1915, was directed by Madame Curie until she was confined to a sanitarium in Switzerland shortly before her death. This was attributed to anemia and depression of the bone marrow from long-term exposure to radium.

1. Curie, M.: *Pierre Curie*, New York: Macmillan Co., 1923.
2. Curie, P., and Curie, S.: A New Radioactive Substance Contained in Pitchblende (Fr), *C R Acad Sci (Paris)* 127:175-178, 1898.
3. Curie, P.; Curie, S.; and Bemont, G.: A New Highly Radioactive Substance Contained in Pitchblende (Fr), *C R Acad Sci (Paris)* 127:1215-1217, 1898.
4. Curie, M., and Debierne, A.: Metallic Radium (Fr), *C R Acad Sci (Paris)* 151:523-525, 1910.
5. The Nobel Prize in Chemistry, in *The Nobel Prize in 1911*, Stockholm: P.-A. Norstedt & Sons, 1912.

Crawford Williamson Long
(1815-1878)

Composite by G. Bako

THE CONTROVERSY OVER THE INITIAL USE OF ETHER for anesthesia has long been resolved in the medical literature, although personal beliefs related to traditional teaching suggest at times that irreconcilable differences persist. Surely, Crawford W. Long, a physician and surgeon practicing in Athens, Georgia, was the first physician to use sulfuric ether for surgical anesthesia; however, William Morton, a young dentist who administered the gas to a patient of John Collins Warren in the Massachusetts General Hospital upon the suggestion of Jackson, physician and chemist, was the first to have his experience proclaimed to the world.

Crawford Long was born in Danielsville, Georgia.[1] His father, a successful merchant, respected student of the law, and an outstanding citizen of Georgia, helped found the academy at Danielsville. Young Long attended Franklin College, later the University of Georgia, and graduated master of arts at the age of 19. He subsequently taught in the academy, read medicine for a time with Dr. George R. Grant of Jefferson, Georgia, and then took to the mountain trails for the medical department of Transylvania University of Lexington, Kentucky. After an academic year at the first medical school established in the West in America, he enrolled in the University of Pennsylvania, Philadelphia, the first medical school founded in the colonies. After graduation, Long spent 18 months walking the wards in the New York hospitals, later returned to Jefferson, Georgia, bought the practice of his preceptor, Dr. Grant, and in 1842, moved to Athens. Country practitioner Long, knowing the exhilarating effects of sulfuric ether, had inhaled it in "ether frolics." Following the "frolics" he had observed bruises on some of the participants, who had been unaware of pain. The next obvious step to one with imagination was the test of ether for its inhibition of pain during a surgical operation. Although this notable event took place in 1842, several years elapsed before the initial experiences by Long were recorded in the medical literature. In Boston, meanwhile, H. J. Bigelow had announced to the world the notable event in the Massachusetts General Hospital. Long's report to the *Southern Medical and Surgical Journal* of 1849 described the procedure.[2]

The ether was introduced: I gave it first to the gentleman who had previously inhaled it, then inhaled it myself, and afterwards gave it to all persons present.

On numerous occasions I have inhaled ether for its exhilarating properties, and would frequently, at some short time subsequent to its inhalation, discover bruised or painful spots on my person, which I had no recollection of causing, and which I felt satisfied were received while under the influence of ether.

The first patient to whom I administered ether in a surgical operation, was Mr. James M. Venable, who then resided within two miles of Jefferson, and at present lives in Cobb county, Georgia. Mr. Venable consulted me on several occasions in regard to the propriety of removing two small tumours situated on the back part of his neck, but would postpone from time to time having the operations performed, from dread of pain. At length I mentioned to him the fact of my receiving bruises while under the influence of the vapour of ether, without suffering, and as I knew him to be fond of, and accustomed to inhale ether, I suggested to him the probability that the operation might be performed without pain, and proposed operating on him while under its influence. He consented to have one tumor removed, and the operation was performed the same evening. The ether was given to Mr. Venable on a towel; and when fully under its influence I extirpated the tumour. It was encysted, and about half an inch in diameter. The patient continued to inhale ether during the time of the operation; and when informed it was over, seemed incredulous, until the tumor was shown him. He gave no evidence of suffering during the operation, and assured me, after it was over, that he did not experience the slightest degree of pain from its performance. *This operation was performed on the 20th March, 1842.*

The second operation I performed upon a patient etherized was on the 6th June, 1842, and was on the same person, for the removal of another small tumour.

The announcement by H. J. Bigelow in the *Boston Medical and Surgical Journal,* Nov 18, 1846, with acclaim for the discovery that was shared later with Long, marked the beginning of a series of investigations, claims, and counterclaims. A group of physicians from the Medical Society of the State of Georgia interviewed Long, investigated his documents, and concluded that he had, in fact, administered ether for surgical anesthesia in 1842. Not content with this inquiry, Jackson, who had suggested ether to Morton, visited Long in 1854 in a private attempt to establish the facts. Morton, meanwhile, had appealed to the Congress of the United States for a handsome award because of the "discovery."

At the time of the April 19th session of the Senate, extended debate was held on Bill No. 210 to recompense the discoverer of practical anesthesia. Morton, Jackson, and Wells by then had each laid claim to the $100,000 to be paid to the person who should be found to have been the discoverer.[3] Horace Wells of Hartford had some justification for his claim, having advocated nitrous oxide gas for extraction of teeth as early as 1844. During the discussion in the Senate, Mr. Dawson of Georgia introduced a resolution that Long's name be included in both sections of the bill, which was eventually passed by each house of Congress but was not signed by the President.

Jackson's letter to the *Boston Medical and Surgical Journal,* based upon his 1854 investigation of Long's claims, did not appear until 1861. Although he did not give full credit to Long, as the latter had wished, the communication leaves no doubt regarding the date and the nature of the performance by the Athens surgeon in 1842.[4]

From the documents shown me by Dr. Long, it appears that he employed sulphuric ether as an anaesthetic agent—

1st, March 30, 1842, when he extirpated a small glandular tumor from the neck of James M. Venable, a boy in Jefferson, Georgia, now dead.

Copies of the letters and depositions proving these operations with ether were shown me by Dr. Long.

I have waited, expecting Dr. Long to publish his statements and evidence in full, and therefore have not before published what I learned from him. He is a very modest and retiring man, and not disposed to bring his claims before any but a medical or scientific tribunal. This he has done in the State Medical Society of Georgia.

Had he written to me in season, I would have presented his claims to the Academy of Sciences of France.

The last important document written during Long's generation was a critique by J. Marion Sims, published in the *Virginia Medical Monthly,* 1877. In the review of the history of anesthesia, Sims noted that Priestley had discovered nitrous oxide gas in 1790; Sir Humphry Davy had experimented with it in 1799, observing that it was capable of destroying physical pain and probably would be of value in surgical operations; that Wells, of Hartford, Conn, had used the gas in the extraction of a tooth in 1844; that Morton had administered ether upon the suggestion of Jackson to a patient of Drs. Warren, Hayward, and Bigelow of Boston in 1846; that Wells, Morton, and Jackson had met cruel fate, but most important that Long had performed his surgery in 1842.[5]

The names of Long, Wells, Morton and Jackson, all Americans, will doubtless be associated, and to these must be added the name of Sir James Y. Simpson, who introduced chloroform and enlarged the domain of anaesthesia.

Sir James received the highest honor from his government in recognition of the great service he had rendered humanity. I wish we could say the same of our benefactors and government. Our great republic too often leaves our discoverers and scientists to rest in obscurity and to starve.

The fate of Wells, Morton, and Jackson is most pitiable.

Wells, disappointed in carrying off the honor of the great discovery of anesthesia, became insane and committed suicide in New York in 1848.

Morton, disappointed at not receiving a pecuniary recognition from Congress, for his labors, fretted himself into a congestion of the brain. In July, 1868, he . . . drove furiously up Broadway, and through Central Park. At the upper end of the Park, he leaped from his buggy, and ran to a lake nearby to cool his burning brain. Being persuaded to get into his buggy again, he drove a short distance, then leaped out, and jumping over a fence, he fell down in a state of insensibility. He was then taken moribund to St. Luke's Hospital, where he died an hour or two later.

Jackson has been for some time in an insane asylum, hopelessly incurable.

How mournful the fate of these men! Let us remember only the good that has resulted from their labors.

Vaccination and Anaesthesia are the greatest boons ever conferred by science on humanity. England gave us the one, America the other.

Honors accorded to Long in the intervening century have been significant but never-theless modest. A shaft in his honor was erected in 1910 in Jefferson. A bronze medallion by Dr. R. Tait McKenzie was hung in the Medical Building of the University of Pennsylvania in 1912. In 1926, a statute to the discoverer of ether was unvailed in Statuary Hall in the United States Capitol. His place of birth, Danielsville, erected a statue to him in 1936; while a commemorative stamp was issued by the Postal Department in 1940.

1. Taylor, F. L.: Crawford Williamson Long, *Ann Med Hist* 7:267-296, 394-424, 1925.

2. Long, C. W.: An Account of the First Use of Sulphuric Ether by Inhalation as an Anaesthetic in Surgical Operations, *Southern Med Surg J* 5(ns):705-713, 1849.

3. *Congressional Globe*, 33 US Congress, first session pt 2, April 19, 1854, pp 943-944.

4. Jackson, C. T.: Letter to the Editor, *Boston Med Surg J* 64:229-231 (April 11) 1861.

5. Sims, J. M.: History of the Discovery of Anaesthesia, *Virginia Med Monthly*, May 1877.

Boston Medical Library

William Thomas Green Morton (1819-1868)

IN THE SUMMER OF 1844, being in the practice of dentistry, and desirous to improve myself in chemical and medical knowledge, I studied in the office of Dr. Charles T. Jackson, of Boston, and in order to employ my time to the utmost advantage, I resided in his family. One day, in casual conversation upon my profession of dentistry, I spoke of the operation of destroying the nerve of a tooth. . . . Dr. Jackson said, in a humorous manner, that I must try some of his tooth-ache drops. . . . Dr. Jackson then added, that as this ether might be applied with advantage to sensitive teeth, he would send me some. The conversation then turned upon the effect of ether upon the system, and he told me how the students at Cambridge used to inhale sulphuric ether from their handkerchiefs, and that it intoxicated them, making them reel and stagger.

The successful application I had made of the ether in destroying the sensibility of a tooth, together with what Dr. Jackson told me of its effects when inhaled by the students at college, awakened my attention, and having free access to Dr. Jackson's books, I began to read on the subject of its effects upon the animal system. I became satisfied there was nothing new or particularly dangerous in the inhaling of ether, that it had long been the toy of professors and students, known as a powerful anti-spasmodic, anodyne and narcotic, capable of intoxicating and stupefying, when taken in sufficient quantity. I found that even the apparatus for inhaling it was described in some treatises, but in most cases it was described as inhaled from a saturated sponge or handkerchief.

In the spring of 1846, . . . I tried an experiment upon a water spaniel, inserting his head in a jar having sulphuric ether at the bottom. . . . After breathing the vapor for some time, the dog completely wilted down in my hands. I then removed the jar. In about three minutes he aroused, yelled loudly, and sprung some ten feet, into a pond of water.

. . . early in August; and it being hot weather, and I being somewhat out of health, I went into the country, and abandoned the experiments until the middle of September. With the autumn and the restoration of health, my ambition led me to resume my experiments.

I . . . waited impatiently for some one upon whom I could make a fuller trial. Toward evening, a man [Eben Frost], residing in Boston, whose certificate is in the appendix, came in, suffering great pain and wishing to have a tooth extracted. He was afraid of the operation and asked if he could be mesmerized. I told him I had something better, and saturating my handkerchief, gave it to him to inhale. He became unconscious almost immediately. It was dark, and Dr. Hayden held the lamp, while I extracted a firmly rooted bicuspid tooth. There was not much alteration in the pulse, and no relaxation of the muscles. He recovered in a minute, and knew nothing of what had been done to him. This was on the 30th of Sept., 1846. This I consider to be the first demonstration of this new fact in science.

The above recounting by Morton[1] of the administration of sulphuric ether was not prepared for publication until a year after the best known public demonstration had taken place—in the surgical amphitheater of the Massachusetts General Hospital—albeit but four years after Crawford Long, in Jackson County, Georgia, had used ether in his country practice. The events surrounding the observations of Morton and Long have been told and retold many times. Although no new evidence or documents have been uncovered to prompt this essay, the Federal Government recently declared the Ether Dome of the Massachusetts General Hospital as a national shrine, to be dedicated appropriately in Boston on Ether Day, Oct 16, 1965.

William Thomas Green Morton was born at Charlton, in Worcester County, Massachusetts, the son of a farmer of that town.[2] He received a common-school education at the Northfield and Leicester Academies and, at the age of 17, went to Boston and held various jobs as a clerk and a salesman. At the age of 21 he began the study of dentistry at the Baltimore College of Dental Surgery. Two years later he settled in Boston, where he built a thriving dental practice in partnership with Horace Wells. In March of 1844, Morton enrolled at Harvard Medical School, meanwhile continuing his dental practice. He completed two terms at Harvard but did not receive a medical degree. While studying medicine he lived with his preceptor, Charles T. Jackson, graduate of Harvard Medical School, chemist, geologist, and state assayer, whose success with ether drops used as a local anesthetic during the filling of teeth was familiar to Morton.

Meanwhile, Morton was relentlessly searching for a nontoxic agent to produce insensibility to pain during extraction of teeth and later for general surgical procedures. By the fall of 1846, Morton was familiar with Wells's employment of nitrous oxide for dental extraction, with Jackson's interest in the local use of ether in dentistry, with the relative harmlessness of sulfuric ether inhalation during "ether frolics," and with the experimental inhalation of ether to induce temporary insensibility in animals. He himself had also inhaled the substance with good effect. Two requirements remained to be satisfied to justify the inhalation of ether for physical insensibility during a surgical operation: a device for the efficient administration of ether as well as a surgical team and a patient for the experiment. Each need was satisfied on Oct 16, 1846. An ether cone was made ready by Mr. Chamberlain, an instrument maker of Boston, just in time for use by Morton at an operation by John Collins Warren, Hersey professor of anatomy and surgery at Harvard Medical School and senior surgeon at the Massachusetts General Hospital. The patient, a young man named Gilbert Abbott, permitted a tumor to be removed from his neck by Warren following Morton's successful induction of insensibility with ether. The surgeon was convinced of the importance of the demonstration, as were the students and physicians in attendance. A painting of the scene, as depicted by Hinckley, with considerable accuracy of detail and verisimilitude many years later, is an acquisition of the Boston (Countway) Medical Library.

The event was described in the Boston newspapers and casually mentioned in the *Boston Medical and Surgical Journal* of Oct 21, 1846, as follows:[3]

> Strange stories are related in the papers of a wonderful preparation, in this city, by administering which, a patient is affected just long enough, and just powerfully enough to undergo a surgical operation without pain.

An extended announcement of the event was read by Henry Jacob Bigelow, a junior surgeon at the hospital, before the Boston Society of Medical Improvement on Nov 9, an abstract having been previously read before the American Academy of Arts and Sciences on Nov 3, 1846. The communication to the *Boston Medical and Surgical Journal* recounts the first and subsequent operations on patients under ether anesthesia[4] and concludes with a short discourse on patent rights and the maintenance of secrecy regarding an agent.

> On the 16th of Oct., 1846, an operation was performed at the hospital, upon a patient who had inhaled a preparation administered by Dr. Morton, a dentist of this city, with the alleged intention of producing insensibility to pain. Dr. Morton was understood to have extracted teeth under similar circumstances, without the knowledge of the patient. The present operation was performed by Dr. Warren, and though comparatively slight,

involved an incision near the lower jaw of some inches in extent. During the operation the patient muttered, as in a semi-conscious state, and afterwards stated that the pain was considerable, though mitigated; in his own words, as though the skin had been scratched with a hoe. There was, probably, in this instance, some defect in the process of inhalation, for on the following day the vapor was administered to another patient with complete success. A fatty tumor of considerable size was removed, by Dr. Hayward, from the arm of a woman near the deltoid muscle. The operation lasted four or five minutes, during which time the patient betrayed occasional marks of uneasiness; but upon subsequently regaining her consciousness, professed not only to have felt no pain, but to have been insensible to surrounding objects, to have known nothing of the operation, being only uneasy about a child left at home. No doubt, I think, existed, in the minds of those who saw this operation, that the unconsciousness was real; nor could the imagination be accused of any share in the production of these remarkable phenomena.

Initially, Morton withheld the chemical nature of the substance, calling it "Letheon," a name which soon lost favor. The true nature of the compound was disclosed and an application for a patent was filed on Oct 28, 1848, and was granted (No. 4848) on Nov 12. One of the provisions permitted certain charitable hospitals to use Letheon free of charge. Upon advice of others, Jackson's name was included as a patentee; however, this legal recognition failed to satisfy Jackson, who created such a local and national furor over priority and recognition that glory for Boston's contribution to anesthesia was outweighed tenfold by bitterness. Furthermore, Morton's great days were soon over. His scientific communications were limited to a small number of treatises on dentistry, the communication to the Academy of Sciences in Paris, a discourse on the comparative value of sulfuric ether and chloroform (in which he declared chloroform a dangerous anesthetic), remarks on the proper mode of administering sulfuric ether by inhalation, and a short-lived privately printed circular, *Morton's Letheon,* which began as a handbill and grew to 88 pages in the fifth edition.

Morton saw military service during the Civil War. He served with General Grant in the Battles in the Wilderness and in the Battle of Spottsylvania Court House, where he administered ether in the field hospitals to over 2,000 wounded. The remainder of his time was devoted to the establishment of priority for the ether discovery.[5] Applications were made to Congress in 1849, 1851, and 1854, and resulted in a bill authorizing an appropriation of $100,000 for the discoverer of anesthesia. Jackson and his supporters plotted and intrigued to divert the funds from Morton. Later, friends of Crawford Long entered his name in the controversy. The Congressional deliberations continued for years, but the bill remained in committee and was never passed.

In addition to whatever personal satisfaction Morton received from his great contribution, he was awarded an honorary MD degree by Washington University of Baltimore and $1,000 by the trustees of the Massachusetts General Hospital. An award of 5,000 francs was offered by the French Academy of Medicine but was refused by Morton since it was made jointly to Morton and Jackson. The last years of Morton's life were spent in agricultural pursuits in Wellesley, Mass; he died in mental anguish in Central Park, New York. Wells took his own life in 1848, and Jackson was committed to an insane asylum in 1873.

1. Morton, W. T. G.: A Memoir to the Academy of Sciences at Paris on a New Use of Sulphuric Ether, translated in *Littell's Living Age* 16:529-571 (March 18) 1848.

2. Packard, F. R.: The Conquest of Surgical Pain, *Amer Philos Soc*, March 27, 1940, pp 5-48.

3. Medical Miscellany, *Boston Med Surg J* 35:247 (Oct) 21) 1846.

4. Bigelow, H. J.: Insensibility During Surgical Operations Produced by Inhalation, *Boston Med Surg J* 35:309-317 (Nov 18) 1846.

5. Rice, N. P.: *Trials of a Public Benefactor, as Illustrated in the Discovery of Etherization*, New York: Pudney & Russell, 1859

Sir George Murray Humphry (1820-1896)

GEORGE MURRAY HUMPHRY was born at Sudbury in Suffolk, the son of a barrister-at-law and distributor of stamps for Suffolk. He was educated at the local grammar schools of Sudbury and Dedham in the days when emphasis on Latin and Greek was traditional. At the age of 16, he began a three year apprenticeship with J. G. Crosse, who housed and fed his pupils and set an example of industry in the study of anatomy

Royal College of Physicians

and the care of the sick. Humphry then entered St. Bartholomew's Hospital, passed the first portion of the MB examination at the University of London with a gold medal in anatomy and physiology, and in 1841 was admitted a member of the Royal College of Surgeons of England. The following year he qualified for licensure in the Society of Apothecaries of London. He was appointed surgeon to Addenbrooke's Hospital in Cambridge and, in his 22nd year, because of a vacancy on the staff and with the support of Sir James Paget, became one of the youngest hospital surgeons in Great Britain.[1] Humphry held the post for more than one-half century, combining an active surgical practice with an academic career. He proceeded to Downing College, Cambridge, in 1847 and was granted the MB in 1852 and the MD in 1859. Lecturing in human anatomy and surgery, which he had begun early in his career and before he received his first degree, was rewarded in 1866 when he was elected professor of human anatomy at the

University, a senior position held until 1883; then he was appointed professor of surgery, without salary. Special honors included election to fellowship in the Royal Society in 1859, knighthood in 1891, and honorary degrees from Edinburgh and Dublin.

Humphry was a keen clinical observer, a skilled technician, and a stimulating teacher who employed the Socratic method at the bedside. He copied John Hunter in his devotion to pathological anatomy. In giving the Hunterian Oration in 1879, Humphry praised his academic ancestor but voiced skepticism over the undue emphasis placed upon the minutiae of human anatomy.[2]

The knowledge of the facts of anatomy, we all admit, are essential to the practice of surgery, and to an appreciation of physiology; and the correct learning of them promotes the habit of attention, and of accuracy which is the associate of attention. Still it may be questioned whether, from an educational, or even from a practical, point of view, the result is proportionate to the time and labour expended in the way in which it is done. Certainly, there is no other subject which men exhibit so much proneness to forget, none of which the overdistended memory so quickly disgorges as soon as the examination ordeal is over, and too frequently before that ordeal begins; and in the summary process the useful is indiscriminately rejected with the superfluous. The knowledge, painfully acquired, is strainingly held and cheerfully let go. Hence the facts of anatomy, being measured by an examination standard and acquired for an examination purpose, are repulsive to most students, are made a drudgery instead of being a pleasure, and become a means of deterring men from scientific pursuit, instead of alluring them to it.

It will not, I am sure, for a moment, be thought that one who has devoted so large a part of life to the study and teaching of anatomy, and who holds a responsible University position in relation to it, would speak disparagingly of it. . . . But, in thus speaking of anatomy, I do not mean an anatomy which taxes memory without stimulating thought; which consists in a collection of naked facts without an appropriate clothing of the varied interest which properly attaches to them, and which renders them attractive and seals them on the memory. I mean an anatomy, not limited to the technical details of the structure of the body, but a science implying an intelligent acquaintance with this the highest and most exquisite of existing forms.

Humphry was a prolific contributor to the scientific periodicals of his day. He was founder and co-editor of the *Journal of* *Anatomy and Physiology,* which later changed its name to the *Journal of Anatomy,* giving way to the *Journal of Physiology* for subjects appropriate to the parallel basic science. His works included *A Treatise on the Human Skeleton,* with 60 illustrations on stone drawn by his wife,[3] *On the Coagulation of Blood in the Venous System During Life,* prepared in part from personal experience with phlebitis, a monograph on *The Human Foot and the Human Hand, Observations in Myology, A Guide to the Town of Cambridge,* and a treatise on *Old Age.* Humphry, teacher, anatomist, and clinical surgeon, will be remembered as one of the founders of the Cambridge University Medical Schools.

1. Rolleston, H. D.: *The Cambridge Medical School,* Cambridge: University Press, 1932.
2. Humphry, G. M.: The Hunterian Oration, *Brit Med J* 1:259-264, 1879.
3. Humphry, G. M.: *A Treatise on the Human Skeleton,* Cambridge: MacMillan and Co., 1858.

Richard von Volkmann (1830-1889)

RICHARD VON VOLKMANN, one of the great German surgeons, was born in Leipzig, and spent six years in the famous Furstenshule at Grimma. At the age of 20 he began the study of medicine at Halle, where his father Alfred Wilhelm Volkmann held the chair of physiology from 1843 until 1877.[1] Richard continued the study of medicine at Giessen and in 1854 presented his inaugural dissertation in Latin, *De Pulmonum Gangraena,* at the University of Berlin. Richard had early shown an interest and aptitude for literature and the classics, as evidenced by the fluent Latin of his dissertation, and, during his later years, by the composition of a widely read book of children's stories—a compilation of troubadour songs and other light nonmedical books. Like his father, Richard spent his prime professional years at the University of Halle. He was appointed privatdocent in surgery in 1856, advanced to professorial status in 1863, and became full professor and head of the surgical clinic in 1867. Previously he had served with the Prussian army in the campaign of 1866 and, in 1870-1871, accompanied the fourth army corps as surgeon-general.

Prior to the Franco-Prussian War, Volkmann had heard of Lister's antisepsis tech-

Composite by G. Bako

nique; however, he achieved little success with it in field hospitals. Not discouraged by his military experiences, upon return to his surgical clinic, he introduced Lister's principles into civilian medicine, especially in the surgical treatment of bones and joints, a subject of particular interest. He simplified the application of Lister's bandages, used large quantities of dilute carbolic acid in the operating theater, and, by writing and acting with a conviction equal to Lister's, found greater support for antisepsis in Germany than Lister had received from his associates in Edinburgh. It is noteworthy that one of Volkmann's early communications on antiseptic osteotomy was prefaced with a note by Lister. The first portion of Lister's comments reproduced below is followed by an excerpt of Volkmann's experience in surgery of the bones and joints.[2]

The following papers by Professor Volkmann of Halle seems to me worthy of the notice of British surgeons, not only on account of the novelty and interest of the method of treatment which it describes, but also from the example which it presents of a surgeon, deservedly occupying a very high position in the profession in Germany, who, appreciating the paramount importance of the antiseptic principle, carries it out with an intelligent care such as can alone ensure success.

Professor Volkmann's confidence . . . is clear proof that he has made himself thoroughly master of the antiseptic method; and the statistical evidence which he adduces of the success of that method in his hands, including the entire banishment of pyaemia from an old and overcrowded hospital, under the most unfavourable hygienic conditions in other respects, will I trust receive the serious attention which it deserves.

Since the introduction of the antiseptic method into my clinique, now exactly two years ago (at the end of November 1872), no single patient suffering from a compound fracture in which conservative treatment was attempted, has died. Amongst this number are included even those cases in which conservative treatment was only resorted to because the patients would not give their consent to amputation, and also those in which we at first underestimated the severity of the injury, and afterwards intermediate or secondary amputation had to be undertaken on account of haemorrhage or gangrene. The number of compound fractures successfully treated without a single fatal result in our hospital, which is old and always overcrowded, and offers the most unhealthy hygienic conditions, amount at present to 31. Amongst these were as many as 19 compound fractures of the leg, in several instances much comminuted and often complicated with most severe bruising and laceration of soft parts. There were also two compound comminuted fractures of the patella, both of which recovered with movable joints. No case of pyaemia has occurred for a year and a half, i.e., since July 1873, although during this period alone about 60 major amputations have taken place.

Volkmann's general surgical interest included wound healing, resection of cancer of the rectum, tumors in those working with paraffin and cold tar products, inflammatory osteoporosis, embolic necrosis of bone following endocarditis, carcinoma of the breast, surgical treatment of tuberculosis of bones, and wound erysipelas. Three of his contributions were translated and published by the New Sydenham Society: "On Lupus and Its Treatment," "On Infantile Paralysis and Paralytic Contractions," and "On Excision of Joints."[3] His discussion of cheilitis glandularis was judged by Shelley and Crissey to be a classic in dermatology, and a translated excerpt is included in their monograph.[4]

Volkmann's "Ischemic Paralysis and Contractures" is one of his lesser contributions but his best known eponym. He discounted the effect on nerves in ischemic paralysis and attributed the harm to rapid disintegration of muscle fibers, deprived of normal nutrients through the blood supply, and subsequent fibrous regeneration.[5]

For years I have called attention to the fact that the pareses and contractures of limbs following application of a tight bandages are caused not by pressure paralysis of nerves, as formerly assumed, but by the rapid and massive deterioration of contractile substance and by the following reactive and regenerative processes.

(1) Paresis and contracture of the forearm and hand, and less often of the lower extremities, following application of tight bandages, should be considered to be of ischemic origin. They are caused by prolonged deprivation of arterial blood. The concurrent venous stasis which often is severe seems only to hasten the onset of paralysis.

(2) Paralysis is caused by death of the primary muscle fibers deprived of oxygen for too long a period. The contractile substance coagulates, then it flakes up, and later it is reabsorbed. The following contracture should be considered simply as death stiffness. The paralyzed and contracted limbs—when all muscles of an extremity or its part are affected, as is usually the case—have an appearance identical to *rigor mortis*.

(3) It is characteristic that the paralysis and contracture set in concurrently or follow one another by a very short interval, whereas in the nervous type of paralysis the contracture sets in slowly and develops much later. Months and years pass before a deformity develops which cannot be displaced by moderate manual pressure.

(4) An ischemic contracture, however, from the beginning offers enormous resistance to a force trying to straighten the extremity. As in *rigor mortis,* the corresponding muscles lose their elasticity and become stiff even in cases which have developed recently.

(5) The prognosis of ischemic paralysis and contracture depends on the number of muscle fibers that have disintegrated. The most severe cases affecting hand and fingers should be considered absolutely incurable. The prognosis is better in the lower extremities.

During the siege of Paris, as a German army officer occupying a French chateau and waiting for the surrender, Volkmann used his leisure time to prepare his *Reveries at French Firesides,* comprising short stories written for children but also widely read by adults.[6] The book was published under the pseudonym Richard Leander, the hellenized form of his name. The tales whose titles of the stories are reminiscent of the Grimm brothers or H. C. Andersen include: "The Magic Organ," "Dream Tree," "Little Black Boy," "The Invisible Kingdom," and "The Little Hunchback." Initially sent home to his children and later published, an American reprinting of the stories was offered in 1908 as a selection of reading matter suitable for the early stages of foreign language study. Volkmann founded the *Sammlung klinischer Vorträge,* a valuable series of monographs from outstanding German clinics.[7] He became Rector of the University of Halle in 1878-1879 and in 1885 was raised to the hereditary nobility.

1. Krause, F.: *In Memory of Richard von Volkmann (Richard Leander)* (Ger), Berlin: A. Hirschwald, 1890.

2. Volkmann, R.: On Two Cases of Anchylosis of the Knee-Joint Treated by Osteotomy, *Edinburgh Med J* 20: 794-799 (Jan) 1875.

3. Volkmann, R.: *Clinical Lectures on Subjects Connected With Medicine, Surgery, and Obstetrics,* London: New Sydenham Society, 1876.

4. Shelley, W. B., and Crissey, J. T.: *Classics in Clinical Dermatology,* Springfield, Ill: C. C Thomas, Publisher, 1953.

5. Volkmann, R.: Ischemic Paralysis and Contractures (Ger), *Centralbl Chir* 8:801-803, 1881.

6. Volkmann, R. (pseudonym—Leander): *Reveries at French Firesides* (Ger), New York: Ginn & Co., 1908.

7. Volkmann, R.: *Collection of Clinical Contributions* (Ger), Leipzig, 1870-1890.

Henry Orlando Marcy (1837-1924)

HENRY O. MARCY, surgeon and gynecologist, was born in Otis, Massachusetts, son of a schoolteacher and a veteran of the War of 1812. He attended Wilbraham Academy and Amherst College and received the MD degree from Harvard Medical School in 1864.[1] Before, as well as after, graduation he served with the Union Army in the Civil War. In the spring of 1863 Marcy was appointed assistant surgeon of the 43rd Massachusetts

Volunteers and, in the fall, surgeon of the first regiment of Negro troops recruited in North Carolina. In this assignment he established classes for the Negroes and did double duty as officer and instructor, a noteworthy task. The following year he was made medical director of Florida, served on Sherman's

Composite by G. Bako

staff in the Carolina campaign, and supervised the sanitary renovation of Charleston, South Carolina.

At the close of the war, Marcy returned to the Boston area and practiced in Cambridge, Massachusetts, until 1869, when he devoted himself to postgraduate work in Europe. He studied with Virchow in Berlin, with Paget and Spencer Wells in London, and finally with Lister in Edinburgh; there he became convinced of the advantages of the antiseptic method of operative surgery. Upon his return to Boston Bigelow refused to allow him to use the antiseptic technique. However, Marcy persisted in Cambridge, where he founded a private hospital for diseases of women and gained an excellent reputation, without benefit of medical school or teaching hospital affiliations. In his clinical laboratory he studied procedures for reconstruction of the inguinal canal and the use of anti-

septic catgut in the management of strangulated hernia.[2]

I must claim at least a favorable consideration, on a legitimate field, for the use of the carbolized catgut ligature, in all cases of strangulated hernia where the wound can be closed. This method does not add to the dangers of the operation, and is probably followed by a cure. In comparing the operation with that usually recommended, of subcutaneously stitching the ring with sutures on any material, it seems apparent that to cut down upon and expose the ring gives much better opportunity of carefully closing it, and thus avoids injury to the spermatic cord, while it does not increase the danger of the patient.

As a capable writer, Marcy contributed a number of clinical reports on general and gynecologic surgery to current periodicals, translated from the Italian the two-volume treatise by Ercolani on the reproductive process, and prepared an outstanding monograph, entitled *The Anatomy and Surgical Treatment of Hernia*.[3] The following are two passages from his address in Detroit in 1892 when he presided at the annual meeting of the American Medical Association. The first relates to the purpose of the association, the second to the official scientific publication.[4]

It was wisely enacted that our Association consist, in large degree, of delegated membership, since this makes it, as by no other plan, a representative body, and, as such, it is not too much for us to claim that we stand as the exponent of the medical thought and progress of our noble profession represented in the United States alone by a membership of nearly one hundred thousand workers.

Modelled in considerable degree upon the constitutional principles of our popular Government, we are supposed to recognize the wants and necessities, and from year to year, to be able to outline and, in a measure, formulate the ever-changing needs and requirements of the public welfare.

The Journal of our Association has already advanced to a position of influence, second to that of no other medical publication in America. With a circulation of over six thousand copies it is now a source of independent income. Under a wise leadership and editorial management it has steadily improved and gives promise of a much greater development. It should be a weekly interchange of thought and the distribution of the latest and best, at a very early future, to a membership of three or four times its present number, an ever increasing bond of union between our members, with whom it should be the pride, as it is at present within our power, to make it the leading journal of the world.

Marcy was active in the Massachusetts Medical Society and became president of the section on gynecology at the 9th International Medical Congress in Washington, 1887. He also assumed an active interest in public affairs. A portion of the property upon which the Massachusetts Institute of Technology on the Charles River bank was constructed was reclaimed by him from marshland. He was instrumental in the decision to build the Harvard Bridge which spanned the Charles River and in the renovation of the Charles River Basin; in addition, Marcy was responsible for the design of the Esplanade Parkway. Amherst College bestowed upon him an honorary AM and Wesleyan University an LLD.

1. Lewis, F. C.: A Tribute to Henry O. Marcy, *J Amer Med Ed Assoc* 5:16-19, 1925.
2. Marcy, H. O.: The Radical Cure of Hernia by the Antiseptic Use of the Carbolized Catgut Ligature, *Trans AMA* 29:295-305, 1878.
3. Marcy, H. O.: *The Anatomy and Surgical Treatment of Hernia*, New York: D. Appleton & Co., 1892.
4. Marcy, H. O.: The President's Address—Evolution of Medicine, *JAMA* 18:725-732 (June 11) 1892.

W. W. Keen (1837-1932)

WILLIAM WILLIAMS KEEN, surgeon of the Woman's Medical College and Jefferson Medical College, is better known for his clinical teaching, surgical skill, and outstanding addresses than for any major scientific contributions in his specialty. He was born in Philadelphia, attended Central High School and Saunders Academy, and in 1859, graduated with collegiate honors from Brown University. He received his medical training at Jefferson Medical College, where he came under the influence of S. Weir Mitchell, and completed requirements for the MD degree in 1862. During his first year in medical school, he spent a few weeks of military service in a camp at Alexandria and saw action in the Battle of Bull Run. Immediately following graduation he was commissioned acting assistant surgeon in the US Army, eventually serving in the Turner Lane Army Hospital; there combatants with nerve injuries were treated, and a patient with Horner's syndrome was observed before the aggregate of symptoms had received the eponymic designation.

College of Physicians, Philadelphia

With the cessation of hostilities, Keen went abroad for two years, spending time in clinics in Paris and with Virchow in Berlin. Upon his return to Philadelphia, he began practice as an associate of Mitchell, lectured on surgical pathology at Jefferson Medical College, and took charge of the private Philadelphia School of Anatomy. From 1876 to 1889, Keen was professor of artistic anatomy at the Philadelphia Academy of Fine Arts and, from 1884 to 1889, was professor of surgery at the Woman's Medical College. Meanwhile, he had developed a large general practice without benefit of a major hospital service. His great capacity for work became apparent at once. Having established good habits in composition, Keen published in 1870 two of his best known surgical works, *Early History of Practical Anatomy* and Practical Anatomy—*Manual of Dissections*. In 1883 and 1887, he updated two editions of *Gray's Anatomy;* in 1892 and 1903, he published his *American Text-Book of Surgery;* his six-volume compendium prepared in collaboration with others, *Surgery, Its*

Principles and Practice, appeared between 1906 and 1921.

While serving with Mitchell and Morehouse in the army hospital he observed a patient under their care with a previously undescribed phenomenon. The soldier had been wounded at Chancellorsville, Virginia, by a shot which penetrated the right neck and led to the development of a group of symptoms and findings, which were described by Horner six years later and which have persisted in the literature with the eponym. The lesion was attributed to damage to the cervical sympathetic nerve and was judged at that time to be the only case on record. The residual symptoms were descriped in the monograph published in 1864, entitled *Gunshot Wounds and Other Injuries of Nerves.*[2]

July 15, 1863—The pupil of the right eye is very small, that of the left eye unusually large. There is slight but very distince ptosis of the right eye, and its outer angle appears as though it were dropped a little lower than the inner angle. The ball of the right eye looks smaller than that of the left. These appearances existed whether the eye was open or closed, and gave to that organ the look of being tilted out of the usual position. The conjunctiva of the right eye is somewhat redder than that of the left, and the pupil of the right eye is a little deformed, oval rather than round. In a dark place, or in half-lights, the difference in the pupils was best seen; but in very bright light, as sunlight, the two pupils became nearly of equal size. The left eye waters a good deal, but has the better vision, the right eye having become myopic. In sunlight he sees well at first, but, after a time, observes red flashes of light in the right eye, and finally, after long exposure, sees the same appearances with the left eye also.

An orderly who was with him on this occasion, remarked to one of the hospital staff upon the singular appearance which his face presented after walking in the heat. It became distinctly flushed on the right side only, and pale on the left.

In 1889, Keen relinquished all previous institutional responsibilities to accept the professorship of the principles of surgery and of clinical surgery at Jefferson Medical College and to concentrate his clinical work in the Jefferson Hospital. In this position he was recognized as one of the leaders of surgery in America, highly regarded teacher, an extensive reader, thorough note-taker, prolific writer, crusader against antivivisec-tion, proponent of experimental medicine, and a deeply religious man. A large number of case reports, presidential or commencement addresses, and general writings for the profession and the laity were published during this tenure. Several of his clinical communications concerned the brain and spinal cord, and his biographers considered him one of the earliest "brain" surgeons in America. He tapped the ventricles, decompressed the skull, devised an electrode for exploring the motor centers in the brain, severed the Gasserian ganglion for tic douloureux, and decompressed the cranial cavity for expanding lesions. In his Presidential Address to the American Medical Association in 1900, he spoke against the antivivisection bill then under discussion in Congress, dwelt upon the endowment of medical schools and the work of the Sections at the Annual Meeting, and presented a useful editorial policy for *The Journal of the American Medical Association* regarding manuscripts presented before the Sections.[3]

The policy of THE JOURNAL, also, in connection with the various papers read before the Sections is an important one. Papers vary greatly in their merit and importance, and it would seem to me that to the trustees and the editor of THE JOURNAL should be confided the entire responsibility of selecting the more important papers for publication in full, and of presenting the less important in longer or shorter abstracts. The example of the *British Medical Journal* may well guide us in this matter.

In the commencement address delivered to the students of Rush Medical College a few days later, Keen described the ideal intellectual life of a preeminent physician of horse and buggy days.[4]

Make it a point not to let your intellectual life atrophy through non-use. Be familiar with the classics of English literature in prose and verse; read the lives of the great men of the past, and keep pace with modern thought in books of travel, history, fiction, science. A varied intellectual life will give zest to your medical studies and enable you to enter not unequipped into such social intercourse as will beget you friends and will relieve the monotony of a purely medical diet. Let music and art shed their radiance upon your too often weary life and find in the sweet cadences of sound or the rich emotions of form and color a refinement which adds polish to the scientific man.

Keen was a member of the surgical team which removed a sarcoma from the mandible of President Grover Cleveland aboard the yacht, *Oneida,* sailing between New York and Newport in 1893. The resection was performed in two stages; it was successful and Mr. Cleveland died 15 years later without a recurrence. During the Spanish American War Keen was commissioned but did not serve out of the country; in World War I, again he was commissioned, but his most important service was performed as a member of the National Research Council. He was president of the American Philosophical Society, the American Surgical Association, and the College of Physicians of Philadelphia; he held honorary fellowship in the Royal College of Surgeons of England, Edinburgh, and Ireland. The Boston Surgical Society awarded him the Henry Jacob Bigelow gold medal. Honorary degrees were granted him by the following universities: Brown, Northwestern, Toronto, Edinburgh, Yale, St. Andrews, Pennsylvania, Uppsala, and Harvard. As an active Baptist parishioner, Keen was a trustee of Crozer Theological Seminary and deacon and trustee of the First Baptist Church of Philadelphia. His interest in his undergraduate school never lagged; he served as trustee of Brown University from 1873 until 1895 and continued to participate in affairs as Fellow until his death.

1. Taylor, W. J.: Memoir of William Williams Keen, M.D., *Trans Coll Physicians Phila* 1(ser 4):lxii-lxvii, 1934.

2. Mitchell, S. W.; Morehouse, G. R.; and Keen, W. W.: *Gunshot Wounds and Other Injuries,* Philadelphia: J. B. Lippincott & Co., 1864.

3. Keen, W. W.: The President's Address, *JAMA* 34:1445-1450 (June 9) 1900.

4. Keen, W. W.: The Ideal Physician, *JAMA* 34:1592-1594 (June 23) 1900.

Theodor Kocher (1841-1917)

KOCHER, whose name is associated with several notable surgical procedures, a surgical clamp, and the testicular-abdominal reflex, received the Nobel Prize in medicine for multiple contributions in his chosen field, but especially for the understanding of the physiology of the thyroid and the treatment of toxic and nontoxic goiter. He was born in Bern, Switzerland, received the MD degree at the University of Bern, and spent his pro-

Composite by G. Bako

fessional days deep in the Swiss Alps. Subsequently, he visited clinics in central Europe and Great Britain, including those of Langenbeck, Billroth, and Lister.[1] Kocher was appointed professor in the university Surgical Clinic at the early age of 31 and held the post for 45 years. A capacity for grasping the significance of broad, general concepts and pursuing them in meticulous detail was matched by a gentle personality in the study and treatment of patients in the Surgical Clinic. Nor is it surprising, with these attributes, to learn that in the surgical amphitheater he operated unhurriedly and with illimitable skill, soundly based on careful anatomical dissection.

In the humanities, Kocher displayed a talent for painting and a deeply religious philosophy handed on from his mother, a descendant of the Moravian Brethren. On the other hand, surgical discipline, which encompassed teaching his pupils, exquisite technical craftsmanship, and warmth for his patients, was his great vocation.

An interest in diseases of the thyroid and particularly endemic goiter seems self-evident for a Bernese surgeon. Colloid goiter, cosmetically unattractive and occasionally impairing health through pressure on vital structures of the neck, was a common finding in the surgical clinic. Kocher's surgical approach in selected patients, which combined precise dissection and restoration of disturbed structures contiguous to the thyroid, led in some instances to postoperative athyreosis. In retrospect, although cretinism had been vaguely associated with function of the thyroid early in Kocher's professional days, the role of the normal thyroid in body economy was poorly understood. Nor was the precise association between complete loss of functioning thyroid tissue and cretinism (myxedema) apparent until athyreosis appeared postoperatively. In his description of postoperative myxedema, called "cachexia strumipriva," no significant clinical findings were omitted. Kocher reported weight gain, slowing of intellect and speech, loss of hair, thickening of the tongue, and abnormal heart sounds, as well as the laboratory findings of anemia and alteration of the white blood cell count.

The mortality in Kocher's first series of thyroidectomies was 12.8%; in an 1898 series of 600 cases, there was only one death. He paid particular attention to the phethoric vascular bed adjacent to the thyroid, to protection of the parathyroids whose loss leads to tetany, and to avoidance of injury to the recurrent laryngeal nerves which might result in impairment of phonation or respiration. The development of cachexia strumipriva was not recognized as a hazard until reports of such iatrogenic complications were brought to his attention and subsequently summarized. In an 1883 communication describing postoperative athyreosis, Kocher gave full credit to others who had made important observations in surgical removal of the thyroid.[2]

What makes particular caution necessary after the veins have been ligated in goiter operations is the preservation of the recurrent laryngeal nerves. Wölfler was the first to emphasize this danger in an exhaustive manner, and explain the reasons.

I must completely agree with him and Billroth, that it is relatively easy to preserve the trunk of the nerve when ligating the inferior thyroid artery. Here it is necessary meticulously to isolate this vessel before one puts a ligature around it, and not to tie its trunk at the point of entrance into the goiter, but to ligate it laterally.

On the basis of the results of goiter extirpation here reported, we maintain that even in this difficult operation we have arrived at the point where we generally recommend the radical operation for goiter as the surest and simplest method of treatment. . . . The second question of importance in regard to the generalized use of surgery for goiter has to do with the physiological importance of the thyroid gland. Unfortunately, the physiologists know almost nothing about it, and this has probably been the main reason why surgeons have simply assumed that the thyroid gland has no function whatever. As soon as it had been learned that from the standpoint of technique total extirpation could be carried out successfully there was no longer reason to hesitate to remove the entire organ when both lobes are diseased.

Of the 18 patients with total excision who presented themselves for examination, only two show a state of health as good as or better than before the operation.

The remaining 16 patients with total excision of the diseased thyroid gland all show more or less severe disturbances in their general condition, the analysis of which has been drawn from precise records in each individual case. The time elapsed since the operation ranges from 3½ months to 9 years and 2 months, and the severity of the symptoms is far graver in the oldest cases. They (symptoms) are obviously progressive. All younger patients who were operated upon more than two years ago show these manifestations to a pronounced degree.

As a rule, soon after discharge from the hospital, but in occasional cases not before the lapse of 4 or 5 months, the patients begin to complain of fatigue, and especially of weakness and heaviness in the extremities.

In addition there is a sensation of coldness in the extremities.

The mental alertness decreases. This is particularly striking in children of school age, inasmuch as they drop in class standing, and the teachers note a progressive diminution of their intellectual capabilities.

Associated with the slowness of thinking, there is gradually increasing slowness of speech and of all other movements.

With the onset of the clumsiness and tiredness in thought and movement swellings appear, sometimes intermittent, involving the face, hands and feet, lasting a few hours and then disappearing.

In the majority of the cases, the swelling is a permanent puffiness of the face. Second only to the clumsiness, it is this which creates the impression among more distant acquaintances that the patient has become an idiot.

The skin shows changes which are associated with the puffiness of certain parts of the body. It is slightly infiltrated, its flexibility lost, and it can be picked up only in thick folds, just as in cases where edematous swellings have existed . . . in two cases there was marked loss of hair.

Anemia is pronounced in advanced cases. . . . The heart sounds are clear but weak, the second aortic, and even more so, the pulmonic are loudly snapping.

If we are to give a name to this picture, we cannot fail to recognize its relation to idiocy and cretinism: the stunted growth, the large head, the swollen nose, thick lips, heavy body, the clumsiness of thought and speech in the presence of a well-developed musculature undoubtedly point to a related evil. It is interesting that the individuals are not really stupid, which has often been emphasized by their families; they are fully conscious of the retardation of their mental capabilities and especially of the slowness of their comprehension, deliberation, and particularly, of their speech.

We prefer, for the time being, to use an entirely innocuous name for this symptom-complex. For the nutritional disturbances which accompany the disappearance of goiters after iodine administration (Virchow), the name goiter cachexia or cachexia iodica has been used; we see no objection for the time being, to the use of the name *cachexia strumipriva*.

The Nobel Prize in medicine was awarded to Kocher, with similar citations in French and Swedish.

The Karolinska Institute of Medicine and Surgery resolved on the 28th of October, 1909 to award the Nobel prize of the year for physiology and medicine to

THEODOR KOCHER

for his work in physiology, pathology and surgery on the thyroid gland.

Kocher conducted a large private practice and performed more than 5,000 thyroidectomies in his extended surgical career. He was modest and unpretentious, eager to learn from others, and willing to abandon his specially designed procedure when a better one was described. The operations associated with his name include excision of the ankle joint, thyroidectomy, excision of the tongue for carcinoma, repair of inguinal hernia, hypophysectomy, and modification of Billroth I gastroduodenostomy. He was responsible also for a procedure for reduction of dislocation of the shoulder joint and for a description of the abdominal reflex following pressure on the testicles.

Kocher's text, *Operative Surgery,* served as a standard reference work for a generation of surgeons. The second edition was translated into English in 1895.[3] At the First International Neurological Congress held in Bern in 1931, Harvey Cushing, in placing a wreath on the tomb of Kocher in the Bern Cemetery, linked Kocher and William S. Halsted as follows:[4]

In my younger days I had the good fortune to come under the influence to two men who were outstanding surgeons of their generation—William S. Halsted and Theodor Kocher. I may couple their names together for they had much in common. They were engaged in similar problems; they were friends and correspondents; they were equally fastidious in their operative craftsmanship and at the same time, by precept and example, exerted a profound influence as investigators on the scientific aspects of their art. They represented the European and American surgery of their day at its very best.

From hard work and responsibility surgeons are prone to burn themselves out comparatively young, but Kocher had been blessed with an imperturbability of spirit or had cultivated these habits of self-control which enabled him to bear his professional labours, his years, and his honours with equal composure to the very end.

1. Bonjour, E.: *Theodor Kocher,* Bern: P. Haupt, 1950.
2. Kocher, T.: Postoperative Results of Extirpation of the Thyroid, *Arch Klin Chir* 29:254-337, 1883, in Zimmerman, L. M., and Veith, I. (trans.): *Great Ideas in the History of Surgery,* Baltimore: Williams & Wilkins Co., 1961.
3. Kocher, T.: *Text-book of Operative Surgery,* H. J. Stiles (trans.), London: A. & C. Black, 1895.
4. Fulton, J. F.: Arnold Klebs and Harvey Cushing at the 1st International Neurological Congress at Bern in 1931, *Bull Hist Med* 8:322-346, 1940.

Ludwig Courvoisier (1843-1918)

LG. COURVOISIER, whose interest in clinical surgery centered about the gallbladder and its ducts, was born in Basel, Switzerland. As a child he enriched his precocious mind with unusual industry and diligence; at the age of seven when his family lived for a short time in Malta, he acquired a particular interest in botany and entomology, and a proficiency in the English language.[1] Upon returning to Basel he studied at the gymnasium and prepared for medicine at the University. His medical education at Basel was interrupted for a year because of a severe attack of typhus fever, for several months during military service in the Austro-Prussian War, and

National Library of Medicine

for a semester while studying at the University of Göttingen. Before passing the state examination, Courvoisier won a prize in competition for his thesis, *The Histology of the Sympathetic Nervous System,* and served as an assistant in the surgical clinic to Professor Socin. The doctorate in medicine was granted with high honors upon the presentation of an inaugural dissertation, entitled *The Microscopic Structure of the Spinal Ganglion.*

Courvoisier's travel year was divided between Vienna, where he was a pupil of Billroth and Czerny, and London, where he studied with William Fergusson, Spencer Wells, and others. The Franco-Prussian War took him from Basel once more, for he served in the German army hospital at Karlsruhe under Socin. At the age of 28, he was appointed clinical director of a new hospital in Riehen, a suburb of Basel, and began building a private practice which grew rapidly and successfully. The proximity to

the University enabled him to maintain close liaison, and in 1880 he received academic status. Courvoisier moved into the city in 1883, strengthened his affiliation with the University, building again a private clinic where he pursued his clinical research. In 1888, he received professorial standing and from 1900 to 1912 served as professor in the University; however, he declined the directorship of the surgical clinic in deference to a younger teacher.

Courvoisier's sign or law, described in his monograph on the biliary tract, differentiated obstruction by stone in the common duct from other causes. If a stone was responsible, the gallbladder was apt to be fibrotic from chronic inflammation, associated with the presence of stones, and was therefore incapable of dilatation. On the other hand, with obstruction due to causes other than stone (principally tumors) the gallbladder, not having been subjected to chronic inflammation, was capable of distension and could be felt on abdominal palpation. Also, diverticuli developed with extraluminal obstruction but not with stones. The description by Courvoisier was correctly presented as a sign—not a law, and applicable to the majority of instances only, and was not to be assumed to be an invariable consequence.[2]

Common duct obstruction reacts differently when caused by different conditions. Among 109 well described cases of dilatation of the gallbladder only 17 were due to impacted stones. The remained were caused by occlusion of the duct (intrinsic tumors 10, obliteration of the duct 8, extraluminal compression 74). Furthermore, dilatation was only moderate when associated with obstruction by stone. In only two instances was the gallbladder unusually large. Diverticuli did not develop following duct obstruction from stones, only from other causes of occlusion.

On the contrary 78 cases showed contraction of the gallbladder with an occluded common duct and a patent cystic duct; the gallbladder was never enlarged, only atrophic. Seventy of this group (90%) were associated with common duct stones; only eight (10%) were caused by a different process.

If one separates the 187 cases into two main groups, there were 87 with obstruction from stones and 100 from other causes. Among those caused by stones, a shrunken gallbladder was present in 80.4% while a dilated gallbladder was present in 19.6%. In obstruction from other causes, the gallbladder was dilated. Thus with stone obstruction of the common duct, dilatation of the gallbladder is rarely observed; the organ has already undergone contraction; with obstruction from other causes, dilatation is to be expected; atrophy exists in only one-twelfth of these cases.

The results of this investigation . . . provide important criteria in differential diagnosis.

Other communications by Courvoisier include a score of contributions on entomology, several editions of a popular treatise on the care of the sick in the home, a monograph on neuroma, a description of posterior gastroenterostomy for carcinoma of the pylorus, and one of the first descriptions of choledocholithotomy. He has been described as an excellent operative surgeon, a natural scientist, and a citizen with demonstrated civic interests. His great herbarium was bequeathed to the botanical Institute and his collection of butterflies to the Natural Museum of Basel. It has been suggested that his best scientific work was in nonmedical fields.

1. Veillon, E.: Professor Dr. med. L. G. Courvoisier (Ger), *Schweiz Med Wschr* 43:1314-1319, 1918.

2. Courvoisier, L. G.: *The Pathology and Surgery of the Biliary Tract* (Ger), Leipzig: F. C. W. Vogel, 1890.

Edoardo Bassini (1844-1924)

OF THE ILLUSTRIOUS GROUP OF SURGEON-ANATOMISTS associated with the radical repair of inguinal hernia, Bassini of Padua is the outstanding member. Camper of Franeker and Gröningen, Scarpa of Pavia, Hesselbach of Würzburg, and Astley Cooper of London each gave the hernia special and anatomical treatment, but each was handicapped in practice by inadequate anesthesia or by postoperative sepsis in the pre-Listerian era. Bassini's technical improvements in the late 1880's, however, comprised the steps for a radical cure clearly defined and achieved through satisfactory anesthesia and control of infection.[1] Marcy of Boston deserves mention, for he advocated ample exposure of the subcutaneous inguinal ring and restoration of the obliquity of the inguinal canal. Halsted of Baltimore agreed with Bassini after less satisfactory procedures were tried and abandoned. Lotheissen of Vienna and Andrews and

Composite by G. Bako

Ferguson of Chicago were also interested in inguinal hernia before the end of the century and are deserving of mention. No major changes have been made in the operative treatment of indirect inguinal hernia in recent generations of surgeons.

Edoardo Bassini was born in Pavia and received his doctorate in medicine from the University of Pavia at the early age of 22. He followed the example of his uncle in joining the liberation forces of Garibaldi as an infantryman in the crusade for unification of Italy and national freedom.[1] In combat during the second campaign, he suffered a bayonet wound of the groin, which became infected and was complicated by a fecal fistula. Following recovery in the surgical clinic of Luigi Porta of the University of Pavia, Bassini returned as a member of the staff in 1868 and resumed his study of anatomy and surgical pathology. His postgraduate training was continued with Billroth in Vienna, Langenbeck in Berlin, Nussbaum in Munich, and with Lister in London. He had hoped to succeed Porta upon the latter's death, but instead he became head of the department of surgery at Spezia. At the age of 38, Bassini was called to the University of Padua as professor of surgical pathology and later advanced to the chair of clinical surgery where he became the greatest Italian surgeon of his generation. During World War I he set up a small field hospital near the front and dispensed moral, medical, and surgical comfort to the wounded. In private life he was unselfish, generous, and charitable to the poor; he enjoyed horseback riding for relaxation. He spent his retired days in Verona.

Although Bassini's most notable contribution was the description of the repair of inguinal hernia, documented with a remarkable series of good results, he published monographs on operative surgery, immobility of the jaw, and the pathological histology of bone. Bassini's initial communication in 1887 on the inguinal hernia was presented to the Italian Society of Surgery. His radical cure was based upon the anatomical and functional restoration of the inguinal canal, a study that he had pursued for more than a decade. The procedure embraced adequate exposure including opening the inguinal canal, mobilization of the spermatic cord, ligation and removal of the sac at the deep inguinal ring, oblique reconstruction of the canal with an anterior and posterior wall, and an internal and external opening. If these steps were taken, the anterior and posterior walls would approximate and the canal would close without any significant increase in abdominal pressure. The initial report included the results with 42 cases.[1] The series was extended to 262 cases, with no deaths among the patients with nonstrangulated hernia, and only seven recurrences in the follow-up period. The 1887 communication in Italian and the 1890 report in German have been reproduced in facsimile, with recent English translations.[2] The following is from the Italian.

This method reconstructs the inguinal canal as it is physiologically, with two rings, one abdominal, the other subcutaneous; and with two walls, one posterior and the other anterior, between which the spermatic cord passes obliquely.

Using deep chloroform anaesthesia and careful antiseptic medication, incise the skin and sub-

cutaneous tissue in the inguino-scrotal region of the hernia and expose the external oblique aponeurosis for a distance corresponding to the hernial opening. Isolate the spermatic cord and the lower portion of the neck of the hernia sac at the external inguinal ring.

This constitutes the first stage of the operation.

In the second stage divide the aponeurosis to the external oblique from the external ring to a point past the internal ring, and detach the entire spermatic cord and the neck of the hernia. With an index finger under these parts, and with blunt instruments, isolate the neck of the hernia sac from the elements of the cord up to the inlet. At this point place a ligature or suture of catgut and cut off the sac distally. As soon as the ligated or sutured peritoneum (sac) is cut, it retracts into the internal iliac fossa. Then remove the sac of the hernia in part, or preferably completely, whether the hernia is congenital or acquired.

The removal of the sac completes the second stage of the operation.

In the third stage displace the isolated spermatic cord upward (if necessary the testicle may be removed from the scrotum) and expose the gutter, which is formed by Poupart's ligament, to one centimeter beyond the point where the spermatic cord emerges from the iliac fossa. Then free the aponeurosis of the external oblique and the preserous adipose tissue from the triple layer of the internal oblique, the transversus muscles and the fascia verticalis of Cooper enough to allow the triple layer to be brought easily to the isolated posterior border of Poupart's ligament.

Having done this, stitch these two parts for a distance of five to seven centimeters, the space between the pubic tubercle and the spermatic cord which is gently retracted laterally.

In this way the third stage of the operation accomplishes reconstruction of the internal or abdominal ring and the posterior wall of the canal.

After this suturing Prof. Bassini tests the fixation of the musculo-aponeurotic triple layer to Poupart's ligament by causing the patient to vomit to see if it remains in place, capable of resisting the increased intra-abdominal pressure.

In the fourth stage return the spermatic cord to its anatomic position and reunite with sutures the external oblique aponeurosis, reestablishing the external opening of the inguinal canal. Place a tube drain and bring it out of the upper angle of the wound. And finally stitch the skin.

In this way the inguinal canal is reconstructed with an internal ring and a posterior wall made up of the triple musculo-aponeurotic layer fastened to Poupart's ligament; and with an anterior wall narrowing the external or cutaneous ring.

1. Austoni, A.: The Life and Work of Edoardo Bassini (Ital), Arch Ital Chir 5:591-620, 1922.

2. Bassini, E.: New Technique for the Treatment of Inguinal Hernia (Ital), Soc Ital Chir 4:379-382, 1887, translated by R. K. Brown; G. Galetti; and K. S. Tumm, J Hist Med 21:401-407 (Oct) 1966.

Charles McBurney (1845-1913)

McBurney, surgeon of Manhattan, described the operative management of acute appendicitis, with and without complications, not long after Fitz suggested the term "appendicitis," and associated clinical symptoms with postmortem findings. McBurney was noted for his deft operative skill, for the recognition of the importance of asepsis in the operating room, for clarity of presentation in lectures, and for the formulation of sound ideas of surgical therapy. He was born in Roxbury, Massachusetts, attended Boston Latin School, received the AB and AM degrees from Harvard University, and the MD from the College of Physicians and Surgeons in New York. Following an internship at Bellevue Hospital, he went to Vienna, Paris, and London for postgraduate study, and began the practice of surgery in New York at the age of 28. At various times he was on the staff of major hospitals in the area: St. Luke's, Bellevue, Presbyterian, New York Hospital, and the Hospital for Ruptured and Crippled, but his allegiance was always to Roosevelt Hospital. He served as professor of surgery at the College of Physicians

and Surgeons from 1889 to 1894 and continued as clinical professor until 1907.[1]

Only three years after Fitz presented his findings on the vermiform appendix to the Association of American Physicians (1886), McBurney described the specific site (McBurney's point) of point tenderness (McBurney's sign) as special diagnostic criteria. The pain on pressure at McBurney's point during inflammation of the appendix is interpreted as a response to reflex irritation on the anterior abdominal wall of the nerve endings of the 11th and 12th dorsal segments. The same nerve segments are stimulated, irrespective of limited migration at times of the diseased appendix from the usual position.[2]

General abdominal pain is often all that the patient will complain of during the first few hours of his attack, and in many cases it requires a careful and pointed examination to determine that the cause of the pain is situated in the iliac fossa. But after the first few hours it becomes more and more evident that the chief seat of pain is at that point, and the general pain then usually subsides. The epigastric region is frequently the point first complained of. . . . The *exact* locality of the greatest sensitiveness to pressure has seemed to me to be usually one of importance. Whatever may be the position of the healthy appendix as found in the dead-house—and I am well aware that its position when uninflamed varies greatly—I have found in all of my operations that it lay, either thickened, shortened, or adherent, very close to its point of attachment to the caecum. This, of course, must, in early stages of the disease, determine the seat of greatest pain *on pressure*. And I believe that in every case the seat of greatest pain, *determined by the pressure of one finger,* has been very exactly between an inch and a half and two inches from the anterior spinous process of the ilium on a straight line drawn from that process to the umbilicus. This may appear to be an affectation of accuracy, but, so far as my experience goes, the observation is correct.

The operative or radical treatment of acute appendicitis, without perforation or before the development of peritonitis, had been carried out before McBurney's time, but it was he who suggested the gridiron procedure (McBurney's incision)—the splitting of the muscle bundles rather than the cutting of the muscle bellies. The operation for acute symptoms was performed in 1888 on a 19-year-old male.[2] The gridiron incision was described in 1894.[3]

The skin incision should be made as already described. The section of the external oblique muscle and aponeurosis should correspond, great care being taken to separate these tissues in the same line, *not cutting any fibres across*. This is easily accomplished.

When the edges of the wound in the external oblique are now strongly pulled apart with retractors, a considerable expanse of the internal oblique muscle is seen, the fibres of which cross somewhat obliquely the opening formed by these retractors. With a blunt instrument, such as the handle of a knife or closed scissors, the fibres of the internal oblique and transversalis muscles can now be *separated*, without cutting more than an occasional fibre, in a line parallel with their course,—that is, nearly at right angles to the incision in the external oblique aponeurosis. Blunt retractors should now be introduced into this in turn and the edges separated.

Skill in standard operative procedures plus experimental study after careful planning contributed to McBurney's reputation and fame. He sought to devise a radical cure for inguinal hernia (also known as McBurney's operation), with less success than other innovations. In the management of dislocation of the humerus complicated by a fracture, he discovered that correction of the dislocation in open reduction was followed by realignment of the fractured fragments. Aware of the inevitable microbiologic agents on the hands of the operator, as well as those harbored on the patient's skin, he began the use of rubber gloves shortly after Halsted of Johns Hopkins recommended them for surgeons and assistants. He related his experience to the New York Surgical Society on March 9, 1898.[4]

April last I began the *constant* use of rubber gloves, and had my first assistant, whose hands especially came in contact with the operation wounds, also use them. At first I thought that the difficulty had been solved, for the wound-healing was remarkably perfect. But in the course of three months there were several imperfect wounds, not serious or dangerous, but positively imperfect. I then made up my mind that my system was not sufficiently complete, for, while my first assistant and I both wore gloves, my other assistants, who handled instruments, ligatures, etc., did not. Since the middle of October, immediately on my return from my summer vacation, I and all my assistants have worn rubber gloves at *every operation of every kind,* and the service has been a daily one of great activity. In private practice I have followed the same plan. The result has been most gratifying. The list of operations includes a large variety, such as for gall-stones, operations upon the intestines, hernias, nephrectomies, extensive breast amputations, thyroidectomies, amputations, resections, for haemorrhoids, harelip, cleft palate, urethral strictures, appendicitis, etc. That is to say, a set of operations such as test the value of methods for avoiding sepsis, and test also the use of the hands and the sensitiveness of the fingers in palpation. All of the cases operated upon, both in hospital and private practice, from October 19 up to the present date, have been carefully observed with a view to the detection of the slightest infection. A large number of the wounds have been immediately closed without other drainage than a small bit of thin rubber tissue inserted at one or at two angles. Solutions of bichloride have not been used in any case, and iodoform has been applied only to wounds already infected before operation and in operations about the rectum. The only douche used has been sterilized salt solution of the strength of 6/10 of 1 per cent. Excepting that rubber gloves have been worn at every operation, and that the hands have been merely washed in soap and water, *no* change in any of the methods or details in connection with operations have been made within a year.

Skilled in surgical diagnosis and in surgical technique, McBurney had a talent for clear exposition, both written and oral; and although an innovator, he remained practical in his selection of cases for teaching. His contributions were sound, if not brilliant, while his presence commanded respect as probably the leading Manhattan surgeon of his generation. Throughout life he maintained an active interest in out-of-door sports. This included sculling on the East River during his student days, and in later years, golf, marksmanship, and fishing.

1. Walsh, J. J.: *History of Medicine in New York,* vol 5, New York: National Americana Society, Inc., 1919, pp 435-437.

2. McBurney, C.: Experience with Early Operative Interference in Cases of Disease of the Vermiform Appendix, *New York Med J* 50:676-684, 1889.

3. McBurney, C.: The Incision Made in the Abdominal Wall in Cases of Appendicitis, with a Description of a New Method of Operating, *Ann Surg* 20:38-43, 1894.

4. McBurney, C.: The Use of Rubber Gloves in Operative Surgery, *Ann Surg* 28:108-119, 1898.

National Library of Medicine

Johann von Mikulicz (1850-1905)

JOHANN MIKULICZ (von Mikulicz-Radecki), sympathetic surgeon, skillful technician, and famous pupil of Billroth of Vienna, was born in Czernowitz, Poland, at that time a part of Austria. His father, an imperial counselor, favored a career in law for his son, and, when this proposal was not accepted, it became necessary for Johann to provide for his own education. This was not an overwhelming obstacle because of a great love and exceptional capacity for music. Johann supported himself at school by giving piano lessons and playing the pipe organ. He received his medical training in Vienna and graduated at the age of 25. The Viennese faculty at that time included Hyrtl in anatomy, Rokitansky in pathology, von Hebra in dermatology, and Billroth in surgery. Following graduation, he assisted Billroth in the surgical clinic in the Allgemeines Krankenhaus, qualifying as assistant and later, as privatdozent. It is reasonable to believe that the musical interest of Mikulicz and Billroth contributed to a firm social and professional frendship.[1]

Mikulicz's first call to a senior academic post was to the chair of surgery at the University of Cracow. He accepted a similar ap-pointment at Königsberg at the age of 37, and, finally, became professor of surgery at the University of Breslau at the age of 40, where he remained until his death.[2] His first scientific contribution on rhinoscleroma was published during the year following graduation. Then followed a series of outstanding contributions, particularly to the surgical literature. He discussed surgery of the nose and throat, radiation therapy, blood transfusions, and selected problems, including the treatment of tuberculosis and hyperthyroidism. An interest in antisepsis early in his surgical career took him to England for firsthand observation of Lister's technique. The use of iodoform for surgical dressing and the employment of a face-mask and cotton gloves while operating were significant aspects of good surgical practice that he adopted.

Mikulicz, like his famous teacher, was a widely respected lecturer in surgery. The presentation was cast from careful observation of the case under study, supported by reasoning from past experience. Any postulates offered were implemented by the fundamentals of surgery derived from laboratory investigation. Mikulicz prepared a treatise for the Chicago exhibition in 1893 on the development of surgery in the German universities, and also discussed German teaching in medicine for the St. Louis World's Fair in 1904. One or more outstanding contributions were made at each of his three senior academic posts. At Cracow he put to practical use a lighted esophagoscope recently invented by Leiter, but Mikulicz failed in his efforts to perfect a rigid gastroscope.[3]

The esophagoscope is an entirely straight tube which is constructed exactly in the manner of Leiter's urethroscope, but larger in all dimensions. It consists of a simple tube of approximately 12- or 13-cm radius, with a stylus, and is closed by its button-like end. When the instrument is inserted into the esophagus, the stylus is wihdrawn and replaced by an instrument for illumination; in this case, this is a flat rod, as small as possible, containing conductors for water and electricity, with a platinum knot on one end protected by a crystal window. If desired, a magnifying lens can be added to enlarge the tissues.

We experimented with a gastroscope, beginning with a straight tube constructed along the lines of Leiter's cystoscope, since we were of the opinion that if the throat and head were in the correct position, a straight instrument might reach into the lower portion of the stomach. We were never successful in this attempt. Whichever way we moved the head and throat, we could never reach the depth of the stomach. In considering this problem, I found this failure was caused by anatomical relations, an opinion confirmed by studies on cadavers.

Also, while at Cracow, Mikulicz was successful in treating carcinoma of the esophagus by resection and plastic reconstruction of the cervical portion. The patient lived 11 months following antiseptic surgery.[4]

All the above-mentioned reasons explain sufficiently why a resection of a cancerous esophagus has not been done more than a dozen times, although Billroth has proved such an operation possible, by animal experiments, 15 years ago; and Czerny performed it successfully 9 years ago. Czerny's patient was a 51-year-old woman, and he resected a portion 6 cm long on the upper end of the esophagus and left an opening through which the patient took nourishment. The patient was still healthy 5 months after the operation but died more than a year later of a recurrence of the cancer.

The operation which I will describe has been done by me successfully. The patient remained free of recurrence for 7 months but died 11 months after the operation from cancer reappearing in the pharynx. Considering that the patient was not able to swallow liquids two days before the operation, I would say this was a good beginning.

On June 10, 1884, the patient was anesthetized and a tracheotomy performed. We put tampons drenched in iodine into the trachea above the tube inserted.

We employed the usual incision for an esophagotomy along the frontal line of the cervical vertebrae, beginning at the superior vertebrae and carrying down to the jugular fossa. I succeeded in exposing the esophagus, which had been replaced by a hard growth one finger thick and 3 cm wide. By retracting tissues and partly turning the throat, we isolated the esophagus without difficulty; but the separation of the cancer from the posterior wall of the cervical vertebrae was difficult and demanded careful ligation. In the upper portion, we proceeded into the area of the pharynx, in the lower portion just above the sterno-clavicular joint, in a manner which required the resection of a ½- to 1-cm wide strip of normal mucous tissue on both sides. The lower end of the esophagus had receded, so that an immediate union of the two ends was impossible. Therefore, I put a few button stiches in the lower operating field and placed a strong rubber tube into the esophagus. Then I filled the wound with gauze drenched in iodine.

At Königsberg, Mikulicz devised and described a procedure for lateral pharyngotomy for malignant lesions of the pharynx, and recommended a simple technique for draining empyema of the maxillary sinus.[5]

It so happened that in the first days of June two more cases of empyema of the antrum were treated by me. In the one case, the empyema had repeatedly perforated the hard palate; in the other case, a fistula has been present in the alveolus of a wisdom tooth for a long time. In both cases I succeeded in perforating Highmore's cavity [maxillary sinus] easily, in the described manner, and the wound healed promptly.

In treating carcinoma of the stomach, Mikulicz was more optimistic than were contemporary gastric surgeons. If resection was accomplished through the uninvolved stomach wall and malignant tissue was avoided in surgical removal, a successful result was anticipated. At Breslau, he described symmetrical inflammation of the lacrimal and salivary glands—Mikulicz's disease—and the Mikulicz-Bloch, two-stage operation for carcinoma of the colon. The mortality at that time in the one-stage resection of the colon was over 40%; in the two-stage Mukulicz procedure, it was reduced to less than 15%. The mesentary and regional lymph nodes were removed with the involved portion of the colon.[6]

The advantages of this procedure are evident. The main operation is shorter than by the single stage method, the peritoneal infection during the operation is absolutely avoided, and one can thus attempt it much earlier on a patient debilitated by the disease. A further advantage is that the operation can be performed in cases of wide extension of the tumor or in deep locations, as for example in the lower part of the sigmoid flexture, where it would be too dangerous to unite the intestine because of too forceful tension on the loops of gut.

Mikulicz's disease, his best-remembered eponymic contribution, was based upon a single case of hypertrophy of the lacrimal and salivary glands. Microscopically, the tissue showed small cell infiltration, which was judged nonmalignant. It is not possible to determine whether this was a premalignant stage since the patient died of peritonitis approximately one year after onset of symptoms. At the patient's death, the glandular adenopathy had largely disappeared, which precluded accurate determination of the etiology. Leukemia, lymphosarcoma, and sarcoidosis have been held responsible for similar lesions in subsequent years. Mikulicz described his findings as follows:[2]

> Both lacrymal glands and all the salivary glands were changed in a symmetrical manner into tumors, which pushed themselves markedly forward from the normal position of these organs and thereby distorted the physiognomy of the patient in a remarkable way. The tumors had arisen gradually; they were at the time of examination of a hard consistency, painless, without trace of inflammatory signs. Moreover, elsewhere there were present no pathological changes in the bearer of these tumors.
>
> The interpretation of this disease placed me in the greatest dilemma, for it occurred nowhere in the list of familiar and recorded diseases up to the present time. Also I found not a single observation similar to mine recorded in the literature. The microscopic examination reveals that the true parenchyma of the glands play an entirely passive role. The increase in size is entirely brought about by a massive, small cell infiltration of the interstitial connective tissue.
>
> It is clear that the microscopic findings alone cannot explain the process. Were a single gland involved in the way depicted, then we would not hesitate to postulate a true tumor. We know well enough that even in the salivary glands, the various tumors of the connective tissue series and, at times, even the round cell sarcoma occur, arising from the interstitial connective tissue. But the histologic finding here does not correspond to a typical round cell sarcoma; moreover, the microscopic and still more the clinical findings speak against the picture of a genuine sarcoma. I refer to the preservation of the borders of the gland and particularly the large and small septa between the lobules of the glands. The histologic nature of the small cell infiltration corresponds primarily to the properties of a tumor of lymphoid tissue. Therefore, one can think histologically of a lymphoma or lymphosarcoma.

1. Sauerbruch, E. F.: Johann v. Mikulicz, *Munich Med Wschr* 52:1297-1300, 1905.
2. Johann von Mikulicz-Radecki, *Med Classics* 2:106-231, 1937-1938.
3. Mikulicz, J.: Gastroscopy and Esophagoscopy (Ger), *Wien Med Presse* 22:1405, 1437, 1473, 1505, 1537, 1573, 1629, 1881, excerpt translated by E. Longar.
4. Mikulicz, J.: A Case of Resection of Carcinoma of the Esophagus (Ger), *Prag Med Wschr* 9:92-95, 1886, excerpt translated by E. Longar.
5. Mikulicz, J.: Operative Management of Empyema of the Accesory Nasal Sinuses (Ger), *Arch Klin Chir* 34: 626-634, 187, excerpt translated by F. Sternthal.
6. Mikulicz, J.: Surgical Experiences with Intestinal Carcinoma, *Arch Klin Chir* 69:28-47, 1903, trans., *Med Classics* 2:210-229, 1937-1938.

National Library of Medicine

William Stewart Halsted (1852-1922)

WILLIAM S. HALSTED, one of the great American surgeons, was born into a socially prominent and industrially successful New York City family of English descent.[1] He prepared at Phillips Andover and took his undergraduate work at Yale, where he showed greater skill in athletics than in scholarship. His selection as captain of his football team when football was in its infancy best demonstrated his physical prowess. Rowing, baseball, boxing, and wrestling, all greatly attracted him. Halsted returned to New York for medical training and graduated from the College of Physicians and Surgeons (Columbia) in 1877, where he led the graduating class and received a prize for scholarship. In medical school Halsted was an assistant to John C. Dalton, professor of physiology. Both before and following graduation he served as surgical intern at Bellevue Hospital. After Bellevue he was house physician for several months in the New York Hospital.

In the fall of 1878 Halsted traveled to Europe for further study. In Vienna he audited courses or attended clinics under Chiari, Fuchs, Arlt, Politzer, Kaposi, Zuckerkandl, Billroth and Mikulicz. In Würzburg he studied embryology and histology with Kölliker and Stoehr and brief periods with Weigert, Thiersch, Volkmann and Esmarch. He returned to the United States in the fall of 1880 and for seven years entered the greatest period of professional activity of his life. He demonstrated anatomy at the College of Physicians and Surgeons, served on the visiting staff at the Charity Hospital, the Immigrant Hospital, Ward's Island, as well as at Bellevue and Presbyterian Hospitals. Graduate courses and practical exercises in the laboratory and at the bedside were organized, and a fruitful period of surgical research was begun.

Halsted was one of the first to employ cocaine for regional anesthesia and nerve blocking; meanwhile he prolonged the effect of the drug by restriction of circulation. Spinal anesthesia was achieved by injecting the drug into the lumbar meninges. However, using himself as an experimental subject, in 1885, his addiction to cocaine brought to an end his clinical career in New York. This turn of fate has been interpreted as a blessing in disguise. After two periods of hospitalization in the attempt to overcome the addiction he was persuaded by William H. Welch to come to Baltimore and work in Welch's temporary laboratory.

In 1892, Halsted assumed the office as professor of surgery in the university and chief of the surgical service in the hospital. In these capacities and for the remainder of his life his personality and performance differed radically from his New York years. In Baltimore, he was shy, relatively antisocial and deeply introspective. He shunned the average student and showered his favors upon his responsive surgical residents. Caring little for private practice, he went full time when the opportunity appeared in 1913. Long hours were spent in the surgical laboratory in contemplation or in experiments on problems that had presented themselves on the wards. He operated only a few times a week and many times abandoned the operation which was finished by his assistants. He conducted unattractive ward rounds for students and was not considered a good teacher or an efficient administrator because he allowed his juniors to conduct the clinical activities according to their best judgment. As if to compensate for the unorthodox performance of a capable surgeon and a distinguished professor, he contributed handsomely to the development of surgical technique, the solution of clinical problems in the laboratory and the design of a residency training program. In the latter, the resident was responsible for the sick in the wards cases, a practice that overlooked the visiting surgeon but which formed a pattern for surgical training in this country.

In the handling of living tissue in the operating room Halsted was meticulous in respect for it but was not a brilliant technician. He practiced exquisite hemostasis, obliterated dead space and insisted on exact approximation of sutures. He demanded strenuous laundering of the hands, extolled the merits of fine silk sutures, demonstrated the importance of the submucosa in the application of suturing in intestinal anastomosis, and applied silver foil over the suture line. Although the antiseptic principles of Lister were known and were available and well recognized, they were in truth, antiseptic. Halstead introduced rubber gloves into the surgical amphitheater, first for his scrub nurse and later for each member of the surgical team. His operation for cancer of the breast and the repair of an inguinal hernia were notable contributions. He was the first to ligate successfully the first portion of the subclavian artery for a natural aneurysm and devised a procedure for the slow constriction of major arteries in the treatment of aneurysms. He was probably more friendly with surgeons in Europe than in America.

One of his first communications after returning from Europe and while assistant surgeon to the Roosevelt Hospital in New York described refusion in carbonic oxide poisoning. A depletory tranfusion in which blood was withdrawn, defibrinated, reoxygenated and returned to the patient, is described as follows.[2]

In carbonic-oxide poisoning, refusion involves an additional factor, viz.: the oxygenation of the poisoned blood employed; and is, therefore, an infusion of the purified, defibrinated for the poisoned, entire blood of the individual.

A 57-year-old patient was taken unconscious to the Chambers Street Hospital where the cannula was introduced into the radial artery. . . .

Through the cannula 512 c.c. of blood were withdrawn, defibrinated, strained, and kept at a temperature of about 37.5 C. in a transfusion apparatus. . . . At 11:32 A.M., 288 c.c. of defibrinated blood, all that could be obtained from the 512 ccm., were refunded through the cannula in the artery toward the heart—centripetal arterial infusion. At 11:45 the injection was completed. . . . The usual post-transfusion rigors lasted for half an hour. 12:35 P.M.: 300 c.c. withdrawn as before, through the cannula, defibrinated and mixed with 128 c.c. of defibrinated blood taken from another patient. 1.05 P.M.: patient's pallor most striking; 192 c.c. of the mixed blood infused. The color returned rapidly to his face when from 80 to 100 c.c. had been injected, the change from a deathly white to a healthy red taking place in a few seconds.

Allowed to go home to Wareham, Mass., about 50 hours after admission. . . . October 24th, have today, 5½ months after the poisoning, interviewed Mr. A.S.G., and ascertained that he has not had a single unpleasant symptom referable to the effect of the gas.

Halsted's law of transplanted endocrin tissue necessitated significant deficiency in the specific endocrine function for the autografts to survive. This was annunciated in his study of Auto- and Isotransplantation, in Dogs, of the Parathyroid Glandules.[3]

1. The autotransplantation of parathyroid glandules into the thyroid gland and behind the musculus rectus abdominis has been successful in sixty-one per cent of the cases in which a deficiency greater than one-half has been created.

2. In no instance has the autotransplantation succeeded without the creation of such deficiency.

3. Isotransplantation has been uniformly unsuccessful.

4. Parathyroid tissue transplanted in excess of what is urgently required by the organism has not lived.

5. One parathyroid autograft may suffice to maintain the animal in good health and spirits for many months and possibly for years.

Ligation of the first portion of the left subclavian artery, then incision of the subclavio-axillary aneurysm was described as follows:[4]

On admission, the patient had an almost spherical, perfectly smooth tumor under the left clavicle. To the touch the tumor was quite solid but elastic and was not easy to feel the feeble expansile pulsation. No pulse could be felt at the wrist or anywhere below the aneurysm.

The next step in the operation was the deligation of the left subclavian artery. This portion of the artery had been drawn down by the tumor, so as to occupy a horizontal position rather than a vertical one. It was entirely concealed by the subclavian vein, and lay below and behind the vein instead of above and behind it. I thought for a moment that it might be necessary to excise a portion of the first rib to expose the artery. Two strong silk ligatures were applied to the artery as it emerged from the chest, and the vessel was divided between them. The deltoid muscle was cut through a little below the clavicle, and the clavicle sawed through at about 2½ cm. from its outer end. The aneurysm, the greater part of the clavicle, a piece of the deltoid muscle and about 6 cm. of the subclavio-axillary vein were then removed in one piece. The vein was intimately adherent to the aneurysm. The axillary artery was ligated at the beginning of its second part. The operation as a whole was a tedious one and consumed 3½ hours. The wound was closed with interrupted buried skin sutures of fine black silk. The large dead space incompletely covered by the skin was bridged over with gutta-percha tissue.

This case is, perhaps, the only successful one of deligation of the first part of either subclavian artery, and the first one of complete extirpation of a subclavio-axillary aneurysm.

Halsted's personal idiosyncrasies were many. He was a gourmet but sophisticated. His shoes were made by a bootmaker in Paris; his dress shirts were sent or hand delivered to London or Paris for laundering. He spent considerable time in avoiding patients and students. While not gregarious he did enjoy a few select friends and associates. He was witty, sarcastic, and sometimes was better appreciated by his understudies after they had departed from Baltimore than when they were members of his department. Halsted's honors include a fellowship in the Royal College of Surgeons of Edinburgh, an LLD from Edinburgh and Yale, and a DSC from Columbia.

1. MacCallum, W. G.: *William Stewart Halsted, Surgeon,* Johns Hopkins Press, Baltimore, 1930.

2. Halsted, W. S.: Refusion in the Treatment of Carbonic Oxide Poisoning, *New York Med J* 38:625-629, 1883.

3. Halsted, W. S.: Auto- and Isotransplantation, in Dogs, of the Parathyroid Glandules, *J Exp Med* 11:175-199, 1909.

4. Halsted, W. S.: Ligation of the First Portion of the Left Subclavian Artery and Excision of a Subclavio-Axillary Aneurism, *Johns Hopk Hosp Bull* 3:93-94, 1892.

Howard A. Kelly (1858-1943)

THE PUBLICATION OF THE BIOGRAPHY of Howard A. Kelly[1] completed the tetralogy of the illustrious men of Johns Hopkins University School of Medicine who built an institution with great accomplishments. Kelly was born in Camden, New Jersey, and lived his 85 years in the environs of Philadelphia and Baltimore. He inherited a deep spiritual insight from his maternal grandfather, a clergyman, and from his mother a lifelong interest in the natural sciences. His father's contributions were spiritual and material—the latter because of his interest in the sugar industry. The University of Pennsylvania claimed Kelly as an undergraduate as well as a medical student. Summers afforded him leisure time for the pursuit of biology and other phases of natural science. A great many hours and days were spent in the out-of-doors. One summer was spent on a ranch in Elbert County in the Colorado Rockies.

Fame and responsibility came to Howard A. Kelly at an early age. He was scarcely 31 years of age when he was invited by President Gilman of Johns Hopkins University to head the department of obstetrics and gynecology in the medical school. Simultaneously he was appointed chief of the clinical departments at the John Hopkins University Hospital. Until he relinquished his academic post at the age of 60, his professional days were prolific in writing, stimulating in developing young men, bountiful in honors, and professionally fruitful as a skilled disciple of Asculepius. He shared a common belief that a gynecologist should be a qualified abdominal surgeon first. This is borne out by the publication in 1905 of his monograph on the vermiform appendix.[5] This followed only a few years his two-volume treatise on operative gynecology.[6] Max Broedel, the medical artist of renown who had been invited to Johns Hopkins from Germany in 1894, illustrated these works.

The Flexner report on medical education appeared in the midst of Kelly's brilliant career. The strong recommendation in support of full-time clinical departments provoked much discussion at Hopkins as it did in many medical schools. Osler as well as Kelly was opposed to the full-time system, athough it is debatable whether the opportunity to collect consultation fees from private patients interfered seriously with the scientific contributions of either teacher. Kelly relinquished his academic post at Hopkins in 1919 and concentrated his professional activities on private practice. His ancillary activities included philanthropy—medical, religious, and academic—motivated by a capacity to raise money from friends and patients for each of these three areas when the need arose.

Kelly's interest in the out-of-doors continued until late in life. At the age of 71 he expressed keen disappointment in being thwarted in his desire to go down the Colorado River by boat, following the pattern of Powell and Dellenbaugh, a half century earlier. The Colorado River is navigable over the treacherous runs late in the spring for a few weeks only. At the time selected for Kelly's party the river was swollen to a dangerous level, and the trip was abandoned.

Many honors came to the "Prince of Gynecology." Probably the most distinguished was the degree of Doctor of Laws *honoris causa,* given by Johns Hopkins. He died in his 85th year, preceding by only a few hours the death of Mrs. Kelly.

1. Davis, A. W.: Dr. Kelly of Hopkins: Surgeon, Scientist, Christian, Baltimore, Johns Hopkins Press, 1959.

2. Cushing, H.: Life of Sir William Osler, New York, Oxford University Press, 1925.

3. Flexner, S. and J. T.: William Henry Welch and The Heroic Age of American Medicine, New York, Viking Press, 1941.

4. Crowe, S. J.: Halsted of Johns Hopkins: The Man and His Men, Springfield, Ill., Charles C Thomas, Publisher, 1957.

5. Kelly, H. A., and Hurdon, E.: *The Vermiform Appendix and Its Diseases*, Philadelphia: W. B. Saunders, 1905.

6. Kelly, H. A.: *Operative Gynecology*, 2 vols, New York: D. Appleton & Co., 1898.

American College of Surgeons

John Benjamin Murphy
(1857-1916)

J. B. MURPHY, one of the great clinical teachers during the maturation of surgery in America and as popular abroad as at home, was born of Irish parents on a farm near Appleton, Winconsin. His father had left County Limerick during the potato famine of the late 1840's.[1] Young Murphy completed seven years of elementary education in a one-room district school with one teacher for all grades; thereafter, he attended the Appleton High School and supplemented his

meager allowance by working part-time at the village pharmacy. He became acquainted with the leading practitioners, H. W. Reilly, first as an interested attendant and later as an apprentice. Access to medical books enabled him to study anatomy and physiology; his curiosity in biology led him to dissect birds, rabbits, and squirrels from the fields. His formal medical education was completed in one year at Rush Medical College, after which he proceeded to intern at the Cook County Hospital, having won first place in competition.

During these formative years, Murphy was fortunate in coming under the influence of Edward Lee, Frank Billings, and especially Christian Fenger, who extolled the virtues of the clinics of central Europe in their years of justified popularity. Inspired by reports of wonderful opportunities in the medical centers of Germany and Austria, Murphy spent 18 months in advanced training under Billroth in Vienna, Schroder in Berlin, and Arnold at Heidelberg. Returning to Chicago in 1884, he entered private practice with Edward Lee and was appointed lecturer in surgery at Rush Medical College.

Endowed with great industry and a fine intellect, trained by great surgeons and pathologists, and relieved of financial worries through marriage to a wealthy Chicago socialite, Murphy's attainments in experimental surgery, surgical techniques, and surgical teaching were not surprising. The majority of his surgical accomplishments were founded upon experimental investigation pursued in the dog laboratory, a shed behind his home where his wife assisted in the scientific endeavors. Although he prepared no medical text and no separately bound treatise, several of his published communications were modest-sized monographs. His Annual Oration, entitled "Surgery of the Lung," delivered at the 49th annual meeting of the American Medical Association in 1898, required more than 50 *JAMA* pages;[2] his presidental address in 1912, "Contributions to the Surgery of Bones, Joints and Tendons," required 60 *JAMA* pages.

Murphy was a general surgeon by definition and performance. He worked in the cranial cavity, the chest, the abdomen, and included the osseous and the peripheral vascular system in his procedural plans. He was the first in Chicago to enter the peritoneum for acute appendicitis, doing so within a few days after a similar procedure by McBurney in New York. In a communication to the Chicago Medical Society in November of 1889, entitled *Perityphlitis,* he described the clinical symptoms and surgical findings of acute appendicitis. Recognizing the dangers of perforation with localized or generalized sepsis, he advised surgical intervention over conservative management. The profession was slow to accept his recommendations, but by 1904 he summarized his deductions from experience with 2,000 operations.

In the development of surgical procedures, Murphy is probably best known for the "Murphy button," a two-piece device designed to effect an artificial anastomosis between two hollow abdominal viscera—a significant improvement upon the technique of Denans of France. The anastomosis button was contrived as a male and female circular bowl to be clipped together after each open end of the viscus was affixed. After testing the expediency of such a device on experimental animals, he proceeded to humans, performing each of the anastomoses mentioned in the title of the monograph published in 1892, *Cholecysto-Intestinal, Gastro-Intestinal, Entero-Intestinal Anastomosis, and Approximation Without Sutures.* By this time, Murphy was professor of clinical surgery at the College of Physicians and Surgeons in Chicago, professor of surgery at the Postgraduate Medical School and Hospital, and attending surgeon and president of the medical staff of Cook County Hospital.

In the initial report Murphy described three cases. The button was recovered in the stool in only one patient, 18 days following surgery. In subsequent communications, the button was passed as early as four days following insertion and delayed for as long as three weeks. The device, long since abandoned, represented a significant contribution to abdominal surgery and undoubtedly permitted surgical intervention in critical situations that would otherwise have ended fatally.[3]

By this, it will be seen, we have two hemispherical bodies held together by invaginating cylinders.

These hemispheres of the button are inserted in slits or ends of the viscera to be operated on. A running thread is placed around the slit in the viscus, so that when it is tied it will draw the cut edges within the clasp of the bowl. A similar running thread is applied to the slit in the viscus into which the other half of the button is inserted, and the bowls are then pressed together. The pressure atrophy at the edge of the bowl is produced by the brass ring supported by the wire spring. The opening left after the button has liberated itself is the size of the button.

This differs from all other previous devices in the following particulars or combinations thereof: 1, It retains its position automatically; 2, it is entirely independent of sutures; 3, it produces a pressure atrophy and adhesion of surfaces at the line of atrophy; 4, it insures a perfect apposition of surfaces without the danger of displacement; 5, it is applicable to the lateral as well as to the end-to-end approximation; 6, it produces a linear cicatrix and thus insures a minimum of contraction; and 7, in the extreme simplicity of its technique, which makes it a specially safe instrument in the hands of the everyday practitioner as well as the more dexterous specialist.

Five years later Murphy published his communication on *Resection of Arteries and Veins Injured in Continuity—End to End Suture.* Although end-to-end anastomosis of veins, lateral suturing of arteries, repair of arteriovenous aneurysms and visceral anastomosis had been described in the literature, Murphy believed that he was the first to record a case in which an artery was sutured after complete division. Proceeding in his usual custom, he tested his skill in repair of major arteries in the laboratory on dogs and farm animals, and at an early opportunity he corrected the sequelae of a bullet wound in the femoral artery in a man. Of his many contributions to the literature, others mentioned are slightly less important: Murphy's slow proctoclysis for administration of saline solution in the treatment of generalized peritonitis,[4] the Murphy drip; his surgical procedure for luxation of the patella, which came to be known as Murphy's operation;[5] and the introduction of nitrogen gas into the pleural cavity for the collapse of the lung in pulmonary tuberculosis. The vascular anastomosis was accomplished as follows:[6]

The adventitia was peeled off the invaginated portion for a distance of one-third inch; a row of sutures was placed around the edge of the overlapping distal end, the sutures penetrating only the media of the proximal portion; the adventitia was then drawn over the line of union and sutured. The clamps were removed. Not a drop of blood escaped at the line of suture. Pulsation was immediately restored in the artery below the line of approximation, and it could be felt feebly in the posterior tibial and dorsalis pedis. The sheath and connective tissue around the artery were then approximated at the position of suture with cat-gut, so as to support the wall of the artery.

A pulsation could be felt in the dorsalis pedis on October 11th, four days after the operation. There were no oedema of the leg and no pain.

Although Murphy attracted many pupils, he founded no school of surgery in the tradition of his German contemporaries. Those who knew him as a teacher described him as an effective lecturer whose clinics were prepared with exquisite detail, under personal supervision. Students were as anxious to see him operate as they were apprehensive of his Socratic pedagogy in the amphitheater or at the bedside. The latter was summarized in his introductory remarks to the 1913, first-year class at Northwestern Medical School as follows:[7]

DR. MURPHY: In our plan of teaching clinical surgery in this clinic the purpose is to get the student *to think,* and to think not only when he is in his seat, but also when he is on his feet, which is a much more difficult proposition. When I press him for words and for answers, remember it is always impersonal; we are not endeavoring to put him in the position of one who does not know, but to get him to think and to get the other members of the class to think with him along the line he is trying to think on. We do not expect a man in the arena to do the best work he is capable of doing. We know he will not answer as well at that time as he is capable of answering on the benches. We ask him questions for the purpose of fixing the attention of the others who are in the seats.

Murphy was equally convinced of the merit of his ideas concerning postgraduate study expressed in his Presidential address before the American Medical Association at the 62nd annual session in Los Angeles in 1911. The address, entitled "Organized Medicine; Its Influence and Its Obligations," included a reference to organized medical societies and specifically the American Medical Association as follows:[8]

When a license to practice has been granted a graduate of a medical school it should be only for a period of, say five to ten years, at the end of which time he should be required to pass an examination or take a prescribed course of study. This provision is necessary to keep the general profession abreast of the times. A few enthusiastic men endeavor to accomplish this result now without the legal license requirement, by attending every year or two a course of postgraduate or clinical instruction, in their own or foreign countries. This would greatly improve the efficiency of the medical profession and the trusting public is entitled to it. This plan is not so novel as it seems, as in both the army and navy services periods of demonstrations of mental as well as physical fitness are required.

The development of postgraduate medical teaching in the country medical societies would be advantageous as an educational factor. . . . No scheme or plan for the betterment of physicians in this country is workable that does not provide for strengthening medical societies—and to be specific—the American Medical Association and its component parts.

Following his early academic appointments, Murphy served as professor of surgery, Northwestern University Medical School (1901-1905); professor of surgery, Rush Medical College (1905-1908); and again professor of surgery, Northwestern Medical School (1908-1916). He was chief of the surgical service of Mercy Hospital, where he conducted his famous clinics from 1895 to his death, continuing meanwhile his association with Cook County Hospital as attending surgeon. Murphy was one of the founders and charter members of the American College of Surgeons and was the first chief of the editorial staff of *Surgery, Gynecology and Obstetrics* and the *International Abstracts of Surgery.* In 1902, Notre Dame University conferred on him the Laetare medal; later in the decade the University of Illinois and the Catholic University of America granted him the honorary LLD, and the University of Sheffield, England, the DSC. In the year of his death, he received the collar and cross of the Order of St. Gregory the Great from the Pope. In addition to membership in several American medical and surgical associations, Murphy held foreign or honorary membership in the German Society for Surgery, the Society of Surgery of Paris, and Fellowship in the Royal College of Surgeons of England.

1. Phalen, J. M.: "John Benjamin Murphy," in *Dictionary of American Biography,* New York: C. Scribner's Sons, 1934, vol 7, pp 353-354.

2. Murphy, J. B.: Surgery of the Lung, *JAMA* 31:151-165 (July 23), 208-216 (July 30), 281-297 (Aug 6), 341-356 (Aug 13) 1898.

3. Murphy, J. B.: Cholecysto-Intestinal, Gastro-Intestinal, Entero-Intestinal Anastomosis, and Approximation Without Sutures, *Med Rec* 42:665-676 (Dec 10) 1892.

4. Murphy, J. B.: Proctoclysis in the Treatment of Peritonitis, *JAMA* 52:1248-1250 (April 17) 1909.

5. Murphy, J. B.: "Congenital Luxation of the Patella," in *The Clinics of John B. Murphy, M.D.*, Philadelphia: W. B. Saunders Co., 1914, vol 3, pp 817-838.

6. Murphy, J. B.—Resection of Arteries and Veins Injured in Continuity—End to End Sutures—Experimental and Clinical Research, *Med Rec* 51:73-88 (Jan 16) 1897.

7. Murphy, J. B.: "Students' Clinics at Opening of Session This Year," in *The Surgical Clinics of John B. Murphy, M.D.*, Philadelphia: W. B. Saunders Co., 1913, vol 2, pp 1061-1065.

8. Murphy, J. B.: Organized Medicine; Its Influence and Its Obligations, *JAMA* 57:1-9 (July 1) 1911.

Composite by G. Bako

Albert John Ochsner
(1858-1925)

A. J. OCHSNER, proponent of conservative management of appendicitis, was born into a pioneer farming family in the small community of Baraboo, Wisconsin, where his father was serving as county treasurer.[1] At the end of the term of office, the family returned to their farm near Honey Creek, Wisconsin. The community was composed largely of German emigrants, with English their second language. In keeping with the current custom, Ochsner attended country school during the winter and worked on the farm at other times. He attended high school in Baraboo and, beginning at the age of 18, after passing the county teachers examination, taught for five winter terms, returning to the farm each summer. In 1881, Ochsner entered the University of Wisconsin, where he completed the four-year course in three with honors and a BS degree. While in college an interest in histology, essentially a new field of scientific development, heightened his desire for the pursuit of a career in medicine. Two years later he received the MD degree from Rush Medical College and began internship at the Presbyterian Hospital in Chicago.

Formal training was followed by a postgraduate year in Europe; there he studied pathology in Berlin and surgery with Billroth in Vienna. Having appeared successfully before a committee of the Royal Microscopic Society in London for Fellowship qualification, he returned to Chicago and sponsored a course in microscopy at Rush at the age of 31. This was followed in two years by appointment as chief surgeon to Augustana Hospital and, at the age of 38, chief surgeon to St. Mary's Hospital. At the age of 42, he accepted the chair of clinical surgery at the University of Illinois, and for the remainder of his career his teaching at Illinois and his clinical work at Augustana were interwoven.

Primarily a practical surgeon, Ochsner was a meticulous operator thoroughly conversant with the principles of surgical management and capable of interpreting these clearly to those who were eager to observe and willing to listen. His written work covered a great variety of subjects. Monographs included: five editions of *Clinical Surgery for the Instruction of Practitioners and Students of Surgery;* two editions of *Handbook of Appendicitis;* two editions of *The Organization, Construction and Management of Hospitals;* and *The Surgery and Pathology of the Thyroid and Parathyroid Glands.* He edited a four-volume encyclopedia by American contributors, *Surgical Diagnosis and Treatment.* Among his many contributions to American and foreign periodicals, "The Conservative Treatment of Acute Appendicitis" is one of his best known. The results of his experience in a relatively short time constituted the basis of the Chairman's Address delivered before the section on surgery and anatomy at the 52nd Annual Meeting of the American Medical Association in St. Paul in 1901. Quotations follow.[2]

From Jan. 1, 1898, to May 1, 1901, I have operated in this hospital upon 565 appendicitis cases, which I have divided into three groups: 1, those who entered the hospital suffering from diffuse peritonitis; 2, those who entered the hospital suffering from gangrenous or perforative appendicitis, and 3, those who entered the hospital suffering from recurrent appendicitis in the interval between attacks or at the beginning of a recurrent attack when the infectious material was still confined to the appendix. Of the first class I treated 18 cases, with 10 deaths, 55.5 per cent. mortality; of the second class I operated 179 cases, with 9 deaths, 5 per cent. mortality; of the third class I operated 368 cases, with one death, ⅓ per cent. mortality. Total, 565 cases, with 20 deaths, 3.5 per cent. mortality.

As a result of my clinical observations I am prepared to formulate the following conclusions:

1. Peristaltic motion of the small intestines is the chief means of carrying the infection from the perforated or gangrenous appendix to the other portions of the peritoneum, changing a circumscribed into a general peritonitis.

2. This can be prevented by prohibiting the use of every kind of food and cathartics by mouth, and by employing gastric lavage in every case in which there are remnants of food in the stomach or in the intestines above the ileocecal valve, as indicated by the presence of nausea or vomiting or meteorism.

3. The patient can be supported by the use of concentrated predigested food administered as enemata not oftener than once in four hours and not in larger quantities than four ounces at a time.

4. This form of treatment, when instituted early, will change the most violent and dangerous form of acute perforative or gangrenous appendicitis into a comparatively mild and harmless form.

Ochsner believed in medical organizations and planned periodic visits to other clinics throughout America in order to observe first-hand their surgical practice. He was president of the Clinical Congress of Surgeons of North America in 1910-1912; one of the founders of the American College of Surgeons, of which he was president in 1923-1924; president of the American Surgical Association in 1924; and an editor of *Surgery, Gynecology and Obstetrics*. During World War II Ochsner served at Base Hospital Unit 11 with the rank of major. He received the LLD degree from the University of Wisconsin and was an honorary fellow of the Royal College of Surgeons of Ireland. Practicing the highest type of professional ethics and endowed with great industry, a kindly manner, a philosophical approach to day-by-day affairs, and a gentle but halting voice, he was quick to command the confidence of his patients and respect from associates and pupils, who came from many parts of the world. He was buried in the Freethinkers cemetery not far from the site of his birth.

1. Kelly, E. C.: Albert John Ochsner, *Med Classics* 4:583-599 (Feb) 1940.

2. Ochsner, A. J.: The Cause of Diffuse Peritonitis Complicating Appendicitis and Its Prevention, *JAMA* 36: 1747-1754 (June 22) 1901.

Composite by G. Bako

Rodolphe Matas (1860-1957)

THIS IS THE NAME OF RUDOLPH MATAS as inscribed on the baptismal certificate in the Jesuit Church in New Orleans on Jan. 31, 1862. The date of birth was given as Sept. 12, 1860. His Catalonian parents emigrated to the New World so that his father could study pharmacy and medicine in the newly-organized New Orleans College of Medicine. In spite of good intentions, the Civil War provided rich opportunities for profiteering, and his swashbuckling father did not pursue continuously his profession as a physician. His efforts were expended in exploiting natural resources and engaging in other nonprofessional activities rather than in caring for the sick. During the first decade of the life of Rudolph Matas, Napoleon III had placed Maximilian II and Carlotta on the throne in Mexico, and the Carlist revolutionists were seeking to oust Isabella from the throne in Spain. Rudolph's mother was 10 years older than his father, an irresponsible parent and husband. The son, on the other hand, developed outstanding traits as a surgeon and medical writer, and was a leading member of the medical community, probably the most outstanding member of his profession in New Orleans for more than half a century. The boyhood days of Rudolph were divided between Brownsville, Texas, a neighboring community, Matamoros, across the Rio Grande in Mexico, and the riverports of the lower Mississippi. He was fluent in Spanish, French, and Cathalonian; his English was acquired in a Brownsville public school. Rudolph contracted typhoid fever while a boy and was treated by his father with a multibladed artificial leech. The scars from this treatment remained on the nape of his neck throughout his life.

The degree of doctor of medicine was granted to Rudolph by the medical college of the University of Louisiana (later Tulane University) in 1880 at the age of 19. A portion of his medical school expenses represented his savings from working in a drugstore in Matamoros. Since he had registered in the medical school as a resident of Mexico, he was temporarily denied an appointment as a resident student in Charity Hospital, open only to citizens of the United States. This condition was corrected only after reference to his baptismal certificate issued by the church not far from the medical college. Yellow fever, a devastating scourge of the South for many years, reached epidemic proportions several times during the early professional years of young Matas. He participated in one expedition to Cuba before grad-

uating from medical school, an expedition which revealed the epidemiology of the malady and contributed greatly to the understanding of the etiology of the fever that killed untold thousands in the subtropics of this country. The National Health Service of the federal government sent a commission to Havana in 1879 to study the cause of yellow fever. The expedition was only partially productive, but just two years later Dr. Carlos Finley reported his studies, which showed that the bite of the female *Culex* mosquito was responsible for the spread of the malady. These studies by Finley were translated in 1882 by Matas, who at that time was the recently appointed editor of the *New Orleans Medical and Surgical Journal*. New Orleans had experienced at least 10 severe epidemics of yellow fever before the disease was stamped out. More than 3500 persons died in one epidemic alone. Rudolph cared for the father of the girl who was to become his wife a number of years later. These and many other items are revealed in the biography prepared by Dr. Isidore Cohn, a devoted friend and pupil of the famous surgeon.[1]

At the age of 22 Matas was appointed editor of the *New Orleans Medical and Surgical Journal,* the first Southern medical periodical, founded in 1844. The masthead read: "Communications relating to medicine invited from every source. Matters of more than ordinary moment are occurring daily to country physicians, brief reports of which this Journal will be glad to get." While editor of the Journal, Matas was called to Brownsville, Texas, to help fight an epidemic of yellow fever. One of the patients he treated there was Dr. William C. Gorgas, later General Gorgas, the conqueror of yellow fever in Cuba and Panama.

The branch of surgery for which Rudolph Matas is best known, vascular surgery, began with the first 'Matas operation' in 1888. He had rejected the operative procedure for surgical correction of an aneurysm recommended by John Hunter and chose instead to suture the vessel wall from within after obliterating the circulation above and below the aneurysm. The second operation for a traumatic aneurysm was not performed until 12 year later. Meanwhile, in 1894, he was appointed professor of surgery at Tulane. The critical steps in the aneurysmorrhaphy of the traumatic aneurysm of the brachial artery was described as follows:[2]

It will be noticed that (1) after the failure of the various measures that had been instituted to diminish the circulation in the sac, (2) the brachial was ligated at what might be called the point of election in the upper third of the arm, just below the origin of the superior profunda and immediately above the sac; that (3) apparent cure followed the deligation of the artery at this point, (Anel's operation); that (4) pulsation returned on the tenth day, and with it all the other aneurismal symptoms; (5) that four days after the return of the aneurismal symptoms a ligature was applied to the brachial at the distal end of the sac; (6) that notwithstanding this ligature the tumor still pulsated and its size remained totally unaffected; (7) that after incising at the same sitting and clearing the sac (old operation) the orifices of three arteries of supply were readily discovered and the inefficiency of the ligatures easily explained, as will be readily understood by referring to the accompanying diagram; (8) the ease and the thoroughness with which the bleeding orifices of the nutrient vessels were sealed by the method employed, viz., *suture;* (9) lastly, the rapid recovery of the patient and the equally prompt healing of the wound in spite of the extensive traumatism inflicted.

Matas was short of stature and if he had been suitably attired he could have passed for Czar Nicholas of Russia. His love for writing shared honors with his love of operative surgery. The latter was responsible for the loss of an eye as a result of opening a gonorrheal tubo-ovarian abscess. During the operation pus squirted over his surgical gown; later he rubbed his face with the contaminated portion of the gown. Infection developed in his eye, and enucleation was carried out three months later. There are two characteristics of his writings. First, he rarely finished a manuscript at the predetermined time; frequently he was months behind the anticipated delivery date. Secondly, his desk was never in order; it was littered with books, pamphlets, reports, letters, and papers. His tardiness in completing promised manuscripts was matched by his failure to keep within the allotted time for his speeches and addresses.

The kudos and glory were his in abundance. The honorary degrees of Doctor of Laws and Doctor of Science were awarded him by five universities. He received innumerable fellowships in medical societies and in foreign organizations. Matas was parsimonious with his pennies but profligate with his dollars. He endowed the library at Tulane Medical School with a legacy of a million dollars. He advised his patients also to contribute handsomely to the university. No one can doubt his qualifications as a vascular surgeon or his dedication to his profession.

1. Cohn, I.: *Rudolph Matas, Biography of the Great Pioneers in Surgery,* New York, Doubleday & Company, Inc., 1960.
2. Matas, R.: Traumatic Aneurism of the Left Brachial Artery, *Med News* (Phil), 53:462-466, 1888.

Composite by G. Bako

Lord Moynihan (1865-1936)

BERKELEY GEORGE ANDREW MOYNIHAN, the only son of Captain Andrew Moynihan, descendant of proud northern Irish parents, was born in Malta, where his father was stationed with the British Army.[1] Captain Moynihan cherished an unusual honor: he became one of the first to receive the Victoria Cross, gained for bravery in the Crimean War. Berkeley Moynihan attended the Royal Naval School with more than casual thought of a military career but, in deference to his mother, turned for professional training to

Leeds Medical School, then associated with Yorkshire College. He qualified in 1887 with the MB at the University of London, studied for a winter term in Berlin, and in 1890, was admitted a fellow in the Royal College of Surgeons of England. Returning to Leeds he initiated a career destined to bring great credit to British surgery. He began teaching anatomy at the Leeds Medical School, eventually becoming professor of surgery. Prospering in the profession, he rose to surgeon in the Leeds General Infirmary. In his senior years he held important administrative positions in national and international societies and for six years president of the Royal College of Surgeons. During his tenure he was created a baron, the first practicing physician since Lister to enter the House of Lords.

Moynihan was especially indebted to three surgeons, each a practitioner in Leeds: A. F. McGill, his first chief at the Infirmary; A. W. M. Robson, whom he first served as house surgeon and later as collaborator in the composition of monographs; and T. R. Jessop, his immediate predecessor as surgeon to the Infirmary and whose daughter he married. In lucrative surgical practice and in the spiritual rewards of teaching surgery, Moynihan emphasized the need for surgical research, stressing the greater significance of knowledge derived from pathology of the living rather than from postmortem examination. He devised advanced techniques in surgery, particularly for abdominal intervention.

His brilliant series of monographs include: *Retro-peritoneal Hernia* (1899), *Gall-stones and Their Surgical Treatment* (1904), *Abdominal Operations* (1905), *Diseases of the Stomach* (Robson and Moynihan, 1901), "Surgery of the Spleen" and "Surgery of the Pancreas in *Keen's Surgery* (1908), *Diseases of the Pancreas* (Robson and Moynihan, 1902), *Diseases of the Stomach* (Robson and Moynihan, 1904), and *Duodenal Ulcer* (1910). Motivated by a deep desire to unify the surgeons of England and those of other countries of the world, he sponsored a new journal for his colleagues, the *British Journal of Surgery*. The initial tissue appeared in 1913 with Moynihan as chairman of the editorial committee. In America he served for the British Empire on the editorial staff of *Surgery, Gynecology and Obstetrics*.

Moynihan's strong body, abundant energy, and a cheerful disposition led to his recognition in maturity as a charming consultant and a preeminent public speaker. His carefully prepared addresses were delivered in a faultless manner without notes. General cultural interests, delightful personality, sound judgment, and enviable surgical technique won him many friends in Europe and America and prompted several invitations to visit the United States. In turn, surgeons from many countries came to witness his skill in the operating amphitheater. In 1903, the American Surgical Association meeting in Philadelphia was honored by his presence; the American College of Surgeons admitted him as an honorary fellow in 1917. Moynihan delivered the first Murphy Memorial Oration in Montreal in 1920 and presented at that time to the American College of Surgeons a ceremonial mace bearing the following inscription:[2] "From the Consulting Surgeons of the British Armies to the American College of Surgeons in Memory of the Mutual Work and Good Fellowship in the Great War 1914-1918."

In Britain, Moynihan is credited with the Arris and Gale Lectures, 1898-1900; he was Hunterian professor, 1919-1920; Hunterian orator to the College of Surgeons in 1927; Romanes lecturer at Oxford in 1932; and Linacre lecturer at Cambridge in 1936. An address on "The Pathology of the Living," delivered before the Ashton-under-Lyne Division of the British Medical Association, was incorporated in a collection of essays published in America. In the preface he presents his thoughts on the value to him of experimental surgery and the importance of learning from living tissue.[3]

The time has come, I think, when the surgeon must cast off some of the shackles by which he has been fettered for so many years. When research into the conditions within the abdomen has been conducted during the course of an operation, the fruits have been judged by the standard set up by the disclosures and by the statistics of the post-mortem room. Differences often of the gravest significance between the evidence offered by the two modes of investigation have not been co-ordinated, or even compared; they have been contrasted to the detraction and the detriment of the surgeon's work. His enquiry has been reckoned as valueless in so far as it opposed the doctrines held as sacred by the pathologist. No recognition has been accorded to the truth that in almost every particular the value of evidence obtained from the living outweighs that which is disclosed upon the post-mortem table.

It is not alone in respect of the pathological changes discovered in the conduct of an abdominal operation that a new knowledge is growing up, but also in reference to the clinical manifestations that are attached to these structural changes. The literature of medicine has been too much concerned with terminal events. It is necessary for us now to devote our closest inquiry to the very earliest disturbances of health so that medical treatment of a condition whose authentic nature is known may be more purposeful, and surgical treatment, when necessary, adopted at an earlier, and in a safer, stage.

From the extensive writing of a successful surgeon, it seems pertinent to quote a triad of commonplace symptoms described by him in differentiating gastric ulcer from duodenal ulcer. He introduced the term, "hunger pain," the first of the triad, which remains a valuable clinical adjunct in the differential diagnosis.

In the differentiation from gastric ulcer there is, as a rule, no great difficulty. If pain after food does not appear for two hours or more, it may be said with reasonable confidence that the ulcer is in the duodenum. I am convinced of the importance of the time-element in cases of gastric and duodenal ulcer. If pain appears early, within an hour or so, the ulcer is certainly in the stomach, probably on the lesser curvature, and to the cardiac side of that sphincter in the stomach which Cunningham has described. If pain comes between one and two hours after food, the ulcer is probably in the pyloric antrum; the long interval of relief is then possibly due to the firm contraction of the muscle at the junction of the storage and grinder portions of the stomach. This tonic action of the sphincter is perhaps more marked in cases of ulcer than in the normal conditions, and it may be that it is protective in character. The period of relief from pain conferred by the taking of a meal is then the first and a chief point to be considered in the differential diagnosis.

Berkeley Moynihan was the most accomplished surgeon in the British Empire during his great days. His skill as an operator and talent as a writer were equaled by his reputation as a teacher. His patients were given meticulous care before and following surgery; gentle handling of tissue was a basic requisite. During World War I, he was first appointed consulting surgeon to the Northern Command and later consulting surgeon to the British Expeditionary Force, with the rank of major-general. The University of Leeds honored him with an LLD in 1924. Knighthood was conferred upon him in 1912; he was made a CB in 1917, a KCMG in 1918, a baronet in 1922, and in 1929, was raised to the peerage as Baron Moynihan of Leeds, an appropriate recognition of his surgical influence and to honor his home, school, and infirmary.

1. Bateman, D.: *Berkeley Moynihan, Surgeon,* New York: MacMillan Co., 1940.
2. Crile, G.: Lord Moynihan, *Bull Amer Coll Surg* 22:24 (Jan) 1937.
3. Moynihan, B. G. A.: *The Pathology of the Living and Other Essays,* Philadelphia: W. B. Saunders Co., 1910.
4. Moynihan, B. G. A.: *Duodenal Ulcer,* Philadelphia: W. B. Saunders Co., 1910.

Composite by G. Bako

Ferdinand Sauerbruch
(1875-1951)

FERDINAND SAUERBRUCH, the famous pupil of von Mikulicz, was one of the most respected as well as most fearsome surgeons of Central Europe in the first half of the 20th century. His significant contributions to the development of techniques made the thoracic cavity as surgically approachable as the abdominal cavity a generation earlier. Ferdinand was born of humble parents in Barmen, Germany. His father, who died of pulmonary tuberculosis two years after his son's birth, was the technical manager of a textile factory; subsequently, his grandfather Hammerschmidt, a master shoemaker, became his guardian. In Ferdinand's early years, as recounted in his autobiography, he suffered more bitterness and frustration than happiness, a fate which may have been reflected by his unusual adjustment to a highly successful professional career.[1]

Sauerbruch studied the natural sciences at the University of Marburg, found them uninteresting, and transferred to the University of Leipzig to begin the study of medicine. Following graduation he practiced in a village near Erfurt, then served on the staff of a Protestant nursing home at Kassel. While in Erfurt, Sauerbruch prepared his first scientific communication on the experimental treatment of intestinal lacerations. This study came to the attention of von Mikulicz, professor of surgery at Breslau, who offered him a voluntary assistantship in one of the outstanding surgical departments in Europe. Although this tour of duty at Breslau was not the first to incite an interest in surgery of the chest, a suggestion from von Mikulicz that a machine be devised to prevent or to control pneumothorax during thoracic surgery proved noteworthy.

He constructed a small experimental chamber for operating under negative pressure, whereby the head of the animal remained at atmospheric pressure. After several successful operations and at least one miserable failure, the principle was judged sound and the device practical. This model for a human chamber was demonstrated at the German Congress for Surgery in Berlin in 1904. While the chamber accommodated patient and operator under negative pressure, the anesthetist and the patient's head were exposed to the normal environment. In describing the demonstration chamber, Sauerbruch referred to a more spacious box designed by von Mikulicz.[2]

The operating room is 14 cubic meters, constructed after the principles of the animal pressure box and made of iron and aluminum . . . a telephone permits communication outside of the chamber. The ventilation and pressure may be adjusted from within the chamber. A pressure lock permits entrance and exit, without losing the negative pressure. Pressure is reduced by a motor pump, supported by an auxiliary hand pump. The head of the patient protrudes through an opening in the wall, sealed with a rubber collar.

Delayed venous return was one disadvantage of the body chamber not encountered in a cylinder that enclosed only the thorax. Sauerbruch concluded that the compartment probably was not the ultimate device in preventing collapse of the lungs during open chest surgery. However, he hoped that it would be a valuable instrument for the experimental physiologist and pathologist and might serve as the base upon which others could build a thoroughly useful machine.

After Breslau there were dreary years for Sauerbruch at Griefswald and Marburg, but finally in 1910 singular recognition of his academic talents and surgical skill came to him—he was called to the chair of surgery as chief of a large clinic at the University of Zürich. To the mountains of Switzerland, dotted with sanitaria, flocked patients in various stages of pulmonary diseases. Sauerbruch's skill in intrathoracic surgery was evidenced by the many successful operations he performed.

While in Zürich, Sauerbruch removed a tumor of the thymus from a patient afflicted with exophthalmic goiter and myasthenia gravis.[3] The relation of the thymus to myasthenia gravis, suspected by Capelle and Bayer and supported by the findings of Sauerbruch, remains an enigma. The photograph of the patient is characteristic of exophthalmic goiter, but the possibility that the profound muscle weakness was an aberrant symptom of hyperthyroidism rather than myasthenia gravis must cause a final conclusion to be held in abeyance.

Unilateral paralysis of the diaphragm and arrest of pulmonary excursion in the treatment of chronic diseases of the lung had been recommended by Forlanini of Italy and rediscovered by Sauerbruch during a thoracic operation that entailed wide exposure. It was clear to Sauerbruch that surgical interruption of the phrenic nerve and physical rest of the lung in the treatment of tuberculosis and other chronic pulmonary infections were logical procedures.[4]

> Five phrenicotomies in humans have shown that this operation is simple to perform and not severe on the patient. Each patient was ambulatory after two or three days. There were neither cardiac nor respiratory difficulties nor irregularities. Even the tachypnea often observed after an injury of the phrenic nerve was absent.
>
> The first patient suffered from advanced tuberculosis on the right side of the lung, with less involvement on the left side. The interruption of the phrenic nerve relieved the annoying compulsive cough, which ceased at once.
>
> Two patients were afflicted with bronchiectasis. A decrease in the sputum from 300 to 150-200 cubic centimeters was observed in one.
>
> In the fourth and fifth cases, both with tuberculosis, the coughing stopped and the sputum decreased after the phrenicotomy.

During World War I, Sauerbruch served as consulting surgeon to the 15th Army Corps of the German Army for several months, commuting weekdays or week-ends between his clinic in Switzerland and the military hospital on the German front. He utilized his military experience and devised prosthetic devices for upper extremity amputees. Following the war he was called to Munich and finally in 1927 was invited by the Prussian Ministry of Education to serve as surgical chief at the Charité Hospital in Berlin. There he became the best-known surgeon in Germany before World War II.

Sauerbruch's personality reflected many of the desirable as well as several of the undesirable features of a geheimrat. He has been described as arrogant, bold, daring, domineering, brilliant, technically skillful, and physically strong; in addition, he was a martinet, a perfectionist, and a popular consultant. Among his famous patients were a young Russian, later known as Lenin, the aging Baron Rothschild, world financier, King Constantine of Greece, and Generals Ludendorff and von Hindenburg. In his autobiography it is difficult to determine whether he was a Nazi at heart or a Nazi by convenience as surgeon-general of Hitler's legions. Irrespective of his conciliation with his conscience, Sauerbruch was interrogated at the denazification trials. One of the judges

inquired as to who would be prepared to speak in his behalf.[5]

> I replied that I thought the countless war wounded and sick people whom I had healed and whose lives I had saved might say a word for me.
>
> I wonder what will happen when I am called before the final tribunal to join the countless legions. Maybe I shall be accused of having paid attention of the major facets of life to the neglect of the minor ones. Will the many bottles I have drunk be counted against me, or the many women I have loved? And then again, I hope I shall be able to bring forward the many whose lives I have made happier by my ministrations. But I shall be very polite, and, for once, meek.

1. Sauerbruch, F.: *That Was My Life*, Bad Wörish-ofen: Kindler and Schiermeyer, 1950.

2. Sauerbruch, F.: The Physiological and Physical Principles of Intrathoracic Procedures in a Pneumatic Operating Chamber (Ger), *Verh Deutsch Ges Chir*, 33rd Congress, 1904, pp 105-115, excerpt translated by E. Longar.

3. Schumacher, and Roth: Thymectomy in a Case of Basedow's Disease with Myasthenia (Ger), *Mitt Grenzgeb Med Chir* 25:746-765, 1913.

4. Sauerbruch, F.: Influence of Paralysis of the Diaphragm (Phrenectomy) on Pulmonary Diseases (Ger), *Münch Med Wschr* 60:625-626, 1913, excerpt translated by E. Longar.

5. Sauerbruch, F.: *Master Surgeon*, F. G. Renier, and A. Cliff, trans., New York: T. Y. Crowell Company, 1953.

Richard Bright (1789-1858)

IT MAY NOT HAVE BEEN NECESSARY to be English-born, Edinburgh-trained, and an associate of Guy's Hospital and responsible for the description of an internal malady to be identified eponymically in medical writing, but, indeed, Richard Bright, Thomas Addison, and Thomas Hodgkin satisfied each of these criteria in the first half of the 19th century in London. Richard Bright has been adjudged the most outstanding of the three. The story of his life, particularly during the years of higher learning and the two golden decades of the clinical preeminence, represents a series of successful accomplishments of a richly endowed and orderly mind. Although his fame surpassed that of Addison and Hodgkin, he was unselfish in recounting his scientific accomplishments and liberal in his credit to associates and subordinates at every opportunity.[1]

Richard Bright was born at Queen's Square, Bristol, in 1789. His father was a successful banker and provided handsomely for the son's education. Following matriculation at Edinburgh at the age of 21, he

Royal College of Physicians

majored in moral philosophy, political economy, and mathematics. As interest in medicine became apparent during the second year when he began the study of anatomy.

After Edinburgh, two terms were spent at Cambridge; Berlin and Vienna were visited later. On his return, Bright passed through Brussels to observe the treatment of the wounded from the battle of Waterloo. A license to practice in London was granted by the College of Physicians in 1816. Four years later he was appointed assistant physician at Guy's. During the next 2 decades, Bright's great contributions to morbid anatomy and clinical medicine were made. He became a full physician in 1824 at the age of 35.

Although Richard Bright was by no means the first physician in modern times to accept the value of a detailed examination of the patient, to record clinical notes at frequent intervals of the natural history of the disease, and to insist upon a complete postmortem examination, these precepts were ever-apparent in his clinical reports. They were the tools with which his clinical investigation was conducted. When Bright entered upon his uninterrupted duties as a clinical investigator, Guy's Hospital, with 500 patients, was considered the best source of morbid material in London. The hospital had been constructed as a single unit a century earlier. Since the patients were assigned to the wards without any attempt at segregation according to disease or treatment, it was necessary to roam the entire hospital for illustrative cases in the clinical-pathological study of the kidney, Bright's disease. Albuminous urine and dropsy during life, together with anatomical changes in the kidney postmortem, constitute the triad. His first postmortem case of chronic nephritis was observed at Guy's in 1811. The first published report (1827) did not appear until untiring years had been devoted in the interim to the clinical-pathological studies. Before this report, kidney disease was considered a rather rare malady, although the association of anasarca, oliguria, and shrunken kidneys had been recognized. Matthew Baillie, wise and industrious at the bedside and in the morgue, reported only one case of chronic renal disease in his experience. On the other hand, Bright reported on 24 cases of kidney disease initially.

Three clinical entities were identified.[3] Although the classification does not correspond precisely with current terminology, it is a remarkable document, as a first approximation. Acute nephritis, subacute nephritis (nephrosis), and chronic nephritis were recognized. Differentiation was also made between glomerulonephritis and interstitial or vascular nephritis. There was a vague suggestion of a malady identified today as essential hypentension. Bright described the glomerular lesion without the advantage of the achromatic microscope.[3]

There are other appearances to which I think too little attention has hitherto been paid. They are those evidences of organic disease which occasionally present themselves in the structure of the *kidney*, and which, whether they are to be considered as the cause of the dropsical effusion or as the consequence of some other disease, cannot be unimportant. Where those conditions of the kidney to which I allude have occurred, I have often found the dropsy connected with the secretion of albuminous urine, more or less coagulable on the application of heat. . . . I have never yet examined the body of a patient dying with dropsy attended with coagulable urine, in whom some obvious derangement was not discovered in the kidneys.

Most commonly when the urine has been exposed to the heat of a candle in a spoon, before it rises quite to the boiling point it becomes clouded, sometimes simply opalescent, at other times almost milky, beginning at the edges of the spoon and quickly meeting in the middle. During some part of the progress of these cases of anasarca, I have in almost all instances found a great tendency to throw off the red particles of the blood by the kidneys, betrayed by various degrees of haematuria, from the simple dingy colour of the urine, which is easily recognized, or the slight brown deposit—to the completely bloody urine. . . . In all cases in which I have observed the albuminous urine, it has appeared to me that the kidney has itself acted a more important part, and has been more deranged both functionally and organically than has generally been imagined. In the latter class of cases I have always found the kidney decidedly disorganized. In the former, when very recent, I have found the kidneys gorged with blood. . . . It is now nearly twelve years since I first observed the altered structure of the kidney in a patient who had died dropsical; and I have still the slight drawing which I then made. It was not, however, till within the last two years that I had an opportunity of connecting these appearances with any particular symptoms, and since that time I have added several observations. I shall now detail a few cases, beginning with the two first, in which I had an opportunity of connecting the fact of the coagulation of the urine with the disorganized state of the kidneys.

The simple test for albumin in the urine—holding a spoonful of urine over a candle and observing the development of coagulum—was one of three diagnostic procedures used by Bright. A decrease in the specific gravity of the urine and an increase in the concentration of urealike substances in the blood were valuable adjuncts devised by Bostock, a chemist-friend of Bright. In the pursuit of his studies on the kidney, Bright left little for subsequent clinicians to add to the syndrome. The symptoms included headache, convulsions, loss of vision, peritonitis, and uremic colitis. An increase in blood pressure and the onset of acute nephritis following scarlatina were also noted.

Bright believed that his work

. . . would not be complete until every disease which influences the natural structure, or originates in its derangements, has been connected with the accompanying organic lesion.

He did not rest on his laurels for his work on the kidney but contributed additional information to such a mission. Other clinical studies embraced his first love, neurology, acute yellow atrophy and cirrhosis of the liver, cardiac infarction with intraventricular thrombi, chronic peritonitis, mesenteric glandular tuberculosis, intestinal lesions in typhoid fever, brain tumor, erysipelas, acute hydrocephalus, pancreatic diabetes, pancreatic steatorrhea, otitic abscess of the brain, laryngeal phthisis, hysteria, whooping cough, hydatid cyst of the abdomen, cerebral vascular sclerosis, spastic paraplegia, Jacksonian epilepsy, cerebral infarction, herpes zoster, and Adams-Stokes syndrome, Bright described a case of Addison's disease but failed to relate the cutaneous pigmentation, weakness, slow pulse, and sudden death with caseation of the adrenals. However, the association of rheumatic fever, chorea, cardiac disease, and pericarditis was noted.

In 1843, Bright became ill and retired from Guy's Hospital shortly after. Meanwhile, however, the authorities of the hospital approved his recommendation that 2 clinical wards, a total of 42 beds, be assigned for male and female cases and devoted exclusively to the study of renal disease. It was a unit for clinical investigation, with wards and a laboratory for the study of patients in a hospital. The "metabolic unit" served a triple purpose. It was used for patient care, patient study, and teaching. Several medical students who worked on the unit with Bright became notable clinicians in later years.[4]

The first experiment which, as far as I know, has yet been made in this country to turn the ample resources of a hospital to the investigation of a particular disease, by bringing the patients labouring under it into one ward, properly arranged for observation.

The remaining years were spent in a leisurely but rewarding consulting practice and travel. As an accomplished artist, he illustrated his early books on travel. He possessed a warmth for associates and patients, was unostentatious in public, and industrious in his profession until his health called a check. He had been aware for some time of an affliction with valvular heart disease, although there is a record of one physician only having examined his heart. Postmortem examination revealed aortitis and an enlarged heart. He died in 1858 at the age of 69, the first and the best-known of the 3 great clinicians of Guy's in the first half of the 19th century. "Bright's disease" is almost a forgotten term today.[4] "Addison's disease" is losing its luster. There are some who are making every effort to relegate to oblivion the term "Hodgkin's disease."

1. Thayer, W. S.: Richard Bright: The Man and the Physician, *Brit Med J* 2:87-93 (July 6) 1927.
2. Wilks, S., and Bettany, G. T.: *A Biographical History of Guy's Hospital*, London: Ward Lock Bowden and Co., 1892.
3. Bright, R.: *Reports of Medical Cases, Selected with a View of Illustrating the Symptoms and Cure of Disease by a Reference to Morbid Anatomy*, Vol. 1, London: Longman, Rees, Orme, Brown, and Green, 1827.
4. Mann, W. N.: Bright's Disease: The Changing Concept of a Century, *Guy Hospt Rep*, 1946, p. 323.

Royal College of Physicians

Thomas Addison (1793-1860)

THOMAS ADDISON, authoritative and perceptive teacher of morbid disease at Guy's Hospital, richly endowed medicine in the middle of the 19th century. Like his famous contemporaries at Guy's, Hodgkin and Bright, his name is identified in specific constitutional deficiencies. Thomas was born of common folk, whose paternal forebears had lived in Cumberland near the old Roman wall, a notable archeologic monument. The village of his birth was Newcastle in nearby Northumberland County. Primary education in Latin was excellent. He became skilled in conversation in this language and later in medical school transcribed his lecture notes in Latin. Although his father would have preferred law, Thomas chose medicine and Edinburgh. His graduation thesis, prepared in Latin, was entitled *De Syphilide et Hydrargyro*.[1]

At the age of 23, Addison began the practice of medicine as a house pupil at Lock Hospital, London. For a considerable period of time, his great interest in dermatology can be attributed to the influence of Bateman, the foremost English dermatologist. A great curiosity for dermatologic afflictions was never lost; the cutaneous manifestations of clinical maladies were described from time to time throughout his professional career. While a house pupil at Lock Hospital, he devised "Addison's pill" (also Guy's or Baillie's pill), compounded from calomel, digitalis, and squill for use in liver insufficiency from syphilis.

The association with Guy's Hospital, which was begun at the age of 27 (or possibly earlier, the record is not clear), was followed by increasing responsibilities for more than 30 years. The first teaching appointment was as assistant physician; the assignment was a series of lectures on materia medica. At the age of 36, in collaboration with John Morgan, Addison prepared the first treatise in English on the action of poisonous agents on the living body. He entered Guy's as a student but remained as a "perpetual physician's pupil." An intense desire to study and examine the patient in detail and in depth was never lost. Sometimes such stern discipline was exasperating to patients and attending students alike.

The best known monograph by Addison describes the eponymic maladies, Addison's anemia and Addison's disease, attributed to a "diseased condition of the supra-renal capsules." The initial communication was presented at the South London Medical Society and published in the *London Medical*

Gazette of 1849.[2] The recorder of the society noted that:

> Dr. Addison, at the request of the President, proceeded to describe a remarkable form of anemia, which although incidently noticed by various writers, had not attracted, as he thought, by any means the attention it really deserved. It was a state of general anemia incident to adult males . . . sometimes proceeding to an extreme degree in a few weeks, but more frequently commencing insidiously, and proceeding very slowly, so as to occupy a period of several weeks. . . . Its approach is first indicated by a certain amount of languor and restlessness, to which presently succeed a manifest paleness of the countenance, loss of muscular strength, general relaxation or feebleness of the whole frame, and indisposition to, or incapacity for, bodily or mental exertion. These symptoms go on increasing with greater or less rapidity; the face, lips, conjunctivae, and external surface of the body, become more and more bloodless; the tongue appears pale and flabby; the heart's action gets exceedingly enfeebled, with a weak, soft usually large, but always strikingly compressible pulse; the appetite may or may not be lost; the patient experiences a distressing and increasing sense of helplessness and faintness; the heart is excited, or rendered tumultuous in its action, the breathing painfully hurried by the slightest exertion, whilst the whole surface bears some resemblance to a bad wax figure; the patient is no longer able to rise from his bed; slight edema perhaps shows itself about the ankles; the feeling of faintness and weakness becomes extreme . . . relaxation and flabbiness, rather than wasting of the flesh, being one of the most remarkable features of the disorder.

The monograph *On the Constitutional and Local Effects of Disease of the Suprarenal Capsules,* published in 1855, clearly defined adrenal insufficiency but did little to penetrate the uncertainty surrounding the clinical syndrome, Addison's anemia. The volume is a slender tome with beautiful lithographs. The preface is introspective and philosophical:[3]

> If Pathology be to disease what Physiology is to health, it appears reasonable to conclude, that in any given structure or organ, the laws of the former will be as fixed and significant as those of the latter; and that the peculiar characters of any structure or organ may be as certainly recognized in the phenomena of disease as in the phenomena of health.

Within a year after this second publication, Armand Trousseau of Paris used the eponym, Addison's disease (*Maladie d'Addison* or bronze disease). There were 11 cases in the 1855 monograph. The postmortem findings were described in each instance. Incomplete clinical observations were given on 4. Five cases would be rejected today as examples of classical Addison's disease. One of the most interesting descriptions was case No. 5, who was admitted to Guy's in 1829, a patient of Richard Bright.[3]

> Her complexion was very dark, her whole person emaciated . . . she had bilious vomiting . . . and occasionally wandering a little in her intellects.

Postmortem examination disclosed tubercles in the lungs in addition to a cerebral abscess, but[3]

> . . . the only marked disease was the renal capsules, both of which were enlarged, lobulated, and the seat of morbid deposits apparently of a scrofulous character. . . . It does not appear that Dr. Bright either entertained a suspicion of the disease of the capsules before death, or was led at any period to associate the colour of the skin with the diseased condition of these organs.

Case No. 6 was an example of vitiligo with pigmentation. The observation of fatty degeneration of the liver in chronic adrenal insufficiency was noted. Particular attention was given to the description of the pigmentations of the skin and the mucous membranes.

The adrenal glands had been mystery organs prior to this time. They were described by Eustachius in 1552, but the copperplates illustrating this observation were not printed until 1714. Casper Bartholin and his son Thomas misnamed the glands "capsule atrabiliarae," in the belief that they purified the black bile in its passage through the kidneys. Within a few months after the publication of the 1855 treatise by Addison, Claude Bernard had formulated and advanced the concept of internal secretion from the ductless glands, and Brown-Séquard had observed the early development of ominous symptoms following extirpation of the adrenal glands in animals. Replacement therapy for adrenal insufficiency was begun early in the 20th century; the effective management of Addison's disease was not available until a century after Addison's initial publication.

But to return to pernicious anemia—in 1872, Anton Biermer of Zürich reported a series of cases on the assumption that this was an original observation. The communication prompted a reinvestigation of the literature and reappraisal of the contributions of Addison and Biermer. Neither investigator had described the condition for the first time. In 1822, James Scarth Combe, a Scottish physician and surgeon, had reported to the Medico-Chirurgical Society of Edinburgh the clinical and postmortem findings of a characteristic case.[4] At least 4 other examples of pernicious anemia were described prior to 1849. Addison never published a separate manuscript on primary or pernicious anemia.

There is ample evidence to document Addison's reputation as a skilled physician in general clinical medicine. Several studies were devoted to morbid conditions of the lungs; in Addison's opinion, these were his most important contributions. Descriptions of sclerema neonatorum, morphea (Addison's keloid), and vitiligoidea (xanthoma) reflected a continuing interest in cutaneous disorders. A case of appendicitis was described in 1839, in a text on *Elements of Practical Medicine* prepared in collaboration with Richard Bright.[5]

. . . he has been suddenly seized with more severe pain, attended with rigors, chills, and sometimes with sickness and violent vomiting. The pain and tenderness become excessive, and extend to the neighbouring parts of the abdomen. A hardness and tumefaction are soon very evident to the hand in the part first affected: this continuing, general symptoms of peritonitis often take place, and terminate fatally; but under careful treatment the inflammation remains circumscribed, and become even less extensive, assuming the form of a local, deep-seated abscess. . . . From numerous dissections it is proved that the faecal abscess thus formed in the right iliac region arises, in a large majority of cases, from disease set up in the appendix caeci.

Addison suffered from attacks of melancholy several years before death; on at least one occasion he was reported to have attempted suicide. The events that surround his death are not entirely clear. No autopsy was performed. Neither the *Lancet* nor the *British Medical Journal* published an obituary notice when he died—only 18 months after Richard Bright. He was never elected to fellowship in the Royal Society; no University awarded him an honorary degree. In perusing the biographical data, it is clear that Addison's superior capacities as a teacher were widely recognized by his contemporaries; his contributions as a clinical pathological investigator were probably not.

1. Thomas Addison, *Med Classics* 2:233 (Nov) 1937.
2. Wilks, S., and Bettany, G. T.: *Biographical History of Guy's Hospital*, London: Ward, Lock, Bowden & Co., 1892, p 221.
3. Addison, T.: *On the Constitutional and Local Effects of Disease of the Supra-renal Capsules*, London: S. Highley, 1855.
4. Jacobs, A.: Pernicious Anemia, 1822-1929, *Arch Int Med (Chicago)* 103:329 (Feb) 1959.
5. Hale-White, W.: "Thomas Addison," in *Guy's Hospital Reports*, vol VI, 4th series, 1926, p 253.

Composite by G. Bako

Thomas Hodgkin (1798-1866)

HODGKIN, one of the renowned physicians of Guy's Hospital, was born at Pentonville in 1798. His father, a grammarian and fashionable tutor to ladies of wealthy families of London, was largely responsible for the education of his children. Comparative philology greatly interested Thomas, as reflected in his skill in Latin, Greek, French, Italian, and German. There is no record of a formal education until he entered Guy's at the age of 21. Sometime later, he visited several medical centers on the Continent and studied under Laennec at the Necker Hospital in Paris. Convinced of the advantages of the stethoscope in auscultation of the chest, upon his return to London he introduced this new device in examination of the patient. Following the practice of Bright and Addison, future associates at Guy's, Hodgkin completed medical training at the University of Edinburgh with the receipt of the doctorate of medicine. The graduation thesis, composed in Latin, discussed the function of absorption in the body. Returning to London, Thomas became licensed through membership in the Royal College of Surgeons, and subsequently (1825) was appointed curator of the museum and lecturer on morbid anatomy. This title must not be interpreted as a reflection of menial responsibility, since the cellular theory had not been defined in the early part of the 19th century. The emphasis upon morbid anatomy and the correlation of structural changes in the morgue with clinical findings antemortem formed the basis of the scientific contributions of the medical teachers of that time.

Under the stimulus of competition to excel after dissolution of the partnership of the United Hospitals of Guy's and St. Thomas', the former utilized every opportunity. The result was the development of Guy's into one of the great teaching centers of medicine in the Old World. The advantages of a pathological museum had been demonstrated by John Hunter to the satisfaction of enlightened physicians. Hodgkin's interest in pathological anatomy made him the logical choice as inspector of the dead. His best remembered, as well as his little known, accomplishments in medicine were made at Guy's while occupying this position. The contributions included the treatise on morbid anatomy,[1] description of diffuse glandular adenopathy (Hodgkin's disease), postmortem recognition of retroversion of the aortic valves in aortic insufficiency, and a discussion of blood cells, prepared with the assistance of J. J. Lister. Hodgkin remained at Guy's for 12 years and accepted an appointment at St. Thomas' only because the hospital of his choice failed to appoint him assistant physician. This transfer of loyalty

and site of study brought to a close the second and most productive portion of his career. The remaining two decades were devoted to a modest practice, manifest interest in philanthropy, and promotion of social reform.

Although Hodgkin is best remembered for the postmortem description of the syndrome associated with the enlargement of the spleen and lymphatic glands, it is not generally recognized that aortic insufficiency was described in 1829, three years before Corrigan's interpretation of the clinical and postmortem findings. The observation by Hodgkin was neither widely appreciated nor generally accepted for a number of years. The correlative contribution, *On Retroversion of the Valves of the Aorta,* was presented in Quaker tongue to the members of the Hunterian Society:[2]

Thou wilt probably recollect having pointed out to me, a few months ago, a particular state of the valves of the Aorta, which, by admitting of their falling back towards the ventricle, unfits them for the performance of their function. The specimen . . . was first observed by thyself, exhibits this derangement in a well-marked manner.

In defining the antemortem findings he noted that

In diseases, of the aortic valves, auscultation often detects a prolonged and perverted sound, such as has been compared to the stroke of a saw, the puff of a pair of bellows or the action of a rasp.

The communication entitled, *On Some Morbid Appearances of the Absorbent Glands and Spleen,* was presented by Robert Lee, secretary to the Medical and Chirurgical Society (Royal Society of Medicine) in 1832. Since Hodgkin was not a member of the society (and never was elected to membership), he was not permitted to appear in person. The communication in 1832 attracted little attention, and it remained for Wilks, in 1856, to rediscover the disease and attach the eponym, "Hodgkin's disease." In the original contribution, six cases from the wards at Guy's were supplemented by additional cases, whose records only were reviewed. There are three, perhaps four of the cases from Guy's, that leave no doubt regarding the diagnosis of Hodgkin's disease. The integral components included splenomegaly, diffuse, nonsuppurative adenopathy, and a chronic but eventually a fatal clinical course. The first case would be recognized today as disseminated tuberculous adenitis. The second case, a 10-year-old male, had been ill for 13 months. He was admitted to the service of Richard Bright. The patient exhibited bilateral cervical adenopathy, an enlarged spleen, distention of the abdomen, and edema of the scrotum. The glands of the neck, when examined postmortem,[3]

. . . exhibited a firm cartilaginous structure of a light colour and very feeble vascularity, but with no appearance of softening or suppuration. Glands similarly affected accompanied the vessels into the chest, where the bronchial and mediastinal glands were in the same state and greatly enlarged. . . . The substance of the lungs was generally healthy.

The mesenteric glands were but slightly enlarged, and but little if at all indurated; but those accompanying the aorta, the splenic artery, and the iliacs were in the same state as the glands of the neck.

The liver contained no tubercles, and its structure was quite healthy. . . . The spleen was enlarged to at least four times its natural size, its surface was mammillated, and its structure thickly sprinkled with tubercles, presenting the same structure as the enlarged glands already described.

Tissues from cases II and IV were preserved in spirits for 82 years and in formalin for an additional 15 years.[4] The pathological report of the spleen 97 years later includes the following:

The general picture of Hodgkin's disease histology is readily recognized, the cell structure well preserved and the nuclei well brought out. . . . Occasional Reed giant cells can clearly be followed. Eosinophilia is absent from both sections. In both occur small foci of necrosis and scarring, at first suggesting the idea of tubercles. However, in none of these are there recognizable Langhan's giant cells, and staining for tubercle bacilli has failed. . . . The cervical glands [revealed] multinucleated cells that could correspond to Reed cells. The tissue is acceptable as Hodgkin's disease.

Case IV was a 50-year old male on the service of Thomas Addison:

. . . not at all wasted, but was rather plump than otherwise. . . . The most remarkable feature in his case was the great enlargement of nearly, if not quite, all of the absorbent glands within reach of examination, but more especially in the axillae and groins Those at the side of the neck were scarcely less so.

The gross examination of the glands showed them to be

. . . of a soft consistence, which might be compared to that of a testicle. They possessed a slight translucence, and were nearly or quite uniform throughout, exhibiting no trace of partial softening or suppuration. . . . The alteration in this case seemed to consist in an interstitial deposit from a morbid hypertrophy of the glandular structure itself, rather than on a new adventitious growth. . . . The glands at the small curvature of the stomach, several in Glisson's capsule, and a large mass of them along the entire course of the abdominal aorta and iliac arteries were greatly enlarged. . . . The spleen was very greatly enlarged, being at least nine inches long, five broad, and proportionally thick. . . . On cutting into it an almost infinite number of small white nearly opake [opaque] spots were seen pervading its substance.

Tissue from this case also was examined 97 years later:

The tissue has not preserved perfectly but one can make out lymph cells, plasma cells, endothelioid cells, and multinucleated cells that correspond in a general way to Reed cells. There are no tubercular areas. There are no Langhans giant cells, no eosinophils (all this tissue stains poorly in eosin). It corresponds, therefore, with the present conception of Hodgkin's disease.

Thomas was born a Quaker, dressed as a Quaker, wrote as a Quaker, and followed the precepts of the Society of Friends in clinical practice and in retirement. Humanitarianism occupied his attention and interests after his service at St. Thomas'. He denounced overcrowding of homes, bad sanitation, "horrible houses," drunkenness, lack of fresh air and exercise, and chimney-sweeping by children. His benevolence extended to American colonization and the emancipation of the Negro. He was one of the founders of the Aborigines Protection Society.

In 1863, Hodgkin journeyed to Morocco on a pleasure and geological excursion. Notes were taken and drawings were prepared at the time, but the monograph of the trip was not published until after his death. The volume is beautifully illustrated with lithographs prepared from his original drawings.[5]

The events that surround his death in the Holy Land are germane to a 40-year friendship with Sir Moses Haim Montefiore, the great Jewish philanthropist, whose wife and he were closely related to the Rothschilds, the international banking family. As in modern times, the itinerary was planned for the travelers to proceed from Alexandria, to Jaffa, and Jerusalem.[6] An epidemic of cholera was exacting its toll in Palestine in 1866. Hodgkin, who had not been in the best of health, was afflicted with dysentery in Jaffa and died shortly after. The possibility of "dysentery" being mistaken for cholera seems reasonable.[7] An obelisk of red Egyptian granite was erected by Montefiore over the grave at Jaffa. It bears the inscription:

Here rests the body of Thomas Hodgkin, M.D., of Bedford Square, London, a man distinguished alike for scientific attainments, medical skill, and self-sacrificing philanthropy. He died at Jaffa, the 4th of April, 1866, in the 68th year of his age, in the faith and hope of the Gospel.

1. Hodgkin, T.: *Lectures on the Morbid Anatomy of the Serous and Mucous Membranes*, vol. 1, London: Shewood, Gilbert, and Piper, 1836; vol. 2, Simpkin, Marshall & Co., 1840.

2. Hodgkin, T.: On the Retroversion of the Values of the Aorta, *London Med Gaz* 3:433-443 (March 7) 1829.

3. Hodgkin, T.: On Some Morbid Appearances of the Absorbent Glands and Spleen, *Med-Chir Trans* 17:68-114, 1832.

4. Fox, H.: Remarks on the Presentation of Microscopical Preparations Made from Some of the Original Tissue Described by Thomas Hodgkin, 1832, *Ann Med Hist* 8:370-374, 1926.

5. Hodgkin, T.: *Narrative of a Journey to Morocco in 1863 and 1864*, London: T. Cautley Newby, 1866.

6. Rosenbloom, J.: An Interesting Friendship—Thomas Hodgkin, M.D., and Sir Moses Montefiore, Bart., *Ann Med Hist* 3:381-386, 1921.

7. Plaschkes, S. J.: The Cholera Epidemic in Palestine in 1886, with Remarks About the Cause of the Death of Thomas Hodgkin, *Acta Med Orient* 16:136-138, 1957.

Robert James Graves
(1796-1853)

PROFESSOR TROUSSEAU OF PARIS credited Graves of Meath Hospital, Dublin, with the initial description of exophthalmic goiter, just as he believed Addison responsible for the initial description of systemic symptoms of chronic adrenal insufficiency. The identification in the first instance remained unchallenged until Osler suggested that hyperthyroidism had been noted in 1786 by Caleb Hillier Parry, a colleague of Edward Jenner. The case report was not published until his posthumous writings appeared in 1825, a decade before Graves' clinical lectures were delivered. The Germans prefer to call the malady von Basedow's disease (1840) in honor of their landsman. Earlier in the century, Flajani (1802) and Demours and Scarpa (1821) had recognized the symptom complex. Nor should one claim priority for any of these observations. A clinical malady with such distinctive features as exophthalmic goiter, which includes tachycardia, nervousness, portruding eyes, and enlarged thyroid, most surely had not escaped the attention of clinicians until the 19th century.

Robert James Graves (1796-1853) was the son of Richard Graves, senior fellow of Trinity College and Regius professor of divinity, Dublin. Robert demonstrated an interest in journalism on two occasions. In his youth he published a weekly school paper; as a clinical teacher he helped found *The Dublin Journal of Medical Science* (1832).[1] The medical degree, with honors, was granted from the University of Dublin in 1818. Following graduation, he studied at London, Berlin, Göttingen, Vienna, Copenhagen, Paris, and in Italy. Graves was as brilliant in foreign languages as in clinical medicine. His faultless German was responsible for his mistaken identity as a German spy in Vienna, and he was confined to prison for a short time. In 1821, at the age of 25, he returned to Dublin to pursue a rewarding medical practice and an enviable career as a teacher at the Meath Hospital, together with Stokes, a colleague only a few years his junior.

When Graves began his clinical teaching, medical students were given little exposure to the sick and were permitted little practical experience on the wards. Book medicine and book surgery were traditional. It was not unusual for the student to appear for the final examination in medicine, having had a minimum of direct contact with patients and with essentially no clinical experience. Neither the Edinburgh system of clinical rounds nor the practice of bedside teaching in vogue in several of the schools on the Continent had been accepted by the medical curriculists in Dublin. Graves advocated reform and insisted that the advanced students assume responsibility for diagnosis, treatment, and care of ward patients—in substance, a "clinical clerkship." Graves judged it self-evident that responsibility for patient care should begin in the teaching hospital, under supervision, and thereby spare the patient the hazards attendant upon acquisition of clinical experience by the unsupervised neophyte. The indigent on the ward suffered especially under the then prevailing system, but the well-to-do did not escape completely.

Three years in Britain and on the Continent provided Graves the experience,

training, and assurance to institute his educational reforms in Dublin. Lectures previously had been delivered in Latin; Graves insisted that English be the academic language. His eloquence in communication contributed to his wide popularity and recognition as an outstanding teacher of medicine. Subsequently he was elected a fellow of the King's and Queen's College of Physicians and at the age of 31, Regius professor of the Institutes of Medicine at Trinity College.[2]

Although Graves is best known for the description of exophthalmic goiter, his clinical interests were many. He believed that his greatest contribution was in fevers, although the difference between typhus and typhoid was not appreciated.[3] Several contributions on cholera were prepared. It was urged that pyrexic patients be treated with food and fluid, in contrast to the current practice of partial starvation. He requested that on his tombstone the statement should be inscribed, "He fed fever." A law was proposed which described the[4]

. . . relapse-periods of ague malaria. . . . This table . . . contained *data* which authorize us in concluding that the law regulating the periodicity of agues applies not only to the succession of paroxysms, but is extended to the free intervals between them—in other words, that the same law of periodicity which governs the disease while it occasions fits, continues likewise to preside over its latent movements during the interval when no fit occurs, and thus the true periodic rate is carried on.

The case I am about to detail possesses likewise several features of practical interest, and serves to shew, that a very obstinate species of ague, accompanied by various complications, may be perfectly cured by the use of quinine alone.

Other subjects discussed included the value of iron and arsenic in clinical medicine, the incidence of yellow fever in Dublin, acidity of the stomach, psoriasis, angioneurotic edema, and hepatic abscess. Attention was drawn to the development of the pin-hole pupil following pontine hemorrhage and the use of the watch for counting the pulse.[5]

The description of hyperthyroidism[6] concerned three cases of

. . . violent and long continued palpitations in females, in each of which the same peculiarity presented itself, viz. enlargement of the thyroid gland; the size of this gland, at all times considerably greater than natural. . . . There was not the slightest evidence of any thing like inflammation of the gland. . . . The palpitations have in all lasted considerably more than a year, and with such violence as to be at times exceedingly distressing, and yet there seems no certain grounds for concluding that organic disease of the heart exists. . . . In one the beating of the heart could be heard during the paroxysm at some distance from the bed, a phenomenon I had never before witnessed, and which strongly excited my attention and curiosity. . . . The well-known connexion which exists between the uterine functions of the female and the development of the thyroid observed at puberty, renders this affection worthy of attention, paricularly when we find it so closely related by sympathy to those palpitations of the heart which are of so frequent occurrence in hysterical and nervous females.

In each of the three cases, exophthalmos was noted. In the first patient:[6]

It was now observed that . . . the eyeballs were apparently enlarged, so that when she slept or tried to shut her eyes, the lids were incapable of closing. When the eyes were open, the white sclerotic could be seen, to a breadth of several lines, all round the cornea.

Trousseau, in speaking of the French translation of the clinical lectures, the students' breviary, noted:[3]

Graves is in my acceptation of the term a perfect clinical teacher. An attentive observer, a profound philosopher, an ingenious artist, an able therapeutist, he commends to our admiration the art whose domain he enlarges, and the practice of which he renders more useful and more fertile.

The scope of Graves' influence as a clinical teacher is reflected in the statement:[1]

. . . the British teacher sits in the centre of a circle far wider than Sweden or Prussia, or Austria or France; his pupils are to be met with practising in every climate, exercising their art in almost every habitable region of the globe . . . to the hardy white settlers of Canada, the aboriginal red skins of North America, the negroes of Jamaica, the Hottentots and Kaffirs of Africa, and the countless tribes of Hindostan.

1. Duncan, J. F.: Life and Labours of Robert James Graves, M.D., *Dublin J Med Sci* 65:1-12, (Jan-June) 1878.

2. Graves, R. J.: *Studies in Physiology and Medicine,* W. Stokes, ed., London: John Churchill & Sons, 1863.

3. Bettany, G. T.: *Eminent Doctors: Their Lives and Their Works,* vol 2, London: John Hogg, 1885.

4. Graves, R. J.: On the Law Which Regulates the Relapse-Periods of Ague, *Dublin Quart J Med Sci* 1:59-76 (Feb 1) 1846.

5. Stellhorn, C. E.: Robert James Graves, *Amer J Surg* 28:183-189 (April-June) 1935.

6. Graves, R. J.: Clinical Lectures, *Lond Med Surg J* 7:513-520 (May 23) 1835.

National Library of Medicine

Gabriel Andral (1797-1876)

ANDRAL OF PARIS, sound clinician, respected teacher, and a founder of clinical hematology, was one of three outstanding figures, with Chomel and Louis, in the golden days of 19th century Parisian medicine. Andral was born in Paris and studied medicine in the capital city but in the interim lived in Italy, where his father was personal physician to Murat, Marshal of the Empire and King of Naples. After two years of study at the lycée Louis-leGrand, Andral enrolled with the Faculté de Médecine in 1815. The first years in medicine appear uneventful until he was attracted one day to the classroom of Lerminier, who was in the midst of an autopsy.[1] The student-teacher conversation was the beginning of a mutually profitable association; but more important, it awakened Andral to the great possibilities of the correlative pursuit of clinical medicine and pathological anatomy—a pursuit developed maximally by the Parisan school of his era. Before finishing formal medical education, he had published several contributions and had begun the compilation of notes that were to form the basis of his *Clinique Médicale,* the first volume of which appeared in 1823.

Three years after graduation Andral qualified as "agrégé" at the Faculté in a brilliant examination and in 1828 was appointed to the professorship of hygiene. Upon the death of Broussais in 1839, he succeeded to the chair of general pathology and therapeutics and remained in the post until 1866. Although an intimate friend and a few years younger than Louis and Chomel, Andral displayed independence as a thinker and teacher. He achieved a wide reputation in his lectures and writings for the analytical description of clinical problems, their correlation with pathological structure, and the confirmation of rigid deductions. He was a firm advocate of Louis' numerical method of case study, referring repeatedly in his scientific communications to figures and statistical percentages. Andral also followed Louis in advocating cold baths for fevers generally and for typhoid fever especially. In his personality and powers of persuasion, however, Louis found a superior.

The works by Andral are clinically significant and characteristic of the best medical practice more than a century ago. His *Essay on the Blood in Disease,*[2] and the *Clinical Reports from the Hospital of la Charité*[3] were favored medical texts in the mid-19th century. The case records were especially noteworthy since they were beautifully presented and highly regarded. His treatise on *Pathological Anatomy* was expanded subsequently to three volumes on *Internal Pathology.* In 1837, his "Lectures on the Grippe, or Epidemic Influenza" contained a number of clinical findings reminiscent of the influenza epidemic of 1917-18.[4] Andral observed that the malady appeared in all ranks of society in various localities and raged with equal violence in the most populous and filthy districts, as well as in those inhabited by the most opulent classes. Symptoms included[4]

. . . cephalalgia, more or less intense, from the onset; . . . and weariness, . . . intellectual facilities presented nothing worthy of remark. . . . In some

individuals labouring under intense fever, a transient momentary delirum was observed. . . . Want of appetite was felt during the period of fever, . . . there were observed very obstinate vomiting and copious diarrhoea. . . . A cough was rarely absent. . . . the skin was burning, sometimes dry . . . dull pains in the limbs. . . . When death did occur it was from the complication of other diseases, as pneumonia, general bronchitis, &c.

The influenza, like all epidemics, was not always accompanied by all its symptoms: some individuals were but slightly affected by it, or presented but an isolated symptom, . . . the autopsical characteristics may be wanting. The influenza is, therefore, a general affection, the nature and cause of which are unknown, as are those of the greater part of epidemics which appear at irregular epochs.

Andral was not content to confine his observations at the bedside; he pursued laboratory studies in blood analysis and participated in the establishment of clinical hematology as a separate branch of pathology. In this endeavor, he enjoyed the advice of the chemist Jean-Baptiste Dumas and the collaboration of Jules Gavarret. Ample quantities of blood for the laboratory studies were available through bloodletting. The microscope was useful in studying the formed elements; chemical procedures were used for the determination of the concentration of solids in the serum and the fibrin content of whole blood. The *Essay on the Blood in Disease,* translated into English and published in 1844, extended the concept of primary blood dyscrasias as well as the effect upon the elements of the blood of nonhemolytic disorders. This led to the integration into clinical medicine of the examination of the blood. In his handbook it is easy to recognize septicemia, polycythemia, anemia in contrast to plethora, and anemia from lead intoxication, respectively.[2]

These three cases prove clearly that pus, in the form of globules, can circulate with the blood in the vessels, and even pass through the lungs from the right to the left side of the heart.

The blood of plethoric persons then differs from ordinary blood in the greater quantity of globules and the much less quantity of water that it contains.

Thus, before coagulation, the blood of plethoric people is remarkable for its high coloration, which is in relation with the large proportion of globules it contains.

The individuals whose blood contains an excess of globules are subject to some peculiar symptoms, of which no one has perhaps up to the present time given a very satisfactory explanation; thus, the vertigo, the dizziness, the tinnitus aurrium, the heat of head that they experience, have been accounted for by congestions of blood towards the brain.

Venesection will certainly modify it, by acting on the blood, whose globules it will infalliby [sic] diminish; but though evidently useful in this point of view, it will have a much less direct influence on the inflammatory alteration which has produced the fever.

Of the Blood in Anemia.

I have just pointed out what may result in the organism, in the state of health and of disease, from an excess of the globular element of the blood. But there are cases also in which this fluid comes to present a character precisely inverse, that is to say when its amount of globules falls much below the physiological mean, and diminishing more and more, reaches a proportion so low that we can scarcely comprehend how, with so few globules in the blood, life can still be maintained.

This diminution, in different degrees, of the globular element of the blood is the fundamental character of anaemia, a condition which, therefore, in regard to the composition of the sanguine fluid, as well as in relation to its symptoms, is the opposite of plethora. According to the degree of the diminution of the globules, this condition is still compatible with a certain amount of health, or it becomes by itself a true morbid state, which may exist alone, or intervene as a complication in all diseases. Thus then, independent of the solids, we find one of the principles of the blood, becoming distinct from all the others, exercising, sometimes by its augmentation, and sometimes by its spontaneous diminution, an influence such as to become the point of departure and the sole appreciable material element of a considerable number of diseases.

When the influence of lead has acted for a long time upon the human constitution, there may result from it the production of a cachectic condition, very well described by Doctor Tanquerel; I have found that, in this condition, the globules of the blood suffer as great a diminution as in spontaneous anaemia, and, as in this latter, the fibrine and other elements of the blood preserve their normal quantity. This effect of the saturnine intoxication repeated or prolonged is certainly very remarkable.

It would be very curious to know whether the globules at the same time that they are diminished in quantity in anaemia, do not become altered also in their structure, and tend to undergo a true destruction.

These excerpts provide ample evidence that Andral accepted the existence of mor-bid states, related primarily to disorders of the blood. Thus, he established clinical hematology as a separate discipline in internal medicine. In his prime years, he rose early and retired late. Not only was his writing marked by a vigorous style, but also his skill in personal communication raised his lectures to a plane seldom, if ever, reached by his senior associates, Chomel and especially Louis, who for more than 25 years held the principal professorships in medicine in the Paris Medical School. Here Andral taught those who came to him from the Continent as well as a number of pupils from the United States who were attracted to Paris, the leading medical center in Europe for postgraduate study.[5] As the 19th century wore on, Parisian medicine dropped from the pinnacle of its earlier glory, and shared honors with the rise of clinical medicine in Eng'and and pathological anatomy and medical research in the German and Austrian universities.

1. Eulogy of Andral, *Gaz Hop* 53:665-671 (July 20) 1880.

2. Andral, G.: *Pathological Haematology: An Essay on the Blood in Disease*, J. F. Meigs and A. Stille, trans., Philadelphia: Lea and Blanchard, 1844.

3. Andral, G.: *Clinique Médicale, ou Choix d'Observations Recueillies a l'Hopital de la charité (Cinique de M. Lerminier)* Brussels Belgium: H. Dumont 1837.

4. Andral, G.: "Lecture on the Grippe, or Epidemic Influenza," in *Medical and Surgical Monographs*, R. Dunglison, ed., Philadelphia: A. Waldie, 1838, pp 143-148.

5. Andral's Death, obituary, *Boston Med Surg J* 94: 313-315 (March 16) 1876.

Karl Adolph von Basedow (1799-1854)

THE TRIAD of exophthalmos, palpitation, and enlargement of the thyroid identified with Parry, Graves, and von Basedow was well documented by the latter, although he was not the first to describe exophthalmic goiter. Von Basedow, familiar with the French, Italian, and his native German literature, introduced his series of cases with historical data.[1] He noted that three instances of proptosis were reported by St. Yves in 1722 and were attributed to accumulation of fluid deep in the orbit. No heed was taken by St. Yves of enlargement of the thyroid. Reference was also made to four cases by P. C. A. Louis (1821) of unilateral

Composite by G. Bako

exophthalmos and enlargement of the thyroid. In 1837, Pauli described a 30-year-old female who showed cessation of menses, irregular heart rhythm, decreasing strength, and exophthalmos following dysentery and prolonged mental stress. Systemic symptoms were relieved by digitalis, but the protruding eyes remained. Several incomplete clinical descriptions of exophthalmic goiter were overlooked: Guiseppe Flajani reported three cases of cardiac palpitation with goiter in 1802; Demours, in 1818, reported a case of unilateral exophthalmos. The most typical example of exophthalmic goiter, antedating Basedow's communication of 1840, was the report of Caleb Hillier Parry of London in 1825.[2] Thirteen cases of goiter associated with tachycardia were described, one with well-developed exophthalmos. A decade later, Robert J. Graves of Dublin described the triad in his Meath Hospital lectures, five years before the communication by Basedow.[1]

Basedow was born in Dessau, Germany, received his medical degree at Halle, and spent two postgraduate years in Paris at the Charité and Hôtel Dieu, concentrating in surgery. In 1822, he established a practice in Merseburg, East Germany, where he remained throughout his professional career. As district physician, he enjoyed an extensive practice in general medicine, surgery, and ophthalmology. Basedow was not content to allow his clinical observations to remain unheralded; consequently, he prepared several contributions on the morbidity of the eye. The most famous was the description of four cases of exophthalmos, with a complete listing of the clinical signs and symptoms of exophthalmic goiter. Included were shortness of breath, a rapid, small pulse, abnormal heart sounds, palpitation, intolerance to heat, insomnia, nervous irritability, loss of weight combined with an excellent appetite, gastrointestinal irritability and, in the female, menstrual irregularity. Excerpts of the first three cases are given:[1]

Mrs. G. became ill again, with a severe case of acute rheumatism, which traveled through all the points. She lost weight, suffered from oedema of the legs, general emaciation, amenorrhoea, palpitation of the heart, fast, small, irregular heart beats, shortness of breath, and a sense of depression about the chest. There was a noticeable protrusion of the eyeballs which were otherwise healthy and functioned completely, although she slept with open eyes. She had a frightened look and was known in our whole town as a crazy woman.

At the same time there was a strumous enlargement of the thyroid gland, presumably the same cellular enlargement that was taking place back of the eyes. The enlargement of the thyroid invited the use of iodine and digitalis. There was, from all appearances, improvement. In the next five years she went through two pregnancies.

Mrs. F., a woman of decided phlegmatic temperament, was subject as a child to articular rheumatism. . . . After weaning [her fourth child in the summer of 1837], her menses returned with only a scanty flow, and then were entirely suppressed through a gross error in her diet. She now felt very weak, had an obstinate diarrhoea, and night sweats. She lost weight; the eyeballs began to protrude from the sockets. The patient complained of shortness of breath and sense of compression of the chest, but she could take deep inspirations. She had a very quick, feeble pulse, a clinking heart sound, could not hold her hands still, and spoke exceedingly fast. She would sit down while she was hot, with naked chest and arms exposed to the cold air.

Her arms, neck, chest, and breasts were very emaciated; in contrast, her abdomen was extraordinary full and fat.

At the neck there appeared a strumous enlargement of the thyroid. The heart impulse now spread out and enlargement noticeable. A sawing sound was heard over the carotids. Her pulse became faster and weaker and the quickness of speech and unnatural gaiety of the patient even more pronounced. She had night sweats of very foul odor, urine scanty and red, appetite always great. Whatever the eyes signified, they protruded so far that one could see the sclera above and below the cornea. The eyelids were spread wide apart and with much force was unable to bring them together, and she slept with wide open eyes.

The pupils were clean. One could not push the tense, bulging eyeballs back. She had to blink often and had a small stream of tears in order to keep the conjunctiva from shrinking, and because of inadequate cooling had eye infections. Her sight remained unaltered except for a nearsightedness present since childhood. The patient now feels fairly well. The first real improvement came from bloodletting and a mineral [containing iodine]. Before that she was given lapis infernalis [silver nitrate]. Now the menses started. The swelling of the legs and the enlarged thyroid disappeared.

In the fall of 1837, the menses stopped again and soon her former pitiable condition returned, and again she was helped by using the baths in *Heilbronn* for 4 four weeks and improved more than before.

In the winter of 1837, she sickened of an epidemic fever attacking the gastric system, survived it against my expectations, but soon afterward fell ill again with all her old complaints. For the third time Adelheidsbrunn worked a miracle, which she used for eight weeks, and whose healing powers she felt already after the third or fourth bottle. The chest, neck, breasts, and arms are well nourished and full. The belly is yet too thick; her digestion is normal, but not her circulation. While her pulse is still rapid and feeble and the impulse of the heart too disseminated, yet she does not complain, after walking or climbing stairs, of shortness of breath, or discomfort. The exophthalmos is not much changed.

The third patient, a 50-year-old male, suffered from many of the symptoms of hyperthyroidism, including neurosis, diarrhoea, intolerance to heat, tightness of the chest, irregular pulse, a full abdomen with a thin body, a large appetite, and exophthalmos. Several medicines were used, including digitalis and iodine applied locally to the neck. First one eye and then the other were enucleated within a year because of ulcers of the cornea. Before the disease had burned itself out, the thyroid had enlarged to a degree that it hindered breathing. The fourth patient, a young mother, had suffered similarly to the second patient; she too benefited from iodine applied to the gland.

A follow-up report eight years later reemphasized the clinical observations and supported Basedow's contentions on treatment, which included the use of calomel, iodine, aloes, and rhubarb.[3] He noted also that Sickel claimed a regression of the exophthalmos with dietary measures and calomel with digitalis and improvement of symptoms with potassium iodide.[4]

The identification of exophthalmic goiter by one of its eponymic terms depends upon the country of one's interest. In Ireland, it should be "Graves' disease"; "Parry's disease" might be preferred in England, whereas in Central Europe, "Basedow's disease," or even the "Merseburg Triad," named after the village where Basedow practiced, has been popular. Such a diverse selection serves to emphasize the disadvantages of eponymism, either accepted or discredited, respectively, by discerning physicians.

1. Basedow, K. A.: Exophthalmos Caused by Hypertrophy of the Connective Tissue in the Orbit, excerpt translated by E. Longar. *Wschr Ges Heilk* no. 13:197-204; 220-228, 1840.

2. Parry, C. E.: *Collections from the Unpublished Writings of Caleb Hillier Parry*, London: Underwoods, 1825.

3. Graves, R. J.: Clinical Lectures, *London Med Surg J* 7:513-520, 1835.

4 Basedow, K. A.: Exophthalmos (Ger), *Wschr Ges Heilk* no. 49:769-777, 1848.

Sir William Gull (1816-1899)

NO PHYSICIAN IN LONDON is more deserving of the title, "Perpetual Pupil" of Guy's, than William Gull. The initial contact with Guy's dates from the age of four, when the family moved to a small village in the Essex Estates, the property of the Thomas Guy's Foundation.[1] William's father, a barge owner and wharfinger, died ten years after William's birth (1816) and left the family in meager circumstances. The widow, a remarkable person, capable and industrious, devoted her life to the care of her fatherless children. William attended the parish school after outgrowing the Dame's school in the village. The influence of the rector, a nephew of Benjamin Harrison and treasurer of Guy's, was fortuitous. Harrison, who ruled the hospital as a beneficent despot

Composite by G. Bako

for 50 years, had much to do in furthering William's medical career. He was encouraged to attend lectures on botany, chemistry, and other premedical subjects, meanwhile learning Greek and mathematics by self-instruction. When William was 21, Harrison created a position for him in the counting-house of the hospital. Thus, his full-time activities at Guy's began. They were continued without interruption until 11 years later, when he married and moved to a home in Finsbury Square.

The initial assignment at the hospital was the cataloguing of the items in the museum that had been prepared by the fine hand of Thomas Hodgkin, the first curator and demonstrator of morbid anatomy in the medical school.[2] This position provided living quarters in the hospital and a salary of £15 per year. At the age of 22, Gull matriculated at the newly founded University of London and became a "perpetual pupil" at Guy's. The duties attendant upon the ap-

pointment represented a significant step in advance of the then common practice of apprenticeship, which demanded little more than menial service at the discretion of the senior physician in the hospital. As a "perpetual pupil," Gull had free access to the clinical material in the wards (similar to a house pupil in the teaching hospital today), meanwhile pursuing formal training in the medical school. An apt scholar, he was awarded most of the hospital prizes. In 1841, the bachelor of medicine degree was granted, with honors in physiology, medicine, and surgery. This was followed by a teaching appointment in materia medica, a lectureship in natural philosophy, and assignment as librarian and medical tutor. The hospital apothecary shared with Gull the care of the patients on the mental ward when the staff members were absent.

The opportunity for a young physician to live with the sick in the hospital day and night, seven days a week, meanwhile entrusted with substantial responsibilities is given to a select few only in any period of medical education. Gull was then a single man without financial or family obligations, a condition which sometimes interferes with complete devotion to clinical medicine. Had he been a student of lesser intellect, the results might have been less fruitful. Fortunately the blending of early advantages, great industry, and a fine intellect enabled Gull to absorb the maximum from the clinical experience. The building stones were well selected—broad and solid. The superstructure could become as vast as clinical medicine permitted in the mid-19th century. Although Gull displayed a singleness of purpose in his professional goal, his interests were many. Leisure time was devoted to some of the great English writers; Shakespeare, Milton, and George Herbert were favorites. Philosophical polemics were to his liking; a ready wit was one of his charms.

At the age of 30, Gull was awarded the doctorate in medicine and a gold medal for the thesis. Appointment as a lecturer in physiology was but a step to the professorship in this subject. The following year he was elected Fullerian professor of physiology at the Royal Institution, simultaneously with Michael Faraday, the contemporary Fullerian professor of chemistry. Other appointments at Guy's were accepted in due time and subsequently the title of full physician in 1858.

Gull's contributions, published mainly in *Guy's Hospital Reports,* contain original observations and cover a variety of clinical subjects. The first published contribution on xanthoma or xanthelasma was prepared with Thomas Addison. Intermittent hematuria was described; excellent results were reported in treating tapeworm with oil of male fern. The arteriocapillary fibrosis of the parenchyma of the kidney in chronic Bright's disease was described, with Sutton as co-author. The communication purported to show that the peripheral vascular system was affected in chronic nephritis and that the malady was not exclusively a local affliction of the kidney. Several reports on neurologic conditions were published. Histological changes in the cord in tabes dorsalis were recognized. One controversy with Brown-Séquard, in which Gull subsequently was proved correct, concerned reflex paraplegia. Gull submitted that paralytic symptoms following disorders of the bladder must be accompanied by histological changes in the spinal cord. He was one of the first to describe anorexia nervosa and was especially interested in hypochondriasis, "a healthy man out of health." Fatty stools in pancreatic disease were recognized. His last important work, "On a Cretinoid State supervening in Adult Life in Women," was one of the first definitive studies of myxedema. The descriptive term selected by Gull even today has certain advantages over the contemporary designation given it by Ord shortly after.[3] The first of five patients discussed by Gull presented the following.[4]

Miss B., after the cessation of the catamenial period, became insensibly more and more languid, with general increase of bulk. This change went on from year to year, her face altering from oval to round, much like the full moon at rising. with a complexion soft and fair, the skin presenting a peculiarly smooth and fine texture was almost porcelainous in aspect, the cheeks tinted of a delicate rose-purple, the cellular tissue under the eyes being loose and folded, and that under the jaws and in the neck becoming heavy, thickened, and folded. The lips large and of a rose-purple, alae nasi thick, cornea and pupil of the eye normal, but the distance between the eyes appearing disproportionately wide, and the rest of the nose depressed, given the whole face a flattened broad character. The hair flaxen and soft, the whole expression of the face remarkably placid. The tongue broad and thick, voice guttural, and the pronunciation as if the tongue were too large for the mouth (cretinoid). The hands peculiarly broad and thick, spade-like, as if the whole textures were infiltrated. The integuments of the chest and abdomen loaded with subcutaneous fat. The upper and lower extremities also large and fat, with slight traces of oedema over the tibiae, but this not distinct, and pitting doubtfully on pressure.

Gull was a "fashionable physician." His extensive private practice included the carriage trade, beginning with the Prince of Wales, who was later to be King Edward VII. Together with William Jenner, he treated the Prince, critically ill with typhoid fever. The hours spent at the royal bedside reflected his philosophy in the care of any patient, irrespective of the stratum of society. Never hurried in a clinical examination, he displayed a fine faculty for creating the appearance of unlimited time and undivided attention to the case under consideration. Such exemplary skill and art was infectious. Similarly, his lectures in the classroom achieved the same degree of excellence as his bedside care and bedside teaching. The need for clinical investigation and the opportunities for advancement in medicine were readily apparent to Gull. He advocated vivisection and took a firm stand against the fanatical zoophilists.[5]

There is no doubt that physiological experiments are useful, useful for animals as well as for man. They are therefore justifiable. . . . Nothing is so cruel as ignorance. . . . How many are now dying of tubercle and scrofula whom a better knowledge of their conditions might rescue? Yet the pursuit of this knowledge is hindered in England by the outcry of cruelty—the cruelty being no more than the inoculation of some of the lower animals with tubercular and scrofulous matter, in order to study the course of the disease and the modes of prevention. The cruelty obviously lies, not in performing these experiments, but in the hindering of progressive knowledge.

The accusation against Gull of therapeutic nihilism has little foundation. The acumen of a skillful physician leads him to differentiate effective therapeutic agents from placebos. Gull was keenly aware that the[5]

. . . great truth that diseases are but perverted life processes, and have for their natural history, not only a beginning, but equally a period of culmination and decline.

He recommended mint water in the treatment of acute rheumatic fever, not as a therapeutic agent, but as a placebo. A sick man was a patient with a disease, not a disease in a patient. Such a concept is emphasized currently. It is probably as old as the practice of thoughtful clinical medicine, it was paraphrased by Francis Peabody[6] in his memorable essay: "The secret of the care of the patient is in caring for the patient."

Many honors came to Gull. The universities of Oxford, Cambridge, and Edinburgh awarded him honorary degrees. He was a member of the General Medical Council and the first physician to sit on the Senate of the University of London. He was a fellow of the Royal Society, and although elected a fellow of the Royal College of Physicians, was never its president. After the recovery of the Prince of Wales, he was knighted by Queen Victoria.

Pleasant holidays were spent in the Highlands of Scotland. Two years before his death (1890) he suffered a mild stroke followed by others. With the first he abandoned the practice of medicine for he did not judge himself clinically competent after this morbid affliction. He was buried in the churchyard of his childhood home, a great physician of England and a leader at Guy's in the 19th century. The memorial tablet in the chapel at Guy's records that[7]

. . . as a teacher, few have exceeded him in the depth and accuracy of his knowledge, in the lucidity and terseness of his language, in the effect produced upon his hearers. As a physician, his almost instinctive insight, his unwearied patience, his exact method and ready resources, and, above all, that hearty sympathy, which seemed concentrated for the time on each patient, placed him in the highest rank in the noble band of British physicians.

1. Wilks, S., and Bettany, G. T.: *A Biographical History of Guy's Hospital*, London: Ward, Lock, Bowden & Co., 1892, pp 261-274.

2. In Memoriam: Sir William Gull, ed. N. Davies-Colley, and W. H. White, *Guy Hosp Rep* 47:xxv-xliii, 1890.

3. Ord, W. M.: On Myxoedema, *Med-Chir Trans* 61:57-78, 1878.

4. Gull, W. W.: On a Cretinoid State supervening in Adult Life in Women, *Trans clin Soc London:* 7:180-185, 1873.

5. Sir William Gull, *Brit Med J* 1:256-262 (Jan.-June) 1890.

6. Peabody, F. W.: *Doctor and Patient*, New York: MacMillan Company, 1930.

7. Leaders in Modern Medicine, III: Sir William Gull, *Practitioner* 79:703-714 (Nov.) 1907.

National Library of Medicine

Robert Adams (1791-1875)

ROBERT ADAMS, best remembered for his contributions in internal medicine; was a member of the surgical group of the great Irish school of medicine in the 19th century. In his native city of Dublin he received his general education and in 1810 entered Trinity College.[1] Combining an apprenticeship in medicine with a liberal schooling, he studied first under William Hartigan, leading surgeon of Dublin, and later with George Stewart, surgeon-general to the English army in Ireland. After receiving the AB degree in 1814, he visited surgical clinics on the Continent. Adams continued his primary interest in surgery, becoming a licentiate of the Irish College of Surgeons in 1815, and a member of the Royal College of Surgeons in Ireland in 1828. He received the MA in 1832 and the MD in 1842 from Dublin University. His hospital affiliations included the Jervis-street Hospital and later the Richmond Hospital, where he served on the surgical staff.

Adams wrote on tumors, fractures and dislocations, hernia, and diseases of the bones and joints, and contributed major sections to Todd's *Cyclopaedia of Anatomy and Physiology*. In medicine he discussed pneumonia, peptic ulcer, apoplexy, vascular disorders, and cutaneous diseases. Outstanding in popular appeal was his *Treatise on Rheumatic Gout* (rehumatoid arthritis),[2] from which he was a sufferer; however, his most important scientific contributions were made in cardiology and the postmortem examination of patients suffering from various cardiac disorders. He associated cerebral symptoms and slowing of the pulse with cardiac disease, as Morgagni before him had done, a phenomenon confirmed two decades later by William Stokes, also a Dublin physician—hence the triple eponym, the Morgagni-Adams-Stokes syndrome.

In a 100-page monograph in the *Dublin Hospital Reports and Communications in Medicine and Surgery* of 1827, Adams presented three important clinical-pathological observations in a series of patients suffering from heart disease. The first excerpt contains significant pathological findings from patients with seizures and a slow pulse, observed when partial auriculoventricular heart block is approaching completion and less frequently in instances of established complete heart block. The second excerpt further discloses his expertness as a clinical cardiologist. Being aware that cardiac incompetence from pericardial adhesions may lead to myocardial hypertrophy, he postulated that pericardial adhesions may stimulate muscular hypertrophy from augmented nutrition through increased vascularity. The third excerpt presents his findings on sclerosis of the coronary vessels in patients with angina pectoris. Adams, however, did not correlate clinical symptoms that we now associate with coronary artery disease and myocardial infarction.[3]

An officer in the revenue, aged 68 years . . . was just then recovering from the effects of an apoplectic attack, which had suddenly seized him three days before. He was well enough to be about his house, and even to go out. But he was oppressed by stupor, having a constant disposition to sleep, and still a very troublesome cough. What most attracted my attention was, the irregularity of his breathing, and remarkable slowness of the pulse, which generally ranged at the rate of 30 in a minute. Mr. Duggan informed me that he had been in almost continual attendance on this gentleman for the last seven years; and that during that period he had seen him, he is quite certain, in not less than twenty apoplectic attacks. Before each of them he was observed, for a day or two, heavy and lethargic, with loss of memory. He would then fall down in a state of complete insensibility, and was on several occasions hurt by the fall. When they attacked him, his pulse would become even slower than usual; his breathing loudly stertorous.

November 4th, 1819, he was suddenly seized with an apopletic attack, which in two hours carried him off, before the arrival of his medical attendant.
. . . apoplexy must be considered less a disease in itself than symptomatic of one, the organic seat of which was in the heart; although during life there was much analogy in their symptoms, the examination of the bodies after death disclosed . . . fat had so accumulated at the expense of the muscular structure, that it was scarcely a line in depth. The explanation of the fact how causes so different could have produced effects nearly similar, will, I imagine, be found in the reflection, that anything occasioning an undue distention of the vessels of the brain, may be followed by apoplexy. This over distention may arise from the impulse a tergo being preternaturally strong, or on the contrary, it may be the result of some obstruction in front, as that arising from a contracted arterial opening, or some state of the ventricle incapacitating it from emptying itself with sufficient quickness to relieve the brain. Indeed, upon considering the latter condition of things, where the heart is slow in transmitting the blood it receives, we find, I imagine, even in this a means of accounting for the lethargy, loss of memory, and vertigo.

No. 11.—Case of Active Enlargement of the Heart without any Valvular Disease.
Although we do not unusually find the heart enlarged where the pericardium is adherent to it this has never been, as far as I know, referred to, as a cause of its inordinate growth; yet when we reflect that in the natural state the heart has no vascular connexion with the surrounding organs, and is only supplied with two small arteries, we can readily conceive what a new impulse its

nutrition must derive from the immense number of vessels which from the adherent pericardium will pass directly into the muscular substance of the heart. Under such circumstances we may as fairly attribute enlargement of the heart to the pericardum, as the unlimited growth of a tumor to the organised cyst which contains it.

Case of Complete Ossification of the Coronary Arteries of the Heart and of the Aortic Valves.

A gentleman, aetat. 68, of a pallid countenance, yet full and corpulent, while exerting himself in arranging some books on a high shelf in a library, suddenly felt severe pain in his chest, extending down his right arm, accompanied by a sensation of numbness; his sight became dim, he had vertigo, but did not fall. From that moment his breathing became oppressed, and in a little time he discovered that his pulse, which was unaccountably weak in his left arm, was altogether imperceptible in the right.

On the following day, the 18th of October, he had still further grounds for alarm; the most careful examination could not detect the least pulsation in any artery in the body; nor was the movement of the heart sensible to the hand laid over the breast; an obscure undulating motion could alone be heard when the ear was for some moments attentively applied to the side of the thorax.

Dissection.

The body was examined the following day. The heart was large, flabby, and of a yellow color from fatty deposition; all its cavities were distended with fluid blood; the semilunar valves of the aorta were completely ossified; but this bony or earthy deposition was not confined to the aorta; it extended to the coronary arteries, which were so completely converted into bone as to be quite solid, having no perceptible cavity except at the distance of an inch from their origin; beyond this these vessels were at intervals completely interrupted by small bony specks.

The syncope which occurs in angina pectoris (an irregular form of which this case is to be considered) I am aware has been ascribed to a temporary spasm of the organ. . . . But while I would suggest that the total failure of the pulse in this instance might have resulted from the defective nutrition and paralysis of the heart, I am not at the same time disinclined to admit that the state of the semilunar valves of the aorta, *in combination* with the ossified condition of the coronary vessels, might have greatly contributed to impede the circulation or rather suppress the pulse; indeed it is evident that there must have been something mechanical in the cause which thus impeded the action of the heart.

Adams was a popular lecturer, well versed in the medicine and surgery of the Continent, and a gregarious person in professional society. He is described as being completely honest in his clinical work. Together with Kirby and Read he founded the Peter-Street School of Medicine; later he dissociated himself and founded the Richmond (subsequently called the Carmichael) School of Medicine and Surgery. The Royal College of Surgeons chose him as their president for three terms, and the Dublin Pathological Society for one term. At the age of 70, Adams was appointed surgeon to Queen Victoria and regius professor of surgery in the University of Dublin.

1. Robert Adams, M.A., M.D., obituary, *Lancet* 1: 145 (Jan 23) 1875.
2. Adams, R.: *A Treatise on Rheumatic Gout, or Chronic Rheumatic Arthritis of All the Joints,* London: J. Churchill, 1857.
3. Adams, R.: Cases of Diseases of the Heart, Accompanied With Pathological Observations, *Dublin Hosp Rep* 4:353-453, 1827.

Composite by G. Bako

James Hope (1801-1841)

THE HOPE OF CARDIOLOGY,[1] London teacher and consultant in diseases of the heart, was born at Stockport, Cheshire, into a wealthy merchant's family, whose fortune affected neither his industry nor his ultimate professional attainments.[2] Unfortunately, a familial incidence of tuberculosis paved the way to an early death. After attending grammar school Hope lived in Oxford for a time, but never was a member of the University. Before settling on medicine, the practice of law held some appeal, and, during the period of indecision, he enlisted in the Yeomanry Lancers and became expert in the lance and the broadsword. At the age of 19, Hope enrolled in the University of Edinburgh where he spent five years; as evidence of his talents and esteem, he served as one of the presidents of the Royal Medical Society of Edinburgh, as well as house physician and house surgeon at the Royal Infirmary. His inaugural dissertation for the MD degree, aneurysm of the aorta, was evidence of a life-long scientific concern for the heart and great vessels. With formal training over, he returned to London, and specifically St. Bartholomew's Hospital, where he qualified for the diploma of the Royal College of Suregons.

The appeal of amenities on the Continent and the methods of teaching medicine drew Hope to Paris. There he became fluent in French, cultivated auscultation at la Charité, and pursued a clinical clerkship in pathological anatomy under Chomel. Then visiting the hospitals in Rome and Florence he added Italian to his language repertory, and completed a two-year postgraduate tour. Upon return to London he satisfied the criteria as a licentiate of the College of Physicians, enrolled as a pupil at St. George's Hospital, and entered into the practice of medicine. He lectured to practitioners privately and to students at St. George's Hospital and subsequently became full physician. The interruption of this assignment because of the contraction of pulmonary tuberculosis, left him with periods of inactivity and led to his death at the age of 40. In the score of years in medicine, however, Hope accomplished much, including election to the Royal Society at the age of 31 and the preparation of two outstanding monographs, the first on cardiovascular diseases, the second on morbid anatomy. While studying in Edinburgh, he began a series of drawings on morbid anatomy—some colored, others in black and white. These and others were reproduced in his *Principles*

and Illustrations of Morbid Anatomy which appeared in 1834.[3] The colored lithographs are exceptional, albeit of limited practical value a century and more later. They were of equal quality with those in Carswell's work of 1830 and did not suffer in comparison with those in Cruveilhier's treatise of 1842.

The first edition of Hope's *A Treatise on the Diseases of the Heart and Great Vessels*[4] was extensively revised in 1835 and again in 1839, with additional evidence in support of the clinical deductions. The first American edition, prepared by Pennock from the third London edition, appeared posthumously in 1842.[5] The passages on cardiac asthma, aortic regurgitation, and mitral insufficiency are excerpted from this edition. Hope's cardiology was based upon bedside observations, physiological experiments, and extensive knowledge of pathological anatomy. He chose the wise policy of accepting the best from his predecessors and contemporaries in the interpretation of sounds of the heart and structural changes in the great vessels. The passage on cardiac asthma, clinically distinguishable from bronchial asthma, contains a dramatic and vivid portrayal of a patient in critical air hunger.[5]

Amongst the diseases of the heart may be justly reckoned one of the forms of the malady termed in common language *asthma*. This has been too much regarded as independent of disease of the heart. Long treatises have even been written upon it without ever mentioning disease of this organ as one of its causes.

From all that has been said, we are now led to the resulting inquiry—what is the essential difference between asthma from disease of the heart and that from disease of the lungs.

The respiration [in severe asthma from disease of the heart], always short, becomes hurried and laborious on the slightest exertion or mental emotion. The effort of ascending a staircase is peculiarly distressing. The patient stops abruptly, grasps at the first object that presents itself, and fixing the upper extremities in order to afford a fulcrum for the muscles of respiration, gasps with an aspect of extreme distress.

Incapable of lying down, he is seen for weeks, and even for months together, either reclining in the semi-erect posture supported by pillows, or sitting with the trunk bent forwards and the elbows or fore-arms resting on the drawn-up knees. The latter position he assumes when attacked by a paroxysm of dyspnoea—sometimes, however, extending the arms against the bed on either side, to afford a firmer fulcrum for the muscles of respiration. With eyes widly expanded and starting, eye-brows raised, nostrils dilated, a ghastly and haggard countenance, and the head thrown back at every inspiration, he casts round a hurried, distracted look of horror; of anguish, and of supplication; now imploring, in plaintive moans, or quick, broken accents, and half-stifled voice, the assistance already often lavished in vain; now upbraiding the impotency of medicine; and now, in an agony of despair, drooping his head on his chest, and muttering a fervent invocation for death to put a period to his sufferings. For a few hours—perhaps only for a few minutes—he tastes an interval of delicious respite, which cheers him with the hope that the worst is over, and that his recovery is at hand. Soon that hope vanishes. From a slumber fraught with the horrors of a hideous dream, he starts up with a wild exclamation that "it is returning." At length, after reiterated recurrences of the same attacks, the muscles of respiration, subdued by efforts of which the instinct of self-preservation alone renders them capable, participate in the general exhustion, and refuse to perform their function. The patient gasps, sinks, and expires.

The investigations into aortic regurgitation included direct observations on the exposed heart of an ass that had been stunned, poisoned, or pithed. Aortic insufficiency was produced experimentally; the auscultatory findings were compared with those produced by disease,[4] and the capillary pulse was described.[5]

The subject of their observations, say the committee, were, in most instances, young asses, from three to six months old, apparently in good health; and the mode of operation was in a few instances, poisoning with woorara; in others stunning by a blow on the head; but in the majority, the animal was pithed.
2. The second sound was more audible over the semilunar valves than at the other parts of the heart, being sometimes distinct at the mouths of the arteries when inaudible on the body of the ventricles.
3. Pressure on the arterial orifices by the fingers or the stethoscope invariably stopped the second sound.
15. A common dissecting hook was passed into the pulmonary artery, so as to prevent the closure of the semilunar valves; the second sound was impaired, and a hissing murmur accompanied it. A hook was passed into the aorta, so as to act in the same way on the aortic valves; the second sound entirely ceased, and was replaced by a prolonged hissing. (Heard by several.)
16. When the hooks were withdrawn, the second sound returned and the hissing ceased.

When there is regurgitation through the perma-

nently open aortic valves, a murmur accompanies the second sound, and its source may be known by the following circumstances:—1. It is louder and more superficial opposite to and above the aortic valves than about the apex of the heart, by which it is distinguished from a murmur in the auricular valves with the second sound. 2. It is louder along the course of the ascending aorta than along that of the pulmonary artery, and down the tract of the left ventricle, than down that of the right; by which circumstances its seat is known to be in the aortic, and not in the pulmonic valves. This inference is strongly corroborated by the state of the pulse, which, when the aortic regurgitation is at all considerable, is singularly and preeminently jerking—the pulse of unfilled arteries. 3. It is distinguished from a systolic murmur in the aortic orifice by its accompanying the second sound; . . . always imparting to it the softness of the bellows-murmur, an inferior degree of loudness, and a lower key, like whispering the word *awe* during inspiration. It often becomes musical.

Similarly, the auscultatory findings in pulmonic and mitral valve involvement were described. According to Hope, disease of the pulmonic valves was not to be suspected unless the signs were well marked. When the mitral valve was permanently impaired and failed to prevent regurgitation, the first sound was attended with a murmur which might be[5]

. . . rough, (rasping,) or smooth, (bellows-murmur,) according to the nature of the contraction. . . . Its key is low,—more or less like whispering *who;* yet it sounds loud and *near* if explored about the apex of the heart, and a little to the sternal side of the nipple. It may thus be easily distinguished from a direct semilunar murmur, which, in this low situation, always sounds feeble and *distant*. The murmur in some cases completely drowns the natural first sound on the left side; in others, the sound can be distinguished at the commencement of the murmur.
I have found a perceptible purring tremor to be produced more frequently by regurgitation through the mitral valve than by any other valvular lesion—especially when the ventricle was hypertrophous and dilated, by which the refluent current was rendered stronger.

1. Flaxman, N.: The Hope of Cardiology, *Bull Inst Hist Med* 6:1-21, 1938.
2. Hope, A.: *Memior of the Late James Hope, M.D.*, ed 4, K. Grant (ed.), London: J. Hatchard and Son, 1848.
3. Hope, J.: *Principles and Illustrations of Morbid Anatomy*, London: Whittaker & Co., 1834.
4. Hope, J.: *A Treatise on the Diseases of the Heart and Great Vessels*, ed 3, London: J. Churchill, 1839.
5. Hope, J.: *A Treatise on the Diseases of the Heart and Great Vessels*, Philadelphia: Lea & Blanchard, 1842.

Composite by G. Bako

Sir Dominic John Corrigan
(1802-1880)

AMONG THE NOTABLE DUBLIN PHYSICIANS and surgeons of the 19th century, it is fitting that the most famous should bear the most Irish name. Adams, Carmichael, Colles, Collins, Graves, and Stokes could be either English or Irish. Corrigan, on the other hand, surely should be Irish-born. The year was 1802, the city Dublin. Dominic received his primary education at the lay College at Maynooth, one of the first modern Catholic educational institutions in Ireland.[1] He was a fine student and especially interested in physical science and natural philosophy as well as in Latin, Greek, and French. As was the custom of the times, the initial phase of medical learning was acquired in apprenticeship. Dr. O'Kelly, the village doctor and school physician at Maynooth, quickly realized the potentiality of youth in his care. The fame and excellence of Edinburgh attracted Corrigan for formal medical training, as it had attracted students from England and Scotland. Dominic took the degree of MD in 1825 at the age of 23. William Stokes (Cheyne-Stokes respiration and Stokes-Adams disease) was a classmate and fellow Dubliner.

Upon return to Dublin, a period of austerity and expectancy was inevitable. Hos-pital appointments were as difficult to obtain as patients. Corrigan was appointed physician to the Jervis Street Hospital, with admission privileges only after the contribution of a sizable sum of money. Six beds only were assigned to Corrigan, but they proved sufficient to insure a sound beginning for his clinical-pathological studies. Although his reputation as consultant, physician, and teacher probably centered on the morbid states of the heart and great vessels, Corrigan was no dogmatic specialist. A review of his bibliography discloses more than 100 communications of a great variety of morbid conditions. Several manuscripts discussed fevers (Corrigan's sign—shallow respiration in fever), with an ill-defined distinction between typhus and typhoid fever. Stricture of the pylorus, syphilitic eruption, apoplexy, caries of the bone, scarlatina, Bright's disease, variola, pemphigus, intestinal ulceration, anemia, strangulation of the intestines, ovarian tumor, carcinoma of the liver, arthritis of the hip, tuberculous peritonitis, copper poisoning (Corrigan's line-sign), and Corrigan's button cautery reflect his interest in general medical subjects. In the communication to the *Dublin Journal of Medical Science* in 1838, cirrhosis of the lung (Corrigan's cirrhosis) was distinguished from tuberculous infection. Displacement of the heart and the mediastinum as a result of the contracting process was also described.

One of Corrigan's early papers (1837) lists aortitis as one of the causes of angina pectoris.[2] Inflammation of the intima of the aorta "is capable of producing the group of symptoms to which we give the name of angina pectoris." Of course, others, including Heberden, in 1772, had made a similar suggestion. In 1846, the year of the great potato famine in Ireland, Corrigan published a communication on famine and fever. The failure of the potato crop was not caused by a new infection. The parasitic fungus, *Phytophthora infestans,* had been present on the potato plant since its introduction from Central America.[3] The economy of Ireland was ruined by the fungus; more than a million persons died of starvation. Corrigan served on the Central Board of Health during these critical years.

Another eponym, Corrigan's sign, identifies the expansile pulsation of an aneurysm of the aortic arch. At the time this communication was submitted to the *Lancet* in 1829, Corrigan was lecturer in the Institutes and Practice of Medicine and one of the physicians of the Sick-Poor Institution of Dublin. The case described was a male who complained of[4]

. . . oppression and straitness in his chest, succeeded by cough, occasionally convulsive . . . presenting the very vigour of health . . . of a florid complexion, and active in his limbs. . . . Questioning him closely, I found that he occasionally felt pain in the left side of his neck and left arm.

On stripping him, the first remarkable appearance that caught the eye, was a singular pulsation of all the arterial trunks of the upper part of the body. . . . Respiration was pure, save in the same place, where, in its stead, existed a most intense "bruit de soufflet," accompanied by indistinct pulsation. . . . On placing him sitting opposite a window, and looking from behind, aslant down his chest, there was a prominence, although very slight, perceptible above the left mamma, where the sound was dull, and the "bruit de soufflet" intense. I had now no doubt as to the nature of the disease, that there was aneurism of the ascending aorta, and that the termination must almost inevitably be fatal.

Since the patient had received a blow to his chest approximately six months before the onset of symptoms, the possibility that this was a traumatic aneurysm must be entertained.

The best known eponyms are associated with aortic regurgitation. In 1832, at the age of 30, Corrigan submitted to the *Edinburgh Medical and Surgical Journal* a contribution entitled: "On Permanent Patency of the Mouth of the Aorta, or Inadequacy of the Aortic Valves." No claim was made for priority. Cooper in 1705, Vieussens in 1715, and Key and Hodgkin, independently in 1829, described postmortem or clinical findings of aortic insufficiency, but the correlation was not appreciated. Corrigan notes that in his initial considerations of aortic insufficiency he had used the designation "inadequacy," but, impressed by the contributions of Dr. Elliotson, he selected "permanent patency of the mouth of the aorta" as a more descriptive identification. On the basis of pathological examination, inade-

quacy could be produced by reticulation or fenestration of the aortic leaflets, rupture of one or more of the valves, fibrosis or contraction of the leaflets, or dilatation of the mouth of the aorta without any recognizable organic lesion.[5]

On the general symptoms that accompany this disease, little is necessary to be said. Like most of those connected with affections of the respiratory and circulating organs, they are uncertain and unsatisfactory. They are frequently convulsive fits of coughing, more or less dyspnoea, sense of straitness and oppression across the chest, palpitations after exercise, sounds of rushing in the ears, and inability to lie down. . . . What is deficient in general symptoms from their obscurity, is, however, amply supplied by the certainty of the physical and stethoscopic signs, which may be referred to the three following indications. *1st,* Visible pulsation of the arteries of the head and superior extremities [Corrigan's pulse]. *2d, Bruit de soufflet* in the ascending aorta, in the carotids, and subclavians. *3d, Bruit de soufflet* and *fremissement,* or a peculiar rushing thrill felt by the finger, in the carotids and subclavians. In conjunction with these may be reckoned the pulse, which is invariably full.

Later in the communication Corrigan described a model composed of a flexible tube through which a current of water of variable force may be passed in order to mimic the changes in pulsations in patients with aortic insufficiency. With these studies and others he properly explained the murmur (*bruit de soufflet*) and the thrill (*fremissement*) of aortic insufficiency. Corrigan noted that no case occurred in very young persons. The youngest was 20, the cause of the disease uncertain. In one case, the symptoms appeared following an attack of acute rheumatism "which had been accompanied with symptoms of *pericarditis,*" most surely acute rheumatic fever. Treatment of aortic insufficiency stressed supportive measures, rather than the debilitating procedures of purging, bleeding, and starvation. Digitalis was contraindicated because it slowed the pulse, in a condition in which an increased pulse rate was judged beneficial.

Although the term "water-hammer pulse" is frequently associated with aortic insufficiency, this physical concept was not stated by name in any of Corrigan's communications. After extensive and impressive bibliographic study, Dock[6] discovered that G. H. Barlow, in 1852, had referred to the physical anomaly as "the splashing or water-hammer pulse." This description followed by 15 years a case report by Thomas Watson in which the "hard, sudden, hammering pulse" was associated with aortic regurgitation. Dock gives an excellent discussion of the origin and infiltration into medical literature of a term that has been accepted for almost a century because it is truly suggestive, "hitting the ear as the pulse hits the finger."

Corrigan was a physician with many interests beyond medicine. He was a founder and subsequently president of the Dublin Pathological Society, president of the Royal Zoological Society of Dublin, physician-in-ordinary to the Queen of Ireland, and a representative of Dublin in the House of Commons. He was created a baronet in 1866. In his later years he suffered from gout, although personal reference to this affliction does not appear in his writings. A statement in his obituary (1880) suggests that the affliction had reached the advanced tophaceous stage:[2]

Those who have not seen him of late years in London, with too many and too evident indications of the ravages of gout on his fine physique, are apt to forget his work as a pathologist and a physician, though his work in both capacities remains standard to this day.

1. Williamson, R. T.: Sir Dominic Corrigan, *Ann Med Hist* 7:354-361 (Dec) 1925.
2. Obituary, Sir Dominic John Corrigan, Bart., M.D., *Brit Med J* 1:266-268, 1880.
3. Dubos, R.: *Mirage of Health,* Garden City, NY, Doubleday & Company, Inc., 1961.
4. Corrigan, D. J.: Aneurism of the Aorta, *Lancet* 1: 586-590, 1829.
5. Corrigan, D. J.: On Permanent Patency of the Mouth of the Aorta, or Inadequacy of the Aortic Valves, *Edinburgh Med Surg J* 37:225-245 (April) 1832.
6. Dock, G.: I. Dominic John Corrigan; His Place in the Development of Our Knowledge of Cardiac Disease; II. The Water-Hammer Pulse, *Ann Med Hist* 6:381-395 (Sept) 1934.

William Stokes (1804-1878)

WILLIAM STOKES was born into a family of political titans, intellectuals, and scientists. During the great moments of his medical career, he shared the leadership in Irish medicine with his associate, Graves. Other physicians who furthered the reputation of the Irish school of medicine in the 19th century, which began with John Cheyne, included Colles, Adams, Corrigan, Wallace, and Rynd. William's father, Whitley Stokes, professor of the practice of medicine in the Royal College of Physicians, was compelled to resign his senior fellowship because of alleged activity with the Society of United Irishmen, an organization whose objects of reform were gained by other than peaceful and constitutional means. Subsequently, his teaching position was restored, followed by the appointment as regius professor of medicine at Dublin University and physician to the Meath Hospital. He was a family man, who cultivated the companionship of his children, especially his son William. The pair loved to roam the Irish hills on archeologic and scientific excursions. William's powers of observation undoubtedly were developed during these formative years while exposed to the natural sciences.

Preparation for a medical career was begun by a study of clinical medicine on his father's service in the Meath Hospital and the pursuit of chemistry in the laboratory at Trinity College. This was followed by further training in chemistry in Glasgow and full-time devotion to medicine at Edinburgh. While a medical student, Stokes published a small volume on the use of the stethoscope, the first English description of this clinical instrument devised by Laennec. The royalties for the publication totaled 70 pounds. In the fall of 1825, having gained the MD degree, he returned to Dublin and accepted the appointment, with financial contingencies, of physician to the Dublin General Dispensary. Lecturing and clinical instruction were assumed shortly after at Meath Hospital. Following recovery from an attack of typhus, he was elected physician to the Meath Hospital, thereby succeeding his father, who had resigned with this expectation.

William Stokes shared with Graves and William Porter editorial responsibility for the *Dublin Journal of Medical Science.* He is credited with founding the Dublin Pathological Society, which later became the Royal Academy of Medicine in Ireland. At the age of 38, he was appointed Regius professor of physic in Dublin, again succeeding his father. He enjoyed an extensive private practice but maintained, meanwhile, a deep interest in detailed observation of the sick as well as in medical writing.

One of the first responsibilities at the Meath Hospital was the reorganization of the clinical teaching, a major task begun a few years earlier by Graves. Rather than assigning passages from texts for memory, he encouraged the students to learn at the bedside under the stimulating guidance of the chief. The acquisition of clinical experience was but one aspect of his desire to provide liberal education in preparation for medicine. Physicians were urged to seek a general education comparable to that required of students of theology or law. At that time, as is the case today, the value of an arts course for medical students was subject to grave doubts. Stokes insisted that

admission requirements for medicine at Dublin University include a degree in arts.[1]

Let us emancipate the student, and give him time and opportunity for the cultivation of his mind, so that in his pupilage he shall not be a puppet in the hands of others, but a self-relying and reflecting being.

Stokes' succinct statement, "My father left me but one legacy, the blessed gift of rising early," emphasizes his habit of beginning the day's work at 4 or 5 A.M. Several hours without interruption were available for study and preparation of manuscripts. Strong of physique and endowed with a resilient mind, his kind personality was as attractive at the close of a harried day as at the beginning.

Among his 144 scientific contributions,[2] two were outstanding. The first, *Diseases of the Chest,* was published at the age of 33; the second, *Diseases of the Heart,* was published at the age of 50. Meanwhile, he had written on intestinal disorders, fevers, diaphragmatic pleurisy, aneurism of the aorta, mediastinal tumors, fatty degeneration of the liver, granular kidney, phlegmasia dolens, jaundice, hydrocephalus, paralysis, smallpox, cancer of the mouth, diphtheria, pemphigus, cerebrospinal meningitis, sarcoma of the scrotum, tapeworms, medical ethics, and diseases of the spleen.

In *Diseases of the Chest,* full credit was given to Laennec and Corvisart as the studies on the physical signs and symptoms of pulmonary diseases were extended.[3]

. . . there is no cavity in the disease of which, when we combine the study of symptoms properly so called with that of physical signs, the determination of the nature, extent, and modification of disease is so easy and certain.

Abnormal action of the respiratory center and depression of the heart rate were described and come to us as eponyms, ie, Cheyne-Stokes respiration and Adams-Stokes syndrome.

In 1818, John Cheyne, a Scotch physician who had established a practice in Dublin, published in the *Dublin Hospital Reports* his observations on rhythmic respiration. In

1854, Stokes extended and popularized the description of this type of breathing.[4]

The symptom was observed by Dr. Cheyne, although he did not connect it with the special lesion of the heart. It consists in the occurrence of a series of inspirations, increasing to a maximum, and then declining in force and length, until an apparent apnoea is established. In this condition the patient may remain for such a length of time as to make his attendants believe that he is dead, when a low inspiration, followed by one more decided, marks the commencement of a new ascending and then decending series of inspirations. This symptom, as occurring in its highest degree, I have only seen during a few weeks previous to the death of the patient.

The Adams-Stokes syndrome was observed first, not by Adams or Stokes, but by Morgagni in 1765. The first patient described by Robert Adams, regius professor of surgery in the University of Dublin, was a 68-year-old officer in the revenue who had been subject, over a period of several years, to at least 20 apoplectic attacks accompanied by a slow pulse. Usually these were associated with complete insensibility. Three case were reported by Adams in 1827, with specific attention directed to the brachycardia. In 1846, Stokes assembled his cases and those of Adams and others that had been brought to his attention for publication in the *Dublin Quarterly Journal of Medical Science*.[5] Stokes' first patient also was 68 years of age. Fainting fits had appeared over a three-year period. They occurred several times during the day and

. . . always left him without any unpleasant effects. . . . The duration of the attack is seldom more than four or five minutes. . . . The pulse has varied from twenty-eight to thirty in the minute.

In *Diseases of the Heart and the Aorta,* other cardiac phenomena were mentioned.[4] A patient with thyrotoxicosis relieved by iodine was described several decades before Plummer's contribution. In spite of Stokes' great interest in heart disease, the use of digitalis in treatment of cardiac maladies is mentioned casually and without enthusiasm. Greater credit was given to mercury (blue pills.) Three types of pericarditis were described: dry, with effusion, and combined pleural-pericardial effusion. In adhesive pericarditis there may be atrophy or hypertrophy of the heart or the heart may be unaltered in its capacity or muscular condition.[4]

Obstruction of the coronary arteries may or may not be present, and is probably not infrequent; but, as a cause of angina, its action is remote, and its existence unnecessary. . . . It is greatly to be doubted that angina pectoris has ever occurred in a patient perfectly free from organic disease of the heart and aorta.

Beyond the field of medicine, Stokes displayed broad interests. References to music and drama appeared repeatedly in the letters of William Stokes. He had a great appreciation for Shakespeare, soft Irish music, landscape painting, and the violin. He traveled extensively throughout Europe, pursuing his antiquarian leanings. Saturday evenings were usually given to music and conversation. On Christmas day, foreigners were invited to his home. He was an unrivaled storyteller, with a pungent wit. He loved to explore the archeology of Ireland—the early Christian or pre-Christian structures to be found in the remote districts. With Philip Crampton, he founded the Dublin Zoo about 1836. His grandson, Henry Stokes, onetime surgeon at the Meath Hospital, in his busiest years, made a notable collection of skeletons of Irish elks, having inherited the family flair for archeology.

Many honors were conferred upon Stokes. Included were honorary degrees from Edinburgh, Oxford, Cambridge, and Dublin. He was an honorary member of the Imperial College of Vienna, the Royal Medical Societies of Berlin and Leipzig, and the National Institute of Philadelphia. Cheyne-Stokes breathing and Adams-Stokes syndrome are familiar terms. Other expressions associated with his name include Stokes' collar (varicosities of the neck), Stokes' disease (exophthalmic goiter), Stokes' expectorant (a combination of ammonium carbonate, senna, squill, and camphorated tincture of opium in syrup of tolu), Stokes' liniment, and Stokes' sign (a severe throbbing in the abdomen, at the right of the umbilicus, in acute enteritis).

1. Bettany, G. T.: *Eminent Doctors: Their Lives and Their Work*, vol. II, London: John Hogg, Paternoster Row, 1885, pp. 188-193.
2. William Stokes, *Med Classics* 3:711-746 (March) 1939.
3. Stokes, W.: *A Treatise on the Diagnosis and Treatment of Diseases of the Chest*, Dublin: Hodges and Smith, 1837.
4. Stokes, W.: *The Diseases of the Heart and the Aorta*, Dublin: Hodges and Smith, 1854.
5. Stokes, W.: Observations on Some Cases of Permanently Slow Pulse, *Dublin Quart J Med Sci* 2:73-85, 1846.

Los Angeles County Medical Library

Joseph Skoda (1805-1881)

JOSEPH SKODA described the drumlike sound in auscultation of the chest in patients suffering from pneumonia and pericardial effuson. As one of the leading teachers in the revitalized Viennese Medical School, he also extended and promoted the pragmatic value of physical examination developed by the physicians of the Parisian school. Joseph was born in Pilsen, Bohemia, the son of a locksmith, who lacked funds to provide higher education for his children.[1] However, it is reasonable to assume that the parents must have passed on a rich intellectual heritage and an urge to excel; for in subsequent years, each of the three sons acquired stature, respect, and an enviable position in society. Joseph and his older brother, Franz, studied medicine, the latter advancing to

public health officialdom and a royal title. The younger brother, Johann, turned to heavy industry and founded the Skoda steel works in Pilsen, one of the great plants in Central Europe.

Joseph studied first at Pilsen, planning to dedicate his life to the Church. Because of special talents in mathematics and physics, however, he turned from theology to the natural sciences. Through the gracious gesture of affluent friends of Franz, he trained for medicine, receiving the MD degree in 1831 from the University of Vienna. He spent a year in Bohemia, dividing his time between practice and the study of cholera before returning to Vienna as an unsalaried assistant in the famous General Hospital.

Although Skoda is best remembered for his observations on auscultation of the lungs, the heart received his first and probably greatest attention in the study of physical aberrations. Heart sounds or functional murmurs were distinguished from organic murmurs, in support of Bouillaud and Rouanet's theory that:[2]

. . . in any disease of the heart, as long as the valves are intact, there is no appreciable alteration in the heart sounds; but in examples of valvular defects there are constant and significant variations; the heart sounds are replaced by completely different (sounds) murmurs.

The heart sounds are clear if the tendinous attachments of the valves are normal; if the cords lose their elasticity, become thickened and contain calcium, the clarity of the sound is affected and it the volume is weak it becomes a murmur; if the volume is strong the sound resembles harsh snoring, grating or a bellows.

As a fitting monument to his service, Skoda gave the world a notable monograph on the heart and the lungs, *A Treatise on Auscultation and Percussion*. He discussed the anatomical location, the time in the cardiac cycle, and the direction of transmission of the bruit, as well as the thrill in organic murmurs. In the development of the clinical significance of percussion and auscultation, he sought a mechanical basis for his findings, believing that an alteration in sound was caused by alteration in the physical properties of the afflicted organ but was not necessarily specific for any disease entity. Laennec, on the other hand, tended to associate alterations in physical findings with organic specificity. While the treatise was coolly received initially, it eventually enjoyed several editions and an English translation. Auscultation phenomena were interpreted under the laws of acoustics. Percussion sounds were arranged into classes and were named according to a physical scale: (1) from full to empty, (2) from clear to dull, (3) from tympanitic to non-tympanitic, and (4) from high to deep. Skodiac resonance was in the third class.[3]

That the lungs partially deprived of air, should yield a tympanitic, and, when the quantity of air in them is increased, a non-tympanitic sound, appears opposed to the laws of physics. The fact however is certain, and is corroborated both by experiments on the dead body (which will be presently referred to), and also by this constant phenomenon, viz.: that when the lower portion of a lung is entirely compressed by any pleuritic effusion, and its upper portion reduced in volume, the percussion-sound at the upper part of the thorax is distinctly tympanitic.

Less than ten years after Skoda's return to Vienna, he was appointed physician to the General Hospital and in another five years professor of internal medicine. The thesis submitted in qualifying for the latter post was prepared in Latin as was the custom of the day, but his lectures were given in German—a break from tradition. In the thesis, the relation of medicine to the other natural sciences was advanced. It was proposed that two important functions of a clinic were to instruct students and to provide the opportunity for direct observation of the sick. In the search for the scientific basis of physical findings, Skoda was more interested in confirming the diagnosis than in exploring useless drugs in treatment. This is not surprising, since a century ago few effective therapeutic agents were available. Therapeutic nihilism was the only critical path to follow in the search for valid findings and probably benefited the patient more than bleeding, leeches, purgation, cupping, blistering, or other nonspecific insults customarily recommended.

Although Skoda lacked the warmth of a "beloved" teacher, he should be judged by his industry, clinical contributions, and devotion of his life to the medical clinic. He

was one of the first to recognize the significance of the observations on puerperal fever made by his associate, Semmelweis. Skoda, a bachelor, suffered from gout and died of heart disease at the age of 76. A wide knowledge of pathological anatomy and great skill in auscultation and percussion made him the renowned diagnostician of Vienna of his day, an outstanding contributor to the flowering of Viennese medicine in the mid-19th century.

1. Sternberg, M.: *Josef Skoda*, Vienna: J. Springer, 1924.
2. Skoda, J.: Heart Sounds and Heart Action, *Med Jahrb Osterr Staates Wien* 13:227-266, 1837, excerpt by Z. Danilevicius.
3. Skoda, J.: *A Treatise on Auscultation and Percussion*, W. O. Markham, trans., London: Highley & Son, 1853.

Composite by G. Bako

Henri-Louis Roger (1809-1891)

HENRI ROGER, student of auscultation and the first physician to present a comprehensive description of asymptomatic interventricular septal defect, was born, studied, and spent his professional life in the city of Paris.[1] He began his internship in the city hospitals in 1833, received a gold medal for scholarship three years later, and in 1839 presented his doctoral thesis on auscultation and the significance of rales in the diagnosis of diseases of the chest. Recast as the first chapter of a monograph, prepared jointly with Barth, entitled *Traite Pratique d'Auscultation,* it went through several French and one English edition.

Following graduation, Roger joined the Central Bureau of hospitals but his main interest lay in academic medicine. In 1847, he received professional standing but never achieved departmental headship, since a chair of pediatrics had not been established. He served on the staffs of the Institute for Foundling Children and later of the Hospital for Sick Children, and from 1860 to 1875 the Hospital of Eugenie. Held in great esteem as a bedside teacher he was less skillful in the amphitheater. An ardent organization man, Roger was an important member of the General Association of Medicine of France and from 1876 until his death held the president's chair. In 1862, he was awarded membership in the Academy of Medicine in the section of pathology and, after performing the duties as secretary for many years, was elected president in 1880.

Following his work on auscultation, Roger prepared a discussion in five parts on the pathologic physiology of temperature of children, a two-volume treatise on the maladies of the child (1872-1883), a small monograph on auscultation of the head, translated into English, and together with Damaschino a monograph on spinal paralysis. Shorter presentations were published on aspiration of the pericardium, contagiousness of diphtheria, croup, and epidemic cholera. Although not the first to describe the bruit of well-developed interventricular septal defect sans symptoms or cyanosis, he was the first to discuss the clinicopathologic observations in a series of cases.

While performing an autopsy on a 12-year-old boy in 1861, Roger discovered a defect in the upper portion of the interventricular area, without accompanying pulmonary artery stenosis. The clinical protocol described a thrill and a systolic murmur in the center of the heart, unaccompanied by cyanosis or impairment of general health. A summary of his findings of the anomaly, among thousands of children examined, was presented to the Academy of Medicine in 1879 as follows:[2]

1. *A developmental defect of the heart occurs* from which *cyanosis* does not ensue in spite of the fact that a communication exists between the cavities of the two ventricles and in spite of the fact that admixture of venous blood and arterial blood occurs. This congenital defect, which is even compatible with a long life, is a simple one, without the association of congenital pulmonary stenosis. It comprises a defect in the interventricular septum.

2. It is necessary to differentiate this anomaly of the heart, which I have recently been the first to study clinically, not only from other malformations, but particularly from acquired disease of the heart. Its presence is revealed only by auscultation, through a physical sign with definite characteristics: this consists of a long loud *murmur* (resulting from the passage of blood through the opening in the interventricular septum and directly into the pulmonary artery or the aorta, the location of which is frequently abnormal in these cases). This murmur is unaccompanied by other murmurs, begins with systole and is so prolonged that it entirely occupies the period of the natural tic-tac (sic) of the normal heart sounds. Its point of maximal intensity is not at the apex (as in the case of lesions of the auriculoventricular orifices), nor at the base on the right side (as in stenosis of the aortic orifice), but over the upper third of the precordial area. It is mainly medial in location like the septum itself, and from this focal point diminishes uniformly in intensity as the stethoscope is moved over the chest. The murmur is not propagated into the vessels. It coincides with no other sign of organic disease with the exception of the *harsh thrill* which accompanies it. This murmur is *the pathognomonic sign of a defect in the interventricular septum.*

3. The differential diagnosis of this malformation (up to the present time either unrecognized or confused with other congenital or acquired lesions) will from now on be rendered simple by careful comparison of the physical signs. These signs vary in number, location, and character in heart disease when structural alterations are multiple, progressive, and changing, while the murmur under discussion, like the permanently fixed lesion responsible for its occurrence, remains unaltered for an indefinite period of time. The same statement holds true when comparing this murmur with the signs of functional disturbances; such signs vary with the changing episodes of heart weakness, and are entirely different in their

acute or chronic characteristics from the unaltered signs of a defective interventricular septum which change inappreciably over the years and increase only very gradually and almost without detection.

4. The consideration of the age of the patient is a noteworthy point in the diagnosis; endocarditis, for example, is rarely seen in infancy, before the age of two years, and furthermore, the anemia of very young children is very seldom associated with a heart murmur. Thus, *a murmur in a nursing infant* is almost always a definite indication of an *anomaly* of the heart or great vessels.

5. The *prognosis* is generally less significant in the abnormality described than in other structural diseases of the heart, in which the danger for children is greater and occurs sooner, permitting hope for not much more than another decade of life. In spite of the existence of an uncomplicated defect of the interventricular septum, patients may attain or even surpass the average span of human life.

6. A definite diagnosis usually demands an active sustained program of *treatment* in heart disease. But, if a congenital anomaly of the heart exists, vigorous treatment is of no avail and may even be harmful. To show, thanks to the accuracy of diagnosis, when to act in one and when to withhold treatment in another, is to be of service not only to physicians but also to patients.

1. Rendu, H.: Henri Roger, obituary (Fr), *Gaz Hop* 65:1-2, 1892.

2. Roger, H.: Researches on the Congenital Communication on the Two Sides of the Heart by Failure of Occlusion of the Interventricular Septum (Fr), *Bull Acad Med* 8:1074-1094; 1189-1191, 1879, translated in Willius, F. A., and Keys, T. E.: *Cardiac Classics*, St. Louis: C. V. Mosby Co., 1941, pp 623-638.

Thomas Bevill Peacock
(1812-1882)

THE STANDARD REFERENCE TREATISE on congenital and acquired malformations of the heart a century ago was prepared by Thomas B. Peacock, physician to St. Thomas' Hospital, London.[1] Thomas was born at York, was apprenticed for five years to John Fothergill, proceeded to University College Hospital, London, for advanced training, and received the MD degree at Edinburgh.[2] He served as surgical dresser at St. George's Hospital and, at the age of 23, qualified as a member of the Royal College of Surgeons and as a licentiate of the Society of Apothecaries. He then served as

ship's surgeon on two voyages to Ceylon. At the age of 37, Peacock was elected assistant physician to St. Thomas' Hospital; in the meantime, he had helped found the

Composite by G. Bako

Pathological Society of London and was a frequent contributor to its *Transactions*. The Victoria Park Hospital for Diseases of the Chest, Liverpool Street, London, was established by Peacock as a dispensary.

Peacock's important writings were based upon a pathological collection, devoted largely to the heart and the great vessels. In 1865, Peacock delivered the Croonian Lecture on valvular disease of the heart. His first monograph, published in 1848, concerned epidemic influenza as observed in the great epidemic of 1847. Many of the afflicted were stricken in early adulthood, similarly to the great influenza epidemic of 1917-1918 in America.

While Peacock was house physician and pathologist at the Edinburgh Royal Infirmary, in preparation for his degree and to ascertain the dynamic effect of injecting fluids between the external and middle coats of an artery, he performed experiments on aortas, removed from cadavers of the young.[3] In the *Transactions of the Pathological Society of London*, 1863, he described three stages in the development of dissecting aneurism as follows.[4]

1. *The incipient stage,* in which there is a rupture, or destruction in some other way, of a part or the whole of the internal coats of the vessel, and an extravasation of blood to a limited extent between the external and middle coat, or, more probably, in the laminae of the latter.

2. In the next, or *early stage of the fully-formed dissecting aneurism,* in addition to the internal rupture or perforation, the blood is found to be extensively extravasated in the coats of the vessel, separating the middle from the external tunic, or the laminae of the middle coat, to a variable extent above the seat of rupture and downwards in the course of the vessel, and not unfrequently along the primary branches.

3. In the *advanced stage of dissecting aneurism* there is found an opening through the internal coats of the vessel, leading into a sac situated within the arterial tunics, and extending to a greater or lesser distance along the course of the vessel. This sac is lined by a distinct membrane very similar to the natural lining membrane of the arteries.

On malformations of the human heart, Peacock's orderly mind treated the subject in five sections, differentiating between arrest of development of the heart at an early period of fetal life, malformations which prevent normal development after birth, and malformations which do not interfere with the function of the heart but lay the foundation for clinical disturbance in later life.[1] In a communication published in the *Transactions,* he described the multiple malformations, to be rediscovered 40 years later by Fallot. Peacock made no claim to an original observation; in fact, the abnormality had been described by others. Currently it is identified by the eponymic term.[5]

In this case there existed extreme contraction of the orifice of the pulmonary artery, with a deficiency in the interventricular septum, and the aorta arose in chief part from the right ventricle. The right auricle and ventricle were of large size, and the walls of the latter thick and very firm. The left ventricle was, on the contrary, small, and its walls thin and flaccid. The left auricle was also small. The foramen ovale and ductus arteriosus were both closed. The heart was taken from a child two years and five months old, who had exhibited well-marked symptoms of cyanosis, which commenced three months after birth. . . . The intensity of the cyanosis, and the duration of life in these cases, bears a general relation to the amount of contraction of the pulmonary orifice and the freedom of communication between the right and left cavities of the heart, through the medium of the open foramen ovale and the aperture in the interventricular septum.

A case of subacute bacterial endocarditis was described in a fireman, who attributed his illness to a cold four months before. The patient complained of shortness of breath, cough, and insomnia. A systolic murmur was audible over the precordium, harsh at the apex, which extended into the left axilla. A distinct musical murmur was heard in diastole at the base of the heart. Albumin was present in the urine and blood in the stool. Pathological examination showed:[6]

The fragments of the destroyed cordae tendineae were covered by vegetations, as was also the under surface of the valve itself, and some of these vegetations were infiltrated with earthy deposit. . . . The liver was large, congested, and somewhat cirrhosed; the spleen was large, pulpy, and contained a partially decolorized fibrinous mass of considerable size; the kidneys were much hypertrophied, weighing together nineteen ounces; they were minutely congested and studded with red, bloody points.

The great interest of the case Dr. Peacock considered to be: 1. The existence of disease both in the aortic and mitral valves, which had been manifested by distinct physical signs, so that a correct diagnosis had been effected during life.

2. The musical character of the murmur heard at the base with the diastole of the heart, and which was clearly traceable to the loose retroverted edge of the posterior semilunar valve.

1. Peacock, T. B.: *On Malformations of the Human Heart,* London: J. Churchill, 1858.
2. Porter, I. H.: The Nineteenth-Century Physician and Cardiologist, Thomas Bevill Peacock, 1812-82. *Med Hist* 6:240, 1962.
3. Peacock, T. B.: An Account of Some Experiments Illustrative of the Mode of Formation of the Dissecting Aneurisms, *Lond Edinburgh J Med Sci* 3:871, 1843.
4. Peacock, T. B.: Report on Cases of Dissecting Aneurism, *Trans Path Soc Lond* 14:87, 1863.
5. Peacock, T. B.: Malformation of the Heart, Consisting in Contraction of the Orifice of the Pulmonary Artery with Deficiency at the Base of the Interventricular Septum, *Trans Path Soc Lond* 1:25, 1846-1847.
6. Peacock, T. B.: Retroversion of One of the Aortic Valves, and Destruction of Some of the Chordae Tendineae of the Mitral Valve, *Trans Path Soc Lond* 12:59, 1861.

Adolf Kussmaul (1822-1902)

ADOLF KUSSMAUL, whose name is associated with the hyperpnea of diabetic coma, was a country practitioner with a fervent desire for a career in academic medicine. This was satisfied in proper time with professorships of medicine at Heidelberg, Erlangen, Freiburg, and Strasbourg, where, in each post, he made one or more notable contributions to clinical medicine.[1] He differentiated symptoms associated with mercurialism from those of syphilis,[2] was the first to use the term "periarteritis nodosa," introduced the concept of paradoxical pulse in the clinical description of obstructive pericarditis, discussed gastric tetany, and prepared a monograph on disorders of speech.

Adolf was born in Baden near Karlsruhe. His grandfather was a surgical dresser and an army surgeon. His father, after serving his time as a military surgeon, took postgraduate training in anatomy, physiology, and clinical medicine. Such an interest in medical practice and medical science was passed on to Adolf. At the age of 18, he began his medical studies at the University of Heidelberg, which boasted Henle, Johannes Müller, Franz Karl Nägele, and others on the medical faculty. Adolf enjoyed the intellectual as well as the social amenities of the University, including membership in the Swabian Student Corps. In his final year at Heidelberg, he prepared a thesis on the color changes in the fundus of the eye, which was awarded a gold medal. Before beginning practice he studied under Hebra, Rokitansky, and Skoda in Vienna and under Oppolzer in Prague—excellent training for the appreciation of the interdependence of pathological anatomy and clinical medicine.

In 1848, Kussmaul accepted his responsibility in the army—as had his grandfather and father—and joined the Baden Battalion, recently alerted for combat in the border skirmishes with the Danes. Upon discharge from the army he returned to Kandern, where he had once been stationed, to begin a country practice and to give without compromise physical and mental energies in the care of the mountain folk and the lowlanders. In spite of a heavy and harried practice, interposed by a severe attack of cerebral spinal meningitis, he found time to remain current with medical literature and to prepare for publication communications on clinical medicine. After four years of practice, he resumed postgraduate training as a pupil of Virchow and received the MD degree in 1854 from the University of Würzburg.

The first academic appointment was as privatdocent in medicine at Heidelberg, where he lectured in materia medica, toxicology, legal medicine, and psychiatry. In 1856, Kussmaul showed that rigor mortis was caused by chemical changes associated with disintegration of the muscle and was not due to death of the nerves. He was called to Erlangen in 1859, and later to Freiburg. The term "periarteritis [polyarteritis] nodosa" was first used by Kussmaul in the description of a patient with vascular changes of the nerves, heart, and bowel. The observations, including caution in recommending a biopsy, were summarized as follows:[3]

(1) There are muscular paralyses which are independent of diphtheria, which start with kidney disease and fever and develop rapidly, with severe pains in the muscles; whose anatomical basis is the granular and waxlike degeneration of the muscular substance. Such paralyses are not the results of trichina, and their cause is not known at the present time.

(2) There is a certain affliction of the arteries, beginning with the bifurcation, which we call periarteritis nodosa and, similar to Virchow's endarteritis nodosa deformans, begins in the intima, alters the contour of the arteries, and sometimes expands the radius in an aneurysmal fashion, and sometimes decreases the lumen and hinders the flow of blood. Such a disease attacks— if such an observation may be taken from a single case—only the smaller arteries of selected organs and systems, to be exact, the inner organs of the lower abdomen, of the heart and voluntary mucles, and may develop acutely. Death may occur in a few weeks after the first sign of serious illness.

(3) The significant diagnostic items include rapid development of a general paralysis of the muscles, with loss of the ability to contract, even when electrically stimulated; severe pains as in trichinosis; symptoms of nephritis and enteritis, and the appearance of small nodules under the skin which can be identified as knotty swellings when excised.

(4) If periarteritis nodosa develops in the wall of the bowel and becomes intensive and widespread, it can produce similar anatomical changes in the mucosa of the bowel as an embolus.

(5) Biopsy for diagnostic purposes in cases of waxy degeneration of the muscles accompanied by degeneration of many capillaries and arteries of the muscles is not an insignificant event because such a wound will heal slowly.

Kussmaul's observations on the value of thoracentesis in the treatment of empyema and pyopneumothorax were published in 1868. A U-tube was inserted in the pleural cavity, and the purulent space irrigated with an antiseptic solution.[4] The use of the stomach tube to alleviate pyloric obstruction was based upon the theory that excessive stimulation of the sympathetic nerves by the acid contents of the stomach was responsible for chronic constriction of the pylorus.[5] Although the stomach pump had been used by others, Kussmaul popularized the device. In the same communication, mention was made also of the esophagoscope, and a gastroscope. One of the first descriptions of gastric tetany was based on the observations in a six-year-old child who was admitted to the hospital because of wailing, fever, and diarrhea.[6]

It was soon suspected that the cause for his screaming was a severe tetany.
He had attacks of tonic spasms in many of the muscles of each of the four extremities, while simultaneously both feet were continuously in contraction, pes equinovarus.

Contractions of the calf muscles during the intervals were so strong that they could not be overcome without fracturing the legs. We did not succeed in bending the feet, even to a right angle, and as soon as passive flexion was released, they returned to their previous position.

One of the most interesting phenomena observed was first discovered by *Trousseau: During the free intervals, tetany could be induced by pressure on the arteries.*

In a communication on *"Rheumatic Tetany and rheumatic tonic spasms combined with albuminuria"* (which I published last year), I remarked that the strange neurosis which *Corvisart* called *Tetany* (though it seems that it was first described by our fellow countryman, Steinheim, in 1830) remained almost unnoticed in Germany and is far less known than it deserves to be. We owe almost all our kowledge of this disease to the French, from whose description *Hasse* and I have traced the picture.
. . . the spasms during the attack spread from the periphery to the center, ie, upwards from the fingers, and this is characteristic of tetany plus the interesting symptom which *Trousseau* discovered, inciting of spasms whenever pressure is exerted on the main artery of a limb.

Paradoxical pulse, a finding associated with chronic obliterating pericarditis or mediastinitis, he described and illustrated it with a case report.[7]

. . . this affliction results in the symptoms associated with chronic infection of the pericardium and obliteration, as well as a special symptom characteristic of sclerosing mediastinitis, a pronounced arterial pulse phenomenon and sometimes an unusual appearance of the veins of the throat.

Inasmuch as the sternum exerts, with each respiration, a dampening pressure on the ascending portion and arch of the aorta through its mediastinal structure, the pulsations of all arteries become smaller or disappear completely in regular intervals and return with expiration; this may be approached during normal heart action. I propose to call this pulse action paradoxical, partly on account of the great discrepancy between heart action and aterial pulse, partly because the pulse, although apparently irregular, is in reality waning and waxing in regular motion.

In the veins of the neck, especially the jugular vein, the pressure from the mediastinal fascia results in a noticeble swelling instead of the normal depression if the respiration is deep enough.

These manifestations suggest . . . a diagnosis of fibrous mediastinitis accompanied by pericarditis.

The hyperpnea associated with diabetic acidosis and coma was described from observations of patients in his clinic in Freiburg.[8]

Since I have seen three diabetics in the course of a year die, with remarkably similar symptoms in which there was a *peculiar comatose condition preceded and accompanied by dyspnoea,* I believe that it is not merely a play of chance, but am of the opinion that it has to do with a form of death in diabetes which is rarely observed.

These conditions, with which all the patients reached the terminal stage, were essentially as follows:

1. A *dyspnoea of an unusual kind.* There is nothing here, as in ordinary dyspnoeas, to indicate that the air has to overcome the slightest obtacle on its way into or out of the lungs; on the contrary, it comes in and out with the greatest ease; the thorax widens itself splendidly in all directions, without any evidence of pulling in of the lower end of the sternum or the intercostal spaces, and a complete inspiration followed each complete respiration; down to the deepest part of the lungs, one hears a pure, loud and sharp vesicular breathing (so-called puerile breathing); and that all points to the highest degree of air hunger (Lufthunger) as does the oppressive pain of which the patient complains, as well as the tremendous activity of the respiratory muscles, which are so readily seen, the loud noise which the mighty respiratory and even stronger expiratory air stream produces in the larynx. . . .

In spite of the great distress, the dyspnoea did not become orthopnoea, because the patients were too weak to hold themselves up. The contrast of the general weakness with the strength of the respiratory movements is one of the most remarkable characteristics in this picture.

1. This dyspnoea is not the product of a reflex excitation of the respiratory centers from the vagus or the laryngeal nerve, but is a result of a direct central stimulation.

2. It is not the result of a lack of oxygen in the respiratory center, either the result of a stagnation of a slow flow of blood in the capillaries or the result of an inability of the red blood cells to hold oxygen.

3. It is not the result of an inordinate increase of carbon dioxide in the blood.

A monograph on speech disturbance published first in 1877, in which the term "word blindness" was used, went through several editions.[9]

We have discovered cases in the literature, which were known as aphasia, but should not be designated as such, inasmuch as the patients were able to express themselves in speaking and writing. They were neither inarticulate (incapable of speech) nor illiterate (incapable of writing); but despite an acute sense of hearing they could no longer comprehend words they heard or, despite good vision, they could no longer read the words they saw. For the sake of brevity these pathologic disabilities are named: *word deafness and word blindness (caecitas et surditas verbalis).*

Kussmaul retired from his post in Strasbourg at the age of 66 and returned to Heidelberg, where he was honored by the University as professor of Medicine emeritus. Here he prepared his autobiography, *Memories of the Youth of an Old Physician,* and continued a consulting practice. The city of Heidelberg formally celebrated his 80th birthday, while the Grand Duke of Baden granted him the title of Real Privy Councilor. Kussmaul was one of the great men of German medicine in the 19th century, when internal medicine based upon pathological anatomy, biochemistry, and bacteriology was reaching maturity.

1. Bast, T. H.: The Life and Time of Adolf Kussmaul, *Ann Med Hist* 8:95-127 (June) 1926.

2. Kussmaul, A.: *Investigations of Constitutional Mercurialism and Its Relation to Constitutional Syphilis* (Ger), Würzburg: Stahel, 1861.

3. Kussmaul, A., and Maier, R.: A Previously Undescribed Arterial Disease (Periarteritis Nodosa) with Bright's Disease and Rapidly Progressive General Muscle Weakness (Ger), *Deutsch Arch Klin Med* 1:484-516, 1866, excerpt translated by E. Longar.

4. Kussmaul, A.: Sixteen Observations on Thoracentesis (Ger), *Deutsch Arch Klin Med* 4:1-32; 173-202, 1868.

5. Kussmaul, A.: Treatment of Hypertrophy of the Stomach Through a New Method Using the Stomach Pump (Ger), *Deutsch Arch Klin Med* 6:455-500, 1869.

6. Kussmaul, A.: The Study of Tetany (Ger), *Klin Wschr* 9:441, 1872, excerpt translated by F. Sternthal.

7. Kussmaul, A.: Mediastinal Pericarditis and Paradoxical Pulse (Ger), *Klin Wschr* 10:433-435, 1873, excerpt translated by E. Longar.

8. Kussmaul, A.: The Study of Diabetes Mellitus, *Deutsch Arch Klin Med* 14:1-46, 1874, in Major, R. H.: Classic Descriptions of Disease, 3rd ed, Springfield, Ill: Charles C Thomas, 1945.

9. Kussmaul, A.: *Speech Disturbances* (Ger), 4th ed, Leipzig: F. C. W. Vogel, 1910, excerpt translated by F. Sternthal.

John C. W. Lever (1811-1858)

JOHN CHARLES WEAVER LEVER, obstetrician of Guy's Hospital, it best remembered for his recognition of the incidence of albuminuria in toxemia of pregnancy complicated by convulsions. Lever, of humble origin, was born at Plumstead, Kent. At the age of 18, he was apprenticed to John Butler of Woolwich, an industrious and highly skilled practitioner, especially of midwifery. In 1832, at the expiration of his indenture,

Guy's Hospital, London

Lever was accepted as a pupil at Guy's Hospital and soon became recognized for his mental and physical capacity. An example of his stamina concerns the reputation of being poor in pocket and of having walked a daily round trip of almost 20 miles from home to lectures for two years to save money. After passing his examinations but not qualifying for the MD degree, he was admitted a member of the Royal College of Surgeons of London and entered general practice at Newington Causeway. Following the path of his preceptor, midwifery and disorders of the female organs became his principal interest, and led to his organizing the obstetrical department of Guy's Hospital, called Lying-in-Charity. In 1842, Lever was appointed to assist in the senior duties of the department, was admitted a licentiate of the Royal College of Physicians of London, and received the MD degree from the University of Giessen. In 1849, he shared responsibilities with Dr. Oldham as physician-accoucheur and lecturer in midwifery at the Lying-in-Charity.

Upon entering the practice of obstetrics and gynecology in the south of London, Lever was not long in gaining an enviable reputation for his clear and practical lectures and for his clinical demeanor in office and hospital practice. He gained the confidence of female patients by his stout stature and skill in practice rather than by obvious social charms. Lever finally began to enjoy the amenities of success; he abandoned his abstinence from alcohol and for a short time became a *bon vivant*. However, when death struck his family, he turned to the church for solace and quickened his general activities for which his premature death has been attributed. Dr. Addison was his attending physician. In addition to the hospital and college appointments, Lever was a fellow of the Medico-Chirurgical Society, an honorary member of the College of Physicians of Philadelphia and the Obstetric Societies of Edinburgh and Dublin, and president of the Hunterian Society in 1851.

Lever did not pose as a scientific physician; rather, he was a critical observer of the sick and prepared only clinical tracts in obstetrics and gynecology. *A Practical Treatise on Organic Diseases of the Uterus* was judged the prize essay by the Medical Society of London and was awarded the Fothergillian medal for 1843. His most notable contribution was the correlation between albuminuria and puerperal convulsions, in which he described a series of patients from his office practice or obstetrical service at Guy's Hospital as follows:[2]

The following Fourteen Cases of Puerperal Convulsions, out of Seven thousand four hundred and four women attended by the Pupils attached to the Lying-in-Charity of Guy's Hospital, have occurred between the years 1834 and 1843.

The symptoms which marked their course, and the principles which guided their treatment, present no new or extraordinary feature; but the coincidence of an albuminous condition of the urine, in nine out of ten cases in which that secretion was examined, is a fact which, so far as my investigations and inquiries have extended, has not been previously remarked.

At first, I was induced to believe that it (albuminuria) was merely a case of pregnancy occurring in a woman affected with granular degeneration of the kidney; but as the traces of albumen became daily more faint (fifth case), until they entirely disappeared on November 3, I was led to suppose that the albuminous condition of the urine depended upon some transient cause probably connected with the state of gestation itself.

To settle this point, I have carefully examined the urine in every case of puerperal convulsions that has since come under my notice, both in the Lying-in-Charity of Guy's Hospital and in private practice; and in *every case, but one,* the urine has been found to be *albuminous* at the time of the convulsions. In the case (10) in which the albumen was wanting, inflammation of the membranes of the brain, with considerable effusion, was detected after death. I further have investigated the condition of the urine in upwards of fifty women, from whom the secretion has been drawn, during labour, by the catheter; great care being taken that none of the vaginal discharges were mixed with the fluid: and the result has been, *that in NO cases have I detected albumen, except in those in which there have been convulsions, or in which symptoms have presented themselves, and which are readily recognised as the precursors of puerperal fits.*

From what I have seen in public and private practice, I am led to the conclusion, that cases of convulsions complicated with an albuminous condition of the urine are divisible into two forms: in the one, the urine is *albuminous during pregnancy;* and there are external evidences, as shewn in the oedema of the face, eyelids, hands, &c. In such cases, the convulsions will be more violent, and will last for a longer time after delivery. The urine also retains its albuminous properties for a longer period than in the second form, or that in which the urine becomes *albuminous during the labour.* In this variety, the urine contains less albumen; the fits are less violent; seldom re-appear after delivery has been completed; and if they do, it is in a milder form, unless complicated with some lesion of the brain. The urine, in this form, very speedily loses all traces of albumen after labour is completed.

1. Wilks, S., and Bettany, G. T.: *A Biographical History of Guy's Hospital,* London: Ward, Lock, Bowden & Co., 1892, pp 374-376.

2. Lever, J. C. W.: Cases of Puerperal Convulsions, With Remarks, *Guy's Hosp* 1:495-517, 1843.

Composite by G. Bako

Eduard Heinrich Henoch (1820-1910)

HENOCH, of Henoch-Schönlein's purpura and pupil of Schönlein, was born in Berlin and received his doctor's degree at the University in 1843. He remained in the capital city, beginning his academic career as assistant in the neurological clinic of his famous uncle Moritz H. Romberg. Henoch was a gentle physician, a wise clinician, and a gifted teacher. These qualities were recognized and rewarded by his appointment, at the age of 40, to the professorship in the University and to the headship of the pediatric polyclinic in the Royal Charité Hospital. As the leading children's physician of Germany and the writer of the authoritative texts of his specialty, the honorable title "Geheimrat" was bestowed on him. The standard treatises were held in high regard by his countrymen and were translated so that other physicians might profit from his professional wisdom and clinical experience.

The description of the first case of non-thrombocytopenic purpura was communicated by Henoch to the Berlin Medical Society on Nov 18, 1863, in a discussion of the relationship of purpura and intestinal dysfunction.[1] A 15-year-old boy, from the private practice of an associate, complained of abdominal colic, arthralgia, slight icterus, and purpura on the arms and legs and in the buccal mucous membranes. The pathogenesis of the purpura was attributed to changes in the small vessels. In considering the etiology, mention was made of Schönlein's peliosis rheumatica, but Henoch rejected classification of his case in this category. Nor did he attribute the malady to an allergic phenomenon. Two case studies from Henoch's clinic at the Charité were noted in the conclusion of the report. The first patient was a seven-year-old boy with purpura and nephritis, which appeared following scarlatina; the second patient was a seven-year-old girl with hematuria and purpura.

In 1874, and again before the Berlin Medical Society, the considerations on purpura were expanded to include the clinical data on four additional patients. Intermittent purpura, arthralgia, and gastrointestinal symptoms were found to be characteristic features.[2] In 1886, purpura fulminans was discussed as a variant of purpura rheumatica, with emphasis on a predisposing severe infection, either a fibrinous (lobar) pneumonia or scarlet fever.[3] The clinical summary of rheumatic purpura (Henoch-Schönlein purpura) was included in his *Lectures on Diseases of Children,* which was published in English in 1882.[2]

Numerous smaller, and larger, dark red, or bluish, round patches are especially noticed on the legs and feet, while the upper portions of the body are free, or present but few specks. They are not changed by pressure, and here and there present in the centre a papular or more diffuse hardness and prominence caused by coagulation of fibrin. Apart from the previously mentioned spontaneous pains, the tibia, small bones of the feet, and the soles are not infrequently tender on pressure, and movements of the joints are painful, . . . Occasionally a wheal-like efflorescence (erythema nodosum) is also present, in the middle of which a bluish extravasation of blood can be seen and felt, and I have not infrequently noticed slight oedema of the dorsum of the foot, though the urine did not contain any albumen.

There is at present no explanation for the undoubted connection of the purpura with the pains and swelling in the limbs and joints. It is questionable whether the term purpura rheumatica is justified, because the influence of cold and wet cannot always be demonstrated. This etiological factor is especially absent in a more complicated form, in which, in addition to the previously mentioned symptoms, vomiting, intestinal hemorrhage, and colic, are also present.

The purpura in these cases was always combined with colic, tenderness of the colon, vomiting, intestinal hemorrhage, and, with one exception, with rheumatic pains, the swelling of the joints being less constant. There was also a characteristic development of the symptoms in exacerbations, with intervals of several days, or even a week, so that the disease was prolonged to three to seven weeks. Fever was not constant, and, when present, was always very moderate. That these symptoms are mutually connected cannot be denied, but how this connection can be explained I am unable to state.

At the time of his retirement, Henoch had extended the observations of Schönlein in describing purpura associated with joint disease, sometimes appearing without a recognized pathogenic agent, at other times complicating a severe infection. In contemporary medicine, lesions in the genitourinary tract, similar to those in the skin and mucous membranes, may lead to transient hematuria or proteinuria. A low mortality rate is observed in the mild form; whereas the outcome frequently is fatal in those severely afflicted. The malady usually appears in children, with a higher incidence in girls than in boys. The syndrome of abdominal crisis and articular distress, in combination with one of the erythemas (multiforme, bullosum, vesiculosum, and nodosum), is placed in the class of allergic purpura.

1. Henoch, E.: The Association of Purpura and Intestinal Disturbance (Ger), *Klin Wschr* 5:517-19, 1868.
2. Henoch, E.: *Lectures on Diseases of Children, a Handbook for Physicians and Students,* New York: William Wood & Co., 1882, pp 315-19.
3 Henoch, E.: Purpura Fulminans (Ger), *Klin Wschr* 24:8-10, 1887.

Austin Flint (1812-1886)

ALTHOUGH A CHAIR IN A MEDICAL SCHOOL is considered to be a relatively stable professional position, a few notable exceptions come to mind. Hans Zinsser wandered from the Department of Bacteriology at Stanford to the College of Physicians and Surgeons of Columbia University in New York, and later to Harvard Medical School. William Dock went from the Department of Pathology at Stanford to Cornell and to the New York Downstate Medical School at Brooklyn. Another notable example of a roving professor was Austin Flint, a friend of W. H. Welch, who held positions in six medical schools. Flint was one of the outstanding professors of medicine in the mid-portion of the 19th century. Following graduation from Harvard Medical School at the age of 21, he practiced medicine in Boston and Northampton, Mass. for three years. He then moved to Buffalo, established a new practice, and subsequently was appointed Health Officer. In 1844, at the age of 32, he was called to Chicago as Professor of Medical Theory and Practice in Rush Medical College. One year later, he returned to Buffalo and established the *Buffalo Medical Journal*

and was its editor for 10 years, even though he did not remain in Buffalo during the entire time. The *Journal* was published with few interruptions until World War I. Flint served as delegate from the Buffalo Medical Association to the National Medical Convention in 1846.[1] He was appointed a member of a committee to report on requirements for the degree of Doctor of Medicine. The National Medical Convention changed its name to the American Medical Association in 1847-48. Meanwhile Flint became the first Professor of the Theory and Practice of Medicine at the University of Buffalo Medical School established in 1847. Hamburg Canal College, Medical and Surgical Institute and Sanitorium, Buffalo College of Rational Medicine, Homeopathic, College of Physicians and Surgeons, Homeopathic, Mohawk Medical College, and Niagara University Medical Department were organized in later years in the Niagara Frontier but eventually were closed by order of the Supreme Court of the state of New York, were dissolved by attrition, or merged. Once more Flint was attracted elsewhere. In this instance he spent one year at the University of Louisville as Professor of Medical Theory and Practice. In 1856, however, he returned to Buffalo as Professor of Pathology and Clinical Medicine.

It is noteworthy that the professorial aspirant currently, at the age of 40, considers himself fortunate to be as far up the academic ladder as to hold an associate professorship. At this age, Flint had already held a full professorship in three medical schools. Two years later he became Professor of Clinical Medicine in the New Orleans School of Medicine and visiting physician to the Charity Hospital. He enjoyed an unusual arrangement with these two most recent assignments. He spent the winter in New Orleans and each summer in Buffalo. In 1860 at the age of 48, he made his last geographic move in academic medicine. He accepted the Professorship of the Principles and Practice of Medicine at Bellevue Hospital. Also, he was Professor of Pathology and Practical Medicine at Long Island College Hospital for several years. He was honored by the Presidency of the American

Medical Association in 1884 at the age of 72.

A number of other noteworthy accomplishments of Flint include studies on auscultation and percussion of the chest[2, 3] and a textbook on medicine,[4] that preceded by 25 years Osler's *Practice and Principles of Medicine*. He coined the term "bronchovesicular breathing." Flint's Law states:

An elevation of pitch always accompanies diminution of resonance in consequence of pulmonary consolidation. In other words, dullness of resonance is never present without the pitch being raised.

This is not to be confused with Flint's Law: "The ontogeny of an organ is the phylogeny of its blood supply." The Austin Flint murmur is "a loud presystolic murmur at the apex in aortic regurgitation." He described it thus:

In some cases in which free aortic regurgitation exists, the left ventricle becoming filled before the auricles contract, the mitral curtains are floated out, and the valve closed when the mitral current takes place, and, under these circumstances, this murmur may be produced by the current just named, although no mitral lesion exists.[5]

Austin Flint was a physician and teacher, a person of many talents and many interests. His epidemiologic studies before the discoveries of Koch, Pasteur, and Lister were pioneer contributions. His early investigations as Health Officer for the city of Buffalo concerned typhoid fever. An outbreak occurred in North Boston a few miles south of Buffalo, deep in the Boston hills where hemlock plank houses with cucumber wood floors were constructed by the early settlers from native timber. The outbreak of typhoid fever, studied by Flint, occurred in 1843, three decades before William Budd's monumental treatise on the subject was published. Flint discovered[6] that the well which supplied Fuller's Tavern attracted seepage from a privy only a few yards away. A number of the residents who used the water from Fuller's well contracted typhoid fever. One family, at odds with Fuller and refused the use of his well, did not contract the fever.

The water from the well was submitted to chemical analysis and was considered chemically pure, except for the presence of sugar. This was attributed to the fact that the jug in which the water was collected had been used previously for the transport of molasses.

A Treatise on the Principles and Practice of Medicine Designed for the Use of Practitioners and Students of Medicine[4] by Flint was published in Philadelphia in 1866. The introductory chapter outlines the scope of medicine and defines pathology and the relationship of pathology to physiology. Part II, a discussion of morbid states, begins with diseases that affect the respiratory system. There are three chapters on pleuritis, two on pneumonitis and one on bronchitis. Section IV discusses diseases of the nervous system including hysteria, catalepsy, ecstasy, somnambulism, and nervous asthenia. The concluding chapter is on scurvy, which is preceded by 16 pages of a discussion of gout.

There were six physicians in the Flint medical dynasty whose practice of medicine in America extended over a period of more than two centuries. The first, the great-grandfather of Austin Flint, began the practice of medicine in Shrewsbury, Massachusetts, in 1733. Austin Flint, Jr., served as Professor of Physiology at the University of Buffalo and later at New York Medical College, at Bellevue Medical College, and Cornell University Medical School. The last Austin Flint was a teacher at Bellevue University Medical School and Professor of Obstetrics and Gynecology at New York University.

1. Evans, A. S.: Austin Flint and His Contributions to Medicine, *Bull Hist Med* 32:224 (May-June) 1958.
2. Middleton, W. S.: Biographical History of Physical Diagnosis, *Ann Med Hist* 6:425-452 (Dec.) 1924.
3. Flint, A.: Analytical Study of Auscultation and Percussion, with Reference to the Distinctive Characters of Pulmonary Signs, *Trans Int Med Congr*, Seventh Session, London 2:130-141, 1881.
4. Flint, A.: *Treatise on the Principles and Practice of Medicine*, Philadelphia: H. C. Lea's Son & Co., 1866.
5. Flint, A.: On Cardiac Murmurs, *Amer J Med Sci* 44:29-54, 1862.
6. Flint, A.: Account of Epidemic Fever Which Occurred at North Boston, Erie County, New York, During the Months of October and November, 1843, *Amer J Med Sci* 10:21-35, 1845.

Composite by G. Bako

Elizabeth Blackwell (1821-1910)

NOT ONLY WAS ELIZABETH BLACKWELL the recipient of the doctorate of medicine from the provincial Geneva Medical College, the first of her sex to become a physician in America, but also she was equally at home in Cincinnati, Philadelphia, New York, London, and Hastings. The family emigrated from her birthplace in Bristol, England, to Cincinnati, prompted by the interest of her father in the cultivation of sugar beets as a substitute for cane sugar.[1] This practical motive was balanced by a zealous ulterior one. He abhorred the subjugation of man, irrespective of race, creed, or color, and fervently hoped to make all men free. While residing temporarily in New York prior to the westward trek, he became an ardent abolitionist. William Lloyd Garrison was a frequent visitor at their home on Long Island.

The father died shortly after the family moved to Cincinnati when Elizabeth was 17. In order to support the family, the three elder sisters established a boarding school for young ladies. Elizabeth, between the ages of 22 and 24, taught school in Henderson, Kentucky. The next teaching position, in Asheville, North Carolina, under Dr. John Dickson, physician and minister, provided

exposure to medicine through the perusal of the Reverend's medical text. Although unconfirmed by concrete evidence, probably she was inclined to a medical career several years earlier. Further uncertainty as to the reason for her spinsterhood may be attributed to a Puritan reluctance to accept male advances, for she was described as an attractive, intelligent, and sparkling young lady. In later years she wrote as an eccentric on sex, masturbation, circumcision, impotence, and continence, with little understanding of the human emotions involved.

At the age of 25 Elizabeth accepted a teaching position at a fashionable boarding academy in Charleston, South Carolina. Her mentor was another Dr. Dickson—Samuel Henry—professor of theory and practice of medicine at Charleston Medical School, a teacher of James Marion Sims and later a member of the faculty of the Jefferson Medical College. She continued to "read" medical books when time permitted. In 1847, Miss Blackwell was determined to enroll in one of the four medical colleges in Philadelphia. Overtures in each instance met with disappointment. A similar fate awaited her in New York City. The last effort led to a volume of correspondence. An earnest appeal was made to a number of the "country colleges" of the Northeastern states. Through a most unusual academic action, she was accepted at Geneva Medical College. The school, one of the pioneer medical schools in upper New York State, was an outgrowth of the Geneva Academy, which had been chartered in 1826.[2] The establishment of the medical college was a retaliatory action, through a nefarious collusion with Rutgers College in New Brunswick, against the College of Physicians and Surgeons of Columbia University. The medical school was identified initially as "Rutgers Medical Faculty, Geneva College, Duane Street, City of New York." The attempt to utilize Geneva's charter for the conferring of medical degrees downstate was short-lived. In 1834, the activities were abandoned in Manhattan and transferred to the upstate community. Little is known about the early years of the College. There were six members of the original faculty, scientists of wide experience and national reputation. The school flourished until 1872. The formation of a medical school in Buffalo in 1846 and the difficulties common to educational institutions during the Civil War contributed to its deterioration and subsequent closing.

But to return to Elizabeth Blackwell—her application for admission was approved not by the trustees nor the faculty but by an almost unanimous vote of the student body. This decision was announced by the resolution dispatched to the applicant:

Resolved, That one of the radical principles of a Republican Government is the universal education of both sexes; that to every branch of scientific education the door should be open equally to all; that the application of Elizabeth Blackwell to become a member of our class meets our entire approbation; and in extending our unanimous invitation we pledge ourselves that no conduct of ours shall cause her to regret her attendance at this institution.

A degree in medicine was granted two years later at the commencement exercises held in the local church.

In the 19th century, and to some extent in the early part of the 20th century, a physician considered postgraduate training in Europe a necessary extension of an adequate medical education. Elizabeth Blackwell went to Paris with the hope of being allowed to study with Pierre Charles Alexandre Louis.[3] But she failed where male physicians succeeded. In consolation, assignment to the school for midwives at La Maternité was gained but only on the same status as the other student midwives. Gonorrheal ophthalmia, contracted from one of the babes, resulted eventually in the loss of vision in one eye. London was the next medical center on her postgraduate circuit. England, more kindly than France, admitted her for study at St. Bartholomew's Hospital. The lectures on surgical pathology by James Paget and the physiological lectures of Senhouse Kirkes proved particularly enjoyable. Friendships were formed with Florence Nightingale and Lady Byron during the London visit. The former may have interested Elizabeth in her subsequent efforts to provide nursing care for the wounded and sick during the Civil War.

Elizabeth returned to New York in 1851 but received a cool welcome. She was denied hospital and dispensary privileges, office space, even a boardinghouse room in which to live. There was no alternative but to establish her own infirmary. The articles of incorporation for the New York Infirmary and College for Women and Children were granted in 1853. In 1857, she was joined by Dr. Marie Zakrzewska and her own sister Emily, a graduate of the Cleveland Medical College of Western Reserve University. She occupied the chair of hygiene when, in 1865, the Woman's Medical College of New York Infirmary was founded: "as a proof of woman's ability to practice medicine, and as a medical center for women, this institution is well worthy of support."[4] In 1899, the College closed, and the students were transferred to Cornell University Medical College, coeducational from its beginning.

Elizabeth returned to London in 1869 for reasons best known to her. It is possible that she was discouraged with her efforts in America. An equally logical explanation was her enduring love for England. Meanwhile, her name had been enrolled in the Medical Register, reputedly through the efforts of Benjamin Brodie. Thus, she became the first duly registered female physician in England as in the United States. Irrespective of the motives for her return to England, she left her sister in New York, began the practice of medicine in London, and became identified with the medical woman's movement and woman's suffrage. Her most important book *Counsel to Parents on the Moral Education of Children* was written in 1876, a strange discussion of metaphysical data.[5] Death came at the age of 89 in Hastings, where Harold was vanquished by William the Conquerer. It was not until 5 decades later (1960) that Jefferson Medical College, the last of American schools to admit women students, accepted the principles for which she fought.

In reading the stories about Elizabeth Blackwell, her autobiography, and biographical sketches, one gains the impression that she was a kind, lovable, and gentle physician, and not a militant suffragette. Probably these two extremes were combined with an outward appearance of graciousness and gentility, but with the spirit of the reformer which sometimes is most effective when least apparent.

1. Robinson, V.: *Pathfinders in Medicine,* 2nd ed, New York: Medical Life Press, 1929.
2. Cushing, H.: *The Medical Career,* Boston: Little, Brown and Company, 1940.
3. Lovejoy, E. P.: *Women Doctors of the World,* New York: MacMillan, 1860.
4. Blackwell, E.: *Medicine as a Profession for Women,* New York, 1860.
5. Blackwell, E.: *Counsel to Parents on the Moral Education of Children,* 1876.

Sir James Paget (1814-1899)

JAMES PAGET, surgeon to St. Bartholomew's Hospital, and one of the first English surgeons to investigate microscopic as well as macroscopic structure, was born in 1814 at Yarmouth, the eighth in a family with 16 siblings. His father—brewer, large ship-owner, and purveyor to his majesty's ships —experienced good fortune and bad. His mother, endowed with an industrious nature and charm, was gracious in prosperity and unwavering in adversity. She collected all types of curiosities and was clever at knitting and painting. James attended a nearby school kept by a Unitarian minister. It was a fair education for what it cost—eight guineas a year. He acquired sufficient comprehension of Latin and Greek for a "commonplace understanding of a Latin or a Greek book."[1] James was not the only distinguished physician in the Paget family. An older brother George obtained a medical fellowship at Gonville and Caius College and later was regius professor of medicine at Cambridge.

Paget was apprenticed to Charles Costerton "to learn the art and mystery of a Surgeon and Apothecary." For four years he performed menial chores in the office, attended outpatients, and prepared drugs and debit statements for Costerton. But the chores were more dull than arduous, and ample time was found for the study of anatomy, reading of the medical books in the office library, sketching, and roaming the country collecting insects and flowers. Paget entered St. Bartholomew's Hospital as a medical student at the age of 20 and passed the examinations at the College of Surgeons 18 months later. During the period of professional study, he showed diligence in the laboratory and in the death house. The identification of specks in the muscles of dissecting room specimens prompted his first published pathological observation. A microscope was borrowed from the botany department of the British Museum. Magnification of the spicules disclosed *Trichina spiralis.* Although Paget made the interpretation, Sir Richard Owen reported the observation to the Abernethian Society in 1835.[2]

For 15 years following graduation, Paget pursued a variety of professional labors. He taught anatomy and physiology, served as sub-editor on the *Medical Gazette,* and reviewed books and prepared articles for the *Penney Cyclopaedia* and the *Biographical Dictionary,* published by the Society for the Diffusion of Useful Knowledge. He translated medical articles from German, French, Dutch, and Italian—languages that had been learned largely on his own. As curator of St. Bartholomew's anatomical museum, at a miserably low salary, he was responsible for procuring bodies for dissection and for the preparation of specimens for the surgery lectures. Later Paget became surgeon at St.

Bartholomew's and professor of anatomy and surgery at the Royal College of Surgeons. His lectures were widely received and highly regarded. He was elected a Fellow of the Royal Society at the age of 37 and at 44 was appointed surgeon-extraordinary to Queen Victoria. At 57 he resigned as surgeon at Bart's and accepted a baronetcy. Five years later he was appointed sergeant-surgeon to Queen Victoria.

An outstanding disappointment at this time was the rejection by a prospective publisher of a prepared treatise on general anatomy. Paget's capacity for writing was phenomenal.[1]

Q. I used to write a leading article every two or three weeks, sometimes more often [for the *Medical Gazette*]; and have been amused, after 40 or more years, to find them generally discreet, not lively or clever.

Descriptions of two eponymic maladies associated with Paget were published after he had resigned his active post at the hospital. Eczema of the nipple, with mammary cancer—Paget's disease of the nipple—was described in *St. Bartholomew's Hospital Reports*.[3]

I believe it has not yet been published that certain chronic affections of the skin of the nipple and areola are very often succeeded by the formation of scirrhous cancer in the mammary gland. I have seen about fifteen cases in which this has happened, and the events were in all of them so similar that one description may suffice. In the majority it had the appearance of a florid, intensely red, raw surface, very finely granular, as if nearly the whole thickness of the epidermis were removed; like the surface of very acute diffuse eczema, or like that of an acute balanitis.

In the cancers themselves, I have seen in these cases nothing peculiar. They have been various in form; some acute, some chronic, the majority following an average course, and all tending to the same end; recurring if removed, affecting lymph-glands and distant parts, showing nothing which might not be written in the ordinary history of cancer of the breast.

Paget's disease of bone, osteitis deformans, is described.[4,5]

I hope it will be agreeable to the Society if I make known some of the results of the study of a rare disease of bones.

At forty-six, from no assigned cause, unless it were that he lived in a rather cold and damp

place in the North of England, he began to be subject to aching pains in his thighs and legs.

I first saw this gentleman in 1856, when these things had been observed for about two years. Except that he was very grey and looked rather old for his age, he might have been considered as in perfect health. He walked with full strength and power, but somewhat stiffly. His left tibia, especially in its lower half, was broad, and felt nodular and uneven, as if not only itself but its periosteum and the integuments over it were thickened. In a much less degree similar changes could be felt in the lower half of the left femur.

Three years later . . . he was in the same good general health, but the left tibia had become larger and had a well-marked anterior curve. . . . The left femur also was now distinctly enlarged, and felt tuberous at the junction of its upper and middle thirds, and was arched forwards and outwards, so that he could not bring the left knee into contact with the right. There was also some appearance of widening of the left side of the pelvis, the nates on this side being flattened and lowered, and the great trochanter projecting nearly half an inch farther from the middle line. The left limb was about a quarter of an inch shorter than the right. The patient believed that the right side of his skull was enlarged, for his hats had become too tight; but the change was not clearly visible.

Notwithstanding these progressive changes, the patient suffered very little; he had lived actively, walking, riding, and engaging in all the usual pursuits of a country gentleman.

In the next seventeen years of his life I rarely saw him, but the story of his disease, of which I often heard, may be briefly told and with few dates, for its progress was nearly uniform and very slow. The left femur and tibia became larger, heavier, and somewhat more curved. Very slowly those of the right limb followed the same course, till they gained very nearly the same size and shape. The limbs thus became nearly symmetrical in their deformity, the curving of the left being only a little more outward than that of the right.

The skull became gradually larger, so that nearly every year, for many years, his hat, and the helmet that he wore as a member of the Yeomanry Corps needed to be enlarged. . . . In its enlargement, however, the head retained its natural shape and, to the last, looked intellectual, though with some exaggeration.

The spine very slowly became curved and almost rigid. The whole of the cervical vertebrae and the upper dorsal formed a strong posterior, not angular, curve; and an anterior curve, of similar shape, was formed by the lower dorsal and lumbar vertebrae. The length of the spine thus seemed lessened, and from a height of six feet one inch he sank to about five feet nine inches. At the same time the chest became contracted, narrow, flattened laterally, deep from before backwards, and the movements of the ribs and of the spine were lessened.

His head was advanced and lowered so that the neck was very short, and the chin, when he held his head at ease, was more than an inch lower than the top of the sternum.

The short narrow chest suddenly widened into a much shorter and broad abdomen, and the pelvis was wide and low. The arms appeared unnaturally long, and, though the shoulders were very high, the hands hung low down by the thighs and in front of them. Altogether, the attitude in standing looked simian, strangely in contrast with the large head and handsome features.

About this time some signs of insufficiency of the mitral valve were observed, but the patient now lived so quietly, and moved with so little speed, that this defect gave him no considerable distress.

In December, 1872, sight was partially destroyed by retinal haemorrhage, first in one eye, then in the other, and at nearly the same time he began to be somewhat deaf.

At postmortem examination, the skull and the long bones were sufficiently soft to be cut with a razor.[4]

. . . the contents of the Haversian canals were seen to consist generally of a homogeneous or granular basis, containing cells of round or oval form about the size and having much the appearance of leucocytes. . . . The presence of new bone was most evident in the periosteum of the tibia, external to the ordinary compact layer of the shaft.

With a medium power the number of lamellae surrounding the Haversian canals was easily seen to be not larger than in normal bone, whilst the arrangement of the intervening space was most complex and totally different from that of a healthy bone.

Three cases of gouty arthritis or familial gout were observed in the series. Paget wrote of gout from personal experience; the malady was inherited from his maternal grandfather.[6]

Paget was a gentleman surgeon, a surgeon and a gentleman. He displayed great capacity for friendship in the profession, outside the profession, and among royalty. Students and patients alike were endeared to him. Friends included Gladstone, Cardinal Newman, Tennyson, Robert Browning, George Eliot, Tyndall, Huxley, Darwin, Pasteur, Virchow, Koch, Charcot, and Florence Nightingale. According to his son, who edited and amplified his memoirs,[1] he made the most of old age, was always happy among friends or family, and held no fear

of death, which occurred in 1899 at the age of 85. He received the last consolation of religion from his son, the Bishop of Oxford. The first portion of the service was held in Westminster Abbey; he was buried in Finchley Cemetery.

1. *Memoirs and Letters of Sir James Paget*, S. Paget, ed., London: Longmans, Green, and Co., 1903.
2. Zoological Society. Newly-Discovered Animal in Human Muscle, *Lond Med Gaz* 16:125-127, 1835.
3. Paget, J.: On Disease of the Mammary Areola Preceding Cancer of the Mammary Gland, *St Bart Hosp Rep* 10:87-89, 1874.
4. Paget, J.: On a Form of Chronic Inflammation of Bones (Osteitis Deformans), *Trans Med Chir Soc,* 2nd series 42:37-63, 1877.
5. Paget, J.: Additional Cases of Osteitis Deformans, *Trans Med Chir Soc* 65:225-236, 1882.
6. Paget, J.: Gouty and Some Other Forms of Phlebitis, *St Bart Hosp Rep* 2:82-92, 1866.

Friedrich Theodor von Frerichs (1819-1885)

FRERICHS, one of the designers in central Europe of bedside instruction, built his reputation upon clinical investigation and diagnostic acumen within a few short years after completion of formal education. Born in Aurich, Germany, of Frisian stock he studied medicine at Göttingen, where he was an illustrious pupil of Wöhler, the synthesizer of urea. Frerichs was interested in ophthalmology and practiced this specialty for a time in his native community; however, his career lay in academic medicine and especially in the critical correlation of findings from the clinical laboratory and the pathological amphitheater with the natural history of morbid states. At the early age of 29, he accepted his first senior appointment, that of professor of medicine on the distinguished faculty of Göttingen, an especially noteworthy appointment for one so young. Two years later Frerichs departed for his next post, the chair of medicine at Kiel. This was followed by an appointment at Breslau; and, finally at the age of 40, he succeeded Schönlein as professor of medicine in Berlin and chief of the medical clinic at Charité Hospital. In each university he made one or more notable contributions.

A selected list of students who came under his influence included brilliant names in clinical medicine, clinical pathology, and fundamental science: Ehrlich, Naunyn, Leyden, von Mering, and Quincke. Frerichs was a diagnostician with great intuition, a lecturer with great histrionic skill, and a consultant with a large following. However, he was austere, frequently insensitive to students and patients, while controversy with his professional associates marked him as one with an inflammable personality. He chose his intellectual equals—Traube, Virchow, Graefe, and Langenbeck—for astute polemics. The pummeling of scientific intercourse reflected upon his productivity in professional maturity, and eventually this merged into a dark period of his clinical life. Subsequently, the bright days returned, and once more he became worthy of the leadership among clinical teachers in Germany.

While in Breslau, Frerichs, in conjunction with Staedeler, identified leucine and tyrosine in the urine of a patient with acute liver atrophy.[1] Also, he prepared the section on digestion for Wagner's *Dictionary of Physiology* and gave one of the first accounts of cerebral sclerosis. Four case reports of the affliction were gleaned from the literature in the historical survey. The integrated findings were described.[2]

It is well known that an increase in the consistency of the brain can often be observed as a result of anemia and after devastating purulent infections, such as puerperal peritonitis, ileotyphus, choleratyphus, etc. The increase in consistency is the result of partial dehydration and never attains a high degree. More pronounced is the sclerosis which accompanies senile atrophy.

The highest degree of hardening is always localized; it is limited to larger or smaller areas and can be caused by several factors. The residue of tubercular infections is not to be considered because it differs from the surrounding brain substance, not the hardening produced by cancerous infiltration, and finally not the advanced brain sclerosis from purulent infections.

There exists another form of brain sclerosis which cannot be traced with certainty to any of the above mentioned cases, and which even pose well founded objections to the infectious theory. This form usually develops in the soft parts above the lateral ventricles and spreads slowly, often over several years. The hardening is sharply delineated and shows a pattern which is different from infectious exudates or pathological lesions. The meninges are not involved, even if the hardening spreads over the whole cortical substance.

At the Kiel clinic, Frerichs published a monograph on the kidney, entitled *Bright's Kidney Diseases and Their Treatment*.[3] He speculated that the symptoms in uremia were related to the formation of ammonium carbonate from the action of an enzyme on urea. A monograph on diseases of the liver, his greatest contribution to medical literature, was prepared while at Breslau. In the preface he disclosed his philosophy of disease and the science of diagnosis and treatment in the mid-19th century.[4]

The main part of the science of disease is of a purely descriptive character; a scientific interpretation of facts and a clear insight into the intimate connection subsisting between different phenomena, which may precede all attempts at a rational method of cure, having been attained in a few instances only. Hence, treatment is still, as heretofore, handed over, for the most part, to empiricism, but not, however, to that traditional so-called experience, which has no clear knowledge of the subject, which is followed by no certain results, and which does not make any rigid discrimination between the heterogeneous elements which are jumbled together, or between one form of disease and another. Therapeutic researchers must be regulated in the same manner as pathological. Scientific medicine, although it has not rendered a rational system of treatment possible, has already furnished us with important data in anticipation of such a system. The more careful tracing of the progress of morbid processes, and the insight into their modes of origin and retrogression, enable us to determine the principles of treatment with greater clearness than formerly; a more accurate diagnosis secures to us the homogenous nature of the quantities that we have to deal with, while the study of pharmacy provides us wih the first materials for an insight into the mode of action of drugs.

The postmortem examination of a 33-year-old pregnant housewife, dead of acute atrophy of the liver, showed crystalline deposits in the tissues similar in structure to those which had been observed in the urine of a patient also afflicted with liver dystrophy. The patient died four days after the onset of overt jaundice. The liver was atrophied, flabby, and shriveled. The identification of leucine and tyrosine crystals within the injured liver cells was described in the appropriate section on acute yellow atrophy.[4]

No trace of the hepatic cells could be detected upon microscopic examination of the hepatic tissue. . . . Amidst this detritus of the secreting apparatus of the liver, there were observed numerous needle-shaped crysals adhering together in bundles, or in radiating masses (tyrosine).

These crystals were found in much greater abundance in the blood of the hepatic veins, which contained a thin reddish fluid, in which, along with normal blood-corpuscles, there floated numberless crystals in bundles and radiating masses. They were entirely absent from the blood of the portal vein and hepatic artery. The liver was washed in cold water, to free it from its adherent blood; it was then cut in pieces, triturated, and boiled. The filtered fluid, upon standing, deposited numerous cystals, adhering partly in bundles, and partly in radiating masses (tyrosine). When farther concentrated, a greyish-yellow film formed at the margins and over the surface of the fluid, and there separated, a large quantity of brown globular masses, made up of concentric layers (leucine).

In 1861, Frerichs described progressive lenticular degeneration in association with cirrhosis of the liver (Kinnier-Wilson's disease) in a ten-year-old boy who had experienced good health and normal mental development until one year prior to the onset of clinical symptoms. These included headache, lassitude, stammering, slowness of speech, and weakness of the extremities. Subsequently, the patient lost all power of speech and was able to swallow only liquid food. Postmortem examination disclosed that:[5]

The substance of the brain was soft, particularly in the fornix and corpus callosum; everywhere it contained much blood. There was nothing abnormal in the lateral ventricles; but, beneath the lining membrane of the fourth ventricle, were extravasations of blood, the size of a linseed.

The medulla oblongata was firmer and more tenacious than in the normal state. The liver was small, and its convex surface was adherent by numerous bands to the diaphragm. Its surface was covered with nodules, varying in size from a pea to a bean, and similar formations could be seen in its interior, where they were separated from one another by broad bands of areolar tissue.

Frerichs' last major contribution to medicine was a monograph on diabetes mellitus.[6] The treatise, which appeared after a fallow period of several years, approached in brilliance his earlier efforts in the description of morbid states. By then he was entitled to be addressed as von Frerichs, an honor bestowed by the Emperor but justly deserved, for his contributions to clinicopathological observation and bedside teaching a century ago.

1. Frerichs, F.: Open Letter to Professor Oppolzer in Vienna (Ger), *Wien Med Wschr* 4:465-470, 1854.
2. Frerichs, F.: Disseminated Sclerosis (Ger), excerpt trans. by E. Longar, *Arch Ges Med* 10:334-350, 1849.
3. Frerichs, F.: *Bright's Kidney Diseases and Their Treatment* (Ger), Braunschweig: F. Vieweg, 1851.
4. Frerichs, F.: *A Clinical Treatise on Diseases of the Liver,* vol 1, C. Murchison, trans., London: New Sydenham Society, 1860.
5. Frerichs, F.: *A Clinical Treatise on Diseases of the Liver,* vol 2, C. Murchison, trans., London: New Sydenham Society, 1861, pp 60-63.
6. von Frerichs, F.: *On Diabetes* (Ger), Berlin: A. Hirschwald, 1884.

Alfred Baring Garrod
(1819-1909)

GOUT AND GARROD have been linked in medical literature for more than a century. This distinguished London physician, born in 1819 at Ipswich, identified uric acid as a normal constituent of the serum of healthy persons and devised a method for detecting its increased concentration in gouty subjects. Alfred attended the local grammar school and, after an apprenticeship with Mr. Charles Hammond, surgeon to the East Suffolk Hospital, entered University College Hospital, London, where he received the

Composite by G. Bako

MD degree in 1843. He placed first in the examinations and was awarded the Galen medal for botany by the Society of Apothecaries. Loyalty to the University College Hospital continued in his postgraduate years, and he enjoyed the ascending progression of responsibility, beginning as assistant physician and ending as full physician and professor of therapeutics and clinical medicine.

His "Observations on Certain Pathological Conditions of the Blood and Urine, in Gout, Rheumatism, and Bright's Disease" was published in 1848, while serving as assistant physician.[1] It is interesting that Garrod grouped and discussed these morbid states in a single treatise. Gout and rheumatism (rheumatoid arthritis) were not always dissociated as separate entities, and Garrod's clinical observations were of help in supporting specific differentiation. On the other hand, gout and Bright's disease were not associated clinically, except for critical degenerative changes in the kidney observed in a small percentage of patients with gout, sometimes under the mistaken premise that the renal findings justified a diagnosis of chronic glomerulonephritis.

Garrod begins the discourse on his discoveries of uric acid metabolism and the pathogenesis of gout, communicated by C. J. B. Williams, senior associate, as follows:[1]

The ancients considered *gout* to depend on the presence of some morbid humour in the blood, which, becoming deposited in weak parts, gave rise to the affections of the joints; as to the nature of this matter their ideas greatly varied. . . . The nature of this change, however, has not been defined, although most agree in regarding it as connected with an excessive formation of uric acid in the system; the frequent presence of chalk-stones or tophaceous deposits in and around the joints, the liability of gouty patients to uric acid deposits in the urine, and the formation of urinary calculi consisting of the same acid, strongly favouring the idea. But as gout sometimes occurs in patients not having such deposits in their urine, and also in broken-down constitutions not generally considered prone to an excessive formation of uric acid, it has been doubted by many whether this substance is the "materies morbi," or only an occasional accompaniment.

Garrod continued with a discussion of the first procedure for the quantitative determination of uric acid in a series of normal and gouty persons:[1]

As far as my experiments regarding the nature of this disease have been prosecuted, they appear to show that—
1st. The blood in gout contains *uric acid* in the form of urate of soda, which salt can be obtained from it, in a crystalline state.
In June 1847, a male patient, R. Hartley, was admitted into the hospital suffering from gout. . . . At this time blood was taken from the arm for the purpose of examination.
1000 grains of the serum were taken for examination, and evaporated to dryness in thin layers in a water-bath. It was then powdered and treated with rectified spirit, boiled for about ten or fifteen minutes, again treated in the same way, and the spirit solutions preserved for examination. After again washing with spirit, the dried serum was exhausted by means of boiling distilled water, the operation being repeated two or three times, and the watery solutions mixed. When a small quantity of this fluid was evaporated with the

addition of nitric acid, and afterwards held over the vapour of ammonia, distinct evidence of the existence of uric acid was afforded by the production of the beautiful purple tint of murexide or purpurate of ammonia. The watery solution was then evaporated till it became slightly thick, and, when cool, was acidulated with pure hydrochloric acid. On standing for some hours, crystals of *uric acid* were deposited, which were afterwards collected, washed with alcohol and weighed.

As judged by current recoveries of uric acid in the serum, Garrod's method was more qualitative than quantitative. When comparison was made, however, with recovery from the serum of non-gouty patients, a significant difference was demonstrated. Thus, Garrod had revealed not only the presence of uric acid in the body fluids of gouty and nongouty persons, but had provided experimental proof of an increased concentration of uric acid in the gouty subject. In the concluding portion of the communication, Garrod speculated that uric acid always can be recovered from the urine of patients with chronic tophaceous gout.

The quantitative procedure was modified shortly after, and a higher yield of uric acid was obtained with small quantities of blood. The new process was named the uric acid "thread test."[2]

Take from one to two fluid drachms of the serum of blood, and put it into a flattened glass dish or capsule; . . . to this is added the strong acetic acid of the London Pharmacopoeia, in the proportion of about six minims to each fluid drachm of the serum; a few bubbles of gas are generally evolved at first, when the fluids are well mixed, a very fine thread is introduced, consisting of from one to three ultimate fibers, from a piece of unwashed huckaback or other linen fabric, about one inch in length, which should be depressed by means of a small rod, as a probe or point of a pencil. The glass is then put aside in a moderately warm place, until the serum is quite set and almost dry; the mantelpiece in a room of the ordinary temperature answers very well, the time varying from eighteen to forty-eight hours, depending on the warmth and dryness of the atmosphere.

Should uric acid be present in the serum in quantities above a certain small amount noticed below, it will crystallise, and during its crystallisation will be attracted to the thread, and assume a form not unlike that presented by stone sugar upon a string.

Abdominal fluid, pericardial fluid, and the fluid of an artificially formed blister were positive for uric acid with the new test. No uric acid was found in the sweat of gouty subjects, an observation currently valid. Minute amounts only are lost from the body through the skin.

Garrod advanced a highly prophetic concept of the function of the kidneys in regard to excretion of uric acid and other solutes:[1]

Thus it appears that the kidneys [in gout] had almost entirely lost their power of excreting uric acid, but not the other solids of the urine.

The results of these experiments on the condition of the blood and urine, prove that uric acid is not a product of the action of the kidneys, as is frequently supposed, but that it is merely excreted from the system by these organs. They also appear to indicate that the excreting function of the kidneys, with regard to the solid portion of the urine, is not simple, but that the urea and uric acid are separately eliminated; also that one of these functions may be impaired or destroyed, the other remaining entire.

Gout would thus appear partly to depend on a loss of power (temporary or permanent) of the "uric-acid-excreting function" of the kidneys; the premonitory symptoms, and those also which constitute the paroxysm, arising from an excess of this acid in the blood, and from the effort to expel the "materies morbi" from the system. Any undue *formation* of this compound would favour the occurrence of the disease; and hence the connection between gout and uric acid, gravel and calculi; . . . This hypothesis would also explain two facts which have been regarded as militating against its humoral pathology; viz. the *hereditary* nature of the affection, . . . for we can understand that the peculiarity of the kidney, with reference to the excretion of uric acid, may be transmitted.

Although the hypothesis that the diminished capacity of the kidney to excrete uric acid was responsible for the increased concentration of uric acid in the serum, received strong support late in the 19th century and early in the 20th century, this explanation lost favor thereafter. In recent years, it is gaining acceptance once more.

Garrod prepared two standard texts; each enjoyed several editions. *Essentials of Materia Medica and Therapeutics,* published first in 1855, went through 13 editions and 3 editors.[3] The *Treatise on Gout and Rheumatic Gout* was published first in 1859.[4] The differential diagnosis between rheumatoid arthritis and gouty arthritis was clearly stated. The discussion of the use of colchicine in the diagnosis and treatment of the acute attack and the role of this drug in the prophylactic regimen remain valid a century later. No increase in uric acid excretion or general diuresis was attributed to the pharmacologic action of cholchicine; whereas the diagnostic and therapeutic value of the drug was self-evident.[4]

> That colchicum in its various forms has a most powerful influence upon the progress of gouty inflammation is undeniable, and this action is not simply limited to the removal of gout when it attacks the joints, but it proves efficacious even in its masked and irregular forms. . . . My own experience fully coincides with that of Sir H. Holland, and I would even go the length of asserting that we may sometimes diagnose gouty inflammation from any form by noting the influence of colchicum upon its progress.
>
> There is some evidence and considerable authority for regarding colchicum as effectual in warding off an attack of gout, especially when an approaching fit is beginning to manifest itself.

By 1851, Garrod had become professor of materia medica, therapeutics and clinical medicine at University College and physician to University College Hospital. In 1863, he moved to King's College Hospital, with similar responsibilities. By then his fame was secure. Subsequent accomplishments consisted of revising his texts and reaping the rewards of a productive professional life. He was knighted in 1887 and appointed physician-extraordinary to Queen Victoria in 1890. The question has been posed on several occasions whether one so interested in a single morbid entity was not attracted to this by his own infirmity. However, there is no evidence that Garrod suffered from gout; he died of natural causes in 1907, at the age of 88. By then his fourth son, Archibald Edward Garrod, the author of *Inborn Errors of Metabolism,* had equaled and later surpassed his father in fame, and in 1920, followed Sir William Osler at Oxford as regius professor of medicine.

1. Garrod, A. B.: Observations on Certain Pathological Conditions of the Blood and Urine in Gout, Rheumatism, and Bright's Disease, *Medicochir Trans* 31:83-97, 1848.
2. Garrod, A. B.: On the Blood and Effused Fluids in Gout, Rheumatism, and Bright's Disease, *Medicochir Trans* 37:49-59, 1854.
3. Garrod, A. B.: *The Essentials of Materia Medica, Therapeutics, and the Pharmacopoeias,* London: Walton and Maberly, 1855.
4. Garrod, A. B.: *A Treatise on Gout and Rheumatic Gout (Rheumatoid Arthritis)* 3rd ed London: Longmans, Green, & Co., 1876.

Composite by G. Bako

W. S. Kirkes (1823-1864)

WILLIAM SENHOUSE KIRKES, recognized in his brief professional career for his text on physiology and a comprehensive description of the sequelae of intracardiac emboli, was born at Holker in North Lancashire, England. He attended grammar school at Cartmel and at the age of 13 was apprenticed to a partnership of three surgeons in Lancaster, with whom he remained five years.[1] He obtained his hospital and medical training at St. Bartholomew's Hospital in London; there he ranked high in chemistry, surgery, medicine, midwifery, medical jurisprudence, and clinical medicine. At the age of 23, Kirkes received the MD degree from the University of Berlin. Four years later he became licentiate of the Royal College of Physicians and, in 1855, was advanced to fellowship. Only two years after receiving his degree, he was appointed medical registrar and demonstrator of morbid anatomy at St. Bartholomew's Hospital, assistant physician in 1854 and, in a close contest only a few months before his premature death, was advanced to physician.

Kirkes was unusually successful with his *Handbook of Physiology,* first published in 1848, and based upon Sir James Paget's lectures on physiology.[2] Later editions were authored solely by Kirkes. The editing was continued posthumously by W. M. Baker, who later was joined by V. D. Harris. Eventually the 17th American edition, renamed *Manual of Physiology,* appeared in 1902, revised by W. H. Rockwell and C. L. Dana.

Kirkes's bedside interest in cardiovascular diseases led to his best-known clinical contribution—the first English communication on emboli from verrucous endocarditis. Although the report appeared after Virchow's discussion of thrombosis and embolism which extended over a decade beginning in 1846, this fact detracts little from Kirkes's observations. Four cases were described, with postmortem findings of critical vascular occlusion by emboli originating from one or more valves of the heart of patients afflicted with rheumatic valvular heart disease. The first case was admitted to St. Bartholomew's Hospital in 1850. Excerpts of the discussion as well as the summary of the report follow.[3]

That the fibrinous principle of the blood may, under certain circumstances, separate from the circulating fluid during life, and be deposited within the vascular system, especially on the valves of the heart, is a fact so clearly established and so generally admitted, that I need only, at the outset of the communication I have the honour to present to this Society, allude to it as a settled truth. . . . It may, however, be premised that the forms of fibrinous concretions to which my observations chiefly apply, are, first, the masses usually described as Laennec's globular excrescences; and, secondly, the granular or warty growths adhering to the valves and presenting innumerable varieties from mere granules to large irregular fungous or cauliflower excrescences projecting into the cavities of the heart.

If of large size and only loosely-adherent, as they often are, one or more masses of even considerable magnitude may at any time be detached from the valves and conveyed with the circulating blood until arrested within some arterial canal which may be completely plugged up by it, and thus the supply of blood to an important part be suddenly cut off, and serious, even fatal results ensue. Or, the deposits on the valves may be detached in smaller masses, and pass on into arteries of much less size, or even into the capillaries, where, being arrested, they may cause congestion, followed by stagnation and coagulation of the blood with all the subsequent changes which blood coagulated within the living body is liable to undergo. In this way are probably induced many singular morbid appearances often observed in internal organs, and rarely well accounted for.

The parts of the vascular system within which these transmitted masses of fibrine may be found will of course depend, in great measure, upon whether they proceeded from the right or left side of the heart. Thus if they have been detached from either the aortic or mitral valves, they will pass into the blood propelled by the left ventricle into the aorta and its subdivisions, and may be arrested in any of the systemic arteries or their ramifications in the various organs, especially those which, like the brain, spleen, and kidneys, receive large supplies of blood directly from the left side of the heart.

If, on the other hand, the fibrinous masses are derived from the pulmonary or tricuspid valves, the pulmonary artery and its subdivisions within the lungs will necessarily become the primary if not the exclusive seat of their subsequent deposition.

The first three cases which I shall offer are in many respects identical; for in each death seemed to ensue from softening of the brain, consequent on obliteration of one of the main cerebral arteries by a mass of fibrinous material, apparently derived directly from warty growths on the left valves of the heart.

Case I.—Margaret Shaw, aet. 34, a pale, weakly-looking woman; admitted into St. Bartholomew's Hospital, under Dr. Roupell, about the middle of July, 1850, on account of pains in her lower limbs, and general debility. A loud systolic murmur was heard all over the cardiac region. No material change ensued in her condition until August 7th, when, while sitting up in bed eating her dinner, she suddenly fell back as if fainting, vomited a little, and when attended to was found speechless, though not unconscious, and partially hemiplegic on the left side.

On examining the body, six hours after death, . . . the right middle cerebral artery just at its commencement was plugged up by a small nodule of firm, whitish, fibrinous-looking substance. . . . The mitral valve was much diseased, the auricular surface of its large cusp being beset with large warty excrescences of adherent blood-stained fibrine.

I am not aware that there has yet been recorded a case in which fatal softening of the brain resulted from a cause like this; therefore in itself this case is one of value.

In conclusion, let me briefly recapitulate the principal points I have endeavoured to establish to the satisfaction of the Society. They are, 1st, the general fact that fibrinous concretions on the valves or the interior of the heart admit of being readily detached during life, and mingled with the circulating blood: 2dly, that if detached and transmitted in large masses, they may suddenly block up a large artery, and so cut off the supply of blood to an important part. . . . 3rdly, that the effects produced and the organs affected will be in great measure determined by the side of the heart from which the fibrinous masses have been detached; for, if the right valves have furnished the source of the fibrine, the lungs will bear the brunt of the secondary mischief, displaying it in coagula in the pulmonary arteries, and various forms of deposit in the pulmonary tissue: but if, as is far more commonly the case, the left valves are affected, the mischief is more widely spread, and may fall on any systemic part, but especially on those organs which, such as the brain, spleen, and kidneys, are largely and directly supplied with blood from the left side of the heart.

Kirkes presented the Gulstonian Lectures at the Royal College of Physicians in 1856. His early death interrupted his plans for a comprehensive treatise on diseases of the heart as well as his duties on a commission appointed by the Admiralty and Horse Guards to inquire into the nature, treatment, and prevention of venereal diseases in the military services. After his death, friends and students at St. Bartholomew's Hospital contributed funds for a gold medal awarded annually to the student with the best examination in the diagnosis and treatment of patients on the medical service. In 1885, Mrs. Kirkes established an endowment which provided a monetary prize . . . to accompany the medal.

1. Moore, N.: William Senhouse Kirkes, *Dictionary of National Biography* 3(suppl 22):69, 1901.
2. Kirkes, W. S.: *Handbook of Physiology*, assisted by J. Paget, London: Taylor, Walton & Maberly, 1848.
3. Kirkes, W. S.: On Some of the Principal Effects Resulting From the Detachment of Fibrinous Deposits From the Interior of the Heart, and Their Mixture With the Circulating Blood, *Medicochir Trans* 35:281-324, 1852.

Ferdinand von Hebra
(1816-1880)

THE RISE AND FALL OF A SEGMENT OF MEDICAL SCIENCE, a specialty in clinical medicine, or a field of scientific endeavor distantly related to medicine is a recurring phenomenon throughout medical history. In some instances, a single individual or a small group of individuals may be responsible for scientific progress, intense development of the subject, and subsequent rise to preeminence. In the first quarter of this century,

the schools of physiology in England were outstanding. In the last quarter of the 19th century, brilliant advances in pathological anatomy radiated from Germany and Austria. Bacteriology approached the zenith in France in the same generation. A similar apogee may be recounted for dermatology in Vienna. There were many influences responsible for the glories of Viennese dermatology; the leader was Ferdinand von Hebra.

The first portion of the 1800's witnessed the beginning of modern dermatology in France.[1] Alibert described mycosis fungoides and recognized the character of keloid. His protégé, Biett, described lupus erythematosus. Famous among their pupils were Cazenave (who first used the term lupus erythematosus), Rayer (physician to Napoleon III), Gibert (pityriasis rosea), Devergie (Devergie's disease—pityriasis rubra pilaris), and Bazin (description of erythema induratum, therapy of scabies, favus, and ringworm). Before the luster of clinical dermatology had faded in Paris, Vienna was prepared to accept the leadership under the aegis of Ferdinand Hebra—a member of the brilliant group of Viennese clinicians and medical scientists associated with the Allgemeines Krankenhaus.

Hebra was born in Brno, Moravia, and received his MD degree from the University of Vienna. Not long after, he became associated with Skoda (Skoda's resonance), a Bohemian, and the chief of the chest service at the Krankenhaus, the section which included diseases of the skin. Rokitansky, also a Bohemian, and chief of pathology, is credited with urging Hebra to develop the new techniques for the study of structure in the classification of cutaneous disorders. The combination of the precepts of clinical medicine gleaned from Skoda and the instigations of Rokitansky in pathology led to a new concept of cutaneous medicine. Others had dabbled in the furtive hope that pathology would contribute to clinical dermatology; Hebra was successful in this pursuit and deserves full credit for the classification of cutaneous disorders on the basis of structural alterations.

Scabies was Hebra's initial problem. When he became assistant to Skoda, the majority of patients on the skin service suffered from scabies. The false belief in humoral pathology had not been completely dispelled. Hebra tended to attribute scabies to the outward manifestation of a systemic disease. His experimental studies, however, convinced him of the fallacy of this reasoning. Clinical experiments revealed that scabies was a local disease produced by the itch mite. His paper *Über die Krätze* appeared in 1844. If a parasite could irritate, chemical agents might have a similar inflammatory effect on the skin. It was concluded that external irritants were responsible for a variety of cutaneous reactions and that many skin conditions might be limited to the outer shell of the body. Although the possibility of a systemic disorder with an outward cutaneous manifestation was not rejected entirely, this concept of dermatology which had been popular in France in preceding generations was deemphasized.[2]

The first treatise on classification, published in 1845, formed the basis of the monumental *Atlas der Hautkrankenheiten,* which appeared between 1856 and 1876. Hebra's interest in clinical dermatology became all-absorbing and presumably left little time to consider the possible role that bacterial infection might play in this field. Although parasites and fungi were recognized as etiologic agents, bacteria and other means of contagion were not considered in his classification of skin diseases.

Notwithstanding, Hebra practiced and taught in an era of therapeutic nihilism; he rediscovered the value of inunctions of mercury in the treatment of syphilis. Early in his career, he described seborrhea congestiva and later agreed with Cazenave that it was a form of lupus erythematosus. Erythema multiforme (Hebra's disease) was based upon his initial description of this malady. He reported the first case of rhinoscleroma.

In lectures and social contacts, he was warm, sympathetic, witty in conversation, and clear in reasoning. He befriended Semmelweis and, although only 2 years older than the discoverer of childbed fever, it was Hebra who brought Semmelweis to the madhouse a few days before the latter's death. The son-in-law of Hebra, Moriz Kaposi (born Moriz Kohn),[3] carried on the tradition and completed Hebra's *Lehrbuch der Hautkrankenheiten,* which was republished in English by the New Sydenham Society between 1866 and 1880.[4] An excerpt from the chapter on scleroderma is especially interesting because of the clarity and validity of the description:

By the term Scleroderma adultorum, we understand an idiopathic, morbid change in the skin which is chiefly known by a diffuse and remarkable induration, rigidity, and comparative shortening of the affected part.

The morbid change appears on various parts of the body, mostly on the upper extremities, less frequently on the lower ones.

Now and then, we find that the symptoms of the scleroderma appear variously characterized on different parts of the body of the same individual; whilst, in others, the whole skin appears uniformly thickened. In these cases, the skin is swollen over a greater or lesser extent, is moderately elevated above the level of the surrounding skin, is smooth and shining or slightly scaly, of a brownish-red or pale white colour, like wax or alabaster, or is pigmented in patches of a brown colour with patches interspersed without pigment.

If the finger is drawn over the diseased skin no permanent depression remains. It feels firm, like a board, rigid and cold, as if it belonged to a frozen corpse. It is difficult or impossible to pinch up a fold of skin, and the latter is not movable on the subjacent tissue. It appears as if it were of one consistence with the subcutaneous tissue, and closely soldered to the muscular fascia (as, for example, on the forearm), or firmly joined to the bone (over the joints). The skin appears, therefore, as if it were shortened, put on the stretch, like a tendinous band, passing over the flexor surface of a joint which, consequently, cannot be extended. The arm and each of the fingers, for this reason, appear in a state of semiflexion, and their position cannot be altered, either actively or passively, in the least, or at any rate only very slightly. If the skin of the face be affected the features are rigid, quite immovable, as if "petrified," like those of a marble bust. Neither pain nor joy causes the "stony" countenance to alter. The skin is changed in the manner described, incapable of wrinkling, contracted. The mouth, for this reason, opens imperfectly, and the alae nasi are tightly stretched.

1. Pusey. W. A.: *History of Dermatology,* Springfield, Ill.: Charles C Thomas, 1933, pp. 98-107.
2. Shelley, W. B., and Crissey, J. T.: *Classics in Clinical Dermatology,* Springfield, Ill.: Charles C Thomas, Publisher, 1953.
3. Robinson, V.: *Pathfinders in Medicine,* New York: Medical Life Press, 1929.
4. Hebra, F., and Kaposi, M.: *On Diseases of the Skin,* Vol. III, translated and edited by Waren Tay, London: New Sydenham Society, 1874.

Emil Vidal (1825-1893)

JEAN BAPTISTE EMILE VIDAL was born in Paris and received his classical training at the lycée Condorcet.[1] With his parents he moved to Tours; there he began medical studies which were completed in the faculty of medicine in Paris. Then followed service as an extern and later as an intern in the city hospitals and the granting of the medical degree in 1855, upon his fulfilling the requirements and submission of a thesis, *Considerations on Chronic Primary Articular Rheumatism.*[2] The title page credits Vidal with a first prize awarded while he was preparing for medicine at Tours, and a silver and bronze medal from the hospitals of Paris. At the time his thesis was presented, the faculty included Cruveilhier as a member of the department of anatomic pathology, Andral in pathology and general therapeutics, Bouillaud and Trousseau in clinical medicine, Velpeau in clinical surgery, and Broca as associate.

Composite by G. Bako

Vidal was appointed physician to the hospitals in 1861 and was assigned a medical service at the Hôpital Saint Louis in 1867. The latter provided the source of much of his patient material for his clinical contributions to general medicine, surgery, and dermatology. As documented in the scientific literature, his interests included splenic leukocythemia, rectal prolapse, isolation of patients with contagious maladies, abolition of maternity wards with replacement by obstetrical polyclinics, and an efficient sewage disposal system for Paris. Vidal's contributions specifically in dermatology and venereal maladies, many of which were published in *Annales de Dermatologie et de Syphiligraphie,* discussed the use of small doses of mercury in syphilis, the treatment of gonorrhea, the destruction of chancroids, the inoculability of impetigo, herpes praeputialis, ecthyma and pemphigus of the newborn, mycosis fungoides, lupus erythematosus, lupus tuberculosis, facial erysipelas, generalized exfoliative dermatitis, and the value of chaulmoogra oil in leprosy.

The doctoral thesis on chronic primary articular rheumatism (rheumatoid arthritis), prepared more than one century ago when the clinical and pathological understanding of rheumatism and arthritis was emerging, is an important study in its specific descriptive statements. Vidal quotes Charcot and others frequently, emphasizes higher sex ratio of females to males in rheumatoid arthritis, differentiates this condition from gouty arthritis and osteoarthritis, notes that some consider the disease incurable and that the malady begins in the synovia with injection of the capillaries, and describes the clinical findings of ulnar deviation, subluxation of the joints, fixation in flexion, muscle wasting, skin changes, and atrophy of the digits. There was much to substantiate his classification of rheumatoid arthritis as chronic atrophic arthritis.[2]

The articulation of the wrist and of the hand is very painful, reacting to the slightest touch. There is considerable deformity. The right forearm is in a position of forced pronation, while supination is impossible. The patient holds his hand towards the ulnar side with the dorsal surface presenting. The wrist seems to be subluxated, the head of the ulna protrudes, and the styloid process is evident under the soft tissues. The carpal bones appear to be pushed forward. The hand is partially flexed on the forearm. All phalanges, except the fixed and immobile little finger, are flexed on the metacarpals and respond slightly to further flexion. The terminal phalanges are slightly flexed and retain some mobility. The phalanges of the little finger are capable of minimal motion.

All joints may be affected, even the spine and the jaw. The shoulder and the hip are less often affected, although one may detect crepitation and varying degrees of rigidity. We have seen instances of atrophy of the shoulder muscles with almost complete immobilization of the shoulder joint.

The elbow is partially flexed or fixed at a right angle with the arm. It is possible to flex it slightly, but it is impossible to extend the joint. The forearm is in pronation. When one attempts to extend the arm, considerable resistance is encountered and the flexor muscles bulge under the skin.

The retraction of the muscles and the tendinous tissues is equally pronounced in the lower extremity, the knee joint tends to hyperflex, while extension is impossible. The joint is often the site of osteophytes or foreign bodies (Adams), and the head of the tibia presents changes similar to the changes in femoral condyli, which protrude forward, leaving the tibia subluxated posteriorly. This joint often crepitates.

The toes are less frequently involved than the fingers and have a tendency to deviate laterally. Most often the great toe turns laterally and subluxates below the other toes, while the head of its metacarpal protrudes onto the inner surface of the foot.

These findings accompany the atrophic type of primary chronic articular rheumatism. The mechanism of its development is different from the other types; it should be distinguished as a separate entity, and it should not be considered a variety of the others.

The skin, almost always moist, usually covered with viscous sweat, is pale, has the color of old wax, shows very few blood-vessels, and seems altered in its structure. In the atrophic form, it is glossy, stretched like a glove, thin, and adherent to the bones. The folds which are normally seen at the joints, and even the small wrinkles, have disappeared. The stiffness, the tightness, and the adherence to the surrounding tissues are all very marked, so that it is impossible to pinch the soft parts covering the fingers. The nail shows no line of demarcation where it meets the skin; the epidermis is not elevated; subcutaneous tissue is lacking. Longitudinal striae and friability of the nail reflect the disease.

Treatment of lupus vulgaris and other appropriate cutaneous disorders by scarification with a many-bladed knife, known as "Vidal's treatment," was one of his favorite therapeutic procedures. Initially, Vidal was opposed to the hypothesis that lupus vulgaris was one manifestation of cutaneous tuberculosis, but later he supported this concept of the pathogenesis. After recommending compounds of potassium iodide and iron salts and other caustics locally for the treatment of lupus (vulgaris), he discussed his modification of scarification, building upon the surgical procedures of Dubini of Milan and Volkmann of Halle.[3]

I do not use general anesthesia; even local anesthesia is used on very sensitive patients only.

The instrument used is a thin, straight blade, 2½ cm long and 2 mm wide, which ends with a triangle of two edges which meet at an angle of 55°. It is mounted on a handle similar to the one used for cataract needles. It is held delicately, as a writing pen, between the fingers without pressure. During the operation one evaluates the consistency of the tissue. The tip penetrates the tubercle, avoiding the normal areas. Parallel incisions are made as close together as possible. This is followed by oblique incisions, thus forming a netlike pattern. Sometimes another row of incisions is made diagonally. It is important to penetrate the tissue as deep as the lupus process, where the characteristic resistance of healthy tissue is detected.

It is necessary to attack the involved areas, including about 5 mm of surrounding normal tissue. After three to four days, the incised area improves; the surface granulates. After five or six scarring sessions, a tendency to heal is noticed. Sometimes this is sufficient. On the average, at least ten scarifications are needed.

Scarification is a less painful procedure than the application of caustics. The pain does not last more than 30 minutes. Moreover, the final results are excellent. If one treats a case of long-standing lupus with the skin well irritated by previous medications, a pink scar is obtained which looks thin and almost has a shiny appearance.

In an investigation of the inoculability of certain cutaneous diseases, Vidal was successful experimentally in transmitting ecthyma, herpes labialis, herpes praeputialis, and epidemic pemphigus of the newborn, but was unable to transmit eczema, herpes zona, and chronic pemphigus.[4] Shelley and Crissey translated his description of keratosis blennorrhagica.[5] Probably Vidal's favorite group of disorders (if one was accorded more of his attention than others) was the lichens, a group to which he contributed descriptions and classification to the literature. Excerpts of acute and chronic lichen simplex follow.[6]

1. Acute form of *lichen simplex*—The acute form of lichen simplex consists of an eruption of small disseminated papules. It starts abruptly, most often during the spring and summer; it affects young people with fine and delicate skin. Patients at times have general malaise, anorexia, and slight fever. But most often it starts without general symptoms. It is accompanied by a prickly sensation and itching which becomes intense. Itching may at times precede the eruptions or it may appear when the eruptions are hardly perceptible. Afterwards numerous pink papules develop—on the elbows, the face, the limbs, and especially on the hands and on the fore-arms. They are small and firm, contain no fluid, and seldom exceed the size of a poppy seed; sometimes they are so small that they give only an impression of roughness when the skin is stroked. Their form usually corresponds to their size: they are pointed or conical when they are small; flat, lenticular, or even hemispheric when they are larger; their surface is dry, rough, and covered with small epidermis scales.

The acute stage of lichen lasts from three weeks to one month. With resolution, the papules become pale, shrink, and tend to disappear; the itching subsides and the eruption ends with a fine scaly desquamation.

2. *Chronic Lichen Simplex*—In some cases, during a course of acute lichen simplex, one can recognize on parts of the body persistent single or multiple circumscribed plaques consisting of groups of papules; then the eruption loses its intensity and tends to disappear. Chronic lichen simplex may start in this manner or it may be chronic from the beginning.

In the latter, the papules are less red than in the originally acute form; they tend to blend together and to form a single plaque; single papules are recognizable only at the edges which are well delineated and raised; the surface of the plaque is uneven and wavy; the surface is granular like the skin of an orange. Fine purplish scales are seen, with criss-crossing grooves, giving the impression of a special design; at times there are signs of excoriations caused by repeated scratching.

This eruption is usually accompanied by burning, itching, and a prickling sensation; in some, the itching is severe and becomes much worse towards evening and during the night.

Vidal is described by his biographers as an excellent clinician, with unusual capacity for uncanny rapidity and great validity in diagnosis of cutaneous disorders. Surrounded by pupils and visting physicians, he held the center of attention and performed admirably in handling patients and managing their maladies. In addition to his prolific writings, he was coauthor with his younger associate, Henri Leloir, of an encyclopedia of diseases of the skin. Seven volumes had already appeared before death closed the project.[7]

1. Brocq, L.: Emile Vidal, 1825-1893 (Fr), *Ann Derm Syph* (Par) 4:805-813, 1893.

2. Vidal, E.: *Considerations on Chronic Primary Articular Rheumatism* (Fr), thesis, Paris, 1855, excerpts translated by Z. Danilevicius.

3. Vidal, E.: Treatment of Lupus (Fr), *Ther Contemp* 2:417-424, 1882, excerpt translated by Z. Danilevicius.

4. Vidal, E.: Inoculability of Several Cutaneous Afflications (Fr), *Ann Derm Syph* (Par) 9:329-344, 1877-1878.

5. Shelley, W. B., and Crissey, J. T.: *Classics in Clinical Dermatology*, Springfield, Ill: C. C Thomas, 1953.

6. Vidal, E.: The Lichens (Fr), *Ann Derm Syph* (Par) 7:133-154, 1836, excerpt translated by Z. Danilevicius.

7. Leloir, H., and Vidal, E.: *Descriptive Treatise of Diseases of the Skin, Symptoms and Pathologic Anatomy* (Fr), vol 1-7, Paris: G. Masson, 1889-1894.

Composite by G. Bako

Maurice Raynaud (1834-1881)

MAURICE RAYNAUD, son of a professor at the University of Paris, prepared for medicine with a classical education in his father's school and trained for practice in the hospitals of Paris.[1] He qualified for his doctorate in medicine in 1862 upon presentation of a thesis, *Local Asphyxia and Symmetrical Gangrene of the Extremities,* which brought him lasting fame and eponymic recognition. Less well known but equal in scholarly achievement was his thesis, *The Asclepiade of Bithynia,* and a historical account of *Physicians in the Time of Molière* (1622-1673), presented for his licentiate (doctoral degree) in letters. Thus, by 1863 when he qualified for a professional appointment, he possessed the equivalent of two earned doctorates as well as silver and gold medals awarded during his internship. With such a brilliant introduction to academic medicine, it might be expected that appointment to a senior post would be inevitable in a matter of time. However, the expectation never became a fact, and, although he was honored by his state as an officer of the Legion of Honor in 1871 and by his associates in the election to the Academy of Medicine in 1879, Raynaud was never offered a senior academic post and especially the cherished chair of the history of medicine. The sincerity of his devotion to the Catholic Church was suggested as one reason for the failure of the University to give adequate recognition to his talents at the bedside and with the pen.

Raynaud's thesis in medicine was published the same year it was presented,[2] supplemented in 1874 with additional case reports and experimental studies.[3] Both contributions were translated by the New Sydenham Society and were published in 1888. In the "Preface," Raynaud accepted credit for the description of a new disease and for the selection of a new name to a group of symptoms which had been observed and described by others in the past. He declined to speculate on the pathological features of the lesion.[4]

To describe a new disease, and especially to give a new name to a group of symptoms which has been long observed and described, is assuredly less difficult than to link together under a common law which dominates them many affections apparently different. In the infinite variety of morbid phenomena which present themselves daily to our observation with a physiognomy always new, it is easy to choose here and there some exceptional facts and to constitute them a common type, omitting the differences which separate them in order to see only the points of contact between them. A little imagination suffices for this task, and positive science has little to profit by it. Also, in spite of the title which I have given to this thesis, I am bound to declare at the outset that I do not aspire to the frivolous and dangerous honour of making an innovation in pathology.

Raynaud included 25 case reports, with eight deaths, in the initial communication; three deaths were attributed to causes unrelated to local asphyxia of the extremities.[2] The majority were females; five were males. The usual onset of symptoms occurred in patients between 18 and 30 years of age. Inciting causes were the lowering of the external temperature; "often an imperceptible change . . . was sufficient, such as the passage from the heat of the bed to the temperature of a warm room," and "suppression of the menses." The following excerpts from the case histories include the significant clinical findings.[4]

Under the influence of a very moderate cold, and even at the height of summer, she [Case I] sees her fingers become ex-sanguine, completely insensible, and of a whitish yellow colour. This phenomenon happens often without reason, lasts a variable time, and terminates by a period of very painful reaction, during which the circulation is reestablished little by little and recurs to the normal state.

On the 8th April, Easter Day, being at chapel, she [Case V] was taken without assignable cause with pains in the hands sufficiently severe to make her cry; in the back she felt as though violently compressed by a vice. I found her in the middle of an attack of cyanosis which had lasted for two hours; the pulse was quite perceptible; the skin of the hands was very cold, and of a violet tint.

The attacks recur now in the feet and in the hands five or six times a day without any periodicity.

Her [Case VI] cheeks and chin were of indigo colour; her hands were as cold as marble.

It was at the extremities of the fingers that the cyanosis and the cold persisted longest. Finally at the end of a quarter or half an hour the whole hand was of a vermilion red; the pulse had regained its force, the warmth of skin was perfectly developed, and a slight sweat had moistened the cutaneous surface. All these phenomena were reproduced each time that Rose was exposed to cool air, whether in the evening, morning, or at the middle of the day.

The possibility that Anna B. [Case IX] presented Raynaud's phenomena as a manifestation of systemic scleroderma, an infrequent sequela, cannot be dismissed lightly. The 30-year-old maidservant died less than two years after the onset of progressive atrophy of the tissue of the fingers and toes, edema of the fingers, ungual infection, decreased appetite, loss of facial expression, pallor, discoloration of the skin, and extreme feebleness.[4]

By degrees the second and first phalanges of the fingers had presented successively the same phenomena, that is to say, sensation of habitual cold, tinglings, slaty tint, incomplete anaesthesia at the moment of the attack, return of sensibility during the intervals, and then acute pains in the region of the punctures which had been made. Soon we saw bullae appear at the extremities of the ungual phalanges; they passed from one to the other, and preceded the fall of all the nails, which came to pass in six weeks' time.

Extreme pallor. The lines of the countenance are flaccid, and expressive of sadness.

So soon as she allows her hands to be exposed to a rather low temperature the fingers become pale, oedematous, half flexed; they are attacked with painful sensations, numbness, and torpor; shortly afterwards they become blue, then black, in their whole extent.

. . . the epidermis is raised by pus, so as to imitate a bulla, which develops, breaks, and leaves the derma naked. Eight days afterwards a cicatrix is formed, and this morbid process is repeated elsewhere.

In discussing pathogenesis, Raynaud referred to the absence of pathological findings in the arteries central to the arterioles, studied the patency of the arterial supply by injection of a limb removed postmortem, and observed with the ophthalmoscope the retina of rabbits following interruption of the cervical sympathetic chain. He postulated that a local reflex was responsible for asphyxia and constriction of the vessels.[4]

Hitherto one might indeed have suspected that the local asphyxia was connected with a spasmodic state of the vessels. But whatever foundation there might be for this supposition, as the digital exploration of the accessible arterial trunks did not reveal in these cases anything special, one was obliged to admit by induction a functional trouble localised to the arterioles immediately contiguous to the capillaries.

The treatise, *Physicians in the Time of Molière,* described 17th century Paris. Molière, one of the most articulate and persistent critics of the medical profession, composed symphonies of satire on physicians that reached their peak in *The Imaginary Invalid.* Raynaud described the practice of medicine two centuries before his time, sometimes apologizing for Molière, but casting an interpretation of his satire most favorable to the physician whenever possible.[5]

Molière condemned that which deserved to be condemned. Most of the absurdities he criticized are, thanks to him, now defunct. Some still survive, and will always survive: Molière is immortal, and the plays stand there, as if to prove him eternally right.

The Faculty of Medicine [Paris in the 17th century] was not necessarily an enemy of progress, as it is believed. But it wanted that progress to proceed from its body and not from outside. No one among mortals can monopolize geniuses or discoveries, and as a consequence the Faculty became the adversary of many useful things: it forced surgery into lowly disputes; it rejected the circulation of the blood because it came from England; it forbade the use of antimony because it came from Montpellier; it condemned quinine because it came from America.

All of the examples of satire which I have taken at random, and which are lost in the gay extravagance of the general action, are a disguise for the most truthful and philosophic exposure of the faults of scholasticism, and the most eloguent declaration in favor of experimentation and practicality, which constituted, perhaps, Molière's constant aspiration. . . . Tradition is no longer legitimate when it becomes routine . . . science lives as long as it progresses; the moment it stops, the moment it presumes to have said the last word, it dies. Progress or die; this is the frightful law that should have been clear to science. Molière, in choosing the doctors for his satirical attacks, did nothing more than follow the examples provided by the long-established tradition of popular farce.

1. Maurice Raynaud, obituary (Fr), *Progr Med (Par)* 9:552-553, 1881, translated by Z. Danilevicius.

2. Raynaud, M.: *Local Asphyxia and Symmetrical Gangrene of the Extremities* (Fr), Paris: L. Leclerc, 1862.

3. Raynaud, M.: New Researches on the Nature and Treatment of Local Asphyxia of the Extremities (Fr), *Arch Gen Med* 1:189-206, 1874.

4. *Selected Monographs: Raynaud's Two Essays on Local Asphyxia*, London: New Sydenham Society, 1888.

5. Raynaud, M.: *Physicians in the Time of Molière* (Fr), Paris: Didier, 1862, excerpt translated by Z. Danilevicius.

Moriz Kaposi (1837-1902)

MORIZ KAPOSI, born Moriz Kohn in Kaposvar, Hungary, of indigent parents, studied medicine at the University of Vienna, where he received his MD degree in 1861.[1] He was immediately appointed assistant in Hebra's clinic at the Allgemeines Krankenhaus and later qualified as privatdocent, with a dissertation on syphilis of the mucous membranes. Subsequently, he married Hebra's daughter and, upon Hebra's death, received his professional mantle as the leading dermatologist in Vienna. Kaposi was a prolific writer, a highly respected teacher, a wise clinician, and a physician capable of luring students and patients from many countries to the Viennese clinic. A generation of practitioners in dermatology was trained by him, and his pupils occupied chairs of dermatology in a number of continental universities. Kaposi collaborated with his father-in-law on a *Handbook of Diseases of the Skin*[2] and prepared his own text on *Pathology and Treatment of Diseases of the Skin*.[3] The success of these texts is evident from the fact that each was translated and readily available in English.

Composite by G. Bako

The initial description of several cutaneous diseases has been attributed to Kaposi. Included are pigmented sarcoma of the skin (Kaposi's sarcoma), 1872; lupus erythematosus, 1872; diabetic dermatitis, 1876; xeroderma pigmentosum, 1882; lymphodermia perniciosa, 1885; lichen ruber planus, 1886; impetigo herpetiformis, 1887; dermatitis papillaris capillitii, 1869; and herpes varicelliform, 1887. The description of multiple idiopathic hemorrhagic sarcoma, Kaposi's sarcoma, appeared first in the *Archiv für Dermatologie und Syphilis* in 1872[4] and was translated in 1895.[3]

(*b*) A second typical form of sarcomatosis of the skin was described by me in 1879 as "*idiopathic multiple pigment sarcoma*." I have seen sixteen cases, all in men, and others have been reported by various writers. It always begins upon both feet and hands, and advances by separate growths along the legs and arms until, at the end of two to three years, it appears upon the face and trunk. We find reddish-brown, later bluish-red, round, moderately firm nodules, from the size of a pea to that of a bean, which are in part separate and irregularly situated, in part arranged in groups and diffuse infiltrations varying from the size of a quarter to that of the palm of the hand. . . . Glandular enlargement does not appear to be peculiar to this type of sarcoma, apart from occasional sympathetic enlargement, as, for example, in gangrene of the foot. Fever, bloody diarrhoea, haemoptysis, and marasmus soon set in at this stage, and are followed by death. At the autopsy similar nodules are found in large numbers in the lungs, liver, spleen, heart, intestinal tract; in the descending colon they are especially dense and apt to be necrotic.

Histologically we find a round-cell sarcoma, except that in a few places the characteristic spindle-cell sarcoma is seen. A peculiarity of this type is the presence of capillary haemorrhages, which explain the later bluish-black pigmentation of the originally bluish-red nodules, and also the excessive hardness of the diffuse infiltrations around the groups of nodules (deposit of fibrin).

Xeroderma pigmentosum was described in several of Kaposi's communications. The following excerpt is from the New Sydenham Society translation.[2]

The skin of the face, ears, throat, neck, shoulders, arms, and of the breast, to the level of the third rib, exhibited a peculiar alteration. It was remarkable, in the first place, owing to its checkered appearance, for it appeared to be abundantly dotted over with pigmented spots of the size of pins' heads or of lentils, and of a yellowish-brown colour; it was also tightly stretched, as if contracted, was pinched up into a fold with difficulty, and felt very thin.

In addition to the parchment-like dryness, thinness, and wrinkling of the epidermis, the checkered pigmentation, and the small dilatations of the vessels, the most remarkable symptoms were the contraction and, at the same time, thinning of the skin. In consequence of the first, the lower eyelids were drawn downwards; on the left side, this was so considerable that the eye could not be closed. As a result, the cornea was ulcerated, and rendered opaque in its lower half, which was always uncovered. The nose, towards its tip, appeared compressed, owing to the shrinking of its skin, and the external ears at their free extremities appeared indented here and there owing to the shrinking. The lips could only be slightly separated from one another.

Lymphodermia perniciosa (mihi) was described in 1885[5] and was translated by Johnston.[3]

In 1885, this disease was first described by me, and has since been observed by a few other writers. It began with the symptoms of a partly diffuse, partly localized, scaling, moist, and intensely itching eczema, which gradually resulted in diffuse, soft swelling and thickening of the affected parts. Then cutaneous and subcutaneous, doughy or firm, in part ulcerating nodules developed, the glands and spleen enlarged, with severe affection of the entire organism, leukaemia set in. . . . At the autopsy the spleen was found to be enlarged fourfold, the marrow of the sternum, vertebrae, metatarsi, and long bones was grayish from the excess of leucocytes, and leukaemic nodules were present in the pleura and lungs. The nodules of the cutis, which were situated mainly in the adipose layer, were also leukaemic tumors.

Lichen ruber moniliformis was discussed in *Vierteljahresschrift für Dermatologie und Syphilis* in 1886[6]; again, the translation was provided by Johnston.[3]

The following is the history of a case of a unique form of lichen ruber planus, which I have termed lichen ruber moniliformis:

A man, aged forty-five, presented a dense eruption covering the neck, the acromial and axillary regions, the bends of the elbows and popliteal spaces, the abdomen and the gluteal region. The efflorescences projected in the shape of threads, ridges, and sausage-like swellings. They were red in color, with a yellowish tinge on their crests, smooth and very firm here and there, but usually notched at regular intervals so as to resemble a coral necklace. The eruption, while similar to xanthoma and keloid, looked like hypertrophic cicatrices from burns. The general direction of efflorescences was parallel to the longitudinal axis of the body, but they were joined together everywhere, especially in the bends of the joints as well as on the neck, by oblique and transverse ridges, here and there forming a very close network. The immediate neighborhood of these networks of spherical swellings, and the fields of skin between the meshes, were covered with dark-red or brownish characteristic nodules of lichen ruber planus, which were partly grouped in dense masses, partly arranged in streaks or disseminated.

The communication on dermatitis papillaris capillitii, one of Kaposi's first clinical descriptions, appeared in the *Archiv für Dermatologie und Syphilis* in 1869[7] and was later translated.[1]

On the neck, close below the hair line, in the region of the sparse hair at the nape, there was a tubercle the entire base of which was irregularly oval, about the size of a thaler, raised some two inches above the level of the skin, sloping off presipitously at the edges, of the same color as the normal skin, very firm, feeling like a hard scar or keloid. Its surface was broken by superficial and deep pits and furrows, and as the result of this, knobby or warty in appearance. The individual papules had the same red color and firm quality as the base of the elevation. A number of hairs, gathered in tufts, projected here and there from the pits and furrows, while the smooth parts of the swelling bore no hair for the most part.

The tubercles were, however, painful either spontaneously or to pressure. They itched moderately at times. Each time the patient scratched open individual points on the papules with the fingernails or with the comb, yellowish gummy crusts were seen, adherent here and there.

Kaposi's description of varicelliform eruption was translated by Shelley and Crissey.[1]

As a very alarming complication of Eczema larvale infantum I have seen, in some cases, an acute eruption of vesicles which are numerous, partly disseminated, arranged in groups and clusters for the most part, lentil sized and somewhat larger, filled with clear serum, transparent, flat, and usually delled as well. Because of the picture described they give the impression of varicella lesions, but they certainly are not. The skin of the face affected in this way, already swollen to various degrees by the eczema, now appears intensely turgid, even stretched taut, more edematous than solid. The little patients run a high fever, up to 40° and more, and are very restless. The eruption appears very acutely, as overnight, in the greater number, and frequently continues for three to four days or even a week with fresh outbreaks while the efflorescence of the first day involute, either dry up or, as is usual, break open and lay the corium bare, or become crusted and fall off.

The course of this peculiar affection in the cases observed so far has been favorable, and has ended with the healing of the vesicles as described and the epithelization of the denuded surfaces in two to three weeks, in which time the fever has subsided in relation to the local affection.

The description of impetigo herpetiformis, which established the status of this disease, appeared in the *Vierteljahresschrift für Dermatologie und Syphilis* and was translated by Johnston.[3]

Fifteen cases [of impetigo herpetiformis] have been observed in our clinic. All occurred in pregnant women, usually in the last months of pregnancy, and terminated fatally, with the exception of the cases which will be mentioned later.

Little pustules, as large as a pin's head, with opaque, later greenish-yellow contents, develop in the groin, at the umbilicus, the breasts and axillae, later in many other parts of the body. They are situated on a red, moderately swollen base, and are at first confined to patches from the size of a lentil to that of a penny. In one or two days they dry into a dirty-brown crust, while

similar ones appear immediately around them in a single, double, or triple circle; the desiccation of the latter enlarges the central crust. . . . At the end of three to four months almost the entire integument is involved; it is swollen, hot, covered with crusts, and contains excoriated and fissured surfaces which are still surrounded, here and there, by circles of pustules.

1. Shelley, W. B., and Crissey, J. T.: *Classics in Clinical Dermatology*, Springfield, Ill: Charles C Thomas, 1948.
2. Hebra, F., and Kaposi, M.: *On Diseases of the Skin*, vol 3, W. Tay, trans-ed., London: New Sydenham Society, 1874.
3. Kaposi, M.: *Pathology and Treatment of Diseases of the Skin*, J. C. Johnston, trans., New York: W. Wood, 1895.
4. Kaposi, M.: Idiopathic Multiple Pigmented Sarcoma of the Skin (Ger), *Arch Derm Syph* 4:265-273, 1872.
5. Kaposi, M.: A New Skin Disease, Lymphodermia Perniciosa (Ger), *Med Jahrb*, pp 129-147, 1885.
6. Kaposi, M.: Lichen ruber Monileformis—Korallenschnurartiger Lichen ruber (Ger), *Vjschr Derm Syph*, pp 571-582, 1886.
7. Kohn, M.: Concerning So-Called Framboesia and Other Kinds of Papillary Tumors of the Skin (Ger), *Arch Derm Syph*, pp 383-403, 1869.

Henri Hallopeau (1842-1919)

FRANCOIS HENRI HALLOPEAU was first a student of the nervous system, later a general pathologist and, only in his prime, was attracted to diseases of the skin, becoming one of the outstanding members of the French school of dermatology of the 19th century.[1] He studied at the Condorcet lycée and matriculated at the Faculty of Medicine of Paris in 1864. Following an internship at the hospitals of Paris, he presented a doctoral thesis on diseases of the spinal cord and, continuing an interest in neurologic disorders, published communications on diffuse myelitis and bulbar paralysis. He was affiliated initially with the hospitals of Tenon and St. Antoine and ultimately became physician to Hôpital Saint Louis in 1884, which was devoted exclusively to the care of patients with diseases of the skin. This was a decisive year: his *Elementary Treatise on General Pathology and Pathological Physiology* appeared,[2] he achieved professorial status at the University of Paris, and, most important, he chose dermatology as the field of concentration.

A remarkable number of communications on cutaneous disorders developed from his study of the patients on his service at the Saint Louis. Syphilis, leprosy, tuberculosis,

Composite by G. Bako

lupus vulgaris, lupus erythematosus, dermatitis herpetiformis, infantile vaccinia, dermatitis, eczema, and the erythematous stage of mycosis fungoids are among his best descriptive reports, which formed the basis of his *Practical Treatise on Dermatology*. The first edition was published in 1900, with assistance from his pupil and junior author Leredde. Communications on acanthosis nigricans, lichen planus atrophicus, acrodermatitis continua, pyodermite végétante, and verruga peruana have been selected for excerpting. One of the first reports of acanthosis nigricans from the French school, described initially by Pollitzer in 1890, was presented by Hallopeau in 1893 to the French Society of Dermatologists at the same meeting at which Darier presented a second and third case.[3]

This rare disease of the skin was observed first by Pollitzer in 1890; later it was described by Janovsky. . . . Darier should be credited with the observation that it coincides with cancers of the abdomen. The relation to carcinoma is not constant, and several cases display no such connection (Hügel). The lesions, always symmetrical, are maximal in certain and constant parts of the body; they are located on the neck, axillary grooves, the region of the breasts, umbilicus, perineogenital area, and the inner surface of the buttocks; less often and with less intensity they affect the face, the ante-cubital area, the popliteal area, the palms, and the soles of the feet. In reality it is a universal dermatosis.

Most often the skin has a general bronze-like discoloration, in others it is pale yellow, anemic and cachectic, as in patients with cancer. One may find, at the level of any selected region, intense pigmentation which is colored grey, swarthy, brown, or black. It decreases gradually at the limits of the lesions.

In the areas in which the alterations are maximal one observes papillomatous lesions of deep primary and secondary ridges. The directions of the ridges in general are determined by the normal lines of the skin.

The presence of gastric carcinoma has been noted in most of the cases. The carcinoma sometimes involves only the stomach, but also can be found in the uterus and other organs.

The first description of lichen planus atrophique, now known as lichen planus sclerosus et atrophicus, was published as a clinical lecture in 1887. The lesions were observed in a patient at Saint Louis, a "neurasthenic" woman in her mid-40's.[4]

Her cutaneous affection occupies chiefly the forearms, the back, and the inguinal folds.

On the volar surface of the left forearm, toward the lower part, a plaque is seen which measures about 5 cm. vertically and 3 cm. transversely. Its sinuous and slightly raised contours appear to be formed from conglomerated papules; some of these papules are clearly isolated, round, slightly raised and measure 2 to 3 mm. in diameter; they show in their centers punctiform depressions which evidently correspond to glandular orifices or to hair follicles, and are identical to those seen in ordinary lichen planus.

In summary, *lichen plan atrophique* begins with the formation of papules which are similar at first to those of ordinary lichen planus, although less highly colored, and, which, like those, give rise to a sensation of pruritus, become pale, involute promptly and form, then, white spots with a cicatrical appearance which are remarkable for the presence of punctiform depressions; these eruptive elements become grouped and confluent in such a way that they produce plaques several centimeters in diameter; their surface is checkered, and riddled with punctiform depressions; their contours are irregular; isolated papules are seen at their periphery, some colorless and involuting, others still rose colored and active.

Three forms of acrodermatitis continua of the digits were described—vesicular, suppurative, and mixed—with the following features.[5]

This eruption [vesicular form] consists of vesicles seated on a red surface; these vesicles are discrete and persist for a certain time after their eruption; each finger is only partially involved at first; the eruption may spread here and there on the palm of the hand, which it affects only as part of its extension.

When the isolated vesicles break, they leave erosions which soon become covered either with crusts or lamellar scales which are more or less thick.

When the scales become detached, the epidermis appears thin, smooth, and shiny; in other areas, on the contrary, the thickness of the skin becomes altered through an exaggeration of the folds.

The nail suffers in its nutrition; it loses its polish and becomes deeply grooved and furrowed vertically; moreover one sees transverse flattening of the nails, and also numerous punctiform depressions measuring a few millimeters in diameter. . . . this form [suppurative] is produced at times, but not always, as a sequel to trauma, either on the palm of the hand or on the end of the finger.

The nailfold soon becomes reddened, thickened and painful, leading to elevation and detachment of the nail. There is discharge of pus; the suppuration then extends to part of the first phalanx, usually to its palmar surface. It may involve the other phalanges successively. . . . beginning at isolated sites the pustules become confluent to form large areas from the surface of which the epidermis has been lost. On a bright red base, numerous flat suppurative areas of variable dimensions with polycyclic contours stand out clearly because of their whitish color; . . . In places islets of epidermis persist within the area of the plaques. The suppuration dries up quickly, forming crusts. Pustules recur continuously for months and even years without going beyond the limits of the hand, and predominating always on the ends of the fingers.

A new form of pustular chronic dermatitis, later called pyodermite végétante by Hallopeau, with a tendency to peripheral extension, and representing a variant of Neumann's pemphigus vegetans, was described in 1889. Groups of pustules appear and reappear about previous sites, progress, and form areas with polycyclical borders. Vegetation is apparent, but, when the lesions subside, scarring is not a sequela.[6]

This disease is characterized by persistent development, not influenced by treatment, of foci of suppuration either on the parts previously normal, or in areas of former suppuration, in the form of the vesicopustular miliary eruptions. These lesions spread eccentrically, accompanied by edema and redness of the skin and intense pruritus, then attain a circular form, and as coalescing polycyclic plaques, begin to subside in the center, but continue to expand peripherally. Finally, they leave no trace except for pigmentation, particularly in hairy regions, such as the scalp, axillae, and pubis, but also in the hairless parts such as the arms, the trunk, and thighs. The lesions are not limited to the skin; the buccal mucosa may be the site of the eruption. The lesions may extend into the subcutaneous tissue and be complicated by cellulitis.

Suppuration is not accompanied by a disturbance of nutrition: the only evidence of a systemic response, when the local disorder is accentuated, is a slight transient elevation of the temperature.

Bacteriologic examination, performed on four different occasions by Mr. L. Wickham, intern in our service, showed staphylococcus and particularly staphylococcus albus. . . . we propose to name the disease chronic pustular focal dermatitis with eccentric progression, to express the characteristics of the disease, a form of pyogenic chronic infection limited to the teguments.

The two forms of verruga peruana were described, one an acute severe process with febrile anemia and high mortality (Oroya fever), and the other, a benign eruptive form (verruga peruana), referring to a contribution by Odriozola from Peru in 1895.[3]

It began with symptoms indicating an infection, in some cases severe and in others moderate. In the acute form, the patient aches all over; then, muscular pains, joint pains, and headaches set in, chills appear, fever is very intense, sometimes steady and sometimes fluctuating. The liver, spleen and lymphatic glands are swollen, and multiple hemorrhages or purpura appear on the body. Severe anemia develops, accompanied by vertigo and syncope, the patient goes into a state of typhoid and into coma, and finally death occurs.

In the attenuated or benign form, the general infection manifests itself by moderate fever, signs of anemia, weakness, anorexia, spells of nervousness, and localized hemorrhages.

Two types of skin eruptions, distinguishable by the extent, are observed. In the *miliary form*, one observes a purpuric spot, a vesicle, a pustule, or white papules. In the advanced stages red elevated papules are found; often purplish blue, and at times are pedunculated. The verrugas are very numerous and, in some cases, are abundant on the extensor surfaces of the extremities, on the face, but not on the trunk. Similar lesions may be found on the conjunctiva and on the buccal mucosa.

The *nodular form* is characterized by larger though less numerous tumors, mostly on the face, arms, and knee.

1. Jeanselme, E.: The Scientific Works of Hallopeau (Fr), *Ann Derm Syph (Par)* 7:233-236, 1918-1919.
2. Hallopeau, H.: *Elementary Treatise on General Pathology and Pathological Physiology* (Fr), Paris: J.-B. Baillière, 1884.
3. Hallopeau, H., and Leredde, L. E.: *Practical Treatise on Dermatology* (Fr), Paris: J.-B. Baillière, 1900, excerpt translated by E. Sieweke.
4. Hallopeau, H.: Lichen Plan Atrophique (Fr), *Union Med* 43:742-747, 1887, translated in Shelley, W. B., and Crissey, J. T.: *Classics in Clinical Dermatology*, Springfield, Ill: Charles C Thomas, 1948.
5. Hallopeau, H.: Acrodermatitis Continua (Fr), *Rev Gen Clin Ther*, 1898, pp 97-101.
6. Hallopeau, H.: A New Form of Pustular Chronic Dermatitis With Eccentric Progression (Fr), *Int Congr Derm Syph, C R*, 1890, pp 344-362, excerpt translated by Z. Danilevicius.

Composite by G. Bako

Domenico Majocchi (1849-1929)

DOMENICO MAJOCCHI, leading Italian dermatologist of his time, was born in Roccalvecce, the son of a city physician.[1] He began his higher education in the seminary at Bagnorea, concentrating on classical language and philosophy. In 1868, he matriculated at la Sapienca in preparation for a medical career but continued his philosophical studies with private tutoring. After taking his degree in 1873 and spending a year in private practice in Roccalvecce, Majocchi returned to Rome and committed himself to dermatology and syphilology, with the aid of vast clinical material at the S. Galligano and S. Giacomo hospitals. In 1880, he was appointed professor of dermatology at the University of Parma and 11 years later accepted a similar post at Bologna—a decision that greatly enhanced the reputation of the school. By then he had become one of the foremost clinicians of Europe.

Within his chosen field Majocchi was a skilled clinician, an excellent teacher, and a careful histopathologist. He favored the Viennese school of dermatology in preference to the French. He used his extensive knowledge of anatomy, histology, and parasitology to advance the science and practice of cutaneous diseases, without showing any preference to a special phase of the field. Generous and kind in his dealings, Majocchi was highly regarded by his pupils and associates.

In addition to numerous contributions to the dermatologic literature, Majocchi, intensely interested in medical history, wrote a scholarly treatise on the fateful campaign of Charles VIII in Italy. Communications on granuloma tricofitico, syphilis of the bone, and purpura annularis telangiectodes[2] are judged to be his best works. Excerpts of the latter with the three clinical stages in a single case follow.[3]

1. Telangiectatic Stage. In relation to time, the first appearance of the illness is characterized by rose-red punctate or streak-forming spots which occasionally are serpiginous or slightly branched, and made up of capillary ectasias which because of their increased size may be seen with the naked eye, although better with a lens. Under a transparent plate which is alternately pressed on and released from the ring-forming lesions one can get a better idea of their composition, and also differentiate easily the hemorrhagic lesions from the capillary ectasias. They are located particularly at the follicles, as one can determine from the presence of a small hair in the center of nearly every spot. They persist for a very long time, until by gradual enlargement they unite with one another, either by becoming confluent or contiguous, and in this way produce the ring-forms described above. Pruritus is usually

lacking throughout the entire course of the dermatosis; only rarely does the patient experience minor annoyance with the eruption of the livid red spots, and this soon yields.

2. Hemorrhagic Pigmented stage. This frequently accompanies the telangiectatic stage; however, extravasation of blood does not take place from every ectasia, although it appears at different points. For this reason the hemorrhages do not form an essential stage of the dermatosis, but are only a feature of it.

Further, the punctate and lenticular hemorrhages form at the follicles or in their neighborhood and persist for a long time, so that one may see in their midst tiny ectatic vessels. After a more or less protracted existence they resolve into pigmentations which disappear completely in time.

3. Atrophic Stage. After the disappearance of the pigmented spots, or even during their presence, an important change in the lesions of the disease takes place. The hairs thin out, that is, become colorless, atrophic and fall out; also, the follicular openings disappear, and only with the aid of a lens can one detect them as tiny points. But after several months one sees no trace of either hair or follicular opening. The skin in the ringed lesions becomes somewhat thinner, shiny, loses its pigment and is traversed by delicate wrinkles. This is the atrophic stage, but also during this time the lesions are growing through eccentric extension of the perifollicular capillary ectasias, at the expense of the neighboring follicles.

Usually the livid red spots appear gradually, as discrete lesions, and their arrangement in circular forms also manifests itself with steady slowness. But what is noteworthy in the course of the disease is the lack of sudden or intermittent paroxysmal-like eruptions as occur frequently in purpura hemorrhagica. . . . As already said, these livid red spots terminate usually in pigmentation and atrophy.

1. Diasio, F. A. Domenico Majocchi: A Biographical Appreciation, *Med Life* 39:597-601, 1932.

2. Majocchi, D.: Concerning an Undescribed Telangectoid Dermatosis-Purpura Annularis-Telangiectasia Folllicularis Annulata: A Clinical Study (Ital), *G Ital Mal Vener* 31:242-260, 1896.

3. Majocchi, D.: Purpura Annularis Telangiectodes, in Shelley, W. B., and Crissey, J. T.: *Classics in Clinical Dermatology,* Springfield, Ill: Charles C Thomas, Publisher, 1953, pp 285-286.

Paul Gerson Unna (1850-1929)

P. G. UNNA, one of the leading dermatologists of central Europe, a prodigious worker and a prolific writer, labored in the vineyard without institutional or academic affiliation. Throughout his career he excelled in the development of dermatologic microscopy, enhanced the clinical description of a number of dermatologic disorders, and enjoyed an enviable status as an outstanding consultant in the diagnosis and

treatment of cutaneous maladies. Unna was born in Hamburg, the son of a physician in a family with a strong medical tradition.[1] His higher education was gained at the universities of Heidelberg, Leipzig, and Strasbourg. Studies at Heidelberg were interruped by the Franco-Prussian War, in which Unna received a serious battle wound. For this service and injury, however, he was granted a pension by his government, which in later years he gave as prizes for students.

Unna's inaugural thesis, suggested by Waldeyer and presented for the MD degree in 1875 at Strasbourg, discussed the embryology of the skin. This was the first of several hundred communications on anatomy, physiology, pathological anatomy and general pathology, staining techniques, bacteriology, mycology, leprosy, clinical studies, therapy, pharmacology, chemistry, and philosophy. Following his formal education and before returning to Hamburg for hospital training, Unna spent several months in Vienna with Hebra and Auspitz. In spite of his interest in the skin so clearly evinced in his writings, he assisted his father in general practice in Hamburg for several years. In 1881, however, he moved to Eimsbüttle, a small suburb of Hamburg, to establish a home and to build a hospital, a laboratory, and a library.

Supplemented by great capability in foreign languages and a desire for liaison with clinical and medical scientists in many lands, Unna participated in national and international dermatologic meetings and communicated his researches to dermatologic journals at home and abroad, including a dissertation on seborrheic eczema given at the Dermatological Section of the Ninth International Medical Congress in Washington.

Not content with existing periodicals, he saw a need for a journal of practical dermatology, and the *Monatshefte für Praktische Dermatologie* was founded in 1882. Endowed with great mental industry, a fine talent for teaching, and a curiosity for research, Unna attracted students in large numbers and enjoyed an outstanding reputation for his clinical courses. Although not connected with a university in his prime years and ineligible for academic recognition, he was given the title of honorary professor in 1907 by the Senate of Hamburg. When the University of Hamburg was founded a decade later, Unna became professor of dermatology, but by then he had reached the mandatory age of retirement. The honorary degree of doctor of philosophy, another late award, was bestowed on him by the University of Bonn in 1927.

Unna prepared several monumental treatises on the skin. His *Histopathology of the Skin* was started in 1889 as the section in histopathology for Orth's systems of pathology. This grew to 1,200 pages by 1894 and was translated in 1896 into English.[2] *Histologic Technique of Leprous Skin*[3] was a summary monograph of work that had been undertaken many years earlier. Unna was one of four editors of the *International Atlas of Rare Skin Diseases,* which appeared with descriptions in German, English, and French.[4] Items well worth excerpting include identification of the plasma cell in

connective tissue, orcein method for demonstrating elastic fibers, a concept of staining based upon difference in chemical response of tissue, the description of seborrheic dermatitis, and the recognition of three varieties of favus. The separation of plasma cells by their differential staining characteristics was summarized in the *Encyclopedia of Microscopic Technique.*[5]

The name plasma cell was first proposed by Waldeyer in 1875 for a special group of connective tissue cells distinguished by a remarkable richness in protoplasm, in contrast to the connective tissue cells described by Virchow, Cohnheim and Ranvier, which are shallow and have little protaplasm. The Waldeyer cell includes different varieties whose varied nature has been recognized. Since then I discovered in several pathological lesions of the skin and by a special staining method, cells which were different in their richness of protoplasm, and, following Waldeyer's definition, I suggested the names of plasma cells for this special cell. The rightness of this decision was recognized by Waldeyer in 1895. "The Unna plasma cells fit very well the definition which I gave in 1875 to the plasma cells; to distinguish the protoplasm poor cells in the connective tissue from other forms rich in protoplasm, I must accept the name given them by Unna."

The plasma cell as defined above is a frequent and important component of the infiltration of the skin in a number of diseases; and as experience has taught us, this is valid for the diseases of the other tissues as well. The plasma cells deserve our attention more than the fatty cells, since they are the mother substance for degenerative forms; in other words, they are important in the histology and history of many skin diseases.

The advantages of the use of orcein for staining elastic fibers in the skin were described in 1891.[6]

The study of histopathology of the skin has benefited immeasurably by staining procedures, not to mention the special interest from the concentration or deficiency of Elastin in the different diseases. The presence of Elstin discloses at once the distribution of the vessels in the skin. . . . It outlines the glands which are recognized by their delicate elastic outer shell. It clearly differentiates the several fibrillar structures, the nerve roots by the absence of elastic substance, even from vessels and glands where an Osmium or Gold technique is without value.

An English translation of Unna's description of seborrheic dermatitis appeared in the *Journal of Cutaneous and Genito-Urinary*

Diseases shortly after the communication in his *Monatshefte.*[7]

Seborrhoeal eczema is quite a different matter; here the skin was not previously very healthy, and a few weeks after birth, there has existed, though often not so as to be noticed, an extensive seborrhoea of the scalp. This often spreads over the ears, forehead and cheeks after it has taken on a moist character, and, without attacking the neighborhood of the eyes, jumps over to the eye-lashes. It spreads upon the shoulders and upper arm in the form of dry, scaly or fatty plaques. This eczema maintains its fatty characteristics in all regions, even moist ones.

The starting point of almost all seborrhoeal eczemas is from the scalp. Very rarely the affection begins with a corresponding affection of the margin of the eyelids, or upon one of the well-known surfaces rich in sudoriparous glands, such as the axilla, the bend of the elbow and the cruro-scrotal fold.

From this point the process may take on one of three characters upon the scalp. Either the scaly masses may be simply increased in quantity, but remain white and only moderately fatty, while little by little an increase in the loss of hair is noticed, and the well-known and characteristic baldness of alopecia pityrodes appears.

In another class of cases the scaliness so increases and persists. that during the whole duration it forms the principal symptom. The scales heap themselves up into fatty crusts between the hairs, which they cause to fall out. There is also a corona seborrhoica, which gives a typical appearance to the patient thus affected.

The third form is that in which the catarrhal appearances are the most pronounced, and in which "weeping" occurs, especially about that portion of the temporal region lying next to the ears, and following a simple pityriasis, with its attendant itching, tension and redness. The fatty scales are lost, and, as is always the case in eczema, the dark red, moist and shining basal horny layer comes into view. In increased weeping, erosions may appear at different points, and the rete be laid bare.

The differential diagnosis is to be made from other forms of chronic eczema, and from psoriasis, which latter disease the author has known to have been confounded with it by careful and able observers.

The original communication on three varieties of favus appeared in 1892 and was published by the New Sydenham Society the following year.[8]

Throughout the numerous inoculation experiments, however, the differences between the scutula formed by each variety were maintained.

Microscopic examination also showed individual peculiarities of growth upon the skin, as well as differences in the filaments of the fungi themselves and their mode of sporing.

For the fungus of No. I the name proposed is "Achorion enthythrix" (*i.e.* possessing straight running hairs). For the disease produced by it the term "Favus griseus" is suggested, on account of the greyish-yellow colour of the scutula. The term "griseus" is apothecary's Latin, but has the advantage of being more easily understood than *ravus,* which would be more classical. No. II the author calls "Achorion dikroön" (not to be confounded with dichroön), on account of the forked ends of the hyphae. The disease will be termed in future "Favus sulphureus tardus," owing to its sulphur colour and slow growth.

For variety No. III the term "Achorion atakton" appears suitable, in consequence of the irregular course of the hyphae; and the disease which it produces receives the name "Favus sulphureus celerior," because the crusts are of a sulphur-yellow colour, and the growth of the disease is relatively quicker than that of No. II.

Some of these distinguishing characteristics are as follows:

Favus griseus.—Scutulum of moderate size, about that of a lentil, and as thick. On the upper surface flat or raised, not cup-shaped. Grey-yellow, like old wash-leather, neither shining nor smooth. Penetrated at all points by the fine and tactile hairs.

Favus sulphureus-tardus.—Scutulum very large, covering the whole cheek, and thick. Cup-shaped on the surface, and covered by small humps, gathered into folds, yellowish white, cream-coloured, smooth as leather, shining in some parts, and pressing back the hairs, which do not penetrate it.

Favus sulphureus-celerior.—Scutulum remains small, about the size of a peppercorn, cup-shaped on its surface, smooth but not shining; of a light ochre-colour towards its periphery, in the centre whiter, and on the folded margin of a horn-like brown. It presses back the finer hairs, but is penetrated by the larger. [A.E.]

1. Delbanco, E., and Unna, Jr., P.: The Life of P. G. Unna, *Derm Wschr* 71:621-638, 1920.

2. Unna, P. G.: "Histopathology of the Skin," in Orth, J.: *Handbook of Special Pathological Anatomy,* Berlin: A. Hirschwald, 1894, translated in Walker, N.: *Histopathology of Diseases of the Skin,* Edinburgh: W. F. Clay, 1896.

3. Unna, P. G.: *Histologic Technique of Leprous Skin,* Hamburg: L. Voss, 1910.

4. Morris, M., Unna, P. G., Duhring, L. A., and Leloir, H. (eds.): *International Atlas of Rare Skin Diseases,* Hamburg: L. Voss, 1889.

5. Unna, P. G.: *Encyclopedia of Microscopic Technique* (Ger), Berlin: Urban & Schwarzenberg, 1910, vol 2, pp 409-410, excerpt translated by E. Longar.

6. Unna, P. G.: Notice, Recounting the Taenzer Orcein Staining of Elastic Tissue (Ger), *Mshft Prak Derm* 12: 394-396, 1891, excerpt translated by E. Longar.

7. Unna, P. G.: Seborrheic Eczema, *Mshft Prak Derm* 6:827-846, 1887, translated in *J Cutan Genitourin Dis* 5:449-459, 1887.

8. Unna, P. G.: Three Forms of Favus, *Mshft Prak Derm* 14:1-16, 1892, translated in Abraham, P. S. (ed.): *Selected Monographs on Dermatology,* London: New Sydenham Society, 1893.

Composite by G. Bako

Gustav Riehl (1855-1943)

GUSTAV RIEHL, recognized in his generation as one of the leaders of Viennese dermatology in particular and German dermatology in general, was born in Vienna, completed his higher education at the university, and received the MD in 1879. After a short internship in Bamberg, he trained in his specialty for four years, first under Hebra and later under Kaposi.[1] In 1896, Riehl was called to Leipzig to direct the recently organized University clinic on skin and venereal diseases; six years later, upon the retirement of Kaposi, he returned to Vienna. In bringing to the outstanding post in dermatology in central Europe the rich heritage of his academic forebears, Riehl added his varied interests which included bacteriology, mycology, histology, and a superlative capacity for diagnosis and treatment. His lec-

tures to undergraduate and graduate students proved very popular; his management of the sick exemplified the kindly physician skilled in the art, as well as in the scientific pursuit, of his profession. He contributed immeasurably as a teacher and a consultant in the great days of Viennese medicine in the first quarter of the 20th century.

The first two excerpts presented in this essay are clinical-pathologic descriptions of dermatologic disorders; the third, advocating the use of whole blood transfusions in the treatment of extensive burns, reflects Riehl's belief that his specialty was but a small segment of the great field of medicine. The discussion of verrucose tuberculosis appeared early in his career—the others during the period of full professional maturity. During his service in the dermatology clinic under Kaposi, a series of patients were observed who presented symptoms and a clinical course different from dermatoses already described and recognized. The lesions were found in either sex, but particularly in the male, and were designated "tuberculosis verrucosa cutis." The plaques usually appeared on the dorsum of the hands, sometimes on the extensor surfaces of the fingers, or on the interdigital folds. On casual inspection they could be mistaken for lupus verrucosus or inflamed warts. When fully developed the plaques were several centimeters in diameter and showed progression from the periphery to the center. The borders were elevated above the central zone but not above the adjacent, unaffected skin. In the center of the lesion, the warty excrescences or papillomas varied in size and also underwent involution. The afflicted person experienced no systemic symptoms; the cutaneous lesions were sensitive only when the morbid process was at its height. Riehl described the histologic findings.[2]

All cases investigated showed identical histologic findings, and the only variations were related to the stage of development of the lesion. In the most highly developed lesion the horny layer over the wart-like papilla was unusually thick, was laminated irregularly over the entire surface, and covered the crypt-like depressions at the base of the papilla as well as the elevated tips. . . . No changes were noted in the stratum lucidum or granulosum except for the frequent absence of the stratum granulosum. The layer of horny cells was generally thicker; the interpapillae shafts were hypertrophied so as to form finger-like depressions. . . . In other areas, particularly near the aggregates of purulent material, the rete malpighi were invaded by round cells. The basal layer showed few changes. The principal alterations were seen in the upper layers of the cutis, involving the papillae and their bases. In contrast, there was scarcely any involvement of the deeper layers of cutis or the subcutaneous tissues. The papillae were increased in all dimensions. . . . Several papillae contained caseous foci; neither the caseous areas nor the zone of epithelioid cells contained blood vessels. Giant cells surrounding caseous material were mostly of the smaller variety, with 12 to 20 nuclei around the outer portion. The infiltrates showed all of the properties of giant cell tubercles.

The process is easily recognized as a particular form of skin tuberculosis. This diagnosis, based on the histologic investigation, showed the constant presence of bacilli in the granulation tissue and the presence of a specific organism where purulent material formed. The bacilli were similar in form and size to tubercle bacilli and gave the appropriate staining reactions. They were found in the giant cells, in the epithelioid cells of the small aggregates and sometimes scattered in the granulation tissue. In the epithelioid giant cells there were usually one, but sometimes two or three bacilli.

The number of tubercle bacilli varied according to the stage of development. Several bacilli were demonstrated in all slides taken from fully developed nodules; in sections taken from areas already in regression, fewer bacilli were found. In the more recently formed tubercular infiltrations, bacilli were always present.

This disease must be considered as a form of tuberculosis of the skin, clinically as well as anatomically, and not identical with any of the known varieties of skin tuberculosis. We have given it the name of "Tuberculosis Verrucosa Cutis" to identify its clinical characteristics.

Riehl's melanosis, recognized by a deep browning of the skin similar to suntan, appeared on protected as well as on exposed portions of the body. The diseased skin was thickened, without atrophy, and with gradual transition from discolored to normal colored skin. Discrete lesions which produced neither pruritus nor sensory changes were noted at the margins; sometimes slightly raised papules appeared around the follicles. The original histologic findings described by Riehl in 1917 follow.[3]

The typical changes are mainly in the upper portions of the corium and the papillary layers.

One observes a dense infiltration of round cells contrasting with the otherwise unchanged corium. The hair follicles appear deeper than usual. The round cells, closely packed in the connective tissue, have large nuclei and little protoplasm and are interspersed with larger cells having an abundance of protoplasm. The infiltration is less dense in the papillary layer, and edema is present.

In the lesions of the skin with deep pigmented cells, the bases of the papillae form a band-like horizontal pattern; the chromatophores in the papillae near the border of the epidermis show long tendrils. The elastic tissue in the area of infiltration shows degeneration similar to the senile skin, with thickening of fibers and formation of aggregates that stain weakly.

The epidermis contains little pigment. In some areas the malpighian cells are surrounded by edema. The other layers of the epidermis are well formed. The deposits of horny cells show flaking and disintegration. Some of the hair follicles have a horny appearance typical of ichthyosis.

The use of whole blood transfusions in the treatment of extensive burns was described in 1925. This was an extension of an earlier interest in "survival" as a function of affected body surface. The average survival time, based on 100 cases observed in Riehl's clinic between 1902 and 1904, was found to be 7 hours if the complete body surface was burned. Life was prolonged to 43 hours if one fourth of the body surface was affected, and to 90 hours if not more than one seventh of the skin was burned. The disastrous results from burning were assumed by Riehl to be associated with resorption of toxic products, which could be inhibited by saline infusions and blood transfusions.[4]

The infusion of large quantities of fluid, mainly a salt solution, as many as 3-4 liters daily, has proved satisfactory. Sometimes a life is saved if not more than one-quarter of the body surface has received a third-degree burn.

The possibility of whole-blood transfusions has been suggested many times. During my internship in 1880 I attempted to persuade the Billroth Hospital to give a whole-blood transfusion to a burned patient. The procedure was too hazardous, however, and might have produced more harm than good. During the last decade improvement in the technique of blood transfusion in America and in Germany places this procedure on a sound biological basis, with little danger.

I have given blood transfusions to two patients with severe burns, with recovery in one case and postponement of death in the other.

Riehl lived to such an old age that he was one of the favored few who experienced the birth of dermatology in central Europe, who brought it international fame through microscopic and bacteriologic study of cutaneous lesions, and who continued to uphold the reputation of Viennese medicine into contemporary times. Riehl's monographic contributions to dermatologic literature include an *Atlas of Skin Diseases*,[5] and *The Radium and Mesothorium Treatment of Skin Diseases*.[6] He served as section editor for dermatology of the *Wiener Klinische Wochenschrift* and received an unusual honor, Rector of the University, for the 1921-1922 term shortly before the statutory retirement age of 71 years.

1. Fuhs, H.: Gustav Riehl (Ger), *Wien Klin Wschr* 56:41-42, 1943, excerpt translated by E. Longar.
2. Riehl, G., and Paltauf, R.: Tuberculosis Verrucosa Cutis (Ger), *Vjschr Derm Syph* 13:19-48, 1886, excerpt translated by E. Longar.
3. Riehl, G.: An Unusual Melanosis (Ger), *Wien Klin Wschr* 30:780-781, 1917, excerpt translated by E. Longar.
4. Riehl, G.: The Therapy of Deep Burns (Ger), *Wien Klin Wschr* 38:933-834, 1925, excerpt translated by E. Longar.
5. Riehl, G., and v. Zumbusch, L.: *Atlas of Skin Diseases*, Leipzig: F. C. W. Vogel, 1925.
6. Riehl, G., and Kumer, L.: *The Radium and Mesothorium Treatment of Skin Diseases*, Berlin: J. Springer, 1924.

Sigmund Pollitzer (1859-1937)

SIGMUND POLLITZER, an American dermatologist with an international reputation, was born in Staten Island and spent his professional years in Manhattan. An intelligent youth, he was familiar with the works of Cicero and Virgil in his early teens. He sought higher education at the College of the City of New York, where his interests included physics, mathematics, and astronomy.[1] He graduated from the college in 1879, with membership in the Phi Beta Kappa society, and continued with higher mathematics, receiving a master's degree. Pollitzer graduated in medicine at Columbia University College of Physicians and Surgeons in 1884. His thesis on temperature sensitivity, an original piece of investiga-

tion, subsequently was published in the British *Journal of Physiology*.[2] The relative sensibility of different parts of the body was challenged, with a constant heat source.

Composite by G. Bako

Although the responses were not constant with each subject, the general order of sensitivity progressed from the tip of the finger to the dorsum of the hand, to the back, to the forearm, to the palm, and to the calf. No consistent relationship between thermosensitiveness and thickness of the epidermis was observed.

Following graduation in medicine, Pollitzer acquired his physiologic knowledge at Heidelberg, his bacteriologic indoctrination in Wiesbaden, and pursued the fields of general pathology in Berlin, and clinical medicine in Vienna. When war broke out between Serbia and Bulgaria in the fall of 1885, he served in a Serbian army hospital and was discharged with the rank of major. Returning to New York, he found the practice of general medicine disheartening. Consequently, he returned to Europe, where he centered his attention on dermatology, choosing Unna's clinic in the suburbs of Hamburg. The selection was mutually satisfactory, for, in subsequent years, Pollitzer became one of the best of Unna's many outstanding pupils. From Germany he went to London and then to Paris. He returned to New York in 1890 and practiced dermatology, having explored in the two European tours the advantages of postgraduate medicine in Austria, Germany, England, and France. At the age of 36 Pollitzer was appointed professor of dermatology at the New York Postgraduate Medical School and Hospital, a post held for 20 years. He took an active part in establishing the dermatologic section of the New York Academy of Medicine and in 1914 served as president of the American Dermatological Association.

In the early decades of this century, with syphilology commanding a significant portion of dermatologists' time, one is not surprised to learn of Pollitzer receiving one of the first batches in America of arsphenamine (Salvarsan) from Ehrlich through the courtesy of Dr. Simon Flexner of the Rockefeller Institute. Pollitzer discussed the serologic diagnosis of syphilis shortly after the introduction of the Wassermann test; in 1911, he outlined the indications for the use of arsphenamine, excluding cases of syphilis with organic disease of the heart and cases with paresis and advanced tabes, but including the following:[3]

. . . a. Cases of recent syphilis in which the rapid sterilization of the lesions is a matter of importance for the entourage of the patient and the safety of the community. b. Cases of extensive syphilitic ulceration to shorten the period of local treatment. c. Cases in which important structures, like the eye, the throat, etc., are threatened. d. Cases of syphilitic cachexia. e. Cases with severe lesions in patients who are oversensitive to mercury or are resistant to mercury—the latter are very few in number. f. Cases of syphilis complicated by tuberculosis in which the effect of mercury on the tuberculosis is bad. g. Cases in an early stage of tabes for the relief of pain or of sphincter troubles. h. Cases of hereditary syphilis in infants. In the last two conditions in small doses only.

A degeneration of the sweat gland epithelium, with external formation of nodules which suppurate, had been described by several in the 19th century, but the disease entity is recognized in this century as hydradenitis destruens suppurativa, Pollitzer's disease, from his correlation of the histologic and clinical findings.[4]

In short, we have a complete chain of evidence, beginning with parenchymatous degeneration of the sweat gland epithelium and its coagulation-necrosis, to the final dissociation of the altered epithelial masses, into fragments resembling giant cells.

As to the starting point of the pathological process, it is clear that the changes affect the sweat glands principally, and that these are the seat of a parenchymatous degeneration. The question, however, to be determined is: Is the parenchymatous degeneration primary or is it secondary, or, in other words, Do the changes in the sweat glands originate in them, or are these organs changed secondarily, and only in consequence of a diffuse inflammatory process involving the entire cutis of which they form a part? The question cannot be answered with absolute certainty, but there is enough evidence to leave but little room for doubt that *the process is primary in the sweat glands*.

Nomenclature.—I have called the disease *Hydradenitis destruens suppurativa*. For an inflammation of a sweat gland there is in accordance with the principles of medical nomenclature only one name possible, that is Hydradenitis (υδωρ, water, and αδλν, a gland.) The qualifying adjective *destruens* was selected to indicate the most characteristic pathological feature, the complete destruction of the affected gland. The term *suppurativa* was added to distinguish this form of hydradenitis from other possible forms which may terminate differently; for it is not unlikely that there are other forms of sweat gland inflammation.

One of the first cases of acanthosis nigricans in contemporary literature was seen by Pollitzer in Unna's clinic in 1889 and was described in Unna's book of rare skin diseases. The patient was admitted shortly after symptoms developed. The disease affected the upper extremities, the neck, the mouth, the trunk, and the genitocrural regions. The patient lived less than a year after onset of symptoms. Although no postmortem was performed, the cause of death was attributed to carcinoma occultum. Pollitzer described the lesions as follows.[5]

The skin of the hands is in general of a dirty brownish colour: on the dorsum manus there are patches of a bluish-grey, somewhat deeper in colour along the courses of the veins. . . . The natural furrows are deeply marked, the skin of the entire hands looking as if it were too large for them. On the back of the proximal phalanx of the thumb there is a patch the size of a shilling in which the dirty discoloration and the prominence of the cuticular areas are especially marked, giving the patch the appearance of a diffuse flat wart. The skin of the entire hand is rough and inelastic. The palms are slightly darker than normal, their furrows and folds are strongly marked and the skin feels dry, hard and thickened.

On the anterior surface of the lower third of the forearm the peculiar discolouration is very striking and numerous small brownish patches (like ephilides) are to be seen. On the dorsal surface of the fore-arms the discoloration is especially marked over and along the course of a vein.

The neck appears as if encircled by a dirty greyish band which sends irregular offshoots downwards toward the sternum, clavicles, shoulders and scapulae, and upwards the face. The skin here shows the changes described as existing on the hands, but in a much more marked degree.

Pollitzer described one of the early cases of rhinoscleroma treated with x-ray, in which the patient was presumably cured three years after therapy. Other notable communications discussed parakeratosis variegata, naevus angiectodes disseminatus, and the xanthomas. A presentation of thirteen cases of various kinds of xanthomas, including xanthoma planum palpebrarum, multiple xanthoma, and diabetic xanthoma, gave him an opportunity to review the differential histologic findings.[6]

The so-called xanthoma cell in xanthoma planum is a degenerated muscle fibre. In examining sections taken from the edge of a growing xanthoma I found a great part of the cutis filled with normal or but little changed striped muscle fibres.

The xanthoma neoplasm [xanthoma tuberosum] is a typical hyperplastic development of connective tissue in which connective-tissue cells develop into fibrous tissue on the one hand, or undergo fatty degeneration on the other in varying proportions.

Xanthoma diabeticorum differs histologically from xanthoma tuberosum in the following non-essential details only: (1) The new formation of connective-tissue cells is not sharply limited to one or more nodules, but is a more diffuse process. (2) The entire process is located more superficially in the cutis. (3) The tendency to fatty degeneration is more marked, and the formation of fibrous tissue less apparent.

1. Wile, U. J.: Obituaries, Sigmund Pollitzer, MD, 1859-1937, *Arch Derm* 37:499-503, 1938.

2. Pollitzer, S.: On the Temperature Sense, a Contribution to the Physiology of the Skin as an Organ of Sense, *J Physiol* 5:143-151, 1884-1885.

3. Pollitzer, S.: Salvarsan (Ehrlich-Hata, "606") in Syphilis, *New York Med J* 93:205-211, 1911.

4. Pollitzer, S.: Hydradenitis Destruens Suppurativa, *J Cutan Genitourin Dis* 10:9-24, 1892.

5. Pollitzer, S.: "Acanthosis Nigricans," in *International Atlas of Rare Skin Diseases,* Hamburg and Leipzig: L. Voss, 1890.

6. Pollitzer, S.: The Nature of the Xanthomata, *New York Med J* 70:73-80, 1899.

Vittorio Mibelli (1860-1910)

VITTORIO MIBELLI, leading Italian dermatologist, was born in Portoferraio on the island of Elba.[1] He studied in Siena and, after taking advanced training at Florence, returned to Siena as prosector, first in the anatomical institute and later as assistant in the dermatology clinic. He gained academic status in 1888 and spent the next year with Unna in Hamburg. In 1890, he was called to Cagliari, as professor and director of the skin clinic; two years later he moved to Parma, where he served as professor of dermatology until his death.

Mibelli was recognized as an excellent teacher. He complemented the capacity for clear exposition in the clinical amphitheater with his great curiosity in mycology and histopathology of the skin. He described the first case of urticaria pigmentosa in Italy and discussed the pathogenesis of alopecia areata, exfoliatio linguae areata, acne keloid, fixed drug eruptions, the trichophytoses, and the histopathology of rhinoscleroma. Although two cutaneous disorders are associated with his name, each had been incompletely described earlier. In the *St. George's Hospital Reports* for 1877-1879, in a presentation of several cases of warty growths, Cottle described hyperkeratosis in a young girl suffering from chilblains, since the age of 14.[2] The lesions of the dorsal surface of the fingers and toes were associated with no constitutional disturbances and no local subjective symptoms. In 1889, Mibelli described similar lesions which he called "angiokeratoma."[3] The description was recorded later in the *International Atlas of Rare Skin Diseases* and was translated into English as follows:[4]

. . . the presence of small red spots could be seen, which resembled telangiectases and were covered already by a slightly elevated and horny epidermis. The gradual development of these spots into the small tumours was observed.

For the purpose of studying the disease no treatment was employed beyond the excision of some of the tumours for histological study. More than a year has passed since these tumours were excised, and there is no sign of recurrence.

The external appearance of the small tumours suggested the diagnosis of keratoma. We must however distinguish what I call Angiokeratoma from simple keratoma (verruca vulgaris). The differential diagnosis is easy when the peculiar colour of the Angiokeratoma is considered—a colour which disappears under pressure and immediately reappears when the pressure is removed, and also the changes which the colour undergoes under the influence of cold.

In 1875, Neumann[5] reported eight cases of an unusual type of skin disease which he called "dermatitis circumscripta herpetiformis." In 1893, Mibelli described as an uncommon form of keratodermia a similar disorder which he chose to call "porokeratosis."[6] Histologically, the lesion shows an atrophic center surrounded by a keratotic wall through which runs a deep groove filled with keratotic material. The clinical findings were confined to lesions on the back of the hands and the posterior internal surface of the right forearm, first noted in the patient at the age of two. They were neither preceded nor accompanied by any other symptoms. The English translation from the *International Atlas* follows.[4]

There was noticed at first without any previous change a small isolated disc on the back of the right hand in the place which is now occupied by the large marginated space. From this primary centre the change spread gradually, and within a period of three years came to occupy all the parts of the back of the hand and forearm which it occupies at present. From the age of 5 years the other isolated patches developed on the same hand and in the course of 9 years two patches showed themselves on the back of the thumb, three on the index and one on the ring finger. At the age of fourteen all the lesions had attained nearly their present development. Afterwards new patches showed themselves on the first, fourth, and fifth digits and in correspondence with the interosseous space between the first and second metacarpal bones.

About the age of 7 similar lesions began to develop on the back of the left hand without any of them showing a tendency to spread like the primary patch on the right hand. At the age of 14 there were only five on the left hand, three of which were near the carpus, one on the thumb and one on the base of the third finger: the others developed during the last few years.

The lesions which have been mentioned manifest themselves in the beginning in the form of a small dry conical projection which slowly increases in size, becoming flat on the top and surrounded by a small raised collaret which afterwards develops further and widens out at the circumference.

The dike surrounding the large zone on the forearm has also shown a tendency for some years back to become less prominent and in some places it looks as if it were slowly disappearing without any treatment. Most of the other lesions that have been mentioned have undergone no change for some years; the most recent of them have a tendency to spread and to become more prominent in a very slow almost insensible manner. No subjective phenomena.

1. Dalla Favera, G. B.: Obituary, *Mh Prakt Derm* 50:521-525, 1910.

2. Cottle, W.: Warty Growths, *St. George's Hosp Rep* 9:753-762, 1877-1879.

3. Mibelli, V.: A New Form of Keratosis, Angiokeratoma (Fr), *C R Cong Int Derm Syph*, 1890, pp 89-911.

4. Morris, M., et al: *Interntional Atlas of Rare Skin Diseases*, London: H. K. Lewis, 1889.

5. Neumann, I.: A Little Known Skin Disorder (Dermatitis Circumscripta Herpetiformis) (Ger), *Vjschr Derm Syph* 2:41-52, 1875.

6. Mibelli, V.: Contributions to the Study of Hyperkeratosis of the Sweat Glands (Porokeratosis) (Ital), *G Ital Mal Vener* 28:313-355, 1893.

Composite by G. Bako

Josef Jadassohn (1863-1936)

JOSEPH JADASSOHN, the leading dermatologist of his generation, was born in Liegnitz, Germany, and studied medicine at the universities of Göttingen, Heidelberg, and Breslau.[1] He remained in Breslau serving first as assistance to Neisser in the university clinic and later as chief of the dermatology division of Allerheiligen Hospital. An experimental approach to the understanding of cutaneous disorders, begun in the early years of his academic life, was sustained for half a century. He devised basic designs for investigating the morbid response of the integument, and was especially concerned with drug reactions, leprosy, eczema, tuberculosis, syphilis, and mycotic infections. His awareness of the social aspects of venereal diseases led to his appointment to the Committee on Hygiene of the League of Nations.

An interest and industry in experimental studies, and his compassion and understanding for patients, gained him acclaim and recognition early in his career. At the age of 33 he was called to the University of Bern as chief of dermatology, where he remained for more than a score of years. He then returned to Breslau to succeed Neisser, remaining in the post until several years after the statutory age of retirement. As an international authority, pupils were attracted to Jadassohn from many parts of the world and were exposed to the noblest traits in clinical medicine and clinical investigation. In addition to preparing a standard text on diseases of the skin and publishing on a variety of subjects, Jadassohn served as editor of the *Archiv für Dermatologie und Syphilis,* the *Zentralblatt für Haut-und Geschlechtskrankheiten,* and of a 41-volume, encyclopedic *Handbuch,* as well as departmental editor of *Dermatologische Wochenshrift* and *Klinische Wochenshrift.*

Jadassohn's interest in positive energy and localized sensitivity and immunization is reflected by the introduction of the patch test for the investigation and diagnosis of cutaneous responses. Several eponyms give credit to his original descriptions, of which Jadassohn's anetoderma and Jadassohn's granulosis rubra nasi are excerpted in this essay. While he was serving as an assistant to Neisser, a report of a case of maculopapular erythroderma (anetoderma erythematosus) was presented to the German Congress of Dermatology. The patient, a 23-year-old woman, had noticed red spots on the elbows five years earlier. The lesions at the time of description were localized on the extensor surface of both arms.[2]

They begin at the wrist and continue to the deltoid area. Their location is not completely symmetrical. The following stages of development can be seen: (1) Bright red spots, round or irregular in shape, the size of a pea or a little larger. These are covered with a slightly wrinkled epidermis and appear to be somewhat depressed. On palpation, the skin is thinner and the palpating finger sinks into a small depression of resilient tissue. (2) Dark, bluish-red spots confined to the elbows. These are larger, completely irregular in shape, and have fibers which appear slightly elevated, running in various directions. The spots may be covered with a scaly, peeling epidermis.

(3) Bright red, irregular groups of lesions similar to newly formed oval striae. (4) On the medial surface of both arms, are fine white strands which also simulate striae.

Histologic sections through the widest area of the lesion showed that the elastic tissue was essentially normal at the periphery. In the middle portion, however, elastic tissue was largely lacking. I was able to locate occasional small islands of elastic substance, but, in general, almost the entire network of the papillary body had disappeared. The atrophy had reached the inner surface of the cutis.

I should like to propose that this group of diseases, characterized by the loss of the elastic fibers, be called "anetodermias" (from the Greek word ανετος meaning loose). With such a designation, we can distinguish the unique clinical findings of this condition from those of scleroderma. It would then be possible to call the condition "anetodermia erythematodes" since the erythematous appearance is the second most important characteristic.

At the Seventh German Congress on Dermatology in Breslau in 1901, Jadassohn discussed the clinical findings of seven cases of granulosis rubra nasi, a malady which had been described previously but had not been named.[4]

On the tip of the nose and on the alae nasi, in many cases mostly on the membranous part of the nose, the skin showed an intensive, sharply circumscribed redness, which on pressure became pale. A few nodules were seen, with a dark red discoloration the size of a pin head, and only slightly elevated from the surface of the surrounding skin.

In the majority of the cases, hyperhidrosis, which varied in intensity from patient to patient and at various times, was present. It always was more pronounced on the skin of the nose, but in a mild degree was present on the skin of the remainder of the face.

All of my patients were children, six girls and one boy; whether or not this sex distribution was coincidental is a question which has to be left to future observations. But the fact that children were affected by this disease is no coincidence.

An adequate symptomatic name, according to the style that is being used in France in naming diseases, would be: dermatitis micropapulosa (or granularis) erythematosa hyperidrotica chronica nasi (infantum); shorter and more convenient would be "granulosis rubra nasi."

The patch test was introduced in 1896 in a discussion of "drug-exanthemata." The term "drug eruption," dermatosis medicamentosis, indicating a local response, was

preferred to exanthemata, associated with a systemic reaction. Jadassohn also pointed out the difference between the dermatoses which followed the external application of drugs and those which appeared after their internal administration. The local response to a patch test in a patient sensitive to mercury was described.[4]

A robust young man consulted me last year for extensive dermatitis, the result of an inunction with gray ointment, which had been prescribed for pediculi pubis, and had caused general disturbance of health. . . . After explaining to my patient the state of affairs, and telling him that in my opinion every effort must be made to accustom him to Hg., I applied a piece of gray plaster (5 cm.²) on the upper part of the left arm. The following day the epidermis under the plaster was raised in a blister, the spot was surrounded by a redness resembling that of scarlatina, extending to the shoulder and the wrist, and also along each side of the thorax. There was very little fever, but serious subjective troubles. The eruption disappeared after a few days.

1. Sulzberger, M. B.: Obituary—Josef Jadassohn, Arch Derm 33:1063-1066, 1936.
2. Jadassohn, J.: A Specific Form of "Atrophia maculosa cutis," Verh Deutsch Derm Ges, 1890-1892, pp 342-358, excerpt translated by Z. Danilevicius.
3. Jadassohn, J.: A Peculiar Disease of the Nasal Mucosa of Children "Granulosia Rubra Nasi," Arch fur Derm Syph 58:145-157, 1901, excerpt translated by Z. Danilevicius.
4. Jadassohn, J.: A Contribution to the Study of Dermatoses Produced by Drugs, Verh Deutsch Derm Ges, 1896, pp 103-129, in Selected Essays and Monographs, L. Elkind (trans.), London: New Sydenham Society, 1900, pp 207-229.

Raymond Sabouraud (1864-1938)

RAYMOND JACQUES ADRIEN SABOURAUD was honored by cryptogamic botanists with their selection of the generic name Sabouraudites for specific ringworm fungi. Born in Nantes, France, he studied medicine in Paris, was appointed an intern in 1889 and became doctor of medicine in 1894. Subsequently he was named director of the laboratory in the Hospital of Saint Louis in 1897.[1] During his training period he had prepared for a career in skin diseases by serving as intern in the services of Besnier and Brocq and by studying microbiology with Roux and Metchnikoff at the Pasteur Institute. Because of his great interest in the plurality of ringworm infestation, Sabouraud was placed in charge of the École Lailler, a combined school and hospital with a capacity of 300

Composite by G. Bako

beds, associated with the Saint Louis Hospital for the care of the young afflicted. Through the introduction of radiation for localized or disseminated epilation of the scalp, the need for hospital beds for this condition was markedly reduced. He described his procedure as follows:[2]

The apparatus which I have established at the Lailler School of the St. Louis Hospital has allowed me to form regulations for the use of the X-rays in the treatment of ringworm. An ordinary current supplies a dynamo of ¾ horsepower, which in turn supplies a static machine with 12 plates. The condensers of this machine collect the electricity produced and conduct it to the two poles of a *Chabaud's* tube, with a *Villars'* osmo-regulator. . . . The tube is enclosed in a lantern of lead foil which allows the X-rays to pass only by a lateral orifice. Around this orifice is a cylinder to limit the emission of rays to a single useful pencil, and to fix the patient's head at a fixed distance of 15 centimetres from the centre of the tube. To complete this preparation, a pastille of platino-cyanide of barium is placed at a distance of 8 centimetres from the centre of the tube at a fixed point of the lantern.

This yellow paper becomes brown under the influence of the X-rays and acts as a control apparatus (radiometer X of *Sabouraud* and *Noiré*). The sitting is then terminated and the scalp of the patient has received the quantity of

X-rays necessary to cause total alopecia of the region exposed, without provoking erythema or radiodermatitis and without preventing restoration later.

A patch of ringworm is thus cured at a single sitting.

Sabouraud's great interest in ringworm infection followed by half a century Gruby's description of a contagious tinea sycosis due to a fungus—an observation largely overlooked in the intervening period. Retrieving this earlier observation, Sabouraud gave appropriate credit to Gruby in his monograph published in 1894. The discussion of trichophytons begins with the description of the cultural characteristics of the medium, later revised and identified as Sabouraud's medium.[3]

Before studying the trichophytoses, from both anatomical-pathological and mycological aspects, we are concerned with two questions and we shall place each of these in proper perspective.
1. Influence of the chemical composition of the medium;
2. The fact that many cryptogamic species may live together; however, only one pathogen is usually responsible for the mycotic lesion which is caused by the Trichophytons.
If the culture medium consists of agar-peptonized and maltosed, by increasing the proportion of maltose from one culture to the next and by successively decreasing the quantity of peptone, one can obtain different aspects of the cultures seeded with the same organism.
A one-month-old culture on agar containing the following is illustrative:

Water	100.00
Agar-agar	1.30
Peptone	0.40
Maltose	3.50

Sabouraud was a master at personal correspondence and displayed related talents for writing in his scientific publications. In addition to the monograph noted previously, he is responsible for the preparation of *Diagnosis and Treatment of Alopecia and Ringworm of Infants* (1895), *Diseases of the Scalp* (1902), and *Pityriasis and Alopecia* (1904). Other contributions included laboratory evidence that seborrhea not sweat was fundamental to the pathogenesis of seborrheic eczema and the acnes, and bacteriologic proof that impetigo contagiosa was caused by a *Streptococcus;* whereas the

Staphylococcus was only the secondary invader.

Surrounded by pupils from many countries, Sabouraud gained great satisfaction from teaching, which he performed simply but nevertheless elegantly, punctuated with pertinent remarks on history, art, and literature. His ancestors for generations had followed either medicine or the arts; in carrying on the tradition Sabouraud displayed outstanding skill in each pursuit. He was an able musician and artist, and sculptured several busts of physicians of the Saint Louis hospital for their museum.

1. Pautrier, L.-M.: Raimond Sabouraud (1864-1938) (Fr), *Ann Derm Syph (Paris)* 9:275-297, 1938.
2. Sabouraud, R.: *Elementary Manual of Regional Topographical Dermatology* (Fr), Paris: Mason & Co., 1905, C. F. Marshall (trans.), New York: Rebman Co., 1906.
3. Sabouraud, R.: *Ringworm Trichophytons and the Ringworm of Gruby* (Fr), Paris: Rueff & Co., 1894, excerpt translated by Z. Danilevicius.

Composite by G. Bako

Erich Urbach (1893-1946)

ERICH URBACH, proponent of the allergic pathogenesis of cutaneous disorders, was born in Prague. There he received his early education, but trained for medicine in Vienna, where he remained to practice.[1] His undergraduate studies were interrupted by four years of honorable service with the Austrian Army in the first World War. His military decorations included the silver Medal of Honor from the Red Cross. Upon graduation from the University of Vienna in 1919, Urbach interned at the Allgemeines Krankenhaus and began his postgraduate studies at the University of Breslau under Jadassohn. He returned to Vienna in 1921, becoming resident in internal medicine; in 1928, he was appointed assistant chief of the department of dermatology and venereal diseases under Kerl. By 1938 the tortures and terrors of Nazi persecution led him as well as many Jewish physicians from central Europe, to come to the United States. Here, in association with his wife, he practiced and taught in the department of dermatology at the University of Pennsylvania and in the Jewish Hospital in Philadelphia.

Urbach was a clinical dermatologist, with limitless energy and great ability as a writer. He attempted to integrate dermatology and allergy[2] wherever possible and stressed the benefit of diet in the management of cutaneous disorders.[3] His bibliography includes a number of laboratory studies of the chemistry and histology of the skin, a monograph on skin disease and nutrition, was translated into English in 1932, another on hay fever, appeared in German, and two monographs in related subjects prepared in the United States.

Urbach's name is associated especially with two metabolic conditions which benefited from his clinical description and histologic findings. Lipoproteosis, a familial malady, was described, with Wiethe as the co-author; while a case of necrobiosis lipoidica diabeticorum was presented by Urbach solely. Lipoid proteinosis, characterized by lipid infiltrations of the skin and nasopharyngeal mucosa, may be associated with elevation of blood lipids or a relative increase in lecithin concentration. The cutaneous deposits appear as nodular or verrucous lesions. The histologic findings include hyperkeratosis, irregular acanthosis, thickening of the corium, and waxy deposits, which stain pale pink with hematoxylin and eosin in the thickened vessel wall or are dispersed through the tissues. In interpreting the lesions, "lipoid proteinosis" seemed the logical term because of the aggregates of lipids combined with protein. Three subgroups of histologic findings corresponded to the three clinical varieties.[4]

1. Yellow nodules in the skin of the face, in the axillae and on the elbows. 2. Verrucous lesions on the fingers. 3. Diffuse deposits on the mucous membranes. Even clinically normal skin and mucosa show pathological changes to a mild degree, sometimes only a slight endothelial growth of subpapillary tissue or homogeneous thickening of the vessel walls with Mallory stain.

The first subgroup in paraffin section with hematoxylin and eosin stain shows two slightly different reactions.

The newer lesions under normal epidermis display a cutis which suggests edema, while in the deeper layers the connective tissue is highly homogenized. . . . Many capillaries are filled with dark red homogeneous masses. In the older sections homogeneous conglomerate and artifacts suggest a diffuse infiltrative process and spaces which seem to be areas containing fat drops before fixation in alcohol. The vessels are thickened with fraying of the endothelium.

The second subgroup is similar to the vessel changes in the newer lesions of the first subgroup. The papillae are broadened with proliferation of the vessels which suggest an angioma. Below the hyperkeratosis the fibrous structure of the cutis is loose and homogeneous. In some areas red stained ribbons are projected from the epidermis.

In the third subgroup flesh colored conglomerates with a hazy periphery are transversed by many capillaries. Many of the vessels have thickened walls containing homogeneous masses.

In the histochemical investigations, it is apparent this type of dermatosis is not a function of cholesterol-infiltration which causes xanthomatosis, but is caused by a penetration of a specific lipid-protein compound not previously described.

Necrobiosis lipoidica diabeticorum, an unusual complication of diabetes mellitus, is characterized by deposits of lipids, which follow degeneration and necrobiosis of collagen from vascular lesions of the small vessels. Grossly, the demarcated patches, yellowish in the center and violaceous peripherally, are confined to the legs. As the center becomes depressed and atrophic, ulcers may form. Irregularly defined areas of necrobiosis of collagen are seen histologically throughout the corium. Perivascular inflammatory infiltrates containing lympho-

cytes, histocytes, and fibroblasts are evident in the areas of necrobiosis. The blood vessels are fibrotic, with proliferation of their endothelium. Either partial or complete occlusion follows. Lipid granules in the areas of collagen degeneration are apparent, with scarlet red stain for fat. Few elastic fibers can be demonstrated.[5]

In the papillary bodies and in the subpapillary zone, edema and the widening of the vessels are apparent. The walls of the vessels are thickened throughout. The intima in some places is proliferating wildly. In the central and deep zones of the cutis, centers of proliferation can be seen and the connective tissue is replaced by fragmented masses which stain irregularly. Lymphocytes and fibroblasts, evidence of regeneration, appear in the periphery of the necrosis; but the reaction of the cells is mild in relation to the gravity of the process. With van Giesen stain these areas are transversed by intensely yellowish stained bundles devoid of nuclei.

We are concerned in this tissue with a lipoid and the proof is the inability to stain with osmic acid. In the slides which were treated with superosmic acid there were no blackened areas; but in the necrotic areas, after alcohol treatment, blackish colored areas appeared.

Benda staining for fatty necrosis confirmed the findings. . . . Staining for amyloid was negative.

We are dealing with a severe degeneration of tissue below the cutis which leads to necrosis and an alteration of the vessels. The necrotic masses are enclosed by a fatlike substance and contain phosphates and calcium carbonate.

1. Stokes, J. H.: Erich Urbach, M.D., obituary, *Arch Derm Syph* 55:545-547, 1947.

2. Urbach, E.: *Allergy,* New York: Grune & Stratton, 1943.

3. Urbach, E.: *Skin Diseases and Nutrition, Including the Dermatoses of Children* (Ger), Vienna: W. Maudrich, 1932, translated by F. R. Schmidt.

4. Urbach, E., and Wiethe, C.: Mucous and Cutaneous Lipoidosis (Ger), *Arch path Anat* 273:285-319, 1929, excert translated by E. Longar.

5. Urbach, E.: A New Metabolic Skin Condition: Nekrobiosis lipoidica diabeticorum (Ger), *Arch Derm Syph* 166:273-285, 1932, excerpt translated by E. Longar.

Composite by G. Bako

Pierre-Carl Potain (1825-1901)

PIERRE-CARL-EDOUARD Potain, outstanding descendant in a long line of physicians, is identified with Paris, where he was born, received his education from his parents and from self-instruction, and served as *interne des hôpitaux*. He received his medical degree from the University of Paris in 1853, presenting an inaugural thesis on vascular murmurs following hemorrhage.[1] Pursuing his academic career, he qualified in 1861 as adjunct professor in the Faculty of Medicine of the University and physician to the hospitals; in 1876, he was advanced to professor of clinical medicine. Working initially under Bouillaud, Potain later became chief of Bouillaud's clinic at la Charité, having been associated earlier with Sainte-Antoine and Necker Hospitals. The only interruption of civilian responsibilities came with the Franco-Prussian War of 1870, in which Potain chose to pass his tour of duty as an infantryman.

Potain's most prominent contributions to medicine concerned cardiovascular subjects and are noteworthy for clarity and significance. The *Dictionnaire Encyclopédique des Sciences Médicales* solicited several of his prepared reports. His clinical observations on the heart, lungs, and vascular system were published in a monograph nearly 1,000 pages long, assembled from the bedside and from postmortem observations at la Charité, in collaboration with C. A. François-Franck and with his pupils, L. H. Vaquez, E. Suchard, and P. J. Teissier.[2]

A posthumous treatise on arterial pressure in man described Potain's observations with the air sphygmomanometer, an improvement of Marey's aneroid device. Also, his mechanical curiosity and skill led to the development of an aspirator for pleural effusion, which enabled the operator to replace fluid slowly as air was introduced into a vacuum. In aortic dilatation he observed increased dullness to the right of the sternum in the upper two intercostal spaces (Potain's sign), and noted the unusual character of the second sound, similar to the sound of a small Arab drum, calling it *bruit de tabourka*.

The two most noteworthy contributions to cardiovascular disease by Potain have been translated into English. In 1876, he prepared a communication on gallop rhythm, a name first introduced by Bouillaud. Potain identified the diastolic timing, attributed it to sudden tension in the ventricular wall, and assumed it could be clinically apparent, particularly under impaired distensibility concomitant with hypertrophy of the myocardium in Bright's disease.[3]

We find in the heart in patients suffering from interstitial nephritis, a special sound which is the bruit designated by Professor Bouillaud with the name "Gallop rhythm" (*bruit de galop*).

This sound results from the abruptness with which the dilation of the ventricle takes place during the pre-systolic period, a period which corresponds to the contraction of the auricle. It appears to be an indirect consequence of the excessive arterial tension which interstitial nephritis produces habitually by a mechanism of which we have a glimpse but which still remains to be determined in a thoroughly accurate manner. It can start us on the way to a diagnosis of the renal disease, and reveal it before any other symptom has attraction to it. It can, consequently, be of service in diagnosis and prognosis, and therefore give useful indications for treatment.

A description of the jugular vein murmurs, published in 1867, one of Potain's earliest and best works, was also one of his longest. Although vascular murmurs were not judged to be pathognomonic of anemia, he assumed that hydremia and corpuscular poor blood could produce such murmurs. Potain concluded the presentation with nine arguments, of which the first five are reproduced.[4]

When one observes carefully the portion of the supraclavicular region which the jugular veins and the carotid artery cross, one may frequently note three distinct phenomena through which are revealed the motion by which the blood is quickened in the vessels: (1) visible oscillations; (2) a thrill sensible to the finger; (3) normal and abnormal sounds revealed by auscultation. Since an analysis of the movements and the peculiarities which the purring fremitus shows may throw some light on the mechanism of the murmurs, I have applied myself to study them with care in a large number of individuals.

1. Two kinds of murmurs are heard in the neck: arterial murmurs and venous murmurs;

2. Arterial murmurs are intermittent; venous murmurs may be continuous, intermittent, or continuous with reinforcements;

3. The reinforcements or repetitions of the venous murmur have no other cause than intermittent accelerations of blood flow in the vein;

4. These accelerations and their relation with reinforcement of the murmur are, moreover, demonstrated in a positive manner by the depression which appears, at the moment they take place, at the point of the region which corresponds to the vein. They result from successive aspirations set up in the venous sytem near the thorax by diastole of the auricle and ventricle, as the sphygmographic tracings show;

5. The murmur appears the more easily in veins in which the blood is poorer in corpuscles.

Potain has been likened to a physician, who, as if to compensate for deficiences in physical charm, was gentle to his patients, kind to his pupils at the bedside, and just in the examination of their wisdom and learning. He became the foremost contemporary clinician in Paris, astute in his observations and noteworthy for his capacity to integrate abnormal form and function with physiological knowledge at the bedside. He was honored by his peers through membership in the Academy of Medicine, the Academy of Science, the Institute of France, and by his government as a Commander of the Legion of Honour.

1. Vaquez, H.: Pierre-Carl Potain (1835-1901), Obituary (Fr), *Bull Acad Med Paris* 97:569-587, 1927.

2. Potain, C.: Clinical Observations from la Charité Medical Clinic (Fr), Paris: G. Masson, 1894.

3. Potain, C.: Concerning the Cardiac Rhythm Called Gallop Rhythm (Fr), *Bull Soc Med Hop Paris* 12:137-166, 1876.

4. Potain, C.: On the Movements and Sounds That Take Place in the Jugular Veins (Fr), *Bull Soc Med Hop Paris* 4:3-27, 1867, in Willius, F. A., and Keys, T. E.: *Cardiac Classics*, St. Louis: C. V. Mosby Co., 1941, pp 534-556.

Paul-Louis Duroziez (1826-1897)

PAUL-LOUIS DUROZIEZ, who described the double murmur of the femoral artery in aortic insufficiency and clarified the pure type of mitral stenosis, was born in Paris, where he spent his entire medical career in practice.[1] His grammar school education was gained at L'Institution Favart followed by training at the lyceum Charlemagne. Although Latin, Greek, and English were his strong subjects, when he graduated in 1844 his degree included bachelor of the sciences as well as letters. Training in medicine was begun at the University of Paris and the associated hospitals. He studied under Velpeau at la Charité, continued under Blache at the Hôpital des Enfants

Malades, and for two years was an extern under Jean-Baptiste Bouillaud at la Charité. In 1850, Duroziez was awarded the Corvisart prize for his investigations of the properties and action of digitalis. In 1853, he received the degree of MD, presenting a thesis based upon the cases studied on Boullaud's service. Three years later he was appointed chief of Bouillaud's clinic and held this position for two years. The major portion of his professional time thereafter was given to clinical practice.

Although a leading cardiologist of Paris in the latter half of the 19th century, Duroziez held no senior academic appointment in a major hospital or university. Secondary assignments included service with the Bureau of Welfare, membership on the Commission of Public Hygiene and Health, and medical inspector of schools, each with the First Ward of Paris, and ambulance duties during the Franco-Prussian War. In 1891, Duroziez was awarded the Montyon Prize by the Institute of France for his clinical treatise on the maladies of the heart, and the Itard Prize by the Academy of Medicine. He was an active member of the Society of Medicine of Paris and served as president in 1882.

In 1861, Duroziez published his two most important contributions to cardiology. The entire bibliography reflects his interest in the auscultation of the heart and the great vessels. The description of pure mitral stenosis, later called "Duroziez's disease," was well documented by a résumé of the investigations of others. In the description he noted a preponderance of females among those inflicted, the early age of development, a tendency to emboli, but a relatively good prognosis. Excerpts from his contribution of 1861 which was reprinted in 1877 are as follows:[2]

In *pure mitral stenosis* no blowing murmur is heard at the apex nor at the axillary line which would indicate mitral insufficiency, nor is there any murmur at the aortic orifice; also rejected are those cases in which a blowing murmur at the lower border of the heart and at the level of the epigastrium indicates tricuspid insufficiency which could depend either on a mitral lesion producing dilatation posteriorly or on an organic lesion of the tricuspid valves. In *pure mitral stenosis* the

left auricle may be dilated, as determined by percussion, without producing any dullness at the level of the second interspace on the left.

In our cases with *pure mitral stenosis* 46 were women and 15 men.

Approximately 50% of the patients admit a history of acute rheumatic fever. In many cases palpitations have preceded articular rheumatism. In some cases we find mitral stenosis at the time the patient enters the hospital because of acute rheumatism.

Pure mitral stenosis causes embolism more often than do other lesions. The blood stagnates in the left atrium and creates conditions for embolism. This is one of the greatest dangers of *pure mitral stenosis.*

Pure mitral stenosis seldom is fatal; autopsies are rare and those that come to postmortem show no dilatation of the auricle.

Pure mitral stenosis is characterized by no murmur, with or without dilatation of the auricle, and no pulmonary lesions. The condition may occur more frequently than has been assumed. It may readily escape detection; the patient may have little difficulty and may not appear to be a heart patient. The heart shows normal dimensions with normal pulsations. The patient appears well developed. The first heart sound is loud. It is often difficult to establish the date of onset of stenosis. The history may date back to infancy. The lesion predisposes the patient to embolism, to aphasia and right hemiparesis. It is more common in women than in men. It carries a good prognosis.

The description by Duroziez of the double femoral murmur in aortic insufficiency received better known eponymic accolade. It is recognized today that pressure over the femoral artery is not always needed to bring out the double murmur. His communication paralleled the preceding report with an historical introduction followed by a large number of patient protocols. In the days before vectorcardiography, electrocardiography, and angiography and when the cardiologist was forced to utilize maximally refinements in diagnosis by the eye, hand, and stethoscope, the auscultation of the great vessels sometimes substantiated the presumptions of the examination of the precordium.[3]

The intermittent double murmur over the femoral arteries was described in aortic insufficiency; but no one, I believe, has given it the significance that it deserves. Everyone has mentioned the murmur occurring in arterial diastole *(souffle de la diastole arterielle)* which quite frequently occurs without compression of the artery; but very few authors mentioned the murmur occurring during systole. Very frequently it does not appear of its own accord, but must be produced and sought for. The first murmur results from the powerful contraction of the ventricle, but as the second murmur is produced by the systole of the arteries in the legs, a less powerful force, its production must be facilitated by compression of the artery.

In cases of uncomplicated aortic insufficiency, wherein the heart beats vigorously and the arteries pulsate and react forcefully, the double murmur is audible; when, contrarily, aortic insufficiency is complicated by a considerable degree of aortic or mitral stenosis, a not uncommon occurrence, the arteries are moderately distended with blood and thus the second murmur is difficult to hear. It must be carefully sought and even then it will not appear regularly; it will not be detected when weak pulsations are present. It appears or disappears in relationship to increased or decreased action of the heart. At times it can be heard over both femorals, at other times only over one; briefly, distention and recoil, adequate systole of the arteries, are required for its presence; a careful examination is indispensable.

The double murmur can be produced in two ways, by means of the stethoscope or by means of the hand. With the stethoscope pressure is exerted to completely compress the artery; at a certain moment the double murmur will appear; only when the second murmur can be readily produced is it possible to place the stethoscope on the artery without pressure and then gradually slight pressure can be exerted with the hand above and below the stethoscope. Pressure above will produce the first murmur, while pressure below will produce the second murmur; it is evident that the second murmur is produced by the arteries of the legs, which propel the blood backwards and in some manner empty the capillaries.

The double intermittent murmur is of interest not only from the standpoint of diagnosis. The reflux of blood explains some of the symptoms occurring in aortic insufficiency and explains the sudden death which is occasionally observed.

1. De Beauvais: Dr. Paul-Louis Duroziez (1826-1897) His Life and Works (Fr), *France Med* 14-15:156-157, 172-175, 188-191, 1898.

2. Duroziez, P.: Pure Mitral Murmur (Fr), *Arch Gen Med* 2:32-54, 1877.

3. Duroziez, P.: The Intermittent Double Femoral Murmur in Aortic Insufficiency (Fr), *Arch Gen Med* 1: 417-443, 588-605, 1861, translated in Willius, F. A., and Keys, T. E.: *Cardiac Classics*, St. Louis: C. V. Mosby Co., 1941, pp 492-496.

Composite by G. Bako

George Harley (1829-1896)

THE ONLY SON OF GEORGE BARCLAY HARLEY and Margaret Macbeath was born at Harley House, Haddington, in East Lothian, when his father was sixty-three and his mother forty.[1] Upon his father's death shortly thereafter he was raised by his mother and grandmother. His education was gained first at the Haddingtonburgh school and Hill Street Institution and later at the University of Edinburgh, where he graduated MD in 1850. After serving as house surgeon and resident physician to the Edinburgh Royal Infirmary, Harley invested in a five-year period of study and research. Several of the best clinics and research institutes in Europe, staffed by outstanding medical scientists, were selected. The laboratories of Dollfus, Verdeil, and Wurtz in Paris were visited first. Here iron was identified as a normal constituent of the urine and the cherry color traced to urohematin.[2]

The effects of nervous stimulation on the production of sugar by the liver were investigated in the physiological laboratory of the Collège de France with Magendie and later with Claude Bernard. Harley was elected president of the Parisian Medical Society, where, at the anniversary dinner,

Sir William Priestley and Dr. Burdon-Sanderson were present. Harley returned to Edinburgh for a short time, but, finding no vacancy among the academic chairs, he continued his tour of the Continent. In this instance, he studied physiological chemistry under Liebig at Giessen, histology under von Kölliker at Berlin, pathology under Virchow at Vienna and with Bunsen at Heidelberg and Scherer at the University of Würzburg.

The unusually long period of foreign study placed Harley in an excellent position for an advanced teaching position when he returned from Padua, his last study center. In 1855, he was appointed a lecturer in practical physiology and histology and curator of the anatomical museum at University College. While the emoluments were attractive the inadequate salary made it necessary to earn a living so he began office practice at Nottingham Place. Three years later he assumed the professorship of medical jurisprudence, followed by the appointment as physician to the University College Hospital. In 1862, Harley received the Triennial Prize of the Royal College of Surgeons of England for his researches into the anatomy and physiology of the suprarenal bodies, and was elected fellow of the Royal College of Physicians in 1864 and fellow of the Royal Society in 1865. His physiological or chemical researches included a study of poisons, particularly the nullifying action of strychnine in the presence of the arrow poison, woorali.

A report of two cases of intermittent hematuria, associated with exposure to a cold environment, was presented before the Royal Medical and Chirurgical Society of London in 1865. Although the first patient suffered from malaria (and the possibility of black-water fever cannot be excluded), the second case surely was a valid example. An excerpt of the protocol of the second case notes the significant items in the history of a 32-year-old blacksmith who considered himself perfectly healthy and who had been able to work at the forge without inconvenience until two years prior to consultation with Harley.[3]

Two years ago he for the first time observed that he occasionally passed urine as dark as brown old ale, while that voided at the preceding and succeeding micturitions possessed the normal colour and transparency.

Twelve months later, that is to say, a year ago, the urine for the first time assumed the colour of blood, a symptom which greatly alarmed him, as it recurred about three times a week during the whole of that winter, except during a fortnight in January, while working in the open air, when it became still more frequent, occurring about once every day.

Sometimes the attack of bloody urine lasted over two micturitions, amounting to a period of from four to five hours. In the spring of last year, as the warm weather advanced, the attacks gradually became less frequent, until from the month of May to September they entirely ceased.

On examination it was found that the specimen passed at 8:30 a.m. was normal in colour, devoid of any sediment, six and a half ounces in quantity, acid in reaction, and of a specific gravity of 1010; it contained 1.75 per cent. of urea, traces of sugar, but no albumen.

That passed at 2 p.m. was dark red, almost black-looking, six ounces in quantity, acid in reaction, of a specific gravity of 1017, and on standing deposited a copious precipitate of dark-coloured urate of soda, leaving the supernatant liquid quite clear, and of a fine rich port-wine colour. This urine contained 2.5 per cent. of urea, was highly coagulable by heat and nitric acid, and gave evidences of traces of sugar.

The almost total absence of blood-corpuscles, notwithstanding the haemorrhagic appearance of the urine, stamps the case as being entirely different from ordinary haematuria, and . . . leads to the conclusion that it was not simply the albumen of the blood-serum, but the haematoglobulin itself, which was extracted by the kidneys.

After becoming attached to the University College Medical School and assuming once more a private practice, it is natural that Harley took up residence on Harley street, the fashionable thoroughfare of the consultants in London. Thackery, Dickens, Faraday, Tyndall, Bence Jones, and Sharpey were social or scientific friends. His daughter, who edited his biography,[1] was a popular writer and composed several travel books on the Scandinavian countries. Harley, an advocate of simplified spelling, published a brochure on the subject, and recommended the omission of duplicated consonants from all words except personal names. Other nonmedical interests included shell musical instruments and anthropology.

In a communication in the *Proceedings of the Royal Society,* Harley made an important observation on the oxygen content of blood. He denied the doctrine that the respired oxygen formed a physical mixture in the blood rather than entering into a chemical combination. He developed a retinal hemorrhage and for many months withdrew from the sunlight, but not society, and eventually made a complete recovery. During this enforced seclusion his last of three monographs, *The Urine and Its Derangements,* was dictated. Although he came of a gouty family and published two unimportant contributions on gout, his extensive writing makes no mention of acute paroxysms or urate lithiasis. Harley, an advocate of the use of animals in experimental physiology, in turn, directed that a postmortem examination be performed to determine the cause of his own death, and that his body be cremated.

1. Tweedie, A.: *George Harley, FRS, The Life of a London Physician,* London: Scientific Press, Limited, 1899.
2. Harley, G.: Researches on the Colouring Principle of Urine—Existence of Iron in That Liquid, *Pharm J* (Sept 28) 1852, pp 243-245.
3. Harley, G.: On Intermittent Haematuria, *Medicochi- Trans* 48 161-173, 1865.

Difficult times were in store in the capital city for those identified with the revolutionaries. Jacobi was arrested upon arrival, sentenced, and held in prison for almost two years, upon the pretext that he was aligned with the losing faction. Following release from prison, and before a planned rearrest

Abraham Jacobi (1830-1919)

ABRAHAM JACOBI began his medical training in Germany in 1848 during the Revolution, left his native land shortly after, and lived a full life in America, advancing the art and science of academic pediatrics into the 20th century. Abraham was born in the village of Hartum-in-Minden in Westphalia, Prussia.[1] Although his father was a shopkeeper with limited means, this was no deterrent to the consummation of high scholastic ambitions. After studying oriental languages at the University of Griefswald, Abraham pursued medicine at Göttingen and Bonn. Göttingen was especially attractive since it was one of the few schools at that time which taught pathological anatomy as a major subject. After receiving the degree in medicine in 1851 from Bonn, Jacobi went to Berlin for state examinations.

by the authorities could be effected, he crossed the border and sought refuge in England. Later he migrated to America, first to Boston and then to New York City, where he entered upon the practice of general medicine in 1853. Although his contributions were largely in pediatrics, he accepted general medicine as a broad field of interest. Teaching in diseases of children was begun in 1857 with a series of lectures to a small group of students at the College of Physicians and Surgeons. After the founding of the New York Infirmary for Women and Children (now the New York Infirmary) by Dr. Elizabeth Blackwell, Jacobi organized a pediatric clinic in conjunction. This was shortly after the publication of a valuable treatise on the diet of infants, coauthored with his wife, Mary Putnam Jacobi. In 1860, he was appointed professor of infantile pathology and therapeutics at the

New York Medical College, founded in 1850 and disbanded in 1864 through the exigencies of the war between the states. A decade later Jacobi was honored as the first clinical professor of the diseases of infancy and childhood at the College of Physicians and Surgeons. In 1873, when offered the chair of pediatrics at the University of Berlin, he declined. Transplantation to America had established firm roots. He chose to remain in his adopted land where he received immediate and delayed honors. The Lenox Hill Hospital established an Abraham Jacobi pediatric division in 1915 and the Roosevelt Hospital, an Abraham Jacobi ward for children in 1898. The most recent memorial is the Abraham Jacobi Hospital, a unit of the Albert Einstein College of Medicine.

Jacobi's interest in allied medical subjects, medical journalism, medical societies, and medical history, were apparent throughout his professional career. The *American Journal of Obstetrics and Diseases of Women and Children* (currently the *American Journal of Obstetrics and Gynecology*) was founded at his instigation. A 52-page discussion by Jacobi of the pathology and treatment of the different forms of croup was presented in the first issue.[2] Congress was urged by him to appropriate funds to publish the *Index Catalogue of the Library of the Surgeon General's Office* under the editorship of John S. Billings. As a dedicated advocate of medical societies, he pressed for regular attendance at stated meetings. In 1880, he supported the establishment of the pediatric section of the American Medical Association, was one of the charter members of the New York Academy of Medicine and in 1896 president of the Association of American Physicians. His presidential address to the American Medical Association in 1912 began:[3]

My principal duty and intense pleasure is to tender my thanks to the House of Delegates which selected me for the highest honor in the gift of the medical profession of America, and to my colleagues of all the fifty [sic] states who were good enough to approve of its choice. . . . I was overjoyed to have reason to believe that I owed my election to my lack of efforts to secure it. . . . I have the confidence that if there be in this or any other cultural assembly anybody looking for the highest office for the sake of power and preferment only, he will be deservedly disappointed. . . . There is only one thing that is and must forever remain first—that is the medical profession of America, as represented in this American Medical Association, and its object, which in all its aims is only one and indivisible. That one and inseparable object is to promote the art and science of medicine, to unite into one compact organization the medical profession of the United States for the purpose of fostering the growth and the diffusion of medical knowledge, of promoting friendly intercourse among American physicians, of safeguarding the material interests of the medical profession, of elevating the standard of medical education, of securing the enactment and enforcement of just medical laws, of enlightening and directing public opinion in regard to the broad problems of hygiene, and of representing to the world the practical accomplishments of scientific medicine.

There were many pediatric problems that profited from Jacobi's interests. The majority of his clinical and scientific communications were published in American periodicals, but a few appeared in German journals. He advocated birth control and the use of boiled milk; the latter probably saved more lives than any other procedure except for the use of antibiotics. He stressed the importance of breast feeding, expressed preference for cane sugar over milk sugar in the formula for infants, and was one of the first in this country to recognize the advantages of intubation over tracheotomy for diphtheritic croup. Although the Klebs-Loeffler bacillus was isolated in 1883, Jacobi did not accept this as the pathogenic agent in diphtheria until some time later. Together with Noeggerath, a comprehensive treatise on obstetrics and gynecology was prepared in 1859.[4] It was a financial failure.[5]

. . . I made a heap of money out of literature, which is remarkable for a medical man, unless he be Weir Mitchell, or Osler, or Holt. It happened this way—perhaps someone wishes to imitate me. Indeed, I believe he should. In 1859, E. Noeggerath and I published a big volume, "Contributions to the Diseases of Women and Children," at an expense to ourselves of $800; a few years afterward we sold the edition as waste paper for sixty-eight dollars, a clear profit—compared with nothing.

His *Intestinal Diseases of Infancy and Childhood,* published in 1887, was probably his best known and one of the most German-like treatises.[6] His writings on medical history included monographs on diphtheria (1880), cerebrospinal meningitis in America (1905), American pediatrics (1902-1913), and pediatrics in New York City (1917). In the preface to his *Contributions to Pediatrics,* Jacobi gave an explanation or an apology for the appearance of the eight-volume system.[5]

For many years friends have encouraged me to write my memoirs. They claimed that the Parcae had not cut the thread in my life only to give me an opportunity to report what I had observed in connection with the history of the profession of the country in a medical practice extending over almost sixty years, as a public teacher of medicine during forty-five years, and a member and an officer in many local, national and international associations. That may be true, but as a memoir writer I have not succeeded in being prolific beyond a few chapters which, with others, may or may not reach the eyes of my friends, and enemies, for a long time to come, if at all. A very good reason for that is intelligible to every New Yorker. We have no time for anything but work; the luxury of leisure we do not possess; and pleasure is enjoyed only, or mostly, by those who find pleasure in work.

So no memoirs could be written, on account of constant, and constantly pressing work. Pegasus wears no harness, and I, like most of you, have always been in harness. Whether that was always an enjoyment or a benefit to others, I cannot tell you. But I believe I may assure my present readers that my . . . professional life, taken all in all, was very successful, if not always lucky or happy.

His autobiography was started in his waning years but the copy of the chapters prepared was destroyed in a night fire at his summer home in Lake George, New York. He died shortly after, in his 89th year.

Abraham Jacobi was born in Germany during the dawn of the golden days of medical science. It is reasonable to suspect that he was disheartened by the failure of the Revolution in his homeland and fled to the New World for political freedom and personal liberty. His courage in maintaining an unpopular viewpoint, even though it meant the loss of prestige, was an outstanding quality. He made no contributions to basic medical science comparable to those of his brilliant German contemporaries, Virchow, Koch, and Müller. However, his contribu-

tions to clinical pediatrics, medical history, medical writing, and to city, state, and national medical societies were many, judged sufficient for the title "Father of American Pediatrics."

1. Robinson, V.: The Life of A. Jacobi, *Med Life* 35:214-306 (May) 1928.
2. Jacobi, A.: On the Pathology and Treatment of the Different Forms of Croup, *Amer J Obstet* 1:13-65, 1859.
3. Jacobi, A.: The Best Means of Combating Infant Mortality, *JAMA* 58:1735-1744 (June 8) 1912.
4. Noeggerath, E., and Jacobi, A.: *Contributions to Midwifery and Diseases of Women and Children, with a Report on the Progress of Obstetrics and Uterine and Infantile Pathology in 1858,* New York: Bailliere Bros., 1859.
5. Jacobi, A.: *Contributions to Pediatrics,* Authors Preface, vol. 1, W. J. Robinson, ed., New York: Critic & Guide, 1909.
6. Jacobi, A.: *The Intestinal Diseases of Infancy and Childhood,* Detroit: George S. Davis, 1887.

Royal College of Physicians

Charles Murchison (1830-1879)

CHARLES MURCHISON, fever physician of London, was born in Jamaica. The small child at the age of three was taken by his father, a physician, back to Scotland; there at the age of 15 he entered the University of Aberdeen. Two years later he commenced the study of medicine at the University of Edinburgh and won several prizes for scholastic excellence.[1] In 1850, he passed the examinations of the College of Surgeons of Edinburgh and became house surgeon to James Syme. A year later he graduated MD and for four years followed several pursuits. These included postgraduate study in Dublin and Paris, service in the Bengal Army of the East India Company and with the expedition to Burma, and teaching at the Medical College, Calcutta. By 1855, Murchison was prepared to establish roots; he became a member of the Royal College of Physicians of London, and began practice in London as a well-trained physician. His reputation brought him a series of staff appointments, which included Westminster General Dispensary, St. Mary's Hospital, King's College Hospital, Middlesex Hospital, London Fever Hospital, and St. Thomas' Hospital. In 1866, Murchison was elected a fellow of the Royal Society; in 1870, he received the honorary degree of LLD from the University of Edinburgh, and in 1873 gave the Croonian lectures. His extracurricular activities included botany, a favorite hobby of his father, and paleontology.

In teaching, practice, and consultation Murchison was noted especially for his interest in fevers. He collected and evaluated extensive epidemiologic data. Meanwhile, he failed to recognize the bacterial pathogenesis of infectious diseases about to stir a complacent medical world. Of more practical significance was the experimental approach to the intravascular treatment of large vessel aneurysms, which was presented in an outstanding monograph.[2] He introduced a fine wire into an eroding aneurysm, the size of a man's fist, in a patient under his care in Middlesex Hospital. Excerpts of the palliative procedures, the recommendation of the attending surgeon, Charles H. Moore, and the postmortem examination five days later are as follows:[2]

Early in January it became obvious, that the bursting of the aneurism through the integuments could not be long delayed. It was accordingly resolved to recommend to the patient Mr. Moore's proposed operation. During the month of December this operation had been carefully considered, but it was then deemed unadvisable to have recourse to it It was now explained to the patient that the procedure in question offered some chance of prolonging his life, although in itself it was not free from danger. The patient at once assented; and the operation was performed on January 7th, at half-past 1 p.m.

The operation consisted in the introduction of a quantity of fine iron wire into the aneurism, with the object of inducing coagulation. A small pointed canula was inserted into the tumour and the wire was passed in through this without difficulty. The operation occupied one hour and the quantity of wire introduced was twenty-six yards. It gave rise to no pain or inconvenience excepting a slight and transient feeling of faintness. The quantity of blood lost did not exceed half a fluid ounce.

An autopsy was performed a few hours after death which happened [five days later]. . . . The interior of the tumor was filled, for the most part, with a fibrinous coagulum, enveloping and imbedded in the coils of wire, and firmly adherent to the surrounding walls.

In his *Clinical Lectures on Diseases of the Liver,* Murchison described a family with hemolytic jaundice and gout, one of the early examples of gouty arthritis secondary to familial jaundice.[3]

On Feb. 18, 1875, I had, through the kindness of Dr. Moxon, an opportunity of seeing the following case.

Robert J – – –, aged 30, says he was born yellow and that he has been jaundiced as long as he can remember. . . . From 27 up to the date of his visit to me he had suffered much from gout in fingers and toes, which had always been relieved by iodide of potassium. Urine had deposited a copious sediment as long as he could remember.

I made following notes: Body fairly nourished, and is leading an active life. Has decided yellowness of skin and conjunctivae. Urine contains abundance of lithates, and presents distinct reaction of bile-pigment. Liver slightly enlarged, measuring 4¾ in. in r. m. l., not tender.

R.J. has a brother, two years and eight months older than himself, who has also been deeply jaundiced all his life, and in Feb 1875 was laid up with gout.

The mother of these two brothers died at age of 54. She had been in habit of drinking malt liquor freely, and for fourteen years before death she had been a great sufferer from gout, her feet and every one of her finger-joints being greatly deformed from it. During same period she had been continuously jaundiced . . . her father had suffered greatly from gout and liver-complaints.

Father of R. J. is still (Oct. 1876) alive and healthy; never had gout nor jaundice.

I learned from Dr. Moxon also that both R. J. and his brother have had several children, all of whom "became deeply jaundiced two days after birth, the colour being—eyes, body, and whole frame—as deep as possible, but disappearing after about a month."

There is little of contemporary interest in his early treatise on continued fever.[4] However in a communication several years later to the Pathological Society,[5] he described an undulating type of fever in a case of lymphadenoma which eventually was associated with Pel and Ebstein in the German literature.

1. Obituary, *Brit Med J* 1:648-650 (April 26) 1879.
2. Moore, C. H., and Murchison, C.: On a New Method of Procuring the Consolidation of Fibrin in Certain Incurable Aneurisms, *Medicochir Trans* 47:129-149, 1864.
3. Murchison, C.: *Clinical Lectures on Diseases of the Liver*, New York: W. Wood & Co., 1885.
4. Murchison, C.: *A Treatise on the Continued Fevers Great Britain*, London: Parker, Son & Bourn, 1862.
5. Murchison, C., 'Case of "lymphadenoma" of Lymphatic System, Spleen, Liver, Lungs, Heart, Diaphragm, Dura Mater, etc.,' *Tr. Path. Soc. London*, 21:372-89, 1870.

Composite by G. Bako

Jacob Da Costa (1833-1900)

JACOB MENDEZ DA COSTA, one of the most revered members of the faculty of Jefferson Medical College, was born on the island of St. Thomas, West Indies.[1] His family, of Spanish and Portuguese extraction, endowed with wealth and culture, left the island when Jacob was four years of age to live in Europe in order to insure private tutoring for the children. Jacob attended a gymnasium in Dresden; there he studied the classics, became fluent in German and French, and later acquired a reading knowledge of Spanish, Portuguese, Italian, and Dutch. Following his mother to America, he entered the office of Professor Mütter, enrolled in Jefferson Medical College at the age of 16, and graduated three years later. Appreciative of the opportunities for postgraduate training in medicine and the amenities of a humanistic culture, Da Costa was drawn back to Europe. He studied in Paris, especially with Trousseau, and in Vienna with Skoda, Rokitansky, Hebra, and others during the great days of Viennese medicine. He returned to Philadelphia in 1853, one of the best educated young men in medicine, accomplished in fencing and dancing, devoted to music and the theater, and capable of entering the practice of medicine as well as instructing students and graduates in physical diagnosis.

Da Costa's lectures were popular and well attended and served as the basis for his first and best known monograph, *Medical Diagnosis,* which appeared in 1864.[2] The treatise was warmly received and came to the attention of the medical profession in this country and abroad. It passed through nine editions during his lifetime and was translated into German, Italian, and Russian. By 1866, he was appointed to the faculty at Jefferson Medical College, an academic appointment long overdue; in 1872, he was elected professor of the theory and practice of medicine, having been appointed visiting physician to the Pennsylvania Hospital in the interim. He kept his hospital appointment to the last but resigned his professorship in 1891.

His writings, based on vast clinical experience, include phantom tumors of the abdomen, starvation fever, the pathological anatomy of acute pneumonia, cancer of the pancreas, treatment of respiratory diseases, cerebral neuralgia, splenic leukemia, treatment of diabetes insipidus with ergot, the use of fluorides in medicine, diseases of the pericardium, Bright's disease, malarial paralysis, and the significance of jaundice in typhoid fever. His best-known clinical contribution, a discussion of irritable heart, has also been described as neurocirculatory asthenia, soldier's heart, effort syndrome, or disordered action of the heart.

While serving as visiting physician to Turner's Lane, the military hospital in Philadelphia, Da Costa observed the functional cardiac malady which developed in soldiers in the Peninsular campaign of the Civil War. His description, mentioned in his *Medical Diagnosis,* was expanded into a long treatise in 1871. He claimed no priority for the observation, noting that a similar condition was observed among the troops in the British Army during the Crimean War and in Havelock's troops in India. Nor was the malady confined to military medicine; it also appeared in civilian practice. Neither the fluoroscope, electrocardiograph, nor the intracardiac catheter had been discovered at that time. His conclusions were based upon a series of more than 300 cases, each included on the basis of history and physical examination. Symptoms might develop in the field of battle or when the soldier was at rest in the barracks. Cardiac pain was often the first indication of the disorder. In some patients, attacks of palpitation lasting several hours and incited by exertion would render the patient insensible. Tachycardia was frequently present, the pulse was easily compressible. Shortness of breath or oppression on exertion was a constant complaint and a prominent symptom during attacks of palpitation. On physical examination, the first sound on auscultation was deficient in volume and similar in quality to the second sound. Murmurs, as a rule, were absent.[3]

COURSE OF THE DISORDER.—Having discussed the symptoms and physical signs, it will be useful to inquire into the course of the malady. This mostly either gradually subsides, or it passes by degrees into cardiac enlargement.

When the disorder yields, the heart becomes less and less irritable, exercise no longer affects it so much, the cardiac pain and soreness disappear, and finally the patient is again able to bear fatigue and undergo exertion; or in other instances, he is well as long as he is not too active, but his heart is always liable to be more disturbed by undue exertion or by excitement than the heart of a healthy person is.

In bringing this inquiry to an end, I may be permitted to point out what I believe to be its chief interest and value To the medical officer it

may be of service as investigating a form of cardiac disorder which every severe or protracted campaign is sure to develop. And from a military point of view, further, it enforces the lessons, how important it is not to send back soldiers just convalescent from fevers or other acute maladies, too soon to active work; it suggests that their equipments be such as will not unnecessarily constrict, and thus retard or prevent recovery; that recruits, especially very young ones, be as far as practicable exercised and trained in marches and accustomed to fatigue before they are called upon to undergo the wear and tear of actual warfare; and it exhibits some of the dangers incident to the rapid and incessant maneuvering of troops.

Da Costa's biographers note that he followed a well-designed plan for an academic career in what has come to be recognized as internal medicine. He developed his skill in pathology and clinical diagnosis before the importance of basic physiology was appreciated. He was a successful teacher, an ideal consultant, and a skillful physician in diagnosis. He was one of the founders of the Pathological Society of Philadelphia, an original member of the Association of American Physicians, which he served as president in 1897, and was twice president of the College of Physicians of Philadelphia. He was elected to membership in many learned societies. Hospital appointments included the Philadelphia and Pennsylvania Hospitals. Honorary LLD degrees were awarded by Jefferson College, the University of Pennsylvania, and Harvard University. He loved books and literature and in his own writing was a purist. Attracting the attention of Samuel Gross, he assisted him in the revision of his treatise, *Elements of Pathological Anatomy.* He was several times requested to address the graduating class at Jefferson. An appraisal of Harvey and his discovery, given as an introductory lecture to the students, was one of his favorite addresses. He twice addressed the Harvard Medical Alumni Association; his first address voiced concern for medical education three quarters of a century ago. The apprehension persists, and one wonders when the ideal medical curriculum will become a fact.[4]

I have often asked myself why it is that medical education is so discussed by the profession, why this never-ceasing upheaval. We do not see the education in law, we do not see the education in theology, a matter of constant dispute and agitation. And I have concluded that the keen interest, the deep feeling, which it engenders, is really due to the state of medicine itself. The agitation is but a sign of the unrest in medicine we see everywhere. It is but a recognition of the spirit of research and investigation that is so conspicuous now, of the enthusiasm that is constantly adding new facts, almost new sciences. Medical education must be discussed, must be recast, since the groundwork on which medicine stands is being from day to day enlarged and strengthened. Let us be, therefore, after all, glad that the subject attracts so much attention. It attracts attention because medicine itself is a most progressive science.

1. Wilson, J. C.: Memoir of J. M. Da Costa, M.D., *Trans Col Physicians Phila* 24-81-92, 1902.
2. Da Costa, J. M.: *Medical Diagnosis, With Special Reference to Practical Medicine*, Philadelphia: J. B. Lippincott & Co., 1864.
3. Da Costa, J. M.: On Irritable Heart; a Clinical Study of a Form of Functional Cardiac Disorder and Its Consequences, *Amer J Med Sci* 61:17-52, 1871.
4. Da Costa, J. M.: *Address Before the Harvard Medical Alumni Association, June 27, 1893*, Boston: G. H. Ellis, 1893.

Ernst von Leyden (1832-1910)

ERNST VON LEYDEN, advocate of comprehensive perspection, in contrast to limited specialization in internal medicine, was born in Danzig, the son of a government official. After attending the gymnasium he began his medical training in the Frederick Wilhelm Institute for Military Medicine in Berlin at 'the age of 17 and took the MD degree in 1853.[1] He fulfilled his military obligations in Dusseldorf, Tübingen, and Königsberg. In 1862, von Leyden returned to Berlin as assistant to Traube at the Charité Hospital, where one of the services was reserved for military officers. At the suggestion of Traube he cultivated a special interest in nervous disorders and soon acquired a reputation for his knowledge of neurology displayed in his monograph, *Diseases of the Spinal Cord*.

In 1865, Leyden severed his army affiliations to become professor of medicine and director of the clinic for internal medicine in Königsberg. Eight years later he accepted a similar assignment at the University of Strasbourg. In 1876, he succeeded Traube in

the second medical service in Berlin, and, upon Frerichs' death, he became director of the first medical clinic. This post was not relinquished until he was 75 years of age.

National Library of Medicine

In 1880, von Leyden founded the *Zeitsch für klinische Medicin* with Frerichs and the following year the Society for Internal Medicine. Leyden was a prolific writer on many subjects, an outstanding clinician, and a critical observer of mankind in sickness or health. His renown brought him patients from many parts of Europe, including the Emperor Alexander III of Russia during the ruler's last illness. After retirement from the clinical post, because of a special interest in cancer, he was made head of the cancer ward especially created for him in the Charité Hospital. The title of Excellency was awarded on his 70th birthday.

Leyden advanced the sensory theory of tabetic ataxia from his clinical-pathological studies on the degenerative changes in the posterior columns of the spinal cord. However, he was incorrect in this pathogenesis and denied the syphilitic cause of tabes. The alterations in the sensory fibers were believed to be associated with the changes in the skin and the deeper structures of the body, such as the bones, joints, and periosteum. Since the posterior columns were assumed to be charged with the conduction of the sentient impulses to the brain, their interruption resulted in ataxia. He noted the following.[1]

The sensory nerves in a coordinated normal response constitute the fundamental reaction and are sufficient to inform us of the position of our limbs. The intensity, the extent, and the persistence of these sensations determine our judgment about the effect of an executed movement. When the sensibility decreases, stronger sensations are needed to produce the same reaction. If a patient thus afflicted wishes to move an arm, he will be conscious of the intention only when the movement has been much overdone; he then observes this overdoing and tries to correct it with a new and opposing motion and overlooks small diversions. In such a manner the movement of the limb becomes unsure, weaving, thrustlike, and as if the afficted is not the master; an aberrant movement which has been interpreted as a loss of coordination appears.

Another contribution to the understanding of tabes was incorporated in his observation in a communication entitled, "Acute Cerebral Ataxia," a subject further explored by Westphal. Leyden's patient, a 54-year-old male, developed ataxia and paralysis rapidly, which mimicked the chronic type, but promptly regressed and the patient experienced a complete recovery. The acute symptoms were described as follows:[2]

There is marked ataxia of all gross movements of the legs. With eyes closed the patient is not able to place the heel of one foot on the knee of the other leg. Foot clonus is not elicited and the skin reflexes are weakened. The cremasteric reflex is absent on the left but present and reduced on the right. Sensibility, including space dissociation and pain, is reduced slightly. If the patient attempts to stand, he collapses. His gait is ataxic; his bladder is weak.
Symptoms are confined to the lower half of the body. The reactions of the arms, the cranial nerves, and the pupils are normal. Normal motor power is retained in the legs. Because of the great similarity to [chronic] tabes one may speak of an acute tabes or better of an acute pseudo-tabes produced by a peripheral neuritis.

Almost at the same time but independent of Charcot and Joffroy, Leyden presented detailed pathological investigations in a case of Duchenne's progressive bulbar paralysis and determined the primary site of the illness in the medulla. Subsequent involvement of the white fibers, with progressive muscle atrophy, was compared with changes in the sensory fibers in tabes. Another example of involvement of the pons and medulla from hemorrhagic infarction has been named "Leyden's paralysis." The form of hemiplegia described in 1856 by Gubler displayed the following symptoms.[3]

1. The paralysis alternans (Gubler) paralysed the facial nerves on the left and the extremities on the right.
2. The sensations were markedly affected.
3. The eyes shifted toward the paralysed side as observed by Magendie.
4. Anarthria and difficulty in swallowing were unrelated to involvement of the hypoglossal nerve.
5. Involvement of the vagus and the phrenic was suspected from the convulsive articulations in the throat and the altered respiration.
We conclude that the hemorrhage of the medulla oblongata occurs in the majority of such cases concurrently with a hemorrhage of the pons.

Leyden's work on the fatty heart was summarized in 1882 in the *Zeitschrift für Klinische Medicin* as follows:[4]

1. The concept "fatty heart" refers to cardiac symptoms in obese individuals in whom it is assumed that they develop as a consequence of obesity.
2. The most frequent and mildest forms of the fatty heart are observed in patients where the complaint comes from the fatty infiltration of the heart while the heart muscle remains normal, powerful, and functioning normally.
3. The grave manifestations of the fatty heart begin with pronounced cardiac complaints, shortness of breath, cardiac asthma, angina pectoris, weakness of the heart, and hydrops. These develop either from complications of weakness of the heart muscle with dilatation of the left ventricle, less often of the right ventricle, or the appearance of arteriosclerosis, especially in the aorta and the coronary arteries. The disease carries a grave prognosis. The diagnosis between arteriosclerosis and a true fatty accumulation with weakening of the heart muscle is not always possible and is based usually on the age of the patient and the condition of the peripheral arteries.

Crystals found in the sputum of patients with bronchial asthma were named "Charcot-Leyden crystals," and, although they had been observed earlier, Leyden was the first to appreciate their significance in asthma.[5]

In the center of the just described cylindric masses we found a great number of very small crystals which were colorless, had a subdued shine, and all showed the form of pointed octahedrons. They varied considerably in size. Their consistency was obviously soft because many appeared broken by the pressure and had split into dice or coneshaped forms adjacent to each other in the natural state; the cleavage planes were smooth and lacked resistance.

These peculiar crystals, which I found in several of the sputum masses in great numbers and in delicate forms, reminded me of others which have been observed earlier. They have been found in the sputum by Friedreich in a case of croup bronchitis with asthma. . . . Earlier than that these crystals had been described by Forster in the sputum of a man suffering from a rapidly progressive bronchitis. Robin and Charcot also found them in 1853 in a leukemic pancreas and had observed similar crystals in the sputum of a case of dry catarrh. Finally, Harting had found them in the sputum and had thought them to be calcium carbonate.

The crystals up to this time appeared to be an accidental finding unrelated to cause. Therefore, it is with interest that I have found these same structures in four cases of the same illness; hence they must be regarded as important and not incidental. Each case was diagnosed as bronchial asthma. After the initial observation, I investigated 11 similar cases. In four I found the same results readily, and in only one instance of the same illness did I fail to find any crystals. . . . Since there is some uncertainty about what constitutes bronchial asthma, it is possible that the casual instance of bronchial catarrh of Forster and dry catarrh of Robin and Charcot were really an attack of bronchial asthma. In Friedreich's case there were asthmatic symptoms in addition to bronchial croup.

Leyden described subdiaphragmatic abscess, showed that endocarditis might be caused by Neisser's *gonococcus* and Frankel's *pneumococcus,* described a form of periodic vomiting, prepared a monograph on poliomyelitis and neuritis, identified large mononuclear phagocytic cells in the ascitic fluid associated with abdominal carcinomatosis, recommended sanitarium care for tubercular patients, and recognized the importance of dietetic methods of management of diseases. And last, it may be noted that von Leyden divided cases of coronary sclerosis into four groups: (1) symptomless sclerosis, (2) acute infarction, (3) chronic

fibrous degeneration of the myocardium, and (4) a combination of fibrosis and acute thrombotic softening.

1. Lewandowsky, M.: Leyden Eulogy (Ger), *Z Neurol Psychiat* 4:1-11, 1910-1911, excerpt translated by E. Longar.

2. Leyden, E.: About Acute Ataxia (Ger), *Z Klin Med* 18:576-587, 1891, excerpt translated by E. Longar.

3. Leyden, E.: *Bleeding Into the Substance of the Spine Marrow* (Ger), 2 vol, Berlin: A. Hirschwald, 1874 and 1875, excerpt translated by E. Longar.

4. Leyden, E.: About Fatty Heart (Ger), *Z Klin Med* 5:1-25, 1882, excerpt translated by E. Longar.

5. Leyden, E.: Contribution to Our Knowledge About Broncial Asthma (Ger), *Archiv Path Anat* 54:325, 1872, excerpt translated by E. Longar.

Composite by G. Bako

William H. Broadbent (1835-1907)

WILLIAM HENRY BROADBENT, clinical cardiologist of London, was born near Huddersfield, Yorkshire, the eldest son of an ardent, converted Wesleyan, woolen manufacturer, and part-time farmer.[1] After day-school education in Longwood and courses at Huddersfield College, William entered his father's business at the age of 15 or 16 in deference to parental desire. After the venture was a failure two years later he convinced his father that a professional career was preferable; however, a contract for a five-year apprenticeship was not entirely to his liking either. It was full of drudgery and left little opportunity for supplementary study in anticipation of examinations at London University. Broadbent subsequently attended Owens College and also spent three years at the Royal School of Medicine in Manchester, where he earned medals in chemistry, botany, materia medica, anatomy, physiology midwifery, surgery, and operative surgery. In 1856, his brilliant scholastic record was rewarded with highest honors at the first MB examination at the University of London and with gold medals in anatomy, physiology, and chemistry.

The following year Broadbent was admitted a member of the Royal College of Surgeons and qualified as licentiate of the Society of Apothecaries. Subsequently, he failed to receive the position of house surgeon at the Manchester Royal Infirmary. Disappointed, he studied for eight months in the hospitals in Paris under Trousseau, Ricord, and Reyer. Having strengthened his clinical experience and acquired fluency in French, Broadbent returned to London for the final MB examination, again winning first-class honors in medicine and a gold medal in obstetrics. Despite the lack of influential friends and other considerable odds, his superior scholastic record enabled him to obtain the post of obstetric officer at St. Mary's Hospital late in 1858. One year later he became resident medical officer.

In 1860, Broadbent was appointed pathologist and lecturer on comparative physiology and zoology in the St. Mary's Hospital medical school, and the University of London awarded him the MD degree. Shortly after, he became a member of the Royal College of Physicians. Broadbent served St. Mary's Hospital in increasingly responsible positions until he retired as senior physician in 1896. From 1860 to 1879, he served the London Fever Hospital as physician, and, in 1863, he accepted an appointment as visiting physician to the Western General Dispensary. Throughout Broadbent's professional years he enjoyed an active practice, although it was not as lucrative in his best years as it might have been, had he taken

full advantage of his outstanding reputation and clinical skill. Broadbent's principal contributions to clinical medicine concerned the examination of the heart and blood vessels and were reported in two monographs, complemented by a number of shorter communications. An early interest in the nervous system led ultimately to formulation of an hypothesis in which he explained immunity from paralysis of the contralateral muscles in hemiplegia. He also advanced a theory of aphasia and, in one of his last publications, discussed the cerebral mechanism of speech production and word blindness. Less fortunate was his search for a cancer cure. Broadbent was misled initially by apparent regression of tumor tissue following injection of acetic acid. Five years later he abandoned the treatment, having gained wide attention in England and on the Continent from his overly optimistic and unsupported preliminary findings.

The stimulus to develop a career in cardiovascular diseases has been attributed to Sibson, a discerning bedside clinician practicing at St. Mary's Hospital when Broadbent was house physician. Broadbent meticulously emulated Sibson's custom of tarrying over a heart murmur or other physical aberrations during the examination of the chest and also Sibson's respect for postmortem examination to emphasize the comprehensive evaluation of the case. Retraction of the posterior-lateral area near the 11th and 12th left ribs, due to pericardial adhesions, was reported in 1895 by his son, Walter,[2] who gave full credit to his father for observing this phenomenon many years earlier. The findings which, admittedly, were not always reliable in diagnosis, have persisted in the literature as Broadbent's sign" and were described subsequently by Sir William in 1898 as follows:[3]

The diagnosis [adherent pericarditis] is arrived at by means of physical signs, and there is no better field for minute observation and careful discrimination. We shall better know what to look for and what value to attach to any deviations from the normal which we may discover if we consider the conditions present.

In the normal state the heart glides over the central tendon of the diaphragm upon which it rests, both with its own systole and diastole and with the respiratory ascent and descent of the diaphragm. When adhesion takes place all shifting and gliding must cease; a given area of the surface of the heart (which will correspond very nearly on the posterior inferior aspect with Sibson's fixed point in the interventricular septum in front) is bound to a definite part of the tendinous expansion. While the heart is thus fixed the respiratory excursion of the central tendon must also be restricted, since the heart is adherent to the pericardium as well as to the diaphragm and the fibrous connections of the former do not allow of its free movement downwards. Now, the triangular space between the diverging costal cartilages is closely associated with the central tendon of the diaphragm, and it is here that we look for evidences of the adherence of the heart thereto. Visible or palpable pulsation does not help us, for we may have either epigastric protrusion or tug in normal conditions. Much more significant is the complete arrest of the slight respiratory movements of this part of the abdominal wall. It has been my practice for more than 20 years to note carefully the indications of adhesion left by general pericarditis in every case which has come under my observation, and this arrest has never been wanting.

A systolic tug of the left false ribs posteriorly communicated by the diaphragm may be conspicuous. The recoil from the drag may be so distinct as to look and feel to the hand like pulsation, and in the first case in which I observed it, now more than 20 years since—a case of left empyema—it was taken for pulsation, and it was supposed that a pulsating tumour of some kind underlay the empyema. A *post-mortem* examination showed that the cause was adherent pericardium. I have often seen this tugging since, and in some cases it can be made to affect the right false ribs by causing the patient in the sitting position to lean over to the left so as to throw the drag of the heart upon the right half of the diaphragm.

Broadbent was honored with a full share of named lectureships.[4] In 1874, he delivered the Lettsomian lectures before the Medical Society of London on "Syphilitic Affections of the Nervous System." The Croonian lectures on "The Pulse," given before the Royal College of Physicians of London in 1887, were reproduced in a monograph of the same name.[5] The lectures before the Harveian Society on "Prognosis in Heart-Disease," and the Lumleian lectures delivered before the Royal College on "Structural Diseases of the Heart Considered From the Point of View of Prognosis" formed the basis of his text on heart disease coauthored with a second son, John F. H. Broadbent, MD.[6] In 1894, Broadbent gave

the Cavendish lecture before the West London Medico-Chirurgical Society on "Some Points in the Treatment of Typhoid Fever" and, in 1903, the Hughlings Jackson lecture for the Neurological Society of London.

One of the leading practitioners of London, Broadbent's patients included the royal family and King George V, then the Duke of York, who was treated by Broadbent during a siege of typhoid fever in 1891. The following year he was appointed physician in ordinary to Edward, then Prince of Wales, and, in 1896, physician extraordinary to Queen Victoria. On the death of the Queen, he served as physician in ordinary to King Edward VII. He was created a baronet in 1893 and KCVO in 1901. Other honors included election to fellowship in the Royal Society, honorary degrees of DSC from the University of Leeds, and the LLD from the universities of Edinburgh and St. Andrews. At the meeting of the British Medical Association in Toronto in 1906, Broadbent was especially honored by the Universities of Toronto and Montreal with an LLD degree from each. His coat of arms is reproduced in a stained glass plaque in the new home of the Royal College of Physicians of London in Regent's Park.

1. Broadbent, M. E.: (ed).: *Life of Sir William Broadbent, Bart., K.C.V.O.,* London: J. Murray, 1909.
2. Broadbent, Walter: An Unpublished Physical Sign, *Lancet* 2:200-201 (July 27) 1895.
3. Broadbent, W. H.: Adherent Pericardium, *Trans Med Soc Lond* 21:109-122, 1898.
4. Broadbent, Walter (ed.): *Selections From the Writings Medical and Neurological of Sir William Broadbent, Bart., K.C.V.O.,* London: H. Frowde, 1908.
5. Broadbent, W. H.: *The Pulse,* London: Carsell & Co., 1890.
6. Broadbent, W. H., and Broadbent, J. F. H.: *Heart Diseases With Special Reference to Prognosis and Treatment,* London: Baillière, Tindall & Cox, 1897.

Composite by G. Bako

Sir Thomas Clifford Albutt
(1836-1925)

SIR THOMAS CLIFFORD ALLBUTT, regius professor of physic at Cambridge, has much in common with Sir William Osler (1849-1919), regius professor of medicine at Oxford and better known in America. Allbutt was born in Yorkshire, the only son of Rev. Thomas Allbutt, then Vicar of Dewsbury. The initial education was entrusted to a private tutor. This was followed by attendance at St. Peters School in York, one of the oldest in the country, founded not later than 627 AD. Classics and mathematics were the subjects in which young Allbutt excelled. At the age of 19, he entered Gonville and Caius College, Cambridge. The following year he gained a classics scholarship but transferred his interest subsequently to chemistry and anatomy. At the age of 22 the medical school of St. George's Hospital, London, received him as a medical clerk of Henry Bence Jones, who, in turn, had been a pupil of Liebig. The customary tour of the Continent followed. In Paris, Allbutt studied under Armand Trousseau and Duchenne and mingled professionally with Bazin (Bazin's disease), Raynaud (Raynaud's syn-

drome), and Ménière (Ménière's syndrome). He returned to London and after a short time decided to settle in Leeds, where he was soon elected to the staff of Leeds' House of Recovery and the General Infirmary. He had taken the MB degree at the age of 33. Two decades later he moved to London and accepted the Commissionership in Lunancy. At the age of 56, he was appointed regius professor of physic at Cambridge.

The titles and honors accorded Allbutt are documented in the memoirs prepared by Sir Humphry Davy Rolleston.[1] Kagan noted that Allbutt received almost every honor available to a medical man in England.[2] But these are of less concern than his professional and avocational accomplishments. The latter embraced Greek and Roman medicine, medical composition, and mountaineering. Among the many clinical subjects treated by Allbutt may be numbered discussions of hyperpiesia (benign hypertension), pericarditis, albuminuria in pregnancy, arteriosclerosis, appendicitis, apoplexy, aortitis, angina pectoris, Bright's disease, tuberculous adenitis, diet in disease, typhoid fever, cerebrospinal syphilis, Paget's disease, pulmonary embolism, smallpox, typhus fever, and the use of the ophthalmoscope.[3] He crossed the boundary line of descriptive internal medicine to criticize psychoanalysis severely.

Allbutt's early classical training has been held responsible for his devotion to medical composition. His *Notes on the Composition of Scientific Papers*[4] recounted his step-by-step method for the preparation of a scientific communication. It was intended primarily to assist Cambridge students, who at that time, had to submit to the regius professor of physic a thesis for both the MB and MD degrees, but they soon enjoyed a wider appeal.

All writers, however, even the least skillful, are, in the degree of their skill, at some care how to begin. An unpractised writer, for sheer helplessness at the outset, may never begin; he may abandon his work in despair. . . . Of ends I will only say, "Do not end anyhow;" let your leave-taking be easy, gracious, and impressive in proportion to the theme; not ponderous, pompous, epigrammatic, or austere.

His free-flowing style is easy to read and uncluttered with extraneous words and phrases. He was particularly fond of "good old words and homely phrases but abhorred trite expressions and overworked clichés. He rejected the use of the word "thing" in reference to a disease. The misuse of the words "type" and "typical" was particularly obnoxious. He ridiculed the use of "pseudo"-compound terms such as "pseudo-angina." I would subscribe to his weakness for making corrections in the galley proof, an exasperation for any editor, but I cannot subscribe to his admonition:[1]

Never compose when tired, nor in the false confidence of tea and late hours. At this hour the composition seems to be beautiful and spontaneous, but it is fairy gold, and in the colder light of the morning it turns to ashes.

For some writers, composition is as spontaneous in the dead of night, with fatigue hovering about, as in the freshness of the new day.

Allbutt's interest in Greek and Roman medicine, which was reflected in his writing from time to time, was summarized in the FitzPatrick Lectures given at the Royal College of Physicians on "Greek Medicine in Rome." The lectures disclose a fine appreciation for the ancients and an expression of scholarship in every line and paragraph of the many printed pages.[5]

To original research I have no pretensions; I am a child in scholarship. Yet in some converse with letters my tastes, if not my talents, have attracted me to the development and propagation of ideas through the long and broken ways of history; and it is in the length and breadth of Roman History that we can knit up tradition into some continuity.

Sir Thomas Clifford Allbutt, KCB, MD, FRS, FRCP (Honorary), DSC, LLD, remained in Cambridge as regius professor until his death at the age of 89. He shared honors with Osler as one of the great internists of modern times, a kindly man whose contributions to the art of medicine were many and varied.

1. Rolleston, H. D.: *The Right Honourable Sir Thomas Clifford Allbutt, K.C.B.,* New York: Macmillan Company, 1929

2. Kagan, S. R.: "Sir Thomas Clifford Allbutt," in *Leaders of Medicine,* Boston: Medico-Historical Press, chap 5, 1941.
3. Chance, B.: Short Studies on the History of Ophthalmology: Sir Clifford Allbutt, the Apostle of Medical Ophthalmoscopy, *Arch Ophthal (Chicago)* 17:819 (May) 1937.
4. Allbutt, T. C.: *Notes on the Composition of Scientific Papers,* London: Macmillan & Co., Ltd., 1904.
5. Allbutt, T. C.: *Greek Medicine in Rome,* London: Macmillan & Co., Ltd., 1921.
6. Talbott, J. H.: "Gout," in Christian, H. A.: *Oxford System of Medicine,* New York: Oxford University Press, 1943.

Composite by G. Bako

Heinrich Irenaeus Quincke
(1842-1922)

HEINRICH QUINCKE, who described disseminated blotchy edema of the skin, was born in Frankfurt-on-Oder, Germany, the son of a successful physician. He prepared for medicine at the universities of Berlin, Würzburg, and Heidelberg under some of the best medical scientists of his day, including Virchow, Müller, Kölliker, Helmholtz, and Bunsen.[1] He served for three years under Frerichs at the Charité in Berlin; at the early age of 30, he was called to Bern as professor of internal medicine following the retirement of Naunyn. Five years later he moved to Kiel, where he remained for 30 years.

Quincke is described as an excellent teacher and a calm and sympathetic physician. His capacities for observation at the bedside were remarkable and embraced a large number of subjects in internal medicine, with several diversions into clinical neurology.[1] He was not a particularly popular consultant but compensated for this lack by a warm and natural compassion for the general practitioner. His observations on capillary and venous pulsations in aortic insufficiency and on aneurysm of the hepatic artery were made in Berlin. The response to the stimulation of the carotid sinus was reported from Bern; whereas his description of angioneurotic edema and the value of arachnoidesis in diseases of the nervous system were communicated from Kiel. Passages from each of these contributions will be excerpted. Other clinical interests included poikilocytosis in pernicious anemia, hemolysis of the erythrocytes, hemosiderosis, caisson disease, iron salts and iron therapy, nutrition in diseases of the gastrointestinal tract, diabetic coma, surgical treatment of pulmonary abscess, the extrarenal cause of nephritic edema, amebic dysentery, heat production, and typhoid fever.

Quincke's observations on capillary and venous pulse were helpful in establishing a diagnosis of aortic insufficiency. He accepted the principle well known from physiological observations that the pulsation in the arterial system which originates in the heart extends to the arterioles, but pulsation in the capillaries is apparent only with a diminished flow of venous blood or with intermittent lowering of arterial pressure. However, there are certain areas of the body, such as the fingernails, where capillary pulsations are evident at times under normal conditions, but readily recognizable in abnormal states and visible to the naked eye.[2]

As far as the capillary pulse is concerned, so can one see it best on his own fingernail, or better, on that of another, in the area between the whitish, blood-poor area and the red injected part of the capillary system of the nail-bed; in the majority of persons examined, there is, with each heartbeat, a forward and backward movement of the margin between the red and white part, and he can convince himself that the increase of the

redness follows a moment later than the apex beat and is still clearly systolic and rather rapid, while the backward movement of the edge of the redness seems to take place more slowly. That is, a lingering in the wave which can be seen by the eye, just as palpation and the sphygmograph show it in the pulse waves of the radial artery.

A large and rapidly falling pulse is seen especially in aortic insufficiency, and for this reason the capillary pulse is especially clear in this condition. Even in a horizontal position of the hand we see a very clear and rapid appearance and disappearance of the margin between the red and white zone and also with an uniform coloration of the nail and lightninglike and evanescent reddening, so that the maner of the appearance and disappearance of the capillary pulse is, for the eye, a characteristic sign of active visibility of the capillary pulse in health, and in addition the transparency of the nails and the proper degree of elasticity of the arteries must be considered.

Lately I had an opportunity of observing the capillary pulse in still another place besides the fingernails, namely in the retina, and it was in one of the two cases of aortic insufficiency already mentioned, in a man who is still under my observation.

An aneurysm of the hepatic artery, confirmed by autopsy, was described in a 25-year-old laborer who developed jaundice following typhoid fever. He was troubled with upper abdominal symptoms, passed bloody stools, and died four months later.[3]

. . . an aneurysm was found approximately the size and shape of a Lambert nut, surrounded by liver parenchyma and located next to the main branch of the hepatic artery, 1½ to 2 cm. from the bifurcation. It was near the right hepatic duct which was displaced by it and enlarged as the other ducts. The circumference of the ductus choledochus, when opened, was 2 cm. and the common hepatic duct 2-3 cm. . . . In that portion of the right lobe of the liver corresponding to the injured duct, soft, reddish brown areas were evident. They were surrounded by irregular and round cells; while the hepatic cells were in various stages of destruction. Partly contained in them, partly free were quantities of yellow, iron-containing pigment masses; in some of the smaller areas orange-colored pigment free of iron was found.

The response of the carotid sinus to stimulation, reported by Czermak in 1865, was studied by Quincke a decade later and the knowledge of the action extended. Slowing of the pulse and decrease of the blood pressure were elicited in the healthy as well as in the susceptibly sensitive person.[4]

. . . lately I have gained the conviction through repeated and careful observations, that the slowing of the pulse when pressure is applied on the carotid is a frequent finding, in healthy as well as in sick persons. With the thumb, the forefinger or the middle finger we searched for the carotid in the neck and applied pressure towards the spine and avoiding its escape. At times this pressure was strong enough to compress it fully, at other times a weaker pressure was sufficient to produce the phenomenon. In selected cases the experiment succeeded even when the pressure was applied on the outer edge of the vessel, when it was exerted only slightly to the side and in any case not significantly narrowed.

Angioneurotic edema, Quincke's disease had been observed by others, and Quincke did not wish to detract from credit due his predecessors in his initial description of the clinical findings.[5]

I wish to identify a skin disease which does not seem to be rare; however, only a few cases of it have been described. This disease appears as oedematous swelling of the skin and the subcutaneous tissue in localized lesions from 2 to 10 cm. or more in diameter. There swellings are most common on the buttocks and on the face, particularly on the lips and eyelids. The swollen parts of the skin are not always *demarcated* from the surrounding tissue which may be pale or translucent or reddened. Patients usually have a sense of tension of the skin—pruritus is not common—localized swellings also appear in the gastrointestinal mucosa producing symptoms. In one case serous effusions in the joints were noted.

The general state of health usually is satisfactory. In some, malaise, a slight headache, chills and oliguria appear. An elevation of temperature was never observed.

Because of its manner of development, acute localized swelling of the skin and mucous membranes, it should be considered as an angioneurosis. It cannot be purely a vasomotor phenomenon, but is probably related to an alteration in the permeabilty of the vascular channels from a nervous influence.

Quincke's development of the spinal puncture for withdrawal of cerebrospinal fluid followed his physiological reasoning that this procedure was indicated in children with hydrocephalus. Early in his career he became interested in formation of cerebrospinal fluid in dogs and later studied the

communication between arachnoid space in the brain and the spinal cord. His findings, diagnostic and therapeutic, were presented to the Congress on Internal Medicine in Wiesbaden in 1891, with similar observations presented by Wynter in England.[6] Quincke quantitated the manometric pressures at the beginning and the conclusion of the puncture, studied the cells, measured the specific gravity and the total protein concentration, observed tubercule bacilli in the pedicle, reported diminution of sugar content in meningitis, and speculated on the cause of red blood cells in the fluid. His initial report on lumbar puncture in hydrocephalus described 22 punctures on 10 patients—five adults and five children. In one patient the procedure was performed six times.

1. Bergmann, G.: Heinrich Quincke Memorial by the Medical Faculty of Medicine in Frankfurt am Main (Ger), Z Klin Med 95:1-21, 1922.
2. Quincke, H.: Observations on Capillary and Venous Pulse, Klin Wschr 5:357-379, 1868, translated in Major, R. H.: Classic Descriptions of Disease, Springfield, Ill: Charles C Thomas, 1932.
3. Quincke, H.: A Case of Aneurysm of the Hepatic Artery (Ger), Klin Wschr 8:349:352, 1871, excerpt translated by E. Longar.
4. Quincke, H.: Vagus Stimulation in Man (Ger), Klin Wschr 12:189-191, 1875, excerpt translated by E. Longar.
5. Quincke, H.: Acute Circumscribed Edema of the Skin (Ger), Monatsh Prakt Derm 1:129-131, 1882, excerpt translated by E. Longar.
6. Quincke, H.: Lumbar Puncture in Hydrocephalus (Ger), Klin Wschr 28:929-933, 965-968, 1891, excerpt translated by E. Longar.

Reginald Heber Fitz
(1843-1913)

PERTINENT FACTS FROM THE CURRICULUM
VITAE of Reginald Heber Fitz exemplify the
path to medical greatness in Boston in the
19th century. Fitz was born in Chelsea,
Mass., in 1843, graduated from Harvard
College at the age of 21, received an appointment as house officer at the Boston
City Hospital at the age of 24, and graduated MD at Harvard Medical School one
year later. Following graduation, he studied
with Rokitansky and Skoda in Vienna and
with Virchow in Berlin for a year. Upon returning to Boston in 1870, he was appointed
instructor in pathology at the Harvard Medical School. At the age of 35, he advanced to
the Shattuck professorship of pathological
anatomy at his alma mater and was placed
in charge of the pathological laboratory at
the Masschusetts General Hospital. A decade later he became visiting physician at the
Massachusetts General Hospital. At the age
of 49, Fitz was appointed professor of medicine at Harvard, occupying the Hersey chair
of the theory and practice of physic, and was
honored with the degree of LLD 13 years
later. He retired from the faculty at the age
of 65 and died at the age of 70. Memorial

addresses given by W. W. Keen of Philadelphia and Charles W. Eliot, president
emeritus of Harvard, paid proper tribute to
a medical Boston Brahmin.[1]

Reginald H. Fitz is probably best remembered for the study published in 1886,
in which he suggested the use of the term
"appendicitis" and recognized the association of clinical symptoms with operative and
postmortem findings in the lesion in the
right lower quadrant of the abdomen. Equal
in significance to the dissertation on acute
appendicitis was the Middleton-Goldsmith
Lecture, delivered before the New York
Pathological Society, Feb 16, 1889, which
summarized his clinical observations on
acute pancreatitis.[2] Consonant with the best
clinical teaching of the day, Fitz was a resolute physician, correlating observations at
the bedside with postmortem findings, never
neglecting the one for the other. His pathological demonstrations were presented with
clarity and meaning. His writings, which
numbered 100, disclosed an excellent knowledge of past and current medical literature,
particularly the pathology literature of the
German school.

Perforating inflammation of the vermiform appendix had been described a number of times before Fitz presented his findings at the first annual session of the Association of American Physicians in Washington, D.C. Nor did Fitz claim priority
several previous communications on the general subject were noted. The affliction had
been described by Jean Fernel more than
three centuries earlier, by Lorenz Heister
and M. Mestivier in the 18th century, and
by Parkinson, Hodgkin, and others in the
early part of the 19th century. The abdominal condition had been identified as perityphlitis, typhlo-enteritis, typhlitis, or paratyphlitis. Fitz assigned a new term, "appendicitis," and described the normal and aberrant positions of the inflamed organ, the
clinical symptoms, complications, and surgical treatment. The report was based upon
a review of 257 cases collected from the
literature.[3]

As a circumscribed peritonitis is simply one
event, although usually the most important, in
the history of inflammation of the appendix, it

seems preferable to use the term appendicitis to express the primary condition.

This peritoneal abscess may then become absorbed, or its contents may escape into the general peritoneal cavity through ruptured or softened adhesions. In the latter event, as a rule, death rapidly follows.

If the case does not terminate as thus stated, the tumor may suddenly diminish in size with the discharge of pus from a hollow organ, as the intestine, bladder, or vagina. The anterior abdominal wall may become perforated and a sinus be established opening in the groin, lumbar region, or at the umbilicus.

The occurrence of disease of remote parts may be alluded to, as abscesses of the liver from pyelophlebitis or portal embolism in consequence of a mesenteric thrombophlebitis near the appendix. . . . The extension of a secondary paratyphlitis may cause perforation of the diaghragm with a consecutive pleurisy or pericarditis.

Sudden, severe abdominal pain is the most constant, first, decided symptom of perforating inflammation of the appendix. It occurred in 216 out of 257 cases, 84 per cent. In most instances it is present in apparently healthy individuals, in a few it follows an attack of diarrhoea.

The pain is usually intense, rarely slight, and is occasionally accompanied by a chill, or nausea and vomiting.

The abdominal pain is followed by fever as the next constant symptom.

The circumscribed swelling in the right iliac fossa now demands consideration. This symptom, when present, is evidently of the utmost value in diagnosis, as its appropriate treatment most favorably modifies the prognosis.

A circumscribed resistance is felt on palpation. As the part is often extremely sensitive to pressure and the abdominal muscles tense, the administration of ether or chloroform may be necessary to confirm the diagnosis. A rectal examination not infrequently permits the recognition of the tumor which abdominal palpation fails to disclose, and should always be made in the latter event.
. . . the presence of the abscess may be expected as early as the third day.

The chief danger from the appendicular peritonitis is that it becomes general.

Differential diagnosis, discussed by Fitz, included a primary perforating inflammation of the caecum, stercoral caecitis, intestinal obstruction from intussusception or strangulation, biliary colic, and ureteral calculus. Caution was urged against the use of a cathartic or a laxative lest it incite a general peritonitis. The address concludes with the following admonitions.[3]

The vital importance of the early recognition of perforating appendicitis is unmistakable.

Its diagnosis, in most cases, is comparatively easy.

Its eventual treatment by laparotomy is generally indispensable.

Urgent symptoms demand immediate exposure of the perforated appendix, after recovery from the shock, and its treatment according to surgical principles.

Three years later, Fitz presented his clinicopathological observations on acute pancreatitis, under three categories: (1) pancreatic hemorrhage, (2) hemorrhagic, suppurative, and gangrenous pancreatitis, and (3) disseminated fat-necrosis. As in the communication on appendicitis, a number of reported cases were discussed, including those by Clässen, Friedreich, Oppolzer, Klebs, Haller and Klob, Chiari, Balser, Spiess, and Zenker. The subject was introduced by the concept of liability of the pancreas to hemorrhage.[2]

We learn that pain was an early symptom in nearly one-half of the cases; that it was usually severe, and might be intense, and was to be found in the abdomen or lower chest. Although mention is made of its presence in the epigastrium in one-fifth of the cases, this region is not conspicuously designated as the seat. On the contrary, there may be little or no pain, or merely a sense of constriction of the chest. Nausea or vomiting is but occasionally mentioned; constipation or a desire for frequent stools are still more rarely noted.

The most constant symptoms are those of collapse, and are more or less intense and more or less prolonged.

Death may take place within a half-hour after the onset of the symptoms, and may be delayed for thirty-six hours.

The appearances found after death are conspicuously the hemorrhage within and near the pancreas.

The gland may be of normal size, or enlarged, and its density may not be modified, or the pancreas may be flaccid, soft, and friable. The hemorrhagic infiltration is to be found in the subperitoneal tissue around the pancreas as well as in the interstitial tissue of the gland.

A normal or subnormal temperature may be present. . . .

The symptoms are essentially those of a peritonitis beginning in the epigastrium and occurring suddenly, during ordinary health, without obvious cause.

The diagnosis, therefore, is based on pain, tenderness, and tympany limited to the region of the pancreas, and on the gradual development of a deep-seated peritonitis in the same place.

It is evident that all treatment, at the onset, can be nothing but palliative. With the formation of pus in the omental cavity comes the opportunity for the surgeon. The possibility of the successful removal of the gangrenous pancreas is suggested by the healthy condition of the patient seventeen years after he had discharged this organ from his bowels.

Intrapleural lipoma, with acute pericarditis and pericardial exploration, was discussed by Fitz in the *American Journal of the Medical Sciences* of 1905. Historical references to Cruveilhier, Rokitansky, Lancereaux, Chiari, Czerny, and Langenbeck were followed by a case report of a 34-year-old fisherman seen at the Massachusetts General Hospital. Physical signs suggested consolidation of the left lung and effusion into the pericardiac sac and the pleural cavity. The postmortem examination by J. H. Wright showed that:[4]

Attached to the pericardium on the left side and apparently continuous with the fat tissue of the superior mediastinum is a large mass of fat tissue of about the volume of a newborn child's head, divided by delicate connective-tissue septa into larger and smaller lobules. It evidently occupied the inferior and anterior portions of the left pleural cavity, the left lung being behind and above it.

Most of Fitz's teaching was conducted at the Massachusetts General Hospital on the Charles River or at the Harvard Medical School. His pathological and clinical investigations were pursued in the pathological amphitheater and at the bedside, not in an experimental laboratory. It is not surprising that, when morphological investigation had reached its zenith and was beginning to be overshadowed by the discoveries in microbiology, his writings were singularly deficient in these new fields of scientific endeavor. Any discussion of the prevalent infections— typhoid fever, lobar pneumonia, dysentery, cholera, and tuberculosis—dwelt lightly upon the pathogenesis or etiology and largely upon the pathological and clinical findings.

A review of the scientific writings of Reginald H. Fitz leads one to accept the fact that he was completely dedicated to medicine, with scant mention of any avocational interests. The exception was the historical recounting of the legislative control of medical practice in Massachusetts. Association membership and professional activities were proper for one of Harvard's best known medical sons. These included the Massachusetts Medical Society, The Boston Society for Medical Observation, the Boston Society for Medical Improvement, the Boston Society of Medical Sciences, the Association of American Physicians, the American Academy of Arts and Sciences, and the Interurban Club. Although not the first to describe the inflammation and complications of abscess of the vermiform appendix, Fitz correlated the clinical and pathological findings, recommended early abdominal exploration, and thereby advanced a new concept that saved many lives in the half century before the discovery of effective antibiotics.

1. *Memorial Addresses, Reginald Heber Fitz, M.D., LL.D., 1843-1913,* Jamaica Plain, N. Y.: Jamaica Printing Co., 1913.
2. Fitz, R. H.: Acute Pancreatitis, a Consideration of Pancreatic Hemorrhage; Hemorrhagic, Suppurative, and Gangrenous Pancreatitis, and of Disseminated Fat-Necrosis, *Boston Med Surg J* 70:181-187 (Feb 21); 205-207 (Feb 28); 229-235 (March 7) 1889.
3. Fitz, R. H.: Perforating Inflammation of the Vermiform Appendix; with Special Reference to Its Early Diagnosis and Treatment, *Trans Assn Amer Physicians,* Philadelphia: W. J. Dornan, 1886.
4. Fitz, R. H.: Intrapleural Lipoma; Acute Pericarditis; Pericardial Exploration, *Amer J Med Sci* 130:785-789, 1905.

Henri Rendu (1844-1902)

HENRI JULES MARIE RENDU, who described familial telangiectasia, was the leading French clinician of his day. He was born in Paris while his father was Inspector of Agriculture. His mother was the daughter of a painter, and one of his great uncles was Grand Master of the University of France. Rendu studied for two years in the Agronomic School in Rennes, intending to follow his father's calling. However, he became interested in geology, botany, and mathematics and in time received the *licencié* in science and prepared for the doctor of science degree with the drafting of a thesis on the tertiary strata of the environs of Rennes. Displaying both a brilliant mind and a prodigious memory, he received early acclamation for his recitation in Greek of the Passion at his first communion.[1] In 1865, he turned to the study of medicine, became

Composite by G. Bako

extern of the Paris hospitals in 1867, and subsequently won high honors as an intern. Service with the French army during the Franco-Prussian War left him determined on an academic career in preference to military service. The medical degree was awarded in 1873 following his presentation of a dissertation on clinical and anatomic-pathological researches in the paralyses of tuberculous meningitis.

Rendu served at the Hôpital Saint Louis where Besnier, a junior member of the staff, later recognized as a great dermatologist, was concerned with the relation of skin diseases and systemic disorders. This early exposure to dermatology may have contributed to Rendu's interest late in his career in the specific malady which is now associated with his name. Rendu was a prolific writer in general medicine, preparing a monograph on spontaneous anesthesia, another on the influence of dysfunctions of the heart and liver, a thesis on chronic nephritis (for advanced academic standing), and shorter communications in his two-volume compendium of clinical lectures, which is divided into sections on general medicine, respiratory diseases, circulatory maladies, gastrointestinal troubles, and diseases of the kidney and nervous system.[2] He was responsible for the section on gout in the *Dictionnaire Encylopédiques des Sciences Médicales* and collaborated with Potain in several other sections. Most of his clinical work was done at l'Hôpital Necker. Rendu actively participated in the Academy of Medicine and the Medical Society of the Hospitals of Paris, of which he was general secretary. His highest academic appointment was *professeur agrégé* of the Faculty of Medicine of Paris, which he attained in 1878.

In 1896, Rendu prepared the report of a case of hereditary hemorrhagic telangiectasia in which he differentiated this condition from hemophilia. Five years later William Osler described three cases in two families, giving credit to Rendu's earlier observations and, in time, Weber enhanced our knowledge regarding the familial features. Recent studies disclose the malady to be familial and hereditary, usually as a simple autosomal dominant and transmitted by either sex. Clinical findings include recurring multiple telangiectasis and angiomas of the skin, multiple dilatations of capillaries and venules of the skin and mucous membranes, with bleeding from the face, tongue, lips, or from the gastrointestinal, respiratory, or genitourinary tracts. The vascular anomalies may be present at birth but usually do not become clinically apparent until puberty or even later.

Rendu's patient, a 52-year-old male, was well developed but pale and weak, with a subicteric tint. Epistaxis was the presenting symptom. The father suffered from dysentery and repeated melena and died at 55 years of age; the mother and brother suffered from copious epistaxis. One can only speculate whether the line of descent was through the mother or the father. A summary of the case follows.[3]

He . . . had his first nose bleeds at the age of 12 years, and throughout his youth he was subject to them, chiefly in the spring and in the warm season. This disposition, far from attenuating with advancing age, became considerably aggravated, and since the age of 35 the hemorrhages have become very frequent, always in the form of epistaxis. Indeed, he has never had hematuria, purpuric spots, or gingival hemorrhages, and it is interesting to note that when he injures or cuts himself he loses no more blood than a normal person. He has had two teeth pulled without having had notable consequent hemorrhages. This is, therefore, no true hemophilia, in spite of the ease with which he loses blood from the nose.

A particularity which recalls to mind the case described by M. Chauffard explains, perhaps, this peculiar localization of the hemorrhages and their frequent repetition.

On the skin of the nose, the cheeks, the upper lip, and the chin, there are small purple spots as large as the head of a pin; the largest reach the size of a lentil; they are true cutaneous hemangiomas, produced by a dilatation of the superficial vessels of the skin. Pressure causes them to blanch, but not to disappear; the blood flows back immediately when compression is released. Angiomas of the same nature are scattered over the neck and chest; there appear to be none on the extremities.

This anatomic disposition is not limited to the skin; it extends also to the mucous membranes, and this fact is of considerable interest from the point of view which concerns us. Indeed, small vascular dilatations, true telangiectatic foci, are present on the inner surface of the lips and the cheeks, on the tongue, and on the soft palate, with characteristics identical to those on the integument, but with a very bright color, owing to the decreased thickness of mucous epidermis.

In the nostrils we have not demonstrated these punctiform angiomas, but it is not irrational to suppose that there are similar ones on the nasal septum or in the nasal mucous membrane that is the seat of the hemorrhages, and why they are so recurrent and copious.

1. Henri Rendu, obituary (Fr), *Bull Soc Med Hop Paris,* 19:1188-1204, 1902.

2. Rendu, H.: *Lessons of Clinical Medicine* (Fr), 2 vol, Paris: O. Doin, 1890.

3. Rendu, H.: Repeated Epistaxis in a Patient Having Small Cutaneous and Mucous Membrane Angiomas, *Gaz Hop* 69:1322-1323, 1896, in Shelley, W. B., and Crissey, J. T. (trans.): *Classics in Clinical Dermatology,* Springeld, Ill: Charles C Thomas, Publisher, 1953.

William Osler (1849-1919)

SIR WILLIAM OSLER, judged by many to be the greatest clinician of our times, was born at Bond Head, Ontario, Canada, the son of English parents who migrated to frontier Upper Canada to take up mission work.[1] Osler was educated at the Anglican school in

Weston; there the warden introduced him to Browne's *Religio Medici,* his lifelong literary companion. Although Osler had intended to take holy orders, he began the study of medicine at the University of Toronto; in 1872, he finished at McGill University. During the following two years he visited medical centers in Europe, with the longest residence in London, where he studied physiology under Burdon-Sanderson at University College. This, the first of a long series of "brain-dusting" excursions back and forth across the Atlantic, made him as much a part of European as American medicine.

Osler returned to Canada intending to enter general practice. However, after a few months he was appointed lecturer in the institutes of medicine at McGill. He taught physiology and pathology to the medical students, comparative pathology to veterinary students, and engaged in research in the pathological laboratory. The following year he was appointed professor of medicine; in 1876, a pathologist to the Montreal General Hospital; and, in 1878, physician to the hospital, with full privileges. After a decade in Montreal, Osler accepted an invitation to the

University of Pennsylvania as professor of clinical medicine. He continued his clinical investigations in an inadequate laboratory and conducted his famous ward walks in Old Blockley, a unit of the Philadelphia Hospital.

Osler's stay in Philadelphia terminated in the fall of 1888. He moved to Baltimore and became the physician-in-chief of the recently organized Johns Hopkins Hospital, the second of the "Hopkins Four," following Welch and preceding Kelly and Halsted. His assignment in the Johns Hopkins medical school, not ready to accept students until four years later, was professor of the principles and practice of medicine. His integrated teaching program for medical students and house staff was centered about instruction of small groups. The students served as clinical clerks on the wards and were responsible for detailed case histories and physical examinations. They carried their problems into the clinical laboratory and were part of the demonstrations in the outpatient department.

The postgraduate years in Europe made Osler familiar with their methods of teaching and research, and, from periodic visits to schools in America, he chose the best features of each. His curriculum standards and practices had a great deal to do with casting a new template for medical education in America early in this century. For the house staff he planned a one-year general internship and a graded whole-time resident staff for those of exceptional promise, with a future directed toward institutional positions in the clinical as well as in the basic science departments.

Concomitant with imaginative planning for a new curriculum for students and house staff was Osler's successful fulfillment of a void in medical pedagogy, ie, a modern text on internal medicine based upon advances in medical science, especially bacteriology, during the preceding 50 years. His resulting peerless treatise, The Principles and Practice of Medicine,[2] was rapidly recognized as the standard text on clinical medicine. Its reputation persisted through many editions without serious competition. It was translated into French, German, Spanish, and Chinese, and, after his death, revisions were carried on by others. The work, departing from the design of previous textbooks of general medicine, exhibited a rigid format with its classification of diseases according to pathogenesis or anatomical position. It remained as the pattern for American textbooks of internal medicine until the appearance of Harrison's Principles of Internal Medicine in 1950, a reversion to emphasis upon general discussions of human biology rather than disease entities.

While in Philadelphia and Baltimore, Osler enjoyed a large consulting practice, carried on clinical investigation in a number of diseases, was active in public health, and became an avid bibliophile. His greatest contribution in medicine, however, lay in the example he set as a bedside teacher and in the stimulation of his young associates. In 1904, just 15 years after the Baltimore assignment, Osler was offered the regius professorship of medicine at Oxford University and a staff appointment at the Radcliffe Infirmary. This appointment was a logical step; Osler was English, oriented by heritage and postgraduate training.

The years at Oxford provided time for the leisurely but also vigorous pursuit of literary and humanistic studies. Osler was one of the founding editors of the Quarterly Journal of Medicine. At his home, 13 Norham Gardens in Oxford, notable American, European, and British friends gathered. As curator of the Bodleian Library, he conversed with learned men of many interests, meanwhile expanding his endeavors as a bibliophile and medical historian. Osler was elected to fellowship in the Royal College of Physicians in 1884 while at McGill, and to fellowship in the Royal Society in 1898 during the Hopkins tenure. Taking full advantage of his Oxford residence, he became a familiar figure at the sessions of various medical societies in London.

Osler was an active investigator of typhoid fever, malaria, pneumonia, amebiasis, tuberculosis, cardiovascular disease, and the relation of gallstones to typhoid, to mention a few. His great demand as a speaker led to printing and binding of several of his addresses in Aequanimitas (1904) and An Alabama Student (1908). The Silliman lectures, given at Yale in 1913 but not published until 1921, were entitled *The Evolution of Modern Medicine*. The clinical contributions excerpted below are exemplary of his style in composition and breadth of clinical interests. In 1874, Osler defined the status of the blood platelets as the third corpuscular element in the circulating blood and their relation to the formation of thrombi.[3]

In many disease conditions of the body, occasionally also in perfectly healthy individuals and in many of the lower animals, careful investigation of the blood proves that, in addition to the usual elements, there exist pale granular masses, which on closer inspection present a corpuscular appearance.

In size they vary greatly from half or quarter that of a white blood-corpuscle, to enormous masses occupying a large area of the field or even stretching completely across it. They usually assume a somewhat round or oval form, but may be elongated and narrow, or, from the existence of numerous projections, offer a very irregular outline. They have a compact solid look, and by focusing are seen to possess considerable depth; while in specimens examined without any reagents the filaments of fibrin adhere to them, and, entangled in their interior, white corpuscles are not unfrequently met with.

In a series of three communications published between 1895 and 1903, Osler discussed the visceral complications of erythema exudative multiforme and thereby enlarged the concept of lupus erythematosus as a systemic disease.[4]

By exudative erythema is understood a disease of unknown etiology with polymorphic skin lesions—hyperaemia, oedema, and hemorrhage—arthritis occasionally, and a variable number of visceral manifestations, of which the most important are gastro-intestinal crises, endocarditis, pericarditis, acute nephritis, and hemorrhage from the mucous surfaces. Recurrence is a special feature of the disease, and attacks may come on month after month, or even throughout a long period of years. Variability in the skin lesions is the rule, and a case may present in one attack the features of an angio-neurotic oedema, in a second of a multiforme or nodose erythema, and in a third those of peliosus rheumatica. The attacks may not be characterized by skin manifestations; the visceral symptoms alone may be present, and to the outward view the patient may have no indications whatever of erythema exudativum.

A family form of recurring epistaxis associated with multiple telangiectasis of the skin and mucous membranes, later known as Rendu-Osler-Weber disease, was described 29 years after Legg and 5 years after Rendu.[5]

The association of epistaxis with angiomata of the nasal septum has long been known; but for the associated condition of multiple telangiectases of other mucous membranes and of the skin, I have been able to find only the following report by Rendu.

In the three cases here described, two belonged to a family in which epistaxis had occurred in seven members. Both of my patients had had bleeding at the nose from childhood, and both presented numerous punctiform angiomata on the skin of the face and of the mucous membrane of the nose, lips, cheeks and tongue.

The third patient had suffered in an unusual degree from recurring epistaxis, and the telangiectasis were most abuundant over the body, and very numerous also on the mucous membranes.

Instances of chronic cyanosis with polycythemia and an enlarged spleen, described in 1903, were judged to be a new clinical entity. Later the priority of Vaquez was acknowledged for the disease now known as polycythemia vera. Several cases were described; red blood cell counts as high as 12,000,000/cu mm were reported.[6]

It is by no means easy to offer a satisfactory explanation of the polycythaemia with cyanosis here under consideration. It does not seem possible to connect it in any way with the moderate grade of enlargement of the spleen, and yet there are one or two observations in the literature which are of great interest in this connection.

A more accurate study of the blood in this class of cases—the volume, the viscosity, the state of the plasma and the serum, the amount of haemoglobin, the specific gravity, and the diameter of the corpuscles. As increased viscosity of the blood, with resulting difficulty of flow, seems the most plausible explanation of cyanosis, it is especially important to test the viscosity by accurate physical methods and to determine the relation of the number of corpuscles to the viscosity of the blood.

The relation of the splenomegaly to the cyanosis and polyglobulism should be carefully observed. It may not be anything more than the effect of the chronic passive congestion.

The tender subcutaneous nodes in subacute bacterial endocarditis (Osler's nodes) were first observed by him in the clinic in

1888 but were not reported in the literature until 1908.[7]

On the other hand, there is a large group of cases in which the endocarditis plays a more important role and the vegetations and ulcerations appear to be directly responsible for the fever and the associated symptoms.

One of the most interesting features of the disease and one to which very little attention has been paid is the occurrence of ephemeral spots of a painful nodular erythema, chiefly in the skin of the hands and feet, the *nodosités cutanées éphémères* of the French.

I have known them to pass away in a few hours, but more commonly they last for a day, or even longer. The commonest situation is near the tip of the finger, which may be slightly swollen.

They are not beneath but in the skin and they are not unlike an ordinary wheal of urticaria. The pads of the fingers and toes, the thenar and hypothenar eminences, the sides of the fingers, and the skin of the lower part of the arm are the most common localities. In one case they were present in the skin of the flank. I have never seen them haemorrhagic, but always erythematous, sometimes of a very vivid pink hue, with a slightly opaque centre.

Osler's influence upon the English-speaking medical world was greater than that of any other physician. His personal charm and warm character equalled his skill as a clinical teacher at the bedside and as a planner for the modern curriculum in medical school and house staff training. His remarkable private library, bequeathed to McGill University, is housed in a separate wing of the medical library. Osler's only son, Revere, was named after Lady Osler's ancestor, Paul Revere, his great-great-grandfather of the famous ride. Revere was killed in Flanders in World War I. Osler was a recipient of many honorary degrees, honorary memberships, and active memberships in medical and other learned societies. He received a baronetcy in 1911 and, at all times, the affection and respect of associates, students, and patients. According to *Lancet,* Osler was the greatest personality in the medical world at the time of his death, an accolade which has remained into contemporary times, half a century after his death.

1. Cushing, H.: *The Life of Sir William Osler,* 2 vol, Oxford, England: Clarendon Press, 1925.
2. Osler, W.: *The Principles and Practice of Medicine,* New York: D. Appleton & Co., 1892.

3. Osler, W.: An Account of Certain Organisms Occurring in the Liquor Sanguinis, *Proc Roy Soc* 22:391-398, 1874.
4. Osler, W.: On the Visceral Complications of Erythema Exudativum Multiforme, *Amer J Med Sci* 110-629-646 (Dec) 1895.
5. Osler, W.: On a Family Form of Recurring Epistaxis, Associated With Multiple Telangiectasis of the Skin and Mucous Membranes, *Bull Hopkins Hosp* 12:333-337 (Jan) 1901.
6. Osler, W.: Chronic Cyanosis, With Polycythaemia and Enlarged Spleen: A New Clinical Entity, *Amer J Med Sci* 126:187-201 (Aug) 1903.
7. Osler, W.: Chronic Infectious Endocarditis, *Quart J Med* 2:219-230 (Jan) 1908-1909.

Composite by G. Bako

Arthur Fallot (1850-1911)

ÉTIENNE-LOUIS ARTHUR FALLOT, born in Cette, France, described one of the best-known eponymic syndromes in cardiology.[1] He was educated at the lycée in Marseille, his home for most of his professional days. The study of medicine was begun at Montpellier in 1867, where he served an externship at the local hospitals until 1871. He then began an internship at Marseille and, in turn, demonstrated anatomy in the medical school. In 1876, he presented a thesis on pneumothorax to the faculty of medicine at Montpellier for the MD degree. Fallot carried on an active practice in Marseille, maintaining a close liaison with the university, first in the department of medicine, later in the department of pathological anatomy. In 1888, he was appointed professor of hygiene and legal medicine, a post that was held until his death.

Because of Fallot's wish that no obituary be prepared, little is known of his life or accomplishments beyond the few postdoctoral contributions. He was responsible for a monograph on organization of legal medicine,[2] a description of the brain of two executed criminals,[3] and a treatise of more than 100 pages on the clinical and pathological findings of patients who had been afflicted since adulthood with cyanotic cardiac disease. The tetralogy was composed of (1) stenosis, or obliteration of the pulmonary artery, (2) hypertrophy of the right ventricle, (3) dilation and deviation of the aorta to the right, and, (4) interventricular septal defect.

Fallot was not the first to describe the pathological findings in the malady, but he analyzed and correlated the clinical with postmortem observations, identified the four gross structural aberrations, and thereby presented to the profession a better description of the entity than others before him. Niels Stensen, clinician turned theologian, whose name is associated with the parotid duct, in 1673, was one of the first to recognize the congenital malformation. He described the characteristic alterations without commenting on right ventricular hypertrophy. This feature of the tetralogy was identified by Sandifort of Leyden in 1777, in his excellent account of the clinical and anatomical findings in a 12-year-old boy. He placed the seat of the trouble in the heart and lungs. During the next century others noted that this particular malformation of the heart was the most frequent of the cardiac anomalies. Fallot published a study in 1888 based upon the cardiac malformation in two patients under his care who had been cyanotic since childhood; a summary is included of more than 50 cases from the literature. Since the tetralogy places no strain upon the heart during fetal life, no enlargement of the heart immediately following delivery is to be expected.

The cyanosis and associated symptoms may not appear even during the first year of life; several patients in his study lived more than 60 years. The treatise concluded with the following.[4]

1. Clinicians have until now considered the precise diagnosis of the anatomic lesions of congenital heart disease with cyanosis (la maladie bleu) as almost impossible and to be expressed in the form of an entirely vague and uncertain hypothesis. From observations that we have assembled it appears on the contrary that congenital heart disease with cyanosis, above all in adults is the result of a small number of perfectly definite cardiac malformations.

2. Of these malformations there is one which in frequency surpasses all others, since we have met it in almost 74 per cent of our observations: it is this malformation then that the clinician will be justified in diagnosing and in so doing the chances of error which he will run will be relatively few.

3. This malformation constitutes a true pathologicanatomic type represented by the following tetralogy: (1) stenosis of the pulmonary artery, (2) interventricular septal defect, (3) deviation of the origin of the aorta to the right and (4) hypertrophy of the right ventricle, almost always concentric in type. At times there is an additional entirely accessory defect; namely, patency of the foramen ovale.

4. One cannot at the present time attribute the maladie bleu to the persistence of the foramen ovale without direct opposition to the great majority of observed facts; when the communication between the two auricles exists alone without any other associated cardiac lesion, cyanosis does not result.

5. From the historical point of view one finds, in the writings of the last century [the eighteenth] and of the beginning of the present, frequent observations of congenital heart disease with cyanosis; the majority present the interesting combination of the various cardiac lesions mentioned above.

6. Finally, from the pathogenic point of view the theory that considers the interventricular communication as a simple phenomenon belonging to the group of recessive anomalies rests only on a superficial and inexact interpretation of the facts; the incompletely developed septum in the victim of the maladie bleu can be considered in no way as the analogue of the false septum of vertebrate animals with communicating ventricles, it appears much more logical and more in keeping with physiological laws to regard the entire series of cardiac anomalies enumerated above as the consequence of the stenosis of the pulmonary artery. As to the cause of this pulmonary stenosis we believe that we should attribute it not to a simple arrest in development, but rather to a pathological process occurring in the region of

the pulmonary valve and of the infundibulum just below it during intrauterine life.

1. Willius, F. A., and Keys, T. E.: *Cardiac Classics*, St. Louis: C. V. Mosby Co., 1941, pp 689-690.

2. Fallot, A.: *Reorganization of Legal Medicine* (Fr), Marseille, France: Barlatier & Barthelet, 1891.

3. Fallot, A.: *The Brain of Criminals* (Fr), Lyon, France: A. Storck, 1889.

4. Fallot, A.: Contributions to the Pathological Anatomy of the Blue Cardiac (Fr), *Marseille Med* 25:77-93, 138-158, 207-223, 270-286, 341-354, 403-420, 1888, in White, P. D. (trans.): *Heart Disease*, New York: Macmillan Co., 1932, p 309.

Composite by G. Bako

Graham Steell (1851-1942)

THE DESCRIPTION OF THE MURMUR associated with pulmonic insufficiency and pulmonary hypertension by Graham Steell, Edinburgh born and trained, was published while he was a staff member of the Royal Infirmary in Manchester and occupant of the chair of clinical medicine at the University of Manchester. Graham was the youngest son of Sir John Steell, sculptor to Queen Victoria. He was educated at Edinburgh Academy and the University of Edinburgh, where he was awarded a gold medal for his thesis on scarlatina, presented for the MD degree.[1] Postgraduate study was pursued in Berlin, London, and Leeds.

Steell attributed his particular interest in cardiology to George Balfour, one of his teachers at the Edinburgh Royal Infirmary. Contributions in this rapidly-developing, special area of clinical interest were made in the description and functional identification of the pulmonic murmur and in the description of heart disease associated with beriberi. Several texts and monographs were written during his long and fruitful career in academic medicine and consultative practice. These included a standard reference volume, *Text Book on Diseases of the Heart*,[2] and monographs entitled, *The Use of the Sphygmograph in Clinical Medicine, Physical Signs of Cardiac Disease,* and *Physical Signs of Thoracic Disease.*

The murmur of high pressure in the pulmonary artery was described in an address to the Manchester Medical Society and was later published in the *Medical Chronicle* in 1888. The murmur was detected with a monaural stethoscope made of boxwood, with a bell-shaped earpiece. The significance of the heart muscle and alterations in the valve in the production of abnormal signs on auscultations were emphasized.[3]

I wish to plead for the admission among the recognised auscultatory signs of disease *of a murmur due to pulmonary regurgitation, such regurgitation occurring independently of disease or deformity of the valves and as the result of long-continued excess of blood pressure in the pulmonary artery.*

In cases of mitral obstruction there is occasionally heard over the pulmonary area (the sternal extremity of the third left costal cartilage), and below this region, for the distance of an inch or two along the left border of the sternum, and rarely over the lowest part of the bone itself, a soft blowing diastolic murmur immediately following, or, more exactly, running off from the accentuated second sound, while the usual indications of aortic regurgitation afforded by the pulse, etc., are absent. The maximum intensity of the murmur may be regarded as situated at the sternal end of the third and fourth intercostal spaces. When the second sound is reduplicated, the murmur proceeds from its latter part. That such a murmur as I have described does exist, there can, I think, be no doubt.

The murmur of high-pressure in the pulmonary artery is not peculiar to mitral stenosis, although it is most commonly met with, as a consequence of this lesion. Any long-continued obstruction in the pulmonary circulation may produce it. The pulmonary valves, like the aortic, do not readily become incompetent, apart from structural change.

Probably no amount of blood-pressure in the pulmonary artery will render them so suddenly, as, at least, theoretically, the mitral valves may be rendered incompetent. Changes in the vessel, with widening of its channel, and, eventually, of its orifice, long precede the occurrence of incompetence of its valves. The pulmonary murmur of high-pressure is probably never persistent at first, and one of its most remarkable features is, as a rule, its variableness in intensity. On some days it will be distinctly heard, on others it will be indistinct, or even inaudible; while extreme accentuation of the pulmonary second sound is always present, the closure of the pulmonary semilunar valves being generally perceptible to the hand placed over the pulmonary area, as a sharp thud. This nonpersistence of the murmur, in the earlier stages, at any rate, is only what the study of dilatation of the aorta and the consequent regurgitation would lead us to expect. Indeed, so common is a soft, blowing murmur, after an accentuated aortic second sound, that extreme accentuation should make us listen, with special care, for a murmur, and even though it be absent on the first occasion the search should not be abandoned. My belief is, that when the aortic second sound is extremely accentuated, regurgitation, to some extent, will probably occur sooner or later. Its supervention in aneurism of the first part of the arch of the aorta is a familiar fact.

The description of an atypical form of cardiac failure, complicating either alcoholic cirrhosis of the liver or beri-beri and associated with peripheral neuritis, was his other important contribution to clinical medicine. It is noteworthy that Steell associated the two conditions now known to be related to vitamin B$_1$ deficiency many years before the identification of nicotinic acid or the discovery of the etiologic relationship between nutrient deficiency and the development of either malady.[2]

Capricious distribution of dropsy is specially apt to occur in cases of the cardiac muscle-failure of beer-drinkers and of the disease known as Beri-Beri, of both of which diseases, it is curious to note, peripheral neuritis is a clinical feature. Under the circumstances, not only is the distribution of the dropsy apt to be capricious, but it is apt to be also very extensive. The subcutaneous tissues of the trunk are specially likely to become involved, and in cases of the kind, pressure with the finger over the sternum, for instance, will often leave a depression of great depth in the oedematous pad that overlies the bone. Curious special localizations of oedema met with, in cases of the kind, have been the scrotum, and together the upper trunk, upper extremities, and

scalp and neck, so that the oedema simulates that resulting from mediastinal tumour.

Steell was troubled with irregularity and frequency of the pulse, regarded by him as auricular fibrillation. Subsequently, he accepted the explanation of showers of extra systoles. He practiced what he taught in regard to physical activity and heart disease. He boxed in his youth and was an expert horseman. He was an especially modest physician, seeking only the glory and fame that follows devotion by appreciative patients, respect from pupils who benefited form bedside teaching, and admiration from practitioners who read or studied his treatises on the function and dysfunction of the cardiovascular system.

1. Bramwell, C.: Graham Steell, *Brit Heart J* 4:115-119, 1942.
2. Steell, G.: *Text Book on Diseases of the Heart*, Manchester: University Press, 1906.
3. Steell, G.: The Murmur of High-Pressure in the Pulmonary Artery, *Med Chron Manchester* 9:182-188, 1888-1889.

Guido Banti (1852-1925)

THE UNCERTAINTY regarding the specificity of Banti's disease (or syndrome) is not entirely resolved by reference to his several contributions to progressive congestive splenomegaly associated with nonleukemic anemia, thrombophlebitis of the splenic vein, and portal cirrhosis of the liver. Included in this essay, in their chronological order, are several excerpts which describe the clinical and pathological findings of an unusual malady, similar to several features, but different, neverthless, from Laennec's cirrhosis of the liver.

Banti was born in Montebicchieri in the lower valley of the Arno, the son of a physician.[1] He studied medicine for four years in Pisa and two years in Florence, where he graduated. Shortly after taking his degree, he won in competition an assistantship at the Institute of Pathological Anatomy in Florence. At the age of 35, he was appointed lecturer in pathology in the medical school and three years later director of the Institute. He was coeditor of *Revista Italiana di Patologia Generale* of Turin and, from the age of 56 until his death, editor of *Pathologica* of Genoa.

Composite by G. Bako

Banti's contributions to the medical literature were notable in the areas of bacteriology, pathology, and clinical problems. He was one of the first to recognize the dissemination of Eberth's bacillus (*Salmonella typhi*) in the absence of typical intestinal lesions. Cultures of the bacilli were prepared from the spleen and mesentery glands of patients with atypical findings.[2] Banti attributed pathological processes in the kidney to infection, and nephritis was classified according to etiology. In the leukemias he investigated the anatomical structure, differentiating the type orginating primarily in the lymphatic system from that arising from the bone marrow. Banti's most productive researches, however, concerned the spleen and the liver. When serving as assistant at the Pathological Institute and as chief physician at the Florentine Hospital of S. Maria Nuova, he prepared the 70-page monograph on splenic anemia.

The clinical manifestations of chronic congestive splenomegaly as described by Banti were divided into the preasctitic, ascitic, and an intermediate stage. The uncertainty in contemporary hematology of the identification of a specific syndrome is related in part to an unpredictable variation in concentration of circulatory thrombocytes, due to the poor methods available to him for counting. In some cases the thrombocytes are reported to be diminished, in others a normal quantity is recorded. Splenectomy has proved to be beneficial in the thrombocytopenic group; in the others an excess of platelets, following splenectomy, leads to repeated thromboses and critical hemorrhage. Considering his entire series of patients, Banti may have included some cases of Laennec's cirrhosis, even though he attempted to exclude them as well as one or two patients with myeloid me'aplasia, a disease soon to be recognized by his contemporaries.

In the initial communication Banti introduced a brief historical account of splenic anemia, rejected unqualifiedly any leukemic association, and finally discussed the use of whole blood transfusions and surgery in treatment. No attempt was made to differentiate between patients who did or did not benefit from splenectomy. The significance of thrombophlebitis in such disorders was recognized later. The first report contains three protocols, two with autopsy observations.[3]

Splenic Anemia is a disease characterized by progressive oligemia of unknown origin. It causes severe disturbance of all organic functions, edema, irregular fever, and hemorrhage. It usually results in death. It is accompanied by a swelling of the spleen and often of the liver, a phenomenon that is independent from any precedent condition or leukemic alteration of the blood. In brief, splenic anemia is a progressive idiopathic anemia, accompanied by idiopathic hypertrophy of the spleen and often of the liver, without leukemia.

It had been previously noted that, while as a rule in pseudoleukemia the lymph nodes and spleen or the lymph nodes alone are affected, in rarer cases the lymph nodes remain normal and only the spleen becomes hypertrophic. These cases had the closest similarity to splenic leukemia, the only difference being the absence of blood alterations, and were grouped to constitute a particular form of pseudoleukemia that was called "splenic," and called by Greisinger "anemia" or "cachexia splenica."

Banti brought his concept of splenic anemia up to date in 1894. The entire communication is translated in *Medical Classics,* here excerpted.[4]

The symptoms of the pre-ascitic stage are: tumefaction of the spleen and anemia.

The disease sets in with splenic hypertrophy, which progresses in an insidious manner, so that when it is noticed by the patient or his physician, the spleen has usually attained a considerable size. The spleen, though hypertrophied, retains its normal shape.

Anaemic symptoms follow upon tumefaction of the spleen and consist, as a rule, in increasing debility, with pallor of the skin and mucous surfaces, dyspnoea and palpitation consequent upon the slightest effort.

Anaemic murmurs are constantly present in the cardiac region. They are systolic and their maximum intensity is found in the auscultation area of the pulmonary orifice. The diminution in the number of red blood-corpuscles is proportional to the intensity of the anaemia; usually there are from 3 to 4 millions in a cubic millimetre. There is poikilocytosis and microcythaemia. The white blood corpuscles are not increased numerically.

The liver presents no modification in size, and is not tender to pressure. There is no trace whatever of collateral venous circulation on the abdominal walls. . . . In the cases with which I have had to deal, the pre-ascitic stage varied in duration from one year to four years and a half.

The intermediate state is characterized by the appearance of dyspnea, intestinal disorders, and sometimes haemorrhoids. . . . This stage lasts a few months.

In the ascitic stage a liquid effusion takes place into the peritoneum. . . . The liver appears to be smaller than under normal conditions; . . . The anaemic symptoms become more and more marked; but the examination of the blood continues to give evidence of a normal number of leucocytes This stage lasts from seven to eight months and ends in death.

Microscopical examination of the splenic juice shows complete absence of nucleated red corpuscles. In specimens prepared by hardening, the Malpighian corpuscles are found to be sclerotic, being gradually transformed into connective-tissue nodules. The veins of the splenic pulp are contracted. . . . The liver presents macroscopical and microscopical charateristics of Laennec's atrophic cirrhosis, with the exception that the connective-tissue rings are. in general. very small and show marked infliltration of round cells.

In an 1898 communication, discoloration of the skin with urobilinuria is described,

and the anatomical findings in the splenic vein were offered in greater detail.[5]

In the transitional stage the characteristics of the urine change. The quantity decreases, it contains generous urates, urobilin, and frequently traces of gall pigments. The skin and the conjunctiva of the patient take on an icteric coloring.

The portal vein with its ramifications is distended in the ascitic stage but in the transitional stage it is normal. In all cases in which I had a chance to perform an examination with this in mind, I found the intima of the splenic vein and the portal vein, from the orifice of the splenic vein to the liver, covered with rigid, raised platelets which might be diffuse or circumscribed and showed all the characteristics of the atheromatous and sclerotic plates of the aorta. In the transitional stage these thickenings were confined to the veins mentioned while the other branches which emptied into the portal vein were normal; in the ascitic stage they extended also to these branches but in lesser degree.

In the splenic vein we find the lesions of sclerotic endophlebitis. The intima showed non-uniform thickening. It consisted of thick bundles of fibres which were slightly fibrinous or showed hyaline proverty as to cells. One can also find actual atheromatous or calcified foci.

Banti, recognized by his biographer as an unduly shy and bashful person, was not accorded by his contemporaries the honor due a distinguished scientist. A cultured gentleman and master of four languages, he was a popular lecturer who communicated his enthusiasm for scientific investigation and original thinking to his students and associates. Always at ease at the bedside, in the pathology laboratory, or lecture hall, Banti adorned Florentine medicine.

1. Furno, A.: Guido Banti (Ital), F. Martinelli (trans.), *G Clin Med* 6:115-120, 1925.

2. Banti, G.: The Septicemia of Typhoid Fever and the Spread of Pseudo-Typhoid (Ital), *Riforma Med* 10:674-680, 1894.

3. Banti, G.: *Dell'Anemia Splenica* (Ital), Firenze: C. Le Monnier, 1882, excerpt translated by F. Martinelli.

4. Banti, G.: Splenomegaly With Cirrhosis of the Liver (Ital), *Sperimentale* 48:407-432, 1894, translated in *Med Classics* 1:907-912, 1937.

5. Banti, G.: Splenomegaly With Cirrhosis of the Liver (Ger), *Beitr Path Anat* 24:21-33, 1898, translated in *Med Classics* 1:913-927, 1937.

Adolph Von Strümpell
(1853-1925)

ERNEST ADOLPH GUSTAV GOTTFRIED VON STRÜMPELL, born in Neu-Autz, Kurland, in the Baltic Province of Russia, in childhood lived in nearby Dorpat, where his father was professor of philosophy, an intellectual among the Teutonic minority in a Slavic land.[1] Adolph studied philosophy and psychology at Prague before he turned to medicine at Dorpat, where Stieda and von Bergmann were on the faculty. He completed his medical studies at Leipzig with Wunderlich, Thiersch, Credé, and Ludwig. Following graduation in 1875, he served as assistant to Wunderlich in internal diseases, studied in Vienna, and qualified privatdocent at Leipzig, where his medical associates included Wagner, Cohnheim, Weigert, and Erb.

In 1883, Strümpell accepted a call to Heidelberg as professor and director of the Medical Polyclinic and completed his text on internal diseases.[2] The treatise was translated into English four years later by Vickery and Knapp with a preface by F. C. Shattuck.[3] From 1886 to 1903, he was chief of internal medicine at Erlangen and from 1903-1909, at Breslau. He returned to Leipzig in 1910 as successor to Curschmann.

Although his best-known eponym is Marie-Strümpell's disease, a neurological sign carries his name, while descriptions of other clinical entities include pseudosclerosis of the brain (Westphal-Strümpell's disease), a generation later identified by Kinnier Wilson with hepatolenticular degeneration, hereditary spastic spinal paralysis, previously described by Erb and Charcot, and acute encephalitis similar to polioencephalomyelitis in children (Strümpell's disease), each based upon precise clinical observations supplemented by critical analysis of disorders of function.

Rheumatoid spondylitis or spondylitic deformans was rediscovered 15 years later by Pierre Marie, hence, Marie-Strümpell spondylitis. The initial report as part of a discussion of typical peripheral rheumatoid arthritis contained a description of spondylitis in two patients with a question posed as to a different etiology.[3]

The polyarticular form is the characteristic one. In most of the typical cases it begins in the small joints of the hand and fingers. At a later period the larger joints are also invaded, one after the other, the invasion taking place symmetrically on both sides of the body, although the disturbance is not infrequently greater on one side than on the other. In severe cases, the joints of the spinal column are also involved. This impairs particularly the movement of the head. The articulation of the lower jaw is usually very little affected, if at all.

In less frequent instances the arthritis is confined principally to the lower extremities, while the upper escape intact for a long while, or even permanently. It is very possible that such cases often have a different aetiology from ordinary arthritis deformans; and the same is true of the cases which are confined mainly to the vertebral column, and are termed spondylitis deformans. A remarkable and, as it seems to us, unique disorder may be mentioned in passing. It leads very gradually and painlessly to a complete anchylosis of the entire spinal column and the hip-joints, so that head, trunk, and thighs are firmly united and completely stiffened, while all the other joints retain their normal mobility. It need scarcely be said that this necessarily causes a peculiar modification of the carriage and gait of the sufferer. We have ourselves seen two cases of this peculiar affection which resembled each other very closely.

In the 1897 *Deutsche Zeitschrift für Nervenheilkunde,*[4] Strümpell refers to observations reported by Bechterew and notes that he had seen a third patient with chronic ankylosing spondylitis. A 39-year-old farmer who admitted no joint symptom in his arms or hands, complained of a fixed spinal column with the exception of the cervical and the upper dorsal vertebra. An illustration shows the patient with anterior flexion and apparent fixation of the lower dorsal and lumbar vertebrae. The joints of the legs and the feet were unaffected.

Strümpell showed great promise as a violinist in his youth; as an adult he played chamber music and knew outstanding artists of his time. He has been described as a professor who believed that teaching was the most precious contribution to be made in the medical sciences. This belief was implemented by his *Textbook of Medicine,* prepared without collaborators, which enjoyed more than 30 editions, many of which were translated into foreign languages. He displayed a broad interest in general culture, was a keen observer, and differentiated psychogenic elements in nervous disorders from organically related components at a time when the former were largely overlooked.

1. Strümpell, A.: *From the Life of a German Clinician* (Ger), Leipzig: Verlag Von F. C. W. Vogel, 1925.

2. Strümpell, A.: *Textbook of Special Pathology and Therapy of Internal Diseases, Diseases of the Nervous System* (Ger), Leipzig: Verlag Von F. C. W. Vogel, 1884, vol 2.

3. Strümpell, A.: *A Textbook of Medicine for Students and Practitioners,* translated by H. F. Vickery and P. C. Knapp, with editorial notes by F. C. Shattuck, New York: D. Appleton & Co., 1887.

4. Strümpell, A.: Observations on the Chronic Ankylosing Inflammation of the Vertebral Column and the Hip Joint (Ger), *Deutsch Z Nervenheilk* 11: 338-342, 1897, excerpt translated by E. Longar.

William Forsyth Milroy (1855-1942)

W. F MILROY, native of New York city and a member of the faculty of Omaha Medical College for almost 50 years, described noninfectious hereditary elephantiasis—a contribution recognized by Osler in eponymic identification in his 8th edition of *Principles and Practice of Medicine*. Milroy attended

National Library of Medicine

the University of Rochester for undergraduate education and received one year of medical training at Johns Hopkins University. Subsequently, he entered the College of Physicians and Surgeons of Columbia University with the class of 1883, and qualified for the degree of doctor of medicine in the fall of 1882.[1] He defended his thesis on acute lobular pneumonia in children before Francis Delafield, who represented the faculty. Milroy's internship was served at New York City Hospital, with further training as resident physician in the Charity and Maternity Hospitals in New York city. In 1884, he journeyed west and established practice in Omaha, where he became demonstrator of anatomy in the recently organized medical college. The following year he was appointed professor of histology, pathology, and lecturer on hygiene. In 1891, Milroy advanced to hold the chair of clinical medicine through the reorganization into the Nebraska College of Medicine in 1901. He retired as professor emeritus and in 1933 left Nebraska to spend his final years in California.

Milroy was a prolific writer for his day and environment. The subjects discussed by him included: cryptogenetic pyemia, mortality from diseases of the kidneys and circulatory system, auscultatory percussion and valvular lesions of the heart, therapeutic value of bed rest, rectal anesthesia, the use of strychnine in pulmonary tuberculosis, hemorrhage from the gastrointestinal tract, abscess of the liver, and epidemic typhoid fever in Omaha. His best-known contribution described chronic edema of the legs in six generations of an afflicted family. The findings were presented at the 24th annual session of the Nebraska State Medical Society in May, 1892, and to the Society of the Alumni of Charity Hospital, New York City, a few weeks later. His report was published in the *New York Medical Journal* near the close of the year; however, in the interim and unknown to Milroy, Nonne of Hamburg, Germany, had described in Virchow's *Archiv* four cases of congenital hereditary elephantiasis in a family traced through four generations.[2]

Milroy's propositus, a 31-year-old clergyman and one-time missionary in India, provided genealogic identification of 97 individuals in six generations. Unilateral or bilateral edema was recognized in 22. The condition entered the family about 1768. The edema was painless, pitted on pressure, was not associated with other physical abnormalities and did not influence longevity. When the malady was well developed, the overlying skin presented a slightly rosy hue; the persistent swelling did not extend above the knee, and there was no tendency to ulceration and no associated varicosities. Edema was present from birth in the patients examined. As the afflicted matured, the edematous parts assumed the same size relationship to the remainder of the body. Milroy deplored the lack of a reference library in Omaha necessary for a literature search for similar cases. Instead, he brought his observations to the attention of his former teacher, Delafield in New York, and W. H. Welch of Baltimore.[3]

The newness of the city and consequent dearth of medical libraries in Omaha is a serious obstacle in the way of the study of pathological and other questions here, and inasmuch as the literature at my command furnished no aid to an understanding of this case, I wrote an incomplete account of it to Professor Francis Delafield, of New York, and also to Professor William H. Welch, of Baltimore.

1. So far as known, in every case, with two exceptions only, the oedema was present at birth.

2. The location of the oedema has in every case been limited to one or both lower extremities.

3. The presence of the oedema is persistent, never having been known to disappear, temporarily or permanently, except in one instance.

4. It has never been attended by constitutional symptoms, barring the two possible exceptional cases in which its first appearance was subsequent to birth.

From these considerations it seems evident that the case under discussion is not one of angeio-neurotic oedema, nor would it seem probable from the history that any functional neurosis could be responsible for the oedema.

It is proper to say in this connection that the account of the case upon which Professor Welch based his suggestion as to diagnosis was too fragmentary to admit a fair judgment of it.

Milroy was a member of the Board of Trustees of Omaha Medical College, a member of the American College of Physicians, and an honorary member of Alpha Omega Alpha Society of the College of Medicine, University of Nebraska. He served as president of the Omaha-Douglas County Medical Society in 1890 and president of the Nebraska Medical Association in 1916.

1. Tyler, A. F., and Auerbach, E. F.: *History of Medicine in Nebraska*, Omaha: Magic City Printing Co., 1928.

2. Nonne, M.: Four Cases of Congenital Hereditary Elephantiasis (Ger), *Arch path Anat* 125:189-196, 1891.

3. Milroy, W. F.: An Undescribed Variety of Hereditary Oedema, *New York Med J* 56:505-508 (Nov 5) 1892.

Sir James Mackenzie
(1853-1925)

JAMES MACKENZIE, master in the art of clinical observation, and especially of cardiovascular dysfunction, was born into a humble but proud family in the Highlands in Scone, Perthshire, the ancient coronation place of Scottish kings. He attended Perth Academy, with an uneventful scholastic record, and for a time was apprenticed to a chemist-pharmacist. At the age of 21, he left the apprenticeship to study medicine at the University of Edinburgh, where he received the MD degree in 1882. After a year as house physician in the Edinburgh Royal Infirmary he began the practice of general medicine, surgery, and obstetrics in Burnley, Lancashire; there he remained for more than one quarter of a century.[1]

A self-trained investigator, lacking the status of a university appointment or the facilities of a research laboratory, Mackenzie explored the mechanism of referred pain and cardiac arrhythmias with commonplace devices. He relied upon superbly-developed sensory perception and a cumbersome polygraph, later replaced by an ink polygraph, for interpreting the pulse waves in the neck and wrist. At the time, he was unaware that Potain in France and Riegel in Germany were engaged in similar pursuits. His general cultural interests and the persistent demands upon his clinical talents made the stolen hours for clinical investigation particularly precious. Nevertheless, Mackenzie contributed regularly to the scientific literature. Even while engaged in general practice in Burnley he found time to prepare his first monograph, *The Study of the Pulse*,[2] in which he distinguished the benign from the critical irregularities of the heart.

Destined to become an international clinical cardiologist, it is surprising to find Mackenzie content to remain so long in a community which lacked the amenities of the capital city. In time, but not until the age of 54, did he move to the medical center of England, and later open an office on Harley Street, London. His fame following the publication of his second monograph, *Diseases of the Heart*,[3] prompted this decision. Then followed in rapid succession such recognition as fellowship in the Royal College of Physicians, fellowship in the Royal Society, and knighthood. Mount Vernon Hospital was Mackenzie's first institutional appointment in London; and, in 1913, he transferred to the London Hospital, assuming charge of the cardiac ward and outpatient department. Immediately following World War I, Mackenzie abandoned cardiac consultation to return to general practice at St. Andrews. There he established an Institute for Clinical Research. As if to compensate other physicians for deficiencies early in his own investigative career, he provided research facilities for a young staff that would have been Utopian for his clinical studies half a century earlier.

Mackenzie, a versatile writer, prepared almost a dozen monographs, some with editions and translations into foreign languages and seemed to be forever searching for broad scientific principles on which to base an understanding of nature. His treatises included *The Basis of Vital Activity, Symptoms and Their Interpretation, Angina Pectoris, Principles of Diagnosis and Treatment in Heart Affections, Heart Disease and Preg-*

nancy and *The Future of Medicine.* A complete bibliography of his writings and a short summary of each of his communications to scientific periodicals was prepared by Montieth shortly after his death.[4] Excerpts from three of the clinical contributions have been selected. Working with pulse wave tracings of disordered rhythms of the heart, Mackenzie attempted to define participation of the heart chambers in the pathogenesis of extra systoles. He observed the failure of the palpating finger to detect the small radial impulse from an early occurring systole; it was assumed the heart had either skipped a beat or had propagated a wave too slight to be felt.[2]

What usually happens is that the ventricle has made a premature systole, but the force has been so small that it has not been able to overcome the pressure in the aorta and open the aortic valves, or that having done so, the wave of blood sent forth has not been of sufficient strength to be felt by the finger. . . . If the heart is auscultated there will be heard the two short, sharp sounds, as already described, occurring at the beginning of the long pause, and caused by the rapid premature systole of the ventricle. When the apex beat is absent the presence of these sounds will often reveal the true nature of the delay in the pulse. Occasionally, however, it happens that the ventricular systole has not sufficient strength to raise the aortic valves, and then only the faint, muffled sound may be detected corresponding to the first sound. Sometimes even this may be absent.

As early as 1890 Mackenzie recognized the irregularity, later known as auricular fibrillation, to be a distinguishable abnormality in heart disease, and furthermore, proved this premise with simultaneous recording of the jugular and radial pulses. One of his patients in Burnley, suffering from rheumatic valvular heart disease, lost her presystolic murmur as the disease worsened; concomitantly the rhythm became irregular, presumably from failure of auricular activity. At autopsy the auricles were dilated and lacked contractile power. Mackenzie identified the disturbance as paralysis of the auricle and attributed the arrhythmia to nodal rhythm, ie, an impulse originating from an ectopic source and proceeding through the auriculoventricular node which had taken over the function of the sinoauricular node. Although Mackenzie did not live to realize the soundness of his initial views on auricular fibrillation, his recounting of the pathogenesis remains valid after temporarily losing favor to the circus-movement postulate. His reasoning and initial incorrect conclusion, as well as tributes to his associate Cushny and pupil Thomas Lewis, are recounted.[3]

With this fact before me, I saw that my previous explanation [nodal rhythm] could not be correct; for the fact that the auricles were hypertrophied, indicated that they must have contracted during the years that I had watched them, and when there had been an absence of all signs of auricular activity. As it was clear that the auricles could not have contracted during the normal period—that is to say, immediately before ventricular systole—the only alternative I could see was that they contacted during ventricular systole. . . . As at this time I could not conceive of any other possibility to explain the facts, I suggested that the stimulus for contraction arose in the auriculoventricular node; and I called the condition "nodal rhythm," under which name the clinical aspects of auricular fibrillation are described in the two editions of this book, the first being published in 1908.

Cushny was the first to suggest that auricular fibrillation might be a factor of clinical importance; and in 1906 he and Edmonds drew attention to the resemblance of the radial tracings in a case of paroxysmal irregularity in the human subject to the tracings from a dog, in which they produced experimental fibrillation of the auricles. On reading this communication, I was struck with the idea; and on a visit Professor Cushny paid to me in Burnley in 1906, he discussed with me the probability of auricular fibrillation being the cause of the irregular heart action in certain cases of "nodal rhythm," and he agreed that certain small waves, which I had recognized in the jugular pulse of one case . . . were due to the fibrillation of the auricle.

I published, in 1907, tracings with this explanation, but I failed to appreciate the real significance of what auricular fibrillation was; I thought it only a passing event; and I practically gave up the idea that it was at the bottom of these cases that went on for years. Lewis had been pursuing an inquiry clinically and by experiment into the nature of cardic irregularities, and had produced experimental fibrillation in the dog. In 1909 he took graphic records of the venous and arterial pulses. With the onset of fibrillation, he found that the arterial pulse became irregular, and the venous pulse changed from the auricular to the ventricular form. Pursing his investigations further, Lewis was able to detect in the electrocardiogram of experimentally produced fibrillation, certain oscillations during ventricular diastole, which were induced by the fibrillating auricle.

Examining more critically the electrocardiograms of typical cases of nodal rhythm which I sent to him, he found these oscillations also present, and demonstrated their correspondence with the small fibrillation waves I had noted in the jugular pulse.

When Lewis placed these facts before me, I had no hesitation in abandoning my views, and accepting the fact that these cases owed their abnormal action to auricular fibrillation; and I now recognize that the reason those evidences of auricular activity, to which I have referred, disappear, is because the auricle ceases to act as a contracting chamber.

A study of referred pain and particularly peripheral somatic distress from cardiac dysfunction was of less significance but was carried on simultaneously with the investigation of arrhythmias. The relation of herpetic eruption to the peripheral distribution of posterior nerve roots suggested to Mackenzie, as it did to others, that each viscus was innervated sufficiently to be capable of causing referred pain when subject to stress. The physiological doctrines of Mackenzie are defined in *Symptoms and Their Interpretation* (1909); his conclusions are summarized in a valedictory monograph, *Angina Pectoris*. His interpretation of anginal pain remains valid, if we accept his term, "primary angina pectoris," distinguishing it from "secondary angina pectoris" which carries a good prognosis. Anginal pain was thought to be caused by contraction of compromised cardiac muscle which, in relaying sensation to the appropriate segments of the spinal cord, leads to pain or hyperesthesia over predicted somatic areas, viscerosensory and visceromotor reflexes.[5]

As all muscular organs are capable of producing pain, and as the heart is a muscular organ, it was reasoned that the pain is due to the contraction of the muscle under such conditions as produce pain in other organs. This suggested a line of inquiry which resulted in demonstrating that pain arises when a muscle is made to contract while the supply of blood is deficient. There was found a definite class of hearts which give rise to pain when the blood supply to the muscle is defective on account of narrowing or obliteration of the coronary artery, or when the heart muscle is so damaged that it is unequal to the task of maintaining an efficient circulation, so that in its endeavour to do this it becomes exhausted and pain results.

The appellation, "The Beloved Physician," also a title of one of his biographies and a phrase which might be applied to many clinicians, was richly deserved by Mackenzie. The patient was to him the fulcrum on which the known and unknown in clinical cardiology were delicately balanced. He was an inveterate worker, equally at ease in the general hospital of an industrial community, a teaching clinic in a great London hospital, or in a research laboratory in a small university society. The many honors bestowed upon him failed to change his discerning but kind personality, to dampen a lifelong zeal in pursuing clinical investigation, or to suppress an outgoing sympathy for the sick. Mackenzie advanced the art and science of cardiology in the generation immediately prior to the development of the electrocardiograph. After his time, the string galvanometer confirmed his hypothesis or contributed to the understanding of phenomena not susceptible to analysis by the senses of the physician aided by simple devices.

1. Wilson, R. N.: *The Beloved Physician, Sir James Mackenzie,* London: J. Murray, 1926.

2. Mackenzie, J.: *The Study of the Pulse,* Edinburgh: Y. J. Pentland, 1902.

3. Mackenzie, J.: *Diseases of the Heart,* ed 3, London: H. Frowde, 1913.

4. Montieth, W. B. R.: *Bibliography with Synopsis of the Original Papers of the Writings of Sir James Mackenzie,* London: Oxford University Press, 1930.

5. Mackenzie, J.: *Angina Pectoris,* London: H. Frowde, 1923.

Augustus Desire Waller
(1856-1922)

AUGUSTUS D. WALLER, one of the founders of modern electrocardiography, was born in Paris. There his father, the distinguished English physiologist and physician, who described the degeneration of nerve fibers when separated from their cells (Wallerian degeneration), was engaged in physiological research. Young Waller attended the Collège de Genève. Following the death of his father in 1870, he moved with his mother to Aberdeen, Scotland, where he matriculated at the university.[1] He graduated MB and CM in 1878 and MD in 1881. His postgraduate work, which began under Burdon-Sanderson in physiology at University College, London, was supported periodically by special grants from the British Medical Association.

Composite by G. Bako

Waller's first teaching appointment was that of lecturer on physiology at the London School of Medicine for Women in 1883; three years later he accepted a similar position at St. Mary's Hospital, where his most outstanding work was done. Finally, in 1902, he was appointed director of the Physiological Laboratory of London University. Sustained by substantial donations for equipment and maintenance from his wife's family, Waller designed the laboratory with a dual purpose. Advanced students were offered opportunities for independent research, and established physiologists were provided a forum for presentation of pertinent observations from their current investigations. Although Waller had only limited experience in the full-time practice of medicine, he was a consultant at Westmoreland Street Heart Hospital (National Hospital for Diseases of the Heart).

Throughout Waller's career, each of his important investigations explored phys-

iological unknowns with clinical implications. His first physiological studies dealt with hemodynamics. Later he quantitated the action of ether and chloroform anesthesia, finding that the percentage of inhaled chloroform vapor was more critical than the total dose administered. Waller utilized electrical methods for the study of emotional states and concluded that anticipation of pain exceeded the critical awareness when pain appeared. Determination of the physiological cost of muscular work, as measured by the volume of expired carbon dioxide, constituted one of his later researches. His most important contribution was the discovery that currents established by the beat of the heart could be recorded from the surface of the intact animals or men—a graphic demonstration of the seduction of the electrical potential of the heart through contact electrodes.

In working with isolated contracting hearts, Waller observed that at the inception of contraction a point of high e'ectrical potential developed at the base of the heart, while the myocardium at the apex was electrically negative. It was assumed that a current in moving from an area of high potential to an area of low potential should be susceptible to measurement by an electrometer or a similar device. Since Waller assumed the heart in the supine man to be positioned diagonally across the midline, with the base directed toward the right upper extremity, leads from selected regions of the body should reflect the difference in potential. The body was divided into lateral halves by an imaginary line from the mouth to the feet. With one electrode of an electrometer in the mouth and the other in the right hand, a weak response was obtained. However, when one electrode recorded from the left hand and the other from the mouth, the response was strong, signifying a measurable difference in potential. The positions of several leads were described in the original report of 1887, including mouth to back and one or both hands to feet. The first electrocardiogram on a human was described as follows.[2]

If a pair of electrodes (zinc covered by chamois leather and moistened with brine) are strapped to the front and back of the chest, and connected with a Lippmann's capillary electrometer, the mercury in the latter will be seen to move slightly but sharply at each beat of the heart. If the movements of the column of mercury are photographed on a travelling plate simultaneously with those of an ordinary cardiographic lever a record is obtained as under (fig 1) in which the upper line *h.h.* indicates the heart's movements and the lower line *e.e.* the level of the mercury in the capillary. Each beat of the heart is seen to be accompanied by an electrical variation.

The first and chief point to determine is whether or no the electrical variation is physiological, and not due to a mechanical alteration of contact between the electrodes and the chest wall caused by the heart's impulse. To ascertain this point accurate time-measurements are necessary; a physiological variation should precede the movement of the heart, while this could not be the case if the variation were due to altered contact. Fig 2 is an instance of such time-measurements taken at as high a speed of the travelling surface as may be used without rendering the initial points of the curves too indeterminate. It shows that the electrical phenomenon begins a little before the cardiographic lever begins to rise. The difference of time is however very small, only about .025", and this amount must further be diminished by .01" which represents the "lost time" of the cardiograph. The actual difference is thus no greater than .015", and the record is therefore, although favourable to the physiological interpretation, not conclusively satisfactory.

That a true electrical variation of the human heart is demonstrable, may further be proved beyond doubt by leading off from the body otherwise than from the chest wall. If the two hands or one hand and one foot be plunged into two dishes of salt solution connected with the two sides of the electrometer, the column of mercury will be seen to move at each beat of the heart, though less than when electrodes are strapped to the chest. The hand and foot act in this case as leading off electrodes from the heart, and by taking simultaneous records of these movements of the mercury and of the movements of the heart it is seen that the former correspond with the latter, slightly preceding them and not succeeding them, as would be the case if they depended upon pulsation in the hand or foot. This is unquestionable proof that the variation is physiological, for there is here of course no possibility of altered contact at the chest wall, and any mechanical alteration by arterial pulsation could only produce an effect .15" to .20" after the cardiac impulse. A similar result is obtained if an electrode be placed in the mouth while one of the extremities serves as the other leading off electrode. The electrical variation precedes the heart's beat as in the other cases mentioned.

Among Waller's personal interests were a friendship for a bulldog kept at his side in the laboratory, a desire to drive that strange contraption, an automobile, and a readiness to display his skill as an orator. His recorded declamations included the Croonian lectures before the Royal Society in 1896, the Hitchcock lectures at the University of California in 1909, and in 1913, both the Oliver-Sharpey lectures before the Royal College of Physicians of London, and the Harvey lecture before the New York Academy of Medicine. Waller served the Royal Institution as Fullerian Professor for one year, was elected a member of the Royal Society as his father had been before him, received the honorary LLD from the University of Edinburgh in 1905, and was recognized by many foreign learned societies. Other honors included Lauréat of the Institute of France and the Aldini prize of the Royal Academy of Science of the Institute of Bologna, given for his work on the electromatic action of the human heart.

1. Augustus D. Waller, M.D., LLD., F.R.S., obituary, *Brit Med J* 1:458-459 (March 18) 1922.
2. Waller, A. D.: A Demonstration on Man of Electromotive Changes Accompanying the Heart's Beat, *J Physiol* 8:229-234, 1887.

Willem Einthoven (1860-1927)

WILLEM EINTHOVEN, physiologist, physicist, and physician, developed the string galvanometer, which has proved to be one of the important instruments in the diagnosis and treatment of heart disease in modern medicine. The first description of the string galvanometer, designed for recording of heart potentials, was published early in this century. Each successive decade has witnessed increasing application of the basic design and its physical evolution beyond the initial clinical value in the diagnosis and management of maladies of the heart.

Willem Einthoven was born in Semarang, Java, Indonesia, where his father was practicing medicine. After his father's death, his mother and siblings settled in Utrecht, Holland, where Willem entered the university and graduated with an MD degree in 1885. Before graduation, he engaged in limited physiological investigation; whereas after graduation he ventured into private practice for a short period. But he was destined for an academic life and, once committed, remained at his post as professor of physiology at the University of Leyden until his death.

Composite by G. Bako

There were other physicists or physiologists who preceded Einthoven in the study of techniques of measurement of currents, graphic registration of heart sounds, and recording of potentials of the heart.[1] Matteucci of Italy, a biophysicist, observed the emanation of electrical forces from a pigeon's heart in 1843. This phenomenon was confirmed by von Kölliker and Müller in Germany, who recorded the electrical current from the contraction of the frog's heart when an exposed nerve, or a nerve-muscle preparation, was placed on the pulsating myocardium. In 1878, Burdon-Sanderson and Page in England, using the Lippmann capillary electrometer, recorded the heart beat on a sensitized photographic plate. In 1887, Waller showed that the action currents of the heart could be recorded from an intact animal by surface electrodes or leads. Two years later this procedure was applied by Waller to man. Einthoven was the first to adopt the term "electrocardiogram" and to recognize the spatial relationship of the action potentials spreading through the myocardial mass.

The capillary electrometer served a useful purpose in the development of the galvanometer, but its value was limited by the inertia of the mercury and the absence of precision or accurate determination of the time and strength of the excursion.[2]

Einthoven began his studies with the basic design of the d'Arsonval galvanometer, then proceeded to the string galvanometer, which had a fixed magnet and a fine wire suspended vertically between the poles of the magnet. With a strong magnetic field, a thin wire, and an optical projection system of high magnification, the string galvanometer came into being—the second major step in the development of clinical electrocardiography. In addition to designing the instrument, Einthoven adopted separate leads, paired the three sets of adjacent angles of an equilateral triangle, and calculated the line of the heart's electrical axis from the resulting curves. The galvanometer, modified for cardiography, was first described in 1901.[3]

The instrument of which we are going to speak in these pages and which might be called a "string galvanometer" will be of service principally in electrophysiological research. In examining the electrical phenomena of muscles, glands, nerves, sense organs—in short, of nearly all the tissues and the living organs—one must keep in mind their great resistance. Insofar as the electromotive forces produced are rather weak, it is usually necessary to use galvanometers that are very sensitive and that possess a great internal resistance, so that currents of 10^{-9} and 10^{-10} amperes may be measured.

What we proposed to do in constructing the string galvanometer was to combine a sensitivity suitable for electrophysiological measurements with a high rate of excursion. The instrument is composed primarily of a mobile conductor, that is, a string, stretched in a suitable manner between the poles of an electromagnet. It will be easier to explain the reasons which led us to construct this instrument by beginning with the present form of the Deprez-d'Arsonval galvanometer and by observing how it could be improved.

In 1903, Einthoven reported on the galvanometeric registration of the human electrocardiogram in the *Proceedings of the Royal Academy of Amsterdam*. The report was expanded and appeared in Pflüger's *Archiv* in the same year.[1]

Up to the present time, the human electrocardiogram discovered by Aug. D. Waller could be recorded only by means of the capillary-electrometer. Simple inspection of the curve inscribed by means of this instrument results in an entirely fallacious representation of the variations of potential, which, as a matter of fact, actually existed. If one desires accurate values of the latter, the form of the registered curve must be corrected for the size of the capillary tube used, the degree of magnification, and the speed of the photosensitive plate. By this method one arrives at the construction of a new curve, the outline of which actually represents the variations of potential.

What holds true for the electrocardiogram, also, in general, holds true for any other curve obtained by the capillary-electrometer, if one wishes to reproduce different changes in potential as occurring rather rapidly. One is obliged in both instances, regardless of the method employed, to construct a new curve from the one originally inscribed, whereby accurate measurements can be determined, which are chiefly concerned with different calculations.

I have sought a method in which, so far as possible, the construction of a new curve could be avoided, and finally, to offer an instrument which primarily would satisfy the requirements of inscribing the electrocardiogram of human beings in approximately, at least, its correct proportions.

This instrument—the string galvanometer—is essentially composed of a thin silver-coated quartz filament, which is stretched like a string, in a strong magnetic field. When an electric current is conducted through this quartz filament, the filament reveals a movement which can be observed and photographed by means of considerable magnification. This movement is similar to the movements of the mercury contained in the capillary-electrometer. It is possible to regulate the sensitivity of the galvanometer very accurately within broad limits by tightening or loosening the string.

In this communication, the letters P, Q, R, S, and T of the electrocardiogram were used, and the three standard leads were described. The P wave was recognized as an expression of atrial action and the Q, R, S, and T complexes reflected ventricular action. Einthoven's triangle became the fundamental basis for electrocardiographic interpretation. He did not use the vacuum tube for amplification since transistors were not available in his time. On the other hand, the cathode ray oscilloscope was based upon his fundamental observations.

Although he pioneered in the study of the abnormal heart and in the registering of heart sounds in the sick,[4] Einthoven left the utilization of this instrument to the cli-

nician; he was more concerned with tachycardia and arrhythmias than with other clinical problems. Sir Thomas Lewis, in London, was one of the first to seize upon the practical application of the electrocardiogram, and, under his brilliant guidance, clinical electrophysiology was established. However, the most important advances were made by later investigators in their studies of myocardial diseases, including ischemia and infarction, in particular.

Einthoven developed no special school as such of pupils, assistants, or associates, but rather he opened his laboratory to investigators from near and far who came to study with him. He has been described as a sincere but direct person; he displayed a child-like humor and experienced great joy from his laboratory work and home life alike. The Royal Society of London elected him a foreign member. He received the Nobel prize in medicine in 1924 and was notified of this honor while delivering the Edward K. Dunham lectures at the Harvard Medical School. In accepting the Nobel prize in Stockholm, Einthoven acknowledged that further understanding of cardiac function and cardiac diseases through use of the string galvanometer was probably a contribution second only to that of Harvey in describing the circulation of blood.

1. Einthoven, W.: The Galvanometric Registration of the Human Electrocardiograms, Likewise a Review of the Use of Capillary-Electrometer in Physiology, *Arch ges Physiol* 99:472-480, 1903, in Willius, F. A., and Keys, T. E.: *Cardiac Classics*, St. Louis: C. V. Mosby, 1941.

2. Gottlieb, L. S.: Willem Einthoven, M.D., Ph.D., 1860-1927, *Arch Int Med* 107:447-449, 1961.

3. Einthoven, W.: A New Galvanometer (Ger), *Arch Neerl Sci Exact Natur* 6:625-633, 1901, excerpt translated by L. Woods.

4. Einthoven, W.: The Registering of the Human Heart Sound by Means of the Galvanometer (Ger), *Arch ges Physiol* 117:461-472, 1907.

Louis Henri Vaquez (1860-1936)

H. VAQUEZ, favorite pupil of Potain and master of clinical cardiology, was born in Paris into a family of silk merchants. He studied at the lycée Condorcet and began his medical training as intern in the hospitals of Paris in 1884.[1] He was early interested in the diseases of the heart and circulation, and, before he had reached academic maturity, he had described in a patient on Potain's service at Charité a special form of

Composite by G. Bako

persistent polycythemia, associated neither with the cyanosis of high altitude nor with congenital heart disease.

Vaquez was appointed physician to the hospitals of Paris in 1895 and became professor agrégé in 1898; but not until 1918 was he promoted to full professor on the faculty. During his long association with San-Antoine hospital, and into his retiring years while on the staff of la Pitié, he studied many clinical subjects. These included sphygmomanometry, the peripheral pulse, nephritis, hypertension and partial adrenalectomy in advanced cases, pheochromocytoma, phlebitis, paroxysmal hemoglobinuria, eclampsia, eosinophilia, erythromelalgia, pleurisy, anemia and other aspects of hematology, chloride metabolism in cardiac failure, Stokes-Adams syndrome, administration of cardiac drugs including strophanthin and ouabain, the theory of the aortic site of anginal pain as opposed to the coronary arteries, and the value of phenylhydrazine in the treatment of polycythemia vera.

Vaquez was one of the first cardiologists in France to utilize the electrocardiograph, collaborated with Bordet in the preparation of a monograph on practical contributions of orthodiagraphy of the heart and great vessels, and extended the observations of Velpeau and Babinski on the association of aortitis and luetic tabes, later known as the Babinski-Vaquez syndrome. The Academy of Medicine of Paris elected him to membership in 1919. Diego Rivera included him in the second of a pair of murals in the Institute of Cardiology in Mexico City, which portrays many of the great contemporary cardiologists.

Vaquez was a prolific writer. He edited the *Archives of the Maladies of the Heart* (Paris) from 1908 to his death and prepared several monographs. The two most important were *Arrhythmias,* which appeared in 1911; while his great text, *Maladies of the Heart,* published in 1921 and translated into English by Laidlaw, was recognized internationally as an outstanding contribution.[2]

Osler-Vaquez disease, described by Vaquez in 1892 (redescribed, in fact, almost rediscovered and called "true polycythemia" by Osler a decade later in the belief he had made an original observation), surely had been observed at some earlier time if not identified as an entity. In the discussion of a special form of cyanosis which accompanies persistent polycythemia, Vaquez mentions similar symptoms associated with residence at high altitudes and patients with congenital heart disease. Hyperactivity of the hematopoietic system was one pathogenic mechanism proposed. Excerpts are as follows:[3]

In order to explain this curious phenomenon of the increase in the number of the red cells, the writers have suggested that it is either the simple effect of the concentration of the blood by the loss of serum or an exaggerated production of red cells by physiological or pathological hyperactivity of the hematopoietic tissue.

The case to which we refer is that of a patient admitted on several occasions on the service of our chief, Professor Potain, and which we have been able to study for two years. This patient, aged 40 years, has never noted any disease, any distress in walking, any shortness of breath, any palpitation, until ten years ago. In 1870, he took part in the campaign, was made prisoner in Germany and endured all the hardship and fatigue of captivity without noticing anything abnormal in his health. Ten years ago, when he was not subjected to any excessive work, he noticed that his extremities became progressively blue, that his veins were filled throughout his entire body, and then followed slowly shortness of breath and palpitations of the heart. At the same time, the functions of his stomach became feeble, dyspeptic phenomena appeared with distress in the right hypochondrium; the patient caught cold more easily and could scarcely get rid of a persistent bronchial catarrh. He remained in this condition until three years ago. At this time, attacks of vertigo commenced to appear, corresponding exactly to the vertigo of Mènière, with buzzing, then whistling in the right ear, a sensation of suffering with turning of objects and vomiting, without loss of consciousness. This time also the gums of the patient were tumefied, became fungoid, bleeding at the slightest contact. When we examine him we find that we are dealing with a man afflicted with a chronic cyanosis, without a trace of edema, with considerable dilation of the veins, with an intense redness of the face, marked injection of the conjunctiva, the whole caused probably in the absence of any other plausible hypothesis, by a congenital lesion of the heart which in any event does not give any certain sign on auscultation. Examination of the blood made by us at this time showed the surprising figure of 8,900,000 red cells, that of the white cells remaining practically normal for this proportion.

Another phenomenon already appreciable for two years, but much plainer at the present moment, strikes us; this was the marked increase in volume of the liver (about 20 cm. on the mammary line) and of the spleen (24 cm.).

For our part we would be inclined to believe that there was a functional hyperactivity of the hematopoietic organs, as the excessive size of the liver and spleen proves. This hyperactivity is not present in all patients suffering from chronic cyanosis.

1. Clerc, A.: Necrology of M. Henri Vaquez (Fr), *Bull Acad Med* 115:685-695, 1936.

2. Vaquez, L. H.: *Maladies of the Heart* (Fr), Paris: J.-B. Baillière, 1921, in Laidlaw, G. F. (trans.-ed.): *Dieases of the Heart*, Philadelphia: W. B. Saunders Co., 1924.

3. Vaquez, L. H.: The Special Form of Cyanosis Accompanying Persistent Hyperglobulinemia (Fr), *C R Soc Biol (Paris)* 44:384-388, 1892, in Major, R. H. (trans.): *Classic Descriptions of Disease*, Springfield, Ill: C. C Thomas, 1932.

Composite by G. Bako

James B. Herrick (1861-1954)

THE "FOREMOST CLINICAL CARDIOLOGIST OF THE MIDWEST IN HIS DAY" was a true son of the prairie whose love for teaching, native ability, and clinical curiosity earned for him this mythical title. James Bryan was born in Oak Park, Ill, a community to which his maternal grandfather traveled overland in a covered wagon, having migrated from England to the United States. He attended the Oak Park High School and the Rock River Seminary at Mount Morris, Ill; liberal arts training was received at the University of Michigan, where he came under the influence of M. C. Tyler, colonial historian and student of Chaucer. This influence has been cited as an important force in Herrick's literary interests, medical and nonmedical, in his professional years.[1] Herrick returned to Illinois, taught school at Peoria and Oak Park, and began the part-time study of medicine at Rush Medical College in 1885, graduating MD in 1888. He served an internship at the Cook County Hospital, followed by private practice in Chicago and teaching at the Presbyterian Hospital, in academic affiliation with his alma mater. He engaged in general practice for a time, but his interests and skill, supplemented by exposure to some of the outstanding medical teachers in central Europe, seemed most suited to a consulting practice in internal medicine. And this was his destiny—to work particularly in diseases of the cardiovascular system. A description of sickle-cell anemia and the clinical conditions of coronary vascular disease are his two outstanding contributions to the medical literature.

A case report of sickling in a Negro was published in the *Archives of Internal Medicine,* although the name "sickle cell anemia" was not proposed until more than a decade later. The clinical correlation of the physiology and the morbid anatomy of the coronary vessels was published in the *Journal of the American Medical Association* slightly more than 50 years ago. Herrick published, in all, more than 30 communications. The particulars of the sickle cell findings included a six-year history of a patient from Grenada, West Indies, whose symptoms began at the age of ten. During adolescence, the patient complained of weakness, palpitation, and shortness of breath, and suffered from icterus and a purulent otitis. When Herrick saw the patient first at the age of 20, he was described as being well developed, but several stigmata of sickle cell anemia were recorded. The observations included glandular adenopathy, deeply pigmented patches of leukodermatitis on the chest and abdomen, scars on the legs, icteric sclera, and pale mucous membranes. A soft systolic murmur was heard over the base of the heart and a faint systolic murmur at the apex. Neither the spleen nor the liver could be palpated. Examination of the blood revealed a red blood cell count of 2,570,000/cu mm and a white blood cell count of 40,000/ cu mm. The color index was 0.78. Microscopic examination of the blood was described as follows:[2]

The red corpuscles varied much in size, many microcytes being seen and some macrocytes. Polychromatophilia was present. Nucleated reds were numerous, 74 being seen in a count of 200 leukocytes, there being about 5,000 to the c.mm. The shape of the reds was very irregular, but what especially attracted attention was the large number of thin, elongated, sickle-shaped and crescent-shaped forms. These were seen in fresh specimens, no matter in what way the blood was spread on the slide and they were seen also in specimens fixed by heat, by alcohol and ether, and stained with the Ehrlich triacid stain as well as

with control stains. They were not seen in specimens of blood taken at the same time from other individuals and prepared under exactly similar conditions. They were surely not artefacts, nor were they any form of parasite. In staining reactions they were exactly like their neighbors, the ordinary red corpuscles, though many took the stain heavily. In a few of the elongated forms a nucleus was seen. In the fresh specimen where there was a slight current in the blood before it had become entirely quiet, all of the red corpuscles, the elongated forms as well as those of ordinary form, seemed to be unusually pliable and flexible, bending and twisting in a remarkable manner as they bumped against each other or crowded through a narrow space and seeming almost rubber-like in their elastic resumption of the former shape. One received the impression that the flattened red discs might by reason of unusual pliability be rolled up as it were into a long narrow bundle. Once or twice I saw a corpuscle of ordinary form turn in such a way as to be seen on edge, when its appearance was suggestive of these peculiar forms.

With supportive treatment and the use of syrup of iodid of iron, the patient improved. The blood at the time of discharge showed a red blood cell count of 3,900,000/cu mm, a white blood cell count of 15,000/cu mm, and the hemoglobin, 58% of the normal. Nucleated red blood cells and the tendency to an unusual crescent configuration of the red blood cells persisted in smaller numbers. Two years later the patient was seen by Dr. Ernest E. Irons, who reported an effusion in the left knee-joint and attributed it to physical trauma. The morphologic findings in the blood persisted. When the case was reported by Herrick, he recognized the unusual hematologic changes but admitted that a definite diagnosis could not be made. It remained for Huck, Sydensticker, and others to identify the entity as a familial malady among Negroes and for Pauling and associates, by electrophoresis, to identify an abnormal hemoglobin (hemoglobin S). This abnormal moiety was found to be characteristic of hemoglobin of patients with sickle cell anemia, thereby establishing the general principle that molecular abnormality in a single portein may be responsible for a disease entity.[3]

Although by no means the first to describe coronary heart disease, Herrick was vitally interested in this subject and gave one of the best descriptions of overt coronary occlusion and angina pectoris early in this century.[4] In the lead article in *JAMA* for December 7, 1912, he reviewed briefly the literature of the preceding 100 years on the clinical and pathological observations in relation to the physiological and anatomical knowledge of the coronary arteries.[5]

No one at all familiar with the clinical, pathologic or experimental features of cardiac disease can question the importance of the coronaries. The influence of sclerosis of these vessels in the way of producing anemic necrosis and fibrosis of the myocardium, with such possible results as aneurysm, rupture of dilatation of the heart, is well known. So also is the relation of the coronaries to many cases of angina pectoris, and to cardiac disturbances rather indefinitely classed as chronic myocarditis, cardiac irregularities, etc. It must be admitted, also, that the reputation of the descending branch of the left coronary as the artery of sudden death is not undeserved.

But there are reasons for believing that even large branches of the coronary arteries may be occluded—at times acutely occluded—without resulting death, at least without death in the immediate future. Even the main trunk may at times be obstructed and the patient live. It is the object of this paper to present a few facts along this line, and particularly to describe some of the clinical manifestations of sudden yet not immediately fatal cases of coronary obstruction.

Before presenting the clinical features of coronary obstruction, it may be well to consider certain facts that go to prove that sudden obstruction is not necessarily fatal. Such proof is afforded by a study of the anatomy of the normal as well as of the diseased heart, by animal experiment and by bedside experience.

Attempts to group these cases of coronary obstruction according to clinical manifestations must be more or less unsatisfactory, yet, imperfect as the groups are, the cases may be roughly classified.

One group will include cases in which death is sudden, seemingly instantaneous and perhaps painless.

A second group includes those cases in which the attack is anginal, the pain severe, the shock profound and death follows in a few minutes or several minutes at the most.

In a third group may be placed non-fatal cases with mild symptoms. Slight anginal attacks without the ordinary causes (such as walking), perhaps some of the stitch pains in the precordia, may well be due to obstruction of small coronary twigs.

In a fourth group are the cases in which the symptoms are severe, are distinctive enough to enable them to be recognized as cardiac, and in which the accident is usually fatal, but not immediately, and perhaps not necessarily so.

Other clinical conditions discussed by Herrick included typhoid fever, hemophilia of the newborn (his first published communication following graduation), rupture of the urinary bladder, malaria, ainhum, pneumonia, polymyositis, peptic ulcer, lymphatic leukemia, chronic nephritis, ulcerative endocarditis, pulmonary tuberculosis, and rheumatoid arthritis. The respect that he enjoyed as a teacher and physician is reflected in the professional and nonmedical positions for which he was chosen. These were working positions in most instances, for he was willing to allocate a portion of his industry where it would be most effective. Herrick served as president of the following organizations: the Chicago Pathological Society, the Chicago Society of Internal Medicine, the Institute of Medicine of Chicago, the Association of American Physicians, the Society of Medical History of Chicago, and the American Heart Association. He was a lecturer of the Harvey Society of New York in 1931. The honorary master of arts in 1907 and the honorary degree of doctor of laws in 1932 were conferred upon him by the University of Michigan. The Association of American Physicians awarded him the George M. Kober medal in 1930 and the American Medical Association, the Distinguished Service medal in 1939, the second award in its history.

In the humanities a lifelong love for Chaucer led him at the age of 70 to discuss the poet before the Chicago Literary Club. Herrick will be remembered by his students, associates, and patients for his warmth of spirit and clinical acumen at the bedside. History will remember him for the description of sickling in the Negro and the clinical correlation of the form and function, normal and abnormal, of the coronary vessels.

1. Herrick, J. B.: *Memories of Eighty Years,* Chicago: Chicago University Press, 1949.

2. Herrick, J. B.: Peculiar Elongated and Sickle-Shaped Red Blood Corpuscles in a Case of Severe Anemia, *Arch Intern Med* 6:517-521, 1910.

3. Pauling, L.; Itano, H. A.; Singer, S. J.; and Wells, I. C.: Sickle Cell Anemia, A Molecular Disease, *Science* 110:543-548 (Nov 25) 1949.

4. Herrick, J. B.: *A Short History of Cardiology,* Springfield, Ill: Charles C Thomas, 1942.

5. Herrick, J. B.: Clinical Features of Sudden Obstruction of the Coronary Arteries, *JAMA* 59:2015-2020 (Dec 7) 1912.

Composite by G. Bako

Abel Ayerza (1861-1918)

AYERZA'S SYNDROME, one of the few familiar eponymic terms honoring a South American clinician, lacks a published communication by the original observer. This deficiency accentuates several other items which surrounds the clinicopathological description. In 1901, Abel Ayerza studied a case of intractable dusky cyanosis showing extensive sclerosis of the pulmonary vessels on postmortem examination. His observations, reported verbally at the time, were duly recorded and published in detail by his pupil Arrillaga[1] a decade later. In the meantime, Marty associated the cardinal features of the unusual protocol with Ayerza's name.[2]

Ayerza, son of a physician, was born in Buenos Aires, received his secondary education in Colegio del Salvador, studied humanities, and obtained his bachelor's degree at the Jesuit College of San José. In 1880, he registered in the Faculty of Medicine in the National University of Buenos Aires.[3] Ayerza served as an extern at the Women's Hospital de Clinicas. His inaugural thesis, *Clinical Observations,* submitted for the MD degree in 1886, disclosed his fundamental interest in empiric observations in contrast to others' reliance on theories or who considered bibliographic references the final

authority. To strengthen his clinical background and enhance his inclination for teaching, he continued his postgraduate training in Paris, then the preferred medical center for students from Central and South America. He audited the clinics of Potain, the outstanding clinical cardiologist, who relied particularly upon auscultatory skill in clinical examination of the heart and lungs in the era before development of the modern diagnostic techniques of radiology and cardiography. He spent additional time with Pean, the leading surgeon of Paris.

Upon Ayerza's return, he received a staff appointment in the Hospital de Clinicas in Buenos Aires and advanced to professor of clinical medicine in the University faculty by 1897. He served for more than 30 years in the Fourth Ward of the hospital. Ayerza placed the clinical examination in its proper perspective in the care and management of the patient. A carefully elicited history and a detailed physical examination, unhurried and critically performed, was basic to his clinical pedagogy and clinical practice.

Since Ayerza left no written protocol, it is impossible to determine his familiarity with extant examples. After Ayerza, others have filled the bibliographic void, notably Arrillaga's thesis of 1912,[1] his monograph of 1925,[4] and an extended summary by Brenner in 1935.[5] Sclerosis of the pulmonary artery had previously been described by Corvisart in his *Essay on the Diseases and Organic Lesions of the Heart and of the Great Vessels.*[6] In several passages he mentions "purple face, purplish almost black appearance of the skin and lips," without specific reference to any disease entity. After noting a case of calcified pulmonary valves described by Morgagni, Corvisart mentions calcification and narrowing of the pulmonary artery.[6]

It would be necessary to find a combination of several symptoms to diagnose narrowing of the pulmonary valves; it would be necessary to find the color of the skin as dark as an ecchymotic area, marked engorgement of the liver, longstanding edema, and enlargement of the right heart.

The first published association of the cardiopulmonary-vascular dysfunction with

Ayerza seems to be that of Marty of Buenos Aires in 1909. In a thesis presented to the National University of Buenos Aires, entitled *Arterial Pressure in Pulmonary Tuberculosis,* he noted:[2]

Most frequently the lungs influence the venous circulation and also the right ventricle, a possibility in all patients with pulmonary disease. A group of conditions merits special attention, in which the prolonged and persistent action of the lung on the right ventricle causes considerable hypertrophy. Pulmonary cirrhosis, commonly called sclerosis, develops first and is apparent especially in chronic bronchial patients. Eight years ago, Professor Ayerza described this type of patient using the term *black cardiacs.* We have had occasion to see such a case presented during one of the conferences held by Dr. Escudero.

Ayerza's case of 1901 was discussed by Arrillaga, the first of the series presented in his inaugural thesis, entitled *Secondary Sclerosis of the Pulmonary Artery and Its Clinical Findings, (Black Cardiacs).*[1] A 38-year-old male had contracted pneumonia in 1883, which left him susceptible to chronic pulmonary infection. Progressively severe edema and dyspnea began a decade before his death. Two months before death, he became bedridden. On physician examination at the last admission, he was cyanotic and edematous. It was impossible to outline the border of the heart by percussion because of advanced pulmonary emphysema. The heart sounds were weak on auscultation. The pulse was regular and the rate 112 per minute. The blood pressure was 150/? mm Hg. The red blood cell count ranged between 5.2 million/cu mm and 7.0 million/cu mm. The white blood cell count was 5,250/cu mm. Postmortem examination showed the pulmonary vessels markedly sclerotic. The heart weighed 480 gm; the right chambers were thickened. The orifice of the tricuspid valve was normal.

Eleven cases of pulmonary sclerosis were presented by Arrillaga. The principal symptoms were low-grade pulmonary infection, dyspnea at rest, somnolence, intense cyanosis, polycythemia, pulmonary hypertension, hypertrophy of the right heart, and dilation of the pulmonary artery as judged radiographically. Aberrant mediastinal venous compression was thought to be the signif-

icant condition to be excluded in the differential diagnosis. Excerpts follow.[1]

The black cardiac is a relatively young individual; the majority are approximately 40 years of age. Pulmonary symptoms begin either with or without antecedent pneumonia and are followed by eight to twenty years of persistent cough, mucous expectoration, and congestive bronchitis.

The characteristic pathology of the black cardiac resides in the lesions of the pulmonary artery and the alterations in the right ventricle secondary to a chronic pulmonary process.

There is nothing in the course of chronic bronchitis or emphysema which enables one to predict the progression into a black cardiac. The only hint is the possibility of a chronic infection such as syphilis or malaria.

The clinical prognosis of a black cardiac differs in no way from other patients with emphysema. For twenty or more years, cough and thick sputum alternate with mucopurulent expectoration during congestive episodes. Suddenly the clinical picture changes; cyanosis appears first in the face; the patient continues his activities until dyspnea on exertion appears. Increasing dyspnea on exertion eventually disables the patient.

Finally cyanosis persists even at rest; cyanosis reaches the extreme limits, which induced Professor Ayerza to identify these patients by the name they are known today.

Although a considerable volume of literature in the past 50 years mentions the eponymic term, general agreement is lacking concerning both the specificity of the syndrome and indeed the necessity of retaining the eponym. Earlier in this century Mac-Callum[7] mentions Ayerza only in reference to a case reported by Warthin. In Warthin's report of 1917, "Syphilis of the Pulmonary Artery,"[8] he considered these cases to fall into the class styled "Ayerza's disease." Two years later, Warthin[9] added another case with a descriptive title and summary which omits essentially nothing of the clinical or pathological observations: "A Case of Ayerza's Disease (Chronic Cyanosis, Chronic Dyspnea, Erythremia, Enlargement of the Liver and Spleen and Hyperplasia of Bone Marrow) Associated with Syphilitic Sclerosis of the Pulmonary Artery." The clinical course was characterized by attacks of angina, hypercyanotica, cyanosis, increasing weakness, drowsiness, edema, asthma, dyspnea, enlargement of the spleen and liver, multiple telangiectasia, and constant erythremia. At postmortem, the findings included extreme atherosclerosis of the pulmonary artery and all its branches, extreme dilation of the right heart, fibrosis and emphysema of the lungs, extreme angiectasia of the entire vascular system, enlargement of the liver and spleen, and hyperplasia of the bone marrow. The microscopic examination showed the presence of a typical syphilitic mesarteritis of the pulmonary artery and aorta, chronic fibroid myocarditis, and changes in the stomach wall suggestive of syphilis.

In the 1930's, Castex and Capdehourat of Buenos Aires, in a series of communications, summarized the pathological-physiological observations of several Argentine investigators of the syndrome.[10] They implicated chronic bronchopulmonary infection in the genesis and considered sclerotic lesions of the pulmonary artery neither necessary nor indispensable for the development of hypertrophy and dilation of the heart, polycythemia, dyspnea, and edema.

The association of sclerosis of the pulmonary vessels with deep cyanosis will probably remain to the credit of Ayerza who, however, failed to record his original case and who, though he published other clinical reports, made no other direct or indirect notable contributions to the medical literature. His pupil Arrillaga corrected the initial deficiency and wrote at length on the pathogenesis of the black cardiac; after considerable vacillation, he concluded that a luetic infection of the pulmonary vessels was the primary pathologic process, admittedly without convincing evidence. His case studies and pathological investigations of the syndrome prompted some to propose the double eponym Ayerza-Arrillaga. Against this suggestion, Luis Ayerza voiced strong objections.[11] Until further evidence is produced, it probably should suffice to identify as Ayerza's syndrome persistent severe dyspnea and deep cyanosis at rest (black cardiac) associated with polycythemia, pulmonary emphysema, pulmonary hypertension, arteriosclerosis of the lesser circulation, and severe right ventricular hypertrophy, without preference for any hypothesis of pathogenesis.

1. Arrillaga, F. C.: Secondary Sclerosis of the Pulmonary Artery and Its Clinical Findings (Black Cardiacs) (Sp), thesis, National University of Buenos Aires: A. G. Buffarini, 1912, excerpt translated by Z. Danilevicius.

2. Marty, C. M.: *Arterial Pressure in Pulmonary Tuberculosis* (Sp), thesis, National University of Buenos Aires, 1909, excerpt translated by Z. Danilevicius.

3. Cranwell, D. J.: *Our Great Physicians* (Sp), Buenos Aires: El Ateneo, 1937, pp 81-91.

4. Arrillaga, F. C.: Pulmonary Arteritis and Its Clinical Picture (Sp), Buenos Aires: El Ateneo, 1925.

5. Brenner, O.: Pathology of the Vessels of the Pulmonary Circulation, Arch Intern Med (Chicago) 56:211-237; 457-497; 724-752; 976-1014; 1189-1241, 1935.

6. Corvisart, J. N.: *Essay on the Diseases and Organic Lesions of the Heart and of the Great Vessels* (Fr), Paris: Migneret, 1806, excerpts translated by Z. Danilevicius.

7. MacCallum, W. G.: Obliterative Pulmonary Arteriosclerosis, Bull Hopkins Hosp 49:37-48, 1931.

8. Warthin, A. S.: Syphilis of the Pulmonary Artery, Amer J Syph 1:693-711 (Oct) 1917.

9. Warthin, A. S.: A Case of Ayerza's Disease, JAMA 73:716 (Aug 30) 1919.

10. Castex, M. R., and Capdehourat, E. L.: Chronology and Interpretation of the Morbid Changes in the "Black Cardiacs" of Ayerza (Fr), Presse Med 42:268-272, 1934.

11. Ayerza, L.: Thoughts on the Terminology of "Ayerza's Disease" (Sp), Semana Med (B Air) 32(2):386-388, 1925.

Composite by G. Bako

Wilhelm His, Jr. (1863-1934)

HIS, THE YOUNGER, best known for his description of the atrioventricular conduction bundle of the heart, was born in Basel, Switzerland, while his father was professor of anatomy at the University. When the family moved to Leipzig, Wilhelm, Jr., studied at the gymnasium in a community famous for music, art, and humanistic amenities, as well as being a focal point for the study and practice of law and medicine. His formative years, having been spent in such an environment as a son of one of the best families, were deeply molded for the best. In his mature years, he was a talented violoncellist and painter as evidenced by his collection of musical instruments and objects of art. Wilhelm attended the universities of Leipzig, Strasbourg, Bern, and Geneva, studying under the brilliant minds of central Europe, and graduated from the University of Leipzig in 1889. He served as an assistant in the medical clinic under Curschmann, where Krehl and Romberg also were assistants. A collection of the studies from Curschmann's clinic, published in 1893, contained the description of the activity of the embryonic heart and its significance in the understanding of the contraction of the adult myocardial mass. As a capable clinician, most of his scientific contributions discussed clinical subjects, of which gout and Volhynia fever will be mentioned later, but his description of the A-V bundle was the most significant and his only journey of depth into embryology and anatomy.[1]

After long search I have succeeded in finding a muscle bundle which unites the auricular and ventricular septal walls, and which, up to now, has escaped observation because of incomplete exposure, for it is visible in its entire extent only when the septa are cut exactly in their longitudinal direction. From such cuts, as well as in serial sections, I was able to recognize the course of the bundle and have demonstrated it in a grown mouse, a newborn dog, two newborn and one adult (30-year-old) human. The bundle arises from the posterior wall of the right auricle, near the auricular septum, in the atrioventricular groove; attaches itself along the upper margin of the ventricular septal muscle by means of numerous fiber exchanges; proceeds on top of this toward the front until near the aorta it forks itself into a right and left limb which latter ends in the base of the aortic cusp of the mitral valve.

Whether this bundle really transmits the impulse from the auricle to the ventricle I am unable to say with certainty since, up to now, I have not attempted any transection experiments of it. Very likely its presence is an argument

against the belief of those who, because of the lack of muscular continuity between auricle and ventricle, seek to prove the necessity of nervous conduction.

In a communication written 30 years later His gave a running account of his discovery, reviewing the events which led to the observation and the critical deductions.[2]

One day I came along as Krehl and Romberg were discussing these questions (enervation of the heart). I had just finished an embryological problem under the direction of my father and, knowing the technique, I suggested an embryological investigation to determine if the heart can beat before it contains nerves and ganglia. Romberg agreed and my father placed at our disposal serial sections of human embryos and the photomicrographic apparatus of the Department of Anatomy. We built models of embryonic hearts by means of Born's wax plate method and we could show that the ganglion cells of the heart belong to the sympathetic system.

They belonged, therefore, to the sensory system and, since the physiologists did not know of any nerve to the heart whose stimulation could elicit a beat, we concluded that the heart ganglia too serve as the afferent limb of the nervous regulation apparatus.

While assisting in the Leipzig clinic and under the influence of his anatomist father, His studied the acousticofacial region in man and the migration of ganglion cells. He served as chief physician at the Friedrich City Hospital of Dresden for a short time and in 1902 became associate professor of internal medicine at Basel, devoting considerable attention in the clinic to the study of gout and related joint diseases. A short tour of duty at the medical clinic at Göttingen was the next step on his academic path. He was appointed professor of internal medicine and director of the first medical clinic at the Charité in Berlin in 1907, succeeding von Leyden.

An interest in gout may be traced to his days at Strasbourg as a student of Schmiedeberg, where he was concerned with the metabolism of pyridin and the solubility of uric acid under the influence of various electrolytes. Lithium salts were found to significantly alter urate solubility.[3] Dietary studies on the incidence of acute attacks of gout led to conservative conclusions. He concluded that low-purin foods were rational and should be given a trial, but that there was little reason for persistence if no clinical effect was apparent within a few weeks or months.[4]

1. Experience shows that gout can in most cases be favorably influenced by diet.

2. Food poor in purin is rational and may be tried if it proves agreeable to the digestive organs.

3. There is no reason why this diet should be persisted in, if there is no distinct effect after a few weeks or months.

4. In that case a simple but varied food with plenty of vegetables and fruit is indicated, digestion permitting.

5. Special dietary directions are required where moderation is not vouchsafed by the intelligence and character of the patient.

6. There should always be moderation in the use of alcoholic beverages, while total abstinence is necessary only in isolated cases. The kind of beverage permitted depends upon the susceptibility of the patient and on the customs of the country.

Although a Swiss citizen, His, Jr., became naturalized in Saxony and joined the German army in World War I under a special appointment as consulting internist. He was sent on missions to Turkey, Asia Minor, Russia, and the Western theater. From his tour of duty in Russia, he described trench fever, naming it "Volhynia Fever" after the district where it was observed. In his retiring years he published a monograph, *A German Doctor at the Front*,[5] in which he recounted his war activities. It is a valuable document of considerable historical interest in military medicine. The description of trench fever appeared in 1916.[6]

Among the armies stationed at the eastern front we have repeatedly encountered an entity which resembles malaria, in that attacks of fever of about 24-hours duration develop suddenly and without prodromal symptoms. The disease differs from malaria by the interval between the attacks of fever; as a rule this is 5 days, often 4 days, and sometimes 6 days. The attacks appear suddenly and with severe general symptoms, headaches, backaches, intensive pain in the calves of the legs and along the tibia. In most of the cases the muscles of the back and thighs are sensitive to pressure. The increase in temperature is often accompanied by chills. After the temperature has persisted for 12 to 24, at the most for 36, hours, it subsides, and the patients feel well again. After

5 or 6 days there is another attack of fever, and later other attacks may follow; generally there are 5 or 6, but in some cases 12, 13, or 14 attacks or more.

The spleen is often enlarged, frequently palpable and occasionally painful. Some patients have gastrointestinal symptoms, such as vomiting and diarrhea with abdominal pains; in one case this led to a diagnosis of dysentery.

Since text-books do not mention this disease it must be regarded as a new entity. Since we observed numerous cases in Volhynia, we call it Volhynia fever or Febris Volhynica (Wolhynica).

1. His, J., W.: The Activity of the Embryonic Human Heart and Its Significance for the Understanding of the Heart Movement in the Adult, *Arb Med Klin Leipzig,* pp 14-49, 1893; Bast, T. H., and Gardner, W. D., trans.: *J Hist Med* 4:289-318, 1949.

2. His, Jr., W.: The Story of the Atrioventricular Bundle with Remarks Concerning Embryonic Heart Activity, *Klin Wschr* 12:569-574, 1933; Bast, T. H., and Gardner, W. D., trans.: *J Hist Med* 4:319-333, 1949.

3. His, Jr., W.: Physical-Chemical Investigations of the Proportion of Uric Acid and the Salts in Solution; II. Contribution, The Decreasing Solubility of Uric Acid in Aqueous Solution of Strong Acids (Ger), *Hoppe Seyler Z Physiol Chem* 31:64-78, 1900.

4. His, Jr., W.: Nutrition Therapy of Gout, *Z Aerztl Fortbild* 6:625-633 (Oct 15) 1909; trans.: *Post-Graduate* 25:23-40 (Jan) 1910.

5. His, Jr., W.: *A German Doctor at the Front,* Blech, G. M., and Kean, J. R., trans., Washington, DC: National Service Publishing Co., 1933.

6. His, Jr., W.: On a New Periodic Febrile Illness (Volhynia Fever) (Ger), *Klin Wschr* 53: 322-3333, 1916, excerpt translated by E. Sieweke.

Composite by G. Bako

Sir Arthur Keith (1866-1955)

ARTHUR KEITH, comparative anatomist, physical anthropologist, embryologist, and champion of Darwinism, was born on a small farm in Aberdeenshire, Scotland.[1] Believing he was drawn to the soil, Keith left school for a time to study farming; however, he soon realized his mistake and began his higher education at Gordon's College at the University of Aberdeen. He studied medicine at Marischal College, graduated MB in 1888, and entered general practice in Mansfield. Subsequently, he succumbed to the temptation of serving as medical officer at a gold mine in Siam. Both before and after the mine failed, he turned to less glamorous work, dissecting indigenous gibbons and monkeys in the surrounding jungle. For his anatomical researches he received, upon his return, the Struthers medal and the anatomy prize at Aberdeen University. After further study at University College, London, and at the University of Leipzig, he received the MD degree, with highest honors, from Aberdeen in 1894; in addition, fellowship in the Royal College of Surgeons was bestowed upon him. Two years later Keith was appointed senior demonstrator of anat-

omy at the London Hospital. In this assignment he stressed the importance to his students of learning the origin and nature of the human structure in order that they would understand and better appreciate their clinical experiences in subsequent years.

During the 13 years Keith was senior demonstrator, he established a reputation as an investigator of structure and function, but he became especially noted for his work on the mechanism of respiration by means of roentgenography, for the exploration of the comparative anatomy of the heart, and for his demonstration of the sinoauricular node of the heart in collaboration with his pupil, Martin Flack. In 1908, Keith was appointed by the Royal College of Surgeons to the coveted post of conservator of the Hunterian anatomical museum, a position which he occupied with great distinction until retirement in 1933, when his health began to fail. As conservator he took full advantage of the opportunity to return to his investigations of biologic evolution and anthropology, begun while he was in Siam and pursued with renewed interest in the discovery of the skull of the Piltdown man. In retirement, Keith was master of the Buckston Browne Research Farm at Downe, Kent, which was preserved as a memorial to Charles Darwin, who had lived on the estate for 40 years, including the period of preparation of his *Origin of Species*.

Keith published a number of books and was deputy editor of the *Journal of Anatomy* from 1916 to 1933. His first treatise, entitled *Introduction to the Study of Anthropoid Apes*, appeared in 1896. His later works carried such titles as *Ancient Types of Man, The Human Body, Nationality and Race, Religion of a Darwinist, Essays on Human Evolution, A New Theory of Evolution, Concerning Man's Origin, Antiquity of Man, Menders of the Maimed*, and his most popular work, *Human Embryology and Morphology*, which passed through several editions.

Keith identified the sinoauricular node in 1906, while investigating a series of hearts from patients who had died with cardiac arrhythmias. It was expected that arrhythmias could be correlated with specific lesions in the auriculoventricular system, which had been recently described by Tawara. In examining the auriculoventricular system of humans and animals, Keith and Flack recognized a collection of specialized cardiac muscle fibers in the wall of the right atrium near the entrance of the superior vena cava. The proof of their inference that this was the site of the pacemaker came several years later from the work of Sir Thomas Lewis. The initial findings were summarized as follows:[2]

I. (a) The muscular connection in the lower hearts between sinus and auricular canal, and in the higher between the parts of the heart representing them, is intimate. In the latter, fibres pass directly from this junction to the vicinity of the a.-v. bundle.

(b) The canalo-auricular junction is marked by a thickening of the heart wall at this point. The muscular connection is diffuse. In the lower forms there is a difference between the fibres of the two parts, but in higher forms the fusion is so intimate that no difference in the type of fibre can be distinguished.

(c) The canalo-ventricular junction decreases in extent from the lower to the higher forms; in the latter it is represented solely by the a.-v. bundle.

(d) The bulbo-ventricular junction is well marked in the lower hearts. In higher forms the ventricular musculature has replaced that of the bulbus.

II. (a) There is a remarkable remnant of primitive fibres persisting at the sino-auricular junction in all the mammalian hearts examined. These fibres are in close connection with the vagus and sympathetic nerves, and have a special arterial supply; in them the dominating rhythm of the heart is believed to normally arise.

(b) No special differentiation of fibres was found at the canalo-auricular and bulbo-ventricular junctions.

III. (a) The Knoten is a part of the primitive auricular ring which has remained undifferentiated.

(b) The main bundle and its branches represent the invaginated portion of the primitive auricular canal.

Keith's great intellectual honesty, combined with humility and skepticism, is illustrated in his conclusions concerning the specimens of the Piltdown man. In three letters to the editor in *Nature* in 1913, he described his reconstruction of the Piltdown skull, demonstrating the error in the original reconstruction. He concluded that the brain cast by Dr. Smith Woodward was too small, that the positioning of the temporal lobe of the brain was inaccurate, and that the foramen magnum was too far forward in the base of the skull. Although Keith produced convincing evidence that his reconstructed brain was not a microcephalic simian type but probably similar to *Homo sapiens,* he accepted in substance the validity of the find until the hoax was exposed more than 40 years later.[3]

I made many experiments to test other possible suppositions, but only when the fragments were placed as in Fig. 2 could I secure symmetry, and at the same time obtain all the anatomical markings in their normal situations. The brain cast obtained from this reconstruction displaces just over 1500 cubic centimetres of water. Dr. Smith Woodward estimated his brain cast provisionally at 1070 c.c.; the replicas of the brain cast which were distributed displaced 1200 c.c. of water; even if the reconstruction carried out by Dr. Smith Woodward is accepted, and the right half is made approximately symmetrical with the left, the brain of Piltdown man will be about 200 c.c. above his original estimate.

Keith was a member of many scientific organizations and received outstanding honors. He served as secretary and Fullerian professor of physiology at the Royal Institution from 1917 to 1923. In 1911, the first and possibly the most coveted of his six honorary degrees, the LLD, was conferred by Aberdeen. The universities of Birmingham and Leeds also gave him the doctor of laws, while the universities of Durham, Manchester, and Oxford honored him with the doctor of science. Keith was elected a member of the Royal Society in 1913 and, from 1930 to 1933, served as rector of the University of Aberdeen. Knighthood was conferred in 1921. His investigations in comparative anatomy and in support of the Darwinian concept amply justified both the wisdom of appointing him conservator of the Hunterian museum and the judgment of the authorities in permitting him to spend his retiring years in Darwin's home.

1. Keith, A.: An Autobiography, London: Watts & Co., 1950.

2. Keith, A., and Flack, M.: The Form and Nature of the Muscular Connections Between the Primary Divisions of the Vertebrate Heart, J Anat Physiol 41:172-189, 1907.

3. Keith, A.: The Piltdown Skull and Brain Cast, Nature (Lond) 92:197-199 (Oct 16) 1913.

Composite by G. Bako

Sir Thomas Lewis (1881-1945)

THOMAS LEWIS brought the string galvanometer of Einthoven and critical criteria for clinical investigation to the bedside and into the clinic. He identified auricular fibrillation as the etiologic mechanism in one type of perpetual irregularity of the pulse, made important observations on the excitation wave in the heart in animals, gave the name "effort syndrome" to a functional heart disorder observed in soldiers from the Western Front, and dealt, by direct observations, with the small blood vessels of the human skin.

Lewis was born in Cardiff, Wales, son of a colliery owner. He was tutored at home because of ill health, and then studied at Clifton College until he entered University College, Cardiff, to begin studies in medicine.[1] His clinical training was completed at the University College Hospital Medical School of London in 1904, qualifying for the MB and BS degrees. Then followed an appointment to the staff of the London Chest Hospital, Victoria Park, and, in 1907, membership in the Royal College of Physicians. By then Lewis had investigated the influence of respiration on the pulse and had begun preparation of a chapter for *Recent Advances in Physiology*. The assignment

brought him into scientific communication with Sir James Mackenzie, the leading cardiologist of Britain, who had attributed auricular fibrillation to nodal rhythm.

Lewis found himself sharing his intellectual talents with research, hospital service, consulting practice, and editorial work, having been asked by Mackenzie to assume the editorship of a new journal, *Heart*. Appointment as Beit Memorial Research Fellow, with accompanying modest laboratory space in the University Hospital, was the deciding factor that his major efforts would henceforth be devoted to clinical research. His great influence on pupils and associates continued throughout a rich scientific career, but clinical investigation remained paramount in his work. He utilized the experimental laboratory and animal investigation to support his theories of the pathogenesis of cardiovascular dysfunction in man.

In the same year that Lewis began the editorship of *Heart,* his interpretation of auricular fibrillation was advanced. The nature of the arterial curves from the polygraph had given rise to the term, "pulsus irregularis perpetuus," from the assumption implying that the rhythm producing it arose in the node of Tawara, hence, "nodal rhythm." Lewis produced the evidence supporting two valid conclusions.[2]

I. That a rhythm arising in the neighbourhood of the node gives rise to a totally different clinical picture. This conclusion is based upon a detailed examination (polygraphic and electrocardiographic) of a case of paroxysmal tachycardia, in which it can be demonstrated that auricle and ventricle contract together. This rhythm is a rare clinical phenomenon.

II. That the irregular pulse of mitral stenosis, etc., already referred to, is due to fibrillation of the auricle.

1. The clinical irregularity presented by arterial and heart apex curves is unique. The rhythm is entirely disorderly, and the sizes of the beats do not correspond to the pauses which precede them. Fibrillation of the auricle results in a similar action of the ventricle, and its action under these circumstances is unique experimentally.

2. Electrocardiograms taken from patients exhibiting the irregularity show a number of irregular waves, apart from the ventricular curve; they are more clearly defined in diastole.

3. The venous curves in the clinical irregularity is of the ventricular type; all the prominent waves occur during ventricular systole, and there is no

wave corresponding to a normal auricular contraction.

The study of the excitation wave in the heart was pursued by Lewis and Rothschild with a "unipolar" lead. The exploring electrode, placed on the dog's heart and paired with a distant electrode, distinguished between the electrical activity of the tissue immediately stimulated and the more remote electrical activity, thereby showing that different points on the epicardium were activated at different times. Deflections immediately beneath the contacts were termed "intrinsic;" whereas the deflections produced by activity of the myocardial tissue at a distance from the contact points were termed "extrinsic." The rate of spread of the excitation was estimated to be 1,000 mm/sec in the atrium, 3,000-5,000 mm/sec in the Purkyně system, and 300-500 mm/sec in the ventricle. Their observations were summarized as follows:[3]

That activity first reveals itself in the region of the sino-auricular node in the neighbourhood of the head of that structure has been shown, we consider, beyond question. It spreads from this node in every direction, progressing to all the margins of the musculature; . . . Flowing through the auricle, the wave reaches the auriculoventricular node where it is delayed, it spreads from this through the bundle and passes to the ventricle. In the muscle of the ventricle conduction is slowest, for its function of distribution is a minor one; rapidity of distribution is provided by the architecture of the special tissues. The main bundle splits into two branches, right and left, and then subdivides into a wide arborisation and communicates with a network which pervades almost the whole subendocardial space. This special system of fibres is endowed with the highest order of conducting power. The final spread through the muscle is by penetration of the whole thickness at innumerable points.

World War I interrupted his activities, and, before arrangements were completed for the command of a Welsh military hospital in Mesopotamia, Lewis was invited by the Medical Research Council to supervise studies on the soldier's heart at Mount Vernon Hospital, Hampstead, and later at Sabraon Military Hospital at Colchester. A series of graded exercises were designed to test the work capacity of soldiers complaining of heart fatigue or "effort syndrome." This led to a more careful appraisal of the criteria for the diagnosis of organic heart disease and a better method for selecting recruits with real or functional heart disease. A monograph, *The Soldier's Heart and the Effort Syndrome,* followed the preliminary communication prepared for the Medical Research Committee.[4]

1. In the treatment of soldiers who suffer from distress upon exertion, a condition to be observed in most of those soldiers hitherto returned as cases of "disordered action of the heart," and in many others with a diagnosis of "valvular disease of the heart," it has been found advantageous, wherever possible, to convince the patients that the heart is free from disease or to direct attention away from this organ. It has also been ascertained that the methods commonly in vogue in the treatment of heart cases are far less suitable for this well-marked group of cases than are general hygienic measures. In the opinion of Dr. Lewis, and he is by no means alone in this, an important obstacle to the achievement of these purposes on a wide scale is the present nomenclature. He believes that the use of the diagnostic term "D.A.H.," is apt to weaken the soldier's faith in his chances of subsequent progress; it is well known that those initials are not so cryptic to soldiers as might be expected. It is considered also by many that the use of this terminology is sometimes likely to influence to some extent, and adversely, the method of treatment adopted by medical officers through whose hands the soldier is subsequently to pass. The invention and the use of a new name for the definite condition to which the term "D.A.H." is mainly applied, seem accordingly to be desirable. In his Report Dr. Lewis suggests the term "effort syndrome," which points to the cardinal symptom of distress upon exertion without prejudging the question of causation.

With the war over, Lewis resumed his studies on electrocardiography, identifying auricular flutter as a circus movement of the excitability wave at the mouths of the great veins. With relatively simple experimental tools he began to study dermatographia and the capillaries of the skin by direct observation. Assisted by a series of collaborators, he investigataed the means by which the resistance of the skin to the flow of blood is maintained in smaller vessels and inquired into the reactions to chemical substances released from the cells of the epidermis by mild injury or irritant stimuli. He observed the sequence of events which followed stroking the sensitive or normal skin with a blunt instrument: the white streak, a red line, a red flush, and finally a wheal. The triple response was attributed to a release of a histamine-like substance from the injured cells. A monograph, *The Blood Vessels of the Human Skin and Their Responses,* incorporated his basic observations described in collaboration with Grant.[5]

The broad features of the reaction to histamine puncture and stroking. The reactions of the skin in urticarial patients in response to stroking . . . consist essentially of (*a*) a central and sharply defined red line restricted to the line of stroke and due to a local dilatation of the superficial capillaries, venules and terminal arterioles, (*b*) a bright red flush having irregular margins, and caused by dilatation of the arterioles, over the surrounding area of skin, and (*c*) the appearance of a raised wheal over the line of stroke. Precisely similar reactions occur after puncturing the skin with histamine.

The reactions to stroke and histamine present similar time relations, and it has been shown that the reaction in each case consists of:—

(*a*) A local dilatation of the minute skin vessels which, since it occurs when the circulation is at a standstill, is a primary dilatation of these vessels. It is not dependent upon simultaneous dilatation of the arterioles.

(*b*) A surrounding flush, which is due to widespread dilatation of the skin arterioles; that is known because the flush is of a bright arterial colour; because it fails to appear if the circulation is occluded; because in its area it abolishes cyanosis produced by congesting the veins of the arm; and because it frequently presents capillary pulsation.

(*c*) An output of fluid into the tissues to constitute a wheal. This fluid comes from the vessels and the rate at which it is thrown out is largely controlled by the rate of blood flow through the tissue.

Lewis' contributions to the literature, which began at an early age, continued without interruption for a full scientific lifetime. *The Mechanism of the Heart Beat,* one of his most important monographs, appeared when he was only 29. His last, *Pain,* appeared several years before he died from coronary disease in 1945. He continued as editor of the journal *Heart,* subsequently named *Clinical Science* in 1933, guiding it to a position of prestige as a clinical periodical. Honors included fellowship in the Royal Society, CBE, and knighthood in 1921. He gave many named lectures in England and received distinguished medals and prizes. His influence on clinical cardiology spread throughout Europe and beyond. Several of his notable pupils from America were Edward F. Bland, Paul Camp, Ashton Graybiel, William Kerr, Eugene M. Landis, Samuel A. Levine, Harold M. Marvin, Arthur M. Master, Alfred M. Wedd, Paul D. White, and Frank Wilson.

1. Pickering, G. W.: Thomas Lewis, obituary, *Lancet* 1:419-420, 1945.

2. Lewis, T.: Auricular Fibrillation: A Common Clinical Condition, *Brit Med J* 2:1528, 1909.

3. Lewis, T., and Rothschild, M. A.: IV. The Excitatory Process in the Dog's Heart, *Philos Trans* 206:181-226, 1915.

4. Lewis, T.: *Report Upon Soldiers Returned as Cases of "Disordered Action of the Heart" (D.A.H.) or "Valvular Disease of the Heart" (V.D.H.),* Medical Research Committee, National Health Service, London: His Majesty's Stationery Office, Feb 14, 1917.

5. Lewis, T., and Grant, R. T.: Vascular Reactions of the Skin to Injury, *Heart* 11:209-265, 1924.

Composite by G. Bako

George Frederick Still
(1868-1941)

THE CLINICAL DESCRIPTION OF JUVENILE RHEUMATOID ARTHRITIS, identified as such by name, was prepared by pediatrician George F. Still before he was 30 years old. At that time, he was medical registrar and pathologist to the Hospital for Sick Children, Great Ormond Street, London. This is Still's lasting contribution to medicine, although his writings in pediatrics marked him as the first and most celebrated pediatrician of his time. Still was born at Holloway, London, the son of a customs clerk, was educated at Merchant Taylor School, and matriculated in classics at Gonville and Caius College, Cambridge. His medical training was pursued at Guy's Hospital, where he served as house physician. His graduation thesis, written for the MD degree from Cambridge, described the juvenile form of rheumatoid arthritis. In 1899, Still was appointed physician for diseases of children at King's College Hospital, the first hospital associated with a medical school to establish a separate pediatric department. Several years later he was elected the first professor of diseases of children in King's College.

The description of juvenile rheumatoid arthritis was received in April, 1897, by the Royal Medical and Chirurgical Society of London, simultaneously with the description by Chauffard and Ramond of France and Bannatyne and Wohlmann of Bath, but in less complete form. Also, Cornil published a case report in 1864 of an adult female who had suffered from rheumatoid arthritis since the age of 12, and Diamentberger reported a series of cases in 1891.

Nevertheless, the eponym Chauffard-Still's disease is retained in current literature and is used synonymously with Still's disease. The report by Still was based on 22 cases, of which 19 were under his personal observation at the Great Ormond Street Hospital. The original description has been enriched subsequently but remains currently acceptable. The characteristic features included fusiform enlargement of the joints, glandular hypertrophy, and splenomegaly. Symptoms almost always appeared before the second dentition; the earliest onset occurred at 15 months. Girls were more often afflicted than boys. The onset was insidious, and the cardinal signs of inflammation usually were absent. The knees, wrists, and cervical spine were affected first. The affliction in the peripheral joints was symmetrical; the muscles adjacent to the diseased joints showed early and marked wasting. Evidence of valvular disease was lacking, but several patients showed adherent pericarditis. Prominence of the eyes, without involvement of the thyroid, was noted occasionally. A few patients experienced a curious regularity to pyrexia. Thickening of the articular capsule, without destruction of the cartilage, was a point of differentiation from adult rheumatoid arthritis. The report was summarized as follows:[1]

> There is a disease, occurring in children, and beginning before the second dentition, which is characterized clinically by elastic fusiform enlargement of joints without bony change, and also by enlargement of glands and spleen.
>
> This disease has hitherto been called rheumatoid arthritis, but it differs from that disease in adults, clinically in the absence of bony change, even when the disease is advanced, and in the enlargement of glands and spleen, and pathologically in the absence, even in an advanced case, of the cartilage changes which are found quite early in that disease, and also in the absence of osteophytic change.

Another notable event early in Still's career was the identification of a gram-negative diplococcus in eight patients suffering from posterior basilar meningitis. As his reputation grew and his practice expanded, he published a textbook, *Common Disorders and Diseases of Childhood,* which enjoyed several editions. At the summit of his career, Still was appointed physician-in-ordinary to the Duke and Duchess of York, and physician-extraordinary to the King. Professional honors included the Gulstonian, Lumleian, and Fitzpatrick lecturerships of the Royal College of Physicians, honorary Doctor of Letters from Edinburgh University, and president of the Third International Paediatric Congress in London. An interest in the classics was retained throughout life. His scholarship found expression in *The History of Pediatrics* which began with the aphorisms of Hippocrates;[2] a lay treatise, *Common Happenings in Childhood,* which included chapters on crying, laughter, temper, and tiredness; and a book of verse concerning children and other things.[3]

During a long professional career, Still found interest in a great number of clinical subjects. These included diphtheria, gumma of the spleen, cystic disease of the liver, hemorrhage into the suprarenal capsules, rheumatic heart disease, tubercular ulcer of the stomach, congenital hypertrophy of the pylorus, biliary colic, infant feeding, mongolism, obesity, suppurative pericarditis, nephritis, convulsive disorders, infantile scurvy, rickets, cerebral palsy, infantile paralysis, dental caries, infantile diarrhea, cleidocranial disostosis, hair ball in the stomach, infantile marasmus, enlarged tonsils and adenoids, pyelitis, epidemic stupor, celiac disease, cephalic bruit, chronic intussusception, arrested respiration in the newborn, cyclic vomiting, scleroderma, congenital anorexia, day terrors, head rolling, enuresis, and fecal incontinence.

1. Still, G. F.: On a Form of Chronic Joint Disease in Children, *Medicochir Trans* 80:47-59, 1897.
2. Still, G. F.: *The History of Pediatrics,* London: Oxford University Press, 1931.
3. Still, G. F.: *Childhood and Other Poems,* London: J. Murray, 1941.

Ray Lyman Wilbur (1875-1949)

RAY LYMAN WILBUR, a son of the Iowa and Dakota prairies, attained distinguished maturity as a leader of California medicine.[1] Wilbur's higher education began at Leland Stanford University and was continued at Cooper Medical College in San Francisco. The experiences gained as an extern at the San Francisco City and County Hospital complemented his natural endowments and strengthened a humanistic philosophy that was readily apparent in his deeds and actions throughout his professional career. Coincidental with an externship, Wilbur practiced medicine as a family physician for a decade before he was invited by David Starr Jordan, the first president of Stanford University, to become Professor of Medicine and subsequenty Dean of the Medical School. Ascendancy to the presidency of Stanford in 1916 was interrupted by service to his country as Secretary of the Interior during the Hoover administration.

The prairie years for Wilbur were associated with cyclones and cyclone cellars,

Composite by G. Bako

homesteaders, dread of croup, and sod cabins. The childhood days were happy, surely by comparison with friends and neighbors. The family was emotionally and financially secure. One of the first books that Wilbur owned was Stanley's *In Darkest Africa. The Decline and Fall of the Roman Empire* and Shakespeare were favorites. The *McGuffey Readers* were his best-remembered school books. George Washington and Abraham Lincoln were his first great heroes. Prairie chickens, plover, migrating fowl, and deer were plentiful in the frontier land. It is not surprising that a natural interest in biology was apparent years before a decision was reached that determined his professional career.

Stanford University admitted the first class in 1891. Wilbur enrolled in the Liberal Arts School the following year. The summer after his freshman year, he was a member of a biological expedition to Arizona. Rattlesnakes and Gila monsters were collected in the giant saquaro cactus forests or in the mesquite bush. Forty years later when Wilbur was Secretary of the Interior, the same barren land along the Colorado River came to life with the construction of the

Hoover Dam. One of the communities in the area whose name holds fascination in adult westerns, Tombstone, was a prosperous mining village half a century ago. By the end of Wilbur's sophomore college year, a firm desire to enter medicine was apparent. This was augmented in the final college year by his appointment as an assistant in physiology, a post that was continued in Cooper Medical College following graduation (1889). Cooper Medical College, the first medical school on the West Coast, was founded in 1858 and consolidated with Stanford University in 1911. Stanford Medical School, similar to Cooper Medical College, was subject to severe growing pains before and after consolidation. Wilbur, probably more than any one individual, led the medical school out of chaos and confusion and endowed it with stature and stability.

Wilbur, now married, held office hours in his home on Scott Street in San Francisco in the evenings as the principal source of income following graduation. During the day he served as an assistant in the Medical Clinic of the Cooper Medical College and as an instructor in physiology. The practice of medicine in California at that time was lax. The first law regulating the profession was not passed until 1901. Prior to that time a manifest interest was sufficient for an individual to engage in practice. Wilbur returned to Palo Alto in 1902 and practiced there until 1909 when he went to Europe for study and to prepare himself for an academic career.

One of the critical problems in directing a medical school, now as 50 years ago, was the arrangement for adequate control by the medical faculty of the teaching in the associated hospitals and outpatient clinics and provision for postgraduate education.

A clinical committee was appointed to make decisions on the types, quality or kinds of medical and nursing services, to determine hospital staff relationships and to place the patients' needs above any other considerations in dealing with the sick.

Medical education has become more expensive, requiring more men of long and expensive training to work in departments. . . . It also meant two kinds of instructors in the medical schools: (1) those with clinical appointments on a nominal salary who, as a side line to their own medical practice, worked in the clinics doing a certain amount of teaching, and (2) the so-called full-time academic professors, some in clinical positions in addition to their regular teaching, on academic salaries.

Education should be a continuing process for everyone, but it is perhaps the most imperative of all for the physician. He must be constantly on the alert to keep up to date, for at any moment it may mean life or death to one of his patients. Certainly the doctor who is working today with the education given him some ten or more years ago is an antique that needs renovation.

Wilbur was elected Chairman of the Section of Pharmacology and Therapeutics of the American Medical Association in 1912. He remained actively identified with organized medicine for the next 30 years. He functioned as President of the A.M.A. from 1923 to 1924 and was a member of the Council on Medical Education and Hospitals between 1920 and 1946, except for the one year as President. He was Chairman of this Council from 1929 to 1946. The year as President of the A.M.A. was considered "about the most important experience of my medical career." The great social processes underway in America and the relationship of medicine to them were cause for thought and contemplation. He was concerned that social experiments "were being tried out *on* us, instead of *by* us." Pressures for the control of health to be taken over by the State were related to the development of preventive medicine and progress in public health and bacteriology:

We must keep individualism in medicine. . . . The minute we allow a bureaucracy to step in between the physician and the patient, we take the one step that will degrade our profession so that we cannot render ideal professional services to patients.

It is inevitable that more and more physicians will work for the various government units, but the great body of the profession should remain free from the control of government or payment by it.

Wilbur functioned also as Chairman of the A.M.A. Committee on the Costs of Medical Care. He was criticized for the conclusions rendered by the committee and especially because he was "an educator that had no practical experience in the practice of medicine." Obviously, this was false. The report of the committee was accused of being socialistic, even savored of Communism. The recommendations of the committee were adopted finally by the House of Delegates in 1946.

In one of the concluding chapters of his biography, Wilbur displays his continued interest in medicine:

The protection and advancement of research [in medicine] is our greatest opportunity, but it is as important to apply the results of research as to foster it. . . . At times during my own lifetime it has looked as though most of the larger medical problems had been solved. But each advance, together with the more minute studies that are being made and the development of new instruments, constantly gives us new horizons and the knowledge of new diseases that have to be met. In fact, even now we can say that only the rough and more easily solved problems have been pretty well dealt with and that there are just as many, if not more, difficult ones to tackle.

1. *The Memoirs of Ray Lyman Wilbur, 1875-1949,* edited by E. E. Robinson and P. C. Edwards, Stanford, Calif.: Stanford University Press, 1960.

Composite by G. Bako

George R. Murray (1865-1939)

GEORGE REDMAYNE MURRAY, one of the first physicians to correct the myxedematous state in humans by administration of animal thyroid, was born in Newcastle-upon-Tyne,

the son of an outstanding physician, William Murray.[1] Young Murray was educated at Eton and then at Trinity College, Cambridge. He graduated with honors and rowed on the Eton crew in the Henley race in 1883. His clinical training was acquired at the University College Hospital, London, where he distinguished himself with gold medals and came under the influence of Sir Victor Horsley. The MB was awarded in 1889 and the MD in 1896, each at Cambridge. Before Murray began teaching and practice at Newcastle-upon-Tyne, he spent two years visiting clinics in Paris and Berlin. Returning to Newcastle in 1891, he was appointed pathologist to the Hospital for Sick Children and lecturer in bacteriology and comparative anatomy at Durham University. In 1893, he advanced to the Heath professorship of comparative pathology and, from 1898 to 1908, served as physician to the Royal Victoria Infirmary. When the chair of medicine became vacant at Victoria University in Manchester, Murray accepted the dual offer of professor in the medical school and physician to the Royal Infirmary. In spite of overt opposition from members of the medical community in Manchester, he carried out his duties with great skill, eventually bringing him great respect.

Murray's best known scientific work was reported immediately upon his return to Newcastle and was published in the *British Medical Journal,* Oct 10, 1891. It concluded a decade of speculation and investigation on the thyroid, which had included Sir Victor Horsley's suggestion of transplanting a portion of the thyroid of a sheep into humans for relief from myxedema. Horsley's therapeutic experiment, tested in a few instances with limited success, was never carried to a practical conclusion as a general procedure for the correction of athyreosis. Nevertheless, it seems reasonable to believe that Horsley very likely discussed with Murray, as well as with other students, his theories and the experiments in this field. Extending this speculation, Murray reasoned that, if transplanted thyroid would help in myxedema, subcutaneous injections of an extract of the gland should also be beneficial. A 46-year-old woman, who had developed the characteristic signs and symptoms of myxedema over a five-year period, was the first patient to receive Murray's preparation.[2]

Now it seems reasonable to suppose that the same amount of improvement might be obtained by simply injecting the juice or an extract of the thyroid gland of a sheep beneath the skin of the patient.

Since suggesting this treatment at the February meeting of the Northumberland and Durham Medical Society, I have been able to carry it out in a well-marked case of myxoedema. Such decided improvement has resulted that the details of the method of treatment employed and the results obtained are worth recording.

The lobe of the thyroid gland of a sheep is removed as soon as possible after the animal has been killed. All the instruments and glass vessels used in the further preparation of the extract should be either sterilised by heat or thoroughly cleansed with a 1 in 20 solution of carbolic acid. The gland is cut up on a glass dish into small pieces, and then placed in a test tube with 1 cubic centimetre of pure glycerine and 1 cubic centimetre of a 0.5 per cent solution of carbolic acid. The mouth of the tube is closed with a plug of cotton-wool, and the mixture allowed to stand in a cool place for twenty-four hours. The mixture is then placed in a fine handkerchief which has previously been placed for a few minutes in boiling water. It is then firmly squeezed by screwing up the handkerchief so as to express as much liquid as possible through the handkerchief. By this means 3 cubic centimetres (50 minims) of a turbid pink liquid are obtained. This preparation, which will keep quite fresh for at least a week, should be kept in a small bottle with a glass stopper. It is best to make the extract fresh each week, so as to avoid any risk of putrefaction taking place. This extract may be given in two equal injections of 1.5 cubic centimetre (25 minims) each during the week, so that at first the patient receives the extract of one lobe of a sheep's thyroid in the course of each week.

July 13th. It is now three months since the treatment was commenced; it has not, however, been carried out continuously all the time, and at first a weaker preparation than that described was used. Extracts of five lobes of sheep's thyroid have been injected, that is altogether equal to the extract of two and a half thyroid glands. The patient has steadily improved since the treatment commenced.

This case is published in the hope that others may be induced to give the treatment a fair trial in myxoedema. It might also be tried in cases where it is found necessary to remove the whole of the thyroid gland to prevent the onset of, or at least modify, the unpleasant train of symptoms known as cachexia strumipriva, which so often follows thyroidectomy.

Although the parenteral administration of the extract of the sheep's thyroid was a clinical success, it was laborious to prepare the active agent and probably produced pain for the patient at the site of injection. In proper time, Murray substituted the oral route for the aqueous extract, with comparable therapeutic results. Finally, oral ingestion of desiccated glands replaced the parenteral preparation, which remains in favor. In 1920, Murray described the 28-year follow-up of the first patient treated parenterally.[3]

After this [initial period] the injections were given at fortnightly intervals, and later on, when the oral administration had been shown by Dr. E. L. Fox and Dr. Hector Mackenzie to be equally efficient, she took 10 minims by the mouth six nights a week, so that 1 drachm was consumed in the course of each week. On this dose she remained in good health, and free from the signs of myxoedema. I have only seen this patient once during the last eleven years, but Dr. Helen Gurney, medical registrar at the Royal Victoria Infirmary, Newcastle, has kindly kept her under observation, and has informed me that she continued to take liquid thyroid extract regularly until early in 1918, when it became difficult to obtain, so that she was given dry thyroid extract in a tablet instead. She enjoyed excellent health until early in 1919, when she developed oedema of the legs and died in May of that year at the age of 74 from cardiac failure.

This patient was thus enabled, by the regular and continued use of thyroid extract, to live in good health for over twenty-eight years after she had reached an advanced state of myxoedema.

Until statutory retirement in 1925, Murray held the post in Manchester, devoting his efforts to teaching, administration, practice, and writing on the clinical aspects of thyroid disease. During World War I he was assigned to the Royal Army Medical Corps and later, in the grade of temporary colonel with the British forces, in Italy as consulting physician. He served his government at home as a member of the Medical Research Committee and of the departmental committee of the Home Office on dust diseases in card-room workers. As a fellow of the Royal College of Physicians of London, he delivered the Goulstonian lectures in 1899, on "Pathology of the Thyroid Gland," and the Bradshaw lecture in 1905, on "Exophthalmic Goitre and Its Treatment." Honorary degrees were conferred on him by Durham and Dublin universities.

1. Spence, J. C.: "George Redmayne Murray," in *Dictionary of National Biography*, London: Oxford University Press, 1949.

2. Murray, G. R.: Note on the Treatment of Myxoedema by Hypodermic Injections of an Extract of the Thyroid Gland of a Sheep, *Brit Med J* 2:796-797, 1891.

3. Murray, G. R.: The Life-History of the First Case of Myxoedema Treated by Thyroid Extract, *Brit Med J* 1:359-360, 1920.

Composite by G. Bako

James Ewing (1866-1943)

JAMES EWING, the first professor of pathology at Cornell University Medical School, was one of the recognized authorities in the United States in the diagnosis and management of neoplastic diseases.[1] He was born in Pittsburgh and attended Amherst College, where he seemed more interested in philosophy than the sciences. He received the MD degree from the College of Physicians and Surgeons of Columbia University, having been especially attracted to pathology under the direction of T. M. Prudden. Ewing received further training in the morphology of malignant tumors from Francis Delafield, whose name is memorialized in the Cancer Hospital in Manhattan. After the completion of clinical training, he spent four years in Prudden's laboratory. At the age of 33, Ewing was called to Cornell as head of the recently organized department of pathology and occupied the chair until 1932.

A great capacity for laboratory pursuits, a limitless concern for instruction, combined with a profound knowledge of gross and microscopic structure that he sought to share with others won for him an enviable measure of admiration and respect. Those were the days when little could be done for the patient with cancer beyond confirmation of the diagnosis (usually at the inoperable stage) and symptomatic management. After a decade of ceaseless industry, compounded by intractable tic douloureux and the early death of his wife, his book on neoplastic diseases was published.[2] This was rapidly and readily recognized as the standard text on the subject in America and was translated for use beyond the English-speaking lands.

Two scientific contributions, each based upon repeated observations, are noteworthy. His description of the reticulum cell sarcoma or reticulosarcoma, a primary tumor of lymphoid tissue sometimes confused with diffuse carcinomatosis of the lymph nodes, was published in 1913 in the *Journal of Medical Research*.[3]

For many years I have been encountering tumors of lymph nodes in subjects presenting no other demonstrable tumor and with whom the subsequent course indicated that no other tumor existed, and in which the structure strongly suggested an endothelial origin. The observation of several tumors of this class within the past year which presented early stages and transitional forms between those previously observed has led to the conclusion that endothelioma of lymph nodes is a rather common neoplasm, that it is usually classed with lymphosarcoma on the one hand and with secondary carcinoma on the other, that the process differs in many histological, anatomical, and clinical features from secondary carcinoma, and that it is usually possible to recognize these features with considerable or complete certainty.

The structure is one that is ordinarily called lymphosarcoma, but its characteristic cell forms, the derivation of these cells from the endothelium of the reticulum which could readily be followed, and the resemblance of the process to sarcomas associated with Hodgkin's granuloma in which the large cells are admittedly of endothelial origin, all go to support the interpretation of the case as endothelial sarcoma.

In the inflammatory hyperplasia of germ centers it is the reticulum cells which multiply by mitosis and replace lymphocytes and in the sinuses these cells proliferate and choke the sinuses. The common interpretation as endothelial, of the large cells which proliferate in granulomatous inflammation of lymph nodes, is fully justified and it is equally clear that tumors arising from these cells are properly called endotheliomas.

Ewing's original description of nonosteogenic tumor of the bone, with clearly defined clinical characteristics, brought him sharp criticism. Some believed that the eponymic tumor, usually found in young persons and susceptible to radiation, failed to satisfy the criteria of a pathological entity. Although the tumors were occasionally multiple, they were not metastatic and were unlike multiple myeloma. In recent years, his original contention of an endothelial tumor, specific in morphology, has been supported.[4]

For some years I have been encountering in material curetted from bone tumors a structure which differed markedly from that of osteogenic sarcoma, which was not identical with any known form of myeloma, and which had to be designated by the vague term "round cell sarcoma" of unknown origin and nature. I had no opportunity of following the course or learning the outcome of these cases, as most of them were treated by amputation of the limb.

Recently a case came under observation at the Memorial Hospital which revealed that this tumor is highly susceptible to radium, a fact that convinced me that the disease was entirely different from osteogenic sarcoma, which resists treatment by the physical agents.

The main point of the present communication lies in the demonstration that there is a rather common tumor occurring in young subjects, commonly identified with osteogenic sarcoma, and usually called round cell sarcoma, which is really of endothelial origin, and which is marked by such peculiar gross anatomical, clinical, and therapeutic features as to constitute a specific neoplastic disease of bone.

In 1913, when Memorial Hospital (originally founded as the New York Cancer Hospital) was affiliated with Cornell University Medical College, Ewing was elected president of the medical board; later he became director of cancer research. Upon retirement from Cornell he was made director of the hospital, a position that he held until retirement in 1939. In 1950, the James Ewing Hospital was built in his memory and was a part of the hospital system of New York City. In 1968, it was renamed the Ewing Pavilion and became a clinical unit of the Memorial Sloan-Kettering Cancer Center. Ewing served on the editorial boards of the *Journal of Cancer Research* and the *Archives of Pathology,* was one of the founders of the American Society for the Control of Cancer and the bone sarcoma registry of the American College of Surgeons. He wore the Distinguished Service Medal of the American Medical Association and carried the gold-headed cane of the American Association of Pathologists and Bacteriologists, which had descended from Harold C. Ernst through Theobald Smith, William H. Welch, and Frank B. Mallory. Academic honors included the DSC degree awarded by his alma mater, by the University of Rochester, the University of Pittsburgh, and Union University, and the LLD bestowed by Kenyon College and Western Reserve University.

1. Stewart, F. W.: James Ewing, M.D., 1866-1943, *Arch Path* 36:325-830, 1943.

2. Ewing, J.: *Neoplastic Diseases,* Philadelphia: W. B. Saunders Company, 1919.

3. Ewing, J.: Endothelioma of Lymph Nodes, *J Med Res* 28:1-39, 1913.

4. Ewing, J.: Diffuse Endothelioma of Bone, *Proc New York Path Soc* 21:17-24, 1921.

Composite by G. Bako

Alfred Fröhlich (1871-1953)

THE ASSOCIATION OF TRUNCAL OBESITY and deficient gonadal development, with ablation of the anterior section of the pituitary gland, was reported by Fröhlich in 1901 in a provincial medical journal. Viennese by birth and education, he pursued cultural and academic interests worthy of his nativity.[1] He was an accomplished pianist, well versed in literature, a stimulating conversationalist, and an outstanding natural scientist, with many international friends. He received an upper class general education in Vienna and in 1895 the MD degree from the university. Initially he joined Nothnagel's department of medicine; later he assisted Basch in experimental pathology and L. Frankl-Hochwart in the neurological clinic. In the interim, he traveled to England to study with Sherrington in Liverpool, where he became acquainted with Cushing, also a student of the pituitary gland; later he worked with Langley in Cambridge.

Fröhlich's first appointment, with tenure, was in the department of pharmacology and toxicology under the direction of H. H. Meyer. He gained professional status in 1912 and from 1919-1939 served as a full professor. A victim of the German-Austrian

Anschluss, he came to America in 1939 and joined the May Institute of Medical Research of the Jewish Hospital in Cincinnati. Here he continued his pharmacologic studies, especially the influence of various therapeutic agents on the central nervous system.

Fröhlich's bibliography discloses few subjects in experimental pharmacology currently attractive at that time which escaped his attention either in short communications or in monographic treatment. Interested in invertebrate as well as vertebrate physiology he worked at times in the marine laboratories at Naples, Helgoland, Germany, and Woods Hole, Mass. He contributed to our understanding of contraction of striated muscle fibers, the pathways for visceral pain, heat narcosis, effect of radon emanation on the amphibian heart, the influence of theophylline on absorption, convulsions as a function of age, the potentiation of adrenalin with cocaine, the excitability of the vegetative nervous system by calcium deprivation, and the effect of pituitrin upon the autonomic nervous system. Together with Frankl-Hochwart, Fröhlich extended the work of Dale on the sensitivity of the uterus of the rabbit to posterior pituitary extract and confirmed the observation that pituitary extract stimulates the nonpregnant uterus and produces powerful contractions on the pregnant uterus. The practical application of pituitrin in delivery was recognized.[2]

In the majority of experiments, especially in lactating or gravid rabbits, the uterus is stimulated by small doses, 0.3 to 0.5 ccm of pituitrin into strong, sometimes persistent contractions with pallor of the organ. Immediately the sympathetic nerves to the uterus, the hypogastric nerves, are easily stimulated by a faradic current and react with a stronger response.

According to our studies pituitrin can be regarded as essentially non-toxic and should be considered by obstetricians and urologists in pertinent cases who might profit from the increased excitability which we have demonstrated in the animal experiments on the bladder and the uterus and use it therapeutically in such instances.

The clinical significance of obesity and delayed genital maturation in children without evidence of acromegaly attributed to a pituitary neoplasm or a lesion in the region of the hypophysis, has undergone considerable modification since Fröhlich's initial description. Although it is recognized currently that a lesion of the hypothalamus alone results in adiposogenitalis, and the majority of obese children subsequently grow and develop at a normal or faster rate than other children, the eponym has served a useful purpose. Excerpts of Fröhlich's case which showed stigma of myxedema as well as genital dystrophy, reported from Nothnagel's clinic, follow.[3]

A boy of 14 years has been under our observation since November 1899. At that time the mother stated that twice a week, sometimes at intervals of 14 days, he came home from school with a headache. He had to go to bed; two hours later vomiting, sometimes vomiting as soon as he came home. . . . Otherwise no subjective complaints.

On the 19th of August [1901] he appeared again, this time with a series of grave symptoms. The mother relates the following: Since March 1899 the patient who was then a thin child, began to increase rapidly in weight. In January 1901, he complained of loss of vision in the left eye. Later vision in the right eye diminished.

The significance of these symptoms causes no great difficulty [in diagnosis]. All point to a process localized at the base of the skull in the optic chiasm. The onset with headache and vomiting, the long course all . . . makes certain the supposition of a new growth of the hypophysis, or to be more exact in the region of the hypophysis.

Since however, as already mentioned, there are no signs of acromegaly, we must be content with a purely topical diagnosis. . . . In the first place I wish to stress the *obesity* in the body of our patient. . . . The fingers are thick with *exception of the terminal phalanges,* the hands are plump. The osseous system is not involved in this increase in size. The most marked collections of fat are in the skin of the trunk especially the abdomen and in the region of the genitalia. There are masses of fat so marked that they bulge out around the genitalia. The penis, which is otherwise normally developed, is so hidden between these masses of fat that the genitalia approach the feminine type. The testicles are palpable in the masses of fat and are infantile. There are collections of fat in the region of the nipples. There are some nodules in the breasts, no fluid can be expressed. There are no hairs in the axillae, there are only a few hairs on the genitalia.

The hairs on the skull are brittle, short, scanty and since the onset of this illness continually falling out.

As a characteristic of the skin should be added that it is dry and somewhat harsh.

From what has been described we can conclude that *with symptoms, which point to a tumor in the neighborhood of the brain stem, with the absence of acromegalic symptoms, the presence of other trophic symptoms, such as rapidly developing obesity or skin changes suggesting myxedema, points to the hypophysis as the point of origin of the tumor.*

The next report of the case was prepared by von Eiselsberg, chief of the surgical clinic, and Frankl-Hochwart.[4] In 1907, von Eiselsberg approached the pituitary space by the nasal route and exposed and removed a cyst that had replaced most of the hypophysis. During convalescence, headache subsided slowly and some vision returned. Thereafter, further improvement ceased, and, at the last report 12 years postoperatively, the infantile habitus persisted.[5]

1. Brücke, F.: Alfred Fröhlich (Ger), *Wien Klin Wschr* 65:306-307, 1953.

2. v. Frankl-Hochwart, L., and Fröhlich, A.: Contribution to the Knowledge of the Effects of Hypophysin (Pituitrins), on the Sympathetic and Autonomic Nervous Systems (Ger), *Arch Exp Path* 63:347-356, 1910.

3. Fröhlich, A.: A Case of Pituitary Tumor Without Acromegaly (Ger), *Wein Klin Rdsch* 15:883-886, 906-908, in Major, R. H.: *Classic Descriptions of Disease,* Springfield, Ill: C. C Thomas, 1932.

4. v. Eiselsberg, A., and v. Frankl-Hochwart, L.: The Operative Management of Tumors of the Hypophysis (Ger), *Neurol Cbl* 26:994-1001, 1907.

5. Bruch, H.: The Fröhlich Syndrome, *Amer J Dis Child* 58:1282-1289, 1939.

New York Academy of Medicine

Louis Arthur Milkman
(1895-1951)

THE NAME OF LOUIS A. MILKMAN, associated with a readily identifiable type of advanced osteomalacia, was born in Scranton, Pennsylvania.[1] He took his medical training at Temple University, receiving the MD degree in 1919. Subsequently he served an internship in the Philadelphia General Hospital and, in 1922, attended several post-graduate classes in roentgenology at the New York Post-Graduate Hospital and Medical School. After a brief term as a member of their faculty, he returned to Scranton to practice radiology. Early in the 1930's Milkman was appointed director of the department of radiology of the Scranton State General Hospital, where he served for more than a decade, and was also a consultant in radiology to several private hospitals in Scranton. He was certified by the American Board of Radiology, and became a member of the American College of Radiology and

a fellow of the American College of Physicians.

The syndrome attributed to Milkman was based initially upon his presentation of a case to the Philadelphia Roentgen Ray Society in 1929, entitled "Pseudofractures (Hunger Osteopathy, Late Rickets, Osteomalacia)."[2] In the published communication he mentions several earlier reports, including Looser's experience in 1920 of cases of pseudofractures with transverse fissures of radioparency sometimes showing evidence of callus formation.[3] Later Milkman's description of his case, with postmortem findings, confirmed his earlier conclusions of osteomalacia; nevertheless, he believed he had described a new disease entity.[4] He erred in failing to accept the primary diagnosis in his patient of a disease belonging to the rachitic-osteomalacic group. In time the eponymic term appeared in the literature. One of the earliest was a French reference.[5] Because of the unusual features of osteomalacia, retention of the term is justified.

The generalized bone disorder is a type of osteomalacia which occurs primarily in middle-aged women. It is recognized radiographically by pseudofractures, with an otherwise normal-appearing skeleton. Symptoms develop insidiously with nothing more specific than pains in the back and in the legs. Later a waddling gait and pains in the chest and abdomen from rib fractures appear. The slow progression continues, and eventually the afflicted becomes confined. The lesions appear roentgenographically as ribbon-like zones of decalcification, many of them symmetrical, and, except for osteoporosis, the remaining osseous structure appears normal. Unknown to Milkman, the disease responds to an adequate calcium and phosphorus intake and supplementary vitamin D.

Milkman's patient died in 1933, eight years after the onset of lameness in the back. The skull and pelvis were not involved. The renal lesions were reported as "diffuse nephritis" and, although not discussed, the clinical history contained a statement of glycosuria and ketonuria with a normal concentration of blood sugar. Three of the four consulting pathologists who examined the lesions histologically suggested the diagnosis of osteomalacia. Selected conclusions from the second communication follow.[4]

1. A New Skeletal disease, which is progressive, fails to respond to medication and may end fatally, is reported.

3. The characteristics of this disease are the disturbance in gait, pains in the back, and peculiar multiple symmetrical involvement of the skeleton.

4. The characteristic roentgenographic appearance is bands or zones of increased transparency seen throughout the involved bones of the skeleton. They are multiple and symmetrical. Forty-three fractures occurred.

5. Differential diagnosis is made between this disease, late rickets, osteomalacia and fragilitas ossium.

8. The etiology is unknown. The postmortem findings of increased vascularity at the transparency zones suggest some trophic disturbance.

1. Dr. Louis Arthur Milkman, obituary, *Ann Intern Med* 36:1579, 1952.

2. Milkman, L. A.: Pseudofractures (Hunger Osteopathy, Late Rickets, Osteomalacia): Report of a Case, *Amer J Roentgen* 24:29-37 (July) 1930.

3. Looser, E.: A Pathological Form of Fractures and Callus Formation in Rickets and Osteomalacia and Other Bone Diseases (Ger), *Zbl Chir* 47:1470-1474, 1920.

4. Milkman, L. A.: Multiple Spontaneous Idiopathic Symmetrical Fractures, *Amer J Roentgen* 32:622-634 (Nov) 1934.

5. Guillain, G.; Lereboullet, J.; and Auzépy, P.: A Case of Milkman's Syndrome (Multiple Symmetrical Striatum and Bone Resorption), Nosographic Considerations (Fr), *Bull Soc Med Hop Paris* 53:879-889, 1937.

Florence Rena Sabin (1871-1953)

FLORENCE RENA SABIN was born in Central City, Colorado, a mining camp with a greater interest in a quick fortune than in scholarship and education. The town was scarcely a favorable environment for a young girl who was destined for a rich career in medical research and as a proponent of equitable rights for women in medicine and politics. Before Florence permanently retired, she had made important contributions in medical investigation and in medical teaching in the East; whereas in her native state she was largely responsible for the drafting and promulgation of public health measures that were desperately needed.[1]

The discovery of gold and silver deposits in the West in the second half of the 19th

Composite by G. Bako

century attracted her father, the son of a New England physician, who came as a mining engineer to Colorado from Vermont. At the death of her mother, a schoolteacher, the child, Florence was placed in boarding schools, first in Colorado, then in Illinois, and finally in an academy in Saxton's River, Vermont. Florence followed the preference of her older sister for Smith College, where mathematics and the laboratory sciences appealed especially to her, graduating with a bachelor of science degree.

The time of decision for medicine as a career is not known, but it probably preceded her graduation. Lacking funds for medical school, Florence taught for two years in Denver and one year in the biology department at Smith College. By then, Johns Hopkins Medical School was accepting students for instruction, women as well as men, if they qualified. Florence was admitted in 1896, the first of her sex, and graduated four years later. As a medical student, she displayed a genuine interest in research and, under the guidance of Franklin Paine Mall, professor of anatomy, prepared a wax model of the brain stem of a newborn child. It was an ingenious as well as an instructive teaching aid. The prototype was copied by a German artisan and was widely used for instruction in neuroanatomy. The model was described in the *Johns Hopkins Hospital Reports* and in an atlas prepared for use in conjunction. Florence served as an interne at Johns Hopkins Hospital under William Osler and once more published in the *Reports;* this time it was a description of periarteritis nodosa from a case on Osler's service, a disease of particular interest to the chief.

Dr. Sabin would have been a successful physician in practice, but she chose a career of teaching and research under the stimulus of Mall. Although not so famous as any of the great clinical four at Hopkins—Welch, Kelly, Halsted, and Osler—Mall was selected as the first professor of anatomy because of his outstanding reputation as a teacher and investigator in the basic sciences. The concept of self-education and student investigation was an integral part of Mall's philosophy of medical education, a philosophy which she accepted and implemented in the classroom and laboratory as she progressed academically and intellectually in the department of anatomy. In 1917, Dr. Sabin was appointed professor of histology at the Johns Hopkins Medical School, another first for her sex. Although she was a successful investigator, she was beloved by her students for her understanding and hospitality, while her warm personality found expression in her flower garden, the theater, music, and the culinary art.

The investigations in her early years encompassed physiological and embryological problems and, especially, the determination of the development of the lymphatics. Although both Langer and Ranvier speculated that the lymphatics were extensions of endothelium from the veins of the embryo, there were others who believed that the lymphatics rose from the tissue spaces and grew toward the veins. "The Origin and Development of the Lymphatic System," published in the *Johns Hopkins Hospital Reports* for 1916, described her studies, which were aided by grants from the Baltimore Association for the Promotion of University Education of Women and the Carnegie Institution of Washington. Dr. Sabin clearly demonstrated that lymphatics arise from veins by budding endothelium, that the sprouts or buds join as they grow outward from the veins, and that the peripheral ends of the lymphatics are closed and do not open into the tissue spaces. The most important result of this study was the emphasis it gave to the significance of the endothelium as a tissue.[2]

> The angioblast is one of the early tissues to be differentiated; it is not an inert lining for vessels, but an actively growing functioning tissue. In its place of growth it is a syncytium of actively amoeboid protoplasm.
> The lymphatic endothelium buds off from the veins. It is always a little different in appearance from the endothelium of the veins, and the lymphatic capillary is different in size and form from the blood capillaries. The growing lymphatic tip has the remarkable characteristic that it avoids the blood capillaries, while it is attracted by other lymphatic capillaries.

Dr. Sabin's interest in embryonic vascular tissue led to the study of the formation of red and white blood cells by means of the vital staining technique. The erythroblast was shown to develop from the angioblast, with characteristic elaboration of hemoglobin as distinct from the types of white blood cells. The monocytes and the granulocytes were seen to form from the mesoderm outside the vessels. The report in the year book of the Carnegie Institution for 1922 notes that:[3]

> With the new technique she has made important observations on the origin and differentiation of blood-cells and has brought the study of the blood into the field of experimental cytology where the anatomist and physiologist may meet on common ground. In her previous study she found in the living chick that on the second day all the primitive blood-cells become erythroblasts and that their genealogy is angioblast directly to erythroblast, or angioblast, endothelium, erythroblast. In carrying the study to older, vitally stained chicks, she finds that the primitive red cell shows a characteristic granulation; on the second and third day it takes the form of vitally stainable specific granules and rods which form a wreath around the nucleus and completely fill the cell. As the cytoplasm increases, this granulation is thinned out and the basophilic, finely granular cytoplasm becomes more and more evident. Some specific granules, however, are found in all of the red cells up to the time of hatching, although the basophilia of the cytoplasm disappears. These reactions give us a specific criterion for distin-

guishing the primitive red cell from the other types of blood cells; furthermore, one can recognize how primitive a given cell is by the amount and arrangement of its granules. This should be of great advantage clinically, where one is studying conditions in which blood is regenerating. It will be necessary now to work out the exact stages of development of the vitally stainable granules in the hyman embryo, and we can then estimate just how primitive are the young cells found in the circulation for each phase of regeneration.

Leaving Baltimore in 1925 for New York at the invitation of Simon Flexner, Florence Sabin became a full-time member of the staff of the Rockefeller Institute for Medical Research and headed one of its research divisions. Under the leadership of Flexner, the Institute had invested heavily in the study of infectious diseases, particularly the nature and pathogenesis of immunity. As a full-time investigator, Dr. Sabin began the study of the cellular phases of immune response to disease. She observed globulin-antibody formation using dye-labeled antigens, which revealed first the stimulation of the plasmocytes of the reticuloendothelial system to a high degree of phagocytosis, later fragmenting the cytoplasm to produce antibodies.[4] In a related area of study, she collaborated in a comprehensive investigation of the tubercle bacilli under the aegis of the National Tuberculosis Association. Large numbers of tubercle bacilli were grown, and chemically fractionated into their lipid, protein, and carbohydrate components. It was hoped to identify a fraction which would produce resistance to tuberculosis in the host. Important observations were described, but the goal was not reached.[5]

At the age of 67, Florence Sabin retired from the Institute and returned to Denver to be with her sister. She had lived a full and exciting life, identified with scholarship, culture, and medical research, on the Eastern seaboard, but had scarcely been identified with the slowly maturing and developing Western states. Her return to Colorado was probably noted and welcomed by only the few who knew her best from her early days there. But those who did know her immediately decided to use her rich talents in the interests of her home state. Upon the urging and recommendation of Frances Wayne of the *Denver Post*, Dr. Sabin was appointed to a post-war planning committee by the governor of Colorado. Her career in public health began at the age when retirement had been mandatory in the East. Colorado, with its great mountains and diversified occupations, had failed to institute measures for the control and prevention of disease. For the next two years, Florence, politically active, stumped the mountains and the prairie counties for corrective legislation, encountered resistance at first, but eventually won support and respect for her views from the enlightened politicians. She suffered only one defeat, the Cow Health Bill. After a vigorous campaign throughout the state, she served for a time as Manager of the Department of Health and Welfare of the city of Denver and continued to be active until her sister's failing health demanded most of her personal attention. In 1953, Florence Rena Sabin died quietly in her chair, watching a world series baseball game.

As the first female professor at Johns Hopkins Medical School and the outstanding female scientist in America of her day, she received many honorary degrees and awards. The Florence R. Sabin Building for Research in Cellular Biology is a unit of the University of Colorado's Medical Center. In 1956, her bust was placed in Statuary Hall in the capitol in Washington, one of two permitted the state of Colorado: "In honor of Florence Rena Sabin—Teacher—Scientist—Citizen," who, born in a mining area in Colorado, brought fame to the Johns Hopkins Medical School, to the Rockefeller Institute for Medical Research, and to her native state, where she completed her career in medicine as a public health counselor and leader.

1. Andriole, V. T.: Florence Rena Sabin—Teacher, Scientist, Citizen, *J Hist Med* 14:320-350 (July) 1959.
2. Sabin, F. R.: The Origin and Development of the Lymphatic System, *Johns Hopkins Hosp Rep* 17:347-429, 1916.
3. Sabin, F. R.: "Vascular System and Chromaffin Glands," in *Carnegie Institution of Washington, Year Book no. 21*, Washington, D.C.: Carnegie Institution of Washington, 1922.
4. Sabin, F. R.: Cellular Reactions to a Dye-Protein with a Concept of the Mechanism of Antibody Formation, *J Exp Med* 70:67-82 (July 1) 1939.
5. Sabin, F. R.: Cellular Reactions to Fractions from Tubercle Bacilli, *Amer Rev Tuberc* 44:415-423 (Oct) 1941.

Composite by G. Bako

George R. Minot (1885-1950)

GEORGE RICHARDS MINOT, associated with Boston culture and Boston medicine for a lifetime, brought the Nobel Prize in Medicine to Harvard for his clinical studies, pursued in collaboration with W. P. Murphy; these studies showed that the feeding of whole liver could effect the regeneration of red blood cells and produce a marked clinical improvement in patients suffering from pernicious anemia.

George Minot was born on Marlborough Street in Boston; his father was a visiting physician to the Massachusetts General Hospital.[1] He was a delicate child, went to private schools in Boston's Back Bay, and, up to his college days, displayed no evidence of scholastic excellence. He was fond of collecting butterflies, loved sailing, and enjoyed many of the amenities of Nature. In his late teens his health as well as school record improved, and he graduated from Harvard College AB cum laude. His future course remained uncertain until shortly before opening of school in the fall term, when he enrolled in Harvard Medical School. Four years later he graduated MD cum laude. During his last year in medical school, he

enrolled in an elective course in clinical pathology under J. Homer Wright (Wright's stain), the first biographic evidence of a latent interest in hematology. Subsequently, Minot's studies produced important contributions to our knowledge of the hematologic diseases such as lymphoma, leukemia, purpura, hemophilia, iron deficiency anemia, scurvy, and idiopathic purpura haemorrhagica.

During Minot's internship at the Massachusetts General Hospital on the East Medical Service, he showed a special interest in blood diseases and dealt at length with the dietary habits of his patients. From Boston he went to Johns Hopkins Hospital, spending a portion of his time as resident physician under William S. Thayer, and the remainder in the laboratory of William H. Howell, whose immediate interest centered in fibrin and the coagulation of blood. Returning to Boston in 1915, Minot was awarded a Dalton Scholarship to continue his researches in hematology at the Massachusetts General Hospital, where he also served on the visiting staff. Meanwhile he conducted a private practice from his Marlborough Street office. In 1923, he was appointed chief of the medical service at the Collis P. Huntington Memorial Hospital in the Harvard Medical School complex. His formal teaching activities were across the street at the Peter Bent Brigham Hospital; there his patients afflicted with pernicious anemia were fed nauseating quantities of cooked calf's or beef liver and, as a result, promptly experienced a remarkable and consistent improvement in the critically low red blood cell levels.

In his Nobel Lecture, Minot traced his curiosity about dietary habits and disease—especially the pathogenesis of pernicious anemia—to his days as a house pupil at the Massachusetts General Hospital. He noted that others had found diets rich in protein and iron to be helpful in various types of anemia, with the prime clue coming from the laboratory of George H. Whipple. Whipple's studies in dogs had shown the value of liver and other meat proteins in the regeneration of blood after the animals had been bled to dangerous levels. Minot was pleased to learn later that Whipple was to share the Nobel honor with Murphy and himself. In their preliminary report, Minot and Murphy described the response to their special diet of 45 patients afflicted with pernicious anemia.[2] Although the special diet was little more than a "balanced diet," with supplementary liver and relatively little fat, Minot described the quantity of each item in specific amounts. He also prescribed rest in bed. He gave most of his patients dilute hydrochloric acid, which is absent from the gastric secretions in pernicious anemia, but noted a favorable red cell response was not specifically related to the exogenous correction of the achlorhydria. The first evidence of a favorable response to the diet was a rapid rise in reticulocyte count, followed within a few days by an increased concentration of red blood cells, and, under persistent forced feeding of liver, the reparation of the hematologic defect. Excerpts from the report, presented as a preliminary communication to the Association of American Physicians in May 1926, and published in Aug 14, 1926.[2]

Following the work of Whipple and Robscheit-Robbins, we made a few observations on patients concerning the influence of a diet containing an abundance of liver and muscle meat on blood regeneration. The effect appeared to be quite similar to that which they obtained in dogs. These observations, together with the information given above, led us to investigate the value of a diet with an abundance of food rich in complete proteins and iron—particularly liver—and relatively low in fat, as a means of treatment for pernicious anemia.

Observations set forth below have been made on forty-five patients with typical pernicious anemia first partaking of such a diet when in a relapse and continuing it to date (except temporarily omitted by three), or from six weeks to two and a half years.

The therapeutic regimen for these forty-five patients, besides the special diet, included rest, usually at first in bed for twenty-four hours a day. All but three also took each day about 15 cc. of diluted hydrochloric acid (U. S. P.). These three, however, improved at least as much as the majority of the others.

Clinical improvement has been obvious usually within two weeks. This has been heralded in the peripheral blood before the end of the first week by the beginning of a most definite rise of the reticulocytes (young red blood corpuscles) of from about 1.0 per cent to usually about 8.0 and even to 15.5 per cent of all the red blood cells. This rise occurred in all fifteen patients that have had such counts made every day or so from one to three weeks before and some weeks after beginning the diet. By the end of the second week, these cells usually had returned close to their normal percentage.

Although the reticulocyte response was described in the initial communication, the significance of the reticulocyte in relation to bone marrow regeneration was apparently overlooked. A decade earlier, Minot, with medical colleague Roger I. Lee and surgical colleague, Beth Vincent, had discussed reticulation of red blood cells.[3]

The percentage of reticulated red cells may perhaps be taken as a measure of the hemapoietic activity of the bone marrow. . . . Curves plotted from frequent observations are reliable indicators of bone marrow activity and are the forerunners of increased red cell counts and of clinical improvements.

At the meeting of the Association of American Physicians in May, 1927, a better understanding of reticulocyte activity was reported. The quantitative response was found to be a valuable guide in determining relative potency of uncooked whole liver or the liver factions prepared in the laboratory of Edwin J. Cohn.[4]

The study of 40 cases of pernicious anemia shows that after the feeding of liver (usually 200 gm. a day) or a certain fraction of it, there occurs with extraordinary regularity a prompt, temporary, often marked increase of the reticulocytes, followed by a rise of the red blood corpuscles, which almost always continues to normal.

Kidneys fed to three patients produced similar results. A diet rich in fat does not inhibit the response of the reticulocytes. Raw-liver pulp may perhaps cause a greater increase of these cells than an equivalent amount of cooked liver.

The behavior of the reticulated red blood cells suggests that liver stimulates maturation of the megaloblasts that crowd the bone-marrow in relapse. In secondary anemia the bone-marrow does not contain masses of megaloblasts and a liver diet produces no significant increase of reticulocytes.

In comparable cases of pernicious anemia the rise of the reticulocytes tends to occur sooner and to be more marked the greater the amount of effective liver substance fed. The reticulocyte increase is approximately inversely proportional to the height of the red blood corpuscle count.

Although other questions remain unanswered, three items not known at the time of Minot and Murphy's original observations have contributed to the understanding of the pathogenesis of pernicious anemia. In 1948, Karl Folkers of Merck & Co. and E. Lester-Smith in Britain, working quite independently, isolated the active principle of mammalian liver as vitamin B-12 in the chemical form of cyanocobalamin. Twenty years before the vitamin was discovered, William B. Castle, pupil, collaborator, and, subsequently, successor to Minot at Thorndike Memorial Laboratory, demonstrated that an "intrinsic factor" secreted by the mucosa of the normal stomach wall, when fed together with an extrinsic factor such as beef, produced in pernicious anemia an effect on the blood-forming mechanism similar to that of liver. The stomachs of patients with pernicious anemia contained little if any of this intrinsic factor, and the deficiency seemed to be essential for the development of pernicious anemia. Without the intrinsic factor, vitamin B-12 in the normal diet cannot be absorbed, and, without the vitamin, bone marrow cannot manufacture sound red blood cells. Beef liver was effective because it contained so much of the B-12 that some of it could be absorbed without the missing stomach factor. After vitamin B-12 was isolated from liver, it was found that small amounts could be isolated also from beef muscle.

Honors in great abundance came to Minot following his magnificent clinical research. In 1928, he was given the honorary DSC degree, and a professorship of medicine by Harvard University, and, in the same year, he was appointed chief of the 4th Medical Service, visiting physician, and director of Thorndike Memorial Laboratory at the Boston City Hospital. Hematologic research in the 1930's and 1940's made this laboratory a rich nucleus for many students from America and from abroad. Minot served as chairman of the Section on the Practice of Medicine of the American Medical Association in 1934-1935, and was awarded the AMA Distinguished Service Award in 1945. In 1949, the Council on Scientific Assembly of the AMA established the George R. Minot lectureship, whereby a distinguished lecturer would speak each year

before the Section on Experimental Medicine and Therapeutics. The Association of American Physicians awarded him the Kober medal in 1928 and elected him their president for 1937-38. Foreign honors included honorary fellowship of the Royal College of Physicians, Edinburgh, the Royal College of Physicians, London, the Royal Society of Medicine, London, and corresponding member of the Royal Academy of Medicine, Belgium. He received the Charles Mickle fellowship from the University of Toronto in 1928, the Cameron prize from the University of Edinburgh, the Moxon medal from the Royal College of Physicians of London, and the John Scott medal from the City of Philadelphia in 1933. These honors in no way spoiled the inquisitive physician who remained friendly and modest—a teacher always devoted to his pupils and associates.

Stricken with diabetes mellitus in 1921, Minot received one of the first batches of insulin sent on to Boston in 1923. Insulin saved his life and enabled him to continue working for many active and productive years. At the age of 64, a cerebrovascular accident crippled him, and the following year he died. Minot was a survivor of the superb cultural tradition of 19th century Harvard who utilized his training in medical science with enviable skill; in so doing he discovered the cure of a disease, even though his monocular microscope, a few cover glasses and glass slides, and a bottle of Wright's stain were the only tools that proved necessary.

1. Rackemann, F. M.: *The inquisitive Physician: The Life and Times of George Richards Minot, A.B., M.D., D.Sc.,* Cambridge, Mass: Harvard University Press, 1956.

2. Minot, G. R., and Murphy, W. P.: Treatment of Pernicious Anemia by a Specialist Diet, *JAMA* 87:470-476, 1926.

3. Lee, R. I.; Minot, G. R.; and Vincent, B.: Splenectomy in Pernicious Anemia, Studies on Bone Marrow Stimulation, *JAMA* 67:719-723, 1916.

4. Minot, G. R., et al: The Feeding of Whole Liver or an Effective Fraction in Pernicious Anemia: the Response of the Reticulocytes, *Trans Assoc Amer Physicians* 42:83-86, 1927.

Frederick Grant Banting
(1891-1941)

F. G. BANTING, senior member of the partnership of Banting and Best, which was responsible for the discovery of insulin, was born on his parents' farm at Alliston, Ontario, of Irish-Scottish extraction. He received his collegiate training at the University of Toronto, spending two years in preparation for the ministry, but ultimately turning to medicine.[1] World War I caused him to change course once more, and, in 1915, he joined the Royal Canadian Army Medical Corps as an enlisted man. Later he was reassigned to the University where he graduated MD in 1916. Upon receiving a commission, he served in England and in France, was wounded in action, and was decorated for bravery under fire at Cambrai only a few months before the Armistice. With the war over, Banting entered upon graduate training in orthopedics at the Hospital for Sick Children in Toronto. The practice of surgery was begun in London, Ontario, in 1920, where time was shared as a part-time academic demonstrator in physiology at the University of Western Ontario.

The inspiration for Banting's investigations of the internal secretion of the pancreas has been attributed to the lectures on this organ assigned to him in the course in physiology. Those who had failed to isolate the hypoglycemic agent in the past had reasoned correctly, but the design of the experiment was deficient. Banting believed that he held the knowledge of the explanation for failure and forthwith set about to prove it in the laboratory of J. J. R. Macleod, professor of physiology at the University of Toronto. The search for the active principle of the islet cells of the pancreas during the next few months is as bewitching a tale as there is to tell of physiological investigation during Banting's generation. The experimental studies in animals were productive, chemical purification was readily achieved, and a product was available for clinical trial less than eight months after work had begun. Only a few months were required for success; whereas others had labored in vain for years.

Various accounts of the critical months of planning and skillful execution, which led to success, have been reported. The version provided by Charles H. Best, the junior member of the team, has been selected.[2] When Banting won his appeal for laboratory space from Macleod, he was joined from the first day by Best, who had just graduated from the physiology and biochemistry course at the University of Toronto. The experimental studies were begun in May 1921, with the ligation of the pancreatic duct of a relatively small number of dogs in proportion to the significance of the results. The physiological phase was followed in proper time by the chemical isolation of an active hypoglycemic principle from the degenerated pancreas. The initial report of the isolation of a potent extract from the animal studies was presented by Banting and Best to the Physiological Journal Club of the University of Toronto, Nov 14, 1921. The first published report followed the presentation by Banting, Best, and Macleod at the meeting of the American Physiological Society, New Haven, Dec 28, 1921.[3]

The hypothesis underlying our experiments was that the usual extracts of pancreas do not satisfactorily demonstrate the presence of an internal secretion acting on carbohydrate metabolism, because this is destroyed by the digestive enzymes also present in such extracts. To circumvent this difficulty we have taken advantage of the fact that the acinous, but not the insular cells become degenerated in seven to ten weeks after ligation of the ducts.

A neutral or faintly acid extract of the degenerated gland, kept at a low temperature, was therefore prepared and its effect on pancreatic diabetes investigated. Ten weeks after ligation of the pancreatic ducts the degenerated gland was removed and extracted with ice-cold Ringer's solution. This extract injected intravenously or subcutaneously invariably caused marked reduction of the percentage of sugar in the blood and the amount of sugar excreted in the urine. Extracts of liver, spleen or boiled extracts of degenerated pancreas have no effect.

Further investigations have shown the following: *a,* incubation of the extract, in alkaline reaction, for 2 hours, with pancreatic juice removes its effect; *b,* glucose given intravenously or per os is retained by diabetic animals if adequate doses of the extract are also administered; *c,* the clinical condition of the animal is improved by the extract; *d,* hemoglobin estimations before and after administration of the extract are identical; *e,* neutral extract kept in cold storage retains its potency for at least seven days; *f,* subcutaneous injections have a less rapid but more prolonged effect. Rectal injections are not effective.

The experiments have been repeated on ten animals several of which were under observation for over 2 weeks.

The need for a biochemist in the chemical purification and processing of the physiological product was satisfied with the addition of J. B. Collip, late in the fall, to the research group. His knowledge of extraction and concentration of biological substances led to the preparation of an extract suitable for parenteral use in patients. The first subject was a boy of 14, who had suffered from severe diabetes mellitus for two years. A low-calorie diet failed to influence his regressing clinical state, and on January 11 he was given the first semipurified extract. A modest decrease in the concentration of blood sugar and a diminution of glycosuria followed, with doubtful clinical benefit. Shortly after, a stronger extract was given at daily intervals, with the cessation of ketonuria, an improvement in glycosuria and

hyperglycemia values, and significant clinical improvement.[4]

This case was one of severe juvenile diabetes with ketosis. Previous to admission, he had been starved without evident benefit. During the first month of his stay in hospital, careful dietetic regulation failed to influence the course of the disease and by January 11th his clinical condition made it evident that he was becoming definitely worse.

The extracts given on January 11th were not as concentrated as those used at a later date, and, other than a slightly lowered sugar excretion and a 25% fall in the blood sugar level, no clinical benefit was evidenced.

Daily injections of the extract were made from January 23rd to February 4th (excepting January 25th and 26th). This resulted in immediate improvement. The excretion of sugar as shown in Chart I became much less. On days of treatment, this varied from 7.5 gms. to 45.1 gms. compared with a previous amount well over 100 gms. daily. The acetone bodies disappeared from the urine. The boy became brighter, more active, looked better and said he felt stronger. No extract was given from February 5th to February 15th. During this time sugar again appeared in the urine in large amounts along with traces of acetone. Administration of extract in smaller doses after February 16th again resulted in lowered sugar excretion and disappearance of acetone from the urine.

The first commercial insulin in the United States was prepared by the Connaught Laboratories of the University of Toronto followed by the Eli Lilly Company in the United States. Modest quantities were available for clinical investigation by the summer of 1922. Elliott Joslin, one of the first to use it in the United States, began his insulin series on Aug 7, 1922. On Oct 15, 1922, insulin was released through regular trade channels.

The glory of the great discovery has lingered for decades. It was Canada's finest medical triumph. The Banting and Best Department of Medical Research was created by an act of the Ontario legislature in 1923, with Banting as head of the department. In the same year a life annuity was granted Banting by the Canadian Parliament. In his honor, there were established at the University of Toronto the Banting Research Foundation, the Banting Institute, and the Banting Memorial Lectureship. The Nobel Prize in medicine was awarded to

Banting and Macleod; Banting shared his honorarium with Best and Macleod with Collip. Banting was elected honorary fellow of the Royal College of Surgeons of England, a fellow of the Royal Society, and an honorary fellow of the Royal College of Physicians. In 1934, he was knighted by the King.

Before World War II interrupted his research, Banting sought to isolate the active principle of the adrenal cortex and devoted some time to cancer research and silicosis. He was interested in early Canadian history and assembled a library of Canadiana and a collection of Indian relics. Although painting was never more than a hobby with him, he did several compositions on the rugged terrain of Canada. With the outbreak of the Second World War, Banting enlisted at once as a pathologist with an active service hospital. Soon, however, he was appointed a member of the National Research Council of Canada and Britain. He died before help could reach him in a crash of a bomber after a forced landing in a remote spot in Newfoundland while commuting to the United Kingdom.

1. Stevenson, L.: *Sir Frederick Banting*, Toronto: Ryerson Press, 1946.

2. Best, C. H.: "Sir Frederick Grant Banting," in *Dictionary of National Biography, 1941-1950*, London: Oxford University Press, 1959-1960, pp 53-55.

3. Banting, F. G.; Best, C. H.; and Macleod, J. J. R.: The Internal Secretion of the Pancreas, *Amer J Physiol* 59:479, 1922.

4. Banting, F. G., et al: Pancreatic Extracts in the Treatment of Diabetes Mellitus, *Canad Med Assoc J* 12:141-146, 1922.

ACKNOWLEDGMENTS

IN ADDITION to a few front page acknowledgements in the Preface, the following reviewed one or more essays or otherwise contributed their knowledge to the accuracy of the presentations.

From Europe and the Middle East

John Apley, Bristol; William Bickers, Beirut; K. Brochner-Mortensen, Copenhagen; Erich G. L. Bywaters, London; F. F. Cartwright, Bristol; Sir John Charles, London; Lord Cohen of Birkenhead; Zachary Cope, London; William S. C. Copeman, London; Macdonald Critchley, London; William Doolin, Dublin; Frankis Evans, London; J. M. Forrester, Calverton; Kenneth J. Franklin, London; F. W. Gibbs, London; S. J. Gudlaugsson, Amsterdam; Donald Guthrie, Edinburgh; Allan Jacobs, London; L. E. den D. deJong, Rotterdam; K. D. Keel, Middlesex; Frantisek Lenoch, Prague; Robert Macintosh, Oxford; Douglas McKie, London; Michael Mathews, Edinburgh; Alfred Meyer, London; J. S. Mitchell, Cambridge; Pierre Nicolle, Paris; Sir George Pickering, Oxford; F. N. L. Poynter, London; Ffrangcon Roberts, Chesham Bucks; Hugh M. Sinclair, London; W. Stanley Sykes, Leeds; Nanna Svartz, Stockholm; Walter Trummert, Munich; Raymond Williamson, Cambridge; L. M. Payne, London; John L. Thornton, London

From the United States and Canada

L. R. C. Agnew; Jerry K. Aikawa; Vincent T. Andriole; D. Murray Angevine; Barry J. Anson; Leslie B. Arey; Wardner D. Ayer; A. Clifford Barger; Walter Bauer; William B. Bean; Henry K. Beecher; Howard T. Behrman; Elmer Belt; E. H. Bensley; Richard D. Berlin; Frank B. Berry; Charles H. Best; Eugene Bliss; Arlie V. Bock; Thomas D. Brock; Estelle Brodman; Marshall Brucer; Roswell K. Brown; Thomas R. Buckman; Vern L. Bullough; George E. Burch; Howard B. Burchell; James J. Burrows; C. Sidney Burwell; Bradford Cannon; Carleton B. Chapman; Edward D. Churchill; Theodore Cianfrani; Edwin Clark; Paul F. Clark; Isidore Cohn; David Cogan; Betsy C. and George W. Corner, Sr.; Paul Cranefield; Gustave J. Dammin; Ward Darley; D. B. Dill; Charles A. Doan; William Dock; Raymond N. Doetsch; Lewis J. Doshay; Geoffrey Edsall; Ray F. Farquharson; Marion Fay; Harold Feil; Alfred P. Fishman; George L. Fite; Reginald H. Fitz; Richard Foregger; Thomas F. Frawley; Walter Freeman; Bruno Gebhard; William C. Gibson; Robert Goodwin; Edgar S. Gordon; John E. Gordon; George C. Griffith; Harold Griffiths; Roy R. Grinker, Sr.; Wallace B. Hamby; Sidney V. Hass; Joseph M. Hayman, Jr.; Oliver S. Hayward; Philip S. Hench; John B. Hickam; Emmet F. Horine; Frank B. Horsfall; Saul Jarcho; Robert E. Johnson; Leon Kabakeris; Robert M. Kark; Jack Kevorkian; Lester S. King; Bruno Kisch; William Kolff; Amos R. Koontz; Carl Kupfer; Jerome S. Leopold; Walter F. Lever; Arthur E. Lyons; J. Howard Means; Victor McKusick; H. Houston Merritt; John Stirling Meyer; Hans J. Mezger; William S. Middleton; Felix Milgrom; Francis D. Moore; Donald P. Murnaghan; Karl Neuberger; Wilder Penfield; O. H. Perry Pepper; Richard S. Pollitzer; Francis M. Rackemann; Hermann Rahn; S. R. M. Reynolds; Dickinson W. Richards; Frank B. Rogers; Fred B. Rogers; Charles G. Roland; Leist Rothman; Mitchell I. Rubin; J. B. deC. M. Saunders; Jerome M. Schneck; Robert E. Schofield; Walter B. Shelley; Leo P. Sherman; Benjamin Spector; Harold Speert; Lloyd G. Stevenson; J. D. Stewart; Byron Stookey; Scott N. Swisher; John A. Talbott; Richard W. Telinde; S. Marsh Tenney; Kornel Terplan; George W. Thorn; Paul Tower; Ullrich Trendelenburg; Frederich Urbach; Edward J. Van Liere; Ilza Veith; Maurice B. Visscher; Selman A. Waksman; Joseph I. Waring; Jerome P. Webster; Israel S. Wechsler; A. Ashley Weech; Paul D. White; Alfred H. Whittaker; Harold C. Wiggers; Dwight L. Wilbur; Ernest Witebsky; Leo M. Zimmerman; L. H. Butterfield; Margaret Currier; John Carey; Wesley Draper; Frederick G. Kilgour; Ruth E. Mier; Jacob Minkin; Genevieve Miller; Dorothy Schullian; James A. Servies; Charles Snyder; Richard Shryock; Madeline Stanton; Helen Young

THE SECRETARIES are listed chronologically by tour of duty; Margaret Bruzas, Mary Sylvester, Sharon Rapp, Margaret Young, Diane Bohigian and Patricia Slater.

My first research assistant in library retrieval was Suzanne W. Klein, who started before she matriculated in college. Since then she has finished medical school and currently is in residency training. She was followed by Mary Lindberg, Catherine Phelps, and Linda Binder. Several translations were prepared by Elizabeth L. Peters, Frederick Sternthal, Monica Borgwardt, Elizabeth Sieweke, Lydia Wood, and Hans Frey. I am also indebted to Mary R. Gardner, Robert W. Mayo, Norman D. Richey, and Thomas J. Handrigan for advice and suggestions regarding style and layout, to F. Joseph Fletcher and Thomas G. Bergman for photographic assistance, and to E. B. Howard, Susan Y. Crawford and Warren Albert for staff assistance.

NAME INDEX

SUBJECT INDEX